facts

holding

reasoning

discussion

questions

CASES AND MATERIALS ON
CONSTITUTIONAL LAW
THEMES FOR THE CONSTITUTION'S THIRD CENTURY

Sixth Edition

■ ■ ■

Daniel A. Farber
Sho Sato Professor of Law
University of California, Berkeley

William N. Eskridge Jr.
John A. Garver Professor of Jurisprudence
Yale University

Philip P. Frickey
Late Alexander F. and May T. Morrison Professor of Law
University of California, Berkeley

Jane S. Schacter
William Nelson Cromwell Professor of Law
Stanford Law School

AMERICAN CASEBOOK SERIES®

WEST ACADEMIC PUBLISHING

In Memory of Philip P. Frickey
1953–2010

D.A.F.
W.N.E. JR.
J.S.S.

PREFACE TO THE SIXTH EDITION

Much has happened since the publication of our last edition. Justice Scalia's death left the Court without his powerful advocacy for originalism. Justice Kennedy's retirement deprived the Court of a very different perspective on many issues. Their replacements, Justices Gorsuch and Kavanaugh, are just beginning to establish their own positions within the Court. Kavanaugh's Senate confirmation was among the most controversial in American history. The net effect of these changes is to move the Court to the right, with Chief Jusitce Roberts now replacing Justice Kennedy as the swing vote. There have also been a slew of major Supreme Court decisions, on subjects ranging from same-sex marriage to immigration bans.

In the meantime, American politics has also shifted dramatically with the election of President Donald Trump. The 2016 election reflected an increasingly polarized polity, which has also raised the tensions surrounding constitutional litigation. President Trump's aggressive use of executive power has already sparked a wave of litigation, which we expect will keep issues of presidential power in the headlines for the remainder of his term.

In the meantime, issues of race, gender, and sexuality will continue to place the Court on the frontlines of key social and political controversies. We also expect to see continuing disputes over federalism, including efforts by more liberal states to push back against the Trump Administration. As always, constitutional law will reflect the forces sweeping American society.

This edition is intended not only to incorporate recent doctrinal developments but also to give students the tools to analyze the developments we expect to see in the next few years. As in past editions, we have tried to achieve a mix of doctrinal materials and theoretical commentary in order to prepare students to deal with future doctrinal evolution.

In preparing this edition, we benefitted from many comments and suggestions made by professors and students. Our institutions have provided us with wonderful support. We thank Deans Erwin Chemerinsky, Heather Gerken, and Elizabeth Magill. Many research assistants did research and proofreading for this new edition, and we appreciate their great work.

We once again dedicate this edition to our late co-author, Philip P. Frickey (1953–2010). He was a legal genius and an academic saint. No one in law teaching during the last generation was a more inspired and generous thinker than Phil Frickey. Two of us spent a professional lifetime under his tutelage, and all three of us treasured his ideas and his spirit of joyous community. This book will always bear his imprint.

DANIEL A. FARBER
WILLIAM N. ESKRIDGE JR.
JANE S. SCHACTER

February 25, 2019

SUMMARY OF CONTENTS

TABLE OF CONTENTS

TABLE OF CASES

The principal cases are in bold type.

CASES AND MATERIALS ON

CONSTITUTIONAL LAW

THEMES FOR THE CONSTITUTION'S THIRD CENTURY

Sixth Edition

CHAPTER 1

A PROLOGUE ON
CONSTITUTIONAL HISTORY

■ ■ ■

Like most legal textbooks, this book primarily uses the case method, which means that much of your time in this course will be devoted to the intensive analysis of particular cases. Individual cases cannot be understood, however, without a knowledge of the broader context of American constitutional law. Some students come to this course having already studied the history of the Supreme Court and theories of judicial review. For others, these topics are new. This chapter is designed as a refresher for the first group of students, and a quick introduction for the second.[1]

Additionally, we will emphasize some of the themes of American history that are particularly relevant to the evolution of our constitutionalism. There is a descriptive thesis lurking in this history. Constitutional law has been responsive to larger changes in American society, especially: (1) the development of a national market and a vigorous capitalism; (2) the rise of the modern administrative state; and (3) the great *social movements* that have swept through American history like tornadoes across the prairie. A social movement is a normative mass movement: its leaders galvanize large numbers of citizens in support of an idea or ideology.[2] Among the movements that have shaped American constitutional law are the Revolutionary generation that secured our independence and drafted our first constitutions; the abolitionist movement that triumphed in the Civil War, as well as the white supremacy movement that swallowed Reconstruction; the labor movement and its law-and-order backlash; the civil rights and other nationalizing movements of the twentieth century; the movement to abolish the death penalty; the pro-choice as well as pro-life movements arrayed around the abortion issue;

---

[1] This chapter is largely drawn from Daniel Farber & Suzanna Sherry, *A History of the American Constitution* (1990), and William Eskridge, Jr., *Some Effects of Identity-Based Social Movements on Constitutional Law in the Twentieth Century*, 100 Mich. L. Rev. 2062 (2002). Useful background materials on many of the cases discussed in this chapter can be found in Louis Fisher & Neal Devins, *Political Dynamics of Constitutional Law* (2d ed. 1996).

[2] For an important introduction to the interconnection of social movement theory and the evolution of public law, see *Symposium: Social Movements and Law Reform*, 150 U. Pa. L. Rev. 1–525 (2001).

and the women's and gay rights movements, whose contests with a traditional family values countermovement closed the century.

One way to understand constitutional doctrine is that, in the medium and long term, it has largely reflected the Supreme Court's institutional response to various economic, intellectual, and social movements. Economically, we have seen the industrialization and urbanization, and later suburbanization, of the United States. Intellectually, the dominant trend has been toward modernization: policies once justified on grounds of religious or status categories must be re-evaluated on the basis of science or individual merit. Nonetheless, individual Justices have affected doctrine in important ways not predetermined by such larger historical forces, and so we also include some biographical information about the most noteworthy Justices. We hope that, besides providing a little "human interest," this biographical information will give you a richer perspective on the Court's history.

The Constitution must first be understood as a document, but a text-based understanding of the document will not answer most current issues of constitutional law. Consider the following six simple but important problems. For each problem identify the potentially relevant constitutional provisions and speculate about the correct interpretation of them given the circumstances. Consider first how each claim would be decided under the main body of the Constitution. Then look for relevant amendments.

1.   Plaintiff, an African-American child, brings suit contending that a state statute requiring racial segregation of the public school she attends is unconstitutional. (Does the Constitution provide that the Supreme Court will have the authority to declare the state law unenforceable on the ground that it is inconsistent with the Constitution?)

2.   Plaintiff, an African-American child living in the District of Columbia, brings suit contending that the federal statute requiring the racial segregation of the public school she attends is unconstitutional. (Hint: this question involves a different constitutional provision from the first question.)

3.   Congress enacts a statute creating the United States Bank, which lends funds to state-chartered banks and controls the money supply. The same statute authorizes the Bank to sue the states in federal court for damages or injunctive relief.

4.   Congress passes a statute making it a federal crime to criticize a member of Congress. A state legislature passes a statute making it a state crime to criticize a member of the state legislature.

5.   After a major terrorist incident in the United States, the President believes the people involved are nationals of the state of Badnikstan and directs the Secretary of the Treasury to freeze the monetary assets within

the jurisdiction of the United States of all persons who are nationals of Badnikstan or who are descended from nationals from Badnikstan.

6.   The Department of Justice detains an American citizen whose parents are from Badnikstan but does not charge that citizen with a crime; she brings a habeas corpus lawsuit challenging her detention as unconstitutional. By executive order, the President suspends the writ of habeas corpus.

Jot down your answers in the margin, and return to them as you consider the following mini-history of constitutional law.

SECTION 1. THE FOUNDING GENERATION: THE CONSTITUTION AND THE BILL OF RIGHTS, 1787–1791

The first great social and political movement in American history was the generational movement of young colonial men who led the American Revolution against British rule, wrote and implemented our nation's first constitution, and then threw out that plan for a new one that remains one of the foundational documents in modern political theory. The generation of George Washington, James Madison, Alexander Hamilton, Thomas Jefferson, John Adams, and John Marshall was the most important in our legal history.[3]

The nation's first constitution, the Articles of Confederation, was adopted in 1778, during the Revolution. The Articles established a unicameral Congress in which each state had one vote. Congress had the authority to manage foreign relations, but needed the consent of the states to obtain revenues and regulate interstate commerce. This weak confederation left the national government unable to respond to the urgent needs of the country in foreign affairs and domestic economic policy, and demands for reform led in 1787 to a "Constitutional Convention" of representatives from each of the states in Philadelphia. What began as a discussion about how to reform the Articles became an effort to create an entirely new constitutional structure. The Constitution drafted that summer in Philadelphia was submitted to state conventions for ratification, and by 1788 the required nine states had ratified the Constitution. In 1791, the first ten amendments to the Constitution (the "Bill of Rights") were ratified by the states. This period, from 1787 to 1791, is the foundational period in our constitutional history.

1.   *Intellectual Background.* The leaders of the American Revolution and the Framers of the Constitution drew on a wide variety of sources, including classical writers, eighteenth century Enlightenment thinkers,

---

[3]   See, e.g., Joseph Ellis, *Founding Brothers: The Revolutionary Generation* (2000).

and a variety of English political theorists.[4] As to the English theorists, the Framers drew upon two traditions. One was the "social contract" tradition of Thomas Hobbes and John Locke. This tradition assumed that people are rational beings who seek to maximize their prosperity and happiness. Unfortunately, when a number of such people live in the same society, they tend to invade each others' prosperity and happiness in pursuing their own. This brutish "state of nature" was an impediment to the prosperity and happiness of all, and to avoid it people agreed to form governments. The purpose of such consensual governments was to prevent people from infringing upon the interests of others. The danger of such governments was that the state would become the infringer rather than the protector of individual liberty.

This "liberal," contractarian tradition is the one most people associate with the founding period. Recent accounts of eighteenth century thought, however, stress another, less well-known intellectual tradition, the "republican" tradition.[5] While rooted in Italian Renaissance political theory, republicanism was accessible to the colonists through the teachings of the seventeenth century Opposition party in England. James Harrington and others were appalled by the Crown's use of political patronage to expand executive power. These Opposition thinkers decried the destruction of the old order, the rise of corruption, and the loss of civic virtue. Ultimately, they argued, the fate of the republic rested on the renewed willingness of individuals to sacrifice their private interests for the sake of the common good.

Before the Revolution, most colonists were confident of the virtue of the people and satisfied that it provided a sufficient basis for democratic government. Hence, the Articles of Confederation left virtually all governance to local assemblies and popular collective action. The disadvantages of localism became apparent in the 1780s, when local uprisings disrupted public order, the states refused to cooperate in contributing money and consent for needed national ventures, and some states became rife with factions motivated by self-interest rather than the common good. As a result of this experience, many early Americans lost faith in public virtue as a sufficient basis for government, and they found contractarian theories of government more pertinent to the needs of the country. The republican influence remained strong, however, particularly among the Anti-Federalists who opposed the new Constitution, but also to some degree among Federalists such as James Madison.

---

[4] See Bernard Bailyn, *The Ideological Origins of the American Revolution* (1967); Gordon Wood, *The Creation of the American Republic: 1776–1787* (1969).

[5] For an excellent summary of the historical literature, see Suzanna Sherry, *The Intellectual Origins of the Constitution: A Lawyers' Guide to the Historical Scholarship*, 5 Const. Comm. 323 (1988).

2. *Drafting the Constitution (1787).* The Constitutional Convention assembled in 1787 with a mandate to recommend revisions to the Articles of Confederation. Instead, it ultimately proposed an entirely new constitutional structure with three distinctive features: (1) an assumption of *popular sovereignty*, whereby political power rested in "We The People" and not in any governmental organ, like Parliament or even the states that formed the union; (2) a *federalist* layer-cake arrangement for the exercise of authority, whereby states retained their regulatory powers and governmental autonomy even as a new national government was vested with broad powers and assured supremacy over state laws; and (3) a *separation of powers* within the national government, whereby each of three departments (legislative, executive, judicial) was vested with specialized duties and was expected to check the abuses of the other departments. Notably missing in the document was an extensive array of individual rights directly protected against infringement by state or national governments. The process by which the Framers came up with the details of this structure was driven by pragmatic negotiations about protecting personal liberty and local autonomy while simultaneously creating an "energetic" national government.[6]

The main question before the Convention was how much to strengthen the federal government. The debates were initially focused on Edmund Randolph's "Virginia Plan," which was strongly nationalist. It gave Congress the power to veto state laws and to legislate "in all cases to which the separate States are incompetent, or in which the harmony of the United States may be interrupted by the exercise of individual Legislation." Anti-nationalists, mostly representing the smaller states, countered with the "New Jersey Plan," which merely augmented the minimal powers of the Congress and added a weak executive. Although the New Jersey Plan was rejected, the delegates remained sharply divided about issues of state prerogatives. Ultimately, the deadlock over states' rights was broken with the "Great Compromise" giving the states equal votes in the Senate but requiring popular representation in the House.

There was relatively little discussion of the specific powers of Congress. Initially, the delegates agreed to give Congress a veto over state laws (as Madison strongly urged), but the provision was rejected after reconsideration. The specific list of congressional powers now found in Article I was written late in the Convention by the Committee on Detail, and there was only brief discussion of the Commerce Clause or other grants

---

[6]   See Jack Rakove, *Original Meanings: Politics and Ideas in the Making of the Constitution* (1996); Wood, *Creation.* See also Julius Goebel, Jr., *Antecedents and Beginnings to 1801* (1971) (vol. 1 of the Oliver Wendell Holmes Devise History of the Supreme Court of the United States); Charles Warren, *The Making of the Constitution* (1928). Most of the contemporary notes of the Convention's proceedings are found in *The Records of the Federal Convention of 1787* (Max Farrand ed., rev. ed. 1987) (4 vols.).

of power. See Chapter 7, § 1, for discussion of the Convention's evolving description of national legislative authority.

The other two branches of the federal government received less attention than the legislature. There was lengthy but largely inconclusive debate about the executive branch, with seemingly endless discussions of whether there should be one chief executive or more, how the executive should be chosen, how long the term should be, whether reelection should be allowed, and so on. As soon as one issue seemed resolved, the debate on another issue would prompt delegates to rethink their positions again. The final upshot was the unitary executive established in Article II. As with Congress, there was much discussion about the structure of the office, but little about its specific powers.

The delegates early on agreed to create a Supreme Court whose members would be appointed for life (subject to impeachment) but disagreed as to whether there should be "inferior" federal courts and what matters federal courts should be empowered to adjudicate. Delegates fearing that federal courts would invade state prerogatives proposed tightly limited bases for federal court jurisdiction (cases involving admiralty, foreign interests, and trade laws). As a result of a series of compromises, the Convention created the expansive heads of jurisdiction now found in Article III, § 1, as well as Article VI's Supremacy Clause, but gave Congress discretion as to the establishment and jurisdiction of "inferior" federal courts and some control over the appellate jurisdiction of the U.S. Supreme Court. The delegates were firm as to the matter of judicial independence (life tenure and no salary diminishment) for all federal judges.

A contentious issue that has remained relevant for subsequent constitutional scholarship was James Madison's proposal that a Council of Revision, consisting of the chief executive and several judges, should have the power to veto congressional legislation, subject to a super-majority override. This proposal surfaced on several occasions but was defeated every time it came to a vote. Six arguments were raised against it: (1) judges' power to expound the laws and determine their constitutionality provided them with a sufficient check against the worst laws; (2) prior involvement in legislation weakens the capacity of judges to decide cases later on; (3) judges have no special expertise as regards policy matters; (4) the Council would improperly mix different powers; (5) judicial participation would weaken the accountability of the executive for vetoing measures and would drain the judiciary of its legitimacy; and (6) the security of popular measures belongs to the political branches.[7]

---

[7] See Rakove, *Original Meanings* 156–60; James Barry III, Comment, *The Council of Revision and the Limits of Judicial Power*, 56 U. Chi. L. Rev. 235 (1989).

Although the word never appears in the document, slavery was an important source of dissension at the Convention. The slave states feared that both the slave trade and the "peculiar institution" itself might be threatened by a strong national government. They were also concerned about the issue of fugitive slaves. Yet another question was how to count slaves for purposes of allocating representatives; the compromise solution was the infamous "three-fifths" rule, which was also applied to certain taxes. As to this latter issue, Gouverneur Morris gave an impassioned and prophetic speech, as reported in Madison's convention notes:

> Mr. Govr. Morris moved to insert "free" before the word inhabitants. Much he said would depend on this point. He never would concur in upholding domestic slavery. It was a nefarious institution. It was the curse of heaven on the States where it prevailed. * * * Upon what principle is it that slaves shall be computed in the representation? Are they men? Then make them Citizens and let them vote. Are they property? Why then is no other property included? * * * The admission of slaves into the Representation when fairly explained comes to this: that the inhabitant of Georgia and S.C. who goes to the Coast of Africa, and in defiance of the most sacred laws of humanity tears away his fellow creatures from their dearest connections & damns them to the most cruel bondages, shall have more votes in a Govt. instituted for the protection of the rights of mankind, than the Citizen of Pa. or N. Jersey who views with a laudable horror, so nefarious a practice.

Morris's views did not carry the day. The Constitution included the three-fifths rule and two other provisions that assumed the continuing viability of and even buttressed the institution of slavery but left the issue open for future legislation; this Sectional Compromise may have been just as important in securing general agreement to the Constitution as the Great Compromise that created the House and Senate as complementary bodies.[8]

3. *The Constitution's Ratification Debates (1787–89).* A distinctive feature of the Constitution was its internal requirement that it be ratified by popular conventions in nine states before it would become operative (Article VII). This procedural feature reflected a substantive theory of popular sovereignty.[9] Starting with Delaware and Pennsylvania, each

---

[8]   Article I, § 2, cl. 3 defined a slave as three-fifths of a free person for purposes of political representation and taxation. Article I, § 9, cl. 1 prevented any legislative interference with the slave trade until 1808. Article IV, § 2, cl. 3 required the return of fugitive slaves to their masters.

[9]   Under the Westminster Model of the United Kingdom (against which we had revolted), not only was Parliament *supreme* as against the judiciary and the Crown, but Parliament was *sovereign*. Our Framers modified the idea of legislative supremacy in their separation of powers thinking but decisively rejected the idea of legislative sovereignty. "We The People" are sovereign,

state assembled a popularly chosen convention which debated (and ratified) the Constitution. Thus, there was no single national debate, but rather a series of local debates about the wisdom of adopting the document.[10] Because the document proposed by those assembled at Philadelphia represented a "consolidation" of power in a central government, closely akin to the kind of centralized authority that the American Revolution and the Declaration of Independence denounced, opposition to the Constitution was fierce, and there was considerable doubt that the plan would be ratified by the requisite number of states.

The Anti-Federalists' primary objection to the Constitution was that its vesting the national government with so much power threatened both individual liberty and the flourishing of state and local republican governance. The Federalist defenders maintained that broad national authority was needed for the energetic governance lacking under the Articles of Confederation and that the Constitution contained enough internal checks and balances to prevent the national government from becoming oppressive. Thus, Congress (the chief organ to be feared) was unlikely to usurp excessive power because of the internal checks of bicameral approval of legislation and presentment of it to the President for approval (Article I, § 7) and the likelihood that the other branches of the national government (Articles II–III) and state governments (federalism) would thwart encroaching congressional enactments with the ample weapons at their disposal.

The most celebrated Federalist arguments were those published in newspapers by Madison and Hamilton in connection with New York's ratification. Their articles (and a few by John Jay) are collectively known as *The Federalist Papers*, some of which we have excerpted in Appendix 2 of this book. The clash of ideas is best captured in *Federalist* No. 10, written by Madison. Inspired by the republican tradition, the Anti-Federalists had argued against a strong central government, on the ground that local government, closer to the people, best fostered public virtue. Madison's response was complex. He denied that small group politics can eliminate the "vices" of faction, whose "latent causes are thus sown in the nature of man." This resonates of Hobbes and Locke. But Madison also invoked the republican concern that government may become nothing more than factional struggle delinked from the common good. The remedy for this concern, Madison argued, was not the faction-ridden localized government

---

not Congress. See generally Martin Flaherty, Note, *The Empire Strikes Back:* Annesley v. Sherlock *and the Triumph of Imperial Parliamentary Sovereignty*, 87 Colum. L. Rev. 593 (1987).

[10] For the state-by-state ratification process, see Goebel, *Antecedents* 292–412; Rakove, *Original Meanings* 94–130. See also Larry Kramer, *Madison's Audience*, 112 Harv. L. Rev. 611 (1999). Primary sources are reprinted in *The Documentary History of the Ratification of the Constitution* (John Kaminski & Gaspare Saladino eds.) (multi-volumes, still in progress); *The Debate on the Constitution: Federalist and Antifederalist Speeches, Articles, and Letters During the Struggle Over Ratification* (Bernard Bailyn ed., 1993) (2 vols.).

of the Articles of Confederation, but instead the large-scale representative national government of the Constitution. To get the full flavor of Madison's argument, read the excerpt of *Federalist* No. 10 found in Appendix 2.

Federalist Nos. 51 by Madison and 78 by Hamilton, both excerpted in Appendix 2, are also important analyses of the Constitution's structural benefits. Number 78 not only provides an influential account of the role of judicial review, but defends the independent judiciary against charges that judges would thwart the will of the people. (It also provides the Framers' most articulate theory of statutory interpretation.) Like Madison in No. 10, Hamilton in No. 78 maintained that the will of temporary majorities should sometimes be thwarted—and added the further point that the risks of life-tenured judges invading the prerogatives of Congress or the states were greatly overstated by opponents.

4.   *The Constitution Ratified and the Bill of Rights as Part of the Deal (1789–91).* Another point of controversy in the ratification debates was the Constitution's failure to guarantee a specific bill of individual rights. Federalists argued that a bill of rights was unnecessary (because the federal government had only limited powers) and potentially harmful (because it would preclude whatever rights were left off the specific list). But these arguments were not fully persuasive. New York and Virginia (the tenth and eleventh states to ratify) called for a bill of rights in their ratification resolutions. So the Federalists agreed to a bill of rights as part of the ratification "deal." The Federalists in the first Congress immediately moved to implement the bargain, as Madison introduced a series of constitutional amendments. Most of these were accepted by Congress, with some modifications.[11]

Madison's speech introducing the amendments (Appendix 3 of this book) gives an important view of his perspective on individual rights. He rejected the Federalist argument that a bill of rights was unnecessary because the federal government had only limited powers: "It is true, the powers of the General Government are circumscribed, they are directed to particular objects, but even if Government keeps within those limits, it has certain discretionary powers with respect to the means, which may admit of abuse to a certain extent, in the same manner as the powers of the State governments under their constitutions * * *." Madison also argued that a bill of rights would serve important purposes:

---

[11]   For detailed background materials on the individual amendments, see *The Complete Bill of Rights: The Drafts, Debates, Sources and Origins* (Neil Cogan ed. 1997). The First Amendment has received much historical attention. Compare Leonard Levy, *Freedom of Speech and Press in Early American History: Legacy of Suppression* (1960) (narrow view of the First Amendment's protections), with David Anderson, *The Origins of the Press Clause*, 30 UCLA L. Rev. 455 (1983) (vigorously disputing Levy's reading of the eighteenth century evidence), and David Rabban, *The Ahistorical Historian: Leonard Levy on Freedom of Expression in Early American History*, 37 Stan. L. Rev. 795 (1985) (highly critical review of the 1985 revised edition of Levy's book).

If [guarantees of individual rights] are incorporated in the Constitution, independent tribunals of justice will consider themselves in a peculiar manner the guardians of those rights; they will be an impenetrable bulwark against every assumption of power in the Legislative or Executive; they will be naturally led to resist every encroachment upon rights expressly stipulated for in the Constitution by the declaration of rights. Besides this security, there is a great probability that such a declaration in the federal system would be enforced; because the State Legislatures will jealously and closely watch the operations of this Government, and be able to resist with more effect every assumption of power, than any other power on earth can do; and the greatest opponents to a Federal Government admit the State Legislatures to be sure guardians of the people's liberty.

Madison was actually less sanguine about state governments than this passage might suggest; earlier in the speech, he had spoken about the need to protect individuals not just from the national legislature, but also from "the abuse of the community."

The Bill of Rights, quickly ratified in 1791, consists of the first ten amendments to the Constitution. These amendments were expected to limit only the national government's exercise of power. Madison's original proposal would have protected individual rights from state abuses as well, providing that "[n]o State shall infringe the equal rights of conscience, nor the freedom of speech, or of the press, nor of the right of trial by jury in criminal cases." This restriction on the states was rejected, however.

5. *Historians and the Founding Period.* Historians have actively discussed this important period, the formal beginning of our constitutional tradition. Initially, "whiggish" historians treated the period simply as a high-minded and brilliant period of creative political structuring. Challenging this vision, Charles Beard's *An Economic Interpretation of the Constitution of the United States* (1913) argued that the drafters and boosters of the Constitution tended to be moneyed interests alarmed by the instability and redistributions they expected to result from decentralized government. Beard suggested that the Constitution was itself a result of the very "factional" capture that Madison had warned against in *Federalist* No. 10. A less cynical view of Beard's thesis would be that the Constitution was responsive to the needs of the aborning capitalist economy for stable expectations, especially as to contractual and property arrangements, and for a powerful central government that could protect American shipping and merchant interests against foreign attacks.

Over the years, historians have come to reject the specific Beard thesis, and to acknowledge that support or opposition to the Constitution cut across class and professional lines.[12] To the limited extent that one can differentiate Federalists from Anti-Federalists, the former tended to be "Young Turks" seeking to instill an energetic, forward-looking vision of polity in a strong national government, while the latter tended to be older, more cautious, and less active in national affairs.[13] It is this later scholarship that inspires our understanding of the Founding Period as the culmination of a normative social movement of like-minded revolutionaries. If it is true that the Founding Generation was united more by ideology than by economic interests, it is even more apparent that its members splintered badly in the 1790s, and more tragic that their divisions seem linked to economic disputes and mundane political interests.

6. *Early Constitutional Debates Within Congress, the Presidency, and the States (1790–1801).* The great debates of the Constitution's first decade were carried out more often within the Washington Administration, Congress, and the states than in the Supreme Courts headed by Chief Justices John Jay (1789–95) and Oliver Ellsworth (1796–1800). The most famous example was the *Decision of 1789.*[14] An initial draft of the bill creating the Department of Foreign Affairs posited that the secretary would be removable by the President, without the advice and consent of the Senate. An objection was raised that this language might be read to suggest that the President did not *already* have that authority under Article II, and the language was removed from that bill and was revoked from other department-establishing statutes. Although the exact motivations of different representatives was quite heterogeneous, this series of votes was interpreted at the time and afterwards as a congressional acceptance of the President's removal power for executive department officers.

Consider another, and very different, issue. On February 12, 1790, Ben Franklin and other Pennsylvania abolitionists laid before the House of Representatives a petition for Congress to discourage the slave trade and promote the abolition of slavery. This petition provoked a great debate in the House, with southerners objecting that the preservation of slavery as well as the slave trade was part of the original deal that created the Union, and northerners claiming that the ownership and trade in human beings was deeply inconsistent with the Declaration of Independence and the

---

[12] See, e.g., Robert Brown, *Charles Beard and the Constitution* (1956) (delegate-by-delegate analysis of the economic interests of those at the Convention shows no correlation between support for strong central government and class interests); Forrest McDonald, *We the People: The Economic Origins of the Constitution* 38–92 (1958) (no fundamental antagonism between creditor and realty interests at Convention, contrary to Beard); *The Reinterpretation of the American Revolution 1763– 1789* (J. Greene ed. 1968) (collection of essays attacking Beard thesis).

[13] See Stanley Elkins & Eric McKitrick, *The Founding Fathers: Young Men of the Revolution*, 76 Pol. Sci. Q. 181 (1961); Cecelia Kenyon, *Men of Little Faith: The Anti-Federalists on the Nature of Representative Government*, 12 Wm. & Mary Q. (3d Ser.) 3 (1955).

[14] The Decision of 1789 is discussed in James Hart, *The American Presidency in Action, 1789: A Study in Constitutional History* (1948). See also Steven Calabresi & Christopher Yoo, *The Unitary Executive: Presidential Power from Washington to Bush* (2008).

premises of the Constitution (Ellis 81–119). Although Madison hijacked the abolitionist proposal and turned it into a House vote in favor of congressional noninterference in the constitutional status quo, it marked the fact that an issue largely submerged during ratification would haunt the American republic for its entire constitutional history.

For another example from the (very busy) first Congress, the House and Senate passed legislation creating a national bank. When the bill arrived on President Washington's desk for signature into law, the President put to his cabinet the question whether Congress had Article I authority to establish a bank.[15] Reflecting a localist and farmer perspective, Secretary of State Thomas Jefferson opined that Congress did not have this authority, because it was not among those specifically enumerated in Article I. Reflecting a pro-capitalist and nationalist agenda, Secretary of Treasury Alexander Hamilton opined that Congress had such authority under the Necessary and Proper Clause of Article I, § 8. The President went with Hamilton and signed into law the bill creating the first United States Bank. This was an important constitutional precedent for the broad powers of Congress to create institutions fostering and managing the emerging capitalist economy.

In 1798, Congress debated and enacted the Adams Administration's proposal of a Sedition Act making it illegal to publish "any false, scandalous and malicious writing or writings against the government" or its officers— or "to excite against them . . . the hatred of the good people of the United States, or to stir up sedition within the United States." In this case, the constitutional debates did not end in Washington. The legislatures of Kentucky and Virginia immediately adopted Resolutions (drafted by Jefferson and Madison, respectively) asserting that the Sedition Act was unconstitutional for a couple of reasons: The federal government had been delegated no authority (in Article I or elsewhere in the Constitution) to regulate private speech or publication, and so the law was outside of Congress's authority; even if within the jurisdiction of Congress to adopt, the Sedition Act was void because it was inconsistent with the prohibitions of the First Amendment. Additionally, the Kentucky and Virginia Resolutions of 1798 asserted both that each state party to the "compact" of union retained all sovereign powers not granted to the national government *and* that each state "has an equal right to judge for itself" as to whether acts of the national government went beyond the constitutional authorizations. In response, North Carolina adopted a Resolution agreeing that the Act was unconstitutional but denying that individual states could nullify a federal law. Rhode Island adopted a Resolution maintaining that Article III courts had the exclusive and ultimate authority to determine the constitutionality of the law. (In prosecutions for violations of the law,

---

[15] See David McGowan, *Ethos in Law and History: Alexander Hamilton,* The Federalist, *and the Supreme Court*, 85 Minn. L. Rev. 755 (2001) (account and analysis of the bank debate).

inferior federal courts, created by the Judiciary Act of 1789, generally ruled that the Sedition Act was constitutional.)

SECTION 2. THE MARSHALL COURT'S NATIONALIST VISION, 1801–1835

The Constitution's text changed very little between the adoption of the Bill of Rights (amendments one through ten) and of the Reconstruction Amendments (numbers thirteen through fifteen).[16] But the Constitution itself developed quite substantially under the guidance of its greatest Chief Justice, John Marshall of Virginia. We view Marshall's constitutional jurisprudence as a highly sophisticated continuation of the nationalizing work of the Founding Generation, especially as interpreted by Hamilton.[17]

For one who so much shaped American constitutional law, it is striking how accidental was this Chief Justice's appointment. John Marshall was President Adams' Secretary of State when Adams and his followers were swept out of office in the 1800 election by Thomas Jefferson and the Democrat-Republicans. Chief Justice Oliver Ellsworth resigned in December 1800. Adams first offered the job to John Jay, the neglected third author of *The Federalist Papers*, the first Chief Justice of the United States (1789–95), and Governor of New York. Jay turned the job down, citing the hardships of riding circuit. Marshall and others pushed the President to elevate Associate Justice William Paterson to be Chief, but Adams chose Marshall instead, partly to avoid naming a replacement for Paterson. Marshall, the oldest of fifteen children, was born in a log cabin on what was then the Virginia frontier. His formal legal training was limited to a year of study under George Wythe at William and Mary, but he was the most celebrated advocate of his era in Virginia. He was a star participant in the state ratification debate. After serving briefly as a diplomat and in the House, he was appointed as Secretary of State, and effectively ran the government while Adams was on vacation in 1799.

---

[16] The Eleventh Amendment, preventing states from being sued by various litigants, was an immediate reaction to the Supreme Court's decision allowing such suits in *Chisholm v. Georgia*, 2 U.S. (2 Dall.) 419 (1793). The presidential election of 1800 generated the Twelfth Amendment, which revamped the electoral college system of electing the President and Vice President. In the election, Thomas Jefferson and Aaron Burr received the same number of votes for President, sending the election into the House of Representatives. There, Burr fought for the office, even though everyone knew that he was the Democrat-Republicans' nominee for Vice President, and that Jefferson was the intended presidential candidate. Alexander Hamilton, Jefferson's rival in President Washington's cabinet, ensured the election of Jefferson because he thought Burr a scoundrel. In any event, the Twelfth Amendment prevents any similar embarrassment by separating the electoral college votes for the two offices. (Burr was, by the way, a scoundrel. But he had a good eye, and he killed Hamilton in a duel over their political and personal differences.)

[17] On Marshall's life and public service, the best source is still Albert Beveridge, *The Life of John Marshall* (1919) (4 vols.). On his transformation of the Court, see G. Edward White, *The Marshall Court and Cultural Change, 1815–35* (1988) (vols. 3–4 of the Oliver Wendell Holmes Devise History of the Supreme Court of the United States).

Marshall's appointment as Chief Justice was part of the Federalists' general strategy to extend their influence beyond 1801 through control of the judicial branch. Thus in 1801, before the Jefferson Republicans took over, the Federalists increased the number of judges and hurriedly appointed Federalists to those positions. Some judges were appointed just before midnight on March 3, the last day of the Adams Administration. Although Marshall himself had been appointed Chief Justice, he stayed up with Adams, in his capacity as Secretary of State, to sign the commissions. These judicial commissions were hurriedly signed, sealed, and delivered, but in the rush, a few commissions for these and other last-minute appointments remained undelivered when Jefferson took office on March 4. President Jefferson and his new Secretary of State, James Madison, refused to deliver the remaining commissions.[18] Some of the disappointed appointees, including William Marbury (named as a District of Columbia justice of the peace), sued Madison in the Supreme Court for delivery of his commission.

The 1803 decision in *Marbury v. Madison*, 5 U.S. (1 Cranch) 137 (Chapter 2, § 2A), was Chief Justice Marshall's first important opinion, in which he all at once (1) criticized the new Administration, (2) averted a constitutional crisis, and (3) added a permanent fixture to our constitutional system—namely, judicial review. Marshall declared that Marbury was entitled to his commission, but that bringing suit in the Supreme Court was not a constitutionally authorized way of obtaining it. He thus chastised Jefferson and Madison while still avoiding issuance of an order that probably would have been ignored. *Marbury* is the first Supreme Court opinion explicitly asserting the power of judicial review, the power to strike down federal statutes that violate the Constitution.[19] Its larger importance was in setting forth, in a dramatic setting, high aspirations for the rule of law in the new nation: although slippery in its reasoning, the Chief Justice's opinion insisted that everyone—including the Jefferson Administration and the Marshall Court—was bound by the legal rules set forth in statutes and the Constitution, and suggested that those rules would be deployed in a predictable way by strictly impartial federal judges.

---

[18] This was the least of their defiant actions. The House voted to impeach Federalist Judge John Pickering and Justice Samuel Chase; the Senate removed Pickering from office but acquitted Chase. More provocatively, Congress abolished the new Article III judges created during the Adams Administration, a move that generated tremendous constitutional debate within Congress. The Marshall Court upheld the abolition against an Article III challenge in *Stuart v. Laird*, 5 U.S. (1 Cranch) 299 (1803).

[19] The statute struck down in *Marbury* was part of the Judiciary Act of 1789, interpreted as giving the Supreme Court original jurisdiction to issue mandamus orders against officials such as Madison. The opinion held that this jurisdiction went beyond that authorized by Article III of the Constitution and thus could not be utilized by the Court. For an exploration of the intellectual context of the decision, see Jack Rakove, *The Origins of Judicial Review: A Plea for New Contexts*, 49 Stan. L. Rev. 1031 (1997); William Michael Treanor, *Judicial Review Before* Marbury, 58 Stan. L. Rev. 455 (2005).

Marshall realized that a *national* rule of law brooked no dissent from the states and their courts (contrary to the Kentucky and Virginia Resolutions). A corollary was the authority of the national judiciary to review *state* statutes and other official action. Again, a complicated procedural tangle led to a significant Supreme Court case. This time, the dispute was over land. Lord Fairfax willed some of his vast northern Virginia land holdings to another British citizen, and the property ultimately devolved to an American, Thomas Martin. The state of Virginia claimed that it owned the land, having confiscated it from Fairfax during the Revolution because he was a British loyalist. Virginia then granted the land to David Hunter, a Virginian. The Peace Treaty of 1783 and the Jay Treaty of 1794 both provided, however, that land owned by British citizens would no longer be confiscated. In its first ruling in the case, the Supreme Court held that Virginia's attempted confiscation violated the 1783 treaty.

The Virginia Supreme Court refused to follow the Supreme Court's ruling, and the Marshall Court responded in *Martin v. Hunter's Lessee*, 14 U.S. (1 Wheat.) 304 (1816). Justice Story wrote a highly nationalistic opinion for the Court, holding that it had the authority to review state court decisions and to determine whether state statutes violated federal law (including the federal Constitution, federal statutes, and treaties).[20] In a sweeping assertion of national and judicial power, *Martin* held that the national Constitution and laws trumped state laws and practice, and that the Supreme Court was the final arbiter over all levels of government. To similar effect was Chief Justice Marshall's opinion in *Cohens v. Virginia*, 19 U.S. (6 Wheat.) 264 (1821).

The Marshall Court rounded out its jurisprudence of activist nationalism in an opinion confirming Hamilton's arguments for a national bank. In 1816, Congress chartered the Second Bank of the United States. The Maryland legislature imposed a punitive tax on all banks not chartered by the state legislature itself. When the Baltimore branch of the Bank of the United States refused to pay the tax, Maryland sued the branch's cashier, James McCulloch. Chief Justice Marshall delivered the unanimous decision of the Court in *M'Culloch v. Maryland*, 17 U.S. (4 Wheat.) 316 (1819) (Chapter 7, § 1), upholding the validity of the Bank and invalidating the state tax as inconsistent with federal supremacy. His eloquent opinion opened with an assertion that—contrary to the Kentucky and Virginia Resolutions—it was the Supreme Court that must ultimately decide whether Congress' exercise of authority was consistent with the Constitution, lest such matters become the source of endless and not

---

[20] Joseph Story was the greatest scholar on the early Court, the author of nine major treatises, including one on constitutional law! With misgivings about Story's ideology, President Madison appointed him to the Court only after two other candidates (one of them John Quincy Adams) declined the honor. Although appointed by a Republican, Story immediately became Marshall's staunch ally in constitutional cases and helped assure Marshall's continued dominance notwithstanding a string of Democrat-Republican Presidents.

"peaceable" contest among the political branches. Echoing arguments for the bank made by Hamilton a generation earlier, Marshall relied on general legal principles, as well as the Necessary and Proper Clause, to find that the Constitution permitted Congress to exercise broad implied powers. In a phrase repeated in cases through today, he found few limits on congressional power:

> Let the end be legitimate, let it be within the scope of the constitution, and all means which are appropriate, which are plainly adapted to that end, which are not prohibited, but consist with the letter and spirit of the constitution, are constitutional.

Interpreting the Constitution any less expansively, he said, would turn the document into "a splendid bauble."[21] See also *Gibbons v. Ogden*, 22 U.S. (9 Wheat.) 1 (1824) (Chapter 7, § 2) (broad interpretation of Congress' power to regulate interstate commerce and to preempt the states' laws to achieve national goals).

Having established the supremacy of national authority over state authority and the breadth of the national authority of Congress and the Court, the remaining contribution of the Marshall Court was to announce specific constitutional limits on the power of the states. In *Barron v. Baltimore*, 32 U.S. (7 Pet.) 243 (1833), the Chief Justice ruled that the Bill of Rights placed no limitations on the states, though these amendments obviously remained limitations on the national power. The main specific limitation on the states was the Contracts Clause of Article I, § 10. In *Dartmouth College v. Woodward*, 17 U.S. (4 Wheat.) 518 (1819), the Chief Justice's opinion for the Court held that the state of New Hampshire could not unilaterally alter the charter of Dartmouth College, whose case was ardently argued by its leading alumnus, Senator Daniel Webster. See also *Sturges v. Crowninshield*, 17 U.S. (4 Wheat.) 122 (1819) (state's retroactive insolvency law violated Contracts Clause and was therefore unenforceable).

In John Marshall, the Federalists found the ideal Justice to cement the nationalizing features of the Constitution, for the Virginian was intelligently loyal to Federalist principles, without taking unnecessary risks with the Court's fragile political capital. In carrying out his agenda,

---

[21] Marshall's "great ends justify expansive means" reasoning had precedent in the actions of his supposed states' rights enemies, Jefferson and Madison, the authors of the Kentucky and Virginia Resolutions. As President in 1816, Madison had cast aside his earlier constitutional difficulties with the Bank and proposed the legislation creating it, because of the nation's fiscal needs. As President in 1803, Jefferson had purchased the Louisiana Territory from France without a congressional authorization or budgetary allocation. Agreeing that he had exceeded his lawful authority, Jefferson defended his actions in 1810: "A strict observance of the written law is doubtless one of the high duties of a good citizen but it is not the highest. The laws of necessity, of self-preservation, of saving our country when in danger, are of higher obligation." Gerald Stourzh, *Alexander Hamilton and the Idea of a Republican Government* 34 (1970) (quoting Jefferson). Acquiring the Louisiana Territory was neither necessary to preserve the nation nor essential to save it from "danger."

Marshall revealed a brilliant and deeply learned legal mind, mustering unanimous Courts in most of the constitutional cases and writing most of the decisions himself. And, not least, he was long-lived. Marshall outlived all of his contemporary adversaries, including his enemy Jefferson, and was determined to outlive populist President Andrew Jackson as well. Only in this last aspiration did the Chief Justice fail. He stubbornly refused to resign, notwithstanding failing health, and in 1835 became the first Chief Justice to die in office. While it was being tolled on the occasion of his death, the Liberty Bell cracked. (Can you beat that for symbolism?)

SECTION 3. STATES' RIGHTS, SLAVERY, AND THE TANEY COURT, 1836–1864

The United States underwent a number of major changes in the first half of the nineteenth century: dramatic expansion of the franchise to most adult white males; tremendous geographic expansion and economic growth; and a fervent movement to abolish slavery, which in turn stimulated the South to a more intense defense of that institution.[22] These developments had important consequences for constitutional law under Chief Justice Marshall's successor, Roger Taney of Maryland. The prevailing constitutional philosophy of Taney's period was *instrumentalist* and *pragmatic*, supporting laws and doctrines that fostered economic development and national unity. Challenging that dominant jurisprudence was the *natural rights* philosophy of the abolitionists, who maintained that all human beings enjoy certain inalienable rights and that the state owes every citizen equal treatment under law.[23] The interplay of these two belief systems set the conceptual stage for the Civil War.

Like President Adams in 1801, President Jackson in 1835 drew his nominee for Chief Justice from his cabinet, Attorney General Roger Taney. As Attorney General, Taney did the heavy lifting in Jackson's campaign against the Bank of the United States. When the Secretary of the Treasury refused to pull federal funds out of the Bank, he was fired, and Taney stepped into his shoes to carry out the order. In 1835, Jackson tried to appoint him to the Court but was unable to get Senate approval. Less than

---

[22] See generally Daniel Walker Howe, *What God Hath Wrought: The Transformation of America, 1815–1848* (2006), as well as Walter McDougall, *Throes of Democracy: The American Civil War Era, 1829–1877* (2005); David Reynolds, *Waking Giant: America in the Age of Jackson* (2008).

[23] See Morton Horwitz, *The Transformation of American Law, 1780–1860* (1977) (nineteenth century legal instrumentalism); William Nelson, *The Impact of the Antislavery Movement upon Styles of Judicial Reasoning in Nineteenth Century America*, 87 Harv. L. Rev. 513 (1974) (abolitionist constitutionalism as a challenge to the prevailing instrumentalism); David A.J. Richards, *Public Reason and Abolitionist Dissent*, 69 Chi.-Kent L. Rev. 787 (1994) (anti-racism and anti-sexism as fundamental natural law precepts at foundation of abolitionist constitutionalism); see also Robert Cover, *Justice Accused: Antislavery and the Judicial Process* (1975) (account of Massachusetts Chief Justice Lemuel Shaw, whose instrumentalist judicial philosophy was inconsistent with his political opposition to slavery).

a year later, Jackson sent his name up again as a replacement to Marshall. A brilliant lawyer (like his predecessor), Taney was in some respects a distinguished Chief Justice, but his reputation is fatally tainted by the *Dred Scott* decision (discussed below).

Although Taney supported state autonomy, his Court did not so much curtail federal power as encourage the states to exercise their own police powers vigorously to promote economic development. For example, in *Proprietors of Charles River Bridge v. Proprietors of Warren Bridge*, 36 U.S. (11 Pet.) 420 (1837), Chief Justice Taney permitted the state of Massachusetts to abrogate a bridge monopoly. The aggrieved monopolist argued that his charter, which had been approved by the legislature, was a contract that could not be changed without violating the Contracts Clause (Art. I., § 10, cl. 1), as interpreted in the Dartmouth College case. Interpreting the company's charter, Taney's opinion refused to read the grant of monopoly as broadly as the company wanted, since such a reading would contravene community interests. But the reasoning was unmistakably an instrumentalist contrast with the rights-based logic of the Dartmouth case. "[I]n a country like ours, free, active and enterprising, continually advancing in numbers and wealth, new channels of communication are daily found necessary, both for travel and trade"—and the states need regulatory flexibility to respond to and guide such development in the interest of the larger community. The new Court would give the states more leeway to regulate private interests than the Marshall Court had contemplated.

Most of the Taney Court's slavery-related decisions deployed similar instrumentalist reasoning in support of federal power over state resistance. Article IV, § 2, cl. 3 of the Constitution required the return of fugitive slaves to their masters. Congress in 1793 implemented this provision with the Fugitive Slave Act—anathema to the emerging abolitionist movement, which hearkened to the Declaration of Independence to support its principle that all men should enjoy basic freedoms. At various points, non-slave states were no longer willing to go along with this kind of regulation. For example, Pennsylvania authorities actually arrested Edward Prigg for capturing an escaped slave. But the Taney Court reversed his conviction in *Prigg v. Pennsylvania*, 41 U.S. (16 Pet.) 539 (1842), on the ground that the states were bound by the original constitutional deal—and that enforcement of the original deal was needed to preserve the union. See also *Jones v. Van Zandt*, 46 U.S. (5 How.) 215 (1847).

Abolitionists denounced *Prigg* as inconsistent with people's natural rights, and state judicial resistance persisted. Wisconsin Justice Abram Smith argued that citizens retained their natural right to assist escaped slaves in securing their needed freedoms—and that the states retained the right to resist the Fugitive Slave Act (updated in 1850), which made this rightful activity a crime. See *In re Booth*, 3 Wis. 145 (1854), recalling the stance of the Kentucky and Virginia Resolutions. Abolitionist constitutionalism required that the Constitution be read against the normative baseline of the Declaration of Independence. The Taney Court emphatically disagreed in *Ableman v. Booth*, 62 U.S. (21 How.) 506 (1859), reaffirming both the Marshall Court's insistence that the states were bound by federal law and *Prigg*'s holding that state cooperation in fugitive slave laws was an essential feature of the original constitutional deal and the continuing viability of the union. The latter point was ironic, as Taney and four Justices had two years earlier handed down a decision that would hasten the break up of that Union.

In the "Missouri Compromise" of 1820, Congress prohibited slavery north and west of Missouri (north of 36° 30′), in return for allowing the rest of the country to follow a local option approach. The odd consequences of this compromise were illustrated in the case of Dred Scott, a slave. Scott was taken from Missouri (a slave state under the 1820 compromise), where he and his owner resided, to Illinois, where slavery was forbidden by the state constitution, and then to Fort Snelling (now in Minnesota), where slavery was forbidden by the 1820 federal statute. After his return to Missouri, Scott sued for his freedom in federal court. He invoked federal jurisdiction by claiming diversity of citizenship (he was a citizen of a different state from the defendant), and his claim for relief rested upon the Illinois Constitution and the 1820 federal statute.[24]

Dred Scott's case reached the Supreme Court, which originally was disposed to decide it on narrow grounds. Justice Samuel Nelson of New York prepared an opinion rejecting Scott's claims on the ground that *Strader v. Graham*, 51 U.S. (10 How.) 82 (1850), had held that a black person's legal status was to be determined by the law of the state in which he resided, and that federal courts were bound by that law. Justice John McLean of Ohio, a devout Methodist layman who considered slavery an abomination, prepared a staunch anti-slavery dissenting opinion, and Justice Benjamin Curtis of Massachusetts was prepared to dissent along similar lines. The five pro-slavery Justices—Chief Justice Taney and Justices John Catron of Tennessee, James Wayne of Georgia, Peter Daniel of Virginia, and John Campbell of Alabama—decided to expand the case to settle once and for all the slavery question. The aged Chief Justice wrote what they hoped would be the opinion for the Court. (As it turned out, each of the nine Justices wrote opinions, but the Taney opinion is widely considered to be the main one, though to this day there is debate about just what portions of his opinion had majority support.)

Taney first ruled that federal courts had no jurisdiction, because Scott was not a "citizen" of Missouri, as he necessarily claimed. The Constitution

---

[24] For further discussion of the case and its background, see Don Fehrenbacher, *The Dred Scott Case* (1978); Paul Finkelman, *The Dred Scott Case, Slavery, and the Politics of Law*, 20 Hamline L. Rev. 1 (1996).

when adopted did not contemplate citizenship for free blacks, for "they were at that time considered as a subordinate and inferior class of beings, who had been subjugated by the dominant race, * * * [having] no rights or privileges but such as those who held the power and the Government might choose to grant them." Given this "fixed and universal" view shared by the Framers, the Chief Justice concluded that neither slaves nor their descendants, even if freed, could be considered "citizens" of any state for jurisdictional purposes. This part of Taney's *Dred Scott* opinion is a classic deployment of "originalism" as a constitutional methodology. Under this method, the interpreter asks how the Framers expected the Constitution to be applied to the issue at hand (original intent) or what the Constitution would have been understood to mean by We the People (original meaning). Chapter 2, § 3A will explore these and other approaches to and criticisms of originalism.

Next, the Chief Justice ruled that even if the lawsuit were properly in federal court, Scott could obtain no relief under the Illinois Constitution, because he was bound by the laws of Missouri. Nor could he obtain relief through the federal statute, for it was unconstitutional. As to the latter point, Taney reasoned as follows: (1) The Fifth Amendment prohibited the federal government from depriving citizens of their property without just compensation and due process of law. (2) Scott's owner had a property interest in Scott; indeed, the "right of property in a slave is distinctly and expressly affirmed in the Constitution" itself, another deployment of original intent as a legitimating methodology. (3) The federal statute's effort to deprive the owner of his property was "void" and unenforceable, because it violated "the rights and privileges of the citizen [as] regularly and plainly defined by the Constitution itself." Note how the instrumentalist and pro-regulatory reasoning Taney deployed in earlier cases vanished in the face of the author's sectional loyalty.

The Court's decision in *Dred Scott v. Sandford*, 60 U.S. (19 How.) 393 (1857), was the second time in its history that the Court had declared a federal statute unconstitutional (*Marbury* was the first). Far from "settling" the slavery issue once and for all, *Dred Scott* fanned the flames of discord. Before the 1850s, abolitionists were divided between those who believed slavery inconsistent with the Constitution, properly understood, and radicals who believed the Constitution itself was corrupt because of its protection of slavery. After *Dred Scott*, the radicals gained the upper hand, and the issue of slavery forced the nation into a constitutional corner: Half the nation believed the Constitution had gone to Hell, while the other half believed it represented their Salvation. That there seemed less room for compromise and accommodation undermined the incoming administration of James Buchanan (who knew about the decision in advance). From a political as well as moral point of view, *Dred Scott* was the greatest disaster in the history of the Court.

SECTION 4. RECONSTRUCTION AND THE AMBIGUOUS TRIUMPH OF ABOLITION, 1864–1896

The election of Abraham Lincoln as President in 1860 brought forth a sea change in American constitutionalism. First, it precipitated the Civil War (1861–65) and raised numerous questions the Constitution addressed ambiguously if at all: the legality of state secession, presidential authority to wage war and to suspend civil liberties, and the power of the national government to finance railroads and other massive projects. Second, Reconstruction after the defeat of the South generated the Thirteenth, Fourteenth, and Fifteenth Amendments, which instantiated at least some of the abolitionist philosophy of individual rights of liberty and equal protection, directly enforceable against the states. Third, the implementation of the Reconstruction Amendments shifted away from the vigorous enforcement demanded by the abolitionist natural rights philosophy, and toward a pragmatic and instrumentalist approach reminiscent of the Taney Court's pre-*Dred Scott* decisions.

1. *The Civil War and the Exercise of Great Power by the Federal Government.* The Civil War necessitated a rethinking of American constitutionalism. The Constitution, after all, said nothing about secession. States' rights thinkers like President Buchanan believed that the North was powerless to oppose secession: If the Constitution was a compact among the states, then why couldn't some of them depart from the arrangement? President Lincoln responded that the Constitution had created an inviolable national community and not a loose confederation whose members could depart at will.[25] Over the course of the war, he and the Republican Party became committed to a fundamental rethinking of national citizenship and individual rights as they struggled with the demands of justice for the southern slaves.

Lincoln's conduct of the war meant that the federal government exercised more power than ever before—and often that power was exercised by the President, without prior authorization by Congress. Within a week of the firing on Fort Sumter (April 12, 1861), President Lincoln had not only called out the militia, but had issued a proclamation blockading Confederate ports and authorizing the seizure of ships carrying goods to the rebels. Shipowners challenged this exercise of essentially legislative power by the executive. Not only was there no legislation authorizing this action, but Congress did not even declare war until July 13. Without a declaration of war by Congress, the blockade violated

---

[25] For important analyses of constitutional problems arising out of the Civil War, see Daniel Farber, *Lincoln's Constitution* (2005); William Duker, *A Constitutional History of Habeas Corpus* 140–49, 167–70 (1980); James Randall, *Constitutional Problems Under Lincoln* (rev. ed. 1965); John Sharer, *Power, Idealism, and Compromise: The Coordinate Branches and the Writ of Habeas Corpus*, 26 Emory L.J. 149 (1977). See generally Phillip Shaw Paludan, *The Presidency of Abraham Lincoln* (1994).

international law, as neutral countries were affected. (But note this conundrum: As a matter of U.S. law, Lincoln treated the South's secession as a nullity, but to satisfy international law Lincoln may have needed a declaration of war, which according to Article I could only be accomplished by Congress.)

A bare majority (5–4) of the Supreme Court found sufficient legislative authorization for the President's action in *The Prize Cases*, 67 U.S. (2 Black) 635 (1863) (Chapter 8, § 1B), but Justice Nelson's dissenting opinion demonstrated that the laws cited by the Court only authorized the President to call out the militia and mobilize the federal armed forces and did not authorize him to blockade ports. Justice Grier's opinion for the Court also suggested that the President had inherent authority to "suppress insurrection against the government of a State or of the United States" and seemed to leave it to the political branches to work out the proper response:

> Whether the President, in fulfilling his duties as Commander-in-chief, in suppressing an insurrection, has met with such armed hostile resistance, and a civil war of such alarming proportions as will compel him to accord to them the character of belligerents, is a question to be decided by *him*, and this court must be governed by the decisions and acts of the Political Department of the government to which this power was intrusted.

On April 27, 1861, President Lincoln authorized Commanding General Winfield Scott to suspend the writ of habeas corpus. Scott deployed this power to arrest John Merryman for asserted anti-Union activities in Maryland. Merryman applied to Chief Justice Taney for habeas relief, which Taney granted. *Ex parte Merryman*, 17 Fed. Cas. 144 (C.C.D. Md. 1861). Because the Constitution's authorization for suspension of the writ is in Article I, § 9, cl. 2, the article defining the powers of *Congress*, Taney concluded that the President could not suspend the writ on his own authority. Indeed, by acting outside of legal authorization, the President was violating his Article II duty to "take care that the laws shall be faithfully executed." Taney ruled that any charges against Merryman had to be subject to ordinary judicial process. Although Merryman was then duly indicted for treason, he was never tried. Lincoln later responded to Taney's legal arguments: Article I, § 9, cl. 2 authorized suspension because there was a "Rebellion" and the "public Safety" required it; the provision says nothing about what organ can suspend the writ—a silence that only a knave would construe so stingily. "[A]s the provision was plainly made for a dangerous emergency, it cannot be believed the framers of the instrument intended, that in every case, the danger should run its course, until Congress could be called together; the very assembling of which might be prevented, as was intended in this case, by the rebellion."

President Lincoln's revolutionary Emancipation Proclamation declared that, by virtue of the President's authority as Commander-in-Chief, "all persons held as slaves" within designated rebel states "are, and henceforward [after January 1, 1863] shall be free." The intended legal effect of this order was ambiguous, and it was never litigated in court, but the Proclamation was much debated. Among its critics was former Justice Curtis, one of the abolitionist dissenters in *Dred Scott*. Under the Constitution, Curtis argued, only Congress—and not the President—can override state laws; the military action against the rebel states did not abrogate the applicability of the Constitution to them. Even if the rebels had absolutely no constitutional rights, all Americans had a public right that the President only act according to the duly established laws of the United States, which Lincoln had not done. (Indeed, the slavery-supportive Fugitive Slave Acts of 1793 and 1850 remained in force until Congress repealed them in June 1864.) Lincoln responded to Curtis and other critics that in cases of "Rebellion or Invasion" the President's Commander-in-Chief powers justified the exercise of quasi-legislative authority over enemy or rebel territory and that the remedy for its abuse was the normal channels of the political process. This kind of reasoning was similar to that invoked by Jefferson to justify the Louisiana Purchase.

2.   *Reconstruction and Abolitionist Constitutionalism, 1865–77.* The South's defeat in the Civil War meant the formal end of slavery in the United States—and an opportunity for the triumphant abolitionists to reshape constitutional law.[26] In 1865, Congress submitted, and a sufficient number of states ratified, the Thirteenth Amendment, which made slavery and any "involuntary servitude" illegal. (This instantiated the abolitionists' central proposition: no person can have a legal or moral right to "own" any

---

[26]   Many legal historians maintain that abolitionist thought was the primary influence on the Reconstruction Amendments. See Jacobus tenBroek, *Equal Under Law* (1965) (originally published as *The Antislavery Origins of the Fourteenth Amendment*) (leading work on the contributions of abolitionists to Reconstruction constitutionalism, arguing inter alia for a broad reading of the Thirteenth Amendment), as well as Michael Kent Curtis, *No State Shall Abridge: The Fourteenth Amendment and the Bill of Rights* 26–56 (1986) (abolitionist natural law theories as the basis for congressional debates surrounding Fourteenth Amendment); David A.J. Richards, *Conscience and the Constitution: History, Theory, and the Law of the Reconstruction Amendments* (1993) (arguing that abolitionist thought and activism directly influenced twentieth century theories of individual rights). Some legal historians emphasize that moderate and conservative Republicans, with little connection to the abolition movement, were more important to the Reconstruction Amendments than were the "radical" Republicans who were the heirs to the abolitionists. E.g., Eric Foner, *Reconstruction: America's Unfinished Revolution, 1863–1877* (1988) (rise and fall of the radical Republicans in the 1860s); William Nelson, *The Fourteenth Amendment: From Political Principle to Judicial Doctrine* (1988) (importance of moderates to Congress' proposing the Fourteenth Amendment). But many of these historians believe that abolitionist thought introduced the key ideas for the Reconstruction Amendments—natural right to freedom and to certain liberties from state infringement, the importance of the franchise and other rights of "national citizenship," the state's obligation to provide equal protection of the law to all persons—and have been under-appreciated by the post-1877 Supreme Court. E.g., Eric Foner, *The Strange Career of the Reconstruction Amendments*, 108 Yale L.J. 2003 (1999); Robert Kaczorowski, *Revolutionary Constitutionalism in the Era of the Civil War and Reconstruction*, 61 NYU L. Rev. 863 (1986).

other human being.) Shortly thereafter, Congress created the Freedman's Bureau to provide clothing, medical care, and relocation for white and black refugees; to assist the transition of freedmen to the status of productive citizens with full contractual rights; and to establish schools to improve literacy and computational skills among the new citizens. Several congressional enactments of the period were explicitly limited to helping people of color. In 1866, Congress passed the first Civil Rights Act, which implemented the abolitionists' equal treatment principle, guaranteeing every citizen the right to make and enforce contracts, to sue, to purchase and convey land, and to enjoy the equal benefit of all laws and proceedings for the security of persons and property. This statute survives as 42 U.S.C. §§ 1981, 1982.

The most important Reconstruction Amendment was the Fourteenth, whose drafting history and ratification (1868) are recounted in Chapter 2, § 1A. Section 1 redefined citizenship and rights. Implementing the abolitionists' principle of *national citizenship*, the first sentence overruled what was left of *Dred Scott* by providing that persons born in the United States are citizens of the country first, and of the states in which they reside second. Tracking the natural rights and equality-before-the-law principles of the abolitionists, the second sentence defined several rights enforceable against the states: "No State shall make or enforce any law which shall abridge the privileges or immunities of citizens of the United States; nor shall any State deprive any person of life, liberty, or property, without due process of law; nor deny to any person within its jurisdiction the equal protection of the laws." Note that the rights protected by § 1 go well beyond the property rights protected in the original Constitution (e.g., the Contracts Clause). Section 5 of the Amendment authorized Congress to enforce the provisions of the Amendment "by appropriate legislation."

The Fourteenth Amendment was immediately followed (in 1870) by the Fifteenth Amendment, which forbade racial discrimination in access to voting. Congress enacted further civil rights statutes in 1870, 1871, and 1875, assuring equal rights for black citizens in jury service, voting, and access to public accommodations. Although the Reconstruction Amendments and statutes did not have nearly as much impact in the South as the Republicans had hoped, they reflected an important transformation of substantive constitutional law. They also represented an important innovation in constitutional lawmaking.

President Johnson, the Tennessee Democrat who succeeded Lincoln after his assassination, had been committed to the Thirteenth Amendment and used his military governors to pressure the Southern states into ratifying the Amendment in 1865 (he was successful in all but Mississippi). But Johnson opposed the Fourteenth Amendment, and the southern and border states, one by one, passed resolutions rejecting it. One would have thought that this would have been the end of the matter under Article V.

But the Radical Republican Congress was adamant about the proposed Fourteenth Amendment and forced a constitutional showdown, first with the recalcitrant states, and then with the President. The Radicals were buoyed by the fact that they convincingly won the elections of 1866, months after the Fourteenth Amendment was submitted to the states.

Armed with the popular mandate, Congress in 1867 passed the first Reconstruction Act, which reconstructed state governments and guaranteed the freed slaves voting rights. Section 5 of the statute denied the southern states the right to send representatives to Congress until they ratified the Fourteenth Amendment! President Johnson denounced the process and did all he could to impede it. The House of Representatives impeached him, and to save his office the President retreated from his anti-Reconstruction campaign. Reconstructed southern governments fell into line and began to ratify the Fourteenth Amendment. In May 1868, Johnson survived his Senate impeachment trial, albeit by only one vote. In July 1868, Secretary of State Seward proclaimed the Fourteenth Amendment ratified.

This procedural history of the Fourteenth Amendment strengthens the impression gleaned from its substantive message, that (to use Bruce Ackerman's felicitous phrase) this was an important "constitutional moment" in our history, on a par with the original framing of the Constitution, and moving the document well beyond the original vision. The precise direction and extent of this constitutional reformation was, of course, left for later generations to define (and redefine). Return to the problems posed at the beginning of this chapter, especially the ones asking about the constitutionality of state rather than federal actions. How does the Fourteenth Amendment change your analysis?

The equal protection guarantee was the most intensely litigated of the new rights enforceable against the states. The Supreme Court applied it in *Strauder v. West Virginia*, 100 U.S. 303 (1879), to strike down a law excluding any but "white persons" from juries. The exclusion violated the central theme of abolitionist jurisprudence, "that the law in the States shall be the same for the black as for the white." In *Yick Wo v. Hopkins*, 118 U.S. 356 (1886) (Chapter 3, § 1B), the Court struck down a law whose enforcement discriminated on the basis of (Chinese) ethnicity rather than race.

In its early decisions, however, the Court was not inclined to give the Fourteenth Amendment much bite when discrimination was not related to race or color. In *The Slaughter House Cases*, 83 U.S. (16 Wall.) 36 (1873) (Chapter 5, § 1), the Court held that the Privileges or Immunities Clause of the Fourteenth Amendment was inapplicable to a state grant of local economic monopolies. Economic regulation was a far cry from the central purpose of the amendment, the Court reasoned. The primary protection for individual rights remained state law, and nothing in any of the Reconstruction Amendments was intended to "degrade the State governments by subjecting them to the control of Congress," nor to change radically "the whole theory of the relations of the State and Federal governments to each other and both of these governments to the people."

The same basic reasoning informed the Court's application of the P & I Clause to laws discriminating on the basis of sex. The Court refused to strike down laws excluding women from the practice of law, see *Bradwell v. Illinois*, 83 U.S. 130 (1873) (Chapter 4, § 2A), or the franchise, see *Minor v. Happersett*, 88 U.S. 162 (1874) (id.). These results were no more surprising than those in the race and color cases, however. The women's movement, which had been galvanized at Seneca Falls in 1848 and which had supported abolition, had been spurned by the Republicans drafting the Reconstruction Amendments, especially the Fifteenth. Some feminists, in turn, opposed one or more of the Reconstruction Amendments. Most feminists focused on efforts to override *Happersett* with an amendment to the Constitution.

3.   *The Nation's Retreat from Reconstruction, 1883–1903.* Reconstruction formally came to an end following a deal made between the Republicans and Democrats in 1877. In return for acquiescing in the contested election of Rutherford Hayes as President, the Democrats won the withdrawal of federal troops from the South—an action which left the newly franchised former slaves at the mercy of white planters eager to reestablish their political, economic, and social hegemony. Although the freed slaves continued to assert political power, they were outnumbered and then outmaneuvered all over the South in the 1880s and 1890s. Southern states adopted laws instantiating apartheid, legally requiring segregation of the races and excluding people of color from the franchise, jury service, and other citizenship rights guaranteed by Reconstruction. Northern Republicans turned a blind eye to a literal reign of terror visited upon the freed slaves and their children.

The Supreme Court more or less followed the emerging political consensus. In *The Civil Rights Cases*, 109 U.S. 3 (1883) (Chapter 7, § 3A), the Court ruled that the Fourteenth Amendment did not reach instances of race discrimination by private actors and that Congress therefore had no § 5 authority to bar public accommodation discrimination. Much of the Civil Rights Act of 1875 was swept away by the decision, and Congress did not enact another civil rights measure until 1957. In *Plessy v. Ferguson*, 163 U.S. 537 (1896) (Chapter 2, § 1), the Court ruled that neither the Thirteenth nor Fourteenth Amendments barred the states from requiring racial segregation in railroad transport. Both cases drew dissenting opinions from Justice John Marshall Harlan, an American original. Although he had been a Kentucky slaveowner, Harlan became an anti-slavery Republican and served in the Union Army. His Supreme Court nomination was the result of his crucial support for Rutherford Hayes at the 1876 Republican convention. As a Justice, Harlan is best remembered for his willingness to view issues from the perspective of the politically marginal. He is also said to have been one of the last Justices to chew tobacco on the bench (though the silver spittoons were still in place late in the twentieth century).

In his dissents in *Plessy* and *The Civil Rights Cases*, Harlan argued, persuasively to modern eyes, that the Court's decisions represented a pragmatic but tragic retreat from the values that gave rise to Reconstruction and urged the Court to stand firmly for the equal citizenship of African Americans. But even Harlan did not dissent when the Court assumed that *Plessy* allowed segregated public schools; indeed, he wrote the opinion for the Court in *Cumming v. Richmond County Bd. of Educ.*, 175 U.S. 528 (1899). Nor did he dissent seven years after *Plessy* when the Court unanimously ruled that a federal judge properly declined to issue an injunction against an Alabama voting official who allegedly refused to register more than 5,000 qualified people of color. *Giles v. Harris*, 189 U.S. 475 (1903).

SECTION 5. THE LABOR MOVEMENT, PROGRESSIVISM, AND RIGHTS FOR WOMEN AND BLACKS, 1896–1937

The period after the Civil War was one of great industrial expansion in the North and Midwest—an expansion that stimulated efforts by workers to improve their lot through collective action (labor unions, strikes, and boycotts) and by the state to regulate "abuses" of the new industrial order, including anti-competitive actions by unions, corporate trusts, and railroads. This was not an era in which the Supreme Court engaged in much productive constitutional leadership. During the tenures of Chief Justices Melville Fuller (1888–1910), Edward White (1910–21), and William Howard Taft (1921–30), the Court was sporadically reactionary but more typically drifted from case to case, with little underlying ideological coherence beyond a mild economic libertarianism and a nostalgia for Jefferson's arcadian republic of farmers and shopkeepers. The socio-economic reality, however, was that the United States was becoming an industrial nation of massive trusts, giant railroads, acrimonious labor disputes, and identity-based social movements.

Notwithstanding the Court, the first third of the twentieth century was a generative period for American constitutionalism—yielding important amendments to the Constitution that provided for a federal income tax (XVI, 1913), the direct election of senators (XVII, 1913), and women's suffrage (XIX, 1920); major advances in the ongoing creation of the modern regulatory state, including the first national antitrust law, a food and drug law, and a federal reserve system to manage the flow of money; and doctrinal innovations (typically by state and lower federal court judges), such as the labor injunction, substantive due process, a broad First Amendment, and national rights of criminal procedure. Many of these developments cut across substantive boundaries, highlighting the big tension between the constitutional liberty of contract jurisprudence favored by many judges and the regulatory state's desire to manage the economy more actively.

1.   *The Labor Movement and Liberty of Contract in the* Lochner *Era.* Industrialization generated great hardship for workers, who sought to organize collectively to obtain better wages and working conditions. Beginning in the 1870s, America witnessed often violent strife between labor unions and management, first in the railroads and later across American industries. In this struggle, state and federal judges, like the legal profession generally, were usually allies of management.[27] And the Supreme Court interpreted the Fourteenth Amendment to protect "liberty of contract" against private coercion and state regulation.

This was not the Court's original view; recall *The Slaughter House Cases*. But dissenting opinions by Justices Stephen Field and Joseph Bradley there argued that arbitrary state interference with people's economic interests constituted a violation of the Fourteenth Amendment's Due Process Clause. While the Court declined to invalidate state laws on *substantive due process* grounds during the tenure of Chief Justice Morrison Waite (1874–88), the Fuller Court used that theory as a sharp weapon for business interests against state regulatory legislation, especially laws protecting workers. Justice Field, joined by his nephew, Justice David Brewer, was able to assemble Court majorities to invalidate several state statutes as violating freedom of contract.[28]

The leading substantive due process case, and one whose name has identified the era, was *Lochner v. New York*, 198 U.S. 45 (1905) (Chapter 5, § 2B). In *Lochner*, a closely divided (5–4) Court struck down a New York law limiting the hours bakers could work. The ruling rested on the statute's interference with "the right of contract between the employer and

---

[27] See Arnold Paul, *Conservative Crisis and the Rule of Law: Attitudes of Bar and Bench, 1887–1895* (1960); William Forbath, *Law and the Shaping of the American Labor Movement* (1991); Felix Frankfurter & Nathan Greene, *The Labor Injunction* (1930).

[28] Stephen Field was one of the more colorful Justices of the Court. The brother of David Dudley Field (the great codifier) and Cyrus Field (who laid the first transatlantic cable), Stephen Field grew up in the East, but moved to California in 1849. President Lincoln appointed Field to the Court in 1863, where he served for 34 years, a record of Supreme Court service broken by Justice Douglas, who served for 36 years. His career was marked by intrigue and scandal, leading to an unsuccessful assassination attempt while he was on the Court. On his philosophy, see Charles McCurdy, *Justice Field and the Jurisprudence of Government-Business Relations: Some Parameters of Laissez-Faire Constitutionalism, 1863–1897*, 61 J. Am. Hist. 970 (1975). David Brewer was Field's nephew, the pious son of missionaries (Brewer was born in Asia Minor). Although not as colorful, Brewer was equally dogmatic in his insistence that economic rights to free contracting were protected by the Constitution.

employees," which is "part of the liberty of the individual protected by [the Due Process Clause of] the Fourteenth Amendment." The Court recognized, as it had in *Plessy*, that the state had wide leeway to enact statutes for the protection of the public welfare. But statutes:

> * * * [L]imiting the hours in which grown and intelligent men may labor to earn their living, are mere meddlesome interferences with the rights of the individual, and they are not saved from condemnation by the claim that they are passed in the exercise of the police power and upon the subject of the health of the individual whose rights are interfered with, unless there be some fair ground, * * * to say that there is material danger to the public health or to the health of the employees, if the hours of labor are not curtailed.

The Court was not persuaded by the extensive evidence that long and continuous exposure to heat, fumes, and dust did in fact impair the health of bakers. "It is impossible for us to shut our eyes to the fact that many of the laws of this character, while passed under what is claimed to be the police power[,] * * * are, in reality, passed from other motives," the Court concluded. Indeed, like dozens of laws of the period, the New York bakers' statute was enacted at the behest of unions seeking to impose on nonunionized (smaller) bakeries the same maximum-hour rule that they were obtaining from unionized bakeries.

All but one of the five Justices in the *Lochner* majority had voted to uphold the apartheid statute challenged in *Plessy*. As in *Plessy*, Justice Harlan dissented in *Lochner*. He pointed to the evidence that long hours harmed bakers' health and safety. The statute was invalid only if it bore "no real or substantial relation" to health or safety. "If there be doubt as to the validity of the statute, that doubt must therefore be resolved in favor of its validity, and the courts must keep their hands off, leaving the legislature to meet the responsibility for unwise legislation."

Justice Oliver Wendell Holmes, Jr., who had been nominated for the Court (after *Plessy*) in part because he was skeptical of anti-labor judicial activism, dissented separately. "This case is decided upon an economic theory [laissez-faire] which a large part of the country does not entertain," Holmes contended. Nothing in the Constitution protects "liberty of contract." Sunday closing laws, prohibition on lotteries, and other established regulations, all of which had been upheld, were no less offensive to that "right" than the New York statute. Why should this regulation be struck down while other similar ones have been sustained? As a general matter, Holmes argued for very lenient judicial review under the Due Process Clause:

> * * * [A] constitution is not intended to embody a particular economic theory, whether of paternalism and the organic relation

of the citizen to the State or of *laissez-faire*. It is made for people of fundamentally differing views, and the accident of our finding certain opinions natural and familiar or novel and even shocking ought not conclude our judgment upon the question whether statutes embodying them conflict with the Constitution of the United States.

* * * I think that the word liberty in the Fourteenth Amendment is perverted when it is held to prevent the natural outcome of a dominant opinion, unless it can be said that a rational and fair man necessarily would admit that the statute proposed would infringe fundamental principles as they have been understood by the traditions of our people and our law.

Holmes's philosophy was acquiescent in the overall growth of government regulation during the Progressive era. Railroads fell under increasingly detailed regulation as the Interstate Commerce Act of 1887 was repeatedly expanded. The Sherman Antitrust Act of 1891, expanded by the Clayton Act of 1914, subjected big business to unprecedented administrative and judicial scrutiny. The Pure Food and Drug Act of 1906 created an inspection system for meats and other foodstuffs. All of these statutes, and hundreds of others, limited businesses' freedom to conduct their affairs as they wanted.

In fact, the large majority of the business-restricting statutes survived *Lochner*. Most liberty of contract challenges reaching the Supreme Court were rejected. E.g., *Muller v. Oregon*, 208 U.S. 412 (1908) (Chapter 4, § 2A) (upholding law fixing maximum hours women could work, but for essentially sex-stereotypical, paternalistic reasons). Yet *Lochner* had more than occasional bite, especially when legislatures were perceived to be redistributing wealth or power from entrepreneurs to labor unions, which were viewed with suspicion by hidebound federal judges. For example, in *Coppage v. Kansas*, 236 U.S. 1 (1915), the Court invalidated a state law barring "yellow dog" employment contracts precluding union membership, on the ground that the law prevented willing employers and workers from voluntarily agreeing to such terms. The Court's sporadic activism had little to do with due process, and much to do with fears within the bench and bar that new forms of collective organization—bigger government, labor unions, business trusts and monopolies—threatened the traditional economic rights of individuals to get ahead.

It is hardly surprising that, during the tenures of Chief Justices Fuller, White, and Taft, the Supreme Court sometimes narrowly construed federal power when it compromised the interests of the propertied classes. Thus the Fuller Court struck down the progressive income tax as a violation of Article I, § 9, see *Pollock v. Farmers' Loan and Trust Co.*, 158 U.S. 601 (1895) (overridden by the Sixteenth Amendment), and a federal law prohibiting yellow dog contracts in railroad employment as a violation of the Due Process Clause of the Fifth Amendment, see *Adair v. United States*, 208 U.S. 161 (1908). In contrast, *In re Debs*, 158 U.S. 564 (1895), held that the federal government had direct authority under the Commerce Clause to obtain injunctions to break the Pullman Strike. The Pullman Strike had been the culmination of a decade of labor unrest, especially on the railroads, and the Department of Justice's intervention crushing the strike was a fait accompli that Justice Brewer (who authored the opinion) was determined to uphold. The White Court struck down the federal child labor law as beyond Congress' power to regulate interstate commerce, see *Hammer v. Dagenhart*, 247 U.S. 251 (1918) (Chapter 7, § 2), and the Taft Court invalidated Congress' subsequent effort to discourage child labor under its taxing power, see *Bailey v. Drexel Furniture Co.*, 259 U.S. 20 (1922) (Chapter 7, § 4A). In contrast, the Taft Court authorized federal judges to regulate union-management relations through notorious labor injunctions that were issued by the cartload in the 1920s.

2. *The Progressive Era and the Emerging First Amendment*. While we view this period as a rather dreary one in the Court's history, it was brightened by the prescient dissenting opinions of Justices Holmes (1902–32) and Brandeis (1916–39), who defended the rights of labor unions to form and carry on their economic activities, of states and the federal government to experiment with novel forms of market regulation, and of unpopular individuals and groups to speak out and carry on their own activities without persecution. Theirs was the voice of the future, and nowhere was that more apparent than in the Court's First Amendment jurisprudence.[29]

Holmes, the son of a well-known Boston essayist, may have been the most broadly intellectual person ever to serve on the Court; his private correspondence pithily discusses European thinkers of the time, and he was a friend of the philosopher William James. His capacity for reflection was tested in the seditious speech cases arising out of opposition to American involvement in World War I. A veteran wounded three times while serving in the Union Army during the Civil War, Holmes personally had no use for pacifists, and he warned anti-war protesters in *Schenck v. United States*, 249 U.S. 47 (1919) (Chapter 6, § 2A), that much speech allowable in peacetime was not so during wartime. Upholding the conviction of a man who mailed leaflets objecting to the draft, Holmes announced the requirement that the federal government had to show that, under the circumstances, the assertedly seditious words created a "clear and present danger" of national harm. Although the test was applied

[29] See David Rabban, *Free Speech in Its Forgotten Years* (1997); David Bogen, *The Free Speech Metamorphosis of Mr. Justice Holmes*, 11 Hofstra L. Rev. 97 (1982). See also Gerald Gunther, *Learned Hand and the Origins of Modern First Amendment Doctrine: Some Fragments of History*, 27 Stan. L. Rev. 719 (1975).

harshly to Schenck, it was a doctrinal innovation, for earlier decisions left it unclear whether the First Amendment had any application beyond barring prior restraints. Recall the Sedition Act of 1798, and see also *Patterson v. Colorado*, 205 U.S. 454 (1907) (Holmes, J.); *Fox v. Washington*, 236 U.S. 273 (1915) (nudist art can be censored).

In *Abrams v. United States*, 250 U.S. 616 (1919) (Chapter 6, § 2A), the Court followed *Schenck* to uphold the convictions of Russian-born dissidents for objecting to the Allies' efforts against the Bolsheviks—but over Holmes's objection that the publication of "a silly leaflet by an unknown man" posed no clear and present danger to the American war effort. In his dissent, Holmes endorsed the idea that the First Amendment protects the "free trade in ideas" as the best way to get at "the truth." Holmes's dissent was joined by Brandeis, the brilliant "people's lawyer" whose fact-filled "Brandeis brief" had been persuasive in *Muller*.[30] The latter wrote for himself and Holmes in *Whitney v. California*, 274 U.S. 357 (1927) (Chapter 6, § 2A), which added a different but complementary justification for an aggressive First Amendment: Essential to a vigorous democracy is the "opportunity to discuss freely supposed grievances and proposed remedies," a rationale that demands considerable breathing room for people to say and publish ideas considered false and even dangerous by the majority. Better the citizenry be engaged in rancorous debate than rendered intellectually inert by the censor. The Holmes-Brandeis approach was adopted by Court majorities in *Herndon v. Lowry*, 301 U.S. 242 (1937), and *DeJonge v. Oregon*, 299 U.S. 353 (1937), and ignited a robust First Amendment tradition in American law. (Note that these later cases involved First Amendment challenges to *state* rather than *federal* actions. The Court in *Gitlow v. New York*, 268 U.S. 652 (1925) (Chapter 6, § 2A), assumed that the First Amendment was applicable to the states under the Due Process Clause of the Fourteenth Amendment.)

The free trade in ideas and democracy arguments for a vigorous First Amendment were hardly unique to Holmes and Brandeis; state and federal judges (especially those in cosmopolitan New York) intervened to protect unpopular speech and press in the 1920s and 1930s. This had broad and unanticipated socio-political ramifications. The birth control movement initiated by Emma Goldman and Margaret Sanger was hounded by state authorities opposed to dissemination of contraceptive devices and information, and both Goldman and Sanger were chased off to Europe during World War I. Sanger returned in triumph when charges were

---

[30] Brandeis's nomination was the subject of bitter Senate opposition, partly because of his liberal views and partly because of anti-Semitism. His opinions were sometimes eloquent, but often so heavily documented and detailed that they make for tedious reading today. Holmes and he generally voted to uphold regulations of business, but for different reasons: Brandeis thought regulation was a good idea, while Holmes thought regulation was a form of stupidity in which the public was entitled to indulge.

dismissed against her, in part for First Amendment reasons.[31] Although state authorities harassed early birth control clinics, the movement inexorably gained a foothold in American society and won some important anti-censorship victories in the 1930s. The Second Circuit ruled in *United States v. Dennett*, 39 F.2d 564 (2d Cir. 1930), that the federal government could not censor sex education materials and in *United States v. One Package*, 86 F.2d 737 (2d Cir. 1936), that federal law (properly narrowed) did not bar transportation of diaphragms across state lines. Both Congress and lower courts protected literature seriously discussing issues of sexuality and gender in the 1930s.

3.   *The Women's and Civil Rights Movements.* The *Lochner* era saw considerable pressure to recognize individual civil rights, and the social movements seeking the right to vote for women and civil rights for people of color yielded more lasting constitutional legacies than *Lochner* did. The most dramatic constitutional moment was the ratification of the Nineteenth Amendment in 1920, the culmination of two generations of political activism.[32] Women emancipated from coverture during the nineteenth century insisted on the civil rights and equal citizenship that the Reconstruction Amendments (as interpreted in *Bradwell* and *Happensett*) had failed to deliver to them as they theoretically had to people of color. Opponents of the amendment argued that women's interests were sufficiently represented by the votes of their husbands and that giving women the right to vote would undermine marriage and the family, which were the proper spheres for women as wives (the theme of a concurring opinion in *Bradwell* (Chapter 4, § 2A)).

Unlike the Fifteenth Amendment, the Nineteenth Amendment was implemented without fuss, and women voted without impediment for Warren Harding in 1920. The amendment had some immediate constitutional ramifications. In its wake, a number of state courts reinterpreted laws requiring jury service by all voters to include previously excluded women. Justice George Sutherland, who as a Republican senator from Utah had voted for the Nineteenth Amendment, invoked it in his opinion for the Court in *Adkins v. Children's Hospital*, 261 U.S. 525 (1923), which invalidated a law prescribing minimum wages for female employees.

---

[31] See Ellen Chesler, *Woman of Valor: Margaret Sanger and the Birth Control Movement in America* 127–29, 138–40 (1992); Rabban, *Forgotten Years* 67–70. The Supreme Court upheld Goldman's deportation in *Goldman v. United States*, 245 U.S. 474 (1918), and dismissed Sanger's appeal of her subsequent conviction for violating New York's obscenity law in *Sanger v. People*, 251 U.S. 537 (1919).

[32] See Aileen Kraditor, *The Ideas of the Woman Suffrage Movement, 1890–1920* (1965); Ellen Carol DuBois, *Outgrowing the Compact of the Fathers: Equal Rights, Woman Suffrage, and the United States Constitution, 1820–1878*, 74 J. Am. Hist. 836 (1987); Reva Siegel, *She the People: The Nineteenth Amendment, Sex Equality, and the Family*, 115 Harv. L. Rev. 947 (2002). Another "constitutional moment" engineered by a women's movement was the adoption of the Eighteenth Amendment, which barred the distribution of alcoholic beverages. See Joseph Gusfield, *Symbolic Crusade: Status Politics and the American Temperance Movement* (2d ed. 1986). This was an ill-fated moment, terminated by the Twenty-First Amendment (1933).

To distinguish *Muller*, where the Court had upheld a maximum hour law needed to protect women and the family, Sutherland suggested that the Nineteenth Amendment put women on an equal footing with men, thereby undermining state arguments that women need to be "protected" against workplace conditions that would be tolerable for men.

Many feminists saw their next constitutional step as full legal equality, and in 1923 supporters introduced an Equal Rights Amendment (ERA) in Congress. Although such a constitutional amendment was introduced in most Congresses after 1923, it went nowhere for decades, in part because women's groups were themselves divided as to the desirability of formal equality.[33] Some feared that the ERA would abrogate labor legislation protecting women, just as *Adkins* had suggested that the Nineteenth Amendment would undercut the authority of *Muller*. Others believed that the ERA would undermine women's special position as the glue binding the family together. Still others strongly supported the ERA.

At the same time women were rectifying one of Reconstruction's gaps with the Nineteenth Amendment, African Americans and their allies were organizing to reclaim the lost legacy of Reconstruction. The National Association for the Advancement of Colored People (NAACP) was formed in 1908 and immediately commenced a litigation campaign against southern abuse of black people.[34] The NAACP and other civil rights groups won several landmark Supreme Court decisions which created national rights for criminal defendants through liberal constructions of the Fourteenth Amendment.[35] Relying on the Fifteenth as well as the Fourteenth Amendment, the NAACP successfully challenged voting exclusions, including the notorious system of "whites only" primaries in the South. See *Nixon v. Herndon*, 273 U.S. 536 (1927). Finally, and most importantly, the NAACP stood opposed to apartheid, resisting its expansion into housing ordinances, *Buchanan v. Warley*, 245 U.S. 60 (1917), and initiating a multifaceted campaign in the 1930s against unequal treatment of blacks in public education (Chapter 2, § 1B).

Unlike women, who had access to an occasionally responsive political process, people of color were blocked from political reform by apartheid in the South and dominance of the U.S. Senate by southern members. (Even such elemental reform as anti-lynching legislation was unobtainable from

---

[33] See Cynthia Harrison, *On Account of Sex: The Politics of Women's Issues, 1945–1968* (1988); Verta Taylor, *Social Movement Continuity: The Women's Movement in Abeyance*, 54 Am. Soc. Rev. 761 (1989).

[34] See Charles Flint Kellogg, *NAACP: A History of the National Association for the Advancement of Colored People* (1967); James McPherson, *The Abolitionist Legacy: From Reconstruction to the NAACP* (1975).

[35] E.g., *Moore v. Dempsey*, 261 U.S. 86 (1923) (trial influenced by outside mob violates due process); *Powell v. Alabama*, 287 U.S. 45 (1932) (defendant has due process right to counsel in capital cases); *Norris v. Alabama*, 294 U.S. 587 (1935) (exclusion of blacks from jury violates equal protection); *Brown v. Mississippi*, 297 U.S. 278 (1936) (due process forbids the use of confessions obtained by police coercion).

the Senate.) Federal courts were the only forum willing to listen to black people's complaints of extraordinary mistreatment. Notably, conservative Justices like William Howard Taft and George Sutherland, as well as moderates like Owen Roberts and Charles Evans Hughes, and progressives like Oliver Wendell Holmes, Louis Brandeis, and Benjamin Cardozo, were all willing to grant relief in cases involving lawless treatment of black criminal defendants. In the 1930s, civil rights cases took on an even greater normative urgency, as many Americans came to realize that apartheid resembled the racist policies of Nazi Germany and that the marginalization of African Americans in the South rendered our contrast between American democracy and Russian and German totalitarianism vulnerable if not hypocritical. Accordingly, the NAACP escalated its litigation campaigns against apartheid and unfair criminal process, to an increasingly receptive Supreme Court.

SECTION 6. THE NEW DEAL, THE COURT-PACKING CONTROVERSY, AND THE *CAROLENE* COURT, 1937–1953

The critical election of 1932 made Franklin Delano Roosevelt President and inaugurated a new era in American politics. The winning political coalition assembled by FDR included labor unions and people of color as well as southerners and (some) businesses. The New Deal's many regulatory experiments expanded the scope of the national government and were irrefutable evidence that the United States was an administrative regulatory state rather than the common law laissez-faire entity presumed by the *Lochner* jurisprudence. World War II, the greatest governmental project of the century, not only confirmed the enormous authority of the central government, but also accelerated social change, stimulating new normative aspirations and then constitutional demands by people of color, women, and gay people. The Supreme Court of Chief Justices Charles Evans Hughes (1930–41), Harlan Fiske Stone (1941–46), and Fred Vinson (1946–53) was swept along by these great changes.

1. *The Four Horsemen and Constitutional Crisis (1934–37).* The New Deal entailed much more substantial federal management of the economy than had been tried before, and some of FDR's innovative programs fell athwart the scrutiny of a Supreme Court consisting of four staunch defenders of the *Lochner* philosophy (McReynolds, VanDevanter, Sutherland, and Butler, collectively dubbed the "Four Horsemen"); three Holmesian liberals (Brandeis, Stone, and Cardozo); and two centrists (Hughes and Roberts).

Perhaps surprisingly, the early returns from the Court were mildly encouraging, as almost all federal and state regulatory legislation survived judicial review in 1934.[36] For example, in *Home Building & Loan Ass'n v. Blaisdell*, 290 U.S. 398 (1934), the Court rejected a Contracts Clause challenge to a state moratorium on mortgage foreclosures and sales. Although he emphasized that "[e]mergency does not increase granted power or remove or diminish the restrictions imposed upon power," Hughes essentially weighed the "vital public interests" pressed by the state against "temporary and conditional" impositions on creditors' rights, a balance calibrated to favor the state. This was the beginning of the Contracts Clause's slow decline.

The Court was more hostile to federal as well as state regulatory measures in 1935, and the axe fell on parts of the New Deal. Thus, the Court invalidated the Railroad Retirement Act in *Railroad Retirement Board v. Alton Railroad Co.*, 295 U.S. 330 (1935) (statute held unrelated to asserted Commerce Clause justification). A key program, the National Industrial Recovery Act, was the next to fall, and to a unanimous Court in *A.L.A. Schechter Poultry Corp. v. United States*, 295 U.S. 495 (1935) (Chapter 8, § 2A) (excessive delegation of congressional power to private groups). In *Carter v. Carter Coal Co.*, 298 U.S. 238 (1936), a divided Court found insufficient federal Commerce Clause power to regulate local coal production. The Agricultural Adjustment Act fell to the Four Horsemen in *United States v. Butler*, 297 U.S. 1 (1936), and the Horsemen served notice that liberty of contract remained a viable limit on government regulation when they (plus Justice Roberts) struck down state minimum wage legislation in *Morehead v. New York ex rel. Tipaldo*, 298 U.S. 587 (1936). Note that the Court's most divisive decisions came in cases where legislatures were redistributing wealth or power from capital to labor, the essential complaint of the old *Lochner* majority.

FDR fumed while the Court dismantled much of his program in 1935–36. But he did more than fume—he took his case to the people, who in 1936 gave him an electoral vote landslide and returned enormous Democratic majorities in both Houses of Congress. Armed and perhaps inflated with this electoral mandate, FDR stunned the legal establishment in February 1937 with his "Court-packing plan." Essentially, the plan was to add one Justice to the Court for each Justice over 70 years old, in order (the President said) to ameliorate the "heavy burden" faced by the Court "handicapped by insufficient personnel with which to meet a growing and more complex business" (reviewing those long and technical New Deal statutes, to be sure). Since there were six Justices older than 70 in 1937,

---

[36] E.g., *Nebbia v. New York*, 291 U.S. 502 (1934). The traditional understanding of the Old Court seeking to thwart the New Deal has been challenged by a more subtle understanding of an Old Court accommodating some but not all of the New Deal program. See Barry Cushman, *Rethinking the New Deal Court: The Structure of a Constitutional Revolution* (1998); Barry Friedman, *The History of the Countermajoritarian Difficulty, Part Four: Law's Politics*, 148 U. Pa. L. Rev. 971 (2000); Richard Friedman, *Switching Time and Other Thought Experiments: The Hughes Court and Constitutional Transformation*, 142 U. Pa. L. Rev. 1891 (1994).

the Court-packing plan would have allowed FDR to appoint Justices who could have been counted on to protect the New Deal against constitutional challenge. One didn't have to be very clever to see what the President was up to. Many of his staunchest supporters were horrified that FDR would "politicize" the Supreme Court.

2. *The "Switch in Time"? Or a Switch in Personnel?* Although the Court-packing plan stirred up a big controversy, the Justices themselves were probably critical in defeating it. A letter from Chief Justice Hughes and Justices Brandeis and VanDevanter to Senator Wheeler in March 1937 dispelled any conceivable argument that the Court needed younger Justices to catch up in its work; the letter noted that the Court was already caught up, thank you, and that increasing the size of the Court would only slow things down. More important, the Court handed down two important pro-New Deal decisions during the debate in the spring of 1937—*NLRB v. Jones & Laughlin Steel Corp.*, 301 U.S. 1 (1937) (Chapter 7, § 2), which sustained the National Labor Relations Act against Commerce Clause challenge, and *West Coast Hotel Co. v. Parrish*, 300 U.S. 379 (1937) (Chapter 5, § 2B), which overruled *Adkins* and deflated substantive due process challenges to state labor legislation. Chief Justice Hughes wrote the opinions in both cases, silently joined by poor Justice Roberts, whose change of heart has been branded by history as "the switch in time that saved nine." The Senate Judiciary Committee officially killed the Court-packing plan in June 1937.

Ironically, the Court-packing plan was ultimately unnecessary. It would have given FDR six immediate appointments, but between 1937 and 1941 he got a chance to appoint seven new Justices because of retirements and deaths. Thus FDR appointed to the Court Senator Hugo Black, one of the New Deal's staunchest allies; Solicitor General Stanley Reed; Professor Felix Frankfurter of the Harvard Law School, a leading member of FDR's brain trust and mentor to many young officials staffing the New Deal; SEC Chair and former Yale Law Professor William O. Douglas; Attorney General Frank Murphy and Senator James Byrnes, both early and ardent political allies of FDR; and Attorney General Robert Jackson. FDR also elevated Justice Harlan Stone, a liberal Republican, to be Chief Justice in 1941. On the whole, the New Deal Justices were young, talented, and loyal to the President who appointed them. They transformed constitutional law.[37]

It is instructive to compare the procedural aspects of the transformation of constitutional law that occurred during the New Deal to

---

[37] See generally William Leuchtenburg, *The Supreme Court Reborn: The Constitutional Revolution in the Age of Roosevelt* (1995); Daniel Farber, *Who Killed* Lochner?, 90 Geo. L.J. 985 (2002) (reviewing G. Edward White, *The Constitution and the New Deal* (2000)); Mark Tushnet, *The New Deal Constitutional Revolution: Law, Politics, or What?*, 66 U. Chi. L. Rev. 1061 (1999) (reviewing Barry Cushman, *Rethinking the New Deal Court* (1998)).

those aspects of an earlier transformative "moment," that of Reconstruction, that were examined earlier. Recall that Reconstruction involved a major textual alteration of the constitutional document (the addition of the Thirteenth, Fourteenth, and Fifteenth Amendments) in the aftermath of a civil war, through a federally coerced ratification process that seems hard to square with the original expectations surrounding Article V. The New Deal transformation strayed even further from constitutional formalism, because it involved no formal amendment to the Constitution at all. In the New Deal, the combined pressure of the President and Congress, plus the coincidences of death, disability, and judicial appointments, led to a fundamental change in constitutional law. A reconstituted Supreme Court decisively changed direction.

3.   *The Revolution of the New Deal Court*: Carolene Products *Footnote Four*. The New Deal Justices reinterpreted the Commerce Clause precedents to vest Congress with broad power not only to regulate economic activities affecting interstate commerce, e.g., *United States v. Darby*, 312 U.S. 100 (1941) (Chapter 7, § 2), but also to aggregate the effects of those activities as a basis for regulation. *Wickard v. Filburn*, 317 U.S. 111 (1942) (same). The New Deal Court halted any serious judicial review of economic legislation and interpreted regulatory laws, especially regulations of labor-management relations, very broadly. For example, the New Deal Court's interpretation of the Norris-LaGuardia Act in *Milk Wagon Drivers' Union v. Lake Valley Farm Products*, 311 U.S. 91 (1940), took federal courts out of the labor injunction business for the next generation. But at the same time it was giving up its role in protecting economic rights, the Court also cautiously began to assume a more aggressive role in protecting individual civil liberties. As much of this book is devoted to a detailed consideration of the Supreme Court's late twentieth-century decisions following in these traditions, we will give only a brief sketch here.

Many of the aspects of the shift from economic rights to civil liberties are evident in *United States v. Carolene Products Co.*, 304 U.S. 144 (1938). Justice Stone's opinion for the Court upheld the constitutionality of a federal statute prohibiting the interstate shipment of "filled milk" (milk from which the butter fat has been extracted and vegetable oil substituted). The Court deferred to a congressional finding that filled milk was "injurious to the public health" because it was not as nourishing as "pure milk." This congressional "finding" is debatable scientifically and in any event seemingly remediable simply by a labeling requirement (e.g., "Contains Filled Milk—Not as Nourishing as Pure Milk, but Less Expensive"). In addition, powerful economic interests had selfish motives for supporting such a statute. Should the Court provide some meaningful scrutiny of statutes that may simply represent political deals among powerful interests, to the detriment of the less powerful, like consumers?

In other words, is this too much abdication of judicial responsibility to review economic regulation?

As *Carolene Products* reduced the degree of judicial scrutiny applicable to economic regulation, it suggested, in its now-famous footnote 4, a new set of roles for the Supreme Court:

> There may be narrower scope for operation of the presumption of constitutionality when legislation appears on its face to be within a specific prohibition of the Constitution, such as those of the first ten amendments, which are deemed equally specific when held to be embraced within the Fourteenth. [Citing First Amendment cases.]

> It is unnecessary to consider now whether legislation which restricts those political processes which can ordinarily be expected to bring about repeal of undesirable legislation, is to be subjected to more exacting judicial scrutiny under the general prohibitions of the Fourteenth Amendment than are most other types of legislation. [Citing cases involving the rights to vote, to disseminate information, to organize politically, and to assemble peaceably.]

> Nor need we enquire whether similar considerations enter into the review of statutes directed at particular religious * * * or national * * * or racial minorities[;] whether prejudice against discrete and insular minorities may be a special condition, which tends seriously to curtail the operation of those political processes ordinarily to be relied upon to protect minorities, and which may call for a correspondingly more searching judicial inquiry * * *.

Justice Stone's new roadmap for judicial review was directly inspired by the civil rights movement's normative claim that the Constitution ought to protect people of color and other minorities against "lawless" or "corrupt" local political processes.[38]

The first paragraph of the footnote (which Stone added at the behest of Chief Justice Hughes) seems uncontroversial after *Marbury*: The Court should apply meaningful scrutiny and strike down legislation that violates express constitutional prohibitions. But *Carolene* assumed that these prohibitions also apply to the states through the Fourteenth Amendment, which was a process the NAACP was steadily advancing in its criminal procedure cases. After *Carolene*, the Supreme Court declined to incorporate all the Bill of Rights into the Due Process Clause, see *Adamson v.*

---

[38] See David Bixby, *The Roosevelt Court, Democratic Ideology, and Minority Rights: Another Look at* United States v. Classic, 90 Yale L.J. 741 (1981), which demonstrates from personal archives that the *Carolene* Justices—especially Stone, Frankfurter, Douglas, and Black—were specifically motivated by the national embarrassment of apartheid and the Nazi-like injustices toward people of color in the South.

California, 332 U.S. 46 (1947) (Chapter 5, § 1), but nonetheless applied particular Bill of Rights protections to state criminal processes. Thus, the Court followed the NAACP's suggestion that due process guaranteed criminal defendants rights not to be convicted on the basis of involuntary confessions, see *Chambers v. Florida*, 309 U.S. 227 (1940); by juries not representative of the community, *Smith v. Texas*, 311 U.S. 128 (1940); and in complex felony proceedings where they were not represented by counsel, *Betts v. Brady*, 316 U.S. 455 (1942). Additionally, the "specific" prohibitions the footnote had in mind, like the First Amendment's protection of speech, are vague and susceptible to any number of judicial constructions. So in *Thornhill v. Alabama*, 310 U.S. 88 (1940), the Court ruled that peaceful picketing was "speech" fully protected by the First Amendment, but just as plausible a construction (and one supported by precedent) would have considered picketing "conduct" not protected by the amendment. For an even more dramatic example, Justice Black's opinion for the Court in *The Steel Seizure Case*, 343 U.S. 579 (1952) (Chapter 8, § 1A), overrode President Truman's seizure of the steel industry during the Korean War on the ground that he was usurping the "legislative" power completely vested in Congress by Article I—but dissenters supported the President's argument that he was carrying out core "executive" duties (given him by Article II), including those vested by the Commander-in-Chief Clause of Article II, § 2. Recall the similar debate over Lincoln's exercise of lawmaking powers during the Civil War, but contrast the different results reached by the Taney and Vinson Courts in *The Prize Cases* and *The Steel Seizure Case*.

The second paragraph of footnote 4 has been more controversial and no easier to apply in practice. This paragraph suggests that judicial deference to statutes such as the one concerning filled milk is based at least in part on a judicial presumption of a fair political playing field. If there is reason to doubt that presumption then there is also less reason to defer to the political process. This justification for undeferential judicial scrutiny might be traced to Madison's observations about local political lock-ins in *Federalist* No. 10 and was justified in the 1930s by reference to the idea that free and open democratic decisionmaking is important for law's legitimacy. See John Hart Ely, *Democracy and Distrust* (1980) (Chapter 2, § 3B), for a more recent articulation. As Justice Brandeis's opinion in *Whitney* had suggested, this was a rationale for a broad view of "speech" protected by the First Amendment: Because picketing is conduct that is "expressive," and a way that workers (and later civil rights demonstrators) can object to the status quo, *Thornhill's* liberal view of "speech" is supportable under paragraph 2. For another example, the illegitimacy of local governments entrenched by restricting the franchise was the NAACP's pitch for strict scrutiny of southern white primaries in *Nixon v. Herndon* and subsequent cases, as well as subsequent "one person, one vote" challenges to state legislative apportionment (Chapter 5, § 3A). One controversial aspect of this approach is that neither the text of the Constitution nor its history explicitly supports it, and thus it is subject to the charge of judicial activism. A narrower objection is the difficulty in defining what structural defects in democracy are important enough to warrant higher judicial scrutiny.

The third paragraph of footnote 4 has also been controversial. It suggests that the strategy of the second paragraph is insufficient, standing alone, to promote fair politics. For example, even if the formal political rules about voting and so on are fair, a "discrete and insular minority" against which the majority is prejudiced is still likely to lose. The key to the third paragraph is "prejudice," a distortion of the political process under which certain minorities are rendered politically powerless. Illustratively, even if minority citizens in some communities in the mid-twentieth century were able to vote and organize politically, school segregation by race would continue if racially biased political leaders did not need any political support from the minority community. Hence, paragraph 3 was inspired in part by the NAACP's early litigation campaign against apartheid, and in part by prejudice-based municipal discrimination against minority religious groups such as the Jehovah's Witnesses. As with paragraph 2, paragraph 3's theory supporting stringent judicial scrutiny can find no constitutional text specifically supporting it. Moreover, note the difficult definitional questions posed by paragraph 3 (e.g., what is a "discrete and insular minority," and what is "prejudice"). A related problem is where to draw the line on political fairness: For example, should consumers be heard about their inability to prevent the adoption of self-serving economic regulation, like a filled milk statute?

The *Carolene* Court of the 1940s was one that sometimes enforced human rights to protect minorities, as the Stone Court did in *West Virginia State Board of Education v. Barnette*, 319 U.S. 624 (1943) (protecting religious minorities against being required to recite the Pledge of Allegiance in school), and as the Vinson Court did in *Shelley v. Kraemer*, 334 U.S. 1 (1948) (Chapter 3, § 2) (barring courts from enforcing racially restrictive covenants in property transfers). Justice Jackson's opinion for the Court in *Barnette* was a particularly eloquent statement of the new regime's efforts to protect human rights. Like Brandeis before him, Jackson tied the liberty-protecting First Amendment rule against coerced speech to the intellectual and spiritual diversity of American democracy—the very democratic values the United States was fighting to preserve in World War II. He closed his opinion: "If there is any fixed star in our constitutional constellation, it is that no official, high or petty, can prescribe what shall be orthodox in politics, nationalism, religion, or other matters of opinion or force citizens to confess by word or act their faith therein."

Other times, however, the Court recognized that *Carolene* values were at stake but declined for pragmatic reasons to enforce them. The best (or worst) example of this phenomenon was the Court's response to the federal government's treatment of Japanese-American citizens during World War II. Citing evidence later revealed to have been incorrect and probably perjured, the Army insisted that the loyalty of such citizens could not be presumed. Based upon such suppositions, the Army imposed a curfew on Japanese Americans and then directed that they be evacuated from their homes and relocated in detention camps. These citizens challenged this racially discriminatory treatment under the Fifth Amendment. In *Hirabayashi v. United States*, 320 U.S. 81 (1943), and *Korematsu v. United States*, 323 U.S. 214 (1944), the Supreme Court recognized that the Due Process Clause of the Fifth Amendment regulates racially discriminatory federal laws and that laws restricting the rights of a single racial group are "immediately suspect" and ought to be subjected to the "most rigid scrutiny." Deferring to the Army's assertions of compelling wartime emergency, however, the Court upheld the federal government's curfew (*Hirabayashi*) and evacuation from their homes (*Korematsu*) of Japanese Americans. In *Ex parte Endo*, 323 U.S. 283 (1944), however, the Court ruled that the Army did *not* have legal authority to detain concededly loyal Japanese-American citizens. Because of the racist motivations for targeting only Japanese Americans for special disability, and the corrupt evidence adduced by the government, *Hirabayashi* and *Korematsu* are two of the most criticized Supreme Court decisions of the twentieth century.

SECTION 7. THE WARREN COURT AND THE TRIUMPH OF THE CIVIL RIGHTS MOVEMENT, 1953–1969

An underlying theme of *Carolene Products* was that centralization of power in the national government (the New Deal, World War II) went hand in glove with advances in the civil rights movement (the NAACP). The apex of these twin developments came after the appointment of Governor Earl Warren of California as Chief Justice in 1953. Warren was a major Republican Party figure (Thomas Dewey's running mate for the White House in 1948), enjoyed virtually unprecedented popularity as Governor of California, and helped Dwight Eisenhower win the Republican nomination for President in 1952. Warren's nomination as Chief Justice was probably President Eisenhower's payback of the marker Warren held for his efforts in 1952. Warren did not come to the position with deep legal erudition, or even unusual analytical ability. But he did bring a sense of justice and a tremendous political ability to lead the Court in new, and sometimes radical and controversial, directions. At oral argument, he was prone to brush aside what he considered legal technicalities and ask lawyers to defend the fairness of their positions.[39]

The Warren Court was committed to the legitimacy of the New Deal and centralization of power in Washington, D.C., as well as protecting individual human rights along the lines suggested in *Carolene*. Within that consensus, there was sometimes fierce debate as to how activist the Court should be; much of the debate was shaped by two New Deal appointees, Justices Hugo Black and Felix Frankfurter. Black grew up in a small town in Alabama and received his law degree from the University of Alabama. He was a part-time police court judge and prosecutor. After serving in the military and practicing law for a few years, he ran for the U.S. Senate. He was a key Roosevelt supporter in Congress. After his appointment to the Court, the public was shocked to learn that he had briefly been a member of the Ku Klux Klan, but Black was a strong supporter of civil rights, at least until near the end of his career. He was famous for carrying a copy of the Constitution with him and consulting it when legal questions arose, giving him the appearance of an unsophisticated rustic, but his library showed that he had also read deeply in American history. Black championed the views that the Bill of Rights applied to the states via the Fourteenth Amendment and that the First Amendment was an "absolute." He defended these clear-cut positions with a stubborn eloquence that eventually moved the Court a long way in his direction. Together with William O. Douglas,[40] Hugo Black was for decades the most outspoken civil libertarian on the Court.

Black and Douglas were often aligned against Felix Frankfurter. Frankfurter was an immigrant who worked his way out of the Lower East Side, through a spectacular career as a law student at Harvard, and rose to become a leading member of the Harvard law faculty. He was a key adviser to FDR, a role he continued even after he was appointed to the Supreme Court in 1939. Frankfurter was a strong believer in doctrines of judicial restraint, such as *stare decisis* (the Court must usually follow its prior interpretations of the Constitution), the rule of law (the Court should normally follow the plain meaning and original intent of statutes), and the avoidance of political questions. His later reputation as an anti-civil libertarian is ironic, since he wrote or joined many libertarian decisions

---

[39] See, e.g., Bernard Schwartz, *Super Chief* (1983); G. Edward White, *Earl Warren: A Public Life* (1982). There were limits to Warren's "sense of justice": He was an important figure supporting the evacuation and detention of Japanese-American citizens during World War II, convened a special session of the California legislature to enact the most aggressively antigay legislation in American history, and during his service on the Court was no particular friend of equal rights for women. See William Eskridge, Jr., *Dishonorable Passions: American Sodomy Law, 1861–2003* (2008) (detailed history of Warren's anti-homosexual record as governor).

[40] Douglas had been a rising young star as a law professor, first at Columbia and then at Yale. He then became the first chair of the Securities and Exchange Commission, and perhaps more important for his future, a poker-playing buddy of FDR. He was appointed in 1939. Over the course of his career, he earned a reputation for both extraordinary brilliance and exceptional carelessness. He was also the most dedicated environmentalist to serve on the Court.

and before his service on the Court was a public supporter of Sacco and Vanzetti, a founder of the American Civil Liberties Union, and an advisor to the NAACP. Nevertheless, by the end of his career on the bench, he was constantly at war with Black and the Warren Court majority over what he perceived as their undue judicial activism. It was only after Frankfurter left the bench that the Warren Court had a solid majority of activist liberals, but Frankfurter continued his judicial restraint campaign from the grave: His intellectual disciple John Marshall Harlan (grandson of the *Plessy* dissenter) took over as the leading dissenter, and many of his law clerks, such as Alexander Bickel, became leading legal scholars and continued his campaign against the Warren Court majority.

1.   *The Triumph of the Civil Rights Movement: The Warren Court vs. Apartheid.* The replacement of Fred Vinson with Earl Warren as Chief Justice reportedly broke the Supreme Court's ambivalence about how to handle the NAACP's massive challenge to segregated public schools in *Brown v. Board of Education*, 347 U.S. 483 (1954) (state segregation), and *Bolling v. Sharpe*, 347 U.S. 497 (1954) (segregation in D.C. schools, challenged under the Fifth Amendment) (Chapter 2, § 1). Warren's unanimous decisions striking down school segregation are, we believe, the most important judicial decisions of the post-World-War II era. They embodied the virtues Warren wanted judicial review to foster: equality of opportunity as the goal, fairness as the guidepost, and public morality as the basis for evaluation. The opinions were also illustrative of the central quandary of judicial review: In a representative democracy, what gives the unelected Court the authority to overturn popular desires? How is *Brown* any more legitimate than *Dred Scott* or *Lochner*? Most of the important constitutional theorizing in the last forty years has been directly or indirectly in response to *Brown*. For that reason, Chapter 2 starts with that case, explores it in some detail, and uses it as an introduction to the "big theories" of judicial review. We then systematically examine the doctrinal and theoretical issues raised by the Equal Protection Clause, first in connection with racial classifications (Chapter 3) and then in connection with gender and other classifications (Chapter 4). This focus on individual rights would have been unlikely before the New Deal, and the focus on equality unthinkable before the Warren Court.

Although Warren's opinion in *Brown* focused on the importance of public education and the baleful effects of *de jure* segregation on black schoolchildren, civil rights attorneys read the case as finally giving bite to the *Hirabayashi* and *Korematsu* dictum that race-based classifications are "odious to a free people." The Warren Court confirmed that interpretation in *Loving v. Virginia*, 388 U.S. 1 (1967) (Chapter 3, § 1A), which struck down a state law barring different-race marriages. The Chief Justice's opinion for the Court recognized what appeared to be a per se rule against race-based classifications rooted in the discredited philosophy of "white supremacy." Implicitly after *Brown* and explicitly after *Loving*, race-based classifications were at least "suspect" in American law and required the most compelling state interest to support them.

Brown had enormous and complicated ramifications for American public law generally. Some historians think that *Brown* encouraged the civil rights movement to ever more aggressive challenges to apartheid.[41] The Montgomery bus boycott of 1955–56 (led by Dr. Martin Luther King and his Southern Christian Leadership Conference) was formally resolved in favor of the opponents of racial segregation when the Supreme Court affirmed a lower court ruling that the challenged regime was unconstitutional. *Gayle v. Browder*, 352 U.S. 903 (1956) (per curiam). As the civil rights movement became a mass social movement, with activism focused outside the courtroom, the Warren Court repeatedly struck down southern efforts to suppress peaceful protests, usually through doctrinal innovation under the First Amendment. Thus, the Court created a "freedom of association" (Chapter 6, § 6) to protect the NAACP against state harassment in *NAACP v. Alabama*, 357 U.S. 449 (1958); extended *Thornhill* to protect mass protest marches in *Edwards v. South Carolina*, 372 U.S. 229 (1963), and *Cox v. Louisiana*, 379 U.S. 559 (1965); and created heightened burdens of proof for convictions of lunch counter sit-in protesters in *Garner v. Louisiana*, 368 U.S. 157 (1961). These cases expanded the First Amendment's reach: Not only was expressive conduct protected by the Speech Clause, but group actions, through associations, sit-ins, and protest marches, were protected as well.

Most scholars believe that, whatever the impact of *Brown*, the greatest payoffs for the civil rights movement were the Civil Rights Act of 1964 and the Voting Rights Act of 1965. These enactments were broad assertions of congressional authority and placed the resources of the federal government behind the anti-segregation principle. The Warren Court upheld these statutes against federalism-based attacks in cases excerpted and discussed in Chapter 7. In the cases upholding the 1964 Act, the Court interpreted the Commerce Clause expansively (Chapter 7, § 2); in the cases upholding the 1965 Act, the Court interpreted congressional power to enforce the Fourteenth and Fifteenth Amendments expansively (id. § 3B). During the 1960s, federalism—which had been the shibboleth for the South's massive resistance to integration—seemed deflated. National policy as well as reformist energy were increasingly focused on the national government.

---

[41] David Garrow, *Bearing the Cross: Martin Luther King, Jr., and the Southern Christian Leadership Conference* (1986); Richard Kluger, *Simple Justice: The History of* Brown v. Board of Education *and Black America's Struggle for Equality* (1975). Compare Gerald Rosenberg, *The Hollow Hope: Can Courts Bring About Social Change?* (1991) (no), with Michael Klarman, Brown, *Racial Change, and the Civil Rights Movement*, 80 Va. L. Rev. 7 (1994) (*Brown* brought about change only indirectly, by triggering hysterical southern opposition), with David Garrow, *Hopelessly Hollow History: Revisionist Devaluing of* Brown v. Board of Education, 80 Va. L. Rev. 151 (1994) (vigorously disputing both Rosenberg and Klarman).

2. *The Evolving Protection of Individual Rights Against Both State and National Infringement.* Responding to cases brought by civil rights groups, the New Deal Court had imported federal criminal procedure standards into the Due Process Clause's assurances of rights in state proceedings. In the 1960s, the Court engaged in a process of *selective incorporation* of most of the specific criminal procedure protections of the Bill of Rights into the Due Process Clause (Chapter 6, § 1); see Jerrold Israel, *Selective Incorporation Revisited*, 71 Geo. L.J. 253 (1982). The Warren Court responded to the terror often visited on people of color by racist police officers (in the North as well as South), and this concern for protecting vulnerable defendants from overbearing police led the Court to expand upon the Bill of Rights' protections in the new due process cases. For example, the Chief Justice ruled in *Miranda v. Arizona*, 384 U.S. 436 (1966), that the police could not interrogate accused persons without telling them of their constitutional rights to remain silent and to speak with an attorney, including an attorney paid for by the state if the accused could not afford one, see *Gideon v. Wainwright*, 372 U.S. 335 (1963). The result of the Court's activism was the creation of a *constitutional code of national criminal procedure* in the 1960s, a code that was trimmed back in the 1970s and 1980s but whose character remains part of American public law to this day. E.g., *Dickerson v. United States*, 530 U.S. 428 (2000) (reaffirming *Miranda* as a constitutional rule binding on federal as well as state law enforcement). Because these cases are usually the subject of a whole course in criminal procedure, this casebook does not treat them in detail.

A second aspect of the Warren Court's Due Process Clause jurisprudence bolstered the void-for-vagueness doctrine. Before 1960, the Court periodically struck down "vague" criminal laws that gave insufficient notice to potential violators. E.g., *Stromberg v. California*, 283 U.S. 359 (1931) (anti-sedition law); *Joseph Burstyn, Inc. v. Wilson*, 343 U.S. 495 (1952) (movie licensing law). After 1960, especially in the civil rights protest cases, the Court emphasized different vices of vague laws: they gave police discretion to go after unpopular persons or groups, thereby chilling their exercise of free speech rights. E.g., *NAACP v. Button*, 371 U.S. 415, 432–33 (1963); *Shuttlesworth v. Birmingham*, 382 U.S. 87, 90–92 (1965); *Cox*, 397 U.S. at 551–52 (Black, J., concurring); see Anthony Amsterdam, Note, *The Void-for-Vagueness Doctrine in the Supreme Court*, 109 U. Pa. L. Rev. 67, 88–90 (1960). Although these protest cases represented the high point of the Court's enforcement of the void-for-vagueness doctrine, it retains bite to this day—primarily for the arbitrary enforcement and chilling effect reasons. See *City of Chicago v. Morales*, 527 U.S. 41 (1999), following *Papachristou v. City of Jacksonville*, 405 U.S. 156 (1972) (Chapter 6, § 5).

Although not always consistent with its general *Carolene* philosophy, the Warren Court was also open to recognizing unenumerated but "fundamental" rights: the right to vote (discussed below); the right to travel, see *Shapiro v. Thompson*, 394 U.S. 618 (1969); and the *right to privacy*. Next to *Brown* and its voting rights decisions, the Warren Court precedent with the greatest legal repercussions may have been *Griswold v. Connecticut*, 381 U.S. 479 (1965) (Chapter 5, § 4A), which struck down a law restricting the use of contraceptives as a violation of a right to personal privacy located within the "penumbras" of the Bill of Rights. The Court as protector of fundamental rights is nothing new, see the Takings Clause of the Fifth Amendment and the *Lochner* era's liberty of contract idea, and the Warren Court argued that the right to privacy had deep roots in American public law. Chapter 5, § 4 explores this issue, focusing on the controversies surrounding *Roe v. Wade*, 410 U.S. 113 (1973) (Chapter 5, § 4B), which provided substantial protection for a woman's right to have an abortion, and *Bowers v. Hardwick*, 478 U.S. 186 (1986) (id. § 4C), which provided no protection for private consensual sex by gay men or lesbians.

Consistent with *Carolene*, the Warren Court expanded the reach of the First Amendment even in non-race cases. For example, the Court gave greater bite to Holmes's "clear and present danger" requirement for state regulation of "seditious" speech. In *Dennis v. United States*, 341 U.S. 494 (1951), the Vinson Court had upheld the Smith Act, which made it illegal for anyone to advocate the overthrow of our form of government. Although the Act was aimed at extinguishing the American Communist Party, the Warren Court held that Smith Act convictions based on abstract advocacy were inconsistent with the First Amendment. *Yates v. United States*, 354 U.S. 298 (1957); *Scales v. United States*, 367 U.S. 203 (1961) (Chapter 6, § 2A). In these and other cases, the Warren Court repudiated the political tradition that had inspired the Sedition Act of 1798.

The Warren Court's philosophy of the Religion Clauses was similarly aggressive and individualist. Enforcing the "wall of separation" suggested in *Everson v. Board of Education*, 330 U.S. 1 (1947) (Chapter 6, § 7B), the Warren Court applied the Establishment Clause strictly, to invalidate compulsory school prayer in *Engel v. Vitale*, 370 U.S. 421 (1962), and *School District of Abington Township v. Schempp,* 374 U.S. 203 (1963), both reaffirmed in *Lee v. Weisman*, 505 U.S. 577 (1992) (Chapter 6, § 7B). These decisions brought upon the Court more sustained public denunciation than any other Warren Court precedents outside of the race area. On the other hand, the Warren Court also gave strong effect to the Free Exercise Clause, construing it to require states to accommodate religious minorities. See *Sherbert v. Verner*, 374 U.S. 398 (1963), limited by *Employment Div'n v. Smith*, 494 U.S. 872 (1990) (Chapter 6, § 7A).

Prior Courts had assumed that libel and obscenity were outside the protections of the First Amendment. The Warren Court reaffirmed the exclusion of obscene speech in *Roth v. United States*, 354 U.S. 476 (1957), but limited obscenity to materials whose predominant appeal is to a "prurient interest, i.e., a shameful or morbid interest in nudity, sex, or excretion." The next generation saw intellectually helpless Justices struggle to determine what racy literature and erotica were protected under this test and amended versions of it (Chapter 6, § 3A). Perhaps more successfully, the Warren Court limited the ability of state libel laws to penalize published falsehoods. In order to assure the existence of a vigorous and unchilled press, the Court ruled in *New York Times v. Sullivan*, 376 U.S. 254 (1964) (Chapter 6, § 2B), that public figures had to demonstrate "actual malice" to recover for libel. Again, the basic test has been refined through subsequent Supreme Court decisions, but unlike the obscenity cases the libel cases have followed a coherent path. Chapter 6 explores these and other doctrinal and theoretical issues implicated in the First Amendment.

3.   *The Supreme Court at the Bar of Politics: The Jurisprudence of Voting.* The primary architect of the Supreme Court's individual rights jurisprudence in the 1960s was not Earl Warren or Hugo Black, but Warren's lieutenant, Justice William Brennan. Although a liberal Democrat, Brennan had caught the attention of the Eisenhower Administration through favorable reviews of his service on the New Jersey Supreme Court. In an act of bipartisanship he soon regretted, Eisenhower in 1956 named Brennan to the Court, where he served until 1990. The author of the Court's cautious opinion in *Roth* and the critical fifth vote to refuse to decide the contraception issue in 1961, Brennan did not start out as a constitutional activist. But in the early 1960s he emerged as the political captain of the liberal activist Justices and served that role for almost 30 years. Justice Brennan was the main sponsor of the idea of selective incorporation of specific Bill of Rights protections into the Due Process Clause and pressed Justice Douglas to rest the right of privacy on the emanations of various protections in the Bill of Rights. His opinions in *Button, Sullivan,* and later cases are liberal constitutional classics.

Probably Brennan's most important opinion was *Baker v. Carr*, 369 U.S. 186 (1962) (Chapter 9, § 1), which held that an equal protection challenge to state electoral apportionment is justiciable and is not a *political question. Baker* remains important as the leading statement of the current political question doctrine: federal courts will ordinarily adjudicate constitutional claims unless the Constitution commits the issue to the political branches, courts lack the expertise or standards to adjudicate the matter, or pragmatic considerations counsel against an adjudication. Generally, federal courts will rarely dismiss a lawsuit under this doctrine, but may well dismiss for lack of standing, which reflects some of the same underlying policies. One legacy of *Baker* was the one-person, one-vote formula the Court adopted in *Reynolds v. Sims*, 377 U.S. 533 (1964) (Chapter 5, § 3A), and subsequent cases. This formula revolutionized state and federal representation, erasing outdated electoral boundaries and the advantages accruing to rural districts and introducing a new politics of decennial gerrymandering. A broader legacy is that the Court has become pervasively embroiled in the political thicket of federal election law—not only monitoring compliance with *Reynolds*, but also regulating political and racial gerrymanders, the deployment of money in politics, the regulation of lobbying, and even the ability of the Census Bureau to estimate population beyond that revealed by actual head counts. A final legacy of *Baker* is one Justice Brennan surely did not anticipate: *Bush v. Gore*, 531 U.S. 98 (2000) (id.), where the Court essentially picked a President in the teeth of apparent constitutional commitment of Electoral College issues to Congress—yet none of the parties or *amici* suggested that these issues constituted a political question.

SECTION 8. THE NIXON-REAGAN COURT: CONSERVATIVE LEGAL PROCESS AND WOMEN'S RIGHTS, 1969–2001

The election of Richard Nixon as President in 1968 ushered in a sea change in American politics and constitutionalism. The Silent Majority that Nixon claimed to represent did not support the apartheid and massive resistance of the Old South but embraced a pragmatic politics critical of the civil rights agenda. Reflecting a new mood among the American people that was skeptical of the central government, Nixon's Court—Chief Justice Warren Burger (1969) and Justices Harry Blackmun (1970), Lewis Powell (1971), and William Rehnquist (1971)—retreated from none of the formal anti-apartheid decisions of the Warren Court but declined to expand on them either. While *de jure* segregation remained taboo, actual integration took a back seat to other constitutional values: federalism, freedom of association, and the perceived institutional limitations of the federal courts. Although the Burger Court went slowly in race cases and was unreceptive to the rights of lesbians and gay men, it was activist in cases involving states' rights, separation of powers at the national level, and the rights of women.

The Supreme Court continued to move in a more conservative direction after President Nixon was forced from office in 1974. The next seven appointments installed Justices more conservative than their predecessors: John Paul Stevens, replacing Justice Douglas in 1975; Sandra Day O'Connor, replacing Justice Stewart in 1981; William Hubbs Rehnquist, replacing Chief Justice Burger in 1986; Antonin Scalia, replacing (Associate) Justice Rehnquist in 1986; Anthony Kennedy, replacing Justice Powell in 1987; David Souter, replacing Justice Brennan in 1990; and Clarence Thomas, replacing Justice Marshall in 1991. Only the Clinton-era appointments of Justices Ruth Bader Ginsburg (1993) and Stephen Breyer (1994) bucked the trend toward conservative appointments. Ironically, the parade of appointments by Presidents promising "strict constructionists" resulted in the most aggressive period of judicial review in the nation's history. During this period, the Court literally struck down more laws than any previous Court in the nation's history.

1. *The Race Cases and a New Understanding of Equal Protection.* Led by Justice Brennan, the early years of the Burger Court continued the Warren Court's insistence on actual integration of formerly segregated public schools, with the high point being the busing order approved in *Swann v. Charlotte-Mecklenburg Bd. of Educ.*, 402 U.S. 1 (1971) (Chapter 2, § 2C1). The Court's opinion rejected pragmatic arguments by *amicus* counsel Lewis Powell, who maintained that forced busing not only violated white people's rights to neighborhood schools, but also would be ineffective because whites would simply relocate to escape too much integration. In *Swann*'s wake, and once Powell was named a Justice, the Burger Court drew lines beyond which lower courts could not go in crafting remedial *Brown* decrees. E.g., *Milliken v. Bradley*, 418 U.S. 717 (1974) (remedial decree cannot require "interdistrict" busing). If the Warren Court was characterized by vision and a sometimes unrealistic focus on equality above other values, the Burger Court was characterized by a cost-benefit mentality which focused closely on the practical efficacy of judicial decrees.

The turning point in the Court's approach to equality issues can be fixed precisely: *San Antonio Independent School District v. Rodriguez*, 411 U.S. 1 (1973) (Chapter 5, § 3B, but you might read this case in connection with the post-*Swann* cases). Mexican-American plaintiffs claimed that Texas's system of financing public schools effectively denied lower-income families anything close to the level of education afforded students in upper-income school districts and sought a remedy under the Equal Protection Clause. Justice Powell's opinion for the Court started with an astute analysis of the institutional limitations federalism imposed upon equality claims: neither the Constitution nor sound principles of democratic governance countenanced dictation of local education decisions by federal judges. Powell saw no justification for extending the Warren Court's voting and travel cases to recognize a new "fundamental right" (education) that would trigger heightened equal protection scrutiny. Finally, Powell was skeptical of plaintiffs' claims that they were being discriminated against on the basis of wealth and, in any event, rejected the idea that wealth should be treated as a classification (like race) triggering heightened scrutiny. (Plaintiffs also claimed that the state policy had race-based effects, a claim which Powell shrugged off on the ground that the state could not be charged with discriminatory effects unless they were "intentional." This aside was to be the basis for a formal holding of the Court in *Washington v. Davis*, 426 U.S. 229 (1976) (Chapter 3, § 1B): State policies having racially discriminatory effects were not subject to strict scrutiny unless those effects were intended.)

Justice Powell's opinion for the Court was met by a dissenting opinion by Justice Thurgood Marshall, not only the Court's first African-American Justice, but also the most successful litigator to have sat on the Court since John Marshall. Thurgood Marshall succeeded Charles Houston as the chief litigating counsel for the NAACP and was the architect of that association's anti-apartheid litigation campaign. Although he is best known for his successful argument in *Brown*, many of his most impressive victories were in the courts of southern and border states, where Marshall represented people of color in venues hostile or at best skeptical toward his claims. During his lengthy service on the Court (1967–91), Marshall's chief interests were equal protection law and civil procedure. The *Rodriguez* dissent was his leading statement in the equal protection area.

Without denigrating the federal arrangement, Marshall emphasized the commitment to equality in educational opportunity that was the formal basis for the Court's decision in *Brown* and argued that plaintiffs ought to be given a chance to make their case. On the merits, Marshall set forth a "sliding scale" theory of equal protection: the level of scrutiny the Court should give to a policy depended on the importance of the right to the people excluded, the historical reliability of the classification deployed, and the quality of the state's justification. Under these criteria, as well as the legacy of *Brown*, plaintiffs had made out a strong case. Although the Supreme Court rejected, by a 5–4 vote, Marshall's arguments, many state supreme courts have accepted them as constructions of their state constitutions (Chapter 5, § 3B).

School desegregation was not the only area of constitutional discourse driven by race. In 1963, the NAACP initiated a litigation campaign against the death penalty, one that bore fruit in *Furman v. Georgia*, 408 U.S. 238 (1972) (per curiam). A bare majority of the Court ruled that broadly discretionary death penalty laws violated the Eighth Amendment; four Justices (Douglas, Brennan, Stewart, Marshall) were influenced by the fact that jury discretion to impose death was disproportionately visited upon defendants of color. *Furman* was not the death knell of capital punishment in the United States, however. Like *Brown*, *Furman* contributed to a fierce death penalty countermovement. States responded with statutes limiting capital punishment to the most serious crimes and providing juries with greater guidance in exercising their judgment. Civil rights groups objected that these new statutes did not solve the problems identified by the *Furman* Justices, but the Supreme Court upheld most of these laws in *Gregg v. Georgia*, 428 U.S. 153 (1976), and its companion cases. *Gregg* by no means ended judicial review of death penalty laws. Because of the high stakes on both sides and the open-textured standards of the Eighth

Amendment, the Court has continued to review death sentences for procedural and substantive errors.[42]

As in the public school cases, Justice Powell was the critical voice on the Court when it addressed the contentious issue of affirmative action in *Regents of the University of California v. Bakke*, 438 U.S. 265 (1978) (Chapter 3, § 3A).[43] Bakke, a white man, challenged the admission plan for the medical school of the University of California at Davis, which had reserved for minority students sixteen of the hundred places in its first-year class. Bakke and his *amici* argued that any race-based state classification was suspect under *Loving* and that state affirmative action programs deprived white people of their equality rights while reenforcing stereotypes about black people. The state and its many *amici* (including the ACLU, the ABA, and the NAACP's Inc. Fund) defended the program as needed to assure diversity in and to remedy centuries of black exclusion from higher education.

The Burger Court fractured. Four Justices (Burger, Stewart, Rehnquist, Stevens) maintained that the admissions quota violated federal statutory law and did not reach Bakke's equal protection claim. Four Justices (Brennan, White, Marshall, Blackmun) maintained that the quota violated neither federal statutory nor constitutional law. Justice Powell wrote only for himself but delivered the judgment of the Court: The race-based program was subject to strict scrutiny; such scrutiny could be satisfied by a program narrowly tailored to improve institutional diversity or remedy the ongoing effects of past discrimination; the quota program did not meet that test, but a program where race is a plus factor could do so. Although Powell's Solomonic opinion did not settle the contentious issue of affirmative action, it was (and is) widely hailed as a workable solution. Importantly, Powell demonstrated how deference to the institutional needs of state governments (the bases for his opposition to *Swann* and his majority opinion in *Rodriguez*) could serve liberal as well as conservative institutional needs.

The Burger Court never achieved a stable majority for the Powell or any other test for affirmative action, but a majority of the Rehnquist Court treated even "benign" or "remedial" race-based classifications as "suspect." See *City of Richmond v. J.A. Croson Co.*, 488 U.S. 469 (1989) (state and municipal plans); *Adarand Constructors, Inc. v. Pena*, 515 U.S. 200 (1995)

---

[42] For some of the Court's busy death penalty jurisprudence, see *Coker v. Georgia*, 433 U.S. 584 (1977) (striking down capital punishment for rape); *McCleskey v. Kemp*, 481 U.S. 279 (1987) (rejecting challenge to regime where crimes against white people were regularly punished by death, but analogous crimes against black people were not); *Atkins v. Virginia*, 536 U.S. 304 (2002) (striking down capital punishment for mentally disabled criminals); *Baze v. Rees*, 553 U.S. 35 (2008) (upholding lethal injection as a permissible method for carrying out the death penalty); *Kennedy v. Louisiana*, 554 U.S. 407 (2008) (striking down death penalty for child rape).

[43] See generally John Calvin Jeffries, Jr., *Justice Lewis F. Powell, Jr. and the Era of Judicial Balance* 455–501 (1994) (Powell's role in the case); Bernard Schwartz, *Behind* Bakke: *Affirmative Action and the Supreme Court* (1988).

(federal plans) (both in Chapter 3, § 3B). Dissenting in *Adarand*, Justice Stevens objected that classifications motivated by remedial motives and benefitting racial minorities ought not receive the same beady-eyed scrutiny as those motivated by white supremacy and racial prejudice (*Loving*). Justice O'Connor's opinion responded that race has been such an unreliable criterion for state policy that it should be presumed inadmissible. Concurring opinions went further, claiming that any kind of state racial classification perpetuates racial stereotypes and prejudice. Like Powell in *Bakke*, O'Connor in *Adarand* also insisted that strict scrutiny not always be fatal scrutiny: A carefully crafted affirmative action plan might pass such scrutiny.

The Rehnquist Court's affirmative action cases de-emphasized the *anti-subordination* goal that the Framers of the Fourteenth Amendment saw as central to the Equal Protection Clause, in favor of the *rationality* goal. That is, the majority Justices viewed the equal protection project as discouraging the state from relying on irrational classifications, rather than improving the status of subordinated classes. They also rejected the *Carolene* paradigm that the Court should only intervene when the political process is dysfunctional. The minority set-aside challenged in *Adarand* was adopted by an overwhelmingly white Congress for the benefit of people of color—in contrast to apartheid measures which had been adopted by white legislatures to marginalize and suppress people of color. See also *Shaw v. Reno*, 509 U.S. 630 (1993) (Chapter 3, § 3C), another opinion by Justice O'Connor opening up equal protection challenges to electoral districts drawn to make it more likely that racial minorities would be elected.

Just as the Court has moved toward a rationality-based but flexible model, where some race-based classifications survived strict scrutiny, so it showed some willingness to give sharper teeth to the standard rational basis test applicable to most classifications challenged under the Equal Protection Clause. In *City of Cleburne v. Cleburne Living Center*, 473 U.S. 432 (1985) (Chapter 4, § 3C), the Court ruled that disability is not suspect like race or quasi-suspect like sex but nevertheless struck down a municipal prohibition of a group home for the mentally disabled on the ground that it was motivated by a "bare . . . desire to harm a politically unpopular group." Without addressing the suspect classification issue, the Rehnquist Court applied the rational basis test in a similar way to strike down a state antigay initiative in *Romer v. Evans*, 517 U.S. 620 (1996) (Chapter 4, § 3D).

Romer is more broadly significant. Just as African Americans and women had organized themselves into social movements powerfully objecting to legal rules excluding or segregating them, thousands of lesbians, gay men, and bisexuals in the 1970s "came out" of their "closets" to resist pervasive state discrimination against them. Outside a few censorship cases, the Warren Court had construed statutes and constitutional precedents expansively to *add to* rather than ameliorate legal discriminations against gay people. E.g., *Boutilier v. INS*, 387 U.S. 118 (1967) (ruling that apparent bisexuality was per se evidence of "psychopathic personality" requiring deportation of alien). The sex-squeamish Burger Court had found ways to avoid full briefing and decision in every gay rights case to come before it—until *Bowers v. Hardwick* (Chapter 5, § 4C), which yielded an opinion sustaining the constitutionality of state criminalization of "homosexual sodomy" that gay people and their friends found too dismissive of their claims to dignified treatment.[44] Even when rebuffing lesbian and gay equality claims, the Rehnquist Court avoided the rhetoric used by its predecessor, and *Romer* suggested the possibility that the Constitution provides at least minimal protections for lesbians, gay men, bisexual, and transgendered people.

2. *Women's Equality and Privacy Rights.* Ironically, just as Nixon's Supreme Court was turning down the intensity of civil rights litigation, it was turning it up in cases involving the rights of women. A new wave of feminist activism had swept the 1960s, and women insisting on legal equality consciously followed the civil rights model: Establish litigating institutions such as the ACLU's Women's Rights Project and challenge sex-based discriminations on equal protection grounds.[45] As head of the ACLU's Women's Rights Project, Ruth Bader Ginsburg pressed the race analogy in the early 1970s: Sex ought to be a suspect classification for the same reasons race was—it was a trait that rarely advanced legitimate state policies, and such classifications disadvantaged women, either directly by excluding them from opportunities men had or indirectly by perpetuating stereotypes of women as civilizing domestics and of men as public actors.

While Ginsburg was seeking strict scrutiny for sex classifications, the states were debating the Equal Rights Amendment, which Congress had passed in 1972. Justice Brennan came within one vote of establishing sex as a suspect classification in *Frontiero v. Richardson*, 411 U.S. 677 (1973) (Chapter 4, § 2B1). In *Craig v. Boren*, 429 U.S. 190 (1976) (id.), he obtained a Court majority for what has become known as "intermediate scrutiny": Sex-based classifications "must serve important governmental objectives and must be substantially related to achievement of those objectives." Although a vague test, the Burger Court applied it to strike down most sex-based rules excluding women from opportunities men had, but not to invalidate sex-based classifications the Justices considered remedial. These and later cases are excerpted in § 2B1 of Chapter 4. As in the race cases also decided in the 1970s, the Burger Court was unwilling to apply heightened scrutiny to sex-neutral laws merely because they had

---

[44] On the antigay jurisprudence of the Warren and Burger Courts, see William Eskridge, Jr., *Gaylaw: Challenging the Apartheid of the Closet* 98–137, 149–72 (1999).

[45] See Harrison, *On Account of Sex*; Susan Hartmann, *The Other Feminists: Activists in the Liberal Establishment* (1998); Serena Mayeri, Note, *"A Common Fate of Discrimination": Race-Gender Analogies in Legal and Historical Perspective*, 110 Yale L.J. 1045 (2001).

discriminatory effects on women, unless it could be shown that the effects were intentional (Chapter 4, § 2B3).

The more conservative Rehnquist Court was, ironically, even more aggressive in enforcing the "no sex discrimination" norm in cases such as *J.E.B. v. Alabama ex rel. T.B.*, 511 U.S. 127 (1994) (regulating peremptory challenges to prospective jurors based on their sex), and *United States v. Virginia*, 518 U.S. 515 (1996) (state cannot run single-sex college) (both in Chapter 4, § 2B1). Indeed, Justice Ruth Bader Ginsburg wrote the opinion for the Court in the latter case, which invalidated Virginia's system of separate schools for men (the Virginia Military Academy) and women (a leadership institute situated in Mary Baldwin College). Justice Scalia's blistering dissent accused the majority of smuggling strict scrutiny for sex-based classifications into the opinion, but the Court applied the intermediate level of scrutiny in a subsequent naturalization case, *Nguyen v. INS,* 533 U.S. 53 (2001).

At the same time the Court was moving toward heightened scrutiny of sex-based classifications, it expanded the right of privacy to assure women the right to abortion. *Griswold* had served as the constitutional basis for a vigorous women's "pro-choice" movement in the 1960s. Sarah Weddington, the lawyer for the pregnant challenger in *Roe v. Wade* (Chapter 5, § 4B), argued that, for most women, pregnancy is one of the most determinative events in their lives. To enjoy the complete freedom to pursue careers, develop as individuals, and plan their families, women need to be able to choose abortions without interference from the state. Surprisingly, these arguments had a very receptive audience among the all-male U.S. Supreme Court—and Harry Blackmun emerged as their advocate within the Court. This was ironic, as Blackmun was appointed as part of President Nixon's promise to name "strict constructionists" to the Court, and indeed Blackmun had been Chief Justice Burger's "Minnesota Twin" in voting to deny judicial relief in the Texas school funding case, the racially disparate impact cases, the early gay rights cases, and the death penalty cases being adjudicated at about the same time. On the other hand, Blackmun had been General Counsel of the Mayo Clinic and was knowledgeable about the medical professional problems with existing state abortion laws (doctors as a class were more opposed to them than were women).

Ultimately, seven Justices joined Blackmun's opinion in *Roe v. Wade.* The opinion recognized women's interest in abortion as a due process right, thereby dislodging the privacy right from the penumbras of the Bill of Rights and re-situating it in the Due Process Clause. Blackmun also ruled that the fetus was not a "person" under the Fourteenth Amendment. Although he recognized that the state had legitimate interests later in a pregnancy to protect the life of the fetus, the holding that fetuses themselves have no legal rights was immediately and strongly contested by the already-emerging "pro-life" movement—a movement greatly energized by *Roe v. Wade*. The pro-life movement has been just as much a social movement as women's liberation and the pro-choice movement. Indeed, a pro-life stance is just as important for some people's identity as being a feminist or pro-choice is for other people. Since January 1973, when the Court handed down *Roe*, this issue has embroiled the body politic and periodically returns to the Supreme Court, as pro-life states try new forms of regulation, sometimes successfully and sometimes not.

Just as the Burger Court had diluted the Court's commitment to the *Carolene* paradigm in the race cases, the women's rights cases suggested that *Carolene* was no longer the driving model for activist judicial review. The Court was not enforcing clear constitutional texts (*Carolene* ¶ 1); according to the critics of *Roe*, the Court was not enforcing any kind of text in the abortion cases. Moreover, the political process was addressing the same issues that the Court was resolving (¶ 2): at the same time the Court handed down *Frontiero* and *Craig*, the states were debating the ERA and repealing sex discriminations from their codes; when *Roe* was decided, many states had reformed their outdated abortion laws (four had repealed them altogether), and others were following. This was hardly surprising: as a majority of the voters, women's concerns were ones to which politicians were attentive. As to *Carolene*'s famous ¶ 3, women are hardly the "discrete and insular minority" that African Americans are; indeed, women are a majority and dispersed throughout the population. Their legal disabilities are less the result of emotional "prejudice" and hatred against them than of "stereotypes" about them.

Other critics of these decisions emphasized their departure from original constitutional text and intent. The most ardent original intent critic of the women's rights decisions, and of the privacy right generally, was Professor Robert Bork, an antitrust expert at the Yale Law School and in the 1980s a judge on the United States Court of Appeals for the D.C. Circuit. When President Reagan nominated Bork to a closely divided Supreme Court in 1987, observers predicted the end of *Roe v. Wade*, a prediction Judge Bork confirmed in his Senate testimony, which roundly condemned the privacy decisions, including *Griswold*. A coalition of women's groups, civil rights associations, and other progressives opposed the nomination in an intense public relations campaign that persuaded a large majority of Americans that Bork should not sit on the Court. The Senate rejected his nomination, 58–42. The eventual nominee, Judge Anthony Kennedy of the Ninth Circuit, was the critical fifth vote to reaffirm (and reinterpret) *Roe* in *Planned Parenthood v. Casey*, 505 U.S. 833 (1992) (Chapter 5, § 4B).

3. *Judicial Activism to Protect Constitutional Structure and Accountability: Separation of Powers and Federalism*. The Burger Court's activism was not limited to the women's rights cases. In some respects, the most sweeping decision of recent times was the Court's near-unanimous

decision in *Immigration and Naturalization Service v. Chadha*, 462 U.S. 919 (1983) (Chapter 8, § 2B), which ruled that vetoes of agency rules by the vote of one chamber in Congress violated the bicameralism and presentment requirements of Article I, § 7. Chief Justice Burger's broadly written opinion for the Court effectively invalidated the "legislative veto" provisions found in over 200 federal statutes. The structural themes of *Chadha* can be traced to *The Federalist Papers* but remain more important in the modern regulatory state than ever before. Structural limits on the power of Congress and the President are explored in Chapter 8 of this book.

Chapter 9 treats structural limits on the power of the Supreme Court, and in this arena the Burger Court was particularly innovative. The Court set strict limits on the cases and controversies federal courts could adjudicate. Most of the cases involved questions of *standing*, a requirement the Court found not only in Article III but inherent in the system of separate powers (Chapter 9, § 2). The Court has required plaintiffs to show "actual injury," namely, real harm directly caused by the defendant's conduct and remediable through a judgment. Thus, generalized injuries suffered by all, such as wrongful government action harming all taxpayers or citizens alike, were precisely the ones best dealt with in the political rather than the judicial process (hence, the old political question doctrine sneaked back into constitutional law). And the Court was stingy about allowing public interest plaintiffs to use the federal courts to monitor executive underenforcement of statutory schemes.

The triumph of centralized national authority during the New Deal and Great Society—and with it tremendous advances in the civil rights movement—has been followed by a period when most Americans were concerned with too much central authority and too many restrictions on their liberties emanating from Washington, D.C. Although states' rights arguments took a beating from the New Deal through the Warren Court, federalism made a comeback during the Burger and, especially, Rehnquist Courts. As the introductory materials in Chapter 7 suggest, the federal arrangement whereby states retain independent regulatory authority and the national government is limited to specified areas of regulation was central to the forming of the Constitution—and is an arrangement many consider admirable today as a matter of governance. Although the Burger Court flip-flopped on the issue of direct federal regulation of the states, see *Garcia v. San Antonio Metropolitan Transit Authority*, 469 U.S. 528 (1985) (overruling *National League of Cities v. Usery*, 426 U.S. 833 (1976) (Chapter 7, § 5B)), a stable majority of the Rehnquist Court concluded that Congress and the Court itself have blurred the lines of *accountability* that are essential to the proper function of local democracy and resolved to enforce federalism-based limits on Congress like no Court had done before.

The accountability theme first showed up in the *Brown II* cases. School boards objecting to extensive remedial orders maintained that the success of public education depended on the intimate involvement of parents in their local schools and the accountability of school boards to those parents. If federal judges made local educational policy, school boards could credibly claim that they were not responsible for ongoing problems. The Supreme Court accepted this argument as a basis for curtailing the authority of federal judges to retain jurisdiction indefinitely to monitor compliance with remedial orders. *Freeman v. Pitts*, 503 U.S. 467 (1992) (Chapter 2, § 2C2). For similar accountability reasons, the Court has ruled that Congress cannot "commandeer" state legislatures, *New York v. United States*, 505 U.S. 144 (1992), or state executive officers, *Printz v. United States*, 521 U.S. 898 (1997) (both in Chapter 7, § 5C). In these cases, the Court was policing the tendency of Congress to take credit for a federal program, while shifting many costs and enforcement responsibilities to the states, thereby distracting state officials from their own primary governance duties.

The accountability idea also animated the Rehnquist Court's Eleventh Amendment jurisprudence. The Court has interpreted Article III's grant of "judicial Power" and the Eleventh Amendment not only to bar any kind of lawsuit against the states in federal courts, but also to bar such lawsuits in state courts, *Alden v. Maine*, 527 U.S. 706 (1999) (Chapter 7, § 3D), and in federal administrative adjudications, *Federal Maritime Comm'n v. South Carolina State Ports Auth.*, 535 U.S. 743 (2002). In *Seminole Tribe of Florida v. Florida*, 517 U.S. 44 (1996) (id.), the Court ruled that Congress has no authority under the Commerce Clause to abrogate states' Eleventh Amendment immunity. Because Congress does have such authority under the Fourteenth Amendment, this holding has stimulated a series of lawsuits to determine whether specific statutes have been properly adopted pursuant to Congress's authority under § 5 of the Fourteenth Amendment.

In its most dramatic decisions, the same five Justices of the Rehnquist Court who formed the majority in the above-cited cases (Rehnquist, O'Connor, Scalia, Kennedy, Thomas) also set firmer limits on Congress's authority under the Commerce Clause and the Fourteenth Amendment. Thus, in *United States v. Lopez*, 514 U.S. 549 (1995) (Chapter 7, § 2), the Court struck down a regulation of private conduct as exceeding Congress's power under the Commerce Clause for the first time in sixty years. (The statute prohibited the possession of guns within a thousand feet of a school.) And in *United States v. Morrison*, 529 U.S. 598 (2000) (Chapter 7, § 3E), the Court ruled that the federal government did not have authority to adopt the Violence Against Women Act provision creating a cause of action for gender-motivated violence by private persons. Chief Justice Rehnquist's opinion for a 5–4 Court held that the Commerce Clause gives Congress very limited authority to regulate noneconomic activities and that the Fourteenth Amendment gives it no authority to regulate private activities.

While the Burger and Rehnquist Courts were enforcing federalism guarantees against the federal government, they were also enforcing them against the states, primarily under the Court's assumed authority to enforce the "Dormant" Commerce Clause. Thus, the Burger Court struck down state regulations that either directly trenched upon interstate commerce, e.g., *City of Philadelphia v. New Jersey*, 437 U.S. 617 (1978) (id. § 6B1), or imposed "undue burdens" on commerce. An example of the latter was *Kassel v. Consolidated Freightways Corp.*, 450 U.S. 662 (1981) (id. § 6B2). Iowa imposed stricter limits on truck lengths than its neighbors, and truckers challenged the policy on the ground that it limited their capacity everywhere (it was hard for them to avoid Iowa). Four Justices voted to strike down the Iowa law because the costs to interstate commerce outweighed state safety interests, realistically viewed. Two Justices voted to strike it down because they found Iowa lawmakers motivated by the desire to discourage interstate commerce and shift the costs of big trucks to other states. Objecting that the Court was essentially making a policy rather than a legal determination, three Justices voted to uphold the law. (Note the relevance of *Carolene* to these cases: local political processes are prone to shift costs (like the wear and tear of big trucks) to other jurisdictions, and the federal judiciary is a needed check to prevent races to the bottom, where all states try to shift costs in an escalating series of regulatory moves.)

SECTION 9. THE MILLENNIAL COURT

The new millennium represents a seismic break for the Court in several respects. In the short term, the Court heralded the new millennium with one of the most controversial decisions in its history, *Bush v. Gore*, 531 U.S. 98 (2000) (Chapter 5, § 3A). In a 5–4 per curiam decision, a Court dominated by conservative Republican "nonactivists" applied unprecedented equal protection scrutiny to overturn the Florida Supreme Court's procedures for recounting that state's votes in the closely contested election between Vice President Al Gore and Texas Governor George W. Bush. As a result of the Court's decision, Gore, a liberal Democrat, had to concede Florida, and with it the Presidency, to Bush, a conservative Republican. Because the majority in *Bush v. Gore* was not able to justify its activism by reference to either original meaning or constitutional precedent, it was subjected to withering critique inside and outside the Court. Nonetheless, the Court's intervention was decisive and paved the way for President Bush—rather than President Gore—to name replacements for Chief Justice Rehnquist and Justice O'Connor in 2005. The new justices—Chief Justice John Roberts and Justice Samuel Alito— were talented lower-court judges whose careers started in the Reagan Administration's Department of Justice. Pundits expected both men to support Federalist Society values during their tenures, and their first several years have, with some notable exceptions, largely validated those predictions. After the election of Barack Obama, Justice David Souter was replaced by Justice Sonia Sotomayor, and John Paul Stevens was replaced by Justice Elena Kagan. It is too soon to make sweeping pronouncements about either of the Court's newest justices, but they do not appear to have dramatically changed the ideological makeup of the Court (and had not been expected to do so).

We hesitate a bit before announcing traits or trends that distinguish the Millennial Court, for we are still in the early years of the new century, and there is a great deal of continuity between the pre-2000 Court and the post-2000 Court. Generally, the Millennial Court has supported conservative values most of the time but progressive constitutional values in a surprising number of cases. On the other hand, since 2005, the Roberts Court has often—but not always—been precedent-respecting. Consider these further themes.

1. *The Court's On-and-Off Embrace of the Imperial First Amendment?* The First Amendment flourished in the twentieth century, and today limits the state's ability to regulate even highly controversial expressive conduct such as flagburning and cross-burning (Chapter 6, §§ 1, 2A); hate speech, including racist and misogynist expression (§ 3B); monetary contributions to political campaigns (§ 2C); offensive expression in the mass media (§ 3B2); commercial speech (§ 3B); festive as well as protest marches (§ 5); and identity speech, including the right of social groups to exclude people some members don't like (§ 6). As the references suggest, we try to cover the high points of the expanding First Amendment in Chapter 6, but please be aware that you will not be able to dig very deeply in an introductory survey course.

Much of the Court's expansion of the First Amendment came through (or was facilitated by) a giant pluralist logroll. Identity-based social movements (especially the birth control, civil rights, and gay rights movements) found the protections of the First Amendment necessary to protect their voices against suppression by the state as they protested the legal status quo. The fact that judges who did not favor birth control, were dubious about protest marches, and considered "homosexuals" a bad lot were willing to protect their free speech and association helped create a strong tradition of a neutral and non-political First Amendment. Once these social movements made normative headway and secured antidiscrimination laws from municipal, state, and national legislatures, their traditionalist opponents and identity-based movements on the right (pro-lifers, traditional family values Americans and their groups) claimed the First Amendment's protections for their expressive activities. So Americans, including judges of a variety of political persuasions, supported a First Amendment that vigorously and neutrally protects speech and association rights of all manner of persons and groups.

For this reason, Chapter 6 gives some emphasis to equality-speech clashes, where the state's equality goal of remedying private discrimination limits the liberty of alleged oppressors. This is the common theme of the cross-burning, feminist pornography, hate speech, and public accommodations cases. A millennial case that illustrates the imperialism of the First Amendment is *Boy Scouts of America v. Dale*, 530 U.S. 640 (2000) (§ 6). James Dale was an assistant scoutmaster expelled from the Boy Scouts when they learned from a media interview that he was an openly gay man. The New Jersey state courts ruled that the Scouts were a "public accommodation" in violation of the state law barring discrimination on the basis of sexual orientation. The Scouts claimed, and a majority of the Court agreed, that the First Amendment protected it against being required to retain members whose presence sent the "wrong message" to the community.

The pluralist deal suggested by *Dale* is that the First Amendment protects people's right to "come out of the closet" as openly gay, but also protects people who do not want to associate with openly gay persons. The deal may be fraying, however. For example, the Roberts Court has declined to read *Dale* and other First Amendment precedents broadly when pro-gay institutions challenge state censorship. Speaking for a unanimous Court, Chief Justice Roberts rejected a First Amendment challenge by gay-friendly law schools to federal fund cutoffs if the schools did not cooperate *fully* with the gay-excluding recruitment efforts that were mandated by the now-repealed "Don't Ask, Don't Tell" policy. *Rumsfeld v. FAIR*, 547 U.S. 47 (2006) (Chapter 6, § 6). The law schools relied on *Dale* to argue that their associational identity as pro-gay was threatened by a federal statute conditioning federal grants on a requirement that law schools provide their best-efforts access to gay-discriminating military recruiters; the Administration's stated justification (in a letter to the Yale Law School) was that law school policy treating military recruiters differently (as by not associating them with the school's official job fair) would be construed by students as a stamp of disapproval by the school. Notwithstanding the apparent effort by the government to stifle dissent—and within an academic context—the Chief Justice distinguished *Dale* and found that there was no significant First Amendment interest posed by the law schools. The Court returned to this arena of conflict in 2010, when it used another strand of First Amendment doctrine to uphold a state law school's policy denying official recognition to a religious student group that excluded those who would not reject homosexuality.

Another case suggesting some erosion of First Amendment protections is *Morse v. Frederick,* 551 U.S. 363 (2007) (Chapter 6, § 4B). The Court has long recognized a First Amendment right of high school students to engage in political expression, even within the school. Students at an Alaskan high school were released from classes so that they could view the Olympic

Torch Relay in 2002. One student waved a huge banner reading "BONG HiTS 4 JESUS." The student was disciplined by the principal, who considered the banner to be advocating drug use. Chief Justice Roberts' opinion for the Court held that it was reasonable for schools to censor pro-drug speech, even outside the school premises. In a concurring opinion, Justice Alito suggested that the Court's allowance might not extend beyond the context of high school anti-drug regimes.

One area in which the Roberts Court has applied the First Amendment with an exclamation point is one in which it also showed its willingness to abandon precedent (see more on that theme below). The early-Millennial Court had upheld most of the Bipartisan Campaign Reform Act of 2002's limitations on soft money and corporate contributions in federal campaigns in *McConnell v. FEC*, 540 U.S. 93 (2003). The Court, however, took a dramatic turn in *Citizens United v. Federal Election Commission*, 558 U.S. 310 (2010). That case overruled not only parts of the relatively-recent precedent of *McConnell*, but a 20 year old holding in *Austin v. Michigan Chamber of Commerce*, 494 U.S. 652 (1990) that itself had upheld a century-old tradition of banning corporations from campaign spending. The Court jolted the political system and the law by holding that the First Amendment entitles corporations to exacting protection from spending limitations.

2. *Precedent and (Conservative) Pragmatism.* Although the Millennial Court contains some stalwart advocates of original meaning (Justices Scalia and Thomas), it is overall a Court whose methodology is common law in style and pragmatic in philosophy—albeit pragmatism with a Federalist Society tilt. Thus, the Court as a whole does not subscribe to one foundational inquiry; the Justices will consider text, original meaning, purpose, and Supreme Court precedent when interpreting the Constitution—with the last source usually driving most of the analysis. The Court both respects precedent *and* interprets it, giving some play to conservative readings of liberal precedents but trying not to overrule anything. (During the 2007 Term, for example, the Roberts Court did not overrule a single precedent.)

Perhaps the best example of this approach is *Gonzales v. Carhart*, 550 U.S. 124 (2007) (Chapter 5, § 4B), where a closely divided (5–4) Court upheld the federal ban on "partial birth abortions" against a constitutional privacy attack. In a previous case, a 5–4 Court had struck down a more vaguely worded state ban, *Stenberg v. Carhart*, 530 U.S. 914 (2000). Although the latter *Carhart* decision carefully distinguished the earlier one, commentators and (apparently) the dissenting Justices believed that the different result owed much to the fact that a pro-life Justice (Alito) had replaced a pro-choice Justice (O'Connor) in the interim. It is also notable that Justice Kennedy's opinion for the Court in *Carhart II* made no noise about overruling *Roe v. Wade*, the super-precedent that President George

W. Bush had vowed to overturn through his appointments to the Court. Ironically, although the Court seems disinclined to overrule *Roe v. Wade*, it did overrule precedent to recognize a privacy right to engage in consensual sodomy in *Lawrence v. Texas*, 539 U.S. 558 (2003), overruling *Bowers v. Hardwick* (both in Chapter 5, § 4C).

Perhaps the most contentious *stare decisis* debates have been in cases involving race-based criteria. The grand debate occurred in *Parents Involved in Community Schools v. Seattle School District No. 1*, 551 U.S. 701 (2007) (Chapter 3, § 3D). Chief Justice Roberts' opinion for the Court (speaking for a 5–4 majority as to most issues) ruled that efforts by the Seattle and Louisville school districts to achieve actual integration ran afoul the Equal Protection Clause because they used racial criteria without sufficient justification. (Justice Kennedy wrote a concurring opinion that would allow more liberal use of such criteria.) Justice Breyer's dissenting opinion lambasted the Roberts opinion for minimizing or disregarding bushels of Supreme Court precedent; the Chief Justice responded by parsing most of those precedents more narrowly than Breyer would and relying on the Court's now-established jurisprudence holding that even "remedial" race-based classifications are subject to strict scrutiny. E.g., *Grutter v. Bollinger*, 539 U.S. 306 (2003) (Chapter 3, § 3C).

Another version of a *stare decisis* debate surfaced in the Court's highly anticipated decision on the constitutionality of the Affordable Care Act. In *National Federation of Independent Business v. Sebelius*, 567 U.S. 519 (2012), Chief Justice Roberts—much to the surprise of nearly all observers—provided the fifth vote to uphold the most salient and controversial legislative achievement of President Obama's first term. The Chief Justice joined the Court's moderates in holding that the health care law was a valid exercise of Congress' power to tax. Yet he and the Court's more conservative justices also surprised many by holding that the Act violated the Commerce Clause and could not be upheld as a valid exercise of that federal power. Given the Court's expansive Commerce Clause precedents, especially the Court's 1942 decision in *Wickard v. Filburn*, many observers had thought the Act would easily survive Commerce Clause review. While the Court did not directly overrule a precedent as it did in *Citizens United*, it applied past precedents narrowly to reach this result.

Another example of the Court's conservative pragmatism is *District of Columbia v. Heller*, 554 U.S. 570 (2008), where the same 5–4 majority as in *Carhart II* invoked the Second Amendment to strike down the District of Columbia's bar to possession of loaded and usable handguns within the home. Although *Heller* read the Second Amendment more broadly than the Court had done in previous cases, it did not overrule any precedent, though it did read them very narrowly. Justice Scalia's *Heller* opinion is the most ambitious deployment of original meaning as the reason to strike down a federal statute in the Court's history, and has already sparked enormous controversy, with even conservative commentators claiming that *Heller* is the originalist's version of *Griswold v. Connecticut* (1965) or *Roe v. Wade* (1973). We present the materials debated among the Justices as a Problem at the end of Chapter 2.

3. *National Security and the War on Terror.* Less than a year after *Bush v. Gore,* on 9/11/2001, international terrorists destroyed both towers of the World Trade Center and destroyed part of the Pentagon. This dramatic attack on landmarks within our borders alarmed the nation, triggered a far-reaching response by the Bush Administration, and fueled a national conversation about the acceptable balance between national security and human rights. The Bush Administration's response to international terrorism raised a host of constitutional issues, from the legality of presidentially approved torture to the constitutionality of the NSA's secret wiretap program. The only issues that have thus far reached the Supreme Court for full briefing and decision have involved the Administration's indefinite detention of suspected terrorists; these cases are assembled in Chapter 8, § 3 of the casebook.

The first major case was *Hamdi v. Rumsfeld*, 542 U.S. 507 (2004) (Chapter 8, § 3), where a fractured Court ruled that the President could detain American citizens who fought against their country abroad, but that the Administration was required to justify continued detention before neutral decisionmakers. (The Court applied the balancing approach for procedural due process established in *Mathews v. Eldridge* (Chapter 5, § 6).) Following *Hamdi*, the Administration established administrative tribunals to determine whether there remained good reason to detain persons alleged to be "illegal enemy combatants." (In a statutory decision with constitutional overtones, the Court in *Hamdan v. Rumsfeld*, 548 U.S. 557 (2006), applied the Steel Seizure framework rule that "military commissions" created by the President to try illegal combatants for war crimes was contrary to statute.)

The Administration persuaded Congress to authorize military tribunals, with limited process review in the D.C. Circuit, in exchange for a congressional abrogation of the habeas corpus rights of persons detained in connection with the war on terror. Detainees held at Camp X-Ray in Guantanamo Bay, Cuba (territory occupied by the United States and administered under a long-term lease from Cuba) sought to overturn this deal as inconsistent with the Habeas Clause of Article I, § 9, cl. 2. Again, a closely divided (5–4) Court agreed with the challengers. In *Boumediene v. Bush*, 553 U.S. 723 (2008) (Chapter 8, § 3), the Court held that these detainees were entitled to habeas corpus hearings before Article III federal judges, and not just the administrative process provided by recent statute. Dissenting Justices warned that the Court was risking American lives under circumstances where the President and the Secretary of Defense were better situated to make judgments.

On February 13, 2016, Justice Scalia unexpectedly died during a trip to Texas. He was widely considered the most influential conservative on the Court, and his writings did much to shape constitutional debates on and off the Court. He wrote some important majority opinions, such as the first decision finding the Second Amendment to be a source of enforceable individual rights. But his influence was perhaps more often felt through his concurrences and dissents, along with his extra-judicial writings and speeches. More than most, Scalia's departure from the bench meant the loss of not only a vote, but also a provocative voice that was a flashpoint for both admirers and detractors. To a considerable degree, Scalia's pointed opinions framed the terms of constitutional debate, both on and off the Court.

President Obama nominated Merrick Garland, a widely respected judge on the D.C. Circuit, to replace Scalia. After the nomination was announced in mid-March, Senate Majority Leader Mitch McConnell announced that the Senate would not hold hearings on the nomination. Instead, he said, the Senate would allow the public to have input via the November election, postponing any action until a new President was in office. This left the Supreme Court with only eight Justices for almost all of its October 2016 Term. President Trump nominated Neil Gorsuch to fill the position. Gorsuch was confirmed by the Senate after a rule change to eliminate filibusters on Supreme Court nominees and allow confirmation on a simple majority vote.

After Justice Kennedy retired in the summer of 2018, President Trump nominated a conservative judge on the D.C. Circuit, Brett Kavanaugh to replace him. Even in a politically polarized era, Kavanaugh's confirmation hearing stood out for its bitterness on both sides. Kavanaugh was accused of having committed sexual assaults against women in his younger years, charges that he vehemently denied. He was confirmed by the Senate in a 50–48 vote.

APPENDIX: RECENT JUSTICES

The Burger Court

We have already discussed Justices Harlan, Douglas, and Black, all of whom served under Chief Justice Burger. After Harlan and Black left the Court, the Burger Court was remarkably stable. Justices marked with an asterisk also served under Chief Justice Rehnquist.

Warren Earl Burger, a Minnesota native, graduated from William Mitchell College of Law in St. Paul, where he attended night school. In 1953, he became an assistant attorney general. He became nationally known after he argued an anti-Communist case in the Supreme Court when the Solicitor General had refused to do so. In 1956, he was appointed to the D.C. Circuit, where he was a conservative voice on what was to become a highly liberal bench. He was appointed Chief Justice by President Nixon in 1969. As Chief Justice, he appears to have been poorly regarded by his colleagues—he seemed to have Earl Warren's uneven legal ability but not his personal charm. He was, however, a very effective administrator. Although he was generally conservative, he was far less consistent than his successor in this regard, and joined (or occasionally even wrote) some liberal decisions.

Lewis Powell* was a corporate lawyer in Richmond, Virginia before joining the Supreme Court. He had also served on the Richmond school board, an experience that helped shape his attitudes toward racial issues. His national reputation was due to a stint as president of the American Bar Association. He was technically a Democrat at the time of his nomination, although there is nothing in his judicial opinions to hint at any great sympathy for the post-1968 Democratic Party. Early in his career on the Court, Powell was flattered by a law review article comparing him to Justice Harlan as a judicial craftsman. He seems to have made a conscious effort to be the moderate "voice of reason" on the Court, with the result that he was often the swing voter on the Burger Court.

Harry Blackmun* was appointed by Nixon. He graduated from Harvard *summa cum laude* in mathematics, went on to Harvard Law School, and then clerked for a judge on the Eighth Circuit. He joined the largest firm in Minneapolis, and then became counsel for the Mayo Clinic until President Eisenhower appointed him to the Eighth Circuit. President Nixon turned to him after he failed to obtain confirmation for Judges Haynsworth (who, in retrospect, would have been a good Justice) and Carswell (who was unqualified). Blackmun and Burger were called the "Minnesota Twins" in their early years on the Court, but Blackmun moved progressively away from Burger and was considered a liberal by the time William Rehnquist became Chief Justice.

William Brennan, Jr.* was appointed to the Court by Eisenhower, but was ultimately to emerge as the liberal spokesman on the Burger Court. He had practiced law in Newark until World War II. After returning to practice after the war, he was appointed as a trial judge, and then ultimately to the state supreme court. On the Warren Court, he played an important but quiet role as a moderate coalition-builder. After Warren left the Court, Brennan found himself increasingly in dissent, but up to the very end, he still enjoyed surprising successes in building majorities for occasional liberal results.

John Paul Stevens* was a prominent Chicago antitrust specialist before he was appointed to the Seventh Circuit. Like Byron White and

William Rehnquist, he had served as a Supreme Court law clerk before entering practice. He had come to public attention by leading an investigation into corruption in the Illinois courts. His nomination to the Supreme Court was assisted by his friendship with Attorney General Edward Levi, who had taught an antitrust course with Stevens at the University of Chicago. Justice Stevens quickly obtained a reputation on the Court as a maverick who joined neither ideological camp. During the Rehnquist and Roberts Courts, however, he has been the least conservative Justice, simply because all the newer appointments have been more conservative. As a senior Justice when the Court ruled in a more liberal direction, Stevens assigned himself important opinions for the Court in landmark cases involving campaign finance, presidential power, and constitutional standing. He was a forceful dissenter in cases where the Court has struck down laws regulating firearms, race-based political gerrymanders, campaign finance regulation, and violence against women.

Thurgood Marshall* played a major role in the *Brown* litigation and is probably the most dramatically successful appellate advocate at the Supreme Court level in our nation's history. We detail his historic role as a civil rights advocate in Chapter 2. He was a Howard Law School graduate and became the head of the NAACP Legal Defense and Education Fund, Inc. in 1940. President Kennedy appointed him to the United States Court of Appeals for the Second Circuit; four years later, he became Solicitor General. In 1967, President Johnson nominated him to the Supreme Court. Because he joined the Court just as Warren was about to leave, Justice Marshall was increasingly at odds with the conservative trend on the Court. He and Brennan were staunch allies. Although Justice Marshall was the Court's leading philosopher of equal protection issues across the board (race, sex, poverty, disability, etc.), he was also the Court's leading expert on issues of civil procedure and wrote leading opinions for the Court establishing and enforcing bright-line rules in this area.

Byron White* was a Rhodes Scholar, top of his class at the Yale Law School, a law clerk to Chief Justice Vinson, and a professional football player. His appointment to the Court resulted from his long-time friendship with John Kennedy, going back to his time as a Rhodes Scholar at Oxford. He was an important member of the Kennedy campaign team, became a deputy attorney general, and then moved up to the Supreme Court. During the Warren Court, he was a moderate swing voter, but he became increasingly conservative as he aged, so that ultimately he was sometimes more conservative than several later Republican nominees. Perhaps as a result of his federal service, he seemed to defer to the position taken by the federal government in important cases.

Sandra Day O'Connor* was, as we assume you know, the first woman ever appointed to the Supreme Court. She grew up on a 160,000-acre family ranch in Arizona. She was a classmate of William Rehnquist at the Stanford Law School, but despite a strong academic record, had trouble finding a job. After becoming a state assistant attorney general, she entered politics and eventually became Republican majority leader in the Arizona Senate, the first woman in the United States to hold such a position, before moving on to become a state judge. Given her career in state politics, it is not surprising that she devoted considerable energy to issues of federalism and was the primary philosopher of the Court's federalism jurisprudence. As a swing vote on the tightly divided Rehnquist Court, Justice O'Connor's voice was critically important on high-voltage issues of race-based affirmative action, gay rights, sex discrimination, campaign finance regulation, and presidential power.

William Hubbs Rehnquist was the most conservative Justice on the Burger Court, but was outflanked by Antonin Scalia and Clarence Thomas during his own Chief Justiceship. He grew up in Milwaukee, graduated first in his class from Stanford Law School, and clerked for Justice Robert Jackson. (Jackson was a brilliant maverick during the Vinson and early Warren Courts, somewhat like Justice Stevens on the Burger Court.) After his clerkship, Rehnquist moved to Arizona and became a supporter of Barry Goldwater. He became the head of the Office of Legal Counsel in the Nixon Justice Department, before being nominated for the Court in 1971. He was strongly but unsuccessfully opposed by liberal groups when he was nominated for Chief Justice.

Potter Stewart was the son of an old Ohio political family. Like White, he was a Yale law school graduate. Eisenhower appointed him to the Sixth Circuit in 1954 and to the Supreme Court in 1958. As a Justice, he had a reputation for solid competence and moderation.

The Rehnquist Court

We have already discussed Chief Justice Rehnquist and the seven Justices who served under both him and Burger. The following are the new Justices appointed during the tenure of Chief Justice Rehnquist.

Anthony Kennedy was President Reagan's third effort at filling the Powell seat after Robert Bork was defeated and a second nomination was withdrawn. Kennedy graduated from Harvard Law School in 1961 and practiced law in Sacramento until his appointment to the Ninth Circuit in 1975. In his first years on the Court, Justice Kennedy started out in Justice Scalia's shadow, but early on their judicial philosophies diverged. He was a moderate conservative who prided himself as the Court's political philosopher. Justice Kennedy took a moderately activist stance in protecting a wide array of constitutional values—from the equal protection and privacy rights of gay people (Chapters 4 and 5); to the First Amendment's protection of speech, even as applied to campaign finance and the internet (Chapter 6); to federalism limitations on congressional power (Chapter 7); to the habeas corpus rights of suspected terrorists held without charges at Camp X-Ray in Guantanamo Bay, Cuba (Chapter 8). As a swing vote on both the Rehnquist and Roberts Courts, Justice Kennedy's nuanced views on the right of a woman to an abortion shaped that constitutional right in important ways (Chapter 5). He retired from the Supreme Court in the summer of 2018.

David Souter was a judge on the New Hampshire Supreme Court and (briefly) the United States Court of Appeals for the First Circuit before his Supreme Court nomination. He graduated from Harvard College in 1961 and Harvard Law School in 1966, and was also a Rhodes Scholar. He was known as the "stealth nominee" because so little was known of his positions at the time of his nomination. Although initially seen as conservative, he was later seen as a moderate and sometimes allied himself with Stevens. Justice Souter was a libertarian and evolutionary historicist in the mold of the second Justice Harlan.

Antonin Scalia was, in some ways, a modern, conservative version of Hugo Black. Like Black, he believed in textualism, favored bright-line rules, and abhorred "balancing tests." He also shared Black's penchant for blunt, memorable prose but (very much unlike the genteel Black) tended to lob *ad hominem* barbs at his colleagues when he disagreed with them. Scalia was one of a group of prominent members of the University of Chicago Law School faculty to be appointed to the federal appellate courts. He was nominated along with Rehnquist's appointment to the Chief Justiceship; liberals made a strategic decision to let Scalia sail through while concentrating their fire on Rehnquist. Scalia was the first person of Italian ancestry to serve on the Court. He was more interested in legal theory than most of his colleagues on the bench. He was a formidable dissenter, whose blunt and colorful prose was usually aimed over the heads of his colleagues and directed to Federalist Society law professors, bloggers, think tanks, and even political leaders.

Clarence Thomas replaced Thurgood Marshall, and is only the second African American to serve on the Court. He graduated from College of the Holy Cross in 1971 and Yale Law School in 1974. His most important pre-judicial experience was as the Chair of the Equal Employment Opportunity Commission. He also served briefly on the D.C. Circuit. Because he disavowed most of his previous statements relating to constitutional issues, and claimed never to have discussed *Roe v. Wade* (the abortion decision) with anyone, his confirmation hearings revolved around issues of character. His supporters stressed his rise from an impoverished background; his detractors were more concerned about allegations of sexual harassment made by Anita Hill, one of his former staff members. The Senate confirmed Thomas by only 52–48, the closest ever for Supreme Court confirmation (a vote margin later tied by the Kavanaugh vote). He and Scalia almost always voted together during the 1990s, but in the new millennium Justice Thomas emerged as a more distinctive voice on the Court. More than any other Justice in the Court's history, he is willing to overrule precedent—often whole lines of precedent—he believes inconsistent with original constitutional meaning.

Ruth Bader Ginsburg was a professor at Columbia University Law School when President Carter tapped her for the D.C. Circuit. She was well known for her role in leading the Women's Rights Project of the ACLU. During the 1970s, she participated either as counsel for a party or as *amicus* in the leading gender discrimination cases of the day, including *Reed v. Reed, Frontiero v. Richardson,* and *Craig v. Boren,* all of which are included in Chapter 4. In light of this background, she surprised many observers by her nonactivist, middle-of-the-road record as a D.C. Circuit judge. At the time of her elevation to the Court, she was widely viewed as the least liberal of the Clinton appointees to the D.C. Circuit. On the Supreme Court, Justice Ginsburg has been a pragmatist, for the most part aligning herself with Justices Stevens and Breyer. In sex discrimination cases, she is a forceful voice for liberal feminist positions she pressed at the ACLU, best illustrated by her scholarly opinion in the landmark case that sex-integrated the Virginia Military Institute (Chapter 4, § 2B1).

Stephen Breyer was appointed to the First Circuit by President Carter in 1980. A former Harvard law professor and chief counsel to the Senate Judiciary Committee, Breyer is a respected scholar, primarily in the fields of administrative law and regulated industries. As a First Circuit judge, he had a reputation as a moderate. Reminiscent of Justice Brandeis, Justice Breyer is a fact-oriented pragmatist. He is strongly interested in questions like, How does the challenged rule actually work? What would be the real-world consequences of different courses of action by the Court? Deferential to the political process, Breyer is reluctant to adopt highly activist stances of either a conservative or liberal dimension. Although he usually votes with the more liberal Justices in constitutional cases, Justice Breyer's cautious and pragmatic philosophy made him a judicial soul mate for Justice O'Connor, whose departure from the Court deprived him of an important conservative ally.

The Roberts Court

Justice O'Connor announced her intention to leave the Court on July 1, 2005, and President George W. Bush appointed Judge John Roberts to succeed her. When Chief Justice Rehnquist died in September 2005, the President nominated Judge Roberts to be the Chief Justice and ultimately nominated Judge Samuel Alito to replace Justice O'Connor. In 2009, Justice Souter left the Court, and President Barack Obama replaced him with Judge Sonia Sotomayor. A year later, when Justice Stevens left after

35 years on the Court, President Obama selected Elena Kagan to take that seat.

John Glover Roberts, Jr. is the seventeenth Chief Justice of the United States. The son of a Bethlehem Steel plant manager, Roberts graduated in 1979 from the Harvard Law School, where he was Managing Editor of the *Harvard Law Review*. After clerking for then-Justice Rehnquist, Roberts was a special assistant to Attorney General William French Smith and was Associate Counsel to President Reagan from 1982–86. In a highly successful career in private practice, Roberts argued 39 cases before the Supreme Court. He was a judge on the D.C. Circuit for two years before his nomination to the Court. His judicial philosophy, clearly articulated in his confirmation hearings and in his judicial opinions, is pragmatic, with a strong Federalist Society tilt. A distinctive feature of the Chief Justice's jurisprudence is his close attention to precedent, and his Court is (thus far) strongly inclined not to overrule even constitutional precedents, though the Chief is inclined to give a narrow reading to liberal Court decisions from earlier Courts.

Samuel Anthony Alito grew up in New Jersey, the son of an Italian immigrant father and Italian-American mother, both schoolteachers. After graduating from Princeton University, he earned his law degree at the Yale Law School in 1975. After Yale, Alito served in the Army and then the Army Reserves, ultimately reaching the rank of captain. He served as assistant to Solicitor General Rex Lee and then to Attorney General Edwin Meese during the Reagan Administration and was a judge of the Third Circuit from 1990 to 2006. Like the Chief Justice, Justice Alito is a pragmatist with a strong Federalist Society tilt. Within the Court, he has earned respect from liberals as well as conservatives for his judicious approach to decisionmaking and his narrowly reasoned opinions that stick closely to legal materials and that avoid the personal attacks and hyperbole characteristic of the modern Court.

Sonia Sotomayor was born and raised in Bronx, New York. Her father was a tool and die worker with a third grade education, and he died when she was nine. Her mother was a nurse. Sotomayor graduated from Princeton University and Yale Law School, and worked as a prosecutor and commercial litigator before becoming a judge. She was a judge on the Second Circuit Court of Appeals when President Obama appointed her to the Supreme Court and made her its first Latina member. Justice Sotomayor was appointed to the federal bench by presidents of both parties, having been nominated to be a judge on the United States District Court for the Southern District of New York by President George H.W. Bush in 1992, and nominated for the Second Circuit six years later by President Bill Clinton. As a judge on these lower courts, Justice Sotomayor's reputation was as a centrist. In her first few years on the

Supreme Court, she has sided with the more moderate wing in many of the most controversial cases.

Elena Kagan Like President Obama's first appointment to the Court (Justice Sotamyor), Elena Kagan added to the Court's gender diversity and was born in New York. Unlike Justice Sotomayor (a lifelong Yankees fan), Kagan roots for the Mets. Kagan was the first Justice since Rehnquist to take a seat on the Court without having prior judicial experience. At the time of her appointment, however, Kagan was the Solicitor General of the United States—a position sometimes referred to as the Supreme Court's "tenth justice." In addition to her service as Solicitor General, Kagan spent several years in senior posts in the Clinton White House. Before she joined the Court, Justice Kagan was probably best known as the first woman dean of Harvard Law School, an institution she led from 2003–2009.

Neil Gorsuch was born in Denver but graduated from high school in Bethesda, Maryland. His mother briefly headed the Environmental Protection Agency under President Reagan. He graduated from Columbia and then Harvard Law School, before receiving a graduate degree at Oxford. He was a law clerk for Justices White and Kennedy before spending a decade as a litigator in private practice. He then served briefly in the Justice Department. In 2006, he was appointed to the Tenth Circuit. Shortly after taking office, President Trump nominated Gorsuch to fill the position vacated by Justice Scalia's unexpected death. Early indications are that Justice Gorsuch will be a staunch conservative vote.

Brett Kavanaugh grew up in the Washington, D.C., area. He is a Yale Law School graduate. After a judicial clerkship in the D.C. Circuit, he worked for the special prosecutor investigating President Bill Clinton. He then served in various staff positions in the Bush Administration. He was appointed to the D.C. Circuit in 2006 by President George W. Bush. He was nominated by President Trump to replace Justice Kennedy. His record on the D.C. Circuit indicated a strong dedication to enforcing the separation of powers. However, his views on federalism issues and many individual rights issues were less clear at the time of his appointment, because the D.C. Circuit's caseload is dominated by cases involving government agencies rather than individual or state's rights claims.

CHAPTER 2

AN INTRODUCTION TO CONSTITUTIONAL DECISIONMAKING

■ ■ ■

What is the source of the Supreme Court's power to declare laws unconstitutional? How should that power be exercised? What are its limits? These three questions are basic to understanding constitutional law. Unfortunately, there are no universally accepted answers. We use *Brown v. Board of Education* as a springboard from which to explore these questions. This chapter introduces you to this great constitutional decision, explores the complex constitutional questions it raises, and relates *Brown* to the theoretical debate over the legitimacy and limits of judicial review. If you have not already done so, it would be useful for you to read Chapter 1, which provides a thumbnail sketch of American constitutional history.

SECTION 1. *BROWN v. BOARD OF EDUCATION*: A CASE STUDY[1]

Like many other American cities in 1951, most important public and private facilities in Topeka, Kansas were segregated by race. There was one hotel for blacks only; the rest served whites exclusively. Downtown restaurants refused to serve blacks or limited them to a take-out menu. One movie theater was for blacks only; another admitted blacks but restricted them to seats in the balcony; the other five movie houses excluded blacks entirely. The swimming pool at a public park was open to blacks—for one day each summer. Banks did not lend money to black-owned businesses, and white-owned businesses hired blacks for predominantly menial jobs. Although the city's junior high and high schools had been ordered integrated under state law, School

---

[1] This story is drawn from Richard Kluger, *Simple Justice: The History of* Brown v. Board of Education *and Black America's Struggle for Equality* (rev. ed. 2004); Mark V. Tushnet, *The NAACP's Legal Strategy Against Segregated Education, 1925–1950* (1987), and *Making Civil Rights Law: Thurgood Marshall and the Supreme Court, 1936–1961* (1994); Justin Driver, *The School-House Gate: Public Education, the Supreme Court,, and the Battle for the American Mind* (2018); Michael J. Klarman, *From Jim Crow to Civil Rights: The Supreme Court and the Struggle for Racial Equality* (2004); Mary Dudziak, *The Limits of Good Faith: Desegregation in Topeka, Kansas, 1950–1956*, 5 Law & Hist. Rev. 351 (1987); Philip Elman, *The Solicitor General's Office, Justice Frankfurter, and Civil Rights Litigation, 1946–1960: An Oral History*, 100 Harv. L. Rev. 817 (1987); Dennis Hutchinson, *Unanimity and Desegregation: Decisionmaking in the Supreme Court, 1948–1958*, 68 Geo. L.J. 1 (1979); Mark V. Tushnet, with Katya Lezin, *What Really Happened in* Brown v. Board of Education, 91 Colum. L. Rev. 1867 (1991).

Superintendent Kenneth McFarland discouraged racial mixing. [Dudziak, *Topeka, Kansas,* 366–68; Kluger, *Simple Justice,* 375–76, 380.]

The city's elementary schools were segregated by state law. The black elementary schools had what the city considered to be comparable facilities to those in white elementary schools, except that they were located further away from the homes of black schoolchildren. Linda Brown, for example, had to leave home at 7:40 a.m. and walk through train-switching yards in order to catch a bus that would get her to school by 9:00 a.m. [Kluger, *Simple Justice,* 409–10.] Oliver Brown, Linda's father, and other parents objected to Topeka's segregated elementary schools. The National Association for the Advancement of Colored People (NAACP) filed suit in federal court on behalf of Brown and similarly situated black parents on February 28, 1951.

The NAACP was seeking invalidation of Topeka's segregated school system on the ground that it was inconsistent with the Equal Protection Clause of the Fourteenth Amendment to the U.S. Constitution (read § 1 of the Fourteenth Amendment, Appendix 1). The NAACP argued that legal segregation of the races in elementary school was tantamount to legalizing a racial caste system harmful to blacks. The NAACP supported its position by introducing studies of the detrimental impact of segregation on black children. Federal District Judge Huxman ruled that this evidence was legally irrelevant to the constitutional issue. Because students of color had roughly equal facilities as those enjoyed by white students, Judge Huxman felt constrained by prior decisions of the United States Supreme Court to reject the NAACP's claim for legal relief. *Brown v. Board of Education,* 98 F. Supp. 797 (D. Kan. 1951) (three-judge court). Judge Huxman surely felt that his decision was regrettable, perhaps even tragic, as a matter of morality and policy. Was his disposition correct, as a matter of law, in 1951? Consider the following materials.

A. THE FOURTEENTH AMENDMENT
AND RACE: 1865–1912

The most important legal development in Reconstruction after the Civil War was the adoption of the Fourteenth Amendment (Chapter 1, §§ 3–4).[2] Congress delegated to a "Joint Committee of Fifteen" the task of drafting a constitutional amendment to protect the slaves freed by the

---

[2]   The story of the Fourteenth Amendment is taken from William E. Nelson, *The Fourteenth Amendment: From Political Principle to Judicial Doctrine* (1988); Alexander M. Bickel, *The Original Understanding and the Segregation Decision,* 69 Harv. L. Rev. 1 (1955). On the intellectual background of the Fourteenth Amendment in abolitionist thought, see Eric Foner, *The Strange Career of the Reconstruction Amendments,* 108 Yale L.J. 2003 (1999); Jacobus tenBroek, *The Antislavery Origins of the Fourteenth Amendment* (1951); Robert Kaczorowski, *Revolutionary Constitutionalism in the Era of the Civil War and Reconstruction,* 61 NYU L. Rev. 863 (1986); David A.J. Richards, *Abolitionist Political and Constitutional Theory and the Reconstruction Amendments,* 25 Loy. (L.A.) L. Rev. 1187 (1992).

Thirteenth Amendment from southern efforts to deprive them of political and civil rights. On January 20, 1866, a subcommittee proposed the following language: "Congress shall have power to make all laws necessary and proper to secure to all citizens of the United States, in every State, the same political rights and privileges; and to all persons in every State equal protection in the enjoyment of life, liberty, and property." After debate, the Joint Committee presented the following language to Congress on February 3:

> The Congress shall have power to make all laws which shall be necessary and proper to secure to the citizens of each State all privileges and immunities of citizens in the several states (Art. 4, Sec. 2); and to all persons in the several states equal protection in the rights of life, liberty and property (5th Amendment).

Note that the February 3 language was inspired by existing constitutional provisions and, further, distinguished between "privileges and immunities" of *citizens* and "rights" of *persons* [Nelson, *Fourteenth Amendment,* 52–53]. This proposal died in March, as the House focused on passing the Civil Rights Act of 1866.[3] Opponents claimed that Congress had no constitutional authority to enact such a statute, and that charge revitalized interest in a new amendment.

Within the Joint Committee, Representative Robert Owen proposed a five-section draft that was to form the framework for the Fourteenth Amendment. Section 1 prohibited "discrimination * * * as to the civil rights of persons because of race, color, or previous condition of servitude." Although adopting Owen's framework, the Joint Committee broadened § 1 as follows:

> No state shall make or enforce any law which shall abridge the privileges or immunities of citizens of the United States; nor shall any state deprive any person of life, liberty or property without due process of law; nor deny to any person within its jurisdiction the equal protection of the laws.

Like the February draft of the amendment, new § 1 relied on existing constitutional terms: *privileges and immunities* (Art. IV), which had been broadly defined to include the common law rights embodied in the 1866 statute, as well as rights to carry on a trade or business, *Corfield v. Coryell,* 6 Fed. Cas. 546 (C.C.E.D. Pa. 1823); and *due process* (Amend. V). It is not clear from the committee's deliberations what the term *equal protection* was meant to add. The equality principle originated among prewar abolitionists, who maintained that a truly neutral government owes the

---

[3]   The Civil Rights Act of 1866 assured "citizens of every race and color" the "same right * * * as is enjoyed by white citizens" to make and enforce contracts, to pursue lawsuits, to hold and alienate or receive property, and to be protected in their personal and material security. 14 Stat. 27, now codified at 42 U.S.C. §§ 1981–1982.

humblest person the same protection of the laws as it owes the high and mighty. The "equal protection" language was taken from the Ohio Constitution of 1851. [William N. Eskridge Jr., *Original Meaning and Marriage Equality*, 52 Hous. L. Rev. 1067 (2015).] The House passed the proposed amendment on May 10 by a vote of 128–37.

Senator Jacob Howard introduced the amendment in the Senate. He characterized § 1's equal protection guarantee this way: "This abolishes all class legislation in the States and does away with the injustice of subjecting one caste of persons to a code not applicable to another. * * * It protects the black man in his fundamental rights as a citizen with the same shield which it throws over the white man." Senator Howard also stated that the Privileges or Immunities Clause of the proposed amendment embodied the protections of the Bill of Rights, as well as other fundamental rights protected by the Privileges and Immunities Clause in Article IV. After a debate generally unilluminating as to § 1, the amendment passed the Senate by a vote of 33–12 and was submitted to the states for ratification on June 16.

The proposed amendment was the central issue in the 1866 congressional elections, and the victory of the pro-amendment Republicans was felt to be a popular endorsement of the amendment. The debates were pitched at a rather general level and rarely focused on the technical meaning of *privileges or immunities* or *equal protection.* Proponents of the amendment emphasized that it would assure former slaves and others their "natural, God-given rights," including an "absolute equality of rights of the whole people, high and low, rich and poor, white and black" [Nelson, *Fourteenth Amendment,* 67, 73]. In the argot of the times, the amendment was seen as protecting against "class legislation" and "unjust and oppressive state laws" [*id.* at 79]. Most historians have argued that the amendment was meant to assure the same kind of *civil rights* guaranteed by the 1866 statute (described in note *c, supra*)—common law rights to contract, own and transfer property, invoke legal process—but not *political rights* such as voting or *social rights* such as private association.[4]

In any event, the proposed amendment was controversial. It was opposed by President Andrew Johnson, many prominent Republicans, and most leading Democrats. Opponents joined with proponents in favoring the equality idea but opposed the amendment on the grounds that it (1) was adopted by an unrepresentative Congress, *i.e.,* without southern state

---

[4] See Michael Les Benedict, *A Compromise of Principle: Congressional Republicans and Reconstruction 1863–1869* (1974); Earl Maltz, *Civil Rights, the Constitution, and Congress, 1863– 1869* (1990). The matter is more complicated, however. Nelson, *Fourteenth Amendment* 126–32 shows that many Republicans supporting the Fourteenth Amendment distinguished between (protected) civil and (unprotected) political rights—but many others did not. By Nelson's account, it is not entirely clear whether the Fifteenth Amendment assuring people of color the right to vote added a new protection to those in the Fourteenth Amendment or confirmed or clarified protections already intended.

representation; (2) compelled equal treatment for African Americans, Native Americans, and the "Mongol race" (Chinese), who were in fact not equal to people of European descent; and (3) centralized power by affording national constitutional rights directly against the states and thereby changed the essential federalism of the Constitution [Nelson, *Fourteenth Amendment*, 91–109]. It took over two years to obtain the approval of three-fourths of the states, and two states tried to revoke their approval. Congress overruled those revocations, and Secretary of State Seward proclaimed the amendment ratified on July 28, 1868 (Chapter 1, § 4). The Fourteenth Amendment was followed by the Fifteenth Amendment (1870), which guaranteed former slaves the right to vote. Congress enacted further civil rights statutes, the most important of which was the 1875 statute, which prohibited racial discrimination by public accommodations such as inns and common carriers such as railroads.

The Reconstruction effort met a discouraging reaction at the state level. When the eleven seceding states rejoined the Union, their constitutions provided equal protection guarantees for former slaves, including assurances of equal educational opportunities in several state constitutions. After federal troops were withdrawn from the South in 1877, however, segregationist whites regained political control. Over time, they adopted laws and practices designed to strip black citizens of their right to vote and to segregate blacks from whites in public schools, accommodations, and transportation. Congress after 1877 did nothing to discourage these "Jim Crow" laws, and the federal courts retreated from the broad rhetoric of the ratification debates.

In *The Slaughter House Cases*, 83 U.S. (16 Wall.) 36 (1873) (Chapter 5, § 1), the Supreme Court read § 1 narrowly. The Court limited the Privileges or Immunities Clause to rights distinctive to national citizenship, such as interstate travel. This holding was a retreat from the apparent meaning of that clause, which the framers expected to protect civil rights such as common law rights to hold property and enter contracts. The *Slaughter House Cases* shifted political and constitutional theorizing to the Equal Protection Clause. In *Strauder v. West Virginia*, 100 U.S. 303 (1879), the Court overturned a West Virginia statute excluding any but "white male persons" from juries—arguably contrary to the Framers' intent *not* to regulate political rights. The Court's opinion reasoned from the "true spirit and meaning" of the Fourteenth Amendment, specifically, its protect-the-freed-slaves purpose. "It ordains * * * that the law in the States shall be the same for the black as for the white; that all persons, whether colored or white, shall stand equal before the laws of the States, and, in regard to the colored race, for whose protection the amendment was primarily designed, that no discrimination shall be made against them by law because of their color." Given this purpose, the exclusion of blacks from juries was unconstitutional because the exclusion "is practically a brand upon them, affixed by the law, an assertion of their inferiority, and a stimulant to that race prejudice which is an impediment to securing to individuals of the race that equal justice which the law aims to secure to all others."

Strauder suggested a potentially far-reaching vision of the Reconstruction Amendments, but in *The Civil Rights Cases*, 109 U.S. 3 (1883) (Chapter 7, § 3A), the Court invalidated as beyond the power of Congress the 1875 Civil Rights Act's federal remedy for private racial discrimination. The Court held that the Fourteenth Amendment was aimed at discriminatory state laws, not discriminatory private action; hence, § 5 of that amendment did not authorize Congress to regulate private activity. Although the Thirteenth Amendment did empower the federal government to regulate private activity directly, the mere refusal to serve blacks "has nothing to do with slavery or involuntary servitude" prohibited by that amendment.

Plessy v. Ferguson
163 U.S. 537, 16 S.Ct. 1138, 41 L.Ed. 256 (1896)

Justice Brown * * * delivered the opinion of the Court.

[An 1890 Louisiana statute required railway companies to provide "equal but separate accommodations for the white and colored races" and made it a crime for passengers to violate the required segregation. In 1892, the state prosecuted Homer Adolph Plessy, whose ancestry was one-eighth African and seven-eighths European, for refusing to leave the car reserved for whites. Plessy argued that he was entitled to sit in the whites-only car and that the state had deprived him of a "property" interest in his whiteness and of the equal protection of the laws. The Court brushed aside the taking-of-property argument and focused on the constitutionality of the Louisiana statute. Writing for seven Justices, Justice Brown ruled that the Thirteenth Amendment was not violated, because "[a] statute which implies merely a legal distinction between the white and colored races—a distinction which is founded in the color of the two races, and which must always exist so long as white men are distinguished from the other race by color—has no tendency to destroy the legal equality of the two races, or reestablish a state of involuntary servitude." The remainder of the opinion addressed the Fourteenth Amendment claim.]

The object of the amendment was undoubtedly to enforce the absolute equality of the two races before the law, but in the nature of things it could not have been intended to abolish distinctions based upon color, or to enforce social, as distinguished from political equality, or a commingling of the two races upon terms unsatisfactory to either. Laws permitting, and even requiring, their separation in places where they are liable to be brought into contact do not necessarily imply the inferiority of either race to the other, and have been generally, if not universally, recognized as within the competency of the state legislatures in the exercise of their police power. The most common instance of this is connected with the establishment of separate schools for white and colored children, which has been held to be a valid exercise of the legislative power even by courts of States where the political rights of the colored race have been longest and most earnestly enforced.

[Justice Brown distinguished between "laws interfering with the political equality of the negro," such as the jury-exclusion law struck down in *Strauder*, and "those requiring the separation of the two races in schools, theatres and railway carriages."]

So far, then, as a conflict with the Fourteenth Amendment is concerned, the case reduces itself to the question whether the statute of Louisiana is a reasonable regulation, and with respect to this there must necessarily be a large discretion on the part of the legislature. In determining the question of reasonableness it is at liberty to act with reference to the established usages, customs and traditions of the people, and with a view to the promotion of their comfort, and the preservation of the public peace and good order. Gauged by this standard, we cannot say that a law which authorizes or even requires the separation of the two races in public conveyances is unreasonable, or more obnoxious to the Fourteenth Amendment than the acts of Congress requiring separate schools for colored children in the District of Columbia, the constitutionality of which does not seem to have been questioned, or the corresponding acts of state legislatures.

We consider the underlying fallacy of the plaintiff's argument to consist in the assumption that the enforced separation of the two races stamps the colored race with a badge of inferiority. If this be so, it is not by reason of anything found in the act, but solely because the colored race chooses to put that construction upon it. * * * The argument also assumes that social prejudices may be overcome by legislation, and that equal rights cannot be secured to the negro except by an enforced commingling of the two races. We cannot accept this proposition. If the two races are to meet upon terms of social equality, it must be the result of natural affinities, a mutual appreciation of each other's merits and a voluntary consent of individuals. * * *

JUSTICE HARLAN dissenting. * * *

In respect of civil rights, common to all citizens, the Constitution of the United States does not, I think, permit any public authority to know the race of those entitled to be protected in the enjoyment of such rights. Every true man has pride of race, and under appropriate circumstances when the rights of others, his equals before the law, are not be affected, it is his privilege to express such pride and to take such action based upon it as to him seems proper. But I deny that any legislative body or judicial tribunal may have regard to the race of citizens when the civil rights of those citizens are involved. [Justice Harlan construed the Thirteenth Amendment as prohibiting "any burdens or disabilities that constitute badges of slavery or servitude," and the Fourteenth Amendment as confirming all other "civil rights that pertain to freedom and citizenship."]

These notable additions to the fundamental law were welcomed by the friends of liberty throughout the world. They removed the race line from our governmental systems. They had, as this court has said, a common purpose, namely, to secure "to a race recently emancipated, a race that through many generations have been held in slavery, all the civil rights that the superior race enjoy." They declared, in legal effect, this court has further said, "that the law in the States shall be the same for the black as for the white; that all persons, whether colored or white, shall stand equal before the laws of the States, and, in regard to the colored race, for whose protection the amendment was primarily designed, that no discrimination shall be made against them by law because of their color." [*Strauder*.] * * *

* * * Every one knows that the statute in question had its origin in the purpose, not so much to exclude white persons from railroad cars occupied by blacks, as to exclude colored people from coaches occupied by or assigned to white persons. * * * The thing to accomplish was, under the guise of giving equal accommodation for whites and blacks, to compel the latter to keep to themselves while travelling in railroad passenger coaches. No one would be so wanting in candor as to assert to the contrary. The fundamental objection, therefore, to the statute is that it interferes with the personal freedom of citizens. * * * If a white man and a black man choose to occupy the same public conveyance on a public highway, it is their right to do so, and no government, proceeding alone on grounds of race, can prevent it without infringing the personal liberty of each. * * *

The white race deems itself to be the dominant race in this country. And so it is, in prestige, in achievements, in education, in wealth and in power. So, I doubt not, it will continue to be for all time, if it remains true to its great heritage and holds fast to the principles of constitutional liberty. But in view of the Constitution, in the eye of the law, there is in this country no superior, dominant, ruling class of citizens. There is no caste here. Our Constitution is color-blind, and neither knows nor tolerates classes among citizens. In respect of civil rights, all citizens are equal before the law. * * *

In my opinion, the judgment this day rendered will, in time, prove to be quite as pernicious as the decision made by this tribunal in the *Dred Scott* case. * * * The present decision, it may well be apprehended, will not only stimulate aggressions, more or less brutal and irritating, upon the admitted rights of colored citizens, but will encourage the belief that it is possible, by means of state enactments, to defeat the beneficent purposes which the people of the United States had in view when they adopted the recent amendments of the Constitution[.] * * * Sixty millions of whites are in no danger from the presence here of eight millions of blacks. The destinies of the two races, in this country, are indissolubly linked together, and the interests of both require that the common government of all shall not permit the seeds of race hate to be planted under the sanction of law. What can more certainly arouse race hate, what more certainly create and perpetuate a feeling of distrust between these races, than state enactments, which, in fact, proceed on the ground that colored citizens are so inferior and degraded that they cannot be allowed to sit in public coaches occupied by white citizens? That, as all will admit, is the real meaning of such legislation as was enacted in Louisiana. * * *

There is a race so different from our own that we do not permit those belonging to it to become citizens of the United States. Persons belonging to it are, with few exceptions, absolutely excluded from this country. I allude to the Chinese race. But by the statute in question, a Chinaman can ride in the same passenger coach with white citizens of the United States, while citizens of the black race in Louisiana, * * * who are entitled, by law, to participate in the political control of the State and nation, * * * are yet declared to be criminals, liable to imprisonment, if they ride in a public coach occupied by citizens of the white race. * * *

[JUSTICE BREWER did not participate in the decision of this case.]

NOTES ON PLESSY AND THE CONSTITUTIONALITY OF STATE-MANDATED RACIAL SEGREGATION

1.   *The Role of Judicial Review in Our Federal System.* There are three overall questions regarding judicial review you might consider as you evaluate *Plessy*. (The answers to these questions were settled by the time *Plessy* was decided.) First, why should legislative enactments be subject to review for consistency with the Constitution? The standard answer to this question is that of *Federalist* No. 78 (excerpted in Appendix 2 to this casebook):

> There is no position which depends on clearer principles, than that every act of a delegated authority, contrary to the tenor of the commission under which it is exercised, is void. No legislative act, therefore, contrary to the Constitution, can be valid. To deny this, would be to affirm, that the deputy is greater than his principal; that the servant is above his master; that the representatives of the people are superior to the people themselves; that men acting by virtue of powers, may do not only what their powers do not authorize, but what they forbid.

This argument might be considered circular in cases like *Plessy*. The Constitution itself derives its authority from "We the People" (see the Preamble). If a legislative enactment is consistent with the desires of "We the

People," as segregation was in the 1890s (the South insisted on it, and the North tolerated it), how can it be said that the legislature is traversing its "delegated authority"? Why should we want to limit the power of the legislature to enact whatever laws "We the People" desire? See *Federalist* No. 10 (App. 2).

Second, assuming that legislative enactments must be consistent with the Constitution, why should federal courts generally, or the Supreme Court in particular, be charged with enforcing this duty? Why not leave it to the legislature or state courts to police constitutional questions? To be sure, one might be suspicious of allowing the Louisiana legislature or judicial system to police local decisionmaking under the circumstances of the Jim Crow regime, but those are not the only alternatives in *Plessy*. Under the Supremacy Clause of Article VI, Congress can pass statutes preempting, or invalidating, state law, assuming those statutes are within Congress' authority delegated by the Constitution. Section 5 of the Fourteenth Amendment provides that "Congress shall have power to enforce, by appropriate legislation, the provisions of this article." Why shouldn't § 5 be considered the primary, or sole, mechanism for enforcing the Fourteenth Amendment?

Third, assuming that the Supreme Court has authority to invalidate state as well as federal legislation, when should that authority be exercised? There may be virtues to the *judicial restraint* shown by *Plessy*: The Justices were not approving of apartheid, but merely saying that the Constitution did not clearly prohibit this form of state action. The most thoughtful constitutional theory of that time was James Bradley Thayer, *The Origin and Scope of the American Doctrine of Constitutional Law*, 7 Harv. L. Rev. 129 (1893), which argued that the power of judicial review is a "remarkable practice" in a democracy, unique to the United States. Conceding the existence of such a power, Thayer maintained that it had traditionally, and properly, been exercised with the greatest restraint:

> [A court] can only disregard the Act when those who have the right to make laws have not merely made a mistake, but have made a very clear one,—so clear that it is not open to rational question. * * * This rule recognizes that * * * much which will seem unconstitutional to one man, or body of men, may reasonably not seem so to another; that the constitution often admits of different interpretations; that there is often a range of choice and judgment; that in such cases the constitution does not impose upon the legislature any one specific opinion, but leaves open this range of choice; and that whatever choice is rational is constitutional.

Id. at 144. Compare Thayer's standard with *Plessy*'s inquiry, i.e., whether the statute "is a reasonable regulation, and with respect to this there must necessarily be a large discretion on the part of the legislature." Was Louisiana's law such a "reasonable regulation"? Or was it a "clear mistake"?

Plessy's judicial restraint may be contrasted with the Court's activism in *Dred Scott v. Sandford*, 60 U.S. 393 (1857), where the Taney Court read the

Due Process Clause to protect the property interests of slaveholders and, further, ruled that free persons of African descent could not constitutionally be "citizens" of any state. To support the latter holding, Chief Justice Taney relied on colonial marriage statutes where "intermarriages between white persons and negroes or mulattoes were regarded as unnatural and immoral, and punished as crimes, not only in the parties, but in the person who joined them in marriage." The Constitution of 1789 reflected "this stigma, of the deepest degradation," that "was fixed upon the whole race." Taney also invoked Congress's early law barring men of color from serving in the armed forces. The Reconstruction Amendments overrode *Dred Scott*'s holdings: Can you see where they do so? Should that rebuke to the Court have supported more aggressive review in *Plessy*?

2. *The Meaning of "Equality" and "Race."* All the Justices sharply distinguished between *social* and *political* equality; neither Justice Brown nor Justice Harlan defended a statute requiring social equality for African Americans. One way to express the differences between the majority and dissent is that the majority characterized the statute as involving *social* and not *political* rights, while the dissent characterized it as involving *civil* and not *social* rights. Most historians believe § 1 was originally meant to assure *civil*, but neither *social* nor *political*, rights. If so, Justice Harlan at least posed the issue in the correct way. But not all the Reconstruction Republicans viewed the matter that way (note 4 above), and *The Slaughter House Cases* and *Strauder* had rejected such an understanding. In that event, the Court may have been right in believing that § 1 policed only political, and not civil, rights.

What does *equality* mean? Both sides had theories of formal and functional equality. Justice Harlan's dissent is particularly interesting. On the one hand, Harlan asserted that the Constitution is "color blind," suggesting that race is no longer a proper *classification* upon which to base public policy. This might be read to suggest a *rationality principle* animating the Equal Protection Clause. On the other hand, Harlan asserted that the Constitution embodied an anti-caste idea, suggesting that race cannot be used to subordinate a particular *class* of people. This might be read to suggest an *anti-subordination principle*. In the context of *Plessy*, both principles pressed in the same direction, but in later cases they do not; this dichotomy is one way of understanding modern debates about affirmative action (Chapter 3, § 3A–B) and efforts to draw electoral lines to facilitate the election of minority representatives (*id.*, § 3E).

Note, finally, the way *race* itself was constructed and deployed. Plessy understood himself as white, but the state insisted he was "colored." Harlan invoked the "superiority of the white race" as a *noblesse oblige* reason to be nice to the black race. Although modern conservatives invoke Harlan's color-blindness rhetoric and liberals his anti-caste rhetoric, Harlan seemed to make an explicitly color-conscious and pro-caste argument: Did he not suggest that, in addition to citizenship, what whites and blacks had in common was the fact that they were not yellow?[5]

3.   *Transportation and Education.* Note the Court's argument that because segregated schools were apparently constitutional, surely segregated transportation must be as well. On the one hand, this was not a foregone conclusion; the case for segregated transportation was constitutionally weaker than that for segregated education. When the Fourteenth Amendment was ratified, most northern states had segregated schools, but none had segregated transportation. The latter did not even enter southern law until 1887. The 1875 Civil Rights Act, adopted to implement the Fourteenth Amendment, prohibited segregation in transportation but said nothing about schools. The common carrier tradition of public transportation made an apartheid policy much more exceptional for that arena than it was for the educational arena. See also *Railroad Co. v. Brown*, 84 U.S. 445 (1873) (applying an anti-discrimination law to bar railroads from segregating the races).

When the Court directly addressed segregation in education, it simply deferred to the practice. Justice Harlan's opinion for the Court in *Cumming v. Richmond County Board of Education*, 175 U.S. 528 (1899), allowed Richmond County, Georgia to close its "colored" high school (leaving minority students with no school), because "the education of the people in schools maintained by state taxation is a matter belonging to the respective states." In *Gong Lum v. Rice*, 275 U.S. 78 (1927), the Court upheld against equal protection attack the segregation of Chinese students in "colored" schools and treated it as settled that federal courts would not intervene in state and local decisions about how to manage their public schools.

B. THE ROAD TO *BROWN*

The promise of national citizenship for African Americans made in the Reconstruction Amendments was all but a dead letter at the dawn of the new century, and none of the organs of government seemed interested in redeeming the situation. Yet in less than two generations *Plessy* was overruled, and the country embarked upon a "Second Reconstruction."

1.   *The NAACP.* In 1905, W.E.B. DuBois and 59 other men founded the "Niagara Movement" dedicated to an "organized determination and aggressive action on the part of men who believe in Negro freedom and growth," including the right to equal education. Four years later, DuBois addressed a biracial committee formed to redress African-American inequality. He explained how the South maintained blacks as a permanent underclass through disenfranchisement by poll taxes, literacy tests, and coercion; through segregated and grossly unequal educational opportunities, consigning blacks at best to vocational training; and through

---

[5]   Gabriel Chin, *The* Plessy *Myth: Justice Harlan and the Chinese Cases*, 82 Iowa L. Rev. 151 (1996). The Court in this period denied American-born Chinese persons American citizenship, see *United States v. Wong Kim Ark*, 169 U.S. 649 (1898), and upheld many other discriminations against them, with Harlan's support.

curtailment of basic civil rights through threats of economic and physical retaliation. The conference and DuBois' speech stimulated the formation of the National Association for the Advancement of Colored People (NAACP) as a biracial coalition to seek racial justice through education, lobbying, and litigation. From the beginning, the NAACP petitioned the courts to relieve African Americans of their continuing servitude.[6]

The NAACP submitted its first brief *amicus curiae* (friend of the court) in *Guinn v. United States*, 238 U.S. 347 (1915). Oklahoma required a literacy test for all voters, except those who were entitled to vote before 1866 (and therefore before the Fifteenth Amendment assured the franchise to former slaves) or who were descended from persons entitled to vote before 1866 (the so-called "grandfather clause"). The NAACP's brief helped the Court understand the invidious racial thrust of the Oklahoma law, and the Court struck it down as inconsistent with the Fifteenth Amendment. See also *Buchanan v. Warley*, 245 U.S. 60 (1917) (NAACP *amicus* brief helped convince the Court to invalidate a Kentucky law requiring residential segregation to prevent "ill-feeling" and "cross-breeding" between the races).

In the early 1920s, the Garland Fund made a $100,000 grant to the NAACP to enable it to pursue a legal campaign against institutionalized racism in the United States. The NAACP used the money to establish a litigation branch, headed by the Dean of the Howard Law Center, Charles Hamilton Houston. In the 1930s, the NAACP defended hundreds of innocent black men against criminal charges and filed dozens of lawsuits seeking equal pay for black schoolteachers and equal resources for black schools. Houston's litigation strategy did not challenge the constitutionality of segregation per se, but instead focused on the implicit requirement in *Plessy* that facilities be "equal" if they be separate. [Kluger, *Simple Justice*, 132–37.] As of 1935, courts had always rejected broad attacks on segregated schools, but were sometimes willing to give relief upon claims of unequal resources and facilities.[7]

---

[6]   See generally Kluger, *Simple Justice*; Charles Flint Kellogg, *NAACP: A History of the National Association for the Advancement of Colored People* (1967); James McPherson, *The Abolitionist Legacy: From Reconstruction to the Founding of the NAACP* (1975).

[7]   Cf. *McCabe v. Atchison, Topeka & Santa Fe Railway*, 235 U.S. 151 (1914), which struck down an Oklahoma statute requiring trains to maintain separate coach sections for blacks and whites but allowing them to have dining and sleeping cars for whites only. Howard University's *Journal of Negro Education Yearbook* published a report on "The Courts and the Negro Separate School" in 1935. By that time, school segregation had been the subject of litigation 113 times in 29 states and the District of Columbia. In 44 cases plaintiffs attacked the constitutionality of segregation, and in 44 cases they lost on the issue. Other evidence, however, suggested that *Plessy*'s requirement of "equal" in the separate-but-equal formula might be the basis for successful litigation. Statistics indicated that the average white schoolchild's education was supported by two and one-half times as much money as that of the average black schoolchild. In 17 of 19 states segregating public education, the state failed to support equivalent graduate and professional education for blacks. The Journal also published articles arguing that segregation established psychological patterns of inferiority in black children. [Kluger, *Simple Justice*, 168–72.]

2.   *Chipping Away at Separate but Equal.* The NAACP won its first Supreme Court victory of the equal-though-separate campaign in *Missouri ex rel. Gaines v. Canada*, 305 U.S. 337 (1938). Missouri denied Lloyd Gaines admission to the state law school; the state argued that he could attend an out-of-state law school and Missouri would provide him financial aid. Houston responded that this was on its face an unequal provision of state education to its black and white citizens, and the Supreme Court agreed. "The basic consideration is not as to what sort of opportunities other States provide, * * * but as to what opportunities Missouri itself furnishes to white students and denies to negroes solely upon the ground of color. * * * By the operation of the laws of Missouri a privilege has been created for white law students which is denied to negroes by reason of their race. * * * That is a denial of the equality of legal right to the enjoyment of the privilege which the State has set up, and the provision for the payment of tuition fees in another State does not remove the discrimination." As a remedy, Missouri created a law school for blacks at Lincoln University.

In 1938, Houston returned to private practice and was succeeded by 30-year-old Thurgood Marshall, his star student at Howard and an attorney who had successfully litigated in Maryland state courts to equalize the salaries of black and white schoolteachers. Marshall presided over the creation of a separate litigation organ, the NAACP Education and Defense Fund, Inc. (the "Inc. Fund"), and a change in the organization's constitutional strategy. In 1947–48, Marshall persuaded the NAACP to authorize him to attack segregation as per se unconstitutional. This new strategy did not reap immediate rewards. In *Sipuel v. Board of Regents*, 332 U.S. 631 (1948), the Court struck down Oklahoma's failure to provide legal education for its black citizens, but without addressing Marshall's argument that *Plessy* be overruled. Reflecting a pattern followed by other southern states, Oklahoma complied with the mandate by roping off an area in the state capitol and calling it a law school. Further appeal to the Supreme Court, challenging this continuing inequality, was unavailing. *Fisher v. Hurst*, 333 U.S. 147 (1948).

One decade after *Gaines*, southern states had built no institution where African Americans could pursue doctoral studies. Excluding Howard University, only one of the 29 medical schools in the South was for blacks, and this was also the pattern for pharmacy (one of 20 schools), law (one of 40), and engineering (none of 36). [Kluger, *Simple Justice,* 257.] Southern school districts still spent twice as much on education for white children as on black children and paid white teachers 30% more than equally qualified black teachers.

Marshall and the Inc. Fund believed that equalization would never come without actual desegregation. Also, there was some evidence that whatever the quality of the facilities might be, African Americans could not hope for true citizenship and political dignity under an apartheid regime.

The most famous study was the "doll tests" of psychologists Kenneth and Mamie Clark. The Clarks showed four dolls (two brown and two white) to black and white children aged three to seven. They asked the children: (1) Give me the white doll. (2) Give me the colored doll. (3) Give me the Negro doll. Three-quarters of the children identified the brown doll with "colored" and "Negro," suggesting to the Clarks that the children were quite aware of racial differences and terminology. The Clarks next asked: (1) Give me the doll you like best. (2) Give me the nice doll. (3) Give me the bad doll. (4) Give me the doll that is a nice color. The Clarks' findings were that 57% of the black children preferred the white doll, as did 89% of the white children. From these results, the Clarks concluded that segregation and its atmosphere were assaults on the self-esteem of black children.[8] The NAACP in the 1940s incorporated studies like these into its litigation documents, and they may have contributed to the Court's ruling in *Shelley v. Kraemer*, 334 U.S. 1 (1948) (Chapter 3, § 2), that the Fourteenth Amendment prohibited the judiciary from enforcing racially restrictive property covenants (agreements not to sell property to non-white persons).

Finally, an increasing number of Americans were questioning the legitimacy of race-based exclusionary laws. On the eve of World War II, several Supreme Court Justices recognized parallels between Nazi and American racism, and the special concern for statutes reflecting prejudice against "discrete and insular minorities" in *United States v. Carolene Products Co.*, 304 U.S. 144, 152 n.4 (1938) (quoted in Chapter 1, § 6) reflected those Justices' openness to constitutional claims by racial minorities.[9] Cf. James W. Whitman, *Hitler's American Model: The United States and the Making of Nazi Race Law* (2017) (Hitler's race policies were inspired, in part, by Amercian apartheid). World War II further problematized racial classifications.[10] Upholding a wartime curfew applicable only to Japanese Americans in *Hirabayashi v. United States*, 320 U.S. 81 (1943), the Court for the first time stated that "racial discriminations are in most circumstances irrelevant and therefore prohibited." Upholding the wartime internment of Japanese Americans, *Korematsu v. United States*, 323 U.S. 214 (1944), said that "all legal

---

[8] See Kenneth Clark and Mamie Clark, *Racial Identification and Preference in Negro Children*, in *Readings in Social Psychology* (T. Newcomb and E. Harley eds. 1947). See also Max Deutscher & Isidor Chein, *The Psychological Effects of Enforced Segregation: A Survey of Social Science Opinion*, 26 J. Psychol. 259 (1948).

[9] David Bixby, *The Roosevelt Court, Democratic Ideology, and Minority Rights: Another Look at* United States v. Classic, 90 Yale L.J. 741, 762–78 (1981); Louis Lusky (the law clerk who drafted footnote four of *Carolene Products*), *Minority Rights and the Public Interest*, 52 Yale L.J. 1 (1942).

[10] In 1941, Philip Randolph organized the March on Washington Movement, petitioning the Roosevelt Administration to end federal discrimination against people of color; FDR issued Executive Order 8802, which barred race discrimination in federal government employment, but not in the armed forces. The hypocrisy of Americans' fighting Nazi racism during World War II, while following racist policies at home, was underlined in Gunnar Myrdal, *An American Dilemma* (1944).

restrictions which curtail the civil rights of a single racial group are immediately suspect."[11]

Skepticism about racial classifications deepened after the war, which both contributed to the NAACP's new anti-apartheid constitutional stance and to the willingness of federal officials to question apartheid. The Court in *Morgan v. Virginia*, 328 U.S. 373 (1946), held that states could not segregate interstate bus transportation; the NAACP brief stressed that the United States had just emerged from a war against "the apostles of racism." The Presidential Commission on Civil Rights condemned segregation in its report, *To Secure These Rights* (1947). The next year, President Truman directed that the armed forces be desegregated. Given these developments, the time was ripe for a frontal assault on American apartheid.

Meanwhile, Latinos were challenging their segregation on grounds of ethnicity. Both segregated school districts and the League of United Latin American Citizens (LULAC) asserted that Latino Americans were racially "white," but LULAC objected that its "white" children were segregated from "white" children of northern European descent and that such segregation was irrational. Indeed, the first successful court challenge to apartheid came in a challenge by Mexican-American families. *Méndez v. Westminster School District*, 64 F.Supp. 544 (C.D. Cal. 1946), aff'd, 161 F.2d 774 (9th Cir. 1947). Responding to *Méndez*, Governor Earl Warren presided over the formal abandonment of the anti-Chicano apartheid regime for California schools.[12]

3.   *The United States Joins the Inc. Fund in Questioning Separate but Equal.* As it had done in *Sipuel*, the Inc. Fund urged the Court to overrule *Plessy* in *Sweatt v. Painter*, 339 U.S. 629 (1950). Heman Sweatt was denied admission to the University of Texas Law School, on the ground that the Prairie View Law School, with a few rented rooms and two adjunct teachers, was an equivalent facility. Marshall argued that racial classifications were per se unreasonable and that a one-person law school was inherently unequal to the University of Texas Law School because of the many intangible benefits and connections accruing from attending the latter. Twelve states submitted briefs supporting Texas' solution. The U.S. Department of Justice, for the first time in a public education case, filed a brief arguing that *Plessy* had been incorrectly decided.

Chief Justice Vinson's opinion in *Sweatt* followed the *Gaines* approach, but with striking differences. To begin with, the Court ordered the University of Texas to admit Sweatt, the first time the Court had been so

---

[11]   *Korematsu* was the last Supreme Court decision to permit overt discrimination against a racial or ethnic minority. It has been overruled in *Trump v. Hawaii*, 138 S.Ct. 2392 (2018).

[12]   On the LULAC challenges to segregation of Mexican-American schoolchildren, see Ian Haney-López, *Race and Colorblindness After* Hernandez *and* Brown, 25 Chicano-Latino L. Rev. 61 (2005); Juan Perea, *Buscando América: Why Integration and Equal Protection Fail to Protect Latinos*, 117 Harv. L. Rev. 1420, 1425 (2004).

specific in its remedy for a violation of *Plessy*. Moreover, the Court recognized the significance of intangible differences in the two schools. "The University of Texas Law School possesses to a far greater degree those qualities which are incapable of objective measurement but which make for greatness in a law school." Hence, the hastily assembled Prairie View Law School could not be an equal facility. Most important, the Court suggested that segregation itself contributed to these intangible differences. "The law school to which Texas is willing to admit petitioner excludes from its student body members of the racial groups which number 85% of the population of the State and include most of the lawyers, witnesses, jurors, judges and other officials with whom petitioner will inevitably be dealing when he becomes a member of the Texas Bar. With such a substantial and significant segment of society excluded, we cannot conclude that the education offered petitioner is substantially equal to that which he would receive if admitted to the University of Texas Law School." See also *McLaurin v. Oklahoma State Regents*, 339 U.S. 637 (1950) (once admitted to previously all-white University of Oklahoma, petitioner could not then be forced to sit in segregated areas of classroom, cafeteria, and library).

In both *Sweatt* and *McLaurin*, the United States filed *amicus* briefs urging the Court not to apply *Plessy* or *Cumming* to graduate education. Urging the Court to bar racial discrimination for railroad dining cars, the Solicitor General[13] at oral argument in *Henderson v. United States*, 339 U.S. 816 (1950), asked the Court to overrule *Plessy*: "Segregation of Negroes, as practiced in this country, is universally understood as imposing on them a badge of inferiority. . . . Forbidding this group of American citizens 'to associate with other citizens in the ordinary course of daily living creates inequality by imposing a caste status on the minority group.'" Although most of the Justices privately agreed with the Solicitor General, a majority of them were also fearful that overruling *Plessy* without more warning would trigger a firestorm in the South [Hutchinson 19–30]. Thus, the Court ruled narrowly in *Henderson*, barring railroad segregation on statutory rather than constitutional grounds.

By 1951, both the NAACP and the Justice Department were publicly committed to (and the Supreme Court was privately leaning toward) ending *de jure* segregation, whose existence seemed increasingly bizarre as well as politically and morally embarrassing. Florida did not permit whites and blacks to use the same editions of certain textbooks. Texas did not allow interracial boxing. Alabama prohibited white nurses from tending to

---

[13] The Solicitor General is the chief attorney representing the federal government before the Supreme Court. Among the men who served in that office during the twentieth century were John W. Davis and Thurgood Marshall, the adversaries in *Brown*; Philip Perlman and Simon Sobeloff, both instrumental in the Department of Justice's effort to press the Court to overrule the segregation decisions; Archibald Cox, the Special Prosecutor who initiated the process that led President Nixon to resign, and Robert Bork, the man who fired Cox; and Kenneth Starr, who later gained fame as the Independent Counsel who investigated President Clinton. Elena Kagan, now a Justice, was the first female Solicitor General, under President Obama.

blacks. North Carolina maintained segregated washrooms in factories, South Carolina segregated washrooms in cotton mills, and four other states required separate washrooms in mines. In eight states, parks, playgrounds, bathing, boating and fishing facilities, amusement parks, racetracks, pool halls, circuses, and theatres were segregated. Eleven states racially segregated their schools for the blind. Fourteen states segregated railroad passengers for trips within their borders. Seventeen states and the District of Columbia segregated public schools. In 11,173 school districts in the United States, African-American children were prohibited by law from attending school with white children. [Kluger, *Simple Justice,* 327.]

If you were litigating the *Brown* case, how would you deal with *Plessy*—its reasoning, its status as a precedent? What post-*Plessy* cases would you find helpful? What kind of evidentiary record could you use in order to attack the factual premises of the *Plessy* doctrine? Before reading about the *Brown* litigation, try drafting a few paragraphs of your own for use in a brief.

C. THE END OF SEPARATE BUT EQUAL

1. *The Lower Court Litigation.* In 1952–53, the Supreme Court accepted for review *Brown* and four other cases in order to reconsider the doctrine of separate-but-equal in public education. After *Brown,* the next case taken on writ of certiorari[14] was *Briggs v. Elliott.* When the Reverend Joseph A. DeLaine, a Methodist minister, mobilized the black community to seek the assistance of the NAACP in challenging segregation in Clarendon, South Carolina, whites retaliated. The school board fired DeLaine from his teaching job. Someone set his house afire; when the firefighters arrived, they stood by as the house burned to the ground. White supervisors fired Harry Briggs, the named plaintiff, from his job at a gas station, and his wife lost her job as a maid at a local motel. Levi Pearson, a plaintiff, watched his crops rot in the fields because banks would not lend him the money to lease harvesters. [Kluger, *Simple Justice,* 21–25, 303.]

---

[14] There are two basic routes to the Supreme Court: "appeal" and "certiorari." At the time of *Brown,* a party losing in the lower court could "appeal" from (1) a U.S. court of appeals decision invalidating a state statute or (2) a state court decision upholding a state statute against a claim that it violates federal constitutional or statutory law. Until the federal statute governing the Supreme Court's jurisdiction was amended in 1988, the Court's jurisdiction over appeals was mandatory; in practice, however, the Court usually dismissed such appeals summarily, for want of a substantial federal question. Today, mandatory jurisdiction has been almost entirely eliminated. See generally Bennett Boskey & Eugene Gressman, *The Supreme Court Bids Farewell to Mandatory Appeals,* 121 F.R.D. 81 (1988). The Court has wholly discretionary "certiorari" power to review (1) a U.S. court of appeals decision in any civil or criminal case, or (2) a state court decision whenever (a) a challenge to a state or federal law is based upon a federal issue, or (b) a federal right, privilege, or immunity is set up or claimed. It takes only four votes to grant certiorari. This "rule of four" means that the Court will sometimes hear a case even if a majority is not initially persuaded of its significance.

Unlike the educational facilities for blacks in Topeka, Kansas at issue in *Brown*, those in Clarendon County, South Carolina flunked the *Plessy* equality test cold. The total value of the buildings, grounds, and furnishings of the two white schools (with 276 children) was four times the value of the same in the three black schools (with 808 children). The white school buildings were brick and stucco; the black buildings were rotting wood. The white schools had one teacher for every 28 students, the black schools one for every 47. One of the black schools had no running water, another had no electricity. The white schools had indoor flush toilets; the black schools had outhouses. [Kluger, *Simple Justice,* 330.] Although the plaintiffs in *Briggs* had winning facts under *Gaines*, they also attacked school segregation as inherently unconstitutional, invoking psychological and statistical evidence. Nonetheless, the three-judge federal court upheld segregation, over a dissent by Judge J. Waties Waring, but the court did enter an injunction that the facilities for blacks had to be equalized (which did not occur).

The third case accepted for Supreme Court review was *Davis v. County School Board of Prince Edward County (Virginia)*. The NAACP's challenge to *Plessy* in this case was supported not only by the Clarks' doll studies, but also by testimony of substantial consensus among psychologists that forced segregation has detrimental psychological effects on members of both the minority and majority populations. Unlike Clarendon County, Prince Edward County disputed the NAACP's social science data. The defense subjected Clark to keen cross-examination questioning the scientific validity of his doll studies and introduced experts who denied that broad conclusions about legal apartheid could be drawn from such studies. Henry Garret, Professor of Psychology at Columbia University, testified that "in terms of heredity, physiology and cultural history, the Negro suffers badly when compared with the white man. * * * Physiologists were finding evidence that the Negro's brain was * * * less fissured, less complex and less thick in the frontal lobes where reasoning and abstract thinking go on." [Kluger 502.] The federal court essentially accepted the school board's evidence in its rejection of the assault on *Plessy*. The court ordered Prince Edward County to equalize the white and black schools, but did not set a timetable. [Kluger 506.]

The Supreme Court "noted probable jurisdiction" in the fourth and fifth cases one month prior to the date it had set to hear oral arguments on the first three cases. The Court, in a rare move, called up *Bolling v. Sharpe* from the lower courts on its own initiative. The plaintiffs had only argued that school segregation in the District of Columbia was per se unconstitutional (although there was plenty of evidence that facilities were also unequal), and the trial court had denied relief because of *Plessy*. The Supreme Court also took the appeal in *Belton v. Gebhart* and *Bulah v. Gebhart*, where Collins Seitz, then a state judge, had not only found that the Wilmington, Delaware school system offered blatantly unequal facilities to black students, but also explicitly accepted the NAACP's social science evidence and ordered the white schools to accept black students.

2. *The First Go-Round in the Desegregation Cases.* Once the Supreme Court accepts a case upon writ of certiorari or by noting probable appellate jurisdiction, the parties are on notice that they must file briefs on the merits with the Court. Given the importance of the issue, and the Court's signal that it might overrule *Plessy*, the case attracted several briefs *amicus curiae*, including a brief from the Department of Justice, which again urged the Court to overrule *Plessy*. The Court heard argument on December 9, 1952. The *Brown* case produced a dull argument, in large part because the Topeka Board of Education was in the process of ending *de jure* segregation in public schools.[15]

In the Clarendon County argument, former Solicitor General John W. Davis argued that the county satisfied *Plessy* by equalizing black and white schools and that there was no basis for overruling the longstanding rule of *Plessy*. In constitutional law, courts are supposed to follow precedent, especially when it has been settled for long periods of time and private persons and public entities have relied on it in their plans and established practices. In the South, *Plessy* was the basis for a whole way of life, and Davis maintained that switching the constitutional rule would have thousands of unpredictable and unsettling effects for everyone, so deeply entrenched was the principle against racial integration in the South. (On reargument the next year, Davis added that there was little reason to believe that overruling *Plessy* would actually help black schoolchildren, so entrenched was that principle. "Would that make the children any happier? * * * Would their lives be more serene?" Davis thought not; "the best is often the enemy of the good.")

Thurgood Marshall, for the appellants, retorted that the time had come for the Court to end legal segregation, for it was at odds with the purpose of the Equal Protection Clause, to "eliminate race distinctions from American law" and to secure equality for people of color. *Plessy* was inconsistent with this purpose—but the Court's twentieth century precedents were not. The Court had already invalidated racial discrimination and segregation in graduate education, by making it impossible to prove equal facilities (*Sweatt*); in housing, by striking down segregationist statutes (*Buchanan*) and by refusing to enforce discriminatory private covenants (*Shelley*); in interstate travel, by striking down state segregationist statutes (*Morgan*); in voting, by removing

---

[15] Kansans were embarrassed that Topeka was allied with openly racist southern districts, and the school board voted not to defend itself on appeal. The Supreme Court instructed the Kansas Attorney General's Office that it had to defend the case, or else concede the invalidity of Kansas' school segregation statute. Ten days prior to oral argument the Attorney General gave the case to his young assistant, Paul Wilson. [Dudziak 370–73.]

impediments designed to prevent black suffrage (*Lane v. Wilson*, 307 U.S. 268 (1939), and *Smith v. Allwright*, 321 U.S. 649 (1944)); in economic and employment relations, by invalidating certain efforts to ruin minority businesses (*Yick Wo v. Hopkins*, 118 U.S. 356 (1886)) and to discriminate against black workers (*Steele v. Louisville & Nashville Railroad*, 323 U.S. 192 (1944)); and in jury service, by striking down whites-only jury laws (*Strauder*). The South had been on notice for some time that their "way of life" had to give way to the Constitution, and now was the time for the Court to deliver what the Fourteenth Amendment had promised: actual and full equality.[16]

The Justices discussed the five cases at their Saturday conference. The Court was fractured—four Justices (Black, Douglas, Burton, and Minton) in favor of overruling *Plessy* immediately, three Justices (Frankfurter, Jackson, Clark) inclined to overrule but uncertain as to how or when the Court should do it, one Justice (Reed) opposed to an overruling, and the Chief Justice (Vinson) uncommitted. [Tushnet, with Lezin, 1902–07.] Given the need for a more united front in light of expected southern resistance, such a fractured Court ought not proceed to a hasty decision. At the suggestion of Justice Frankfurter, the Court announced on June 9, 1953, that the five cases would be reargued and that the parties must submit briefs discussing the "original intent" of the Fourteenth Amendment regarding segregation in education.

3. *The Second Go-Round in the Desegregation Cases.* Most of the parties duly filed briefs arguing that the Framers of the Fourteenth Amendment either did (the NAACP's brief) or did not (the defendants' briefs) expect the amendment's equal protection guarantees to disallow race-based segregation in public schools. The Justice Department argued that the original intent was indeterminate but that other considerations favored the overruling of *Plessy*.

When the parties reargued the cases on October 12, they were speaking to a different Supreme Court. Between order and reargument, Chief Justice Vinson died and was succeeded by California Governor Earl Warren, who had led the way toward integrated schools in his state. In conference after the second argument, the new Chief Justice forcefully stated his intent to overrule *Plessy*. Together with mounting pressure from the media and intellectuals outside the Court, Warren's leadership tipped an unsteady Court toward decisive action. The Chief's pitch was immediately seconded by Justice Black (who was the senior Justice and

---

[16] The briefs filed by the NAACP included a further argument, developed in their appendix, "The Effects of Segregation and the Consequences of Desegregation: A Social Science Statement." The statement maintained that law-endorsed segregation had pervasive and harmful psychological effects on people of color. Such laws undermine the dignity of those stigmatized, contribute to rigid and authoritarian personalities among white children, and perpetuate stereotypes and racial animosity among all children. The 32 eminent scientists who signed the statement concluded that race ought not be the basis for legal exclusions or segregations.

spoke immediately after the Chief) and then by Justices Douglas, Burton, and Minton. Justices Frankfurter, Jackson, and Clark expressed concerns about the political nature and ramifications of the decision; Warren gently assuaged their concerns, in part by agreeing to address only the constitutionality of *de jure* segregation and postponing decision of remedy (what the school districts must do to comply with the Court's mandate) for the next year. Justice Reed, from Kentucky, remained unpersuaded that the "separate but equal" doctrine should have been abrogated, but Warren talked him out of filing a dissenting opinion, which (Warren argued) would undermine the Court's institutional ability to stand behind its decrees.

On May 17, 1954, Chief Justice Warren read his opinion to a hushed gallery. A few days earlier his Court had ruled that states could not exclude Mexican Americans from juries. Warren's opinion for the Court in *Hernandez v. Texas*, 347 U.S. 475 (1954), emphasized the arbitrary lines drawn in anti-Chicano apartheid and ruled that the state could not enforce or deploy them in constructing jury venires. The Chief Justice followed a similar line of reasoning—also for a unanimous Court—in *Brown*. Given the legal arguments in the case and its political sensitivity, how would you have drafted the Court's opinion? (You might jot down an outline before reading Warren's opinion below.)

BROWN V. BOARD OF EDUCATION
347 U.S. 483, 74 S.Ct. 686, 98 L.Ed. 873 (1954)

CHIEF JUSTICE WARREN delivered the opinion of the Court.

[The Chief Justice described the cases, how they came to the Court, and the claims common to the plaintiffs in all the state cases—that the "separate but equal" doctrine of *Plessy* did not satisfy the Fourteenth Amendment's requirement that black schoolchildren be afforded equal protection of the laws.]

Reargument was largely devoted to the circumstances surrounding the adoption of the Fourteenth Amendment in 1868. It covered exhaustively consideration of the Amendment in Congress, ratification by the states, then existing practices in racial segregation, and the views of proponents and opponents of the Amendment. This discussion and our own investigation convince us that, although these sources cast some light, it is not enough to resolve the problem with which we are faced. At best, they are inconclusive. The most avid proponents of the post-War Amendments undoubtedly intended them to remove all legal distinctions among "all persons born or naturalized in the United States." Their opponents, just as certainly, were antagonistic to both the letter and the spirit of the Amendments and wished them to have the most limited effect. What others in Congress and the state legislatures had in mind cannot be determined with any degree of certainty.

An additional reason for the inconclusive nature of the Amendment's history, with respect to segregated schools, is the status of public education at that time. In the South, the movement toward free common schools, supported by general taxation, had not yet taken hold. Education of white children was largely in the hands of private groups. Education of Negroes was almost nonexistent, and practically all of the race were illiterate. In fact, any education of Negroes was forbidden by law in some states. Today, in contrast, many Negroes have achieved outstanding success in the arts and sciences as well as in the business and professional world. It is true that public school education at the time of the Amendment had advanced further in the North, but the effect of the Amendment on Northern States was generally ignored in the congressional debates. Even in the North, the conditions of public education did not approximate those existing today. The curriculum was usually rudimentary; ungraded schools were common in rural areas; the school term was but three months a year in many states; and compulsory school attendance was virtually unknown. As a consequence, it is not surprising that there should be so little in the history of the Fourteenth Amendment relating to its intended effect on public education.

In the first cases in this Court construing the Fourteenth Amendment, decided shortly after its adoption, the Court interpreted it as proscribing all state-imposed discriminations against the Negro race. *Slaughter House Cases*; *Strauder*. The doctrine of "separate but equal" did not make its appearance in this Court until 1896 in *Plessy*, involving not education but transportation. American courts have since labored with the doctrine for over half a century. In this Court, there have been six cases involving the "separate but equal" doctrine in the field of public education. In [*Cumming*] the validity of the doctrine itself was not challenged. In more recent cases, all on the graduate school level, inequality was found in that specific benefits enjoyed by white students were denied to Negro students of the same educational qualifications. *Gaines*; *Sipuel*; *Sweatt*; *McLaurin*. In none of these cases was it necessary to re-examine the doctrine to grant relief to the Negro plaintiff. And in *Sweatt* the Court expressly reserved decision on the question whether *Plessy* should be held inapplicable to public education.

In the instant cases, that question is directly presented. Here, unlike *Sweatt*, there are findings below that the Negro and white schools involved have been equalized, or are being equalized, with respect to buildings, curricula, qualifications and salaries of teachers, and other "tangible" factors. Our decision, therefore, cannot turn on merely a comparison of these tangible factors in the Negro and white schools involved in each of the cases. We must look instead to the effect of segregation itself on public education.

In approaching this problem, we cannot turn the clock back to 1868 when the Amendment was adopted, or even to 1896 when *Plessy* was written. We must consider public education in the light of its full development and its present place in American life throughout the Nation. Only in this way can it be determined if segregation in public schools deprives these plaintiffs of the equal protection of the laws.

Today, education is perhaps the most important function of state and local governments. Compulsory school attendance laws and the great expenditures for education both demonstrate our recognition of the importance of education to our democratic society. It is required in the performance of our most basic public responsibilities, even service in the armed forces. It is the very foundation of good citizenship. Today it is a principal instrument in awakening the child to cultural values, in preparing him for later professional training, and in helping him to adjust normally to his environment. In these days, it is doubtful that any child may reasonably be expected to succeed in life if he is denied the opportunity of an education. Such an opportunity, where the state has undertaken to provide it, is a right which must be made available to all on equal terms.

We come then to the question presented: Does segregation of children in public schools solely on the basis of race, even though the physical facilities and other "tangible" factors may be equal, deprive the children of the minority group of equal educational opportunities? We believe that it does.

In *Sweatt*, in finding that a segregated law school for Negroes could not provide them equal educational opportunities, this Court relied in large part on "those qualities which are incapable of objective measurement but which make for greatness in a law school." In *McLaurin* the Court, in requiring that a Negro admitted to a white graduate school be treated like all other students, again resorted to intangible considerations: ". . . his ability to study, to engage in discussions and exchange views with other students, and, in general, to learn his profession." Such considerations apply with added force to children in grade and high schools. To separate them from others of similar age and qualifications solely because of their race generates a feeling of inferiority as to their status in the community that may affect their hearts and minds in a way unlikely ever to be undone. The effect of this separation on their educational opportunities was well stated by a finding in the Kansas case by a court which nevertheless felt compelled to rule against the Negro plaintiffs:

> Segregation of white and colored children in public schools has a detrimental effect upon the colored children. The impact is greater when it has the sanction of the law; for the policy of separating the races is usually interpreted as denoting the inferiority of the negro group. A sense of inferiority affects the

motivation of a child to learn. Segregation with the sanction of law, therefore, has a tendency to [retard] the educational and mental development of negro children and to deprive them of some of the benefits they would receive in a [racially] integrated school system.

Whatever may have been the extent of psychological knowledge at the time of *Plessy*, this finding is amply supported by modern authority.[11] Any language in *Plessy* contrary to this finding is rejected.

We conclude that in the field of public education the doctrine of "separate but equal" has no place. Separate educational facilities are inherently unequal. Therefore, we hold that the plaintiffs and others similarly situated for whom the actions have been brought are, by reason of the segregation complained of, deprived of the equal protection of the laws guaranteed by the Fourteenth Amendment. This disposition makes unnecessary any discussion whether such segregation also violates the Due Process Clause of the Fourteenth Amendment.

Because these are class actions, because of the wide applicability of this decision, and because of the great variety of local conditions, the formulation of decrees in these cases presents problems of considerable complexity. On reargument, the consideration of appropriate relief was necessarily subordinated to the primary question—the constitutionality of segregation in public education. We have now announced that such segregation is a denial of the equal protection of the laws. In order that we may have the full assistance of the parties in formulating decrees, the cases will be restored to the docket, and the parties are requested to present further argument on Questions 4 and 5 previously propounded by the Court for the reargument this Term.[12] The Attorney General of the United States

---

[11] K.B. Clark, Effect of Prejudice and Discrimination on Personality Development (Midcentury White House Conference on Children and Youth, 1950); Witmer and Kotinsky, Personality in the Making (1952), c. VI; Deutscher and Chein, The Psychological Effects of Enforced Segregation: A Survey of Social Science Opinion, 26 J. Psychol. 259 (1948); Chein, What are the Psychological Effects of Segregation Under Conditions of Equal Facilities?, 3 Int. J. Opinion and Attitude Res. 229 (1949); Brameld, Educational Costs, in Discrimination and National Welfare (MacIver ed. 1949), 44–48; Frazier, The Negro in the United States (1949), 674–681. And see generally Myrdal, An American Dilemma (1944).

[12] "4. Assuming it is decided that segregation in public schools violates the Fourteenth Amendment

"(a) would a decree necessarily follow providing that, within the limits set by normal geographic school districting, Negro children should forthwith be admitted to schools of their choice, or

"(b) may this Court, in the exercise of its equity powers, permit an effective gradual adjustment to be brought about from existing segregated systems to a system not based on color distinctions?

"5. On the assumption on which questions 4 (a) and (b) are based, and assuming further that this Court will exercise its equity powers to the end described in question 4 (b),

"(a) should this Court formulate detailed decrees in these cases;

"(b) if so, what specific issues should the decrees reach;

is again invited to participate. The Attorneys General of the states requiring or permitting segregation in public education will also be permitted to appear as amici curiae upon request to do so by September 15, 1954, and submission of briefs by October 1, 1954. It is so ordered.

Bolling v. Sharpe

347 U.S. 497 (1954)

The Court handled the District of Columbia case in a separate opinion, also authored by **Chief Justice Warren**. "The Fifth Amendment, which is applicable in the District of Columbia, does not contain an equal protection clause as does the Fourteenth Amendment which applies only to the states. But the concepts of equal protection and due process, both stemming from our American ideal of fairness, are not mutually exclusive. The 'equal protection of the laws' is a more explicit safeguard of prohibited unfairness than 'due process of law,' and, therefore, we do not imply that the two are always interchangeable phrases. But, as this Court has recognized, discrimination may be so unjustifiable as to be violative of due process.

"Classifications based solely upon race must be scrutinized with particular care, since they are contrary to our traditions and hence constitutionally suspect. As long ago as 1896, this Court declared the principle 'that the Constitution of the United States, in its present form, forbids, so far as civil and political rights are concerned, discrimination by the General Government, or by the States, against any citizen because of his race.' [*Gibson v. Mississippi,* 162 U.S. 565, 591 (1896).] And in *Buchanan v. Warley*, the Court held that a statute which limited the right of a property owner to convey his property to a person of another race was, as an unreasonable discrimination, a denial of due process of law.

"Although the Court has not assumed to define 'liberty' with any great precision, that term is not confined to mere freedom from bodily restraint. Liberty under law extends to the full range of conduct which the individual is free to pursue, and it cannot be restricted except for a proper governmental objective. Segregation in public education is not reasonably related to any proper governmental objective, and thus it imposes on Negro children of the District of Columbia a burden that constitutes an arbitrary deprivation of their liberty in violation of the Due Process Clause.

"In view of our decision that the Constitution prohibits the states from maintaining racially segregated public schools, it would be unthinkable that the same Constitution would impose a lesser duty on the Federal Government. We hold that racial segregation in the public schools of the District of Columbia

---

"(c)   should this Court appoint a special master to hear evidence with a view to recommending specific terms for such decrees;

"(d)   should this Court remand to the courts of first instance with directions to frame decrees in these cases, and if so what general directions should the decrees of this Court include and what procedures should the courts of first instance follow in arriving at the specific terms of more detailed decrees?"

is a denial of the due process of law guaranteed by the Fifth Amendment to the Constitution."

NOTES ON BROWN, BOLLING, AND THE
ROLE OF JUDICIAL REVIEW

1. *Stare Decisis in Constitutional Cases.* Under the principle of *stare decisis* (Latin for "let the decisions stand"), once the Supreme Court has made a decision, it will follow that decision in future cases and not overrule it. Thus, in *Federalist* No. 78 (App. 2), Alexander Hamilton said: "To avoid an arbitrary discretion in the courts, it is indispensable that they should be bound down by strict rules and precedents which serve to define and point out their duty in every particular case that comes before them." *Stare decisis* was the main basis for John W. Davis's argument in the Clarendon County case.

How can the *Brown* decision be squared with *stare decisis*? To begin with, one might observe that *Brown* did not quite "overrule" *Plessy*, which was a transportation case (*Plessy*'s discussion of segregation of schools was "dictum" not necessary to its result). The Court found that *de jure* segregation has a "detrimental effect" on black children and then "rejected" reasoning in *Plessy* "contrary to this finding." That doesn't provide an escape hatch from *stare decisis*, however. The Court overruled an assumption of *Cumming*, which rejected a public education race discrimination claim, and an assumption or holding of *Gong Lum*, which upheld the segregation of Chinese students. Moreover, by rejecting reasoning essential to *Plessy*'s result, *Brown* was overruling part of the earlier Court's holding. Citing only *Brown*, the Court issued a series of summary opinions invalidating public segregation in public parks, facilities, and transportation.[17]

A defense of *Brown*'s willingness to overrule prior constitutional precedents is that the rule of *stare decisis* is not an absolute rule, and in constitutional cases the Court has tended to follow the approach in *Burnet v. Coronado Oil & Gas Co.*, 285 U.S. 393, 406–07 (1932) (Brandeis, J., dissenting):

> Stare decisis is usually the wise policy, because in most matters it is more important that the applicable rule of law be settled than that it be settled right. * * * This is commonly true even where the error is a matter of serious concern, provided correction can be had by legislation. But in cases involving the Federal Constitution, where correction through legislative action is practically impossible, this court has often overruled its earlier decisions.

Does this rationale for relaxed *stare decisis* in constitutional cases apply to *Brown*? It would not have taken a constitutional amendment to have overruled *Plessy* (the tactic Justice Brandeis described as "practically impossible") if

---

[17] See *Mayor & City Council of Baltimore City v. Dawson*, 350 U.S. 877 (1955) (public bathhouses and beaches); *Holmes v. Atlanta*, 350 U.S. 879 (1955) (municipal golf course); *Gayle v. Browder*, 352 U.S. 903 (1956) (city buses, giving the Southern Christian Leadership Conference a victory in its Montgomery, Alabama bus boycott); *New Orleans City Park Improvement Ass'n v. Detiege*, 358 U.S. 54 (1958) (municipal parks and golf course).

Congress, under its Fourteenth Amendment powers, might have outlawed *de jure* segregation at the state level. Congress certainly could have outlawed segregation in the District of Columbia. See U.S. Const., art. I, § 8, cl. 17 (Congress's plenary authority over the District). Since "correction [could have been] had by legislation," should the Court have decided *Bolling* differently from *Brown*? Even if *stare decisis* is not absolute, should the Court feel free to overrule established precedent like *Plessy* without special justification? To what extent was it important that decisions prior to *Brown* had already undermined *Plessy*?

2. *The Court's Reasoning in* Brown. Surely, the Supreme Court should have strong justification when it declares a statute unconstitutional, and especially when the Court must overrule its own precedents to do so. Did *Brown* provide such weighty justification? The Court relied on neither the text nor the "inconclusive" original intent of the Fourteenth Amendment. What is left for the Court to rely on? The Court stated that segregation of blacks in elementary school "generates a feeling of inferiority as to their status in the community." For support, the Court cited a finding of fact made by the district court in *Brown* but ignored contrary findings made by the district court in *Davis* and, further, invoked the "modern authority" collected in footnote 11. Is this persuasive? Social scientists have been skeptical.[18]

Many believe that the evidence was not rigorously scientific. The Clarks' doll tests did not demonstrate that the choice of a white doll by a black child really proved that the child felt inferior, nor could they demonstrate that any feelings of inferiority were "caused" by segregated schools. [Kluger, *Simple Justice*, 321.] Indeed, because children in sometimes integrated northern schools had significantly more negative feelings toward the black dolls than did children in segregated southern schools, the doll studies may undermine *Brown*'s proposition that *de jure* school segregation contributes to feelings of stigma and inferiority? Most important, it may have been imprudent to link an important development in the law to preliminary scientific findings, as Kenneth Clark himself later confessed.[19]

3. *Alternate Grounds for* Brown? As you will see throughout this casebook, Supreme Court opinions are not sacrosanct—and we today might be able to write more satisfactory decisions, with the benefit of hindsight of course. Thus, Chief Justice Warren might have argued that the Harlan dissent in *Plessy* accurately interpreted the Fourteenth Amendment, and *Brown* could have adopted his reasoning: Apartheid undermined the general goal of the Reconstruction Amendments, which was to integrate African Americans into

---

[18] E.g., Harold Gerard, *School Desegregation: The Social Science Role*, 38 Am. Psychol. 869, 870–72 (1983); Ernest Van den Haag, *Social Science Testimony in the Desegregation Cases—A Reply to Professor Kenneth Clark*, 6 Vill. L. Rev. 69 (1960); Symposium, *The Courts, Social Science and School Desegregation*, 38 L. & Contemp. Probs. (Winter/Spring 1975). See John Monahan & Laurens Walker, *Social Science in Law: Cases and Materials* 194–209 (9th ed. 2017).

[19] Kenneth Clark, *Brown Plus Thirty: Perspectives on Desegregation* 18 (1986); see Monahan & Walker, *Social Science in Law*, 207–08; cf. Jacqueline Jordan Irvine, *Black Students and School Failure: Policies, Practices, and Prescriptions* 9–12 (1990) (integration brought with it other forms of racial humiliation and subordination).

the country as equal citizens, and created a politically unhealthy "caste" system. Consider also the arguments made by Thurgood Marshall: Apartheid had been shown to be unworkable, and the Court had backed away from it at every opportunity; the time had come to end that social experiment. Put together a legal argument that would have supported an overruling of *Plessy*. For some academic efforts along these lines, see Jack M. Balkin, editor, *What* Brown v. Board of Education *Should Have Said* (2002) (collecting decisions by various legal academics).

NOTE ON THE INFLUENCE OF BROWN ON OTHER SOCIAL MOVEMENTS

Not only has *Brown v. Board of Education* become a landmark constitutional super-precedent, but the civil rights movement that prepared the country for *Brown* and litigated the cases has become an inspiration and model for other social movements. Specifically, the civil rights movement contributed (1) personnel, (2) ideas, (3) grass-roots tactics, (4) institutional strategies, (5) social norms, and (6) legal precedents that contributed to the success of other social movements. Most of the constitutional doctrine in Chapters 2–6 and much of it in Chapters 7–9 was responsive to social movements following the civil rights model.[20]

Equal rights for women was an idea that predated the civil rights movement—but that movement jump-started serious progress toward an equal protection jurisprudence with teeth. One landmark statute—the Civil Rights Act of 1964—included job protections for women early on. One of the great theorists of the civil rights movement became a great theorist of the women's rights movement: Pauli Murray, who suggested that the same reasoning that justified strict scrutiny for race-based classifications also justified such scrutiny for sex-based classifications. Kathryn Shulz, *The Many Lives of Pauli Murray*, The New Yorker, April 17, 2017. We shall examine Murray's arguments in Chapter 4, § 2B.[21] The creation of an ongoing campaign of grass-roots mobilization, public education, alliance formation, and impact litigation required permanent institutions, and women's groups flourished like azaleas in April. Another civil rights leader, Bayard Rustin, later became an important

---

[20] David S. Meyer & Steven A. Boutcher, *Signals and Spillover: Brown v. Board of Education and Other Social Movements,* 5 Perspectives on Politics (March 2007); see also Symposium, *Social Movements and Law Reform,* 150 U. Pa. L. Rev. 1–525 (2001) (articles on the civil rights model applied to the environmental, women's, gay and lesbian rights movements); William N. Eskridge Jr., *Some Effects of Identity-Based Social Movements on Constitutional Law in the Twentieth Century,* 100 Mich. L. Rev. 2062 (2002) (doctrinal responses to civil rights, women's rights, and gay rights movements).

[21] Serena Mayeri, *Reasoning from Race: Feminism, Law, and the Civil Rights Movement* (2011); Pauli Murray, "A Proposal to Reexamine the Applicability of the Fourteenth Amendment to State Laws and Practices Which Discriminate on the Basis of Sex Per Se" (Dec. 1962), in President's Commission on the Status of Women Papers, Schlesinger Library, Box 8, Folder 62; Pauli Murray & Mary Eastwood, *Jane Crow and the Law: Sex Discrimination and Title VII,* 34 Geo. Wash. L. Rev. 232 (1965–66). See also Sarah Azaransky, *The Dream is Freedom: Pauli Murray and American Democratic Faith* (2011); Patricia Bell-Scott, *The Firebrand and the First Lady* (2016).

theorist for the gay rights movement. See John D'Emilio, *Lost Prophet: The Life and Times of Bayard Rustin* (2003).

Especially in the wake of *Brown*, southern states harassed and some tried of outlaw civil rights organizations—and those groups and their ACLU allies won landmark Supreme Court decisions strongly protecting the right of citizens to associate for political and social purposes. E.g., *NAACP v. Alabama*, 357 U.S. 449 (1958). Those precedents redounded to the benefit of homophile and later gay rights organizations, abortion rights groups, and associations pressing the rights of Spanish-speaking minorities and immigrants. Even states with strong public animosity toward those associations knew that federal judges would intervene if they tried to close them down. See Richard Posner, *Ask, Tell*, New Republic, Oct. 1999. Many of the free speech and press rights examined in Chapter 6 were civil rights decisions that protected speech of other minority groups.

Institutionally, other social movements have replicated the civil rights movement's innovation of creating different organizations—the NAACP Inc. Fund for impact litigation, the SCLC and other groups for grass-roots campaigns, and the NAACP and other organizations for lobbying and political action—which then coordinate in a mega-campaign. Each mega-campaign sought to change social, legal, and constitutional norms. The targets were norms treating the social group's defining trait (race, ethnicity, sex, sexual orientation) as "naturally" inferior or even malignant. The goal was to persuade Americans, including judges, that variation along lines of race, ethnicity, sex, sexual orientation is either tolerable or, better, entirely benign. Race, ethnicity, sex, sexual orientation ought to be irrelevant to government policy. The norm of benign racial variation undergirded the Inc. Fund's campaign against apartheid, but notice that *Brown* does not address the classification issue. (Chapter 3 will develop the line of cases holding that race is a constitutionally "suspect" classification, and Chapter 4 will continue with other social groups and their traits.)

Social movements and the influence of *Brown* are not limited to long-disadvantaged minorities, but also include groups that were traditionally empowered but who view their empowerment at risk. The most notorious example was the "states' rights" (or, more provocatively, the "white supremacy") movement that formed in response to the civil rights movement and desegregation. Although this movement is widely disparaged in educated circles today, Professor Driver has demonstrated that its leaders articulated a coherent philosophy of localism, gradual change/evolution, and individual liberty. See Justin Driver, *Supremacies and the Southern Manifesto*, 92 Tex. 1053 (2014).

Perhaps a better example of a status quo-protecting movement has been what we'd call the "corporate rights" movement. On the eve of his appointment to the Supreme Court, Lewis Powell in 1971 wrote an influential memorandum for the Chamber of Commerce. The Powell Memorandum directed businesses to work the political system to protect their position and the capitalist system generally. Politics included stepping up the business game in lobbying, campaign contributions, and forming organizations to press the business agenda in legislatures and courts. See Steven Teles, *The Rise of a Conservative Legal Movement: The Battle for the Control of the Law* (2008); Amanda Shanor, *The New* Lochner, 2016 Wis. L. Rev. 133, 154–64. The Chamber of Commerce expanded its political activities, the Business Roundtable was formed to lobby for capitalism-enhancing policies, and an assortment of litigation groups have successfully pressed for doctrinal innovations such as increasing First Amendment for commercial speech and for political speech by corporations and corporate-friendly rules and interpretations in civil procedure.[22]

An even more successful deployment of the civil rights model of constitutional rights rhetoric combined with coordinated lobbying, grass-roots, and litigation efforts has been the gun rights movement (or the Second Amendment movement). Even though barely regulated firearms are taking a horrific toll on American children and innocent bystanders, gun ownership has prevailed in constitutional litigation across the country and in the Supreme Court.[23] Problem 2-4, below, examines in detail the leading case for gun rights and the constitutional argumentation supporting and opposing the Court's holding in *Heller v. United States* (2008).

Spanish-speaking minorities have effectively deployed the civil rights model to seek constitutional protection. Indeed, an important precursor to *Brown* was the victory of the League of Latin-American Citizens in *Hernandez v. Texas,* 347 U.S. 475 (1954), which invalidated the exclusion of Latino-Americans from juries.[24] Today, one social group that has been generally vilified has been undocumented immigrants (many of them Spanish-speaking) and their children. Another group has been Muslims. Salem Sayyid & Abdoolkarim Vakil, *Thinking Through Islamophobia: Global Perspectives* (2010). If you were a social movement theorist, steeped in the lessons of the civil rights movement, what advice would you give representatives of each group? What challenges does each group face that would make their task harder than that faced by people of color in the mid-twentieth century?

SECTION 2. THE SUPREME COURT'S ROLE IN OUR POLITICAL SYSTEM

Our notes to *Plessy* and *Brown* have raised issues extending beyond the holdings and ramifications of those decisions: Does the Constitution

---

[22] See Sean Farhang & Stephen B. Burbank, *Rights and Retrenchment: The Counter-Revolution Against Federal Litigation* (2017) (arguing that business interests have been way more successful in securing pro-corporate rules from courts than from legislatures).

[23] See Susan Koniak, *When the Law Risks Madness,* 8 Cardozo Stud. Law & Lit. 65 (1996) (chilling examination of the philosophy of the common law militia movement); Reva Siegel, *Dead or Alive: Originalism as Popular Constitutionalism in* Heller, 122 Harv. L. Rev. 191 (2008) (NRA as a social movement).

[24] Ian Haney-López, *Race and Colorblindness After* Hernandez *and* Brown, 25 Chicano-Latino L. Rev. 61 (2005); Juan Perea, *Buscando América: Why Integration and Equal Protection Fail to Protect Latinos,* 117 Harv. L. Rev. 1420, 1425 (2004).

contemplate "judicial review," which effectively nullifies statutes adopted by state legislatures or Congress? If the Constitution does contemplate such a power, what responsibilities does that power suggest for the Supreme Court in constitutional cases? In this Section, we want to pursue these issues more systematically, through analysis of the decision establishing judicial review, *Marbury v. Madison*, and of the modern Court's expansion of *Marbury* to require southern states to implement *Brown* (a decision they believed to be unconstitutional) in *Cooper v. Aaron*. This Section will conclude with what is probably the hardest issue arising under *Brown*: To what extent, and how long, may a federal court monitor the operation of local schools in order to assure desegregation?

A. BASES FOR JUDICIAL REVIEW

Marbury v. Madison is the leading case supporting the Court's power to declare statutes unconstitutional. The plaintiff, William Marbury, had been appointed justice of the peace in the District of Columbia for a five-year term by outgoing Federalist President John Adams and confirmed by the Senate one day before the Democrat-Republicans took power on March 4, 1801. The new Jefferson Administration obtained a repeal of the statute creating the D.C. courts and refused to deliver Marbury's commission. Marbury sued Secretary of State James Madison in the Supreme Court itself—*not* in some lower court whose decision could then be appealed to the Supreme Court. He asked the Court to order Madison to deliver the commission; this was a request for a writ of mandamus—Latin for "we command." For Marbury to obtain this remedy, he had to show (1) that the Supreme Court had been vested with "jurisdiction" (authority) to adjudicate Marbury's lawsuit, *and* (2) that Madison had in fact violated a binding federal statutory or constitutional rule when he withheld Marbury's commission, *and* (3) that mandamus was an appropriate remedy to redress Marbury's legal injury.

Chief Justice John Marshall's opinion for the unanimous Court did not address the issues in the order that we have listed them. He first focused on issue 2, ruling that Marbury had a "vested legal right" in the commission for its five-year term; that legal right was not "revocable." Marshall next decided issue 3, ruling that under a "government of laws, and not men," a person whose vested legal right is being injured "has a right to resort to the laws of his country for a remedy." Mandamus was a proper remedy, because Marbury had no remedy at law and the officer at whom it was directed, Madison, had no discretion to deprive Marbury of his vested right to the commission. Marshall's opinion at this point carefully distinguished cases which today would be called "political questions," namely, matters which have been reserved by the Constitution to the discretion of the executive department or the President (Chapter 9, § 1). "Where the head of a department acts in a case, in which the executive discretion is to be exercised; in which he is the mere organ of executive will; it is again repeated, that any application to a court to control, in any respect, his conduct, would be rejected without hesitation. But where he is directed by law to do a certain act affecting the absolute rights of individuals, in the performance of which he is not placed under the particular discretion of the President, and the performance of which, the President cannot lawfully forbid, and therefore is never presumed to have forbidden * * * in such cases, it is not perceived on what ground the courts of the country are further excused from the duty of giving judgment."

Issue 1, the jurisdictional issue, is the heart of the case, as Marshall posed it, and this is the only portion of the opinion excerpted below. Marshall's opinion analyzed that issue as three questions: (A) Has Congress vested the Supreme Court with "original" (as opposed to appellate) jurisdiction in mandamus cases, pursuant to § 13 of the Judiciary Act of 1789? (B) If so, is that grant of original jurisdiction inconsistent with Article III of the Constitution? (C) If so, what is the responsibility of the Court? May the Court exercise jurisdiction granted by a statute that is inconsistent with the Constitution? Note that these three questions involve (A) an interpretation of a federal statute, (B) an interpretation of a specific constitutional provision, and (C) an interpretation of the constitutional "scheme" or structure.

MARBURY V. MADISON
5 U.S. (1 Cranch) 137 (1803)

CHIEF JUSTICE MARSHALL delivered the Opinion of the Court. * * *

This, then, is a plain case for a mandamus, either to deliver the commission, or a copy of it from the record; and it only remains to be inquired,

Whether it can issue from this court.

The act to establish the judicial courts of the United States authorizes the supreme court "to issue writs of mandamus, in cases warranted by the principles and usages of law, to any courts appointed, or persons holding office, under the authority of the United States."[25]

---

[25] *Editors' note:* Section 13 of the Judiciary Act provided in its entirety:

And be it further enacted, That the Supreme Court shall have exclusive jurisdiction of all controversies of a civil nature, where the state is a party, except between a state and its citizens; and except also between a state and citizens of other states, or aliens, in which latter case it shall have original but not exclusive jurisdiction. And shall have exclusively all such jurisdiction of suits or proceedings against ambassadors, or other public ministers, or their domestics, or domestic servants, as a court of law can have or exercise consistently with the law of nations; and original, but not exclusive jurisdiction of all suits brought by ambassadors or other public ministers, or in which a consul, or vice consul, shall be a party. And the trial of issues of fact in the Supreme Court, in all actions at law against citizens of the United States, shall be by jury. The Supreme Court shall also have appellate jurisdiction from the circuit courts and courts of the several states, in cases

The secretary of state, being a person holding an office under the authority of the United States, is precisely within the letter of the description; and if this court is not authorized to issue a writ of mandamus to such an officer, it must be because the law is unconstitutional, and therefore absolutely incapable of conferring the authority, and assigning the duties which its words purport to confer and assign.

The constitution vests the whole judicial power of the United States in one supreme court, and such inferior courts as congress shall, from time to time, ordain and establish. This power is expressly extended to all cases arising under the laws of the United States; and, consequently, in some form, may be exercised over the present case; because the right claimed is given by a law of the United States.

In the distribution of this power it is declared that "the supreme court shall have original jurisdiction in all cases affecting ambassadors, other public ministers and consuls, and those in which a state shall be a party. In all other cases, the supreme court shall have appellate jurisdiction."

It has been insisted, at the bar, that as the original grant of jurisdiction, to the supreme and inferior courts, is general, and the clause, assigning original jurisdiction to the supreme court, contains no negative or restrictive words; the power remains to the legislature, to assign original jurisdiction to that court in other cases than those specified in the article which has been recited; provided those cases belong to the judicial power of the United States.

If it had been intended to leave it to the discretion of the legislature to apportion the judicial power between the supreme and inferior courts according to the will of that body, it would certainly have been useless to have proceeded further than to have defined the judicial powers, and the tribunals in which it should be vested. The subsequent part of the section is mere surplusage, is entirely without meaning, if such is to be the construction. If congress remains at liberty to give this court appellate jurisdiction, where the constitution has declared their jurisdiction shall be original; and original jurisdiction where the constitution has declared it shall be appellate; the distribution of jurisdiction, made in the constitution, is form without substance.

Affirmative words are often, in their operation, negative of other objects than those affirmed; and in this case, a negative or exclusive sense must be given to them, or they have no operation at all.

---

herein after specially provided for; and shall have power to issue writs of prohibition to the district courts, when proceeding as courts in admiralty and maritime jurisdiction, and writs of mandamus, in cases warranted by the principles and usages of law, to any court appointed, or persons holding office, under the authority of the United States.

It cannot be presumed that any clause in the constitution is intended to be without effect; and, therefore, such a construction is inadmissible, unless the words require it. * * *

It is the essential criterion of appellate jurisdiction, that it revises and corrects the proceedings in a cause already instituted, and does not create that cause. Although, therefore, a mandamus may be directed to courts, yet to issue such a writ to an officer for the delivery of a paper, is in effect the same as to sustain an original action for that paper, and therefore, seems not to belong to appellate, but to original jurisdiction. Neither is it necessary in such a case as this, to enable the court to exercise its appellate jurisdiction.

The authority, therefore, given to the supreme court, by the act establishing the judicial courts of the United States, to issue writs of mandamus to public officers, appears not to be warranted by the constitution; and it becomes necessary to inquire whether a jurisdiction so conferred can be exercised.

The question, whether an act, repugnant to the constitution, can become the law of the land, is a question deeply interesting to the United States; but, happily, not of an intricacy proportioned to its interest. It seems only necessary to recognize certain principles, supposed to have been long and well established, to decide it.

That the people have an original right to establish, for their future government, such principles as, in their opinion, shall most conduce to their own happiness is the basis on which the whole American fabric has been erected. The exercise of this original right is a very great exertion; nor can it, nor ought it to be frequently repeated. The principles, therefore, so established, are deemed fundamental. And as the authority from which they proceed is supreme, and can seldom act, they are designed to be permanent.

This original and supreme will organizes the government, and assigns to different departments, their respective powers. It may either stop here, or establish certain limits not to be transcended by those departments.

The government of the United States is of the latter description. The powers of the legislature are defined and limited; and that those limits may not be mistaken, or forgotten, the constitution is written. To what purpose are powers limited, and to what purpose is that limitation committed to writing, if these limits may, at any time, be passed by those intended to be restrained? The distinction between a government with limited and unlimited powers is abolished, if those limits do not confine the persons on whom they are imposed, and if acts prohibited and acts allowed, are of equal obligation. It is a proposition too plain to be contested, that the constitution controls any legislative act repugnant to it; or, that the legislature may alter the constitution by an ordinary act.

Between these alternatives there is no middle ground. The constitution is either a superior, paramount law, unchangeable by ordinary means, or it is on a level with ordinary legislative acts, and, like other acts, is alterable when the legislature shall please to alter it.

If the former part of the alternative be true, then a legislative act contrary to the constitution is not law: if the latter part be true, then written constitutions are absurd attempts, on the part of the people, to limit a power in its own nature illimitable.

Certainly all those who have framed written constitutions contemplate them as forming the fundamental and paramount law of the nation, and, consequently, the theory of every such government must be, that an act of the legislature, repugnant to the constitution, is void.

This theory is essentially attached to a written constitution, and, is consequently, to be considered, by this court, as one of the fundamental principles of our society. It is not therefore to be lost sight of in the further consideration of this subject.

If an act of the legislature, repugnant to the constitution, is void, does it, notwithstanding its invalidity, bind the courts, and oblige them to give it effect? Or, in other words, though it be not law, does it constitute a rule as operative as if it was a law? This would be to overthrow in fact what was established in theory; and would seem, at first view, an absurdity too gross to be insisted on. It shall, however, receive a more attentive consideration.

It is emphatically the province and duty of the judicial department to say what the law is. Those who apply the rule to particular cases, must of necessity expound and interpret that rule. If two laws conflict with each other, the courts must decide on the operation of each.

So if a law be in opposition to the constitution; if both the law and the constitution apply to a particular case, so that the court must either decide that case conformably to the law, disregarding the constitution; or conformably to the constitution, disregarding the law; the court must determine which of these conflicting rules governs the case. This is of the very essence of judicial duty.

If, then, the courts are to regard the constitution, and the constitution is superior to any ordinary act of the legislature, the constitution, and not such ordinary act, must govern the case to which they both apply.

Those then who controvert the principle that the constitution is to be considered, in court, as a paramount law, are reduced to the necessity of maintaining that courts must close their eyes on the constitution, and see only the law.

This doctrine would subvert the very foundation of all written constitutions. It would declare that an act which, according to the principles and theory of our government, is entirely void, is yet, in practice, completely obligatory. It would declare that if the legislature shall do what is expressly forbidden, such act, notwithstanding the express prohibition, is in reality effectual. It would be giving to the legislature a practical and real omnipotence, with the same breath which professes to restrict their powers within narrow limits. It is prescribing limits, and declaring that those limits may be passed at pleasure.

That it thus reduces to nothing what we have deemed the greatest improvement on political institutions, a written constitution, would of itself be sufficient, in America, where written constitutions have been viewed with so much reverence, for rejecting the construction. But the peculiar expressions of the constitution of the United States furnish additional arguments in favor of its rejection.

The judicial power of the United States is extended to all cases arising under the constitution.

Could it be the intention of those who gave this power, to say that in using it the constitution should not be looked into? That a case arising under the constitution should be decided without examining the instrument under which it arises?

This is too extravagant to be maintained.

In some cases, then, the constitution must be looked into by the judges. And if they can open it at all, what part of it are they forbidden to read, or to obey?

There are many other parts of the constitution which serve to illustrate this subject.

It is declared that "no tax or duty shall be laid on articles exported from any state." Suppose a duty on the export of cotton, of tobacco, or of flour; and a suit instituted to recover it. Ought judgment to be rendered in such a case? Ought the judges to close their eyes on the constitution, and only see the law?

The constitution declares that "no bill of attainder or *ex post facto* law shall be passed."

If, however, such a bill should be passed and a person should be prosecuted under it; must the court condemn to death those victims whom the constitution endeavors to preserve?

"No person," says the constitution, "shall be convicted of treason unless on the testimony of two witnesses to the same overt act, or on confession in open court."

Here the language of the constitution is addressed especially to the courts. It prescribes, directly for them, a rule of evidence not to be departed from. If the legislature should change that rule, and declare *one* witness, or a confession *out* of court, sufficient for conviction, must the constitutional principle yield to the legislative act?

From these, and many other selections which might be made, it is apparent, that the framers of the constitution contemplated that instrument as a rule for the government of *courts*, as well as of the legislature.

Why otherwise does it direct the judges to take an oath to support it? This oath certainly applies, in an especial manner, to their conduct in their official character. How immoral to impose it on them, if they were to be used as the instruments, and the knowing instruments, for violating what they swear to support!

The oath of office, too, imposed by the legislature, is completely demonstrative of the legislative opinion on the subject. It is in these words: "I do solemnly swear that I will administer justice without respect to persons, and do equal right to the poor and to the rich; and that I will faithfully and impartially discharge all the duties incumbent on me as _____ according to the best of my abilities and understanding, agreeably to *the constitution*, and laws of the United States."

Why does a judge swear to discharge his duties agreeably to the constitution of the United States, if that constitution forms no rule for his government? If it is closed upon him, and cannot be inspected by him?

If such be the real state of things, this is worse than solemn mockery. To prescribe, or to take this oath, becomes equally a crime.

It is also not entirely unworthy of observation, that in declaring what shall be the *supreme* law of the land, the *constitution* itself is first mentioned; and not the laws of the United States generally, but those only which shall be made in *pursuance* of the constitution, have that rank.

Thus, the particular phraseology of the constitution of the United States confirms and strengthens the principle, supposed to be essential to all written constitutions, that a law repugnant to the constitution is void; and that *courts*, as well as other departments, are bound by that instrument.

NOTES ON MARBURY *AND THE* POWER OF JUDICIAL REVIEW

1. *The Reasoning of* Marbury. The Chief Justice's opinion in *Marbury* has tortured generations of law students, because it raises more questions than it answers. See William Van Alstyne, *A Critical Guide to* Marbury v. Madison, 1969 Duke L.J. 1, for an excellent analysis. See also Louise Weinberg, *Our Marbury*, 89 Va. L. Rev. 1235 (2003). Consider some preliminary technical questions raised by the opinion:

(a) *Why Was the Jurisdictional Question Not Answered First?* Marshall's opinion started with the merits of Marbury's claim, before moving to the issue of the Supreme Court's jurisdiction to hear the case. But if the Court does not have the "authority" (jurisdiction) to hear the case in the first place, one might argue that the Court's reaching the merits is inconsistent with the "judicial Power" vested by Article III. In *Hayburn's Case*, 2 U.S. (2 Dall.) 408 (1792), an annotation indicated that it is beyond the "judicial Power" for the Court to issue "advisory opinions," that is, the Court's interpretation of federal law when not in response to a real and live "case or controversy" before the Court. The situation in *Marbury* was similar: In a sense the first part of the Court's opinion was only "advisory," having no legal effect because the Court lacked jurisdiction to do anything in the case. For this reason, the typical practice of the Court is to ascertain that it has jurisdiction before adjudicating the parties' legal and constitutional claims on their merits.

(b) *Does § 13 Give the Court Original Jurisdiction in Mandamus Cases?* In declaring § 13 unconstitutional, Marshall "interpreted" § 13 to be an affirmative grant of original jurisdiction to the Court to issue a mandamus against Madison. Is his interpretation of the statute justifiable? Note the structure of § 13, quoted in the editors' footnote. Its first two sentences relate to the Court's original, and sometimes its exclusive, jurisdiction. Sentence three assures jury trials. Sentence four, containing the mandamus clause at its end, seems to relate to the Court's appellate jurisdiction. The structure suggests that mandamus is simply a power given to the Court in aid of its appellate jurisdiction. (The last clause on mandamus and writs of prohibition might also be read as ancillary powers for the Court whatever the nature of its jurisdiction.) Assuming this reading of § 13 is correct, the Chief Justice should have dismissed Marbury's lawsuit on the ground that the statute did not provide for it to be brought in the Supreme Court; Marbury might be able to sue in a lower court to enforce his rights under the justice-of-the-peace statute, with appeal to the Supreme Court, which could then issue a mandamus to Madison. Even if § 13 were ambiguous, courts ought to choose the interpretation that avoids rather than invites constitutional infirmity.[26]

(c) *As Interpreted, Was § 13 Unconstitutional?* Marshall found § 13 inconsistent with Article III, § 2, cl. 2: Congress cannot go beyond the grant of original jurisdiction specifically delineated in the first sentence. Under this reading, clause 2 divides the Court's jurisdiction into two worlds: the two categories where the Court has original jurisdiction, and all other cases, which Congress can assign to the Court's appellate jurisdiction. Any other reading, says the Chief Justice, would render clause 2 "without effect." But there are plausible readings of clause 2 that could give it effect without invalidating § 13. The meaning of clause 2 could be that Congress cannot restrict the Court's

---

[26] This canon of interpretation is based on a desire to avoid unnecessary friction between the legislative and judicial branches. See generally William Eskridge, Jr., Philip Frickey, Elizabeth Garrett, and James J. Brudney, *Cases and Materials on Legislation and Regulation: Statutes and the Creation of Public Policy* 829–49 (5th ed. 2014). This rule is not applicable when the Court reviews state laws, as in the *Brown* litigation, because state courts are the authoritative interpreters of state law.

original jurisdiction in the two enumerated categories (as to which "the supreme Court shall have original Jurisdiction") but otherwise has a great deal of freedom (to regulate and except from the Court's appellate jurisdiction, which could include adding some appellate matters to the Court's original jurisdiction). In short, clause 2 sets up the starting point, from which Congress can add and subtract under the "Exceptions, and * * * Regulations" language.

As to this and the previous question we posed, note an historical anomaly: The Chief Justice says that the first Congress, in 1789, enacted a jurisdictional statute which, for no apparent reason, violated a command of the just-ratified Constitution. But 51 of the 92 Members of the first Congress had been at the Philadelphia Convention or one of the state ratifying conventions. The drafter and sponsor of the Judiciary Act, Senator Oliver Ellsworth, had been a leading figure at the Convention and was the Chief Justice before John Marshall. The Court later upheld another provision in § 13 against constitutional attack, with the observation that it "was passed by the first Congress assembled under the Constitution, many of whose members had taken part in framing that instrument, and is contemporaneous and weighty evidence of its true meaning." *Wisconsin v. Pelican Ins. Co.*, 127 U.S. 265, 297 (1888). See also *Ames v. Kansas*, 111 U.S. 449, 463 (1884).

2. Marbury's *Justifications for Judicial Review*. The Court's reasoning in support of the authority of Article III courts to review legislation to determine its constitutionality poses its own set of mysteries.

(a) *Was the Power of Judicial Review Already Settled?* Before the Constitution was adopted, state courts had exercised power to declare statutes invalid, and there is every reason to believe that the Framers contemplated some kind of power of judicial review.[27] The Supreme Court had struck down a state law under the Supremacy Clause in *Ware v. Hylton*, 3 U.S. (3 Dall.) 199 (1796). Yet when one reads Marshall's opinion, one has the impression that he was writing on a clean slate, citing none of the prior decisions, or even Hamilton's essay in *Federalist* No. 78 (App. 2), from which the Chief Justice drew some of his arguments.

(b) *Does the Constitution's Structure Contemplate the Power of Judicial Review?* The Chief Justice's argument is simple: The written Constitution is the supreme law of the land; any statute contrary to the supreme law is void; in saying what the law is, courts cannot apply a statute when it is trumped by the supreme law of the land. But other countries with "supreme law" do not have traditions where judges make independent evaluations of statutory validity.[28] Where in our Constitution do courts find the authority to make an *independent* evaluation of a statute's constitutionality?

---

[27] See William Michael Treanor, *Judicial Review Before* Marbury, 58 Stan. L. Rev. 455 (2005) (state and federal judges struck down statues in 31 cases between 1783 and 1803).

[28] See Mario Cappelletti & William Cohen, *Comparative Constitutional Law* 74 (1979). Note that an increasing number of industrialized countries have been adopting judicially-enforceable constitutions along American lines in the last generation. See Vicki C. Jackson & Mark V. Tushnet, *Comparative Constitutional Law* (3d ed. 2015).

Marshall posited that specific constitutional provisions contemplate a role for judicial review. But the admonitions that "no tax or duty shall be laid on articles exported from any state," U.S. Const. Art. 1, § 9, cl. 3, are addressed specifically to legislatures, not to courts. Indeed, the admonitions are found in Article I (legislative power). The admonition in Article III, § 3, cl. 1, that "[n]o person shall be convicted of Treason unless on the Testimony of two Witnesses to the same overt Act, or on Confession in open Court," is addressed to courts, in striking contrast. Hence, one might argue that only the provisions in Article III are directions to courts; the directions in Article I are for legislatures. (*Marbury* of course construed Article III; perhaps its holding could be limited to statutes requiring the Court to violate Article III.) Are there persuasive arguments for the broader position that Marshall takes?

(c) *Does Judicial Review Include Review of Federal Statutes?* There is a structural argument Marshall didn't consider. One problem with the Articles of Confederation was that the national government didn't have the power to enforce uniform national policies on the states, and this led to many difficulties. If the Constitution were to remedy this problem, it had to vest authority in the national legislature to make laws and assess taxes, binding on the whole nation and enforceable through the national executive and courts. This is the best explanation of Article III's "arising under" jurisdiction, especially in light of the Supremacy Clause of Article VI. Judicial review of state laws was thus necessary as part of a coherent scheme to create a unified national government. Indeed, § 25 of the Judiciary Act of 1789 authorized the Supreme Court to review lower court decisions adjudicating the constitutionality of state statutes.[29] Most of the pre-*Marbury* exercises of judicial review saw state or federal judges strike down state laws. William Michael Treanor, *Judicial Review Before* Marbury, 58 Stan. L. Rev. 455 (2005).

But national uniformity does not require the U.S. Supreme Court to review federal statutes. Uniformity could be better achieved by everyone's deferring to whatever rules Congress laid down; consistent with this idea, § 25 gave the Court jurisdiction to review state court decisions invalidating national statutes or treaties. This kind of argument would support judicial review in *Brown* (state statutes), but not in *Marbury* (federal statute). Most of the important constitutional decisions in this book—particularly in the chapters regarding individual rights—involve state rather than federal statutes. Of course, believers in "states' rights" might question whether Congress should be the sole judge of its own powers. And, as Dean Treanor has shown, judges were before *Marbury* especially keen on striking down federal as well as state statutes that encroached upon judicial authority, as Congress was assertedly doing in the Judiciary Act of 1789 (Treanor, *Review Before* Marbury, 496–97, 508–18, 533–41).

---

[29] Section 25 gave the Supreme Court jurisdiction to review "a final judgment * * * in the highest court of law or equity of a State * * * where is drawn in question the validity of a treaty or statute of * * * the United States, and the decision is against their validity; or where is drawn in question the validity of a statute of * * * any State, on the ground of their being repugnant to the constitution, treaties or laws of the United States."

Marshall believed that the Court could strike down federal statutes and that the Court could order the Secretary of State to perform essentially ministerial functions. Note how the odd structure of his opinion allowed him to make both points without getting into overwhelming political trouble. The Democrat-Republicans were irate at the Federalists' last-minute shenanigans. Not only did they repeal the Circuit Court Act, but they revoked the December 1801 Term of the Court and impeached Federalist Justice Chase in 1802 (he was acquitted by the Senate). President Jefferson's hatred for John Marshall was well-known, and he had Spencer Roane of Virginia in mind to replace the Chief Justice. Writing *Marbury* the way he did, Marshall was able to embarrass the President (by showing his administration to be lawless), to assert judicial power over executive officials in appropriate cases (but without actually risking a Supreme Court order that Secretary of State Madison would probably have ignored), and to establish the authority of the Court to invalidate unconstitutional legislation (and proving the Court's impartiality as well, since it was Federalist legislation being struck down).

B. THE COURT'S SUPREMACY IN CONSTITUTIONAL INTERPRETATION?

Brown I did not decide what "relief" (remedy) was to be afforded plaintiffs. The relief usually granted by the Supreme Court when it reverses lower court judgments (as the Court did in all but the Delaware litigation) is simply to remand to the lower court to enter a new judgment consistent with the Supreme Court's decision. In *Brown v. Board of Education*, 349 U.S. 294 (1955) (*Brown II*), the Court remanded the cases to the lower courts to fashion equitable relief, namely, injunctions requiring the school boards to make a "prompt and reasonable start toward full compliance" with *Brown I*. The lower courts were instructed to retain jurisdiction over the litigation and "enter such orders and decrees * * * as are necessary and proper to admit to public schools on a racially nondiscriminatory basis and with all deliberate speed the parties to the cases." Compare *Florida ex rel. Hawkins v. Board of Control*, 350 U.S. 413 (1956) (blacks were entitled to immediate admission to state-run graduate and professional schools).

Brown II's "all deliberate speed" formula was questioned by integrationists as a retreat from the right recognized in *Brown I* and by segregationists as proof that *Brown I* was an invasion of states' rights. Actual implementation of *Brown* was uneven, to say the least. Topeka confessed to the *Brown II* Court that the formerly segregated black schools generally remained all-black and would probably remain segregated, because they were located in mostly black residential areas and because white families had the option of keeping their children in the previously (and still substantially) all-white schools.[30] Although compliance was

---

[30] See Mary Dudziak, *The Limits of Good Faith: Desegregation in Topeka, Kansas: 1950–1956*, 5 Law & Hist. Rev. 351, 379–80 (1987). On remand, the three-judge court approved the

imperfect in Kansas, *Bolling* was seriously implemented in the District of Columbia, and *Brown* was implemented in part in the border states.

On the other hand, the South fiercely objected to the decision. In March 1956, southerners in Congress issued a "Southern Manifesto" denouncing *Brown* as a "clear abuse of judicial power." Justin Driver, *Supremacies and the Southern Manifesto*, 92 Tex. 1053 (2014). Southern states enacted hundreds of laws seeking to impede the implementation of *Brown II*.[31] Prince Edward County, Virginia, for example, closed down its schools rather than comply with the Court's mandate. Some districts agreed to token plans for complying with *Brown*. Most districts, however, simply ignored or defied the decision, and state governments enacted statutes encoding the "segregation now, segregation forever" philosophy. One defiant district was Little Rock, Arkansas. Governor Orval Faubus and the Arkansas Legislature took the position that *Brown* was inconsistent with fundamental constitutional precepts of federalism, with the original intent of the Framers of the Fourteenth Amendment, and with precedent (*Plessy*). Because its leaders' understanding of the Constitution was different from the Court's, Little Rock asked to stay the judicial order requiring limited school integration pursuant to *Brown*. Were the state leaders bound by the Court's interpretation of the Constitution, even if it was "wrong"? The court of appeals held the local authorities to the original decree. The Supreme Court assembled in a special session to decide an appeal by the local officials; the day after it heard the case, the Court issued its mandate affirming the court of appeals and requiring Little Rock officials to proceed with the original plan for partial integration. The decision below, signed by every Justice to show the Court's solidarity, was issued later.

COOPER V. AARON
358 U.S. 1, 78 S.Ct. 1401, 3 L.Ed.2d 5 (1958)

Opinion of the Court by THE CHIEF JUSTICE [WARREN], JUSTICE BLACK, JUSTICE FRANKFURTER, JUSTICE DOUGLAS, JUSTICE BURTON, JUSTICE CLARK, JUSTICE HARLAN, JUSTICE BRENNAN, and JUSTICE WHITTAKER.

As this case reaches us it raises questions of the highest importance to the maintenance of our federal system of government. It necessarily involves a claim by the Governor and Legislature of a State that there is

---

Topeka plan as meeting the Supreme Court's order. "Desegregation does not mean that there must be intermingling of the races in all school districts. It means only that they may not be prevented from intermingling or going to school together because of race or color." *Brown v. Board of Education*, 139 F. Supp. 468, 470 (D. Kan. 1955).

[31] See Numan Bartley, *The Rise of Massive Resistance: Race and Politics in the South During the 1950's* (1969); Francis Wilhoit, *The Politics of Massive Resistance* (1973); J. Harvie Wilkinson III, *From* Brown *to Bakke: The Supreme Court and School Integration, 1954–1978*, at 78–102 (1979) (describing transition from massive resistance to token compliance with *Brown II*).

no duty on state officials to obey federal court orders resting on this Court's considered interpretation of the United States Constitution. Specifically it involves actions by the Governor and Legislature of Arkansas upon the premise that they are not bound by our holding in *Brown*. That holding was that the Fourteenth Amendment forbids States to use their governmental powers to bar children on racial grounds from attending schools where there is state participation through any arrangement, management, funds or property. We are urged to uphold a suspension of the Little Rock School Board's plan to do away with segregated public schools in Little Rock until state laws and efforts to upset and nullify our holding in *Brown* have been further challenged and tested in the courts. We reject these contentions.

[The Court affirmed the appellate court's decision holding the parties to the original judicial decree. Then the Court added, in what might be considered dictum, the following general discussion.] Article VI of the Constitution makes the Constitution the "supreme Law of the Land." In 1803, Chief Justice Marshall, speaking for a unanimous Court, referring to the Constitution as "the fundamental and paramount law of the nation," declared in the notable case of *Marbury v. Madison* that "It is emphatically the province and duty of the judicial department to say what the law is." This decision declared the basic principle that the federal judiciary is supreme in the exposition of the law of the Constitution, and that principle has ever since been respected by this Court and the Country as a permanent and indispensable feature of our constitutional system. It follows that the interpretation of the Fourteenth Amendment enunciated by this Court in the *Brown* case is the supreme law of the land, and Art. VI of the Constitution makes it of binding effect on the States "any Thing in the Constitution or Laws of any State to the Contrary notwithstanding." Every state legislator and executive and judicial officer is solemnly committed by oath taken pursuant to Art. VI, cl. 3, "to support this Constitution." Chief Justice Taney, speaking for a unanimous Court in 1859, said that this requirement reflected the Framers' "anxiety to preserve it [the Constitution] in full force, in all its powers, and to guard against resistance to or evasion of its authority, on the part of a State. . . ." *Ableman v. Booth*, 21 How. 506, 524.

No state legislator or executive or judicial officer can war against the Constitution without violating his undertaking to support it. Chief Justice Marshall spoke for a unanimous Court in saying that: "If the legislatures of the several states may, at will, annul the judgments of the courts of the United States, and destroy the rights acquired under those judgments, the constitution itself becomes a solemn mockery. . . ." *United States v. Peters*, 5 Cranch 115, 136. A Governor who asserts a power to nullify a federal court order is similarly restrained. If he had such power, said Chief Justice Hughes, in 1932, also for a unanimous Court, "it is manifest that the fiat of a state Governor, and not the Constitution of the United States, would be the supreme law of the land; that the restrictions of the Federal Constitution upon the exercise of state power would be but impotent phrases. . . ." *Sterling v. Constantin*, 287 U.S. 378, 397–398. * * *

[The concurring opinion of **JUSTICE FRANKFURTER** is omitted.]

Edwin Meese, III, *The Law of the Constitution*

61 Tul. L. Rev. 979 (1987)[32]

Attorney General Meese agreed with the essential holding of *Cooper*, that judicial interpretation of the Constitution "binds the parties to the case and also the executive branch for whatever enforcement is necessary. But such a decision does not establish a supreme law of the land that is binding on all persons and parts of government henceforth and forevermore." As examples, the Attorney General invoked *Plessy*, which the Court itself had reconsidered in *Brown*, as well as *Dred Scott*, which was debated by Stephen Douglas and Abraham Lincoln in the 1858 Illinois Senate race: the former urged obedience to the decision as supreme law, the latter urged nullification.

SCOTUS can Overturn Own Precedent

"The Supreme Court * * * is not the only interpreter of the Constitution. Each of the three coordinate branches of government created and empowered by the Constitution—the executive and legislative no less than the judicial—has a duty to interpret the Constitution in the performance of its official functions. In fact, every official takes an oath precisely to that effect."

Meese rejected the *Cooper* dictum excerpted above. "[T]he implication of the dictum that everyone would have to accept its judgments uncritically, that they are judgments from which there is no appeal, was astonishing; the language recalled what Stephen Douglas said about *Dred Scott*. In one fell swoop, the Court seemed to reduce the Constitution to the status of ordinary constitutional law, and to equate the judge with the lawgiver. * * * [The] logic of the dictum in *Cooper v. Aaron* was, and is, at war with the Constitution, at war with the basic principles of democratic government, and at war with the very meaning of the rule of law."

NOTE ON WHETHER OFFICIALS ARE REQUIRED TO FOLLOW THE SUPREME COURT'S INTERPRETATION OF THE CONSTITUTION?

Cooper was an easy case on its facts: The school district was under a direct court order to follow *Brown*. As Attorney General Meese contended, however, *Cooper*'s dictum raises issues not resolved by *Marbury*. Public officials have long asserted a power and a responsibility to make their own determinations as to what the Constitution requires.[33] Is there anything in the Constitution to

---

[32] Edwin Meese III, The Law of the Constitution, originally published in 61 TUL. L. REV. 979–90 (1987). Reprinted with the permission of the Tulane Law Review Association.

[33] Thus, in 1798–99, Kentucky and Virginia passed resolutions objecting to the federal Alien and Sedition Acts (making criticism of the Federalist government a crime) as essentially unconstitutional; in 1812–14, New England states objected to our war against England; in the

refute this understanding? The Supremacy Clause, invoked in *Cooper*, only applies to state judges—not to state governors, municipal councils, or national legislators or administrators.

Larry Alexander and Frederick Schauer defend the *Cooper* dictum as required by the rule-of-law features of the "judicial Power."[34] A central role for law is the authoritative settlement of what the rules are. Law thereby provides a content-independent basis for our actions; we will follow the rule because the law requires it. The Supreme Court follows wrongheaded precedent for this reason, too—it is better that things are settled finally than that they are settled correctly. The settlement function of law supports not only *consistency over time*, but also *consistency across institutions*. All other public officials should defer to the Supreme Court's interpretation of the Constitution for the same reason we all defer to the Constitution itself. Is this argument persuasive?

Consider a related historical and institutional argument made by Barry Friedman and Erin Delaney.[35] In a federal system, the Supreme Court's constitutional rulings have got to trump contrary views of state officials— including state governors and legislators as well as the judges covered by the Supremacy Clause. As a practical matter, once the President and Congress bond with the Court in support of its "vertical supremacy," it is harder for those institutions to resist the Court's eventual claim to "horizontal supremacy" as well. Indeed, the civil rights era was the perfect period for the Court to make the claim made in *Cooper*. Because they were allied with the Court on the enforcement of *Brown* injunctions against state and local officials, neither Congress nor the Eisenhower Administration was going to dispute the broader-than-needed assertion of horizontal supremacy in *Cooper*. (Note the strategic similarity to *Marbury*, where the Court went out of its way to confirm its power of judicial review on an issue as to which the Jefferson Administration was not likely to disagree.)

Notwithstanding these arguments, many of the commentators believe that Attorney General Meese has the better view in the post-civil rights era.[36] Thus, the President and Members of Congress take oaths to uphold and defend the Constitution. Does the Constitution's separation of powers authorize or

---

middle part of the century some state courts refused to follow federal legislative and constitutional fugitive slave provisions; President Lincoln considered *Dred Scott* incorrect and acted consistently with that belief, though he also said it was binding on the parties; President F.D. Roosevelt refused to accept many of the Court's *Lochner*-type decisions.

[34] Larry Alexander & Frederick Schauer, *On Extrajudicial Constitutional Interpretation*, 110 Harv. L. Rev. 1359 (1997). Also see Daniel A. Farber, *The Supreme Court and the Rule of Law: Cooper v. Aaron Revisited*, 1982 U. Ill. L. Rev. 387.

[35] See Barry Friedman & Erin F. Delaney, *Becoming Supreme: The Federal Foundation of Judicial Supremacy*, 111 Colum. L. Rev. 1137 (2011).

[36] See Larry Kramer, *The People Themselves: Popular Constitutionalism and Judicial Review* (2004); Saikrishna Bangalore Prakash, *Imperial from the Beginning: The Constitution of the Original Executive* (2015); Neal Devins & Saikrishna Prakash, *The Indefensible Duty to Defend*, 112 Colum. L. Rev. 507, 509 (2012); Sanford Levinson, *Could Meese Be Right This Time?*, 61 Tul. L. Rev. 1071 (1987); Robert Nagel, *Name-Calling and the Clear Error Rule*, 88 Nw. U.L. Rev. 193 (1993); Michael Stokes Paulsen, *The Most Dangerous Branch: Executive Power to Say What the Law Is*, 83 Geo. L.J. 217 (1994); David Strauss, *Presidential Interpretation of the Constitution*, 15 Cardozo L. Rev. 113 (1993).

even require each branch to make its own constitutional determinations? This reading of the Constitution is consistent with *Marbury*: The Court can and should refuse to apply an unconstitutional statute to cases before it, but the President can rely on the statute if she or he has a good faith belief in its constitutionality. See generally Saikrishna Bangalore Prakash, *Imperial from the Beginning: The Constitution of the Original Executive* (2015). Only in cases of a court order directed to the President or an executive branch official is deference required, as Attorney General Meese argued. Are Friedman and Delaney wrong to say that the President's interests are so closely aligned with the Court's vertical supremacy that he or she is unlikely to directly challenge the Court's horizontal supremacy?

Abraham Lincoln, the ultimate nationalist, ran for President on a platform that denounced the Court's *Dred Scott* decision, discussed in the notes after *Plessy*. Was Lincoln not correct to reject Supreme Court decisions whose wrongness goes to the very foundations of a civilized polity? Recall that *Cooper* cited and relied on *Ableman v. Booth*, 62 U.S. (21 How.) 506 (1859), a harbinger for *Dred Scott*. The Wisconsin Supreme Court had upheld a state writ of habeas corpus for a prisoner convicted of violating federal law making it a crime to assist fugitive slaves. *In re Booth*, 3 Wis. 145 (1854). Justice Abram Smith, concurring, argued that the states retained the right to protect the civil liberties of their citizens against disagreeable federal laws. Against the federal interest in uniformity, "it should be remembered that where one will rules, there can be no freedom for the many. The imposition of uniformity is but another name or process for usurpation or tyranny." On the eve of the South's own act of ultimate nullification, the Supreme Court reversed, in *Abelman v. Booth*. Did President Lincoln owe the same deference to *Dred Scott* that Wisconsin owed to *Abelman*? Indeed, could Lincoln not have disrespected *Abelman* and encouraged states like Wisconsin to ignore the Fugitive Slave Act?

C. AFTER *BROWN*: EVALUATION AND CRITIQUE

1. From *Brown II* to *Swann*

Implementation of the Court's decision in *Brown* involved an unprecedented amount of ongoing remedial activity by the federal judiciary and has yielded effects that can be viewed as encouraging, distressing, or incoherent.[37] Most federal judges initially followed the example of Topeka, where the judge accepted a school board plan that left segregation largely in place, and not of Little Rock, where the judge stirred up a hornet's nest by requiring actual integration. As a result, integration proceeded slowly. In the 1964–65 school year, only 2.3% of black school children in the South were attending integrated schools. (Because of desegregation in California after *Méndez*, Mexican-American and Puerto Rican students were more

---

[37] For the discussion that follows, see Justin Driver, *The School-House Gate: Public Education, the Supreme Court, and the Battle for the American Mind* 242–314 (2017); Wilkinson, *From* Brown *to* Bakke.

integrated into public schools than blacks in the South, but Texas schools remained segregated on grounds of ethnicity.) Pressed by constitutional challenges brought by the NAACP and supported by the Department of Justice, the Supreme Court in the 1960s showed open signs of impatience with local foot-dragging. In *Watson v. Memphis*, 373 U.S. 526 (1963), the Court ordered immediate desegregation of municipal recreation facilities, holding *Brown II*'s formula inapplicable and further warning that "*Brown* never contemplated that the concept of 'deliberate speed' would countenance indefinite delay in elimination of racial barriers in schools." Where the *Brown II* formula did apply, the Court began to give it teeth by invalidating half-hearted plans to desegregate. In *Goss v. Board of Education*, 373 U.S. 683 (1963), the Court held that a one-way transfer plan (students could transfer from schools where they were a minority into ones where they were a majority) lent itself to "perpetuation of segregation" and hence was invalid. In *Griffin v. County School Board*, 377 U.S. 218 (1964), the Court held that Prince Edward County, Virginia's closing of its public schools violated the Equal Protection Clause.

At the same time southern whites were dragging their feet, people of color were marching with theirs. Peaceful civil rights protests all over the South, often suppressed by violent white policemen and their attack dogs, culminated in Dr. Martin Luther King's galvanizing 1963 March on Washington. One consequence of civil rights activism was enactment of the Civil Rights Act of 1964, which brought the authority of Congress and the Presidency more directly to bear on resistance to school desegregation. Title IV authorized the Department of Justice to bring desegregation lawsuits, and Title VI prohibited racial discrimination in any program receiving federal financial assistance. The Elementary and Secondary Education Act of 1965 linked federal educational funding to compliance with *Brown*. As implemented by tough guidelines promulgated by the Department of Health, Education and Welfare ("HEW"), the link between federal money and school desegregation pushed toward greater compliance. By the 1968–69 school year, 32% of southern black school children were in integrated schools, a fifteen-fold increase from 1964.

Encouraged by political support, the Supreme Court pressed compliance more aggressively; the Court read the *Brown II* mandate to require actual *integration*, and not just *desegregation*. (The distinction may not have been merely remedial and may have reflected a stronger understanding of the substantive right in anti-subordination and not just colorblindness terms.) In *Green v. New Kent County School Board*, 391 U.S. 430 (1968), the local school board adopted a plan allowing pupils to choose which of two schools they would enter; under this plan, the district's schools remained essentially segregated. Supported by the Solicitor General, the NAACP's Inc. Fund challenged this plan. The Supreme Court, in an opinion by Justice Brennan, held that this plan was not "a sufficient step to 'effectuate a transition' to a unitary school system." The Court cast upon the school board the burden of coming "forward with a plan that promises realistically to work, and promises realistically to work *now*." The test for an acceptable plan was whether it would convert the school system to one "without a 'white' school and a 'Negro' school, but just schools." Federal judges took *Green* as a signal to require more affirmative local action to eliminate school segregation "root and branch," as *Green* suggested. Thus, after *Green*, the Fifth Circuit struck down continuing segregation of Mexican-American students in Texas schools.

Swann v. Charlotte-Mecklenburg Board of Education

402 U.S. 1 (1971)

A large majority of the African-American students in the Charlotte-Mecklenburg school system attended schools that were 99–100% black, and a plaintiff class successfully sued. Invoking *Green*, District Judge McMillan rejected plans offered by the school board, in favor of a plan developed by the court-appointed expert, Dr. John Finger. The Finger Plan rezoned high school districts in ways that distributed black students to previously white schools, and required in addition that 300 African-American students be bused to nearly all-white Independence High School. The Finger Plan for junior high schools created nine "satellite" zones, whereby inner-city black students were assigned by attendance zones to nine outlying predominately white junior high schools; this would substantially desegregate every junior high school in the system. For elementary schools, the Finger Plan relied on rezoning school districts and grouping two or three outlying white schools with one black inner-city school, resulting in extensive busing of grade school students, but also in substantial integration. Most schools would have student bodies with 9% to 38% minority populations. The issue on appeal was whether Judge McMillan had erred in adopting the Finger Plan, which not only rezoned school districts and created racial pairings and groups of schools, but required the extensive busing of schoolchildren, sometimes far from their homes. **Chief Justice Burger**'s opinion for a unanimous Court affirmed McMillan's decree.

"The objective today remains to eliminate from the public schools all vestiges of state-imposed segregation. Segregation was the evil struck down by *Brown I* as contrary to the equal protection guarantees of the Constitution. That was the violation sought to be corrected by the remedial measures of *Brown II*. That was the basis for the holding in *Green* that school authorities are 'clearly charged with the affirmative duty to take whatever steps might be necessary to convert to a unitary system in which racial discrimination would be eliminated root and branch.'

"If school authorities fail in their affirmative obligations under these holdings, judicial authority may be invoked. Once a right and a violation have been shown, the scope of a district court's equitable powers to remedy past wrongs is broad, for breadth and flexibility are inherent in equitable remedies."

See Hecht Co. v. Bowles, 321 U.S. 321, 329–30 (1944), cited in Brown II. The Chief Justice considered various challenges to the district court's plan. Judge McMillan sought approximately a 71%/29% white/black balance in as many schools as possible. "If we were to read the holding of the District Court to require, as a matter of substantive constitutional right, any particular degree of racial balance or mixing, that approach would be disapproved and we would be obliged to reverse. The constitutional command to desegregate schools does not mean that every school in every community must always reflect the racial composition of the school system as a whole." The Court found, however, that the 71/29 ratio "was no more than a starting point in the process of shaping a remedy, rather than an inflexible requirement." Important in the Court's toleration of such a ratio was the finding of fact that Charlotte-Mecklenburg had operated a dual school system and then had not responded in good faith to the court's request for a remedy effective in the Green sense.

"[I]n a system with a history of segregation the need for remedial criteria of sufficient specificity to assure a school authority's compliance with its constitutional duty warrants a presumption against schools that are substantially disproportionate in their racial composition. Where the school authority's proposed plan for conversion from a dual to a unitary system contemplates the continued existence of some schools that are all or predominately of one race, they have the burden of showing that such school assignments are genuinely nondiscriminatory. * * *

"Absent a constitutional violation there would be no basis for judicially ordering assignment of students on a racial basis. All things being equal, with no history of discrimination, it might well be desirable to assign pupils to schools nearest their homes. But all things are not equal in a system that has been deliberately constructed and maintained to enforce racial segregation. The remedy for such segregation may be administratively awkward, inconvenient, and even bizarre in some situations and may impose burdens on some; but all awkwardness and inconvenience cannot be avoided in the interim period when remedial adjustments are being made to eliminate the dual school systems." Based upon this reasoning, the Court accepted Judge McMillan's order to the school system to rezone, pair inner-city and outlying schools, and bus students.

IN SWANN'S WAKE: NOTES ON AFFIRMATIVE REMEDIES IN PUBLIC RIGHTS LITIGATION

1. *The Significance of Affirmative Remedies.* The most important point to be drawn from *Swann* is its least controversial: The district court judge has substantial discretion to fashion a remedy. Hence, one judge might order busing to achieve a unitary school system, while another in a similar situation might accept the school board's proposal to build a new school that would draw from both black and white neighborhoods. If each judge makes plausible findings that her particular remedy is a sufficient step toward creating a unitary school system and the overall order is not an "abuse of discretion," both

judges should be upheld on appeal. What is more controversial about *Swann* is how far the Court would permit district judges to go in imposing equity-based remedies on a school system that is moving too slowly.

For example, the Court upheld Judge McMillan's use of racial quotas as a starting point for evaluating the school board's progress and his assignment of students to schools on a racial basis. In *North Carolina State Board of Education v. Swann*, 402 U.S. 43 (1971), the Court invalidated a state statute prohibiting assignment on the basis of race in order to create a racial balance in the schools. This is anomalous: *Brown*'s mandate to end a classification based upon race (segregation) has begotten an array of classifications based upon race (racial quotas and assignments). How might Chief Justice Burger defend this apparent anomaly?

2. *A Public Rights Model for Constitutional Adjudication and Rights.* The litigation implementing *Brown* gave new prominence to public law litigation:[38] The traditional understanding of constitutional litigation—the *Marbury* understanding, not questioned in *Brown*—is that an aggrieved plaintiff sues the government to redress her particular constitutional injury, through damages or a prohibitory injunction. The post-*Brown* understanding—reflected in *Swann*—is that a minority group sues to redress an ongoing, pervasive constitutional injury, through an affirmative or even structural injunction. We explore the new public law model of litigation in Chapter 9. Consider the ways constitutional litigation changes when group rights, rather than individual rights, are at stake:

Marbury Litigation	*Swann* Litigation
Litigation arises out of isolated violation of *individual* rights and is needed to restore the status quo through a prohibitory injunction.	Litigation arises out of systematic violation of *group* rights and is needed to transform the status quo through a structural injunction.
Operation of law is limited to parties. Court's involvement ends with the issuance of the injunction.	Operation of law is polycentric, with impact on nonparties. Court retains jurisdiction after issuing injunction.
Role of the judge is *umpireal*. Law is neutral and external to the parties. Litigation applies the rules of law.	Role of the judge is *managerial*. Law is generated internally among parties, public, and judge. Litigation creates public values.

Do these differences justify concern under Article III?

3. *Structural Constitutional Issues in* Swann. Was the intrusiveness of Judge McMillan's remedy consistent with the structure of the Constitution?

---

[38] See Owen Fiss, *The Civil Rights Injunction* (1978); Abram Chayes, *The Role of the Judge in Public Law Litigation*, 89 Harv. L. Rev. 1281 (1976); Frank Coffin, *The Frontier of Remedies: A Call for Exploration*, 67 Cal. L. Rev. 983 (1979); Paul Gewirtz, *Choice in the Transition: School Desegregation and the Corrective Ideal*, 86 Colum. L. Rev. 728, 751 (1986).

First, was it appropriate for a *federal* official to dictate the details of local school zones, pupil assignment, and clustering of schools? Federalism might be offended by the detailed remedy imposed on the local authority. In an *amicus* brief authored by Lewis Powell and filed in *Swann*, Virginia argued that, for public schools, the values of localism trumped the values of speedy integration. Specifically, Judge McMillan's plan would undermine the institution of neighborhood schools. Because parental involvement in their children's education (an important variable in student achievement) was most keen when the children attended schools close to their homes, this development would hurt public education for everyone.

Second, should a federal *court* be making essentially legislative or executive judgments in its remedial order? Key to the constitutional design is the separation of legislative, executive, and judicial powers, see, *e.g.*, *Federalist* No. 47 (App. 2) (applying Montesquieu's defense of separate powers to support the Constitution). A danger of the structural injunction and ongoing judicial involvement in the remedy phase of *Brown* litigation is that the judge might be drawn into rulemaking and policymaking—essentially legislative judgments. E.g., *Brown v. Plata*, 563 U.S. 493, 554–59 (2011) (Scalia, J., dissenting, based upon this meta-critique of structural injunctions in prison litigation). Under this critique, Judge McMillan's decree went beyond traditional adjudication (barring the school district from unconstitutional practices) and crossed the line into policymaking (such as reconfiguring student and teacher placement rules and setting racial goals).

Third, is it within the Article III "judicial Power" for a court to involve itself in "polycentric" problems, such as social restructuring? *Marbury* and *Federalist* No. 78 (App. 2), the leading defenses of judicial review, assume a reactive rather than "proactive" court, one that solves particular "Cases or Controversies," a requirement reflected in the Supreme Court's justiciability case law (see Chapter 9, § 2). Powell's *amicus* brief in *Swann* made this point: Judge McMillan's busing order was at best a short-term fix for the problem of ongoing segregation; once a busing order was in place, there would be "white flight" to private schools and to suburbs not reached by the busing order. Because a federal judge could not control important variables—parental decisions about where to live and whether to send their children to private schools—judicial efforts to instantiate good social policy were doomed to failure. Accord, *Plata* (Scalia's dissent, joined by Thomas and Alito).[39]

2. Drawing the Line: From *Swann* to *Pitts*

Green and *Swann* emboldened federal judges in the South to enter strong remedial orders, which contributed to desegregation in that region. According to the U.S. Commission on Civil Rights, 38% of the nation's black

---

[39] One response in the context of *Swann* is that Charlotte (big city) and Mecklenburg (surrounding county) were combined for public school jurisdictional purposes; hence, it would have been harder for white flight to occur. Most big cities with large minority populations are not part of the same school district as their surrounding suburbs, however. How should the Inc. Fund respond to this kind of argument? Is it appropriate in a constitutional case?

schoolchildren (44% in the South) were attending majority-white schools by 1978—compared with 23% (18% in the South) ten years before.[40] Dr. Jay Robinson, the Superintendent of the Charlotte-Mecklenburg School System, told Congress in 1981 that *Swann* had not only established an integrated school system, but had been a very positive experience for students and parents of all races.[41]

The Court extended the principles of *Brown* and *Green* to northern schools in *Keyes v. School District No. 1*, 413 U.S. 189 (1973), a development that also contributed to the higher level of integration in 1978. Justice Brennan's opinion for the Court held that *de facto* racial segregation (segregation resulting from purely private decisionmaking) in public schools does not violate the Equal Protection Clause; only *de jure* racial segregation (that attributable to the state) is actionable. This holding was of momentous but ambiguous importance to the application of *Brown I* outside the South. On the one hand, because most northern school districts had not been segregated as a matter of law, it might be difficult or at least complicated to establish the state action required by the Court's ruling. On the other hand, state action could be shown by evidence short of a formal apartheid regime. The trial court in *Keyes* had found that Denver had manipulated part of its school system to maintain racially segregated schools, which the Court held was sufficient to satisfy the state action requirement. Indeed, once some state action was found to have contributed to segregation in part of the Denver school district, the Court ruled that the trial court could consider city-wide remedies and remanded to the trial court to consider whether a city-wide busing plan would be appropriate under *Swann*.

After *Swann* and *Keyes*, popular interest in, and disapproval of, *Green* decrees increased; many white parents were unwilling to have their children bused outside their neighborhood and into integrated schools. Their concerns, moreover, had a new audience within the Court—the four Justices named by President Nixon, especially Justice Lewis Powell, who had headed the Richmond, Virginia School Board and authored the anti-busing *amicus* brief in *Swann*. Rejecting equal protection claims by Mexican Americans that Texas's system of school financing had the effect of discriminating against the poor and people of color (Latinos as well as blacks), Powell's opinion for the Court in *San Antonio Indep. Sch. Dist. v. Rodriguez*, 411 U.S. 1 (1973) (Chapter 5, § 3B, but you might read this case now), set forth a legal process rationale for judicial restraint in public education cases. According to Powell, the constitutional baseline in such

---

[40] School Desegregation: Hearings Before the Subcomm. on Civil and Constitutional Rights of the House Comm. on the Judiciary, 97th Cong., 1st Sess. 255 (1981) (testimony of Dr. Flemming).

[41] *Id.* at 17–21; see *id.* at 382 (testimony of Robert Crain, Johns Hopkins Univ.) (empirical studies suggest that school integration is very helpful for children of color and helpful or neutral for white children); *id.* at 159 (Prof. Gary Orfield, Univ. of Illinois) (similar).

cases is that the local democratic process must be the primary decisionmaker; intervention from the judiciary can only be justified by "extraordinary" circumstances; and when the judiciary does intervene it ought not intrude too deeply into local governance. Principles of federalism limited the capacity of the courts to address inequalities in local education. In *Rodriguez*, the Court declined to recognize a constitutional cause of action; in the next case, the Court applied similar principles to limit *Brown II* remedies.

Milliken v. Bradley

418 U.S. 717 (1974)

The federal district judge found that the Detroit Board of Education had created and perpetuated a system of racially segregated schools; as an entity created by Michigan, the Board's unconstitutional acts were attributable to the state, ruled the trial judge. Under *Keyes* and *Swann*, the judge rejected the Board's proposed remedy, which would have integrated the city's schools, on the ground that there would still have been "racially identifiable" schools (e.g., inner-city schools 75–90% black). The court determined that there was no effective remedy without busing schoolchildren from inner city (largely black) neighborhoods into the (largely white) Detroit suburbs, and vice-versa. The Supreme Court, in an opinion by **Chief Justice Burger** (joined by the other three Nixon Justices and Justice Stewart, the same majority as in *Rodriguez*), overturned the district court's decree. The Court held that busing between separate school districts is only justified when "racially discriminatory acts of the state or local school districts, or of a single school district have been a substantial cause of interdistrict segregation."

The Chief Justice rebuked the lower court for reading *Swann* to require fairly precise racial balance in a unitary school system, but the court's primary error was its disregard of school district boundaries. "Boundary lines may be bridged where there has been a constitutional violation calling for interdistrict relief, but the notion that school district lines may be casually ignored or treated as a mere administrative convenience is contrary to the history of public education in our country. No single tradition in public education is more deeply rooted than local control over the operation of schools; local autonomy has long been thought essential both to the maintenance of community concern and support for public schools and to quality of the educational process. Thus, in *San Antonio School District v. Rodriguez*, we observed that local control over the educational process affords citizens an opportunity to participate in decisionmaking, permits the structuring of school programs to fit local needs, and encourages 'experimentation, innovation, and a healthy competition for educational excellence.'"

The Chief Justice concluded that the district court's remedy would violate the integrity of this local structure. The decree's requirement that 54 independent school districts be consolidated into a "super district" would generate a host of operational problems that the court would be ill-equipped to resolve—and any resolution would undermine the local electorate's governance of their own school system. Because *Keyes, Swann*, and *Green* had involved single school districts, they did not justify the lower court's activism, and Chief Justice Burger set forth guidance for future judges. "Before the boundaries of separate and autonomous school districts may be set aside by consolidating the separate units for remedial purposes or by imposing a cross-district remedy, it must first be shown that there has been a constitutional violation within one district that produces a significant segregative effect in another district. Specifically, it must be shown that racially discriminatory acts of the state or local school districts, or of a single school district have been a substantial cause of interdistrict segregation. Thus an interdistrict remedy might be in order where the racially discriminatory acts of one or more school districts caused racial segregation in an adjacent district, or where district lines have been deliberately drawn on the basis of race."

Dissenting opinions by **Justices White** and **Marshall** (and joined by Justices Douglas and Brennan, the other two dissenters in *Rodriguez*) maintained that the trial court's finding of fact that state agencies participated in Detroit's scheme to create and perpetuate a racially segregated school system justified interdistrict relief even under the Court's assumptions. More fundamentally, the dissenters argued that the Court's view of judges' equity powers was at odds with the strongly purposive opinions in *Brown, Green*, and *Swann*. See also *Wright v. Council of the City of Emporia*, 407 U.S. 451 (1972) (refusing to allow the creation of a new school district that would "impede the process of dismantling a dual system"); *Reynolds v. Sims*, 377 U.S. 533 (1964) (requiring state to redraw legislative districts to meet the equal protection one-person, one-vote standard). "Until today," Justice White objected, "the permissible contours of the equitable authority of the district courts to remedy the unlawful establishment of a dual school system have been extensive, adaptable, and fully responsive to the ultimate goal of achieving 'the greatest possible degree of actual desegregation.'"

The Chief Justice responded that all of the precedents—from *Brown* to *Keyes*—involved single school districts and delineated the rights of black students in that specific context; *Green*'s remedial goal of a "unitary" school system cannot be understood without reference to that narrow understanding of what the right is. Concluded Burger: "The constitutional right of the Negro respondents residing in Detroit is to attend a unitary school system in that district. Unless petitioners drew the district lines in a discriminatory fashion, or arranged for white students residing in the Detroit District to attend schools in Oakland and Macomb Counties, they were under no constitutional duty to make provisions for Negro students to do so." The dissenters had a completely different view of the underlying constitutional rights and their violation. "The Court's remedy, in the end, is essentially arbitrary and will leave serious violations of the Constitution essentially unremedied." For a continuation of this debate within the Court, see *Pasadena Board of Education v. Spangler*,

427 U.S. 424 (1976) (overturning lower court order periodically adjusting geographic boundaries for schools to take account of "white flight").

On remand, the district judge in *Milliken* abandoned his effort to produce an integrated school system within Detroit; instead, he ordered massive reform of the inner-city system, including remedial programs, counseling and career guidance, and other measures to be paid for by the state. The Supreme Court affirmed this order in *Milliken v. Bradley (II)*, 433 U.S. 267 (1977), holding that remedial orders may include expenditure of state funds. After *Milliken II*, the Inc. Fund shifted its focus from interdistrict remedies to state and local funding to make urban schools attractive enough to generate integrated student bodies as a matter of choice. E.g., *Missouri v. Jenkins*, 495 U.S. 33 (1990) (Chapter 9, § 3) (district judge may order state and local governments to raise taxes in order to fund programs that remedy *Brown* violations by creating magnet schools attracting students of all races). Neo-federalists of the Reagan era opposed these measures, on the ground that they unduly infringed the principle of local control of public schools.

The *Milliken* decisions rested upon the principle that equitable remedies must be tailored to the violation. The Court required a nexus between the violation and the remedy. Besides the geographic dimension featured in *Milliken*, the tailoring principle might have a temporal dimension. The original nexus between violation and remedy may erode over time, so much that continued remedial intervention would become unjustified. In 1986 the Norfolk, Virginia school district was the first to be given permission by a federal court to end its desegregation plan, and other districts clamored to escape the regulation under *Green/Swann* decrees. In *Board of Education v. Dowell*, 498 U.S. 237 (1991), Solicitor General Kenneth Starr and former Solicitor General Rex Lee filed *amicus* briefs arguing that school districts in the 1990s were no longer accountable for segregationist policies that ended in the 1960s. Substantially agreeing with Starr and Lee, the Court held that the principle of local control of education requires a district court to dissolve a remedial decree "after the local authorities have operated in [good faith] compliance with it for a reasonable period of time." (In *Dowell*, the original finding of *de jure* segregation had been made in 1961, the remedial order entered in 1972, and the order dissolved in 1985.) Dissenting, Justice Thurgood Marshall—the advocate who won *Brown*—argued that *Brown* remedial orders should not be dissolved until *Green's* unitary school system had been achieved.

Freeman v. Pitts

503 U.S. 467 (1992)

The DeKalb County School System (DCSS), located outside Atlanta, was under a *Brown II* consent decree starting in 1969. The district court found in 1981 that student reassignments, magnet schools, and active recruitment of minority faculty pursuant to the decree had disestablished the prior dual school system, but that teacher assignments and funding still reflected the dual system. The court also found that continued segregation, with identifiably black and white schools, was "caused" by changing residential patterns (white flight) and not by anything the local government had done. Hence, the court directed DCSS to deal with remaining teacher-assignment problems but relinquished jurisdiction over student assignment and other issues. Emphasizing the continued existence of racial segregation, the court of appeals reversed and directed the district court to consider the aggressive remedies found effective in *Swann* (pairing of schools, gerrymandering school zones, busing). The Supreme Court, in an opinion by **Justice Kennedy**, reversed the court of appeals. As it had done in *Dowell*, the Court in *Pitts* remanded to the district court, to determine whether the school district had shown a "good faith commitment to the entirety of a desegregation plan," including a plan to remedy ongoing violations.

"A federal court in a school desegregation case has the discretion to order an incremental or partial withdrawal of its supervision and control." This ruling was grounded on the tailoring principle for equitable relief, on *Swann's* premise that "judicial powers may be exercised only on the basis of a constitutional violation" and that "the nature of the violation determines the scope of the remedy," and on the "vital national tradition" favoring "local autonomy of school districts." In an important passage embracing the neo-federalist emphasis on *local accountability*, Justice Kennedy said: "Returning schools to the control of local authorities at the earliest practicable date is essential to restore their true accountability in our governmental system. When the school district and all state entities participating with it in operating the schools make decisions in the absence of judicial supervision, they can be held accountable to the citizenry, to the political process, and to the courts in the ordinary course. * * * [O]ne of the prerequisites to relinquishment of control in whole or in part is that a school district has demonstrated its commitment to a course of action that gives full respect to the equal protection guarantees of the Constitution. Yet it must be acknowledged that the potential for discrimination and racial hostility is still present in our country, and its manifestations may emerge in new and subtle forms after the effects of *de jure* desegregation have been eliminated. It is the duty of the State and its subdivisions to ensure that such forces do not shape or control the policies of its school systems. Where control lies, so too does responsibility. * * *

"The Court of Appeals was mistaken in ruling that our opinion in *Swann* requires 'awkward,' 'inconvenient,' and 'even bizarre' measures to achieve racial balance in student assignments in the late phases of carrying out a decree, when the imbalance is attributable neither to the prior *de jure* system nor to a later violation by the school district but rather to independent demographic forces. In *Swann* we undertook to discuss the objectives of a comprehensive desegregation plan and the powers and techniques available to a district court in designing it at the outset. We confirmed that racial balance in school assignments was a necessary part of the remedy in the circumstances there presented. In the case before us the District Court designed a comprehensive plan for desegregation of DCSS in 1969, one that included racial balance in student assignments. The desegregation decree was designed to achieve maximum practicable desegregation. Its central remedy was the closing of black schools and the reassignment of pupils to neighborhood schools, with attendance zones that achieved racial balance. The plan accomplished its objective in the first year of operation, before dramatic demographic changes altered residential patterns. * * *

"That there was racial imbalance in student attendance zones was not tantamount to a showing that the school district was in noncompliance with the decree or with its duties under the law. Racial balance is not to be achieved for its own sake. It is to be pursued when racial imbalance has been caused by a constitutional violation. Once the racial imbalance due to the *de jure* violation has been remedied, the school district is under no duty to remedy imbalance that is caused by demographic factors. If the unlawful *de jure* policy of a school system has been the cause of the racial imbalance in student attendance, that condition must be remedied. The school district bears the burden of showing that any current imbalance is not traceable, in a proximate way, to the prior violation." Justice Kennedy credited the district court's factual findings that resegregation occurred because of population shifts (white flight) that could not be attributed to the state.

"Where resegregation is a product not of state action but of private choices, it does not have constitutional implications. It is beyond the authority and beyond the practical ability of the federal courts to try to counteract these kinds of continuous and massive demographic shifts. To attempt such results would require ongoing and never-ending supervision by the courts of school districts simply because they were once *de jure* segregated. * * * As the *de jure* violation becomes more remote in time and these demographic changes intervene, it becomes less likely that a current racial imbalance in a school district is a vestige of the prior *de jure* system. The causal link between current conditions and the prior violation is even more attenuated if the school district has demonstrated its good faith." Although upholding the district court's authority to divest jurisdiction over some features of the school system, Justice Kennedy ruled that the district court must first assure itself that the area of continuing violation (teacher assignment) does not require attention to other areas (student assignment) that are related. The Court also directed the lower court to make sure that the school district "has an affirmative commitment to comply in good faith with the entirety of a desegregation plan."

Justice Scalia concurred with the observation that the Court "should consider laying aside the extraordinary, and increasingly counterfactual, presumption of *Green*" that school districts bear some responsibility for continuing patterns of segregation. In contrast, concurring **Justices Souter, Blackmun, Stevens**, and **O'Connor** interpreted *Green* as requiring district courts in *Brown II* cases to consider whether previous *de jure* segregation or other school policies contributed to ongoing segregated residential patterns and, before relinquishing jurisdiction over part of the case, to consider whether schools are racially identifiable and therefore vulnerable to resegregation.

Justices Blackmun, Stevens, and O'Connor concurred only in the judgment, because they felt the Court paid insufficient attention to *Swann* and the connection between schools and housing. "This interactive effect between schools and housing choices may occur because many families are concerned about the racial composition of a prospective school and will make residential decisions accordingly. Thus, schools that are demonstrably black or white provide a signal to these families, perpetuating and intensifying the residential movement." The district court left this issue unexamined: DCSS might have encouraged white flight "by assigning faculty and principals so as to identify some schools as intended respectively for black students or white students. Nor did the court consider how the placement of schools, the attendance zone boundaries, or the use of mobile classrooms might have affected residential movement."

NOTE ON THE FUTURE OF BROWN I *&* II

Pitts reflects a duel between state and private responsibility that has bedeviled the Court since *Brown II*. See also Chapter 9, § 3. *Pitts'* premise is consistent with constitutional doctrine prominent since *The Civil Rights Cases* (Chapter 3, § 2): The Constitution generally applies just to state and not private action. In order to find a constitutional violation, therefore, courts have been forced to look backwards to earlier acts of intentional state discrimination. The basic rationale, as in *Pitts*, is that a history of state discrimination has had continuing effects, which the court must now remedy under the tailoring principle. This rationale places a serious, far-reaching judicial remedy on an increasingly tenuous empirical foundation. Even twenty years ago, sympathetic critics questioned whether the causal linkage was strong enough to carry this load, see, *e.g.*, Owen Fiss, *The Jurisprudence of Busing*, 39 L. & Contemp. Prob. 194, 207 (1975). Time has only compounded this uncertainty. But Justice Kennedy's *Pitts* opinion is not the only way to understand the meaning of *Brown I* and the future of *Brown II*. Consider some different approaches:

1. *Everything Is Connected with State (Educational and Housing) Policies*. Another approach would understand "private" decisions about where to live as pervasively connected with "public" policies, including housing as well as educational policies.[42] Accordingly, the persistence of a dual school system (with identifiably black and white schools) reinforces white people's obsession with the racial composition of schools and thereby facilitates white flight (*Pitts* concurring opinions). Something like this approach recognizes the central role of education in either perpetuating or dealing with racism, and possibly in both.[43] Against this approach is the argument that ongoing judicial

---

[42] This is the view of the NAACP's Inc. Fund and many social scientists. See "School Segregation and Residential Segregation: A Social Science Statement," appendix to Brief for Respondents, *Columbus Bd. of Educ. v. Penick* (No. 78–610); "School Desegregation: A Social Science Statement," appendix to Brief of the NAACP [et al.] as *Amicus Curiae* in Support of Respondents, *Freeman v. Pitts* (No. 89–1290).

[43] See James Liebman, *Desegregating Politics: "All-Out" School Desegregation Explained*, 90 Colum. L. Rev. 1463 (1990). "[O]ne of the most important lessons that the American public schools teach is that the diverse ethnic, cultural, and national backgrounds that have been brought

control of local school systems is inconsistent with federalism and separation of powers and, partly for that reason, a sisyphesian task for courts. Another counterargument is that white flight was caused by court-ordered busing rather than by the school system's decisions, but this link is subject to dispute, as we will see.

2. *Integration as a Constitutional Mandate*? Maybe the problem is not with the remedy but with the basic definition of the right, a point made by the Burger opinion in *Milliken I*. Rather than conducting a speculative hunt for historical violations and their continuing effects, perhaps we should just say that schools are under an affirmative duty to use reasonable efforts to achieve and maintain racial integration. Although the Court has never taken this position, it was endorsed by Justice Powell in his separate opinion in *Keyes*. Moreover, although the Court has always demanded a causal link, it has allowed use of evidentiary presumptions to establish the link, see Fiss, *supra*, at 207, so the practical effect of the Court's current theory may not be vastly different from the alternative.

The most prominent critic of the foregoing understanding is Justice Clarence Thomas. In *United States v. Fordice*, 505 U.S. 717 (1992), the Court ruled that Mississippi could not leave in place "policies rooted in its prior officially-segregated system that serve to maintain the racial identifiability of its universities if those policies can practicably be eliminated without eroding sound educational policies." Concurring, Justice Thomas argued that the Court's opinion did not compel "the elimination of all observed racial imbalance," and thereby allowed traditionally black colleges to survive. He seemed to endorse the idea that the state could "operate a diverse assortment of institutions—including historically black institutions—open to all on a race-neutral basis, but with traditions and programs that might disproportionately appeal to one race or another."

In *Missouri v. Jenkins (III)*, 515 U.S. 70 (1995) (Chapter 9, § 3), Thomas went further. Invoking *Milliken I*, the Court overturned the trial court's order requiring the state to fund inner-city schools in order to attract white students from the suburbs. In a concurring opinion, Justice Thomas charged the lower court (and perhaps the four Justices in dissent) with stereotyped thinking in its efforts to attract white students to black schools. "It never ceases to amaze me that the courts are so willing to assume that anything that is predominantly black must be inferior," Thomas objected. He then rejected the social science basis for *Brown*: "Segregation was not unconstitutional because it might have caused psychological feelings of inferiority." It was unconstitutional because the state classified the students based on race. So long as the state is neutral, there is nothing constitutionally or pedagogically wrong with single-race public schools; "there is no reason to believe that black

_____

together in our famous 'melting pot' do not identify essential differences among the human beings that inhabit our land. It is one thing for a white child to be taught by a white teacher that color, like beauty, is only 'skin deep'; it is far more convincing to experience that truth on a day-to-day basis during the routine, ongoing learning process." *Wygant v. Jackson Board of Education*, 476 U.S. 267, 315 (1986) (Stevens, J., dissenting).

students cannot learn as well when surrounded by members of their own race as when they are in an integrated environment." This conservative voice of color decidedly rejects an integrationist reading of the Equal Protection Clause as both illiberal and disrespectful to black culture.

3. *Nearing the End of the* Brown *Regime?* Consistent with Justice Thomas's later stance, Justice Scalia's *Pitts* concurrence suggested that *Brown*'s time has passed and that actual desegregation is a goal beyond the power of courts to require and school districts to attain. During the 1990s, many large school districts, including Denver, Savannah, Buffalo, Dallas, and Wilmington (one of the *Brown* cases), were granted unitary status. Busing ended in the school district where it had first begun—Charlotte-Mecklenburg (*Swann*)—when the Supreme Court refused to hear an appeal from parents who wanted to keep the district under a desegregation order. In September 2002, the Little Rock school district (*Cooper*) was held to be a unitary system freed from judicial supervision.

Consider the subsequent history of the Topeka school system. In the 1980s, African-American parents (including Linda Brown Smith) moved to reopen the original *Brown* litigation. At trial in the new litigation, it was established that the Topeka school system was substantially segregated (eight schools were overwhelmingly nonwhite, five overwhelmingly white). The district court found in *Brown v. Board of Education*, 671 F. Supp. 1290 (D. Kan. 1987), that these racial imbalances were the result of residential patterns rather than actions by the state. The Tenth Circuit reversed, holding that the district had not proved its compliance with *Brown* by demonstrating a unitary school system. *Brown v. Board of Education*, 892 F.2d 851 (10th Cir. 1989). After *Pitts*, the Supreme Court vacated the judgment and remanded the case back to the district court. *Board of Education v. Brown*, 503 U.S. 978 (1992). The Tenth Circuit reinstated its earlier opinion rejecting unitary status, however. See *Brown v. Board of Education*, 978 F.2d 585 (10th Cir. 1992), *cert. denied*, 509 U.S. 903 (1993). It was not until 1999 that the district court concluded that unitary status had been achieved. See *Brown v. Unified School District No. 501*, 56 F. Supp. 2d 1212 (D. Kan. 1999). Meanwhile, over a generation of students had made their way through the Topeka schools.

Pitts may be the swan song for Brown II remedial orders. Although some districts continue to operate pursuant to desegregation plans, between 1991 and 2009 at least 200 significant-seized school districts were relieved of judicial supervision under Brown II remedial orders. Sean F. Reardon et al., Brown *Fades: The End of Court-Order School Desegregation and the Resegregation of American Public Schools*, J. Pol'y Analysis & Management (2012).[44] And the criticisms keep piling up. Some object that *Swann*-type remedies (especially

---

[44] See Stephan Thernstrom & Abigail Thernstrom, *America in Black and White: One Nation, Indivisible* 315–16 (1997) (1995 survey of 103 school districts found that 45% were under court-ordered desegregation plans, and several more had voluntary plans); Wendy Parker, *The Future of School Desegregation*, 94 Nw. U.L. Rev. 1157, 2007 (2000) (only 13% of the school desegregation cases in the Fifth and Eleventh Circuits had been granted unitary status).

busing) are coercive against the victim class.[45] For example, a group of eighteen black parents sought to intervene in *Pitts* to oppose busing. These parents "believe there's nothing wrong with schools that are nearly all black as long as the quality of education is high."[46] Would a *Plessy* regime where "separate but equal" really meant *equal* be preferable to a *Brown* regime where resegregation occurs because of private choices and resegregated black schools are substantially inferior to white schools? See Sonya Ramsey, *The Troubled History of American Education After the* Brown *Decision,* Process, Feb. 7, 2017 (lamenting the loss of schools run by black professionals); Michael Seidman, Brown *and* Miranda, 80 Cal. L. Rev. 673 (1992) (a truly enforced *Plessy* regime might be better), and the following materials.

3.   Has *Brown* Made a Difference? A Good Difference?

By many accounts, *Brown* has been a success. It has been vindicated over time by a near-consensus rejection of *de jure* segregation and by a fair amount of actual integration. By 1981, almost half of the African-American school children in the South attended majority-white schools. Empirical studies have evaluated the effect of school desegregation on schoolchildren: None showed any harm to the educational experience of white schoolchildren, and many showed a statistically significant and positive effect on the educational experience of black schoolchildren.[47] Gains for black schoolchildren were particularly significant when there was substantial racial integration from the beginning of the children's education. Also during this period of steady desegregation, standardized test scores for black students rose much faster than test scores for white students, substantially narrowing the "achievement gap" between the races. See David Grissmer et al., *Why Did the Black-White Score Gap Narrow in the 1970s and 1980s?*, in *The Black-White Test Score Gap* 182–226 (Christopher Jencks & Meredith Philips eds. 1998).

Some studies have found that racial prejudice has been ameliorated by school integration. The U.S. Commission on Civil Rights in *Racial Isolation in the Public Schools* (1967) analyzed data for over 75,000 students in grades nine through twelve in the Northeast. It found a preference by students for desegregated schools and interracial friendships to be positively correlated with *both* the number of years such students had attended desegregated schools *and* the degree of desegregation in their current classrooms. But see Nancy St. John, *School Desegregation Outcomes for Children* 64–86 (1975) (reporting that desegregation

---

[45] E.g., Charles Cooper, *The Coercive Remedies Paradox*, 9 Harv. J.L. & Pub. Pol. 77, 81 (1986).

[46] See Robert Anthony, "Stakes High in DeKalb School Desegregation Case," *Atlanta Const.*, Oct. 6, 1991, at A18.

[47] E.g., Janet Ward Schofield, *Review of Research on School Desegregation's Impact on Elementary and Secondary School Students*, in *Handbook of Research on Multicultural Education* 597–617 (James Banks & Cherry McGee Banks eds. 1995).

sometimes had these effects but sometimes promoted stereotyping and interracial conflict).

Students of color educated in desegregated schools have been significantly more likely to attend desegregated colleges, to work in integrated workplaces, and to enjoy racially mixed social and professional networks. According to some in-depth studies, the best results for students of color have come when they attend schools that are not only racially integrated, but predominantly middle class. A case study of the St. Louis consent decree found that students of color who traveled to suburban schools had significantly higher test scores and graduation rates, were much more likely to attend college, and were (qualitatively) more confident and goal-oriented than students who attended city schools, including magnet schools. See Amy Stuart Wells & Robert Crain, *Stepping Over the Color Line: African-American Students in White Suburban Schools* (1997).

An analysis of a voluntary cross-district transfer program in Boston found that almost all past participants (88% of them) believed the program (inaugurated in 1966) was valuable because it enabled them to bridge black-white gulfs and tap into social and informational networks otherwise unavailable to them. See Susan Eaton, *The Other Boston Busing Story: What's Won and Lost Across the Boundary Line* (2001). A study of Chicago's interdistrict relocation program found that students of color who attended school in largely white suburbs were more likely to attend college and less likely to drop out of high school than students who remained in city schools; they were also much more likely to have jobs and higher pay than their counterparts. See Leonard Rubinowtiz & James Rosenbaum, *Crossing the Class and Color Lines: From Public Housing to White Suburbia* (2000). (These interdistrict programs have been copied in other cities, but under *Miliken I* courts cannot impose them as remedies for constitutional violations of *Brown*.)

Empirical studies for this period (1950–80) provide some further evidence that *Brown* and allied legal developments yielded beneficial economic as well as educational consequences for African Americans. Between 1940 and 1980, the average black man doubled his years in school (from 4.70 to 10.96 years) and saw his wages rise from 43.3% of a white man's wage to 72.6%; the wage increase was largely due to the reduction in the black-white education deficit. See James Smith & Finis Welch, *Black Economic Progress After Myrdal*, 27 J. Econ. Lit. 519, 538–39 (1989).

This is the rosy scenario—but it is only half of the story.

Political scientist Gerald Rosenberg maintains that *Brown* itself did not "cause" the advances noted above, which were the result of national legislative and executive pressures; that *Brown* instead contributed to white backlash against black progress; and that *Brown* did little good even in the school districts under direct judicial supervision. Gerald Rosenberg,

The Hollow Hope: Can Courts Bring About Social Change? (2d ed. 2008). The first claim is particularly controversial; by other accounts, *Brown* figured prominently in the evolution of the civil rights movement, which was responsible for the civil rights statutes of the 1960s.[48]

What is not contested is that American public schools have substantially resegregated. The nation's schools, including those in the South, steadily desegregated between 1964 and 1978.[49] This process stagnated in the 1980s and reversed course by the end of the decade. After the Supreme Court in *Dowell* and *Pitts* encouraged district courts to be open to the possibility that *Brown* remedies were no longer needed, steady and significant resegregation has occurred.[50] In the South, the proportion of black school children attending schools with a majority of minority students has returned to pre-*Swann* levels. Today, most of the progress made in integrating the South after 1964 has been lost. Latino Americans, now the largest minority group in the country, are even more segregated than African Americans, and their isolation has been increasing.

In Mecklenberg County, for example, a federal judge who had been a leading opponent of busing dissolved the *Swann* requirement that racial balance be considered in pupil assignment. His 1999 order was affirmed on appeal, and the *Swann* regime was replaced by a "family choice plan," where most students would attend neighborhood schools. Roslyn Arlin Mickelson et al., editors, *Yesterday, Today, and Tomorrow: School Desegregation and Resegregation in Charlotte* (2015). The result was an immediate resegregation of schools, and the draining of talented faculty away from the "black" schools. A report on the consequences by a former judge declared that the new regime was, in its effect, "academic genocide" for the county's low-income, at-risk students. See Clint Smith, *The Desegregation and Resegreation of Charlotte's Schools,* The New Yorker, Oct. 3, 2016.

Desegregation decrees have been undermined by "white flight"—the migration of white families away from school systems having a large percentage of African-American students. The exact "causes" of white flight

---

[48] See David Garrow, *Hopelessly Hollow History: Revisionist Devaluing of* Brown v. Board of Education, 80 Va. L. Rev. 151 (1994) (leading historian of the civil rights movement arguing that *Brown* directly contributed to its success); Michael J. Klarman, *How* Brown *Changed Race Relations: The Backlash Thesis,* 81 J. Am. Hist. 81 (1994) (*Brown* indirectly contributed to success of civil rights movement by fueling southern violence that elevated race discrimination to a major place on the national political agenda).

[49] To be sure, progress was uneven. Public schools in the District of Columbia and Wilmington, desegregated as a matter of law by *Bolling* and *Brown*, resegregated as a matter of fact, as the percentage of black students in the two districts went from 60.8% and 27.1% in 1954 to 95.3% and 84.7% in 1975. See Raymond Wolters, *The Burden of* Brown: *Thirty Years of School Desegregation* 16, 182 (1984).

[50] The factual materials that follow are taken from recent studies from the Harvard Civil Rights Project. See Gary Orfield & John T. Yun, *Resegregation in American Schools* (June 1999); Gary Orfield & Chungmei Lee, *Historic Reversals, Accelerating Resegregation, and the Need for New Integration Strategies* (Aug. 2007).

are hard to figure. As Lewis Powell first argued in his *Swann amicus* brief, desegregation plans themselves may cause (or significantly exacerbate) white flight, with mandatory ones triggering the most flight. See also David Armour, *Forced Justice: School Desegregation and the Law* 174–80 (1995). Others argue that "flight" would have occurred in any event because of low white birth rates and high levels of migration; these scholars also believe that metropolitan-wide (interdistrict) desegregation plans can do much to mitigate the trend (Orfield & Lee, *Historic Reversals*). Also, white flight began before *Brown* remedies in most cities (such as Wilmington and the District of Columbia) and occurred in some cities with no desegregation plans.

The editors of *Yesterday, Today, and Tomorrow* (the history of school desegregation and resegregation in Mecklenberg County) think that the abandonment of Judge McMillan's remedial order and the creation of the family choice plan *created* white flight in that county. With children assured attendance at "neighborhood" schools, white parents flocked to white-majority neighborhoods, making them whiter and other neighborhoods blacker. Civil rights advocates have found the experience of Mecklenberg County ultimately very discouraging.

Because of white flight, residential housing patterns, and the Supreme Court's limitations on courts' remedial powers, most school children in America today attend substantially segregated schools. See Emma Brown, *The Overwhelming Whiteness of U.S. Private Schools,* Wash. Post, March 29, 2016; Will Stancil, *School Segregation Is Not a Myth*, The Atlantic, March 14, 2018. Additionally, even when children attend schools that are technically "integrated," they are often "resegregated" within the school. Administrators sometimes assign students to essentially segregated classrooms, or assign minority school children in disproportionate numbers to lower "tracks" within the school system. See Roy Brooks, *Rethinking the American Race Problem* 77–78 (1990).

Trends in achievement scores have followed the same pattern as desegregation. After decades of narrowing, the black-white achievement gap in test scores began to widen again in the late 1980s—just as resegregation was occurring.[51] Some students of color suffer even in integrated schools; several studies have suggested that some black students may lose confidence and perform more poorly in integrated schools than in all-black schools, because of discriminatory tracking programs and resegregation, poor teacher attitudes, lack of role models, and biases in the curriculum and its administration. Jacqueline Jordan

---

[51] Armour, *Forced Justice* 91–98, argues that the gap is explainable by socioeconomic factors alone and suggests that changes in socioeconomic factors can explain changes in the achievement gap. Stephan and Abigail Thernstrom, *America in Black and White* 357–59, disagree with Armour's conclusion because the achievement gap widened in the 1990s even though the black middle class was not shrinking. They believe that increased violence and disorder in public schools have contributed to the widening gap. *Id.* at 359, 376–81.

Irvine, *Black Students and School Failure: Policies, Practices, and Prescriptions* 9–12 (1990). This argument turns the rationale of *Brown* on its head: While segregation marginalized and stigmatized blacks by excluding them from white school systems, integration can and sometimes does marginalize and stigmatize blacks by including them within white school systems that are unreceptive to their needs, interests, and concerns.

Parents Involved in Community Schools v. Seattle School District No. 1

551 U.S. 701 (2007)

Many school districts have sought further *de facto* integration through voluntary plans. In *Parents Involved*, the Supreme Court invalidated plans adopted in Seattle and Louisville, based upon the Court's recent affirmative action jurisprudence, which is excerpted and discussed in detail in Chapter 3, § 3A–C of this casebook. *Parents Involved* is excerpted and discussed in § 3D, but you may want to read the case here.

A NOTE ON CONSTITUTIONAL LAW AND LEGAL EDUCATION

The study of *Brown* suggests that constitutional law is not just a system of immutable rules that can be objectively discovered through lawyerly craft. Indeed, the NAACP's efforts to overturn *Plessy* indicate that both constitutional law and the role of the attorney herself are creative, interactive, and nonmechanical. Consider the views of (former) Judge Richard Posner, *The Problems of Jurisprudence* 100 (1990):

> The most important thing that law school imparts to its students is a feel for the outer bounds of permissible legal argumentation at the time when the education is being imparted. (Later those bounds will change, of course.) What "thinking like a lawyer" means is not the use of special analytic powers but an awareness of approximately how plastic law is at the frontiers—neither infinitely plastic, * * * nor rigid and predetermined, as many laypersons think—and of the permissible "moves" in arguing for, or against, a change in the law. It is neither method nor doctrine, but a repertoire of acceptable arguments and a feel for the degree and character of doctrinal stability, or, more generally, for the contours of a professional culture—a professional culture lovable to some, hateful to others.

As Judge Posner would admit, there is a predictable component to constitutional law, but it cannot be grasped by merely searching for the apparent holdings of decided cases and compiling them into an outline of rules.

We believe it is best to confront the fuzzy edges of constitutional law at the outset of this course, before you seek to master particular doctrinal areas. Accordingly, our next section takes up the central question of constitutional law introduced by *Brown*: By what method(s) should the Supreme Court give meaning to the Constitution? To use Judge Posner's terms, in "thinking like a lawyer" about "how plastic [constitutional] law is at the frontiers," a central task is to identify and evaluate a variety of potential theories by which the Supreme Court can ascertain constitutional meaning. Unsurprisingly, each potential technique of constitutional interpretation is controversial. The goal is not to announce what we consider to be the "correct" approach to solving the fundamental problems of constitutional law but instead, as Judge Posner puts it, to provide you with the skills to begin thinking like a lawyer about them. Whatever your views, we invite you to bring vigor, even passion, to the enterprise.

SECTION 3. *BROWN* AND THEORIES OF CONSTITUTIONAL DECISIONMAKING

Marbury held that the Constitution is the supreme law of the land and, as interpreted in *Cooper*, that the Supreme Court's constructions of the Constitution are binding on the other branches of the national as well as state governments. *Brown* is an example of the exercise of this power of judicial review—the power to invalidate the acts of a democratically elected legislature as inconsistent with the Constitution. In a democracy, however, it is troubling that nine unelected judges with life tenure have this authority. In *The Least Dangerous Branch: The Supreme Court at the Bar of Politics* (1962), Alexander M. Bickel expressed this problem as the "countermajoritarian difficulty": The power of judicial review is in tension with our commitment to representative democracy.[52] *Marbury* and *Cooper*, if correctly decided, answer Bickel's question as to the Court's authority to displace majoritarian law. But those precedents do not answer other important questions: By what criteria does the Court evaluate the constitutionality of laws? What limits are there on judicial decisionmaking, lest we substitute judicial tyranny for legislative tyranny?

These are questions that arose in our discussion of *Plessy* and *Brown*. An early academic theory of judicial review, by James Bradley Thayer, maintained that courts should invalidate statutes only when there is no reasonable doubt as to their constitutionality. This theory lends some support to *Plessy* and problematizes *Brown*, either as to its precise result (which is now virtually beyond question in American constitutional law) or as to the possibility of generalizing from it (about which there is no consensus). "*Brown* represented one of the most agonizing moments in American jurisprudence. In some sense, all of American constitutional law * * * has revolved around trying to justify the judicial role in *Brown* while trying simultaneously to show that such a course will not lead to another

---

[52] As Barry Friedman has shown, the countermajoritarian difficulty was not a primary concern with judicial review before the New Deal era, but has become an obsession with critics of the Court in the last third of the twentieth century. Barry Friedman, *The History of the Countermajoritarian Difficulty, Part One: The Road to Judicial Supremacy*, 73 NYU L. Rev. 333 (1998), and *The Birth of an Academic Obsession: The History of the Countermajoritarian Difficulty, Part Five*, 112 Yale L.J. 153 (2002).

Lochner era,"[53] where activist judicial review of labor legislation and ultimately the New Deal did the country no good and got the Supreme Court into political trouble (Chapter 1, §§ 4–5).

The remainder of this chapter introduces you to the leading theories justifying, guiding, and constraining judicial review. Original meaning theories (Part A) posit that the Court's authority rests upon the consent of "We the People" who entered into the Constitution, our social contract. Current majorities can only be overruled, under the Constitution, if they thwart the will of the founding super-majority, as expressed in the Constitution and its amendments. The lodestar for originalist theories is the "original meaning" of constitutional provisions. Legal process theories (Part B) maintain that the Supreme Court must consider its institutional advantages and limitations when exercising its power of judicial review. One prominent theory, for example, infers from the structure and principles of the Constitution as well as the capacities of judges that judicial review is appropriate when the political process has been dysfunctional or procedurally flawed. Theories of popular constitutionalism (Part C) maintain that the Constitution must be read dynamically and should reflect new norms (such as the notion that the state cannot discriminate against citizens because of their race) which our constitutional culture accepts as fundamental. Although there are many such academic theories, we focus on those grounded in the republican tradition, newer critical theory, and common law reasoning—and we explore each in the context of *Brown*. Even if you reject *Brown* as a litmus test and choose to treat it as simply exceptional, the following materials will provide a coherent overview of current constitutional theory.

A. ORIGINAL MEANING THEORIES OF JUDICIAL REVIEW

Historically, judicial review has been justified on the ground that it enforces the original social contract, created in a moment of supermajoritarian popular consent. As the Supremacy Clause suggests and *Marbury* held, the Constitution is a supervening authority, trumping federal and state laws inconsistent with it. If a law can be shown to be inconsistent with the Constitution, then it is invalid, and a federal court will require parties in a case or controversy to disregard that law (*Cooper*). Under this analysis, a court is only enforcing the "original deal," for which there is ongoing consent, and its action is neither countermajoritarian nor violative of the consent of the governed.

Originalists seek to construct a foundation for judicial review that is consistent with the consent of the people, that is intersubjective (does not

---

[53] Morton Horwitz, *The Jurisprudence of* Brown *and the Dilemmas of Liberalism*, 14 Harv. C.R.-C.L. L. Rev. 599, 602 (1979).

depend upon the judge's own values), and that can be applied in a predictable manner. What this entails, and how the theory is expressed, have evolved in the last generation.[54] In the 1970s, scholars such as Raoul Berger and Robert Bork challenged Warren Court precedents as inconsistent with the *original intent* of the Framers. H. Jefferson Powell, *The Original Understanding of Original Intent*, 98 Harv. L. Rev. 885 (1985), however, demonstrated that the Framers did not "intend" that their "intent" would be binding on future generations. Powell's article did not slow down the advance of originalist thinking but did impel a shift in vocabulary, toward the notion of *original understanding*—the understanding of the Constitution that would have been shared by those who ratified what the Framers drafted.[55] In the wake of Jack Rakove, *Original Meanings: Politics and Ideas in the Making of the Constitution* (1996), another linguistic shift occurred, away from original understanding toward *original meaning*.[56] In the new millennium, original (public) meaning is the dominant concept for these theorists and judges: What meaning did constitutional language have for We the People—the public, as well as the ratifiers and the Framers? See Steven G. Calabresi & Andrea Matthews, *Originalism and* Loving v. Virginia, 2012 BYU L. Rev. 1393; Henry Monaghan, *Stare Decisis and Constitutional Adjudication*, 88 Colum. L. Rev. 723 (1988).

In figuring out "original meaning," an interpreter might consider (1) the text of the Constitution, including its structure and other provisions bearing on the issue; (2) the context within which that text was drafted, debated, and ratified, including legal background and traditions; and (3) the original goals and norms that were accepted by those ratifying (and perhaps those framing) the constitutional provision(s) in question. Note that the original meaning inquiry may be conducted at various different levels of generality. Most narrowly, the interpreter might ask whether a modern law is inconsistent with the particular meaning a constitutional provision had in 1789. E.g., Antonin Scalia, *Originalism: The Lesser Evil*, 57 U. Cin. L. Rev. 849 (1989). More broadly, the interpreter might ask what general principle a constitutional provision reflected in 1789, and then further inquire how that principle ought to be translated into constitutional doctrine. E.g., Jack M. Balkin, *Living Originalism* (2011);

---

[54] See Vasan Kesavan & Michael Stokes Paulsen, *The Interpretive Force of the Constitution's Secret Drafting History*, 91 Geo. L.J. 1113 (2003).

[55] Compare John Yoo, *The Continuation of Politics by Other Means: The Original Understanding of War Powers*, 84 Cal. L. Rev. 167 (1996), with William Michael Treanor, *Fame, the Founding, and the Power to Declare War*, 82 Cornell L. Rev. 695 (1997).

[56] For examples of original meaning methodology in action, compare Saikrishna Prakash & Michael Ramsey, *The Executive Power over Foreign Affairs*, 111 Yale L.J. 231 (2001), with Curtis Bradley & Martin Flaherty, *Executive Power Essentialism and Foreign Affairs*, 102 Mich. L. Rev. 545 (2004). And compare Saikrishna Prakash, *Unleashing the Dogs of War: What the Constitution Means by "Declare War,"* 93 Cornell L. Rev. 45 (2007), with Robert Delahunty & John Yoo, *Making War*, 93 Cornell L. Rev. 123 (2007), and Michael Ramsey, *The President's Power to Respond to Attacks*, 93 Cornell L. Rev. 169 (2007).

John F. Manning, *The Supreme Court, 2013 Term—Foreword: The Means of Constitutional Power,* 128 Harv. L. Rev. 1 (2014).

As you read these materials, keep in mind some general difficulties with originalist, consent-based theories of judicial review: (a) *The dead-hand of the past problem*: Is it appropriate to assume that there is an ongoing implicit consent to the original Constitution, which was negotiated and ratified by only a tiny minority of the population who could not possibly have envisioned much of what our world would be like?[57] (b) *The indeterminacy problem*: How can one ever know what more than a handful of founding era people thought about an issue? Can it be seriously maintained that there is a knowable "original meaning" as to issues that the framing generation could not have anticipated?[58] (c) *The cognitive dissonance problem*: For normatively charged issues of constitutional law, can any judge remain genuinely objective? Or will judges sift through evidence of original meaning, cherry-picking sources that support their own perspective and ignoring the rest?[59]

1. Constitutional Text

Text is the most relevant evidence when interpreting any legal document. It is the starting point and usually the ending point for interpreting contracts, wills, and statutes. Unfortunately, the Constitution is a relatively short document, filled with open-textured terms (like "equal protection" and "due process"), most of which were drafted more than 200 years ago. How can such a document address any of the important modern problems of governance? There are a number of judges and theorists who have propounded useful textualist approaches to constitutional decisionmaking.[60] Consider some techniques of textual exegesis:

(a) *Clause-Bound Textualism: What is the "plain meaning" of the constitutional language? How would a reasonable person in the Framers' era have understood the language?* An obvious textual approach would ask

---

[57] See Randy E. Barnett, *Restoring the Lost Constitution: The Presumption of Liberty* (2004) (criticizing social contract theory as an unrealistic view of what makes government legitimate); Dorothy Roberts, *The Meaning of Blacks' Fidelity to the Constitution*, 65 Fordham L. Rev. 1761 (1997) (noting that the social contract did not reflect the input of women and minorities).

[58] Paul Brest, *The Misconceived Quest for the Original Understanding*, 60 B.U. L. Rev. 204 (1980); Mark V. Tushnet, *Following the Rules Laid Down: A Critique of Interpretivism and Neutral Principles*, 96 Harv. L. Rev. 781 (1983); Michael Dorf & Laurence Tribe, *Levels of Generality in the Definition of Rights*, 57 U. Chi. L. Rev. 1057 (1990); Martin Flaherty, *History "Lite" in Modern American Constitutionalism*, 95 Colum. L. Rev. 523 (1995).

[59] For evidence that original meaning jurisprudence, in action, is like looking out over the crowd and picking out your friends, see, e.g., Peter Smith, *Sources of Federalism: An Empirical Analysis of the Court's Quest for Original Meaning*, 52 UCLA L. Rev. 217 (2004).

[60] E.g., Charles Black, *Structure and Relationship in Constitutional Law* (1969); Antonin Scalia, *A Matter of Interpretation: Federal Courts and the Law* (1997); Akhil Reed Amar, *America's Constitution, A Biography* (2005); John F. Manning, *The Eleventh Amendment and the Reading of Precise Constitutional Texts*, 113 Yale L.J. 1663 (2004); Nicholas Quinn Rozenkranz, *The Subjects of the Constitution*, 62 Stan. L. Rev. 1209 (2010), and *The Objects of the Constitution*, 63 Stan. L. Rev. 1055 (2011).

how a normal reader of the English language would construe the provision in question, bringing to bear the conventional tools of grammar and word meaning into play.[61] This was the approach Chief Justice Marshall followed to construe Article III, § 2, clause 2 in *Marbury*. Sentence 1 gave the Supreme Court original jurisdiction but did not include the mandamus action Marbury was pressing; therefore, as a matter of ordinary inference, the Constitution did not authorize Congress to give the Court original jurisdiction in mandamus cases. Recall, however, that the meaning of Article III is not as "plain" as Marshall claimed. Thus, clause 2 could be limited to the proposition that Congress cannot restrict the Court's original jurisdiction in the enumerated categories but otherwise has a great deal of freedom to create "Regulations" and "Exceptions" for the Court's jurisdiction. *Marbury* thus exemplifies the key problem with textualism as a constitutional methodology: The text may not be clear. *Marbury* itself is unusual, insofar as it involves a constitutional provision that is relatively directive, specific, and focused. The constitutional provisions providing details for the structure of government are generally much easier to apply than the broader, "open-textured" provisions such as the Equal Protection Clause interpreted in *Brown*.

Marbury's textual reasoning involved more than grammar and word meaning. Marshall's interpretation rested upon an interpretive *convention*: If I authorize you to do "x", I am implicitly not authorizing you to do "y" as well. The maxim *inclusio unius est exclusio alterius* (inclusion of one thing implies exclusion of all others) is a widely accepted common law presumption for construing legal instruments. Other textualist conventions include the notions that

- the meaning of words not defined in a legal document can be ascertained by consulting authoritative dictionaries and considering other sources of ordinary usage or terms of art;

- a term is presumed to have the same meaning throughout a legal document (rule of consistent use), and the use of a different term suggests a different meaning (the rule of meaningful variation);

- one part of a sentence should not be construed in such a way that it renders another part unnecessary (the rule against surplusage).[62]

---

[61] Oliver Wendell Holmes, Jr., *The Theory of Legal Interpretation*, 12 Harv. L. Rev. 417 (1899) ("normal speaker of English" is the standard for legal interpretation), embraced and elaborated in Scalia, *Matter of Interpretation*.

[62] On textual canons, see William N. Eskridge, Jr., Philip P. Frickey, Elizabeth Garrett & James J. Brudney, *Cases and Materials on Legislation and Regulation: Statutes and the Creation of Public Policy* ch. 8, § 1 (5th ed. 2014); William N. Eskridge Jr., *Interpreting Law: A Primer on How to Read Statutes and the Constitution* (2016); Antonin Scalia & Bryan A. Garner, *Reading Law: The Interpretation of Legal Texts* (2012).

These conventions are controversial. If Mother tells Sally, "Don't hit or kick your sister Anne," is Sally authorized to pinch little sister? Or hit sister Martha? (Hint: no!) At most, these conventions are presumptions; some academics would abolish them altogether.

Should a textualist limit her inquiry to meanings and conventions as they would have been understood at the time of the framing of the original Constitution or of a relevant amendment? The answer to that question sometimes makes a difference. The term "commerce" used in Article I, § 8 probably had a narrower meaning in 1787–89, when the Constitution was ratified, than it has today. See *United States v. Lopez*, 514 U.S. 549, 585–87 (1995) (Thomas, J., concurring) (surveying dictionaries of the time as well as ratification debates to show that "commerce" only included trade or barter and did not involve manufacturing). Most judicial textualists prefer "original meanings" to current ones, but are open to reasonable updating. The Framers of the Second Amendment's right "to keep and bear arms" could not have imagined modern firearms, but the Supreme Court has held that the right is not limited to weapons existing in 1791. *District of Columbia v. Heller*, 554 U.S. 570, 580–85 (2008).

In the same vein, original meaning would construe terms in accord with settled legal or constitutional meanings they had when added to the Constitution. The Fourteenth Amendment terms *privileges or immunities* and *due process* had established constitutional meanings in 1868; those should presumptively be followed. Note that this suggests that *The Slaughter House Cases* were wrongly decided, insofar as they gave the Privilege or Immunities Clause of the Fourteenth Amendment a different and narrower reading (inapplicable to state restrictions of occupation) than the then-established reading of a similar clause in Article IV. This suggests a dilemma for the modern textualist: Under what circumstances, if any, should the Court overrule important precedents because they are inconsistent with (original) constitutional plain meaning? *McDonald v. City of Chicago*, 561 U.S. 742 (2010) (plurality opinion) (declining to overrule *Slaughter House Cases*, notwithstanding very strong history-based refutation of the Court's controversial holding); Scalia, *Originalism* (*stare decisis* usually requires him to follow nonoriginalist precedents, the probable reason for his joining the plurality opinion in *McDonald*).

(b) *Holistic Interpretation: Read the provision in light of the whole document.* The Constitution can be read "holistically," as a coherent document, where all parts are presumed to fit together in a consistent whole.[63] Like the Bible, the Constitution should be read, where possible (or

---

[63] See Akhil Reed Amar, *Intratextualism*, 112 Harv. L. Rev. 747 (1999), and *The Bill of Rights: Creation and Reconstruction* (1998), and John F. Manning, *The Supreme Court, 2013 Term—Foreword: The Means of Constitutional Power*, 128 Harv. L. Rev. 1 (2014), as well as Scalia & Garner, *Reading Law*, 167–233 (detailed examination of holistic canons). Professor Amar's intratextual approach is criticized as too narrow by William Michael Treanor, *Taking Text Too Seriously: Modern Textualism, Original Meaning, and the Case of Amar's* Bill of Rights, 106 Mich.

not absurd), as if it had a single author. Akhil Amar provides a justification: "The American People ratified the Philadelphia Convention not clause by clause, but as a single document. Later generations of Americans have added amendments one by one, but no amendment stands alone as a discrete legal regime. Each amendment aims to fit with, and be read as part of, the larger document."[64]

Holistic interpretation can be a means of determining constitutional plain meaning. Consider the issue debated in Washington's Cabinet in 1790 and resolved in *M'Culloch v. Maryland*, 17 U.S. (4 Wheat.) 316 (1819) (Chapter 7, § 1): Is Congress authorized to charter a national bank? Secretary of Treasury Hamilton and, later, Chief Justice Marshall opined that Congress had such authority under the Article I, § 8 powers of Congress to lay and collect taxes, to borrow money etc., and to make all laws "necessary and proper" for carrying out those activities. A plain meaning problem with the Hamilton-Marshall view is that a national bank does not seem "essential"—the primary meaning of "necessary" then and now—to the enumerated Article I, § 8 activities.

Hamilton and Marshall responded with the Constitution's deployment of the term "necessary" elsewhere. Where the Constitution meant to limit governments strictly, as in Article I, § 10, it limited their actions to that which "may be *absolutely* necessary" to achieve stated goals. In contrast, Article II, § 3 authorizes the President to propose legislation to Congress "as he shall judge necessary and expedient." There, it is clear that "necessary" means something like "useful to attaining a goal" (the secondary definition) rather than "essential." See also U.S. Const. art. IV, § 3, cl. 2 ("needful"); id. art. V ("necessary"). Given the holistic presumption that a document uses the same term consistently throughout, a textualist might conclude that the Necessary and Proper Clause authorizes statutes useful, rather than absolutely essential, to the many activities specifically enumerated for Congress.[65]

The holistic presumption that a term means the same thing everywhere it appears in the Constitution is at odds with *Bolling v. Sharpe*, interpreting the Fifth Amendment's Due Process Clause to have an equal

---

L. Rev. 487 (2007); Adrian Vermeule & Ernest Young, *Hercules, Herbert, and Amar: The Trouble with Intratextualism*, 113 Harv. L. Rev. 730 (2000).

[64] Akhil Reed Amar, *The Supreme Court, 1999 Term: Foreword—The Document and the Doctrine*, 114 Harv. L. Rev. 26, 29–30 (2000). But see Treanor, *Taking Text Too Seriously*, 106 Mich. L. Rev. at 507–43, who argues that such an approach is not consistent with original "public" meaning and is prone to the idiosyncrasies of particular drafters, namely, Gouverneur Morris (Constitution of 1789) and James Madison (Bill of Rights).

[65] There are also intratextual arguments against the Hamilton-Marshall interpretation. The Tenth Amendment's command that "powers not delegated to the United States by the Constitution, nor prohibited by it to the States, are reserved to the States respectively, or to the people" can be read as a constitutional principle of interpretation: construe Congress's enumerated powers narrowly rather than broadly—a rule that is violated by Hamilton and Marshall's elastic construction of the Necessary and Proper Clause.

protection component. Why does the Fourteenth Amendment have an Equal Protection as well as Due Process Clause, if unequal treatment is actionable under the latter? This is an intratextual conundrum, and violates the rule against surplusage to boot: What does the Equal Protection Clause "add" to the Fourteenth Amendment if the Due Process Clause means what *Bolling* says?

Another holistic precept is that a judge should not construe one constitutional provision in a way plainly inconsistent with another current provision or its underlying assumptions. The Supreme Court in *The Insular Cases* (1901) rejected arguments that the Constitution prohibits Congress from acquiring and governing territories (The Philippines, Guam, and Puerto Rico) that it does not intend to assimilate into the United States as new states over time. The Court rejected a simple dichotomy between "domestic" (part of the United States) and "foreign" territories, in part because such a dichotomy is inconsistent with the text-based assumptions of the Thirteenth Amendment's prohibition of involuntary servitude "within the United States, or in any place subject to their jurisdiction." *Downes v. Bidwell*, 182 U.S. 244, 251 (1901).

Justice Scalia rejected constitutional attacks on capital punishment, because he read the Fifth Amendment's Grand Jury and Due Process Clauses as contemplating the existence of the death penalty. Cf. U.S. Const. art. III, § 3 (Treason Clauses; normal punishment for treason in the eighteenth century was death). If one part of the Constitution contemplates capital punishment, another part, the Eighth Amendment, surely cannot prohibit it, argued Justice Scalia. *Query*: Because the Eighth Amendment was added *later*, might it not change the original constitutional assumptions?

Another example is the Second Amendment's guarantee that "the *people*'s right to keep and bear Arms, shall not be infringed." Arguing from the Second Amendment's prefatory clause ("A well-regulated Militia, being necessary to the security of a free State"), some have claimed that the right to bear arms is only a collective right held by We the People as a group, and not an enforceable individual right. The Supreme Court unanimously rejected this intratextual argument based upon a holistic analysis. Justice Scalia's opinion for the Court in *Heller* argued that because rights recognized for "the people" in the First, Fourth, and Ninth Amendments are enforceable individual rights, the Second Amendment ought to be read the same way. *Heller*, 554 U.S. 579–81; *id.* at 636 (Stevens, J., dissenting, but agreeing on this point).

(c) *Structuralism: Read the text in light of overall constitutional principles.* A textualist who follows the aforementioned precepts might well dissent in *Bolling*, and it is unclear how she can support the overruling of precedent in *Brown*. Yet über-textualist Justice Scalia was sure that

Brown was correctly decided, on the ground that the Reconstruction Amendments reflect a legal commitment to complete formal equality for the freed slaves. *Rutan v. Republican Party of Illinois*, 497 U.S. 62, 96 n.1 (1990) (Scalia, J., dissenting). This might not resolve the interpretive dilemma, as *Plessy* presented its separate-but-equal formula as satisfying the requirements of formal equality. To attack *Plessy*, the textualist might need to ratchet up his theory one generality notch: Rather than looking just at the plain meaning of the Constitution, the interpreter should also consider how competing constructions fit with the *principles* instinct in the Constitution.[66] Those principles include democratic representation and accountability of representatives to their constituents, as well as the text-based notion that accidents of birth ought not make a difference in state policy.[67]

Once the textualist attends to these constitutional principles, she has available to her some new defenses of *Brown*, for an understanding of equality that rejects state-supported racial segregation comports well with most theories of democracy and is strongly supported by the "accidents of birth" principle. But the southern opponents of *Brown* also had a structural argument based upon federalism and a holistic argument based on the Fourteenth Amendment's vesting (primary?) enforcement authority with Congress. This reflects a problem with structural or principle-based textualism: principles instinct in the Constitution often cut in different directions in a given case, and they are set at such a high level of generality that even the same principle is often susceptible of application either way regarding contested issues.

If *Brown* is correct, moreover, Justice Scalia might have had a principled basis for joining *Bolling*. Chief Justice Warren's opinion in that case centrally relied on notions of coherence: It would be "unthinkable that the same Constitution would impose a lesser duty on the Federal Government" in a matter of such importance as apartheid. As Vicki Jackson and Akhil Amar have suggested, the constitutional commitment to national citizenship and equal protection represented by the Fourteenth Amendment might, under a structural understanding of the Constitution, be "read into" the Fifth Amendment.[68] See also *Adarand Constructors, Inc. v. Pena*, 515 U.S. 200 (1995) (Chapter 3, § 3) (applying the principle of

---

[66] See Balkin, *Living Originalism*, 21–22; Black, *Structure and Relationship*; Akhil Reed Amar, *America's Constitution, a Biography* (2005); Vicki Jackson, *Holistic Interpretation: Fitzpatrick v. Bitzer and Our Bifurcated Constitution*, 53 Stan. L. Rev. 1259 (2001).

[67] Amar, *America's Constitution*, 124–27, 380–85; *Adarand Constructors, Inc. v. Pena*, 515 U.S. 200, 239 (1995) (Scalia, J., concurring), both recognizing a general principle, reflected in the Constitution's bars to "Title[s] of Nobility" (Art. I, § 9, Cl. 8), and to "Corruption of Blood" (Art. III, § 3, Cl. 2), that counsels against any race-based discrimination in American law.

[68] Jackson, *Holistic Interpretation*, 1279–81 & n.91; Amar, *Intratextualism*, 766–73; see also Akhil Reed Amar, *The Bill of Rights and the Fourteenth Amendment*, 101 Yale L.J. 1193, 1277–82 (1992) (Fourteenth Amendment had a "feedback effect" on First Amendment, not only pressing it against the states, but also transforming its application to the federal government).

"congruence" to interpret equal protection guarantees of the Fifth and Fourteenth Amendments in a similar fashion).

The broader point is that the original meanings of the Constitution of 1787 and the Bill of Rights must, as a matter of formal law, be updated by reference to the transformations of the Reconstruction Amendments. For example, in *Fitzpatrick v. Bitzer*, 427 U.S. 445 (1976), the Court read the Fourteenth Amendment to modify the original meaning of the Eleventh: When acting under its authority to enforce the Fourteenth Amendment, Congress may abrogate state immunity which it cannot do under its Article I powers (Chapter 7, § 3D). See also *Adkins v. Children's Hospital*, 261 U.S. 525, 552–53 (1923) (updating Court's interpretation of Due Process Clause to allow labor legislation protecting women, in light of Nineteenth Amendment, giving women the right to vote and suggesting women are not a class needing special protections).

2. Original Context for Constitutional Text

Purely textual analysis of the Constitution will only get the interpreter so far, and Dean William Treanor has cautioned that examining only the text will often lead to *misreading* original meaning.[69] He says the originalist must also consider context. But what counts as valid context? For example, we have extensive notes of the Framers' debates at Philadelphia and public reports of debates at the state conventions ratifying the original Constitution, including the celebrated *Federalist Papers*. There is a vigorous debate among scholars and judges as to whether the secret deliberations at Philadelphia or public congressional deliberations as to constitutional amendments ought to be consulted in determining original meaning.[70] Those materials probably ought to be consulted, but the ratifying materials are more important for a practical reason. Ratification of the Constitution of 1789 and some of the amendments involved a process of give and take where the public understanding of the provisions "evolved" (or was "clarified") during the course of the debate.[71]

---

[69] William Michael Treanor, *Taking Text Too Seriously: Modern Textualism, Original Meaning, and the Case of Amar's Bill of Rights*, 106 Mich. L. Rev. 487 (2007).

[70] Compare Ronald Rotunda, *Original Intent, the View of the Framers, and the Role of the Ratifiers*, 41 Vand. L. Rev. 507 (1988) (arguing against consideration of the Philadelphia Convention's secret drafting history), with Vasan Kesavan & Michael Stokes Paulsen, *The Interpretive Force of the Constitution's Secret Drafting History*, 91 Geo. L.J. 1113 (2003) (arguing for such consideration). See also *District of Columbia v. Heller*, 554 U.S. 570 (2008), where dissenting Justice Stevens relied on Congress's drafting history of the Second Amendment, which was belittled by Justice Scalia, writing for the Court; *City of Boerne v. Flores*, 521 U.S. 507 (1997), where Justice Kennedy's opinion for the Court relied on Congress's drafting history for the Fourteenth Amendment, over objection from Justice Scalia.

[71] E.g., John Yoo, *The Powers of War and Peace: The Constitution and Foreign Affairs After 9/11* (2005) (evolving Federalist position on war powers); William N. Eskridge, Jr., *All About Words: Early Understandings of the "Judicial Power" in Statutory Interpretation, 1776–1806*, 101 Colum. L. Rev. 990 (2001) (evolving Federalist position on Article III judicial power).

For complex issues or those whose contours have changed over time, an approach true to original understanding might be "imaginative reconstruction": How would the Framers have answered this question if it had been posed to them? Leading legal historians, such as Martin Flaherty, William Treanor, and Saikrishna Prakash, have suggested the proper historicist methodology for reconstructing original meaning: The interpreter must consider not just the drafting deliberations and the state ratification debates, but also the background legal context and the conceptual framework of the Framers.[72] Consider the excerpt that follows, which is also a leading attack on nonoriginalist judicial review of the sort Chief Justice Warren followed in *Brown*.

ROBERT H. BORK,
The Tempting of America: The Political Seduction of the Law
75, 76–77, 143–45, 154–55 (1990)[73]

Brown was a great and correct decision, but it must be said in all candor that the decision was supported by a very weak opinion. Those two facts, taken together, have caused an enormous amount of trouble in the law. [The opinion was weak, indeed disingenuous, in several ways. It failed to deal with the fact that the drafters and ratifiers of the Fourteenth Amendment did not think it outlawed state-required segregation in any aspect of society, especially in education. The Court refused to admit, forthrightly, that much of the originalist evidence cut against its holding. The opinion's reliance on social science evidence about the alleged impact of segregation on black children's self-esteem was nonsense. No one believed it critical for the decision, and the Court immediately proved the cynics correct by summarily invalidating state-required segregation in public accommodations and parks, upon the authority of *Brown*. Clearly, the decision rested upon a broader, more principled foundation than doll studies.]

But the combined disingenuousness of the *Brown* opinion and the obvious moral rightness of its result had, I believe, a calamitous effect upon the law. This was massively ironic, because the result in *Brown* is consistent with, indeed is compelled by, the original understanding of the fourteenth amendment's equal protection clause. The disastrous fact was that the Supreme Court did not think so. The Court, judging by its opinion, thought that it had departed from the original understanding in order to

---

[72] Compare, e.g., John Yoo, *Globalism and the Constitution: Treaties, Non-Self-Execution, and the Original Understanding*, 99 Colum. L. Rev. 1955 (1999), with Martin Flaherty, *History Right? Historical Scholarship, Original Understanding, and Treaties as "Supreme Law of the Land,"* 99 Colum. L. Rev. 2095 (1999).

[73] Reprinted and edited with the permission of The Free Press, a Division of Simon & Schuster Inc., from THE TEMPTING OF AMERICA: The Political Seduction of the Law by Robert H. Bork. Copyright © 1990 by Robert H. Bork. All rights reserved.

do the socially desirable thing. What is more, the Court triumphed over intense political opposition despite that fact.

[Worse, the Court's reputation not only survived its lawless opinion and the controversy it aroused, but was enhanced for a generation of citizens, including future constitutional theorists, who found the Court's moral triumph over narrow "law" inspiring. Worst, when those budding constitutionalists started writing about constitutional theory they marched lock-step away from original understanding: Because *Brown* was the high ground, no constitutional theory that did not explain *Brown* could be legitimate. Because original understanding so dramatically flunked the *Brown* test, it could not be an acceptable constitutional theory. But, argues Bork, *Brown* is defensible under a proper application of original understanding, and even if *Brown* were not consistent with original understanding, its inconsistency could not negate that as the only acceptable philosophy, which follows.]

When we speak of "law," we ordinarily refer to a rule that we have no right to change except through prescribed procedures. That statement assumes that the rule has a meaning independent of our own desires. Otherwise there would be no need to agree on procedures for changing the rule. Statutes, we agree, may be changed by amendment or repeal. The Constitution may be changed by amendment pursuant to the procedures set out in article V. It is a necessary implication of the prescribed procedures that neither statute nor Constitution should be changed by judges. Though that has been done often enough, it is in no sense proper.

What is the meaning of a rule that judges should not change? It is the meaning understood at the time of the law's enactment. Though I have written of the understanding of the ratifiers of the Constitution, since they enacted it and made it law, that is actually a shorthand formulation, because what the ratifiers understood themselves to be enacting must be taken to be what the public of that time would have understood the words to mean. It is important to be clear about this. The search is not for a subjective intention. If someone found a letter from George Washington to Martha telling her that what he meant by the power to lay taxes was not what other people meant, that would not change our reading of the Constitution in the slightest. * * * Law is a public act. Secret reservations or intentions count for nothing. All that counts is how the words used in the Constitution would have been understood at the time. The original understanding is thus manifested in the words used and in secondary materials, such as debates at conventions, public discussion, newspaper articles, dictionaries in use at the time, and the like. * * *

[Original meaning is the methodology for constitutional interpretation that best assures *neutrality* in the deriving, defining, and applying of constitutional   principle.   Without   neutrality   in   constitutional decisionmaking, the Court becomes nothing but a naked power organ, Bork argues. The Court becomes an arbiter of political rather than legal rights and duties.]

The structure of government the Founders of this nation intended most certainly did not give courts a political role. The debates surrounding the Constitution focused much more upon theories of representation than upon the judiciary, which was thought to be a comparatively insignificant branch. There were, however, repeated attempts at the Constitutional Convention in Philadelphia to give judges a policymaking role. The plan of the Virginia delegation, which, amended and expanded, ultimately became the Constitution of the United States, included a proposal that the new national legislature be controlled by placing a veto power in a Council of Revision consisting of the executive and "a convenient number of the National Judiciary." That proposal was raised four times and defeated each time. Among the reasons, as reported in James Madison's notes, was the objection raised by Elbridge Gerry of Massachusetts that it "was quite foreign from the nature of ye. office to make them judges of policy of public measures." Rufus King, also of Massachusetts, added that judges should "expound the law as it should come before them, free from the bias of having participated in its formulation." Judges who create new constitutional rights are judges of the policy of public measures and are biased by having participated in the policy's formulation. * * *

Even if evidence of what the Founders thought about the judicial role were unavailable, we would have to adopt the rule that judges must stick to the original meaning of the Constitution's words. If that method of interpretation were not common in the law, if James Madison and Justice Joseph Story had never endorsed it, if Chief Justice John Marshall had rejected it, we would have to invent the approach of original understanding in order to save the constitutional design. No other method of constitutional adjudication can confine courts to a defined sphere of authority and thus prevent them from assuming powers whose exercise alters, perhaps radically, the design of the American Republic. The philosophy of original understanding is thus a necessary inference from the structure of government apparent on the face of the Constitution.

PROBLEM 2-1:
IS BROWN CONSISTENT WITH THE ORIGINAL MEANING OF THE FOURTEENTH AMENDMENT?

The Supreme Court directed both sides in *Brown* to take original meaning seriously for purposes of the reargument in the case, because the original "intent" of the drafters of the Fourteenth Amendment was the stated agenda of the reargument. This problem presents the evidence pro and con, then concludes with some methodological questions.

(a) Originalist evidence that Brown was wrong.[74]

(i) *Segregationist attitudes and laws in or around 1868.* Segregation was the norm in 1868 [Kelly, *School Segregation,* 539]: An overwhelming majority of the black children in the North attended segregated schools or attended no public school at all; although several states formally desegregated their schools after the Civil War, most did not, and eight states (California, Kansas, Kentucky, Indiana, Maryland, Missouri, Nevada, West Virginia) enacted laws creating or recognizing segregated schools after the Fourteenth Amendment took effect; the rebel states of the South reentered the union with constitutions having no such provision, but they all quickly adopted laws or policies of school segregation soon after 1868. In 1862, Congress established racially segregated schools in Washington, D.C., over which Congress has plenary jurisdiction. 12 Stat. 407. A month after Congress passed the Fourteenth Amendment, it provided that an 1864 statute should be construed to require Washington and Georgetown to pay over certain funds for the support of separate schools. 14 Stat. 216 (also *id.* at 343). The Senate galleries were racially segregated in 1866, when Congress was drafting and debating the Fourteenth Amendment.

There was an underlying intellectual structure behind the country's willingness to assure African Americans "equality" and its disinclination to require "integration."[75] Most Americans, including many of the supporters of radical Reconstruction, believed that "mixing the races" was not desirable, based upon stereotypes about African Americans and fears that racial mixing would lead to racial dilution. Many supporters of the Fourteenth Amendment also seem to have had a different conception of equality than the one many of us share today: Civil equality only assured rights of formal access to courts, contracting, and property ownership, not any kind of social equality. *Plessy,* therefore, may have been an accurate reflection of one strand of the Framers' notions about equality.

(ii) *Drafting history and debates.* The supporters of the Fourteenth Amendment said little about what § 1 would prohibit, but they did emphasize its similarities to the Civil Rights Act of 1866. Representative George Latham said that "the 'civil rights bill' which is now a law * * * covers exactly the same ground as the [proposed] amendment," and many others agreed. What did the 1866 statute have to say about school segregation? Opponents of the proposed statute attacked it for opening up segregated schools to federal question.

---

[74] See Raoul Berger, *Government by Judiciary: The Transformation of the Fourteenth Amendment* 22–27, 117–27 (1977); Andrew Kull, *The Color-Blind Constitution* (1992); Earl Maltz, *Civil Rights, the Constitution, and Congress, 1863–1869* (1990); Alfred Avins, *De Facto and De Jure School Segregation: Some Reflected Light On the Fourteenth Amendment From the Civil Rights Act of 1875,* 38 Miss. L.J. 179 (1967); Alfred Kelly, *The Congressional Controversy Over School Segregation, 1867–1875,* 64 Am. Hist. Rev. 537 (1959). Support for this account can also be drawn from two accounts that find evidence on both sides of the issue: William E. Nelson, *The Fourteenth Amendment: From Political Principle to Judicial Doctrine* (1988), and Alexander M. Bickel, *The Original Understanding and the Segregation Decision,* 69 Harv. L. Rev. 1 (1955).

[75] See generally Herbert Hovenkamp, *Social Service and Segregation Before* Brown, 1985 Duke L.J. 624, 637–51.

Supporters first denied it would have any such effect[76] and, then, narrowed the proposal to drop language prohibiting "discrimination" against civil rights and immunities. Historians have read this as a deliberate choice to put the school segregation issue entirely to rest [Berger, *Government by Judiciary,* 119; Bickel, *Segregation Decision,* 56–57]. That it was not revisited, even by opponents, during debate on the proposed constitutional amendment, may confirm that it was thought to be politically settled once and for all.

(iii) *Post-amendment practice and construction.* Between 1868 and 1883, nine northern state high courts addressed the validity of school segregation. Five courts upheld segregation against state and federal constitutional attack;[77] four courts invalidated segregation under state law;[78] no court held that school segregation violated the Fourteenth Amendment.[79] In southern and border states, there were neither federal nor state court lawsuits challenging the *de facto*, and then *de jure*, school segregation practiced after 1868. Justice Thomas Cooley of the Michigan Supreme Court, an opponent of school segregation, wrote in his influential *General Principles of Constitutional Law* 230–31 (1880), that it was "admissible" under the Fourteenth Amendment "to require colored persons to attend separate schools, provided the schools are equal in advantages."

Congressional practice was to the same effect. In 1871, the Senate's District of Columbia Committee reported a bill to abolish racial segregation in the District's schools. Cong. Globe, 41st Cong., 3d Sess. 1054 (1871). Anti-apartheid Senator Charles Sumner insisted that this was required by the equality principle in the Fourteenth Amendment. *Id.* at 1055, 1056, 1058. None of the bill's opponents disputed this, but the bill never proceeded to a vote in the Senate; a parallel bill was voted down, 71–88, in the House. *Id.* at 1367. Sumner introduced similar bills later in 1871 and in 1873. His 1873 bill passed the Senate but not the House. Congress continued, without interruption, to fund the D.C. school system, which had been formally and continuously segregated by race since 1862.

Enacting the Civil Rights Act of 1875, Congress rejected the provision in Sumner's original bill that would have required "equal and impartial enjoyment" of facilities furnished by "common schools and other public institutions of learning." Cong. Globe, 42d Cong., 2d Sess. 244 (Dec. 20, 1871).

---

[76]   Representative Wilson, the House manager for the bill, explicitly said that the "civil rights" protected by the bill "do not mean that all citizens shall sit on juries, or that their children shall attend the same schools." Cong. Globe, 39th Cong., 1st Sess. 1117 (Mar. 1, 1866). This reflected the well-known distinction among *civil rights* (to sue, to contract) protected by the bill, and *political rights* (to vote) and *social rights* (to associate) not protected.

[77]   See *State ex rel. Garnes v. McCann*, 21 Ohio St. 198 (1871); *State ex rel. Stoutmeyer v. Duffy*, 7 Nev. 342 (1872); *Ward v. Flood*, 48 Cal. 36 (1874); *Cory v. Carter*, 48 Ind. 327 (1874); *People ex rel. King v. Gallagher*, 93 N.Y. 438 (1883).

[78]   See *Clark v. Board of Directors*, 24 Iowa 266 (1868); *People v. Board of Educ.*, 18 Mich. 400 (1869); *Chase v. Stephenson*, 71 Ill. 383 (1874); *Board of Educ. v. Tinnon*, 26 Kan. 1 (1881).

[79]   J. Morgan Kousser, *Dead End: The Development of Nineteenth-Century Litigation on Racial Discrimination in Schools* 22 (1986) reports an 1881 lower court decision in Pennsylvania ruling that education is a privilege or immunity protected under § 1 of the Fourteenth Amendment and that segregation was therefore invalid.

Proponents of the bill emphasized that legalized segregation was tantamount to creating a "caste" system, where African Americans were treated as degraded second-class citizens, or legal "lepers," as Representative Rainey put it. *Id.* app. 16 (Feb. 3, 1872). Opponents of the Sumner bill, led by Senator Lyman Trumbull, the author of the 1866 Civil Rights Act, argued that "the right to go to school is not a civil right," of the sort the 1866 statute and the Fourteenth Amendment were aimed at protecting. *Id.* at 3189–90 (May 8, 1872). Schooling was a matter of local discretion, not federal rights. After Sumner's death, the Senate deleted the schools provision from the bill. Before it was invalidated in *The Civil Rights Cases* in 1883, the 1875 Act's requirement of "equal access" to public accommodations was immediately and pervasively interpreted *not* to mean integrated access.[80] According to those federal judges, even if the schools provision had remained in the bill and the statute had not been invalidated, *Plessy* would just have arrived twenty years earlier as an interpretation of the statute itself.

(b) Originalist evidence that Brown *was right.*[81]

(i) *State recognition that segregated schools violated the original meaning of the Fourteenth Amendment.* The Equal Protection Clause was taken from the same clause in the Ohio Constitution of 1850, and in 1866–68 such a provision was widely understood to mean what Charles Sumer had said in 1849: no class of persons should be treated as second-class or degraded, and presumptively the state should treat all social classes the same (Eskridge, *Original Meaning*). Other scholars think the original meaning of "privileges or immunities" was to the same effect. Either way, contemporaries recognized the broad equalizing effect of the Fourteenth Amendment's text.

Before they could rejoin the union, the rebel states of the South had to submit state constitutions conforming to the U.S. Constitution, including the Fourteenth Amendment. Almost all the southerners who spoke to the issue said that a state constitution separating the races in public education would flunk the Fourteenth Amendment; no state constitution had such a provision, and those of Louisiana and South Carolina explicitly barred school segregation. [Frank & Munro, *Original Understanding,* 459.] Ambiguous but apparently prohibitory provisions were in the constitutions of Florida and Alabama, and three other states (Mississippi, Texas, Virginia) were readmitted upon a federal statutory stipulation that their constitutions could never be amended to deprive any class of citizens of "school rights and privileges." [McConnell, *Desegregation Decisions,* 963–65.] The northern states came to recognize the inconsistency of school segregation and racial equality. After 1855, when

---

[80] See *Charge to Grand Jury—The Civil Rights Act,* 30 Fed. Cas. 999, 1000 (C.C. W.D.N.C. 1875) (No. T8,258); Stephen Riegel, *The Persistent Career of Jim Crow: Lower Federal Courts and the "Separate But Equal" Doctrine, 1865–1896,* 28 Am. J. Legal Hist. 17 (1984).

[81] See Steven Calabresi & Michael Perl, *Originalism and* Brown v. Board of Education, 2014 Mich. St. L. Rev. 429; William N. Eskridge Jr., *Original Meaning and Marriage Equality,* 52 Hous. L. Rev. 1067 (2015); John Frank & Robert Munro, *The Original Understanding of "Equal Protection of the Laws,"* 1972 Wash. U.L.Q. 421; Michael W. McConnell, *Originalism and the Desegregation Decisions,* 81 Va. L. Rev. 947 (1995); Note, *Is Racial Segregation Consistent with Equal Protection of the Laws? Plessy v. Ferguson Reexamined,* 49 Colum. L. Rev. 629 (1949).

Massachusetts repealed its segregation law, none of the New England states had such a law. Although some states enacted school segregation statutes after 1868, most went in the other direction: New Jersey, Michigan, and Illinois desegregated right after ratifying the Fourteenth Amendment; New York, Pennsylvania, Ohio, California, and other states followed, in some instances overriding court decisions allowing segregation. [McConnell, *Desegregation Decisions,* 968–75.]

It may be relevant that, in 1868, almost all state constitutions guaranteed a right of free public education to all children in the state. Some scholars maintain that state constitutional consensus as to fundamental rights of state citizenship were broadened into national rights by the Privileges or Immunities Clause of the Fourteenth Amendment. E.g., Steven G. Calabresi & Sarah E. Agudo, *Individual Rights Under State Constitutions When the Fourteenth Amendment Was Ratified,* 87 Tex. L. Rev. 7 (2008).

(ii) *Congressional recognition that school segregation violated the Fourteenth Amendment.* While Congress funded segregated schools in the District, the decision to segregate was made in 1862–64, before the Reconstruction Congress, whose main sin was one of omission, failing to take a direct vote on Sumner's proposal to desegregate. The post-1868 debate treated the issue as one of policy, and no one focused on the Fourteenth Amendment, which, of course, does not apply to the District. [McConnell, *Desegregation Decisions,* 977–80.] After 1870, Sumner focused attention on his more ambitious national bill.

The 1870 Sumner bill banning segregation in schools, common carriers, and public accommodations was inspired by constitutional values: Sumner and his supporters—the same people who had pushed for the Fourteenth Amendment—maintained that the bill was an effort to enforce the guarantees of § 1 of the Fourteenth Amendment under Congress' § 5 powers.[82] Thus, the proponents believed that school segregation was already illegal; their proposal would simply provide a federal court remedy for rights unenforced by state courts, especially in the South. [McConnell, *Desegregation Decisions,* 990–1005.] The Democrats and some Republicans opposed the bill, and their arguments anticipated those accepted in *Plessy*: segregation is not racial "inequality," as each race is equally affected, and education is a social right rather than a civil right. [*Id.* at 1005–29.] The Senate decisively and repeatedly rejected these arguments and passed the bill in 1874, soon after Sumner's death, but the bill died in the House. When Congress reconvened for its lame-duck session in 1875, after the Democrats had won the 1874 election, the House and Senate passed the Sumner bill, but without the controversial education provision. The wind then went out of the sails of Reconstruction, and Jim Crow came to power in the South.

(iii) *The clear error of* Plessy. Whatever might be the case with segregated schools (the *Brown* issue), segregated transportation (the *Plessy* issue) was

---

[82] Sumner and his supporters generally believed that § 5 did not permit legislation that went beyond § 1, a theory ratified by the Court in *City of Boerne v. Flores* (Chapter 7, § 3C).

clearly outlawed by the Fourteenth Amendment. Interstate travel was a civil right and not just a social right as understood by the Framers; Congress and even the states repeatedly legislated against racial segregation in transportation, with the 1875 Act confirming that principle. [McConnell, *Desegregation Decisions,* 1029–36.] If *Plessy* was wrong, then arguably everything building upon *Plessy* (including the school cases, *Cumming* and *Gong Lum*) was wrong as well.

(c) Methodological problems with original meaning scholarship.

For original meaning to subserve its core goals—respecting the terms of the social contract and constraining the discretion of judges—its methodology must generate predictable results in the hands of a broad array of jurists. Critics claim that changed circumstances render the original deal either an incoherent aspiration or impossible to discover in a neutral way; hence, original meaning jurisprudence is indeterminate and does not constrain interpreters. Some key points made by the critics:

(i) *The problem of the counterfactual.* Because the Constitution and most of its amendments are old, their Framers failed to discuss or anticipate a lot of the issues in which we are interested today. For example, the debates about the Fourteenth Amendment focused on the now-forgotten §§ 2 and 3, which were of immediate concern in the context of Reconstruction but had no lasting importance. Section 1 of the amendment, which today looms larger in judicial application than any other provision of the Constitution, received only the most cursory attention. Because neither the Congress that proposed the amendment nor the states that ratified it focused on the issue of school segregation, originalists like McConnell and Maltz—the main adversaries on the *Brown* issue—must argue from other contemporary sources, which are as plentiful as they are indirect.

Because of changed circumstances, most issues of constitutional interpretation are even more speculative than that in *Brown.* Who can tell how the Framers would have expected the Fourth Amendment to apply to wiretapping, the First Amendment to apply to television and radio, and so forth? Public education in 1868 was not as widely available as it is today, and providing even segregated education for blacks in the South was a major breakthrough. Shouldn't that affect the way we answer the *Brown* question? Unanticipated constitutional circumstances more dramatically illustrate the counterfactual nature of the originalist inquiry. The Reconstruction Congress was surprised when the Supreme Court gave a narrow construction to the Privileges or Immunities Clause in *The Slaughter House Cases* (1872), an event that elevated the Equal Protection Clause to a critical place in our constitutional tradition. The *Brown* question then becomes: How would Framers who thought of education as a possible privilege of national citizenship conceptualize education in equal protection terms?

(ii) *Aggregation problems.* How can individual views, even if on point, be aggregated to establish "public meaning" in 1868? Note how the *Brown* debaters make all kinds of speculative leaps—from the intent of senators in

1874 to those in 1866 and from Congress in 1866 to ratifying states in 1868 (Michael McConnell), from the intent of Congress as to D.C. schools in 1862–66 to the intent of Congress on segregation in southern states in 1866 (Raoul Berger), and from the intent of Congress in passing the 1866 Civil Rights Act to the intent of Congress in proposing the Fourteenth Amendment (Alexander Bickel). No one can actually demonstrate that *two-thirds of each chamber in Congress* and *three-quarters of the states* even thought about the application of the Fourteenth Amendment to the issue of public school segregation, much less agreed that the amendment prohibited—or allowed—separate but equal segregation. Nor can anyone say with assurance what We the People thought about these topics.

These problems are just as acute, if not more so, for the original Constitution. For instance, it cannot be demonstrated that the views of the Philadelphia Convention delegates were known to the public or the state ratifying conventions, or were even accurately recorded by James Madison. The oft-cited *Federalist Papers* are even worse in this regard: They represented the views of Madison and Hamilton, and were read by the New York ratifiers, but they have little determinate value for figuring out what most of the Philadelphia delegates thought about issues, what other ratifying states thought, what the New York delegates thought, or perhaps even what Madison and Hamilton thought (the two main authors had different views as to some issues; the papers were written with strategic purposes in mind).

(iii) *Level of generality problems.* A lot turns on how the level of generality at which the interpretive question is posed to the "Framers" or the "Public" as a group. Rather than asking, "How would the Framers or the Public have addressed this precise issue?" (a specific question), the interpreter might ask, "What goals were We the People pursuing in this provision, and which interpretation best meets the goals in the context of this case?" (a more general question), or even, "How did We the People expect interpreters to go about applying this provision?" (a meta-question). See Balkin, *Living Originalism*, 21–22, 45, who defends a *framework originalism* that reasons from general constitutional principles and standards established by the Framers in the original document.

Judge Bork faults *Brown* for ignoring original meaning, but recall that the Court sought and received extensive briefing on the original meaning of the Fourteenth Amendment. Having read our summary of the evidence, was Chief Justice Warren so far off base when he announced that the originalist evidence was not decisive, at least as to the specific question? One way to read *Brown* is that the Court moved to a higher level of generality and decided the case based upon the general purpose of the Equal Protection Clause. If it was unclear at the time of *Plessy* whether a separate-but-equal regime was a kind of "caste" legislation, it was pellucidly clear by 1954. And that spelled the doom for apartheid. Is this not an original meaning approach?

Consider a meta-critique of original meaning as a methodology, a critique resting upon a deep tension between disciplines.[83] Professional historians, the "experts" in a true original meaning enterprise, tend to understand past events as complicated, evolving, and multifaceted. Lawyers and judges wielding original meaning tend to view the same past events as simple, perseverant, and single-focused. The former accuse the latter of engaging in "law office history," while the latter grumble that the former threaten to render our rich history a dead and unuseful exercise.

NOTE ON PRAGMATIC ARGUMENTS FOR ORIGINAL MEANING

Libertarian constitutionalist Randy Barnett announced his conversion to original meaning in *An Originalism for Nonoriginalists*, 45 Loy. L. Rev. 611 (1999). Many constitutional debates today start with, and often end with, originalist arguments. In the Clinton impeachment proceedings of 1998, the battle for Florida's electoral votes in the 2000 election, and debates in 2002 over presidential power to invade Iraq without congressional authorization, law professors, lawyers, and pundits emphasized the consistency of their views with those of the Framers. After years touting "noninterpretivism," many progressive legal theorists have embraced originalist methodologies. E.g., Balkin, *Living Originalism,* whose "originalist" methodology generates predictably liberal constitutional doctrine. The pragmatic lesson of recent experience: When you want to *persuade* those who may not share your politics, argue originalism!

Barnett offers two additional, pragmatic reasons for adopting an "original meaning" approach to constitutional interpretation. The first emphasizes that the Constitution is *written.* Though lacking the unanimous consent that contracts require, a constitution, like a contract, is put into writing to "lock in" a particular arrangement. Contracts are put in writing and interpreted according to their meaning *at the time of formation* to gain certain practical advantages—reliable evidence as to terms, channeling of those who wish to modify the terms to preexisting procedures for change, and incentives for drafters to work out the details of their relationship before signing off on the document. These pragmatic virtues apply to written constitutions as well. Indeed, in *Constitutional Legitimacy*, 103 Colum. L. Rev. 111 (2003), Barnett posits the legitimacy of the Constitution along pragmatic rather than social contract lines: a constitution is legitimate, even in the absence of consent, if it provides procedural assurances that the commands it imposes on the people are likely to be both necessary and proper.

In *Restoring the Lost Constitution: The Presumption of Liberty* (2004), Professor Barnett provides another pragmatic argument for originalism. If a constitution is supposed to be the law governing law makers, then it cannot be remade by the very parties—legislatures, courts, or executive branch

---

[83] William N. Eskridge, Jr., *Sodomy and Guns: "Tradition" in Constitutional Interpretation*, Harv. J.L. & Pol'y (2008); Martin Flaherty, *"History Lite" in Modern American Constitutionalism*, 95 Colum. L. Rev. 523 (1995); Mark V. Tushnet, *Interdisciplinary Legal Scholarship: The Case of History-in-Law*, 71 Chi.-Kent L. Rev. 909, 917–18 (1996).

officials—upon whom it is imposed. The practical benefits and protections of placing legal constraints on the government could not be obtained if those who are subject to the Constitution's restrictions, such as legislators and judges, could escape these bonds and alter its meaning on their own. For this reason, *the meaning of the Constitution must remain the same until it is properly changed* and some "outside" procedure for change must exist, such as the procedures specified in Article V.

3. Original Purpose

ROBERT H. BORK,
The Tempting of America: The Political Seduction of the Law
81–82 (1990)[84]

[Following Alexander M. Bickel, *The Original Understanding of the Segregation Decision*, 69 Harv. L. Rev. 1 (1955), Judge Bork concedes that the Framers of the Fourteenth Amendment did not intend to invalidate state-enforced racial segregation immediately. Like Bickel, though, Bork advances an originalist theory in support of the *Brown* result.]

Let us suppose that *Plessy v. Ferguson* correctly represented the original understanding of the fourteenth amendment, that those who ratified it intended black equality, which they demonstrated by adopting the equal protection clause. But they also assumed that equality and state-compelled separation of the races were consistent, an assumption which they demonstrated by leaving in place various state laws segregating the races. Let us also suppose, along with the Court in *Plessy*, as I think we must, that the ratifiers had no objection to the psychological harm segregation inflicted. If those things are true, then it is impossible to square the *opinion* in *Brown* with the original understanding. It is, however, entirely possible to square the *result* in *Brown* with that understanding.
* * *

By 1954, when *Brown* came up for decision, it had been apparent for some time that segregation rarely if ever produced equality. Quite aside from any question of psychology, the physical facilities provided for blacks were not as good as those provided for whites. That had been demonstrated in a long series of cases. The Supreme Court was faced with a situation in which the courts would have to go on forever entertaining litigation about primary schools, secondary schools, colleges, washrooms, golf courses, swimming pools, drinking fountains, and the endless variety of facilities that were segregated, or else the separate-but-equal doctrine would have to be abandoned. Endless litigation, aside from the burden on the courts,

---

also would never produce the equality the Constitution promised. The Court's realistic choice, therefore, was either to abandon the quest for equality by allowing segregation or to forbid segregation in order to achieve equality. There was no third choice. Either choice would violate one aspect of the original understanding, but there was no possibility of avoiding that. Since equality and segregation were mutually inconsistent, though the ratifiers did not understand that, both could not be honored. When that is seen, it is obvious that the Court must choose equality and prohibit state-imposed segregation. The purpose that brought the fourteenth amendment into being was equality before the law, and equality, not separation, was written into the text.

Had the *Brown* opinion been written that way, its result would have clearly been rooted in the original understanding, and its legitimacy would have been enhanced for those troubled by the way in which the Court arrived at a moral result without demonstrating its mooring in the historic Constitution. There might have been an even more important benefit. The Court might not have been encouraged to embark on more adventures in policymaking, which is what it thought it had done in *Brown*, and academic constitutional lawyers might not have gone on to construct the apparently endless set of theories that not only attempt to justify *Brown* on grounds other than the original understanding but, in order to do so, advance arguments that necessarily justify departure from the historic Constitution in general. Perhaps constitutional theory would be in a far happier state today if *Brown* had been written, as it could have been, in terms of the original understanding."

[Although *Brown* could have come out the same way under an originalist approach, *Bolling v. Sharpe* could not, according to Judge Bork.]

NOTE ON ORIGINAL PURPOSE AND TRANSLATING GOALS FROM ONE ERA TO THE NEXT

Judge Bork maintains that the Framers of the Fourteenth Amendment accepted state-enforced segregation generally, and school segregation specifically. Yet he ultimately argues that *Brown* was correctly decided, essentially based upon carrying out the original goal once circumstances have changed. Is this really "original meaning"? Recall that, except for the Radicals, the Framers of the Fourteenth Amendment were not committed to racial equality across the board; most of them favored equality only as to "civil rights," which they understood as not including public schooling. One problem with Bork's "originalist" argument is that he seems to abandon the Framers' understanding of equality for one based on contemporary moral criteria.

An important source of the original meaning of the Equal Protection Clause was the oration of Charles Sumner in a Massachusetts desegregation case. He set forth the meta-purpose of a constitutional democracy, as well as of equality clauses in state constitutions:

Here is the Great Charter of every human being drawing the vital breath upon this soil, whatever may be his condition and whoever may be his parents. He may be poor, weak, humble, or black; he may be of Caucasian, Jewish, Indian, or Ethiopian race; he may be of French, German, English, or Irish extraction, but before the Constitution of Massachusetts all these distinctions disappear. He is not poor, weak, humble, or black nor is he Caucasian, Jew, Indian, or Ethiopian nor is he French, German, English, or Irish; he is a Man, the equal of all his fellow men. *He is one of the children of the State, which, like an impartial parent, regards all its offspring with an equal care.* To some it may justly allot higher duties, according to higher capacities, but it welcomes all to its equal, hospitable board.

Charles Sumner, *Equality before the Law: Unconstitutionality of Separate Colored Schools in Massachusetts.* Argument of Charles Sumner, Esq., Before the Supreme Court of Massachusetts In The Case of *Sarah C. Roberts v. City of Boston* 7 (Washington: F. & J. Rives & Geo. A. Bailey, 1870). Introducing the proposed Fourteenth Amendment in Congress, Senator Jacob Howard said that the clause "establishes equality before the law, and * * * gives to the humblest, the poorest, and most despised * * * the same rights and the same protection before the law as it gives to the most powerful, the most wealthy, or the most haughty." It plainly "abolishes all class legislation in the States and does away with the injustice of subjecting one caste of persons to a code not applicable to another." The public debate for state ratification confirmed this reading of the amendment's language—but also confirmed the accepted precept that the principle against class legislation did not apply to laws classifying people based upon traits relevant to regulation that serves the public good or prevents harm.[85]

Is there a good reason to prefer Judge Bork's understanding of the amendment's purpose, over that articulated by Senator Sumner? Paul Brest, *The Fundamental Rights Controversy: The Essential Contradictions of Normative Constitutional Scholarship*, 90 Yale L.J. 1063 (1981), argues that the original principle implicated in the Equal Protection Clause can be stated at several levels of generality: equality for the freed slaves; equality for African Americans generally; equality for people of all races; equality simpliciter. There is no neutral way to choose which level of generality for one's constitutional inquiry. It is also a matter of judgment and not routine for a judge to figure out how the chosen principle applies in the context of the case. Judge Bork responds that "a judge should state the principle at the level of generality that the text and the historical evidence warrant." *Tempting of America* 149; accord, Balkin, *Living Originalism,* 21–22. But Bork seems to violate that precept, as the original evidence does not support the high level of generality Bork has chosen, and even at a high level of generality Bork seems

---

[85] William Nelson, *The Fourteenth Amendment: From Political Principle to Judicial Doctrine* 67, 73, 79 (1988); Steven Calabresi & Julia Rickert, *Originalism and Sex Discrimination*, 90 Tex. L. Rev. 1, 35–42 (2011); William Eskridge Jr., *Original Meaning and Marriage Equality*, 52 Hous. L. Rev. 1067 (2015).

to get the purpose wrong, from an originalist perspective. How can the judge be justified in disregarding that original understanding simply because circumstances have changed? Aren't changed circumstances supposed to be handled, as Bork argues elsewhere in the book, by constitutional amendments under Article V?

Consider similarities between Bork's argument and Mark Tushnet's idea that *Brown* can be defended as the Court's *translation* of the nineteenth century's understanding of civil rights into the modern regulatory state era, when civil rights most naturally mean equal treatment in important state programs, the most important of which is public education.[86] If the Framers of the Fourteenth Amendment intended to ensure equality for all "civil rights," their idea applied in 1868 might be different from application in 1954 because cultural or political facts have changed. As a descriptive matter, public education was not routinely provided by governments in 1868—but it was by 1954. As a normative matter, public education was not considered central to citizenship in 1868—but it was by 1954. Can an originalist theory swallow Tushnet's translation idea without creating a "Living Constitution"? Cf. Charles Reich, *Mr. Justice Black and the Living Constitution*, 76 Harv. L. Rev. 673, 733 (1963). If not, should an honest originalist reject Judge Bork's own dynamic interpretation defending the result in *Brown?*

PROBLEM 2-2:
DOES THE ORIGINAL MEANING OF THE FOURTEENTH AMENDMENT BAR SEX-BASED DISCRIMINATIONS?

For most of American history, states and the federal government have restricted women's employment possibilities. In 1868 and for decades thereafter, states barred women from becoming lawyers and entering other occupations. The Supreme Court unfailingly upheld these laws against Fourteenth Amendment attack. E.g., *Goesaert v. Cleary*, 335 U.S. 464 (1948) (Chapter 4, § 2), where the Court upheld a statute barring women from working as bartenders, unless they were the wife or daughter of the bar owner.

Construct an argument that such laws violate the original meaning of the Fourteenth Amendment. In constructing such an argument, you should consider the text of § 1 of the Fourteenth Amendment, the purpose of the Amendment and its particular clauses, the structure and principles embodied in the Amendment, and the Nineteenth Amendment. Sources of illumination include Robin L. West, *Progressive Constitutionalism: Reconstructing the Fourteenth Amendment* (1994); Steven G. Calabresi & Julia T. Rickert,

---

[86] Mark V. Tushnet, *Following the Rules Laid Down: A Critique of Interpretivism and Neutral Principles*, 96 Harv. L. Rev. 781, 800–01 (1983); accord. Paul Brest, *The Misconceived Quest for the Original Understanding*, 60 B.U.L. Rev. 204 (1980); Lawrence Lessig, *Fidelity in Translation*, 71 Tex. L. Rev. 1165, 1171–72 n.32 (1993) (listing scholars who deploy the translation metaphor); *id.* at 1242–47 (applying translation theory to *Brown*). Although translation has an originalist component, most originalists consider translation too dynamic to qualify as a good theory of original meaning. E.g., Steven G. Calabresi, *The Tradition of the Written Constitution: A Comment on Professor Lessig's Theory of Translation*, 65 Fordham L. Rev. 1435 (1997).

Originalism and Sex Discrimination, 90 Tex. L. Rev. 1 (2011); Reva Siegel, *She the People: The Nineteenth Amendment, Sex Equality, Federalism, and the Family,* 115 Harv. L. Rev. 947 (2002).

Once you have constructed an excellent originalist case, think about whether it could overcome the *stare decisis* effect of *Goesaert* and other precedents. Would your originalist case be persuasive to a judge who was not already committed to a skeptical view of state sex discrimination? Would the originalist case be fatally undermined by evidence that the framers of the Fourteenth and Fifteenth Amendments rejected pleas from feminist abolitionists to cover exclusions of women from the franchise and other important rights? Cf. Calabresi & Rickert, *Originalism* (arguing that such constitutional inaction does not prevent the Court from finding an original meaning critical of laws excluding women from legal benefits).

B. LEGAL PROCESS THEORIES OF JUDICIAL REVIEW

"Legal process" theory views the rule of law from an *institutionalist* and *procedural* perspective.[87] That is, the rule of law is not just a law of rules, but is an institutional and procedural structure by which recognizable legal rules are made and changed in an orderly way, with each institution contributing to the project in ways that reflect its comparative competence. Under our Constitution, the overall structure is easy to understand in principle, but complicated in operation. Law's legitimacy owes as much to the process by which it is enacted as its formal pedigree. Hence, statutes are legitimate not only because they have formally met the Article I, § 7 requirements, but also because they have been adopted in an open and deliberative way by representatives elected by the people and accountable to them. The legitimacy of judicial decisions overturning such laws is trickier and must be considered in light of the proper institutional role that courts play in our constitutional system. That proper role depends, in turn, on (1) judges' special *institutional competence*, the things that the judiciary as an institution does really well; (2) the institutional limitations that justified Hamilton's referring to the judiciary as the "least dangerous branch"; and (3) the judiciary's *comparative* competence and limitations—the same issues viewed against the strengths and limitations of the legislative and executive branches. Consider some legal process theories of judicial review.

1. Neutral Principles and Representation-Reinforcement Theory

Legal process thinkers like Felix Frankfurter, Henry Hart, and Lon Fuller understood adjudication as the "reasoned elaboration" of principles

---

[87] For an introduction to this school of thought, see William N. Eskridge, Jr. & Philip P. Frickey, *An Historical and Critical Introduction to* The Legal Process, in Henry M. Hart, Jr. & Albert M. Sacks, *The Legal Process: Basic Problems in the Making and Application of Law* li-cxxxix (Eskridge & Frickey eds. 1994) (1958 tent. ed.).

and policies as applied to particular cases. Seizing upon this idea, Herbert Wechsler, *Toward Neutral Principles of Constitutional Law*, 73 Harv. L. Rev. 1 (1959), maintained that, in constitutional adjudication, the Court has a responsibility to issue decisions that are "genuinely principled, resting with respect to every step that is involved in reaching judgment on analysis and reasons quite transcending the immediate result that is achieved. * * * A principled decision * * * is one that rests on reasons with respect to all the issues in the case, reasons that in their generality and their neutrality transcend any immediate result that is involved."

Wechsler criticized *Brown* as unprincipled. "[*Brown*] must have rested on the view that racial segregation is, in principle, a denial of equality to the minority against whom it is directed * * *. In the context of a charge that segregation *with equal facilities* is a denial of equality, is there not a point in *Plessy* in the statement that if 'enforced separation stamps the colored race with a badge of inferiority' it is solely because its members choose 'to put that construction upon it?' Does enforced separation of the sexes discriminate against females merely because it may be the females who resent it and it is imposed by judgments predominantly male? Is a prohibition of miscegenation a discrimination against the [minority] member of the couple who would like to marry?

"For me, assuming equal facilities, the question posed by state-enforced segregation is not one of discrimination at all. Its human and its constitutional dimensions lie entirely elsewhere, in the denial by the state of freedom to associate, a denial that impinges in the same way on any groups or races that may be involved. * * * But if freedom of association is denied by segregation, integration forces an association upon those for whom it is unpleasant or repugnant. * * * Given a situation where the state must practically choose between denying the association to those individuals who wish it or imposing it on those who would avoid it, is there any basis in neutral principles for holding that the Constitution demands that the claims for association should prevail? I should like to think there is, but I confess that I have not yet written the opinion. To write it is for me the challenge of the school-segregation cases."

Wechsler's article triggered sharp attacks because of his perceived insensitivity to the appeal of *Brown* and to the injustice of segregation,[88] but his article was also a challenge to legal scholars to justify *Brown* along lines of traditional, consent-based theories of democracy: Even if *Brown* could not be defended by reference to the Framers' original intent, the Court could still be loyal to consent-based theory by grounding its result upon constitutional principles. Scholars struggled to come up with a

---

[88] E.g., Charles Black, *The Lawfulness of the Segregation Decisions*, 69 Yale L.J. 421 (1960); Louis Pollak, *Racial Discrimination and Judicial Integrity: A Reply to Professor Wechsler*, 108 U. Pa. L. Rev. 1 (1959). See generally Gary Peller, *Neutral Principles in the 1950's*, 21 U. Mich. J.L. Reform 561 (1989).

principled defense of *Brown*. Arguably, the most successful effort was the "representation reinforcing" approach to judicial review developed by Professor John Hart Ely. He argued that certain provisions of the Constitution, including the Equal Protection Clause, are too elastic to constrain the Supreme Court—indeed, are so "open-textured" as to invite dynamic interpretation over time. To provide meaning to these clauses, Ely argued that judges should supply answers "derived from the general themes of the entire constitutional document and not from some source entirely beyond its four corners." In Ely's view, those themes are best captured by footnote four of *Carolene Products* (quoted in Chapter 1, § 6).

JOHN HART ELY,
Democracy and Distrust: A Theory of Judicial Review
88–103 (1980)[89]

[Ely starts with the observation that the complaints giving rise to the American Revolution emphasized "participational themes * * * that (1) their input into the process by which they were governed was insufficient, and that (partly as a consequence) (2) they were being denied what others were receiving." Continuing those same themes, the original Constitution] is devoted almost entirely to structure, explaining who among the various actors—federal government, state government, Congress, executive, judiciary—has authority to do what, and going on to fill in a good bit of detail about how these persons are to be selected and to conduct their business. Even provisions that at first glance might seem primarily designed to assure or preclude certain substantive results seem on reflection to be principally concerned with process. Thus, for example, the provision that treason "shall consist only in levying War against [the United States], or in adhering to their Enemies, giving them Aid and Comfort," appears at least in substantial measure to have been a precursor of the First Amendment, reacting to the recognition that persons in power can disable their detractors by charging disagreement as treason. The prohibitions against granting titles of nobility seem rather plainly to have been designed to buttress the democratic ideal that all are equals in government. The Ex Post Facto and Bill of Attainder Clauses prove on analysis to be separation of powers provisions, enjoining the legislature to act prospectively and by general rule (just as the judiciary is implicitly enjoined by Article III to act retrospectively and by specific decree). And * * * the Privileges and Immunities Clause of Article IV, and at least in one aspect—the other being a grant of congressional power—the Commerce Clause as well, function as equality provisions, guaranteeing virtual representation to the politically powerless. * * *

---

[89] Reprinted by permission of the publisher from DEMOCRACY AND DISTRUST: A THEORY OF JUDICIAL REVIEW by John Hart Ely, pp. 88–103, Cambridge, Mass.: Harvard University Press, Copyright © 1980 by the President and Fellows of Harvard College.

* * * [M]y claim is only that the original Constitution was principally, indeed I would say overwhelmingly, dedicated to concerns of process and structure and not to the identification and preservation of specific substantive values. Any claim that it was exclusively so conceived would be ridiculous (as would any comparable claim about any comparably complicated human undertaking). And indeed there are other provisions in the original document that seem almost entirely value-oriented, though my point, of course, is that they are few and far between. Thus "corruption of blood" is forbidden as a punishment for treason. Punishing people for their parents' transgressions is outlawed as a substantively unfair outcome: it just can't be done, irrespective of procedures and also irrespective of whether it is done to the children of all offenders. The federal government, along with the states, is precluded from taxing articles exported from any state. Here too an outcome is simply precluded; what might be styled a value, the economic value of free trade among the states, is protected. This short list, however, covers just about all the values protected in the original Constitution—save one. And a big one it was. Although an understandable squeamishness kept the word out of the document, *slavery* must be counted a substantive value to which the original Constitution meant to extend unusual protection from the ordinary legislative process, at least temporarily. Prior to 1808, Congress was forbidden to prohibit the slave trade into any state that wanted it, and the states were obliged to return escaping slaves to their "homes."

The idea of a bill of rights was not even brought up until close to the end of the Constitutional Convention, at which time it was rejected. The reason is not that the framers were unconcerned with liberty, but rather that by their lights a bill of rights did not belong in a constitution, at least not in the one they had drafted. As Hamilton explained in *Federalist* 84, * * * "The additional securities to republican government, to liberty, and to property, to be derived from the adoption of the plan under consideration, consist chiefly in the restraints which the preservation of the Union will impose on local factions . . . in the express guarantee of a republican form of government to each [state]; in the absolute and universal exclusion of titles of nobility . . . "

Of course a number of the state ratifying conventions remained apprehensive, and a bill of rights did emerge. Here too, however, the data are unruly. The expression-related provisions of the First Amendment * * * were centrally intended to help make our governmental processes work, to ensure the open and informed discussion of political issues, and to check our government when it gets out of bounds. We can attribute other functions to freedom of expression, and some of them must have played a role, but the exercise has the smell of the lamp about it: the view that free expression per se, without regard to what it means to the process of government, is our pre-eminent right has a highly elitist cast. [Moreover,] the linking of the politically oriented protections of speech, press, assembly, and petition is highly informative.

The First Amendment's religious clauses—"Congress shall make no law respecting an establishment of religion, or prohibiting the free exercise thereof"—are a different matter. Obviously part of the point of combining these cross-cutting commands was to make sure the church and the government gave each other breathing space: the provision thus performs a structural or separation of powers function. But we must not infer that because one account fits the data it must be the only appropriate account, and here the obvious cannot be blinked: part of the explanation of the Free Exercise Clause has to be that for the framers religion was an important substantive value they wanted to put significantly beyond the reach of at least the federal legislature.

[The Second Amendment (right to bear arms) and the Third Amendment (no quartering of troops) may sound like substantive amendments in part, but have been construed very narrowly. The Fifth through Eighth Amendments tend to be most relevant during lawsuits, and so we think of them as procedural, for the most part. For each amendment, Ely notes an arguable substantive feature, such as the Fifth Amendment's anti-self-incrimination privilege and the Fourth Amendment's privacy protection, but maintains that the primary role of each amendment is procedural, to assure fair trials.]

With one important exception, the Reconstruction Amendments do not designate substantive values for protection from the political process. The Fourteenth Amendment's Due Process Clause, we have seen, is concerned with process writ small, the processes by which regulations are enforced against individuals. Its Privileges or Immunities Clause is quite inscrutable, indicating only that there should exist some set of constitutional entitlements not explicitly enumerated in the document: it is one of the provisions for which we are seeking guides to construction. The Equal Protection Clause is also unforthcoming with details, though it at least gives us a clue: by its explicit concern with equality among the persons within a state's jurisdiction it constitutes the document's clearest, though not sole, recognition that technical access to the process may not always be sufficient to guarantee good-faith representation of all those putatively represented. The Fifteenth Amendment, forbidding abridgment of the right to vote on account of race, opens the process to persons who had previously been excluded and thus by another strategy seeks to enforce the representative's duty of equal concern and respect. The exception, of course, involves a value I have mentioned before, slavery. The Thirteenth Amendment can be forced into a "process" mold—slaves don't participate effectively in the political process—and it surely significantly reflects a concern with equality as well. Just as surely, however, it embodies a substantive judgment that human slavery is simply not morally tolerable.

Thus at no point has the Constitution been neutral on this subject. Slavery was one of the few values the original document singled out for protection from the political branches; *non*slavery is one of the few values it singles out for protection now.

What has happened to the Constitution in the second century of our nationhood, though ground less frequently plowed, is most instructive on the subject of what jobs we have learned our basic document is suited to. There were no amendments between 1870 and 1913, but there have been eleven since. Five of them have extended the franchise: the Seventeenth extends to all of us the right to vote for our Senators directly, the Twenty-Fourth abolishes the poll tax as a condition of voting in federal elections, the Nineteenth extends the vote to women, the Twenty-Third to residents of the District of Columbia, and the Twenty-Sixth to eighteen-year-olds. Extension of the franchise to groups previously excluded has therefore been the dominant theme of our constitutional development since the Fourteenth Amendment, and it pursues both of the broad constitutional themes we have observed from the beginning: the achievement of a political process open to all on an equal basis and a consequent enforcement of the representative's duty of equal concern and respect to minorities and majorities alike. Three other amendments—the Twentieth, Twenty-Second, and Twenty-Fifth—involve Presidential eligibility and succession. The Sixteenth, permitting a federal income tax, adds another power to the list of those that had previously been assigned to the central government. That's it, save two, and indeed one of those two did place a substantive value beyond the reach of the political process. The amendment was the Eighteenth, and the value shielded was temperance. It was, of course, repealed fourteen years later by the Twenty-First Amendment, precisely, I suggest, because such attempts to freeze substantive values do not belong in a constitution. In 1919 temperance obviously seemed like a fundamental value; in 1933 it obviously did not.

What has happened to the Constitution's other value-enshrining provisions is similar, and similarly instructive. Some surely have survived, but typically because they are so obscure that they don't become issues (corruption of blood, quartering of troops) or so interlaced with procedural concerns they seem appropriate in a constitution (self-incrimination, double jeopardy). Those sufficiently conspicuous and precise to be controvertible have not survived. The most dramatic examples, of course, were slavery and prohibition. Both were removed by repeal, in one case a repeal requiring unprecedented carnage. Two other substantive values that at least arguably were placed beyond the reach of the political process by the Constitution have been "repealed" by judicial construction—the right of individuals to bear arms, and freedom to set contract terms without significant state regulation. Maybe in fact our forebears did not intend very seriously to protect those values, but the fact that the Court, in the face of what must be counted at least plausible contrary arguments, so readily read these values out of the Constitution is itself instructive of American expectations of a constitution. Finally, there is the value of religion, still protected by the Free Exercise Clause. Something different has happened here. In recent years that clause has functioned primarily to protect what must be counted as discrete and insular minorities, such as the Amish, Seventh Day Adventists, and Jehovah's Witnesses. Whatever the original conception of the Free Exercise Clause, its function during essentially all of its effective life has been one akin to the Equal Protection Clause and thus entirely appropriate to a constitution.

Don't get me wrong: our Constitution has always been substantially concerned with preserving liberty. If it weren't, it would hardly be worth fighting for. The question that is relevant to our inquiry here, however, is how that concern has been pursued. The principal answers to that, we have seen, are by a quite extensive set of procedural protections, and by a still more elaborate scheme designed to ensure that in the making of substantive choices the decision process will be open to all on something approaching an equal basis, with the decision-makers held to a duty to take into account the interests of all those their decisions affect. (Most often the document has proceeded on the assumption that assuring access is the best way of assuring that someone's interests will be considered, and so in fact it usually is. Other provisions, however—centrally but not exclusively the Equal Protection Clause—reflect a realization that access will not always be sufficient.) The general strategy has therefore not been to root in the document a set of substantive rights entitled to permanent protection. The Constitution has instead proceeded from the quite sensible assumption that an effective majority will not inordinately threaten its own rights, and has sought to assure that such a majority not systematically treat others less well than it treats itself—by structuring decision processes at all levels to try to ensure, first, that everyone's interests will be actually or virtually represented (usually both) at the point of substantive decision, and second, that the processes of individual application will not be manipulated so as to reintroduce in practice the sort of discrimination that is impermissible in theory. We have noted a few provisions that do not comfortably conform to this pattern. But they're an odd assortment, the understandable products of particular historical circumstances—guns, religion, contract, and so on—and in any event they are few and far between. To represent them as a dominant theme of our constitutional document one would have to concentrate quite single-mindedly on hopping from stone to stone and averting one's eyes from the mainstream.

The American Constitution has thus by and large remained a constitution properly so called, concerned with constitutive questions. What has distinguished it, and indeed the United States itself, has been a process of government, not a governing ideology. Justice Linde has written:

"As a charter of government a constitution must prescribe legitimate processes, not legitimate outcomes, if like ours (and unlike more ideological documents elsewhere) it is to serve many generations through changing times."

As I have tried to be scrupulous about indicating, the argument from the general contours of the Constitution is necessarily a qualified one. In fact the documentary dictation of particular substantive outcomes has been rare (and generally unsuccessful), but our Constitution is too complex a document to lie still for *any* pat characterization. Beyond that, the premise of the argument, that aids to construing the more open-ended provisions are appropriately found in the nature of the surrounding document, though it is a premise that seems to find acceptance on all sides, is not one with which it is impossible to disagree. Thus the two arguments that follow, each overtly normative, are if anything more important than the one I have just reviewed. The first is entirely obvious by now, that unlike an approach geared to the judicial imposition of "fundamental values," the representation-reinforcing orientation whose contours I have sketched and will develop further is not inconsistent with, but on the contrary is entirely supportive of, the American system of representative democracy. It recognizes the unacceptability of the claim that appointed and life-tenured judges are better reflectors of conventional values than elected representatives, devoting itself instead to policing the mechanism by which the system seeks to ensure that our elected representatives will actually represent. There may be an illusion of circularity here: my approach is more consistent with representative democracy because that's the way it was planned. But of course it isn't any more circular than setting out to build an airplane and ending up with something that flies.

The final point worth serious mention is that (again unlike a fundamental-values approach) a representation-reinforcing approach assigns judges a role they are conspicuously well situated to fill. My reference here is not principally to expertise. Lawyers *are* experts on process writ small, the processes by which facts are found and contending parties are allowed to present their claims. And to a degree they are experts on process writ larger, the processes by which issues of public policy are fairly determined: lawyers do seem genuinely to have a feel, indeed it is hard to see what other special value they have, for ways of insuring that everyone gets his or her fair say. But too much shouldn't be made of this. Others, particularly the fulltime participants, can also claim expertise on how the political process allocates voice and power. And of course many legislators are lawyers themselves. So the point isn't so much one of expertise as it is one of perspective.

The approach to constitutional adjudication recommended here is akin to what might be called an "antitrust" as opposed to a "regulatory" orientation to economic affairs—rather than dictate substantive results it intervenes only when the "market," in our case the political market, is systemically malfunctioning. (A referee analogy is also not far off: the referee is to intervene only when one team is gaining unfair advantage, not because the "wrong" team has scored.) Our government cannot fairly be said to be "malfunctioning" simply because it sometimes generates outcomes with which we disagree, however strongly (and claims that it is reaching results with which "the people" really disagree—or would "if they understood"—are likely to be little more than self-deluding projections). In a representative democracy value determinations are to be made by our elected representatives, and if in fact most of us disapprove we can vote them out of office. Malfunction occurs when the process is undeserving of trust, when (1) the ins are choking off the channels of political change to ensure that they will stay in and the outs will stay out, or (2) though no one is actually denied a voice or a vote, representatives beholden to an effective majority are systematically disadvantaging some minority out of simple hostility or a prejudiced refusal to recognize commonalities of interest, and thereby denying that minority the protection afforded other groups by a representative system.

Obviously our elected representatives are the last persons we should trust with identification of either of these situations. Appointed judges, however, are comparative outsiders in our governmental system, and need worry about continuance in office only very obliquely. This does not give them some special pipeline to the genuine values of the American people: in fact it goes far to ensure that they won't have one. It does, however, put them in a position objectively to assess claims—though no one could suppose the evaluation won't be full of judgment calls—that either by clogging the channels of change or by acting as accessories to majority tyranny, our elected representatives in fact are not representing the interests of those whom the system presupposes they are.

NOTES ON REPRESENTATION REINFORCEMENT AND THEORIES OF POLITICAL DYSFUNCTION

Ely's theory, if robust, solves the *Brown* problem: Apartheid is questionable because it flunks both of Ely's representation-reinforcing concerns—the "ins" were disadvantaging a discrete and insular minority out of prejudice and were blocking channels of change or liberation. Moreover, Ely solves the *Brown* puzzle in a way that is faithful to the principles of the Constitution and that limits the amount of spillover judicial activism (it would not lead to another *Lochner* era), Wechsler's two concerns. Or does it?[90]

---

[90] Critiques of Ely's theory include Laurence Tribe, *The Puzzling Persistence of Process-Based Constitutional Theories*, 89 Yale L.J. 1063 (1980); Mark V. Tushnet, *Darkness on the Edge of the Town: The Contributions of John Hart Ely to Constitutional Theory*, 89 Yale L.J. 1037 (1980); Archibald Cox, Book Review, 94 Harv. L. Rev. 700 (1981).

1.   *The Substance-Procedure Problem.* Is Ely right in characterizing the Constitution as a proceduralist document? Many of the provisions that might be viewed that way can also be viewed as protecting substantive rights. For example, the First Amendment's protection of free speech contributes to lively public debate and criticism, but also protects personal rights of individuals. Is it not odd to think that we fought a Revolution and a Civil War to obtain nothing but procedure? Are there no rights so fundamental that courts should not protect them? How about a right to personal privacy, which seems implicated in the First, Fourth, and Fifth Amendments? If a majority of blacks voted for educational segregation, would that be constitutional under Ely's analysis?

Even if the Constitution is largely procedural, applying it Ely's way might involve more substantive judgment than Ely suggests. Key to his theory is the *Carolene* judicial role of protecting "discrete and insular minorities" against the operation of "prejudice" in the political system. In 1954, southerners and many northerners believed that segregation rested on practical grounds, and not "prejudice." Today, Americans remain divided on whether lesbians and gay families and unions should be treated exactly the same. "Prejudice"? Or "Traditional Family Values"?[91]

2.   *The Indeterminacy Problem. Brown* is not as easy a case for representation-reinforcement review as might first appear. While blacks were excluded from the political process in the South, they were not in Kansas, where *Brown* arose. Topeka was abandoning *de jure* segregation through the democratic process in 1954–55. How, then, does Ely's theory support *Brown*? The easiest way would be to show that even though blacks were not formally excluded from the political process in Topeka, they were marginalized politically and were the objects of stereotype and prejudice. Indeed, there was substantial evidence at trial that segregation itself contributed to this marginalization and reified it in the hearts of its intended victims. The difficulty with this type of argument is that once Ely's thesis encompasses functional problems with our democracy, judicial review becomes potentially broad. Poor people are systematically marginalized from local political systems today just as blacks were in Topeka in 1951. Should judicial review tackle the many economic decisions made by the government that hurt the poor, or fail to help them?

While the genius of Ely's theory is that it appears to tie much of the Warren Court's constitutional activism to a primary constitutional policy, it may tend toward judicial activism once one starts evaluating the system of representation functionally. If one abandons functional analysis and only looks at the formal system of representation, then Ely's theory tends toward little judicial review at all, enhancing the danger of legislative tyranny.

---

[91] William N. Eskridge Jr. & Christopher Riano, *From Outlaws to Inlaws: The Marriage Debate, 1967–2017* (forthcoming from Yale Univ. Press, 2020); Daniel Ortiz, *Pursuing a Perfect Politics: The Allure and Failure of Process Theory,* 77 Va. L. Rev. 721 (1991).

3. *The Public Choice Problem.* An appeal of Ely's theory is its focus on protecting discrete and insular minorities, because they will find it hard to protect themselves in the political process. This thesis may be undermined by "public choice theory," the application of economic insights to political behavior.[92] According to public choice, legislation is the result of a political market, with demand and supply features. Interest groups demand legislation, and legislators supply it. Hence, the ability of an identifiable group to secure advantages in the political process depends upon the group's ability to mobilize, to organize its members into an interest group that becomes a political player (lobbying, campaign contributions, political action committees). This, in turn, depends upon the ability of the group to overcome the "free rider problem." Political advantages available to a group are usually available to every member of the group, whether or not she contributed to its procurement (it is a "public good"). As a result, individual members of the group have incentives not to contribute to the formation of the public good, and instead to "free ride" on the efforts of others. The problem is that if everyone, or most people, take this attitude, not much of the public good will be provided.

Given the plethora of interest groups in our society, the free rider problem can often be overcome. Some groups, such as farmers and labor unions, have pre-existing economic organizations that can be turned to political purposes, with a coercive mechanism for getting contributions from its members (*e.g.*, union dues). Absent such historical or organizational features, however, it is hard for large, diffuse groups of people to overcome the free rider problem, because it is impossible to monitor free riders. The smaller the group (*e.g.*, three big auto manufacturers rather than 40 million car buyers) the more likely it is to organize effectively, because the small group can monitor free riders (often by excluding them from the public good) and form a consensus without undue transactions costs. The more a group feels a unique sense of identity (its members see themselves primarily as members of that one group and less as members of other groups and society), the more likely it is to organize, because the impulse to free ride is overridden by the community feeling.

The paradox suggested by public choice theory is that "discrete and insular minorities" are precisely those groups that ought to organize and protect themselves in the political process. See Bruce Ackerman, *Beyond Carolene Products*, 98 Harv. L. Rev. 713, 722–31 (1985). While some discrete and insular minorities may be the objects of special prejudice, once the formal barriers to their political participation are removed, they tend systematically to become active in the political process. Having been the object of prejudice actually helps break down the free rider problem, and often they will bloc vote to maximize their power. If public choice theory is right about this, then Ely's

---

[92] See William N. Eskridge, Jr., Philip P. Frickey, Elizabeth Garrett & James J. Brudney, *Cases and Materials on Legislation and Regulation: Statutes and the Creation of Public Policy* ch. 1 (5th ed. 2014); Daniel A. Farber & Philip P. Frickey, *Law and Public Choice: A Critical Introduction* (1991); Einer Elhauge, *Does Interest Group Theory Justify More Intrusive Judicial Review?*, 101 Yale L.J. 31 (1991).

theory is less progressive than it might otherwise seem. *Brown* is right, insofar as it broke down formal barriers to political participation, but perhaps there is not much of a "representation-reinforcement" reason to remain concerned about such issues in the new millennium.[93] If things such as a resurgence of prejudice and the continuing effects of slavery and apartheid trouble you, representation-reinforcement theory may not help you attack them.

On the other hand, Ely's theory could be more radical than he suspected. Among groups excluded from the political process are those that tend to be "discrete and anonymous," such as gay men and lesbians; "diffuse and noninsular," such as women; and "diffuse and anonymous," such as the poor. It is harder for these groups to organize politically. Large diffuse groups (such as women and the poor) are particularly subject to the free rider problem, especially to the extent that they do not have monetary resources. Anonymous groups (such as closeted gay people) are also subject to the free rider problem because many people are physically and professionally afraid to "come out," and societal prejudice against such groups may undermine their effectiveness even when they are organized. If we take seriously Ely's point that judicial review might correct for inequities in the political system, we should protect the interests of those against whom the political process reflects systematic "prejudice," as emphasized in *Carolene*. Yet one person's "prejudice" against gay people is another person's moral "principle." Ultimately, therefore, a representation-reinforcing theory might have to make substantive determinations of value that Ely says are not properly part of the Constitution.

PROBLEM 2-3:
REPRESENTATION-REINFORCING JUDICIAL REVIEW

(a) Sex Discrimination. How would Professor Ely's theory suggest that the Supreme Court resolve constitutional challenges to state laws excluding women from certain occupations, such as the law described in Problem 2-2? Would it make a difference that the law was adopted after the Nineteenth Amendment, which assured women the right to vote?

(b) Gay Marriage Bars. How would Ely's theory evaluate discrimination against lesbian and gay couples in most state marriage laws? Are gay people a *Carolene* group, for whom representation-reinforcing judges should be solicitous? Would it make a difference to Professor Ely that a discriminating state has enacted a broad law protecting sexual minorities against private as well as public discrimination? That such a state has adopted a law recognizing lesbian and gay "civil unions" and according such unions all the legal rights and benefits of marriage? Compare *Perry v. Brown*, 671 F.3d 1052 (9th Cir. 2012) (evaluating a marriage bar in a state barring sexual orientation discrimination and providing almost all of the legal benefits of marriage in the form of domestic partnership), with *Obergefell v. Hodges,* 135 S.Ct. 2584 (2015)

---

[93] For an argument that the predictions of public choice do not reflect African-American political power, see Daniel A. Farber & Philip P. Frickey, *Is* Carolene Products *Dead? Reflections on Affirmative Action and the Dynamics of Civil Rights Legislation*, 79 Cal. L. Rev. 685 (1991).

(evaluating marriage bars that included non-marital relationshops in states with no statewide discrimination or relationship protections). Paradoxically, in the context of marriage equality litigation in the state courts, judges in LGBT-friendly states were *more* likely to see gay people as politically powerless than judges in states with no anti-discrimination protections. See Jane S. Schacter, *Ely at the Altar: Political Process Theory Through the Lens of the Marriage Debate*, 109 Mich. L. Rev. 1363 (2011). Moreover, federal and state judges in 2013–15, when public opinion had turned decisively in favor of gay marriage, were *more* likely to see gay people as politically powerless and *less* likely to defer to the political process than judges in 1996, when gay people were reviled from coast to coast. Compare Richard A. Posner, *Should There Be Homosexual Marriage? If So, Who Should Decide?*, 95 Mich. L. Rev. 1578 (1997) (reviewing Eskridge's representation-reinforcing case for gay marriage and concluding: you have to be kidding!), with *Baskin v. Bogan*, 766 F.3d 648 (7th Cir. 2014) (Posner, J.) (arguments against same-sex marriage are "so full of holes" that they "cannot be taken seriously"), and Posner, *Eighteen Years On: A Re-Review*, 125 Yale L.J. 533 (2015) (oops, Eskridge had it right in 1996).

(c) Discrimination Against Bilingual Jurors. Prosecutors in criminal cases can strike jurors from the venire without providing reasons, but if it appears that prosecutorial strikes are race-based, the prosecutor must provide a race-neutral explanation. If the judge finds the explanation unpersuasive, the entire jury selection process must start over; an appellate court will overturn the conviction of a defendant whose jury is tainted with race discrimination in this way. E.g., *Batson v. Kentucky*, 476 U.S. 79 (1986). In a case against a Latino-American defendant, the prosecutor strikes several Latino jurors; upon defense objection, the prosecutor explains that it was because much testimony in the trial would be in Spanish, with an official translator for the jury. Should the *Batson* doctrine be applied to invalidate this conviction? See *Hernandez v. New York*, 500 U.S. 352 (1991) (Chapter 4, § 3B); Juan Perea, *Buscando América: Why Integration and Equal Protection Fail to Protect Latinos*, 117 Harv. L. Rev. 1420 (2004).

2. Institutional Competence and Theories of Judicial Restraint

Some kinds of actions should be taken only by entities with special democratic legitimacy, and courts might police the "structures through which policies are both formed and applied."[94] The idea is that major policy decisions in a representative democracy should be made by elected officials and not by administrators or perhaps even more local representatives. For example, the Court has invalidated agency decisions that reflect major policy choices more legitimately made by the President or Congress, *Hampton v. Mow Sun Wong*, 426 U.S. 88 (1976) (invalidating Civil Service bar to federal employment by noncitizens but inviting President or Congress to act); presidential or executive department decisions raising

---

[94]   Laurence Tribe, *Structural Due Process*, 10 Harv. C.R.-C.L. L. Rev. 269 (1975).

constitutional problems that should be addressed by Congress, e.g., *Kent v. Dulles*, 357 U.S. 116 (1958) (Secretary of State cannot deny passport because of political beliefs without more specific congressional authorization); or local decisions that are better made at the state or national level, e.g., *Regents of the Univ. of Calif. v. Bakke*, 438 U.S. 265 (1978) (opinion of Powell, J.) (Board of Regents is not the best institution to adopt racial quotas for university; statewide elected officials would be more legitimate decisionmakers).

Under most legal process theories of judicial review, a key role for the Court is to enforce constitutional rules of jurisdiction. Former Oregon Supreme Court Justice Hans Linde argued that "the central function of judicial review" is "to guarantee the democratic legitimacy of political decisions by establishing essential rules of the political process."[95] This has been a neglected source of review at the federal level until recently, as the Rehnquist Court has revived interest in enforcing the rules of federalism (Chapter 7). The most sweeping judicial activism of the last generation may have been the Court's decision invalidating hundreds of legislative vetoes, as inconsistent with the bicameralism and presentment requirements of Article I, § 7, *Immigration & Naturalization Service v. Chadha*, 462 U.S. 919 (1982) (Chapter 8, § 2A). State constitutions tend to have more procedural requirements for lawmaking than the U.S. Constitution does, and some state supreme courts vigorously enforce those requirements. See, e.g., *Department of Educ. v. Lewis*, 416 So. 2d 455 (Fla. 1982) (enforcing state single-subject rule to invalidate substantive rider in appropriations bill).

Finally, and most generally, the Court might encourage the deliberative, republican government instinct in the Constitution and expressly contemplated by some of its Framers, see *Federalist* No. 10 (App. 2). Thus, the Court might follow Thayer's "give the legislature the benefit of the doubt" approach to statutes that reflect a reasoned, factually based, openly debated policy choice, and a more scrutinizing approach to undeliberated choices. Compare *Romer v. Evans*, 517 U.S. 620 (1996) (Chapter 4, § 3D) (invalidating state initiative targeting gay people based upon open appeal to prejudice), with *Bowers v. Hardwick*, 478 U.S. 186 (1986) (Chapter 5, § 4C) (upholding state sodomy law reflecting longstanding, deliberate state policy).

Alexander M. Bickel, *The Least Dangerous Branch: The Supreme Court at the Bar of Politics*

(1962)

Like Ely's theory, the foregoing discussion has suggested process-based justifications for active judicial review, situations where the Supreme Court

---

[95] Hans Linde, *Due Process of Lawmaking*, 55 Neb. L. Rev. 197, 251 (1976).

should intervene in the political process and reverse the burden of inertia (i.e., require a political response, considering the judicial input). A different kind of legal process theory is that developed by Professor Bickel's book, which famously discussed the Court's "passive virtues," its "techniques of 'not doing,' devices for disposing of a case while avoiding judgment on the constitutional issue it raises." In some cases, the Supreme Court has a constitutional obligation to avoid decision. The Case or Controversy requirement of Article III disables the Court from adjudicating cases where the plaintiff lacks standing to sue, the case is moot, or the issue is not ripe or is reserved for the political processes by the Constitution (Chapter 9, § 2).

Bickel maintained that there are instances where the Court is authorized to adjudicate a constitutional question, but should choose not to decide it. The Court has many procedural devices at its disposal that allow it to avoid exercising its *Marbury* power: (1) declining to hear a case altogether, by denying review or certiorari and leaving the lower court decision in place; (2) dismissing an appeal or petition on grounds of "prudential" ripeness, standing, mootness, or political question even though the dispute satisfies the Case or Controversy requirements of Article III; or (3) deciding the case on narrow grounds, usually as a matter of statutory interpretation that avoids the constitutional question. Declining to decide a constitutional issue properly presented to the Court is a "passive virtue," deployed as a matter of wise judging or even constitutional politics, rather than as a matter of constitutional principle. The passive virtues are most needed in cases where the Court is not prepared to invalidate legislation, but the effect of upholding the legislation would be to legitimate it in ways that would be lamentable. Instead, the Court stays its hand, allowing the political process to continue to work on the problem, and perhaps develop the factual contours of it.

The *Brown* line of cases illustrates Bickel's theory. Before 1954, the Supreme Court repeatedly ducked the question whether it should overrule *Plessy*, as the Justices invalidated segregated education under the criteria of the earlier decision, while accumulating evidence that separate was never equal. In the course of the *Brown* litigation, the Court asked for further briefing (on an issue that ultimately made no difference to any Justice) because the Justices needed more time to resolve their personal and collective uncertainties. Bickel also defended the Court's judgment in *Naim v. Naim*, 350 U.S. 985 (1956), where it dismissed an appeal from the Virginia Supreme Court, which had upheld the state's law criminalizing different-race marriages. The state law was explicitly premised upon the policy of "White Supremacy" and was surely inconsistent with whatever principle animated *Brown*. Yet the Court ducked the issue on a trumped-up technicality, because it feared, with justification, that invalidating different-race marriage bans would embroil the Court in too much controversy and would undermine the needed political support for *Brown* (Bickel, *Least Dangerous Branch*, 174). The Court invalidated the law in *Loving v. Virginia*, 388 U.S. 1 (1967), after the political climate lent more support to its action, and after almost all states outside the South had repealed their miscegenation statutes.

NOTE ON THE PASSIVE VIRTUES AND OTHER
THEORIES OF JUDICIAL RESTRAINT

Gerald Gunther, *The Subtle Vices of the "Passive Virtues"—A Comment on Principle and Expediency in Judicial Review*, 64 Colum. L. Rev. 1 (1964), objected that Bickel's theory was neither passive nor virtuous. It was not passive, as it required judges to manipulate existing procedural doctrines, often in pursuit of a long-term goal of invalidating laws enjoying popular support. It was not virtuous, as it required judges to lie. Bickel might have responded that some strategic behavior is needed to assure the efficacy of our constitutional rule of law: Constitutional rules will not "stick" if the political culture revolts against them;[96] applying bad constitutional rules to avoid the backlash is even worse; the "least bad" option is to follow one of the avoidance strategies. Although he died a generation ago, Professor Bickel's theory of cautious constitutionalism has inspired a new generation of legal academics.

In the spirit of Bickel, we have suggested that the Court will be passive in enforcing constitutional values when there is a political consensus to the contrary, will be cautious and incremental once political consensus dissolves or is in flux, and will be bold only when it can implement its constitutional understanding with the support of the political culture. See William N. Eskridge Jr. & Philip P. Frickey, *The Supreme Court, 1993 Term—Foreword: Law as Equilibrium*, 108 Harv. L. Rev. 26 (1994). Thus, the post-Reconstruction Court abdicated any responsibility for enforcing the Equal Protection Clause against apartheid (*Plessy*), but once African Americans and their allies made the national political culture nervous about apartheid the Court had room to enforce equality guarantees at important margins (*Buchanan, Herndon, Gaines*). When the Truman and Eisenhower Administrations signaled their strong support for overruling *Plessy*, the Court was emboldened to act decisively to denounce apartheid (*Brown I*)—but not to demand immediate desegregation (*Brown II*, following the remedial strategy suggested in the Eisenhower Administration's *amicus* brief). It was not until the 1960s, when Congress as well as the President moved decisively toward actual integration (the Civil Rights Act of 1964 and other initiatives) that the Supreme Court demanded immediate implementation of unitary school systems (*Green*). Our largely descriptive theory does make a normative claim: A Supreme Court that moved too far "ahead" of the political culture would not only have a hard time implementing its decrees, but would lose much of its overall political capital or legitimacy.

Also elaborating on Bickelian themes, Cass R. Sunstein, *The Supreme Court, 1995 Term—Foreword: One Case at a Time*, 110 Harv. L. Rev. 4 (1996), argues for a *minimalist* approach to judicial review most of the time. "Minimalism is best understood as an effort to leave things open by limiting the width and depth of judicial judgments. Minimalist judges try to keep their

---

[96] For a demonstration that appellate courts must consider the possibility that their directives will not be respected or enforced, see Dan Kahan, *Gentle Nudges vs. Hard Shoves: Solving the Sticky Norms Problem*, 67 U. Chi. L. Rev. 607 (2000).

judgments as narrowly and as incompletely theorized as possible, consistent with the obligation to offer reasons. They are enthusiastic about avoiding constitutional questions; they like to use doctrines of justiciability, and their authority over their docket, to limit the occasions for judicial intervention into politically contentious areas; the ban on advisory opinions guides much of their work. They try * * * to minimize the risks of error introduced by broad rules and abstract theories, and to maximize the space for democratic deliberation about basic political and moral issues. Minimalist courts also respond to the sheer practical problem of obtaining consensus amidst pluralism."

"Whether minimalism makes sense cannot be decided in the abstract. The answer has a great deal to do with costs of decisions and costs of error. The case for minimalism is strongest when courts lack information that would justify confidence in a comprehensive ruling; when the need for planning is not especially insistent; when the decision costs of an incremental approach do not seem high; and when minimalist judgments not do create a serious risk of unequal treatment. Thus minimalism is usually the appropriate course when circumstances are changing rapidly or when the Court cannot be confident that a broad rule would make sense in future cases." See also Sunstein, *One Case at a Time: Judicial Minimalism on the Supreme Court* (2001). Was *Brown II* a minimalist decision that complemented *Brown I*'s maximalist symbolism? How would a neo-Bickelian respond to the charge that *Brown II*'s minimalism was both a retreat from a great principle and a practical failure?

3. Common Law Constitutionalism

Because it involves the interpretation of written texts, constitutional law is usually considered more analogous to statutory interpretation than to common law decisionmaking. That analogy may be misleading. See David Strauss, *The Living Constitution* (2012), and *Common Law Constitutional Interpretation*, 88 Colum. L. Rev. 723 (1988); Henry Monaghan, *Stare Decisis and Constitutional Adjudication*, 88 Colum. L. Rev. 723 (1988). Many constitutional decisions, including *Brown*, have a casual relationship to the text of the Constitution—and some of them, including *Bolling* and *Marbury*, seem contrary to the text. Much constitutional doctrine, including liberty of contract (Chapter 5, § 2) and the right to privacy (id. § 4), has no text-based anchor at all, while some texts (such as the First Amendment) have assumed a primacy not apparent from their place in the Constitution or from the ratification debates. Like the common law, modern constitutional law is less concerned with divining the expectations of the Framers than with applying precedent in new factual settings.[97]

---

[97] The list of precedents that are hard to defend based solely on constitutional text and original meaning is arguably a long one—the affirmative action and the racial gerrymandering cases (Chapter 3, § 3); the sex discrimination cases (Chapter 4, § 2); the selective incorporation cases (Chapter 5, § 1); the contraception and abortion cases (Chapter 5, § 4); the flagburning cases (Chapter 6, § 1); the freedom of association cases (Chapter 6, § 6); the "dormant" Commerce Clause

Descriptively, there seems to be little doubt that a great deal of constitutional law is common law with bite. Is this normatively defensible? Justice Scalia denounces such an approach as undemocratic, and his followers claim that judges are institutionally incompetent to carry out common law reasoning where the stakes are so high.[98] On the other hand, there are normative virtues of a common law approach, as Professor Ernest Young argues below.

ERNEST YOUNG,
Rediscovering Conservatism: Burkean Political
Theory and Constitutional Interpretation
72 N.C. L. Rev. 619, 689–90, 691–93, 701–03 (1994)[99]

The political thought of Edmund Burke valorized a polity's traditions as a source of norms superior to the contingent rationalizations of human decisionmakers. A Burkean constitutionalism would interpret foundational texts in an incremental common law manner, respecting without fetishizing original meaning, majority decisionmaking, and bright-line rules. [A] common-law model fairly describes much of what courts actually do when interpreting the Constitution, and * * * such interpretation would generally be more successful if the common-law model were more candidly acknowledged and more broadly employed.

By common-law model, I mean a process that attempts to emulate Burke's rejection of abstract theory and his corresponding emphasis on tradition and incremental change. * * * [N]one of the generally accepted modes of constitutional argument are ruled out; arguments from the constitutional text, the intent of the framers, judicial precedent, the broader philosophical purposes of the constitution, moral philosophy, and social policy may all be relevant in any given case. Given a Burkean set of assumptions, however, some of these arguments are more persuasive than others. For example, even the most fervent nonoriginalists tend to concede that originalist history is an important factor for judges to consider. For the Burkean, that history is primarily valuable as an aid in ascertaining the tradition as a whole as it has evolved from the original period to the present. Similarly, a Burkean judge will tend to reject arguments based on abstract moral theory except insofar as that theory can be shown to reflect and clarify the moral intuitions of society at large. * * *

In a jurisprudence of doctrine, the primary tool of constitutional interpretation will be judicial precedent rather than originalist history or abstract moral theory. This approach mirrors the reality of constitutional

---

cases (Chapter 7, § 6B) and some of the regular Commerce Clause cases (Chapter 7, § 2); and the voting rights cases (Chapter 5, § 3A and Chapter 9, § 1).

[98] Antonin Scalia, *A Matter of Interpretation: Federal Courts and the Law* (1997); Adrian Vermeule, *Judging Under Uncertainty: An Institutional Theory of Legal Interpretation* (2006).

[99] Reprinted by permission of the North Carolina Law Review.

advocacy; although lawyers may make arguments about original understanding or moral philosophy to courts, they generally emphasize the requirements of doctrine as articulated in prior decisions. [Eds.: Recall the NAACP Inc. Fund's argumentation in *Brown*.] Many precedents, of course, will themselves rely in whole or in part upon arguments about the original understanding. By incorporating originalism in this indirect way, however, adherence to precedent also takes account of a constitutional provision's line of growth from the original period down to the present. * * * Use of precedent in this way allows the judge to tap into a cumulative wisdom that transcends his own rationality. As Dean Brest observes, a doctrine that survives over a period of time has the approval of a court composed, in effect, of all the judges who have ever had occasion to consider and apply it. [*The Misconceived Quest for the Original Understanding*, 60 B.U. L. Rev. 204, 228 (1980).] * * *

When specific precedents cannot directly determine a result, judges pursuing the common-law model are nonetheless constrained to some extent by the conventions of legal argument and reasoning. These considerations confine the range of arguments presented to courts by advocates. * * * An important part of this shared vision of what it means to argue like a lawyer is a commitment to the method of analogical reasoning, which Professor Sunstein describes as our legal culture's most characteristic way of proceeding. [*On Analogical Reasoning*, 106 Harv. L. Rev. 741 (1993).] According to Sunstein, the doctrine of stare decisis means that a certain number of outcomes must be respected as starting points for further reasoning; as a result, within the legal culture, analogical reasoning imposes a certain discipline that can help courts to reach determinate results even in the absence of widespread moral or political consensus." Judges are also constrained by norms and procedures of adjudication, including a focus on the facts of particular cases and the need to justify decisions by reasons that could persuade a neutral observer, including judges at the top of the hierarchy or in the future.

Tradition is critical to a common-law constitutionalism—but what of "bad traditions"? "It is true that, in 1954, it was possible to make traditionalist arguments for segregation. Nonetheless, * * * it was possible to make better traditionalist arguments against it.

The first step in such an argument is based on the observation that abstract principles can serve as a source of progressive pressure. These principles are not the product of metaphysical theory; rather, they are simply the traditions of a society taken at a higher level of generality. * * * Any institution of even moderate complexity will also have an aspirational component—it will reflect certain ideals and be oriented toward the attainment of certain values that are never fully realized in practice. The existence of this aspirational component means that one can always argue that the currently prevailing interpretation of an institution's ideals is faulty or incomplete, and attempt to show that from the standpoint of a more adequate interpretation, certain of the institution's existing features must be judged wanting and in need of reform. * * *

This fact is nowhere more evident than in the struggle against slavery and racism * * *. Although some elements of the civil rights movement rejected American liberalism in favor of more radical ideologies, the more successful groups—both within and without the African-American community—grounded their arguments in an appeal to the classical liberal ideals of freedom and equality. * * * Dr. Martin Luther King, Jr. was able to strengthen his moral appeal by drawing on the democratic elements of the American political tradition. * * *

The philosophy of the struggle against racism in America is, of course, more complicated than this thumbnail sketch can convey. It is striking, however, that the opponents of segregation were able to tap into the traditions of the establishment they were fighting. What is equally striking, moreover, is that the defenders of segregation were cut off from those democratic traditions, and forced to fall back on the naked fact of segregation's existence without any way of justifying the institution itself in terms of shared American values. * * * [T]he history of resistance to racism in this country shows the liberating potential of tradition at work, constantly undermining the claims of unjust institutions and providing a consensual basis for arguments in favor of reform.

Query: Professor Young left out traditions that powerfully supported the South in its intense campaign to preserve apartheid—federalism's commitment to local decisionmaking (*Brown I*) and the separation of powers aversion to judicial policymaking (*Brown II*). How does the common law judge arbitrate these different traditions? Consider the next Note.

NOTE ON PRAGMATISM AS ANOTHER RESOURCE FOR COMMON LAW CONSTITUTIONALISM

Pragmatism follows Burke in rejecting the dogmatic assertions of "foundationalist" theories that posit a single template (original intent, representation-reinforcement) and deduce "right" answers to all cases from it. Unlike Burke, these commentators do not give priority to tradition. Following William James, pragmatic legal thought is interested in the consequences of different interpretations. Pragmatic legal scholars attempt to define a mediating path between foundational theory (thinking too big) and deciding each case on its facts without concern about the overall development of the law (thinking too small). Like Ernie Young, legal pragmatists find the common law method to be the appropriate approach for "construct[ing] midlevel theories drawing out the patterns governing large areas of decisions" in constitutional law.[100]

In place of searches for *the* right answer, the pragmatist proposes eclectic—but by no means unfamiliar—methodologies to construct the best answer available. A supportable answer may sometimes descend from deductive analysis alone. More often, such an answer will ascend from a combination of arguments, none of which standing alone would constitute a sufficient justification. Such "supporting arguments" operate more like the legs of a chair than the links of a chain. The leading pragmatic, or eclectic, theories of constitutional law posit that the following considerations are relevant: (1) the constitutional text, especially if focused and not open-textured; (2) original semantic or structural meaning, to the extent determinable; (3) precedent and historical practice; (4) the original or evolved purpose of the provision; (5) practicality and potential resistance; and (6) ethical and political (*e.g.*, representation-reinforcement) norms.[101] As we and others have argued, the listing is also a hierarchy: The first items are more authoritative than the last. For example, a strong textual argument will trump an equally strong original intent or purpose argument.

Although the above factors are taken from legal *practice* and therefore lack the sharp normative edge of critical or republican theory, they may offer greater normative bite or constraint than foundationalist theories. Practical reason's freedom from the necessity of foundationalist justifications makes many cases easy to decide. Even in close cases, moreover, some objective standards of evaluation are available. In this view, then, "the tyranny of the judiciary" is neither inherent in all exercises of judicial review nor beyond

---

[100] The account in text is taken from Daniel A. Farber & Philip P. Frickey, *Practical Reason and the First Amendment*, 34 UCLA L. Rev. 1615, 1645–56 (1987). On the common law as a pragmatic, workable method, consider this:

> It is the merit of the common law that it decides the case first and determines the principle afterwards. Looking at the forms of logic it might be inferred that when you have a minor premise and a conclusion, there must be a major, which you are also prepared then and there to assert. But in fact lawyers * * * frequently see well enough how they ought to decide on a given state of facts without being very clear as to the *ratio decidendi*. In cases of first impression Lord Mansfield's often-quoted advice to the business man who was suddenly appointed judge, that he should state his conclusions and not give his reasons, as his judgment would probably be right and the reasons certainly wrong, is not without its application to more educated courts. It is only after a series of determinations on the same subject-matter, that it becomes necessary to "reconcile the cases," as it is called, that is, by a true induction to state the principle which has until then been obscurely felt. And this statement is often modified more than once by new decisions before the abstracted general rule takes its final shape. A well settled legal doctrine embodies the work of many minds, and has been tested in form as well as substance by trained critics whose practical interest it is to resist it at every step. These are advantages the want of which cannot be supplied by any faculty of generalization, however brilliant * * *.

Oliver Wendell Holmes, Jr., *Codes, and the Arrangement of the Law*, 44 Harv. L. Rev. 725, 725 (1931) (reprinting Holmes, *Codes, and the Arrangement of the Law*, 5 Am. L. Rev. 1 (1870)).

[101] This list is taken from William Eskridge, Jr. & Philip Frickey, *Statutory Interpretation as Practical Reasoning*, 42 Stan. L. Rev. 321 (1990), and is generally similar to the constitutional theories in Philip Bobbitt, *Constitutional Interpretation* (1991), and Richard Fallon, *A Constructivist Coherence Theory of Constitutional Interpretation*, 100 Harv. L. Rev. 1189 (1987).

evaluation in individual cases. The reasoned exercise of limited judicial discretion may not satisfy the purist, but it can hardly be considered a form of tyranny.

Richard A. Posner, *The Problems of Jurisprudence*

302–09 (1990)[102]

Judge Posner says that because the language of the Equal Protection Clause "is not obviously incompatible with a system of segregated schools" and because the Framers of the Fourteenth Amendment perhaps did not intend "to bring about true equality between whites and blacks, * * * the ultimate justification for the *Brown* decision must be sought not in technical legal materials but in such political and ethical desiderata as improving the position of blacks; adopting a principle of racial (and implicitly also religious and ethnic) equality to vindicate the ideals for which World War II had recently been fought; raising public consciousness about racial injustice; promoting social peace through racial harmony; eradicating an institution that was an embarrassment to America's foreign policy; reducing the social and political autonomy of the South ('completing the work of the Civil War'); finding a new institutional role for the Supreme Court to replace the discredited one of protecting economic liberty; breathing new life into the Equal Protection Clause."

"In addition to (but related to) the natural law justification offered earlier (*Brown* as vindication of a moral norm that was influential then and that now commands a consensus), consider what we would think of a decision by the Supreme Court overruling *Brown* tomorrow on the ground that the decision was an incorrect interpretation of the Fourteenth Amendment. We would pronounce such a decision wrong even if we agreed that it rested on a defensible theory of constitutional interpretation. The decision would be an enormous provocation, stirring racial fears and hostilities in a nation more rather than less racially heterogeneous than when *Brown* was decided; it would be promptly overruled by Congress in the exercise of its powers under § 5 [of the Fourteenth Amendment] or the commerce clause; it would unsettle all of constitutional law, most of which rests on interpretive grounds no more powerful (and often much less so) than those of *Brown*; and whatever its actual motivations it would be thought to bespeak the politicization of the Court. It would in short be socially, politically, and legally destabilizing.

"The example suggests that our legal certitudes are pragmatically rather than analytically grounded. The strongest defense of *Brown* is that the consequences of overruling it would be untoward. To borrow William James's formula, we believe that *Brown* is correct because that is a good, a useful, thing to believe. This may be true of most judicial decisions whose authority we are

---

[102] Reprinted by permission of the publisher from THE PROBLEMS OF JURISPRUDENCE by Richard A. Posner, pp. 303, 304, 308, 309, Cambridge, Mass.: Harvard University Press, Copyright © 1990 by the President and Fellows of Harvard College.

not disposed to question, whether they are ostensibly interpretive decisions or are leading cases in common law fields."

In response to the criticism that *Brown* rested on faulty social psychological research, Posner maintains that "there are firmer grounds" for *Brown*, but they "are matters of facts and consequence too, not matters of legal theory or distinctive legal materials. They are not grounds that hit one between the eyes after a careful reading of the equal protection clause and the debates that preceded its enactment and ratification. They are grounds based on political history, common sense and common knowledge, and ethical insight." Is Judge Posner's account a cogent one? A cogent *legal* account of *Brown*?

C. CIVIC REPUBLICANISM AND POLYCENTRIC CONSTITUTIONALISM

Both original meaning and legal process theories of constitutional law assume that the Constitution embodies a liberal understanding of government, as a social contract among self-interested individuals willing to give up their liberties only through the established organs of majority rule, namely, legislation by elected representatives. Alongside the liberal tradition, however, a "republican" tradition has animated American constitutionalism from Madison through Lincoln through *Brown*.[103] Unlike the liberal conception of government, republicanism does not start with atomistic individuals bargaining to form the state, but instead starts with a conception of civic virtue, in which citizens would work for the common good of the republic, from which they would derive a form of "public happiness" (philosopher Hannah Arendt's term) or civic virtue.

For republicans, the role of government is not to cut deals among interest groups, but rather to deliberate for the common good. Liberals, of course, also seek the common good, often defined in terms of overall social utility (typically defined in a materialistic way). The republican has a different focus: citizens are enriched through their participation in politics and self-governance, whose goal is to create *security* for all citizens, so that they and their families can pursue flourishing lives. Liberals usually consider people's preferences to be *exogenous* (outside) the political process; republicans consider them *endogenous*, that is, shaped and transformed by the political process.

Dialogue and discussion among the citizenry are the means by which people go beyond their narrow interests and perspectives and seek to solve

---

[103] See Michael Sandel, *Democracy's Discontent: America in Search of a Public Philosophy* (1996); *Debating* Democracy's Discontent: *Essays on American Politics, Law, and Public Philosophy* (Anita Allen & Milton Regan, Jr. eds., 1998). See also William N. Eskridge, Jr. & John Ferejohn, *A Republic of Statutes: The New American Constitution* ch. 2 (2010); Bruce A. Ackerman, *The Storrs Lectures: Discovering the Constitution*, 93 Yale L.J. 1013 (1984); Tracy Higgins, *Democracy and Feminism*, 110 Harv. L. Rev. 1657 (1997); Frank I. Michelman, *The Supreme Court, 1985 Term—Foreword: Traces of Self-Government*, 100 Harv. L. Rev. 4 (1986); Cass R. Sunstein, *Interest Groups in American Public Law*, 38 Stan. L. Rev. 29 (1985).

social problems and advance the general interest of the republic as a whole. Debate in which all views are considered is likely to result in a better solution than closed discussion, and republicans have great faith in the ability of education to bring about agreement. Decisionmaking by consensus is preferred over coercive majority-vote wins. See *Federalist* 10 (App. 2 to this casebook).

A republican reading of *Federalist* 78 would be different from a liberal understanding of judicial review such as that in *Marbury* (and may explain why Marshall did not refer to *Federalist* 78 in his opinion). A republican reading would emphasize that the Constitution's system of checks and balances sought to yield a system of deliberative democracy in which a number of different institutional filters would weed out measures that did not pursue the common good—filters that include not just bicameralism, the presidential veto, and possible state resistance, but also judicial review. Likewise, the Constitution provides We the People with different institutional forms of access to political participation, not just through elected legislators, but also through the nationally elected President and the unelected judiciary. While Hamilton cautioned that judges should exercise "judgment" and not "will" in striking down laws, he left it to the Court to devise standards of review that would discourage—ex ante (before the fact, as an incentive) as well as ex post (after the fact)—legislative action that was unjust or oppressive.

Republicanism also values perspective. Unlike many liberal theories which insist that the Constitution has an acontextual meaning stable over time, modern republican theorists insist that meaning is influenced by perspective, and that a variety of perspectives must be considered. Feminists and race theorists maintain that constitutional law cannot be "neutral" so long as the constitutional text and history are viewed only from insider (e.g., white male) perspectives.[104] Although people of color were not generally treated as full citizens before the Reconstruction Amendments nor were women before the Nineteenth Amendment, the Constitution should be construed in ways that reflect their full citizenship today. Judges and other public servants should emulate Justice Harlan, who viewed Jim Crow laws from the standpoint of Homer Plessy and through his eyes was able to see how deeply apartheid undermined the norms of Reconstruction.[105]

---

[104] See Derrick Bell, *And We Are Not Saved* (1987); Catharine MacKinnon, *Toward a Feminist Theory of the State* (1989); Katharine Bartlett, *Feminist Legal Methods*, 103 Harv. L. Rev. 829 (1990); Mary Coombs, *Outsider Scholarship: The Law Review Stories*, 63 U. Colo. L. Rev. 683 (1992); Richard Delgado, *Storytelling for Oppositionists and Others: A Plea for Narrative*, 87 Mich. L. Rev. 2411 (1989); Mari Matsuda, *When the First Quail Calls: Multiple Consciousness as Jurisprudential Method*, 11 Women's Rts. L. Rep. 7 (1989); Suzanna Sherry, *Civic Virtue and the Feminine Voice in Constitutional Adjudication*, 72 Va. L. Rev. 543 (1986).

[105] See Martha Minow, *The Supreme Court, 1986 Term—Foreword: Justice Engendered*, 101 Harv. L. Rev. 10, 59–60 (1987).

CH. 2 DECISIONMAKING 187

1. Social Movements as Engines for Civic Republican Engagement

A civic republican understanding of constitutionalism immediately stimulates the rejoinder that, however energized they were in 1776, Americans today are not civically engaged. They are consumers and observers of politics, not agents of political change and fervor. Indeed, most public choice theorists presume that Americans' preferences are exogenously determined, usually by material self-interest, the antithesis of the republican vision. There is much force to these observations, but such a starkly liberal view of politics is punctuated by a great deal of civic republican engagement—starting with the ferocious debates between the Jeffersonians and the Federalists in the 1790s, continuing with the Jacksonian assault on the U.S. Bank and the abolitionists' assault on slavery, reaching a tremendous apex during and after the Civil War, continuing during the Progressive Era, the New Deal, the Great Society, and the post-9/11 era.

Throughout American history, civic engagement has dramatically occurred through *social movements* (mass mobilizations of citizens supporting a norm change), which drive most evolution in constitutional law, in our view. (Social movements do not drive all evolution, as wars, external threats, and technological change trigger and motivate significant constitutional change as well.) The American Revolution itself was a social movement, the brash revolt of a younger generation of colonists unwilling to be treated by Parliament and King George III like pampered children rather than as full and equal citizens. Other social movements important to constitutional change have been the abolitionist (Reconstruction Amendments), temperance (XVIII Amendment), women's rights (XIX Amendment; Chapters 4 & 5), civil rights for African and Latino Americans (Chapters 2–4 & 6), lesbian and gay rights (Chapter 4, § 3D), pro-choice and right-to-life (Chapter 5, §§ 3 & 4) movements. Consider some of the ways that social movements influence formal constitutional law as well as informal constitutional culture.

William N. Eskridge Jr., *Some Effects of Identity-Based Social Movements on Constitutional Law in the Twentieth Century*

100 Mich. L. Rev. 2062, 2064–68 (2002)[106]

"What motivated big changes in constitutional law doctrine during the twentieth century? Rarely did important constitutional doctrine or theory change because of formal amendments to the document's text, and rarer still because scholars or judges 'discovered' new information about the Constitution's original meaning. Precedent and common law reasoning were the mechanisms by which changes occurred rather than their driving force. My

---

[106] Reprinted with permission of the author.

thesis is that most twentieth century changes in the constitutional protection of individual rights were driven by or in response to the great identity-based social movements (IBSMs) of the twentieth century.

"Race, sex, and sexual orientation were markers of social inferiority and legal exclusion throughout the twentieth century. People of color, women, and gay people all came to resist their social and legal disabilities in the civil rights movement seeking to end apartheid; various feminist movements seeking women's control over their own bodies and equal rights with men; and the gay rights movement, seeking equal rights for [lesbian, gay,] and transgendered people. * * * [T]hese IBSMs became involved in constitutional litigation as part of three different kinds of politics in which they were engaged: their own *politics of protection* against state-sponsored threats to the life, liberty, and property of its members; their *politics of recognition*, seeking to end legal discriminations and exclusions of group members and to establish legal protections against private discrimination; and a *politics of remediation*, to rectify material as well as stigmatic legacies of previous state discrimination. At every stage, but particularly the last, these IBSMs were confronted with a *politics of preservation*, whereby countermovements sought to limit or roll back legal protections won or sought by the social movement. Each kind of politics offered opportunities for different kinds of constitutional arguments. The politics of protection most successfully invoked the First Amendment and the Due Process Clauses of the U.S. Constitution; the politics of recognition was most closely associated with the Equal Protection Clause; and the politics of preservation invoked arguments based upon constitutional federalism, separation of powers, and various libertarian doctrines.

"IBSMs and their countermovements brought constitutional litigation that required the Court to apply old constitutional texts and precedents to new circumstances, not just in a single case, but in a string of cases that ran like a chain novel whose audience shifted in the course of narration. Moreover, IBSMs transformed the normative context in which these cases were decided, either by linking the new cases with established norms or by persuading society and its judges to change the normative context in which social traits were evaluated. As to the latter, IBSMs have moved public norms away from understanding race, sex, and (to a lesser extent) sexual orientation as *malign variations* toward understanding them as *tolerable* and (for race and sex) *benign variations*. Finally, as these social movements and countermovements have become institutionalized players in American constitutional litigation and politics, they have become ongoing constituencies for particular ways of thinking about certain provisions of the Constitution. Thus, the oxymoronic notion of 'substantive' due process has become an established part of constitutional jurisprudence because of the importance of the privacy right to women and sexual minorities; waves of minority groups' politics of recognition have transformed the Equal Protection Clause from the last resort to the cutting edge of individual rights claims; and the First Amendment's imperialism in constitutional law owes much to its ability to protect speech and expressive activities most dear to traditionalists as well as gay people; pro-life protesters as well as pro-choice advocates; and racial segregationists as well as people of color. IBSMs and their allies did not single-handedly work these transformations, but they have provided impetus and then support for judges when they have moved in the direction of those stances."

IBSM counsel originated and persuaded the Court to adopt particular doctrines as well, including the strict scrutiny standard in equal protection cases (Chapters 3–4) as well as the alternative sliding scale approach (Chapter 5, § 3); the incorporation of most of the Bill of Rights guarantees against the states through the Fourteenth Amendment (Chapter 5, § 1); the fundamental rights to vote, travel, and privacy (Chapter 5, §§ 2–4); an Imperial First Amendment (Chapter 6); the expansion of congressional authority to enforce the Reconstruction Amendments (Chapter 7, § 3); and the enforcement of human rights limits against the President's conduct of war (Chapter 8, § 3). Although not covered in this casebook, the Eighth Amendment's death penalty jurisprudence is substantially a creation of the civil rights movement.

Judges adopting these constitutional transformations have usually not accepted the IBSM perspective uncritically or without amendment, however. Judges have rejected the most radical proposals, such as a bar to the death penalty, and have diluted other proposals, such as a robust de novo review of state criminal convictions by federal judges, an anti-subordination reading of the Equal Protection Clause, and strong First Amendment protection for sexual speech. Even when judges have accepted IBSM constitutional visions and doctrines, the constitutional transformations movement lawyers argued for have had limited utility for actual minority group members. Some IBSM-inspired doctrines have been turned to the advantage of countermovements. Examples include heightened scrutiny for suspect classifications, which has discouraged open affirmative action measures [Chapter 5, § 3], and the First Amendment rights of expressive conduct and association, which now protect enclaves of exclusion against state anti-discrimination laws [Chapter 6].

"The fate of particular proposals and doctrines has depended on context, but one rule stands out: judges are rarely willing to insist on massive transfers of social or economic entitlements in American society, and when they have—as with school desegregation and abortion—they have been incompletely successful. This rule owes much to the institutional limits of the federal judiciary. Judges do not have the resources to undertake initiatives requiring administrative capacity, nor do they have the political legitimacy to engage in much actual activism not otherwise acceptable to the political system. * * *

"In addition, IBSMs were the key impulse supporting a global shift in the way the Supreme Court applied the Constitution in the twentieth century. The shift was away from the *structural* Constitution of the founding generation and the *vested property/contract rights* Constitution of the *Lochner* era and toward the *Carolene* Constitution, which justified judicial activism along legal process lines. Under the *Carolene* Constitution, the role of the Court is to protect the integrity of the pluralist political process, and especially to check the political process' tendency toward self-perpetuation and persecution or suppression of minorities. This entails protecting despised minority groups against state *Kulturkampfs*, assuring groups that are able to organize themselves into mass movements that they will be integrated into the political process, and protecting traditionalists from excessive state burdens once a formerly subordinated minority has become part of the political mainstream."

Finally, Professor Eskridge explores the inevitable disappointments of IBSMs in constitutional litigation, which has fueled a vigorous *constitutional skepticism*. Theoretically, the origins of skepticism can be expressed in this way: social movement progressives are thoroughgoing civic republicans who aim to revolutionize social as well as political preferences, but constitutional litigation not only limits their agenda to whatever rights against the state that liberal judges are willing to grant, but also tends to channel the social movement's energies in a liberal, universalizing direction. Moreover, because successful countermovements (such as pro-life and traditional values movements) also influence the evolution of constitutional law, the resulting rules are not only incomplete from the progressive point of view, but are often counterproductive. This has given rise to *constitutional law drop-out* as well as *popular constitutionalism* approaches.

Robin L. West, *Constitutional Skepticism*

72 B.U.L. Rev. 765–66, 774–78 (1992)[107]

"[T]he prominence of the debate over the Constitution's *meaning*, whether it can be said to have one, and the implications for the coherence of liberalism that these questions of interpretation seem to raise, has pushed to the background an older and possibly more important debate about the Constitution's *value*. By asking relentlessly whether the Constitution's meaning can be made sufficiently determinate to serve the Rule of Law—by focusing almost exclusively on whether constitutionalism is *possible* within liberal theory and whether liberalism is possible, given an indeterminate Constitution—we have neglected to ask whether our Constitution is *desirable*. Does it further the 'good life' for the individuals, communities, and subcommunities it governs?"

In answering the question of the Constitution's value, Professor West contrasts a "progressive" constitutional vision from a traditional "liberal" one: Both seek personal flourishing and interconnection. "What *distinguishes* progressives from liberals is that while liberals tend to view the dangers of an over-oppressive state as the most serious obstacle to the attainment of such a world, progressives * * * argue that *for the most part* the most serious impediments emanate from unjust concentrations of *private* power—the social power of whites over blacks, the intimate power of men over women, the economic power of the materially privileged over the materially deprived. * * * [I]t is those concentrations of private power that must be targeted, challenged, and reformed by progressive political action. That action, in turn, will often

---

[107] Reprinted with permission of the Boston University Law Review.

involve state intervention into the private spheres within which hierarchies of private power are allowed to thrive, and that simple fact will commonly pit the progressive strategy of ending private domination against the liberal goal of minimizing the danger of an oppressive state.

"This difference between progressives and liberals largely accounts for the degree of conflict between their respective analyses and goals. For example, liberals and progressives generally agree, and lament, that the freedom of gays and lesbians to form and maintain nurturing intimate relationships is threatened by discriminatory state action. At the same time, progressives, far more than liberals, are sensitive to the degree to which that freedom is threatened by the continuing and seemingly unshakable hegemonic rage of an intolerant, abusive, and often violent minority of heterosexual private citizens. That hegemonic rage, not just state action, must somehow be challenged and transformed if gays and lesbians are to thrive." West makes the same point for women and people of color: Private sexism and racism rather than public discrimination is an ongoing problem that is severely disabling and dangerous for women and people of color. * * *

"If [the] progressive insight is basically correct, then at least two problems exist with the scheme of individual rights and liberties protected by the Constitution. First, the Constitution does not prohibit the abuse of private power that interferes with the equality or freedom of subordinated peoples. The Constitution simply does not reach private power, and therefore cannot possibly prohibit its abuse. Even the most far reaching liberal interpretations of the Reconstruction Amendments—the only amendments that *seemingly* reach private power—refuse or fail to find either a constitutional prohibition of private societal racism, intimate sexual violence, or economic coercion or a constitutional imperative that the states take affirmative action to eradicate it. Justice Harlan's famous liberal dissent in *Plessy v. Ferguson*, for example, made painfully clear that, even on his reading of the amendment (which, of course, would have outlawed Jim Crow laws), the Fourteenth Amendment does not challenge the sensed or actual cultural and social superiority of the white race. * * *

"The incompatibility, however, of progressivism and the Constitution goes deeper. Not only does the Constitution fail to prohibit subordinating abuses of private power, but, at least a good deal of the time, in the name of guaranteeing constitutional protection of individual freedom, it also aggressively *protects* the very hierarchies of wealth, status, race, sexual preference, and gender that facilitate those practices of subordination." West notes the Constitution's protection of hate speech, pornography, misogynistic religion, patriarchal family structures, and class- and race-constructed notions of meritocracy.

Professor West maintains that "this incompatibility of the Constitution with progressive ideals is neither momentary nor contingent." First, it rests upon the Constitution's negative vision of liberty (freedom from state interference), which not only fails to protect positive liberty (empowerment) but also stands in the way of the positive liberty of women, gays, the poor, and people of color.

"Second, the Fourteenth Amendment's mandate of equality, rather than being a limit to the Constitution's celebration of liberty, is also a bar to progressive progress, the heroic efforts of progressive litigators, judges, and commentators to prove the contrary notwithstanding. The 'equal protection of the laws' guaranteed by the Fourteenth Amendment essentially guarantees that one's membership in a racially or sexually defined group will not adversely affect one's treatment by the state. As such, the mandate powerfully reinforces the liberal understanding that the only attributes that matter to the state are those shared universally by all members of the community: the possession of equal dignity, the power to form one's own plan of life, and the universal aspirations to autonomy and so forth. Precisely this understanding of equality, grounded in the liberal claim and promise of universality and equal treatment, however, renders the Equal Protection Clause an obstacle to progressive progress. The need to acknowledge and compensate for the individual's membership in profoundly non-universal subordinate groups—whether racially, sexually, or economically defined—is what distinguishes the progressive political impulse from the liberal. It is precisely that membership in non-universal groups, and the centrality of the non-universal attributes that distinguish them, that both liberalism and the liberally defined constitutional mandate of equality are poised not simply to ignore, but also to oppose. It is, then, both unsurprising and inevitable that the Fourteenth Amendment's Equal Protection Clause is understood as not requiring, and indeed forbidding, the state and public interventions into private, intimate, and economic spheres of life needed to interrupt the patterns of domination, subordination, and inequality that continue to define the lives of those within these protected private realms."

NOTE ON PROGRESSIVE CONSTITUTIONALISM

Notwithstanding the critical account in the foregoing excerpt, Professor West believes that progressives should not submit to disabling *constitutional skepticism* and should remain actively engaged among the *constitutional faithful*. Drawing from radical feminist and critical race theories, as well as West's own work, consider these important features of progressive constitutionalism.

1. *An Anti-Subordination Understanding of the Constitution.* An important critical theme is that the Fourteenth Amendment embodies an *anti-subordination* norm, and that this norm must inform the entire constitutional enterprise. The anti-subordination norm posits that the central goal of the Reconstruction Amendments was to overturn laws and practices that unfairly subordinated social groups and to assure all persons the same protection of law that white males have traditionally enjoyed. Although the Supreme Court has occasionally paid lip-service to this goal, its analytical approach, especially after 1968, has been dominated by a *rationality* goal that the Justices have attributed to the Reconstruction Amendments.

Catharine A. MacKinnon, *Reflections on Sex Equality under the Law*, 100 Yale L.J. 1281 (1991), suggests how the judiciary's rationality model has operated doctrinally: "[C]ourts in racial equality cases have largely confined themselves to the Aristotelian framework [where equality means treating like things alike]: qualification for admission into liberal humanity implicitly meant being like the white man. In *Plessy v. Ferguson*, for example, where segregation with equal facilities was held to be equality, the reason given was that Blacks were different from whites, so could be treated differently. When *Brown v. Board of Education* repudiated *Plessy* and held that educational segregation with equal facilities was inherently unequal, what changed was that *Brown* implicitly considered Blacks to be the same as whites. At least, Black school children were potentially so. This was a substantive shift in the political and ideological ground beneath the case law, not a pure doctrinal development. What was different was now the same. Difference could still justify differentiation, presumably including exclusion and subordination as well as segregation (maybe even affirmative action). Being the same as the dominant group remained the equality test."

Several consequences of this doctrinal structure have worried critical theorists. This kind of thinking allows—and perhaps invites—the modernization of anti-minority norms.[108] Thus, the Court's *Brown* jurisprudence disallows arguments that people of color should be excluded because of white prejudice and stereotypes about racial minorities, but it allows continued exclusion based on modern standards of performance and cultural familiarity that many minorities do not meet, in part because of the effects of prior discrimination. This analytic not only permits continued subordination of minorities, but also cloaks it in an aura of enhanced legitimacy. This kind of thinking also has an assimilative effect. To win an equal protection case, minorities and women must show (à la Aristotle) that they are similar to the unspoken white male norm. This means that women and minorities who are already most like the norm will have the greatest success in equal protection cases; their success in court may translate into status within their cohort, a phenomenon which might press toward indirect suppression of distinctive minority cultures.

2. *Affirmative, Not Just Negative, State Responsibilities.* The Supreme Court's articulation of constitutional values sometimes imposes *limitations* on state action, but almost never on private action; the Court rarely imposes *duties* on the state to provide affirmative protections for citizens. Even the desegregation cases have this feature, especially after *Milliken*, when the Court has diluted state responsibility for the ongoing consequences of slavery and apartheid to the libertarian presumption that white people ought to be able to avoid "too much integration" by moving away from people of color. Critics have also objected to the Court's failure to sustain the *Green-Swann*

---

[108] Kimberlé Crenshaw, *Race, Reform, and Retrenchment: Transformation and Legitimation in Antidiscrimination Law*, 101 Harv. L. Rev. 1331 (1988); see also Charles Lawrence, III, *The Id, the Ego, and Equal Protection: Reckoning with Unconscious Racism*, 39 Stan. L. Rev. 317 (1987); Reva Siegel, *"The Rule of Love": Wife Beating as Prerogative and Privacy*, 105 Yale L.J. 2117 (1996).

idea that the state has an affirmative obligation to reconstitute once-unconstitutional systems "root and branch" and to work toward a functionally and not just formally fair and equal system. Chapter 3 will show how the Court has not only refused to hold the state responsible for deeper remedial obligations, but has invalidated some of the remedial responses that state and local governments have made.

Judges would say they are just applying the libertarian Constitution as it is written—but the Constitution is filled with admonitions that demand *affirmative* assistance and not just noninterference from government.[109] Reading the Equal Protection Clause both literally and in light of its abolitionist roots, Professor West maintains that it requires the state to *protect* women and minorities to the same effect that it protects white men. Robin L. West, *Progressive Constitutionalism* (1994). For feminist theorists, it is important that most violence against women occurs within the home or the family and is committed by men whom they know—an arena the law has not policed with the vigor it has exercised in protecting property and assaults by strangers. Both critical race and feminist theorists have urged the state to regulate hate speech and other forms of oppressive conduct that the Supreme Court has protected from regulation under a libertarian reading of the First Amendment.[110]

The Equal Protection Clause is not the only part of the Constitution that, on its face, imposes affirmative obligations on government. Among them are the General Welfare Clause of the Preamble, the Commander-in-Chief Clause of Article II, the Vesting Clause of Article III, the Property Protection and Guarantee Clauses of Article IV, and the Debt Assumption and Oath of Office Clauses of Article VI. From a progressive, republican point of view, the Constitution is a libertarian document *not* because it is written that way, or because such was the original goal of the Framers (quite the opposite), but because *judges* have read the Constitution that way. The primary explanation for such a slanted reading is the institutional limitations of the "least dangerous branch" (*Federalist* No. 78). For that reason, progressive constitutionalism must emphasize affirmative legislative and executive protections and not primarily judicial ones. See Robin L. West, *From Choice to Reproductive Justice: De-Constitutionalizing Abortion Rights,* 118 Yale L.J. 1394 (2009).

3.   *Rejection of Dichotomies Between Liberty and Equality, Public and Private.* The Supreme Court has resisted—sometimes passively (*Plessy*), sometimes aggressively (*Civil Rights Cases*)—progressive arguments that longstanding status alignments should be changed significantly. Primary doctrinal mechanisms for the resistance have been the public-private

---

[109] E.g., U.S. Const., preamble (We the People form the Constitution in order to advance "the general Welfare"); *id.,* art. IV (Congress has a responsibility to preserve and protect national property and to assure each state a "Republican form of government").

[110] Mari Matsuda, *Public Response to Racist Speech: Considering the Victim's Story,* 87 Mich. L. Rev. 2320 (1989); see Charles Lawrence, III, *If He Hollers Let Him Go: Regulating Racist Speech on Campus,* 1990 Duke L.J. 431.

distinction and a preference for liberty over equality. The former prevents courts from applying constitutional norms to social practices (Chapter 3, § 2), and the second prevents courts from imposing equality norms on state actors and invalidates state equalization measures (e.g., Chapter 6, § 5). Both moves are contrary to the anti-subordination norm that critical theorists find in the Reconstruction Amendments.

Critical theorists also find fault in the Court's reliance on and manipulation of such categories. The distinction between state action and private choice, they argue, cannot be neutrally drawn. As the NAACP and its Inc. Fund have maintained, "white flight" cannot be understood as simply a matter of private choice, for white people's housing choices are framed by governmental decisions leaving identifiably white and black schools in place and facilitating gated communities by protective zoning and other property regulations. Even white prejudice against some people of color cannot be understood without reference to centuries of state support for the institutions of slavery and apartheid. And white efforts to avoid integration typically depend on state property and contract law to give effect to their preferences.[111]

Likewise, the liberty-equality distinction is overdrawn, according to the critics. As Mari Matsuda has argued to justify regulation of hate speech, the First Amendment has egalitarian as well as libertarian features: Not only does the First Amendment flatly reject content-based discriminations, but it has sometimes been deployed to allow state regulations that enhance the ability of marginalized people to feel empowered to speak (Matsuda, *Racist Speech*). Although mainstream scholars may question *Bolling*'s holding that the Fifth Amendment's Due Process Clause has an equal protection component, an outsider perspective suggests its cogency: Due process has always included a nonarbitrariness feature: What could be more arbitrary than blanket denial of state benefits or even respect simply because of one's minority trait?[112]

NOTE ON INTEREST CONVERGENCE THEORY

Critical theory recognizes practical problems with its normative aspirations. A founder of Critical Race Theory, Professor Derrick Bell argued in a landmark article that social movements tend to succeed only when their demands coincide with mainstream economic or ideological interests. Thus, he explained *Brown v. Board of Education* (1954) not as a great triumph of judicial compassion for an obscenely treated minority, but rather as the convergence of the interests of people of color with the interests of the white military-industrial establishment fearing that apartheid was holding the country back

---

[111] There is no logical reason why the availability of state remedies cannot be considered sufficient to meet the state action requirement. See *Shelley v. Kraemer*, 334 U.S. 1 (1948) (Chapter 3, § 2) (state court enforcement of a racially restrictive covenant is state action); Mark V. Tushnet, *Shelley v. Kraemer* and Theories of Equality, 33 N.Y.L. Sch. L. Rev. 383 (1988).

[112] See Kenneth L. Karst, *The Supreme Court, 1976 Term—Foreword: Equal Citizenship Under the Fourteenth Amendment*, 91 Harv. L. Rev. 1 (1977) (both due process and equal protection must be understood as guarantees of national citizenship); William N. Eskridge, Jr., *Destabilizing Due Process and Evolutive Equal Protection*, 47 UCLA L. Rev. 1183 (2000).

in the Cold War and in economic development. "The interest of blacks in achieving racial equality will be accommodated only when it converges with the interests of whites." Derrick A. Bell Jr., Brown v. Board of Education *and the Interest-Convergence Dilemma*, 93 Harv. L. Rev. 518, 523 (1980).

Interest convergence theory does not claim that majority attitudes are static nor that *Brown* had no effect on America, but it does claim that the main audience for the symbolism of ending separate but equal was the white majority and, even more, the world-wide Cold War audience that saw the United States as little different from apartheid-era South Africa. Mary L. Dudziak, *Cold War Civil Rights: Race and the Image of American Democracy* (2011). The arguments that prevailed in *Brown* had been around for a long time, and Justice Harlan's *Plessy* dissent had been a cogent constitutional critique since its publication, but more mainstream Americans found them persuasive in 1954 than in 1896. Without reducing everything to a crude class analysis, Professor Bell asks the question: Why would so many thoughtful Americans have found these arguments unpersuasive in 1924 or 1934, while so many more found them compelling in 1954?

Constitutional doctrine, one might argue, encourages interest convergence. Doctrine considers "discrimination" (in violation of the equal protection mandate) to be treatment of *similar* things *differently*. To succeed, therefore, the minority must persuade the majority that they are "just the same" as the majority and, implicitly, that the majority's interests converge with integrating the minority into the status quo.

The flip side of the interest convergence thesis is that if the mainstream does not believe the minority's interests really do converge with theirs, rights will not be granted. Thus, once *Brown*'s implicit mandate of truly equal education for children of color faced white parental anxiety about actual integration, the political process produced a Supreme Court that slowly but methodically reconsidered the *Brown II* mandate and that was not moved by the plight of schoolchildren facing resegregation. See Derrick A. Bell Jr., *Silent Covenants:* Brown v. Board of Education *and the Unfulfilled Hopes for Racial Reform* (2004).

Professor Bell's theory generates insights for other social movements. See Justin Driver, *Rethinking the Interest-Convergence Thesis,* 105 Nw. U.L. Rev. 149 (2011). For example, the welfare-rights social movement of the late 1960s and early 1970s rested upon a robust moral theory of decent treatment, generated enormous media publicity, and enjoyed support among academics, but fizzled and may even have set the cause of welfare recipients back politically. Martha Davis, *Brutal Need: Lawyers and the Welfare Rights Movement, 1960–1973* (1995). Once any social movement's goals are persuasively translated into zero-sum games by opponents, the social movement will be slowed down or thwarted.

For another example, consider the movement of marriage equality for lesbians, gay men, bisexuals, transgender and intersex persons (Chapters 4 and 5). So long as ordinary Americans considered "homosexual marriage" a

Pandora's box, whose opening could hurt their families and tempt their children, marriage equality made no headway. But once one state opened Pandora's box and Hope but not Demons and Disease emerged, many more Americans accepted "the gays" as "just like us." With corporations solidly in support of marriage equality and millions of families realizing for the first time that they had lesbian, gay, transgender, bisexual, and intersex relatives, the Supreme Court repeatedly gave it a boost (*Lawrence, Windsor*) and imposed nationwide marriage equality in *Obergefell v. Hodges,* 135 S.Ct. 2584 (2015) (Chapter 5, § 4D). But marriage equality primarily benefitted LGBT Americans who were "like straight" Americans in their aspiration to link their relationships to civil and social marriage; many gay and transgender persons involved in non-marital relationships believe they were left behind.[113]

2. Polycentric Constitutionalism

The primary civic republican response to constitutional skepticism and the interest convergence thesis is *politics.* See Robin L. West, *Toward the Study of the Legislated Constitution,* 72 Ohio St. L.J. 1343 (2011). The guarded success story surrounding *Brown*—widespread rejection of state-imposed racial segregation and general support for the value of racial diversity—is to a great extent the product of the civil rights movement's successes in Congress during the 1960s. William N. Eskridge Jr. & John Ferejohn, *A Republic of Statutes: The New American Constitution* 1–24 (2010). The Civil Rights Act of 1964 elevated the anti-discrimination norm to widely accepted national policy, and the Elementary and Secondary Education Act of 1965 provided federal funds to school districts, with the stipulation (from the 1964 Act) that segregated districts could not receive such needed monies.

The general point suggested by this experience is that the Constitution (or simply our small "c" political constitution) should be viewed as an authorization and encouragement for the political process, after deliberation where everyone is represented, to create rules and structures that provide security and guarantee civic engagement for all citizens. Examples of republican constitutionalism along these lines include the Sherman Act of 1890 and the Clayton Act of 1914; the Social Security act of 1935 and the Medicare Act of 1965; the Voting Rights Act of 1965; the Clean Air Act Amendments of 1970 and the Clean Water Act of 1970, as well as other environmental-protective laws; and so forth.[114]

---

[113] See Eskridge & Riano, *From Outlaws to Inlaws,* chs. 18 & 22; Anthony Michael Kreis, *Gay Gentrification: Whitewashed Fictions of LGBT Privilege and the New Interest-Convergence Dilemma,* 3 Law & Inequality 117 (2012); Neo Khuu, Comment, Obergefell v. Hodges: *Kinship Formation, Interest Convergence, and the Future of LGBTQ Rights,* 64 UCLA L. Rev. 184 (2017).

[114] These "super-statutes" and their normative evolution are examined in Eskridge & Ferejohn, *Republic of Statutes* chs. 1 (Civil Rights Act), 2 (Voting Rights Act), 3 (Sherman Act), 4 (Social Security Act), and 6 (Clean Water Act).

Bruce Ackerman has expanded upon this idea and has sought to give it a formal grounding as Large "C" Constitutional Law.[115] He has suggested that there have been three big "Constitutional Moments": the Founding, Reconstruction, and the New Deal. Although the third did not produce Constitutional text, the texts produced by the first two were of questionable pedigree,[116] and the New Deal's regulatory statism was ratified by a similar process as the other two moments: a political crisis, followed by an intense period of high-politics debate, followed by a popular electoral ratification of a new order of governance (the ratifying conventions of 1787–89, the election of 1866, the election of 1936). Note how this theory sidesteps Article V, which most Constitutionalists consider the only formal mechanism by which the Constitution can be amended.

Once Constitutional law is viewed as having three rather than two Constitutional Moments, *Brown* and *Bolling* become an exercise, not just in translating the precepts of the Founding in light of Reconstruction, but also in translating precepts of Reconstruction in light of the New Deal. Ackerman terms this a process of *synthesis*, whereby the meaning of the Constitution and the Bill of Rights must be accommodated to reflect the normative changes wrought by the Reconstruction Amendments *and* by the New Deal. (Note the similarity of constitutional synthesis with structural interpretation.)

Bruce A. Ackerman, *Constitutional Politics / Constitutional Law*

99 Yale L.J. 453, 531–36 (1989)[117]

Justice Brown gave two reasons for rejecting Plessy's attack on Jim Crow laws. The first reason was that "in the nature of things" the Fourteenth Amendment "could not have been intended * * * to enforce social, as distinguished from political equality." This was the thinking in the 1890s, but "the great constitutional debate of the 1930s was defined precisely by the Old Court's effort to insist that twentieth-century Americans could not legitimately use state power to pursue 'social, as distinguished from political equality' by requiring the payment of a minimum wage, or the recognition of a labor union, or the guarantee of a retirement pension. Given the New Deal's embrace of activist government in the late 1930s, the Warren Court could hardly respond to the petitioner's complaint about school segregation in *Brown* by reaffirming Justice Brown's assertion that 'the nature of things' precluded a reading of

---

[115] Bruce Ackerman, *We The People: Foundations* (1991).

[116] The original Constitution provided that it would take effect when nine states ratified it, contrary to the Articles of Confederation, which required unanimity to amend or supersede. The Fourteenth Amendment's ratification was owing to Congress' refusal to readmit rebel southern states unless they ratified the amendment and to recognize the effort by two states to rescind their ratifications.

[117] Reprinted with permission of the Yale Law Journal.

'equal protection' that demanded something more than a thin political equality."

Justice Brown's second reason was that any "badge of inferiority" Homer Plessy drew from forced segregation "is not by reason of anything found in the act, but solely because the colored race chooses to put that construction upon it." This reason was more metaphysical: government in nineteenth century thinking could not be held responsible for "choices" like that which Plessy made. "Rather than participating actively in the construction of public understandings, the state stands to one side and allows social groups to give any meaning they 'choose' to the state's treatment of them. * * *

"Once again, whatever the legal plausibility of this claim in 1896, such a view was judicially untenable after the New Deal. It is precisely the Old Court's insistence that the state must not intervene to alter the result of private 'choices' in the economy that precipitated the constitutional struggle of the 1930s that decisively legitimated activist government. In repudiating *Lochner*, the modern Court recognized that the government was an important actor in the process by which groups made their 'choices' in American society." Exemplary of the modern rejection of *Lochner* was compulsory public education (a notion in its infancy in 1896), positing that parents as well as children could be required to submit to a community process of education and inculcation. "Public schools exemplified the newly-legitimated claims of the activist state to shape the conditions under which individual citizens ultimately come to make their mature choices. * * *

"Within this activist setting, it was absurd to accept Justice Brown's assurance that the meaning of segregated schools was up to the 'choices' of 'the colored race.' Was not the state in the business of public education precisely because children were in no position to make an informed 'choice' about the meaning of social reality? Rather than standing passively to one side, the activist state was now intimately involved in the way children—both black and white—would interpret the fact that they were being bussed to different schools on the basis of race."

NOTE ON THE CIVIL RIGHTS REVOLUTION AS A CONSTITUTIONAL MOMENT

The process of what Ackerman calls *higher lawmaking* (his term for widespread civic republican engagement by We the People) is what connects both Reconstruction and the New Deal as Constitutionally transformative. The formal Ackermanian model is this: Interbranch Impasse → Decisive Election → Reformist Challenge to Conservative Branch → Switch in Time.[118] In recent

---

[118] Ackerman, *We the People*, 49–50. The precise parallels: President Johnson vetoed the Civil Rights Act of 1866, the Old Court voided early New Deal legislation; the Radical Republicans triumphed over Johnson in the realigning 1866 election, the New Deal triumphed over the Old Court in the realigning 1936 election; the Republicans tried to impeach Johnson, Roosevelt tried to pack the Court; Johnson backed down, the Old Court backed down. In each case the country moved on, but was permanently transformed in its foundational assumptions about the structure

work, Ackerman argues that the civil rights laws of the 1960s constituted another Constitutional Moment: Congress at an impasse in the 1950s, unable to adopt needed civil rights laws → 1960 Election and the Kennedy Assassination (1963) generate civil rights momentum → civil rights leaders gain important allies (President Johnson) to challenge South-dominated Senate → Senate backs down and goes along with landmark legislation (1964–68).[119] Indeed, Ackerman's 2006 Holmes Lectures identify *eight* periods of Constitutional transformation in American history—the original three plus the civil rights era plus four more. Ackerman, *Living Constitution.*

Critics have pointed to several dangers. There is an increasing fuzziness as to exactly what makes a Constitutional Moment. Conservative critics suspect that Ackerman is at bottom just trying to transform the good old Constitution into liberalism's last stand.[120] For example, Ackerman scoffs at the notion that the Reagan Revolution of the 1980s was a Constitutional Moment, even though his model seems to invite that thesis.[121] Critics of all sorts worry that making so many things constitutional moments risks entrenching too many contingent commitments or diluting what it means to be "constitutional," or both.[122]

Reva Siegel, *She the People: The Nineteenth Amendment, Sex Equality, Federalism, and the Family*, 115 Harv. L. Rev. 947 (2002), extends the Constitutional Moment theory to sex discrimination. She argues that the great national debate that gave women the right to vote in the Nineteenth Amendment (1920) was a referendum on whether women's place should be rooted in the domestic sphere. Professor Siegel views the defeat of traditionalists on the franchise issue as a larger affirmation that women ought to be considered full and equal citizens in the public sphere. Although the Nineteenth Amendment does not fit the Ackerman model, because it was a formal addition to the Constitution, Siegel reads the amendment using the Ackermanian *synthesis* idea: the Fourteenth Amendment needs to be reinterpreted in light of the Nineteenth Amendment's rejection of women's

---

of official power. For a much more complicated model, see Bruce Ackerman, *We the People 2: Transformations* 359–60 (1998).

[119] Bruce Ackerman, *The Living Constitution*, 120 Harv. L. Rev. 1737 (2007) (delivered as the Oliver Wendell Holmes, Jr. Lectures); Bruce Ackerman & Jennifer Nou, *Canonizing the Civil Rights Revolution: The People and the Poll Tax*, 103 Nw. U.L. Rev. (2009).

[120] Richard A. Posner, *Overcoming Law* (1995); Michael Gerhardt, *Ackermania: The Quest for a Common Law of Higher Lawmaking*, 40 Wm. & Mary L. Rev. 1731 (1999); Suzanna Sherry, *The Ghost of Liberalism Past*, 105 Harv. L. Rev. 918 (1992).

[121] Like Roosevelt, Reagan won a landslide election on a platform that promised bold new policies and implemented many of them in the first term of his presidency. Just as Roosevelt faced down the Old Republican Court with labor and security laws, Reagan faced down the Old Democrat House with laws returning power to the states and private individuals. Roosevelt won a smashing reelection in 1936, similar to Reagan's decisive reelection in 1984. Both Presidents were succeeded by like-minded but one-term Vice-Presidents (Truman and Bush 41). Even when the opposing party recaptured the presidency (in 1952 and 1992, respectively), it did so with me-too candidates (Eisenhower and Clinton) who declined to challenge the New Deal and the Reagan Revolution. And the me-too Presidents were in turn succeeded by administrations (Kennedy-Johnson and Bush-Cheney) that pressed the New Deal and the Reagan Revolution even further.

[122] Eskridge & Ferejohn, *Republic of Statutes*, ch. 1.

confinement to domestic roles. Hence, the Equal Protection Clause should, since 1920, be understood to bar traditional sex discriminations on the part of the state. The problem with this view is that immediately after the Nineteenth Amendment was adopted, feminists started pressing for an Equal Rights Amendment (ERA) that specifically addressed that issue—and the ERA languished for decades before Congress in 1972 sent it to the states for ratification, and then an insufficient number of states ratified (Chapter 4, § 2B1). Consider a somewhat different approach to Constitutional sex equality.

Robert Post & Reva Siegel, *Legislative Constitutionalism and Section Five Power: Policentric Interpretation of the Family and Medical Leave Act*

112 Yale L.J. 1943, 1946–47, 1951, 2022–23 (2003)

The Family and Medical Leave Act of 1993 (FMLA) is the kind of constitutionalism that Professor West and other progressives support, for it pro-actively responds to the sexist stereotyping in American workplaces and imposes affirmative duties on public and private employers to accommodate family responsibilities for both male and female employees. But precisely as West argues, this progressive measure came under fire from liberal constitutionalism, because its application to public employers went well beyond what the Supreme Court had been willing to do under § 1 of the Fourteenth Amendment. In a move that surprised many constitutionalists, the Supreme Court upheld Congress's § 5 power to "enforce" the Fourteenth Amendment in *Nevada Department of Human Resources v. Hibbs*, 538 U.S. 721 (2003) (Chapter 7, § 3). This is another instance where IBSMs have exercised strong influence on the Court's jurisprudence, but Professors Siegel and Post explore another dimension of this case.

"Our Constitution contains a variety of structures and arrangements that facilitate [the] necessary connections between constitutional law and constitutional culture. These mechanisms range from the amendment procedures of Article V to the political appointment of Article III judges. § 5 is best conceived as another such mechanism." These also illustrate the general theory of what Post and Siegel call *policentric constitutional interpretation*, whereby "the Constitution should be regarded as having multiple interpreters, both political and legal." Recall Attorney General Meese's analysis of *Cooper v. Aaron* and his departmentalist notion that each branch should decide for itself how the Constitution should be interpreted.

Thus, the dismantling of apartheid was polycentric (our preferred spelling): The Supreme Court announced a new constitutional regime in *Brown*, but it was not until Congress and the President implemented the regime with monetary inducements as well as legal penalties that desegregation actually occurred and the Supreme Court itself actually announced a more positive norm of integration. Siegel and Post flip the account for the dismantling of state sex discrimination. The Supreme Court left state discriminations alone until Congress enacted a series of anti-sex-discrimination measures between 1963 and 1972, culminating in its passage of the ERA. Indeed, the Court *relied* on Congress's constitutional activism in *Frontiero v. Richardson,* 411 U.S. 677 (1973) (plurality opinion) (Chapter 4, § 2B1). "It was only after Congress used its lawmaking powers to validate the [women's] movement's understanding of equality that the Court proved willing to modify its own Section 1 doctrine to protect citizens against state action that discriminates on the basis of sex. The Court altered its jurisprudence to reflect the evolving constitutional culture of the country, as that culture was evidenced by congressional lawmaking."

Professors Post and Siegel call this model "policentric," referring to "the distribution of constitutional interpretation in our legal system across multiple institutions, many of which are political in character. A central premise of the policentric model is that both Congress and the Court should be regarded as having independent authority to ascertain constitutional meaning for purposes of delineating the parameters of § 5 power. The policentric model holds that Congress can exercise § 5 power to enact legislation establishing statutory rights (Rs), even when Congress is acting to enforce an understanding of constitutional rights (Rc) that differs from judicial interpretations of constitutional rights (Rj). The policentric model holds that courts can also act upon their own constitutional understandings (Rj) to subject § 5 legislation to judicial review. Courts can invalidate § 5 legislation that violates judicially enforceable rights or that impermissibly impairs other constitutional values such as federalism. The policentric model insists, however, that congressional enforcement of Rc is not itself a sufficient reason to render § 5 legislation unconstitutional as a violation of separation of powers."

Query: Under what circumstances should the Supreme Court's "legal" understanding of § 5 (or any other constitutional provision) be influenced by legislative interpretations?

3. Taking the Constitutional Away from the Courts?

Constitutional skepticism blossomed into an academic mini-movement to eliminate judicial review altogether. What a reversal of *Brown*! The antecedents to such an impulse lie in the nineteenth century, as revealed by the following excerpt.

James Bradley Thayer, *John Marshall*

103–04, 106, 107 (1901)

In his 1893 law review article, Thayer had propounded a "rule of administration" limiting judicial review to statutes that no reasonable person could consider consistent with the Constitution. Although the Supreme Court had followed his rule in *Plessy,* the Court violated it in other cases, impelling Thayer to offer this further argument in favor of judicial leniency when reviewing legislative decisions: "The legislatures are growing accustomed to this distrust [stimulated by activist judicial review] and more and more readily incline to justify it, and to shed the consideration of constitutional restraints,—

certainly as concerning the exact extent of these restrictions,—turning that subject over to the courts; and, what is worse, they insensibly fall into a habit of assuming that whatever they can constitutionally do they may do,—as if honor and fair dealing and common honesty were not relevant to their inquiries.

"The people, all this while, become careless as to whom they send to the legislature; too often they cheerfully vote for men whom they would not trust with an important private affair, and when these unfit persons are found to pass foolish and bad laws, and the courts step in and disregard them, the people are glad that these few wiser gentlemen on the bench are so ready to protect them against their more immediate representatives. * * *

" * * * [I]t should be remembered that the exercise of [judicial review], even when unavoidable, is always attended with a serious evil, namely, that the correction of legislative mistakes comes from the outside, and the people thus lose the political experience, and the moral education and stimulus that come from fighting the question out in the ordinary way, and correcting their own errors. * * *

"The tendency of a common and easy resort to this great function, now lamentably too common, is to dwarf the political capacity of the people, and to deaden its sense of moral responsibility. It is no light thing to do that."

Mark Tushnet, *Taking the Constitution Away from the Courts*

11–12, 182–83 (1999)

Professor Tushnet starts with a distinction between the *thin* Constitution and the "thick" (full) Constitution of 1789, as amended and interpreted. The idea originates in "an obscure note written by Abraham Lincoln, describing '[t]he Union and the Constitution' as 'the picture of silver,' the 'frame[ ],' around the 'apple of gold,' the principles of the Declaration of Independence: 'The picture was made for the apple—not the apple for the picture.' The project the Constitution established for the people of the United States, Lincoln believed, was the vindication of the Declaration's principles: the principle that all people were created equal, the principle that all had inalienable rights. This is the Thin Constitution. * * *

"Populist constitutional law vindicates the thin Constitution. [As] Lincoln knew, ordinary people could be committed to the thin Constitution in ways they could never be committed to the thick Constitution. And the thin Constitution is indeed admirable in ways the thick Constitution is not. The thin Constitution protects rights that it has taken centuries of struggle for people to appreciate as truly fundamental. Perhaps more important, the nation's commitment to the thin Constitution constitutes us as the people of the United States, and constituting a people is a morally worthy project."

So long as the Supreme Court is the primary (or exclusive) authority on what the Constitution means, the thin Constitution will always be subordinated to the thick (legalized) Constitution. Tushnet argues that progressives ought to support the return of constitutional discourse to "We the People" rather than "We the Court." Tushnet joins former Attorney General Meese in rejecting the doctrine of judicial supremacy suggested by dicta in *Cooper v. Aaron*; urges legislators and citizens to form their own constitutional conclusions independent of what the Supreme Court has said; recommends that the Constitution be amended to abrogate the Court's *Marbury* power of judicial review; and urges that constitutional law be reconceived as *populist*. Populist constitutionalism "treats constitutional law not as something in the hands of lawyers and judges but in the hands of the people themselves."

"Constitutional law creates the people of the United States *as a people* by providing a narrative that connects us to everyone who preceded us." Its project would take the Declaration of Independence, the Preamble to the Constitution, and the great constitutional principles such as equality and free speech (the thin Constitution) and elaborate upon them by application to the problems facing the modern regulatory state. These days, such problems include the validity of the federal government's indefinite detention of suspected terrorists, the legitimacy of race- or sex-based affirmative action, and the proper scope of state regulation of a woman's pregnancy. "One advantage of the thin Constitution is that it leaves a wide range [of fundamental issues] open for resolution through principled political discussions—principled because they are oriented toward the Declaration's principles. In this way the thin Constitution may constitute us as a people."

NOTE ON TAKING THE CONSTITUTION AWAY FROM THE COURTS

Professor Tushnet's idea has had a receptive audience among law professors[123] and, ironically, almost no interest among We the People! Contrary to Tushnet, it is not clear that the Court has taken the Constitution away from We the People.

Conistent with Professor Bell's interest convergence theory, political scientists have found that Supreme Court dispositions in important constitutional decisions typically track public opinion.[124] There is no perfect convergence of course. Sometimes, as with the famous *Miranda* warning, the Court is "ahead" of and shapes public opinion; sometimes, as in the "homosexual sodomy" cases, the Court lags somewhat behind public opinion; in a majority of constitutional cases, especially those involving technical issues such as full faith and credit for interstate judgments, there is no strong public

---

[123] E.g., Larry Kramer, *The People Themselves: Popular Constitutionalism and Judicial Review* (2004) (urging drastic curtailment of judicial review); Jeremy Waldron, *Law and Disagreement* (1999) (abolition); Adrian Vermeule, *Judging Under Uncertainty: An Institutional Theory of Legal Interpretation* (2006) (drastic curtailment).

[124] Nathan Persily, Jack Citrin & Patrick Egan, *Public Opinion and Constitutional Controversy* (2008); William Mishler & Reginald S. Sheehan, *The Supreme Court as a Countermajoritarian Institution? The Impact of Public Opinion on Supreme Court Opinions*, 87 Am. Pol. Sci. Rev. 87 (1993). For a recent exploration of our constitutional history in light of this phenomenon, see Barry Friedman, *The Will of the People: How Public Opinion Has Influenced the Supreme Court and Shaped the Meaning of the Constitution* (2009).

opinion. But there is usually rough parallelism: Constitutional law, as announced by the Supreme Court, almost never trumps entrenched constitutional arrangements, rarely ventures beyond public consensus, and seldom corrects "injustices" that the political system wants to preserve. See Persily et al., *Public Opinion and Constitutional Controversy* (documenting this convergence across an impressive range of issues). If the Supreme Court is already tracking public opinion, is there a need for Tushnet's proposal?

On the other hand, is it really the case that the Court's activism is usually "wrong" from a progressive point of view? In *Brown*, the Court not only contributed mightily to public deliberations about the injustice of racial segregation, but also had an important political effect: by *reversing the burden of inertia*, the Court forced the political system to deal with an issue it had been avoiding for decades.[125] Another civic republican virtue of judicial review, even by conservative judges, is that it provides a portal into the governance structure for groups excluded from local politics (as African Americans were in the South) and unable to get the attention of Congress.

Imagine what American government, politics, and constitutional law would be like without the Supreme Court as the arbiter. You need to perform this thought experiment *now*, because after a few chapters of study from this book, you will find it harder to imagine the Constitution *without* the Court. In conducting such a thought experiment, you might start with the Constitution of Guns.

PROBLEM 2-4:
THE CONSTITUTIONALITY OF GUN CONTROL LAWS: AN EXERCISE IN CONSTITUTIONAL METHODOLOGY

In 2008, the District of Columbia required a license for anyone to own a handgun, and other District regulations made it virtually impossible to procure a license for most ordinary residents and homeowners. Moreover, the lawful owner of a firearm was required to keep his weapon "unloaded and disassembled or bound by a trigger lock or similar device" unless it was kept at his place of business or being used for lawful recreational purposes. See D.C. Code § 7–2507.02. Thus, even if registered, a handgun stored at home could not be immediately operational (as by children).

Police officer Dick Heller felt insecure in his own home because he could not have and use his (police-issued) weapon there. Heller sued the District to overturn its regulation as a violation of his Second Amendment right as a law-abiding citizen to possess a firearm in his own home for self-defense. A majority of the Supreme Court, in an opinion by Justice Scalia, agreed with this argument. *District of Columbia v. Heller*, 554 U.S. 570 (2008), followed and applied to the states in *McDonald v. City of Chicago*, 561 U.S. 742 (2010). Writing for four dissenters, Justice Stevens argued that the Second

---

[125] On the important role of courts in "reversing the burden of inertia," see Eskridge & Ferejohn, *Republic of Statutes*, ch. 8 & postscript.

Amendment's protection was limited to Heller's participation in a citizen militia and did not extend to his home use of a firearm.

Try to set aside your own political views and analyze this constitutional issue in light of the following evidence. Is all of this evidence relevant? If not, what would you consider? What relevant evidence ought to be most weighty? And how does the evidence cut? Purely as a matter of constitutional *law,* how would you vote?

(a) *Constitutional Text and Structure.* The Second Amendment says: "A well regulated Militia, being necessary to the security of a free State, *the right of the people to keep and bear Arms, shall not be infringed.*" The italicized portion is the operative clause; the other portion is the prefatory clause. No other rights-conferring provision of the Constitution has this structure. Justice Scalia read the operative clause to be broader than the prefatory clause and read it liberally. Justice Stevens read the operative clause to be limited to the concerns of the prefatory clause. Which is more linguistically sound? Which is better linked to the meaning of the terms the framers used?

The 1773 edition of Samuel Johnson's *Dictionary of the English Language* (4th ed.) defined *arms* as "weapons of offence, or armour of defence." Accord, Noah Webster, *American Dictionary of the English Language* (1828). "By *arms,* we understand those instruments of offence generally made use of in war; such as firearms, swords, & c." 1 J. Trusler, *The Distinction Between Words Esteemed Synonymous in the English Language* 37 (1794). The same dictionaries defined *keep* as "hav[ing] in custody" and *bear* as "to carry." *Bear arms* comes from the Latin *arma ferre,* which means "to bear [*ferre*] war equipment [*arma*]." Brief for Professors of Linguistics and English as *Amici Curiae,* at 19, *Heller.* Virginia's military law directed that "every one of the said officers, non-commissioned officers, and privates, shall constantly *keep* the aforesaid arms, accoutrements, and ammunition, ready to be produced whenever called for by his commanding officer." Act for Regulating and Disciplining the Militia, 1785 Va. Acts ch. 1, § 3.

As for the prefatory clause, *militia* in the eighteenth century meant both the state-organized militia, but also "all males physically capable of acting in concert for the common defense." *United States v. Miller,* 307 U.S. 174, 179 (1939). The "security of a Free state" referred to the notion that a citizen "militia," i.e., an armed populace, "is the natural defence of a free country." Joseph Story, *Commentaries on the Constitution of the United States* § 189 (4th ed. 1873).

Justice Scalia said that the ordinary linguistic meaning of the Second Amendment's operative clause is the regular law-abiding citizen's right to possess and deploy weapons (especially firearms). Justice Stevens said the ordinary meaning is the right of the citizen to maintain and bear weapons in the context of his service to the militia. Like most historical linguists, Justice Stevens treated "keep and bear arms" as a phrase that had an established term of art meaning in 1791, namely, readiness to mobilize as part of the militia.

(b) *Background, Drafting, Ratification History, and Original Purpose.* Between the Restoration (1661) and the Glorious Revolution (1688), the Stuart Kings suppressed dissent, in part by disarming opponents of their regime and by deploying militias loyal to them. See Joyce Lee Malcolm, *To Keep and Bear Arms: The Origins of an American Right* 103–06 (1994). After King James II was deposed, the Parliament secured an assurance from the new monarchs, William of Orange and Mary Stuart, in the Declaration of Right (codified as the English Bill of Rights): "That the subjects which are Protestants may have arms for their defense suitable to their conditions and as allowed by law." 1 W. & M., c. 2, § 7, in 3 Eng. Stat. at Large 441 (1689). Blackstone considered "the right of having and using arms for self-preservation and defence" in the Bill of Rights to be one of the fundamental rights of Englishmen. *Commentaries on the Laws of England* vol. 1, at 139–40 (1765); see also Thomas Hobbes, *Leviathan* (1651), who argued for a retained right of self-defense as instinct in the social contract.

One of the American grievances against George III was his effort to disarm the colonists. "It is a natural right which the people have reserved to themselves, confirmed by the Bill of Rights, to keep arms for their own defence." *N.Y. Journal*, Supp. 1, Apr. 13, 1769. It is not clear how widely held a view this was, but in the wake of the Revolution several state constitutions had constitutional protections for citizens to keep and bear arms. Pennsylvania's Declaration of Rights (1776) said, in § XIII: "That the people have a right to bear arms for the defence of themselves and the state." North Carolina's Declaration of Rights (1776), § XVII, stated: "That the people have a right to bear arms, for the defence of the State." The Massachusetts Constitution (1780), First Part, Art. XVII, said: "The people have a right to keep and to bear arms for the common defence."

The Constitution presented for ratification gave Congress and the President authority over the national armed forces and the authority to call forth the militia in Article I, § 8, clause 16; the same clause vested the training of the militia with the states. During ratification, most states expressed concern about the strong national authority over armed citizens, and several states proposed (nonbinding) amendments to the document they ratified. George Mason expressed this objection: "The militia may be here destroyed by that method which has been practiced in other parts of the world before; that is, by rendering them useless—by disarming them. Under various pretences, Congress may neglect to provide for arming and disciplining the militia; and the state governments cannot do it, for Congress has the exclusive right to arm them."

Virginia ratified over Mason's objection but included the following proposals for amending the Constitution (*Elliott's Debates* 659):

> 17th, That the people have a right to keep and bear arms; that a well regulated Militia composed of the body of the people trained to arms is the proper, natural and safe defence of a free State. That standing armies are dangerous to liberty, and therefore ought to be avoided,

as far as the circumstances and protection of the Community will admit; and that in all cases the military should be under strict subordination to and be governed by the civil power.

19th. That any person religiously scrupulous of bearing arms ought to be exempted, upon payment of an equivalent to employ another to bear arms in his stead.

North Carolina adopted exactly the same language, and New York similar language ("keep and bear arms") in proposing amendments after ratifying. Similar concerns were expressed in amendments proposed by New Hampshire and Massachusetts; Maryland rejected similar amendments, as did Pennsylvania.

The drafter of the Bill of Rights, James Madison was aware of these amendments and was intimately familiar with the Virginia debates and the amendment proposed there. His initial draft of what became the Second Amendment was as follows: "The right of the people to keep and bear arms shall not be infringed; a well armed, and well regulated militia being the best security of a free country; but no person religiously scrupulous of bearing arms, shall be compelled to render military service in person." *The Complete Bill of Rights: The Drafts, Debates, Sources, and Origins* 183 (Neil H. Cogan ed. 1997). Madison later dropped the last clause and simplified the language into the Second Amendment now in the Constitution.

Is the drafting history relevant to determining original meaning? Does it make a difference that we do not know why Madison rewrote the amendment the way he did? Are the Virginia and other proposed amendments relevant? If so, how do they cut? Based on the foregoing materials, how would you view the purpose of the amendment? How broad?

(c) *Contemporaneous Construction*. There is much debate in *Heller* regarding the understanding of contemporaries. Should this be relevant? Here are some of the materials bruited about by the Justices.

St. George Tucker's American edition of Blackstone's *Commentaries* (1803) included as Note "D" Tucker's "View of the Constitution of the United States." As to the Second Amendment, Tucker (a prominent Anti-Federalist) said: "This may be considered as the true palladium of liberty. . . . The right to self-defence is the first law of nature: in most governments it has been the study of rulers to confine the right within the narrowest limits possible. Wherever standing armies are kept up, and the right of the people to keep and bear arms is, under any colour or pretext whatsoever, prohibited, liberty, if not already annihilated, is on the brink of destruction." Vol. 1, App. 300. Tucker believed that the English game laws had abridged the right by prohibiting "keeping a gun or other engine for the destruction of game." *Id.* He grouped the Second Amendment right with some of the individual rights included in the First Amendment and enforceable through judicial review. *Id.,* App. 357.

Originally published in 1833, Justice Joseph Story's *Commentaries* include discussion of the Second Amendment. In § 189, Story equated the

Second Amendment with the arms provision in the English Declaration (Bill) of Rights. The most relevant portion is worth extensive quotation:

> The importance of [the Second Amendment] will scarcely be doubted by any persons who have duly reflected upon the subject. The militia is the natural defence of a free country against sudden foreign invasions, domestic insurrections, and domestic usurpations of power by rulers. It is against sound policy for a free people to keep up large military establishments and standing armies in time of peace, both from the enormous expenses with which they are attended and the facile means which they afford to ambitious and unprincipled rulers to subvert the government, or trample upon the rights of the people. The right of the citizens to keep and bear arms has justly been considered as the palladium of the liberties of a republic, since it offers a strong moral check against the usurpation and arbitrary power of rulers, and will generally, even if these are successful in the first instance, enable the people to resist and triumph over them. And yet, though this truth would seem so clear, and the importance of a well-regulated militia would seem so undeniable, it cannot be disguised that, among the American people, there is a growing indifference to any system of militia discipline, and a strong disposition, from a sense of its burdens, to be rid of all regulations. How it is practicable to keep the people duly armed without some organization, it is difficult to see. There is certainly no small danger that indifference may lead to disgust, and disgust to contempt; and thus gradually undermine all the protection intended by the clause of our national bill of rights.

Consider a different view: "The provision of the constitution, declaring the right of the people to keep and bear arms, & c. was probably intended to apply to the right of the people to bear arms for such [militia-related] purposes only, and not to prevent congress or the legislatures of the different states from enacting laws to prevent the citizens from always going armed. A different construction however has been given to it." Benjamin L. Oliver, *The Rights of an American Citizen* 177 (1832).

(d) *Post-Enactment Understanding and History.* Recall that the challengers in *Brown*, and ultimately the Court itself, argued that whatever ambiguities there might have been at the time of the Fourteenth Amendment's framing, they had disappeared by 1954. One might argue that ambiguities as to the ambit of the Second Amendment might be clarified by practice after 1791 (when the amendment was adopted). Under almost all theories of constitutional interpretation, this kind of evidence is much weaker than constitutional text, original (and contemporaneous) understanding and purpose, and judicial precedent. Some theories would discount the following information entirely.

Between 1789 and 1820, nine States adopted Second Amendment analogues. Four (Kentucky, Ohio, Indiana, and Missouri) recognized the right of the people to "bear arms in defence of themselves and the State." Another three (Mississippi, Connecticut, and Alabama) found that each citizen has the "right to bear arms in defence of himself and the State." Two (Tennessee and Maine) followed the "common defence" language of the 1780 Massachusetts Constitution.

A number of state courts gave federal or state constitutional protections for the right to bear arms a broad reading in the nineteenth century. In *Nunn v. State*, 1 Ga. 243, 251 (1846), the Georgia Supreme Court invalidated a state ban on open carrying of pistols based upon the defendant's Second Amendment "*natural* right of self-defence." Consider the court's broad rhetoric:

> The right of the whole people, old and young, men, women and boys, and not militia only, to keep and bear *arms* of every description, and not *such* merely as are used by the *militia*, shall not be *infringed*, curtailed, or broken in upon, in the smallest degree; and all this for the important end to be attained: the rearing up and qualifying a well-regulated militia, so vitally necessary to the security of a free State. Our opinion is, that any law, State or Federal, is repugnant to the Constitution, and void, which contravenes this *right*, originally belonging to our forefathers, trampled under foot by Charles I. and his two wicked sons and successors, re-established by the revolution of 1688, conveyed to this land of liberty by the colonists, and finally incorporated conspicuously in our own Magna Charta!

Accord, *State v. Chandler*, 5 La. Ann. 489, 490 (La. 1850) (right of citizens to carry arms openly). On the other hand, the Tennessee Supreme Court in *Aymette v. State*, 21 Tenn. 154 (1840), held that the state constitutional guarantee of the right to "bear" arms did not prohibit the banning of concealed weapons. The court read that right to refer only to "protect[ion of] the public liberty" and "keep[ing] in awe those in power."

After the Civil War, advocates for rights of the freed slaves assumed broad readings of the Second Amendment when they cited state restrictions on gun use by people of color as an example of southern deprivation of constitutional liberties. See Stephen Halbrook, *Freedman, the Fourteenth Amendment, and the Right to Bear Arms, 1866–1876* (1998). Section 14 of the Freedmen's Bureau Act on July 16, 1866, 14 Stat. at 176–77, said this:

> [T]he right ... to have full and equal benefit of all laws and proceedings concerning personal liberty, personal security, and the acquisition, enjoyment, and disposition of estate, real and personal, including the constitutional right to bear arms, shall be secured to and enjoyed by all the citizens ... without respect to race or color, or previous condition of slavery. . . .

It was assumed during congressional debate that the founding generation "were for every man bearing his arms about him and keeping them in his house, his castle, for his own defense." Cong. Globe, 39th Cong., 1st Sess., 362, 371 (1866) (Sen. Davis, an opponent of the 1866 Act).

In debating the Fourteenth Amendment, Congress referred to the right to keep and bear arms as a fundamental right protected by the amendment against state infringement. Senator Samuel Pomeroy described as fundamental a man's "right to bear arms for the defense of himself and family and his homestead. And if the cabin door of the freedman is broken open and the intruder enters for purposes as vile as were known to slavery, then should a well-loaded musket be in the hand of the occupant to send the polluted wretch to another world, where his wretchedness will forever remain complete." 39th Cong. Glob 1182 (1867).

Thomas Cooley, *General Principles of Constitutional Law* 271 (1880) (leading constitutional law treatise), described the Second Amendment:

> The meaning of the provision undoubtedly is, that the people, from whom the militia must be taken, shall have the right to keep and bear arms; and they need no permission or regulation of law for the purpose. But this enables government to have a well-regulated militia; for to bear arms implies something more than the mere keeping; it implies the learning to handle and use them in a way that makes those who keep them ready for their efficient use; in other words, it implies the right to meet for voluntary discipline in arms, observing in doing so the laws of public order.

Other nineteenth century commentators generally followed Cooley, but by the twentieth century the Second Amendment (like the state militias) seemed to recede in debates about public policy and constitutional law.

The first two federal laws directly restricting civilian use and possession of firearms—the 1927 Act prohibiting mail delivery of "pistols, revolvers, and other firearms capable of being concealed on the person," Ch. 75, 44 Stat. 1059, and the 1934 Act prohibiting the possession of sawed-off shotguns and machine guns—were enacted over minor Second Amendment objections dismissed by legislators who participated in the debates. After the New Deal, Congress, state legislatures, and city councils have adopted hundreds of gun control laws. In adopting gun control laws, however, Congress has *always* steered clear of or exempted homeowners' use of guns for self-defense. See 27 Stat. 116 (1892) (crime to carry concealed pistol in the District except in one's place of business or "dwelling house"); Pub. L. No. 275, § 4, 47 Stat. 650, 651 (1932) (same); Pub. L. No. 274, 55 Stat. 742 (1941) (eve-of-war property requisition law, with prominent exception disallowing requisitioning of guns held for one's "personal use or sport"); Pub. L. No. 90–618, § 101, 82 Stat. 1213 (1968) (similar exclusion from the leading gun control statute); Pub. L. No. 99–308, 100 Stat. 449 (1986) (amending 1968 law to further protect people's Second Amendment rights).[126]

(e) *Precedent and Stare Decisis.* In terms of authority, Supreme Court precedent is second only to constitutional text as a matter of legal authority.

---

[126] Stephen Halbrook, *Congress Interprets the Second Amendment,* 62 Tenn. L. Rev. 597 (1995); Brief for *Amici Curiae* 55 Members of the U.S. Senate, the President of the U.S. Senate, and 250 Members of the U.S. House of Representatives in Support of Respondent, *District of Columbia v. Heller* (Supreme Court, Docket No. 07–290), authored by Halbrook.

We treat this evidence here because that's how it best fits chronologically. In *United States v. Cruikshank*, 92 U. S. 542 (1876), the Court sustained a challenge to convictions under the Enforcement Act of 1870 for conspiring to deprive any individual of "any right or privilege granted or secured to him by the constitution or laws of the United States." Counts 2 and 10 of the indictment related to defendants' alleged efforts to restrict the lawful use of weapons by other citizens; the Court declined to view this activity by the defendants as raising a constitutional concern:

> The right there specified [in the indictment] is that of "bearing arms for a lawful purpose." This is not a right granted by the Constitution. Neither is it in any manner dependent on that instrument for its existence. The second amendment declares that it shall not be infringed; but this, as has been seen, means no more than that it shall not be infringed by Congress. This is one of the amendments that has no other effect than to restrict the powers of the national government.

Other nineteenth century Supreme Court cases took a narrow view of the Second Amendment, but none was primarily concerned with that amendment. E.g., *Presser v. Illinois,* 116 U.S. 252 (1886) (the right to keep and bear arms was not violated by a law that forbade "bodies of men to associate together as military organizations, or to drill or parade with arms in cities and towns unless authorized by law").

In *United States v. Miller*, 307 U.S. 174 (1939), the Court upheld a conviction for transporting a double-barreled shotgun in violation of the National Firearms Act of 1934. Rejecting the defendant's Second Amendment argument, Justice McReynolds' opinion ruled that the amendment's operative clause had to be construed in light of the prefatory clause. This was fatal for the defendant's individual rights claim:

> In the absence of any evidence tending to show that possession or use of a 'shotgun having a barrel of less than eighteen inches in length' at this time has some reasonable relationship to the preservation or efficiency of a well regulated militia, we cannot say that the Second Amendment guarantees the right to keep and bear such an instrument. Certainly it is not within judicial notice that this weapon is any part of the ordinary military equipment or that its use could contribute to the common defense. (307 U.S. at 178.)

Miller was the last Supreme Court decision directly addressing individual rights claims under the Second Amendment, and that precedent has been treated as binding interpretation. E.g., *Lewis v. United States*, 445 U.S. 55, 65–66 n.8 (1980) (following *Miller* for the proposition that the Second Amendment guarantees no right to keep and bear a firearm that does not have "some reasonable relationship to the preservation or efficiency of a well regulated militia"). Should *Miller* be overruled? If you agree with Justice Scalia in *Heller,* is there another way to handle *Miller*, rather than overruling the precedent?

(f) *Norms*. Norms come into play at two points: Is there a constitutional interest in possessing handguns in your home, or elsewhere? If so, what state interests justify regulation of guns, and what kinds of regulations are constitutionally permissible?

As to the first issue, there has been a normative shift in the United States as the result of a social movement very different from the civil rights movement that brought *Brown* and other race discrimination cases to the Supreme Court. Represented most effectively in the National Rifle Association (NRA), the right to own and use guns has gained significant traction in the United States in the last generation—at the same time women's rights, gay rights, and disability rights movements have also been successful in changing public opinion as to a broad range of issues. In the middle of the New Deal, when gun control was widely accepted, a Second Amendment right outside the militia context was largely unthinkable to conservative as well as progressive judges—but by 2008 all nine Justices agreed that there is an individual right to gun ownership, and the main debate among the Justices were how broadly to define that right. Justice Scalia did not believe the right extended to "dangerous and unusual weapons" or to weapons used for illegal or harmful purposes.

All nine Justices also accepted the New Deal norm that the public interest can justify extensive state regulation of handguns. Justice Scalia explicitly said that he would not question the constitutionality of "longstanding prohibitions on the possession of firearms by felons and the mentally ill, or laws forbidding the carrying of firearms in sensitive places such as schools and government buildings, or laws imposing conditions and qualifications on the commercial sale of arms." He did not take a clear position on what level of scrutiny he would apply to laws regulating handguns used outside the home or other than for self-defense. Cf. Adam Winkler, *Scrutinizing the Second Amendment,* 105 Mich. L. Rev. 683, 687, 716–718 (2007) (describing hundreds of gun-law decisions issued in the last half-century by supreme courts in 42 states, which courts with "surprisingly little variation" have adopted a standard more deferential than strict scrutiny).

Justice Breyer (in a separate dissent) would have gone considerably further, based in part on founding era precedent. A 1783 Massachusetts law forbade the residents of Boston to "take into" or "receive into" "any Dwelling House, Stable, Barn, Out-house, Ware-house, Store, Shop or other Building" loaded firearms, and permitted the seizure of any loaded firearms that "shall be found" there. Act of Mar. 1, 1783, ch. 13, 1783 Mass. Acts p. 218. Notwithstanding that state's constitutional protection for firearm possession, this statute was similar to the District of Columbia law banning loaded firearms in one's home.

Justice Breyer had a broader concern. The D.C. Council found in 1976 that the proliferation of guns in the District contributed directly to increased levels of violence and death and further concluded that a ban on private possession of firearms was the best way of dealing with this problem of social and personal security. Post-1976 evidence suggests uncertainty whether a firearm ban serves this purpose (especially because Virginia and Maryland, bordering the District, allow gun ownership). Some studies suggest the ban has had no effect, others say that it has had some retarding effect. Why not allow legislatures to experiment in this way, and see over the longer term what works? Is it not irresponsible "judicial activism" to overturn the District's relatively far-reaching law, based upon speculative original meaning evidence?

Theoretical Queries. (1) *Original Meaning.* Which interpretation best reflects "original constitutional meaning," as applied to the District's ban of handguns in the home for self-defense? The constitutional text addresses this issue more specifically than we usually find in individual rights cases: At what level of generality should the historical materials be understood? That is, should the interpretive focus be on the broad constitutional policy embodied in the Second Amendment? Or is there an unambiguous plain meaning of the amendment as applied to the District's law? What historical context is legally relevant to the original meaning inquiry? Are the nineteenth century legal commentaries relevant to an inquiry into original meaning?

Jot down your thoughts now, and then consult the Justices' debate over original meaning in *Heller* and (later) *McDonald.* Do the original materials prevent the Justices from reading their own values into the Constitution? Is *Heller* an example of Jack Balkin's *Living Originalism*? If so, does *Heller* illustrate the virtues of *Living Originalism*? Or its vices? For critiques of *Heller* as a violation of the rule of law, see Richard A. Posner, *In Defense of Looseness: The Supreme Court and Gun Control,* The New Republic, Aug. 27, 2008 (denouncing the Court's opinion as exactly the opposite of what original meaning would have dictated); J. Harvie Wilkinson III, *Of Guns, Abortion, and the Unraveling Rule of Law,* 95 Va. L. Rev. 253 (2009) (raising concerns that the Court was not evaluating the legal evidence in a neutral manner).

(2) *Common Law, Burkean Constitutionalism.* Assume that Professor Ernest Young decides to write a law review article explaining how the Supreme Court should resolve the constitutional issue in *Heller*—and how the majority should explain their reasons. Provide a roadmap for him to follow, given his Burkean pragmatism. Does the case-by-case approach of the common law provide a useful way of approaching an emotional issue (gun control) such as this one? Should a Burkean pragmatist consider the constitutional deliberations of Congress, starting with its debates about the protections of the proposed Fourteenth Amendment (see Justice Alito's plurality opinion in *McDonald*) and continuing through the New Deal and afterwards? See William N. Eskridge Jr., *Sodomy and Guns: Tradition as Democratic Deliberation and Constitutional Interpretation,* 32 Harv. J.L. & Pol'y 193 (2009) (arguing that the legislative debates normatively drove the majority's analysis in *Heller*).

(3) *Popular and Polycentric Constitutionalism.* One might read *Heller* as an example of Professor Tushnet's thesis, that the conservative Supreme Court is taking constitutional discourse away from We the People by barring the kind of gun control experiment reflected in the District's broad law. Cf. Mark V. Tushnet, *Out of Range: Why the Constitution Can't End the Battle over Guns*

(2007). But the narrowness of the Court's holding better fits with Professor Persily's argument that the Court rarely strays far from popular opinion: Americans have a strong right to keep firearms to protect their families within their own homes, a highly popular privacy-based right, but nothing in *Heller* says that the District or the United States cannot regulate firearms in ways that enjoy much greater popular support—such as concealed weapons bans, background checks for firearm sales, and rules barring gun possession by convicted felons, minors, and persons with mental disabilities. See, e.g., *Kachalsky v. County of Westchester,* 701 F.3d 81 (2d Cir. 2012) (upholding against Second Amendment attack, a law severely restricting rights to carry weapons in public).

Heller is also an example of the influence of social movements on constitutional law. This issue would never have reached the Supreme Court absent the gun rights social movement, spearheaded by the NRA. Note the ironic juxtaposition of musty-sounding original meaning jurisprudence, with a modern and highly dynamic understanding of gun-owners rights sponsored by the NRA. See Reva Siegel, *Dead or Alive: Originalism as Popular Constitutionalism in* Heller, 122 Harv. L. Rev. 191 (2008).

Professors Eskridge and Ferejohn argue that *Heller* is an example of polycentric constitutionalism, where congressional deliberation about public values and small "c" constitutional rights framed the judicial deliberations and emboldened the majority Justices to guarantee rights to home use of guns— but without questioning federal or state regulations of assault weapons and other dangerous firearms, regulations of the sale of firearms, requirements that owners register their guns, and bans on public carrying of weapons (concealed or otherwise). Eskridge & Ferejohn, *Republic of Statutes,* 438–43. By crafting an "original meaning" constitutional decision that echoed repeated congressional support for home use of firearms, the Court confirmed its dynamic role as the Constitution's authoritative interpreter—but without risking popular backlash and media attention to judicial "usurpation" along the lines that are the basis for Tushnet's complaint.

Eskridge and Ferejohn close their discussion of *Heller* with the Court's missed Bickelian opportunity to deploy the congressional deliberations in a way that would not have closed off political experimentation for this issue. In 1906, Congress authorized the District to enact "all such usual and reasonable police regulations [as the District] may deem necessary for the regulation of firearms." 34 Stat. 808 (1906). In light of twentieth-century congressional support for exempting home use of firearms from strong regulatory laws, the Court could easily—and lawfully—have interpreted the 1906 statute to bar the District's intrusive regulation. See Eskridge & Ferejohn, *Republic of Statutes,* 464. Such a ruling would have had the virtue of announcing a constitutional value—but without terminating political debate and experimentation on this issue. If the Court was right about the meaning of the Second Amendment, was there a compelling reason to avoid a broad ruling, however?

CHAPTER 3

THE CONSTITUTION AND RACIAL DISCRIMINATION

■ ■ ■

Since *Brown*, the Court has developed an elaborate approach to resolving racial discrimination cases. Section 1 of this chapter considers judicial review of statutes that disproportionally disadvantage racial minorities. Section 1 first analyzes current doctrine concerning such statutes that on their face take race into account, and then turns to the different approach taken to facially neutral statutes. Section 2 considers the important limitation upon federal power to outlaw racial discrimination imposed by the state action doctrine, which restricts the coverage of the Equal Protection Clause to governmental conduct rather than private behavior. In Section 3, we turn to how "affirmative action"—the use of a racial classification to benefit historically disadvantaged minorities—is scrutinized. By way of introduction, consider three sets of issues.

1. *Race and the Equal Protection Clause.* The Equal Protection Clause does not mention racial discrimination. Its context and history, however, establish that it was intended to target discrimination against African Americans. For example, the Court in *Strauder v. West Virginia*, 100 U.S. 303 (1879), held that the state's exclusion of African-American men from juries violated the equal protection of the laws (see Chapter 2, § 1A). One way to understand the result in *Brown* is that the states' segregation had to overcome a strong presumption against distinctions grounded upon race, and the states never overcame that presumption. (This may seem more persuasive than Chief Justice Warren's reliance on social science studies.)

Given the origins of the Equal Protection Clause, should it only be concerned with racial discrimination against African Americans? In *The Slaughter House Cases*, 83 U.S. (16 Wall.) 36 (1872), the Court said that it "doubt[ed] very much whether any action of a state not directed by way of discrimination against the negroes as a class, or on account of their race, will ever be held to come within the purview of this provision." Yet in 1886, in *Yick Wo v. Hopkins* (§ 1B of this chapter), the Supreme Court forcefully applied the Equal Protection Clause to strike down municipal practices discriminating against citizens of China living in the United States.

Indeed, current doctrine concerning discrimination against African Americans is derived in part from two cases involving Asian Americans. During World War II, the federal government forcibly evacuated from the West Coast residents of Japanese ancestry, including those who were American citizens. (Earl Warren, later the Chief Justice, was then Governor of California and enthusiastically helped implement this program.) *Hirabayashi v. United States*, 320 U.S. 81 (1943), unanimously upheld the criminal conviction of an American citizen for refusing to obey a curfew order requiring all persons of Japanese ancestry to remain in their homes from 8:00 p.m. to 6:00 a.m. daily. *Korematsu v. United States*, 323 U.S. 214 (1944), by a 6–3 vote, upheld the criminal conviction of an American citizen who refused to leave the West Coast and be relocated. The subjects of intense criticism to this day, *Hirabayashi* and *Korematsu* seem impossible to defend from the current perspective, for the government programs appear to have been based on racist notions about the lack of loyalty of citizens of Japanese extraction. (German-Americans and Italian-Americans were not subjected to such severe wartime treatment.)[1]

As the Court often does in uncomfortable cases, the opinions in *Hirabayashi* and *Korematsu* tried to put a good face on a bad situation. These cases articulated what has become known as the "strict scrutiny" approach to racial discrimination claims. *Hirabayashi* stated that "[d]istinctions between citizens solely because of their ancestry are by their very nature odious to a free people whose institutions are founded upon the doctrine of equality. * * * [R]acial discriminations are in most circumstances irrelevant and therefore prohibited[.]" *Korematsu* elaborated on this theme:

> [A]ll legal restrictions which curtail the civil rights of a single racial group are immediately suspect. That is not to say that all such restrictions are unconstitutional. It is to say that courts must subject them to the most rigid scrutiny. Pressing public necessity may sometimes justify the existence of such restrictions; racial antagonism never can.

Although *Brown* did not cite *Hirabayashi* or *Korematsu*, the strict scrutiny approach growing out of those cases has become the test for judging (and invalidating) statutes that disadvantage racial minorities through the overt use of racial criteria, as § 1A of this chapter explains.

---

[1] Indeed, in 1988 Congress enacted legislation apologizing for the relocation and internment program and awarding $20,000 to each surviving internee. See Civil Liberties Act of 1988, 50 U.S.C. app. § 1989b–4(a)(1) (1988). In 1987 a federal appeals court vacated Hirabayashi's conviction because of a showing that the federal government had concealed evidence supporting his claim that the prosecution was rooted in racial prejudice rather than military necessity. See *Hirabayashi v. United States*, 828 F.2d 591 (9th Cir. 1987). A few years earlier a district court had vacated Korematsu's conviction for the same reason. See *Korematsu v. United States*, 584 F. Supp. 1406 (N.D. Cal. 1984).

For many years, *Korematsu* has been consigned to the "anticanon" of reviled cases in constitutional law, along with *Dred Scott* and *Plessy*. See, e.g., Jamal Greene, *The Anticanon*, 125 Harv. L. Rev. 379 (2011). But it had never been formally overruled. In 2018, in the course of an opinion upholding the constitutionality of the Trump Administration's travel ban, Chief Justice Roberts said the following:

> Whatever rhetorical advantage the dissent may see in [analogizing the travel ban to the internment and evacuation policy], *Korematsu* has nothing to do with this case. The forcible relocation of U.S. citizens to concentration camps, solely and explicitly on the basis of race, is objectively unlawful and outside the scope of Presidential authority. But it is wholly inapt to liken that morally repugnant order to a facially neutral policy denying certain foreign nationals the privilege of admission. The entry suspension is an act that is well within executive authority and could have been taken by any other President—the only question is evaluating the actions of this particular President in promulgating an otherwise valid Proclamation.

> The dissent's reference to *Korematsu,* however, affords this Court the opportunity to make express what is already obvious: *Korematsu* was gravely wrong the day it was decided, has been overruled in the court of history, and—to be clear—"has no place in law under the Constitution." [*Korematsu*,] 323 U.S. at 248 (Jackson, J., dissenting).

Trump v. Hawaii, 138 S.Ct. 2392, 2423 (2018) (The travel ban and the decision upholding it are addressed in Chapter 8).

2.   *Why Race? What Is Race?* Perhaps the most curious thing about equal protection law is that it proceeds without any reflection on why it is focusing on certain categories, such as race. Biologists tell us that there is a human "race" and that otherwise the term is pretty much a social construction: Human genetic variability among the populations of Europe, Africa, and Asia is not significantly different from the ethnic variations within the so-called racial groups associated with each continent. See Anthony Appiah, *The Uncompleted Argument: DuBois and the Illusion of Race*, 12 Crit. Inquiry, Aut. 1985, at 21. In its *Statement on Race* published in 1998, the American Anthropological Association said this:

> In the United States both scholars and the general public have been conditioned to viewing human races as natural and separate divisions within the human species based on visible physical differences. With the vast expansion of scientific knowledge in this century, however, it has become clear that human populations are not unambiguous, clearly demarcated, biologically distinct groups. Evidence from the analysis of genetics

(e.g., DNA) indicates that most physical variation, about 94%, lies within so-called racial groups. Conventional geographic "racial" groupings differ from one another only in about 6% of their genes. This means that there is greater variation within "racial" groups than between them. In neighboring populations there is much overlapping of genes and their phenotypic (physical) expressions. Throughout history whenever different groups have come into contact, they have interbred. The continued sharing of genetic materials has maintained all of humankind as a single species.

Physical variations in any given trait tend to occur gradually rather than abruptly over geographic areas. And because physical traits are inherited independently of one another, knowing the range of one trait does not predict the presence of others. For example, skin color varies largely from light in the temperate areas in the north to dark in the tropical areas in the south; its intensity is not related to nose shape or hair texture. Dark skin may be associated with frizzy or kinky hair or curly or wavy or straight hair, all of which are found among different indigenous peoples in tropical regions. These facts render any attempt to establish lines of division among biological populations both arbitrary and subjective.

Historical research has shown that the idea of "race" has always carried more meanings than mere physical differences; indeed, physical variations in the human species have no meaning except the social ones that humans put on them. Today scholars in many fields argue that "race" as it is understood in the United States of America was a social mechanism invented during the 18th century to refer to those populations brought together in colonial America: the English and other European settlers, the conquered Indian peoples, and those peoples of Africa brought in to provide slave labor.

https://www.americananthro.org/ConnectWithAAA/Content.aspx?ItemNumber=2583.

Yet the history of the United States is a history of race obsession—as revealed not only in the institution of slavery and its repercussions, but also our country's treatment of Indians, the servitude of Asians in the West, and the reaction to a growing Latino population.[2]

---

[2] Theoretical analysis of the ways in which a dominant group uses labeling to create patterns of domination and marginalization can be found in Mary McIntosh, *The Homosexual Role*, 16 Soc. Probs. 182–93 (1968), reprinted in *The Forms of Desire: Sexual Orientation and the Social Constructionist Controversy* ch. 3 (Edward Stein ed. 1990), and Michel Foucault, *The Subject and Power*, in *Michel Foucault: Beyond Structuralism and Hermeneutics* 208 (Hebert Dreyfuss & Paul Rabinow eds. 1982).

The obsession with race has also generated peculiar constructions of racial and ethnic categories. People like Homer Plessy, who had but one African ancestor, were classified as "black" in American culture (and still are to some extent), even when they were genetically much more ethnically white. The dominant culture tends to classify anyone with a Spanish-sounding last name or with a Cuban, Mexican, Central American, Puerto Rican, or South American parent as "Hispanic," even though such a classification cuts across various ethnic and racial categories internalized by people in the various groups. One consequence of this complexity is that virtually any legal discussion about race and ethnicity will be oversimplified. We apologize in advance for our own sacrifices of precision to space considerations.

3.   *The Legacy of* Brown. This chapter considers the struggle over the meaning of *Brown v. Board of Education*, for African Americans in particular, but also for other racial and ethnic groups. As we discovered in Chapter 2, *Brown* is vulnerable to criticism, which became more intense as *Brown* was implemented (Chapter 2, § 2) and applied to other problems implicating race and ethnicity (this chapter). The struggle to understand *Brown* has focused on determining the meaning of the antidiscrimination principle.

Civil rights movement lawyers and their allies focused on the *anti-subordination* feature of equality and the *affirmative responsibilities* of the state.[3] For Thurgood Marshall and his colleagues at the Inc. Fund, the process initiated by *Brown* was a "Second Reconstruction," whereby the state would not only recognize the full citizenship of a class of Americans who had been treated as second-class citizens by the state and stigmatized by racism, but would also attack the vestiges and effects of apartheid through an affirmative remedial program. The first, a politics of recognition, yielded *Brown I* and entailed a campaign against state policies having racially discriminatory effects, including many criminal laws, the operation of the death penalty, some employment testing, and other requirements. The second, a politics of remediation, yielded *Brown II* and then *Green*—cases requiring the state to dismantle segregated schools and affirmatively integrate them. It entailed a campaign in favor of state policies restructuring race-tainted institutions, barring private parties from discriminating, and redistributing state resources toward people of color. Some of these policies, such as the remedial decree in *Swann* and affirmative action programs, were themselves race-based.

---

[3]   See, e.g., Derrick Bell, Jr., *Race, Racism, and American Law* (6th ed. 2008); Kimberlé Crenshaw, *Race, Reform, and Retrenchment: Transformation and Legitimation in Antidiscrimination Law*, 101 Harv. L. Rev. 1331 (1988); Ruth Colker, *Anti-Subordination Above All: Sex, Race, and Equal Protection*, 61 NYU L. Rev. 1003 (1986); Neil Gotanda, *A Critique of "Our Constitution Is Color-Blind,"* 44 Stan. L. Rev. 1 (1991).

Libertarians, including many who had opposed apartheid as well as (former) supporters of racial segregation, focused on the *basis for using a racial classification* and the *negative responsibilities* of the state.[4] The author of an important memorandum to Justice Frankfurter supporting the Inc. Fund in *Brown*, Alexander Bickel (whose later scholarly work is discussed throughout Chapter 2), personally agreed that race-based statutory classifications were suspect, mainly because they were not relevant to rational state policies; once the state purged itself of the baseless classifications, the equality principle was satisfied. The state had the freedom but not the responsibility to enact laws prohibiting discrimination by private persons and firms. But most libertarians were not willing to go along with eliminating rational state policies because of their race-based effects, and most were skeptical of new race-based policies seeking to remediate the legacy of apartheid. Indeed, Bickel believed that race-based affirmative action deepened the evil legacy of apartheid by reinforcing negative stereotypes about black people and fanning racist prejudices.[5]

Consider these competing visions of equality and state responsibility as you read the materials in this chapter. Consider also how the original meaning of the Fourteenth Amendment, the institutional limits of the judiciary (including Bickel's passive virtues), and precedents as well as common law values should influence the way these different visions were received by Supreme Court Justices who were neither strongly egalitarian nor absolutely libertarian in their approach to these issues.

SECTION 1. RACIAL CLASSIFICATIONS AFTER BROWN

A. FACIAL RACIAL CLASSIFICATIONS THAT DISADVANTAGE MINORITIES OR EVIDENCE RACIAL HOSTILITY

All statutes overtly classify people on the basis of one or more criteria. For example, driver's license regulations classify people on the basis of eyesight, written test results, and so on. In considering modern equal protection doctrine concerning racial discrimination, it is first necessary to distinguish statutes that *on their face* classify on the basis of race or national origin ("it shall be unlawful for any person of Japanese ancestry to fail to . . . ") and those that are facially neutral concerning race or

---

[4]   See, e.g., Thomas Sowell, *Civil Rights: Rhetoric or Reality?* (1984) (excerpted in § 3A of this chapter); Walter Williams, *The State Against Blacks* (1982); Jim Chen, *Diversity and Damnation*, 43 UCLA L. Rev. 1839 (1996); Charles Fried, Metro Broadcasting v. FCC: *Two Concepts of Equality*, 104 Harv. L. Rev. 107 (1990).

[5]   See Brief of the Anti-Defamation League of B'nai B'rith *Amicus Curiae*, *DeFunis v. Odegaard* (U.S. Supreme Court, No. 73–235) (*amicus* brief filed by Bickel and Philip Kurland in Supreme Court's first constitutional affirmative action case).

national origin ("it shall be unlawful for any person to assist a country at war with the United States by . . . "). The governmental orders attacked in *Korematsu* and *Hirabayashi* contained facial national-origin classifications; the school segregation statutes in *Brown* contained facial racial classifications.

The facial classifications in *Korematsu* and *Hirabayashi* disadvantaged a national-origin minority. *Brown*, too, fits this pattern of facial classification and selective disadvantage once the Court accepted the proposition that segregated public schools are inherently unequal and therefore selectively harmful to African Americans. Following *Brown*, the Court, through *per curiam* summary orders without accompanying opinions, applied the antidiscrimination principle to outlaw segregation in other public facilities.[6]

In the 1960s, the Court began facing a somewhat different problem with statutes containing facial racial classifications. Consider *Anderson v. Martin*, 375 U.S. 399 (1964), in which the Court struck down a Louisiana statute that required that election ballots indicate the race of the candidates. The statute applied equally to all candidates, white and non-white alike, and thus was not like the Japanese relocation and curfew orders. Nonetheless, are there arguments flowing from *Brown* that could justify invalidating the law? Similarly, in *McLaughlin v. Florida*, 379 U.S. 184 (1964), the Court struck down a statute prohibiting an unmarried interracial couple from "habitually liv[ing] in and occupy[ing] in the nighttime the same room." The Court noted that this behavior was not a crime if engaged in by a man and woman of the same race. Finally, consider *Loving v. Virginia* in this light.

LOVING V. VIRGINIA

388 U.S. 1, 87 S.Ct. 1817, 18 L.Ed.2d 1010 (1967)

CHIEF JUSTICE WARREN delivered the opinion of the Court.

[In 1958, an African-American woman and a white man, both residents of Virginia, got married in the District of Columbia. Upon returning to Virginia and making their home there, they were prosecuted for violating the state antimiscegenation law. After they pleaded guilty in 1959, the Virginia trial judge imposed a one-year jail sentence, but suspended it for 25 years on condition that the Lovings leave Virginia and not return together for 25 years. The state courts later denied the Lovings' motion to

---

[6]   See *Schiro v. Bynum*, 375 U.S. 395 (1964) (municipal auditorium); *New Orleans City Park Improvement Ass'n v. Detiege*, 358 U.S. 54 (1958) (municipal golf course and parks); *Gayle v. Browder*, 352 U.S. 903 (1956) (city buses); *Holmes v. Atlanta*, 350 U.S. 879 (1955) (municipal golf course); *Mayor & City Council of Baltimore City v. Dawson*, 350 U.S. 877 (1955) (public bathhouses and beaches).

vacate the conviction and sentence on the ground that the antimiscegenation law was unconstitutional.]

Virginia is now one of 16 States which prohibit and punish marriages on the basis of racial classifications.[5] Penalties for miscegenation arose as an incident to slavery and have been common in Virginia since the colonial period. The present statutory scheme dates from the adoption of the Racial Integrity Act of 1924, passed during the period of extreme nativism which followed the end of the First World War. * * *

I.   In upholding the constitutionality of these provisions in the decision below, the Supreme Court of Appeals of Virginia referred to its 1955 decision in *Naim v. Naim*, 197 Va. 80, 87 S.E.2d 749. * * * In *Naim*, the state court concluded that the State's legitimate purposes were "to preserve the racial integrity of its citizens," and to prevent "the corruption of blood," "a mongrel breed of citizens," and "the obliteration of racial pride," obviously an endorsement of the doctrine of White Supremacy. * * *

States Interest

* * * [T]he State argues that the meaning of the Equal Protection Clause, as illuminated by the statements of the Framers, is only that state penal laws containing an interracial element as part of the definition of the offense must apply equally to whites and Negroes in the sense that members of each race are punished to the same degree. Thus, the State contends that, because its miscegenation statutes punish equally both the white and the Negro participants in an interracial marriage, these statutes, despite their reliance on racial classifications do not constitute an invidious discrimination based upon race. The second argument advanced by the State assumes the validity of its equal application theory. The argument is that, if the Equal Protection Clause does not outlaw miscegenation statutes because of their reliance on racial classifications, the question of constitutionality would thus become whether there was any rational basis for a State to treat interracial marriages differently from other marriages. On this question, the State argues, the scientific evidence is substantially in doubt and, consequently, this Court should defer to the wisdom of the state legislature in adopting its policy of discouraging interracial marriages.

Because we reject the notion that the mere "equal application" of a statute containing racial classifications is enough to remove the classifications from the Fourteenth Amendment's proscription of all invidious racial discriminations, we do not accept the State's contention that these statutes should be upheld if there is any possible basis for concluding that they serve a rational purpose. The mere fact of equal application does not mean that our analysis of these statutes should follow the approach we have taken in cases involving no racial discrimination

---

[5]   * * * Over the past 15 years, 14 states have repealed laws outlawing interracial marriages.
* * *

where the Equal Protection Clause has been arrayed against a statute discriminating between the kinds of advertising which may be displayed on trucks in New York City, *Railway Express Agency, Inc. v. New York* [Chapter 4, § 1], or an exemption in Ohio's ad valorem tax for merchandise owned by a non-resident in a storage warehouse, *Allied Stores of Ohio, Inc. v. Bowers*, 358 U.S. 522 (1959). In these cases, involving distinctions not drawn according to race, the Court has merely asked whether there is any rational foundation for the discriminations, and has deferred to the wisdom of the state legislatures. In the case at bar, however, we deal with statutes containing racial classifications, and the fact of equal application does not immunize the statute from the very heavy burden of justification which the Fourteenth Amendment has traditionally required of state statutes drawn according to race.

The State argues that statements in the Thirty-ninth Congress about the time of the passage of the Fourteenth Amendment indicate that the Framers did not intend the Amendment to make unconstitutional state miscegenation laws. Many of the statements alluded to by the State concern the debates over the Freedmen's Bureau Bill, which President Johnson vetoed, and the Civil Rights Act of 1866, 14 Stat. 27, enacted over his veto. While these statements have some relevance to the intention of Congress in submitting the Fourteenth Amendment, it must be understood that they pertained to the passage of specific statutes and not to the broader, organic purpose of a constitutional amendment. As for the various statements directly concerning the Fourteenth Amendment, we have said in connection with a related problem, that although these historical sources "cast some light" they are not sufficient to resolve the problem; "[a]t best, they are inconclusive. The most avid proponents of the post-War Amendments undoubtedly intended them to remove all legal distinctions among 'all persons born or naturalized in the United States.' Their opponents, just as certainly, were antagonistic to both the letter and the spirit of the Amendments and wished them to have the most limited effect." *Brown*. We have rejected the proposition that the debates in the Thirty-ninth Congress or in the state legislatures which ratified the Fourteenth Amendment supported the theory advanced by the State, that the requirement of equal protection of the laws is satisfied by penal laws defining offenses based on racial classifications so long as white and Negro participants in the offense were similarly punished. *McLaughlin*.

The State finds support for its "equal application" theory in the decision of the Court in *Pace v. Alabama*, 106 U.S. 583 (1883). In that case, the Court upheld a conviction under an Alabama statute forbidding adultery or fornication between a white person and a Negro which imposed a greater penalty than that of a statute proscribing similar conduct by members of the same race. The Court reasoned that the statute could not be said to discriminate against Negroes because the punishment for each participant in the offense was the same. However, as recently as the 1964 Term, in rejecting the reasoning of that case, we stated *"Pace* represents a limited view of the Equal Protection Clause which has not withstood analysis in the subsequent decisions of this Court." *McLaughlin.* As we there demonstrated, the Equal Protection Clause requires the consideration of whether the classifications drawn by any statute constitute an arbitrary and invidious discrimination. The clear and central purpose of the Fourteenth Amendment was to eliminate all official state sources of invidious racial discrimination in the States.

There can be no question but that Virginia's miscegenation statutes rest solely upon distinctions drawn according to race. The statutes proscribe generally accepted conduct if engaged in by members of different races. Over the years, this Court has consistently repudiated "[d]istinctions between citizens solely because of their ancestry" as being "odious to a free people whose institutions are founded upon the doctrine of equality." *Hirabayashi.* At the very least, the Equal Protection Clause demands that racial classifications, especially suspect in criminal statutes, be subjected to the "most rigid scrutiny," *Korematsu,* and, if they are ever to be upheld, they must be shown to be necessary to the accomplishment of some permissible state objective, independent of the racial discrimination which it was the object of the Fourteenth Amendment to eliminate. * * *

There is patently no legitimate overriding purpose independent of invidious racial discrimination which justifies this classification. The fact that Virginia prohibits only interracial marriages involving white persons demonstrates that the racial classifications must stand on their own justification, as measures designed to maintain White Supremacy.[11] We have consistently denied the constitutionality of measures which restrict the rights of citizens on account of race. There can be no doubt that restricting the freedom to marry solely because of racial classifications violates the central meaning of the Equal Protection Clause.

II. These statutes also deprive the Lovings of liberty without due process of law in violation of the Due Process Clause of the Fourteenth

---

[11] Appellants point out that the State's concern in these statutes, as expressed in the words of the 1924 Act's title, "An Act to Preserve Racial Integrity," extends only to the integrity of the white race. While Virginia prohibits whites from marrying any nonwhite (subject to the exception for the descendants of Pocahontas), Negroes, Orientals, and any other racial class may intermarry without statutory interference. Appellants contend that this distinction renders Virginia's miscegenation statutes arbitrary and unreasonable even assuming the constitutional validity of an official purpose to preserve "racial integrity." We need not reach this contention because we find the racial classifications in these statutes repugnant to the Fourteenth Amendment, even assuming an even-handed state purpose to protect the "integrity" of all races. [*Editors' note*: The Virginia statutes stated that "the term 'white person' shall apply only to such person as has no trace whatever of any blood other than Caucasian; but persons who have one-sixteenth or less of the blood of the American Indian and have no other non-Caucasic blood shall be deemed to be white persons." In an earlier footnote, Chief Justice Warren explained this exception by quoting a 1925 publication by a state official, who wrote that it reflected "the desire of all to recognize as an integral and honored part of the white race the descendants of John Rolfe and Pocahontas."]

Amendment. The freedom to marry has long been recognized as one of the vital personal rights essential to the orderly pursuit of happiness by free men. Marriage is one of the "basic civil rights of man," fundamental to our very existence and survival. *Skinner v. State of Oklahoma* [Chapter 5, § 1]. To deny this fundamental freedom on so unsupportable a basis as the racial classifications embodied in these statutes, classifications so directly subversive of the principle of equality at the heart of the Fourteenth Amendment, is surely to deprive all the State's citizens of liberty without due process of law. * * * [Reversed.]

[The concurring opinion of Justice Stewart is omitted.]

NOTES ON LOVING AND GOVERNMENT ACTIONS CLASSIFYING BY RACE

1. *Different Avenues to Attack the Virginia Statutes.* The state faced at least three hurdles in defending the laws involved in *Loving*: (1) If the statutes embodied racial discrimination, *Brown* would subject them to close judicial examination under the Equal Protection Clause. (2) Even if the statutes were not racially discriminatory, the state acknowledged that they violated equal protection if no rational basis could be discerned for the distinctions among persons found in them. (3) By burdening the liberty to marry, the statutes potentially violated the Due Process Clause. Each theory is discussed below.

2. *Defining and Invalidating Racial Discrimination.* Virginia contended that its statutes were not subject to close constitutional examination because persons of all races were equally disadvantaged. This argument attempts to distinguish statutes that *classify* on the basis of race from statutes that *discriminate* on the basis of race. As footnote 11 suggests, the "equal application" argument would have been sounder factually if all miscegenation had been outlawed. *Loving* makes clear, though, that even such an across-the-board approach would run afoul of the "central meaning" of the Equal Protection Clause. Why? Because it is inconsistent with the text of the Fourteenth Amendment or the intentions of its Framers? (See note 8 below.) Because, under appropriate theories of justice, race, an immutable characteristic, should be always irrelevant in appropriate governmental decisionmaking? Another avenue of analysis would harken back to footnote 4 of *Carolene Products* (Chapter 1, § 6), which suggested a special role for the Supreme Court in protecting "discrete and insular minorities" against prejudice, and the representation-reinforcement theory of Professor Ely (Chapter 2, § 3B). Under this approach, should the statutes be struck down because they were adopted during a period in which African Americans were politically powerless in Virginia? Because the statutes were adopted out of hostility toward African Americans or stigmatized them as inferior? Because race is an immutable characteristic? Do any (or all) of these theories necessarily follow from *Brown*?

3. *Colorblindness Versus Prejudice.* Consider *Palmore v. Sidoti*, 466 U.S. 429 (1984). Upon the divorce of a white couple, the state judge awarded

the mother custody of their daughter under the usual "best interests of the child" standard applicable to child custody. Later, when the mother married a black man, the state court reconsidered the best interests of the girl and concluded that her father should have custody. The state judge said that, despite improvement in race relations, it was inevitable that the girl would suffer social stigmatization if she lived in the home of a racially mixed marriage. A unanimous Supreme Court held that the judge's order violated equal protection. The Court acknowledged that the child "may be subject to a variety of pressures and stresses not present if the child were living with parents of the same racial or ethnic origin," but concluded that these were not permissible considerations for the state judge: Such private "biases may be outside the reach of the law, but the law cannot, directly or indirectly, give them effect." Was the problem with the judge's actions that they took race into account—that the judge was not colorblind—or that they deferred to private biases against racial minorities?

4. *Racial Classification and Harmed Groups.* The distinction between an equal protection theory based on colorblindness and one based on prejudice is often drawn by examining the groups benefitted or harmed by a racial classification. All criteria used to classify people create two or more affected groups—for example:

Government Regulation	Criterion	Ideology/Purpose	Allegedly Harmed Group
antimiscegenation laws (*Loving*)	race	white supremacy	stigmatizing people of color
affirmative action by state university (*Bakke, Grutter, Fisher II,* this chapter, § 3A)	race	remediation of social disadvantages and/or promotion of diverse institutions	white people
exclusion of women from state military college (VMI case, Chapter 4, § 2B1)	sex	separate spheres	women
vision test for driver's license	visual acuity	traffic safety	poorly sighted

The *Loving* opinion emphasized the suspect *classification*, which had the effect of harming a subordinated *class* by reinforcing the *ideology* of white supremacy. The ideas that the state should not racially classify without a legitimate reason to do so, and should not use race to subordinate or stigmatize people of color, pressed in the same directions here—as they later would in the VMI case, which struck down a sex-based classification excluding women from a state military college on the basis of a separate-spheres ideology (men =

warriors protecting women, who tend the home fires). An easy case in the opposite direction is the vision test for driver's licenses: The criterion of good vision is a rational one in this context, and the purpose of preventing traffic accidents is a splendid basis for state policy. Unlike the other items in the chart, affirmative action disaggregates the anti-classification (focus on the fishy classification) and anti-subordination (focus on the harmed class) features of the Equal Protection Clause. Consider also Problem 3-1, which follows these notes.

5.   *Current Formulation of the "Strict Scrutiny" Standard: A Means/ Ends Inquiry.* Although the Court does not always use precisely the same words in formulating the strict scrutiny standard derived from *Korematsu*, it has indicated that the variations are not legally significant. See, e.g., *In re Griffiths*, 413 U.S. 717, 721–22 & n.9 (1973). An illustrative formulation, taken from *Palmore, supra,* says that racial classifications "are subject to the most exacting scrutiny; to pass constitutional muster, they must be justified by a compelling governmental interest and must be 'necessary * * * to the accomplishment' of their legitimate purpose."

Note that this approach first says that the goal, or end, of the legislation must be "compelling," which presumably means something more than "permissible" or even "important." Recall *Korematsu*'s use of the phrase "[p]ressing public necessity." *Palmore,* for example, specifically held that satisfying widely held popular prejudices (against interracial households, in that case and in *Loving*) does not qualify as a compelling government interest. The approach then requires that the means chosen be "necessary" to effectuate the goal. Thus, merely a rational relationship between ends and means will not do, and presumably even a "significant" relationship is not good enough. The "means" scrutiny is designed to strike down statutes that create a greater burden than is necessary to achieve admittedly important goals. Note how this formulation would work in *Loving*: The statutes in question would be unconstitutional because the goal of racial integrity is not a compelling governmental interest; even if it were, as footnote 11 of the opinion indicates, the means chosen were hardly necessary to effectuate the goal.

6.   *Rational Basis Review.* As noted above, the attorneys representing Virginia conceded that the Equal Protection Clause provided some limitation even on state legislation that did not constitute racial discrimination. This "rational basis" inquiry is discussed in Chapter 4, § 1. For present purposes, note the distinction in *Loving* between invidious racial discrimination (however that is defined), which is subject to heightened equal protection scrutiny, and discrimination in economic regulation, which *Loving* indicates is subject to deferential review inquiring only whether there is a rational connection between the goal of the statute and the means chosen to effectuate that goal.

7.   *Judicial Restraint and the Right to Marry.* In only one paragraph, the Court struck down the Virginia statutes as violating the right to marry provided by the Due Process Clause of the Fourteenth Amendment. This part

of *Loving* later became a regular part of debates about same-sex marriage, and we will discuss such fundamental rights in Chapter 5. For present purposes, though, ask yourself: Why did the Chief Justice include Part II of the opinion, when he had already struck down the statutes in Part I? Should the Court ever decide more questions than are necessary to dispose of a case? Is there something about a *constitutional* question that especially suggests that the Court should decide it only if necessary? If the Court should engage in this kind of judicial restraint, how should it pick which dispositive ground—in *Loving*, equal protection or fundamental right/due process—to invoke? A similar point can be made about the equal protection issue in *Loving*: As footnote 11 demonstrates, the Court could have avoided deciding whether the "equal application" argument could save the statutes by holding that the statutes really did not equally apply to persons of all races. Should the Court have done this?

8.   *The Complexities of History.* As he had done in *Brown*, Chief Justice Warren concluded that the intentions of the Framers of the Fourteenth Amendment were sufficiently unclear so that they could be set aside in *Loving*. This may be problematic. Herbert Hovenkamp, *Social Science and Segregation Before* Brown, 1985 Duke L.J. 624, argues that before the mid-twentieth century, the prevailing culture in the United States believed in strict separation of the races. In the nineteenth century, even "progressives," such as many of the Radical Republicans who pushed through the Fourteenth Amendment, often believed that the white race was different and superior to the black race and that "mixing of the races" was a bad idea mainly because it would lead to interracial marriages, which were widely considered to produce defective children and even to "dilute" the white race. Under this view of nineteenth century ideology, any doubts about educational integration would have been pale in comparison with marital integration.[7] If this historical analysis is correct, should that change the result in *Loving*? If not, when should such evidence of original intent ever be relevant? See generally Problem 2-1, *Is* Brown *Consistent with the Original Intent of the Fourteenth Amendment?*, Chapter 2, § 3A.

9.   *Implementing* Brown: *Federal Antidiscrimination Legislation.* The antidiscrimination principle of *Brown* and its progeny has been implemented most broadly not by judges under the Constitution, but by Congress under its authority to pass civil rights legislation. (The sources of, and limitations on, this congressional power are examined in Chapter 7.) One of the most important statutes implementing *Brown* is the Civil Rights Act of 1964. For

---

[7]   In 1956, the Supreme Court dismissed on seemingly unsupportable jurisdictional grounds the appeal in *Naim v. Naim*, 350 U.S. 985 (1956), discussed in *Loving*. Alexander Bickel conceded that affirmance of *Naim* would have been "unthinkable" after *Brown*, but justified what the Court did on practical grounds: "[W]ould it have been wise, at a time when the Court had just pronounced its new integration principle, when it was subject to scurrilous attack by men who predicted that integration of the schools would lead to 'mongrelization of the race' and that this was the result the Court had really willed, * * * to declare that the states may not prohibit racial intermarriage?" Alexander Bickel, *The Least Dangerous Branch* 174 (1962). *Naim* suggests the power, as late as the 1950s, of fears of interracial marriage.

instance, Title VI of this statute provides that "No person in the United States shall, on the ground of race, color, or national origin, be excluded from participation in, be denied the benefits of, or be subjected to discrimination under any program or activity receiving Federal financial assistance." Title VII forbids certain employers from engaging in employment discrimination on account of race and other specified criteria, such as gender.

PROBLEMS INVOLVING RACIAL CLASSIFICATIONS IN LAW ENFORCEMENT AND ADOPTION

Problem 3-1: *Prudential uses of race in the criminal justice system?* (1) May a state law enforcement agency take race into account in determining what officers to assign to work undercover as purported members of a gang defined by race (e.g., to infiltrate the Klu Klux Klan)? (2) Assume that a large city has a substantial community of persons of color, and that there have been serious racial tensions between members of that community and the police force. May the police chief order the reassignment of officers so that more officers who are persons of color are responsible for patrolling areas with high minority population? (3) Same city: May the police chief adjust the department's hiring criteria, if need be, to ensure that a higher percentage of new officers will be persons of color? (4) May prison officials, immediately following a prison riot triggered by racial tension among inmates, racially segregate the inmates for a cooling-off period? (5) Same prison system: If after months of problems the officials decide that the best way to protect inmates from violence is to segregate all inmates by race for the indefinite future, is that constitutional? Cf. *Johnson v. California*, 543 U.S. 499 (2005) (placing new inmates in cells with persons of same race during initial evaluation period is subject to strict scrutiny); *Lee v. Washington*, 390 U.S. 333 (1968) (striking down state statutes requiring ongoing racial segregation of prisons and jails). (6) What if law enforcement officials believe there is a correlation between race and the commission of certain kinds of crimes in certain places? May race be part of a "profile" used to identify suspects? On these general issues, see, e.g., *Brown v. City of Oneonta, New York*, 221 F.3d 329 (2d Cir. 2000) (police did not violate the Equal Protection Clause when using race as part of description of a criminal suspect that led to stops); David Harris, *The Stories, the Statistics, and the Law: Why "Driving While Black" Matters*, 84 Minn. L. Rev. 265 (1999).[8]

Problem 3-2: *Race-matching in adoption?* Under *Loving* and *Palmore*, is it constitutional for a state-run adoption agency to follow a policy of "race matching," whereby the agency prefers to place children in homes of racially similar parents—children of color with parents of color, biracial children with different-race parents, white children in white homes? See, e.g., Elizabeth

---

[8] In *United States v. Brignoni-Ponce*, 422 U.S. 873 (1975), the Court stated that "the characteristic appearance of persons who live in Mexico [such as] the mode of dress and haircut" could be a factor, but not the only factor, used by the Border Patrol in stopping and questioning possible illegal immigrants near the Mexican border. No Justice disagreed with this conclusion, which was based on an analysis of the factors that can provide "reasonable suspicion" justifying an investigative "stop" for Fourth Amendment purposes. Would, or should, the analysis be any different if the issue were viewed as one of equal protection?

Bartholet, *Where Do Black Children Belong? The Politics of Race Matching in Adoption*, 139 U. Pa. L. Rev. 1163 (1991).[9]

Problem 3-3: *Colorblindness in adoption?* Assume that it would be unconstitutional for adoption agencies to follow a policy of race matching. Would it also be constitutionally required for the state agency not to reveal the racial background of children to prospective parents? It is apparently true that a large majority of prospective parents, knowing the racial background of the children, will choose a child whose background is the same as theirs. It is also true that such discrimination has a disproportionate impact on children of color. There are many more children of color (especially African-American children) available for adoption than there are interested parents of color. Compare R. Richard Banks, *The Color of Desire: Fulfilling Adoptive Parents' Racial Preferences Through Discriminatory State Action*, 107 Yale L.J. 875 (1998), with Elizabeth Bartholet, Correspondence, *Private Race Preferences in Family Formation*, 107 Yale L.J. 2351 (1998).

B. FACIALLY NEUTRAL CLASSIFICATIONS (DISCRIMINATORY INTENT AND EFFECT)

In *Brown* and *Loving*, the racial nature of the statute was plainly evident on the face of the statute. Could a statute or practice that is facially neutral concerning race nonetheless violate the Equal Protection Clause? Consider the following cases. The first case involves a facially neutral statute that was enforced in a discriminatory way.

YICK WO V. HOPKINS
118 U.S. 356, 6 S.Ct. 1064, 30 L.Ed. 220 (1886)

JUSTICE MATTHEWS delivered the opinion of the Court.

[In 1880, the San Francisco Board of Supervisors adopted a series of ordinances providing that a laundry located in a building constructed of material other than brick or stone could be operated only by obtaining the consent of the Board. Yick Wo, a citizen of China, was imprisoned for operating a laundry in a wood building without the Board's consent, and he brought this action for habeas corpus relief. He demonstrated that he had operated his laundry in the same location for 22 years and had been licensed to do so by the board of fire wardens. It was conceded that in 1880

---

[9]   Cf. the Indian Child Welfare Act, 25 U.S.C. § 1901 et seq., which in some circumstances mandates tribal-court rather than state-court jurisdiction over the placement of Indian children and otherwise strongly prefers that such children be in Indian homes. The statute defines "Indian child" as someone (1) who is a member of a federally recognized Indian tribe or (2) who is eligible for membership in such a tribe and is the biological child of a member of such a tribe. Are classifications based on membership in a federally recognized Indian tribe "racial" classifications? See *Morton v. Mancari*, 417 U.S. 535 (1974) (such classifications are "political," not racial). Many tribes define their membership at least in part by blood quantum (e.g., a tribe might require that, to be eligible to enroll as a member, the person must be the child of a tribal member and have at least a certain percentage of her lineage traceable to this tribe). Should that make any difference in the analysis?

"there were about 320 laundries in [San Francisco], of which about 240 were owned and conducted by subjects of China, and of the [320], about 310 were constructed of wood, the same material that constitutes nine-tenths of the houses in [San Francisco]." Moreover, all the applications of the approximately 200 Chinese who had applied for permits had been denied; with only one exception, all the 80 or so applications of non-Chinese had been granted. The California state courts denied the application for habeas corpus.]

The Fourteenth Amendment to the Constitution is not confined to the protection of citizens. It says: "Nor shall any State deprive any person of life, liberty, or property without due process of law; nor deny to any person within its jurisdiction the equal protection of the laws." These provisions are universal in their application, to all persons within the territorial jurisdiction, without regard to any differences of race, of color, or of nationality; and the equal protection of the laws is a pledge of the protection of equal laws. * * *

It is contended on the part of the petitioners that the ordinances for violations of which they are severally sentenced to imprisonment are void on their face, as being within the prohibitions of the Fourteenth Amendment; and, in the alternative, if not so, that they are void by reason of their administration, operating unequally, so as to punish in the present petitioners what is permitted to others as lawful, without any distinction of circumstances—an unjust and illegal discrimination, it is claimed, which, though not made expressly by the ordinances is made possible by them.

* * * In the present cases we are not obliged to reason from the probable to the actual, and pass upon the validity of the ordinances complained of, as tried merely by the opportunities which their terms afford, of unequal and unjust discrimination in their administration. For the cases present the ordinances in actual operation, and the facts shown establish an administration directed so exclusively against a particular class of persons as to warrant and require the conclusion that, whatever may have been the intent of the ordinances as adopted, they are applied by the public authorities charged with their administration, and thus representing the State itself, with a mind so unequal and oppressive as to amount to a practical denial by the State of that equal protection of the laws which is secured to the petitioners, as to all other persons, by the broad and benign provisions of the Fourteenth Amendment to the Constitution of the United States. Though the law itself be fair on its face and impartial in appearance, yet, if it is applied and administered by public authority with an evil eye and an unequal hand, so as practically to make unjust and illegal discriminations between persons in similar circumstances, material to their rights, the denial of equal justice is still within the prohibition of the Constitution. * * *

The present cases, as shown by the facts disclosed in the record, are within this class. It appears that both petitioners have complied with every requisite, deemed by the law or by the public officers charged with its administration, necessary for the protection of neighboring property from fire, or as a precaution against injury to the public health. No reason whatever, except the will of the supervisors, is assigned why they should not be permitted to carry on, in the accustomed manner, their harmless and useful occupation, on which they depend for a livelihood. And while this consent of the supervisors is withheld from them and from 200 others who have also petitioned, all of whom happen to be Chinese subjects, 80 others, not Chinese subjects, are permitted to carry on the same business under similar conditions. The fact of this discrimination is admitted. No reason for it is shown, and the conclusion cannot be resisted, that no reason for it exists except hostility to the race and nationality to which the petitioners belong, and which in the eye of the law is not justified. The discrimination is, therefore, illegal, and the public administration which enforces it is a denial of the equal protection of the laws and a violation of the Fourteenth Amendment of the Constitution. The imprisonment of the petitioners is, therefore, illegal, and they must be discharged.

NOTES ON YICK WO AND DISCRIMINATORY INTENT

1.   *Contemporary Context for Yick Wo.* Consider the applicability of *Yick Wo* to the kind of litigation identified in Problem 3-1, above. Objections to disproportionate stops of African-American drivers, for example, have clear parallels with *Yick Wo.* As in *Yick Wo,* the relevant statute (authorizing police to stop motorists) is race-neutral. As in *Yick Wo,* the focus is not on the original enactment of that statute, but rather on how it is enforced. And the allegedly-discriminatory actors are not those who wrote the law, but those who decide how to implement it. Some lower courts have noted the applicability of *Yick Wo* for a range of questions about discriminatory policing. See, e.g., *Brown v. City of Oneonta, New York*, 221 F.3d 329, 337 (2d Cir. 2000) (citing *Yick Wo* and noting in the context of a racial profiling claim that one of the ways for plaintiffs to prevail is to "identify a facially neutral law or policy that has been applied in an intentionally discriminatory manner"); *Floyd v. City of New York*, 959 F. Supp. 2d 540 (S.D.N.Y. 2013) (same for claim of discriminatory stops and frisks on the street). In a case alleging discriminatory traffic stops, how large a statistical disparity would a plaintiff have to show? How much weight would *Yick Wo* carry if the statistics were not as overwhelming as they were in that case? What other factors would be relevant to a judicial assessment of whether traffic stops were being made in an "intentionally discriminatory manner"?

2.   *The Relevance of Discriminatory Purposes for Enactment.* In *Yick Wo,* the Court did not need to address what motivated the passage of the law in question because it was clear that the law had been *implemented*

discriminatorily.[10] But suppose Yick Wo had contacted an attorney the day after the law had been enacted, suspecting that the Board of Supervisors had adopted it for the purpose of driving Chinese laundries out of business. How could you prove the Board's evil intent? And even if you could prove that discriminatory reasons motivated the passage of the ordinances, should evil intent, standing alone, justify striking down these facially neutral laws? There has been a longstanding debate throughout American constitutional history about whether enactment of legislation for bad reasons, standing alone, could justify judicial invalidation.

problems of proof

Consider Chief Justice Marshall's discussion in *Fletcher v. Peck*, 10 U.S. (6 Cranch.) 87 (1810), a case in which a Georgia statute that had provided for the sale of public land was said to be the result of fraud and undue influence on the state legislature. Chief Justice Marshall cautioned against consideration of legislative motives:

intent irrelevant

> [That] impure motives should contribute to the passage of a law [is] most deeply to be deplored. * * * [Nonetheless, it] may well be doubted how far the validity of a law depends upon the motives of its framers * * *. If the principle be conceded, that an act of the supreme sovereign power may be declared null by a court, in consequence of the means which procured it, still would there be much difficulty in saying to what extent those means must be applied to produce this effect. * * * Must the vitiating cause operate on a majority, or on what number of the members? Would the act be null, whatever might be the wish of the nation, or would its * * * nullity depend upon the public sentiment?

> If the majority of the legislature be corrupted, it may well be doubted, whether it be within the province of the judiciary to control their conduct, and, if less than a majority act from impure motives, the principle by which judicial interference would be regulated, is not clearly discerned.

Many years later, in *Gomillion v. Lightfoot*, 364 U.S. 339 (1960), the Court considered an Alabama statute that altered the boundaries of the City of Tuskegee from the shape of a square to an irregular 28-sided figure. Justice Frankfurter's unanimous opinion for the Court noted that "the essential inevitable effect of this [statute] is to remove from the city all save only four or five of its 400 Negro voters while not removing a single white voter or resident." Consistent with the concerns mentioned in *Fletcher v. Peck*, may the Constitution be invoked to attack this racial gerrymander? Without citing *Fletcher*, *Gomillion* held that such a gerrymander was unconstitutional:

intent + effect

---

[10] This is the usual understanding of the case. But see Gabriel Chin, *Unexplainable on Grounds of Race: Doubts about* Yick Wo (unpublished paper, Dec. 2007) (properly understood historically, case actually turned on property right to operate laundry, not race discrimination).

The result of the Act is to deprive the Negro petitioners discriminatorily of the benefits of residence in Tuskegee, including, *inter alia*, the right to vote in municipal elections.

These allegations, if proven, would abundantly establish that Act 140 was not an ordinary geographic redistricting measure even within familiar abuses of gerrymandering. If these allegations upon a trial remained uncontradicted or unqualified, the conclusion would be irresistible, tantamount for all practical purposes to a mathematical demonstration, that the legislation is solely concerned with segregating * * * voters by fencing Negro citizens out of town so as to deprive them of their pre-existing municipal vote.

It is difficult to appreciate what stands in the way of adjudging a statute having this inevitable effect invalid in light of the principles by which this Court must judge, and uniformly has judged, statutes that, howsoever speciously defined, obviously [racially] discriminate[.] "The [Fifteenth] Amendment nullifies sophisticated as well as simple-minded modes of discrimination." *Lane v. Wilson*, 307 U.S. 268, 275. * * *

* * * According to the allegations here made, the Alabama Legislature has not merely redrawn the Tuskegee city limits with incidental inconvenience to the petitioners; it is more accurate to say that it has deprived the petitioners of the municipal franchise and consequent rights and to that end it has incidentally changed the city's boundaries. While in form this is merely an act redefining metes and bounds, if the allegations are established, the inescapable human effect of this essay in geometry and geography is to despoil [blacks, and only blacks], of their theretofore enjoyed voting rights. * * *

What is the basis for the holding in *Gomillion*—discriminatory intent, discriminatory effect, or some combination of the two?

In *Palmer v. Thompson*, 403 U.S. 217 (1971), the Court returned to the issue of discriminatory motives for facially-neutral legislation. In 1962, Jackson, Mississippi operated five public segregated swimming pools: four for whites, one for blacks. Following a lawsuit in which this segregation was declared illegal, the city council simply closed down all the pools. Writing for a five-member majority in *Palmer*, Justice Black stated that "no case in this Court has held that a legislative act may violate equal protection solely because of the motivations of the men who voted for it." Alluding to Chief Justice Marshall's admonitions in *Fletcher v. Peck*, Justice Black assayed the "hazards of declaring a law unconstitutional because of the motivations of its sponsors":

* * * [P]etitioners have argued that the Jackson pools were closed because of ideological opposition to racial integration in swimming pools. Some evidence in the record appears to support this argument. On the other hand the courts below found that the pools were closed because the city felt they could not be operated safely and

economically on an integrated basis. There is substantial evidence in the record to support this conclusion. It is difficult or impossible for any court to determine the "sole" or "dominant" motivation behind the choices of a group of legislators. Furthermore, there is an element of futility in a judicial attempt to invalidate a law because of the bad motives of its supporters. If the law is struck down for this reason, rather than because of its facial content or effect, it would presumably be valid as soon as the legislature or relevant governing body repassed it for different reasons.

It is true there is language in some of our cases interpreting the Fourteenth and Fifteenth Amendments which may suggest that the motive or purpose behind a law is relevant to its constitutionality. *Griffin v. County School Board*, [377 U.S. 218 (1964)]; *Gomillion*. But the focus in those cases was on the actual effect of the enactments, not upon the motivation which led the States to behave as they did. In *Griffin*[,] the State was in fact perpetuating a segregated public school system by financing segregated "private" academies. And in *Gomillion* the Alabama Legislature's gerrymander of the boundaries of Tuskegee excluded virtually all Negroes from voting in town elections. Here the record indicates only that Jackson once ran segregated public swimming pools and that no public pools are now maintained by the city. Moreover, there is no evidence in this record to show that the city is now covertly aiding the maintenance and operation of pools which are private in name only. It shows no state action affecting blacks differently than whites.

Is this consistent with *Gomillion*? *Loving*?

3.   *Discriminatory Intent or Effect? Hawkins v. Town of Shaw*, 437 F.2d 1286 (5th Cir. 1971), *aff'd en banc*, 461 F.2d 1171 (5th Cir. 1972), illustrates one way in which judges could react to *Palmer*. Consider the facts:

The town of Shaw, Mississippi, was incorporated in 1886 and is located in the Mississippi Delta. Its population * * * consists of about 2,500 people—1,500 black and 1,000 white residents. Residential racial segregation is almost total. There are 451 dwelling units occupied by blacks in town, and, of these, 97% (439) are located in neighborhoods in which no whites reside. That the town's policies in administering various municipal services have led to substantially less attention being paid to the black portion of town is clear.

Nearly 98% of all homes that front on unpaved streets in Shaw are occupied by blacks. Ninety-seven percent of the homes not served by sanitary sewers are in black neighborhoods. Further, while the town has acquired a significant number of medium and high intensity mercury vapor street lighting fixtures, every one of them has been installed in white neighborhoods. The record further discloses [similar] statistical evidence of grave disparities in both the level and kinds of services offered regarding surface water drainage, water mains, fire hydrants, and traffic control apparatus * * *.

After *Palmer*, should these facts constitute an equal protection violation? Judge Tuttle's panel opinion, written just prior to *Palmer*, concluded that the facts amounted to "a prima facie case of racial discrimination," that the only remaining question was whether "these disparities can possibly be justified by any compelling state interests," and that no such compelling state interests were revealed by the record. Judge Tuttle continued:

> Yet, despite the fact that we conclude that no compelling state interests can justify the disparities * * *, it may be argued that this result was not intended. That is to say, the record contains no direct evidence aimed at establishing bad faith, ill will or an evil motive on the part of the Town of Shaw and its public officials. We feel, however, that the law on this point is clear. In a civil rights suit alleging racial discrimination in contravention of the Fourteenth Amendment, actual intent or motive need not be directly proved, for * * *

> * * * "equal protection of the laws" means more than merely the absence of governmental action designed to discriminate; . . . we now firmly recognize that the arbitrary quality of thoughtlessness can be as disastrous and unfair to private rights and the public interest as the perversity of a willful scheme. [Citing other lower court cases.]

Fletcher, *Gomillion*, *Palmer*, and *Hawkins* suggest a dilemma about using the Equal Protection Clause to attack facially neutral statutes that have a disproportionate racial impact. *Fletcher* and *Palmer* suggest at least three reasons why courts should not inquire whether the adoption of such statutes was discriminatorily motivated: (1) *deference to legislatures*: labeling a co-equal branch (Congress) or a state or local legislature "wicked" raises serious separation of powers problems; (2) *evidentiary problems*: what kind of proof should be admissible, and how much proof is enough; (3) *remedial problems and judicial futility*: the same statute if reenacted with pure motives would be valid. But doesn't common sense suggest that the core purpose of the Reconstruction Amendments was to forbid intentional discrimination against racial minorities? Moreover, there seems to be only one obvious alternative to a discriminatory-intent approach if the courts are to nullify "sophisticated as well as simple-minded modes of discrimination"—a discriminatory-effects approach, as in *Hawkins*, where courts balance the degree of discriminatory effects against any plausible public policies that might support retaining the statute in question. But that kind of balancing will strike many as a quintessential legislative, not judicial, function.

Unlike *Yick Wo*, the next case did not involve discriminatory enforcement of a law. It instead posed a different—and larger—question about intent and effect, and has become one of the most important cases in shaping the modern jurisprudence of race and equal protection.

WASHINGTON V. DAVIS

426 U.S. 229, 96 S.Ct. 2040, 48 L.Ed.2d 597 (1976)

JUSTICE WHITE delivered the opinion of the Court.

[Plaintiffs, African Americans whose applications for the District of Columbia police department were rejected, alleged that the department's hiring practices were racially discriminatory because they included a written personnel test, "Test 21," that operated to exclude a disproportionate number of African-American applicants. Plaintiffs based their claim on federal civil service laws and on the equal protection component of the Due Process Clause of the Fifth Amendment (recall *Bolling v. Sharpe*, Chapter 2, § 1C), since at the time of their lawsuit Title VII of the 1964 Civil Rights Act, which prohibits employment discrimination on account of race, did not apply to the federal government. The court of appeals looked to the primary case interpreting Title VII, *Griggs v. Duke Power Co.*, 401 U.S. 424 (1971), and held that the *Griggs* standard for proving employment discrimination under Title VII should also be the constitutional standard. The court of appeals held that Test 21 violated the Fifth Amendment because a far greater proportion of African Americans than whites failed the test and defendants had not shown that the test was an adequate measure of job performance.]

As the Court of Appeals understood Title VII, employees or applicants proceeding under it need not concern themselves with the employer's possibly discriminatory purpose but instead may focus solely on the racially differential impact of the challenged hiring or promotion practices. This is not the constitutional rule. * * *

The central purpose of the Equal Protection Clause * * * is the prevention of official conduct discriminating on the basis of race. * * * [O]ur cases have not embraced the proposition that a law or other official act, without regard to whether it reflects a racially discriminatory purpose, is unconstitutional *solely* because it has a racially disproportionate impact. * * *

The school desegregation cases * * * adhered to the basic equal protection principle that the invidious quality of a law claimed to be racially discriminatory must ultimately be traced to a racially discriminatory purpose. That there are both predominantly black and predominantly white schools in a community is not alone violative of the Equal Protection Clause. The essential element of *de jure* segregation is "a current condition of segregation resulting from intentional state action." *Keyes v. School District No. 1*, 413 U.S. 189 (1973). "The differentiating factor between *de jure* segregation and so-called *de facto* segregation . . . is *purpose* or *intent* to segregate." The Court has also recently rejected allegations of racial discrimination based solely on the statistically disproportionate racial impact of various provisions of the Social Security Act because "[t]he acceptance of appellants' constitutional theory would render suspect each difference in treatment among the grant classes, however lacking in racial motivation and however otherwise rational the treatment might be." *Jefferson v. Hackney*, 406 U.S. 535 (1972). * * *

This is not to say that the necessary discriminatory racial purpose must be express or appear on the face of the statute, or that a law's disproportionate impact is irrelevant in cases involving Constitution-based claims of racial discrimination. A statute, otherwise neutral on its face, must not be applied so as invidiously to discriminate on the basis of race. *Yick Wo.* * * *

Necessarily, an invidious discriminatory purpose may often be inferred from the totality of the relevant facts, including the fact, if it is true, that the law bears more heavily on one race than another. It is also not infrequently true that the discriminatory impact—in the jury cases for example, the total or seriously disproportionate exclusion of Negroes from jury venires—may for all practical purposes demonstrate unconstitutionality because in various circumstances the discrimination is very difficult to explain on nonracial grounds. Nevertheless, we have not held that a law, neutral on its face and serving ends otherwise within the power of government to pursue, is invalid under the Equal Protection Clause simply because it may affect a greater proportion of one race than of another. Disproportionate impact is not irrelevant, but it is not the sole touchstone of an invidious racial discrimination forbidden by the Constitution. Standing alone, it does not trigger the rule that racial classifications are to be subjected to the strictest scrutiny and are justifiable only by the weightiest of considerations.

There are some indications to the contrary in our cases. In *Palmer v. Thompson*, the city of Jackson, Miss., following a court decree to this effect, desegregated all of its public facilities save five swimming pools which had been operated by the city and which, following the decree, were closed by ordinance pursuant to a determination by the city council that closure was necessary to preserve peace and order and that integrated pools could not be economically operated. Accepting the finding that the pools were closed to avoid violence and economic loss, this Court rejected the argument that the abandonment of this service was inconsistent with the outstanding desegregation decree and that the otherwise seemingly permissible ends served by the ordinance could be impeached by demonstrating that racially invidious motivations had prompted the city council's action. The holding was that the city was not overtly or covertly operating segregated pools and was extending identical treatment to both whites and Negroes. The opinion warned against grounding decision on legislative purpose or motivation, thereby lending support for the proposition that the operative effect of the law rather than its purpose is the paramount factor. But the holding of the case was that the legitimate purposes of the ordinance to preserve peace and avoid deficits were not open to impeachment by evidence that the councilmen were actually motivated by racial considerations. Whatever dicta the opinion may contain, the decision did not involve, much less invalidate, a statute or ordinance having neutral purposes but disproportionate racial consequences. * * *

That [*Palmer* was not] understood to have changed the prevailing rule is apparent from *Keyes*, where the principal issue in litigation was whether and to what extent there had been purposeful discrimination resulting in a partially or wholly segregated school system. * * *

* * * [V]arious Courts of Appeals have held in several contexts, including public employment, that the substantially disproportionate racial impact of a statute or official practice standing alone and without regard to discriminatory purpose, suffices to prove racial discrimination violating the Equal Protection Clause absent some justification going substantially beyond what would be necessary to validate most other legislative classifications.[12] The cases impressively demonstrate that there is another side to the issue; but * * * we are in disagreement.

As an initial matter, we have difficulty understanding how a law establishing a racially neutral qualification for employment is nevertheless racially discriminatory and denies "any person . . . equal protection of the laws" simply because a greater proportion of Negroes fail to qualify than members of other racial or ethnic groups. Had respondents, along with all others who had failed Test 21, whether white or black, brought an action claiming that the test denied each of them equal protection of the laws as compared with those who had passed with high enough scores to qualify them as police recruits, it is most unlikely that their challenge would have been sustained. Test 21, which is administered generally to prospective Government employees, concededly seeks to ascertain whether those who take it have acquired a particular level of verbal skill; and it is untenable that the Constitution prevents the Government from seeking modestly to upgrade the communicative abilities of its employees rather than to be satisfied with some lower level of competence, particularly where the job requires special ability to communicate orally and in writing. Respondents, as Negroes, could no more successfully claim that the test denied them equal protection than could white applicants who also failed. The conclusion would not be different in the face of proof that more Negroes than whites had been disqualified by Test 21. That other Negroes also failed to score well would, alone, not demonstrate that respondents individually were being denied equal protection of the laws by the application of an otherwise valid qualifying test being administered to prospective police recruits.

---

[12]   [Justice White cited a number of decisions, including *Hawkins v. Town of Shaw*.]

Nor on the facts of the case before us would the disproportionate impact of Test 21 warrant the conclusion that it is a purposeful device to discriminate against Negroes and hence an infringement of the constitutional rights of respondents as well as other black applicants. As we have said, the test is neutral on its face and rationally may be said to serve a purpose the Government is constitutionally empowered to pursue. Even agreeing with the District Court that the differential racial effect of Test 21 called for further inquiry, we think the District Court correctly held that the affirmative efforts of the Metropolitan Police Department to recruit black officers, the changing racial composition of the recruit classes and of the force in general, and the relationship of the test to the training program negated any inference that the Department discriminated on the basis of race[.] * * *

Under Title VII, Congress provided that when hiring and promotion practices disqualifying substantially disproportionate numbers of blacks are challenged, discriminatory purpose need not be proved, and that it is an insufficient response to demonstrate some rational basis for the challenged practices. It is necessary, in addition, that they be "validated" in terms of job performance in any one of several ways, perhaps by ascertaining the minimum skill, ability, or potential necessary for the position at issue and determining whether the qualifying tests are appropriate for the selection of qualified applicants for the job in question. However this process proceeds, it involves a more probing judicial review of, and less deference to, the seemingly reasonable acts of administrators and executives than is appropriate under the Constitution where special racial impact, without discriminatory purpose, is claimed. We are not disposed to adopt this more rigorous standard for the purposes of applying the Fifth and the Fourteenth Amendments * * *.

A rule that a statute designed to serve neutral ends is nevertheless invalid, absent compelling justification, if in practice it benefits or burdens one race more than another would be far reaching and would raise serious questions about, and perhaps invalidate, a whole range of tax, welfare, public service, regulatory, and licensing statutes that may be more burdensome to the poor and to the average black than to the more affluent white.[14]

Given that rule, such consequences would perhaps be likely to follow. However, in our view, extension of the rule beyond those areas where it is already applicable by reason of statute, such as in the field of public employment, should await legislative prescription. [The Court also held

---

[14] * * * [D]isproportionate-impact analysis might invalidate "tests and qualifications for voting, draft deferment, public employment, jury service, and other government-conferred benefits and opportunities . . . ; [s]ales taxes, bail schedules, utility rates, bridge tolls, license fees, and other state-imposed charges." It has also been argued that minimum wage and usury laws as well as professional licensing requirements would require major modifications in light of the unequal-impact rule. * * *

that, assuming that the applicable federal civil service statutes incorporated Title VII prohibitions against employment discrimination, plaintiffs had not satisfied Title VII standards for invalidating Test 21.]

JUSTICE STEVENS, concurring.

[Frequently] the most probative evidence of intent will be objective evidence of what actually happened rather than evidence describing the subjective state of mind of the actor. For normally the actor is presumed to have intended the natural consequences of his deeds. This is particularly true in the case of governmental action which is frequently the product of compromise, of collective decisionmaking, and of mixed motivation. It is unrealistic, on the one hand, to require the victim of alleged discrimination to uncover the actual subjective intent of the decisionmaker or, conversely, to invalidate otherwise legitimate action simply because an improper motive affected the deliberation of a participant in the decisional process. A law conscripting clerics should not be invalidated because an atheist voted for it.

My point [is] that the line between discriminatory purpose and discriminatory impact is not nearly as bright, and perhaps not quite as critical, as the reader of the Court's opinion might assume. I agree, of course, that a constitutional issue does not arise every time some disproportionate impact is shown. On the other hand, when the disproportion is as dramatic as in *Gomillion* or *Yick Wo* it really does not matter whether the standard is phrased in terms of purpose or effect. Therefore, although I accept the statement of the general rule in the Court's opinion, I am not yet prepared to indicate how that standard should be applied in the many cases which have formulated the governing standard in different language. * * *

[JUSTICE BRENNAN, joined by JUSTICE MARSHALL, dissented on the statutory issue, but did not address the Court's constitutional holding.]

NOTES ON DAVIS AND PROVING DISCRIMINATORY INTENT

1.   *Constitutional Theory and* Washington v. Davis. *Washington v. Davis* did not turn on the text and ratification debates surrounding the Equal Protection Clause. Consider other factors: (a) *Precedent.* Neither *Brown* nor *Loving* answers the question as to which approach to equality—the anti-classification or the anti-subordination theory—should prevail when a seemingly rational classification has the effect of disadvantaging a historically subordinated class of citizens. *Palmer v. Thompson,* and the century of case law it reflects, certainly cut against the Court's approach. On the other hand, the Court in the public school cases of the early 1970s distinguished sharply between intentional discrimination remediable under the Equal Protection Clause and unintended but discriminatory effects, which were not. See *San Antonio Indep. Sch. Dist. v. Rodriguez* (Chapter 5, § 3B), where the Court

implicitly rejected a claim that Texas's school funding scheme violated the Equal Protection Clause because it had discriminatory effects against Mexican—as well as African-American school children. *Jefferson v. Hackney*, cited in the Court's opinion, involved a dramatic showing that Texas's welfare policies systematically benefitted white over black and Latino recipients; that the Court was unwilling to find an equal protection claim under those circumstances was a precedent-based reason not to do so in *Davis*. But did these recent precedents justify departing from the older ones like *Fletcher v. Peck*?

(b) *Institutional Competence and Capacity*. As Justice White's reference to *Keyes* (a school desegregation case) suggests, the Justices were worried that the federal judiciary was already overextended with the *Brown II* cases and were unprepared to open up another arena of equal protection litigation requiring courts to monitor local policies. (According to Justice Brennan's notes, this was the stated reason Justices Blackmun and Powell were opposed to recognizing the equality claims in *Rodriguez*.) Should Professor Bickel's passive virtues approach to cautious judicial review (Chapter 3, § 3) extend this far—denying relief in a whole class of cases, rather than temporarily as to one issue, where equality might be served?

(c) *Constitutional Principles: Federalism and Separation of Powers*. Although *Davis* involved a Fifth Amendment claim against the federal government (which controls the District of Columbia), the Court was concerned about the federalism implications of any holding that racially discriminatory effects would be subject to strict scrutiny. A huge number of state and local policies would be litigable under such a constitutional regime, which would place a large burden on state and local governments and incorporate federal judges into their decisionmaking—at a point in time when a majority of the Court may have felt that judges had already gone too far. An oddity of the case was that the Court in 1971 had interpreted Title VII to render employers liable for policies having a racially discriminatory effect (unless the employer could show the policy served a valid business purpose) and Congress in 1972 had extended Title VII to cover federal, state, and local governments.[11] Because the Court had to address the Title VII question (and did so, resolving it against the challengers), it was unnecessary to have ruled that the Equal Protection Clause and Title VII rules were different—unless the Court majority was trying to make an important constitutional point. It is possible that the broad coverage of Title VII gave the Court cover for its narrow ruling: The unelected Court would not subject state and local governments to broad liability, but this might be accomplished in certain areas by Congress, where state governments were well-represented by senators, the party system, and powerful lobbyists.

---

[11] The lower court had granted the challengers relief only on Title VII grounds, and the petitioners relied only on Title VII. At oral argument, Justices Rehnquist and Powell fed the counsel their winning equal protection argument—and the attorneys rejected it, reaffirming their position that Title VII and the Equal Protection Clause provided the same assurances against policies having race-based effects but arguing that the local employment policy was justified for good business reasons.

2.   Arlington Heights *and Proving Discriminatory Intent and Effect.* Later cases have understood *Washington v. Davis* as requiring a showing of both discriminatory purpose and discriminatory effect. See, e.g., *United States v. Armstrong*, 517 U.S. 456 (1996). The "effects" prong seems clear enough—it compels proof of disproportionate impact. The "intent" prong is murkier. In *Village of Arlington Heights v. Metropolitan Housing Development Corp.*, 429 U.S. 252 (1977), an important case, the Court explained the evidentiary burdens concerning intent that are imposed by *Davis*:

> *Davis* made it clear that official action will not be held unconstitutional solely because it results in a racially disproportionate impact. * * * *Davis* does not require a plaintiff to prove that the challenged action rested solely on racially discriminatory purposes. Rarely can it be said that a legislature or administrative body operating under a broad mandate made a decision motivated solely by a single concern, or even that a particular purpose was the "dominant" or "primary" one. In fact, it is because legislators and administrators are properly concerned with balancing numerous competing considerations that courts refrain from reviewing the merits of their decisions, absent a showing of arbitrariness or irrationality. But racial discrimination is not just another competing consideration. When there is proof that a discriminatory purpose has been a motivating factor in the decision, this judicial deference is no longer justified.

> Determining whether invidious discriminatory purpose was a motivating factor demands a sensitive inquiry into such circumstantial and direct evidence of intent as may be available. The impact of the official action—whether it "bears more heavily on one race than another," *Davis*—may provide an important starting point. Sometimes a clear pattern, unexplainable on grounds other than race, emerges from the effect of the state action even when the governing legislation appears neutral on its face. *Yick Wo.* The evidentiary inquiry is then relatively easy. But such cases are rare. Absent a pattern as stark as that in *Yick Wo*, impact alone is not determinative, and the Court must look to other evidence.

> The historical background of the decision is one evidentiary source, particularly if it reveals a series of official actions taken for invidious purposes. The specific sequence of events leading up to the challenged decision also may shed some light on the decisionmaker's purposes. * * * Departures from the normal procedural sequence also might afford evidence that improper purposes are playing a role. Substantive departures too may be relevant, particularly if the factors usually considered important by the decisionmaker strongly favor a decision contrary to the one reached.

> The legislative or administrative history may be highly relevant, especially where there are contemporary statements by members of

the decisionmaking body, minutes of its meetings, or reports. In some extraordinary instances the members might be called to the stand at trial to testify concerning the purpose of the official action, although even then such testimony frequently will be barred by privilege.

At the end of this discussion, the Court said, in a footnote:

> This Court has recognized, ever since *Fletcher v. Peck*, that judicial inquiries into legislative or executive motivation represent a substantial intrusion into the workings of other branches of government. Placing a decisionmaker on the stand is therefore "usually to be avoided."

Two years later, in a gender discrimination case, *Personnel Administrator v. Feeney*, 442 U.S. 256 (1979), the Court further elaborated:

> The appellee's ultimate argument rests upon the presumption, common to the criminal and civil law, that a person intends the natural and foreseeable consequences of his voluntary actions. * * * "Discriminatory purpose," however, implies more than intent as volition or intent as awareness of consequences. It implies that the decisionmaker * * * selected or reaffirmed a particular course of action at least in part "because of," not merely "in spite of," its adverse effects upon an identifiable group.

In a footnote, the Court continued:

> This is not to say that the inevitability or foreseeability of consequences of a neutral rule has no bearing upon the existence of discriminatory intent. Certainly, when the adverse consequences of a law upon an identifiable group are [plainly] inevitable * * *, a strong inference that the adverse effects were desired can reasonably be drawn. But in this inquiry * * * an inference is a working tool, not a synonym for proof. When * * * the impact is essentially an unavoidable consequence of legislative policy that has in itself always been deemed to be legitimate, and when * * * the statutory history and all of the available evidence effectively demonstrate the opposite, the inference simply fails to ripen into proof.

Do these cases require a showing of outright racial animus? Reconsider *Palmer*. Assume that the Jackson city council was ideologically opposed to integration. Would proof along those lines satisfy the *Feeney* standard? What if the Jackson city council was ideologically neutral about integration, but decided to close the swimming pools because of a justifiable fear that violence would result from integrated swimming? Dicta in *Davis*, discussing *Palmer*, suggests that this purpose might survive equal protection review. But wouldn't this theory allow the city council to maintain segregated swimming pools in the first place, if the council could demonstrate that was the only way to allow safe public swimming? And isn't that inconsistent with *Cooper v. Aaron* (Chapter 2, § 2B), which refused to allow local officials to postpone compliance with a *Brown II* order based on a fear of backlash? Compare *Palmore v. Sidoti* (note 3 following *Loving* in § 1A of this chapter), where the Court invalidated a state judge's order revoking a divorced white mother's custody of her white child when she married a black man because the judge feared that the child would suffer because of societal prejudice. Can the *Davis* dicta concerning *Palmer* be squared with *Palmore*?

Consider a different problem. Assume that a city council decides to build an interstate highway bypass through an African-American neighborhood, knowing that the project will dislocate hundreds of families. When asked why, council members point out that this was the least expensive place to route the bypass. Is there any way, under *Davis* and its progeny, to attack that decision? In answering this question, consider Paul Brest, *In Defense of the Antidiscrimination Principle*, 90 Harv. L. Rev. 1, 6 (1976):

> * * * [T]he antidiscrimination principle disfavors race-dependent decisions and conduct—at least when they selectively disadvantage the members of a minority group. By race-dependent, I mean decisions and conduct * * * that would have been different but for the race of those benefited or disadvantaged by them.

Under *Davis* and the later cases, is it relevant to inquire, as Brest suggested, whether the city council would have put the bypass through a white neighborhood, had that been the cheapest route? *Should* this inquiry be relevant to any meaningful approach based on discriminatory intent? Consider Brest's concept of "racially selective sympathy and indifference"—"the unconscious failure to extend to a minority the same recognition of humanity, and hence the same sympathy and care, given as a matter of course to one's own group." Does *Feeney* make it impossible to attack decisions rooted in racial indifference rather than racial hostility? Consider this additional language from *Feeney*: "When there is no 'reason to infer antipathy' * * * it is presumed that 'even improvident decisions will eventually be rectified by the democratic process.'"

3. *More Problems of Proof: Failure to Act and Partial Motivation.* If an official fails to act because of discriminatory reasons, can this inaction violate the Fourteenth Amendment? In *Rogers v. Lodge*, 458 U.S. 613 (1982), the Court accepted the lower courts' finding that an at-large voting scheme in a Georgia county had been *maintained* for discriminatory reasons and then invalidated the scheme even though it assumed that at-large elections had been adopted for valid reasons. Conversely, may a legislature refuse to repeal a statute that was adopted for discriminatory reasons and that continues to have a discriminatory effect if the refusal to repeal is motivated by nondiscriminatory factors? Consider *Hunter v. Underwood*, 471 U.S. 222 (1985), which invalidated a provision in the Alabama Constitution of 1901 that disenfranchised a person convicted of any crime "involving moral turpitude," which had been interpreted broadly to include minor offenses like presenting a bad check. The Court concluded that "the delegates to the all-white [constitutional] convention were not secretive about their purpose" for this provision, which was largely to disenfranchise African Americans, and that at present the statute continued

to disenfranchise them disproportionately. Does *Hunter* suggest an affirmative duty to repeal legislation that was enacted for discriminatory reasons and that has a discriminatory effect, even if today's legislators think the statute serves legitimate contemporary purposes? How can this be, if the state legislature could constitutionally respond to *Hunter* by enacting a law containing the same substance so long as its motive is simply to limit voting to persons of high moral character? Note that state statutes disenfranchising persons convicted of certain kinds of crimes are common throughout the United States.[12]

In footnote 21 in *Arlington Heights*, the Court stated that proof of improper motivation shifts to the defendant decisionmaker "the burden of establishing that the same decision would have resulted even had the impermissible purpose not been considered. If this were established, the complaining party * * * no longer fairly could attribute the injury complained of to improper consideration of a discriminatory purpose." In *Hunter*, the Court stated that even if the "real purpose" of the constitutional provision was to disenfranchise poor whites as well as blacks, the provision was nonetheless unconstitutional because discriminatory animus against blacks was a but-for motivation for the enactment of the provision.

The proof problems explored in these notes, and the sense that *Davis* represents a retreat from *Brown*, have made *Davis* a highly controversial case from the time it was decided.[13]

PROBLEM CONCERNING PRESIDENTIAL SPEECH AND DISCRIMINATORY INTENT

Problem 3-4: Review Problem 8-10(c) on the Trump Travel Ban in § 3 of Chapter 8. Focus on Travel Ban 2.0, which restricted travel to the United States from Iran, Libya, Somalia, Sudan, Syria and Yemen. Suppose that, instead of making derogatory comments about Muslims in the lead up to the travel ban, the President had made similar comments about what he called "the Arab race." Assume, in other words, that his comments treated the category "Arab" as a matter of race or ethnic descent, and disparaged those with that identity. He later made a written finding that allowing travel from those six countries would be detrimental to national security, and his finding was silent on ethnicity and race. Although there are ethnic and cultural differences between and among the six covered countries, all are or have been

---

[12] See *Richardson v. Ramirez*, 418 U.S. 24, 54 (1974) (upholding ban of voting by convicted felons on the ground that "the exclusion of felons from the vote has an affirmative sanction in § 2 of the Fourteenth Amendment"). Challenges to felon disenfranchisement under the Voting Rights Act have generally failed as well, but in recent years several states have softened their disenfranchisement statutes. See, e.g., *Developments in the Law—One Person, No Vote: The Laws of Felon Disenfranchisement*, 115 Harv. L. Rev. 1939 (2002).

[13] Influential early critiques include Derrick Bell, *Foreword: Equal Employment Law and the Continuing Need for Self-Help*, 8 Loy. U. Chi. L.J. 681 (1977); Michael Selmi, *Proving Intentional Discrimination: The Reality of Supreme Court Rhetoric*, 86 Geo. L.J. 279 (1997); David Strauss, *Discriminatory Intent and the Taming of Brown*, 56 U. Chi. L. Rev. 935 (1989). See generally *Colloquium on Legislative and Administrative Motivation in Constitutional Law*, 15 San Diego L. Rev. 925 (1978). For later critiques focusing on issue of implicit bias, see § 1C of this chapter.

members of the Arab League and are commonly regarded as Arab nations. There are, of course, many other nations that are members of the Arab League that are not covered by the ban.

Assume that plaintiffs of Arab descent challenged this hypothetical version of the travel ban as unconstitutional discrimination based on race and ethnicity. These plaintiffs include American citizens with family members in the banned countries who are now unable to travel to the U.S. Would the President's public comments denigrating "Arabs" be taken into account to determine whether the policy had a discriminatory intent? Should they be? Do such comments fit within the scope of the *Arlington Heights* factors? Would it matter whether the comments were made before or after the President was elected? Are campaign statements especially problematic because of the context in which they are made and the possible variation in what a candidate says on a subject at different points or venues?

A question something like this was before the Supreme Court in *Trump v. Hawaii*, 138 S.Ct. 2392 (2018). In that case (addressed at length in Chapter 8), the Court upheld the Trump Administration's travel ban. The Supreme Court rejected a claim that the ban discriminated on the basis of religion notwithstanding numerous presidential statements indicating a specific intent to target Muslims. The question whether such presidential speech should be considered by courts as evidence a discriminatory intent is explored in Katherine Shaw, *Beyond the Bully Pulpit*, 96 Tex. L. Rev. 71 (2017).

C. CONCLUDING THOUGHTS ABOUT STATUTES WITH DISCRIMINATORY EFFECTS

The cases we have examined seem to divide the world of statutes into two categories. Statutes that on their face take race into account are subject to strict scrutiny, even if they equally disadvantage whites and blacks, at least so long as the use of race can be traced to hostility toward a racial minority or the view that the minority is inferior. *Loving*. Facially neutral statutes that have a disparate impact upon persons of color are subject to strict scrutiny only if *Davis* discriminatory intent can be shown; without that showing, as explained in Chapter 4, § 1, such statutes are subject only to rational-basis review, the most minimal form of equal protection scrutiny.

To prove a *Davis* claim, *Feeney* requires a showing that the decisionmaker acted at least in part because of a desire to harm a protected minority; foreseeable harmful effects upon a protected minority are not unconstitutional so long as the decision was made in spite of, not because of, them. So understood, these cases seem to view the Equal Protection Clause as designed primarily to root out the evil decisionmaker and to protect individuals against the stigma of disadvantage flowing from hostility or visions of inferiority based on race, and not against disadvantage flowing from more general social conditions.

Similarly, *Davis* and its progeny may be seen as designed to perfect the political process. Footnote 4 of *Carolene Products* (Chapter 1, § 6) spoke of how prejudice against discrete and insular minorities distorts the political process. Racially discriminatory motives result in harms to individuals that would not occur if the political process were cleansed of those motives. As *Feeney* said, if there is no reason to infer antipathy, the Court will presume that even improvident decisions will be rectified by the political process. Outright racial animus is a political distortion that the Equal Protection Clause invalidates; other distortions of the political process do not count.[14]

One problem with this approach is that it cannot attack the perpetuation of past discrimination. Choosing public employees based on civil service examinations will have a discriminatory impact because of the nation's history of inferior and segregated public educational opportunities for racial minorities. Although by using standardized tests the government is not using race impermissibly in a *Brown* sense (it is not overtly segregating) or a *Davis* sense (it did not choose the test because it wished to exclude racial minorities), real harm with a disproportionate racial impact results nonetheless. Not having the job, or not getting into a professional school, may strike many as a much more concrete form of disadvantage than the psychological harm of stigma and the barriers to political influence that *Davis* considers important.[15] In short, *Davis* looks

---

[14] In a few contexts, the Court has been more willing to infer discriminatory purpose from a showing of discriminatory effects. See *Dayton Board of Educ. v. Brinkman*, 443 U.S. 526 (1979) (school desegregation); *Columbus Board of Educ. v. Penick*, 443 U.S. 449 (1979) (same); *Castaneda v. Partida*, 430 U.S. 482 (1977) (jury selection); *Rogers v. Lodge, supra* (racial vote dilution). Professor Daniel Ortiz argues in *The Myth of Intent in Equal Protection*, 41 Stan. L. Rev. 1105, 1137 (1989), that in all the cases since *Washington v. Davis* "[i]ntent takes into account not only the invidiousness of the government's classification but also the importance of the individual interest at stake." Thus, the important thing about *Davis, Arlington Heights,* and *Feeney* is that the individual interest at stake in them (employment, housing) is of less constitutional significance than jury composition for a criminal defendant (*Castaneda*), voting (*Rogers*), and public education (the school desegregation cases cited above). Ortiz acknowledges that this hierarchy of values is controversial and explains it by suggesting that the Court has essentially embraced a free-market allocational system and its associated disparities in wealth except where our society has not relegated an area to market control—thus, a distinction between "ordinary" social and economic goods (jobs and housing) and political, criminal, and educational "rights."

[15] Consider this criticism:

[W]hite people tend to view intent as an essential element of racial harm; nonwhites do not. The white perspective can be, and frequently is, expressed succinctly and without any apparent perceived need for justification: "[W]ithout concern about past and present intent, racially discriminatory effects of legislation would be quite innocent." For black people, however, the fact of racial oppression exists largely independent of the motives or intentions of its perpetrators. Second, both in principle and in application the *Davis* rule presupposes the existence of race-neutral decisionmaking. Whites' level of confidence in race neutrality is much greater than nonwhites'; a skeptic (nonwhite, more likely than not) would not adopt a rule that presumes the neutrality of criteria of decision absent the specific intent to do racial harm. Finally, retaining the intent requirement in the face of its demonstrated failure to effectuate substantive racial justice is indicative of a complacency concerning, or even a commitment to, the racial status quo that can only be enjoyed by those who are its beneficiaries—by white people.

for evil decisionmakers who have harmed identifiable people because of their race, rather than government decisions that disadvantage historically subordinated racial groups. See Alan Freeman, *Legitimating Racial Discrimination Through Antidiscrimination Law: A Critical Review of Supreme Court Doctrine*, 62 Minn. L. Rev. 1049 (1978).

A contrary vision might try to avoid this all-or-nothing approach to laws that have discriminatory effects. Consider the following argument.

CHARLES LAWRENCE, III, *The Id, the Ego, and Equal Protection: Reckoning with Unconscious Racism*

39 Stan. L. Rev. 317, 319–24, 366–67 (1987)[16]

* * * [The critics of *Washington v. Davis*] advance two principal arguments. The first is that a motive-centered doctrine of racial discrimination places a very heavy, and often impossible, burden of persuasion on the wrong side of the dispute. Improper motives are easy to hide. And because behavior results from the interaction of a multitude of motives, government officials will always be able to argue that racially neutral considerations prompted their actions. Moreover, where several decisionmakers are involved, proof of racially discriminatory motivation is even more difficult.

The second objection to the *Davis* doctrine is more fundamental. It argues that the injury of racial inequality exists irrespective of the decisionmakers' motives. Does the black child in a segregated school experience less stigma and humiliation because the local school board did not consciously set out to harm her? * * *

Supporters of the intent requirement * * * echo the four main arguments that the Court itself set forth in *Davis*: (1) A standard that would subject all governmental action with a racially disproportionate impact to strict scrutiny would cost too much * * *; (2) a disproportionate impact standard would make innocent people bear the costs of remedying a harm in which they played no part; (3) an impact test would be inconsistent with equal protection values, because the judicial decisionmaker would have to explicitly consider race; and (4) it would be inappropriate for the judiciary to choose to remedy the racially disproportionate impact of otherwise neutral governmental actions at the expense of other legitimate social interests.

Barbara Flagg, *"Was Blind, But Now I See": White Race Consciousness and the Requirement of Discriminatory Intent*, 91 Mich. L. Rev. 953, 968–69 (1993).

[16] Copyright © 1987 by the Board of Trustees of the Leland Stanford Junior University. For an interesting retrospective of this article, see Charles Lawrence III, *Unconscious Racism Revisited: Reflections on the Impact and Origins of "the Id, the Ego, and Equal Protection,"* 40 Conn. L. Rev. 931 (2008).

My own sympathies lie with the critics * * *

Scholarly and judicial efforts to explain the constitutional significance of disproportionate impact and government motive in cases alleging racial discrimination treat these two categories as mutually exclusive. * * * [T]he Court thinks of facially neutral actions as either [1] intentionally and unconstitutionally or [2] unintentionally and constitutionally discriminatory.

I argue this is a false dichotomy. Traditional notions of intent do not reflect the fact that decisions about racial matters are influenced in large part by factors that can be characterized as neither intentional—in the sense that certain outcomes are self-consciously sought—nor unintentional—in the sense that the outcomes are random, fortuitous, and uninfluenced by the decisionmaker's beliefs, desires, and wishes.* * *

[T]he theory of cognitive psychology states that the culture—including, for example, the media and an individual's parents, peers, and authority figures—transmits certain beliefs and preferences. Because these beliefs are so much a part of the culture, they are not experienced as explicit lessons. Instead, they seem part of the individual's rational ordering of her perceptions of the world. The individual is unaware, for example, that the ubiquitous presence of a cultural stereotype has influenced her perception that blacks are lazy or unintelligent. Because racism is so deeply ingrained in our culture, it is likely to be transmitted by tacit understandings: Even if a child is not told that blacks are inferior, he learns that lesson by observing the behavior of others. These tacit understandings, because they have never been articulated, are less likely to be experienced at a conscious level.

In short, requiring proof of conscious or intentional motivation as a prerequisite to constitutional recognition that a decision is race-dependent ignores much of what we understand about how the human mind works. It also disregards both the irrationality of racism and the profound effect that the history of American race relations has had on the individual and collective unconscious. * * * The equal protection clause requires the elimination of governmental decisions that take race into account without good and important reasons. Therefore, equal protection doctrine must find a way to come to grips with unconscious racism.

In pursuit of that goal, this article proposes a new test to trigger judicial recognition of race-based behavior. [This test would] evaluate governmental conduct to determine whether it conveys a symbolic message to which the culture attaches racial significance. A finding that the culture thinks of an allegedly discriminatory governmental action in racial terms would also constitute a finding regarding the beliefs and motivations of the governmental actors: The actors are themselves part of the culture and presumably could not have acted without being influenced by racial considerations, even if they were unaware of their racist beliefs. Therefore, the court would apply strict scrutiny.

[Professor Lawrence applies his test to some easy cases, like *Brown*, where there is a direct historical link between slavery, the black codes, and Jim Crow laws, including educational segregation; forcing black and white children into different schools had a cultural significance—subordination of blacks—that was inescapable. Also an easy case for Professor Lawrence would be a city's increase in a railway fare; even if blacks were relatively less able to absorb the increased cost, this would not be suspicious unless there were a history of using fares as a way to harm African Americans.

[Consider how Professor Lawrence, in the next paragraph, applies his test to *Arlington Heights*, note 2 following *Davis* earlier in this chapter, where the zoning board denied a developer's request to build an integrated townhouse project in an all-white neighborhood.]

Several kinds of evidence would be available to demonstrate that denying the zoning variance in these circumstances has a cultural meaning that demeans blacks. Initially, plaintiffs could present evidence of the historical and contemporaneous meaning of residential segregation in the culture as a whole. This would include the history of statutorily mandated housing segregation as well as the use of restrictive covenants among private parties that aim to prevent blacks from purchasing property in white neighborhoods. Studies of racially segregated housing patterns throughout the United States and in the areas surrounding Arlington Heights as well as data and attitudinal surveys on residential segregation and "white flight" would also be relevant. Such studies * * * agree substantially on the prominence of race in the minds of both those who flee and those who stay. They also note whites' continuing aversion to housing integration.

The body of evidence that documents our culture's frequent attachment of racial meaning to the very existence of segregated housing is extensive and should be more than sufficient to establish the cultural meaning of the Arlington Heights city officials' action. We live in segregated neighborhoods because whites have believed that living with or close to blacks lowers their own status. Where one lives is an important index of one's status in our culture, and to live in proximity to those who are looked down upon is to be looked down upon oneself.

NOTE ON THE COGNITIVE TURN AND IMPLICIT BIAS

Professor Lawrence's influential article relies in part on cognitive psychology. Since he wrote in 1987, there has been an explosion of research into what he called "unconscious racism" and what is often called "implicit bias" in contemporary parlance. While Lawrence emphasized Freudian dynamics and the processes by which cultural attitudes and stereotypes are transmitted and given meaning, the newer work focuses on the dynamics of cognition and its implications for problems of discrimination. Professor Lawrence's framework was updated in the logic and language of social cognition theory in Eva Paterson, Kimberly Thomas Rapp & Sara Jackson, *The Id, the Ego and Equal Protection in the 21st Century: Building Upon Charles Lawrence's Vision to Mount a Contemporary Challenge to the Intent Doctrine*, 40 Conn. L. Rev. 1175 (2008). The authors consider how stereotyping and perceptions of "outgroups" as an "undifferentiated mass" are part of unconscious bias. There is now a voluminous literature on the question of implicit bias, with many scholars calling for a "behavioral realism" that rejects the assumption that individuals are colorblind. Principal contributions to this body of research, and the critiques that have been launched against it, are traced in Jerry Kang and Kristin Lane, *Seeing Through Colorblindness: Implicit Bias and the Law*, 58 U.C.L.A. L. Rev. 465 (2010); see also Gregory Mitchell and Philip Tetlock, *Antidiscrimination Law and the Perils of Mindreading*, 67 Ohio St. L.J. 1023 (2006) (criticizing implicit bias findings); Samuel R. Bagenstos, *Implicit Bias, 'Science' and Antidiscrimination Law*, 1 Harv. L. & Pol'y Rev. 477 (2007) (defending research).

What are the implications of this research for the idea of discriminatory intent? Can the idea of discriminatory intent meaningfully take into account implicit bias? If so, how? Can behavioral realism be reconciled with the framework adopted by the Court in *Washington v. Davis*, or must that framework be replaced? If so, what might and should a doctrinal replacement look like? For thoughtful reflections on these problems, see Kang and Lane, above; *Symposium on Behavioral Realism*, 94 Cal. L. Rev. 945 (2006); Linda Hamilton Krieger, *The Content of Our Categories: A Cognitive Bias Approach to Discrimination and Equal Employment Opportunity*, 47 Stan. L. Rev. 1161 (1995). For a collection of judicial decisions accepting and rejecting evidence of implicit bias, see the appendices in Erik J. Girvan, *When Our Reach Exceeds Our Grasp: Remedial Realism in Antidiscrimination Law*, 95 Or. L. Rev. 359 (2016).

PROBLEMS CONCERNING DISCRIMINATORY INTENT

Problem 3-5: *Unequal Application of Death Penalty*. Under Georgia law, a jury may impose the death penalty for murder only if the crime involved certain aggravating circumstances (*e.g.*, prior conviction for a capital felony; murder occurred in the commission of certain specified crimes; defendant greatly risked death of more than one person by means of weapon; murder for hire; murder of judicial official or member of her family; murder was "outrageously or wantonly vile, horrible, or inhuman in that it involved torture, depravity of mind, or an aggravated battery"). An African-American criminal defendant alleged that the death penalty assessed to him by a jury for the murder of a white victim violated the Equal Protection Clause. The argument was based on statistical evidence. An empirical study examined over 2,000 murder cases arising in Georgia in the 1970s. The death penalty was imposed "in 22% of the cases involving black defendants and white victims; 8% of the cases involving white defendants and white victims; 1% of the cases involving black defendants and black victims; and 3% of the cases involving white defendants and black victims. * * * [P]rosecutors sought the death penalty in 70% of the cases involving black defendants and white victims; 32% of the cases involving white defendants and white victims; 15% of the cases involving black defendants and black victims; and 19% of the cases involving white defendants and black victims." After statistical analysis of variables that could explain these disparities on nonracial grounds, the study suggested that "defendants charged with killing white victims were 4.3 times as likely to receive a death sentence as defendants charged with killing blacks. [B]lack defendants were 1.1 times as likely to receive a death sentence as other defendants. Thus, [the study] indicates that black defendants, like [petitioner], who kill white victims have the greatest likelihood of receiving the death penalty." The author of the study testified: "[W]hen the cases become tremendously aggravated so that everybody would agree that if we're going to have a death sentence, these are the cases that should get it, the race effects go away. It's only in the mid-range of cases where the decision makers have a real choice as to what to do. If there's room for the exercise of discretion, then the [racial] factors begin to play a role."

Assuming that petitioner's case falls in this "mid-range" of aggravating factors, should the Court find an equal protection violation and invalidate his death sentence? Should the Court consider other factors bearing on motivation, such as the racial composition of his jury? Or should the Court take more clear-cut action—either invalidating the capital punishment statutes themselves because of their disparate impact, or holding the statistical evidence irrelevant? See *McCleskey v. Kemp*, 481 U.S. 279 (1987). How should the case come out under Professor Lawrence's approach? See generally David Baldus, George Woodworth & Charles Pulaski, Jr., *Equal Justice and the Death Penalty: A Legal and Empirical Study* (1990); Randall Kennedy, *Race, Crime, and the Law* 328–50 (1997). For recent reflections on *McCleskey* and statistical evidence in the context of discrimination and criminal justice, see Symposium: *"A Fear of Too Much Justice"? Equal Protection and the Social Sciences Thirty Years After* McCleskey v. Kemp, 112 Nw. U. L. Rev. 1259, et seq. (2018).

Problem 3-6: *Prosecutorial Discretion and Punishment for Crack Cocaine Offenses Versus Powder Cocaine Offenses.* Suppose that, under state law, possession of three grams of "crack cocaine" (a crystalline form of the substance) carries a penalty of up to 20 years in prison, while possession of a similar amount of powder cocaine carries only a sentence of up to 5 years. If defendants, who are African American, show that 96.6% of all defendants in the state charged with crack cocaine possession are African American, while only 20.4% of all state defendants charged with powder cocaine are African American, have they demonstrated a violation of the federal Equal Protection Clause? If not, should a state supreme court invoke the state constitution's equality clause to strike down the disparity? See *State v. Russell*, 477 N.W.2d 866 (Minn. 1991).

Would it change your analysis if an African-American crack-cocaine defendant charged by the United States in the Central District of California demonstrated that federal penalties for crack-cocaine possession were more severe than state penalties, that all 24 crack-cocaine cases brought by the United States Attorney for the Central District of California in the last year were against African Americans, and that criminal defense attorneys were willing to testify as expert witnesses that non-African Americans involved in alleged cocaine offenses were being prosecuted in state rather than federal court? Would you at least allow the defendant to obtain discovery on recent cocaine cases in the District, including the race of the defendants, and to require the United States Attorney to explain her criteria for deciding whom to prosecute? See *United States v. Armstrong*, 517 U.S. 456 (1996). How would these cases come out under Professor Lawrence's theory of "unconscious racism"? See generally Randall Kennedy, *supra*, at 357–59, 364–86; David Sklansky, *Cocaine, Race, and Equal Protection*, 47 Stan. L. Rev. 1283 (1995).

Finally, how much of a racial disparity in sentencing results is constitutionally permissible in this area? Against a background in which there was a whopping 100:1 crack-powder disparity in federal sentences, Congress passed the Fair Sentencing Act of 2010. It did so by means of a facially race-neutral bill that changed mandatory minimum sentences for crack cocaine. The effect was to reduce the disparity to 16:1. Could an equal protection challenge to that statute be mounted? Would it succeed? The history of federal sentencing in this area is recounted in *Dorsey v. United States*, 567 U.S. 260 (2012), a statutory interpretation case about the retroactivity of the Fair Sentencing Act. The Court in that case found the 2010 legislation partially retroactive, and the 2018 First Step Act expanded that retroactivity. In the course of dissenting in *Dorsey*, however, Justice Scalia, joined by the Chief Justice and Justices Thomas and Alito, was dismissive of potential constitutional questions about even the heftier pre-Fair Sentencing Act 100:1 sentencing disparity, saying that "only *intentional* discrimination may violate the equal protection component of the Fifth Amendment's Due Process Clause." Id. at 296.

SECTION 2. THE STATE ACTION DOCTRINE AS A LIMIT ON THE JUDICIAL POWER TO ADDRESS RACIAL DISCRIMINATION

Washington v. Davis holds that racially discriminatory effects are subject to heightened scrutiny only if they result from intentional discrimination by the state. The materials that we just examined suggest why the Court required a showing of *discriminatory intent*. In this section, we address why it is only discrimination *by the state*, and not by private persons, that implicates the Equal Protection Clause.

A. INTRODUCTION

At first glance, the question concerning whether the Equal Protection Clause reaches private conduct seems easily answered by its text. After all, the provision says that "no state," rather than "no person," shall deny anyone the equal protection of the laws. Compare the language of the Thirteenth Amendment, which by providing that "[n]either slavery nor involuntary servitude . . . shall exist within the United States" directly prohibits a certain kind of private conduct.[17]

In addition to this textualist point, there are other strong arguments against applying the Fourteenth Amendment to private persons. The regulation of private conduct has always been the domain of the common law, supplemented by statutes, and it would seem surprising if the framers of the Fourteenth Amendment would have intended to alter this fundamental aspect of our legal regime. Moreover, applying constitutional prohibitions to private parties would drastically increase the degree to which the government would be regulating private life. It would also greatly shift the responsibility of determining the appropriateness of private conduct from state judges (applying the common law and interpreting state statutes) and state legislators (considering whether to adopt new statutory provisions) to federal judges (interpreting the Constitution) and to Congress (considering whether to exercise its legislative power, under Section 5 of the Fourteenth Amendment, to enforce the amendment by appropriate legislation).

To take an obvious example: If, as in *Yick Wo*, government officials close down the businesses of a certain ethnic group out of animus toward such persons, that seems an obvious violation of the government's responsibility of providing equal protection of the laws. In contrast, the common law has always assumed that a private person has the freedom to contract with whomever she wishes, and if she decides not to take her clothes to a laundry because she is biased against its owners, that is within her freedom of choice. If she does more than that—for example, burning down the business out of spite—the common law and state criminal statutes provide remedies.

It is thus unsurprising that the Supreme Court has always understood the Fourteenth Amendment as targeting state governmental conduct, not private activity. In *The Civil Rights Cases*, 109 U.S. 3 (1883), the Court held that the Fourteenth Amendment only regulated "State action of a particular character."[18] Justice Bradley explained:

> [C]ivil rights, such as are guaranteed by the Constitution against State aggression, cannot be impaired by the wrongful acts

---

[17] See *United States v. Reynolds*, 235 U.S. 133 (1914) (Thirteenth Amendment forbids compelling someone to work for another to pay off a debt); *The Civil Rights Cases*, 109 U.S. 3 (1883) (Thirteenth Amendment "by its own unaided force and effect . . . abolished slavery").

[18] We excerpt more of *The Civil Rights Cases* in Chapter 7, § 3A. Note that for purposes of this requirement the state includes all of its formal governmental subdivisions. Thus, the actions of a city, a county, a public school board, and so on—whether by formal lawmaking, such as the adoption of an ordinance, or by the actions of their employees—are subject to the Fourteenth Amendment.

of individuals, unsupported by State authority in the shape of laws, customs, or judicial or executive proceedings. The wrongful act of an individual, unsupported by any such authority, is simply a private wrong, or a crime of that individual; an invasion of the rights of the injured party, it is true * * * but if not sanctioned in some way by the State, or not done under State authority, his rights remain in full force, and may presumably be vindicated by resort to the laws of the State for redress. * * *

Some civil rights lawyers and Justices have urged that this precedent should suffer the same fate as *Plessy*, because a rigid state action doctrine prevents the Court from protecting racial minorities from the systemwide discriminatory effects of racism. But the Supreme Court has never overruled or even limited this holding of the case—for some of the same libertarian, federalism, and institutional reasons that animated the Court's decision in *Washington v. Davis* in the previous section.

But neither has the Court been capable of applying the doctrine with any degree of consistency. The essential problem is conceptual in nature. The state action principle is designed to limit the reach of the Constitution, but it is an analytically limitless concept. In every instance, the state, through its common law and statutes, is prohibiting conduct, requiring conduct, or permitting persons to choose whether to engage in conduct. There is no such thing as a pre-political "state of nature" existing prior to the application of a state regulatory regime.

For example, if a homeowner orders a visitor to leave because of the visitor's race and gets police assistance to expel her if she refuses to leave, the homeowner is discriminating with the assistance of state (police) action. Even if the visitor goes quietly without police intervention, that action operates against a backdrop of the state's legal rule that property owners may exclude anyone they wish and obtain state assistance in doing so. In this sense, even the most seemingly private of personal choices is infused with state authority.

Many things can be attributed in part to state action, yet applying the Constitution to all private conduct seems inconsistent with constitutional text, the value of personal autonomy, and the primary state legislative and judicial responsibility to regulate private conduct. For this reason, courts have an analytically challenging task when they try to make sense of the state action doctrine. The general approach is clear enough: The Fourteenth Amendment is usually triggered only by the actions of government officials. Yet in some cases, to which we now turn, the Supreme Court has applied the Fourteenth Amendment to the conduct of private parties—those who seem to be exercising *de facto* governmental power, or to be intertwined with the government, to such an extent that it is deemed important to impose constitutional limitations upon their activities. The cases are "a conceptual disaster area,"[19] so do not expect bright-line distinctions and logical consistency. Instead, attempt to identify the values that are being balanced and to appreciate the difficulty of this enterprise.

B. THE PUBLIC/PRIVATE DISTINCTION TODAY

1. Private Actors and Public Functions

The doctrinal developments involving *private actors performing public functions* and thereby being subjected to constitutional constraint began in response to the racism of the Texas Democratic Party in the early twentieth century, when Texas was effectively a one-party, Democratic state. In *Nixon v. Herndon*, 273 U.S. 536 (1927), the Court struck down Texas statutes that excluded blacks from voting in Democratic Party primary elections. The state action requirement was easily satisfied by the presence of state statutes compelling discrimination by a private organization (a political party is in form a private association, not a branch of the state government). Texas then responded by granting the executive committee of the party the authority to decide who could vote in the primary. Discriminatory Democratic Party rules adopted pursuant to this authority were struck down in *Nixon v. Condon*, 286 U.S. 73 (1932). The Court in *Condon* concluded that the inherent authority to regulate membership lies with a state political party's convention, not the executive committee, and therefore when the executive committee acted to adopt the rules in question it was acting as the agent of the state, not of the convention.

Ever determined to discriminate, the Texas Democratic Party convention then adopted racially exclusionary rules. The Court first held that the party convention's conduct was not state action, *Grovey v. Townsend*, 295 U.S. 45 (1935), but nine years later overruled *Grovey* in *Smith v. Allwright*, 321 U.S. 649 (1944). *Smith* stated:

> [S]tate delegation to a party of the power to fix the qualifications of primary elections is delegation of a state function that may make the party's action the action of the state. * * * If the State requires a certain electoral procedure, prescribes a general election ballot made up of party nominees so chosen and limits the choice of the electorate in general elections for state offices, practically speaking, to those whose names appear on such a ballot, it endorses, adopts and enforces the discrimination against Negroes, practiced by a party entrusted by Texas law with the determination of the qualifications of participants in the primary. This is state action within the meaning of the Fifteenth Amendment.

---

[19] Charles Black, *The Supreme Court, 1966 Term—Foreword, "State Action," Equal Protection, and California's Proposition 14*, 81 Harv. L. Rev. 69, 95 (1967).

The shift from *Grovey* to *Smith* reflected both a change in Court personnel and in social context. Between 1935 and 1943, President Roosevelt remade the Court, and the New Deal Justices were open to the kind of anti-apartheid activism suggested in *Carolene Products* (Chapter 1, § 6). Similarly, the values associated with apartheid were under fire, as the civil rights movement was gaining steam and an increasing number of thoughtful people (including the Justices) were embarrassed by the similarities between American apartheid and Nazi racism.

Undaunted, Texas Democrats then turned to yet another technique, relying on private groups formally independent of the Democratic Party that effectively controlled the slating of candidates for the Democratic primary. As explained in *Terry v. Adams*, 345 U.S. 461 (1953):

> * * * This case raises questions concerning the constitutional power of a Texas county political organization called the Jaybird Democratic Association or Jaybird Party to exclude Negroes from its primaries on racial grounds. The Jaybirds deny that their racial exclusions violate the Fifteenth Amendment. They contend that the Amendment applies only to elections or primaries held under state regulation, that their association is not regulated by the state at all, and that it is not a political party but a self-governing voluntary club. * * *

> * * * The Jaybird Association or Party was organized in 1889. Its membership was then and always has been limited to white people; they are automatically members if their names appear on the official list of county voters. It has been run like other political parties with an executive committee named from the county's voting precincts. Expenses of the party are paid by the assessment of candidates for office in its primaries. Candidates for county offices submit their names to the Jaybird Committee in accordance with the normal practice followed by regular political parties all over the country. Advertisements and posters proclaim that these candidates are running subject to the action of the Jaybird primary. While there is no legal compulsion on successful Jaybird candidates to enter Democratic primaries, they have nearly always done so and with few exceptions since 1889 have run and won without opposition in the Democratic primaries and the general elections that followed. Thus the party has been the dominant political group in the county since organization, having endorsed every county-wide official elected since 1889.

It may seem difficult to distinguish the Jaybird Association from other local political groups, such as a business owners' association, that slate candidates. Nonetheless, although the Court could not muster a majority opinion, it did hold that the conduct of the Jaybird Association was state action. Speaking for himself and Justices Douglas and Burton, Justice Black said:

> For a state to permit such a duplication of its election processes is to permit a flagrant abuse of those processes to defeat the purposes of the Fifteenth Amendment. * * * It violates the Fifteenth Amendment for a state, by such circumvention, to permit within its borders the use of any device that produces an equivalent of the prohibited election.

Justice Frankfurter, writing for himself only, found the "vital component" of "State responsibility" in the "practical politics" of the situation, including participation by state officials in the Jaybird primary. Four other Justices said that the Jaybird Association operated "as an auxiliary of the local Democratic Party organization."

With no majority opinion and no clear consensus in the separate opinions about the nature of the crucial factors in the case, *Terry v. Adams* may have little precedential force outside its facts. It is an important case, nonetheless, because (if we may be a bit irreverent) the Court essentially adopted what might be called the "duck" test: If it walks like a duck, quacks like a duck, etc., it will be treated as a duck. The test in *Terry* can be difficult to apply, but without it, the protections of the Reconstruction Amendments could be eroded through subterfuge. *Terry* is a rare case in which the Court seemingly suggested that "private" power, if great enough, can erode constitutional values so much that, as a practical matter, the Constitution must be brought to bear on it. Moreover, *Terry* must be understood as the culmination of a series of cases about political racism in Texas, not as an isolated case announcing an analytically pure principle of state action.

These "white primary" cases exemplify our first category of state action cases, those involving *public functions* (like elections) that will be subject to the Constitution even if carried out by putatively private entities. Probably the broadest application of this approach is *Marsh v. Alabama*, 326 U.S. 501 (1946), involving a "company town." Chicasaw, a suburb of Mobile, Alabama, was owned by Gulf Shipbuilding Corp. It looked and functioned pretty much like any other town; it had a main street with merchants, residential streets, and so on. A Mobile County deputy sheriff, paid by the company, provided police protection. Marsh, a Jehovah's Witness, attempted to distribute religious material on the sidewalk near the post office. After she declined the request that she leave town, she was arrested and convicted of trespassing. Justice Black's majority opinion held that her conviction violated her First Amendment rights, made applicable to this "state action" by virtue of the Due Process Clause of the Fourteenth Amendment:

The more an owner, for his advantage, opens up his property for use by the public in general, the more do his rights become circumscribed by the statutory and constitutional rights of those who use it. Thus, the owners of privately held bridges, ferries, turnpikes, and railroads may not operate them as freely as a farmer does his farm. Since these facilities are built and operated primarily to benefit the public and since their operation is essentially a public function, it is subject to state regulation. * * *

We do not think it makes any significant constitutional difference as to the relationship between the rights of the owner and those of the public that here the State, instead of permitting the corporation to operate a highway, permitted it to use its property as a town. * * * Whether a corporation or a municipality owns or possesses the town the public in either case has an identical interest in the functioning of the community in such manner that the channels of communication remain free.

In *Marsh*, Justice Black acknowledged that he was "balanc[ing] the Constitutional rights of owners of property against those of the people to enjoy freedom of press and religion." He justified the result by noting that the many persons living in company towns were, like everyone else, "free citizens of their State and country" who "must make decisions which affect the welfare of community and nation." "To act as good citizens they must be informed. In order to enable them to be properly informed their information must be uncensored. There is no more reason for depriving these people of the liberties guaranteed by the First and Fourteenth Amendments than there is for curtailing these freedoms with respect to any other citizen."

This kind of balancing approach, where the interest in individual autonomy protected by the state action doctrine is weighed against the societal interest in avoiding erosion of constitutional rights by private actors performing public functions, has not overtly been a factor in most recent cases. In fact, after the liberal Warren Court, the Supreme Court has declined to apply the public function exception broadly. It is no coincidence that most of the refusals have *not* involved racial equal protection claims. For example, *Hudgens v. National Labor Relations Board*, 424 U.S. 507 (1976), overruled a 1968 decision holding that, by analogy to *Marsh*, a private shopping center was subject to the Constitution.[20] In *Jackson v. Metropolitan Edison Co.*, 419 U.S. 345 (1974),

---

[20] *PruneYard Shopping Center v. Robins*, 447 U.S. 74 (1980), is the flip side of *Hudgens*. The California Supreme Court held that, under the state constitution, peaceful picketers could not be excluded from a private shopping center. The U.S. Supreme Court found no federal constitutional infirmity with the state constitution as interpreted. The general point is that a state constitution may provide persons in the state more rights than granted by the federal Constitution so long as the state-created rights do not violate any federal constitutional protection (for example, the

the Court held that an privately owned utility with a state-granted monopoly on providing electricity to a locale was not a "state actor" and therefore could terminate services without providing a hearing or otherwise concerning itself with due process requirements. The Court distinguished *Terry* and *Marsh* as cases that "found state action present in the exercise by a private entity of powers traditionally exclusively reserved to the State"; providing electricity, the Court said, was an essential public service, but "is not traditionally the exclusive prerogative of the State."

A similar case is *Flagg Brothers v. Brooks*, 436 U.S. 149 (1978), which involved a provision of the Uniform Commercial Code adopted in many states that provides that a warehouse company may sell goods in its possession to satisfy unpaid storage charges. The Court held that such conduct of the warehouse company was not state action, and thus not subject to any procedural limitations that might otherwise have been required by the Due Process Clause of the Fourteenth Amendment. The Court said that it "has never held that a State's mere acquiescence in a private action converts that action into that of the State," and that it makes no difference if the State "has embodied its decision not to act in statutory form." It made no difference that the state statute seemingly delegated much of the authority to resolve a private dispute to one of the private parties involved, for the majority referred to *Terry* and *Marsh* as involving functions "exclusively reserved to the State" and explained that commercial disputes between private persons are subject to resolution in a variety of private ways. Thus, *Flagg Brothers* and *Metropolitan Edison* indicate that it is not the functional importance of the interest sought to be protected, but the presence of some exclusive state attribute, that today will render putatively private conduct to be state action under the "public function" theory. Cf. *Lugar v. Edmondson Oil Co.*, 457 U.S. 922 (1982) (state action present when creditor obtained a prejudgment writ of attachment from state court clerk and county sheriff executed the writ and seized debtor's property).[21]

---

shopping center owner in *PruneYard* argued that the California Constitution as interpreted violated its federal constitutional free speech and property rights).

[21] As the Note on State Action Under State Constitutions at the end of this section suggests, the *Marsh* kind of balancing has been more popular in cases adjudicated under some state constitutions. In addition to *PruneYard Shopping Center, supra*, where the California Supreme Court held that state constitutional guarantees of free expression applied to a shopping mall, that court also applied state constitutional guarantees to a sidewalk owned by a grocery store, *In re Lane*, 71 Cal. 2d 872, 457 P.2d 561, 79 Cal. Rptr. 729 (1969), and to a train station, *In re Hoffman*, 67 Cal. 2d 845, 434 P.2d 353, 64 Cal. Rptr. 97 (1967), in both cases protecting people's right to leaflet in "public spaces" owned by private parties. In *Sharrock v. Dell Buick-Cadillac, Inc.*, 45 N.Y.2d 152, 379 N.E.2d 1169, 408 N.Y.S.2d 39 (1978), the New York Court of Appeals invalidated on due process grounds the private sale of a person's car pursuant to New York's lien law (which did not require prior notice to the owner). The court recognized that *Flagg Brothers* probably precluded its reaching the merits of the plaintiff's federal law claim, but held that New York constitutional law offered broader protection, in part because its state due process clause did not have a state action requirement on its face. Because state law authorized otherwise illegal conduct (selling someone's car without her consent), state involvement was present. The court further

2. State Encouragement of or Entanglement with Private Actors

Two other categories of state action cases are worth exploring. Sometimes, state action has been found when the state encouraged or reinforced private conduct that would violate the Constitution if done by the state directly. *Shelley v. Kraemer* is the principal case, and, as the trite adage goes, it raises many more questions than it answers. The other category involves situations in which the state has intertwined itself with a private entity. *Moose Lodge No. 107 v. Irvis* illustrates this problem.

SHELLEY V. KRAEMER
334 U.S. 1, 68 S.Ct. 836, 92 L.Ed. 1161 (1948)

CHIEF JUSTICE VINSON delivered the opinion of the Court.

[In 1911, thirty property owners on an avenue in St. Louis entered into a "racially restrictive covenant": an agreement binding them and their successors to restrict the occupancy of their property for the next fifty years to white persons. In 1945 the Shelleys, a black couple, bought one of the parcels of land covered by this agreement. Shortly thereafter, several neighboring landowners filed suit, alleging that the Shelleys' purchase was void because it violated the covenant. The Supreme Court of Missouri granted the relief sought, rejecting the Shelleys' argument that judicial enforcement of the restrictive covenant constituted state action violating the Equal Protection Clause. Chief Justice Vinson's opinion disposed of *Shelley* as well as a similar case from Michigan.]

I.   * * * Here the particular patterns of discrimination and the areas in which the restrictions are to operate, are determined, in the first instance, by the terms of agreements among private individuals. Participation of the State consists in the enforcement of the restrictions so defined. The crucial issue * * * is whether this distinction removes these cases from the operation of the * * * Fourteenth Amendment.

Since [*The Civil Rights Cases*, 109 U.S. 3 (1883)] the principle has become firmly embedded in our constitutional law that the action inhibited by the first section of the Fourteenth Amendment is only such action as may fairly be said to be that of the States. That Amendment erects no shield against merely private conduct, however discriminatory or wrongful.

We conclude, therefore, that the restrictive agreements standing alone cannot be regarded as violative of any rights guaranteed to petitioners by

---

emphasized (in contrast to *Flagg Brothers*) that the lienor in that situation is performing functions traditionally performed by a sheriff, and therefore traditional limitations on the state, such as the due process requirement of prior notice, were appropriate.

In recent years, governments have hired private contractors to carry out many governmental functions. On the problematic reach of the Constitution in such instances, see Gillian Metzger, *Privatization as Delegation*, 103 Colum. L. Rev. 1367 (2003).

the Fourteenth Amendment. So long as the purposes of those agreements are effectuated by voluntary adherence to their terms, it would appear clear that there has been no action by the State * * *.

But here there was more. These are cases in which the purposes of the agreements were secured only by judicial enforcement by state courts of the restrictive terms of the agreements. The respondents urge that judicial enforcement of private agreements does not amount to state action; or, in any event, the participation of the State is so attenuated in character as not to amount to state action within the meaning of the Fourteenth Amendment. Finally, it is suggested, even if the States in these cases may be deemed to have acted in the constitutional sense, their action did not deprive petitioners of rights guaranteed by the Fourteenth Amendment. We move to a consideration of these matters.

II.   * * * [T]he examples of state judicial action which have been held by this Court to violate the Amendment's commands are not restricted to situations in which the judicial proceedings were found in some manner to be procedurally unfair. It has been recognized that the action of state courts in enforcing a substantive common-law rule formulated by those courts, may result in the denial of rights guaranteed by the Fourteenth Amendment, even though the judicial proceedings in such cases may have been in complete accord with the most rigorous conceptions of procedural due process. * * *

The short of the matter is that from the time of the adoption of the Fourteenth Amendment until the present, it has been the consistent ruling of this Court that the action of the States to which the Amendment has reference, includes action of state courts and state judicial officials. * * * [I]t has never been suggested that state court action is immunized from the operation of those provisions simply because the act is that of the judicial branch of the state government.

III. Against this background of judicial construction, extending over a period of some three-quarters of a century, we are called upon to consider whether enforcement by state courts of the restrictive agreements in these cases may be deemed to be the acts of those States; and, if so, whether that action has denied these petitioners the equal protection of the laws which the Fourteenth Amendment was intended to insure.

We have no doubt that there has been state action in these cases in the full and complete sense of the phrase. The undisputed facts disclose that petitioners were willing purchasers of properties upon which they desired to establish homes. The owners of the properties were willing sellers; and contracts of sale were accordingly consummated. It is clear that but for the active intervention of the state courts, supported by the full panoply of state power, petitioners would have been free to occupy the properties in question without restraint.

These are (not cases,) as has been suggested, in which the States have merely abstained from action, leaving private individuals free to impose such discriminations as they see fit. Rather, these are cases in which the States have made available to such individuals the full coercive power of government to deny to petitioners, on the grounds of race or color, the enjoyment of property rights in premises which petitioners are willing and financially able to acquire and which the grantors are willing to sell. The difference between judicial enforcement and nonenforcement of the restrictive covenants is the difference to petitioners between being denied rights of property available to other members of the community and being accorded full enjoyment of those rights on an equal footing.

The enforcement of the restrictive agreements by the state courts in these cases was directed pursuant to the common-law policy of the States as formulated by those courts in earlier decisions. In the Missouri case, enforcement of the covenant was directed in the first instance by the highest court of the State after the trial court had determined the agreement to be invalid for want of the requisite number of signatures. In the Michigan case, the order of enforcement by the trial court was affirmed by the highest state court. The judicial action in each case bears the clear and unmistakable imprimatur of the State. We have noted that previous decisions of this Court have established the proposition that judicial action is not immunized from the operation of the Fourteenth Amendment simply because it is taken pursuant to the state's common-law policy. Nor is the Amendment ineffective simply because the particular pattern of discrimination, which the State has enforced, was defined initially by the terms of a private agreement. * * *

Respondents urge, however, that since the state courts stand ready to enforce restrictive covenants excluding white persons from the ownership or occupancy of property covered by such agreements, enforcement of covenants excluding colored persons may not be deemed a denial of equal protection of the laws to the colored persons who are thereby affected. This contention does not bear scrutiny. The parties have directed our attention to no case in which a court, state or federal, has been called upon to enforce a covenant excluding members of the white majority from ownership or occupancy of real property on grounds of race or color. But there are more fundamental considerations. The rights created by the first section of the Fourteenth Amendment are, by its terms, guaranteed to the individual. The rights established are personal rights. It is, therefore, no answer to these petitioners to say that the courts may also be induced to deny white persons rights of ownership and occupancy on grounds of race or color. Equal protection of the laws is not achieved through indiscriminate imposition of inequalities.

Nor do we find merit in the suggestion that property owners who are parties to these agreements are denied equal protection of the laws if denied access to the courts to enforce the terms of restrictive covenants and to assert property rights which the state courts have held to be created by such agreements. The Constitution confers upon no individual the right to demand action by the State which results in the denial of equal protection of the laws to other individuals. And it would appear beyond question that the power of the State to create and enforce property interests must be exercised within the boundaries defined by the Fourteenth Amendment. Cf. *Marsh*. * * * [Reversed.]

[JUSTICES REED, JACKSON, and RUTLEDGE took no part in the consideration or decision of these cases.]

NOTES ON SHELLEY

1. *State   Support / Encouragement / Ratification   of   Private Discrimination*. On the surface, *Shelley* may appear to be an easy case for finding state action, as it involves an act of a state judge. But consider some questions suggested earlier. To return to an earlier example, is there state action if a landowner orders someone off her property solely because she does not like the person's race? What if, when the trespasser refuses, (a) the police arrive at the behest of the landowner and arrest the person, or (b) the landowner obtains an injunction ordering the person to leave? It is unlikely that today's Court would find state action in either instance.[22] Why should it make a difference that in *Shelley* third parties are interfering with a willing buyer and seller, where in the questions asked above the unwilling property owner is allowed to discriminate? The problem may boil down to this inquiry: Consistent with both the goals of the Equal Protection Clause and the purpose of the state action doctrine (which is designed to preserve a distinction between the public and private spheres of life), where should the power to assert individual autonomy lie? Should the personal autonomy of Shelley and the seller be preferred to that of the complaining neighbors? Should the personal autonomy of the landowner be preferred to that of the trespasser?

In all these examples, there is obvious action by the state (the judge or police intervening in the private dispute; the baseline of state common law empowering a property owner to eject an unwanted intruder); the hard question is whether this should constitute "state action" for Fourteenth Amendment purposes. In this sense, "the state action doctrine" is a very misleading term, for, as was stressed earlier, in every circumstance the state either forbids conduct, requires conduct, or allows the person to decide whether

---

[22] In the sit-in cases of the early 1960s, the Supreme Court found state action when lunch counter owners were following state or local laws prohibiting nondiscriminatory service, e.g., *Peterson v. City of Greenville*, 373 U.S. 244 (1963), and in one case where there was no such ordinance the Court found official encouragement. *Lombard v. Louisiana*, 373 U.S. 267 (1963). The Court has read these precedents narrowly. See *Adickes v. S.H. Kress Co.*, 398 U.S. 144 (1970). See also *Bell v. Maryland*, 378 U.S. 226 (1964), in which three Justices stated that the Equal Protection Clause should apply where a business owner refuses to serve blacks because of local custom. These Justices said that they would not take the same position with respect to discrimination by a homeowner; they saw the business as a quasi-public entity.

to engage in conduct, and state officers stand ready to enforce these rules. In the first and second instances, where the state compulsion is obvious, state action seems obvious. The problem of "state action" generally arises in the third category, when a private person is allowed by law to exercise freedom of choice and undertakes a course of conduct that would be forbidden by the Constitution if done by the government. Maybe the doctrine should be renamed "the state responsibility doctrine" and focus on the unusual situations in which the state is deemed to bear sufficient responsibility associated with the exercise of private choice that constitutional limitations should be imposed. Consider the next note.

2. *Explaining* Shelley *and Narrowing Its Implications.* One way to justify the outcome in *Shelley* without expanding the state action concept is to note that the common law disfavored restraints on alienation like the covenant involved in *Shelley*, but had an exception allowing racial covenants. This exception giving preferred status to racial covenants seems impossible to defend in the twenty-first century and appears to be state encouragement or ratification of private discrimination.

Another rather narrow way to view *Shelley* is to note that the racially restrictive covenant involved quite a large area of land. When the covenant was enforced by the Missouri courts, it operated much like a zoning ordinance—and there is no doubt that a zoning ordinance forbidding the sale of certain property to blacks violates equal protection.

A third narrowing understanding of *Shelley* would posit that the state actor in the case, the judge, should be "colorblind." A "colorblind" judge could convict the trespasser in the hypothetical above because her race would be legally irrelevant, but could not enforce the covenant because the judge would need to know the race of the buyer.

All of these rationales for *Shelley* would still allow a private homeowner to distinguish among guests on the basis of race and allow the homeowner to get state actors (police, a judge) to assist in excluding someone on the basis of race. Perhaps the essential difference is one of "baselines." The common law has always considered it the right of a landowner to exclude persons for almost any reason. The idea of a common law baseline against which to measure state action is incoherent to some extent, since (as we have continually stressed) the common law is judge-created and therefore reliance on common law rights by private persons could always be seen as state action. But if we move away from technicalities and ask "in this situation, is the state doing anything *extraordinary* to encourage, or even ratify, racial discrimination," we may be asking the relevant practical question. State encouragement might be seen if the state uses its coercive power to allow persons tangential to a transaction (the complaining neighbors in *Shelley*) for facially racially discriminatory reasons to prevent a transaction between a willing, nondiscriminatory buyer and seller. State encouragement might be even more apparent if the judge-made common law disfavors certain agreements but allows them if they are for racist purposes.

3.   Shelley *as a Balancing Test*. The inquiry suggested in the previous note is essentially a balancing test focusing on the impact and appearance of holding one way or the other on the state action question. Perhaps what the Equal Protection Clause requires is that the state avoid the appearance as well as the reality of state-endorsed racial superiority. The Jaybird Case (*Terry v. Adams*) is a hard case theoretically, but as a practical matter a result contrary to the one reached there would have solidified the politics of racial superiority in Texas. In effect, Texas had an affirmative duty (a "responsibility") not to allow white primaries, and the Court had the authority to strike them down under the Equal Protection Clause or the Fifteenth Amendment. A contrary result in *Shelley* would have allowed bigots to take advantage of a racist exception in the common law to carve out huge residential areas for whites only and would have required judges to order facially racist results.

In contrast, if the police remove a trespasser from land because the owner dislikes the trespasser's race, the state could be seen as simply vindicating the individual autonomy of the owner (however misguided) and preserving a realm of private conduct within which the individual may be accorded freedom of association. This result places no affirmative obligation on the state to attack "private" discrimination in this context. The state legislature would, however, have authority under its police power to enact legislation forbidding many kinds of private discrimination.[23] Essentially, the inquiry we are suggesting focuses on whether on the facts the antidiscrimination principle is so threatened that direct judicial intervention is necessary, or whether it is enough to allow the state or federal legislature discretion about whether to outlaw the "private" discrimination in question.

The line we are suggesting is drawn more on the basis of pragmatics than of theory. It assumes that the essential task is promoting the antidiscrimination principle without destroying individual autonomy. Under this view, state action questions in race cases should be resolved by overall considerations of equal protection, rather than by some unified theory of state action that applies to all cases, including those outside the equal protection arena. See generally Robert Glennon & John Nowak, *A Functional Analysis of the Fourteenth Amendment "State Action" Requirement*, 1976 Sup. Ct. Rev. 221.

Recall, however, that recent cases have not been willing overtly to engage in a balancing inquiry like the one suggested above. See Mark Tushnet, Shelley v. Kraemer *and Theories of Equality*, 33 N.Y. L. Sch. L. Rev. 383 (1988). Nonetheless, their outcomes might be supportable by a balancing approach. For example, *Metropolitan Edison* and *Flagg Brothers* presented the issue

---

[23] Although we know of no state laws forbidding discrimination by the owner of one private home, many states and cities have open-housing laws that require those renting or selling multiple units to avoid racial discrimination. The federal Fair Housing Act of 1968 also forbids private racial discrimination in housing in some contexts, and a Reconstruction-era federal statute, 42 U.S.C. § 1982, has been interpreted as outlawing a racially discriminatory refusal to sell a home, see *Jones v. Alfred H. Mayer Co.* (Chapter 7, § 3A). If a state statute attempted to prohibit the owner of a family home from racially discriminating in the choice of guests, the owner could argue that the state law violated the owner's federal constitutional property rights and privacy rights.

whether the actions of private entities should be regulated by due process requirements, which often mandate notice and a hearing before someone may be deprived of "property" or "liberty." Absent legislative guidance, the judiciary might reasonably be hesitant to apply procedural due process guarantees to wide sections of the private sector, for fear that the economy could grind to a halt. Had Metropolitan Edison responded to an energy shortage by shutting off power only to black customers, could the Court have possibly reached the same result about state action? Of course, this hypothetical is unlikely to arise, even if the utility were operated by racists, considering the heavy regulation to which public utilities are now subjected by state law.

On the whole, do the state action cases suggest that the Court was willing to engage in balancing in racial discrimination cases where allowing the "private" conduct would seriously threaten implementation of the antidiscrimination principle, whereas in more recent cases arising outside the Equal Protection Clause the Court has more rigidly attempted to preserve a wide sphere of private autonomy? Would it be unacceptable if state action means different things in different contexts?[24]

MOOSE LODGE NO. 107 v. IRVIS
407 U.S. 163, 92 S.Ct. 1965, 32 L.Ed.2d 627 (1972)

JUSTICE REHNQUIST delivered the opinion of the Court.

[A member of Moose Lodge No. 107 in Harrisburg, Pennsylvania, invited Irvis, an African American, to dine there. The club refused to serve him, consistent with rules of its national organization that limited membership to white males and allowed members to have only white guests.]

Moose Lodge is a private club in the ordinary meaning of that term. It is a local chapter of a national fraternal organization having well-defined requirements for membership. It conducts all of its activities in a building that is owned by it. It is not publicly funded. * * *

Appellee [Irvis], while conceding the right of private clubs to choose members upon a discriminatory basis, asserts that the licensing of Moose Lodge to serve liquor by the Pennsylvania Liquor Control Board amounts to such state involvement with the club's activities as to make its discriminatory practices forbidden by the Equal Protection Clause of the Fourteenth Amendment. The relief sought and obtained by appellee in the District Court was an injunction forbidding the licensing by the liquor authority of Moose Lodge until it ceased its discriminatory practices. * * *

---

[24] For a thorough examination of the attempts to rationalize the *Shelley* result and a suggested reformulation under which *Shelley* could be understood as arising in a setting implicating the Thirteenth Amendment's prohibition on the badges and incidents of slavery even when private action is involved, see Mark Rosen, *Was* Shelly v. Kramer *Incorrectly Decided? Some New Answers*, 95 Cal. L. Rev. 451 (2007).

Our cases make clear that the impetus for the forbidden discrimination need not originate with the State if it is state action that enforces privately originated discrimination. *Shelley*. The Court held in [*Burton v. Wilmington Parking Authority*, 365 U.S. 715 (1961)] that a private restaurant owner who refused service because of a customer's race violated the Fourteenth Amendment, where the restaurant was located in a building owned by a state-created parking authority and leased from the authority. The Court * * * concluded that the [parking authority] had "so far insinuated itself into a position of interdependence with Eagle [the restaurant operator] that it must be recognized as a joint participant in the challenged activity, which, on that account, cannot be considered to have been so 'purely private' as to fall without the scope of the Fourteenth Amendment."

The Court has never held, of course, that discrimination by an otherwise private entity would be violative of the Equal Protection Clause if the private entity receives any sort of benefit or service at all from the State, or if it is subject to state regulation in any degree whatever. Since state-furnished services include such necessities of life as electricity, water, and police and fire protection, such a holding would utterly emasculate the distinction between private as distinguished from state conduct * * *. Our holdings indicate that where the impetus for the discrimination is private, the State must have "significantly involved itself with invidious discriminations," *Reitman v. Mulkey*, 387 U.S. 369 (1967), in order for the discriminatory action to fall within the ambit of the constitutional prohibition.

Our prior decisions dealing with discriminatory refusal of service in public eating places are significantly different factually from the case now before us. *Peterson v. City of Greenville*, 373 U.S. 244 (1963), dealt with the trespass prosecution of persons who "sat in" at a restaurant to protest its refusal of service to Negroes. There the Court held that although the ostensible initiative for the trespass prosecution came from the proprietor, the existence of a local ordinance requiring segregation of races in such places was tantamount to the State having "commanded a particular result." With one exception, which is discussed *infra*, there is no suggestion in this record that the Pennsylvania statutes and regulations governing the sale of liquor are intended either overtly or covertly to encourage discrimination.

In *Burton*, the Court's full discussion of the facts in its opinion indicates the significant differences between that case and this: "The land and building were publicly owned. As an entity, the building was dedicated to public uses in performance of the Authority's 'essential governmental functions.' The costs of land acquisition, construction, and maintenance are defrayed entirely from donations by the City of Wilmington, from loans and revenue bonds and from the proceeds of rentals and parking services out of which the loans and bonds were payable. Assuming that the distinction would be significant, the commercially leased areas were not surplus state property, but constituted a physically and financially integral and, indeed, indispensable part of the State's plan to operate its project as a self-sustaining unit. Upkeep and maintenance of the building, including necessary repairs, were responsibilities of the Authority and were payable out of public funds. It cannot be doubted that the peculiar relationship of the restaurant to the parking facility in which it is located confers on each an incidental variety of mutual benefits. Guests of the restaurant are afforded a convenient place to park their automobiles, even if they cannot enter the restaurant directly from the parking area. Similarly, its convenience for diners may well provide additional demand for the Authority's parking facilities. Should any improvements effected in the leasehold by Eagle become part of the realty, there is no possibility of increased taxes being passed on to it since the fee is held by a tax-exempt government agency. Neither can it be ignored, especially in view of Eagle's affirmative allegation that for it to serve Negroes would injure its business, that profits earned by discrimination not only contribute to, but also are indispensable elements in, the financial success of a governmental agency."

Here there is nothing approaching the symbiotic relationship between lessor and lessee that was present in *Burton*, where the private lessee obtained the benefit of locating in a building owned by the state-created parking authority, and the parking authority was enabled to carry out its primary public purpose of furnishing parking space by advantageously leasing portions of the building constructed for that purpose to commercial lessees such as the owner of the Eagle Restaurant. Unlike *Burton*, the Moose Lodge building is located on land owned by it, not by any public authority. Far from apparently holding itself out as a place of public accommodation, Moose Lodge quite ostentatiously proclaims the fact that it is not open to the public at large. Nor is it located and operated in such surroundings that although private in name, it discharges a function or performs a service that would otherwise in all likelihood be performed by the State. In short, while Eagle was a public restaurant in a public building, Moose Lodge is a private social club in a private building.

With the exception hereafter noted, the Pennsylvania Liquor Control Board plays absolutely no part in establishing or enforcing the membership or guest policies of the club that it licenses to serve liquor. There is no suggestion in this record that Pennsylvania law, either as written or as applied, discriminates against minority groups either in their right to apply for club licenses themselves or in their right to purchase and be served liquor in places of public accommodation. The only effect that the state licensing of Moose Lodge to serve liquor can be said to have on the right of any other Pennsylvanian to buy or be served liquor on premises other than those of Moose Lodge is that for some purposes club licenses are counted in the maximum number of licenses that may be issued in a given municipality.

Basically each municipality has a quota of one retail license for each 1,500 inhabitants. Licenses issued to hotels, municipal golf courses, and airport restaurants are not counted in this quota, nor are club licenses until the maximum number of retail licenses is reached. Beyond that point, neither additional retail licenses nor additional club licenses may be issued so long as the number of issued and outstanding retail licenses remains at or above the statutory maximum.

The District Court was at pains to point out in its opinion what it considered to be the "pervasive" nature of the regulation of private clubs by the Pennsylvania Liquor Control Board. As that court noted, an applicant for a club license must make such physical alterations in its premises as the board may require, must file a list of the names and addresses of its members and employees, and must keep extensive financial records. The board is granted the right to inspect the licensed premises at any time when patrons, guests, or members are present.

However detailed this type of regulation may be in some particulars, it cannot be said to in any way foster or encourage racial discrimination. Nor can it be said to make the State in any realistic sense a partner or even a joint venturer in the club's enterprise. The limited effect of the prohibition against obtaining additional club licenses when the maximum number of retail licenses allotted to a municipality has been issued, when considered together with the availability of liquor from hotel, restaurant, and retail licensees, falls far short of conferring upon club licensees a monopoly in the dispensing of liquor in any given municipality or in the State as a whole. We therefore hold that, with the exception hereafter noted, the operation of the regulatory scheme enforced by the Pennsylvania Liquor Control Board does not sufficiently implicate the State in the discriminatory guest policies of Moose Lodge to make the latter "state action" within the ambit of the Equal Protection Clause of the Fourteenth Amendment.

The District Court found that the regulations of the Liquor Control Board adopted pursuant to statute affirmatively require that "[e]very club licensee shall adhere to all of the provisions of its Constitution and By-Laws." Appellant argues that the purpose of this provision "is purely and simply and plainly the prevention of subterfuge," pointing out that the bona fides of a private club, as opposed to a place of public accommodation masquerading as a private club, is a matter with which the State Liquor Control Board may legitimately concern itself. * * * [T]he label "private club" can be and has been used to evade both regulations of state and local liquor authorities, and statutes requiring places of public accommodation to serve all persons without regard to race, color, religion, or national origin. * * *

Even though the Liquor Control Board regulation in question is neutral in its terms, the result of its application in a case where the constitution and bylaws of a club required racial discrimination would be to invoke the sanctions of the State to enforce a concededly discriminatory private rule. * * * *Shelley* makes it clear that the application of state sanctions to enforce such a rule would violate the Fourteenth Amendment. * * *

Appellee was entitled to a decree enjoining the enforcement of § 113.09 of the regulations promulgated by the Pennsylvania Liquor Control Board insofar as that regulation requires compliance by Moose Lodge with provisions of its constitution and bylaws containing racially discriminatory provisions. He was entitled to no more.

[Reversed and remanded.]

JUSTICE DOUGLAS, with whom JUSTICE MARSHALL joins, dissenting.

* * * Liquor licenses in Pennsylvania, unlike driver's licenses, or marriage licenses, are not freely available to those who meet racially neutral qualifications. There is a complex quota system * * * [, and] the quota for Harrisburg, where Moose Lodge No. 107 is located, has been full for many years. No more club licenses may be issued in that city.

This state-enforced scarcity of licenses restricts the ability of blacks to obtain liquor, for liquor is commercially available *only* at private clubs for a significant portion of each week. Access by blacks to places that serve liquor is further limited by the fact that the state quota is filled. A group desiring to form a nondiscriminatory club which would serve blacks must purchase a license held by an existing club, which can exact a monopoly price for the transfer. The availability of such a license is speculative at best, however, for, as Moose Lodge itself concedes, without a liquor license a fraternal organization would be hard pressed to survive. Thus, the State of Pennsylvania is putting the weight of its liquor license, concededly a valued and important adjunct to a private club, behind racial discrimination. * * *

[The dissent of JUSTICE BRENNAN, joined by JUSTICE MARSHALL, is omitted.]

NOTES ON MOOSE LODGE

1.   *State Action in* Moose Lodge. Was the Court correct in deciding to prefer individual autonomy to the antidiscrimination principle in *Moose Lodge*? Is *Burton* legitimately distinguishable? Note the two arguments for finding state action in *Moose Lodge*: (1) The quota on liquor licenses means that the discrimination of Moose Lodge, although done in a narrowly defined private context, has potentially broad external racially discriminatory effects. (2) Under the Twenty-First Amendment, the states have nearly plenary

authority to regulate liquor. According to the district court in *Moose Lodge*, the Pennsylvania Liquor Control Board pervasively regulated liquor licensees. For example, the Board could order physical alterations to the premises and could inspect the premises at any time during business hours. The licensee was required to file a list of its employees, to conform its financial arrangements to statutory requirements, to keep extensive records, not to permit persons of "ill repute" to frequent the club or allow any "lewd, immoral or improper entertainment." The court concluded that "[i]t would be difficult to find a more pervasive interaction of state authority with personal conduct." Yet the state failed to forbid racial discrimination by licensees. As an advocate, how would you articulate and use these two theories to support state action here, and how should your opposing counsel respond?

2. *Unified Versus Contextual Concepts of State Action.* If state action means the same thing in all constitutional contexts—that is, if procedural due process cases, free speech cases, and equal protection cases all must approach state action the same way—then maybe *Moose Lodge* is correctly decided.[25] It might seem silly to say that an employee dismissed by the lodge could argue that she was entitled to "due process"—notice and the opportunity to be heard—prior to the dismissal as a matter of federal constitutional law, or that her firing violated the First Amendment because it was in retaliation for her criticisms of the lodge or for her religion. These problems are perhaps best handled by sources of law other than the Constitution—*i.e.*, by federal and state statutes, supplemented by state common law. Only by approaching state action as a question of judicial authority under specific constitutional provisions, rather than as a unitary concept limiting all constitutional provisions uniformly, could *Moose Lodge* be decided differently in the equal protection context and the due process or free speech context. For example, consider whether the state's failure to prevent racial discrimination by liquor licensees is any greater a federal concern than its failure to provide procedural protections to employees of licensees when they are discharged.

David Strauss, in *State Action After the Civil Rights Era*, 10 Const. Comm. 409 (1993), elaborated upon this point as a historical perspective on the state action cases. *Shelley*, the white primary cases, and *Burton* involved someone directly discriminating on the basis of race in a context in which no statute prohibited the act. Congress and the state legislatures not only had failed to outlaw racial discrimination, some state legislatures had actually engaged in it systematically with Jim Crow laws. Waiting for legislative reform seemed futile: Neither Congress nor many state legislatures were capable of

---

[25] In cases that do not involve equal protection, the trend since *Moose Lodge* has been to find no state action. See *National Collegiate Athletic Association v. Tarkanian*, 488 U.S. 179 (1988) (procedural due process claim against private athletic association that strongly encouraged state university to discipline coach); *Blum v. Yaretsky*, 457 U.S. 991 (1982) (procedural due process claim against privately owned nursing homes extensively regulated and subsidized by the state); *Rendell-Baker v. Kohn*, 457 U.S. 830 (1982) (free speech and procedural due process objections to termination of employees by heavily regulated and subsidized private school). *Cf. DeShaney v. Winnebago County Social Services Department*, 489 U.S. 189 (1989) (denying due process claim against county for failure of social workers to protect child against abusive parent).

addressing the issue for political reasons (*e.g.*, avoiding a "hot potato"; structural problems that lead to legislative deadlock such as filibusters and malapportionment). If a law were to attack this racial discrimination, it would have to be the Equal Protection Clause, and thus the requirement of state action became "the enemy" of racial progress, a picky formalism that stood in the way of federal judges performing an important social role. Moreover, in many contexts, especially in the South—the white primary cases are perhaps the most obvious example—there was a substantial blurring of the "public" and the "private," situations in which the same elite whites ruled both the government and the social and business realms and drew little practical distinction among them, imposing government regulation or private pressure or social custom based simply on which seemed the most expedient. In such a context, it might well make sense to avoid formalistic applications of the state action doctrine. In contrast, one might suggest that today, in changed circumstances—Congress and the state legislatures are more able to respond to such social problems, and many current legal issues lack the clear moral imperative of those found in the earlier civil rights era—invoking the state action doctrine to limit the reach of the Constitution may often be more justified; it allows Congress and the state legislatures greater capacity to experiment and find different local solutions to problems, and it allows the private marketplace to have a role as well.

3. *Routine Versus Extraordinary Intertwining with the State. Burton*, discussed in *Moose Lodge*, seemingly held that a private actor can be subjected to the Constitution if it is symbiotically intertwined with the state. But *Moose Lodge* and *Metropolitan Edison* indicate that state licensing and regulation are not enough to render the private entity a state actor. Moreover, *Moose Lodge* states that private entities are entitled to receive the general benefits of all citizens or taxpayers (police and fire protection, for example) without thereby subjecting themselves to the Constitution.

Norwood v. Harrison, 413 U.S. 455 (1973), involved a Mississippi program, in effect since 1940, under which the state provided free textbooks to all students in the state. The Court held that the state could not constitutionally lend textbooks to students attending racially discriminatory private schools:

> Textbooks are a basic educational tool [and] are to be distinguished from generalized services government might provide to schools in common with others. Moreover, the textbooks * * * are a form of assistance readily available from sources entirely independent of the State—unlike, for example, "such necessities of life as electricity, water, and police and fire protection." * * * [T]he Constitution does not permit the State to aid discrimination even when there is no precise causal relationship between state financial aid to a private school and the continued well-being of that school. A State may not grant the type of tangible financial aid here involved if that aid has a significant tendency to facilitate, reinforce, and support private discrimination.

How can *Norwood* be distinguished from *Moose Lodge*, where the state's granting of a liquor license can be considered a subsidy? Given the *Norwood* Court's focus on effects rather than purpose, is *Norwood* good law after *Washington v. Davis*? Could it be defended on the ground that Mississippi had earlier engaged in *de jure* school segregation?

4.   *An Analogy to the Establishment of Religion?* The First Amendment forbids government from establishing a state religion (Chapter 6, § 7). In many ways, Establishment Clause questions (for example, whether a state may provide free textbooks to religious private schools, whether a state may display a creche at Christmas) are similar to state action questions, in that both ask the Court to draw a line between the public and private sectors. Justice O'Connor has proposed an "endorsement" test in religion cases that asks, essentially, whether the government policy has the purpose or effect of conveying a message "that religion or a particular religious belief is favored or preferred." See *Wallace v. Jaffree*, 472 U.S. 38, 70 (1985) (O'Connor, J., concurring in the judgment). How many of the principal state action cases we have examined—the white primary cases, *Marsh*, *Hudgens*, *Metropolitan Edison*, *Flagg Brothers*, *Shelley*, *Moose Lodge*, *Burton*, and *Norwood*—could be explained by an endorsement test?

5.   *Contrasting State Court Approaches.* Even when state courts purport to follow federal state action doctrines, they often apply them differently. Consider *Gay Law Students Association v. Pacific Telegraph & Telephone*, 24 Cal. 3d 458, 595 P.2d 592, 156 Cal. Rptr. 14 (1979), in which gay men and lesbians challenged the utility's policy excluding them from employment. The California Supreme Court held that its state equal protection provision (Article I, § 7(a)) applied to state-licensed utilities and that their discrimination on grounds of sexual orientation was actionable. The court held that the California equal protection guarantee does not always require the presence of a state actor to be applicable and, further, that under traditional public function analysis (*Metropolitan Edison*) the utility was a public actor because of the monopoly power granted it by the state. The court distinguished its result from that in *Metropolitan Edison* on the ground that a utility's decision to cut off a customer's electricity was an ad hoc decision that did not implicate the utility's monopoly power so much as a blanket policy of discriminating against gays and lesbians. Is this persuasive, or is the court implicitly suggesting that it would have decided *Metropolitan Edison* differently under the state constitution?

6.   *A Substantive Theory of State Action.* Consider this theory of state action: Every private dispute involves state action, because the parties rely upon state-created interests—*e.g.*, a property right, a tort duty, predictable rules on how a contract will be read. Where one party is claiming a violation of equal protection, she can always articulate her claim as in *Shelley*: The state's protection of the other private party through a common law or regulatory rule undermines constitutional values. Where racial distinctions are not being made (as in *Flagg Brothers*), the state regulation is subject to a very low level of scrutiny and will usually be upheld; the state action doctrine is a convenient

(if confusing) surrogate for review on the merits that such statutes almost always pass. Where racial distinctions are made by state law (either explicitly as in *Brown* or by obvious implication as in *Shelley* and the white primary cases), the state action requirement falls away. Where race distinctions are not obvious and are only indirectly the result of state law (as in *Moose Lodge*), the state action requirement reemerges as a convenience. As Mark Tushnet has argued, the state action requirement in this third set of cases allows the Supreme Court to avoid the appearance that it is endorsing discrimination against African Americans. See Mark Tushnet, Shelley v. Kraemer *and Theories of Equality*, 33 N.Y.L. Sch. L. Rev. 383 (1988).

Recall the state cases we have discussed in this chapter, especially the California cases such as *PruneYard* and *Gay Law Students Association*. This theory would suggest that the California court's expansive treatment of state action in those cases merely reflects a more expansive vision of free expression and equal protection than that held by the U.S. Supreme Court. Or would it be more plausible to attribute the federal Court's more restrictive view to federalism concerns (preserving the authority of the state itself to address these issues), which do not enter the state courts' analysis? Might some combination of these factors be at work?

3. The Special Context of the Courtroom

In *Batson v. Kentucky*, the Court held that a prosecutor may not use peremptory challenges in a criminal case for the purpose of excluding racial minorities from the jury. This seems to be a straightforward application of *Washington v. Davis*: A state actor intentionally used race in a way that disadvantages persons of color (even if the defendant is not a person of color, excluding people of color from the jury is a cognizable racial harm). Notice how this fits the *Davis* intentional discrimination model: even though the prosecutor has discretion to use her peremptory challenges to exclude anyone from a jury without having to show cause why the person should be excluded, she may not use this authority granted by the courts for racially discriminatory reasons.

A much more difficult conceptual setting arose in *Edmonson v. Leesville Concrete Co.*, 500 U.S. 614 (1991). In this civil case, defense counsel used two of its three peremptory challenges to remove African-American persons from the prospective jury. Of course, defense counsel in a civil case is not a government officer, so state action is not clearly involved. Nonetheless, the majority of the Court, per Justice Kennedy, concluded that state action was present. First, the Court emphasized that the power of defense counsel to exercise the peremptory challenge flowed from state authority: "Peremptory challenges are permitted only when the government, by statute or decisional law, deems it appropriate to allow parties to exclude a given number of persons who otherwise would satisfy the requirements for service on the petit jury." Second, the Court concluded that it was appropriate to consider the private individual (defense counsel) a government actor. In evaluating this issue, the Court seemingly breathed life into precedents that many had considered dormant:

> Our precedents establish that, in determining whether a particular action or course of conduct is governmental in character, it is relevant to examine the following: the extent to which the actor relies on governmental assistance and benefits, see *Tulsa Professional Collection Services, Inc. v. Pope*, 485 U.S. 478 (1988); *Burton v. Wilmington Parking Authority*; whether the actor is performing a traditional governmental function, see *Terry v. Adams*; *Marsh v. Alabama*; and whether the injury caused is aggravated in a unique way by the incidents of governmental authority, see *Shelley v. Kraemer*.

As for the first factor, the Court stressed that, "without the overt, significant participation of the government, the peremptory challenge system, as well as the jury trial system of which it is a part, simply could not exist." It also emphasized the appearance to potential jurors of extensive state involvement in jury selection: the role of the court clerk in summoning them and requiring them to complete jury questionnaires, the use of the open courtroom for voir dire, the presence and activity of the judge, who (rather than counsel) dismisses jurors challenged peremptorily, and so on.

As for the second factor, the Court concluded that the jury is a "quintessential governmental body," so that the process of comprising it should be viewed as a traditional governmental function. "If a government confers on a private body the power to choose the government's employees or officials, the private body will be bound by the constitutional mandate of race-neutrality. At least a plurality of the Court recognized this principle in *Terry v. Adams*."

Concerning the third factor, the Court stated:

> Finally, we note that the injury caused by the discrimination is made more severe because the government permits it to occur within the courthouse itself. Few places are a more real expression of the constitutional authority of the government than a courtroom, where the law itself unfolds. Within the courtroom, the government invokes its laws to determine the rights of those who stand before it. In full view of the public, litigants press their cases, witnesses give testimony, juries render verdicts, and judges act with the utmost care to ensure that justice is done.

> Race discrimination within the courtroom raises serious questions as to the fairness of the proceedings conducted there. Racial bias mars the integrity of the judicial system and prevents the idea of democratic government from becoming a reality. In the many times we have addressed the problem of racial bias in our

system of justice, we have not "questioned the premise that racial discrimination in the qualification or selection of jurors offends the dignity of persons and the integrity of the courts." To permit racial exclusion in this official forum compounds the racial insult inherent in judging a citizen by the color of his or her skin.

Justice O'Connor, joined by Chief Justice Rehnquist and Justice Scalia, dissented, contending that the peremptory challenge was "an enclave of private action in a government-managed proceeding" and that "[t]he entirety of the Government's actual participation in the peremptory process boils down to a single fact: 'When a lawyer exercises a peremptory challenge, the judge advises the juror he or she has been excused.'" This, she said, is a far cry from active governmental participation in, much less encouragement of, discrimination. She distinguished *Shelley* as a case where judicial power was exercised to enforce a facially discriminatory contract so as to compel discrimination on the part of those who did not wish to discriminate. Here, in contrast, no one was compelled to discriminate, and the peremptory challenge was merely an unexplained (not facially objectionable) request to excuse a juror. Did Justice O'Connor persuasively distinguish *Shelley*? How did the Court—and how can a court generally—measure how much governmental participation is "significant"? Isn't this lack of a precise or easily applied standard present in all of the state action cases you have read?

Justice O'Connor also argued that the exercise of a peremptory challenge is not a traditional governmental function because:

> Whatever reason a private litigant may have for using a peremptory challenge, it is not the government's reason. The government otherwise establishes its requirements for jury service, leaving to the private litigant the unfettered discretion to use the strike for any reason. This is not part of the government's function in establishing the requirements for jury service.

While the majority seemed to focus on resolution of disputes by jury trial as a traditional governmental function, Justice O'Connor viewed the function in question here much more narrowly (the exercise of peremptory challenges). She stressed that "[t]he peremptory challenge forms no part of the *government's* responsibility in selecting a jury." Moreover, pointing out that the "peremptory challenge is a practice of ancient origin, part of our common law heritage in criminal trials," and harkening back to the "exclusivity" requirement of *Metropolitan Edison*, she contended that:

> [i]n order to constitute state action under [the traditional governmental function doctrine,] private conduct must not only comprise something that the government traditionally does, but something that *only* the government traditionally does. Even if one could fairly characterize the use of a peremptory strike as the

performance of the traditional government function of jury selection, it has never been exclusively the function of the government to select juries; peremptory strikes are older than the Republic.

How could the majority respond?[26]

PROBLEM ON STATE ACTION: ENTWINEMENT REVISITED

Problem 3-7: The Tennessee Secondary School Athletic Association (TSSAA), formed in 1925, is a not-for-profit membership corporation that regulates interscholastic sport among the private and public high schools that belong to it. The great majority of public schools in the state are members; 55 private schools also belong. According to its rules, absent a waiver, a member school's team may play or scrimmage only against the team of another member. The Tennessee State Board of Education at one time officially designated TSSAA as the organization to supervise public school athletics, but in recent years the State Board dropped the official designation and merely acknowledged TSSAA's role "in coordinating interscholastic athletic competition" and "authorized" public schools to join TSSAA. TSSAA staff members are not paid by the state, but are eligible to join the state's public employee retirement system. TSSAA's revenue comes from dues from member schools and gate receipts at athletic tournaments. TSSAA found that Brentwood Academy, a private parochial school and member, had violated association rules against exercising "undue influence" in recruiting athletes when the Academy wrote to incoming students and their parents about spring football practice. TSSAA imposed sanctions upon Brentwood's athletic program (e.g., barring teams from participating in state playoffs for two years). When these penalties were imposed, all the members of TSSAA's governing bodies were public school administrators. Should the penalties be subject to constitutional review? See *Brentwood Academy v. TSSAA*, 531 U.S. 288 (2001).

SECTION 3. THE AFFIRMATIVE ACTION CONTROVERSY: BENIGN RACIAL CLASSIFICATIONS OR REVERSE DISCRIMINATION?

A. AN INTRODUCTION TO THE DEBATE

Following *Brown*, a state university law school that limited the number of racial minorities it admitted would surely violate the Equal Protection Clause. To return to an earlier theme (see notes 3 and 4 following *Loving*), that practice would be unconstitutional regardless of whether heightened scrutiny is triggered merely by the use of a racial

---

[26] See also *Georgia v. McCollum*, 505 U.S. 42 (1992) (*Batson* applies to peremptory challenges by counsel for a criminal defendant). For a recent case finding a violation of the *Batson* standard, see *Snyder v. Louisiana*, 552 U.S. 472 (2008).

classification, or alternatively by only those racial classifications that disadvantage a racial minority. The first approach turns on a strong presumption that race is never relevant to government decisionmaking (a "race neutrality" approach). Under the second approach, the government might sometimes have legitimate reasons to consider race, but not when the group disadvantaged by the classification is a racial minority—a comparatively powerless group that has suffered a history of prejudice and thus cannot be expected to defend itself adequately in the political process. This approach might be called the "discrete and insular minority" approach, based on its linkage to *Carolene Products* footnote 4 (Chapter 1, § 6) and the representation-reinforcement theory of Professor Ely (Chapter 2, § 3B). In addition, the second approach might be defended not on the basis of political power, but on the ground that the government has, at least in theory, an affirmative obligation to attack racial subordination. Even if courts will not enforce this obligation by compelling the government to act, courts should not interfere when the government does in fact act consistent with the obligation.

Sometimes, as in the law school example above, it makes no difference which theory is chosen. But if a state law school set aside a minimum, rather than maximum, number of places for racial minorities, the constitutional treatment of the admissions plan would vary greatly depending upon which of these two approaches was invoked. In cases where it makes a difference, which approach should be used?

Some of the cases we have examined, such as *Washington v. Davis*, seem premised on the second approach—that heightened scrutiny is reserved to protect those most likely to be disadvantaged because of prejudice. Other cases, such as *Loving*, contain language supporting a colorblind or race-neutrality approach. But in none of these cases was it necessary to choose between the two approaches because they all involved discrimination against a racial minority. Beginning in the 1970s, the Court faced a series of cases in which affirmative action—the overt use of racial criteria to benefit racial minorities—was challenged, and accordingly the Court had to choose between the two approaches.

We use the famous *Bakke* case, from 1978, to introduce this debate. Justice Powell's opinion in the case has had a formative influence on the doctrine in the area. We then consider the issue in a larger theoretical framework, and finally examine the most recent decisions.

Regents of the University of California v. Bakke

438 U.S. 265 (1978)

The University of California at Davis medical school reserved sixteen of the 100 places in its class for minority group members (defined as "Blacks, Chicanos, Asians, and American Indians"). Alan Bakke, a rejected white applicant with arguably better "paper credentials" than some minority students who had been admitted, brought suit. Four Justices (**Burger**, **Stewart**, **Rehnquist**, and **Stevens**) concluded that the admissions program violated Title VI of the Civil Rights Act of 1964 because it constituted racial discrimination by a recipient of federal financial assistance, and accordingly these Justices did not reach the constitutional issue. The other five Justices concluded that Title VI forbids only those racial classifications that would violate the Equal Protection Clause, and accordingly they considered the meaning of equal protection in this context. In a joint opinion, four Justices (**Brennan**, **White**, **Marshall**, and **Blackmun**) would have upheld the program; **Justice Powell** concluded that the program violated equal protection. Thus, a majority of five Justices (Justice Powell and the four who rested their decision on Title VI) held the program illegal, but no rationale had the support of a majority of the Court. The debate between Justice Powell and the "Brennan four" on the constitutional issue illustrates many central issues concerning affirmative action.

1. *Nature of Discrimination and Level of Scrutiny.* Justice Powell argued that strict scrutiny should apply regardless of whether whites are a "discrete and insular minority" under *Carolene Products* footnote 4:

> [T]he white "majority" itself is composed of various minority groups, most of which can lay claim to a history of prior discrimination at the hands of the State and private individuals. * * * There is no principled basis for deciding which groups would merit "heightened judicial solicitude" and which would not. Courts would be asked to evaluate the extent of the prejudice and consequent harm suffered by various minority groups. * * * As these preferences began to have their desired effect, and the consequences of past discrimination were undone, new judicial rankings would be necessary. The kind of variable sociological and political analysis necessary to produce such rankings simply does not lie within the judicial competence—even if they otherwise were politically feasible and socially desirable.

He suggested that even seemingly "benign" preferences might simply be a product of racial politics, that such preferences might reinforce "common stereotypes holding that certain groups are unable to achieve success without special protection based on a factor having no relationship to individual worth," and that "innocent" persons like Bakke should not bear the burdens of redressing wrongs not of their making. Ultimately, he took it as axiomatic that strict scrutiny should apply in these circumstances.

According to the "Brennan four," strict scrutiny was inappropriate for "benign" racial classifications, which they defined as those that do not stigmatize those disadvantaged by the classification. The Davis plan was not based on the assumption that those disadvantaged by it were inferior, much less on racial hatred or separatism. Ultimately, they opted for "intermediate scrutiny."

2.   *Applying Strict Scrutiny: Justice Powell.* Justice Powell concluded that remedying societal discrimination was too amorphous a "concept of injury that may be ageless in its reach into the past." Nor was the Davis program justified by the goal of improving the delivery of health care to underserved communities, since there was no evidence that the program was "either needed or geared to promote that goal."

Justice Powell did conclude that ameliorating the effects of identified past discrimination would be a constitutionally permissible purpose for affirmative action. But even if the Davis program were designed to achieve this purpose, it could not pass constitutional muster under the "means" portion of strict scrutiny analysis. Justice Powell stated that the Court had never "approved a classification that aids persons perceived as members of relatively victimized groups at the expense of other innocent individuals in the absence of judicial, legislative, or administrative findings of constitutional or statutory violations."

Most significantly for future case law, Justice Powell accepted, as a constitutionally sufficient purpose, "the attainment of a diverse student body," which he saw as linked to creating the best academic environment for the school. Again, however, the Davis plan failed to be a constitutionally acceptable means of promoting this purpose: "The diversity that furthers a compelling state interest encompasses a far broader array of qualifications and characteristics of which racial or ethnic origin is but a single though important element." Powell favorably compared the admissions program at Harvard College, where race may be deemed a "plus" but "does not insulate the individual from comparison with all other candidates for the available seats. * * * This kind of program treats each applicant as an individual in the admissions process."

3.   *Applying "Intermediate Scrutiny": The Brennan Four.* The Brennan four concluded that Davis's "purpose of remedying the effects of past societal discrimination" is "sufficiently important to justify the use of race-conscious admissions programs where there is a sound basis for concluding that minority underrepresentation is substantial and chronic, and that the handicap of prior discrimination is impeding access of minorities to the Medical School."

Justice Marshall wrote separately to emphasize the deep and pervasive historical discrimination against African Americans in this country. **Justice Blackmun**'s separate opinion suggested that "to get beyond racism, we must first take account of race. There is no other way."

NOTES ON AFFIRMATIVE ACTION IN A BROADER THEORETICAL CONTEXT

How would the following theories suggest that *Bakke* be decided?

1.   *Original Intent Theories.* Return to our brief history of the Fourteenth Amendment in Chapter 2, §§ 1A, 3A. Would the original drafters of the Fourteenth Amendment have disapproved of state or municipal preferences benefitting only African Americans or other racial minorities? Recall that the

Reconstruction Congress passed the Fourteenth Amendment in part to protect the constitutionality of the Civil Rights Act of 1866, which was viewed by its critics as partial to the freed slaves. Also, between 1866 and 1871, Congress adopted eight reconstructive measures that established programs benefitting primarily African Americans; the Freedman's Bureau Act of 1866, 14 Stat. 173, was the most important of these.[27]

2.   *Representation-Reinforcing   Theories.*   Recall   Professor   Ely's representation-reinforcing theory of judicial review (Chapter 2, § 3B). How would he analyze *Bakke*? See John Hart Ely, *The Constitutionality of Reverse Racial Discrimination*, 41 U. Chi. L. Rev. 723 (1974).

Consider two competing views about the appropriateness of adopting racial preferences benefitting traditional minority groups.

THOMAS SOWELL,
Civil Rights: Rhetoric or Reality?
37, 42, 50–53, 118–19 (1984)[28]

The very meaning of the phrase "civil rights" has changed greatly since the *Brown* decision in 1954. * * * Initially, civil rights meant, quite simply, that all individuals should be treated the same under the law, regardless of their race, religion, sex or other such social categories. For blacks, especially, this would have represented a dramatic improvement in those states where law and public policy mandated racially separate institutions and highly discriminatory treatment.

Many Americans who supported the initial thrust of civil rights * * * later felt betrayed as the original concept of equal individual *opportunity* evolved toward the concept of equal group *results.* * * *

Those who carry the civil rights vision to its ultimate conclusion see no great difference between promoting equality of opportunity and equality of results. If there are not equal results among groups presumed to have equal genetic potential, then some inequality of opportunity must have intervened somewhere, and the question of precisely where is less important than the remedy of restoring the less fortunate to their just position. The fatal flaw in this kind of thinking is that there are many reasons, besides genes and discrimination, why groups differ in their economic performances and rewards. Groups differ by large amounts demographically, culturally, and geographically—and all of these differences have profound effects on incomes and occupations.

---

[27] Contrasting views of original intent on this issue are offered by Robert Bork, *The Tempting of America: The Political Seduction of the Law* 101–10 (1989), and Eric Schnapper, *Affirmative Action and the Legislative History of the Fourteenth Amendment*, 71 Va. L. Rev. 753 (1985).

[28] Copyright © 1984 by THOMAS SOWELL. Reprinted by permission of HarperCollins Publishers.

[Sowell argues that many of the apparent statistical disparities between the economic success of different racial and ethnic groups (especially African-Americans and whites) are the result of differing age and geographic distributions of the people in the different groups, the culture and goals that have been inculcated into people, and the choices they tend to have made. He argues, therefore, that it is indeterminate exactly how much of blacks' economic disadvantage *vis-a-vis* whites is due to discrimination of any sort. He further argues that the gap between earnings of blacks and whites narrowed before blacks gained efficacious remedies for discrimination in the Civil Rights Act of 1964.]

* * * Those blacks with less education and less job experience—the truly disadvantaged—have been falling farther and farther behind their white counterparts under affirmative action, during the very same years when blacks with more education and job experience have been advancing economically, both absolutely and relative to their white counterparts. First, the disadvantaged: Black male high school dropouts with less than six years of work experience earned 79% of the income of white male high school dropouts with less than six years of work experience in 1967 (before affirmative action quotas) and this *fell* to 69% by 1978 (after affirmative action quotas). Over these very same years, the income of black males who had completed college and had more than six years of work experience *rose* from 75% of the income of their white counterparts to 98%.

assertion of argument

Affirmative action hiring pressures make it costly to have no minority employees, but continuing affirmative action pressures at the promotion and discharge phases also make it costly to have minority employees who do not work out well. The net effect is to increase the demand for highly qualified minority employees while decreasing the demand for less qualified minority employees or for those without a sufficient track record to reassure employers. * * *

* * * Among the [dangers of affirmative action] are the undermining of minority * * * self-confidence by incessant reiteration of the themes of pervasive discrimination, hypocritical standards, and shadowy but malign enemies relentlessly opposing their progress. * * * [I]t also obscures the urgency of acquiring economically meaningful skills or developing the attitudes to apply them with the best results. Pride of achievement is also undermined by the civil rights vision that assumes credit for minority * * * advancement. This makes minority * * * achievement suspect in their own eyes and in the eyes of the larger society.

The more acute dangers are longer run. The spread of hate organizations may be a symptom of much more unorganized sentiment among people * * *. The dangers of continually adding to those resentments are all the greater the more heedlessly preferential doctrines are pushed in the courts, in the federal bureaucracy and by activists.

PATRICIA WILLIAMS,
Metro Broadcasting, Inc. v. FCC:
Regrouping in Singular Times

104 Harv. L. Rev. 525, 541–44 (1990)[29]

* * * [A] student recently demanded of me, "Don't you think affirmative action is what creates a David Duke?" (David Duke is the former Ku Klux Klan leader who recently lost a race for U.S. Senator from Louisiana—but only narrowly, with sixty percent of the white vote and, according to one estimate, seventy percent of the white male vote.) Blacks are positioned in this query as responsible for the bitterest backlash against them, an eerie repeat of the responses (one being the founding of the Ku Klux Klan) to black gains * * * during Reconstruction.

In fact, affirmative action and minority set-aside programs are vastly more complicated than this "you're in, I'm out" conception suggests. Nothing in this rigid win-loss dichotomy permits the notion that everyone could end up a beneficiary, that expansion rather than substitution might be possible, and that the favoring of multiple cultures is enhancement of the total rather than a sweepingly reflexive act of favoritism for anything other than the monolithic purity of an all-white nation.

This particular evocation, of a corrupt system of favoritism seesawing between "the deserving" and "the preferred," caters to an assumption that those who are included by the grace of affirmative action systems are therefore *un*deserving. I want to underscore that I do mean that it "*caters to,*" rather than *creates*, an assumption of inferiority, for the assumption of inferiority has a life that precedes and, unfortunately, will probably outlive affirmative action programs. The subtlety of this distinction has terrified even some few blacks into distorting historic assumptions of blacks as inferior into their weird acceptance of their exclusion as its cure. Sitting on university admissions committees, for example, I have seen black candidates who write on their applications comments such as, "Don't admit me if you have to lower your standards." I have never seen the same acutely self-conscious disavowals from students who are admitted because they meet some geographic criterion * * * or who are older re-entry students, or football heroes, or alumni children. I think this is so because these latter inclusionary categories are thought to indicate group life experiences * * * that "enrich" rather than "lower."

The question, then, becomes not how to undo the inclusionary affirmative action programs, but how to undo the stigma of inferiority that resides not merely in the label or designation of race, but that, according to our national symbology, is actually *embodied* in black presence. * * *

The tenacity of this devalued condition is perhaps captured by something I saw not long ago in a five-and-dime store: a huge bin of identically molded plastic sets of mother and father dolls. Some dolls in the bin were priced at $3.99 a set. Others had been originally priced at $2.99, now marked down to the "Must Sacrifice!" price of $1.99 a set. As a neutral market phenomenon, this obviously makes little sense, and one would assume that a rational vendor would quickly adjust one way or another for the discrepancy. As a less-than-neutral observer, however, I should add that although all the dolls were obviously cast from the same mold, they had not been privileged to share the same dye lot. The higher-priced dolls were white; the dolls priced for sacrificial sale were black. I was struck by how central the information about color was to my analysis of this situation: in a color-blind frame, the pricing was so irrational that I might comfortably assume a laissez-faire approach, confident that market pressures would assure a rapid adjustment. Knowing the dolls' color, however, exposed a more grim social reality: the irrationality of racism not only perpetuated, but also made "rational" by market forces. The absolute necessity of a corrective response to the silent tenacity of this status quo is the heart of what affirmative action is all about. * * *

* * * [T]he idea that an egalitarian society can be achieved or maintained through the mechanism of blind neutrality is fallacious. Racial discrimination is powerful precisely because of its frequent invisibility, its felt neutrality. * * * Racism inscribes culture with generalized preferences and routinized notions of propriety. It is aspiration as much as condemnation; it is an aesthetic. It empowers the mere familiarity and comfort of the status quo by labeling that status quo as "natural." If we are to reach the deep roots of this legacy, antidiscrimination must be a commitment not merely to undo the words of this forced division, but also to undo the consequences of oppressive acts. As in the old saw about the two horses given "equal" opportunity to run a race, but one of whom has a stone in his shoe, the failure to take into account history and context can radically alter whether mere neutrality can be deemed just.

NOTES ON SPECIFIC ARGUMENTS IN THE AFFIRMATIVE ACTION DEBATE

These excerpts only scratch the surface of the affirmative action debate. As you consider them and read the cases that follow, keep in mind some core questions:

- *What conception of equality should prevail in this area?* As noted at the beginning of this chapter, scholars such as Dr. Sowell, who emphasize colorblindness, work within a very different ideological framework than those such as Professor Williams, who emphasize historical subordination. The former speak in terms of formal equality and emphasize the importance of equal process; the latter speak in terms of functional equality and emphasize equal results. Put differently, Dr. Sowell adopts an "anti-classification" approach and Professor Williams an "anti-subordination" approach. Obviously, one's views are not necessarily connected to one's own race or ethnicity. For example, Dr. Sowell and Professor Williams are both African American, and each claims adherents within that community.

- *Should affirmative action be justified based on the past or the future?* Some advocates of affirmative action premise such programs on a backward-looking approach, reasoning that affirmative action is a remedy for past discrimination, especially against African Americans. By contrast, others urge a forward-looking approach to affirmative action. On the latter view, such programs might be justified based on considerations like the instrumental value of diversity in the workplace or classroom, the functional need to have more people of color occupy certain jobs, or the need to offer role models to young people of color.

- *How should the effects of affirmative action be measured?* As you can see in the Sowell-Williams arguments, and as you will note in the cases that follow, proponents and opponents of the policy have strikingly different beliefs about the effects of affirmative action. Proponents tend to point to the positive consequences they expect to flow from the policy, such as greater equalization of key opportunities that can shape life chances, greater fairness, a more probing assessment of what "merit" means," or the practical effects of teaching people of all races to work with those from a different background. Opponents, however, typically have a more jaundiced view of the effects. In addition to worrying (as Dr. Sowell suggested) that affirmative action favors those members of minority groups who are already more advantaged, they fear stigmatization of beneficiaries, backlash, and balkanization. How should these contrasting accounts of affirmative action's effects be measured? Are the ideas inherently ideological or can they yield to reliable empirical assessment?

- *Beyond the racial binary.* Originally, affirmative action programs were conceptualized in terms of blacks and whites. Increasingly, however, affirmative action programs, both state and private, provide preferences not only to African-Americans, but also to Latinos (usually quite vaguely defined), Asians, and Native Americans; many programs also include or focus on women, discussed in Chapter 4. One is immediately struck by the disparate experiences of the various groups. The historical treatment of Native Americans, for example, is quite distinctive. See, e.g., Rennard Strickland, *Genocide-at-Law: An Historic and Contemporary View of the Native American Experience*, 34 Kan.

L. Rev. 713 (1986). Note that if affirmative action programs are justified by the instrumental, forward-looking value of diversity, rather than the remediation of past harms, comparison between and among historical experiences is less relevant. On the other hand, for forward-looking purposes, variations in the current situations and trajectories of different groups might be seen as more relevant.

B. THE EVOLUTION OF THE MODERN CASE LAW AND THE ROAD TO STRICT SCRUTINY, 1980–1995

As was the case in *Bakke*, in the 1980s the Supreme Court remained deeply divided over the question of affirmative action and was unable to produce any majority opinions that significantly clarified the issue. Adding to the disarray in the Court was whether affirmative action adopted by Congress should be treated differently from affirmative action at the state or local level. By 1995, however, after the Court had changed composition, a clearer constitutional approach had emerged.

1. *Fullilove.* In *Fullilove v. Klutznick,* 448 U.S. 448 (1980), six justices voted to uphold against a facial challenge a 1977 federal statute providing federal funds to state and local government building projects that required that, absent an administrative waiver, at least 10% of the money had to be spent procuring goods or services from minority business enterprises ("MBEs"). MBEs were defined as businesses owned or controlled by "citizens of the United States who are Negroes, Spanish-speaking, Orientals, Indians, Eskimos, and Aleuts." Three justices concluded that the statute survived the "intermediate scrutiny" approach that they had favored in *Bakke*, while three others also voted to uphold the statute, but did not identify a standard of review, stating only that the use "of racial or ethnic criteria, even in a remedial context, calls for close examination." Several justices expressed the view that Congress had particularly expansive remedial power to enforce the guarantees of equal protection. Two of the three dissenters argued the Constitution required governmental colorblindness.

[margin handwritten note: Ok to use fed. $ to remedy past discrimination]

2. *Croson.* In 1989, the Court took a major step toward adopting strict scrutiny as the relevant standard for review of affirmative action plans. In *City of Richmond v. J.A. Croson Co.*, 488 U.S. 469 (1989), the Court addressed the constitutionality of a plan adopted by the Richmond, Virginia City Council in 1983. The City's "Minority Business Utilization Plan" required non-minority prime contractors receiving city construction contracts "to subcontract at least 30% of the dollar amount of the contract to one or more Minority Business Enterprises (MBEs)." The Plan declared that its 30% set-aside was 'remedial' in nature, and enacted 'for the purpose of promoting wider participation by minority business enterprises in the construction of public projects.' " Supporters relied on the fact that, "while

the general population of Richmond was 50% black, only .67% of the city's prime construction contracts had been awarded to minority businesses in the 5-year period from 1978 to 1983."

The city relied heavily on *Fullilove*, but Justice O'Connor, in an opinion joined by three justices, rejected the argument, noting that the fact that "Congress may identify and redress the effects of society-wide discrimination does not mean that, *a fortiori*, the States and their political subdivisions are free to decide that such remedies are appropriate. Section 1 of the Fourteenth Amendment is an explicit constraint on state power, and the States must undertake any remedial efforts in accordance with that provision." Justice Scalia made a similar point in his concurrence.

[handwritten margin note: ok for Congress but not States]

On the question whether strict scrutiny should apply, Justice O'Connor said the following:

> The Richmond Plan denies certain citizens the opportunity to compete for a fixed percentage of public contracts based solely upon their race. To whatever racial group these citizens belong, their "personal rights" to be treated with equal dignity and respect are implicated by a rigid rule erecting race as the sole criterion in an aspect of public decisionmaking.

> Absent searching judicial inquiry into the justification for such race-based measures, there is simply no way of determining what classifications are "benign" or "remedial" and what classifications are in fact motivated by illegitimate notions of racial inferiority or simple racial politics. Indeed, the purpose of strict scrutiny is to "smoke out" illegitimate uses of race by assuring that the legislative body is pursuing a goal important enough to warrant use of a highly suspect tool. The test also ensures that the means chosen "fit" this compelling goal so closely that there is little or no possibility that the motive for the classification was illegitimate racial prejudice or stereotype.

> Classifications based on race carry a danger of stigmatic harm. Unless they are strictly reserved for remedial settings, they may in fact promote notions of racial inferiority and lead to a politics of racial hostility. *See Bakke* (opinion of Powell, J). We thus reaffirm the view expressed by the plurality in [*Wygant v. Jackson*, 476 U.S. 267 (1986)] that the standard of review under the Equal Protection Clause is not dependent on the race of those burdened or benefitted by a particular classification.

Justice O'Connor continued by invoking the principles of representation-reinforcement developed by John Hart Ely:

> Even were we to accept a reading of the guarantee of equal protection under which the level of scrutiny varies according to

the ability of different groups to defend their interests in the representative process, heightened scrutiny would still be appropriate in the circumstances of this case. One of the central arguments for applying a less exacting standard to "benign" racial classifications is that such measures essentially involve a choice made by dominant racial groups to disadvantage themselves. If one aspect of the judiciary's role under the Equal Protection Clause is to protect "discrete and insular minorities" from majoritarian prejudice or indifference, see *Carolene Products* n.4, some maintain that these concerns are not implicated when the "white majority" places burdens upon itself. *See* J. Ely, Democracy and Distrust 170 (1980).

In this case, blacks comprise approximately 50% of the population of the city of Richmond. Five of the nine seats on the City Council are held by blacks. The concern that a political majority will more easily act to the disadvantage of a minority based on unwarranted assumptions or incomplete facts would seem to militate for, not against, the application of heightened judicial scrutiny in this case.

Finally, Justice O'Connor emphasized how exacting strict scrutiny must be:

> [A] generalized assertion that there has been past discrimination in an entire industry provides no guidance for a legislative body to determine the precise scope of the injury it seeks to remedy. * * * "Relief" for such an ill-defined wrong could extend until the percentage of public contracts awarded to MBEs in Richmond mirrored the percentage of minorities in the population as a whole. * * *

> While there is no doubt that the sorry history of both private and public discrimination in this country has contributed to a lack of opportunities for black entrepreneurs, this observation, standing alone, cannot justify a rigid racial quota in the awarding of public contracts in Richmond, Virginia. * * *

> It is sheer speculation how many minority firms there would be in Richmond absent past societal discrimination, just as it was sheer speculation how many minority medical students would have been admitted to the medical school at Davis absent past discrimination in educational opportunities. Defining these sorts of injuries as "identified discrimination" would give local governments license to create a patchwork of racial preferences based on statistical generalizations about any particular field of endeavor. * * *

[I]t is almost impossible to assess whether the Richmond Plan is narrowly tailored to remedy prior discrimination since it is not linked to identified discrimination in any way. We limit ourselves to two observations in this regard.

First, there does not appear to have been any consideration of the use of race-neutral means to increase minority business participation in city contracting. * * *

Second, the 30% quota cannot be said to be narrowly tailored to any goal, except perhaps outright racial balancing. It rests upon the "completely unrealistic" assumption that minorities will choose a particular trade in lockstep proportion to their representation in the local population.

Justice Marshall, joined by Justices Brennan and Blackmun, dissented. Marshall argued that the Richmond plan passed the "intermediate scrutiny" he would apply to affirmative action measures. The city had two important governmental interests—eradicating the present effects of past racial discrimination and ensuring that the city's money did not perpetuate those effects—that, he contended, were adequately supported by the record. He stressed that minority-owned businesses received only "one-seventy-fifth the public contracting funds that other businesses receive." The means chosen were reasonable because they were similar to those approved in *Fullilove*. He contended that, since the Civil War Amendments were adopted because of fears that states would inadequately respond to "racial violence or discrimination against newly freed slaves," "[t]o interpret any aspect of these Amendments as proscribing state remedial measures * * * turns the Amendments on their heads."

3. *Metro Broadcasting*. In *Metro Broadcasting, Inc. v. Federal Communications Commission*, 497 U.S. 547 (1990), the Court—somewhat surprisingly in the wake of *Croson*—upheld a federal policy designed to increase minority ownership of television and radio stations. Justice Brennan's majority opinion, joined by Justices White, Marshall, Blackmun, and Stevens, concluded that *Fullilove* had not imposed strict scrutiny upon the federal program challenged there, and then adopted the less rigorous "intermediate scrutiny" as the appropriate standard for assessing "benign" racial classifications adopted by the *federal* government. The majority distinguished *Croson*, which had applied strict scrutiny to state and local government plans.

Justice O'Connor, joined by Chief Justice Rehnquist and Justices Scalia and Kennedy, issued a long and vigorous dissenting, arguing that *Croson* required the application of strict scrutiny to federal policies, as well. Five years later, in the next case, that view prevailed.

ADARAND CONSTRUCTORS, INC. V. PENA
515 U.S. 200, 115 S.Ct. 2097, 132 L.Ed.2d 158 (1995)

JUSTICE O'CONNOR announced the judgment of the Court and delivered an opinion with respect to Parts I, II, III-A, III-B, III-D, and IV, which is for the Court except insofar as it might be inconsistent with the views expressed in JUSTICE SCALIA's concurrence, and an opinion with respect to Part III-C in which JUSTICE KENNEDY joins.

[The federal government awarded the prime contract for a highway construction project to Mountain Gravel & Construction Co. Mountain Gravel solicited bids from subcontractors for a portion of the work. Adarand Constructors submitted the low bid. Mountain Gravel chose Gonzales Construction Co., however, because Mountain Gravel would receive additional compensation from the federal government for hiring subcontractors, such as Gonzales Construction, certified as small businesses controlled by "socially and economically disadvantaged persons." "Social disadvantage" referred to those "subjected to racial or ethnic prejudice or cultural bias because of their identity as a member of a group without regard to their individual qualities"; "economic disadvantage" referred to "those socially disadvantaged individuals whose ability to compete in the free enterprise system has been impaired due to diminished capital and credit opportunities as compared to others in the same business area who are not socially disadvantaged." Women and racial minorities were presumed to be socially and economically disadvantaged, but this presumption was subject to rebuttal by a third party. A subcontractor who was not a woman or a racial minority could nonetheless qualify by proving social disadvantage "on the basis of clear and convincing evidence" and then by proving economic disadvantage as well. Adarand challenged this scheme as unconstitutional.]

III.A.   [Justice O'Connor traced at length the history of the Court's cases reading an equal protection component into the Fifth Amendment and thus obligating the federal government to comply with the dictates of the equal protection clause. She emphasized cases noting that "the Equal Protection Clause demands that racial classifications . . . be subjected to the 'most rigid scrutiny,'" and that the "Court's approach to Fifth Amendment equal protection claims has always been precisely the same as to equal protection claims under the Fourteenth Amendment."]

III.B.   With *Croson*, the Court finally agreed that the Fourteenth Amendment requires strict scrutiny of all race-based action by state and local governments. But *Croson* of course had no occasion to declare what standard of review the Fifth Amendment requires for such action taken by the Federal Government. * * * Thus, some uncertainty persisted with respect to the standard of review for federal racial classifications.

Despite lingering uncertainty in the details, however, the Court's cases through *Croson* had established three general propositions with respect to governmental racial classifications. First, skepticism: " '[a]ny preference based on racial or ethnic criteria must necessarily receive a most searching examination.' " Second, consistency: "the standard of review under the Equal Protection Clause is not dependent on the race of those burdened or benefitted by a particular classification," *i.e.*, all racial classifications reviewable under the Equal Protection Clause must be strictly scrutinized. And third, congruence: "[e]qual protection analysis in the Fifth Amendment area is the same as that under the Fourteenth Amendment[.]" Taken together, these three propositions lead to the conclusion that any person, of whatever race, has the right to demand that any governmental actor subject to the Constitution justify any racial classification subjecting that person to unequal treatment under the strictest judicial scrutiny. * * *

[Justice O'Connor then criticized as a "surprising turn" the Court's post-*Croson* holding in *Metro Broadcasting*, which held that "benign" federal racial classifications need only satisfy intermediate scrutiny. She argued that *Metro Broadcasting* undermined] the basic principle that the Fifth and Fourteenth Amendments to the Constitution protect *persons*, not *groups*. It follows from that principle that all governmental action based on race—a *group* classification long recognized as "in most circumstances irrelevant and therefore prohibited,"—should be subjected to detailed judicial inquiry to ensure that the *personal* right to equal protection of the laws has not been infringed. * * * Accordingly, we hold today that all racial classifications, imposed by whatever federal, state, or local governmental actor, must be analyzed by a reviewing court under strict scrutiny. In other words, such classifications are constitutional only if they are narrowly tailored measures that further compelling governmental interests. To the extent that *Metro Broadcasting* is inconsistent with that holding, it is overruled. * * *

Justice Stevens chides us for our "supposed inability to differentiate between 'invidious' and 'benign' discrimination," because it is in his view sufficient that "people understand the difference between good intentions and bad." [But] the point of strict scrutiny is to "differentiate between" permissible and impermissible governmental use of race. And Justice Stevens himself has already explained in his dissent in *Fullilove* why "good intentions" alone are not enough to sustain a supposedly "benign" racial classification: "[E]ven though it is not the actual predicate for this legislation, a statute of this kind inevitably is perceived by many as resting on an assumption that those who are granted this special preference are less qualified in some respect that is identified purely by their race. Because that perception—*especially when fostered by the Congress of the United States*—can only exacerbate rather than reduce racial prejudice, it will delay the time when race will become a truly irrelevant, or at least insignificant, factor. *Unless Congress clearly articulates the need and basis for a racial classification, and also tailors the classification to its justification*, the Court should not uphold this kind of statute." [Emphasis added] * * * [This passage makes] a persuasive case for requiring strict scrutiny of congressional racial classifications.

Perhaps it is not the standard of strict scrutiny itself, but our use of the concepts of "consistency" and "congruence" in conjunction with it, that leads Justice Stevens to dissent. According to Justice Stevens, our view of consistency "equate[s] remedial preferences with invidious discrimination" and ignores the difference between "an engine of oppression" and an effort "to foster equality in society," or, more colorfully, "between a 'No Trespassing' sign and a welcome mat." It does nothing of the kind. The principle of consistency simply means that whenever the government treats any person unequally because of his or her race, that person has suffered an injury that falls squarely within the language and spirit of the Constitution's guarantee of equal protection. It says nothing about the ultimate validity of any particular law; that determination is the job of the court applying strict scrutiny. The principle of consistency explains the circumstances in which the injury requiring strict scrutiny occurs. The application of strict scrutiny, in turn, determines whether a compelling governmental interest justifies the infliction of that injury. * * *

Justice Stevens also claims that we have ignored any difference between federal and state legislatures. But requiring that Congress, like the States, enact racial classifications only when doing so is necessary to further a "compelling interest" does not contravene any principle of appropriate respect for a co-equal Branch of the Government. * * *

III.D.   * * * We think that requiring strict scrutiny is the best way to ensure that courts will consistently give racial classifications that kind of detailed examination, both as to ends and as to means. *Korematsu* demonstrates vividly that even "the most rigid scrutiny" can sometimes fail to detect an illegitimate racial classification * * * Any retreat from the most searching judicial inquiry can only increase the risk of another such error occurring in the future.

Finally, we wish to dispel the notion that strict scrutiny is "strict in theory, but fatal in fact." The unhappy persistence of both the practice and the lingering effects of racial discrimination against minority groups in this country is an unfortunate reality, and government is not disqualified from acting in response to it. * * * When race-based action is necessary to further a compelling interest, such action is within constitutional constraints if it satisfies the "narrow tailoring" test this Court has set out in previous cases. [The Court remanded the case for application of the strict-scrutiny standard.]

JUSTICE SCALIA, concurring in part and concurring in the judgment.

I join the opinion of the Court, except Part III-C, and except insofar as it may be inconsistent with the following: In my view, government can never have a "compelling interest" in discriminating on the basis of race in order to "make up" for past racial discrimination in the opposite direction. Individuals who have been wronged by unlawful racial discrimination should be made whole; but under our Constitution there can be no such thing as either a creditor or a debtor race. * * * To pursue the concept of racial entitlement—even for the most admirable and benign of purposes— is to reinforce and preserve for future mischief the way of thinking that produced race slavery, race privilege and race hatred. In the eyes of government, we are just one race here. It is American. * * *

JUSTICE THOMAS, concurring in part and concurring in the judgment.

* * * I [disagree] with the premise underlying [the dissents]: that there is a racial paternalism exception to the principle of equal protection. I believe that there is a "moral [and] constitutional equivalence," *post* (Stevens, J., dissenting), between laws designed to subjugate a race and those that distribute benefits on the basis of race in order to foster some current notion of equality. Government cannot make us equal; it can only recognize, respect, and protect us as equal before the law. * * *

These programs * * * undermine the moral basis of the equal protection principle. Purchased at the price of immeasurable human suffering, the equal protection principle reflects our Nation's understanding that such classifications ultimately have a destructive impact on the individual and our society. * * * [T]here can be no doubt that racial paternalism and its unintended consequences can be as poisonous and pernicious as any other form of discrimination. So-called "benign" discrimination teaches many that because of chronic and apparently immutable handicaps, minorities cannot compete with them without their patronizing indulgence. Inevitably, such programs engender attitudes of superiority or, alternatively, provoke resentment among those who believe that they have been wronged by the government's use of race. These programs stamp minorities with a badge of inferiority and may cause them to develop dependencies or to adopt an attitude that they are "entitled" to preferences. * * *

JUSTICE STEVENS, with whom JUSTICE GINSBURG joins, dissenting.

The Court's concept of "consistency" assumes that there is no significant difference between a decision by the majority to impose a special burden on the members of a minority race and a decision by the majority to provide a benefit to certain members of that minority notwithstanding its incidental burden on some members of the majority. * * * [But] [t]here is no moral or constitutional equivalence between a policy that is designed to perpetuate a caste system and one that seeks to eradicate racial subordination. Invidious discrimination is an engine of oppression, subjugating a disfavored group to enhance or maintain the power of the majority. Remedial race-based preferences reflect the opposite impulse: a desire to foster equality in society. No sensible conception of the Government's constitutional obligation to "govern impartially" should ignore this distinction. * * *

The consistency that the Court espouses would disregard the difference between a "No Trespassing" sign and a welcome mat. It would treat a Dixiecrat Senator's decision to vote against Thurgood Marshall's confirmation in order to keep African Americans off the Supreme Court as on a par with President Johnson's evaluation of his nominee's race as a positive factor. It would equate a law that made black citizens ineligible for military service with a program aimed at recruiting black soldiers. An attempt by the majority to exclude members of a minority race from a regulated market is fundamentally different from a subsidy that enables a relatively small group of newcomers to enter that market. An interest in "consistency" does not justify treating differences as though they were similarities.

The Court's explanation for treating dissimilar race-based decisions as though they were equally objectionable is a supposed inability to differentiate between "invidious" and "benign" discrimination. But the term "affirmative action" is common and well understood. Its presence in everyday parlance shows that people understand the difference between good intentions and bad. * * * [O]ur equal protection jurisprudence has identified a critical difference between state action that imposes burdens on a disfavored few and state action that benefits the few "in spite of" its adverse effects on the many. * * *

The Court's concept of "congruence" assumes that there is no significant difference between a decision by the Congress of the United States to adopt an affirmative-action program and such a decision by a State or a municipality. In my opinion that assumption is untenable. It ignores important practical and legal differences between federal and state or local decisionmakers. * * * [Because oppression by faction is less likely to occur at the national level, see *Federalist* 10 (Madison) (App. 2), Congress could be trusted more than the legislatures of the states and localities. Moreover, the Congress is elected by all Americans, "whereas a state or local program may have an impact on nonresident entities who played no part in the decision to enact it. Thus, in the state or local context, individuals who were unable to vote for the local representatives who enacted a race-conscious program may nonetheless feel the effects of that program."] * * *

[The dissent of **JUSTICE SOUTER**, joined by **JUSTICES GINSBURG** and **BREYER**, and the dissent of **JUSTICE GINSBURG**, joined by **JUSTICE BREYER**, are omitted.]

NOTE ON APPLYING STRICT SCRUTINY TO THE FEDERAL GOVERNMENT

Adarand: *Formalism and Precedent.* The Constitution contains no Equal Protection Clause applicable to the federal government, and thus there is no obvious textual support for Justice O'Connor's "congruence" argument. Moreover, following the Civil War, in the Freedman's Bureau Acts, Congress engaged in race-based affirmative action by providing land, education, medical care, and other benefits to the newly freed former slaves. This historical record calls into question any argument that the Framers of the Fourteenth Amendment thought that their handiwork expressly or impliedly forbade *federal* usage of benign racial classifications. Moreover, to reach its result in *Adarand* the majority had to overcome the traditional presumption of *stare decisis* and overrule *Fullilove* and *Metro Broadcasting*. With all these formalist (textualist, originalist, precedential) arguments cutting against the result in *Adarand*, it seems odd to see that the Justices most inclined toward formalist arguments are in the majority. What arguments support the majority in *Adarand*?

To understand *Adarand*, consider the legacy of *Bolling*, *Korematsu*, and *Hirabayashi*. *Bolling*, which considered school segregation in the District of Columbia, stated: "In view of our decision that the Constitution prohibits the states from maintaining racially segregated schools, it would be unthinkable that the same Constitution would impose a lesser duty on the Federal Government." Is it equally "unthinkable" that the city council of Richmond, Virginia, and the Congress of the United States should be subjected to differing constitutional standards concerning the "benign" usage of race? Maybe it is "unthinkable" only when these two governments are operating similarly—*i.e.*, governing a city (Richmond; Washington, D.C.), and not when the Congress legislates on a nationwide basis. But would that mean that *Korematsu* and *Hirabayashi* were correctly decided? On *Bolling* and its progeny, see, e.g., Richard Primus, Bolling *Alone*, 104 Colum. L. Rev. 975 (2004); Peter Rubin, *Taking its Proper Place in the Constitutional Canon:* Bolling v. Sharpe, Korematsu, *and the Equal Protection Component of Fifth Amendment Due Process*, 92 Va. L. Rev. 1879 (2006).

NOTE ON THE POTENTIAL IMPLICATIONS OF APPLYING STRICT SCRUTINY TO STATUTES DESIGNED TO BENEFIT VICTIMS OF RACIAL DISCRIMINATION

Recall that in *Washington v. Davis* (see § 3B of this chapter), the Court ruled that discriminatory racial effects alone do not trigger strict scrutiny and that discriminatory intent must be shown. In the course of his majority opinion, Justice White noted that a plaintiff *can* prevail on a discriminatory impact theory under Title VII of the Civil Rights Act of 1964, but argued that the same standard is not appropriate for constitutional claims. It has long been assumed that legislatures may elect to enact laws, like Title VII, that permit recovery for discriminatory impact. In recent years, however, some members of the Court have suggested that this assumption may not be correct. These suggestions have given rise to questions about whether the application of strict scrutiny might create equal protection problems for statutes that allow claims for discriminatory impact.

In *Ricci v. DeStefano*, 557 U.S. 557 (2009), the Court addressed the claim of a white firefighter who had taken a written test for promotion and objected when the city of New Haven later decided not to use the results of that test. Had the test results been used, only whites and Hispanics—and no African Americans—would have been promoted. The City was threatened with a lawsuit if it used these test scores to allocate promotions, as well as a *different* lawsuit if, based on the racially disparate results, the city elected *not* to use the test. When the city ultimately declined to use the test, it was sued by both white and Hispanic firefighters who claimed they were denied promotion in violation both of Title VII of the Civil Rights Act of 1964 and the Equal Protection Clause. In a 5–4 opinion, the Court ruled that the city's action violated Title VII. While the majority did not reach the equal protection question, it did suggest it had concerns about disparate impact claims and would therefore impose a high bar for an employer that wants to take action to address the racially disparate effects of its policies, as New Haven had sought to do with this written test. The Court said:

> Congress has imposed liability on employers for unintentional discrimination in order to rid the workplace of 'practices that are fair in form, but discriminatory in operation.' But it has also prohibited employers from taking adverse employment actions 'because of' race. Applying the strong-basis-in-evidence standard to Title VII gives effect to both the disparate-treatment and disparate-impact provisions, allowing violations of one in the name of compliance with the other only in certain, narrow circumstances. * * * [This] standard appropriately constrains employers' discretion in making race-based decisions: It limits that discretion to cases in which there is a strong basis in evidence of disparate-impact liability, but it is not so restrictive that it allows employers to act only when there is a provable, actual violation. * * * We conclude there is no strong basis in evidence to establish that the test was deficient in either of these respects.

Justice Scalia concurred, and suggested that statutory disparate impact liability itself might violate equal protection:

> [The Court's] resolution of this dispute merely postpones the evil day on which the Court will have to confront the question: Whether, or to what extent, are the disparate-impact provisions of Title VII of the

Civil Rights Act of 1964 consistent with the Constitution's guarantee of equal protection? The question is not an easy one. * * *

The difficulty is this: Whether or not Title VII's disparate-treatment provisions forbid 'remedial' race-based actions when a disparate-impact violation would *not* otherwise result—the question resolved by the Court today—it is clear that Title VII not only permits but affirmatively *requires* such actions when a disparate-impact violation *would* otherwise result. But if the Federal Government is prohibited from discriminating on the basis of race, then surely it is also prohibited from enacting laws mandating that third parties—*e.g.*, employers, whether private, state, or municipal—discriminate on the basis of race. As the facts of these cases illustrate, Title VII's disparate-impact provisions place a racial thumb on the scales, often requiring employers to evaluate the racial outcomes of their policies, and to make decisions based on (because of) those racial outcomes. That type of racial decisionmaking is, as the Court explains, discriminatory. * * *

[T]he war between disparate impact and equal protection will be waged sooner or later, and it behooves us to begin thinking about how—and on what terms—to make peace between them.

You will note that Justice Scalia's rationale is not framed in terms of constitutional text or original understanding, which might well provide support for the federal creation of disparate impact liability (For historical background, see Chapter 2, § 1A). His argument is instead rooted in judicially developed doctrine on race.

Six years later, in *Texas Department of Housing Community Affairs v. Inclusive Communities Project, Inc.,* __ U.S. ___, 135 S.Ct. 2507 (2015), the Court ruled that plaintiffs may claim disparate impact under the federal Fair Housing Act. Writing for a 5-member majority, Justice Kennedy reached the result as a matter of statutory interpretation. The post-*Ricci* decision to interpret the Act to allow disparate impact liability would seem to take some of the steam out of the constitutional threat Justice Scalia had issued six years earlier. See, e.g., Samuel Bagenstos, *Disparate Impact and the Role of Classification and Motivation in Equal Protection Law After* Inclusive Communities, 101 Cornell L. Rev. 1115 (2016). But at several points in the opinion, Justice Kennedy alluded to the need to narrow disparate impact liability under the statute because of lurking constitutional concerns of the kind flagged in *Ricci*. He noted, for example, that "disparate-impact liability has always been properly limited in key respects that avoid the serious constitutional questions that might arise under the FHA, for instance, if such liability were imposed based solely on a showing of a statistical disparity."

After you have read *Fisher v. University Texas* (*Fisher II*) in the next section, consider whether the dissenters' apparent acceptance of the Texas Top Ten Percent Plan for admissions offers some indirect evidence that constitutional skepticism about disparate impact, in some form, may have receded. The dissenters seem to endorse the idea that a percentage plan can be used for purpose of addressing the disparate racial impact of existing admissions processes.

C. REVISITING THE DIVERSITY RATIONALE AND ADMISSION TO STATE UNIVERSITY PROFESSIONAL SCHOOLS

GRUTTER V. BOLLINGER
539 U.S. 306, 123 S.Ct. 2325, 156 L.Ed.2d 304 (2003)

JUSTICE O'CONNOR delivered the opinion of the Court.

[The University of Michigan Law School] ranks among the Nation's top law schools. It receives more than 3,500 applications each year for a class of around 350 students. Seeking to "admit a group of students who individually and collectively are among the most capable," the Law School looks for individuals with "substantial promise for success in law school" and "a strong likelihood of succeeding in the practice of law and contributing in diverse ways to the well-being of others." More broadly, the Law School seeks "a mix of students with varying backgrounds and experiences who will respect and learn from each other." * * *

The hallmark of [the law school's admissions policy, adopted in 1992,] is its focus on academic ability coupled with a flexible assessment of applicants' talents, experiences, and potential "to contribute to the learning of those around them." The policy requires admissions officials to evaluate each applicant based on all the information available in the file, including a personal statement, letters of recommendation, and an essay describing the ways in which the applicant will contribute to the life and diversity of the Law School. In reviewing an applicant's file, admissions officials must consider the applicant's undergraduate grade point average (GPA) and Law School Admissions Test (LSAT) score because they are important (if imperfect) predictors of academic success in law school. The policy stresses that "no applicant should be admitted unless we expect that applicant to do well enough to graduate with no serious academic problems."

The policy makes clear, however, that even the highest possible score does not guarantee admission to the Law School. Nor does a low score automatically disqualify an applicant. Rather, the policy requires admissions officials to look beyond grades and test scores to other criteria that are important to the Law School's educational objectives. So-called " 'soft' variables" such as "the enthusiasm of recommenders, the quality of the undergraduate institution, the quality of the applicant's essay, and the areas and difficulty of undergraduate course selection" are all brought to bear in assessing an "applicant's likely contributions to the intellectual and social life of the institution."

The policy aspires to "achieve that diversity which has the potential to enrich everyone's education and thus make a law school class stronger than the sum of its parts." The policy does not restrict the types of diversity contributions eligible for "substantial weight" in the admissions process, but instead recognizes "many possible bases for diversity admissions." The policy does, however, reaffirm the Law School's longstanding commitment to "one particular type of diversity," that is, "racial and ethnic diversity with special reference to the inclusion of students from groups which have been historically discriminated against, like African-Americans, Hispanics and Native Americans, who without this commitment might not be represented in our student body in meaningful numbers." By enrolling a " 'critical mass' of [underrepresented] minority students," the Law School seeks to "ensur[e] their ability to make unique contributions to the character of the Law School."

The policy does not define diversity "solely in terms of racial and ethnic status." Nor is the policy "insensitive to the competition among all students for admission to the [L]aw [S]chool." Rather, the policy seeks to guide admissions officers in "producing classes both diverse and academically outstanding, classes made up of students who promise to continue the tradition of outstanding contribution by Michigan Graduates to the legal profession."

Petitioner Barbara Grutter is a white Michigan resident who applied to the Law School in 1996 with a 3.8 grade point average and 161 LSAT score[, who was rejected for admission. She brought suit challenging the constitutionality of the admissions policy. The district court found the admissions program unconstitutional, but a sharply divided en banc court of appeals reversed.] * * *

Since this Court's splintered decision in *Bakke*, Justice Powell's opinion announcing the judgment of the Court has served as the touchstone for constitutional analysis of race-conscious admissions policies. Public and private universities across the Nation have modeled their own admissions programs on Justice Powell's views on permissible race-conscious policies. * * * [T]oday we endorse Justice Powell's view that student body diversity is a compelling state interest that can justify the use of race in university admissions. * * *

[Justice O'Connor noted that under *Adarand* all racial classifications receive strict scrutiny review, but that strict scrutiny is not "strict in theory, but fatal in fact."] Not every decision influenced by race is equally objectionable and strict scrutiny is designed to provide a framework for carefully examining the importance and the sincerity of the reasons advanced by the governmental decisionmaker for the use of race in that particular context.

With these principles in mind, we turn to the question whether the Law School's use of race is justified by a compelling state interest. * * * [T]he Law School asks us to recognize, in the context of higher education, a compelling state interest in student body diversity.

We first wish to dispel the notion that the Law School's argument has been foreclosed, either expressly or implicitly, by our affirmative-action cases decided since *Bakke*. It is true that some language in those opinions might be read to suggest that remedying past discrimination is the only permissible justification for race-based governmental action. See, e.g., *Croson* (plurality opinion) (stating that unless classifications based on race are "strictly reserved for remedial settings, they may in fact promote notions of racial inferiority and lead to a politics of racial hostility"). But we have never held that the only governmental use of race that can survive strict scrutiny is remedying past discrimination. Nor, since *Bakke*, have we directly addressed the use of race in the context of public higher education. Today, we hold that the Law School has a compelling interest in attaining a diverse student body.

The Law School's educational judgment that such diversity is essential to its educational mission is one to which we defer. The Law School's assessment that diversity will, in fact, yield educational benefits is substantiated by respondents and their *amici*. Our scrutiny of the interest asserted by the Law School is no less strict for taking into account complex educational judgments in an area that lies primarily within the expertise of the university. * * *

We have long recognized that, given the important purpose of public education and the expansive freedoms of speech and thought associated with the university environment, universities occupy a special niche in our constitutional tradition. In announcing the principle of student body diversity as a compelling state interest, Justice Powell invoked our cases recognizing a constitutional dimension, grounded in the First Amendment, of educational autonomy: "The freedom of a university to make its own judgments as to education includes the selection of its student body." From this premise, Justice Powell reasoned that by claiming "the right to select those students who will contribute the most to the 'robust exchange of ideas,'" a university "seek[s] to achieve a goal that is of paramount importance in the fulfillment of its mission." Our conclusion that the Law School has a compelling interest in a diverse student body is informed by our view that attaining a diverse student body is at the heart of the Law School's proper institutional mission, and that "good faith" on the part of a university is "presumed" absent "a showing to the contrary."

As part of its goal of "assembling a class that is both exceptionally academically qualified and broadly diverse," the Law School seeks to "enroll a 'critical mass' of minority students." [Quoting law school's brief.]

The Law School's interest is not simply "to assure within its student body some specified percentage of a particular group merely because of its race or ethnic origin." *Bakke* (opinion of Powell, J.). That would amount to outright racial balancing, which is patently unconstitutional. Rather, the Law School's concept of critical mass is defined by reference to the educational benefits that diversity is designed to produce.

These benefits are substantial. As the District Court emphasized, the Law School's admissions policy promotes "cross-racial understanding," helps to break down racial stereotypes, and "enables [students] to better understand persons of different races." These benefits are "important and laudable," because "classroom discussion is livelier, more spirited, and simply more enlightening and interesting" when the students have "the greatest possible variety of backgrounds." [Quoting district court opinion.]

These benefits are not theoretical but real, as major American businesses have made clear that the skills needed in today's increasingly global marketplace can only be developed through exposure to widely diverse people, cultures, ideas, and viewpoints. Brief for 3M et al. as *Amici Curiae* 5; Brief for General Motors Corp. as *Amicus Curiae* 3–4. What is more, high-ranking retired officers and civilian leaders of the United States military assert that, "[b]ased on [their] decades of experience," a "highly qualified, racially diverse officer corps . . . is essential to the military's ability to fulfill its principle mission to provide national security." Brief for Julius W. Becton, Jr. et al. as *Amici Curiae* 27. The primary sources for the Nation's officer corps are the service academies and the Reserve Officers Training Corps (ROTC), the latter comprising students already admitted to participating colleges and universities. At present, "the military cannot achieve an officer corps that is *both* highly qualified *and* racially diverse unless the service academies and the ROTC used limited race-conscious recruiting and admissions policies." *Ibid.* (emphasis in original). * * *

We have repeatedly acknowledged the overriding importance of preparing students for work and citizenship, describing education as pivotal to "sustaining our political and cultural heritage" with a fundamental role in maintaining the fabric of society. *Plyler v. Doe*. This Court has long recognized that "education . . . is the very foundation of good citizenship." *Brown v. Board of Education*. * * * Effective participation by members of all racial and ethnic groups in the civic life of our Nation is essential if the dream of one Nation, indivisible, is to be realized.

Moreover, universities, and in particular, law schools, represent the training ground for a large number of our Nation's leaders. Individuals with law degrees occupy roughly half the state governorships, more than half the seats in the United States Senate, and more than a third of the seats in the United States House of Representatives. The pattern is even more striking when it comes to highly selective law schools. A handful of these schools accounts for 25 of the 100 United States Senators, 74 United States Courts of Appeals judges, and nearly 200 of the more than 600 United States District Court judges.

In order to cultivate a set of leaders with legitimacy in the eyes of the citizenry, it is necessary that the path to leadership be visibly open to talented and qualified individuals of every race and ethnicity. All members of our heterogeneous society must have confidence in the openness and integrity of the educational institutions that provide this training. As we have recognized, law schools "cannot be effective in isolation from the individuals and institutions with which the law interacts." See *Sweatt v. Painter*. Access to legal education (and thus the legal profession) must be inclusive of talented and qualified individuals of every race and ethnicity, so that all members of our heterogeneous society may participate in the educational institutions that provide the training and education necessary to succeed in America.

The Law School does not premise its need for critical mass on "any belief that minority students always (or even consistently) express some characteristic minority viewpoint on any issue." To the contrary, diminishing the force of such stereotypes is both a crucial part of the Law School's mission, and one that it cannot accomplish with only token numbers of minority students. Just as growing up in a particular region or having particular professional experiences is likely to affect an individual's views, so too is one's own, unique experience of being a racial minority in a society, like our own, in which race unfortunately still matters. The Law School has determined, based on its experience and expertise, that a "critical mass" of underrepresented minorities is necessary to further its compelling interest in securing the educational benefits of a diverse student body.

[Justice O'Connor then turned to the second element of strict scrutiny: the narrow tailoring requirement.] To be narrowly tailored, a race-conscious admissions program cannot use a quota system—it cannot "insulat[e] each category of applicants with certain desired qualifications from competition with all other applicants." *Bakke* (opinion of Powell, J.). Instead, a university may consider race or ethnicity only as a " 'plus' in a particular applicant's file," without "insulat[ing] the individual from comparison with all other candidates for the available seats." *Id.* In other words, an admissions program must be "flexible enough to consider all pertinent elements of diversity in light of the particular qualifications of each applicant, and to place them on the same footing for consideration, although not necessarily according them the same weight." *Ibid.*

We find that the Law School's admissions program bears the hallmarks of a narrowly tailored plan. * * * We are satisfied that the Law School's admissions program, like the Harvard plan described by Justice

Powell, does not operate as a quota. Properly understood, a "quota" is a program in which a certain fixed number or proportion of opportunities are "reserved exclusively for certain minority groups." *Croson.* * * * In contrast, "a permissible goal . . . require[s] only a good-faith effort . . . to come within a range demarcated by the goal itself," and permits consideration of race as a "plus" factor in any given case while still ensuring that each candidate "compete[s] with all other qualified applicants." * * *

The Law School's goal of attaining a critical mass of underrepresented minority students does not transform its program into a quota. As the Harvard plan described by Justice Powell recognized, there is of course "some relationship between numbers and achieving the benefits to be derived from a diverse student body, and between numbers and providing a reasonable environment for those students admitted." "[S]ome attention to numbers," without more, does not transform a flexible admissions system into a rigid quota. *Ibid.* Nor, as JUSTICE KENNEDY posits, does the Law School's consultation of the "daily reports," which keep track of the racial and ethnic composition of the class (as well as of residency and gender), "suggest [ ] there was no further attempt at individual review save for race itself" during the final stages of the admissions process. See *post* (dissenting opinion). To the contrary, the Law School's admissions officers testified without contradiction that they never gave race any more or less weight based on the information contained in these reports. Moreover, * * * between 1993 and 2000, the number of African-American, Latino, and Native-American students in each class at the Law School varied from 13.5 to 20.1 percent, a range inconsistent with a quota.

THE CHIEF JUSTICE believes that the Law School's policy conceals an attempt to achieve racial balancing, and cites admissions data to contend that the Law School discriminates among different groups within the critical mass. *Post* (dissenting opinion). But * * * the number of underrepresented minority students who ultimately enroll in the Law School differs substantially from their representation in the applicant pool and varies considerably for each group from year to year.

That a race-conscious admissions program does not operate as a quota does not, by itself, satisfy the requirement of individualized consideration. When using race as a "plus" factor in university admissions, a university's admissions program must remain flexible enough to ensure that each applicant is evaluated as an individual and not in a way that makes an applicant's race or ethnicity the defining feature of his or her application. The importance of this individualized consideration in the context of a race-conscious admissions program is paramount. See *Bakke* (opinion of Powell, J.) (identifying the "denial . . . of th[e] right to individualized consideration" as the "principal evil" of the medical school's admissions program).

Here, the Law School engages in a highly individualized, holistic review of each applicant's file, giving serious consideration to all the ways an applicant might contribute to a diverse educational environment. * * * Unlike the program at issue in *Gratz v. Bollinger*, the Law School awards no mechanical, predetermined diversity "bonuses" based on race or ethnicity. Like the Harvard plan, the Law School's admissions policy "is flexible enough to consider all pertinent elements of diversity in light of the particular qualifications of each applicant, and to place them on the same footing for consideration, although not necessarily according them the same weight." *Bakke* (opinion of Powell, J.).

We also find that, like the Harvard plan Justice Powell referenced in *Bakke*, the Law School's race-conscious admissions program adequately ensures that all factors that may contribute to student body diversity are meaningfully considered alongside race in admissions decisions. * * *

[T]he 1992 policy makes clear "[t]here are many possible bases for diversity admissions," and provides examples of admittees who have lived or traveled widely abroad, are fluent in several languages, have overcome personal adversity and family hardship, have exceptional records of extensive community service, and have had successful careers in other fields. * * * All applicants have the opportunity to highlight their own potential diversity contributions through the submission of a personal statement, letters of recommendation, and an essay describing the ways in which the applicant will contribute to the life and diversity of the Law School.

What is more, the Law School actually gives substantial weight to diversity factors besides race. The Law School frequently accepts nonminority applicants with grades and test scores lower than underrepresented minority applicants (and other nonminority applicants) who are rejected. This shows that the Law School seriously weighs many other diversity factors besides race that can make a real and dispositive difference for nonminority applicants as well. By this flexible approach, the Law School sufficiently takes into account, in practice as well as in theory, a wide variety of characteristics besides race and ethnicity that contribute to a diverse student body. JUSTICE KENNEDY speculates that "race is likely outcome determinative for many members of minority groups" who do not fall within the upper range of LSAT scores and grades. *Post* (dissenting opinion). But the same could be said of the Harvard plan discussed approvingly by Justice Powell in *Bakke*, and indeed of any plan that uses race as one of many factors. See *Bakke* (" 'When the Committee on Admissions reviews the large middle group of applicants who are "admissible" and deemed capable of doing good work in their courses, the race of an applicant may tip the balance in his favor' ").

Petitioner and the United States argue that the Law School's plan is not narrowly tailored because race-neutral means exist to obtain the educational benefits of student body diversity that the Law School seeks. We disagree. Narrow tailoring does not require exhaustion of every conceivable race-neutral alternative. Nor does it require a university to choose between maintaining a reputation for excellence or fulfilling a commitment to provide educational opportunities to members of all racial groups. Narrow tailoring does, however, require serious, good faith consideration of workable race-neutral alternatives that will achieve the diversity the university seeks.

* * * The District Court took the Law School to task for failing to consider race-neutral alternatives such as "using a lottery system" or "decreasing the emphasis for all applicants on undergraduate GPA and LSAT scores." But these alternatives would require a dramatic sacrifice of diversity, the academic quality of all admitted students, or both.

The Law School's current admissions program considers race as one factor among many, in an effort to assemble a student body that is diverse in ways broader than race. Because a lottery would make that kind of nuanced judgment impossible, it would effectively sacrifice all other educational values, not to mention every other kind of diversity. So too with the suggestion that the Law School simply lower admissions standards for all students, a drastic remedy that would require the Law School to become a much different institution and sacrifice a vital component of its educational mission. The United States advocates "percentage plans," recently adopted by public undergraduate institutions in Texas, Florida, and California to guarantee admission to all students above a certain class-rank threshold in every high school in the State. The United States does not, however, explain how such plans could work for graduate and professional schools. Moreover, even assuming such plans are race-neutral, they may preclude the university from conducting the individualized assessments necessary to assemble a student body that is not just racially diverse, but diverse along all the qualities valued by the university. We are satisfied that the Law School adequately considered race-neutral alternatives currently capable of producing a critical mass without forcing the Law School to abandon the academic selectivity that is the cornerstone of its educational mission.

We acknowledge that "there are serious problems of justice connected with the idea of preference itself." *Bakke* (opinion of Powell, J.). Narrow tailoring, therefore, requires that a race-conscious admissions program not unduly harm members of any racial group. Even remedial race-based governmental action generally "remains subject to continuing oversight to assure that it will work the least harm possible to other innocent persons competing for the benefit." To be narrowly tailored, a race-conscious admissions program must not "unduly burden individuals who are not members of the favored racial and ethnic groups."

We are satisfied that the Law School's admissions program does not. Because the Law School considers "all pertinent elements of diversity," it can (and does) select nonminority applicants who have greater potential to enhance student body diversity over underrepresented minority applicants. See *Bakke* (opinion of Powell, J.). As Justice Powell recognized in *Bakke*, so long as a race-conscious admissions program uses race as a "plus" factor in the context of individualized consideration, a rejected applicant

> will not have been foreclosed from all consideration for that seat simply because he was not the right color or had the wrong surname. . . . His qualifications would have been weighed fairly and competitively, and he would have no basis to complain of unequal treatment under the Fourteenth Amendment.

* * * We are mindful, however, that "[a] core purpose of the Fourteenth Amendment was to do away with all governmentally imposed discrimination based on race." *Palmore v. Sidoti*. Accordingly, race-conscious admissions policies must be limited in time. This requirement reflects that racial classifications, however compelling their goals, are potentially so dangerous that they may be employed no more broadly than the interest demands. Enshrining a permanent justification for racial preferences would offend this fundamental equal protection principle. We see no reason to exempt race-conscious admissions programs from the requirement that all governmental use of race must have a logical end point. The Law School, too, concedes that all "race-conscious programs must have reasonable durational limits." Brief at 32.

In the context of higher education, the durational requirement can be met by sunset provisions in race-conscious admissions policies and periodic reviews to determine whether racial preferences are still necessary to achieve student body diversity. Universities in California, Florida, and Washington State, where racial preferences in admissions are prohibited by state law, are currently engaged in experimenting with a wide variety of alternative approaches. Universities in other States can and should draw on the most promising aspects of these race-neutral alternatives as they develop. * * *

We take the Law School at its word that it would "like nothing better than to find a race-neutral admissions formula" and will terminate its race-conscious admissions program as soon as practicable. See Brief for law school; *Bakke* (opinion of Powell, J.) (presuming good faith of university officials in the absence of a showing to the contrary). It has been 25 years since Justice Powell first approved the use of race to further an interest in student body diversity in the context of public higher education. Since that time, the number of minority applicants with high grades and test scores has indeed increased. We expect that 25 years from now, the use of racial preferences will no longer be necessary to further the interest approved today.

[JUSTICE GINSBURG, with whom JUSTICE BREYER joined, concurred, agreeing that affirmative action must have a logical stopping point but expressing concern that, in light of ongoing discrimination and social inequality, the Court's suggestion of a 25-year sunset on affirmative action might be optimistic.]

CHIEF JUSTICE REHNQUIST, with whom JUSTICE SCALIA, JUSTICE KENNEDY, and JUSTICE THOMAS join, dissenting.

* * * From 1995 through 2000, the Law School admitted between 1,130 and 1,310 students. Of those, between 13 and 19 were Native American, between 91 and 108 were African-Americans, and between 47 and 56 were Hispanic. If the Law School is admitting between 91 and 108 African-Americans in order to achieve "critical mass," thereby preventing African-American students from feeling "isolated or like spokespersons for their race," one would think that a number of the same order of magnitude would be necessary to accomplish the same purpose for Hispanics and Native Americans. Similarly, even if all of the Native American applicants admitted in a given year matriculate, which the record demonstrates is not at all the case, how can this possibly constitute a "critical mass" of Native Americans in a class of over 350 students? In order for this pattern of admission to be consistent with the Law School's explanation of "critical mass," one would have to believe that the objectives of "critical mass" offered by respondents are achieved with only half the number of Hispanics and one-sixth the number of Native Americans as compared to African-Americans. But respondents offer no race-specific reasons for such disparities. Instead, they simply emphasize the importance of achieving "critical mass," without any explanation of why that concept is applied differently among the three underrepresented minority groups. * * *

Only when the "critical mass" label is discarded does a likely explanation for these numbers emerge. The Court states that the Law School's goal of attaining a "critical mass" of underrepresented minority students is not an interest in merely " 'assur[ing] within its student body some specified percentage of a particular group merely because of its race or ethnic origin.' " *Ante* (quoting *Bakke* (opinion of Powell, J.)). The Court recognizes that such an interest "would amount to outright racial balancing, which is patently unconstitutional." The Court concludes, however, that the Law School's use of race in admissions, consistent with Justice Powell's opinion in *Bakke*, only pays " '[s]ome attention to numbers.' "

But the correlation between the percentage of the Law School's pool of applicants who are members of the three minority groups and the percentage of the admitted applicants who are members of these same groups is far too precise to be dismissed as merely the result of the school paying "some attention to [the] numbers." * * * [F]rom 1995 through 2000 the percentage of admitted applicants who were members of these minority groups closely tracked the percentage of individuals in the school's applicant pool who were from the same groups. * * *

I do not believe that the Constitution gives the Law School such free rein in the use of race. The Law School has offered no explanation for its actual admissions practices and, unexplained, we are bound to conclude that the Law School has managed its admissions program, not to achieve a "critical mass," but to extend offers of admission to members of selected minority groups in proportion to their statistical representation in the applicant pool. But this is precisely the type of racial balancing that the Court itself calls "patently unconstitutional."

Finally, I believe that the Law School's program fails strict scrutiny because it is devoid of any reasonably precise time limit on the Law School's use of race in admissions. * * *

[**JUSTICE KENNEDY**, dissenting, endorsed Justice Powell's approach in *Bakke* but believed that the majority was not true to it, engaging in "nothing short of perfunctory" review that was too accepting of the Law School's assurances that its admissions process satisfied constitutional requirements, when in fact "the Law School's pursuit of critical mass mutated into the equivalent of a quota."]

[**JUSTICE SCALIA** filed a short dissenting statement contending, among other things, that the majority's work will lead to further confusion and litigation about the constitutionality of affirmative action.]

[**JUSTICE THOMAS**, joined by **JUSTICE SCALIA**, lampooned Michigan's supposed compelling state interest as simply one seeking to maintain a prestigious law school that uses admissions criteria that disproportionally disadvantage racial minorities. He suggested that the law school could achieve its goal of a more racially diverse student body by using nonracial means: for example, it could expand the class size or simply drop some of its elite admissions criteria (e.g., stop using LSAT scores, which are generally lower for minority applicants). Even if diversity is a compelling government interest, he argued that narrow tailoring would require the use of such neutral criteria before considering engaging in race-based means of achieving diversity.]

Gratz v. Bollinger

539 U.S. 244 (2003)

In a companion case to *Grutter*, disappointed white applicants challenged the affirmative action policy used for admission to the undergraduate college of liberal arts and sciences of the University of Michigan. Out of a scheme with 150 total points and in which 100 points guaranteed admission, the program automatically awarded 20 points to any underrepresented minority applicant. **Chief Justice Rehnquist**, joined by **Justices O'Connor**, **Scalia**, **Kennedy**, and **Thomas**, struck down the program as failing to provide the individualized evaluation of each applicant required by *Grutter* and the Powell opinion in *Bakke*. The approach amounted to a practical quota because, as the majority understood the facts, it resulted in the admission of virtually any minimally qualified minority applicant. Thus, even though under *Grutter* educational diversity is a compelling government interest, the undergraduate admissions plan flunked the narrow-tailoring requirement. The majority was unmoved by the university's argument that it could not easily provide individualized consideration to the large number of applications it received. **Justice O'Connor** concurred, stressing the differences between the mechanical, nonindividualized process for undergraduate admissions and the individualized approach her majority opinion approved in the law-school case. **Justice Breyer** concurred in the judgment and expressed agreement with Justice O'Connor's views. Among the dissenting opinions, the most relevant for current concerns were filed by **Justice Souter** and by **Justice Ginsburg**. Justice Souter stressed that, even under the automatic process of awarding 20 points to minority applicants, all applicants contended for all seats in the class, and nonminority applicants could easily obtain admission over minority applicants by gaining more points based on other criteria (grades, test scores, strength of high school, quality of course of study, residence, alumni relationships, leadership, personal character, socioeconomic disadvantage, athletic ability, and quality of a personal essay). Thus, in his view the program operated more like a plus-factor scheme than a quota. Justice Ginsburg suggested that, in light of ongoing racial inequality and the distinction between benign and pernicious racial preferences, colleges and universities should continue to have ways to attempt to ameliorate racial differences in admissions. In her view, it is better to do this forthrightly, as Michigan had done, than to encourage applicants and admissions officers to do it by "resort to camouflage":

> Seeking to improve their chances for admission, applicants may highlight the minority group associations to which they belong, or the Hispanic surnames of their mothers or grandparents. In turn, teachers' recommendations may emphasize who a student is as much as what he or she has accomplished. * * * If honesty is the best policy, surely Michigan's accurately described, fully disclosed College affirmative action program is preferable to achieving similar numbers through winks, nods, and disguises.

NOTES ON THE MICHIGAN CASES

1.   *Why Revive Justice Powell's Approach Concerning the "Compelling" Nature of the Diversity Rationale?* The majority of the deeply divided Court settles on embracing Justice Powell's approach in *Bakke* but then divides on what that approach entails—for example, the narrow-tailoring point at which a plus factor becomes a quota. Strictly speaking, *stare decisis* in no way compels this outcome, as Justice Powell was writing only for himself, and in any event the current Court certainly has the authority to overrule the holding or implications of an earlier decision. What factors seem to have led Justice O'Connor to endorse the Powell approach, noting along the way that the *Croson* plurality opinion (written by her) had suggested that only remedial purposes could serve as compelling government interests in the affirmative action context?

In prior cases, one government interest found by a majority of the Court to be "compelling" was remedying past illegal discrimination (*Swann* and the *de jure* segregation cases involving busing as a remedy, cf. dictum in the *Croson* and *Adarand* cases regarding the capacity of government to consider taking race into account to remedy past illegal discrimination in the contracting industry). There is no suggestion in the Michigan cases that the University engaged in past illegal discrimination against persons of color in admissions. The other governmental interest found by a majority of the Court to be compelling is national security (*Korematsu*; *Hirabayashi*). This might have suggested that, outside the context of past illegality, a "compelling" government interest justifying the use of a racial classification must amount to something analogous to self-defense or the necessity defense in tort law and criminal law—a compulsion to act to save life or limb that authorizes the use of conduct (even deadly force in tort and criminal law) that society almost always otherwise forbids. (An arguable context would be separation of the races in a prison following a race riot.) In the Michigan cases, there is no contention that colorblind law school admissions will cause the University to unravel or result in lethal results to the citizenry. So what is "compelling" about the diversity rationale, in the context of law school admissions?

Despite *Croson*'s and *Adarand*'s insistence that strict scrutiny does not vary regardless of whether the use of race is hostile toward a racial minority or "benign," can the Michigan cases be explained in any way other than that a majority of the Court (embodied in the swing vote of Justice O'Connor) truly became comfortable that race was used here in a "benign" way in which the public interest in a future society that is both more racially integrated and racially compatible greatly outweighs the harm caused to non-minority law school applicants? Has strict scrutiny turned into a balancing test, not very different from the intermediate scrutiny approach (important government interest achieved by reasonable means)?

What exactly is/are the compelling interest(s)? Diversity of viewpoints and experiences in the educational milieu? Diversifying the legal profession? Diversifying the elite segment of the legal profession? Diversifying the professions, generally? As for that, consider all the professionals trained by state universities—how might *Grutter* affect the constitutionality of admissions to state university programs that train, e.g., accountants, architects, doctors, engineers, military officers, morticians, pharmacists, psychologists (those who provide mental health counseling), optometrists, nurses, and social workers? To what extent, if any, does the socioeconomic status the person might attain or the power the person might wield in society, regardless of whether she is in a profession, make a difference (note that Justice O'Connor cited the amicus brief filed by big business (3M et al.) supporting the diversity rationale)? To what extent does the racial composition of the profession or industry play a role (note that she cited the amicus brief by retired high-ranking military officers, which argued that diversifying the officer corps was essential to the effective functioning of the military)? Does any of this have anything to do with undergraduate admissions?

2. *Narrow Tailoring?* Is there any important difference between the law school's "holistic" review of applications and the undergraduate college's review of all applications with some applicants getting an automatic 20 points and others not? Focusing on the law school, is there any good response to the Chief Justice's contention that "critical mass" is a hollow concept that is a cover for loose proportional representation? Or to Justice Thomas's argument that race-neutral means (e.g., a lottery) should have been used before race-conscious means were considered?

3. *Nature of the Harm and Causation.* No Justice quarreled with the assumption that Ms. Grutter had suffered an injury that entitled her to have standing to object to the consideration of race in the law school admissions policy. But note that there is a serious question of causation: had the law school used a colorblind policy, there is no way to know whether she would have been admitted. Thus, the harm that she suffered is not that she was wrongfully denied admission (though had she prevailed, she could have attempted to prove that on remand); the harm must be that she was denied some sort of "equal treatment" in the admissions process.

Schuette v. Coalition to Defend Affirmative Action

572 U.S. 291 (2014)

After the Supreme Court's decisions in the Michigan cases, political forces opposed to the University's policy mounted a ballot initiative to eliminate affirmative action by state constitutional amendment. "Proposal 2" was modeled after a similar initiative that passed in California in 1996.[30]

The Michigan measure provided that state universities, and the state generally, "shall not discriminate against, or grant preferential treatment to,

---

[30] As of 2018, six other states also have such a policy. *See* Ariz. Const., art. II, § 36 (Arizona); Neb. Const., art. I, § 30(1) (Nebraska); Okla. Const., art. II, § 36(A) (Oklahoma); Wash. Rev. Code § 49.60.400(1) (Washington); N.H. Rev. Stat. § 187–A:16–a (New Hampshire); Fla. Exec. Order No. 99–281 (Florida).

any individual or group on the basis of race, sex, color, ethnicity or national origin in the operation of public employment, public education, or public contracting." Proposal 2 passed with 58% of the vote. Drawing on *Washington v. Seattle School Dist. No. 1*, 458 U. S. 457 (1981), *Hunter v. Erickson*, 393 U.S. 385 (1969), and related cases about racially discriminatory "restructuring" of the political process, the challengers argued that Proposal 2 violated equal protection because it modified the political process along racial lines. Michigan, the challengers argued, subjected only racial minorities to the onerous political burden of amending the state constitution in order to secure favorable policy on university admissions or other matters covered by the measure, while other groups could use the ordinary political process to seek desired change. The Supreme Court rejected this challenge. There was no majority opinion for the Court. Justice Kennedy's plurality, joined by the Chief Justice and Justice Alito, emphasized two points. One was to distinguish the political restructuring cases:

> Those cases were ones in which the political restriction in question was designed to be used, or was likely to be used, to encourage infliction of injury by reason of race. What is at stake here is not whether injury will be inflicted but whether government can be instructed not to follow a course that entails, first, the definition of racial categories and, second, the grant of favored status to persons in some racial categories and not others. The electorate's instruction to governmental entities not to embark upon the course of race-defined and race-based preferences was adopted, we must assume, because the voters deemed a preference system to be unwise, on account of what voters may deem its latent potential to become itself a source of the very resentments and hostilities based on race that this Nation seeks to put behind it.

The plurality's second point was to underscore the importance of allowing citizens to debate about whether they want to adopt affirmative action policies in their states. On this point, Justice Kennedy argued that:

> Were the Court to rule that the question addressed by Michigan voters is too sensitive or complex to be within the grasp of the electorate; or that the policies at issue remain too delicate to be resolved save by university officials or faculties, acting at some remove from immediate public scrutiny and control; or that these matters are so arcane that the electorate's power must be limited because the people cannot prudently exercise that power even after a full debate, that holding would be an unprecedented restriction on the exercise of a fundamental right held not just by one person but by all in common. It is the right to speak and debate and learn and then, as a matter of political will, to act through a lawful electoral process.

In a lengthy and impassioned dissent that was joined by Justice Ginsburg, Justice Sotomayor argued that the Michigan initiative did, in fact, violate the Equal Protection Clause by creating a separate and more burdensome political path for supporters of affirmative action. More broadly, she made a plea for greater realism about the corrosive effects of race in the lives of individuals and the nation:

> Race matters. Race matters in part because of the long history of racial minorities' being denied access to the political process. * * * And although we have made great strides, "voting discrimination still exists; no one doubts that." *Shelby County.*

> Race also matters because of persistent racial inequality in society—inequality that cannot be ignored and that has produced stark socioeconomic disparities. * * *

> And race matters for reasons that really are only skin deep, that cannot be discussed any other way, and that cannot be wished away. Race matters to a young man's view of society when he spends his teenage years watching others tense up as he passes, no matter the neighborhood where he grew up. Race matters to a young woman's sense of self when she states her hometown, and then is pressed, "No, where are you *really* from?", regardless of how many generations her family has been in the country. Race matters to a young person addressed by a stranger in a foreign language, which he does not understand because only English was spoken at home. Race matters because of the slights, the snickers, the silent judgments that reinforce that most crippling of thoughts: "I do not belong here."

> In my colleagues' view, examining the racial impact of legislation only perpetuates racial discrimination. This refusal to accept the stark reality that race matters is regrettable. The way to stop discrimination on the basis of race is to speak openly and candidly on the subject of race, and to apply the Constitution with eyes open to the unfortunate effects of centuries of racial discrimination. As members of the judiciary tasked with intervening to carry out the guarantee of equal protection, we ought not sit back and wish away, rather than confront, the racial inequality that exists in our society. It is this view that works harm, by perpetuating the facile notion that what makes race matter is acknowledging the simple truth that race *does* matter.

FISHER V. UNIVERSITY OF TEXAS AT AUSTIN
579 U.S. ___, 136 S.Ct. 2198, 195 L.Ed.2d 511 (2016)

JUSTICE KENNEDY delivered the opinion of the Court.

[In 1996, the Fifth Circuit ruled in *Hopwood v. Texas*, 78 F.3d 932 (5th Cir. 1996) that the University of Texas at Austin's use of race in admissions was unconstitutional. In the wake of *Hopwood*, the University stopped considering race. The state legislature later adopted the Top Ten Percent Law, granting automatic admission to students in the top 10% of their class at a Texas high school. After the Supreme Court decided *Grutter* and *Gratz*, the University developed a plan to supplement the racial diversity produced by the percentage plan with a policy inspired by the approach upheld in *Grutter*. Abigail Fisher, a white student, applied for admission to the class entering the University of Texas in 2008. She was denied, and then challenged the University's admission policy as violating the equal protection clause. Most of those admitted to the University when Fisher was rejected were in the top 10% of their high school class and admitted on that basis alone. The University admitted the remainder of its class through a holistic set of factors that included race. Fisher was not in the top 10% of her class and did not challenge that aspect of the Texas policy. She argued that the use of race in admitting the remainder of the class was unconstitutional. Citing *Grutter*, the District Court and Fifth Circuit upheld the policy. In 2013, by a 7–1 vote (with Justice Kagan recused and only Justice Ginsburg dissenting), the Supreme Court decided *Fisher I*, holding that the circuit court had misapplied strict scrutiny by deferring excessively to the University. On the narrow-tailoring prong of strict scrutiny, the Court wrote, "the University receives no deference." It remanded, emphasizing that a court should not accept "a school's assertion that its admission process uses race in a permissible way without a court giving close analysis to the evidence of how the process works in practice." After the remand and further proceedings, the Fifth Circuit again upheld the University's policy. The case came back to the Supreme Court as *Fisher II*, and was decided by a vote of 4–3 with Justice Kagan again recused and Justice Scalia passing away between the oral argument and the decision.]

In the wake of *Grutter,* the University embarked upon a year-long study seeking to ascertain whether its admissions policy was allowing it to provide "the educational benefits of a diverse student body . . . to all of the University's undergraduate students." The University concluded that its admissions policy was not providing these benefits. * * *

Although the University's new admissions policy was a direct result of *Grutter,* it is not identical to the policy this Court approved in that case. Instead, consistent with the State's legislative directive, the University continues to fill a significant majority of its class through the Top Ten Percent Plan (or Plan). Today, up to 75 percent of the places in the freshman class are filled through the Plan. As a practical matter, this 75 percent cap, which has now been fixed by statute, means that, while the Plan continues to be referenced as a "Top Ten Percent Plan," a student actually needs to finish in the top seven or eight percent of his or her class in order to be admitted under this category.

The University did adopt an approach similar to the one in *Grutter* for the remaining 25 percent or so of the incoming class. This portion of the class continues to be admitted based on a combination of their [Academic Index, which combines test scores and high school performance and

Personal Achievement Index] scores. Now, however, race is given weight as a subfactor within the PAI. The PAI is a number from 1 to 6 (6 is the best) that is based on two primary components. The first component is the average score a reader gives the applicant on two required essays. The second component is a full-file review that results in another 1-to-6 score, the "Personal Achievement Score" or PAS. The PAS is determined by a separate reader, who (1) rereads the applicant's required essays, (2) reviews any supplemental information the applicant submits (letters of recommendation, resumes, an additional optional essay, writing samples, artwork, etc.), and (3) evaluates the applicant's potential contributions to the University's student body based on the applicant's leadership experience, extracurricular activities, awards/honors, community service, and other "special circumstances."

"Special circumstances" include the socioeconomic status of the applicant's family, the socioeconomic status of the applicant's school, the applicant's family responsibilities, whether the applicant lives in a single-parent home, the applicant's SAT score in relation to the average SAT score at the applicant's school, the language spoken at the applicant's home, and, finally, the applicant's race. * * *

Race enters the admissions process [at] one stage and one stage only—the calculation of the PAS.

Therefore, although admissions officers can consider race as a positive feature of a minority student's application, there is no dispute that race is but a "factor of a factor of a factor" in the holistic-review calculus. 645 F.Supp.2d 587, 608 (W.D.Tex.2009). Furthermore, consideration of race is contextual and does not operate as a mechanical plus factor for underrepresented minorities. There is also no dispute, however, that race, when considered in conjunction with other aspects of an applicant's background, can alter an applicant's PAS score. Thus, race, in this indirect fashion, considered with all of the other factors that make up an applicant's AI and PAI scores, can make a difference to whether an application is accepted or rejected. * * *

Fisher I set forth three controlling principles relevant to assessing the constitutionality of a public university's affirmative-action program. First, "because racial characteristics so seldom provide a relevant basis for disparate treatment," *Richmond v. J.A. Croson Co.* (1989), "[r]ace may not be considered [by a university] unless the admissions process can withstand strict scrutiny." Strict scrutiny requires the university to demonstrate with clarity that its " 'purpose or interest is both constitutionally permissible and substantial, and that its use of the classification is necessary . . . to the accomplishment of its purpose.' "

Second, *Fisher I* confirmed that "the decision to pursue 'the educational benefits that flow from student body diversity' . . . is, in substantial measure, an academic judgment to which some, but not complete, judicial deference is proper." A university cannot impose a fixed quota or otherwise "define diversity as 'some specified percentage of a particular group merely because of its race or ethnic origin.'" Once, however, a university gives "a reasoned, principled explanation" for its decision, deference must be given "to the University's conclusion, based on its experience and expertise, that a diverse student body would serve its educational goals."

Third, *Fisher I* clarified that no deference is owed when determining whether the use of race is narrowly tailored to achieve the university's permissible goals. * * * Though "[n]arrow tailoring does not require exhaustion of every conceivable race-neutral alternative" or "require a university to choose between maintaining a reputation for excellence [and] fulfilling a commitment to provide educational opportunities to members of all racial groups," it does impose "on the university the ultimate burden of demonstrating" that "race-neutral alternatives" that are both "available" and "workable" "do not suffice." *Fisher I.*

The University's program is *sui generis*. Unlike other approaches to college admissions considered by this Court, it combines holistic review with a percentage plan. This approach gave rise to an unusual consequence in this case: The component of the University's admissions policy that had the largest impact on petitioner's chances of admission was not the school's consideration of race under its holistic-review process but rather the Top Ten Percent Plan. Because petitioner did not graduate in the top 10 percent of her high school class, she was categorically ineligible for more than three-fourths of the slots in the incoming freshman class. It seems quite plausible, then, to think that petitioner would have had a better chance of being admitted to the University if the school used race-conscious holistic review to select its entire incoming class, as was the case in *Grutter*.

Despite the Top Ten Percent Plan's outsized effect on petitioner's chances of admission, she has not challenged it. For that reason, throughout this litigation, the Top Ten Percent Plan has been taken, somewhat artificially, as a given premise.

Petitioner's acceptance of the Top Ten Percent Plan complicates this Court's review. In particular, it has led to a record that is almost devoid of information about the students who secured admission to the University through the Plan. The Court thus cannot know how students admitted solely based on their class rank differ in their contribution to diversity from students admitted through holistic review. * * *

[T]he University lacks any authority to alter the role of the Top Ten Percent Plan in its admissions process. The Plan was mandated by the Texas Legislature in the wake of [*Hopwood, v. Texas*] so the University, like petitioner in this litigation, has likely taken the Plan as a given since its implementation in 1998. * * *

Under the circumstances of this case, then, a remand would do nothing more than prolong a suit that has already persisted for eight years and cost the parties on both sides significant resources. Petitioner long since has graduated from another college, and the University's policy—and the data on which it first was based—may have evolved or changed in material ways.

* * * Through regular evaluation of data and consideration of student experience, the University must tailor its approach in light of changing circumstances, ensuring that race plays no greater role than is necessary to meet its compelling interest. The University's examination of the data it has acquired in the years since petitioner's application, for these reasons, must proceed with full respect for the constraints imposed by the Equal Protection Clause. The type of data collected, and the manner in which it is considered, will have a significant bearing on how the University must shape its admissions policy to satisfy strict scrutiny in the years to come. Here, however, the Court is necessarily limited to the narrow question before it: whether, drawing all reasonable inferences in her favor, petitioner has shown by a preponderance of the evidence that she was denied equal treatment at the time her application was rejected.

In seeking to reverse the judgment of the Court of Appeals, petitioner makes four arguments. First, she argues that the University has not articulated its compelling interest with sufficient clarity. According to petitioner, the University must set forth more precisely the level of minority enrollment that would constitute a "critical mass." Without a clearer sense of what the University's ultimate goal is, petitioner argues, a reviewing court cannot assess whether the University's admissions program is narrowly tailored to that goal.

As this Court's cases have made clear, however, the compelling interest that justifies consideration of race in college admissions is not an interest in enrolling a certain number of minority students. Rather, a university may institute a race-conscious admissions program as a means of obtaining "the educational benefits that flow from student body diversity." As this Court has said, enrolling a diverse student body "promotes cross-racial understanding, helps to break down racial stereotypes, and enables students to better understand persons of different races." Equally important, "student body diversity promotes learning outcomes, and better prepares students for an increasingly diverse workforce and society."

Increasing minority enrollment may be instrumental to these educational benefits, but it is not, as petitioner seems to suggest, a goal that can or should be reduced to pure numbers. Indeed, since the

University is prohibited from seeking a particular number or quota of minority students, it cannot be faulted for failing to specify the particular level of minority enrollment at which it believes the educational benefits of diversity will be obtained.

On the other hand, asserting an interest in the educational benefits of diversity writ large is insufficient. A university's goals cannot be elusory or amorphous—they must be sufficiently measurable to permit judicial scrutiny of the policies adopted to reach them.

[Justice Kennedy noted that University articulated various diversity-based rationales for its admissions policy, including promotion of cross-racial understanding, preparation for the workforce, and a robust exchange of ideas. The University also documented how the inadequacy of race-neutral alternatives were unsuccessful in achieving these goals.]

Second, petitioner argues that the University has no need to consider race because it had already "achieved critical mass" by 2003 using the Top Ten Percent Plan and race-neutral holistic review. Petitioner is correct that a university bears a heavy burden in showing that it had not obtained the educational benefits of diversity before it turned to a race-conscious plan. The record reveals, however, that, at the time of petitioner's application, the University could not be faulted on this score. * * *

The record itself contains significant evidence, both statistical and anecdotal, in support of the University's position. [Justice Kennedy reviewed evidence showing "consistent stagnation in terms of the percentage of minority students enrolling at the University from 1996 to 2002," and said that while numbers are "by no means dispositive, they do have some value as a gauge of the University's ability to enroll students who can offer underrepresented perspectives."]

In addition to this broad demographic data, the University put forward evidence that minority students admitted under the *Hopwood* regime experienced feelings of loneliness and isolation. This anecdotal evidence is, in turn, bolstered by further, more nuanced quantitative data. * * * [O]nly 21 percent of undergraduate classes with five or more students in them had more than one African-American student enrolled. Twelve percent of these classes had no Hispanic students, as compared to 10 percent in 1996. Though a college must continually reassess its need for race-conscious review, here that assessment appears to have been done with care, and a reasonable determination was made that the University had not yet attained its goals.

Third, petitioner argues that considering race was not necessary because such consideration has had only a " 'minimal impact' in advancing the [University's] compelling interest." Again, the record does not support this assertion. [Justice Kennedy tracked data showing "that consideration of race has had a meaningful, if still limited, effect on the diversity of the University's freshman class."]

In any event, it is not a failure of narrow tailoring for the impact of racial consideration to be minor. The fact that race consciousness played a role in only a small portion of admissions decisions should be a hallmark of narrow tailoring, not evidence of unconstitutionality.

Petitioner's final argument is that "there are numerous other available race-neutral means of achieving" the University's compelling interest. A review of the record reveals, however, that, at the time of petitioner's application, none of her proposed alternatives was a workable means for the University to attain the benefits of diversity it sought. [I]n the wake of *Hopwood,* the University spent seven years attempting to achieve its compelling interest using race-neutral holistic review. None of these efforts succeeded, and petitioner fails to offer any meaningful way in which the University could have improved upon them at the time of her application. * * *

[Petitioner suggests that the University] cap the Top Ten Percent Plan, and admit more—if not all—the University's students through a percentage plan. As an initial matter, petitioner overlooks the fact that the Top Ten Percent Plan, though facially neutral, cannot be understood apart from its basic purpose, which is to boost minority enrollment. Percentage plans are "adopted with racially segregated neighborhoods and schools front and center stage." *Fisher I,* 570 U.S., at ___ (Ginsburg, J., dissenting). "It is race consciousness, not blindness to race, that drives such plans." *Ibid.* Consequently, petitioner cannot assert simply that increasing the University's reliance on a percentage plan would make its admissions policy more race neutral.

Even if, as a matter of raw numbers, minority enrollment would increase under such a regime, petitioner would be hard-pressed to find convincing support for the proposition that college admissions would be improved if they were a function of class rank alone. That approach would sacrifice all other aspects of diversity in pursuit of enrolling a higher number of minority students. * * *

Class rank is a single metric, and like any single metric, it will capture certain types of people and miss others. This does not imply that students admitted through holistic review are necessarily more capable or more desirable than those admitted through the Top Ten Percent Plan. It merely reflects the fact that privileging one characteristic above all others does not lead to a diverse student body. Indeed, to compel universities to admit students based on class rank alone is in deep tension with the goal of educational diversity as this Court's cases have defined it. At its center, the Top Ten Percent Plan is a blunt instrument that may well compromise the University's own definition of the diversity it seeks. * * *

A university is in large part defined by those intangible "qualities which are incapable of objective measurement but which make for greatness." *Sweatt v. Painter*. Considerable deference is owed to a university in defining those intangible characteristics, like student body diversity, that are central to its identity and educational mission. But still, it remains an enduring challenge to our Nation's education system to reconcile the pursuit of diversity with the constitutional promise of equal treatment and dignity.

In striking this sensitive balance, public universities, like the States themselves, can serve as "laboratories for experimentation." The University of Texas at Austin has a special opportunity to learn and to teach. The University now has at its disposal valuable data about the manner in which different approaches to admissions may foster diversity or instead dilute it. The University must continue to use this data to scrutinize the fairness of its admissions program; to assess whether changing demographics have undermined the need for a race-conscious policy; and to identify the effects, both positive and negative, of the affirmative-action measures it deems necessary.

The Court's affirmance of the University's admissions policy today does not necessarily mean the University may rely on that same policy without refinement. It is the University's ongoing obligation to engage in constant deliberation and continued reflection regarding its admissions policies.

Justice Alito, with whom **The Chief Justice** and **Justice Thomas** join, dissenting.

Something strange has happened since our prior decision in this case. See *Fisher v. University of Tex. at Austin*, 570 U.S. ___ (2013) (*Fisher I*). In that decision, we held that strict scrutiny requires the University of Texas at Austin (UT or University) to show that its use of race and ethnicity in making admissions decisions serves compelling interests and that its plan is narrowly tailored to achieve those ends. Rejecting the argument that we should defer to UT's judgment on those matters, we made it clear that UT was obligated (1) to identify the interests justifying its plan with enough specificity to permit a reviewing court to determine whether the requirements of strict scrutiny were met, and (2) to show that those requirements were in fact satisfied. On remand, UT failed to do what our prior decision demanded. The University has still not identified with any degree of specificity the interests that its use of race and ethnicity is supposed to serve. Its primary argument is that merely invoking 'the educational benefits of diversity' is sufficient and that it need not identify any metric that would allow a court to determine whether its plan is needed to serve, or is actually serving, those interests. This is nothing less than the plea for deference that we emphatically rejected in our prior decision. Today, however, the Court inexplicably grants that request. * * *

At times, UT has claimed that its plan is needed to achieve a 'critical mass' of African-American and Hispanic students, but it has never explained what this term means. * * * UT tells us that it will let the courts know when the desired end has been achieved. This is a plea for deference—indeed, for blind deference—the very thing that the Court rejected in *Fisher I*.

UT has also claimed at times that the race-based component of its plan is needed because the Top Ten Percent Plan admits *the wrong kind* of African-American and Hispanic students, namely, students from poor families who attend schools in which the student body is predominantly African-American or Hispanic. As UT put it in its brief in *Fisher I*, the race-based component of its admissions plan is needed to admit '[t]he African-American or Hispanic child of successful professionals in Dallas.'

After making this argument in its first trip to this Court, UT apparently had second thoughts, and in the latest round of briefing UT has attempted to disavow ever having made the argument. See Brief for Respondents 2 ('Petitioner's argument that UT's interest is favoring 'affluent' minorities is a fabrication'); see also *id.*, at 15. But it did, and the argument turns affirmative action on its head. Affirmative-action programs were created to help *disadvantaged* students. * * *

It is important to understand what is and what is not at stake in this case. *What is not at stake* is whether UT or any other university may adopt an admissions plan that results in a student body with a broad representation of students from all racial and ethnic groups. UT previously had a race-neutral plan that it claimed had 'effectively compensated for the loss of affirmative action,' and UT could have taken other steps that would have increased the diversity of its admitted students without taking race or ethnic background into account.

What is at stake is whether university administrators may justify systematic racial discrimination simply by asserting that such discrimination is necessary to achieve 'the educational benefits of diversity,' without explaining—much less proving—why the discrimination is needed or how the discriminatory plan is well crafted to serve its objectives. Even though UT has never provided any coherent explanation for its asserted need to discriminate on the basis of race, and even though UT's position relies on a series of unsupported and noxious racial assumptions, the majority concludes that UT has met its heavy burden. This conclusion is remarkable—and remarkably wrong.

Because UT has failed to satisfy strict scrutiny, I respectfully dissent.

[An additional dissenting opinion by **JUSTICE THOMAS** is omitted.]

NOTES

1. *Strict Scrutiny?* Did the Court retreat in *Fisher II* from its insistence in *Fisher I* that universities should get no deference on the narrow tailoring prong of strict scrutiny? Or do the majority's repeated cautions about the University's continuing obligation to review and refine its policy indicate that it expects judicial scrutiny to be meaningful and to continue?

2. *Critical Mass.* The notion of "critical mass" has been notoriously difficult to define in this context. Does *Fisher II* add greater clarity? How does the case define it? Who gets the better of the exchange between Justices Kennedy and Alito on this point?

3. *Combatting Racial Isolation?* In his opinion, Justice Kennedy noted that the University was aware of "loneliness and isolation" suffered by minority students. When you read *Parents Involved in Community Schools v. Seattle School District No. 1*, 551 U.S. 701 (2007) in the next section, you will notice that Kennedy's influential concurrence identifies a "compelling state interest" in "avoiding racial isolation." Does *Fisher II* suggest this might be an interest distinct from diversity that could justify affirmative action programs?

4. *Justice Kennedy's Position. Fisher II* reflects the only time that Justice Kennedy voted to uphold an affirmative action plan. What might explain that? Note that his majority opinion calls the circumstances of *Fisher II* "*sui generis.*" Given that the case involved only three years in the past, and that Texas uses the holistic review challenged in this case to supplement the percentage plan, the plan examined in the case is, in fact, unique in important respects. Moreover, the percentage plan is consistent with the sort of facially neutral policy that Kennedy has favored in the past, including the facially race-neutral means of combatting racial isolation that Kennedy endorsed in his *Parents Involved* concurrence. Might Kennedy have been more willing to tolerate race-consciousness in *Fisher II* because it supplemented a race-neutral plan and made race only "a factor of a factor of a factor"? Do these characteristics limit the effect of *Fisher II* going forward? Given that Kennedy provided the fifth vote in this case, his retirement puts very much in question the constitutionality of race-conscious admissions going forward.

5. *Limits?* Does *Fisher II* modify *Grutter*? What limits does *Fisher II* place on affirmative action plans? The majority says, for example, that "[f]ormalistic racial classifications can sometimes fail to capture diversity in all its dimensions, and when used in a divisive manner, could undermine the educational benefits the University values." What does that mean? How about the majority's statement that the University must "reconcile its pursuit of diversity with the constitutional promise of equal treatment and dignity"?

PROBLEMS ON FACIALLY NEUTRAL UNIVERSITY ADMISSIONS PROGRAMS DESIGNED TO BENEFIT RACIAL MINORITIES

Problem 3-8: *The "10% Solution."* What is the status of percentage plans after *Fisher II*? Should it matter if the reason why this method was chosen is that it will make admission possible for more students of color? Note that Justice Kennedy's opinion adopts the view, first expressed by Justice Ginsburg, that such plans are, in fact, race conscious, even if not facially so. Does that mean a percentage plan would trigger strict scrutiny under an *Arlington Heights*-type approach? Or does the fact that the plan does not classify individuals based on race shield it from strict scrutiny? If the Texas percentage plan was challenged by a rejected white applicant to the University of Texas in the future, what do you think the Court would and should conclude about the constitutionality of the plan? For pre-*Fisher II* analyses, see, e.g., Michelle Adams, *Isn't It Ironic? The Central Paradox at the Heart of "Percentage Plans,"* 62 Ohio St. L.J. 1729 (2001); Brian Fitzpatrick, *Strict Scrutiny of Facially Race-Neutral State Action and the Texas Ten Percent Plan*, 53 Baylor L. Rev. 289 (2001). For analysis in the wake of Fisher II, see, e.g., Elise C. Boddie, *The Constitutionality of Racially Integrative Purpose*, 38 Cardozo L. Rev. 531 (2016).

Problem 3-9: *Affirmative Action Based on Low Socioeconomic Status.* Suppose that, in the aftermath of Gratz, a state university gave an automatic 20 points in the admission calculus to persons on the basis of very low socioeconomic status. Assuming this was motivated at least in large part to increase the enrollment of persons of color, should the approach be subject to strict scrutiny? See, e.g., Richard Fallon, *Affirmative Action Based on Economic Disadvantage*, 43 UCLA L. Rev. 1913 (1996); Kim Forde-Mazrui, *The Constitutional Implications of Race-Neutral Affirmative Action*, 88 Geo. L.J. 2331 (2000). For broader perspectives on class-based affirmative action, see, e.g., Khiara M. Bridges, *The Deserving Poor, the Undeserving Poor, and Class-Based Affirmative Action*, 66 Emory L.J. 1049 (2017); Richard Kahlenberg, *Affirmative Action Should Be Based on Class, Not Race*, The Economist (Sept. 4, 2018), https://www.economist.com/open-future/2018/09/04/affirmative-action-should-be-based-on-class-not-race; William Kidder, *How Workable are Class-Based and Race-Neutral Alternatives at Leading American Universities?*, 64 UCLA L. Rev. Disc. 100 (2016).

D. STUDENT ASSIGNMENT IN K–12 PUBLIC EDUCATION

PARENTS INVOLVED IN COMMUNITY SCHOOLS V. SEATTLE SCHOOL DISTRICT NO. 1

551 U.S. 701, 127 S.Ct. 2738, 168 L.Ed.2d 508 (2007)

CHIEF JUSTICE ROBERTS announced the judgment of the Court, and delivered the opinion of the Court with respect to Parts I, II, III-A, and III-C, and an opinion with respect to Parts III-B and IV, in which JUSTICES SCALIA, THOMAS, and ALITO join.

The school districts in these cases voluntarily adopted student assignment plans that rely upon race to determine which public schools certain children may attend. The Seattle[, Washington] school district classifies children as white or nonwhite; the Jefferson County [Kentucky] school district as black or "other." In Seattle, this racial classification is used to allocate slots in oversubscribed high schools. In Jefferson County, it is used to make certain elementary school assignments and to rule on transfer requests. In each case, the school district relies upon an individual student's race in assigning that student to a particular school, so that the racial balance at the school falls within a predetermined range based on the racial composition of the school district as a whole. Parents of students denied assignment to particular schools under these plans solely because of their race brought suit, contending that allocating children to different public schools on the basis of race violated the Fourteenth Amendment guarantee of equal protection. The Courts of Appeals below upheld the plans. We granted certiorari, and now reverse. ← violation of 14th

[I] Both cases present the same underlying legal question—whether a public school that had not operated legally segregated schools or has been found to be unitary may choose to classify students by race and rely upon that classification in making school assignments. Although we examine the plans under the same legal framework, the specifics of the two plans, and the circumstances surrounding their adoption, are in some respects quite different.

[The Chief Justice described the two plans and their backgrounds. Seattle's school district had never been segregated by law, but concern with racial imbalances led the district in 1998 to adopt the following plan (in effect 1999–2002). Students would submit a list of high schools they preferred to attend. If too many students choose the same high schools, as is typically the case, the district adopted several tiebreaker rules: (1) the applicant has a sibling enrolled in that school; (2) for schools that are more than 10% off the city's overall racial balance (41% "white" and 59% "nonwhite") the applicant gets in if he or she helps bring the school into racial balance; and (3) geographic proximity.

[Jefferson County (where Louisville is located) had maintained a de jure segregated public school system which was adjudged unconstitutional in 1973. The schools operated under this decree until 2000, when the District Court dissolved the decree after finding that the district had achieved unitary status by eliminating "[t]o the greatest extent practicable" the vestiges of its prior policy of segregation. In 2001, the County adopted a voluntary program seeking to maintain racial balance (overall, about 66% of the district's schoolchildren are white, 34% nonwhite). Parents of kindergartners, first-graders, and students new to the district may submit an application indicating a first and second choice among the schools within their cluster; students who do not submit such an application are assigned within the cluster by the district. Decisions to assign students to schools within each cluster are based on available space within the schools and the racial guidelines in the District's current student assignment plan. If a school has reached the "extremes of the racial guidelines" (15% minimum black enrollment, 50% maximum), a student whose race would contribute to the school's racial imbalance will not be assigned there. After assignment, students at all grade levels are permitted to apply to transfer between nonmagnet schools in the district. A similar system works for middle and high schools.

[In Part II of his opinion, the Chief Justice rejected Seattle's objections that Parents Involved lacks standing to litigate their equal protection claims.]

[III.A] It is well established that when the government distributes burdens or benefits on the basis of individual racial classifications, that action is reviewed under strict scrutiny. *Grutter.* As the Court recently reaffirmed, " 'racial classifications are simply too pernicious to permit any but the most exact connection between justification and classification.' " *Gratz.* In order to satisfy this searching standard of review, the school districts must demonstrate that the use of individual racial classifications in the assignment plans here under review is "narrowly tailored" to achieve a "compelling" government interest. *Adarand.*

Without attempting in these cases to set forth all the interests a school district might assert, it suffices to note that our prior cases, in evaluating the use of racial classifications in the school context, have recognized two interests that qualify as compelling. The first is the compelling interest of remedying the effects of past intentional discrimination. See *Freeman v. Pitts.* Yet the Seattle public schools have not shown that they were ever segregated by law, and were not subject to court-ordered desegregation decrees. The Jefferson County public schools were previously segregated by law and were subject to a desegregation decree entered in 1975. In 2000, the District Court that entered that decree dissolved it, finding that Jefferson County had "eliminated the vestiges associated with the former policy of segregation and its pernicious effects," and thus had achieved "unitary" status. Jefferson County accordingly does not rely upon an interest in remedying the effects of past intentional discrimination in defending its present use of race in assigning students.

Nor could it. We have emphasized that the harm being remedied by mandatory desegregation plans is the harm that is traceable to segregation, and that "the Constitution is not violated by racial imbalance in the schools, without more." *Milliken.* Once Jefferson County achieved unitary status, it had remedied the constitutional wrong that allowed race-based assignments. Any continued use of race must be justified on some other basis.[10]

---

[10] The districts point to dicta in a prior opinion in which the Court suggested that, while not constitutionally mandated, it would be constitutionally permissible for a school district to seek racially balanced schools as a matter of "educational policy." See *Swann.* * * * [But] *Swann,*

The second government interest we have recognized as compelling for purposes of strict scrutiny is the interest in diversity in higher education upheld in *Grutter*. The specific interest found compelling in *Grutter* was student body diversity "in the context of higher education." The diversity interest was not focused on race alone but encompassed "all factors that may contribute to student body diversity." We described the various types of diversity that the law school sought:

> [The law school's] policy makes clear there are many possible bases for diversity admissions, and provides examples of admittees who have lived or traveled widely abroad, are fluent in several languages, have overcome personal adversity and family hardship, have exceptional records of extensive community service, and have had successful careers in other fields.

The Court quoted the articulation of diversity from Justice Powell's opinion in *Bakke*, noting that "it is not an interest in simple ethnic diversity, in which a specified percentage of the student body is in effect guaranteed to be members of selected ethnic groups, that can justify the use of race." Instead, what was upheld in *Grutter* was consideration of "a far broader array of qualifications and characteristics of which racial or ethnic origin is but a single though important element."

The entire gist of the analysis in *Grutter* was that the admissions program at issue there focused on each applicant as an individual, and not simply as a member of a particular racial group. The classification of applicants by race upheld in *Grutter* was only as part of a "highly individualized, holistic review." As the Court explained, "[t]he importance of this individualized consideration in the context of a race-conscious admissions program is paramount." The point of the narrow tailoring analysis in which the *Grutter* Court engaged was to ensure that the use of racial classifications was indeed part of a broader assessment of diversity, and not simply an effort to achieve racial balance, which the Court explained would be "patently unconstitutional."

In the present cases, by contrast, race is not considered as part of a broader effort to achieve "exposure to widely diverse people, cultures, ideas, and viewpoints"; race, for some students, is determinative standing alone. The districts argue that other factors, such as student preferences, affect assignment decisions under their plans, but under each plan when race comes into play, it is decisive by itself. It is not simply one factor weighed with others in reaching a decision, as in *Grutter*; it is *the* factor. Like the University of Michigan undergraduate plan struck down in *Gratz*, the plans here "do not provide for a meaningful individualized review of

---

evaluating a school district engaged in court-ordered desegregation, had no occasion to consider whether a district's voluntary adoption of race-based assignments in the absence of a finding of prior *de jure* segregation was constitutionally permissible, an issue that was again expressly reserved in *Washington v. Seattle School Dist. No. 1*, 458 U.S. 457, 472, n. 15 (1982). * * *

applicants" but instead rely on racial classifications in a "nonindividualized, mechanical" way. *Id.* (O'Connor, J., concurring).

Even when it comes to race, the plans here employ only a limited notion of diversity, viewing race exclusively in white/nonwhite terms in Seattle and black/"other" terms in Jefferson County. The Seattle "Board Statement Reaffirming Diversity Rationale" speaks of the "inherent educational value" in "[p]roviding students the opportunity to attend schools with diverse student enrollment." But under the Seattle plan, a school with 50 percent Asian-American students and 50 percent white students but no African-American, Native-American, or Latino students would qualify as balanced, while a school with 30 percent Asian-American, 25 percent African-American, 25 percent Latino, and 20 percent white students would not. It is hard to understand how a plan that could allow these results can be viewed as being concerned with achieving enrollment that is " 'broadly diverse,' " *Grutter*. * * *

In upholding the admissions plan in *Grutter*, * * * this Court relied upon considerations unique to institutions of higher education, noting that in light of "the expansive freedoms of speech and thought associated with the university environment, universities occupy a special niche in our constitutional tradition." See also *Bakke* (opinion of Powell, J.). The Court explained that "[c]ontext matters" in applying strict scrutiny, and repeatedly noted that it was addressing the use of race "in the context of higher education." *Grutter*. The Court in *Grutter* expressly articulated key limitations on its holding—defining a specific type of broad-based diversity and noting the unique context of higher education—but these limitations were largely disregarded by the lower courts in extending *Grutter* to uphold race-based assignments in elementary and secondary schools. The present cases are not governed by *Grutter*.

[III.B] Perhaps recognizing that reliance on *Grutter* cannot sustain their plans, both school districts assert additional interests, distinct from the interest upheld in *Grutter,* to justify their race-based assignments. In briefing and argument before this Court, Seattle contends that its use of race helps to reduce racial concentration in schools and to ensure that racially concentrated housing patterns do not prevent nonwhite students from having access to the most desirable schools. Jefferson County has articulated a similar goal, phrasing its interest in terms of educating its students "in a racially integrated environment." Each school district argues that educational and broader socialization benefits flow from a racially diverse learning environment, and each contends that because the diversity they seek is racial diversity—not the broader diversity at issue in *Grutter*—it makes sense to promote that interest directly by relying on race alone.

The parties and their *amici* dispute whether racial diversity in schools in fact has a marked impact on test scores and other objective yardsticks or achieves intangible socialization benefits. The debate is not one we need to resolve, however, because it is clear that the racial classifications employed by the districts are not narrowly tailored to the goal of achieving the educational and social benefits asserted to flow from racial diversity. In design and operation, the plans are directed only to racial balance, pure and simple, an objective this Court has repeatedly condemned as illegitimate.

The plans are tied to each district's specific racial demographics, rather than to any pedagogic concept of the level of diversity needed to obtain the asserted educational benefits. In Seattle, the district seeks white enrollment of between 31 and 51 percent (within 10 percent of "the district white average" of 41 percent), and nonwhite enrollment of between 49 and 69 percent (within 10 percent of "the district minority average" of 59 percent). In Jefferson County, by contrast, the district seeks black enrollment of no less than 15 or more than 50 percent, a range designed to be "equally above and below Black student enrollment systemwide," based on the objective of achieving at "all schools . . . an African-American enrollment equivalent to the average district-wide African-American enrollment" of 34 percent. In Seattle, then, the benefits of racial diversity require enrollment of at least 31 percent white students; in Jefferson County, at least 50 percent. There must be at least 15 percent nonwhite students under Jefferson County's plan; in Seattle, more than three times that figure. This comparison makes clear that the racial demographics in each district—whatever they happen to be—drive the required "diversity" numbers. The plans here are not tailored to achieving a degree of diversity necessary to realize the asserted educational benefits; instead the plans are tailored, in the words of Seattle's Manager of Enrollment Planning, Technical Support, and Demographics, to "the goal established by the school board of attaining a level of diversity within the schools that approximates the district's overall demographics."

The districts offer no evidence that the level of racial diversity necessary to achieve the asserted educational benefits happens to coincide with the racial demographics of the respective school districts—or rather the white/nonwhite or black/"other" balance of the districts, since that is the only diversity addressed by the plans. Indeed, in its brief Seattle simply assumes that the educational benefits track the racial breakdown of the district. When asked for "a range of percentage that would be diverse," however, Seattle's expert said it was important to have "sufficient numbers so as to avoid students feeling any kind of specter of exceptionality." The district did not attempt to defend the proposition that anything outside its range posed the "specter of exceptionality." Nor did it demonstrate in any way how the educational and social benefits of racial diversity or avoidance of racial isolation are more likely to be achieved at a school that is 50 percent white and 50 percent Asian-American, which would qualify as diverse under Seattle's plan, than at a school that is 30 percent Asian-American, 25 percent African-American, 25 percent Latino, and 20 percent white, which under Seattle's definition would be racially concentrated. [The same was true of Jefferson County.]

In *Grutter,* the number of minority students the school sought to admit was an undefined "meaningful number" necessary to achieve a genuinely diverse student body. Although the matter was the subject of disagreement on the Court, the majority concluded that the law school did not count back from its applicant pool to arrive at the "meaningful number" it regarded as necessary to diversify its student body. Here the racial balance the districts seek is a defined range set solely by reference to the demographics of the respective school districts.

This working backward to achieve a particular type of racial balance, rather than working forward from some demonstration of the level of diversity that provides the purported benefits, is a fatal flaw under our existing precedent. We have many times over reaffirmed that "[r]acial balance is not to be achieved for its own sake." *Freeman.* See also *Croson*; *Bakke* (opinion of Powell, J.) ("If petitioner's purpose is to assure within its student body some specified percentage of a particular group merely because of its race or ethnic origin, such a preferential purpose must be rejected . . . as facially invalid"). *Grutter* itself reiterated that "outright racial balancing" is "patently unconstitutional."

Accepting racial balancing as a compelling state interest would justify the imposition of racial proportionality throughout American society, contrary to our repeated recognition that "[a]t the heart of the Constitution's guarantee of equal protection lies the simple command that the Government must treat citizens as individuals, not as simply components of a racial, religious, sexual or national class." *Miller v. Johnson*, 515 U.S. 900, 911 (1995) (quoting *Metro Broadcasting* (O'Connor, J., dissenting)).[14] Allowing racial balancing as a compelling end in itself would "effectively assur[e] that race will always be relevant in American life, and that the 'ultimate goal' of 'eliminating entirely from governmental decisionmaking such irrelevant factors as a human being's race' will never be achieved." *Croson* (plurality opinion of O'Connor, J.). An interest "linked to nothing other than proportional representation of various races . . . would support indefinite use of racial classifications, employed first to

---

[14] In contrast, Seattle's website formerly described "emphasizing individualism as opposed to a more collective ideology" as a form of "cultural racism," and currently states that the district has no intention "to hold onto unsuccessful concepts such as [a] . . . colorblind mentality." Harrell, School Web Site Removed: Examples of Racism Sparked Controversy, Seattle Post-Intelligencer, June 2, 2006, pp. B1, B5. Compare *Plessy v. Ferguson* (Harlan, J., dissenting) ("Our Constitution is color-blind, and neither knows nor tolerates classes among citizens. In respect of civil rights, all citizens are equal before the law").

obtain the appropriate mixture of racial views and then to ensure that the [program] continues to reflect that mixture." *Metro Broadcasting* (O'Connor, J., dissenting).

The validity of our concern that racial balancing has "no logical stopping point," *Croson; see also Grutter,* is demonstrated here by the degree to which the districts tie their racial guidelines to their demographics. As the districts' demographics shift, so too will their definition of racial diversity. See App. in No. 05-908, at 103a (describing application of racial tiebreaker based on "*current* white percentage" of 41 percent and "*current* minority percentage" of 59 percent (emphasis added)). * * *

The principle that racial balancing is not permitted is one of substance, not semantics. Racial balancing is not transformed from "patently unconstitutional" to a compelling state interest simply by relabeling it "racial diversity." While the school districts use various verbal formulations to describe the interest they seek to promote—racial diversity, avoidance of racial isolation, racial integration—they offer no definition of the interest that suggests it differs from racial balance. See, *e.g.,* App. in No. 05-908, at 257a ("Q. What's your understanding of when a school suffers from racial isolation? A. I don't have a definition for that"); *id.,* at 228a–229a ("I don't think we've ever sat down and said, 'Define racially concentrated school exactly on point in quantitative terms.' I don't think we've ever had that conversation"); Tr. in *McFarland I,* at 190 (Dec. 8, 2003) ("Q. How does the Jefferson County School Board define diversity. . . ?" "A. Well, we want to have the schools that make up the percentage of students of the population"). * * *

The en banc Ninth Circuit declared that "when a racially diverse school system is the goal (or racial concentration or isolation is the problem), there is no more effective means than a consideration of race to achieve the solution." For the foregoing reasons, this conclusory argument cannot sustain the plans. However closely related race-based assignments may be to achieving racial balance, that itself cannot be the goal, whether labeled "racial diversity" or anything else. To the extent the objective is sufficient diversity so that students see fellow students as individuals rather than solely as members of a racial group, using means that treat students solely as members of a racial group is fundamentally at cross-purposes with that end.

[III.C] The districts assert, as they must, that the way in which they have employed individual racial classifications is necessary to achieve their stated ends. The minimal effect these classifications have on student assignments, however, suggests that other means would be effective. Seattle's racial tiebreaker results, in the end, only in shifting a small number of students between schools. Approximately 307 student assignments were affected by the racial tiebreaker in 2000–2001; the district was able to track the enrollment status of 293 of these students. Of these, 209 were assigned to a school that was one of their choices, 87 of whom were assigned to the same school to which they would have been assigned without the racial tiebreaker. Eighty-four students were assigned to schools that they did not list as a choice, but 29 of those students would have been assigned to their respective school without the racial tiebreaker, and 3 were able to attend one of the oversubscribed schools due to waitlist and capacity adjustments. In over one-third of the assignments affected by the racial tiebreaker, then, the use of race in the end made no difference, and the district could identify only 52 students who were ultimately affected adversely by the racial tiebreaker in that it resulted in assignment to a school they had not listed as a preference and to which they would not otherwise have been assigned. [A similarly minimal effect came from Jefferson County's use of racial classifications.]

While we do not suggest that *greater* use of race would be preferable, the minimal impact of the districts' racial classifications on school enrollment casts doubt on the necessity of using racial classifications. * * *

The districts have also failed to show that they considered methods other than explicit racial classifications to achieve their stated goals. Narrow tailoring requires "serious, good faith consideration of workable race-neutral alternatives," *Grutter*, and yet in Seattle several alternative assignment plans—many of which would not have used express racial classifications—were rejected with little or no consideration. Jefferson County has failed to present any evidence that it considered alternatives, even though the district already claims that its goals are achieved primarily through means other than the racial classifications. Compare *Croson* (Kennedy, J., concurring in part and concurring in judgment) (racial classifications permitted only "as a last resort").

[In Part IV, Chief Justice Roberts responds to Justice Breyer's dissent. The Chief Justice contends that Justice Breyer errs in relying upon precedents recognizing the compelling interest in remedying past intentional discrimination, because in these cases the Seattle school district never engaged in such discrimination, and the Louisville district remedied its past discrimination and achieved unitary status before adopting the plan in question. The Chief Justice also responds that Justice Breyer unduly relies upon mere dicta from *Swann*. Furthermore, "[w]e simply do not understand how Justice Breyer can maintain that classifying every schoolchild as black or white, and using that classification as a determinative factor in assigning children to achieve pure racial balance, can be regarded as 'less burdensome, and hence more narrowly tailored' than the consideration of race in *Grutter*, when the Court in *Grutter* stated that '[t]he importance of . . . individualized consideration' in the program was 'paramount,' and consideration of race was one factor in a 'highly individualized, holistic review.'" The Chief Justice contends that Justice Breyer is simply resisting the Court's precedents in *Adarand* and other cases that hold that all racial classifications, including "benign" ones, must be subjected to strict scrutiny. He quotes Justice O'Connor's dissent in *Metro Broadcasting* (" '[B]enign' carries with it no independent meaning, but reflects only acceptance of the current generation's conclusion that a politically acceptable burden, imposed on particular citizens on the basis of race, is reasonable."). "Accepting Justice Breyer's approach would do no more than move us from 'separate but equal' to 'unequal but benign.' *Metro Broadcasting* (Kennedy, J., dissenting)." Furthermore, Chief Justice Roberts states, Justice Breyer, in speaking of bringing the races together, ignores that the Equal Protection Clause " 'protects *persons*, not *groups*,' " quoting *Adarand* (emphasis in original) and referring to similar language in *Brown II*.]

JUSTICE BREYER's position comes down to a familiar claim: The end justifies the means. He admits that "there is a cost in applying 'a state-mandated racial label,' " but he is confident that the cost is worth paying. Our established strict scrutiny test for racial classifications, however, insists on "detailed examination, both as to ends *and* as to means." *Adarand* (emphasis added). Simply because the school districts may seek a worthy goal does not mean they are free to discriminate on the basis of race to achieve it, or that their racial classifications should be subject to less exacting scrutiny. * * *

If the need for the racial classifications embraced by the school districts is unclear, even on the districts' own terms, the costs are undeniable. "[D]istinctions between citizens solely because of their ancestry are by their very nature odious to a free people whose institutions are founded upon the doctrine of equality." *Adarand*. Government action dividing us by race is inherently suspect because such classifications promote "notions of racial inferiority and lead to a politics of racial hostility," *Croson,* "reinforce the belief, held by too many for too much of our history, that individuals should be judged by the color of their skin," *Shaw v. Reno*, and "endorse race-based reasoning and the conception of a Nation divided into racial blocs, thus contributing to an escalation of racial hostility and conflict." *Metro Broadcasting* (O'Connor, J., dissenting). As the Court explained in *Rice v. Cayetano*, 528 U.S. 495, 517 (2000), "[o]ne of the principal reasons race is treated as a forbidden classification is that it demeans the dignity and worth of a person to be judged by ancestry instead of by his or her own merit and essential qualities."

All this is true enough in the contexts in which these statements were made—government contracting, voting districts, allocation of broadcast licenses, and electing state officers—but when it comes to using race to assign children to schools, history will be heard. In *Brown I*, we held that segregation deprived black children of equal educational opportunities regardless of whether school facilities and other tangible factors were equal, because government classification and separation on grounds of race themselves denoted inferiority. It was not the inequality of the facilities but the fact of legally separating children on the basis of race on which the Court relied to find a constitutional violation in 1954. The next Term, we accordingly stated that "full compliance" with *Brown I* required school districts "to achieve a system of determining admission to the public schools *on a nonracial basis.*" *Brown II* (emphasis added).

The parties and their *amici* debate which side is more faithful to the heritage of *Brown,* but the position of the plaintiffs in *Brown* was spelled out in their brief and could not have been clearer: "[T]he Fourteenth Amendment prevents states from according differential treatment to American children on the basis of their color or race." Brief for Appellants in Nos. 1, 2, and 4 and for Respondents in No. 10 on Reargument in *Brown I,* O.T.1953, p. 15 (Summary of Argument). What do the racial classifications at issue here do, if not accord differential treatment on the basis of race? As counsel who appeared before this Court for the plaintiffs in *Brown* put it: "We have one fundamental contention which we will seek to develop in the course of this argument, and that contention is that no State has any authority under the equal-protection clause of the Fourteenth Amendment to use race as a factor in affording educational opportunities among its citizens." Tr. of Oral Arg. in *Brown I,* p. 7 (Robert L. Carter, Dec. 9, 1952). There is no ambiguity in that statement. And it was that position that prevailed in this Court, which emphasized in its remedial opinion that what was "[a]t stake is the personal interest of the plaintiffs in admission to public schools as soon as practicable *on a nondiscriminatory basis,*" and what was required was "determining admission to the public schools *on a nonracial basis.*" *Brown II* (emphasis added). What do the racial classifications do in these cases, if not determine admission to a public school on a racial basis?

Before *Brown,* schoolchildren were told where they could and could not go to school based on the color of their skin. The school districts in these cases have not carried the heavy burden of demonstrating that we should allow this once again—even for very different reasons. For schools that never segregated on the basis of race, such as Seattle, or that have removed the vestiges of past segregation, such as Jefferson County, the way "to achieve a system of determining admission to the public schools on a nonracial basis," *Brown II*, is to stop assigning students on a racial basis. The way to stop discrimination on the basis of race is to stop discriminating on the basis of race.

JUSTICE KENNEDY, concurring in part and concurring in the judgment.

[Justice Kennedy faulted the Jefferson County assignment plan as internally contradictory and confusing, qualities immediately fatal under the strict scrutiny required by *Adarand* and the Court's other precedents. Seattle did a better job of explaining its plan.] The district, nevertheless, has failed to make an adequate showing in at least one respect. It has failed to explain why, in a district composed of a diversity of races, with fewer than half of the students classified as "white," it has employed the crude racial categories of "white" and "non-white" as the basis for its assignment decisions.

The district has identified its purposes as follows: "(1) to promote the educational benefits of diverse school enrollments; (2) to reduce the potentially harmful effects of racial isolation by allowing students the opportunity to opt out of racially isolated schools; and (3) to make sure that racially segregated housing patterns did not prevent non-white students from having equitable access to the most popular over-subscribed schools." Yet the school district does not explain how, in the context of its diverse student population, a blunt distinction between "white" and "non-white" furthers these goals. As the Court explains, "a school with 50 percent Asian-American students and 50 percent white students but no African-American, Native-American, or Latino students would qualify as balanced, while a school with 30 percent Asian-American, 25 percent African-American, 25 percent Latino, and 20 percent white students would not." Far from being narrowly tailored to its purposes, this system threatens to defeat its own ends, and the school district has provided no convincing explanation for its design. * * * As the district fails to account for the classification system it has chosen, despite what appears to be its ill fit, Seattle has not shown its plan to be narrowly tailored to achieve its own ends; and thus it fails to pass strict scrutiny.

* * * [P]arts of the opinion by The Chief Justice imply an all-too-unyielding insistence that race cannot be a factor in instances when, in my view, it may be taken into account. The plurality opinion is too dismissive of the legitimate interest government has in ensuring all people have equal opportunity regardless of their race. The plurality's postulate that "[t]he way to stop discrimination on the basis of race is to stop discriminating on the basis of race" is not sufficient to decide these cases. Fifty years of experience since *Brown I* should teach us that the problem before us defies so easy a solution. School districts can seek to reach *Brown*'s objective of equal educational opportunity. The plurality opinion is at least open to the interpretation that the Constitution requires school districts to ignore the problem of *de facto* resegregation in schooling. I cannot endorse that conclusion. To the extent the plurality opinion suggests the Constitution

mandates that state and local school authorities must accept the status quo of racial isolation in schools, it is, in my view, profoundly mistaken.

The statement by Justice Harlan that "[o]ur Constitution is color-blind" was most certainly justified in the context of his dissent in *Plessy v. Ferguson* [Chapter 2, § 1A]. The Court's decision in that case was a grievous error it took far too long to overrule. *Plessy,* of course, concerned official classification by race applicable to all persons who sought to use railway carriages. And, as an aspiration, Justice Harlan's axiom must command our assent. In the real world, it is regrettable to say, it cannot be a universal constitutional principle.

In the administration of public schools by the state and local authorities it is permissible to consider the racial makeup of schools and to adopt general policies to encourage a diverse student body, one aspect of which is its racial composition. If school authorities are concerned that the student-body compositions of certain schools interfere with the objective of offering an equal educational opportunity to all of their students, they are free to devise race-conscious measures to address the problem in a general way and without treating each student in different fashion solely on the basis of a systematic, individual typing by race.

School boards may pursue the goal of bringing together students of diverse backgrounds and races through other means, including strategic site selection of new schools; drawing attendance zones with general recognition of the demographics of neighborhoods; allocating resources for special programs; recruiting students and faculty in a targeted fashion; and tracking enrollments, performance, and other statistics by race. These mechanisms are race conscious but do not lead to different treatment based on a classification that tells each student he or she is to be defined by race, so it is unlikely any of them would demand strict scrutiny to be found permissible. Executive and legislative branches, which for generations now have considered these types of policies and procedures, should be permitted to employ them with candor and with confidence that a constitutional violation does not occur whenever a decisionmaker considers the impact a given approach might have on students of different races. Assigning to each student a personal designation according to a crude system of individual racial classifications is quite a different matter; and the legal analysis changes accordingly.

Each respondent has asserted that its assignment of individual students by race is permissible because there is no other way to avoid racial isolation in the school districts. Yet, as explained, each has failed to provide the support necessary for that proposition. [I]ndividual racial classifications employed in this manner may be considered legitimate only if they are a last resort to achieve a compelling interest.

In the cases before us it is noteworthy that the number of students whose assignment depends on express racial classifications is limited. I join Part III-C of the Court's opinion because I agree that in the context of these plans, the small number of assignments affected suggests that the schools could have achieved their stated ends through different means. These include the facially race-neutral means set forth above or, if necessary, a more nuanced, individual evaluation of school needs and student characteristics that might include race as a component. The latter approach would be informed by *Grutter,* though of course the criteria relevant to student placement would differ based on the age of the students, the needs of the parents, and the role of the schools.

[Justice Kennedy suggested that the state may have compelling interests that go beyond remedying past discrimination (*Swann*) or creating educational diversity (*Grutter*).] This Nation has a moral and ethical obligation to fulfill its historic commitment to creating an integrated society that ensures equal opportunity for all of its children. A compelling interest exists in avoiding racial isolation, an interest that a school district, in its discretion and expertise, may choose to pursue. Likewise, a district may consider it a compelling interest to achieve a diverse student population. Race may be one component of that diversity, but other demographic factors, plus special talents and needs, should also be considered. What the government is not permitted to do, absent a showing of necessity not made here, is to classify every student on the basis of race and to assign each of them to schools based on that classification. Crude measures of this sort threaten to reduce children to racial chits valued and traded according to one school's supply and another's demand.

That statement, to be sure, invites this response: A sense of stigma may already become the fate of those separated out by circumstances beyond their immediate control. But to this the replication must be: Even so, measures other than differential treatment based on racial typing of individuals first must be exhausted.

The decision today should not prevent school districts from continuing the important work of bringing together students of different racial, ethnic, and economic backgrounds. Due to a variety of factors—some influenced by government, some not—neighborhoods in our communities do not reflect the diversity of our Nation as a whole. Those entrusted with directing our public schools can bring to bear the creativity of experts, parents, administrators, and other concerned citizens to find a way to achieve the compelling interests they face without resorting to widespread governmental allocation of benefits and burdens on the basis of racial classifications.

[The concurring opinion of **JUSTICE THOMAS** and the dissenting opinion of **JUSTICE STEVENS** are omitted. Both Justices' views are discussed in the Notes following the case. The dissenting opinion of **JUSTICE BREYER**, joined by **JUSTICE STEVENS, JUSTICE SOUTER,** and **JUSTICE GINSBURG**, is summarized in the Notes as well.]

NOTES ON THE SEATTLE AND LOUISVILLE SCHOOL CASES

1. *Justice Stevens' Dissent.* Justice Stevens called it a "cruel irony" to invoke *Brown* as mandating color-blindness when in the case it was only African-American children who suffered segregation by race. The Court of the 1960s and 1970s was truer to the real meaning of *Brown* than the current Court, he argued. He concluded: "It is my firm conviction that no Member of the Court that I joined in 1975 would have agreed with today's decision."

2. *Justice Breyer's Dissent.* The dissent runs 77 pages and cannot be easily digested or summarized. Students especially interested in any of the following points should consult the opinion directly.

(a) *Precedent and Practice.* In *Swann*, decided in 1971, the opinion for the Court by Chief Justice Burger stated in dictum:

> School authorities are traditionally charged with broad power to formulate and implement educational policy and might well conclude, for example, that in order to prepare students to live in a pluralistic society each school should have a prescribed ratio of Negro to white students reflecting the proportion for the district as a whole. *To do this as an educational policy is within the broad discretionary powers of school authorities.* (Emphasis added).

Justice Breyer stressed that this language provided a basis for much innovation over three decades, both by judges and by school boards, to tackle the difficult problem of racial isolation in public schools, whether easily traceable to *de jure* segregation or not. Congress, too, has enacted numerous race-conscious statutes in the context of schools. See, *e.g.,* 20 U.S.C. § 6311(b)(2)(C)(v) (No Child Left Behind Act); § 1067 *et seq.* (authorizing aid to minority institutions).

(b) *The Reality of Racial Isolation in Public Schools.* "Between 1968 and 1980, the number of black children attending a school where minority children constituted more than half of the school fell from 77% to 63% in the Nation (from 81% to 57% in the South) but then reversed direction by the year 2000, rising from 63% to 72% in the Nation (from 57% to 69% in the South). Similarly, between 1968 and 1980, the number of black children attending schools that were more than 90% minority fell from 64% to 33% in the Nation (from 78% to 23% in the South), but that too reversed direction, rising by the year 2000 from 33% to 37% in the Nation (from 23% to 31% in the South). As of 2002, almost 2.4 million students, or over 5% of all public school enrollment, attended schools with a white population of less than 1%. Of these, 2.3 million were black and Latino students, and only 72,000 were white. In recent years, more than one in six black children attend a school that is 99–100% minority. In light of the evident risk of a return to school systems that are in fact (though not in law) resegregated, many school districts have felt a need to maintain or to extend their integration efforts."

(c) *The Murkiness of the De Jure/De Facto Distinction.* No law ever required segregation of the Seattle schools, but they were highly segregated in fact and in practice (white students were routinely allowed to transfer out of majority-black schools). Ultimately the NAACP brought suit, contending that the government building and teacher-assignment policies perpetuated the segregation. The parties settled after the school district pledged to undertake a desegregation plan. The district then implemented a plan requiring race-based transfers and busing. In response to concerns from the Department of Education, the district agreed to remedy racially imbalanced schools through mandatory busing, starting in 1978. The Supreme Court protected the busing plan against a state constitutional amendment in *Washington v. Seattle School Dist. No. 1,* 458 U.S. 457, 461–466 (1982). Subsequently, in an effort to achieve school integration without busing, the district adopted race-based student assignment plans, culminating in the 1998 plan challenged in this litigation. Justice Breyer queried: Was Seattle's school system *de jure* or *de facto*? Why should it matter whether a federal district court had adjudicated the matter? "Are courts really to treat as merely *de facto* segregated those school districts that avoided a federal order by voluntarily complying with *Brown*'s requirements?"

(d) *The Complexity of Reducing Racial Isolation.* "[School] boards work in communities where demographic patterns change, where they must meet traditional learning goals, where they must attract and retain effective teachers, where they should (and will) take account of parents' views and maintain *their* commitment to public school education, where they must adapt to court intervention, where they must encourage voluntary student and parent action—where they will find that their own good faith, their knowledge, and their understanding of local circumstances are always necessary but often insufficient to solve the problems at hand.

"These facts and circumstances help explain why in this context, as to means, the law often leaves legislatures, city councils, school boards, and voters with a broad range of choice, thereby giving 'different communities' the opportunity to 'try different solutions. . . .' "

(e) *The Nature of the Compelling Government Interest.* Justice Breyer identified the government interest as "the school districts' interest in eliminating school-by-school racial isolation and increasing the degree to which racial mixture characterizes each of the district's schools and each individual student's public school experience." He posited three elements to this interest:

(1) remediating prior conditions of segregation, including "an interest in continuing to combat the remnants of segregation caused in whole or in part by [school-related] policies, which have often affected not only schools, but also housing patterns, employment practices, economic conditions, and social attitudes. It is an interest in maintaining hard-won gains. And it has its roots in preventing

what gradually may become the *de facto* resegregation of America's public schools."

(2) "an interest in overcoming the adverse educational effects produced by and associated with highly segregated schools. Studies suggest that children taken from those schools and placed in integrated settings often show positive academic gains."

(3) "a democratic element: an interest in producing an educational environment that reflects the 'pluralistic society' in which our children will live. *Swann.* It is an interest in helping our children learn to work and play together with children of different racial backgrounds. It is an interest in teaching children to engage in the kind of cooperation among Americans of all races that is necessary to make a land of three hundred million people one Nation.

" * * * [T]his Court from *Swann* to *Grutter* has treated these civic effects as an important virtue of racially diverse education. In *Grutter,* in the context of law school admissions, we found that these types of interests were, constitutionally speaking, 'compelling.' See *Grutter* (recognizing that Michigan Law School's race-conscious admissions policy 'promotes cross-racial understanding, helps to break down racial stereotypes, and enables [students] to better understand persons of different races,' and pointing out that 'the skills needed in today's increasingly global marketplace can only be developed through exposure to widely diverse people, cultures, ideas, and viewpoints').

"In light of this Court's conclusions in *Grutter,* the 'compelling' nature of these interests in the context of primary and secondary public education follows here *a fortiori*. Primary and secondary schools are where the education of this Nation's children begins, where each of us begins to absorb those values we carry with us to the end of our days. * * *

"The compelling interest at issue here, then, includes an effort to eradicate the remnants, not of general 'societal discrimination,' but of primary and secondary school segregation; it includes an effort to create school environments that provide better educational opportunities for all children; it includes an effort to help create citizens better prepared to know, to understand, and to work with people of all races and backgrounds, thereby furthering the kind of democratic government our Constitution foresees. If an educational interest that combines these three elements is not 'compelling,' what is?"

(f)   *The Question of Narrow Tailoring.* "[First,] the defining feature of both plans is greater emphasis upon student choice. In Seattle, for example, in more than 80% of all cases, that choice alone determines which high schools Seattle's ninth graders will attend. After ninth grade, students can decide voluntarily to transfer to a preferred district high school (without any consideration of race-conscious criteria). *Choice,* therefore, is the 'predominant factor' in these plans. *Race* is not.'

"Indeed, the race-conscious ranges at issue in these cases often have no effect, either because the particular school is not oversubscribed in the year in question, or because the racial makeup of the school falls within the broad range, or because the student is a transfer applicant or has a sibling at the school. * * *

"Second, broad-range limits on voluntary school choice plans are less burdensome, and hence more narrowly tailored, see *Grutter,* than other race-conscious restrictions this Court has previously approved. See, *e.g., Swann.* Indeed, the plans before us are *more narrowly tailored* than the race-conscious admission plans that this Court approved in *Grutter.* Here, race becomes a factor only in a fraction of students' non-merit-based assignments—not in large numbers of students' merit-based applications. Moreover, the effect of applying race-conscious criteria here affects potentially disadvantaged students *less severely,* not more severely, than the criteria at issue in *Grutter.* Disappointed students are not rejected from a State's flagship graduate program; they simply attend a different one of the district's many public schools, which in aspiration and in fact are substantially equal. And, in Seattle, the disadvantaged student loses at most one year at the high school of his choice. One will search *Grutter* in vain for similarly persuasive evidence of narrow tailoring as the school districts have presented here.

"Third, the manner in which the school boards developed these plans itself reflects 'narrow tailoring.' Each plan was devised to overcome a history of segregated public schools. Each plan embodies the results of local experience and community consultation. Each plan is the product of a process that has sought to enhance student choice, while diminishing the need for mandatory busing. And each plan's use of race-conscious elements is *diminished* compared to the use of race in preceding integration plans. * * *

"Experience in Seattle and Louisville is consistent with experience elsewhere. In 1987, the U.S. Commission on Civil Rights studied 125 large school districts seeking integration. It reported that most districts—92 of them, in fact—adopted desegregation policies that combined two or more highly race-conscious strategies, for example, rezoning or pairing.

"Having looked at dozens of *amicus* briefs, public reports, news stories, and the records in many of this Court's prior cases, which together span 50 years of desegregation history in school districts across the Nation, I have discovered many examples of districts that sought integration through explicitly race-conscious methods, including mandatory busing. Yet, I have found no example or model that would permit this Court to say to Seattle and to Louisville: 'Here is an instance of a desegregation plan that is likely to achieve your objectives and also makes less use of race-conscious criteria than your plans.' And, if the plurality cannot suggest such a model—and it cannot—

then it seeks * * * to impose a 'narrow tailoring' requirement that in practice would never be met.

" * * * Why does Seattle's plan group Asian-Americans, Hispanic-Americans, Native-Americans, and African-Americans together, treating all as similar minorities? The majority suggests that Seattle's classification system could permit a school to be labeled 'diverse' with a 50% Asian-American and 50% white student body, and no African-American students, Hispanic students, or students of other ethnicity.

"The 50/50 hypothetical has no support in the record here; it is conjured from the imagination. In fact, Seattle apparently began to treat these different minority groups alike in response to the federal Emergency School Aid Act's requirement that it do so. Moreover, maintaining this federally mandated system of classification makes sense insofar as Seattle's experience indicates that the relevant circumstances in respect to each of these different minority groups are roughly similar, *e.g.,* in terms of residential patterns, and call for roughly similar responses. This is confirmed by the fact that Seattle has been able to achieve a desirable degree of diversity without the *greater* emphasis on race that drawing fine lines among minority groups would require. Does the plurality's view of the Equal Protection Clause mean that courts must give no weight to such a board determination? Does it insist upon especially strong evidence supporting inclusion of multiple minority groups in an otherwise lawful government minority-assistance program? If so, its interpretation threatens to produce divisiveness among minority groups that is incompatible with the basic objectives of the Fourteenth Amendment. Regardless, the plurality cannot object that the constitutional defect is the individualized use of race and simultaneously object that not enough account of individuals' race has been taken."

3.   *What Is the Holding of the Seattle and Louisville Cases?* Note that there was no majority *judgment* for the Court, so the *holding* of these cases would appear no broader than what would be allowed by Justice Kennedy's concurrence. This fact led many to assume that Justice Kennedy was, for practical purposes, the key judicial decisionmaker for efforts to desegregate and diversify K–12 school populations. With Justice Kennedy's retirement, the concurrence may no longer have that significance. If the newest justices do not subscribe to the views set out in that concurrence, what approach should fill that vacuum?

4.   *Theories of Judicial Review.* Can the striking down of the chosen policies of democratically elected school boards here be justified by any theory of judicial review? Consider factors discussed in Chapter 2, *supra:*

(a)   *Original Meaning.* In passages we have omitted, the Chief Justice makes some appeal to the Constitution's original meaning, but Justice Breyer responds that the Reconstruction Congress itself engaged in race-conscious programs to assist people of color after the Civil War. Justice Thomas, in the concurring opinion we have omitted, responds:

What the dissent fails to understand, however, is that the color-blind Constitution does not bar the government from taking measures to remedy past state-sponsored discrimination—indeed, it requires that such measures be taken in certain circumstances. Race-based government measures during the 1860's and 1870's to remedy *state-enforced slavery* were therefore not inconsistent with the color-blind Constitution.

Note, however, that the Reconstruction statutes were usually not narrowly tailored, that is, limited to former slaves alone; any person of color could take advantage of their largesse.

Is there a better way to make an original meaning argument for the Court's result? The plurality Justices, especially Justices Thomas (who writes a strong colorblindness concurring opinion) and Scalia (who in *Adarand* made a similar point), believe that the Constitution as a coherent document lends support to elements of Justice Harlan's famous *Plessy* dissent, which is a leading precedent for colorblindness. See if you can construct such an argument from the Constitution, as it was changed by the Reconstruction (and perhaps other amendments).

(b)   *Representation-Reinforcement.* Representation-reinforcement theories have generally supported the Breyer position in cases such as this one. Professor Ely was openly critical of judicial invalidation when the state was deploying race for remedial or other problem-solving "benign" reasons. Justice Stevens made this kind of argument in his *Adarand* dissent as well.

One possible argument for the Court along these lines is the pluralism argument originally suggested by Professors Bickel and Kurland in the *DeFunis* case. Bickel and Kurland argued that "benign" affirmative action would stigmatize racial minorities and create animosities against them—contributing to social anxieties and political polarization. Justices Scalia and Thomas seemed persuaded by this kind of point in earlier cases, such as *Adarand*. Indeed, progressive academics are now making a similar point. Arguing from the social constructionist philosophy of Michel Foucault, Professor Richard Ford argues that when the state creates race-based categories, it is perpetuating and intensifying a discourse of racial line-drawing that has the effect of socially hard-wiring race into American culture, often to the disadvantage of "racial" minorities. *See* Ford, *Racial Culture: A Critique* (2005). Although Ford supports affirmative action and is probably sympathetic to Breyer's arguments in the Seattle and Louisville School Cases, his theory provides a postmodern edge to the Bickel and Kurland argument.

(c)   *Pragmatism.* Justice Breyer does not have a monopoly on pragmatic arguments. Although Justice Thomas's position is based upon the colorblindness principle of *Plessy*'s dissent and original meaning (as he understands it), he responded at some length to Justice Breyer's pragmatic points in the Seattle and Louisville School Cases.

According to Justice Thomas, there is no hard, rigorous empirical evidence that racial integration in schools *causes* populations to achieve greater understanding or attain better educations. Thus, even according to one of Breyer's main sources, "the main reason white and minority students perform better academically in majority white schools is likely that these schools provide greater opportunities to learn. In other words, it is not desegregation per se that improves achievement, but rather the learning advantages some desegregated schools provide." Hallinan, *Diversity Effects on Student Outcomes: Social Science Evidence*, 59 Ohio St. L.J. 733, 744 (1998). Conversely, students of color often achieve *better* educations in segregated environments. Indeed, Seattle maintains a school aimed at black students (99% of the student body, by design), for that very reason.

Justice Thomas sharply disputes Justice Breyer's argument that integrated education will contribute to greater racial harmony in society and politics. First, he points out that there is little evidence of a causal link between school integration and harmony. Although many social scientists believe there is a link, others do not.

Some studies have even found that a deterioration in racial attitudes seems to result from racial mixing in schools. See N. St. John, School Desegregation Outcomes for Children 67–68 (1975) ("A glance at [the data] shows that for either race positive findings are less common than negative findings"); Stephan, The Effects of School Desegregation: An Evaluation 30 Years After Brown, in Advances in Applied Social Psychology 183–186 (M. Saks & L. Saxe eds.1986).

Third, Thomas points out that even when students of different races attend the same schools, they are often educationally and socially resegregated within the schools.

5.   *The Legacy of* Brown: *Chief Justice Roberts and Justice Breyer.* As our excerpt indicates, Chief Justice Roberts claimed that his opinion was true to the legacy of *Brown*, but so did Justice Breyer in dissent. For Breyer, *Brown* was "this Court's finest hour," which "held out a promise . . . of true racial equality—not as a matter of fine words on paper, but as a matter of everyday life in the Nation's cities and schools." He applauded the racial progress in the 50 years since *Brown* and deplored the majority's holding taking from school districts "the instruments they have used to rid their schools of racial segregation, instruments that they believe are needed to overcome the problems of cities divided by race and poverty."[31]

Without unduly stressing the point, it could be suggested that these widely different invocations of *Brown* are evidence that people tend to rewrite

---

[31] For discussion of such diverse, competing, and common invocations of *Brown* as involving either a principle of racial antisubordination (Justice Breyer's position) or a principle forbidding racial classification (Chief Justice Roberts' position), see, e.g., Goodwin Liu, *"History Will Be Heard": An Appraisal of the* Seattle/Louisville *Decision*, 2 Harv. Law & Policy Rev. 53 (2008); Reva Siegel, *Equality Talk: Antisubordination and Anticlassification Values in Constitutional Struggles over* Brown, 117 Harv. L. Rev. 1470 (2004).

history to suit their own fundamental commitments, that such rewriting is especially keen to appropriate and reinterpret canonical texts (*Brown* as much as the Constitution) to celebrate and cement one's own vision for America, and that those canonical texts are susceptible to such interpretive appropriations and revisions. Indeed, one of the features, shared by *Brown* and the Constitution, that enables a text to *become* canonical is its articulation of a simple but powerful principle at a level of generality that defies easy cabining.

6.   *The Legacy of* Brown: *Justice Thomas*. In this process of claiming the legacy of *Brown*, Justice Thomas's concurring opinion makes a distinctive contribution. Part III of his opinion lays out the ways in which the arguments made by the Seattle and Jefferson County school districts and Justice Breyer may echo the arguments made by the *de jure* segregated school districts in South Carolina and Virginia more than 50 years ago in *Brown*:[32]

- Justice Breyer says that "[e]ach plan embodies the results of local experience and community consultation," the same appeal to local practice and mores made by the segregationists;

- "weight [must be given] to a local school board's knowledge, expertise, and concerns," the same appeal that the segregationists made for deference to the expertise of elected school boards;

- the Court's decision "threatens to substitute for present calm a disruptive round of race-related litigation" and "risks serious harm to the law and for the Nation," echoes of the segregationists' claims that desegregation would generate violence and turmoil in the South;

- Justice Breyer wraps his dissent in many older precedents and complains that the majority has abandoned them for newer ones, the same charge made by the segregationists in 1952–55;

- states using race-based criteria for good goals and with benign motives should not be judged harshly, the same attitude taken by the segregationists, who saw themselves as benignly inspired and even protective of minority interests; and

- "just as the dissent argues that the need for these programs will lessen over time, the segregationists claimed that reliance on segregation was lessening and might eventually end."

"What was wrong in 1954 cannot be right today," concluded Justice Thomas. Is there a good answer to him?[33]

---

[32]   All of the quotations are from Justice Breyer's dissent, until the last one, which is from Justice Thomas's opinion. Each parallel for the segregationists' arguments in 1952–55 is massively supported by references to the *Brown I* and *Brown II* briefs and arguments.

[33]   For commentary on the Seattle and Louisville decisions, see, e.g., Heather Gerken, *Justice Kennedy and the Domains of Equal Protection*, 121 Harv. L. Rev. 104 (2007); James Ryan, *The Supreme Court and Voluntary Integration*, 121 Harv. L. Rev. 131 (2007); J. Harvie Wilkinson III, *The Seattle and Louisville School Cases: There Is No Other Way*, 121 Harv. L. Rev. 158 (2007).

PROBLEMS ON REDUCING RACIAL
ISOLATION IN PUBLIC SCHOOLS

Apply the Seattle and Louisville cases to the following circumstances:

Problem 3-10: School district is completely segregated by race (all "nonwhite" schools have 0% whites, all "white" schools have 0% nonwhites) and adopts a plan allowing "integrative" transfers, i.e., only those breaking down segregated patterns. (This example is similar to the plan Seattle adopted in 1963, in response to complaints from the NAACP.)

Problem 3-11: School district faces substantial racial segregation (most children are in 80% segregated schools) and adopts a plan that places children in schools based upon a balance for each child, including where she lives, where her sibling(s) are in school, specialized educational opportunities available at magnet schools, and the pupil's own race (race being a plus when diluting segregated patterns). (The example is similar to the plan Seattle adopted in 1998, but adapted to be more like the balance-of-factors approach the Court approved in *Grutter*.)

Problem 3-12: School district faces substantial racial segregation (most children are in 80% segregated schools) and adopts a plan that creates new schools and populates those schools by a selective admissions process that considers students' race and aims at a balance in the new schools reflecting the racial population of the city. (The example bears some similarities to the plan Seattle adopted in the 1970s, in response to the NAACP's lawsuit against the school district.)

Would it make a difference if the district had been legally segregated before 1954, and that experts believe the current segregation can be traced to housing patterns, etc., created by that earlier regime? Note that the plurality Justices, and apparently also Justice Kennedy, are strongly resistant to Justice Breyer's criticism of the *de jure/de facto* distinction; rooted in the state action doctrine, the distinction strikes Breyer as fuzzy and indeterminate as applied to Seattle.

E. FACIALLY NEUTRAL CLASSIFICATIONS DESIGNED TO BENEFIT RACIAL MINORITIES

1. Introduction

In the affirmative action cases, the Supreme Court considered the governmental use of race to be highly suspicious. In this context of a *facial racial classification*, the Court rejected the idea that a desire to help minorities is legally distinct from a desire to harm whites.

Would the Court be equally suspicious of all *facially neutral* classifications attributable at least in part to racial considerations? *Washington v. Davis*, combined with *Adarand*'s "consistency" axiom, may suggest that all such facially neutral classifications trigger strict scrutiny because they are racial classifications in disguise. The question may be a good deal more complicated than that, however.

In *Davis* and similar cases, the statutory scheme had a disparate impact on minorities. Because the statute was facially neutral, *Brown* and its progeny did not require applying strict scrutiny. *Davis* held that this discriminatory impact creates no serious constitutional problem unless the government adopted the law at least in part out of a desire to achieve those effects; "selective racial indifference" is not enough to state a claim. Thus, the practical harm caused by the statute (in *Davis*, failure to get a government job) must be linked to another kind of injury to be actionable. Why such racial motivation is the right kind of extra harm is left unclear in *Davis*.

One explanation is that *Davis* adopts an intentional tort model: Injury is not actionable unless the actor intended it to occur. Thus, the government's negligence or selective racial indifference—*i.e.*, failure to focus upon and avoid foreseeable racially discriminatory effects through reasonable steps—provides no basis for relief. This *mens rea* requirement may be supportable in many ways, but we will identify two that seem particularly relevant here.

First, perhaps the injury should not legally "count" as racial unless there is a realization that the government intended it to happen. This explanation links *Davis* to the *Brown* tradition through the requirement of "stigma." *Brown* suggested that the problem with "separate but equal" school segregation was stigma—the "brand of inferiority" that it placed upon even those African-American children receiving an otherwise allegedly equal education. School segregation sent a message of the inferiority of African-American children, even of the antipathy of white society toward them. The presence of *Davis* intent surrounding the adoption of a government employment test signals similar antipathy or stereotypes of inferiority, causing stigma to the excluded individual and assaulting her dignity. When no *Davis* intent is shown, the injury hurts less and is just one of those disappointments that must be borne in a complex society.

This conclusion about the "individuation" of the cause of action in *Davis*, whereby group effects are beside the point (except where they are so dramatic as to suggest wrongful intent) and individual disappointment must be linked with individual psychological harm, is suggested by a passage in *Davis* (reprinted earlier in this chapter). After noting that no one has a constitutional claim just because she fails the employment test, the Court continued:

> The conclusion would not be different in the face of proof that more Negroes than whites had been disqualified by Test 21. That other Negroes also failed to score well would, alone, not

demonstrate that respondents individually were being denied equal protection of the laws by the application of an otherwise valid qualifying test being administered to prospective police recruits.

Although this passage leaves obscure exactly why illicit intent would demonstrate an equal protection violation, it does suggest that there must be some harm to the individual beyond the loss of the job. One understanding of that additional injury is a requirement of dignitary harm.

Second, from the perspective of the government, the *Davis* approach avoids imposing limitations upon governmental decisionmaking that may be unrealistic. The government often finds itself in "zero sum" situations where helping one group disadvantages another. Scarce resources prevent the government from addressing all social problems. Moreover, the government has an interest in expeditious decisionmaking. Holding the government responsible for "negligent failure to take reasonable steps to avoid racially discriminatory effects" could seriously intrude upon these interests, perhaps to the point of suggesting separation of powers concerns about courts invading the legislative domain. Moreover, the "negligent failure" theory would place in constitutional jeopardy all sorts of government actions. This political-process and "slippery slope" defense of *Davis* also resonates well with footnote 14 in the case and the paragraph to which it is attached.

This reading of *Davis* is in tension with *Croson* (and with its federal offspring, *Adarand*). The Court in *Croson* did not inquire whether the minority set-aside program caused dignitary harm to the white contractors. Moreover, the Court seemed troubled by the appearance of "selective racial indifference" on the part of the Richmond city council.

One could maintain both *Davis* and *Croson* by drawing a bright line between them. When a facial racial classification is used, a "red flag" goes up, concerns about stigma vanish, and strict scrutiny is invoked. In contrast, when the classification is facially neutral, the plaintiff must show both practical injury (failure to get a government job) and dignitary harm. Would it make sense to draw this bright line? Consider an example.

Assume that a city council is considering two bills appropriating funds for a job-training program. One would define the qualifications for spots in the program to assist the retraining of skilled workers who have lost their jobs. The majority of skilled workers are unionized, and thus labor unions are promoting the bill. The majority of skilled workers are also white, but many minorities would benefit from it as well. The second bill would use economic status to define the qualifications for getting into the program; only the very poor would qualify. This bill is being promoted by a variety of community groups, including the African-American Alliance, which is concerned about the disproportionate poverty and unemployment of African Americans.

If the city council adopts the first bill and an African American who cannot qualify for its benefits brings suit, a straightforward application of *Davis* would result in the denial of relief. The plaintiff could not show that the city council adopted the bill at least in part because of a desire disproportionately to exclude African Americans from its coverage. The city council will defend itself by noting that the ordinance is facially neutral and was adopted for bona fide reasons. All African Americans who are skilled workers may enjoy the benefits of the bill, and the thought never entered anyone's mind that it was a way to engage in hateful racial exclusion. "We weren't trying to hurt anyone, just trying to help skilled, unemployed people."

If the city council adopts the second bill and an unemployed, skilled worker who is white and above the poverty line (because of spousal income, for example) brings suit, a similarly straightforward application of *Davis* should result in the denial of relief as well. Again, the classification is facially neutral (all people defined as "poor" qualify, which includes many whites), and the city council did not adopt this ordinance because of antipathy toward whites or stereotypes about their inferiority.

These are hardly controversial examples. But the reasons that real-world analogues to them are not controversial may be subtle. We will suggest two. First, even a facially neutral classification that disproportionately benefits racial minorities usually benefits a greater absolute number of whites. When Congress adopts a statute benefitting the poor, the statute may well disproportionately benefit racial minorities (because they are disproportionately poor), but in absolute terms a greater number of whites than minorities are benefitted (because there are also lots of poor whites, and so many more whites than minorities generally). Thus, upon cursory examination, the statute does not resemble a racial preference at all.

Second, and relatedly, when legislators adopt such a statute, it is easy to view them as being motivated by a desire to help a class of people not defined by race (the poor), and not being motivated by a desire to harm anyone. True, the money allocated to this project is unavailable for competing proposals to help the non-poor; true, the bill disproportionately helps racial minorities, who may have lobbied for it on that basis. The legislature's action, however, seems benevolent—"benign" toward all and rooted in antipathy or visions of inferiority toward none, including those who are not benefitted by the statute and perhaps even lobbied against it in favor of proposals that would have helped them.

Both of these reasons why a facially neutral statute infrequently generates hostility from the general community are easy to destroy, however. In some situations, at least, it is possible to craft the legislation in a way that helps a larger aggregate number of minorities than whites. Imagine a state law school establishing a minimum quota (subject to some grade point average and LSAT requirements) for graduates of "inner city public high schools," defined as those located in the fifteen or twenty largest cities in the United States. If a law school did that, would its intent still be viewed as "benign," desiring only to help a certain class not defined by race? (Note that many whites would benefit from this classification as well.) If your intuitions about constitutionality change when the comparative number of beneficiaries according to racial makeup is flipped, why?

All of this becomes more complicated when it is recognized that, at least sometimes, government cannot avoid considering racial impact. When the city council in the hypothetical above chooses between the union-promoted bill and the bill designed to help the poor, its members not only know the racially differential effects of the choice, that racial impact has been thrust upon them by lobbyists as well. "Help our people," say the lobbyists for the African-American community. Is that somehow an illicit lobbying campaign? (If you think so, you might want to peek ahead to Chapter 6, on the First Amendment.) If a councilmember votes that way, does the councilmember have the kind of illicit motivation condemned by *Davis*? Or may she say, "I was simply trying to help one part of the community, and the bill helps lots of other kinds of people as well"? Should it matter whether the councilmember votes that way for political reasons (to pick up minority votes for reelection) or for high-minded reasons of promoting social progress?

2. The Context of Electoral Redistricting

Probably the starkest context in which elected officials simply cannot avoid racial considerations is electoral redistricting. As explained in Chapter 5, § 3A, the Constitution requires state legislatures and the federal House of Representatives to be reapportioned on a "one person, one vote" basis following each decennial census. The state legislature reapportions itself as well as the state's federal congressional districts. Reapportionment is an intensely political affair in which the majority party tries to maximize its influence, the minority party fights back, and incumbents of both parties hope for district configurations favorable for reelection.

In America, of course, the racial composition of an area affects its politics. Thus, a reapportionment involves racial considerations. Moreover, racial minorities may argue that some "majority-minority" districts (*e.g.*, ones with a majority of African Americans) be created, because otherwise, in the presence of racial bloc voting by both whites and African Americans, the latter can neither elect a candidate of their choice nor hope for much responsiveness from the white candidate who is elected.

In areas covered by the Voting Rights Act, legislative consideration of race in the reapportionment context became even more inevitable. The original Act covered jurisdictions that had low voter turnout and a "test or device" as a prerequisite to voting. (See Chapter 7, § 3B.) In such a jurisdiction, any change in voting structure, like a reapportionment, required federal "preclearance" under § 5 of the Act—that is, the approval of either the federal Justice Department or the federal District Court for the District of Columbia based on a finding that the change had neither the purpose nor the effect of diminishing minority voting strength. Since 1982, § 2 of the Act has provided an independent, nationwide prohibition on electoral structures that "result" in the dilution of the minority vote. Thus, under the original Act as it was amended in 1982, a jurisdiction covered by the Act had to reapportion in a way that did not diminish minority political power from the pre-existing baseline (§ 5) and did not result in minority political power being manifestly lower than it could be under other districting (§ 2).

But in *Shelby County v. Holder,* 570 U.S. 529 (2013) (addressed at length in Chapter 7), a 5–4 majority rendered § 5 unenforceable. In his opinion for the Court, Chief Justice Roberts wrote that § 4(b), the coverage formula that determined which jurisdictions were subject to § 5 preclearance requirements, was unconstitutional. The majority ruled that because the coverage formula was based on decades-old data and practices that had been eradicated, § 4(b) could no longer be justified in the face of concerns regarding federalism and the equal treatment of the states by the federal government. "In 1965, the States could be divided into two group: those with a recent history of voting tests and low voter registration and turnout, and those without those characteristics. Congress based its coverage formula on that distinction. Today the Nation is no longer divided along those lines, yet the Voting Rights Act continues to treat it as if it were." The opinion left open the possibility for Congress to construct a new coverage formula that reflected modern conditions. That has not happened, however, so for all practical purposes, previously covered jurisdictions were freed from the preclearance requirement.

Justice Ginsburg, joined by Justices Breyer, Sotomayor, and Kagan, dissented, arguing that "[t]hrowing out preclearance when it has worked and is continuing to work to stop discriminatory changes is like throwing away your umbrella in a rainstorm because you are not getting wet."

Complicating the Court's doctrine on race and redistricting is the fact that a reapportionment is facially neutral: The statute drawing district lines says nothing about race on its face. The next case was important in inaugurating a line of doctrine in this area that has addressed—and sometimes invalidated—facially neutral redistricting schemes designed to benefit minority voters.

Shaw v. Reno

509 U.S. 630 (1993)

The North Carolina General Assembly's reapportionment of the state's twelve seats in the federal House of Representatives based on the 1990 census included one majority-black congressional district. After the federal Attorney General objected to the plan pursuant to § 5 of the Voting Rights Act, the General Assembly revised the plan and created a second majority-black district. "The first of the two majority-black districts contained in the revised plan, District 1, is somewhat hook shaped. Centered in the northeast portion of the State, it moves southward until it tapers to a narrow band; then, with finger-like extensions, it reaches far into the southern-most part of the State near the South Carolina border. District 1 has been compared to a 'Rorschach ink-blot test' and a 'bug splattered on a windshield.'

"The second majority-black district, District 12, is even more unusually shaped. It is approximately 160 miles long and, for much of its length, no wider than the I-85 corridor. It winds in snake-like fashion through tobacco country, financial centers, and manufacturing areas 'until it gobbles in enough enclaves of black neighborhoods.' * * * Northbound and southbound drivers on I-85 sometimes find themselves in separate districts in one county, only to 'trade' districts when they enter the next county. Of the 10 counties through which District 12 passes, five are cut into three different districts; even towns are divided. At one point the district remains contiguous only because it intersects at a single point with two other districts before crossing over them."

The majority opinion of **Justice O'Connor** held that strict scrutiny applied to this redistricting. She upheld as constitutionally cognizable the plaintiffs' complaint "that the deliberate segregation of voters into separate districts on the basis of race violated their constitutional right to participate in a 'color-blind' electoral process. * * * What appellants object to is redistricting legislation that is so extremely irregular on its face that it rationally can be viewed only as an effort to segregate the races for purposes of voting, without regard for traditional districting principles and without sufficiently compelling justification. * * *

"[W]e believe that reapportionment is one area in which appearances do matter. A reapportionment plan that includes in one district individuals who belong to the same race, but who are otherwise widely separated by geographical and political boundaries, and who may have little in common with one another but the color of their skin, bears an uncomfortable resemblance to political apartheid. It reinforces the perception that members of the same racial group—regardless of their age, education, economic status, or the community in which they live—think alike, share the same political interests, and will prefer the same candidates at the polls. We have rejected such perceptions elsewhere as impermissible racial stereotypes. By perpetuating such notions, a racial gerrymander may exacerbate the very patterns of racial bloc voting that majority-minority districting is sometimes said to counteract.

"The message that such districting sends to elected representatives is equally pernicious. When a district obviously is created solely to effectuate the perceived common interests of one racial group, elected officials are more likely to believe that their primary obligation is to represent only the members of that group, rather than their constituency as a whole. This is altogether antithetical to our system of representative democracy. * * *

"The state appellees suggest that a covered jurisdiction may have a compelling interest in creating majority-minority districts in order to comply with the Voting Rights Act." Justice O'Connor acknowledged that § 5 of the Voting Rights Act forbade preclearance of a reapportionment "if it will lead to 'a retrogression in the position of racial minorities with respect to their effective exercise of the electoral franchise.'" She cautioned, however, against reading the Court's "§ 5 cases to give covered jurisdictions *carte blanche* to engage in racial gerrymandering in the name of nonretrogression. A reapportionment plan would not be narrowly tailored to the goal of avoiding retrogression if the State went beyond what was reasonably necessary to avoid retrogression." She noted that on remand the state could attempt to prove that the plan was necessary to "avoid dilution of black voting strength in violation of § 2."

"The state appellees alternatively argue that the General Assembly's plan advanced a [different] compelling interest. * * * We previously have recognized a significant state interest in eradicating the effects of past racial discrimination. But the State must have a 'strong basis in evidence for [concluding] that remedial action [is] necessary.' *Croson*." The Court remanded for consideration of the state's defenses.

Justices White, Blackmun, Stevens, and **Souter** dissented. For them, it blinked reality to think that a redistricting could be done without race being considered. Redistricting is inherently partisan, with politically salient factors such as race inevitably taken into account. In addition, the plaintiffs had not demonstrated any cognizable harm from the redistricting (everyone in the district had the same right to vote, for example). Moreover, Justice White explained, "[w]hites constitute roughly 76 percent of the total population and 79 percent of the voting age population in North Carolina. Yet, under the State's plan, they still constitute a voting majority in 10 (or 83 percent) of the 12 congressional districts. Though they might be dissatisfied at the prospect of casting a vote for a losing candidate—a lot shared by many, including a disproportionate number of minority voters—surely they cannot complain of discriminatory treatment."

Justice Souter maintained that, "[u]nlike other contexts in which we have addressed the State's conscious use of race, see, *e.g.*, *Croson* (city contracting); *Wygant* (teacher layoffs), electoral districting calls for decisions that nearly always require some consideration of race for legitimate reasons where there is a racially mixed population. As long as members of racial groups have the commonality of interest implicit in our ability to talk about concepts like "minority voting strength" and "dilution of minority votes," and as long as racial bloc voting takes place, legislators will have to take race into account in order to avoid dilution of minority voting strength in the districting plans they adopt. One need look no further than the Voting Rights Act to understand that this may be required * * *.

"A second distinction between districting and most other governmental decisions in which race has figured is that those other decisions using racial criteria characteristically occur in circumstances in which the use of race to the advantage of one person is necessarily at the obvious expense of a member of a different race. Thus, for example, awarding government contracts on a racial basis excludes certain firms from competition on racial grounds. See *Croson.* * * *

"In districting, by contrast, the mere placement of an individual in one district instead of another denies no one a right or benefit provided to others. All citizens may register, vote, and be represented. In whatever district, the individual voter has a right to vote in each election, and the election will result in the voter's representation. As we have held, one's constitutional rights are not violated merely because the candidate one supports loses the election or because a group (including a racial group) to which one belongs winds up with a representative from outside that group. It is true, of course, that one's vote may be more or less effective depending on the interests of the other individuals who are in one's district, and our cases recognize the reality that members of the same race often have shared interests. 'Dilution' thus refers to the effects of districting decisions not on an individual's political power viewed in isolation, but on the political power of a group. * * *

"Our different approaches to equal protection in electoral districting and nondistricting cases reflect these differences. There is a characteristic coincidence of disadvantageous effect and illegitimate purpose associated with the State's use of race in those situations in which it has immediately triggered at least heightened scrutiny (which every Member of the Court to address the issue has agreed must be applied even to race-based classifications designed to serve some permissible state interest). Presumably because the legitimate consideration of race in a districting decision is usually inevitable under the Voting Rights Act when communities are racially mixed, however, and because, without more, it does not result in diminished political effectiveness for anyone, we have not taken the approach of applying the usual standard of such heightened 'scrutiny' to race-based districting decisions."

————

Limitations of length preclude our full exploration of the cases following *Shaw v. Reno*. For present purposes, it should suffice to note the following:

- *The nature of the harm.* Justice O'Connor, in her plurality opinion in *Bush v. Vera*, 517 U.S. 952 (1996), wrote that some majority-minority districts "cause constitutional harm insofar as they convey the message that political identity is, or should be, predominantly racial." She labeled this an "expressive harm," which Justice Souter, in dissent, defined as "one that 'results from the idea or attitudes expressed through a governmental action, rather than from the more tangible or material consequences the action brings about.'" Why is expressive harm, rather than more concrete harm, sufficient in this context to constitute a constitutional claim? Compare Professor Lawrence's argument (§ 1C of this chapter) for modifying the *Washington v. Davis* approach to bring within constitutional cognizance those governmental acts that send a racist message. If expressive harm counts in *Shaw*, should it count in the contexts identified by Professor Lawrence as well?

- *Bizarre shape?* In *Miller v. Johnson*, 515 U.S. 900 (1995), the majority held that "[s]hape is relevant not because bizarreness is a necessary element of the constitutional wrong or a threshold requirement of proof, but because it may be persuasive circumstantial evidence that race for its own sake, and not other districting principles, was the legislature's dominant and controlling rationale in drawing its district lines. The logical implication * * * is that parties may rely on evidence other than bizarreness to establish race-based districting."

- *Predominant motive.* Recall that under *Washington v. Davis*, racially discriminatory intent need not be the predominant motive; it is actionable if it is a substantial factor. But when it is recognized that racial considerations will play a role in any redistricting, the majority of Justices who support *Shaw v. Reno* limited its cause of action to situations of predominant motive. In *Miller*, the Court stated: "The plaintiff's burden is to show, either through circumstantial evidence of a district's shape and demographics or more direct evidence going to legislative purpose, that race was the predominant factor motivating the legislature's decision to place a significant number of voters within or without a particular district. To make this showing, a plaintiff must prove that the legislature subordinated traditional race-neutral districting principles, including but not limited to compactness, contiguity, respect for political subdivisions or communities defined by actual shared interests, to racial considerations. Where these or other race-neutral considerations are the basis for redistricting legislation, and are not subordinated to race, a state can 'defeat a claim that a district has been gerrymandered on racial lines.'" As one might imagine, the requirement of "predominant motive" has proved bedeviling in practice because of the close correlation of racial and political considerations in redistricting.

Oppressing

- *The decline and re-emergence of* Shaw *claims.* In the years since *Shaw*, the Supreme Court's race and redistricting doctrine has taken a winding path. Initially, after *Easley v. Cromartie*, 532 U.S. 234 (2001), it appeared that *Shaw*-type claims would be significantly less likely to succeed. *Easley* once again involved a racial gerrymandering challenge to North Carolina's 12th congressional district. Yet this time, Justice O'Connor joined Justice Breyer's majority opinion, which set aside the district court's conclusion as clearly erroneous. The majority concluded that because African-American Democrats in the state were far more likely to vote for Democratic candidates, the legislature's tendency to create safe Democratic districts by concentrating African-Americans within them was not necessarily motivated predominantly by race rather than by politics. *Easley*'s rationale appeared to arm state legislatures with a "politics not race" trump card against future claims of racial gerrymandering. But in 2017, the Court issued a pair of decisions that breathed new life into *Shaw*-type litigation. In *Bethune-Hill v. Virginia State Board of Elections*, 580 U.S. ___, the Court held that plaintiffs need not show that a challenged district's makeup was inconsistent with traditional redistricting criteria. Even though a district otherwise adhered to such criteria, plaintiffs could establish that race was the predominant factor in shaping the district through other direct and circumstantial evidence. More to the point, in *Cooper v. Harris*, 581 U.S. ___, the Court stated in a footnote that trial courts may find proof of unconstitutional racial gerrymandering "when legislators have 'place[d] a significant number of voters within or without' a district predominantly because of their race, regardless of their ultimate objective in taking that step. * * * [T]he sorting of voters on the grounds of their race remains suspect even if race is meant to function as a proxy for other (including political) characteristics."

F. A CONCLUDING THOUGHT: THE ROAD FROM *BROWN*

As you conclude this chapter, review the path the Supreme Court has charted from *Brown v. Board of Education* (Chapter 2) to the most recent cases on race. *Parents Involved* featured a pitched battle over the legacy of

Brown, but was mostly about the specific issue of school integration. Think more broadly about the road from *Brown*. In some of the principal decisions you have read—*Washington v. Davis*, *Croson/Adarand*, *Grutter* and *Fisher II, Parents Involved*—do you think the Court has redeemed or betrayed the basic promise of *Brown*? How would you define that promise? Is this an empirical question (dependent on data about how African Americans and other racial minorities are faring?) Or is it a normative question implicating basic ideas about racial justice? You may wish to revisit this question after reading *Shelby Counter v. Holder* in Chapter 7, the case that struck down a key portion of the Voting Rights Act. Some would argue that *Shelby County* is as central a part of the Court's jurisprudence on race in America, and reveals as much about the contemporary Court's views on that question, as anything in this chapter.

CHAPTER 4

SEX AND GENDER DISCRIMINATION AND OTHER EQUAL PROTECTION CONCERNS

■ ■ ■

In *The Slaughter-House Cases*, 83 U.S. (16 Wall.) 36 (1872), the first Supreme Court case to interpret the Fourteenth Amendment, the Court said that it "doubt[ed] very much whether any action of a state not directed by way of discrimination against the negroes as a class, or on account of their race, will ever be held to come within the purview of this provision." This prediction proved to be inaccurate, as the Court held discrimination against Chinese Americans to violate the Equal Protection Clause in *Yick Wo v. Hopkins*, 118 U.S. 356 (1886) (Chapter 3, § 1B), and suggested in *Strauder v. West Virginia*, 100 U.S. 303 (1879) (Chapter 2, § 1A) that national origin discrimination (against, for example, "Celtic Irishmen") would violate the clause. By the turn of the century, the Equal Protection Clause had been construed as a general protection against arbitrary classifications, requiring "some reasonable ground—some difference which bears a just and proper relation to the attempted classification." *Gulf, C. & S.F. Ry. v. Ellis*, 165 U.S. 150 (1897). Today, the clause is read in accord with its broad plain meaning—to apply to any state classification. As § 1 of this chapter indicates, however, the requirement of a "rational basis" for the state's line-drawing is typically an easy test for a statute to pass.

Race-based classifications, of course, trigger strict scrutiny (recall Chapter 3). An important question is when, if ever, something more stringent than rational-basis review should be applied to classifications other than race or national origin. A note at the end of § 1 of this chapter traces the Supreme Court's consideration of this issue for statutory discrimination along lines of alienage, illegitimacy, age, and wealth. The most important line of cases deals with discrimination based upon sex or gender (§ 2 of this chapter).[1] Recall that African Americans earlier engaged in a constitutionalized politics of recognition that transformed the Equal Protection Clause by creating a higher standard for race as a "suspect

---

[1]   The terms "sex" and "gender" are sometimes used synonymously, but can have different meanings. "Sex" often refers to biological classifications *man* and *woman*, and "gender" to characteristics associated with being a man (*masculine*) and a woman (*feminine*). But courts are not uniform in their terminology. For fruitful discussion, see Mary Anne Case, *Disaggregating Gender from Sex and Sexual Orientation: The Effeminate Man in the Law and Feminist Jurisprudence*, 105 Yale L.J. 1 (1995); Richard Epstein, *Gender Is for Nouns*, 41 DePaul L. Rev. 981 (1992); Katherine Franke, *The Central Mistake of Sex Discrimination Law: The Disaggregation of Sex from Gender*, 144 U. Pa. L. Rev. 1 (1995).

classification" (Chapter 3, § 1A). The women's movement engaged in a similar constitutional campaign in the 1970s, seeking recognition of sex as another suspect classification.[2] Because the Framers of the Fourteenth Amendment did not specifically intend to protect against sex classifications as they did for at least some racial classifications, one needs a different theory of equal protection to justify its expansion. Is there a special justification for subjecting sex or gender classifications to stricter scrutiny than the rational-basis test? If so, should such classifications be scrutinized as severely as classifications based upon race?

Other identity-based social movements, most notably the disability rights and gay liberation movements, sought similar equal protection scrutiny to sweep away hundreds of statutory discriminations. Section 3 of this chapter traces the Court's ambiguous response to these movements. Without subjecting either classification to strict scrutiny (like race) or intermediate scrutiny (like sex), the Supreme Court has on a few occasions invalidated disability and sexual orientation classifications under some version of rational-basis review. This not only creates potential problems for the many disability and sexual orientation discriminations in American law, but raises the question whether the so-called "double standard" (rational basis = easy to pass; strict scrutiny = bound to fail) still holds in equal protection cases or is being (and should be) replaced by a sliding-scale approach such as that proposed by Thurgood Marshall, the greatest social movement lawyer of the last century.[3]

SECTION 1. MINIMAL EQUAL PROTECTION SCRUTINY (THE RATIONAL-BASIS TEST)

The Equal Protection Clause speaks in general language, protecting "any person" against the denial of "the equal protection of the laws." Just as equal protection has not been limited to race claims, so also it cannot practically require the state to treat all persons the same. People differ in many ways relevant to public policy. A sensible way to begin thinking about equal protection as a generalized requirement is to consider whether, as a federal constitutional matter, a state must treat *all similarly situated people similarly*.[4] For purposes of driving an automobile, the blind and the sighted are not similarly situated; people with blue eyes and people with brown eyes are.

---

[2] The historical parallels are explored in Serena Mayeri, *Constitutional Choices: Legal Feminism and the Historical Dynamics of Change,* 92 Calif. L. Rev. 755 (2004).

[3] Justice Marshall's most elaborate statement of this approach was in his dissent in *San Antonio Ind. School Dist. v. Rodriguez* (Chapter 5, § 3B), discussed in William Eskridge, Jr., *Some Effects of Identity-Based Social Movements on Constitutional Law in the Twentieth Century*, 100 Mich. L. Rev. 2062, 2269–79 (2002).

[4] This understanding of the Equal Protection Clause (and the over-and underinclusion analysis in the next paragraph) was classically articulated in Joseph Tussman & Jacobus tenBroek, *The Equal Protection of the Laws*, 37 Calif. L. Rev. 341 (1949).

A state that wishes to prevent dangerous drivers from operating motor vehicles might start by requiring that all drivers have a certain level of visual acuity. Standing alone, this requirement is *underinclusive*: It would eliminate only one of a variety of kinds of dangerous drivers. At first glance, the problem of underinclusion may not seem important, for the person complaining about underinclusion has been properly identified as contributing to the problem the state is attempting to remedy. States ought to be able to pursue partial remedies rather than be compelled to take an all-or-nothing approach; reform may be taken "one step at a time." But if equal protection requires even a minimal degree of fairness in regulation, underinclusion can be troubling. Imagine that California must reduce auto emissions by 40%, and the state responds by revoking the licenses of all persons who make less than $15,000 a year. These persons were contributing to the air pollution problem—perhaps even disproportionally, if they tend to have older autos with less effective emissions controls—but picking out these people and forcing them to bear the full brunt of a general societal problem seems grossly unfair. These persons also are probably less politically powerful than the class of drivers left untouched by the remedy, which may heighten our concerns.

Overinclusion is the flip side of the equal protection coin. A statute that forbids a driver's license to someone with poor eyesight will probably keep off the road some drivers who can operate a vehicle safely despite their poor visual acuity, and if so, the statute is overinclusive. If these persons could demand a driving test, they might well pass it. In some ways, we may be more sympathetic with the victims of overinclusive statutes than with the victims of underinclusive statutes, for the former are not even contributing to the problem the state is attempting to remedy. The state, however, has a legitimate interest in adopting regulatory approaches that are administratively convenient and cost effective; allowing anyone to demand a driver's test before a license could be denied would be inefficient and costly (and sometimes even dangerous).

Many of the cases involving arguments about underinclusion and overinclusion concern economic regulation. From the beginning of this century until the late 1930s, the Supreme Court took an activist posture in protecting economic interests from "unfair" regulation, pursuant to the Due Process Clause (the *Lochner* case, discussed in Chapter 1, § 5, and Chapter 5, § 2B). The Court treated the Due Process Clause's protection against a deprivation of (economic) "liberty" without due process of law as forbidding the government from regulating where the goal of the regulation was either deemed illegitimate or too minor compared to the importance of the liberty to the person being regulated. The person being regulated could and often did also make an equal protection challenge to the regulation based on underinclusion or overinclusion. For example, if the government decided to promote workplace health by forbidding bakers from working more than sixty hours each week, a bakery or its employees could argue that due process was violated because the goal (promoting employee health) was insufficient when weighed against the employer's and employee's interests in being free to choose how long the work week should be. Alternatively, they could argue that equal protection was violated because the statute was *underinclusive* (it did not limit the work week in other occupations such as mining or cotton-mill work, where long hours pose a greater threat to worker health than in the bakery trade) and *overinclusive* (most bakery workers could work more than sixty hours per week and suffer no discernible deterioration in health).

By the late 1930s, the Court had abandoned rigorous review of economic regulation under either the Due Process or Equal Protection Clauses. Indeed, one of the principal cases announcing the Court's new refusal to review such statutes vigorously was *Carolene Products*, in which Justice Stone inserted his famous footnote 4 containing dictum about a potential new judicial role: protecting "discrete and insular minorities" (Chapter 1, § 6; Chapter 2, § 3B). The next case demonstrates the general approach the Court has taken to equal protection review of economic regulation since the late 1930s.

RAILWAY EXPRESS AGENCY, INC. v. NEW YORK
336 U.S. 106, 69 S.Ct. 463, 93 L.Ed. 533 (1949)

JUSTICE DOUGLAS delivered the opinion of the Court.

Section 124 of the Traffic Regulations of the City of New York promulgated by the Police Commissioner provides: "No person shall operate, or cause to be operated, in or upon any street an advertising vehicle; provided that nothing herein contained shall prevent the putting of business notices upon business delivery vehicles, so long as such vehicles are engaged in the usual business or regular work of the owner and not used merely or mainly for advertising."

Appellant is engaged in a nation-wide express business. It operates about 1,900 trucks in New York City and sells the space on the exterior sides of these trucks for advertising. That advertising is for the most part unconnected with its own business. It was convicted in the magistrate's court and fined. The judgment of conviction was sustained in the Court of Special Sessions. The Court of Appeals affirmed without opinion by a divided vote. The case is here on appeal. * * *

The Court of Special Sessions concluded that advertising on vehicles using the streets of New York City constitutes a distraction to vehicle drivers and to pedestrians alike and therefore affects the safety of the public in the use of the streets. We do not sit to weigh evidence on the due process issue in order to determine whether the regulation is sound or appropriate; nor is it our function to pass judgment on its wisdom. We would be trespassing on one of the most intensely local and specialized of all municipal problems if we held that this regulation had no relation to the traffic problem of New York City. It is the judgment of the local authorities that it does have such a relation. And nothing has been advanced which shows that to be palpably false. *deference*

The question of equal protection of the laws is pressed more strenuously on us. It is pointed out that the regulation draws the line between advertisements of products sold by the owner of the truck and general advertisements. It is argued that unequal treatment on the basis of such a distinction is not justified by the aim and purpose of the regulation. It is said, for example, that one of appellant's trucks carrying the advertisement of a commercial house would not cause any greater distraction of pedestrians and vehicle drivers than if the commercial house carried the same advertisement on its own truck. Yet the regulation allows the latter to do what the former is forbidden from doing. It is therefore contended that the classification which the regulation makes has no relation to the traffic problem since a violation turns not on what kind of advertisements are carried on trucks but on whose trucks they are carried.

That, however, is a superficial way of analyzing the problem, even if we assume that it is premised on the correct construction of the regulation. The local authorities may well have concluded that those who advertised their own wares on their trucks do not present the same traffic problem in view of the nature or extent of the advertising which they use. It would take a degree of omniscience which we lack to say that such is not the case. If that judgment is correct, the advertising displays that are exempt have less incidence on traffic than those of appellants.

We cannot say that that judgment is not an allowable one. Yet if it is, the classification has relation to the purpose for which it is made and does not contain the kind of discrimination against which the Equal Protection Clause affords protection. It is by such practical considerations based on experience rather than by theoretical inconsistencies that the question of equal protection is to be answered. And the fact that New York City sees fit to eliminate from traffic this kind of distraction but does not touch what may be even greater ones in a different category, such as the vivid displays on Times Square, is immaterial. It is no requirement of equal protection that all evils of the same genus be eradicated or none at all. *No violation*

JUSTICE RUTLEDGE acquiesces in the Court's opinion and judgment, *dubitante* on the question of equal protection of the laws.

JUSTICE JACKSON, concurring.

The burden should rest heavily upon one who would persuade us to use the due process clause to strike down a substantive law or ordinance. Even its provident use against municipal regulations frequently disables all government—state, municipal and federal—from dealing with the conduct in question because the requirement of due process is also applicable to State and Federal Governments. Invalidation of a statute or an ordinance on due process grounds leaves ungoverned and ungovernable conduct which many people find objectionable.

Invocation of the equal protection clause, on the other hand, does not disable any governmental body from dealing with the subject at hand. It merely means that the prohibition or regulation must have a broader impact. I regard it as a salutary doctrine that cities, states and the Federal Government must exercise their powers so as not to discriminate between their inhabitants except upon some reasonable differentiation fairly related to the object of regulation. This equality is not merely abstract justice. The framers of the Constitution knew, and we should not forget today, that there is no more effective practical guaranty against arbitrary and unreasonable government than to require that the principles of law which officials would impose upon a minority must be imposed generally. Conversely, nothing opens the door to arbitrary action so effectively as to allow those officials to pick and choose only a few to whom they will apply legislation and thus to escape the political retribution that might be visited upon them if larger numbers were affected. Courts can take no better measure to assure that laws will be just than to require that laws be equal in operation.

This case affords an illustration. Even casual observations from the sidewalks of New York will show that an ordinance which would forbid all advertising on vehicles would run into conflict with many interests, including some, if not all, of the great metropolitan newspapers, which use that advertising extensively. Their blandishment of the latest sensations is not less a cause of diverted attention and traffic hazard than the commonplace cigarette advertisement which this truck-owner is forbidden to display. But any regulation applicable to all such advertising would require much clearer justification in local conditions to enable its enactment than does some regulation applicable to a few. I do not mention this to criticize the motives of those who enacted this ordinance, but it dramatizes the point that we are much more likely to find arbitrariness in the regulation of the few than of the many. Hence, for my part, I am more receptive to attack on local ordinances for denial of equal protection than for denial of due process, while the Court has more often used the latter clause.

In this case, if the City of New York should assume that display of any advertising on vehicles tends and intends to distract the attention of persons using the highways and to increase the dangers of its traffic, I should think it fully within its constitutional powers to forbid it all. The same would be true if the City should undertake to eliminate or minimize the hazard by any generally applicable restraint, such as limiting the size, color, shape or perhaps to some extent the contents of vehicular advertising. Instead of such general regulation of advertising, however, the City seeks to reduce the hazard only by saying that while some may, others may not exhibit such appeals. The same display, for example, advertising cigarettes, which this appellant is forbidden to carry on its trucks, may be carried on the trucks of a cigarette dealer and might on the trucks of this appellant if it dealt in cigarettes. And almost an identical advertisement, certainly one of equal size, shape, color and appearance, may be carried by this appellant if it proclaims its own offer to transport cigarettes. But it may not be carried so long as the message is not its own but a cigarette dealer's offer to sell the same cigarettes. * * *

The question in my mind comes to this. Where individuals contribute to an evil or danger in the same way and to the same degree, may those who do so for hire be prohibited, while those who do so for their own commercial ends but not for hire be allowed to continue? I think the answer has to be that the hireling may be put in a class by himself and may be dealt with differently than those who act on their own. But this is not merely because such a discrimination will enable the lawmaker to diminish the evil. That might be done by many classifications, which I should think wholly unsustainable. It is rather because there is a real difference between doing in self-interest and doing for hire, so that it is one thing to tolerate action from those who act on their own and it is another thing to permit the same action to be promoted for a price.

NOTES ON RAILWAY EXPRESS AND THE RATIONAL-BASIS STANDARD

1. *Some Rational Basics.* Any equal protection standard evaluating whether there is a rational basis for a classification must somehow identify a goal for the statute and decide whether the means chosen in the statute to effectuate that goal are rational. This is simply a much weaker form of means/ends scrutiny than the strict scrutiny applied to racial discrimination (which we analyzed in means/ends terms in the notes following *Loving* in Chapter 3). The Court has phrased the standard for minimal equal protection scrutiny in a variety of ways. A weak formulation is found in *Lindsley v. Natural Carbonic Gas Co.*, 220 U.S. 61 (1911):

> 1.   The equal protection clause * * * does not take from the State the power to classify in the adoption of police laws, but admits the exercise of a wide scope of discretion in that regard, and avoids what is done only when it is without any reasonable basis and therefore is purely arbitrary. 2. A classification having some rational basis does not offend against that clause merely because it is not made with mathematical nicety or because in practice it results in some inequality. 3. When the classification in such a law is called in question, if any state of facts reasonably can be conceived that would sustain it, the existence of that state of facts at the time the law was

enacted must be assumed. 4. One who assails the classification in such a law must carry the burden of showing that it does not rest upon any reasonable basis, but is essentially arbitrary.

A stronger standard is set forth in *Royster Guano Co. v. Virginia*, 253 U.S. 412 (1920):

> The classification must be reasonable, not arbitrary and must rest upon some ground of difference having a fair and substantial relation to the object of the legislation, so that all persons similarly circumstanced shall be treated alike.

Note some of the important differences in these formulations, as well as some broader possibilities. *Goals*: Should any goal or end for the statute suffice, even one dreamed up by counsel, after the fact, to put a good face on the statute? Or should the Court consider only the goal the legislature actually had in mind? How can the Court determine the actual goal? Should the Court require the legislature to say what the goal is? *Means*: May counsel, after the fact, justify the means chosen by pointing to evidence not before the legislature? Is it enough to find some minimal rational connection between goals and means, or must the rationality of the statute be substantial?

2. *Theories of Economic Legislation and Judicial Review. Railway Express* is a lenient (minimalist) application of the rational-basis test, upholding an ordinance that was highly underinclusive and entailed lines drawn to avoid hurting powerful interests. Whether such a lenient approach is defensible depends upon theories of legislation as well as judicial review. Consider some possibilities:

(a) *Public-Spirited Legislatures and Cautious Courts.* Most of the *Railway Express* Justices seemed to be optimistic that legislatures would deliberate in the public interest most of the time and skeptical that courts were institutionally competent to second-guess most policy judgments made by legislatures. This is the legal process vision that prevailed during the New Deal and is still influential today.[5]

(b) *Unprincipled Legislatures and Cautious Courts.* Justice Jackson took a more beady-eyed view of the legislature in this case, viewing the ordinance as a political compromise, whereby lines were drawn to exempt powerful interests from regulation. A cautious court would still uphold such a regulation, as Jackson did, because there are no principles by which the court can draw better lines, and dealmaking among interest groups is part of the normal political process. Pure policy decisions and line-drawing—including special interest deals and compromises—should be left to the legislature.[6]

(c) *Rent-Seeking Legislatures and Representation-Reinforcing Courts.* According to public choice theory (Chapter 2, § 3B), many laws are not just

---

[5] See Henry Hart, Jr. & Albert Sacks, *The Legal Process: Materials on the Making and Application of Law* (William Eskridge, Jr. & Philip Frickey eds. 1994) (1958 tent. ed.).

[6] See Alexander Bickel, *The Least Dangerous Branch: The Supreme Court at the Bar of Politics* (1962).

deals, but are "rent-seeking" distributions of public funds or authority to special interest groups without a public-regarding justification. The New York law might have drawn its regulatory lines to provide a competitive advantage for local companies over interstate ones, for example. A court following Ely's representation-reinforcing theory (Chapter 2, § 3B) might consider rent-seeking laws to be political dysfunctions which independent courts could correct.[7]

3. *Equal Protection Scrutiny: An Underenforced Constitutional Norm?* In economic regulation cases, the Court usually finds a way to uphold the regulation in question.[8] The Court has upheld some apparent special-interest laws by deploying the rational basis test in a highly lenient manner: (a) accepting counsel's post-hoc justifications or supplying the Court's own "plausible reasons" for the legislature's line-drawing, *e.g., United States Railroad Retirement Bd. v. Fritz*, 449 U.S. 166 (1980); *Williamson v. Lee Optical*, 348 U.S. 483 (1955); (b) deferring to legislative assertion of an "at least debatable" connection between a legitimate end and the means chosen by the legislature, *e.g., Minnesota v. Clover Leaf Creamery Co.*, 449 U.S. 456 (1981); and (c) accepting "administrative convenience" or general "public sentiment" as a rational state goal.

Recent formulations of the standard of review reflect the expectation of substantial deference. For example, in *Federal Communications Commission v. Beach Communications, Inc.*, 508 U.S. 307 (1993), the Court upheld federal regulation of cable and satellite television that exempted certain types of buildings from franchising requirements. In doing so, the Court noted that review of economic regulation should generally be a "paradigm of restraint." Such regulation, the Court noted, is to be upheld if there is "any reasonably conceivable state of affairs that could provide a rational basis for the classification" because "the Constitution presumes that, absent some reason to infer antipathy, even improvident decisions will eventually be rectified by the democratic process." Although the many decisions in this area are not easy to aggregate into any simple test, perhaps at a minimum they stand for the proposition that equal protection in the economic arena is an "underenforced constitutional norm."[9] Under this view, state officials, who are duty-bound to follow the federal Constitution, are required by the Equal Protection Clause to treat similarly situated people similarly with respect to all manner of

---

[7] Other approaches along these lines are animated by republican theory. See, e.g., Bruce Ackerman, *Beyond* Carolene Products, 98 Harv. L. Rev. 713 (1985); Cass Sunstein, *Interest Groups in American Law*, 38 Stan. L. Rev. 29 (1985).

[8] For the occasional modern exception, see *Metropolitan Life Ins. Co. v. Ward*, 470 U.S. 869 (1985) (impermissible for state to encourage growth of in-state insurance industry by taxing in-state companies at much lower rate than out-of-state companies doing business in state); *Logan v. Zimmerman Brush Co.*, 455 U.S. 422 (1982) (irrational for statute to bar employment discrimination complaint simply because state agency with which complaint was filed did not schedule hearing before statutory time period for relief expired).

[9] See Lawrence Sager, *Fair Measure: The Legal Status of Underenforced Constitutional Norms*, 91 Harv. L. Rev. 1212 (1978); Stephen Ross, *Legislative Enforcement of Equal Protection*, 72 Minn. L. Rev. 311 (1987). Much the same point could be made about the discriminatory-intent requirement of *Washington v. Davis*, 426 U.S. 229 (1976) (Chapter 3, § 1B).

regulation, including economic. Federal judges should not, however, second-guess state officials concerning economic regulation, both for normative reasons (the latter, but not the former, are elected) and for practical reasons (the difficulty of developing workable standards for evaluating and enforcing equal protection in the sphere of economic regulation). Under this construct, one might say that the New York officials might have acted unconstitutionally in imposing the regulation in *Railway Express*, but the Supreme Court properly refused to invalidate it.

One reason for underenforcing the rationality norm is federalism: National courts should defer to local regulations not having interstate ramifications. In that event, state courts might—and in fact often do—apply rational-basis review with greater bite to state legislation under state, rather than federal, constitutional law.[10] Thus, the New York courts could apply the state constitutional protections against arbitrary legislative line-drawing with more bite than the U.S. Supreme Court did in *Railway Express*.

Another reason for underenforcing the rationality norm is that it might often duplicate routine review of administrative decisions. For example, when a zoning variance is denied, the property owner may be able to identify seemingly similar properties that were allowed a similar variance. Is it possible to distinguish honest but inept or arbitrary state or local administrative decisions, for which the remedy perhaps should simply be found under state law, from violations of the constitutional rationality requirement? In *Village of Willowbrook v. Olech*, 528 U.S. 562 (2000) (*per curiam*), which involved local zoning, the Court concluded that its decisions:

> [H]ave recognized successful equal protection claims brought by a 'class of one,' where the plaintiff alleges that she has been intentionally treated differently from others similarly situated and that there is no rational basis for the difference in treatment. In so doing, we have explained that 'the purpose of the equal protection clause * * * is to secure every person within the State's jurisdiction against intentional and arbitrary discrimination, whether occasioned by express terms of a statute or by its improper execution through duly constituted agents.' "

The Court did not address an alternative theory advanced by the Court of Appeals, which relied upon plaintiff's allegation that the local officials had been motivated solely by a spiteful effort to "get" her. Justice Breyer, concurring in the judgment, stressed that this additional factor of illegitimate animus was "sufficient to minimize any concern about transforming run-of-the-mill zoning cases into cases of constitutional right."

---

[10] See William Brennan, *State Constitutions and the Protection of Individual Rights*, 90 Harv. L. Rev. 489 (1977); *Developments in the Law—The Interpretation of State Constitutional Rights*, 95 Harv. L. Rev. 1324, 1463–93 (1982).

PROBLEM 4-1:
APPLYING RATIONAL-BASIS SCRUTINY TO DRIVER'S LICENSING

Under the cases you have read thus far, including the cases in Chapters 2 and 3, is it a denial of the equal protection of the laws if the state forbids issuance of a driver's license to:

(a)   any person on public welfare or with an income at a defined poverty level, based upon a statistical showing that such persons have been engaged in a disproportionate number of auto accidents;

(b)   men under the age of 18 and women under the age of 16, with the sex differential based upon insurance studies showing that young men aged 16–18 are two times more likely than young women aged 16–18 to have a serious auto accident;

(c)   any person who is not an American citizen, based upon a legislative finding that such people are not as likely to understand English (needed to read road signs, etc.);

(d)   gay men and lesbians, based upon the announced legislative policy to discourage and not to "promote the homosexual lifestyle" in the state;

(e)   any person who has ever had a diagnosed instance of epilepsy or "any mental disease or emotional disturbance," based upon a legislative finding that such people are more likely to cause accidents;

(f)   any person who was "born out of wedlock," based upon a legislative policy to encourage people to procreate within the institution of marriage.

Work through each of these exclusions, with an eye toward whether each policy meets the rational basis test of *Railway Express* and *Beach Communications* (addressed in note 3, above). Should some of the classifying criteria used be subjected to a stricter examination? How does the array of results you reach fit together? The remainder of this chapter describes some of the lines the Supreme Court has drawn.

NOTE ON THE COURT'S APPLICATION OF HEIGHTENED SCRUTINY TO NON-RACE CLASSIFICATIONS: A "DOUBLE STANDARD"?

Gerald Gunther wrote in 1972 that the Supreme Court had developed a "double standard" in equal protection cases: easy-to-pass rational-basis review for economic and most other classifications, contrasted with automatically lethal strict scrutiny for race, ethnicity, and a few other classifications.[11] Under such an approach, the key was whether a classification triggered strict rather than rational basis scrutiny. Accordingly, lawyers petitioned the Court to recognize other classifications as similarly "suspect." Consider the Court's

---

[11] Gerald Gunther, *The Supreme Court, 1971 Term—Foreword: In Search of Evolving Doctrine on a Changing Court: A Model for a Newer Equal Protection*, 86 Harv. L. Rev. 1 (1972).

analysis of the following classifications, and see if criteria emerge that justify elevating a classification to strict scrutiny (also, revisit your answers to Problem 4-1).

1. *Alienage.* Under longstanding precedent, the federal authority over foreign relations and immigration has included nearly plenary power over "aliens." Thus, federal regulation of noncitizens is ordinarily subject at most to the most lenient rationality review when challenged on equal protection grounds.[12] For the same federal plenary authority reasons, however, the states have less justification for treating noncitizens differently from citizens, and the Supreme Court has reviewed their discriminations more strictly.[13] In *Graham v. Richardson*, 403 U.S. 365 (1971), the Court held that states could not, without substantial justification, deny welfare benefits to noncitizens lawfully present in the country. "[C]lassifications based on alienage, like those based on nationality or race, are inherently suspect and subject to close judicial scrutiny. Aliens as a class are a prime example of a 'discrete and insular' minority (see *Carolene Products* n.4) for whom such heightened judicial solicitude is appropriate."[14]

After *Graham*, the Court struck down across-the-board rules excluding all noncitizens from employment in the state civil service, *Sugarman v. Dougall*, 413 U.S. 634 (1973), and from admission to the state bar, *In re Griffiths*, 413 U.S. 717 (1973). The Court has backed away from strict-meaning-fatal scrutiny in this context, however. States are allowed to bar noncitizens from certain state positions that are involved in the governance or functioning of the state as a political entity. In *Foley v. Connelie*, 435 U.S. 291 (1978), for example, the Court upheld a state law excluding noncitizens from the state police force.[15] Although the noncitizen cases are not easy to aggregate into any simple formula, it appears that the Court has attempted to apply a pragmatic

---

[12] See, e.g., *Mathews v. Diaz*, 426 U.S. 67 (1976). Cf. *Hampton v. Mow Sun Wong*, 426 U.S. 88 (1976) (invalidating Civil Service Commission bar to federal employment of noncitizens on ground that only President or Congress is institutionally competent to make such policy judgments; after the Court's decision, President issued a similar bar, which was upheld by the lower courts).

[13] In *Oyama v. California*, 332 U.S. 633 (1948), and *Takahashi v. Fish & Game Comm'n*, 334 U.S. 410, 420 (1948), the Court struck down California statutes discriminating against aliens and their children. For theoretical support of the Court's higher standard for reviewing state alienage classifications, see Gerald Neuman, *Aliens as Outlaws: Government Services, Proposition 187, and the Structure of Equal Protection Doctrine*, 42 UCLA L. Rev. 1425 (1995); Michael Wishnie, *Laboratories of Bigotry? Devolution of the Immigration Power, Equal Protection and Federalism*, 76 NYU L. Rev. 493 (2001); Note, *The Equal Treatment of Aliens: Preemption or Equal Protection?*, 31 Stan. L. Rev. 1069 (1979).

[14] Louis Lusky, the law clerk who drafted the celebrated footnote four in *Carolene Products*, believed that noncitizens are not discrete and insular minorities because "many of them, who are anglophones, pass unnoticed, and many if not most others fit into the social scene with little difficulty." Lusky, *Footnote Redux: A* Carolene Products *Reminiscence*, 82 Colum. L. Rev. 1093, 1105 n.72 (1982).

[15] Other such decisions upholding exclusionary state laws include *Cabell v. Chavez-Salido*, 454 U.S. 432 (1982) (probation officers); *Ambach v. Norwick*, 441 U.S. 68 (1979) (public school teachers). Compare *Bernal v. Fainter*, 467 U.S. 216 (1984) (striking down requirement that notary public be citizen because official functions are clerical and do not go "to the heart of representative government").

distinction between state statutes that are economically protectionist—that reserve economic benefits for citizens (*Graham*)—and ones that are deemed to be rationally related to reserving sovereign functions for citizens (*Foley*).

2. *Birth Outside Marriage.* Historically, many state laws have treated children born outside of marriage less favorably than marital children, particularly in such areas as inheritance rights. Beginning in 1968, when the Court struck down two Louisiana statutes, *Levy v. Louisiana*, 391 U.S. 68 (1968) (equal protection violated when state allowed marital, but not nonmarital, child to sue for damages for wrongful death of mother); *Glona v. American Guarantee & Liability Ins. Co.*, 391 U.S. 73 (1968) (equal protection violated when state allowed parent to sue for wrongful death of marital, but not nonmarital, child), something more than *Railway Express* rationality review has been applied to classifications based upon parental status. The Court has rejected the argument that statutes penalizing a child for the status of her parents are a justified means of encouraging marriage. "[N]o child is responsible for his birth and penalizing the illegitimate child is an ineffective— as well as an unjust—way of deterring the parent." *Weber v. Aetna Casualty & Surety Co.*, 406 U.S. 164 (1972). In essence, the decisions are based on the premise that persons born outside of marriage have suffered from irrational societal prejudice that imposes burdens upon them bearing no relation to their own responsibility or wrongdoing.

The more recent precedents apply an "intermediate" level of scrutiny, *e.g., Clark v. Jeter*, 486 U.S. 456 (1988). The Court's path has been anything but straightforward, and it has upheld some distinctions between children of marital and nonmarital birth. A common problem has concerned the situation where a man dies intestate (without a will) and someone comes forward and claims to be his child for purposes of inheriting his property. The Court has held that a state may not categorically deny intestate inheritance to children born out of marriage, *Trimble v. Gordon*, 430 U.S. 762 (1977), but may limit intestate inheritance to persons who, during the life of the deceased, were adjudged by a state court to be his children, *Lalli v. Lalli*, 439 U.S. 259 (1978).

3. *Age.* Age is different in nature from other potentially sensitive equal protection classifications: Everybody is young once, and—notwithstanding 1960s rock music dictum to the contrary—few hope to die before they get old. But the very young are formally politically powerless (they have no vote), and there is a history of discrimination against older workers, who have suffered the loss of employment to make way for younger, more modestly paid substitutes. On the other hand, some elderly persons—such as many federal judges and members of Congress—wield considerable power, and in recent years groups such as the American Association of Retired Persons have lobbied effectively in Congress and the state legislatures.

The Court has been unwilling to apply any form of heightened scrutiny to age classifications. It has upheld mandatory retirement laws for state and federal employees. See *Massachusetts Board of Retirement v. Murgia*, 427 U.S. 307 (1976) (upholding 50-year-old retirement age for state police); *Vance v.*

Bradley, 440 U.S. 93 (1979) (upholding 60-year-old retirement age for federal foreign service personnel).[16] More recently, the Court found no equal protection violation in a municipal ordinance that allowed only persons between the ages of fourteen and eighteen to be admitted to certain dance halls. *Dallas v. Stanglin*, 490 U.S. 19 (1989). See also *Kimel v. Florida Board of Regents*, 528 U.S. 62 (2000) (applying the *Murgia* principle to limit Congress's Fourteenth Amendment authority to "enforce" norms against age discrimination).

United States Department of Agriculture v. Moreno

413 U.S. 528 (1973)

The Food Stamp Act of 1964, as amended in 1971, 84 Stat. 2048, created a program of subsidized food for the poor. Excluded from participation was any household containing an individual unrelated to any other member of the household. Ermina Sanchez and her three children were threatened with termination of the food stamps they needed, because they shared their home with Jacinta Moreno, a 56-year-old diabetic whom Sanchez cared for. The Court, in an opinion by **Justice Brennan**, held that the "statutory classification (households of related persons versus households containing one or more unrelated persons) is clearly irrelevant to the stated purposes of the Act," which were to assure minimal nutrition and alleviate hunger, as well as distribution of agricultural surpluses. 7 U.S.C. § 2011.

The legislative history suggested that the 1971 amendment was meant to prevent "hippie communes" from taking advantage of the food stamp program, but Justice Brennan ruled that this was an impermissible purpose. "For if the constitutional conception of 'equal protection of the laws' means anything, it must at the very least mean that a bare congressional desire to harm a politically unpopular group cannot constitute a *legitimate* government interest." Justice Brennan rejected government arguments that the classification was an effort to regulate morality, for that would raise serious constitutional problems under the right to privacy (Chapter 5, § 4), or to prevent fraud, for the classification would have been very under-as well as overinclusive for such a purpose.

Justice Rehnquist, joined by **Chief Justice Burger**, dissented. They found the classification not quite so irrational as the Court did and pointed to *Dandridge v. Williams*, 397 U.S. 471 (1970), where the Court upheld a state limit on the amount of welfare a single family could receive. The limit upheld

---

[16] In *Murgia*, the Court explained that "unlike, say, those who have been discriminated against on the basis of race or national origin," the aged "have not experienced a 'history of purposeful unequal treatment' or been subjected to unique disabilities on the basis of stereotyped characteristics not truly indicative of their abilities." Moreover, "old age does not define a 'discrete and insular' group, *Carolene Products* n.4, in need of 'extraordinary protection from the majoritarian political process.' Instead, it marks a stage that each of us will reach if we live out our normal span." The federal Age Discrimination in Employment Act of 1967, as amended, 29 U.S.C. § 621 et seq., provides statutory protection against age discrimination in the workplace. In some senses, *Murgia* is like *Washington v. Davis* (Chapter 3, § 1B), in that both cases refused to adopt stringent constitutional approaches to employment discrimination when Congress had already statutorily addressed the problem to some extent.

in *Dandridge* burdened large families in a similar way that the limit struck down in *Moreno* disadvantaged unrelated families, and for a similar rational basis: conservation of scarce state monies allocated for helping poor people. How can *Moreno* and *Dandridge* be reconciled?[17] Note that these cases illustrate a broader equal protection puzzle: What *conditions* can *constitutionally* be imposed upon the receipt of government benefits?

SECTION 2. SEX- AND GENDER-BASED DISCRIMINATION

Law has long treated women differently from men. For most of our history this has not been considered constitutionally problematic, but viewed as justified by differences between men and women rooted in biology and social roles. This traditional "jurisprudence of difference" was the basis for the Court's early application of the Fourteenth Amendment to statutes making sex-based distinctions (Part A).

In the last hundred years many women's rights advocates have argued for a "jurisprudence of equal treatment," which posits that men and women, as equal citizens of this country, are entitled to be treated by precisely the same legal rules. Part B traces the impact of this line of thought upon equal protection doctrine, which in the 1970s began to scrutinize gender-based discrimination more strictly and to invalidate such statutes. Many of the Supreme Court cases invalidated statutes that seemingly gave women advantages over men.

Throughout the last century, some women's rights advocates have questioned the jurisprudence of sameness, on the ground that by seeking to treat women the "same" as men, the jurisprudence accepts "men" as the norm and perpetuates structural inequality between women and men in American society. Recent theorists have worked toward a new "jurisprudence of difference," which rejects the fundamental structure of equal protection law ("similarly situated" women must be treated the same as men) and argues for a new constitutional baseline where women actually enjoy the equal *protection* of the laws. Part C summarizes this line of theory and contrasts it with the jurisprudence of formal equality.

A. WOMEN OUTSIDE THE CONSTITUTION: THE TRADITIONAL JURISPRUDENCE OF DIFFERENCE

The role of women in colonial society was not an elevated one. They had no right to vote, did not serve on juries, had few economic rights if they were married, and were assigned economic and family roles that were rarely better than drudgery. From the birth of our nation, some women have had a vision of a different society. In 1776, for example, Abigail Adams

---

[17] For one effort at reconciliation, see Lynn Baker, *The Prices of Rights: Toward a Positive Theory of Unconstitutional Conditions*, 75 Cornell L. Rev. 1185 (1990).

urged her husband John to "Remember the Ladies, and be more generous and favourable to them than your ancestors," in crafting laws for the emerging republic. "Do not put such unlimited power into the hands of the Husbands. Remember all Men would be tyrants if they could. If particular care and attention is not paid to the Ladies we are determined to foment a Rebellion, and will not hold ourselves bound by any laws in which we have no voice, or Representation."[18] Within months of this letter, the Continental Congress adopted the Declaration of Independence and its precept that "all men are created equal." The "Ladies" were not "Remembered."

The Constitution and the Bill of Rights were little more sensitive to the political rights of women, though they were written in a gender-neutral fashion that assured some formal rights to women as well as men. For example, women as well as men were assured freedom of religion by the First Amendment. On the other hand, the background assumption, completely unchanged by the Constitution, was that women were not part of the public citizenry. They were considered submerged in the family unit headed by the husband.[19] Like slaves and poor men, women were not entitled to vote.

Notwithstanding their subordination in both the family and the polity, women in the early United States (especially those in the upper classes) asserted their personal and political rights against the traditional claims of their "inferiority."[20] Women gained important political experience as leaders in the abolitionist and temperance movements of the early and mid-nineteenth century. Leaders included Lucretia Mott, Elizabeth Cady Stanton, and Harriet Tubman in the abolitionist movement and Susan B. Anthony in the temperance movement. Led by Mott and Stanton, an assembly of women and men at Seneca Falls, New York (Stanton's home) issued a "Declaration of Sentiments" on July 19, 1848, which asserted the formal human equality of men and women (tracking the language of the Declaration of Independence but expanding it to include women) and

---

[18] Letter from Abigail Adams to John Adams (March 31, 1776), in 1 *Adams Family Correspondence* 369–71 (L. Butterfield ed. 1963). John treated it as a lark: "As to your extraordinary Code of Laws, I cannot but laugh. We have been told that our Struggle has loosened the bands of Government every where. That Children and Apprentices were disobedient—that schools and Colleges were grown turbulent—that Indians slighted their Guardians and Negroes grew insolent to their Masters. But your Letter was the first Intimation that another Tribe more numerous and powerful than all the rest were grown discontented.—This is rather too coarse a Compliment but you are so saucy, I wont blot it out." Letter from John Adams to Abigail Adams (Apr. 14, 1776), in *id.* at 381. Abigail replied: "[W]hilst you are proclaiming peace and good will to Men, Emancipating all Nations, you insist upon retaining an absolute power over Wives. But you must remember that Arbitrary power is like most other things which are very hard, very liable to be broken * * *." Letter from Abigail Adams to John Adams (May 7, 1776), in *id.* at 401.

[19] See Sir William Blackstone, *Commentaries on the Laws of England* book I, ch. XV (1765) (no separate legal existence of wife apart from her husband). On the confining features of early marriage law, see Nancy Cott, *Public Vows: A History of Marriage and the Nation* 9–55 (2000).

[20] See, e.g., Mary Wollstonecraft, *Vindication of the Rights of Women* (1792); Sarah Grimke, *Letters on the Equality of the Sexes* (1838).

protested the "entire disenfranchisement of one-half the people of this country."

Although women were among the leading abolitionists, and many abolitionist leaders such as Stanton and Frederick Douglass called for suffrage for women as well as the former slaves, the male chiefs of the movement abandoned female suffrage after the Civil War and focused their attention on the former *male* slaves. Thus the Fifteenth Amendment to the Constitution said nothing about women's right to vote, and § 2 of the Fourteenth Amendment explicitly wrote "male" into the Constitution. Bitterly disappointed by the betrayal of their supposed male abolitionist and Republican allies, Anthony and Stanton emerged as voices urging women to take direct action against oppression. "Reconstruction politics shattered feminists' dependence on abolitionism and opened the way for woman suffrage to develop into an organized movement of women, ultimately one of mass proportions."[21] It took a half century for that movement to find its way into the Constitution (the Nineteenth Amendment (1920)) and a century for it to be reflected in Supreme Court opinions concerning the Fourteenth Amendment (*Reed v. Reed* (1971)). Consider the inauspicious beginnings.

Bradwell v. Illinois

83 U.S. (16 Wall.) 130 (1873)

Myra Bradwell's application for a license to practice law had been denied by the Illinois Supreme Court solely because she was a married woman. The U.S. Supreme Court affirmed this judgment with only one dissent.[22] **Justice Miller**'s opinion for the majority addressed Bradwell's argument that she was denied a constitutional "privilege or immunity": Because Bradwell was a citizen of Illinois, the Privileges and Immunities Clause of Article IV was inapplicable to her claim; because admission to the bar of a state is not one of the privileges and immunities of United States citizenship, the Fourteenth Amendment (as interpreted in *The Slaughter House Cases* (Chapter 5, § 1), decided the day before) did not secure the asserted right either.   *pre-incorporation*

Justice Bradley, who dissented in *The Slaughter House Cases*, concurred in the judgment on broader grounds, reflecting a theory of gender:

> [T]he civil law, as well as nature herself, has always recognized a wide difference in the respective spheres and destinies of man and woman. Man is, or should be, woman's protector and defender. The natural and proper timidity and delicacy which belongs to the female sex evidently unfits it for many of the occupations of civil life. The constitution of the family organization, which is founded in the divine ordinance, as well as in the nature of things, indicates the domestic

---

[21] See, e.g., id.

[22] Bradwell was subsequently admitted to the Illinois bar anyway, by additional legislation.

sphere as that which properly belongs to the domain and functions of womanhood. The harmony, not to say identity, of interests and views which belong, or should belong, to the family institution is repugnant to the idea of a woman adopting a distinct and independent career from that of her husband. So firmly fixed was this sentiment in the founders of the common law that it became a maxim of that system of jurisprudence that a woman had no legal existence separate from her husband. * * *

It is true that many women are unmarried and not affected by any of the duties, complications, and incapacities arising out of the married state, but these are exceptions to the general rule. The paramount destiny and mission of woman are to fulfil the noble and benign offices of wife and mother. This is the law of the Creator. And the rules of civil society must be adapted to the general constitution of things, and cannot be based upon exceptional cases.

The humane movements of modern society, which have for their object the multiplication of avenues for woman's advancement, and of occupations adapted to her condition and sex, have my heartiest concurrence. But I am not prepared to say that it is one of her fundamental rights and privileges to be admitted into every office and position, including those which require highly special qualifications and demanding special responsibilities. In the nature of things it is not every citizen of every age, sex, and condition that is qualified for every calling and position. It is the prerogative of the legislator to prescribe regulations founded on nature, reason, and experience for the due admission of qualified persons to professions and callings demanding special skill and confidence. This fairly belongs to the police power of the State; and, in my opinion, in view of the peculiar characteristics, destiny, and mission of woman, it is within the province of the legislature to ordain what offices, positions, and callings shall be filled and discharged by men, and shall receive the benefit of those energies and responsibilities, and that decision and firmness which are presumed to predominate in the sterner sex.

In *Minor v. Happersett*, 88 U.S. (21 Wall.) 162 (1874), the Supreme Court ruled that the right to vote was not among the "privileges and immunities of United States citizenship." Consequently, the states were not inhibited by the Constitution from committing "that important trust to men alone." But the Court also said that women are "persons" and may be "citizens" within the meaning of the Fourteenth Amendment. In 1878, the National Women's Suffrage Association voted to fight for a constitutional amendment assuring women the right to vote. For the next two generations, feminists campaigned for such an amendment, arguing that women ought to be considered autonomous and equal citizens—a norm requiring that they be given the right to vote.[23] Opponents argued that (1) women were not in fact autonomous and ought to be happy ruling over their natural province, the domestic sphere (the Bradley stance in *Bradwell*); (2) recognition of women's citizenship by assuring women the right to vote would undermine the family and introduce discord into husband-wife relations; and (3) the normative arguments were best resolved on a state-by-state basis rather than by a blanket national constitutional rule. After decades of debate, Congress propounded the Nineteenth Amendment, and three-quarters of the states ratified it in 1920.

At the same time women were seeking the right to vote, they were petitioning the Supreme Court for interpretations of the Due Process and Equal Protection Clauses protecting against sex-exclusionary legislation. In this campaign, feminists came up empty-handed; whatever the basis of constitutional challenges, the Court followed the prevailing jurisprudence of difference accepted by the American legal establishment.

Due Process. Most of the due process cases involved industry attacks on legislation providing workplace protections for women. Early in the women's rights movement, Stanton and Anthony had advocated equal pay for equal work, eight-hour days, and better workplace conditions for women, but most legislation "protecting" women in the workplace was adopted for other reasons.[24] Unions sought maximum hour laws for women and children, arguably as a way to prevent women from competing on equal terms with men in the workplace. As a result of this and many other factors, women—who constituted about one-fifth of the workforce at the turn of the century—tended to be segregated into "women's work," jobs reflecting home-based values (teaching and helping, subordinate as well as nurturing).

When Oregon's law setting maximum hours for women was challenged by employers in *Muller v. Oregon*, 208 U.S. 412 (1908), the Supreme Court unanimously upheld the law, based upon the state's important interest in protecting women:

> That woman's physical structure and the performance of maternal functions place her at a disadvantage in the struggle for subsistence is obvious. * * * [B]y abundant testimony of the medical fraternity continuance for a long time on her feet at work, repeating this from day to day, tends to injurious effects upon the body, and as healthy mothers are essential to vigorous offspring, the physical well-being of woman becomes an object of public interest and care in order to preserve the strength and vigor of the race.

---

[23] See Aileen Kraditor, The Ideas of the Woman Suffrage Movement, 1890–1920 (1965); Ellen Carol DuBois, Outgrowing the Compact of the Fathers: Equal Rights, Woman Suffrage, and the United States Constitution, 1820–1878, 74 J. Am. Hist. 836 (1987); Reva Siegel, *She the People: The Nineteenth Amendment, Sex Equality, and the Family*, 115 Harv. L. Rev. 947 (2002).

[24] On women in the workplace, male resistance, and gendered labor laws, see Alice Kessler-Harris, *Out to Work: A History of Wage-Earning Women in the United States* 201–02 (1982); Philip Foner, *Women and the American Labor Movement* (1979); Julie Matthei, *An Economic History of Women in America* (1982); Elizabeth Brandeis, *Labor Legislation*, in 3 *History of Labor in the United States* 462 (John Commons et al. eds. 1935).

Still again, history discloses the fact that woman has always been dependent upon man. * * * As minors * * * she has been looked upon in the courts as needing especial care that her rights may be preserved. * * * Differentiated by these matters from the other sex, she is properly placed in a class by herself, and legislation designed for her protection may be sustained even when like legislation is not necessary for men and could not be sustained. It is impossible to close one's eyes to the fact that she still looks to her brother and depends upon him. * * *

Most middle-class progressive groups applauded the decision in *Muller*, and the National Consumers' League's brief, filed by Louis Brandeis, containing detailed empirical policy arguments became a new standard for influencing the Court (the so-called "Brandeis brief"). Progressives were more ambivalent about decisions upholding other "protective" legislation that effectively closed off employment options for women. See *Radice v. New York*, 264 U.S. 292 (1924) (upholding law forbidding nightwork for waitresses but exempting female entertainers and ladies' room attendants); *Bosley v. McLaughlin*, 236 U.S. 385 (1915) (rejecting challenge by female pharmacist to 8-hour law preventing her employment with hospital).

In the wake of cases like *Radice*, many women came to oppose "protective" legislation, arguing that "unequal wages and bad factory conditions, and not special laws for adult women workers, are the things in which we should all interest ourselves. . . . When we limit women's opportunities to work, we simply create more poverty, and we postpone the day when equal pay for equal work will be universal."[25] They invoked the Nineteenth Amendment's implicit recognition of women's equal citizenship as a basis for criticizing protective legislation. Accepting a Nineteenth Amendment argument made by employers, the Supreme Court in *Adkins v. Children's Hospital*, 261 U.S. 525 (1923), struck down a federal statute fixing minimum wages for women and children in the District of Columbia. Although *Adkins* was primarily a *Lochner*-style liberty of contract decision, it also reflected society's and the Court's tentative movement away from complete acceptance of the separate spheres philosophy and the jurisprudence of natural difference.

Equal Protection. The early equal protection cases generally involved efforts by men to overturn laws that discriminated in favor of women—without success, because of the jurisprudence of difference embedded in *Muller*. For example, in *Quong Wing v. Kirkendall*, 223 U.S. 59 (1912), the Court upheld against equal protection attack a statute that imposed a $10 licensing charge for laundries but exempted any laundry operation of two or fewer women. Justice Holmes wrote for the Court, finding the legislature's "ground of distinction in sex . . . not without precedent," citing *Muller*. "If Montana deems it advisable to put a lighter burden upon women than upon men with regard to an employment that our people commonly regard as more appropriate for the former, the Fourteenth Amendment does not interfere by creating a

---

[25] Views of Rheta Childe Dorr, *Good Housekeeping*, Sept. 1925, at 156 ff.

fictitious equality where there is a real difference." See also *Breedlove v. Suttles*, 302 U.S. 277 (1937) (upholding Georgia statute exempting nonvoting women from state poll tax "[i]n view of burdens necessarily borne by them for the preservation of the race").

Later cases were brought by women seeking to overturn statutes segregating them from job opportunities. There was particular enthusiasm for these efforts after World War II, during which many women moved into the workplace, doing traditionally "men's work" as well as serving in the armed forces. The second wave of feminism began after the war, but the Supreme Court remained deaf to women's voices. For example, in *Goesaert v. Cleary*, 335 U.S. 464 (1948), the Court upheld a statute allowing a woman to work as a bartender only if she was the wife or daughter of the bar owner. *Goesaert* approached the problem as simply a matter of *Railway Express* rationality review: "The fact that women may now have achieved the virtues that men have long claimed as their prerogatives and now indulge in vices that men have long practiced, does not preclude the State from drawing a sharp line between the sexes," certainly in such matters as the regulation of the liquor traffic.[26] The Constitution does not require legislatures to reflect sociological insight, or shifting social standards, any more than it requires them to keep abreast of the latest scientific standards. The Court rejected the sex discrimination claim on the basis of deference (*Railway Express*) rather than the old separate spheres idea (*Muller*).

Also reflecting the erosion of the public separate spheres ideology was erosion in traditional state exclusions of women from jury service. Before World War I, all states excluded women, but as the nation entered World War II, only 13 states required the same jury service of women that they required of men; 15 states allowed women to opt out of compulsory jury service; 20 states disqualified women as a class. After the war, the situation shifted rapidly, and the Supreme Court gave it a push in 1946. Relying on a statute regulating federal jury service, the Court overturned the conviction of defendants, because the federal judge excluded women from the jury venire in *Ballard v. United States*, 329 U.S. 187 (1946). In response to the government's argument that the discrimination was not prejudicial to defendants' jury trial rights, Justice Douglas responded that women and men are "not fungible; a community made up exclusively of one is different from a community composed of both." He then posed the question: "[I]f the shoe were on the other foot, who would claim that a jury was truly representative of the community if all men were intentionally and systematically excluded from the panel?" A Court majority declined to constitutionalize that principle in *Fay v. New York*, 332 U.S. 261 (1947), but four dissenters maintained that a "blue ribbon" jury substantially excluding women and working class people violated the Equal Protection Clause.

---

[26] Note the possible influence of the Twenty-First Amendment, which was later construed as granting the states extraordinary authority, for example, to censor expressive conduct that would otherwise be protected by the First Amendment. See *California v. LaRue*, 409 U.S. 109 (1972).

B. THE JURISPRUDENCE OF EQUAL TREATMENT AND HEIGHTENED SCRUTINY OF SEX-BASED DISTINCTIONS

The erosion of separate spheres was not immediately accompanied by a single positive feminist vision of equal protection. Between 1920 and 1960, the women's rights movement was deeply divided between feminists like Eleanor Roosevelt who accepted natural differences between men and women and supported female-protective legislation, and those who rejected that jurisprudence and insisted on the autonomy of women and their complete equality with men.[27] Feminists and their allies in the latter camp pressed for the adoption of an Equal Rights Amendment, which was first introduced in Congress in 1923 but which made little progress because of the opposition of women and their allies in the former group.

After World War II, political and constitutional activism among women moved slowly toward the full equality stance. Exemplifying this shift was the ACLU's alliance with ERA feminists in the jury cases. By 1961, only three states retained complete exclusions of women from juries, and three others permitted women to serve only if they opted in. Gwendolyn Hoyt killed her husband in Florida, one of the states in the latter group. A jury of 12 men found her guilty of murder, and she appealed on the ground that the Equal Protection Clause prohibited the exclusion of women from the jury that convicted her. Dorothy Kenyon's *amicus* brief for the ACLU (its first in a sex discrimination case) argued that representation on juries is an important civil right, as illustrated by the experience of blacks, who did not achieve genuine citizenship until the Court required that they be invited to its burdens such as jury service. The same was true of women. They continued to be excluded, either by law or in practice, because "the thinking of older times, when women were no part of the body politic" persisted and suggested that jury service would detract from women's "primary duties" of housekeeping and childrearing within the home. This rationale was anachronistic, as "a revolution has taken place in the lives and status of women." Not only was the discrimination against all women therefore unreasonable, but it was a discrimination that the "fully emancipated, fully enfranchised woman citizen" would no longer tolerate.

The Supreme Court unanimously rejected these arguments, holding in *Hoyt v. Florida*, 368 U.S. 57 (1961), that an opt-in system did not clearly discriminate against women's service on juries in the way that the Court had criticized in an earlier statutory case about women and juries. *Hoyt* cast into bold relief the fact that the Supreme Court had never struck down a sex discrimination as unconstitutional. Civil rights activist Pauli Murray

---

[27] See Cynthia Harrison, On Account of Sex: The Politics of Women's Issues, 1945–1968 (1988); Ruth Rosen, The World Split Wide Open: How the Modern Women's Movement Changed America 27, 66 (2000); Verta Taylor, Social Movement Continuity: The Women's Movement in Abeyance, 54 Am. Soc. Rev. 761 (1989).

argued that the Equal Protection Clause could be interpreted to question sex-based discriminations for the same reasons the Court had deployed it against race-based discriminations: Sex discriminations (like race discriminations) rested upon a natural law understanding of "inherent differences" that had been deployed to support disadvantages and the social inferiority of women; the naturalized view of sex differences rested upon unproven stereotypes or myths about women that were usually an irrational basis for subordinating them; like blacks, women needed to mobilize against pervasive state discrimination through the formation of an organization like the NAACP.[28]

Murray's arguments persuaded President Kennedy's Commission on the Status of Women to proclaim that "equality of rights under the law for all persons, male or female, is so basic to democracy and its commitment to the ultimate value of the individual that it must be reflected in the fundamental law of the land." Moreover, Murray's memorandum helped bridge the concerns of various civil rights activists: Her Fourteenth Amendment strategy sought equality for women (desired by liberal ERA feminists), but without sacrificing laws genuinely remedying women's disadvantages in the workplace (desired by labor feminists and ERA opponents). Murray, an African American active in the civil rights movement, also sought to unite blacks and women in a common campaign against prejudice and discrimination.

Murray's arguments found their way into the congressional debates over the addition of "sex discrimination" to the jobs title of the Kennedy Administration's civil rights bill. Although the amendment was propounded by anti-civil rights (but pro-ERA) Representative Howard Smith of Virginia, Murray and other feminists supported it and ensured that it was preserved in the final statute. The EEOC, however, refused to make sex discrimination a priority in its enforcement of the new law, a stance that drew strong protests. When officials ignored their complaints at a 1966 conference on women's status, Murray, Betty Friedan, and other feminists stormed out in protest and founded the National Organization for Women (NOW). The feminist political energy harnessed by NOW sought a relatively unified political agenda: serious enforcement of the Equal Pay Act and Title VII by the EEOC to assure equality in the workplace; liberalization or repeal of restrictive abortion laws; adoption of legislation barring sex discrimination in education, accomplished with the enactment of Title IX in 1972; and adoption of the ERA, which would assure constitutional equality.[29]

---

[28] Pauli Murray, A Proposal to Reexamine the Applicability of the Fourteenth Amendment to State Laws and Practices Which Discriminate on the Basis of Sex Per Se (Dec. 1962), discussed in Harrison, *On Account of Sex* 126–34.

[29] See generally Serena Mayeri, *Constitutional Choices: Legal Feminism and the Historical Dynamics of Change*, 92 Calif. L. Rev. 755, 761–801 (2004).

The last point underscores a conscious decision made by these groups, based upon their experience and upon feminist theory: The jurisprudence of difference embedded in *Bradwell* and *Muller* should be repudiated, because it subordinated women as humans and citizens. Even when gender differences "protected" or "benefitted" women, special treatment of women only perpetuated gender stereotypes of women as the "weaker sex" who need protection at the grace of men. Aside from this critique of the jurisprudence of difference, women's rights groups developed an affirmative vision of equal protection, a "jurisprudence of equal treatment." A good statement of this jurisprudence from one of the main women's rights lawyers of the 1970s is Wendy Webster Williams' article (excerpted immediately below). In the remainder of this part, following the Williams excerpt, we shall trace the Supreme Court's reaction to the various strands of the equal-treatment argument.

WENDY WEBSTER WILLIAMS,
Equality's Riddle: Pregnancy and the Equal Treatment/Special Treatment Debate
13 N.Y.U. Rev. L. & Soc. Change 325, 329–31 (1984–85)[30]

The first proposition essential to this analysis is that sex-based generalizations are generally impermissible whether derived from physical differences such as size and strength, from cultural role assignments such as breadwinner or homemaker, or from some combination of innate and ascribed characteristics, such as the greater longevity of the average woman compared to the average man. Instead of classifying on the basis of sex, lawmakers and employers must classify on the basis of the trait or function or behavior for which sex was used as a proxy. Strength, not maleness, would be the criterion for certain jobs; economic dependency, not femaleness, the criterion for alimony upon divorce. The basis for this proposition is a belief that a dual system of rights inevitably produces gender hierarchy and, more fundamentally, treats women and men as statistical abstractions rather than as persons with individual capacities, inclinations and aspirations—at enormous cost to women and not insubstantial cost to men.

The second essential proposition is that laws and rules which do not overtly classify on the basis of sex, but which have a disproportionately negative effect upon one sex, warrant, under appropriate circumstances, placing a burden of justification upon the party defending the law or rule in court. In the view of its proponents, the proposition is an essential companion to the first proposition and is necessary for the ultimate equality of the sexes. Society has been tailored to predefined sex roles not only through overt gender classifications, but also through laws and rules

---

[30] Reprinted by permission from vol. 13 (1984), N.Y.U. Rev. L. & Soc. Change.

neutral on their face but inspired by the same assumptions, stereotypes and ideologies as sex-based classifications.

The goal of the feminist legal movement that began in the early seventies is not and never was the integration of women into a male world any more than it has been to build a separate but better place for women. Rather, the goal has been to break down the legal barriers that restricted each sex to its predefined role and created a hierarchy based on gender. The ability to challenge covert as well as overt gender sorting laws is essential both for challenging in court a male defined set of structures and institutions and for requiring their reconstitution to reflect the full range of our human concerns. The first proposition (sex classifications are generally impermissible) facilitates the elimination of legislation that overtly classifies by sex. The second proposition (perpetrators of rules with a disparate effect must justify them) provides a doctrinal tool with which to begin to squeeze the male tilt out of a purportedly neutral legal structure and thus substitute genuine for merely formal gender neutrality.

1. From Rational Basis to Intermediate Scrutiny (and Beyond?) in Gender Cases

Like the NAACP before it, NOW established a Legal Defense and Education Fund to litigate issues of women's equality. Also, the ACLU in 1971 established its Women's Rights Project, headed by Ruth Bader Ginsburg. Representing a new generation of litigators, Ginsburg followed Kenyon and Murray in pressing the Court to rule that women should have all the same legal rights and duties as men. These lawyers had filed constitutional challenges to statutory sex discriminations, and state and federal judges found many of the challenged policies unconstitutional—notwithstanding *Hoyt.* E.g., *White v. Crook*, 251 F. Supp. 401 (M.D. Ala. 1966) (three-judge court) (state exclusion of women from juries violates the Equal Protection Clause) (not appealed); *Sail'er Inn, Inc. v. Kirby*, 485 P.2d 529 (Cal. 1971) (applying heightened equal protection scrutiny to exclusion of women from employment as bartenders).

In *Reed v. Reed*, the ACLU attorneys—Kenyon, Murray, and Ginsburg—urged the Court to renounce the constitutional philosophy of *Muller*, *Goesaert*, and *Hoyt.* In their brief, counsel announced that "a new appreciation of women's place has been generated in the United States." Feminists "of both sexes" were pressing for women's "full membership" in the benefits and duties of constitutional citizenship:

> "But the distance to equal opportunity for women—in the face of the pervasive social, cultural, and legal roots of sex-based discrimination—remains considerable. In the absence of a firm constitutional foundation for equal treatment of men and women

by the law, women seeking to be judged on their individual merits will continue to encounter law-sanctioned obstacles."

Accordingly, the ACLU lawyers maintained that sex was a suspect classification for the same reasons race was: Both were natural traits that the dominant culture treated as a badge of inferiority and stigmatized legally, based upon inaccurate stereotypes about the group defined by the trait. Consider the Court's response in *Reed* and in the next case, *Frontiero v. Richardson*, where the ACLU reiterated its arguments for strict scrutiny in an *amicus* brief.

Reed v. Reed

404 U.S. 71 (1971)

Idaho statutes provided a "tie-breaker" preference for males over females of equal degrees of relationship to be appointed to administer an estate. (Thus, a son would be preferred over a daughter to administer a deceased parent's estate.) A unanimous Supreme Court, per **Chief Justice Burger**, struck down the statute under the rational basis standard. The Court relied upon the *Royster Guano* formulation (note 1 following *Railway Express*), under which the classification "must be reasonable, not arbitrary, and must rest upon some ground of difference having a fair and substantial relation to the object of the legislation, so that all persons similarly circumstanced shall be treated alike." The state relied upon the justification of administrative convenience: In general, men are more likely than women to have the sophistication in business affairs needed to administer an estate, and by eliminating one area of controversy where two or more persons seek to be appointed administrator, probate courts avoid time-consuming issues. Rejecting this argument, the Court stated: "To give a mandatory preference to members of either sex over members of the other, merely to accomplish the elimination of hearings on the merits, is to make the very kind of arbitrary legislative choice forbidden by the Equal Protection Clause." *Query*: Is this really an example of *Railway Express* rational-basis scrutiny? Even *Moreno* scrutiny?

FRONTIERO V. RICHARDSON
411 U.S. 677, 93 S.Ct. 1764, 36 L.Ed.2d 583 (1973)

JUSTICE BRENNAN announced the judgment of the Court in an opinion in which **JUSTICE DOUGLAS**, **JUSTICE WHITE**, and **JUSTICE MARSHALL** join.

[Pursuant to 37 U.S.C. §§ 401, 403, and 10 U.S.C. §§ 1072, 1076, a serviceman could claim his wife as a "dependent" without regard to whether she was in fact dependent upon him for any part of her support. A servicewoman, on the other hand, could not claim her husband as a "dependent" under these programs unless he was in fact dependent upon her for over one-half of his support. Rejecting the Frontieros' equal protection attack, the lower court held that Congress might reasonably have concluded that, since the husband in our society is generally the "breadwinner" in the family—and the wife typically the "dependent" partner—"it would be more economical to require married female members claiming husbands to prove actual dependency than to extend the presumption of dependency to such members." The Supreme Court reversed.]

At the outset, appellants contend that classifications based upon sex, like classifications based upon race, alienage, and national origin, are inherently suspect and must therefore be subjected to close judicial scrutiny. We agree and, indeed, find at least implicit support for such an approach in our unanimous decision only last Term in *Reed v. Reed.* [In *Reed*], the Court implicitly rejected appellee's apparently rational explanation of the statutory scheme, and concluded that, by ignoring the individual qualifications of particular applicants, the challenged statute provided "dissimilar treatment for men and women who are . . . similarly situated." The Court therefore held that, even though the State's interest in achieving administrative efficiency "is not without some legitimacy," "[t]o give a mandatory preference to members of either sex over members of the other, merely to accomplish the elimination of hearings on the merits, is to make the very kind of arbitrary legislative choice forbidden by the [Constitution.]" This departure from "traditional" rational-basis analysis with respect to sex-based classifications is clearly justified.

There can be no doubt that our Nation has had a long and unfortunate history of sex discrimination. Traditionally, such discrimination was rationalized by an attitude of "romantic paternalism" which, in practical effect, put women, not on a pedestal, but in a cage. [As an example of such a "paternalistic attitude," Justice Brennan quoted from Justice Bradley's concurring opinion in *Bradwell, supra*.]

As a result of notions such as these, our statute books gradually became laden with gross, stereotyped distinctions between the sexes and, indeed, throughout much of the 19th century the position of women in our society was, in many respects, comparable to that of blacks under the pre-Civil War slave codes. Neither slaves nor women could hold office, serve on juries, or bring suit in their own names, and married women traditionally were denied the legal capacity to hold or convey property or to serve as legal guardians of their own children. And although blacks were guaranteed the right to vote in 1870, women were denied even that right * * * until adoption of the Nineteenth Amendment half a century later.

It is true, of course, that the position of women in America has improved markedly in recent decades. Nevertheless, it can hardly be doubted that, in part because of the high visibility of the sex characteristic, women still face pervasive, although at times more subtle, discrimination in our educational institutions, in the job market and, perhaps most conspicuously, in the political arena.[31]

Moreover, since sex, like race and national origin, is an immutable characteristic determined solely by the accident of birth, the imposition of special disabilities upon the members of a particular sex because of their sex would seem to violate "the basic concept of our system that legal burdens should bear some relationship to individual responsibility. . . ." And what differentiates sex from such non-suspect statuses as intelligence or physical disability, and aligns it with the recognized suspect criteria, is that the sex characteristic frequently bears no relation to ability to perform or contribute to society. As a result, statutory distinctions between the sexes often have the effect of invidiously relegating the entire class of females to inferior legal status without regard to the actual capabilities of its individual members.

We might also note that, over the past decade, Congress has itself manifested an increasing sensitivity to sex-based classifications. In Tit. VII of the Civil Rights Act of 1964, for example, Congress expressly declared that no employer, labor union, or other organization subject to the provisions of the Act shall discriminate against any individual on the basis of "race, color, religion, *sex*, or national origin." Similarly, the Equal Pay Act of 1963 provides that no employer covered by the Act "shall discriminate . . . between employees on the basis of *sex*." And § 1 of the Equal Rights Amendment, passed by Congress on March 22, 1972, and submitted to the legislatures of the States for ratification, declares that "[e]quality of rights under the law shall not be denied or abridged by the United States or by any State on account of sex." Thus, Congress itself has concluded that classifications based upon sex are inherently invidious, and this conclusion of a coequal branch of Government is not without significance to the question presently under consideration. *Cf. Oregon v. Mitchell* (opinion of Brennan, White, and Marshall, JJ.); *Katzenbach v. Morgan* [both cases in Chapter 7, § 3B].

With these considerations in mind, we can only conclude that classifications based upon sex, like classifications based upon race, alienage, or national origin, are inherently suspect, and must therefore be subjected to strict judicial scrutiny. Applying the analysis mandated by that stricter standard of review, it is clear that the statutory scheme now before us is constitutionally invalid.

---

[31] It is true, of course, that when viewed in the abstract, women do not constitute a small and powerless minority. Nevertheless, in part because of past discrimination, women are vastly underrepresented in this Nation's decisionmaking councils. There has never been a female President, nor a female member of this Court. Not a single woman presently sits in the United States Senate, and only 14 women hold seats in the House of Representatives. And, as appellants point out, this underrepresentation is present throughout all levels of our State and Federal Government.

[On their face, the statutes commanded "dissimilar treatment for men and women who are . . . similarly situated," *Reed*, and the government conceded that the differential treatment accorded men and women under these statutes serves no purpose other than mere "administrative convenience." But the government offered no evidence that the differential treatment actually saved it money. "In order to satisfy the demands of strict judicial scrutiny, the Government must demonstrate, for example, that it is actually cheaper to grant increased benefits with respect to *all* male members, than it is to determine which male members are in fact entitled to such benefits and to grant increased benefits only to those members whose wives actually meet the dependency requirement. Here, however, there is substantial evidence that, if put to the test, many of the wives of male members would fail to qualify for benefits." Moreover, administrative convenience, even if established, cannot support a statutory classification under strict scrutiny. "On the contrary, any statutory scheme which draws a sharp line between the sexes, *solely* for the purpose of achieving administrative convenience, necessarily commands 'dissimilar treatment for men and women who are . . . similarly situated,' and therefore involves the 'very kind of arbitrary legislative choice forbidden by the [Constitution]. . . .' *Reed*." Justice Brennan found the statutory policy violative of the equal protection component of the Fifth Amendment.]

JUSTICE STEWART concurring in the judgment, agreed that the statutes before the Court function as an invidious discrimination in violation of the Constitution. *Reed*.

JUSTICE REHNQUIST dissented for the reasons stated by Judge Rives in his opinion for the District Court[.]

JUSTICE POWELL, with whom **THE CHIEF JUSTICE [BURGER]** and **JUSTICE BLACKMUN** join, concurring in the judgment.

I agree that the challenged statutes constitute an unconstitutional discrimination against servicewomen in violation of the Due Process Clause of the Fifth Amendment, but I cannot join the opinion of Justice Brennan, which would hold that all classifications based upon sex, "like classifications based upon race, alienage, and national origin," are "inherently suspect and must therefore be subjected to close judicial scrutiny." It is unnecessary for the Court in this case to characterize sex as a suspect classification, with all of the far-reaching implications of such a holding. *Reed*, which abundantly supports our decision today, did not add sex to the narrowly limited group of classifications which are inherently suspect. In my view, we can and should decide this case on the authority of *Reed* and reserve for the future any expansion of its rationale.

There is another, and I find compelling, reason for deferring a general categorizing of sex classifications as invoking the strictest test of judicial scrutiny. The equal rights amendment, which if adopted will resolve the substance of this precise question, has been approved by the Congress and submitted for ratification by the States. If this Amendment is duly adopted, it will represent the will of the people accomplished in the manner prescribed by the Constitution. By acting prematurely and unnecessarily, as I view it, the Court has assumed a decisional responsibility at the very time when state legislatures, functioning within the traditional democratic process, are debating the proposed Amendment. It seems to me that this reaching out to pre-empt by judicial action a major political decision which is currently in process of resolution does not reflect appropriate respect for duly prescribed legislative processes.

NOTES ON THE RACE ANALOGY AND WHETHER SEX-BASED CLASSIFICATIONS SHOULD BE SUBJECT TO STRICT SCRUTINY

1.   *Objections to the Race-Sex Analogy—and the Issue of Immutability.* Justice Brennan's plurality opinion maintained, as the ACLU had argued, that sex-based classifications are enough "like" race-based classifications to require strict scrutiny; the opinion points to pervasive past and continuing discrimination against women, the immutability of sex, and its typical irrelevance to legitimate state goals. Note, initially, that some feminists believe the ACLU's race analogy was the wrong strategy for arguing women's equality.[32] To begin with, the strategy accepted the traditional equal protection trope that "similarly situated people should be treated similarly." In a society where "man is the measure of all things," this approach unfairly required women to demonstrate that they are "similarly situated" to men and failed to meet women's particular needs. Moreover, women's rights counsel were analogizing sex to race at precisely the point in time when the Court was reinterpreting the race cases to foreclose most constitutional claims based upon the disparate impact of state policies on racial minorities (Chapter 3, § 1B). As Wendy Williams's article emphasized, women's equality required heightened scrutiny of policies not deploying sex-based classifications but still directly affecting women—most notably policies discriminating on the basis of pregnancy. The race analogy undermined women's arguments in the pregnancy cases, as Williams immediately learned in *Geduldig v. Aiello* (§ 2B3 below).

Finally, and perhaps most interestingly, the ACLU and the plurality both emphasized the immutability of sex as a key factor motivating heightened scrutiny. Is immutability a necessary *or* sufficient condition to trigger strict scrutiny? Alienage is not immutable (many aliens can become citizens), yet it had just been recognized as a suspect classification, at least for state laws. Neither the civil rights movement nor the Warren Court gave any emphasis to immutability as a reason to treat race as a suspect classification, and with good reason: Race is not as immutable as some people assume, because one's race

---

[32]   For an excellent analysis of the pitfalls of the race analogy for women's rights, see Serena Mayeri, Note, *"A Common Fate of Discrimination": Race-Gender Analogies in Legal and Historical Perspective*, 110 Yale L.J. 1045 (2001).

depends upon context and the person's presentation. Homer Plessy thought himself "white," but the state deemed him "colored." Nor is immutability a sufficient criterion for strict scrutiny. If it could be shown that most shoplifters act out of an "immutable" compulsion (kleptomania), could they challenge discrimination against them in those criminal laws?

Note how the immutability criterion in *Frontiero* disaggregates *sex* and *gender*. Sex is viewed as natural, prepolitical, *immutable*, while gender is treated as socially created, political, *mutable*. This is a feminist "advance" over the traditional jurisprudence of difference, which viewed both sex and gender as natural and immutable—but why treat sex as immutable?[33] Some transgender persons, for example, feel that their gender identity but not their sex is fixed, and may pursue gender-confirmation procedures, including the possibility of surgery. Is that relevant to thinking about the standard of review for sex discrimination? (Issues relating to gender identity and discrimination are addressed in Problem 4-2). In general, the disaggregation of sex and gender links up with the analytical structure of the Court's cases: A law classifying on the basis of *sex* will be most questionable when it subserves traditional *gender* "stereotypes." How would the Court analyze the issue if it considered *both* sex and gender social constructs?

2. *Original Intent and the De Facto ERA.* The Framers of the Fourteenth Amendment were particularly solicitous of protecting the rights of the former slaves; thus, heightened scrutiny could be limited to classifications based upon race and ethnicity, as the majority suggested in *The Slaughter House Cases*. These Framers turned their backs on their former allies in the women's movement and rejected proposals for "equal treatment" for women. As a matter of original intent, one might argue that the Court should not read extra protections into the Constitution that the Framers considered but left out, nor should the Court overrule precedents without better originalist evidence.[34] Ruth Bader Ginsburg later conceded that "[b]oldly dynamic interpretation, departing radically from the original understanding, is required to tie to the fourteenth amendment's equal protection clause a command that government treat men and women as individuals equal in rights, responsibilities and opportunities."[35] She invoked *Loving v. Virginia* (Chapter 3, § 1A) and *Brown v. Board of Education* (Chapter 2, § 1), to argue that the Equal Protection Clause *should* be dynamically interpreted. Again, note the race-sex analogy and the implicit argument that the Court should update the Constitution to recognize women's full equal citizenship for the same reasons that motivated the Court to recognize the full equal citizenship for people of color. But because the core goal of the Fourteenth Amendment was to assure black people full citizenship, the originalist case for sex

---

[33] See Katherine Franke, *The Central Mistake of Sex Discrimination Law: The Disaggregation of Sex from Gender*, 144 U. Pa. L. Rev. 1 (1995) (detailed critique of this disaggregation).

[34] See Earl Maltz, *Gender Discrimination and the Original Understanding*, 18 Harv. J.L. & Pub. Pol'y 415 (1995).

[35] Ruth Bader Ginsburg, *Sexual Equality under the Fourteenth and Equal Rights Amendments*, 1979 Wash. U.L.Q. 161, 161.

discrimination dynamism is much weaker than that for race discrimination dynamism.

Moreover, the 1789 Framers intended that the mechanism for "updating" the Constitution be the amendment process outlined in Article V, a procedure under way when Ginsburg sought a judicial updating. In 1972, Congress submitted the Equal Rights Amendment (ERA) to the states. Section 1 said: "Equality of rights under the law shall not be denied or abridged by the United States or by any State on account of sex." Within months of its submission, the ERA was ratified by half of the 38 states needed for amendment of the Constitution, but then it became stalled by opposition. In 1978, Congress extended the deadline for ratification until 1982, by which point the ERA still only had 35 of the 38 states needed, and the amendment died. Is it appropriate for the Court to "amend" the Constitution on its own, or anticipate an amendment's passage, while the amendment is pending under the procedures sanctioned by Article V? The four concurring Justices in *Frontiero* thought not; some scholars have concluded that the *Frontiero* plurality's willingness to adopt a "*de facto* ERA" through interpretation is inconsistent with Article V and the rule of law.[36]

Other scholars have been friendly to the Court's creation of a *de facto* ERA.[37] One of us suggests this caveat: there was normative significance to the *reasons* Americans agreed with Phyllis Schlafly and STOP-ERA. Schlafly charged that the ERA would (1) sweep away legislation *protecting* women, including statutory rape laws, labor and tax benefits for working wives and mothers, and exemption from military service; (2) destroy traditional family values by "liberating" husbands from alimony obligations and pregnant women from restrictions on abortion; and (3) impose homosexual marriage and the rest of the "homosexual agenda" on the nation. Most Americans, including most women, did *not* want all the logical consequences of a totally sex-blind jurisprudence, and even ERA supporters denied the ERA would have these effects. Our suggestion is that these counter-arguments molded the Supreme Court's sex discrimination jurisprudence from the very beginning: Unlike in the race cases, where the Court has pressed a colorblind perspective, the Court in the sex cases has allowed a lot of sex-based distinctions, precisely along the lines advocated by Schlafly.[38] Does this hypothesis render the *de facto* ERA more legitimate?

---

[36] E.g., Henry Monaghan, *We the People[s], Original Understanding, and Constitutional Amendment*, 96 Colum. L. Rev. 121 (1996); David Dow, *When Words Mean What We Believe They Say: The Case of Article V*, 76 Iowa L. Rev. 1 (1990). See also Akhil Reed Amar, *The Consent of the Governed: Constitutional Amendment Outside Article V*, 94 Colum. L. Rev. 457 (1994) (Constitution can also be amended by a national referendum).

[37] Michael Dorf, *Equal Protection Incorporation*, 88 Va. L. Rev. 951 (2002); William Eskridge, Jr., *Some Effects of Identity-Based Social Movements on Constitutional Law in the twentieth Century*, 100 Mich. L. Rev. 2062, 2130–38 (2002); Reva Siegel, *Constitutional Culture, Social Movement Conflict and Constitutional Change*, 94 Calif. L. Rev. 1323 (2006); David Strauss, *The Irrelevance of Constitutional Amendments*, 114 Harv. L. Rev. 1457, 1476–78 (2001).

[38] Eskridge, *Identity-Based Social Movements*, 100 Mich. L. Rev. at 2138–56. On the reasons for the ERA's defeat, see Jane Mansbridge, *Why We Lost the ERA* (1986); Donald Mathews & Jane Sherron De Hart, *Sex, Gender, and the Politics of the ERA: A State and the Nation* (1990).

3. *Was There a Political Need for the Court to Intervene? Women as a Discrete and Dispersed Majority.* Recall the *Carolene Products* idea that special constitutional protection might be extended to "discrete and insular minorities" (like blacks) whose problems will not be fairly addressed by a biased political process (Chapter 1, § 6). Women, however, are discrete but not insular (wherever you find men in our society, you also find women) and are certainly not a minority, as they constitute a majority of our population. After the Nineteenth Amendment, women have potentially great political power. Not only does the race-sex analogy break down, but a representation-reinforcing Supreme Court has much less incentive to protect women against discriminations; such problems ought to be remedied in the political process, yes?

John Hart Ely, *Democracy and Distrust: A Theory of Judicial Review* 164–70 (1980), makes these points but notes that women might be appropriate beneficiaries of his representation-reinforcement interpretation of the Constitution (Chapter 2, § 3B). Women have long been victims of laws that reflect invidious stereotypes, many of which were enacted in periods when women had no political representation (before 1920), and even after women could vote their political participation was hampered by the continuing effects of their traditional subordination. Sex discrimination is based upon a "highly visible" trait that "lends itself to a system of thought dominated by stereotype, which automatically consigns an individual to a general category (such as race or gender), often implying the inferiority of the person so categorized."[39]

Conceding all this, Ely argues that women are more than capable of being heard politically, and that if the political process fails to correct such outdated statutes it is more because women as a group are ambivalent about some of them or don't organize against them. Also, the success of the ERA, the adoption of equal rights amendments in sixteen state constitutions, and the enactment of Title VII of the Civil Rights Act and other laws assuring women's rights all suggest that women in the 1960s and 1970s were a political force who overcame the stigmatization of gender stereotypes by their own efforts. Ely's theory suggests that, although "older" statutes (especially those enacted before women had the right to vote) might be strictly scrutinized, newer statutes (such as the one in *Frontiero*, which was adopted in 1967) might be left alone.

CRAIG V. BOREN
429 U.S. 190, 97 S.Ct. 451, 50 L.Ed.2d 397 (1976)

JUSTICE BRENNAN delivered the opinion of the Court.

[An Oklahoma statute prohibited the sale of 3.2% beer to males under the age of 21 and to females under the age of 18; it did not prohibit the possession or consumption of such beer by males aged 18–20. A male in the 18–20 age group and a bar owner filed suit for declaratory and injunctive

---

[39] Kenneth Karst, *The Supreme Court, 1976 Term—Foreword: Equal Citizenship under the Fourteenth Amendment*, 91 Harv. L. Rev. 1, 23 (1977).

relief, alleging that the law was unconstitutional. The three-judge district court upheld the statute.]

Analysis may appropriately begin with the reminder that *Reed* emphasized that statutory classifications that distinguish between males and females are "subject to scrutiny under the Equal Protection Clause." To withstand constitutional challenge, previous cases establish that classifications by gender must serve important governmental objectives and must be substantially related to achievement of those objectives. Thus, in *Reed*, the objectives of "reducing the workload on probate courts" and "avoiding intrafamily controversy" were deemed of insufficient importance to sustain use of an overt gender criterion in the appointment of administrators of intestate decedents' estates. Decisions following *Reed* similarly have rejected administrative ease and convenience as sufficiently important objectives to justify gender-based classifications. *See, e.g., Stanley v. Illinois*, 405 U.S. 645 (1972); *Frontiero; cf. Schlesinger v. Ballard*. And only two Terms ago, *Stanton v. Stanton*, 421 U.S. 7 (1975), expressly stating that *Reed v. Reed* was "controlling," held that *Reed* required invalidation of a Utah differential age-of-majority statute, notwithstanding the statute's coincidence with and furtherance of the State's purpose of fostering "old notions" of role typing and preparing boys for their expected performance in the economic and political worlds.[6]

Reed v. Reed has also provided the underpinning for decisions that have invalidated statutes employing gender as an inaccurate proxy for other, more germane bases of classification. Hence, "archaic and overbroad" generalizations, *Ballard*, concerning the financial position of servicewomen, *Frontiero*, and working women, *Weinberger v. Wiesenfeld*, 420 U.S. 636 (1975), could not justify use of a gender line in determining eligibility for certain governmental entitlements. Similarly, increasingly outdated misconceptions concerning the role of females in the home rather than in the "marketplace and world of ideas" were rejected as loose-fitting characterizations incapable of supporting state statutory schemes that were premised upon their accuracy. *Stanton*. In light of the weak congruence between gender and the characteristic or trait that gender purported to represent, it was necessary that the legislatures choose either to realign their substantive laws in a gender-neutral fashion, or to adopt procedures for identifying those instances where the sex-centered generalization actually comported with fact. * * *

We accept for purposes of discussion the District Court's identification of the objective underlying [the statute] as the enhancement of traffic

---

[6] *Kahn v. Shevin* and *Schlesinger v. Ballard*, upholding the use of gender-based classifications, rested upon the Court's perception of the laudatory purposes of those laws as remedying disadvantageous conditions suffered by women in economic and military life. Needless to say, in this case Oklahoma does not suggest that the age-sex differential was enacted to ensure the availability of 3.2% beer for women as compensation for previous deprivations.

safety. Clearly, the protection of public health and safety represents an important function of state and local governments. However, appellees' statistics in our view cannot support the conclusion that the gender-based distinction closely serves to achieve that objective and therefore the distinction cannot under *Reed* withstand equal protection challenge.

[handwritten margin note: not narrowly tailored]

The appellees introduced a variety of statistical surveys. First, an analysis of arrest statistics for 1973 demonstrated that 18–20-year-old male arrests for "driving under the influence" and "drunkenness" substantially exceeded female arrests for that same age period. Similarly, youths aged 17–21 were found to be overrepresented among those killed or injured in traffic accidents, with males again numerically exceeding females in this regard. Third, a random roadside survey in Oklahoma City revealed that young males were more inclined to drive and drink beer than were their female counterparts. Fourth, Federal Bureau of Investigation nationwide statistics exhibited a notable increase in arrests for "driving under the influence." Finally, statistical evidence gathered in other jurisdictions, particularly Minnesota and Michigan, was offered to corroborate Oklahoma's experience by indicating the pervasiveness of youthful participation in motor vehicle accidents following the imbibing of alcohol. Conceding that "the case is not free from doubt," the District Court nonetheless concluded that this statistical showing substantiated "a rational basis for the legislative judgment underlying the challenged classification."

[handwritten margin notes: more male arrests; more male deaths; more males likely drink & drive]

Even were this statistical evidence accepted as accurate, it nevertheless offers only a weak answer to the equal protection question presented here. The most focused and relevant of the statistical surveys, arrests of 18–20 year-olds for alcohol-related driving offenses, exemplifies the ultimate unpersuasiveness of this evidentiary record. Viewed in terms of the correlation between sex and the actual activity that Oklahoma seeks to regulate—driving while under the influence of alcohol—the statistics broadly establish that .18% of females and 2% of males in that age group were arrested for that offense. While such a disparity is not trivial in a statistical sense, it hardly can form the basis for employment of a gender line as a classifying device. Certainly if maleness is to serve as a proxy for drinking and driving, a correlation of 2% must be considered an unduly tenuous "fit." Indeed, prior cases have consistently rejected the use of sex as a decisionmaking factor even though the statutes in question certainly rested on far more predictive empirical relationships than this.[13]* * *

---

[13] For example, we can conjecture that in *Reed*, Idaho's apparent premise that women lacked experience in formal business matters (particularly compared to men) would have proved to be accurate in substantially more than 2% of all cases. And in both *Frontiero* and *Wiesenfeld*, we expressly found appellees' empirical defense of mandatory dependency tests for men but not women to be unsatisfactory, even though we recognized that husbands are still far less likely to be dependent on their wives than vice versa.

There is no reason to belabor this line of analysis. * * * Suffice to say that the showing offered by the appellees does not satisfy us that sex represents a legitimate, accurate proxy for the regulation of drinking and driving. In fact, when it is further recognized that Oklahoma's statute prohibits only the selling of 3.2% beer to young males and not their drinking the beverage once acquired (even after purchase by their 18–20-year-old female companions), the relationship between gender and traffic safety becomes far too tenuous to satisfy *Reed*'s requirement that the gender-based difference be substantially related to achievement of the statutory objective.

JUSTICE STEVENS, concurring.

There is only one Equal Protection Clause. It requires every State to govern impartially. It does not direct the courts to apply one standard of review in some cases and a different standard in other cases. Whatever criticism may be leveled at a judicial opinion implying that there are at least three such standards applies with the same force to a double standard.

I am inclined to believe that what has become known as the two-tiered analysis of equal protection claims does not describe a completely logical method of deciding cases, but rather is a method the Court has employed to explain decisions that actually apply a single standard in a reasonably consistent fashion. I also suspect that a careful explanation of the reasons motivating particular decisions may contribute more to an identification of that standard than an attempt to articulate it in all-encompassing terms. It may therefore be appropriate for me to state the principal reasons which persuaded me to join the Court's opinion.

In this case, the classification is not as obnoxious as some the Court has condemned,[1] nor as inoffensive as some the Court has accepted. It is objectionable because it is based on an accident of birth, because it is a mere remnant of the now almost universally rejected tradition of discriminating against males in this age bracket, and because, to the extent it reflects any physical difference between males and females, it is actually perverse.[4] The question then is whether the traffic safety justification put forward by the State is sufficient to make an otherwise offensive classification acceptable.

The classification is not totally irrational. For the evidence does indicate that there are more males than females in this age bracket who drive and also more who drink. Nevertheless, there are several reasons why I regard the justification as unacceptable. It is difficult to believe that

---

[1] Men as a general class have not been the victims of the kind of historic, pervasive discrimination that has disadvantaged other groups.

[4] Because males are generally heavier than females, they have a greater capacity to consume alcohol without impairing their driving ability than do females.

the statute was actually intended to cope with the problem of traffic safety, since it has only a minimal effect on access to a not very intoxicating beverage and does not prohibit its consumption. Moreover, the empirical data submitted by the State accentuate the unfairness of treating all 18—21-year-old males as inferior to their female counterparts. The legislation imposes a restraint on 100% of the males in the class allegedly because about 2% of them have probably violated one or more laws relating to the consumption of alcoholic beverages. It is unlikely that this law will have a significant deterrent effect either on that 2% or on the law-abiding 98%. But even assuming some such slight benefit, it does not seem to me that an insult to all of the young men of the State can be justified by visiting the sins of the 2% on the 98%.

[We have omitted the opinions of **JUSTICE POWELL**, concurring; of **JUSTICE BLACKMUN**, concurring in part; of **JUSTICE STEWART**, concurring in the judgment; and of **CHIEF JUSTICE BURGER**, dissenting.]

JUSTICE REHNQUIST, dissenting.

Most obviously unavailable to support any kind of special scrutiny in this case, is a history or pattern of past discrimination, such as was relied on by the plurality in *Frontiero* to support its invocation of strict scrutiny. There is no suggestion in the Court's opinion that males in this age group are in any way peculiarly disadvantaged, subject to systematic discriminatory treatment, or otherwise in need of special solicitude from the courts. * * *

The Court's conclusion that a law which treats males less favorably than females "must serve important governmental objectives and must be substantially related to achievement of those objectives" apparently comes out of thin air. The Equal Protection Clause contains no such language, and none of our previous cases adopt that standard. I would think we have had enough difficulty with the two standards of review which our cases have recognized—the norm of "rational basis," and the "compelling state interest" required where a "suspect classification" is involved—so as to counsel weightily against the insertion of still another "standard" between those two. How is this Court to divine what objectives are important? How is it to determine whether a particular law is "substantially" related to the achievement of such objective, rather than related in some other way to its achievement? Both of the phrases used are so diaphanous and elastic as to invite subjective judicial preferences or prejudices relating to particular types of legislation, masquerading as judgments whether such legislation is directed at "important" objectives or whether the relationship to those objectives is "substantial" enough.

NOTE ON THE COURT'S "MIDDLE TIER" SCRUTINY

Since *Craig*, it has appeared that we have three tiers of equal protection scrutiny, with *Craig* establishing "intermediate scrutiny" for a "semi-suspect classification." Is Justice Stevens correct in his concurring opinion in *Craig* that the same standard explains the outcomes in all equal protection cases? What justifications—based upon original intent, representation reinforcement, or justice-based theories—might there be for the majority's approach? What difference does the level of scrutiny make? The Oklahoma statute would have passed the rational basis test, because there was an empirical connection between a legitimate state goal (safety) and the classification chosen by the state (young men statistically threatened the goal more than young women). How is Justice Brennan's application of intermediate scrutiny materially different from strict scrutiny? Consider this angle: Although the federal ERA died in 1982, at least sixteen state constitutions have ERAs protecting against discrimination because of sex.[40] Assuming that an ERA would require strict rather than intermediate scrutiny, in what sort of case would strict scrutiny invalidate, but *Craig*'s intermediate scrutiny affirm, a statute containing a sex-based classification?

Craig settled on intermediate review for gender classifications as a formal matter, but many questions have remained about how demanding that level of review should be and, indeed, to what kinds of laws it should apply. Bear these themes in mind as you read on.

RICHARD EPSTEIN,
THE RULE OF SEX-BLIND JURISPRUDENCE ISN'T ALWAYS FAIR
Wall Street Journal, July 21, 1993, at A15[41]

In connection with Ruth Bader Ginsburg's nomination to the Court, Professor Epstein evaluated several cases where she had won Supreme Court rulings to invalidate sex discriminations. Epstein felt that *Reed v. Reed* was defensible, because the state made no showing that decedents generally preferred men to women as executors. He cautioned, however, that the sex discrimination would have been rational if the state had made such a showing, because the state ought to have the authority to set up "a default rule that best mirrors the preferences of ordinary citizens who have the right to choose executors of their choice."

---

[40] See Alaska Const. art. I, § 3; Colorado Const. art. II, § 29; Connecticut Const. art. I, § 20; Hawaii Const. art. I, § 3; Illinois Const. art. I, § 18; Louisiana Const. art. I, § 3; Maryland Const., Declaration of Rights, art. 46; Massachusetts Const. pt 1, art. I; Montana Const. art. II, § 4; New Mexico Const. art. II, § 18; Pennsylvania Const. art. I, § 28; Texas Const. art. I, § 3a; Utah Const. art. IV, § 1; Virginia Const. art. I, § 11; Washington Const. art. XXXI, § 1; Wyoming Const. art. I, § 3. Half of these provisions were modeled on the proposed federal Equal Rights Amendment. Other states as well as the District of Columbia have statutes protecting against discrimination because of sex in employment and other arenas.

[41] Materials reprinted with permission of Professor Richard Epstein.

As for *Craig v. Boren*, Epstein argued: "The social gain of denying alcohol to males at 18 is far greater than the gain from denying it to females at 18. A rule that keeps women from drinking until 21 imposes unnecessary deprivation; a rule that allows men to drink at 18 creates unnecessary risk. Clearly the law is not designed to oppress or stigmatize men, and nothing in the Constitution forbids this sensible accommodation."

From the foregoing analysis, Epstein concluded that a "rigid" sex-equality jurisprudence saddled the country with "inferior social outcomes for the small benefit of striking down sex-based statutes that are likely to fall anyhow of their own political weight." Does his analysis undervalue the goals of the Court's sex discrimination jurisprudence? Is his analysis persuasive as a matter of neutral cost-benefit economics? Compare Mary Anne Case, *Of Richard Epstein and Other Radical Feminists*, 18 Harv. J.L. & Pub. Pol'y 369, 382–85 (1995). How would Epstein's treat-like-cases-alike analysis resolve the next case, where the sex discrimination served a remedial goal?

Califano v. Webster

430 U.S. 313 (1977)

Until it was amended in 1972, the Social Security Act provided for old-age benefits to be calculated on the basis of the wage earner's "average monthly wage" (AMW) for a specified number of years (to be chosen by the employee, hence, her or his highest earning years). The AMW for male and female wage earners was calculated differently, such that female earners could exclude more low-earning years from the formula than male earners could. Will Webster claimed this formula discriminated against him under the *Craig* test and was inconsistent with *Wiesenfeld* and *Califano v. Goldfarb*, 430 U.S. 199 (1977) (invalidating a federal law providing for different survivors' benefits for widows and widowers).

The Court, in a *per curiam* opinion, disagreed. It read *Ballard* and *Kahn v. Shevin*, 416 U.S. 351 (1974) (upholding state statute allowing widows but not widowers a property tax exemption) for the proposition that "[r]eduction of the disparity in economic condition between men and women caused by the long history of discrimination against women [is] an important governmental objective" under *Craig*. But " 'the mere recitation of a benign, compensatory purpose is not an automatic shield which protects against any inquiry into the actual purposes underlying a statutory scheme,' " as *Wiesenfeld* held. The Court found the provision more analogous to *Ballard* and *Kahn* than to *Wiesenfeld* and *Goldfarb*. "The more favorable treatment of the female wage earner enacted here was not a result of 'archaic and overbroad generalizations' about women, *Ballard*, or of 'the role-typing society has long imposed' upon women, *Stanton*, such as casual assumptions that women are 'the weaker sex' or are more likely to be child-rearers or dependents. Rather 'the only discernible purpose of [this statute's more favorable treatment is] the permissible one of redressing our society's longstanding disparate treatment of women.' *Goldfarb*."

The Court found in the legislative history of the 1956 statute evidence that Congress was responding to the well-documented fact that women's wages and economic opportunities were wrongfully depressed by traditionalist attitudes; the differential of the statute was defended and tailored to rectify some of this past discrimination. (Significantly, *Wiesenfeld* and *Goldfarb* struck down provisions that disadvantaged female wage earners, though they advantaged female survivors, while the *Webster* provision advantaged female wage earners as well as their spouses.) Congress repealed the favorable treatment in 1972 prospectively, because statutes prohibiting sex discrimination in the workplace made remediation less necessary.

Chief Justice Burger, joined by **Justices Stewart, Blackmun**, and **Rehnquist**, concurred in the judgment, but believed the result inconsistent with *Goldfarb*, from which he had dissented. "I question whether certainty in the law is promoted by hinging the validity of important statutory schemes on whether five Justices view them to be more akin to the 'offensive' provisions struck down in *Wiesenfeld* and *Frontiero*, or more like the 'benign' provisions upheld in *Ballard* and *Kahn*." Compare these Justices' tolerance for remedial sex-based classifications in *Webster* with their objection (except for Blackmun) to remedial race-based classifications in *Bakke* (Chapter 3, § 3A), decided the next Term of the Court.

J.E.B. v. Alabama ex rel. T.B.

511 U.S. 127 (1994)

In a state action to establish J.E.B.'s paternity, the state exercised nine of its ten peremptory challenges to strike male jurors; although J.E.B. used all but one of his challenges to strike female jurors, the jury ended up all-female. The Supreme Court declared the process inconsistent with the Equal Protection Clause and extended *Batson*, prohibiting discriminatory use of race-based peremptory challenges, to prohibit sex-based peremptory challenges. **Justice Blackmun**'s opinion for the Court noted that sex-discriminating peremptory challenges were only recently the subject of challenge, because women were long excluded from jury service, even longer than African Americans (see *Hoyt*). Indeed, the stereotypes invoked to exclude women from juries were similar to those invoked by the state to strike male jurors: Women will empathize with the jilted complainant, while men will be skeptical of her charges. Blackmun cited empirical studies casting doubt on generalizations that women will vote differently on juries than men and, more pointedly, maintained that sex or gender stereotypes are no more defensible than race stereotypes.

> Discrimination in jury selection, whether based on race or on gender, causes harm to the litigants, the community, and the individual jurors who are wrongfully excluded from participation in

the judicial process. The litigants are harmed by the risk that the prejudices which motivated the discriminatory selection of the jury will infect the entire proceedings. The community is harmed by the State's participation in the perpetuation of invidious group stereotypes and the inevitable loss of confidence in our judicial system that state-sanctioned discrimination in the courtroom engenders.

The Court insisted on the same protections as in *Batson* for race-based challenges: The party alleging gender discrimination must make a prima facie showing of intentional discrimination, and the party challenged must then explain the basis for the strike; the explanation need not rise to the level of for-cause challenges but must persuade the judge that the strike was motivated by non-gender reasons.

Justice Scalia, writing for himself and **Chief Justice Rehnquist** and **Justice Thomas**, dissented. His initial point was that the discrimination in question was *sex discrimination* (men were excluded), not *gender discrimination* (masculine people were not at issue). His second point was that he didn't understand how it is sex discrimination when each side is free to exercise offsetting peremptory challenges: J.E.B. struck women, the state struck men. Why isn't the system as a whole satisfactory under ideas of functional as well as formal equality? His third point was that group-based characteristics are the whole point of peremptory challenges, and extending *Batson* to sex-based challenges further undermines their role in an adversarial system. Is there any principled reason why *J.E.B.* should not be extended to religion-based challenges? Ethnicity- or alienage-based? Non-speakers of the English language? Sexual orientation? See *People v. Garcia*, 92 Cal. Rptr. 2d 339 (App. 2000) (extending state constitutional rule to monitor peremptory exclusion of lesbians, gay men, and bisexuals from juries).

argument

Mississippi University for Women v. Hogan

458 U.S. 718 (1982)

The Mississippi University for Women (MUW) was created in 1884 to provide higher education for white women, who before 1882 were excluded from the state university (which did not encourage women to attend until 1920) and all other state colleges. MUW remained all-female until Joe Hogan applied to its School of Nursing. The Supreme Court ruled that the exclusion of men violated the Equal Protection Clause. **Justice O'Connor**'s opinion for the Court summarized the precedents as establishing that

> [T]he party seeking to uphold a statute that classifies individuals on the basis of their gender must carry the burden of showing an 'exceedingly persuasive justification for the classification.' *Kirchberg v. Feenstra*, 450 U.S. 455 (1981). The burden is met only by showing at least that the classification serves 'important governmental objectives and that the discriminatory

means employed' are 'substantially related to the achievement of those objectives.' *Wengler v. Druggists Mut. Ins. Co.*, 446 U.S. 142 (1980).

Justice O'Connor found the state justification, compensation for workplace discrimination against women, unsupported. "In limited circumstances, a gender-based classification favoring one sex can be justified if it intentionally and directly assists members of the sex that is disproportionately burdened," as in *Webster* and *Ballard*. But where the "benign, compensatory purpose" is no more than a shield for archaic gender norms, it cannot save the statute, as in *Wiesenfeld*. The Court found that women in Mississippi lacked no opportunities to become nurses; at all points in the last generation, more than 90% of the nurses in the state have been female. "Rather than compensate for discriminatory barriers faced by women, MUW's policy of excluding males from admission to the School of Nursing tends to perpetuate the stereotyped view of nursing as an exclusively woman's job. By assuring that Mississippi allots more openings in its state-supported nursing schools to women than it does to men, MUW's admissions policy lends credibility to the old view that women, not men, should become nurses, and makes the assumption that nursing is a field for women a self-fulfilling prophecy."

Four dissenting Justices (**Chief Justice Burger** and **Justices Blackmun, Powell, Rehnquist**) lamented the possibility that the Court was threatening educational diversity. Specifically, the dissenters eulogized all-female schools, which experts had found useful in creating a preferable learning environment for women who found coeducational schools unfriendly to women and dominated by men. (See Problem 4-3: Is Sex Segregation in Schools Ever Constitutional?)

NOTE ON THEORIES OF CULTURAL FEMINISM AND SOCIOBIOLOGY

Carol Gilligan, *In a Different Voice: Psychological Theory and Women's Development* (1982), argued that female and male children develop differently in our society. Her prototypical children, Jake and Amy, approached problem-solving differently. In response to the dilemma of a man whose wife was dying and the medicine needed to treat her was beyond his ability to pay, Jake reasoned deductively that the man should steal the needed drugs, because the wife's death was more lamentable than the theft. Amy, in contrast, resisted the question and wondered whether there were ways of accommodating the two values (life and property); perhaps the man could work out a deal with a druggist whereby he could obtain the needed medicine in return for working extra hours for the druggist. Gilligan maintained that girls approach a wide range of issues looking for connection, empathy, and accommodation, while boys are more likely to view issues and problems in the abstract and as yes/no propositions. Girls tend to embrace an "ethic of care," boys an "ethic of rights."

Cultural feminism has been controversial within feminist thought, with some feminists urging the ethic of care as a different and more productive way of analyzing legal problems generally,[42] and other feminists worrying that Gilligan's dichotomy replicates traditional stereotypes about women.[43] Gilligan responded to her critics in *Making Connections: The Relational Worlds of Adolescent Girls at Emma Willard School* (1990). She denied taking the position that the Jake/Amy dichotomy is hard-wired into male and female children, but insisted that, under the particular circumstances of our culture today, boys and girls tend to reason differently and that Amy's ethic of care should be more widely appreciated.

Scientific theories of evolutionary psychology or "sociobiology" likewise point to differences between men and women.[44] According to such theories, gender differences are the result of evolutionary adaptation. Sexual differentiation results from, or is strongly influenced by, the different reproductive roles of men and women. Men have the ability to engage in rivalrous, aggressive, and promiscuous behavior and have less incentive to stick around for the rearing of offspring as women, whose pregnancies incapacitate them as well as connect them with their offspring. Natural selection would be expected to favor females whose character is nurturant and loyal, and males whose character is bold and aggressive (Posner, *Sex and Reason,* 93).

These descriptive features of evolutionary psychology are subject to argument and dispute, and even more controversial are the normative conclusions sometimes drawn from them by legal scholars. Richard Epstein, for example, cautions that "men and women are more comfortable in playing the roles that are congenial to their biological roles, and will find themselves uneasy with powerful social [or legal] conventions that dictate a parity in social roles in courtship, marriage, and parenting" (Epstein, *Two Challenges,* 336). Although such scholars concede that nature is not a sure guide to regulation, the general thrust of their prescriptive arguments is that legal regulations

---

[42] See Katharine Bartlett, *Feminist Legal Methods*, 103 Harv. L. Rev. 829 (1990); Carrie Menkel-Meadow, *Portia in a Different Voice: Speculations on a Woman's Lawyering Process*, 1 Berkeley Women's L.J. 39 (1985); Suzanna Sherry, *Civic Virtue and the Feminine Voice in Constitutional Adjudication*, 72 Va. L. Rev. 543 (1986); Robin West, *Jurisprudence and Gender*, 55 U. Chi. L. Rev. 1 (1988). See also Martha Minow, *The Supreme Court, 1986 Term—Foreword: Justice Engendered*, 101 Harv. L. Rev. 10 (1987).

[43] See, e.g., Catharine MacKinnon, *Feminism Unmodified: Discourses on Life and Law* (1987); Christine Littleton, *Reconstructing Sexual Equality*, 75 Calif. L. Rev. 1279 (1987); Joan Williams, *Deconstructing Gender*, 87 Mich. L. Rev. 797 (1989).

[44] Sociobiology classics include Edward Wilson, *Sociobiology: The New Synthesis* (1976); Richard Dawkins, *The Selfish Gene* (1976); Jerome Barkow, Leda Cosmides & John Tooby, *The Adapted Mind: Evolutionary Psychology and the Generation of Culture* (1992). An excellent journalistic account is Robert Wright, *The Moral Animal—Why We Are the Way We Are: The New Science of Evolutionary Psychology* (1994). Leading applications of sociobiology to legal regulatory issues include Richard Posner, *Sex and Reason* 88–98 (1992), reviewed by Gillian Hadfield, *Flirting with Science: Richard Posner on the Bioeconomics of Sexual Man*, 106 Harv. L. Rev. (1992), and by Jane Larson, *The New Home Economics*, 10 Const. Comm. 443 (1993); Richard Epstein, *Two Challenges for Feminist Thought*, 18 Harv. J.L. & Pub. Pol'y 321 (1995), with a response in Mary Anne Case, *Of Richard Epstein and Other Radical Feminists, id.* at 369.

cutting against the grain of evolutive imperative are doomed to expensive failure, just as are legal regulations cutting against the grain of free markets.

Notwithstanding their profound intellectual differences, both cultural feminists and sociobiologists would seem presumptively open to the idea of same-sex schooling, an issue unresolved in *Hogan*. Their different-yet-similar takes on gender were on vivid display in the litigation surrounding the sex integration of two all-male public paramilitary colleges, The Citadel in South Carolina and Virginia Military Institute in Virginia. The latter generated the following Supreme Court decision. How does Justice Ginsburg respond to the general points raised by cultural feminism and evolutionary psychology?

UNITED STATES V. VIRGINIA

518 U.S. 515, 116 S.Ct. 2264, 135 L.Ed.2d 735 (1996)

JUSTICE GINSBURG delivered the opinion of the Court.

[Virginia Military Institute (VMI) was the sole single-sex school among Virginia's public institutions of higher learning. VMI's distinctive mission was to produce "citizen-soldiers," men prepared for leadership in civilian life and in military service. Using an "adversative," or constantly challenging and doubting, method of training not available elsewhere in Virginia,[45] VMI endeavored to instill physical and mental discipline in its cadets. The United States sued Virginia and VMI, alleging that VMI's exclusively male admission policy violated the Equal Protection Clause, as construed in *Hogan*. The Fourth Circuit agreed and ordered Virginia to remedy the constitutional violation. In response, Virginia proposed a parallel program for women: Virginia Women's Institute for Leadership (VWIL), located at Mary Baldwin College, a private liberal arts school for women. In lieu of VMI's adversative method, the VWIL Task Force favored "a cooperative method which reinforces self-esteem." In addition to the standard bachelor of arts program offered at Mary Baldwin, VWIL students would take courses in leadership, complete an off-campus leadership externship, participate in community service projects, and assist in arranging a speaker series. The lower courts found this parallel program provided "substantively comparable" benefits and held it met equal protection requirements. The Supreme Court reversed.]

To summarize the Court's current directions for cases of official classification based on gender: Focusing on the differential treatment or denial of opportunity for which relief is sought, the reviewing court must determine whether the proffered justification is "exceedingly persuasive."

---

[45] *Editors' note*: According to the record in the case, the adversative model of education features "[p]hysical rigor, mental stress, absolute equality of treatment, absence of privacy, minute regulation of behavior, and indoctrination in desirable values." The cadets live in spartan barracks where surveillance is constant and privacy nonexistent; they wear uniforms, eat together in the mess hall, and regularly participate in drills. Freshmen students are exposed to the rat line, comparable in intensity to Marine Corps boot camp.

The burden of justification is demanding and it rests entirely on the State. See *Hogan*. The State must show "at least that the [challenged] classification serves 'important governmental objectives and that the discriminatory means employed' are 'substantially related to the achievement of those objectives.'" *Id*. The justification must be genuine, not hypothesized or invented *post hoc* in response to litigation. And it must not rely on overbroad generalizations about the different talents, capacities, or preferences of males and females.

[Sex is not a proscribed classification, however.] "Inherent differences" between men and women, we have come to appreciate, remain cause for celebration, but not for denigration of the members of either sex or for artificial constraints on an individual's opportunity. Sex classifications may be used to compensate women "for particular economic disabilities [they have] suffered," *Webster*, to "promot[e] equal employment opportunity," to advance full development of the talent and capacities of our Nation's people.[7] But such classifications may not be used, as they once were, to create or perpetuate the legal, social, and economic inferiority of women. * * *

[Virginia asserted two justifications in defense of VMI's exclusion of women. The Court agreed that the first justification, diversity of educational benefits, is a benign goal (*Webster*), but not one of the "actual state purposes" that motivated the policy. Justice Ginsburg's review of the record of single-sex education in Virginia revealed that it originated in the state's belief that only men would benefit from higher education. Virginia persisted in that belief much longer than other states; its public university, the University of Virginia, did not admit female students until 1970. The state only came to its diversity purpose for VMI after the Supreme Court called such policies into question in *Hogan*; that was too late to save the state justification, however.

[Justice Ginsburg then addressed the state's second justification: Preserving the adversative method of education. The District Court forecast from expert witness testimony that coeducation would materially affect physical training, the absence of privacy, and the adversative approach. The lower court found, as matters of fact, that women developed differently from men, that men "tend to need an atmosphere of adversativeness," while women "tend to thrive in a cooperative atmosphere," but also that some women desired VMI's adversative method and would benefit from it.] The notion that admission of women would

---

[7] Several *amici* have urged that diversity in educational opportunities is an altogether appropriate governmental pursuit and that single-sex schools can contribute importantly to such diversity. Indeed, it is the mission of some single-sex schools "to dissipate, rather than perpetuate, traditional gender classifications." See Brief for Twenty-Six Private Women's Colleges as *Amici Curiae* 5. We do not question the State's prerogative evenhandedly to support diverse educational opportunities. * * * Cf. *Hogan* [Mississippi had no other single-sex college except the nursing school].

downgrade VMI's stature, destroy the adversative system and, with it, even the school, is a judgment hardly proved, a prediction hardly different from other "self-fulfilling prophec[ies]," see *Hogan*, once routinely used to deny rights or opportunities. When women first sought admission to the bar and access to legal education, concerns of the same order were expressed. For example, in 1876, the Court of Common Pleas of Hennepin County, Minnesota, explained why women were thought ineligible for the practice of law. Women train and educate the young, the court said, which

> forbids that they shall bestow that time (early and late) and labor, so essential in attaining to the eminence to which the true lawyer should ever aspire. It cannot therefore be said that the opposition of courts to the admission of females to practice . . . is to any extent the outgrowth of . . . "old fogyism[.]" . . . [I]t arises rather from a comprehension of the magnitude of the responsibilities connected with the successful practice of law, and a desire to *grade up* the profession (emphasis added).

[Similar fears were voiced by law schools refusing to admit women in the early twentieth century. The medical profession and the military academies made the same kinds of arguments. None of the fears about debasing the legal, medical, or military professions came to pass after women were admitted to those careers.]

The State's misunderstanding and, in turn, the District Court's, is apparent from VMI's mission: to produce "citizen-soldiers," individuals

> imbued with love of learning, confident in the functions and attitudes of leadership, possessing a high sense of public service, advocates of the American democracy and free enterprise system, and ready . . . to defend their country in time of national peril. [Quoting Mission Study Committee of the VMI Board of Visitors, Report, May 16, 1986.]

Surely that goal is great enough to accommodate women, who today count as citizens in our American democracy equal in stature to men. Just as surely, the State's great goal is not substantially advanced by women's categorical exclusion, in total disregard of their individual merit, from the State's premier "citizen-soldier" corps. Virginia, in sum, "has fallen far short of establishing the 'exceedingly persuasive justification,'" *Hogan*, that must be the solid base for any gender-defined classification.

[Justice Ginsburg then turned to the remedial plan, whose constitutionality had been upheld in the lower courts. The Supreme Court's race discrimination precedents establish that the remedial decree must closely fit the constitutional violation; it must be shaped to place persons unconstitutionally denied an opportunity or advantage in "the position they would have occupied in the absence of [discrimination]." See *Milliken v. Bradley*, 433 U.S. 267, 280 (1977). Justice Ginsburg found that the

different + inferior

establishment of the VWIL did not practically remedy the discrimination, in large part because the women's program was qualitatively different and quantitatively inferior to that retained for males at VMI. Tangible differences included fewer courses for VWIL students, less qualified faculty members, lower admissions standards for students, no comparable athletic facilities, a much smaller educational endowment, and incomplete access to VMI's impressive alumni network. Intangible differences included loss of the adversative method and the bonding it seems to achieve. Virginia defended its solution based upon "real differences" in the preference most women have for a more cooperative, and less competitive, learning environment.]

[G]eneralizations about "the way women are," estimates of what is appropriate for *most women*, no longer justify denying opportunity to women whose talent and capacity place them outside the average description. Notably, Virginia never asserted that VMI's method of education suits *most men*. * * *

Virginia's VWIL solution is reminiscent of the remedy Texas proposed 50 years ago, in response to a state trial court's 1946 ruling that, given the equal protection guarantee, African Americans could not be denied a legal education at a state facility. See *Sweatt v. Painter*, 339 U.S. 629 (1950) [Chapter 2, § 1B]. Reluctant to admit African Americans to its flagship University of Texas Law School, the State set up a separate school for Heman Sweatt and other black law students. As originally opened, the new school had no independent faculty or library, and it lacked accreditation.

[Although the lower courts found the parallel law school "substantially equivalent" to the whites' law school, the Supreme Court struck down the remedy on the ground that the tangible facilities and faculty of the new law school were distinctly inferior and that there was an even greater disparity for intangible elements such as reputation.] In line with *Sweatt*, we rule here that Virginia has not shown substantial equality in the separate educational opportunities the State supports at VWIL and VMI. * * *

A prime part of the history of our Constitution * * * is the story of the extension of constitutional rights and protections to people once ignored or excluded. VMI's story continued as our comprehension of "We the People" expanded. There is no reason to believe that the admission of women capable of all the activities required of VMI cadets would destroy the Institute rather than enhance its capacity to serve the "more perfect Union."

[JUSTICE THOMAS took no part in the consideration of this case. Although objecting to the Court's apparently "strict" scrutiny, CHIEF JUSTICE REHNQUIST concurred in the judgment.]

JUSTICE SCALIA, dissenting.

Much of the Court's opinion is devoted to deprecating the closed-mindedness of our forebears with regard to women's education, and even with regard to the treatment of women in areas that have nothing to do with education. Closed-minded they were—as every age is, including our own, with regard to matters it cannot guess, because it simply does not consider them debatable. The virtue of a democratic system with a First Amendment is that it readily enables the people, over time, to be persuaded that what they took for granted is not so, and to change their laws accordingly. That system is destroyed if the smug assurances of each age are removed from the democratic process and written into the Constitution. So to counterbalance the Court's criticism of our ancestors, let me say a word in their praise: they left us free to change. The same cannot be said of this most illiberal Court, which has embarked on a course of inscribing one after another of the current preferences of the society (and in some cases only the counter-majoritarian preferences of the society's law-trained elite) into our Basic Law. Today it enshrines the notion that no substantial educational value is to be served by an all-men's military academy—so that the decision by the people of Virginia to maintain such an institution denies equal protection to women who cannot attend that institution but can attend others. Since it is entirely clear that the Constitution of the United States—the old one—takes no sides in this educational debate, I dissent.

* * * [I]n my view the function of this Court is to *preserve* our society's values regarding (among other things) equal protection, not to *revise* them; to prevent backsliding from the degree of restriction the Constitution imposed upon democratic government, not to prescribe, on our own authority, progressively higher degrees. For that reason it is my view that, whatever abstract tests we may choose to devise, they cannot supersede—and indeed ought to be crafted *so as to reflect*—those constant and unbroken national traditions that embody the people's understanding of ambiguous constitutional texts. More specifically, it is my view that "when a practice not expressly prohibited by the text of the Bill of Rights bears the endorsement of a long tradition of open, widespread, and unchallenged use that dates back to the beginning of the Republic, we have no proper basis for striking it down." *Rutan v. Republican Party of Ill.*, 497 U.S. 62, 95 (1990) (Scalia, J., dissenting). The same applies, *mutatis mutandis*, to a practice asserted to be in violation of the post-Civil War Fourteenth Amendment. * * *

[Justice Scalia then made the following arguments: The Court was silently replacing the intermediate scrutiny standard traditionally applied in sex-discrimination cases with a strict scrutiny standard akin to that in race-discrimination cases; the Court's requirement that VMI must open its adversative method to women so long as there are any women who would benefit from it imported a least-restrictive-means requirement characteristic only of strict scrutiny and not of intermediate scrutiny as articulated in precedents such as *Hogan*; and the Court's approach destabilized equal protection law without any firm theoretical basis. With respect to his last charge, Justice Scalia adverted to *Carolene Products'* justification for judicial review when "prejudice against discrete and insular minorities may be a special condition, which tends seriously to curtail the operation of those political processes ordinarily to be relied upon to protect minorities, and which may call for a correspondingly more searching judicial inquiry."]

* * * It is hard to consider women a "discrete and insular minorit[y]" unable to employ the "political processes ordinarily to be relied upon," when they constitute a majority of the electorate. And the suggestion that they are incapable of exerting that political power smacks of the same paternalism that the Court so roundly condemns. Moreover, a long list of legislation proves the proposition false. See, *e.g.*, Equal Pay Act of 1963, 29 U.S.C. § 206(d); Title VII of the Civil Rights Act of 1964, 42 U.S.C. § 2000e–2; Title IX of the Education Amendments of 1972, 20 U.S.C. § 1681; Women's Business Ownership Act of 1988, Pub. L. 100–533, 102 Stat. 2689; Violence Against Women Act of 1994, Pub. L. 103–322, Title IV, 108 Stat. 1902.

[Justice Scalia also criticized the Court for ignoring the lower court findings of fact that women and men do, on the whole, have different educational needs that are adequately reflected in the different designs of VMI and VWIL. He lamented the sacrifice of educational diversity that the Court's opinion required and concluded with quotations from the *Code of a Gentleman* the Court, in his view, was destroying.]

NOTES ON VMI

1.   Two Justices in the VMI case (Rehnquist and Scalia) felt the Court's analysis departed from *Craig*'s intermediate scrutiny. The suggestion is that the *Frontiero* plurality opinion, which adopted attorney Ruth Bader Ginsburg's effort to read the ERA into the Equal Protection Clause, had been furtively adopted by now-Justice Ginsburg's opinion for the Court. On the one hand, Justice Ginsburg framed her test almost exclusively from Justice O'Connor's opinion in *Hogan*, which struck down a sex segregation that disadvantaged men. Indeed, it is Justice Scalia's approach that seems inconsistent with the Court's precedents, for it was specifically rejected by Court majorities in *Hogan* and *J.E.B.* On the other hand, note how tightly Justice Ginsburg's opinion held the state to the policies that had actually motivated its exclusion of women, which focused the debate on stereotype-ridden reasons that dominated Virginian education a hundred years ago and deflected the diversity justification offered by *amici* (note 7 of the Court's opinion). Note also how Ginsburg's opinion closely associated the Court's sex and race discrimination jurisprudence on the matter of remedy (*Sweatt*).

2.   The VMI case also illustrates this pattern in the Court's jurisprudence: However the Justices verbally articulate the test for review of laws deploying a sex-based classification, they generally strike down laws that deny women opportunities that men have (*Reed*; *Stanton*; *Kirchberg*; VMI) or that deny men opportunities that women have when the state was motivated by archaic stereotypes (*Craig*; *Hogan*), but uphold laws benefitting women when the Court believes the state was motivated by remedial justifications rather than archaic stereotypes (*Ballard*; *Kahn*; *Webster*). Unfortunately, this neat categorization does not capture three other kinds of cases, where a sex-based law (1) is plausibly tied to the "inherent differences" between men and women that even Ginsburg "celebrat[ed]" in her VMI opinion; (2) has been adopted under circumstances where the Court for institutional reasons "defers" to other branches of government; or (3) advantages neither women nor men systematically. Examples of all three phenomena appear in the next subpart; most of these cases reflect the normative compromises entailed in a *de facto* ERA adopted without strong public consensus favoring a purely sex-blind jurisprudence.

3.   Fifteen years before VMI, the Court addressed another issue implicating the role of women in military settings. In *Rostker v. Goldberg*, 453 U.S. 57 (1981), the Court upheld the constitutionality of the law that requires men, but not women, to register for the draft. The Court called for substantial deference to Congress in this area and also reasoned that the policy was justified because women were, at the time, excluded from combat duty. The latter part of the Court's reasoning was overtaken in January 2013, when the Department of Defense, citing a recommendation from the Joint Chiefs of Staff, announced that it would be changing the regulation excluding women from combat. The effects of excluding women from combat positions included their exclusion from some leadership positions, lower salaries, fewer opportunities, and a general need for fewer women in the armed forces. Some scholars have contended that, because "combat is a synonym for power," the reason women are excluded is to preserve male power, and even to preserve fragile conceptions of "manhood" itself, as uniquely involving fighting and protecting home and family from invaders[46]—a justification that would seem unacceptable under the VMI case. The armed forces have traditionally maintained that men are better suited for combat roles (*i.e.*, they are stronger) than women.[47] This kind of argument has seemed increasingly inconsistent with the realities of modern warfare, which relies less and less on muscle power and more and more on firepower and technology. Moreover, the VMI decision suggests that the military's need for strong soldiers is not a valid reason for having a sex-based exclusion, because the military could (and does) exclude people who do not meet minimal strength requirements.

---

[46]   See Helen Rogan, Mixed Company: Women in the Modern Army 296 (1981); Karst, Pursuit of Manhood; Kornblum, Women Warriors.

[47]   See Brian Mitchell, Weak Link: Feminization of the American Military (1989). Contrast Female Soldiers; Jill Laurie Goodman, Women, War, and Equality: An Examination of Sex Discrimination in the Military, 5 Women's Rts. L. Rptr. 243 (1979).

4.   In light of the Obama era policy opening combat positions to women, should *Rostker v. Goldberg* still be regarded as good law? Note that the permanence of that policy change is not certain; some skeptical comments during the Trump Administration have raised questions about whether women will necessarily remain eligible for service in combat. Lolita Baldor, *Mattis: Jury is Out on Women in Succeeding in Combat Jobs*, Military Times, Sept. 25, 2018. In the realm of *gender identity*-based discrimination in the military, the Trump Administration has already reversed its predecessor's policy opening service to transgender soldiers, and the new restrictive policy has been challenged as unconstitutional in several lawsuits. See Jessica Gresko, *Appeals Court Sides with Trump in Transgender Military Case*, Jan. 4, 2019, https://www.apnews.com/2f2fe27025b5401688486f3b7d5080e2   (describing policy and litigation against it).

2.   Deference to Traditional Gender Classifications Based upon "Real Differences"

The Supreme Court has accepted most of the jurisprudence of equal treatment, as outlined by Justice Ginsburg and Professor Williams. But others, such as Justice Scalia and Professor Epstein, believed that the Court has not sufficiently defended its new level of equal protection scrutiny to justify using it as a sharp tool against controversial targets. Indeed, two lines of thought have existed side by side: the principle of equal treatment, and the exception for "real differences," a phrase used in *Ballard* and echoed in *United States v. Virginia*.

The intellectual debate about real differences between men and women assumes, as all the opinions in *Frontiero* did, that sex is biologically fixed, perhaps even immutable. As you read the following cases, note these further inquiries: (1) The biggest "real difference" is assumed to be women's ability to be pregnant and bear children. Is this a general difference, or is it one affecting only some women? (2) For each case, separate the examination of whether there is a real difference between men and women from the examination of the regulatory strategy the state has adopted. Is the strategy a rational and gender-neutral response to sex differences, or is it gendered in ways that reinforce unproductive stereotypes? (3) Baselines make a big difference. Someone who follows sociobiology or natural law and thinks sex differences are relatively hard-wired may be much more open to sex-based regulations than someone who follows most strands of feminist theory and thinks that many supposed sex differences are just gender stereotypes.

Michael M. v. Superior Court of Sonoma County

450 U.S. 464 (1981)

Section 261.5 of California's Penal Code included as unlawful sexual intercourse "an act of sexual intercourse accomplished with a female not the wife of the perpetrator, where the female is under the age of 18 years." The statute made men alone criminally liable for the act of statutory rape. Michael M., a 17½-year-old male charged with statutory rape of Sharon, a 16½-year-old female, moved to have § 261.5 invalidated as unlawful sex discrimination, an effort rebuffed by the California courts. Following cases where it had upheld laws "where the gender classification is not invidious, but rather realistically reflects the fact that the sexes are not similarly situated in certain circumstances," the Supreme Court affirmed.

Justice Rehnquist's plurality opinion, joined by three other Justices, reasoned that the statutory sex discrimination was substantially related to the goal of preventing illegitimate pregnancy, an important state interest. "We need not be medical doctors to discern that young men and young women are not similarly situated with respect to the problems and the risks of sexual intercourse. Only women may become pregnant, and they suffer disproportionately the profound physical, emotional, and psychological consequences of sexual activity. The statute at issue here protects women from sexual intercourse at an age when those consequences are particularly severe. * * *

"Because virtually all of the significant harmful and inescapably identifiable consequences of teenage pregnancy fall on the young female, a legislature acts well within its authority when it elects to punish only the participant who, by nature, suffers few of the consequences of his conduct. It is hardly unreasonable for a legislature acting to protect minor females to exclude them from punishment. Moreover, the risk of pregnancy itself constitutes a substantial deterrence to young females. No similar natural sanctions deter males. A criminal sanction imposed solely on males thus serves to roughly 'equalize' the deterrents on the sexes. * * *

"In any event, we cannot say that a gender-neutral statute would be as effective as the statute California has chosen to enact. The State persuasively contends that a gender-neutral statute would frustrate its interest in effective enforcement. Its view is that a female is surely less likely to report violations of the statute if she herself would be subject to criminal prosecution. In an area already fraught with prosecutorial difficulties, we decline to hold that the Equal Protection Clause requires a legislature to enact a statute so broad that it may well be incapable of enforcement."

Justice Blackmun concurred only in the judgment. He pointed out that Sharon "appears not to have been an unwilling participant in at least the initial stages of the intimacies that took place the night of June 3, 1978." As evidence, Justice Blackmun pointed to Sharon's testimony at the preliminary hearing:

> "Yeah. We was laying there and we were kissing each other, and then he asked me if I wanted to walk him over to the park; so we walked over to the park and we sat down on a bench and then he started kissing me again and we were laying on the bench. And he told me to take my pants off.

"I said, 'No,' and I was trying to get up and he hit me back down on the bench and then I just said to myself, 'Forget it,' and I let him do what he wanted to do * * *."

Michael's and Sharon's "nonacquaintance with each other before the incident; their drinking; their withdrawal from the others of the group; their foreplay, in which she willingly participated and seems to have encouraged; and the closeness of their ages (a difference of only one year and 18 days) are factors that should make this case an unattractive one to prosecute at all, and especially to prosecute as a felony, rather than as a misdemeanor chargeable under § 261.5."

Justice Brennan, in dissent, argued that California had presented no evidence that a gender-neutral statutory rape law (such as the laws adopted by 37 other states) would be less enforceable or less effective in deterring minor females from having intercourse than its males-only statute. "Until very recently, no California court or commentator had suggested that the purpose of California's statutory rape law was to protect young women from the risk of pregnancy. Indeed, the historical development of § 261.5 demonstrates that the law was initially enacted on the premise that young women, in contrast to young men, were to be deemed legally incapable of consenting to an act of sexual intercourse. Because their chastity was considered particularly precious, those young women were felt to be uniquely in need of the State's protection. In contrast, young men were assumed to be capable of making such decisions for themselves; the law therefore did not offer them any special protection."

NOTES ON MICHAEL M.

1. After the Court's decision, California amended its statutory rape law to be gender-neutral. Over time, the other states that limited protection as California had followed suit. In addition to having been eclipsed by these legislative changes, was *Michael M.* effectively overruled by the VMI case, where the Court insisted upon considering only the *actual, historical purposes* of the exclusion of women, not (as the Court did in *Michael M.*) current justifications? Many feminists criticized *Michael M.* for upholding a law that rested upon gender stereotypes like those in *Bradwell* and *Craig*.[48] Has their point of view been accepted by the VMI Court?

2. With statutory rape law having faded as an issue of gender equality, contemporary debates about gender, sexuality and consent among teens and young adults are most prominent in the realm of Title IX of the Education Amendments of 1972, which addresses sexual assaults at schools and colleges. Those debates include, among other things, disputes about what constitutes meaningful consent to sexual activity, and these disputes raise questions about Justice Blackmun's analysis of whether Sharon was a "willing participant" in

---

[48] See Frances Olsen, *Statutory Rape: A Feminist Critique of Rights Analysis*, 63 Tex. L. Rev. 387 (1984); Wendy Webster Williams, *The Equality Crisis: Reflections on Culture, Courts and Feminism*, 7 Women's Rts. L. Rep. 175, 181–82 (Spring 1982).

sexual activity. For an analysis of the complex questions of consent in this realm, see Aya Gruber, *Consent Confusion*, 38 Cardozo L. Rev. 415 (2016).

Nguyen v. INS

533 U.S. 53 (2001)

The Supreme Court rejected a challenge to a federal statute, 8 U.S.C. § 1409(a)(4), that accorded American citizenship automatically, upon birth, to a child born out of wedlock in a foreign country to an American mother, but denied citizenship to such a child whose only American parent was her father, unless the child were legally legitimated or paternity were established in a court of law or by paternal oath before the child's eighteenth birthday. In *Miller v. Albright*, 523 U.S. 420 (1998), a divided Court had failed to resolve the constitutionality of § 1409(a)(4), essentially because two Justices believed that the child plaintiff seeking a declaration of citizenship did not have standing to raise her father's sex discrimination claim. In *Nguyen*, both the child and the father were plaintiffs, so there was no problem of standing.

Justice Kennedy's opinion for the Court found the sex discrimination justified by two governmental interests. "The first governmental interest to be served is the importance of assuring that a biological parent-child relationship exists. In the case of the mother, the relation is verifiable from the birth itself. The mother's status is documented in most instances by the birth certificate or hospital records and the witnesses who attest to her having given birth.

"In the case of the father, the uncontestable fact is that he need not be present at the birth. If he is present, furthermore, that circumstance is not incontrovertible proof of fatherhood. See *Lehr v. Robertson*, 463 U.S. 248 (1983). Fathers and mothers are not similarly situated with regard to the proof of biological parenthood. The imposition of a different set of rules for making that legal determination with respect to fathers and mothers is neither surprising nor troublesome from a constitutional perspective. Section 1409(a)(4)'s provision of three options for a father seeking to establish paternity—legitimation, paternity oath, and court order of paternity—is designed to ensure an acceptable documentation of paternity. * * *

"[T]o require Congress to speak without reference to the gender of the parent with regard to its objective of ensuring a blood tie between parent and child would be to insist on a hollow neutrality. * * * Congress could have required both mothers and fathers to prove parenthood within 30 days or, for that matter, 18 years, of the child's birth. Given that the mother is always present at birth, but that the father need not be, the facially neutral rule would sometimes require fathers to take additional affirmative steps which would not be required of mothers, whose names will appear on the birth certificate as a result of their presence at the birth, and who will have the benefit of witnesses to the birth to call upon. The issue is not the use of gender specific terms instead of neutral ones. Just as neutral terms can mask discrimination that is unlawful, gender specific terms can mark a permissible distinction. The equal protection question is whether the distinction is lawful. Here, the use of gender specific terms takes into account a biological difference between the parents. The differential treatment is inherent in a sensible statutory scheme, given the unique relationship of the mother to the event of birth.

"The second important governmental interest furthered in a substantial manner by § 1409(a)(4) is the determination to ensure that the child and the citizen parent have some demonstrated opportunity or potential to develop not just a relationship that is recognized, as a formal matter, by the law, but one that consists of the real, everyday ties that provide a connection between child and citizen parent and, in turn, the United States. In the case of a citizen mother and a child born overseas, the opportunity for a meaningful relationship between citizen parent and child inheres in the very event of birth, an event so often critical to our constitutional and statutory understandings of citizenship. The mother knows that the child is in being and is hers and has an initial point of contact with him. There is at least an opportunity for mother and child to develop a real, meaningful relationship.

"The same opportunity does not result from the event of birth, as a matter of biological inevitability, in the case of the unwed father. Given the 9-month interval between conception and birth, it is not always certain that a father will know that a child was conceived, nor is it always clear that even the mother will be sure of the father's identity. This fact takes on particular significance in the case of a child born overseas and out of wedlock. One concern in this context has always been with young people, men for the most part, who are on duty with the Armed Forces in foreign countries." Justice Kennedy finally concluded that the statutory differentiation was narrowly enough tailored to fit this asserted interest, as well as the first.

Justice Scalia, joined by **Justice Thomas**, concurred in the Court's opinion but reiterated their view, stated in *Miller*, that Congress has plenary and unreviewable power in the arena of immigration and naturalization.

Justice O'Connor, joined by **Justices Souter**, **Ginsburg**, and **Breyer**, dissented. Justice O'Connor maintained that the Court's approach deviated from the heightened scrutiny its precedents bound it to apply in sex discrimination cases, such as the VMI case. Specifically, she criticized the Court's first justification (proof of parental relationship) as insufficient because (1) there was scant evidence that this was the actual reason for the sex-based classification; (2) the requirements of § 1409(a)(4) add nothing to what § 1409(a)(1) already requires, namely, a blood test showing a parental relationship between the American father and the child claiming citizenship; and (3) sex-neutral criteria, such as the blood-test requirement of § 1409(a)(1) for the child-claimant whatever the sex of its American parent, would fully serve the asserted governmental interest. Justice O'Connor suggested that the Court's willingness to attribute a rational goal to Congress and to allow much leeway in the fit between the statutory criterion and the valid state interest was more characteristic of rational basis review than heightened scrutiny as required by the VMI Case and other precedents.

Justice O'Connor made two of the same criticisms of the Court's second justification (opportunity of the American parent and foreign-born child to develop a relationship): It was hypothetical and could be met by a more direct—and ungendered—statutory criterion (*e.g.*, the child and the parent, whatever the gender, have enjoyed a relationship). By stressing an "opportunity" for a relationship, the Court was more successful in creating a closer fit between the end and the means—but at the expense of creating an end that is not sufficiently important to justify a statutory sex discrimination.

"The claim that § 1409(a)(4) substantially relates to the achievement of the goal of a 'real, practical relationship' thus finds support not in biological differences but instead in a stereotype—*i.e.*, 'the generalization that mothers are significantly more likely than fathers . . . to develop caring relationships with their children.' *Miller* (Breyer, J., dissenting). Such a claim relies on 'the very stereotype the law condemns,' *J.E.B.*, 'lends credibility' to the generalization, *Hogan*, and helps to convert that 'assumption' into 'a self-fulfilling prophecy,' *ibid.* Indeed, contrary to this stereotype, Boulais [the father] has reared Nguyen, while Nguyen apparently has lacked a relationship with his mother. * * *

"In denying petitioner's claim that § 1409(a)(4) rests on stereotypes, the majority articulates a misshapen notion of 'stereotype' and its significance in our equal protection jurisprudence. The majority asserts that a 'stereotype' is 'defined as a frame of mind resulting from irrational or uncritical analysis.' This Court has long recognized, however, that an impermissible stereotype may enjoy empirical support and thus be in a sense 'rational.' See, e.g., *J.E.B.* ('We have made abundantly clear in past cases that gender classifications that rest on impermissible stereotypes violate the Equal Protection Clause, even when some statistical support can be conjured up for the generalization'); *Craig* (invalidating a sex-based classification even though the evidence supporting the distinction was 'not trivial in a statistical sense'). Indeed, the stereotypes that underlie a sex-based classification 'may hold true for many, even most, individuals.' *Miller* (Ginsburg, J., dissenting). But in numerous cases where a measure of truth has inhered in the generalization, 'the Court has rejected official actions that classify unnecessarily and overbroadly by gender when more accurate and impartial functional lines can be drawn.' *Ibid.*"

Sessions v. Morales-Santana

137 S.Ct. 1678 (2017)

In 2017, the Court returned to the issue of gender-based differences in the transmission of U.S. citizenship, but this time reached a different conclusion. The case addressed the citizenship of children born outside the United States where only one parent is a U.S. citizen. Under the law in effect at the time of this case, where the parents were married, the citizen-parent must have had ten years' physical presence in the United States before the child's birth, at least five of which were after that parent reached the age of 14. If the parents were not married, however, the rules differed based on the gender of the citizen-parent. Under section 1409(a) of the statute, where the citizen-parent was the father, the same rules that govern married couples applied. But if the citizen-parent was the mother, she must merely have lived continuously in the United States for one year before the child's birth. These gendered rules were challenged by Luis Ramon Morales-Santana, whom the government sought to deport based on criminal convictions. Morales asserted that he could not be deported because he acquired U.S. citizenship through his citizen-father. Morales' father, however, moved to the Dominican Republic 20 days before he turned 19, thus falling short of the requirement that he have five years' physical presence in the United States after the age of 14. Morales challenged the constitutionality of this rule and prevailed in the court of appeals, which ruled that he should be given citizenship.

Justice Ginsburg wrote an opinion for the Court, in which she was joined by five other justices (with Justices Thomas and Alito concurring in the judgment, and Justice Gorsuch not participating). The Court affirmed in part and reversed in part. The majority opinion noted that the statutory provisions "date from an era when the lawbooks of our Nation were rife with overbroad generalizations about the way men and women are. Today, laws of this kind are subject to review under the heightened scrutiny that now attends 'all gender-based classifications.'" * * *

Addressing the standard of review, she noted that the "defender of legislation that differentiates on the basis of gender must show 'at least that the [challenged] classification serves important governmental objectives and that the discriminatory means employed are substantially related to the achievement of those objectives.' Moreover, the classification must substantially serve an important governmental interest *today,* for 'in interpreting the [e]qual [p]rotection [guarantee], [we have] recognized that new insights and societal understandings can reveal unjustified inequality . . . that once passed unnoticed and unchallenged.' *Obergefell v. Hodges.* Here, the Government has supplied no 'exceedingly persuasive justification,' *Virginia,* for § 1409(a) and (c)'s 'gender-based' and 'gender-biased' disparity.

"History reveals what lurks behind § 1409. Enacted in the Nationality Act of 1940 (1940 Act), § 1409 ended a century and a half of congressional silence on the citizenship of children born abroad to unwed parents. During this era, two once habitual, but now untenable, assumptions pervaded our Nation's citizenship laws and underpinned judicial and administrative rulings: In marriage, husband is dominant, wife subordinate; unwed mother is the natural and sole guardian of a nonmarital child.* * *

"At common law, the mother, and only the mother, was 'bound to maintain [a nonmarital child] as its natural guardian.'" The Court went on to note that, in 1940, Congress "codified the mother-as-sole-guardian perception regarding unmarried parents," and then observed: "This unwed-mother-as-natural-guardian notion renders § 1409's gender-based residency rules understandable. Fearing that a foreign-born child could turn out 'more alien than American in character,' the administration believed that a citizen parent with lengthy ties to the United States would counteract the influence of the alien parent. Concern about the attachment of foreign-born children to the United States explains the treatment of unwed citizen fathers, who, according to the familiar stereotype, would care little about, and have scant contact with, their nonmarital children. For unwed citizen mothers, however, there was no need for a prolonged residency prophylactic: The alien father, who might transmit foreign ways, was presumptively out of the picture. * * *

"Unlike the paternal-acknowledgment requirement at issue in *Nguyen*. . . the physical-presence requirements now before us relate solely to the duration of the parent's prebirth residency in the United States, not to the parent's filial tie to the child. As the Court of Appeals observed in this case, a man needs no more time in the United States than a woman 'in order to have assimilated citizenship-related values to transmit to [his] child.' And unlike *Nguyen*'s parental-acknowledgment requirement, § 1409(a)'s age-calibrated physical-presence requirements cannot fairly be described as 'minimal.' * * *

"Underlying [the apparent statutory] design is the assumption that the alien father of a nonmarital child born abroad to a U.S.-citizen mother will not accept parental responsibility. For an actual affiliation between alien father and nonmarital child would create the 'competing national influence' that, according to the Government, justifies imposing on unwed U.S.-citizen fathers, but not unwed U.S.-citizen mothers, lengthy physical-presence requirements. Hardly gender neutral, that assumption conforms to the long-held view that unwed fathers care little about, indeed are strangers to, their children. Lump characterization of that kind, however, no longer passes equal protection inspection.

"Accepting, *arguendo,* that Congress intended the diverse physical-presence prescriptions to serve an interest in ensuring a connection between the foreign-born nonmarital child and the United States, the gender-based means scarcely serve the posited end. The scheme permits the transmission of citizenship to children who have no tie to the United States so long as their mother was a U.S. citizen continuously present in the United States for one year at any point in her life *prior* to the child's birth. The transmission holds even if the mother marries the child's alien father immediately after the child's birth and never returns with the child to the United States. At the same time, the legislation precludes citizenship transmission by a U.S.-citizen father who falls a few days short of meeting § 1401(a)(7)'s longer physical-presence requirements, even if the father acknowledges paternity on the day of the child's birth and raises the child in the United States. One cannot see in this driven-by-gender scheme the close means-end fit required to survive heightened scrutiny."

The Court went on to consider and reject the other justification proffered by the government—that the policy would reduce the risk of statelessness, finding that "there is little reason to believe that a statelessness concern prompted the diverse physical-presence requirements. Nor has the

Government shown that the risk of statelessness disproportionately endangered the children of unwed mothers."

The Court closed by confronting the issue of remedy. "There are 'two remedial alternatives,' our decisions instruct, when a statute benefits one class (in this case, unwed mothers and their children), as § 1409(c) does, and excludes another from the benefit (here, unwed fathers and their children). '[A] court may either declare [the statute] a nullity and order that its benefits not extend to the class that the legislature intended to benefit, or it may extend the coverage of the statute to include those who are aggrieved by exclusion.' '[W]hen the "right invoked is that to equal treatment," the appropriate remedy is a mandate of equal treatment, a result that can be accomplished by withdrawal of benefits from the favored class as well as by extension of benefits to the excluded class.' * * *

"The choice between these outcomes is governed by the legislature's intent, as revealed by the statute at hand. * * *

"Ordinarily, we have reiterated, 'extension, rather than nullification, is the proper course.' Illustratively, in a series of cases involving federal financial assistance benefits, the Court struck discriminatory exceptions denying benefits to discrete groups, which meant benefits previously denied were extended. Here, however, the discriminatory exception consists of *favorable* treatment for a discrete group (a shorter physical-presence requirement for unwed U.S.-citizen mothers giving birth abroad). Following the same approach as in those benefits cases—striking the discriminatory exception—leads here to extending the general rule of longer physical-presence requirements to cover the previously favored group. * * *

"Although extension of benefits is customary in federal benefit cases, all indicators in this case point in the opposite direction. Put to the choice, Congress, we believe, would have abrogated § 1409(c)'s exception, preferring preservation of the general rule. * * *

"Going forward, Congress may address the issue and settle on a uniform prescription that neither favors nor disadvantages any person on the basis of gender. In the interim, as the Government suggests, § 1401(a)(7)'s now-five-year requirement should apply, prospectively, to children born to unwed U.S.-citizen mothers."

NOTES ON NGUYEN AND MORALES-SANTANA

1. *Whither* Nguyen? Note that the Court distinguishes *Nguyen*. But does *Morales-Santana* implicitly suggest that *Nguyen* was wrongly decided? Don't both cases involve the same stereotypical assumptions about unmarried mothers and fathers? Setting aside the factual differences, did the Court apply the same version of intermediate scrutiny in *Morales-Santana* as it had in *Nguyen*? Recall that Justice Ginsburg joined Justice O'Connor's dissent in *Nguyen* criticizing the weak form of review applied there.

2.   Obergefell. The majority imports into its analysis ideas of evolving norms and dignity that it traces to *Obergefell v. Hodges* (see chapter 5). Does this signal that these ideas, and the related "synergy" between equality and liberty emphasized by Justice Kennedy, have taken root in the realm of constitutional sex equality law? What might the implications of that move be for sex equality doctrine going forward?

3.   *Remedy.* The Court leaves the successful plaintiff with no remedy. Was the Court right to level down, rather than level up?

B. THE JURISPRUDENCE OF EQUAL TREATMENT AND HEIGHTENED SCRUTINY OF SEX-BASED DISTINCTIONS

3. Classifications That Have a Disparate Impact upon Women

Many feminists have been just as opposed to policies that have a discriminatory impact upon women as to those that discriminate on their face. Both before and after *Craig*, however, such policies proved impervious to constitutional attack, even though they had pervasive discriminatory effects on women's opportunities in the workplace. Note the parallel to *Washington v. Davis* (Chapter 3, § 1B) in the race discrimination context. Is there a persuasive reason not to follow the *Davis* approach in either of the following cases?

Geduldig v. Aiello

417 U.S. 484 (1974)

California's disability insurance program paid benefits to persons temporarily disabled from work, but excluded pregnancy-related disabilities from coverage. Challenging the pregnancy-based discrimination, Wendy Williams maintained that "the individual who receives a benefit or suffers a detriment because of a physical characteristic unique to one sex benefits or suffers because he or she belongs to one or the other sex"—which was sex discrimination, because men were treated differently (Brief for Appellees, at 31, *Geduldig* (No. 73–640)). Moreover, men were treated more favorably than women, and for exactly the reasons rejected in *Reed* and *Frontiero* (and later in *Craig*): men were privileged and women were denigrated in the public and workplace sphere because of women's unique ability to bear children and the concomitant special responsibility for rearing them in the domestic sphere. "Those who would make these unique physical differences a touchstone for unscrutinized differential treatment offer nothing other than the modern version of the historical rationales which were for so long the source of women's second class citizenship under the law." (Id. at 36.) Indeed, "[t]his last prejudice—that women are not serious and permanent members of the workforce and that lurking somewhere in each woman's life is a man fully able to support her—underlies and reinforces discrimination against women in all realms of their lives." (Id. at 39–40.)

But the nine men on the Court were not persuaded that this was the right focus. According to Justice Douglas's conference notes, most of the Justices agreed with Chief Justice Burger's complaint that the pregnancy exclusion involves "a different kind of risk than illness covered by [the] Act. [P]rostate problem is covered—as is hysterectomy—different from pregnancy." **Justice Stewart**'s opinion for the Court ruled that the pregnancy exclusion was rationally related to the insurance program's self-supporting goals; benefits are covered by premiums, and some lines have to be drawn. Three dissenting Justices argued that such lenient rational basis review was inappropriate under either *Reed* or the just-decided *Frontiero*, which required more exacting scrutiny for sex-based classifications. Justice Stewart responded that the exclusion was not "gender discrimination as such": It does not divide the world into men and women, but merely classifies the world into men-plus-nonpregnant-women and pregnant women. Indeed, there was not necessarily a sex-discriminatory impact on men, as the annual claim rate and cost were higher for women than men in California.

Personnel Administrator of Massachusetts v. Feeney

442 U.S. 256 (1979)

Massachusetts General Laws, ch. 31, § 23 (originally enacted 1884), provided that all veterans who qualified for state civil service positions be given a preference over nonveterans. During her 12-year tenure as a public employee, Helen Feeney took and passed several competitive civil service exams. In 1971, she received the second highest score on an exam for a job with the Board of Dental Examiners, but she was ranked sixth behind five male veterans on the Dental Examiner list because of the veterans' preference; a lower-scoring veteran got the job. In 1973, she received the third highest score on an exam for an administrative assistant position with a mental health center but was placed twelfth on the hiring list, behind eleven male veterans with lower scores. This pattern of getting high scores but losing the job to lower-scoring male veterans recurred. Feeney challenged the veterans' preference as a violation of equal protection.

In the 1970s, over 98% of the veterans in Massachusetts were male; only 1.8% were female. Between 1963 and 1973, when Feeney was competing for state merit jobs, 47,005 new permanent appointments were made, 43% women and 57% men. Of the women appointed, 1.8% were veterans, while 54% of the men had veteran status. A large unspecified percentage of the female appointees were serving in lower paying positions for which males traditionally had not applied. On each of 50 sample eligible lists that are part of the record in this case, one or more women who would have been certified as eligible for appointment on the basis of test results were displaced by veterans whose test scores were lower.

The Court, in another opinion by **Justice Stewart**, upheld the statutory classification. It relied on *Washington v. Davis* and *Arlington Heights* (Chapter 3, § 1B) for the proposition that "even if a neutral law has a disproportionately adverse effect upon a racial minority [or, in Feeney's case, women], it is unconstitutional under the Equal Protection Clause only if that impact can be traced to a discriminatory purpose."

The trial court found, as a matter of fact, that the veterans' preference "was not established for the purpose of discriminating against women." The key issue was whether Feeney had shown "that a gender-based discriminatory purpose has, at least in some measure, shaped the Massachusetts veterans' preference legislation." Feeney first argued that the preference was inherently sex-biased because it favored a status reserved under federal military policy primarily for men. The Court rejected this argument as inconsistent with Feeney's concession that some kind of veterans' preference would be allowable: If a more limited "sex-biased" preference were okay, why not a broad one? Feeney also argued that the state had to have realized that an extensive invocation of a veterans' preference would naturally exclude women from the better state jobs; indeed, the statute until 1971 exempted from operation of the preference jobs "especially calling for women," namely secretarial and other "women's work." The Court found this to be the most weighty argument but was unpersuaded.

" 'Discriminatory purpose,' however, implies more than intent as volition or intent as awareness of consequences. It implies that the decisionmaker, in this case a state legislature, selected or reaffirmed a particular course of action at least in part 'because of,' not merely 'in spite of,' its adverse effects upon an identifiable group. Yet nothing in the record demonstrates that this preference for veterans was originally devised or subsequently re-enacted because it would accomplish the collateral goal of keeping women in a stereotypic and predefined place in the Massachusetts Civil Service.

"To the contrary, the statutory history shows that the benefit of the preference was consistently offered to 'any person' who was a veteran. That benefit has been extended to women under a very broad statutory definition of the term veteran. The preference formula itself, which is the focal point of this challenge, was first adopted—so it appears from this record—out of a perceived need to help a small group of older Civil War veterans. It has since been reaffirmed and extended only to cover new veterans. When the totality of legislative actions establishing and extending the Massachusetts veterans' preference are considered, the law remains what it purports to be: a preference for veterans of either sex over nonveterans of either sex, not for men over women."

Justice Marshall, joined by **Justice Brennan**, dissented. Under *Arlington Heights* (Chapter 3, § 1B), a discriminatory purpose can be inferred by looking at the "degree, inevitability, and foreseeability of any disproportionate impact as well as the alternatives reasonably available." The district court's finding that the veterans' preference essentially supplanted test results as the determinant of upper-level civil service appointments underscored the overwhelming impact of the preference upon women. Given the armed forces' longstanding exclusion of women from service (until World War I) and from combat and other positions, such an overwhelming impact was inevitable and foreseeable. "Although neutral in form, the statute is anything but neutral in application. It inescapably reserves a major sector of public employment to 'an already established class which, as a matter of historical fact, is 98% male.' Where the foreseeable impact of a facially neutral policy is so disproportionate, the burden should rest on the State to establish that sex-based considerations played no part in the choice of the particular legislative scheme." Indeed, the statute's exclusion of traditional women's work from the veterans' preference revealed that it embodied the same "archaic assumptions about women's roles" the Court invoked to invalidate statutes in *Craig* and *Wiesenfeld*.

NOTES ON FEENEY AND DISCRIMINATORY IMPACT ON WOMEN

1. *Application of the Discriminatory Intent Test to Issues of Jobs and Abortion.* Recall the argument that the *Washington v. Davis/Arlington Heights* discriminatory-intent test should be softened, so that it may be satisfied by a showing of "selective racial indifference." See Chapter 3, § 1B. Could Massachusetts have been any more indifferent to the interests of women seeking civil service employment and promotion? Also consider whether Professor Lawrence's arguments about "unconscious racism" (Chapter 3, § 1C) can be applied to issues of "unconscious sexism" in cases like *Feeney*.

Consider also state regulation of abortion. The issue has traditionally been analyzed under fundamental rights theories (see Chapter 5, § 4B), but can also be viewed as a violation of a woman's right to be treated equally.[49] By analogy, consider *Bray v. Alexandria Women's Health Clinic*, 506 U.S. 263 (1993). There, the Court rejected the claim that barriers to abortion access qualify as discrimination against women under a federal civil rights statute, but Justice Stevens, in dissent, argued that allowing anti-abortion protests was indeed class-based discrimination for purposes of that law. Note that if *Geduldig* and *Feeney* had invalidated their respective state classifications (pregnancy and nonveteran status) because of their disparate impact upon women, the same kind of equal protection argument could easily have been raised against all abortion restrictions. Would such restrictions survive middle-tier scrutiny, as applied in the VMI case?

---

[49] See, e.g., Ruth Bader Ginsburg, *Some Thoughts on Autonomy and Equality in Relation to Roe v. Wade*, 63 N.C. L. Rev. 375 (1985); Kenneth Karst, *Women's Constitution*, 1984 Duke L.J. 447; Sylvia Law, *Rethinking Sex and the Constitution*, 132 U. Pa. L. Rev. 955 (1984); Catharine MacKinnon, *Reflections on Sex Equality Under Law*, 100 Yale L.J. 1281 (1991); Frances Olsen, *Unraveling Compromise*, 103 Harv. L. Rev. 105 (1989); Reva Siegel, *Reasoning from the Body: A Historical Perspective on Abortion Regulation and Questions of Equal Protection*, 44 Stan. L. Rev. 261 (1992); cf. Kenji Yoshino, *The New Equal Protection*, 124 Harv. L. Rev. 747 (2011) (examining *Bray* and equal protection in the realm of abortion legislation and noting how liberty-based claims have offered something of an end-run around equal protection cases).

2.   Geduldig, Feeney, *and the Court's Theory of Equal Protection*. These cases reflect several features of the Court's philosophy for interpreting the Equal Protection Clause. Most important, the Court has suppressed the anti-subordination goal, perhaps even more in the sex cases than in the race cases. See generally Ruth Colker, *Anti-Subordination Above All: Sex, Race, and Equal Protection*, 61 NYU L. Rev. 1003 (1986). Compare *Craig* with *Feeney*. In the former case, where the sex-based discrimination inconvenienced young men, the Court struck it down because it appeared on the face of the statute. In the latter case, where the sex-based discrimination severely disadvantaged women, the Court upheld it because the sex differential was not "intended" and the veteran-based classification was rational. (Yet one reason the sex discrimination was an inevitable consequence is the traditional discrimination against women by the military, which has been embodied in facial classifications. See note 3 following the VMI case.)

Also, Court majorities have been reluctant, for institutional reasons, to require states to rearrange their workplace policies, absent invidious motivation. The Court's baseline is that state governments should be given leeway to make the complicated allocative judgments required for disability plans such as the one in *Geduldig* and personnel policies such as that in *Feeney*. While open and invidious sex- or race-based criteria trump such a baseline, it snaps back into place when challengers are "merely" asserting disparate impact. Finally, as Justice Stewart said in *Feeney*, "when there is no 'reason to infer antipathy,' it is presumed that 'even improvident decisions will eventually be rectified by the democratic process.'" Recall that women are a majority of the voting public. Public choice theory, however, would suggest that a statute benefitting veterans, a tightly (male-) bonded and well organized group, would be hard to change in the democratic process; even though they might be outnumbered by the Helen Feeneys, as well as the male victims, of the veterans preference, they have legislative inertia on their side.[50]

3.   *Disparate Impact on Women under State Constitutional Law*. Recall that many states have state constitutional equal rights amendments. One is Massachusetts: "Equality under the law shall not be denied *or abridged* because of sex, race, color, creed or national origin" (emphasis added).[51] Feeney challenged the veterans preference only under the U.S. Constitution in federal court. Would she have been more successful bringing her lawsuit in state court and invoking the state constitution as well?

---

[50]   For other ironies of the case, see Michael Seidman, *Public Principle and Private Choice: The Uneasy Case for a Boundary Maintenance Theory of Constitutional Law*, 96 Yale L.J. 1006 (1987). For an argument that the traditional distinction between discriminatory intent and impact is one among several elements of the Court's equal protection doctrine that has begun to fray in the realm of gender and beyond, see Holning Lau and Hillary Li, *American Equal Protection and Global Convergence*, 86 Fordham L. Rev. 1251 (2017).

[51]   The ERAs in Maryland, Pennsylvania, Washington say that "equality of rights shall not be abridged or denied because of sex," and there is similar language in the ERAs of three other states (Colorado, Hawaii, Texas).

NOTE ON STATUTORY RIGHTS AGAINST SEX AND PREGNANCY DISCRIMINATION IN PRIVATE AND PUBLIC EMPLOYMENT

SHOULD GEDULDIG *BE OVERRULED?*

Congress in Title VII of the Civil Rights Act of 1964 prohibited private job discrimination or adverse job classification "because of" an employee's "race, color, religion, sex, or national origin." 42 U.S.C. § 2000e–2(a)(1)–(2). The sex discrimination component was neither thoroughly considered by Congress nor vigorously enforced at the outset, but it was an unmistakable command that Congress extended to state and local employers in the statute's 1972 amendments. Moreover, the Supreme Court construed the statute to prohibit employment policies having an unjustified "disparate impact" on employees because of their race, sex, etc., *Griggs v. Duke Power Co.*, 401 U.S. 424 (1971)— precisely the kind of claim that the Court refused to constitutionalize five years later in *Washington v. Davis*. Note that Title VII as amended would seemingly require a different result in *Feeney*—were it not for the fact that § 712 preserves federal, state, and local veterans' preferences. 42 U.S.C. § 2000e–11. Recall the public choice point in the previous Note.

Griggs would also suggest that Title VII as amended would require a different result in *Geduldig*, at least as applied to insurance programs tied to state employment, but the Court followed *Geduldig* rather than *Griggs* in *General Electric v. Gilbert*, 429 U.S. 125 (1976), upholding an employer disability plan which excluded disability arising from pregnancy. The Court found that the exclusion of pregnancy was not a statutory discrimination "because of * * * sex" (it's because of pregnancy!) and that the whole package of disability benefits was not worth more to men than to women. The attorneys in *Gilbert*, Professors Wendy Webster Williams and Susan Deller Ross, lobbied Congress to override the Court, on the ground that pregnancy-based discriminations have traditionally been a barrier to women obtaining certain jobs and advancing up employment ladders. Congress agreed and overrode the Court with the Pregnancy Discrimination Act of 1978 (PDA), which defined "sex" in Title VII to include "pregnancy, childbirth, or related medical conditions"; the PDA further provided that "women affected by pregnancy, childbirth, or related medical conditions shall be treated the same for all employment-related purposes, including receipt of benefits under fringe benefit programs, as other persons not so affected but similar in their ability or inability to work." 42 U.S.C. § 2000e(k). The Supreme Court has applied the PDA to invalidate on statutory grounds employer policies disqualifying pregnant women from certain jobs the employer considered potentially harmful to the fetus. See *United Auto Workers v. Johnson Controls*, 499 U.S. 187 (1991).

In *Price Waterhouse v. Hopkins*, 490 U.S. 228 (1989), the Court held that it is sex discrimination if an employer disadvantages an employee because she violates traditional gender roles. The plaintiff, Ann Hopkins, had allegedly been denied partnership at Price Waterhouse on the ground that some partners felt she was "macho" and uncharming; even her supporters urged her to "walk more femininely, talk more femininely," etc. Again, Congress picked up on this idea when it enacted the Family and Medical Leave Act of 1993 (FMLA). One purpose of the FMLA was to require employers to provide such leaves to *both* male and female employees, for it was often assumed that only female employees wanted such leaves, a classic gender stereotype that Congress believed held women back in the workplace.

In *Nevada Department of Human Resources v. Hibbs*, 538 U.S. 721 (2003) (reproduced in Chapter 7, § 3F), the Supreme Court ruled that Congress in the FMLA was attacking sex discrimination along the following lines: "Historically, denial or curtailment of women's employment opportunities has been traceable directly to the pervasive presumption that women are mothers first, and workers second. This prevailing ideology about women's roles has in turn justified discrimination against women when they are mothers or mothers-to-be." (Quoting the FMLA's legislative history.) The Court held that it was a violation of the Equal Protection Clause for state employers to provide family leave only to female employees or to administer such leaves in a discriminatory manner. The Court also said that this was the problem Congress was trying to address, with incomplete success, in the PDA. The Court further said that it was a violation of equal protection for states to offer no family leave at all, as "such a policy would exclude far more women than men from the workplace." This was precisely the argument that the Court rejected in *Geduldig*. Should *Geduldig* be overruled?

PROBLEM 4-2:
SEX DISCRIMINATION AND GENDER IDENTITY

How should the principles the Court has developed for constitutional sex discrimination apply to claims of discrimination based on gender identity? This question has been coming to the fore over the last several years, as courts grapple with claims brought by transgender individuals. Clashes over equal access to bathrooms have been especially salient. The following problem is based on a series of events in North Carolina in 2016 and 2017 that made national news.

(a) In 2016, the state enacted, as an "emergency" measure, H.B. 2, a law pushing back against Charlotte's new ordinance barring discrimination because of sexual orientation or gender identity. One provision of the law imposed this requirement on public school boards: "Local boards of education shall require every multiple occupancy bathroom or changing facility that is designated for student use to be designated for and used only by students based on their biological sex." N.C. Gen. Stat. § 115C–521.2(b). The law allowed school boards to provide single-occupancy bathrooms, *id.* § 115C–521.2(c), and contained exceptions for custodial, maintenance, medical, and other exceptional purposes. Id. § 115C–521.2(d).

Suppose that, while the law was in effect, a male-to-female transgender high school student, Kim P., asked the school principal for permission to use the girls' restroom in the local North Carolina high school. After consultation with teachers, student groups, and staff, the principal agreed and notified everyone in the school. The local school board vetoed that plan, based upon the new law. The board issued this statement: "We have no discretion to allow access to a school restroom that does not match the student's 'biological sex.' "

If the student sued the school board, claiming a violation of the Equal Protection Clause, how would the District Court evaluate her claim: Is this a "sex discrimination" that triggers the heightened scrutiny of *Craig v. Boren*? If not, does the school board have a "rational basis" for the discrimination? What is the board's best justification? Would it pass *Craig*'s heightened scrutiny?

(b) In 2017, the North Carolina legislature repealed H.B. 2. But it replaced the bill with H.B. 142, a new law that preempted (1) any state agency, university, local board of education or other political subdivision of the state from regulating access to multiple occupancy restrooms, showers, or changing facilities, except in accordance with an act of the state legislature; and (2) any local government in the state from enacting or amending, before an identified date, any ordinance regulating private employment or public accommodations. The upshot of the replacement bill seems to be that no public entity can regulate to mandate access for transgender students to use the restroom that matches their gender identity unless the state legislature has done so. In addition, no local entity can add new protections against discrimination in employment or public accommodations, including protections based on gender identity, before that same identified date. If Kim P.'s school board took the same position on restroom access that it took in section (a) above, would the adoption of the new law change the equal protection analysis in Kim's lawsuit? If so, how? As you consider this question, assume that the state legislature has not enacted any law protecting transgender students' access to restrooms matching their gender identity.

Note: After you have read *Romer v. Evans* (Sec. 3.D below), you may want to revisit the second provision of HB 142, barring the enactment of new local anti-discrimination protections before a stated date.

On the question of whether gender identity-based discrimination is a form of sex discrimination under either the Equal Protection Clause or federal statutory law, compare the conflicting approaches in *Glenn v. Brumby*, 663 F.3d 1312 (11th Cir. 2011) (gender identity discrimination is a form of sex discrimination) with *Etsitty v. Utah Transit Auth.*, 502 F.3d 1215 (10th Cir. 2007) (gender identity discrimination is not a form of sex discrimination). After the materials on sexual orientation, Problem 4-6 will ask you to assess whether discrimination against transgender people should be accorded heightened scrutiny, independent of whether a court would see it as a form of sex discrimination.

C. CRITIQUES OF ABSTRACT EQUALITY AND THE EMERGENCE OF A JURISPRUDENCE OF DIFFERENCE

For a number of feminist legal scholars, the litigation strategy adopted by women's groups in the 1970s, and reflected in many of the Court's decisions, erroneously glorified abstract principle over concrete result.

"Formal equality * * * can effect only limited change. It cannot, for example, ensure that jobs are structured so that female workers and male workers are equally able to combine wage work and parenthood. Nor can it ensure that social security, unemployment compensation, and other safety nets are structured so as to provide for women's financial security as well as they provide for men's. Moreover, women, especially ordinary mothers and wives, have been harmed by the changes effected to date by the movement towards formal equality." Mary Becker, *Prince Charming: Abstract Equality*, 1987 Sup. Ct. Rev. 201, 247.[52] Because some of the most harmful discriminations against women were sex-neutral, such as those in *Geduldig* and *Feeney*, formal equality failed to address the big issues. Because men were often the plaintiffs, some of the feminist "victories" took away preferences women enjoyed in law. Consider three areas of concern:

1.   *Alimony and Child Support*. The Court in *Orr v. Orr*, 440 U.S. 268 (1979), invalidated state laws imposing alimony (or, by implication, child support) payments on husbands but not wives. The Court found the sex-based classification grounded in gender stereotypes (the woman is always the dependent) and rejected Alabama's claim that it was remedial (the only women helped by the classification were well-to-do). Although defensible under *Craig*, *Orr* came at a time when many wives were impoverished by the no-fault divorce revolution, which allowed men so inclined to abandon their supportive spouses more readily and, often, without easily enforceable alimony and child support obligations.[53]

2.   *Benefit and Tax Statutes*. Women's groups persuaded the Court to strike down (or Congress to change) most of the sex-based distinctions in federal statutes setting Social Security and other work-related benefits. Yet the beneficiaries of these victories are usually men (the widowers in *Wiesenfeld* and *Goldfarb*), who continue to earn a lot more on average than female wage earners. More important, sex-based classifications on the face of the statute are not the problem for most women. "[T]he major problem with social security was *and is* its treatment of ordinary women, women

---

[52] For other critiques of equality feminism, see Ann Freedman, *Sex Equality, Sex Differences, and the Supreme Court*, 92 Yale L.J. 913 (1983); Christine Littleton, *Reconstructing Sexual Equality*, 75 Calif. L. Rev. 1279 (1987). An effort at synthesis is Elizabeth Schneider, *The Dialectic of Rights and Politics: Perspectives from the Women's Movement*, 61 N.Y.U. L. Rev. 589 (1986). A scholarly review of the equality problems still facing women in the workplace, the home, and elsewhere can be found in Deborah Rhode, *Justice and Gender: Sex Discrimination and the Law* chs. 6–11 (1989), with a concluding essay on the sameness/difference debates within feminism.

[53] See generally *Symposium: Divorce and Feminist Legal Theory*, 82 Geo. L.J. 2119–2569 (1994).

who are primarily responsible for domestic production and reproduction and who often participate, on a limited basis, in wage employment. The social security system is structured to afford greater financial security in old age to breadwinners than to full or part-time homemakers. Thus, the major problem from the perspective of women's inequality is not, as the cases suggest, that the social security system has treated the atypical woman differently from a similar man, but rather that it gives less effective old-age financial security to typical women than to typical men."[54]

3. *Preferences for Women.* Equality theory has arguably put women in the same bind the NAACP's victories put blacks in: By problematizing sex-based classifications at the very point when women were gaining real political clout, equal protection theory became a sharp tool to criticize, and perhaps overturn, statutes seeking to remedy the functional barriers to women's equal participation in society and the economy and to address women's unique experiences and problems. That is why some feminist legal scholars argue for a jurisprudence of difference: "[P]regnancy, abortion, reproduction, and creation of another human being *are* special—very special. Women have these experiences. Men do not. An equality doctrine that ignores the unique quality of these experiences implicitly says that women can claim equality only insofar as they are like men. Such doctrine demands that women deny an important aspect of who they are." Sylvia Law, *Rethinking Sex and the Constitution*, 132 U. Pa. L. Rev. 955, 1007 (1984).

The debate over formal equality shows up most sharply in cases where a recently enacted statute draws sex-based distinctions that benefit women, but usually in response to a traditional inequity. E.g., *California Fed. Savs. & Loan Ass'n v. Guerra*, 479 U.S. 272 (1987) (ruling that Title VII did not preempt a state law ensuring family leave time for female but not male employees).

PROBLEM 4-3:
IS SEX SEGREGATION IN SCHOOLS EVER CONSTITUTIONAL?

(A) *All-Girls' Elementary School.* In a series of publications informed by expert surveys, the American Association of University Women (AAUW) concluded that girls as early as third grade are disadvantaged by being educated with boys. See AAUW, *How Schools Shortchange Girls* (1992), and *Achieving Gender Equity in the Classroom and on the Campus: The Next Steps* (1995). Reasons may include greater teacher (including female teacher) attention to the boys, an overwhelming male focus in the teaching materials, and the channeling of the girls' social attention toward the boys. Some studies have found that girls in single-sex schools score a half-grade above their

---

[54] Mary Becker, *Obscuring the Struggle: Sex Discrimination, Social Security, and Stone, Seidman, Sunstein & Tushnet's* Constitutional Law, 89 Colum. L. Rev. 264, 276 (1989).

coeducational counterparts on four academic ability tests, and a full grade higher on science tests.[55] Following school boards in New York, California, Virginia, and other states, a local school board finds these theories to have merit and wants to apply them in a single school, open to female but not male applicants from the county school system. Is this constitutional after the VMI case? For lower court cases considering issues of this kind, see *Garrett v. Board of Educ.*, 775 F. Supp. 1004 (E.D. Mich. 1991) (all-male academies in inner city are unconstitutional); *A.N.A. ex rel. S.F.A. v. Breckinridge Cty. Board of Educ.*, 833 F. Supp. 2d 673 (W.D. Ky. 2011) (providing students the option to take single-gender classes is constitutional); *Doe v. Wood Cty. Board of Educ.*, 888 F. Supp. 2d 771 (W.D. W.Va. 2012) (students' challenge of opt-in—as opposed to opt-out—single-sex public middle schools was likely to succeed on equal protection grounds).

(B) *All-Girls' Schools Revisited?* Would your answer to the previous inquiry change in light of the AAUW's later study, *Separated by Sex: A Critical Look at Single-Sex Education for Girls* (1998), which concluded that "there is no evidence in general that single-sex education works or is better for girls than coeducation." The second AAUW study specifically found: (1) "girls and boys succeed" wherever and whenever elements of a good education are present, like small classes and schools, equitable teaching practices, and focused academic curriculum; (2) while "some kinds of single-sex programs produce positive results" for some girls, including a preference for math and science, increased risk-taking, and increased confidence, it was unclear whether these benefits "derive from factors unique to single-sex programs or factors that promote good education such as small classes," etc.; (3) there is no escape from sexism, even in single-sex schools and classes, which have drawbacks of their own, such as depriving girls of the social benefits of coeducation. On the other hand, the Department of Education has come down the other way, concluding that single-sex education is better for many girls and proposing that federal law explicitly acknowledge that (controversial) conclusion. 67 Fed. Reg. 31,098 (May 8, 2002).

(C) *Sex-Segregated Sports.* Almost all public schools maintain athletic programs that are sex-segregated. Swanson Junior High School has a boys' but not a girls' football team. Jane Doe is an athletic girl who wants to play football; sports medical experts tell the school that she is as qualified as the boys to play several positions, and she has in fact played in recreational leagues. The school refuses to allow her to compete for a position on the boys' team. Constitutional? *Compare O'Connor v. Board of Educ.*, 449 U.S. 1301 (1980) (Stevens, J., as circuit Justice, denying an application to vacate a stay that favored the school in seeking to maintain sex-segregated sports); *Beattie v. Line Mountain Sch. Dist.*, 992 F. Supp. 2d 384 (M.D. Pa. 2014) (granting preliminary injunction against schools that would not allow a female student to participate on all male wrestling team); *Kleczek v. Rhode Island Interscholastic League, Inc.*, 768 F. Supp. 951 (D.R.I. 1991) (denying preliminary injunction against school that

---

[55] See Note, *Inner-City Single-Sex Schools: Educational Reform or Invidious Discrimination?*, 105 Harv. L. Rev. 1741, 1757 (1992).

would not allow a male student to play on the girls' field hockey team). Should Justice Stevens' disposition be revisited in light of the VMI case? Suppose a school has football for boys and soccer for girls. Should a boy be allowed to compete for a spot on the soccer team?

CATHARINE A. MACKINNON,
Toward a Feminist Theory of the State
220–22, 225–27, 232, 244–45 (1991)[56]

The philosophy underlying the sameness/difference approach applies liberalism to women. Sex is a natural difference, a division, a distinction, beneath which lies a stratum of human commonality, sameness. The moral thrust of the sameness branch of the doctrine conforms normative rules to empirical reality by granting women access to what men have: to the extent women are no different from men, women deserve what men have. The differences branch, which is generally regarded as patronizing and unprincipled but necessary to avoid absurdity, exists to value or compensate women for what they are or have become distinctively as women—by which is meant, unlike men, or to leave women as "different" as equality law finds them.

Most scholarship on sex discrimination law concerns which of these paths to sex equality is preferable in the long run * * * as if they were all there is. As a prior matter, however, treating issues of sex equality as issues of sameness and difference is to take a particular approach. This approach is here termed the sameness/difference approach because it is obsessed with the sex difference. Its main theme is: "we're the same, we're the same, we're the same." Its counterpoint theme (in a higher register) goes: "but we're different, but we're different, but we're different." * * *

Concealed is the substantive way in which man has become the measure of all things. Under the sameness rubric, women are measured according to correspondence with man, their equality judged by proximity to his measure. Under the difference rubric, women are measured according to their lack of correspondence from man, their womanhood judged by their distance from his measure. Gender neutrality is the male standard. The special protection rule is the female standard. Masculinity or maleness is the referent for both. * * *

The sameness standard has mostly gotten men the benefit of those few things women have historically had—for all the good they did. Under gender neutrality, the law of custody and divorce has shifted once again, giving men what is termed an equal chance at custody of children and at alimony. Men often look like better parents under gender-neutral rules like level of income and presence of nuclear family, because men make more money and * * * initiate the building of family units. They also have greater

---

[56] Reprinted with permission of Professor Catharine MacKinnon, the copyright holder.

credibility and authority in court. Under gender neutrality, men are in effect granted a preference as parents because society advantages them before they get to court. * * *

Missing in sex equality law is what Aristotle missed in his empiricist notion that equality means treating likes alike and unlikes unlike. * * * Why should one have to be the same as a man to get what a man gets simply because he is one? Why does maleness provide an original entitlement * * * ?

The women that gender neutrality benefits, and there are some, expose this method in highest relief. They are mostly women who have achieved a biography that somewhat approximates the male norm, at least on paper. They are the qualified, the least of sex discrimination's victims. When they are denied a man's chance, it looks the most like sex bias. [*E.g., Hopkins.*] * * *

The special benefits side of the sameness/difference approach has not compensated women for being second class. Its double standard does not give women the dignity of the single standard, nor does it suppress the gender of its referent: female. The special benefits rule is the only place in mainstream sex equality doctrine where one can identify as a woman and not have that mean giving up all claim to equal treatment. But it comes close. Originally, women were permitted to be protected in the workforce, with dubious benefit. Then, under its double standard, women who stood to inherit something when their husbands died were allowed to exclude a small percentage of inheritance tax, Justice Douglas waxing eloquent about the difficulties of all women's economic situation. [*Kahn.*] If women are going to be stigmatized as different, the compensation should at least fit the disparity. Women have also gotten three more years than men get before being advanced or kicked out of the military hierarchy. [*Ballard.*] This is to compensate them for being precluded from combat, the usual way to advance. [*Rostker.*] Making exceptions for women, as if they are a special case, often seems preferable to correcting the rule itself, even when women's "specialness" is dubious or shared or statutorily created. * * *

The result of gender neutrality is that at the same time that very few women gain access to the preconditions effectively to assert equality on male terms, women created in society's traditional mold lose the guarantees of those roles to men asserting sex equality. Women asking courts to enforce the guarantees that have been part of the bargain of women's roles receive less and less, while also not receiving the benefits of the social changes that would qualify them for rights on the same terms as men. This is not a transitional problem. Abstract equality necessarily reinforces the inequalities of the status quo to the extent that it evenly reflects an unequal social arrangement. The law of sex discrimination has largely refused to recognize that it is women who are unequal to men, and has called this refusal the equality principle. * * *

* * * [This analysis] does challenge the view that neutrality, specifically gender neutrality as an expression of objectivity, is adequate to the nonneutral objectified social reality women experience. If differentiation were the problem, gender neutrality would make sense as an approach to it. Since hierarchy is the problem, it is not only inadequate, it is perverse. * * * [C]urrent law to rectify sex inequality is premised upon, and promotes, its continued existence.

The analytical point of departure and return of sex discrimination law is thus the liberal one of gender differences, understood rationally or irrationally to create gender inequalities. The feminist issue, by contrast, is gender hierarchy, which not only produces inequalities but shapes the social meaning, hence legal relevance, of the sex difference. * * *

* * * Can women, demanding actual equality through law, be part of changing the state's relation to women and women's relation to men?

The first step [toward an adequate sex equality argument] is to claim women's concrete reality. Women's inequality occurs in a context of unequal pay, allocation to disrespected work, demeaned physical characteristics, targeting for rape, domestic battery, sexual abuse as children, and systematic sexual harassment. Women are daily dehumanized, used in denigrating entertainment, denied reproductive control, and forced by the conditions of their lives into prostitution. These abuses occur in a legal context historically characterized by disenfranchisement, preclusion from property ownership, exclusion from public life, and lack of recognition of sex-specific injuries. Sex inequality is thus a social and political institution.

The next step is to recognize that male forms of power over women are affirmatively embodied as individual rights in law. When men lose power, they feel they lose rights. Often they are not wrong. Examples include the defense of mistaken belief in consent in the rape law, which legally determines whether or not a rape occurred from the rapists' perspective; freedom of speech, which gives pimps rights to torture, exploit, use, and sell women to men through pictures and words, and gives consumers rights to buy them; the law of privacy, which defines home and sex as presumptively consensual and protects the use of pornography in the home; the law of child custody, which purports gender neutrality while applying a standard of adequacy of parenting based on male-controlled resources and male-defined norms, sometimes taking children away from women but more generally controlling women through the threat and fear of loss of their children. Real sex equality under law would qualify or eliminate these powers of men, hence men's current "rights" to use, access, possess, and traffic women and children.

NOTES ON RADICAL AND CRITICAL FEMINIST THEORIES

As the MacKinnon excerpt suggests, it can be argued that, notwithstanding judicial decisions striking down "archaic" sex-based classifications and purporting to deliver formal equality, women are not equal citizens in the United States. Women make less money than similarly qualified males, are sexually harassed on the job and in the classroom, and are subject to rape by dates and spouses as well as by strangers.[57] Arguably, the statutory or constitutional reforms only nibble at the margins—treating women like men for purposes of drinking (*Craig*), alimony (*Orr*), property (*Reed*), survivors' benefits (*Wiesenfeld*), education (the VMI case), and a few minor compensatory measures (*Ballard, Webster, Guerra*). By lining up marginal victories that mean little, perhaps legal feminism has deflected attention from the real problems that remain. See also Robin West, *Progressive Constitutionalism: Restructuring the Fourteenth Amendment* (1994), which makes similar constitutional arguments for the affirmative responsibilities of the state to address private violence and discrimination against women. How would liberal feminists respond to such critique? Scholars influenced by sociobiology? Consider also some larger questions of constitutional theory raised by MacKinnon and West:

1.   *Transforming Law.* If law is thoroughly gendered, law needs to be rethought from the ground up, not just at the margins (the mistake of equality feminism) or with special remedial exceptions (the mistake of difference feminism). Radical feminism insists that a state founded on male baselines is not constitutionally legitimate for the non-male majority. To sustain its legitimacy in a polity where women are full and equal citizens, law needs to be reconceived from women's point of view.

Consider a radical approach to the VMI case. The Court interrogated the historical arguments for sex-segregated colleges and thereby exposed their sexist philosophy—but then failed to interrogate the linkages between VMI's pedagogy and its all-male culture. Such an interrogation might have exposed a sexist philosophy underlying the adversarial method and the ritual (fraternity-like) hazing entailed in that culture. In that event, the remedy sought by the Department of Justice and accepted by the Court might be shallow, for it might leave VMI as an institution profoundly hostile to women and it might have female taxpayers fund an institution that almost none of them would want to attend. Under a radical critique, the VMI Court's analogy to *Sweatt* was telling, for that was a race case where the Court simply ordered a person of color admitted to an extremely inhospitable white institution, with no protection for the minority nor any requirement that the institution protect the student from inevitable harassment. Just as tellingly, the VMI Court did not invoke *Green* or *Swann*, desegregation cases where the Department of

---

[57] See generally Justice Souter's dissent in *United States v. Morrison*, Chapter 7, § 3E (summarizing extensive congressional findings regarding the high level of violence against women in the United States); Susan Estrich, *Sex at Work*, 43 Stan. L. Rev. 813 (1991) (pervasive sexual harassment of women in the workplace); Vicki Schultz, *Life's Work*, 100 Colum. L. Rev. 1881 (2000) (continuing sex segregation and employment discrimination against women).

Justice requested, and the Court required, long-segregated state institutions to take affirmative steps to restructure themselves.

Recall the liberal feminist critique of *Michael M.*, reflected in Justice Brennan's dissent: The gendered rape law was invalid because it rested on traditional notions of female virginity as valuable and the older male as the only responsible actor. MacKinnon has criticized the dissent for being more concerned "with avoiding the stereotyping attendant to the ideological message the law communicated than with changing the facts that make the stereotype largely true. In the interest of opposing facial distinctions and debunking the supposed myth of male sexual aggression, the fact that it is overwhelmingly girls who are sexually victimized by older males for reasons wholly unrelated to their capacity to become pregnant was completely obscured. * * * Underage girls form a credible disadvantaged group for equal protection purposes when the social facts of sexual assault are faced, facts which prominently feature one-sided sexual aggression by older males." Catharine MacKinnon, *Reflections on Sex Equality Under Law*, 100 Yale L.J. 1281, 1305 (1991). If you agree with MacKinnon's critique, how would you vote to uphold the sex-based law in *Michael M*? Does MacKinnon's critique run the risk of perpetuating a view of adolescent girls as fragile creatures in need of protection from predatory boys? Consider the next Note.

2. *Equality and Liberty.* Radical feminists argue that the Supreme Court overemphasizes the libertarian features of the original Constitution, which they maintain has been modified or even trumped by the egalitarian features of the Reconstructed Constitution and the Nineteenth Amendment. These are *not* just another set of amendments—they rescued the original Constitution from illegitimacy in a polity where people of color and, later, women are citizens whose interests must be respected. For women, equality values are particularly important, and traditional liberty values must give way through the kind of constitutional holism or synthesis described in Chapter 2, § 3C.

Accordingly, Professor MacKinnon, *Francis Biddle's Sister: Pornography, Civil Rights, and Speech*, in *Feminism Unmodified* 163 (1987), argues that the state must suppress misogynistic pornography, because it perpetuates a culture where women are sexualized and therefore objectified. This is not a culture where women *can* be equal citizens. MacKinnon recognizes the obvious response, that such suppression would infringe on men's First Amendment liberties. She replies that this kind of liberty for men cannot justify more serious deprivations of liberty for women (whom she claims suffer sexual assaults as a result of pornography). When two kinds of liberty are at stake, a "neutral" Court cannot cogently prefer the liberty of those who are inclined to *commit* the violence over the liberty of those who will *suffer* it. If women's equal citizenship is to mean anything, it has got to mean that the state can suppress violence-inducing "speech."

MacKinnon's critique of pornography has called forth vigorous feminist responses. By defining women too much by male sexual oppression against them, pro-sex feminists such as Carole Vance argue that MacKinnon's brand of feminism denies women's personal and sexual agency.[58] MacKinnon's dominance thesis, they maintain, oversimplifies women's experience and denies women a resource needed for self-understanding and even resistance. Robin West, *The Difference in Women's Hedonic Lives: A Phenomenological Critique of Feminist Legal Theory*, 3 Wis. Women's L.J. 81 (1987), criticizes MacKinnon for not attending to women's own accounts of pleasure and fulfillment. Just as some women apparently want to attend VMI and participate in its culture of ritualized hazing, so some women enjoy dominance forms of sexual intercourse popularized in soft-core pornography. It is a departure from feminist method, West argues, to elevate abstract conceptions of women's equality above concrete experiences women consider valuable as a matter of their own sexual liberty.

West's article also criticizes liberal constitutionalism for its assumption that citizens are autonomous, utility-maximizing agents. Liberal constitutionalism seeks to prevent the state from unduly restricting people's range of choices and from coercing choices. Drawing from cultural feminist thought, West argues that this rests upon male-centered and thereby biased assumptions. Women are more relational than men; they often "choose" options because of the benefits that flow to people with whom they feel connected (children, spouses, friends). So giving them more choices (the goal of liberalism) will not necessarily benefit women, and the fact that they have the same formal choices as men does not mean that women are being treated equally by the state. The *circumstances* of choice are more important than the *possibility* of choice. If the circumstances offer women few realistic choices, because of continuing sexist structures and ideology, women will lose rather than exercise liberty through choice, which is perverse. From these Westian ideas, formulate a possible defense for the constitutionality of the sex-based law in *Michael M.* Is *Nguyen* defensible under her theory?

3.   *Feminist Critique of the Public-Private Distinction and the State Action Doctrine.* For libertarian and institutionalist reasons, the state action requirement plays a central role in the Supreme Court's narrow enforcement of the Equal Protection Clause (Chapter 3, § 2). The Court's constitutionalism reaches the conduct of "public" but not "private" actors. An expansive state action doctrine is objectionable from a feminist perspective. Most violence and discrimination against women are carried out by private actors; such violence and discrimination harm women and deny them both genuine liberty and full equality. The Constitution ought to be concerned about this—but the traditional state action doctrine has been the doctrinal basis for judicial abnegation. The state action doctrine, and not the Constitution, ought to give way.[59]

---

[58]   See *Pleasure and Danger: Exploring Female Sexuality* (Carole Vance ed., 2d ed. 1992); *Powers of Desire: The Politics of Sexuality* (Anne Snitow et al. eds. 1983); Kathryn Abrams, *Sex Wars Redux: Agency and Coercion in Feminist Legal Theory*, 95 Colum. L. Rev. 304 (1995).

[59]   See Ruth Gavison, *Feminism and the Public/Private Distinction*, 45 Stan. L. Rev. 1 (1992); Frances Olsen, *Statutory Rape: A Feminist Critique of Rights Analysis*, 63 Tex. L. Rev. 387 (1984).

One feminist approach would be to view the idea of state action expansively, as the NAACP's Inc. Fund and its allies did in the lunch counter sit-in cases. See *Lombard v. Louisiana*, 373 U.S. 267 (1963) (refusal of lunch place to serve people of color can be attributed to the state because of the state's long support of racist attitudes through apartheid). State entanglement theories could justify attributing some private action to the state. Another approach would be to take an expansive view of state responsibility for failing to act. Robin West, *Equality Theory, Marital Rape, and the Promise of the Fourteenth Amendment*, 42 Fla. L. Rev. 45 (1990), makes this kind of argument: State laws long exempted domestic rape and violence against women from sexual assault statutes and still exempt marital rape under some circumstances; state police and prosecutors do not vigorously enforce the laws that do exist; these policies of state neglect as well as action give rise to state responsibility for domestic violence against women. To be sure, American courts generally do not take the state to task for its inaction—but this is another legacy of the Constitution's original sexism. As before, the baseline should be the Reconstructed Constitution: Just as the state in *Green* and *Swann* had an obligation to restructure a status quo founded on racist policies, so the state now has an obligation to restructure a status quo founded on sexist policies.

Some feminists deny the constitutional imperative of the state action doctrine through an expansive reading of the Thirteenth Amendment. Thus, one might argue that private as well as public obstacles to women's exercising their right to choose abortions constitute efforts to impose "involuntary servitude" on women that is directly actionable under the Thirteenth Amendment. Other feminists undercut the state action requirement through a literal reading of the Fourteenth Amendment that dovetails with its anti-subordination purpose. Kenneth Karst, *The Supreme Court, 1976 Term—Foreword: Equal Citizenship Under the Fourteenth Amendment*, 91 Harv. L. Rev. 1 (1977), maintains that the Fourteenth Amendment must be read in light of its first sentence, the Citizenship Clause, which does not have a state action requirement. Robin West argues in *Progressive Constitutionalism* (1994) that the state's obligation, in the second sentence, to assure "equal protection of the laws" *literally* requires the state to protect women where they are most vulnerable (within the family) at least as strongly as the state protects men in the public sphere (streets, business).

Under Karst's or West's theory, the state has an obligation to adopt statutory rape laws to protect girls against sexual assault. Justice Rehnquist's *Michael M.* arguments are enriched by this line of thought: If the state has reason to believe (as Rehnquist claimed) that a sex-neutral statutory rape law would discourage female minors from reporting assaults by male minors, the efficacy of the law would be undermined; under those circumstances, the state has a strong equal *protection* interest in defining the crime in gendered terms. If the factual predicate of this argument is correct, is this argument a cogent defense of *Michael M.*? Was the case rightly decided?

SECTION 3. WHAT LEVEL OF SCRUTINY FOR OTHER "SUSPICIOUS" CLASSIFICATIONS?

A central lesson of the race discrimination cases, amplified in the sex discrimination cases, was that a group could sweep away almost all formal state discriminations stigmatizing its members if social movement lawyers could persuade the Supreme Court to recognize the trait marking the group's members as a "suspect" or "quasi-suspect" classification. For reasons of federalism, institutional legitimacy, and the capacity of the judiciary to handle large numbers of claims, the Court after 1976 was leery of creating more such classifications. In this section, we examine the claims of several social movements and the Court's responses. Consider, also, the Court's uncertainty as to what criteria should determine which classifications should be subjected to strict scrutiny. Finally, reflect on the thesis, first advanced by Justice Thurgood Marshall, that the "double standard" of strict and usually fatal scrutiny for a few classifications and rational basis and easy-to-pass scrutiny for all others, has never adequately explained the Court's actual decisionmaking and that the Court does and should follow a context-specific approach where it considers the reliability of the classification, the importance of the state benefit discriminatorily apportioned, and the cogency of the state justification for the particular discrimination. *San Antonio Indep. Sch. Dist. v. Rodriguez* (Marshall, J., dissenting) (Chapter 5, § 3B).[60]

A. WEALTH

Early American history was filled with statutes discriminating on the basis of wealth; property ownership, for example, was often a requirement for the exercise of the franchise. Since the Civil War, most laws formally excluding or discriminating against people on the basis of wealth have disappeared. But countless statutes have the effect of excluding or discriminating against people without much money. A law requiring a couple to pay a state fee to obtain a marriage license may not formally bar poor people from getting married, but it would have the effect of discouraging some poor people from being able to take advantage of the institution of civil marriage. From the perspective of the person without much money, the statutes are equivalent. In the world of *Washington v. Davis* (Chapter 3, § 1B), their constitutional status might be different.

---

[60] Academics have been especially receptive to Justice Marshall's functional (anti-tiers) approach. See Suzanne Goldberg, *Equality Without Tiers,* 77 S. Cal. L. Rev. 481 (2004); Toni Massaro, *Gay Rights, Thick and Thin,* 49 Stan. L. Rev. 45 (1996), as well as Leslie Friedman Goldstein, *Between the Tiers: The New(est) Equal Protection and* Bush v. Gore, 4 U. Pa. J. Const. L. 372 (2002); Peter Smith, Note, *The Demise of Three-Tier Review: Has the United States Supreme Court Adopted a "Sliding Scale" Approach Toward Equal Protection Jurisprudence?,* J. Contemp. L. 475 (1997).

For a time, the Court seemed to apply heightened scrutiny to statutes disadvantaging the poor by imposing a charge for governmental services or, even more broadly, failing to provide support for the necessary expenditures of life. For example, the Court held that in most circumstances a poor person charged with a crime has a right to free counsel at trial and on appeal, *Gideon v. Wainwright*, 372 U.S. 335 (1963) (right to counsel in felony cases); *Argersinger v. Hamlin*, 407 U.S. 25 (1972) (right to counsel in misdemeanor cases if a prison term is imposed), and that the state may not impose appellate filing fees or a charge for a transcript on appeal if that would preclude access to the appellate process. *Griffin v. Illinois*, 351 U.S. 12 (1956) (felony cases); *Mayer v. Chicago*, 404 U.S. 189 (1971) (misdemeanor cases). Another case outlawed imposing a filing fee on a poor person seeking to file a divorce action. *Boddie v. Connecticut*, 401 U.S. 371 (1971). In the course of invalidating a poll tax— a tax on the privilege of voting—the Court said that "[l]ines drawn on the basis of wealth or property, like those of race, are traditionally disfavored." *Harper v. Virginia Board of Elections*, 383 U.S. 663 (1966). These cases helped fuel a welfare rights movement that sought protections for affirmative state benefits for poor people. See *Goldberg v. Kelly*, 397 U.S. 254 (1970) (requiring the state to provide a due process hearing before depriving recipients of welfare benefits, which the Court treated as an "entitlement" rather than a "privilege").[61]

In the early 1970s, however, the Court rejected the proposition that wealth-based classifications and access fees are suspect. In *San Antonio Independent School District v. Rodriguez*, 411 U.S. 1 (1973) (Chapter 5, § 3B), the Court rejected a challenge to Texas' funding of public education on the ground that it distinguished between rich and poor neighborhoods and areas. Anticipating *Washington v. Davis*, Justice Powell's opinion for the Court noted that wealth-based equal protection claimants like those in *Rodriguez* typically challenge policies that only have discriminatory effects on the poor and do not formally exclude them from state services. Without evidence of invidious intent, such claims cannot succeed, Powell concluded. He also ruled that wealth as a classification had "none of the indicia of suspectness: the class is not saddled with such disabilities, or subjected to a history of purposeful unequal treatment, or relegated to such a position of political powerlessness as to command extraordinary protection from the majoritarian political process." Justice Marshall's dissenting opinion witheringly criticized this reasoning. See also *Dandridge v. Williams*, 397 U.S. 471 (1970). It is very doubtful that *Rodriguez* provides any support for the proposition that the state can provide important services like education only to people who own property or have a certain income, but it probably

---

[61] On the background for *Goldberg*, and a wonderful introduction to much of the welfare rights social movement, see Martha Davis, *Brutal Need: Lawyers and the Welfare Rights Movement, 1960–1973* (1993).

allows states to provide a better quality education for students who live in high-income districts than to those in low-income ones.

In *United States v. Kras*, 409 U.S. 434 (1973), the Court held that you can be too poor to go bankrupt. Justice Blackmun's opinion upheld an across-the-board filing fee for bankruptcy proceedings and admonished the petitioner that the modest cost (as prorated over several months, the cost of a movie each week) was something he ought to be able to pay. The Court in *Ortwein v. Schwab*, 410 U.S. 656 (1973) (per curiam), held that *Griffin*'s waiver of criminal appeal filing fees for the indigent did not extend to civil cases generally: There was no due process right to appeal, nor was there an equal protection violation for state charges that discriminated against the indigent. On the other hand, where the state imposes special, and costly, procedural requirements on only one class of litigants, the Court has scrutinized more vigorously. See *Lindsey v. Normet*, 405 U.S. 56 (1972) (invalidating a double-bond requirement imposed only on tenants appealing their evictions).

Just as the Court seemed to be confining *Griffin* to criminal cases, another arena for challenge opened up in litigation involving parental rights. Thus, in *Lassiter v. Department of Soc. Servs.*, 452 U.S. 18 (1981), the Court ruled that parents were sometimes entitled to attorneys paid for by the state, and in *Little v. Streater*, 452 U.S. 1 (1981), the Court required the state to pay for blood tests to enable an indigent defendant to contest a paternity claim.

M.L.B. v. S.L.J.

519 U.S. 102 (1996)

The Mississippi chancery court terminated the parental rights of M.L.B., who was unable to appeal because she could not afford the $2,352.36 in fees required by the state to prepare a record for appeal. The U.S. Supreme Court, in an opinion by **Justice Ginsburg**, ruled that the state could not constitutionally apply the fee requirement to M.L.B. Justice Ginsburg recognized that the precedents involved both equal protection and due process concerns. "The equal protection concern relates to the legitimacy of fencing out would-be appellants based solely on their inability to pay core costs. *Griffin* (Frankfurter, J., concurring in the judgment). The due process concern homes in on the essential fairness of the state-ordered proceedings anterior to adverse state action." Because due process does not require the state to provide an appeal (*Ortwein*), Ginsburg focused on the equal protection feature of M.L.B.'s claim. In line with the precedents, she considered "the character and intensity of the individual interest at stake, on the one hand, and the State's justification for its exaction, on the other." Even more than in *Mayer*, where the stakes of a lost appeal for the misdemeanor offender (in his case, loss of professional opportunities but not of liberty) outweighed the state's mere pecuniary costs, M.L.B.'s stakes (the loss of her children) were most severe and greatly outweighed the state pecuniary interest (further diluted by the state interest in correcting lower court errors).

Justice Kennedy concurred only in the judgment; he believed the fee invalid as an undue burden on the fairest possible process when family relations are under state control. **Justice Thomas**, joined by **Chief Justice Rehnquist** and **Justice Scalia**, dissented. Those Justices would have overruled *Griffin* and its line of cases in light of *Washington v. Davis* and *Feeney*. The Equal Protection Clause, warned Justice Thomas, "is not a panacea for perceived social or economic inequity; it seeks to 'guarante[e] equal laws, not equal results.' *Feeney*."

NOTES ON POVERTY AND ACCESS TO COURT

1.   *M.L.B.* affirmed that a majority of the Court still adhered to the *Griffin* line of cases, at least in some circumstances. More recently, the Court returned to the issue in the context of whether due process guarantees counsel to an indigent party confronted with a loss of liberty in a civil proceeding based on being a "deadbeat dad." *Turner v. Rogers*, 564 U.S. 431 (2011). Reflecting persistent doctrinal uncertainties in this area, the Court dealt with *Turner* as a procedural due process case, not as one in the *Griffin-M.L.B* line. In that context, the Court vacated the lower court's contempt finding and said that, short of appointing counsel, "substitute" procedural safeguards were required to ensure that the defendant had a "fundamentally fair" opportunity to show his inability to pay the award that led to the contempt finding against him. The decision was, thus, something of a split decision for those arguing that indigent litigants face unfair obstacles in court.

2.   More recently, advocates for low-income litigants have launched a "Civil *Gideon*" drive to try to secure greater right to appointed counsel in civil cases—rights comparable to those guaranteed in criminal cases under the landmark case of *Gideon v. Wainwright*, 332 U.S. 335 (1963). This movement has yielded some successes in state courts, as well as state legislatures. For an overview and varying perspectives on the issue, see Clare Pastore, *A Civil Right to Counsel: Closer to Reality*, 42 Loyola L.A. L. Rev. 1065 (2009); Benjamin H. Barton, *Against Civil* Gideon (*and for* Pro Se *Court Reform*), 62 Fla. L. Rev. 1227 (2010).

3.   With the steady rise of economic inequality, scholars have increasingly asserted that such inequality ought to be seen as a distinctively *constitutional* problem. Arguments of this kind have become more forceful since the economic crash of 2008. For salient contributions, see Symposium: *The Constitutional and Economic Inequality*, 94 Tex. L. Rev. 1287, et seq. (2016); Kate Andrias, *The Fortification of Inequality: Constitutional Doctrine and the Political Economy*, 93 Ind. L. J. 5 (2018); Joseph Fishkin & William E. Forbath, *The Anti-Oligarchy Constitution*, 94 B.U. L. Rev. 669 (2014); Ganesh Sitaraman, *The Puzzling Absence of Economic Power in Constitutional Theory*, 101 Cornell L. Rev. 1445 (2016).

B. LANGUAGE AND ETHNICITY

It is typically forgotten that southern apartheid extended to Mexican as well as African Americans in states like Texas. Outside the South, state discrimination against Mexican Americans was pervasive in California, Arizona, and New Mexico; New York discriminated in some respects against Puerto Ricans.[62] Recall that *Yick Wo v. Hopkins* (Chapter 3, § 1) had held that state discrimination on grounds of (Chinese) ethnicity could violate the Equal Protection Clause.

As we noted in Chapter 2, the first successful court challenge to apartheid came in a challenge by Mexican American families. *Méndez v. Westminster School District*, 64 F.Supp. 544 (C.D. Cal. 1946), aff'd, 161 F.2d 774 (9th Cir. 1947). On the eve of *Brown,* the Supreme Court ruled that states could not exclude Mexican Americans from juries in *Hernandez v. Texas*, 347 U.S. 475 (1954). Ironically, both the defendant (represented by the League of United Latin American Citizens, LULAC) and the state treated Mexican Americans as "white" in the jury case. Hence, the Court treated the exclusion as nonracial and invalidated it on the basis of analogy to race. "Community prejudices are not static," wrote Chief Justice Warren (who as Governor of California had presided over legal desegregation of the public schools for Latinos). Warren catalogued the José Crow regime that Texas had constructed for Mexican Americans and concluded that "persons of Mexican descent constitute a separate class . . . distinct from 'whites.' "[63]

Pure and open ethnicity-based discriminations have gradually melted away, yet Latinos still face what many thoughtful observers consider pervasive discrimination. Today, Latino Americans are more de facto segregated in schools, housing, and jobs than any other big ethnic or racial group, outside Native Americans. Why is that? Is constitutional equality at stake?

JUAN PEREA,
Buscando América: Why Integration and Equal Protection Fail to Protect Latinos
117 Harv. L. Rev. 1420, 1425, 1432–34 (2004)[64]

Professor Perea's argument is that de jure as well as de facto language discrimination is at the heart of the ongoing discrimination against

---

[62] E.g., Thomas Carter, *Mexican Americans in School: A History of Educational Neglect* (1970); Gilbert González, *Segregation and the Education of Mexican Children, 1900–1940*, in José Moreno, ed., *The Elusive Quest for Equality: 150 Years of Chicano-Chicana Education* 53 (1999).

[63] See Ian Haney-López, *Race and Colorblindness After* Hernandez *and* Brown, 25 Chicao-Latino L. Rev. 61 (2005). Unlike California, Texas continued de jure discrimination long after *Brown.* As late as the 1970s, Latinos were challenging de jure school discrimination on the basis of Mexican ethnicity. E.g., *Alvarado v. El Paso Independent School District*, 326 F.Supp. 674 (S.D. Tex. 1971), rev'd, 445 F.2d 1011 (5th Cir. 1971).

[64] Reprinted with permission of the Harvard Law Review.

Latinos. According to the 2000 Census, 17.9% of American residents speak a language other than English at home; 10.7% speak Spanish at home. "I argue that the Equal Protection Clause, as currently implemented through assimilation and integration, actually denies equality to Latinos, many of whom are native or bilingual Spanish speakers.

"Negative social valuations are attributed to native speakers of Spanish and certain other non-English languages. Historically, native speakers of languages other than English have been viewed as threatening to the safety of the state." Slaves were forced to give up their African languages, German and other immigrants were derided by the Framers, and nineteenth century nativist movements are all examples.

"Bilinguals deviate from the norm of English monolingualism and are often 'raced' because of it. Majoritarian fears of disloyalty, loss of control, and exclusion are directed at bilinguals who speak their native, non-English languages in the presence of English monolinguals. * * * Many teachers further devalue these students and their language abilities by presuming that they are of low intelligence and that their knowledge of Spanish constitutes no knowledge at all, and by adopting educational goals that include the elimination of the native Spanish."

"Language difference itself, independent of skin color and other physical features that we usually equate with race, often triggers racism and discrimination." Perea invokes the standard notion that race is a social rather than biological construction, "a concept which signifies and symbolizes social conflicts and interests by referring to different types of human bodies." Michael Omi & Howard Winant, *Racial Formation in the United States* 55 (2d ed. 1994). "Because language differences are used to subordinate members of Latino and other language minority communities—in employment, in education, and more generally in the assignment of low prestige and dignity—language should be understood as part of a dynamic understanding of race itself.

"A secondary argument is that language discrimination is analogous to the more commonly understood notion of race discrimination. The Equal Protection Clause forbids intentional discrimination based on race. Since intentional discrimination based on language or accent often functions like race discrimination, it should be redressable in the same way. Language discrimination functions like race discrimination when employees are fired or disciplined for speaking Spanish in the workplace, when language qualifications are imposed that bear no relation to legitimate government or employment requirements, and when language regulations are used to deny equal education to, or disparage the native cultures of, language minority students. This argument from analogy, however, is weaker than the more direct argument outlined above because, given a general lack of understanding of bilingualism and language discrimination, judges often miss or reject the analogy."

HERNANDEZ V. NEW YORK
500 U.S. 352, 111 S.Ct. 1859, 114 L.Ed.2d 395 (1991)

JUSTICE KENNEDY announced the judgment of the Court and delivered an opinion in which THE CHIEF JUSTICE [REHNQUIST], JUSTICE WHITE and JUSTICE SOUTER join.

[Dionisio Hernandez was convicted of attempted murder and possession of a weapon. After nine jurors had been impaneled, defense counsel objected to the prosecutor's striking several Latino jurors. In response, the prosecutor volunteered his reasons for striking the jurors in question:

> * * * I felt there was a great deal of uncertainty as to whether they could accept the interpreter as the final arbiter of what was said by each of the witnesses, especially where there were going to be Spanish-speaking witnesses, and I didn't feel, when I asked them whether or not they could accept the interpreter's translation of it, I didn't feel that they could. They each looked away from me and said with some hesitancy that they would try, not that they could, but that they would try to follow the interpreter, and I feel that in a case where the interpreter will be for the main witnesses, they would have an undue impact upon the jury.

The issue was whether the prosecutor's explanation provided a race-neutral explanation for his peremptory strikes or constituted discriminatory challenges in violation of the Equal Protection Clause as interpreted in *Batson v. Kentucky*, 476 U.S. 79 (1986).]

The prosecutor here offered a race-neutral basis for these peremptory strikes. As explained by the prosecutor, the challenges rested neither on the intention to exclude Latino or bilingual jurors, nor on stereotypical assumptions about Latinos or bilinguals. The prosecutor's articulated basis for these challenges divided potential jurors into two classes: those whose conduct during *voir dire* would persuade him they might have difficulty in accepting the translator's rendition of Spanish-language testimony and those potential jurors who gave no such reason for doubt. Each category would include both Latinos and non-Latinos. While the prosecutor's criterion might well result in the disproportionate removal of prospective Latino jurors, that disproportionate impact does not turn the prosecutor's actions into a *per se* violation of the Equal Protection Clause. * * *

Once the prosecutor offers a race-neutral basis for his exercise of peremptory challenges, "[t]he trial court then [has] the duty to determine if the defendant has established purposeful discrimination." *Batson*. While the disproportionate impact on Latinos resulting from the prosecutor's criterion for excluding these jurors does not answer the race-neutrality inquiry, it does have relevance to the trial court's decision on this question. "[A]n invidious discriminatory purpose may often be inferred from the totality of the relevant facts, including the fact, if it is true, that the [classification] bears more heavily on one race than another." *Washington v. Davis*. If a prosecutor articulates a basis for a peremptory challenge that results in the disproportionate exclusion of members of a certain race, the trial judge may consider that fact as evidence that the prosecutor's stated reason constitutes a pretext for racial discrimination.

In the context of this trial, the prosecutor's frank admission that his ground for excusing these jurors related to their ability to speak and understand Spanish raised a plausible, though not a necessary, inference that language might be a pretext for what in fact were race-based peremptory challenges. This was not a case where by some rare coincidence a juror happened to speak the same language as a key witness, in a community where few others spoke that tongue. If it were, the explanation that the juror could have undue influence on jury deliberations might be accepted without concern that a racial generalization had come into play. But this trial took place in a community with a substantial Latino population, and petitioner and other interested parties were members of that ethnic group. It would be common knowledge in the locality that a significant percentage of the Latino population speaks fluent Spanish, and that many consider it their preferred language, the one chosen for personal communication, the one selected for speaking with the most precision and power, the one used to define the self.

The trial judge can consider these and other factors when deciding whether a prosecutor intended to discriminate. For example, though petitioner did not suggest the alternative to the trial court here, Spanish-speaking jurors could be permitted to advise the judge in a discreet way of any concerns with the translation during the course of trial. A prosecutor's persistence in the desire to exclude Spanish-speaking jurors despite this measure could be taken into account in determining whether to accept a race-neutral explanation for the challenge. [But the trial judge believed the prosecutor's race-neutral explanation for striking the two jurors in question, and the Court held that appeals courts must defer to trial court findings under *Batson*. The Court found such deference particularly appropriate because *Batson* cases will turn on the credibility of prosecutors and their explanations.]

Language permits an individual to express both a personal identity and membership in a community, and those who share a common language may interact in ways more intimate than those without this bond. Bilinguals, in a sense, inhabit two communities, and serve to bring them closer. Indeed, some scholarly comment suggests that people proficient in two languages may not at times think in one language to the exclusion of the other. The analogy is that of a high-hurdler, who combines the ability to sprint and to jump to accomplish a third feat with characteristics of its own, rather than two separate functions. This is not to say that the cognitive processes and reactions of those who speak two languages are susceptible of easy generalization, for even the term "bilingual" does not describe a uniform category. It is a simple word for a more complex phenomenon with many distinct categories and subdivisions. Sanchez, Our Linguistic and Social Context, in Spanish in the United States 9, 12 (J. Amastae & Elias-Olivares 1982); Dodson, Second Language Acquisition and Bilingual Development: A Theoretical Framework, 6 J. Multilingual & Multicultural Development 325, 326–327 (1985).

Our decision today does not imply that exclusion of bilinguals from jury service is wise, or even that it is constitutional in all cases. It is a harsh paradox that one may become proficient enough in English to participate in trial, see, e.g., 28 U.S.C. §§ 1865(b)(2), (3) (English-language ability required for federal jury service), only to encounter disqualification because he knows a second language as well. As the Court observed in a somewhat related context: "Mere knowledge of [a foreign] language cannot reasonably be regarded as harmful. Heretofore it has been commonly looked upon as helpful and desirable." *Meyer v. Nebraska*, 262 U.S. 390 (1923).

Just as shared language can serve to foster community, language differences can be a source of division. Language elicits a response from others, ranging from admiration and respect, to distance and alienation, to ridicule and scorn. Reactions of the latter type all too often result from or initiate racial hostility. In holding that a race-neutral reason for a peremptory challenge means a reason other than race, we do not resolve the more difficult question of the breadth with which the concept of race should be defined for equal protection purposes. We would face a quite different case if the prosecutor had justified his peremptory challenges with the explanation that he did not want Spanish-speaking jurors. It may well be, for certain ethnic groups and in some communities, that proficiency in a particular language, like skin color, should be treated as a surrogate for race under an equal protection analysis. Cf. *Yu Cong Eng v. Trinidad*, 271 U.S. 500 (1926) (law prohibiting keeping business records in other than specified languages violated equal protection rights of Chinese businessmen); *Meyer v. Nebraska* (striking down law prohibiting grade schools from teaching languages other than English). And, as we make clear, a policy of striking all who speak a given language, without regard to the particular circumstances of the trial or the individual responses of the jurors, may be found by the trial judge to be a pretext for racial discrimination. But that case is not before us.

[**JUSTICE O'CONNOR**, with whom **JUSTICE SCALIA** joined, concurred in the judgment. Her view was that the plurality opinion contained dicta unnecessary to the decision which invited language-based challenges to jury venires.]

JUSTICE STEVENS, with whom JUSTICE MARSHALL joins, dissenting. [JUSTICE BLACKMUN dissented, "essentially" for the reasons in Part II of this dissent.]

[I.] An avowed justification that has a significant disproportionate impact will rarely qualify as a legitimate, race-neutral reason sufficient to rebut the prima facie case because disparate impact is itself evidence of discriminatory purpose. *Arlington Heights*; *Washington v. Davis*. An explanation based on a concern that can easily be accommodated by means less drastic than excluding the challenged venireperson from the petit jury will also generally not qualify as a legitimate reason because it is not in fact "related to the particular case to be tried." *Batson*. And, as in any other equal protection challenge to a government classification, a justification that is frivolous or illegitimate should not suffice to rebut the prima facie case.

If any explanation, no matter how insubstantial and no matter how great its disparate impact, could rebut a prima facie inference of discrimination provided only that the explanation itself was not facially discriminatory, "the Equal Protection Clause 'would be but a vain and illusory requirement.'" *Batson*. The Court mistakenly believes that it is compelled to reach this result because an equal protection violation requires discriminatory purpose. The Court overlooks, however, the fact that the "discriminatory purpose" which characterizes violations of the Equal Protection Clause can sometimes be established by objective evidence that is consistent with a decisionmaker's honest belief that his motive was entirely benign. "Frequently the most probative evidence of intent will be objective evidence of what actually happened," *Washington v. Davis* (Stevens, J., concurring), including evidence of disparate impact. See, e.g., *Yick Wo v. Hopkins*; *Gomillion v. Lightfoot*. The line between discriminatory purpose and discriminatory impact is neither as bright nor as critical as the Court appears to believe.

The Court therefore errs in focusing the entire inquiry on the subjective state of mind of the prosecutor. In jury selection challenges, the requisite invidious intent is established once the defendant makes out a prima facie case. No additional evidence of this intent is necessary unless the explanation provided by the prosecutor is sufficiently powerful to rebut the prima facie proof of discriminatory purpose. By requiring that the prosecutor's explanation itself provide additional, direct evidence of discriminatory motive, the Court has imposed on the defendant the added requirement that he generate evidence of the prosecutor's actual subjective intent to discriminate. Neither *Batson* nor our other equal protection holdings demand such a heightened quantum of proof.

[II.] The prosecutor's explanation was insufficient for three reasons. First, the justification would inevitably result in a disproportionate disqualification of Spanish-speaking venirepersons. An explanation that is "race-neutral" on its face is nonetheless unacceptable if it is merely a proxy for a discriminatory practice. Second, the prosecutor's concern could easily have been accommodated by less drastic means. As is the practice in many jurisdictions, the jury could have been instructed that the official translation alone is evidence; bilingual jurors could have been instructed to bring to the attention of the judge any disagreements they might have with the translation so that any disputes could be resolved by the court. Third, if the prosecutor's concern was valid and substantiated by the record, it would have supported a challenge for cause. The fact that the prosecutor did not make any such challenge should disqualify him from advancing the concern as a justification for a peremptory challenge.

NOTES ON LANGUAGE- & ETHNICITY-BASED DISCRIMINATION

1.   *Juror Selection.* Professor Perea objects to the Court's approach in *Hernandez.* Because "[b]ilinguals understand and think in two languages simultaneously and interdependently," the prosecutor "was asking the impossible." And he was making a demand of potential Latino jurors—to ignore their own judgment of the truth—that no one was making of Anglo jurors. The only jurors excused for bilingual ability, here and in other cases, are Latinos. There was nothing race-neutral about the prosecutor's actions. Perea, *Buscando América*, 117 Harv. L. Rev. at 1436.

Might Justice Kennedy have decided/voted differently if the record reflected that the prosecutor *only* asked Latinos whether they were bilingual and (then) whether they could accept the official translation? Many non-Latino Americans are bilingual; many speak Spanish. If these questions were never asked of non-Latino jurors, would that be sufficient evidence of *race* discrimination to satisfy *Batson*? Ought it be sufficient?

2.   *Workplace.* Most workplace discrimination based on language has been analyzed under Title VII, which makes discrimination on the basis of "national origin" actionable. Courts have been reluctant to view language-based discrimination as actionable, e.g., *Garcia v. Gloor*, 618 F.2d 264 (5th Cir.1980). Responding to *Garcia,* the EEOC developed guidelines presuming that English-only workplace rules are national origin discrimination; employers can rebut the presumption if they can show a business necessity for the English-only policy. See 29 C.F.R. § 1606.7 (2007). Such complaints comprise a rapidly increasing part of the EEOC's workload, though few lawsuits have been successful. See Cristina Rodriguez, *Language Diversity in the Workplace*, 100 Nw. U.L. Rev. 1689 (2006). For public employers (covered by Title VII), is the EEOC's guideline a fair statement of the equal protection requirement, or does the Constitution demand less than Title VII?

3.   *Voting.* Again, this is an arena regulated by statute. The Voting Rights Act Amendments of 1975, Pub. L. No. 94–73, title III, 89 Stat. 402

(1975), codified as amended at 42 U.S.C. § 1973aa–1a, protect language-minority voters against discrimination and assure most such voters access to voting materials in their language.[65] Congress was acting under its authority to "enforce" the Fifteenth Amendment. As you will see in Chapter 7, § 3, Congress can only adopt laws that redress problems the Supreme Court would consider constitutional violations; if Congress and the Court are on the same page as to a constitutional violation, Congress has significant discretion in crafting a remedial statute addressing the problem. So is there a constitutional problem when language-minority citizens with limited command of English (thus, *not* bilinguals like the jurors in *Hernandez*) cannot understand the ballot and the state provides them with no assistance?[66]

PROBLEM 4-4:
CONSTITUTIONALITY OF ENGLISH-ONLY LAWS?

Over half the states have enacted some type of English-only law. Many laws just declare English as the "official" language of the state, without imposing specific legal rules to implement this symbolism. How should a state attorney general respond to equal protection questions about such a law? See Cristina Rodriguez, *Language and Participation*, 94 Calif. L. Rev. 687, 751–54 (2006). Would it matter whether a state's law mandated that public employees speak only English while on the job? That bilingual education be banned? That the law was passed by ballot measure? For perspectives on equal protection in this area, see Cristina Rodriguez, *Accommodating Linguistic Difference: Toward a Comprehensive Theory of Language Rights in the United States*, 36 Harv. C.R.-C.L. L. Rev. 133 (2001); Juan Perea, *Demography and Distrust: An Essay on American Languages, Cultural Pluralism, and Official English*, 77 Minn. L. Rev. 269 (1992).

C. PHYSICAL OR MENTAL DISABILITY

Disability-based discrimination is deeply rooted in American history. Individuals with mental and physical disabilities have been routinely denied marriage licenses, excluded from classrooms and workplaces by law or official practice, institutionalized for indefinite periods of time, and even sterilized. In *Buck v. Bell*, 274 U.S. 200 (1927) (Chapter 5, § 1), Justice Holmes, in a flippant opinion, dismissed an equal protection challenge to a sterilization law. For decades after *Buck v. Bell*, no one raised constitutional arguments against disability-based classifications. Although there were a number of organizations dedicated to protective legislation, it was not until the 1970s that people with disabilities and their allies were energized into a mass social movement demanding dignified treatment for

---

[65] The Voting Rights Act of 1965, § 4(e), imposed language assistance for Puerto Rican voters under certain circumstances and was the basis for a federalism challenge in *Katzenbach v. Morgan* (excerpted and discussed in Chapter 7, § 3B).

[66] We use the present tense, because the Voting Rights Act was renewed in 2006, with the language-assistance provision intact (after strong opposition).

disabled citizens.[67] The Rehabilitation Act of 1973, which formally banned discrimination by reason of one's handicap, was left unimplemented until disability rights activists engaged in civil disobedience and political protest and established a lobbying organization in Washington, D.C. The Carter Administration finally issued strong implementing regulations in 1977.

The new grass roots movement was normative as well as political. Disability has traditionally been viewed as malignant—unnatural, medically degenerate, socially disruptive, at best pitiable. The movement not only rejected those characterizations, but maintained that the governmental and societal discrimination they engendered were more disabling than the physical or mental variations themselves. By working against those barriers, the disability rights movement has sought to advance the self-determination, independence, and equal citizenship of its members. Like the other identity-based social movements, the disability rights movement created litigating institutions that have sought constitutional protections. Specifically, those organizations sought judicial recognition that disability is a suspect or quasi-suspect classification like race or sex—a recognition that would have called into question hundreds of state and local laws formally discriminating against people with disabilities.

CITY OF CLEBURNE V. CLEBURNE LIVING CENTER
473 U.S. 432, 105 S.Ct. 3249, 87 L.Ed.2d 313 (1985)

JUSTICE WHITE delivered the opinion of the Court.

[Cleburne Living Center attempted to establish a group home for the developmentally disabled in Cleburne, Texas. Under that city's zoning regulations applicable to the proposed site of the home, a special use permit was required for the construction of "[h]ospitals for the insane or feeble-minded, or alcoholic [sic] or drug addicts, or penal or correctional institutions." The city classified the proposed home as one for the "feeble-minded," and after a hearing the city council voted to deny a special use permit. The federal court of appeals overturned the city's action, concluding that the developmentally disabled are a "quasi-suspect class" and that, under intermediate scrutiny, the city's zoning regulation was invalid both on its face and as applied. Justice White's opinion began by surveying the cases applying minimal scrutiny to economic regulation; strict scrutiny to classifications based on race, alienage, or national origin; intermediate scrutiny for classifications based on gender or illegitimacy; and the Court's

---

[67] For the history of this social movement, see Doris Zames Fleischer & Freda Zames, *The Disability Rights Movement: From Charity to Confrontation* (2001); Richard Scotch, *From Good Will to Civil Rights: Transforming Federal Disability Policy* (2d ed. 2001); Joseph Shapiro, *No Pity: People with Disabilities Forging a New Civil Rights Movement* (1993).

refusal in *Murgia* (see § 1, *supra*) "to extend heightened scrutiny to differential treatment based on age."]

The lesson of *Murgia* is that where individuals in the group affected by a law have distinguishing characteristics relevant to interests the State has the authority to implement, the courts have been very reluctant, as they should be in our federal system and with our respect for the separation of powers, to closely scrutinize legislative choices as to whether, how, and to what extent those interests should be pursued. In such cases, the Equal Protection Clause requires only a rational means to serve a legitimate end.

Against this background, we conclude for several reasons that the Court of Appeals erred in holding mental retardation a quasi-suspect classification calling for a more exacting standard of judicial review than is normally accorded economic and social legislation. First, * * * those who are mentally retarded have a reduced ability to cope with and function in the everyday world. * * * [T]hey range from those whose disability is not immediately evident to those who must be constantly cared for. They are thus different, immutably so, in relevant respects, and the States' interest in dealing with and providing for them is plainly a legitimate one. How this large and diversified group is to be treated under the law is a difficult and often a technical matter, very much a task for legislators guided by qualified professionals and not by the perhaps ill-informed opinions of the judiciary. Heightened scrutiny inevitably involves substantive judgments about legislative decisions, and we doubt that the predicate for such judicial oversight is present where the classification deals with mental retardation.

erred in applying heightened scrutiny —

rational basis appropriate

Second, the distinctive legislative response, both national and state, to the plight of those who are mentally retarded demonstrates not only that they have unique problems, but also that the lawmakers have been addressing their difficulties in a manner that belies a continuing antipathy or prejudice and a corresponding need for more intrusive oversight by the judiciary. Thus, the Federal Government has not only outlawed discrimination against the mentally retarded in federally funded programs, see § 504 of the Rehabilitation Act of 1973, but it has also provided the retarded with the right to receive "appropriate treatment, services, and habilitation" in a setting that is "least restrictive of [their] personal liberty." [Developmental Disabilities Assistance and Bill of Rights Act.]

[Justice White discussed other federal and Texas legislation designed to help the developmentally disabled. These affirmative rights would come into question if the Court made disability a suspect classification.] Even assuming that many of these laws could be shown to be substantially related to an important governmental purpose, merely requiring the legislature to justify its efforts in these terms may lead it to refrain from acting at all. Much recent legislation intended to benefit the retarded also assumes the need for measures that might be perceived to disadvantage them. The Education of the Handicapped Act, for example, requires an "appropriate" education, not one that is equal in all respects to the education of nonretarded children. * * * Especially given the wide variation in the abilities and needs of the retarded themselves, governmental bodies must have a certain amount of flexibility and freedom from judicial oversight in shaping and limiting their remedial efforts.

Third, the legislative response, which could hardly have occurred and survived without public support, negates any claim that the mentally retarded are politically powerless in the sense that they have no ability to attract the attention of the lawmakers. Any minority can be said to be powerless to assert direct control over the legislature, but if that were a criterion for higher level scrutiny by the courts, much economic and social legislation would now be suspect.

Fourth, if the large and amorphous class of the mentally retarded were deemed quasi-suspect * * *, it would be difficult to find a principled way to distinguish a variety of other groups who have perhaps immutable disabilities setting them off from others, who cannot themselves mandate the desired legislative responses, and who can claim some degree of prejudice from at least part of the public at large. One need mention in this respect only the aging, the disabled, the mentally ill, and the infirm. We are reluctant to set out on that course, and we decline to do so.

Doubtless, there have been and there will continue to be instances of discrimination against the retarded that are in fact invidious, and that are properly subject to judicial correction under constitutional norms. But the appropriate method of reaching such instances is not to create a new quasi-suspect classification and subject all governmental action based on that classification to more searching evaluation. Rather, we should look to the likelihood that governmental action premised on a particular classification is valid as a general matter, not merely to the specifics of the case before us. Because mental retardation is a characteristic that the government may legitimately take into account in a wide range of decisions, and because both State and Federal Governments have recently committed themselves to assisting the retarded, we will not presume that any given legislative action, even one that disadvantages retarded individuals, is rooted in considerations that the Constitution will not tolerate.

Our refusal to recognize the retarded as a quasi-suspect class does not leave them entirely unprotected from invidious discrimination. To withstand equal protection review, legislation that distinguishes between the mentally retarded and others must be rationally related to a legitimate governmental purpose. This standard, we believe, affords government the latitude necessary both to pursue policies designed to assist the retarded in realizing their full potential, and to freely and efficiently engage in activities that burden the retarded in what is essentially an incidental manner. The State may not rely on a classification whose relationship to an asserted goal is so attenuated as to render the distinction arbitrary or irrational. See *Zobel v. Williams*, 457 U.S. 55 (1982); *Moreno*. Furthermore, some objectives—such as "a bare . . . desire to harm a politically unpopular group," *Moreno*—are not legitimate state interests. * * *

[Rather than first entertain a *facial* challenge to the requirement of a special-use permit for homes for the developmentally disabled, the Court chose first to consider whether requiring a special-use permit for this home was, on the facts of the case, an "as applied" violation of equal protection.] The City does not require a special use permit in an R-3 zone for apartment houses, multiple dwellings, boarding and lodging houses, fraternity or sorority houses, dormitories, apartment hotels, hospitals, sanitariums, nursing homes for convalescents or the aged (other than for the insane or feeble-minded or alcoholics or drug addicts), private clubs or fraternal orders, and other specified uses. * * * May the city require the permit for this facility when other care and multiple dwelling facilities are freely permitted?

It is true, as already pointed out, that the mentally retarded as a group are indeed different from others not sharing their misfortune, and in this respect they may be different from those who would occupy other facilities that would be permitted in an R-3 zone without a special permit. But this difference is largely irrelevant unless the Featherston home and those who would occupy it would threaten legitimate interests of the city in a way that other permitted uses such as boarding houses and hospitals would not. Because in our view the record does not reveal any rational basis for believing that the Featherston home would pose any special threat to the city's legitimate interests, we affirm the judgment below insofar as it holds the ordinance invalid as applied in this case.

The District Court found that the City Council's insistence on the permit rested on several factors. First, the Council was concerned with the negative attitude of the majority of property owners located within 200 feet of the Featherston facility, as well as with the fears of elderly residents of the neighborhood. But mere negative attitudes, or fear, unsubstantiated by factors which are properly cognizable in a zoning proceeding, are not permissible bases for treating a home for the mentally retarded differently from apartment houses, multiple dwellings, and the like. * * * "Private biases may be outside the reach of the law, but the law cannot, directly or indirectly, give them effect." *Palmore v. Sidoti* [Chapter 3, § 1 of this casebook].

Second, the Council had two objections to the location of the facility. It was concerned that the facility was across the street from a junior high school, and it feared that the students might harass the occupants of the Featherston home. But the school itself is attended by about 30 mentally retarded students, and denying a permit based on such vague, undifferentiated fears is again permitting some portion of the community to validate what would otherwise be an equal protection violation. The other objection to the home's location was that it was located on "a five hundred year flood plain." This concern with the possibility of a flood, however, can hardly be based on a distinction between the Featherston home and, for example, nursing homes, homes for convalescents or the aged, or sanitariums or hospitals, any of which could be located on the Featherston site without obtaining a special use permit. The same may be said of another concern of the Council—doubts about the legal responsibility for actions which the mentally retarded might take. If there is no concern about legal responsibility with respect to other uses that would be permitted in the area, such as boarding and fraternity houses, it is difficult to believe that the groups of mildly or moderately mentally retarded individuals who would live at 201 Featherston would present any different or special hazard.

Fourth, the Council was concerned with the size of the home and the number of people that would occupy it. The District Court found, and the Court of Appeals repeated, that "[i]f the potential residents of the Featherston Street home were not mentally retarded, but the home was the same in all other respects, its use would be permitted under the city's zoning ordinance." Given this finding, there would be no restrictions on the number of people who could occupy this home as a boarding house, nursing home, family dwelling, fraternity house, or dormitory. The question is whether it is rational to treat the mentally retarded differently. It is true that they suffer disability not shared by others; but why this difference warrants a density regulation that others need not observe is not at all apparent. At least this record does not clarify how, in this connection, the characteristics of the intended occupants of the Featherston home rationally justify denying to those occupants what would be permitted to groups occupying the same site for different purposes. * * * In the words of the Court of Appeals, "[T]he City never justifies its apparent view that other people can live under such 'crowded' conditions when mentally retarded persons cannot." * * *

The short of it is that requiring the permit in this case appears to us to rest on an irrational prejudice against the mentally retarded.

JUSTICE STEVENS, with whom **THE CHIEF JUSTICE [BURGER]** joins, concurring. [Justice Stevens reiterated his view, first expressed in *Craig*, that equal protection review involves a "continuum" of responses rather than "tiers" of review. "Rationality" always insists that the sovereign's line-drawing be defensible by reference to criteria that are "neutral" and "legitimate."]

In every equal protection case, we have to ask certain basic questions. What class is harmed by the legislation, and has it been subjected to a "tradition of disfavor" by our laws? What is the public purpose that is being served by the law? What is the characteristic of the disadvantaged class that justifies the disparate treatment? In most cases the answer to these questions will tell us whether the statute has a "rational basis." The answers will result in the virtually automatic invalidation of racial classifications and in the validation of most economic classifications, but they will provide differing results in cases involving classifications based on alienage, gender, or illegitimacy. But that is not because we apply an "intermediate standard of review" in these cases; rather it is because the characteristics of these groups are sometimes relevant and sometimes irrelevant to a valid public purpose, or, more specifically, to the purpose that the challenged laws purportedly intended to serve.

Every law that places the mentally retarded in a special class is not presumptively irrational. The differences between mentally retarded persons and those with greater mental capacity are obviously relevant to certain legislative decisions. An impartial lawmaker—indeed, even a member of a class of persons defined as mentally retarded—could rationally vote in favor of a law providing funds for special education and special treatment for the mentally retarded. A mentally retarded person could also recognize that he is a member of a class that might need special supervision in some situations, both to protect himself and to protect others. * * *

Even so, the Court of Appeals correctly observed that through ignorance and prejudice the mentally retarded "have been subjected to a history of unfair and often grotesque mistreatment." The discrimination against the mentally retarded that is at issue in this case is the city's decision to require an annual special use permit before property in an apartment house district may be used as a group home for persons who are mildly retarded. The record convinces me that this permit was required because of the irrational fears of neighboring property owners, rather than for the protection of the mentally retarded persons who would reside in respondent's home.

[JUSTICE MARSHALL, joined by JUSTICES BRENNAN and BLACKMUN, concurred in the judgment in part and dissented in part. Justice Marshall applied the "sliding scale" approach to equal protection developed in his dissent in *San Antonio Independent School District v. Rodriguez* (Chapter 5, § 3B), under which the "substantiality of the state interests to be served" and "the reasonableness of the means by which the State has sought to advance its interests" are crucial factors. "Differences in the application of this test [are] a function of the constitutional importance of the interests at stake and the invidiousness of the particular classification." Applying this approach in *Cleburne*, Justice Marshall maintained that developmentally disabled people, like blacks and women in the past, are subject to laws that discriminate on their face against them, based upon irrational prejudices. Justice Marshall invoked the *Carolene Products* idea that citizens have no firm equality baseline as regards economic legislation but are assured substantial equality in other arenas by the Fourteenth Amendment.

[Where legislatures have systematically ignored those baselines in the past, the Court has been justified in conducting a "more searching judicial inquiry" of such frequently invoked, but typically irrational, classifications.] Heightened scrutiny does not allow courts to second-guess reasoned legislative or professional judgments tailored to the unique needs of a group like the retarded, but it does seek to assure that the hostility or thoughtlessness with which there is reason to be concerned has not carried the day. By invoking heightened scrutiny, the Court recognizes, and compels lower courts to recognize, that a group may well be the target of the sort of prejudiced, thoughtless, or stereotyped action that offends principles of equality found in the Fourteenth Amendment. Where classifications based on a particular characteristic have done so in the past, and the threat that they may do so remains, heightened scrutiny is appropriate.[9]

In light of the scrutiny that should be applied here, Cleburne's ordinance sweeps too broadly to dispel the suspicion that it rests on a bare desire to treat the retarded as outsiders, pariahs who do not belong in the community. The Court, while disclaiming that special scrutiny is necessary

---

[9]   No single talisman can define those groups likely to be the target of classifications offensive to the Fourteenth Amendment and therefore warranting heightened or strict scrutiny; experience, not abstract logic, must be the primary guide. The "political powerlessness" of a group may be relevant, but that factor is neither necessary, as the gender cases demonstrate, nor sufficient, as the example of minors illustrates. Minors cannot vote and thus might be considered politically powerless to an extreme degree. Nonetheless, we see few statutes reflecting prejudice or indifference to minors, and I am not aware of any suggestion that legislation affecting them be viewed with the suspicion of heightened scrutiny. Similarly, immutability of the trait at issue may be relevant, but many immutable characteristics, such as height or blindness, are valid bases of governmental action and classifications under a variety of circumstances. The political powerlessness of a group and the immutability of its defining trait are relevant insofar as they point to a social and cultural isolation that gives the majority little reason to respect or be concerned with that group's interests and needs. Statutes discriminating against the young have not been common nor need be feared because those who do vote and legislate were once themselves young, typically have children of their own, and certainly interact regularly with minors. Their social integration means that minors, unlike discrete and insular minorities, tend to be treated in legislative arenas with full concern and respect, despite their formal and complete exclusion from the electoral process.

The discreteness and insularity warranting a "more searching judicial inquiry," *Carolene Products* n.4., must therefore be viewed from a social and cultural perspective as well as a political one. To this task judges are well suited, for the lessons of history and experience are surely the best guide as to when, and with respect to what interests, society is likely to stigmatize individuals as members of an inferior caste or view them as not belonging to the community. Because prejudice spawns prejudice, and stereotypes produce limitations that confirm the stereotype on which they are based, a history of unequal treatment requires sensitivity to the prospect that its vestiges endure. In separating those groups that are discrete and insular from those that are not, as in many important legal distinctions, "a page of history is worth a volume of logic." *New York Trust Co. v. Eisner*, 256 U.S. 345 (1921) (Holmes, J.).

or warranted, reaches the same conclusion. Rather than striking the ordinance down, however, the Court invalidates it merely as applied to respondents. I must dissent from the novel proposition that "the preferred course of adjudication" is to leave standing a legislative act resting on "irrational prejudice," thereby forcing individuals in the group discriminated against to continue to run the act's gauntlet.

The Court appears to act out of a belief that the ordinance might be "rational" as applied to some subgroup of the retarded under some circumstances, such as those utterly without the capacity to live in a community, and that the ordinance should not be invalidated *in toto* if it is capable of ever being validly applied. But the issue is not "whether the city may never insist on a special use permit for the mentally retarded in an R-3 zone." The issue is whether the city may require a permit pursuant to a blunderbuss ordinance drafted many years ago to exclude all the "feebleminded," or whether the city must enact a new ordinance carefully tailored to the exclusion of some well defined subgroup of retarded people in circumstances in which exclusion might reasonably further legitimate city purposes. * * *

To my knowledge, the Court has never before treated an equal protection challenge to a statute on an as-applied basis. When statutes rest on impermissibly overbroad generalizations, our cases have invalidated the presumption on its face. We do not instead leave to the courts the task of redrafting the statute through an ongoing and cumbersome process of "as applied" constitutional rulings.

NOTE ON CLEBURNE AND EQUAL PROTECTION TIERS

1.   *Is There an Additional Level of Scrutiny (Rational Basis with Bite) for Disability-Based Classifications?* In *Cleburne*, the six Justices who joined the opinion for the Court seem to have accepted *four* tiers of scrutiny: (1) "anything goes" rational basis (*Railway Express*); (2) rational basis "with teeth" (*Cleburne*); (3) intermediate scrutiny (*Craig*); (4) strict scrutiny (the race cases). One reason *Cleburne* seems not to be an example of ordinary rational basis review is that Justice White was unwilling to attribute legitimate goals to the governmental decision, such as protection of property values or even safety concerns, because they were not documented in the public record.

It is hard to tell how broadly to read *Cleburne*. According to Justice Brennan's notes of the first *Cleburne* conference, the Justices were evenly split on whether to uphold the ordinance, with four Justices voting to strike under heightened scrutiny and four voting to uphold under rational basis. On reargument, Justice Powell broke the tie: No heightened scrutiny, but the ordinance as applied fell on rational basis grounds. But what, exactly, was irrational about the decision? The Court in *Board of Trustees v. Garrett*, 531 U.S. 356 (2001) (Chapter 7, § 3D3), interpreted *Cleburne* as *not* resting on improper (prejudice- or stereotype-based) motives alone; the negative attitudes must be accompanied by a showing that the local decision did not rest on other, legitimate bases, the Court said in *Garrett*. It is possible that *Cleburne* could be limited to cases where the legislative record contains evidence of improper bias and no evidence of legitimate considerations. In that event, would it be too easy for prejudice-based laws to withstand scrutiny? Would judicial review then have any value for people with disabilities?

One way of articulating a new (*Cleburne*) tier of scrutiny is this: Heightened scrutiny in the race and sex discrimination cases starts with a presumption of unconstitutionality, shifts the burden of justification to the government, and limits the kinds of arguments the government can make. Ordinary rational basis review starts with a presumption of constitutionality, which the challenger can rebut only by demonstrating that there is no reasonable connection with any plausible state goal. *Cleburne*-style rational basis review also starts with a presumption of validity, but might be understood to allow the challenger to create a prima facie case of invalidity by showing no rational fit with the asserted purpose or by demonstrating antipathy. Such a prima facie case would shift the burden to the state to demonstrate a rational and neutral justification for its discrimination.

2.   *Should the Court Abandon the Tiers Approach and Follow a Single Unified Standard in Equal Protection Cases?* Five *Cleburne* Justices (the three dissenters and the two concurring Justices) seemingly endorsed a balancing approach rather than the tiers approach. Elaborating on his earlier *Rodriguez* dissent, Justice Marshall argued for a sliding scale. Elaborating on his concurring opinion in *Craig*, Justice Stevens argued for a single standard asking mostly the same questions Marshall had laid out in *Rodriguez*. How would this work? In the spirit of Dan Ortiz's recharacterization of the role of intent in equal protection law, one of us has structured the Marshall-Stevens balancing approach in the following way.[68]

Almost all laws have arguable purposes that can be expressed in terms of the public interest, but the statutory criteria are usually both overinclusive (regulating activities not needed to meet the statute's rational goals) and underinclusive (failing to regulate some activities inconsistent with the goals). Where the state is regulating the market and the classification is a purely economic one, courts will not be interested in the actual, typically messy, motivations of the legislature and will be willing to attribute plausible public interests to such laws; additionally, they will tolerate a great deal of over-and underinclusion in the choice of statutory criteria. Where important rights are involved and the classification one that has been found consistently invidious, courts will attribute irrational motives (prejudice and stereotypes) to the legislature and may strike down the law on that ground alone, as the Court did in *Loving*. The hardest cases are those where important rights are involved and the classification somewhat fishy but not meeting all the criteria for suspectness the Court laid out in *Frontiero* and *Cleburne*. In those cases, the

---

[68] William Eskridge, Jr., *Some Effects of Identity-Based Social Movements on Constitutional Law in the Twentieth Century*, 100 Mich. L. Rev. 2062 (2002), drawing from Daniel Ortiz, *The Myth of Intent in Equal Protection*, 41 Stan. L. Rev. 1105 (1989).

Court will follow a presumption of validity that can be trumped by evidence of prejudice—or stereotype—based motivation. Such evidence makes the Court reluctant to attribute legitimate governmental goals not found in the record and unwilling to tolerate much over-or underinclusion. Does this standard make sense? Note its similarity with some of the analysis in the previous Note: Does that suggest the substantial irrelevance of the verbal formulation of the equal protection test?

3.   *The Disability Rights Movement and the Goals of the Equal Protection Clause.* Like earlier identity movements, the disability rights movement has challenged disability-based discriminations and exclusions. In contrast to the initial focus of those earlier movements, the disability rights movement from the beginning has viewed benign neglect as just as big a problem for its members as formal discrimination and has demanded not just formal equality but functional equality as well: The state must not only admit disabled people into its programs, but must also take reasonable measures to accommodate the needs of the disabled.[69] The *Cleburne* Justices probably did not perceive this, but they would surely have rejected it, for the same institutional and ideological reasons they were unwilling to press hard for *Brown II* remedies or accept the remedial ideas of radical feminists. Like *Freeman v. Pitts* (Chapter 2, § 2C2), *Cleburne* assumes the primacy of the rationality goal of the Fourteenth Amendment and slights its anti-subordination goal. Given the disability rights constitutional vision, therefore, *Cleburne* was a significant defeat—notwithstanding the fact that the challengers won a remand. Consider the next case.

Heller v. Doe

509 U.S. 312 (1993)

Kentucky statutes provided for the involuntary institutionalization of persons with mental illness, as well as those with what the statute called "mental retardation." Both groups could be involuntarily committed only upon a showing that they were dangerous to themselves or others, that they could reasonably benefit from treatment, and that no less restrictive alternative existed. For the mentally ill, the burden of proof for these factors was "beyond a reasonable doubt"; for those in the second group—those with what are today more commonly called developmental or cognitive disabilities—the burden was the less demanding standard of "clear and convincing evidence." Thus, it was easier for the state to institutionalize a person with developmental disabilities. **Justice Kennedy**'s opinion for the Court accepted the apparent legislative assumptions that, in comparison to mental illness, such disabilities can be more easily diagnosed and provide a basis for more reliable predictions of future dangerousness. These differences justified different standards of proof because of the plausibly different " 'risk of error' faced by the subject of the proceedings." Justice Kennedy also relied on the gravity of erroneous

---

[69]   See Arlene Mayerson & Sylvia Yee, *The ADA and Models of Equality*, 62 Ohio St. L.J. 535 (2001).

institutionalization: Because treatment methods for developmentally disabled persons are "much less invasive" than those for the mentally ill, it was rational for the state to believe that the liberty deprivation would be much more grievous for the wrongfully institutionalized mentally ill person than the wrongfully institutionalized person with a developmental disability.

Justice Souter, joined by **Justices Blackmun** and **Stevens**, dissented on *Cleburne* grounds.

> While the Court cites *Cleburne* once, and does not purport to overrule it, neither does the Court apply it, and at the end of the day *Cleburne*'s status is left uncertain. I would follow *Cleburne* here. * * * Without plausible justification, Kentucky is being allowed to draw a distinction that is difficult to see as resting on anything other than the stereotypical assumption that the retarded are 'perpetual children,' an assumption that has historically been taken to justify the disrespect and 'grotesque mistreatment' to which the retarded have been subjected.

Justice Blackmun also dissented on the ground that the statutory distinction could not survive heightened scrutiny.

Do you agree with the dissent that the majority opinion is inconsistent with *Cleburne*?

D. SEXUAL ORIENTATION

Unlike race, sex, wealth, and disability classifications, sexual orientation classifications are relatively new to American statutory history; the concept of "homosexuality" was not developed until around 1890.[70] Although criminal laws proscribed certain sex acts as sodomy, the concept of "homosexuals" as a defined class of people was not developed until the late 19th century. In the early twentieth century, cities and states adopted rules to suppress and exclude "degenerates" and "sexual inverts." After World War II, anti-homosexual laws, rules, and state practices exploded in a Kulturkampf seeking to purge public life of "homosexuals and sex perverts," as a Senate investigating subcommittee deemed these people in 1950. They were barred from the state and federal civil service and from the armed forces, hunted and exposed by the FBI and several state investigatory commissions, rounded up and deported by the INS, expelled from state colleges and universities, denied or stripped of professional licenses and certifications, prohibited from congregating together or from being served in bars, harassed and arrested by the police in large numbers for cross-dressing and alleged sexual solicitations, beaten and raped by police officers, incarcerated in state prisons and mental hospitals, and made the objects of state-sponsored medical experiments, castrations,

---

[70] See Jonathan Ned Katz, Gay American History (1976), as well as Lillian Faderman, Surpassing the Love of Men: Romantic Friendship and Love Between Women, from the Renaissance to the Present (1981).

sterilizations, and electrical shock treatments—all because of their (perceived) sexual orientation or their (supposed) private consensual activities.[71]

Like other stigmatized minorities, some lesbians, gay men, and bisexuals came to resist state persecution and asserted, initially, that homosexuality is a tolerable variation from the norm and, later, that it is a benign variation ("Gay is Good"). The June 1969 riots outside New York City's Stonewall Inn, when gay and transgender people fought back against police violence, galvanized thousands of gays to "come out" of their "closets" and organize themselves politically and legally. Several decades of political activism and court challenges have eliminated many antigay laws and policies, but questions remain about the scope of equal protection rights that may be asserted in this area. In addition, in perhaps the most significant legislative achievement in the history of the gay rights movement, Congress in 2011 repealed the Don't Ask, Don't Tell policy that had barred gay people from serving openly in the military. The policy was not lifted at that time in relation to transgender people, however, and a later Obama-era policy permitting transgender people to serve was revoked by the Trump Administration. While legal battles over equal access to the military are likely to continue in the context of gender identity-based discrimination, the end of Don't Ask, Don't Tell marked the end of decades of legal and political struggle for gay people who wanted to serve. That and other successes, however, were met with a normative traditional family values countermovement that sought not only to preserve prior antigay laws, but to introduce new ones. The battle became particularly salient in the context of same-sex marriage laws.

We trace in the remainder of this chapter the development of equal protection law in this area, beginning with the foundational Supreme Court decision on sexual orientation discrimination.

ROMER V. EVANS
517 U.S. 620, 116 S.Ct. 1620, 134 L.Ed.2d 855 (1996)

JUSTICE KENNEDY delivered the opinion of the Court.

[In 1992, Colorado for Family Values (CFV) proposed Amendment 2 to the state constitution:

> Neither the State of Colorado, through any of its branches or departments, nor any of its agencies, political subdivisions, municipalities or school districts, shall enact, adopt or enforce any statute, regulation, ordinance or policy whereby homosexual,

---

[71] On the anti-homosexual Kulturkampf of 1946–61, see William Eskridge, Jr., Dishonorable Passions: Sodomy Laws in America, 1861–2003, at 73–108 (2008); David Johnson, The Lavender Scare: The Cold War Persecution of Gays and Lesbians in the Federal Government (2004).

lesbian or bisexual orientation, conduct, practices or relationships shall constitute or otherwise be the basis of or entitle any person or class of persons to have or claim any minority status, quota preferences, protected status or claim of discrimination.

Before Amendment 2 was proposed, the cities of Aspen, Boulder, and Denver, Colorado had adopted ordinances prohibiting private as well as public workplace, housing, and public accommodations discrimination on the basis of sexual orientation.

[In Colorado, as in most states, the voters can amend the state constitution through a majority vote for "initiatives" like Amendment 2. Gay rights groups and their allies opposed the initiative on the ground that it would preempt important local protections and subject gay people to affirmative and unfair state discrimination.

[Typical of the initiative process, CFV prepared a ballot pamphlet setting forth its case for Amendment 2, "equal rights—not special rights."[72] The pamphlet made the following arguments: (1) "Homosexuals" are not a "disadvantaged minority" meriting anti-discrimination protections, as they are much wealthier than average citizens, have never been subject to legal segregation, and are marked by immoral behavior rather than immutable traits such as race, sex, and disability. Instead, "special class status for gays threaten[s] the hard-won gains of disadvantaged minorities." (2) "Target: Children." Pedophilia, said CFV, "is actually an accepted part of the homosexual community!" "Homosexuals" account for more than one-third of all child molestations. And "Homosexual indoctrination in the schools? It's Happening in Colorado," through educational materials that "try and convince children—maybe even your own—that they should consider homosexuality!" (3) "Homosexuals" are sexually promiscuous. " 'Monogamy' is virtually unknown in the homosexual lifestyle." Gay men tend to be afflicted with AIDS: "Gays have been unwilling (or unable) to curb their voracious, unsafe sex practices in the face of AIDS." Even those not afflicted with AIDS die young; according to CFV, the average reported age of death for gay men is 42 years old, lesbians 45 years old. (4) "To this angry, alienated minority, the family is the symbol of everything they attack." "Militant" gay rights people want to destroy the family and the state's churches. (5) "Homosexuality" is a choice and not an innate trait. (6) " 'Gay-rights' destroys basic freedoms." The freedom of "your child" at the University of Colorado not to have a gay roommate has been taken away by Boulder's anti-discrimination law. Gay rights will suppress free speech and deny straight people jobs they ought to have. A cartoon depicted a day care center telling a rejected applicant that he cannot be hired because "we haven't filled our quota of homosexuals."

---

[72] The ballot materials are reproduced as an appendix to Robert Nagel, *Playing Defense*, 6 Wm. & Mary Bill of Rights L.J. 167 (1997).

[Gay rights advocates claimed that most of these factual assertions are false, and none could be empirically supported. Colorado voters approved the initiative 54%–46%, but it was challenged as a violation of the Equal Protection Clause before it could go into effect.]

One century ago, the first Justice Harlan admonished this Court that the Constitution "neither knows nor tolerates classes among citizens." *Plessy v. Ferguson*, 163 U.S. 537, 559 (1896) (dissenting opinion). Unheeded then, those words now are understood to state a commitment to the law's neutrality where the rights of persons are at stake. The Equal Protection Clause enforces this principle and today requires us to hold invalid a provision of Colorado's Constitution [Amendment 2, quoted above]. * * *

The State's principal argument in defense of Amendment 2 is that it puts gays and lesbians in the same position as all other persons. So, the State says, the measure does no more than deny homosexuals special rights. This reading of the amendment's language is implausible. [The Colorado Supreme Court interpreted the amendment as repealing local protections for gay people and preventing further protections from being adopted unless the state constitution were first amended.]

Sweeping and comprehensive is the change in legal status effected by this law. So much is evident from the ordinances that the Colorado Supreme Court declared would be void by operation of Amendment 2. Homosexuals, by state decree, are put in a solitary class with respect to transactions and relations in both the private and governmental spheres. The amendment withdraws from homosexuals, but no others, specific legal protection from the injuries caused by discrimination, and it forbids reinstatement of these laws and policies.

The change that Amendment 2 works in the legal status of gays and lesbians in the private sphere is far-reaching, both on its own terms and when considered in light of the structure and operation of modern anti-discrimination laws. [Justice Kennedy explained that the common law afforded no protection against discrimination by public accommodations because of race, sex, etc. The common law also placed few, if any, restrictions on employment discrimination. The Aspen, Boulder, and Denver ordinances are typical of antidiscrimination regulations adopted in hundreds of jurisdictions filling this gap in the common law. Additionally, those regulations, like others, prohibit discrimination on the basis of criteria that have not triggered constitutional strict scrutiny, including age, military status, marital status, pregnancy, parenthood, custody of a minor child, political affiliation, physical or mental disability of an individual or of his or her associates, and sexual orientation. The effect of Amendment 2 was to deprive gay people of those protections in public accommodations, housing, sale of real estate, insurance, health and welfare services, private education, and employment.]

Amendment 2's reach may not be limited to specific laws passed for the benefit of gays and lesbians. It is a fair, if not necessary, inference from the broad language of the amendment that it deprives gays and lesbians even of the protection of general laws and policies that prohibit arbitrary discrimination in governmental and private settings. See, *e.g.*, Colo. Rev. Stat. § 24–4–106(7) (1988) (agency action subject to judicial review under arbitrary and capricious standard); § 18–8–405 (making it a criminal offense for a public servant knowingly, arbitrarily or capriciously to refrain from performing a duty imposed on him by law); * * * 4 Colo. Code of Regulations 801–1, Policy 11–1 (1983) (prohibiting discrimination in state employment on grounds of specified traits or "other non-merit factor"). At some point in the systematic administration of these laws, an official must determine whether homosexuality is an arbitrary and thus forbidden basis for decision. Yet a decision to that effect would itself amount to a policy prohibiting discrimination on the basis of homosexuality, and so would appear to be no more valid under Amendment 2 than the specific prohibitions against discrimination the state court held invalid.

If this consequence follows from Amendment 2, as its broad language suggests, it would compound the constitutional difficulties the law creates. [The Colorado Supreme Court made the limited observation that the amendment is not intended to affect many anti-discrimination laws protecting non-suspect classes, but the state court's construction left open the possibility of broader application. Justice Kennedy specifically rejected the view that Amendment 2's prohibition on specific legal protections does no more than deprive homosexuals of special rights.] We find nothing special in the protections Amendment 2 withholds. These are protections taken for granted by most people either because they already have them or do not need them; these are protections against exclusion from an almost limitless number of transactions and endeavors that constitute ordinary civic life in a free society. * * *

Amendment 2 fails, indeed defies, [rational basis] inquiry. First, the amendment has the peculiar property of imposing a broad and undifferentiated disability on a single named group, an exceptional and, as we shall explain, invalid form of legislation. Second, its sheer breadth is so discontinuous with the reasons offered for it that the amendment seems inexplicable by anything but animus toward the class that it affects; it lacks a rational relationship to legitimate state interests.

Taking the first point, even in the ordinary equal protection case calling for the most deferential of standards, we insist on knowing the relation between the classification adopted and the object to be attained. The search for the link between classification and objective gives substance to the Equal Protection Clause; it provides guidance and discipline for the legislature, which is entitled to know what sorts of laws it can pass; and it marks the limits of our own authority. In the ordinary case, a law will be sustained if it can be said to advance a legitimate government interest, even if the law seems unwise or works to the disadvantage of a particular group, or if the rationale for it seems tenuous. [Citing, *inter alia*, *Railway Express*.] By requiring that the classification bear a rational relationship to an independent and legitimate legislative end, we ensure that classifications are not drawn for the purpose of disadvantaging the group burdened by the law.

Amendment 2 confounds this normal process of judicial review. It is at once too narrow and too broad. It identifies persons by a single trait and then denies them protection across the board. The resulting disqualification of a class of persons from the right to seek specific protection from the law is unprecedented in our jurisprudence. The absence of precedent for Amendment 2 is itself instructive; "[d]iscriminations of an unusual character especially suggest careful consideration to determine whether they are obnoxious to the constitutional provision."

[handwritten margin note: reading class / doesn't remove this protection from any other class]

It is not within our constitutional tradition to enact laws of this sort. Central both to the idea of the rule of law and to our own Constitution's guarantee of equal protection is the principle that government and each of its parts remain open on impartial terms to all who seek its assistance. "'Equal protection of the laws is not achieved through indiscriminate imposition of inequalities.'" *Sweatt v. Painter*, 339 U.S. 629, 635 (1950) (quoting *Shelley v. Kraemer*, 334 U.S. 1, 22 (1948)). Respect for this principle explains why laws singling out a certain class of citizens for disfavored legal status or general hardships are rare. A law declaring that in general it shall be more difficult for one group of citizens than for all others to seek aid from the government is itself a denial of equal protection of the laws in the most literal sense. * * *

A second and related point is that laws of the kind now before us raise the inevitable inference that the disadvantage imposed is born of animosity toward the class of persons affected. "[I]f the constitutional conception of 'equal protection of the laws' means anything, it must at the very least mean that a bare . . . desire to harm a politically unpopular group cannot constitute a *legitimate* governmental interest." *Moreno*. Even laws enacted for broad and ambitious purposes often can be explained by reference to legitimate public policies which justify the incidental disadvantages they impose on certain persons. Amendment 2, however, in making a general announcement that gays and lesbians shall not have any particular protections from the law, inflicts on them immediate, continuing, and real injuries that outrun and belie any legitimate justifications that may be claimed for it. We conclude that, in addition to the far-reaching deficiencies of Amendment 2 that we have noted, the principles it offends, in another sense, are conventional and venerable; a law must bear a rational relationship to a legitimate governmental purpose, and Amendment 2 does not.

[handwritten margin note: See Cleburne— absent animus, wouldn't have this rule]

The primary rationale the State offers for Amendment 2 is respect for other citizens' freedom of association, and in particular the liberties of landlords or employers who have personal or religious objections to homosexuality. Colorado also cites its interest in conserving resources to fight discrimination against other groups. The breadth of the Amendment is so far removed from these particular justifications that we find it impossible to credit them. We cannot say that Amendment 2 is directed to any identifiable legitimate purpose or discrete objective. It is a status-based enactment divorced from any factual context from which we could discern a relationship to legitimate state interests; it is a classification of persons undertaken for its own sake, something the Equal Protection Clause does not permit. "[C]lass legislation . . . [is] obnoxious to the prohibitions of the Fourteenth Amendment. . . ." *Civil Rights Cases.*

JUSTICE SCALIA, with whom **THE CHIEF JUSTICE [REHNQUIST]** and **JUSTICE THOMAS** join, dissenting.

The Court has mistaken a Kulturkampf for a fit of spite. The constitutional amendment before us here is not the manifestation of a " 'bare . . . desire to harm' " homosexuals, but is rather a modest attempt by seemingly tolerant Coloradans to preserve traditional sexual mores against the efforts of a politically powerful minority to revise those mores through use of the laws. That objective, and the means chosen to achieve it, are not only unimpeachable under any constitutional doctrine hitherto pronounced (hence the opinion's heavy reliance upon principles of righteousness rather than judicial holdings); they have been specifically approved by the Congress of the United States and by this Court. * * *

[Justice Scalia criticized the Court for suggesting that Amendment 2 had a potentially broad impact upon gay people, for the Colorado Supreme Court authoritatively construed Amendment 2 "only to prevent the adoption of antidiscrimination laws intended to protect gays, lesbians, and bisexuals."] The amendment prohibits *special treatment* of homosexuals, and nothing more. It would not affect, for example, a requirement of state law that pensions be paid to all retiring state employees with a certain length of service; homosexual employees, as well as others, would be entitled to that benefit. But it would prevent the State or any municipality from making death-benefit payments to the "life partner" of a homosexual when it does not make such payments to the long-time roommate of a non-homosexual employee. Or again, it does not affect the requirement of the State's general insurance laws that customers be afforded coverage without discrimination unrelated to anticipated risk. Thus, homosexuals could not be denied coverage, or charged a greater premium, with respect to auto collision insurance; but neither the State nor any municipality could require that distinctive health insurance risks associated with homosexuality (if there are any) be ignored.

Despite all of its hand-wringing about the potential effect of Amendment 2 on general antidiscrimination laws, the Court's opinion ultimately does not dispute all this, but assumes it to be true. The only denial of equal treatment it contends homosexuals have suffered is this: They may not obtain *preferential* treatment without amending the state constitution. That is to say, the principle underlying the Court's opinion is that one who is accorded equal treatment under the laws, but cannot as readily as others obtain *preferential* treatment under the laws, has been denied equal protection of the laws. If merely stating this alleged "equal protection" violation does not suffice to refute it, our constitutional jurisprudence has achieved terminal silliness. * * *

I turn next to whether there was a legitimate rational basis for the substance of the constitutional amendment—for the prohibition of special protection for homosexuals. It is unsurprising that the Court avoids discussion of this question, since the answer is so obviously yes. The case most relevant to the issue before us today is not even mentioned in the Court's opinion: In *Bowers v. Hardwick* [Chapter 5, § 4C], we held that the Constitution does not prohibit what virtually all States had done from the founding of the Republic until very recent years—making homosexual conduct a crime. That holding is unassailable, except by those who think that the Constitution changes to suit current fashions. But in any event it is a given in the present case: Respondents' briefs did not urge overruling *Bowers*, and at oral argument respondents' counsel expressly disavowed any intent to seek such overruling. If it is constitutionally permissible for a State to make homosexual conduct criminal, surely it is constitutionally permissible for a State to enact other laws merely *disfavoring* homosexual conduct. * * * And *a fortiori* it is constitutionally permissible for a State to adopt a provision *not even* disfavoring homosexual conduct, but merely prohibiting all levels of state government from bestowing *special protections* upon homosexual conduct. Respondents (who, unlike the Court, cannot afford the luxury of ignoring inconvenient precedent) counter *Bowers* with the argument that a greater-includes-the-lesser rationale cannot justify Amendment 2's application to individuals who do not engage in homosexual acts, but are merely of homosexual "orientation." * * *

But assuming that, in Amendment 2, a person of homosexual "orientation" is someone who does not engage in homosexual conduct but merely has a tendency or desire to do so, *Bowers* still suffices to establish a rational basis for the provision. If it is rational to criminalize the conduct, surely it is rational to deny special favor and protection to those with a self-avowed tendency or desire to engage in the conduct. Indeed, where criminal sanctions are not involved, homosexual "orientation" is an acceptable stand-in for homosexual conduct. * * * Just as a policy barring the hiring of methadone users as transit employees does not violate equal protection simply because *some* methadone users pose no threat to passenger safety, see *New York City Transit Authority v. Beazer*, 440 U.S. 568 (1979), and just as a mandatory retirement age of 50 for police officers does not violate equal protection even though it prematurely ends the careers of many policemen over 50 who still have the capacity to do the job, see *Murgia*, Amendment 2 is not constitutionally invalid simply because it could have been drawn more precisely so as to withdraw special antidiscrimination protections only from those of homosexual "orientation" who actually engage in homosexual conduct. * * *

* * * The Court's opinion contains grim, disapproving hints that Coloradans have been guilty of "animus" or "animosity" toward homosexuality, as though that has been established as Unamerican. Of course it is our moral heritage that one should not hate any human being or class of human beings. But I had thought that one could consider certain conduct reprehensible—murder, for example, or polygamy, or cruelty to animals—and could exhibit even "animus" toward such conduct. Surely that is the only sort of "animus" at issue here: moral disapproval of homosexual conduct, the same sort of moral disapproval that produced the centuries-old criminal laws that we held constitutional in *Bowers*. The Colorado amendment does not, to speak entirely precisely, prohibit giving favored status to people who are *homosexuals*; they can be favored for many reasons—for example, because they are senior citizens or members of racial minorities. But it prohibits giving them favored status *because of their homosexual conduct*—that is, it prohibits favored status *for homosexuality*.

[Justice Scalia maintained that Colorado had, in fact, engaged in a measured response to homosexuality. The state in 1971 repealed its law making consensual sodomy a crime, but that repeal was not intended to connote an approval of homosexuality.] The problem (a problem, that is, for those who wish to retain social disapprobation of homosexuality) is that, because those who engage in homosexual conduct tend to reside in disproportionate numbers in certain communities, see Record, Exh. MMM, have high disposable income, see *ibid.*; App. 254 (affidavit of Prof. James Hunter), and of course care about homosexual-rights issues much more ardently than the public at large, they possess political power much greater than their numbers, both locally and statewide. Quite understandably, they devote this political power to achieving not merely a grudging social toleration, but full social acceptance, of homosexuality. * * *

That is where Amendment 2 came in. It sought to counter both the geographic concentration and the disproportionate political power of homosexuals by (1) resolving the controversy at the statewide level, and (2) making the election a single-issue contest for both sides. It put directly, to all the citizens of the State, the question: Should homosexuality be given special protection? They answered no. The Court today asserts that this most democratic of procedures is unconstitutional. Lacking any cases to establish that facially absurd proposition, it simply asserts that it *must* be unconstitutional, because it has never happened before. [This is completely false, says Justice Scalia. In the late nineteenth century, the federal government enacted a series of statutes singling out polygamists for special criminal, civil, and juridical treatment; the Court upheld all the legal disabilities, including one that disenfranchised not only polygamists, but also people who taught or counseled polygamy. *Davis v. Beason*, 133 U.S. 333 (1890). Although abstract advocacy cannot today be punished, *Beason* remains good for the proposition that disapproved status can be the basis for civil penalty.] Has the Court concluded that the perceived social harm of polygamy is a "legitimate concern of government," and the perceived social harm of homosexuality is not? [Justice Scalia concluded his opinion:]

When the Court takes sides in the culture wars, it tends to be with the knights rather than the villeins—and more specifically with the Templars, reflecting the views and values of the lawyer class from which the Court's Members are drawn. How that class feels about homosexuality will be evident to anyone who wishes to interview job applicants at virtually any of the Nation's law schools. The interviewer may refuse to offer a job because the applicant is a Republican; because he is an adulterer; because he went to the wrong prep school or belongs to the wrong country club; because he eats snails; because he is a womanizer; because she wears real-animal fur; or even because he hates the Chicago Cubs. But if the interviewer should wish not to be an associate or partner of an applicant because he disapproves of the applicant's homosexuality, *then* he will have violated the pledge which the Association of American Law Schools requires all its member-schools to exact from job interviewers: "assurance of the employer's willingness" to hire homosexuals. This law-school view of what "prejudices" must be stamped out may be contrasted with the more plebeian attitudes that apparently still prevail in the United States Congress, which has been unresponsive to repeated attempts to extend to homosexuals the protections of federal civil rights laws, see, *e.g.*, Employment Non-Discrimination Act of 1994, S. 2238, 103d Cong., 2d Sess. (1994); Civil Rights Amendments of 1975, H.R. 5452, 94th Cong., 1st Sess. (1975), and which took the pains to exclude them specifically from the Americans With Disabilities Act of 1990, see 42 U.S.C. § 12211(a) (1988 ed., Supp. V).

NOTES ON ROMER *AND ITS IMPLICATIONS FOR JUDICIAL REVIEW OF ANTIGAY STATE POLICIES*

1.   *What Is the Holding of* Romer? What exactly was wrong with Amendment 2? Some possibilities:

(a) it deprived gay people of the right to participate equally in the political process;[73]

(b) the law was a denial of the "equal protection of the laws" in the most literal sense, as it closed off state process to one vulnerable group;[74]

(c) the law may not draw moral distinctions based upon sexual practices between consenting adults (therefore overruling *Hardwick*);[75]

(d) the state cannot, without justification, single out one social group for "pariah" status by creating a constitutional right to discriminate against that group,[76] or the state has an obligation to remedy pervasive discrimination against a vulnerable group similar to those the state does protect;[77]

(e) the law's goal—state action reflecting widespread animus against gay people—was impermissible;[78]

(f) the measure, unprecedented in its sweep, was extremely overbroad.[79]

Which basis is the *best* (most persuasive) basis for *Romer*? Does the best reading of the case meet Justice Scalia's criticisms that the result is inconsistent with *Hardwick* and with the general precepts underlying rational basis review?

2. *The War of Analogies; Classification Versus Class.* Justice Scalia argued that a state that can discourage polygamy by penalizing "polygamosexuals" is a state that can discourage sodomy by penalizing "homosexuals." Would equal protection law allow the state to deny fundamental rights to people who identified themselves as polygamosexuals? Justice Kennedy invoked a counter-analogy, *Plessy*. Is it fair to analogize racial apartheid, a pervasive and violent state regime, with the regime of Amendment 2? Note the potential power of race-based analogies in equal protection law—but it is a power that can backfire if the analogy is incorrect or even insulting as Justice Scalia argued in dissent. Like Colorado for Family Values, Scalia depicted gays as a group earning high incomes and wielding

---

[73] This was the theory followed by the Colorado Supreme Court, *Evans v. Romer*, 854 P.2d 1270 (1993), and has been viewed by some commentators as essentially the Court's theory. See Pamela Karlan, *Just Politics? Five Not So Easy Pieces of the 1995 Term*, 34 Houston L. Rev. 289, 296 (1997); Nicholas Zeppos, *The Dynamics of Democracy: Travel, Premature Predation, and the Components of Political Identity*, 50 Vand. L. Rev. 445 (1997).

[74] Brief by Laurence Tribe et al., in *Romer*, the so-called "Scholars' Brief" filed in the case.

[75] Robert Bork, *Slouching Towards Gomorrah* 112–14 (1996) (disapproving); Ronald Dworkin, *Sex, Death, and the Courts*, N.Y. Rev. Books, Aug. 8, 1996, at 49 (approving); Cass Sunstein, *The Supreme Court, 1995 Term—Foreword: Leaving Things Undecided*, 110 Harv. L. Rev. 4, 62 (1996) (approving).

[76] Daniel Farber & Suzanna Sherry, *The Pariah Principle*, 13 Const. Comm. 257 (1996), as well as Akhil Amar, *Attainder and Amendment 2:* Romer's *Rightness*, 95 Mich. L. Rev. 203 (1996).

[77] Louis Michael Seidman, Romer's *Radicalism: The Unexpected Revival of Warren Court Activism*, 1996 Sup. Ct. Rev. 67.

[78] Eskridge, *Gaylaw* 205–18; Andrew Koppelman, Romer v. Evans *and Invidious Intent*, 6 Wm. & Mary Bill of Rights J. (1997).

[79] Richard Duncan, *The Narrow and Shallow Bite of* Romer *and the Eminent Rationality of Dual-Gender Marriage: A (Partial) Response to Professor Koppelman*, 6 Wm. & Mary Bill of Rights J. 147 (1997).

political power much greater than their numbers would suggest. He characterized the result as "special rights" legislation, such as the ordinances prohibiting sexual orientation discrimination. Justice Kennedy rejected this rhetoric and treated gays and lesbians as a group beset by "animus" which threatened to close them out of the Colorado political process. Which view is more accurate?[80]

Justice Kennedy's focus on the "classification" (sexual orientation) contrasts with Justice Scalia's focus on the "class" ("homosexuals"). Recall *Loving v. Virginia* (Chapter 3). Although *Carolene Products* and Ely's "representation-reinforcing" theory (Chapter 2, § 3B) make the discriminated-against class the focus, like Justice Scalia did, others believe that Justice Kennedy's is the better approach in general. An advantage of the classification-oriented approach would be to escape the implicit issue of whether a particular group is sufficiently "victimized" to merit heightened scrutiny of an invidious classification. Can such an inquiry really be avoided, though? Which is more consistent with the sex discrimination cases such as VMI? Which focus (if either) is most conceptually attractive?

3.   One effect of *Romer's* focus on "animus" has been to transform public discourse about homosexuality. Proponents of laws and initiatives that discriminate against gay people have increasingly focused on neutral policies; to minimize the chance of a successful equal protection challenge, they have abstained from arguments which demonize gay people or which make wild claims about them. *Romer* and equal protection law *channel* antigay discourse into more tolerant tropes.[81] Antigay policies are now justified as preventing harm to third parties or as signaling that the state should *tolerate* "homosexuals" but should *not promote* "homosexuality."

NOTE ON JUDICIAL REVIEW OF POPULAR INITIATIVES AND REFERENDA

State constitutions are routinely subject to amendment by ballot proposal, and in about half the states citizens may adopt ordinary legislation by initiative as well. The Supreme Court has rarely reviewed the constitutionality of such direct lawmaking, and until *Romer* its review had largely focused on initiatives having a race-based impact.[82] With few dissenting voices, scholars have urged the Court to scrutinize popular initiatives for equal protection violations more vigorously than the Court reviews ordinary statutes adopted

---

[80]   M.V. Lee Badgett, *The Wage Effects of Sexual Orientation Discrimination*, 48 Indus. & Labor Rel. Rev. 726 (1995), analyzed pooled data from a national random sample, and found that bisexual and gay male workers earned 11–27% less money than heterosexual workers with the same experience, education, occupation, etc. Badgett found that lesbians and bisexual women earned less than heterosexual women, but the difference was not statistically significant.

[81]   See William Eskridge, Jr., *No Promo Homo: The Sedimentation of Antigay Discourse and the Channeling Effect of Judicial Review*, 75 NYU L. Rev. 1327 (2000).

[82]   See *Reitman v. Mulkey*, 387 U.S. 369 (1967); *Hunter v. Erickson*, 393 U.S. 385 (1969); *James v. Valtierra*, 402 U.S. 137 (1971); *Washington v. Seattle Sch. Dist. No. 1*, 458 U.S. 457 (1982); *Crawford v. Board of Educ.*, 458 U.S. 527 (1982). In all but *James* and *Crawford*, the Court invalidated the initiative because it impaired racial minority equality.

by legislatures.[83] *Romer* might be an example of that realist argument. If so, it and the other cases are vulnerable to the argument from democracy: Perhaps courts should be more rather than less reluctant to overturn legislation when it is clearly responsive to majority preferences.

The main argument for heightened review is that the Constitution adopts a "republican" structure rather than direct democracy (see *Federalist* 10 [App. 2]) for the national government and expresses a preference for the same at the state level (see U.S. Const., Art. IV, § 4, requiring Congress to "guarantee to every State [a] Republican Form of Government"). The reason for the Constitution's policy is the greater preference for the status quo and for deliberation assured by republican governance. Before a bill becomes law, it must pass through two legislative chambers and a possible executive veto. This assures more opportunities for affected minorities to block or ameliorate the harm to them from representative than popular legislation. Possibilities for distortion and emotional appeals are more likely in direct democracy, where voters are often confused by the phrasing of initiatives and subject to demagogy by professional politicians or grass-roots organizers. Also, because voting is open and public in the representative but not initiative process, critics of direct democracy fear that prejudice will be more readily expressed in the latter than the former.

Other scholars reject or caution against this academic conventional wisdom.[84] Initiatives are an intrinsically fair way for the voting population to focus on an issue that concerns them—and are often a better path to active citizen engagement in substantive issues. Public choice theory, for example, suggests that legislators have incentives not to confront or resolve conflictual issues, and this may have been the reason the Colorado legislature ducked the issue of sexual orientation protections at the local level. Moreover, the same kinds of questions raised against direct democracy—the inability of minorities to win, the lack of genuine deliberation, private interests winning over the common good—have been posed by public choice theorists criticizing representative democracy.

One context in which ballot propositions figured prominently is the debate over same-sex marriage. Beginning in the 1990s, when it first seemed plausible that a state would legalize same-sex marriage, many states in this country enacted ballot propositions to ban same-sex couples from marrying. Over time, equal protection-based challenges to these marriage bans were litigated all

---

[83] Among the scholars urging such heightened scrutiny are Derrick Bell, Jr., *The Referendum: Democracy's Barrier to Racial Equality*, 54 Wash. L. Rev. 1 (1978); Julian Eule, *Judicial Review of Direct Democracy*, 99 Yale L.J. 1503 (1990); Daniel Lowenstein, *California Initiatives and the Single-Subject Rule*, 30 UCLA L. Rev. 936 (1983) (state constitutional review); Lawrence Sager, *Insular Majorities Unabated:* Warth v. Seldin *and* City of Eastlake v. Forest City Enterprises, Inc., 91 Harv. L. Rev. 1373 (1978). Along the same lines, see Philip P. Frickey, *Interpretation on the Borderline: Constitution, Canons, Direct Democracy*, 1996 Ann. Surv. Am. L. 477 (urging narrow interpretation of ballot measures).

[84] See Lynn Baker, *Direct Democracy and Discrimination: A Public Choice Perspective*, 67 Chi-Kent L. Rev. 707 (1991); Richard Briffault, *Distrust of Democracy*, 63 Tex. L. Rev. 1347 (1985) (book review); Clayton Gillette, *Plebiscites, Participation, and Collective Action in Local Government Law*, 86 Mich. L. Rev. 930 (1988).

over the country. In addition, a constitutional challenge was brought seeking to invalidate the federal Defense of Marriage Act ("DOMA"), a statute that, among other things, prohibited the federal government from recognizing same-sex marriages even if a state did accord such recognition. The Supreme Court struck down this portion of DOMA in a landmark decision in *United States v. Windsor*, to which we will shortly turn. Before the Court ruled, however, there was great uncertainty about what tier of review should be applied to the DOMA ban on federal recognition. In 2011, the Obama Administration weighed in on this question with a memorandum addressed in the following problem.

PROBLEM 4-5:
WHAT TIER OF SCRUTINY FOR SEXUAL ORIENTATION CLAIMS?

Section 3 of DOMA provided as follows:

> In determining the meaning of any Act of Congress, or of any ruling, regulation, or interpretation of the various administrative bureaus and agencies of the United States, the word "marriage" means only a legal union between one man and one woman as husband and wife, and the word "spouse" refers only to a person of the opposite sex who is a husband or a wife.

Ordinarily, the federal government treats as married any couple that is married under the law of the relevant state. DOMA created a new rule of exclusion for same-sex couples. Once states began marrying same-sex couples, these couples were denied federal rights to which they would otherwise have been entitled—such as tax, immigration, and social security benefits, among many others. Several challenges to the constitutionality of DOMA were filed in federal courts around the country. Initially, the Department of Justice defended these suits. In February 2011, however, Attorney General Eric Holder, Jr. announced that the Department of Justice believed that heightened scrutiny should be applied to distinctions based on sexual orientation and, on that basis, would decline to defend section 3 of DOMA in circuits that had not already established rational basis as the relevant level of scrutiny. In February 2011, a letter from Eric Holder to Speaker of the House John Boehner set out the in detail DOJ's arguments for heightened scrutiny:

> After careful consideration, including review of a recommendation from me, the President of the United States has made the determination that Section 3 of the Defense of Marriage Act ("DOMA"), 1 U.S.C. § 7, as applied to same-sex couples who are legally married under state law, violates the equal protection component of the Fifth Amendment. * * *

> Previously, the Administration has defended Section 3 in jurisdictions where circuit courts have already held that classifications based on sexual orientation are subject to rational basis review, and it has advanced arguments to defend DOMA Section 3 under the binding standard that has applied in those cases.

These new lawsuits, by contrast, will require the Department to take an affirmative position on the level of scrutiny that should be applied to DOMA Section 3 in a circuit without binding precedent on the issue. As described more fully below, the President and I have concluded that classifications based on sexual orientation warrant heightened scrutiny and that, as applied to same-sex couples legally married under state law, Section 3 of DOMA is unconstitutional.

The Supreme Court has yet to rule on the appropriate level of scrutiny for classifications based on sexual orientation. It has, however, rendered a number of decisions that set forth the criteria that should inform this and any other judgment as to whether heightened scrutiny applies: (1) whether the group in question has suffered a history of discrimination; (2) whether individuals "exhibit obvious, immutable, or distinguishing characteristics that define them as a discrete group"; (3) whether the group is a minority or is politically powerless; and (4) whether the characteristics distinguishing the group have little relation to legitimate policy objectives or to an individual's "ability to perform or contribute to society." See Bowen v. Gilliard, 483 U.S. 587, 602–03 (1987); City of Cleburne v. Cleburne Living Ctr., 473 U.S. 432, 441–42 (1985).

Each of these factors counsels in favor of being suspicious of classifications based on sexual orientation. First and most importantly, there is, regrettably, a significant history of purposeful discrimination against gay and lesbian people, by governmental as well as private entities, based on prejudice and stereotypes that continue to have ramifications today. Indeed, until very recently, states have "demean[ed] the[ ] existence" of gays and lesbians "by making their private sexual conduct a crime." Lawrence v. Texas, 539 U.S. 558, 578 (2003).

Second, while sexual orientation carries no visible badge, a growing scientific consensus accepts that sexual orientation is a characteristic that is immutable, see Richard A. Posner, Sex and Reason 101 (1992); it is undoubtedly unfair to require sexual orientation to be hidden from view to avoid discrimination, see Don't Ask, Don't Tell Repeal Act of 2010, Pub. L. No. 111–321, 124 Stat. 3515 (2010).

Third, the adoption of laws like those at issue in Romer v. Evans, 517 U.S. 620 (1996), and Lawrence, the longstanding ban on gays and lesbians in the military, and the absence of federal protection for employment discrimination on the basis of sexual orientation show the group to have limited political power and "ability to attract the [favorable] attention of the lawmakers." Cleburne, 473 U.S. at 445. And while the enactment of the Matthew Shepard Act and pending repeal of Don't Ask, Don't Tell indicate that the political process is not closed entirely to gay and lesbian people, that is not the standard by which the Court has judged "political powerlessness." Indeed, when the Court ruled that gender-based classifications were subject to heightened scrutiny, women already had won major political victories such as the Nineteenth Amendment (right to vote) and protection under Title VII (employment discrimination).

Finally, there is a growing acknowledgment that sexual orientation "bears no relation to ability to perform or contribute to society." *Frontiero v. Richardson*, 411 U.S. 677, 686 (1973) (plurality). Recent evolutions in legislation (including the pending repeal of Don't Ask, Don't Tell), in community practices and attitudes, in case law (including the Supreme Court's holdings in *Lawrence* and *Romer*), and in social science regarding sexual orientation all make clear that sexual orientation is not a characteristic that generally bears on legitimate policy objectives. *See, e.g.,* Statement by the President on the Don't Ask, Don't Tell Repeal Act of 2010 ("It is time to recognize that sacrifice, valor and integrity are no more defined by sexual orientation than they are by race or gender, religion or creed.")

To be sure, there is substantial circuit court authority applying rational basis review to sexual-orientation classifications. We have carefully examined each of those decisions. Many of them reason only that if consensual same-sex sodomy may be criminalized under *Bowers v. Hardwick*, then it follows that no heightened review is appropriate—a line of reasoning that does not survive the overruling of *Bowers* in *Lawrence v. Texas*, 538 U.S. 558 (2003). Others rely on claims regarding "procreational responsibility" that the Department has disavowed already in litigation as unreasonable, or claims regarding the immutability of sexual orientation that we do not believe can be reconciled with more recent social science understandings. And none engages in an examination of all the factors that the Supreme Court has identified as relevant to a decision about the appropriate level of scrutiny. Finally, many of the more recent decisions have relied on the fact that the Supreme Court has not recognized that gays and lesbians constitute a suspect class or the fact that the Court has applied rational basis review in its most recent decisions addressing classifications based on sexual orientation, *Lawrence* and *Romer*. But neither of those decisions reached, let alone resolved, the level of scrutiny issue because in both the Court concluded that the laws could not even survive the more deferential rational basis standard.

* * * [U]nder heightened scrutiny, the United States cannot defend Section 3 by advancing hypothetical rationales, independent of the legislative record, as it has done in circuits where precedent mandates application of rational basis review. Instead, the United States can defend Section 3 only by invoking Congress' actual justifications for the law.

Moreover, the legislative record underlying DOMA's passage contains discussion and debate that undermines any defense under heightened scrutiny. The record contains numerous expressions reflecting moral disapproval of gays and lesbians and their intimate and family relationships—precisely the kind of stereotype-based thinking and animus the Equal Protection Clause is designed to guard against. *See Cleburne*, 473 U.S. at 448 ("mere negative attitudes, or fear" are not permissible bases for discriminatory treatment); *see also Romer*, 517 U.S. at 635 (rejecting rationale that law was supported by "the liberties of landlords or employers who have personal or religious objections to homosexuality"); *Palmore v. Sidoti*, 466 U.S. 429, 433 (1984) ("Private biases may be outside the reach of the law, but the law cannot, directly or indirectly, give them effect.").

As you know, the Department has a longstanding practice of defending the constitutionality of duly-enacted statutes if reasonable arguments can be made in their defense, a practice that accords the respect appropriately due to a coequal branch of government. However, the Department in the past has declined to defend statutes despite the availability of professionally responsible arguments, in part because the Department does not consider every plausible argument to be a "reasonable" one. . . . This is the rare case where the proper course is to forgo the defense of this statute . . . * * *

Review each element of the doctrine addressed by the Attorney General and determine whether you find the DOJ's arguments persuasive. What counter-arguments could be made on each point?

When the Holder Memorandum was written, marriage equality advocates had begun to have successes in state legislatures and ballot measures. Should that success have borne on the application of heightened scrutiny? Why or why not? (Recall the discussion of Ely and representation-reinforcement in Chapter 2 § 3.)

What do you make of the Attorney General staking out this position? Is it a laudable exercise of "popular constitutionalism" for the Executive to assert these views? Or is it a kind of abdication to refuse to defend the statute in this fashion? How should executive officials make these decisions?

In the next case, the justices addressed the constitutionality of DOMA.

UNITED STATES V. WINDSOR

570 U.S. 744, 133 S.Ct. 2675, 186 L.Ed.2d 808 (2013)

JUSTICE KENNEDY delivered the opinion of the Court.

In 1996, as some States were beginning to consider the concept of same-sex marriage, and before any State had acted to permit it, Congress enacted the Defense of Marriage Act (DOMA). DOMA contains two operative sections: Section 2, which has not been challenged here, allows States to refuse to recognize same-sex marriages performed under the laws of other States.

Section 3 is at issue here. It amends the Dictionary Act in Title 1, § 7, of the United States Code to provide a federal definition of "marriage" and "spouse." Section 3 of DOMA provides as follows:

> In determining the meaning of any Act of Congress, or of any ruling, regulation, or interpretation of the various administrative bureaus and agencies of the United States, the word 'marriage' means only a legal union between one man and one woman as husband and wife, and the word 'spouse' refers only to a person of the opposite sex who is a husband or a wife.

The definitional provision does not by its terms forbid States from enacting laws permitting same-sex marriages or civil unions or providing state benefits to residents in that status. The enactment's comprehensive definition of marriage for purposes of all federal statutes and other regulations or directives covered by its terms, however, does control over 1,000 federal laws in which marital or spousal status is addressed as a matter of federal law.

[The Court then traced the relationship between Edith Windsor and Thea Spyer, who began a long-term relationship in the early 1960s and, when Spyer became seriously ill, travelled to Canada in 2007 to marry. It noted that their home state, New York, deemed their Canadian marriage valid. After Spyer died in 2009, she left her estate to Windsor. DOMA precluded federal recognition of the marriage and thus barred Windsor from the marital exemption to the federal estate tax. Because of this, Windsor was subject to a tax of $363,053 that a heterosexual spouse would not have had to pay. She thus "commenced this refund suit, [contending] that DOMA violates the guarantee of equal protection, as applied to the Federal Government through the Fifth Amendment."]

It seems fair to conclude that, until recent years, many citizens had not even considered the possibility that two persons of the same sex might aspire to occupy the same status and dignity as that of a man and woman in lawful marriage. For marriage between a man and a woman no doubt had been thought of by most people as essential to the very definition of that term and to its role and function throughout the history of civilization. That belief, for many who long have held it, became even more urgent, more cherished when challenged. For others, however, came the beginnings of a new perspective, a new insight. Accordingly some States concluded that same-sex marriage ought to be given recognition and validity in the law for those same-sex couples who wish to define themselves by their commitment to each other. The limitation of lawful marriage to heterosexual couples, which for centuries had been deemed both necessary and fundamental, came to be seen in New York and certain other States as an unjust exclusion.

Slowly at first and then in rapid course, the laws of New York came to acknowledge the urgency of this issue for same-sex couples who wanted to affirm their commitment to one another before their children, their family, their friends, and their community. And so New York recognized same-sex marriages performed elsewhere; and then it later amended its own marriage laws to permit same-sex marriage. * * *

DOMA seeks to injure the very class New York seeks to protect. By doing so it violates basic due process and equal protection principles applicable to the Federal Government [citing the Fifth Amendment]. The Constitution's guarantee of equality "must at the very least mean that a bare congressional desire to harm a politically unpopular group cannot" justify disparate treatment of that group. In determining whether a law is motivated by an improper animus or purpose, " '[d]iscriminations of an unusual character' " especially require careful consideration (quoting *Romer*). DOMA cannot survive under these principles. The responsibility of the States for the regulation of domestic relations is an important indicator of the substantial societal impact the State's classifications have in the daily lives and customs of its people. DOMA's unusual deviation from the usual tradition of recognizing and accepting state definitions of marriage here operates to deprive same-sex couples of the benefits and responsibilities that come with the federal recognition of their marriages. This is strong evidence of a law having the purpose and effect of disapproval of that class. * * *

The history of DOMA's enactment and its own text demonstrate that interference with the equal dignity of same-sex marriages, a dignity conferred by the States in the exercise of their sovereign power, was more than an incidental effect of the federal statute. It was its essence. The House Report announced its conclusion that "it is both appropriate and necessary for Congress to do what it can to defend the institution of traditional heterosexual marriage. . . . H.R. 3396 is appropriately entitled the 'Defense of Marriage Act.' The effort to redefine 'marriage' to extend to homosexual couples is a truly radical proposal that would fundamentally alter the institution of marriage." H.R.Rep. No. 104–664, pp. 12–13 (1996). The House concluded that DOMA expresses "both moral disapproval of homosexuality, and a moral conviction that heterosexuality better comports with traditional (especially Judeo-Christian) morality." * * *

The particular case at hand concerns the estate tax, but DOMA is more than a simple determination of what should or should not be allowed as an estate tax refund. Among the over 1,000 statutes and numerous federal regulations that DOMA controls are laws pertaining to Social Security, housing, taxes, criminal sanctions, copyright, and veterans' benefits.

DOMA's principal effect is to identify a subset of state-sanctioned marriages and make them unequal. * * * The differentiation demeans the couple, whose moral and sexual choices the Constitution protects, see *Lawrence*, and whose relationship the State has sought to dignify. And it humiliates tens of thousands of children now being raised by same-sex couples. The law in question makes it even more difficult for the children to understand the integrity and closeness of their own family and its concord with other families in their community and in their daily lives. * * *

[The Court went on to note the financial harm DOMA visited on the children of same-sex couples].

The liberty protected by the Fifth Amendment's Due Process Clause contains within it the prohibition against denying to any person the equal protection of the laws. While the Fifth Amendment itself withdraws from Government the power to degrade or demean in the way this law does, the equal protection guarantee of the Fourteenth Amendment makes that Fifth Amendment right all the more specific and all the better understood and preserved. * * *

By seeking to displace [the protection granted by states allowing same-sex marriage] and treating those persons as living in marriages less respected than others, the federal statute is in violation of the Fifth Amendment. This opinion and its holding are confined to those lawful marriages.

CHIEF JUSTICE ROBERTS, dissenting.

The majority [points] out that the Federal Government has generally (though not uniformly) deferred to state definitions of marriage in the past. That is true, of course, but none of those prior state-by-state variations had involved differences over something—as the majority puts it—"thought of by most people as essential to the very definition of [marriage] and to its role and function throughout the history of civilization." That the Federal Government treated this fundamental question differently than it treated variations over consanguinity or minimum age is hardly surprising—and hardly enough to support a conclusion that the "principal purpose," of the 342 Representatives and 85 Senators who voted for it, and the President who signed it, was a bare desire to harm. Nor do the snippets of legislative history and the banal title of the Act to which the majority points suffice to make such a showing. At least without some more convincing evidence that the Act's principal purpose was to codify malice, and that it furthered *no* legitimate government interests, I would not tar the political branches with the brush of bigotry.

But while I disagree with the result to which the majority's analysis leads it in this case, I think it more important to point out that its analysis leads no further. The Court does not have before it, and the logic of its opinion does not decide, the distinct question whether the States, in the exercise of their "historic and essential authority to define the marital relation," may continue to utilize the traditional definition of marriage. * * *

The dominant theme of the majority opinion is that the Federal Government's intrusion into an area "central to state domestic relations law applicable to its residents and citizens" is sufficiently "unusual" to set off alarm bells. I think the majority goes off course, as I have said, but it is undeniable that its judgment is based on federalism. * * *

JUSTICE SCALIA, with whom JUSTICE THOMAS joins, and with whom THE CHIEF JUSTICE joins as to part I, dissenting. * * *

[II.][I]f this is meant to be an equal-protection opinion, it is a confusing one. The opinion does not resolve and indeed does not even mention what had been the central question in this litigation: whether, under the Equal Protection Clause, laws restricting marriage to a man and a woman are reviewed for more than mere rationality. That is the issue that divided the parties and the court below. In accord with my previously expressed skepticism about the Court's "tiers of scrutiny" approach, I would review this classification only for its rationality. As nearly as I can tell, the Court agrees with that; its opinion does not apply strict scrutiny, and its central propositions are taken from rational-basis cases like *Moreno*. But the Court certainly does not *apply* anything that resembles that deferential framework. * * *

The penultimate sentence of the majority's opinion is a naked declaration that "[t]his opinion and its holding are confined" to those couples "joined in same-sex marriages made lawful by the State." I have heard such "bald, unreasoned disclaimer[s]" before. When the Court declared a constitutional right to homosexual sodomy, we were assured that the case had nothing, nothing at all to do with "whether the government must give formal recognition to any relationship that homosexual persons seek to enter." (citing *Lawrence*). Now we are told that DOMA is invalid because it "demeans the couple, whose moral and sexual choices the Constitution protects,"—with an accompanying citation of *Lawrence*. It takes real cheek for today's majority to assure us, as it is going out the door, that a constitutional requirement to give formal recognition to same-sex marriage is not at issue here—when what has preceded that assurance is a lecture on how superior the majority's moral judgment in favor of same-sex marriage is to the Congress's hateful moral judgment against it. I promise you this: The only thing that will "confine" the Court's holding is its sense of what it can get away with.

I do not mean to suggest disagreement with THE CHIEF JUSTICE'S view that lower federal courts and state courts can distinguish today's case when the issue before them is state denial of marital status to same-sex couples—

or even that this Court could *theoretically* do so. Lord, an opinion with such scatter-shot rationales as this one (federalism noises among them) can be distinguished in many ways. And deserves to be. State and lower federal courts should take the Court at its word and distinguish away.

[The separate dissent of Justices Alito, joined by Justice Thomas, is omitted].

NOTES

1.   Notice that the Court does not resolve, or even address, the tier-of-scrutiny question that was so central to the Holder Memorandum. Why might this be so? Is this a sign that the tiers of scrutiny are fading in importance?

2.   *The Dissenters' Critiques.* In dissents (including some portions not excerpted above), several criticisms were levelled against the majority opinion in *Windsor*:

> (a)   that the opinion is missing key doctrinal elements, such as the standard of review it is applying, as well as a clear statement of whether the opinion relies on "liberty" as a means of imposing equal protection on the federal government (as suggested by the citations to *Bolling v. Sharpe*, Casebook p. 98) or means to invoke liberty as an independent constitutional norm;

> (b)   that the Court ought to leave the question of marriage equality to the political branches and public debate, which have been heavily engaged with the question in recent years;

> (c)   that the majority wrongly imputes bias and animus to those who enacted DOMA, rather than a good faith difference of opinion; and

> (d)   that, contrary to the disclaimer at the end of the majority opinion, the majority's rationale is unlikely to be limited to DOMA, as opposed to state laws that bar same-sex marriage.

Obergefell v. Hodges (Chapter 5) demonstrated that point (d) was correct. Do you find merit in any of the other critiques? Did Justice Kennedy answer them satisfactorily? Could a stronger opinion have been written in support of the result the Court reached? If so, how?

3.   *Dignity.* The majority emphasized its view that DOMA undermines the dignity of same-sex couples who are married under state law. Indeed, some form of the word "dignity" was used no fewer than ten times in Justice Kennedy's full opinion. What does he mean by dignity? How ought a claim of dignitary harm be demonstrated? Does the idea of dignity merit a special place in Fourteenth Amendment jurisprudence? How might it apply in other contexts, such as disputes over abortion and affirmative action? Note that human dignity is a key concept in some other constitutions, such as Germany's Basic Law. The term is not used in the U.S. Constitution, but is the concept implicit?

4. *Connections to* Romer *and* Lawrence. Compare Justice Kennedy's opinion to the opinions he wrote previously in *Romer* and *Lawrence*. Do you notice similarities? Among other things, consider the *Windsor* majority opinion's repeated emphasis on the idea of respect for gay persons (a theme stressed in *Lawrence*) and on the unfair singling out of gay persons alone for a broadly-drawn legal disability (a theme stressed in *Romer*).

———

Two years to the day after *Windsor*, in an opinion once again authored by Justice Kennedy, the Court returned to the issue of same-sex marriage in the landmark case of *Obergefell v. Hodges*, ___ U.S. ___, 135 S.Ct. 2584 (2015). *Obergefell* declared a broad right of marriage equality applicable in every state. The Court placed principal emphasis not on equal protection, but on the fundamental right to marry. For that reason, the case appears in Chapter 5. While the *Obergefell* opinion focuses on due process, you will note that the majority invokes the equal protection clause as part of its analysis.

PROBLEM 4-6:
A BAN ON LESBIAN, GAY OR TRANSGENDER
GRADE SCHOOL TEACHERS

Suppose a state enacts a law banning gay, lesbian, or transgender persons from becoming public school teachers in kindergarten through fifth grade classes. The state cites as its justification its desire to shield young children for as long as possible from the complex issues of sexual orientation and gender identity. Gay, lesbian, and transgender teachers challenge the law as a violation of equal protection. Consider the following questions.

(a) What tier of scrutiny will be applied to this policy? Would a court distinguish the restriction on gay and lesbian teachers from the restriction on transgender teachers? Should it?

(b) With respect to the ban on gay and lesbian teachers, review the argument for heightened scrutiny in the context of sexual orientation-based discrimination made in the Holder Letter on the federal Defense of Marriage Act. If you have read the *Obergefell* opinion, consider what, if anything, the majority opinion in the case adds on the issue of heightened scrutiny. Is it significant that Justice Kennedy's opinion in that case twice characterizes sexual orientation as immutable? That he begins his opinion by reviewing in detail the history of how American law has regarded homosexuality? Do you find anything else in the opinion that might bear on the tier of scrutiny a court would use?

(c) With respect to the ban on transgender teachers, review Problem 4-2 and consider whether it sheds any light. How would this part of the policy on teachers fare under the constitutional standard for sex discrimination? Would it matter if some affected teachers considered themselves "gender-fluid"? To the extent that discrimination against transgender teachers is not considered a form of sex discrimination, is there an independent basis to argue for heightened scrutiny of gender identity classifications under the criteria invoked in the Holder letter? If not, how would an animus argument fare? For arguments about the level of scrutiny for gender identity discrimination, see Kevin M. Barry, Brian Farrell, Jennifer L. Levi and Neelima Vanguri, *A Bare Desire to Harm: Transgender People and the Equal Protection Clause*, 57 B.C. L. REV. 507 (2016).

CONCLUDING NOTE ON EQUAL PROTECTION

Having traveled from equal protection review of one tier (rational basis), to two tiers (adding strict scrutiny), to three tiers (adding intermediate scrutiny, most prominently for gender classifications), to four tiers (adding *Cleburne's* "rational basis with attitude") and possibly beyond (*Romer, Windsor*), evaluate the utility of "tiered analysis" in this area. What factors explain why judges seem to want tiers of scrutiny? Among other things, presumably the impetus here is to provide predictability and certainty in law, both for the benefit of the citizenry and the lower courts. Are those goals satisfied by the materials you have read? Are there other reasons for the creation and maintenance of the tiered approach? What factors seem to inhibit the success of the approach?

Have we progressed much beyond the obvious? Although equal protection requires the government to treat "similarly situated" people "similarly," the definition and application of the two quoted terms in this phrase are exceedingly difficult and normatively charged. Does this suggest that a return to originalism would be in order, to promote greater predictability and certainty? The cases in this chapter reflect the fact that originalism has had little impact in the contemporary interpretation of the Equal Protection Clause. Should it? What are the implications of originalism for sex discrimination? For LGBT rights? Does the answer depend on what variety of originalism is used?

Finally, consider *Carolene Products* footnote 4 and the "discrete and insular minority" theory. To what extent does this theory explain the presence of the tiers or the outcomes when that approach is applied? Does there remain any necessary relationship between political powerlessness and heightened judicial scrutiny of classifications disadvantaging the group in question? Hasn't increased judicial solicitude actually paralleled the *increase* in political power of the affected group (*Frontiero* and the women's movement, *Romer* and the gay rights movement, and so on)?

Indeed, does the story of this chapter boil down to the lesson that judges will sometimes attempt to promote progress, as viewed by the elite segment of society in which they reside? Recall Justice Scalia's dissenting arguments in the VMI and *Romer* cases about the differences in attitude between the "law-trained elite" and the society at large. It's easy, in the abstract, to attack judges as both unauthorized and poorly equipped to be vanguards of social change. Do

Chapters 2–4 validate this criticism as a practical matter, or have the judges done pretty well at it, all things considered? Or does this social/political perspective miss important other factors? The next chapter continues the consideration of this problem, but in the context of the identification and enforcement of constitutional rights not easily linked to constitutional text— the most prominent example being *Roe v. Wade*, the landmark abortion decision.

CHAPTER 5

PROTECTING FUNDAMENTAL RIGHTS

■ ■ ■

From the right to free speech to the right to bear arms to the right against self-incrimination, the Constitution directly provides a rich mix of rights against governmental intrusion. Other rights are indirectly protected in terms of equal treatment. The Constitution provides no absolute right to vote, for example. But when voting is the method selected for choosing a public official, the vote must be *equally* open to racial minorities as well as whites (the Fifteenth Amendment), to women as well as men (the Nineteenth Amendment), and to those aged eighteen years as well as those who are older (the Twenty-Sixth Amendment).

Yet, there are important interests the Framers did not specifically protect. Nowhere is there any express right to subsistence or education, to engage in intimate personal relationships, or to run for office. Is the Supreme Court precluded from declaring that any such interests have constitutional status? Are other forms of liberty protected by the Constitution? And if so, how? Those questions are the subject of this chapter.

SECTION 1. SHOULD COURTS EVER ENFORCE UNENUMERATED RIGHTS?

Before considering whether specific rights are "fundamental," it behooves us to consider whether courts should ever enforce rights that are not specifically designated in the Constitution. The issue is obviously controversial, and you will have to form your own conclusion. We begin by considering the historical origins of today's "fundamental rights" jurisprudence.

NOTE ON THE HISTORICAL ROOTS OF UNENUMERATED RIGHTS

American thought in the revolutionary period was permeated with natural-rights concepts.[1] The most notable embodiment of this view is the Declaration of Independence itself, which speaks of a right "to life, liberty, and happiness" not because the government granted it, but because all people

---

[1] For discussion of this history, see Thomas Grey, *Origins of the Unwritten Constitution: Fundamental Law in American Revolutionary Thought*, 30 Stan. L. Rev. 843 (1978).

naturally have it simply because they are people. Another example is James Otis's argument against the power of Parliament to authorize unreasonable searches:

> As to Acts of Parliament, an Act against the Constitution is void; an Act against natural Equity is void; and if an Act of Parliament should be made, in the very Words of this Petition, it would be void. The Executive Courts must pass such Acts into disuse.

Similarly, in protesting the Stamp Act, the Whigs turned to the courts for support, contending that the act was unconstitutional and therefore void.

Some scholars suggest that this belief in natural law as a judicially enforceable restriction on legislatures persisted into the early nineteenth century.[2] On this view, enforcement of natural rights by courts would not even require a textual basis. Alternatively, the Ninth Amendment might provide such a textual basis for fundamental rights.

There is also some historical evidence that the natural-law tradition influenced the drafters of the Fourteenth Amendment. The idea of "higher law" was deeply embedded in the jurisprudence of the time, particularly in what was then called the "law of nations," a term that included a variety of subjects such as public international law, conflict of laws, and even parts of commercial law.[3] Anti-slavery Republicans, including Abraham Lincoln, placed a great deal of emphasis on the Declaration of Independence, with its natural-law philosophy. Although the legislative history of the Fourteenth Amendment is sparse, there was extensive debate on the closely related Civil Rights Act of 1866, in which fundamental rights figured prominently.[4] For example, Senator Trumbull, in a major speech defending the bill after President Johnson's veto, asserted that

> [t]o be a citizen of the United States carries with it some rights; * * * They are those inherent, fundamental rights which belong to free citizens or free men in all countries, such as the rights enumerated in this bill, and they belong to them in all the States of the Union. The right of American citizenship means something. [Cong. Globe, 39th Cong., 1st Sess. 1757 (1866).]

The fundamental rights idea has also been a recurring theme in Supreme Court decisions. Early nineteenth century decisions by Chief Justice Marshall and others had a strong natural-law tinge. Later in the nineteenth century (and consistently through the present day), the Court has viewed the Due Process Clause as embodying those rights fundamental to citizens in a free country. This formulation received its most notable modern phrasing in Justice Cardozo's opinion in *Palko v. Connecticut*, 302 U.S. 319 (1937) (reprinted in this chapter), which held that the test for incorporation under the Fourteenth

---

[2]   See Suzanna Sherry, *The Founders' Unwritten Constitution*, 54 U. Chi. L. Rev. 1127 (1987).

[3]   See Daniel Farber & Suzanna Sherry, *A History of the Constitution* ch. 9 (1990).

[4]   Remnants of this statute survive as 42 U.S.C. §§ 1981 and 1982. See *Jones v. Alfred H. Mayer Co.* and accompanying text (Chapter 7, § 3A).

Amendment is whether a right found in the Bill of Rights is "implicit in the concept of ordered liberty." As we shall see, this test became the basis for the selective incorporation doctrine, under which most provisions of the Bill of Rights were read into the Due Process Clause of the Fourteenth Amendment and thereby made applicable to state as well as federal action.

It may seem odd that a provision regarding "process" has come to protect "substance." Nevertheless, history seems to have settled that issue. The provisions of the Bill of Rights have been applied to the states by way of the Due Process Clause for many years. The Privileges or Immunities Clause of the Fourteenth Amendment might have provided a more appropriate textual anchor for substantive rights, but the following case seems to have foreclosed that possibility.

The Slaughter House Cases

83 U.S. 36 (1873)

A Louisiana law banned slaughter houses within the New Orleans city limits but made an exception for the Crescent City Company, which was thereby essentially given a monopoly. In an opinion by **Justice Miller**, the Supreme Court rejected a broad-gauged attack on the statute brought by New Orleans butchers. One of the butchers' arguments was based on the Privileges or Immunities Clause of the Fourteenth Amendment, which they asserted protected their fundamental right to work at their trade. The Court held, however, that this clause protected only a limited set of national privileges, such as the right of access to federal agencies and the right to use navigable waters.

In limiting the Fourteenth Amendment "P or I Clause" to protecting a limited set of national rights, the Court stressed that the language of the Fourteenth Amendment says that no state shall abridge "the privileges or immunities *of citizens of the United States*." Justice Miller contrasted this language to that found in the Privileges and Immunities Clause of Article IV, which refers to the privileges and immunities of citizens of a state. The Article IV clause had been held to protect nonresidents from discrimination affecting a broad range of significant interests, such as the right to own property or the right to protection by the government. The right to pursue a trade was probably within the range of interests protected by the Article IV clause, but that clause applied only to discrimination against nonresidents. If the same interests were protected by the Fourteenth Amendment against state abridgement, then the effect would be a massive transfer of power to the federal government:

> For not only are these rights subject to the control of Congress whenever in its discretion any of them are supposed to be abridged by State legislation, but that body may also pass laws in advance, limiting and restricting the exercise of legislative power by the States, in their most ordinary and usual functions, as in its judgment it may think proper on all such subjects. And still further, such a

construction followed by the reversal of the judgments of the Supreme Court of Louisiana in these cases, would constitute this court a perpetual censor upon all legislation of the States, on the civil rights of their own citizens, with authority to nullify such as it did not approve as consistent with those rights, as they existed at the time of the adoption of this amendment. * * * We are convinced that no such results were intended by the Congress which proposed these amendments, nor by the legislatures of the States which ratified them.

Justice Field, joined by **Chief Justice Chase** and **Justices Swayne** and **Bradley**, argued in dissent for a broad reading of the P or I Clause. What the Article IV clause did to protect citizens against discrimination by other states, "the fourteenth amendment does for the protection of every citizen of the United States against hostile and discriminating legislation against him in favor of others, whether they reside in the same or in different States." In particular, Field said, "all pursuits, all professions, all avocations are open" to American citizens equally. "The State may prescribe such regulations for every pursuit and calling of life as will promote the public health, secure the good order and advance the general prosperity of society, but when once prescribed, the pursuit or calling must be free to be followed by every citizen who is within the conditions designated, and will conform to the regulations."

NOTES ON THE AFTERMATH OF THE
SLAUGHTER HOUSE CASES

1. *Incorporation and the P or I Clause.* Interestingly, Justice Miller listed among the national privileges and immunities the rights to "peaceably assemble and petition for redress of grievances." Thus, his interpretation left open the possibility that the Bill of Rights might be incorporated into the P or I Clause. There is also some support for this view in the debates on the Fourteenth Amendment—and also support for the view, so emphatically rejected by Justice Miller, that the Fourteenth Amendment clause was meant to protect the same rights as the Article IV clause.[5] For example, in introducing the amendment in the Senate, Senator Howard explained the P or I Clause by reading at length from an opinion broadly construing the Article IV Clause. He then went on to say:

> Such is the character of the privileges and immunities spoken of in the second section of the fourth article of the Constitution. To these privileges and immunities, whatever they may be—for they are not and cannot be fully defined in their entire extent and precise nature— to those should be added the personal rights guaranteed and secured

---

[5] See Bryan Wildenthal, *The Lost Compromise: Reassessing the Early Understanding in Court and Congress on Incorporation of the Bill of Rights in the Fourteenth Amendment*, 61 Ohio St. L.J. 1053 (2000); Daniel Farber & Suzanna Sherry, *A History of the American Constitution* ch. 11 (1990); John Harrison, *Reconstructing the Privileges or Immunities Clause*, 101 Yale L.J. 1385 (1992).

by the first eight amendments of the Constitution [which he then proceeded to list].

2.   *The Due Process Clause and the* Slaughter House Cases. After the *Slaughter House Cases*, the P or I Clause became essentially defunct. The decision was less successful, however, in disposing of the Due Process Clause. According to Justice Miller, due process provides only procedural protections— not an unreasonable reading, given the language of the clause. (At least one prominent pre-Fourteenth Amendment case had viewed a state due process clause as providing substantive protection for property, however, so it is conceivable that the Framers of the Fourteenth Amendment did have more than procedural protections in mind.[6]) By the time it decided *Mugler v. Kansas*, 123 U.S. 623 (1887), however, the Court had concluded that due process protects more than procedure—that someone is deprived of their property without due process of *law* if the deprivation is based on an arbitrary legislative fiat.

Some cases raised issues of both substance and procedure. In *Twining v. New Jersey*, 211 U.S. 78 (1908), the Court rejected defendant's claim that the Fifth Amendment's privilege against self-incrimination applies in state criminal proceedings as a matter of due process. The Court's methodology was historicist: Because such rights were not widely recognized at the time of the Fourteenth Amendment, they would not be read into its Due Process Clause.

3.   *The Civil Rights Campaign to Save the Lives of Black Defendants.* The NAACP and other civil rights groups deliberately sought to loosen up the *Twining* approach, by showing the Justices that southern trials of black men were mockeries of due process and needed to be monitored. The civil rights strategy was to invoke federal standards as the basis for rights that the Due Process Clause ought to protect in state courts. They were remarkably successful, persuading Justices of all ideologies to recognize due process rights to counsel in capital cases, *Powell v. Alabama*, 287 U.S. 45 (1932); against the use of coerced or involuntary confessions in their trials, *Brown v. Mississippi*, 297 U.S. 278 (1936); and to juries drawn from a cross-section of the community, *Smith v. Texas*, 311 U.S. 128 (1940). These cases, and the dozens of follow-up appeals, left several Supreme Court Justices receptive to the long-rejected idea that the Due Process Clause "incorporates" all or most of the specific guarantees of the Bill of Rights. The Justices debated that issue in the next two cases, the latter of which was another black defendant case.

PALKO V. CONNECTICUT
302 U.S. 319, 58 S.Ct. 149, 82 L.Ed. 288 (1937)

JUSTICE CARDOZO delivered the opinion of the Court.

[Palko had been indicted for first-degree murder. The jury found him guilty of second-degree murder, and he received a life sentence. The state

---

[6]   The state cases are reviewed in Edward Corwin, *The Doctrine of Due Process of Law Before the Civil War*, 24 Harv. L. Rev. 460 (1911).

appealed, as allowed by a Connecticut statute, contending that the trial judge had erred in excluding certain evidence and had wrongly instructed the jury on the difference between first-degree and second-degree murder. The Connecticut Supreme Court of Errors agreed with the state and ordered a new trial. Palko objected that a new trial would place him twice in jeopardy for the same offense, which he claimed would violate the Fourteenth Amendment. The state trial court overruled the objection; this time the jury convicted him of first-degree murder, and he was sentenced to death.

[Justice Cardozo assumed that, in a federal prosecution, allowing the appeal and retrial in these circumstances would violate the privilege against double jeopardy found in the Fifth Amendment. The case turned on whether, as Palko claimed, "the Fourteenth Amendment is to be taken as embodying the prohibitions of the Fifth," and more generally whether "[w]hatever would be a violation of the original bill of rights (Amendments I to VIII) if done by the federal government is now equally unlawful by force of the Fourteenth Amendment if done by a state." The Court held that "[t]here is no such general rule," and then continued in the following passages, from which citations to precedent have been removed:]

The Fifth Amendment provides, among other things, that no person shall be held to answer for a capital or otherwise infamous crime unless on presentment or indictment of a grand jury. This court has held that, in prosecutions by a state, presentment or indictment by a grand jury may give way to informations at the instance of a public officer. The Fifth Amendment provides also that no person shall be compelled in any criminal case to be a witness against himself. This court has said that, in prosecutions by a state, the exemption will fail if the state elects to end it. The Sixth Amendment calls for a jury trial in criminal cases and the Seventh for a jury trial in civil cases at common law where the value in controversy shall exceed $20. This court has ruled that consistently with those amendments trial by jury may be modified by a state or abolished altogether. * * *

On the other hand, the due process clause of the Fourteenth Amendment may make it unlawful for a state to abridge by its statutes the freedom of speech which the First Amendment safeguards against encroachment by the Congress or the like freedom of the press, or the free exercise of religion, or the right of peaceable assembly, without which speech would be unduly trammeled, or the right of one accused of crime to the benefit of counsel. In these and other situations immunities that are valid as against the federal government by force of the specific pledges of particular amendments have been found to be implicit in the concept of ordered liberty, and thus, through the Fourteenth Amendment, become valid as against the states.

The line of division may seem to be wavering and broken if there is a hasty catalogue of the cases on the one side and the other. Reflection and analysis will induce a different view. There emerges the perception of a rationalizing principle which gives to discrete instances a proper order and coherence. The right to trial by jury and the immunity from prosecution except as the result of an indictment may have value and importance. Even so, they are not of the very essence of a scheme of ordered liberty. To abolish them is not to violate a "principle of justice so rooted in the traditions and conscience of our people as to be ranked as fundamental." Few would be so narrow or provincial as to maintain that a fair and enlightened system of justice would be impossible without them. What is true of jury trials and indictments is true also, as the cases show, of the immunity from compulsory self-incrimination. This too might be lost, and justice still be done. Indeed, today as in the past there are students of our penal system who look upon the immunity as a mischief rather than a benefit, and who would limit its scope, or destroy it altogether.[7] No doubt there would remain the need to give protection against torture, physical or mental. Justice, however, would not perish if the accused were subject to a duty to respond to orderly inquiry. The exclusion of these immunities and privileges from the privileges and immunities protected against the action of the States has not been arbitrary or casual. It has been dictated by a study and appreciation of the meaning, the essential implications, of liberty itself.

We reach a different plane of social and moral values when we pass to the privileges and immunities that have been taken over from the earlier articles of the Federal Bill of Rights and brought within the Fourteenth Amendment by a process of absorption. These in their origin were effective against the federal government alone. If the Fourteenth Amendment has absorbed them, the process of absorption has had its source in the belief that neither liberty nor justice would exist if they were sacrificed. This is true, for illustration, of freedom of thought and speech. Of that freedom one may say that it is the matrix, the indispensable condition, of nearly every other form of freedom. With rare aberrations a pervasive recognition of that truth can be traced in our history, political and legal. So it has come about that the domain of liberty, withdrawn by the Fourteenth Amendment from encroachment by the states, has been enlarged by latter-day judgments to include liberty of the mind as well as liberty of action. The extension became, indeed, a logical imperative when once it was recognized, as long ago it was, that liberty is something more than exemption from physical restraint, and that even in the field of substantive rights and duties the legislative judgment, if oppressive and arbitrary, may be overridden by the courts. Fundamental too in the concept of due process, and so in that of

---

[7]   See, e.g., Bentham, *Rationale of Judicial Evidence*, Book IX, Pt. 4, c.III[.] Compulsory self-incrimination is part of the established procedure in the law of Continental Europe.

liberty, is the thought that condemnation shall be rendered only after trial. The hearing, moreover, must be a real one, not a sham or a pretense. For that reason, ignorant defendants in a capital case were held to have been condemned unlawfully when in truth, though not in form, they were refused the aid of counsel. The decision did not turn upon the fact that the benefit of counsel would have been guaranteed to the defendants by the provisions of the Sixth Amendment if they had been prosecuted in a federal court. The decision turned upon the fact that in the particular situation laid before us in the evidence the benefit of counsel was essential to the substance of a hearing.

[The Court concluded that allowing the state to appeal, when a defendant had been acquitted due to a legal error at trial, did not violate any fundamental principle of justice.]

ADAMSON V. CALIFORNIA
332 U.S. 46, 67 S.Ct. 1672, 91 L.Ed. 1903 (1947)

JUSTICE REED delivered the opinion of the Court.

[Adamson was convicted of murder in a California court. He challenged the constitutionality of California provisions that allowed the judge and the prosecutor to point out to the jury that he did not testify and thus made no effort to explain or to deny the evidence against him. Justice Reed first assumed that such practices would violate the Fifth Amendment's privilege against self-incrimination if done in federal court.]

Such an assumption does not determine appellant's rights under the Fourteenth Amendment. It is settled law that the clause of the Fifth Amendment, protecting a person against being compelled to be a witness against himself, is not made effective by the Fourteenth Amendment as a protection against state action on the ground that freedom from testimonial compulsion is a right of national citizenship, or because it is a personal privilege or immunity secured by the Federal Constitution as one of the rights of man that are listed in the Bill of Rights. * * *

Appellant secondly contends that if the privilege against self-incrimination is not a right protected by the privileges and immunities clause of the Fourteenth Amendment against state action, this privilege, to its full scope under the Fifth Amendment, inheres in the right to a fair trial. A right to a fair trial is a right admittedly protected by the due process clause of the Fourteenth Amendment. Therefore, appellant argues, the due process clause of the Fourteenth Amendment protects his privilege against self-incrimination. The due process clause of the Fourteenth Amendment, however, does not draw all the rights of the federal Bill of Rights under its protection. That contention was made and rejected in *Palko.* * * * Nothing has been called to our attention that either the framers of the Fourteenth Amendment or the states that adopted intended its due process clause to draw within its scope the earlier amendments to the Constitution. *Palko* held that such provisions of the Bill of Rights as were "implicit in the concept of ordered liberty" became secure from state interference by the clause. But it held nothing more.

[The Court concluded that, although the Due Process Clause of the Fourteenth Amendment forbade compulsion to testify through torture or other coercion, the California procedure at issue here did not violate "the concept of ordered liberty." The Court was impressed that the California procedure did not compel the jury to find guilt or even create a rebuttable presumption of guilt, but merely "was a method for advising the jury in the search for truth."]

JUSTICE FRANKFURTER, concurring.

Between the incorporation of the Fourteenth Amendment into the Constitution and the beginning of the present membership of the Court—a period of 70 years—the scope of that Amendment was passed upon by 43 judges. Of all these judges, only one, who may respectfully be called an eccentric exception, ever indicated the belief that the Fourteenth Amendment was a shorthand summary of the first eight Amendments theretofore limiting only the Federal Government, and that due process incorporated those eight Amendments as restrictions upon the powers of the States. Among these judges were not only those who would have to be included among the greatest in the history of the Court, but—it is especially relevant to note—they included those whose services in the cause of human rights and the spirit of freedom are the most conspicuous in our history. It is not invidious to single out Miller, Davis, Bradley, Waite, Matthews, Gray, Fuller, Holmes, Brandeis, Stone and Cardozo (to speak only of the dead) as judges who were alert in safeguarding and promoting the interests of liberty and human dignity through law. But they were also judges mindful of the relation of our federal system to a progressively democratic society and therefore duly regardful of the scope of authority that was left to the States even after the Civil War. And so they did not find that the Fourteenth Amendment, concerned as it was with matters fundamental to the pursuit of justice, fastened upon the States procedural arrangements which, in the language of Mr. Justice Cardozo, only those who are "narrow or provincial" would deem essential to "a fair and enlightened system of justice." *Palko.* To suggest that it is inconsistent with a truly free society to begin prosecutions without an indictment, to try petty civil cases without the paraphernalia of a common law jury, to take into consideration that one who has full opportunity to make a defense remains silent is, in de Tocqueville's phrase, to confound the familiar with the necessary. * * *

A construction which gives to due process no independent function but turns it into a summary of the specific provisions of the Bill of Rights would, as has been noted, tear up by the roots much of the fabric of law in the several States, and would deprive the States of opportunity for reforms in legal process designed for extending the area of freedom. It would assume that no other abuses would reveal themselves in the course of time than those which had become manifest in 1791. Such a view not only disregards the historic meaning of "due process." It leads inevitably to a warped construction of specific provisions of the Bill of Rights to bring within their scope conduct clearly condemned by due process but not easily fitting into the pigeon-holes of the specific provisions. It seems pretty late in the day to suggest that a phrase so laden with historic meaning should be given an improvised content consisting of some but not all of the provisions of the first eight Amendments, selected on an undefined basis, with improvisation of content for the provisions so selected.

And so, when, as in a case like the present, a conviction in a State court is here for review under a claim that a right protected by the Due Process Clause of the Fourteenth Amendment has been denied, the issue is not whether an infraction of one of the specific provisions of the first eight Amendments is disclosed by the record. The relevant question is whether the criminal proceedings which resulted in conviction deprived the accused of the due process of law to which the United States Constitution entitled him. Judicial review of that guaranty of the Fourteenth Amendment inescapably imposes upon this Court an exercise of judgment upon the whole course of the proceedings in order to ascertain whether they offend those canons of decency and fairness which express the notions of justice of English-speaking peoples even toward those charged with the most heinous offenses. These standards of justice are not authoritatively formulated anywhere as though they were prescriptions in a pharmacopoeia. But neither does the application of the Due Process Clause imply that judges are wholly at large. The judicial judgment in applying the Due Process Clause must move within the limits of accepted notions of justice and is not to be based upon the idiosyncrasies of a merely personal judgment. The fact that judges among themselves may differ whether in a particular case a trial offends accepted notions of justice is not disproof that general rather than idiosyncratic standards are applied. An important safeguard against such merely individual judgment is an alert deference to the judgment of the State court under review.

JUSTICE BLACK, dissenting.

I am attaching to this dissent, an appendix which contains a resume, by no means complete, of the Amendment's history. In my judgment that history conclusively demonstrates that the language of the first section of the Fourteenth Amendment, taken as a whole, was thought by those responsible for its submission to the people, and by those who opposed its submission, sufficiently explicit to guarantee that thereafter no state could deprive its citizens of the privileges and protections of the Bill of Rights.

Whether this Court ever will, or whether it now should, in the light of past decisions, give full effect to what the Amendment was intended to accomplish is not necessarily essential to a decision here. However that may be, [prior decisions] do not prevent our carrying out that purpose, at least to the extent of making applicable to the states, not a mere part, as the Court has, but the full protection of the Fifth Amendment's provision against compelling evidence from an accused to convict him of crime. And I further contend that the "natural law" formula which the Court uses to reach its conclusion in this case should be abandoned as an incongruous excrescence on our Constitution. I believe that formula to be itself a violation of our Constitution, in that it subtly conveys to courts, at the expense of legislatures, ultimate power over public policies in fields where no specific provision of the Constitution limits legislative power. * * *

[Justice Black here contended that the Court had subverted the Fourteenth Amendment in two ways. First, in decisions such as *Lochner v. New York* (§ 2B of this chapter), it held that "the Fourteenth Amendment guarantees the liberty of all persons under 'natural law' to engage in their chosen business or vocation." Justice Black considered this an unjustified expansion of the Fourteenth Amendment, which he believed was not designed to interfere with state regulation of property rights or business practices. Second, the Court imported this natural law/balancing approach to decide cases involving alleged state infringement of "individual liberties enumerated in the Bill of Rights," such as in *Twining* and the present case. This, Justice Black contended, was an unjustified contraction of the Fourteenth Amendment that made cases turn on "this Court's notions of 'civilized standards,' 'canons of decency,' and 'fundamental justice[.]'" Justice Black also noted that, despite the language of precedent suggesting that reliance upon the Bill of Rights was precluded in deciding what "due process" meant in the Fourteenth Amendment, in a series of cases the Court had already held that the following rights were "fundamental" and therefore applicable to the states through the Fourteenth Amendment: Right to counsel in some criminal cases; freedom of assembly; the rights to be free from certain kinds of cruel and unusual punishment and from double jeopardy; the right of a criminal defendant to be informed of the charge against him; the right to just compensation when private property is taken for public use; and First Amendment guarantees generally.]

I cannot consider the Bill of Rights to be an outworn 18th Century "strait jacket" * * *. Its provisions may be thought outdated abstractions by some. And it is true that they were designed to meet ancient evils. But they are the same kind of human evils that have emerged from century to century wherever excessive power is sought by the few at the expense of the many. In my judgment the people of no nation can lose their liberty so long as a Bill of Rights like ours survives and its basic purposes are conscientiously interpreted, enforced and respected so as to afford continuous protection against old, as well as new, devices and practices which might thwart those purposes. I fear to see the consequences of the Court's practice of substituting its own concepts of decency and fundamental justice for the language of the Bill of Rights as its point of departure in interpreting and enforcing that Bill of Rights. * * * I would follow what I believe was the original purpose of the Fourteenth Amendment—to extend to all the people of the nation the complete protection of the Bill of Rights. To hold that this Court can determine what, if any, provisions of the Bill of Rights will be enforced, and if so to what degree, is to frustrate the great design of a written Constitution.

JUSTICE DOUGLAS joins in this opinion.

[The appendix to Justice Black's dissent, in which he made his historical argument about the original meaning of the Fourteenth Amendment, is not excerpted, but is discussed in the notes following this case.]

JUSTICE MURPHY, with whom JUSTICE RUTLEDGE concurs, dissenting.

While in substantial agreement with the views of Justice Black, I have one reservation and one addition to make.

I agree that the specific guarantees of the Bill of Rights should be carried over intact into the first section of the Fourteenth Amendment. But I am not prepared to say that the latter is entirely and necessarily limited by the Bill of Rights. Occasions may arise where a proceeding falls so far short of conforming to fundamental standards of procedure as to warrant constitutional condemnation in terms of a lack of due process despite the absence of a specific provision in the Bill of Rights.

That point, however, need not be pursued here inasmuch as the Fifth Amendment is explicit in its provision that no person shall be compelled in any criminal case to be a witness against himself. That provision, as Justice Black demonstrates, is a constituent part of the Fourteenth Amendment.

NOTES ON THE INCORPORATION DEBATE

1. *Justice Black's Historical Argument.* Justice Black's dissent touched off a substantial scholarly dispute about whether he accurately described the intentions of the Framers of the Fourteenth Amendment.[8] Suffice it to say that

---

[8] See Charles Fairman, *Does the Fourteenth Amendment Incorporate the Bill of Rights? The Original Understanding*, 2 Stan. L. Rev. 5 (1949), for arguments by a leading historian that the Due Process Clause does not incorporate the Bill of Rights. For a critique of Fairman's analysis, see Richard Aynes, *On Misreading John Bingham and the Fourteenth Amendment*, 103 Yale L.J. 57, 61 (1993) (arguing that Fairman "misread critical sources, relied on information taken out of context, ignored important contemporary materials, and buttressed his argument with a flawed legal theory").

the scholars are still divided and that the Supreme Court never accepted Justice Black's theory as a matter of constitutional interpretation.

Consider Justice Black's best evidence, contained in a speech by Senator Howard presenting to the Senate the joint resolution proposing the Fourteenth Amendment. Senator Howard said that, under the proposed amendment, "privileges and immunities" included whatever rights were secured by the Privileges and Immunities Clause of Article IV of the original Constitution. He then continued:

> * * * [T]o these should be added the personal rights guarantied and secured by the first eight amendments of the Constitution; such as the freedom of speech and of the press; the right of the people peaceably to assemble and petition the Government for a redress of grievances, a right appertaining to each and all the people; the right to keep and to bear arms; the right to be exempted from the quartering of soldiers in a house without the consent of the owner; the right to be exempt from unreasonable searches and seizures, and from any search or seizure except by virtue of a warrant issued upon a formal oath or affidavit; the right of an accused person to be informed of the nature of the accusation against him, and his right to be tried by an impartial jury of the vicinage; and also the right to be secure against excessive bail and against cruel and unusual punishments.

How much weight should be given to Howard's statement? Black's critics suggest that (a) Senator Howard was not a key player in formulating the Fourteenth Amendment (he presented the proposal because the Senate chairman of the joint committee was ill); (b) such a major proposal as full incorporation would have been discussed and debated frequently and thoroughly (which it wasn't); and (c) subsequent congressional practice was inconsistent with incorporation (Congress admitted some states whose constitutions did not embody all Bill of Rights protections, and Congress considered some federal constitutional amendments that would have been superfluous had full incorporation been encompassed within the Fourteenth Amendment).

2.   *The Judicial Reception of Incorporation.* As *Adamson* indicates, *The Slaughter House Cases* are usually read as rejecting the argument that the P or I Clause of the Fourteenth Amendment incorporates Bill of Rights guarantees. Even though the Supreme Court never accepted Justice Black's argument, it has accomplished much the same thing by essentially incorporating the important protections of the Bill of Rights on a case-by-case basis. This so-called "selective incorporation" technique, which Justice Black disparaged in *Adamson*, asked the Court to consider whether the Bill of Rights guarantee in question was "fundamental." In the 1960s especially, the Supreme Court incorporated into the Due Process Clause virtually all of the

provisions of the Bill of Rights.[9] Along the way the Court modified its incorporation inquiry from whether the right was "implicit in the concept of ordered liberty" (*Palko*) to whether it was "fundamental to the American scheme of justice" (*Duncan v. Louisiana*, 391 U.S. 145 (1968))—a change that shifted the focus from whether the right was necessary in any system of democratic government to whether it was important in American society. See Jerold Israel, *Selective Incorporation Revisited*, 71 Geo. L.J. 253 (1982). See also William Eskridge, Jr., *Some Effects of Identity-Based Social Movements on Constitutional Law in the Twentieth Century*, 100 Mich. L. Rev. 2062 (2002) (continuing role of the race cases in creating a national code of criminal procedure).

3. *"Incorporation Plus."* Justice Murphy in *Adamson* believed that the Due Process Clause of the Fourteenth Amendment could be *broader* than the original Bill of Rights. Later in this chapter, we will trace developments along these lines that, ironically, flowed in part from the *Palko* formulation about values "implicit in the concept of ordered liberty." As originally conceived, this standard was a way to avoid applying to the states certain rights that the Bill of Rights provided against federal action. But because of the way it was phrased, this standard is not necessarily linked to the Bill of Rights—anything sufficiently important, whether recognized as such by the Bill of Rights, would seem to qualify.

In 2010, the incorporation debate reappeared as the Court incorporated a new provision of the Bill of Rights for the first time in 40 years. As you read the next case, consider the implications of the different views expressed for incorporation doctrine, as well as for approaches to unenumerated constitutional rights more generally.

McDONALD V. CITY OF CHICAGO
561 U.S. 742, 130 S.Ct. 3020, 177 L.Ed.2d 894 (2010)

JUSTICE ALITO announced the judgment of the Court and delivered the opinion of the Court with respect to Parts I, II-A, II-B, II-D, III-A, and III-B, in which the **CHIEF JUSTICE, JUSTICE SCALIA, JUSTICE KENNEDY,** and **JUSTICE THOMAS** join, and an opinion with respect to Parts II-C, IV,

---

[9] In particular: The Fourth Amendment right to be free from unreasonable searches and seizures, *Mapp v. Ohio*, 367 U.S. 643 (1961); the Fifth Amendment right against self-incrimination, *Griffin v. California*, 380 U.S. 609 (1965), and *Malloy v. Hogan*, 378 U.S. 1 (1964) (overruling *Adamson*), and its prohibition against double jeopardy, *Benton v. Maryland*, 395 U.S. 784 (1969) (overruling *Palko*); the Sixth Amendment rights to counsel, *Gideon v. Wainwright*, 372 U.S. 335 (1963), to a speedy and public trial, *Klopfer v. North Carolina*, 386 U.S. 213 (1967), to confrontation of opposing witnesses, *Pointer v. Texas*, 380 U.S. 400 (1965), to compulsory process for obtaining witnesses, *Washington v. Texas*, 388 U.S. 14 (1967), and to a jury trial in criminal cases, *Duncan v. Louisiana*, 391 U.S. 145 (1968); and the Eighth Amendment prohibitions against cruel and unusual punishment, *Robinson v. California*, 370 U.S. 660 (1962), and excessive bail, *Schilb v. Kuebel*, 404 U.S. 357 (1971). (Well before *Adamson*, the First Amendment rights of free speech, press, and religion and the Fifth Amendment right to just compensation had been applied to the states through the Due Process Clause.) Today, the few Bill of Rights guarantees that have not been applied to the states include the Fifth Amendment requirement of grand-jury indictment for major crimes and the Seventh Amendment right to jury trial in civil cases.

and V, in which the CHIEF JUSTICE, JUSTICE SCALIA, and JUSTICE KENNEDY join.

Two years ago, in *District of Columbia* v. *Heller,* 554 U.S. ___ (2008), we held that the Second Amendment protects the right to keep and bear arms for the purpose of self-defense, and we struck down a District of Columbia law that banned the possession of handguns in the home. The city of Chicago (City) and the village of Oak Park, a Chicago suburb, have laws that are similar to the District of Columbia's, but Chicago and Oak Park argue that their laws are constitutional because the Second Amendment has no application to the States. We have previously held that most of the provisions of the Bill of Rights apply with full force to both the Federal Government and the States. Applying the standard that is well established in our case law, we hold that the Second Amendment right is fully applicable to the States. * * *

III. [Following reviews of the facts and of the incorporation debate by the Court,] we now turn directly to the question whether the Second Amendment right to keep and bear arms is incorporated in the concept of due process. In answering that question * * * we must decide whether the right to keep and bear arms is fundamental to *our* scheme of ordered liberty, or as we have said in a related context, whether this right is "deeply rooted in this Nation's history and tradition," *Washington* v. *Glucksberg,* 521 U.S. 702, 721 (1997) (internal quotation marks omitted).

A. Our decision in *Heller* points unmistakably to the answer. Self-defense is a basic right, recognized by many legal systems from ancient times to the present day, and in *Heller,* we held that individual self-defense is "the *central component*" of the Second Amendment right. * * *

IV

Municipal respondents' remaining arguments are at war with our central holding in *Heller*: that the Second Amendment protects a personal right to keep and bear arms for lawful purposes, most notably for self-defense within the home. Municipal respondents, in effect, ask us to treat the right recognized in *Heller* as a second-class right, subject to an entirely different body of rules than the other Bill of Rights guarantees that we have held to be incorporated into the Due Process Clause.

Municipal respondents' main argument is nothing less than a plea to disregard 50 years of incorporation precedent and return (presumably for this case only) to a bygone era. Municipal respondents submit that the Due Process Clause protects only those rights " 'recognized by all temperate and civilized governments, from a deep and universal sense of [their] justice.' " *city's argument* * * * Therefore, the municipal respondents continue, because such countries as England, Canada, Australia, Japan, Denmark, Finland, Luxembourg, and New Zealand either ban or severely limit handgun ownership, it must follow that no right to possess such weapons is protected by the Fourteenth Amendment.

This line of argument is, of course, inconsistent with the long-established standard we apply in incorporation cases. * * *

We likewise reject municipal respondents' argument that we should depart from our established incorporation methodology on the ground that making the Second Amendment binding on the States and their subdivisions is inconsistent with principles of federalism and will stifle experimentation. Municipal respondents point out—quite correctly—that conditions and problems differ from locality to locality and that citizens in different jurisdictions have divergent views on the issue of gun control. Municipal respondents therefore urge us to allow state and local governments to enact any gun control law that they deem to be reasonable, including a complete ban on the possession of handguns in the home for self-defense.

There is nothing new in the argument that, in order to respect federalism and allow useful state experimentation, a federal constitutional right should not be fully binding on the States. This argument was made repeatedly and eloquently by Members of this Court who rejected the concept of incorporation and urged retention of the two-track approach to incorporation. Throughout the era of "selective incorporation," Justice Harlan in particular, invoking the values of federalism and state experimentation, fought a determined rearguard action to preserve the two-track approach.

Time and again, however, those pleas failed. Unless we turn back the clock or adopt a special incorporation test applicable only to the Second Amendment, municipal respondents' argument must be rejected. Under our precedents, if a Bill of Rights guarantee is fundamental from an American perspective, then, unless *stare decisis* counsels otherwise, that guarantee is fully binding on the States and thus *limits* (but by no means eliminates) their ability to devise solutions to social problems that suit local needs and values. As noted by the 38 States that have appeared in this case as *amici* supporting petitioners, "[s]tate and local experimentation with reasonable firearms regulations will continue under the Second Amendment.

JUSTICE SCALIA, concurring.

I join the Court's opinion. Despite my misgivings about Substantive Due Process as an original matter, I have acquiesced in the Court's incorporation of certain guarantees in the Bill of Rights "because it is both long established and narrowly limited." This case does not require me to reconsider that view, since straightforward application of settled doctrine suffices to decide it.

I write separately only to respond to some aspects of Justice Stevens' dissent. * * *

Justice Stevens' response to this concurrence, makes the usual rejoinder of "living Constitution" advocates to the criticism that it empowers judges to eliminate or expand what the people have prescribed: The traditional, historically focused method, he says, reposes discretion in judges as well. Historical analysis can be difficult; it sometimes requires resolving threshold questions, and making nuanced judgments about which evidence to consult and how to interpret it.

I will stipulate to that. But the question to be decided is not whether the historically focused method is a *perfect means* of restraining aristocratic judicial Constitution-writing; but whether it is the *best means available* in an imperfect world. Or indeed, even more narrowly than that: whether it is demonstrably much better than what Justice Stevens proposes. I think it beyond all serious dispute that it is much less subjective, and intrudes much less upon the democratic process. It is less subjective because it depends upon a body of evidence susceptible of reasoned analysis rather than a variety of vague ethico-political First Principles whose combined conclusion can be found to point in any direction the judges favor. In the most controversial matters brought before this Court—for example, the constitutionality of prohibiting abortion, assisted suicide, or homosexual sodomy, or the constitutionality of the death penalty—*any* historical methodology, under *any* plausible standard of proof, would lead to the same conclusion. Moreover, the methodological differences that divide historians, and the varying interpretive assumptions they bring to their work, are nothing compared to the differences among the American people (though perhaps not among graduates of prestigious law schools) with regard to the moral judgments Justice Stevens would have courts pronounce. And whether or not special expertise is needed to answer historical questions, judges most certainly have no "comparative . . . advantage" in resolving moral disputes. What is more, his approach would not eliminate, but multiply, the hard questions courts must confront, since he would not *replace* history with moral philosophy, but would have courts consider *both*.

And the Court's approach intrudes less upon the democratic process because the rights it acknowledges are those established by a constitutional history formed by democratic decisions; and the rights it fails to acknowledge are left to be democratically adopted or rejected by the people, with the assurance that their decision is not subject to judicial revision. Justice Stevens' approach, on the other hand, deprives the people of that power, since whatever the Constitution and laws may say, the list of protected rights will be whatever courts wish it to be. After all, he notes, the people have been wrong before, and courts may conclude they are wrong in the future. Justice Stevens abhors a system in which "majorities or powerful interest groups always get their way," but replaces it with a system in which unelected and life-tenured judges always get their way. That such usurpation is effected unabashedly—with "the judge's cards . . . laid on the table"—makes it even worse. In a vibrant democracy, usurpation should have to be accomplished in the dark. It is Justice Stevens' approach, not the Court's, that puts democracy in peril.

JUSTICE THOMAS, concurring in part and concurring in the judgment.

I agree with the Court that the Fourteenth Amendment makes the right to keep and bear arms set forth in the Second Amendment "fully applicable to the States." I write separately because I believe there is a more straightforward path to this conclusion, one that is more faithful to the Fourteenth Amendment's text and history.

Applying what is now a well-settled test, the plurality opinion concludes that the right to keep and bear arms applies to the States through the Fourteenth Amendment's Due Process Clause because it is "fundamental" to the American "scheme of ordered liberty," and " 'deeply rooted in this Nation's history and tradition,.' " I agree with that description of the right. But I cannot agree that it is enforceable against the States through a clause that speaks only to "process." Instead, the right to keep and bear arms is a privilege of American citizenship that applies to the States through the Fourteenth Amendment's Privileges or Immunities Clause. * * *

As a consequence of this Court's marginalization of the [Privileges or Immunities] Clause, litigants seeking federal protection of fundamental rights turned to the remainder of § 1 in search of an alternative fount of such rights. They found one in a most curious place—that section's command that every State guarantee "due process" to any person before depriving him of "life, liberty, or property." * * *

All of this is a legal fiction. The notion that a constitutional provision that guarantees only "process" before a person is deprived of life, liberty, or property could define the substance of those rights strains credulity for even the most casual user of words. Moreover, this fiction is a particularly dangerous one. The one theme that links the Court's substantive due process precedents together is their lack of a guiding principle to distinguish "fundamental" rights that warrant protection from nonfundamental rights that do not. * * *

I acknowledge the volume of precedents that have been built upon the substantive due process framework, and I further acknowledge the importance of *stare decisis* to the stability of our Nation's legal system. But *stare decisis* is only an "adjunct" of our duty as judges to decide by our best lights what the Constitution means. It is not "an inexorable command."* * * I believe this case presents an opportunity to reexamine, and begin the process of restoring, the meaning of the Fourteenth Amendment agreed upon by those who ratified it.

JUSTICE STEVENS, dissenting.

The first, and most basic, principle established by our cases is that the rights protected by the Due Process Clause are not merely procedural in nature. At first glance, this proposition might seem surprising, given that the Clause refers to "process." But substance and procedure are often deeply entwined. Upon closer inspection, the text can be read to "impos[e] nothing less than an obligation to give substantive content to the words 'liberty' and 'due process of law,'" lest superficially fair procedures be permitted to "destroy the enjoyment" of life, liberty, and property, *Poe v. Ullman*, 367 U. S. 497, 541 (1961) (Harlan, J., dissenting), and the Clause's prepositional modifier be permitted to swallow its primary command. Procedural guarantees are hollow unless linked to substantive interests; and no amount of process can legitimize some deprivations.

I have yet to see a persuasive argument that the Framers of the Fourteenth Amendment thought otherwise. To the contrary, the historical evidence suggests that, at least by the time of the Civil War if not much earlier, the phrase "due process of law" had acquired substantive content as a term of art within the legal community. This understanding is consonant with the venerable "notion that governmental authority has implied limits which preserve private autonomy, a notion which predates the founding and which finds reinforcement in the Constitution's Ninth Amendment. The Due Process Clause cannot claim to be the source of our basic freedoms—no legal document ever could—but it stands as one of their foundational guarantors in our law. * * *

The second principle woven through our cases is that substantive due process is fundamentally a matter of personal liberty. For it is the liberty clause of the Fourteenth Amendment that grounds our most important holdings in this field. It is the liberty clause that enacts the Constitution's "promise" that a measure of dignity and self-rule will be afforded to all persons. It is the liberty clause that reflects and renews "the origins of the American heritage of freedom [and] the abiding interest in individual liberty that makes certain state intrusions on the citizen's right to decide how he will live his own life intolerable." Our substantive due process cases have episodically invoked values such as privacy and equality as well, values that in certain contexts may intersect with or complement a subject's liberty interests in profound ways. But as I have observed on numerous occasions, "most of the significant [20th-century] cases raising Bill of Rights issues have, in the final analysis, actually interpreted the word 'liberty' in the Fourteenth Amendment."

It follows that the term "incorporation," like the term "unenumerated rights," is something of a misnomer. Whether an asserted substantive due process interest is explicitly named in one of the first eight Amendments to the Constitution or is not mentioned, the underlying inquiry is the same: We must ask whether the interest is "comprised within the term liberty." As the second Justice Harlan has shown, ever since the Court began considering the applicability of the Bill of Rights to the States, "the Court's usual approach has been to ground the prohibitions against state action squarely on due process, without intermediate reliance on any of the first eight Amendments." * * *

[A] rigid historical methodology is unfaithful to the Constitution's command. For if it were really the case that the Fourteenth Amendment's guarantee of liberty embraces only those rights "so rooted in our history, tradition, and practice as to require special protection," then the guarantee would serve little function, save to ratify those rights that state actors have *already* been according the most extensive protection. Cf. *Duncan*, 391 U. S., at 183 (Harlan, J., dissenting) (critiquing "circular[ity]" of historicized test for incorporation). That approach is unfaithful to the expansive principle Americans laid down when they ratified the Fourteenth Amendment and to the level of generality they chose when they crafted its language; it promises an objectivity it cannot deliver and masks the value judgments that pervade any analysis of what customs, defined in what manner, are sufficiently "'rooted'"; it countenances the most revolting injustices in the name of continuity, for we must never forget that not only slavery but also the subjugation of women and other rank forms of discrimination are part of our history; and it effaces this Court's distinctive role in saying what the law is, leaving the development and safekeeping of liberty to majoritarian political processes. It is judicial abdication in the guise of judicial modesty.

No, the liberty safeguarded by the Fourteenth Amendment is not merely preservative in nature but rather is a "dynamic concept. Its dynamism provides a central means through which the Framers enabled the Constitution to "endure for ages to come," *McCulloch* v. *Maryland*, 4 Wheat. 316, 415 (1819), a central example of how they "wisely spoke in general language and left to succeeding generations the task of applying that language to the unceasingly changing environment in which they would live," Rehnquist, The Notion of a Living Constitution, 54 Tex. L. Rev. 693, 694 (1976). "The task of giving concrete meaning to the term 'liberty,'" I have elsewhere explained at some length, "was a part of the work assigned to future generations." The judge who would outsource the interpretation of "liberty" to historical sentiment has turned his back on a task the Constitution assigned to him and drained the document of its intended vitality. * * *

Although Justice Scalia aspires to an "objective," "neutral" method of substantive due process analysis, his actual method is nothing of the sort. Under the "historically focused" approach he advocates, numerous threshold questions arise before one ever gets to the history. At what level of generality should one frame the liberty interest in question? What does it mean for a right to be " 'deeply rooted in this Nation's history and tradition' "? By what standard will that proposition be tested? Which types of sources will count, and how will those sources be weighed and aggregated? There is no objective, neutral answer to these questions. There is not even a theory—at least, Justice Scalia provides none—of how to go about answering them. * * *

The malleability and elusiveness of history increase exponentially when we move from a pure question of original meaning, as in *Heller*, to Justice Scalia's theory of substantive due process. * * * In conducting this rudderless, panoramic tour of American legal history, the judge has more than ample opportunity to "look over the heads of the crowd and pick out [his] friends."

* * * My point is simply that Justice Scalia's defense of his method, which holds out objectivity and restraint as its cardinal—and, it seems, only—virtues, is unsatisfying on its own terms. For a limitless number of subjective judgments may be smuggled into his historical analysis. Worse, they may be *buried* in the analysis. At least with my approach, the judge's cards are laid on the table for all to see, and to critique. The judge must exercise judgment, to be sure. When answering a constitutional question to which the text provides no clear answer, there is always some amount of discretion; our constitutional system has always depended on judges' filling in the document's vast open space. But there is also transparency.

JUSTICE BREYER, with whom **JUSTICE GINSBURG** and **JUSTICE SOTOMAYOR** join, dissenting.

In my view, taking *Heller* as a given, the Fourteenth Amendment does not incorporate the Second Amendment right to keep and bear arms for purposes of private self-defense. Under this Court's precedents, to incorporate the private self-defense right the majority must show that the right is, *e.g.*, "fundamental to the American scheme of justice." And this it fails to do. * * *

[I] think it proper, above all where history provides no clear answer, to look to other factors in considering whether a right is sufficiently "fundamental" to remove it from the political process in every State. I would include among those factors the nature of the right; any contemporary disagreement about whether the right is fundamental; the extent to which incorporation will further other, perhaps more basic, constitutional aims; and the extent to which incorporation will advance or hinder the Constitution's structural aims, including its division of powers among different governmental institutions (and the people as well). Is incorporation needed, for example, to further the Constitution's effort to ensure that the government treats each individual with equal respect? Will it help maintain the democratic form of government that the Constitution foresees? In a word, will incorporation prove consistent, or inconsistent, with the Constitution's efforts to create governmental institutions well suited to the carrying out of its constitutional promises?

Finally, I would take account of the Framers' basic reason for believing the Court ought to have the power of judicial review. Alexander Hamilton feared granting that power to Congress alone, for he feared that Congress, acting as judges, would not overturn as unconstitutional a popular statute that it had recently enacted, as legislators. The Federalist No. 78 ("This independence of the judges is equally requisite to guard the constitution and the rights of individuals from the effects of those ill humours, which" can, at times, lead to "serious oppressions of the minor part in the community"). Judges, he thought, may find it easier to resist popular pressure to suppress the basic rights of an unpopular minority. See *United States v. Carolene Products Co.*, 304 U. S. 144, 152, n. 4 (1938). That being so, it makes sense to ask whether that particular comparative judicial advantage is relevant to the case at hand. See, *e.g.,* J. Ely, Democracy and Distrust (1980). * * *

Consider too that countless gun regulations of many shapes and sizes are in place in every State and in many local communities. Does the right to possess weapons for self-defense extend outside the home? To the car? To work? What sort of guns are necessary for self-defense? Handguns? Rifles? Semiautomatic weapons? When is a gun semi-automatic? Where are different kinds of weapons likely needed? Does time-of-day matter? Does the presence of a child in the house matter? Does the presence of a convicted felon in the house matter? Do police need special rules permitting patdowns designed to find guns? When do registration requirements become severe to the point that they amount to an unconstitutional ban? Who can possess guns and of what kind? Aliens? Prior drug offenders? Prior alcohol abusers? How would the right interact with a state or local government's ability to take special measures during, say, national security emergencies? As the questions suggest, state and local gun regulation can become highly complex, and these "are only a few uncertainties that quickly come to mind."

The difficulty of finding answers to these questions is exceeded only by the importance of doing so. Firearms cause well over 60,000 deaths and injuries in the United States each year. Those who live in urban areas, police officers, women, and children, all may be particularly at risk. And gun regulation may save their lives. Some experts have calculated, for example, that Chicago's handgun ban has saved several hundred lives, perhaps close to 1,000, since it was enacted in 1983. Other experts argue that stringent gun regulations "can help protect police officers operating on the front lines against gun violence," have reduced homicide rates in

Washington, D. C., and Baltimore, and have helped to lower New York's crime and homicide rates. * * *

[I] cannot find a historical consensus with respect to whether the right described by *Heller* is "fundamental" as our incorporation cases use that term. Nor can I find sufficient historical support for the majority's conclusion that that right is "deeply rooted in this Nation's history and tradition." Instead, I find no more than ambiguity and uncertainty that perhaps even expert historians would find difficult to penetrate. And a historical record that is so ambiguous cannot itself provide an adequate basis for incorporating a private right of self-defense and applying it against the States.

NOTES ON MCDONALD'S *MULTIPLE APPROACHES*

1.   *Counting Votes.* Note that eight Justices reject the argument that the Second Amendment applies to the states through the Privileges or Immunities Clause (everyone but Thomas). Five Justices reject the argument that the Due Process Clause incorporates the Second Amendment (Thomas plus the dissenters). McDonald wins even though a majority of judges rejects each of his arguments—not unprecedented in the Court's history, although not usually something that occurs in cases of such importance. Is it troubling that the Court is making such an important decision without agreeing on the rationale?

2.   *The Privileges or Immunities Clause.* None of the other Justices responded to Justice Thomas's historical argument. Justice Thomas reasserted his view in a recent case in which the Court was unanimous in holding that the Eighth Amendment's Excessive Fines Clause applied to the states. *Timbs v. Indiana*, ___ U.S. ___, 139 S.Ct. 682 (2019). The majority relied on the Due Process Clause and no justice joined the lengthy argument for applying the Privileges or Immunities Clause in Justice Thomas' concurrence in the judgment. Justice Gorsuch indicated support for the Thomas view that "as an original matter, the appropriate vehicle for incorporation may well be the Fourteenth Amendment's Privileges or Immunities Clause," but concurred in the majority opinion, noting that "nothing in this case turns on that question." Justice Thomas obviously gives very little weight to precedent, viewing *stare decisis* as more akin to a mild suggestion than an inexorable command. Would the Court do better to return to first principles more frequently rather than following precedent?

3.   *Judicial Methodology.* The debate between Justice Stevens and Justice Scalia exposes themes that will continue throughout this chapter. In a number of the cases we will read, Justice Kennedy sides with Justice Stevens in terms of methodology (and often outcome). When you get to *Casey*, consider why Justice Kennedy and Stevens were on opposite sides here but not in that case.

4.   *Originalism. McDonald* is a sequel to *Heller*, which held that the Second Amendment forbids the federal government from banning handguns in

the District of Columbia. In both cases, the Justices disagreed vehemently about the historical record. If the Court is going to rely so heavily on history, should historians be asked to testify as expert witnesses at trial? Is Justice Scalia right that originalism is the best available method to limit politicization of the judicial process?

5.   *The Scope of the Second Amendment.* As the dissent notes, *Heller* and *McDonald* leave many questions open about the scope of gun rights. The Court declines to adopt a balancing test to resolving the questions. How then should it resolve them—purely through historical analysis or through some other technique? Also, one might wonder to what extent the holding could be affected by technological change. If an equally effective but non-lethal method of home self-defense became widely available, could handguns be banned?

SKINNER V. OKLAHOMA EX REL. WILLIAMSON
316 U.S. 535, 62 S.Ct. 1110, 86 L.Ed. 1655 (1942)

JUSTICE DOUGLAS delivered the opinion of the Court.

This case touches a sensitive and important area of human rights. Oklahoma deprives certain individuals of a right which is basic to the perpetuation of a race—the right to have offspring. * * *

[Oklahoma's Habitual Criminal Sterilization Act] defines an "habitual criminal" as a person who, having been convicted two or more times for crimes "amounting to felonies involving moral turpitude," either in an Oklahoma court or in a court of any other State, is thereafter convicted of such a felony in Oklahoma and is sentenced to a term of imprisonment in an Oklahoma penal institution. Machinery is provided for the institution by the Attorney General of a proceeding against such a person in the Oklahoma courts for a judgment that such person shall be rendered sexually sterile. Notice, an opportunity to be heard, and the right to a jury trial are provided. The issues triable in such a proceeding are narrow and confined. If the court or jury finds that the defendant is an "habitual criminal" and that he "may be rendered sexually sterile without detriment to his or her general health," then the court "shall render judgment to the effect that said defendant be rendered sexually sterile" by the operation of vasectomy in case of a male, and of salpingectomy in case of a female. [The Act] provides that "offenses arising out of the violation of the prohibitory laws, revenue acts, embezzlement, or political offenses, shall not come or be considered within the terms of this Act."

[Between 1926–34, Skinner had been convicted twice for robbery with firearms and once for stealing chickens.] In 1936 the Attorney General instituted proceedings against him. Petitioner in his answer challenged the Act as unconstitutional by reason of the Fourteenth Amendment. A jury trial was had. The court instructed the jury that the crimes of which petitioner had been convicted were felonies involving moral turpitude, and that the only question for the jury was whether the operation of vasectomy could be performed on petitioner without detriment to his general health. The jury found that it could be. A judgment directing that the operation of vasectomy be performed on petitioner was affirmed by the Supreme Court of Oklahoma by a five to four decision.

Several objections to the constitutionality of the Act have been pressed upon us. It is urged that the Act cannot be sustained as an exercise of the police power, in view of the state of scientific authorities respecting inheritability of criminal traits. It is argued that due process is lacking because, under this Act, unlike the Act upheld in *Buck v. Bell*, 274 U.S. 200 [1927], the defendant is given no opportunity to be heard on the issue as to whether he is the probable potential parent of socially undesirable offspring. It is also suggested that the Act is penal in character and that the sterilization provided for is cruel and unusual punishment and violative of the Fourteenth Amendment. We pass those points without intimating an opinion on them, for there is a feature of the Act which clearly condemns it. That is, its failure to meet the requirements of the equal protection clause of the Fourteenth Amendment.

We do not stop to point out all of the inequalities in this Act. A few examples will suffice. In Oklahoma, grand larceny is a felony. Larceny is grand larceny when the property taken exceeds $20 in value. Embezzlement is punishable "in the manner prescribed for feloniously stealing property of the value of that embezzled." Hence, he who embezzles property worth more than $20 is guilty of a felony. A clerk who appropriates over $20 from his employer's till and a stranger who steals the same amount are thus both guilty of felonies. If the latter repeats his act and is convicted three times, he may be sterilized. But the clerk is not subject to the pains and penalties of the Act no matter how large his embezzlements nor how frequent his convictions. * * * [T]he nature of the two crimes is intrinsically the same and they are punishable in the same manner. Furthermore, the line between them follows close distinctions. * * *[10]

It was stated in *Buck v. Bell,* that the claim that state legislation violates the equal protection clause of the Fourteenth Amendment is "the usual last resort of constitutional arguments." Under our constitutional system the States in determining the reach and stope of particular legislation need not provide "abstract symmetry." * * * Thus, if we had here only a question as to a State's classification of crimes, such as

---

[10] *Editors' note*: One "close distinction" noted by Justice Douglas was that under Oklahoma law an employee who receives personal property intended for his employer but converts the property for his own use commits larceny by fraud if at the time of receipt he intended to convert the property, but is guilty of embezzlement if his intent to convert arises later. "Whether a particular act is larceny by fraud or embezzlement thus turns not on the intrinsic quality of the act but on when the felonious intent arose[.]"

embezzlement or larceny, no substantial federal question would be raised. * * *

But * * * [w]e are dealing here with legislation which involves one of the basic civil rights of man. Marriage and procreation are fundamental to the very existence and survival of the race. The power to sterilize, if exercised, may have subtle, far-reaching and devastating effects. In evil or reckless hands it can cause races or types which are inimical to the dominant group to wither and disappear. There is no redemption for the individual whom the law touches. Any experiment which the State conducts is to his irreparable injury. He is forever deprived of a basic liberty. We mention these matters not to reexamine the scope of the police power of the States. We advert to them merely in emphasis of our view that strict scrutiny of the classification which a State makes in a sterilization law is essential, lest unwittingly, or otherwise, invidious discriminations are made against groups or types of individuals in violation of the constitutional guaranty of just and equal laws. The guaranty of "equal protection of the laws is a pledge of the protection of equal laws." *Yick Wo v. Hopkins* [Chapter 3, § 1B]. When the law lays an unequal hand on those who have committed intrinsically the same quality of offense and sterilizes one and not the other, it has made as invidious a discrimination as if it had selected a particular race or nationality for oppressive treatment. Sterilization of those who have thrice committed grand larceny, with immunity for those who are embezzlers, is a clear, pointed, unmistakable discrimination. Oklahoma makes no attempt to say that he who commits larceny by trespass or trick or fraud has biologically inheritable traits which he who commits embezzlement lacks. Oklahoma's line between larceny by fraud and embezzlement is determined "with reference to the time when the fraudulent intent to convert the property to the taker's own use" arises. We have not the slightest basis for inferring that that line has any significance in eugenics, nor that the inheritability of criminal traits follows the neat legal distinctions which the law has marked between those two offenses. In terms of fines and imprisonment, the crimes of larceny and embezzlement rate the same under the Oklahoma code. Only when it comes to sterilization are the pains and penalties of the law different. The equal protection clause would indeed be a formula of empty words if such conspicuously artificial lines could be drawn.

[The concurring opinions of CHIEF JUSTICE STONE and JUSTICE JACKSON are omitted.]

NOTES ON SKINNER *AND* PROTECTING *IMPLIED* FUNDAMENTAL *RIGHTS*

1. *Equal Protection.* Is *Skinner*'s approach at all similar to any you have seen in earlier equal protection cases? This doesn't seem to be the normal rational basis test, or even the *Cleburne* version of that test (Chapter 4, § 3C).

Regarding issues of empirical uncertainty, such as whether certain behavioral traits are inherited, it matters a good deal whether the Court adopts a rational-basis test (under which the factual basis for the regulation is presumed, with plaintiff bearing the burden of demonstrating the contrary) or some form of higher scrutiny (which has the effect of shifting the burden of justification to the state). Since proof either way is probably not available, the standard of review essentially dictates the outcome.

2.   *Examining the Potential Theories in* Skinner. In this chapter, we will discuss some cases involving voting and education, in which the Court has based its recognition of an implied fundamental right upon the Equal Protection Clause. This chapter also considers the alternative theory of substantive due process and concludes with some consideration of procedural due process. As in *Skinner*, in the other cases in this chapter there might be an explicit constitutional right—like the right to be free from "cruel and unusual punishment"—that could be invoked. In each instance, sort out how the potential theories might apply. For example, had *Skinner* been decided on cruel and unusual punishment grounds, could it have any bearing on whether a state might sterilize developmentally disabled adults who reside in state institutions? Does the actual holding in *Skinner* prevent a state from sterilizing such persons? How would you make a "substantive due process" or "procedural due process" argument against such a state practice concerning such developmentally disabled adults?

A WORLD WITHOUT IMPLIED FUNDAMENTAL RIGHTS: A NOTE ON THE SOCIAL CONTEXT OF BUCK V. BELL *AND* SKINNER

It is easy to indict *Skinner* and other fundamental rights cases as exercises in improper judicial activism. Consider the facts of *Skinner*. Can the result be justified under any approach we have mentioned to the problem of judicial review? Reconsider your answer after considering the following.

In the early part of the twentieth century, state legislatures embraced the notion that compulsory sterilization was an appropriate strategy to rid our society of "defective people." Although today the idea seems repulsive, for many people prior to World War II it seemed like a progressive reform.[11] *Buck v. Bell*,

---

[11] See generally Daniel Kevles, *In the Name of Eugenics: Genetics and the Uses of Human Heredity* (1985). Consider Stephen Jay Gould, *Carrie Buck's Daughter*, 2 Const. Comm. 331, 332 (1985):

>   The movement for compulsory sterilization began in earnest during the 1890s, abetted by two major factors—the rise of eugenics as an influential political movement and the perfection of safe and effective operations * * * to replace castration and other obvious mutilation. Indiana passed the first sterilization act based on eugenic principles in 1907. * * * Like so many others to follow, it provided for sterilization of afflicted people residing in the state's "care," either as inmates of mental hospitals and homes for the feebleminded or as inhabitants of prisons. Sterilization could be imposed upon those judged insane, idiotic, imbecilic, or moronic, and upon convicted rapists or criminals when recommended by a board of experts.

>   By the 1930s, more than thirty states had passed similar laws, often with an expanded list of so-called hereditary defects, including alcoholism and drug addiction in some states, and even blindness and deafness in others. It must be said that these laws

274 U.S. 200 (1927), cited in *Skinner*, lent legitimacy to the practice. Indeed, the Chief Justice at the time of *Buck v. Bell*, William Howard Taft, was a former U.S. president who favored some eugenics reforms and publicly supported some of the movement's leaders.[12] Justice Holmes' opinion for the Court upheld a Virginia statute that established a process for the sterilization of developmentally disabled persons in state institutions. The statute was based on the assumptions that developmental disability is inheritable; that reproduction by such adults is against society's interests; and that if sterilized some of these persons could be discharged from state institutions and, free from state supervision, could become self-supporting contributors to society. The state invoked the statute against Carrie Buck, an institutionalized woman. According to findings made by the state trial court, Ms. Buck was developmentally disabled, as were both her mother and her nonmarital child. Because the Virginia practice allowed some procedural protections before sterilization could be performed, Buck argued that the statute was unconstitutional only because it intruded into her bodily integrity in violation of substantive due process and, in applying only to institutionalized persons, the statute was so underinclusive as to violate equal protection.

Justice Holmes dismissed both arguments. Finding a sufficient state interest in promoting the public welfare to justify the statute against substantive due process attack, Justice Holmes relied upon *Jacobson v. Massachusetts*, 197 U.S. 11 (1905), which upheld a state law requiring people to submit to vaccination against infectious disease. In language that became notorious, Justice Holmes said:

> It is better for all the world, if instead of waiting to execute degenerate offspring for crime, or to let them starve for their imbecility, society can prevent those who are manifestly unfit from continuing their kind. The principle that sustains compulsory vaccination is broad enough to cover cutting the Fallopian tubes. *Jacobson.* Three generations of imbeciles are enough.

Turning to Buck's second contention, Justice Holmes labeled the Equal Protection Clause "the usual last resort of constitutional arguments" and said that "the answer is that the law does all that is needed when it does all that it can, indicates a policy, applies it to all within the lines, and seeks to bring within the lines all similarly situated so far and so fast as its means allow."

As Chapters 2–4 indicate, however, the Equal Protection Clause has become far more than the constitutional doormat it was in Justice Holmes's day. Still, questions persist about when and how to apply it, along with questions we will track in the remainder of this chapter about whether the due

---

were continually challenged and rarely enforced in most states; only California and Virginia applied them zealously. By January 1935, some 20,000 forced "eugenic" sterilizations had been performed in the United States, nearly half in California.

[12] Paul Lombardo, *Three Generations, No Imbeciles: Eugenics, the Supreme Court and* Buck v. Bell 158 (2008).

process clause should be read to afford protections beyond those that are purely procedural.

Buried beneath the constitutional theory operating in *Buck v. Bell* are tragic facts that remained hidden for a half-century [see Gould, *supra*; Lombardo, *supra*]. In 1980, a Virginia official found Carrie Buck still alive, living near Charlottesville with her sister Doris, who had also been sterilized (she had been told that the operation was for appendicitis). Carrie Buck was found to be a woman of normal intelligence. She had been shunted off to the state institution by her foster parents when she became pregnant (apparently the result of rape by a relative of her foster parents). Some of those in the legal system in a position to protect Bell had sympathies with the eugenics movement. Indeed, her own lawyer appears to have been one of them. The only evidence he presented at her commitment hearing came from her foster parents. Later, she and her mother were administered an IQ test, which purported to show that both were developmentally disabled. During the trial on whether Carrie Buck could be sterilized, the only evidence put forward concerning the supposed developmental disabilities of her daughter—who at that time was *seven months old*—came from a social worker who said that "there is a look about [the baby] that is not quite normal, but just what it is, I can't tell." The daughter later received adequate grades in elementary school before dying at the age of eight from an illness.

The compulsory sterilization movement, as exposed by the real facts of *Buck v. Bell*, was concerned essentially with eliminating the genes of "the most worthless one-tenth of our present population," to use the language of the movement's leader, Harry Laughlin. Indeed, Laughlin's report on the Buck family, used in the litigation, began: "These people belong to the shiftless, ignorant, and worthless class of anti-social whites of the South." According to Stephen Jay Gould, the case really stands for the proposition that "[t]wo generations of bastards are enough." [Gould 336–37.]

For lawyers, the problem is that our constitutional document says nothing that clearly protects the Carrie Bucks of the world on these facts. Her sterilization was not in punishment for crime, and thus could not be considered an Eighth Amendment problem. The Virginia statute did provide her some procedural protections, but people like her are unlikely to be able to afford an attorney, and even if an attorney is provided, he or she might have been unable to find enough scientific evidence to counter the prevailing wisdom of the day. A flat prohibition on sterilization for eugenic purposes—or at least a strong presumption against it, with the state bearing a high burden of justification— may be the only practical way to protect society against such fundamental abuses. And yet the judge who entertains creating such a fundamental constitutional right will surely be criticized for usurping the legislative function.

A final lesson of *Buck v. Bell* is that the Constitution, as construed by the Court, rarely provides more than marginal protection for the victims of such policy fads as the eugenics movement—until public norms change. The case of

J.L. Skinner illustrates this idea. He was convicted and sentenced to sterilization in 1930s Oklahoma, when legislators, prosecutors, and ordinary people were anxious about the perpetuation of so-called "degenerates." But as the case made its way up the appellate system, the eugenics policy encountered increased skepticism. Scientists in the 1930s cast doubt on these theories, and national policymakers by the end of the decade were acutely aware of the philosophical similarities between American and Nazi eugenics. Once the case reached the Supreme Court, scientific experts, elite lawyers, and national policymakers had set their minds against sterilization and other eugenics policies.

Review Justice Douglas's opinion and see if you can detect Nazi Germany in the background. The concern is more explicit in Justice Jackson's concurring opinion in *Skinner*, which we have omitted. Jackson stated in part:

> There are limits to the extent to which a legislatively represented majority may conduct biological experiments at the expense of the dignity and personality and natural powers of a minority—even those who have been guilty of what the majority define as crimes. But this Act falls down before reaching this problem, which I mention only to avoid the implication that such a question may not exist because not discussed.

Note the tension between this language and Jackson's concurring opinion in *Railway Express*, decided seven years later, in which he scorned substantive due process review in favor of somewhat searching equal protection analysis. Also note that Justice Black, who condemned judicial creation of rights beyond the constitutional text in *Adamson*, silently joined the majority opinion in *Skinner*, presumably because the clever equal-protection rationale avoided the need to address whether compulsory sterilization violated substantive due process.

As we turn to substantive due process, consider what basis there is for courts to protect rights that are not specifically enumerated in the constitutional text. What are the strongest arguments for and against implying rights not expressly provided for in the text? Does it depend on the importance of the interests for which protection is sought? Their recognition in history? Something else?

SECTION 2. PROTECTING ECONOMIC LIBERTY AND PROPERTY

A. HISTORICAL INTRODUCTION

The state of New York enacts a law restricting the hours that bakers can work and another law restricting the owners' use of designated historic buildings. Such statutes regulate important economic interests. What federal constitutional restrictions apply? This is an unexpectedly complicated question.

If the first law were applied to rewrite existing labor-management contracts, it might fall athwart the Contracts Clause of Article I, § 10, which says that "[n]o State shall * * * pass any * * * Law impairing the Obligation of Contracts." The Contracts Clause was originally aimed at debtor-relief legislation by the states and was liberally applied in the early nineteenth century. Thus, in *Fletcher v. Peck*, 10 U.S. (6 Cranch) 87 (1810), the Marshall Court refused to allow Georgia to rescind land grants that had been obtained by bribing the state legislature, because rescission would impair vested rights that the ultimate purchasers had acquired by contract. In the *Dartmouth College Case*, 17 U.S. (4 Wheat.) 518 (1819), the Court struck down a New Hampshire law changing the provisions of the college's state charter, which the Court viewed as a contract. The same principle was applied by the Marshall Court to limit state regulation of business corporations.

The Taney Court (1836–64) retreated from the Marshall Court's broad use of the Contracts Clause, however. In *Charles River Bridge v. Warren Bridge*, 36 U.S. (11 Pet.) 420 (1837), the Court upheld the right of Massachusetts to adopt new policies in derogation of a public charter granted to a ferry company. Justice Story (a Marshall Court holdover) adamantly objected that the Court was sanctioning a violation of the Contracts Clause and undermining vested rights. But Chief Justice Taney's opinion for the Court insisted that "contract" rights should not be needlessly constructed when they would derogate from the public interest. This was obviously a different attitude toward state regulation of private property than that followed by the Marshall Court. A broadly utilitarian justification for state regulation of private property is set forth in Chief Judge Lemuel Shaw's opinion in *Commonwealth v. Alger*, 61 Mass. 53 (1851).[13]

What Chief Justice Taney did to the Contracts Clause in *Charles River* Justice Miller did to the Privileges or Immunities Clause in *The Slaughter House Cases* (described above)—substantially removing both as federal constitutional protections against state regulation of "vested" private rights, whether expressed in contract or in property. Justice Miller's decision also dismissed due process objections to state regulation, indicating that the Fourteenth Amendment's Due Process Clause spoke only to procedural requirements of state actions. But before the ink was dry on *The Slaughter House Cases*, the state courts were interpreting the Due Process Clause to protect liberty of private contracting and the sanctity of private property.[14]

---

[13] On the ideological features of judicial approaches to economic regulation in this period, see Morton Horwitz, *The Transformation of American Law, 1780–1860* (1977).

[14] In *Bertholf v. O'Reilly*, 74 N.Y. 509, 511 (1878), the New York Court of Appeals recognized that due process "right to liberty [includes] the right to exercise his faculties and to follow a lawful avocation for the support of life; the right to property [includes] the right to acquire possession and enjoy it in any way consistent with the equal rights of others." For other authorities to the same

Some of the state court judges who saw the Due Process Clause in economic terms—Judges David Brewer of the Kansas Supreme Court (1871–84) and Rufus Peckham of the New York Court of Appeals (1886–95)—were later appointed to the U.S. Supreme Court. In the 1890s they transformed American constitutional law, under cover of the Due Process Clause. The primary innovation of the state cases in the 1880s, e.g., *In re Jacobs*, 98 N.Y. 98 (1885) (a leading case), and of the Supreme Court cases in the 1890s, was their recognition of a "liberty of contract" right in the Due Process Clause. "So long as any single man, the humblest and the weakest in the land, may not enter into business or engage in labor such as his means will permit and his inclination determine, just so long is personal liberty an unaccomplished fact." Justice Brewer, *The Liberty of Each Individual* (address, July 4, 1893). This line of cases is explored in Part B.

A second innovation adopted by the Supreme Court during this period was an embryonic version of the incorporation doctrine. *Chicago, Burlington & Quincy Railroad v. Chicago*, 166 U.S. 226 (1897), which held the Fifth Amendment's Takings Clause applicable to the states through the Fourteenth Amendment's Due Process Clause, was the Court's first incorporation of a Bill of Rights guarantee to the states.

B. THE RISE AND DECLINE OF LIBERTY OF CONTRACT AND SUBSTANTIVE DUE PROCESS REVIEW

In *Allgeyer v. Louisiana*, 165 U.S. 578 (1897), the Court struck down a Louisiana law requiring all insurance on Louisiana property to be issued by insurers registered to do business in the state. The Court characterized the law as an infringement on the right of out-of-state brokers to pursue their livelihoods and subjected the law to strict scrutiny, which it flunked. In contrast, in *Holden v. Hardy*, 169 U.S. 366 (1898), the Court, over the dissent of Justices Brewer and Peckham, upheld against due process attack a Utah statute which limited mining and smelting workers to eight-hour days. Although the Court recognized that the statute limited employers' and employees' freedom of contract, it found the regulation justified in order to protect the health and safety of those working in such hazardous jobs.

Between 1898 and 1905, the U.S. Supreme Court upheld a series of state laws limiting freedom of contract, sometimes relying upon an idea suggested in *Holden* that placing an employer and employee on a more equal footing was itself a sufficient state interest to justify labor regulation. E.g., *Knoxville Iron Co. v. Harbison*, 183 U.S. 13 (1901). The state courts

---

effect, see *Hanson v. Vernon*, 27 Iowa 28, 73 (1869); *Carew v. Rutherford*, 106 Mass. 1, 10–15 (1870); *People v. Salem*, 20 Mich. 452, 484–85 (1870); Thomas Cooley, *A Treatise on the Constitutional Limitations Which Rest Upon Legislative Power of the States of the American Union* (1868).

grew more moderate in their application of substantive due process review after the late 1890s, as illustrated by the New York Court of Appeals' decision in *State v. Lochner*, 177 N.Y. 145 (1904). Justice Peckham's former court had been at the forefront in strictly scrutinizing economic regulations, but under the leadership of Chief Judge Alton Parker the court upheld the New York "bakers' law," which prohibited employers from requiring bakers to work more than 60 hours in one week. Chief Judge Parker relied on *Holden*. The U.S. Supreme Court disagreed and reversed, in a landmark decision.

LOCHNER V. NEW YORK

198 U.S. 45, 25 S.Ct. 539, 49 L.Ed. 937 (1905)

JUSTICE PECKHAM delivered the opinion of the Court.

[Lochner was charged with violating a New York statute that prohibited employers from requiring bakers to work over sixty hours in a week.] The statute necessarily interferes with the right of contract between the employer and employees, concerning the number of hours in which the latter may labor in the bakery of the employer. The general right to make a contract in relation to his business is part of the liberty of the individual protected by the Fourteenth Amendment of the Federal Constitution. *Allgeyer*. Under that provision no State can deprive any person of life, liberty or property without due process of law. The right to purchase or to sell labor is part of the liberty protected by this amendment, unless there are circumstances which exclude the right. There are, however, certain powers, existing in the sovereignty of each State in the Union, somewhat vaguely termed police powers, the exact description and limitation of which have not been attempted by the courts. Those powers, broadly stated and without, at present, any attempt at a more specific limitation, relate to the safety, health, morals and general welfare of the public. Both property and liberty are held on such reasonable conditions as may be imposed by the governing power of the State in the exercise of those powers, and with such conditions the Fourteenth Amendment was not designed to interfere. * * *

It must, of course, be conceded that there is a limit to the valid exercise of the police power by the State. There is no dispute concerning this general proposition. Otherwise the Fourteenth Amendment would have no efficacy and the legislatures of the States would have unbounded power, and it would be enough to say that any piece of legislation was enacted to conserve the morals, the health or the safety of the people; such legislation would be valid, no matter how absolutely without foundation the claim might be. The claim of the police power would be a mere pretext—become another and delusive name for the supreme sovereignty of the State to be exercised free from constitutional restraint. This is not contended for. In every case that comes before this court, therefore, where legislation of this character is concerned and where the protection of the Federal Constitution is sought, the question necessarily arises: Is this a fair, reasonable and appropriate exercise of the police power of the State, or is it an unreasonable, unnecessary and arbitrary interference with the right of the individual to his personal liberty or to enter into those contracts in relation to labor which may seem to him appropriate or necessary for the support of himself and his family? Of course the liberty of contract relating to labor includes both parties to it. The one has as much right to purchase as the other to sell labor.

This is not a question of substituting the judgment of the court for that of the legislature. If the act be within the power of the State it is valid, although the judgment of the court might be totally opposed to the enactment of such a law. But the question would still remain: Is it within the police power of the State? and that question must be answered by the court.

The question whether this act is valid as a labor law, pure and simple, may be dismissed in a few words. There is no reasonable ground for interfering with the liberty of person or the right of free contract, by determining the hours of labor, in the occupation of a baker. There is no contention that bakers as a class are not equal in intelligence and capacity to men in other trades or manual occupations, or that they are not able to assert their rights and care for themselves without the protecting arm of the State, interfering with their independence of judgment and of action. They are in no sense wards of the State. Viewed in the light of a purely labor law, with no reference whatever to the question of health, we think that a law like the one before us involves neither the safety, the morals nor the welfare of the public, and that the interest of the public is not in the slightest degree affected by such an act. The law must be upheld, if at all, as a law pertaining to the health of the individual engaged in the occupation of a baker. * * *

We think the limit of the police power has been reached and passed in this case. There is, in our judgment, no reasonable foundation for holding this to be necessary or appropriate as a health law to safeguard the public health or the health of the individuals who are following the trade of a baker. If this statute be valid, and if, therefore, a proper case is made out in which to deny the right of an individual, sui juris, as employer or employee, to make contracts for the labor of the latter under the protection of the provisions of the Federal Constitution, there would seem to be no length to which legislation of this nature might not go.

* * * We think that there can be no fair doubt that the trade of a baker, in and of itself, is not an unhealthy one to that degree which would authorize the legislature to interfere with the right to labor, and with the right of free contract on the part of the individual, either as employer or

employee. In looking through statistics regarding all trades and occupations, it may be true that the trade of a baker does not appear to be as healthy as some other trades, and is also vastly more healthy than still others. To the common understanding the trade of a baker has never been regarded as an unhealthy one. * * * It is unfortunately true that labor, even in any department, may possibly carry with it the seeds of unhealthiness. But are we all, on that account, at the mercy of legislative majorities? A printer, a tinsmith, a locksmith, a carpenter, a cabinetmaker, a dry goods clerk, a bank's, a lawyer's or a physician's clerk, or a clerk in almost any kind of business, would all come under the power of the legislature, on this assumption. No trade, no occupation, no mode of earning one's living, could escape this all-pervading power, and the acts of the legislature in limiting the hours of labor in all employments would be valid, although such limitation might seriously cripple the ability of the laborer to support himself and his family. * * *

It is manifest to us that the limitation of the hours of labor as provided for in this section of the statute under which the indictment was found, and the plaintiff in error convicted, has no such direct relation to and no such substantial effect upon the health of the employee, as to justify us in regarding the section as really a health law. It seems to us that the real object and purpose were simply to regulate the hours of labor between the master and his employees (all being men, sui juris), in a private business, not dangerous in any degree to morals or in any real and substantial degree, to the health of the employees. Under such circumstances the freedom of master and employee to contract with each other in relation to their employment, and in defining the same, cannot be prohibited or interfered with, without violating the Federal Constitution.

JUSTICE HOLMES, dissenting.

This case is decided upon an economic theory which a large part of the country does not entertain. If it were a question whether I agreed with that theory, I should desire to study it further and long before making up my mind. But I do not conceive that to be my duty, because I strongly believe that my agreement or disagreement has nothing to do with the right of a majority to embody their opinions in law. It is settled by various decisions of this court that state constitutions and state laws may regulate life in many ways which we as legislators might think as injudicious or if you like as tyrannical as this, and which equally with this interfere with the liberty to contract. Sunday laws and usury laws are ancient examples. A more modern one is the prohibition of lotteries. The liberty of the citizen to do as he likes so long as he does not interfere with the liberty of others to do the same, which has been a shibboleth for some well-known writers, is interfered with by school laws, by the Post Office, by every state or municipal institution which takes his money for purposes thought desirable, whether he likes it or not. The Fourteenth Amendment does not enact Mr. Herbert Spencer's Social Statics. The other day we sustained the Massachusetts vaccination law. United States and state statutes and decisions cutting down the liberty to contract by way of combination are familiar to this court. Two years ago we upheld the prohibition of sales of stock on margins or for future delivery in the constitution of California. The decision sustaining an eight hour law for miners is still recent. Some of these laws embody convictions or prejudices which judges are likely to share. Some may not. But a constitution is not intended to embody a particular economic theory, whether of paternalism and the organic relation of the citizen to the State or of Laissez faire. It is made for people of fundamentally differing views, and the accident of our finding certain opinions natural and familiar or novel and even shocking ought not to conclude our judgment upon the question whether statutes embodying them conflict with the Constitution of the United States.

General propositions do not decide concrete cases. The decision will depend on a judgment or intuition more subtle than any articulate major premise. But I think that the proposition just stated, if it is accepted, will carry us far toward the end. Every opinion tends to become a law. I think that the word "liberty" in the Fourteenth Amendment is perverted when it is held to prevent the natural outcome of a dominant opinion, unless it can be said that a rational and fair man necessarily would admit that the statute proposed would infringe fundamental principles as they have been understood by the traditions of our people and our law. It does not need research to show that no such sweeping condemnation can be passed upon the statute before us. A reasonable man might think it a proper measure on the score of health. Men whom I certainly could not pronounce unreasonable would uphold it as a first installment of a general regulation of the hours of work. Whether in the latter aspect it would be open to the charge of inequality I think it unnecessary to discuss.

JUSTICE HARLAN, with whom **JUSTICE WHITE** and **JUSTICE DAY** concurred, dissenting.

It is plain that this statute was enacted in order to protect the physical well-being of those who work in bakery and confectionery establishments. It may be that the statute had its origin, in part, in the belief that employers and employees in such establishments were not upon an equal footing, and that the necessities of the latter often compelled them to submit to such exactions as unduly taxed their strength. Be this as it may, the statute must be taken as expressing the belief of the people of New York that, as a general rule, and in the case of the average man, labor in excess of sixty hours during a week in such establishments may endanger the health of those who thus labor. Whether or not this be wise legislation it is not the province of the court to inquire. * * *

Professor Hirt in his treatise on the "Diseases of the Workers" has said: "The labor of the bakers is among the hardest and most laborious imaginable, because it has to be performed under conditions injurious to the health of those engaged in it. It is hard, very hard work, not only because it requires a great deal of physical exertion in an overheated workshop and during unreasonably long hours, but more so because of the erratic demands of the public, compelling the baker to perform the greater part of his work at night thus depriving him of an opportunity to enjoy the necessary rest and sleep, a fact which is highly injurious to his health." Another writer says: "The constant inhaling of flour dust causes inflammation of the lungs and of the bronchial tubes. The eyes also suffer through this dust, which is responsible for the many cases of running eyes among the bakers. The long hours of toil to which all bakers are subjected produce rheumatism, cramps and swollen legs. The intense heat in the workshops induces the workers to resort to cooling drinks, which together with their habit of exposing the greater part of their bodies to the change in the atmosphere, is another source of a number of diseases of various organs. Nearly all bakers are pale-faced and of more delicate health than the workers of other crafts, which is chiefly due to their hard work and their irregular and unnatural mode of living, whereby the power of resistance against disease is greatly diminished. The average age of a baker is below that of other workmen; they seldom live over their fiftieth year, most of them dying between the ages of forty and fifty. During periods of epidemic diseases the bakers are generally the first to succumb to the disease[.]" * * *

I do not stop to consider whether any particular view of this economic question presents the sounder theory. What the precise facts are it may be difficult to say. It is enough for the determination of this case, and it is enough for this court to know, that the question is one about which there is room for debate and for an honest difference of opinion. There are many reasons of a weighty, substantial character, based upon the experience of mankind, in support of the theory that, all things considered, more than ten hours' steady work each day, from week to week, in a bakery or confectionery establishment, may endanger the health, and shorten the lives of the workmen, thereby diminishing their physical and mental capacity to serve the State, and to provide for those dependent upon them.

If such reasons exist that ought to be the end of this case, for the State is not amenable to the judiciary, in respect of its legislative enactments, unless such enactments are plainly, palpably, beyond all question, inconsistent with the Constitution of the United States. We are not to presume that the State of New York has acted in bad faith. Nor can we assume that its legislature acted without due deliberation, or that it did not determine this question upon the fullest attainable information, and for the common good. We cannot say that the State has acted without reason nor ought we to proceed upon the theory that its action is a mere sham.

NOTES ON LOCHNER AND THE HEYDAY OF SUBSTANTIVE DUE PROCESS

1. *What's Wrong with* Lochner? Justice Peckham's decision came as something of a surprise to the legal world, and in fact depended upon an unexplained shift in position by Justice Brown, the author of *Holden v. Hardy*. The decision was criticized when it was handed down (though not so much as other anti-labor decisions of the Fuller Court, 1888–1910), and the level of criticism has only grown over time. Consider these ways to disagree with the Court.

(a) Justice Holmes' dissent might be read for the proposition that the Court should afford only minimal scrutiny to socio-economic regulations adopted by the legislature. Recall Thayer, *The Origin and Scope of the American Doctrine of Constitutional Law*, 7 Harv. L. Rev. 129 (1883) (Chapter 2 § 1). Justice Holmes challenged the Court to justify its adoption of a particular theory of economics (laissez faire) when it recognized invasions of "liberty of contract" as a basis for strict scrutiny of labor legislation.

(b) Justice Harlan's dissent might be read for the proposition that the Court overlooked legitimate state justifications for its intrusion into the parties' liberty of contract—either the health and safety of bakers (more thoroughly documented in the encyclopedic opinion by Chief Judge Parker of the New York Court of Appeals) or the disparity in bargaining power between workers and employers (*Holden*).

(c) A more recent attack on *Lochner* focuses on its assumption that there is a "private" sphere of worker-management "liberty" into which the state should presumptively not intrude. But the state is already there, for the possibility of worker-management contracting is premised upon the state's standing ready to enforce the terms of that contract—as it frequently did in the 1890s when employers would call upon the police and the courts to enjoin "unlawful" strikes. Hence, the private sphere is already infected with public participation, and there is no neutral reason for the Court to presume against state regulation of contracting activity.[15]

2. *Defense of* Lochner. Arguably the New York bakers' statute was not really enacted as a health measure, nor did it reflect inequality of bargaining position; instead, it was possibly rent-seeking by unions and employers.[16] The bakers' unions in the 1890s obtained maximum hour rules from the major employers, but small-time bakeries that were not unionized then had a competitive advantage over the big bakeries that were, because the former had

---

[15] See Gary Peller, *The Metaphysics of American Law*, 73 Cal. L. Rev. 1151 (1985) (retrieving this insight from the work of the legal realists); Cass Sunstein, Lochner's Legacy, 87 Colum. L. Rev. 873 (1987) (reinterpreting *Lochner* in light of this insight).

[16] See Sidney Tarrow, Lochner v. New York: *A Political Analysis*, 5 Labor History 277 (1964).

lower labor costs per hour. The *Lochner* statute was a measure by which the unions and the big bakeries could raise the labor costs—and incidentally the prices charged to consumers—of the small bakeries, so that they would not outsell the big bakeries. Some theories of economics suggest that this might be economically inefficient, and some theories of public choice suggest that the state is often the cover for precisely this sort of rent-seeking.[17]

3. Lochner's *Aftermath.* The Court's decision in *Lochner* signaled a reinvigorated judicial hostility (at both the state and federal level) to legislation enacted at the behest of labor unions. Most prominently, *Lochner* was the basis for subsequent invalidation of state laws making "yellow dog contracts" (whereby the employer would require a promise by employees that they not join a union) unlawful. See *Coppage v. Kansas*, 236 U.S. 1 (1915); *People v. Marcus*, 185 N.Y. 257 (1906); see also *Adair v. United States*, 208 U.S. 161 (1908) (invalidating federal law as beyond Congress's Commerce Clause power). On the other hand, the Supreme Court refused to apply *Lochner* to strike down a law regulating the hours women could work, see *Muller v. Oregon*, 208 U.S. 412 (1908) (Chapter 4, § 2A), and in *Bunting v. Oregon*, 243 U.S. 426 (1917), refused to follow *Lochner* in upholding a state law generally restricting work days to ten hours. Any implication that *Bunting* overruled the *Lochner* approach was dispelled, however, in *Adkins v. Children's Hospital of the District of Columbia*, 261 U.S. 525 (1923), which struck down a minimum wage law for female employees.

Lochner, as well as other cases that limited the authority of Congress and the state legislatures, caused a constitutional crisis in the 1930s, when the Great Depression led to tremendous political pressure for more national and state economic regulation (Chapter 1, §§ 4–5). See *Home Building & Loan Ass'n v. Blaisdell*, 290 U.S. 398 (1934) (upholding a temporary moratorium on mortgage foreclosures). President Franklin Roosevelt's Court-packing plan may have had something to do with the "switch in time that saved nine." In any event, changes in composition of the Court coupled with the crushing economic realities of the time led a majority of the Justices to abandon *Lochner*. *Nebbia v. New York*, 291 U.S. 502 (1934), a 5–4 decision that upheld a New York law allowing a state board to fix minimum and maximum retail prices for milk, was the first major signal of a retreat from economic substantive due process. See Daniel Farber, *Who Killed* Lochner?, 90 Geo. L.J. 985 (2002). The doctrine was firmly interred in the next two cases. The first case decisively rejects the constitutional baseline at the heart of *Lochner*; the second goes quite far in deferring to potentially protectionist economic regulation.

4. Lochner's *Symbolism.* Before turning to the cases that decisively ended the *Lochner* era, it is worth noting that *Lochner* remains a potent symbol of the problem of judicial activism. As we will see in § 4D of this chapter, Chief Justice Roberts deployed it as the rhetorical core of his extended dissent in *Obergefell v. Hodges*, the high-profile case finding that same-sex couples have

---

[17] See generally Bernard Siegan, *Economic Liberties and the Constitution* (1980); Richard Epstein, *Toward a Revitalization of the Contract Clause*, 51 U. Chi. L. Rev. 703 (1984).

a fundamental right to marry. Roberts compared what he saw as the Court's overreach in *Obergefell* to that exemplified by *Lochner*. Despite this critique, however, some scholars argue that the Roberts Court has inaugurated a "new *Lochner*" doctrine through controversial rulings enlisting the First Amendment to protect business interests. Some of this scholarship is collected in Chapter 6 (see note 3, p. 721).

West Coast Hotel v. Parrish

300 U.S. 379 (1937)

In a 5–4 decision, **Chief Justice Hughes** upheld a state law establishing a minimum wage for women, overruling the *Lochner*-like *Adkins v. Children's Hospital, supra.* The opinion stated that "[t]he Constitution does not speak of freedom of contract. It speaks of liberty and prohibits the deprivation of liberty without due process of law. [Regulation] which is reasonable in relation to its subject and is adopted in the interests of the community is due process." The opinion stressed that the legislature "was clearly entitled to consider the situation of women in employment, the fact that they are in the class receiving the least pay, that their bargaining power is relatively weak, and that they are the ready victims of those who would take advantage of their necessitous circumstances. The legislature was entitled to adopt measures to reduce the evils of the 'sweating system,' the exploiting of workers at wages so low as to be insufficient to meet the bare cost of living, thus making their very helplessness the occasion of a most injurious competition. * * * The adoption of similar requirements by many States evidences a deep-seated conviction both as to the presence of the evil and as to the means adopted to check it. Legislative response to that conviction cannot be regarded as arbitrary or capricious, and that is all we have to decide. Even if the wisdom of the policy be regarded as debatable and its effects uncertain, still the legislature is entitled to its judgment." The opinion then seemingly junked the baseline of *Lochner*: "There is an additional and compelling consideration which recent economic experience has brought into a strong light. The exploitation of a class of workers who are in an unequal bargaining position with respect to bargaining power and are thus relatively defenseless against the denial of a living wage is not only detrimental to their health and well being but casts a direct burden for their support upon the community. What these workers lose in wages the taxpayers are called upon to pay. The bare cost of living must be met. We may take judicial notice of the unparalleled demands for relief which arose during the recent period of depression. * * * The community is not bound to provide what is in effect a subsidy for unconscionable employers. The community may direct its law-making power to correct the abuse which springs from their selfish disregard of the public interest."

Williamson v. Lee Optical

348 U.S. 483, 75 S.Ct. 461, 99 L.Ed. 563 (1955)

An Oklahoma statute prohibited opticians from duplicating or replacing lenses without a written prescription from an ophthalmologist or optometrist, even though opticians have the expertise and equipment to take a whole (or, frequently, even broken) lens and determine the prescription for it. The Court, per **JUSTICE DOUGLAS**, conceded that the statute was perhaps "a needless, wasteful requirement in many cases" and that the law was "not in every respect logically consistent with its aims." Nevertheless, the statute did not violate due process: "[I]t is for the legislature, not the courts, to balance the advantages and disadvantages. * * * The legislature might have concluded that the frequency of occasions when a prescription is necessary was sufficient to justify this regulation, [or] the legislature may have concluded that eye examinations were so critical, not only for correction of vision but also for detection of latent ailments or diseases, that every change in frames and every duplication of a lens should be accompanied by a prescription from a medical expert. * * * It is enough that there is an evil at hand for correction, and that it might be thought that the particular legislative measure was a rational way to correct it. The day is gone when this Court uses the Due Process Clause * * * to strike down state laws, regulatory of business and industrial conditions, because they may be unwise, improvident, or out of harmony with a particular school of thought. * * * 'For protection against abuses by legislatures the people must resort to the polls, not to the courts.'" The Court also rejected an equal protection challenge, for reasons similar to those accepted in the majority opinion in *Railway Express* (Chapter 4).

SECTION 3. EQUAL PROTECTION AND "FUNDAMENTAL INTERESTS"

In Chapters 3 and 4, we considered equal protection as concerned with the fair allocation of governmental benefits or detriments, not with the underlying question of whether the government has the authority to regulate the benefit or detriment in the first place. Moreover, the allocation of benefits or detriments generally need only be minimally rational to pass equal protection scrutiny. From the cases we have seen, heightened scrutiny under the Equal Protection Clause is warranted only if the government action overtly classifies people on the basis of a sensitive criterion (e.g., race) or, although facially neutral, is rooted in intentional discrimination against such a group.

For a simple illustration, consider three state statutes: One outlaws the ownership of guns by anyone; the second outlaws the ownership of guns by convicted felons; the third outlaws the ownership of guns by women. The first statute probably does not even raise any conventional equal protection problems. (It has no underinclusion or overinclusion at all unless the goal is not just to regulate guns but to regulate dangerous objects generally, and even then it easily survives equal protection review.) The second statute is clearly overinclusive (some convicted felons won't harm people if they own guns). It is also underinclusive—it does nothing about convicted felons who possess but don't own guns, and in any event lots of non-felons are bad bets to own guns, from society's standpoint. Nonetheless, the second statute survives equal protection review because under the Court's decisions only rational-basis scrutiny is available, and the statute clearly passes muster under that standard. The third statute violates equal protection, because the Court's precedents prescribe higher scrutiny for statutes that overtly disadvantage women. Under conventional theory, each of these equal protection inquiries is *egalitarian* in nature, focusing on the extent of overinclusion and underinclusion and the degree to which our norms of equal treatment are offended by the nature of the group disadvantaged (e.g., felons, women) or by the criterion used to classify (e.g., felony convictions, sex).

Of course, even if the statute in question survives conventional equal protection review, it may well be unconstitutional for some other reason. For example, the Court has recently interpreted the Second Amendment to protect the liberty to own guns (recall the recent decisions in *Heller* and *McDonald*). And, even absent explicit protection, the Court might have inquired whether there was implicit protection for owning a gun (e.g., as an aspect of the "liberty" protected against deprivation without "due process of law" by the Fourteenth Amendment). In contrast to the egalitarian inquiry of classic equal protection, the Second Amendment or due process argument here is *libertarian* and "rights oriented" in nature: It contends that people have a "right" to be free from government regulation of gun ownership even if the government regulation in question is fairly drawn from an egalitarian standpoint. Again, note that the libertarian argument, which focuses on the personal interest being deprived or regulated (e.g., gun ownership), is not a part of the classic equal protection approach.

Now consider a statute that gives veterans of the armed services special preferences. If the preference the state has granted violates an independent constitutional right—such as giving only veterans the right to speak on foreign policy issues—then of course the statute is unconstitutional under the libertarian, rights-oriented approach to which we will soon turn our attention. If, however, no independent constitutional right is involved, our materials so far suggest that the usual challenge will be based on the Equal Protection Clause. But note that our hypothetical statute does not use race, sex, or other established "sensitive factors" to classify people. Also, let us assume that the legislature had no covert intent to discriminate against such a class. It might seem that the only thing left to do under the Equal Protection Clause is apply minimal scrutiny for underinclusion and overinclusion, which the statute will almost surely survive.

Under this analysis, if only "constitutional gratuities" are involved— things to which no one has a constitutional right—the nature of the particular privilege or detriment is irrelevant, and the only questions from the equal protection standpoint are whether the statute (1) flunks higher scrutiny because it overtly or covertly embodies discrimination on the basis of race, gender, and so on; or (2) is so irrationally overinclusive or underinclusive as to flunk minimal scrutiny. This is the conventional approach to equal protection, based on Justice Jackson's concurring opinion in *Railway Express* and on the tiers of higher scrutiny for race, gender, and so on that have arisen since the Jackson opinion.

What the conventional approach ignores, however, is that our fundamental norms about equality are sometimes hard to divorce from a consideration of the particular interests being regulated. For example, our basic sense of equal treatment may not be violated by a law that gives veterans a special preference in getting state jobs. (Even that, of course, is controversial, given the impact of this preference on women, as discussed in *Feeney* (Chapter 4, § 2B).) But surely we would have graver doubts about a law that gives a veteran more than one vote in state judicial elections or that gives only the children of veterans the right to a free public education. Even though such laws might serve the rational purpose of encouraging and rewarding military service, we might well demand a stronger justification for a state decision touching on such important interests.

If we wish to subject these hypothetical veterans' preferences to heightened scrutiny, there are three reasons why we might want to look to equal protection rather than due process or some other libertarian constitutional provision as a basis. First, to some extent, our objection to these laws is based on equality—that in giving veterans extra votes or the exclusive right to educate their children free of charge, the government is essentially treating the rest of the populace as second-class citizens. Giving one group certain crucial benefits while depriving others creates a hierarchy that may offend our notion of equality.

Second, a libertarian approach may not work as a source of protection here. How can the Constitution be said to guarantee the right to vote in state judicial elections, given the undisputed power of the government to abolish judicial elections entirely in favor of appointment by the governor? Similarly, it is far from clear that the Constitution requires the state to establish public schools at all. Hence, if state power is limited, it must be on the basis of some kind of equal-treatment principle, rather than by a substantive individual right.

Third, equal protection is a lesser intrusion on legislative autonomy. It leaves to the state, for example, the question of whether to appoint or elect judges, merely requiring that if the electoral route is taken the state must give everyone an equal vote. Similarly, the decision to establish public education may be left to the states even though the courts might police arbitrary exclusions from the public schools.

Despite these potential attractions, equal protection has only sporadically served as a basis for protecting "fundamental interests" that are not independent constitutional rights. One of the relatively few cases is *Skinner* (this Chapter, § 1). Another is *Harper v. Virginia Board of Elections*, 383 U.S. 663 (1966). *Harper* struck down, as violating equal protection, a Virginia statute that imposed a poll tax not exceeding $1.50 upon each voter. The opinion was wonderfully ambiguous, both casually referring to voting as a fundamental right and stating that "[l]ines drawn on the basis of wealth or property, like those of race are traditionally disfavored." Nowhere does the Constitution expressly provide an individual right to vote, however, and probably the Framers of both the original Constitution and the Reconstruction Amendments considered it the prerogative of the states to set the basic requirements for voting. Nor, despite language in *Harper*, has the Court ever held that the poor are a suspect class for equal protection purposes. Since the poll tax statute had a rational basis—more than just raising revenue, the statute could be said to encourage voting only by those persons who consider voting important enough to pay a little something for the privilege—*Harper* is difficult to square with the classical approach to equal protection. Contrast *Lassiter v. Northampton County Board of Elections*, 360 U.S. 45 (1959), where the Court upheld a statute requiring literacy as a precondition to voting.

In this section, we will trace the current developments in voting and wealth discrimination cases. Be careful to examine precisely how the Court defines what is protected in each case, and then consider whether the Equal Protection Clause is the appropriate locus in the Constitution for the protection involved.

A. VOTING

Throughout much of the twentieth century, many state legislatures failed to reapportion their seats in light of shifting population. Because this was a period of urbanization, legislative districts in urban areas tended to have increasingly more voters in them than did rural districts. Could an urban voter challenge the failure to reapportion as unconstitutionally diluting her voting power in the state legislature? One obvious problem with this type of challenge is finding some constitutional provision to serve as its basis. To be sure, as with any governmental allocation of benefits, the Equal Protection Clause can be invoked to challenge this distribution of legislative seats. Unless something more than rational-basis review can be invoked, however, the failure to reapportion would survive traditional equal protection review, since it is probably "rational" for a legislature to accord increased political power to rural residents (for example, to offset the inherent power of urban economic centers). Another textual basis for the challenge might be the Guarantee Clause, Art. IV, § 4, which provides that "[t]he United States shall guarantee to every State in this Union a Republican Form of Government." A severely malapportioned legislature might not seem "republican." A problem with this theory is, however, that under longstanding precedent the Court has held that issues under the Guarantee Clause are nonjusticiable "political questions." See *Luther v. Borden*, 48 U.S. (7 How.) 1 (1849) (Chapter 9, § 1).[18] Indeed, no matter what the constitutional theory, the Court had traditionally seemed very reluctant to address malapportionment claims, considering them "political thickets" that were not amenable to judicial remedy.

All this changed with the cases brought by the NAACP Inc. Fund challenging voting practices in the South that excluded or diluted the votes of African Americans. Building on their earlier Supreme Court decisions which intruded deeply into southern voting rules, the Inc. Fund and the ACLU persuaded the Supreme Court in *Gomillion v. Lightfoot*, 364 U.S. 339 (1960), to adjudicate and invalidate a gerrymander that effectively diluted the votes of blacks in Tuskegee. Once the Court had crossed the political Rubicon in *Gomillion*, it was easier to decide *Baker v. Carr*, 369 U.S. 186 (1962) (Chapter 9, § 1), which held that allegations that a state legislature was malapportioned were justiciable and were properly conceptualized as equal protection claims. In *Gray v. Sanders*, 372 U.S. 368 (1963), the Court invoked the Equal Protection Clause to invalidate the Georgia "county unit system" used in state primary elections for statewide offices, under which a candidate who received the highest number of votes in a county received two votes for each representative the county had in the lower state legislative chamber. The winner of the primary was the candidate who received the most county unit votes. Because counties were represented in the lower state house on a basis other than population, counties with only about a third of the state's population could control the primary election outcome. *Wesberry v. Sanders*, 376 U.S. 1 (1964), struck down a Georgia statute allocating that state's districts in the federal House of Representatives under which some districts had more than twice the population of others. *Wesberry* was based upon Article I, § 2, not the Equal Protection Clause. Then came the following case.

---

[18] In *Luther v. Borden*, Chapter 9, § 1, the Court refused to decide which of two competing groups constituted the lawful government of Rhode Island, which was in a state of some insurrection. The Court thought that the Guarantee Clause contained no judicially manageable standards for determining whether a government was republican and suggested that the clause was enforceable only by the Congress or the President.

REYNOLDS V. SIMS
377 U.S. 533, 84 S.Ct. 1362, 12 L.Ed.2d 506 (1964)

CHIEF JUSTICE WARREN delivered the opinion of the Court.

[Notwithstanding provisions in the Alabama Constitution requiring the state legislature to reapportion its seats in response to the federal census taken every ten years, the last reapportionment of the legislature apparently was based on the 1900 census. Since 1900, the population of Alabama had grown substantially in urban, but not rural, areas, resulting in many more persons in urban than in rural legislative districts. "Under the existing provisions, applying 1960 census figures, only 25.1% of the State's total population resided in districts represented by a majority of the members of the Senate, and only 25.7% lived in counties which could elect a majority of the members of the House of Representatives. Population-variance ratios of up to about 41-to-1 existed in the Senate, and up to about 16-to-1 in the House. Bullock County, with a population of only 13,462, and Henry County, with a population of only 15,286, each were allocated two seats in the Alabama House, whereas Mobile County, with a population of 314,301, was given only three seats, and Jefferson County, with 634,864 people, had only seven representatives. With respect to senatorial apportionment, because the pertinent Alabama constitutional provisions had been consistently construed as prohibiting the giving of more than one Senate seat to any one county, Jefferson County, with over 600,000 people, was given only one senator, as was Lowndes County, with a 1960 population of only 15,417, and Wilcox County, with only 18,739 people."

[In a suit by residents of a large Alabama county against state officials and political party officers, the federal district court concluded that the population inequality among districts violated the Equal Protection Clause, rejected as inadequate two reapportionment plans proposed by the legislature, and developed its own reapportionment plan for the 1962 elections.]

Undeniably the Constitution of the United States protects the right of all qualified citizens to vote, in state as well as in federal elections. A consistent line of decisions by this Court in cases involving attempts to deny or restrict the right of suffrage has made this indelibly clear. [Here Chief Justice Warren cited Fifteenth Amendment cases involving racial gerrymandering or other racially exclusionary tactics and cases involving prosecutions under federal criminal statutes designed to protect the right to vote for federal elected officials or to protect against racial discrimination in voting.] And history has seen a continuing expansion of the scope of the right of suffrage in this country.[19] The right to vote freely for the candidate

---

[19] The Fifteenth, Seventeenth, Nineteenth, Twenty-third and Twenty-fourth Amendments to the Federal Constitution all involve expansions of the right of suffrage. Also relevant, in this regard, is the [voting] rights legislation enacted by Congress in 1957 and 1960.

of one's choice is of the essence of a democratic society, and any restrictions on that right strike at the heart of representative government. And the right of suffrage can be denied by a debasement or dilution of the weight of a citizen's vote just as effectively as by wholly prohibiting the free exercise of the franchise. * * *

Legislators represent people, not trees or acres. Legislators are elected by voters, not farms or cities or economic interests. As long as ours is a representative form of government, and our legislatures are those instruments of government elected directly by and directly representative of the people, the right to elect legislators in a free and unimpaired fashion is a bedrock of our political system. It could hardly be gainsaid that a constitutional claim had been asserted by an allegation that certain otherwise qualified voters had been entirely prohibited from voting for members of their state legislature. And, if a State should provide that the votes of citizens in one part of the State should be given two times, or five times, or 10 times the weight of votes of citizens in another part of the State, it could hardly be contended that the right to vote of those residing in the disfavored areas had not been effectively diluted. * * * Of course, the effect of state legislative districting schemes which give the same number of representatives to unequal numbers of constituents is identical. * * *

* * * [R]epresentative government is in essence self-government through the medium of elected representatives of the people, and each and every citizen has an inalienable right to full and effective participation in the political processes of his State's legislative bodies. Most citizens can achieve this participation only as qualified voters through the election of legislators to represent them. Full and effective participation by all citizens in state government requires, therefore, that each citizen have an equally effective voice in the election of members of his state legislature. * * *

We are told that the matter of apportioning representation in a state legislature is a complex and many-faceted one. We are advised that States can rationally consider factors other than population in apportioning legislative representation. We are admonished not to restrict the power of the States to impose differing views as to political philosophy on their citizens. We are cautioned about the dangers of entering into political thickets and mathematical quagmires. Our answer is this: a denial of constitutionally protected rights demands judicial protection; our oath and our office require no less of us. * * * Population is, of necessity, the starting point for consideration and the controlling criterion for judgment in legislative apportionment controversies. A citizen, a qualified voter, is no more nor no less so because he lives in the city or on the farm. * * * The Equal Protection Clause demands no less than substantially equal state legislative representation for all citizens, of all places as well as of all races. * * *

Since neither of the houses of the Alabama Legislature, under any of the three plans considered by the District Court, was apportioned on a population basis, we would be justified in proceeding no further. However, one of the proposed plans * * * at least superficially resembles the scheme of legislative representation followed in the Federal Congress [because each county got one representative in the state senate, while the house was apportioned on the basis of population]. * * *

* * * [We] find the federal analogy inapposite and irrelevant to state legislative districting schemes. * * * The original constitutions of 36 of our States provided that representation in both houses of the state legislatures would be based completely, or predominantly, on population. And the Founding Fathers clearly had no intention of establishing a pattern or model for the apportionment of seats in state legislatures when the system of representation in the Federal Congress was adopted. Demonstrative of this is the fact that the Northwest Ordinance, adopted in the same year, 1787, as the Federal Constitution, provided for the apportionment of seats in territorial legislatures solely on the basis of population.

The system of representation in the two Houses of the Federal Congress is one ingrained in our Constitution, as part of the law of the land. It is one conceived out of compromise and concession indispensable to the establishment of our federal republic. Arising from unique historical circumstances, it is based on the consideration that in establishing our type of federalism a group of formerly independent States bound themselves together under one national government. * * *

* * * [N]either history alone, nor economic or other sorts of group interests, are permissible factors in attempting to justify disparities from population-based representation. Citizens, not history or economic interests, cast votes. Considerations of area alone provide an insufficient justification for deviations from the equal-population principle. Again, people, not land or trees or pastures, vote. * * *

A consideration that appears to be of more substance in justifying some deviations from population-based representation in state legislatures is that of insuring some voice to political subdivisions, as political subdivisions. * * * Local governmental entities are frequently charged with various responsibilities incident to the operation of state government. In many States much of the legislature's activity involves the enactment of so-called local legislation, directed only to the concerns of particular political subdivisions. And a State may legitimately desire to construct districts along political subdivision lines to deter the possibilities of gerrymandering. However, permitting deviations from population-based representation does not mean that each local governmental unit or political subdivision can be given separate representation, regardless of population. Carried too far, a scheme of giving at least one seat in one house to each political subdivision (for example, to each county) could easily result, in many States, in a total subversion of the equal-population principle in that legislative body. * * *

We do not consider here the difficult question of the proper remedial devices which federal courts should utilize in state legislative apportionment cases. Remedial techniques in this new and developing area of the law will probably often differ with the circumstances of the challenged apportionment and a variety of local conditions. It is enough to say now that, once a State's legislative apportionment scheme has been found to be unconstitutional, it would be the unusual case in which a court would be justified in not taking appropriate action to insure that no further elections are conducted under the invalid plan. However, under certain circumstances, such as where an impending election is imminent and a State's election machinery is already in progress, equitable considerations might justify a court in withholding the granting of immediately effective relief in a legislative apportionment case, even though the existing apportionment scheme was found invalid.

[The opinion of **JUSTICE CLARK**, concurring in the affirmance, the separate opinion of **JUSTICE STEWART**, and the dissenting opinion of **JUSTICE HARLAN** are omitted.]

NOTES ON REYNOLDS AND THE "FUNDAMENTAL RIGHT" TO VOTE

1. *Defining the Right.* How does *Reynolds* define the protection the Equal Protection Clause accords voting? Why not adopt a weaker standard, such as the one proposed in a separate opinion by Justice Stewart, who suggested that the Equal Protection Clause be read as outlawing only differences in voting strength that are not rationally defensible or that "permit the systematic frustration of the will of a majority of the electorate of the State"? After all, political influence can be asserted in many ways, not just through the ballot. Moreover, techniques such as providing that one state legislative chamber (like the federal Senate) be smaller than the other and apportioned on some basis other than population could be rational attempts to provide some insulation from the influence of faction (the dominant political currents that Madison feared might overwhelm minority rights).

Following *Wesberry*, the Court has applied the one person, one vote requirement very strictly in the context of apportionment of the House of Representatives, relying upon Article I, § 2, cl. 1. See *Karcher v. Daggett*, 462 U.S. 725 (1983) (invalidating apportionment that had a maximum population deviation of only .7%). The Court has been considerably more flexible under *Reynolds* in reviewing the apportionment of state and local legislative bodies, allowing political subdivision lines and other factors to influence apportionment to some extent. Although generalizations are not simple to construct, it appears that the Court will uphold state and local apportionment plans that contain less than 10% maximum population deviation among districts. For a particularly lenient decision, see *Brown v. Thomson*, 462 U.S. 835 (1983).

2. *History.* In *Reynolds*, Justice Harlan in dissent contended that the Framers of the Fourteenth Amendment did not intend the Equal Protection Clause to be applied to voting.[20] Indeed, the constitutional text itself raises some hard questions about *Reynolds*. Why would the Framers of the Fourteenth Amendment have included § 2 of the Fourteenth Amendment if, as *Reynolds* suggests, the Equal Protection Clause in § 1 outlaws discrimination in voting? Moreover, why adopt the Fifteenth Amendment shortly thereafter if the Equal Protection Clause applied to voting? The legislative history of the Fourteenth Amendment also provides support for Harlan's position. Representative Bingham, a primary congressional sponsor, stated that "[t]he amendment does not give, as the second section shows, the power to Congress of regulating suffrage in the several states." Representative Garfield expressed "profound regret" that the right to vote had not been included in the Amendment, but remarked that "I am willing * * * when I cannot get all I wish to take what I can get." In introducing the Amendment in the Senate, Howard said that § 1 "does not give to either of these classes the right of voting," because voting is not one of the "privileges or immunities" secured by the Constitution but is "merely the creature of law." The conclusion that discrimination in voting rights was not covered by the Amendment seems startling today, but was consistent with the distinction drawn at the time between "political" and "civil" rights.[21] If this is a correct rendition of the original understanding, should the Court overrule *Reynolds v. Sims* (not to mention *Shaw v. Reno* and its successors, Chapter 3, § 3E)?

3. *Denial of the Vote.* In a variety of circumstances, the Supreme Court has held that the Equal Protection Clause forbids a state from denying the vote to otherwise qualified citizens. The principal cases include *Kramer v. Union Free School District*, 395 U.S. 621 (1969) (state may not limit vote in school district election only to those who own or lease taxable real property in the district or who have children enrolled in the school), and *Carrington v. Rash*, 380 U.S. 89 (1965) (state may not bar members of military service from voting in state elections). Recall also *Harper v. Virginia Board of Elections*, the poll tax case mentioned earlier in this Section.

NOTE ON POLITICAL GERRYMANDERING

In *Karcher v. Daggett*, 462 U.S. 725 (1983), the plaintiffs seeking a declaratory judgment that the New Jersey congressional districting was unconstitutional included all the Republican members of the federal House of Representatives from New Jersey. Among other arguments, they contended

---

[20] See also William Van Alstyne, *The Fourteenth Amendment, the "Right" to Vote, and the Understanding of the Thirty-ninth Congress*, 1965 Sup. Ct. Rev. 33.

[21] See Daniel Farber & Suzanna Sherry, *A History of the American Constitution* 310–11, 314, 365 (1990).

that "the bizarre configuration of New Jersey's Congressional districts is sufficient to demonstrate that the plan was not adopted in 'good faith.' This argument [is] a claim that the district boundaries are unconstitutional because they are the product of political gerrymandering." *Id.* (Stevens, J., concurring). Invoking the Equal Protection Clause, Justice Stevens, in a concurring opinion in *Karcher*, was willing to strike down the redistricting based solely upon the taking of partisan advantage, and to consider the noncompact shape of district configurations and "extensive deviation from established political boundaries" as evidence of illicit political gerrymandering. (Justice Powell voiced similar concerns in a separate opinion in *Karcher*.) Justice Stevens also stated:

A procedural standard * * * may also be enlightening. If the process for formulating and adopting a plan excluded divergent viewpoints, openly reflected the use of partisan criteria, and provided no explanation of the reasons for selecting one plan over another, it would seem appropriate to conclude that an adversely affected plaintiff group is entitled to have the majority explain its action. On the other hand, if neutral decisionmakers developed the plan on the basis of neutral criteria, if there was an adequate opportunity for the presentation and consideration of differing points of view, and if the guidelines used in selecting a plan were explained, a strong presumption of validity should attach to whatever plan such a process produced. * * *

A glance at the [districting] map * * * shows district configurations well deserving the kind of descriptive adjectives— "uncouth" and "bizarre"—that have traditionally been used to describe acknowledged gerrymanders. * * * In addition [to] disregarding geographical compactness, the redistricting scheme wantonly disregards county boundaries. For example, in the words of a commentator: "In a flight of cartographic fancy, the Legislature packed New Jersey Republicans into a new district many call 'the Swan.' Its long neck and twisted body stretch from the New York suburbs to the rural upper reaches of the Delaware River." That district, the Fifth, contains segments of at least seven counties. The same commentator described the Seventh District, comprised of parts of five counties, as tracing "a curving partisan path through industrial Elizabeth, liberal, academic Princeton and largely Jewish Marlboro in Monmouth County. The resulting monstrosity was called 'the Fishhook' by detractors." 40 Cong.Q. 1193–1195 (1982).

Such a map prompts an inquiry into the process that led to its adoption. The plan was sponsored by the leadership in the Democratic Party, which controlled both houses of the state legislature as well as the Governor's office, and was signed into law the day before the inauguration of a Republican Governor. The legislators never formally explained the guidelines used in formulating their plan or in selecting it over other available plans. Several [other plans] contained districts that were more nearly equal in population, more compact, and more consistent with subdivision boundaries. * * * [T]he record indicates that the decisionmaking process leading to adoption of the challenged plan was far from neutral. It was designed to increase the number of Democrats, and to decrease the number of Republicans, that New Jersey's voters would send to Congress in future years.

Should this amount to a violation of Article I, § 2 of the Equal Protection Clause? Cf. *Davis v. Bandemer*, 478 U.S. 109 (1986); Samuel Issacharoff, *Judging Politics: The Elusive Quest for Judicial Review of Political Fairness*, 71 Tex. L. Rev. 1643 (1993).

Since *Karcher*, the Court has been asked repeatedly to rule on the constitutionality of political gerrymandering, but has continued to issue rulings that avoid the core question. In *Vieth v. Jubelirer*, 541 U.S. 267 (2004), four members of the Court agreed that such claims are nonjusticiable, but there was no majority opinion. In *League of United Latin American Citizens v. Perry*, 548 U.S. 399 (2006), the Court again left the justiciability question unresolved. Even as objections to political gerrymandering have grown more heated in recent years, the Court's pattern of avoiding the difficult questions continued. In 2018, the Court decided two cases that offered the opportunity to determine whether political gerrymandering is subject to meaningful judicial review and, if it is, to identify the governing standard. In neither case did the Court do so. Instead, both cases were decided on procedural questions. See *Gill v. Whitford*, ___ U.S. ___, 138 S.Ct. 1916 (2018) (remanding for determination whether plaintiffs have standing under principles identified in opinion); *Benisek v. Lamone*, ___ U.S. ___, 138 S.Ct. 1942 (2018) (affirming lower court ruling that had declined to preliminarily enjoin the disputed map). Shortly before this edition of the casebook went to press, *Benisek*, which involves a Maryland district, came back to the Supreme Court, 586 U.S. ___ (No. 18-726, Jan. 4, 2019), along with *Rucho v. Common Cause*, 586 U.S. ___ (No. 18-422 Jan. 4, 2019), a case challenging districts drawn in North Carolina. The Court accepted these cases for review and will have yet another opportunity to decide whether partisan gerrymandering claims are justiciable.

With the Court's repeated side-stepping of the issue, action by the states has filled the vacuum in some cases. In a significant ruling in 2018, for example, Pennsylvania's high court ruled that congressional districts drawn by the state legislature violated the state constitution, and the Supreme Court declined to review objections that the state court ruling offended the federal Constitution. *League of Women Voters v. Commonwealth of Pennsylvania*, 175 A.3d 282 (Pa. 2018), cert. denied *Turzai v. Brandt*, ___ U.S. ___, 139 S.Ct. 445 (2018). The Pennsylvania court ruled that the state legislature's congressional redistricting plan deprived voters of their state constitutional right to free and equal elections. Because Pennsylvania often figures prominently in elections for the presidency and control of Congress, this ruling attracted substantial public attention. But the state's court is not alone in addressing redistricting issues. In recent years, there has been increased engagement by state courts on these issues, and some scholars have argued that state court enforcement of state constitutional provisions have an important role to play here. See, e.g., Christopher S. Elmendorf, *From Educational Adequacy to Representational Adequacy: A New Template for Legal Attacks on Partisan Gerrymanders*, 59 Wm. & Mary L. Rev. 1601, 1675–79 (2018); James A. Gardner, *Foreword: Representation Without Party: Lessons From State Constitutional Attempts to Control Gerrymandering*, 27 Rutgers L. Rev. 881, 970 (2006) (noting limited record of success on some theories, but suggesting availability of state constitutional "provisions that might be understood to constitutionalize principles of equality, fair representation, or fair politics").[22] There are a range of unanswered questions about the role for state courts, including about regulating elections of federal officials. But if the Supreme Court were to conclusively rule partisan gerrymandering claims non-justiciable, calls for state courts to fill the void might accelerate.

One other mechanism some states have used to control political gerrymandering is the creation of independent commissions to handle redistricting. The voters in Arizona pursued this course in 2000 by passing a state constitutional amendment that reallocated authority from the state legislature to the Arizona Independent Redistricting Commission. The state legislature challenged this measure as a violation of the Elections Clause, Art. I, § 4, cl. 1, which provides that the "Times, Places and Manner of holding Elections for Senators and Representatives shall be prescribed in each State by the *Legislature* thereof." (emphasis added). In *Arizona State Legislature v. Arizona Independent Redistricting Comm'n*, ___ U.S. ___, 135 S.Ct. 2652 (2015), the Court by a 5–4 majority rejected this challenge. The case turned on how to interpret the word "legislature" in the Clause. Justice Ginsburg's opinion for the Court reasoned that when the legislative power of a state is given by state constitution to the people, acting through the initiative process, they constitute the "legislature" for purposes of the Elections Clause. The opinion emphasized the norm of self-government (noting that direct democracy is consistent with the idea of popular sovereignty that underlies the Constitution's creation of republican government) and the policy consequences that would flow from a contrary ruling (noting that many election-related laws passed directly by voters around the country would be jeopardized). In a vigorous dissent, Chief Justice Roberts argued that Senators were chosen by state legislatures, not popular vote, under the original Constitution. If judges could legitimately read the word legislature in the Elections Clause to include the people acting in a legislative capacity, he suggested, there would have been no need for the Seventeenth Amendment because even a change as consequential as popular election of Senators could have been accomplished by an act of simple judicial interpretation. With more states adopting independent redistricting commissions by ballot measure, it bears watching whether the

---

[22] Elmendorf notes parallels between gerrymandering and educational finance litigation, such as concerns about judicial manageability and the presence of more specifically relevant text in the state than the federal constitution. As you will see in section 3.B of this chapter, the Supreme Court's reluctance to address interdistrict disparities in education funding as a matter of federal constitutional concern was followed by state courts stepping into the arena and becoming the primary forum for litigation.

changes in membership on the Court since 2015 might bring more support for the Chief Justice's view.

BUSH V. GORE
531 U.S. 98, 121 S.Ct. 525, 148 L.E.2d 388 (2000)

PER CURIAM.

[This case arose out of the hotly contested election of 2000. Al Gore emerged with a slight lead in the national popular vote, but the electoral college vote depended on Florida, where George W. Bush had a razor-thin margin on the initial count (about 1,700 votes out of roughly six million cast). Because Bush's margin was less than .5%, an automatic machine recount was conducted, which showed Bush still winning but by a smaller margin. Pursuant to Florida law, Gore then demanded manual recounts in four counties. A dispute arose about the deadline for local canvassing boards to submit their returns to the Secretary of State. The Florida Supreme Court overturned the Secretary's refusal to extend the deadline, but the U.S. Supreme Court remanded that decision for further consideration. Since Article II, § 1, cl. 2 requires presidential electors to be selected in "such Manner as the [state legislature] may direct," the Court sought further clarification on whether the Florida court's decision was based on ordinary principles of construing state statutes adopted by the legislature or, instead, was based on the state constitution's guarantee of the right to vote. In the meantime, the Florida court's new deadline had expired, and the state electoral commission had declared Bush the victor. Gore then filed a state court complaint, pursuant to a state statute providing that "[r]eceipt of a number of illegal votes or rejection of a number of legal votes sufficient to change or place in doubt the result of the election" is grounds for contesting the result. In response, the Florida Supreme Court ordered a statewide manual recount under the supervision of a single trial judge. To complicate matters further, a federal statute purported to give a presumption of validity to the state's electors if the state finally determined the validity of its returns by December 12. The Supreme Court stayed the Florida decision on December 9 by a 5–4 vote.]

The individual citizen has no federal constitutional right to vote for electors for the President of the United States unless and until the state legislature chooses a statewide election as the means to implement its power to appoint members of the electoral college. U.S. Const., Art. II, § 1. This is the source for the statement in *McPherson v. Blacker,* 146 U.S. 1 (1892), that the State legislature's power to select the manner for appointing electors is plenary; it may, if it so chooses, select the electors itself, which indeed was the manner used by state legislatures in several States for many years after the framing of our Constitution. History has now favored the voter, and in each of the several States the citizens themselves vote for Presidential electors. When the state legislature vests the right to vote for President in its people, the right to vote as the legislature has prescribed is fundamental; and one source of its fundamental nature lies in the equal weight accorded to each vote and the equal dignity owed to each voter. The State, of course, after granting the franchise in the special context of Article II, can take back the power to appoint electors. See *id.* ("[T]here is no doubt of the right of the legislature to resume the power at any time, for it can neither be taken away nor abdicated").

The right to vote is protected in more than the initial allocation of the franchise. Equal protection applies as well to the manner of its exercise. Having once granted the right to vote on equal terms, the State may not, by later arbitrary and disparate treatment, value one person's vote over that of another. It must be remembered that "the right of suffrage can be denied by a debasement or dilution of the weight of a citizen's vote just as effectively as by wholly prohibiting the free exercise of the franchise." *Reynolds v. Sims.*

There is no difference between the two sides of the present controversy on these basic propositions. Respondents say that the very purpose of vindicating the right to vote justifies the recount procedures now at issue. The question before us, however, is whether the recount procedures the Florida Supreme Court has adopted are consistent with its obligation to avoid arbitrary and disparate treatment of the members of its electorate.

Much of the controversy seems to revolve around ballot cards designed to be perforated by a stylus but which, either through error or deliberate omission, have not been perforated with sufficient precision for a machine to register the perforations. In some cases a piece of the card—a chad—is hanging, say, by two corners. In other cases there is no separation at all, just an indentation.

The Florida Supreme Court has ordered that the intent of the voter be discerned from such ballots. For purposes of resolving the equal protection challenge, it is not necessary to decide whether the Florida Supreme Court had the authority under the legislative scheme for resolving election disputes to define what a legal vote is and to mandate a manual recount implementing that definition. The recount mechanisms implemented in response to the decisions of the Florida Supreme Court do not satisfy the minimum requirement for nonarbitrary treatment of voters necessary to secure the fundamental right. Florida's basic command for the count of legally cast votes is to consider the "intent of the voter." This is unobjectionable as an abstract proposition and a starting principle. The problem inheres in the absence of specific standards to ensure its equal application. The formulation of uniform rules to determine intent based on these recurring circumstances is practicable and, we conclude, necessary.

The law does not refrain from searching for the intent of the actor in a multitude of circumstances; and in some cases the general command to ascertain intent is not susceptible to much further refinement. In this instance, however, the question is not whether to believe a witness but how to interpret the marks or holes or scratches on an inanimate object, a piece of cardboard or paper which, it is said, might not have registered as a vote during the machine count. The factfinder confronts a thing, not a person. The search for intent can be confined by specific rules designed to ensure uniform treatment.

The want of those rules here has led to unequal evaluation of ballots in various respects. As seems to have been acknowledged at oral argument, the standards for accepting or rejecting contested ballots might vary not only from county to county but indeed within a single county from one recount team to another. * * *

The recount process, in its features here described, is inconsistent with the minimum procedures necessary to protect the fundamental right of each voter in the special instance of a statewide recount under the authority of a single state judicial officer. Our consideration is limited to the present circumstances, for the problem of equal protection in election processes generally presents many complexities.

The question before the Court is not whether local entities, in the exercise of their expertise, may develop different systems for implementing elections. Instead, we are presented with a situation where a state court with the power to assure uniformity has ordered a statewide recount with minimal procedural safeguards. When a court orders a statewide remedy, there must be at least some assurance that the rudimentary requirements of equal treatment and fundamental fairness are satisfied. * * *

The Supreme Court of Florida has said that the legislature intended the State's electors to "participat[e] fully in the federal electoral process," as provided in 3 U.S.C. § 5. That statute, in turn, requires that any controversy or contest that is designed to lead to a conclusive selection of electors be completed by December 12. That date is upon us, and there is no recount procedure in place under the State Supreme Court's order that comports with minimal constitutional standards. Because it is evident that any recount seeking to meet the December 12 date will be unconstitutional for the reasons we have discussed, we reverse the judgment of the Supreme Court of Florida ordering a recount to proceed.

Seven Justices of the Court agree that there are constitutional problems with the recount ordered by the Florida Supreme Court that demand a remedy [citing the dissents by Justices Souter and Breyer, agreeing that the Florida procedure raised equal protection concerns.] The only disagreement is as to the remedy. Because the Florida Supreme Court has said that the Florida Legislature intended to obtain the safe-harbor benefits of 3 U.S.C. § 5, Justice Breyer's proposed remedy—remanding to the Florida Supreme Court for its ordering of a constitutionally proper contest until December 18—contemplates action in violation of the Florida Election Code, and hence could not be part of an "appropriate" order authorized by Fla. Stat. § 102.168(8) (2000). [The majority concluded that remand would not be appropriate.]

None are more conscious of the vital limits on judicial authority than are the Members of this Court, and none stand more in admiration of the Constitution's design to leave the selection of the President to the people, through their legislatures, and to the political sphere. When contending parties invoke the process of the courts, however, it becomes our unsought responsibility to resolve the federal and constitutional issues the judicial system has been forced to confront.

[CHIEF JUSTICE REHNQUIST, joined by JUSTICES SCALIA and THOMAS, concurred on the ground that the Florida Supreme Court had so blatantly misapplied Florida election law as to violate the mandate of Article II that the election be conducted in the manner dictated by the state legislature.]

JUSTICE STEVENS, with whom JUSTICE GINSBURG and JUSTICE BREYER join, dissenting.

The Constitution assigns to the States the primary responsibility for determining the manner of selecting the Presidential electors. See Art. II, § 1, cl. 2. When questions arise about the meaning of state laws, including election laws, it is our settled practice to accept the opinions of the highest courts of the States as providing the final answers. On rare occasions, however, either federal statutes or the Federal Constitution may require federal judicial intervention in state elections. This is not such an occasion. * * *

Nor are petitioners correct in asserting that the failure of the Florida Supreme Court to specify in detail the precise manner in which the "intent of the voter" is to be determined rises to the level of a constitutional violation. We found such a violation when individual votes within the same State were weighted unequally, but we have never before called into question the substantive standard by which a State determines that a vote has been legally cast. And there is no reason to think that the guidance provided to the factfinders, specifically the various canvassing boards, by the "intent of the voter" standard is any less sufficient—or will lead to results any less uniform—than, for example, the "beyond a reasonable doubt" standard employed every day by ordinary citizens in courtrooms across this country.

Admittedly, the use of differing substandards for determining voter intent in different counties employing similar voting systems may raise serious concerns. Those concerns are alleviated—if not eliminated—by the fact that a single impartial magistrate will ultimately adjudicate all objections arising from the recount process. Of course, as a general matter, "[t]he interpretation of constitutional principles must not be too literal. We must remember that the machinery of government would not work if it were not allowed a little play in its joints." If it were otherwise, Florida's decision to leave to each county the determination of what balloting system to employ—despite enormous differences in accuracy—might run afoul of equal protection. So, too, might the similar decisions of the vast majority of state legislatures to delegate to local authorities certain decisions with respect to voting systems and ballot design.

Even assuming that aspects of the remedial scheme might ultimately be found to violate the Equal Protection Clause, I could not subscribe to the majority's disposition of the case. As the majority explicitly holds, once a state legislature determines to select electors through a popular vote, the right to have one's vote counted is of constitutional stature. As the majority further acknowledges, Florida law holds that all ballots that reveal the intent of the voter constitute valid votes. Recognizing these principles, the majority nonetheless orders the termination of the contest proceeding before all such votes have been tabulated. Under their own reasoning, the appropriate course of action would be to remand to allow more specific procedures for implementing the legislature's uniform general standard to be established. * * *

What must underlie petitioners' entire federal assault on the Florida election procedures is an unstated lack of confidence in the impartiality and capacity of the state judges who would make the critical decisions if the vote count were to proceed. Otherwise, their position is wholly without merit. The endorsement of that position by the majority of this Court can only lend credence to the most cynical appraisal of the work of judges throughout the land. It is confidence in the men and women who administer the judicial system that is the true backbone of the rule of law. Time will one day heal the wound to that confidence that will be inflicted by today's decision. One thing, however, is certain. Although we may never know with complete certainty the identity of the winner of this year's Presidential election, the identity of the loser is perfectly clear. It is the Nation's confidence in the judge as an impartial guardian of the rule of law.

[Dissenting opinions by JUSTICES GINSBURG, SOUTER, and BREYER are omitted.]

NOTES ON BUSH V. GORE

1. *The Equality/Substantive Right Distinction. Bush* dramatically illustrates the difference between a substantive claim and an equality claim. Because the right to vote for President is fundamental only for equality purposes, completely abolishing the right—either for all voters, or merely for those whose ballots were poorly marked—would seem to raise no federal

constitutional problem. (Recall that the President is formally elected by the Electoral College, and electors are chosen in such manner as the state legislatures provide.) But using different methods in different counties to decipher poorly marked ballots raises an equality issue. Thus, it would seem, by mandating that none of the votes be counted unless all can be counted alike, the Court vindicates the fundamental right to vote. That, at least, is the theory of the opinion.

2.   *Political and Jurisprudential Implications. Bush v. Gore* produced some of the strongest popular and scholarly reaction to a Supreme Court decision in many years. For a sampling of academic views, see Bush v. Gore: *The Question of Legitimacy* (Bruce Ackerman ed. 2002); *A Badly Flawed Election: Debating* Bush v. Gore, *the Supreme Court, and American Democracy* (Ronald Dworkin ed. 2002); Richard Posner, *Breaking the Deadlock: The 2000 Election, the Constitution, and the Courts* (2001); *The Vote: Bush, Gore, and the Supreme Court* (Cass Sunstein & Richard Epstein eds. 2001); Jack Balkin, Bush v. Gore *and the Boundary Between Law and Politics*, 110 Yale L.J. 1407 (2001); Jesse Choper, *Why the Supreme Court Should Not Have Decided the Presidential Election of 2000*, 18 Const. Comm. 335 (2002); Symposium, *The Law of Presidential Elections: Issues in the Wake of Florida 2000*, 29 Fla. State U. L. Rev. (2001). (Comprehensive background on the case can be found in Samuel Issacharoff, Pamela Karlan & Richard Pildes, *When Elections Go Bad: The Law of Democracy and the Presidential Election of 2000* (2001).) Defenders of the Court tend to proclaim that the Florida vote-counting process had become unconscionably arbitrary or biased and that the Court properly stepped in to end what was becoming a national political catastrophe. Opponents argue, among other things, that the Court should have remanded the case so that the Florida trial court could have attempted to achieve compliance with the new requirements. More broadly, opponents tend to condemn the Court for taking the issue away from the political process (a contested election would have been resolved in the U.S. House of Representatives) on flimsy doctrinal grounds and writing an opinion seemingly designed to apply to no other situation. Opponents also note the irony that the five Justices in the majority that deprived the Florida courts of authority are the five Justices who routinely vote to limit federal intrusions into state affairs (see Chapter 7). One response to such complaints might be to say that *Bush v. Gore* is simply the same sort of activism as *Roe v. Wade*, just to different political and social ends.

Crawford v. Marion County Election Bd.

553 U.S. 181 (2008)

A coalition of plaintiffs challenged an Indiana law, which had passed on a party-line vote in the state legislature, that required persons seeking to vote to present a government-issued photo identification. **Justice Stevens**, joined by **Chief Justice Roberts** and **Justice Kennedy**, concluded that the law was not susceptible to a facial challenge. Stevens applied a balancing test and concluded that the statute was facially justified by the state's interest in preventing voter fraud and instilling confidence in the electoral process. The Stevens opinion left open the possibility that a narrower attack on the statute's application to specific groups might be sustainable on a different factual record.

Justice Scalia, joined by **Justices Thomas** and **Alito**, maintained that "weighing the burden of a nondiscriminatory voting law upon each voter and concomitantly requiring exceptions for vulnerable voters would effectively turn back decades of equal-protection jurisprudence. A voter complaining about such a law's effect on him has no valid equal-protection claim because, without proof of discriminatory intent, a generally applicable law with disparate impact is not unconstitutional." Justice Scalia continued:

> * * * This is an area where the dos and don'ts need to be known in advance of the election, and voter-by-voter examination of the burdens of voting regulations would prove especially disruptive. A case-by-case approach naturally encourages constant litigation. Very few new election regulations improve everyone's lot, so the potential allegations of severe burden are endless. * * *

> That sort of detailed judicial supervision of the election process would flout the Constitution's express commitment of the task to the States. See Art. I, § 4. It is for state legislatures to weigh the costs and benefits of possible changes to their election codes, and their judgment must prevail unless it imposes a severe and unjustified overall burden upon the right to vote, or is intended to disadvantage a particular class. Judicial review of their handiwork must apply an objective, uniform standard that will enable them to determine, *ex ante*, whether the burden they impose is too severe.

Justice Souter, joined by **Justice Ginsburg**, dissented. Justice Souter maintained that the statute failed the balancing test because it "threatens to impose nontrivial burdens on the voting right of tens of thousands of the State's citizens, and a significant percentage of those individuals are likely to be deterred from voting." **Justice Breyer** also dissented. Curiously, none of the opinions in the case cited *Bush v. Gore*, which seems to have had little or no precedential impact.

Lawsuits about the legality of voter identification have proliferated since *Crawford*. This spate of litigation is, at least in part, attributable to the Court's decision five years later in *Shelby County v. Holder*, 570 U.S. 529 (2013) (Chapter 7). *Shelby County* struck down the formula used to determine which jurisdictions need federal preclearance to make voting law changes. The effect of that ruling was to free jurisdictions with problematic voting rights histories to enact new voter identification rules, as well as other voting law changes, without getting the advance authorization from the federal government that once was required. The Supreme Court has not revisited the issue addressed in *Crawford*, and lower courts have divided on constitutional challenges, as well as claims that voter identification rules violate section 2 of the Voting

Rights Act. For a collection of cases litigating the legality of voter identification laws, see https://moritzlaw.osu.edu/electionlaw/litigation/index.

B. BASIC RIGHTS FOR THE LEAST ADVANTAGED

Once the NAACP's Inc. Fund had substantially won its campaign against apartheid, its focus shifted from policies discriminating on the basis of race to those having racially disproportionate effects. A big variable correlating with race was poverty; state policies shortchanging the poor typically harmed Latinos and African Americans the most. Progressive attorneys in the Inc. Fund, ACLU, and other public interest groups brought lawsuits to recognize rights of poor people—including "welfare rights," a minimal standard of living for all Americans.[23] In 1970, the welfare rights movement won a surprising victory in *Goldberg v. Kelly* (§ 6A of this chapter), which held that welfare recipients have a constitutional entitlement that cannot be taken away without notice and a right to be heard. *Goldberg*, however, was the movement's high-water point. Once all four Nixon Justices were in place, the Court trimmed back welfare rights, rejecting claims that state welfare programs discriminated against certain kinds of poor families. See *Dandridge v. Williams*, 397 U.S. 471 (1970) (rejecting challenge to Maryland's policy of capping family grants regardless of family size); *Jefferson v. Hackney*, 406 U.S. 535 (1972) (rejecting challenge to Texas's policy of underfunding family grants, which had a hugely disproportionate effect on Latino and African American welfare recipients). Confirming that the Court was closing the doors to at least most challenges to state policies hurting the poor, the Burger Court applied those precedents to the field of education in the following case. Was there a limit to what states could do?

SAN ANTONIO INDEPENDENT SCHOOL DISTRICT V. RODRIGUEZ

411 U.S. 1, 93 S.Ct. 1278, 36 L.Ed.2d 16 (1973)

JUSTICE POWELL delivered the opinion of the Court.

[In this suit attacking the Texas system of financing public education, Mexican-American parents whose children attended schools in the Edgewood Independent School District in San Antonio brought a class action on behalf of schoolchildren throughout the State who are members of minority groups or who are poor and live in school districts having a low property tax base.]

---

[23] See generally Martha Davis, *Brutal Need: Lawyers and the Welfare Rights Movement, 1960–1973* (1994); Elizabeth Bussiere, *(Dis)Entitling the Poor: The Warren Court, Welfare Rights, and the American Political Tradition* (1997); Shep Melnick, *Between the Lines: Interpreting Welfare Rights* (1994).

[Edgewood District] has been compared throughout this litigation with the Alamo Heights Independent School District[, a] comparison between the least and most affluent districts in the San Antonio area [that] serves to illustrate the manner in which the dual system of finance operates and to indicate the extent to which substantial disparities exist despite the State's impressive progress in recent years. Edgewood is one of seven public school districts in the metropolitan area. Approximately 22,000 students are enrolled in its 25 elementary and secondary schools. The district is situated in the core-city sector of San Antonio in a residential neighborhood that has little commercial or industrial property. The residents are predominantly of Mexican-American descent: approximately 90% of the student population is Mexican-American and over 6% is Negro. The average assessed property value per pupil is $5,960—the lowest in the metropolitan area—and the median family income ($4,686) is also the lowest. At an equalized tax rate of $1.05 per $100 of assessed property— the highest in the metropolitan area—the district contributed $26 to the education of each child for the 1967–1968 school year above its Local Fund Assignment for the [Texas State] Minimum Foundation Program. The Foundation Program contributed $222 per pupil for a state-local total of $248. Federal funds added another $108 for a total of $356 per pupil.

Alamo Heights is the most affluent school district in San Antonio. Its six schools, housing approximately 5,000 students, are situated in a residential community quite unlike the Edgewood District. The school population is predominantly "Anglo," having only 18% Mexican-Americans and less than 1% Negroes. The assessed property value per pupil exceeds $49,000, and the median family income is $8,001. In 1967–1968 the local tax rate of $.85 per $100 of valuation yielded $333 per pupil over and above its contribution to the Foundation Program. Coupled with the $225 provided from that Program, the district was able to supply $558 per student. Supplemented by a $36 per-pupil grant from federal sources, Alamo Heights spent $594 per pupil. * * *

* * * [Substantial interdistrict] disparities, largely attributable to differences in the amounts of money collected through local property taxation, * * * led the District Court to conclude that Texas' dual system of public school financing violated the Equal Protection Clause. * * * Finding that wealth is a "suspect" classification and that education is a "fundamental" interest, the District Court held that the Texas system could be sustained only if the State could show that it was premised upon some compelling state interest. On this issue the court concluded that "[n]ot only are defendants unable to demonstrate compelling state interests * * * they fail even to establish a reasonable basis for these classifications."

[The Court rejected the wealth-discrimination argument for two reasons: "First, in support of their charge that the system discriminates against the 'poor,' appellees have made no effort to demonstrate that it operates to the peculiar disadvantage of any class fairly definable as indigent, or as composed of persons whose incomes are beneath any designated poverty level. Indeed, there is reason to believe that the poorest families are not necessarily clustered in the poorest property districts." And second: "The argument here is not that the children in districts having relatively low assessable property values are receiving no public education; rather, it is that they are receiving a poorer quality education than that available to children in districts having more assessable wealth. Apart from the unsettled and disputed question whether the quality of education may be determined by the amount of money expended for it, a sufficient answer to appellees' argument is that, at least where wealth is involved, the Equal Protection Clause does not require absolute equality or precisely equal advantages."]

In *Brown v. Board of Education*, a unanimous Court recognized that "education is perhaps the most important function of state and local governments." * * *

Nothing this Court holds today in any way detracts from our historic dedication to public education. We are in complete agreement with the conclusion of the three-judge panel below that "the grave significance of education both to the individual and to our society" cannot be doubted. But the importance of a service performed by the State does not determine whether it must be regarded as fundamental for purposes of examination under the Equal Protection Clause. Mr. Justice Harlan, dissenting from the Court's application of strict scrutiny to a law impinging upon the right of interstate travel, admonished that "[v]irtually every state statute affects important rights." *Shapiro v. Thompson*[, 394 U.S. 618 (1969)] (Harlan, J., dissenting). In his view, if the degree of judicial scrutiny of state legislation fluctuated, depending on a majority's view of the importance of the interest affected, we would have gone "far toward making this Court a ' "super-legislature.' " We would, indeed, then be assuming a legislative role and one for which the Court lacks both authority and competence. * * *

The lesson of these cases in addressing the question now before the Court is plain. It is not the province of this Court to create substantive constitutional rights in the name of guaranteeing equal protection of the laws. Thus, the key to discovering whether education is "fundamental" is not to be found in comparisons of the relative societal significance of education as opposed to subsistence or housing. Nor is it to be found by weighing whether education is as important as the right to travel. Rather, the answer lies in assessing whether there is a right to education explicitly or implicitly guaranteed by the Constitution. * * * *Dunn v. Blumstein*, 405 U.S. 330 (1972);[24] * * * *Skinner v. Oklahoma*.[25]

Education, of course, is not among the rights afforded explicit protection under our Federal Constitution. Nor do we find any basis for saying it is implicitly so protected. * * * It is appellees' contention, however, that education is distinguishable from other services and benefits provided by the State because it bears a peculiarly close relationship to other rights and liberties accorded protection under the Constitution. Specifically, they insist that education is itself a fundamental personal right because it is essential to the effective exercise of First Amendment freedoms and to intelligent utilization of the right to vote. In asserting a nexus between speech and education, appellees urge that the right to speak is meaningless unless the speaker is capable of articulating his thoughts intelligently and persuasively. The "marketplace of ideas" is an empty forum for those lacking basic communicative tools. Likewise, they argue that the corollary right to receive information becomes little more than a hollow privilege when the recipient has not been taught to read, assimilate, and utilize available knowledge.

A similar line of reasoning is pursued with respect to the right to vote. Exercise of the franchise, it is contended, cannot be divorced from the educational foundation of the voter. The electoral process, if reality is to conform to the democratic ideal, depends on an informed electorate * * *.

* * * [W]e have never presumed to possess either the ability or the authority to guarantee to the citizenry the most *effective* speech or the most *informed* electoral choice. That these may be desirable goals of a system of freedom of expression and of a representative form of government is not to be doubted. * * * But they are not values to be implemented by judicial intrusion into otherwise legitimate state activities.

Even if it were conceded that some identifiable quantum of education is a constitutionally protected prerequisite to the meaningful exercise of either right, we have no indication that the present levels of educational expenditures in Texas provide an education that falls short. * * * Whatever merit appellees' argument might have if a State's financing system occasioned an absolute denial of educational opportunities to any of its children, that argument provides no basis for finding an interference with fundamental rights where only relative differences in spending levels are involved and where—as is true in the present case—no charge fairly could

---

[24] *Dunn* fully canvasses this Court's voting rights cases and explains that "this Court has made clear that a citizen has a *constitutionally protected right* to participate in elections on an equal basis with other citizens in the jurisdiction." (Emphasis supplied.)

[25] *Skinner* applied the standard of close scrutiny to a state law permitting forced sterilization of "habitual criminals." Implicit in the Court's opinion is the recognition that the right of procreation is among the rights of personal privacy protected under the Constitution. See *Roe v. Wade*, 410 U.S. 113 (1973).

be made that the system fails to provide each child with an opportunity to acquire the basic minimal skills necessary for the enjoyment of the rights of speech and of full participation in the political process.

[The concurring opinion of **JUSTICE STEWART**, the dissenting opinion of **JUSTICE BRENNAN**, and the dissenting opinion of **JUSTICE WHITE**, joined by **JUSTICES DOUGLAS** and **BRENNAN**, are omitted.]

JUSTICE MARSHALL, joined by **JUSTICE DOUGLAS**, dissenting.

The Court apparently seeks to establish today that equal protection cases fall into one of two neat categories which dictate the appropriate standard of review—strict scrutiny or mere rationality. But this Court's decisions in the field of equal protection defy such easy categorization. A principled reading of what this Court has done reveals that it has applied a spectrum of standards in reviewing discrimination allegedly violative of the Equal Protection Clause. This spectrum clearly comprehends variations in the degree of care with which the Court will scrutinize particular classifications, depending, I believe, on the constitutional and societal importance of the interest adversely affected and the recognized invidiousness of the basis upon which the particular classification is drawn. I find in fact that many of the Court's recent decisions embody the very sort of reasoned approach to equal protection analysis for which I previously argued—that is, an approach in which "concentration [is] placed upon the character of the classification in question, the relative importance to individuals in the class discriminated against of the governmental benefits that they do not receive, and the asserted state interests in support of the classification." *Dandridge* ([Marshall's] dissenting opinion).

I therefore cannot accept the majority's labored efforts to demonstrate that fundamental interests, which call for strict scrutiny of the challenged classification, encompass only established rights which we are somehow bound to recognize from the text of the Constitution itself. To be sure, some interests which the Court has deemed to be fundamental for purposes of equal protection analysis are themselves constitutionally protected rights. Thus, discrimination against the guaranteed right of freedom of speech has called for strict judicial scrutiny. See *Police Dept. of Chicago v. Mosley*, 408 U.S. 92 (1972). Further, every citizen's right to travel interstate, although nowhere expressly mentioned in the Constitution, has long been recognized as implicit in the premises underlying that document: the right "was conceived from the beginning to be a necessary concomitant of the stronger Union the Constitution created." *United States v. Guest*, 383 U.S. 745, 758 (1966). * * * But it will not do to suggest that the "answer" to whether an interest is fundamental for purposes of equal protection analysis is always determined by whether that interest "is a right . . . explicitly or implicitly guaranteed by the Constitution."

I would like to know where the Constitution guarantees the right to procreate, *Skinner*, or the right to vote in state elections, e. g., *Reynolds*, or the right to an appeal from a criminal conviction, e. g., *Griffin v. Illinois*, 351 U.S. 12 (1956). These are instances in which, due to the importance of the interests at stake, the Court has displayed a strong concern with the existence of discriminatory state treatment. But the Court has never said or indicated that these are interests which independently enjoy full-blown constitutional protection. * * *

[T]he right to vote in state elections has been recognized as a "fundamental political right," because the Court concluded very early that it is "preservative of all rights." *Yick Wo*; see also *Reynolds*. * * *

The majority is, of course, correct when it suggests that the process of determining which interests are fundamental is a difficult one. But I do not think the problem is insurmountable. And I certainly do not accept the view that the process need necessarily degenerate into an unprincipled, subjective "picking-and-choosing" between various interests or that it must involve this Court in creating "substantive constitutional rights in the name of guaranteeing equal protection of the laws." Although not all fundamental interests are constitutionally guaranteed, the determination of which interests are fundamental should be firmly rooted in the text of the Constitution. The task in every case should be to determine the extent to which constitutionally guaranteed rights are dependent on interests not mentioned in the Constitution. As the nexus between the specific constitutional guarantee and the nonconstitutional interest draws closer, the nonconstitutional interest becomes more fundamental and the degree of judicial scrutiny applied when the interest is infringed on a discriminatory basis must be adjusted accordingly. Thus, it cannot be denied that interests such as procreation, the exercise of the state franchise, and access to criminal appellate processes are not fully guaranteed to the citizen by our Constitution. But these interests have nonetheless been afforded special judicial consideration in the face of discrimination because they are, to some extent, interrelated with constitutional guarantees. Procreation is now understood to be important because of its interaction with the established constitutional right of privacy. The exercise of the state franchise is closely tied to basic civil and political rights inherent in the First Amendment. And access to criminal appellate processes enhances the integrity of the range of rights implicit in the Fourteenth Amendment guarantee of due process of law. Only if we closely protect the related interests from state discrimination do we ultimately ensure the integrity of the constitutional guarantee itself. This is the real lesson that must be taken from our previous decisions involving interests deemed to be fundamental. [Justice Marshall compared this process of analogy to the process the Court has used to determine which classifications should trigger heightened equal protection scrutiny.]

In summary, it seems to me inescapably clear that this Court has consistently adjusted the care with which it will review state discrimination in light of the constitutional significance of the interests affected and the invidiousness of the particular classification. In the context of economic interests, we find that discriminatory state action is almost always sustained, for such interests are generally far removed from constitutional guarantees. * * * But the situation differs markedly when discrimination against important individual interests with constitutional implications and against particularly disadvantaged or powerless classes is involved. The majority suggests, however, that a variable standard of review would give this Court the appearance of a "superlegislature." I cannot agree. Such an approach seems to me a part of the guarantees of our Constitution and of the historic experiences with oppression of and discrimination against discrete, powerless minorities which underlie that document.

Plyler v. Doe

457 U.S. 202 (1982)

By a 1975 amendment to state education statutes, the Texas legislature refused to provide state funds to local school districts for the education of children not "legally admitted" into the United States, and school districts were authorized to deny enrollment to such children. In several class actions brought by school-age children of Mexican descent living in Texas who could not document legal immigration status, the lower courts concluded that this statute violated the Equal Protection Clause. In an opinion by **Justice Brennan**, a sharply divided Court affirmed. Justice Brennan began with the premise that the "Equal Protection Clause was intended to work nothing less than the abolition of all caste-based and invidious class-based legislation." The Court rejected the claim that "illegal aliens" are a "suspect class" for two reasons: Illegal entry is a voluntary action, and it is not in general a "constitutional irrelevancy" (given the government's power to control access to the United States). "At the least, those who elect to enter our territory by stealth and in violation of our law should be prepared to bear the consequences, including, but not limited to, deportation." But their children are not "comparably situated," having no control over the situation; thus, the legislation violated the fundamental premise that " 'no child is responsible for his birth and penalizing the * * * child is an ineffectual—as well as unjust— way of deterring the parent' " (quoting a case involving discrimination against nonmarital children). Moreover, although public education is not a fundamental right, "neither is it merely some governmental 'benefit' indistinguishable from other forms of social welfare legislation." The statute "imposes a lifetime hardship on a discrete class of children not accountable for their disabling status," because the "stigma of illiteracy will mark them for the rest of their lives." Thus, the discrimination "can hardly be considered rational unless it furthers some substantial goal of the State." Justice Brennan found no legitimate state interest.

Two members of the *Rodriguez* majority wrote concurring opinions in *Plyler*. **Justice Blackmun** argued that classifications "involving the complete denial of education are in a sense unique, for they strike at the heart of equal protection values by involving the State in the creation of permanent class distinctions," thereby being analogous to a deprivation of the vote. **Justice Powell** agreed that a "legislative classification that threatens the creation of an underclass of future citizens and residents cannot be reconciled with one of the fundamental purposes of the Fourteenth Amendment." He found *Rodriguez* distinguishable: "in *Rodriguez* no group of children was singled out by the State and then penalized because of their parents' status," "[n]or * * * was any group of children totally deprived of all education as in these cases."

The four dissenters, led by **Chief Justice Burger**, applied a simple syllogism: "Once it is conceded—as the Court does—that illegal aliens are not a suspect class, and that education is not a fundamental right," the only issue logically was whether "the legislative classification at issue bears a rational relationship to a legitimate state purpose." Without "laboring what will undoubtedly seem obvious to many, it simply is not 'irrational' for a state to conclude that it does not have the same responsibility to provide benefits for persons whose very presence in the state and this country is illegal as it does to provide for persons lawfully present." That the majority's motives "are noble and compassionate does not alter the fact that the Court distorts our constitutional function to make amends for the defaults of others."

NOTES ON RODRIGUEZ *AND* PLYLER

1.   *Quo Vadis Fundamental Interests?* Jot down a list of "fundamental" interests that the *Rodriguez* majority would accept as justifying heightened equal protection scrutiny. Do the same for the dissenters. Which interests are on both lists? Which are only on the dissent's list?

After *Rodriguez*, one would expect the Court not to recognize more fundamental interests as a mechanism for equal protection heightened scrutiny. So, for example, even though, as we shall see, the Court recognized the right to choose an abortion as a fundamental due process right, it did not subject state medical and hospital plans to heightened scrutiny when they refused to cover abortion. See *Maher v. Roe*, 432 U.S. 464 (1977) (Medicaid programs can refuse to fund abortions); *Poelker v. Doe*, 432 U.S. 519 (1977) (per curiam) (municipal hospital could refuse to provide abortion services). On the other hand, the Court in *Zablocki v. Redhail*, 434 U.S. 374 (1978), recognized the right to marry as a fundamental right and struck down a state law barring remarriages by people with outstanding family support obligations (the proverbial deadbeat dads). Marshall wrote the opinion; Powell concurred. Is the "right to marry" any more "in" the Constitution than the right to an education? Is it more "preservative" of other rights?

2. *Rights and Remedies.* Keep in mind that the Court deciding *Rodriguez* was a Court struggling with the difficulty of judicial remediation of school segregation. Justice Blackmun spoke for all four Nixon Justices when he reportedly said in conference on *Rodriguez*, "if we affirm, federal courts will destroy the state systems; we cannot legislate equality in education." Justice Powell had been chair of the Richmond School Board and was a powerful voice in conference for minimal judicial "interference" with local school systems. Any Justice who felt that the federal judiciary was overextended in the school desegregation cases would have been aghast at the prospect of parallel litigation over school financing. Note that Justices Blackmun and Powell were both in the *Plyler* majority, in part because remediation was much easier: the Texas law was struck down, and the children of aliens could attend school. That there was little need for ongoing judicial supervision made it easier for those Justices to join Justice Brennan's opinion. We will discuss remedial issues in more depth in Chapter 9.

Even more difficult was the question of what the constitutional standard would be for determining whether a school system violated the rights articulated in the *Rodriguez* dissent. In the voting cases, one problem with a less expansive right—such as the one Justice Stewart suggested in his separate opinion in *Reynolds*, which would protect against only irrational allocations of political power that absolutely frustrate the preferences of a majority of citizens—is that figuring out whether it had been violated would require much more difficult judicial judgment calls than the simple standard of *Reynolds* (which in light of later cases amounts to something like "one person, one vote, plus or minus 10%"). Note, too, that Justice Stewart's approach in *Reynolds* and the approach to education rejected in *Rodriguez* would create difficult problems of implementation and remedy, while *Reynolds* and *Plyer* were remedially simple.

3. *How to Explain* Plyler? Given the powerful forces generating the result in *Rodriguez*, how does one explain *Plyler*, an activist result by a much more conservative Court? Probably the best explanation is that Texas's law looked punitive and short-sighted to the Court. According to Brennan's conference notes, the Justices were deeply troubled that Texas was engaging in renegade immigration politics which penalized "helpless" children (Powell's phrase, echoing Marshall's arguments at conference) and risked creating a "permanent underclass" (Blackmun and Stevens). Burger and O'Connor expressed dismay at the law and opined that the political process was unresponsive to this unfairness. The strongest statement at conference in favor of the law was Rehnquist's: Illegal immigration was "an intractable problem in the southwest." Whatever doctrinal difficulties Justice Brennan had on cobbling together an opinion,[26] he had at least five Justices who wanted to join it. Brennan was aided by the fact that *Rodriguez* had language leaving the door

---

[26] Cf. Mark Tushnet, *The Optimist's Tale*, 132 U. Pa. L. Rev. 1257 (1989) (Brennan's opinion cobbled together different theories appealing to different Justices in order to get five votes).

open to claims that some children had been excluded from receiving a minimum level of education.

A complementary explanation for *Plyler* is that it illustrates the "sliding scale" that Marshall articulated in his *Rodriguez* dissent (and that we saw in his and Stevens' opinions in *Cleburne*, Chapter 4, § 3C). Marshall anticipated *Plyler* when he maintained that the Court should be particularly militant against laws discriminating "against important individual interests with constitutional implications and against particularly disadvantaged or powerless classes." Marshall's might be a more accurate descriptive theory of the Court's case law in this area, for it also helps us understand cases like *Cleburne* and *Romer v. Evans* (Chapter 4, § 3C & D). But the spirit in which this kind of equal protection review has been carried out has unquestionably been that of Justice Powell's philosophy—cautious in its definition of "rights" and deferential to well-motivated state policies and even experiments, pragmatic and attentive to institutional concerns before engaging the Court in activist review, but open to selective interventions when apparently ill-motivated policies hurt people who are not well represented in the political process.

EDGEWOOD INDEPENDENT SCHOOL DISTRICT V. KIRBY
777 S.W.2d 391 (Supreme Court of Texas, 1989)

MAUZY, JUSTICE.

At issue is the constitutionality of the Texas system for financing the education of public school children. * * *

There are approximately three million public school children in Texas. The legislature finances the education of these children through a combination of revenues supplied by the state itself and revenues supplied by local school districts which are governmental subdivisions of the state. Of total education costs, the state provides about forty-two percent, school districts provide about fifty percent, and the remainder comes from various other sources including federal funds. School districts derive revenues from local ad valorem property taxes, and the state raises funds from a variety of sources including the sales tax and various severance and excise taxes. * * *

Because of the disparities in district property wealth, spending per student varies widely, ranging from $2,112 to $19,333. Under the existing system, an average of $2,000 more per year is spent on each of the 150,000 students in the wealthiest districts than is spent on the 150,000 students in the poorest districts.

The lower expenditures in the property-poor districts are not the result of lack of tax effort. Generally, the property-rich districts can tax low and spend high while the property-poor districts must tax high merely to spend low. In 1985–86, local tax rates ranged from $.09 to $1.55 per $100 valuation. The 100 poorest districts had an average tax rate of 74.5 cents and spent an average of $2,978 per student. The 100 wealthiest districts had an average tax rate of 47 cents and spent an average of $7,233 per student. * * *

The amount of money spent on a student's education has a real and meaningful impact on the educational opportunity offered that student. High-wealth districts are able to provide for their students broader educational experiences including more extensive curricula, more up-to-date technological equipment, better libraries and library personnel, teacher aides, counseling services, lower student-teacher ratios, better facilities, parental involvement programs, and drop-out prevention programs. They are also better able to attract and retain experienced teachers and administrators. * * *

Article VII, section 1 of the Texas Constitution provides:

A general diffusion of knowledge being essential to the preservation of the liberties and rights of the people, it shall be the duty of the Legislature of the State to establish and make suitable provision for the support and maintenance of an efficient system of public free schools.

* * * [T]he language of article VII, section 1 imposes on the legislature an affirmative duty to establish and provide for the public free schools. This duty is not committed unconditionally to the legislature's discretion, but instead is accompanied by standards. By express constitutional mandate, the legislature must make "suitable" provision for an "efficient" system for the "essential" purpose of a "general diffusion of knowledge." While these are admittedly not precise terms, they do provide a standard by which this court must, when called upon to do so, measure the constitutionality of the legislature's actions. We do not undertake this responsibility lightly and we begin with a presumption of constitutionality. * * *

The Texas Constitution derives its force from the people of Texas. This is the fundamental law under which the people of this state have consented to be governed. In construing the language of article VII, section 1, we consider "the intent of the people who adopted it." In determining that intent, "the history of the times out of which it grew and to which it may be rationally supposed to have direct relationship, the evils intended to be remedied and the good to be accomplished, are proper subjects of inquiry." However, because of the difficulties inherent in determining the intent of voters over a century ago, we rely heavily on the literal text. We seek its meaning with the understanding that the Constitution was ratified to function as an organic document to govern society and institutions as they evolve through time. * * *

Considering "the general spirit of the times and the prevailing sentiments of the people," it is apparent from the historical record that those who drafted and ratified article VII, section 1 never contemplated the possibility that such gross inequalities could exist within an "efficient" system. At the Constitutional Convention of 1875, delegates spoke at length on the importance of education for *all* the people of this state, rich and poor alike. The chair of the education committee, speaking on behalf of the majority of the committee, declared:

> [Education] must be classed among the abstract rights, based on apparent natural justice, which we individually concede to the State, for the general welfare, when we enter into a great compact as a commonwealth. I boldly assert that it is for the general welfare of all, rich and poor, male and female, that the means of a common school education should, if possible, be placed within the reach of every child in the State.

Other delegates recognized the importance of a diffusion of knowledge among the masses not only for the preservation of democracy, but for the prevention of crime and for the growth of the economy. * * *

* * * The economic development of the state has not been uniform. Some cities have grown dramatically, while their sister communities have remained static or have shrunk. Formulas that once fit have been knocked askew. Although local conditions vary, the constitutionally imposed state responsibility for an efficient education system is the same for all citizens regardless of where they live.

We conclude that, in mandating "efficiency," the constitutional framers and ratifiers did not intend a system with such vast disparities as now exist. Instead, they stated clearly that the purpose of an efficient system was to provide for a "*general* diffusion of knowledge." (Emphasis added.) The present system, by contrast, provides not for a diffusion that is general, but for one that is limited and unbalanced. The resultant inequalities are thus directly contrary to the constitutional vision of efficiency. * * *

Some have argued that reform in school finance will eliminate local control, but this argument has no merit. An efficient system does not preclude the ability of communities to exercise local control over the education of their children. It requires only that the funds available for education be distributed equitably and evenly. An efficient system will actually allow for more local control, not less. It will provide property-poor districts with economic alternatives that are not now available to them. Only if alternatives are indeed available can a community exercise the control of making choices.

Our decision today is not without precedent. Courts in nine other states with similar school financing systems have ruled those systems to be unconstitutional for varying reasons. * * *

Although we have ruled the school financing system to be unconstitutional, we do not now instruct the legislature as to the specifics of the legislation it should enact; nor do we order it to raise taxes. The legislature has primary responsibility to decide how best to achieve an efficient system. We decide only the nature of the constitutional mandate and whether that mandate has been met. Because we hold that the mandate of efficiency has not been met, we reverse the judgment of the court of appeals. The legislature is duty-bound to provide for an efficient system of education, and only if the legislature fulfills that duty can we launch this great state into a strong economic future with educational opportunity for all.

NOTES ON EDGEWOOD, STATE CONSTITUTIONAL PROTECTIONS, AND CONSTITUTIONAL BALANCING

1.   *State Constitutional Rights in a Federal System.* A decision of a state supreme court on state law is definitive, except in exceptional circumstances where a blatant misinterpretation of state law might undermine the enforcement of a federal constitutional right. Thus, the Supreme Court of the United States may not review whether the Supreme Court of Texas properly interpreted the Texas Constitution in *Edgewood*. Indeed, since no federal issue is found in *Edgewood*, the Supreme Court of the United States may not review the case at all. See U.S. Const., art. III, § 2. Because state constitutions can expand (but not contract) the rights of state citizens beyond those they hold as a matter of federal law, students in Texas public schools have a broader right to equality in school finance than do students in states where the state constitution provides no more protection than the federal Constitution, as interpreted in *Rodriguez*. Indeed, it is precisely this facet of state constitutional law that once led Justice Brennan to suggest that attorneys consider whether litigation attempting to establish new individual rights might have a better chance of success if based on a state constitutional claim rather than a federal one. See William Brennan, *State Constitutions and the Protection of Individual Rights*, 90 Harv. L. Rev. 489 (1977).

Many state judiciaries have addressed the *Rodriguez* issue, with a majority having granted some kind of relief. For a survey and critical analysis, see William S. Koski, *Of Fuzzy Standards and Institutional Constraints: A Re-Examination of the Jurisprudential History of Educational Finance Reform Litigation*, 43 Santa Clara L. Rev. 1185 (2003); James Ryan, *Schools, Race, and Money*, 109 Yale L.J. 249 (1999). The state courts are divided on whether the goal should be to equalize funding (the issue in *Rodriguez*) or assure every child access to a minimally adequate education (as arguably required by the language of many state constitutions' education clauses).

2.   *The Openly Utilitarian Reasoning in* Edgewood: *Arguments for Balancing.* Recall the theories of judicial review discussed at the end of Chapter 2: Textualism, originalism, process theory (exemplified by representation reinforcement), progressivism, and practical reason. Do any of

them resemble the approach taken to the Texas Constitution in *Edgewood*? The text of the Texas Constitution provides a source of argument in the case, but does it compel the outcome?

One way to view *Edgewood* is the following: Utilitarianism views with suspicion policies that distribute a lot more resources to the rich than to the poor (classification based upon wealth) or that deprive poor people of an important public good (education, a fundamental public right). Why? Because in such circumstances moving one dollar from a rich district to a poor district would presumably have a higher marginal payoff, and the total social utility would be higher. If the state is making such an obvious sacrifice of aggregate social utility, it is not adequately doing its job of serving the "general welfare," and the court might usefully step in.

The judicial process arguably might have three types of institutional advantages in making utility-maximizing social and economic policy.[27] Consider the strengths and weaknesses of the following arguments:

(a) *The problem of inertia.* Much social policy is the result of legislative and executive inertia and inactivity rather than continuing choice. Because they often do not get sufficient credit for addressing vexing social problems and, indeed, often must make unpleasant allocational choices, legislators often have incentives to avoid tinkering with outdated policies. And because the legislature is not required to act on proposed measures (which can be bottled up indefinitely in committee), obsolescent policies can linger unchanged for long periods of time. Unlike the legislature, a court cannot control its agenda: It must decide the case before it, and must justify its decision by reasons (also in some contrast to legislative failures to act). Hence, courts will be willing to correct inefficient policies in a number of cases where the legislature is content to be inactive, and judicial review can serve "action-forcing" functions even when the legislature must ultimately make the utilitarian judgments. State funding of school districts is a conflictual issue that the Texas legislature perhaps wanted to avoid, and *Edgewood* was a good way to put the issue on the political agenda.

(b) *The problem of rent-seeking.* When they do focus on social problems, the legislature and agencies often seem to favor the interests of well-organized groups, arguably at the expense of the general welfare. Economists call this "rent-seeking" (a group or individual extracts money or a privilege from the state, which is not justified on utilitarian/efficiency grounds for the polity as a whole). Legislative earmarks, bloated defense contracts, monopolistic licensing arrangements, tobacco subsidies (paying farmers to grow stuff that kills us) are all examples of rent-seeking legislative policy. Precisely because judges either have life tenure (in the federal system) or serve long, relatively insulated terms (the norm in state systems), they are somewhat free from interest group

---

[27] The following discussion is drawn from Guido Calabresi, *A Common Law for the Age of Statutes* (1982); Daniel Farber & Philip Frickey, *Law and Public Choice: A Critical Introduction* (1991); William Eskridge, Jr., *Politics Without Romance: Implications of Public Choice Theory for Statutory Interpretation*, 74 Va. L. Rev. 274 (1988).

pressures and bring to bear a more scrutinizing perspective upon these issues. Even if Texas's legislature had seriously considered the school funding issue, well-heeled parent groups would have been powerful impediments to major reform. The same socio-economic inequities that yielded different expenditures in Edgewood and Alamo Heights also would yield different political clout in Austin.

(c)   *The problem of prejudice.* An underlying issue in both the *Edgewood* and *Serrano* cases, politely submerged by the courts in each state, is race and ethnicity. Alamo Heights is overwhelmingly white as well as affluent. Many of the poor school districts in Texas are predominantly African American or Latino. The failure of the Texas legislature to provide more funding for the poor districts might have been in part due to their racial and ethnic composition. "Have not" groups tend to lose in our political system, and when they are of a different skin color they tend to lose more often. One lesson of *Brown* is that courts can be a means of forcing the legislature to treat "discrete and insular" minority groups more fairly. But do courts in the broad range of cases protect groups that are truly politically powerless? One might suggest that courts are more likely to become involved when the group in question begins to have enhanced political power and a capacity to place issues on the public agenda. Consider, for example, when the Court intervened in the school segregation controversy in *Brown*, when it began providing more meaningful scrutiny of sex classifications in *Reed* and *Frontiero* (Chapter 4, § 2B), and when it struck down a measure disadvantaging lesbians and gay males in *Romer v. Evans* (Chapter 4, § 3D).

3.   *Problems with Judicial Balancing.* Some of the problems with "balancing" as a technique of judicial review are suggested in T. Alexander Aleinikoff, *Constitutional Law in the Age of Balancing*, 96 Yale L.J. 943 (1987). The problem that looms largest is the indeterminacy problem: It is not clear that utilitarian analysis—balancing—can be anything but indeterminate. Consider some of the questions unaddressed in *Edgewood* and *Serrano*:

(a)   *What interests should be considered?* The *Edgewood* majority mainly considers the interest in equality of resources, but without much consideration of the traditional interest in local control and fiscal management of school districts. Once those interests are considered, the balance becomes less clear.

(b)   *How can the various interests be measured and compared? Serrano* makes a case for valuing educational equality quite highly, which *Edgewood* seems to accept, and both cases assume a low valuation for local control (though there is little justification in the opinions). But the Alamo Hills people might value their local control quite highly, and indeed also derive a lot of satisfaction out of spending a lot more money than Edgewood does. For all the Court tells us, their total satisfaction might indeed be higher than the aggregate dissatisfaction of the Edgewood people with their system of local control but fewer resources.

(c)   *What would be the effect of the court's decision upon the interests it is balancing?* The court's result has an intuitive appeal—splitting up a limited pie more evenly might yield overall greater utility because of the greater marginal utility of each dollar for the poor as opposed to the rich districts. But that assumes a static analysis. What if the court's result has consequences for the size of the pie? One benefit of local control might be an incentive for school districts to engage in a competition with one another to put more resources into education, to make their local communities relatively attractive. If the funding of education becomes a completely statewide decision, then the local efforts may diminish, and with it the overall quality of education in the state—defeating the goal of greatest happiness for the greatest number.

If you believe that the balancing inquiry is essentially indeterminate, you might be more likely to defer to the legislative judgment; at least its balancing (which may be equally indeterminate) is done by elected representatives, and therefore is subject to some external check. If the elected representatives compromise overall social utility, they might be voted out of office.

Finally, Aleinikoff suggests that balancing is "transforming constitutional discourse into a general discussion of the reasonableness of governmental conduct." He finds this troubling:

> Balancing opinions give one the eerie sense that constitutional law as a distinct form of discourse is slipping away. The balancing drum beats the rhythm of reasonableness, and we march to it because the cadence seems so familiar, so sensible. But our eyes are no longer focused on the Constitution. If each constitutional provision, every constitutional value, is understood simply as an invitation for a discussion of good social policy, it means little to talk of constitutional "theory."[28]

PROBLEM 5-1:
RACIAL DISPARITIES AND STATE CONSTITUTIONAL LAW

The State of Westland's constitution provides for an "adequate and efficient educational system." Under state law, school districts are funded exclusively by the state government, and every district gets the same funding per pupil. The major city in Westland is Metropolis. Students in Metropolis have much lower test scores and higher drop-out rates than those elsewhere in the state. They are also disproportionately people of color. Suburban schools with higher performance indicators do not accept transfers from outside their own districts. Moreover, school segregation has increased because the local public housing district has constructed all of its public housing within the Metropolis city limits rather than the suburbs. A civil rights group files suit in state court based on these allegations (but not alleging any racial animus). The group seeks (a) an order directing the state legislature to devote additional resources to Metropolis schools in light of the more difficult problems of those schools, (b) an order requiring suburban schools to accept inner-city transfer

---

[28] For a more recent analysis and partial defense of balancing approaches, see Richard Fallon, *The Supreme Court, 1996 Term—Foreword: Implementing the Constitution*, 111 Harv. L. Rev. 54, 77–83 (1997).

students, and (c) an order that the public housing authority build new projects outside of the city limits. Should the court find any violation of the state constitution? If so, what would be the appropriate remedial order?

C. THE RIGHT TO TRAVEL

Shapiro v. Thompson

394 U.S. 618 (1969)

The Court struck down rules in several states and the District of Columbia that denied welfare assistance to residents who had not resided in the jurisdiction for at least one year. The decision said it was based on the Equal Protection Clause, and thus it fueled the debate (prior to *Dandridge* and *Rodriguez*) whether the poor could be a suspect class, wealth could be a suspect classification, or welfare could be a fundamental right. The opinion in *Shapiro* also alluded to a right of interstate travel, however:

> This Court long ago recognized that the nature of our Federal Union and our constitutional concepts of personal liberty unite to require that all citizens be free to travel throughout the length and breadth of our land uninhibited by statutes, rules, or regulations which unreasonably burden or restrict this movement.

The Court noted that its precedents have not "ascribed the source of this right to * * * a particular constitutional provision," and in a footnote stated that some cases linked the right to the Privileges and Immunities Clause of Article IV, § 2, other cases tied it to the Privileges or Immunities Clause of the Fourteenth Amendment, and yet other cases saw it connected to the Commerce Clause. See the debate within the Court in *Edwards v. California*, 314 U.S. 160 (1941), as well as *Crandall v. Nevada*, 73 U.S. (6 Wall.) 35 (1868).

Having recognized a right to travel, the Court demanded a compelling state interest to justify its residence requirement. **Justice Brennan**'s opinion held that the apparent purpose of deterring in-migration of poor people "cannot serve as justification * * * since that purpose is constitutionally impermissible" as a penalty chilling people's exercise of their constitutional rights. His opinion recognized that planning the state budget, having an objective test for apportioning welfare benefits, and minimizing fraud were permissible state purposes, but held that these interests were not constitutionally compelling.

It was not clear whether *Shapiro* is a fundamental rights/equal protection case or (as *Rodriguez* interpreted it) a penalty-on-interstate-travel case. No matter how it is characterized, *Shapiro* has had a robust legacy in several lines of cases. To begin, the right to travel has been the basis for invalidating state benefit schemes that discriminate based upon residence in the state. In *Zobel v. Williams*, 457 U.S. 55 (1982), the Court struck down Alaska's statute distributing its oil and gas windfalls to its citizens, with the rebate dependent upon length of residency in Alaska. The Court relied on the Equal Protection Clause and invoked *Shapiro* to dismiss the state's rationale that the statute rewarded citizens for their "past contributions." Justice Brennan, the author of *Shapiro*, wrote a concurring opinion arguing that "it is difficult to escape from the recognition that underlying any scheme of classification on the basis of duration of residence, we shall almost invariably find the unstated premise that 'some citizens are more equal than others,'" a premise starkly inconsistent with the Equal Protection Clause. The Court followed *Zobel* to invalidate benefit statutes based upon residency criteria in *Attorney General of New York v. Soto-Lopez*, 476 U.S. 898 (1986), and *Hooper v. Bernalillo County Assessor*, 472 U.S. 612 (1985).

The right to travel has been the main basis for striking down one-year residence requirements for voting, see *Dunn v. Blumstein*, 405 U.S. 330 (1972), but not a 50-day period, see *Marston v. Lewis*, 410 U.S. 679 (1973) (*per curiam*). The right has also been invoked to strike down a one-year residence requirement for receiving nonemergency medical care at public expense, see *Memorial Hospital v. Maricopa County*, 415 U.S. 250 (1974), but was not sufficient to invalidate a one-year residence requirement for bringing a divorce action against a nonresident, see *Sosna v. Iowa*, 419 U.S. 393 (1975). See if you can figure out a rationale to reconcile *Sosna* with the other cases.

Additionally, consider whether some of these cases should not have been decided on grounds of the Privileges and Immunities Clause of Article IV, which Justice O'Connor believed was the soundest basis for *Zobel* (she concurred in the Court's result but did not join its right-to-travel discussion). See also *Supreme Court of New Hampshire v. Piper*, 470 U.S. 274 (1985) (relying on Article IV to strike down state residence requirement for admission to the bar).

SAENZ V. ROE
526 U.S. 489, 119 S.Ct. 1518, 143 L.Ed.2d 689 (1999)

JUSTICE STEVENS delivered the opinion of the Court.

In 1992, California enacted a statute [§ 11450.03] limiting the maximum welfare benefits available to newly arrived residents. The scheme limits the amount payable to a family that has resided in the State for less than 12 months to the amount payable by the State of the family's prior residence. The questions presented by this case are whether the 1992 statute was constitutional when it was enacted and, if not, whether an amendment to the Social Security Act enacted by Congress in 1996 affects that determination. * * *

The "right to travel" discussed in our cases embraces at least three different components. It protects the right of a citizen of one State to enter and to leave another State, the right to be treated as a welcome visitor rather than an unfriendly alien when temporarily present in the second State, and, for those travelers who elect to become permanent residents, the right to be treated like other citizens of that State.

* * * Given that § 11450.03 imposed no obstacle to respondents' entry into California, we think the State is correct when it argues that the statute does not directly impair the exercise of the right to free interstate movement. For the purposes of this case, therefore, we need not identify the source of that particular right in the text of the Constitution. The right of "free ingress and regress to and from" neighboring States, which was expressly mentioned in the text of the Articles of Confederation, may simply have been "conceived from the beginning to be a necessary concomitant of the stronger Union the Constitution created."

The second component of the right to travel is, however, expressly protected by the text of the Constitution. The first sentence of Article IV, § 2, provides:

> The Citizens of each State shall be entitled to all Privileges and Immunities of Citizens in the several States.

Thus, by virtue of a person's state citizenship, a citizen of one State who travels in other States, intending to return home at the end of his journey, is entitled to enjoy the "Privileges and Immunities of Citizens in the several States" that he visits. * * *

What is at issue in this case [is the] third aspect of the right to travel— the right of the newly arrived citizen to the same privileges and immunities enjoyed by other citizens of the same State. That right is protected not only by the new arrival's status as a state citizen, but also by her status as a citizen of the United States. That additional source of protection is plainly identified in the opening words of the Fourteenth Amendment:

> All persons born or naturalized in the United States, and subject to the jurisdiction thereof, are citizens of the United States and of the State wherein they reside. No State shall make or enforce any law which shall abridge the privileges or immunities of citizens of the United States;. . . .

Despite fundamentally differing views concerning the coverage of the Privileges or Immunities Clause of the Fourteenth Amendment, most notably expressed in the majority and dissenting opinions in the *Slaughter-House Cases* [§ 1 of this chapter], it has always been common ground that this Clause protects the third component of the right to travel. * * *

It is undisputed that respondents and the members of the class that they represent are citizens of California and that their need for welfare benefits is unrelated to the length of time that they have resided in California. We thus have no occasion to consider what weight might be given to a citizen's length of residence if the bona fides of her claim to state citizenship were questioned. Moreover, because whatever benefits they receive will be consumed while they remain in California, there is no danger that recognition of their claim will encourage citizens of other

States to establish residency for just long enough to acquire some readily portable benefit, such as a divorce or a college education, that will be enjoyed after they return to their original domicile. * * *

Disavowing any desire to fence out the indigent, California has instead advanced an entirely fiscal justification for its multitiered scheme. The enforcement of § 11450.03 will save the State approximately $10.9 million a year. The question is not whether such saving is a legitimate purpose but whether the State may accomplish that end by the discriminatory means it has chosen. An evenhanded, across-the-board reduction of about 72 cents per month for every beneficiary would produce the same result. But our negative answer to the question does not rest on the weakness of the State's purported fiscal justification. It rests on the fact that the Citizenship Clause of the Fourteenth Amendment expressly equates citizenship with residence: "That Clause does not provide for, and does not allow for, degrees of citizenship based on length of residence." It is equally clear that the Clause does not tolerate a hierarchy of 45 subclasses of similarly situated citizens based on the location of their prior residence.[20] Thus § 11450.03 is doubly vulnerable: Neither the duration of respondents' California residence, nor the identity of their prior States of residence, has any relevance to their need for benefits. Nor do those factors bear any relationship to the State's interest in making an equitable allocation of the funds to be distributed among its needy citizens. * * * In short, the State's legitimate interest in saving money provides no justification for its decision to discriminate among equally eligible citizens.

The question that remains is whether congressional approval of durational residency requirements in the 1996 amendment to the Social Security Act somehow resuscitates the constitutionality of § 11450.03. That question is readily answered, for we have consistently held that Congress may not authorize the States to violate the Fourteenth Amendment. Moreover, the protection afforded to the citizen by the Citizenship Clause of that Amendment is a limitation on the powers of the National Government as well as the States.

CHIEF JUSTICE REHNQUIST, with whom **JUSTICE THOMAS** joins, dissenting.

I agree with the proposition that a "citizen of the United States can, of his own volition, become a citizen of any State of the Union by a *bona fide* residence therein, with the same rights as other citizens of that State." [*Slaughter-House Cases*.]

---

[20] See Cohen, Discrimination Against New State Citizens: An Update, 11 *Const. Comm.* 73, 79 (1994) ("[J]ust as it would violate the Constitution to deny these new arrivals state citizenship, it would violate the Constitution to concede their citizenship in name only while treating them as if they were still citizens of other states").

But I cannot see how the right to become a citizen of another State is a necessary "component" of the right to travel, or why the Court tries to marry these separate and distinct rights. A person is no longer "traveling" in any sense of the word when he finishes his journey to a State which he plans to make his home. Indeed, under the Court's logic, the protections of the Privileges or Immunities Clause recognized in this case come into play only when an individual *stops* traveling with the intent to remain and become a citizen of a new State. * * *

The Court today recognizes that States retain the ability to determine the bona fides of an individual's claim to residence, but then tries to avoid the issue. It asserts that because respondents' need for welfare benefits is unrelated to the length of time they have resided in California, it has "no occasion to consider what weight might be given to a citizen's length of residence if the bona fides of her claim to state citizenship were questioned." But I do not understand how the absence of a link between need and length of residency bears on the State's ability to objectively test respondents' resolve to stay in California. There is no link between the need for an education or for a divorce and the length of residence, and yet States may use length of residence as an objective yardstick to channel their benefits to those whose intent to stay is legitimate.

JUSTICE THOMAS, with whom **THE CHIEF JUSTICE [REHNQUIST]** joins, dissenting.

The colonists' repeated assertions that they maintained the rights, privileges, and immunities of persons "born within the realm of England" and "natural born" persons suggests that, at the time of the founding, the terms "privileges" and "immunities" (and their counterparts) were understood to refer to those fundamental rights and liberties specifically enjoyed by English citizens and, more broadly, by all persons. Presumably members of the Second Continental Congress so understood these terms when they employed them in the Articles of Confederation, which guaranteed that "the free inhabitants of each of these States, paupers, vagabonds and fugitives from justice excepted, shall be entitled to all privileges and immunities of free citizens in the several States." Art. IV. The Constitution, which superseded the Articles of Confederation, similarly guarantees that "[t]he Citizens of each State shall be entitled to all Privileges and Immunities of Citizens in the several States." Art. IV, § 2, cl. 1.

Justice Bushrod Washington's landmark opinion in *Corfield v. Coryell*, 6 F. Cas. 546 (No. 3, 230) (CCED Pa. 1825), reflects this historical understanding. In *Corfield*, a citizen of Pennsylvania challenged a New Jersey law that prohibited any person who was not an "actual inhabitant and resident" of New Jersey from harvesting oysters from New Jersey waters. Justice Washington, sitting as Circuit Justice, rejected the argument that the New Jersey law violated Article IV's Privileges and Immunities Clause. He reasoned, "we cannot accede to the proposition . . . that, under this provision of the constitution, the citizens of the several states are permitted to participate in all the rights which belong exclusively to the citizens of any other particular state, merely upon the ground that they are enjoyed by those citizens." * * * Washington rejected the proposition that the Privileges and Immunities Clause guaranteed equal access to all public benefits (such as the right to harvest oysters in public waters) that a State chooses to make available. Instead, he endorsed the colonial-era conception of the terms "privileges" and "immunities," concluding that Article IV encompassed only *fundamental* rights that belong to all citizens of the United States.

Justice Washington's opinion in *Corfield* indisputably influenced the Members of Congress who enacted the Fourteenth Amendment. When Congress gathered to debate the Fourteenth Amendment, Members frequently, if not as a matter of course, appealed to *Corfield*, arguing that the Amendment was necessary to guarantee the fundamental rights that Justice Washington identified in his opinion. For just one example, in a speech introducing the Amendment to the Senate, Senator Howard explained the Privileges or Immunities Clause by quoting at length from *Corfield*. Furthermore, it appears that no Member of Congress refuted the notion that Washington's analysis in *Corfield* undergirded the meaning of the Privileges or Immunities Clause.

That Members of the 39th Congress appear to have endorsed the wisdom of Justice Washington's opinion does not, standing alone, provide dispositive insight into their understanding of the Fourteenth Amendment's Privileges or Immunities Clause. Nevertheless, their repeated references to the *Corfield* decision, combined with what appears to be the historical understanding of the Clause's operative terms, supports the inference that, at the time the Fourteenth Amendment was adopted, people understood that "privileges or immunities of citizens" were fundamental rights, rather than every public benefit established by positive law. Accordingly, the majority's conclusion—that a State violates the Privileges or Immunities Clause when it "discriminates" against citizens who have been domiciled in the State for less than a year in the distribution of welfare benefits—appears contrary to the original understanding and is dubious at best.

NOTES ON SAENZ

1. *Alignment of the Justices.* The alignment of the Justices in *Saenz* is of some interest. On the one hand, Justice Scalia joined the majority, apparently untroubled by Justice Thomas's appeal to the original understanding. On the other hand, Chief Justice Rehnquist joined Thomas's

call for a possibly fundamental rethinking of the Fourteenth Amendment, giving central place to the "P or I" clause.

2. *Has the P or I Clause Been Resurrected?* The majority's interpretation of the clause is hardly fully fleshed out. Shortly after it was decided, *Saenz* was hailed for resurrecting the P or I clause as a formidable constitutional provision. See Akhil Amar, "Lost Clause," *New Republic*, June 14, 1999, at 14. While Justice Thomas wants to see a P or I revival, it is unclear whether the majority's holding necessarily engaged the broader issues about the clause discussed by Thomas. Thomas focuses on the "nationally protected rights" covered by the clause. At one point, the majority speaks of two separate prongs, the right to equal treatment for new state residents, and the "nationally protected" rights covered by the clause. Perhaps the implication is that the second, potentially much more expansive prong (the part discussed by Justice Thomas), remains dormant; only the first prong is resurrected by *Saenz*. On the other hand, the P or I clause itself draws no such distinction, and speaks only of certain national rights ("the privileges or immunities of citizens of the United States"). A more natural reading of the clause might be that the right to equal treatment as a new resident is simply one of the nationally protected "privileges or immunities."

Perhaps the Court meant to base its ruling on the residence-based definition of state citizenship in the first sentence of the Fourteenth Amendment, which it also quotes, rather than simply the P or I clause. It would not be too much of a stretch to read the grant of state citizenship to mean a grant of *equal* state citizenship, regardless of duration; otherwise, the southern states could have discriminated against African Americans by creating disabilities for individuals who had only recently acquired state citizenship. The Court's opinion at least hints at this, and it provides a limiting principle that may have made Justice Scalia more comfortable about joining. In any event, whatever the Court may have intended, the two decades since *Saenz* have seen no full-blown revival of the P or I clause. Other than Justice Thomas' argument that the clause offers a better basis than the due process clause for incorporation (see note 2 following *McDonald v. Chicago*, in § 1, above), the Court has had little to say about the P or I clause since *Saenz*.

SECTION 4. FUNDAMENTAL PRIVACY RIGHTS

In the first three sections of this chapter we saw how the Constitution might protect rights necessary to "ordered liberty," rights of private property and economic freedom, and equal rights to vote, to receive a public education, and to travel. In this section we explore rights of privacy. The earliest cases involving this right were decided during the *Lochner* era. Note how the Court's approach to substantive due process with respect to economic regulation might have influenced its analysis of privacy.

MEYER V. NEBRASKA

262 U.S. 390, 43 S.Ct. 625, 67 L.Ed. 1042 (1923)

[A Nebraska law prohibited teaching young children in any public or private school in any language other than English. Writing for the Court, **JUSTICE MCREYNOLDS** ruled this law inconsistent with the Due Process Clause.]

While this court has not attempted to define with exactness the liberty thus guaranteed [by the Due Process Clause], the term has received much consideration and some of the included things have been definitely stated. Without doubt, it denotes not merely freedom from bodily restraint but also the right of the individual to contract, to engage in any of the common occupations of life, to acquire useful knowledge, to marry, establish a home and bring up children, to worship God according to the dictates of his own conscience, and generally to enjoy those privileges long recognized at common law as essential to the orderly pursuit of happiness by free men. [Citing many cases, including *Lochner* and *Adkins v. Children's Hospital*.] The established doctrine is that this liberty may not be interfered with, under the guise of protecting the public interest, by legislative action which is arbitrary or without reasonable relation to some purpose within the competency of the state to effect. Determination by the Legislature of what constitutes proper exercise of police power is not final or conclusive but is subject to supervision by the courts.

The American people have always regarded education and acquisition of knowledge as matters of supreme importance which should be diligently promoted. * * *

Practically, education of the young is only possible in schools conducted by especially qualified persons who devote themselves thereto. The calling always has been regarded as useful and honorable, essential, indeed, to the public welfare. Mere knowledge of the German language cannot reasonably be regarded as harmful. Heretofore it has been commonly looked upon as helpful and desirable. Plaintiff in error taught this language in school as part of his occupation. His right thus to teach and the right of parents to engage him so to instruct their children, we think, are within the liberty of the amendment.

The challenged statute forbids the teaching in school of any subject except in English; also the teaching of any other language until the pupil has attained and successfully passed the eighth grade, which is not usually accomplished before the age of twelve. The Supreme Court of the state has held that "the so-called ancient or dead languages" are not "within the spirit or the purpose of the act." Latin, Greek, Hebrew are not proscribed; but German, French, Spanish, Italian, and every other alien speech are within the ban. Evidently the Legislature has attempted materially to interfere with the calling of modern language teachers, with the opportunities of pupils to acquire knowledge, and with the power of parents to control the education of their own.

It is said the purpose of the legislation was to promote civic development by inhibiting training and education of the immature in foreign tongues and ideals before they could learn English and acquire American ideals, and "that the English language should be and become the mother tongue of all children reared in this state." It is also affirmed that the foreign born population is very large, that certain communities commonly use foreign words, follow foreign leaders, move in a foreign atmosphere, and that the children are thereby hindered from becoming citizens of the most useful type and the public safety is imperiled.

That the state may do much, go very far, indeed, in order to improve the quality of its citizens, physically, mentally and morally, is clear; but the individual has certain fundamental rights which must be respected. The protection of the Constitution extends to all, to those who speak other languages as well as to those born with English on the tongue. Perhaps it would be highly advantageous if all had ready understanding of our ordinary speech, but this cannot be coerced by methods which conflict with the Constitution—a desirable end cannot be promoted by prohibited means. * * *

The desire of the Legislature to foster a homogeneous people with American ideals prepared readily to understand current discussions of civic matters is easy to appreciate. Unfortunate experiences during the late war and aversion toward every character of truculent adversaries were certainly enough to quicken that aspiration. But the means adopted, we think, exceed the limitations upon the power of the state and conflict with rights assured to plaintiff in error. The interference is plain enough and no adequate reason therefor in time of peace and domestic tranquility has been shown.

The power of the state to compel attendance at some school and to make reasonable regulations for all schools, including a requirement that they shall give instructions in English, is not questioned. Nor has challenge been made of the state's power to prescribe a curriculum for institutions which it supports. Those matters are not within the present controversy. Our concern is with the prohibition approved by the Supreme Court. * * * We are constrained to conclude that the statute as applied is arbitrary and without reasonable relation to any end within the competency of the state.

As the statute undertakes to interfere only with teaching which involves a modern language, leaving complete freedom as to other matters, there seems no adequate foundation for the suggestion that the purpose was to protect the child's health by limiting his mental activities. It is well known that proficiency in a foreign language seldom comes to one not instructed at an early age, and experience shows that this is not injurious to the health, morals or understanding of the ordinary child.

[Dissenting opinion of **JUSTICE HOLMES**, joined by **JUSTICE SUTHERLAND** is omitted.]

NOTE: WHAT KINDS OF "LIBERTY" ARE SUBSTANTIVELY PROTECTED BY THE DUE PROCESS CLAUSE?

Following *Meyer*, the Court in *Pierce v. Society of Sisters*, 268 U.S. 510 (1925), ruled that the state could not require all children to attend public schools. The Due Process Clause barred the state from using compulsory education laws to suppress private, especially religious, schools. Today, *Pierce* and *Meyer* could be defended on First Amendment grounds, but as written they stand for the proposition that the Constitution protects certain zones of "privacy" from state control.[29] There were in the 1920s a number of different ways one could understand these zones of privacy:[30] (1) *Privacy as Family Governance.* Presumptively, the state cannot interfere in the individual's choices as to marriage and the married couple's choices as to how to raise its family. *Meyer* and *Pierce* might also be read to support the notion of parental rights to govern their children, without "excessive" state "protection" of the children. Cf. *Hammer v. Dagenhart* (Chapter 7, § 2) (striking down federal law aimed at stopping child labor). (2) *Privacy as Life Choices. Meyer*'s list of common law privileges "essential to the orderly pursuit of happiness by free men" boil down to certain kinds of life choices with which the state cannot readily interfere. Indeed, the facts of *Meyer*—the state during World War I was disrespecting German-American communities—suggest that activities and knowledge that help bind together minority groups are entitled to some protection against state suppression. (3) *Privacy as Inaccessibility. Meyer* starts with the proposition that liberty naturally includes "freedom from bodily restraint." The Court in *Union Pacific Railroad v. Botsford*, 141 U.S. 250 (1891) (essentially overruled by *Sibbach v. Wilson & Co.*, 312 U.S. 1 (1941)), held that the state could not require a personal injury plaintiff to submit to a medical examination. *Skinner* is an application of this privacy right. Presumptively, one's body is inaccessible to the state—as is one's home. See *Boyd v. United States*, 116 U.S. 616, 630 (1886) (Fourth Amendment protects the "sanctities of a man's home and the privacies of his life"); see also Anita Allen, *Uneasy Access: Privacy for Women in a Free Society* (1988).

The cases in this section will explore the Court's application of the nascent privacy right. As you read the cases, consider (1) the legitimacy of the Court's

---

[29] These cases did not explicitly rely on the right to be let alone articulated in Louis Brandeis & Samuel Warren, *The Right to Privacy,* 4 Harv. L. Rev. 193 (1890), which was mainly about what we would call "informational privacy," the tort right to avoid publicity. On the early cases and their ambiguous relationship to the right to be let alone, see Ken Gormley, *One Hundred Years of Privacy*, 1992 Wis. L. Rev. 1335.

[30] See William Eskridge, Jr., *Some Effects of Identity-Based Social Movements on Constitutional Law in the Twentieth Century*, 100 Mich. L. Rev. 2062 (2002), for the analysis that follows.

jurisprudence, (2) exactly what the Court considers to be "privacy," and (3) how issues of sex and gender discrimination relate to the privacy reasoning.

A. CONTRACEPTION, MARRIAGE, AND FAMILY

By World War I, most states and the federal government made it a crime to distribute articles of contraception, and almost half the states criminalized a doctor's providing contraceptive information to patients.[31] These laws bore harshly on women, and feminists such as Emma Goldman and Margaret Sanger objected that these laws not only threatened women's health, but also deprived them of life choices. The state went after both women, deporting Goldman and arresting Sanger, her sister, and even her husband. New York closed her birth control clinic in 1916, and Sanger appealed the conviction to the U.S. Supreme Court. Her argument was that the state's suppression of birth control information and devices was a severe and unacceptable intrusion into a woman's due process liberties, specifically, her right to protect her own health and her right to make important life choices without state interference. By thwarting reproductive choice, the state was essentially controlling the entire lives of women. *"The State has no more right to compel 'motherhood' than the individual has to compel [sexual] relations."* Brief on Behalf of the Plaintiff in Error, at 31, *Sanger v. People* (1919 Term, No. 75) (emphasis in original). Although Sanger made her argument in the substantive due process argot the Court would accept in *Meyer*, the Court dismissed her appeal on the ground that it raised no substantial federal question. *Sanger v. People*, 251 U.S. 537 (1919) (per curiam). Notwithstanding the Court's deaf ear, Sanger and Planned Parenthood (which she founded) engaged in a relentless and ultimately successful campaign to nullify state and federal anti-contraception laws, usually through legislative amendment or repeal and administrative construction, but sometimes through judicial review.[32]

The Connecticut statute criminalizing birth control was before the Supreme Court as early as 1943. In the 1943 case, a physician argued that the statute prevented him from providing birth-control advice to patients whose health would be threatened by pregnancy and birth. The Court refused to address whether the statute violated the Fourteenth Amendment. The Court avoided the issue because, it said unanimously, the doctor did not have "standing" in this situation: He had alleged no injury to himself caused by the statute, and he could not get into court merely by asserting the standing of other persons, such as his patients. *Tileston v. Ullman*, 318 U.S. 44 (1943) *(per curiam)*.

---

[31] See generally Janet Farrell Brodie, *Contraception and Abortion in Nineteenth-Century America* (1994); Thomas Dienes, *Law, Politics, and Birth Control* (1974).

[32] See Ellen Chesler, *Woman of Valor: Margaret Sanger and the Birth Control Movement in America* (1992); Carole McCann, *Birth Control Politics in the United States* 1916–1945 (1994); see also David Garrow, *Liberty and Sexuality: The Right of Privacy and the Making of* Roe v. Wade (1994) (useful combination of social movement and legal history).

POE V. ULLMAN
367 U.S. 497, 81 S.Ct. 1752, 6 L.Ed.2d 989 (1961)

[Not quite two decades after *Tileston* a new lawsuit was brought that avoided the standing problem. The plaintiffs included married women who allegedly had a medical need for, but could not receive, birth-control advice because of the statute. The Court again ducked the issue, this time concluding that the lawsuit was not "ripe." Essentially, a bare majority (five Justices) thought there was no practical dispute. Apparently only one prosecution for violation of the statute had been brought since its adoption in 1879, and in that case the prosecutor eventually refused to proceed. Contraceptives were readily available in Connecticut drug stores, notwithstanding the statute. As Justice Frankfurter explained for four Justices, "[t]he undeviating policy of nullification by Connecticut of its anti-contraceptive laws throughout all the long years that they have been on the statute books bespeaks more than prosecutorial paralysis." Justice Brennan, who provided the crucial fifth vote not to hear the case, stated that he was not convinced that plaintiffs "as individuals are truly caught in an inescapable dilemma." Justice Harlan's dissent provided an important opening chapter to the privacy debate.]

JUSTICE HARLAN, dissenting.

[P]recisely because it is the Constitution alone which warrants judicial interference in sovereign operations of the State, the basis of judgment as to the Constitutionality of state action must be a rational one, approaching the [constitutional] text which is the only commission for our power not in a literalistic way, as if we had a tax statute before us, but as the basic charter of our society, setting out in spare but meaningful terms the principles of government. *McCulloch v. Maryland* [Chapter 7, § 1]. But as inescapable as is the rational process in Constitutional adjudication in general, nowhere is it more so than in giving meaning to the prohibitions of the Fourteenth Amendment and, where the Federal Government is involved, the Fifth Amendment, against the deprivation of life, liberty or property without due process of law.

It is but a truism to say that this provision of both Amendments is not self-explanatory. As to the Fourteenth, which is involved here, the history of the Amendment also sheds little light on the meaning of the provision. It is important to note, however, that two views of the Amendment have not been accepted by this Court as delineating its scope. * * *

Were due process merely a procedural safeguard it would fail to reach those situations where the deprivation of life, liberty or property was accomplished by legislation which by operating in the future could, given even the fairest possible procedure in application to individuals, nevertheless destroy the enjoyment of all three. [Citing, *inter alia*, *Korematsu v. United States*, 323 U.S. 214 (1944).] Thus the guaranties of due process, though having their roots in Magna Carta's *"per legem terrae"* and considered as procedural safeguards "against executive usurpation and tyranny," have in this country "become bulwarks also against arbitrary legislation."

However it is not the particular enumeration of rights in the first eight Amendments which spells out the reach of Fourteenth Amendment due process, but rather, as was suggested in another context long before the adoption of that Amendment, those concepts which are considered to embrace those rights "which are . . . *fundamental*; which belong . . . to the citizens of all free governments," *Corfield v. Coryell*, Fed.Cas.No. 3,230, 4 Wash.C.C. 371, 380, for "the purposes [of securing] which men enter into society," *Calder v. Bull*, 3 Dall. 386, 388, 1 L.Ed. 648. Again and again this Court has resisted the notion that the Fourteenth Amendment is no more than a shorthand reference to what is explicitly set out elsewhere in the Bill of Rights. [Citing, *inter alia, Slaughter-House Cases* and *Palko*.] Indeed the fact that an identical provision limiting federal action is found among the first eight Amendments, applying to the Federal Government, suggests that due process is a discrete concept which subsists as an independent guaranty of liberty and procedural fairness, more general and inclusive than the specific prohibitions. [Citing, *inter alia, Bolling v. Sharpe* (Chapter 2, § 1C).]

Due process has not been reduced to any formula; its content cannot be determined by reference to any code. The best that can be said is that through the course of this Court's decisions it has represented the balance which our Nation, built upon postulates of respect for the liberty of the individual, has struck between that liberty and the demands of organized society. If the supplying of content to this Constitutional concept has of necessity been a rational process, it certainly has not been one where judges have felt free to roam where unguided speculation might take them. The balance of which I speak is the balance struck by this country, having regard to what history teaches are the traditions from which it developed as well as the traditions from which it broke. That tradition is a living thing. A decision of this Court which radically departs from it could not long survive, while a decision which builds on what has survived is likely to be sound. No formula could serve as a substitute, in this area, for judgment and restraint.

It is this outlook which has led the Court continuingly to perceive distinctions in the imperative character of Constitutional provisions, since that character must be discerned from a particular provision's larger context. And inasmuch as this context is one not of words, but of history and purposes, the full scope of the liberty guaranteed by the Due Process Clause cannot be found in or limited by the precise terms of the specific guarantees elsewhere provided in the Constitution. This "liberty" is not a series of isolated points pricked out in terms of the taking of property; the freedom of speech, press, and religion; the right to keep and bear arms; the freedom from unreasonable searches and seizures; and so on. It is a rational continuum which, broadly speaking, includes a freedom from all substantial arbitrary impositions and purposeless restraints, and which also recognizes, what a reasonable and sensitive judgment must, that certain interests require particularly careful scrutiny of the state needs asserted to justify their abridgment. Cf. *Skinner*; *Bolling v. Sharpe*.

[Justice Harlan endorsed *Meyer* and *Pierce*.] I do not think it was wrong to put those decisions on "the right of the individual to . . . establish a home and bring up children," *Meyer*, or on the basis that "The fundamental theory of liberty upon which all governments in this Union repose excludes any general power of the State to standardize its children by forcing them to accept instruction from public teachers only," *Pierce*. I consider this so, even though today those decisions would probably have gone by reference to the concepts of freedom of expression and conscience assured against state action by the Fourteenth Amendment, concepts that are derived from the explicit guarantees of the First Amendment against federal encroachment upon freedom of speech and belief. For it is the purposes of those guarantees and not their text, the reasons for their statement by the Framers and not the statement itself, see *Palko*, which have led to their present status in the compendious notion of "liberty" embraced in the Fourteenth Amendment.

Each new claim to Constitutional protection must be considered against a background of Constitutional purposes, as they have been rationally perceived and historically developed. Though we exercise limited and sharply restrained judgment, yet there is no "mechanical yard-stick," no "mechanical answer." The decision of an apparently novel claim must depend on grounds which follow closely on well-accepted principles and criteria. The new decision must take "its place in relation to what went before and further [cut] a channel for what is to come." The matter was well put in *Rochin v. California*, 342 U.S. 165, 170–171:

> The vague contours of the Due Process Clause do not leave judges at large. We may not draw on our merely personal and private notions and disregard the limits that bind judges in their judicial function. Even though the concept of due process of law is not final and fixed, these limits are derived from considerations that are fused in the whole nature of our judicial process. . . . These are considerations deeply rooted in reason and in the compelling traditions of the legal profession.

[For Justice Harlan, the intrusion into the privacy of the "most intimate details of the marital relation with the full force of the criminal law" was of constitutional significance because marital privacy is an aspect of the privacy of the home, expressly protected against certain governmental intrusions by the Third and Fourth Amendments and more generally protected, under a series of precedents, by the "principle of liberty" found in the Due Process Clause "against all unreasonable intrusion of whatever character." He conceded that the state may regulate to promote public morality, and even that perhaps a state might reasonably view the use of contraceptives as immoral. But he concluded:]

Adultery, homosexuality and the like are sexual intimacies which the State forbids altogether, but the intimacy of husband and wife is necessarily an essential and accepted feature of the institution of marriage, an institution which the State not only must allow, but which always and in every age it has fostered and protected. It is one thing when the State exerts its power either to forbid extra-marital sexuality altogether, or to say who may marry, but it is quite another when, having acknowledged a marriage and the intimacies inherent in it, it undertakes to regulate by means of the criminal law the details of that intimacy.

In sum, even though the State has determined that the use of contraceptives is as iniquitous as any act of extra-marital sexual immorality, the intrusion of the whole machinery of the criminal law into the very heart of marital privacy, requiring husband and wife to render account before a criminal tribunal of their uses of that intimacy, is surely a very different thing indeed from punishing those who establish intimacies which the law has always forbidden and which can have no claim of social protection.

[Justice Harlan therefore concluded that "a closer scrutiny and stronger justification" for the statute was required than merely a rational relationship to a proper state purpose; that even the state itself apparently conceded that the moral judgment underlying the statute was not an important one, or the means chosen to effectuate that judgment appropriate, because it was not enforcing the statute against individual marital users; and that the infirmity of the statute was confirmed by the fact that no other state or the federal government has ever made use of contraceptives a crime.]

GRISWOLD V. CONNECTICUT
381 U.S. 479, 85 S.Ct. 1678, 14 L.Ed.2d 510 (1965)

JUSTICE DOUGLAS delivered the opinion of the Court.

[Estelle Griswold was Executive Director of the Planned Parenthood League of Connecticut. Another appellant, Lee Buxton, was a professor at the Yale Medical School who served as Medical Director for Planned Parenthood at its Center in New Haven. They gave information, instruction, and medical advice to married couples about birth control. They examined the wife and prescribed the best contraceptive device or material for her use. Fees were usually charged, although some couples received free service. No statute prohibited the sale of birth control devices. But it was a crime to use "any drug, medicinal article or instrument for the purpose of preventing conception," and they were charged as accessories to that offense.]

Coming to the merits, we are met with a wide range of questions that implicate the Due Process Clause of the Fourteenth Amendment. Overtones of some arguments suggest that *Lochner* should be our guide. But we decline that invitation. * * * We do not sit as a super-legislature to determine the wisdom, need, and propriety of laws that touch economic problems, business affairs, or social conditions. This law, however, operates directly on an intimate relation of husband and wife and their physician's role in one aspect of that relation.

The association of people is not mentioned in the Constitution nor in the Bill of Rights. The right to educate a child in a school of the parents' choice—whether public or private or parochial—is also not mentioned. Nor is the right to study any particular subject or any foreign language. Yet the First Amendment has been construed to include certain of those rights. [The Court then reviewed *Meyer* and *Pierce*, as well as First Amendment cases dealing with freedom of association.]

The foregoing cases suggest that specific guarantees in the Bill of Rights have penumbras, formed by emanations from those guarantees that help give them life and substance. *See Poe v. Ullman* (dissenting opinion). Various guarantees create zones of privacy. The right of association contained in the penumbra of the First Amendment is one, as we have seen. The Third Amendment in its prohibition against the quartering of soldiers "in any house" in time of peace without the consent of the owner is another facet of that privacy. The Fourth Amendment explicitly affirms the "right of the people to be secure in their persons, houses, papers, and effects, against unreasonable searches and seizures." The Fifth Amendment in its Self-Incrimination Clause enables the citizen to create a zone of privacy which government may not force him to surrender to his detriment. The Ninth Amendment provides: "The enumeration in the Constitution, of certain rights, shall not be construed to deny or disparage others retained by the people."

The Fourth and Fifth Amendments were described in *Boyd v. United States*, 116 U.S. 616, 630, as protection against all governmental invasions "of the sanctity of a man's home and the privacies of life." We recently referred in *Mapp v. Ohio*, 367 U.S. 643, 656, to the Fourth Amendment as creating a "right to privacy, no less important than any other right carefully and particularly reserved to the people." * * *

The present case, then, concerns a relationship lying within the zone of privacy created by several fundamental constitutional guarantees. And it concerns a law which, in forbidding the use of contraceptives rather than regulating their manufacture or sale, seeks to achieve its goals by means having a maximum destructive impact upon that relationship. Such a law cannot stand in light of the familiar principle, so often applied by this Court, that a "governmental purpose to control or prevent activities constitutionally subject to state regulation may not be achieved by means which sweep unnecessarily broadly and thereby invade the area of protected freedoms." *NAACP v. Alabama*, 377 U.S. 288, 307. Would we allow the police to search the sacred precincts of marital bedrooms for telltale signs of the use of contraceptives? The very idea is repulsive to the notions of privacy surrounding the marriage relationship.

We deal with a right of privacy older than the Bill of Rights—older than our political parties, older than our school system. Marriage is a coming together for better or for worse, hopefully enduring, and intimate to the degree of being sacred. It is an association that promotes a way of life, not causes; a harmony in living, not political faiths; a bilateral loyalty, not commercial or social projects. Yet it is an association for as noble a purpose as any involved in our prior decisions.

JUSTICE GOLDBERG, whom **THE CHIEF JUSTICE [WARREN]** and **JUSTICE BRENNAN** join, concurring.

This Court, in a series of decisions, has held that the Fourteenth Amendment absorbs and applies to the States those specifics of the first eight amendments which express fundamental personal rights. The language and history of the Ninth Amendment reveal that the Framers of the Constitution believed that there are additional fundamental rights, protected from governmental infringement, which exist alongside those fundamental rights specifically mentioned in the first eight constitutional amendments.

The Ninth Amendment reads, "The enumeration in the Constitution, of certain rights, shall not be construed to deny or disparage others retained by the people." The Amendment is almost entirely the work of James Madison. It was introduced in Congress by him and passed the House and Senate with little or no debate and virtually no change in language. It was proffered to quiet expressed fears that a bill of specifically enumerated rights could not be sufficiently broad to cover all essential rights and that the specific mention of certain rights would be interpreted as a denial that others were protected.

In presenting the proposed Amendment, Madison said:

> It has been objected also against a bill of rights, that, by enumerating particular exceptions to the grant of power, it would disparage those rights which were not placed in that enumeration; and it might follow by implication, that those rights which were not singled out, were intended to be assigned into the hands of the General Government, and were consequently insecure. This is one

of the most plausible arguments I have ever heard urged against the admission of a bill of rights into this system; but, I conceive, that it may be guarded against. I have attempted it, as gentlemen may see by turning to the last clause of the fourth resolution [the Ninth Amendment]. * * *

[This statement by Madison makes] clear that the Framers did not intend that the first eight amendments be construed to exhaust the basic and fundamental rights which the Constitution guaranteed to the people. * * *

While this Court has had little occasion to interpret the Ninth Amendment, "[i]t cannot be presumed that any clause in the constitution is intended to be without effect." *Marbury v. Madison.* In interpreting the Constitution, "real effect should be given to all the words it uses." The Ninth Amendment to the Constitution may be regarded by some as a recent discovery and may be forgotten by others, but since 1791 it has been a basic part of the Constitution which we are sworn to uphold. To hold that a right so basic and fundamental and so deep-rooted in our society as the right of privacy in marriage may be infringed because that right is not guaranteed in so many words by the first eight amendments to the Constitution is to ignore the Ninth Amendment and to give it no effect whatsoever. Moreover, a judicial construction that this fundamental right is not protected by the Constitution because it is not mentioned in explicit terms by one of the first eight amendments or elsewhere in the Constitution would violate the Ninth Amendment, which specifically states that "[the] enumeration in the Constitution, of certain rights, shall not be *construed* to deny or disparage others retained by the people." (Emphasis added.)

* * * I do not mean to imply that the Ninth Amendment is applied against the States by the Fourteenth. Nor do I mean to state that the Ninth Amendment constitutes an independent source of rights protected from infringement by either the States or the Federal Government. Rather, the Ninth Amendment shows a belief of the Constitution's authors that fundamental rights exist that are not expressly enumerated in the first eight amendments and an intent that the list of rights included there not be deemed exhaustive. * * * [Justice Goldberg endorsed the view that fundamental rights are those rooted in the traditions of our people.] "Liberty" also "gains content from the emanations of . . . specific [constitutional] guarantees" and "from experience with the requirements of a free society." *Poe v. Ullman* (dissenting opinion of Justice Douglas). * * *

Although the Constitution does not speak in so many words of the right of privacy in marriage, I cannot believe that it offers these fundamental rights no protection. The fact that no particular provision of the Constitution explicitly forbids the State from disrupting the traditional relation of the family—a relation as old and as fundamental as our entire civilization—surely does not show that the Government was meant to have the power to do so. Rather, as the Ninth Amendment expressly recognizes, there are fundamental personal rights such as this one, which are protected from abridgment by the Government though not specifically mentioned in the Constitution. * * *

The logic of the dissents would sanction federal or state legislation that seems to me even more plainly unconstitutional than the statute before us. Surely the Government, absent a showing of a compelling subordinating state interest, could not decree that all husbands and wives must be sterilized after two children have been born to them. Yet by their reasoning such an invasion of marital privacy would not be subject to constitutional challenge because, while it might be "silly," no provision of the Constitution specifically prevents the Government from curtailing the marital right to bear children and raise a family. While it may shock some of my Brethren that the Court today holds that the Constitution protects the right of marital privacy, in my view it is far more shocking to believe that the personal liberty guaranteed by the Constitution does not include protection against such totalitarian limitation of family size, which is at complete variance with our constitutional concepts. Yet, if upon a showing of a slender basis of rationality, a law outlawing voluntary birth control by married persons is valid, then, by the same reasoning, a law requiring compulsory birth control also would seem to be valid. In my view, however, both types of law would unjustifiably intrude upon rights of marital privacy which are constitutionally protected. * * *

Finally, it should be said of the Court's holding today that it in no way interferes with a State's proper regulation of sexual promiscuity or misconduct. As my Brother Harlan so well stated in his dissenting opinion in *Poe v. Ullman*[:]

> Adultery, homosexuality and the like are sexual intimacies which the State forbids . . . but the intimacy of husband and wife is necessarily an essential and accepted feature of the institution of marriage, an institution which the State not only must allow, but which always and in every age it has fostered and protected. It is one thing when the State exerts its power either to forbid extra-marital sexuality . . . or to say who may marry, but it is quite another when, having acknowledged a marriage and the intimacies inherent in it, it undertakes to regulate by means of the criminal law the details of that intimacy.

In sum, I believe that the right of privacy in the marital relation is fundamental and basic—a personal right "retained by the people" within the meaning of the Ninth Amendment. Connecticut cannot constitutionally abridge this fundamental right, which is protected by the Fourteenth

Amendment from infringement by the States. I agree with the Court that petitioners' convictions must therefore be reversed.

JUSTICE HARLAN, concurring in the judgment.

[Justice Harlan followed his *Poe* dissent to find that the statute violated the Due Process Clause. He then responded to Justice Black's contention that his approach lacked judicial restraint and that judicial restraint requires limiting the reach of the Fourteenth Amendment's Due Process Clause to those rights expressly found in the Bill of Rights.]

While I could not more heartily agree that judicial "self restraint" is an indispensable ingredient of sound constitutional adjudication, I do submit that the formula suggested for achieving it is more hollow than real. "Specific" provisions of the Constitution, no less than "due process," lend themselves as readily to "personal" interpretations by judges whose constitutional outlook is simply to keep the Constitution in supposed "tune with the times." * * *

Judicial self-restraint will not, I suggest, be brought about in the "due process" area by the historically unfounded incorporation formula long advanced by my Brother Black, and now in part espoused by my Brother Stewart. It will be achieved in this area, as in other constitutional areas, only by continual insistence upon respect for the teachings of history, solid recognition of the basic values that underlie our society, and wise appreciation of the great roles that the doctrines of federalism and separation of powers have played in establishing and preserving American freedoms. See *Adamson v. California* (Justice Frankfurter, concurring). Adherence to these principles will not, of course, obviate all constitutional differences of opinion among judges, nor should it. Their continued recognition will, however, go farther toward keeping most judges from roaming at large in the constitutional field than will the interpolation into the Constitution of an artificial and largely illusory restriction on the content of the Due Process Clause.

JUSTICE WHITE, concurring in the judgment.

In my view this Connecticut law as applied to married couples deprives them of "liberty" without due process of law, as that concept is used in the Fourteenth Amendment. I therefore concur in the judgment of the Court reversing these convictions under Connecticut's aiding and abetting statute. * * *

As I read the opinions of the Connecticut courts and the argument of Connecticut in this Court, the State claims but one justification for its anti-use statute. There is no serious contention that Connecticut thinks the use of artificial or external methods of contraception immoral or unwise in itself, or that the anti-use statute is founded upon any policy of promoting population expansion. Rather, the statute is said to serve the State's policy against all forms of promiscuous or illicit sexual relationships, be they premarital or extramarital, concededly a permissible and legitimate legislative goal.

Without taking issue with the premise that the fear of conception operates as a deterrent to such relationships in addition to the criminal proscriptions Connecticut has against such conduct, I wholly fail to see how the ban on the use of contraceptives by married couples in any way reinforces the State's ban on illicit sexual relationships. Connecticut does not bar the importation or possession of contraceptive devices; they are not considered contraband material under state law, and their availability in that State is not seriously disputed. The only way Connecticut seeks to limit or control the availability of such devices is through its general aiding and abetting statute whose operation in this context has been quite obviously ineffective and whose most serious use has been against birth-control clinics rendering advice to married, rather than unmarried, persons. Cf. *Yick Wo v. Hopkins*. Indeed, after over 80 years of the State's proscription of use, the legality of the sale of such devices to prevent disease has never been expressly passed upon, although it appears that sales have long occurred and have only infrequently been challenged. This "undeviating policy . . . throughout all the long years . . . bespeaks more than prosecutorial paralysis." *Poe v. Ullman*. Moreover, it would appear that the sale of contraceptives to prevent disease is plainly legal under Connecticut law.

JUSTICE BLACK, with whom **JUSTICE STEWART** joins, dissenting.

The Court talks about a constitutional "right of privacy" as though there is some constitutional provision or provisions forbidding any law ever to be passed which might abridge the "privacy" of individuals. But there is not. There are, of course, guarantees in certain specific constitutional provisions which are designed in part to protect privacy at certain times and places with respect to certain activities. Such, for example, is the Fourth Amendment's guarantee against "unreasonable searches and seizures." * * *

The due process argument which my Brothers Harlan and White adopt here is based, as their opinions indicate, on the premise that this Court is vested with power to invalidate all state laws that it considers to be arbitrary, capricious, unreasonable, or oppressive, or on this Court's belief that a particular state law under scrutiny has no "rational or justifying" purpose, or is offensive to a "sense of fairness and justice." If these formulas based on "natural justice," or others which mean the same thing, are to prevail, they require judges to determine what is or is not constitutional on the basis of their own appraisal of what laws are unwise or unnecessary. The power to make such decisions is of course that of a legislative body. * * *

* * * [The Ninth] Amendment was passed, not to broaden the powers of this Court or any other department of "the General Government," but, as every student of history knows, to assure the people that the Constitution in all its provisions was intended to limit the Federal Government to the powers granted expressly or by necessary implication. If any broad, unlimited power to hold laws unconstitutional because they offend what this Court conceives to be the "[collective] conscience of our people" is vested in this Court by the Ninth Amendment, the Fourteenth Amendment, or any other provision of the Constitution, it was not given by the Framers, but rather has been bestowed on the Court by the Court. This fact is perhaps responsible for the peculiar phenomenon that for a period of a century and a half no serious suggestion was ever made that the Ninth Amendment, enacted to protect state powers against federal invasion, could be used as a weapon of federal power to prevent state legislatures from passing laws they consider appropriate to govern local affairs. Use of any such broad, unbounded judicial authority would make of this Court's members a day-to-day constitutional convention. * * *

The late Judge Learned Hand, after emphasizing his view that judges should not use the due process formula suggested in the concurring opinions today or any other formula like it to invalidate legislation offensive to their "personal preferences," made the statement, with which I fully agree, that:

"For myself it would be most irksome to be ruled by a bevy of Platonic Guardians, even if I knew how to choose them, which I assuredly do not."

So far as I am concerned, Connecticut's law as applied here is not forbidden by any provision of the Federal Constitution as that Constitution was written, and I would therefore affirm.

JUSTICE STEWART, whom **JUSTICE BLACK** joins, dissenting.

Since 1879 Connecticut has had on its books a law which forbids the use of contraceptives by anyone. I think this is an uncommonly silly law. As a practical matter, the law is obviously unenforceable, except in the oblique context of the present case. As a philosophical matter, I believe the use of contraceptives in the relationship of marriage should be left to personal and private choice, based upon each individual's moral, ethical, and religious beliefs. As a matter of social policy, I think professional counsel about methods of birth control should be available to all, so that each individual's choice can be meaningfully made. But we are not asked in this case to say whether we think this law is unwise, or even asinine. We are asked to hold that it violates the United States Constitution. And that I cannot do.

NOTES ON GRISWOLD AND THE RIGHT OF PRIVACY

1. *Alternative Methods in* Griswold. What is a "penumbra" and how does it generate rights? (No fair to answer, "Only the Shadow knows!") See generally Paul Kauper, *Penumbras, Peripheries, Emanations, Things Fundamental and Things Forgotten: The* Griswold *Case*, 64 Mich. L. Rev. 235 (1965). Of the Justices writing in support of the majority decision, who has the strongest arguments? What sources do they suggest that the Court should examine to determine whether a given right is fundamental? For a skeptical survey, see John Hart Ely, *The Supreme Court, 1977 Term—Foreword: On Discovering Fundamental Values*, 92 Harv. L. Rev. 5 (1978).

2. *Linking* Griswold, *the Incorporation Doctrine, and the "Reverse Incorporation" Problem.* Justice Harlan again invoked *Palko* to define what substantive due process rights are provided by the Due Process Clause of the Fourteenth Amendment. Justice Goldberg, in a footnote we have not reproduced, asserted that the Court "has never held that the Bill of Rights or the Fourteenth Amendment protects only those rights that the Constitution specifically mentions by name." As you would expect, he cited *Meyer* and *Pierce*; in addition, he cited *Bolling v. Sharpe*, the companion case to *Brown* in which the Court held that school segregation in the District of Columbia violated the Due Process Clause of the Fifth Amendment. Does the "reverse incorporation" holding in *Bolling* lend any support to *Griswold*? Note how Justice Harlan deployed *Palko* and *Bolling v. Sharpe* in his *Poe* dissent.

3. *Equal Protection as an Alternative?* It is clear that in Connecticut the women who had the most difficulty receiving birth-control information and supplies were poor women, who had to rely upon birth-control clinics. Should the Court have based its result on these facts, invoking the Equal Protection Clause? The statute's harm to the poor was perpetuated in Connecticut because of continued support for the statute by the Roman Catholic Church— suggesting the statute served a "sectarian" religious purpose and not even a minimal secular one. Might this explain Justice White's position in *Griswold*?

Because women obviously bear disproportionate burdens from unwanted pregnancies, the Connecticut law had a strikingly disparate impact on women. Recall *Yick Wo v. Hopkins* (Chapter 3, § 1B). Should this have influenced the outcome in *Griswold*?

4. *Unmarried People and the Expanding Ambit of the Right of Privacy.* Griswold involved only the rights of married couples to use birth control. In *Eisenstadt v. Baird*, 405 U.S. 438 (1972), the Court struck down a law prohibiting the sale of contraceptives to unmarried individuals. The majority decision, by Justice Brennan, purported to apply "rational basis" equal protection analysis. According to Justice Brennan, the state surely could not have meant to make the threat of unwanted pregnancy a punishment for non-marital sex (which is almost surely what the state in fact did mean to do). (Might Justice Brennan have implicitly rejected this purpose as embodying sex discrimination, since the effect of the "punishment" would fall primarily on women?) Having refused to consider the statute's most probable purpose, the

Court then examined a variety of trumped-up justifications, not surprisingly finding all of them to be unconvincing.

Eisenstadt said: "If the right of privacy means anything, it is the right of the *individual*, married or single, to be free from unwarranted governmental intrusion into matters so fundamentally affecting a person as the decision whether to bear or beget a child." Although *Griswold* articulated the privacy right in *family governance* terms, *Eisenstadt* rearticulated it in terms of the individual's *life choices*. This libertarian rearticulation was important in the next cases, involving abortions and regulation of contraceptives by minors, as both decisions certainly viewed privacy in *inaccessibility* terms.

5. *Minors.* In a later contraception case, *Carey v. Population Services International*, 431 U.S. 678 (1977), the Court considered the sale of contraceptives to minors. Justice Brennan's plurality opinion concluded that restrictions on such sales infringed minors' right to privacy. Three concurring Justices made it clear that they did not believe that minors had a constitutional right to be sexually active, but instead that denying them access to birth control was an inappropriate means of deterring sexual activity. Concurring, Justice Stevens remarked that "[i]t is as though a State decided to dramatize its disapproval of motorcycles by forbidding the use of safety helmets." Dissenting alone, Justice Rehnquist observed that if the men who struggled to establish the Constitution or the Reconstruction Amendments "could have lived to know that their efforts had enshrined in the Constitution the right of commercial vendors of contraceptives to peddle them to unmarried minors, [it] is not difficult to imagine their reaction."

6. *A Right of "Sexual" Privacy?* Echoing Margaret Sanger's 1919 appeal, Professor Fowler Harper's brief for Planned Parenthood in *Poe* argued that "sexual pleasure" is an important end in human life, and that frustration of one's preferred sexual outlet, by the state or otherwise, is psychologically harmful to the individual as well as the entire family. This was an open appeal for the Court to recognize the important role of sexuality in people's lives—but the Justices ducked *Poe* and dodged the issue in subsequent cases. Justice Brennan's opinion in *Eisenstadt* pretended that the state was not trying to regulate nonmarital sexuality, and his opinion in *Carey* conceded that the Court had never ruled that a particular sexual act is constitutionally protected. Richard Posner, *Sex and Reason* 331 (1992), reads *Eisenstadt* for the proposition that "unmarried persons have a constitutional right to engage in sexual intercourse." Would the Supreme Court agree? If it did, could the state continue to criminalize adultery, namely, sexual intercourse between a man and a woman, at least one of whom is married to someone else? Incest, or intercourse between two closely related persons? Sex between first cousins, which many states consider incest? Sex with animals? Where does precedent draw the line? Where would you draw the line if you were a legislator? Are the two lines notably different?

ROBERT H. BORK,
Neutral Principles and Some First Amendment Problems
47 Ind. L.J. 1, 8–9 (1971)[33]

[In *Griswold,* Justice Douglas] performed a miracle of transubstantiation. He called the first amendment's penumbra a protection of "privacy" and then asserted that other amendments create "zones of privacy." He had no better reason to use the word "privacy" than that the individual is free within these zones, free to act in public as well as in private. None of these penumbral zones—from the first, third, fourth or fifth amendments, all of which he cited, along with the ninth—covered the case before him. One more leap was required. Justice Douglas asserted that these various "zones of privacy" created an independent right of privacy, a right not lying within the penumbra of any specific amendment. He did not disclose, however, how a series of specified rights combined to create a new and unspecified right.

The *Griswold* opinion fails every test of neutrality. The derivation of the principle was utterly specious, and so was its definition. In fact, we are left with no idea of what the principle really forbids. Derivation and definition are interrelated here. Justice Douglas called the amendments and their penumbras "zones of privacy," though of course they are not that at all. They protect both private and public behavior and so would more properly be labelled "zones of freedom." If we follow Justice Douglas in his next step, these zones would then add up to an independent right of freedom, which is to say, a general constitutional right to be free of legal coercion, a manifest impossibility in any imaginable society.

Griswold, then, is an unprincipled decision, both in the way in which it derives a new constitutional right and in the way it defines that right, or rather fails to define it. We are left with no idea of the sweep of the right of privacy and hence no notion of the cases to which it may or may not be applied in the future. The truth is that the Court could not reach its result in *Griswold* through principle. The reason is obvious. Every clash between a minority claiming freedom and a majority claiming power to regulate involves a choice between the gratifications of the two groups. When the Constitution has not spoken, the Court will be able to find no scale, other than its own value preferences, upon which to weigh the respective claims to pleasure. Compare the facts in *Griswold* with a hypothetical suit by an electric utility company and one of its customers to void a smoke pollution ordinance as unconstitutional. The cases are identical.

In *Griswold* a husband and wife assert that they wish to have sexual relations without fear of unwanted children. The law impairs their sexual gratifications. The State can assert, and at one stage in that litigation did

---

assert, that the majority finds the use of contraceptives immoral. Knowledge that it takes place and that the State makes no effort to inhibit it causes the majority anguish, impairs their gratifications.

The electrical company asserts that it wishes to produce electricity at low cost in order to reach a wide market and make profits. Its customer asserts that he wants a lower cost so that prices can be held low. The smoke pollution regulation impairs his and the company's stockholders' economic gratifications. The State can assert not only that the majority prefer clean air to lower prices, but also that the absence of the regulation impairs the majority's physical and aesthetic gratifications.

Neither case is covered specifically or by obvious implication in the Constitution. Unless we can distinguish forms of gratification, the only course for a principled Court is to let the majority have its way in both cases. It is clear that the Court cannot make the necessary distinction. There is no principled way to decide that one man's gratifications are more deserving of respect than another's or that one form of gratification is more worthy than another. Why is sexual gratification more worthy than moral gratification? Why is sexual gratification nobler than economic gratification? There is no way of deciding these matters other than by reference to some system of moral or ethical values that has no objective or intrinsic validity of its own and about which men can and do differ. Where the Constitution does not embody the moral or ethical choice, the judge has no basis other than his own values upon which to set aside the community judgment embodied in the statute. That, by definition, is an inadequate basis for judicial supremacy. The issue of the community's moral and ethical values, the issue of the degree of pain an activity causes, are matters concluded by the passage and enforcement of the laws in question. The judiciary has no role to play other than that of applying the statutes in a fair and impartial manner.

One of my colleagues refers to this conclusion, not without sarcasm, as the "Equal Gratification Clause." The phrase is apt, and I accept it, though not the sarcasm. Equality of human gratifications, where the document does not impose a hierarchy, is an essential part of constitutional doctrine because of the necessity that judges be principled. To be perfectly clear on the subject, I repeat that the principle is not applicable to legislatures. Legislation requires value choice and cannot be principled in the sense under discussion. Courts must accept any value choice the legislature makes unless it clearly runs contrary to a choice made in the framing of the Constitution.

It follows, of course, that broad areas of constitutional law ought to be reformulated. Most obviously, it follows that substantive due process, revived by the *Griswold* case, is and always has been an improper doctrine. Substantive due process requires the Court to say, without guidance from the Constitution, which liberties or gratifications may be infringed by majorities and which may not. This means that *Griswold's* antecedents were also wrongly decided, *e.g., Meyer v. Nebraska*, which struck down a statute forbidding the teaching of subjects in any language other than English; *Pierce v. Society of Sisters*, which set aside a statute compelling all Oregon school children to attend public schools; *Adkins v. Children's Hospital*, which invalidated a statute of Congress authorizing a board to fix minimum wages for women and children in the District of Columbia; and *Lochner v. New York*, which voided a statute fixing maximum hours of work for bakers. With some of these cases I am in political agreement, and perhaps *Pierce's* result could be reached on acceptable grounds, but there is no justification for the Court's methods. In *Lochner*, Justice Peckham, defending liberty from what he conceived as a mere meddlesome interference, asked, "[A]re we all . . . at the mercy of legislative majorities?" The correct answer, where the Constitution does not speak, must be "yes."

———

Professor Bork's suggestion that *Griswold* was not good law generated controversy when President Reagan nominated then-Judge Bork to be a Justice on the Supreme Court. When Bork refused to back away from his principled opposition to a general constitutional right of privacy, large majorities of Americans viewed his nomination in a negative light, and the Senate rejected it on a bipartisan 58–42 vote.[34] Bork's obedience to principle is admirable, but is it fair to say that the Constitution's text says *nothing* relevant to the issue? Consider the following Notes.

NOTES ON THE NINTH AMENDMENT

1. *The Text.* There is a maxim of interpretation that the expression of certain things implies the exclusion of all other things (in lawyer's Latin, *expressio unius est exclusio alterius*). To take a simple example, when a parent sends a child to the corner store with a grocery list, the listing of certain items implies that the child is not to buy anything else. Read the Ninth Amendment carefully, for it seems to embody an instruction that at least some parts of the Constitution are *not* to be interpreted according to this maxim.

Justice Goldberg in *Griswold* argued that the amendment commands that *expressio unius* is not an appropriate method of interpreting the Bill of Rights. To be specific, his argument is that, according to the Ninth Amendment, the existence of a list of express rights (Amendments 1–8) is not to be taken as creating a negative implication about the existence of other, unexpressed rights. On this reading, the Ninth Amendment does not itself protect any unenumerated rights; it simply assumes that such rights exist and are to be

---

[34] See generally Ethan Bronner, *Battle for Justice: How the Bork Nomination Shook America* (1989). Bork's unapologetic response is *The Tempting of America: The Political Seduction of the Law* (1990), excerpted in Chapter 2, § 3A.

protected by courts in the same way as listed rights. There is some historical evidence that the authors of the Ninth Amendment intended to refer to unwritten "natural rights." See Daniel Farber, Retained by the People (2008); Suzanna Sherry, *The Founders' Unwritten Constitution*, 54 U. Chi. L. Rev. 1127 (1987).

Even on Goldberg's reading, does the use of the word "retained" in the Ninth Amendment restrict the meaning of it to those freedoms that have always been fundamental in our traditions, or at least were fundamental in 1791, thus making the extension of *Griswold* to unmarried persons and minors quite problematic? More dramatically, could "rights retained by the people" simply mean that those rights already provided under state law (state constitutional law, statutory law, or common law) continue after the adoption of the Bill of Rights unless and until they are modified or abolished by the state, by an act of Congress constitutionally preempting the state law, or by a judicial declaration that the state law is unconstitutional? This reading of the Ninth Amendment would completely undercut Justice Goldberg's approach. But this reading seems merely to duplicate the Tenth Amendment, which appears to make clear that states remain free to define individual rights not otherwise guaranteed by the federal Constitution.

Contrast Justice Black's approach in *Griswold*. He contended that the Ninth Amendment is designed to refute any implication that the expression of certain rights against federal action (Amendments 1–8) indicates that the federal government, which is limited to exercising the powers delegated to it under the original Constitution (see Article I), had been transformed by the existence of the Bill of Rights into a government that can do anything not expressly prohibited in the Bill of Rights. Is Black's reading of the Amendment as compatible with its words as Goldberg's reading? Does Black's reading of the Ninth Amendment just duplicate the Tenth Amendment?

Consider Bork's attack on *Griswold*. Does he violate his own interpretive model by, in effect, reading the word "not" out of the Ninth Amendment?[35]

2. *The Historical Context.* Justices Goldberg and Black reformulated their textual disagreement into a disagreement about original intentions as well. Consider their disagreement, as well as the third approach identified above, in terms of constitutional originalism:

(1) *The Goldberg view.* Goldberg argued that the Framers of the Bill of Rights intended to rebut the *expressio unius* negative implication about the existence of unenumerated *rights*.

---

[35] In his Senate confirmation hearings concerning his nomination to the Supreme Court, Judge Bork was asked about the Ninth Amendment. He responded:

> I do not think that you can use the ninth amendment unless you know something of what it means. For example, if you had an amendment that says "Congress shall make no" and then there is an ink blot and you cannot read the rest of it and that is the only copy you have, I do not think the court can make up what might be under the ink blot.

Nomination of Robert H. Bork to be Associate Justice of the Supreme Court of the United States: Hearings Before the Senate Comm. on the Judiciary, 100th Cong., 1st Sess. 249 (1987).

(2) *The Black view.* Black contended that, to the contrary, the Framers intended to rebut the *expressio unius* negative implication about the existence of unenumerated federal *powers.*

(3) *The state-law view.* The third argument noted above—that the Ninth Amendment was designed simply to preserve rights recognized under state law—is also subscribed to by some scholars.[36]

During the period in which the Constitution was ratified, it and its Framers were attacked for failing to include a Bill of Rights against federal action. Supporters of the Constitution argued in defense that, under the document they drafted, a Bill of Rights was unnecessary: The federal government was already quite limited, as its authority was confined to those powers delegated to it.[37] The defenders also contended that including a Bill of Rights could work mischief. James Iredell, a supporter of the Constitution, argued in the North Carolina ratifying convention:

> [I]t would be not only useless, but dangerous, to enumerate a number of rights which are not intended to be given up; because it would be implying, in the strongest manner, that every right not included in the exception might be impaired by the government without usurpation; and it would be impossible to enumerate every one. Let any one make what collection or enumeration of rights he pleases, I will immediately mention twenty or thirty more rights not contained in it.[38]

Iredell's speech typified the sentiments of supporters of the Constitution. One way to read Iredell's argument is Justice Black's: Adding a Bill of Rights might create ambiguity about whether the federal government remained one solely of enumerated, delegated powers. Another way to read the argument is compatible with Justice Goldberg's views: Adding a Bill of Rights would

---

[36] See, e.g., Russell Caplan, *The History and Meaning of the Ninth Amendment*, 69 Va. L. Rev. 223 (1983). For a discussion of the overall problem, see generally Daniel Farber, *Retained by the People* (2007); Thomas McAffee, *The Original Meaning of the Ninth Amendment*, 90 Colum. L. Rev. 1215 (1990).

An illustration of this argument is provided in McAffee, supra, at 1227:

> * * * The objection that the Constitution should include a bill of rights was first raised near the end of the Convention, in August and September of 1787. Even after the Convention had rejected the call to form a committee to draft a bill of rights, on September 14, just three days before the Convention adjourned, Charles Pinckney and Elbridge Gerry moved to insert a provision for freedom of the press. But Roger Sherman * * * argued that the proposal was "unnecessary" because "[t]he power of Congress does not extend to the Press."

[37] *Roth's* discussion of *Wisconsin v. Constantineau* might suggest that personal reputation is also a liberty interest. In *Paul v. Davis*, 424 U.S. 693 (1976), however, the Court held that due process was not triggered when police circulated a flyer to merchants that labeled a person a shoplifter. *Paul* concluded that injury to reputation, without some other injury, did not qualify as a deprivation of a liberty interest. (*Constantineau* thus could be conceptualized as involving an injury to reputation plus a ban on the purchase of liquor.) *Paul* is perhaps explicable as an attempt to avoid equating common law torts (e.g., libel) with due process liberty interests.

[38] North Carolina Ratifying Convention (July 29, 1788), in 4 Jonathan Elliot, *Debates in the Several State Conventions on the Adoption of the Federal Constitution* 167 (1891). See Daniel Farber & Suzanna Sherry, *A History of the American Constitution* 224–25, 230 (1990).

endanger the unwritten individual rights already "retained" by the people. Which is the more plausible understanding? Whichever reading you accept explains what the Ninth Amendment was supposed to guard against.

In part, the historical record is somewhat ambiguous because of a lack of clarity about what "rights" meant in this context. One could say, with Justice Goldberg, that the Framers understood "rights retained by the people" as those individual rights found in natural law. There was a strong tradition of natural law in colonial America, which is reflected in the Declaration of Independence ("all men have certain inalienable rights, including life, liberty, and the pursuit of happiness") and in the early state constitutions. Whether this tradition of natural law continued unabated into the framing of the Constitution is more debatable, however. In any event, even if many of the Framers believed in natural law, in our contemporary, skeptical world many intellectuals reject the idea—they would contend that natural law is just some sort of quasi-religious superstition, or that we cannot hope to ascertain what list of rights the Framers thought were contained in natural law and that the contents of it are too debatable and subjective to be left to the Supreme Court. Thus, even if Goldberg was right about the historical context, some would argue that our contemporary context is so different that we ought to ignore the Ninth Amendment.

An alternative reading of the historical context fits Justice Black's understanding. For the drafters of the Constitution, one can argue, "the scheme of limited government embodied in the system of enumerated powers was a means of reserving rights to the people." [McAffee 1219]. Here "right" is not being used in the contemporary sense of a specific limitation on otherwise lawful governmental power—as we would say today, for example, that Congress has the power to regulate interstate commerce, but cannot exercise that power in a way that violates the First Amendment. Rather, on this reading "right" means the absence of governmental authority to operate in the first place—the unenumerated rights are those "retained" by the simple device of enumerating a list of limited powers. This, of course, raises again the question whether this reading of the Ninth Amendment simply duplicates the Tenth Amendment—why would the Framers have inserted one amendment dealing with "rights" and one with "powers" if the two terms had the same effect?

We cannot hope to give you any way to resolve the historical dispute. We can give you one potential source of historical understanding, however. Appendix 3 reproduces an edited version of James Madison's speech to the House of Representatives presenting his draft of the Bill of Rights (including the Ninth Amendment). Read it and see what you think.

3.   *Alternatives.* Consider Randy Barnett, *Reconceiving the Ninth Amendment*, 74 Cornell L. Rev. 1, 37 (1988):

> As a practical matter, we must choose between two fundamentally different constructions of the Constitution, each resting on a different presumption. We either accept the presumption that in pursuing happiness persons may do whatever is not justly

prohibited or we are left with a presumption that the government may do whatever is not expressly prohibited. The presence of the Ninth Amendment in the Constitution strongly supports the first of these two presumptions. According to this interpretation of the Ninth Amendment, the Constitution established what Steven Macedo has called islands of governmental powers "surrounded by a sea of individual rights." It did not establish "islands [of rights] surrounded by a sea of governmental powers."

On this reading, is there any way to distinguish between unenumerated economic rights and unenumerated personal rights? Should there be? How might Bork respond?

B. ABORTION

ROE V. WADE
410 U.S. 113, 93 S.Ct. 705, 35 L.Ed.2d 147 (1973)

JUSTICE BLACKMUN delivered the opinion of the Court.

[Jane Roe, an unmarried pregnant woman, brought a class action challenging the constitutionality of the Texas criminal abortion laws. Texas prohibited all abortions except for the purpose of saving the pregnant woman's life. The Court undertook a detailed examination of the history of abortion law, beginning with the ancient Greeks. The Court observed that "the restrictive criminal abortion laws in effect in a majority of States today are of relatively recent vintage," generally dating from the second half of the nineteenth century. In contrast, the common law did not prohibit abortion before "quickening"—the first noticeable movement of the fetus, usually around the seventeenth week of pregnancy:

> It is thus apparent that at common law, at the time of the adoption of our Constitution, and throughout the major portion of the 19th century, abortion was viewed with less disfavor than under most American statutes currently in effect. Phrasing it another way, a woman enjoyed a substantially broader right to terminate a pregnancy than she does in most States today. At least with respect to the early stage of pregnancy, and very possibly without such a limitation, the opportunity to make this choice was present in this country well into the 19th century. Even later, the law continued for some time to treat less punitively an abortion procured in early pregnancy.

The Court noted that the move toward more severe abortion laws seems to have been caused by medical concerns about the risks to women posed by abortions under the medical technology of the time. After a lengthy discussion of this background, the Court turned to the constitutional issues.]

The Constitution does not explicitly mention any right of privacy. In a line of decisions, however, going back perhaps as far as *Union Pacific R. Co. v. Botsford*, 141 U.S. 250, 251 (1891), the Court has recognized that a right of personal privacy, or a guarantee of certain areas or zones of privacy, does exist under the Constitution. In varying contexts, the Court or individual Justices have, indeed, found at least the roots of that right in the First Amendment, in the Fourth and Fifth Amendments, in the penumbras of the Bill of Rights [citing *Griswold*], in the Ninth Amendment, or in the concept of liberty guaranteed by the first section of the Fourteenth Amendment. These decisions make it clear that only personal rights that can be deemed "fundamental" or "implicit in the concept of ordered liberty," *Palko*, are included in this guarantee of personal privacy. They also make it clear that the right has some extension to activities relating to marriage, procreation, contraception, family relationships, and child rearing and education.

This right of privacy, whether it be founded in the Fourteenth Amendment's concept of personal liberty and restrictions upon state action, as we feel it is, or, as the District Court determined, in the Ninth Amendment's reservation of rights to the people, is broad enough to encompass a woman's decision whether or not to terminate her pregnancy. The detriment that the State would impose upon the pregnant woman by denying this choice altogether is apparent. Specific and direct harm medically diagnosable even in early pregnancy may be involved. Maternity, or additional offspring, may force upon the woman a distressful life and future. Psychological harm may be imminent. Mental and physical health may be taxed by child care. There is also the distress, for all concerned, associated with the unwanted child, and there is the problem of bringing a child into a family already unable, psychologically and otherwise, to care for it. In other cases, as in this one, the additional difficulties and continuing stigma of unwed motherhood may be involved. All these are factors the woman and her responsible physician necessarily will consider in consultation.

On the basis of elements such as these, appellant and some *amici* argue that the woman's right is absolute and that she is entitled to terminate her pregnancy at whatever time, in whatever way, and for whatever reason she alone chooses. With this we do not agree. Appellant's arguments that Texas either has no valid interest at all in regulating the abortion decision, or no interest strong enough to support any limitation upon the woman's sole determination, are unpersuasive. The Court's decisions recognizing a right of privacy also acknowledge that some state regulation in areas protected by that right is appropriate. [A] State may properly assert important interests in safeguarding health, in maintaining medical standards, and in protecting potential life. At some point in pregnancy, these respective interests become sufficiently compelling to sustain regulation of the factors that govern the abortion decision. The privacy right involved, therefore, cannot be said to be absolute. In fact, it is not clear to us that the claim asserted by some *amici* that one has an unlimited right to do with one's body as one pleases bears a close relationship to the right of privacy previously articulated in the Court's decisions. The Court has refused to recognize an unlimited right of this kind in the past. *Jacobson v. Massachusetts*, 197 U.S. 11 (1905) (vaccination); *Buck v. Bell* (sterilization).

We, therefore, conclude that the right of personal privacy includes the abortion decision, but that this right is not unqualified and must be considered against important state interests in regulation. [Justice Blackmun found this approach consistent with the trend in the lower courts and concluded that, where " 'fundamental rights' are involved, * * * regulation limiting these rights may be justified only by a 'compelling state interest,' and that legislative enactments must be narrowly drawn to express only the legitimate state interests at stake," citing *Griswold*.]

The appellee and certain *amici* argue that the fetus is a "person" within the language and meaning of the Fourteenth Amendment. In support of this, they outline at length and in detail the well-known facts of fetal development. If this suggestion of personhood is established, the appellant's case, of course, collapses, for the fetus' right to life is then guaranteed specifically by the Amendment. The appellant conceded as much on reargument. On the other hand, the appellee conceded on reargument that no case could be cited that holds that a fetus is a person within the meaning of the [Amendment].

The Constitution does not define "person" in so many words. Section 1 of the Fourteenth Amendment contains three references to "person." The first, in defining "citizens," speaks of "persons born or naturalized in the United States." The word also appears both in the Due Process Clause and in the Equal Protection Clause. "Person" is used in other places in the Constitution. But in nearly all these instances, the use of the word is such that it has application only postnatally. None indicates, with any assurance, that it has any possible pre-natal application.

All this, together with our observation that throughout the major portion of the 19th century prevailing legal abortion practices were far freer than they are today, persuades us that the word "person," as used in the Fourteenth Amendment, does not include the unborn. This is in accord with the results reached in those few cases where the issue has been squarely presented. * * *

This conclusion, however, does not of itself fully answer the contentions raised by Texas, and we pass on to other considerations.

The pregnant woman cannot be isolated in her privacy. She carries an embryo and, later, a fetus, if one accepts the medical definitions of the developing young in the human uterus. The situation therefore is inherently different from marital intimacy, or bedroom possession of obscene material, or marriage, or procreation, or education, with which [prior cases] were respectively concerned. As we have intimated above, it is reasonable and appropriate for a State to decide that at some point in time another interest, that of health of the mother or that of potential human life, becomes significantly involved. The woman's privacy is no longer sole and any right of privacy she possesses must be measured accordingly.

Texas urges that, apart from the Fourteenth Amendment, life begins at conception and is present throughout pregnancy, and that, therefore, the State has a compelling interest in protecting that life from and after conception. We need not resolve the difficult question of when life begins. When those trained in the respective disciplines of medicine, philosophy, and theology are unable to arrive at any consensus, the judiciary, at this point in the development of man's knowledge, is not in a position to speculate as to the answer. * * *

In view of all this, we do not agree that, by adopting one theory of life, Texas may override the rights of the pregnant woman that are at stake. We repeat, however, that the State does have an important and legitimate interest in preserving and protecting the health of the pregnant woman, whether she be a resident of the State or a nonresident who seeks medical consultation and treatment there, and that it has still *another* important and legitimate interest in protecting the potentiality of human life. These interests are separate and distinct. Each grows in substantiality as the woman approaches term and, at a point during pregnancy, each becomes "compelling."

With respect to the State's important and legitimate interest in the health of the mother, the "compelling" point, in the light of present medical knowledge, is at approximately the end of the first trimester. This is so because of the now-established medical fact * * * that until the end of the first trimester mortality in abortion may be less than mortality in normal childbirth. It follows that, from and after this point, a State may regulate the abortion procedure to the extent that the regulation reasonably relates to the preservation and protection of maternal health. Examples of permissible state regulation in this area are requirements as to the qualifications of the person who is to perform the abortion; as to the licensure of that person; as to the facility in which the procedure is to be performed, that is, whether it must be a hospital or may be a clinic or some other place of less-than-hospital status; as to the licensing of the facility; and the like.

This means, on the other hand, that, for the period of pregnancy prior to this "compelling" point, the attending physician, in consultation with his patient, is free to determine, without regulation by the State, that, in his medical judgment, the patient's pregnancy should be terminated. If that decision is reached, the judgment may be effectuated by an abortion free of interference by the State.

With respect to the State's important and legitimate interest in potential life, the "compelling" point is at viability. This is so because the fetus then presumably has the capability of meaningful life outside the mother's womb. State regulation protective of fetal life after viability thus has both logical and biological justifications. If the State is interested in protecting fetal life after viability, it may go so far as to proscribe abortion during that period, except when it is necessary to preserve the life or health of the mother. * * *

This holding, we feel, is consistent with the relative weights of the respective interests involved, with the lessons and examples of medical and legal history, with the lenity of the common law, and with the demands of the profound problems of the present day. The decision leaves the State free to place increasing restrictions on abortion as the period of pregnancy lengthens, so long as those restrictions are tailored to the recognized state interests. The decision vindicates the right of the physician to administer medical treatment according to his professional judgment up to the points where important state interests provide compelling justifications for intervention. Up to those points, the abortion decision in all its aspects is inherently, and primarily, a medical decision, and basic responsibility for it must rest with the physician. If an individual practitioner abuses the privilege of exercising proper medical judgment, the usual remedies, judicial and intra-professional, are available.

[Concurring opinions by **CHIEF JUSTICE BURGER**, **JUSTICE DOUGLAS**, and **JUSTICE STEWART** are omitted, as is the dissenting opinion of **JUSTICE WHITE**.]

JUSTICE REHNQUIST, dissenting.

The Court's opinion brings to the decision of this troubling question both extensive historical fact and a wealth of legal scholarship. While the opinion thus commands my respect, I find myself nonetheless in fundamental disagreement with those parts of it that invalidate the Texas statute in question, and therefore dissent. * * *

* * * I have difficulty in concluding, as the Court does, that the right of "privacy" is involved in this case. Texas, by the statute here challenged, bars the performance of a medical abortion by a licensed physician on a plaintiff such as Roe. A transaction resulting in an operation such as this is not "private" in the ordinary usage of that word. Nor is the "privacy" that the Court finds here even a distant relative of the freedom from searches and seizures protected by the Fourth Amendment to the Constitution, which the Court has referred to as embodying a right to privacy.

* * * The test traditionally applied in the area of social and economic legislation is whether or not a law such as that challenged has a rational relation to a valid state objective. *Williamson v. Lee Optical Co.* The Due Process Clause of the Fourteenth Amendment undoubtedly does place a limit, albeit a broad one, on legislative power to enact laws such as this. If the Texas statute were to prohibit an abortion even where the mother's life is in jeopardy, I have little doubt that such a statute would lack a rational relation to a valid state objective under the test stated in *Williamson.* But the Court's sweeping invalidation of any restrictions on abortion during the first trimester is impossible to justify under that standard, and the conscious weighing of competing factors that the Court's opinion apparently substitutes for the established test is far more appropriate to a legislative judgment than to a judicial one. * * *

To reach its result, the Court necessarily has had to find within the scope of the Fourteenth Amendment a right that was apparently completely unknown to the drafters of the Amendment. As early as 1821, the first state law dealing directly with abortion was enacted by the Connecticut Legislature. By the time of the adoption of the Fourteenth Amendment in 1868, there were at least 36 laws enacted by state or territorial legislatures limiting abortion. While many States have amended or updated their laws, 21 of the laws on the books in 1868 remain in effect today. Indeed, the Texas statute struck down today was, as the majority notes, first enacted in 1857 and "has remained substantially unchanged to the present time."

There apparently was no question concerning the validity of this provision or of any of the other state statutes when the Fourteenth Amendment was adopted. The only conclusion possible from this history is that the drafters did not intend to have the Fourteenth Amendment withdraw from the States the power to legislate with respect to this matter.

NOTES ON ROE AND THE ABORTION CONTROVERSY

1. *Should the Statute's Age Make a Difference?* In a companion case, *Doe v. Bolton*, 410 U.S. 179 (1973), the Court invalidated a more modern abortion statute that required abortions to be performed in hospitals and set up special procedures for hospital approval of abortions, on the ground that such procedures unduly restricted the exercise of the *Roe* right. Should the more modern statute, adopted after women obtained the right to vote, have been treated differently than the nineteenth century Texas law in *Roe*?

2. *Did the Court Act Too Soon? Was the Political Process Working?* Consider whether the Court would have done better to follow its own example in the contraception cases and try to establish a dialogue with the legislatures before attempting a definitive statement about abortion rights. Such a dialogue might well have been productive. In 1962, the influential American Law Institute, in its Model Penal Code, proposed liberalizing criminal abortion

statutes. Beginning in 1968, thirteen states had softened their abortion statutes to allow abortions not only if the woman's life was threatened, but also if the pregnancy seriously endangered her physical or mental health, if the child would have major physical or mental abnormalities, or if the pregnancy resulted from rape. Four states essentially allowed abortion on demand if performed early in the pregnancy. Both the American Bar Association and the American Medical Association had gone on record favoring a liberalization of access to abortion. Although in the early 1970s many states continued to have restrictive approaches to abortion, the trend in the states, if left unimpeded, might well have led to a national consensus or at least to much wider availability of abortion through state legislation. Indeed, in 1973 immediately following *Roe*, 52% of those polled in a national survey said that they approved of *Roe*'s holding, which was described to them as "making abortions up to three months of pregnancy legal."[39]

3. *Aggressive Rational Basis Review as an Alternative.* As with the birth-control statute in *Griswold*, many of the abortion statutes on the books in the early 1970s were a century old, adopted in a different time and climate, both moral and political. The primary purpose for the statutes apparently was to protect the life and health of the mother from the comparative dangers of abortion instead of childbirth. By 1973, the medical basis for the criminal statutes had evaporated: Abortion in the early stages of pregnancy had become safer than carrying the fetus to term. These facts led one thoughtful lower-court judge to contend that the old abortion statutes should be invalidated because there was no longer any logical connection between the nineteenth century legislature's purpose and the means chosen to effectuate that purpose. See *Abele v. Markle*, 342 F. Supp. 800, 809 (D. Conn. 1972) (three-judge court) (Newman, J., concurring in the result). Should the Court have taken this more limited tack in *Roe*? Or would it have been ducking its constitutional responsibilities if it had done so? How would this analysis be affected by considering the law's disproportionate effect on women? (Note that Justice White, who concurred in *Griswold* on rational basis grounds, dissented in *Roe*.)

4. *Revisiting* Lochner. Is *Roe* just *Lochner* in feminist garb, or is there a principled reason for viewing abortion as a fundamental right? Consider how *Roe* would be decided by a judge applying originalism, representation reinforcement,[40] or normative interpretation.[41] Does it matter whether we phrase the question in terms of "abortion" or "control over reproduction"?

5. *The Role of the Physician.* In his concurring opinion, Chief Justice Burger stressed that the Court was not simply endorsing abortion on demand,

---

[39] See Eric Uslander & Ronald Weber, *Public Support for Pro-Choice Abortion Policies in the Nation and States: Changes and Stability After the* Roe *and* Doe *Decisions*, 77 Mich. L. Rev. 1772, 1775 (1979). See also Garrow, *Liberty and Sexuality, supra.*

[40] See John Hart Ely, *The Wages of Crying Wolf: A Comment on* Roe v. Wade, 82 Yale L.J. 920 (1973).

[41] See Sylvia Law, *Rethinking Sex and the Constitution*, 132 U. Pa. L. Rev. 955 (1984); Michael Perry, *Abortion, the Public Morals, and the Police Power: The Ethical Function of Substantive Due Process*, 23 UCLA L. Rev. 689 (1976). Compare Michael Perry, *The Constitution, the Courts, and Human Rights* 94 (1982) (author changes his mind about normative consensus).

because the physician's independent medical judgment remained a crucial element in the abortion decision. Would an independent medical judgment be desirable, or would it in fact give undue control of women's lives to their (at the time, at least) predominantly male doctors? In any event, the creation of abortion clinics seems to have undercut whatever expectation of direct patient-physician dialogue the *Roe* majority may have expected as a barrier to on-demand abortions.

REVA SIEGEL,
Reasoning from the Body: A Historical Perspective on Abortion Regulation and Questions of Equal Protection
44 Stan. L. Rev. 261, 276–77, 350–51 (1992)[42]

[*Roe*] holds that the state has an interest in potential life which becomes compelling at the point of viability. It defines this regulatory interest in potential life physiologically, without reference to the sorts of constitutional considerations that normally attend the use of state power against a citizen. In the Court's reasoning, facts concerning the physiological development of the unborn provide "logical and biological justifications" both limiting and legitimating state action directed against the pregnant woman. Because *Roe* analyzes an exercise of state power from a medical, rather than a social, point of view, it authorizes state action against the pregnant woman on the basis of physiological criteria, requiring no inquiry into the state's reasons for acting against the pregnant woman, or the impact of its actions on her. Indeed, *Roe* analyzes the state's interest in potential life as a benign exercise of state power for the protection of the unborn, and not as a coercive exercise of state power against pregnant women, often reasoning as if the state's interest in protecting potential life scarcely pertained to the pregnant woman herself. Thus, in the course of justifying its decision to protect the abortion decision as a right of privacy, the Court recognized an antagonistic state interest in restricting women's access to abortion on which it imposed temporal, but few principled, restraints.

To the extent that *Roe* relied upon physiological reasoning to define the state's interest in potential life, it unleashed a legal discourse of indeterminate content and scope—one legitimating boundless regulation of women's reproductive lives should the Court abandon the trimester framework that presently constrains it. In recognizing the state's interest in potential life, the Court ignored a simple social fact that should be of critical constitutional significance: When a state invokes an interest in potential life to justify fetal-protective regulation, the proposed use of public power concerns not merely the unborn, but women as well. Abortion-restrictive regulation is sex-based regulation, the use of public power to force women to bear children. Yet, the Court has never described the state's interest in protecting potential life as an interest in forcing women to bear children. *Roe*'s physiological reasoning obscures that simple social fact. "[I]f one accepts the medical definitions of the developing young in the human uterus" as a sufficient, objective, and authoritative framework for evaluating the state's regulatory interest in abortion—as *Roe* did—state action compelling women to perform the work of motherhood can be justified without ever acknowledging that the state is enforcing a gender status role. In part, this is because analyzing abortion-restrictive regulation within physiological paradigms obscures its social logic, but also, and as importantly, it is because physiological reasons for regulating women's conduct are already laden with socio-political import: Facts about women's bodies have long served to justify regulation enforcing judgments about women's roles.

Abortion-restrictive regulation is state action compelling pregnancy and motherhood, and this simple fact cannot be evaded by invoking nature or a woman's choices to explain the situation in which the pregnant woman subject to abortion restrictions finds herself. A pregnant woman seeking an abortion has the practical capacity to terminate a pregnancy, which she would exercise but for the community's decision to prevent or deter her. If the community successfully effectuates its will, it is the state, and not nature, which is responsible for causing her to continue the pregnancy. * * *

When abortion-restrictive regulation is analyzed as state action compelling motherhood, it presents equal protection concerns that *Roe*'s physiological reasoning obscures.

NOTE ON ABORTION REGULATION AS SEX DISCRIMINATION

Was the Due Process Clause the best place to ground an argument against abortion statutes? Would the Equal Protection Clause have been preferable? What doctrinal obstacles were there? (See Chapter 4, § 2.)[43]

Ruth Bader Ginsburg, *Some Thoughts on Autonomy and Equality in Relation to* Roe v. Wade, 63 N.C. L. Rev. 375, 382–83 (1985)[44], suggests that *Roe* might have been more firmly grounded "had the Court placed the woman alone, rather than the woman tied to her physician, at the center of its attention":

It is not a sufficient answer to charge it all to women's anatomy—a natural, not man-made, phenomenon. Society, not

---

[43] Is it relevant to this argument that public opinion polls show that women favor restricting abortion slightly more than men? See Daniel Farber, *Legal Pragmatism and the Constitution*, 72 Minn. L. Rev. 1331, 1369 n.186 (1988).

[44] Reprinted with permission.

anatomy, "places a greater stigma on unmarried women who become pregnant than on the men who father their children." Society expects, but nature does not command, that "woman take the major responsibility * * * for child care" and that they will stay with their children, bearing nurture and support burdens alone, when fathers deny paternity or otherwise refuse to provide care or financial support for unwanted offspring.

I do not pretend that, if the Court had added a distinct sex discrimination theme to its medically oriented opinion, the storm *Roe* generated would have been less furious. I appreciate the intense divisions of opinion on the moral question and recognize that abortion today cannot fairly be described as nothing more than birth control delayed. The conflict, however, is not simply one between a fetus' interests and a woman's interests, narrowly conceived, nor is the overriding issue state versus private control of a woman's body for a span of nine months. Also in the balance is a woman's autonomous charge of her full life's course—as Professor Karst put it, her ability to stand in relation to man, society, and the state as an independent, self-sustaining, equal citizen.

The conceptualization of abortion as forcing a burden on women is expressed in a well-known philosophical article, Judith Jarvis Thompson, *A Defense of Abortion*, 1 Phil. & Pub. Aff. 47 (1971). Professor Thompson asks the reader to consider the possibility of being kidnapped and hooked up to a blood circulation machine in order to save the life of a famous violinist. After nine months, the violinist will be well enough to be unplugged. This would plainly be an invasion of your moral rights, and Thompson argues by analogy that (even if the fetus is a person) coercing a woman's participation in the pregnancy is no different than the violinist hypothetical. See also Judith Jarvis Thompson, *The Realm of Rights* 289–93 (1990) (what claims does a "fertilized egg" have against a woman?). Is this argument persuasive, or is the violinist analogy contrived?

Some of these arguments illustrate the importance of baselines. Is the pregnant woman being required to confer a benefit to the fetus, or is she being prevented from harming it? This depends on whether the baseline is a world in which women control their pregnancies, or one where pregnancies proceed to term. (Compare the problem of picking baselines in an economic substantive due process case (§ 2B of this chapter) and in a Takings Clause case.) Which is the proper baseline?

NOTE: THE ABORTION RIGHT FROM ROE *TO* CASEY

Just as the Equal Rights Amendment was to generate an anti-ERA politics seeking to preserve traditional gender roles against state liberalization, so the pro-choice movement triggered a "pro-life" countermovement seeking to preserve traditional ideas about family and the origins of human life.[45] *Roe v. Wade* energized the countermovement, which persuaded state legislatures to adopt numerous measures to make abortions more difficult for women, including (1) rules against abortions for minors without parental consent or (2) for wives without their husbands' consent; (3) requirements that women be given state-specified information (meant to discourage this choice) and (4) be required to wait for a period of time before they could have abortions; (5) refusal to fund abortions in state Medicaid and employee health insurance programs; and (6) closure of municipal hospitals to abortions. Reread *Roe*. Which of these new state policies would you expect the Court to invalidate as inconsistent with *Roe*? Jot down your answer and then read the following account.

In the wake of *Roe*, the Court invalidated most of the new restrictions. In *Planned Parenthood v. Danforth*, 428 U.S. 52 (1976), the Court invalidated requirements of parental consent for minors and spousal consent for wives. Justice Blackmun's opinion for the Court ruled that parents and husbands cannot have vetoes over a right personal to the pregnant woman. The pregnancy of minors troubled most of the Justices, however. Although invalidating a less restrictive parental consent law as an "undue burden" on the minor's right to choose in *Bellotti v. Baird*, 443 U.S. 622 (1979), Justice Powell's plurality opinion recognized "the peculiar vulnerability of children; their inability to make critical decisions in an informed, mature manner; and the importance of the parental role in child rearing." In dictum, Powell opined that states could require parents to consent so long as there were a judicial procedure available for the minor to petition in lieu of a parental dialogue. Thus, it was no great surprise when the Court in *Planned Parenthood v. Ashcroft*, 462 U.S. 476 (1983), upheld a state law requiring a minor to obtain either parental consent or judicial approval of her choice to abort.

In *Akron v. Akron Center for Reproductive Health*, 462 U.S. 416 (1983), the Court struck down a requirement that dilation-and-evacuation abortions be performed in hospitals, because the ban imposed a heavy and unnecessary burden on women's access to a relatively inexpensive, otherwise accessible, and safe abortion procedure in clinics. The Court also invalidated the government's blanket determination that *all* minors under the age of 15 are too immature to make an abortion decision or that an abortion never may be in the minor's best interests without parental approval. The statute did not provide any opportunity for case-by-case evaluations of the maturity of pregnant minors. The Court was similarly unsympathetic with an "informed consent" requirement. By requiring the attending physician to give the woman a lengthy and inflexible list of information, and by imposing a twenty-four-hour waiting period, the state had placed a burden on abortions that was not reasonably related to health or safety. See also *Thornburgh v. American College of Obstetricians and Gynecologists*, 476 U.S. 747 (1986) (striking down a similar informed-consent law).

---

[45] See generally Dallas Blanchard, *The Anti-Abortion Movement and the Rise of the Religious Right: From Polite to Firey Protest* (1994) (institutional history and ideology of pro-life movement).

For poor women, the rights granted in theory by *Roe* were not necessarily available in practice. In *Maher v. Roe*, 432 U.S. 464 (1977), and *Harris v. McRae*, 448 U.S. 297 (1980), the Court held that the government has no affirmative obligation to pay for abortions, even if it does pay for childbirth. *Maher* found no violation of substantive due process because the government was imposing no "unduly burdensome interference" with the freedom to decide whether to terminate the pregnancy. On the equal protection front, the Court applied only a rational basis test, because wealth is not a suspect class and because the Court had already determined that no fundamental right was infringed. A sufficient rational basis was present because of the government's legitimate (though not always, according to *Roe*, compelling) interest in protecting the potential life of the fetus.

The Reagan Administration mounted a constitutional attack on *Roe*. In *Akron* and *Thornburgh*, the Solicitor General urged the Court to abandon *Roe*'s "rigid" trimester framework and adopt *Maher*'s "undue burden" approach. The Solicitor General maintained that *Roe* created a fundamental right that was not supported by constitutional text, intent, or traditions; denigrated the state's interest in potential human life without any legal or moral basis; and engaged in judicial activism in the teeth of popular demands for regulation of this controversial activity.

Webster v. Reproductive Health Services, 492 U.S. 490 (1989), involved a challenge to a Missouri law requiring doctors to determine viability before performing an abortion after the twentieth week of pregnancy. The state of Missouri, dozens of amici, and the Solicitor General asked the Court to overturn *Roe*. The Court declined to do so, with Chief Justice Rehnquist writing in a plurality opinion that the abortion right involved some "liberty interest protected by the Due Process Clause." The Court upheld the testing requirement, with Justice O'Connor concurring on a basis that presaged a coming change in the constitutional law of access to abortion—the idea that the Missouri law could stand because it imposed no "undue burden" on women seeking to end a pregnancy.

———

When Justices Brennan and Marshall were replaced by Justices Souter and Thomas, the future of *Roe* looked even dimmer. When *Casey*, excerpted below, was argued, the Solicitor General for the George H. W. Bush Administration and the State of Pennsylvania both asked the Court to overrule *Roe*. Planned Parenthood, which challenged the state restrictions on abortion, asked the Court to overrule *Roe* if it was not willing to give the right real bite. Consider the Court's response.

PLANNED PARENTHOOD OF SOUTHEASTERN PENNSYLVANIA V. CASEY

505 U.S. 833, 112 S.Ct. 2791, 120 L.Ed.2d 674 (1992)

JUSTICE O'CONNOR, JUSTICE KENNEDY, and JUSTICE SOUTER announced the judgment of the Court and delivered the opinion of the Court with respect to Parts I, II, and III. [This is referred to by the other Justices and in our Notes as the "Joint Opinion."]

[Pennsylvania required a woman seeking an abortion to wait 24 hours (except in a medical emergency), so that she could consider information regarding the nature and risks of the procedure and the probable gestational age of the fetus, which the law required the physician to provide. The law required minors to obtain the consent of one parent, with a judicial-bypass option. Married women were required to notify their spouses, subject to the exceptions set out in note 1, below, following the decision.]

I.   Liberty finds no refuge in a jurisprudence of doubt. Yet 19 years after our holding that the Constitution protects a woman's right to terminate her pregnancy in its early stages, *Roe v. Wade*, that definition of liberty is still questioned. Joining the respondents as *amicus curiae*, the United States, as it has done in five other cases in the last decade, again asks us to overrule *Roe*. * * *

After considering the fundamental constitutional questions resolved by *Roe*, principles of institutional integrity, and the rule of *stare decisis*, we are led to conclude this: the essential holding of *Roe v. Wade* should be retained and once again reaffirmed.

It must be stated at the outset and with clarity that *Roe*'s essential holding, the holding we reaffirm, has three parts. First is a recognition of the right of the woman to choose to have an abortion before viability and to obtain it without undue interference from the State. Before viability, the State's interests are not strong enough to support a prohibition of abortion or the imposition of a substantial obstacle to the woman's effective right to elect the procedure. Second is a confirmation of the State's power to restrict abortions after fetal viability, if the law contains exceptions for pregnancies which endanger a woman's life or health. And third is the principle that the State has legitimate interests from the outset of the pregnancy in protecting the health of the woman and the life of the fetus that may become a child. These principles do not contradict one another; and we adhere to each.

II.   Constitutional protection of the woman's decision to terminate her pregnancy derives from the Due Process Clause of the Fourteenth Amendment. It declares that no State shall "deprive any person of life, liberty, or property, without due process of law." The controlling word in

PROTECTING FUNDAMENTAL RIGHTS

the case before us is "liberty." Although a literal reading of the Clause might suggest that it governs only the procedures by which a State may deprive persons of liberty, for at least 105 years * * * the Clause has been understood to contain a substantive component as well, one "barring certain government actions regardless of the fairness of the procedures used to implement them." * * * "[T]he guaranties of due process, though having their roots in Magna Carta's *'per legem terrae'* and considered as procedural safeguards 'against executive usurpation and tyranny,' have in this country 'become bulwarks also against arbitrary legislation.'" *Poe v. Ullman* (Harlan, J., dissenting from dismissal on jurisdictional grounds).

The most familiar of the substantive liberties protected by the Fourteenth Amendment are those recognized by the Bill of Rights. We have held that the Due Process Clause of the Fourteenth Amendment incorporates most of the Bill of Rights against the States. It is tempting, as a means of curbing the discretion of federal judges, to suppose that liberty encompasses no more than those rights already guaranteed to the individual against federal interference by the express provisions of the first eight amendments to the Constitution. See *Adamson* (Black, J., dissenting). But of course this Court has never accepted that view.

It is also tempting, for the same reason, to suppose that the Due Process Clause protects only those practices, defined at the most specific level, that were protected against government interference by other rules of law when the Fourteenth Amendment was ratified. See *Michael H. v. Gerald D.*, 491 U.S. 110, 127–128, n.6 (1989) (opinion of Scalia, J.). But such a view would be inconsistent with our law. It is a premise of the Constitution that there is a realm of personal liberty which the government may not enter. We have vindicated this principle before. Marriage is mentioned nowhere in the Bill of Rights and interracial marriage was illegal in most States in the 19th century, but the Court was no doubt correct in finding it to be an aspect of liberty protected against state interference by the substantive component of the Due Process Clause in *Loving.* * * *

Neither the Bill of Rights nor the specific practices of States at the time of the adoption of the Fourteenth Amendment marks the outer limits of the substantive sphere of liberty which the Fourteenth Amendment protects. See U.S. Const., Amend. 9. [The Joint Opinion then quoted extensively from Justice Harlan's dissent in *Poe v. Ullman*].* * *

It is settled now, as it was when the Court heard arguments in *Roe v. Wade*, that the Constitution places limits on a State's right to interfere with a person's most basic decisions about family and parenthood, as well as bodily integrity.

The inescapable fact is that adjudication of substantive due process claims may call upon the Court in interpreting the Constitution to exercise that same capacity which by tradition courts always have exercised: reasoned judgment. Its boundaries are not susceptible of expression as a simple rule. That does not mean we are free to invalidate state policy choices with which we disagree; yet neither does it permit us to shrink from the duties of our office.

Men and women of good conscience can disagree, and we suppose some always shall disagree, about the profound moral and spiritual implications of terminating a pregnancy, even in its earliest stage. Some of us as individuals find abortion offensive to our most basic principles of morality, but that cannot control our decision. Our obligation is to define the liberty of all, not to mandate our own moral code. The underlying constitutional issue is whether the State can resolve these philosophic questions in such a definitive way that a woman lacks all choice in the matter, except perhaps in those rare circumstances in which the pregnancy is itself a danger to her own life or health, or is the result of rape or incest.

It is conventional constitutional doctrine that where reasonable people disagree the government can adopt one position or the other. That theorem, however, assumes a state of affairs in which the choice does not intrude upon a protected liberty. Thus, while some people might disagree about whether or not the flag should be saluted, or disagree about the proposition that it may not be defiled, we have ruled that a State may not compel or enforce one view or the other.

Our law affords constitutional protection to personal decisions relating to marriage, procreation, contraception, family relationships, child rearing, and education. Our cases recognize "the right of the *individual*, married or single, to be free from unwarranted governmental intrusion into matters so fundamentally affecting a person as the decision whether to bear or beget a child." *Eisenstadt v. Baird* (emphasis in original). Our precedents "have respected the private realm of family life which the state cannot enter." These matters, involving the most intimate and personal choices a person may make in a lifetime, choices central to personal dignity and autonomy, are central to the liberty protected by the Fourteenth Amendment. At the heart of liberty is the right to define one's own concept of existence, of meaning, of the universe, and of the mystery of human life. Beliefs about these matters could not define the attributes of personhood were they formed under compulsion of the State.

These considerations begin our analysis of the woman's interest in terminating her pregnancy but cannot end it, for this reason: though the abortion decision may originate within the zone of conscience and belief, it is more than a philosophic exercise. Abortion is a unique act. It is an act fraught with consequences for others: for the woman who must live with the implications of her decision; for the persons who perform and assist in the procedure; for the spouse, family, and society which must confront the knowledge that these procedures exist, procedures some deem nothing short of an act of violence against innocent human life; and, depending on one's beliefs, for the life or potential life that is aborted. Though abortion is conduct, it does not follow that the State is entitled to proscribe it in all instances. That is because the liberty of the woman is at stake in a sense unique to the human condition and so unique to the law. The mother who carries a child to full term is subject to anxieties, to physical constraints, to pain that only she must bear. That these sacrifices have from the beginning of the human race been endured by woman with a pride that ennobles her in the eyes of others and gives to the infant a bond of love cannot alone be grounds for the State to insist she make the sacrifice. Her suffering is too intimate and personal for the State to insist, without more, upon its own vision of the woman's role, however dominant that vision has been in the course of our history and our culture. The destiny of the woman must be shaped to a large extent on her own conception of her spiritual imperatives and her place in society.

It should be recognized, moreover, that in some critical respects the abortion decision is of the same character as the decision to use contraception, to which *Griswold v. Connecticut, Eisenstadt v. Baird*, and *Carey v. Population Services International* afford constitutional protection. We have no doubt as to the correctness of those decisions. They support the reasoning in *Roe* relating to the woman's liberty because they involve personal decisions concerning not only the meaning of procreation but also human responsibility and respect for it.* * *

While we appreciate the weight of the arguments made on behalf of the State in the case before us, arguments which in their ultimate formulation conclude that *Roe* should be overruled, the reservations any of us may have in reaffirming the central holding of *Roe* are outweighed by the explication of individual liberty we have given combined with the force of *stare decisis*. We turn now to that doctrine.

III. The obligation to follow precedent begins with necessity, and a contrary necessity marks its outer limit. With Cardozo, we recognize that no judicial system could do society's work if it eyed each issue afresh in every case that raised it. Indeed, the very concept of the rule of law underlying our own Constitution requires such continuity over time that a respect for precedent is, by definition, indispensable. At the other extreme, a different necessity would make itself felt if a prior judicial ruling should come to be seen so clearly as error that its enforcement was for that very reason doomed. * * *

So in this case we may inquire whether *Roe*'s central rule has been found unworkable; whether the rule's limitation on state power could be removed without serious inequity to those who have relied upon it or significant damage to the stability of the society governed by the rule in question; whether the law's growth in the intervening years has left *Roe's* central rule a doctrinal anachronism discounted by society; and whether *Roe's* premises of fact have so far changed in the ensuing two decades as to render its central holding somehow irrelevant or unjustifiable in dealing with the issue it addressed. [Addressing each of these factors, the Court concluded that *Roe* remains "viable."]

The sum of the precedential inquiry to this point shows *Roe's* underpinnings unweakened in any way affecting its central holding. While it has engendered disapproval, it has not been unworkable. An entire generation has come of age free to assume *Roe's* concept of liberty in defining the capacity of women to act in society, and to make reproductive decisions; no erosion of principle going to liberty or personal autonomy has left *Roe's* central holding a doctrinal remnant; *Roe* portends no developments at odds with other precedent for the analysis of personal liberty; and no changes of fact have rendered viability more or less appropriate as the point at which the balance of interests tips. Within the bounds of normal *stare decisis* analysis, then, and subject to the considerations on which it customarily turns, the stronger argument is for affirming *Roe's* central holding, with whatever degree of personal reluctance any of us may have, not for overruling it. * * *

* * * Where, in the performance of its judicial duties, the Court decides a case in such a way as to resolve the sort of intensely divisive controversy reflected in *Roe* and those rare, comparable cases, its decision has a dimension that the resolution of the normal case does not carry. It is the dimension present whenever the Court's interpretation of the Constitution calls the contending sides of a national controversy to end their national division by accepting a common mandate rooted in the Constitution.

The Court is not asked to do this very often, having thus addressed the Nation only twice in our lifetime, in the decisions of *Brown* and *Roe*. But when the Court does act in this way, its decision requires an equally rare precedential force to counter the inevitable efforts to overturn it and to thwart its implementation. Some of those efforts may be mere unprincipled emotional reactions; others may proceed from principles worthy of profound respect. But whatever the premises of opposition may be, only the most convincing justification under accepted standards of precedent could suffice to demonstrate that a later decision overruling the first was anything but a surrender to political pressure, and an unjustified repudiation of the principle on which the Court staked its authority in the first instance. So to overrule under fire in the absence of the most compelling reason to reexamine a watershed decision would subvert the Court's legitimacy beyond any serious question. Cf. *Brown II* ("[I]t should go without saying that the vitality of th[e] constitutional principles [announced in *Brown I*] cannot be allowed to yield simply because of disagreement with them"). * * *

The Court's duty in the present case is clear. In 1973, it confronted the already-divisive issue of governmental power to limit personal choice to undergo abortion, for which it provided a new resolution based on the due process guaranteed by the Fourteenth Amendment. Whether or not a new social consensus is developing on that issue, its divisiveness is no less today than in 1973, and pressure to overrule the decision, like pressure to retain it, has grown only more intense. A decision to overrule *Roe*'s essential holding under the existing circumstances would address error, if error there was, at the cost of both profound and unnecessary damage to the Court's legitimacy, and to the Nation's commitment to the rule of law. It is therefore imperative to adhere to the essence of *Roe*'s original decision, and we do so today.

IV. From what we have said so far it follows that it is a constitutional liberty of the woman to have some freedom to terminate her pregnancy. We conclude that the basic decision in *Roe* was based on a constitutional analysis which we cannot now repudiate. The woman's liberty is not so unlimited, however, that from the outset the State cannot show its concern for the life of the unborn, and at a later point in fetal development the State's interest in life has sufficient force so that the right of the woman to terminate the pregnancy can be restricted.

That brings us, of course, to the point where much criticism has been directed at *Roe*, a criticism that always inheres when the Court draws a specific rule from what in the Constitution is but a general standard. We conclude, however, that the urgent claims of the woman to retain the ultimate control over her destiny and her body, claims implicit in the meaning of liberty, require us to perform that function. Liberty must not be extinguished for want of a line that is clear. And it falls to us to give some real substance to the woman's liberty to determine whether to carry her pregnancy to full term.

We conclude the line should be drawn at viability, so that before that time the woman has a right to choose to terminate her pregnancy. We adhere to this principle for two reasons. First * * * is the doctrine of *stare decisis*. Any judicial act of line-drawing may seem somewhat arbitrary, but *Roe* was a reasoned statement, elaborated with great care. We have twice reaffirmed it in the face of great opposition. *Thornburgh*; *Akron*.

The second reason is that the concept of viability, as we noted in *Roe*, is the time at which there is a realistic possibility of maintaining and nourishing a life outside the womb, so that the independent existence of the second life can in reason and all fairness be the object of state protection that now overrides the rights of the woman. Consistent with other constitutional norms, legislatures may draw lines which appear arbitrary without the necessity of offering a justification. But courts may not. We must justify the lines we draw. And there is no line other than viability which is more workable. To be sure, * * * there may be some medical developments that affect the precise point of viability, but this is an imprecision within tolerable limits given that the medical community and all those who must apply its discoveries will continue to explore the matter. The viability line also has, as a practical matter, an element of fairness. In some broad sense it might be said that a woman who fails to act before viability has consented to the State's intervention on behalf of the developing child.

The woman's right to terminate her pregnancy before viability is the most central principle of *Roe v. Wade*. It is a rule of law and a component of liberty we cannot renounce.

On the other side of the equation is the interest of the State in the protection of potential life. The *Roe* Court recognized the State's "important and legitimate interest in protecting the potentiality of human life." The weight to be given this state interest, not the strength of the woman's interest, was the difficult question faced in *Roe*. We do not need to say whether each of us, had we been Members of the Court when the valuation of the State interest came before it as an original matter, would have concluded, as the *Roe* Court did, that its weight is insufficient to justify a ban on abortions prior to viability even when it is subject to certain exceptions. The matter is not before us in the first instance, and coming as it does after nearly 20 years of litigation in *Roe*'s wake we are satisfied that the immediate question is not the soundness of *Roe*'s resolution of the issue, but the precedential force that must be accorded to its holding. And we have concluded that the essential holding of *Roe* should be reaffirmed.

Yet it must be remembered that *Roe v. Wade* speaks with clarity in establishing not only the woman's liberty but also the State's "important and legitimate interest in potential life." That portion of the decision in *Roe* has been given too little acknowledgment and implementation by the Court in its subsequent cases. Those cases decided that any regulation touching upon the abortion decision must survive strict scrutiny, to be sustained only if drawn in narrow terms to further a compelling state interest. Not all of the cases decided under that formulation can be reconciled with the holding in *Roe* itself that the State has legitimate interests in the health of the woman and in protecting the potential life within her. In resolving this tension, we choose to rely upon *Roe*, as against the later cases.

Roe established a trimester framework to govern abortion regulations. Under this elaborate but rigid construct, almost no regulation at all is permitted during the first trimester of pregnancy; regulations designed to protect the woman's health, but not to further the State's interest in potential life, are permitted during the second trimester; and during the third trimester, when the fetus is viable, prohibitions are permitted provided the life or health of the mother is not at stake. Most of our cases since *Roe* have involved the application of rules derived from the trimester framework. * * *

We reject the trimester framework, which we do not consider to be part of the essential holding of *Roe*. See *Webster*. Measures aimed at ensuring that a woman's choice contemplates the consequences for the fetus do not necessarily interfere with the right recognized in *Roe*, although those measures have been found to be inconsistent with the rigid trimester framework announced in that case. A logical reading of the central holding in *Roe* itself, and a necessary reconciliation of the liberty of the woman and the interest of the State in promoting prenatal life, require, in our view, that we abandon the trimester framework as a rigid prohibition on all previability regulation aimed at the protection of fetal life. The trimester framework suffers from these basic flaws: in its formulation it misconceives the nature of the pregnant woman's interest; and in practice it undervalues the State's interest in potential life, as recognized in *Roe*.

As our jurisprudence relating to all liberties save perhaps abortion has recognized, not every law which makes a right more difficult to exercise is, *ipso facto*, an infringement of that right. An example clarifies the point. We have held that not every ballot access limitation amounts to an infringement of the right to vote. Rather, the States are granted substantial flexibility in establishing the framework within which voters choose the candidates for whom they wish to vote.

The abortion right is similar. Numerous forms of state regulation might have the incidental effect of increasing the cost or decreasing the availability of medical care, whether for abortion or any other medical procedure. The fact that a law which serves a valid purpose, one not designed to strike at the right itself, has the incidental effect of making it more difficult or more expensive to procure an abortion cannot be enough to invalidate it. Only where state regulation imposes an undue burden on a woman's ability to make this decision does the power of the State reach into the heart of the liberty protected by the Due Process Clause. * * *

A finding of an undue burden is a shorthand for the conclusion that a state regulation has the purpose or effect of placing a substantial obstacle in the path of a woman seeking an abortion of a nonviable fetus. A statute with this purpose is invalid because the means chosen by the State to further the interest in potential life must be calculated to inform the woman's free choice, not hinder it. And a statute which, while furthering the interest in potential life or some other valid state interest, has the effect of placing a substantial obstacle in the path of a woman's choice cannot be considered a permissible means of serving its legitimate ends. To the extent that the opinions of the Court or of individual Justices use the undue burden standard in a manner that is inconsistent with this analysis, we set out what in our view should be the controlling standard. In our considered judgment, an undue burden is an unconstitutional burden. Understood another way, we answer the question, left open in previous opinions discussing the undue burden formulation, whether a law designed to further the State's interest in fetal life which imposes an undue burden on the woman's decision before fetal viability could be constitutional. The answer is no.

Some guiding principles should emerge. What is at stake is the woman's right to make the ultimate decision, not a right to be insulated from all others in doing so. Regulations which do no more than create a structural mechanism by which the State, or the parent or guardian of a minor, may express profound respect for the life of the unborn are permitted, if they are not a substantial obstacle to the woman's exercise of the right to choose. Unless it has that effect on her right of choice, a state measure designed to persuade her to choose childbirth over abortion will be upheld if reasonably related to that goal. Regulations designed to foster the health of a woman seeking an abortion are valid if they do not constitute an undue burden. * * *

[V. The Joint Opinion upheld the informed consent, 24-hour waiting period, and one-parent consent provisions of the Pennsylvania law (see notes 1 and 2 following the case). In holding that the state can require the physician to provide the woman seeking abortion with truthful information about the procedure, the health risks, and the probable gestational age of the fetus, the Joint Opinion overruled *Akron* and *Thornburgh* to the extent they held to the contrary. Chief Justice Rehnquist and Justices White, Scalia, and Thomas concurred with the Joint Opinion on these points. The Joint Opinion ruled that the spousal notification provision was an undue, and therefore unconstitutional, burden on the right to abortion. Justices Blackmun and Stevens concurred with the Joint Opinion on this point.]

VI. Our Constitution is a covenant running from the first generation of Americans to us and then to future generations. It is a coherent succession. Each generation must learn anew that the Constitution's written terms embody ideas and aspirations that must survive more ages than one. We accept our responsibility not to retreat from interpreting the full meaning of the covenant in light of all of our precedents. We invoke it once again to define the freedom guaranteed by the Constitution's own promise, the promise of liberty.

[**JUSTICES BLACKMUN** and **STEVENS** filed concurring opinions, applauding Parts I through III of the Joint Opinion, but arguing that the *Roe* trimester system should be retained.]

[**CHIEF JUSTICE REHNQUIST**, joined by **JUSTICES WHITE, SCALIA,** and **THOMAS**, concurred in the portions of the judgment upholding most of Pennsylvania's law, but dissented from the reaffirmance of *Roe*. The Chief Justice argued that the right to abortion fails the "implicit in the concept of ordered liberty" test of *Palko*: Abortion is *sui generis*—and therefore different from parenting (*Meyer* and *Pierce*), contraception (*Griswold*), and marriage (*Loving*)—because it involves the "purposeful termination of potential life. * * * Nor do the historical traditions of the American people support the view that the right to terminate one's pregnancy is 'fundamental.' The common law which we inherited from England made abortion after 'quickening' an offense. At the time of the adoption of the Fourteenth Amendment, statutory prohibitions or restrictions on abortion were commonplace; in 1868, at least 28 of the then-37 States and 8 Territories had statutes banning or limiting abortion. By the turn of the century virtually every State had a law prohibiting or restricting abortion on its books. By the middle of the present century, a liberalization trend had set in. But 21 of the restrictive abortion laws in effect in 1868 were still in effect in 1973 when *Roe* was decided, and an overwhelming majority of the States prohibited abortion unless necessary to preserve the life or health of the mother. On this record, it can scarcely be said that any deeply rooted tradition of relatively unrestricted abortion in our history supported the classification of the right to abortion as 'fundamental' " for due process purposes.]

JUSTICE SCALIA, with whom THE CHIEF JUSTICE, JUSTICE WHITE, and JUSTICE THOMAS join, concurring in the judgment in part and dissenting in part.

Laws against bigamy, for example—which entire societies of reasonable people disagree with—intrude upon men and women's liberty to marry and live with one another. But bigamy happens not to be a liberty specially "protected" by the Constitution.

That is, quite simply, the issue in this case: not whether the power of a woman to abort her unborn child is a "liberty" in the absolute sense; or even whether it is a liberty of great importance to many women. Of course it is both. The issue is whether it is a liberty protected by the Constitution of the United States. I am sure it is not. I reach that conclusion not because of anything so exalted as my views concerning the "concept of existence, of meaning, of the universe, and of the mystery of human life." [Quoting Joint Opinion.] Rather, I reach it for the same reason I reach the conclusion that bigamy is not constitutionally protected—because of two simple facts: (1) the Constitution says absolutely nothing about it, and (2) the longstanding traditions of American society have permitted it to be legally proscribed.[46]

---

[46] The Court's suggestion that adherence to tradition would require us to uphold laws against interracial marriage is entirely wrong. Any tradition in [*Loving*] was contradicted *by a text*—an Equal Protection Clause that explicitly establishes racial equality as a constitutional value. See *Loving v. Virginia* ("In the case at bar, . . . we deal with statutes containing racial classifications, and the fact of equal application does not immunize the statute from the very heavy burden of justification which the Fourteenth Amendment has traditionally required of state statutes drawn according to race"). The enterprise launched in *Roe*, by contrast, sought to *establish*—in the teeth of a clear, contrary tradition—a value found nowhere in the constitutional text.

The Court destroys the proposition, evidently meant to represent my position, that "liberty" includes "only those practices, defined at the most specific level, that were protected against government interference by other rules of law when the Fourteenth Amendment was ratified," [citing *Michael H.*]. That is not, however, what *Michael H.* says; it merely observes that, in defining "liberty," we may not disregard a specific, "relevant tradition protecting, or denying protection to, the asserted right." But the Court does not wish to be fettered by any such limitations on its preferences. The Court's statement that it is "tempting" to acknowledge the authoritativeness of tradition in order to "cur[b] the discretion of federal judges" is of course rhetoric rather than reality; no government official is "tempted" to place restraints upon his own freedom of action, which is why Lord Acton did not say "Power tends to purify." The Court's temptation is in the quite opposite and more natural direction—towards systematically eliminating checks upon its own power; and it succumbs. * * *

Assuming that the question before us is to be resolved at such a level of philosophical abstraction, in such isolation from the traditions of American society, as by simply applying "reasoned judgment," I do not see how that could possibly have produced the answer the Court arrived at in *Roe v. Wade*. Today's opinion describes the methodology of *Roe*, quite accurately, as weighing against the woman's interest the State's " 'important and legitimate interest in protecting the potentiality of human life.' " But "reasoned judgment" does not begin by begging the question, as *Roe* and subsequent cases unquestionably did by assuming that what the State is protecting is the mere "potentiality of human life." The whole argument of abortion opponents is that what the Court calls the fetus and what others call the unborn child *is a human life*. Thus, whatever answer *Roe* came up with after conducting its "balancing" is bound to be wrong, unless it is correct that the human fetus is in some critical sense merely potentially human. There is of course no way to determine that as a legal matter; it is in fact a value judgment. Some societies have considered newborn children not yet human, or the incompetent elderly no longer so.

The authors of the joint opinion, of course, do not squarely contend that *Roe v. Wade* was a *correct* application of "reasoned judgment"; merely that it must be followed, because of *stare decisis*. But in their exhaustive discussion of all the factors that go into the determination of when *stare decisis* should be observed and when disregarded, they never mention "how wrong was the decision on its face?" Surely, if "[t]he Court's power lies . . .

There is, of course, no comparable tradition barring recognition of a "liberty interest" in carrying one's child to term free from state efforts to kill it. For that reason, it does not follow that the Constitution does not protect childbirth simply because it does not protect abortion. The Court's contention that the only way to protect childbirth is to protect abortion shows the utter bankruptcy of constitutional analysis deprived of tradition as a validating factor. It drives one to say that the only way to protect the right to eat is to acknowledge the constitutional right to starve oneself to death.

in its legitimacy, a product of substance and perception," [quoting Joint Opinion], the "substance" part of the equation demands that plain error be acknowledged and eliminated. *Roe* was plainly wrong—even on the Court's methodology of "reasoned judgment," and even more so (of course) if the proper criteria of text and tradition are applied.

The emptiness of the "reasoned judgment" that produced *Roe* is displayed in plain view by the fact that, after more than 19 years of effort by some of the brightest (and most determined) legal minds in the country, after more than 10 cases upholding abortion rights in this Court, and after dozens upon dozens of *amicus* briefs submitted in this and other cases, the best the Court can do to explain how it is that the word "liberty" *must* be thought to include the right to destroy human fetuses is to rattle off a collection of adjectives that simply decorate a value judgment and conceal a political choice. The right to abort, we are told, inheres in "liberty" because it is among "a person's most basic decisions," it involves a "most intimate and personal choic[e]," it is "central to personal dignity and autonomy," it "originate[s] within the zone of conscience and belief," it is "too intimate and personal" for state interference, it reflects "intimate views" of a "deep, personal character," it involves "intimate relationships," and notions of "personal autonomy and bodily integrity," and it concerns a particularly " 'important decisio[n].' " But it is obvious to anyone applying "reasoned judgment" that the same adjectives can be applied to many forms of conduct that this Court (including one of the Justices in today's majority, see *Bowers v. Hardwick*) has held are *not* entitled to constitutional protection—because, like abortion, they are forms of conduct that have long been criminalized in American society. Those adjectives might be applied, for example, to homosexual sodomy, polygamy, adult incest, and suicide, all of which are equally "intimate" and "deep[ly] personal" decisions involving "personal autonomy and bodily integrity," and all of which can constitutionally be proscribed because it is our unquestionable constitutional tradition that they are proscribable. It is not reasoned judgment that supports the Court's decision; only personal predilection.
* * *

[W]hether it would "subvert the Court's legitimacy" or not, the notion that we would decide a case differently from the way we otherwise would have in order to show that we can stand firm against public disapproval is frightening. It is a bad enough idea, even in the head of someone like me, who believes that the text of the Constitution, and our traditions, say what they say and there is no fiddling with them. But when it is in the mind of a Court that believes the Constitution has an evolving meaning; that the Ninth Amendment's reference to "othe[r]" rights is not a disclaimer, but a charter for action; and that the function of this Court is to "speak before all others for [the people's] constitutional ideals" unrestrained by meaningful text or tradition—then the notion that the Court must adhere to a decision for as long as the decision faces "great opposition" and the Court is "under fire" acquires a character of almost czarist arrogance. We are offended by these marchers who descend upon us, every year on the anniversary of *Roe*, to protest our saying that the Constitution requires what our society has never thought the Constitution requires. These people who refuse to be "tested by following" must be taught a lesson. We have no Cossacks, but at least we can stubbornly refuse to abandon an erroneous opinion that we might otherwise change—to show how little they intimidate us. * * *

We should get out of this area, where we have no right to be, and where we do neither ourselves nor the country any good by remaining.

NOTES ON CASEY *AND THE RIGHT TO ABORTION*

1.   *Spousal Notification.* The Pennsylvania statute required a married woman to sign a statement indicating that she had notified her husband of the abortion decision, but also provided that "[t]he woman has the option of providing an alternative signed statement certifying that her husband is not the man who impregnated her; that her husband could not be located; that the pregnancy is the result of spousal sexual assault which she has reported; or that the woman believes that notifying her husband will cause him or someone else to inflict bodily injury upon her." Regarding the spousal notice provision, the majority had this to say:

> There was a time, not so long ago, when a different understanding of the family and of the Constitution prevailed. In *Bradwell v. Illinois*, 16 Wall. 130 (1873), three Members of this Court reaffirmed the common-law principle that "a woman had no legal existence separate from her husband, who was regarded as her head and representative in the social state; and, notwithstanding some recent modifications of this civil status, many of the special rules of law flowing from and dependent upon this cardinal principle still exist in full force in most States." Only one generation has passed since this Court observed that "woman is still regarded as the center of home and family life," with attendant "special responsibilities" that precluded full and independent legal status under the Constitution. *Hoyt v. Florida*, 368 U.S. 57, 62 (1961). These views, of course, are no longer consistent with our understanding of the family, the individual, or the Constitution.

> In keeping with our rejection of the common-law understanding of a woman's role within the family, the Court held in *Danforth* that the Constitution does not permit a State to require a married woman to obtain her husband's consent before undergoing an abortion. The principles that guided the Court in *Danforth* should be our guides today. For the great many women who are victims of abuse inflicted by their husbands, or whose children are the victims of such abuse, a spousal notice requirement enables the husband to wield an effective veto over his wife's decision. Whether the prospect of notification

itself deters such women from seeking abortions, or whether the husband, through physical force or psychological pressure or economic coercion, prevents his wife from obtaining an abortion until it is too late, the notice requirement will often be tantamount to the veto found unconstitutional in *Danforth*. The women most affected by this law—those who most reasonably fear the consequences of notifying their husbands that they are pregnant—are in the gravest danger.

The husband's interest in the life of the child his wife is carrying does not permit the State to empower him with this troubling degree of authority over his wife. The contrary view leads to consequences reminiscent of the common law. A husband has no enforceable right to require a wife to advise him before she exercises her personal choices. If a husband's interest in the potential life of the child outweighs a wife's liberty, the State could require a married woman to notify her husband before she uses a postfertilization contraceptive. Perhaps next in line would be a statute requiring pregnant married women to notify their husbands before engaging in conduct causing risks to the fetus. After all, if the husband's interest in the fetus' safety is a sufficient predicate for state regulation, the State could reasonably conclude that pregnant wives should notify their husbands before drinking alcohol or smoking. Perhaps married women should notify their husbands before using contraceptives or before undergoing any type of surgery that may have complications affecting the husband's interest in his wife's reproductive organs. And if a husband's interest justifies notice in any of these cases, one might reasonably argue that it justifies exactly what the *Danforth* Court held it did not justify—a requirement of the husband's consent as well. A State may not give to a man the kind of dominion over his wife that parents exercise over their children.

Section 3209 embodies a view of marriage consonant with the common-law status of married women but repugnant to our present understanding of marriage and of the nature of the rights secured by the Constitution. Women do not lose their constitutionally protected liberty when they marry. * * *

Is this a fair characterization of the Pennsylvania statute? If marriage is a "bilateral loyalty," as *Griswold* said, why doesn't the husband have a colorable interest in notification? On this point, is it relevant that the statute created the several exceptions to spousal notification quoted above?

Chief Justice Rehnquist's dissenting opinion argued that this provision should be upheld:

The question before us is therefore whether the spousal notification requirement rationally furthers any legitimate state interests. We conclude that it does. First, a husband's interests in procreation within marriage and in the potential life of his unborn child are certainly substantial ones. The State itself has legitimate interests both in protecting these interests of the father and in protecting the potential life of the fetus, and the spousal notification requirement is reasonably related to advancing those state interests. By providing that a husband will usually know of his spouse's intent to have an abortion, the provision makes it more likely that the husband will participate in deciding the fate of his unborn child, a possibility that might otherwise have been denied him. This participation might in some cases result in a decision to proceed with the pregnancy. As Judge Alito observed in his dissent below, "[t]he Pennsylvania legislature could have rationally believed that some married women are initially inclined to obtain an abortion without their husbands' knowledge because of perceived problems—such as economic constraints, future plans, or the husbands' previously expressed opposition—that may be obviated by discussion prior to the abortion."

Is the Chief Justice's position sufficiently attentive to the concern that the husband may attempt to coerce the wife, through violence or threats, to forego her right to abortion?[47] Are the statutory exceptions sufficient to address this threat?

2. *Waiting Periods*. The Pennsylvania statute required a twenty-four hour waiting period after a doctor provided specified information about abortion. Parallel requirements had been invalidated in *Akron*. Nevertheless, the Joint Opinion concluded that these provisions were valid. Requiring information about the fetus was acceptable as part of informed consent:

> We also see no reason why the State may not require doctors to inform a woman seeking an abortion of the availability of materials relating to the consequences to the fetus, even when those consequences have no direct relation to her health. An example illustrates the point. We would think it constitutional for the State to require that in order for there to be informed consent to a kidney transplant operation the recipient must be supplied with information about risks to the donor as well as risks to himself or herself.

Can this overruling of *Akron* be squared with the Joint Opinion's ode to *stare decisis*? Was there something about *Akron* that made it less important than *Roe* for purposes of *stare decisis*? Justices Blackmun and Stevens argued that the waiting period was a gratuitous burden on the woman's choice and reflected a disturbing distrust of the ability of women to make considered decisions on their own.

---

[47] Cf. American Medical Association Council on Scientific Affairs, *Violence Against Women* 7 (1991): "Researchers on family violence agree that the true incidence of partner violence is probably * * * four million severely assaulted women per year. Studies suggest that from one-fifth to one-third of all women will be physically assaulted by a partner or ex-partner during their lifetime."

3.   *Parental Consent (with Judicial Bypass).* On the authority of *Hodgson v. Minnesota*, 497 U.S. 417 (1990) (two-parent notice requirement was unconstitutional unless it included a judicial bypass option) and *Akron*, the Joint Opinion held that the state may require a minor seeking abortion to obtain the consent of a parent, so long as there was the opportunity for a judicial bypass (where the minor could explain to a judge her reasons for not notifying her parents). Yet there was strong evidence in *Hodgson* and *Casey* (and findings of fact by the trial judge in *Hodgson*) that (1) many adolescent girls legitimately fear violence or coercion from their fathers[48] and (2) therefore fear notifying them or their mothers, and often (3) are too intimidated and humiliated to tell their fears and reasons to a judicial stranger. The Joint Opinion found spousal *notification* an "undue burden." Why was parental *consent* not also an "undue burden," given documented dangers of coercion?

4.   *The Fetus as a Person.* Most laypeoples' evaluation of *Roe* probably turns on their view of the status of the fetus: If they believe that the fetus is a person, they oppose *Roe*; otherwise, they probably favor some degree of free choice regarding abortion. A more sophisticated critique of *Roe* does not depend on the status of the fetus, but rather on the absence of a sufficient foundation for rejecting the state's judgment about the undesirability of abortion. In *Roe* itself, Justice Blackmun avoided the issue, concluding that the fetus is not a "person" protected by the Fourteenth Amendment, and that when life begins is a philosophical question beyond judicial resolution.

Interestingly, in *Casey* this issue seems to have reemerged as a focal point of debate. Arguing that abortion is not a protected right, Chief Justice Rehnquist contended that abortion is *sui generis* because of the effect on potential human life, quoting a statement from an earlier case that to look "at the act which is assertedly the subject of a liberty interest in isolation from its effect upon other people [is] like inquiring whether there is a liberty interest in firing a gun where the case at hand happens to involve its discharge into another person's body." This analogy rather loses its force without the comparison between the fetus and "another person's body." Even more pointedly, Justice Scalia says:

> The whole argument of abortion opponents is that what the Court calls the fetus and what others call the unborn child *is a human life.* Thus, whatever answer *Roe* came up with after conducting its "balancing" is bound to be wrong, unless it is correct that the human fetus is in some critical sense merely potentially human. There is of course no way to determine that as a legal matter; it is in fact a value judgment. Some societies have considered newborn children not yet human, or the incompetent elderly no longer so.

---

[48] See also the sources collected in William Eskridge, Jr. & Nan Hunter, *Sexuality, Gender, and the Law* 190–202 (1997).

In response to Justice Scalia, Justice Stevens pointed to the *Roe* Court's holding that unborn children are not "persons" within the meaning of the Fourteenth Amendment:

> From this holding, there was no dissent; indeed, no member of the Court has ever questioned this fundamental proposition. Thus, as a matter of federal constitutional law, a developing organism that is not yet a "person" does not have what is sometimes described as a "right to life." This has been and, by the Court's holding today, remains a fundamental premise of our constitutional law governing reproductive autonomy.

5. *Conservation and Tradition.* Given the general trend toward conservative dominance of the Court in recent years, the schism between the authors of the Joint Opinion and the four dissenters may turn out to have permanent importance. One particularly interesting point is the differing views of tradition expressed by the Joint Opinion and Justice Scalia's dissent. Justice Scalia views tradition as consisting of a number of discrete, static practices and beliefs. These traditions play something of the role of "trade usages" in construing contracts. Under Scalia's view, just as we know that the word "dozen" in a contract between bakers does not mandate twelve donuts because of a consistent history of past performances, so we know that the word "liberty" does not include abortion because of a consistent history of past legislation. Similarly, Justice Scalia views the tradition of public nonsectarian prayer as putting a gloss on the phrase "establishment of religion" found in the First Amendment (see his dissent in *Lee v. Weisman*, Chapter 6, § 7B).

In stark contrast, the Joint Opinion, like Justice Frankfurter (in *Adamson*) and Justice Harlan (in *Poe* and *Griswold*), portrays tradition as subject to growth and reconsideration. (Cf. Ernest Young's Burkean defense of evolutive judicial review in Chapter 2, § 3B3.) This view of tradition parallels the Joint Opinion's concern about *stare decisis*. The common law, with its deep respect for precedent but also its historic ability to evolve, provides a model that connects both living tradition and *stare decisis*. In this light, the Joint Opinion seems to be a quintessential act of common law judging. Moreover, to determine the scope of "liberty," the Joint Opinion relies on common law techniques like analogy with other precedents, rather than on the kind of clear deductive logic that Justice Scalia demands in his dissent. Thus, the two conservative camps seem to be separated by a deep jurisprudential gulf.

To an extraordinary degree, the jurisprudential debate in *Casey* is reminiscent of the debate between Justices Black and Frankfurter in *Adamson*. Like Frankfurter, the authors of the Joint Opinion rely on the common law tradition to define the scope of protected liberty under the Fourteenth Amendment. Like Scalia, Black was intensely skeptical of what he saw to be the subjectivity of this enterprise. Also like Scalia, Black relied on text and history to construct clear legal rules as barriers to subjectivity. Both feared an "imperial judiciary."

———

In 2000, the Supreme Court in *Stenberg v. Carhart*, 530 U.S. 914 (2000), struck down a Nebraska ban on a form of dilation and extraction (D & X) abortion in the later stages of pregnancy that is sometimes called "partial-birth abortion." As defined by the statute, this is a procedure in which the doctor "partially delivers vaginally a living unborn child before killing the unborn child," meaning "intentionally delivering into the vagina a living unborn child, or a substantial portion thereof, for the purpose of performing a procedure that the [abortionist] knows will kill the unborn child and does kill the unborn child." By a 5–4 vote, the Court ruled the ban unconstitutional because it lacked an exception when the procedure is necessary to protect a woman's life or health, and because its wording could ban other forms of abortion. Seven years later, the Court returned to the issue in the next case.

GONZALES V. CARHART
550 U.S. 124, 127 S.Ct. 1610, 167 L.Ed.2d 480 (2007)

JUSTICE KENNEDY delivered the opinion of the Court.

[In the usual second-trimester abortion procedure, "dilation and evacuation" (D & E), the doctor dilates the cervix and then inserts surgical instruments into the uterus in order to separate portions of the fetus and remove them one by one. A variation of the standard D & E, usually termed an "intact D & E," and sometimes called "dilation and extraction" (D & X), requires a doctor to extract the fetus intact or largely intact with only a few passes, pulling out its entire body instead of ripping it apart. In order to allow the head to pass through the cervix, the doctor typically pierces or crushes the skull.

[After *Stenberg,* Congress passed a national Partial-Birth Abortion Ban Act of 2003. The federal statute prohibits "knowingly perform[ing] a partial-birth abortion . . . that is [not] necessary to save the life of a mother." There is no exclusion for the mother's health. The statute defines a partial-birth abortion as a procedure in which the doctor: "(A) deliberately and intentionally vaginally delivers a living fetus until, in the case of a head-first presentation, the entire fetal head is outside the [mother's] body . . . , or, in the case of breech presentation, any part of the fetal trunk past the navel is outside the [mother's] body . . . , for the purpose of performing an overt act that the person knows will kill the partially delivered living fetus"; and "(B) performs the overt act, other than completion of delivery, that kills the fetus."

[I. As he and Justice Thomas had done in their *Stenberg* dissenting opinions, Justice Kennedy began his *Carhart* majority opinion with a detailed description of the D & E and intact D & E (or D & X) procedures. Justice Kennedy started with an "abortion doctor's clinical description," followed by "another description from a nurse who witnessed the same method performed on a 26½-week fetus and who testified before the Senate Judiciary Committee:

> 'Dr. Haskell went in with forceps and grabbed the baby's legs and pulled them down into the birth canal. Then he delivered the baby's body and the arms—everything but the head. The doctor kept the head right inside the uterus. . . .

> 'The baby's little fingers were clasping and unclasping, and his little feet were kicking. Then the doctor stuck the scissors in the back of his head, and the baby's arms jerked out, like a startle reaction, like a flinch, like a baby does when he thinks he is going to fall.

> 'The doctor opened up the scissors, stuck a high-powered suction tube into the opening, and sucked the baby's brains out. Now the baby went completely limp. . . 'He cut the umbilical cord and delivered the placenta. He threw the baby in a pan, along with the placenta and the instruments he had just used.'

[Based upon testimony such as this, Congress found that "[a] moral, medical, and ethical consensus exists that the practice of performing a partial-birth abortion . . . is a gruesome and inhumane procedure that is never medically necessary and should be prohibited." Congressional Findings, 117 Stat. 1202, notes following 18 U.S.C. § 1531.]

II.   The principles set forth in the joint opinion in *Casey* did not find support from all those who join the instant opinion. Whatever one's views concerning the *Casey* joint opinion, it is evident a premise central to its conclusion—that the government has a legitimate and substantial interest in preserving and promoting fetal life—would be repudiated were the Court now to affirm the judgments of the Courts of Appeals. * * *

We assume the following principles for the purposes of this opinion. Before viability, a State "may not prohibit any woman from making the ultimate decision to terminate her pregnancy." *Casey* (plurality opinion). It also may not impose upon this right an undue burden, which exists if a regulation's "purpose or effect is to place a substantial obstacle in the path of a woman seeking an abortion before the fetus obtains viability." On the other hand, "[r]egulations which do no more than create a structural mechanism by which the State, or the parent or the guardian of a minor, may express profound respect for the life of the unborn are permitted, if they are not a substantial obstacle to the woman's exercise of the right to choose." *Casey*, in short, struck a balance. The balance was central to its holding. We now apply its standard to the cases at bar.

[In Section III.B, the Court concluded that the Act was not unconstitutionally vague on its face because (1) the "Act's anatomical landmarks provide doctors with objective standards," such that "doctors performing D & E will know that if they do not deliver a living fetus to an anatomical landmark they will not face criminal liability; (2) the Act required proof of intent as a condition of liability; and (3) the Act did not encourage discriminatory or arbitrary enforcement.]

C.   We next determine whether the Act imposes an undue burden, as a facial matter, because its restrictions on second-trimester abortions are too broad. A review of the statutory text discloses the limits of its reach. The Act prohibits intact D & E; and, notwithstanding respondents' arguments, it does not prohibit the D & E procedure in which the fetus is removed in parts. * * *

The Act excludes most D & Es in which the fetus is removed in pieces, not intact. If the doctor intends to remove the fetus in parts from the outset, the doctor will not have the requisite intent to incur criminal liability. A doctor performing a standard D & E procedure can often "tak[e] about 10–15 'passes' through the uterus to remove the entire fetus." Removing the fetus in this manner does not violate the Act because the doctor will not have delivered the living fetus to one of the anatomical landmarks or committed an additional overt act that kills the fetus after partial delivery. § 1531(b)(1).

A comparison of the Act with the Nebraska statute struck down in *Stenberg* confirms this point. The statute in *Stenberg* prohibited " 'deliberately and intentionally delivering into the vagina a living unborn child, or a substantial portion thereof, for the purpose of performing a procedure that the person performing such procedure knows will kill the unborn child and does kill the unborn child.' " The Court concluded that this statute encompassed D & E because "D & E will often involve a physician pulling a 'substantial portion' of a still living fetus, say, an arm or leg, into the vagina prior to the death of the fetus." The Court also rejected the limiting interpretation urged by Nebraska's Attorney General that the statute's reference to a "procedure" that " 'kill[s] the unborn child' " was to a distinct procedure, not to the abortion procedure as a whole. [Justice Kennedy concluded that the language of the new statute avoided these concerns.]

[IV. Finally, Justice Kennedy considered the *Casey*-based argument that the Act imposed a substantial obstacle to late-term but pre-viability abortions.]

A.   The Act's purposes are set forth in recitals preceding its operative provisions. A description of the prohibited abortion procedure demonstrates the rationale for the congressional enactment. The Act proscribes a method of abortion in which a fetus is killed just inches before completion of the birth process. Congress stated as follows: "Implicitly approving such a brutal and inhumane procedure by choosing not to prohibit it will further coarsen society to the humanity of not only newborns, but all vulnerable and innocent human life, making it increasingly difficult to protect such life." Congressional Findings. The Act expresses respect for the dignity of human life. * * *

Respect for human life finds an ultimate expression in the bond of love the mother has for her child. The Act recognizes this reality as well. Whether to have an abortion requires a difficult and painful moral decision. *Casey*. While we find no reliable data to measure the phenomenon, it seems unexceptionable to conclude some women come to regret their choice to abort the infant life they once created and sustained. See Brief for Sandra Cano et al. as *Amici Curiae*. Severe depression and loss of esteem can follow. See *ibid*.

In a decision so fraught with emotional consequence some doctors may prefer not to disclose precise details of the means that will be used, confining themselves to the required statement of risks the procedure entails. From one standpoint this ought not to be surprising. Any number of patients facing imminent surgical procedures would prefer not to hear all details, lest the usual anxiety preceding invasive medical procedures become the more intense. This is likely the case with the abortion procedures here in issue.

It is, however, precisely this lack of information concerning the way in which the fetus will be killed that is of legitimate concern to the State. *Casey* (plurality opinion). The State has an interest in ensuring so grave a choice is well informed. It is self-evident that a mother who comes to regret her choice to abort must struggle with grief more anguished and sorrow more profound when she learns, only after the event, what she once did not know: that she allowed a doctor to pierce the skull and vacuum the fast-developing brain of her unborn child, a child assuming the human form.

It is a reasonable inference that a necessary effect of the regulation and the knowledge it conveys will be to encourage some women to carry the infant to full term, thus reducing the absolute number of late-term abortions. The medical profession, furthermore, may find different and less shocking methods to abort the fetus in the second trimester, thereby accommodating legislative demand. The State's interest in respect for life is advanced by the dialogue that better informs the political and legal systems, the medical profession, expectant mothers, and society as a whole of the consequences that follow from a decision to elect a late-term abortion.

It is objected that the standard D & E is in some respects as brutal, if not more, than the intact D & E, so that the legislation accomplishes little. What we have already said, however, shows ample justification for the regulation. Partial-birth abortion, as defined by the Act, differs from a standard D & E because the former occurs when the fetus is partially outside the mother to the point of one of the Act's anatomical landmarks. It was reasonable for Congress to think that partial-birth abortion, more than standard D & E, "undermines the public's perception of the appropriate role of a physician during the delivery process, and perverts a process during which life is brought into the world." [citing Congressional Findings]. There would be a flaw in this Court's logic, and an irony in its jurisprudence, were we first to conclude a ban on both D & E and intact D & E was overbroad and then to say it is irrational to ban only intact D & E because that does not proscribe both procedures. In sum, we reject the contention that the congressional purpose of the Act was "to place a substantial obstacle in the path of a woman seeking an abortion." *Casey* (plurality opinion).

B.   The Act's furtherance of legitimate government interests bears upon, but does not resolve, the next question: whether the Act has the effect of imposing an unconstitutional burden on the abortion right because it does not allow use of the barred procedure where " 'necessary, in appropriate medical judgment, for [the] preservation of the . . . health of the mother.' " [W]hether the Act creates significant health risks for women has been a contested factual question. The evidence presented in the trial courts and before Congress demonstrates both sides have medical support for their position.

[For example, "abortion doctors" testified that intact D & E is safer for the pregnant woman, because it poses less risk of cervical laceration or uterine perforation and of leaving fetal material in the uterus. On the other hand, Justice Kennedy pointed to trial and congressional testimony "by other doctors" that D & E is "always" a safe alternative to intact D & E. "There is documented medical disagreement whether the Act's prohibition would ever impose significant health risks on women."]

The question becomes whether the Act can stand when this medical uncertainty persists. The Court's precedents instruct that the Act can survive this facial attack. The Court has given state and federal legislatures wide discretion to pass legislation in areas where there is medical and scientific uncertainty.

This traditional rule is consistent with *Casey*, which confirms the State's interest in promoting respect for human life at all stages in the pregnancy. Physicians are not entitled to ignore regulations that direct them to use reasonable alternative procedures. The law need not give abortion doctors unfettered choice in the course of their medical practice, nor should it elevate their status above other physicians in the medical community. * * *

Medical uncertainty does not foreclose the exercise of legislative power in the abortion context any more than it does in other contexts. The medical uncertainty over whether the Act's prohibition creates significant health risks provides a sufficient basis to conclude in this facial attack that the Act does not impose an undue burden.

The conclusion that the Act does not impose an undue burden is supported by other considerations. Alternatives are available to the prohibited procedure. As we have noted, the Act does not proscribe D & E. One District Court found D & E to have extremely low rates of medical complications. In addition the Act's prohibition only applies to the delivery of "a living fetus." 18 U.S.C. § 1531(b)(1)(A). If the intact D & E procedure is truly necessary in some circumstances, it appears likely an injection that kills the fetus is an alternative under the Act that allows the doctor to perform the procedure. * * *

In reaching the conclusion the Act does not require a health exception we reject certain arguments made by the parties on both sides of these cases. On the one hand, the Attorney General urges us to uphold the Act on the basis of the congressional findings alone. Although we review congressional factfinding under a deferential standard, we do not in the circumstances here place dispositive weight on Congress' findings. The Court retains an independent constitutional duty to review factual findings where constitutional rights are at stake.

As respondents have noted, and the District Courts recognized, some recitations in the Act are factually incorrect. Whether or not accurate at the time, some of the important findings have been superseded. Two examples suffice. Congress determined no medical schools provide instruction on the prohibited procedure. The testimony in the District Courts, however, demonstrated intact D & E is taught at medical schools. Congress also found there existed a medical consensus that the prohibited procedure is never medically necessary. The evidence presented in the District Courts contradicts that conclusion. Uncritical deference to Congress' factual findings in these cases is inappropriate.

On the other hand, relying on the Court's opinion in *Stenberg*, respondents contend that an abortion regulation must contain a health exception "if 'substantial medical authority supports the proposition that banning a particular procedure could endanger women's health.'" As illustrated by respondents' arguments and the decisions of the Courts of Appeals, *Stenberg* has been interpreted to leave no margin of error for legislatures to act in the face of medical uncertainty.

A zero tolerance policy would strike down legitimate abortion regulations, like the present one, if some part of the medical community were disinclined to follow the proscription. This is too exacting a standard to impose on the legislative power, exercised in this instance under the Commerce Clause, to regulate the medical profession. Considerations of marginal safety, including the balance of risks, are within the legislative competence when the regulation is rational and in pursuit of legitimate ends. When standard medical options are available, mere convenience does not suffice to displace them; and if some procedures have different risks than others, it does not follow that the State is altogether barred from imposing reasonable regulations. The Act is not invalid on its face where there is uncertainty over whether the barred procedure is ever necessary to preserve a woman's health, given the availability of other abortion procedures that are considered to be safe alternatives.

V. The considerations we have discussed support our further determination that these facial attacks should not have been entertained in the first instance. In these circumstances the proper means to consider exceptions is by as-applied challenge. The Government has acknowledged that pre-enforcement, as-applied challenges to the Act can be maintained. This is the proper manner to protect the health of the woman if it can be shown that in discrete and well-defined instances a particular condition has or is likely to occur in which the procedure prohibited by the Act must be used. In an as-applied challenge the nature of the medical risk can be better quantified and balanced than in a facial attack. * * *

Respondents have not demonstrated that the Act, as a facial matter, is void for vagueness, or that it imposes an undue burden on a woman's right to abortion based on its overbreadth or lack of a health exception. For these reasons the judgments of the Courts of Appeals for the Eighth and Ninth Circuits are reversed.

[**JUSTICE THOMAS**, joined by **JUSTICE SCALIA**, concurred. They reiterated their view that "the Court's abortion jurisprudence, including *Casey* and *Roe v. Wade*, has no basis in the Constitution." Justice Thomas also noted that the parties had not raised the question of whether the statute exceeded Congress's Article I powers and, therefore, that the validity of Congress's exercising authority over this issue was not before the Court.]

JUSTICE GINSBURG, with whom **JUSTICE STEVENS**, **JUSTICE SOUTER**, and **JUSTICE BREYER** join, dissenting.

Today's decision is alarming. It refuses to take *Casey* and *Stenberg* seriously. It tolerates, indeed applauds, federal intervention to ban nationwide a procedure found necessary and proper in certain cases by the American College of Obstetricians and Gynecologists (ACOG). It blurs the line, firmly drawn in *Casey*, between previability and postviability abortions. And, for the first time since *Roe*, the Court blesses a prohibition with no exception safeguarding a woman's health.

I dissent from the Court's disposition. Retreating from prior rulings that abortion restrictions cannot be imposed absent an exception safeguarding a woman's health, the Court upholds an Act that surely would not survive under the close scrutiny that previously attended state-decreed limitations on a woman's reproductive choices.

I.   As *Casey* comprehended, at stake in cases challenging abortion restrictions is a woman's "control over her own destiny." * * * [L]egal challenges to undue restrictions on abortion procedures do not seek to vindicate some generalized notion of privacy; rather, they center on a woman's autonomy to determine her life's course, and thus to enjoy equal citizenship stature. See, e.g., Siegel, Reasoning from the Body: A Historical Perspective on Abortion Regulation and Questions of Equal Protection, 44 Stan. L. Rev. 261 (1992); Law, Rethinking Sex and the Constitution, 132 U. Pa. L. Rev. 955, 1002–28 (1984).

In keeping with this comprehension of the right to reproductive choice, the Court has consistently required that laws regulating abortion, at any stage of pregnancy and in all cases, safeguard a woman's health. *Stenberg.*

[Justice Ginsburg noted that the federal statute had no health exception, based upon incorrect assumptions, such as the congressional finding that "[t]here is no credible medical evidence that partial-birth abortions are safe or are safer than other abortion procedures." Yet ACOG and other medical associations attested to Congress and the trial courts that "intact D & E carries meaningful safety advantages over other methods." Intact D & E minimizes the number of times a physician must insert instruments through the cervix and into the uterus, a minimization that helps the woman avoid risks of tearing and infection. Intact D & E reduces the risk that fetal material will be left in the uterus, which can cause infection, hemorrhage, and infertility. Intact D & E diminishes the chances of exposing the woman's tissues to sharp bony fragments sometimes resulting from dismemberment of the fetus. Intact D & E takes less operating time, thereby reducing risks of complications relating to anesthesia. Justice Ginsburg maintained that there was no reasonable basis to believe otherwise, as reflected in the trial records.]

II.   The Court offers flimsy and transparent justifications for upholding a nationwide ban on intact D & E *sans* any exception to safeguard a women's health. Today's ruling, the Court declares, advances "a premise central to [*Casey*'s] conclusion"—*i.e.,* the Government's "legitimate and substantial interest in preserving and promoting fetal life." But the Act scarcely furthers that interest: The law saves not a single fetus from destruction, for it targets only a *method* of performing abortion. And surely the statute was not designed to protect the lives or health of pregnant women. In short, the Court upholds a law that, while doing nothing to "preserv[e] . . . fetal life," bars a woman from choosing intact D & E although her doctor "reasonably believes [that procedure] will best protect [her]."

* * * Ultimately, the Court admits that "moral concerns" are at work, concerns that could yield prohibitions on any abortion. Notably, the concerns expressed are untethered to any ground genuinely serving the

Government's interest in preserving life. By allowing such concerns to carry the day and case, overriding fundamental rights, the Court dishonors our precedent.

Revealing in this regard, the Court invokes an antiabortion shibboleth for which it concededly has no reliable evidence: Women who have abortions come to regret their choices, and consequently suffer from "[s]evere depression and loss of esteem." Because of women's fragile emotional state and because of the "bond of love the mother has for her child," the Court worries, doctors may withhold information about the nature of the intact D & E procedure. The solution the Court approves, then, is *not* to require doctors to inform women, accurately and adequately, of the different procedures and their attendant risks. Instead, the Court deprives women of the right to make an autonomous choice, even at the expense of their safety.

This way of thinking reflects ancient notions about women's place in the family and under the Constitution—ideas that have long since been discredited.

Though today's majority may regard women's feelings on the matter as "self-evident," this Court has repeatedly confirmed that "[t]he destiny of the woman must be shaped . . . on her own conception of her spiritual imperatives and her place in society." *Casey.* * * *

III. If there is anything at all redemptive to be said of today's opinion, it is that the Court is not willing to foreclose entirely a constitutional challenge to the Act. "The Act is open," the Court states, "to a proper as-applied challenge in a discrete case." But the Court offers no clue on what a "proper" lawsuit might look like. Nor does the Court explain why the injunctions ordered by the District Courts should not remain in place, trimmed only to exclude instances in which another procedure would safeguard a woman's health at least equally well. Surely the Court cannot mean that no suit may be brought until a woman's health is immediately jeopardized by the ban on intact D & E. A woman "suffer[ing] from medical complications" needs access to the medical procedure at once and cannot wait for the judicial process to unfold.

The Court appears, then, to contemplate another lawsuit by the initiators of the instant actions. In such a second round, the Court suggests, the challengers could succeed upon demonstrating that "in discrete and well-defined instances a particular condition has or is likely to occur in which the procedure prohibited by the Act must be used." One may anticipate that such a preenforcement challenge will be mounted swiftly, to ward off serious, sometimes irremediable harm, to women whose health would be endangered by the intact D & E prohibition. * * *

IV. As the Court wrote in *Casey,* "overruling *Roe*'s central holding would not only reach an unjustifiable result under principles of *stare* *decisis*, but would seriously weaken the Court's capacity to exercise the judicial power and to function as the Supreme Court of a Nation dedicated to the rule of law." * * *

Though today's opinion does not go so far as to discard *Roe* or *Casey*, the Court, differently constituted than it was when we last considered a restrictive abortion regulation, is hardly faithful to our earlier invocations of the "rule of law" and the "principles of *stare decisis*." * * *

* * * In candor, the Act, and the Court's defense of it, cannot be understood as anything other than an effort to chip away at a right declared again and again by this Court—and with increasing comprehension of its centrality to women's lives.

WHOLE WOMAN'S HEALTH V. HELLERSTEDT
___ U.S. ___, 136 S.Ct. 2292, 195 L.Ed.2d 665 (2016)

JUSTICE BREYER delivered the opinion of the Court.

In *Planned Parenthood of Southeastern Pa. v. Casey*, a plurality of the Court concluded that there "exists" an "undue burden" on a woman's right to decide to have an abortion, and consequently a provision of law is constitutionally invalid, if the "*purpose or effect*" of the provision "*is to place a substantial obstacle* in the path of a woman seeking an abortion before the fetus attains viability." (Emphasis added.) The plurality added that "[u]nnecessary health regulations that have the purpose or effect of presenting a substantial obstacle to a woman seeking an abortion impose an undue burden on the right."

We must here decide whether two provisions of Texas' House Bill 2 violate the Federal Constitution as interpreted in *Casey*. The first provision, which we shall call the "*admitting-privileges requirement*," says that

> "[a] physician performing or inducing an abortion . . . must, on the date the abortion is performed or induced, have active admitting privileges at a hospital that . . . is located not further than 30 miles from the location at which the abortion is performed or induced." Tex. Health & Safety Code Ann. § 171.0031(a) (West Cum. Supp. 2015).

This provision amended Texas law that had previously required an abortion facility to maintain a written protocol "for managing medical emergencies and the transfer of patients requiring further emergency care to a hospital." 38 Tex. Reg. 6546 (2013).

The second provision, which we shall call the "*surgical-center requirement*," says that "the minimum standards for an abortion facility must be equivalent to the minimum standards adopted under [the Texas Health and Safety Code section] for ambulatory surgical centers." Tex. Health & Safety Code Ann. § 245.010(a).

We conclude that neither of these provisions confers medical benefits sufficient to justify the burdens upon access that each imposes. Each places a substantial obstacle in the path of women seeking a previability abortion, each constitutes an undue burden on abortion access, and each violates the Federal Constitution.

I.   [The Court reviewed the procedural history of the Texas legislation. The admitting privileges requirement was first challenged in court in 2013. The District Court enjoined the measure, but the Fifth Circuit upheld it. After that ruling, a group of abortion providers, some of whom had participated in the first lawsuit, filed a new challenge and pointed to changed circumstances since the first lawsuit was filed. This second lawsuit challenged the admitting privileges requirement as applied to physicians at two abortion facilities, and added new claims challenging the surgical center requirement. The District Court held a bench trial to determine the constitutionality of the requirements. The District Court's factual findings included the following:]

1.   Of Texas' population of more than 25 million people, "approximately 5.4 million" are "women" of "reproductive age," living within a geographical area of "nearly 280,000 square miles."

2.   "In recent years, the number of abortions reported in Texas has stayed fairly consistent at approximately 15–16% of the reported pregnancy rate, for a total number of approximately 60,000–72,000 legal abortions performed annually."

3.   Prior to the enactment of H.B. 2, there were more than 40 licensed abortion facilities in Texas, which "number dropped by almost half leading up to and in the wake of enforcement of the admitting-privileges requirement that went into effect in late-October 2013."

4.   If the surgical-center provision were allowed to take effect, the number of abortion facilities, after September 1, 2014, would be reduced further, so that "only seven facilities and a potential eighth will exist in Texas."

5.   Abortion facilities "will remain only in Houston, Austin, San Antonio, and the Dallas/Fort Worth metropolitan region." These include "one facility in Austin, two in Dallas, one in Fort Worth, two in Houston, and either one or two in San Antonio."

6.   [Based on certain assumptions,] it is foreseeable that over 1,200 women per month could be vying for counseling, appointments, and follow-up visits at some of these facilities."

7. The suggestion "that these seven or eight providers could meet the demand of the entire state stretches credulity."

8. "Between November 1, 2012 and May 1, 2014," that is, before and after enforcement of the admitting-privileges requirement, "the decrease in geographical distribution of abortion facilities" has meant that the number of women of reproductive age living more than 50 miles from a clinic has doubled (from 800,000 to over 1.6 million); those living more than 100 miles has increased by 150% (from 400,000 to 1 million); those living more than 150 miles has increased by more than 350% (from 86,000 to 400,000); and those living more than 200 miles has increased by about 2,800% (from 10,000 to 290,000). After September 2014, should the surgical-center requirement go into effect, the number of women of reproductive age living significant distances from an abortion provider will increase as follows: 2 million women of reproductive age will live more than 50 miles from an abortion provider; 1.3 million will live more than 100 miles from an abortion provider; 900,000 will live more than 150 miles from an abortion provider; and 750,000 more than 200 miles from an abortion provider.

9. The "two requirements erect a particularly high barrier for poor, rural, or disadvantaged women."

10. "The great weight of evidence demonstrates that, before the act's passage, abortion in Texas was extremely safe with particularly low rates of serious complications and virtually no deaths occurring on account of the procedure."

11. "Abortion, as regulated by the State before the enactment of House Bill 2, has been shown to be much safer, in terms of minor and serious complications, than many common medical procedures not subject to such intense regulation and scrutiny[, including colonoscopies, vasectomy, endometrial biopsy, and plastic surgery]."

12. "Additionally, risks are not appreciably lowered for patients who undergo abortions at ambulatory surgical centers as compared to nonsurgical-center facilities."

13. "[W]omen will not obtain better care or experience more frequent positive outcomes at an ambulatory surgical center as compared to a previously licensed facility."

14. "[T]here are 433 licensed ambulatory surgical centers in Texas," of which "336 . . . are apparently either 'grandfathered' or enjo[y] the benefit of a waiver of some or all" of the surgical-center "requirements."

15. The "cost of coming into compliance" with the surgical-center requirement "for existing clinics is significant," "undisputedly approach[ing] 1 million dollars," and "most likely exceed[ing] 1.5 million dollars," with "[s]ome . . . clinics" unable to "comply due to physical size

limitations of their sites." The "cost of acquiring land and constructing a new compliant clinic will likely exceed three million dollars." * * *

[The Court reviewed and rejected the state's argument that that petitioners' constitutional claims were barred by principles of res judicata. It then turned to the merits].

III. *Undue Burden—Legal Standard*

We begin with the standard, as described in *Casey.* We recognize that the "State has a legitimate interest in seeing to it that abortion, like any other medical procedure, is performed under circumstances that insure maximum safety for the patient." But, we added, "a statute which, while furthering [a] valid state interest, has the effect of placing a substantial obstacle in the path of a woman's choice cannot be considered a permissible means of serving its legitimate ends." Moreover, "[u]nnecessary health regulations that have the purpose or effect of presenting a substantial obstacle to a woman seeking an abortion impose an undue burden on the right."* * *

The Court of Appeals' articulation of the relevant standard is incorrect. The first part of the Court of Appeals' test may be read to imply that a district court should not consider the existence or nonexistence of medical benefits when considering whether a regulation of abortion constitutes an undue burden. The rule announced in *Casey,* however, requires that courts consider the burdens a law imposes on abortion access together with the benefits those laws confer. And the second part of the test is wrong to equate the judicial review applicable to the regulation of a constitutionally protected personal liberty with the less strict review applicable where, for example, economic legislation is at issue. See, *e.g., Williamson v. Lee Optical of Okla., Inc.* The Court of Appeals' approach simply does not match the standard that this Court laid out in *Casey,* which asks courts to consider whether any burden imposed on abortion access is "undue."

The statement that legislatures, and not courts, must resolve questions of medical uncertainty is also inconsistent with this Court's case law. Instead, the Court, when determining the constitutionality of laws regulating abortion procedures, has placed considerable weight upon evidence and argument presented in judicial proceedings. In *Casey,* for example, we relied heavily on the District Court's factual findings and the research-based submissions of *amici* in declaring a portion of the law at issue unconstitutional. 505 U.S., at 888–894 (opinion of the Court) (discussing evidence related to the prevalence of spousal abuse in determining that a spousal notification provision erected an undue burden to abortion access). And, in *Gonzales* the Court, while pointing out that we must review legislative "factfinding under a deferential standard," added that we must not "place dispositive weight" on those "findings." *Gonzales* went on to point out that the "*Court retains an independent constitutional duty to review factual findings where constitutional rights are at stake."* *Ibid.* (emphasis added). Although there we upheld a statute regulating abortion, we did not do so solely on the basis of legislative findings explicitly set forth in the statute, noting that "evidence presented in the District Courts contradicts" some of the legislative findings. In these circumstances, we said, "[u]ncritical deference to Congress' factual findings . . . is inappropriate."

Unlike in *Gonzales,* the relevant statute here does not set forth any legislative findings. Rather, one is left to infer that the legislature sought to further a constitutionally acceptable objective (namely, protecting women's health). For a district court to give significant weight to evidence in the judicial record in these circumstances is consistent with this Court's case law. As we shall describe, the District Court did so here. It did not simply substitute its own judgment for that of the legislature. It considered the evidence in the record—including expert evidence, presented in stipulations, depositions, and testimony. It then weighed the asserted benefits against the burdens. We hold that, in so doing, the District Court applied the correct legal standard.

IV. *Undue Burden—Admitting-Privilege Requirement*

Turning to the lower courts' evaluation of the evidence, we first consider the admitting-privileges requirement. Before the enactment of H.B. 2, doctors who provided abortions were required to "have admitting privileges *or* have a working arrangement with a physician(s) who has admitting privileges at a local hospital in order to ensure the necessary back up for medical complications." (emphasis added). The new law changed this requirement by requiring that a "physician performing or inducing an abortion . . . must, on the date the abortion is performed or induced, have active admitting privileges at a hospital that . . . is located not further than 30 miles from the location at which the abortion is performed or induced." * * *

The purpose of the admitting-privileges requirement is to help ensure that women have easy access to a hospital should complications arise during an abortion procedure. But the District Court found that it brought about no such health-related benefit. The court found that "[t]he great weight of evidence demonstrates that, before the act's passage, abortion in Texas was extremely safe with particularly low rates of serious complications and virtually no deaths occurring on account of the procedure." Thus, there was no significant health-related problem that the new law helped to cure.

[The Court noted the evidence on which the district court relied, including peer-reviewed studies and expert testimony indicating that abortion complications are extremely rare in both the first and second trimester and that most such complications occur in the days after the abortion, not on the spot.] We have found nothing in Texas' record evidence that shows that, compared to prior law (which required a "working arrangement" with a doctor with admitting privileges), the new law advanced Texas' legitimate interest in protecting women's health.* * *

At the same time, the record evidence indicates that the admitting-privileges requirement places a "substantial obstacle in the path of a woman's choice." *Casey* (plurality opinion). The District Court found, as of the time the admitting-privileges requirement began to be enforced, the number of facilities providing abortions dropped in half, from about 40 to about 20. Eight abortion clinics closed in the months leading up to the requirement's effective date. Eleven more closed on the day the admitting-privileges requirement took effect.

Other evidence helps to explain why the new requirement led to the closure of clinics. We read that other evidence in light of a brief filed in this Court by the Society of Hospital Medicine. That brief describes the undisputed general fact that "hospitals often condition admitting privileges on reaching a certain number of admissions per year." Returning to the District Court record, we note that, in direct testimony, the president of Nova Health Systems, implicitly relying on this general fact, pointed out that it would be difficult for doctors regularly performing abortions at the El Paso clinic to obtain admitting privileges at nearby hospitals because "[d]uring the past 10 years, over 17,000 abortion procedures were performed at the El Paso clinic [and n]ot a single one of those patients had to be transferred to a hospital for emergency treatment, much less admitted to the hospital." In a word, doctors would be unable to maintain admitting privileges or obtain those privileges for the future, because the fact that abortions are so safe meant that providers were unlikely to have any patients to admit. * * *

In our view, the record contains sufficient evidence that the admitting-privileges requirement led to the closure of half of Texas' clinics, or thereabouts. Those closures meant fewer doctors, longer waiting times, and increased crowding.

V.   *Undue Burden—Surgical-Center Requirement*

The second challenged provision of Texas' new law sets forth the surgical-center requirement. Prior to enactment of the new requirement, Texas law required abortion facilities to meet a host of health and safety requirements. * * * These requirements are policed by random and announced inspections, at least annually, as well as administrative penalties, injunctions, civil penalties, and criminal penalties for certain violations.

There is considerable evidence in the record supporting the District Court's findings indicating that the statutory provision requiring all abortion facilities to meet all surgical-center standards does not benefit patients and is not necessary. The District Court found that "risks are not appreciably lowered for patients who undergo abortions at ambulatory surgical centers as compared to nonsurgical-center facilities." The court added that women "will not obtain better care or experience more frequent positive outcomes at an ambulatory surgical center as compared to a previously licensed facility." And these findings are well supported.

The record makes clear that the surgical-center requirement provides no benefit when complications arise in the context of an abortion produced through medication. That is because, in such a case, complications would almost always arise only after the patient has left the facility. The record also contains evidence indicating that abortions taking place in an abortion facility are safe—indeed, safer than numerous procedures that take place outside hospitals and to which Texas does not apply its surgical-center requirements. * * *

Moreover, many surgical-center requirements are inappropriate as applied to surgical abortions. [The opinion described extensive requirements designed to prevent infection]. But abortions typically involve either the administration of medicines or procedures performed through the natural opening of the birth canal, which is itself not sterile. Nor do provisions designed to safeguard heavily sedated patients (unable to help themselves) during fire emergencies provide any help to abortion patients, as abortion facilities do not use general anesthesia or deep sedation. Further, since the few instances in which serious complications do arise following an abortion almost always require hospitalization, not treatment at a surgical center, surgical-center standards will not help in those instances either. * * *

At the same time, the record provides adequate evidentiary support for the District Court's conclusion that the surgical-center requirement places a substantial obstacle in the path of women seeking an abortion. The parties stipulated that the requirement would further reduce the number of abortion facilities available to seven or eight facilities, located in Houston, Austin, San Antonio, and Dallas/Fort Worth. In the District Court's view, the proposition that these "seven or eight providers could meet the demand of the entire State stretches credulity." We take this statement as a finding that these few facilities could not "meet" that "demand." * * *

More fundamentally, in the face of no threat to women's health, Texas seeks to force women to travel long distances to get abortions in crammed-to-capacity superfacilities. Patients seeking these services are less likely to get the kind of individualized attention, serious conversation, and emotional support that doctors at less taxed facilities may have offered. * * *

We agree with the District Court that the surgical-center requirement, like the admitting-privileges requirement, provides few, if any, health benefits for women, poses a substantial obstacle to women seeking abortions, and constitutes an "undue burden" on their constitutional right to do so. * * *

JUSTICE GINSBURG, concurring.

Many medical procedures, including childbirth, are far more dangerous to patients, yet are not subject to ambulatory-surgical-center or hospital admitting-privileges requirements. Given those realities, it is beyond rational belief that H.B. 2 could genuinely protect the health of women, and certain that the law "would simply make it more difficult for them to obtain abortions." When a State severely limits access to safe and legal procedures, women in desperate circumstances may resort to unlicensed rogue practitioners, *faute de mieux,* at great risk to their health and safety. So long as this Court adheres to *Roe v. Wade* and *Planned Parenthood of Southeastern Pa. v. Casey*, Targeted Regulation of Abortion Providers laws like H.B. 2 that "do little or nothing for health, but rather strew impediments to abortion," cannot survive judicial inspection.

JUSTICE THOMAS, dissenting.

I remain fundamentally opposed to the Court's abortion jurisprudence. Even taking *Casey* as the baseline, however, the majority radically rewrites the undue-burden test. * * *

First, the majority's free-form balancing test is contrary to *Casey*. * * * *Casey* did not balance the benefits and burdens of Pennsylvania's spousal and parental notification provisions[ ]. Pennsylvania's spousal notification requirement, the plurality said, imposed an undue burden because findings established that the requirement would "likely . . . prevent a significant number of women from obtaining an abortion"—not because these burdens outweighed its benefits. * * *

Second, by rejecting the notion that "legislatures, and not courts, must resolve questions of medical uncertainty," the majority discards another core element of the *Casey* framework. Before today, this Court had "given state and federal legislatures wide discretion to pass legislation in areas where there is medical and scientific uncertainty." This Court emphasized that this "traditional rule" of deference "is consistent with *Casey*." This Court underscored that legislatures should not be hamstrung "if some part of the medical community were disinclined to follow the proscription." And this Court concluded that "[c]onsiderations of marginal safety, including the balance of risks, are within the legislative competence when the regulation is rational and in pursuit of legitimate ends." This Court could not have been clearer: Whenever medical justifications for an abortion restriction are debatable, that "provides a sufficient basis to conclude in [a] facial attack that the [law] does not impose an undue burden." *Gonzales*. Otherwise, legislatures would face "too exacting" a standard.

Finally, the majority overrules another central aspect of *Casey* by requiring laws to have more than a rational basis even if they do not substantially impede access to abortion. "Where [the State] *has a rational basis to act* and it does not impose an undue burden," this Court previously held, "the State may use its regulatory power" to impose regulations "in furtherance of its legitimate interests in regulating the medical profession in order to promote respect for life, including life of the unborn." *Gonzales*. No longer. Though the majority declines to say how substantial a State's interest must be, one thing is clear: The State's burden has been ratcheted to a level that has not applied for a quarter century. * * *

The majority's undue-burden test looks far less like our post-*Casey* precedents and far more like the strict-scrutiny standard that *Casey* rejected, under which only the most compelling rationales justified restrictions on abortion. One searches the majority opinion in vain for any acknowledgment of the "premise central" to *Casey's* rejection of strict scrutiny: "that the government has a legitimate and substantial interest in preserving and promoting fetal life" from conception, not just in regulating medical procedures. Meanwhile, the majority's undue-burden balancing approach risks ruling out even minor, previously valid infringements on access to abortion. * * *

The majority's furtive reconfiguration of the standard of scrutiny applicable to abortion restrictions also points to a deeper problem. The undue-burden standard is just one variant of the Court's tiers-of-scrutiny approach to constitutional adjudication. And the label the Court affixes to its level of scrutiny in assessing whether the government can restrict a given right—be it "rational basis," intermediate, strict, or something else— is increasingly a meaningless formalism. As the Court applies whatever standard it likes to any given case, nothing but empty words separates our constitutional decisions from judicial fiat.

Though the tiers of scrutiny have become a ubiquitous feature of constitutional law, they are of recent vintage. Only in the 1960's did the Court begin in earnest to speak of "strict scrutiny" versus reviewing legislation for mere rationality, and to develop the contours of these tests. See Fallon, Strict Judicial Scrutiny, 54 UCLA L. Rev. 1267, 1274, 1284– 1285 (2007). * * *

The illegitimacy of using "made-up tests" to "displace longstanding national traditions as the primary determinant of what the Constitution means" has long been apparent. The Constitution does not prescribe tiers of scrutiny. The three basic tiers—"rational basis," intermediate, and strict scrutiny—"are no more scientific than their names suggest, and a further element of randomness is added by the fact that it is largely up to us which test will be applied in each case."

But the problem now goes beyond that. If our recent cases illustrate anything, it is how easily the Court tinkers with levels of scrutiny to achieve its desired result. * * *

Today's decision will prompt some to claim victory, just as it will stiffen opponents' will to object. But the entire Nation has lost something essential. The majority's embrace of a jurisprudence of rights-specific exceptions and balancing tests is "a regrettable concession of defeat—an acknowledgement that we have passed the point where 'law,' properly speaking, has any further application." Scalia, The Rule of Law as a Law of Rules, 56 U. Chi. L. Rev. 1175, 1182 (1989). I respectfully dissent.

[**JUSTICE ALITO**, joined by **JUSTICE THOMAS** and the **CHIEF JUSTICE (ROBERTS)**, wrote a dissent that focused on the res judicata issue and then contested the factual sufficiency of the case against both Texas requirements].

NOTES

1. *Whole Woman's Health* was decided nearly 25 years after *Casey*. During those years, state legislatures skeptical about abortion had passed scores of so-called Targeted Regulation of Abortion Provider (TRAP) laws all over the country. Unlike laws that directly restrict women's access to abortion, these laws regulate abortion providers in ways that are claimed to safeguard women's health, while also reducing access to abortion. See Linda Greenhouse and Reva B. Siegel, *Casey and the Clinic Closings: When Protecting "Women's Health" Obstricts Choice*, 125 Yale L. J. 1428 (2016). Notice the fact-intensive nature of Justice Breyer's majority opinion. Going forward, what limits has this case placed on TRAP laws? Does the Court's approach suggest that trial courts will play a particularly significant role? That expert witnesses will be important?

2. On the state's factual basis for regulating abortion, compare Justice Breyer's approach in this case to Justice Kennedy's in *Gonzales v. Carhart*, the Court's last major opinion on abortion. On the subject of women coming to regret abortions, Kennedy said in *Gonzales* that "[w]hile we find no reliable data to measure the phenomenon, it seems unexceptionable to conclude that some women come to regret their choice to abort the infant life they once created and sustained" (citing an amicus brief). Does Justice Breyer's detailed approach to the evidence suggest that states will now have to be more data-driven if they seek to justify abortion regulation as a way to protect women's interests?

3. Consider the debate between Justices Breyer and Thomas as to whether or not the "undue burden" test imposed by *Casey* requires courts to consider the benefits of an abortion regulation to women or just the burdens the law imposes. In light of your reading of *Casey*, who has the better of this

argument? Does the word "undue" itself suggest that a court must consider the justification for a law in order to determine whether its burden is unlawfully imposed or not? To the extent that *Casey* had not clearly resolved the question, do you think Justice Breyer's approach makes sense?

4.   Perhaps the most doctrinally significant aspect of the case is how it resolves questions about the standard of review courts should use in assessing the necessity for an abortion regulation. The Court rejected the argument— pressed by the state and the Fifth Circuit—that courts should separate their review of medical necessity from the question of undue burden, and should consider the necessity issue under the forgiving standard of rationality. What standard did the Court substitute in place of rational basis? In this aspect of the analysis, did the Court depart from the approach to legislative beliefs about medical facts that was employed in *Gonzales v. Carhart*? What do you make of Justice Thomas' argument that the Court functionally reinstated the strict scrutiny of *Roe* or something close to it? Had the Court given the clear endorsement of rational-basis review for medical necessity that Justice Thomas favored, would it have amounted to a silent overruling of *Roe* in its entirety?

5.   Justice Ginsburg's concurrence was brief and pointed. Although not all of it is reproduced here, it consisted of only one long paragraph. Is her concurrence suggesting that the very purpose of TRAP laws is to create an obstacle to abortion? Recall that *Casey* says a law creates an undue burden if it has the purpose *or* effect of creating an obstacle to abortion. Would the majority have been justified in focusing less on effects and concluding, instead, that the purpose of the Texas requirements was to reduce access to abortion? For an illustration of this more aggressive approach, see Judge Richard Posner's conclusion about a similar admitting privilege requirement imposed in Wisconsin. *Planned Parenthood of Wis., Inc. v. Schimel*, 806 F.3d 908, 921 (7th Cir. 2015) ("Opponents of abortion reveal their true objectives when they procure legislation limited to a medical procedure—abortion—that rarely produces a medical emergency").

6.   Justice Kennedy's retirement in 2018 has created widespread uncertainty about the Court's future abortion jurisprudence. See, e.g., Julie Hirschfeld Davis, *Departure of Kennedy, 'Firewall for Abortion Rights,' Could End* Roe v. Wade, N.Y. Times, June 27, 2018. While media attention has focused on whether *Roe v. Wade* will be overruled, it seems likely that Justice Kavanaugh's appointment to the Court will lead to change in this area even if *Roe* is retained. The replacement of Kennedy puts sharply in relief the question whether there remain five votes for the approach and outcome of *Whole Women's Health*.

PROBLEM 5-2:
REGULATING ABORTIONS

Consider the constitutionality of the following regulations on abortion.

(A) In some cultures, it is common for couples to abort female fetuses in order to increase their chances of male offspring. This phenomenon may occur in some subcultures of our own society. In addition, couples whose children are all of one gender might abort a fetus of that gender in the hope that a new pregnancy will give them a more diverse brood. There are no available statistics about sex-specific abortions in America. Having heard testimony about such incidents, however, the Eastland legislature passes a law making it unlawful for a physician to perform any abortion if he knows that the abortion is motivated by the sex of the fetus. It is a misdemeanor to perform such an abortion before viability but a felony if the physician knows that the fetus is viable. The legislation does not impose any duty on the physician to inquire into the parents' motivation, but he or she must inform any pregnant woman seeking an abortion that under state law, she is not supposed to consider the gender of the fetus in making a decision about abortion. Furthermore, a state court may not issue a by-pass order for a minor whose parents have not consented to the abortion, if the court finds that the abortion is sex-motivated.

(B) Suppose that the Eastland legislature enacts another bill requiring that abortions after the gestational age of 19 weeks are banned based on a legislative finding that a fetus can feel pain at that age. This finding is sharply disputed in the relevant scientific literature, but was endorsed at a legislative hearing by a physician who heads a group of medical professionals opposed to abortion.

How should a court rule on each of these provisions under current law? Would a court rule differently under an equal protection approach to abortion?

C. CONSENSUAL SEXUAL ACTIVITY

In 1961 (*Poe*) and 1965 (*Griswold*), almost all gay men, lesbians, and bisexuals were deeply closeted, and their venues for socialization (bars, restaurants) regularly harassed by police and state regulators. After the celebrated Stonewall riots of June 1969, many gay people "came out" of their closets and challenged state and federal laws criminalizing their consensual conduct and discriminating against them in government employment, immigration, state licensing and censorship, police surveillance, child custody proceedings, recognition of families, educational programs, and so forth.[49] Central to the "gay rights" efforts was the repeal or nullification of state laws prohibiting consensual "sodomy." By 1986, the laws of twenty-five states had been repealed or judicially nullified under

---

[49] See William Eskridge, Jr., *Challenging the Apartheid of the Closet: Establishing Conditions for Lesbian and Gay Intimacy*, Nomos, and Citizenship, 25 Hofstra L. Rev. 817 (1997).

Griswold and its progeny. Does the *Griswold* line of cases *require* the state to allow private same-sex intimacy?

Bowers v. Hardwick

478 U.S. 186 (1986)

Hardwick challenged the Georgia statute criminalizing sodomy[50] by committing that act with another adult male in the bedroom of respondent's home. **Justice White** delivered the opinion of the Court. The Court rejected Hardwick's substantive due process claim on the following grounds:

> Sodomy was a criminal offense at common law and was forbidden by the laws of the original 13 States when they ratified the Bill of Rights. In 1868, when the Fourteenth Amendment was ratified, all but 5 of the 37 States in the Union had criminal sodomy laws. In fact, until 1961, all 50 States outlawed sodomy, and today, 24 States and the District of Columbia continue to provide criminal penalties for sodomy performed in private and between consenting adults. Against this background, to claim that a right to engage in such conduct is "deeply rooted in this Nation's history and tradition" or "implicit in the concept of ordered liberty" is, at best, facetious.

In the years following *Bowers*, many state sodomy laws were repealed, invalidated by a court, or interpreted very narrowly. In a few states, state constitutional challenges failed. One such failed challenge, *Lawrence v. State*, 41 S.W.3d 349 (Tex. App. 2001), then reached the U.S. Supreme Court.

LAWRENCE V. TEXAS
539 U.S. 558, 123 S.Ct. 2472, 156 L.Ed.2d 508 (2003)

JUSTICE KENNEDY delivered the opinion of the Court.

Liberty protects the person from unwarranted government intrusions into a dwelling or other private places. In our tradition the State is not omnipresent in the home. And there are other spheres of our lives and existence, outside the home, where the State should not be a dominant presence. Freedom extends beyond spatial bounds. Liberty presumes an autonomy of self that includes freedom of thought, belief, expression, and

---

[50] Georgia Code Ann. § 16–6–2 (1984) provides, in pertinent part, as follows:

"(a) A person commits the offense of sodomy when he performs or submits to any sexual act involving the sex organs of one person and the mouth or anus of another. . . .

"(b) A person convicted of the offense of sodomy shall be punished by imprisonment for not less than one nor more than 20 years. . . ."

certain intimate conduct. The instant case involves liberty of the person both in its spatial and more transcendent dimensions.

[Acting on a reported weapons disturbance, the Harris County Police entered the apartment of John Lawrence and found him engaging in anal sex with another adult man, Tyron Garner. The police arrested and detained the men overnight for violating Texas's "Homosexual Conduct Law." Tex. Penal Code § 21.06(a) (2003). The law provides: "A person commits an offense if he engages in deviate sexual intercourse with another individual of the same sex." The statute defines deviate sexual intercourse to include oral and anal sex. The defendants pleaded *nolo contendere*, were fined $200 apiece (plus court costs of $141.25), and appealed their convictions, on the ground that the Homosexual Conduct Law was unconstitutional. The Texas courts rejected their federal constitutional claims, largely on the authority of *Bowers v. Hardwick*. The Supreme Court reversed.]

II.   The Court began its substantive discussion in *Bowers* as follows: "The issue presented is whether the Federal Constitution confers a fundamental right upon homosexuals to engage in sodomy and hence invalidates the laws of the many States that still make such conduct illegal and have done so for a very long time." That statement, we now conclude, discloses the Court's own failure to appreciate the extent of the liberty at stake. To say that the issue in *Bowers* was simply the right to engage in certain sexual conduct demeans the claim the individual put forward, just as it would demean a married couple were it to be said marriage is simply about the right to have sexual intercourse. The laws involved in *Bowers* and here are, to be sure, statutes that purport to do no more than prohibit a particular sexual act. Their penalties and purposes, though, have more far-reaching consequences, touching upon the most private human conduct, sexual behavior, and in the most private of places, the home. The statutes do seek to control a personal relationship that, whether or not entitled to formal recognition in the law, is within the liberty of persons to choose without being punished as criminals.

This, as a general rule, should counsel against attempts by the State, or a court, to define the meaning of the relationship or to set its boundaries absent injury to a person or abuse of an institution the law protects. It suffices for us to acknowledge that adults may choose to enter upon this relationship in the confines of their homes and their own private lives and still retain their dignity as free persons. When sexuality finds overt expression in intimate conduct with another person, the conduct can be but one element in a personal bond that is more enduring. The liberty protected by the Constitution allows homosexual persons the right to make this choice.

Having misapprehended the claim of liberty there presented to it, and thus stating the claim to be whether there is a fundamental right to engage in consensual sodomy, the *Bowers* Court said: "Proscriptions against that conduct have ancient roots." In academic writings, and in many of the scholarly *amicus* briefs filed to assist the Court in this case, there are fundamental criticisms of the historical premises relied upon by the majority and concurring opinions in *Bowers*. Brief for Cato Institute as *Amicus Curiae* 16–17; Brief for American Civil Liberties Union et al. as *Amici Curiae* 15–21; Brief for Professors of History et al. as *Amici Curiae* 3–10. We need not enter this debate in the attempt to reach a definitive historical judgment, but the following considerations counsel against adopting the definitive conclusions upon which *Bowers* placed such reliance.

At the outset it should be noted that there is no longstanding history in this country of laws directed at homosexual conduct as a distinct matter. [Both English and early American "crime against nature" laws regulated relations between men and women as well as between men and men.] The absence of legal prohibitions focusing on homosexual conduct may be explained in part by noting that according to some scholars the concept of the homosexual as a distinct category of person did not emerge until the late 19th century. * * *

It was not until the 1970's that any State singled out same-sex relations for criminal prosecution, and only nine States have done so. [Citing Arkansas, Kansas, Kentucky, Missouri, Montana, Nevada, Tennessee, and Texas statutes]; see also *Post v. State*, 715 P. 2d 1105 (Okla. Crim. App. 1986) (sodomy law invalidated as applied to different-sex couples). Post-*Bowers* even some of these States did not adhere to the policy of suppressing homosexual conduct. Over the course of the last decades, States with same-sex prohibitions have moved toward abolishing them.

In summary, the historical grounds relied upon in *Bowers* are more complex than the majority opinion and the concurring opinion by Chief Justice Burger indicate. Their historical premises are not without doubt and, at the very least, are overstated.

It must be acknowledged, of course, that the Court in *Bowers* was making the broader point that for centuries there have been powerful voices to condemn homosexual conduct as immoral. The condemnation has been shaped by religious beliefs, conceptions of right and acceptable behavior, and respect for the traditional family. For many persons these are not trivial concerns but profound and deep convictions accepted as ethical and moral principles to which they aspire and which thus determine the course of their lives. These considerations do not answer the question before us, however. The issue is whether the majority may use the power of the State to enforce these views on the whole society through operation of the criminal law. "Our obligation is to define the liberty of all, not to mandate our own moral code." *Casey.* * * *

The sweeping references by Chief Justice Burger to the history of Western civilization and to Judeo-Christian moral and ethical standards did not take account of other authorities pointing in an opposite direction. A committee advising the British Parliament recommended in 1957 repeal of laws punishing homosexual conduct. The Wolfenden Report: Report of the Committee on Homosexual Offenses and Prostitution (1963). Parliament enacted the substance of those recommendations 10 years later. Sexual Offences Act 1967, § 1.

Of even more importance, almost five years before *Bowers* was decided the European Court of Human Rights considered a case with parallels to *Bowers* and to today's case. An adult male resident in Northern Ireland alleged he was a practicing homosexual who desired to engage in consensual homosexual conduct. The laws of Northern Ireland forbade him that right. He alleged that he had been questioned, his home had been searched, and he feared criminal prosecution. The court held that the laws proscribing the conduct were invalid under the European Convention on Human Rights. *Dudgeon v. United Kingdom*, 45 Eur. Ct. H. R. (1981) ¶ 52. Authoritative in all countries that are members of the Council of Europe (21 nations then, 45 nations now), the decision is at odds with the premise in *Bowers* that the claim put forward was insubstantial in our Western civilization.

In our own constitutional system the deficiencies in *Bowers* became even more apparent in the years following its announcement. The 25 States with laws prohibiting the relevant conduct referenced in the *Bowers* decision are reduced now to 13, of which 4 enforce their laws only against homosexual conduct. In those States where sodomy is still proscribed, whether for same-sex or heterosexual conduct, there is a pattern of nonenforcement with respect to consenting adults acting in private. The State of Texas admitted in 1994 that as of that date it had not prosecuted anyone under those circumstances. *State v. Morales*, 869 S. W. 2d 941, 943.

Two principal cases decided after *Bowers* cast its holding into even more doubt. In *Casey*, the Court reaffirmed the substantive force of the liberty protected by the Due Process Clause. The *Casey* decision again confirmed that our laws and tradition afford constitutional protection to personal decisions relating to marriage, procreation, contraception, family relationships, child rearing, and education. In explaining the respect the Constitution demands for the autonomy of the person in making these choices, we stated as follows:

> These matters, involving the most intimate and personal choices a person may make in a lifetime, choices central to personal dignity and autonomy, are central to the liberty protected by the

Fourteenth Amendment. At the heart of liberty is the right to define one's own concept of existence, of meaning, of the universe, and of the mystery of human life. Beliefs about these matters could not define the attributes of personhood were they formed under compulsion of the State.

Persons in a homosexual relationship may seek autonomy for these purposes, just as heterosexual persons do. The decision in *Bowers* would deny them this right.

The second post-*Bowers* case of principal relevance is *Romer v. Evans* (Chapter 4, § 3D). There the Court struck down class-based legislation directed at homosexuals as a violation of the Equal Protection Clause. *Romer* invalidated an amendment to Colorado's constitution which named as a solitary class persons who were homosexuals, lesbians, or bisexual either by "orientation, conduct, practices or relationships," and deprived them of protection under state antidiscrimination laws. We concluded that the provision was "born of animosity toward the class of persons affected" and further that it had no rational relation to a legitimate governmental purpose. * * *

To the extent *Bowers* relied on values we share with a wider civilization, it should be noted that the reasoning and holding in *Bowers* have been rejected elsewhere. The European Court of Human Rights has followed not *Bowers* but its own decision in *Dudgeon v. United Kingdom*. See *P.G. & J.H. v. United Kingdom*, App. No. 00044787/98, ¶ 56 (Eur. Ct. H. R., Sept. 25, 2001); *Modinos v. Cyprus*, 259 Eur. Ct. H. R. (1993); *Norris v. Ireland*, 142 Eur. Ct. H. R. (1988). Other nations, too, have taken action consistent with an affirmation of the protected right of homosexual adults to engage in intimate, consensual conduct. See Brief for Mary Robinson et al. as *Amici Curiae* 11–12. The right the petitioners seek in this case has been accepted as an integral part of human freedom in many other countries. There has been no showing that in this country the governmental interest in circumscribing personal choice is somehow more legitimate or urgent.

The doctrine of *stare decisis* is essential to the respect accorded to the judgments of the Court and to the stability of the law. It is not, however, an inexorable command. In *Casey* we noted that when a Court is asked to overrule a precedent recognizing a constitutional liberty interest, individual or societal reliance on the existence of that liberty cautions with particular strength against reversing course. The holding in *Bowers*, however, has not induced detrimental reliance comparable to some instances where recognized individual rights are involved. Indeed, there has been no individual or societal reliance on *Bowers* of the sort that could counsel against overturning its holding once there are compelling reasons to do so. *Bowers* itself causes uncertainty, for the precedents before and after its issuance contradict its central holding.

The rationale of *Bowers* does not withstand careful analysis. In his dissenting opinion in *Bowers* Justice Stevens came to these conclusions:

> Our prior cases make two propositions abundantly clear. First, the fact that the governing majority in a State has traditionally viewed a particular practice as immoral is not a sufficient reason for upholding a law prohibiting the practice; neither history nor tradition could save a law prohibiting miscegenation from constitutional attack. Second, individual decisions by married persons, concerning the intimacies of their physical relationship, even when not intended to produce offspring, are a form of "liberty" protected by the Due Process Clause of the Fourteenth Amendment. Moreover, this protection extends to intimate choices by unmarried as well as married persons.

Justice Stevens' analysis, in our view, should have been controlling in *Bowers* and should control here.

Bowers was not correct when it was decided, and it is not correct today. It ought not to remain binding precedent. *Bowers v. Hardwick* should be and now is overruled.

The present case does not involve minors. It does not involve persons who might be injured or coerced or who are situated in relationships where consent might not easily be refused. It does not involve public conduct or prostitution. It does not involve whether the government must give formal recognition to any relationship that homosexual persons seek to enter. The case does involve two adults who, with full and mutual consent from each other, engaged in sexual practices common to a homosexual lifestyle. The petitioners are entitled to respect for their private lives. The State cannot demean their existence or control their destiny by making their private sexual conduct a crime. Their right to liberty under the Due Process Clause gives them the full right to engage in their conduct without intervention of the government. "It is a promise of the Constitution that there is a realm of personal liberty which the government may not enter." *Casey.* The Texas statute furthers no legitimate state interest which can justify its intrusion into the personal and private life of the individual.

Had those who drew and ratified the Due Process Clauses of the Fifth Amendment or the Fourteenth Amendment known the components of liberty in its manifold possibilities, they might have been more specific. They did not presume to have this insight. They knew times can blind us to certain truths and later generations can see that laws once thought necessary and proper in fact serve only to oppress. As the Constitution endures, persons in every generation can invoke its principles in their own search for greater freedom.

[JUSTICE O'CONNOR concurred in the judgment. She had joined the Court's opinion in *Bowers* and was not willing to join the Court's opinion overruling that precedent. But, she concluded, the Texas Homosexual Conduct Law did violate the Equal Protection Clause because it branded all homosexuals as criminals.]

JUSTICE SCALIA, with whom THE CHIEF JUSTICE [REHNQUIST] and JUSTICE THOMAS join, dissenting.

"Liberty finds no refuge in a jurisprudence of doubt." *Casey.* That was the Court's sententious response, barely more than a decade ago, to those seeking to overrule *Roe v. Wade.* The Court's response today, to those who have engaged in a 17-year crusade to overrule *Bowers v. Hardwick*, is very different. The need for stability and certainty presents no barrier.

Most of the rest of today's opinion has no relevance to its actual holding—that the Texas statute "furthers no legitimate state interest which can justify" its application to petitioners under rational-basis review. Though there is discussion of "fundamental proposition[s]" and "fundamental decisions," nowhere does the Court's opinion declare that homosexual sodomy is a "fundamental right" under the Due Process Clause; nor does it subject the Texas law to the standard of review that would be appropriate (strict scrutiny) if homosexual sodomy *were* a "fundamental right." Thus, while overruling the *outcome* of *Bowers*, the Court leaves strangely untouched its central legal conclusion: "[R]espondent would have us announce . . . a fundamental right to engage in homosexual sodomy. This we are quite unwilling to do." Instead the Court simply describes petitioners' conduct as "an exercise of their liberty"—which it undoubtedly is—and proceeds to apply an unheard-of form of rational-basis review that will have far-reaching implications beyond this case. * * *

Today's opinion is the product of a Court, which is the product of a law-profession culture, that has largely signed on to the so-called homosexual agenda, by which I mean the agenda promoted by some homosexual activists directed at eliminating the moral opprobrium that has traditionally attached to homosexual conduct. I noted in an earlier opinion the fact that the American Association of Law Schools (to which any reputable law school *must* seek to belong) excludes from membership any school that refuses to ban from its job-interview facilities a law firm (no matter how small) that does not wish to hire as a prospective partner a person who openly engages in homosexual conduct. See *Romer* [dissenting opinion]. * * *

The matters appropriate for this Court's resolution are only three: Texas's prohibition of sodomy neither infringes a "fundamental right" (which the Court does not dispute), nor is unsupported by a rational relation to what the Constitution considers a legitimate state interest, nor denies the equal protection of the laws. I dissent.

JUSTICE THOMAS, dissenting.

I write separately to note that the law before the Court today "is . . . uncommonly silly." *Griswold v. Connecticut* (Stewart, J., dissenting). If I were a member of the Texas Legislature, I would vote to repeal it. Punishing someone for expressing his sexual preference through noncommercial consensual conduct with another adult does not appear to be a worthy way to expend valuable law enforcement resources.

Notwithstanding this, I recognize that as a member of this Court I am not empowered to help petitioners and others similarly situated. My duty, rather, is to "decide cases 'agreeably to the Constitution and laws of the United States.' " [*Id.*] And, just like Justice Stewart, I "can find [neither in the Bill of Rights nor any other part of the Constitution a] general right of privacy," [*id.*], or as the Court terms it today, the "liberty of the person both in its spatial and more transcendent dimensions."

NOTES ON LAWRENCE AND THE FUTURE OF THE RIGHT OF PRIVACY

1.   Stare Decisis *in Constitutional Cases.* Two authors of the joint opinion in *Casey* (Justices Kennedy and Souter) voted to overrule *Bowers.* As he candidly signaled in his *Casey* and *Carhart* dissents, Justice Scalia considers *stare decisis* no big obstacle to overruling wrongly decided constitutional precedents—but in *Lawrence* he chided the majority Justices for giving nothing more than lip service to the principle that, they said, saved the abortion right from being overruled in *Casey.* (Scalia's criticism does not apply to Justice O'Connor, who took *stare decisis* just as seriously in *Lawrence* as she did in *Casey.*) The majority didn't say much in response, but consider some possible defenses:

(a)   *The Libertarian Presumption.* The Constitution is a highly libertarian document, and its structural protection of people's freedom to act in their own interests without state interference was buttressed in the Bill of Rights and then in the Fourteenth Amendment. *Roe v. Wade*, a precedent protecting a liberty interest, gets more *stare decisis* support than *Bowers v. Hardwick*, a precedent declining to protect a liberty interest. Moreover, it cannot be ignored that the invasions of liberty were in criminal statutes, which have long been subjected to different, and more stringent, liberty-protective limitations than civil statutes. Note that the same argument could be applied to efforts by progressives to overrule the Court's Second Amendment holdings.

(b)   Stare Decisis *Cuts Both Ways. Bowers'* holding that anti-homosexual sentiment is a rational basis for a law criminalizing "homosexual sodomy" is inconsistent with *Romer'*s holding that antigay "animus" is not a rational basis for a potentially sweeping anti-civil rights measure. Unless the rational basis test applies differently for the Due Process and Equal Protection Clauses—a proposition Justice O'Connor seems to accept—these two holdings cannot logically coexist. The Court chose *Romer* over *Bowers*, which is not only defensible but also supported by the litigation posture in the case: Harris County did not ask the Court to reconsider *Romer*, while Lawrence and dozens of *amici* asked the Court to reconsider and overrule *Bowers*.

(c) *Social Movements and Emerging National Consensus.* By 1992, the pro-choice movement had been successful in persuading substantial majorities of Americans that women have a right to abortion—but not an unlimited right. This was a script *Casey* followed carefully: The *Roe* right was reaffirmed, but state regulatory authority was expanded (and several recent decisions were overruled to do so). By 2003, the gay rights movement had been successful in persuading substantial majorities of Americans that lesbians, gay men, and bisexuals were an acceptable minority whose so-called "lifestyles" should be "tolerated" by the state—and that it was ridiculous for the state to criminalize their private intimate activities. This was a script *Lawrence* followed carefully: Criminal sodomy laws were invalidated, but the majority disclaimed any endorsement of same-sex marriage or gays in the military, for example.

Do any of these theories (or a combination) justify the different deployment of *stare decisis* in the two cases?

2. *History and Political Theory: The Constitution as a Mechanism for Moderating Culture Wars.* Recall that Justice Scalia demands a long and unbroken history of affirmative protection before he will acknowledge some kind of fundamental right protection—but that view of the relationship between history and substantive due process was rejected in *Griswold, Roe* and *Casey,* and *Loving v. Virginia*. Justice Kennedy demonstrates that there can be relatively objective benchmarks for evolving tradition—the ALI's Model Penal Code, the adoption of its deregulatory principle in the next generation of state legislative and judicial deliberation, the experience of other Western countries. All point in the same direction: Consensual sodomy laws unnecessarily intrude into people's private lives.

Underlying Kennedy's and O'Connor's approach is *not* the idea that the Court decides great moral issues, but that the Court and its constitutional discourse contribute to a well-managed pluralism. America is a nation of social groups, and they constantly come into conflict. The political process is the arena where their conflicts are worked out, most of the time. But constitutionalism can serve a useful purpose of managing and channeling intergroup conflict. On the one hand, constitutionalism can prevent the state from being deployed as a means whereby a minority is turned into an outlaw group. That is not only an unfair deployment of the state, but creates resentments and the risk that the outlaws (and the "in-laws") will go outside normal politics to fight. On the other hand, constitutionalism can protect groups against excessive state intrusion into their own bonding needs. Freedom of religion, of association, the sanctity of the home, and the right of privacy are examples. Keep these arguments in mind when considering related issues in Chapter 6.

3.   *Can State Morals Laws Survive* Lawrence? Justice Scalia also predicted in his dissent that *Lawrence* is the end of state morals regulation. This is an echo of Lord Patrick Devlin's famous attack on the Wolfenden Report urging the United Kingdom to decriminalize consensual sodomy; like Scalia, Devlin defended state morals regulation as an expression of popular norms. Scalia's list of morals laws that would fall if "homosexual sodomy" were deregulated is even an adaptation of Devlin's list in *On the Enforcement of Morals* (1959). H.L.A. Hart famously responded to Devlin in *Law, Liberty, and Morality* (1963). His argument was that however repugnant "homosexual sodomy" was, the state should not regulate private activities not harming third parties, the principle best articulated in John Stuart Mill, *On Liberty* ch. 4 (1857).

Lawrence does not purport to decide the constitutionality of other laws regulating morals, but lower courts will now have to adjudicate such challenges, if only because the dissenting opinion will inspire lawyers to bring them. The most obvious criterion for evaluating the laws is the Mill-Hart inquiry: Does this private conduct harm third parties? Consider the following array of morals legislation, loosely based on Justice Scalia's list. Which of these laws must fall after *Lawrence*? Which are easily defensible?

(1)   Use of sex toys on oneself or on another person (yes, several states do outlaw the sale of such devices);

(2)   Fornication: Sexual intercourse between two people who are not married;

(3)   Adult incest between first cousins (could it be made illegal if the incest were between adult siblings?; would it matter whether such incest increases the risk of birth defects to offspring?);

(4)   Prostitution;

(5)   Bestiality;

(6)   Adultery: Sex between two adults, at least one of whom is married to someone else.

4.   The Court's reference to European human rights decisions on the same issue was highly controversial. Is it appropriate for a U.S. court to rely on foreign decisions in construing the American Constitution? For an argument in favor of this practice, see Daniel Farber, *The Supreme Court, the Law of Nations, and Citations of Foreign Law: The Lessons of History*, 95 Cal. L. Rev. 1335 (2007).

D. THE RIGHT TO MARRY

Griswold spoke of marriage as "an association for as noble a purpose as any involved in our prior decisions." *Loving v. Virginia* is best known as a case about racial equality, but identified a right to marry found in the Due Process Clause as an alternative ground for the Court's decision striking down laws prohibiting different-race marriage (Chapter 3, § 1A).

Indeed, many constitutional debates about marriage, including the contemporary debate over same-sex marriage addressed in Chapter 4, involve both equal protection and due process claims.

In *Zablocki v. Redhail*, 434 U.S. 374 (1978), the Court invalidated Wisconsin's law precluding the issuance of marriage licenses to people with outstanding support obligations to children from a previous marriage. Justice Thurgood Marshall's opinion for the Court started with the proposition that the "right to marry" is a fundamental right:

> It is not surprising that the decision to marry has been placed on the same level of importance as decisions relating to procreation, childbirth, child rearing, and familial relationships. As the facts of these cases illustrate, it would make little sense to recognize a right to privacy with respect to other matters of family life and not with respect to the decision to enter into a relationship that is the foundation of the family in our society.

Justice Marshall then reasoned that any state discrimination in allocating the right to marry must be scrutinized strictly under the Equal Protection Clause. "When a statutory classification significantly interferes with the exercise of a fundamental right, it cannot be upheld unless it is supported by sufficiently important state interests and is closely tailored to effectuate only those interests." The Wisconsin statute flunked this stringent test. Although ensuring collection of support obligations owed one's children is an important state interest, the state has other, less constitutionally intrusive, ways of effectuating that interest.

In *Turner v. Safley*, 482 U.S. 78 (1987), a unanimous Court, per Justice O'Connor, struck down a state regulation barring the ability of prisoners to marry. The Court held that the right to marry was implicated even in prison settings, where sex with outsiders is normally prohibited:

> First, inmate marriages, like others, are expressions of emotional support and public commitment. These elements are an important and significant aspect of the marital relationship. In addition, many religions recognize marriage as having spiritual significance; for some inmates and their spouses, therefore, the commitment of marriage may be an exercise of religious faith as well as an expression of personal dedication. Third, most inmates eventually will be released by parole or commutation, and therefore most inmate marriages are formed in the expectation that they will be fully consummated. Finally, marital status often is a precondition to the receipt of government benefits (e.g., Social Security benefits), property rights (e.g., tenancy by the entirety, inheritance rights), and other, less tangible benefits (e.g., legitimation of children born out of wedlock). These incidents of marriage, like the religious and personal aspects of the marriage

commitment, are unaffected by the fact of confinement or the pursuit of legitimate corrections goals.

Because of the prison setting, Justice O'Connor applied the Court's precedents requiring a "reasonable relationship" between a prison regulation and legitimate penological objectives. Another part of her opinion (joined only by five Justices) upheld prison surveillance of inmate mail, usually protected under the First Amendment. Unlike opening inmate mail, preventing inmate marriages did not narrowly serve legitimate penological purposes, Justice O'Connor reasoned.

Goodridge v. Department of Public Health, 440 Mass. 309, 798 N.E. 2d 941 (2003), became the first appellate decision to find that same-sex couples had a right to marry, grounded in the state constitution. But the first appellate decision in the United States to recognize what it called a "fundamental right to marry" for lesbian and gay couples was *In re Marriage Cases*, 43 Cal. 4th 757, 183 P.3d 384, 76 Cal. Rptr. 3d 683 (2008). In that case, the Court ruled that the state's exclusion of lesbian and gay couples from civil marriage violated the state constitution's privacy right and was an additional reason why the exclusion was subject to strict scrutiny under the state equal protection right. However, the fundamental right to marry recognized in *In re Marriage Cases* was eliminated later that same year by California's voters, who passed Proposition 8 at the polls. The marriages of 18,000 same-sex couples who were wed after the decision, but before Prop 8, were undisturbed, but no new same-sex marriages were permitted. Prop 8 was ultimately struck down by a federal district court after a trial and extensive findings of fact. *Perry v. Schwarzenegger*, 704 F. Supp. 2d 921 (N.D. Cal. 2010). The Ninth Circuit subsequently upheld the district court in striking down Prop 8, and the Supreme Court appeared poised to decide the question when it granted *certiorari*. Instead, the Court held that those supporting Prop 8 lacked standing to pursue an appeal where the state was no longer defending the measure. *Hollingsworth v. Perry*, 570 U.S. 693 (2013), is addressed in Chapter 9.

The issue came back to the Supreme Court in 2015. At this point, the Court had struck down the federal Defense of Marriage Act (DOMA) in *United States v. Windsor* (addressed in Chapter 4), but had expressly reserved in that case the question whether it was constitutional for *states* to ban same-sex marriage, as California had sought to do with Prop 8. Between *Windsor* and the next case, numerous federal courts had struck down state marriage bans as unconstitutional. When the Sixth Circuit bucked the trend and upheld such bans, the Court agreed to decide the issue. The next case seems destined to become one of the most significant cases in a generation or more. It inspired a heated debate among the justices about the appropriate role of courts.

OBERGEFELL V. HODGES
___ U.S. ___, 135 S.Ct. 2584, 192 L.Ed.2d 609 (2015)

[Voters in Michigan, Kentucky, Ohio, and Tennessee enacted state constitutional amendments defining marriage as a union between one man and one woman. Same-sex couples challenged the denial of their right to marry and to have out-of-state marriages that were valid where performed recognized in any of these states. The Sixth Circuit upheld the bans in 2014. That decision conflicted with decisions of several federal appellate courts in favor of marriage equality. Two terms after it had struck down the federal Defense of Marriage Act as unconstitutional in *United States v. Windsor* (Chapter 4, § 3D), the Supreme Court granted review to decide whether the Fourteenth Amendment requires states to license a marriage between two people of the same sex and/or to recognize a same-sex marriage licensed in another state.]

JUSTICE KENNEDY delivered the opinion of the Court.

[II.] From their beginning to their most recent page, the annals of human history reveal the transcendent importance of marriage. The lifelong union of a man and a woman always has promised nobility and dignity to all persons, without regard to their station in life. Marriage is sacred to those who live by their religions and offers unique fulfillment to those who find meaning in the secular realm. Its dynamic allows two people to find a life that could not be found alone, for a marriage becomes greater than just the two persons. Rising from the most basic human needs, marriage is essential to our most profound hopes and aspirations.

The centrality of marriage to the human condition makes it unsurprising that the institution has existed for millennia and across civilizations. Since the dawn of history, marriage has transformed strangers into relatives, binding families and societies together. * * *

The petitioners acknowledge this history but contend that these cases cannot end there. * * * Far from seeking to devalue marriage, the petitioners seek it for themselves because of their respect—and need—for its privileges and responsibilities. And their immutable nature dictates that same-sex marriage is their only real path to this profound commitment.

[**Justice Kennedy** described in detail the plaintiffs, who included 14 same-sex couples and two men whose partners are deceased.]

The ancient origins of marriage confirm its centrality, but it has not stood in isolation from developments in law and society. The history of marriage is one of both continuity and change. That institution—even as confined to opposite-sex relations—has evolved over time.

For example, marriage was once viewed as an arrangement by the couple's parents based on political, religious, and financial concerns; but by the time of the Nation's founding it was understood to be a voluntary contract between a man and a woman. As the role and status of women changed, the institution further evolved. Under the centuries-old doctrine of coverture, a married man and woman were treated by the State as a single, male-dominated legal entity. As women gained legal, political, and property rights, and as society began to understand that women have their own equal dignity, the law of coverture was abandoned. These and other developments in the institution of marriage over the past centuries were not mere superficial changes. Rather, they worked deep transformations in its structure, affecting aspects of marriage long viewed by many as essential. * * *

These new insights have strengthened, not weakened, the institution of marriage. Indeed, changed understandings of marriage are characteristic of a Nation where new dimensions of freedom become apparent to new generations, often through perspectives that begin in pleas or protests and then are considered in the political sphere and the judicial process.

This dynamic can be seen in the Nation's experiences with the rights of gays and lesbians. Until the mid-20th century, same-sex intimacy long had been condemned as immoral by the state itself in most Western nations, a belief often embodied in the criminal law. * * * Even when a greater awareness of the humanity and integrity of homosexual persons came in the period after World War II, the argument that gays and lesbians had a just claim to dignity was in conflict with both law and widespread social conventions. Same-sex intimacy remained a crime in many States. Gays and lesbians were prohibited from most government employment, barred from military service, excluded under immigration laws, targeted by police, and burdened in their rights to associate.

For much of the 20th century, moreover, homosexuality was treated as an illness. When the American Psychiatric Association published the first Diagnostic and Statistical Manual of Mental Disorders in 1952, homosexuality was classified as a mental disorder, a position adhered to until 1973. Only in more recent years have psychiatrists and others recognized that sexual orientation is both a normal expression of human sexuality and immutable.

In the late 20th century, following substantial cultural and political developments, same-sex couples began to lead more open and public lives and to establish families. This development was followed by a quite extensive discussion of the issue in both governmental and private sectors and by a shift in public attitudes toward greater tolerance. As a result, questions about the rights of gays and lesbians soon reached the courts, where the issue could be discussed in the formal discourse of the law.

[**Justice Kennedy** first recounted the history of the Court's cases addressing "the legal status of homosexuals" in *Bowers v. Hardwick*, *Romer v. Evans*, and *Lawrence v. Texas*. He then reviewed the history of the major cases over the course of the same-sex marriage debate]. After years of litigation, legislation, referenda, and the discussions that attended these public acts, the States are now divided on the issue of same-sex marriage.

[III.]   Under the Due Process Clause of the Fourteenth Amendment, no State shall "deprive any person of life, liberty, or property, without due process of law." The fundamental liberties protected by this Clause include most of the rights enumerated in the Bill of Rights. In addition these liberties extend to certain personal choices central to individual dignity and autonomy, including intimate choices that define personal identity and beliefs. The identification and protection of fundamental rights is an enduring part of the judicial duty to interpret the Constitution. That responsibility, however, "has not been reduced to any formula." *Poe v. Ullman* (Harlan, J., dissenting). Rather, it requires courts to exercise reasoned judgment in identifying interests of the person so fundamental that the State must accord them its respect. That process is guided by many of the same considerations relevant to analysis of other constitutional provisions that set forth broad principles rather than specific requirements. History and tradition guide and discipline this inquiry but do not set its outer boundaries. See *Lawrence*. That method respects our history and learns from it without allowing the past alone to rule the present.

The nature of injustice is that we may not always see it in our own times. The generations that wrote and ratified the Bill of Rights and the Fourteenth Amendment did not presume to know the extent of freedom in all of its dimensions, and so they entrusted to future generations a charter protecting the right of all persons to enjoy liberty as we learn its meaning. When new insight reveals discord between the Constitution's central protections and a received legal stricture, a claim to liberty must be addressed.

Applying these established tenets, the Court has long held the right to marry is protected by the Constitution. [The Court then reviewed *Loving*, *Zablocki* and *Turner*]. * * *

The four principles and traditions to be discussed demonstrate that the reasons marriage is fundamental under the Constitution apply with equal force to same-sex couples.

A first premise of the Court's relevant precedents is that the right to personal choice regarding marriage is inherent in the concept of individual autonomy. This abiding connection between marriage and liberty is why *Loving* invalidated interracial marriage bans under the Due Process Clause. Like choices concerning contraception, family relationships, procreation, and childrearing, all of which are protected by the Constitution, decisions concerning marriage are among the most intimate that an individual can make. * * *

A second principle in this Court's jurisprudence is that the right to marry is fundamental because it supports a two-person union unlike any other in its importance to the committed individuals. This point was central to *Griswold v. Connecticut,* which held the Constitution protects the right of married couples to use contraception. * * *

The right to marry thus dignifies couples who "wish to define themselves by their commitment to each other." *Windsor.* Marriage responds to the universal fear that a lonely person might call out only to find no one there. It offers the hope of companionship and understanding and assurance that while both still live there will be someone to care for the other. * * *

Lawrence confirmed a dimension of freedom that allows individuals to engage in intimate association without criminal liability [but], it does not follow that freedom stops there. Outlaw to outcast may be a step forward, but it does not achieve the full promise of liberty.

A third basis for protecting the right to marry is that it safeguards children and families and thus draws meaning from related rights of childrearing, procreation, and education. See *Pierce v. Society of Sisters*; *Meyer v. Nebraska.* * * *

As all parties agree, many same-sex couples provide loving and nurturing homes to their children, whether biological or adopted. And hundreds of thousands of children are presently being raised by such couples. Most States have allowed gays and lesbians to adopt, either as individuals or as couples, and many adopted and foster children have same-sex parents. This provides powerful confirmation from the law itself that gays and lesbians can create loving, supportive families.

Excluding same-sex couples from marriage thus conflicts with a central premise of the right to marry. Without the recognition, stability, and predictability marriage offers, their children suffer the stigma of knowing their families are somehow lesser. They also suffer the significant material costs of being raised by unmarried parents, relegated through no fault of their own to a more difficult and uncertain family life. The marriage laws at issue here thus harm and humiliate the children of same-sex couples.

That is not to say the right to marry is less meaningful for those who do not or cannot have children. An ability, desire, or promise to procreate is not and has not been a prerequisite for a valid marriage in any State. In light of precedent protecting the right of a married couple not to procreate, it cannot be said the Court or the States have conditioned the right to marry on the capacity or commitment to procreate. The constitutional marriage right has many aspects, of which childbearing is only one.

Fourth and finally, this Court's cases and the Nation's traditions make clear that marriage is a keystone of our social order. * * *

[J]ust as a couple vows to support each other, so does society pledge to support the couple, offering symbolic recognition and material benefits to protect and nourish the union. Indeed, while the States are in general free to vary the benefits they confer on all married couples, they have throughout our history made marriage the basis for an expanding list of governmental rights, benefits, and responsibilities. These aspects of marital status include: Taxation; inheritance and property rights; rules of intestate succession; spousal privilege in the law of evidence; hospital access; medical decisionmaking authority; adoption rights; the rights and benefits of survivors; birth and death certificates; professional ethics rules; campaign finance restrictions; workers' compensation benefits; health insurance; and child custody, support, and visitation rules. Valid marriage under state law is also a significant status for over a thousand provisions of federal law. See *Windsor*. The States have contributed to the fundamental character of the marriage right by placing that institution at the center of so many facets of the legal and social order.

There is no difference between same- and opposite-sex couples with respect to this principle. Yet by virtue of their exclusion from that institution, same-sex couples are denied the constellation of benefits that the States have linked to marriage. This harm results in more than just material burdens. * * * It demeans gays and lesbians for the State to lock them out of a central institution of the Nation's society. Same-sex couples, too, may aspire to the transcendent purposes of marriage and seek fulfillment in its highest meaning.

Objecting that this does not reflect an appropriate framing of the issue, the respondents refer to *Washington v. Glucksberg,* which called for a " 'careful description' " of fundamental rights. They assert the petitioners do not seek to exercise the right to marry but rather a new and nonexistent "right to same-sex marriage." *Glucksberg* did insist that liberty under the Due Process Clause must be defined in a most circumscribed manner, with central reference to specific historical practices. Yet while that approach may have been appropriate for the asserted right there involved (physician-assisted suicide), it is inconsistent with the approach this Court has used in discussing other fundamental rights, including marriage and intimacy. *Loving* did not ask about a "right to interracial marriage"; *Turner* did not ask about a "right of inmates to marry"; and *Zablocki* did not ask about a "right of fathers with unpaid child support duties to marry." Rather, each case inquired about the right to marry in its comprehensive sense, asking if there was a sufficient justification for excluding the relevant class from the right.

That principle applies here. If rights were defined by who exercised them in the past, then received practices could serve as their own continued justification and new groups could not invoke rights once denied. This Court has rejected that approach, both with respect to the right to marry and the rights of gays and lesbians. See *Loving*; *Lawrence*. * * *

The right of same-sex couples to marry that is part of the liberty promised by the Fourteenth Amendment is derived, too, from that Amendment's guarantee of the equal protection of the laws. The Due Process Clause and the Equal Protection Clause are connected in a profound way, though they set forth independent principles. Rights implicit in liberty and rights secured by equal protection may rest on different precepts and are not always co-extensive, yet in some instances each may be instructive as to the meaning and reach of the other. In any particular case one Clause may be thought to capture the essence of the right in a more accurate and comprehensive way, even as the two Clauses may converge in the identification and definition of the right. This interrelation of the two principles furthers our understanding of what freedom is and must become. * * *

[**JUSTICE KENNEDY** then argued that *Loving* and *Zablocki* illustrated the synergy between liberty and equal protection].

Indeed, in interpreting the Equal Protection Clause, the Court has recognized that new insights and societal understandings can reveal unjustified inequality within our most fundamental institutions that once passed unnoticed and unchallenged. To take but one period, this occurred with respect to marriage in the 1970's and 1980's. Notwithstanding the gradual erosion of the doctrine of coverture, invidious sex-based classifications in marriage remained common through the mid-20th century. These classifications denied the equal dignity of men and women. One State's law, for example, provided in 1971 that "the husband is the head of the family and the wife is subject to him; her legal civil existence is merged in the husband, except so far as the law recognizes her separately, either for her own protection, or for her benefit." Responding to a new awareness, the Court invoked equal protection principles to invalidate laws imposing sex-based inequality on marriage. [Justice Kennedy collected here a set of gender discrimination cases decided in the 1970s and 1980s]. * * *

[*Lawrence* also] drew upon principles of liberty and equality to define and protect the rights of gays and lesbians, holding the State "cannot demean their existence or control their destiny by making their private sexual conduct a crime." * * *

These considerations lead to the conclusion that the right to marry is a fundamental right inherent in the liberty of the person, and under the Due Process and Equal Protection Clauses of the Fourteenth Amendment couples of the same-sex may not be deprived of that right and that liberty. The Court now holds that same-sex couples may exercise the fundamental right to marry. No longer may this liberty be denied to them. * * *

[IV].   There may be an initial inclination in these cases to proceed with caution—to await further legislation, litigation, and debate. The respondents warn there has been insufficient democratic discourse before deciding an issue so basic as the definition of marriage. In its ruling on the cases now before this Court, the majority opinion for the Court of Appeals made a cogent argument that it would be appropriate for the respondents' States to await further public discussion and political measures before licensing same-sex marriages. Yet there has been far more deliberation than this argument acknowledges. [The majority noted here the many "referenda, legislative debates, and grassroots campaigns, as well as countless studies, papers, books, and other popular and scholarly writings," and the scores of amicus briefs filed in *Obergefell* itself. Justice Kennedy also attached to the opinion two appendices that listed state and federal litigation addressing, and state legislation legalizing, same-sex marriage.]

Of course, the Constitution contemplates that democracy is the appropriate process for change, so long as that process does not abridge fundamental rights. * * *

[But t]he idea of the Constitution "was to withdraw certain subjects from the vicissitudes of political controversy, to place them beyond the reach of majorities and officials and to establish them as legal principles to be applied by the courts." This is why "fundamental rights may not be submitted to a vote; they depend on the outcome of no elections." It is of no moment whether advocates of same-sex marriage now enjoy or lack momentum in the democratic process. * * *

The petitioners' stories make clear the urgency of the issue they present to the Court. * * *

The respondents also argue allowing same-sex couples to wed will harm marriage as an institution by leading to fewer opposite-sex marriages. This may occur, the respondents contend, because licensing same-sex marriage severs the connection between natural procreation and marriage. That argument, however, rests on a counterintuitive view of opposite-sex couple's decisionmaking processes regarding marriage and parenthood. Decisions about whether to marry and raise children are based on many personal, romantic, and practical considerations; and it is unrealistic to conclude that an opposite-sex couple would choose not to marry simply because same-sex couples may do so. * * * Indeed, with respect to this asserted basis for excluding same-sex couples from the right to marry, it is appropriate to observe these cases involve only the rights of two consenting adults whose marriages would pose no risk of harm to themselves or third parties.

Finally, it must be emphasized that religions, and those who adhere to religious doctrines, may continue to advocate with utmost, sincere conviction that, by divine precepts, same-sex marriage should not be condoned. The First Amendment ensures that religious organizations and persons are given proper protection as they seek to teach the principles that are so fulfilling and so central to their lives and faiths, and to their own deep aspirations to continue the family structure they have long revered. The same is true of those who oppose same-sex marriage for other reasons. In turn, those who believe allowing same-sex marriage is proper or indeed essential, whether as a matter of religious conviction or secular belief, may engage those who disagree with their view in an open and searching debate. The Constitution, however, does not permit the State to bar same-sex couples from marriage on the same terms as accorded to couples of the opposite sex.

[V. The Court then held that the same reasons cited for affording same-sex couples the right to marry also affords them the right to have an out-of-state marriage recognized.] * * *

It would misunderstand [the plaintiffs] to say they disrespect the idea of marriage. Their plea is that they do respect it, respect it so deeply that they seek to find its fulfillment for themselves. Their hope is not to be condemned to live in loneliness, excluded from one of civilization's oldest institutions. They ask for equal dignity in the eyes of the law. The Constitution grants them that right.

CHIEF JUSTICE ROBERTS, with whom **JUSTICE SCALIA** and **JUSTICE THOMAS** join, dissenting.

Petitioners make strong arguments rooted in social policy and considerations of fairness. They contend that same-sex couples should be allowed to affirm their love and commitment through marriage, just like opposite-sex couples. That position has undeniable appeal; over the past six years, voters and legislators in eleven States and the District of Columbia have revised their laws to allow marriage between two people of the same sex.* * *

Although the policy arguments for extending marriage to same-sex couples may be compelling, the legal arguments for requiring such an extension are not. The fundamental right to marry does not include a right to make a State change its definition of marriage. * * *

[T]he Court invalidates the marriage laws of more than half the States and orders the transformation of a social institution that has formed the basis of human society for millennia, for the Kalahari Bushmen and the

Han Chinese, the Carthaginians and the Aztecs. Just who do we think we are? * * *

[I.] [The] universal definition of marriage as the union of a man and a woman is no historical coincidence. Marriage did not come about as a result of a political movement, discovery, disease, war, religious doctrine, or any other moving force of world history—and certainly not as a result of a prehistoric decision to exclude gays and lesbians. It arose in the nature of things to meet a vital need: ensuring that children are conceived by a mother and father committed to raising them in the stable conditions of a lifelong relationship. * * *

The human race must procreate to survive. Procreation occurs through sexual relations between a man and a woman. When sexual relations result in the conception of a child, that child's prospects are generally better if the mother and father stay together rather than going their separate ways. Therefore, for the good of children and society, sexual relations that can lead to procreation should occur only between a man and a woman committed to a lasting bond.

Society has recognized that bond as marriage. And by bestowing a respected status and material benefits on married couples, society encourages men and women to conduct sexual relations within marriage rather than without. * * *

[II.] Petitioners' "fundamental right" claim falls into the most sensitive category of constitutional adjudication. Petitioners do not contend that their States' marriage laws violate an *enumerated* constitutional right, such as the freedom of speech protected by the First Amendment. There is, after all, no "Companionship and Understanding" or "Nobility and Dignity" Clause in the Constitution. They argue instead that the laws violate a right *implied* by the Fourteenth Amendment's requirement that "liberty" may not be deprived without "due process of law." * * *

The need for restraint in administering the strong medicine of substantive due process is a lesson this Court has learned the hard way. The Court first applied substantive due process to strike down a statute in *Dred Scott*. There the Court invalidated the Missouri Compromise on the ground that legislation restricting the institution of slavery violated the implied rights of slaveholders. The Court relied on its own conception of liberty and property in doing so. * * *

Dred Scott's holding was overruled on the battlefields of the Civil War and by constitutional amendment after Appomattox, but its approach to the Due Process Clause reappeared. In a series of early 20th-century cases, most prominently *Lochner v. New York,* this Court invalidated state statutes that presented "meddlesome interferences with the rights of the individual," and "undue interference with liberty of person and freedom of contract." In *Lochner* itself, the Court struck down a New York law setting maximum hours for bakery employees, because there was "in our judgment, no reasonable foundation for holding this to be necessary or appropriate as a health law."

The dissenting Justices in *Lochner* explained that the New York law could be viewed as a reasonable response to legislative concern about the health of bakery employees, an issue on which there was at least "room for debate and for an honest difference of opinion." (opinion of Harlan, J.). The majority's contrary conclusion required adopting as constitutional law "an economic theory which a large part of the country does not entertain." (opinion of Holmes, J.). As Justice Holmes memorably put it, "The Fourteenth Amendment does not enact Mr. Herbert Spencer's Social Statics," a leading work on the philosophy of Social Darwinism. The Constitution "is not intended to embody a particular economic theory. . . . It is made for people of fundamentally differing views, and the accident of our finding certain opinions natural and familiar or novel and even shocking ought not to conclude our judgment upon the question whether statutes embodying them conflict with the Constitution."

In the decades after *Lochner,* the Court struck down nearly 200 laws as violations of individual liberty, often over strong dissents contending that "[t]he criterion of constitutionality is not whether we believe the law to be for the public good." * * *

Eventually, the Court recognized its error and vowed not to repeat it. * * * [I]t has become an accepted rule that the Court will not hold laws unconstitutional simply because we find them "unwise, improvident, or out of harmony with a particular school of thought." *Williamson v. Lee Optical of Okla., Inc.* * * *

None of the laws at issue in [the cases cited by the majority finding a fundamental right to marry] purported to change the core definition of marriage as the union of a man and a woman. * * *

Perhaps recognizing how little support it can derive from precedent, the majority goes out of its way to jettison the "careful" approach to implied fundamental rights taken by this Court in *Glucksberg*. It is revealing that the majority's position requires it to effectively overrule *Glucksberg,* the leading modern case setting the bounds of substantive due process. At least this part of the majority opinion has the virtue of candor. Nobody could rightly accuse the majority of taking a careful approach. * * *

It is striking how much of the majority's reasoning would apply with equal force to the claim of a fundamental right to plural marriage. If "[t]here is dignity in the bond between two men or two women who seek to marry and in their autonomy to make such profound choices," why would there be any less dignity in the bond between three people who, in exercising their autonomy, seek to make the profound choice to marry? If a same-sex couple has the constitutional right to marry because their children would otherwise "suffer the stigma of knowing their families are somehow lesser," why wouldn't the same reasoning apply to a family of three or more persons raising children? * * *

Near the end of its opinion, the majority offers perhaps the clearest insight into its decision. Expanding marriage to include same-sex couples, the majority insists, would "pose no risk of harm to themselves or third parties." * * *

[T]his assertion of the "harm principle" sounds more in philosophy than law. The elevation of the fullest individual self-realization over the constraints that society has expressed in law may or may not be attractive moral philosophy. But a Justice's commission does not confer any special moral, philosophical, or social insight sufficient to justify imposing those perceptions on fellow citizens under the pretense of "due process." There is indeed a process due the people on issues of this sort—the democratic process. Respecting that understanding requires the Court to be guided by law, not any particular school of social thought. As Judge Henry Friendly once put it, echoing Justice Holmes's dissent in *Lochner,* the Fourteenth Amendment does not enact John Stuart Mill's On Liberty any more than it enacts Herbert Spencer's Social Statics. And it certainly does not enact any one concept of marriage. * * *

[III.]   [The Chief Justice then argued that the majority's argument about the " 'synergy between' " the Equal Protection Clause and the Due Process Clause," was "frankly difficult to follow."* * *

People denied a voice are less likely to accept the ruling of a court on an issue that does not seem to be the sort of thing courts usually decide. As a thoughtful commentator observed about another issue, "The political process was moving . . . , not swiftly enough for advocates of quick, complete change, but majoritarian institutions were listening and acting. Heavy-handed judicial intervention was difficult to justify and appears to have provoked, not resolved, conflict." Ginsburg, Some Thoughts on Autonomy and Equality in Relation to *Roe* v. *Wade,* 63 N.C.L.Rev. 375, 385–386 (1985) (footnote omitted). Indeed, however heartened the proponents of same-sex marriage might be on this day, it is worth acknowledging what they have lost, and lost forever: the opportunity to win the true acceptance that comes from persuading their fellow citizens of the justice of their cause. And they lose this just when the winds of change were freshening at their backs. * * *

Respect for sincere religious conviction has led voters and legislators in every State that has adopted same-sex marriage democratically to include accommodations for religious practice. The majority's decision imposing same-sex marriage cannot, of course, create any such accommodations. The majority graciously suggests that religious believers may continue to "advocate" and "teach" their views of marriage. The First

Amendment guarantees, however, the freedom to *"exercise"* religion. Ominously, that is not a word the majority uses.* * *

If you are among the many Americans—of whatever sexual orientation—who favor expanding same-sex marriage, by all means celebrate today's decision. Celebrate the achievement of a desired goal. Celebrate the opportunity for a new expression of commitment to a partner. Celebrate the availability of new benefits. But do not celebrate the Constitution. It had nothing to do with it.

JUSTICE SCALIA, with whom JUSTICE THOMAS joins, dissenting.

When the Fourteenth Amendment was ratified in 1868, every State limited marriage to one man and one woman, and no one doubted the constitutionality of doing so. That resolves these cases. When it comes to determining the meaning of a vague constitutional provision—such as "due process of law" or "equal protection of the laws"—it is unquestionable that the People who ratified that provision did not understand it to prohibit a practice that remained both universal and uncontroversial in the years after ratification. * * *

Judges are selected precisely for their skill as lawyers; whether they reflect the policy views of a particular constituency is not (or should not be) relevant. Not surprisingly then, the Federal Judiciary is hardly a cross-section of America. Take, for example, this Court, which consists of only nine men and women, all of them successful lawyers who studied at Harvard or Yale Law School. Four of the nine are natives of New York City. Eight of them grew up in east- and west-coast States. Only one hails from the vast expanse in-between. Not a single Southwesterner or even, to tell the truth, a genuine Westerner (California does not count). Not a single evangelical Christian (a group that comprises about one quarter of Americans), or even a Protestant of any denomination. The strikingly unrepresentative character of the body voting on today's social upheaval would be irrelevant if they were functioning as *judges,* answering the legal question whether the American people had ever ratified a constitutional provision that was understood to proscribe the traditional definition of marriage. But of course the Justices in today's majority are not voting on that basis; *they say they are not.* And to allow the policy question of same-sex marriage to be considered and resolved by a select, patrician, highly unrepresentative panel of nine is to violate a principle even more fundamental than no taxation without representation: no social transformation without representation.

[II.] But what really astounds is the hubris reflected in today's judicial Putsch. The five Justices who compose today's majority are entirely comfortable concluding that every State violated the Constitution for all of the 135 years between the Fourteenth Amendment's ratification and Massachusetts' permitting of same-sex marriages in 2003. They have discovered in the Fourteenth Amendment a "fundamental right" overlooked by every person alive at the time of ratification, and almost everyone else in the time since. * * *

JUSTICE THOMAS, with whom JUSTICE SCALIA joins, dissenting.

As used in the Due Process Clauses, "liberty" most likely refers to "the power of locomotion, of changing situation, or removing one's person to whatsoever place one's own inclination may direct; without imprisonment or restraint, unless by due course of law." 1 W. Blackstone, Commentaries on the Laws of England 130 (1769) (Blackstone). That definition is drawn from the historical roots of the Clauses and is consistent with our Constitution's text and structure. * * *

Even assuming that the "liberty" in those Clauses encompasses something more than freedom from physical restraint, it would not include the types of rights claimed by the majority. In the American legal tradition, liberty has long been understood as individual freedom *from* governmental action, not as a right *to* a particular governmental entitlement.

The founding-era understanding of liberty was heavily influenced by John Locke, whose writings "on natural rights and on the social and governmental contract" were cited "[i]n pamphlet after pamphlet" by American writers. * * * Because [the] state of nature left men insecure in their persons and property, they entered civil society, trading a portion of their natural liberty for an increase in their security. Upon consenting to that order, men obtained civil liberty, or the freedom "to be under no other legislative power but that established by consent in the commonwealth; nor under the dominion of any will or restraint of any law, but what that legislative shall enact according to the trust put in it." * * *

Petitioners cannot claim, under the most plausible definition of "liberty," that they have been imprisoned or physically restrained by the States for participating in same-sex relationships. To the contrary, they have been able to cohabitate and raise their children in peace. They have been able to hold civil marriage ceremonies in States that recognize same-sex marriages and private religious ceremonies in all States. They have been able to travel freely around the country, making their homes where they please. Far from being incarcerated or physically restrained, petitioners have been left alone to order their lives as they see fit. * * *

Instead, the States have refused to grant them governmental entitlements. Petitioners claim that as a matter of "liberty," they are entitled to access privileges and benefits that exist solely *because of* the government. They want, for example, to receive the State's *imprimatur* on their marriages—on state issued marriage licenses, death certificates, or other official forms. And they want to receive various monetary benefits, including reduced inheritance taxes upon the death of a spouse, compensation if a spouse dies as a result of a work-related injury, or loss of consortium damages in tort suits. But receiving governmental recognition and benefits has nothing to do with any understanding of "liberty" that the Framers would have recognized. * * *

[IV.]   Human dignity has long been understood in this country to be innate. When the Framers proclaimed in the Declaration of Independence that "all men are created equal" and "endowed by their Creator with certain unalienable Rights," they referred to a vision of mankind in which all humans are created in the image of God and therefore of inherent worth. That vision is the foundation upon which this Nation was built.

The corollary of that principle is that human dignity cannot be taken away by the government. Slaves did not lose their dignity (any more than they lost their humanity) because the government allowed them to be enslaved. Those held in internment camps did not lose their dignity because the government confined them. And those denied governmental benefits certainly do not lose their dignity because the government denies them those benefits. The government cannot bestow dignity, and it cannot take it away. * * *

JUSTICE ALITO, with whom JUSTICE SCALIA and JUSTICE THOMAS join, dissenting.

[The decision] will be used to vilify Americans who are unwilling to assent to the new orthodoxy. In the course of its opinion, the majority compares traditional marriage laws to laws that denied equal treatment for African-Americans and women. The implications of this analogy will be exploited by those who are determined to stamp out every vestige of dissent.

Perhaps recognizing how its reasoning may be used, the majority attempts, toward the end of its opinion, to reassure those who oppose same-sex marriage that their rights of conscience will be protected. We will soon see whether this proves to be true. I assume that those who cling to old beliefs will be able to whisper their thoughts in the recesses of their homes, but if they repeat those views in public, they will risk being labeled as bigots and treated as such by governments, employers, and schools.

The system of federalism established by our Constitution provides a way for people with different beliefs to live together in a single nation. If the issue of same-sex marriage had been left to the people of the States, it is likely that some States would recognize same-sex marriage and others would not. It is also possible that some States would tie recognition to protection for conscience rights. The majority today makes that impossible. By imposing its own views on the entire country, the majority facilitates the marginalization of the many Americans who have traditional ideas. Recalling the harsh treatment of gays and lesbians in the past, some may think that turnabout is fair play. But if that sentiment prevails, the Nation will experience bitter and lasting wounds. * * *

NOTES

1. *Possible Rationales.* The parties and amici in *Obergefell* presented the Court with several ways to find bans on same-sex marriage unconstitutional under the Fourteenth Amendment. The principal theories argued that the bans:

- Violated the fundamental right to marry grounded in the Due Process Clause;

- Violated the fundamental right to marry (or interest in marriage) grounded in the Equal Protection Clause;

- Violated the Equal Protection Clause by discriminating against same-sex couples based on their sexual orientation (whether under heightened scrutiny or under rational basis with bite, as deployed in prior LGBT rights cases); and

- Violated the Equal Protection Clause by discriminating against same-sex couples based on gender.

The first of these alternatives plainly forms a core part of the opinion, which says explicitly that same-sex couples have a fundamental right to marry as part of the liberty protected by the Due Process Clause. Given Justice Kennedy's invocation of equal protection, as well, do you read the opinion to bring in any of the other rationales? Do you think Justice Kennedy chose the strongest framing for the right vindicated in the case? Why might he have chosen to emphasize the fundamental right to marry and avoid unambiguous reliance on equal protection?

2. *Strict Scrutiny?* As you consider the fundamental right to marry identified in the opinion, recall that under established doctrine, a finding that a right is fundamental triggers strict scrutiny. Strict scrutiny, in turn, requires the reviewing court to determine whether the state has a compelling interest and has used the least restrictive alternative in the challenged policy. Puzzlingly, there is no explicit application of strict scrutiny in the opinion. Note that the opinion, in section IV, does discuss what might be seen as three state interests: The interest in allowing a state's democratic process to define marriage; the interest in linking marriage to procreation as a way to channel birth parents into marriage; and the interest in protecting the religious liberties of those opposing same-sex marriage. Is the first of these three—letting majorities decide—a cognizable state "interest" at all? As to all three, does the majority's rejection of them serve as a version of strict, or at least heightened, scrutiny? If so, does it matter that the relevant doctrinal language about compelling interests and narrow tailoring is never used? What should lower courts take away from this approach? Is this what heightened scrutiny in the realm of due process now looks like? Recall that *Lawrence* and *Windsor*

were also doctrinally idiosyncratic, although *Obergefell* is clearer than they were in saying unambiguously that a fundamental right is involved.

3. *Synergy Between Liberty and Equality*. What does Justice Kennedy mean when he links due process and equal protection in the opinion and speaks of a "synergy" between them? This is not a new idea, as his discussion of *Loving* and *Lawrence*, among others, suggests. [51] Indeed, Justice Ginsburg at her 1993 confirmation hearing said, when asked about the constitutional basis for the abortion right:

> [Y]ou asked me about my thinking about equal protection versus individual autonomy, and my answer to you is it's both. This is something central to a woman's life, to her dignity. It's a decision that she must make for herself.

The Supreme Court; Excerpts From Senate Hearing on the Ginsburg Nomination, N.Y. Times, July 22, 1993, https://www.nytimes.com/1993/07/22/us/the-supreme-court-excerpts-from-senate-hearing-on-the-ginsburg-nomination.html.

How, if at all, does Justice Kennedy's use of equal protection language change the due process holding in this case? Does it suggest that the Court has now embraced a new understanding of liberty itself? Does the liberty-equality synergy implicate any of the other rationales listed in note 1 above?

4. *Role of Justice Kennedy*. It is both striking and unusual that Justice Kennedy wrote all four of the major LGBT rights opinions decided by the Supreme Court since *Romer*, in 1996. *Obergefell* contains some of the hallmarks of the jurisprudence he has created through *Romer*, *Lawrence*, and *Windsor*, especially his focus on rejecting laws that demean gays and lesbians and protecting the dignity of this group. From the institutional perspective of the Court, would it be preferable for more than one justice to write major opinions in a highly salient and controversial area like this one? What will his retirement in 2018 mean for future decisions in this area?

5. *Praise of Marriage*. Justice Kennedy is lavish in his praise of marriage as an institution, calling it, for example, of "transcendent importance," "sacred," "offer[ing] unique fulfillment," "essential to our most profound hopes and aspirations," and a "keystone of our social order." Does he go too far? Is he overreaching when he twice casts marriage as the antidote to "loneliness"? Does the rhetoric in the opinion stigmatize those who are not married?

6. *Links to* Roe. Given the Chief Justice's emphasis on the perils of "Lochnerizing," is it surprising that he did not invoke *Roe v. Wade* (or its

---

[51] For scholarly elaborations of this idea before *Obergefell*, see Rebecca L. Brown, *Liberty, the New Equality*, 77 N.Y.U. L. Rev. 1491 (2002); Cary Franklin, *Marrying Liberty and Equality: The New Jurisprudence of Gay Rights*, 100 Va. L. Rev. 817 (2014); Reva B. Siegel, *Dignity and the Politics of Protection: Abortion Restrictions Under Casey/Carhart*, 117 Yale L.J. 1694 (2008); Laurence H. Tribe, Lawrence v. Texas: *The "Fundamental Right" that Dare Not Speak Its Name*, 117 Harv. L. Rev. 1893 (2004); Kenji Yoshino, *The New Equal Protection*, 124 Harv. L. Rev. 747 (2011).

successor, *Casey*) as an example of this danger? Abortion, after all, has been the most controversial issue in modern substantive due process. (And, indeed, a year later, Justice Thomas alluded to *Lochner* in a portion of his dissent from *Whole Woman's Health* that is not reproduced above.) The closest the Chief comes is citing an article by Justice Ginsburg suggesting how the Court could have avoided some of the controversy generated by *Roe*. How do you think Justice Ginsburg might respond to the parallel Roberts draws here? Do you think *Obergefell* will be controversial in the way *Roe* has been? Is it relevant to consider the rapid recent shift of public opinion in favor of marriage equality, and, especially, the strong generational tilt in favor? See Chris Cillizza, *How Unbelievably Quickly Public Opinion Changed on Gay Marriage, in 5 Charts*, Washington Post, June 26, 2015 (http://www.washingtonpost.com/blogs/the-fix/wp/2015/06/26/how-unbelievably-quickly-public-opinion-changed-on-gay-marriage-in-6-charts/).

7. *Bitterness on the Court.* After *Obergefell* was decided, various observers, including former Solicitor Generals from both parties, noted that some of the dissents contained particularly bitter language. See Nina Totenberg, *Liberal Minority Won Over Conservatives in Historic Supreme Court Term*, July 6, 2015, http://www.npr.org/sections/itsallpolitics/2015/07/06/420289254/liberal-minority-won-over-conservatives-in-historic-supreme-court-term (quoting Charles Fried, who served in the Reagan Administration and Walter Dellinger, who served in the Clinton Administration). In addition to what is in the excerpts above, the dissents by Chief Justice Roberts and Justice Scalia both called the majority opinion "pretentious," and Scalia said he would "hide [his] head in a bag" before joining any opinion with such language. Former Solicitor General Fried suggested that Justice Kennedy might have helped to provoke that reaction by aiming more for poetry than precedent laid out in a straightforward way. Does the heated rhetoric suggest that not much is left to the norm of civility on the Court, at least on the part of some Justices? Or is the problem merely a reflection of growing polarization in society as a whole? Or, perhaps, an indication that Justices may be directing parts of their opinions at a public (rather than professional) audience? And is the problem merely an issue of etiquette or something that may affect the Court's institutional functioning and legitimacy?

8. *Theories of Interpretation.* The opinions in the case offer a rich basis for exploring theories of constitutional interpretation. The justices divide along familiar jurisprudential lines; the majority espouses the virtues of living constitutionalism, while the dissents counter with arguments grounded in originalism and excoriate what they see as illegitimate judicial activism. Two of us have examined how the marriage debate can be understood in terms of a range of constitutional theories. For an argument that there is an unappreciated originalist case *in favor of* marriage equality, see William N. Eskridge, Jr., The Nineteenth Annual Frankel Lecture, *Original Meaning and Marriage Equality*, 52 Houston L. Rev. 1067 (2015); see also Steven G. Calabresi and Hannah Begley, *Originalism and Same-Sex Marriage*, 70 U. Miami. L. Rev. 648 (2016). For an argument about the interlocking roles of

popular and living constitutionalism in the debate, see Jane S. Schacter, Commentary, *What Marriage Equality Can Tell Us About Popular Constitutionalism (and Vice-Versa),* 52 Houston L. Rev. 1147 (2015).

9. The Court's most significant post-*Obergefell* decision relating to marriage equality is *Masterpiece Cakeshop v. Colorado Civil Rights Comm'n,* 138 S.Ct. 1719 (2018). *Masterpiece* is a religious liberty case that involves not the right to marry itself, but the obligation of vendors to provide goods and services for same sex weddings. In the decision, the Court sustained the claim of a baker who objected, based on religious reasons, to providing a wedding cake to a same-sex couple celebrating a commitment ceremony (before same-sex marriage was legal in Colorado). As addressed in Chapter 6, *Masterpiece* was a narrow ruling that left many questions unanswered. The dispute at the heart of the case has emerged as a prominent part of the same-sex marriage debate, but it implicates larger tensions between religious liberty and equality measures. For a lively exchange of views on the broader issues, see the diverse views of various scholars collected in William N. Eskridge, Jr. & Robin Fretwell Wilson, *Religious Freedom, LGBT Rights and Prospects for Common Ground* (Cambridge 2018).

10. Since the decision in *Obergefell* in 2015, Justices Scalia and Kennedy have been replaced by Justices Gorsuch and Kavanaugh respectively. If, as is widely surmised, the two new justices think that *Obergefell* was wrongly decided, should they vote to overrule it? Why or why not? How does and should the decision's relative recency cut in terms of *stare decisis*?

PROBLEM 5-3:
PLURAL MARRIAGE

In 1878, the Supreme Court rejected a challenge to a federal ban on bigamy. In *Reynolds v. United States,* 98 U.S. 145 (1879), the Court ruled that this ban did not violate the free exercise rights of Mormon men who, at the time, wished to have multiple wives. Chief Justice Roberts's *Obergefell* dissent argues that the logic of Justice Kennedy's majority opinion entails constitutional protection under the Fourteenth Amendment for plural marriage. The dissent cited a newspaper story about three lesbians who consider themselves married, and who plan to raise together the baby carried by one of them. See *Married Lesbian "Throuple" Expecting First Child,* N.Y. Post, Apr. 23, 2014. Two of the women were legally married in Massachusetts, but the three cohabitate, divide household labor, are supported by the wages of one, and intend to co-parent. Suppose these three women seek to be recognized as married to one another, and challenge as unconstitutional Massachusetts law permitting only two persons to be recognized as legal spouses. What arguments will each side make under *Obergefell,* and how do you think a court would and should rule? After you set out your arguments, you may wish to consult recent scholarly analysis of this question. See *Symposium: Polygamous Unions? Charting the Contours of Marriage Law's Frontier,* 64 Emory L.J. 1669 et seq. (2015). The Roberts dissent cited an article from this collection: Otter, *Three May Not Be a Crowd: The Case for a Constitutional Right to Plural Marriage*, 64 Emory L.J.1977 (2015).

SECTION 5. THE "RIGHT TO DIE"

WASHINGTON V. GLUCKSBERG
521 U.S. 702, 117 S.Ct. 2258, 138 L.Ed.2d 772 (1997)

CHIEF JUSTICE REHNQUIST delivered the opinion of the Court.

[This case involved Washington State's prohibition against causing or aiding a suicide. Such prohibitions are long-standing and practically universal. Also, a recent federal statute bans use of federal funds to finance physician-assisted suicide. The suit was brought by several doctors who treat terminally ill patients in extreme pain, as well as three terminally ill patients who died while the case was on appeal, and by Compassion in Dying, an organization that counsels people considering physician assisted suicide. In an en banc opinion, the federal court of appeals held the Washington ban on assisted suicide unconstitutional as applied to terminally ill, mentally competent patients. The Supreme Court reversed.[52]]

The Due Process Clause guarantees more than fair process, and the "liberty" it protects includes more than the absence of physical restraint. The Clause also provides heightened protection against government interference with certain fundamental rights and liberty interests. In a long line of cases, we have held that, in addition to the specific freedoms protected by the Bill of Rights, the "liberty" specially protected by the Due Process Clause includes the rights to marry, *Loving*; to have children, *Skinner*; to direct the education and upbringing of one's children, *Meyer*; *Pierce*; to marital privacy, *Griswold*; to use contraception, ibid; *Eisenstadt*; to bodily integrity, *Rochin v. California*, 342 U.S. 165 (1952), and to abortion, *Casey*. We have also assumed, and strongly suggested, that the Due Process Clause protects the traditional right to refuse unwanted lifesaving medical treatment. *Cruzan* [*v. Director, Missouri Dept. of Health*, 497 U.S. 261 (1990)].

---

[52] *Editors' note*: In a companion case, *Vacco v. Quill*, 521 U.S. 793 (1997), the Court reviewed an equal protection challenge to a similar New York law. The federal court of appeals had found it irrational for the state to distinguish between active physician assistance to terminate a patient's life and removing life support with the same purpose and effect. After concluding, in reliance on *Glucksberg*, that the case did not involve a fundamental right, the *Quill* Court concluded that the New York statute easily survived rational basis review. The Court relied on the overwhelming number of state statutes and judicial decisions making this distinction and found ample justification for the statute, "including prohibiting intentional killing and preserving life; preventing suicide; maintaining physicians' role as their patients' healers; protecting vulnerable people from indifference, prejudice, and psychological and financial pressure to end their lives and avoiding a possible slide toward euthanasia."

But we "ha[ve] always been reluctant to expand the concept of substantive due process because guideposts for responsible decisionmaking in this unchartered area are scarce and open-ended." By extending constitutional protection to an asserted right or liberty interest, we, to a great extent, place the matter outside the arena of public debate and legislative action. We must therefore "exercise the utmost care whenever we are asked to break new ground in this field," lest the liberty protected by the Due Process Clause be subtly transformed into the policy preferences of the members of this Court.

Our established method of substantive-due-process analysis has two primary features: First, we have regularly observed that the Due Process Clause specially protects those fundamental rights and liberties which are, objectively, "deeply rooted in this Nation's history and tradition," and "implicit in the concept of ordered liberty," such that "neither liberty nor justice would exist if they were sacrificed." Second, we have required in substantive-due-process cases a "careful description" of the asserted fundamental liberty interest. Our Nation's history, legal traditions, and practices thus provide the crucial "guideposts for responsible decisionmaking" that direct and restrain our exposition of the Due Process Clause. As we stated recently[,] the Fourteenth Amendment "forbids the government to infringe . . . 'fundamental' liberty interests *at all*, no matter what process is provided, unless the infringement is narrowly tailored to serve a compelling state interest."

Justice Souter, relying on Justice Harlan's dissenting opinion in *Poe v. Ullman*, would largely abandon this restrained methodology, and instead ask "whether [Washington's] statute sets up one of those 'arbitrary impositions' or 'purposeless restraints' at odds with the Due Process Clause of the Fourteenth Amendment." In our view, however, the development of this Court's substantive-due-process jurisprudence * * * has been a process whereby the outlines of the "liberty" specially protected by the Fourteenth Amendment—never fully clarified, to be sure, and perhaps not capable of being fully clarified—have at least been carefully refined by concrete examples involving fundamental rights found to be deeply rooted in our legal tradition. This approach tends to rein in the subjective elements that are necessarily present in due-process judicial review. In addition, by establishing a threshold requirement—that a challenged state action implicate a fundamental right—before requiring more than a reasonable relation to a legitimate state interest to justify the action, it avoids the need for complex balancing of competing interests in every case.

Turning to the claim at issue here, the Court of Appeals stated that "[p]roperly analyzed, the first issue to be resolved is whether there is a liberty interest in determining the time and manner of one's death," or, in other words, "[i]s there a right to die?" Similarly, respondents assert a "liberty to choose how to die" and a right to "control of one's final days," and describe the asserted liberty as "the right to choose a humane, dignified death," and "the liberty to shape death." * * *.

We now inquire whether this asserted right has any place in our Nation's traditions. Here * * * we are confronted with a consistent and almost universal tradition that has long rejected the asserted right, and continues explicitly to reject it today, even for terminally ill, mentally competent adults. To hold for respondents, we would have to reverse centuries of legal doctrine and practice, and strike down the considered policy choice of almost every State.

Respondents contend, however, that the liberty interest they assert *is* consistent with this Court's substantive-due-process line of cases, if not with this Nation's history and practice. Pointing to *Casey* and *Cruzan*, respondents read our jurisprudence in this area as reflecting a general *Counter* tradition of "self-sovereignty," and as teaching that the "liberty" protected by the Due Process Clause includes "basic and intimate exercises of personal autonomy." According to respondents, our liberty jurisprudence, and the broad, individualistic principles it reflects, protects the "liberty of competent, terminally ill adults to make end-of-life decisions free of undue government interference." The question presented in this case, however, is whether the protections of the Due Process Clause include a right to commit suicide with another's assistance. With this "careful description" of respondents' claim in mind, we turn to *Casey* and *Cruzan*.

In *Cruzan*, we considered whether Nancy Beth Cruzan, who had been severely injured in an automobile accident and was in a persistive vegetative state, "ha[d] a right under the United States Constitution which would require the hospital to withdraw life-sustaining treatment" at her parents' request. We began with the observation that "[a]t common law, even the touching of one person by another without consent and without legal justification was a battery." We then discussed the related rule that "informed consent is generally required for medical treatment." After reviewing a long line of relevant state cases, we concluded that "the common-law doctrine of informed consent is viewed as generally encompassing the right of a competent individual to refuse medical treatment." Next, we reviewed our own cases on the subject, and stated that "[t]he principle that a competent person has a constitutionally protected liberty interest in refusing unwanted medical treatment may be inferred from our prior decisions." Therefore, "for purposes of [that] case, we assume[d] that the United States Constitution would grant a competent person a constitutionally protected right to refuse lifesaving hydration and nutrition." We concluded that, notwithstanding this right, the Constitution permitted Missouri to require clear and convincing evidence of an incompetent patient's wishes concerning the withdrawal of life-sustaining treatment.

* * * The right assumed in *Cruzan*, however, was not simply deduced from abstract concepts of personal autonomy. Given the common-law rule that forced medication was a battery, and the long legal tradition protecting the decision to refuse unwanted medical treatment, our assumption was entirely consistent with this Nation's history and constitutional traditions. The decision to commit suicide with the assistance of another may be just as personal and profound as the decision to refuse unwanted medical treatment, but it has never enjoyed similar legal protection. Indeed, the two acts are widely and reasonably regarded as quite distinct. In *Cruzan* itself, we recognized that most States outlawed assisted suicide—and even more do today—and we certainly gave no intimation that the right to refuse unwanted medical treatment could be somehow transmuted into a right to assistance in committing suicide. * * *

The Court of Appeals, like the District Court, found *Casey* " 'highly instructive' " and " 'almost prescriptive' " for determining " 'what liberty interest may inhere in a terminally ill person's choice to commit suicide' ":

> Like the decision of whether or not to have an abortion, the decision how and when to die is one of "the most intimate and personal choices a person may make in a lifetime," a choice "central to personal dignity and autonomy."

Similarly, respondents emphasize the statement in *Casey* that:

> At the heart of liberty is the right to define one's own concept of existence, of meaning, of the universe, and of the mystery of human life. Beliefs about these matters could not define the attributes of personhood were they formed under compulsion of the State.

By choosing this language, the Court's opinion in *Casey* described, in a general way and in light of our prior cases, those personal activities and decisions that this Court has identified as so deeply rooted in our history and traditions, or so fundamental to our concept of constitutionally ordered liberty, that they are protected by the Fourteenth Amendment. The opinion moved from the recognition that liberty necessarily includes freedom of conscience and belief about ultimate considerations to the observation that "though the abortion decision may originate within the zone of conscience and belief, it is *more than a philosophic exercise*." [emphasis added] That many of the rights and liberties protected by the Due Process Clause sound in personal autonomy does not warrant the sweeping conclusion that any and all important, intimate, and personal decisions are so protected. *Rodriguez* [this chapter, § 3B], and *Casey* did not suggest otherwise.

The history of the law's treatment of assisted suicide in this country has been and continues to be one of the rejection of nearly all efforts to permit it. That being the case, our decisions lead us to conclude that the asserted "right" to assistance in committing suicide is not a fundamental liberty interest protected by the Due Process Clause. The Constitution also requires, however, that Washington's assisted-suicide ban be rationally related to legitimate government interests. This requirement is unquestionably met here. As the court below recognized,[53] Washington's assisted-suicide ban implicates a number of state interests.

[The lower court struck down Washington's assisted-suicide ban only "as applied to competent, terminally ill adults who wish to hasten their deaths by obtaining medication prescribed by their doctors." The Supreme Court was concerned, however, that any such limitations on the right to die might be eroded.]

This concern is further supported by evidence about the practice of euthanasia in the Netherlands. The Dutch government's own study revealed that in 1990, there were 2,300 cases of voluntary euthanasia (defined as "the deliberate termination of another's life at his request"), 400 cases of assisted suicide, and more than 1,000 cases of euthanasia without an explicit request. In addition to these latter 1,000 cases, the study found an additional 4,941 cases where physicians administered lethal morphine overdoses without the patients' explicit consent. This study suggests that, despite the existence of various reporting procedures, euthanasia in the Netherlands has not been limited to competent, terminally ill adults who are enduring physical suffering, and that regulation of the practice may not have prevented abuses in cases involving vulnerable persons, including severely disabled neonates and elderly persons suffering from dementia. * * * Washington, like most other States, reasonably ensures against this risk by banning, rather than regulating, assisting suicide.

We need not weigh exactingly the relative strengths of these various interests. They are unquestionably important and legitimate, and Washington's ban on assisted suicide is at least reasonably related to their promotion and protection. We therefore hold that [Washington law] does not violate the Fourteenth Amendment, either on its face or "as applied to competent, terminally ill adults who wish to hasten their deaths by obtaining medication prescribed by their doctors."[54]

---

[53] The court identified and discussed six state interests: (1) preserving life; (2) preventing suicide; (3) avoiding the involvement of third parties and use of arbitrary, unfair, or undue influence; (4) protecting family members and loved ones; (5) protecting the integrity of the medical profession; and (6) avoiding future movement toward euthanasia and other abuses.

[54] Justice Stevens states that "the Court does conceive of respondents' claim as a facial challenge—addressing not the application of the statute to a particular set of plaintiffs before it, but the constitutionality of the statute's categorical prohibition. . . ." We emphasize that we today reject the Court of Appeals' specific holding that the statute is unconstitutional "as applied" to a particular class. Justice Stevens agrees with this holding, but would not "foreclose the possibility that an individual plaintiff seeking to hasten her death, or a doctor whose assistance was sought, could prevail in a more particularized challenge." Our opinion does not absolutely foreclose such a claim. However, given our holding that the Due Process Clause of the Fourteenth Amendment does not provide heightened protection to the asserted liberty interest in ending one's life with a physician's assistance, such a claim would have to be quite different from the ones advanced by respondents here.

Throughout the Nation, Americans are engaged in an earnest and profound debate about the morality, legality, and practicality of physician-assisted suicide. Our holding permits this debate to continue, as it should in a democratic society. The decision of the en banc Court of Appeals is reversed, and the case is remanded for further proceedings consistent with this opinion.

JUSTICE O'CONNOR, concurring.[55]

Death will be different for each of us. For many, the last days will be spent in physical pain and perhaps the despair that accompanies physical deterioration and a loss of control of basic bodily and mental functions. Some will seek medication to alleviate that pain and other symptoms.

The Court frames the issue in this case as whether the Due Process Clause of the Constitution protects a "right to commit suicide which itself includes a right to assistance in doing so," and concludes that our Nation's history, legal traditions, and practices do not support the existence of such a right. I join the Court's opinions because I agree that there is no generalized right to "commit suicide." But respondents urge us to address the narrower question whether a mentally competent person who is experiencing great suffering has a constitutionally cognizable interest in controlling the circumstances of his or her imminent death. I see no need to reach that question in the context of the facial challenges to the New York and Washington laws at issue here. The parties and *amici* agree that in these States a patient who is suffering from a terminal illness and who is experiencing great pain has no legal barriers to obtaining medication, from qualified physicians, to alleviate that suffering, even to the point of causing unconsciousness and hastening death. In this light, even assuming that we would recognize such an interest, I agree that the State's interests in protecting those who are not truly competent or facing imminent death, or those whose decisions to hasten death would not truly be voluntary, are sufficiently weighty to justify a prohibition against physician-assisted suicide.

JUSTICE STEVENS, concurring in the judgments.

There may be little distinction between the intent of a terminally-ill patient who decides to remove her life-support and one who seeks the assistance of a doctor in ending her life; in both situations, the patient is seeking to hasten a certain, impending death. The doctor's intent might also be the same in prescribing lethal medication as it is in terminating life support. A doctor who fails to administer medical treatment to one who is dying from a disease could be doing so with an intent to harm or kill that patient. Conversely, a doctor who prescribes lethal medication does not

---

[55] JUSTICE GINSBURG concurs in the Court's judgments substantially for the reasons stated in this opinion. JUSTICE BREYER joins this opinion except insofar as it joins the opinion of the Court.

necessarily intend the patient's death—rather that doctor may seek simply to ease the patient's suffering and to comply with her wishes. The illusory character of any differences in intent or causation is confirmed by the fact that the American Medical Association unequivocally endorses the practice of terminal sedation—the administration of sufficient dosages of pain-killing medication to terminally ill patients to protect them from excruciating pain even when it is clear that the time of death will be advanced. The purpose of terminal sedation is to ease the suffering of the patient and comply with her wishes, and the actual cause of death is the administration of heavy doses of lethal sedatives. This same intent and causation may exist when a doctor complies with a patient's request for lethal medication to hasten her death.

Thus, although the differences the majority notes in causation and intent between terminating life-support and assisting in suicide support the Court's rejection of the respondents' facial challenge, these distinctions may be inapplicable to particular terminally ill patients and their doctors. Our holding today in *Vacco v. Quill* that the Equal Protection Clause is not violated by New York's classification, just like our holding in *Washington v. Glucksberg* that the Washington statute is not invalid on its face, does not foreclose the possibility that some applications of the New York statute may impose an intolerable intrusion on the patient's freedom.

JUSTICE SOUTER, concurring in the judgment.

In my judgment, the importance of the individual interest here, as within that class of "certain interests" demanding careful scrutiny of the State's contrary claim, cannot be gainsaid. Whether that interest might in some circumstances, or at some time, be seen as "fundamental" to the degree entitled to prevail is not, however, a conclusion that I need draw here, for I am satisfied that the State's interests described in the following section are sufficiently serious to defeat the present claim that its law is arbitrary or purposeless.

The State has put forward several interests to justify the Washington law as applied to physicians treating terminally ill patients, even those competent to make responsible choices: protecting life generally, discouraging suicide even if knowing and voluntary, and protecting terminally ill patients from involuntary suicide and euthanasia, both voluntary and nonvoluntary.

It is not necessary to discuss the exact strengths of the first two claims of justification in the present circumstances, for the third is dispositive for me. That third justification is different from the first two, for it addresses specific features of respondents' claim, and it opposes that claim not with a moral judgment contrary to respondents', but with a recognized state interest in the protection of nonresponsible individuals and those who do not stand in relation either to death or to their physicians as do the patients whom respondents describe. * * * The State thus argues, essentially, that respondents' claim is not as narrow as it sounds, simply because no recognition of the interest they assert could be limited to vindicating those interests and affecting no others. The State says that the claim, in practical effect, would entail consequences that the State could, without doubt, legitimately act to prevent. * * *

Respondents propose an answer to all this, the answer of state regulation with teeth. Legislation proposed in several States, for example, would authorize physician-assisted suicide but require two qualified physicians to confirm the patient's diagnosis, prognosis, and competence; and would mandate that the patient make repeated requests witnessed by at least two others over a specified time span; and would impose reporting requirements and criminal penalties for various acts of coercion.

But at least at this moment there are reasons for caution in predicting the effectiveness of the teeth proposed. Respondents' proposals, as it turns out, sound much like the guidelines now in place in the Netherlands, the only place where experience with physician-assisted suicide and euthanasia has yielded empirical evidence about how such regulations might affect actual practice. Dutch physicians must engage in consultation before proceeding, and must decide whether the patient's decision is voluntary, well considered, and stable, whether the request to die is enduring and made more than once, and whether the patient's future will involve unacceptable suffering. There is, however, a substantial dispute today about what the Dutch experience shows. Some commentators marshal evidence that the Dutch guidelines have in practice failed to protect patients from involuntary euthanasia and have been violated with impunity. The day may come when we can say with some assurance which side is right, but for now it is the substantiality of the factual disagreement, and the alternatives for resolving it, that matter. They are, for me, dispositive of the due process claim at this time.

JUSTICE BREYER, concurring in the judgments.

I believe that Justice O'Connor's views, which I share, have greater legal significance than the Court's opinion suggests. I join her separate opinion, except insofar as it joins the majority. And I concur in the judgments. I shall briefly explain how I differ from the Court. * * *

Justice Harlan concluded that marital privacy was such a "special interest[ ]" [which "require[s] particularly careful scrutiny of the state needs asserted to justify [its] abridgment."] He found in the Constitution a right of "privacy of the home"—with the home, the bedroom, and "intimate details of the marital relation" at its heart—by examining the protection that the law had earlier provided for related, but not identical, interests described by such words as "privacy," "home," and "family." The respondents here essentially ask us to do the same. They argue that one can find a "right to die with dignity" by examining the protection the law has provided for related, but not identical, interests relating to personal dignity, medical treatment, and freedom from state-inflicted pain.

I do not believe, however, that this Court need or now should decide whether or not such a right is "fundamental." That is because, in my view, the avoidance of severe physical pain (connected with death) would have to comprise an essential part of any successful claim and because, as Justice O'Connor points out, the laws before us do not force a dying person to undergo that kind of pain. Rather, the laws of New York and of Washington do not prohibit doctors from providing patients with drugs sufficient to control pain despite the risk that those drugs themselves will kill. And under these circumstances the laws of New York and Washington would overcome any remaining significant interests and would be justified, regardless.

Medical technology, we are repeatedly told, makes the administration of pain-relieving drugs sufficient, except for a very few individuals for whom the ineffectiveness of pain control medicines can mean, not pain, but the need for sedation which can end in a coma. We are also told that there are many instances in which patients do not receive the palliative care that, in principle, is available, but that is so for institutional reasons or inadequacies or obstacles, which would seem possible to overcome, and which do *not* include *a prohibitive set of laws.*

This legal circumstance means that the state laws before us do not infringe directly upon the (assumed) central interest (what I have called the core of the interest in dying with dignity) as, by way of contrast, the state anticontraceptive laws at issue in *Poe* did interfere with the central interest there at stake—by bringing the State's police powers to bear upon the marital bedroom.

Were the legal circumstances different—for example, were state law to prevent the provision of palliative care, including the administration of drugs as needed to avoid pain at the end of life—then the law's impact upon serious and otherwise unavoidable physical pain (accompanying death) would be more directly at issue. And as Justice O'Connor suggests, the Court might have to revisit its conclusions in these cases.

NOTES ON THE "RIGHT TO DIE" CASE

1. *The Holding and the Role of Precedent.* What exactly is the holding of this case? Note the seeming presence of two majorities: Five Justices (Rehnquist, O'Connor, Scalia, Kennedy, Thomas) join the opinion of the Court broadly dismissing right-to-die arguments, but five Justices (O'Connor, Stevens, Souter, Ginsburg, Breyer) write separately to reserve a number of issues. Under what circumstances, if any, has the Court left room for a potential constitutional claim? Would it matter if the risk of abuse was

particularly small in a particular case? Would it matter if the individual's pain was not capable of being controlled by medication? One medical observer suggests that, in effect, by endorsing potentially lethal sedation of terminal patients (which is normally accompanied by withholding of hydration and nutrition), the Court has rejected assisted suicide only to embrace euthanasia. See David Orentlicher, *The Supreme Court and Physician-Assisted Suicide*, 337 New England J. of Med. 1236 (1997).

One intriguing aspect of this case was the handling of precedent. Chief Justice Rehnquist sidestepped any criticism of *Roe* or *Casey* (perhaps to retain the votes of Justices Kennedy and O'Connor). He also conspicuously avoided any reliance on *Bowers*, which had not yet been overruled. The concurring Justices seemed to feel no need to deal with that precedent, either. At this point, is the case law on substantive due process internally consistent, or has the Court been weaving from one side to the other?

2.   *Approaches to Substantive Due Process.* The dispute between the majority and Justice Souter over methodology deserves careful attention. Which most adequately channels judicial discretion? Most effectively protects individual liberty? To what extent is the quality of public deliberation on the issue relevant to the constitutional question? Consider the observation that the "earnestness, profundity, and widespread nature of the debate [over assisted suicide] reduced and perhaps eliminated the Court's relative advantage over legislatures in formulating relevant principles and bringing these principles to bear on contested general issues." Richard Fallon, *The Supreme Court, 1996 Term—Foreword: Implementing the Constitution*, 111 Harv. L. Rev. 54, 145 (1997).

3.   *A Coda to* Glucksberg *in Washington.* In November 2008, the voters in Washington passed the "Death With Dignity" initiative by a 59% vote. The measure allows physician-assisted suicide in some circumstances. A mentally competent adult resident of the state who has less than six months to live may request and receive a prescription to hasten death. As this edition of the Casebook goes to press, five other states (California, Colorado, Hawaii, Oregon, and Vermont), as well as the District of Columbia, have adopted laws that allow physician aid in dying. Bills have been introduced in several other states. For a review of the state laws, see https://www.deathwithdignity.org/learn/death-with-dignity-acts/. Does the passage of such laws vindicate the Court's approach to leave this policy to the democratic process? Or did the Court undervalue the protected liberty interest when it failed to accord constitutional protection? Is it problematic or desirable to allow states to choose their own policies in this area?

4.   *Effect of* Obergefell *on* Glucksberg. What is left of *Glucksberg* after *Obergefell*? The case was not overruled, but was apparently limited in Justice Kennedy's opinion. The core principle of *Glucksberg* is its emphasis on the normative weight of history and tradition in substantive due process analysis. But the *Obergefell* majority said that "history and tradition guide and discipline this inquiry but do not set its outer boundaries." The *Obergefell*

majority also said that while the *Glucksberg* approach "may have been appropriate for the asserted right there involved (physician-assisted suicide), it is inconsistent with the approach this Court has used in discussing other fundamental rights, including marriage and intimacy." Does this mean *Glucksberg* no longer has force beyond the context of end-of-life decisions? Might the retirement of Justice Kennedy figure in the future vitality of *Glucksberg*?

PROBLEM 5-4:
HUMAN CLONING

Many countries have banned reproductive cloning. In the context of human beings, such cloning would mean making an identical genetic copy or duplicate of an existing person. Although no one has yet successfully cloned a human, efforts to do so continue. Should the United States ban human cloning? Critics argue that cloning would have some clinical uses:

> [Consider] a couple each carrying a recessive gene for a serious disorder. Cloning would allow them to avoid conceiving an embryo with the disorder and facing selective abortion. In another case, a woman might carry a dominant gene for a disorder. Cloning would permit her to avoid genetic contribution from an egg donor and thus would keep the genetic parenting between the woman and her partner, something of value to many couples. Other cases would include a couple entirely lacking gametes.

Susan Wolf, *Ban Cloning? Why NAC Is Wrong*, 27 Hastings Center Report, Sept.-Oct. 1997, at 12, 13. Under the substantive due process caselaw reviewed in this chapter, how would you analyze whether a complete ban on human reproductive cloning would be unconstitutional?

SECTION 6. PROCEDURAL DUE PROCESS

A. INTRODUCTORY NOTES ON PROCEDURAL DUE PROCESS

1. *Procedural Versus Substantive Due Process.* Whatever force there might be to the criticism that "substantive due process" is logically an oxymoron and without support in the Constitution's text and history, the Due Process Clauses of the Fifth and Fourteenth Amendments clearly have *some* content. Both amendments state that a person is entitled to "due process of law" before she is deprived of certain important interests by the government. Even if this language is given a purely procedural definition, it could still be an important source of protection against governmental abuse.

2. *Due Process Values.* One important aspect of due process is a guarantee of procedural fairness in adjudication, whether in the courts or in trial-like hearings before administrative agencies. In *Marshall v.*

Jerrico, Inc., 446 U.S. 238 (1980), the Supreme Court explained some of the significant values underlying procedural due process:

> The Due Process Clause entitles a person to an impartial and disinterested tribunal in both civil and criminal cases. This requirement of neutrality in adjudicative proceedings safeguards the two central concerns of procedural due process, the prevention of unjustified or mistaken deprivations and the promotion of participation and dialogue by affected individuals in the decisionmaking process. The neutrality requirement helps to guarantee that life, liberty, or property will not be taken on the basis of an erroneous or distorted conception of the facts or the law. At the same time, it preserves both the appearance and reality of fairness, "generating the feeling, so important to a popular government, that justice has been done," by ensuring that no person will be deprived of his interests in the absence of a proceeding in which he may present his case with assurance that the arbiter is not predisposed to find against him.

Consider the "two central concerns of procedural due process" identified in *Jerrico*. The first is utilitarian—the government should not deprive a person of an important interest unless the correct understanding of the facts and the law allows it to do so. The second is normative and is often called the "dignitary" or "intrinsic" value to due process—even if the government may lawfully deprive someone of an important interest, respect for that individual demands that she have the opportunity to be heard by a neutral decisionmaker. In other words, one concern relates to the actuality of justice, and the other involves the appearance of justice.

3. *Rules Versus Adjudications.* Note that these two concerns of procedural due process make the most sense when a judge or administrative official is enforcing a governmental directive in an individualized manner. The utilitarian concern suggests that the individual should be allowed to show that the deprivation is not justified under the governmental directive. The normative concern highlights the individual's dignitary interest in observing and participating in a procedure that has singled her out for a potentially grievous loss. In contrast, the Supreme Court has held that due process does not require any special procedural protections when a governmental lawmaking body adopts a statute or rule of general application The notion is that the lawmaking process provides all the process that is due. See *Bi-Metallic Investment Co. v. State Board of Equalization*, 239 U.S. 441 (1915) (state agency may increase the valuation of all taxable property in a jurisdiction without providing hearing).

This distinction may be clarified by an example. Suppose the legislature imposes a tax on everyone who owns more than two cars. In passing the statute, the legislature is under no duty to conduct hearings of any kind. But imposing the tax is a different story. A taxpayer must be given some opportunity to establish that she does not in fact own more than two cars. In short, legislative policy decisions (should car owners be taxed?) are not generally subject to procedural due process. (The idea of legislative due process (Chapter 2, § 3B), is an unconventional effort to impose some process restrictions on legislation, but even so, nothing like a conventional trial-type hearing is contemplated.) On the other hand, individualized fact-determinations (how many cars does Jane Doe own?) are usually subject to some due process requirements.

4. *Critical Definitional Issues.* The Due Process Clause leaves all of its terms undefined. Consider another simple example. Assume that someone receiving public assistance from the state gets a letter informing him that his benefits will be cut off at the end of the month. This is the first time he learns that any questions had been raised about his eligibility. Upon phoning the welfare office, he is informed that the only avenue of relief available to him is to write a letter of protest, which will be reviewed administratively at some point (perhaps months) in the future.

How do the words of the Due Process Clause apply to this situation? The man is certainly a person, and the state is taking away from (and therefore arguably "depriving") him of a benefit he has been enjoying. Beyond that, many questions arise. It is hard to consider his deprivation one of "life"—but what if he starves as a result of the loss of welfare? Should "liberty" include the ability to continue to rely upon governmental benefits? Could the benefits be considered "property"? Assuming he has suffered a deprivation of life, liberty, or property, the inquiry then turns to what "process" is "due." Here the questions relate to the formality and complexity of the required procedures. Must the state engage in trial-like proceedings before cutting off his benefits? If trial-like proceedings are unnecessary, what kind of process short of them will suffice? For instance, is there a right to confront and cross-examine adverse witnesses?

Note that in considering what process is due, the two values identified in *Jerrico* can point in different directions. The utilitarian concern might suggest that the determination of what process is due should be done by cost/benefit analysis (balancing the cost of additional procedures against their utilitarian value—i.e., the product of the likelihood that they would prevent erroneous deprivations and the magnitude of those deprivations). The dignitary or intrinsic value to due process might suggest that better procedures are required as long as they do not unduly burden the government and foster the appearance of justice or reduce psychological harm.[56]

---

[56] For example, suppose that you believe that you did far better on a law school examination than the grade awarded for your performance. Assuming that some process should be available to you in these circumstances (maybe your "contract" with the law school constitutes a "property"

5. *The Interplay Between Federal and State Law.* Before we turn to a consideration of current doctrine, we should alert you to an issue that many students find confusing: The interplay between federal and state law in procedural due process cases. Eligibility for state programs is generally a matter of state law. Thus, for example, it is up to the state to decide the requirements for revoking a driver's license. Consequently, we have to look to *state law* to answer the following question: "What facts, if any, are required to justify terminating eligibility for this benefit?" The character of the inquiry changes, however, when we switch from the question of standards for driver's licenses to whether denial of a driver's license triggers procedural due process at all and if so, whether the state's procedures are sufficient. At this point, *federal law* takes over with the following two questions: First, given the way the state has structured the rules, does a driver's license amount to the kind of "liberty" or "property" protected by the Due Process Clause? Second, if the Due Process Clause does apply, do the state-established procedures for awarding or taking away a license provide "enough of a hearing"?

6. *Introduction to the Doctrinal Debate.* Prior to the 1960s, the Supreme Court tended to look to the common law for guidance in defining what constituted a "liberty" or "property" interest. If one of these interests was present, the Court ordinarily assumed that the "process" that was "due" included notice and an opportunity to be heard before the deprivation occurred.

The common law considered government benefits (public employment, welfare, and so on) mere privileges rather than rights. Thus, due process was not triggered when a public employee lost her job or a recipient of governmental benefits like welfare or social security was cut off from those funds. Professor Charles Reich argued in a pathbreaking article, *The New Property*, 73 Yale L.J. 733 (1964), that the promised receipt of state benefits constituted an "entitlement" that is the "new property" characteristic of life in the modern regulatory state. The nascent welfare rights movement seized upon this idea as the basis for arguing that the state could not arbitrarily cut off welfare benefits. Their efforts bore almost immediate doctrinal fruit.

---

interest and contains an implied term of fair grading), is it enough for the school to require the professor to provide you a short written, truthful response, such as "I graded the exam according to my usual grading processes, which include anonymous grading, and thus you were treated just like everyone else"? Or should the professor be required to discuss the exam with you, or even regrade it? The written response might satisfy the utilitarian value of due process, since requiring any additional procedure is very unlikely to result in a change of grade and would involve some burden to the professor. The dignitary or intrinsic value of due process is premised on the notion that you'll justifiably feel better if, at a minimum, the professor stares you in the eye and tells you personally, even if your grade remains the same.

Goldberg v. Kelly

397 U.S. 254 (1970)

Welfare recipients challenged the termination of their benefits without a prior evidentiary hearing. Citing Reich's article, **Justice Brennan**'s opinion for the Court ruled that the continued receipt of welfare benefits is *property* whose deprivation triggers the protections of the Due Process Clause. "Such benefits are a matter of statutory entitlement for persons qualified to receive them. Their termination involves state action that adjudicates important rights."

As to the *process* that is *due*, Brennan suggested:

The extent to which procedural due process must be afforded the recipient is influenced by the extent to which he may be 'condemned to suffer grievous loss,' *Joint Anti-Fascist Refugee Committee v. McGrath*, 341 U.S. 123, 168 (1951) (Frankfurter, J., concurring), and depends upon whether the recipient's interest in avoiding that loss outweighs the governmental interest in summary adjudication." * * * [T]the crucial factor in this context * * * is that termination of aid pending resolution of a controversy over eligibility may deprive an eligible recipient of the very means by which to live while he waits." Moreover, "important governmental interests are promoted by affording recipients a pre-termination evidentiary hearing. From its founding the Nation's basic commitment has been to foster the dignity and well-being of all persons within its borders. We have come to recognize that forces not within the control of the poor contribute to their poverty. This perception, against the background of our traditions, has significantly influenced the development of the contemporary public assistance system. * * * Public assistance, then, is not mere charity, but a means to 'promote the general Welfare, and secure the Blessings of Liberty to ourselves and our Posterity.' The same governmental interests that counsel the provision of welfare, counsel as well its uninterrupted provision to those eligible to receive it; pre-termination evidentiary hearings are indispensable to that end." The state's justification, resting on the conservation of "fiscal and administrative resources," could not offset these interests.

Chief Justice Burger and **Justices Black** and **Stewart** dissented. Justice Black objected to the essentially legislative nature of the Court's balancing:

I would have little, if any, objection to the majority's decision in this case if it were written as the report of the House Committee on Education and Labor, but as an opinion ostensibly resting on the language of the Constitution I find it woefully deficient. * * * Although the majority attempts to bolster its decision with limited quotations from prior cases, it is obvious that today's result does not depend on the language of the Constitution itself or the principles of other decisions, but solely on the collective judgment of the majority as to what would be a fair and humane procedure in this case.

Invoking his famous debate with Justice Frankfurter in *Adamson* (§ 1 of this chapter), Justice Black charged that "fairness" approaches to the Due Process Clause, unmoored to the constitutional text or original intent, were invitations to judicial tyranny.

———

Goldberg was, as Justice Black feared, a potentially revolutionary opinion. But once the four Nixon Justices were in place, the *Goldberg* revolution was tamed at both ends of its analysis—what government benefits were entitlements triggering due process protection (Part B of this section) and what protection would be triggered (Part C). As you read the following materials, consider whether they meet Justice Black's demand that the Due Process Clause be construed by reference to standards that "mean something definite and have an explicit content."

B.   DEFINING "LIBERTY" AND "PROPERTY"

Almost all law schools have parking problems. Suppose an employee of a state law school arrives at work one morning and discovers that his parking permit has been canceled. Presumably, the right to a workplace parking space is not "fundamental to ordered liberty," even under the most generous conception of that concept. But is the employee at least entitled to an explanation of the decision or a chance to contest it? It would seem in the abstract that the answer might be influenced by either an evaluation of the importance of the employee's interest and the utility of providing some procedures, or whether the law school's rules limit the administrator's discretion in lifting the permit, so the employee might be able to force a favorable decision at the hearing. It might also be relevant if the school gave a damaging explanation for the decision—for instance, perhaps the employee should get some kind of hearing before the school issued an interoffice memo announcing that the permit was lifted because the employee was a drunken driver. Consider, in light of the following materials, whether the Court has picked the right factors for determining whether the right to due process exists in a given situation.

BOARD OF REGENTS V. ROTH
408 U.S. 564, 92 S.Ct. 2701, 33 L.Ed.2d 548 (1972)

JUSTICE STEWART delivered the opinion of the Court.

[Roth was hired to teach at a state university for one year, and he lacked "tenure" under state law. The university president informed him that he would not be rehired, giving no reason for the decision and providing Roth no opportunity to challenge it. The president's action complied with state law and university rules. Roth contended that the failure to provide him a statement of reasons and a hearing violated due process. The Supreme Court ruled against Roth's claim.]

The requirements of procedural due process apply only to the deprivation of interests encompassed by the Fourteenth Amendment's protection of liberty and property. When protected interests are implicated, the right to some kind of prior hearing is paramount.[57] But the range of interests protected by procedural due process is not infinite.

The District Court decided that procedural due process guarantees apply in this case by assessing and balancing the weights of the particular interests involved. It concluded that the respondent's interest in re-employment at [the University] outweighed the University's interest in denying him re-employment summarily. Undeniably, the respondent's re-employment prospects were of major concern to him—concern that we surely cannot say was insignificant. And a weighing process has long been a part of any determination of the *form* of hearing required in particular situations by procedural due process. But, to determine whether due process requirements apply in the first place, we must look not to the "weight" but to the *nature* of the interest at stake. We must look to see if the interest is within the Fourteenth Amendment's protection of liberty and property.

* * * [T]he Court has fully and finally rejected the wooden distinction between "rights" and "privileges" that once seemed to govern the applicability of procedural due process rights. The Court has also made clear that the property interests protected by procedural due process extend well beyond actual ownership of real estate, chattels, or money. By the same token, the Court has required due process protection for deprivations of liberty beyond the sort of formal constraints imposed by the criminal process. * * *

There might be cases in which a State refused to reemploy a person under such circumstances that interests in liberty would be implicated. But this is not such a case. [Justice Stewart stressed that it would be "a different case" if the State had made "any charge against him that might seriously damage his standing and associations in his community," because " '[w]here a person's good name, reputation, honor, or integrity is at stake because of what the government is doing to him, notice and an opportunity to be heard are essential.' *Wisconsin v. Constantineau*, 400 U.S. 433, 437 (1971)." There was also "no suggestion that the State, in declining to re-employ the respondent, imposed on him a stigma or other disability that

---

[57] Before a person is deprived of a protected interest, he must be afforded opportunity for some kind of a hearing, "except for extraordinary situations where some valid governmental interest is at stake that justifies postponing the hearing until after the event." *Boddie v. Connecticut*, 401 U.S. 371, 379 [1971]. * * *

foreclosed his freedom to take advantage of other employment opportunities."]

The Fourteenth Amendment's procedural protection of property is a safeguard of the security of interests that a person has already acquired in specific benefits. These interests—property interests—may take many forms.

Thus, the Court has held that a person receiving welfare benefits under statutory and administrative standards defining eligibility for them has an interest in continued receipt of those benefits that is safeguarded by procedural due process. *Goldberg v. Kelly.* Similarly, in the area of public employment, the Court has held that a public college professor dismissed from an office held under tenure provisions, and college professors and staff members dismissed during the terms of their contracts have interests in continued employment that are safeguarded by due process. * * *

* * * To have a property interest in a benefit, a person clearly must have more than an abstract need or desire for it. He must have more than a unilateral expectation of it. He must, instead, have a legitimate claim of entitlement to it. It is a purpose of the ancient institution of property to protect those claims upon which people rely in their daily lives, reliance that must not be arbitrarily undermined. It is a purpose of the constitutional right to a hearing to provide an opportunity for a person to vindicate those claims.

Property interests, of course, are not created by the Constitution. Rather, they are created and their dimensions are defined by existing rules or understandings that stem from an independent source such as state law—rules or understandings that secure certain benefits and that support claims of entitlement to those benefits. Thus, the welfare recipients in *Goldberg* had a claim of entitlement to welfare payments that was grounded in the statute defining eligibility for them. The recipients had not yet shown that they were, in fact, within the statutory terms of eligibility. But we held that they had a right to a hearing at which they might attempt to do so.

Just as the welfare recipients' "property" interest in welfare payments was created and defined by statutory terms, so the respondent's "property" interest in employment at [the University] was created and defined by the terms of his appointment. Those terms secured his interest in employment up to June 30, 1969. But the important fact in this case is that they specifically provided that the respondent's employment was to terminate on June 30. They did not provide for contract renewal absent "sufficient cause." Indeed, they made no provision for renewal whatsoever.

Thus, the terms of the respondent's appointment secured absolutely no interest in re-employment for the next year. They supported absolutely no possible claim of entitlement to re-employment. Nor, significantly, was there any state statute or University rule or policy that secured his interest in re-employment or that created any legitimate claim to it. In these circumstances, the respondent surely had an abstract concern in being rehired, but he did not have a *property* interest sufficient to require the University authorities to give him a hearing when they declined to renew his contract of employment.

[JUSTICE POWELL took no part in the decision. The concurring opinion of CHIEF JUSTICE BURGER and the dissenting opinions of JUSTICES DOUGLAS, BRENNAN, and MARSHALL are omitted.]

NOTES ON DEFINING "PROPERTY" AND "LIBERTY"

1.   *Defining "Property": Entitlements. Roth* rejected one plausible interpretation of *Goldberg* (which was followed by the lower court in *Roth*): That "property" in the administrative state might include all of the many important economic interests flowing from the government. *Roth* did not go all the way back to the old common law right/privilege distinction, however. At common law a public employee had no right to employment, and his or her working terms were purely a matter of contract. *Roth* recognizes that a bona fide expectation of continuing employment arising from state law is "property" for due process purposes.[58] After *Roth*, does an applicant for welfare who is not currently receiving benefits qualify for due process protection? (Hint: Note how *Roth* conceptualizes the interests safeguarded by "[t]he Fourteenth Amendment's procedural protection of property," just before it discusses *Goldberg*. This is just dictum, however, and the Court has never definitively resolved the issue.) Determining whether state law creates an "entitlement" is no easy task. Compare, e.g., *Bishop v. Wood*, 426 U.S. 341 (1976) (police officer held job at will of city despite being classified as "permanent employee") with *Goss v. Lopez*, 419 U.S. 565 (1975) (school children were deprived of a property interest by their temporary suspension from school because state law stated that students could be suspended only for "misconduct").

2.   *The Purposes of a Hearing.* In the introduction to this section, we remarked that policy decisions normally do not require due process, but individualized fact-finding does. *Roth* can be seen as resting on a similar concept. If a person is an "employee at will," the decision of whether to retain him or her is essentially an open-ended policy decision, in which individual traits, financial considerations, and institutional priorities may all factor in. Indeed, at common law, an employee at will could be discharged for any reason or no reason at all ("I felt like it" is an adequate legal justification for the employer). On the other hand, a tenured employee can only be discharged on specific grounds, and thus the discharge will involve narrowly focused factual inquiries. Or, to put it another way, the tenured employee can prevail by

---

[58]   In a companion case, *Perry v. Sindermann*, 408 U.S. 593 (1972), the Court held that a professor had a property interest in continued employment, even if his college had no formal contractual tenure system, so long as the college and he had a mutual expectation that his employment would be renewed each year.

proving certain facts at the hearing, while the untenured employee can be fired no matter what facts she can prove at the hearing. So the hearing serves a clear instrumental purpose for the tenured employee, but not for the employee at will.

3. *The Consequences of Finding "Property": A Rejection of "the Bitter with the Sweet" Argument.* If the entitlement under state law is shown, then "property" is present and procedural due process applies notwithstanding any procedural conditions found in the employee's contract. *Cleveland Board of Education v. Loudermill*, 470 U.S. 532 (1985), demonstrates how this approach works. An employee fired by the school board contended that he should have been granted a pretermination hearing. The Supreme Court first asked whether he had a "property" interest for procedural due process purposes. It concluded that he did because Ohio statutes provided that "classified civil service employees" like him were entitled to retain their positions "during good behavior and efficient service" and could not be dismissed except for "misfeasance, malfeasance, or nonfeasance in office." Next, the Court asked whether the procedures accorded him complied with procedural due process, and it concluded that they did not. But the same Ohio statutes that created an entitlement to future employment also purported to specify the procedures for termination. Should this matter—should the claimant have to accept the "bitter" (procedural limitations) with the "sweet" (the entitlement)? Rejecting the plurality opinion in *Arnett v. Kennedy*, 416 U.S. 134 (1974), the Court considered it irrelevant that the school board had followed the statutory procedures:

> [T]he "bitter with the sweet" approach misconceives the constitutional guarantee. * * * [T]he Due Process Clause provides that certain substantive rights—life, liberty, and property—cannot be deprived except pursuant to constitutionally adequate procedures. The categories of substance and procedure are distinct. Were the rule otherwise, the Clause would be reduced to a mere tautology. "Property" cannot be defined by the procedures provided for its deprivation any more than can life or liberty. The right to due process "is conferred, not by legislative grace, but by constitutional guarantee. While the legislature may elect not to confer a property interest in [public] employment, it may not constitutionally authorize the deprivation of such an interest, once conferred, without appropriate procedural safeguards."

4. *Liberty Interests.* Many government actions do not directly deprive an individual of property, even in the broad form of government assistance, and yet cause substantial hardship. Some of these government actions invade "liberty interests," as defined for procedural due process purposes. Prior to *Roth* the courts relied upon common law conceptions (e.g., false imprisonment, battery) for guidance in defining "liberty." Hence, the government may accomplish physical restraint (e.g., imprisonment) or physical intrusion only if

appropriate procedures are followed.[59] Speaking more broadly, in general an individual has been deprived of a "liberty interest" for procedural due process purposes if she is the subject of a coercive government order prohibiting her from engaging in previously lawful activity. (In *Roth*, the Court found no such liberty interest when a person "simply is not rehired in one job but remains free as before to seek another." Contrast this with an order disbarring an attorney, who is then unable to seek a job in the field in which she is trained.) In some situations, a liberty interest might encompass a status, such as marriage or parental custody. Such a status will be considered a liberty interest if it has constitutional protection as a fundamental right. (Note the quotation from *Meyer* in *Roth*.)

For example, suppose the state allows the mother of a nonmarital child to be deprived of parental rights whenever that decision is in "the best interests of the child," as determined by a judge after an *ex parte* hearing. She could make a substantive claim that the "best interests" standard is unconstitutional (because of her fundamental right relating to parenting, see again the excerpt from *Meyer* in *Roth*) and that the state must instead prove her unfitness to be a parent. She can also make a procedural claim that, whatever the substantive standard, an *ex parte* hearing violates her right to be heard before being deprived of such an important liberty interest. In practice, of course, she would usually want to make both claims: The only permissible substantive standard is unfitness, and the only permissible procedure is an adversary hearing.

C. DEFINING "WHAT PROCESS IS DUE"

It is all very well to have the right to "due process" in a given situation, but this begs the question of what process is actually required. In various circumstances, the state might argue that anything from an informal phone call to a full-blown trial constituted the appropriate process. The following case is the leading authority on how to determine which procedures are required by due process. (Don't forget, however, that you must always consider the antecedent question raised above—whether *any* procedures *at all* are required by due process in a given situation.)

MATHEWS V. ELDRIDGE
424 U.S. 319, 96 S.Ct. 893, 47 L.Ed.2d 18 (1976)

JUSTICE POWELL delivered the opinion of the Court.

[The Social Security Act provides benefits to workers while they are disabled. When the state agency responsible for investigating ongoing eligibility believes that a recipient is no longer "disabled," it informs him or her that benefits may be terminated and that he or she may respond in writing and may furnish new evidence. If the agency decides to terminate

---

[59] A post-*Roth* example is *Ingraham v. Wright*, 430 U.S. 651 (1977) (paddling of public school children implicates liberty interest).

benefits, a federal official must approve it before it takes effect. If benefits are terminated, there is a statutory right to an evidentiary hearing, and if the termination is shown to be erroneous the worker may receive benefits retroactively. Subsequent judicial review is also available. In this case, a worker whose benefits were terminated contended that the absence of a pretermination evidentiary hearing violated due process. The government conceded that these benefits were "property" for procedural due process purposes, but argued that the procedures in place provided all the process that was constitutionally due.]

This Court consistently has held that some form of hearing is required before an individual is finally deprived of a property interest. * * * The fundamental requirement of due process is the opportunity to be heard "at a meaningful time and in a meaningful manner." * * * [This] dispute centers upon what process is due prior to the initial termination of benefits, pending review. * * *

* * * "[D]ue process is flexible and calls for such procedural protections as the particular situation demands." Accordingly, resolution of the issue whether the administrative procedures provided here are constitutionally sufficient requires analysis of the governmental and private interests that are affected. More precisely, our prior decisions indicate that identification of the specific dictates of due process generally requires consideration of three distinct factors: First, the private interest that will be affected by the official action; second, the risk of an erroneous deprivation of such interest through the procedures used, and the probable value, if any, of additional or substitute procedural safeguards; and finally, the Government's interest, including the function involved and the fiscal and administrative burdens that the additional or substitute procedural requirement would entail. See, e.g., *Goldberg*. * * *

Since a recipient whose benefits are terminated is awarded full retroactive relief if he ultimately prevails, his sole interest is in the uninterrupted receipt of this source of income pending final administrative decision on his claim. * * *

[*Goldberg* is the only case in which] the Court [has] held that due process requires an evidentiary hearing prior to a temporary deprivation. It was emphasized there that welfare assistance is given to persons on the very margin of subsistence. * * * Eligibility for disability benefits, in contrast, is not based upon financial need [but rather upon the worker's average monthly earnings during the period prior to disability, his age, and other factors not directly related to financial need that are specified by statute].

As *Goldberg* illustrates, the degree of potential deprivation that may be created by a particular decision is a factor to be considered in assessing the validity of any administrative decisionmaking process. The potential deprivation here is generally likely to be less than in *Goldberg*, although the degree of difference can be overstated. * * * [T]o remain eligible for benefits a recipient must be "unable to engage in substantial gainful activity." 42 U.S.C. § 423. Thus, * * * there is little possibility that the terminated recipient will be able to find even temporary employment to ameliorate the interim loss.

* * * "[T]he possible length of wrongful deprivation of * * * benefits [also] is an important factor in assessing the impact of official action on the private interests." The Secretary concedes that the delay between a request for a hearing before an administrative law judge and a decision on the claim is currently between 10 and 11 months. Since a terminated recipient must first obtain a reconsideration decision as a prerequisite to invoking his right to an evidentiary hearing, the delay between the actual cutoff of benefits and final decision after a hearing exceeds one year.

In view of the torpidity of this administrative review process and the typically modest resources of the family unit of the physically disabled worker, the hardship imposed upon the erroneously terminated disability recipient may be significant. Still, the disabled worker's need is likely to be less than that of a welfare recipient. In addition to the possibility of access to private resources, other forms of government assistance will become available where the termination of disability benefits places a worker or his family below the subsistence level. In view of these potential sources of temporary income, there is less reason here than in *Goldberg* to depart from the ordinary principle, established by our decisions, that something less than an evidentiary hearing is sufficient prior to adverse administrative action.

An additional factor to be considered here is the fairness and reliability of the existing pretermination procedures, and the probable value, if any, of additional procedural safeguards. Central to the evaluation of any administrative process is the nature of the relevant inquiry. In order to remain eligible for benefits the disabled worker must demonstrate by means of "medically acceptable clinical and laboratory diagnostic techniques" that he is unable "to engage in any substantial gainful activity by reason of any *medically determinable* physical or mental impairment . . ." In short, a medical assessment of the worker's physical or mental condition is required. This is a more sharply focused and easily documented decision than the typical determination of welfare entitlement. * * *

[T]he decision whether to discontinue disability benefits will turn, in most cases, upon "routine, standard, and unbiased medical reports by physician specialists" concerning a subject whom they have personally examined. * * * To be sure, credibility and veracity may be a factor in the ultimate disability assessment in some cases. But procedural due process rules are shaped by the risk of error inherent in the truthfinding process as applied to the generality of cases, not the rare exceptions. The potential value of an evidentiary hearing, or even oral presentation to the decisionmaker, is substantially less in this context than in *Goldberg.* * * *

[A]*mici* point to the significant reversal rate for appealed cases as clear evidence that the current process is inadequate. Depending upon the base selected and the line of analysis followed, the relevant reversal rates urged by the contending parties vary from a high of 58.6% for appealed reconsideration decisions to an overall reversal rate of only 3.3%. Bare statistics rarely provide a satisfactory measure of the fairness of a decision-making process. Their adequacy is especially suspect here since the administrative review system is operated on an open file basis. A recipient may always submit new evidence, and such submissions may result in additional medical examinations. Such fresh examinations were held in approximately 30% to 40% of the appealed cases in fiscal 1973, either at the reconsideration or evidentiary hearing stage of the administrative process. In this context, the value of reversal rate statistics as one means of evaluating the adequacy of the pretermination process is diminished. * * *

In striking the appropriate due process balance the final factor to be assessed is the public interest. This includes the administrative burden and other societal costs that would be associated with requiring, as a matter of constitutional right, an evidentiary hearing upon demand in all cases prior to the termination of disability benefits. The most visible burden would be the incremental cost resulting from the increased number of hearings and the expense of providing benefits to ineligible recipients pending decision. No one can predict the extent of the increase, but the fact that full benefits would continue until after such hearings would assure the exhaustion in most cases of this attractive option. Nor would the theoretical right of the Secretary to recover undeserved benefits result, as a practical matter, in any substantial offset to the added outlay of public funds. The parties submit widely varying estimates of the probable additional financial cost. We only need say that experience with the constitutionalizing of government procedures suggests that the ultimate additional cost in terms of money and administrative burden would not be insubstantial.

Financial cost alone is not a controlling weight in determining whether due process requires a particular procedural safeguard prior to some administrative decision. But the Government's interest, and hence that of the public, in conserving scarce fiscal and administrative resources is a factor that must be weighed. At some point the benefit of an additional safeguard to the individual affected by the administrative action and to society in terms of increased assurance that the action is just, may be outweighed by the cost. Significantly, the cost of protecting those whom the preliminary administrative process has identified as likely to be found undeserving may in the end come out of the pockets of the deserving since resources available for any particular program of social welfare are not unlimited.

But more is implicated in cases of this type than ad hoc weighing of fiscal and administrative burdens against the interests of a particular category of claimants. The ultimate balance involves a determination as to when, under our constitutional system, judicial-type procedures must be imposed upon administrative action to assure fairness. We reiterate the wise admonishment of Mr. Justice Frankfurter that differences in the origin and function of administrative agencies "preclude wholesale transplantation of the rules of procedure, trial, and review which have evolved from the history and experience of courts." The judicial model of an evidentiary hearing is neither a required, nor even the most effective, method of decisionmaking in all circumstances. The essence of due process is the requirement that "a person in jeopardy of serious loss [be given] notice of the case against him and opportunity to meet it." All that is necessary is that the procedures be tailored, in light of the decision to be made, to "the capacities and circumstances of those who are to be heard," *Goldberg*, to insure that they are given a meaningful opportunity to present their case. In assessing what process is due in this case, substantial weight must be given to the good-faith judgments of the individuals charged by Congress with the administration of social welfare programs that the procedures they have provided assure fair consideration of the entitlement claims of individuals. This is especially so where, as here, the prescribed procedures not only provide the claimant with an effective process for asserting his claim prior to any administrative action, but also assure a right to an evidentiary hearing, as well as to subsequent judicial review, before the denial of his claim becomes final.

[**JUSTICE STEVENS** took no part in the consideration or decision of this case. The dissenting opinion of **JUSTICE BRENNAN**, joined by **JUSTICE MARSHALL**, is omitted.]

NOTES ON DEFINING "WHAT PROCESS IS DUE"

1.   *Utilitarianism and Due Process.* Does *Eldridge* slight the dignitary or intrinsic value of due process?[60] Note that the loss of disability benefits can be devastating. (Justice Brennan's dissent noted that because of the loss of benefits "there was a foreclosure upon the Eldridge home and the family's furniture was repossessed, forcing Eldridge, his wife, and their children to sleep in one bed.") Wouldn't the termination of benefits have far more legitimacy, at least in the eyes of the Eldridge family, if they had been heard in person before the cutoff occurred? From the standpoint of legal process

---

[60] See Jerry Mashaw, *The Supreme Court's Due Process Calculus for Administrative Adjudication in* Mathews v. Eldridge: *Three Factors in Search of a Theory of Value*, 44 U. Chi. L. Rev. 28 (1976).

values (e.g., creating judicially manageable standards, discouraging continuous litigation on an issue), would a more categorical approach be preferable to case-by-case application of the *Eldridge* balancing approach? In considering questions of efficiency, fairness, and individual dignity, one should not ignore the possibility that the greater the procedural rights accorded, the greater will be the state's expenses in administering a program, which may reduce the amount of benefits available for bona fide claimants.

2. *Determining "What Process Is Due."* In considering "what process is due," several central questions arise. One is the question of *timing*: May a prompt post-deprivation hearing suffice, or must there be a hearing prior to the deprivation? Another is the question of *formality*: The possibilities for a hearing extend from an oral, evidentiary trial before a neutral tribunal to a decision by a government official involved in the dispute based on a written or brief oral record, with none of the rights described above. As one would predict in light of *Eldridge*, the Court has answered the question of "what process is due" on a case-by-case basis, and it seems impossible to generalize about the issue in the space available to us. At one extreme remains *Goldberg v. Kelly*, which requires that a welfare recipient be allowed to retain an attorney (at his or her own expense) and receive "timely and adequate notice detailing the reasons for a proposed termination, and an effective opportunity to defend by confronting any adverse witnesses and by presenting his own arguments and evidence orally."

At the other end of the continuum are cases in which the Court found a liberty or property interest but nonetheless almost entirely deferred to the existing state scheme. For example, in *Ingraham v. Wright*, 430 U.S. 651 (1977), the Court concluded that the "paddling" of students in public schools involved a liberty interest, but said that the availability of a later tort action under state law to obtain damages provided "what process is due" in these circumstances. Another illustration is *Goss v. Lopez*, 419 U.S. 565 (1975). In *Goss*, the Court held that suspension of students from public schools for disciplinary reasons involved both a property interest (because state law said that students could be suspended only for "misconduct") and a liberty interest. Yet the process "due" in these circumstances was only a conversation before the suspension in which the school official told the student of the charge against her, informed her of the evidence supporting the charge, and provided her an opportunity to give her side of the events.

3. *Due Process and Especially Sensitive Areas of Liberty.* Although most of the "action" in recent years has involved accommodating procedural due process to the modern administrative state, other decisions have considered what process is due outside the administrative context. For example, in addition to retaining the longstanding "beyond a reasonable doubt" approach to the burden of proof in criminal cases, the Court has held that "clear and convincing evidence" rather than a mere preponderance of the evidence is the required burden of proof in other sensitive areas of loss of liberty. See *Santosky v. Kramer*, 455 U.S. 745 (1982) (termination of parental rights with respect to child requires clear and convincing evidence of statutory criteria); *Addington*

v. Texas, 441 U.S. 418 (1979) (involuntary commitment of adult to mental hospital requires clear and convincing evidence that person is dangerous to him/herself or to others).

In *Little v. Streater*, 452 U.S. 1 (1981), the Supreme Court ruled that due process required the state to provide indigent male defendants in paternity suits with free paternity testing. But the same day, the Court ruled that the Due Process Clause does not assure an indigent mother free counsel in an adversary proceeding initiated by the state to terminate her parental rights. Justice Stewart's opinion for the Court in *Lassiter v. Department of Social Servs.*, 452 U.S. 18 (1981), noted that a man accused of a misdemeanor cannot constitutionally be sentenced to one day in jail without representation by appointed counsel. But this reflects a presumption that an indigent litigant has a right to appointed counsel only when, if he loses, he may be deprived of his physical liberty. The indigent mother, the Court concluded, was entitled to counsel only if the *Eldridge* factors—the private interest at stake, the government's interest, and the risk that the procedures used will lead to erroneous decisions—were satisfied. Because the parent's interest in the accuracy and justice of the decision to terminate parental status is a "commanding" one, the state shares with the parent an interest in a correct decision and has a relatively weak pecuniary interest in avoiding the expense of appointed counsel and the cost of the lengthened proceedings his presence may cause; and judges as well as litigants believe that appointed counsel would both facilitate parental termination hearings and prevent arbitrary terminations, the Court ruled that *in some cases* the *Eldridge* factors would be able to overcome the presumption against counsel. But the Court found the added value of counsel insufficient to overcome the presumption in Lassiter's case.

PROBLEM 5-5:
ISSUES OF PROCEDURAL DUE PROCESS

(a)   Under state law, it is illegal in some circumstances to discharge an employee because of a physical disability. Logan filed a claim with the state agency, which triggered the agency's obligation to begin a proceeding within 120 days. The agency scheduled the proceeding five days after that period, and the state courts held that the failure to start the procedure in a timely fashion deprived the agency of jurisdiction. Assess whatever constitutional claims Logan might have. See *Logan v. Zimmerman Brush Co.*, 455 U.S. 422 (1982).

(b)   A school board requires pregnant schoolteachers to take an unpaid maternity leave, commencing five months before the expected birth. A school teacher objects that the board's "irrebuttable presumption" of incapacity to teach violates her due process rights. The board responds that the rule is substantive (*Lochner*-like) and not procedural (*Goldberg*-ish). Who wins? See *Cleveland Board of Education v. LaFleur*, 414 U.S. 632 (1974).

(c)   A more dramatic due process question: In 2002, an American citizen was arrested as he entered the country. He was allegedly connected with a terrorist organization and was seeking to assemble a "dirty bomb" (one that would spread radioactive contaminants). Suppose that the government seeks to detain him indefinitely, both to allow questioning and to keep him from carrying through on the plan. Assume for present purposes that such a detention is not per se unconstitutional. Under the Due Process Clause, does he have the right to some kind of a hearing regarding the allegations? If so, what procedures are required? [See *Hamdan v. Rumsfeld*, Chapter 8.]

CAPERTON V. A.T. MASSEY COAL COMPANY, INC.
556 U.S. 868, 129 S.Ct. 2252, 173 L.Ed.2d 1208 (2009)

[A coal company was the defendant in a $50 million lawsuit. After a jury verdict against it, the company's chairman gave $3 million to support the campaign of Brent Benjamin for a seat on the West Virginia Supreme Court. His $3 million in contributions exceeded the total amount spent by all other Benjamin supporters and by Benjamin's own committee. Benjamin won by fewer than 50,000 votes. He refused to recuse himself from hearing the coal company's appeal, which was successful before the state supreme court.]

JUSTICE KENNEDY delivered the opinion of the Court.

Under our precedents there are objective standards that require recusal when "the probability of actual bias on the part of the judge or decisionmaker is too high to be constitutionally tolerable." Applying those precedents, we find that, in all the circumstances of this case, due process requires recusal. * * *

It is axiomatic that "[a] fair trial in a fair tribunal is a basic requirement of due process." As the Court has recognized, however, "most matters relating to judicial disqualification [do] not rise to a constitutional level." The early and leading case on the subject is *Tumey v. Ohio*, 273 U.S. 510 (1927). There, the Court stated that "matters of kinship, personal bias, state policy, remoteness of interest, would seem generally to be matters merely of legislative discretion."

The *Tumey* Court concluded that the Due Process Clause incorporated the common-law rule that a judge must recuse himself when he has "a direct, personal, substantial, pecuniary interest" in a case. This rule reflects the maxim that "[n]o man is allowed to be a judge in his own cause; because his interest would certainly bias his judgment, and, not improbably, corrupt his integrity." Under this rule, "disqualification for bias or prejudice was not permitted"; those matters were left to statutes and judicial codes. Personal bias or prejudice "alone would not be sufficient basis for imposing a constitutional requirement under the Due Process Clause."

As new problems have emerged that were not discussed at common law, however, the Court has identified additional instances which, as an objective matter, require recusal. These are circumstances "in which experience teaches that the probability of actual bias on the part of the judge or decisionmaker is too high to be constitutionally tolerable." To place the present case in proper context, two instances where the Court has required recusal merit further discussion.

The first involved the emergence of local tribunals where a judge had a financial interest in the outcome of a case, although the interest was less than what would have been considered personal or direct at common law.

This was the problem addressed in *Tumey*. There, the mayor of a village had the authority to sit as a judge (with no jury) to try those accused of violating a state law prohibiting the possession of alcoholic beverages. Inherent in this structure were two potential conflicts. First, the mayor received a salary supplement for performing judicial duties, and the funds for that compensation derived from the fines assessed in a case. No fines were assessed upon acquittal. The mayor-judge thus received a salary supplement only if he convicted the defendant. Second, sums from the criminal fines were deposited to the village's general treasury fund for village improvements and repairs.

The Court held that the Due Process Clause required disqualification "both because of [the mayor-judge's] direct pecuniary interest in the outcome, and because of his official motive to convict and to graduate the fine to help the financial needs of the village." It so held despite observing that "[t]here are doubtless mayors who would not allow such a consideration as $12 costs in each case to affect their judgment in it." * * *

This concern with conflicts resulting from financial incentives was elaborated in *Ward v. Monroeville,* 409 U.S. 57 (1972), which invalidated a conviction in another mayor's court. In *Monroeville,* unlike in *Tumey,* the mayor received no money; instead, the fines the mayor assessed went to the town's general fisc. The Court held that "[t]he fact that the mayor [in *Tumey*] shared directly in the fees and costs did not define the limits of the principle." The principle, instead, turned on the " 'possible temptation' " the mayor might face; the mayor's "executive responsibilities for village finances may make him partisan to maintain the high level of contribution [to those finances] from the mayor's court." * * *

The Court in [*Aetna Life Ins. Co. v. Lavoie,* 475 U.S. 813 (1986)] further clarified the reach of the Due Process Clause regarding a judge's financial interest in a case. There, a justice had cast the deciding vote on the Alabama Supreme Court to uphold a punitive damages award against an insurance company for bad-faith refusal to pay a claim. At the time of his vote, the justice was the lead plaintiff in a nearly identical lawsuit pending in Alabama's lower courts. His deciding vote, this Court surmised, "undoubtedly 'raised the stakes'" for the insurance defendant in the justice's suit. * * *

We turn to the influence at issue in this case. Not every campaign contribution by a litigant or attorney creates a probability of bias that requires a judge's recusal, but this is an exceptional case. We conclude that there is a serious risk of actual bias—based on objective and reasonable perceptions—when a person with a personal stake in a particular case had a significant and disproportionate influence in placing the judge on the case by raising funds or directing the judge's election campaign when the case was pending or imminent. The inquiry centers on the contribution's relative size in comparison to the total amount of money contributed to the campaign, the total amount spent in the election, and the apparent effect such contribution had on the outcome of the election. * * *

Our decision today addresses an extraordinary situation where the Constitution requires recusal. Massey and its *amici* predict that various adverse consequences will follow from recognizing a constitutional violation here—ranging from a flood of recusal motions to unnecessary interference with judicial elections. We disagree. The facts now before us are extreme by any measure. The parties point to no other instance involving judicial campaign contributions that presents a potential for bias comparable to the circumstances in this case.

It is true that extreme cases often test the bounds of established legal principles, and sometimes no administrable standard may be available to address the perceived wrong. But it is also true that extreme cases are more likely to cross constitutional limits, requiring this Court's intervention and formulation of objective standards. This is particularly true when due process is violated.

CHIEF JUSTICE ROBERTS, with whom **JUSTICE SCALIA**, **JUSTICE THOMAS**, and **JUSTICE ALITO** join, dissenting.

Until today, we have recognized exactly two situations in which the Federal Due Process Clause requires disqualification of a judge: when the judge has a financial interest in the outcome of the case, and when the judge is trying a defendant for certain criminal contempts. Vaguer notions of bias or the appearance of bias were never a basis for disqualification, either at common law or under our constitutional precedents. Those issues were instead addressed by legislation or court rules.

Today, however, the Court enlists the Due Process Clause to overturn a judge's failure to recuse because of a "probability of bias." Unlike the established grounds for disqualification, a "probability of bias" cannot be defined in any limited way. The Court's new "rule" provides no guidance to judges and litigants about when recusal will be constitutionally required. This will inevitably lead to an increase in allegations that judges are biased, however groundless those charges may be. The end result will do far more to erode public confidence in judicial impartiality than an isolated failure to recuse in a particular case. Chief Justice Roberts listed forty questions about the scope of the Court's holding as applied to other cases, such as "How much money is too much money?" and "What if the supporter is not a party to the pending or imminent case, but his interests will be affected by the decision?".]

These are only a few uncertainties that quickly come to mind. Judges and litigants will surely encounter others when they are forced to, or wish to, apply the majority's decision in different circumstances. Today's opinion requires state and federal judges simultaneously to act as political scientists (why did candidate X win the election?), economists (was the financial support disproportionate?), and psychologists (is there likely to be a debt of gratitude?). * * *

It is an old cliché, but sometimes the cure is worse than the disease. I am sure there are cases where a "probability of bias" should lead the prudent judge to step aside, but the judge fails to do so. Maybe this is one of them. But I believe that opening the door to recusal claims under the Due Process Clause, for an amorphous "probability of bias," will itself bring our judicial system into undeserved disrepute, and diminish the confidence of the American people in the fairness and integrity of their courts. I hope I am wrong.

[A separate dissent by **JUSTICE SCALIA** is omitted].

Williams v. Pennsylvania

136 S.Ct. 1899 (2016)

This decision involved a criminal prosecution that had begun when one of the state court's current justices had been a state's attorney. Although he had given formal approval to seek the death penalty, he had not been otherwise involved in the prosecution. The criminal defendant later filed a postconviction challenge, arguing that the prosecution team (but not the state's attorney himself) had concealed favorable evidence and presented false testimony. By the time that this issue came before the state supreme court, the former prosecutor in the case had been appointed to the court. The state supreme court overturned a decision by a lower court in favor of the defendant. With **Justice Kennedy** again writing the majority opinion, the Court held that the state court's judgment was invalid because the former prosecutor's participation in the decision "gave rise to an unacceptable risk of actual bias." The constitutional violation was not rendered harmless by the fact that the former prosecutor did not supply the critical vote to reverse the lower court. **Chief Justice Roberts**, **Justice Alito**, and **Justice Thomas** dissented.

NOTES ON WILLIAMS V. PENNSYLVANIA

1.   *Judicial Elections and the Presumption of Impartiality.* The dissenters in both *Caperton* and *Williams* correctly observe that those two opinions go well beyond prior precedents in applying due process analysis to judicial recusal. Both opinions make a point of mentioning judicial campaigns—*Caperton* in terms of campaign expenditures and *Williams* in terms of the judge's campaign platform. Could the shift in the Court's stance be related to growing concerns about how the increased politicization of state judicial elections might impair judicial objectivity? Is that a realistic concern for the Court to consider?

2.   *The Floodgates Argument and Other Problems.* Recusal motions take place all the time anyway. Prosecutors presumably do not make campaign contributions to judges, so it is hard to see how *Caperton* claims would arise in criminal cases. Williams' claims also seem relatively unlikely. In federal cases, recusal motions are also made without regard to *Caperton*. A collateral attack on a civil judgment via a § 1983 action is almost certain to fail because of res judicata. Thus, successful claims of unconstitutional bias are likely to be rare.

3.   *Recusal Boundaries.* Is the Court in the process of constitutionalizing the judicial ethical code? Would this be an undesirable development? Or is the Court is in the process of evolving its own common law of judicial bias—a process that could leave judges up in the air for a considerable time about constitutional recusal requirements? Or alternatively, is the Court simply drawing an outer boundary to deal with very rare cases where a failure to recuse by a state supreme court judge seems far out of bounds—a kind of "shock the conscience test"?

CHAPTER 6

THE FIRST AMENDMENT

■ ■ ■

One of our themes has been the role of social and political movements in helping to shape constitutional law. But constitutional law also helps create the legal context in which these movements function. It plays that role with respect to religious groups, voluntary associations, media, and political groups. The First Amendment sets limits on government intrusions into these important aspects of civil society and limits government intrusion into public debate. In the course of providing this protection, however, it may leave some groups vulnerable to forms of discourse that can help more entrenched dominant groups. In addition, as we will see, the Court has used the First Amendment to limit regulation of campaign finance, strengthening the role of the wealthy and corporations in the political process.

Some key aspects of First Amendment law bear on democracy and the political process:

- Dissident political groups can vehemently attack the government and other groups, so long as a communication does not pose an imminent risk of violence.

- The media, as well as other groups, can criticize public officials and public figures without restraint, so long as they do not make knowingly false statements of fact.

- Some forms of economic influence on the political process (such as corporate expenditures to support a candidate) are constitutionally protected from regulation, whereas others are subject to significant government regulations (such as direct candidate contributions).

The First Amendment also limits the ability of government to shape group relations by regulating speech that offends the members of particular groups. It sharply limits the ability of the government to prohibit verbal attacks on groups, speech that group members find demeaning, or speech that might encourage discrimination. In the cultural realm, groups are left free to act toward each other as they will, without any requirement of civility. And where religious groups are concerned, the First Amendment provides some protection of religious practices (but not much), while limiting the ability of government to channel assistance to religious education or other church activities. Thus, the First Amendment plays an important role in deregulating some aspects of group relations, while imposing special regulations on how religious groups and government can interact.

Notably, although the First Amendment does a lot to set the ground rules for collective activities, the Court is much more prone to discuss the First Amendment in terms of *individual* rights. As you read this chapter, consider whether this emphasis is helpful or whether it obscures the First Amendment's role in setting ground rules for civil society.

SECTION 1. FREE SPEECH AND COMPETING VALUES

The Supreme Court has decided several hundred First Amendment cases, the great majority of them since 1970. They deal with a wide range of factual and legal issues, from copyright law to nude dancing. It would be impossible to examine fully this enormous, complex body of case law, and we make no pretense of doing so. Instead, this chapter covers key aspects of First Amendment doctrine, while emphasizing applications that connect with the book's major themes.

Because the doctrine is so intricate, it is easy to become lost in the details. A brief overview may be helpful before we begin. Historically, the central struggle in free speech doctrine involved subversive speech. It was only in the 1960s that the Supreme Court finally resolved that issue. At around the same time, the Court began giving serious attention to other categories of speech. Previously, obscenity, commercial advertising, and defamation had all been relegated to outlaw status, completely lacking in First Amendment protection. Today, the government still has authority to regulate speech falling into these categories, but that authority is subject to substantial restrictions.[1] With regard to speech falling *outside* of these historic categories, the Court is extremely suspicious of government efforts to ban harmful messages. But the Court is much more forgiving of laws that ignore content completely and regulate only the time, place, or manner of speech.

The Court has also confronted a number of problems that do not fit neatly within this framework. First, there are several settings where the government has a special relationship with the speaker, providing a distinctive reason for it to address the content of speech. The Court has developed special doctrines to deal with many of these settings, involving speech by public employees, students, recipients of government grants,

---

[1] For commentary on the categorical approach, see Gregory P. Magarian, *The Marrow of Tradition: The Roberts Court and Categorical First Amendment Speech* Exclusions, 56 Wm. & Mary L. Rev. 1339 (2015); Alexander Tsesis, *The Categorical Free Speech Doctrine and Contextualization*, 65 Emory L. Rev. 495 (2015).

broadcasters, and others. These doctrines give the government more control over these speakers than it is allowed to exercise over the general public. Second, the Court has developed another set of doctrines dealing with the form (rather than the substance) of government regulations. These doctrines require an unusual degree of precision in laws regulating speech. They also favor after-the-fact sanctions over before-the-fact restrictions on speech. Third, the Court has recognized a right of freedom of association, connected with (but distinct from) the right to free expression.

NOTE ON THE ORIGINAL UNDERSTANDING OF FREEDOM OF SPEECH

As we saw in Chapter 2, there is considerable dispute about just how important original meaning should be in constitutional interpretation, but almost no one denies its relevance. We begin our study of the First Amendment, then, with a quick look at its historical context.[2]

When the printing press was invented, governments were quick to respond. The new ability to circulate thousands of copies of a work threatened social stability and government authority. The response was a system of licensing for authors and printers. The poet John Milton was a prominent early critic of the sweeping censorship of the period. See Vincent Blasi, *Milton's Areopagitica and the Modern First Amendment*, 13 Comm. Lawyer 1 (1996). By the mid-eighteenth century, however, the English were proud of themselves for having abolished this system. Indeed, for at least some, the absence of licensing was pretty much the definition of free speech. As Blackstone said, "the liberty of the press" consists of "laying no previous restraints upon publication," rather than "freedom from censure for criminal matter when published." Licensing makes a single censor the absolute authority over what is said. But punishing "any dangerous writings, which, when published, shall on a fair and impartial trial be adjudged of a pernicious tendency, is necessary for the preservation of peace and good order, of government and religion, the only solid foundations of civil liberty."

Even in England, Blackstone's definition of free speech was not universally accepted. Opposition writers (so-called because they opposed the group in power) emphasized that freedom of speech was a check on the power of tyrants. The opposition writers found a ready audience in the New World, where their theories helped provide the intellectual framework for the American Revolution. In the colonies, efforts to repress dissent were less frequent than in England. Probably the most notable was the Zenger trial. The governor of New York, whom Zenger had criticized, charged him with seditious libel. Contrary to existing English practice, his lawyers argued that he had a right to have the jury determine the truth of his remarks. One of his lawyers

---

[2]   For background on this history, see Leonard Levy's books, *Legacy of Suppression: Freedom of Speech and Press in Early American History* (1960) and *Emergence of a Free Press* (1985), along with William Van Alstyne's review of the latter in 99 Harv. L. Rev. 1089 (1986).

proclaimed the right "publicly to remonstrate the abuse of power in the strongest terms, to put their neighbors upon their guard against the craft of open violence of men in authority." The jury disobeyed its instructions from the judge and acquitted Zenger, to the accompaniment of loud cheers from the audience.

Unfortunately, the incomplete materials concerning the legislative history of the amendment shed little light about just what was meant by freedom of speech and of the press. The upshot is that the modern Supreme Court's interpretations of the First Amendment have drawn from this history, but the Court has rarely found decisive historical evidence on the issues before it. Instead, it has been guided largely by its interpretation of the First Amendment's purposes, with some deference to historical practices such as long-established limitations on obscenity and slander.

Before we begin any serious doctrinal exploration, it is important to consider the fundamental issues of why speech receives special constitutional protection and to what degree other values should be sacrificed in the name of free speech. The following two cases raise those issues. We will then take a look at the content neutrality rule that has become the cornerstone of current doctrine.

TEXAS V. JOHNSON
491 U.S. 397, 109 S.Ct. 2533, 105 L.Ed.2d 342 (1989)

JUSTICE BRENNAN delivered the opinion of the Court.

After publicly burning an American flag [near the Republican National Convention] as a means of political protest, Gregory Lee Johnson was convicted of desecrating a flag in violation of Texas law.[3] This case presents the question whether his conviction is consistent with the First Amendment. We hold that it is not. * * *

Texas claims that its interest in preventing breaches of the peace justifies Johnson's conviction for flag desecration. However, no disturbance of the peace actually occurred or threatened to occur because of Johnson's burning of the flag. * * * The only evidence offered by the State at trial to show the reaction to Johnson's actions was the testimony of several persons who had been seriously offended by the flag-burning.

The State's position, therefore, amounts to a claim that an audience that takes serious offense at particular expression is necessarily likely to

---

[3] *Editors' note*: The Texas statute, entitled "Desecration of Venerated Object," provided:

(a) A person commits an offense if he intentionally or knowingly desecrates . . . a state or national flag.

(b) For purposes of this section, "desecrate" means deface, damage, or otherwise physically mistreat in a way that the actor knows will seriously offend one or more persons likely to observe or discover his action.

(c) An offense under this section is a Class A misdemeanor.

disturb the peace and that the expression may be prohibited on this basis. Our precedents do not countenance such a presumption. On the contrary, they recognize that a principal "function of free speech under our system of government is to invite dispute. It may indeed best serve its high purpose when it induces a condition of unrest, creates dissatisfaction with conditions as they are, or even stirs people to anger." It would be odd indeed to conclude *both* that "if it is the speaker's opinion that gives offense, that consequence is a reason for according it constitutional protection," *and* that the Government may ban the expression of certain disagreeable ideas on the unsupported presumption that their very disagreeableness will provoke violence. * * *

Texas' focus on the precise nature of Johnson's expression, moreover, misses the point of our prior decisions: their enduring lesson, that the Government may not prohibit expression simply because it disagrees with its message, is not dependent on the particular mode in which one chooses to express an idea. If we were to hold that a State may forbid flag-burning wherever it is likely to endanger the flag's symbolic role, but allow it wherever burning a flag promotes that role—as where, for example, a person ceremoniously burns a dirty flag—we would be saying that when it comes to impairing the flag's physical integrity, the flag itself may be used as a symbol—as a substitute for the written or spoken word or a "short cut from mind to mind"—only in one direction. We would be permitting a State to "prescribe what shall be orthodox" by saying that one may burn the flag to convey one's attitude toward it and its referents only if one does not endanger the flag's representation of nationhood and national unity.

[The concurring opinion of **JUSTICE KENNEDY** is omitted.]

CHIEF JUSTICE REHNQUIST, with whom **JUSTICE WHITE** and **JUSTICE O'CONNOR** join, dissenting.

The Court decides that the American flag is just another symbol, about which not only most opinions pro and con be tolerated, but for which the most minimal public respect may not be enjoined. The government may conscript men into the Armed Forces where they must fight and perhaps die for the flag, but the government may not prohibit the public burning of the banner under which they fight. I would uphold the Texas statute as applied in this case.

[**JUSTICE STEVENS'** dissenting opinion is omitted.]

R.A.V. v. CITY OF ST. PAUL
505 U.S. 377, 112 S.Ct. 2538, 120 L.Ed.2d 305 (1992)

JUSTICE SCALIA delivered the opinion of the Court.

In the predawn hours of June 21, 1990, petitioner and several other teenagers allegedly assembled a crudely-made cross by taping together broken chair legs. They then allegedly burned the cross inside the fenced yard of a black family that lived across the street from the house where petitioner was staying. Although this conduct could have been punished under any of a number of laws, one of the two provisions under which respondent city of St. Paul chose to charge petitioner (then a juvenile) was the St. Paul Bias-Motivated Crime Ordinance, which provides:

> Whoever places on public or private property a symbol, object, appellation, characterization or graffiti, including, but not limited to, a burning cross or Nazi swastika, which one knows or has reasonable grounds to know arouses anger, alarm or resentment in others on the basis of race, color, creed, religion or gender commits disorderly conduct and shall be guilty of a misdemeanor.

* * *The First Amendment generally prevents government from proscribing speech, or even expressive conduct because of disapproval of the ideas expressed. Content-based regulations are presumptively invalid. From 1791 to the present, however, our society, like other free but civilized societies, has permitted restrictions upon the content of speech in a few limited areas, which are "of such slight social value as a step to truth that any benefit that may be derived from them is clearly outweighed by the social interest in order and morality." We have recognized that "the freedom of speech" referred to by the First Amendment does not include a freedom to disregard these traditional limitations. [Editors' note: These exceptions include defamation, obscenity, and fighting words. According to the "fighting words" doctrine of *Chaplinsky v. New Hampshire*, 315 U.S. 568 (1942), the First Amendment does not protect personal insults against the audience that are likely to cause retaliation.] * * *

In other words, the exclusion of "fighting words" from the scope of the First Amendment simply means that, for purposes of that Amendment, the unprotected features of the words are, despite their verbal character, essentially a "nonspeech" element of communication. Fighting words are thus analogous to a noisy sound truck: Each is, as Justice Frankfurter recognized, a "mode of speech," both can be used to convey an idea; but neither has, in and of itself, a claim upon the First Amendment. As with the sound truck, however, so also with fighting words: The government may not regulate use based on hostility—or favoritism—towards the underlying message expressed. * * *

Even the prohibition against content discrimination that we assert the First Amendment requires is not absolute. It applies differently in the context of proscribable speech than in the area of fully protected speech. * * *

When the basis for the content discrimination consists entirely of the very reason the entire class of speech at issue is proscribable, no significant danger of idea or viewpoint discrimination exists. Such a reason, having been adjudged neutral enough to support exclusion of the entire class of speech from First Amendment protection, is also neutral enough to form the basis of distinction within the class. To illustrate: A State might choose to prohibit only that obscenity which is the most patently offensive *in its prurience*—*i.e.*, that which involves the most lascivious displays of sexual activity. But it may not prohibit, for example, only that obscenity which includes offensive *political* messages. * * *

Another valid basis for according differential treatment to even a content-defined subclass of proscribable speech is that the subclass happens to be associated with particular "secondary effects" of the speech, so that the regulation is "*justified* without reference to the content." *Renton v. Playtime Theatres, Inc.* [this chapter, § 3A]. A State could, for example, permit all obscene live performances except those involving minors. * * * Thus, for example, sexually derogatory "fighting words," among other words, may produce a violation of Title VII's general prohibition against sexual discrimination in employment practices. Where the government does not target conduct on the basis of its expressive content, acts are not shielded from regulation merely because they express a discriminatory idea or philosophy.

These bases for distinction refute the proposition that the selectivity of the restriction is "even arguably 'conditioned upon the sovereign's agreement with what a speaker may intend to say.'" There may be other such bases as well. Indeed, to validate such selectivity (where totally proscribable speech is at issue) it may not even be necessary to identify any particular "neutral" basis, so long as the nature of the content discrimination is such that there is no realistic possibility that official suppression of ideas is afoot. * * *

Applying these principles to the St. Paul ordinance, we conclude that, even as narrowly construed by the Minnesota Supreme Court, the ordinance is facially unconstitutional. Although the phrase in the ordinance, "arouses anger, alarm or resentment in others," has been limited by the Minnesota Supreme Court's construction to reach only those symbols or displays that amount to "fighting words," the remaining, unmodified terms make clear that the ordinance applies only to "fighting words" that insult, or provoke violence, "on the basis of race, color, creed, religion or gender." Displays containing abusive invective, no matter how vicious or severe, are permissible unless they are addressed to one of the specified disfavored topics. Those who wish to use "fighting words" in connection with other ideas—to express hostility, for example, on the basis of political affiliation, union membership, or homosexuality—are not covered. The First Amendment does not permit St. Paul to impose special prohibitions on those speakers who express views on disfavored subjects.

In its practical operation, moreover, the ordinance goes even beyond mere content discrimination, to actual viewpoint discrimination. Displays containing some words—odious racial epithets, for example—would be prohibited to proponents of all views. But "fighting words" that do not themselves invoke race, color, creed, religion, or gender—aspersions upon a person's mother, for example—would seemingly be usable *ad libitum* in the placards of those arguing *in favor* of racial, color, etc. tolerance and equality, but could not be used by that speaker's opponents. One could hold up a sign saying, for example, that all "anti-Catholic bigots" are misbegotten; but not that all "papists" are, for that would insult and provoke violence "on the basis of religion." St. Paul has no such authority to license one side of a debate to fight freestyle, while requiring the other to follow Marquis of Queensbury Rules.

JUSTICE WHITE, with whom **JUSTICE BLACKMUN** and **JUSTICE O'CONNOR** join, and with whom **JUSTICE STEVENS** joins [in part], concurring in the judgment.

The majority's observation that fighting words are "quite expressive indeed" is no answer. Fighting words are not a means of exchanging views, rallying supporters, or registering a protest; they are directed against individuals to provoke violence or to inflict injury. Therefore, a ban on all fighting words or on a subset of the fighting words category would restrict only the social evil of hate speech, without creating the danger of driving viewpoints from the marketplace. [Although Justice White disagreed with the Court's reasoning, he agreed that the ordinance was invalid because it was "overbroad." The overbreadth doctrine is discussed later in this chapter.]

[**JUSTICE BLACKMUN**'s opinion concurring in the judgment is omitted.]

JUSTICE STEVENS, with whom **JUSTICE WHITE** and **JUSTICE BLACKMUN** join as to Part I, concurring in the judgment.

Just as Congress may determine that threats against the President entail more severe consequences than other threats, so St. Paul's City Council may determine that threats based on the target's race, religion, or gender cause more severe harm to both the target and to society than other threats. This latter judgment—that harms caused by racial, religious, and gender-based invective are qualitatively different from that caused by other fighting words—seems to me eminently reasonable and realistic.

NOTES ON JOHNSON AND R.A.V.

1.   *Dissenting Speech.* Flag burning, almost by definition, is not a form of mainstream expression. It derives its emotional punch from the very fact that the larger culture invests meaning in the flag. For some groups, such as veterans, this use of a venerated symbol may seem assaultive. Why is the Court

unwilling to allow Congress to regulate this means of expression? Should it matter if this kind of expression is used by dissident groups to assault majority values rather than being used by dominant groups against marginalized ones?

2.   *The Content Distinction.* Both the *Johnson* and *R.A.V.* stress that particular types of communication have been singled out for regulation because of their content. Suppose the defendants in these two cases had been prosecuted for starting an outdoor fire without a permit. Should enforcement of such laws against speakers be subject to anything more than the rationality test?

3.   *Why Do We Protect Speech?* Would society be the poorer if it were illegal to burn flags or crosses? Why do we bother protecting speech that offends what many consider to be basic national values?

NOTES ON FIRST AMENDMENT VALUES

1.   *First Amendment Values.* There is a large academic literature on the overall values served by the First Amendment. The following values are most frequently invoked. How well do they hold up? Do the flag-burning and cross-burning cases subserve the values that hold up?

(a)   *The "marketplace of ideas" and the search for truth.* Truth cannot be decided by the fiat of a government authority, but only by a free and open debate. From the competition of ideas, truth will emerge. This is the teaching of John Stuart Mill, *On Liberty* (1859), and is important to both the decisions we have reproduced. But how do burning a cross on someone's lawn or burning a flag contribute to free and open debate, or to the search for truth?

(b)   *Systemic political values.* If We the People are to govern, they must first be informed. Hence, the channels of communication about political and social issues must be unimpaired. This is the teaching of Alexander Meiklejohn, *Free Speech and Its Relation to Self-Government* (1948), who analogized the First Amendment's protection of informative public speech to the free flow of debate in a town meeting. (Is this a realistic vision?) Other systemic political values have been argued as a basis for privileging the First Amendment. For example, human beings have a tendency to be intolerant of people who are different from themselves or who espouse unfamiliar ideas. By carving out arenas where society restrains itself from suppressing not only disagreement but offensive behavior, the First Amendment encourages our polity to consider tolerance as a norm that might be fruitful elsewhere.[4] The cluster of values relating broadly to political life can be combined under the rubric of participatory democracy. See Robert C. Post, *Participatory Democracy and Free Speech*, 97 Va. L. Rev. 477 (2011); James Weinstein, *Participatory Democracy as the Basis of American Free Speech Doctrine: A Reply*, 97 Va. L. Rev. 633 (2011).

---

[4]   This is the teaching of Lee Bollinger, *The Tolerant Society: Freedom of Speech and Extremist Speech in America* (1986), criticized in David Strauss, *Why Be Tolerant?*, 53 U. Chi. L. Rev. 1485 (1986).

(c) *Individualism and autonomy values.* Speech is a primary method for people to express their individuality and personhood. A libertarian would argue that the state must leave the individual alone when she is engaged in speech, unless there is compelling evidence of harm to the autonomy of others.[5] Others might argue that the state should be encouraging individualism, anti-authoritarianism, and nonconformity.[6] Does either formulation support the right of R.A.V. to burn a cross in the middle of the night? What about Johnson's right to burn a stolen flag?

2. *"Slippery Slopes," Absolutism, and Balancing.* While "slippery slope" arguments are found in other areas of the law, they are particularly prevalent in First Amendment cases, as *Johnson* illustrates. Part of the debate in *Johnson* involves the feasibility of treating flag burning differently from other forms of conduct. Justice Brennan argues that allowing a ban on flag burning will open the door to other forms of repression; Chief Justice Rehnquist believes that flag burning can be properly singled out for special treatment. (Note that Justice Scalia sided with Justice Brennan in *Johnson*, perhaps because he is a strong believer in "bright line" rules.) At mid-century, the major debate was between First Amendment "absolutists" and "balancers." Although the rhetoric was somewhat different, the methodological issue was similar: To what extent should speech be protected by broad categorical rules as opposed to more finely tuned, fact-sensitive standards?

The argument for broad categorical rules is based on the dynamics of censorship. It runs as follows: Once allowed to operate at all, censorship gains acceptability and will tend to expand. Because the application of fact-sensitive doctrines is unpredictable, self-censorship will silence even those who might ultimately win if their cases were litigated. Moreover, the First Amendment is most needed in times of public hysteria, when careful weighing of the facts is most difficult, and when judges will be under the most pressure to bend to popular fears. Even in normal times, First Amendment cases often will involve the most despised members of society, and judges will often be tempted to give way to their own prejudices. Only categorical rules can protect against the ultimate erosion of First Amendment protection.

The counter-argument is that no set of rules can be effective if we do not trust the judges who administer them. If we trust the judges, we ought to give them leeway to consider the full range of facts relevant to a particular case, rather than limiting them with oversimplistic rules. First Amendment cases

---

[5] See Edwin Baker, *Autonomy and Free Speech*, 27 Const. Comm. 251 (2011); Seanna Valentine Shiffrin, *A Thinker-Based Approach to Freedom of* Speech, 27 Const. Comm. 283 (2011); Martin Redish, *The Value of Free Speech*, 130 U. Pa. L. Rev. 591 (1982).

[6] See Steven Shiffrin, *The First Amendment, Democracy, and Romance* (1990). Later, Shiffrin stressed dissent as the core concern of the First Amendment. See Steven Shiffrin, *Dissent, Injustice, and the Meanings of America* (1999).

often involve conflicts between important social values, to which categorical rules simply cannot do justice.[7]

As applied to *Johnson*, which set of arguments is more convincing? Is it possible to give both viewpoints some credence, by using categorical rules in some areas and fact-sensitive balancing in others? In the *R.A.V.* situation, can we draw a workable line between cross-burning and other forms of "speech"?[8]

If the government steers away from speech having significant value, should it have a free hand in regulating? Maybe not, according to the following case.

United States v. Stevens

559 U.S. 460 (2010)

A federal statute banned any visual or auditory depiction "in which a living animal is intentionally maimed, mutilated, tortured, wounded, or killed," if that conduct violates federal or state law where the creation, sale, or possession takes place. Another clause exempted depictions with "serious religious, political, scientific, educational, journalistic, historical, or artistic value." In support of the statute, the government argued that "[w]hether a given category of speech enjoys First Amendment protection depends upon a categorical balancing of the value of the speech against its societal cost." In the course of invalidating the statute, **Chief Justice Roberts**'s opinion for the Court rejected this "highly manipulable balancing test" and seemingly limited the categories of unprotected speech to those "historically unprotected." The Court went to hold the statute overbroad but left open the question of whether a ban limited to "depictions of extreme animal cruelty" would be constitutional.

—————

What is the First Amendment value of movies depicting abuse of animals? If a type of speech causes more social harm than its value, why shouldn't society be able to regulate it? Is the only problem the "manipulability" of this standard? Would raising the burden of proof solve that problem?

As *R.A.V.* indicates, whether the government can punish speech depends not only whether the speech is "protected" by the First Amendment, but on type of regulation that the government is enforcing. *R.A.V.* invalidated a particular regulation applying to unprotected speech.

—————

[7] For discussions of these issues, see Frederick Schauer, *The Second-Best First Amendment*, 31 Wm. & Mary L. Rev. 1 (1989); Kathleen Sullivan, *Post-Liberal Judging: The Roles of Categorization and Balancing*, 63 U. Colo. L. Rev. 293 (1992).

[8] For a discussion of *R.A.V.* and the evolution of the categorical approach, see Keith Werhan, *The Liberalization of Freedom of Speech on a Conservative Court*, 80 Iowa L. Rev. 51 (1994).

Can some types of regulation be applied to punish expression that would otherwise be protected? Consider the following case.

United States v. O'Brien

391 U.S. 367 (1968)

One of the major issues in *Johnson* is the extent to which the Constitution protects "symbolic speech"—that is, the use of nonverbal methods of expression. *O'Brien*, which involved draft-card burning, is the leading case on this issue. In an opinion by **Chief Justice Warren**, the Court upheld O'Brien's conviction for burning his draft card at an anti-war rally, on the ground that the government had valid reasons for protecting draft cards that had nothing to do with O'Brien's message. It was clear from the legislative history, however, that Congress's motive was to target dissenters; nevertheless, in this pre-*Washington v. Davis* decision, the Court said that legislative motivation was irrelevant. In the course of the opinion, the Court laid down the following four-part test to be applied when " 'speech' and 'non-speech' elements are combined in the same course of conduct":

> [A] government regulation is sufficiently justified [1] if it is within the constitutional power of the Government; [2] if it furthers an important or substantial governmental interest; [3] if the governmental interest is unrelated to the suppression of free expression; [4] and if the incidental restriction on alleged First Amendment freedoms is no greater than is essential to the furtherance of that interest.

At the time, *O'Brien* was mostly considered to be a "symbolic speech" case, although its test has now been applied in many other contexts. *O'Brien* and subsequent cases distinguish sharply between content-based restrictions and content-neutral regulations.[9]

The distinction between content-neutral and content-based discrimination has become increasingly pivotal in First Amendment analysis. The Court refined the test for content neutrality in the following case.

Reed v. Town of Gilbert

135 S.Ct. 2218 (2015)

A town adopted a sign ordinance, which identified various categories of signs based on based on the type of information they convey, and then subjected each category to different restrictions. One of the categories was

---

[9]   For efforts to justify the distinction, see Elena Kagan, *Private Speech, Public Purpose: The Role of Governmental Motive in First Amendment Doctrine*, 63 U. Chi. L. Rev. 413 (1996); Geoffrey Stone, *Content Regulation and the First Amendment*, 25 Wm. & Mary L. Rev. 189 (1983). For the contrary view, see Martin Redish, *The Content Distinction in First Amendment Analysis*, 34 Stan. L. Rev. 113 (1981). A more recent contribution to the debate is Leslie Kendrick, *Content Discrimination Revisited*, 98 Va. L. Rev. 231 (2012) (defending the content distinction against charges of incoherence).

"Temporary Directional Signs Relating to a Qualifying Event," defined as signs directing the public to a meeting of a nonprofit group. The ordinance imposed more stringent restrictions on these signs than it does on signs conveying other messages. Signs with ideological or political messages were treated most favorably.

In an opinion by **Justice Thomas**, the court held that these provisions were content-based regulations of speech that could not survive strict scrutiny. He defined content regulation as follows:

> Government regulation of speech is content based if a law applies to particular speech because of the topic discussed or the idea or message expressed. This commonsense meaning of the phrase "content based" requires a court to consider whether a regulation of speech "on its face" draws distinctions based on the message a speaker conveys. Some facial distinctions based on a message are obvious, defining regulated speech by particular subject matter, and others are more subtle, defining regulated speech by its function or purpose. Both are distinctions drawn based on the message a speaker conveys, and, therefore, are subject to strict scrutiny.

Thomas also identified another prong of content neutrality:

> Our precedents have also recognized a separate and additional category of laws that, though facially content neutral, will be considered content-based regulations of speech: laws that cannot be " 'justified without reference to the content of the regulated speech,' " or that were adopted by the government "because of disagreement with the message [the speech] conveys." Those laws, like those that are content based on their face, must also satisfy strict scrutiny.

Applying this test, he found the sign ordinance to be content-based on its face because the categories were defined on the basis of communicative content. Use of these categories was not justified by the city's compelling interesting in traffic safety.

NOTES ON REED

1. *Defining Content Neutrality.* The majority defines content neutrality very narrowly. To be content neutral, a law must neither (a) draw any distinctions based on communicative content, nor (b) have a purpose related to communicative content. Any other regulation of private speech is subject to strict scrutiny. Absent a compelling interest, if the state allows any category of messages, it must allow all categories of messages equally, even if there seems to be a commonsense justification for treating some messages (such as address signs) differently.

2. *Why Not Allow Commonsense Content Distinctions?* Consider a law that allows owners to illuminate their house numbers but not other kinds of signs. Why should that be subject to strict scrutiny? Is the reason that there might be some discriminatory intent behind theses seemingly innocuous

distinctions that would be difficult to establish more directly? (Perhaps the city wanted to prevent illumination of some other particular kind of sign in drawing this distinction?) Or is the reason that cities are likely to want to allow addresses to be illuminated and that an anti-discrimination rule will then provide an opportunity for other signs to be illuminated, increasing the possibilities for communication? (Notice that these reasons are quite different: one is an effort to smoke out hidden discrimination while the other one is an effort to open up broader channels of communication.) Or is the reason that there is something intrinsically unjust about distinctions based on communicative message, no matter how trivial they may seem? Or, finally, do we not trust judges to decide when a particular type of content distinction poses no threat to public discourse? Lower courts do not seem to have applied *Reed* broadly, perhaps because it would subject so many apparently innocuous laws to strict scrutiny. See Note, *Free Speech Doctrine After Reed v. Town of Gilbert*, 129 Harv. L. Rev. 1981 (2017).

The Supreme Court has continued to make aggressive use of the doctrine of content neutrality, brushing aside arguable exceptions. Consider the following case.

NATIONAL INSTITUTE OF FAMILY AND LIFE ADVOCATES [NIFLA] V. BECERRA
___ U.S. ___, 138 S.Ct. 2361, 201 L.Ed.2d 835 (2018)

JUSTICE THOMAS delivered the opinion of the Court.

The California Reproductive Freedom, Accountability, Comprehensive Care, and Transparency Act (FACT Act) requires clinics that primarily serve pregnant women to provide certain notices. Cal. Health & Safety Code Ann. § 123470 et seq. (West 2018). Licensed clinics must notify women that California provides free or low-cost services, including abortions, and give them a phone number to call. Unlicensed clinics must notify women that California has not licensed the clinics to provide medical services. The question in this case is whether these notice requirements violate the First Amendment. We first address the licensed notice.[2]

The licensed notice is a content-based regulation of speech. By compelling individuals to speak a particular message, such notices "alte[r] the content of [their] speech." Here, for example, licensed clinics must provide a government-drafted script about the availability of state-sponsored services, as well as contact information for how to obtain them. One of those services is abortion—the very practice that petitioners are devoted to opposing. By requiring petitioners to inform women how they can obtain state-subsidized abortions—at the same time petitioners try to

---

[2] Petitioners raise serious concerns that both the licensed and unlicensed notices discriminate based on viewpoint. Because the notices are unconstitutional either way, as explained below, we need not reach that issue.

dissuade women from choosing that option—the licensed notice plainly "alters the content" of petitioners' speech.

Although the licensed notice is content based, the Ninth Circuit did not apply strict scrutiny because it concluded that the notice regulates "professional speech." Some Courts of Appeals have recognized "professional speech" as a separate category of speech that is subject to different rules. So defined, these courts except professional speech from the rule that content-based regulations of speech are subject to strict scrutiny.

But this Court has not recognized "professional speech" as a separate category of speech. Speech is not unprotected merely because it is uttered by "professionals." This Court has "been reluctant to mark off new categories of speech for diminished constitutional protection." This Court's precedents do not permit governments to impose content-based restrictions on speech without " 'persuasive evidence . . . of a long (if heretofore unrecognized) tradition' ": to that effect.

This Court's precedents do not recognize such a tradition for a category called "professional speech." This Court has afforded less protection for professional speech in two circumstances—neither of which turned on the fact that professionals were speaking. First, our precedents have applied more deferential review to some laws that require professionals to disclose factual, noncontroversial information in their "commercial speech." Second, under our precedents, States may regulate professional conduct, even though that conduct incidentally involves speech. But neither line of precedents is implicated here.

This Court's precedents have applied a lower level of scrutiny to laws that compel disclosures in certain contexts. In *Zauderer [v. Office of Disciplinary Counsel of Supreme Court of Ohio*, 471 U.S. 626, 651, 105 S.Ct. 2265, 85 L.Ed.2d 652 (1985)], for example, this Court upheld a rule requiring lawyers who advertised their services on a contingency-fee basis to disclose that clients might be required to pay some fees and costs. Noting that the disclosure requirement governed only "commercial advertising" and required the disclosure of "purely factual and uncontroversial information about the terms under which . . . services will be available," the Court explained that such requirements should be upheld unless they are "unjustified or unduly burdensome."

The *Zauderer* standard does not apply here. Most obviously, the licensed notice is not limited to "purely factual and uncontroversial information about the terms under which . . . services will be available." The notice in no way relates to the services that licensed clinics provide. Instead, it requires these clinics to disclose information about state-sponsored services—including abortion, anything but an "uncontroversial" topic. Accordingly, *Zauderer* has no application here.

In addition to disclosure requirements under *Zauderer*, this Court has upheld regulations of professional conduct that incidentally burden speech. "[T]he First Amendment does not prevent restrictions directed at commerce or conduct from imposing incidental burdens on speech," and professionals are no exception to this rule. Longstanding torts for professional malpractice, for example, "fall within the traditional purview of state regulation of professional conduct." While drawing the line between speech and conduct can be difficult, this Court's precedents have long drawn it.

In *Planned Parenthood of Southeastern Pa. v. Casey*, for example, this Court upheld a law requiring physicians to obtain informed consent before they could perform an abortion. Pennsylvania law required physicians to inform their patients of "the nature of the procedure, the health risks of the abortion and childbirth, and the 'probable gestational age of the unborn child.'" The law also required physicians to inform patients of the availability of printed materials from the State, which provided information about the child and various forms of assistance.

The joint opinion in *Casey* rejected a free-speech challenge to this informed-consent requirement. It described the Pennsylvania law as "a requirement that a doctor give a woman certain information as part of obtaining her consent to an abortion," which "for constitutional purposes, [was] no different from a requirement that a doctor give certain specific information about any medical procedure." The joint opinion explained that the law regulated speech only "as part of the practice of medicine, subject to reasonable licensing and regulation by the State." Indeed, the requirement that a doctor obtain informed consent to perform an operation is "firmly entrenched in American tort law."

The licensed notice at issue here is not an informed-consent requirement or any other regulation of professional conduct. The notice does not facilitate informed consent to a medical procedure. In fact, it is not tied to a procedure at all. It applies to all interactions between a covered facility and its clients, regardless of whether a medical procedure is ever sought, offered, or performed. If a covered facility does provide medical procedures, the notice provides no information about the risks or benefits of those procedures. Tellingly, many facilities that provide the exact same services as covered facilities—such as general practice clinics, see § 123471(a)—are not required to provide the licensed notice. The licensed notice regulates speech as speech. * * *

In sum, neither California nor the Ninth Circuit has identified a persuasive reason for treating professional speech as a unique category that is exempt from ordinary First Amendment principles. We do not foreclose the possibility that some such reason exists. We need not do so because the licensed notice cannot survive even intermediate scrutiny.

[The Court argued that the notice was a poor fit with its asserted goal of providing low-income women with information about state-sponsored services. Assuming that this is a substantial state interest, the licensed notice is not sufficiently drawn to achieve it, since it included only family planning and pregnancy-related services and excluded federal clinics. Moreover, California could achieve its goal in less intrusive ways, such as advertising about free medical services.]

We next address the unlicensed notice. The parties dispute whether the unlicensed notice is subject to deferential review under *Zauderer*. We need not decide whether the *Zauderer* standard applies to the unlicensed notice. Even under *Zauderer,* a disclosure requirement cannot be "unjustified or unduly burdensome." Our precedents require disclosures to remedy a harm that is "potentially real not purely hypothetical," and to extend "no broader than reasonably necessary." Otherwise, they risk "chilling" protected speech." Importantly, California has the burden to prove that the unlicensed notice is neither unjustified nor unduly burdensome. It has not met its burden. [The Court concluded that "California has not demonstrated any justification for the unlicensed notice that is more than "purely hypothetical." The state's only asserted justification was informing women when they are getting care from licensed professionals, but there was no evidence to show that women were unaware of that fact.]

The application of the unlicensed notice to advertisements demonstrates just how burdensome it is. The notice applies to all "print and digital advertising materials" by an unlicensed covered facility. These materials must include a government-drafted statement that "[t]his facility is not licensed as a medical facility by the State of California and has no licensed medical provider who provides or directly supervises the provision of services." * * * As California conceded at oral argument, a billboard for an unlicensed facility that says "Choose Life" would have to surround that two-word statement with a 29-word statement from the government, in as many as 13 different languages. In this way, the unlicensed notice drowns out the facility's own message. More likely, the "detail required" by the unlicensed notice "effectively rules out" the possibility of having such a billboard in the first place.

For all these reasons, the unlicensed notice does not satisfy Zauderer, assuming that standard applies. California has offered no justification that the notice plausibly furthers. It targets speakers, not speech, and imposes an unduly burdensome disclosure requirement that will chill their protected speech. Taking all these circumstances together, we conclude that the unlicensed notice is unjustified and unduly burdensome under Zauderer. We express no view on the legality of a similar disclosure requirement that is better supported or less burdensome.

[A concurring opinion by JUSTICE KENNEDY, joined by CHIEF JUSTICE ROBERTS and JUSTICES ALITO and GORSUCH, flagged the risk that the law was viewpoint based because it focused on anti-abortion groups.]

JUSTICE BREYER, joined by Justices GINSBURG, SOTOMAYOR, and KAGAN, dissenting.

Because much, perhaps most, human behavior takes place through speech and because much, perhaps most, law regulates that speech in terms of its content, the majority's approach at the least threatens considerable litigation over the constitutional validity of much, perhaps most, government regulation. Virtually every disclosure law could be considered "content based," for virtually every disclosure law requires individuals "to speak a particular message." Thus, the majority's view, if taken literally, could radically change prior law, perhaps placing much securities law or consumer protection law at constitutional risk, depending on how broadly its exceptions are interpreted. * * *

Precedent does not require a test such as the majority's. Rather, in saying the Act is not a longstanding health and safety law, the Court substitutes its own approach—without a defining standard—for an approach that was reasonably clear. Historically, the Court has been wary of claims that regulation of business activity, particularly health-related activity, violates the Constitution. Ever since this Court departed from the approach it set forth in *Lochner v. New York*, 198 U.S. 45, 25 S.Ct. 539, 49 L.Ed. 937 (1905), ordinary economic and social legislation has been thought to raise little constitutional concern. As Justice Brandeis wrote, typically this Court's function in such cases "is only to determine the reasonableness of the Legislature's belief in the existence of evils and in the effectiveness of the remedy provided." * * *

Even during the *Lochner* era, when this Court struck down numerous economic regulations concerning industry, this Court was careful to defer to state legislative judgments concerning the medical profession. The Court took the view that a State may condition the practice of medicine on any number of requirements, and physicians, in exchange for following those reasonable requirements, could receive a license to practice medicine from the State. Medical professionals do not, generally speaking, have a right to use the Constitution as a weapon allowing them rigorously to control the content of those reasonable conditions. In the name of the First Amendment, the majority today treads into territory where the pre-New Deal, as well as the post-New Deal, Court refused to go. * * *

* * *

Of course, one might take the majority's decision to mean that speech about abortion is special, that it involves in this case not only professional medical matters, but also views based on deeply held religious and moral beliefs about the nature of the practice. To that extent, arguably, the speech here is different from that at issue in *Zauderer*. But assuming that is so, the law's insistence upon treating like cases alike should lead us to reject the petitioners' arguments that I have discussed. This insistence, the need for evenhandedness, should prove particularly weighty in a case involving abortion rights. * * * For this reason too a Constitution that allows States to insist that medical providers tell women about the possibility of adoption should also allow States similarly to insist that medical providers tell women about the possibility of abortion.

NOTES ON NIFLA V. BECARRA

1. *Is the Majority Content Neutral?* The dissent accuses the majority of favoring anti-abortion requirements over those designed to increase access to abortions. Suppose the state requirement had been set up differently, so as to require all medical personnel offering pregnancy-related services to inform patients at the time of the service about the availability of abortion. Would such a requirement be valid under the majority's approach?

2. *A Class of Perspectives.* Much of First Amendment doctrine embodies the assumption that people will react rationally to any information they receive. But cognitive psychologists and behavioral economists have increasingly documented ways in which this rationality assumption is unjustified. Regulators, too, have increasingly tried to address problems through regulating the form and content of information, along with the way individual decision are framed. See Richard H. Thaler and Case R. Sunstein, *Nudge: Improving Decisions About Health, Wealth, and Happiness* (rev. ed. 2009). Thus, developments in regulation and social policy seem to be on a collision force with trends in First Amendment doctrine. It remains to see how this potential conflict will be resolved.

3. Lochner *and the First Amendment.* First Amendment doctrine requires more rigorous scrutiny than is typically applied to economic regulations today. But as the scope of First Amendment coverage expands, there is correspondingly less room for states to engage in regulation of subjects that they traditionally regulated. For scholarly arguments framing expanded speech protections for businesses as the Roberts Court's "new *Lochner*," see, e.g., Jeremy Kessler, *The Early Years for First Amendment Lochnerism,* 116 Colum. L. Rev. 1915 (2016); Robert Post and Amanda Shanor, *Adam Smith's First Amendment,* 128 Harv. L. Rev. F. 165 (2015); Amanda Shanor, *The New Lochner,* 2016 Wis. L. Rev. 133 (2016).

PROBLEM 6-1

In 2012, California passed SB 1172, a law that forbids any licensed health care provider from engaging in "sexual orientation change efforts" with a person under the age of 18. This term is defined to include any effort by "mental health providers" that seeks to change an individual's sexual orientation, "including efforts to change behaviors or gender expressions, or to eliminate or reduce sexual or romantic attractions or feelings toward individuals of the same sex." The law, which contains extensive legislative findings about problems with such efforts at changing sexual orientation, applies to mental health providers licensed by the state such as physicians or clinical psychologists.

In *Pickup v. Brown*, 740 F.3d 1208 (9th Cir. 2014), the court upheld the statute on the theory that it "regulates only treatment, while leaving mental health providers free to discuss and recommend" sexual orientation change efforts, the court, concluded that any effect it might have on free speech interests was merely incidental. Hence, the court upheld the law under the rational basis test.

How would you analyze this issue after *NIFLA*? Is it distinguishable from the abortion-related disclosures struck down in *NIFLA*? What standard of review applies? And more broadly, to what extent can the government regulate various forms of professional advice and communication?

SECTION 2. REGULATION OF POLITICAL EXPRESSION

It is commonly agreed that political speech is at the "core" of the First Amendment. Indeed, some theorists would provide protection only to political speech. In this section, we consider the circumstances under which such speech is protected and those in which, despite its core status, it can nevertheless be regulated. We begin by reviewing some history, including some classical opinions that are universally classed as part of the First Amendment canon.

A. ILLEGAL ADVOCACY

Historically, the most stringent controls on speech have been imposed during periods of national emergency to prevent subversion. For an early example, the Sedition Act of 1798, 1 Stat. 596, criminalized "false, scandalous, and malicious writing or writings against the government of the United States," as well as against Congress and the President, "with intent to defame [them]; or to bring them [into] contempt or disrepute." Although the Supreme Court never adjudicated the constitutionality of the Act, several Justices applied it sitting on circuit, and there is some reason to believe that it would have been upheld.[10]

Between the Sedition Act of 1798 and the Espionage Act of 1917, the federal and state governments continued to repress speech, especially in periods of emergency. For example, southern states suppressed abolitionist

---

[10] See generally Leonard Levy, *Legacy of Suppression* (1960); Walter Berns, *Freedom of the Press and the Alien and Sedition Laws: A Reappraisal*, 1970 Sup. Ct. Rev. 109; Philip Hamburger, *The Development of the Law of Seditious Libel and the Control of the Press*, 37 Stan. L. Rev. 661 (1985).

literature and speech before the Civil War, both North and South stifled dissent during the Civil War, the Reconstruction as well as the Jim Crow South suppressed opposition political activity, and courts as well as executive officers brutally suppressed workers and labor leaders seeking to better their lot. The nineteenth century was in fact filled with repression of speech, and much of it was litigated and written about. See David Rabban, *The First Amendment in Its Forgotten Years* (1997). Nonetheless, the First Amendment did not "come into its own" until World War I. Consider the following case, decided almost a century ago.

The Twentieth Century development of First Amendment doctrine remains important today for several reasons. First, it is important to realize that modern doctrine has evolved through a common law process. Originalists like Justice Scalia have freely admitted that it is not directly traceable to the Amendment's original meaning. Second, these decisions establish both a "canon" (consisting of the rousing dissents of Justices Holmes and Brandeis) and an "anti-canon" of results to be avoided, in the form of the anti-subversive statutes that were upheld in those days. And third, even though some of these cases involve what now seems like extraordinary suppression of dissent, the United States did have a functioning democracy and raucous public debate.

Masses Publishing Co. v. Patten

244 Fed. 535 (S.D.N.Y. 1917), *rev'd*, 246 Fed. 24 (2d Cir. 1917)

The case arose when the post office refused to mail a magazine called "The Masses" on the ground that its contents would hamper the war effort. The Espionage Act of 1917 barred publications from the mail if they made false statements with the intent of hindering the war effort, willfully caused military insubordination, or obstructed military recruiting. **Judge Learned Hand** construed the statute narrowly to criminalize only speech or writings that on their face constituted a "direct incitement to violent resistance" to the law. For example, he had the following to say about the provision regarding causing insubordination:

> [The government's position] is that to arouse discontent and disaffection among the people with the prosecution of the war and with the draft tends to promote a mutinous and insubordinate temper among the troops. This, too, is true; men who become satisfied that they are engaged in an enterprise dictated by the unconscionable selfishness of the rich, and effectuated by a tyrannous disregard for the will of those who must suffer and die, will be more prone to insubordination than those who have faith in the cause and acquiesce in the means. Yet to interpret the word "cause" so broadly would * * * involve necessarily as a consequence the suppression of all hostile criticism, and of all opinion except what encouraged and supported the existing policies, or which fell within the range of temperate

argument. It would contradict the normal assumption of democratic government that the suppression of hostile criticism does not turn upon the justice of its substance or the decency and propriety of its temper. Assuming that the power to repress such opinion may rest in Congress in the throes of a struggle for the very existence of the state, its exercise is so contrary to the use and wont of our people that only the clearest expression of such a power justified the conclusion that it was intended.

Similarly, with regard to the draft-resistance provision, Hand distinguished between language that might "arouse a seditious disposition," which was not forbidden as he interpreted the law, and "language that directly advocated resistance to the draft," which was illegal. As we will see below, the Supreme Court did not adopt Hand's statutory analysis, though his analysis did ultimately influence later opinions such as *Brandenburg v. Ohio* (this chapter, *infra*).[11]

Schenck v. United States

249 U.S. 47 (1919)

Schenck had mailed a leaflet to draft-age men arguing that the draft violated the Thirteenth Amendment. **Justice Holmes**, for the Court, first concluded that the leaflet Schenck distributed "would not have been sent unless it had been intended to have some effect, and we do not see what effect it could be expected to have upon persons subject to the draft except to influence them to obstruct the carrying of it out." Then Holmes announced the "clear and present danger test" and found it satisfied on the facts:

> We admit that in many places and in ordinary times the defendants in saying all that was said in the circular would have been within their constitutional rights. But the character of every act depends upon the circumstances in which it is done. The most stringent protection of free speech would not protect a man in falsely shouting fire in a theatre and causing a panic. * * * The question in every case is whether the words used are used in such circumstances and are of such a nature as to create a clear and present danger that they will bring about the substantive evils that Congress has a right to prevent. It is a question of proximity and degree. When a nation is at war many things that might be said in time of peace are such a hindrance to its effort that their utterance will not be endured so long as men fight, and that no Court could regard them as protected by any constitutional right. It seems to be admitted that if an actual obstruction of the recruiting service were proved, liability for words that produced that effect might be enforced. [The Espionage Act] punishes conspiracies to obstruct as well as actual obstruction. If the

---

[11] See Gerald Gunther, *Learned Hand and the Origins of Modern First Amendment Doctrine: Some Fragments of History*, 27 Stan. L. Rev. 719 (1975).

act (speaking, or circulating a paper), its tendency and the intent with which it is done are the same, we perceive no ground for saying that success alone warrants making the act a [crime].

Justice Holmes deployed the clear and present danger test in *Schenck* to justify a restriction on speech. A third case, also decided in 1919, marked a turning point in First Amendment law. While the majority continued to brush aside First Amendment concerns, Justice Holmes' dissent announced a bold new perspective on freedom of speech, using the same test to expand protection of speech.

ABRAMS V. UNITED STATES
250 U.S. 616, 40 S.Ct. 17, 63 L.Ed. 1173 (1919)

JUSTICE CLARKE delivered the opinion of the Court.

[The defendants were charged with violating the 1917 Espionage Act by using language that was "disloyal, scurrilous and abusive . . . about the form of Government of the United States," "intended to bring the form of Government of the United States into contempt, scorn, contumely and disrepute"; and "intended to incite, provoke and encourage resistance to the United States in said war." The two leaflets in question attacked the Allied invasion of Russia, which was intended to quash the Bolsheviks and bring Russia back into World War I on the Allies' side. One leaflet accused President Wilson of "cowardly silence" about the intervention in Russia. The other pamphlet warned workers that munitions might be used not to fight the Germans but to fight the Bolsheviks. Neither pamphlet supported the Germans, and the first one said "[w]e hate and despise German militarism. . . ."]

On the record thus described it is argued, somewhat faintly, that the acts charged against the defendants were not unlawful because within the protection of that freedom of speech and of the press which is guaranteed by the First Amendment to the Constitution of the United States, and that the entire Espionage Act is unconstitutional because in conflict with that Amendment.

This contention is sufficiently discussed and is definitely negatived in [*Schenck*] and in *Frohwerk v. United States*, 249 U.S. 204 [1919].[12] * * *

It will not do to say, as is now argued, that the only intent of these defendants was to prevent injury to the Russian cause. Men must be held to have intended, and to be accountable for, the effects which their acts were likely to produce. Even if their primary purpose and intent was to aid

---

[12] *Editors' note*: Justice Holmes wrote for the Court in *Frohwerk*, upholding the conviction of publishers of a German-language newspaper for criticizing the sending of troops to France and deploring the pathetic condition of the drafted American soldier. See also *Debs v. United States*, 249 U.S. 211 (1919) (upholding Debs' conviction for obstructing the recruitment of American soldiers).

the cause of the Russian Revolution, the plan of action which they adopted necessarily involved, before it could be realized, defeat of the war program of the United States, for the obvious effect of this appeal, if it should become effective, as they hoped it might, would be to persuade persons of character such as those whom they regarded themselves as addressing, not to aid government loans and not to work in ammunition factories, where their work would produce "bullets, bayonets, cannon" and other munitions of war, the use of which would cause the "murder" of Germans and Russians.

JUSTICE HOLMES, dissenting.

I never have seen any reason to doubt that the questions of law that alone were before this Court in the cases of *Schenck*, *Frohwerk* and *Debs*, 249 U.S. 47, 204, 211, were rightly decided. I do not doubt for a moment that by the same reasoning that would justify punishing persuasion to murder, the United States constitutionally may punish speech that produces or is intended to produce a clear and imminent danger that it will bring about forthwith certain substantive evils that the United States constitutionally may seek to prevent. The power undoubtedly is greater in time of war than in time of peace because war opens dangers that do not exist at other times.

But as against dangers peculiar to war, as against others, the principle of the right to free speech is always the same. It is only the present danger of immediate evil or an intent to bring it about that warrants Congress in setting a limit to the expression of opinion where private rights are not concerned. Congress certainly cannot forbid all effort to change the mind of the country. Now nobody can suppose that the surreptitious publishing of a silly leaflet by an unknown man, without more, would present any immediate danger that its opinions would hinder the success of the government arms or have any appreciable tendency to do so. Publishing those opinions for the very purpose of obstructing however, might indicate a greater danger and at any rate would have the quality of an attempt. So I assume that the second leaflet if published for the purposes alleged in the fourth count might be punishable. But it seems pretty clear to me that nothing less than that would bring these papers within the scope of this law. An actual intent in the sense that I have explained is necessary to constitute an attempt, where a further act of the same individual is required to complete the substantive crime * * *. It is necessary where the success of the attempt depends upon others because if that intent is not present the actor's aim may be accomplished without bringing about the evils sought to be checked. An intent to prevent interference with the revolution in Russia might have been satisfied without any hindrance to carrying on the war in which we were engaged. * * *

Persecution for the expression of opinions seems to me perfectly logical. If you have no doubt of your premises or your power and want a certain result with all your heart you naturally express your wishes in law and sweep away all opposition. To allow opposition by speech seems to indicate that you think the speech impotent, as when a man says that he has squared the circle, or that you do not care whole-heartedly for the result, or that you doubt either your power or your premises. But when men have realized that time has upset many fighting faiths, they may come to believe even more than they believe the very foundations of their own conduct that the ultimate good desired is better reached by free trade in ideas—that the best test of truth is the power of the thought to get itself accepted in the competition of the market, and that truth is the only ground upon which their wishes safely can be carried out. That at any rate is the theory of our Constitution. It is an experiment, as all life is an experiment. Every year if not every day we have to wager our salvation upon some prophecy based upon imperfect knowledge. While that experiment is part of our system I think that we should be eternally vigilant against attempts to check the expression of opinions that we loathe and believe to be fraught with death, unless they so imminently threaten immediate interference with the lawful and pressing purposes of the law that an immediate check is required to save the country. I wholly disagree with the argument of the Government that the First Amendment left the common law as to seditious libel in force. History seems to me against the notion. I had conceived that the United States through many years had shown its repentance for the Sedition Act of 1798, by repaying fines that it imposed. Only the emergency that makes it immediately dangerous to leave the correction of evil counsels to time warrants making any exception to the sweeping command, "Congress shall make no law . . . abridging the freedom of speech." Of course I am speaking only of expressions of opinion and exhortations, which were all that were uttered here, but I regret that I cannot put into more impressive words my belief that in their conviction upon this indictment the defendants were deprived of their rights under the Constitution of the United States.

JUSTICE BRANDEIS concurs with the foregoing opinion.

A NOTE ON SUBVERSIVE SPEECH FROM 1920–1960

Note the transformation of Justice Holmes' views from *Schenck, Frohwerk,* and *Debs,* where he wrote opinions for the Court upholding convictions that don't seem much different from the majority opinion in *Abrams,* where he dissented. Essentially, Holmes moved toward the libertarian approach urged by Professor Zechariah Chafee, who believed it important to carve out an arena of protected speech.[13] Holmes' clear and

---

[13] The story of the change in Holmes' thinking is told in David Bogen, *The Free Speech Metamorphosis of Mr. Justice Holmes,* 11 Hofstra L. Rev. 97 (1982), and in David Rabban, *The Emergence of Modern First Amendment Doctrine,* 50 U. Chi. L. Rev. 1205 (1983). See also Fred Ragan, *Justice Oliver Wendell Holmes, Jr., Zechariah Chafee, Jr., and the Clear and Present Danger Test for Free Speech: The First Year, 1919,* 58 J. Am. Hist. 24 (1971).

present danger approach in *Abrams* is different from the incitement approach taken by Hand in *Masses*, even though Chafee influenced both judges. Hand was critical of the Holmes approach as too subjective to constrain lemming-like judges in times of national crisis. See Gunther, *supra* note *b*, 27 Stan. L. Rev. at 749 (Hand's criticism of Holmes' dissent).

Consider the irony of the next case, in which a decision upholding repression subjected a new body of government actors to First Amendment constraints.

Gitlow v. New York

268 U.S. 652 (1925)

The Court upheld the conviction of Benjamin Gitlow for violating New York's law prohibiting the advocacy of criminal anarchy. His offense was helping to publish a "Left Wing Manifesto," which advocated worldwide class struggle, mass industrial revolts and strikes, and the establishment of a "revolutionary dictatorship of the proletariat." This is the first opinion where the Court applied the guarantees of the First Amendment to the states as protections assured by the Due Process Clause of the Fourteenth Amendment. The Court held that "utterances inciting to the overthrow of organized government by unlawful means present a sufficient danger of substantive evil" to justify legislative prohibition. "A single revolutionary spark may kindle a fire that, smoldering for a time, may burst into a sweeping and destructive conflagration."

Justice Holmes, joined by **Justice Brandeis**, dissented. Holmes responded to the majority's "incitement" rationale: "Every idea is an incitement. It offers itself for belief, and, if believed, it is acted on unless some other belief outweighs it, or some failure of energy stifles the movement at its birth. * * * If, in the long run, the beliefs expressed in proletarian dictatorship are destined to be accepted by the dominant forces of the community, the only meaning of free speech is that they should be given their chance and have their way."

Whitney v. California

274 U.S. 357 (1927)

In this case, the majority upheld the conviction for "criminal syndicalism" of a member of the Communist Labor Party, whose only individual activities had been attending meetings. **Justice Brandeis'** opinion was technically a concurrence but rejected the majority's reasoning entirely. One of the most famous passages in First Amendment law comes from that Brandeis opinion:

> Those who won our independence believed that the final end of the State was to make men free to develop their faculties; and that in its government the deliberative forces should prevail over the arbitrary. They valued liberty both as an end and as a means. They

believed liberty to be the secret of happiness and courage to be the secret of liberty. They believed that freedom to think as you will and to speak as you think are means indispensable to the discovery and spread of political truth; that without free speech and assembly discussion would be futile; that with them, discussion affords ordinarily adequate protection against the dissemination of noxious doctrine; that the greatest menace to freedom is an inert people; that public discussion is a political duty; and that this should be a fundamental principle of the American government.[14] They recognized the risks to which all human institutions are subject. But they knew that order cannot be secured merely through fear of punishment for its infraction; that it is hazardous to discourage thought, hope and imagination; that fear breeds repression; that repression breeds hate; that hate menaces stable government; that the path of safety lies in the opportunity to discuss freely supposed grievances and proposed remedies; and that the fitting remedy for evil counsels is good ones. Believing in the power of reason as applied through public discussion, they eschewed silence coerced by law—the argument of force in its worst form. Recognizing the occasional tyrannies of governing majorities, they amended the Constitution so that free speech and assembly should be guaranteed.

Fear of serious injury cannot alone justify suppression of free speech and assembly. Men feared witches and burnt women. It is the function of speech to free men from the bondage of irrational fears. To justify suppression of free speech there must be reasonable ground to fear that serious evil will result if free speech is practiced. There must be reasonable ground to believe that the danger apprehended is imminent. * * *

Those who won our independence by revolution were not cowards. They did not fear political change. They did not exalt order at the cost of liberty. To courageous, self-reliant men, with confidence in the power of free and fearless reasoning applied through the processes of popular government, no danger flowing from speech can be deemed clear and present, unless the incidence of the evil apprehended is so imminent that it may befall before there is opportunity for full discussion. If there be time to expose through discussion the falsehood and fallacies, to avert the evil by the processes of education, the remedy to be applied is more speech, not enforced silence. Only an emergency can justify repression. Such

---

[14] In a footnote at this point, Justice Brandeis added the following historical reference: "Compare Thomas Jefferson: 'We have nothing to fear from the demoralizing reasonings of some, if others are left free to demonstrate their errors and especially when the law stands ready to punish the first criminal act produced by the false reasonings; these are safer corrections than the conscience of the judge.' Quoted by Charles A. Beard, The Nation, July 7, 1926, vol. 123, p. 8. Also in first Inaugural Address: 'If there be any among us who would wish to dissolve this union or change its republican form, let them stand undisturbed as monuments of the safety with which error of opinion may be tolerated where reason is left free to combat it.' "

must be the rule if authority is to be reconciled with freedom. Such, in my opinion, is the command of the Constitution. It is therefore always open to Americans to challenge a law abridging free speech and assembly by showing that there was no emergency justifying it.

This may be a somewhat idealized portrait of the Framers, but it is one that has helped inspire modern First Amendment jurisprudence.

During the post-war "red scare," the Court continued to uphold state repression. By the 1930s, however, a majority of the Court had been converted to the more libertarian position espoused by Brandeis and Holmes and used their approach to invalidate convictions under state "syndicalism" laws. See *De Jonge v. Oregon*, 299 U.S. 353 (1937); *Herndon v. Lowry*, 301 U.S. 242 (1937). The Court then adopted the "clear and present danger" test as a general standard for First Amendment cases. When the Court returned to free speech issues after World War II, it continued to apply the test.

Dennis v. United States

341 U.S. 494 (1951)

After World War II, the country again was faced with a period of serious repression. In what is now called the McCarthy era (but which actually began before Senator Joseph McCarthy attained national prominence), sweeping actions were taken to suppress "Communist influences." The Court gave its backing to these efforts by upholding the convictions of leading Communist Party figures for violating the Smith Act, which made it unlawful for any person "to knowingly or willfully advocate, abet, advise, or teach the duty, necessity, or propriety of overthrowing or destroying any government in the United States by force or violence." Following the lead of Chief Judge Learned Hand's opinion for the Second Circuit affirming the convictions, the Court in an opinion by **Chief Justice Vinson** watered down the clear and present danger test, saying that the immediacy and probability of the harm were only factors to be offset against its gravity. Apparently, since an eventual Communist revolution would be such a disaster, not much was required in the way of present risk to justify suppression of the party.[15] **Justices Black** and **Douglas** wrote stinging dissents in this and other McCarthy-era cases.

The Court's application of the clear and present danger test in *Dennis* raised considerable doubt about whether that test offered sufficient protection to subversive speech. After the McCarthy era, though, the test was applied with greater bite. See *Watts v. United States*, 394 U.S. 705 (1969); *Bond v. Floyd*, 385 U.S. 116 (1966). At the end of the Warren Court era, in the following case, the Court revamped the test, creating the standard that currently applies to advocacy of illegal action.

---

[15] But see Richard Posner, *Free Speech in an Economic Perspective*, 20 Suffolk U. L. Rev. 1, 34–35 (1986) (court should have discounted to present value the cost of a future revolution).

BRANDENBURG V. OHIO

395 U.S. 444, 89 S.Ct. 1827, 23 L.Ed.2d 430 (1969)

PER CURIAM.

The appellant, a leader of a Ku Klux Klan group, was convicted under the Ohio Criminal Syndicalism statute for "advocat[ing] . . . the duty, necessity, or propriety of crime, sabotage, violence, or unlawful methods of terrorism as a means of accomplishing industrial or political reform" and for "voluntarily assembl[ing] with any society, group, or assemblage of persons formed to teach or advocate the doctrines of criminal syndicalism." He was fined $1,000 and sentenced to one to 10 years' imprisonment. [Brandenburg was convicted on the basis of events at Klan rallies filmed by a television reporter.]

One film showed 12 hooded figures, some of whom carried firearms. They were gathered around a large wooden cross, which they burned. No one was present other than the participants and the newsmen who made the film. Most of the words uttered during the scene were incomprehensible when the film was projected, but scattered phrases could be understood that were derogatory of Negroes and, in one instance, of Jews.[1]

Another scene on the same film showed the appellant, in Klan regalia, making a speech. The speech, in full, was as follows:

> This is an organizers' meeting. We have had quite a few members here today which are—we have hundreds, hundreds of members throughout the State of Ohio. I can quote from a newspaper clipping from the Columbus, Ohio Dispatch, five weeks ago Sunday morning. The Klan has more members in the State of Ohio than does any other organization. We're not a revengent organization, but if our President, our Congress, our Supreme Court, continues to suppress the white, Caucasian race, it's possible that there might have to be some revengeance taken.

> We are marching on Congress July the Fourth, four hundred thousand strong. From there we are dividing into two groups, one group to march on St. Augustine, Florida, the other group to march into Mississippi. Thank you.

* * * The Ohio Criminal Syndicalism Statute was enacted in 1919. From 1917 to 1920, identical or quite similar laws were adopted by 20 States and two territories. In 1927, this Court sustained the constitutionality of California's Criminal Syndicalism Act, the text of which is quite similar to that of the laws of Ohio. *Whitney v. California.* The Court

---

[1] The significant portions that could be understood were: "How far is the nigger going to—yeah." "This is what we are going to do to the niggers." "A dirty nigger." "Send the Jews back to Israel." "Let's give them back to the dark garden." "Save America." "Let's go back to constitutional betterment." "Bury the niggers." "We intend to do our part." "Give us our state rights." "Freedom for the whites." "Nigger will have to fight for every inch he gets from now on."

upheld the statute on the ground that, without more, "advocating" violent means to effect political and economic change involves such danger to the security of the State that the State may outlaw it. But *Whitney* has been thoroughly discredited by later decisions. *See Dennis v. United States.* These later decisions have fashioned the principle that the constitutional guarantees of free speech and free press do not permit a State to forbid or proscribe advocacy of the use of force or of law violation except where such advocacy is directed to inciting or producing imminent lawless action and is likely to incite or produce such action.[2] As we said in *Noto v. United States*, 367 U.S. 290, 297–298 (1961), "the mere abstract teaching . . . of the moral propriety or even moral necessity for a resort to force and violence, is not the same as preparing a group for violent action and steeling it to such action." A statute which fails to draw this distinction impermissibly intrudes upon the freedoms guaranteed by the First and Fourteenth Amendments. It sweeps within its condemnation speech which our Constitution has immunized from governmental control.

Measured by this test, Ohio's Criminal Syndicalism Act cannot be sustained. The Act punishes persons who "advocate or teach the duty, necessity, or propriety" of violence "as a means of accomplishing industrial or political reform"; or who publish or circulate or display any book or paper containing such advocacy; or who "justify" the commission of violent acts "with intent to exemplify, spread or advocate the propriety of the doctrines of criminal syndicalism"; or who "voluntarily assemble" with a group formed "to teach or advocate the doctrines of criminal syndicalism." Neither the indictment nor the trial judge's instructions to the jury in any way refined the statute's bald definition of the crime in terms of mere advocacy not distinguished from incitement to imminent lawless action.

Accordingly, we are here confronted with a statute which, by its own words and as applied, purports to punish mere advocacy and to forbid, on pain of criminal punishment, assembly with others merely to advocate the described type of action. Such a statute falls within the condemnation of the First and Fourteenth Amendments. The contrary teaching of *Whitney v. California* cannot be supported, and that decision is therefore overruled.

[The concurring opinions of **JUSTICE BLACK** and **JUSTICE DOUGLAS** are omitted.]

---

[2] It was on the theory that the Smith Act embodied such a principle and that it had been applied only in conformity with it that this Court sustained the Act's constitutionality. *Dennis.* That this was the basis for *Dennis* was emphasized in *Yates v. United States*, 354 U.S. 298, 320–324 (1957), in which the Court overturned convictions for advocacy of the forcible overthrow of the Government under the Smith Act, because the trial judge's instructions had allowed conviction for mere advocacy, unrelated to its tendency to produce forcible action.

NOTES ON BRANDENBURG

1. *"Clear and Present Danger."* How does *Brandenburg* modify the clear and present danger test? Is the modification justified? Note how the first element of the *Brandenburg* test ("advocacy is directed to inciting") follows Hand's *Masses* opinion (discussed above) in distinguishing direct incitement from mere advocacy. Does *Brandenburg* essentially overrule *Abrams, Gitlow*, and *Dennis*, as well as *Whitney*?[16]

Even as recast in *Brandenburg*, the clear and present danger test allows radical political expression to be suppressed as soon as it shows signs of becoming effective.[17] Justice Douglas' concurring opinion argued that the test should be whether the inciting speech is accompanied by "overt acts" violating the law. For example, yelling "fire" in a theatre is "speech brigaded with action" and can be regulated under his approach.

2. *The Flag Salute Case.* What about the use of affirmative mandates to display loyalty, such as requiring children to salute the flag? During World War II, the Court overruled a case decided just three years earlier and held that compulsory flag salutes violated the First Amendment. *West Virginia State Bd. of Education v. Barnette*, 319 U.S. 624 (1943). Justice Jackson's opinion for the Court contained some eloquent passages reminiscent of Brandeis in *Whitney*:

> The case is made difficult not because the principles of its decision are obscure but because the flag involved is our own. * * * [F]reedom to differ is not limited to things that do not matter much. That would be a mere shadow of freedom. The test of its substance is the right to differ as to things that touch the heart of the existing order.

> If there is any fixed star in our constitutional constellation, it is that no official, high or petty, can prescribe what shall be orthodox in politics, nationalism, religion, or other matters of opinion or force citizens to confess by word or act their faith therein. If there are any circumstances which permit an exception, they do not now occur to us.

Note that in *Brandenburg*, the speech in question involved threats against minority groups, as opposed to earlier cases in which the threats had been directed against the government. The Court seems to assume that the same test should apply to both kinds of speech. Do you agree? Or should the government have greater power to protect minority groups from threatening speech? Recall the *R.A.V.* case and consider the following opinion:

---

[16] See Hans Linde, *"Clear and Present Danger" Reexamined: Dissonance in the* Brandenburg *Concerto*, 22 Stan. L. Rev. 1163 (1970).

[17] See Thomas Emerson, *First Amendment Doctrine and the Burger Court*, 68 Cal. L. Rev. 422 (1980).

VIRGINIA V. BLACK

538 U.S. 343, 123 S.Ct. 1536, 155 L.Ed.2d 535 (2003)

JUSTICE O'CONNOR announced the judgment of the Court and delivered the opinion of the Court with respect to Parts I, II, and III, and an opinion with respect to Parts IV and V, in which CHIEF JUSTICE REHNQUIST, JUSTICE STEVENS, and JUSTICE BREYER join.

I.   Respondents Barry Black, Richard Elliott, and Jonathan O'Mara were convicted separately of violating Virginia's cross-burning statute, [which] provides:

> It shall be unlawful for any person or persons, with the intent of intimidating any person or group of persons, to burn, or cause to be burned, a cross on the property of another, a highway or other public place. Any person who shall violate any provision of this section shall be guilty of a Class 6 felony.

> Any such burning of a cross shall be prima facie evidence of an intent to intimidate a person or group of persons.

[Black led a Ku Klux Klan rally attended by around thirty people. The rally was located on private property in an open field near a state highway. At the conclusion of the rally, the crowd circled around a 25- to 30-foot cross. The cross was between 300 and 350 yards away from the road. According to the sheriff, the cross "then all of a sudden . . . went up in a flame. In a separate case, two other defendants attempted to burn a cross on the yard of an African-American. The two defendants drove a truck onto the neighbor's property, planted a cross, and set it on fire. Their apparent motive was to "get back" at the neighbor for complaining about shooting in their backyard.]

[Part II of the opinion is devoted to a review of the history of cross burning. It concludes: "In sum, while a burning cross does not inevitably convey a message of intimidation, often the cross burner intends that the recipients of the message fear for their lives. And when a cross burning is used to intimidate, few if any messages are more powerful."]

[III.]   "True threats" encompass those statements where the speaker means to communicate a serious expression of an intent to commit an act of unlawful violence to a particular individual or group of individuals. The speaker need not actually intend to carry out the threat. Rather, a prohibition on true threats "protect[s] individuals from the fear of violence" and "from the disruption that fear engenders," in addition to protecting people "from the possibility that the threatened violence will occur." Intimidation in the constitutionally proscribable sense of the word is a type of true threat, where a speaker directs a threat to a person or group of persons with the intent of placing the victim in fear of bodily harm or death. Respondents do not contest that some cross burnings fit within this meaning of intimidating speech, and rightly so. As noted in Part II, the history of cross burning in this country shows that cross burning is often intimidating, intended to create a pervasive fear in victims that they are a target of violence. * * *

[Furthermore,] Virginia's statute does not run afoul of the First Amendment insofar as it bans cross burning with intent to intimidate. Unlike the statute at issue in *R.A.V.*, the Virginia statute does not single out for opprobrium only that speech directed toward "one of the specified disfavored topics." It does not matter whether an individual burns a cross with intent to intimidate because of the victim's race, gender, or religion, or because of the victim's "political affiliation, union membership, or homosexuality." Moreover, as a factual matter it is not true that cross burners direct their intimidating conduct solely to racial or religious minorities. Indeed, in the case of Elliott and O'Mara, it is at least unclear whether the respondents burned a cross due to racial animus.

The First Amendment permits Virginia to outlaw cross burnings done with the intent to intimidate because burning a cross is a particularly virulent form of intimidation. Instead of prohibiting all intimidating messages, Virginia may choose to regulate this subset of intimidating messages in light of cross burning's long and pernicious history as a signal of impending violence. Thus, just as a State may regulate only that obscenity which is the most obscene due to its prurient content, so too may a State choose to prohibit only those forms of intimidation that are most likely to inspire fear of bodily harm. A ban on cross burning carried out with the intent to intimidate is fully consistent with our holding in *R.A.V.* and is proscribable under the First Amendment.

[In Parts IV and V of her plurality opinion, Justice O'Connor concluded that the state's prima facie evidence provision was facially unconstitutional because of its indiscriminate coverage. Since the instruction was given in Black's case, the plurality voted to reverse his conviction, but it remanded the convictions of Elliott and O'Mara to determine whether the prima facie evidence provision was severable or whether it was subject to a narrowing construction. In a partial concurrence, Justice Scalia (joined by Justice Thomas) argued that the provision had such a modest potential impact on prosecutions that it should not be subject to a facial attack].

[The concurring opinion of **JUSTICE STEVENS**, as well as the opinion of **JUSTICE SCALIA**, joined in part by **JUSTICE THOMAS**, concurring in part and dissenting in part, are omitted.]

JUSTICE SOUTER, with whom **JUSTICE KENNEDY** and **JUSTICE GINSBURG** join, concurring in the judgment in part and dissenting in part.

The majority's approach could be taken as recognizing an exception to *R.A.V.* when circumstances show that the statute's ostensibly valid reason for punishing particularly serious proscribable expression probably is not a ruse for message suppression, even though the statute may have a greater (but not exclusive) impact on adherents of one ideology than on others.

My concern here, in any event, is not with the merit of a pragmatic doctrinal move. For whether or not the Court should conceive of exceptions to *R.A.V.*'s general rule in a more practical way, no content-based statute should survive even under a pragmatic recasting of *R.A.V.* without a high probability that no "official suppression of ideas is afoot." I believe the prima facie evidence provision stands in the way of any finding of such a high probability here.

JUSTICE THOMAS, dissenting.

That in the early 1950s the people of Virginia viewed cross burning as creating an intolerable atmosphere of terror is not surprising: Although the cross took on some religious significance in the 1920's when the Klan became connected with certain southern white clergy, by the postwar period it had reverted to its original function "as an instrument of intimidation." * * *

It strains credulity to suggest that a state legislature that adopted a litany of segregationist laws self-contradictorily intended to squelch the segregationist message. Even for segregationists, violent and terroristic conduct, the Siamese twin of cross burning, was intolerable. The ban on cross burning with intent to intimidate demonstrates that even segregationists understood the difference between intimidating and terroristic conduct and racist expression. It is simply beyond belief that, in passing the statute now under review, the Virginia legislature was concerned with anything but penalizing conduct it must have viewed as particularly vicious.

Accordingly, this statute prohibits only conduct, not expression. And, just as one cannot burn down someone's house to make a political point and then seek refuge in the First Amendment, those who hate cannot terrorize and intimidate to make their point. In light of my conclusion that the statute here addresses only conduct, there is no need to analyze it under any of our First Amendment tests.

NOTES ON VIRGINIA V. BLACK

1. *Distinguishing* R.A.V. Notice that Elliott and O'Mara's conduct was strikingly similar to R.A.V.'s. Why the difference in results? While cross-burning may be among the most virulent forms of threats, are there any other threats that are equally virulent? If so, does the state's decision to punish one subcategory of the super-virulent threats but not the others fit within the *R.A.V.* exception?

2. *Law and Social Meaning. Virginia v. Black* stresses the historical context of cross-burning and the ways in which this symbol is understood by observers. We will see this concern with social meaning again at the end of the chapter, when we discuss the Court's jurisprudence regarding public religious symbols. Are the Court's perceptions of social meaning a valuable assist to decisionmaking or an unreliable guide? For reflections on how the Court should think about these issues, see Kenneth L. Karst, *Threats and Meanings: How the Facts Govern First Amendment Doctrine*, 58 Stan. L. Rev. 1337 (2006); Frederick Schauer, *Intentions, Conventions, and the First Amendment*, 2003 Sup. Ct. Rev. 197 (2004).

———

In the aftermath of *Brandenberg*, few prosecutions have been based on the connection between speech and threats against national security. But the issue did reemerge in the following case as part of the "war on terror."

Holder v. Humanitarian Law Project

561 U.S. 1 (2010)

It is a federal crime to knowingly provide material support or resources to a foreign terrorist organization. The Secretary of State maintains a list of such organizations, and organizations have the right to challenge their inclusion on the list. The term "material support" is defined broadly to include "expert advice or assistance." Thus, the statute directly regulates speech. The plaintiffs wanted to support the nonviolent, lawful activities of some listed organizations, while opposing their terrorist efforts. For instance, they wanted to train organization members in how to use international law to resolve disputes peacefully and to teach them how to petition the UN for relief.

In an opinion by **Chief Justice Roberts**, the Court held that the law applied to these activities and that the First Amendment would not bar prosecution. The Court stressed that support for a terrorist organization's lawful activities would free up resources for its violent ones and would also help legitimize the organization. Notably, however, the Court declined the government's invitation to use the *O'Brien* standard:

> [A]s applied to plaintiffs the conduct triggering coverage under the statute consists of communicating a message. As we explained in *Texas v. Johnson*, '[I]f the [Government's] regulation is not related to expression, then the less stringent standard we announced in *United States v. O'Brien* for regulations of noncommunicative conduct controls. If it is, then we are outside of *O'Brien's* test, and we must [apply] a more demanding standard."

In upholding the law, the Court emphasized that "the Government's interest in combating terrorism is an urgent objective of the highest order."

Chief Justice Roberts noted three limitations to the holding. First, "we in no way suggest that a regulation of independent speech would pass constitutional muster, even if the Government were to show that such speech benefits foreign terrorist organizations." Second, the Court also did "not suggest that Congress could extend the same prohibition on material support at issue here to domestic organizations." Third, the statute did not prohibit mere membership in an organization in the absence of additional material support.

In dissent, **Justice Breyer**, joined by **Justices Ginsburg** and **Sotomayor**, argued that the statute should not be interpreted to apply to the plaintiffs' proposed activities. Justice Breyer emphasized that all of the activities "involve the communication and advocacy of political ideas and lawful means of achieving political ends," such as addressing the U.S. Congress. Justice Breyer also criticized the majority for excessive deference to the political branches.

B. DEFAMATION AND OTHER TORTS

Political speech can contain falsehoods, deliberately or otherwise, and it can involve discussion of otherwise private aspects of a person's life. This section considers the use of tort law to discipline such speech, and the role of the First Amendment in constraining tort law.

NEW YORK TIMES CO. V. SULLIVAN
376 U.S. 254, 84 S.Ct. 710, 11 L.Ed.2d 686 (1964)

JUSTICE BRENNAN delivered the opinion of the Court.

We are required in this case to determine for the first time the extent to which the constitutional protections for speech and press limit a State's power to award damages in a libel action brought by a public official against critics of his official conduct.

Respondent L. B. Sullivan is one of the three elected Commissioners of the City of Montgomery, Alabama. He testified that he was "Commissioner of Public Affairs and the duties are supervision of the Police Department, Fire Department, Department of Cemetery and Department of Scales." He brought this civil libel action against the four individual petitioners, who are Negroes and Alabama clergymen, and against petitioner the New York Times Company, a New York corporation which publishes the New York Times, a daily newspaper. A jury in the Circuit Court of Montgomery County awarded him damages of $500,000, the full amount claimed, against all the petitioners, and the Supreme Court of Alabama affirmed.

Respondent's complaint alleged that he had been libeled by statements in a full-page advertisement that was carried in the New York Times on March 29, 1960. Entitled "Heed Their Rising Voices," the advertisement began by stating that "As the whole world knows by now, thousands of Southern Negro students are engaged in widespread non-violent demonstrations in positive affirmation of the right to live in human dignity as guaranteed by the U.S. Constitution and the Bill of Rights." It went on to charge that "in their efforts to uphold these guarantees, they are being met by an unprecedented wave of terror by those who would deny and negate that document which the whole world looks upon as setting the pattern for modern freedom. . . ." Succeeding paragraphs purported to illustrate the "wave of terror" by describing certain alleged events. The text concluded with an appeal for funds for three purposes: support of the student movement, "the struggle for the right-to-vote," and the legal defense of Dr. Martin Luther King, Jr., leader of the movement, against a perjury indictment then pending in Montgomery.

[The text contained several references to police brutality in Montgomery. Although Sullivan wasn't named, the state courts said these were sufficient as a reference to him as police commissioner. Also, the text contained some minor and largely irrelevant inaccuracies.]

[W]e consider this case against the background of a profound national commitment to the principle that debate on public issues should be uninhibited, robust, and wide-open, and that it may well include vehement, caustic, and sometimes unpleasantly sharp attacks on government and public officials. The present advertisement, as an expression of grievance and protest on one of the major public issues of our time, would seem clearly to qualify for the constitutional protection. The question is whether it forfeits that protection by the falsity of some of its factual statements and by its alleged defamation of respondent.

Authoritative interpretations of the First Amendment guarantees have consistently refused to recognize an exception for any test of truth—whether administered by judges, juries, or administrative officials—and especially one that puts the burden of proving truth on the speaker. The constitutional protection does not turn upon "the truth, popularity, or social utility of the ideas and beliefs which are offered." *N.A.A.C.P. v. Button*, 371 U.S. 415, 445. As Madison said, "Some degree of abuse is inseparable from the proper use of every thing; and in no instance is this more true than in that of the press." * * *

That erroneous statement is inevitable in free debate, and that it must be protected if the freedoms of expression are to have the "breathing space" that they "need . . . to survive," *N.A.A.C.P. v. Button*, was also recognized by the Court of Appeals for the District of Columbia Circuit in *Sweeney v. Patterson*, 76 U.S. App. D.C. 23, 24, 128 F. 2d 457, 458 (1942), *cert. denied*, 317 U.S. 678. Judge Edgerton spoke for a unanimous court which affirmed the dismissal of a Congressman's libel suit based upon a newspaper article charging him with anti-Semitism in opposing a judicial appointment. He said:

> Cases which impose liability for erroneous reports of the political conduct of officials reflect the obsolete doctrine that the governed must not criticize their governors. . . . The interest of the public here outweighs the interest of appellant or any other individual. The protection of the public requires not merely discussion, but information. Political conduct and views which some respectable people approve, and others condemn, are constantly imputed to Congressmen. Errors of fact, particularly in regard to a man's mental states and processes, are inevitable. . . . Whatever is added to the field of libel is taken from the field of free debate.

Injury to official reputation affords no more warrant for repressing speech that would otherwise be free than does factual error. Where judicial officers are involved, this Court has held that concern for the dignity and reputation of the courts does not justify the punishment as criminal contempt of criticism of the judge or his decision. This is true even though the utterance contains "half-truths" and "misinformation." Such repression can be justified, if at all, only by a clear and present danger of the obstruction of justice. If judges are to be treated as "men of fortitude, able to thrive in a hardy climate," surely the same must be true of other government officials, such as elected city commissioners.[14] Criticism of their official conduct does not lose its constitutional protection merely because it is effective criticism and hence diminishes their official reputations.

If neither factual error nor defamatory content suffices to remove the constitutional shield from criticism of official conduct, the combination of the two elements is no less inadequate. This is the lesson to be drawn from the great controversy over the Sedition Act of 1798, which first crystallized a national awareness of the central meaning of the First Amendment. * * * The Act allowed the defendant the defense of truth, and provided that the jury were to be judges both of the law and the facts. Despite these qualifications, the Act was vigorously condemned as unconstitutional in an attack joined in by Jefferson and Madison. In the famous Virginia Resolutions of 1798, the General Assembly of Virginia resolved that * * * [the Sedition Act] exercises . . . a power not delegated by the Constitution, but, on the contrary, expressly and positively forbidden by one of the amendments thereto—a power which, more than any other, ought to

---

[14] The climate in which public officials operate, especially during a political campaign, has been described by one commentator in the following terms: "Charges of gross incompetence, disregard of the public interest, communist sympathies, and the like usually have filled the air; and hints of bribery, embezzlement, and other criminal conduct are not infrequent." Noel, *Defamation of Public Officers and Candidates*, 49 Col. L. Rev. 875 (1949). * * *

produce universal alarm, because it is levelled against the right of freely examining public characters and measures, and of free communication among the people thereon, which has ever been justly deemed the only effectual guardian of every other right."

Madison prepared the Report in support of the protest. His premise was that the Constitution created a form of government under which "The people, not the government, possess the absolute sovereignty." The structure of the government dispersed power in reflection of the people's distrust of concentrated power, and of power itself at all levels. This form of government was "altogether different" from the British form, under which the Crown was sovereign and the people were subjects. "Is it not natural and necessary, under such different circumstances," he asked, "that a different degree of freedom in the use of the press should be contemplated?" Earlier, in a debate in the House of Representatives, Madison had said: "If we advert to the nature of Republican Government, we shall find that the censorial power is in the people over the Government, and not in the Government over the people." Of the exercise of that power by the press, his Report said: "In every state, probably, in the Union, the press has exerted a freedom in canvassing the merits and measures of public men, of every description, which has not been confined to the strict limits of the common law. On this footing the freedom of the press has stood; on this foundation it yet stands. . . ." The right of free public discussion of the stewardship of public officials was thus, in Madison's view, a fundamental principle of the American form of government.

Although the Sedition Act was never tested in this Court, the attack upon its validity has carried the day in the court of history. Fines levied in its prosecution were repaid by Act of Congress on the ground that it was unconstitutional. * * * The invalidity of the Act has also been assumed by Justices of this Court. These views reflect a broad consensus that the Act, because of the restraint it imposed upon criticism of government and public officials, was inconsistent with the First Amendment. * * *

The constitutional guarantees require, we think, a federal rule that prohibits a public official from recovering damages for a defamatory falsehood relating to his official conduct unless he proves that the statement was made with "actual malice"—that is, with knowledge that it was false or with reckless disregard of whether it was false or not. * * *

[The concurring opinion of **JUSTICE BLACK**, joined by **JUSTICE DOUGLAS**, is omitted.]

Gertz v. Robert Welch, Inc.

418 U.S. 323 (1974)

This case involved an article accusing the plaintiff of organizing a "communist frameup" of a policeman. The police officer was convicted of killing a youth, and the plaintiff, an attorney, had represented the family in a damage suit. The Court, per **Justice Powell**, held that the *New York Times v. Sullivan* rule did not apply because the plaintiff was neither a public official nor a public figure. The Court laid down two rules governing liability in such cases:

> "[S]o long as they do not impose liability without fault, the States may define for themselves the appropriate standard of liability for a publisher or broadcaster of defamatory falsehood injurious to a private individual." Thus, the plaintiff need only prove negligence.

> "It is necessary to restrict defamation plaintiffs who do not prove knowledge of falsity or reckless disregard for the truth to compensation for actual injury." Thus, to recover "presumed" or punitive damages, the plaintiff must satisfy the *New York Times* test even if he is a private figure.

NOTES ON POST-NEW YORK TIMES DEVELOPMENTS IN DEFAMATION LAW

The Supreme Court has been faced with a plethora of cases requiring it to apply the New York Times rule in various factual settings. For this reason, a rich body of constitutional doctrine has evolved that defines the limits of the rule. Consider several critical issues.

1.   *Who Is a Public Figure?* A few years after New York Times, the Court was faced with the question whether it applied to other prominent individuals who were not on the state payroll. In two tandem cases, the Court ruled that at least some such individuals were covered by the rule.[18] One of the cases involved allegations of misconduct by the athletic director at a state university, who was technically an employee of a privately incorporated athletic association. The other involved a retired general who had become active in national politics, and was accused of haranguing a mob to resist a desegregation order. As "public figures," these plaintiffs were covered by the same rule as public officials.

Later cases make it clear that the category of public figures is limited. For example, involvement in well-publicized litigation is not enough to make a person a public figure.[19] Nor does a lawyer become a public figure by representing a client in civil rights litigation.[20] Similarly, a government researcher was not considered a public figure when a U.S. Senator attacked

---

[18] See *Curtis Publishing Co. v. Butts*, 388 U.S. 130 (1967) (also presenting the opinion in the companion case of *Associated Press v. Walker*).

[19] See *Wolston v. Reader's Digest Ass'n*, 443 U.S. 157 (1979); *Time, Inc. v. Firestone*, 424 U.S. 448 (1976).

[20] See *Gertz v. Robert Welch, Inc.*, 418 U.S. 323 (1974).

his work as a waste of public funds, since he had not assumed any role of public prominence in debate over government research expenditures and had not otherwise invited a high level of public attention.[21]

2. *What Is Defamatory?* In *Milkovich v. Lorain Journal Co.*, 497 U.S. 1 (1990), the plaintiff was a high-school wrestling coach whose team was placed on probation for misconduct. The local courts overturned the ruling against the team. The coach sued because of press coverage implying that he had lied at the hearing. The Court rejected the argument that this was merely a matter of opinion and therefore not defamatory under the *New York Times* rule. Rather than using the "opinion" label, the Court preferred to ask whether a statement has provably false factual implications, and whether it used language in a loose, figurative, or hyperbolic sense that might dispel the factual implications. Although *Milkovich* rejects the idea of a separate privilege for "opinion," it provides the functional equivalent of such a privilege by careful tailoring of the plaintiff's duty to prove falsity.

3. *What Is Malice?* In common usage, malice means personal animosity. This is clearly not the meaning of the term under *New York Times v. Sullivan*. Rather, the plaintiff must prove by clear and convincing evidence that the defendant knew the statement was false or acted with reckless disregard of the truth. And "recklessness" here means something more than a high degree of negligence, as the cases also indicate.[22]

4. *Private Libels.* As we saw in *Gertz*, the *New York Times* rule does not apply to claims of defamation brought by private citizens (as opposed to public figures). *Gertz* and other libel cases have emphasized the identity of the plaintiff rather than other potentially relevant factors. Some of these other factors have, however, occasionally been pivotal.[23] Thus, although the *New*

---

[21] See *Hutchinson v. Proxmire*, 443 U.S. 111 (1979).

[22] In *Harte-Hanks Communications v. Connaughton*, 491 U.S. 657 (1989), the Court held that a showing of "highly unreasonable conduct constituting an extreme departure from the standards of investigation and reporting ordinarily adhered to by responsible publishers" is not enough to show malice. Thus, as the Court indicated in another case, the crucial point is whether in fact the publisher had serious doubts about the accuracy of the statement, not whether a prudent publisher would have had such doubts. See *St. Amant v. Thompson*, 390 U.S. 727 (1968). To show malice, it is not enough to show that the journalist knew that a story was not literally accurate in all regards. See *Masson v. New Yorker Magazine*, 501 U.S. 496 (1991).

[23] The concept of "public concern" surfaced in *Dun & Bradstreet, Inc. v. Greenmoss Builders, Inc.*, 472 U.S. 749 (1985), in which a credit reporting agency had erroneously informed some of its clients that the plaintiff corporation was bankrupt. Finding the kind of speech involved in the case to be peripheral to the First Amendment, like commercial speech, the plurality could find "no credible argument that this type of credit reporting requires special protection to ensure that 'debate on public issues [will] be uninhibited, robust, and wide-open.'." Chief Justice Burger and Justice White concurred on the ground that *Gertz* was wrongly decided anyway.

One point that had clear majority support in *Dun & Bradstreet* is that the media enjoy no special privileges under libel law. But this point too has been called into question. In *Philadelphia Newspapers, Inc. v. Hepps*, 475 U.S. 767 (1986), the Court considered whether in a private libel case, the state may apply the common law rule that puts the burden of proof on the defendant to establish truth as a defense. Rejecting the common law rule, the Court said that to "ensure that true speech on matters of public concern is not deterred, we hold that the common-law presumption that defamatory speech is false cannot stand when a plaintiff seeks damages against a media defendant for speech of public concern."

York Times rule seems to be well settled, the situation for private libel is less clear. There seems to be a broad consensus that at least some private defamation cases should be subject to constitutional restraints. What is unclear is whether there are some examples of defamation that are so truly private, and so far removed from public discourse, that they should be exempted from these restraints.

————

The following case raises questions about the scope of the rationale for the *New York Times* rule and the extent to which it applies to non-defamatory, false speech. Do all false statements of fact fall outside the boundaries of the First Amendment, or only some?

United States v. Alvarez

567 U.S. 709 (2012)

In 2007, Alvarez attended his first public meeting as a board member of a water district. He introduced himself as follows: "I'm a retired marine of 25 years. I retired in the year 2001. Back in 1987, I was awarded the Congressional Medal of Honor. I got wounded many times by the same guy." None of this was true. The Stolen Valor Act makes it a crime to falsely claim receipt of military medals and provides an enhanced penalty if the Congressional Medal of Honor is involved.]

Justice Kennedy announced the judgment of the Court and delivered the plurality opinion. He argued that even false statements of fact are not entirely outside the protection of the First Amendment:

> The Act by its plain terms applies to a false statement made at any time, in any place, to any person. It can be assumed that it would not apply to, say, a theatrical performance. Still, the sweeping, quite unprecedented reach of the statute puts it in conflict with the First Amendment. Here the lie was made in a public meeting, but the statute would apply with equal force to personal, whispered conversations within a home. The statute seeks to control and suppress all false statements on this one subject in almost limitless times and settings. And it does so entirely without regard to whether the lie was made for the purpose of material gain.

> Permitting the government to decree this speech to be a criminal offense, whether shouted from the rooftops or made in a barely audible whisper, would endorse government authority to compile a list of subjects about which false statements are punishable. That governmental power has no clear limiting principle.

Justice Breyer, joined by **Justice Kagan,** concurred in the judgment. He said he "must concede, as the Government points out, that this Court has frequently said or implied that false factual statements enjoy little First

Amendment protection." He considered those statements over-simplifications, however:

> [F]ew statutes, if any, simply prohibit without limitation the telling of a lie, even a lie about one particular matter. Instead, in virtually all these instances limitations of context, requirements of proof of injury, and the like, narrow the statute to a subset of lies where specific harm is more likely to occur. * * *

> The statute before us lacks any such limiting features. It may be construed to prohibit only knowing and intentional acts of deception about readily verifiable facts within the personal knowledge of the speaker, thus reducing the risk that valuable speech is chilled. But it still ranges very broadly. And that breadth means that it creates a significant risk of First Amendment harm.

Justice Alito dissenting, joined by **Justice Scalia** and **Justice Thomas**. He maintained that the speech banned by the statute had no First Amendment value:

> In stark contrast to hypothetical laws prohibiting false statements about history, science, and similar matters, the Stolen Valor Act presents no risk at all that valuable speech will be suppressed. The speech punished by the Act is not only verifiably false and entirely lacking in intrinsic value, but it also fails to serve any instrumental purpose that the First Amendment might protect. Tellingly, when asked at oral argument what truthful speech the Stolen Valor Act might chill, even respondent's counsel conceded that the answer is none.

NOTES ON ALVAREZ

1. *Why Is Defamation Unprotected?* Although *Alvarez* is not a defamation case, it raises questions about the basis for *New York Times v. Sullivan* and later cases. The dissent argued that false statements receive no constitutional protection except where needed to prevent chilling truthful speech. There is language in *New York Times* that seems to take this approach. But the plurality opinion and the concurrence rejected that premise. Both Breyer and Kennedy seemed to think that false statements may have some residual First Amendment value. Justice Kennedy suggested that defamation is unprotected primarily because the tort has a long historical pedigree, with secondary support from the low value of false speech. Thus, other types of false speech are presumptively protected unless they fall into some other well-recognized category such as fraud or perjury. But the Breyer concurrence viewed falsity as relevant across a category of cases, applies intermediate scrutiny, and places less emphasis on a history of regulation. Consider how these views translate into varying rationales for the *New York Times* rule.

2. *Whatever Happened to* R.A.V.? Even if false statements were unprotected speech, *R.A.V.* might suggest the Stolen Valor Act is a content-

based distinction within that category and therefore subject to strict scrutiny. How might Justice Alito have attempted to distinguish *Alvarez* and *R.A.V.*?

As the following three cases show, tort-related concepts also intersect the First Amendment outside of defamation law. The Court has repeatedly encountered the question whether the First Amendment protects certain invasions of privacy and with international infliction of emotional distress.

Bartnicki v. Vopper

532 U.S. 514 (2001)

The chief negotiator for a local teachers union used the cell phone in her car to call the union's president. In the process of discussing the negotiations, the president said, "If they're not gonna move for three percent, we're gonna have to go to their, their homes. . . . To blow off their front porches, we'll have to do some work on some of those guys." The school district later accepted a proposal favorable to the teachers. In connection with news reports about the settlement, the defendant played a tape of the intercepted conversation on his radio talk show. The union negotiator sued under a federal anti-wiretapping law. Section 2511(1)(a) of the statute prohibits interception of certain communications, including cell phone calls. Section 2511(1)(c) prohibits disclosure of the contents of any illegally intercepted material. The statute provides a private cause of action. In its presentation of the facts, the Court stressed three aspects of the facts: the defendant had nothing to do with the interception and did not even know the name of the person responsible; the tapes were obtained legally by the radio station; and the tapes involved a matter of public concern.

In an opinion by **Justice Stevens**, the Court held that the First Amendment shielded the radio station from liability. Justice Stevens concluded that "the enforcement of that provision in these cases, however, implicates the core purposes of the First Amendment because it imposes sanctions on the publication of truthful information of public concern." The court did not find a sufficiently weighty public interest on the facts of the case to justify imposing liability. **Justice Breyer**, joined by **Justice O'Connor**, filed a concurring opinion, stressing that the Court's holding was limited to "the special circumstances present here: (1) the radio broadcasters acted lawfully (up to the time of final public disclosure); and (2) the information publicized involved a matter of unusual public concern, namely a threat of potential physical harm to others." **Chief Justice Rehnquist** dissented, joined by **Justices Scalia** and **Thomas**.

Hustler Magazine v. Falwell

485 U.S. 46 (1988)

In a heavy-handed parody, *Hustler* portrayed Jerry Falwell, a well-known minister and commentator on public affairs, as having committed incest with his mother in an outhouse. Falwell sued for libel and intentional infliction of emotional distress. The jury found that the parody could not be reasonably understood as purporting to communicate facts and so did not constitute libel, but did find *Hustler* liable for intentional infliction of emotional distress. In an opinion by **Chief Justice Rehnquist**, the Court held that a public figure cannot recover damages for emotional distress without satisfying *New York Times*, and that the plaintiff had failed to prove that the parody constituted a false "statement of fact." The Court rejected the argument that a malicious motive should be a basis for liability: "Were we to hold otherwise, there can be little doubt that political cartoonists and satirists would be subject to damage awards. * * * The appeal of the political cartoon or caricature is often based on exploration of unfortunate physical traits or politically embarrassing events—an exploration often calculated to injure the feelings of the subject of the portrayal." The Court also rejected "outrageousness" as a standard for liability:

> Respondent contends, however, that the caricature in question here was so "outrageous" as to distinguish it from more traditional political cartoons. * * * If it were possible by laying down a principled standard to separate the one from the other, public discourse would probably suffer little or no harm. But we doubt that there is any such standard, and we are quite sure that the pejorative description "outrageous" does not supply one. "Outrageousness" in the area of political and social discourse has an inherent subjectiveness about it which would allow a jury to impose liability on the basis of the jurors' tastes or views, or perhaps on the basis of their dislike of a particular expression. An "outrageousness" standard thus runs afoul of our longstanding refusal to allow damages to be awarded because the speech in question may have an adverse emotional impact on the audience.

Snyder v. Phelps

562 U.S. 443 (2011)

Fred Phelps, who founded the Westboro Baptist church, and six members of the church picketed the funeral of a Marine who was killed in Iraq in the line of duty. The picketing took place on public land approximately 1,000 feet from the church where the funeral was held. The picketers peacefully displayed their signs—"Thank God for Dead Soldiers," "Fags Doom Nations," "America is Doomed," "Priests Rape Boys," and "You're Going to Hell"—for about thirty minutes before the funeral began. The Marine's father saw the tops of the picketers' signs when driving to the funeral, but did not learn what was written on the signs until watching the news later that night. He sued for intentional infliction of emotional distress, and a jury awarded multi-million dollar damages.

In an opinion by **Chief Justice Roberts**, the Court held that Phelps was engaged in protected speech. While the signs "may fall short of refined social or political commentary, the issues they highlight—the political and moral conduct of the United States and its citizens, the fate of our Nation, homosexuality in the military, and scandals involving the Catholic clergy—are matters of public import." Even though some signs ("You're Going to Hell" and "God Hates You") may have been addressed to the Marine and his family, "that would not change the fact that the overall thrust and dominant theme of Westboro's demonstration spoke to broader public issues." As in *Hustler*, the jury's finding that the speech was outrageous could not be used to strip it of its constitutional protection. The Court also rejected the argument that the funeral-goers were a captive audience, given the facts. Roberts left open the possibility, however, that the state might limit all speech within a certain distance of funerals.

In dissent, **Justice Alito** argued that the Marine's family were not public figures, that infliction of emotional distress on them was central to Phelps's activities, and that "funerals are unique events at which special protection against emotional assaults is in order."

————

With few exceptions, the Justices appear to be willing to protect speech they find personally appalling. First Amendment doctrine seems to reflect a kind of bargain between liberals and conservatives to protect speech one side finds offensive and the other does not, in return for similar protection on the other side. In this bargain, has the Court gone too far to allow unacceptable forms of conduct? Should human dignity be considered a countervailing interest?

C. CAMPAIGN EXPENDITURES

Campaign finance reform became a major issue as a result of scandals during the Nixon Administration. In 1974, Congress passed its first major campaign finance legislation, the Federal Election Campaign Act (FECA). The FECA was immediately challenged on First Amendment grounds. Like its successors, the FECA contained special fast-track provisions, intended to move the constitutional issues up to the Supreme Court as quickly as possible. The Court's ensuing landmark decision has determined the shape of current campaign finance law.

Buckley v. Valeo

424 U.S. 1 (1976)

This was a facial challenge to the FEC. has determined the shape of current campaign finance law. One of the most important holdings was the validity of public funding for campaigns, even when subject to some conditions on candidates who chose to accept the funds. The Court's response to direct restrictions on campaign spending, however, was much more mixed.

The *Buckley* Court distinguished sharply between limits on expenditures and limits on contributions. The Court found the interests invoked by the government to be insufficient to justify the spending restrictions. The majority scorned the argument that the expenditure limits were necessary to neutralize the effects of wealth on political campaigns. According to the Court, "the concept that government may restrict the speech of some elements of our society in order to enhance the relative voice of others is wholly foreign to the First Amendment," which was intended "to secure 'the widest possible dissemination of information from diverse and antagonistic sources' and 'to assure unfettered interchange of ideas for the bringing about of political and social changes desired by the people.' "

The Court was more receptive to the contribution restrictions. Unlike restrictions on a person's expenditures, a contribution limitation places "little direct restraint on his political communication, for it permits the symbolic expression of support evidenced by a contribution but does not in any way infringe the contributor's freedom to discuss candidates and issues." In short, the Court seemed to consider contribution restrictions as mostly involving associational rather than speech rights, and as burdening those rights only marginally. The Court found ample justification for the restriction:

> To the extent that large contributions are given to secure a political *quid pro quo* from current and potential office holders, the integrity of our system of representative democracy is undermined. Although the scope of such pernicious practices can never be reliably ascertained, the deeply disturbing examples surfacing after the 1972 election demonstrate that the problem is not an illusory one.

"Of almost equal concern," the Court added, was the "appearance of corruption" due to public awareness of the potential for abuse created by large contributions.

NOTE ON CAMPAIGN FINANCE REGULATION
AFTER BUCKLEY V. VALEO

Some commentators on campaign finance speak of the hydraulic effect, where blocking campaign spending in one area just causes it to pop up somewhere else. There is some historical support for the hydraulics theory. One effect of *Buckley* was to increase the importance of campaign spending by organizations such as political action committees (PACs), corporations, and other groups. PACs are organizations that are designed to receive contributions from some group of people for election purposes. They therefore provide an alternative pathway for individuals to aggregate their election spending, outside of political parties or direct contributions to candidates. The upshot of the cases is that PACs can spend unlimited amounts of money, so long as no individual contributor gave more than $5,000. See *California Medical Ass'n v. Federal Election Comm'n*, 453 U.S. 182 (1981); *Federal Election Comm'n v. National Conservative PAC,* 470 U.S. 480 (1985).

In the 1990s, the flood of campaign funding jumped into a different channel called "soft money." To an increasing extent, contributions from corporations, unions, and other large donors were funneled through political parties, which then used the money to support the election of their party candidates. Typically, the money was used to increase voter registration and election turnout by party members or people thought to be sympathetic to the party. The Court held that the First Amendment shielded "independent" expenditures by political parties, just as it would shield independent expenditures by individuals, but that soft money can be treated a candidate contributions when the party pays for certain campaign ads over which the candidate has some degree of control. *Colorado Republican Fed. Campaign Comm. v. FEC*, 518 U.S. 604 (1996) (*Colorado Republicans I*); *FEC v. Colorado Republican Fed. Campaign Comm.*, 533 U.S. 431 (2001) (*Colorado Republicans II*).

The only deviation from the pattern of upholding contribution limits and invalidating expenditure limits was in the area of corporate speech, where the Court's approach wobbled. In terms of contributions, the Court in *First National Bank v. Bellotti,* 435 U.S. 765 (1978), struck down a statute prohibiting corporations from spending money to influence referendums on subjects unrelated to their business. Federal law has long prohibited corporations from making campaign contributions to candidates, however, and the Court has found sufficient potential for corruption to justify such restrictions. See *FEC v. National Right to Work Comm.*, 459 U.S. 197 (1982).

These cases do fit the *Buckley* pattern, but the next decision took a different turn. In *Austin v. Michigan Chamber of Commerce,* 494 U.S. 652 (1990), the Court upheld a state prohibition on corporate expenditures in political campaigns except through special political action funds. The Court found that the statute burdened the corporation's First Amendment rights. Nevertheless, the Court upheld the statute because it was supported by the compelling state interest in preventing corporations from channeling funds obtained from consumers and investors into political campaigns. Rather than being aimed at corruption, the ban on partisan corporate expenditures was designed to end "the corrosive and distorting effects of immense aggregations of wealth that are accumulated with the help of the corporate form and that have little or no correlation to the public's support for the corporation's political ideas." Instead of attempting to equalize the relative influence of speakers—a purpose found to be illegitimate in *Buckley*—the corporate expenditure ban "ensures that expenditures reflect actual public support for the political ideas espoused by corporations" by forcing the corporation to raise money for political expenditures separately.

This brings us to 2002, when Congress passed its most important campaign finance legislation in three decades, the Bipartisan Campaign Reform Act (BCRA). BCRA is a massive, complex piece of legislation (leading to an equally massive, complex set of opinions by the Justices). Our focus will be on two of the main provisions. Section 323 attempts to eliminate "soft money" donations. It prohibits national political parties from soliciting, receiving or spending any money except in compliance with federal funding limits—in effect, forcing them to rely entirely on "hard money" that is subject to federal regulation. Section 203 attempted to deal with a problem created by *Buckley* concerning corporate speech. Congress had attempted to ban all use of corporate and union funds (except through PACs) for campaign ads. But the *Buckley* Court, in order to avoid overbreadth concerns, had construed the statute narrowly to apply only to ads containing "express advocacy" of a candidate. Section 203 expanded the ban to include all "electioneering communications," whether or not they explicitly told the audience to vote for or against a candidate.

Like the original 1974 statute, the 2002 version was immediately challenged on First Amendment grounds. Many observers expected the Court to strike down substantial portions of BCRA, if not the entire statute. Some even anticipated a decision overruling *Buckley* and striking down all limits on contributions.

McCONNELL v. FEDERAL ELECTION COMMISSION
540 U.S. 93, 124 S.Ct. 619, 157 L.Ed.2d 491 (2003)

JUSTICE STEVENS and **JUSTICE O'CONNOR** delivered the opinion of the Court.[24]

The Government defends § 323(a)'s ban on national parties' involvement with soft money as necessary to prevent the actual and apparent corruption of federal candidates and officeholders. Our cases have made clear that the prevention of corruption or its appearance constitutes a sufficiently important interest to justify political contribution limits. We have not limited that interest to the elimination of cash-for-votes exchanges. * * *

Of "almost equal" importance has been the Government's interest in combating the appearance or perception of corruption engendered by large campaign contributions. Take away Congress' authority to regulate the

---

[24] Due to the complexity of the case, there were actually multiple "opinions of the Court," authored by different Justices. We will focus only on the lead opinion, which dealt with the soft money and electioneering issues. (Challenges to others aspects of the statute were covered in opinions for the Court written by Chief Justice Rehnquist and Justice Breyer.) Unusually, the lead opinion is co-authored, probably in order to expedite the process so that the case could be handed down before the 2004 campaign began in earnest. There were also multiple dissenting and concurring opinions, some of which will be partially excerpted.

appearance of undue influence and "the cynical assumption that large donors call the tune could jeopardize the willingness of voters to take part in democratic governance." And because the First Amendment does not require Congress to ignore the fact that "candidates, donors, and parties test the limits of the current law," *Colorado II*, these interests have been sufficient to justify not only contribution limits themselves, but laws preventing the circumvention of such limits.

* * * For nearly 30 years, FECA has placed strict dollar limits and source restrictions on contributions that individuals and other entities can give to national, state, and local party committees for the purpose of influencing a federal election. The premise behind these restrictions has been, and continues to be, that contributions to a federal candidate's party in aid of that candidate's campaign threaten to create—no less than would a direct contribution to the candidate—a sense of obligation. This is particularly true of contributions to national parties, with which federal candidates and officeholders enjoy a special relationship and unity of interest. This close affiliation has placed national parties in a unique position, "whether they like it or not," to serve as "agents for spending on behalf of those who seek to produce obligated officeholders." As discussed below, rather than resist that role, the national parties have actively embraced it.

The question for present purposes is whether large *soft-money* contributions to national party committees have a corrupting influence or give rise to the appearance of corruption. Both common sense and the ample record in these cases confirm Congress' belief that they do. [T]he FEC's allocation regime has invited widespread circumvention of FECA's limits on contributions to parties for the purpose of influencing federal elections. Under this system, corporate, union, and wealthy individual donors have been free to contribute substantial sums of soft money to the national parties, which the parties can spend for the specific purpose of influencing a particular candidate's federal election. It is not only plausible, but likely, that candidates would feel grateful for such donations and that donors would seek to exploit that gratitude.

The evidence in the record shows that candidates and donors alike have in fact exploited the soft-money loophole, the former to increase their prospects of election and the latter to create debt on the part of officeholders, with the national parties serving as willing intermediaries. * * *

The evidence from the federal officeholders' perspective is similar. For example, one former Senator described the influence purchased by nonfederal donations as follows:

> Too often, Members' first thought is not what is right or what they believe, but how it will affect fundraising. Who, after all, can

seriously contend that a $100,000 donation does not alter the way one thinks about—and quite possibly votes on—an issue? . . . When you don't pay the piper that finances your campaigns, you will never get any more money from that piper. Since money is the mother's milk of politics, you never want to be in that situation.

* * *

By bringing soft-money donors and federal candidates and officeholders together, "[p]arties are thus necessarily the instruments of some contributors whose object is not to support the party's message or to elect party candidates across the board, but rather to support a specific candidate for the sake of a position on one narrow issue, or even to support any candidate who will be obliged to the contributors."

Plaintiffs argue that without concrete evidence of an instance in which a federal officeholder has actually switched a vote (or, presumably, evidence of a specific instance where the public believes a vote was switched), Congress has not shown that there exists real or apparent corruption. But the record is to the contrary. The evidence connects soft money to manipulations of the legislative calendar, leading to Congress' failure to enact, among other things, generic drug legislation, tort reform, and tobacco legislation. To claim that such actions do not change legislative outcomes surely misunderstands the legislative process.

More importantly, plaintiffs conceive of corruption too narrowly. Our cases have firmly established that Congress' legitimate interest extends beyond preventing simple cash-for-votes corruption to curbing "undue influence on an officeholder's judgment, and the appearance of such influence." Many of the "deeply disturbing examples" of corruption cited by this Court in *Buckley* to justify FECA's contribution limits were not episodes of vote buying, but evidence that various corporate interests had given substantial donations to gain access to high-level government officials. Even if that access did not secure actual influence, it certainly gave the "appearance of such influence."

The record in the present case is replete with similar examples of national party committees peddling access to federal candidates and officeholders in exchange for large soft-money donations. * * * So pervasive is this practice that the six national party committees actually furnish their own menus of opportunities for access to would-be soft-money donors, with increased prices reflecting an increased level of access. * * *

In sum, there is substantial evidence to support Congress' determination that large soft-money contributions to national political parties give rise to corruption and the appearance of corruption. * * *

BCRA § 203's Prohibition of Corporate and Labor Disbursements for Electioneering Communications

Since our decision in *Buckley,* Congress' power to prohibit corporations and unions from using funds in their treasuries to finance advertisements expressly advocating the election or defeat of candidates in federal elections has been firmly embedded in our law. The ability to form and administer separate segregated funds [PACs] has provided corporations and unions with a constitutionally sufficient opportunity to engage in express advocacy. That has been this Court's unanimous view, and it is not challenged in this litigation.

Section 203 of BCRA [extends] this rule, which previously applied only to express advocacy, to all "electioneering communications" covered by the definition of that term in amended FECA § 304(f)(3). [That subsection defines electioneering communications as any broadcast, cable, or satellite communication that clearly identifies a candidate, airs within sixty days of a general election or thirty days of a primary, and is targeted at the relevant electorate.] Thus, under BCRA, corporations and unions may not use their general treasury funds to finance electioneering communications, but they remain free to organize and administer segregated funds, or PACs, for that purpose. Because corporations can still fund electioneering communications with PAC money, it is "simply wrong" to view the provision as a "complete ban" on expression rather than a regulation.

Rather than arguing that the prohibition on the use of general treasury funds is a complete ban that operates as a prior restraint, plaintiffs instead challenge the expanded regulation on the grounds that it is both overbroad and underinclusive. [The Court concluded, however, that issues about the exact scope of the provision were not troublesome because "corporations and unions may finance genuine issue ads during those time frames by simply avoiding any specific reference to federal candidates, or in doubtful cases by paying for the ad from a segregated fund."]

[Dissenting opinions are omitted, but follow the lines set out in the majority opinion in the next case.]

NOTES ON MCCONNELL

1. *Fracture Lines Within the Court.* One of the fracture lines within the Court concerned the status of speech by corporations and unions. Are there legitimate reasons for allowing greater regulation of speech by these entities? See Richard L. Hasen, *Buckley is Dead, Long Live Buckley: the New Campaign Finance Incoherence of McConnell v. Federal Election Commission*, 153 U. Pa. L. Rev. 31 (2004). A second fracture line concerned the meaning of corruption. Loosely, the majority thinks corruption includes "influence peddling," while the dissent defines it as bribery. Is the grant of access as a reward for political contributions and expenditures something that we should be worried about?

Or is it an inevitable component of democracy? Just what does "corruption" mean in this context?

2. *Decisions Between* McConnell *and* Citizens United. Cases after *McConnell* were less receptive to campaign finance regulation. First, in *Randall v. Sorrell*, 548 U.S. 230 (2006), the Court struck down a 1997 Vermont law that imposed especially stringent limits on contributions and campaign expenditures. Notably, Chief Justice Roberts joined a portion of Justice Breyer's decision that refused to overrule *Buckley*'s limits on expenditures, but that spoke more broadly about adherence to *Buckley*.

Second, in *Federal Election Comm'n v. Wisconsin Right to Life*, 551 U.S. 44 (2007), a closely divided Court sharply contracted the prohibition on union and corporate advertising during the so-called blackout period before elections.

Third, in *Davis v. Federal Election Commission*, 554 U.S. 724 (2008), the Court struck down the so-called "Millionaire's Amendment." This amendment raised the ceiling on expenditures by candidates receiving public financing when the opposing candidate finances his or her campaign out of personal wealth. Justice Alito's opinion for the Court rejected as illegitimate any government interest in providing a level playing field between wealthy and less affluent candidates.

Finally, in *Arizona Free Enterprise Club's Freedom Club PAC v. Bennett*, 564 U.S. 721 (2011), the Court struck down an effort to make public financing more attractive by providing matching funds when an opponent who is not receiving public funding spends more than the amount granted in public funding. Those four cases presaged a major revision of campaign finance law in the following case.

CITIZENS UNITED V. FEDERAL ELECTION COMMISSION
558 U.S. 310, 130 S.Ct. 876, 175 L.Ed.2d 753 (2010)

JUSTICE KENNEDY delivered the opinion of the Court.

Federal law prohibits corporations and unions from using their general treasury funds to make independent expenditures for speech defined as an "electioneering communication" or for speech expressly advocating the election or defeat of a candidate. Limits on electioneering communications were upheld in *McConnell*. The holding of *McConnell* rested to a large extent on an earlier case, *Austin* [discussed supra, p. 750.] *Austin* had held that political speech may be banned based on the speaker's corporate identity.

In this case we are asked to reconsider *Austin* and, in effect, *McConnell*. It has been noted that "*Austin* was a significant departure from ancient First Amendment principles" * * * We agree with that conclusion and hold that *stare decisis* does not compel the continued acceptance of *Austin*. The Government may regulate corporate political speech through disclaimer and disclosure requirements, but it may not suppress that speech altogether. We turn to the case now before us. * * *

The law before us is an outright ban, backed by criminal sanctions. Section 441b makes it a felony for all corporations—including nonprofit advocacy corporations—either to expressly advocate the election or defeat of candidates or to broadcast electioneering communications within 30 days of a primary election and 60 days of a general election. Thus, the following acts would all be felonies under § 441b: The Sierra Club runs an ad, within the crucial phase of 60 days before the general election, that exhorts the public to disapprove of a Congressman who favors logging in national forests; the National Rifle Association publishes a book urging the public to vote for the challenger because the incumbent U.S. Senator supports a handgun ban; and the American Civil Liberties Union creates a Web site telling the public to vote for a Presidential candidate in light of that candidate's defense of free speech. These prohibitions are classic examples of censorship.

Section 441b is a ban on corporate speech notwithstanding the fact that a PAC created by a corporation can still speak. A PAC is a separate association from the corporation. So the PAC exemption from § 441b's expenditure ban, does not allow corporations to speak. * * *

Premised on mistrust of governmental power, the First Amendment stands against attempts to disfavor certain subjects or viewpoints. Prohibited, too, are restrictions distinguishing among different speakers, allowing speech by some but not others. As instruments to censor, these categories are interrelated: Speech restrictions based on the identity of the speaker are all too often simply a means to control content.

Quite apart from the purpose or effect of regulating content, moreover, the Government may commit a constitutional wrong when by law it identifies certain preferred speakers. By taking the right to speak from some and giving it to others, the Government deprives the disadvantaged person or class of the right to use speech to strive to establish worth, standing, and respect for the speaker's voice. The Government may not by these means deprive the public of the right and privilege to determine for itself what speech and speakers are worthy of consideration. The First Amendment protects speech and speaker, and the ideas that flow from each.

The Court has upheld a narrow class of speech restrictions that operate to the disadvantage of certain persons, but these rulings were based on an interest in allowing governmental entities to perform their functions. The corporate independent expenditures at issue in this case, however, would not interfere with governmental functions, so these cases are inapposite. These precedents stand only for the proposition that there are certain governmental functions that cannot operate without some restrictions on particular kinds of speech. By contrast, it is inherent in the nature of the political process that voters must be free to obtain information from diverse sources in order to determine how to cast their votes. At least before *Austin,* the Court had not allowed the exclusion of a class of speakers from the general public dialogue.

We find no basis for the proposition that, in the context of political speech, the Government may impose restrictions on certain disfavored speakers. Both history and logic lead us to this conclusion. * * *

If the First Amendment has any force, it prohibits Congress from fining or jailing citizens, or associations of citizens, for simply engaging in political speech. If the antidistortion rationale were to be accepted, however, it would permit Government to ban political speech simply because the speaker is an association that has taken on the corporate form. The Government contends that *Austin* permits it to ban corporate expenditures for almost all forms of communication stemming from a corporation. If *Austin* were correct, the Government could prohibit a corporation from expressing political views in media beyond those presented here, such as by printing books. The Government responds "that the FEC has never applied this statute to a book," and if it did, "there would be quite [a] good as-applied challenge." This troubling assertion of brooding governmental power cannot be reconciled with the confidence and stability in civic discourse that the First Amendment must secure. * * *

There is simply no support for the view that the First Amendment, as originally understood, would permit the suppression of political speech by media corporations. The Framers may not have anticipated modern business and media corporations. Yet television networks and major newspapers owned by media corporations have become the most important means of mass communication in modern times. The First Amendment was certainly not understood to condone the suppression of political speech in society's most salient media. It was understood as a response to the repression of speech and the press that had existed in England and the heavy taxes on the press that were imposed in the colonies. The great debates between the Federalists and the Anti-Federalists over our founding document were published and expressed in the most important means of mass communication of that era—newspapers owned by individuals. At the founding, speech was open, comprehensive, and vital to society's definition of itself; there were no limits on the sources of speech and knowledge. The Framers may have been unaware of certain types of speakers or forms of communication, but that does not mean that those speakers and media are entitled to less First Amendment protection than those types of speakers and media that provided the means of communicating political ideas when the Bill of Rights was adopted. * * *

The censorship we now confront is vast in its reach. The Government has "muffle[d] the voices that best represent the most significant segments of the economy." And "the electorate [has been] deprived of information, knowledge and opinion vital to its function." By suppressing the speech of manifold corporations, both for-profit and nonprofit, the Government prevents their voices and viewpoints from reaching the public and advising voters on which persons or entities are hostile to their interests. Factions will necessarily form in our Republic, but the remedy of "destroying the liberty" of some factions is "worse than the disease." Factions should be checked by permitting them all to speak, and by entrusting the people to judge what is true and what is false. * * *

The appearance of influence or access, furthermore, will not cause the electorate to lose faith in our democracy. By definition, an independent expenditure is political speech presented to the electorate that is not coordinated with a candidate. The fact that a corporation, or any other speaker, is willing to spend money to try to persuade voters presupposes that the people have the ultimate influence over elected officials. This is inconsistent with any suggestion that the electorate will refuse " 'to take part in democratic governance' " because of additional political speech made by a corporation or any other speaker. * * *

We need not reach the question whether the Government has a compelling interest in preventing foreign individuals or associations from influencing our Nation's political process. Section 441b is not limited to corporations or associations that were created in foreign countries or funded predominately by foreign shareholders. Section 441b therefore would be overbroad even if we assumed, *arguendo,* that the Government has a compelling interest in limiting foreign influence over our political process. * * *

Citizens United argues that the disclaimer requirements in § 311 are unconstitutional as applied to its ads. It contends that the governmental interest in providing information to the electorate does not justify requiring disclaimers for any commercial advertisements, including the ones at issue here. We disagree. The ads fall within BCRA's definition of an "electioneering communication": They referred to then-Senator Clinton by name shortly before a primary and contained pejorative references to her candidacy. * * * At the very least, the disclaimers avoid confusion by making clear that the ads are not funded by a candidate or political party.

CHIEF JUSTICE ROBERTS, with whom **JUSTICE ALITO** joins, concurring.

The Government urges us in this case to uphold a direct prohibition on political speech. It asks us to embrace a theory of the First Amendment that would allow censorship not only of television and radio broadcasts, but of pamphlets, posters, the Internet, and virtually any other medium that corporations and unions might find useful in expressing their views on matters of public concern. Its theory, if accepted, would empower the Government to prohibit newspapers from running editorials or opinion pieces supporting or opposing candidates for office, so long as the newspapers were owned by corporations—as the major ones are. First Amendment rights could be confined to individuals, subverting the vibrant public discourse that is at the foundation of our democracy.

JUSTICE STEVENS, with whom **JUSTICE GINSBURG**, **JUSTICE BREYER**, and **JUSTICE SOTOMAYOR** join, concurring in part and dissenting in part.

The real issue in this case concerns how, not if, the appellant may finance its electioneering. Citizens United is a wealthy nonprofit corporation that runs a political action committee (PAC) with millions of dollars in assets. Under the Bipartisan Campaign Reform Act of 2002 (BCRA), it could have used those assets to televise and promote *Hillary: The Movie* wherever and whenever it wanted to. It also could have spent unrestricted sums to broadcast *Hillary* at any time other than the 30 days before the last primary election. Neither Citizens United's nor any other corporation's speech has been "banned." All that the parties dispute is whether Citizens United had a right to use the funds in its general treasury to pay for broadcasts during the 30-day period. The notion that the First Amendment dictates an affirmative answer to that question is, in my judgment, profoundly misguided. Even more misguided is the notion that the Court must rewrite the law relating to campaign expenditures by *for-profit* corporations and unions to decide this case.

The basic premise underlying the Court's ruling is its iteration, and constant reiteration, of the proposition that the First Amendment bars regulatory distinctions based on a speaker's identity, including its "identity" as a corporation. While that glittering generality has rhetorical appeal, it is not a correct statement of the law. Nor does it tell us when a corporation may engage in electioneering that some of its shareholders oppose. It does not even resolve the specific question whether Citizens United may be required to finance some of its messages with the money in its PAC. The conceit that corporations must be treated identically to natural persons in the political sphere is not only inaccurate but also inadequate to justify the Court's disposition of this case.

In the context of election to public office, the distinction between corporate and human speakers is significant. Although they make enormous contributions to our society, corporations are not actually members of it. They cannot vote or run for office. Because they may be managed and controlled by nonresidents, their interests may conflict in fundamental respects with the interests of eligible voters. The financial resources, legal structure, and instrumental orientation of corporations raise legitimate concerns about their role in the electoral process. Our lawmakers have a compelling constitutional basis, if not also a democratic duty, to take measures designed to guard against the potentially deleterious effects of corporate spending in local and national races. * * *

The Framers thus took it as a given that corporations could be comprehensively regulated in the service of the public welfare. Unlike our colleagues, they had little trouble distinguishing corporations from human beings, and when they constitutionalized the right to free speech in the First Amendment, it was the free speech of individual Americans that they had in mind. While individuals might join together to exercise their speech rights, business corporations, at least, were plainly not seen as facilitating such associational or expressive ends. Even "the notion that business corporations could invoke the First Amendment would probably have been quite a novelty," given that "at the time, the legitimacy of every corporate activity was thought to rest entirely in a concession of the sovereign." * * * In light of these background practices and understandings, it seems to me implausible that the Framers believed "the freedom of speech" would extend equally to all corporate speakers, much less that it would preclude legislatures from taking limited measures to guard against corporate capture of elections. * * *

The Court's blinkered and aphoristic approach to the First Amendment may well promote corporate power at the cost of the individual and collective self-expression the Amendment was meant to serve. It will undoubtedly cripple the ability of ordinary citizens, Congress, and the States to adopt even limited measures to protect against corporate domination of the electoral process. Americans may be forgiven if they do not feel the Court has advanced the cause of self-government today. * * *

At bottom, the Court's opinion is thus a rejection of the common sense of the American people, who have recognized a need to prevent corporations from undermining self-government since the founding, and who have fought against the distinctive corrupting potential of corporate electioneering since the days of Theodore Roosevelt. It is a strange time to repudiate that common sense. While American democracy is imperfect, few outside the majority of this Court would have thought its flaws included a dearth of corporate money in politics.

NOTES ON THE FIRST AMENDMENT
AND CAMPAIGN FINANCE LAWS

1. *Equal Respect for Corporate Persons.* Justice Kennedy says, "By taking the right to speak from some and giving it to others, the Government deprives the disadvantaged person or class of the right to use speech to strive to establish worth, standing, and respect for the speaker's voice." Does that argument apply to corporations? Are artificial legal persons entitled to "worth,

standing, and respect"? If not, does that undermine Justice Kennedy's argument that corporations are entitled to equal speech rights?

2. *The Issue of Foreign Influence.* The Court's left open the issue of regulation of contribution from foreign individuals and corporations. Would the Court in fact hold reduction of foreign influence to be a compelling interest? Could it be argued that foreign entities (individual, corporate, or governmental) *should* have the right to voice their views in U.S. elections since the outcome of those elections (especially in terms of the presidency) may affect people around the world? Could *Citizens United* serve as the basis for internationalizing U.S. politics?

3. *Would a Different Factual Record Matter?* The Montana Supreme Court concluded that there was stronger evidence about the dangers of corporate corruption in Montana than considered the evidence about national corruption in *Citizens United*, but the Supreme Court summarily reversed this effort to distinguish *Citizens United* in *American Tradition Partnership, Inc. v. Bullock*, 567 U.S. 516 (2012). Justice Breyer, joined by Ginsburg, Sotomayor, and Kagan, argued that the Court should have heard the case. In response, the majority said only: "Montana's arguments in support of the judgment below either were already rejected in *Citizens United*, or fail to meaningfully distinguish that case."

4. *Critiques and Defenses. Citizens United* gave rise to heated scholarly debate. For a sample of the initial responses, see Lucian A. Bebchuck and Robert J. Jackson, Jr., *Corporate Political Speech: Who Decides?*, 124 Harv. L. Rev. 83 (2010); Samuel Issacharoff, *On Political Corruption*, 124 Harv. L. Rev. 118 (2010); Kathleen M. Sullivan, *Two Concepts of Freedom of Speech*, 124 Harv. L. Rev. 143 (2010); Richard L. Hasen, *Citizens United and the Illusion of Coherence*, 109 Mich. L. Rev. 581 (2011).

5. *Rolling Back One Prong of Buckley.* In a later case, *McCutcheon v. Federal Election Commission*, 572 U.S. 185 (2014), the Court reversed one aspect of *Buckley v. Valeo. Buckley* upheld a limit on the total contributions that an individual can make to federal candidates during an election cycle, as well the limits on contributions to individual candidates. In *McCutcheon*, the Court struck down the aggregate limit. Chief Justice Roberts's plurality opinion (joined by Scalia, Kennedy and Alito) focused on whether the aggregate limit was necessary to prevent quid pro quo corruption, which it considered the only valid purpose for campaign regulation. The plurality concluded that the risk of quid pro quo corruption was adequately addressed by the limit on contributions to each individual candidate. Because of anti-circumvention regulations adopted since *Buckley* was decided, the plurality dismissed the government's argument that the aggregate limit was necessary to prevent schemes evading the individual candidate limit. Justice Thomas concurred in the judgment, arguing that *Buckley* should be overruled outright. In dissent, Justice Breyer (joined by Justices Ginsburg, Sotomayor, and Kagan), argued as in *Citizens United* that corruption included broader forms of influence peddling than simple bribery, and that the aggregate limit was in fact required

to prevent circumvention of the individual limits. Breyer also chided the majority for deciding factual issues about the potential for circumvention without any evidentiary hearing in the lower court, while Roberts responded that the parties had not pressed for a remand on this basis.

6.   *A Different Rules for Judges?* A 2015 case was a departure from the strong trend of invalidating campaign finance regulations under the Roberts Court. In *Williams-Yulee v. Florida Bar*, ___ U.S. ___, 135 S.Ct. 1656, 191 L.Ed.2d 570 (2015), the Court upheld a limit on solicitation of campaign contributions by judges in judicial elections in an opinion by Chief Justice Roberts. His opinion speaks of the "vital state interest" in safeguarding "public confidence in the fairness and integrity of the nation's elected judges." Unlike elected officials, Roberts emphasized, judges are not supposed to be responsive to the preferences of their constituents, and allowing them to solicit campaign contributions would create a temptation to sway decisions in favor of prospective donors.

The dissenters argued that the majority did not seem to be demanding as much precision in the fit between ends and means as in some other cases of strict scrutiny. On the other hand, once avoiding the appearance of partiality is accepted as a compelling state interest, is it possible to draw rules as precise as those that the dissenters demanded?

The dissenters seemed sanguine about the possibility that judges might become as responsive to contributors as other office-holders. To the extent that the governmental interest is public confidence in the institutions of government, isn't the dissent right that this interest is neither more nor less important as applied to judges as to others? On the other hand, could the majority argue that there is a special interest in giving litigants (as opposed to the general public) confidence that there cases are being decided impartially?

SECTION 3. CULTURAL DISCOURSE AND INTERGROUP RELATIONS

People can come to identify themselves as part of groups in various ways, including the way that the culture identifies and characterizes individuals and their behaviors. Challenging, transgressing, or defending these characterizations is an important aspect of public discourse, and the contestants often call upon government assistance. For instance, sex-related expression can help define how people think about men, women, and sexuality. In response, religious groups call for regulation of obscenity in order to defend traditional understandings of sex roles, while some feminists call for regulation of pornography in order to change attitudes and behavior toward women. Similar disputes arise with respect to ethnic, language, and racial minorities. Overlayed on these debates is the question of how to structure the public sphere, so that on the one hand all groups are free to use it for self-expression but on the other hand all groups can navigate it freely.

A. SEXUALITY AND GENDER

When the First Amendment was ratified, all fourteen states made either blasphemy or profanity a statutory crime, and some of the states made it a crime to promulgate "any filthy, obscene, or profane song, pamphlet, libel or mock sermon," *Mass. Bay Colony Charters and Laws* 399 (1814). In the first half of the nineteenth century, most states and many municipalities adopted laws criminalizing the promulgation of obscene printed materials—but never defining what was meant by obscenity. Materials advertising contraceptives, describing the biology of human reproduction, advocating tolerance of homosexuality, or recounting episodes of fornication or sodomy were seized as obscene, without any noticeable judicial resistance until the 1930s.

Although the Supreme Court in *Roth v. United States*, 354 U.S. 476 (1957), held for the first time that obscenity was not protected by the First Amendment, the Court rejected the "tends to deprave vulnerable minds" test followed since the 1880s and redefined obscenity as material which, if considered as a whole, predominantly appeals to "prurient interest, i.e., a shameful or morbid interest in nudity, sex, or excretion." During the 1960s, the Court expanded and sought to refine the *Roth* definition, but could never obtain the agreement of five Justices for any precise formulation. Then, in 1973, the Court finally handed down two decisions that commanded five-Justice majority opinions.

Miller v. California

413 U.S. 15 (1973)

The Court held in an opinion by **Chief Justice Burger** that "the basic guidelines for the trier of fact must be: (a) whether 'the average person, applying contemporary community standards' would find that the work, taken as a whole, appeals to the prurient interest; (b) whether the work depicts or describes, in a patently offensive way, sexual conduct specifically defined by the applicable state law; and (c) whether the work, taken as a whole, lacks serious literary, artistic, political, or scientific value." As the Court explained:

> Sex and nudity may not be exploited without limit by films or pictures exhibited or sold in places of public accommodation any more than live sex and nudity can be exhibited or sold without limit in such public places. At a minimum, prurient, patently offensive depiction or description of sexual conduct must have serious literary, artistic, political, or scientific value to merit First Amendment protection. For example, medical books for the education of physicians and related personnel necessarily use graphic illustrations and descriptions of human anatomy. In resolving the inevitably sensitive questions of fact and law, we must continue to rely on the jury system, accompanied by the safeguards that judges, rules of evidence,

presumption of innocence, and other protective features provide, as we do with rape, murder, and a host of other offenses against society and its individual members.

———

In a companion case, *Paris Adult Theatre I v. Slaton*, 413 U.S. 49 (1973), the Court rejected the argument that the First Amendment protects the right of consenting adults to purchase obscene materials. The Court held that the government had valid regulatory interests, including "the interest of the public in the quality of life and the total community environment, the tone of commerce in the great city centers, and, possibly, the public safety itself." The Court also noted that "there is at least an arguable correlation between obscene material and crime." Although (then as now) the empirical evidence was at least subject to dispute, the Court concluded that the legislature was entitled to assume that obscene materials were harmful.

Some feminists have criticized the Court's approach based on the possible harm of pornography to women. See Professor Catharine A. MacKinnon, *Francis Biddle's Sister: Pornography, Civil Rights, and Speech*, in *Feminism Unmodified* 163 (1987). Based upon empirical studies, published stories, and testimony at hearings on her proposed anti-pornography ordinance in Minneapolis, MacKinnon argued that pornography plays a critical role in subordinating women. According to MacKinnon, children as well as women are coerced into performing in pornographic films, sometimes physically and sometimes psychologically, as through blackmail. Furthermore, she argued, pornography directly causes sexual abuse, particularly against women. "Some rapes are performed by men with paperback books in their pockets." Experimental studies, MacKinnon wrote, show that exposure to pornography as defined in the proposed ordinance "cause[s] measurable harm to women through increasing men's attitudes and behaviors of discrimination in both violent and nonviolent forms."[25] Third, MacKinnon argued that pornography contributes generally to women's inequality. MacKinnon's views are discussed in more detail in Chapter 4.

These arguments led several city councils to pass ordinances banning pornography without regard to the *Miller* test. This effort did not receive a favorable judicial reaction. See *American Booksellers Ass'n v. Hudnut*, 771 F.2d 323 (7th Cir. 1985) (Easterbrook, J.), *aff'd mem.*, 475 U.S. 1001 (1986)

———

[25] Other examinations of research on possible linkages between pornography and violence or oppression against women include James Weinstein, *Hate Speech, Pornography, and the Radical Attack on Free Speech Doctrine* 191–217 (1999); Richard Posner, *Sex and Reason* 366–73 (1992); Frederick Schauer, *Causation Theory and the Causes of Sexual Violence*, 1987 Am. Bar Found. Res. J. 737 (analyzing the results of the Report of the Attorney General's Commission on Pornography, on which Schauer served); Cass Sunstein, *Pornography and the First Amendment*, 1986 Duke L.J. 589.

(reviewing a similar ordinance). Thus, the *Miller* test remains the law today. The following notes explore doctrinal developments relating to its scope.

NOTES ON REGULATING SEXUALLY EXPLICIT WRITINGS AND VIDEOS

1. *Privacy*. In connection with *Paris Adult Theatre*, consider *Stanley v. Georgia*, 394 U.S. 557 (1969), in which the Court reversed a conviction for possession of obscene films. The police had discovered the films during a search of the defendant's home for evidence of illegal gambling. Justice Marshall's opinion for the Court held that the regulations for regulating obscenity do not reach into the privacy of the home: "If the First Amendment means anything, it means that a State has no business telling a man, sitting alone in his own house, what books he may read or what films he may watch." Apparently, under *Stanley*, the government cannot arrest a person for possessing a videotape of an obscene movie, but under *Paris Adult Theatre*, it can prosecute the store that sold the tape.

2. *Local Communities and the Internet*. In *Ashcroft v. ACLU*, 535 U.S. 564 (2002), the Court grappled with the question of how to apply the "community standard" portion of *Miller* to the Internet. In response to *Reno v. ACLU*, 521 U.S. 844 (1997), which struck down Congress' first effort to shield children from pornographic material on the Internet, Congress passed the Child Online Protection Act, which restricts only commercial material on the World Wide Web that is "harmful to minors." The statute incorporates the *Miller* test. The lower court held that using contemporary community standards made the statute unconstitutional on its face, since it would in effect limit the entire country to whatever material was acceptable to the most restrictive local community. The case produced such a badly fractured Court that we are reluctant to attempt a summary. The only thing that almost everyone on the Court did agree about was that the lower court's first effort was unsatisfactory. On remand, the lower courts issued a permanent injunction, which the Court declined to review.

3. *Child Pornography*. The Court has made only one significant departure from the *Miller* obscenity test. In *New York v. Ferber*, 458 U.S. 747 (1982), the Court upheld a statute banning "child pornography," which was defined as sexual material involving children as models or actors. The Court found that the state's interest in protecting children from participating in the production of these materials was strong enough to justify banning the materials themselves, so as to dry up the market. In *Ashcroft v. The Free Speech Coalition*, 535 U.S. 234 (2002), the Court considered whether to expand *Ferber* to encompass "virtual child pornography"—pornography in which adult actors portray juveniles or in which computer images appearing like real children are used. Justice Kennedy's opinion for the Court emphasized that "*Ferber's* judgment about child pornography was based upon how it was made, not on what it communicated." To the government's argument that virtual

pornography encourages pedophiles, the Court responded that the government "cannot constitutionally premise legislation on the desirability of controlling a person's private thoughts. . . . First Amendment freedoms are most in danger when the government seeks to control thought or to justify its laws for that impermissible end. "The government also argued that makers of real child pornography would evade conviction if they were allowed to offer a "virtual pornography" defense. But the Court said that banning protected speech in order to expedite the prosecution of unprotected speech "turns the First Amendment on its head."

Expression related to sexuality seems to be subject to an unusual amount of acceptable regulation in the Court's eyes, as illustrated by the following decisions. In considering these cases, ask whether the Courts would have upheld similar restraints on political expression.

City of Renton v. Playtime Theatres, Inc.

475 U.S. 41 (1986)

A city ordinance in Renton, Washington, prohibited adult movie theaters within 1,000 feet of any residence, church, park, or school. The plaintiffs had purchased two theatres with the intention of exhibiting adult films. In an opinion by **Chief Justice Rehnquist**, the Court upheld the ordinance, reasoning that "at least with respect to businesses that purvey sexually explicit materials, zoning ordinances designed to combat the undesirable secondary effects of such businesses are to be reviewed under the standards applicable to 'content-neutral' time, place, and manner regulations." The ordinance satisfied this standard, in the Court's view. The Court was unimpressed by the facts that Renton had relied entirely on the experience of other cities to show that adult businesses would cause harm rather than presenting evidence relating specifically to its own situation, and that the ordinance left open very few sites that were actually commercially available.[26]

Barnes v. Glen Theatre, Inc.

501 U.S. 560 (1991)

This case involved the application of Indiana's ban on public nudity to barroom dancing. **Chief Justice Rehnquist**'s plurality opinion accepted the premise that nude dancing was sufficiently expressive to receive some First Amendment protection. He considered the state's interest in preventing public

---

[26] *Renton* purports to leave open the opportunity to operate an adult bookstore or movie theater, though subjecting these activities to special land-use restrictions. In practice, however, administrators might either delay issuing permits or arbitrarily deny them, in effect turning what is supposed to be a system of zoning into a flat prohibition. *City of Littleton v. Z.J. Gifts D-4, L.L.C.*, 541 U.S. 774 (2004), considers what procedural safeguards are required to prevent this abuse. *City of Littleton* held that the state's "ordinary judicial review procedures suffice as long as the courts remain sensitive to the need to prevent First Amendment harms and administer those procedures accordingly. And whether the courts do so is a matter normally fit for case-by-case determination rather than a facial challenge."

nudity to be content neutral and upheld the ordinance under the *O'Brien* test. **Justice Scalia**, concurring in the judgment, argued that a general law regulating conduct (and not targeted at expressive conduct) should not be subject to First Amendment scrutiny at all. ("Were it the case that Indiana *in practice* targeted only expressive nudity, while turning a blind eye to nude beaches and unclothed purveyors of hot dogs and machine tools, it might be said that what posed as a regulation of conduct in general was in reality a regulation of only communicative conduct.") **Justice Souter** also concurred in the judgment, on the basis that the state had a "substantial interest in combating the secondary effects of adult entertainment establishments" such as prostitution and sexual assaults. **Justice White**, joined by **Justices Marshall**, **Blackmun**, and **Stevens**, dissented, arguing that the statute was aimed at the "communicative aspect of the erotic dance" and therefore was not content-neutral.

City of Erie v. Pap's A.M.

529 U.S. 277 (2000)

This case presented the Court with the opportunity to clarify its holding in *Barnes*, but the Justices once again proved unable to agree on a rationale. The plaintiff operated an adult entertainment establishment featuring nude dancing. Erie passed an ordinance against nude dancing, with language tracking the ordinance upheld in *Barnes*, thus requiring that the dancers wear pasties and G-strings. The introduction to the ordinance recited the city's concern about the secondary effects of nude dancing establishments like the plaintiff's. Once again, the Court upheld the ban on nude dancing, but with no consensus on the reasoning. According to the plurality opinion by **Justice O'Connor**, the propensity of adult entertainment establishments to attract crime and prostitution is a content-neutral secondary effect that the city could validly seek to suppress. Consequently, she found that the *O'Brien* test was applicable and was satisfied by the ordinance. **Justices Scalia** and **Thomas** once again concluded that a general ban on public nudity regulates conduct rather than speech, and is therefore immune from First Amendment scrutiny. In dissent, **Justice Souter** found an inadequate factual record to support the city's concerns. In another dissent, **Justice Stevens**, joined by **Justice Ginsburg**, argued that the ban was content-based since it was aimed entirely at erotic dancing rather than other nude dancing—the city having conceded that it had not applied the ordinance to serious theatrical productions such as the play "Equus."

What exactly is the state's interest in banning public nudity where only consenting adults are involved? How is it different from the state's interest in banning photographs of nude individuals, which clearly would not be subject to the *O'Brien* test?

The state courts had indicated that the ban did not apply to theatrical performances. Is there any constitutional obstacle to applying the ban in that context? If not, why should the state have the power to ban a live performance involving nudity, but not the power to ban a movie showing exactly the same thing?

B. FIGHTING WORDS, CAPTIVE AUDIENCES, AND HATE SPEECH

COHEN V. CALIFORNIA
403 U.S. 15, 91 S.Ct. 1780, 29 L.Ed.2d 284 (1971)

JUSTICE HARLAN delivered the opinion of the Court.

This case may seem at first blush too inconsequential to find its way into our books, but the issue it presents is of no small constitutional significance.

Appellant Paul Robert Cohen was convicted [of] "maliciously and willfully disturb[ing] the peace or quiet of any neighborhood or person . . . by . . . offensive conduct . . . " He was given 30 days' imprisonment. The facts upon which his conviction rests are detailed in the opinion of the Court of Appeal of California, Second Appellate District, as follows:

> On April 26, 1968, the defendant was observed in the Los Angeles County Courthouse in the corridor outside of division 20 of the municipal court wearing a jacket bearing the words "Fuck the Draft" which were plainly visible. There were women and children present in the corridor. The defendant was arrested. The defendant testified that he wore the jacket knowing that the words were on the jacket as a means of informing the public of the depth of his feelings against the Vietnam War and the draft.

> The defendant did not engage in, nor threaten to engage in, nor did anyone as the result of his conduct in fact commit or threaten to commit any act of violence. The defendant did not make any loud or unusual noise, nor was there any evidence that he uttered any sound prior to his arrest. * * *

In order to lay hands on the precise issue which this case involves, it is useful first to canvass various matters which this record does *not* present. * * *

In the first place, Cohen was tried under a statute applicable throughout the entire State. Any attempt to support this conviction on the ground that the statute seeks to preserve an appropriately decorous atmosphere in the courthouse where Cohen was arrested must fail in the absence of any language in the statute that would have put appellant on notice that certain kinds of otherwise permissible speech or conduct would nevertheless, under California law, not be tolerated in certain places. No fair reading of the phrase "offensive conduct" can be said sufficiently to inform the ordinary person that distinctions between certain locations are thereby created.[27]

In the second place, as it comes to us, this case cannot be said to fall within those relatively few categories of instances where prior decisions have established the power of government to deal more comprehensively with certain forms of individual expression simply upon a showing that such a form was employed. * * *

This Court has also held that the States are free to ban the simple use, without a demonstration of additional justifying circumstances, of so-called "fighting words," those personally abusive epithets which, when addressed to the ordinary citizen, are, as a matter of common knowledge, inherently likely to provoke. While the four-letter word displayed by Cohen in relation to the draft is not uncommonly employed in a personally provocative fashion, in this instance it was clearly not "directed to the person of the hearer." No individual actually or likely to be present could reasonably have regarded the words on appellant's jacket as a direct personal insult. Nor do we have here an instance of the exercise of the State's police power to prevent a speaker from intentionally provoking a given group to hostile reaction. There is, as noted above, no showing that anyone who saw Cohen was in fact violently aroused or that appellant intended such a result.

Finally, in arguments before this Court much has been made of the claim that Cohen's distasteful mode of expression was thrust upon unwilling or unsuspecting viewers, and that the State might therefore legitimately act as it did in order to protect the sensitive from otherwise unavoidable exposure to appellant's crude form of protest. Of course, the mere presumed presence of unwitting listeners or viewers does not serve automatically to justify curtailing all speech capable of giving offense. While this Court has recognized that government may properly act in many situations to prohibit intrusion into the privacy of the home of unwelcome views and ideas which cannot be totally banned from the public dialogue, we have at the same time consistently stressed that "we are often 'captives' outside the sanctuary of the home and subject to objectionable speech." The ability of government, consonant with the Constitution, to shut off discourse solely to protect others from hearing it is, in other words, dependent upon a showing that substantial privacy interests are being invaded in an essentially intolerable manner. Any broader view of this authority would effectively empower a majority to silence dissidents simply as a matter of personal predilections. * * *

Against this background, the issue flushed by this case stands out in bold relief. It is whether California can excise, as "offensive conduct," one

---

[27] It is illuminating to note what transpired when Cohen entered a courtroom in the building. He removed his jacket and stood with it folded over his arm. Meanwhile, a policeman sent the presiding judge a note suggesting that Cohen be held in contempt of court. The judge declined to do so and Cohen was arrested by the officer only after he emerged from the courtroom.

particular scurrilous epithet from the public discourse, either upon the theory of the court below that its use is inherently likely to cause violent reaction or upon a more general assertion that the States, acting as guardians of public morality, may properly remove this offensive word from the public vocabulary.

The rationale of the California court is plainly untenable. At most it reflects an "undifferentiated fear or apprehension of disturbance [which] is not enough to overcome the right to freedom of expression." We have been shown no evidence that substantial numbers of citizens are standing ready to strike out physically at whoever may assault their sensibilities with execrations like that uttered by Cohen. There may be some persons about with such lawless and violent proclivities, but that is an insufficient base upon which to erect, consistently with constitutional values, a governmental power to force persons who wish to ventilate their dissident views into avoiding particular forms of expression. The argument amounts to little more than the self-defeating proposition that to avoid physical censorship of one who has not sought to provoke such a response by a hypothetical coterie of the violent and lawless, the States may more appropriately effectuate that censorship themselves.

Admittedly, it is not so obvious that the First and Fourteenth Amendments must be taken to disable the States from punishing public utterance of this unseemly expletive in order to maintain what they regard as a suitable level of discourse within the body politic. We think, however, that examination and reflection will reveal the shortcomings of a contrary viewpoint.

At the outset, we cannot overemphasize that, in our judgment, most situations where the State has a justifiable interest in regulating speech will fall within one or more of the various established exceptions, discussed above but not applicable here, to the usual rule that governmental bodies may not prescribe the form or content of individual expression. Equally important to our conclusion is the constitutional backdrop against which our decision must be made. The constitutional right of free expression is powerful medicine in a society as diverse and populous as ours. It is designed and intended to remove governmental restraints from the arena of public discussion, putting the decision as to what views shall be voiced largely into the hands of each of us, in the hope that use of such freedom will ultimately produce a more capable citizenry and more perfect polity and in the belief that no other approach would comport with the premise of individual dignity and choice upon which our political system rests. *See Whitney v. California* (Brandeis, J., concurring).

To many, the immediate consequence of this freedom may often appear to be only verbal tumult, discord, and even offensive utterance. These are, however, within established limits, in truth necessary side effects of the broader enduring values which the process of open debate permits us to achieve. That the air may at times seem filled with verbal cacophony is, in this sense not a sign of weakness but of strength. We cannot lose sight of the fact that, in what otherwise might seem a trifling and annoying instance of individual distasteful abuse of a privilege, these fundamental societal values are truly implicated. That is why "[w]holly neutral futilities . . . come under the protection of free speech as fully as do Keats' poems or Donne's sermons," and why "so long as the means are peaceful, the communication need not meet standards of acceptability."

[JUSTICE WHITE's dissenting opinion is omitted.]

JUSTICE BLACKMUN, with whom THE CHIEF JUSTICE [BURGER] and JUSTICE BLACK join, dissenting.

Cohen's absurd and immature antic, in my view, was mainly conduct and little speech. The California Court of Appeal appears so to have described it, and I cannot characterize it otherwise. Further, the case appears to me to be well within the sphere of *Chaplinsky v. New Hampshire*, where Justice Murphy, a known champion of First Amendment freedoms, wrote for a unanimous bench. As a consequence, this Court's agonizing over First Amendment values seems misplaced and unnecessary.

NOTES ON COHEN AND OFFENSIVE SPEECH

1. *The Distinction Between Profanity and Fighting Words*. Justice Harlan's decision suggests that even if fighting words can be regulated, ordinarily profanity cannot. Should there be such a wide distinction drawn between these two categories of expression? Presumably *Cohen* would have greatly surprised the Framers, who operated against the backdrop of state laws criminalizing blasphemy and other forms of profanity. Should state actions clearly allowable at the time of the Framers be restricted? Are the purposes or values of the First Amendment more implicated in profanity cases than in fighting-words cases?

The regulation of both fighting words and profanity relates to the maintenance of public civility.[28] By protecting profanity and narrowly construing the fighting-words doctrine, *Cohen* reduces the state's ability to maintain such civility. If that is a good idea, why not overrule *Chaplinsky*?

Could the Court be wrong in suggesting that profanity has fewer third-party effects than fighting words? In cases where profanity is not also fighting words, the listeners might often be vulnerable people (e.g., children, the

---

[28] For explorations of this question, see Walter Berns, *The First Amendment and the Future of American Democracy* (1976); Daniel Farber, *Civilizing Public Discourse: An Essay on Professor Bickel, Justice Harlan, and the Enduring Significance of* Cohen v. California, 1980 Duke L.J. 283. A more recent appraisal of *Cohen* can be found in Thomas G. Krattenmaker, *Looking Back at Cohen v. California: A 40-Year Retrospective from Inside the Court*, 20 Wm. & Mary Bill of Rights Journal 651 (2012).

elderly) unable to escape the onslaught. Is Justice Harlan undervaluing parents' interest in protecting children from foul language? On the other hand, if you can burn a flag or a cross with the intent of upsetting targeted persons, perhaps the display of language in *Cohen* is tame by comparison.

2. *May the State Regulate Harassing Expression?* In *Plummer v. City of Columbus*, 414 U.S. 2 (1973), the Court struck down an ordinance prohibiting "menacing, insulting, slanderous, or profane language." The defendant was a taxicab driver who addressed a female passenger with a series of "vulgar, suggestive, and abhorrent, sexually-oriented statements." In *State v. Harrington*, 67 Or. App. 608, 680 P.2d 666 (1984), the Oregon Supreme Court interpreted its state constitution to overturn a conviction for uttering racial epithets in violation of a harassment law. The court ruled that "abusive language spoken with intent to annoy or alarm" could not constitutionally be regulated. Should the U.S. Supreme Court carry *Cohen* that far?

1. An Exception for Hate Speech?

Constitutional protection for hate speech can be criticized—and distinguished from *Cohen*—by invoking an antisubordination principle suggested by the equal protection cases (Chapters 2–4) and by critical theory of the sort outlined by Professor Robin West (Chapter 2). Mari Matsuda, *Public Response to Racist Speech: Considering the Victim's Story*, 87 Mich. L. Rev. 2320 (1989), argues for a reading of the First Amendment that accounts for such an antisubordination principle. She defines hate speech to include only that which contains a message of racial inferiority, directed against a historically oppressed group and is persecutory and hateful in its message. Is her reconciliation of free speech and equal protection precepts a persuasive one?

Beauharnais v. Illinois

343 U.S. 250 (1952)

Defendant Beauharnais was the president of the White Circle League. He was prosecuted for distributing a leaflet calling for white citizens of Chicago "to halt the further encroachment, harassment and invasion of white people, their property, neighborhoods and person by the Negro" and to unite "to prevent the white race from becoming mongrelized by the negro." The legal basis for the prosecution was an Illinois law making it a crime to distribute a publication that "portrays depravity, criminality, unchastity, or lack of virtue of a class of citizens, of any race, color, creed or religion" or which "exposes the citizens of any race, color, creed or religion to contempt, derision, or obloquy or which is productive of breach of the peace or riots." The trial judge did not allow Beauharnais to put on evidence of the truth of the statements.

A divided (5–4) Supreme Court affirmed the conviction. **Justice Frankfurter**'s opinion for the Court ruled that (1) libel is not speech protected by the First Amendment, (2) "collectivities" as well as individuals can be libeled, and (3) it was within the realm of reasonable legislative choice to create such a law to ease racial tensions in the state. "[T]he Illinois Legislature may warrantably believe that a man's job and his educational opportunities and the dignity accorded him may depend as much on the reputation of the racial and religious group to which he willy-nilly belongs, as on his own merits. This being so, we are precluded from saying that speech concededly punishable when immediately directed at individuals cannot be outlawed if directed at groups with whose position and esteem in society the affiliated individual may be inextricably involved."

————

Some lower courts have suggested that Justice Frankfurter's ruling did not survive *New York Times v. Sullivan* (§ 2B, *supra*). See, e.g., *Collin v. Smith*, 578 F.2d 1197 (7th Cir. 1978) (Illinois town of Skokie could not constitutionally prevent white supremacist, anti-Semitic Nazi Party march; *Beauharnais* no longer good law). *R.A.V.* seems even more contrary to *Beauharnais*. Does *R.A.V.* draw into question a law making only some group libels illegal? Or a rule protecting against race-based animus? Consider the next case.

Wisconsin v. Mitchell

508 U.S. 476 (1993)

In this case, the Court explored the implications of the Court's holding in *R.A.V., supra*. After seeing a movie in which a white man had beaten a young black, the defendant, who was black, asked his friends, "Do you all feel hyped up to move on some white people?" Soon afterward, at the defendant's direction, the group beat up a young white. The defendant was convicted of aggravated battery, but his sentence was increased under a statute providing extra punishment for "hate crimes" (that is, crimes in which the victim was selected on the basis of a prohibited criterion, such as race). The Court affirmed the enhanced sentence in an opinion by **Chief Justice Rehnquist**. He distinguished *R.A.V.* as follows:

> [Defendant] argues that the Wisconsin penalty-enhancement statute is invalid because it punishes the defendant's discriminatory motive, or reason, for acting. But motive plays the same role under the Wisconsin statute as it does under federal and state antidiscrimination laws, which we have previously upheld against constitutional challenge. * * * [I]n *R.A.V.*, we cited Title VII (as well as [other federal antidiscrimination statutes]) as an example of a permissible content-neutral regulation of conduct.

> Nothing in our decision last Term in *R.A.V.* compels a different result here. * * * Because the ordinance only proscribed a class of 'fighting words' deemed particularly offensive by the city—*i.e.*, those 'that contain . . . messages of "bias-motivated" hatred'—we held that

it violated the rule against content-based discrimination. But whereas the ordinance struck down in *R.A.V.* was explicitly directed at expression (*i.e.*, 'speech' or 'messages'), the statute in this case is aimed at conduct unprotected by the First Amendment.

Moreover, the Wisconsin statute singles out for enhancement bias-inspired conduct because this conduct is thought to inflict greater individual and societal harm. For example, according to the State and its *amici*, bias-motivated crimes are more likely to provoke retaliatory crimes, inflict distinct emotional harms on their victims, and incite community unrest. The State's desire to redress these perceived harms provides an adequate explanation for its penalty-enhancement provision over and above mere disagreement with offenders' beliefs or biases.

NOTE ON THE HATE SPEECH DEBATE

What are the implications of *Mitchell*? Suppose that the sentence enhancement was applied in a case where the crime was "making terroristic threats"? Valid under *Mitchell*? Under *R.A.V.* itself? How do you fit *Virginia v. Black* (the "true threats" cross-burning case) into the analysis?

Hate speech in general and proposals to regulate it in particular have received a great deal of attention from commentators. A complete discussion of the scholarship on the subject is precluded by space limitations. Our goal here is simply to give you a flavor of the contending positions. A sample of more recent viewpoints can be found in *Symposium: Hate Speech and Political Legitimacy*, 32 Const. Commentary 527–782 (2017).

Richard Delgado, *Campus Antiracism Rules: Constitutional Narratives in Collision*, 85 Nw. U.L. Rev. 343 (1991), argued that hate speech does little to promote First Amendment values:

Uttering racial slurs may afford the racially troubled speaker some immediate relief, but hardly seems essential to self-fulfillment in any ideal sense. Indeed, social science writers hold that making racist remarks impairs, rather than promotes, the growth of the person who makes them, by encouraging rigid, dichotomous thinking and impeding moral development. * * *

Additionally, slurs contribute little to the discovery of truth. Classroom discussion of racial matters and even the speech of a bigot aimed at proving the superiority of the white race might move us closer to the truth. But one-on-one insults do not. They neither state nor attack a proposition; they are like a slap in the face. * * * "More speech" is rarely a solution. Epithets often strike suddenly, immobilizing their victim and rendering her speechless. Often they are delivered in cowardly, anonymous fashion—for example, in the form of a defaced poster or leaflet slipped under a student's door, or hurled by a group against a single victim, rendering response foolhardy.

Turning to an equality perspective, Delgado observes that regulation of hate speech "may be necessary for full effectuation of the values of equal personhood we hold equally dear."[29]

Charles Lawrence III, *Acknowledging the Victim's Cry*, Academe 10 (November–December 1990), draws an intriguing analogy between hate speech regulation and the *Brown* decision:

> [*Brown*] speaks directly to the psychic injury inflicted by racist speech by noting that the symbolic message of segregation affected "the hearts and minds" of African-American children "in a way unlikely ever to be undone." Racial epithets and harassment often cause deep emotional scarring and feelings of anxiety and fear that pervade every aspect of a victim's life.

> *Brown* also recognized that African-American children did not have an equal opportunity to learn and participate in the school's community when they bore the additional burden of being subject to the humiliation and psychic assault contained in the message of segregation. * * *

> African-Americans and other people of color are skeptical about the argument that even the most injurious speech must remain unregulated because, in an unregulated marketplace of ideas, the best ones will rise to the top and gain acceptance. Experience tells quite the opposite. People of color have seen too many demagogues elected by appealing to America's racism. * * *

> Whenever we decide that racist speech must be tolerated because of the importance of maintaining societal tolerance for all unpopular speech, we are asking African-Americans and other subordinated groups to bear the burden of the good of all. We must be careful that the ease with which we strike the balance against the regulation of racist speech is in no way influenced by the fact that the cost will be borne by others. We must be certain that those who will pay that price are fairly represented in our deliberations and that they are heard.[30]

In a response to Professor Lawrence, Gerald Gunther, *Freedom for the Thought We Hate*, Academe 10 (November–December 1990), argued:

> Lest it be thought that I am insensitive to the pain imposed by expressions of racial or religious hatred, let me say that I have

---

[29] For a summary of Delgado's views, see Richard Delgado, *Toward a Legal Realist View of the First Amendment*, 113 Harv. L. Rev. 778 (2000) (book review). For a critique of this line of argument, see Gary Goodpaster, *Equality and Free Speech: The Case Against Substantive Equality,* 82 Iowa L. Rev. 645 (1997).

[30] See also Charles Lawrence, III, *If He Hollers Let Him Go: Regulating Racist Speech on Campus*, 1990 Duke L.J. 431.

suffered that pain and empathize with others under similar verbal assault. My deep belief in the principles of the First Amendment arises in part from my own experiences. I received my elementary education in a public school in a very small town in Nazi Germany. There I was subject to vehement anti-Semitic remarks from my teacher, classmates, and others—Judensau (Jew pig) was far from the harshest. I can assure you that they hurt.

More generally, I lived in a country where ideological orthodoxy reigned and where the opportunity for dissent was severely limited.

The lesson I have drawn from my childhood in Nazi Germany and my happier adult life in this country is the need to walk the sometimes difficult path of denouncing the bigots' hateful ideas with all my power, yet at the same time challenging any community's attempt to suppress hateful ideas by force of law. * * *

[S]peech should not and cannot be banned simply because it is "offensive" to substantial parts or a majority of the community. The refusal to suppress offensive speech is one of the most difficult obligations the free speech principle imposes upon all of us; yet it is also one of the First Amendment's greatest glories—indeed, it is a central test of a community's commitment to free speech.[31]

Like Professor Gunther, Nadine Strossen, *Regulating Racist Speech on Campus: A Modest Proposal?*, 1990 Duke L.J. 484, argues that hate speech cannot be banned consistent with existing First Amendment analysis. She also argues that hate speech regulation has a tendency to backfire, harming minority groups:

The first reason that laws censoring racist speech may undermine the goal of combating racism flows from the discretion such laws inevitably vest in prosecutors, judges, and the other individuals who implement them. One ironic, even tragic, result of this discretion is that members of minority groups themselves—the very people whom the law is intended to protect—are likely targets of punishment. For example, among the first individuals prosecuted under the British Race Relations Act of 1965 were black power leaders. Their overtly racist messages undoubtedly expressed legitimate anger at real discrimination, yet the statute drew no such fine lines, nor could any similar statute possibly do so. * * *

The British experience * * * parallels the experience in the United States under the one [hate speech] rule that has led to a judicial decision. During the approximately one year that [the rule] was in effect, there were more than twenty cases of whites charging blacks with racist speech. More importantly, the only two instances

---

[31] Other notable responses to Professors Delgado, Lawrence, and Matsuda include James Weinstein, *Hate Speech, Pornography, and the Radical Attack on Free Speech Doctrine* (1999), and Robert Post, *Racist Speech, Democracy, and the First Amendment*, 32 Wm. & Mary L. Rev. 267 (1991).

in which the rule was invoked to sanction racist speech (as opposed to sexist and other forms of hate speech) involved the punishment of speech by or on behalf of black students. Additionally, the only student who was subject to a full-fledged disciplinary hearing * * * was a black student accused of homophobic and sexist expression. * * * Likewise, the student who recently brought a lawsuit challenging the University of Connecticut's hate speech policy, under which she had been penalized for an allegedly homophobic remark, was Asian-American.[32]

The debate continues today. The legal philosopher Jeremy Waldron argues that speech can be regulated with meaningful intrusion into democratic freedoms. See Jeremy Waldron, *Dignity and Defamation: The Visibility of Hate*, 123 Harv. L. Rev. 1596 (2010). On the other hand, opponents of some existing regulation now hold important positions in the U.S. government. In 2018 the U.S. Secretary of Education and the Attorney General warned that free speech was threatened by universities seeking to shield students from offensive or hurtful ideas. The Justice Department has filed "statements of interest" in support of some students challenging campus speech restrictions in court. See Megan Keller, *Sessions: DOJ Concerned About Suppression of Free Speech on College Campuses*, THE HILL (Sept. 18, 2018).

PROBLEM 6-2:
UNIVERSITY REGULATION OF DISCRIMINATORY HARASSMENT

Indiana University prohibits discriminatory harassment, which is defined as follows:

> Discriminatory harassment is defined as conduct that targets an individual based upon age, color, religion, disability, race, ethnicity, national origin, sex, gender, gender identity, sexual orientation, marital status, or veteran's status and that adversely affects a term or condition of an individual's education, housing, or participation in a university activity; or has the purpose or effect of unreasonably creating an intimidating, hostile, or offensive environment for academic pursuits, housing, or participation in university activities.

http://studentcode.iu.edu/rights/harassment.html. Consider whether this provision would apply to communications such as a professor's tweet, "Why is White America so reluctant to identify White college males as a problem population?", or a Facebook post that Nation of Islam Minister Louis

---

[32] For responses to Strossen and other critics of hate speech regulation, see W. Bradley Wendel, *"Certain Fundamental Truths": A Dialectic on Negative and Positive Liberty in Hate-Speech Cases*, 65 Law & Contemp. Probs. 33 (2002) (presenting a thoughtful dialogue on the issue); Jean Stefancic & Richard Delgado, *A Shifting Balance: Freedom of Expression and Hate-Speech Restriction*, 78 Iowa L. Rev. 737 (1993).

Farrakhan was correct that "Israeli and Zionist Jews" played "key roles in the 9/11 attack."[33]

The rationale for restricting racial speech on campus (and by extension, speech aimed at other vulnerable groups) was explained in Professor Matsuda's article:

> Official tolerance of racist speech in this setting is more harmful than generalized tolerance in the community-at-large. It is harmful to student perpetrators in that it is a lesson in getting-away-with-it that will have lifelong repercussions. It is harmful to targets, who perceive the university as taking sides through inaction, and who are left to their own resources in coping with the damage wrought. Finally, it is a harm to the goals of inclusion, education, development of knowledge, and ethics that universities exist and stand for. Lessons of cynicisms and hate replace lessons in critical thought and inquiry.

Mari Matsuda, *Public Response to Racist Speech: Considering the Victim's Story*, 87 MICH. L. REV. 2310, 2370–71 (1989). A different perspective, more skeptical of such rules, is presented by Peter Byrne, *Racial Insults and Free Speech Within the University*, 79 Geo. L.J. 399 (1991).

(1) Would Professor Matsuda consider the Indiana University provision sufficient to deal with racist or similar speech on campus? Is there an argument for broadening the definition of discriminatory harassment?

(2) Are there situations where the existing Indiana University provision arguably applies to protected speech? As some possible examples, consider a tweet (from a professor at another school) that Twitter: "Why is White America so reluctant to identify White college males as a problem population?"

If you have identified arguable applications to protected speech, could you suggest drafting changes to strengthen the provision's prospects in court?

Could you suggest drafting changes or alternative types of regulation that might make the regulation less vulnerable to challenge? Should First Amendment doctrine be realigned, as Professor Matsuda suggests, to eliminate constitutional protection for hate speech—defined as messages of racial inferiority, directed against a historically oppressed group, and characterized as persecutorial, hateful, and degrading?

For purposes of this problem, assume that the state does not have any special power to regulate speech merely because it owns and operates the University. We will reconsider that assumption later.

2. Offensive Speech in the Electronic Media

The precepts of *Cohen* and *R.A.V.* apply with full force to print media such as newspapers, but not necessarily to electronic media, such as

---

[33] These examples, which involved faculty at other universities, are cited in Alexander Tseis, *The Categorical Free Speech Doctrine and Contextualization*, 65 Emory L. Rev. 495 (2015).

television or radio. *Red Lion Broadcasting Co. v. Federal Communications Commission*, 395 U.S. 367 (1969), upheld the FCC's fairness doctrine, which required radio and television to provide equal time to opposing viewpoints on important political issues. Such a holding, unthinkable for newspaper regulation, was justified for television regulation by the scarcity of possible channels. Cf. *Turner Broadcasting Sys. v. FCC*, 512 U.S. 622 (1994) (conceding that this rationale has been overtaken by changed circumstances). Consider the different rationale for allowing regulation of dirty words on the airwaves.

Federal Communications Commission v. Pacifica Foundation

438 U.S. 726 (1978)

George Carlin recorded a monologue which featured "seven dirty words" that you couldn't say on the airwaves; the comic point of the monologue was Carlin's mocking and defying the ban by iterating the seven dirty words in a variety of contexts. Pacifica's New York radio station played the monologue. In response to complaints from a father whose son was exposed to it, the FCC ruled it "patently offensive" but not obscene and banned it pursuant to 18 U.S.C. § 1464, which forbids the use of "any obscene, indecent, or profane language by means of radio communication." A fractured Supreme Court upheld the FCC action.

Justice Stevens wrote a plurality opinion emphasizing the special nature of radio transmissions. "Patently offensive, indecent material presented over the airwaves confronts the citizen, not only in public, but also in the privacy of the home, where the individual's right to be left alone plainly outweighs the First Amendment rights of an intruder." Additionally, "broadcasting is uniquely accessible to children, even those too young to read. Although Cohen's written message might have been incomprehensible to a first grader, Pacifica's broadcast could have enlarged a child's vocabulary in an instant. Other forms of offensive expression may be withheld from the young without restricting the expression at its source. Bookstores and motion picture theaters, for example, may be prohibited from making indecent material available to children."

Justice Powell, joined by **Justice Blackmun**, concurred in that portion of Justice Stevens' opinion. They emphasized the Commission's factual findings, the intrusion into the home, and the exposure of children to the monologue. But they stated that state censorship would not necessarily be permissible against radio broadcasts late at night, when children were not likely to be listening, or against sale of the monologue in record form.

Four Justices dissented. **Justice Brennan**'s dissenting opinion, joined by **Justice Marshall**, argued that the Court's result was inconsistent with *Cohen*'s rule that the state cannot silence speech to protect others from hearing it, unless substantial privacy interests are being invaded in an intolerable manner. "[A]n individual's actions in switching on and listening to communications transmitted over the public airways and directed to the public at large do not implicate fundamental privacy interests, even when engaged in within the home. * * * [U]nlike other intrusive modes of communication, such as sound trucks, '[t]he radio can be turned off.'" More pointedly, Justice Brennan argued that the majority displayed a "depressing inability to appreciate that in our land of cultural pluralism, there are many who think, act, and talk differently from the Members of this Court, and who do not share their fragile sensibilities. It is only an acute ethnocentric myopia that enables the Court to approve the censorship of communications solely because of the words they contain."

NOTE ON SEXUAL CONTENT IN ELECTRONIC MEDIA

Notwithstanding *Pacifica*, a unanimous Court in *Sable Communications, Inc. v. Federal Communications Commission*, 492 U.S. 115 (1989), invalidated a 1988 federal law that criminally prohibited "sexually oriented pre-recorded [dial-a-porn] telephone messages" that were either indecent or obscene. Justice White's opinion for the Court held that indecent but nonobscene speech is protected by the First Amendment and presumptively cannot be banned. He distinguished *Pacifica* as involving only a partial ban on programming that intruded into the home without prior warning as to indecent content. Placing a telephone call requires affirmative choice by the listener as to precisely what she or he wants to hear. The danger that children would be exposed to indecent material did not justify a total ban, because less restrictive means—special access codes, blocking porn numbers at parents' request—could achieve substantially the same end.

After *Sable*, it was accepted that Congress could not completely ban indecency on cable television. A plurality opinion in *Denver Area Educational Telecommunications Consortium v. Federal Communications Commission*, 518 U.S. 727 (1996), adopted a balancing approach to legislation authorizing the FCC and cable operators to censor indecent material. The law allowed cable operators to bar "sexually explicit" as well as obscene material on leased access and public access channels, for which such operators normally have no editorial discretion.

The next year, the application of the First Amendment to the Internet came before the Supreme Court. In *Reno v. American Civil Liberties Union*, 521 U.S. 844 (1997), the Supreme Court invalidated provisions of the Communications Decency Act (CDA) of 1996 prohibiting transmission of indecent communications to persons under age eighteen on the Internet. Justice Stevens' opinion for the Court ruled that cyberspace is subject to normal First Amendment precepts, which were automatically fatal to the Act's content-based regulation of indecency. The Internet is not as invasive as radio or television, nor can a user come upon sexually explicit materials by accident and without prior warning. Hence, the Court said, the statutory regulation was much more like that in *Sable* than in *Pacifica*. The Act was overbroad, for it suppressed speech adults are entitled to send and receive, and the statutory goal of protecting minors could be achieved through less restrictive means, as in *Denver Area*.

The Court revisited the issue of indecent speech in the electronic media in *United States v. Playboy Entertainment Group*, 529 U.S. 803 (2000). The Telecommunications Act required cable operators either to scramble sexually explicit channels in full or to limit programming on those channels to certain hours, because of the possibility that "signal bleed" from incomplete scrambling would allow children to see portions of the programming. Justice Kennedy's opinion for the Court held the provision to be content-based and struck it down. He emphasized that the statute was concerned with the "direct impact that speech has on its listeners" rather than on secondary effects. The plaintiff had offered a "plausible, less restrictive alternative": requiring cable operators to block undesired channels at the request of individual households, combined with advertising and other efforts to notify households of this option. The government failed to show that this alternative would be ineffective at protecting children. Justice Kennedy emphasized that current technology "expands the capacity to choose; and it denies the potential of this revolution if we assume the Government is best positioned to make these choices for us."

After remand, the Court upheld a ruling by the district court that the plaintiffs were likely to prevail on the merits of their claim. *Ashcroft v. ACLU*, 542 U.S. 656 (2004). Justice Kennedy's opinion for the Court stressed that upon remand for trial the government would have a full opportunity to demonstrate that the district court's initial conclusions about less restrictive alternatives were incorrect. He also emphasized that five years had passed since the district court's decision, suggesting that a new examination was in order in light of the rapidly evolving nature of Internet technology. Finally, he concluded that leaving the preliminary injunction in place guarded against chilling effect and self-censorship threatened by the statute pending final resolution of the case.

So far, the discussion has involved explicit erotic communications. But what about other types of speech that offend current norms, such as graphic violence in children's products? The following case is noteworthy because it considers whether other forms of speech can be treated like erotic speech, and because it required the Court to encounter for the first time the constitutional status of videogames.

BROWN V. ENTERTAINMENT MERCHANTS ASSOCIATION
564 U.S. 786, 131 S.Ct. 2729, 180 L.Ed.2d 708 (2011)

JUSTICE SCALIA delivered the opinion of the Court.

We consider whether a California law imposing restrictions on violent video games comports with the First Amendment. [A California statute prohibits the sale or rental of "violent video games" to minors, and requires their packaging to be labeled "18." [The Act, which was designed to parallel the *Miller* test for obscenity, covers games "in which the range of options available to a player includes killing, maiming, dismembering, or sexually assaulting an image of a human being, if those acts are depicted" in a manner that "[a] reasonable person, considering the game as a whole, would find appeals to a deviant or morbid interest of minors," that is "patently offensive to prevailing standards in the community as to what is suitable for minors," and that "causes the game, as a whole, to lack serious literary, artistic, political, or scientific value for minors."]

California correctly acknowledges that video games qualify for First Amendment protection. The Free Speech Clause exists principally to protect discourse on public matters, but we have long recognized that it is difficult to distinguish politics from entertainment, and dangerous to try. "Everyone is familiar with instances of propaganda through fiction. What is one man's amusement, teaches another's doctrine." Like the protected books, plays, and movies that preceded them, video games communicate ideas—and even social messages—through many familiar literary devices (such as characters, dialogue, plot, and music) and through features distinctive to the medium (such as the player's interaction with the virtual world). That suffices to confer First Amendment protection. * * *

Last Term, in *Stevens*, we held that new categories of unprotected speech may not be added to the list by a legislature that concludes certain speech is too harmful to be tolerated. *Stevens* concerned a federal statute purporting to criminalize the creation, sale, or possession of certain depictions of animal cruelty. * * * A saving clause largely borrowed from our obscenity jurisprudence exempted depictions with "serious religious, political, scientific, educational, journalistic, historical, or artistic value." We held that statute to be an impermissible content-based restriction on speech. There was no American tradition of forbidding the *depiction of* animal cruelty—though States have long had laws against *committing* it.

The Government argued in *Stevens* that lack of a historical warrant did not matter; that it could create new categories of unprotected speech by applying a "simple balancing test" that weighs the value of a particular category of speech against its social costs and then punishes that category of speech if it fails the test. We emphatically rejected that "startling and dangerous" proposition. "Maybe there are some categories of speech that have been historically unprotected, but have not yet been specifically identified or discussed as such in our case law." But without persuasive evidence that a novel restriction on content is part of a long (if heretofore unrecognized) tradition of proscription, a legislature may not revise the "judgment [of] the American people," embodied in the First Amendment, "that the benefits of its restrictions on the Government outweigh the costs."

That holding controls this case. As in *Stevens*, California has tried to make violent-speech regulation look like obscenity regulation by appending a saving clause required for the latter. That does not suffice. Our cases have been clear that the obscenity exception to the First Amendment does not cover whatever a legislature finds shocking, but only depictions of "sexual conduct." [I]t is of no consequence that California's statute mimics the New York statute regulating obscenity-for-minors that we upheld in *Ginsberg v. New York,* 390 U.S. 629 (1968). That case approved a prohibition on the sale to minors of *sexual* material that would be obscene from the perspective of a child. We held that the legislature could "adjus[t] the definition of obscenity 'to social realities by permitting the appeal of this type of material to be assessed in terms of the sexual interests . . . of . . . minors." The California Act is something else entirely. It does not adjust the boundaries of an existing category of unprotected speech to ensure that a definition designed for adults is not uncritically applied to children. California does not argue that it is empowered to prohibit selling offensively violent works *to adults*—and it is wise not to, since that is but a hair's breadth from the argument rejected in *Stevens.* Instead, it wishes to create a wholly new category of content-based regulation that is permissible only for speech directed at children.

That is unprecedented and mistaken. "[M]inors are entitled to a significant measure of *First Amendment* protection, and only in relatively narrow and well-defined circumstances may government bar public dissemination of protected materials to them." No doubt a State possesses legitimate power to protect children from harm, but that does not include a free-floating power to restrict the ideas to which children may be exposed. "Speech that is neither obscene as to youths nor subject to some other legitimate proscription cannot be suppressed solely to protect the young from ideas or images that a legislative body thinks unsuitable for them."

California's argument would fare better if there were a longstanding tradition in this country of specially restricting children's access to depictions of violence, but there is none. Certainly the *books* we give children to read—or read to them when they are younger—contain no shortage of gore. Grimm's Fairy Tales, for example, are grim indeed. As her just deserts for trying to poison Snow White, the wicked queen is made to dance in red hot slippers "till she fell dead on the floor, a sad example of envy and jealousy." * * *

California's effort to regulate violent video games is the latest episode in a long series of failed attempts to censor violent entertainment for minors. While we have pointed out above that some of the evidence brought forward to support the harmfulness of video games is unpersuasive, we do not mean to demean or disparage the concerns that underlie the attempt to regulate them—concerns that may and doubtless do prompt a good deal of parental oversight. We have no business passing judgment on the view of the California Legislature that violent video games (or, for that matter, any other forms of speech) corrupt the young or harm their moral development. Our task is only to say whether or not such works constitute a "well-defined and narrowly limited clas[s] of speech, the prevention and punishment of which have never been thought to raise any Constitutional problem," and if not, whether the regulation of such works is justified by that high degree of necessity we have described as a compelling state interest (it is not). Even where the protection of children is the object, the constitutional limits on governmental action apply.

JUSTICE ALITO, joined by CHIEF JUSTICE ROBERTS, concurring in the judgment.

The California statute that is before us in this case represents a pioneering effort to address what the state legislature and others regard as a potentially serious social problem: the effect of exceptionally violent video games on impressionable minors, who often spend countless hours immersed in the alternative worlds that these games create. Although the California statute is well intentioned, its terms are not framed with the precision that the Constitution demands, and I therefore agree with the Court that this particular law cannot be sustained.

I disagree, however, with the approach taken in the Court's opinion. In considering the application of unchanging constitutional principles to new and rapidly evolving technology, this Court should proceed with caution. * * * The opinion of the Court exhibits none of this caution.

In the view of the Court, all those concerned about the effects of violent video games—federal and state legislators, educators, social scientists, and parents—are unduly fearful, for violent video games really present no serious problem. Spending hour upon hour controlling the actions of a character who guns down scores of innocent victims is not different in "kind" from reading a description of violence in a work of literature.

The Court is sure of this; I am not. There are reasons to suspect that the experience of playing violent video games just might be very different from reading a book, listening to the radio, or watching a movie or a television show. [However, Justice Alito concurred in the judgment on the ground that the statutory definition was unconstitutionally vague, despite its resemblance to the *Miller* standard, because the threshold reference to violent acts failed to narrow the statute's scope sufficiently.]

JUSTICE THOMAS, dissenting.

In my view, the "practices and beliefs held by the Founders" reveal another category of excluded speech: speech to minor children bypassing their parents. The historical evidence shows that the founding generation believed parents had absolute authority over their minor children and expected parents to use that authority to direct the proper development of their children. It would be absurd to suggest that such a society understood "the freedom of speech" to include a right to speak to minors (or a corresponding right of minors to access speech) without going through the minors' parents. The founding generation would not have considered it an abridgment of "the freedom of speech" to support parental authority by restricting speech that bypasses minors' parents.

JUSTICE BREYER, dissenting.

California's law imposes no more than a modest restriction on expression. The statute prevents no one from playing a video game, it prevents no adult from buying a video game, and it prevents no child or adolescent from obtaining a game provided a parent is willing to help. All it prevents is a child or adolescent from buying, without a parent's assistance, a gruesomely violent video game of a kind that the industry *itself* tells us it wants to keep out of the hands of those under the age of 17. * * *

Ginsberg makes clear that a State can prohibit the sale to minors of depictions of nudity; today the Court makes clear that a State cannot prohibit the sale to minors of the most violent interactive video games. But what sense does it make to forbid selling to a 13-year-old boy a magazine with an image of a nude woman, while protecting a sale to that 13-year-old of an interactive video game in which he actively, but virtually, binds and gags the woman, then tortures and kills her? What kind of First Amendment would permit the government to protect children by restricting sales of that extremely violent video game *only* when the woman—bound, gagged, tortured, and killed—is also topless?

This anomaly is not compelled by the First Amendment. It disappears once one recognizes that extreme violence, where interactive, and *without literary, artistic, or similar justification*, can prove at least as, if not more, harmful to children as photographs of nudity. And the record here is more than adequate to support such a view. That is why I believe that *Ginsberg* controls the outcome here *a fortiori*. And it is why I believe California's law is constitutional on its face.

NOTE ON ENTERTAINMENT MERCHANTS

Justice Breyer finds it bizarre that a video game containing graphic violence can be sold to children, but not one with nudity. The issue is interesting in its own right but also because it connects with broader questions about constitutional methodology. Justice Scalia's response is that legal restrictions on sexual expression are part of a traditional category of restricted speech. Why should this matter one way or the other? (And does it make sense for the constitutionality of a regulation of a novel technology to depend on whether the regulation fits a traditional category?) One can imagine several rationales for the tradition requirement: (a) traditional forms of government regulation reflect consensus values that should receive legal recognition; (b) the existing categories of unprotected speech are justified only by precedent and should not be expanded; (c) traditions reflect the original understanding (but what then of Justice Thomas's view?); (d) it would be politically too costly for the Court to uproot entrenched practices but novel ones risk less of a backlash; or (e) the Justices themselves agree that sexual speech is more dangerous to minors than violent speech.

Which of these justifications seems to underlie the majority view? Are you convinced or do you agree with Justice Breyer that history alone cannot justify such a constitutional distinction?

As the previous case show, the Court has been willing to extend traditional First Amendment protections to electronic media without significant dilution. That trend is also exemplified by the following case.

Packingham v. North Carolina

137 S.Ct. 1730 (2017)

North Carolina law made it a felony for a registered sex offender "to access a commercial social networking Web site where the sex offender knows that the site permits minor children to become members or to create or maintain personal Web pages." The statute exempted websites that "[p]rovid[e] only one of the following discrete services: photo-sharing, electronic mail, instant messenger, or chat room or message board platform." The law also exemped websites that have as their "primary purpose the facilitation of commercial transactions involving goods or services between [their] members or visitors." The statute applied to about 20,000 people in North Carolina and the State had prosecuted over 1,000 people for violating it.

Justice Kennedy's opinion for the Court began by emphasizing the importance of the Internet:

> While in the past there may have been difficulty in identifying the most important places (in a spatial sense) for the exchange of views, today the answer is clear. It is cyberspace—the "vast democratic forums of the Internet" in general, and social media in particular. Seven in ten American adults use at least one Internet social networking service. One of the most popular of these sites is Facebook, the site used by petitioner leading to his conviction in this case. According to sources cited to the Court in this case, Facebook has 1.79 billion active users. This is about three times the population of North America.

Given the importance of access to social media, Justice Kennedy said, the statute could not stand even if it was considered content neutral:

> [T]he statute here enacts a prohibition unprecedented in the scope of First Amendment speech it burdens. Social media allows users to gain access to information and communicate with one another about it on any subject that might come to mind. By prohibiting sex offenders from using those websites, North Carolina with one broad stroke bars access to what for many are the principal sources for knowing current events, checking ads for employment,

speaking and listening in the modern public square, and otherwise exploring the vast realms of human thought and knowledge.

To round out the casebook's coverage of the categories of speech that have traditional been considered unprotected, we will now briefly discuss a final such "less protected" category, which consists of commercial adevertising and similar types of speech.

NOTES ON COMMERCIAL SPEECH

1. *Constitutional Protection for Commercial Speech.* Commercial advertising was long considered to be outside the scope of First Amendment protection. That rule changed in *Virginia State Board of Pharmacy v. Virginia Citizens Consumer Council*, 425 U.S. 748 (1976). In striking down a state ban on price advertising by pharmacists, Justice Blackmun's opinion for the Court rejected the traditional doctrine for several reasons. First, the fact that the advertiser's interest was economic did not eliminate First Amendment protection, because the Court had long held that the First Amendment protected the speech of both sides in labor disputes. Second, the consumer interest in obtaining the information was high: "When drug prices vary as strikingly as they do, information as to who is charging what becomes more than a convenience. It could mean the alleviation of physical pain or the enjoyment of basic necessities." Advertising is the "dissemination of information as to who is producing and selling what product, for what reason, and at what price" and it is a matter of public interest that market decisions be "intelligent and well informed." which requires the free flow of commercial information.

The rationale for the state regulation was the price regulation would lead to a race to the bottom-cheaper prices but a loss of professionalism. Justice Blackmun found this rationale to be unacceptable because it rests on the paternalistic assumption that consumers will foolishly make decisions based purely on price rather than considering quality:

> There is, of course, an alternative to this highly paternalistic approach. That alternative is to assume that this information is not in itself harmful, that people will perceive their own best interests if only they are well enough informed, and that the best means to that end is to open the channels of communication rather than to close them. If they are truly open, nothing prevents the "professional" pharmacist from marketing his own assertedly superior product, and contrasting it with that of the low-cost, high-volume prescription drug retailer. But the choice among these alternative approaches is not ours to make or the Virginia General Assembly's. It is precisely this kind of choice, between the dangers of suppressing information, and the dangers of its misuse if it is freely available, that the First Amendment makes for us. * * *

Nevertheless, Justice Blackmun said, commercial speech remained subject to greater regulation than other forms of protected speech. In the concluding part of the opinion, the Court stressed that it was not precluding time, place, and manner regulations; restrictions on false or misleading advertising; or bans on advertising for illegal products or services.

2. *The Current Test. Central Hudson Gas & Electric Corp. v. Public Service Comm'n*, 447 U.S. 557 (1980), involved a state regulation that banned public utility ads promoting the use of electricity. The Court struck down the ban, despite the state's attempt to rely on energy conservation as a justification. In the course of the decision, the Court set forth a four-part test for regulations of commercial speech:

> At the outset we must determine whether the expression is protected by the First Amendment. For commercial speech to come within that provision, it at least must concern lawful activity and not be misleading. Next we ask whether the asserted governmental interest is substantial. If both inquiries yield positive answers, we must determine whether the regulation directly advances the governmental interest asserted, and whether it is not more extensive than is necessary to serve that interest.[34]

Presumably this test would yield the same result the Court reached in *Virginia Board*. Reconsider *Railway Express* (Chapter 4, § 1) in light of this approach. Would New York City's restriction of advertising on vehicles pass muster?

3. *Advertising by Lawyers.* Lawyers have been traditionally prohibited from soliciting business by advertising or otherwise. "Ambulance chasing" is a long-standing basis for disbarment. Soon after *Virginia Board*, however, the Court made it clear that the First Amendment also covered advertising by lawyers. *Bates v. State Bar*, 433 U.S. 350 (1977). Since then, the state bars have attempted to continue as much regulation of legal advertising as possible, resulting in a spate of later Supreme Court opinions.

4. *Regulation of Truthful Information.* In *44 Liquormart, Inc. v. Rhode Island*, 517 U.S. 484 (1996), two liquor stores filed suit to challenge a Rhode Island statute banning price advertising for alcoholic beverages except at the place of sale. The Justices were unanimous in agreeing to strike down the law, but badly divided in terms of the rationale. The lead opinion was by Justice Stevens. He read *Central Hudson* as requiring "special care" in reviewing a "blanket ban" on truthful, nonmisleading speech about a lawful product for reasons unrelated to consumer protection. Justice O'Connor, joined by Chief Justice Rehnquist and Justices Souter and Breyer, applied *Central Hudson* and concluded that the statute was unconstitutional. Finally, Justice Scalia indicated an inclination to revisit the entire area of commercial speech in some later case. Although the Court has decided several commercial speech cases since *44 Liquormart*, in each case it invalidated the government regulation

---

[34] The final factor has been interpreted as a "reasonableness" or "narrow tailoring" test, rather than as a more stringent test requiring the least restrictive alternative. See *Board of Trustees v. Fox*, 492 U.S. 469 (1989).

under the *Central Hudson* test, without revisiting the question of the test's validity.

SECTION 4. SPEECH WITH A GOVERNMENT NEXUS

The government may relate to civil society in a variety of ways. In the previous sections, we have considered situations in which the government's role was purely regulatory. Often, however, non-governmental actors want more from government than being free from regulation. They may want to use government-owned streets and parks for demonstrations, parades, or leafletting. They may want government funding for some of their activities. Or they may want to mobilize public employees, students, or other participants in government institutions. In this section, we consider the extent to which the government may foreclose the use of these avenues for expression or condition their use on restrictions on speech.

A. PUBLIC FORUM DOCTRINE

The government may have additional powers to regulate speech when it is not only acting as a regulator but also as an employer, property owner, or source of funding. Indeed, at one time, it was thought that the government's proprietary activities were simply outside the scope of the First Amendment, just like the activities of firms in the private sector. See *Commonwealth v. Davis*, 162 Mass. 510, 39 N.E. 113 (1895) (Holmes, J.), *aff'd*, 167 U.S. 43 (1897). The unarticulated premise may have been that constitutional restrictions should apply only when the government is using its unique power of legal coercion, rather than when it is engaging in the same kinds of conduct also found in the private sector. Today, that position has clearly been rejected, but First Amendment protection is sometimes weaker when speech has a government nexus.

A classic example involves speech on government property. *Hague v. Committee for Industrial Organization*, 307 U.S. 496 (1939), suggested an approach for reviewing government regulation of expressive activities in streets and parks:

> [T]hey have immemorially * * * been used for purposes of assembly, communicating thoughts between citizens, and discussing public questions. * * * The privilege of a citizen of the United States to use the streets and parks for communication of views on national questions may be regulated in the interest of all; it is not absolute, but relative, and must be exercised in subordination to the general comfort and convenience, and in consonance with peace and good order; but it must not, in the guise of regulation, be abridged or denied.

See also *Schneider v. State*, 308 U.S. 147 (1939).

Hague contained the outlines of the public forum doctrine: State property traditionally open for expressive purposes may not be closed off or abridged for reasons relating to the content of the proposed expression, but the state may impose reasonable "time, place, and manner" restrictions on the use of public property. See *Cox v. New Hampshire*, 312 U.S. 569 (1941).

UNITED STATES V. GRACE
461 U.S. 171, 103 S.Ct. 1702, 75 L.Ed.2d 736 (1983)

JUSTICE WHITE delivered the opinion of the Court.

In this case we must determine whether 40 U.S.C. § 13k, which prohibits, among other things, the "display [of] any flag, banner, or device designed or adapted to bringing into public notice any party, organization, or movement" in the United States Supreme Court building and on its grounds, violates the First Amendment. [The Court construed the "bring into public notice" clause to apply to "almost any sign or leaflet carrying a communication."]

* * * The sidewalks comprising the outer boundaries of the Court grounds are indistinguishable from any other sidewalks in Washington, D.C., and we can discern no reason why they should be treated any differently. Sidewalks, of course, are among those areas of public property that traditionally have been held open to the public for expressive activities and are clearly within those areas of public property that may be considered, generally without further inquiry, to be public forum property. The inclusion of the public sidewalks within the scope of § 13k's prohibition, however, results in the destruction of public forum status that is at least presumptively impermissible. Traditional public forum property occupies a special position in terms of First Amendment protection and will not lose its historically recognized character for the reason that it abuts government property that has been dedicated to a use other than as a forum for public expression. Nor may the government transform the character of the property by the expedient of including it within the statutory definition of what might be considered a nonpublic forum parcel of property. The public sidewalks forming the perimeter of the Supreme Court grounds, in our view, are public forums and should be treated as such for First Amendment purposes. * * *

Based on its provisions and legislative history, it is fair to say that the purpose of the Act was to provide for the protection of the building and grounds and of the persons and property therein, as well as the maintenance of proper order and decorum. [Section 13k] was one of the provisions apparently designed for these purposes. At least, no special reason was stated for its enactment.

We do not denigrate the necessity to protect persons and property or to maintain proper order and decorum within the Supreme Court grounds, but we do question whether a total ban on carrying a flag, banner, or device on the public sidewalks substantially serves these purposes. * * * A total ban on that conduct is no more necessary for the maintenance of peace and tranquility on the public sidewalks surrounding the building than on any other sidewalks in the city. Accordingly, § 13k cannot be justified on this basis.

The United States offers another justification for § 13k that deserves our attention. * * * Courts are not subject to lobbying, judges do not entertain visitors in their chambers for the purpose of urging that cases be resolved one way or another, and they do not and should not respond to parades, picketing, or pressure groups. Neither, the Government urges, should it appear to the public that the Supreme Court is subject to outside influence or that picketing or marching, singly or in groups, is an acceptable or proper way of appealing to or influencing the Supreme Court. Hence, we are asked to hold that Congress was quite justified in preventing the conduct in dispute here from occurring on the sidewalks at the edge of the Court grounds.

As was the case with the maintenance of law and order on the Court grounds, we do not discount the importance of this proffered purpose for § 13k. But, again, we are unconvinced that the prohibitions of § 13k that are at issue here sufficiently serve that purpose to sustain its validity insofar as the public sidewalks on the perimeter of the grounds are concerned. Those sidewalks are used by the public like other public sidewalks. There is nothing to indicate to the public that these sidewalks are part of the Supreme Court grounds or are in any way different from other public sidewalks in the city. We seriously doubt that the public would draw a different inference from a lone picketer carrying a sign on the sidewalks around the building than it would from a similar picket on the sidewalks across the street.

Hill v. Colorado

530 U.S. 703 (2000)

This case illustrates the difficulty the Court has sometimes encountered in applying the principle of content neutrality. A Colorado statute made it unlawful for anyone within 100 feet of a healthcare facility to "knowingly approach" within eight feet of another person, without that person's consent, in order to pass out leaflets, display a sign, or engage in "oral protest, education, or counseling." The statute was prompted by anti-abortion activities at clinics offering abortions.

In an opinion by **Justice Stevens**, the Court upheld the statute as a valid time, place or manner regulation. As to why the statute should be considered content-neutral, the Court stressed that it applied on its face to all viewpoints and subjects. The fact that the statute did not cover routine social interactions (such as asking the time) was not enough to make it suspect, nor was the fact that the impetus for the statute came from demonstrations supporting a particular viewpoint. Having found the statute content-neutral, the Court upheld it because it left open many methods of communicating with pedestrians near clinics, and because it was narrowly tailored to the permissible statutory purpose of protecting unwilling listeners from unwanted communications.

Accusing the majority of favoritism toward abortion, **Justice Scalia**, joined by **Justice Thomas**, argued that it was obvious that the statute was targeted at anti-abortion demonstrators and that it distinguished on the basis of content by singling out protest, education, and counseling. He also denied that the state had a legitimate interest in protecting individuals from unwanted speech in a public forum. **Justice Kennedy** also considered the statute unconstitutional, though he did not join the Scalia dissent. In a passionate dissent of his own, he asserted that the majority had denied "these protesters, in the face of what they consider to be one of life's gravest moral crises, even the opportunity to try to offer a fellow citizen a little pamphlet, a handheld paper seeking to reach a higher law."

McCULLEN V. COAKLEY

573 U.S. 464, 134 S.Ct. 2518, 189 L.Ed.2d 502 (2014)

CHIEF JUSTICE ROBERTS delivered the opinion of the Court.

A Massachusetts statute makes it a crime to knowingly stand on a "public way or sidewalk" within 35 feet of an entrance or driveway to any place, other than a hospital, where abortions are performed. Petitioners are individuals who approach and talk to women outside such facilities, attempting to dissuade them from having abortions. The statute prevents petitioners from doing so near the facilities' entrances. The question presented is whether the statute violates the First Amendment. * * *

Petitioners at all three clinics claim that the buffer zones have considerably hampered their counseling efforts. Although they have managed to conduct some counseling and to distribute some literature outside the buffer zones—particularly at the Boston clinic—they say they have had many fewer conversations and distributed many fewer leaflets since the zones went into effect.

The second statutory exemption allows clinic employees and agents acting within the scope of their employment to enter the buffer zones. Relying on this exemption, the Boston clinic uses "escorts" to greet women as they approach the clinic, accompanying them through the zones to the clinic entrance. Petitioners claim that the escorts sometimes thwart petitioners' attempts to communicate with patients by blocking petitioners from handing literature to patients, telling patients not to "pay any

attention" or "listen to" petitioners, and disparaging petitioners as "crazy."
* * *

Petitioners contend that the Act is not content neutral for two independent reasons: First, they argue that it discriminates against abortion-related speech because it establishes buffer zones only at clinics that perform abortions. Second, petitioners contend that the Act, by exempting clinic employees and agents, favors one viewpoint about abortion over the other. If either of these arguments is correct, then the Act must satisfy strict scrutiny—that is, it must be the least restrictive means of achieving a compelling state interest. Respondents do not argue that the Act can survive this exacting standard. * * *

The Act applies only at a "reproductive health care facility," defined as "a place, other than within or upon the grounds of a hospital, where abortions are offered or performed." Given this definition, petitioners argue, "virtually all speech affected by the Act is speech concerning abortion," thus rendering the Act content based.

We disagree. To begin, the Act does not draw content-based distinctions on its face. The Act would be content based if it required "enforcement authorities" to "examine the content of the message that is conveyed to determine whether" a violation has occurred. But it does not. Whether petitioners violate the Act "depends" not "on what they say," but simply on where they say it. Indeed, petitioners can violate the Act merely by standing in a buffer zone, without displaying a sign or uttering a word. * * *

We have previously deemed the foregoing concerns to be content neutral. Obstructed access and congested sidewalks are problems no matter what caused them. A group of individuals can obstruct clinic access and clog sidewalks just as much when they loiter as when they protest abortion or counsel patients. * * *

Petitioners do not really dispute that the Commonwealth's interests in ensuring safety and preventing obstruction are, as a general matter, content neutral. But petitioners note that these interests "apply outside every building in the State that hosts any activity that might occasion protest or comment," not just abortion clinics. By choosing to pursue these interests only at abortion clinics, petitioners argue, the Massachusetts Legislature evinced a purpose to "single[ ] out for regulation speech about one particular topic: abortion."

We cannot infer such a purpose from the Act's limited scope. The broad reach of a statute can help confirm that it was not enacted to burden a narrower category of disfavored speech. At the same time, however, "States adopt laws to address the problems that confront them. The First Amendment does not require States to regulate for problems that do not exist." The Massachusetts Legislature amended the Act in 2007 in response

to a problem that was, in its experience, limited to abortion clinics. There was a record of crowding, obstruction, and even violence outside such clinics. There were apparently no similar recurring problems associated with other kinds of healthcare facilities, let alone with "every building in the State that hosts any activity that might occasion protest or comment."
* * *

Even though the Act is content neutral, it still must be "narrowly tailored to serve a significant governmental interest." The tailoring requirement does not simply guard against an impermissible desire to censor. The government may attempt to suppress speech not only because it disagrees with the message being expressed, but also for mere convenience. Where certain speech is associated with particular problems, silencing the speech is sometimes the path of least resistance. But by demanding a close fit between ends and means, the tailoring requirement prevents the government from too readily "sacrific[ing] speech for efficiency."

For a content-neutral time, place, or manner regulation to be narrowly tailored, it must not "burden substantially more speech than is necessary to further the government's legitimate interests." Such a regulation, unlike a content-based restriction of speech, "need not be the least restrictive or least intrusive means of" serving the government's interests. But the government still "may not regulate expression in such a manner that a substantial portion of the burden on speech does not serve to advance its goals."

As noted, respondents claim that the Act promotes "public safety, patient access to healthcare, and the unobstructed use of public sidewalks and roadways." Petitioners do not dispute the significance of these interests. We have, moreover, previously recognized the legitimacy of the government's interests in "ensuring public safety and order, promoting the free flow of traffic on streets and sidewalks, protecting property rights, and protecting a woman's freedom to seek pregnancy-related services." The buffer zones clearly serve these interests.

At the same time, the buffer zones impose serious burdens on petitioners' speech. At each of the three Planned Parenthood clinics where petitioners attempt to counsel patients, the zones carve out a significant portion of the adjacent public sidewalks, pushing petitioners well back from the clinics' entrances and driveways. The zones thereby compromise petitioners' ability to initiate the close, personal conversations that they view as essential to "sidewalk counseling." * * *

The buffer zones burden substantially more speech than necessary to achieve the Commonwealth's asserted interests. At the outset, we note that the Act is truly exceptional: Respondents and their *amici* identify no other State with a law that creates fixed buffer zones around abortion clinics.

That of course does not mean that the law is invalid. It does, however, raise concern that the Commonwealth has too readily forgone options that could serve its interests just as well, without substantially burdening the kind of speech in which petitioners wish to engage.

That is the case here. * * * If Massachusetts determines that broader prohibitions along the same lines are necessary, it could enact legislation similar to the federal Freedom of Access to Clinic Entrances Act of 1994 (FACE Act), 18 U.S.C. § 248(a)(1), which subjects to both criminal and civil penalties anyone who "by force or threat of force or by physical obstruction, intentionally injures, intimidates or interferes with or attempts to injure, intimidate or interfere with any person because that person is or has been, or in order to intimidate such person or any other person or any class of persons from, obtaining or providing reproductive health services." Some dozen other States have done so. If the Commonwealth is particularly concerned about harassment, it could also consider an ordinance such as the one adopted in New York City that not only prohibits obstructing access to a clinic, but also makes it a crime "to follow and harass another person within 15 feet of the premises of a reproductive health care facility." * * *

JUSTICE SCALIA, with whom **JUSTICE KENNEDY** and **JUSTICE THOMAS** join, concurring in the judgment.

The majority points only to the statute's stated purpose of increasing " 'public safety' " at abortion clinics, and to the additional aims articulated by respondents before this Court—namely, protecting " 'patient access to healthcare . . . and the unobstructed use of public sidewalks and roadways.' " Really? Does a statute become "justified without reference to the content of the regulated speech" simply because the statute itself and those defending it in court *say* that it is? Every objective indication shows that the provision's primary purpose is to restrict speech that opposes abortion. [Justice Scalia stressed that the law covered all abortion clinics in the state, although only the Boston clinic had faced serious problems in maintaining order and access. He argued that this undermined the credibility of the state's claimed interest.]

There is not a shadow of a doubt that the assigned or foreseeable conduct of a clinic employee or agent can include both speaking in favor of abortion rights and countering the speech of people like petitioners. * * *

In sum, the Act should be reviewed under the strict-scrutiny standard applicable to content-based legislation. That standard requires that a regulation represent "the least restrictive means" of furthering "a compelling Government interest." Respondents do not even attempt to argue that subsection (b) survives this test. "Suffice it to say that if protecting people from unwelcome communications"—the actual purpose of the provision—"is a compelling state interest, the First Amendment is a dead letter."

Having determined that the Act is content based and does not withstand strict scrutiny, I need not pursue the inquiry [into whether the statute is narrowly tailored.] I suppose I *could* do so, * * * and if I did, I suspect I would agree with the majority that the legislation is not narrowly tailored to advance the interests asserted by respondents. But I prefer not to take part in the assembling of an apparent but specious unanimity. I leave both the plainly unnecessary and erroneous half and the arguably correct half of the Court's analysis to the majority.

[**JUSTICE ALITO** concurred in the judgment on the ground that the exemption for clinic employees constituted viewpoint discrimination, but agreed with the majority that in any event the statute was not narrowly tailored.]

NOTES ON MCCULLEN

1. *Realism and Judicial Review.* Whose version of the statute's purpose and effect seems most plausible—the majority's or Justice Scalia's? Note that neither side offers direct evidence about the intentions of the legislatures. Both purport to infer purpose from the face of the statute and the context, but with an important difference: the majority takes the statute as it is written, while Justice Scalia is willing to make inferences about the political dynamics. Which approach is preferable?

2. *Harassment or Outreach?* A traditional argument for protecting speech involves the ability to speakers to reach willing listeners without government interference. But the Court valorizes public forums for the ability of speakers to reach listeners who would prefer to be left alone. Should there be a constitutional right to avoid unwanted communications?

3. *Sauce for the Goose Versus Sauce for the Gander?* There is a large buffer zone excluding from the Supreme Court's grounds, including the plaza in front of the building, the following activities: "demonstrations, picketing, speechmaking, marching, holding vigils or religious services and all other like forms of conduct that involve the communication or expression of views or grievances, engaged in by one or more persons, the conduct of which is reasonably likely to draw a crowd of onlookers." Is this buffer zone constitutional?

NOTES ON GRACE, HILL, *AND THE* TRADITIONAL PUBLIC FORUM

Consistent with the famous statement in *Hague*, the *Grace* opinion stresses the special constitutional status of sidewalks as a traditional "public forum." But *why* do these places have special status?[35] Is it because history has

---

[35] See generally Ronald Cass, *First Amendment Access to Government Facilities*, 65 Va. L. Rev. 1287 (1979); Robert Post, *Between Governance and Management: The History and Theory of the Public Forum*, 34 UCLA L. Rev. 1713 (1987); Geoffrey Stone, *Fora Americana: Speech in Public Places*, 1974 Sup. Ct. Rev. 233.

given the public a sort of constitutional easement? Or because these places are especially well suited for these purposes? Or simply because there has to be *someplace* where people can exercise their First Amendment rights?

What kinds of limitations can the state place on our use of a public forum? Contrast *Grace* with *Cox v. Louisiana*, 379 U.S. 559 (1965), which upheld a Louisiana statute prohibiting picketing "near" a courthouse with the intent to influence the administration of justice.[36] The Louisiana statute had been modeled on a federal statute, which was passed in 1950 as a response to picketing of federal courthouses to protest the trials of Communist Party leaders. Does *Grace* overrule *Cox* sub silentio? If not, does *Grace* mean that people have the constitutional right to picket on the sidewalk in front of the Court only if their message doesn't relate to the Court's business?

WARD V. ROCK AGAINST RACISM
491 U.S. 781, 109 S.Ct. 2746, 105 L.Ed.2d 661 (1989)

JUSTICE KENNEDY delivered the opinion of the Court.

In the southeast portion of New York City's Central Park, about 10 blocks upward from the park's beginning point at 59th Street, there is an amphitheater and stage structure known as the Naumberg Acoustic Bandshell. The bandshell faces west across the remaining width of the park. In close proximity to the bandshell, and lying within the directional path of its sound, is a grassy open area called the Sheep Meadow. The city has designated the Sheep Meadow as a quiet area for passive recreations like reclining, walking, and reading. Just beyond the park, and also within the potential sound range of the bandshell, are the apartments and residences of Central Park West.

This case arises from the city's attempt to regulate the volume of amplified music at the bandshell so the performances are satisfactory to the audience without intruding upon those who use the Sheep Meadow or live on Central Park West and in its vicinity.

The city's regulation requires bandshell performers to use sound-amplification equipment and a sound technician provided by the city. [The sound technician controls both the volume and the mix of sound—that is, the way the sound from various microphones and instruments is combined. The city adopted this regulation after considering various alternatives, and also after prolonged difficulties with concerts by Rock Against Racism, at one of which the police ultimately "pulled the plug" after issuing noise citations.] The challenge to this volume control technique comes from the sponsor of a rock concert. * * *

---

[36] See Harry Kalven, *The Concept of the Public Forum:* Cox v. Louisiana, 1965 Sup. Ct. Rev. 1.

Music is one of the oldest forms of human expression. From Plato's discourse in the Republic to the totalitarian state in our own times, rulers have known its capacity to appeal to the intellect and to the emotions, and have censored musical compositions to serve the needs of the state. The Constitution prohibits any like attempts in our own legal order. Music, as a form of expression and communication, is protected under the First Amendment. In the case before us the performances apparently consisted of remarks by speakers, as well as rock music, but the case has been presented as one in which the constitutional challenge is to the city's regulation of the musical aspects of the concert; and, based on the principle we have stated, the city's guidelines must meet the demands of the First Amendment. The parties do not appear to dispute that proposition.

We need not here discuss whether a municipality which owns a band stand or stage facility may exercise, in some circumstances, a proprietary right to select performances and control their quality. Though it did demonstrate its own interest in the effort to insure high quality performance by providing the equipment in question, the city justifies its guideline as a regulatory measure to limit and control noise. Here the bandshell was open, apparently, to all performers; and we decide the case as one in which the bandshell is a public forum for performances in which the government's right to regulate expression is subject to the protections of the First Amendment. Our cases make clear, however, that even in a public forum the government may impose reasonable restrictions on the time, place, or manner of protected speech, provided the restrictions "are justified without reference to the content of the regulated speech, that they are narrowly tailored to serve a significant governmental interest, and that they leave open ample alternative channels for communication of the information." *Clark v. Community for Creative Non-Violence*, 468 U.S. 288, 293 (1984). We consider these requirements in turn.

It is undeniable that the city's substantial interest in limiting sound volume is served in a direct and effective way by the requirement that the city's sound technician control the mixing board during performances. Absent this requirement, the city's interests would have been served less well, as is evidenced by the complaints about excessive volume generated by respondent's past concerts. The alternative regulatory methods hypothesized by the Court of Appeals reflect nothing more than a disagreement with the city over how much control of volume is appropriate or how that level of control is to be achieved. The Court of Appeals erred in failing to defer to the city's reasonable determination that its interest in controlling volume would be best served by requiring bandshell performers to utilize the city's sound technician.

[The Court also upheld the city's second justification, to ensure "that the sound amplification [is] sufficient to reach all listeners within the defined concert ground." In response to Rock Against Racism's argument that the guideline was overbroad (requiring a city technician when the sponsor had equally expert personnel), the Court relied on the lower court's finding that the city's technician was able to accommodate all sponsor needs. Finally, the Court found that the guidelines left ample alternative means of communication, since it did not restrict access to the bandshell but merely reduced volume.]

NOTES ON ROCK AGAINST RACISM AND TIME, PLACE AND MANNER REGULATION

1. *Content Neutrality. Rock Against Racism* highlights the importance of the content distinction in First Amendment analysis. Content-neutral regulations receive lower scrutiny. See *O'Brien*. But is there ever such a thing as a *truly* content-neutral regulation? Even in *Rock Again Racism*, is the noise level completely unrelated to the "message" of the music? Don't some forms of music rely on their loudness as part of their impact?

2. *Completely Foreclosing a Mode of Communication.* Normally, content-neutral regulations survive review with little difficulty, given the leniency of the test. The primary exception seems to be for regulations that shut off a traditional mode of communication. In *City of Ladue v. Gilleo*, 512 U.S. 43 (1994), the Court struck down a local ordinance banning lawn signs, as applied to a woman who wanted to post a sign protesting the Persian Gulf War on her front lawn. The Court was unpersuaded that "adequate substitutes exist for the important medium of speech" that the city had closed: "especially for persons of modest means or limited mobility, a yard or window sign may have no practical substitute."

3. *Other Government Property.* We have already considered the government's (quite limited) ability to restrict speech on some government-owned property. Government ownership of streets, parks, and sidewalks seems to add only marginally to its regulatory power. But the Court has also had occasion to consider speech activities involving other types of government property. In *Widmar v. Vincent*, 454 U.S. 263 (1981), for example, the Court held that the government could not exclude religious groups from using university classrooms for after-hours meetings, since other student groups were allowed to use the rooms. On the other hand, in *United States Postal Service v. Greenburgh Civic Ass'ns*, 453 U.S. 114 (1981), the Court held that the government could ban civic groups from putting leaflets in home mailboxes without paying for postage, and in *City Council v. Taxpayers for Vincent*, 466 U.S. 789 (1984), the Court upheld a municipal ban against posting signs on public property.

Perry Educ. Ass'n v. Perry Local Educators' Ass'n

460 U.S. 37 (1983)

The issue before the Court in *Perry* was whether an insurgent faculty union could have access to school mailboxes. The Court held that the faculty mailboxes constituted a nonpublic forum and that restricting access to the recognized union was reasonable. The Court attempted to provide a framework for analyzing speech restrictions on government property. *Perry* created a tri-partite framework for evaluating regulations of speech on government property. The degree of scrutiny depends on whether the property in question is (1) a traditional public forum such as a park, (2) a "limited" forum that the government has expressly dedicated to speech purposes, or (3) other government property ("nonpublic forum").

Perry allows different forms of regulation in different types of forums. In a traditional forum, time, place, and manner regulations are allowed, but the government cannot close the forum to expressive activities, and it has no more power to regulate on the basis of content than it has on private property. The rules for a "limited" forum are the same, except that the government can close the forum to expressive activity altogether if it chooses. In a nonpublic forum, the government can impose any reasonable regulation so long as it avoids discriminating on the basis of viewpoint. The Court decided that the faculty mail boxes were a nonpublic forum, though the dissent argued that the school had made little attempt to control access and really objected to the pro-union viewpoint.

Applying the *Perry* test to public spaces is not always easy. The difficulties are compounded, however, when the test is applied to metaphorical forums: opportunities for speech that are not defined by location. *Arkansas Educational Television Comm'n v. Forbes*, 523 U.S. 666 (1998), is illustrative. A public television decided that Forbes was not a serious candidate and excluded him from a televised debate. The Court decided that candidate debates should be treated as nonpublic forums, allowing reasonable, non-viewpoint restrictions on access. The Court concluded, however, that the decision to exclude Forbes had been made on neutral grounds. How useful is forum analysis here? Would it have been better for the Court to simply analyze candidate debates as sui generis rather than applying *Perry*? Are you convinced that the Court was successful in *Citizens United* in distinguishing earlier cases like *Forbes* involving speech restrictions tied to the identity of the speaker?

Note that a public forum is an actual or metaphorical space that the government provides for the use of private speakers. This must be distinguished from speech by the government itself. In many cases, the nature of government speech is obvious. But it can sometimes be difficult to determine whether the government is offering its own message or providing space for the messages of others. In *Walker v. Texas Division, Sons of Confederate Veterans*, ___ U.S. ___, 135 S.Ct. 2239, 192 L.Ed.2d 274 (2015), Texas refused to approve a vanity license plate featuring a Confederate flag. The Court upheld the state's refusal in an opinion by Justice Breyer on the theory that license plates are government speech. License plates have long conveyed messages from state government, such as state slogans, and a plate is a "government article serving the governmental purposes of vehicle registration and identification and the state owns the designs on its license plates. The dissent pooh-poohed this argument, pointing out the diversity of plates allowed by Texas, including fraternities, soft drinks, and private organization. If you sat by the side of a highway and studied these plates, the dissent asked,

> [W]ould you really think that the sentiments reflected in these specialty plates are the views of the State of Texas and not those of the owners of the cars? If a car with a plate that says "Rather Be Golfing" passed by at 8:30 am on a Monday morning, would you think: "This is the official policy of the State—better to golf than to work?" * * * And when a car zipped by with a plate that reads "NASCAR—24 Jeff Gordon," would you think that Gordon (born in California, raised in Indiana, resides in North Carolina) is the official favorite of the State government?

In the following case, the Court refused to extend the government-speech rationale and seemed to retreat from the holding in *Walker*:

MATAL v. TAM
__ U.S. __, 137 S.Ct. 1744, 198 L.Ed.2d 366 (2017)

JUSTICE ALITO announced the judgment of the Court and delivered the opinion of the Court with respect to Parts I, II, and III-A, and an opinion with respect to Parts III-B, III-C, and IV, in which the **CHIEF JUSTICE**, **JUSTICE THOMAS**, and **JUSTICE BREYER** join.

This case concerns a dance-rock band's application for federal trademark registration of the band's name, "The Slants." "Slants" is a derogatory term for persons of Asian descent, and members of the band are Asian-Americans. But the band members believe that by taking that slur as the name of their group, they will help to "reclaim" the term and drain its denigrating force.

The Patent and Trademark Office (PTO) denied the application based on a provision of federal law prohibiting the registration of trademarks that may "disparage . . . or bring . . . into contemp[t] or disrepute" any "persons, living or dead." 15 U.S.C. § 1052(a). We now hold that this provision violates the Free Speech Clause of the First Amendment. It offends a bedrock First Amendment principle: Speech may not be banned on the ground that it expresses ideas that offend. * * *

[Part I of the opinion reviews federal trademark law and the facts of the case. Part II rejects a statutory argument against applying § 1052(a) to trademarks that disparage racial or ethnic groups.]

[III] Because the disparagement clause applies to marks that disparage the members of a racial or ethnic group, we must decide whether the clause violates the Free Speech Clause of the First Amendment. And at the outset, we must consider three arguments that would either eliminate any First Amendment protection or result in highly permissive rational-basis review. Specifically, the Government contends (1) that trademarks are government speech, not private speech, (2) that trademarks are a form of government subsidy, and (3) that the constitutionality of the disparagement clause should be tested under a new "government-program" doctrine. We address each of these arguments below.

[III.A. For the Court.] The First Amendment prohibits Congress and other government entities and actors from "abridging the freedom of speech"; the First Amendment does not say that Congress and other government entities must abridge their own ability to speak freely. And our cases recognize that "[t]he Free Speech Clause . . . does not regulate government speech." As we have said, "it is not easy to imagine how government could function" if it were subject to the restrictions that the First Amendment imposes on private speech. " '[T]he First Amendment forbids the government to regulate speech in ways that favor some viewpoints or ideas at the expense of others," but imposing a requirement of viewpoint-neutrality on government speech would be paralyzing. When a government entity embarks on a course of action, it necessarily takes a particular viewpoint and rejects others. The Free Speech Clause does not require government to maintain viewpoint neutrality when its officers and employees speak about that venture.

Here is a simple example. During the Second World War, the Federal Government produced and distributed millions of posters to promote the war effort. There were posters urging enlistment, the purchase of war bonds, and the conservation of scarce resources. These posters expressed a viewpoint, but the First Amendment did not demand that the Government balance the message of these posters by producing and distributing posters encouraging Americans to refrain from engaging in these activities. But while the government-speech doctrine is important—indeed, essential—it is a doctrine that is susceptible to dangerous misuse. If private speech could be passed off as government speech by simply affixing a government seal of approval, government could silence or muffle the expression of disfavored viewpoints. For this reason, we must exercise great caution before extending our government-speech precedents.

At issue here is the content of trademarks that are registered by the PTO, an arm of the Federal Government. The Federal Government does not dream up these marks, and it does not edit marks submitted for registration. Except as required by the statute involved here, an examiner may not reject a mark based on the viewpoint that it appears to express. * * * Moreover, once a mark is registered, the PTO is not authorized to remove it from the register unless a party moves for cancellation, the registration expires, or the Federal Trade Commission initiates proceedings based on certain grounds. * * *

For example, if trademarks represent government speech, what does the Government have in mind when it advises Americans to "make.believe" (Sony), "Think different" (Apple), "Just do it" (Nike), or "Have it your way" (Burger King)? Was the Government warning about a coming disaster when it registered the mark "EndTime Ministries"? * * *

This brings us to the case on which the Government relies most heavily, *Walker*, which likely marks the outer bounds of the government-speech doctrine. Holding that the messages on Texas specialty license plates are government speech, the *Walker* Court cited three factors * * * . First, license plates have long been used by the States to convey state messages. Second, license plates "are often closely identified in the public mind" with the State, since they are manufactured and owned by the State, generally designed by the State, and serve as a form of "government ID." Third, Texas "maintain[ed] direct control over the messages conveyed on its specialty plates." As explained above, none of these factors are present in this case. * * *

[In Part III(B) of his opinion, Justice Alito argued for a plurality that the Court's prior cases dealing with government subsidies were distinguishable because "all involved cash subsidies or their equivalent." In Part III(C), he rejected the government's request that the Court recognize a new doctrine for "government programs," merging government speech cases and subsidy cases.]

[The parties disputed whether trademarks are commercial speech, but the Court, in Part IV of the Alito opinion, found it unnecessary to resolve that dispute because it found that the disparagement clause did not survive even under the standards applying to commercial speech.] Under *Central Hudson*, a restriction of speech must serve "a substantial interest," and it must be "narrowly drawn." This means, among other things, that "[t]he regulatory technique may extend only as far as the interest it serves." The disparagement clause fails this requirement.

It is claimed that the disparagement clause serves two interests. The first is phrased in a variety of ways in the briefs. * * * But no matter how the point is phrased, its unmistakable thrust is this: The Government has an interest in preventing speech expressing ideas that offend. And, as we have explained, that idea strikes at the heart of the First Amendment. Speech that demeans on the basis of race, ethnicity, gender, religion, age, disability, or any other similar ground is hateful; but the proudest boast of our free speech jurisprudence is that we protect the freedom to express "the thought that we hate."

The second interest asserted is protecting the orderly flow of commerce. Commerce, we are told, is disrupted by trademarks that "involv[e] disparagement of race, gender, ethnicity, national origin, religion, sexual orientation, and similar demographic classification." Such trademarks are analogized to discriminatory conduct, which has been recognized to have an adverse effect on commerce. A simple answer to this argument is that the disparagement clause is not "narrowly drawn" to drive out trademarks that support invidious discrimination. * * *

The clause is far too broad in other ways as well. The clause protects every person living or dead as well as every institution. Is it conceivable that commerce would be disrupted by a trademark saying: "James Buchanan was a disastrous president" or "Slavery is an evil institution"?

There is also a deeper problem with the argument that commercial speech may be cleansed of any expression likely to cause offense. The commercial market is well stocked with merchandise that disparages prominent figures and groups, and the line between commercial and non-commercial speech is not always clear, as this case illustrates. If affixing the commercial label permits the suppression of any speech that may lead to political or social "volatility," free speech would be endangered.

JUSTICE GORSUCH took no part in the consideration or decision of this case.

[JUSTICES KENNEDY, with whom JUSTICE GINSBURG, JUSTICE SOTOMAYOR, and JUSTICE KAGAN join, concurred in part and concurred in the judgment, arguing that the statute engaged in viewpoint discrimination because it only restricted speech conveying a negative perspective about a group.]

NOTES ON THE IMPLICATIONS OF MATAL

1. *Limiting* Walker *to Its Facts?* Note that the Court sets on outer boundary on the government speech cases by calling the case the "outer limit" of the government speech doctrine. This is generally a sign that a case is no longer to be considered a precedent for other rulings, which suggests that the Court has doubts about its validity without going so far as to overrule it. It is a bit surprising to see such a recent precedent given such short shrift, suggesting that perhaps some of the Justices who joined it may be having second thoughts.

2. *How Strong Is the Prohibition on Viewpoint Discrimination?* Although we have called Alito's the "plurality opinion" for convenience in those sections where he did not have a majority, in fact the Court was equally divided on those sections given that Gorsuch did not participate. The division seems to represent a division on the Court regarding the degree to which viewpoint discrimination is forbidden across the board, including areas like commercial speech where regulations are generally subject to lower scrutiny. The group led by Justice Alito seems unwilling to take that step, whereas the group led by Justice Kennedy seems unwilling to allow regulation on this basis

(including the offensiveness of speech) in any context other than government speech.

3. *Campus Restrictions on Hate Speech and Micro Aggressions.* The government's asserted interests in preventing disparagement of racial groups in trademarks involved the impact of this type of speech on minorities. How broad are the implications of the opinion for other types of efforts to protect minorities from similar impacts? The Kennedy opinion seems to imply that any restriction on speech based on the effect of speech on its audience could be at risk of being considered viewpoint discrimination and hence impermissible unless government speech is involved. The Alito opinion does not seem to rule out government consideration of audience effect in commercial speech and perhaps other areas where speech is subject to reduced protection. Neither opinion expresses any strong endorsement of the government's purposes. Lower courts will be left with the problem of sorting out the implications for regulation of speech in campus settings.

B. GOVERNMENT-SUPPORTED SPEECH

A pervasive issue in constitutional law is the extent to which the government can use its financial resources to obtain results that it could not obtain through direct regulation. For instance, although *Roe* and *Casey* restrict governmental regulation of abortion, whether the government has to fund abortions may be a different matter. The issue of "unconstitutional conditions" has been particularly significant in the area of free speech. We begin with the relatively straightforward situation in which the financial leverage takes the form of a government paycheck, and then consider the more general problems of restrictions on government funding.

NOTE ON PUBLIC EMPLOYEE SPEECH

The speech in *Perry* was doubly subject to regulation: not only were the mailboxes government property, but the speakers were employees and their would-be union representatives. The government has a greater interest in limiting the speech of its employees than that of the general public. The government has no legitimate interest in restricting the street-corner speaker who says the governor is an idiot; it does have an interest in eliminating members of his own staff who are openly insulting at the office.

In *Pickering v. Board of Education,* 391 U.S. 563 (1968), a teacher had been fired for writing a newspaper letter criticizing the school board's fiscal policies. The Court saw its task as finding "a balance between the interests of the teacher, as a citizen, in commenting upon matters of public concern and the interest of the State, as an employer, in promoting the efficiency of the public services it performs through its employees." The teacher's statements obviously related to matters of public concern. Because the letter was not shown to undermine the performance of his teaching duties or otherwise interfere with the operation of the schools, the school had no more interest in restricting this speech than that of any citizen. Although the letter did contain some factual misstatements, they did not rise to the level of unprotected defamation under the *New York Times* test. Hence, the letter was protected speech.

One issue left open by *Pickering* was the role of subject matter in the analysis. Although the Court characterized the speech as relating to matters of public concern, it was not clear whether this was essential to the holding. Also, it was not clear how broadly this term swept—recall that in defamation law only a narrow category of speech has been excluded from the "public concern" category. In *Connick v. Myers,* 461 U.S. 138 (1983), the Court made it clear that *Pickering* only applies to matters of public concern, and that the term is defined somewhat narrowly.

Connick involved a disgruntled assistant district attorney who circulated a questionnaire to fellow workers. The questions covered office transfer policy (her particular gripe), office morale, the need for a grievance committee, confidence in supervisors, and whether employees felt pressured to work in political campaigns. She was fired for insubordination. The Court attempted to draw a line between matters of public concern and "matters of only personal interest" such as "employee grievances." With the possible exception of the "most unusual circumstances," the Court said, "a federal court is not the appropriate forum in which to review the wisdom of a personnel decision" relating to employee grievances that lack public concern.

In *Garcetti v. Ceballos,* 547 U.S. 410 (2006), the Court further limited *Pickering* by holding that "when public employees make statements pursuant to their official duties, the employees are not speaking as citizens for First Amendment purposes, and the Constitution does not insulate their communications from employer discipline." The employee was a district attorney who was fired in retaliation for informing his superiors and later testifying in court about an invalid warrant. The court viewed this conduct as part of his job as a state lawyer and therefore outside the bounds of constitutional protection. We will return later to the idea that speech is subject to plenary government if the speaker can be construed to be acting as an agent of the state.

In the following case, reversing a forty-year-old precedent, the Court also used the First Amendment to restrict funding for public employee unions.

Janus v. American Federation of State, County, and Municipal Employees

138 S.Ct. 2448 (2018)

Under Illinois law, when a majority of public employees vote to form a union, that union becomes the exclusive bargaining agent for all employees, including nonmembers. Nonmembers are required to pay a fee for the union's collective bargaining and related activities. The Court upheld a similar law in *Abood v. Detroit Bd. of Ed.,* 431 U.S. 209, 97 S.Ct. 1782, 52 L.Ed.2d 261 (1977). **Justice Alito** wrote for the majority, overruling *Abood*. He stressed that, in addition to the values involved generally in restrictions on free speech, compelled speech places at risk additional values:

> When speech is compelled, however, additional damage is done. In that situation, individuals are coerced into betraying their convictions. Forcing free and independent individuals to endorse ideas they find objectionable is always demeaning, and for this reason, one of our landmark free speech cases said that a law commanding "involuntary affirmation" of objected-to beliefs would require "even more immediate and urgent grounds" than a law demanding silence.

Because Illinois law required non-union members to pay for speech by the union in collective bargaining with which they disagreed, it was subject to strict scrutiny. The *Abood* Court had found such laws to be constitutional based on the state's interest in "labor peace," but the Court concluded that collective bargaining by unions could function well without requiring non-members' financial support. The Court also rejected an alternative justification, holding that the state's interest in preventing non-members from free riding on the union's activities on their behalf was not compelling.

Justice Kagan's dissent on behalf of the four liberal Justices stressed *stare decisis*:

> Rarely if ever has the Court overruled a decision—let alone one of this import—with so little regard for the usual principles of *stare decisis*. There are no special justifications for reversing *Abood*. It has proved workable. No recent developments have eroded its underpinnings. And it is deeply entrenched, in both the law and the real world. More than 20 States have statutory schemes built on the decision. Those laws underpin thousands of ongoing contracts involving millions of employees. Reliance interests do not come any stronger than those surrounding *Abood*. And likewise, judicial disruption does not get any greater than what the Court does today.

The dissent closed by identifying *Janus* as part of a trend:

> And maybe most alarming, the majority has chosen the winners by turning the First Amendment into a sword, and using it against workaday economic and regulatory policy. Today is not the first time the Court has wielded the First Amendment in such an aggressive way. And it threatens not to be the last. Speech is everywhere—a part of every human activity (employment, health care, securities trading, you name it). For that reason, almost all economic and regulatory policy affects or touches speech. So the majority's road runs long. And at every stop are black-robed rulers overriding citizens' choices. The First Amendment was meant for better things. It was meant not to undermine but to protect democratic governance—including over the role of public-sector unions.

———

As the foregoing materials show, the First Amendment establishes limits on how the government treats its employees. (See also the procedural due process rights of state employees, Chapter 5, § 6B.) May the government employee *waive* these rights? Although most personal constitutional rights—such as the right not to incriminate oneself, the right to counsel, and the right to a jury trial in civil or criminal cases—may be waived by the recipient, the weight of scholarly opinion is to the effect that the public employee cannot waive all or most of her First Amendment rights.[37] The best reasons against allowing total waivers is the social benefit of protecting these rights of public employees—such as the assurance of meritocracy and robust public discussion, not to mention the possibility of whistleblowing.

Now, expand the inquiry: If the government may not ordinarily condition public employment upon the waiver of First Amendment rights, may it condition the payment of other benefits upon the recipient's waiver of her First Amendment rights? Is there a class of cases where the government cannot control speech *directly*, through criminal bars or license requirements or injunctions, but can influence speech *indirectly*, through subsidies and grants conditioned upon nonspeech? Consider also the restrictions the First Amendment places on the government's ability to condition the use of government property upon the user's conformity to state guidelines.

RUST V. SULLIVAN
500 U.S. 173, 111 S.Ct. 1759, 114 L.Ed.2d 233 (1991)

CHIEF JUSTICE REHNQUIST delivered the opinion of the Court.

[Title X of the Public Health Services Act established funding for family-planning services. Section 1008 of the Act provided that none of the funds "shall be used in programs where abortion is a method of family planning." In 1989, the Department of Health and Human Services (HHS) issued new regulations implementing the statute. Under the 1989 regulations, Title X projects must refer every pregnant client "for appropriate prenatal and/or social services by furnishing a list of available providers that promote the welfare of the mother and the unborn child." The list may not be used indirectly to encourage or promote abortion, "such as by weighing the list of referrals in favor of health care providers which perform abortions, by including on the list of referral providers health care providers whose principal business is the provision of abortions, by excluding available providers who do not provide abortions, or by 'steering'

---

[37] See Daniel Farber, *Free Speech Without Romance: Public Choice and the First Amendment*, 105 Harv. L. Rev. 554 (1991). On the tougher question of whether a public employee may be held to contracts promising confidentiality, compare Frank Easterbrook, *Insider Trading, Secret Agents, Evidentiary Privileges, and the Production of Information*, 1981 Sup. Ct. Rev. 309, with Cass Sunstein, *Government Control of Information*, 74 Cal. L. Rev. 889 (1986).

clients to providers who offer abortion as a method of family planning."
Title X projects are expressly prohibited from referring a pregnant woman
to an abortion provider, even upon specific request. One permissible
response to such an inquiry is that "the project does not consider abortion
an appropriate method of family planning and therefore does not counsel
or refer for abortion."]

The challenged regulations implement the statutory prohibition by
prohibiting counseling, referral, and the provision of information regarding
abortion as a method of family planning. They are designed to ensure that
the limits of the federal program are observed. The Title X program is
designed not for prenatal care, but to encourage family planning. A doctor
who wished to offer prenatal care to a project patient who became pregnant
could properly be prohibited from doing so because such service is outside
the scope of the federally funded program. The regulations prohibiting
abortion counseling and referral are of the same ilk; "no funds appropriated
for the project may be used in programs where abortion is a method of
family planning," and a doctor employed by the project may be prohibited
in the course of his project duties from counseling abortion or referring for
abortion. This is not a case of the Government "suppressing a dangerous
idea," but of a prohibition on a project grantee or its employees from
engaging in activities outside of its scope. * * *

[H]ere the government is not denying a benefit to anyone, but is
instead simply insisting that public funds be spent for the purposes for
which they were authorized. The Secretary's regulations do not force the
Title X grantee to give up abortion-related speech; they merely require that
the grantee keep such activities separate and distinct from Title X
activities. Title X expressly distinguishes between a Title X *grantee* and a
Title X *project*. The grantee, which normally is a health care organization,
may receive funds from a variety of sources for a variety of purposes. The
grantee receives Title X funds, however, for the specific and limited
purpose of establishing and operating a Title X project. The regulations
govern the scope of the Title X *project*'s activities, and leave the grantee
unfettered in its other activities. The Title X *grantee* can continue to
perform abortions, provide abortion-related services, and engage in
abortion advocacy; it simply is required to conduct those activities through
programs that are separate and independent from the project that receives
Title X funds.

In contrast, our "unconstitutional conditions" cases involve situations
in which the government has placed a condition on the *recipient* of the
subsidy rather than on a particular program or service, thus effectively
prohibiting the recipient from engaging in the protected conduct outside
the scope of the federally funded program. * * *

[T]his Court has recognized that the existence of a Government "subsidy," in the form of Government-owned property, does not justify the restriction of speech in areas that have "been traditionally open to the public for expressive activity," or have been "expressly dedicated to speech activity." Similarly, we have recognized that the university is a traditional sphere of free expression so fundamental to the functioning of our society that the Government's ability to control speech within that sphere by means of conditions attached to the expenditure of Government funds is restricted by the vagueness and overbreadth doctrines of the First Amendment. It could be argued by analogy that traditional relationships such as that between doctor and patient should enjoy protection under the First Amendment from government regulation, even when subsidized by the Government. We need not resolve that question here, however, because the Title X program regulations do not significantly impinge upon the doctor-patient relationship. Nothing in them requires a doctor to represent as his own any opinion that he does not in fact hold. * * * The doctor is always free to make clear that advice regarding abortion is simply beyond the scope of the program. In these circumstances, the general rule that the Government may choose not to subsidize speech applies with full force.

JUSTICE BLACKMUN, with whom JUSTICE MARSHALL joins, and with whom JUSTICE STEVENS joins [as to the portions excerpted here], dissenting.

Until today, the Court never has upheld viewpoint-based suppression of speech simply because that suppression was a condition upon the acceptance of public funds. Whatever may be the Government's power to condition the receipt of its largess upon the relinquishment of constitutional rights, it surely does not extend to a condition that suppresses the recipient's cherished freedom of speech based solely upon the content or viewpoint of that speech. * * *

Remarkably, the majority concludes that "the Government has not discriminated on the basis of viewpoint; it has merely chosen to fund one activity to the exclusion of another." But the majority's claim that the Regulations merely limit a Title X project's speech to preventive or preconceptional services rings hollow in light of the broad range of non-preventive services that the Regulations authorize Title X projects to provide. By refusing to fund those family-planning projects that advocate abortion *because* they advocate abortion, the Government plainly has targeted a particular viewpoint. The majority's reliance on the fact that the Regulations pertain solely to funding decisions simply begs the question. Clearly, there are some bases upon which government may not rest its decision to fund or not to fund. For example, the Members of the majority surely would agree that government may not base its decision to support an activity upon considerations of race. As demonstrated above, our cases make clear that ideological viewpoint is a similarly repugnant ground upon which to base funding decisions. * * *

[The dissents of **JUSTICES STEVENS** and **O'CONNOR** are omitted.]

AGENCY FOR INTERNATIONAL DEVELOPMENT V. ALLIANCE FOR OPEN SOCIETY INT'L, INC.
570 U.S. 205, 133 S.Ct. 2321, 186 L.Ed.2d 398 (2013)

CHIEF JUSTICE ROBERTS delivered the opinion of the Court.

The United States Leadership Against HIV/AIDS, Tuberculosis, and Malaria Act of 2003 (Leadership Act), 22 U.S.C. § 7601 et seq., outlined a comprehensive strategy to combat the spread of HIV/AIDS around the world. As part of that strategy, Congress authorized the appropriation of billions of dollars to fund efforts by nongovernmental organizations to assist in the fight. The Act imposes two related conditions on that funding: First, no funds made available by the Act "may be used to promote or advocate the legalization or practice of prostitution or sex trafficking." § 7631(e). And second, no funds may be used by an organization "that does not have a policy explicitly opposing prostitution and sex trafficking." § 7631(f). This case concerns the second of these conditions, referred to as the Policy Requirement. The question is whether that funding condition violates a recipient's First Amendment rights. * * *

Respondents are a group of domestic organizations engaged in combating HIV/AIDS overseas. In addition to substantial private funding, they receive billions annually in financial assistance from the United States, including under the Leadership Act. Their work includes programs aimed at limiting injection drug use in Uzbekistan, Tajikistan, and Kyrgyzstan, preventing mother-to-child HIV transmission in Kenya, and promoting safer sex practices in India. Respondents fear that adopting a policy explicitly opposing prostitution may alienate certain host governments, and may diminish the effectiveness of some of their programs by making it more difficult to work with prostitutes in the fight against HIV/AIDS. They are also concerned that the Policy Requirement may require them to censor their privately funded discussions in publications, at conferences, and in other forums about how best to prevent the spread of HIV/AIDS among prostitutes. * * *

The Policy Requirement mandates that recipients of Leadership Act funds explicitly agree with the Government's policy to oppose prostitution and sex trafficking. It is, however, a basic First Amendment principle that "freedom of speech prohibits the government from telling people what they must say." *Rumsfeld v. Forum for Academic and Institutional Rights, Inc.*, 547 U.S. 47 (2006) (citing *West Virginia Bd. of Ed. v. Barnette*, 319 U.S. 624 (1943), and *Wooley v. Maynard*, 430 U.S. 705 (1977)). "At the heart of the First Amendment lies the principle that each person should decide for himself or herself the ideas and beliefs deserving of expression, consideration, and adherence." *Turner Broadcasting System, Inc. v. FCC,* 512 U.S. 622 (1994). Were it enacted as a direct regulation of speech, the Policy Requirement would plainly violate the First Amendment. The question is whether the Government may nonetheless impose that requirement as a condition on the receipt of federal funds. * * *

As a general matter, if a party objects to a condition on the receipt of federal funding, its recourse is to decline the funds. This remains true when the objection is that a condition may affect the recipient's exercise of its First Amendment rights. See, e.g., *United States v. American Library Assn., Inc.,* 539 U.S. 194 (2003) (plurality opinion) (rejecting a claim by public libraries that conditioning funds for Internet access on the libraries' installing filtering software violated their First Amendment rights, explaining that "[t]o the extent that libraries wish to offer unfiltered access, they are free to do so without federal assistance"); *Regan v. Taxation With Representation of Wash.,* 461 U.S. 540, 546 (1983) (dismissing "the notion that First Amendment rights are somehow not fully realized unless they are subsidized by the State" (internal quotation marks omitted)).

At the same time, however, we have held that the Government " 'may not deny a benefit to a person on a basis that infringes his constitutionally protected . . . freedom of speech even if he has no entitlement to that benefit.' " In some cases, a funding condition can result in an unconstitutional burden on First Amendment rights.

The dissent thinks that can only be true when the condition is not relevant to the objectives of the program (although it has its doubts about that), or when the condition is actually coercive, in the sense of an offer that cannot be refused. See post (opinion of SCALIA, J.). Our precedents, however, are not so limited. In the present context, the relevant distinction that has emerged from our cases is between conditions that define the limits of the government spending program—those that specify the activities Congress wants to subsidize—and conditions that seek to leverage funding to regulate speech outside the contours of the program itself. The line is hardly clear, in part because the definition of a particular program can always be manipulated to subsume the challenged condition. We have held, however, that "Congress cannot recast a condition on funding as a mere definition of its program in every case, lest the First Amendment be reduced to a simple semantic exercise." *Legal Services Corporation v. Velazquez,* 531 U.S. 533, 547 (2001). * * *

Our decision in *Rust v. Sullivan* elaborated on the approach reflected in *Regan* and *League of Women Voters.* In *Rust,* we considered Title X of the Public Health Service Act, a Spending Clause program that issued grants to nonprofit health-care organizations "to assist in the establishment and operation of voluntary family planning projects [to] offer a broad range of acceptable and effective family planning methods and services." The organizations received funds from a variety of sources other than the Federal Government for a variety of purposes. The Act, however, prohibited the Title X federal funds from being "used in programs where abortion is a method of family planning." Ibid. (internal quotation marks omitted). To enforce this provision, HHS regulations barred Title X projects from advocating abortion as a method of family planning, and required grantees to ensure that their Title X projects were " 'physically and financially separate' " from their other projects that engaged in the prohibited activities—group of Title X funding recipients brought suit, claiming the regulations imposed an unconstitutional condition on their First Amendment rights. We rejected their claim.

We explained that Congress can, without offending the Constitution, selectively fund certain programs to address an issue of public concern, without funding alternative ways of addressing the same problem. In Title X, Congress had defined the federal program to encourage only particular family planning methods. The challenged regulations were simply "designed to ensure that the limits of the federal program are observed," and "that public funds [are] spent for the purposes for which they were authorized."

In making this determination, the Court stressed that "Title X expressly distinguishes between a Title X grantee and a Title X project." The regulations governed only the scope of the grantee's Title X projects, leaving it "unfettered in its other activities." I "The Title X grantee can continue to . . . engage in abortion advocacy; it simply is required to conduct those activities through programs that are separate and independent from the project that receives Title X funds." Because the regulations did not "prohibit[ ] the recipient from engaging in the protected conduct outside the scope of the federally funded program," they did not run afoul of the First Amendment.

As noted, the distinction drawn in these cases—between conditions that define the federal program and those that reach outside it—is not always self-evident. As Justice Cardozo put it in a related context, "Definition more precise must abide the wisdom of the future." *Steward Machine Co. v. Davis*, 301 U.S. 548, 591 (1937). Here, however, we are confident that the Policy Requirement falls on the unconstitutional side of the line.

To begin, it is important to recall that the Leadership Act has two conditions relevant here. The first—unchallenged in this litigation—prohibits Leadership Act funds from being used "to promote or advocate the legalization or practice of prostitution or sex trafficking." 22 U.S.C. § 7631(e). The Government concedes that § 7631(e) by itself ensures that federal funds will not be used for the prohibited purposes

The Policy Requirement therefore must be doing something more—and it is. The dissent views the Requirement as simply a selection criterion by which the Government identifies organizations "who believe in its ideas to carry them to fruition." As an initial matter, whatever purpose the Policy Requirement serves in selecting funding recipients, its effects go beyond selection. The Policy Requirement is an ongoing condition on recipients' speech and activities, a ground for terminating a grant after selection is complete. In any event, as the Government acknowledges, it is not simply seeking organizations that oppose prostitution. Rather, it explains, "Congress has expressed its purpose 'to eradicate' prostitution and sex trafficking, 22 U.S.C. § 7601(23), and it wants recipients to adopt a similar stance." This case is not about the Government's ability to enlist the assistance of those with whom it already agrees. It is about compelling a grant recipient to adopt a particular belief as a condition of funding.

By demanding that funding recipients adopt—as their own—the Government's view on an issue of public concern, the condition by its very nature affects "protected conduct outside the scope of the federally funded program." A recipient cannot avow the belief dictated by the Policy Requirement when spending Leadership Act funds, and then turn around and assert a contrary belief, or claim neutrality, when participating in activities on its own time and dime. By requiring recipients to profess a specific belief, the Policy Requirement goes beyond defining the limits of the federally funded program to defining the recipient.

The Government contends that the affiliate guidelines, established while this litigation was pending, save the program. Under those guidelines, funding recipients are permitted to work with affiliated organizations that do not abide by the condition, as long as the recipients retain "objective integrity and independence" from the unfettered affiliates. The Government suggests the guidelines alleviate any unconstitutional burden on the respondents' First Amendment rights by allowing them to either: (1) accept Leadership Act funding and comply with Policy Requirement, but establish affiliates to communicate contrary views on prostitution; or (2) decline funding themselves (thus remaining free to express their own views or remain neutral), while creating affiliates whose sole purpose is to receive and administer Leadership Act funds, thereby "cabin[ing] the effects" of the Policy Requirement within the scope of the federal program.

Neither approach is sufficient. When we have noted the importance of affiliates in this context, it has been because they allow an organization bound by a funding condition to exercise its First Amendment rights outside the scope of the federal program. Affiliates cannot serve that purpose when the condition is that a funding recipient espouse a specific belief as its own. If the affiliate is distinct from the recipient, the arrangement does not afford a means for the recipient to express its beliefs.

If the affiliate is more clearly identified with the recipient, the recipient can express those beliefs only at the price of evident hypocrisy. The guidelines themselves make that clear.

The Government suggests that the Policy Requirement is necessary because, without it, the grant of federal funds could free a recipient's private funds "to be used to promote prostitution or sex trafficking." That argument assumes that federal funding will simply supplant private funding, rather than pay for new programs or expand existing ones. The Government offers no support for that assumption as a general matter, or any reason to believe it is true here. And if the Government's argument were correct, *League of Women Voters* would have come out differently, and much of the reasoning of *Regan* and *Rust* would have been beside the point.
* * *

Pressing its argument further, the Government contends that "if organizations awarded federal funds to implement Leadership Act programs could at the same time promote or affirmatively condone prostitution or sex trafficking, whether using public or private funds, it would undermine the government's program and confuse its message opposing prostitution and sex trafficking." But the Policy Requirement goes beyond preventing recipients from using private funds in a way that would undermine the federal program. It requires them to pledge allegiance to the Government's policy of eradicating prostitution. As to that, we cannot improve upon what Justice Jackson wrote for the Court 70 years ago: "If there is any fixed star in our constitutional constellation, it is that no official, high or petty, can prescribe what shall be orthodox in politics, nationalism, religion, or other matters of opinion or force citizens to confess by word or act their faith therein."

The Policy Requirement compels as a condition of federal funding the affirmation of a belief that by its nature cannot be confined within the scope of the Government program. In so doing, it violates the First Amendment and cannot be sustained.

KAGAN, J., took no part in the consideration or decision of this case.

JUSTICE SCALIA, with whom JUSTICE THOMAS joins dissenting.

The Leadership Act provides that "any group or organization that does not have a policy explicitly opposing prostitution and sex trafficking" may not receive funds appropriated under the Act. 22 U.S.C. § 7631(f). This Policy Requirement is nothing more than a means of selecting suitable agents to implement the Government's chosen strategy to eradicate HIV/AIDS. That is perfectly permissible under the Constitution.
* * *

The Court's opinion contains stirring quotations * * * . They serve only to distract attention from the elephant in the room: that the Government is not forcing anyone to say anything. What Congress has done here—requiring an ideological commitment relevant to the Government task at hand—is approved by the Constitution itself. Americans need not support the Constitution; they may be Communists or anarchists. But "[t]he Senators and Representatives . . . , and the Members of the several State Legislatures, and all executive and judicial Officers, both of the United States and of the several States, shall be bound by Oath or Affirmation, to support [the] Constitution." U.S. Const., Art. VI, cl. 3. The Framers saw the wisdom of imposing affirmative ideological commitments prerequisite to assisting in the government's work. And so should we.

NOTES

1.   *A Unified Test.* In *AID*, the Court finally seems to have settled on a First Amendment test for funding conditions relating to speech. The downside is that, as Chief Justice Roberts concedes, applying the test may not always be difficult. We've already seen a similar problem before, where we saw that subject matter limits in defining a limited public forum are fine, but subject matter carve-outs from the forum are not. Yet, the distinction between the two situations can be elusive. But at least the Court has now provided a framework in which to conduct the argument.

2.   *Should Coercion Be the Test?* Justice Scalia argues that, at least when the condition is relevant to the goal of a government program, the text should be coercion. But he does not explain why as a general matter coercion should be the test for funding conditions. After all, the word "coercion" does not appear in the First Amendment. Instead, it forbids abridging the freedom of speech. Is it implausible to say that a person's freedom of speech has been "abridged" if they are required express a view or refrain from expressing a view in order to participate in a government program?

3.   *The Oath of Office as an Analogy.* How good an analogy is the oath of office? Employees have a duty of loyalty toward their employers, and this is especially true for the employers' officers and directors. But this isn't true of independent contractors. Also, doesn't the new regulation allowing the use of affiliates underlie this argument? After all, this mechanism is designed to allow grants to go to recipients who actually do not share the government's purpose but are willing to go through a charade to meet the law's requirements. So the regulation seems ill-suited to test for genuine enthusiasm about the abortion funding restriction.

PROCESS-BASED PROTECTIONS FOR SPEECH

To get a complete view of free speech doctrine, it is necessary to understand not only the substantive restrictions on speech regulation, but also the special process-based protections that apply to speech. Even if a speech restriction would otherwise be permissible, it may be struck down because it takes the form of a prior restraint or because it is badly drafted. In this section, we briefly touch upon these process-based protections.

Prior Restraints. As noted at the beginning of this chapter, Blackstone identified the "liberty of the press" with the absence of prior restrictions on publication such as licensing. So long as the press was able to publish what it wanted, the government could impose a suitable punishment after the fact for abuses. An early opinion by Justice Holmes suggested a Blackstonian interpretation of the First Amendment. The defendant had been held in contempt of court for publishing an editorial and cartoon questioning the motives of the Colorado Supreme Court. Holmes said that the main purpose of the First Amendment was to "prevent all such *previous restraints* upon publication as had been practiced by other governments," not the "subsequent punishment of such as may be deemed contrary to the public welfare." *Patterson v. People of State of Colorado ex rel. Attorney General*, 205 U.S. 454 (1907). By the end of World War I, however, Holmes had clearly changed his mind about this point, and today's Court endorses his later view. Later decisions, for example, limit the use of contempt citations to actual violations of court orders or out-of-court conduct that presents a "clear and present danger" to the integrity of pending judicial proceedings. See *Wood v. Georgia*, 370 U.S. 375 (1962); *Bridges v. California*, 314 U.S. 252 (1941). Thus, the First Amendment is clearly not limited to prior restraints. Nevertheless, it does apply to them with particular vigor.[38]

Near v. Minnesota, 283 U.S. 697 (1931), is the leading case on prior restraints. A newspaper had charged that certain public officials had been protecting local gangsters and called for a special grand jury. Acting under a state statute, the government obtained an injunction forbidding the defendants from circulating "any publication whatsoever which is a malicious, scandalous or defamatory newspaper." Chief Justice Hughes wrote the opinion of the Court. He emphasized that "unless the owner or publisher is able and disposed to bring competent evidence to satisfy the judge that the charges are true and are published with good motives and for justifiable ends, his newspaper or periodical is suppressed and further publication is made punishable as a contempt." Thus, the state had instituted the equivalent of a licensing system, covering only the defendants. "This," said Hughes, "is of the essence of censorship." He stressed the powerful objections to prior restraints voiced by Blackstone, as well as later history: "The fact that for approximately one hundred and fifty years there has been almost an entire absence of attempts to impose previous restraints upon publications relating to the malfeasance of public officers is significant of the deep-seated convictions that such restraints would violate constitutional right."

Hughes did admit that the rule against prior restraints was not absolute, but the rule applied except in a few special cases: "[N]o one would question but that a government might prevent actual obstruction to its recruiting service or

---

[38] For commentary, see Stephen Barnett, *The Puzzle of Prior Restraint*, 29 Stan. L. Rev. 539 (1977); Thomas Emerson, *The Doctrine of Prior Restraint*, 20 Law & Contemp. Probs. 648 (1955); Paul Freund, *The Supreme Court and Civil Liberties*, 4 Vand. L. Rev. 533 (1951); William Mayton, *Toward a Theory of First Amendment Process: Injunctions of Speech, Subsequent Punishment, and the Costs of the Prior Restraint Doctrine*, 67 Cornell L. Rev. 245 (1982); Marin Scordato, *Distinction Without a Difference: A Reappraisal of the Doctrine of Prior Restraint*, 68 N.C. L. Rev. 1 (1989).

the publication of the sailing dates of transports or the number or location of troops. On similar grounds, the primary requirements of decency may be enforced against obscene publications. The security of the community life may be protected against incitements to acts of violence."

Shuttlesworth v. City of Birmingham, 394 U.S. 147 (1969), illustrates how the prior restraint concept can be used to challenge permit systems as well as injunctions. Civil rights marchers were convicted under an ordinance that gave complete discretion to city officials over parade permits. In an opinion by Justice Stewart, the Court reversed the convictions for violating the ordinance: "This ordinance as it was written, therefore, fell squarely within the ambit of the many decisions of this Court over the last 30 years, holding that a law subjecting the exercise of First Amendment freedoms to the prior restraint of a license, without narrow, objective, and definite standards to guide the licensing authority, is unconstitutional. And our decisions have made clear that a person faced with such an unconstitutional licensing law may ignore it and engage in impunity in the exercise of the right of free expression." The state unsuccessfully argued that the ordinance had been cured by a later interpretation of the state supreme court, limiting the discretion of the municipal officials.

New York Times Co. v. United States

403 U.S. 713 (1971)

The most famous prior-restraint case, *The Pentagon Papers Case*, arose out of the Vietnam War. To make a long story short, the *New York Times* and *Washington Post* had obtained copies of a classified study entitled *History of U.S. Decision-Making Process on Viet Nam Policy* (also known as "the Pentagon Papers"). The study indicated that the government had concealed important facts or actively misled the public with respect to decisions to escalate the war. The government sought an injunction against publication of the study. In a short *per curiam*, accompanied by lengthy concurring opinions, the Court rejected the government's arguments. The *per curiam* contains one paragraph explaining the Court's rationale, which (apart from citations) reads as follows:

> 'Any system of prior restraints of expression comes to this Court bearing a heavy presumption against its constitutional validity.' The Government 'thus carries a heavy burden of showing justification for the imposition of such a restraint.' The District Court for the Southern District of New York in the *New York Times* case and the Court of Appeals for the District of Columbia Circuit in the *Washington Post* case held that the government had not yet met that burden. We agree.

In addition to the *per curiam*, every Justice wrote a separate opinion, six concurring in the judgment and three dissenting. Justices Black, Douglas, Brennan, and Marshall would have summarily reversed all the lower court orders staying the newspapers' publication. Justice Black (joined by Douglas) stated that "every moment's continuance of the injunctions against these newspapers amounts to a flagrant, indefensible, and continuing violation of the First Amendment." **Justices Stewart and White** were more cautious. Justice Stewart ruled against the government because he could not say that disclosure of any of the "Pentagon Papers" would "surely result in direct, immediate, and irreparable damage to our Nation or its people." Justice White joined Stewart's opinion, but also wrote a concurrence of his own (which was joined by Stewart). Justice White emphasized that there were a number of criminal statutes that were "potentially relevant to these cases." Finally, Chief Justice Burger, Justice Harlan, and Justice Blackmun dissented on the ground that the Court should not have heard and decided the case so hastily, ruling only a week after the lower courts entered their orders.

Under some circumstances, however, the Court has allowed injunctions against speech when the injunctions are based on disruptive conduct rather than the message conveyed. In *Madsen v. Women's Health Center, Inc.*, 512 U.S. 753 (1994), a state trial court enjoyed picketers outside a Florida abortion clinic from blocking access or physically abusing people entering or leaving the clinic. Despite the initial injunction, the trial court found, protesters continued to impede access to the clinic, creating a high level of noise with loudspeakers and bullhorns, and they also picketed the homes of clinic workers. Concluding that the initial injunction had been ineffective, the trial court issued a new, more detailed injunction. Among other provisions, the injunction created a 36-foot buffer zone around the clinic in which picketing was banned, limiting the noise level, and prohibiting any uninvited approach to clinic patients within 300 feet of the clinic. In an opinion by Chief Justice Rehnquist, the Court held that this injunction should be scrutinized under a standard somewhere between strict scrutiny and *O'Brien* content neutrality: "We must ask instead whether the challenged provisions of the injunction burden no more speech than necessary to serve a significant government interest." Applying this standard, the Court upheld the 36-foot buffer zone in front of the clinic and the noise restrictions as burdening "no more speech than necessary to accomplish the governmental interest at stake." But several portions of the injunction were invalidated: the restriction on approaching patients within 300 feet of the clinic, a prohibition on using images "visible within the clinic," and the 300-foot buffer zone around the residences of clinic workers.

Justice Scalia protested in dissent that the "entire injunction in this case departs so far from the established course of our jurisprudence that in any other context it would have been regarded as a candidate for summary reversal." He attributed the result to the Court's favoritism toward abortion.

Vagueness Doctrine. The Supreme Court has frequently invalidated broadly written statutes on the ground that they are "void for vagueness." Traditionally, the Court has understood the void-for-vagueness doctrine in due process terms: criminal laws must "give a person of ordinary intelligence fair notice that his contemplated conduct is forbidden by statute." *United States v. Harriss*, 347 U.S. 612, 617 (1954); accord, *Lanzetta v. New Jersey*, 306 U.S. 451

(1939); *Stromberg v. California*, 283 U.S. 359 (1931). The doctrine is also an example of a structural approach to due process: the important moral judgments made in the criminal law must be made by the legislature, directly accountable to the people, and not by the police, prosecutors, or even judges. See *Grayned v. Rockford*, 408 U.S. 104 (1972); Chapter 8, § 2A (the nondelegation doctrine). Most of the Justices in *Roe v. Wade* (Chapter 5, § 4B) thought the nineteenth century Texas abortion law was void-for-vagueness, and Justice Blackmun's original draft opinion invalidated the law only on those grounds. Consider the advantages of an opinion in that case that would have left the states free to adopt more precise abortion laws, which could then have been reviewed on privacy grounds with a more complete record of the evidence and public opinion.

In response to the civil rights cases of the 1960s, the Court rethought the doctrine along equal protection lines: another vice of vague statutes is that they give enforcement authorities (e.g., southern police) too much discretion to apply criminal sanctions arbitrarily.[39]

The leading case for this newer problem with vague statutes was *Papachristou v. City of Jacksonville*, 405 U.S. 156 (1972). Jacksonville made it a crime to be "vagabonds," "lewd, wanton and lascivious persons," "habitual loafers," and so forth. The lead defendants were two white women and two black men who were doing nothing more sinister than riding around together in an automobile. On appeal of their conviction to the Supreme Court, they argued that the state and local "vagrancy laws are archaic vestiges of long-past economic conditions and social philosophies" which posed risks of arbitrary enforcement. According to Justice Douglas's conference notes, the Justices were less concerned about notice than about the discretion these laws gave "police or judges . . . to go after anyone they do not like." A secondary theme of Justices at the conference was the obsolescence of these laws. Justice Douglas's opinion for a unanimous Court ruled that the "archaic" law was unconstitutionally vague, because it "makes criminal actions which by modern standards are normally innocent," and which are indeed fundamental freedoms traditionally enjoyed by Americans; was "not intelligible to the poor among us, the minorities, the average householder"; and seemed to be enforced mainly against "nonconformists" and "suspicious persons."

---

[39] This idea was advanced by Anthony Amsterdam, *The Void-for-Vagueness Doctrine in the Supreme Court*, 109 U. Pa. L. Rev. 67 (1960) (student note), and its influence on the civil rights cases is developed in William Eskridge, Jr., *Some Effects of Identity-Based Social Movements on Constitutional Law in the Twentieth Century*, 100 Mich. L. Rev. 501 (2002) (Part II.A.3 of the article). Thus, obstruction of sidewalk laws were enforced against civil rights protesters and not white citizens, see *Cox v. Louisiana*, 379 U.S. 536, 551–52 (1965); *id.* at 579 (Black, J.); disturbing the peace laws tended to spring into action only when racial minorities were engaged in peaceful protests, see *Shuttlesworth v. Birmingham*, 382 U.S. 87, 90–92 (1968); "crime against nature" laws were used only against gay or bisexual men (even though straight men and women engaged in equally unconventional acts), see *Wainwright v. Stone*, 414 U.S. 21 (1973); "lewd vagrancy" and cross-dressing laws were deployed only against lesbians, gay men, and transgendered people, see *Pryor v. Municipal Court*, 599 P.2d 636 (Cal. 1979); *City of Columbus v. Rogers*, 324 N.E.2d 563 (Ohio 1975); and "psychopathic personality" bars were applied only to gay and bisexual people. See *Boutilier v. INS*, 387 U.S. 118 (1967).

Papachristou confirmed the conventional wisdom that two bases for the void-for-vagueness doctrine were fair notice and preventing arbitrary enforcement, but expanded the lesson of the protest cases of the 1960s: the Court will be particularly vigilant when broad, ill-defined statutes touch upon any fundamental rights. This concern has been particularly strong when broadly written laws can be applied to activities protected under the First Amendment. In *NAACP v. Button*, 371 U.S. 415 (1963), the Court struck down a Virginia law barring organizations from retaining counsel to represent persons in litigation as to which the organizations had no direct interest. On its face, the law seemed justified on grounds of legal ethics (as Justice Harlan maintained in his dissent), but a Court suspicious of the legislature's (anti-NAACP) motives struck it down because of concern that it could be deployed to penalize protected speech and association. Justice Brennan's opinion urged courts to err against censorship, lest citizens and their associations not have the "breathing space" they need to exercise their First Amendment rights. This was the origin of the famous "chilling effect" argument: Because citizens do not know exactly where the statutory line is drawn between permitted and prohibited expression, they will typically err on the side of caution and refrain from exercising their expressive rights.

Overbreadth. The introduction to Chapter 4 discussed the idea of overinclusiveness or *overbreadth*, which occurs when a statute's prohibition sweeps beyond its stated purpose. In ordinary equal protection cases, some overbreadth is not fatal to the statute's constitutionality; one hallmark of strict scrutiny, where the statutory classification is suspect (like race) or impinges a fundamental interest (like voting), is that it does not tolerate much overbreadth. Similarly, statutes impinging fundamental First Amendment interests are not allowed much overbreadth. The rationales for the overbreadth doctrine are similar to those of the vagueness doctrine just examined: (a) minimizing official discretion in the enforcement of statutes that might curtail speech, (b) expanding the range of people who can bring constitutional challenges, and (c) minimizing the chilling effect of rules on people's willingness to engage in expression.[40]

On the other hand, a chilling effect may not be fatal. In *Broadrick v. Oklahoma*, 413 U.S. 601 (1973), a closely divided Court upheld a state law restricting political activities by public employees. Although the law seemed to reach core First Amendment activities that posed no danger to state policies (e.g., display of campaign buttons or bumper stickers), the Court declined to strike down the law. Justice White's opinion required that overbreadth "must not only be real, but substantial as well," to justify invalidation. *Broadrick* suggests that there may also be costs to the overbreadth doctrine, such as dangers that (a) it becomes too easy for courts to invalidate statutes, (b) it can invalidate statutes whose harms may be more hypothetical than real, and (c) it slights legitimate state policies.

---

[40] See Richard Fallon, Jr., *Making Sense of Overbreadth*, 100 Yale L.J. 853 (1991); Kenneth Karst, *Equality as a Central Principle in the First Amendment*, 43 U. Chi. L. Rev. 20 (1975); Note, *The First Amendment Overbreadth Doctrine*, 83 Harv. L. Rev. 844 (1970).

Board of Airport Commissioners v. Jews for Jesus, 482 U.S. 569, 107 S.Ct. 2568, 96 L.Ed.2d 500 (1987), provides a striking example of overbreadth. The Board of Airport Commissioners of Los Angeles adopted a resolution banning all "First Amendment activities" within the "Central Terminal Area" at Los Angeles International Airport (LAX). After an airport officer told a minister affiliated with Jews for Jesus that he must stop distributing religious literature in the Central Terminal Area, the plaintiff commenced this action, contending that the resolution was unconstitutional on its face. The Court noted that on its face, the resolution "reaches the universe of expressive activity, and, by prohibiting all protected expression, purports to create a virtual 'First Amendment Free Zone' at LAX."

Was the L.A. ordinance in *Jews for Jesus* overbroad, or is it vague? If read literally, it's certainly overbroad, since it forbids people from reading books in the terminal. But obviously no one would really apply the ordinance that way, so just what kind of activities are actually covered by the ordinance? As a practical matter, doesn't the ordinance really mean that expressive activities will be allowed in the terminal at the discretion of various state officials? On this reading, doesn't it fall afoul of *Shuttlesworth*?

If a defendant's own conduct is constitutionally protected, she doesn't need the overbreadth doctrine (or a vagueness challenge, for that matter). On the other hand, if her conduct isn't protected, why should she escape prosecution because the statute is overbroad and infringes other people's rights? Normally, standing rules only allow people to litigate their own rights, not someone else's (see Chapter 9, § 1). So what *is* the basis of overbreadth analysis? See Henry Monaghan, *Third Party Standing*, 84 Colum. L. Rev. 277 (1984).

The Court has typically been unwilling to apply overbreadth or vagueness analysis to regulations that apply purely to commercial speech. Is this just another reflection of the "second class" status of commercial speech, or is there some principled justification? Recall the earlier discussion of commercial speech as being less of a public good economically, and therefore less at risk of overdeterrence.

The Court distinguished between standing and overbreadth analysis in *Virginia v. Hicks*, 539 U.S. 113 (2003). The case involved regulations by the Richmond housing authority, which allowed the police to serve notice on any person lacking "a legitimate business or social purpose" for being on the premises and to arrest for trespassing any person who remains or returns after having been given this notice. Allegedly, an unwritten rule required advance permission from the management for leafleting and demonstrations. Hicks was given written notice barring him from the residence. When he was arrested after his return to the premises, he challenged the regulation as facially overbroad, although he himself had not engaged in *any* speech-related activities. The state supreme court ruled in his favor. The Court held that it had jurisdiction because the state had standing to appeal the ruling against it, regardless of whether Hicks would have had standing to bring a First Amendment challenge in the first place in federal court. On the merits, it rejected the overbreadth argument on the ground that any invalid application to speech activities was not substantial compared with the breadth of the rule's legitimate applications to nonspeech activities (such as Hicks').

SECTION 5. FREEDOM OF ASSOCIATION

Most of the Court's decisions regarding freedom of association have involved politically oriented organizations. Freedom of association first received explicit constitutional protection in cases involving the efforts of southern states to harass the NAACP. The leading case was *NAACP v. Alabama ex rel. Patterson*, 357 U.S. 449 (1958), in which Justice Harlan wrote for a unanimous Court in holding that the NAACP couldn't be required to turn over its membership list to the state. See also *NAACP v. Button*, 371 U.S. 415 (1963) (striking down Virginia law prohibiting organizations like the NAACP from retaining lawyers in connection with litigation to which it was not a party). On the other hand, in *Federal Trade Commission v. Superior Court Trial Lawyers Ass'n*, 493 U.S. 411 (1990), the Court upheld the application of the antitrust laws to another boycott. That boycott was organized by lawyers in private practice who acted as court-appointed counsel for indigents in criminal cases in the District of Columbia. They were protesting the low fees for criminal representation.

Besides the freedom to associate, there is also the freedom *not* to associate. In *Abood v. Detroit Bd. of Ed.*, 431 U.S. 209 (1977), the Court held that school teachers could not be forced to join a union as a condition of employment, nor could they be required to pay for the union's social or political programs. Another aspect of *Abood* was overruled in *Janus*, which held that government employees cannot even be required to pay for collective bargaining activities that directly benefit them.

NAACP v. Claiborne Hardware Co.

458 U.S. 886 (1982)

This case arose from a boycott of white stores by African Americans in Claiborne County, Mississippi. The boycott was intended to force business and civic leaders to agree to a series of civil rights demands. Although the boycott was largely peaceful, there were some violent episodes. In a state antitrust action, some of the merchants recovered over $1 million in damages against the boycott organizers. Applying the principles of *Scales* (§ 2A, *supra*), **Justice Stevens** concluded on behalf of a unanimous Court that liability cannot be imposed simply because an individual belonged to a group that also contained some violent members; instead, "it is necessary to establish that the group itself possessed unlawful goals and that the individual held a specific intent to further those illegal aims." The opinion closed with some general observations about "guilt by association":

In litigation of this kind the stakes are high. Concerted action is a powerful weapon. History teaches that special dangers are associated with conspiratorial activity. And yet one of the foundations of our society is the right of individuals to combine with other persons in pursuit of a common goal by lawful means. * * *

The taint of violence colored the conduct of some of the petitioners. They, of course, may be held liable for the consequences of their violent deeds. The burden of demonstrating that it colored the entire collective effort, however, is not satisfied by evidence that violence occurred or even that violence contributed to the success of the boycott. A massive and prolonged effort to change the social, political, and economic structure of a local environment cannot be characterized as a violent conspiracy simply by reference to the ephemeral consequences of relatively few violent acts. * * * A court must be wary of a claim that the true color of forest is better revealed by reptiles hidden in the weeds than by the foliage of countless freestanding trees.

BOARD OF DIRECTORS OF ROTARY INTERNATIONAL v. ROTARY CLUB OF DUARTE
481 U.S. 537, 107 S.Ct. 1940, 95 L.Ed.2d 474 (1987)

JUSTICE POWELL delivered the opinion of the Court.

[The international Rotary organization revoked the charter of a local Rotary Club because it had admitted women. The local club and two of its women members filed suit in state court challenging the action as a violation of California's Unruh Civil Rights Act (so called by reference to the name of its legislative sponsor).]

In *Roberts v. United States Jaycees*, 468 U.S. 609 (1984), we upheld against First Amendment challenge a Minnesota statute that required the Jaycees to admit women as full voting members. *Roberts* provides the framework for analyzing appellants' constitutional claims. As we observed in *Roberts*, our cases have afforded constitutional protection to freedom of association in two distinct senses. First, the Court has held that the Constitution protects against unjustified government interference with an individual's choice to enter into and maintain certain intimate or private relationships. Second, the Court has upheld the freedom of individuals to associate for the purpose of engaging in protected speech or religious activities. In many cases, government interference with one form of protected association will also burden the other form of association. In *Roberts* we determined the nature and degree of constitutional protection by considering separately the effect of the challenged state action on individuals' freedom of private association and their freedom of expressive association. We follow the same course in this case.

The Court has recognized that the freedom to enter into and carry on certain intimate or private relationships is a fundamental element of liberty protected by the Bill of Rights. Such relationships may take various forms, including the most intimate. * * * We have emphasized that the First Amendment protects those relationships, including family relationships, that presuppose "deep attachments and commitments to the necessarily few other individuals with whom one shares not only a special community of thoughts, experiences, and beliefs but also distinctively personal aspects of one's life." *Roberts*. But in *Roberts* we observed that "[d]etermining the limits of state authority over an individual's freedom to enter into a particular association . . . unavoidably entails a careful assessment of where that relationship's objective characteristics locate it on a spectrum from the most intimate to the most attenuated of personal attachments." In determining whether a particular association is sufficiently personal or private to warrant constitutional protection, we consider factors such as size, purpose, selectivity, and whether others are excluded from critical aspects of the relationship.

The evidence in this case indicates that the relationship among Rotary Club members is not the kind of intimate or private relation that warrants constitutional protection. The size of local Rotary Clubs ranges from fewer than 20 to more than 900. There is no upper limit on the membership of any local Rotary Club. About ten percent of the membership of a typical club moves away or drops out during a typical year. * * * To be sure, membership in Rotary Clubs is not open to the general public. But each club is instructed to include in its membership "all fully qualified prospective members located within its territory," to avoid "arbitrary limits on the number of members in the club," and to "establish and maintain a membership growth pattern."

Many of the Rotary Clubs' central activities are carried on in the presence of strangers. Rotary Clubs are required to admit any member of any other Rotary Club to their meetings. Members are encouraged to invite business associates and competitors to meetings. At some Rotary Clubs, the visitors number "in the tens and twenties each week." Joint meetings with the members of other organizations, and other joint activities, are permitted. The clubs are encouraged to seek coverage of their meetings and activities in local newspapers. In sum, Rotary Clubs, rather than carrying on their activities in an atmosphere of privacy, seek to keep their "windows and doors open to the whole world." We therefore conclude that application of the Unruh Act to local Rotary Clubs does not interfere unduly with the members' freedom of private association.

The Court also has recognized that the right to engage in activities protected by the First Amendment implies "a corresponding right to associate with others in pursuit of a wide variety of political, social, economic, educational, religious, and cultural ends." *Roberts*. For this reason, "[i]mpediments to the exercise of one's right to choose one's associates can violate the right of association protected by the First Amendment. . . ." In this case, however, the evidence fails to demonstrate that admitting women to Rotary Clubs will affect in any significant way the existing members' ability to carry out their various purposes.

As a matter of policy, Rotary Clubs do not take positions on "public questions," including political or international issues. To be sure, Rotary Clubs engage in a variety of commendable service activities that are protected by the First Amendment. But the Unruh Act does not require the clubs to abandon or alter any of these activities. * * *

Even if the Unruh Act does work some slight infringement on Rotary members' right of expressive association, that infringement is justified because it serves the State's compelling interest in eliminating discrimination against women. * * * In *Roberts* we recognized that the State's compelling interest in assuring equal access to women extends to the acquisition of leadership skills and business contacts as well as tangible goods and services. The Unruh Act plainly serves this interest. We therefore hold that application of the Unruh Act to California Rotary Clubs does not violate the right of expressive association afforded by the First Amendment.

Boy Scouts of America v. Dale

530 U.S. 640 (2000)

The Boy Scouts of America (BSA) is a private, not-for-profit organization engaged in instilling its system of values in boys. James Dale, a former Eagle Scout, was an Assistant Scoutmaster as an adult until the BSA expelled him on the ground that he was an "avowed homosexual and gay rights activist." Dale sued BSA for violating a New Jersey statute that prohibits discrimination by public accommodations on the basis of sexual orientation. The New Jersey state appellate courts ruled that BSA was a public accommodation covered by the law and that application of the statute did not unconstitutionally infringe BSA's First Amendment rights of free speech and expressive association. In a majority opinion by **Chief Justice Rehnquist**, the U.S. Supreme Court reversed, holding that the state violated BSA's right of expressive association.

Chief Justice Rehnquist found that the BSA was an intensely expressive association, seeking to inculcate Scout values in boys, and that exclusion of gay people from BSA leadership positions was consistent with their expressive purpose. "The Scout Oath and Law includes a vow '[t]o keep myself physically strong, mentally awake, and morally straight.' Although this oath does not explicitly speak to issues of sexuality, '[t]he Boy Scouts asserts that it "teach[es] that homosexual conduct is not morally straight," ' and that it does 'not want to promote homosexual conduct as a legitimate form of behavior.' We accept the Boy Scouts' assertion. We need not inquire further to determine the nature of the Boy Scouts' expression with respect to homosexuality. This message would be impaired if Dale was allowed to be an assistant scout master:

As we give deference to an association's assertions regarding the nature of its expression, we must also give deference to an association's view of what would impair its expression. That is not to say that an expressive association can erect a shield against antidiscrimination laws simply by asserting that mere acceptance of a member from a particular group would impair its message. But here Dale, by his own admission, is one of a group of gay Scouts who have 'become leaders in their community and are open and honest about their sexual orientation.' * * *

The Chief Justice distinguished cases such as *Rotary Club*, where the Court allowed states to apply their public accommodations laws to commercial organizations for the compelling interest of eliminating discrimination against women. "But in each of these cases we went on to conclude that the enforcement of these statutes would not materially interfere with the ideas that the organization sought to express." As in *Hurley*, the state regulation directly interfered with the organization's ideas. As to the state's justification for burdening BSA's expressive rights, the Chief Justice simply said: "The state interests embodied in New Jersey's public accommodations law do not justify such a severe intrusion on the Boy Scouts' rights to freedom of expressive association. That being the case, we hold that the First Amendment prohibits the State from imposing such a requirement through the application of its public accommodations law."

Four Justices joined a dissenting opinion authored by **Justice Stevens**. Three of those Justices (all but Stevens) also joined a dissent by **Justice Souter**.

NOTE: CAN ROTARY/ROBERTS *AND* DALE *BE RECONCILED?*

Dale seems to support the proposition that an expressive association has a First Amendment right to exclude people who would dilute or undermine its message. But the Jaycees (in *Roberts*) made similar arguments supporting their exclusion of women, to no avail. Why the different results? Some possibilities: (1) The Court viewed the Boy Scouts as a truly "expressive" association, and the Jaycees and Rotary as social clubs. As Justice Stevens's dissent argued, however, the Boy Scouts were "expressive" only in the same apple-pie sense that the Jaycees and Rotary Clubs were. And in one sense, the latter were more expressive, for their exclusionary policies were articulated in their foundational documents, while the Boy Scouts' exclusion of gay people was ad hoc and its justifications substantially coined by their Supreme Court counsel. (2) The Court viewed the state interest in combatting sex discrimination as compelling in *Roberts* and *Rotary*, in contrast to the state interest in opposing discrimination against gay people in *Hurley* and *Dale*. Recall that the Court views sex-based classifications as quasi-suspect; while the Court has not formally ruled on the level of scrutiny for sexual orientation classifications, it had regularly upheld every antigay discrimination that has ever come before it until *Romer v. Evans* (Chapter 4, § 3D). Is either theory a persuasive justification for deciding *Roberts/Rotary* differently from *Hurley/Dale*? Can you think of other justifications?[41]

As this book was going to press, the Boy Scouts announced that it would allow gays to be Scouts but not to hold leadership positions. Does acceptance of gays as Scouts cast doubt on the organization's previous assertion that it had an anti-gay message?

You may recall that in Chapter 4, Justice Scalia referred several times to the stance taken by an association of law schools regarding anti-gay practices by law firms. The following case involves one aspect of the association's policy.

RUMSFELD V. FORUM FOR ACADEMIC AND INSTITUTIONAL RIGHTS (FAIR)
547 U.S. 47, 126 S.Ct. 1297, 164 L.Ed.2d 156 (2006)

[FAIR was an association of law schools and law faculties. Its members opposed discrimination based on sexual orientation. At the time, the military followed a "don't ask, don't tell" policy toward homosexuality. The law schools had rules that prohibited use of their recruiting facilities by employers who engaged in such discrimination. Under these rules, the military's anti-gay policies would disqualify it from recruiting on campus. A federal statute, the Solomon Amendment, cuts off federal funding to universities that deny military recruiters access equal to that provided other recruiters. The court of appeals had declared the Solomon Amendment unconstitutional.]

CHIEF JUSTICE ROBERTS delivered the opinion of the Court [joined by all members of the Court, except for Justice Alito, who did not participate].

[The Court rejected the argument that the Solomon Amendment forced law schools to endorse speech that they disagreed with or impaired the ability of schools to communicate their own views about anti-gay discrimination. It then turned to the issue of expressive association.]

FAIR argues that the Solomon Amendment violates law schools' freedom of expressive association. According to FAIR, law schools' ability to express their message that discrimination on the basis of sexual orientation is wrong is significantly affected by the presence of military recruiters on campus and the schools' obligation to assist them. Relying heavily on our decision in *Dale,* the Court of Appeals agreed.

---

[41] *Dale* gave rise to considerable controversy. For discussion of the decision and its implications for freedom of association, see Evelyn Broady, *Entrance, Voice, and Exit: The Constitutional Bounds of the Right of Association,* 35 U.C. Davis L. Rev. 821 (2002); Dale Carpenter, *Expressive Association and Anti-Discrimination Law After* Dale*: A Tripartite Approach,* 85 Minn. L. Rev. 1515 (2001); Daniel Farber, *Speaking in the First Person Plural: Expressive Associations and the First Amendment,* 85 Minn. L. Rev. 1483 (2001); David McGowan, *Making Sense of* Dale, 18 Const. Comm. 121 (2001).

In *Dale,* we held that the Boy Scouts' freedom of expressive association was violated by New Jersey's public accommodations law, which required the organization to accept a homosexual as a scoutmaster. After determining that the Boy Scouts was an expressive association, that "the forced inclusion of Dale would significantly affect its expression," and that the State's interests did not justify this intrusion, we concluded that the Boy Scout's First Amendment rights were violated.

The Solomon Amendment, however, does not similarly affect a law school's associational rights. To comply with the statute, law schools must allow military recruiters on campus and assist them in whatever way the school chooses to assist other employers. Law schools therefore "associate" with military recruiters in the sense that they interact with them. But recruiters are not part of the law school. Recruiters are, by definition, outsiders who come onto campus for the limited purpose of trying to hire students—not to become members of the school's expressive association. This distinction is critical. Unlike the public accommodations law in *Dale,* the Solomon Amendment does not force a law school " 'to accept members it does not desire.' " * * *

FAIR correctly notes that the freedom of expressive association protects more than just a group's membership decisions. For example, we have held laws unconstitutional that require disclosure of membership lists for groups seeking anonymity, or impose penalties or withhold benefits based on membership in a disfavored group. Although these laws did not directly interfere with an organization's composition, they made group membership less attractive, raising the same First Amendment concerns about affecting the group's ability to express its message.

The Solomon Amendment has no similar effect on a law school's associational rights. Students and faculty are free to associate to voice their disapproval of the military's message; nothing about the statute affects the composition of the group by making group membership less desirable. The Solomon Amendment therefore does not violate a law school's First Amendment rights. A military recruiter's mere presence on campus does not violate a law school's right to associate, regardless of how repugnant the law school considers the recruiter's message.

NOTE ON FAIR

To what extent does *FAIR* limit the implications of *Dale?* Suppose Congress banned discrimination against members of the military in law school admissions or against the hiring of reservists as faculty members. Are students or faculty "spokesmen" as in *Dale* or are they more like the recruiters in *FAIR?* Would your answer be the same if Congress banned discrimination against gays in hiring or admissions?

The Court says that an organization cannot satisfy *Dale* by simply saying that association would impair its message. What made the Boy Scouts' claim that Dale's presence as a Scoutmaster would impair its message more credible than the law schools' claim in *FAIR*?

Notice that FAIR involved a funding condition that allegedly impaired freedom of expressive association. Since the Court found that expressive association was not implicated, it had no reason to consider the scope of the unconstitutional conditions doctrine. That issue was more squarely raised in the following case.

Christian Legal Society Chapter v. Martinez

561 U.S. 661 (2010)

A law school (Hastings) required that, as a condition of receiving school funds, an organization had to open eligibility for membership and leadership to all students. The school denied funding to a student religious group that required leaders to endorse certain religious teachings, including rejection of homosexuality. The Court upheld the funding condition in an opinion by **Justice Ginsburg**, viewing the law school's financial support as equivalent to a limited public forum:

> [T]his case fits comfortably within the limited-public-forum category, for CLS, in seeking what is effectively a state subsidy, faces only indirect pressure to modify its membership policies; CLS may exclude any person for any reason if it forgoes the benefits of official recognition. The expressive-association precedents on which CLS relies, in contrast, involved regulations that *compelled* a group to include unwanted members, with no choice to opt out.

> In diverse contexts, our decisions have distinguished between policies that require action and those that withhold benefits. Application of the less-restrictive limited-public-forum analysis better accounts for the fact that Hastings, through its RSO program, is dangling the carrot of subsidy, not wielding the stick of prohibition

The majority concluded that the school's all-comers requirements was a reasonable definition of the funding "forum" because it served several university interests: (1) it "ensures that no Hastings student is forced to fund a group that would reject her as a member"; (2) it helps the school "police the written terms of its Nondiscrimination Policy without inquiring into an RSO's motivation for membership restrictions"; (3) by bringing together students with diverse backgrounds and beliefs, it encourages "encourages tolerance, cooperation, and learning among students"; and (4) it "conveys the Law School's decision 'to decline to subsidize with public monies and benefits conduct of which the people of California disapprove [violation of discrimination policies]." The Court also considered the all-comers policy to be viewpoint neutral.

Justice Alito, joined by the **Chief Justice, Justice Scalia,** and **Justice Thomas** join, dissented. Much of the dissent is devoted to arguing that Hasting was not actually following an "an all-comers" policy but was instead enforcing another policy that banned discrimination based on religion or sexual orientation. The dissent also argued that the application of Hastings' policies was pretextual, motivated by disapproval of the Christian Legal Society's viewpoint. The majority left the issue of pretext open on remand. The dissent also argued that the forum was defined in terms of all noncommercial student groups, not all noncommercial groups accepting all students.

NOTES ON CHRISTIAN LEGAL SOCIETY *AND THE LIMITED PUBLIC FORUM*

1. *The Puzzle of the Limited Forum.* The conceptual point of disputes between the majority and dissent is whether the "all comers" policy is part of the definition of the limited forum or whether it is a restriction on groups that do qualify under the forum's definition. More concretely, is being a recognized student group a "forum" open to every "non-commercial student group" (the dissent's view) or is it a forum for every "non-commercial group open to all students" (the majority's view)? The difference is whether the Christian Legal Society was precluded from being recognized group because it did not meet the qualification, or whether it was *ex*cluded even though it did meet the qualifications.

The distinction between forum definition and forum exclusion is elusive in much the same way as the difference between conditions subsequent or precedent, or between losing a benefit versus suffering a penalty. Nevertheless, under public forum doctrine, the distinction drives the analysis and the outcome. Once the school has defined and opened the forum, it has no more power to regulate expression or association than society has in a traditional public forum. On the other hand, the school can use any reasonable, non-viewpoint criterion to define the scope of a limited public forum. The trouble is that there's really no functional difference between the two, and the Court has never explained how to make the distinction.

Note that a similar distinction also drove the analysis in *Rust*. There, the Court divided on whether the government was subsidizing reproductive services but then censoring abortion information, or had simply defined the activity that it wanted to subsidize as contraceptive advice. Consider some possible factors that the Court could use to make this distinction: the history of the forum; the existence of a formal written definition of the forum; the motivation of the government officials; the message conveyed by the government's action; and the extent of the burden or viewpoint impact of the restriction. Would these factors or others provide sufficient guidance? Or should the whole idea of the "limited public forum" be abandoned as hopelessly incoherent?

2. *Anti-Discrimination Rules.* The Court dodged the question of whether a law school could apply its nondiscrimination rules to deny funding rather

than a more general "all comers" policies. (The difference would arise only if a group excluded members for some reason not covered by the anti-discrimination rules, such as political affiliation.) Suppose that the Women's Law Society at some school is only open to women? Could the group constitutionally be denied status as a recognized student group because it is violating an anti-discrimination rule even if the school allows other kinds of membership restrictions?

SECTION 6. THE RELIGION CLAUSES

Religion is an important component of civil society. In this section, we will consider the government's relationship with religious groups. Although the trend has been to loosen the restrictions, significant constitutional restrictions still apply to laws that hinder religious practices, provide financial assistance to the activities of religious groups, or endorse religious symbols.

The Framers of the Bill of Rights held a variety of views about the relation of religion and the state, according to Arlin Adams & Charles Emmerich, *A Nation Dedicated to Religious Liberty: The Constitutional Heritage of the Religion Clauses* (1990).[42] Pietistic separatists (e.g., John Witherspoon) followed the traditions of the Pennsylvania Quakers and Rhode Island's Roger Williams, who believed in the "wall of separation between the garden of the Church and the wilderness of the world," *id.* at 6 (quoting Williams), and embraced a confessional pluralism that left every person free to pursue his or her own faith. Enlightenment separatists (e.g., Tom Paine, Thomas Jefferson) were not conventionally religious and saw religious liberty as an individual right; in the Lockean tradition; they taught liberty of conscience and plurality of religions. Political centrists such as George Washington and John Adams favored state nonintrusion, mainly because they "believed that religion was an essential cornerstone for morality, civic virtue and democratic government." *Id.* at 26. Hence, this group favored government fostering of a religious attitude (e.g., Thanksgiving Day prayers), but not state intrusion.

Adams and Emmerich do not believe that any one of these schools dominated in the framing of the Religion Clauses of the First Amendment but instead believe the clauses a result of a dialogue among all three views. All the views strongly supported religious liberty but sought to protect that liberty in different ways—precluding the establishment of a state church (as in England), refraining from regulations that unnecessarily burden people's exercise of their faiths, requiring state neutrality, and avoiding

---

[42] Helpfully reviewed by John Witte, Jr., *The Integration of Religious Liberty*, 90 Mich. L. Rev. 1363 (1992). See also William Miller, *The First Liberty: Religion and the American Republic* (1986); Laurence Tribe, *American Constitutional Law* 1158–60 (2d ed. 1988); Michael McConnell, *The Origins and Historical Understanding of the Free Exercise of Religion*, 103 Harv. L. Rev. 1410 (1990). See generally *Church and State in America: A Bibliographical Guide* (John Wilson ed. 1986).

favoritism for or discrimination against different religions. At least some of the Framers believed that these protections not only assured people their freedom of faith, but also served as a more general protection of liberty for all, because flourishing churches and religious groups could serve as buffers between the individual and the state, and as contributors to the marketplace of ideas.

The lesson Adams and Emmerich draw from history is that the different goals of the Religion Clauses must be integrated with one another and not viewed in isolation. For example, they argue that Justices who emphasize a "wall of separation" between church and state marginalize the Free Exercise Clause, while those who emphasize state accommodation to religious practices marginalize the Establishment Clause. The tension is most acute in cases where a religion seeks an exemption on religious grounds from the courts or from the government itself: granting the exemption seems to privilege the religious practice, raising establishment concerns, while denying the exemption burdens the religion, raising free exercise concerns. Read the following materials and see if you can do the job better than the Court has done. Then consider the material at the end of this section, which presents a modern theory of religious pluralism and its implications for liberty/equality clashes, such as those raised in *Rotary* and *Hurley*, *supra*.

We will devote most of our attention to the Free Exercise Clause, which has been increasingly deployed in efforts to shield opponents from regulations and anti-discrimination laws. Because of space limitations, we will only touch on the Establishment Clause. The following case poses some basic questions about protection for religion.

Stansbury v. Marks

2 Dall. 213 (Pa. 1793)

In this case (which was tried on Saturday, the 5th of April), the defendant offered Jonas Phillips, a Jew, as a witness; but he refused to be sworn, because it was his Sabbath. The court, therefore, fined him 10£; but the defendant, afterwards, waived the benefit of his testimony, and he was discharged from the fine.

NOTES ON STANSBURY

1. *State Constitutional Rights.* The foregoing is the complete report of the case—possibly the shortest judicial opinion you will ever read. In evaluating the opinion, consider the language of the Pennsylvania Constitution of 1790, Art. IX, § 3, which was in effect at the time of the decision:

> That all men have a natural and indefeasible right to worship
> Almighty God according to the dictates of their own consciences; that
> no man can of right be compelled to attend, erect, or support any place

of worship, or maintain any ministry, against his consent; that no human authority can, in any case whatever, control or interfere with their rights of conscience; and that no preference shall ever be given, by law, to any religious establishment or modes of worship.

Compare this provision with the language of the First Amendment. Which is more protective of religious freedom?

2. *Values in the Free Exercise of Religion.* In light of this introductory history and modern constitutional theory, what values does the Free Exercise Clause protect? There are a number of possibilities:[43] (a) *Autonomy.* An important element of our personal autonomy is our faith (or lack thereof), and the state shouldn't be able to coerce or penalize us for our faith. (b) *Pluralism and Representation-Reinforcement.* Communities of faith contribute to the pluralist richness of the United States, but there may also be a tendency of the majority to "pick on" minority faiths (this has been the experience of Jews, Mormons, Amish, Muslims, and Jehovah's Witnesses at various points in our history). The Free Exercise Clause provides a bulwark for such "discrete and insular" minority communities against majoritarian oppression. (c) *Tolerant Society.* The Free Exercise Clause enforces norms of tolerance in a diverse society, which can carry over into other areas of society as well.

Query: In light of these values, how much does or should a (state or federal constitutional) Free Exercise Clause add to a Speech Clause, which provides an independent (but perhaps weaker) justification for a challenge to the requirement that Jonas Phillips testify?

3. *Neutrality Versus Accommodation.* Assuming that the Free Exercise Clause embodies important constitutional values, how strongly should they be enforced? Consider some analogies. Paralleling the Court's interpretation of the Equal Protection Clause to prohibit only intentional state discrimination (and not state action having discriminatory effects), see *Washington v. Davis* (Chapter 3, § 1B), the Free Exercise Clause might be applied only against state policies intentionally harming one group's free exercise of religion, but not against state laws whose infringement on religion is only incidental and unintended. (Recall the language of the clause: "Congress shall make no law . . . *prohibiting* the free exercise" of religion.)

Under this view, the requirement in *Stansbury* might seem permissible, so long as the Saturday trial day was not intended to harass Jonas Phillips. But the representation-reinforcement rationale for the Free Exercise Clause suggests that the majority's insensitivity to the genuine needs of religious minorities may result in major deprivations that would be imperfectly policed by an intent approach. The better analogy might be to the Speech Clause of the First Amendment. (But note the different text: "Congress shall make no law

[43] See Lee Bollinger, *The Tolerant Society* (1986); Frederick Gedicks & Roger Hendrix, *Democracy, Autonomy, and Values: Some Thoughts on Religion and Law in Modern America*, 60 S. Cal. L. Rev. 1579 (1987); Robert Rodes, *Sub Deo et Lege: A Study of Free Exercise*, 4 Relig. & Pub. Order 3 (1968); Michael Sandel, *Religious Liberty—Freedom of Conscience or Freedom of Choice?*, 1989 Utah L. Rev. 597 (1989).

... *abridging* the freedom of speech," versus "prohibiting" the free exercise of religion.) A rule such as the mandatory equipment-and-technician rule in *Rock Against Racism* (§ 4A of this chapter) might not be intended to chill speech, but the speaker can still challenge it if it has the effect of burdening speech and is not supported by a legitimate state interest that is also "neutral" toward religion.

Was the law requiring the attendance of witnesses "neutral" in its effect on religion? True, the law does not distinguish on its face between religious beliefs, but of course trials were never held on Sunday, so that compulsory attendance would never burden those whose Sabbath was on Sunday. So perhaps Jonas Phillips could not constitutionally be required to testify on his Sabbath. But consider *McGowan v. Maryland*, 366 U.S. 420 (1961), in which the Court rejected attacks on Sunday closing laws. Chief Justice Warren's opinion for the Court held that the laws originally had a religious purpose, but now have the secular purpose of providing a "uniform day of rest for all citizens." In *Braunfeld v. Brown*, 366 U.S. 599 (1961), the Court rejected a challenge to a Sunday closing law by Orthodox Jews, who argued that the law placed them at a competitive disadvantage because their religion required them to close on Saturday as well. The Court concluded that there was no less burdensome alternative, since allowing exemptions for Saturday Sabbatarians would cause enforcement problems and undermine the purpose of providing a noncommercial day of rest for the entire population. Doesn't this statute favor one religion over another? See also *Goldman v. Weinberger*, 475 U.S. 503 (1986) (divided Court permitted Air Force to prohibit the wearing of a Jewish yarmulke by military officer who was an orthodox Jew and ordained rabbi). Can these cases be distinguished from *Stansbury*?

Wisconsin v. Yoder

406 U.S. 205 (1972)

Defendants, who were members of the Old Order Amish religion, were convicted for refusing to send their children to school after eighth grade, violating the state-law requirement that children attend school until age 16. The evidence showed that Amish children received vocational training at home and that the defendants believed that attending high school would destroy the Amish way of life. The defendants offered expert testimony in support of their view that a high school education was unnecessary for their agrarian way of life and that the public schools transmitted values such as competitiveness and independence that were inconsistent with their culture.

In an opinion by **Chief Justice Burger**, the Court upheld their free exercise claim. The Court found that conclusion "inescapable that secondary schooling, by exposing Amish children to worldly influences in terms of attitudes, goals, and values contrary to beliefs, and by substantially interfering with the way of life of the Amish faith community at the crucial adolescent stage of development, contravenes the basic religious tenets and practice of the Amish faith, both as to the parent and the child." Under the circumstances of the case, the Court did not find any compelling interest in requiring continued school attendance, finding that an eighth-grade education was ample to prepare Amish children for life in their community, and that the history of the Amish showed the viability of their way of life. The Court also rejected the state's asserted interest in protecting the interests of Amish children who might ultimately decide to leave the community: "when the interests of parenthood are combined with a free exercise claim of the nature revealed by this record," a particularly strong showing on the part of the state was required.

NOTES ON YODER AND RELIGIOUS EXEMPTIONS

1. *A Special Rule for the Amish*? Consider how the holding of *Yoder* would apply in the following two situations:

(a) A commune pursuing an agrarian way of life like that of the Amish, but based on the reading of secular writers.

(b) A small religious community established in 1985 by a group professing allegiance to a belief in a new sect, embracing a way of life similar to that of the Amish but without the history of Amish culture.

Would *Yoder* protect either of these groups? If not, has the Court violated the Establishment Clause by giving the Amish special status?

2. *Unemployment Compensation. Yoder* finds its strongest doctrinal support in *Sherbert v. Verner*, 374 U.S. 398 (1963), the first case in which the Supreme Court held that the Free Exercise Clause was a limitation on state laws independent of the other provisions of the First Amendment. *Sherbert* involved the denial of unemployment benefits to a Sabbatarian who refused to work on Saturdays. The Court held that the denial of benefits "force[d] her to choose between following the precepts of her religion and forfeiting benefits, on the one hand, and abandoning of the precepts of her religion in order to accept work, on the other hand. Governmental imposition of such a choice puts the same kind of burden upon the free exercise of religion as would a fine." Hence, the *Sherbert* Court applied a compelling interest test. Is *Sherbert* consistent with *Rust v. Sullivan* in its treatment of funding denials? See Richard Epstein, *The Supreme Court, 1987 Term—Foreword: Unconstitutional Conditions, State Power, and the Limits of Consent*, 102 Harv. L. Rev. 4, 83–85 (1988) (defending *Sherbert*). If the state gives unemployment compensation to a woman who refuses to take a job for religious reasons, but denies compensation to one who refuses a job for equally firm secular reasons, isn't the state subsidizing religion?

3. *Applications of* Yoder *and* Sherbert. Consider the following possible applications of the Court's precedents:

(a) Lee is an Old Order Amish self-employed farmer who employed other Amish on his farm. He did not pay social security taxes for his employees, because Amish faith considers the social security system unnecessary for their people, who take seriously their moral responsibility to care for the elderly.

Assume that this factual claim is true. Can the government nevertheless require Lee to pay the taxes? See *United States v. Lee*, 455 U.S. 252 (1982).

(b) The Forest Service proposed to permit timber harvesting and road building in a portion of the National Forest System that is considered sacred by Native American tribes, and where they have held religious rituals. Can the tribes prevent this intrusion? See *Lyng v. Northwest Indian Cemetery Protective Association*, 485 U.S. 439 (1988).

EMPLOYMENT DIVISION, DEPARTMENT OF HUMAN RESOURCES V. SMITH
494 U.S. 872, 110 S.Ct. 1595, 108 L.Ed.2d 876 (1990)

JUSTICE SCALIA delivered the opinion of the Court.

[Smith and Black were fired by a private drug rehabilitation organization because they used peyote, a hallucinogen, at a ceremony of the Native American Church. Their applications for unemployment compensation were denied under a state law disqualifying employees discharged for work-related "misconduct." When the case was first brought before the Supreme Court, the Court remanded for a determination of whether sacramental peyote use violates Oregon's criminal law. On remand, the Oregon court held that the criminal statute did apply to their conduct.]

It is no more necessary to regard the collection of a general tax, for example, as "prohibiting the free exercise [of religion]" by those citizens who believe support of organized government to be sinful, than it is to regard the same tax as "abridging the freedom . . . of the press" of those publishing companies that must pay the tax as a condition of staying in business. It is a permissible reading of the text, in the one case as in the other, to say that if prohibiting the exercise of religion (or burdening the activity of printing) is not the object of the tax but merely the incidental effect of a generally applicable and otherwise valid provision, the First Amendment has not been offended.

Our decisions reveal that the latter reading is the correct one. We have never held that an individual's religious beliefs excuse him from compliance with an otherwise valid law prohibiting conduct that the State is free to regulate. On the contrary, the record of more than a century of our free exercise jurisprudence contradicts that proposition. * * *

The only decisions in which we have held that the First Amendment bars application of a neutral, generally applicable law to religiously motivated action have involved not the Free Exercise Clause alone, but the Free Exercise Clause in conjunction with other constitutional protections, such as freedom of speech and of the press, see *Cantwell v. Connecticut*, 310 U.S. 296 (1940) (invalidating a licensing system for religious and charitable solicitations under which the administrator had discretion to deny a license to any cause he deemed nonreligious); *Murdock v. Pennsylvania*, 319 U.S. 105 (1943) (invalidating a flat tax on solicitation as applied to the dissemination of religious ideas); *Follett v. McCormick*, 321 U.S. 573 (1944) (same), or the right of parents, acknowledged in *Pierce v. Society of Sisters*, 268 U.S. 510 (1925), to direct the education of their children, see *Wisconsin v. Yoder* (invalidating compulsory school-attendance laws as applied to Amish parents who refused on religious grounds to send their children to school). Some of our cases prohibiting compelled expression, decided exclusively upon free speech grounds, have also involved freedom of religion. And it is easy to envision a case in which a challenge on freedom of association grounds would likewise be reinforced by Free Exercise Clause concerns. * * *

The present case does not present such a hybrid situation, but a free exercise claim unconnected with any communicative activity or parental right. Respondents urge us to hold, quite simply, that when otherwise prohibitable conduct is accompanied by religious convictions, not only the convictions but the conduct itself must be free from governmental regulation. We have never held that, and decline to do so now. * * *

Respondents argue that even though exemption from generally applicable criminal laws need not automatically be extended to religiously motivated actors, at least the claim for a religious exemption must be evaluated under the balancing test set forth in *Sherbert v. Verner*, 374 U.S. 398 (1963). Under the *Sherbert* test, governmental actions that substantially burden a religious practice must be justified by a compelling governmental interest. Applying that test we have, on three occasions, invalidated state unemployment compensation rules that conditioned the availability of benefits upon an applicant's willingness to work under conditions forbidden by his religion. We have never invalidated any governmental action on the basis of the *Sherbert* test except the denial of unemployment compensation. Although we have sometimes purported to apply the *Sherbert* test in contexts other than that, we have always found the test satisfied. In recent years we have abstained from applying the *Sherbert* test (outside the unemployment compensation field) at all. * * *

Even if we were inclined to breathe into *Sherbert* some life beyond the unemployment compensation field, we would not apply it to require exemptions from a generally applicable criminal law. The *Sherbert* test, it must be recalled, was developed in a context that lent itself to individualized governmental assessment of the reasons for the relevant conduct. [A] distinctive feature of unemployment compensation programs is that their eligibility criteria invite consideration of the particular circumstances behind an applicant's unemployment * * *

Whether or not the decisions are that limited, they at least have nothing to do with an across-the-board criminal prohibition on a particular form of conduct. Although, as noted earlier, we have sometimes used the *Sherbert* test to analyze free exercise challenges to such laws, we have never applied the test to invalidate one. We conclude today that the sounder approach, and the approach in accord with the vast majority of our precedents, is to hold the test inapplicable to such challenges. * * * To make an individual's obligation to obey such a law contingent upon the law's coincidence with his religious beliefs, except where the State's interest is "compelling"—permitting him, by virtue of his beliefs, "to become a law unto himself"—contradicts both constitutional tradition and common sense.

JUSTICE O'CONNOR, concurring in the judgment. [Although JUSTICE BRENNAN, JUSTICE MARSHALL, and JUSTICE BLACKMUN joined parts of this opinion, they did not concur in the judgment.]

The Court today gives no convincing reason to depart from settled First Amendment jurisprudence. There is nothing talismanic about neutral laws of general applicability or general criminal prohibitions, for laws neutral toward religion can coerce a person to violate his religious conscience or intrude upon his religious duties just as effectively as laws aimed at religion. Although the Court suggests that the compelling interest test, as applied to generally applicable laws, would result in a "constitutional anomaly," the First Amendment unequivocally makes freedom of religion, like freedom from race discrimination and freedom of speech, a "constitutional nor[m]," not an "anomaly." Nor would application of our established free exercise doctrine to this case necessarily be incompatible with our equal protection cases. We have in any event recognized that the Free Exercise Clause protects values distinct from those protected by the Equal Protection Clause. As the language of the Clause itself makes clear, an individual's free exercise of religion is a preferred constitutional activity. A law that makes criminal such an activity therefore triggers constitutional concern—and heightened judicial scrutiny—even if it does not target the particular religious conduct at issue. Our free speech cases similarly recognize that neutral regulations that affect free speech values are subject to a balancing, rather than categorical, approach. *See, e.g., United States v. O'Brien*; *City of Renton v. Playtime Theatres, Inc.* The Court's parade of horribles not only fails as a reason for discarding the compelling interest test, it instead demonstrates just the opposite: that courts have been quite capable of applying our free exercise jurisprudence to strike sensible balances between religious liberty and competing state interests.

[Justice O'Connor argued, however, that the government had a compelling health interest in forbidding peyote use. JUSTICE BLACKMUN, joined by JUSTICES BRENNAN and MARSHALL, dissented; in their view,

the fact that almost half the states exempted ceremonial use of peyote
established that there was no compelling interest.]

NOTES ON SMITH AND FREE EXERCISE

1.   *Is Religious Freedom Disfavored?* Does *Smith* give religious practices
the same degree of protection given free speech? (Note that in *Barnes*, one of
the nude dancing cases discussed earlier in this chapter, *supra*, Justice Scalia
was alone in his view that *Smith* should extend to free speech claims.) How
does the protection given religious minorities under the First Amendment
compare with that given racial minorities under the Equal Protection Clause?
If some relatively minor legal prohibition makes the practice of a religion into
a crime, without serving any important government purpose, why shouldn't
the courts require an exemption? How much bite is left in the Free Exercise
Clause after *Smith*? See Douglas Laycock, *The Remnants of Free Exercise*, 1990
Sup. Ct. Rev. 1.

2.   *Airport Terminals Revisited.* Krishna Consciousness is a religion, and
adherents are required to solicit funds for it publicly. If such persons seek to
solicit funds at public airports, would McConnell require that this be allowed?
(If Krishna Consciousness were the majority religion, wouldn't airports have
been designed with plenty of room for this practice? Note that the airport does
have a chapel for those with more conventional religions.) What is the result
under *Smith*? Could this be considered a "hybrid" claim based on both free
exercise and free speech rights?

3.   Smith v. Sherbert. The majority in *Smith* distinguishes
unemployment compensation (in *Sherbert*) as a unique setting, but don't forget
that *Smith* itself involves unemployment compensation. What difference does
it make that Oregon also has a criminal penalty for religious use of peyote?
Why couldn't another state say that it will allow religious use but that it won't
encourage such use by giving users state benefits when they lose their jobs?
This isn't a rhetorical question: we're puzzled about it ourselves. Should
Sherbert be overruled?

NOTE ON THE HISTORICAL DEBATE OVER
SMITH IN THE BOERNE OPINIONS

In response to *Smith*, Congress adopted the Religious Freedom
Restoration Act of 1993 (RFRA), 42 U.S.C. §§ 2000bb–2000bb–4, which sought
to "restore" federal law to the strict-scrutiny approach found in pre-*Smith*
precedents to judge the legality of incidental burdens on religious freedom.

In *City of Boerne v. Flores* (Chapter 7, § 3C), the Supreme Court in 1997
invalidated those portions of RFRA applying to state and local governments,
concluding that Congress lacked the authority to adopt these provisions under
§ 5 of the Fourteenth Amendment. *Boerne* also provided the occasion for an
important debate over the original understanding of the Free Exercise Clause.
In her dissent in *Boerne*, Justice O'Connor mustered much of the historical

evidence against *Smith*, drawing on the work of legal scholars.[44] For instance, several state constitutions protected religious exercise except when it harmed specific state interests. In New York, the exception was for "acts of licentiousness" and "practices inconsistent with the peace or safety of this State." In Maryland, it was any disturbance of "the good order, peace or safety of the State," infringement of "the laws of morality," or injury to "others, in their natural, civil, or religious rights." The Northwest Ordinance provided that no person "demeaning himself in a peaceable and orderly manner" shall be "molested on account of his mode of worship or religious sentiments."

Justice O'Connor devoted particular attention to James Madison's views, appropriately enough given his central role in the adoption of the First Amendment. In the debates over the Virginia Declaration of Rights, Madison's proposed language would have safeguarded the "full and free exercise" of religion, "unless under color of religion the preservation of equal liberty, and the existence of the State be manifestly endangered." Later, in supporting a Bill for Establishing Religious Freedom drafted by Jefferson, Madison drafted his famous "Memorial and Remonstrance Against Religious Assessments." In the "Memorial and Remonstrance," Madison argued that free exercise entails a "duty toward the Creator":

> This duty is precedent both in order of time and degree of obligation to the claims of Civil Society . . . [E]very man who becomes a member of any Civil Society, [must] do it with a saving of his allegiance to the Universal Sovereign. We maintain therefore that in matters of Religion, no man's right is abridged by the institution of Civil Society, and that Religion is wholly exempt from its cognizance.

Similarly, Jefferson held that the federal government was constitutionally forbidden "from intermeddling with religious institutions, their doctrines, discipline, or exercises."

Justice O'Connor also observed that the "practice of the colonies and early States bears out the conclusion that, at the time the Bill of Rights was ratified, it was accepted that government should, when possible, accommodate religious practice." For examples, Quakers were often exempted from the duty to swear an oath of allegiance, and most legislators exempted conscientious objectors from conscription. In addition, she noted, "North Carolina and Maryland excused Quakers from the requirement of removing their hats in courts; Rhode Island exempted Jews from the requirements of the state marriage laws; and Georgia allowed groups of European immigrants to organize whole towns according to their own faith."

Justice Scalia responded to Justice O'Connor in his *Boerne* concurrence, making the following points: The early state constitutions typically applied only to state actions taken "for," "in respect of," or "on account of" religion, a description that Scalia said did not apply to neutral laws of general application.

---

[44] See Adams & Emmerich, A Nation Dedicated to Religious Liberty, supra; Leonard Levy, Judgments: Essays on American Constitutional History (1972).

Moreover, the provisos about "good order" and so forth could be read broadly, since "peace" and "order" were often taken to encompass the obligations to obey general laws in eighteenth century usage. Nor, in Scalia's view, are the religious exemptions granted by legislatures decisive, since they do not show that the legislators felt constitutionally obligated to provide the exemptions.[45]

Thus, the debate on *Smith* and the original understanding continues. Note that, as the next two cases illustrate, the free exercise clause does retain *some* relevance, despite *Smith*.

Church of the Lukumi Babalu Aye, Inc. v. Hialeah

508 U.S. 520 (1993)

Hialeah, Florida, passed a series of ordinances that, though facially neutral, were targeted against the church's use of animal sacrifice, a religious ritual central to the church's religious practice. All nine Justices concluded that the ordinances were unconstitutional. The majority opinion of **Justice Kennedy** applied the *Smith* standard, found that the ordinances were not "neutral and of general applicability" but rather were enacted with the intention and had the effect of suppressing a religion, and accordingly applied strict scrutiny. The ordinances flunked rigid review because they were underinclusive with respect to the two interests advanced in support of them—protecting public health and preventing cruelty to animals. Few killings of animals were regulated at all unless the death was through religious ritual. **Justice Scalia**, joined by **Chief Justice Rehnquist**, filed a separate statement agreeing with much of the majority opinion, but objecting to the inquiry concerning the subjective motivations of the city council.

Justice Blackmun, joined by **Justice O'Connor**, concurred in the judgment, writing separately to continue to express his disagreement with the *Smith* test. **Justice Souter** also wrote separately and voiced his disapproval of *Smith* (which was decided before he came to the Court). Perhaps because of his strong endorsement of *stare decisis* in the *Casey* abortion decision (Chapter 5, § 4B), Justice Souter wrote at length concerning why he believed *Smith* could be reconsidered.

Presumably, the Free Exercise Clause, if it does nothing else, prohibits discrimination against religion. The preceding case adds a sort of *Washington v. Davis* intent gloss to the clause. But in the following case, the Court finds a free-exercise violation even though the law is facially neutral and there is no claim of discrimination.

---

[45] Accord, Philip Hamburger, *A Constitutional Right of Religious Exemption: An Historical Perspective*, 60 Geo. Wash. L. Rev. 915 (1992).

Hosanna-Tabor Evangelical Lutheran Church and School v. EEOC

565 U.S. 171 (2012)

A church classified teachers at its schools into two categories: "called" and "lay." To be eligible to be considered "called," a teacher must complete certain academic requirements, including a course of theological study. Called teachers had the formal title "Minister of Religion, Commissioned." "Lay" teachers are not required to be trained by even to belong to the Church. Although lay and called teachers at Hosanna-Tabor generally performed the same duties, lay teachers were hired only when called teachers were unavailable. Cheryl Perich was designated as a commissioned minister. In addition to teaching secular subjects, she taught a religion class, led her students in daily prayer and devotional exercises, and took her students to a weekly school-wide chapel service. Perich led the chapel service herself about twice a year. After she developed a chronic condition, she threatened to file suit against the school for failing to accommodate her disability. She was then fired for insubordination. The EEOC charged the school with unlawfully firing her in retaliation for claiming her rights under federal law. **Chief Justice Roberts** delivered the opinion of the Court. He held that religious groups are entitled to a ministerial exception from anti-discrimination laws:

> The members of a religious group put their faith in the hands of their ministers. Requiring a church to accept or retain an unwanted minister, or punishing a church for failing to do so, intrudes upon more than a mere employment decision. Such action interferes with the internal governance of the church, depriving the church of control over the selection of those who will personify its beliefs. By imposing an unwanted minister, the state infringes the Free Exercise Clause, which protects a religious group's right to shape its own faith and mission through its appointments. According the state the power to determine which individuals will minister to the faithful also violates the Establishment Clause, which prohibits government involvement in such ecclesiastical decisions.

Roberts rejected the argument that the appropriate analysis was under the *Dale* approach to freedom of association. He could not accept "the remarkable view that the Religion Clauses have nothing to say about a religious organization's freedom to select its own ministers." He also rejected the applicability of *Smith*:

> It is true that the ADA's prohibition on retaliation, like Oregon's prohibition on peyote use, is a valid and neutral law of general applicability. But a church's selection of its ministers is unlike an individual's ingestion of peyote. *Smith* involved government regulation of only outward physical acts. The present case, in contrast, concerns government interference with an internal church decision that affects the faith and mission of the church itself. The contention that *Smith* forecloses recognition of a ministerial exception rooted in the Religion Clauses has no merit.

Having concluded that there is a ministerial exception grounded in the religion clauses, the Court held that "called teachers" were appropriately considered ministers. The Court emphasized "the formal title given Perich by the Church, the substance reflected in that title, her own use of that title, and the important religious functions she performed for the Church."

NOTES ON HOSANNA-TABOR

1. *What Are the Implications for* Smith*?* The Court distinguishes *Smith* as involving only "outward actions" rather than the internal affairs of the church. In what sense is a religious sacrament an "outward action"? Is the implication that the Free Exercise Clause gives more protection to churches as institutions than to the religious practices of their members? Would it have been better for the Court to have reached the same result by applying the hybrid rights prong of *Smith* (with freedom of association serving as the hybridized right)?

2. *Who Is Covered by the Ministerial Exemption?* Suppose that Perich had not become a "called" teacher. She still might have performed exactly the same functions at the school. Under the majority view, would the school have retained its exemption from anti-discrimination laws? Is it significant that non-members of the church could also be hired as lay teachers?

3. *What Actions Are Exempt?* The Court emphasizes the Church's right to select its ministers. But suppose that the dispute does not involve hiring or firing? Suppose that the employee is only suing for a pay raise or promotion? Or suppose the argument is that the church should be liable for knowingly appointing a minister with a history of child sexual abuse? Does the ministerial exemption apply? Just how far does *Hosanna-Tabor* sweep? For varying views on the decision's implications, see Ashutosh Bhagwat, *Religious Associations: Howanna-Tabor and the Instrumental Value of Religious Groups*, 92 Wash. U. L. Rev. 73 (2015); Christopher C. Lund, *Free Exercise Reconceived: The Logic and Limits of* Hosanna-Tabor, 108 Nw. U. L. Rev. 1183 (2014).

Recall that in the aftermath of *Smith*, Congress passed the Religious Freedom Restoration Act, which the Court then declared unconstitutional as applied to the states. RFRA does, however, remain in effect with regard to the federal government. In *Burwell v. Hobby Lobby Stores*, 573 U.S. 682 (2014), a five-Justice majority held that RFRA immunized a closely held corporation from being required to provide contraception coverage to female employees. The majority concluded that RFRA protected the religious scruples of the owners, who sincerely objected to providing insurance for actions by employees that violated their religious views. The majority found that the government had a less restrictive alternative: extending to for-profit corporations an optional mechanism already provided to non-profit religious organizations. Justice Kennedy concurred to emphasize the narrowness of the decision in applying only to contraception (indeed, on the facts, only to forms of contraception that operate after intercourse has already occurred). He also stressed the existence of the off-the-rack accommodation already devised by the government. The four dissenters expressed concern that the Court had opened the door for corporations to object to coverage for a wide range of medical procedures and to claim religious exemptions from anti-discrimination and other laws. They also suggested that publicly held corporations might well try to take advantage of the ruling.

Burwell makes it clear that, as a practical matter, *Smith* has no significance as applied to the federal government, given the existence of RCRA. State governments, however, may retain more discretion regarding religious exemptions. But this does not mean they are entitled to excluded religious groups from programs unrelated to religion, as the following case indicates.

Trinity Lutheran Church of Columbia, Inc. v. Comer, 137 S.Ct. 2012 (2017). A Lutheran childcare center, which had merged with a church, applied for funding as part of a state program to install safer surfaces made of recycled tires at playgrounds at nonprofits. The government rejected the ground because of its strict policy against providing any funding to churches. In an opinion by **Chief Justice Roberts**, the Court held that this government policy was unconstitutional. According to the Court, because the policy "expressly discriminates against otherwise eligible recipients by disqualifying them from a public benefit solely because of their religious character," it was subject to "the most exacting scrutiny." The opinion concluded:

> The Missouri Department of Natural Resources has not subjected anyone to chains or torture on account of religion. And the result of the State's policy is nothing so dramatic as the denial of political office. The consequence is, in all likelihood, a few extra scraped knees. But the exclusion of Trinity Lutheran from a public benefit for which it is otherwise qualified, solely because it is a church, is odious to our Constitution all the same, and cannot stand.

Footnote 3 of the opinion, which was joined only by the Roberts, Kennedy, Alito, and Kagan, limited the scope of the opinion: "This case involves express discrimination based on religious identity with respect to playground resurfacing. We do not address religious uses of funding or other forms of discrimination." **Justices Thomas** and **Justice Gorsuch** wrote separately to express disapproval of this footnote. Justice Breyer, concurring in the judgement, emphasized the health and safety nature of the benefit in the case.

In dissent, **Justice Sotomayor** (joined by **Justice Ginsberg**), argued that the decision represented an important breach in the separation of church and state:

> To hear the Court tell it, this is a simple case about recycling tires to resurface a playground. The stakes are higher. This case is about nothing less than the relationship between religious institutions and the civil government—that is, between church and state. The Court today profoundly changes that relationship by holding, for the first time, that the Constitution requires the government to provide public funds directly to a church. Its decision

slights both our precedents and our history, and its reasoning weakens this country's longstanding commitment to a separation of church and state beneficial to both.

The biggest immediate question posed by *Trinity Lutheran* relates to school voucher programs. The Court had previously held that it is constitutional to include religious schools in such programs. After *Trinity Lutheran*, is it constitutional to *exclude* religious schools from such programs?

————

In the following case, the Court returned to the issue of anti-religious animus, perhaps opening the door to widespread challenges to the enforcement of anti-discrimination laws against members of religious groups.

MASTERPIECE CAKESHOP V. COLORADO CIVIL RIGHTS COMM'N
___ U.S. ___, 138 S.Ct. 1719, 201 L.Ed.2d 35 (2018)

JUSTICE KENNEDY delivered the opinion of the Court.

In 2012 a same-sex couple visited Masterpiece Cakeshop, a bakery in Colorado, to make inquiries about ordering a cake for their wedding reception. The shop's owner told the couple that he would not create a cake for their wedding because of his religious opposition to same-sex marriages—marriages the State of Colorado itself did not recognize at that time. The couple filed a charge with the Colorado Civil Rights Commission alleging discrimination on the basis of sexual orientation in violation of the Colorado Anti-Discrimination Act.

The Commission determined that the shop's actions violated the Act and ruled in the couple's favor. The Colorado state courts affirmed the ruling and its enforcement order, and this Court now must decide whether the Commission's order violated the Constitution.

The case presents difficult questions as to the proper reconciliation of at least two principles. The first is the authority of a State and its governmental entities to protect the rights and dignity of gay persons who are, or wish to be, married but who face discrimination when they seek goods or services. The second is the right of all persons to exercise fundamental freedoms under the First Amendment, as applied to the States through the Fourteenth Amendment.

The freedoms asserted here are both the freedom of speech and the free exercise of religion. The free speech aspect of this case is difficult, for few persons who have seen a beautiful wedding cake might have thought of its creation as an exercise of protected speech. This is an instructive example, however, of the proposition that the application of constitutional freedoms in new contexts can deepen our understanding of their meaning.

One of the difficulties in this case is that the parties disagree as to the extent of the baker's refusal to provide service. If a baker refused to design a special cake with words or images celebrating the marriage—for instance, a cake showing words with religious meaning—that might be different from a refusal to sell any cake at all. In defining whether a baker's creation can be protected, these details might make a difference.

The same difficulties arise in determining whether a baker has a valid free exercise claim. A baker's refusal to attend the wedding to ensure that the cake is cut the right way, or a refusal to put certain religious words or decorations on the cake, or even a refusal to sell a cake that has been baked for the public generally but includes certain religious words or symbols on it are just three examples of possibilities that seem all but endless.

Whatever the confluence of speech and free exercise principles might be in some cases, the Colorado Civil Rights Commission's consideration of this case was inconsistent with the State's obligation of religious neutrality. The reason and motive for the baker's refusal were based on his sincere religious beliefs and convictions. The Court's precedents make clear that the baker, in his capacity as the owner of a business serving the public, might have his right to the free exercise of religion limited by generally applicable laws. Still, the delicate question of when the free exercise of his religion must yield to an otherwise valid exercise of state power needed to be determined in an adjudication in which religious hostility on the part of the State itself would not be a factor in the balance the State sought to reach. That requirement, however, was not met here. When the Colorado Civil Rights Commission considered this case, it did not do so with the religious neutrality that the Constitution requires. * * *

The neutral and respectful consideration to which Phillips was entitled was compromised here, however. The Civil Rights Commission's treatment of his case has some elements of a clear and impermissible hostility toward the sincere religious beliefs that motivated his objection.

That hostility surfaced at the Commission's formal, public hearings, as shown by the record. On May 30, 2014, the seven-member Commission convened publicly to consider Phillips' case. At several points during its meeting, commissioners endorsed the view that religious beliefs cannot legitimately be carried into the public sphere or commercial domain, implying that religious beliefs and persons are less than fully welcome in Colorado's business community. One commissioner suggested that Phillips can believe "what he wants to believe," but cannot act on his religious beliefs "if he decides to do business in the state." A few moments later, the commissioner restated the same position: "[I]f a businessman wants to do business in the state and he's got an issue with the—the law's impacting his personal belief system, he needs to look at being able to compromise." Standing alone, these statements are susceptible of different interpretations. On the one hand, they might mean simply that a business cannot refuse to provide services based on sexual orientation, regardless of the proprietor's personal views. On the other hand, they might be seen as inappropriate and dismissive comments showing lack of due consideration for Phillips' free exercise rights and the dilemma he faced. In view of the comments that followed, the latter seems the more likely.

On July 25, 2014, the Commission met again. This meeting, too, was conducted in public and on the record. On this occasion another commissioner made specific reference to the previous meeting's discussion but said far more to disparage Phillips' beliefs. The commissioner stated:

> "I would also like to reiterate what we said in the hearing or the last meeting. Freedom of religion and religion has been used to justify all kinds of discrimination throughout history, whether it be slavery, whether it be the holocaust, whether it be—I mean, we—we can list hundreds of situations where freedom of religion has been used to justify discrimination. And to me it is one of the most despicable pieces of rhetoric that people can use to—to use their religion to hurt others."

To describe a man's faith as "one of the most despicable pieces of rhetoric that people can use" is to disparage his religion in at least two distinct ways: by describing it as despicable, and also by characterizing it as merely rhetorical—something insubstantial and even insincere. The commissioner even went so far as to compare Phillips' invocation of his sincerely held religious beliefs to defenses of slavery and the Holocaust. This sentiment is inappropriate for a Commission charged with the solemn responsibility of fair and neutral enforcement of Colorado's antidiscrimination law—a law that protects discrimination on the basis of religion as well as sexual orientation.

The record shows no objection to these comments from other commissioners. And the later state-court ruling reviewing the Commission's decision did not mention those comments, much less express concern with their content. Nor were the comments by the commissioners disavowed in the briefs filed in this Court. For these reasons, the Court cannot avoid the conclusion that these statements cast doubt on the fairness and impartiality of the Commission's adjudication of Phillips' case. Members of the Court have disagreed on the question whether statements made by lawmakers may properly be taken into account in determining whether a law intentionally discriminates on the basis of religion. In this case, however, the remarks were made in a very different context—by an adjudicatory body deciding a particular case.

Another indication of hostility is the difference in treatment between Phillips' case and the cases of other bakers who objected to a requested cake on the basis of conscience and prevailed before the Commission.

[O]n at least three other occasions the Civil Rights Division considered the refusal of bakers to create cakes with images that conveyed disapproval of same-sex marriage, along with religious text. Each time, the Division found that the baker acted lawfully in refusing service. It made these determinations because, in the words of the Division, the requested cake included "wording and images [the baker] deemed derogatory."

The treatment of the conscience-based objections at issue in these three cases contrasts with the Commission's treatment of Phillips' objection. The Commission ruled against Phillips in part on the theory that any message the requested wedding cake would carry would be attributed to the customer, not to the baker. Yet the Division did not address this point in any of the other cases with respect to the cakes depicting anti-gay marriage symbolism. Additionally, the Division found no violation of CADA in the other cases in part because each bakery was willing to sell other products, including those depicting Christian themes, to the prospective customers. But the Commission dismissed Phillips' willingness to sell "birthday cakes, shower cakes, [and] cookies and brownies," to gay and lesbian customers as irrelevant. The treatment of the other cases and Phillips' case could reasonably be interpreted as being inconsistent as to the question of whether speech is involved, quite apart from whether the cases should ultimately be distinguished. In short, the Commission's consideration of Phillips' religious objection did not accord with its treatment of these other objections.

Before the Colorado Court of Appeals, Phillips protested that this disparity in treatment reflected hostility on the part of the Commission toward his beliefs. He argued that the Commission had treated the other bakers' conscience-based objections as legitimate, but treated his as illegitimate—thus sitting in judgment of his religious beliefs themselves. The Court of Appeals addressed the disparity only in passing and relegated its complete analysis of the issue to a footnote. There, the court stated that "[t]his case is distinguishable from the Colorado Civil Rights Division's recent findings that [the other bakeries] in Denver did not discriminate against a Christian patron on the basis of his creed" when they refused to create the requested cakes. In those cases, the court continued, there was no impermissible discrimination because "the Division found that the bakeries . . . refuse[d] the patron's request . . . because of the offensive nature of the requested message."

A principled rationale for the difference in treatment of these two instances cannot be based on the government's own assessment of offensiveness. Just as "no official, high or petty, can prescribe what shall be orthodox in politics, nationalism, religion, or other matters of opinion," it is not, as the Court has repeatedly held, the role of the State or its officials to prescribe what shall be offensive. The Colorado court's attempt to account for the difference in treatment elevates one view of what is offensive over another and itself sends a signal of official disapproval of Phillips' religious beliefs. The court's footnote does not, therefore, answer the baker's concern that the State's practice was to disfavor the religious basis of his objection.

[JUSTICE KAGAN, joined by JUSTICE BREYER, concurred and added that the bakers who refused to bake anti-gay messaging cakes were not discriminating because of "religion": they would have refused to bake such cakes for anyone. JUSTICE GORSUCH, joined by JUSTICE ALITO, argued that similar reasoning would indicate that he was not discriminating because of "sexual orientation" either, They observed that Phillips refused to make a gay wedding cake for the (straight) mother of one of the grooms, so It violates equal protection or freedom of religion for the state to deny relief to adherents to traditional values because the inquiry is set narrowly (focus only on the identity of the customer), while giving relief to gay claimants because the inquiry is set broadly (focus on the overall "gay wedding" framework).]

JUSTICE THOMAS, joined by JUSTICE GORSUCH, concurring.

* * * Although public-accommodations laws generally regulate conduct, particular applications of them can burden protected speech. When a public-accommodations law "ha[s] the effect of declaring . . . speech itself to be the public accommodation," the First Amendment applies with full force. *Hurley*; accord, *Boy Scouts v. Dale*. * * *

The parade in *Hurley* was an example of what this Court has termed "expressive conduct." This Court has long held that "the Constitution looks beyond written or spoken words as mediums of expression," and that "[s]ymbolism is a primitive but effective way of communicating ideas," Thus, a person's "conduct may be 'sufficiently imbued with elements of communication to fall within the scope of the First and Fourteenth Amendments.'" *Texas v. Johnson*. Applying this principle, the Court has recognized a wide array of conduct that can qualify as expressive, including nude dancing, burning the American flag, flying an upside-down American flag with a taped-on peace sign, wearing a military uniform, wearing a black armband, conducting a silent sit-in, refusing to salute the American flag, and flying a plain red flag. [The state can only regulate expressive conduct if needed to advance a "compelling" public interest.]

The conduct that the Colorado Court of Appeals ascribed to Phillips—creating and designing custom wedding cakes—is expressive. Phillips considers himself an artist. The logo for Masterpiece Cakeshop is an artist's paint palette with a paintbrush and baker's whisk. Behind the counter

Phillips has a picture that depicts him as an artist painting on a canvas. Phillips takes exceptional care with each cake that he creates—sketching the design out on paper, choosing the color scheme, creating the frosting and decorations, baking and sculpting the cake, decorating it, and delivering it to the wedding. [When Phillips does a custom wedding cake, he is an active participant in the wedding plans.]

Wedding cakes do, in fact, communicate this message. A tradition from Victorian England that made its way to America after the Civil War, "[w]edding cakes are so packed with symbolism that it is hard to know where to begin." M. Krondl, Sweet Invention: A History of Dessert 321 (2011) (Krondl); see also *ibid.* (explaining the symbolism behind the color, texture, flavor, and cutting of the cake). If an average person walked into a room and saw a white, multi-tiered cake, he would immediately know that he had stumbled upon a wedding. The cake is "so standardised and inevitable a part of getting married that few ever think to question it." Charsley, Interpretation and Custom: The Case of the Wedding Cake, 22 Man 93, 95 (1987). Almost no wedding, no matter how spartan, is missing the cake. * * * The cake's purpose is to mark the beginning of a new marriage and to celebrate the couple. [Justice Thomas rejected the various defenses, including the heckler's veto.]

JUSTICE GINSBURG, joined by **JUSTICE SOTOMAYOR,** dissenting.

[The dissenters found the gay wedding cake case and the three Bible cake cases entirely different. William Jack had asked three bakers to make cakes in the shape of a Bible, decorated with provocative references, such as Leviticus 20-13, which says that "men lying with men" should be put to death. Hence, the Commission's different treatment was no evidence of discrimination.]

The bakers would have refused to make a cake with Jack's requested message for any customer, regardless of his or her religion. And the bakers visited by Jack would have sold him any baked goods they would have sold anyone else. The bakeries' refusal to make Jack cakes of a kind they would not make for any customer scarcely resembles Phillips' refusal to serve Craig and Mullins: Phillips would *not* sell to Craig and Mullins, for no reason other than their sexual orientation, a cake of the kind he regularly sold to others. When a couple contacts a bakery for a wedding cake, the product they are seeking is a cake celebrating *their* wedding—not a cake celebrating heterosexual weddings or same-sex weddings—and that is the service Craig and Mullins were denied. Colorado, the Court does not gainsay, prohibits precisely the discrimination Craig and Mullins encountered. Jack, on the other hand, suffered no service refusal on the basis of his religion or any other protected characteristic. He was treated as any other customer would have been treated—no better, no worse. * * *

Nor was the Colorado Court of Appeals' "difference in treatment of these two instances . . . based on the government's own assessment of offensiveness." Phillips declined to make a cake he found offensive where the offensiveness of the product was determined solely by the identity of the customer requesting it. The three other bakeries declined to make cakes where their objection to the product was due to the demeaning message the requested product would literally display. As the Court recognizes, a refusal "to design a special cake with words or images . . . might be different from a refusal to sell any cake at all." The Colorado Court of Appeals did not distinguish Phillips and the other three bakeries based simply on its or the Division's finding that messages in the cakes Jack requested were offensive while any message in a cake for Craig and Mullins was not. The Colorado court distinguished the cases on the ground that Craig and Mullins were denied service based on an aspect of their identity that the State chose to grant vigorous protection from discrimination. [The dissenters also dismissed the significance of statements by two of the seven commissioners. The Court has never inferred institutional "intent" from random statements like that.]

NOTES ON RELIGIOUS LIBERTY-LGBTQI EQUALITY CLASHES

1. *Evidence of Discriminatory Intent?* How persuasive is the evidence that the decision was tainted by religious prejudice? Recall from Chapters 3 and 4, that evidence of discriminatory race-based or sex-based or sexual orientation-based intent is very hard or impossible for some judges to see, yet relatively easy for others. We see this here. The majority attributes anti-religious animus to the Commission, based in large part on the statements of two of the seven, buttressed by the different treatment of the two sets of discrimination complaints. See the Gorsuch concurring opinion for a deep and sensitive exploration that makes a good case for anti-religious bias. The test of a Justice's neutrality is this: Would he have been so thorough if gay people were complaining? Women? People of color?

Striking is the contrast between Justice Kennedy's opinion in *Masterpiece* and the Court's opinion (joined by Kennedy) the next month in *Trump v. Hawaii,* 138 S.Ct. 3892 (2018) (end of Chapter 8). There was a lot of evidence that President Trump won the presidency on a promise to issue a "Muslim travel ban," and he did so. See Problem 8-10(c) for a small sample. Travel Ban 3.0 did not use the word Muslim and targeted only some majority-Muslim countries. The Court majority found no violation of the Religion Clauses. Can that result be reconciled with *Masterpiece*?

2. *What Is Discrimination Because of Sexual Orientation? Religion?* The Gorsuch opinion suggests that "discrimination" depends on one's frame of reference. If a straight woman asks for a wedding cake for her gay son's wedding, the baker has not "discriminated" against her in the sense that she is straight—but it has discriminated in the sense that she is asking that gay people be treated the same. Flip the analysis to religion, for this allows Gorsuch

to respond to Ginsburg's argument that there was only message-based discrimination in the Jack cases. Any customer who asks for a Bible-verse wedding cake is revealing to the baker that she or he is a fundamentalist Jew or Christian—just like any customer who asks for a cake for a gay wedding is revealing his sexual orientation or that of his or her relative.

Every discrimination claim could arguably be analyzed in this way. The service provider's *conduct* (refusal to serve) is based upon the interaction between the *identity* of the customer (gay, fundamentalist) and the *expression* associated with service to the customer (gay wedding, anti-gay speech). Differential treatment based on either the classification or the expression can be discrimination. Usually, the two work together:

Conduct = Identity Classification ↔ Expression

Sometimes, there is a gap, but the interaction still arguably suggests discrimination. Thus, if the heterosexual mother of a gay groom asks for a wedding cake for their ceremony, a refusal to serve constitutes sexual orientation discrimination. Likewise, if a secular wedding planner asks for a wedding cake with Levitical condemnations on it, a refusal to serve arguably constitutes religion-based discrimination. (But what if the seller would have also rejected a cake with a secular message of condemnation?) See William N. Eskridge Jr., *Noah's Curse: How Religion Often Conflates Status, Belief, and Conduct to Resist Antidiscrimination Norms*, 45 Ga. L. Rev. 657 (2011).

The foregoing strengthens the Gorsuch claim that the Jack cases were similar to the Phillips case. How might Justice Ginsburg respond?

3.   *How Ought the Court to Limit a First Amendment Right of Expressive Conduct?* The expressive conduct issue will return to the Court (see the problems that follow). How can ADF/Thomas reconcile their reading of the First Amendment with *FAIR*? A unanimous Court said that the government can impose anti-gay accommodation requirements on universities that have an "incidental" effect on their pro-gay expression. The Court distinguished *Hurley*, because the effect on the Boston parade's speech was not incidental to a regulation of conduct, and because "the complaining speaker's own message was affected by the speech it was forced to accommodate." Under *Hurley* and *FAIR*, a state public accommodations law cannot tell a parade what marchers and banners to include—but it can tell a business that offers parade-planning services to the public that it cannot discriminate against gay people or Catholics in providing its services. Should Justice Thomas call for the overruling of *FAIR*? Or is there a better way to read *Hurley* and *FAIR* as consistent?

Assume that the ADF/Thomas reading of the First Amendment is doctrinally plausible. What ought to be its limits? Scholars have weighed in on this matter. Douglas Laycock, for example, would exempt any small business providing any same-sex marriage or wedding services (so flowers and photography as well as cakes), where the owner has a faith-based objection. Reflecting a different balance, Kent Greenawalt would exempt only those businesses where the religious owner is directly involved with the wedding ceremony: so the baker and the florist usually have no free speech/free exercise allowance, but the photographer and caterer do. Michael McConnell would exempt any commercial provider who has a sincere religious objection to participating in or facilitating a particular service. Douglas NeJaime and Reva Siegel would not exempt any religious provider if it would harm a third party (customer) in a dignitary or financial manner. All of these theories are set forth in chapters in William N. Eskridge Jr. & Robin Fretwell Wilson, *Religious Freedom, LGBT Rights, and Prospects for Common Ground* (Cambridge 2018).

Is any of the foregoing theories actually suggested by First Amendment doctrine? Is there a theory you think best derived from First Amendment principles? Should the Supreme Court be drawing this line? Consider some hard questions.

PROBLEM 6-3
FIRST AMENDMENT RIGHTS OF RELIGIOUS TRADITIONALISTS?

(A) *Faithful Word Baptist Church, Tempe Arizona.* Reverend Steve Anderson of Faithful Word preaches that "homosexuals" are bad child-molesting people, and God would be happy if they were all dead. One of his famous catch phrases is that LGBTQ stands for "Let God Burn Them Quickly."[46] Parishioner Fred Faithful goes to a Tempe bakery to make a wedding cake with that logo as its decoration. The baker refuses, as do all other bakers (most of them religious persons) in Tempe. Representing the upset couple, Anderson files a complaint with the state civil rights commission, based on a state law bar to discrimination because of religion. Assume state law covers all the bakers.

The commission dismisses the complaint, ruling that "the phrase 'LGBTQ: Let God Burn Them Quickly' is hate speech and not genuine religious expression." Hence there was no discrimination because of religion. Relying on the *Masterpiece* majority, Anderson argues on appeal that this is an open discrimination based on religion. If the animal sacrifice religion in *Lukumi Babalu Aye* is entitled to First Amendment protection, then surely Levitical Christianity is so entitled. (Leviticus 20:13 says that "men lying with men" should be put to death.) Are Anderson and Faithful entitled to judgment under binding Sureme Court precedent?

(B) *Jack Phillips, Revisited.* As Jack Phillips puts it, his troubles had only just begun with the gay wedding cake controversy. "On the same day that the Supreme Court announced it would hear my case, a Colorado lawyer [Autumn Scardino] called my shop and requested a cake that I've never before created. It was a cake with a pink interior and blue exterior that the lawyer said was to represent and celebrate a gender transition. Because I believe that each person's sex—whether male or female—is given by God and cannot be chosen or changed, the requested message is not one that I can express through my

---

[46] "Pastor Steven Anderson's Genocide of Homosexuals," video clips available at https://www.youtube.com/watch?v=gVseLfwfCMA (viewed Jan. 2, 2019).

cake art. But my shop still told the caller that we'd be happy to sell them other items or design cakes with other messages." Jack Phillips, *Despite My Court Win, Colorado Civil Rights Commission Is Coming After Me Again*, USA Today, Aug. 16, 2018.

Scardino has filed a complaint with the Commission. Phillips' ADF counsel from are making both free exercise (*Masterpiece* majority and Gorsuch concurrence) and free speech (Thomas concurrence) arguments. How should the Commission rule? If the Commission finds a violation and doesn't make the same mistake it made before, would the Supreme Court reverse? Specifically, would the Court find a violation of the Speech Clause?

(C) *How Does This Apply to Race?* Assume that in the second Phillips Case ADF wins a Supreme Court decision along the lines laid out in Justice Thomas's *Masterpiece* opinion. The baker has a First Amendment right to "expressive conduct," disassociating himself from collaborating with activities that violate the Word of the Lord as he sees it. The next case involves a baker who will not serve an interracial couple who want to marry. Like hundreds of thousands of Americans who read the Bible to bar such unions, see Eskridge, *Noah's Curse*, the baker claims the same free speech right as Phillips. Under the Thomas approach, can the First Amendment "discriminate" between racist readings of Scripture and anti-gay readings? Would the Supreme Court grant relief to the Noah's Curse baker? Cf. *Newman v. Piggie Park Ents.*, 256 F. Supp. 941, 945 (D.S.C. 1966), *rev'd*, 377 F.2d 433, 437–38 (4th Cir. 1967), *aff'd*, 390 U.S. 400, 402 n.5 (1968) (all judges rejecting as frivolous the free exercise argument, grounded in Noah's Curse, for a drive-in and sandwich shop to segregate customers).

The complaint in *Masterpiece Cake* was that the state violated the Constitution by disfavoring religion. The Establishment Clause involves the contrary complaint that the state violated the Constitution by favoring religion. Such claims arise in a wide variety of contexts, from religious activities in public schools to receipt of government funding by religious groups. Our goal here is not to plumb the doctrinal issues but only to give a sense of the main fault lines between different interpretations of the clause. Those fault lines may also have implications for accommodation cases such as *Masterpiece Cake*.

EVERSON V. BOARD OF EDUCATION
330 U.S. 1, 67 S.Ct. 504, 91 L.Ed. 711 (1947)

JUSTICE BLACK delivered the opinion of the Court.

[A New Jersey statute authorized local school districts to pay for transportation of children to and from school (both public and private). The issue in the case was whether a local school district violated the Establishment Clause by reimbursing parents for transportation of their children to Catholic parochial schools.]

Whether this New Jersey law is one respecting the "establishment of religion" requires an understanding of the meaning of that language, particularly with respect to the imposition of taxes. Once again, therefore, it is not inappropriate briefly to review the background and environment of the period in which that constitutional language was fashioned and adopted.

A large proportion of the early settlers of this country came here from Europe to escape the bondage of laws which compelled them to support and attend government favored churches. The centuries immediately before and contemporaneous with the colonization of America had been filled with turmoil, civil strife, and persecutions, generated in large part by established sects determined to maintain their absolute political and religious supremacy. With the power of government supporting them, at various times and places, Catholics had persecuted Protestants, Protestants had persecuted Catholics, Protestant sects had persecuted other Protestant sects, Catholics of one shade of belief had persecuted Catholics of another shade of belief, and all of these had from time to time persecuted Jews. In efforts to force loyalty to whatever religious group happened to be on top and in league with the government of a particular time and place, men and women had been fined, cast in jail, cruelly tortured, and killed. Among the offenses for which these punishments had been inflicted were such things as speaking disrespectfully of the views of ministers of government-established churches, non-attendance at those churches, expressions of non-belief in their doctrines, and failure to pay taxes and tithes to support them.

These practices of the old world were transplanted to and began to thrive in the soil of the new America. The very charters granted by the English Crown to the individuals and companies designated to make the laws which would control the destinies of the colonials authorized these individuals and companies to erect religious establishments which all, whether believers or non-believers, would be required to support and attend. An exercise of this authority was accompanied by a repetition of many of the old-world practices and persecutions. Catholics found themselves hounded and proscribed because of their faith; Quakers who followed their conscience went to jail; Baptists were peculiarly obnoxious to certain dominant Protestant sects; men and women of varied faiths who happened to be in a minority in a particular locality were persecuted because they steadfastly persisted in worshipping God only as their own consciences dictated. And all of these dissenters were compelled to pay tithes and taxes to support government-sponsored churches whose ministers preached inflammatory sermons designed to strengthen and consolidate the established faith by generating a burning hatred against dissenters.

These practices became so commonplace as to shock the freedom-loving colonials into a feeling of abhorrence. The imposition of taxes to pay ministers' salaries and to build and maintain churches and church property aroused their indignation. It was these feelings which found expression in the First Amendment. No one locality and no one group throughout the Colonies can rightly be given entire credit for having aroused the sentiment that culminated in adoption of the Bill of Rights' provisions embracing religious liberty. But Virginia, where the established church had achieved a dominant influence in political affairs and where many excesses attracted wide public attention, provided a great stimulus and able leadership for the movement. The people there, as elsewhere, reached the conviction that individual religious liberty could be achieved best under a government which was stripped of all power to tax, to support, or otherwise to assist any or all religions, or to interfere with the beliefs of any religious individual or group.

The movement toward this end reached its dramatic climax in Virginia in 1785–86 when the Virginia legislative body was about to renew Virginia's tax levy for the support of the established church. Thomas Jefferson and James Madison led the fight against this tax. Madison wrote his great Memorial and Remonstrance against the law. In it, he eloquently argued that a true religion did not need the support of law; that no person, either believer or non-believer, should be taxed to support a religious institution of any kind; that the best interest of a society required that the minds of men always be wholly free; and that cruel persecutions were the inevitable result of government-established religions. Madison's Remonstrance received strong support throughout Virginia, and the Assembly postponed consideration of the proposed tax measure until its next session. When the proposal came up for consideration at that session, it not only died in committee, but the Assembly enacted the famous "Virginia Bill for Religious Liberty" originally written by Thomas Jefferson. The preamble to that Bill stated among other things that

> Almighty God hath created the mind free; that all attempts to influence it by temporal punishments, or burdens, or by civil incapacitations, tend only to beget habits of hypocrisy and meanness, and are a departure from the plan of the Holy author of our religion, who being Lord both of body and mind, yet chose not to propagate it by coercions on either . . . ; that to compel a man to furnish contributions of money for the propagation of opinions which he disbelieves, is sinful and tyrannical; that even the forcing him to support this or that teacher of his own religious persuasion, is depriving him of the comfortable liberty of giving his contributions to the particular pastor, whose morals he would make his pattern. * * *

And the statute itself enacted

That no man shall be compelled to frequent or support any religious worship, place, or ministry whatsoever, nor shall be enforced, restrained, molested, or burthened in his body or goods, nor shall otherwise suffer on account of his religious opinions or belief. . . .

This Court has previously recognized that the provisions of the First Amendment, in the drafting and adoption of which Madison and Jefferson played such leading roles, had the same objective and were intended to provide the same protection against governmental intrusion on religious liberty as the Virginia statute. * * *

The "establishment of religion" clause of the First Amendment means at least this: Neither a state nor the Federal Government can set up a church. Neither can pass laws which aid one religion, aid all religions, or prefer one religion over another. Neither can force nor influence a person to go to or to remain away from church against his will or force him to profess a belief or disbelief in any religion. No person can be punished for entertaining or professing religious beliefs or disbeliefs, for church attendance or non-attendance. No tax in any amount, large or small, can be levied to support any religious activities or institutions, whatever they may be called, or whatever form they may adopt to teach or practice religion. Neither a state nor the Federal Government can, openly or secretly, participate in the affairs of any religious organizations or groups and *vice versa*. In the words of Jefferson, the clause against establishment of religion by law was intended to erect "a wall of separation between Church and State." * * *

Measured by these standards, we cannot say that the First Amendment prohibits New Jersey from spending tax-raised funds to pay the bus fares of parochial school pupils as a part of a general program under which it pays the fares of pupils attending public and other schools. It is undoubtedly true that children are helped to get to church schools. There is even a possibility that some of the children might not be sent to the church schools if the parents were compelled to pay their children's bus fares out of their own pockets when transportation to a public school would have been paid for by the State. The same possibility exists where the state requires a local transit company to provide reduced fares to school children including those attending parochial schools, or where a municipally owned transportation system undertakes to carry all school children free of charge. * * *

The First Amendment has erected a wall between church and state. That wall must be kept high and impregnable. We could not approve the slightest breach. New Jersey has not breached it here.

[The dissenting opinion of **JUSTICE JACKSON**, joined by **JUSTICE FRANKFURTER**, and the dissenting opinion of **JUSTICE RUTLEDGE**, joined by **JUSTICES FRANKFURTER, JACKSON**, and **BURTON** are omitted.]

Wallace v. Jaffree

472 U.S. 38 (1985)

This case involved a state law mandating a moment of silence "for meditation or voluntary prayer" in public classrooms. In an opinion by **Justice Stevens**, the Court held the statute unconstitutional because its purpose was to foster school prayer, rejecting the argument that the Establishment Clause prohibits only government discrimination between various sects:

> Just as the right to speak and the right to refrain from speaking are complementary components of a broader concept of individual freedom of mind, so also the individual's freedom to choose his own creed is the counterpart of his right to refrain from accepting the creed established by the majority. At one time it was thought that this right merely proscribed the preference of one Christian sect over another, but would not require equal respect for the conscience of the infidel, the atheist, or the adherent of a non-Christian faith such as Islam or Judaism. But when the underlying principle has been examined in the crucible of litigation, the Court has unambiguously concluded that the individual freedom of conscience protected by the First Amendment embraces the right to select any religious faith or none at all. This conclusion derives support not only from the interest in respecting the individual's freedom of conscience, but also from the conviction that religious beliefs worthy of respect are the product of free and voluntary choice by the faithful, and from recognition of the fact that the political interest in forestalling intolerance extends beyond intolerance among—or even intolerance among 'religions'—to encompass intolerance of the disbeliever and the uncertain."

In dissent, **Justice Rehnquist** argued that the Court's Establishment Clause jurisprudence has been warped by Jefferson's misleading "wall of separation" metaphor:

> James Madison was undoubtedly the most important architect among the Members of the House of the Amendments which became the Bill of Rights, but it was James Madison speaking as an advocate of sensible legislative compromise, not as an advocate of incorporating the Virginia Statute of Religious Liberty into the United States Constitution. * * * His original language 'nor shall any national religion be established' obviously does not conform to the 'wall of separation' between church and State idea which latter-day commentators have ascribed to him. His explanation on the floor of the meaning of his language—"that Congress should not establish a religion, and enforce the legal observation of it by law" is of the same

ilk. When he replied to Huntington in the debate over the proposal which came from the Select Committee of the House, he urged that the language 'no religion shall be established by law' should be amended by inserting the word 'national' in front of the word "religion."

NOTES ON EVERSON, JAFFREE, AND ESTABLISHMENT CLAUSE ANALYSIS

1. *The Debate over Justice Black's History of the Religion Clauses.* In their book *A Nation Dedicated to Religious Liberty, supra,* Adams and Emmerich object to historical theories, like Justice Black's, that emphasize only one historical value (wall of separation) to the exclusion of others (equal treatment). Of course, the actual holding in *Everson* upheld the New Jersey bus fare program. Other historians fault Justice Black for an ahistorical reading of what early Americans meant by "wall of separation." Anticipating the views of the pietistic separatists, Roger Williams himself (who coined the phrase) believed that the wall prevented the state from interfering with religion but not from fostering religion generally. Jefferson and the other Enlightenment separatists wanted a wall that worked both ways—protecting church from state and state from church. See Laurence Tribe, *American Constitutional Law* 1158–60 (2d ed. 1988). But both pietistic groups and Enlightenment thinkers may have shared an avowal of the critical value of liberty of conscience and its incompatibility with religious establishment. See Noah Feldman, *The Intellectual Origins of the Establishment Clause*, 77 NYU L. Rev. 346 (2002).

Robert Cord, *Separation of Church and State* (1982), takes on some of Justice Black's specific evidence to argue that few of the Framers absolutely opposed state aid to religion, and most believed that nondiscriminatory state aid was fine. For example, he argues that Madison's Memorial and Remonstrance objected that the statute was discriminatory, by privileging one religion, Christianity, and that Madison did not object to general state fostering of religious attitudes. Additionally, the United States during Madison's and Jefferson's presidential terms (1801–17) entered into treaties agreeing to subsidize schools for Native Americans run by several different Christian groups—without recorded objection from either Jefferson or Madison, and without recorded court challenges.

2. *Applying General Lessons of History to Specific Problems.* The dissenters in *Everson* protested that upholding the school busing statute was inconsistent with Justice Black's general theory of the Establishment Clause. The Court's decisions about aid to parochial schools have continued to produce some very odd line drawing. For example, while *Everson* allows the state to bus students to parochial schools, the state may not supply them with transportation for field trips; it can give them textbooks but cannot provide classroom maps or charts. See *Wolman v. Walter*, 433 U.S. 229 (1977). If this makes any sense to you, you're ahead of most of the scholars in the field.

Based on his *Jaffree* dissent, would Chief Justice Rehnquist allow the state to subsidize purely religious events (e.g., Sunday school classes), so long as the subsidy was open to members of all religions? (What counts as a religion, by the way—could the "United Church of Atheism" qualify?)

3. *Does History Solve Cases Like* Everson *and* Jaffree? In connection with the dispute over the original understanding of the religion clauses, consider *Marsh v. Chambers*, 463 U.S. 783 (1983), a challenge to the practice of opening state legislative sessions each day with a prayer by a state-paid chaplain. Chief Justice Burger's opinion for the Court upheld the practice based on its unique historical roots, because legislators since the time of the first Congress had followed the practice without challenge. Note, here, the dispute over the level of generality at which original intent is to be determined, which parallels that in the racial discrimination area. Within an originalist approach, is there any systematic way of deciding these issues?

NOTE ON ESTABLISHMENT CLAUSE TESTS

In 1971, the Court attempted a synthesis of its case law in *Lemon v. Kurtzman*.[47] *Lemon* struck down two state laws providing partial funding for teacher salaries at parochial schools. In an effort to make sense of the prior cases, the Court announced a three-part test: "First, the statute must have a secular legislative purpose; second, its principal or primary effect must be one that neither advances nor inhibits religion; finally, the statute must not foster 'an excessive government entanglement with religion.'" The salary supplements were unconstitutional because they involved excessive entanglement. In order to ensure that the money did not go for religious instruction, the state had to engage in intrusive supervision of parochial school activities. Moreover, the legislation also caused religious issues to become entangled in politics due to bitter disputes over this novel form of assistance to church-related activities.

For most of the next twenty years, *Lemon* was clearly the governing test. But its current status is unclear. To date, it has never been overruled, and it still receives favorable mention in some majority opinions. But sometimes the Court seems to forget about it entirely. The Rehnquist Court's approach seemed quite different in spirit from Burger Court opinions such as *Lemon* and the Roberts Court seems likely to hew to that path. The entanglement prong of the *Lemon* test seems to be fading from the scene. The Court no longer seems worried about political divisiveness as such, and seems willing to deal with problems of government supervision as they arise. But the secular purpose and effect prongs seem more viable.

The Equal Protection Clause prohibits statutes that are facially neutral but actually designed to discriminate against racial minorities. Discriminatory intent is not a permissible basis for legislation. By the same token, a desire to further religion seems inconsistent with the Establishment Clause. For

---

[47] 403 U.S. 602 (1971).

example, it would seem to be unconstitutional for the government to pass a law forbidding the raising of hogs in order to promote Jewish and Islamic religious practices. For just the same reason, a law mandating the eating of pork, passed in order to punish members of those religions, would violate the Free Exercise Clause even under *Smith* because of its motivation.

Nevertheless, the purpose requirement has its problems. First, establishing the motivation of a collective body is a difficult undertaking, and some have argued that it is essentially impossible. Second, much of criminal law and family law were originally supported by religious beliefs, and still may draw support from that source. Yet it cannot be illegitimate for legislators to support laws that are otherwise valid merely because they also have religious motivations. Third, it is unclear what counts as a secular purpose. In particular, if the legislature believes that it is merely compensating for a burden on religious practice, it is unclear whether this should be considered a purpose to further religion or merely an attempt to remain neutral.

A somewhat similar problem attends the secular effect prong of *Lemon*. Consider a law providing free eye and ear tests for students in all public and private schools. Is the primary effect of the New York program to provide services to all children regardless of their school choices, or is it to underwrite parochial schooling for certain children? One factor is the net effect of the program as a whole. If inclusion of parochial schools merely offsets a competitive advantage that the program gives other schools, it may be accommodationist. But if the net effect of including parochial schools in a program is to make them more attractive relative to other public or private schools than they would be if the program did not exist at all, the program appears preferential. This test would allow special education programs to be extended to religious schools, but probably not tuition vouchers. Another factor is whether the program provides an incentive for anyone to adopt a religious affiliation in order to qualify. More broadly, we could consider the program to have a secular purpose so long as it applies equally to secular and religious entities. This would allow both special education and vouchers. The Court moved in that direction in *Zelman v. Simmons-Harris*, 536 U.S. 639 (2002), which upheld an Ohio school voucher program even though the benefits of the program flowed primarily to parochial schools.

Perhaps the greatest problem with the *Lemon* is not conceptual but practical. It turned out to be hard for different judges to agree on how to apply the test to particular circumstances. Also, the test did not seem particularly helpful in dealing with religious symbolism, where "purpose and effect" seem intangible. For this reason, Justice O'Connor proposed an alternative test. In her concurring opinion in *Lynch v. Donnelly*,[48] a religious symbolism case, she laid out her endorsement test. Her premise was that the Establishment Clause "prohibits government from making adherence to a religion relevant in any way to a person's standing in the political community." Although entanglement can result from this connection between religion and political standing, the

---

[48] 465 U.S. 668 (1984).

primary and "more direct infringement is government endorsement or disapproval of religion," which "sends a message to nonadherents that they are outsiders, not full members of the political community, and an accompanying message to adherents that they are insiders, favored members of the political community."

This test has some appeal. Surely it is basic to our understanding of democracy that all citizens are equal without regard to religion. Also, the endorsement test does seem responsive to the problem of religious symbols. Suppose the Minnesota legislature passed a resolution making Lutheranism the "official state religion"—perhaps a dubious honor, given that the legislature has also seen fit to make blueberry the "official state muffin." The purpose might be nonreligious (merely to commemorate the historic role of Lutheranism in Minnesota history) and the practical effects seem unclear. Yet such a declaration seems quite contrary to the Establishment Clause. The endorsement test fits these facts neatly.

Yet, the test has serious problems. First, it has proved difficult to apply. It has an unavoidably subjective aspect, which is especially unfortunate because this particular subjective reaction probably varies with a person's religious standpoint. Whose reaction determines whether the message is one of endorsement? It is not easy to specify what kind of person operates as the bellwether (the reasonable member of a minority religion? the average citizen? the most sensitive person?), or what information they have available (in particular, how well do they understand the legal context?). Second, although the endorsement test is not really precluded by Establishment Clause history, endorsement does not seem to have been the primary concern of the Framers. Third, like *Lemon*, the endorsement test has difficulty evaluating issues of religious accommodation.

As an alternative to the endorsement test, several Justices have proposed a focus on coercion. As explained by Justice Kennedy in another religious symbolism case, the principle is that "government may not coerce anyone to support or participate in any religion or its exercise."[49] Again, this is an appealing principle: surely it is at least part of the core of the Establishment Clause. This theory also helps explain why the Establishment Clause applies to the states. Like other parts of the First Amendment, the Establishment Clause is incorporated into the concept of "liberty" under the Fourteenth Amendment. Incorporation is harder to explain if we think of the Clause as pertaining primarily to the secular nature of government rather than to individual freedom. Nevertheless, the coercion approach, too, has significant problems.

The first problem is defining coercion. Of course, we could limit "coercion" to mean a direct mandate to engage in a religious practice subject to criminal penalty or civil fine. But this definition is unappealingly narrow. For instance, it does not cover the use of general tax receipts to subsidize a particular church (paying a general tax isn't a religious practice). Yet we know that the use of

---

[49]   County of Allegheny v. ACLU, 492 U.S. 573 (1989).

taxes to support religion was at the core of the original concept of establishment. Justice Kennedy dealt with this problem by adding a separate prohibition on "direct benefits to religion in such a degree that it in fact 'establishes a [state] religion or religious faith, or tends to do so.'"

Also, at least in its narrower sense, coercion does not readily cover other practices now commonly thought to violate the Establishment Clause, such as state-supplied prayers for use in the classroom (provided participation is voluntary). To avoid these problems, Kennedy expanded his view of coercion to include psychological pressures and economic incentives, as well as instances of "[s]ymbolic recognition or accommodation of religious faith" that would "place the government's weight behind an obvious effort to proselytize on behalf of a particular religion." But at this point, the meaning of "coercion" starts becoming a bit misty.

A second possible criticism is that under this interpretation, the Establishment Clause seems to verge on being superfluous. After all, the Free Exercise Clause already prohibits religious coercion. One explanation might be that free exercise covers coercion to refrain from religious conduct and establishment covers coercion to engage in religious conduct. But we know that the Free Speech Clause guarantees not only the right to speak but the right to refrain from speaking. Similarly, it would seem that the Free Exercise Clause should cover not only the right to engage in religious practices but the right to refrain from doing so. But then, what is the Establishment Clause for? At most, under this interpretation, it merely seems to serve as an adjunct to the Free Exercise Clause, reinforcing the rule against state coercion of religion.

Finally, in part because the concept of coercion is pliable, the test has not always been easy to apply. Reasonable people may differ on what is coercive, and where the majority group sees only an invitation, a religious minority may see an offer it cannot refuse.

There seems to be an inherent tension between the two clauses: one imposes special protections for the benefit of minority groups, whereas the other forbids special treatment for those groups. The position of the Roberts Court on the Establishment Clause has not yet crystalized. But given the Court's increasingly enthusiasm for Free Exercise, we expect it take a narrow view of the Establishment Clause.

CHAPTER 7

FEDERALISM: CONGRESSIONAL POWER AND STATE AUTHORITY

■ ■ ■

SECTION 1. ENUMERATED FEDERAL POWER, RESERVED STATE AUTHORITY: INTRODUCTION

Our constitutional system contemplates two levels of power, the national power and that of the individual states.[1] According to Supreme Court doctrine, three different types of constitutional issues derive from the federal structure of our government. First, under what circumstances can the national government act? The structure of the Constitution and the expectations of the Framers suggest that Congress could only act pursuant to one of the "enumerated powers," almost all of which are set forth in Article I. As a result, decisions about the reach of the national government's power involve a categorization game, in which proponents try to fit the exercise into one of the enumerated cubbyholes, and opponents argue that no cubbyhole will accommodate the exercise.[2] We trace the history of the most extensive such "game," that involving the Commerce Clause and the regulation of economic activity, in Section 2. Section 3 considers the congressional authority to enact civil rights legislation, which requires an examination of the powers delegated to Congress under the Thirteenth, Fourteenth, and Fifteenth Amendments. Section 4 briefly examines several other potential sources of wide-ranging congressional authority.

Second, how does this federal power relate to state power? The traditional understanding is that the states delegated only limited power to the federal government and retained (or "reserved," if you will) general regulatory power—sometimes called the "local police power"—over their geographic domains and the persons within them. It is inevitable under such a federal structure that conflicting claims of state and national power will arise. The Supremacy Clause of Article VI tells us that a constitutional

---

[1]   A third layer of government exists in areas within the sovereignty of Indian tribes. The complex questions of federal Indian law are beyond the scope of this course, but we do introduce them briefly in the Note on Triadic Federalism: Indian Tribal Sovereignty, at the end of this chapter.

[2]   Compare Richard Primus, *The Limits of Enumeration,* 124 Yale L.J. 576 (2014) (arguing that the enumerated powers precept is not inconsistent with Congress's enjoying general regulatory jurisdiction), with Kurt T. Lash, *The Sum of All Delegated Power: A Response to Richard Primus, The Limits of Enumeration,* 124 Yale L.J. F. 180 (2014) (supporting the traditional reading, that enumerated powers connote limited powers).

exercise of congressional power is the supreme law of the land, displacing any state laws inconsistent with it. This "preemption" doctrine is discussed in Section 6, but has important implications throughout the chapter. For instance, many of the cases examined in Sections 2, 3, and 4 consider claims that the supremacy of federal power must be carefully confined to its constitutionally defined spheres, lest Congress run roughshod over appropriate state authority to regulate the persons found within their borders. As a further protection of state autonomy from federal encroachment, the Supreme Court has found an implicit "intergovernmental immunity doctrine," which limits congressional power to regulate the states themselves (and not merely persons found within the states). Section 5 explore this line of cases.

Third, in what ways does the Constitution limit the exercise of state power? Earlier chapters considered several important such limitations found in the First, Fourteenth, and Fifteenth Amendments. Section 6 of this chapter considers several more limitations upon state power that are more directly related to our federal structure of shared power between the national and state governments. In addition to the preemption doctrine briefly explained above, Section 6 traces approaches that sometimes prevent the states from taking advantage of our federal structure to benefit their citizens at the expense of citizens of other states. It considers an express constitutional limitation to this effect, the Privileges and Immunities Clause of Article IV, and an implicit limitation, the so-called "Dormant Commerce Clause," which seeks to prevent states from regulating interstate commerce in ways that discriminate in favor of in-state economic interests.

All three of these issues are implicated in our opening case, *McCulloch v. Maryland*, which many consider "the greatest decision John Marshall ever handed down." Robert McCloskey, *The American Supreme Court* 66 (1960). The case also illustrates key themes of constitutional decisionmaking—reasoning from the constitutional structure, the role of original intent in constitutional decisionmaking, and the representation-reinforcement theory of judicial review. Think more broadly. What exactly is the nature of the "federalist" arrangement? What goals does that arrangement advance?

McCULLOCH V. MARYLAND
17 U.S. (4 Wheat.) 316, 4 L.Ed. 579 (1819)

CHIEF JUSTICE MARSHALL delivered the opinion of the Court.

[Congress created the Second Bank of the United States in 1816 to provide loans to the national government and assist in the collection of taxes (see Note 1 following this case for background history). The Bank was blamed for the economic recession of 1818, and several states sought to tax it. One was Maryland, which sued James McCulloch, cashier of the Baltimore branch of the Bank,[3] when the Bank refused to pay. Maryland argued that the Bank's charter was itself invalid legislation and that, in any event, the states have authority to tax national instrumentalities such as the Bank.]

The first question made in the cause is, has Congress power to incorporate a bank?

It has been truly said, that this can scarcely be considered as an open question, entirely unprejudiced by the former proceedings of the nation respecting it. The principle now contested was introduced at a very early period of our history, has been recognized by many successive legislatures, and has been acted upon by the judicial department, in cases of peculiar delicacy, as a law of undoubted obligation.

It will not be denied, that a bold and daring usurpation might be resisted, after an acquiescence still longer and more complete than this. But it is conceived, that a doubtful question, one on which human reason may pause, and the human judgment be suspended, in the decision of which the great principles of liberty are not concerned, but the respective powers of those who are equally the representatives of the people, are to be adjusted; if not put at rest by the practice of the government, ought to receive a considerable impression from that practice. An exposition of the constitution, deliberately established by legislative acts, on the faith of which an immense property has been advanced, ought not to be lightly disregarded.

The power now contested was exercised by the first Congress elected under the present constitution. The bill for incorporating the [first] bank of the United States did not steal upon an unsuspecting legislature, and pass unobserved. Its principle was completely understood, and was opposed with equal zeal and ability. After being resisted, first in the fair and open field of debate, and afterwards in the executive cabinet, with as much persevering talent as any measure has ever experienced, and being supported by arguments which convinced minds as pure and as intelligent as this country can boast, it became a law. The original act was permitted to expire; but a short experience of the embarrassments to which the refusal to revive it exposed the government, convinced those who were most prejudiced against the measure of its necessity, and induced the passage of the present law. It would require no ordinary share of intrepidity to assert that a measure adopted under these circumstances was a bold and plain usurpation, to which the constitution gave no countenance. * * *

---

[3] *Editors' note:* McCulloch was himself a controversial figure, hated in Maryland as an important lobbyist for the Bank in Washington and suspected of looting the Bank by making unsecured loans to cronies. He was removed from office shortly after his case was decided. Later he was unsuccessfully criminally prosecuted by Maryland.

In discussing this question, the counsel for the State of Maryland have deemed it of some importance, in the construction of the constitution, to consider that instrument not as emanating from the people, but as the act of sovereign and independent States. The powers of the general government, it has been said, are delegated by the States, who alone are truly sovereign; and must be exercised in subordination to the States, who alone possess supreme dominion.

It would be difficult to sustain this proposition. The Convention which framed the constitution was indeed elected by the State legislatures. But the instrument, when it came from their hands, was a mere proposal, without obligations, or pretensions to it. * * * [This] instrument was submitted to the people. They acted upon it in the only manner in which they can act safely, effectively, and wisely, on such a subject, by assembling in Convention [, from which] the constitution derives its whole authority. The government proceeds directly from the people. * * *

The government of the Union, then, * * * is, emphatically, and truly, a government of the people. In form and in substance it emanates from them. Its powers are granted by them, and are to be exercised directly on them, and for their benefit.

This government is acknowledged by all to be one of enumerated powers. The principle, that it can exercise only the powers granted to it, * * * is now universally admitted. But the question respecting the extent of the powers actually granted, is perpetually arising, and will probably continue to arise, as long as our system shall exist. * * *

If any one proposition could command the universal assent of mankind, we might expect it would be this—that the government of the Union, though limited in its powers, is supreme within its sphere of action. This would seem to result necessarily from its nature. It is the government of all; its powers are delegated by all; it represents all, and acts for all. Though any one State may be willing to control its operations, no State is willing to allow others to control them. The nation, on those subjects on which it can act, must necessarily bind its component parts. But this question is not left to mere reason: the people have, in express terms, decided it, by saying, "this constitution, and the laws of the United States, which shall be made in pursuance thereof," "shall be the supreme law of the land," and by requiring that the members of the State legislatures, and the officers of the executive and judicial departments of the States, shall take the oath of fidelity to it.

Among the enumerated powers, we do not find that of establishing a bank or creating a corporation. But there is no phrase in the instrument which, like the articles of confederation, excludes incidental or implied powers; and which requires that everything granted shall be expressly and minutely described. Even the 10th amendment, which was framed for the purpose of quieting the excessive jealousies which had been excited, omits the word "expressly," and declares only that the powers "not delegated to the United States, nor prohibited to the States, are reserved to the States or to the people;" thus leaving the question, whether the particular power which may become the subject of contest has been delegated to the one government, or prohibited to the other, to depend on a fair construction of the whole instrument. The men who drew and adopted this amendment had experienced the embarrassments resulting from the insertion of this word in the articles of confederation, and probably omitted it to avoid those embarrassments. A constitution, to contain an accurate detail of all the subdivisions of which its great powers will admit, and of all the means by which they may be carried into execution, would partake of the prolixity of a legal code, and could scarcely be embraced by the human mind. It would probably never be understood by the public. Its nature, therefore, requires, that only its great outlines should be marked, its important objects designated, and the minor ingredients which compose those objects be deduced from the nature of the objects themselves. That this idea was entertained by the framers of the American constitution, is not only to be inferred from the nature of the instrument, but from the language. Why else were some of the limitations, found in the ninth section of the 1st article, introduced? It is also, in some degree, warranted by their having omitted to use any restrictive term which might prevent its receiving a fair and just interpretation. In considering this question, then, we must never forget, that it is a *constitution* we are expounding.

Although, among the enumerated powers of government, we do not find the word "bank" or "incorporation," we find the great powers to lay and collect taxes; to borrow money; to regulate commerce; to declare and conduct a war; and to raise and support armies and navies. The sword and the purse, all the external relations, and no inconsiderable portion of the industry of the nation, are entrusted to its government. It can never be pretended that these vast powers draw after them others of inferior importance, merely because they are inferior. Such an idea can never be advanced. But it may with great reason be contended, that a government, entrusted with such ample powers, on the due execution of which the happiness and prosperity of the nation so vitally depends, must also be entrusted with ample means for their execution. The power being given, it is the interest of the nation to facilitate its execution. It can never be their interest, and cannot be presumed to have been their intention, to clog and embarrass its execution by withholding the most appropriate means. Throughout this vast republic, from the St. Croix to the Gulf of Mexico, from the Atlantic to the Pacific, revenue is to be collected and expended, armies are to be marched and supported. The exigencies of the nation may require that the treasure raised in the north should be transported to the south, that raised in the east conveyed to the west, or that this order should be reversed. Is that construction of the constitution to be preferred which would render these operations difficult, hazardous, and expensive? Can we adopt that construction, (unless the words imperiously require it,) which would impute to the framers of that instrument, when granting these powers for the public good, the intention of impeding their exercise by withholding a choice of means? If, indeed, such be the mandate of the constitution, we have only to obey; but that instrument does not profess to enumerate the means by which the powers it confers may be executed; nor does it prohibit the creation of a corporation, if the existence of such a being be essential to the beneficial exercise of those powers. It is, then, the subject of fair inquiry, how far such means may be employed.

It is not denied, that the powers given to the government imply the ordinary means of execution. That, for example, of raising revenue, and applying it to national purposes, is admitted to imply the power of conveying money from place to place, as the exigencies of the nation require, and of employing the usual means of conveyance. * * *

But the constitution of the United States has not left the right of Congress to employ the necessary means, for the execution of the powers conferred on the government, to general reasoning. To its enumeration of powers is added that of making "all laws which shall be necessary and proper, for carrying into execution the foregoing powers, and all other powers vested by this constitution, in the government of the United States, or in any department thereof."

The counsel for the State of Maryland have urged various arguments, to prove that this clause, though in terms a grant of power, is not so in effect; but is really restrictive of the general right, which might otherwise be implied, of selecting means for executing the enumerated powers. * * *

[The] argument on which most reliance is placed, is drawn from the peculiar language of this clause. Congress is not empowered by it to make all laws, which may have relation to the powers conferred on the government, but such only as may be *necessary and proper* for carrying them into execution. The word *"necessary,"* is considered as controlling the whole sentence, and as limiting the right to pass laws for the execution of the granted powers, to such as are indispensable, and without which the power would be nugatory. That it excludes the choice of means, and leaves to Congress, in each case, that only which is most direct and simple.

Is it true, that this is the sense in which the word "necessary" is always used? Does it always import an absolute physical necessity, so strong, that one thing, to which another may be termed necessary, cannot exist without that other? * * * To employ the means necessary to an end, is generally understood as employing any means calculated to produce the end, and not as being confined to those single means, without which the end would be entirely unattainable. * * * The word "necessary" * * * has not a fixed character peculiar to itself. It admits of all degrees of comparison; and is often connected with other words, which increase or diminish the impression the mind receives of the urgency it imports. A thing may be necessary, very necessary, absolutely or indispensably necessary. To no mind would the same idea be conveyed, by these several phrases. This comment on the word is well illustrated, by the passage cited at the bar, from the 10th section of the 1st article of the constitution. It is, we think, impossible to compare the sentence which prohibits a State from laying "imposts, or duties on imports or exports, except what may be *absolutely* necessary for executing its inspection laws," with that which authorizes Congress "to make all laws which shall be necessary and proper for carrying into execution" the powers of the general government, without feeling a conviction that the convention understood itself to change materially the meaning of the word "necessary," by prefixing the word "absolutely." This word, then, like others, is used in various senses; and, in its construction, the subject, the context, the intention of the person using them, are all to be taken into view.

* * * It must have been the intention of those who gave these powers, to insure, as far as human prudence could insure, their beneficial execution. This could not be done by confiding the choice of means to such narrow limits as not to leave it in the power of Congress to adopt any which might be appropriate, and which were conducive to the end. This provision is made in a constitution intended to endure for ages to come, and, consequently, to be adapted to the various *crises* of human affairs. To have prescribed the means by which government should, in all future time, execute its powers, would have been to change, entirely, the character of the instrument, and give it the properties of a legal code. It would have been an unwise attempt to provide, by immutable rules, for exigencies which, if foreseen at all, must have been seen dimly, and which can be best provided for as they occur. * * * If we apply this principle of construction to any of the powers of the government, we shall find it so pernicious in its operation that we shall be compelled to discard it. * * *

So, with respect to the whole penal code of the United States: whence arises the power to punish in cases not prescribed by the constitution? All admit that the government may, legitimately, punish any violation of its laws; and yet, this is not among the enumerated powers of Congress. The right to enforce the observance of law, by punishing its infraction, might be denied with the more plausibility, because it is expressly given in some cases. Congress is empowered "to provide for the punishment of counterfeiting the securities and current coin of the United States," and "to define and punish piracies and felonies committed on the high seas, and offences against the law of nations." The several powers of Congress may exist, in a very imperfect state to be sure, but they may exist and be carried into execution, although no punishment should be inflicted in cases where the right to punish is not expressly given.

Take, for example, the power "to establish post offices and post roads." This power is executed by the single act of making the establishment. But, from this has been inferred the power and duty of carrying the mail along the post road, from one post office to another. And, from this implied power, has again been inferred the right to punish those who steal letters from the post office, or rob the mail. It may be said, with some plausibility, that the right to carry the mail, and to punish those who rob it, is not indispensably necessary to the establishment of a post office and post road. This right is indeed essential to the beneficial exercise of power, but not indispensably necessary to its existence. * * *

In ascertaining the sense in which the word "necessary" is used in this clause of the constitution, we may derive some aid from that with which it is associated. Congress shall have power "to make all laws which shall be necessary and proper to carry into execution" the powers of the government. If the word "necessary" was used in that strict and rigorous sense for which the counsel for the State of Maryland contend, it would be an extraordinary departure from the usual course of the human mind, as exhibited in composition, to add a word, the only possible effect of which is to qualify that strict and rigorous meaning; to present to the mind the idea of some choice of means of legislation not straitened and compressed within the narrow limits for which gentlemen contend.

But the argument which most conclusively demonstrates the error of the construction contended for by the counsel for the State of Maryland, is founded on the intention of the Convention, as manifested in the whole clause. To waste time and argument in proving that, without it, Congress might carry its powers into execution, would be not much less idle than to hold a lighted taper to the sun. * * * We think so for the following reasons:

1st. The clause is placed among the powers of Congress, not among the limitations on those powers.

2nd. Its terms purport to enlarge, not to diminish the powers vested in the government. It purports to be an additional power, not a restriction on those already granted. No reason has been, or can be assigned for thus concealing an intention to narrow the discretion of the national legislature under words which purport to enlarge it. * * *

The result of the most careful and attentive consideration bestowed upon this clause is, that if it does not enlarge, it cannot be construed to restrain the powers of Congress, or to impair the right of the legislature to exercise its best judgment in the selection of measures to carry into execution the constitutional powers of the government. If no other motive for its insertion can be suggested, a sufficient one is found in the desire to remove all doubts respecting the right to legislate on that vast mass of incidental powers which must be involved in the constitution, if that instrument be not a splendid bauble.

We admit, as all must admit, that the powers of the government are limited, and that its limits are not to be transcended. But we think the sound construction of the constitution must allow to the national legislature that discretion, with respect to the means by which the powers it confers are to be carried into execution, which will enable that body to perform the high duties assigned to it, in the manner most beneficial to the people. Let the end be legitimate, let it be within the scope of the constitution, and all means which are appropriate, which are plainly adapted to that end, which are not prohibited, but consist with the letter and spirit of the constitution, are constitutional. * * *

If a corporation may be employed indiscriminately with other means to carry into execution the powers of the government, no particular reason can be assigned for excluding the use of a bank, if required for its fiscal operations. To use one, must be within the discretion of Congress, if it be an appropriate mode of executing the powers of government. That it is a convenient, a useful, and essential instrument in the prosecution of its fiscal operations, is not now a subject of controversy. * * *

But, were its necessity less apparent, none can deny its being an appropriate measure; and if it is, the degree of its necessity, as has been very justly observed, is to be discussed in another place. Should Congress, in the execution of its powers, adopt measures which are prohibited by the constitution; or should Congress, under the pretext of executing its powers, pass laws for the accomplishment of objects not entrusted to the government; it would become the painful duty of this tribunal, should a case requiring such a decision come before it, to say that such an act was not the law of the land. But where the law is not prohibited, and is really calculated to effect any of the objects entrusted to the government, to undertake here to inquire into the degree of its necessity, would be to pass the line which circumscribes the judicial department, and to tread on legislative ground. This court disclaims all pretensions to such a power. * * *

It being the opinion of the Court, that the act incorporating the bank is constitutional; and that the power of establishing a branch in the State of Maryland might be properly exercised by the bank itself, we proceed to inquire—

2. Whether the State of Maryland may, without violating the constitution, tax that branch?

That the power of taxation is one of vital importance; that it is retained by the States; that it is not abridged by the grant of a similar power to the government of the Union; that it is to be concurrently exercised by the two governments: are truths which have never been denied. But, such is the paramount character of the constitution that its capacity to withdraw any subject from the action of even this power, is admitted. The States are expressly forbidden to lay any duties on imports or exports, except what may be absolutely necessary for executing their inspection laws. If the obligation of this prohibition must be conceded—if it may restrain a State from the exercise of its taxing power on imports and exports—the same paramount character would seem to restrain, as it certainly may restrain, a State from such other exercise of this power, as is in its nature incompatible with, and repugnant to, the constitutional laws of the Union. A law, absolutely repugnant to another, as entirely repeals that other as if express terms of repeal were used.

On this ground the counsel for the bank place its claim to be exempted from the power of a State to tax its operations. There is no express provision for the case, but the claim has been sustained on a principle which so entirely pervades the constitution, is so intermixed with the materials which compose it, so interwoven with its web, so blended with its texture, as to be incapable of being separated from it without rending it into shreds.

This great principle is, that the constitution and the laws made in pursuance thereof are supreme; that they control the constitution and laws of the respective States, and cannot be controlled by them. * * *

That the power to tax involves the power to destroy; that the power to destroy may defeat and render useless the power to create; that there is a plain repugnance, in conferring on one government a power to control the constitutional measures of another, which other, with respect to those very measures, is declared to be supreme over that which exerts the control, are propositions not to be denied. But all inconsistencies are to be reconciled by the magic of the word *confidence*. Taxation, it is said, does not necessarily and unavoidably destroy. To carry it to the excess of destruction would be an abuse, to presume which, would banish that confidence which is essential to all government.

But is this a case of confidence? Would the people of any one State trust those of another with a power to control the most insignificant operations of their State government? We know they would not. Why then, should we suppose that the people of any one State should be willing to trust those of another with a power to control the operations of a government to which they have confided the most important and most valuable interests? In the legislature of the Union alone, are all represented. The legislature of the Union alone, therefore, can be trusted by the people with the power of controlling measures which concern all, in the confidence that it will not be abused. This, then, is not a case of confidence, and we must consider it as it really is. * * *

If the States may tax one instrument, employed by the government in the execution of its powers, they may tax any and every other instrument. They may tax the mail; they may tax the mint; they may tax patent-rights; they may tax the papers of the custom-house; they may tax judicial process, they may tax all the means employed by the government, to an excess which would defeat all the ends of government. This was not intended by the American people. They did not design to make their government dependent on the States. * * *

It has also been insisted, that, as the power of taxation in the general and State governments is acknowledged to be concurrent, every argument which would sustain the right of the general government to tax banks chartered by the States, will equally sustain the right of the States to tax banks chartered by the general government.

But the two cases are not on the same reason. The people of all the States have created the general government, and have conferred upon it the general power of taxation. The people of all the States, and the States themselves, are represented in Congress, and, by their representatives, exercise this power. When they tax the chartered institutions of the States, they tax their constituents; and these taxes must be uniform. But, when a State taxes the operations of the government of the United States, it acts upon institutions created, not by their own constituents, but by people over whom they claim no control. It acts upon the measures of a government created by others as well as themselves, for the benefit of others in common with themselves. The difference is that which always exists, and always must exist, between the action of the whole on a part, and the action of a part on the whole—between the laws of a government declared to be supreme, and those of a government which, when in opposition to those laws, is not supreme.

But if the full application of this argument could be admitted, it might bring into question the right of Congress to tax the State banks, and could not prove the right of the States to tax the Bank of the United States.

The court has bestowed on this subject its most deliberate consideration. The result is a conviction that the States have no power, by taxation or otherwise to retard, impede, burden, or in any manner control the operations of the constitutional laws enacted by Congress to carry into execution the powers vested in the general government. This is, we think, the unavoidable consequence of that supremacy which the constitution has declared.

We are unanimously of opinion that the law passed by the legislature of Maryland, imposing a tax on the Bank of the United States, is unconstitutional and void.

This opinion does not deprive the States of any resources which they originally possessed. It does not extend to a tax paid by the real property of the bank, in common with the other real property within the State, nor to a tax imposed on the interest which the citizens of Maryland may hold in this institution, in common with other property of the same description throughout the State. But this is a tax on the operations of the bank, and is, consequently, a tax on the operation of an instrument employed by the government of the Union to carry its powers into execution. Such a tax must be unconstitutional. * * *

NOTES ON CONSTITUTIONAL REASONING IN McCULLOCH: ORIGINAL INTENT OR MEANING, CONSTITUTIONAL STRUCTURE, REPRESENTATION REINFORCEMENT

1. *Original Intent or Meaning: The Curious Role of History in the Bank Case.* During the Philadelphia Convention in 1787, Madison proposed that Congress in Article I, § 8, be empowered "to grant charters of incorporation," but the Convention rejected this suggestion. Chief Justice Marshall does not mention this argument, and slides by the question of original intent by invoking something like a constitutional rule of adverse possession: Because the political system has acquiesced in the Bank's constitutionality for so long, it would require extremely strong arguments to invalidate the Bank. Why isn't the rejection of the power to incorporate banks at the Philadelphia Convention precisely the sort of strong argument needed to rebut the long acquiescence? Consider the following history of the argument from the rejected proposal.[4]

Before signing the bank bill, which had sailed through Congress, President Washington asked for the advice of his cabinet. Secretary of State Thomas Jefferson opposed the Bank, at least in part on constitutional grounds. He read the Tenth Amendment and the Necessary and Proper Clause to conclude that "the Constitution allows only the means which are necessary, not merely 'convenient,' for effecting the enumerated powers. If such a latitude of construction be allowed to this phrase as to give any non-enumerated power [to Congress], it would swallow up all the delegated powers, and reduce the whole to one power." 19 *Papers of Thomas Jefferson* 275, 278 (1974) ("Opinion on the Constitutionality of the Bill for Establishing a National Bank").

Attorney General Edmund Randolph and Secretary of Treasury Alexander Hamilton rejected the relevance of arguments based upon original intent and argued that the text of the Constitution gave firm support to the validity of the Bank charter. Hamilton claimed that the Bank charter had "a relation more or less direct to the power of collecting taxes; to that of borrowing money; to that of regulating trade between the states; and to those of raising, supporting & maintaining fleets and armies." If more confirmation were needed, Hamilton argued, it came from the Necessary and Proper Clause. Against Jefferson, Hamilton argued that the term "necessary" means "no more than needful, requisite, incidental, useful, or conducive to." 8 *Papers of Alexander Hamilton* 97 (1965) ("Opinion on the Constitutionality of an Act to Establish a Bank"). The President signed the Bank bill into law.

---

[4] See Paul Finkelman, *The Constitution and the Intentions of the Framers: The Limits of Historical Analysis*, 50 U. Pitt. L. Rev. 349, 358–71 (1989); David McGowan, *Ethos in Law and History: Alexander Hamilton*, The Federalist, *and the Supreme Court*, 85 Minn. L. Rev. 794, 804–19 (2001).

Congress declined to recharter the bank in 1811, but the War of 1812 fueled a ruinous inflation that impelled Congress to pass a new charter in 1815. Although he had opposed the Bank for constitutional reasons in 1790, President Madison vetoed it for policy reasons in 1815. The earlier objections were "precluded by repeated recognitions under varied circumstances of the validity of such an institution in acts of the legislative, executive, and judicial branches of the Government." Within a year, Congress passed a bill that President Madison could sign, and the second Bank was established in 1816. What conclusions might you draw about constitutional theory from the debates about the Bank's constitutionality in 1790, and the lack of debate in 1815–16? About *McCulloch* generally?

2.   *The Text: Structural Arguments*. Notice how deftly the Chief Justice dodged the technical argument that there is no clause in Article I, § 8 listing the chartering of banks as an enumerated power of Congress. Can the Chief Justice's opinion be read to free Congress of the categorization game that the jurisprudence of enumerated powers seems to entail? What did Marshall mean when he said "that it is a *constitution* we are expounding"? Did he mean that, unlike a statute, a constitution should be interpreted flexibly over time to subserve its purposes of an organizationally flourishing government?

On the other hand, *McCulloch* paid careful attention to the constitutional text and, especially, structure—especially the Necessary & Proper Clause, which Marshall interpreted liberally to mean "useful." Are his arguments persuasive? Consider the view of Professor Natelson, who maintains that "necessary and proper" was a term of art taken from the eighteenth century law of trusts and estates. Natelson maintains that the key word is "proper"; in trust instruments, "proper" entailed compliance with "then-prevailing fiduciary norms," such as "proceeding in good faith, maintaining undivided loyalty to the principal, accounting to the principal, and proceeding with due care." Gary Lawson, Geoffrey P. Miller, Robert G. Natelson & Guy I. Seidman, *The Origins of the Necessary and Proper Clause* 78–79 (2010). Does this analysis defeat the Chief Justice's reasoning?

Marshall's textual arguments became more abstract in the second part of his opinion, dealing with the federal immunity from state taxation. There is no precise clause to analyze here, but Marshall created his own text by seizing upon "a principle which so entirely pervades the constitution" that it must be considered as important as the actual written text. The great principle is the supremacy of the national power from state interference. Where did the Chief Justice find that principle in the Constitution? How did it support his holding that Maryland cannot tax the operations of the Bank?

3.   *Representation-Reinforcement Argument*. The most celebrated argument in *McCulloch* is the representation-reinforcement one at the end: The United States and its instrumentalities are vulnerable to attack by the state political processes, because they are not "represented" therein, and hence the Court has a special duty to protect the United States against potentially oppressive laws. The obverse, however, is not true: The United States can tax

the states (so long as such taxation is "uniform"), which are well represented in the national legislature.

Is this distinction persuasive? Why should we care that the United States is not "well represented" in state legislatures, as Congress can simply preempt state legislation that unduly penalizes it? Why isn't that an adequate political process check on the states? Also, as a policy matter, shouldn't the states be able to tax U.S. instrumentalities on a non-discriminatory basis? *McCulloch* can be read to suggest that even non-discriminatory taxes are invalid, as the opinion emphasized the destructive potential of taxation, but the representation-reinforcement rationale ought not apply when there is no indication that the state is treating the United States' instrumentality any differently from other corporations.

Consider, also, that the *McCulloch* formulation is asymmetrical, protecting the United States against state taxation but not necessarily vice versa. Are the states really protected against unfair treatment because they are "represented" in the national legislature? Did the Chief Justice's argument depend upon the fact that before the Seventeenth Amendment the state legislatures elected U.S. senators (Art. I, § 3, cl. 1)? If so, what about today, when senators are elected directly by the people?

U.S. Term Limits, Inc. v. Thornton

514 U.S. 779 (1995)

In 1992, Arkansas voters amended the state constitution to prevent certification as a candidate for the U.S. House from Arkansas any person already elected to three or more House terms, and as a candidate for the U.S. Senate from Arkansas any person already elected to two or more Senate terms. Read the Constitution. Do its text and structure suggest that these limtis are constitutional? The Supreme Court was passionately divided on this issue, with five Justices voting to invalidate the amendment. Apart from a debate about the originalist sources, the case generated a debate over the nature of the federalist arrangement, because one's resolution of the interpretive issue depended in large part upon the normative baseline about federal/state sovereignty from which one started.

Proponents of state-imposed term limits on federal officials argued that because the Constitution does not expressly prohibit them, the states are authorized to impose them. The opinion for the Court by **Justice Stevens** followed Chief Justice Marshall's opinion in *Sturges v. Crowninshield*, 4 Wheat. 122, 193 (1819) (as well as *McCulloch*), and Hamilton's *Federalist* No. 32, to read the Constitution and the Tenth Amendment to stand for the proposition that the states retained all the rights of sovereignty they had before 1789, except those divested of the states by the Constitution. The national government, in turn, owed its sovereignty, not to the states, but directly to "We the People."

Under this view of federal/state sovereignty, Stevens rejected the proponents' argument on the grounds that the power to add qualifications was not within the original powers of the pre-Constitution states, and that the Framers intended that the Constitution be the exclusive source of qualifications for members of Congress. As to the first reason, Justice Stevens interpreted *McCulloch* to stand for the proposition that, before the federal government existed, the states had no original power to tax federal entities (*McCulloch*) or to regulate federal representatives (*U.S. Term Limits*). As to the second reason, the Constitution generally and the Qualifications Clauses in particular assured that for the "National Government, representatives owe primary allegiance not to the people of a State, but to the people of the Nation." See also Art. I, § 5, cl. 1; § 6. Compare Art. II, § 1, cl. 2; *Powell v. McCormack*, 395 U.S. 486 (1969) (surveying originalist evidence).

Justice Thomas, joined by Chief Justice Rehnquist and Justices O'Connor and Scalia, dissented. He started with a different baseline for thinking about federal sovereignty: "The ultimate source of the Constitution's authority is the consent of the people of each individual State, not the consent of the undifferentiated people of the Nation as a whole.

"The ratification procedure erected by Article VII makes this point clear. The Constitution took effect once it had been ratified by the people gathered in convention in nine different States. But the Constitution went into effect only 'between the States so ratifying the same,' Art. VII; it did not bind the people of North Carolina until they had accepted it. In Madison's words, the popular consent upon which the Constitution's authority rests was 'given by the people, not as individuals composing one entire nation, but as composing the distinct and independent States to which they respectively belong.' *The Federalist* No. 39."

Because the federal government is a creature of state agreement, its powers are narrowly limited to those enumerated in the Constitution; conversely, state powers remain plenary, unlimited except insofar as the Constitution limits them. "In each State, the remainder of the people's powers—'[t]he powers not delegated to the United States by the Constitution, nor prohibited by it to the States,' Amdt. 10—are either delegated to the state government or retained by the people. The Federal Constitution does not specify which of these two possibilities obtains; it is up to the various state constitutions to declare which powers the people of each State have delegated to their state government. As far as the Federal Constitution is concerned, then, the States can exercise all powers that the Constitution does not withhold from them. The Federal Government and the States thus face different default rules: where the Constitution is silent about the exercise of a particular power—that is, where the Constitution does not speak either expressly or by necessary implication—the Federal Government lacks that power and the States enjoy it."

Justice Kennedy concurred in the opinion for the Court and wrote a separate opinion responding to Justice Thomas's theory of federal/state sovereignty. "Federalism was our Nation's own discovery. The Framers split the atom of sovereignty. It was the genius of their idea that our citizens would have two political capacities, one state and one federal, each protected from incursion by the other. The resulting Constitution created a legal system unprecedented in form and design, establishing two orders of government, each with its own direct relationship, its own privity, its own set of mutual rights and obligations to the people who sustain it and are governed by it. *McCulloch*." Because the Arkansas amendment directly affected the unique federal right to vote, a right also implicating the First Amendment, Justice Kennedy believed it crossed the line. But his concurring opinion emphasized, contrary to *McCulloch*, that the states must be equally well-protected against federal incursions.

United States v. Comstock

560 U.S. 126 (2010)

A federal civil-commitment statute authorizes a federal district court to order the civil commitment of an individual who is currently "in the custody of the [Federal] Bureau of Prisons," 18 U.S.C. § 4248, if that individual "suffers from a serious mental illness, abnormality, or disorder," or satisfies other conditions. § 4247(a). The defendant claimed that Congress did not have the Article I authority to pass such a law. Writing for the Court, **Justice Breyer** concluded that Congress had such authority under the Necessary and Proper Clause.

The Court read *McCulloch* broadly, to allow a great deal of constitutional bootstrapping. Although with one minor exception (offenses against the law of nations), there is no enumerated power to make conduct a federal crime, Congress has that authority as necessary and proper to regulating commerce or protecting civil rights. Because the civil-commitment statute constituted "a modest addition to a set of federal prison-related mental-health statutes that have existed for many decades" *and* operated on persons already in federal custody (whom Congress had an implicit obligation to protect and to restrain if they pose a continuing public danger upon release) *and* "took sufficient account of state interests," Justice Breyer found ample justification for Congress's exercise of power under the Necessary and Proper Clause.

Concurring in the Court's judgment, **Justice Alito** rejected that *McCulloch* premise but believed that "§ 4248 satisfies that requirement because it is a necessary and proper means of carrying into execution the enumerated powers that support the federal criminal statutes under which the affected prisoners were convicted." **Justice Kennedy** also concurred in the judgment. He objected to the Court's broad, potentially limitless, reading of the Necessary and Proper Clause but upheld the law because "essential attributes of state sovereignty" were not "compromised by the assertion of federal power."

Joined by Justice Scalia in dissent and similar to Justice Alito, **Justice Thomas** took the position that the Necessary and Proper Clause only justifies federal regulation in support of an explicitly enumerated power. As James Madison put it at the Virginia Convention, "the sweeping clause . . . only extend[s] to the enumerated powers." Hamilton's *Federalist* No. 33 and other ratifying discussions were to the same effect.

NOTES ON THEORIES OF FEDERAL/STATE SOVEREIGNTY AND ON THE ADVANTAGES OF A FEDERAL ARRANGEMENT

Step back from the debate over the precise powers at issue in the National Bank, Term Limits, and Civil Commitment Cases. In analyzing the issues throughout this chapter, the baseline matters. As reflected in his *Term Limits* and *Comstock* dissents, Justice Thomas starts with the Article VII baseline: the Constitution was an agreement among sovereign states, each of which was giving up some but not all of its sovereign authority; because sovereign grants are traditionally (and should be) construed strictly, assertions of national authority need to be demonstrated by precise reference to explicit constitutional grants, construed reasonably but not expansively. Federalism, under this approach, rests upon dual sovereignty, where the federal government and state government each has sole authority within its own domain. Every congressional power case requires a categorization analysis: Does the statute rest upon an explicit grant of authority?

But the majority opinions in *Term Limits* and *Comstock* rest upon a different baseline, inspired by the Preamble: the Constitution created a national government, authorized by We the People, and that charter of government ought to be applied pragmatically, with limits primarily enforced by the political process and not by the Court. These opinions seem to go beyond *McCulloch* in their willingness to infer broad congressional authority that reached beyond the strictly defined enumerated powers. Indeed, scholars have argued that federalism today rests upon the organizational benefits of multiple centers of governmental power. E.g., Malcolm Feeley & Edward Rubin, *Federalism: Political Identity & Tragic Compromise* (2008); Robert Schapiro, *Polyphonic Federalism: Toward the Protection of Fundamental Rights* (2009).

Which understanding of the constitutional baseline is "best," as a legal matter? Is there a middle way that is most legally defensible? In resolving this issue in your own mind, you might consider, first, the text and debates behind the Constitution of 1789. Most of the relevant sources are in appendices to this casebook: the Constitution, of course (App. 1); the letter from George Washington, president of the Convention, speaking for the Convention on these issues (App. 2); and *Federalist* No. 51 (App. 2). Which view of federal/state sovereignty do these sources support?[5]

---

[5] For speculations in different directions, compare Richard Primus, *The Limits of Enumeration,* 124 Yale L.J. 576 (2014), with Kurt T. Lash, *The Sum of All Delegated Power: A Response to Richard Primus, The Limits of Enumeration*, 124 Yale L.J. F. 180 (2014) with Daniel A. Farber, *The Constitution's Forgotten Cover Letter: An Essay on the New Federalism and the Original Understanding*, 94 Mich. L. Rev. 615 (1995), and with Charles Fried, *Federalism—Why Should We Care?*, 6 Harv. J.L. & Pub. Pol'y 1 (1982).

A second source of materials might be the Reconstruction Amendments to the Constitution and their debating history, recounted in Chapter 2. Do the Civil War and the Reconstruction Amendments reflect a victory of Lincoln's view, which was even more nationalistic than Marshall's in *McCulloch*? Or do they leave in place the separate sovereign spheres that modern federalists say prevailed during the Constitution's Founding? If you accept Bruce Ackerman's thesis that the New Deal was a third great *constitutional moment*, you are more likely to reject the separate-sovereign-spheres argument entirely and view federalism as an administrative mechanism. If you believe the New Deal was a constitutional betrayal of federalism limits, you are likely to reject or read the expansive national power precedents narrowly.[6]

A third possible source of insight involves an inquiry into the *values or goals* federalism is supposed to play or might productively play in our polity.[7] At least three goals can be identified:

(1) *Protecting Liberty*. Madison in *Federalist* No. 51 argued that the federal arrangement would assure a "double security" for citizen liberty, because the states would protect citizens against federal overregulation or tyranny. See also Clarence Thomas, *Why Federalism Matters*, 48 Drake L. Rev. 231 (2000). States can accomplish this because they have an independent lobbying voice in the nation's capital, are needed to administer most national programs, and are the building blocks of national political parties (Merritt, *State Autonomy*). If the states balk at bad national regulation or executive overreaching, they can stop it or ameliorate its harms by bargaining or ongoing resistance. See Jessica Bulman-Pozen, *Federalism as a Safeguard of the Separation of Powers*, 112 Colum. L. Rev. 459, 461 (2012). The federal arrangement also provides libertarian sanctuaries for people mistreated in their home states. Racial and sexual minorities brutalized by the police in repressive states could and did move in large numbers to more tolerant states.

On the other hand, the federal arrangement protects both the policies and perhaps also the locked-in political structures of the so-called "repressive" states. See David A. Super, *Laboratories of Destitution: Democratic Experimentalism and the Failure of Antipoverty Law*, 157 U. Pa. L. Rev. 541, 582–83 (2008) (describing states' hesitation to experiment with welfare policies due to population mobility). Indeed, Madison in *Federalist* No. 10 warned that

---

[6] For example, Robert H. Bork, *The Tempting of America: The Political Seduction of the Law* 52–58 (1990); Randy E. Barnett, *No Small Feat: Who Won the Health Care Case (and Why Did so Many Law Professors Miss the Boat)?*, 65 Fla. L. Rev. 1331 (2013) (even if the New Deal precedents are valid, original meaning suggests they should not be expanded).

[7] *Gregory v. Ashcroft*, 501 U.S. 452 (1991); *FERC v. Mississippi*, 456 U.S. 742 (1982) (O'Connor, J., dissenting). For the values of a federalist arrangement, see Randy E. Barnett, *Our Republican Constitution: Securing the Liberty and Sovereignty of We the People* (2016); Paul Peterson, *The Price of Federalism* (1995); Akhil Reed Amar, Of Sovereignty and Federalism, 96 Yale L.J. 1425 (1987); Heather K. Gerken, *The Supreme Court, 2009 Term—Foreword: Federalism All the Way Down*, 124 Harv. L. Rev. 4 (2010); Deborah Jones Merritt, *Three Faces of Federalism: Finding a Formula for the Future*, 47 Vand. L. Rev. 1563 (1994); Ernest A. Young, *The Conservative Case for Federalism*, 74 Geo. Wash. L. Rev. 874 (2006). For critiques, see Rubin & Feeley, *Federalism*; Sheryll D. Cashin, *Federalism, Welfare Reform, and the Minority Poor: Accounting for the Tyranny of State Majorities*, 99 Colum. L. Rev. 552 (1999).

tyranny was more likely in a smaller republic and that this was a republican advantage of a strong national government. Are states likely to protect us against federal overregulation, with the federal government protecting us against state overregulation? Or is there an off-setting danger that a double layer of government (state/federal) will impose a double layer of regulation—a double risk of tyranny? Is the Fourteenth Amendment relevant to our understanding of the states' role in protecting, or threatening, liberty?

(2) *Republicanism and Legitimacy.* Because citizens are more likely to be politically active at the local level, federalism "assures a decentralized government that will be more sensitive to the diverse needs of a heterogeneous society; it increases opportunity for citizen involvement in the political process; it allows for more innovation and experimentation in government." *Gregory v. Ashcroft*, 501 U.S. 451, 458 (1991); see Amar, *Sovereignty and Federalism*; Merritt, *Three Faces.* Opinion polls suggest that most Americans identify with the states in which they live and trust their state governments a lot more than they trust the national government. Ernest Young, *Federalism as a Constitutional Principle*, 83 U. Cin. L. Rev. 1057, 1080–81 (2015).

Most political groups in American history—from Irish and Italian immigrants early in the century, to African Americans after World War II, to women and gay people today—started their political participation and gained a measure of political respectability at the state and local level before becoming nationally significant. On the other hand, Ed Rubin and Malcolm Feeley ask: Is constitutional *federalism* necessary or even useful for fostering local autonomy in an era where major metropolitan areas cross state boundaries in some regions? Rubin & Feeley, *Federalism: Tragic Compromise.* Moreover, as *Federalist* No. 10 suggested, local governments might also be more prone to ossification and interest-group capture than the national government.

(3) *Efficiency and Diversity.* A third value is efficiency. A federal arrangement allows better satisfaction of peoples' preferences. Assume a unitary state with 100 people, 60 of whom prefer Policy *A* and 40 prefer Policy *B*. Under majority rule, the state will choose Policy *A*, leaving 40 citizens unhappy. If the state were a federation, more citizen preferences could usually be satisfied. Divide up the hypothetical polity in this way (Gordon Tullock, *Federalism: Problems of Scale*, 6 Pub. Choice 19 (1969)):

	Prefer Policy A	*Prefer Policy B*
Province 1	50	10
Province 2	10	30

Under this scenario, the policies adopted by the different provinces would satisfy the preferences of 80 citizens, a net gain in overall citizen happiness. If some citizens of each polity "voted with their feet" and moved to satisfy their preferences, even greater satisfaction could be achieved. Finally, the two provinces over time could gauge the relative effectiveness of their different policies, and one policy might prove superior and then be adopted by both.

This simple game dynamic suggests one possible argument that allocative and distributive policies (the traditional police powers) are best left to the control of local governments: such governments have an incentive to do the job well, lest they lose citizens to more efficient local governments (Peterson, *Price of Federalism*). This game dynamic also suggests that the federal arrangement can serve the equal citizenship and diversity goals advanced by identity-based social movements. Federalism has had a bad odor because southern supporters of apartheid rallied under the constitutional banner of "states rights," but one reason for the success of the civil rights movement was that southern blacks relocated in northern cities, where they were able to exercise political power. Persecuted by the federal government, gay people flourished in states like California and Massachusetts, where the local political processes protected them against private discrimination and violence and recognized their relationships as partnerships and marriages.[8]

Diversity and efficiency of administration have assumed a new dimension with the Affordable Care Act of 2010 (ACA). Abbe R. Gluck & Nicole Huberfield, *What Is Federalism in Healthcare For?*, 70 Stan L Rev 1689 (2018). The nation's most ambitious regulatory initiative, the ACA relies on state exchanges (where established by the states) and state Medicaid programs to achieve its objective of greater health care coverage. Like environmental law since the 1970s, "ObamaCare" advances the goals of federalism through a wide array of state-federal interactions. The Gluck and Huberfield study demands that scholars rethink categorical treatment of federalism issues. In light of their study and the insights of Schapiro, *Polyphonic Federalism,* is it important that *courts* enforce federalism limits on congressional power?

PROBLEM 7-1:
FEDERAL INSURANCE REGULATION

Assume that Congress decides that health insurance companies have been unfairly denying coverage to people with preexisting conditions. Does Congress have the authority to adopt a statute barring insurance companies participating in interstate commerce from discriminating against potential insureds because of preexisting conditions? If so, does Congress have the further authority to require all Americans to secure health insurance, upon the theory that the anti-discrimination rule would bankrupt insurance companies if they could not have an expanded pool of insureds? How would Justices Thomas, Breyer, and Roberts approach these issues? Do the following materials on the Framers' discussions of Article I's enumeration of congressional authority change your thinking?

---

[8] William N. Eskridge Jr. & Christopher Riano, *From Outlaws to Inlaws: The Marriage Debate, 1967–2017* (forthcoming 2019); Heather K. Gerken, *Dissenting by Deciding,* 56 Stan. L. Rev. 1745 (2005); Ernest **A.** Young, *Exit, Voice, and Loyalty as Federalism Strategies: Lessons from the Same-Sex Marriage Debate,* 85 U. Colo. L. Rev. 1133 (2014).

NOTE ON THE FRAMERS' DISCUSSIONS
OF CONGRESS'S POWERS

One central purpose of the Philadelphia Convention was to create a government that could act more decisively in the national interest than the Articles of Confederation government had been able to do.[9] Edmund Randolph of Virginia expressed his view of the defects of the Articles on May 29, 1787: (1) They offered little "security against foreign invasion," because the national government lacked the power to tax and raise armies and because the states were free to provoke foreign conflicts. (2) "That there were many advantages, which the U.S. might acquire, which were not attainable under the confederation," especially regulation of interstate and international commerce. (3) The federal government could not resolve conflicts among the states, could not defend itself against state encroachment, and was not even supreme over state constitutions. II Max Farrand, *The Records of Federal Constitution of 1787*, at 19 (1911) [hereinafter "Farrand"].

With relative consensus that the national government had to be more powerful, the debate at the Convention dealt with how to define the national authority. On May 29, the Convention voted for the Sixth Resolution: "That the national legislature ought to be empowered to enjoy the legislative rights vested in Congress by the Confederation; and moreover To legislate in all cases to which the separate States are incompetent or in which the harmony of the United States may be interrupted by the exercise of individual legislation." I Farrand 47. Part of the debate is reported in Madison's notes:

Mr. Pinckney [S. Car.] & Mr. Rutledge [S. Car.] objected to the vagueness of the term *incompetent*, and said they could not well decide how to vote until they should seen an exact enumeration of the powers comprehended by this definition.

Mr. Butler [S. Car.] repeated his fear that we were running into an extreme in taking away the powers of the States, and called on Mr. Randolph for the extent of his meaning.

Mr. Randolph [Va.] disclaimed any intention to give indefinite powers to the national Legislature, declaring that he was entirely opposed to such an inroad of the State jurisdictions, and that he did not think any considerations whatever could ever change his determination. His opinion was fixed on this point.

Mr. Madison [Va.] said that he had brought with him into the Convention a strong bias in favor of an enumeration and definition of the powers necessary to be exercised by the national Legislature; but had also brought doubts concerning its practicability. His wishes

---

[9] On the discussions about federalism at the Convention and the ratifying debates, see generally Raoul Berger, *Federalism: The Founders' Design* (1987); Randy E. Barnett, *The Original Meaning of the Commerce Clause*, 68 U. Chi. L. Rev. 101 (2001); Daniel A. Farber & Suzanna Sherry, *A History of the American Constitution* (1990); Daniel A. Farber, *The Constitution's Forgotten Cover Letter: An Essay on the New Federalism and the Original Understanding*, 94 Mich. L. Rev. 615 (1995). The original sources are cited in the text of our explication that follows.

remained unaltered; but his doubts had become stronger. What his opinion might ultimately be he could not yet tell. But he should shrink from nothing which should be found essential to such a form of Govt. as would provide for the safety, liberty and happiness of the Community. * * *

(The States then voted 9–0, with one divided state, in favor of the proposition.)

Later, the Convention considered amending the second clause of the Sixth Resolution. One amendment, which read as follows, failed by a 2–8 vote:

> To make laws binding on the People of the United States in all cases which may concern the common interests of the Union; but not to interfere with the government of the individual States in any matters of internal policy, which respect the government of such States only, and wherein the general welfare of the United States is not concerned.

A second amendment to the same clause was adopted by an 8–2 vote:

> and moreover to legislate in all cases for the general interests of the Union, and also in those to which the States are separately incompetent, or in which the harmony of the United States may be interrupted by the exercise of individual legislation.

A third amendment to the same clause was then adopted: "(and moreover) to legislate in all cases for the general interests of the Union, and also in those to which the States are separately incompetent (or in which the harmony of the U. States may be interrupted by the exercise of individual Legislation)."

On August 6, the Committee of Detail reported a draft Constitution based upon the Resolutions passed by the Convention. Section 1 of Article VII listed 18 enumerated powers of the "Legislature of the United States," very similar to the enumerated powers in the ultimately adopted Article I, § 8. On August 16, the Convention adopted the Committee's recommendation that the Legislature be permitted "To regulate commerce with foreign nations, and among the several States." Southern states subsequently objected that the clause would enable Northern states to obtain advantageous commercial laws, to the detriment of southern states, and sought to amend the clause to require a two-thirds vote of Congress to enact commercial regulations. The motion was defeated on August 28. Some of the debate (II Farrand 449–53):

> Mr. Sherman [Conn.], alluding to Mr. Pinckney's enumeration of particular interests, as requiring a security agst. abuse of the power; observed that, the diversity was of itself a security, adding that to require more than a majority to decide a question was always embarrassing as had been experience in cases [under the Articles of Confederation] requiring the votes of nine States of Congress. * * *

> Mr. Madison [Va.] went into pretty full view of the subject. He observed that the disadvantage to the S. States from a navigation act, lay chiefly in a temporary rise of freight, attended however with an

increase of Southern. as well as Northern Shipping—with the emigration of Northern seamen & merchants to the Southern States—& with a removal of the existing & injurious retaliations among States (on each other). The power of foreign nations to obstruct our retaliating measures on them by a corrupt influence would also be less if a majority shd. be made competent than if 2/3 of each House shd. be required to legislative acts in this case. An abuse of the power would be qualified with all these good effects. But he thought an abuse was rendered improbable by the provision of 2 branches—by the independence of the Senate, by the negative of the Executive, by the interest of Connecticut & New Jersey which were agricultural, not commercial States; by the interior interest which was also agricultural in the most commercial States—by the accession of Western States which wd. be altogether agricultural. He added that the Southern States would derive an essential advantage in the general security afforded by the increase of our maritime strength. * * *

These excerpts, as well as *Federalist* Nos. 45–47 & 78 (Numbers 47 and 78 are in Appendix 2 to this Casebook), give some flavor of the original discussions surrounding the nature and scope of the national legislative authority. The discussions suggest that Congress was expected to exercise only those powers delegated to it, and the Tenth Amendment confirmed that all other powers were reserved to the states or to the people. It is less clear from these original sources how the Framers expected these structural limitations to operate. For example, some debate among the Framers indicated a desire to treat Congress' powers as rather open-ended. Moreover, attempts to modify the language of the Tenth Amendment more clearly to cabin congressional power, by stating that "the powers not *expressly* delegated" to the federal government belonged to the states or the people, failed (Farber & Sherry, *Constitution* 134–42, 241–42).

Our discussion of the powers of the national Congress in this chapter will be selective, focusing on the Commerce Clause (Section 2) and Congress's authority to enact civil rights legislation (Section 3), which have shown the most interesting development. We shall next turn to the Taxing and Spending Clause and the problem of unconstitutional conditions, along with a brief look at the Treaty Power (Section 4). Our treatment of national authority will culminate with the Affordable Care Act Case (Section 5). We shall not deal with other powers of Congress in this chapter, although several of them are involved in our discussion of *McCulloch*. (Chapter 8 will explore Congress' war and foreign affairs powers, especially as they have fallen into competition with those of the President.)

SECTION 2. CONGRESSIONAL POWER UNDER THE COMMERCE CLAUSE

The federal commerce power clearly provides a grant of legislative authority to Congress. It has also been judicially construed to create an implied limitation upon state legislative authority to burden interstate commerce. Congressional power is our primary topic in this section; we turn to implied limits on the states in Section 6 of this chapter.

PROBLEM 7-2:
REGULATION OF PUBLIC ACCOMMODATIONS

Consider a federal statute that makes it unlawful for a public accommodation, such as a restaurant, to refuse to serve people on the basis of their race or ethnic background. Assuming that the statute was enacted under Congress' Commerce Clause powers, could it be constitutionally applied to (a) Trader Rick's, a restaurant in a northern Virginia suburb of Washington, D.C., located in a posh hotel and catering to customers from out-of-town, especially tourists; (b) The Greasy Spoon, a restaurant in Paw Paw, West Virginia, located off a state road and catering to a local clientele, though occasionally an out-of-stater wanders in; (c) Leslie's Lemonade Stand in Richmond, Virginia, operated by an eight-year-old entrepreneur and serving only a local clientele. Based upon the language of the clause and the Framers' discussions, could Congress regulate any of these businesses under the Commerce Clause? Reconsider your answer after you read each of the major cases reproduced below, namely, *Gibbons v. Ogden*, *Hammer v. Dagenhart*, *United States v. Darby*, *Katzenbach v. McClung*, and *United States v. Lopez*.

GIBBONS V. OGDEN
22 U.S. (9 Wheat.) 1, 6 L.Ed. 23 (1824)

CHIEF JUSTICE MARSHALL delivered the opinion of the Court.

[In 1803, the New York legislature granted Robert Livingston and Robert Fulton an exclusive license to operate steamships in New York waters. Livingston and Fulton assigned Aaron Ogden the right to operate a ferry between New York City and Elizabethtown Point, New Jersey. Thomas Gibbons, a competing ferry operator, technically violated the New York license, because he entered New York waters. But Gibbons' ferries were licensed as "vessels [in] the coasting trade" pursuant to a 1793 federal statute. Ogden obtained an injunction in New York state courts, prohibiting Gibbons from operating his vessels in New York waters. Gibbons appealed, claiming the judgment was inconsistent with the Commerce Clause.]

The subject to be regulated is commerce; and our constitution being, as was aptly said at the bar, one of enumeration, and not of definition, to ascertain the extent of the power, it becomes necessary to settle the meaning of the word. The counsel for the appellee would limit it to traffic, to buying and selling, or the interchange of commodities, and do not admit that it comprehends navigation. This would restrict a general term, applicable to many objects, to one of its significations. Commerce, undoubtedly, is traffic, but it is something more; it is intercourse. It describes the commercial intercourse between nations, and parts of nations, in all its branches, and is regulated by prescribing rules for carrying on that intercourse. The mind can scarcely conceive a system for regulating commerce between nations, which shall exclude all laws concerning navigation, which shall be silent on the admission of the vessels of the one nation into the ports of the other, and be confined to prescribing rules for the conduct of individuals, in the actual employment of buying and selling, or of barter.

If commerce does not include navigation, the government of the Union has no direct power over that subject, and can make no law prescribing what shall constitute American vessels, or requiring that they shall be navigated by American seamen. Yet this power has been exercised from the commencement of the government, has been exercised with the consent of all, and has been understood by all to be a commercial regulation. All America understands, and has uniformly understood, the word "commerce" to comprehend navigation. It was so understood, and must have been so understood when the constitution was framed. The power over commerce, including navigation, was one of the primary objects for which the people of America adopted their government, and must have been contemplated in forming it. The convention must have used the word in that sense; because all have understood it in that sense, and the attempt to restrict it comes too late.

If the opinion that "commerce" as the word is used in the constitution, comprehends navigation also, requires any additional confirmation, that additional confirmation is, we think, furnished by the words of the instrument itself. * * * The 9th section of the 1st article declares, that "no preference shall be given, by any regulation of commerce or revenue, to the ports of one state over those of another." This clause cannot be understood as applicable to those laws only which are passed for the purposes of revenue, because it is expressly applied to commercial regulations; and the most obvious preference which can be given to one port over another, in regulating commerce, relates to navigation. But the subsequent part of the sentence is still more explicit. It is, "nor shall vessels bound to or from one state, be obliged to enter, clear, or pay duties, in another." These words have a direct reference to navigation.

The universally acknowledged power of the government to impose embargoes, must also be considered as showing that all America is united

in that construction which comprehends navigation in the word commerce.
* * *

The word used in the constitution, then, comprehends, and has been always understood to comprehend, navigation within its meaning; and a power to regulate navigation, is as expressly granted, as if that term had been added to the word "commerce."

To what commerce does this power extend? The constitution informs us, to commerce "with foreign nations, and among the several States, and with the Indian tribes."

It has, we believe, been universally admitted that these words comprehend every species of commercial intercourse between the United States and foreign nations. No sort of trade can be carried on between this country and any other, to which this power does not extend. It has been truly said, that commerce, as the word is used in the constitution, is a unit, every part of which is indicated by the term.

If this be the admitted meaning of the word, in its application to foreign nations, it must carry the same meaning throughout the sentence, and remain a unit, unless there be some plain intelligible cause which alters it.

The subject to which the power is next applied, is to commerce "among the several states." The word "among" means intermingled with. A thing which is among others, is intermingled with them. Commerce among the states cannot stop at the external boundary line of each state, but may be introduced into the interior. It is not intended to say that these words comprehend that commerce, which is completely internal, which is carried on between man and man in a State, or between different parts of the same State, and which does not extend to or affect other states. Such a power would be inconvenient, and is certainly unnecessary.

Comprehensive as the word "among" is, it may very properly be restricted to that commerce which concerns more States than one. The phrase is not one which would probably have been selected to indicate the completely interior traffic of a State, because it is not an apt phrase for that purpose; and the enumeration of the particular classes of commerce to which the power was to be extended, would not have been made had the intention been to extend the power to every description. The enumeration presupposes something not enumerated; and that something, if we regard the language or the subject of the sentence, must be the exclusively internal commerce of a state. The genius and character of the whole government seem to be, that its action is to be applied to all the external concerns of the nation, and to those internal concerns which affect the States generally; but not to those which are completely within a particular state, which do not affect other states, and with which it is not necessary to interfere, for the purpose of executing some of the general powers of the government.

The completely internal commerce of a state, then, may be considered as reserved for the state itself.

But, in regarding commerce with foreign nations, the power of Congress does not stop at the jurisdictional lines of the several states. It would be a very useless power, if it could not pass those lines. The commerce of the United States with foreign nations, is that of the whole United States. Every district has a right to participate in it. The deep streams which penetrate our country in every direction, pass through the interior of almost every state in the Union, and furnish the means of exercising this right. If Congress has the power to regulate it, that power must be exercised whenever the subject exists. If it exists within the States, if a foreign voyage may commence or terminate at a port within a State, then the power of Congress may be exercised within a State. * * *

We are now arrived at the inquiry—What is this power?

It is the power to regulate; that is, to prescribe the rule by which commerce is to be governed. This power, like all others vested in Congress, is complete in itself, may be exercised to its utmost extent, and acknowledges no limitations, other than are prescribed in the constitution. These are expressed in plain terms, and do not affect the questions which arise in this case, or which have been discussed at the bar. If, as has always been understood, the sovereignty of Congress, though limited to specified objects, is plenary as to those objects, the power over commerce with foreign nations, and among the several States is vested in Congress, as absolutely as it would be in a single government, having in its constitution the same restrictions on the exercise of the power as are found in the constitution of the United States. The wisdom and the discretion of Congress, their identity with the people, and the influence which their constituents possess at election, are, in this, as in many other instances, as that, for example, of declaring war, the sole restraints on which they have relied, to secure them from its abuse. They are the restraints on which the people must often rely solely, in all representative governments.

The power of Congress, then, comprehends navigation, within the limits of every state in the Union; so far as that navigation may be, in any manner, connected with "commerce with foreign nations, or among the several States, or with the Indian tribes." It may, of consequence, pass the jurisdictional line of New York, and act upon the very waters to which the prohibition now under consideration applies.

[Thus, Chief Justice Marshall concluded that Congress's commerce power was expansive enough to enact the federal statute in question. In the remainder of the opinion, Chief Justice Marshall considered how to resolve the conflict between the federal statute and the state grant of monopoly, and also discussed whether the state monopoly would be lawful in the absence of any federal statute covering the same subject. This portion of the opinion is reproduced at the beginning of Section 6.]

NOTES ON GIBBONS AND COMMERCE CLAUSE LIMITS ON NATIONAL POWER

1. *Should the Supreme Court Enforce the Article I, § 8 Limits on National Power?* A premise of Chief Justice Marshall's opinion is that Ogden wins the case if the federal statute is not within the powers enumerated in Article I, § 8. This assumes that the reach of the Commerce Clause (and other enumerated powers) is a limitation on national power that should be enforced by the courts. Although this assumption pervades the cases in this part, it does not necessarily follow from the original expectations of the Framers.

In *Federalist* Nos. 45–46, Madison refuted the Anti-Federalists' charge that the stronger national government in the Constitution will swallow up the state governments. Madison's argument was that the people's first loyalty will always be to the states (the governments closer to the people), that the Constitution was written to ensure the states' participation in the national government (as by election of senators and the President), and that the states would have several means to resist unlawful or unjust encroachments against them by the national government. If this argument is correct, should the Supreme Court in cases like *Gibbons* assume—presumptively or irrebuttably—that Congress has acted properly in adopting statutes, and that the chief or only protection against congressional usurpation is objection and resistance by the states?

Updating Madison's arguments, several modern scholars have read the Constitution to suggest that the Article I limits on national power should be enforced only through the political process.[10] Such authors argue that the Supreme Court should not decide constitutional questions arising out of the national government's alleged usurpation of state authority, on the ground that the states are well represented in the national political process. (Recall Chief Justice Marshall's discussion in *McCulloch*. Why was a similar argument not made in *Gibbons*?) Note that a similar argument could be made as to the enforcement of some of the individual rights treated in earlier chapters. For example, because the press is extremely well-represented in the state as well as national political process, should the protections of *New York Times v. Sullivan* (Chapter 6, § 2B) be diluted or not enforced? Has the Supreme Court been justified in lenient review of state policies having racially significant

---

[10] Herbert Wechsler, *The Political Safeguards of Federalism*, in *Principles, Politics and Fundamental Law* 49–82 (1954) (§ 5B of this chapter); see Larry Kramer, *The People Themselves: Popular Constitutionalism and Judicial Review* (2005); Jesse Choper, *Judicial Review and the National Political Process* 171–259 (1980). For commentary suggesting the many ways state governments can influence national political decisions, see Larry Kramer, *Understanding Federalism*, 45 Vand. L. Rev. 1485 (1994) (political parties as conduit of influence); Deborah Jones Merritt, *The Guarantee Clause and State Autonomy: Federalism for a Third Century*, 88 Colum. L. Rev. 1 (1988).

effects (see *Washington v. Davis*, Chapter 3, § 1B), on the ground that racial minorities are well-represented in state and local political processes?

2.   *Theories for Limiting Congress' Commerce Clause Power.* On the issue of Congress' power under the Commerce Clause, *Gibbons* seems like an easy case, for interstate navigation was contemplated as the clause's object by the Framers. Yet Congress presumably cannot do anything it wants under the aegis of the Commerce Clause; several possible limitations on that power were suggested in *Gibbons* and were then elaborated in subsequent Supreme Court cases.

(a)   *"Commerce."* Marshall's opinion suggested that an activity not falling within a commonly accepted notion of commerce would not be within Congress' power. Randy E. Barnett, *The Original Meaning of the Commerce Clause,* 68 U. Chi. L. Rev. 101 (2001). In *Paul v. Virginia*, 75 U.S. (8 Wall.) 168 (1868), the Court held that federal law could not regulate insurance contracts. "Issuing a policy of insurance is not a transaction of commerce," because the policy is a contract, not something offered in barter and trade.

(b)   *"Among the Several States."* *Gibbons* stated: "The completely internal commerce of a State, then, may be considered as reserved for the State itself." Thus, the Court in *Federal Baseball Club v. National League*, 259 U.S. 200 (1922), held that the Sherman Act (prohibiting conspiracies to monopolize trade or commerce "among the several states") did not apply to organized baseball, whose "exhibitions" were held to be "purely state affairs." The Court rejected the argument that transportation of players across state lines rendered the sport interstate in nature, because "the transport is a mere incident, not the essential thing." (The Court also seemed to rely on the "commerce" requirement, for it suggested that the "personal effort" involved in baseball is not commerce.)

(c)   *"Regulate."* Finally, Congress can only "regulate" interstate commerce. Several early Presidents believed that it prevented Congress from passing legislation that "facilitated" (rather than "regulated") interstate commerce. In 1817, President Madison vetoed the Internal Improvement Bill because " '[t]he power to regulate commerce among the several States,' cannot include a power to construct roads and canals, and to improve the navigation of water courses, in order to facilitate, promote, and secure such a commerce, without a latitude of construction departing from the ordinary import of the terms, strengthened by the known inconveniences which doubtless led to the grant of this remedial power to Congress." II *Messages and Papers of the Presidents* 569, 570 (1897).

3.   *Congress' Efforts to Regulate New Problems Under Its Commerce Clause Power, 1887–1920.* The analytical structure in *Gibbons* was not often tested in the early nineteenth century, because Congress did not engage in much economic regulation.[11] Congress's regulatory activity expanded after the

---

[11]   Congress fought pirates, regulated rivers and harbors, established safety standards for steamboats, and engaged in other activities that did not raise serious Commerce Clause questions.

Civil War. The advent of railroads, large-scale manufacturing, the telephone and telegraph, labor unions, and cartels introduced social and economic issues that could not be adequately dealt with at the state level. National legislation of three sorts was adopted pursuant to Congress' Commerce Clause power.

(a)   *Impediments to an Efficient National Market.* Once markets became national, market abuses could no longer be effectively addressed by the states acting singly or even in concert.[12] The Interstate Commerce Act of 1887 established a regulatory structure (the Interstate Commerce Commission) to respond to unfair railroad practices, such as price discrimination and rebates to certain customers. The act ensured a smoothly functioning interstate transportation system. The Sherman Anti-Trust Act of 1890 prohibited, in § 1, any contract, combination, or conspiracy "in restraint of trade or commerce among the several states" and, in § 2, any effort or conspiracy to "monopolize any part of the trade or commerce among the several states."

(b)   *Interstate and International Contagion.* With increased mobility of people and goods came fears of migrating people and evils. National immigration regulations began in earnest in the 1880s, to keep out "undesirable" persons, defined by race, sexuality, and class.[13] Other statutes tried to prevent the interstate transmission of vice. The Comstock Act of 1873 criminalized using the U.S. mails for sending "obscene" material, including contraception and abortion information. The Mann Act of 1910 prohibited the transportation of women in interstate or foreign commerce for "immoral purposes." Yet other statutes were concerned with interstate disease and health menaces. The Pure Food & Drugs Act of 1906 prohibited the interstate transportation of adulterated or unsafe foods and drugs and established an agency to set standards.

(c)   *National Standards of Safety and Fairness.* Congress also adopted statutes setting national standards for safety and fairness. National standards could be useful *focal points* for private activity, channeling it in ways that could improve safety and even efficiency. Thus in 1893, Congress required all common carriers engaged in interstate commerce to have a power driving wheel brake system and to have couplers between the cars that worked automatically (so that workers need not risk injury by going between the cars). Additionally, national standards could be useful to avoid local *races to the bottom*, by which individual states decline to adopt needed business regulations out of fear that businesses will "vote with their feet" by relocating

---

See Jerry Mashaw, *Administration and "The Democracy": Administrative Law from Jackson to Lincoln, 1829–1861,* 117 Yale L.J. 1568 (2008).

[12] As § 6 details, states were probably prohibited by the Commerce Clause itself from exercising much, if any, jurisdiction outside their individual borders, for the defensible reason that states would create a cacophony of regulations and might create self-seeking ones. One solution would have been for the states to form interstate agreements, allowed under Art. I, § 10, cl. 3 if consented to by Congress, but collective action problems have made that difficult.

[13] Immigration statutes were enacted under Congress' "Naturalization" authority of Article I, § 8, cl. 4, which has been broadly construed to permit Congress virtually unlimited power to limit entry by noncitizens.

to more lenient jurisdictions.[14] In an important application of this idea, the Child Labor Act of 1916 prohibited the transportation in interstate commerce of goods produced in factories employing children under the age of fourteen or employing children aged fourteen to sixteen for more than eight hours a day, for six days a week, or for nighttime work.

NOTE ON ENUMERATED POWERS AND DUAL FEDERALISM AS STRONG LIMITATIONS ON CONGRESSIONAL AUTHORITY

Many of the laws described in the previous note were questionable under the Court's traditional conception of the restrictions on congressional power. Not only did they have a less certain connection with *commerce* than the law upheld in *Gibbons*, but they regulated matters that seemed to be *intrastate* as well as *interstate*. This was a big problem for a Court committed to the conceptual framework of *dual federalism*. "There are certain matters over which the National Government has absolute control, and no action of the State can interfere therewith, and there are others in which the State is supreme, and in respect to them the National Government is powerless. To preserve the even balance between the two governments and hold each in its separate sphere is the peculiar duty of all courts." *South Carolina v. United States*, 199 U.S. 437, 448 (1905). Consider how the following decisions by the Court accommodated or sacrificed that principle.

In *United States v. E.C. Knight*, 156 U.S. 1 (1895), the Court ruled that the Sherman Act could not constitutionally apply to break up the Sugar Trust (a monopoly of the production of sugar), on the ground that this was a regulation of *manufacturing*, rather than *commerce*. Although refined sugar was shipped in interstate commerce, it was just *incidental* to the manufacturing monopoly that the government alleged.[15] But in *Champion v. Ames (The Lottery Case)*, 188 U.S. 321 (1903), the Court upheld the constitutionality of the federal Lottery Act, which outlawed carrying lottery tickets across state lines. Although the dissenters objected that the interstate traffic in lottery tickets was incidental to their local purposes (as in *E.C. Knight*), Justice Harlan (a dissenter in the previous case) viewed the issue functionally. State statutes could not reach the interstate market in lotteries; hence, there was a justification for national regulation. The same relaxed

---

[14] A race to the bottom is a standard prisoners' dilemma game, whereby two players are collectively better off by cooperating but, acting not in concert, will tend to cheat on one another, yielding a result that is poorer for both. Thus, each of two states has strong incentives to pollute the atmosphere, even though it is in their joint interest to reduce overall pollution. See Richard Musgrave, *The Theory of Public Finance* 132–33 (1959); Wallace Oates, *An Economist's Perspective on Fiscal Federalism*, in *The Political Economy of Fiscal Federalism* 3 (Oates ed. 1977); Daniel A. Farber, *Environmental Federalism in a Global Economy*, 83 Va. L. Rev. 1283 (1997).

[15] *E.C. Knight* was a controversial decision, and the Court retreated from such a broad position. In *Addyston Pipe & Steel Co. v. United States*, 175 U.S. 211 (1899), the Court upheld a Sherman Act suit against iron pipe companies conspiring to fix prices, which the Court characterized as not only a manufacturing restraint, but also a "direct restraint upon interstate commerce." The Court liberally applied the Sherman Act to a labor union boycott in *Loewe v. Lawlor*, 208 U.S. 274 (1908); see also *Coronado Coal Co. v. United Mine Workers*, 268 U.S. 295 (1925).

ends/means test was applied to uphold the Pure Food & Drugs Act in *Hipolite Egg Co. v. United States*, 220 U.S. 45 (1911), and the Mann Act in *Hoke v. United States*, 227 U.S. 308 (1913).

At the same time, the Court applied the Commerce Clause to authorize congressional regulation of intrastate as well as interstate activities. In *Swift & Co. v. United States*, 196 U.S. 375 (1905), the Court upheld a Sherman Act injunction against price-fixing by meat-packers. Against objection that this was federal regulation of intrastate commerce, the opinion for the Court by Justice Holmes responded: "When cattle are sent for sale from a place in one State, with the expectation that they will end their transit, after purchase in another, and when in effect they do so, with only the interruption necessary to find a purchaser at the stockyard, and when this is a typical, constantly recurring course, the current thus existing is a current of commerce among the States, and the purchase of the cattle is a part and incident of such commerce."

Swift was followed in *Stafford v. Wallace*, 258 U.S. 495 (1922), which upheld regulation of animal stockyards because they were in a "stream of commerce" that Congress could surely regulate. According to Chief Justice Taft's opinion for the Court in *Stafford*, a reasonable fear by Congress that a course of conduct "usually lawful and affecting only intrastate commerce when considered alone, will probably and more or less constantly be used in conspiracies against interstate commerce or constitute a direct and undue burden on it," could serve "the same purpose as the intent charged in the Swift indictment to bring acts of a similar character into the current of interstate commerce for federal restraint." Taft also emphasized that the Court should defer to Congress's judgment as to the nature and extent of the connection between apparently local acts and interstate commerce. Yet the Court did not defer to Congress in *The First Employers' Liability Cases*, 207 U.S. 463 (1908) (invalidating a requirement that railroads insure employees against accidents), and *Adair v. United States*, 208 U.S. 161 (1908) (overturning a federal prohibition of yellow-dog contracts between railroads and their employees).

Likewise, the Court in *Houston, East & West Texas Railway v. United States (The Shreveport Rate Case)*, 234 U.S. 342 (1914), ruled that the Interstate Commerce Commission could regulate intrastate as well as interstate portions of railroad operations. Justice Hughes' opinion for the Court reasoned that congressional "authority, extending to these interstate carriers as instruments of interstate commerce, necessarily embraces the right to control their operations in all matters having such a close and substantial relation to interstate traffic that the control is essential or appropriate to the security of that traffic, to the efficiency of the interstate service, and to the maintenance of conditions under which interstate commerce may be conducted upon fair terms and without molestation or hindrance."

In a major precedent, ***Hammer v. Dagenhart, 247 U.S. 251 (1918)***, the Court held that Congress had no Commerce Clause power to prohibit interstate transportation of goods made by child labor. Congress relied on *Ames*, *Hipolite*, and *Hoke*, where the Court allowed Congress to prohibit disapproved items from entering interstate commerce. **Justice Day**'s opinion for the Court distinguished these precedents: "In each of these instances the use of interstate transportation was necessary to the accomplishment of harmful results," while the Child Labor Act was not really a regulation of commerce, as its aim was "to standardize the ages at which children may be employed in mining and manufacturing within the States. The goods shipped are of themselves harmless."

Justice Day argued that this was a case of federal regulation of manufacture, rather than commerce, and so *E.C. Knight* governed. "The far reaching result of upholding the act cannot be more plainly indicated than by pointing out that if Congress can thus regulate matters entrusted to local authority by prohibition of the movement of commodities in interstate commerce, all freedom of commerce will be at an end, and the power of the States over local matters may be eliminated, and thus our system of government be practically destroyed."

Justice Holmes dissented. "The statute confines itself to prohibiting the carriage of certain goods in interstate or foreign commerce. Congress is given power to regulate such commerce in unqualified terms. It would not be argued today that the power to regulate does not include the power to prohibit." Thus, Congress had authority to pass the law based upon *The Lottery Case*, as well as *Hoke*, where a unanimous Court said: "Let an article be debased by adulteration, let it be misrepresented by false branding, and Congress may exercise its prohibitive power. It may be that Congress could not prohibit the manufacture of the article in a state. It may be that Congress could not prohibit in all of its conditions its sale within a state. But Congress may prohibit its transportation between the states, and by that means defeat the motive and evils of its manufacture." Commentators agreed with Holmes that a product of child labor was just as much an "outlaw of commerce" as adulterated food (*Hipolite Egg*) or lottery tickets (*The Lottery Case*).[16]

Like some of the earlier Commerce Clause decisions, The Child Labor Case may be viewed as substantive rather than purely jurisdictional. Unlike *Hoke* and *The Lottery Case,* the Child Labor Case involved labor law and the family. The same Justices who applied substantive due process to strike down state employee protections in *Lochner v. New York* (1906) and state interference with parental control over children in *Meyer v. Nebraska* (1923) would have been unenthusiastic about the regulatory objective in the Child Labor Act.[17]

---

[16] None of the important contemporary commentators thought the Court had adequate answers to Holmes' dissent. E.g., Thurlow Gordon, *The Child Labor Law Case*, 32 Harv. L. Rev. 45 (1918); William Carey Jones, *The Child Labor Decision*, 6 Calif. L. Rev. 395 (1918); William Sutherland, *The Child Labor Cases & the Constitution*, 8 Cornell L.Q. 338 (1923).

[17] See Lawrence Berger & S. Rayan Johansson, *Child Health in the Workplace: The Supreme Court in* Hammer v. Dagenhart, 5 J. Health Politics, Policy & Law 81 (1980).

NOTE ON THE NEW DEAL'S EARLY DIFFICULTIES MEETING COMMERCE CLAUSE SCRUTINY, 1934–36

President Franklin Roosevelt's plan to bring the country out of the Great Depression of 1929 involved unprecedented national direction of the economy, through national standards for conditions of labor, fair business practices, unionizing, social welfare and insurance, and so forth. These new kinds of statutes were more creative invocations of the Commerce Clause than the Child Labor Act. Because the Court for the first four years of the New Deal (1933–37) was populated entirely with pre-New Deal Justices committed to the line-drawing of cases like the *Child Labor Case* or the *Shreveport Rate Case*, there was bound to be trouble. And trouble there was.[18]

In *Railroad Retirement Board v. Alton Railroad*, 295 U.S. 330 (1935), the Court by a 5–4 vote struck down the Railroad Retirement Act of 1934. Although Congress had the power to regulate railroad transportation and safety under the Commerce Clause, that power did not extend to establishment of a mandatory retirement plan for railroad workers, which Justice Roberts' opinion for the Court characterized as "essentially related to the social welfare of the worker, and therefore remote from any regulation of commerce as such." This was an invalid Commerce Clause goal under the *Child Labor Case*.

Three weeks after *Alton Railroad*, the Court in *A.L.A. Schechter Poultry Corp. v. United States*, 295 U.S. 495 (1935), invalidated the National Industry Recovery Act's (NIRA) labor rules for the New York poultry market. NIRA authorized the President to establish codes of fair competition for various industries, to be written by experts within those industries, a move which the Court in *Panama Refining Co. v. Ryan*, 293 U.S. 388 (1935), invalidated as an excessive delegation of congressional power to the President (and in turn to private parties (see Chapter 8, § 2A)). In *Schechter*, the Court held that the Poultry Code—prohibiting child labor, setting a minimum wage and maximum hours, and assuring workers the right to unionize—was an excessive delegation *and* was beyond Congress' Commerce Clause power, even though the Code only applied to "transaction[s] in or affecting interstate commerce." Schechter argued, however, that the Code was applied to his business, which only sold chickens in New York.

Because chickens generally were shipped across state lines, the government argued that the poultry industry was part of a current of commerce that could be regulated (*Swift*) and that defects in the industry "directly affected" commerce (the *Shreveport Rate Case*). In an opinion by Chief Justice Hughes, the Court rejected the current of commerce argument because the wage and work week limitations did not relate to commerce and only applied to slaughterhouse and sales work performed locally, after the chickens had arrived in New York. The Court rejected the affecting-commerce argument

---

[18] See Barry Cushman, *Rethinking the New Deal Court: The Structure of a Constitutional Revolution* (1998); Peter Irons, *The New Deal Lawyers* (1982); G. Edward White, *The Constitution and the New Deal* (2000); Robert Stern, *The Commerce Clause and the National Economy, 1933–1946*, 59 Harv. L. Rev. 645 (1946).

on the ground that the regulations' effect on commerce was "indirect" and not "direct." *Schechter* concluded with a classic statement of the formalist position (in response to the government's overall argument that the nation as a practical matter needed national wage and hour rules to climb out of the Depression): "It is not the province of this Court to consider the economic advantages or disadvantages of such a centralized system. It is sufficient to say that the Federal Constitution does not provide for it."

Stung but undaunted, the New Deal Congress continued to legislate, immediately adopting the National Labor Relations Act to assure workers' rights to organize and bargain and the Bituminous Coal Conservation Act, which established an NIRA-type Code for the coal industry. In *Carter v. Carter Coal Co.*, 298 U.S. 238 (1936), the Court by a 6–3 vote struck down the Coal Conservation Act. The government again relied on the flow of coal in interstate commerce and the effects of the market collapse; the Court (per Sutherland, J.) again rebuffed the arguments, based on *Schechter*: "The only perceptible difference between that case and this is that in the *Schechter* case the federal power was asserted with respect to commodities which had come to rest after their interstate transportation; while here, the case deals with commodities at rest before interstate commerce has begun. That difference is without significance." Chief Justice Hughes concurred; Justices Cardozo, Stone, and Brandeis dissented on the ground that there was a sufficient connection between the Code's price controls and interstate commerce.[19]

The decisions in *Schechter* and *Carter Coal* precipitated FDR's 1937 Court-packing plan described in Chapter 1, § 5. Court-packing aroused significant opposition, as a usurpation of power by the President and an unconstitutional infringement upon the Article III independence of the Court. In any event, the plan was derailed by action within the Court. First, Justice VanDevanter retired in 1937 (ultimately to be replaced by Justice Hugo Black, a New Deal Senator from Alabama). Second, in two important cases the Court indicated a more pragmatic approach to economic regulation. In *West Coast Hotel Co. v. Parrish*, 300 U.S. 379 (1937), the Court, by a five-to-four vote, upheld a state minimum wage statute. While the "Four Horsemen" (VanDevanter, McReynolds, Butler, Sutherland)—the Justices most committed to formalism under the Commerce Clause—dissented, Justices historically committed to flexibility under the Commerce Clause (Brandeis, Stone, and Cardozo) were joined by Chief Justice Hughes and Justice Owen

---

[19] Nor was the Court willing to allow Congress to use its taxing and spending powers, rather than its commerce power, to regulate such matters as agricultural production. In *United States v. Butler*, 297 U.S. 1 (1936), the Court struck down a federal tax on processors of agricultural commodities that was designed to fund a program paying farmers to reduce their productive acreage. The Court concluded that the tax violated the Tenth Amendment by "invad[ing] the reserved rights of the states. It is a statutory plan to regulate and control agricultural production, a matter beyond the powers delegated to the federal government." This was so even though Article I, § 8, in defining Congress's taxing and spending powers, contains no limitation to interstate or national matters other than the "general welfare." Thus, *Butler* was based on the proposition that the Tenth Amendment, and more generally the structures of federalism built into the Constitution, operated as an independent barrier to congressional regulation. The current status of this congressional power is considered in § 4, *infra*.

Roberts.[20] After the "switch in time that saved nine," the Court-packing bill died in Congress.

National Labor Relations Board v. Jones & Laughlin Steel Corp.

301 U.S. 1 (1937)

Speaking for five Justices, **Chief Justice Hughes** upheld the application of the NLRA's labor-management provisions to a national steel company. Relying on *E.C. Knight* and *Carter Coal*, Jones & Laughlin argued that Congress could not regulate manufacturing. The government replied, first, that because the steel company was a large, vertically integrated enterprise, disruption of manufacturing operations would disrupt the stream of interstate commerce (*Swift*) and, in the alternative, that disruption of intrastate manufacturing by labor strife would directly affect commerce and that Congress can act to prevent obstructions to the free flow of commerce (the *Shreveport Rate Case*).

Answering Jones & Laughlin's broad facial attack on the statute, the Chief Justice ruled that the law was written in a constitutional manner and could be limited to contexts "affecting commerce." "It is a familiar principle that acts which directly burden or obstruct interstate or foreign commerce, or its free flow, are within the reach of the congressional power. Acts having that effect are not rendered immune because they grow out of labor disputes. [It] is the effect upon commerce, not the source of the injury, which is the criterion." Applying that test, the Chief Justice addressed the steel company's argument that the NLRA could not be applied to its local manufacturing workers.

Hughes avoided taking a position on the government's stream of commerce theory but accepted its affecting commerce theory. "The congressional authority to protect interstate commerce from burdens and obstructions is not limited to transactions which can be deemed to be an essential part of a 'flow' of interstate or foreign commerce. * * * Although activities may be intrastate in character when separately considered, if they have such a close and substantial relation to interstate commerce that their control is essential or appropriate to protect that commerce from burdens and obstructions, Congress has the power to exercise that control." The Court laid to rest the *E.C. Knight* idea that manufacturing could not be regulated under the Commerce Clause. "[T]hat the employees here concerned were engaged in production is not determinative. The question remains as to the effect upon interstate commerce of the labor practice involved."

---

[20] Justice Roberts's vote was dubbed the "switch in time that saved nine." He had voted in *Morehead v. New York ex rel. Tipaldo*, 298 U.S. 587 (1936), to invalidate a state minimum wage law for women, and seemed to change his mind one year later in *West Coast Hotel*. But Roberts had voted in *West Coast Hotel* before Roosevelt submitted his Court-packing plan, and later claimed that he had joined the majority in *Morehead* only because the dissenters had not faced the fact that they had to overrule earlier precedents to sustain the minimum wage law (which Roberts claimed to be willing to do). Richard Friedman, *Switching Time and Other Thought Experiments: The Hughes Court and Constitutional Transformation*, 142 U. Pa. L. Rev. 1891 (1994).

"Giving full weight to the [company's] contention with respect to a break in the complete continuity of the 'stream of commerce' by reason of [its] manufacturing operations, the fact remains that the stoppage of these operations by industrial strife would have a most serious effect upon interstate commerce. In view of [the company's] far-flung activities, it is idle to say that the effect would be indirect and remote. It is obvious that it would be immediate and might be catastrophic. * * * We have often said that interstate commerce itself is a practical conception. It is equally true that interferences with that commerce must be appraised by a judgment that does not ignore actual experience."

Writing for four dissenters, **Justice McReynolds** objected to "this chain of indirect and progressively remote events" by which the government and the Court justified NLRA jurisdiction over a dispute in which but ten men were discharged, because the unfair labor practice affected interstate commerce. Justice McReynolds' dissenting colleagues then left the Court seriatim: VanDevanter in 1937 (replaced by New Deal Senator Hugo Black), Sutherland in 1938 (replaced by New Deal Solicitor General Stanley Reed), and Butler in 1939 (replaced by New Deal Michigan Governor Frank Murphy). McReynolds himself retired in 1941, shortly before the next major Commerce Clause precedent was handed down—by a unanimous Court populated mostly by New Deal Justices.

United States v. Darby

312 U.S. 100 (1941)

The Fair Labor Standards Act of 1938 regulated hours, wages, and other conditions of employment. Darby, who manufactured lumber in Georgia and shipped some of it to customers in other states, was indicted for violating the Act, but the district court quashed the indictment on the ground that the statute was unconstitutional under *Hammer v. Dagenhart*. In an opinion by **Chief Justice Stone**, the Supreme Court reversed.

"The prohibition of shipment of the proscribed goods in interstate commerce. * * * While manufacture is not of itself interstate commerce, the shipment of manufactured goods interstate is such commerce and the prohibition of such shipment by Congress is indubitably a regulation of the commerce. The power to regulate commerce is the power "to prescribe the rule by which commerce is governed." *Gibbons.* It extends not only to those regulations which aid, foster and protect the commerce, but embraces those which prohibit it. It is conceded that the power of Congress to prohibit transportation in interstate commerce includes noxious articles, stolen articles, kidnapped persons, and articles such as intoxicating liquor or convict made goods, traffic in which is forbidden or restricted by the laws of the state of destination.

But it is said that the present prohibition falls within the scope of none of these categories; that while the prohibition is nominally a regulation of the commerce its motive or purpose is regulation of wages and hours of persons engaged in manufacture, the control of which has been reserved to the states and upon which Georgia and some of the states of destination have placed no restriction; that the effect of the present statute is not to exclude the proscribed articles from interstate commerce in aid of state regulation, but instead, under the guise of a regulation of interstate commerce, it undertakes to regulate wages and hours within the state contrary to the policy of the state which has elected to leave them unregulated. * * *

Such regulation is not a forbidden invasion of state power merely because either its motive or its consequence is to restrict the use of articles of commerce within the states of destination; and is not prohibited unless by other Constitutional provisions. It is no objection to the assertion of the power to regulate interstate commerce that its exercise is attended by the same incidents which attend the exercise of the police power of the states. * * *

In the more than a century which has elapsed since the decision of *Gibbons v. Ogden*, these principles of constitutional interpretation have been so long and repeatedly recognized by this Court as applicable to the Commerce Clause, that there would be little occasion for repeating them now were it not for the decision of this Court twenty-two years ago in *Hammer v. Dagenhart*. In that case it was held by a bare majority of the Court over the powerful and now classic dissent of Mr. Justice Holmes setting forth the fundamental issues involved, that Congress was without power to exclude the products of child labor from interstate commerce. The reasoning and conclusion of the Court's opinion there cannot be reconciled with the conclusion which we have reached, that the power of Congress under the Commerce Clause is plenary to exclude any article from interstate commerce subject only to the specific prohibitions of the Constitution.

Hammer v. Dagenhart has not been followed. The distinction on which the decision was rested that Congressional power to prohibit interstate commerce is limited to articles which in themselves have some harmful or deleterious property—a distinction which was novel when made and unsupported by any provision of the Constitution—has long since been abandoned. The thesis of the opinion that the motive of the prohibition or its effect to control in some measure the use or production within the states of the article thus excluded from the commerce can operate to deprive the regulation of its constitutional authority has long since ceased to have force. *Lottery Case*. And finally we have declared "The authority of the federal government over interstate commerce does not differ in extent or character from that retained by the states over intrastate commerce."

The conclusion is inescapable that *Hammer v. Dagenhart* was a departure from the principles which have prevailed in the interpretation of the Commerce Clause both before and since the decision and that such vitality, as a precedent, as it then had has long since been exhausted. It should be and now is overruled.

Validity of the wage and hour requirements. * * * As the Government seeks to apply [§ 15(a)(2)] in the indictment, and as the court below construed the phrase "produced for interstate commerce," it embraces at least the case where an employer engaged, as is appellee, in the manufacture and shipment of goods in filling orders of extrastate customers, manufactures his product with the intent or expectation that according to the normal course of his business all or some part of it will be selected for shipment to those customers.

Without attempting to define the precise limits of the phrase, we think the acts alleged in the indictment are within the sweep of the statute. * * *

There remains the question whether such restriction on the production of goods for commerce is a permissible exercise of the commerce power. The power of Congress over interstate commerce is not confined to the regulation of commerce among the states. It extends to those activities intrastate which so affect interstate commerce or the exercise of the power of Congress over it as to make regulation of them appropriate means to the attainment of a legitimate end, the exercise of the granted power of Congress to regulate interstate commerce. See *McCulloch*. * * *

* * * [T]he power of Congress to regulate interstate commerce extends to the regulation through legislative action of activities intrastate which have a substantial effect on the commerce or the exercise of the Congressional power over it. * * *

Congress, having by the present Act adopted the policy of excluding from interstate commerce all goods produced for the commerce which do not conform to the specified labor standards, it may choose the means reasonably adapted to the attainment of the permitted end, even though they involve control of intrastate activities. [Thus] Congress may require inspection and preventive treatment of all cattle in a disease infected area in order to prevent shipment in interstate commerce of some of the cattle without the treatment. And we have recently held that Congress in the exercise of its power to require inspection and grading of tobacco shipped in interstate commerce may compel such inspection and grading of all tobacco sold at local auction rooms from which a substantial part but not all of the tobacco sold is shipped in interstate commerce. *Currin v. Wallace*, [306 U.S. 1]. * * *

The means adopted by § 15(a)(2) for the protection of interstate commerce by the suppression of the production of the condemned goods for interstate commerce is so related to the commerce and so affects it as to be within the reach of the commerce power. Congress, to attain its objective in the suppression of nationwide competition in interstate commerce by goods produced under substandard labor conditions, has made no distinction as to the volume or amount of shipments in the commerce or of production for commerce by any particular shipper or producer. It recognized that in present day industry, competition by a small part may affect the whole and that the total effect of the competition of many small producers may be great. The legislation aimed at a whole embraces all its parts.

So far as *Carter Coal Co.* is inconsistent with this conclusion, its doctrine is limited in principle by the decisions under the Sherman Act and the National Labor Relations Act, which we have cited and which we follow.

Our conclusion is unaffected by the Tenth Amendment. * * * The amendment states but a truism that all is retained which has not been surrendered. There is nothing in the history of its adoption to suggest that it was more than declaratory of the relationship between the national and state governments as it had been established by the Constitution before the amendment or that its purpose was other than to allay fears that the new national government might seek to exercise powers not granted, and that the states might not be able to exercise fully their reserved powers.

Wickard v. Filburn

317 U.S. 111 (1942)

The Court applied the new learning on the Commerce Clause (*Darby*) to uphold the Agricultural Adjustment Act's quota on agricultural production. Under the Act, the Secretary of Agriculture imposed a quota on the production of wheat because, he concluded, the total supply of wheat would exceed domestic and export needs, driving down prices. Filburn had a dairy farm and grew small amounts of wheat to feed to his animals and for other purposes. He exceeded his quota and was fined. Even though the federal regulation of Filburn had nothing like a "direct" effect on interstate commerce, **Justice Jackson**'s opinion for a unanimous Court viewed the regulation as the federal government's effort to stabilize national wheat prices by limiting the supply. "That appellee's own contribution to the demand for wheat may be trivial by itself is not enough to remove him from the scope of federal regulation where, as here, his contribution, taken together with that of many others similarly situated, is far from trivial." *Darby*.

"It is well established by decisions of this Court that the power to regulate commerce includes the power to regulate the prices at which commodities in that commerce are dealt in and practices affecting such prices. One of the primary purposes of the Act in question was to increase the market price of wheat, and to that end to limit the volume thereof that could affect the market. It can hardly be denied that a factor of such volume and variability as home-consumed wheat would have a substantial influence on price and market conditions. This may arise because being in marketable condition such wheat overhangs the market and, if induced by rising prices, tends to flow into the market and check price increases. But if we assume that it is never marketed, it supplies a need of the man who grew it which would otherwise be reflected by purchases in the open market. Home-grown wheat in this sense competes with wheat in commerce. The stimulation of commerce is a use of the regulatory function quite as definitely as prohibitions or restrictions thereon. This record leaves us in no doubt that Congress may properly have considered that wheat consumed on the farm where grown, if wholly outside the scheme of regulation, would have a substantial effect in defeating and obstructing its purpose to stimulate trade therein at increased prices.

"It is said, however, that this Act, forcing some farmers into the market to buy what they could provide for themselves, is an unfair promotion of the markets and prices of specializing wheat growers. It is of the essence of regulation that it lays a restraining hand on the self-interest of the regulated and that advantages from the regulation commonly fall to others. The conflicts of economic interest between the regulated and those who advantage by it are wisely left under our system to resolution by the Congress under its more flexible and responsible legislative process. Such conflicts rarely lend themselves to judicial determination. And with the wisdom, workability, or fairness, of the plan of regulation we have nothing to do."

NOTE ON CIVIL RIGHTS AND FEDERALISM

After being associated with *Lochner*'s liberty of contract jurisprudence before 1937, federalism became most closely associated with *Plessy*'s jurisprudence of apartheid after 1937. Representing Clarendon County, South Carolina in *Brown I*, John W. Davis's main argument was that racial segregation was a matter of local custom to which the Court should defer. In *Brown II*, southern states insisted, from federalist premises, that federal trial judges should defer to local political processes in determining the manner and speed of school desegregation. When the Supreme Court rejected their stance in *Brown I* and *II*, the South denounced the Court's actions as violating the federal arrangement.[21] States rights became the shibboleth for die-hard opposition to racial integration and for the constitutional right of localities to choose apartheid. In contrast, the civil rights movement was associated with national human rights trumping localism.

This was just as apparent in the political as in the constitutional arena. Rejecting states rights arguments, Congress adopted the Civil Rights Act of 1964 to make the anti-discrimination norm applicable on a national and uniform basis. Title II of the new law prohibited specified public accommodations (such as motels and restaurants) from discriminating on the basis of race. The law was immediately challenged. The jurisdictional statement of Moreston Rolleston Jr., representing the Heart of Atlanta Motel, presented an odd amalgam of federalist and original meaning arguments. "George Washington," he argued, "did not intend that the new Constitution would provide any rights of personal freedom for his Negro slaves and certainly not the right to use the taverns and inns in which George Washington slept." Solicitor General Archibald Cox defended Title II as an exercise of Congress's Commerce Clause powers and rejected his advisers' plea to rely also on

---

[21] See Numan Bartley, *The Rise of Massive Resistance: Race and Politics in the South in the 1950's* (1969); Francis Wilhoit, *The Politics of Massive Resistance* (1973); Justin Driver, *Supremacies and the Southern Manifesto*, 92 Tex. L. Rev. 1053 (2014).

Congress's power under the Fourteenth Amendment (which is examined in Section 3 of this chapter).[22]

HEART OF ATLANTA MOTEL V. UNITED STATES
379 U.S. 241, 85 S.Ct. 348, 13 L.Ed.2d 258 (1964)

JUSTICE CLARK delivered the opinion of the Court.

[Title II of the Civil Rights Act of 1964 assures that "[a]ll persons shall be entitled to the full and equal enjoyment of the goods, services, facilities, privileges, advantages, and accommodations of any place of public accommodation," free of discrimination because of race (§ 201(a)). Section 201(b) lists four classes of business establishments, each of which "serves the public" and "is a place of public accommodation" within the meaning of the title "if its operations affect commerce, or if discrimination or segregation by it is supported by State action." The covered establishments include "(1) any inn, hotel, motel, or other establishment which provides lodging to transient guests." Section 201(c) declares that "any inn, hotel, motel, or other establishment which provides lodging to transient guests" affects commerce *per se*. The Heart of Atlanta was a 216-room motel located close to posh Peachtree Street in Atlanta, as well as major state and national highways. The motel refused to accommodate African Americans. Conceding that it fell within § 201, the motel sought an order invalidating Title II as applied to its business.]

The sole question posed is, therefore, the constitutionality of the Civil Rights Act of 1964 as applied to these facts. The legislative history of the Act indicates that Congress based the Act on § 5 and the Equal Protection Clause of the Fourteenth Amendment as well as its power to regulate interstate commerce. * * *

While the Act as adopted carried no congressional findings the record of its passage through each house is replete with evidence of the burdens that discrimination by race or color places upon interstate commerce. * * * This testimony included the fact that our people have become increasingly mobile with millions of people of all races travelling from State to State; that Negroes in particular have been the subject of discrimination in transient accommodations, having to travel great distances to secure the same; that often they have been unable to obtain accommodations and have had to call upon friends to put them up overnight, * * *; and that these conditions had become so acute as to require the listing of available lodging for Negroes in a special guidebook [the "Green Book"] which was itself "dramatic testimony to the difficulties" Negroes encounter in travel. * * *

---

[22] An excellent account of the litigation and the Justices' deliberation is Richard Cortner, *Civil Rights and Public Accommodations: The* Heart of Atlanta Motel *and* McClung *Cases* (2001).

[T]he determinative test of the exercise of power by the Congress under the Commerce Clause is simply whether the activity sought to be regulated is "commerce which concerns more States than one" and has a real and substantial relation to the national interest. Let us now turn to this facet of the problem.

That the "intercourse" of which the Chief Justice [Marshall] spoke [in *Gibbons*] included the movement of persons through more States than one was settled as early as 1849. * * * Nor does it make any difference whether the transportation is commercial in character. * * *

The same interest in protecting interstate commerce which led Congress to deal with segregation in interstate carriers and the white-slave traffic has prompted it to extend the exercise of its power to gambling, *Lottery Case*, * * * and to racial discrimination by owners and managers of terminal restaurants, *Boynton v. Virginia*, 364 U.S. 454 (1960).

That Congress was legislating against moral wrongs in many of these areas rendered its enactments no less valid. In framing Title II of this Act Congress was also dealing with what it considered a moral problem. But that fact does not detract from the overwhelming evidence of the disruptive effect that racial discrimination has had on commercial intercourse. It was this burden which empowered Congress to enact appropriate legislation, and, given this basis for the exercise of its power, Congress was not restricted by the fact that the particular obstruction to interstate commerce with which it was dealing was also deemed a moral and social wrong.

It is said that the operation of the motel here is of a purely local character. But, assuming this to be true, "[i]f it is interstate commerce that feels the pinch, it does not matter how local the operation which applies the squeeze." *United States v. Women's Sportswear Mfrs. Assn.*, 336 U.S. 460, 464 (1949). * * *

We, therefore, conclude that the action of the Congress in the adoption of the Act as applied here to a motel which concededly serves interstate travelers is within the power granted it by the Commerce Clause of the Constitution, as interpreted by this Court for 140 years. * * *

[**JUSTICE DOUGLAS**'s concurring opinion stated that he was reluctant to rest solely on the Commerce Clause because of his belief that the right of people to be free of state action that discriminates against them because of race "occupies a more protected position in our constitutional system than does the movement of cattle, fruit, steel and coal across state lines." He would also have relied upon § 5 of the Fourteenth Amendment. **JUSTICES BLACK** and **GOLDBERG** filed concurring opinions. All of these opinions also applied to the following case.]

Katzenbach v. McClung

379 U.S. 294 (1964)

Under Title II, any restaurant "principally engaged in selling food for consumption on the premises" was subject to the Act "if it serves or offers to serve interstate travelers or a substantial portion of the food which it serves * * * has moved in interstate commerce." This case involved Ollie's Barbecue, a Birmingham, Alabama, restaurant specializing in barbecued meats and homemade pies. Ollie's had a seating capacity of 220. It was located on a state highway, 11 blocks from an interstate. Although two-thirds of its employees were African American, Ollie's refused to serve African Americans. The district court found that, if forced to serve African Americans, the restaurant would lose a substantial amount of business.

A unanimous Court held that Title II constitutionally applied to Ollie's. **Justice Clark**'s opinion emphasized the "impressive array of testimony" during the 1963–64 congressional hearings "that discrimination in restaurants had a direct and highly restrictive effect upon interstate travel by Negroes. This resulted, it was said, because discriminatory practices prevent Negroes from buying prepared food served on the premises while on a trip * * *. This obviously discourages travel and obstructs interstate commerce for one can hardly travel without eating."

The Court also emphasized that "this testimony afforded ample basis for the conclusion that established restaurants in such areas sold less interstate goods because of the discrimination, * * * that business in general suffered and that many new businesses refrained from establishing there as a result of [the discrimination]." During the twelve months prior to the Civil Rights Act of 1964, Ollie's purchased about $150,000 worth of food, $69,683 of which was meat that had been shipped interstate. "It goes without saying that, viewed in isolation, the volume of food purchased by Ollie's Barbecue from sources supplied from out of state was insignificant when compared with the total foodstuffs moving in commerce. But, as our late Brother Jackson said for the Court in *Wickard v. Filburn*: 'That appellee's own contribution to the demand for wheat may be trivial by itself is not enough to remove him from the scope of federal regulation where, as here, his contribution, taken together with that of many others similarly situated, is far from trivial.'"

Justice Black concurred, with some hesitation about the breadth of the Court's opinion. "I recognize too that some isolated and remote lunchroom which sells only to local people and buys almost all its supplies in the locality may possibly be beyond the reach of the power of Congress to regulate commerce, just as such an establishment is not covered by the present Act." **Justices Douglas** and **Goldberg** also concurred separately, arguing that Congress also had authority to enact Title II under § 5 of the Fourteenth Amendment.

NOTE ON THE POST-NEW DEAL COMMERCE CLAUSE AND CIVIL RIGHTS DECISIONS

The post-*Darby* precedents can be read to demolish many of the old Commerce Clause limitations:

- The Tenth Amendment has been reduced to a "truism" (*Darby*), the dual federalism idea underlying *E.C. Knight* has been abandoned, and formal distinctions as to subject matter marginalized (*Heart of Atlanta*).

- Congress can regulate anything once it actually enters commerce, under the outlaws-of-commerce theory (*Lottery Case*), and even beforehand under the current-of-commerce theory (*Swift*).

- Congress can regulate intrastate activities by showing a substantial effect on interstate commerce (*Darby*), and to show such effect Congress can aggregate lots of little transactions (*Wickard*) and even search through trash cans and food bins (*McClung*).

In *Perez v. United States*, 402 U.S. 146 (1971), the Court upheld a federal statute prohibiting "extortionate credit transactions" (*i.e.*, loan-sharking enforced by threats of violence). Perez was convicted without any showing that his loan-sharking affected interstate commerce in any way, but the Court upheld the law as applied to him, because he was "clearly a *member of the class* which engages in 'extortionate credit transactions' * * *. Where the *class of activities* is regulated and that *class* is within the reach of federal power, the courts have no power 'to excise, as trivial, individual instances' of the class."

After *Perez*, was there any basis left for Commerce Clause review? Compare *Hodel v. Virginia Surface Mining & Reclamation Ass'n*, 452 U.S. 264 (1981) (deferring to congressional findings that linked the regulation to interstate commerce), with *United States v. Bass*, 404 U.S. 336 (1971) (interpreting a criminal statute to require a connection between the defendant's possession of a firearm was connected with interstate commerce). Do these precedents essentially negate the original meaning of Article I's enumerated powers precept?

UNITED STATES V. LOPEZ

514 U.S. 549, 115 S.Ct. 1624, 131 L.Ed.2d 626 (1995)

CHIEF JUSTICE REHNQUIST delivered the opinion of the Court.

[Alfonso Lopez, a twelfth-grade student, was arrested for carrying a concealed .38 caliber handgun. He was originally charged under Texas law with firearm possession on school premises. The state charges were dismissed after federal agents charged Lopez with violating the federal Gun-Free School Zones Act of 1990, 18 U.S.C. § 922(q), which made it a federal offense "for any individual knowingly to possess a firearm at a place that the individual knows, or has reasonable cause to believe, is a school zone." The term "school zone" was defined as "in, or on the grounds of, a public, parochial or private school" or "within a distance of 1,000 feet from the grounds of a public, parochial or private school." Lopez challenged the authority of Congress to legislate concerning local gun possession.]

We start with first principles. The Constitution creates a Federal Government of enumerated powers. See U.S. Const., Art. I, § 8. As James Madison wrote, "[t]he powers delegated by the proposed Constitution to the federal government are few and defined. Those which are to remain in the State governments are numerous and indefinite." *The Federalist* No. 45. This constitutionally mandated division of authority "was adopted by the Framers to ensure protection of our fundamental liberties." *Gregory v. Ashcroft*, 501 U.S. 452, 458 (1991). "Just as the separation and independence of the coordinate branches of the Federal Government serves to prevent the accumulation of excessive power in any one branch, a healthy balance of power between the States and the Federal Government will reduce the risk of tyranny and abuse from either front." *Ibid.*

[The Chief Justice then traced the history of the Court's analysis of Congress' power under the Commerce Clause: *Gibbons* as the foundational case; *E.C. Knight* and the other turn-of-the-century cases seeking principled limits, culminating with "the watershed case of *Jones & Laughlin*"; *Darby* and *Wickard*, "which ushered in an era of Commerce Clause jurisprudence that greatly expanded the previously defined authority of Congress."]

But even these modern-era precedents which have expanded congressional power under the Commerce Clause confirm that this power is subject to outer limits. In *Jones & Laughlin*, the Court warned that the scope of the interstate commerce power "must be considered in the light of our dual system of government and may not be extended so as to embrace effects upon interstate commerce so indirect and remote that to embrace them, in view of our complex society, would effectually obliterate the distinction between what is national and what is local and create a completely centralized government." Since that time, the Court has heeded that warning and undertaken to decide whether a rational basis existed for concluding that a regulated activity sufficiently affected interstate commerce. [Citing *Hodel, Perez, McClung, Heart of Atlanta Motel*.] * * *

Consistent with this structure, we have identified three broad categories of activity that Congress may regulate under its commerce power. First, Congress may regulate the use of the channels of interstate commerce. See, *e.g.*, *Darby*; *Heart of Atlanta Motel*. Second, Congress is empowered to regulate and protect the instrumentalities of interstate commerce, or persons or things in interstate commerce, even though the threat may come only from intrastate activities. See, *e.g.*, *Shreveport Rate Case*. Finally, Congress' commerce authority includes the power to regulate those activities having a substantial relation to interstate commerce, *Jones & Laughlin*, *i.e.*, those activities that substantially affect interstate commerce. [Section 922(q) could be sustained only under the third category.]

Even *Wickard*, which is perhaps the most far reaching example of Commerce Clause authority over intrastate activity, involved economic activity in a way that the possession of a gun in a school zone does not. [The Agricultural Adjustment Act of 1938 required small farmers like Roscue Filburn to curtail his production of wheat for home consumption.] The Act was designed to regulate the volume of wheat moving in interstate and foreign commerce in order to avoid surpluses and shortages, and concomitant fluctuation in wheat prices, which had previously obtained. [In sustaining the Act, the Court stressed that home-grown and-consumed wheat affected the interstate market price of wheat because its use obviated the need to buy that wheat on the market.]

Section 922(q) is a criminal statute that by its terms has nothing to do with "commerce" or any sort of economic enterprise, however broadly one might define those terms.[3] Section 922(q) is not an essential part of a larger regulation of economic activity, in which the regulatory scheme could be undercut unless the intrastate activity were regulated. It cannot, therefore, be sustained under our cases upholding regulations of activities that arise out of or are connected with a commercial transaction, which viewed in the aggregate, substantially affects interstate commerce.

Second, § 922(q) contains no jurisdictional element which would ensure, through case-by-case inquiry, that the firearm possession in question affects interstate commerce. For example, in *United States v. Bass*, 404 U.S. 336 (1971), the Court interpreted former 18 U.S.C. § 1202(a), which made it a crime for a felon to "receiv[e], posses[s], or transpor[t] in commerce or affecting commerce . . . any firearm." The Court interpreted the possession component of § 1202(a) to require an additional nexus to interstate commerce both because the statute was ambiguous and because "unless Congress conveys its purpose clearly, it will not be deemed to have significantly changed the federal-state balance." The *Bass* Court set aside the conviction because although the Government had

---

[3] Under our federal system, the " 'States possess primary authority for defining and enforcing the criminal law.' " When Congress criminalizes conduct already denounced as criminal by the States, it effects a " 'change in the sensitive relation between federal and state criminal jurisdiction.' " The Government acknowledges that § 922(q) "displace[s] state policy choices in . . . that its prohibitions apply even in States that have chosen not to outlaw the conduct in question." Brief for United States 29, n.18; see also Statement of President George Bush on Signing the Crime Control Act of 1990, 26 Weekly Comp. of Pres. Doc. 1944, 1945 (Nov. 29, 1990) ("Most egregiously, section [922(q)] inappropriately overrides legitimate state firearms laws with a new and unnecessary Federal law. The policies reflected in these provisions could legitimately be adopted by the States, but they should not be imposed upon the States by Congress").

demonstrated that Bass had possessed a firearm, it had failed "to show the requisite nexus with interstate commerce." The Court thus interpreted the statute to reserve the constitutional question whether Congress could regulate, without more, the "mere possession" of firearms. Unlike the statute in *Bass*, § 922(q) has no express jurisdictional element which might limit its reach to a discrete set of firearm possessions that additionally have an explicit connection with or effect on interstate commerce.

Although as part of our independent evaluation of constitutionality under the Commerce Clause we of course consider legislative findings, and indeed even congressional committee findings, regarding effect on interstate commerce, the Government concedes that "[n]either the statute nor its legislative history contain[s] express congressional findings regarding the effects upon interstate commerce of gun possession in a school zone." Brief for United States 5–6. We agree with the Government that Congress normally is not required to make formal findings as to the substantial burdens that an activity has on interstate commerce. But to the extent that congressional findings would enable us to evaluate the legislative judgment that the activity in question substantially affected interstate commerce, even though no such substantial effect was visible to the naked eye, they are lacking here.[4] * * *

The Government's essential contention, *in fine*, is that we may determine here that § 922(q) is valid because possession of a firearm in a local school zone does indeed substantially affect interstate commerce. The Government argues that possession of a firearm in a school zone may result in violent crime and that violent crime can be expected to affect the functioning of the national economy in two ways. First, the costs of violent crime are substantial, and, through the mechanism of insurance, those costs are spread throughout the population. Second, violent crime reduces the willingness of individuals to travel to areas within the country that are perceived to be unsafe. Cf. *Heart of Atlanta Motel*. The Government also argues that the presence of guns in schools poses a substantial threat to the educational process by threatening the learning environment. A handicapped educational process, in turn, will result in a less productive citizenry. That, in turn, would have an adverse effect on the Nation's economic well-being. As a result, the Government argues that Congress could rationally have concluded that § 922(q) substantially affects interstate commerce.

We pause to consider the implications of the Government's arguments. The Government admits, under its "costs of crime" reasoning, that

---

[4]   We note that on September 13, 1994, President Clinton signed into law the Violent Crime Control and Law Enforcement Act of 1994, Pub.L. 103–322, 108 Stat. 1796. Section 320904 of that Act amends § 922(q) to include congressional findings regarding the effects of firearm possession in and around schools upon interstate and foreign commerce. The Government does not rely upon these subsequent findings as a substitute for the absence of findings in the first instance.

Congress could regulate not only all violent crime, but all activities that might lead to violent crime, regardless of how tenuously they relate to interstate commerce. Similarly, under the Government's "national productivity" reasoning, Congress could regulate any activity that it found was related to the economic productivity of individual citizens: family law (including marriage, divorce, and child custody), for example. Under the theories that the Government presents in support of § 922(q), it is difficult to perceive any limitation on federal power, even in areas such as criminal law enforcement or education where States historically have been sovereign. Thus, if we were to accept the Government's arguments, we are hard-pressed to posit any activity by an individual that Congress is without power to regulate. * * *

To uphold the Government's contentions here, we would have to pile inference upon inference in a manner that would bid fair to convert congressional authority under the Commerce Clause to a general police power of the sort retained by the States. Admittedly, some of our prior cases have taken long steps down that road, giving great deference to congressional action. The broad language in these opinions has suggested the possibility of additional expansion, but we decline here to proceed any further. To do so would require us to conclude that the Constitution's enumeration of powers does not presuppose something not enumerated, and that there never will be a distinction between what is truly national and what is truly local. This we are unwilling to do.

[**JUSTICE KENNEDY**, with whom **JUSTICE O'CONNOR** joined, wrote a concurring opinion emphasizing that it was important for the Court to follow precedent in this arena, because Congress and the nation have relied on the evolving authority found in the Commerce Clause. "*Stare decisis* operates with great force in counseling us not to call in question the essential principles now in place respecting the congressional power to regulate transactions of a commercial nature. That fundamental restraint on our power * * * mandates against returning to the time when congressional authority to regulate undoubted commercial activities was limited by a judicial determination that those matters had an insufficient connection to an interstate system. Congress can regulate in the commercial sphere on the assumption that we have a single market and a unified purpose to build a stable national economy."]

[**JUSTICE THOMAS** wrote a concurring opinion. "In an appropriate case, I believe that we must further reconsider our 'substantial effects' test with an eye toward constructing a standard that reflects the text and history of the Commerce Clause without totally rejecting our more recent Commerce Clause jurisprudence." Drawing from eighteenth century dictionaries etc., Justice Thomas opined that "[a]t the time the original Constitution was ratified, 'commerce' consisted of selling, buying, and bartering, as well as transporting for these purposes." It was synonymous with trade and was used in contrast to productive activities such as manufacturing and agriculture. See *Federalist* Nos. 21, 36, 74; see U.S. Const., Art. I, § 9, cl. 6 (Port Preference Clause uses the term "Commerce" in a manner that suggests only trade, and not business more generally). Finally, "much if not all of Art. I, § 8 * * * would be surplusage if Congress had been given authority over matters that substantially affect interstate commerce. An interpretation of cl. 3 that makes the rest of § 8 superfluous simply cannot be correct."]

[The dissenting opinions of **JUSTICES STEVENS** and **SOUTER** have been omitted.]

JUSTICE BREYER, with whom **JUSTICE STEVENS, JUSTICE SOUTER,** and **JUSTICE GINSBURG** join, dissenting.

* * * I apply three basic principles of Commerce Clause interpretation. First, the power to "regulate Commerce . . . among the several States" encompasses the power to regulate local activities insofar as they significantly affect interstate commerce. See, *e.g., Gibbons; Wickard.* As the majority points out, the Court, in describing how much of an effect the Clause requires, sometimes has used the word "substantial" and sometimes has not. Compare, *e.g., Wickard* ("substantial economic effect") with *Hodel* ("affects interstate commerce").* * * I use the word "significant" because the word "substantial" implies a somewhat narrower power than recent precedent suggests. See, *e.g., Perez.*

Second, in determining whether a local activity will likely have a significant effect upon interstate commerce, a court must consider, not the effect of an individual act (a single instance of gun possession), but rather the cumulative effect of all similar instances (i.e., the effect of all guns possessed in or near schools). See, *e.g., Wickard.* * * *

Third, the Constitution requires us to judge the connection between a regulated activity and interstate commerce, not directly, but at one remove. Courts must give Congress a degree of leeway in determining the existence of a significant factual connection between the regulated activity and interstate commerce—both because the Constitution delegates the commerce power directly to Congress and because the determination requires an empirical judgment of a kind that a legislature is more likely than a court to make with accuracy. The traditional words "rational basis" capture this leeway. Thus, the specific question before us, as the Court recognizes, is not whether the "regulated activity sufficiently affected interstate commerce," but, rather, whether Congress could have had "*a rational basis*" for so concluding. * * *

* * * Could Congress rationally have found that "violent crime in school zones," through its effect on the "quality of education," significantly (or substantially) affects "interstate" or "foreign commerce"? 18 U.S.C.A. §§ 922(q)(1)(F), (G). As long as one views the commerce connection, not as

a "technical legal conception," but as "a practical one," *Swift & Co.*, the answer to this question must be yes. Numerous reports and studies—generated both inside and outside government—make clear that Congress could reasonably have found the empirical connection that its law, implicitly or explicitly, asserts.

[Justice Breyer compendiously documented the extent to which guns in and around schools have become widespread and have contributed to increased school violence, with a concomitant decline in the learning environment.] Having found that guns in schools significantly undermine the quality of education in our Nation's classrooms, Congress could also have found, given the effect of education upon interstate and foreign commerce, that gun-related violence in and around schools is a commercial, as well as a human, problem. Education, although far more than a matter of economics, has long been inextricably intertwined with the Nation's economy. [A quarter of America's economic growth in the early twentieth century was traceable to better education. The link between secondary education and business has become more important in recent decades, owing to increased emphasis on technology and service in the economy, global competition, and firm preferences for areas with good educational facilities.]

The economic links I have just sketched seem fairly obvious. Why then is it not equally obvious, in light of those links, that a widespread, serious, and substantial physical threat to teaching and learning *also* substantially threatens the commerce to which that teaching and learning is inextricably tied? That is to say, guns in the hands of six percent of inner-city high school students and gun-related violence throughout a city's schools must threaten the trade and commerce that those schools support. The only question, then, is whether the latter threat is (to use the majority's terminology) "substantial." And, the evidence of (1) the *extent* of the gun-related violence problem, (2) the *extent* of the resulting negative effect on classroom learning, and (3) the *extent* of the consequent negative commercial effects, when taken together, indicate a threat to trade and commerce that is "substantial." At the very least, Congress could rationally have concluded that the links are "substantial."

Specifically, Congress could have found that gun-related violence near the classroom poses a serious economic threat (1) to consequently inadequately educated workers who must endure low paying jobs, and (2) to communities and businesses that might (in today's "information society") otherwise gain, from a well-educated work force, an important commercial advantage of a kind that location near a railhead or harbor provided in the past. * * * Congress has written that "the occurrence of violent crime in school zones" has brought about a "decline in the quality of education" that "has an adverse impact on interstate commerce and the foreign commerce of the United States." 18 U.S.C.A. §§ 922(q)(1)(F), (G). The violence-related facts, the educational facts, and the economic facts, taken together, make this conclusion rational. And, because under our case law the sufficiency of the constitutionally necessary Commerce Clause link between a crime of violence and interstate commerce turns simply upon size or degree, those same facts make the statute constitutional. * * *

The majority's holding—that § 922 falls outside the scope of the Commerce Clause—creates three serious legal problems. First, the majority's holding runs contrary to modern Supreme Court cases that have upheld congressional actions despite connections to interstate or foreign commerce that are less significant than the effect of school violence. [Specifically, *Perez*, where Congress found a link between local loansharking, violence, and commerce, and *McClung*, where Congress found a link between prejudicial discrimination, interstate travel, and economic integration.]

The second legal problem the Court creates comes from its apparent belief that it can reconcile its holding with earlier cases by making a critical distinction between "commercial" and noncommercial "transaction[s]." That is to say, the Court believes the Constitution would distinguish between two local activities, each of which has an identical effect upon interstate commerce, if one, but not the other, is "commercial" in nature. As a general matter, this approach fails to heed this Court's earlier warning not to turn "questions of the power of Congress" upon "formula[s]" that would give "controlling force to nomenclature such as 'production' and 'indirect' and foreclose consideration of the actual effects of the activity in question upon interstate commerce." *Wickard*. See also *Darby* (overturning the Court's distinction between "production" and "commerce" in the child labor case, *Hammer v. Dagenhart*). * * * Although the majority today attempts to categorize *Perez, McClung*, and *Wickard* as involving intrastate "economic activity," the Courts that decided each of those cases did *not* focus upon the economic nature of the activity regulated. Rather, they focused upon whether that activity *affected* interstate or foreign commerce. In fact, the *Wickard* Court expressly held that Wickard's consumption of home grown wheat, "though it may not be regarded as commerce," could nevertheless be regulated—"whatever its nature"—so long as "it exerts a substantial economic effect on interstate commerce."

More importantly, if a distinction between commercial and noncommercial activities is to be made, this is not the case in which to make it. The majority clearly cannot intend such a distinction to focus narrowly on an act of gun possession standing by itself, for such a reading could not be reconciled with *McClung* or *Perez*—in each of those cases the specific transaction (the race-based exclusion, the use of force) was not itself "commercial." And, if the majority instead means to distinguish generally among broad categories of activities, differentiating what is educational from what is commercial, then, as a practical matter, the line becomes almost impossible to draw. Schools that teach reading, writing, mathematics, and related basic skills serve both social and commercial purposes, and one cannot easily separate the one from the other. American industry itself has been, and is again, involved in teaching. When, and to what extent, does its involvement make education commercial? * * * Even if one were to ignore these practical questions, why should there be a theoretical distinction between education, when it significantly benefits commerce, and environmental pollution, when it causes economic harm? * * *

The third legal problem created by the Court's holding is that it threatens legal uncertainty in an area of law that, until this case, seemed reasonably well settled. Congress has enacted many statutes (more than 100 sections of the United States Code), including criminal statutes (at least 25 sections), that use the words "affecting commerce" to define their scope, and other statutes that contain no jurisdictional language at all, see, e.g., 18 U.S.C. § 922(o)(1) (possession of machine guns). Do these, or similar, statutes regulate noncommercial activities? If so, would that alter the meaning of "affecting commerce" in a jurisdictional element? More importantly, in the absence of a jurisdictional element, are the courts nevertheless to take *Wickard* (and later similar cases) as inapplicable, and to judge the effect of a single noncommercial activity on interstate commerce without considering similar instances of the forbidden conduct? However these questions are eventually resolved, the legal uncertainty now created will restrict Congress' ability to enact criminal laws aimed at criminal behavior that, considered problem by problem rather than instance by instance, seriously threatens the economic, as well as social, well-being of Americans. * * *

NOTES ON LOPEZ AND THE COMMERCE CLAUSE'S NEW TEETH

1.   *Reconciling the Precedents?* How can *Lopez* be distinguished from *Perez*, *McClung*, and *Wickard*? The educational setting? That gun-toting is not as obviously "commercial" as loan-sharking, restaurants, and farming? The absence of congressional findings in the 1990 statute? The absence of a jurisdictional feature to the statute? Is there any answer to Justice Breyer's charge that the gun-control statute can be factually connected with commerce at least as persuasively as the statutes upheld in some earlier cases? His argument that there is no reason to believe that the Court's new test will work any better than the failed tests of the past?

Justice Thomas's concurring opinion can be read as suggesting that *Perez* and the other precedents should be read narrowly (perhaps some overruled), because a broad reading would press the Court's Commerce Clause jurisprudence further from the original meaning. Scholars are divided as to whether Justice Thomas is right about the original meaning of the Commerce Clause. Compare Grant E. Nelson & Robert J. Pushaw Jr., *Rethinking the*

Commerce Clause, 85 Iowa L. Rev. 1 (1999) (arguing that "commerce" meant any "gainful activity"), with Randy E. Barnett, *The Original Meaning of the Commerce Clause,* 68 U. Chi. L. Rev. 101 (2001) (finding that the framing discussions almost universally referred to "commerce" only in its narrow sense as "trade"). If Justice Thomas is correct, which precedents should be overruled?

2.   *Institutional Concerns.* Justice Souter worried that the new bout of line-drawing and litigation that *Lopez* will stimulate threatens a new *Lochner* era, in which the Court will trump democratic values without appropriate reference to a valid or even administrable constitutional principle. Justice Breyer argued that the commercial/noncommercial principle cannot be neutrally or predictably administered.[23] The majority believed that if such a weak statute were upheld against Commerce Clause attack, Congress would view itself as essentially unlimited, thereby usurping more and more state terrain and wasting the potential benefits of federalism. An opinion affirming this much of a congressional reach would also raise a *commitment problem*: Why should states continue to have enthusiasm for the federal arrangement if they see the federal government as unlimited? *Lopez* might be a "constitutional wake-up call," where the Court reminds Congress that it must attend to jurisdictional limits when it adopts legislation.[24] Under this view, the Court could still be lenient in reviewing congressional enactments but will not make up reasons for Congress, as Justice Breyer was willing to do.

3.   *Justifying National Regulation Under the Commerce Clause.* Professor Donald Regan criticizes the Court's post-New Deal decisions for failing to ask whether the regulation should or should not come from the federal government.[25] Given the presumptive state regulation of allocative and developmental projects such as education, police, and fire protection, he argues that national regulation of such issues must be affirmatively, and deliberately, justified along the lines suggested above, i.e., facilitating an efficient national market, creating public goods, and avoiding races to the bottom. Could *Darby*, *Wickard*, and *McClung* all be defended under this revised line of inquiry? If Justice Breyer's opinion had been written into the statute and its legislative history, would it have passed this test?

---

[23]   For an argument that the Court's line-drawing in Commerce Clause cases is no worse than its line-drawing in individual rights cases, see Lynn Baker & Ernest Young, *Federalism and the Double Standard of Judicial Review,* 51 Duke L.J. 75, 94–100 (2001).

[24]   See Jenna Bednar & William N. Eskridge Jr., *Steadying the Court's "Unsteady Path": A Theory of Judicial Enforcement of Federalism,* 68 S. Cal. L. Rev. 1447 (1995).

[25]   See Donald Regan, *How To Think About the Federal Commerce Power and Incidentally Rewrite* United States v. Lopez, 94 Mich. L. Rev. 554 (1995). For other scholarly discussions of *Lopez* and its implications, see, e.g., Ann Althouse, *Enforcing Federalism After* United States v. Lopez, 38 Ariz. L. Rev. 793 (1996); Steven G. Calabresi, *"A Government of Limited and Enumerated Powers": In Defense of* United States v. Lopez, 94 Mich. L. Rev. 752 (1995); Symposium, 46 Case Western Res. L. Rev. 633 (1996).

PROBLEM 7-3:
THE REACH OF COMMERCE CLAUSE POWER AFTER LOPEZ

(a) *Medical Marijuana.* Angel Raich, a California resident suffering from serious medical conditions, grows and uses marijuana for medical purposes, as allowed by state law. Federal agents seize Raich's cannabis plants, because even their private production violates the Controlled Substances Act (CSA). The California law does not protect Raich against prosecution if the CSA is a proper use of Congress's Commerce Clause power. After *Lopez*, does Congress have the authority to regulate private production of marijuana? For the *[yes]* Supreme Court's post-*Lopez* answer, see *Gonzales v. Raich*, 545 U.S. 1 (2005).

(b) *Partial Birth Abortion.* Congress enacted the Partial Birth Abortion Act of 2003, P.L. 108–105: "Any physician who, in or affecting interstate or foreign commerce, knowingly performs a partial-birth abortion and thereby kills a human fetus shall be fined under this title or imprisoned not more than 2 years, or both." The Supreme Court rejected a constitutional privacy challenge to the law. *Gonzales v. Carhart*, 523 U.S. 124 (2007) (Chapter 5, § 2). *[no?]* After *Lopez*, does Congress have Commerce Clause power to enact such a law?

(c) *Compulsory Health Insurance.* Congress enacts a law barring health insurance providers from denying coverage to applicants because of preexisting conditions. These consumer-protection rules are expensive—so Congress also includes a requirement that most Americans must secure health insurance coverage. (This increases the insured pool enough to cushion the health insurance companies against the costs of the new consumer-protective rules.) Congress is acting under its Commerce Clause (and Necessary and Proper Clause) authority. Is forcing Americans to purchase a product a constitutional exercise of Congress's Article I authority? See *National Federation of Indep.* *[yes]* *Business v. Sebelius*, 567 U.S. 519 (2012) (§ 5 of this chapter).

SECTION 3. CONGRESSIONAL AUTHORITY TO PROMOTE CIVIL RIGHTS

After *Lopez*, Congress was on notice that the Commerce Clause no longer served as the source of a virtually limitless national police power. *Heart of Atlanta* and *McClung* are probably safe from post-*Lopez* reconsideration, as both deal with the refusal to enter into a commercial transaction (renting a hotel room, buying food in a restaurant). But other civil rights measures may lack this obvious economic connection and so might not be defensible under the Commerce Clause. Natural sources of congressional power for civil rights legislation are the enforcement provisions of the Reconstruction Amendments (§ 2 of the Thirteenth and Fifteenth Amendments and § 5 of the Fourteenth Amendment). A limit upon congressional power is the Eleventh Amendment, which, as interpreted by the Court, sometimes forbids Congress from authorizing a suit by a private party against a state. This section examines such civil rights laws in chronological order, starting with the post-Civil War statutes, then turning to the major cases that arose under the Voting Rights Act and later enactments. We end with the Court's consideration of the Violence Against Women Act, where Commerce Clause and civil-rights-enforcement rationales were both invoked in defense of the statute.

A. CONGRESSIONAL AUTHORITY VESTED BY THE RECONSTRUCTION AMENDMENTS

Recall the discussion of the adoption of the Reconstruction Amendments following the Civil War in Chapter 1, § 4 and Chapter 2, § 1. Read § 2 of the Thirteenth and Fifteenth Amendments and § 5 of the Fourteenth Amendment carefully. What should it mean for Congress "to enforce" these provisions "by appropriate legislation"?

In 1866, when only the Thirteenth Amendment had been ratified, Congress enacted the Civil Rights Act of 1866. In addition to providing criminal penalties for the deprivation of federal rights under color of state law, the statute, as currently codified, contains two important protections. 42 U.S.C. § 1981(a) provides: "All persons within the jurisdiction of the United States shall have the same right in every State and Territory to make and enforce contracts, to sue, be parties, give evidence, and to the full and equal benefit of all laws and proceedings for the security of persons and property as is enjoyed by white citizens." 42 U.S.C. § 1982 sets forth similar civil rights "to inherit, purchase, lease, sell, hold, and convey real and personal property." Serious questions were raised concerning whether the 1866 statute was within Congress's enumerated legislative power under § 2 of the Thirteenth Amendment.

Much of the impetus for the Fourteenth Amendment was to make certain that the 1866 Act was constitutional—and even more so, to protect those rights by constitutional text so that they would not be subject to repeal by a later Congress. Read § 1 of the Fourteenth Amendment and compare it to the language of the 1866 Act. The Framers of the Fourteenth Amendment viewed Congress, through the enactment of legislation pursuant to § 5, and not the courts, through the interpretation of § 1, as the primary institutional enforcement of the Amendments.[26] Indeed, Congress adopted new civil rights measures in 1870 and 1871. The latter provided a federal cause of action for violations of federal rights by state officers. Now codified as 42 U.S.C. § 1983, this important provision states:

> Every person who, under color of any statute, ordinance, regulation, custom, or usage, of any State or Territory, subjects, or causes to be subjected, any citizen of the United States or other persons with the jurisdiction thereof to the deprivation of any rights, privileges or immunities secured by the Constitution and

---

[26] See, e.g., Steven Engel, Note, *The* McCulloch *Theory of the Fourteenth Amendment:* City of Boerne v. Flores *and the Original Understanding of Section 5*, 109 Yale L.J. 115 (1999).

laws, shall be liable to the person injured in an action at law, suit in equity, or other proper proceeding for redress.[27]

The last federal civil rights statute adopted during Reconstruction, the Civil Rights Act of 1875, provided that "all persons within the jurisdiction of the United States," regardless of "race or color," should without discrimination enjoy any and all public accommodations, such as inns and restaurants. Violation of the statute was a misdemeanor, and persons whose rights were violated could recover $500 for every offense.

THE CIVIL RIGHTS CASES
109 U.S. 3, 3 S.Ct. 18, 27 L.Ed. 835 (1883)

JUSTICE BRADLEY delivered the opinion of the Court.

[It was conceded that Congress lacked any such power to pass the 1875 Act under Article I. The Court rejected an argument based on § 5 of the Fourteenth Amendment. The Court understood § 1 of the Amendment only to reach state action, not private action like that of the defendants in the case. (Recall the discussion of the state action doctrine in Chapter 3, § 2.) Accordingly, the Court reasoned, § 5's authorization of legislative power to enforce § 1 allows Congress] to adopt appropriate legislation for correcting the effects of such prohibited State law and State acts, and thus to render them effectually null, void, and innocuous. This is the legislative power conferred upon Congress, and this is the whole of it. It does not invest Congress with power to legislate upon subjects which are within the domain of State legislation; but to provide modes of relief against State legislation, or State action, of the kind referred to. It does not authorize Congress to create a code of municipal law for the regulation of private rights; but to provide modes of redress against the operation of State laws, and the action of State officers, executive or judicial, when these are subversive of the fundamental rights specified in the amendment. * * *

If this legislation is appropriate for enforcing the prohibitions of the amendment, it is difficult to see where it is to stop. Why may not Congress, with equal show of authority, enact a code of laws for the enforcement and vindication of all rights of life, liberty, and property? * * * The truth is, that the implication of a power to legislate in this manner is based upon the assumption that if the States are forbidden to legislate or act in a particular way on a particular subject, and power is conferred upon Congress to enforce the prohibition, this gives Congress power to legislate generally upon that subject, and not merely power to provide modes of redress against such State legislation or action. The assumption is certainly unsound. It is repugnant to the Tenth Amendment of the Constitution, which declares that powers not delegated to the United States by the

---

[27] An important additional remedy available to prevailing plaintiffs in § 1983 cases is the award of reasonable attorneys' fees. See 42 U.S.C. § 1988.

Constitution, nor prohibited by it to the States, are reserved to the States respectively or to the people. * * *

In this connection it is proper to state that civil rights, such as are guarantied by the Constitution against State aggression, cannot be impaired by the wrongful acts of individuals, unsupported by State authority in the shape of laws, customs, or judicial or executive proceedings. The wrongful act of an individual, unsupported by any such authority, is simply a private wrong, or a crime of that individual; an invasion of the rights of the injured party, it is true, whether they affect his person, his property, or his reputation; but if not sanctioned in some way by the State, or not done under State authority, his rights remain in full force, and may presumably be vindicated by resort to the laws of the State for redress. An individual cannot deprive a man of his right to vote, to hold property, to buy and to sell, to sue in the courts, or to be a witness or a juror; he may, by force or fraud, interfere with the enjoyment of the right in a particular case; * * * but, unless protected in these wrongful acts by some shield of State law or State authority, he cannot destroy or injure the right; he will only render himself amenable to satisfaction or punishment; and amenable therefor to the laws of the State where the wrongful acts are committed. Hence, in all those cases where the Constitution seeks to protect the rights of the citizen against discriminative and unjust laws of the State by prohibiting such laws, it is not individual offenses, but abrogation and denial of rights, which it denounces, and for which it clothes the Congress with power to provide a remedy. This abrogation and denial of rights, for which the States alone were or could be responsible, was the great seminal and fundamental wrong which was intended to be remedied. And the remedy to be provided must necessarily be predicated upon that wrong. It must assume that in the cases provided for, the evil or wrong actually committed rests upon some State law or State authority for its excuse and perpetration. * * *

By its own unaided force and effect [the Thirteenth Amendment] abolished slavery, and established universal freedom. Still, legislation may be necessary and proper to meet all the various cases and circumstances to be affected by it, and to prescribe proper modes of redress for its violation in letter or spirit. And such legislation may be primary and direct in its character; for the amendment is not a mere prohibition of State laws establishing or upholding slavery, but an absolute declaration that slavery or involuntary servitude shall not exist in any part of the United States.

It is true that slavery cannot exist without law, any more than property in lands and goods can exist without law; and, therefore, the Thirteenth Amendment may be regarded as nullifying all State laws which establish or uphold slavery. But it has a reflex character also, establishing and decreeing universal civil and political freedom throughout the United States; and it is assumed that the power vested in Congress to enforce the article by appropriate legislation, clothes Congress with power to pass all laws necessary and proper for abolishing all badges and incidents of slavery in the United States; and upon this assumption it is claimed that this is sufficient authority for declaring by law that all persons shall have equal accommodations and privileges in all inns, public conveyances, and places of amusement; the argument being, that the denial of such equal accommodations and privileges is, in itself, a subjection to a species of servitude within the meaning of the amendment. * * *

The only question * * * is, whether the refusal to any persons of the accommodations of an inn, or a public conveyance, or a place of public amusement, by an individual, and without any sanction or support from any State law or regulation, does inflict upon such persons any manner of servitude, or form of slavery, as those terms are understood in this country? Many wrongs may be obnoxious to the prohibitions of the Fourteenth Amendment which are not, in any just sense, incidents or elements of slavery. Such, for example, would be the taking of private property without due process of law; or allowing persons who have committed certain crimes (horse-stealing, for example) to be seized and hung by the *posse comitatus* without regular trial; or denying to any person, or class of persons, the right to pursue any peaceful avocations allowed to others. * * *

Now, conceding, for the sake of the argument, that the admission to an inn, a public conveyance, or a place of public amusement, on equal terms with all other citizens, is the right of every man and all classes of men, is it any more than one of those rights which the States by the Fourteenth Amendment are forbidden to deny to any person? And is the Constitution violated until the denial of the right has some State sanction or authority? Can the act of a mere individual, the owner of the inn, the public conveyance or place of amusement, refusing the accommodation, be justly regarded as imposing any badge of slavery or servitude upon the applicant, or only as inflicting an ordinary civil injury, properly cognizable by the laws of the State, and presumably subject to redress by those laws until the contrary appears?

After giving to these questions all the consideration which their importance demands, we are forced to the conclusion that such an act of refusal has nothing to do with slavery or involuntary servitude, and that if it is violative of any right of the party, his redress is to be sought under the laws of the State; or if those laws are adverse to his rights and do not protect him, his remedy will be found in the corrective legislation which Congress has adopted, or may adopt, for counteracting the effect of State laws, or State action, prohibited by the Fourteenth Amendment. It would be running the slavery argument into the ground to make it apply to every act of discrimination which a person may see fit to make as to the guests he will entertain, or as to the people he will take into his coach or cab or car, or admit to his concert or theater, or deal with in other matters of intercourse or business. Innkeepers and public carriers, by the laws of all the States, so far as we are aware, are bound, to the extent of their facilities, to furnish proper accommodation to all unobjectionable persons who in good faith apply for them. If the laws themselves make any unjust discrimination, amenable to the prohibitions of the Fourteenth Amendment, Congress has full power to afford a remedy under that amendment and in accordance with it.

When a man has emerged from slavery, and by the aid of beneficent legislation has shaken off the inseparable concomitants of that state, there must be some stage in the progress of his elevation when he takes the rank of a mere citizen, and ceases to be the special favorite of the laws, and when his rights as a citizen, or a man, are to be protected in the ordinary modes by which other men's rights are protected. There were thousands of free colored people in this country before the abolition of slavery, enjoying all the essential rights of life, liberty, and property the same as white citizens; yet no one, at that time, thought that it was any invasion of their personal status as freemen because they were not admitted to all the privileges enjoyed by white citizens, or because they were subjected to discriminations in the enjoyment of accommodations in inns, public conveyances, and places of amusement. Mere discriminations on account of race or color were not regarded as badges of slavery. * * *

JUSTICE HARLAN, dissenting.

* * * I do not contend that the Thirteenth Amendment invests Congress with authority, by legislation, to define and regulate the entire body of the civil rights which citizens enjoy, or may enjoy, in the several States. But I hold that since slavery, as the court has repeatedly declared, was the moving or principal cause of the adoption of that amendment, and since that institution rested wholly upon the inferiority, as a race, of those held in bondage, their freedom necessarily involved immunity from, and protection against, all discrimination against them, because of their race, in respect of such civil rights as belong to freemen of other races. Congress, therefore, under its express power to enforce that amendment, by appropriate legislation, may enact laws to protect that people against the deprivation, *because of their race*, of any civil rights granted to other freemen in the same State; and such legislation may be of a direct and primary character, operating upon States, their officers and agents, and, also, upon, at least, such individuals and corporations as exercise public functions and wield power and authority under the State.

[Justice Harlan then discussed cases holding that common carriers, inns, and places of public amusement have been given special privileges by the law and, under the common law, owe special duties to the public beyond those owed by other privately owned establishments.]

* * * Congress has not, in [this statute], entered the domain of State control and supervision. It does not assume to prescribe the general conditions and limitations under which inns, public conveyances, and places of public amusement, shall be conducted or managed. It simply declares, in effect, that since the nation has established universal freedom in this country, for all time, there shall be no discrimination, based merely upon race or color, in respect of the accommodations and advantages of public conveyances, inns, and places of public amusement.

I am of the opinion that such discrimination practised by corporations and individuals in the exercise of their public or quasi-public functions is a badge of servitude the imposition of which Congress may prevent under its power, by appropriate legislation, to enforce the Thirteenth Amendment. * * *

The assumption that [the Fourteenth Amendment] consists wholly of prohibitions upon State laws and State proceedings in hostility to its provisions, is unauthorized by its language. The first clause of the first section—"All persons born or naturalized in the United States, and subject to the jurisdiction thereof, are citizens of the United States, and of the State wherein they reside"—is of a distinctly affirmative character. In its application to the colored race, previously liberated, it created and granted, as well as citizenship of the United States, citizenship of the State in which they respectively resided. * * *

The citizenship thus acquired, by that race, in virtue of an affirmative grant from the nation, may be protected, not alone by the judicial branch of the government, but by Congressional legislation of a primary direct character; this, because the power of Congress is not restricted to the enforcement of prohibitions upon State laws or State action. It is, in terms distinct and positive, to enforce "the *provisions* of *this article*" of amendment; not simply those of a prohibitive character, but the provisions—*all* of the provisions—affirmative and prohibitive, of the amendment. It is, therefore, a grave misconception to suppose that the fifth section of the amendment has reference exclusively to express prohibitions upon State laws or State action. * * *

But what was secured to colored citizens of the United States—as between them and their respective States—by the national grant to them of State citizenship? With what rights, privileges, or immunities did this grant invest them? There is one, if there be no others—exemption from race discrimination in respect of any civil right belonging to citizens of the white race in the same State. * * * [S]uch must be their constitutional right, in their own State, unless the recent amendments be "splendid baubles," thrown out to delude those who deserved fair and generous treatment at the hands of the nation. Citizenship in this country necessarily imports at least equality of civil rights among citizens of every race in the same State.

It is fundamental in American citizenship that, in respect of such rights, there shall be no discrimination by the State, or its officers, or by individuals, or corporations exercising public functions or authority, against any citizen because of his race or previous condition of servitude. * * *

* * * I agree that government has nothing to do with social, as distinguished from technically legal, rights of individuals. * * * Whether one person will permit or maintain social relations with another is a matter with which government has no concern. * * * What I affirm is that no State, nor the officers of any State, nor any corporation or individual wielding power under State authority for the public benefit or the public convenience, can, consistently either with the freedom established by the fundamental law, or with that equality of civil rights which now belongs to every citizen, discriminate against freemen or citizens, in those rights, because of their race, or because they once labored under the disabilities of slavery imposed upon them as a race. * * *

My brethren say, that when a man has emerged from slavery, and by the aid of beneficent legislation has shaken off the inseparable concomitants of that State, there must be some stage in the progress of his elevation when he takes the rank of a mere citizen, and ceases to be the special favorite of the laws, and when his rights as a citizen, or a man, are to be protected in the ordinary modes by which other men's rights are protected. It is, I submit, scarcely just to say that the colored race has been the special favorite of the laws. * * * Today, it is the colored race which is denied, by corporations and individuals wielding public authority, rights fundamental in their freedom and citizenship. At some future time it may be that some other race will fall under the ban of racial discrimination. If the constitutional amendments be enforced, according to the intent with which, as I conceive, they were adopted, there cannot be, in this republic, any class of human beings in practical subjection to another class, with power in the latter to dole out to the former just such privileges as they may choose to grant. * * *

NOTES ON THE CIVIL RIGHTS CASES

1. *Relationship Between the Substantive and Enforcement Sections, Between Judicial and Congressional Power.* In *The Civil Rights Cases*, the majority narrowly construed § 1 of both the Thirteenth and Fourteenth Amendments (the former limited to the badges and incidents of slavery, the latter limited to state rather than private misconduct). Even if those are defensible interpretations, does it follow that the enforcement provisions of both amendments grant Congress no power to create statutory civil rights transcending those limitations? For example, is it unimaginable that *judicial* power to reach private conduct through constitutional interpretation should be so circumspect, but that *congressional* power could be more expansive?

Read the text of § 2 of the Thirteenth Amendment and of § 5 of the Fourteenth Amendment: Can the words be reasonably understood more broadly than the Court read them in *The Civil Rights Cases*? Where did Congress get those words? (Hint: *McCulloch* formulates the test for congressional authority under the Necessary and Proper Clause this way: "Let the end be legitimate, let it be within the scope of the constitution, and all means which are appropriate, which are plainly adapted to that end, which are not prohibited, but consist with the letter and spirit of the constitution, are constitutional.")

Even under this unitary view of judicial and congressional authority— under which Congress seems to have legislative authority only "to enforce" whatever the judiciary says § 1 of the amendments mean—the constitutionality of 42 U.S.C. § 1983 (the basic civil rights enforcement provision quoted earlier) is not in doubt. This statute simply provides commonplace legal remedies (damages, injunctive relief) for conduct that the judiciary defines as violating § 1 of the amendments and thus easily fits under congressional power to "enforce" the (judicially defined) amendments. In addition, note that the "under color of state law" element of § 1983 accommodates the Court's requirement of state action to trigger the Fourteenth Amendment.

2.   *Section 5 of the Fourteenth Amendment: From* The Civil Rights Cases *to* United States v. Guest. *The Civil Rights Cases* were decided after Reconstruction had ended and after the Compromise of 1877, in which the Republicans effectively abandoned the interests of the freed slaves to accommodate the resurgent whites in the South. In such a climate, Justice Bradley's opinion was a precursor to *Plessy*. Although decided more than a decade later, *Plessy* bears many similarities to *The Civil Rights Cases*: Both decisions denied any state responsibility for redressing private discrimination against the freed slaves, and both found Justice Harlan in solo dissent, arguing that the remedial agenda of Reconstruction was betrayed. The civil rights movement of the twentieth century challenged *Plessy* but neglected *The Civil Rights Cases*, largely because Congresses dominated by southern Democrats enacted no civil rights law between 1875 and 1957. Because *The Civil Rights Cases* had never been revisited, the Justice Department relied on Congress's spending and commerce powers to justify the 1964 Civil Rights Act, and the Solicitor General defended Title II in *Heart of Atlanta* and *McClung* only on Commerce Clause grounds. Within the Court, however, there were three Justices (Black, Douglas, Goldberg) prepared to overrule *The Civil Rights Cases*. (Ironically, the staunchest supporter of the precedent was Justice John Harlan, the grandson of the 1883 dissenter.) Was it appropriate, these Justices wondered, for the Court to uphold the nation's landmark civil rights legislation under Congress's Commerce Clause rather than Fourteenth Amendment authority?

In *United States v. Guest*, 383 U.S. 745 (1966), the Court ruled that § 5 authorized Congress to make it a crime for white supremacists to conspire to deprive African Americans of their civil rights. Justice Stewart's majority opinion rested upon the allegation that the defendants had acted in concert with state officials, thereby satisfying *The Civil Rights Cases* (liberally construed). But six Justices joined Justice Brennan's concurring statement that § 5 empowers Congress "to enact laws punishing *all* conspiracies to interfere with the exercise of Fourteenth Amendment rights, whether or not state officers or others acting under the color of state law are implicated in the conspiracy." *Id.* at 782 (Brennan, joined by Warren and Douglas); see *id.* at 762 (Clark, Black, and Fortas, joining the Brennan statement). Although *Guest* did not formally overrule *The Civil Rights Cases* as to Congress's § 5 powers, it did suggest the votes were there for such an overruling.

3. *Section 2 of the Thirteenth Amendment: From* The Civil Rights Cases *to* Jones v. Alfred Mayer. Unlike the Fourteenth, the Thirteenth Amendment reaches private activities. Like *Plessy*, *The Civil Rights Cases* took a narrow view of the rights recognized by § 1 of the Thirteenth Amendment and Congress's authority under § 2. In the early twentieth century, the Supreme Court recognized that the Thirteenth Amendment justified judicial relief and congressional legislation against "peonage" practices in the South, whereby poor people (typically people of color) became indentured to plantation owners to pay off debts owed them. E.g., *Bailey v. Alabama*, 219 U.S. 219 (1911). The Justice Department in the late 1930s and early 1940s asserted a broader federal power to attack private violence against as well as economic control over poor blacks in the South, but those efforts were stymied by southern influence in the New Deal and (ironically) by the Justice Department's focus on the anti-apartheid campaign under the Fourteenth Amendment after World War II. The Thirteenth Amendment lay in desuetude until the 1960s, when civil rights lawyers and the Justice Department sought to enforce the Civil Rights Act of 1866 against private parties. Their campaign led to the decision that follows.

Jones v. Alfred H. Mayer Co.

392 U.S. 409 (1968)

A part of the Civil Rights Act of 1866, now codified as 42 U.S.C. § 1982, provides: "All citizens of the United States shall have the same right, in every State and Territory, as is enjoyed by white citizens thereof to inherit, purchase, lease, sell, hold, and convey real and personal property." Plaintiffs, who were African American, contended that a real estate developer refused to sell them a home because of race. **Justice Stewart**'s opinion for the Court held that § 1982 constitutionally bars all racial discrimination, including private discrimination, in the sale or rental of property.

Unlike the Fourteenth Amendment, the Thirteenth Amendment's Enabling Clause vests Congress with the power to enact laws "direct and primary, operating upon the acts of individuals, whether sanctioned by State legislation or not." *The Civil Rights Cases*. "[T]he majority leaders in Congress—who were, after all, the authors of the Thirteenth Amendment— had no doubt that its Enabling Clause contemplated the sort of positive legislation that was embodied in the 1866 Civil Rights Act. Their chief spokesman, Senator Trumbull of Illinois, the Chairman of the Judiciary Committee, had brought the Thirteenth Amendment to the floor of the Senate in 1864. In defending the constitutionality of the 1866 Act, he argued[:] * * *

> * * * I have no doubt that under this provision * * * we may destroy all these discriminations in civil rights against the black man; and if we cannot, our constitutional amendment amounts to nothing. It was for that purpose that the second clause of that amendment was adopted, which says that Congress shall have authority, by appropriate legislation, to carry into effect the article prohibiting slavery. Who is to decide what that appropriate legislation is to be? The Congress of the United States; and it is for Congress to adopt such appropriate legislation as it may think proper, so that it be a means to accomplish the end.

"Surely Senator Trumbull was right. Surely Congress has the power under the Thirteenth Amendment rationally to determine what are the badges and the incidents of slavery, and the authority to translate that determination into effective legislation. Nor can we say that the determination Congress has made is an irrational one. For this Court recognized long ago that, whatever else they may have encompassed, the badges and incidents of slavery—its 'burdens and disabilities'—included restraints upon 'those fundamental rights which are the essence of civil freedom, namely, the same right . . . to inherit, purchase, lease, sell and convey property, as is enjoyed by white citizens.' *The Civil Rights Cases.* Just as the Black Codes, enacted after the Civil War to restrict the free exercise of those rights, were substitutes for the slave system, so the exclusion of Negroes from white communities became a substitute for the Black Codes. And when racial discrimination herds men into ghettos and makes their ability to buy property turn on the color of their skin, then it too is a relic of slavery.

"Negro citizens, North and South, who saw in the Thirteenth Amendment a promise of freedom—freedom to 'go and come at pleasure' and to 'buy and sell when they please'—would be left with 'a mere paper guarantee' if Congress were powerless to assure that a dollar in the hands of a Negro will purchase the same thing as a dollar in the hands of a white man. At the very least, the freedom that Congress is empowered to secure under the Thirteenth Amendment includes the freedom to buy whatever a white man can buy, the right to live wherever a white man can live. If Congress cannot say that being a free man means at least this much, then the Thirteenth Amendment made a promise the Nation cannot keep."

Justice Harlan (joined by Justice White) dissented.

NOTE ON ALFRED H. MAYER AND CONGRESS'S THIRTEENTH AMENDMENT POWER

Jones v. Alfred H. Mayer is a very aggressive reading of Congress's Thirteenth Amendment enforcement authority.[28] The case was decided in 1968, four years after *Heart of Atlanta* and *McClung*. Had the chronology been reversed, and *Alfred H. Mayer* was a precedent Congress could have considered in enacting Title II of the 1964 Civil Rights Act, should Congress have relied upon § 2 of the Thirteenth Amendment rather than (or in addition to) the commerce power? Contrast Title VII of the 1964 Act, which forbids private employment discrimination on such factors as race and gender—while the former might come within an expansive view of § 2 power, it is difficult to make the case for the latter.

NOTE ON THE VOTING RIGHTS ACT OF 1965

For a century, the promise of § 1 of the Fifteenth Amendment—that African Americans shall have access to voting without racial discrimination—remained largely unfulfilled. Large majorities of African-American citizens were effectively barred from voting by poll taxes, literacy tests that were applied in a discriminatory manner, social pressure and threats of violence, and administrative intransigence. Federal legislation adopted in 1957, 1960, and 1964 created and expanded the authority of the Attorney General to seek injunctive relief against racial voting discrimination and of the federal courts to provide relief. Litigation under these statutes had, however, been largely ineffectual, because it had proved too slow, too expensive, and too cumbersome, and because a decree outlawing a discriminatory device could easily be circumvented simply by adopting a different method of discrimination. E.g., *United States v. Mississippi*, 380 U.S. 128 (1965) (surveying the series of discriminatory measures, starting with literacy tests, that Mississippi whites used to block voters of color from exercising the franchise).[29]

Congress responded to this kind of evidence by adopting the Voting Rights Act of 1965, codified as amended at 42 U.S.C. § 1973 *et seq.* See Brian Landsberg, *Free at Last to Vote: The Alabama Origins of the Voting Rights Act* (2007). The Act had two essential strategies for jurisdictions having low minority voting rates: to remove barriers to registering and voting by racial

---

[28] Many scholars believe that the Court went well beyond the (state) conduct that Congress in 1866 was targeting. E.g., Barry Sullivan, *Historical Reconstruction: Reconstruction History and the Proper Scope of Section 1981*, 98 Yale L.J. 541, 546 n.36 (1989) (reviewing division among historians on this issue). Nonetheless, the Court stuck with the *Jones* approach in *Runyon v. McCrary*, 427 U.S. 160 (1976), which interpreted 42 U.S.C. § 1981, another provision derived from the 1866 Civil Rights Act, as reaching race discrimination in the making and enforcement of private contracts.

[29] For an example of discriminatory application of a "read and understand" requirement, see *United States v. Louisiana*, 225 F. Supp. 353, 384 (E.D. La. 1963) (3-judge court), *aff'd*, 380 U.S. 145 (1965). In one instance "FRDUM FOOF SPETGH" was an acceptable response from a white voter to the request to interpret the Louisiana Constitution's protection of freedom of speech, while intelligent analyses of much more difficult provisions were rejected by registrars when people of color tried to register.

minorities and then to protect them against future attempts to dilute their new voting power. Accordingly, the Act first outlawed or suspended "tests and devices" prerequisite to voting, such as literacy tests. Second, § 5 of the Act provided that no change in voting qualifications or procedures could be implemented without the prior determination of either the Attorney General or the United States District Court for the District of Columbia (*not* by the local district court that would ordinarily have jurisdiction over such matters) that the change did not have the purpose *and* would not have the effect of causing a retrogression in minority voting strength.

The Act was adopted eleven years before the Court decided *Washington v. Davis* (Chapter 3, § 1B), which held that, for equal protection purposes, facially neutral laws with disparate racial impact are unconstitutional only upon a showing that they are contaminated by discriminatory intent. By outlawing discriminatory effects even when discriminatory intent is not present, the Voting Rights Act might seem vulnerable to constitutional objection, as violating *The Civil Rights Cases* model by which congressional authority to adopt civil rights legislation pursuant to the enforcement clauses of the Reconstruction Amendments is limited by the judicial understanding of what the substantive provisions of those amendments outlaw. Watch for this problem as we proceed through these materials.

The provisions of the Voting Rights Act noted above did not apply nationwide. They reached only those jurisdictions that on November 1, 1964, maintained any "test or device" and had less than 50% of the voting-age population registered to vote or in which less than 50% of such persons voted in the presidential election of 1964. Although the coverage formula was written in neutral terms, the Act was designed to have, and did have, the effect of bringing the Deep South within its coverage. The 1965 Act was drafted as a temporary remedy, having a five-year life span.

South Carolina v. Katzenbach

383 U.S. 301 (1966)

In upholding the constitutionality of the Voting Rights Act against a facial challenge, **Chief Justice Warren** relied upon the *McCulloch* test for congressional power. The Court first concluded that the statute's remedies, which apply without the need for prior adjudication, were an appropriate response to the demonstrated ineffectiveness of case-by-case adjudication. Second, notwithstanding principles of federalism, the Act could constitutionally apply only to certain regions of the country in light of the "local evils" found there. Moving to the heart of the statute, the Court upheld the dual strategy of suspending "tests and devices" for five years and using federal preclearance to prevent erosion of the minority vote by new discriminatory techniques.

"South Carolina assails the temporary suspension of existing voting qualifications, reciting the rule laid down by *Lassiter v. Northampton County*

Bd. of Elections, 360 U.S. 45 [1959], that literacy tests and related devices are not in themselves contrary to the Fifteenth Amendment. In that very case, however, the Court went on to say, 'Of course a literacy test, fair on its face, may be employed to perpetuate that discrimination which the Fifteenth Amendment was designed to uproot.' * * *

"The Act suspends literacy tests and similar devices for a period of five years from the last occurrence of substantial voting discrimination. * * * Underlying [this approach] was the feeling that States and political subdivisions which had been allowing white illiterates to vote for years could not sincerely complain about 'dilution' of their electorates through the registration of Negro illiterates. Congress knew that continuance of the tests and devices in use at the present time, no matter how fairly administered in the future, would freeze the effect of past discrimination in favor of unqualified white registrants. Congress permissibly rejected the alternative of requiring a complete re-registration of all voters, believing that this would be too harsh on many whites who had enjoyed the franchise for their entire adult lives.

"The Act suspends new voting regulations pending scrutiny by federal authorities to determine whether their use would violate the Fifteenth Amendment. This may have been an uncommon exercise of congressional power, as South Carolina contends, but the Court has recognized that exceptional conditions can justify legislative measures not otherwise appropriate. Congress knew that some of the [covered States] had resorted to the extraordinary stratagem of contriving new rules of various kinds for the sole purpose of perpetuating voting discrimination in the face of adverse federal court decrees. Congress had reason to suppose that these States might try similar maneuvers in the future in order to evade the remedies for voting discrimination contained in the Act itself. Under the compulsion of these unique circumstances, Congress responded in a permissibly decisive manner."

KATZENBACH V. MORGAN

384 U.S. 641, 86 S.Ct. 1717, 16 L.Ed.2d 828 (1966)

JUSTICE BRENNAN delivered the opinion of the Court.

[Section 4(e) of the 1965 Act provided that no person who had completed the sixth grade in school in Puerto Rico in which the language of instruction was other than English could be denied the right to vote on account of inability to read or write English. This provision was aimed primarily at stopping New York City from using the New York state literacy test to prevent American citizens of Puerto Rican descent from voting. New York argued that because a court would not have invalidated the literacy requirement prohibited by § 4(e), Congress's Fourteenth Amendment authority did not reach such tests.]

* * * A construction of § 5 that would require a judicial determination that the enforcement of the state law precluded by Congress violated the Amendment, as a condition of sustaining the congressional enactment,

would depreciate both congressional resourcefulness and congressional responsibility for implementing the Amendment. It would confine the legislative power in this context to the insignificant role of abrogating only those state laws that the judicial branch was prepared to adjudge unconstitutional, or of merely informing the judgment of the judiciary by particularizing the "majestic generalities" of § 1 of the Amendment. * * *

By including § 5 the draftsmen sought to grant to Congress, by a specific provision applicable to the Fourteenth Amendment, the same broad powers expressed in the Necessary and Proper Clause, Art. I, § 8, cl. 18. * * * Thus the *McCulloch v. Maryland* standard is the measure of what constitutes "appropriate legislation" under § 5 of the Fourteenth Amendment. Correctly viewed, § 5 is a positive grant of legislative power authorizing Congress to exercise its discretion in determining whether and what legislation is needed to secure the guarantees of the Fourteenth Amendment. * * * 10

There can be no doubt that § 4(e) may be regarded as an enactment to enforce the Equal Protection Clause. Congress explicitly declared that it enacted § 4(e) "to secure the rights under the fourteenth amendment of persons educated in American-flag schools in which the predominant classroom language was other than English." * * * § 4(e) may be viewed as a measure to secure for the Puerto Rican community residing in New York nondiscriminatory treatment by government—both in the imposition of voting qualifications and the provision or administration of governmental services, such as public schools, public housing and law enforcement.

Section 4(e) may be readily seen as "plainly adapted" to furthering these aims of the Equal Protection Clause. The practical effect of § 4(e) is to prohibit New York from denying the right to vote to large segments of its Puerto Rican community. Congress has thus prohibited the State from denying to that community the right that is "preservative of all rights." This enhanced political power will be helpful in gaining nondiscriminatory treatment in public services for the entire Puerto Rican community. * * * It was well within congressional authority to say that this need of the Puerto Rican minority for the vote warranted federal intrusion upon any state interests served by the English literacy requirement. It was for Congress, as the branch that made this judgment, to assess and weigh the various conflicting considerations—the risk or pervasiveness of the discrimination in governmental services, the effectiveness of eliminating

---

10 Contrary to the suggestion of the dissent, § 5 does not grant Congress power to exercise discretion in the other direction and to enact "statutes so as in effect to dilute equal protection and due process decisions of this Court." We emphasize that Congress' power under § 5 is limited to adopting measures to enforce the guarantees of the Amendment; § 5 grants Congress no power to restrict, abrogate, or dilute these guarantees. Thus, for example, an enactment authorizing the States to establish racially segregated systems of education would not be—as required by § 5—a measure "to enforce" the Equal Protection Clause since that clause of its own force prohibits such state laws.

the state restriction on the right to vote as a means of dealing with the evil, the adequacy or availability of alternative remedies, and the nature and significance of the state interests that would be affected by the nullification of the English literacy requirement as applied to residents who have successfully completed the sixth grade in a Puerto Rican school. It is not for us to review the congressional resolution of these factors. It is enough that we be able to perceive a basis upon which the Congress might resolve the conflict as it did. There plainly was such a basis to support § 4(e) in the application in question in this case. Any contrary conclusion would require us to be blind to the realities familiar to the legislators.

* * * We are told that New York's English literacy requirement originated in the desire to provide an incentive for non-English speaking immigrants to learn the English language and in order to assure the intelligent exercise of the franchise. Yet Congress might well have questioned, in light of the many exemptions provided, and some evidence suggesting that prejudice played a prominent role in the enactment of the requirement, whether these were actually the interests being served. Congress might have also questioned whether denial of a right deemed so precious and fundamental in our society was a necessary or appropriate means of encouraging persons to learn English, or of furthering the goal of an intelligent exercise of the franchise. Finally, Congress might well have concluded that as a means of furthering the intelligent exercise of the franchise, an ability to read or understand Spanish is as effective as ability to read English for those to whom Spanish-language newspapers and Spanish-language radio and television programs are available to inform them of election issues and governmental affairs. * * * [I]t is enough that we perceive a basis upon which Congress might predicate a judgment that the application of New York's English literacy requirement to deny the right to vote to a person with a sixth grade education in Puerto Rican schools in which the language of instruction was other than English constituted an invidious discrimination in violation of the Equal Protection Clause.

There remains the question whether the congressional remedies adopted in § 4(e) constitute means which are not prohibited by, but are consistent "with the letter and spirit of the constitution." The only respect in which appellees contend that § 4(e) fails in this regard is that the section itself works an invidious discrimination in violation of the Fifth Amendment by prohibiting the enforcement of the English literacy requirement only for those educated in American-flag schools (schools located within United States jurisdiction) in which the language of instruction was other than English, and not for those educated in schools beyond the territorial limits of the United States in which the language of instruction was also other than English. This is not a complaint that Congress, in enacting § 4(e), has unconstitutionally denied or diluted anyone's right to vote but rather that Congress violated the Constitution by not extending the relief effected in § 4(e) to those educated in non-American-flag schools. [The Court concluded that failing to extend relief to those educated in non-American-flag schools did not violate the equal protection component of the Fifth Amendment because reform measures such as § 4(e) may take a one-step-at-a-time approach.]

[The separate statement of **JUSTICE DOUGLAS** is omitted.]

JUSTICE HARLAN, with whom **JUSTICE STEWART** joins, dissenting.

When recognized state violations of federal constitutional standards have occurred, Congress is of course empowered by § 5 to take appropriate remedial measures to redress and prevent the wrongs. But it is a judicial question whether the condition with which Congress has thus sought to deal is in truth an infringement of the Constitution, something that is the necessary prerequisite to bringing the § 5 power into play at all. * * *

* * * The question here is not whether the statute is appropriate remedial legislation to cure an established violation of a constitutional command, but whether there has in fact been an infringement of that constitutional command. * * * That question is one for the judicial branch ultimately to determine. Were the rule otherwise, Congress would be able to qualify this Court's constitutional decisions under the Fourteenth and Fifteenth Amendments, let alone those under other provisions of the Constitution, by resorting to congressional power under the Necessary and Proper Clause. In view of this Court's holding in *Lassiter* that an English literacy test is a permissible exercise of state supervision over its franchise, I do not think it is open to Congress to limit the effect of that decision as it has undertaken to do by § 4(e). In effect the Court reads § 5 of the Fourteenth Amendment as giving Congress the power to define the *substantive* scope of the Amendment. If that indeed be the true reach of § 5, then I do not see why Congress should not be able as well to exercise its § 5 "discretion" by enacting statutes so as in effect to dilute equal protection and due process decisions of this Court. In all such cases there is room for reasonable men to differ as to whether or not a denial of equal protection or due process has occurred, and the final decision is one of judgment. Until today this judgment has always been one for the judiciary to resolve.

I do not mean to suggest in what has been said that a legislative judgment of the type incorporated in § 4(e) is without any force whatsoever. Decisions on questions of equal protection and due process are based not on abstract logic, but on empirical foundations. To the extent "legislative facts" are relevant to a judicial determination, Congress is well equipped to investigate them, and such determinations are of course entitled to due respect. In *South Carolina v. Katzenbach* such legislative findings were made to show that racial discrimination in voting was actually occurring. * * *

But no such factual data provide a legislative record supporting § 4(e)[9] by way of showing that Spanish-speaking citizens are fully as capable of making informed decisions in a New York election as are English-speaking citizens. * * *

Thus, we have here not a matter of giving deference to a congressional estimate, based on its determination of legislative facts, bearing upon the validity *vel non* of a statute, but rather what can at most be called a legislative announcement that Congress believes a state law to entail an unconstitutional deprivation of equal protection. * * *

NOTE ON THE REMEDIAL VS. THE SUBSTANTIVE THEORY OF CONGRESS'S ENFORCEMENT POWER

Consider a distinction between a *remedial* theory and a *substantive* theory of § 5 power. Under the former, the judiciary has a monopoly on the substantive meaning of § 1 of the amendment, such that Congress may provide statutory remedies only for violations of § 1 as it is judicially understood. Under the latter, Congress and the Court have a shared interpretive power over the substantive meaning of § 1, such that, for example, Congress may enact legislation under § 5 providing remedies for what Congress believes are equal protection violations even if the Court would not read the Equal Protection Clause that way. Justice Harlan, in dissent, argued that the logic of the majority opinion would allow Congress to dilute rights as easily as expand them. The majority's response, in footnote 10, is that Congress may only expand, not contract, constitutional rights. The footnote is sometimes called the "one-way-ratchet" theory of congressional power (§ 5 is a tool that allows Congress to "turn" § 1 meaning in only one direction). Is footnote 10 defensible? Can the substantive theory be defended under the theories of constitutional interpretation earlier examined: text and original meaning (Chapter 2, § 3A); representation-reinforcement (Chapter 2, § 3B)?

Oregon v. Mitchell

400 U.S. 112 (1970)

A fractured Court, with no majority opinion, upheld one key provision and struck down another of the Voting Rights Act Amendments of 1970. First, the amendments expanded the suspension of literacy tests beyond the jurisdictions covered by the original Voting Rights Act to include all state and national elections throughout the United States. The Court unanimously held that the nationwide ban on such tests was constitutional, but no opinion commanded a majority of the Court. **Justice Douglas** opined that the statute was constitutional under § 5 of the Fourteenth Amendment; the other eight Justices, in four separate opinions, concluded that it was appropriate legislation under § 2 of the Fifteenth Amendment. The Justices all stressed

---

[9]   There were no committee hearings or reports referring to this section, which was introduced from the floor during debate on the full Voting Rights Act.

that Congress had evidence before it showing that literacy tests reduced voter participation in a discriminatory manner. **Justice Harlan** said: "Despite the lack of evidence of specific instances of discriminatory application or effect, Congress could have determined that racial prejudice is prevalent throughout the Nation, and that literacy tests unduly lend themselves to discriminatory application, either conscious or unconscious. This danger of violation of § 1 of the Fifteenth Amendment was sufficient to authorize the exercise of congressional power under § 2." Harlan added: "[t]he legislative history of the Voting Rights Act Amendments contains sufficient evidence to this effect, if any be needed."

Section 302 of the amendments lowered the minimum age for voting in state and national elections from 21 to 18. **Justice Black** concluded that the statute was constitutional as applied to federal, but not state, elections. Although he wrote only for himself, his conclusion controlled the outcome, because the other eight justices were evenly divided. Four Justices (**Burger, Harlan, Stewart, Blackmun**) would have struck down § 302 in its entirety. In *Morgan,* **Justice Stewart** reasoned, the "Court upheld the statute on two grounds: that Congress could conclude that enhancing the political power of the Puerto Rican community by conferring the right to vote was an appropriate means of remedying discriminatory treatment in public services; and that Congress could conclude that the New York statute was tainted by the impermissible purpose of denying the right to vote to Puerto Ricans. But it is necessary to go much further to sustain § 302. The state laws that it invalidates do not invidiously discriminate against any discrete and insular minority. Unlike the statute considered in *Morgan,* § 302 is valid only if Congress has the power not only to provide the means of eradicating situations that amount to a violation of the Equal Protection Clause, but also to determine as a matter of substantive constitutional law what situations fall within the ambit of the clause."

Justices Douglas, Brennan, White, and **Marshall** would have upheld § 302 in all respects. The *joint opinion* of the latter three argued: "We believe there is a serious question whether a statute granting the franchise to citizens 21 and over while denying it to those between the ages of 18 and 21 could * * * withstand present scrutiny under the Equal Protection Clause. Regardless of the answer to this question, however, it is clear to us that proper regard for the special function of Congress in making determinations of legislative fact compels this Court to respect those determinations unless they are contradicted by evidence far stronger than anything that has been adduced in these cases."

The joint opinion noted that equal protection review by judges started with "the presumption that the legislature has, as it should, acted within constitutional limitations." But "this limitation on judicial review of state legislative classifications is a limitation stemming, not from the Fourteenth Amendment itself, but from the nature of judicial review," and the institutional limitation of courts, which are "an inappropriate forum for the determination of complex factual questions of the kind so often involved in constitutional adjudication. * * *

"Limitations stemming from the nature of the judicial process, however, have no application to Congress. * * * Should Congress, pursuant to [§ 5 of the Fourteenth Amendment], undertake an investigation in order to determine whether the factual basis necessary to support a state legislative discrimination actually exists, it need not stop once it determines that some reasonable men could believe the factual basis exists. Section 5 empowers Congress to make its own determination on the matter. See *Morgan*. It should hardly be necessary to add that if the asserted factual basis necessary to support a given state discrimination does not exist, § 5 of the Fourteenth Amendment vests Congress with power to remove the discrimination by appropriate means." Judges ought to uphold such congressional findings and conclusions so long as legislators "have a rational basis for finding a chosen regulatory scheme necessary" to remedy a constitutional problem.

Justice Harlan responded to the joint opinion of Justices Brennan, Marshall, and White. "To allow a simple majority of Congress to have final say on matters of constitutional interpretation is * * * fundamentally out of keeping with the constitutional structure," which required deference to state legislatures as to matters of voting qualification. "The sole distinction between Congress and the Court in this regard is that Congress, being an elective body, presumptively has popular authority for the value judgment it makes. But since the state legislature has a like authority, this distinction between Congress and the judiciary falls short of justifying a congressional veto on the state judgment. The perspectives and values of national legislators on the issue of voting qualifications are likely to differ from those of state legislators, but I see no reason *a priori* to prefer those of the national figures, whose collective decision, applying nationwide, is necessarily less able to take account of peculiar local conditions. Whether one agrees with this judgment or not, it is the one expressed by the Framers in leaving voter qualifications to the States."

NOTE ON THE VOTING RIGHTS ACT'S EFFECTS TEST

The Voting Rights Act requires covered jurisdictions to submit electoral changes made after 1964 for preclearance either to the Department of Justice or to the federal District Court for the District of Columbia. Under the Act, preclearance is granted only if the jurisdiction proves the absence of both discriminatory intent and discriminatory effect. Rome, Georgia, persuaded the district court that a variety of electoral changes (described in note 1 following this case) had not been discriminatorily motivated. The court nonetheless denied preclearance because the changes would have a discriminatory impact.

On the same day the Court decided *Mobile v. Bolden*, 446 U.S. 55 (1980), that the Fifteenth Amendment only reached intentional discrimination, the Court ruled in ***City of Rome v. United States***, 446 U.S. 156 (1980), that Congress appropriately used its § 2 power to outlaw voting practices that are discriminatory in effect. **Justice Marshall**'s opinion for the Court relied on

South Carolina v. Katzenbach, which the Court read to "make[ ] clear that Congress may, under the authority of § 2 of the Fifteenth Amendment, prohibit state action that, though in itself not violative of § 1, perpetuates the effects of past discrimination." Accord, *Katzenbach v. Morgan; Oregon v. Mitchell*, both of which upheld Voting Rights Act provisions regulating discriminatory effects.

"It is clear, then, that under § 2 of the Fifteenth Amendment Congress may prohibit practices that in and of themselves do not violate § 1 of the Amendment, so long as the prohibitions attacking racial discrimination in voting are 'appropriate[.]' In the present case, we hold that the Act's ban on electoral changes that are discriminatory in effect is an appropriate method of promoting the purposes of the Fifteenth Amendment, even if it is assumed that § 1 of the Amendment prohibits only intentional discrimination in voting. Congress could rationally have concluded that, because electoral changes by jurisdictions with a demonstrable history of intentional racial discrimination in voting create the risk of purposeful discrimination, it was proper to prohibit changes that have a discriminatory impact."

Justice Rehnquist dissented, on the ground that if Congress wanted to regulate hard-to-prove discriminatory intents, it may shift the burden of proof in such cases. But Rome had shown that it did not have a discriminatory intent, and so Congress had no authority to "enforce" the Fifteenth Amendment in that case. "Absent other circumstances, it would be a topsy-turvy judicial system which held that electoral changes which have been affirmatively proved to be permissible under the Constitution nonetheless violate the Constitution." Consider three different responses the majority might have made to Justice Rehqnuist's point:

1. *Remedial theory: Congress may paint with a broad brush and adopt a prophylactic rule.* Where there's smoke there's fire, the adage goes. By analogy, where there are discriminatory effects, we might well worry whether there is also discriminatory intent, especially because such intent is hard to prove. In some situations, we might adopt a broad, prophylactic rule that forbids smoke-causing behavior that often (although not always) is related to the threat of fire. This may explain how the Court in *South Carolina* and *Oregon* upheld a federal statutory ban on literacy tests even though, under *Lassiter*, literacy tests are not unconstitutional per se. Indeed, the electoral changes made in Rome were to replace a city commission where each commissioner had to reside in the ward from which he or she was elected and could win with a plurality of the vote, with a commission where three commissioners were elected from each of just three wards and had to win by a majority. Although the district court found that these changes were not improperly motivated, its opinion suggested room for debate.[30] The main problem with a prophylactic approach is overbreadth: Should Congress be

---

[30] The district court was suspicious that the new voting rules were adopted right after the VRA went into effect, were a well-known mechanism for diluting the black vote, and were supported by a false assertion about the requirements of Georgia voting law. On the other hand, the city persuaded the district court of its clean hands through sworn statements of participants at every stage in this process that their actions were not motivated by race.

authorized to interfere with the sovereignty of the states by prohibiting quite a bit of constitutional state action (action that produces discriminatory effects in voting but not for reasons of discriminatory intent) so that it can prevent a largely unmeasurable degree of unconstitutional state action (action that produces such effects because of such intent)?

2. *Substantive theory: Congress may update the protections of the Civil War Amendments.* This approach would build upon *Morgan*. But by 1980, a Court majority appointed by Presidents Nixon and Ford would have been skeptical of this approach, for the reasons articulated by Justices Harlan and Stewart.

3. *Legal process theory: Congress is the most competent institution to enforce an "underenforced constitutional norm."* The joint opinion in *Oregon v. Mitchell* (Brennan, Marshall, and White) suggested that the anti-discrimination rule of the Fourteenth and Fifteenth Amendments was an "underenforced constitutional norm"—a norm that the judiciary will enforce only narrowly because of institutional limitations.[31] The Court in both *Washington v. Davis* and *Mobile v. Bolden* was reluctant to give full force to the anti-discrimination rule when plaintiffs could not show that the racially discriminatory effects were the intended result of state action. Because constitutionalizing a "discriminatory effects" approach would create a permanent right that not only burdened states but also could prove hard for judges to administer, the Court was reluctant to enforce the Fifteenth Amendment in that way. By engaging in its own factfinding and deliberation, which would consider the interests of the states as well as minority persons and could fine-tune the rights and remedies involved so that they would be easier for courts to administer, Congress can provide precisely the kind of legitimacy and certitude that the Court, as an institution, cannot.

In the abstract, which of the foregoing theories makes the best constitutional sense of the precedents from *South Carolina* to *Rome*? Now, apply your theory to the next problem.

PROBLEM 7-4:
LEGISLATIVE FACTFINDING: FOURTEENTH AMENDMENT "PERSONS"

In *Roe v. Wade* (Chapter 5, § 4B), which struck down state laws outlawing abortion as violating the Fourteenth Amendment, the Court stated that it did not need to "resolve the difficult question of when life begins." Suppose that Congress holds extensive hearings and, in response, adopts statutory findings that "present-day scientific evidence indicates a significant likelihood that actual human life exists from conception" and then legislates, under its § 5 power, "that for the purpose of enforcing the obligation of the States under the fourteenth amendment not to deprive persons of life without due process of

---

[31] See Lawrence Gene Sager, *Fair Measure: The Legal Status of Underenforced Constitutional Norms*, 91 Harv. L. Rev. 1212 (1978).

law, human life shall be deemed to exist from conception, without regard to race, sex, age, health, defect, or condition of dependency; and for this purpose 'person' shall include all human life as defined herein." Is the statute constitutional? How would you vote, based upon the theory you just adopted in connection with *Rome v. United States*?

NOTE ON THE RELIGIOUS FREEDOM RESTORATION ACT OF 1993

As Problem 7-4 illustrates, Congress's authority under the Fourteenth Amendment is not limited to remedying race discrimination. Congress's most sweeping legislation along these lines was a statute enforcing the Free Exercise Clause. In many ways, the Free Exercise Clause raises similar questions to those that arise under the Equal Protection Clause, for both clauses are fatal to state laws that discriminate on the basis of race or religion on their face or by clear legislative intent—but neither has been applied to invalidate laws that have a discriminatory impact that was not intended.

Several Supreme Court precedents had suggested that the Free Exercise Clause might subject to strict scrutiny some facially neutral regulations that inhibited religious freedom. In *Employment Division, Department of Human Resources v. Smith* (Chapter 6, § 7), however, a closely divided Supreme Court held that, at least in the context of criminal statutes, a facially neutral regulation of conduct that incidentally inhibits a religious practice is not subject to any stringent constitutional standard.

Smith met with criticism from religious and civil libertarian communities. Congress responded by passing the Religious Freedom Restoration Act (RFRA) of 1993, 42 U.S.C. §§ 2000bb–2000bb–4. Under RFRA, facially neutral laws that "substantially burden a person's exercise of religion" are legal only if the Government demonstrates "that application of the burden to the person" is "in furtherance of a compelling governmental interest" and "is the least restrictive means of furthering that compelling governmental interest." Congress invoked its legislative authority under § 5 of the Fourteenth Amendment to impose this approach upon state and local governments. The Free Exercise Clause applies to the states through the Due Process Clause of the Fourteenth Amendment (see Chapter 5, § 1), so Congress maintained that it was applying RFRA to state and local governments to enforce that Fourteenth Amendment provision. How should the Supreme Court have responded to this legislative gambit?

CITY OF BOERNE V. FLORES
521 U.S. 507, 117 S.Ct. 2157, 138 L.Ed.2d 624 (1997)

JUSTICE KENNEDY delivered the opinion of the Court.[32]

[The Archbishop of San Antonio applied for a building permit to enlarge St. Peter Catholic Church in Boerne, Texas. City authorities denied

---

[32] *Editors' note:* **JUSTICE SCALIA** joined all but Part III-A-1 of this opinion.

the application because, under a local historic preservation ordinance, the church was within a historic district. The Archbishop then brought suit, arguing that the permit denial violated RFRA. The city responded that RFRA was unenforceable because it was unconstitutional as applied to state and local governments.]

II.   Congress enacted RFRA in direct response to the Court's decision in *Smith*. There we considered a Free Exercise Clause claim brought by members of the Native American Church who were denied unemployment benefits when they lost their jobs because they had used peyote. Their practice was to ingest peyote for sacramental purposes, and they challenged an Oregon statute of general applicability which made use of the drug criminal. In evaluating the claim, we declined to apply the balancing test set forth in *Sherbert v. Verner*, 374 U.S. 398 (1963), under which we would have asked whether Oregon's prohibition substantially burdened a religious practice and, if it did, whether the burden was justified by a compelling government interest. * * * The application of the *Sherbert* test, the *Smith* decision explained, would have produced an anomaly in the law, a constitutional right to ignore neutral laws of general applicability. [Four Justices disagreed and offered a broader understanding of the Free Exercise Clause.]

These points of constitutional interpretation were debated by Members of Congress in hearings and floor debates. Many criticized the Court's reasoning, and this disagreement resulted in the passage of RFRA. [In RFRA,] Congress announced:

(1)   [T]he framers of the Constitution, recognizing free exercise of religion as an unalienable right, secured its protection in the First Amendment to the Constitution;

(2)   laws "neutral" toward religion may burden religious exercise as surely as laws intended to interfere with religious exercise;

(3)   governments should not substantially burden religious exercise without compelling justification;

(4)   in [*Smith*] the Supreme Court virtually eliminated the requirement that the government justify burdens on religious exercise imposed by laws neutral toward religion; and

(5)   the compelling interest test as set forth in prior Federal court rulings is a workable test for striking sensible balances between religious liberty and competing prior governmental interests.

The Act's stated purposes are:

(1)   to restore the compelling interest test as set forth in [*Sherbert*] and *Wisconsin v. Yoder*, 406 U.S. 205 (1972) and to

guarantee its application in all cases where free exercise of religion is substantially burdened; and

(2) to provide a claim or defense to persons whose religious exercise is substantially burdened by government.

RFRA prohibits "[g]overnment" from "substantially burden[ing]" a person's exercise of religion even if the burden results from a rule of general applicability unless the government can demonstrate the burden "(1) is in furtherance of a compelling governmental interest; and (2) is the least restrictive means of furthering that compelling governmental interest." The Act's mandate applies to [both the federal government and state and local governments]. * * *

[IIIA.]   Legislation which deters or remedies constitutional violations can fall within the sweep of Congress' enforcement power even if in the process it prohibits conduct which is not itself unconstitutional and intrudes into "legislative spheres of autonomy previously reserved to the States." For example, the Court upheld a suspension of literacy tests and similar voting requirements under Congress' parallel power to enforce the provisions of the Fifteenth Amendment, as a measure to combat racial discrimination in voting, *South Carolina v. Katzenbach*, despite the facial constitutionality of the tests under *Lassiter*. We have also concluded that other measures protecting voting rights are within Congress' power to enforce the Fourteenth and Fifteenth Amendments, despite the burdens those measures placed on the States. *South Carolina v. Katzenbach*; *Katzenbach v. Morgan*; *Oregon v. Mitchell*; *City of Rome v. United States*.

It is also true, however, that "[a]s broad as the congressional enforcement power is, it is not unlimited." *Oregon v. Mitchell* (opinion of Black, J.). In assessing the breadth of § 5's enforcement power, we begin with its text. Congress has been given the power "to enforce" the "provisions of this article." We agree with respondent, of course, that Congress can enact legislation under § 5 enforcing the constitutional right to the free exercise of religion. The "provisions of this article," to which § 5 refers, include the Due Process Clause of the Fourteenth Amendment. Congress' power to enforce the Free Exercise Clause follows from our holding in *Cantwell v. Connecticut*, 310 U.S. 296, 303 (1940), that the "fundamental concept of liberty embodied in [the Fourteenth Amendment's Due Process Clause] embraces the liberties guaranteed by the First Amendment."

Congress' power under § 5, however, extends only to "enforc[ing]" the provisions of the Fourteenth Amendment. The Court has described this power as "remedial," *South Carolina v. Katzenbach*. The design of the Amendment and the text of § 5 are inconsistent with the suggestion that Congress has the power to decree the substance of the Fourteenth Amendment's restrictions on the States. Legislation which alters the meaning of the Free Exercise Clause cannot be said to be enforcing the Clause. Congress does not enforce a constitutional right by changing what the right is. It has been given the power "to enforce," not the power to determine what constitutes a constitutional violation. Were it not so, what Congress would be enforcing would no longer be, in any meaningful sense, the "provisions of [the Fourteenth Amendment]."

While the line between measures that remedy or prevent unconstitutional actions and measures that make a substantive change in the governing law is not easy to discern, and Congress must have wide latitude in determining where it lies, the distinction exists and must be observed. There must be a congruence and proportionality between the injury to be prevented or remedied and the means adopted to that end. Lacking such a connection, legislation may become substantive in operation and effect. * * *

[In Part III-A-1, Justice Kennedy supported his conclusion by contending that "[t]he Fourteenth Amendment's history confirms the remedial, rather than substantive, nature of the Enforcement Clause." The first draft of the Fourteenth Amendment, reported by Rep. Bingham (R-OH), provided:

> The Congress shall have power to make all laws which shall be necessary and proper to secure to the citizens of each State all privileges and immunities of citizens in the several States, and to all persons in the several States equal protection in the rights of life, liberty, and property.

"Members of Congress from across the political spectrum criticized the Amendment, and the criticisms had a common theme: The proposed Amendment gave Congress too much legislative power at the expense of the existing constitutional structure." In response, the draft was taken off the table and replaced by a new version, which was adopted as the Fourteenth Amendment. "Under the revised Amendment, Congress' power was no longer plenary but remedial. Congress was granted the power to make the substantive constitutional prohibitions against the States effective. Representative Bingham said the new draft would give Congress 'the power . . . to protect by national law the privileges and immunities of all the citizens of the Republic . . . whenever the same shall be abridged or denied by the unconstitutional acts of any State.' Representative Stevens described the new draft Amendment as 'allow[ing] Congress to correct the unjust legislation of the States.'"]

The design of the Fourteenth Amendment has proved significant also in maintaining the traditional separation of powers between Congress and the Judiciary. The first eight Amendments to the Constitution set forth self-executing prohibitions on governmental action, and this Court has had primary authority to interpret those prohibitions. The Bingham draft, some thought, departed from that tradition by vesting in Congress primary power to interpret and elaborate on the meaning of the new Amendment through legislation. Under it, "Congress, and not the courts, was to judge whether or not any of the privileges or immunities were not secured to citizens in the several States." [H. Flack, The Adoption of the Fourteenth Amendment 64 (1908).] While this separation of powers aspect did not occasion the widespread resistance which was caused by the proposal's threat to the federal balance, it nonetheless attracted the attention of various Members. As enacted, the Fourteenth Amendment confers substantive rights against the States which, like the provisions of the Bill of Rights, are self-executing. The power to interpret the Constitution in a case or controversy remains in the Judiciary.

The remedial and preventive nature of Congress' enforcement power, and the limitation inherent in the power, were confirmed in our earliest cases on the Fourteenth Amendment [i.e., *The Civil Rights Cases*]. * * * Recent cases have continued to revolve around the question of whether § 5 legislation can be considered remedial. [Justice Kennedy invoked *South Carolina v. Katzenbach* as a precedent where the Court's willingness to sustain Congress's use of its Fourteenth Amendment authority was premised on its understanding that the statutory rules were "remedies aimed at areas where voting discrimination has been most flagrant" and necessary to "banish the blight of racial discrimination in voting, which has infected the electoral process in parts of our country for nearly a century."]

Any suggestion that Congress has a substantive, non-remedial power under the Fourteenth Amendment is not supported by our case law. In *Oregon v. Mitchell*, a majority of the Court concluded Congress had exceeded its enforcement powers by enacting legislation lowering the minimum age of voters from 21 to 18 in state and local elections. The five [Justices] who reached this conclusion explained that the legislation intruded into an area reserved by the Constitution to the States. Four of these five were explicit in rejecting the position that § 5 endowed Congress with the power to establish the meaning of constitutional provisions. [Chief Justice Burger and Justices Harlan, Stewart, Blackmun.]

There is language in our opinion in *Morgan* which could be interpreted as acknowledging a power in Congress to enact legislation that expands the rights contained in § 1 of the Fourteenth Amendment. This is not a necessary interpretation, however, or even the best one. [Justice Kennedy noted the Court's explanation that Congress was trying to give Puerto Ricans "enhanced political power" that would be "helpful in gaining nondiscriminatory treatment in public services for the entire Puerto Rican community." Section 4(e) thus could be justified as a remedial measure to deal with "discrimination in governmental services." The Court also perceived a factual basis on which Congress could have concluded that New York's literacy requirement "constituted an invidious discrimination in violation of the Equal Protection Clause."] Both rationales for upholding § 4(e) rested on unconstitutional discrimination by New York and Congress' reasonable attempt to combat it. As Justice Stewart explained in *Oregon v. Mitchell*, interpreting *Morgan* to give Congress the power to interpret the Constitution "would require an enormous extension of that decision's rationale."

If Congress could define its own powers by altering the Fourteenth Amendment's meaning, no longer would the Constitution be "superior paramount law, unchangeable by ordinary means." It would be "on a level with ordinary legislative acts, and, like other acts, . . . alterable when the legislature shall please to alter it." *Marbury v. Madison*. Under this approach, it is difficult to conceive of a principle that would limit congressional power. Shifting legislative majorities could change the Constitution and effectively circumvent the difficult and detailed amendment process contained in Article V. * * *

[III.B] Respondent contends that RFRA is a proper exercise of Congress' remedial or preventive power. The Act, it is said, is a reasonable means of protecting the free exercise of religion as defined by *Smith*. It prevents and remedies laws which are enacted with the unconstitutional object of targeting religious beliefs and practices. See *Church of the Lukumi Babalu Aye, Inc. v. Hialeah* [Chapter 6, § 7] ("[A] law targeting religious beliefs as such is never permissible"). To avoid the difficulty of proving such violations, it is said, Congress can simply invalidate any law which imposes a substantial burden on a religious practice unless it is justified by a compelling interest and is the least restrictive means of accomplishing that interest. If Congress can prohibit laws with discriminatory effects in order to prevent racial discrimination in violation of the Equal Protection Clause, see *City of Rome*, then it can do the same, respondent argues, to promote religious liberty.

While preventive rules are sometimes appropriate remedial measures, there must be a congruence between the means used and the ends to be achieved. The appropriateness of remedial measures must be considered in light of the evil presented. Strong measures appropriate to address one harm may be an unwarranted response to another, lesser one.

A comparison between RFRA and the Voting Rights Act is instructive. In contrast to the record which confronted Congress and the judiciary in the voting rights cases, RFRA's legislative record lacks examples of modern instances of generally applicable laws passed because of religious bigotry. The history of persecution in this country detailed in the hearings mentions no episodes occurring in the past 40 years. [Citing various statements made in legislative history.] The absence of more recent episodes stems from the fact that, as one witness testified, "deliberate persecution is not the usual problem in this country." House Hearings [on RFRA] 334 (statement of

Douglas Laycock). Rather, the emphasis of the hearings was on laws of general applicability which place incidental burdens on religion. Much of the discussion centered upon anecdotal evidence of autopsies performed on Jewish individuals and Hmong immigrants in violation of their religious beliefs, and on zoning regulations and historic preservation laws (like the one at issue here), which as an incident of their normal operation, have adverse effects on churches and synagogues. It is difficult to maintain that they are examples of legislation enacted or enforced due to animus or hostility to the burdened religious practices or that they indicate some widespread pattern of religious discrimination in this country. Congress' concern was with the incidental burdens imposed, not the object or purpose of the legislation. This lack of support in the legislative record, however, is not RFRA's most serious shortcoming. Judicial deference, in most cases, is based not on the state of the legislative record Congress compiles but "on due regard for the decision of the body constitutionally appointed to decide." *Oregon v. Mitchell* (opinion of Harlan, J.). As a general matter, it is for Congress to determine the method by which it will reach a decision.

Regardless of the state of the legislative record, RFRA cannot be considered remedial, preventive legislation, if those terms are to have any meaning. RFRA is so out of proportion to a supposed remedial or preventive object that it cannot be understood as responsive to, or designed to prevent, unconstitutional behavior. It appears, instead, to attempt a substantive change in constitutional protections. Preventive measures prohibiting certain types of laws may be appropriate when there is reason to believe that many of the laws affected by the congressional enactment have a significant likelihood of being unconstitutional. See *City of Rome* (since "jurisdictions with a demonstrable history of intentional racial discrimination . . . create the risk of purposeful discrimination" Congress could "prohibit changes that have a discriminatory impact" in those jurisdictions). Remedial legislation under § 5 "should be adapted to the mischief and wrong which the [Fourteenth] [A]mendment was intended to provide against." *The Civil Rights Cases.*

RFRA is not so confined. Sweeping coverage ensures its intrusion at every level of government, displacing laws and prohibiting official actions of almost every description and regardless of subject matter. RFRA's restrictions apply to every agency and official of the Federal, State, and local Governments. 42 U.S.C. § 2000bb–2(1). RFRA applies to all federal and state law, statutory or otherwise, whether adopted before or after its enactment. § 2000bb–3(a). RFRA has no termination date or termination mechanism. Any law is subject to challenge at any time by any individual who alleges a substantial burden on his or her free exercise of religion.

The reach and scope of RFRA distinguish it from other measures passed under Congress' enforcement power, even in the area of voting rights. In *South Carolina v. Katzenbach*, the challenged provisions were confined to those regions of the country where voting discrimination had been most flagrant and affected a discrete class of state laws, *i.e.*, state voting laws. Furthermore, to ensure that the reach of the Voting Rights Act was limited to those cases in which constitutional violations were most likely (in order to reduce the possibility of overbreadth), the coverage under the Act would terminate "at the behest of States and political subdivisions in which the danger of substantial voting discrimination has not materialized during the preceding five years." *Id.* The provisions restricting and banning literacy tests, upheld in *Katzenbach v. Morgan* and *Oregon v. Mitchell*, attacked a particular type of voting qualification, one with a long history as a "notorious means to deny and abridge voting rights on racial grounds." In *City of Rome*, the Court rejected a challenge to the constitutionality of a Voting Rights Act provision which required certain jurisdictions to submit changes in electoral practices to the Department of Justice for preimplementation review. The requirement was placed only on jurisdictions with a history of intentional racial discrimination in voting. Like the provisions at issue in *South Carolina v. Katzenbach*, this provision permitted a covered jurisdiction to avoid preclearance requirements under certain conditions and, moreover, lapsed in seven years. This is not to say, of course, that § 5 legislation requires termination dates, geographic restrictions or egregious predicates. Where, however, a congressional enactment pervasively prohibits constitutional state action in an effort to remedy or to prevent unconstitutional state action, limitations of this kind tend to ensure Congress' means are proportionate to ends legitimate under § 5.

The stringent test RFRA demands of state laws reflects a lack of proportionality or congruence between the means adopted and the legitimate end to be achieved. If an objector can show a substantial burden on his free exercise, the State must demonstrate a compelling governmental interest and show that the law is the least restrictive means of furthering its interest. Claims that a law substantially burdens someone's exercise of religion will often be difficult to contest. * * * Laws valid under *Smith* would fall under RFRA without regard to whether they had the object of stifling or punishing free exercise. * * * [RFRA] is a considerable congressional intrusion into the States' traditional prerogatives and general authority to regulate for the health and welfare of their citizens.

The substantial costs RFRA exacts, both in practical terms of imposing a heavy litigation burden on the States and in terms of curtailing their traditional general regulatory power, far exceed any pattern or practice of unconstitutional conduct under the Free Exercise Clause as interpreted in *Smith*. Simply put, RFRA is not designed to identify and counteract state laws likely to be unconstitutional because of their treatment of religion. In most cases, the state laws to which RFRA applies are not ones which will have been motivated by religious bigotry. If a state law disproportionately burdened a particular class of religious observers, this circumstance might be evidence of an impermissible legislative motive. Cf. *Washington v. Davis*. RFRA's substantial burden test, however, is not even a discriminatory effects or disparate impact test. It is a reality of the modern regulatory state that numerous state laws, such as the zoning regulations at issue here, impose a substantial burden on a large class of individuals. When the exercise of religion has been burdened in an incidental way by a law of general application, it does not follow that the persons affected have been burdened any more than other citizens, let alone burdened because of their religious beliefs. In addition, the Act imposes in every case a least restrictive means requirement—a requirement that was not used in the pre-*Smith* jurisprudence RFRA purported to codify—which also indicates that the legislation is broader than is appropriate if the goal is to prevent and remedy constitutional violations. * * *

Our national experience teaches that the Constitution is preserved best when each part of the government respects both the Constitution and the proper actions and determinations of the other branches. When the Court has interpreted the Constitution, it has acted within the province of the Judicial Branch, which embraces the duty to say what the law is. *Marbury*. When the political branches of the Government act against the background of a judicial interpretation of the Constitution already issued, it must be understood that in later cases and controversies the Court will treat its precedents with the respect due them under settled principles, including *stare decisis*, and contrary expectations must be disappointed. RFRA was designed to control cases and controversies, such as the one before us; but as the provisions of the federal statute here invoked are beyond congressional authority, it is this Court's precedent, not RFRA, which must control. * * *

[We omit the concurring opinion of **JUSTICE STEVENS**; the opinion of **JUSTICE SCALIA**, joined by **JUSTICE STEVENS**, concurring in part; the dissenting opinion of **JUSTICE O'CONNOR**, joined in large part by **JUSTICE BREYER**; the dissenting opinion of **JUSTICE SOUTER**; and the dissenting opinion of **JUSTICE BREYER**.]

NOTES ON BOERNE AND CONGRESSIONAL POWER TO ENFORCE THE FOURTEENTH AMENDMENT

1. *Possible Objections to the Court's Rejection of Congressional Power to Protect the Free Exercise of Religion.* Although some academics had correctly predicted the demise of RFRA,[33] the Supreme Court's lopsided rejection of the

---

[33] See, e.g., Christopher Eisgruber & Lawrence Gene Sager, *Why the Religious Freedom Restoration Act Is Unconstitutional*, 69 NYU L. Rev. 437 (1994); William Van Alstyne, *The Failure of the Religious Freedom Restoration Act Under Section 5 of the Fourteenth Amendment*, 46 Duke L.J. 291 (1996).

statute came as something of a constitutional surprise.[34] It is remarkable that even the dissenters in *Boerne* pretty much conceded the Court's view that § 5 did not authorize Congress to override *Smith* and argued, instead, that *Smith* should be reconsidered. Are there good arguments for the proposition that § 5 of the Fourteenth Amendment gives Congress the authority to adopt RFRA?

Does *Boerne* commit the Court to a purely remedial theory of congressional enforcement authority? If the Court for institutional reasons "underenforces" individual rights, might Congress have some latitude to enforce those norms? This provides one account of *South Carolina v. Katzenbach.* Even if the Court refused to recognize its own institutional caution as a reason to give Congress leeway, it might do so as part of an inter-branch dialogue about the meaning of the Free Exercise Clause. *Boerne* has been criticized for rejecting any substantive role for Congress in defining the rights protected by the Fourteenth Amendment.[35] Recall the critique developed in our notes after *Cooper v. Aaron* (Chapter 2, § 2B): Commentators from a variety of perspectives dispute the Supreme Court's insistence that it must always have the last word as to the meaning of the Constitution. Indeed, *Boerne* may be a more aggressive deployment of the judicial supremacy idea than *Cooper* was. *Smith* was a decision that not only divided the Court, but was immediately and overwhelmingly repudiated by Congress, while *Brown* was a unanimous decision of the Court that Congress did not try to override.

2. *The Court, Congress, and Social Movements.* Admittedly, following the precedents on congressional authority to enforce the Reconstruction Amendments is a challenge. The path from *The Civil Rights Cases* to *Boerne* was anything but straightforward. Consider the discussion in Chapter 1 of the possible relationship between social movements and the evolution of constitutional doctrine. After Reconstruction ended, the Court narrowly interpreted congressional power to legislate under the Reconstruction Amendments (*The Civil Rights Cases*); during the "second Reconstruction" of the civil rights movement of the 1960s, the Court accorded Congress very expansive power in this area (*South Carolina v. Katzenbach* and, especially, *Katzenbach v. Morgan*). The cases in the next decade or so did not quarrel with this Court/Congress equilibrium, especially when Congress was legislating concerning a core, historical aspect of Reconstruction (race: *Rome*) rather than an issue of equality outside that core (age: *Oregon v. Mitchell*).

In the 1990s, however, a Court composed of a different set of Justices has shattered the earlier equilibrium of deference to congressional power.[36] *Lopez* is the paradigm-shifting Commerce Clause decision, although it purports to overrule no precedent; *Boerne* takes a similar, but even bolder tack to congressional authority to enforce the Reconstruction Amendments, as it does

---

[34] See, e.g., Robert Drinan, S.J., *Reflections on the Demise of the Religious Freedom Restoration Act*, 86 Geo. L.J. 101 (1997).

[35] See David Cole, *The Value of Seeing Things Differently:* City of Boerne v. Flores *and Congressional Enforcement of the Bill of Rights*, 1997 S.Ct. Rev. 31.

[36] See, e.g., Robert Post & Reva Siegel, *Equal Protection by Law: Federal Antidiscrimination Legislation After* Morrison *and* Kimel, 110 Yale L.J. 441 (2000).

expressly repudiate the substantive theory of *Morgan*. What is driving the Court to undo what might have been thought to be the settled expectations concerning congressional power? Consider three possibilities.

(a) *Federalism concerns*. The current majority of the Court considers federalism a core constitutional principle and does not trust Congress to respect it and stay within its constitutional boundaries. Nor have "the political safeguards of federalism" been sufficient to prevent congressional overreaching. For instance, how could states lobby against forbidding guns in schools, or the promotion of religious liberty? The Court sees itself as the only institution that can effectively protect the states against congressional encroachment. The earlier apparent equilibrium about congressional authority under the Commerce Clause and the Reconstruction Amendments gave Congress *carte blanche*, in effect a national police power contrary to constitutional text, to the historical expectations of the Framers, and to good policy (recall the values of federalism).

(b) *Separation of powers concerns*. Since *Marbury*, it has been emphatically the province of the judiciary, not of Congress, to say what the law is. Questions such as whether a statute concerns something substantially related to interstate commerce or is designed to remedy constitutional violations are questions of law for courts, not questions of policy for Congress. The earlier equilibrium involved an improper shift of judicial power to the legislative branch. In this regard, note that the congressional strategy with RFRA—lambasting the Court for misconstruing the Free Exercise Clause— and the very title to the statute, suggesting that religious liberty has been lost (through judicial foolishness) and must be "restored," are direct challenges to the Court. Note how this account is diametrically opposed to arguments contending that the Court should accord Congress some enforcement-power discretion based on Congress's better fact-finding capacity and on the notion that an inter-branch dialogue about constitutional meaning can be productive.

(c) *Easy cases and political appearances*. If the Court were ever to strike down anything as beyond the commerce power, *Lopez* was the perfect case, for there was no obvious connection between the statute and interstate commerce, there was no evidence that state regulation was insufficient, and Congress may have been engaged in symbolic legislation for political purposes. *Boerne* can be seen as similar. Assuming there is no *Morgan*-like substantive power, the statute was vulnerable to constitutional attack because, RFRA's legislative history did not demonstrate that local governments were intentionally but furtively discriminating against religious free exercise—in contrast to the VRA's legislative history, which demonstrated how southern registrars pervasively discriminated against potential black voters. The Justices may have thought that Congress responded to political pressure from a powerful political lobby, the religious community, rather than carefully evaluated public need.

Were these changes potentially affected by a major shift in political equilibrium? Certainly federal policy from the Reagan Administration onward has been to devolve increasing authority to the states. In 1994, Republicans took control of the House of Representatives on a campaign platform called "The Contract with America," which included a promise to respect state prerogatives (e.g., to avoid unfunded federal mandates, which require states or local governments to do certain things but provide no federal funds to pay for these activities).

3. Boerne *as Precedent: The Congruence and Proportionality Test.* What does the Court mean by "congruence"? "Proportionality"? This test has been crucial in the post-*Boerne* cases, to which we now turn.

B. CONGRESSIONAL POWER AND THE ELEVENTH AMENDMENT

1. An Overview of the Eleventh Amendment

In addition to truncating the commerce power in *Lopez* and the civil rights enforcement power in *Boerne*, the Court in the 1990s took a third step to cabin congressional authority: a persistent majority interpreted the Eleventh Amendment to deny Congress the authority to subject unconsenting states to suit in federal court for violations of federal statutes adopted pursuant to Congress's Article I powers. The intricacies of the Eleventh Amendment are beyond the scope of this book (most Federal Courts courses offer deeper coverage). For present purposes, a short overview should suffice.

As a matter of federal common law (with possible constitutional roots), the United States cannot be sued in the federal courts without its consent (a consent that has been given in a series of federal statutes partially waiving immunity). See *United States v. Nordic Village*, 503 U.S. 30 (1992). A similar immunity generally protects states from lawsuits in their own courts unless they have consented to suit. During the first decade of the Constitution, the question arose whether and under what circumstances the states might be sued in federal court.

In *Chisholm v. Georgia*, 2 U.S. (2 Dall.) 419 (1793), the Supreme Court took original jurisdiction in a lawsuit against the state of Georgia by a South Carolina creditor seeking payment for goods purchased by Georgia during the Revolution. Georgia argued that the Supreme Court did not have jurisdiction over the controversy. Four Justices read Article III's grant of jurisdiction over "Controversies * * * between a State and Citizens of another State" to embrace cases where the State is a defendant as well as those where it is a plaintiff. Only Justice Iredell dissented, primarily on statutory grounds.

Chisholm created a sensation, because several states were under pressure by creditors to pay their debts incurred during the Revolution, which the states were not in a position to do. Within a year, Congress proposed the Eleventh Amendment to the Constitution as a response to this problem, and the states ratified it.[37] The amendment provides: "The Judicial power of the United States shall not be construed to extend to any suit in law or equity, commenced or prosecuted against one of the United States by Citizens of another State, or by Citizens or Subjects of any Foreign State."

In *Hans v. Louisiana*, 134 U.S. 1 (1890), the Court gave this amendment a decidedly nonliteral interpretation by holding that it forbids a suit against an unconsenting state not only by a citizen of another state or foreign country, but also by one of its own citizens. In brief, the Court thought it would be "anomalous" if the state, without its consent, could be sued by one of its own citizens but not by others. In essence, the Court read the Eleventh Amendment as reflecting a broad principle, perhaps implicit in the original Constitution as well, that states generally have sovereign immunity when sued in federal court.

Hans seems at war with the text of the Constitution, for it reads the Eleventh Amendment to afford state immunity in cases not covered by its precise terms. Chief Justice Hughes rescued constitutional state immunity from this textualist embarrassment in *Monaco v. Mississippi*, 292 U.S. 313 (1934), which extended state immunity to cases brought by a foreign state. Hughes explained the state immunity not as an interpretation of the Eleventh Amendment, but instead as a construction of the "judicial Power" conferred by Article III, which the Eleventh Amendment had enforced by overriding *Chsiholm*. Given the sovereign immunity the common law invariably recognized as a defense from lawsuits, the Framers surely did not intend for Article III to confer jurisdiction against the states (or the United States) without their consent.

Hans (supplemented by *Monaco*) had the potential to destroy the capacity of federal courts to hear claims, including constitutional claims, against state action. The Court has addressed this concern. First, a federal suit may proceed against a state officer in her official capacity implementing an unconstitutional state statute, on the ground that the state is not the defendant. See *Ex parte Young*, 209 U.S. 123 (1908). Such suits may be for prospective injunctive relief, but not for retrospective money damages. See *Edelman v. Jordan*, 415 U.S. 651 (1974). Second, the Court has recognized that a state may waive the immunity and allow itself to be sued, although for the waiver to be effective the state statute or state constitutional provision must clearly specify the state's intention to allow suits against it in federal court (thus, a general waiver of immunity in its own state courts is insufficient). *Edelman*. Third, the United States may sue a state in federal court notwithstanding the Eleventh Amendment.

---

[37] Oddly enough, the purpose of the Eleventh Amendment seems to be to allow the states to engage in the very "impairments of contracts" supposedly forbidden by the Contract Clause (unless, of course, the Contract Clause applies only to private contracts).

E.g., *United States v. Mississippi*, 380 U.S. 128 (1965). The Eleventh Amendment does not bar suits against municipalities, counties, or other subdivisions of a state. E.g., *Lincoln County v. Luning*, 133 U.S. 529 (1890).

2. May Congress Abrogate States' Eleventh Amendment (or Article III) Immunity?

Like Article III, the text of the Eleventh Amendment is all about the jurisdiction of federal courts and tells us nothing about Congress's power to enact legislation that would alter or remove the jurisdictional bar. In *Fitzpatrick v. Bitzer*, 427 U.S. 445 (1976), the Court held that § 5 of the Fourteenth Amendment authorizes Congress to abrogate state Eleventh Amendment immunity. *Bitzer* emphasized the transformation of American federalism accomplished by the Reconstruction Amendments and ruled that the Eleventh Amendment had to be read in light of the subsequent-in-time Fourteenth Amendment.[38] As with state waivers, the Court has required a crystal-clear statement of abrogation on the face of a statute before it will find that Congress has exercised its *Bitzer* authority. E.g., *Quern v. Jordan*, 440 U.S. 332 (1979).

Bitzer did not address the question whether Congress could abrogate the states' immunity pursuant to its antecedent-in-time Article I powers. One argument in favor of such power is the following: Sovereign immunity is a common law doctrine that can be overridden by statute; therefore, the Supremacy Clause authorizes Congress to abrogate state sovereign immunity by a law adopted under any of its authorized powers, including those in Article I. Consistent with this common law notion of state immunity, in *Pennsylvania v. Union Gas Co.*, 491 U.S. 1 (1989), the Court ruled that Congress's legislative powers under Article I, such as the commerce power, also include the authority to subject states to suit in federal court. But *Union Gas* was a 5–4 decision with no majority opinion, and the Court turned around on this issue seven years later.

Seminole Tribe of Florida v. Florida

517 U.S. 44 (1996)

The Court invalidated the provision of the Indian Gaming Regulatory Act that allowed Indian tribes to sue states in federal court to enforce the statutory duty to negotiate in good faith to create Indian gaming enclaves. The Court, per **Chief Justice Rehnquist**, ruled that the "Indian Commerce Clause" does not authorize Congress to abrogate state Eleventh Amendment immunity. To reach that result, the Court overruled *Union Gas*.

To support its departure from *stare decisis*, the Court noted that there was no majority opinion in *Union Gas*; the fifth Justice (White) concurred only in

---

[38] See Vicki Jackson, *Holistic Interpretation:* Fitzpatrick v. Bitzer *and Our Bifurcated Constitution*, 53 Stan. L. Rev. 1259 (2001); Chapter 2, § 3A1.

the result and rejected the plurality opinion's rationale. This disarray within the Court majority created confusion among lower courts, which had difficulty applying the decision. More important, the Chief Justice criticized the plurality opinion in *Union Gas* because it "departed sharply from our established federalism jurisprudence and essentially eviscerated our decision in *Hans*," which had been followed for one hundred years until *Union Gas*. The Chief Justice maintained that the Court has always held that "the Eleventh Amendment stood for the constitutional principle that state sovereign immunity limited the federal courts' jurisdiction in Art. III. * * * And our decisions since *Hans* had been equally clear that the Eleventh Amendment reflects 'the fundamental principle of sovereign immunity [that] limits the grant of judicial authority under Article III.' *Pennhurst State Sch. & Hosp. v. Halderman*, 465 U.S. 89, 97–98 (1984). As the dissent in *Union Gas* recognized, the plurality's conclusion—that Congress could under Article I expand the scope of the federal courts' jurisdiction under Article III—'contradict[ed] our unvarying approach to Article III as setting forth the *exclusive* catalog of permissible federal court jurisdiction.'" Hence, *stare decisis* cut both ways in *Seminole Tribe*.

Finally, the Court rejected the notion that state immunity from suit was nothing more than a common law doctrine. Entering the union as independent sovereigns, the states retained their immunity as part of the Constitution's plan. Thus, it was a fundamental constitutional " 'postulate that States of the Union, still possessing attributes of sovereignty, shall be immune from suits, without their consent, save where there has been a "surrender of this immunity in the plan of the [C]onvention." ' " *Monaco*. The Chief Justice distinguished *Bitzer* on the ground that "the Fourteenth Amendment, by expanding federal power at the expense of state autonomy, had fundamentally altered the balance of state and federal power struck by the Constitution." Thus, although Congress could not abrogate the states' Eleventh Amendment immunity under Article I (part of the original constitutional plan), Congress could do so under its legislative power under § 5 of the later-in-time Fourteenth Amendment.

Four Justices—**Stevens**, **Souter**, **Ginsburg**, and **Breyer**—dissented. In an opinion by Souter, the latter three argued that *Hans*, rather than *Union Gas*, should be narrowed if not overruled. Souter maintained that, as a matter of the Framers' original expectations, state sovereign immunity in 1789 was entirely unclear, and whatever immunity the states had was terminated by the Constitution, as *Chisholm* held for diversity cases and everyone assumed for federal question cases (such as *Seminole Tribe*). The plain language of the Eleventh Amendment reflected its purpose: to divest federal courts of diversity jurisdiction when an out-of-stater sues a state. Conversely, the amendment left federal question jurisdiction alone, and *Hans* was wrong to hold otherwise. "In sum, reading the Eleventh Amendment solely as a limit on citizen-state diversity jurisdiction has the virtue of coherence with this Court's practice, with the views of John Marshall, with the history of the Amendment's drafting, and with its allusive language," concluded Justice Souter. In light of this evidence, and *Hans*' own misreading of the common law and the Framers' expectations, Justice Souter objected to any extension of *Hans*. (The Chief Justice vigorously disagreed: no precedent of the Court has questioned *Hans*, which has been the foundational precedent.)

Last of all, Justice Souter explored the relationship between immunity and sovereignty. The Founding rejected the idea of *indivisible sovereignty*, for the Constitution created an arrangement where both state and national governments were sovereign, within their respective spheres. (To the extent sovereignty remained indivisible, it rested with We the People.) Following Akhil Reed Amar, *Of Federalism and Sovereignty*, 96 Yale L.J. 1425 (1987), Souter argued that the logical implication of divided sovereignty was that each government would retain immunity only within its respective sphere, and would be subject to suit where acting outside its constitutional authority. "When individuals sued States to enforce federal rights, the Government that corresponded to the 'sovereign' in the traditional common-law sense was not the State but the National Government, and any state immunity from the jurisdiction of the Nation's courts would have required a grant from the true sovereign, the people, in their Constitution, or from the Congress that the Constitution had empowered."

Alden v. Maine

527 U.S. 706 (1999)

State probation officers and juvenile caseworkers sued the state to enforce the overtime-pay requirements of the Fair Labor Standards Act. *Seminole Tribe* required dismissal of their federal court lawsuit, but the state workers refiled in state court, upon the theory that the Eleventh Amendment only regulates *federal* jurisdiction and does not affect the Supremacy Clause obligation of state courts to enforce federal law. The U.S. Supreme Court ruled that, although the Eleventh Amendment was not technically applicable (because the suit was in state court), the principle underlying *Hans* and *Seminole Tribe* barred the state lawsuit as well as the federal one. **Justice Kennedy**'s opinion for the Court (the same five Justices who formed the majority in *Seminole Tribe*) relied on the common law notion, universally accepted at the Founding, that sovereigns are immune from lawsuits to which they have not expressly consented. Thus, *Hans*' reading of the Eleventh Amendment and *Monaco*'s reading of Article III "do not exhaust the constitutional importance of the sovereign immunity baseline. That principle would be defeated if state immunity were lost for lawsuits filed in state courts."

Indeed, "a congressional power to authorize private suits against nonconsenting States in their own courts would be even more offensive to state sovereignty than a power to authorize the suits in a federal forum. Although the immunity of one sovereign in the courts of another has often depended in part on comity or agreement, the immunity of a sovereign in its own courts has always been understood to be within the sole control of the sovereign itself." This constitutional symmetry was reinforced, Justice Kennedy reasoned, by functional considerations, particularly the "political accountability so essential to our liberty and republican form of government" which would be compromised by allowing the federal government to commandeer the states' courts against the states: "This case at one level concerns the formal structure of federalism, but in a Constitution as resilient as ours form mirrors substance. Congress has vast power but not all power. When Congress legislates in matters affecting the States, it may not treat these sovereign entities as mere prefectures or corporations."

Speaking for the same four Justices who dissented in *Seminole Tribe*, **Justice Souter** objected to the Court's hardwiring the eighteenth century concept of sovereign immunity into the Constitution. Not only is the concept unmentioned in the Constitution's text, but the Framers themselves were silent about its role in the new government, and none of the opinions in *Chisholm* mentioned it. Nor did Justice Souter find any tangible basis for the principle in the "structure" of the Constitution. Several different conceptions of sovereign immunity would be perfectly consistent with the Constitution and the Bill of Rights. "[T]here is much irony in the Court's profession that it grounds its opinion on a deeply rooted historical tradition of sovereign immunity, when the Court abandons a principle nearly as inveterate, and much closer to the hearts of the Framers: that where there is a right there must be a remedy." See *Marbury v. Madison*.

NOTES ON THE ELASTIC ELEVENTH AMENDMENT

1. *Constitutional Theory*. The most remarkable thing about these decisions is how much they have rendered the actual text of the Eleventh Amendment irrelevant to the constitutional immunity. See John F. Manning, *The Eleventh Amendment and the Reading of Precise Constitutional Texts,* 113 Yale L.J. 1663 (2004) (critical of the Court's nontextual activism). *Hans* commenced that process, by extending Eleventh Amendment immunity beyond the diversity cases targeted by the amendment; subsequent Supreme Court decisions extended the immunity to admiralty cases, see *Ex parte New York*, 256 U.S. 490 (1921), and cases where foreign states sued the states. *Monaco* (interpreting Article III). In effect, those cases lopped off "by Citizens of another State, or by Citizens or Subjects of any Foreign State" from the end of the Eleventh Amendment. *Alden* extended the constitutional immunity to suits to enforce federal statutes against the states in their own state courts. *Alden* is based on supposedly fundamental (unwritten) constitutional principles of dual federalism rather than on the Eleventh Amendment per se, but in practical effect it lopped off "of the United States" from the amendment. Following *Alden*, the Court in *Federal Maritime Comm'n (FMC) v. South Carolina State Ports Auth.*, 535 U.S. 743 (2002), held that dual federalism protects the states against being hailed before federal agencies performing adjudicative functions. Again, although the Eleventh Amendment was not the basis for this decision, it in effect rewrote "The Judicial Power" in the amendment to mean "Any Adjudicatory Power."

The Court has relied on the original understanding by the Framers of the Constitution of 1789 as the basis for broadly construing state sovereign immunity. Because the common law recognized immunity of governments to lawsuits as to which they have not consented, that principle was assumed in the Constitution (*Monaco*; *Seminole*; *Alden*). Hamilton in *Federalist* No. 81 explicitly promised the states that they would retain their full immunity (*FMC*), and Madison and Marshall similarly defended the Constitution against attacks that it would deprive states of their immunity from private lawsuits (*Alden*). Do the representations of Hamilton, Madison, and Marshall, made after eight states had ratified the Constitution, bind the Framers? Justice Souter argued in his *Seminole* and *Alden* dissents that sovereign immunity was a highly unsettled concept among the colonists, and some states explicitly recognized lawsuits against their governments. Also, Framers such as Edmund Randolph and James Wilson assumed that the states would be giving up any immunity not retained when they ratified the Constitution. *Thornton, supra* (the term limits case). Finally, when they ratified, several states proposed that the Constitution be clarified or amended to protect states against suit—hardly the appropriate stance if immunity was already written into the Constitution.

The *Chisholm* Court—filled with important Framers (James Wilson wrote the lead opinion, James Iredell dissented)—believed that the states had surrendered most of their immunities. The constitutional override of *Chisholm* by the adoption of the Eleventh Amendment was limited to diversity cases in federal court and was so read by the Founding Generation, represented by Chief Justice Marshall. In *FMC*, Justice Stevens' dissent added this historical argument: *Chisholm* held that states were not immune from service of process in a federal lawsuit *and* that federal courts had subject matter jurisdiction over lawsuits between a state and citizens of another state. The first bill responding to *Chisholm*, introduced the day after the decision was handed down, would have overridden both holdings; the amendment Congress ultimately submitted to the states overrode only the subject matter jurisdiction holding.

The Court's ultimate theory for this line of cases is that they are consistent with the federalist structure adopted in the Constitution.[39] But the same Constitution that adopted a federalist structure also created a powerful national government whose statutes are the supreme law of the land, to be faithfully applied by state as well as federal judges. U.S. Const. art. VI. *Alden*'s invigoration of state governments comes at the price of Maine's obligation to obey the directives of the Fair Labor Standards Act. *FMC*'s extension of *Alden* comes at the price of South Carolina's obligation to obey the Shipping Act. Is there a neutral way to justify this trade-off from the structure of the Constitution?

The four Justices who dissented in *Seminole* and *Alden* charged the five-Justice majority with judicial activism. Justice Stevens' dissent in *Florida*

---

[39] The *Seminole/Alden/FMC* line of cases might be defended by reference to precedent going back as far as *Hans*. But as Vicki Jackson, *The Supreme Court, the Eleventh Amendment, and State Sovereign Immunity*, 98 Yale L.J. 1 (1988), has demonstrated, precedent cuts both ways. Since *Cohens v. Virginia*, 19 U.S. 264 (1821), the Supreme Court has reviewed state court judgments in actions against the states under its federal question authority, without any mention of the Eleventh Amendment. That should have been a strong precedent-based argument against the result in *Alden*, yet the Court did not even mention *Cohens*.

Prepaid Postsecondary Education Expense Fund v. College Savings Bank, 527 U.S. 627 (1999), a companion case to *Alden*, said that the Court created a version of sovereign immunity "defined only by the present majority's perception of constitutional penumbras rather than constitutional text." Recall *Griswold v. Connecticut* (Chapter 5, § 4A). Stevens' charge, of course, can be turned around: If federalism and privacy are both robust ideas for a healthy polity, why not create constitutional space out of penumbras and background principles for both, just as the Rehnquist Court has done? A Court deciding both *Casey* (Chapter 5, § 4B) and *Alden* is not a passive Court, but that may not make it a bad Court.

2. *The Court's Theory of Strict Accountability.* A theory of political accountability inspires the Court's activism in *Seminole*, *Alden*, and *FMC*, and probably *Lopez* and *Boerne* as well. (See also *Freeman v. Pitts*, a recent *Brown II* case (Chapter 2, § 2C2).) The allocation of scarce resources among competing needs is fundamental to the political process. State officials must make hard choices as to priorities—and they are accountable to the voters for unsatisfactory choices at election time. This political accountability is sacrificed whenever the federal government asserts authority over the state's political processes or highjacks part of the state budget for its own goals. The underlying and broad purpose of the Eleventh Amendment was to prevent the distortions of state politics that would occur were the states suable for nonpayment of their debts. This accountability rationale applies regardless of whether the lawsuit is in state rather than federal court (*Alden*) or an administrative adjudication rather than a court case (*FMC*). Is this a cogent theory of politics and governance in a federal system? Is it cogent enough to trump the Supremacy Clause goals in these circumstances? Under what meta-principle do you choose between the two great constitutional goal?

3. *When States Can Be Sued, Notwithstanding the Eleventh Amendment.* Recall that, notwithstanding the Eleventh Amendment, the states can be sued if they waive their immunity, when the plaintiff is the United States, or if Congress has abrogated their immunity pursuant to its Fourteenth Amendment authority (*Bitzer*). Although *Seminole Tribe* explicitly reaffirms it, might *Bitzer* be revisited after *Alden*? Or is *Bitzer* insulated as a longstanding precedent upon which Congress has relied?

Indeed, in *Central Virginia Community College v. Katz*, 546 U.S. 356 (2006), the Court ruled that Congress has authority to abrogate state immunity pursuant to the Bankruptcy Clause, authorizing the establishment of "uniform Laws on the subject of Bankruptcies throughout the United States." According to Justice Stevens's opinion, the Framers designed the Bankruptcy Clause to allow Congress to create a uniform, integrated national bankruptcy system to replace the inconsistent state approaches to the discharge of debts and the refusal of states to respect one another's discharge orders. Inherent in the constitutional plan was congressional authority to treat states as other creditors are treated. In dissent, Justice Thomas, joined by Chief Justice Roberts, Justice Scalia, and Justice Kennedy, argued that this holding was inconsistent with *Seminole Tribe* and earlier Eleventh Amendment decisions.

3. Congress's Fourteenth Amendment Authority to Abrogate State Eleventh Amendment Immunity After *Boerne*

Now let us apply the foregoing principles to concrete situations. Title VII of the 1964 Civil Rights Act (as amended), the Age Discrimination in Employment Act (as amended), and the Americans with Disabilities Act forbid states from discriminating against their employees on certain grounds (race, gender, age, disability) and provide that prevailing plaintiffs may recover damages. These statutes are within Congress' commerce power, as they regulate an economic relationship (that of employer and employee). But under *Seminole Tribe*, Congress has no authority under the Commerce Clause to abrogate the states' immunity to suit. Plaintiffs therefore argue that these statutes are also justified by Congress' authority to enforce the Reconstruction Amendments, and so such statutes may apply to the states, as in *Bitzer*. This argument has not fared well in the post-*Boerne* era.

Thus, in ***Kimel v. Florida Board of Regents***, 528 U.S. 62 (2000), the five federalism-enforcing Justices held that the Age Discrimination in Employment Act (ADEA) could not be applied to state employers under Congress's authority to enforce the Fourteenth Amendment and, therefore, that Congress could not abrogate the states' immunity from suit. **Justice O'Connor**'s opinion for the Court started with the proposition that the Fourteenth Amendment imposes only a minimal rationality requirement on state rules discriminating on the basis of age. See *Massachusetts Bd. of Retirement v. Murgia* (Chapter 4, § 1). "Judged against the backdrop of our equal protection jurisprudence, it is clear that the ADEA is 'so out of proportion to a supposed remedial or preventive object' that it cannot be understood as responsive to, or designed to prevent, unconstitutional behavior.' *Boerne*. The Act, through its broad restriction on the use of age as a discriminating factor, prohibits substantially more state employment decisions and practices than would likely be held unconstitutional under the applicable equal protection, rational basis standard."

Justice O'Connor examined the ADEA's legislative record and found the extension of the statute to the states was "an unwarranted response to a perhaps inconsequential problem. Congress never identified any pattern of age discrimination by the States, much less any discrimination whatsoever that rose to the level of constitutional violation. The evidence compiled by petitioners to demonstrate such attention by Congress to age discrimination by the States falls well short of the mark. That evidence consists almost entirely of isolated sentences clipped from floor debates and legislative reports." Given the indiscriminate scope of the ADEA's substantive requirements, the dearth of evidence for widespread and unconstitutional age discrimination by the states brought the case within *Boerne*'s rule of invalidity. See also *Florida Prepaid Postsecondary Education Expense Board v. College Sav. Bank*, 527 U.S. 627 (1999) (ruling that a federal patent remedy statute could not be applied against state patent violators, because there was no pattern of unconstitutional behavior by the states to establish this as a "proportional and congruent" congressional enforcement response).

In *Board of Trustees v. Garrett,* 531 U.S. 356 (2001), the Court, by the same 5–4 vote as in *Seminole* and *Kimel*, held that Congress had exceeded its § 5 power when it enacted the provisions of the Americans with Disabilities Act (ADA) forbidding states from engaging in employment discrimination against the disabled, which included a requirement that states take affirmative steps to accommodate disabled employees. In some senses, the case resembled *Kimel*, in that discrimination on the basis of disability, like age discrimination, draws only rational-basis review under the Equal Protection Clause. *Garrett* presented two factors not present in *Kimel*, however. First, unlike with age discrimination, the Court has found a violation of the Equal Protection Clause in the context of disability discrimination, concluding that a city's refusal to allow the construction of a group home for the developmentally disabled was motivated by irrational animus. See *Cleburne v. Cleburne Living Center* (Chapter 4, § 3C). Thus, rational-basis review in this context seems to be a more aggressive judicial scrutiny than the "anything goes" review accorded to age classifications. Second, the text of the ADA and its legislative history contained elaborate findings and information seemingly documenting widespread disability discrimination.

Chief Justice Rehnquist's opinion for the Court first rejected the contention that *Cleburne* established a special kind of rationality review for disability claims. He also found that Congress had failed to document "a pattern of irrational state discrimination in employment against the disabled." Because the Eleventh Amendment shields only states, and not local governments or private parties, from suit in federal court, the majority considered irrelevant all information in the legislative history concerning supposed discrimination by any entity other than states. All that remained were half a dozen examples from the record that did involve alleged state discrimination. If, as Congress found, more than 43 million Americans suffer from disabilities, this record of state discrimination was surprisingly modest and did not come close to meeting the *Boerne* congruence and proportionality test. In dissent, Justice Breyer (joined by Stevens, Ginsburg, and Souter) added a number of other examples of state discrimination—which the Court dismissed as "unexamined, anecdotal accounts of 'adverse, disparate treatment by state officials.'" Justice Breyer complained that the majority was "reviewing the congressional record as if it were an administrative agency record."

Academics have been critical of *Garrett*, in part because the Court applied to Congress a requirement of factual documentation that Congress cannot easily satisfy.[40] *Garrett* may go even further, imposing an additional requirement that Congress duly deliberate and conscientiously determine that the facts justify invoking its § 5 power. Thus, even if Congress could gather sufficient information—which interest groups supporting legislation invoking the § 5 power now have every incentive to give to Congress—the *Garrett* majority might not be satisfied unless the congressional record revealed a kind of deliberative, objective quality similar to the way a federal district judge is supposed to apply the assembled facts to the legal standards developed by the Supreme Court.[41]

This represents a subtle transformation of the *Boerne* test. In *Boerne,* the Court considered gross disproportionality and lack of congruity to be reasons why a statute could not plausibly be viewed as remedial. In these later cases, the Court has placed a strong burden on Congress to demonstrate a significant level of congruence and proportionality.

Some scholars read *Lopez, Boerne, Seminole,* and *Garrett* as a repudiation of the cooperative relationship forged by the Court with Congress to implement the equality values of *Brown v. Board of Education.*[42] But note how carefully the majorities have distinguished the civil rights cases. Consider the following hypothesis: Because southern apartheid was entrenched and inconsistent with core constitutional values (democracy as well as equality), and because drastic measures were called for, the civil rights precedents were exceptional. But legislators, judges, and commentators have taken the civil rights cases at face value and then expanded upon them to justify more aggressive congressional legislation for the benefit of other social groups—religious minorities (*Boerne*), the aged (*Kimel*), and the disabled (*Garrett*). The Court believes that the normal political process is sufficient to protect these minorities (*Smith; Murgia; Cleburne*). Hence, the need for congressional action was not as great as it was for people of color in the 1960s, and if the Court went along with these new congressional exercises of power there would be no limit to that power. Federalism is a core constitutional value, and it has been of enormous utility as well. Hence, the time has come for the Court to reassert

---

[40] See, e.g., William W. Buzbee & Robert A. Schapiro, *Legislative Record Review*, 54 Stan. L. Rev. 87 (2001); Ruth Colker & James J. Brudney, *Dissing Congress*, 100 Mich. L. Rev. 80 (2001).

[41] For the argument that any requirement of due deliberation fundamentally misconceives how Congress (or any other legislature) operates, see Philip P. Frickey & Steven S. Smith, *Judicial Review, The Congressional Process, and the Federalism Cases: An Interdisciplinary Critique*, 111 Yale L.J. 1707 (2002). By treating Congress like a lower court, *Garrett* "is demanding more than a statute, which is a legislative *outcome*, that meets constitutional standards. It is requiring that a bargaining *process* have the major features of a hypothetical rational policymaking process. It is demanding that the legislative process become something it is not and cannot be in a system of competitive parties operating through several institutions with shared policymaking responsibilities." *Id.* at 1745.

[42] See, e.g., Brudney & Colker, *supra*; Robert Post & Reva Siegel, *Equal Protection by Law: Federal Antidiscrimination Legislation After* Morrison *and* Kimel, 110 Yale L.J. 441 (2000).

limitations on Congress's authority, under the Fourteenth Amendment as well as Article I. Persuasive?

C. CONGRESSIONAL POWER TO RESPOND TO DISCRIMINATION AGAINST WOMEN AND TO PROTECT FUNDAMENTAL RIGHTS

UNITED STATES V. MORRISON
529 U.S. 598, 120 S.Ct. 1740, 146 L.Ed.2d 658 (2000)

CHIEF JUSTICE REHNQUIST delivered the opinion of the Court.

[Petitioner Christy Brzonkala, a student at Virginia Polytechnic Institute (Virginia Tech), complained that respondents Antonio Morrison and James Crawford, football-playing students at Virginia Tech, assaulted and repeatedly raped her. Brzonkala filed a complaint against respondents under Virginia Tech's Sexual Assault Policy. During the school-conducted hearing on her complaint, Morrison admitted having sexual contact with her despite the fact that she had twice told him "no." After the hearing, Virginia Tech's Judicial Committee found insufficient evidence to punish Crawford, but found Morrison guilty of sexual assault and sentenced him to immediate suspension for two semesters. Virginia Tech's vice president later set this aside as excessive punishment. Brzonkala dropped out of the university and sued it and the male students under the Violence Against Women Act, 42 U.S.C. § 13981, which provides a federal cause of action for the victim of a "crime of violence motivated by gender" against the perpetrator. The Court considered whether either the Commerce Clause or § 5 of the Fourteenth Amendment authorized Congress to create this new cause of action. The Court first ruled that the Commerce Clause, as construed in *Lopez*, did not authorize the private VAWA remedy.]

[A] fair reading of *Lopez* shows that the noneconomic, criminal nature of the conduct at issue was central to our decision in that case. *Lopez*'s review of Commerce Clause case law demonstrates that in those cases where we have sustained federal regulation of intrastate activity based upon the activity's substantial effects on interstate commerce, the activity in question has been some sort of economic endeavor. [*Lopez* also emphasized that the gun-free school zone law lacked a jurisdictional element tying the offense to interstate commerce and congressional findings regarding the effects of gun possession in a school zone on interstate commerce. Overall, the Court was worried that if the attenuated connection between guns in school zones and interstate commerce were accepted, Congress "could regulate any activity that it found was related to the economic productivity of individual citizens: family law (including marriage, divorce, and child custody), for example."]

With these principles underlying our Commerce Clause jurisprudence as reference points, the proper resolution of the present cases is clear. Gender-motivated crimes of violence are not, in any sense of the phrase, economic activity. While we need not adopt a categorical rule against aggregating the effects of any noneconomic activity in order to decide these cases, thus far in our Nation's history our cases have upheld Commerce Clause regulation of intrastate activity only where that activity is economic in nature.

Like the Gun-Free School Zones Act at issue in *Lopez*, § 13981 contains no jurisdictional element establishing that the federal cause of action is in pursuance of Congress' power to regulate interstate commerce. Although *Lopez* makes clear that such a jurisdictional element would lend support to the argument that § 13981 is sufficiently tied to interstate commerce, Congress elected to cast § 13981's remedy over a wider, and more purely intrastate, body of violent crime.

In contrast with the lack of congressional findings that we faced in *Lopez*, § 13981 *is* supported by numerous findings regarding the serious impact that gender-motivated violence has on victims and their families. But the existence of congressional findings is not sufficient, by itself, to sustain the constitutionality of Commerce Clause legislation. As we stated in *Lopez*, " '[S]imply because Congress may conclude that a particular activity substantially affects interstate commerce does not necessarily make it so.' " Rather, " '[w]hether particular operations affect interstate commerce sufficiently to come under the constitutional power of Congress to regulate them is ultimately a judicial rather than a legislative question, and can be settled finally only by this Court.' " *Lopez* n.2 (quoting *Heart of Atlanta* (Black, J., concurring)).

In these cases, Congress' findings are substantially weakened by the fact that they rely so heavily on a method of reasoning that we have already rejected as unworkable if we are to maintain the Constitution's enumeration of powers. Congress found that gender-motivated violence affects interstate commerce

> "by deterring potential victims from traveling interstate, from engaging in employment in interstate business, and from transacting with business, and in places involved in interstate commerce; . . . by diminishing national productivity, increasing medical and other costs, and decreasing the supply of and the demand for interstate products." H. R. Conf. Rep. No. 103–711, at 385.

Given these findings and petitioners' arguments, the concern that we expressed in *Lopez* that Congress might use the Commerce Clause to completely obliterate the Constitution's distinction between national and local authority seems well founded. The reasoning that petitioners advance seeks to follow the but-for causal chain from the initial occurrence of violent crime (the suppression of which has always been the prime object of the States' police power) to every attenuated effect upon interstate commerce. If accepted, petitioners' reasoning would allow Congress to regulate any crime as long as the nationwide, aggregated impact of that crime has substantial effects on employment, production, transit, or consumption. Indeed, if Congress may regulate gender-motivated violence, it would be able to regulate murder or any other type of violence since gender-motivated violence, as a subset of all violent crime, is certain to have lesser economic impacts than the larger class of which it is a part.

Petitioners' reasoning, moreover, will not limit Congress to regulating violence but may, as we suggested in *Lopez*, be applied equally as well to family law and other areas of traditional state regulation since the aggregate effect of marriage, divorce, and childrearing on the national economy is undoubtedly significant. Congress may have recognized this specter when it expressly precluded § 13981 from being used in the family law context. See 42 U.S.C. § 13981(e)(4). Under our written Constitution, however, the limitation of congressional authority is not solely a matter of legislative grace. See *Lopez* (Kennedy, J., concurring); *Marbury*.

We accordingly reject the argument that Congress may regulate noneconomic, violent criminal conduct based solely on that conduct's aggregate effect on interstate commerce. The Constitution requires a distinction between what is truly national and what is truly local. In recognizing this fact we preserve one of the few principles that has been consistent since the Clause was adopted. The regulation and punishment of intrastate violence that is not directed at the instrumentalities, channels, or goods involved in interstate commerce has always been the province of the States. See, *e.g.*, *Cohens v. Virginia*, 6 Wheat. 264, 426, 428 (1821) (Marshall, C.J.) (stating that Congress "has no general right to punish murder committed within any of the States," and that it is "clear . . . that congress cannot punish felonies generally"). Indeed, we can think of no better example of the police power, which the Founders denied the National Government and reposed in the States, than the suppression of violent crime and vindication of its victims.

* * * Petitioners' § 5 argument is founded on an assertion that there is pervasive bias in various state justice systems against victims of gender-motivated violence. This assertion is supported by a voluminous congressional record. Specifically, Congress received evidence that many participants in state justice systems are perpetuating an array of erroneous stereotypes and assumptions. Congress concluded that these discriminatory stereotypes often result in insufficient investigation and prosecution of gender-motivated crime, inappropriate focus on the behavior and credibility of the victims of that crime, and unacceptably lenient punishments for those who are actually convicted of gender-motivated

violence. Petitioners contend that this bias denies victims of gender-motivated violence the equal protection of the laws and that Congress therefore acted appropriately in enacting a private civil remedy against the perpetrators of gender-motivated violence to both remedy the States' bias and deter future instances of discrimination in the state courts.

[The state action requirement of the Fourteenth Amendment extends to remedies Congress is authorized to adopt under § 5. *The Civil Rights Cases.* Petitioners argued that *United States v. Guest*, 383 U.S. 745 (1966) implicitly overruled the *Civil Rights Cases.* Although six concurring Justices expressed such a view in two separate statements, the opinion for the Court did not. It would require more than magic mathematics to dislodge the established rule of the *Civil Rights Cases.*]

Petitioners alternatively argue that, unlike the situation in the *Civil Rights Cases,* here there has been gender-based disparate treatment by state authorities, whereas in those cases there was no indication of such state action. There is abundant evidence, however, to show that the Congresses that enacted the Civil Rights Acts of 1871 and 1875 had a purpose similar to that of Congress in enacting § 13981: There were state laws on the books bespeaking equality of treatment, but in the administration of these laws there was discrimination against newly freed slaves. * * *

But even if that distinction were valid, we do not believe it would save § 13981's civil remedy. For the remedy is simply not "corrective in its character, adapted to counteract and redress the operation of such prohibited [s]tate laws or proceedings of [s]tate officers." *Civil Rights Cases.* Or, as we have phrased it in more recent cases, prophylactic legislation under § 5 must have a "'congruence and proportionality between the injury to be prevented or remedied and the means adopted to that end.'" *Florida Prepaid*, quoting *Boerne.* Section 13981 is not aimed at proscribing discrimination by officials which the Fourteenth Amendment might not itself proscribe; it is directed not at any State or state actor, but at individuals who have committed criminal acts motivated by gender bias.

In the present cases, for example, § 13981 visits no consequence whatever on any Virginia public official involved in investigating or prosecuting Brzonkala's assault. The section is, therefore, unlike any of the § 5 remedies that we have previously upheld. [The Voting Rights Act remedies in *Katzenbach v. Morgan* and *South Carolina v. Katzenbach* were imposed upon the states, consistent with *The Civil Rights Cases.*]

Section 13981 is also different from these previously upheld remedies in that it applies uniformly throughout the Nation. Congress' findings indicate that the problem of discrimination against the victims of gender-motivated crimes does not exist in all States, or even most States. By contrast, the § 5 remedy upheld in *Katzenbach v. Morgan* was directed only to the State where the evil found by Congress existed, and in *South Carolina v. Katzenbach*, the remedy was directed only to those States in which Congress found that there had been discrimination. * * *

[JUSTICE THOMAS concurred in the Court's opinion but also expressed his view that the very notion of a 'substantial effects' test under the Commerce Clause is inconsistent with the original understanding of Congress' powers and with this Court's early Commerce Clause cases."]

JUSTICE SOUTER, with whom JUSTICE STEVENS, JUSTICE GINSBURG, and JUSTICE BREYER join, dissenting. * * *

I.   Our cases, which remain at least nominally undisturbed, stand for the following propositions. Congress has the power to legislate with regard to activity that, in the aggregate, has a substantial effect on interstate commerce. See *Wickard v. Filburn*. The fact of such a substantial effect is not an issue for the courts in the first instance, but for the Congress, whose institutional capacity for gathering evidence and taking testimony far exceeds ours. By passing legislation, Congress indicates its conclusion, whether explicitly or not, that facts support its exercise of the commerce power. The business of the courts is to review the congressional assessment, not for soundness but simply for the rationality of concluding that a jurisdictional basis exists in fact. Any explicit findings that Congress chooses to make, though not dispositive of the question of rationality, may advance judicial review by identifying factual authority on which Congress relied. Applying those propositions in these cases can lead to only one conclusion.

One obvious difference from *Lopez* is the mountain of data assembled by Congress, here showing the effects of violence against women on interstate commerce. Passage of the Act in 1994 was preceded by four years of hearings, which included testimony from physicians and law professors; from survivors of rape and domestic violence; and from representatives of state law enforcement and private business. The record includes reports on gender bias from task forces in 21 States, and we have the benefit of specific factual findings in the eight separate Reports issued by Congress and its committees over the long course leading to enactment. Compare *Hodel* (noting "extended hearings," "vast amounts of testimony and documentary evidence," and "years of the most thorough legislative consideration").

With respect to domestic violence, Congress received evidence for the following findings:

"Three out of four American women will be victims of violent crimes sometime during their life." H.R. Rep. No. 103–395 p. 25 (1993).

"Violence is the leading cause of injuries to women ages 15 to 44. . . ." S. Rep. No. 103–138, p. 38 (1993). * * *

"Between 2,000 and 4,000 women die every year from [domestic] abuse." S. Rep. No. 101–545, at 36.

"[A]rrest rates may be as low as 1 for every 100 domestic assaults." S. Rep. No. 101–545, at 38.

"Partial estimates show that violent crime against women costs this country at least 3 billion—not million, but billion—dollars a year." S. Rep. No. 101–545, at 33. * * *

" '[A]n individual who commits rape has only about 4 chances in 100 of being arrested, prosecuted, and found guilty of any offense.' " S. Rep. No. 101–545, at 33, n. 30. * * *

Based on the data thus partially summarized, Congress found that

"crimes of violence motivated by gender have a substantial adverse effect on interstate commerce, by deterring potential victims from traveling interstate, from engaging in employment in interstate business, and from transacting with business, and in places involved, in interstate commerce . . . [,] by diminishing national productivity, increasing medical and other costs, and decreasing the supply of and the demand for interstate products. . . ." H. R. Conf. Rep. No. 103–711, p. 385 (1994).

Congress thereby explicitly stated the predicate for the exercise of its Commerce Clause power. Is its conclusion irrational in view of the data amassed? True, the methodology of particular studies may be challenged, and some of the figures arrived at may be disputed. But the sufficiency of the evidence before Congress to provide a rational basis for the finding cannot seriously be questioned.

Indeed, the legislative record here is far more voluminous than the record compiled by Congress and found sufficient in two prior cases upholding Title II of the Civil Rights Act of 1964 against Commerce Clause challenges. In *Heart of Atlanta Motel* and *McClung*, the Court referred to evidence showing the consequences of racial discrimination by motels and restaurants on interstate commerce. Congress had relied on compelling anecdotal reports that individual instances of segregation cost thousands to millions of dollars. Congress also had evidence that the average black family spent substantially less than the average white family in the same income range on public accommodations, and that discrimination accounted for much of the difference.

While Congress did not, to my knowledge, calculate aggregate dollar values for the nationwide effects of racial discrimination in 1964, in 1994 it did rely on evidence of the harms caused by domestic violence and sexual assault, citing annual costs of $3 billion in 1990 and $5 to $10 billion in 1993. Equally important, though, gender-based violence in the 1990's was shown to operate in a manner similar to racial discrimination in the 1960's in reducing the mobility of employees and their production and consumption of goods shipped in interstate commerce. Like racial discrimination, "[g]ender-based violence bars its most likely targets— women—from full partic[ipation] in the national economy." * * *

II. The Act would have passed muster at any time between *Wickard* in 1942 and *Lopez* in 1995, a period in which the law enjoyed a stable understanding that congressional power under the Commerce Clause, complemented by the authority of the Necessary and Proper Clause, Art. I. § 8 cl. 18, extended to all activity that, when aggregated, has a substantial effect on interstate commerce. [In the post-*Lopez* era, the Court seems to be applying something more than "rational basis" review of congressional findings. The "substantial effects" analysis is one where the Court will second-guess the empirical rigor of congressional evidence. This hard-look judicial review is inconsistent with the Court's precedents and is not required by the enumerated-powers feature of Congress's authority.]

[Justice Souter also took issue with the Court's newest categorical test for limiting Congress's authority under the Commerce Clause.] Obviously, it would not be inconsistent with the text of the Commerce Clause itself to declare "noncommercial" primary activity beyond or presumptively beyond the scope of the commerce power. That variant of categorical approach is not, however, the sole textually permissible way of defining the scope of the Commerce Clause, and any such neat limitation would at least be suspect in the light of the final sentence of Article I, § 8, authorizing Congress to make "all Laws . . . necessary and proper" to give effect to its enumerated powers such as commerce. Accordingly, for significant periods of our history, the Court has defined the commerce power as plenary, unsusceptible to categorical exclusions, and this was the view expressed throughout the latter part of the 20th century in the substantial effects test. These two conceptions of the commerce power, plenary and categorically limited, are in fact old rivals, and today's revival of their competition summons up familiar history * * *. [Justice Souter surveyed the Court's vacillating approach, starting with *Gibbons*, which he interpreted as encompassing a broad understanding of Congress' power and anticipating the approach followed after the New Deal. The New Deal Court rejected earlier cases which had experimented, unsuccessfully, with various limiting principles.]

Since adherence to these formalistically contrived confines of commerce power in large measure provoked the judicial crisis of 1937, one might reasonably have doubted that Members of this Court would ever again toy with a return to the days before *NLRB v. Jones & Laughlin Steel Corp.*, which brought the earlier and nearly disastrous experiment to an end. And yet today's decision can only be seen as a step toward recapturing the prior mistakes. Its revival of a distinction between commercial and noncommercial conduct is at odds with *Wickard*, which repudiated that analysis, and the enquiry into commercial purpose, first intimated by the *Lopez* concurrence, see *Lopez* (opinion of *Kennedy*, J.), is cousin to the intent-based analysis employed in *Hammer*, but rejected for Commerce Clause purposes in *Heart of Atlanta* and *Darby*.

Why is the majority tempted to reject the lesson so painfully learned in 1937? An answer emerges from contrasting *Wickard* with one of the predecessor cases it superseded. It was obvious in *Wickard* that growing wheat for consumption right on the farm was not "commerce" in the common vocabulary, but that did not matter constitutionally so long as the aggregated activity of domestic wheat growing affected commerce substantially. Just a few years before *Wickard*, however, it had certainly been no less obvious that "mining" practices could substantially affect commerce, even though *Carter Coal Co.* had held mining regulation beyond the national commerce power. When we try to fathom the difference between the two cases, it is clear that they did not go in different directions because the *Carter Coal* Court could not understand a causal connection that the *Wickard* Court could grasp; the difference, rather, turned on the fact that the Court in *Carter Coal* had a reason for trying to maintain its categorical, formalistic distinction, while that reason had been abandoned by the time *Wickard* was decided. The reason was laissez-faire economics, the point of which was to keep government interference to a minimum. The Court in *Carter Coal* was still trying to create a laissez-faire world out of the 20th-century economy, and formalistic commercial distinctions were thought to be useful instruments in achieving that object. The Court in *Wickard* knew it could not do any such thing and in the aftermath of the New Deal had long since stopped attempting the impossible. Without the animating economic theory, there was no point in contriving formalisms in a war with Chief Justice Marshall's conception of the commerce power.

If we now ask why the formalistic economic/noneconomic distinction might matter today, after its rejection in *Wickard*, the answer is not that the majority fails to see causal connections in an integrated economic world. The answer is that in the minds of the majority there is a new animating theory that makes categorical formalism seem useful again. Just as the old formalism had value in the service of an economic conception, the new one is useful in serving a conception of federalism. It is the instrument by which assertions of national power are to be limited in favor of preserving a supposedly discernible, proper sphere of state autonomy to legislate or refrain from legislating as the individual States see fit. The legitimacy of the Court's current emphasis on the noncommercial nature of regulated activity, then, does not turn on any logic serving the text of the Commerce Clause or on the realism of the majority's view of the national economy. The essential issue is rather the strength of the majority's claim to have a constitutional warrant for its current conception of a federal relationship enforceable by this Court through limits on otherwise plenary commerce power. This conception is the subject of the majority's second categorical discount applied today to the facts bearing on the substantial effects test.

[Justice Souter also maintained that the Framers expected the relations between state and national authority to be regulated more by political than judicial checks. See *The Federalist* No. 46 (Madison); *Gibbons*; *Garcia* (§ 5B of this Chapter). He also found it ironic that, in the name of federalism, the Court was striking down a statute supported by attorneys general representing 38 states, who admitted that local remedies for violence against women were insufficient and insisted upon the need for a national regulatory response. Thirty-six states joined an amicus brief supporting the statute in this case; only one state has argued the unconstitutionality of the law.] It is, then, not the least irony of these cases that the States will be forced to enjoy the new federalism whether they want it or not. For with the Court's decision today, Antonio Morrison, like *Carter Coal*'s James Carter before him, has "won the states' rights plea against the states themselves." R. Jackson, The Struggle for Judicial Supremacy 160 (1941). * * *

JUSTICE BREYER, joined by JUSTICE STEVENS, dissenting. [We have omitted that portion of the dissent joined also by Justices Souter and Ginsburg.]

[Justice Breyer believed that Congress's authority under the Commerce Clause was sufficient for this statute.] Given my conclusion on the Commerce Clause question, I need not consider Congress' authority under § 5 of the Fourteenth Amendment. Nonetheless, I doubt the Court's reasoning rejecting that source of authority. The Court points out that * * * § 5 does not authorize Congress to use the Fourteenth Amendment as a source of power to remedy the conduct of *private persons*. That is certainly so. The Federal Government's argument, however, is that Congress used § 5 to remedy the actions of *state actors*, namely, those States which, through discriminatory design or the discriminatory conduct of their officials, failed to provide adequate (or any) state remedies for women injured by gender-motivated violence—a failure that the States, and Congress, documented in depth. * * *

But why can Congress not provide a remedy against private actors? Those private actors, of course, did not themselves violate the Constitution. But this Court has held that Congress at least sometimes can enact remedial "[l]egislation ... [that] prohibits conduct which is not itself unconstitutional." *Boerne*; see also *Katzenbach v. Morgan*; *South Carolina v. Katzenbach*. The statutory remedy does not in any sense purport to "determine what constitutes a constitutional violation." *Boerne*. It intrudes little upon either States or private parties. It may lead state actors to improve their own remedial systems, primarily through example. It restricts private actors only by imposing liability for private conduct that is, in the main, already forbidden by state law. Why is the remedy "disproportionate"? And given the relation between remedy and violation— the creation of a federal remedy to substitute for constitutionally inadequate state remedies—where is the lack of "congruence"? * * *

NOTES ON MORRISON AND THE VALUES OF FEDERALISM

1. *The Need for This Limiting Principle?* In its Commerce Clause holding, *Morrison* applies the *Lopez* limiting principle—but the dissenters claim that it does so in an unprincipled way. *Morrison* reveals the dark side of limiting principles: if a constitutional principle designed to constrain Congress is applied flexibly, then it becomes a means for the Court itself to escape constitutional constraint. Why not go all the way, as Justice Thomas suggested in *Lopez*, and limit Congress to regulating activities that are mainly "commercial," rather than more broadly economic? Justice Thomas's approach has a closer relationship to the constitutional text and may be easier to administer than the Chief Justice's approach. Conversely, why not follow the dissenters' suggestion that judicial review of congressional decisions under Article I should be only process-oriented: So long as Congress has openly deliberated and made appropriate findings relating to interstate commerce, the Court should defer to its judgment. Is this essentially no more than the leave-it-to-the-political-process approach?

As for a limiting principle for Congress's § 5 authority, the majority sticks with the state-action doctrine and finds evidence of state bias insufficient to support a remedy against a private actor under the *Boerne* congruence and proportionality test. Notice that none of the dissenters pushes back hard against the Court's § 5 analysis. What would be the consequences of expanding upon the precept accepted by six Justices in *Guest*? If states have failed to provide equal protection to women against sexual assaults, why isn't it proper for Congress to remedy the default by providing needed additional protections, as it did in VAWA?

2. Morrison *and the Purposes of Federalism.* Consider the VAWA Case and its limiting principle in light of the purposes of federalism. As to the particular statute, the libertarian benefits of federalism are purchased at a high libertarian price. That is, the Court protects accused rapists like Antonio Morrison from "excessive" regulation: he and his friend were subject to three levels of regulation (the school's administrative proceeding, possible state prosecution or a tort suit in state court, the federal VAWA lawsuit), one of which the Supreme Court stripped away. From Morrison's point of view, he was being *over-regulated*. But from Christy Brzonkala's point of view, Morrison and those like him—whom the local and state authorities are unlikely to punish—are *under-regulated* without the VAWA remedy, and women's liberty that is sacrificed in the name of "libertarian" federalism. How should the libertarian risks of over-and under-regulation be balanced in this circumstance?

Consider a different perspective. VAWA is premised in part on the notion that local politics—in *Morrison*, the university officials and the county prosecutors—is unresponsive to the plight of rape victims and that the only way to break through these local lock-ins is through federal litigation such as that provided by VAWA. Congress found—and the Court did not deny—that local political lock-ins prevented effective enforcement of sexual assault laws and that those lock-ins were resistant to change through voting-with-their-feet and other mechanisms. Under these circumstances, why shouldn't Congress have authority to regulate? In any event, relegating victims of local oppression to the vote-with-your-feet remedy seems hopelessly inconsistent with the Court's race cases.

3. Morrison *and the Costs of Federalism. Morrison* is a costly decision, both in terms of risking that rapists will escape punishment and that a new generation of women (and men) will be subjected to gender-motivated sexual assault without effective remedies. The majority Justices understand federalism limitations on Congress's authority to be a matter of constitutional imperative. Failure to enforce those rules would be a default in the rule of law itself. From this point of view, *Morrison* may be a *constitutional tragedy*—the application of the rule of law yields not only undesirable consequences but horrible and tragic ones. But the judge charged with applying the rule of law has no choice, and she imposes its iron rule regardless of consequences. Robert Bolt's *A Man for All Seasons* (1962) portrays Sir Thomas More as such a tragic figure. He refused to bend the law to forward favored policies or persons or to punish persons he and his friends thought were "bad." When questioned whether he would apply the law to protect The Devil, he replied that he would. If the law were bent to get Satan, then the law can be similarly bent to get you and me. More died in support of his unbending view of the rule of law. See Lawrence Alexander, *Constitutional Tragedies and Giving Refuge to the Devil,* in *Constitutional Stupidities/Constitutional Tragedies* (William N. Eskridge Jr. & Sanford Levinson eds. 1997).

From the dissenters' point of view, however, *Morrison* is a *constitutional stupidity*—a terrible result unjustified by the rule of law, especially the post-New Deal precedents concerning the extent of congressional power. In the post-legal realist world of law, there is always play in the hard cases. From this fact, Justice Souter argues that the majority Justices must defend their choice to strike down a much-needed federal statute. They cannot. Federalism gave way during the New Deal. And it gave way some more during the Civil Rights Revolution of the 1960s. Why should it not accommodate the Women's Rights Revolution in law of the last generation?

From yet another point of view, *Morrison* may represent a critique of the political process. Perhaps the Court simply did not buy the factual premise of VAWA (that local jurisdictions throughout the country routinely neglect or refuse to provide women victims with equal protection of the law) or the logic of its remedy (that a tort action in federal court that duplicates the tort action such victims would have in state court would deter or remedy such violations of equal protection). Under this view, *Morrison* is similar to *Lopez*: both involve symbolic legislation eagerly passed for political reasons by Members of Congress that merely duplicates the local police power. There are insufficient political safeguards for federalism, and the Court is left as the only institution that can provide meaningful review. Is this kind of thinking too much like *Lochner*, where a business-protecting Court questioned the pro-labor redistributive motives of the New York legislature?

Nevada Department of Human Resources v. Hibbs

538 U.S. 721 (2003)

The Family and Medical Leave Act of 1993, 29 U.S.C. § 2612(a)(1)(C), provides employees with the right to take up to twelve weeks of unpaid leave from work annually to care for a newborn child or for a spouse, child, or parent with a serious health condition. The statute applies to the states as employers and provides a cause of action for equitable relief and damages. In this case, a former employee sought damages from the state for the alleged violation of the statute. In an opinion by **Chief Justice Rehnquist**, the Court upheld the application of the FMLA to state employers.

"The FMLA aims to protect the right to be free from gender-based discrimination in the workplace." The Chief Justice chronicled the long history of state laws restricting women's job opportunities, such as the laws upheld in *Bradwell* and *Muller*, as well as others examined in Chapter 4, § 2B. Congress responded to this history with Title VII of the Civil Rights Act of 1964, which the Court applied to state employers in *Fitzpatrick v. Bitzer*. But Title VII did not address all forms of sex discrimination. "According to evidence that was before Congress when it enacted the FMLA, States continue to rely on invalid gender stereotypes in the employment context, specifically in the administration of leave benefits. Reliance on such stereotypes cannot justify the States' gender discrimination in this area. *Virginia*. The long and extensive history of sex discrimination prompted us to hold that measures that differentiate on the basis of gender warrant heightened scrutiny; here, as in *Fitzpatrick,* the persistence of such unconstitutional discrimination by the States justifies Congress' passage of prophylactic § 5 legislation."

For example, a 1990 Bureau of Labor Statistics (BLS) survey found that 37% of surveyed private-sector employees were covered by maternity leave policies, while only 18% were covered by paternity leave policies. S. Rep. No. 103–3, pp. 14–15 (1993). A 50-state survey also before Congress demonstrated that "[t]he proportion and construction of leave policies available to public sector employees differs little from those offered private sector employees." The Parental and Medical Leave Act of 1986: Joint Hearing before the Subcommittee on Labor-Management Relations and the Subcommittee on Labor Standards of the House Committee on Education and Labor, 99th Cong., 2d Sess., 33 (1986) (statement of Meryl Frank, Director of the Yale Bush Center Infant Care Leave Project). Thus, the Court concluded, "stereotype-based beliefs about the allocation of family duties remained firmly rooted, and employers' reliance on them in establishing discriminatory leave policies remained widespread."

Congress also heard testimony that "[p]arental leave for fathers . . . is rare. Even . . . [w]here child-care leave policies do exist, men, *both in the public and private sectors,* receive notoriously discriminatory treatment in their requests for such leave." States routinely offered women extended maternity leave that far exceeded the typical 4-to-8 week period of physical disability due to pregnancy and childbirth, but very few states granted men a parallel benefit. "This and other differential leave policies were not attributable to any differential physical needs of men and women, but rather to the pervasive sex-role stereotype that caring for family members is women's work." Finally, Congress had evidence that, even where state laws and policies were not facially discriminatory, they were applied in discriminatory ways, and this contributed to "an environment where [sex] discrimination is rampant."

"In sum, the States' record of unconstitutional participation in, and fostering of, gender-based discrimination in the administration of leave benefits is weighty enough to justify the enactment of prophylactic § 5 legislation." The Chief Justice contrasted *Garrett* and *Kimel*, which involved age and disability discrimination, where the Court's equal protection jurisprudence required a "widespread pattern" of irrational reliance on such criteria. *Kimel.* The ADEA and ADA legislative records did not satisfy this requirement.

Because the standard for demonstrating the constitutionality of a gender-based classification is more difficult to meet than our rational-basis test, it was easier for Congress to show a pattern of state constitutional violations, making Hibbs' case more like *South Carolina v. Katzenbach.* In the FMLA, Congress credibly determined that "denial or curtailment of women's employment opportunities has been traceable directly to the pervasive presumption that women are mothers first, and workers second. This prevailing ideology about women's roles has in turn justified discrimination against women when they are mothers or mothers-to-be."

"Stereotypes about women's domestic roles are reinforced by parallel stereotypes presuming a lack of domestic responsibilities for men. Because employers continued to regard the family as the woman's domain, they often denied men similar accommodations or discouraged them from taking leave. These mutually reinforcing stereotypes created a self-fulfilling cycle of discrimination that forced women to continue to assume the role of primary family caregiver, and fostered employers' stereotypical views about women's commitment to work and their value as employees. Those perceptions, in turn, Congress reasoned, lead to subtle discrimination that may be difficult to detect on a case-by-case basis."

Based upon the foregoing review of the congressional record, the Court found that the family-care leave provision of the FMLA, was "congruent and proportional to the targeted violation." Congress had already tried unsuccessfully to address this problem through Title VII and the amendment of Title VII by the Pregnancy Discrimination Act, 42 U.S.C. § 2000e(k). Here, as in *South Carolina v. Katzenbach,* Congress again confronted a "difficult and intractable proble[m]," *Kimel,* where previous legislative attempts had failed. Such problems may justify added prophylactic measures in response.

"By creating an across-the-board, routine employment benefit for all eligible employees, Congress sought to ensure that family-care leave would no longer be stigmatized as an inordinate drain on the workplace caused by female employees, and that employers could not evade leave obligations simply by hiring men. By setting a minimum standard of family leave for *all* eligible employees, irrespective of gender, the FMLA attacks the formerly state-sanctioned stereotype that only women are responsible for family caregiving, thereby reducing employers' incentives to engage in discrimination by basing hiring and promotion decisions on stereotypes."

Joined by Justices Scalia and Thomas, **Justice Kennedy** dissented. He found the FMLA to be a "substantive entitlement program" rather than a remedial statute because it established a floor of 12 weeks' leave. To be proportional and congruent with the documented harm of stereotype-based sex discrimination by state employers, Congress had § 5 power to simply proscribe such discrimination. But, the Court responded. *Kimel* confirmed the lesson of the voting rights precedents that Congress "is not confined to the enactment of legislation that merely parrots the precise wording of the Fourteenth Amendment," but may prohibit "a somewhat broader swath of conduct, including that which is not itself forbidden by the Amendment's text." As in those precedents, Congress has § 5 authority to adopt prophylactic measures.

Thus, "mandated gender equality in the administration of leave benefits, would not have achieved Congress' remedial object. Such a law would allow States to provide for no family leave at all," which would have had devastating effects for women in the workplace. The Court also credited Congress's narrow targeting of "the fault line between work and family—precisely where sex-based overgeneralization has been and remains strongest—and affects only one aspect of the employment relationship." And Congress limited its remedy to longer-term and non-managerial employees, which the Court found helpful to establish a narrow tailored remedy. "Moreover, the cause of action under the FMLA is a restricted one: The damages recoverable are strictly defined and measured by actual monetary losses, and the accrual period for backpay is limited by the Act's 2-year statute of limitations (extended to three years only for willful violations)."

Tennessee v. Lane

541 U.S. 509 (2004)

Title II of the Americans with Disabilities Act provides that "no qualified individual with a disability shall, by reason of such disability, be excluded from participation in or be denied the benefits of the services, programs or activities of a public entity." Two physically handicapped persons who used wheelchairs for mobility brought suit for damages and equitable relief against the state and several of its counties on the ground that, because of physical barriers, they were denied access to state courts. To answer criminal charges against him, at his first appearance George Lane crawled up two flights of stairs to get to the courtroom; he refused to do so for a second hearing and also refused to be carried by officers and then was arrested and jailed for failure to appear. Beverly Jones, a certified court reporter, alleged that she could not get to several courtrooms and thereby was denied employment opportunities as well as the right to access to judicial proceedings. Lane and Jones claimed that the state was in violation of the ADA; the state responded that it was immune under the Eleventh Amendment and that Congress had not lawfully abrogated that immunity because Congress had no Fourteenth Amendment authority to enact Title II, like Title I evaluated in *Garrett*.

Justice Stevens' opinion for the Court noted that *Garrett* had only ruled that ADA Title I (employment discrimination) had not abrogated state immunity and had expressly withheld judgment regarding ADA Titles II and III (public accommodations). Justice Stevens distinguished Title II from Title I in two important ways. First, Title I is an anti-discrimination provision seeking to enforce equal protection guarantees. Title II also seeks to outlaw irrational disability discrimination, but it also seeks to enforce "a variety of other basic constitutional guarantees, infringements of which are subject to more searching judicial review." The Confrontation Clause of the Sixth Amendment, protecting the right of a criminal defendant to be present at all important stages of proceedings, was relevant to Lane's case. More generally, all litigants have due process rights to notice and the opportunity to be heard in court and First Amendment rights of access to judicial proceedings.

Moreover, the legislative record was stronger for Title II. "With respect to the particular services at issue in this case, Congress learned that many individuals, in many States across the country, were being excluded from courthouses and court proceedings by reason of their disabilities. A report before Congress showed that some 76% of public services and programs housed in state-owned buildings were inaccessible to and unusable by persons with disabilities, even taking into account the possibility that the services and programs might be restructured or relocated to other parts of the buildings. Congress itself heard testimony from persons with disabilities who described the physical inaccessibility of local courthouses. And its appointed task force heard numerous examples of the exclusion of persons with disabilities from state judicial services and programs, including exclusion of persons with visual impairments and hearing impairments from jury service, failure of state and local governments to provide interpretive services for the hearing impaired, failure to permit the testimony of adults with developmental disabilities in abuse cases, and failure to make courtrooms accessible to witnesses with physical disabilities."

Justice Stevens concluded that the record of state constitutional violations was stronger in this case than it had been in *Hibbs*. "Title II is aimed at the enforcement of a variety of basic rights, including the right of access to the courts at issue in this case, that call for a standard of judicial review at least as searching, and in some cases more searching, than the standard that applies to sex-based classifications." Supporting the conclusion that Title II was a "congruent and proportional" response to constitutional violations was the fact that Title II's remedy was a "reasonable accommodation" by public accommodations for people with disabilities. This gave states and their organs flexible options for providing access.

"This duty to accommodate is perfectly consistent with the well-established due process principle that, 'within the limits of practicability, a State must afford to all individuals a meaningful opportunity to be heard' in its courts. Our cases have recognized a number of affirmative obligations that flow from this principle: the duty to waive filing fees in certain family-law and criminal cases, the duty to provide transcripts to criminal defendants seeking review of their convictions, and the duty to provide counsel to certain criminal defendants. Each of these cases makes clear that ordinary considerations of cost and convenience alone cannot justify a State's failure to provide individuals with a meaningful right of access to the courts. Judged against this backdrop, Title II's affirmative obligation to accommodate persons with disabilities in the administration of justice cannot be said to be "so out of proportion to a supposed remedial or preventive object that it cannot be understood as responsive to, or designed to prevent, unconstitutional behavior." *Boerne.* It is, rather, a reasonable prophylactic measure, reasonably targeted to a legitimate end." In a footnote, Justice Stevens stated: "Because this case implicates the right of access to the courts, we need not consider whether Title II's duty to accommodate exceeds what the Constitution requires in the class of cases that implicate only *Cleburne*'s prohibition on irrational discrimination. See *Garrett.*"

Dissenting and arguing that Title II was not a valid exercise of Congress's Fourteenth Amendment authority, **Chief Justice Rehnquist** (joined by Justices Kennedy and Thomas) distinguished *Hibbs* because it involved sex discrimination, where the standard of scrutiny was higher.

Justice Scalia dissented in a separate opinion. Confessing that he had reluctantly joined the majority in *Boerne,* he repudiated his acceptance of the congruence and proportionality test, which has been too "malleable" and subject to "individual judges' policy preferences," and has made the Court too much "Congress's taskmaster" in second-guessing legislative handiwork. Returning to the narrowness of *The Civil Rights Cases,* Justice Scalia would have limited § 5 to simply "enforc[ing]" § 1 of the Fourteenth Amendment. Congress could, for example, provide a cause of action against a violation of § 1, could make such violations federal crimes, and could impose reporting obligations on the states to facilitate the enforcement of the Fourteenth Amendment, but Congress would have no prophylactic authority. Acknowledging that "[t]he major impediment" to this approach was *stare decisis,* Justice Scalia would have accorded a broader authority to congressional power to attack racial discrimination—what he saw as at the core of § 1 and which was the subject matter of the expansive § 5 precedents (*South Carolina*, *Morgan*, *Rome*, *Alfred H. Mayer Co.*).

Coleman v. Court of Appeals of Maryland

566 U.S. 30 (2012)

An employee may take leave under the FMLA for: (A) "the birth of a son or daughter . . . in order to care for such son or daughter," (B) the adoption or foster-care placement of a child with the employee, (C) the care of a "spouse . . . son, daughter, or parent" with "a serious health condition," and (D) the employee's own serious health condition when the condition interferes with the employee's ability to perform at work. 29 U.S.C. § 2612(a)(1). The Court in *Hibbs* upheld subparagraph (C) as applied to state employers, but in *Coleman* the Court ruled that subparagraph (D) could not be constitutionally applied to state employers.

Justice Kennedy delivered a plurality opinion joined by Chief Justice Roberts and Justices Thomas and Alito. At the time the FMLA was enacted, almost all state employees were covered by paid sick care plans, and there was no evidence that states discriminated in any way against women in these plans, nor was there evidence of stereotyping. Indeed, Congress found that "men and women are out on medical leave approximately equally." H.R.Rep. No. 101–28, pt. 1, p. 15 (1989).

"Without widespread evidence of sex discrimination or sex stereotyping in the administration of sick leave, it is apparent that the congressional purpose in enacting the self-care provision is unrelated to these supposed wrongs. The legislative history of the self-care provision reveals a concern for the economic burdens on the employee and the employee's family resulting from illness-related job loss and a concern for discrimination on the basis of illness, not sex. In the findings pertinent to the self-care provision, the statute makes no reference to any distinction on the basis of sex. See 29 U.S.C. § 2601(a)(4) ('[T]here is inadequate job security for employees who have serious health conditions that prevent them from working for temporary periods'). By contrast, with regard to family care [the provision upheld in *Hibbs*], Congress invoked concerns related to gender. See § 2601(a)(5) ('[D]ue to the nature of the roles of men and women in our society, the primary responsibility for family caretaking often falls on women, and such responsibility affects the working lives of women more than it affects the working lives of men').

"It is true the self-care provision offers some women a benefit by allowing them to take leave for pregnancy-related illnesses; but as a remedy, the provision is not congruent and proportional to any identified constitutional violations. At the time of the FMLA's enactment, 'ninety-five percent' of state employees had paid sick-leave plans at work, and 'ninety-six percent' had short-term disability protection. Texas Brief 13–14 (citing BLS Rept. 17–26). State employees presumably could take leave for pregnancy-related illnesses under these policies, and Congress did not document any pattern of States excluding pregnancy-related illnesses from sick-leave or disability-leave policies. 'Congress . . . said nothing about the existence or adequacy of state remedies.' *Florida Prepaid.* It follows that abrogating the States' immunity from suits for damages for failure to give self-care leave is not a congruent and proportional remedy if the existing state leave policies would have sufficed.

Justice Scalia concurred only in the Court's judgment; after *Lane,* he would only sustain Congress's § 5 authority when it was aimed at state action that *itself* violated the Fourteenth Amendment.

Justice Ginsburg wrote a dissenting opinion. In footnote 1, joined by Justice Breyer, she maintained that *Seminole Tribe* was wrongly decided and therefore that Congress had authority under the Commerce Clause to abrogate the state's Eleventh Amendment immunity. In the remainder of her dissent, joined by Justices Breyer, Sotomayor, and Kagan, Justice Ginsburg argued that the self-care provision, like the family-care provision upheld in *Hibbs,* satisfied the Court's congruence and proportionality test. Both provisions were responsive to pervasive state discrimination against pregnant female workers.

Specifically, Congress heard evidence that state employers pervasively discriminated against pregnant employees, denying them sufficient leave time to recover from their pregnancies. Both the self-care and the family-leave provisions in the FMLA were responsive to this pervasive sex discrimination and, hence, satisfied the *Boerne/Hibbs* test. Justice Ginsburg conceded that *Geduldig v. Aiello* (Chapter 4, § 2) ruled that pregnancy discrimination is not sex discrimination, but she urged the Court to overrule that clearly erroneous precedent.

Even if *Geduldig* were not overruled, the self-care provision satisfied *Boerne,* because Congress accepted the evidence offered by the Chamber of Commerce and many other sources that a statute requiring only family-care (*Hibbs*) and not self-care (*Coleman*) leave would be perceived as making female workers much more expensive than male workers. To head off the possibility that the FMLA would actually fuel new sex discriminations, Congress included the self-care leave that everyone agreed would be used by men as well as women.

Although Justice Ginsburg dissented from the Court's application of *Seminole Tribe* to exempt the state from monetary damages, she observed that the FMLA's self-care provision is still binding on state employers and that employees can sue the state for injunctive relief, pursuant to *Ex parte Young,* 209 U.S. 123 (1908). Also, the Department of Labor may bring an action against a state for violating the self-care provision and recover monetary relief on an employee's behalf. 29 U.S.C. § 2617(b)(2)–(3), (d).

NOTES ON HIBBS, LANE, AND COLEMAN

1. *Liberal Readings of the Record.* The debates in these recent cases turn on how sympathetically the Court ought to read the congressional record of constitutional violations. This is particularly notable in *Hibbs,* where Justice

Kennedy's dissenting opinion picked apart the record to demonstrate that there were few hard constitutional violations found by Congress. His charges against the Chief Justice's sympathetic reading included the following: (a) The Court's focus was too broad. The FMLA was not a response to general sex discrimination in the workplace, but was responding only to alleged discrimination in the granting of family and medical leaves. (b) The only evidence that state as well as private sector employers discriminated came in conclusory form from two witnesses to the 1986 precursor bill, which was very different from the FMLA. There was no empirical basis for Congress's conclusion. (c) Indeed, the states led the way. Thirty states had parental and medical leave statutes before Congress enacted the FMLA in 1993. At most, three states had "discriminatory" policies, because they had programs women but not men could take advantage of. These were troubling criticisms. Why were they not persuasive to the Chief Justice?[43]

Contrast *Coleman*, where Justice Kennedy wrote for the Court and gave the congressional record the same close and unforgiving read. After the departures of both Chief Justice Rehnquist and Justice O'Connor (both in the *Hibbs* majority), Justice Ginsburg's generous reading of the record garnered only four votes. Her best argument was that the self-care provision was needed to prevent the FMLA from becoming a reason not to hire women: Why was that not more persuasive to other Justices? We confess some astonishment that four Justices read the ADA record so stingily in *Lane*, especially in light of the due process and First Amendment rights implicated in a disabled person's access to court. Why was *Lane* not an easy case under *Boerne*?

2. *Feminism and Federalism. Coleman* was the third recent federalism decision that involved congressional responses to violence against women and workplace inequality. Consider the views of Robin West (Chapter 2, § 3) and Catharine MacKinnon (Chapter 4, § 2), that homes and workplaces, and not the state, have been the primary situses of violence and discrimination against women. Given this social fact, aggressive state responses are needed to provide women the literal "equal protection of the law" that men enjoy. Notice that, in *Coleman*, all three female Justices found that point persuasive, while five of the six male Justices did not. (The three female Justices are all Democratic appointees, but even GOP Justice O'Connor was a key vote for the expansive majority opinion in *Hibbs*.)

Putting *Hibbs* and *Coleman* together, female state employees are not protected by the FMLA when they are pregnant—but they are protected after pregnancy, if they want to take care of their offspring. This recalls the sameness-difference debate within feminist jurisprudence (Chapter 4, § 2). Liberal feminists such as Justice Ginsburg say that women are pretty much like men, and when they are treated differently that is subject to heightened scrutiny. *Hibbs* reflects this point of view: the FMLA is justified because it offsets the tendency of employers to consider women as family caregivers first

---

[43] For a cogent account, see Reva Siegel, *You've Come a Long Way, Baby: Rehnquist's New Approach to Pregnancy Discrimination in* Hibbs, 58 Stan. L. Rev. 1871 (2006).

and employees second. Difference feminists say that women are actually different from men; as a descriptive matter, women tend to be caregivers, and as a normative matter the state ought to be supporting their caregiving. When the Supreme Court has agreed with difference feminists, however, it has used those "real differences" to deny rights rather than insist on them, as in *Coleman*.

The conservative exploitation of "real differences" jurisprudence provides one angle for understanding *Coleman*. The majority Justices were unwilling to view employer pregnancy policies as a matter of "discrimination," perhaps because they viewed the matter as naturalized rather than social. For them, it was not discrimination to treat different things differently, and pregnancy was different from anything else and so had its own distinctive jurisprudence. In contrast, the dissenting Justices connected pregnancy with social practices of stereotyping and, hence, viewed it as deeply connected with the anti-discrimination project. Should it make a difference that Congress agreed with Justice Ginsburg? It seemed to make a difference in *Lane* as well as *Hibbs*, but not in *Coleman*.

3. *The Court's Narrow Understanding of Legislative Constitutionalism.* *Coleman* was an important rejection of strong versions of "legislative constitutionalism" (Chapter 2, § 3C). Not only did Congress have to follow the Supreme Court's understanding of the Equal Protection Clause (*Boerne*), but the Court reviewed Congress's linkage between factual findings and constitutional violations with the beady-eyed scrutiny usually reserved for conclusions of law by lower court judges (*Garrett* and *Kimel*).

What of the race cases? The majority Justices cabined legislative constitutionalism to the race cases of the 1960s: the Court let Congress do that to combat race discrimination, but the Court was not willing to let Congress do this again against other forms of discrimination. After Justice O'Connor wasbeen replaced by the more conservative Justice Alito, would the Roberts Court dare to revisit the legislative constitutionalism of the 1960s?

SHELBY COUNTY, ALABAMA V. HOLDER
570 U.S. 529, 133 S.Ct. 2612, 186 L.Ed.2d 651 (2013)

CHIEF JUSTICE ROBERTS delivered the opinion of the Court.

[As illustrated in the *Katzenbach* Cases and *City of Rome*, § 5 of the Voting Rights Act of 1965 imposed preclearance requirements on jurisdictions defined in § 4(b), namely, those states or political subdivisions that on November 1, 1964 maintained a test or device that limited voting *and* had voting levels lower than 50% of the eligible voters in the 1964 election. Congress reauthorized the Act with minimal changes to the § 4(b) coverage formula in 1970 and 1975 (notably, to include language barriers to the definition of tests or devices limiting voting opportunities, which added Texas, Arizona, and Alaska to the roster of covered jurisdictions), and with no changes to the formula in 1982 and 2006. In 2006, Congress significantly expanded the § 5 preclearance restrictions. Shelby County fell under the coverage formula of § 4(b) but objected to preclearance on the ground that this portion of the Voting Rights Act was unconstitutional.]

Nearly 50 years later, [the § 5 preclearance requirements for covered jurisdictions] are still in effect; indeed, they have been made more stringent, and are now scheduled to last until 2031. There is no denying, however, that the conditions that originally justified these measures no longer characterize voting in the covered jurisdictions. By 2009, "the racial gap in voter registration and turnout [was] lower in the States originally covered by § 5 than it [was] nationwide." *Northwest Austin Municipal Util. Dist. No. One* v. *Holder*, 557 U.S. 193, 203–204 (2009).[44] Since that time, Census Bureau data indicate that African-American voter turnout has come to exceed white voter turnout in five of the six States originally covered by § 5,with a gap in the sixth State of less than one half of one percent. See Dept. of Commerce, Census Bureau, Reported Voting and Registration, by Sex, Race and Hispanic Origin, for States (Nov. 2012) (Table 4b). * * *

[II.] In *Northwest Austin*, we stated that "the Act imposes current burdens and must be justified by current needs." And we concluded that "a departure from the fundamental principle of equal sovereignty requires a showing that a statute's disparate geographic coverage is sufficiently related to the problem that it targets." *Ibid.* These basic principles guide our review of the question before us. [The Chief Justice set forth the well-established federalist structure of government and the substantial "autonomy" the states have in structuring their electoral processes, especially in state elections.]

Not only do States retain sovereignty under the Constitution, there is also a "fundamental principle of *equal* sovereignty" among the States. *Northwest Austin* (emphasis added). Over a hundred years ago, this Court explained that our Nation "was and is a union of States, equal in power, dignity and authority." *Coyle* v. *Smith*, 221 U.S. 559, 567 (1911). Indeed, "the constitutional equality of the States is essential to the harmonious operation of the scheme upon which the Republic was organized." *Id.,* at 580. *Coyle* concerned the admission of new States, and *Katzenbach* rejected the notion that the principle operated as a *bar* on differential treatment outside that context. At the same time, as we made clear in *Northwest Austin*, the fundamental principle of equal sovereignty remains highly pertinent in assessing subsequent disparate treatment of States.

---

[44] [Eds.] In *Northwest Austin*, the Court faced a "serious" constitutional challenge to §§ 4–5 but declined to address it, because there was a statutory ground for giving relief to a local government objecting to preclearance. To avoid the serious constitutional problems with §§ 4(b) and 5, the Court interpreted the "bailout" provision in § 4(a) broadly. Shelby County did not seek bailout under § 4(a), and so its challenge did not offer the Court a statutory solution.

The Voting Rights Act sharply departs from these basic principles. It suspends "*all* changes to state election law—however innocuous—until they have been precleared by federal authorities in Washington, D.C." States must beseech the Federal Government for permission to implement laws that they would otherwise have the right to enact and execute on their own, subject of course to any injunction in a § 2 action. The Attorney General has 60 days to object to a preclearance request, longer if he requests more information. See 28 CFR §§ 51.9, 51.37. If a State seeks preclearance from a three judge court, the process can take years.

And despite the tradition of equal sovereignty, the Act applies to only nine States (and several additional counties). While one State waits months or years and expends funds to implement a validly enacted law, its neighbor can typically put the same law into effect immediately, through the normal legislative process. [Invoking these background principles, the Chief Justice explained that *Katzbenbach*'s willingness to uphold the extraordinary requirements in §§ 4–5 was premised upon their temporary remedial features.]

Nearly 50 years later, things have changed dramatically. Shelby County contends that the preclearance requirement, even without regard to its disparate coverage, is now unconstitutional. Its arguments have a good deal of force. In the covered jurisdictions, "[v]oter turnout and registration rates now approach parity. Blatantly discriminatory evasions of federal decrees are rare. And minority candidates hold office at unprecedented levels." *Northwest Austin*. The tests and devices that blocked access to the ballot have been forbidden nationwide for over 40 years. See § 6, 84 Stat. 315; § 102, 89 Stat. 400. [The Chief Justice summed up the progress by reference to data on voting turn-out, by race, that was compiled by the House and Senate Judiciary Committees for the 2006 reauthorization:]

	1965			2004		
	White	Black	Gap	White	Black	Gap
Alabama	69.2	19.3	49.9	73.8	72.9	0.9
Georgia	62.[6]	27.4	35.2	63.5	64.2	− 0.7
Louisiana	80.5	31.6	48.9	75.1	71.1	4.0
Mississippi	69.9	6.7	63.2	72.3	76.1	− 3.8
South Carolina	75.7	37.3	38.4	74.4	71.1	3.3
Virginia	61.1	38.3	22.8	68.2	57.4	10.8

See S. Rep. No. 109–295, p. 11 (2006); H. R. Rep. No. 109–478, at 12.

[In light of these data, the Chief Justice found Congress's reauthorization of the Voting Rights Act, with no change in the coverage formula, in 1982 and 2006 astonishing. In Part III of his opinion, the Chief Justice explained that applying the old 1965 formula to impose preclearance obligations on states, like Alabama, that had not used voting tests since 1965 and that now had virtually complete parity in racial voting levels over several election cycles, was constitutionally unsustainable. The Fifteenth Amendment was intended to ensure voting rights now and in the future, not to punish jurisdictions for past discriminations.]

[The government argued that Congress compiled an extensive record of continuing evasions by the covered jurisdictions.] The court below and the parties have debated what that record shows * * *. Regardless of how to look at the record, however, no one can fairly say that it shows anything approaching the "pervasive," "flagrant," "widespread," and "rampant" discrimination that faced Congress in 1965, and that clearly distinguished the covered jurisdictions from the rest of the Nation at that time. *Katzenbach*; *Northwest Austin*.

But a more fundamental problem remains: Congress did not use the record it compiled to shape a coverage formula grounded in current conditions. It instead reenacted a formula based on 40-year-old facts having no logical relation to the present day. The dissent relies on "second generation barriers," which are not impediments to the casting of ballots, but rather electoral arrangements that affect the weight of minority votes. That does not cure the problem. Viewing the preclearance requirements as targeting such efforts simply highlights the irrationality of continued reliance on the § 4 coverage formula, which is based on voting tests and access to the ballot, not vote dilution. We cannot pretend that we are reviewing an updated statute, or try our hand at updating the statute ourselves, based on the new record compiled by Congress. Contrary to the dissent's contention, we are not ignoring the record; we are simply recognizing that it played no role in shaping the statutory formula before us today. [The Chief Justice concluded with an invitation to Congress to reconsider the coverage formula and enact one that remedies current rather than historical impediments to exercise of the franchise by racial minorities.]

[**JUSTICE THOMAS** wrote a concurring opinion agreeing with the Chief Justice that the coverage formula in § 4 went beyond Congress's Fifteenth Amendment authority, but also arguing that the preclearance requirements of § 5 were unconstitutional as well. The "extraordinary" burdens imposed by § 5 would be unconstitutional even if § 4 could be more narrowly tailored, Justice Thomas concluded.]

JUSTICE GINSBURG, with whom **JUSTICE BREYER, JUSTICE SOTOMAYOR,** and **JUSTICE KAGAN** join, dissenting.

In the Court's view, the very success of § 5 of the Voting Rights Act demands its dormancy. Congress was of another mind. Recognizing that large progress has been made, Congress determined, based on a voluminous record, that the scourge of discrimination was not yet extirpated. The question this case presents is who decides whether, as currently operative, § 5 remains justifiable, this Court, or a Congress charged with the obligation to enforce the post-Civil War Amendments "by appropriate legislation." [XV Am., § 2.] With overwhelming support in both Houses, Congress concluded that, for two prime reasons, § 5 should continue in force, unabated. First, continuance would facilitate completion of the impressive gains thus far made; and second, continuance would guard against backsliding. Those assessments were well within Congress' province to make and should elicit this Court's unstinting approbation. * * *

After considering the full legislative record, Congress made the following findings: The VRA has directly caused significant progress in eliminating first-generation barriers to ballot access, leading to a marked increase in minority voter registration and turnout and the number of minority elected officials. 2006 Reauthorization § 2(b)(1). But despite this progress, "second generation barriers constructed to prevent minority voters from fully participating in the electoral process" continued to exist, as well as racially polarized voting in the covered jurisdictions, which increased the political vulnerability of racial and language minorities in those jurisdictions. §§ 2(b)(2)–(3). Extensive "[e]vidence of continued discrimination," Congress concluded, "clearly show[ed] the continued need for Federal oversight" in covered jurisdictions. §§ 2(b)(4)–(5). The overall record demonstrated to the federal lawmakers that, "without the continuation of the Voting Rights Act of 1965 protections, racial and language minority citizens will be deprived of the opportunity to exercise their right to vote, or will have their votes diluted, undermining the significant gains made by minorities in the last 40 years." § 2(b)(9).

Based on these findings, Congress reauthorized preclearance for another 25 years, while also undertaking to reconsider the extension after 15 years to ensure that the provision was still necessary and effective. [These findings, supported by exhaustive legislative hearings and factual materials assembled for Congress, are entitled to the Court's deference, argued Justice Ginsburg. This is particularly true where Congress is implementing the Fifteenth Amendment, whose text borrows the expansive language of § 2. Cf. *McCulloch* (an example of liberal construction for Congress's discretion in implementing core constitutional grants of authority).]

I begin with the evidence on which Congress based its decision to continue the preclearance remedy. The surest way to evaluate whether that remedy remains in order is to see if preclearance is still effectively preventing discriminatory changes to voting laws. See *City of Rome* (identifying "information on the number and types of submissions made by covered jurisdictions and the number and nature of objections interposed by the Attorney General" as a primary basis for upholding the 1975 reauthorization). On that score, the record before Congress was huge. In fact, Congress found there were *more* DOJ objections between 1982 and 2004 (626) than there were between 1965 and the 1982 reauthorization (490). 1 Voting Rights Act: Evidence of Continued Need, Hearing before the Subcommittee on the Constitution of the House Committee on the Judiciary, 109th Cong., 2d Sess., p. 172 (2006) (hereinafter Evidence of Continued Need).

All told, between 1982 and 2006, DOJ objections blocked over 700 voting changes based on a determination that the changes were discriminatory. H.R. Rep. No. 109–478, at 21. Congress found that the majority of DOJ objections included findings of discriminatory intent, and that the changes blocked by preclearance were "calculated decisions to keep minority voters from fully participating in the political process." H.R. Rep. 109–478, at 21. On top of that, over the same time period the DOJ and private plaintiffs succeeded in more than 100 actions to enforce the § 5 preclearance requirements. 1 Evidence of Continued Need 186, 250. [Likewise, the record established that the covered jurisdictions had to alter or withdraw an unprecedented number of proposed changes in the post-1982 period.]

The number of discriminatory changes blocked or deterred by the preclearance requirement suggests that the state of voting rights in the covered jurisdictions would have been significantly different absent this remedy. Surveying the type of changes stopped by the preclearance procedure conveys a sense of the extent to which § 5 continues to protect minority voting rights. [For example, in 1995, Mississippi sought to reenact a dual voter registration system, "which was initially enacted in 1892 to disenfranchise Black voters," and for that reason, was struck down by a federal court in 1987. H.R. Rep. No. 109–478, at 39. See also *League of United Latin American Citizens* v. *Perry*, 548 U.S. 399, 440 (2006) (blocking discriminatory voting proposals from Texas). These examples, and others invoked by Justice Ginsburg, were only the "tip of the iceberg," as Congress received and credited ample evidence that covered jurisdictions evaded the VRA through subtle as well as blatant measures. Justice Ginsburg then considered evidence that § 4(b)'s coverage formula still addressed current and not just historical needs for remedy.]

There is no question, moreover, that the covered jurisdictions have a unique history of problems with racial discrimination in voting.

Consideration of this long history, still in living memory, was altogether appropriate. The Court criticizes Congress for failing to recognize that "history did not end in 1965." But the Court ignores that "what's past is prologue." W. Shakespeare, The Tempest, act 2, sc. 1. And "[t]hose who cannot remember the past are condemned to repeat it." 1 G. Santayana, The Life of Reason 284 (1905). Congress was especially mindful of the need to reinforce the gains already made and to prevent backsliding. 2006 Reauthorization § 2(b)(9).

Of particular importance, even after 40 years and thousands of discriminatory changes blocked by preclearance, conditions in the covered jurisdictions demonstrated that the formula was still justified by "current needs." *Northwest Austin*. Congress learned of these conditions through a report, known as the Katz study, that looked at § 2 suits between 1982 and 2004. To Examine the Impact and Effectiveness of the Voting Rights Act: Hearing before the Subcommittee on the Constitution of the House Committee on the Judiciary, 109th Cong., 1st Sess., pp. 964–1124 (2005). Because the private right of action authorized by § 2 of the VRA applies nationwide, a comparison of § 2 lawsuits in covered and noncovered jurisdictions provides an appropriate yardstick for measuring differences between covered and noncovered jurisdictions. If differences in the risk of voting discrimination between covered and noncovered jurisdictions had disappeared, one would expect that the rate of successful § 2 lawsuits would be roughly the same in both areas. The study's findings, however, indicated that racial discrimination in voting remains "concentrated in the jurisdictions singled out for preclearance." *Northwest Austin*.

Although covered jurisdictions account for less than 25 percent of the country's population, the Katz study revealed that they accounted for 56 percent of successful § 2 litigation since 1982. Controlling for population, there were nearly *four* times as many successful § 2 cases in covered jurisdictions as there were in noncovered jurisdictions. The Katz study further found that § 2 lawsuits are more likely to succeed when they are filed in covered jurisdictions than in noncovered jurisdictions. From these findings—ignored by the Court—Congress reasonably concluded that the coverage formula continues to identify the jurisdictions of greatest concern.

[Justice Ginsburg also invoked evidence before Congress that voting in the covered jurisdictions was more racially polarized than elsewhere in the country. H.R. Rep. No. 109–478, at 34–35. And she observed that the § 4 coverage regime was far from static, contrary to the Court's suggestions. Section 4(a), expanded in 1982, allows jurisdictions to bail out of § 4(b)'s coverage if they can demonstrate a history of voting regularity. Indeed, more than 200 jurisdictions have bailed out of the VRA since the 1982 Reauthorization.

[Justice Ginsburg took the Court to task for its treatment of the Court's own precedents for analyzing constitutional issues. Shelby County's challenge was a facial one: under the Court's precedents, such a challenge can succeed *only* if the challenger can show there is "no set of circumstances" to which the statute can constitutionally be applied. *United States* v. *Salerno*, 481 U.S. 739, 745 (1987). Why did the Court not engage the *Salerno* analysis? Apparently because Alabama was the classic case where the "old" formula applied in full force.]

Although circumstances in Alabama have changed, serious concerns remain. Between 1982 and 2005, Alabama had one of the highest rates of successful § 2 suits, second only to its VRA-covered neighbor Mississippi. In other words, even while subject to the restraining effect of § 5, Alabama was found to have "deni[ed] or abridge[d]" voting rights "on account of race or color" more frequently than nearly all other States in the Union. * * * Alabama's sorry history of § 2 violations alone provides sufficient justification for Congress' determination in 2006 that the State should remain subject to § 5's preclearance requirement. [Two recent Supreme Court decisions confirmed the perseverance of "purposeful racial discrimination in Alabama."]

A recent FBI investigation provides a further window into the persistence of racial discrimination in state politics. See *United States* v. *McGregor*, 824 F.Supp.2d 1339, 1344–1348 (MD Ala. 2011). Recording devices worn by state legislators cooperating with the FBI's investigation captured conversations between members of the state legislature and their political allies. The recorded conversations are shocking. Members of the state Senate derisively refer to African-Americans as "Aborigines" and talk openly of their aim to quash a particular gambling-related referendum because the referendum, if placed on the ballot, might increase African-American voter turnout. *Id.*, at 1345–1346 (internal quotation marks omitted). See also *id.*, at 1345 (legislators and their allies expressed concern that if the referendum were placed on the ballot, " '[e]very black, every illiterate' would be 'bused [to the polls] on HUD financed buses' "). These conversations occurred not in the 1870's, or even in the 1960's, they took place in 2010. * * *

The sad irony of today's decision lies in its utter failure to grasp why the VRA has proven effective. The Court appears to believe that the VRA's success in eliminating the specific devices extant in 1965 means that preclearance is no longer needed. With that belief, and the argument derived from it, history repeats itself. The same assumption—that the problem could be solved when particular methods of voting discrimination are identified and eliminated—was indulged and proved wrong repeatedly prior to the VRA's enactment. Unlike prior statutes, which singled out particular tests or devices, the VRA is grounded in Congress' recognition of the "variety and persistence" of measures designed to impair minority voting rights. *Katzenbach*. In truth, the evolution of voting discrimination into more subtle second-generation barriers is powerful evidence that a remedy as effective as preclearance remains vital to protect minority voting rights and prevent backsliding. * * *

NOTES ON SHELBY COUNTY

1. *The Doctrinal Debate.* Does the Chief Justice have satisfactory answers to the doctrinal issues raised by Justice Ginsburg's dissenting opinion? Consider the Court's failure to engage Justice Ginsburg's charge that the majority was violating the doctrine established by *United States* v. *Salerno*, 481 U.S. 739, 745 (1987). That is, Shelby County's challenge to the VRA was a facial challenge; under *Salerno,* the challenger was required to show that there was "no set of circumstances" to which the VRA could constitutionally be applied. This seems hard to accomplish, as Justice Ginsburg demonstrated. How should the Chief Justice have responded?

The Chief Justice's opinion in *Shelby County* is now a citation for a constitutional norm that all states must, presumptively, be treated the same. What is the legal source of this norm? It does not appear anywhere in the Constitution, or even in *The Federalist*. The Chief Justice cited *Coyle* v. *Smith* but immediately conceded that *Coyle* created the "equal footing doctrine," relating to the admission of new states under U.S. Const., art. IV, § 3, cl. 1; see Sonia Sotomayor de Noonen, Note, *Statehood and the Equal Footing Doctrine: The Case for Puerto Rican Seabed Rights*, 88 Yale L.J. 825 (1979) (demonstrating that the equal footing doctrine does not prevent different treatment for new states, grounded upon demonstrated need). Does this norm have a solid "footing" in the Constitution's text? Structure? Original meaning?

How far does the Court's state equal treatment precept extend? For example, if Congress decided that all nuclear waste materials would be stored in Nevada, over the objections of its citizens, would *Shelby County* stand in the way? Would the Court require Congress to spread the waste proportionately among all 50 states? Article I, § 9, cl. 4 of the Constitution imposes a proportionality requirement upon "direct" taxation by the federal government: Why, then, is there need for a Direct Taxation Clause in the Constitution of 1789 if it already embodied a background norm of state equal treatment? The Sixteenth Amendment negated the Direct Taxation Clause: How does this affect the willingness of a strict textualist to create a norm of state equal treatment?

2. *The End of the Second Reconstruction?* Note the parallel to the Court's evolving *Brown II* jurisprudence, set forth in Chapter 2, § 2C2 of the Casebook. Justices Scalia and Thomas have insisted in the *Brown II* cases that there is a laches limitation to constitutional remedies: once extraordinary remedies have been implemented for a period of time, and jurisdictions have formally acquiesced in them, courts must relinquish jurisdiction, even if (de facto) racial segregation continues. See also *Parents Involved in Community*

Schools v. Seattle School District No. 1, where the Court rebuked local efforts to create integrated schools through race-sensitive criteria.

In *Shelby County*, the Court majority revealed a similar impatience with longstanding remediation by Congress (rather than the Court) and terminated the process upon a finding that covered jurisdictions have formally acquiesced in the remedies. As in the school segregation cases, the liberal Justices dissented, on the ground that there was evidence of continuing exclusions based upon race. In the school context, the winding down of judicial monitoring has coincided with rising levels of segregation—precisely the phenomenon Justice Ginsburg warned will happen in the voting context. Is this process a judicial renunciation of the Reconstruction Amendments? Or just a retreat from the deployment of significant governmental resources to solve a problem that seems intractable.

According to the Brennan Institute, *Shelby County* did open some floodgates to state laws curtailing voting rights in ways that disproportionately disadvantage minority voters. "Voters in 23 states will face tougher restrictions [in 2018] than they did in 2010. The most common restrictions involve voter ID laws, but they also include additional burdens on registration, cutbacks to early voting and absentee voting, and reduced voting access for people with past criminal convictions. If these laws remain in effect, they have the potential to make it harder for millions of Americans to vote." Wendy R. Weiser & Max Feldman, Brennan Center for Justice, NYU Law, *The State of Voting 2018* p. 5 (June 5, 2018). Reports from the 2016 and 2018 elections suggest a renewed voting gap between white and minority voters, especially in the South, and the Center for American Progress suggests that the new racial voting gap owes much to the new voter-suppression laws, which are concentrated in the South. Danielle Roof & Adam Barclay, *Voter Suppression During the 2018 Midterm Elections* (CAP Nov. 20, 2018).

3. *The North Carolina Vote Fraud Law.* When *Shelby County* was decided, the North Carolina Legislature was considering legislation to require voters to present IDs, although there was virtually no evidence of voter fraud in recent elections. Within weeks of the Court's decision, HB 589 was expanded and then passed by the legislature. The new law instituted a strict photo ID requirement; curtailed early voting; eliminated same day registration; restricted pre-registration; ended annual voter registration drives; and eliminated the authority of county boards of elections to keep polls open for an additional hour. The litany of restrictions in this bill was the most restrictive bill passed immediately after *Shelby County*.

DOJ did not have to preclear the new rules under VRA § 5, but they were immediately challenged as franchise restrictions inconsistent with VRA § 2: the new restrictions not only had a disparate racial impact, *i.e.*, preventing people of color from voting, but were intended to do so. Given North Carolina's history of racial exclusion, the close connection between the new restrictions and the ability of minority voters to participate, and the dearth of evidence that voting fraud was occurring, the Fourth Circuit agreed with the challengers and enjoined the operation of the law. Judge Diana Gribbon Motz wrote that "the new provisions target African Americans with almost surgical precision," and that state legislators' concerns about too many black Democratic voters were "what comes as close to a smoking gun as we are likely to see in modern times." *North Carolina State Conference of NAACP v. McCrory*, 831 F.3d 204 (4th Cir. 2016). Split 4–4, the U.S. Supreme Court declined to stay the ruling. 137 S.Ct. 1399 (May 2017).

The Fourth Circuit declined to invoke its authority under VRA § 3, which permits a remedy for § 2 violations to impose a judicially mandated preclearance requirement on the offending jurisdiction. See Travis Crum, Note, *The Voting Rights Act's Secret Weapon: Pocket Trigger Litigation and Dynamic Preclearance,* 119 Yale L.J. 1992 (2010). District Court Judge Lee Rosenthal found that Pasadena, Texas intentionally violated the VRA and imposed § 3 preclearance as part of her remedial order. Pasadena withdrew its appeal. Do §§ 2–3 serve as an adequate substitute for §§ 4–5 preclearance? Are there any advantages to the former?

SECTION 4. BEYOND THE COMMERCE AND CIVIL RIGHTS ENFORCEMENT POWERS

In this section, we examine three other sources of congressional authority that might provide Congress a way around the limitations on the commerce power and the civil rights enforcement power that are found in the recent cases we just examined.

A. TAXING POWER

In the Child Labor Case (*Hammer v. Dagenhart*), the Court ruled that Congress could not prevent manufacturers from using child labor, under its Commerce Clause power. After *Hammer*, Congress enacted the Child Labor Tax Law, which imposed tax assessments on companies employing child labor. If the employer used child labor (defined in detail by the Act), it was required to pay the government 10% of its entire net business income. There was no plan to apportion the tax according to the extent of the employer's violation of the no-child-labor requirement, although the tax was not levied if the employer was actually unaware it was using child labor. Congress asserted authority for the law under Article I, § 8, cl. 1, namely it "Power To lay and collect Taxes, Duties, Imposts, and Excises, to pay the Debts and provide for the common Defence and general Welfare of the United States."

Although a transparent effort around the Child Labor Case, Congress had substantial authority for accomplishing its goal by the less controversial taxing authority. In *McCray v. United States*, 195 U.S. 27 (1904), the Court upheld a blatantly discriminatory tax of ten cents on yellow (looks like butter) oleomargarine and one one-quarter of a cent on white (doesn't look like butter). The Court refused to examine the possibly illicit motives of Congress in that case, and in *United States v. Doremus*, 249 U.S. 86 (1919), which upheld not only a special tax on opium, but set up a special inspection apparatus. Notwithstanding these precedents, the Supreme Court in *Bailey v. Drexel Furniture Co.* (The Child Labor Tax Case), 259 U.S. 20 (1922), invalidated the tax scheme, upon the ground that it was a "penalty" and not a "tax." "Where the sovereign enacting the law has power to impose both tax and penalty the difference between revenue production and mere regulation may be immaterial, but not so when one sovereign can impose a tax only, and the power of regulation rests in another. * * * [T]here comes a time in the extension of the penalizing features of the so-called tax when it loses its character as such and becomes a mere penalty with the characteristics of regulation and punishment." Interestingly, Justice Holmes and Brandeis (dissenters in the Child Labor Case) joined Chief Justice Taft's opinion.[45]

As in the Commerce Clause cases, the New Deal Court was prepared to give Congress wider discretion under the Taxing Clause. See *Steward Machine Co. v. Davis*, 301 U.S. 548 (1937) (upholding the unemployment compensation provisions of the Social Security Act of 1935; discussed below); *United States v. Kahriger*, 345 U.S. 22 (1953) (upholding a special tax on persons involved in the business of accepting wagers, i.e., "bookies"). Although the Court in both cases brushed aside arguments that Congress was motivated by regulatory rather than fundraising needs, the Court continued to cite the Child Labor Tax Case for this proposition: "Penalty provisions in tax statutes added for breach of a regulation concerning activities in themselves subject only to state regulation have caused this Court to declare the enactments invalid. Unless there are provisions extraneous to any tax need, courts are without authority to limit the exercise of the taxing power." *Kahriger*.

B. SPENDING POWER

The Child Labor Tax Act relied on the coercive portion of Article I, § 8, cl. 1, namely, its taxing power. What if Congress had relied on the inducement portion, its spending power? For example, Congress could have voted a substantial subsidy to all American businesses, to enable them to pay for adult labor; hence, the subsidy would not be payable to businesses employing child labor. Would this have passed constitutional muster before 1937? Perhaps not.

In *United States v. Butler*, 297 U.S. 1 (1936), the Court invalidated the Agricultural Adjustment Act of 1933, which was designed to encourage farmers to reduce their production so as to raise market prices. The Act conditioned farm subsidies upon farmers' agreements to curtail production

---

[45] Cf. Alexander M. Bickel, *The Unpublished Opinions of Mr. Justice Brandeis* 3–4, 18–19 (1957) (Justice Brandeis sometimes failed to file dissents for strategic reasons, perhaps here to avoid offending the new Chief Justice).

in line with federal guidelines. In turn, the subsidies were paid from a fund financed by a "processing tax" on farm products. Thus, farmers were indirectly taxed to pay for subsidies to reduce their production. The Court held that Congress' taxing and spending power was an independent enumerated power, limited only by the requirement that the tax and expenditure be "in the General welfare." Thus, the Court rejected the view, held by Madison among others, that the taxing and spending powers could only be invoked in support of other enumerated powers of Congress. Nevertheless, the Court reasoned that the statute "invades the reserved rights of the states" and treated matters "beyond the powers delegated to the federal government. The tax, the appropriation of the funds raised, and the direction for their disbursement, are but parts of the plan. They are but means to an unconstitutional end. * * * If the taxing power may not be used as the instrument to enforce a regulation of matters of state concern with respect to which Congress has no authority to interfere [e.g., the Child Labor Tax Case], may it, as in the present case, be employed to raise the money necessary to purchase a compliance which the Congress is powerless to command?" The Court said "no," while dissenting Justices Stone, Brandeis, and Cardozo said "yes."

As in the Commerce Clause and Tax Clause cases, the post-*Butler* has been substantially more lenient in upholding Congress' authority to condition its grants upon the recipient's compliance with detailed substantive regulations. In *Steward Machine Company v. Davis*, 301 U.S. 548 (1937), the Court upheld the unemployment compensation provisions of the Social Security Act of 1935. Those provisions established a federal taxing and conditional spending program to encourage the states to adopt federal unemployment compensation standards. The Act imposed a federal payroll tax on employers, but the employer received a tax credit for any contributions made to a qualifying state plan. Among other requirements, a state plan had to place its contributions in a federal trust fund. Justice Cardozo's opinion for the Court in *Steward* found no invasion of the states' Tenth Amendment rights, because there was no "coercion," only "inducement" for the states to adopt progressive laws. His opinion openly praised the object of the Social Security Act: to encourage states to make their unemployment compensation plans more responsive to the suffering during the Great Depression.

As we saw in Chapter 6, § 4B, in connection with *Rust v. Sullivan*, the Court's interest in individual rights during and after the 1960s stimulated renewed interest in "unconstitutional conditions" as a limitation on the federal spending power.[46] To what extent may Congress use federal money

---

[46] See, e.g., Mitchell N. Berman, *Coercion Without Baselines: Unconstitutional Conditions in Three Dimensions*, 90 Geo. L.J. 1 (2001); Thomas R. McCoy & Barry Friedman, *Conditional Spending: Federalism's Trojan Horse*, 1988 Sup. Ct. Rev. 85; Kathleen M. Sullivan, *Unconstitutional Conditions*, 102 Harv. L. Rev. 1413 (1989).

to induce persons or entities (like the states) to forego their constitutional protections? Consider the following case in light of the unconstitutional conditions doctrine—and in light of the Court's new (post-*Lopez*) federalism jurisprudence.

SOUTH DAKOTA V. DOLE

483 U.S. 203, 107 S.Ct. 2793, 97 L.Ed.2d 171 (1987)

CHIEF JUSTICE REHNQUIST delivered the opinion of the Court.

[In 1984, Congress enacted 23 U.S.C. § 158, which directs the Secretary of Transportation to withhold 5% of the federal highway funds otherwise payable to states from any state which permits purchase or public possession of any alcoholic beverage by a person less than 21 years old. South Dakota, which permitted persons 19 years of age or older to purchase 3.2% beer, sought a declaratory judgment that § 158 violates constitutional limits on the congressional spending power and also violates the Twenty-first Amendment. The lower federal courts rejected these claims, and the Supreme Court affirmed. The Supreme Court found this legislative effort within constitutional bounds even if Congress could not regulate drinking ages directly.]

* * * Incident to [the spending] power, Congress may attach conditions on the receipt of federal funds, and has repeatedly employed the power "to further broad policy objectives by conditioning receipt of federal moneys upon compliance by the recipient with federal . . . directives." The breadth of this power was made clear in *Butler*. * * * Thus, objectives not thought to be within Article I's "enumerated legislative fields" may nevertheless be attained through the use of the spending power and the conditional grant of federal funds.

The spending power is of course not unlimited, but is instead subject to several general restrictions articulated in our cases. The first of these limitations is derived from the language of the Constitution itself: the exercise of the spending power must be in pursuit of "the general welfare." In considering whether a particular expenditure is intended to serve general public purposes, courts should defer substantially to the judgment of Congress. Second, we have required that if Congress desires to condition the States' receipt of federal funds, it "must do so unambiguously . . . , enabl[ing] the States to exercise their choice knowingly, cognizant of the consequences of their participation." Third, our cases have suggested (without significant elaboration) that conditions on federal grants might be illegitimate if they are unrelated "to the federal interest in particular national projects or programs." Finally, we have noted that other constitutional provisions may provide an independent bar to the conditional grant of federal funds.

South Dakota does not seriously claim that § 158 is inconsistent with any of the first three restrictions mentioned above. * * * [T]he State itself, rather than challenging the germaneness of the condition to federal purposes, admits that it "has never contended that the congressional action was . . . unrelated to a national concern in the absence of the Twenty-first Amendment." Indeed, the condition imposed by Congress is directly related to one of the main purposes for which highway funds are expended—safe interstate travel. This goal of the interstate highway system had been frustrated by varying drinking ages among the States. * * * By enacting § 158, Congress conditioned the receipt of federal funds in a way reasonably calculated to address this particular impediment to a purpose for which the funds are expended.

The remaining question about the validity of § 158—and the basic point of disagreement between the parties—is whether the Twenty-first Amendment constitutes an "independent constitutional bar" to the conditional grant of federal funds. Petitioner, relying on its view that the Twenty-first Amendment prohibits *direct* regulation of drinking ages by Congress, asserts that "Congress may not use the spending power to regulate that which it is prohibited from regulating directly under the Twenty-first Amendment." But our cases show that this "independent constitutional bar" limitation on the spending power is not of the kind petitioner suggests. *Butler*, for example, established that the constitutional limitations on Congress when exercising its spending power are less exacting than those on its authority to regulate directly.

We have also held that a perceived Tenth Amendment limitation on congressional regulation of state affairs did not concomitantly limit the range of conditions legitimately placed on federal grants. In *Oklahoma v. Civil Service Comm'n*, 330 U.S. 127 (1947), the Court considered the validity of the Hatch Act insofar as it was applied to political activities of state officials whose employment was financed in whole or in part with federal funds. The State contended that an order under this provision to withhold certain federal funds unless a state official was removed invaded its sovereignty in violation of the Tenth Amendment. Though finding that "the United States is not concerned with, and has no power to regulate, local political activities as such of state officials," the Court nevertheless held that the Federal Government "does have power to fix the terms upon which its money allotments to states shall be disbursed." The Court found no violation of the State's sovereignty because the State could, and did, adopt "the 'simple expedient' of not yielding to what she urges is federal coercion. The offer of benefits to a state by the United States dependent upon cooperation by the state with federal plans, assumedly for the general welfare, is not unusual."

These cases establish that the "independent constitutional bar" limitation on the spending power is not, as petitioner suggests, a prohibition on the indirect achievement of objectives which Congress is not empowered to achieve directly. Instead, we think that the language in our earlier opinions stands for the unexceptionable proposition that the power may not be used to induce the States to engage in activities that would themselves be unconstitutional. Thus, for example, a grant of federal funds conditioned on invidiously discriminatory state action or the infliction of cruel and unusual punishment would be an illegitimate exercise of the Congress' broad spending power. But no such claim can be or is made here. * * *

Our decisions have recognized that in some circumstances the financial inducement offered by Congress might be so coercive as to pass the point at which "pressure turns into compulsion." [*Steward Machine.*] Here, however, Congress has directed only that a State desiring to establish a minimum drinking age lower than 21 lose a relatively small percentage of certain federal highway funds. Petitioner contends that the coercive nature of this program is evident from the degree of success it has achieved. We cannot conclude, however, that a conditional grant of federal money of this sort is unconstitutional simply by reason of its success in achieving the congressional objective. * * *

Here Congress has offered relatively mild encouragement to the States to enact higher minimum drinking ages than they would otherwise choose. But the enactment of such laws remains the prerogative of the States not merely in theory but in fact. Even if Congress might lack the power to impose a national minimum drinking age directly, we conclude that encouragement to state action found in § 158 is a valid use of the spending power.

[The dissenting opinion of **JUSTICE BRENNAN** is omitted.]

JUSTICE O'CONNOR, dissenting.

* * * [Section 158] is not a condition on spending reasonably related to the expenditure of federal funds and cannot be justified on that ground. Rather, it is an attempt to regulate the sale of liquor, an attempt that lies outside Congress' power to regulate commerce because it falls within the ambit of § 2 of the Twenty-first Amendment.

* * * [T]he Court's application of the requirement that the condition imposed be reasonably related to the purpose for which the funds are expended is cursory and unconvincing. We have repeatedly said that Congress may condition grants under the spending power only in ways reasonably related to the purpose of the federal program. In my view, establishment of a minimum drinking age of 21 is not sufficiently related to interstate highway construction to justify so conditioning funds appropriated for that purpose. * * *

* * * [T]he Court asserts the reasonableness of the relationship between the supposed purpose of the expenditure—"safe interstate travel"—and the drinking age condition. The Court reasons that Congress wishes that the roads it builds may be used safely, that drunken drivers threaten highway safety, and that young people are more likely to drive while under the influence of alcohol under existing law than would be the case if there were a uniform national drinking age of 21. It hardly needs saying, however, that if the purpose of § 158 is to deter drunken driving, it is far too over-and under-inclusive. It is over-inclusive because it stops teenagers from drinking even when they are not about to drive on interstate highways. It is under-inclusive because teenagers pose only a small part of the drunken driving problem in this Nation.

When Congress appropriates money to build a highway, it is entitled to insist that the highway be a safe one. But it is not entitled to insist as a condition of the use of highway funds that the State impose or change regulations in other areas of the State's social and economic life because of an attenuated or tangential relationship to highway use or safety. Indeed, if the rules were otherwise, the Congress could effectively regulate almost any area of a State's social, political, or economic life on the theory that use of the interstate transportation system is somehow enhanced. If, for example, the United States were to condition highway moneys upon moving the state capital, I suppose it might argue that interstate transportation is facilitated by locating local governments in places easily accessible to interstate highways—or, conversely, that highways might become overburdened if they had to carry traffic to and from the state capital. In my mind, such a relationship is hardly more attenuated than the one which the Court finds supports § 158.

There is a clear place at which the Court can draw the line between permissible and impermissible conditions on federal grants. It is the line identified in the Brief for the National Conference of State legislatures et al. as *Amici Curiae*:

> Congress has the power to *spend* for the general welfare, it has the power to *legislate* only for delegated purposes. * * *

The appropriate inquiry, then, is whether the spending requirement or prohibition is a condition on a grant or whether it is regulation. The difference turns on whether the requirement specifies in some way how the money should be spent, so that Congress' intent in making the grant will be effectuated. Congress has no power under the Spending Clause to impose requirements on a grant that go beyond specifying how the money should be spent. A requirement that is not such a specification is not a condition, but a regulation, which is valid only if it falls within one of Congress' delegated regulatory powers.

This approach harks back to *United States v. Butler*. The *Butler* Court saw the Agricultural Adjustment Act for what it was—an exercise of regulatory, not spending, power. The error in *Butler* was not the Court's conclusion that the Act was essentially regulatory, but rather its crabbed view of the extent of Congress' regulatory power under the Commerce Clause. The Agricultural Adjustment Act was regulatory but it was regulation that today would likely be considered within Congress' commerce power.

While *Butler*'s authority is questionable insofar as it assumes that Congress has no regulatory power over farm production, its discussion of the spending power and its description of both the power's breadth and its limitations remain sound. The Court's decision in *Butler* also properly recognizes the gravity of the task of appropriately limiting the spending power. If the spending power is to be limited only by Congress' notion of the general welfare, the reality, given the vast financial resources of the Federal Government, is that the Spending Clause gives "power to the Congress to tear down the barriers, to invade the states' jurisdiction, and to become a parliament of the whole people, subject to no restrictions save such as are self-imposed." *Butler*. This, of course, as *Butler* held, was not the Framers' plan and it is not the meaning of the Spending Clause. * * *

Of the other possible sources of congressional authority for regulating the sale of liquor only the commerce power comes to mind. But in my view, the regulation of the age of the purchasers of liquor, just as the regulation of the price at which liquor may be sold, falls squarely within the scope of those powers reserved to the States by the Twenty-first Amendment. * * * Accordingly, Congress simply lacks power under the Commerce Clause to displace state regulation of this kind.

The immense size and power of the Government of the United States ought not obscure its fundamental character. It remains a Government of enumerated powers. *McCulloch*. Because § 158 cannot be justified as an exercise of any power delegated to the Congress, it is not authorized by the Constitution. * * *

NOTES ON DOLE AND CONDITIONAL FEDERAL SPENDING

1. *Another Relic of a Bygone Era?* There is good reason to question whether the deferential approach reflected in *South Dakota v. Dole* will preclude tougher review in the future. *Dole*'s deference to congressional intermeddling in states' affairs is inconsistent with the Court's more scrutinizing review in *Lopez*, *Boerne*, and *Morrison*. "[I]f the Spending Clause is simultaneously interpreted to permit Congress to seek otherwise forbidden regulatory aims indirectly through a conditional offer of federal funds to the states, the notion of a 'federal government of enumerated powers' will have no

meaning,"[47] precisely the argument that motivated the Court's aggressive review in *Morrison*. Could Congress condition receipt of federal monies for state programs upon the states' agreement to abide by federal anti-discrimination rules of the sort that were struck down in *Kimel* and *Garrett*? To enact laws similar to the VAWA? (Would it make a constitutional difference that such a requirement were linked to the monies Congress is already providing the states under other portions of the VAWA?)

Additionally, some legal scholars who have examined the historical record believe the Framers intended that Congress is authorized to spend only for the "general Welfare" and that this limitation is one the Framers expected to be enforced through judicial review.[48] Additionally, Congress's conditional deployment of its Spending Clause power may be its greatest threat to state autonomy and the values of federalism. Almost 30% of state budgets now come from federal contributions, and this gives the federal government potentially enormous leverage to nationalize policies that might be better handled locally.[49]

If *Dole* were narrowed, what approach should the Court adopt for reviewing congressional conditions? To begin with, the Court already construes statutory conditions narrowly, see *Pennhurst State School & Hosp. v. Halderman*, 451 U.S. 1 (1981), and the rule of narrow construction might be applied with even greater rigor in cases where Congress is essentially trying to regulate local affairs.[50] As Justice O'Connor argued in her dissent, the Court might also apply *Dole*'s germaneness requirement more strictly, perhaps in the way the Court is now reviewing statutes enacted under Congress's Fourteenth Amendment authority. Rather than the lenient (rational basis) scrutiny of *Morgan* and *Dole*, the Court could carefully examine the connection between the condition on the states and the purpose of the federal spending and demand a tight fit, as the Court required in *Kimel* and *Garrett*. In addition, *Dole*'s suggestion that some federal offers are so "coercive" that they would violate the Spending Clause might be explored, as Justice Scalia suggested in *College Savs. Bank v. Florida Prepaid Postsecondary Educ. Expense Bd.*, 527 U.S. 666, 692 (1999). Lynn Baker has urged the Court to abandon the *Dole* framework altogether and adopt a new test, under which courts would presume invalid conditional offers of federal funds to the states that would regulate them in ways Congress could not directly mandate.[51]

2. *Or, Congress's Last Best Chance?* On the other hand, there are good arguments supporting the lenient approach taken in *Dole*, not the least of

---

[47] Lynn A. Baker, *Conditional Federal Spending After* Lopez, 95 Colum. L. Rev. 1911, 1920 (1995).

[48] See John Eastman, *Restoring the "General" to the General Welfare Clause*, 4 Chapman L. Rev. 63 (2001); David Engdahl, *The Basis of the Spending Power*, 18 Seattle U.L. Rev. 215 (1995).

[49] See Ilya Somin, *Closing the Pandora's Box of Federalism: The Case for Judicial Restriction of Federal Subsidies to State Governments*, 90 Geo. L.J. 461 (2002).

[50] See William N. Eskridge Jr. & Philip P. Frickey, *Quasi-Constitutional Law: Clear Statement Rules as Constitutional Lawmaking*, 45 Vand. L. Rev. 593 (1992).

[51] Lynn Baker, *Conditional Federal Spending and States' Rights*, 574 Annals 104 (2001).

which is *stare decisis*.[52] As *Dole* reflects, some of the pro-federalism Justices are reluctant to second-guess federal spending decisions and hence are not inclined toward aggressive review for unconstitutional conditions. E.g., *National Endowment for the Arts v. Finley*, 524 U.S. 569 (1998) (Scalia, J., joined by Thomas, J., concurring) (urging narrow First Amendment review of federal spending on the arts). Indeed, it is not clear what standard can be adopted that will sharply limit congressional meddling in state affairs through conditional spending and can be predictably applied by the lower courts. Surely lower courts could apply Professor Baker's even stricter rule (that the condition is presumptively unconstitutional unless Congress has an independent ground for regulation) as well as they can apply *Lopez* and *Boerne*—but the Court might not be willing to go that far, especially if it means overruling *Dole*. Could *Dole*'s germaneness and no-coercion requirements, if beefed up along the lines suggested by Justice O'Connor, be predictably applied?

3. *Federalism, the Public/Private Distinction, and Conditional Spending.* Titles VI and IX of the Civil Rights Act require recipients of federal financial assistance (including private entities, like private colleges and universities) to avoid racial and gender discrimination. Thus, conditional federal spending not only provides Congress the opportunity to conflate the national and state governments (as in *Dole*), but to conflate the public and the private spheres as well. Is one conflation more of a threat to liberty than the other? What of the values of federalism, versus the values of private autonomy? Is it more appropriate to reach private entities through conditional funding than through direct regulation under the Commerce Clause?

PROBLEM 7-5:
SPENDING CLAUSE AND THE SOLOMON AMENDMENT

As amended in 2004, the Solomon Amendment provides that if any part of an institution of higher education denies military recruiters access equal to that provided other recruiters, the entire institution would lose designated federal funds. 10 U.S.C. § 983. The purpose of the Amendment was to discipline universities whose law schools were refusing to allow Judge Advocate General recruiters to participate fully in their career services programs, because the armed forces by law could not enlist openly lesbian, gay, or bisexual lawyers (this exclusion has recently been ended by congressional and executive action). Law schools challenged the Solomon Amendment as an "unconstitutional condition" in violation of the First Amendment, an argument unanimously rejected in *Rumsfeld v. Forum for Academic & Institutional Rights, Inc.*, 547 U.S. 47 (2006).

Consider a different kind of challenge. Polytech University is science-oriented and receives $100 million in science research funds from the federal government. Because Polytech's law school does not allow military recruiters to participate fully in its career services program, the federal government

---

[52] E.g., Richard Fallon, *The "Conservative" Paths of the Rehnquist Court's Federalism Decisions*, 69 U. Chi. L. Rev 429 (2002).

terminates all its research money. Not one penny of those funds came from the Department of Defense or any other military-related agency; all of the money was for medical research, and most of it came from the Department of Health & Human Services. Polytech argues that the Solomon Amendment violates the Spending Clause because there is no "nexus" between the medical research funds it receives and the military programs Congress is trying to protect. Is this a tenable argument under *Dole*? Under the O'Connor dissenting opinion? Should the plaintiffs in *FAIR* (above) have made this argument? Why did they not make it?

C. THE TREATY POWER

Not all of the federal government's enumerated powers are in Article I. Article III empowers Congress to establish federal courts, and the Sixteenth Amendment empowers Congress to "lay and collect taxes on incomes." Several of the constitutional amendments empower Congress to enforce their mandates by appropriate legislation, as we saw in our detailed look at congressional authority to enforce the Reconstruction Amendments. Not the least of non-Article I powers is the authority in Article II, § 2, cl. 2, for the President and the Senate to make treaties.

Query: After being rebuffed in the Child Labor Case, and then again in the Child Labor Tax Case, the federal government (through the President and the Senate) enters into a treaty with foreign countries, wherein the signatories agree to abolish child labor in their respective jurisdictions. By now, you might consider this to be an easy case (the treaty is invalid, until *Hammer* is overruled), but consider the following case, which is still the leading case concerning the national treaty power.

MISSOURI V. HOLLAND
252 U.S. 416, 40 S.Ct. 382, 64 L.Ed. 641 (1920)

JUSTICE HOLMES delivered the opinion of the Court.

This is a bill in equity brought by the State of Missouri to prevent a game warden of the United States from attempting to enforce the Migratory Bird Treaty Act of July 3, 1918, and the regulations made by the Secretary of Agriculture in pursuance of the same. The ground of the bill is that the statute is an unconstitutional interference with the rights reserved to the States by the Tenth Amendment, and that the acts of the defendant done and threatened under that authority invade the sovereign right of the State and contravene its will manifested in statutes. The State also alleges a pecuniary interest, as owner of the wild birds within its border and otherwise, admitted by the Government to be sufficient, but it is enough that the bill is a reasonable and proper means to assert the alleged quasi sovereign rights of a State. A motion to dismiss was sustained by the District Court on the ground that the act of Congress is constitutional. The State appeals.

On December 8, 1916, a treaty between the United States and Great Britain was proclaimed by the President. It recited that many species of birds in their annual migrations traversed certain parts of the United States and of Canada, that they were of great value as a source of food and in destroying insects injurious to vegetation, but were in danger of extermination through lack of adequate protection. It therefore provided for specified close seasons and protection in other forms, and agreed that the two powers would take or propose to their law-making bodies the necessary measures for carrying the treaty out. The above mentioned Act of July 3, 1918, entitled an act to give effect to the convention, prohibited the killing, capturing or selling any of the migratory birds included in the terms of the treaty except as permitted by regulations compatible with those terms, to be made by the Secretary of Agriculture. * * *

To answer this question it is not enough to refer to the Tenth Amendment, reserving the powers not delegated to the United States, because by Article II, § 2, the power to make treaties is delegated expressly, and by Article VI treaties made under the authority of the United States, along with the Constitution and laws of the United States made in pursuance thereof, are declared the supreme law of the land. If the treaty is valid there can be no dispute about the validity of the statute under Article I, § 8, as a necessary and proper means to execute the powers of the Government. The language of the Constitution as to the supremacy of treaties being general, the question before us is narrowed to an inquiry into the ground upon which the present supposed exception is placed.

It is said that a treaty cannot be valid if it infringes the Constitution, that there are limits, therefore, to the treaty-making power, and that one such limit is that what an act of Congress could not do unaided, in derogation of the powers reserved to the States, a treaty cannot do. An earlier act of Congress that attempted by itself and not in pursuance of a treaty to regulate the killing of migratory birds within the States had been held bad in the District Court. *United States v. Shauver*, 214 Fed. Rep. 154[;] *United States v. McCullagh*, 221 Fed. Rep. 288. Those decisions were supported by arguments that migratory birds were owned by the States in their sovereign capacity for the benefit of their people, and that under cases like *Geer v. Connecticut*, 161 U.S. 519, this control was one that Congress had no power to displace. The same argument is supposed to apply now with equal force.

Whether the two cases cited were decided rightly or not they cannot be accepted as a test of the treaty power. Acts of Congress are the supreme law of the land only when made in pursuance of the Constitution, while treaties are declared to be so when made under the authority of the United

States. It is open to question whether the authority of the United States means more than the formal acts prescribed to make the convention. We do not mean to imply that there are no qualifications to the treaty-making power; but they must be ascertained in a different way. It is obvious that there may be matters of the sharpest exigency for the national well being that an act of Congress could not deal with but that a treaty followed by such an act could, and it is not lightly to be assumed that, in matters requiring national action, "a power which must belong to and somewhere reside in every civilized government" is not to be found. * * * [W]hen we are dealing with words that also are a constituent act, like the Constitution of the United States, we must realize that they have called into life a being the development of which could not have been foreseen completely by the most gifted of its begetters. It was enough for them to realize or to hope that they had created an organism; it has taken a century and has cost their successors much sweat and blood to prove that they created a nation. The case before us must be considered in the light of our whole experience and not merely in that of what was said a hundred years ago. The treaty in question does not contravene any prohibitory words to be found in the Constitution. The only question is whether it is forbidden by some invisible radiation from the general terms of the Tenth Amendment. We must consider what this country has become in deciding what that Amendment has reserved.

The State as we have intimated founds its claim of exclusive authority upon an assertion of title to migratory birds, an assertion that is embodied in statute. No doubt it is true that as between a State and its inhabitants the State may regulate the killing and sale of such birds, but it does not follow that its authority is exclusive of paramount powers. To put the claim of the State upon title is to lean upon a slender reed. Wild birds are not in the possession of anyone; and possession is the beginning of ownership. The whole foundation of the State's rights is the presence within their jurisdiction of birds that yesterday had not arrived, tomorrow may be in another State and in a week a thousand miles away. If we are to be accurate we cannot put the case of the State upon higher ground than that the treaty deals with creatures that for the moment are within the state borders, that it must be carried out by officers of the United States within the same territory, and that but for the treaty the State would be free to regulate this subject itself.

As most of the laws of the United States are carried out within the States and as many of them deal with matters which in the silence of such laws the State might regulate, such general grounds are not enough to support Missouri's claim. Valid treaties of course "are as binding within the territorial limits of the States as they are elsewhere throughout the dominion of the United States." No doubt the great body of private relations usually fall within the control of the State, but a treaty may override its power. * * *

Here a national interest of very nearly the first magnitude is involved. It can be protected only by national action in concert with that of another power. The subject-matter is only transitorily within the State and has no permanent habitat therein. But for the treaty and the statute there soon might be no birds for any powers to deal with. We see nothing in the Constitution that compels the Government to sit by while a food supply is cut off and the protectors of our forests and our crops are destroyed. It is not sufficient to rely upon the States. The reliance is vain, and were it otherwise, the question is whether the United States is forbidden to act. We are of opinion that the treaty and statute must be upheld.

JUSTICE VANDEVANTER and JUSTICE PITNEY dissent.

NOTES ON THE TREATY POWER AND ORIGINAL MEANING

Missouri v. Holland is a "nationalist" reading of the Treaty Clause: Treaty obligations entered into by the President, with the advice and consent of the Senate, create domestic law under the Supremacy Clause (Art. VI, cl. 2) even if not supported by an independent Article I ground for federal authority.[53] Through most of our history, there has been a countervision of the Treaty Clause, a "states' rights" reading: Treaty obligations are not the law of the land unless they fall under one of the powers delegated to the national government under Article I.[54] As a matter of law, which reading is correct?

Consider the Constitution's text. The Tenth Amendment "reserves" to the states those powers "not delegated to the United States" and reflects the fact that the federal government is one of limited powers. But Article II seems to create an explicit delegation of power that Article VI explicitly gives the same supremacy as it gives Article I statutes; unlike Article I, however, Article II does not set out limits as to what treaties may touch upon. If a treaty were self-executing, intended by the President and Senate to be operative law, it would presumably trump state law under Article VI. But most treaties (now) are *not* self-executing, and if they are to be the law of the land they must be implemented by legislation.[55] The migratory bird treaty apparently had this feature.

Can Congress enact such an implementing statute without an Article I foundation? Justice Holmes says yes, and he cites the Necessary and Proper Clause, which allows Congress "[t]o make all Laws which shall be necessary and proper for carrying into Execution the foregoing Powers [those in Article I], and all other Powers vested by this Constitution in the Government of the

---

[53] David M. Golove, *Treaty-Making and the Nation: The Historic Foundations of the Nationalist Conception of the Treaty Power*, 98 Mich. L. Rev. 1075 (2000).

[54] Curtis A. Bradley, *The Treaty Power and American Federalism*, 97 Mich. L. Rev. 391 (1998).

[55] See *Medellín v. Texas*, 552 U.S. 491 (2008), excerpted in Chapter 8, § 1B3.

United States," including Article II's Treaty Clause. As Nicholas Rosenkranz has argued, if you put these clauses together, you have the following power of Congress: "To make all Laws which shall be necessary and proper for carrying into Execution * * * [the] Power * * * to make Treaties."[56] Rosenkranz says that the plain meaning of the Constitution reveals that Justice Holmes was flat wrong: the migratory birds statute was *not* needed to carry into execution Congress's power to "make Treaties." Instead, it was a congressional implementation of a treaty already made, but without any basis (in 1921) in the Constitution's delegation of limited authority to Congress. Can the Holmes position be salvaged? David Golove and Louis Henkin, among others, believe that original meaning supports *Missouri v. Holland*. Curtis Bradley and Nick Rosenkranz do not. Consider the evidence.

1.   *Pre-1787 Practice*. In eighteenth-century England, treaties were made by the King, and they were binding on the nation. The Articles of Confederation vested the exclusive right to enter into treaties with Congress, with the proviso that no commercial treaty could interfere with state legislative power to impose equal taxes on foreigners as they impose on their own citizens or from regulating trade in goods or commodities (Art. IX). The Articles also prohibited the states from imposing imposts or duties inconsistent with treaties proposed for France and Spain (Art. VI). These limitations, explicitly recognizing state power as a limit on the national treaty power, bedeviled American negotiators of the Treaty of Peace entered into with Great Britain in 1782. The nationalist-versus-states' rights debate over the treaty power began during this period. Most of the statesmen in the national government— including Jefferson and Madison—took the nationalist position, that Congress could accrue new commerce-regulatory powers through treaties than it was otherwise vested with by the Articles (Golove, *Treaty-Making*). Statesmen at the local level tended to disagree; Virginia, for example, insisted it was not bound to enforce the Treaty of Peace provision enforcing debt obligations to the British. But see *Ware v. Hylton*, 3 U.S. 199 (1796) (upholding Art. IV of the Peace Treaty, requiring restitution of confiscated debts to British citizens). Moreover, other countries doubted the United States had this power either, and refused to enter into commercial treaties with the new country for that reason.

2.   *The Philadelphia Convention and the Ratifying Debates*. The frustrations of the Articles period created consensus at Philadelphia supporting a rule that the national treaty power trumps state law, but there was also a consensus that the national government would be one of limited authority, confined to those powers delegated to it by the Constitution. It is not apparent that anyone gave thought to the proposition that a treaty power in Article II could reach subjects about which Article I did not authorize Congress to legislate. Louis Henkin argues that an early draft of the Necessary and Proper Clause explicitly included the power to "enforce treaties," but that language was struck because it was "superfluous." Rosenkranz responds that

---

[56]   Nicholas Quinn Rosenkranz, *Executing the Treaty Power*, 118 Harv. L. Rev. 1867 (2005).

the language struck was from the Militia Clause and that the Necessary and Proper Clause never had language relating to treaties.[57]

During the state ratifying debates, Anti-Federalists attacked the Constitution's treaty power on the ground that it was unbounded—and therefore represented an important threat to the viability of autonomous states (Golove, *Treaty-Making*). Of particular concern was the possibility that the President and Senate might cede territorial rights over individual state objections. In the Virginia ratifying debates, Madison confessed that the treaty power under both the Articles and the Constitution gave no power of "dismembering" the country, "or alienating any part of it," because that was not a treaty power recognized by the law of nations. The opponents, particularly Patrick Henry, also argued that the treaty power could override individual rights. The Federalists generally denied that this would be legal, but without detailed reasoning from their constitutional text—except for this defense by George Nicholas: The President and Senate can "make no treaty which shall be repugnant to the spirit of the Constitution, or inconsistent with the delegated powers." Scholars vigorously debate how Nicholas' statement should be interpreted and how broadly to attribute it to other Federalists.[58]

3. *Early Interpretation and Practice.* The Jay Treaty with Great Britain ignited a great debate between the nationalist and states' rights visions of the treaty power. Article 9 of the treaty overrode state law to assure property rights of British subjects in the American states, and opponents argued that this was beyond the authority of the President and Senate to accomplish. These arguments were rejected by President Washington, who upon the advice of Hamilton signed and supported the treaty; by two-thirds of the Senate, which ratified the treaty; by a slender majority in the House, which voted to give the treaty effect (Golove, *Treaty-Making,* 1154–61); and by the U.S. Supreme Court in *Martin v. Hunter's Lessee*, 14 U.S. 304 (1816), which applied the treaty to override state law. On the other hand, some supporters of the Constitution opined that the treaty power did not authorize national action beyond the powers delegated by Article I. Jefferson opposed the Jay Treaty on this ground and wrote his view into the Senate's earliest manual of parliamentary practice, which said that the treaty power could not extend to objects not normally regulated by treaties, to matters where the Constitution vested the House with a role, or to matters "reserved to the States: for surely the President and Senate cannot do by treaty what the whole government is interdicted from doing in any way" (Bradley, *Treaty Power*, 415, quoting the manual). As President, however, Jefferson was not so particular about the treaty power when he used it to make the Louisiana Purchase (Golove, *Treaty-Making*, 1188–95).

Bottom line: Was *Missouri v. Holland* wrongly decided? Should it be overruled? Can *stare decisis* save *Holland*?

---

[57] Compare Louis Henkin, *Foreign Affairs and the Constitution* 481 n.111 (2d ed. 1996), with Rosenkranz, *Executing the Treaty Power*, 1912–18.

[58] Compare Bradley, *Treaty Power,* 413, with Golove, *Treaty-Making*, 1148.

Bond v. United States

572 U.S. 844 (2014)

In 1997, the Senate ratified the Convention on the Prohibition of the Development, Production, Stockpiling, and Use of Chemical Weapons and on Their Destruction. S. Treaty Doc. No. 103–21, 1974 U. N. T. S. 317. To fulfill the United States' obligations under the Convention, Congress enacted the Chemical Weapons Convention Implementation Act of 1998. 112 Stat. 2681–856. The Act forbids any person knowingly "to develop, produce, otherwise acquire, transfer directly or indirectly, receive, stockpile, retain, own, possess, or use, or threaten to use, any chemical weapon." 18 U.S.C. § 229(a)(1). It defines "chemical weapon" in relevant part as "[a] toxic chemical and its precursors, except where intended for a purpose not prohibited under this chapter as long as the type and quantity is consistent with such a purpose." § 229F(1)(A).

When Carol Anne Bond, a microbiologist, learned that her best friend was pregnant with a child whose father was her own husband, Bond spread an arsenic-based chemical on the other woman's car door, the front door of her house, and her mailbox. Bond's hope was to harass the cheating friend and make her sick, but the only injury sustained by the other woman was a slight burn on one finger. Because the chemical was "toxic," however, federal prosecutors charged Bond with two counts of violating the 1998 Implementation Act. Bond responded that Congress had no authority to adopt this statute. On appeal, the Government relied on Congress's Treaty Power, as understood in *Missouri v. Holland*. Bond urged the Court to overrule *Holland*.

Writing for the Court, **Chief Justice Roberts** declined to rule on the constitutional issue, because a statutory issue resolved the case: Bond did not fall within the ambit of the statute. To be sure, she had used a chemical considered "toxic" under the Convention and as defined by the Implementation Act, but a literal application of the statute "would 'dramatically intrude[ ] upon traditional state criminal jurisdiction,' and we avoid reading statutes to have such reach in the absence of a clear indication that they do. *United States* v. *Bass*, 404 U.S. 336, 350 (1971)." The Court ruled that "chemical weapons" regulated by the treaty-implementing statute does not cover "purely local," garden-variety crimes involving toxic materials.

Joined by Justices Thomas and Alito, **Justice Scalia** rejected the Court's interpretation of the statute, for it clearly covered Bond's vengeful activities. But Justice Scalia (joined by Justice Thomas) concurred in the Court's judgment on the ground that the Treaty Clause vests no authority in Congress to adopt statutes that do not fall within one of its enumerated powers (such as the Commerce Clause power, which had been waived as a basis for the statute in this appeal). Justices Scalia and Thomas would have overruled *Missouri v. Holland*.

Justice Scalia rejected the Government's *Holland*-based argument that the 1998 Implementation Act was "necessary and proper" to carry out

Congress's and the President's exercise of the Treaty Power set forth in Article II. Under the Necessary and Proper Clause, Congress has the authority to facilitate treaty-making, such as funding presidential treaty negotiators. "But a power to help the President *make* treaties is not a power to *implement* treaties already made. See generally Rosenkranz, Executing the Treaty Power, 118 Harv. L. Rev. 1867 (2005). Once a treaty has been made, Congress's power to do what is 'necessary and proper' to assist the making of treaties drops out of the picture. To legislate compliance with the United States' treaty obligations, Congress must rely upon its independent (though quite robust) Article I, § 8, powers."

Justice Scalia warned that strict compliance with the Constitution's structure is especially important in an era when treaties have become multilateral regulatory regimes, requiring signatories to regulate private businesses and persons as well as public activities. The constitutional limitations protecting private persons against federal governmental regulation, such as the limits enforced in *Lopez* and *Morrison*, would be easily negated under the Government's reading of *Missouri v. Holland*.

In a separate concurring opinion, **Justice Thomas** (joined by Justices Scalia and Alito) argued for a narrow understanding of the Treaty Power: the President and the Senate have no authority to enter into a treaty that does not have a "nexus to foreign relations." Such a limitation on the Federal Government's treaty power is needed not only to preserve "the basic constitutional distinction between domestic and foreign powers, see *Curtiss-Wright Export Corp.*," but also to protect the personal liberties that derive from the Constitution's diffusion of sovereign power. "And a treaty-based police power would pose an even greater threat when exercised through a self-executing treaty because it would circumvent the role of the House of Representatives in the legislative process."

Justice Thomas surveyed the leading pre-1789 treatises by Grotius, Pufendorf, and Vattel, as well as contemporary dictionaries and practice. When they adopted the Constitution in 1789, We the People would have understood the power to make "treaties" to have been a power to enter into agreements relating to "international intercourse" (i.e., war and peace, alliances with other countries, foreign trade) and *not* a power to regulate domestic activities. Justice Thomas argued that this original meaning was consistent with the actual ratifying debates as well. E.g., *Federalist* No. 45 (Madison) (treaty power "will be exercised principally on external objects, as war, peace, negotiation, and foreign commerce"). Indeed, *Missouri v. Holland* is consistent with this understanding of the Treaty Power, for the treaty in that case covered only *migratory birds,* namely, those traversing national borders.

In his concurring opinion, **Justice Alito** found that the 1998 Implementation Act reached Bond's conduct but concurred in the Court's judgment because he found the statute unconstitutional. He did not have to reach the issue of overruling *Missouri v. Holland,* because he agreed with

Justice Thomas that the Treaty Power was limited to matters of "international intercourse."

Query: The United States has entered into various treaties and conventions creating customary international law barring discrimination against women. See Catherine A. MacKinnon, *The Supreme Court, 1999 Term—Comment: Disputing Male Sovereignty: On* United States v. Morrison, 114 Harv. L. Rev. 135, 167 (2000). Does Congress have the *Missouri v. Holland* authority to reenact the VAWA private cause of action invalidated in *Morrison*? How would the Chief Justice rule in an appeal by men sued for violating VAWA? Justices Thomas and Alito? Based purely on rule of law considerations, how would you advise Justices Gorsuch and Kavanaugh to rule?

SECTION 5. INTERGOVERNMENTAL IMMUNITIES AND CONGRESSIONAL POWER

The existence of the federal and state levels of sovereignty in this country might impose additional limitations on the ability of each level to act, apart from the division of responsibilities entailed in the limited but supreme powers of the national government and the plenary but subordinate powers of state governments. *McCulloch* illustrates this phenomenon, whereby the Court inferred from the Constitution's structure a prohibition against state taxation of a national entity. *McCulloch* has been extended to prohibit other state regulations of or burdens on the national government.[59]

McCulloch suggests in dicta that national regulation of or burdens on state governments do not justify the same, or perhaps any, level of judicial enforcement. In addition to national *taxation* of the states, either directly imposed on the states or indirectly imposed, as by taxing the interest on state bonds, national intrusions might include:

- national *regulations* applicable to the states, either nondiscriminatory (regulations applicable to all, including the states) or discriminatory (Part A of this section);

- national *commandeering* of state legislatures or state officers to help administer national programs (Part B); or

- *jurisdiction* over the states in federal courts (the Eleventh Amendment, § 3D of this chapter).

We do not read *McCulloch* for the proposition that the values of federalism are not threatened by possible national impositions on state governments—for such impositions theoretically do pose threats to the federal arrangement.[60] And nothing in *McCulloch* denies that the national

---

[59] See generally Laurence Tribe, *American Constitutional Law* § 6–33 (3d ed. 2000).

[60] To the contrary, such threats can be just as serious. Most federations (Yugoslavia, U.S.S.R.) have dissolved because of the commitment problem identified in Jenna Bednar &

government has obvious incentives to impose burdens on state governments, namely, to satisfy interest groups benefitting from federal legislation, to achieve national goals at a lower cost through reliance on state resources, and to assure state accountability for obeying national policies. Might these actions by the national government—direct taxation or regulation, commandeering, federal jurisdiction—be just as destructive of federalism as Congress' overreaching its Commerce Clause powers? Commandeering, in particular, might be especially destructive because it not only interferes with the operation of and imposes potentially large costs upon state governance, but blurs lines of accountability by allowing national officials to take credit for work done by the states.

The reasons for possible judicial passivity in the face of national encroachments, those suggested by Chief Justice Marshall, are what we today call legal process limits, similar to the representation-reinforcement theory of John Hart Ely (Chapter 2, § 3B), which *McCulloch* anticipates. But *McCulloch* poses the issue without definitively resolving it. Are the states well-enough represented in the national political process to obviate the need for judicial protection? Is the Court institutionally capable of developing administrable limitations on national regulation? If so, what exactly are those standards?

A. STATE IMMUNITY FROM DIRECT NATIONAL REGULATION

National League of Cities v. Usery

426 U.S. 833 (1976)

The Fair Labor Standards Act (FLSA) upheld in *Darby* was amended in 1961 and 1966 to apply to certain classes of state employees who had since 1938 been excluded from the statute's minimum wage and other guarantees. The Supreme Court sustained this regulation of the terms and conditions of state employment in *Maryland v. Wirtz*, 392 U.S. 183 (1968). After Congress further expanded the statute's application to state employees in 1974, the Court not only invalidated the 1974 amendments, but overruled *Maryland v. Wirtz*. **Justice Rehnquist**'s opinion for the Court ruled that "there are limits upon the power of Congress to override state sovereignty, even when exercising its otherwise plenary powers to tax or to regulate commerce which are conferred by Art. I of the Constitution." He continued with this quotation from *Fry v. United States*, 421 U.S. 542 (1975):

William N. Eskridge Jr., *Steadying the Court's "Unsteady Path": A Theory of Judicial Enforcement of Federalism*, 68 S. Cal. L. Rev. 1447 (1995). If states are not assured that their ability to govern is protected against national burdens, they might lose enthusiasm for the federal arrangement. In Canada, separatist movements became serious only after the British House of Lords ceased reviewing federalism issues for that country in the 1950s, and almost all national assertions of jurisdiction were upheld, in contrast to frequent invalidations before 1949. See Katharine Swinton, *The Supreme Court and Canadian Federalism: The Laskin-Dickson Years* (1990).

While the Tenth Amendment has been characterized as a "truism," stating merely that "all is retained which has not been surrendered," *Darby*, it is not without significance. The Amendment expressly declares the constitutional policy that Congress may not exercise power in a fashion that impairs the States' integrity or their ability to function effectively in a federal system. See also *New York v. United States*, 326 U.S. 572 (1946); *Coyle v. Oklahoma*, 221 U.S. 559 (1911) (national government cannot, for example, tell state government where its seat of power shall be located).

"One undoubted attribute of state sovereignty is the States' power to determine the wages which shall be paid to those whom they employ in order to carry out their governmental functions, what hours those persons will work, and what compensation will be provided where these employees may be called upon to work overtime. The question we must resolve here, then, is whether these determinations are 'functions essential to separate and independent existence,' *Coyle*, so that Congress may not abrogate the States' otherwise plenary authority to make them." National League of Cities' complaint alleged "substantial costs which will be imposed upon them by the 1974 amendments," which revealed "a significant impact on the functioning of the governmental bodies involved.

"Quite apart from the substantial costs imposed upon the States and their political subdivisions, the Act displaces state policies regarding the manner in which they will structure delivery of those governmental services which their citizens require. The Act, speaking directly to the States *qua* States, requires that they shall pay all but an extremely limited minority of their employees the minimum wage rates currently chosen by Congress." This decision, Justice Rehnquist reasoned, "will impermissibly interfere with the integral governmental functions of these bodies" and will "significantly alter or displace the States' abilities to structure employer-employee relationships in such areas as fire prevention, police protection, sanitation, public health, and parks and recreation," core functions that state and local governments perform for citizens. "We hold that insofar as the challenged amendments operate to directly displace the States' freedom to structure integral operations in areas of traditional governmental functions, they are not within the authority granted Congress by Art. I, § 8, cl. 3."

Justice Blackmun joined the Court's opinion upon the understanding that it adopted a "balancing approach" that "does not outlaw federal power in areas such as environmental protection, where the federal interest is demonstrably greater and where state facility compliance with imposed federal standards would be essential." **Justices Brennan**, **White**, **Marshall**, and **Stevens** dissented.

NOTE ON THE CONSTITUTIONAL EXPERIMENT
IN NATIONAL LEAGUE OF CITIES

Most constitutional commentators were surprised by *National League of Cities*, not least because this was the first time since the 1930s that the Court had invalidated a federal statute as beyond Congress' enumerated powers.[61] Some believed that the decision rested upon a less than firm constitutional foundation, the Tenth Amendment, which had been consigned to "truism" status by *Darby*. Compounding these difficulties was the fuzziness of the actual limitation on federal authority, which the Court clarified in *Hodel v. Virginia Surface Mining & Reclamation Ass'n*, 452 U.S. 264, 287–88 (1981), announcing that to be unconstitutional under *National League of Cities*, a statute must meet all of the following requirements: "First, there must be a showing that the challenged statute regulates the 'States as States.' Second, the federal regulation must address matters that are indisputably 'attribute[s] of state sovereignty.' And third, it must be apparent that the States' compliance with the federal law would directly impair their ability 'to structure integral operations in areas of traditional governmental functions.'"

In no case did the Court invalidate a statute based upon the *Hodel* test. The regulation in *Hodel* itself was permissible because it only regulated private mining companies, and not the states as states (first prong). In *United Transportation Union v. Long Island Railroad*, 455 U.S. 678 (1982), the Court unanimously held that federal labor relations rules could be applied to state-owned railroads, because operating a railroad has traditionally been a function of private industry, not state action, and therefore not a "traditional" state function (third prong). Hence, federal regulation of state-owned railroads "does not impair a state's ability to function as a state." The Court in *Equal Employment Opportunity Commission v. Wyoming*, 460 U.S. 226 (1983), upheld the application of federal prohibitions against compulsory retirement to state park employees. While management of parks is a traditional state function, the third prong of the *Hodel* test was not met, because federal regulation had a marginal effect on the state's ability to operate its parks efficiently.

GARCIA V. SAN ANTONIO METROPOLITAN
TRANSIT AUTHORITY
469 U.S. 528, 105 S.Ct. 1005, 83 L.Ed.2d 1016 (1985)

JUSTICE BLACKMUN delivered the opinion of the Court.

[This case involved whether the San Antonio Metropolitan Transit Authority (SAMTA) was subject to the minimum-wage and overtime requirements of the FLSA. The district court ruled that SAMTA was

---

[61] See, e.g., Sotirios Barber, National League of Cities v. Usery: *New Meaning for the Tenth Amendment?*, 1976 Sup. Ct. Rev. 161. Subsequent commentators were less critical of the decision. See Philip Bobbitt, *Constitutional Fate* 191–95 (1982); Robert Nagel, *Federalism as a Fundamental Value:* National League of Cities *in Perspective*, 1981 Sup. Ct. Rev. 81.

immune from FLSA regulation under *National League of Cities* and *Long Island Railroad*. The Supreme Court reversed, and in the process overruled *National League of Cities*.]

The controversy in the present cases has focused on the third *Hodel* requirement—that the challenged federal statute trench on "traditional governmental functions." The District Court voiced a common concern: "Despite the abundance of adjectives, identifying which particular state functions are immune remains difficult." Just how troublesome the task has been is revealed by the results reached in other federal cases. Thus, [lower] courts have held that regulating ambulance services, licensing automobile drivers, operating a municipal airport, performing solid waste disposal, and operating a highway authority are functions *protected* under *National League of Cities*. At the same time, [lower] courts have held that issuance of industrial development bonds, regulation of intrastate natural gas sales, regulation of traffic on public roads, regulation of air transportation, operation of a telephone system, leasing and sale of natural gas, operation of a mental health facility, and provision of in-house domestic services for the aged and handicapped are *not* entitled to immunity. We find it difficult, if not impossible, to identify an organizing principle that places each of the cases in the first group on one side of a line and each of the cases in the second group on the other side. The constitutional distinction between licensing drivers and regulating traffic, for example, or between operating a highway authority and operating a mental health facility, is elusive at best.

Thus far, this Court itself has made little headway in defining the scope of the governmental functions deemed protected under *National League of Cities*. In that case the Court set forth examples of protected and unprotected functions, but provided no explanation of how those examples were identified. The only other case in which the Court has had occasion to address the problem is *Long Island*. * * * We relied in large part there on "the *historical reality* that the operation of railroads is not among the functions *traditionally* performed by state and local governments," but we simultaneously disavowed "a static historical view of state functions generally immune from federal regulation." (first emphasis added; second emphasis in original) We held that the inquiry into a particular function's "traditional" nature was merely a means of determining whether the federal statute at issue unduly handicaps "basic state prerogatives," but we did not offer an explanation of what makes one state function a "basic prerogative" and another function not basic. Finally, having disclaimed a rigid reliance on the historical pedigree of state involvement in a particular area, we nonetheless found it appropriate to emphasize the extended historical record of *federal* involvement in the field of rail transportation.

Many constitutional standards involve "undoubte[d] . . . gray areas," and, despite the difficulties that this Court and other courts have encountered so far, it normally might be fair to venture the assumption that case-by-case development would lead to a workable standard for determining whether a particular governmental function should be immune from federal regulation under the Commerce Clause. A further cautionary note is sounded, however, by the Court's experience in the related field of state immunity from federal taxation. [The Court had ruled the states immune from federal taxation in *Collector v. Day*, 78 U.S. (11 Wall.) 113 (1871). In *South Carolina v. United States*, 199 U.S. 437 (1905), the Court held that *Day*'s state tax immunity extended only to the "ordinary" and "strictly governmental" instrumentalities of state governments and not to instrumentalities "used by the State in the carrying on of an ordinary private business." The Court in *New York v. United States*, 326 U.S. 572 (1946), found that the distinction between "governmental" and "proprietary" functions was "untenable" and abandoned it.]

The distinction the Court discarded as unworkable in the field of tax immunity has proved no more fruitful in the field of regulatory immunity under the Commerce Clause. Neither do any of the alternative standards that might be employed to distinguish between protected and unprotected governmental functions appear manageable. We rejected the possibility of making immunity turn on a purely historical standard of "tradition" in *Long Island*, and properly so. The most obvious defect of a historical approach to state immunity is that it prevents a court from accommodating changes in the historical functions of States, changes that have resulted in a number of once-private functions like education being assumed by the States and their subdivisions. At the same time, the only apparent virtue of a rigorous historical standard, namely, its promise of a reasonably objective measure for state immunity, is illusory. Reliance on history as an organizing principle results in line-drawing of the most arbitrary sort; the genesis of state governmental functions stretches over a historical continuum from before the Revolution to the present, and courts would have to decide by fiat precisely how longstanding a pattern of state involvement had to be for federal regulatory authority to be defeated.

A nonhistorical standard for selecting immune governmental functions is likely to be just as unworkable as is a historical standard. The goal of identifying "uniquely" governmental functions, for example, has been rejected by the Court in the field of government tort liability in part because the notion of a "uniquely" governmental function is unmanageable. Another possibility would be to confine immunity to "necessary" governmental services, that is, services that would be provided inadequately or not at all unless the government provided them. The set of services that fits into this category, however, may well be negligible. The fact that an unregulated market produces less of some service than a State deems desirable does not mean that the State itself must provide the service; in most if not all cases, the State can "contract out" by hiring private firms to provide the service or simply by providing subsidies to existing suppliers. It also is open to question how well equipped courts are to make this kind of determination about the workings of economic markets.

We believe, however, that there is a more fundamental problem at work here, a problem that explains why the Court was never able to provide a basis for the governmental/proprietary distinction in the intergovernmental tax immunity cases and why an attempt to draw similar distinctions with respect to federal regulatory authority under *National League of Cities* is unlikely to succeed regardless of how the distinctions are phrased. The problem is that neither the governmental/proprietary distinction nor any other that purports to separate out important governmental functions can be faithful to the role of federalism in a democratic society. The essence of our federal system is that within the realm of authority left open to them under the Constitution, the States must be equally free to engage in any activity that their citizens choose for the common weal, no matter how unorthodox or unnecessary anyone else— including the judiciary—deems state involvement to be. Any rule of state immunity that looks to the "traditional," "integral," or "necessary" nature of governmental functions inevitably invites an unelected federal judiciary to make decisions about which state policies it favors and which ones it dislikes. * * * [T]he States cannot serve as laboratories for social and economic experiment, if they must pay an added price when they meet the changing needs of their citizenry by taking up functions that an earlier day and a different society left in private hands. * * *

We therefore now reject, as unsound in principle and unworkable in practice, a rule of state immunity from federal regulation that turns on a judicial appraisal of whether a particular governmental function is "integral" or "traditional." Any such rule leads to inconsistent results at the same time that it disserves principles of democratic self-governance, and it breeds inconsistency precisely because it is divorced from those principles. If there are to be limits on the Federal Government's power to interfere with state functions—as undoubtedly there are—we must look elsewhere to find them. We accordingly return to the underlying issue that confronted this Court in *National League of Cities*—the manner in which the Constitution insulates States from the reach of Congress' power under the Commerce Clause. * * *

The States unquestionably do "retai[n] a significant measure of sovereign authority." They do so, however, only to the extent that the Constitution has not divested them of their original powers and transferred those powers to the Federal Government. In the words of James Madison to the Members of the First Congress: "Interference with the power of the States was no constitutional criterion of the power of Congress. If the power was not given, Congress could not exercise it; if given, they might exercise it, although it should interfere with the laws, or even the Constitution of the States." * * *

* * * With rare exceptions, like the guarantee, in Article IV, § 3, of state territorial integrity, the Constitution does not carve out express elements of state sovereignty that Congress may not employ its delegated powers to displace. * * *

* * * Apart from the limitation on federal authority inherent in the delegated nature of Congress' Article I powers, the principal means chosen by the Framers to ensure the role of the States in the federal system lies in the structure of the Federal Government itself. It is no novelty to observe that the composition of the Federal Government was designed in large part to protect the States from overreaching by Congress. The Framers thus gave the States a role in the selection both of the Executive and the Legislative Branches of the Federal Government. The States were vested with indirect influence over the House of Representatives and the Presidency by their control of electoral qualifications and their role in presidential elections. U.S. Const., Art. I, § 2, and Art. II, § 1. They were given more direct influence in the Senate, where each State received equal representation and each Senator was to be selected by the legislature of his State. Art. I, § 3. The significance attached to the States' equal representation in the Senate is underscored by the prohibition of any constitutional amendment divesting a State of equal representation without the State's consent. Art. V. * * * The effectiveness of the federal political process in preserving the States' interests is apparent even today in the course of federal legislation. * * * [T]he States have been able to direct a substantial proportion of federal revenues into their own treasuries in the form of general and program-specific grants in aid.

* * * We realize that changes in the structure of the Federal Government have taken place since 1789, not the least of which has been the substitution of popular election of Senators by the adoption of the Seventeenth Amendment in 1913, and that these changes may work to alter the influence of the States in the federal political process. Nonetheless, against this background, we are convinced that the fundamental limitation that the constitutional scheme imposes on the Commerce Clause to protect the "States as States" is one of process rather than one of result. * * *

Insofar as the present cases are concerned, we need go no further than to state that we perceive nothing in the overtime and minimum-wage requirements of the FLSA, as applied to SAMTA, that is destructive of state sovereignty or violative of any constitutional provision. SAMTA faces nothing more than the same minimum-wage and overtime obligations that hundreds of thousands of other employers, public as well as private, have to meet. * * *

Of course, we continue to recognize that the States occupy a special and specific position in our constitutional system and that the scope of Congress' authority under the Commerce Clause must reflect that position. But the principal and basic limit on the federal commerce power is that inherent in all congressional action—the built-in restraints that our system provides through state participation in federal governmental action. The political process ensures that laws that unduly burden the States will not be promulgated. In the factual setting of these cases the internal safeguards of the political process have performed as intended.

JUSTICE POWELL, with whom THE CHIEF JUSTICE [BURGER], JUSTICE REHNQUIST, and JUSTICE O'CONNOR join, dissenting.

More troubling than the logical infirmities in the Court's reasoning is the result of its holding, *i.e.*, that federal political officials, invoking the Commerce Clause, are the sole judges of the limits of their own power. This result is inconsistent with the fundamental principles of our constitutional system. At least since *Marbury v. Madison* it has been the settled province of the federal judiciary "to say what the law is" with respect to the constitutionality of acts of Congress. In rejecting the role of the judiciary in protecting the States from federal overreaching, the Court's opinion offers no explanation for ignoring the teaching of the most famous case in our history.

In our federal system, the States have a major role that cannot be preempted by the National Government. As contemporaneous writings and the debates at the ratifying conventions make clear, the States' ratification of the Constitution was predicated on this understanding of federalism. Indeed, the Tenth Amendment was adopted specifically to ensure that the important role promised the States by the proponents of the Constitution was realized.

[All eight States voting for the Constitution only after proposing amendments to be adopted after ratification included among their recommendations some version of what later became the Tenth Amendment. Justice Powell essentially charged the Court with acquiescing in a constitutional "bait and switch": a necessary inducement to states' ratification of the Constitution being taken away years after the fact by judicial fait.]

[We omit the separate dissenting opinions of JUSTICE O'CONNOR and JUSTICE REHNQUIST. The latter conceded that there was no consensus as to exactly what the *National League of Cities* test should be but maintained that "under any one of these approaches the judgment in this case should be affirmed, and I do not think it incumbent on those of us in dissent to spell out further the fine points of a principle that will, I am confident, in time again command the support of a majority of this Court."]

NOTE ON GARCIA: SHOULD THE COURT ABSTAIN FROM ENFORCING FEDERALISM-BASED LIMITS ON CONGRESS?

Garcia followed Herbert Wechsler, *The Political Safeguards of Federalism*, in *Principles, Politics, and Fundamental Law* 49–82 (1961), in leaving enforcement of federalism-based limitations to the political process. See also *Federalist* Nos. 45–46; Jesse Choper, *Judicial Review and the National Political Process* (1980). Like Chief Justice Marshall in *McCulloch*, Wechsler thought that intergovernmental immunities should be asymmetrical for political process reasons: The national government is vulnerable to state predation and so requires judicial protection, but states are well represented in the national process and thus can protect themselves against federal intrusion. Consider some criticisms of this approach.[62]

1. *Original Meaning: The Bait and Switch Problem*. Would the states have ratified the Constitution if they had known that the Court would not enforce federalism limits on Congress *and* would not protect the states themselves against national intrusion? Is *Garcia* an example of constitutional "bait-and-switch"? In a twist on Wechsler, Larry Kramer argues not. By his account, the Constitution's drafters and the delegates at the ratifying conventions did not expect courts to enforce jurisdictional limits on Congress. "It was the legislature's delegated responsibility to decide whether a proposed law was constitutionally authorized, subject to oversight by the people. Courts simply had nothing to do with it, and they were acting as interlopers if they tried to second-guess the legislature's decision."[63] Others who have examined the original evidence disagree with Kramer. In addition to the support for judicial review found in *Federalist* No. 78 (which Kramer dismisses as a pamphlet almost no one read), other examinations of the historical evidence have concluded that the Framers expected courts to enforce the jurisdictional limits on Congress's power (e.g., Prakash & Yoo, *Puzzling Persistence*).

---

[62] For critiques of *Garcia* and Wechsler's "political safeguards" thesis, see Lynn A. Baker, *Putting the Safeguards Back into the Political Safeguards of Federalism*, 46 Vill. L. Rev. 951 (2001); Steven G. Calabresi, *"A Government of Limited and Enumerated Powers": In Defense of United States v. Lopez*, 94 Mich. L. Rev. 752, 790–99 (1995); John O. McGinnis & Ilya Somin, *Federalism v. States Rights: A Defense of Judicial Review in a Federal System*, 99 Nw. U.L. Rev. 89 (2004); Saikrishna B. Prakash & John C. Yoo, *The Puzzling Persistence of Process-Based Federalism Theories*, 79 Tex. L. Rev. 1459 (2001); Andrzej Rapaczynski, *From Sovereignty to Process: The Jurisprudence of Federalism After Garcia*, 1985 Sup. Ct. Rev. 341; Martin Redish & Karen Drizin, *Constitutional Federalism and Judicial Review: The Role of Textual Analysis*, 62 NYU L. Rev. 1 (1987); William Van Alstyne, *The Second Death of Federalism*, 83 Mich. L. Rev. 1709 (1985). Defenses of *Garcia* include Martha Field, Garcia v. San Antonio Metropolitan Transit Authority: *The Demise of a Misguided Doctrine*, 99 Harv. L. Rev. 84 (1985); Larry Kramer, *Putting the Politics Back into the Political Safeguards of Federalism*, 100 Colum. L. Rev. 215 (2000); Robert Mikos, *The Populist Safeguards of Federalism*, 68 Ohio St. L.J. 1669 (2007). See also Bradford R. Clark, *Separation of Powers as a Safeguard of Federalism*, 79 Tex. L. Rev. 1321 (2001).

[63] Larry Kramer, *The Supreme Court, 2000 Term—Foreword: We the Court*, 115 Harv. L. Rev. 4, 49 (2001); see *id.* at 65–70 (surveying the original evidence); Kramer, *Political Safeguards of Federalism*.

2. *The Political Process Problem.* Does the political structure really protect the "states *qua* states," especially now that state legislatures no longer elect senators and the state-oriented electoral college is only a formality in electing the President? Consider the FLSA, which was amended in 1974 to include all state employees. Senators would have been under great pressure from public employee unions, and indeed unions in general, to support such legislation, and those unions can turn out votes and contribute money and volunteers for (or against) the Senator at election time. Can her state do anything similar to affect her reelection chances? Nonetheless, states do seem to be an effective lobbying group in the nation's capital.[64] Within a year of *Garcia*, for example, Congress amended the FLSA to allow public employers some ability to substitute compensatory time off for costly overtime pay. The states *qua* states also have clout through the national political parties, which are organized at the state level, and through the national government's reliance on state cooperation to carry out most programs (Kramer, *Political Safeguards*).

Finally, note that the Court can tip the political process in favor of the states by the way it interprets potentially intrusive federal statutes. The Court took this step in *Gregory v. Ashcroft*, 501 U.S. 452 (1991), where it held that general federal legislation does not apply to core state governmental operations unless the statute contains a clear statement to that effect. Thus, because the Age Discrimination in Employment Act says nothing directly about whether it applies to appointed state judges, states may maintain their mandatory retirement rules for such judges even though mandatory retirement age is ordinarily considered a prima facie violation of the statute and the judges seemed to fall within the general coverage provisions of the Act. Is this revival of the Rehnquist approach in *National League of Cities* as a statutory-interpretation rather than constitutional approach a useful compromise in accommodating state sovereignty while maintaining congressional supremacy (because Congress can always amend the statute to make it clear that particular state operations are covered)?

3. *The Rotten Federalism Argument.* Especially in times of governmental scarcity, the national government has every incentive to enact regulatory programs whose cost is borne mainly by private businesses and by the states. Private businesses can pass on many of these costs to consumers or resist their imposition through lobbying, but the states are less able to do so, because their taxpayers are increasingly resistant to tax increases. This is pretty rotten federalism: In the olden days (the sixties), the federal government followed a carrot approach—if the states took federal money (under the spending power), they had to abide by federal policy conditions. At least the states had a choice and got some assistance. Later, the federal government began to follow a stick approach—it just told the states they have to do federal

---

[64] See William N. Eskridge Jr., *Overriding Supreme Court Statutory Interpretation Decisions*, 101 Yale L.J. 331 (1991); Carol Lee, *The Political Safeguards of Federalism? Congressional Responses to Supreme Court Decisions on State and Local Liability*, 20 Urb. Law. 301 (1988).

bureaucratic chores or adopt within their governments preferred federal policies.

If *Garcia* fell by the constitutional wayside, what approach should the Court take? The Rehnquist approach in *National League of Cities*? A balancing approach? *Hodel*? Redish & Drizin, *Textual Analysis*, argue that both *National League of Cities* and *Garcia* are inconsistent with the text of the Constitution: The Tenth Amendment imposes no additional limits on Congress' power (contra *National League of Cities*) beyond the judicially enforceable limits mandated by the enumerated powers in Article I (contra *Garcia*). They argue that the best that can be done is to give some teeth to the Commerce Clause, by requiring a truly "rational basis" for Congress' exercise of powers thereunder (anticipating *Lopez*).

Field, *Misguided Doctrine*, cheered the overruling of *National League of Cities*, but also suggested a limiting principle: "A more satisfactory version of a 'core governmental functions' test would include traditional and nontraditional roles alike and would restrict immunity to essentially internal state activities. Such internal matters would include the organization of state and local governments, the treatment of the states' own employees, and other activities that fall under the rubric of housekeeping functions. Immunity would end where state actions impinge directly upon the outside world, however traditional the activity or slight the impact." Hence, Professor Field would immunize state employee rules and render FLSA essentially inapplicable to the states (thus the result in *National League of Cities* would survive).

NOTE ON INTERGOVERNMENTAL TAX IMMUNITIES

McCulloch's rule against state taxation of federal entities has never been questioned. Indeed, it was expanded by the Court to immunize indirect as well as direct state burdens on the federal government. Thus, the Court exempted from state taxation, interest from federal bonds, *Weston v. City Council of Charleston*, 2 Pet. 449 (1829); wages paid federal employees, *Dobbins v. Commissioners of Erie County*, 16 Pet. 435 (1842); and even income derived from a federal lease, *Gillespie v. Oklahoma*, 257 U.S. 501 (1922).

Although *McCulloch* suggested reasons why federal immunity from state taxation did not require state immunity from federal taxation, the Court later held not only that the federal government cannot tax the states directly, but cannot burden them indirectly, as by taxing the wages of state employees, *Collector v. Day*, 78 U.S. (11 Wall.) 113 (1871), or the income from the lease of lands to the state, *Burnet v. Coronado Oil Co.*, 285 U.S. 393 (1932). In *Pollock v. Farmers' Loan & Trust Co.*, 157 U.S. 429 (1895), the Court narrowly invalidated a federal tax on the interest earned on state bonds. (*Pollock* also invalidated the federal income tax, a holding that was overridden by the Seventeenth Amendment.)

The New Deal Court cut back on intergovernmental immunity restrictions. In *Graves v. New York ex rel. O'Keefe*, 306 U.S. 466 (1939), the Court repudiated the theory that a tax on income is constitutionally equivalent to a tax on its source (the state or federal government). Such taxes are incident to the normal operation of modern administrative governance, to be borne by both state and federal governments. Thus, the New Deal Court allowed federal taxation of state employee wages, *Helvering v. Gerhardt*, 304 U.S. 405 (1938), as well as state taxation of federal employee wages, *Graves*. All of the old indirect tax cases were overruled by *Graves* and its progeny, except *Pollock*.

The federal government itself remained immune from state taxation, but for a time state immunity from federal taxation was limited to state governmental, but not proprietary, activities. See *South Carolina v. United States*, 199 U.S. 437 (1905); *Helvering v. Powers*, 293 U.S. 214 (1934). This test was abandoned in *New York v. United States*, 326 U.S. 572 (1946), but without a majority opinion. Two Justices in that case believed that any nondiscriminatory tax on a state was constitutional, even if directly collected. A plurality of four Justices upheld the tax before them as constitutional, even though it was directly levied against the state, but left open the possibility that a tax "impair[ing] the sovereign status" of a state might be vulnerable.

In *First Agricultural Bank v. State Tax Commission*, 392 U.S. 339 (1968), the Court reaffirmed the *McCulloch* holding that federal banks are immune from state taxation—over a dissent by Justice Marshall, who argued that intergovernmental tax immunities should not be read easily into federal statutes, because the doctrine itself has no textual support in the Constitution and is inconsistent with the premises of the modern regulatory state.

South Carolina v. Baker

485 U.S. 505 (1988)

In 1982, Congress removed the federal income tax exemption for interest on state bonds unless they are issued in registered form; this effectively eliminated bearer bonds, which the IRS found contributed to tax evasion. Although the statute had a direct effect on state tax policy, the opinion for the Court by **Justice Brennan** ruled that there was no process defect in the statute, the only ground for Tenth Amendment challenge left by *Garcia*. "It suffices to observe that South Carolina has not even alleged that it was deprived of any right to participate in the national political process or that it was singled out in a way that left it politically isolated and powerless. Cf. *Carolene Products*, n.4. Rather, South Carolina argues that the political process failed here because [the provision] was 'imposed by the vote of an uninformed Congress relying upon incomplete information.' But nothing in *Garcia* or the Tenth Amendment authorizes courts to second-guess the substantive basis for congressional legislation."

The Court agreed with South Carolina that the effect of the law was to impose a tax upon interest earned on a state bond, which had been declared immune from national taxation in *Pollock*, discussed in the previous note. The *Pollock* rule was merely "one application of the more general rule that neither the federal nor the state governments could tax income an individual derived from *any* contact with another government," including income by state or federal employees (*Collector v. Day*). That rationale was repudiated by the New Deal Court, which considered such taxes constitutionally acceptable even if they had the indirect effect of increasing governmental costs. *E.g., Graves.* "Subsequent cases have consistently reaffirmed the principle that a nondiscriminatory tax collected from private parties contracting with another government is constitutional even though part or all the financial burden falls on the other government." Justice Brennan applied this principle to overrule *Pollock.*

Only **Justice O'Connor** dissented from both parts of the Court's holding, viewing the 1982 statute as unacceptable congressional nibbling away at state sovereignty. **Chief Justice Rehnquist** and **Justice Scalia** concurred in the judgment but declined to join the Court's *Garcia* analysis.

B. STATE IMMUNITY FROM NATIONAL COMMANDEERING

The Supremacy Clause of Article VI contemplates that state judges can be commandeered to apply national law, see *Testa v. Katt*, 330 U.S. 386 (1947), but national commandeering of state legislatures or even executive officials was viewed as potentially threatening to state sovereignty during the *National League of Cities* era. In *FERC v. Mississippi*, 456 U.S. 742 (1982), the Court recognized this problem but upheld a federal law requiring state utility commissions to hold fact-finding hearings and carry out certain national energy policy tasks. In dissent, Justice O'Connor argued that this was commandeering contrary to the rule of *National League of Cities* and core values of federalism. "If Congress routinely required the state legislatures to debate bills drafted by congressional committees, it could hardly be questioned that the practice would affect an attribute of state sovereignty. [This statute], which sets the agendas of agencies exercising delegated legislative power in a specific field, has a similarly intrusive effect." Recall the "rotten federalism" point above. *Query*: After *Garcia* and *South Carolina v. Baker*, is a commandeering claim relegated to the political process, and the Court severely limited in its review?

NEW YORK V. UNITED STATES
505 U.S. 144, 112 S.Ct. 2408, 120 L.Ed.2d. 120 (1992)

JUSTICE O'CONNOR delivered the opinion of the Court.

[Low-level radioactive waste is commonplace, and when disposed it must be isolated from people for long periods of time. The dominant public sentiment on the issue is "NIMBY"—"Not In My Back Yard." Every state wants to engage in the activities producing this waste; no one wants it stored in their state. Since 1979, only three disposal sites had been in operation, and the nation's waste had been shipped to them. In 1980, Congress enacted legislation encouraging states to enter into regional compacts creating disposal sites. By 1985, only three compacts had been approved, and they were formed around the already-existing South Carolina, Nevada, and Washington sites; under the 1980 statute these three compacts were authorized to exclude waste from nonmembers starting in 1986. In response, Congress enacted the Low-Level Radioactive Waste Policy Amendments Act of 1985. The statute was designed to solve the NIMBY problem.

[Based largely upon a proposal of the National Governors' Association, the 1985 statute was a compromise between sited and unsited states (those containing or not containing disposal sites). The sited states agreed to accept waste for another seven years, and the unsited states agreed to handle their own waste by 1992. The statute provided three kinds of incentives to encourage states to tackle this problem, along with a series of deadlines that the states were expected to meet as they did so. *First*, the sited states were authorized to charge gradually increasing fees for waste from unsited states. One quarter of these surcharges went to the federal Department of Energy, which used these funds to make payments to states that met their deadlines. *Second*, states that failed to meet certain deadlines could be charged higher surcharges and, eventually, could be denied access to disposal facilities altogether. *Third*, the so-called "take title" provision told states that eventually they would literally own the problem themselves if they didn't cooperate. It provided:

If a State (or, where applicable, a compact region) in which low-level radioactive waste is generated is unable to provide for the disposal of all such waste generated within such State or compact region by January 1, 1996, each State in which such waste is generated, upon the request of the generator or owner of the waste, shall take title to the waste, be obligated to take possession of the waste, and shall be liable for all damages directly or indirectly incurred by such generator or owner as a consequence of the failure of the State to take possession of the waste as soon after January 1, 1996, as the generator or owner notifies the State that the waste is available for shipment.

[New York joined no regional compact. It complied with the initial requirements of the statute by enacting legislation providing for the siting of a facility in the state. Residents of the two counties containing potential sites opposed the state's choice of location—a classic example of the NIMBY syndrome. Fearing that it could not comply with the statutory deadlines, New York and these two counties brought suit, contending that the statute was inconsistent with the Tenth Amendment and with the Guaranty Clause of Article IV.]

[Federalism] questions can be viewed in either of two ways. In some cases the Court has inquired whether an Act of Congress is authorized by one of the powers delegated to Congress in Article I of the Constitution. See, *e.g.*, *McCulloch*. In other cases the Court has sought to determine whether an Act of Congress invades the province of state sovereignty reserved by the Tenth Amendment. See, *e.g.*, *Garcia*. * * *

It is in this sense that the Tenth Amendment "states but a truism that all is retained which has not been surrendered." *Darby*. * * *

Congress exercises its conferred powers subject to the limitations contained in the Constitution. Thus, for example, under the Commerce Clause Congress may regulate publishers engaged in interstate commerce, but Congress is constrained in the exercise of that power by the First Amendment. The Tenth Amendment likewise restrains the power of Congress, but this limit is not derived from the text of the Tenth Amendment itself, which, as we have discussed, is essentially a tautology. Instead, the Tenth Amendment confirms that the power of the Federal Government is subject to limits that may, in a given instance, reserve power to the States. The Tenth Amendment thus directs us to determine, as in this case, whether an incident of state sovereignty is protected by a limitation on an Article I power. * * *

Petitioners do not contend that Congress lacks the power to regulate the disposal of low level radioactive waste. Space in radioactive waste disposal sites is frequently sold by residents of one State to residents of another. Regulation of the resulting interstate market in waste disposal is therefore well within Congress' authority under the Commerce Clause. Petitioners * * * do not dispute that under the Supremacy Clause Congress could, if it wished, pre-empt state radioactive waste regulation. Petitioners contend only that the Tenth Amendment limits the power of Congress to regulate in the way it has chosen. Rather than addressing the problem of waste disposal by directly regulating the generators and disposers of waste, petitioners argue, Congress has impermissibly directed the States to regulate in this field.

Most of our recent cases interpreting the Tenth Amendment have concerned the authority of Congress to subject state governments to generally applicable laws. The Court's jurisprudence in this area has traveled an unsteady path. [Citing *Maryland v. Wirtz*, *National League of Cities*, *Garcia*.] This case presents no occasion to apply or revisit the holdings of any of these cases, as this is not a case in which Congress has subjected a State to the same legislation applicable to private parties.

This case instead concerns the circumstances under which Congress may use the States as implements of regulation; that is, whether Congress may direct or otherwise motivate the States to regulate in a particular field or a particular way. * * *

* * * While Congress has substantial powers to govern the Nation directly, including in areas of intimate concern to the States, the Constitution has never been understood to confer upon Congress the ability to require the States to govern according to Congress' instructions. The Court has been explicit about this distinction. "Both the States and the United States existed before the Constitution. The people, through that instrument, established a more perfect union by substituting a national government, acting, with ample power, *directly upon the citizens*, instead of the Confederate government, which acted with powers, greatly restricted, only upon the States." [*Lane County v. Oregon*, 7 Wall. 71, 76 (1869) (emphasis added).] The Court has made the same point with more rhetorical flourish, although perhaps with less precision, on a number of occasions. In Chief Justice Chase's much-quoted words, "the preservation of the States, and the maintenance of their governments, are as much within the design and care of the Constitution as the preservation of the Union and the maintenance of the National government. The Constitution, in all its provisions, looks to an indestructible Union, composed of indestructible States." *Texas v. White*, 7 Wall. 700, 725 (1869). * * *

In the end, the [Philadelphia] Convention opted for a Constitution in which Congress would exercise its legislative authority directly over individuals rather than over States * * *. This choice was made clear to the subsequent state ratifying conventions. Oliver Ellsworth, a member of the Connecticut delegation in Philadelphia, explained the distinction to his State's convention: "This Constitution does not attempt to coerce sovereign bodies, states, in their political capacity. . . . But this legal coercion singles out the . . . individual." Charles Pinckney, another delegate at the Constitutional Convention, emphasized to the South Carolina House of Representatives that in Philadelphia "the necessity of having a government which should at once operate upon the people, and not upon the states, was conceived to be indispensable by every delegation present." Rufus King, one of Massachusetts' delegates, returned home to support ratification by recalling the Commonwealth's unhappy experience under the Articles of Confederation and arguing: "Laws, to be effective, therefore, must not be laid on states, but upon individuals." * * * At North Carolina's convention, Samuel Spencer recognized that "all the laws of the Confederation were binding on the states in their political capacities, . . . but now the thing is entirely different. The laws of Congress will be binding on individuals."

In providing for a stronger central government, therefore, the Framers explicitly chose a Constitution that confers upon Congress the power to regulate individuals, not States. As we have seen, the Court has consistently respected this choice. We have always understood that even where Congress has the authority under the Constitution to pass laws requiring or prohibiting certain acts, it lacks the power directly to compel the States to require or prohibit those acts. The allocation of power contained in the Commerce Clause, for example, authorizes Congress to regulate interstate commerce directly; it does not authorize Congress to regulate state governments' regulation of interstate commerce.

This is not to say that Congress lacks the ability to encourage a State to regulate in a particular way, or that Congress may not hold out incentives to the States as a method of influencing a State's policy choices. Our cases have identified a variety of methods, short of outright coercion, by which Congress may urge a State to adopt a legislative program consistent with federal interests. Two of these methods are of particular relevance here.

First, under Congress' spending power, "Congress may attach conditions on the receipt of federal funds." *South Dakota v. Dole.* Such conditions must (among other requirements) bear some relationship to the purpose of the federal spending; otherwise, of course, the spending power could render academic the Constitution's other grants and limits of federal authority. Where the recipient of federal funds is a State, as is not unusual today, the conditions attached to the funds by Congress may influence a State's legislative choices. *Dole* was one such case: The Court found no constitutional flaw in a federal statute directing the Secretary of Transportation to withhold federal highway funds from States failing to adopt Congress' choice of a minimum drinking age. Similar examples abound.

Second, where Congress has the authority to regulate private activity under the Commerce Clause, we have recognized Congress' power to offer States the choice of regulating that activity according to federal standards or having state law pre-empted by federal regulation. This arrangement, which has been termed "a program of cooperative federalism," is replicated in numerous federal statutory schemes. * * *

By either of these two methods, as by any other permissible method of encouraging a State to conform to federal policy choices, the residents of the State retain the ultimate decision as to whether or not the State will comply. If a State's citizens view federal policy as sufficiently contrary to local interests, they may elect to decline a federal grant. If state residents would prefer their government to devote its attention and resources to problems other than those deemed important by Congress, they may choose to have the Federal Government rather than the State bear the expense of a federally mandated regulatory program, and they may continue to supplement that program to the extent state law is not preempted. Where Congress encourages state regulation rather than compelling it, state governments remain responsive to the local electorate's preferences; state officials remain accountable to the people.

By contrast, where the Federal Government compels States to regulate, the accountability of both state and federal officials is diminished. If the citizens of New York, for example, do not consider that making provision for the disposal of radioactive waste is in their best interest, they may elect state officials who share their view. That view can always be preempted under the Supremacy Clause if it is contrary to the national view, but in such a case it is the Federal Government that makes the decision in full view of the public, and it will be federal officials that suffer the consequences if the decision turns out to be detrimental or unpopular. But where the Federal Government directs the States to regulate, it may be state officials who will bear the brunt of public disapproval, while the federal officials who devised the regulatory program may remain insulated from the electoral ramifications of their decision. Accountability is thus diminished when, due to federal coercion, elected state officials cannot regulate in accordance with the views of the local electorate in matters not pre-empted by federal regulation. * * *

[The Court upheld the Act's provision authorizing sited states to impose a surcharge on waste received from other states. As discussed above, these charges were intended to provide financial incentives for states to cooperate with the waste disposal scheme. The Court called this provision "an unexceptional exercise of Congress' power to authorize the states to burden interstate commerce." The Court also upheld the provision under which the federal government would collect a portion of this surcharge and place it into an escrow account, calling it "no more than a federal tax on interstate commerce." The Court also held valid the provision under which states achieving a series of milestones in combating radioactive waste receive portions of these federally collected funds, calling it a "conditional exercise of Congress' authority under the Spending Clause" consistent with *South Dakota v. Dole.*

[The Court also upheld the provision authorizing states and regional compacts with disposal sites to increase the costs of access to those sites, and deny access altogether, to waste generated in states that do not meet federal guidelines. This was viewed as a "conditional exercise of Congress' commerce power."] Where federal regulation of private activity is within the scope of the Commerce Clause, we have recognized the ability of Congress to offer states the choice of regulating that activity according to federal standards or having state law pre-empted by federal regulation. This is the choice presented to nonsited States by the Act's second set of incentives: States may either regulate the disposal of radioactive waste according to federal standards by attaining local or regional self-sufficiency, or their residents who produce radioactive waste will be subject to federal regulation authorizing sited States and regions to deny access to their disposal sites. The affected States are not compelled by Congress to regulate, because any burden caused by a State's refusal to regulate will fall on those who generate waste and find no outlet for its disposal, rather than on the State as a sovereign. A State whose citizens do not wish it to attain the Act's milestones may devote its attention and its resources to issues its citizens deem more worthy; the choice remains at all times with the residents of the State, not with Congress. The State need not expend any funds, or participate in any federal program, if local residents do not view such expenditures or participation as worthwhile. Nor must the State abandon the field if it does not accede to federal direction; the State may continue to regulate the generation and disposal of radioactive waste in any manner its citizens see fit.

The take title provision is of a different character. This * * * offers States, as an alternative to regulating pursuant to Congress' direction, the option of taking title to and possession of the low level radioactive waste generated within their borders and becoming liable for all damages waste generators suffer as a result of the States' failure to do so promptly. In this provision, Congress has crossed the line distinguishing encouragement from coercion. * * *

The take title provision offers state governments a "choice" of either accepting ownership of waste or regulating according to the instructions of Congress. Respondents do not claim that the Constitution would authorize Congress to impose either option as a freestanding requirement. On one hand, the Constitution would not permit Congress simply to transfer radioactive waste from generators to state governments. Such a forced transfer, standing alone, would in principle be no different than a congressionally compelled subsidy from state governments to radioactive waste producers. The same is true of the provision requiring the States to become liable for the generators' damages. Standing alone, this provision would be indistinguishable from an Act of Congress directing the States to assume the liabilities of certain state residents. Either type of federal action would "commandeer" state governments into the service of federal regulatory purposes, and would for this reason be inconsistent with the Constitution's division of authority between federal and state governments. On the other hand, the second alternative held out to state governments—regulating pursuant to Congress' direction—would, standing alone, present a simple command to state governments to implement legislation enacted by Congress. As we have seen, the Constitution does not empower Congress to subject state governments to this type of instruction. * * *

The take title provision appears to be unique. No other federal statute has been cited which offers a state government no option other than that of implementing legislation enacted by Congress. Whether one views the take title provision as lying outside Congress' enumerated powers, or as infringing upon the core of state sovereignty reserved by the Tenth

Amendment, the provision is inconsistent with the federal structure of our Government established by the Constitution.

Respondents raise a number of objections to this understanding of the limits of Congress' power.

First, the United States argues that the Constitution's prohibition of congressional directives to state governments can be overcome where the federal interest is sufficiently important to justify state submission. This argument contains a kernel of truth: In determining whether the Tenth Amendment limits the ability of Congress to subject state governments to generally applicable laws, the Court *has* in some cases stated that it will evaluate the strength of federal interests in light of the degree to which such laws would prevent the State from functioning as a sovereign; that is, the extent to which such generally applicable laws would impede a state government's responsibility to represent and be accountable to the citizens of the State. See, *e.g.*, *National League of Cities*; *Garcia*. But whether or not a particularly strong federal interest enables Congress to bring state governments within the orbit of generally applicable *federal* regulation, no Member of the Court has ever suggested that such a federal interest would enable Congress to command a state government to enact *state* regulation. No matter how powerful the federal interest involved, the Constitution simply does not give Congress the authority to require the States to regulate. The Constitution instead gives Congress the authority to regulate matters directly and to pre-empt contrary state regulation. Where a federal interest is sufficiently strong to cause Congress to legislate, it must do so directly; it may not conscript state governments as its agents.

Second, the United States argues that the Constitution does, in some circumstances, permit federal directives to state governments. Various cases are cited for this proposition, but none support it. * * * Federal statutes enforceable in state courts do, in a sense, direct state judges to enforce them, but this sort of federal "direction" of state judges is mandated by the text of the Supremacy Clause. No comparable constitutional provision authorizes Congress to command state legislatures to legislate.

The sited State respondents focus their attention on the process by which the Act was formulated. They correctly observe that public officials representing the State of New York lent their support to the Act's enactment. A Deputy Commissioner of the State's Energy Office testified in favor of the Act. Senator Moynihan of New York spoke in support of the Act on the floor of the Senate. Respondents note that the Act embodies a bargain among the sited and unsited States, a compromise to which New York was a willing participant and from which New York has reaped much benefit. Respondents then pose what appears at first to be a troubling question: How can a federal statute be found an unconstitutional infringement of State sovereignty when state officials consented to the statute's enactment?

The answer follows from an understanding of the fundamental purpose served by our Government's federal structure. The Constitution does not protect the sovereignty of States for the benefit of the States or state governments as abstract political entities, or even for the benefit of the public officials governing the States. To the contrary, the Constitution divides authority between federal and state governments for the protection of individuals. State sovereignty is not just an end in itself: "Rather, federalism secures to citizens the liberties that derive from the diffusion of sovereign power." "Just as the separation and independence of the coordinate Branches of the Federal Government serve to prevent the accumulation of excessive power in any one Branch, a healthy balance of power between the States and the Federal Government will reduce the risk of tyranny and abuse from either front." *Gregory v. Ashcroft.* [Hence, the Court concluded, state officials "cannot consent to the enlargement of the powers of Congress beyond those enumerated in the Constitution."

[Finally, the Court turned to New York's argument that the Act violated the Guarantee Clause. The Court noted that disputes under the clause are ordinarily considered nonjusticiable, see generally Chapter 9, § 1, and concluded that even if the issue were justiciable, "neither the monetary incentives provided by the Act nor the possibility that a State's waste producers may find themselves excluded from the disposal sites of another State can reasonably be said to deny any State a republican form of government. As we have seen, these two incentives represent permissible conditional exercises of Congress' authority under the Spending and Commerce Clauses respectively, in forms that have now grown commonplace. Under each, Congress offers the States a legitimate choice rather than issuing an unavoidable command. The States thereby retain the ability to set their legislative agendas; state government officials remain accountable to the local electorate. The twin threats imposed by the first two challenged provisions of the Act—that New York may miss out on a share of federal spending or that those generating radioactive waste within New York may lose out-of-state disposal outlets—do not pose any realistic risk of altering the form or the method of functioning of New York's government."]

JUSTICE WHITE, with whom **JUSTICE BLACKMUN** and **JUSTICE STEVENS** join, concurring in part and dissenting in part.

Curiously absent from the Court's analysis is any effort to place the take title provision within the overall context of the legislation. * * * Congress could have pre-empted the field by directly regulating the disposal of this waste pursuant to its powers under the Commerce and Spending Clauses, but instead it *unanimously* assented to the States' request for congressional ratification of agreements to which they had acceded. * * * [T]he States wished to take the lead in achieving a solution to this problem and agreed among themselves to the various incentives and penalties implemented by Congress to insure adherence to the various deadlines and goals. The chief executives of the States proposed this approach, and I am unmoved by the Court's vehemence in taking away Congress' authority to sanction a recalcitrant unsited State now that New York has reaped the benefits of the sited States' concessions. * * *

The Court's distinction between a federal statute's regulation of States and private parties for general purposes, as opposed to a regulation solely on the activities of States, is unsupported by our recent Tenth Amendment cases. In no case has the Court rested its holding on such a distinction. Moreover, the Court makes no effort to explain why this purported distinction should affect the analysis of Congress' power under general principles of federalism and the Tenth Amendment. * * * An incursion on state sovereignty hardly seems more constitutionally acceptable if the federal statute that "commands" specific action also applies to private parties. * * *

Ultimately, I suppose, the entire structure of our federal constitutional government can be traced to an interest in establishing checks and balances to prevent the exercise of tyranny against individuals. But these fears seem extremely far distant to me in a situation such as this. We face a crisis of national proportions in the disposal of low-level radioactive waste, and Congress has acceded to the wishes of the States by permitting local decisionmaking rather than imposing a solution from Washington. New York itself participated and supported passage of this legislation at both the gubernatorial and federal representative levels, and then enacted state laws specifically to comply with the deadlines and timetables agreed upon by the States in the 1985 Act. For me, the Court's civics lecture has a decidedly hollow ring at a time when action, rather than rhetoric, is needed to solve a national problem.

[The opinion of **JUSTICE STEVENS**, concurring in part and dissenting in part, is omitted.]

NOTES ON NEW YORK AND PROCESS FEDERALISM

1. *Federalism and Prisoners' Dilemmas*. In *New York*, as in many other federalism cases, the states were caught in a game of prisoners' dilemma. The states are all better off collectively if waste disposal sites are available, yet each individual state would prefer to opt out of the disposal process, dumping their waste on other states that have been responsible enough to develop their own waste disposal programs. Without some coordination scheme and some sanction for defectors, the rational strategy is for every state to produce waste and for no one to establish disposal sites. The Court's decision seems to undermine the availability of a national remedy for such dilemmas and, worse,

to validate New York's predatory strategy toward states that attempted to implement the statute in good faith.

Justice O'Connor might respond that direct federal regulation can cure the coordination problem, but without interfering with state autonomy. To the extent that the effect of the decision is to require the federal government to displace more state regulation, however, it is unclear how state autonomy is served. In any event, is it likely that New York citizens were any more confused about responsibility for radioactive waste control than about the relative responsibility of the state, federal courts, and Congress regarding school desegregation, or about the responsibility of the state, the federal Environmental Protection Agency, and Congress regarding air pollution?

2. *State Autonomy, Republicanism, and Federalism*. Professor Deborah Merritt defends the anti-commandeering principle generally, and *New York* in particular, as required by the Guarantee Clause of Article IV, which assures the states a republican form of government and, therefore, governmental autonomy.[65] On this reading, state governments exist as organs representative of and accountable to local communities. For citizens of other states (via the national government) to seize control of a state's legislative process destroys the special relationship between the state government and its own citizens. This is important, not because it protects the individual rights of these citizens, but because it eliminates the nexus which gives their community a legal voice. A republican interpretation might provide a more powerful normative basis for O'Connor's opinion. One might wonder, however, whether this is an overly romanticized view of the nature of state governments. Compare Sheryll Cashin, *Federalism, Welfare Reform, and the Minority Poor: Accounting for the Tyranny of State Majorities*, 99 Colum. L. Rev. 552 (1999) (state and, especially, local governments are not responsive to racial minorities and, to the contrary, serve as mechanisms for resegregation).

3. *Structural Limits and Individual Rights*. First Amendment rights are subject to a compelling interest test (Chapter 6), as is the right to be free from racial discrimination (Chapter 3). Apparently, however, the right of state officials to be free from federally mandated enforcement is *absolute*, and would not be subject to modification even where national survival is at stake. The Court's rationale is that there will always be a temptation to bend structural limits in pursuit of whatever a given era regards as compelling national interests. Obviously, however, the same temptation also exists with respect to individual rights. Is the result to place structural limits on a higher plane than fundamental human rights? If, as Justice O'Connor suggests in *New York*, federalism is an indirect method of protecting human rights, why should this indirect mechanism be treated as more sacrosanct than the rights it is designed to protect? (Incidentally, it is far from clear that federalism was initially

---

[65] See Deborah Jones Merritt, *The Guarantee Clause and State Autonomy: Federalism for a Third Century*, 88 Colum. L. Rev. 1 (1988); Merritt, *Three Faces of Federalism: Finding a Formula for the Future*, 47 Vand. L. Rev. 1563 (1994). For a similar suggestion that Justice O'Connor's opinion in the *Croson* affirmative action case (Chapter 3, § 3B), is essentially republican, see Daniel A. Farber, Richmond *and Republicanism*, 41 U. Fla. L. Rev. 623 (1989).

designed for this purpose, rather than for protecting provincial economic and social interests—most notably slavery—from potential federal interference.)

Saikrishna Prakash, *Field Office Federalism*

79 Va. L. Rev. 1957 (1993)

In our editing of *New York v. United States*, we omitted the historical debate between Justices O'Connor and Stevens over the original understanding the Framers had about commandeering. Professor Prakash's article presents a thoughtful review of that complicated topic. We summarize his conclusions, drawn from examination of the American experience during the Articles of Confederation, the drafting of the Constitution at Philadelphia, and the ratification debates:

The Framers were hostile to national commandeering of state legislatures. Unlike the Articles, the Constitution did not give Congress authority to "requisition" state legislatures, directing them to provide the national government with monies and men. A primary reason the Philadelphia Convention rejected the New Jersey Plan was its effort to continue the Articles' requisition system, and proponents of the Virginia Plan such as Edmond Randolph and James Madison made opposition to national requisitioning of state legislatures a central argument against the New Jersey Plan. Hamilton's *Federalist* No. 15 heartily criticized the Articles for their allowing coercion of state governments. Prakash concludes, after a balanced analysis of *The Federalist Papers*, that their authors advertised the Constitution as creating a federal government that acted directly upon individuals, and not states, and that this authority was a substitute for the old and unworkable requisitioning power.

The Framers were open to national commandeering of state magistracy (executive and judicial officers). The Continental Congress under the Articles assumed that it had authority to direct state executive officers, and none of the discussions at Philadelphia disputed this power, in contrast to the sharp dispute about the power to commandeer state legislatures. *The Federalist Papers*, by and large, continued that assumption. Madison, for example, responded to Anti-Federalist fears of a dual (and doubly oppressive) set of tax collectors by observing that federal tax collection "will generally be made by the officers, and according to the rules, appointed by the several States." *Federalist* No. 45. Hamilton's *Federalist* No. 27 was the most extensive discussion, insisting that the Constitution "will enable the government to employ the ordinary magistracy of each [state], in the execution of its laws." Most speakers at the ratification debates (whose views were recorded) agreed with Madison and Hamilton.

Professor Prakash argues that the distinction was grounded in *sovereignty*: The national government could not regulate the direct voices of state sovereignty (the legislatures), but could commandeer administrative individuals, including state judges as well as executives. Compare Evan

Caminker, *State Sovereignty and Subordinacy: May Congress Commandeer State Officers to Implement Federal Law?*, 95 Colum. L. Rev. 1001 (1995) (arguing that Framers expected Congress to be able to commandeer both state legislatures and administrators). Consider how these arguments about the original understanding played out in the next case.

PRINTZ V. UNITED STATES
521 U.S. 898, 117 S.Ct. 2365, 138 L. Ed. 2d 914 (1997)

JUSTICE SCALIA delivered the opinion of the Court.

[The Gun Control Act of 1968 (GCA), 18 U.S.C. § 921 *et seq.*, prohibits firearms dealers from transferring handguns to any person under 21, to anyone not resident in the dealer's state, to convicted felons, and to certain others. In 1993, the Brady Act amended the GCA to require the Attorney General to establish a national instant background check system by November 30, 1998, Pub. L. 103–159, note following 18 U.S.C. § 922, and immediately put in place certain interim provisions until that system becomes operative. Under the interim provisions, a firearms dealer who proposes to transfer a handgun must (1) receive from the transferee a statement (the Brady Form), containing data on the proposed transferee, (2) verify the identity of the transferee, and (3) provide the "chief law enforcement officer" (CLEO) of the transferee's residence with the Brady Form. With some exceptions, the dealer must then wait five business days before consummating the sale, unless the CLEO earlier notifies the dealer that he has no reason to believe the transfer would be illegal. The Brady Act creates two significant alternatives to the foregoing scheme. A dealer may sell a handgun immediately if the purchaser possesses a state handgun permit issued after a background check or if state law provides for an instant background check. In states that have not rendered one of these alternatives applicable to all gun purchasers, CLEOs must "make a reasonable effort to ascertain within 5 business days whether receipt or possession would be in violation of the law." The Act does not require the CLEO to take any particular action if he determines that a pending transaction would be unlawful; he may notify the firearms dealer to that effect, but is not required to do so. If, however, the CLEO notifies a gun dealer that a prospective purchaser is ineligible to receive a handgun, he must, upon request, provide the would-be purchaser with a written statement of the reasons for that determination.]

[Three CLEOs challenged the statute, claiming that] congressional action compelling state officers to execute federal laws is unconstitutional. Because there is no constitutional text speaking to this precise question, the answer to the CLEOs' challenge must be sought in historical understanding and practice, in the structure of the Constitution, and in the jurisprudence of this Court. * * *

Petitioners contend that compelled enlistment of state executive officers for the administration of federal programs is, until very recent years at least, unprecedented. The Government contends, to the contrary, that "the earliest Congresses enacted statutes that required the participation of state officials in the implementation of federal laws." The Government's contention demands our careful consideration, since early congressional enactments "provid[e] 'contemporaneous and weighty evidence' of the Constitution's meaning." Indeed, such "contemporaneous legislative exposition of the Constitution . . . , acquiesced in for a long term of years, fixes the construction to be given its provisions." *Myers v. United States*, 272 U.S. 52, 175 (1926) (citing numerous cases). Conversely if, as petitioners contend, earlier Congresses avoided use of this highly attractive power, we would have reason to believe that the power was thought not to exist.

The Government observes that statutes enacted by the first Congresses required state courts to record applications for citizenship, to transmit abstracts of citizenship applications and other naturalization records to the Secretary of State, and to register aliens seeking naturalization and issue certificates of registry. * * * Other statutes of that era apparently or at least arguably required state courts to perform functions unrelated to naturalization, such as resolving controversies between a captain and the crew of his ship concerning the seaworthiness of the vessel, hearing the claims of slave owners who had apprehended fugitive slaves and issuing certificates authorizing the slave's forced removal to the State from which he had fled, taking proof of the claims of Canadian refugees who had assisted the United States during the Revolutionary War, and ordering the deportation of alien enemies in times of war.

These early laws establish, at most, that the Constitution was originally understood to permit imposition of an obligation on state *judges* to enforce federal prescriptions, insofar as those prescriptions related to matters appropriate for the judicial power. [But such laws are consistent with the Supremacy Clause, which explicitly requires state *judges* to give effect to federal law in their courts. Indeed, the existence of many statutes commandeering state judges contrasts with virtually no statute commandeering state administrators, suggesting an absence of congressional power to impose obligations on the latter.]

In addition to early legislation, the Government also appeals to other sources we have usually regarded as indicative of the original understanding of the Constitution. It points to portions of *The Federalist* which reply to criticisms that Congress's power to tax will produce two sets of revenue officers—for example, "Brutus's" assertion in his letter to the *New York Journal* of December 13, 1787, that the Constitution "opens a door to the appointment of a swarm of revenue and excise officers to prey upon the honest and industrious part of the community, eat up their substance, and riot on the spoils of the country." "Publius" responded that Congress will probably "make use of the State officers and State regulations, for collecting" federal taxes, *The Federalist* No. 36 (Hamilton), and predicted that "the eventual collection [of internal revenue] under the immediate authority of the Union, will generally be made by the officers, and according to the rules, appointed by the several States," *id.*, No. 45 (J. Madison). The Government also invokes the *Federalist*'s more general observations that the Constitution would "enable the [national] government to employ the ordinary magistracy of each [State] in the execution of its laws," *id.*, No. 27, at 176 (A. Hamilton), and that it was "extremely probable that in other instances, particularly in the organization of the judicial power, the officers of the States will be clothed in the correspondent authority of the Union," *id.*, No. 45, at 292 (J. Madison). But none of these statements necessarily implies—what is the critical point here—that Congress could impose these responsibilities without the consent of the States. They appear to rest on the natural assumption that the States would consent to allowing their officials to assist the Federal Government, an assumption proved correct by the extensive mutual assistance the States and Federal Government voluntarily provided one another in the early days of the Republic, including voluntary federal implementation of state law, see, e.g., Act of Apr. 2, 1790, ch. 5, § 1, 1 Stat. 106 (directing federal tax collectors and customs officers to assist in enforcing state inspection laws).

Another passage of *The Federalist* reads as follows:

> It merits particular attention . . . , that the laws of the Confederacy as to the *enumerated* and *legitimate* objects of its jurisdiction will become the SUPREME LAW of the land; to the observance of which all officers, legislative, executive, and judicial in each State will be bound by the sanctity of an oath. Thus, the legislatures, courts, and magistrates, of the respective members will be incorporated into the operations of the national government as far as its just and constitutional authority extends; and will be rendered auxiliary to the enforcement of its laws.

The Federalist No. 27 (A. Hamilton) (emphasis in original).

[Justice Scalia rejected any implication that this passage supports any federal commandeering of state executive officers, as Justice Souter maintained in his dissenting opinion.] First, the consequences in question ("incorporated into the operations of the national government" and "rendered auxiliary to the enforcement of its laws") are said in the quoted passage to flow automatically from the officers' oath to observe the "the laws of the Confederacy as to the enumerated and legitimate objects of its jurisdiction." Thus, if the passage means that state officers must take an active role in the implementation of federal law, it means that they must do so without the necessity for a congressional directive that they implement it. But no one has ever thought, and no one asserts in the present litigation, that that is the law. The second problem with Justice Souter's reading is that it makes state legislatures subject to federal direction. (The passage in question, after all, does not include legislatures merely incidentally, as by referring to "all state officers"; it refers to legislatures specifically and first of all.) We have held, however, that state legislatures are not subject to federal direction. *New York v. United States.*

These problems are avoided, of course, if the calculatedly vague consequences the passage recites—"incorporated into the operations of the national government" and "rendered auxiliary to the enforcement of its laws"—are taken to refer to nothing more (or less) than the duty owed to the National Government, on the part of all state officials, to enact, enforce, and interpret state law in such fashion as not to obstruct the operation of federal law, and the attendant reality that all state actions constituting such obstruction, even legislative acts, are ipso facto invalid. * * *

[Justice Scalia next examined the most relevant constitutional principle—the assurance that the states retained "a residuary and inviolable sovereignty," *The Federalist* No. 39 (J. Madison), a principle reflected in the Constitution's prohibition on any involuntary reduction or combination of a State's territory, Art. IV, § 3; the Judicial Power Clause, Art. III, § 2, and the Privileges and Immunities Clause, Art. IV, § 2, which speak of the "Citizens" of the States; Article V, which requires the votes of three-fourths of the States to amend the Constitution; the Guarantee Clause, Art. IV, § 4, which "presupposes the continued existence of the states and . . . those means and instrumentalities which are the creation of their sovereign and reserved rights," *Helvering v. Gerhardt*, 304 U.S. 405, 414–415 (1938); and of course the enumeration of congressional powers in Article I and reservation of other powers to the states in the Tenth Amendment. Justice Scalia quoted Justice Kennedy's concurring opinion in *U.S. Term Limits* for its claim that the Framers' great innovation was that "our citizens would have two political capacities, one state and one federal, each protected from incursion by the other"—"a legal system unprecedented in form and design, establishing two orders of government, each with its own direct relationship, its own privity, its own set of mutual rights and obligations to the people who sustain it and are governed by it." See also *The Federalist* No. 51, at 323. "The power of the Federal Government would be augmented immeasurably if it were able to impress into its service—and at no cost to itself—the police officers of the 50 States," reasoned Justice Scalia.]

The dissent of course resorts to the last, best hope of those who defend ultra vires congressional action, the Necessary and Proper Clause. * * * When a "La[w] . . . for carrying into Execution" the Commerce Clause violates the principle of state sovereignty reflected in the various constitutional provisions we mentioned earlier, it is not a "La[w] . . . proper for carrying into Execution the Commerce Clause," and is thus, in the words of *The Federalist*, "merely [an] ac[t] of usurpation" which "deserve[s] to be treated as such." *The Federalist* No. 33 (A. Hamilton). We in fact answered the dissent's Necessary and Proper Clause argument in *New York*: "[E]ven where Congress has the authority under the Constitution to pass laws requiring or prohibiting certain acts, it lacks the power directly to compel the States to require or prohibit those acts. . . . [T]he Commerce Clause, for example, authorizes Congress to regulate interstate commerce directly; it does not authorize Congress to regulate state governments' regulation of interstate commerce." * * *

The Government also maintains that requiring state officers to perform discrete, ministerial tasks specified by Congress does not violate the principle of *New York* because it does not diminish the accountability of state or federal officials. This argument fails even on its own terms. By forcing state governments to absorb the financial burden of implementing a federal regulatory program, Members of Congress can take credit for "solving" problems without having to ask their constituents to pay for the solutions with higher federal taxes. And even when the States are not forced to absorb the costs of implementing a federal program, they are still put in the position of taking the blame for its burdensomeness and for its defects. See Merritt, *Three Faces of Federalism: Finding a Formula for the Future*, 47 Vand. L. Rev. 1563, 1580, n.65 (1994). Under the present law, for example, it will be the CLEO and not some federal official who stands between the gun purchaser and immediate possession of his gun. And it will likely be the CLEO, not some federal official, who will be blamed for any error (even one in the designated federal database) that causes a purchaser to be mistakenly rejected. * * *

Finally, the Government puts forward a cluster of arguments that can be grouped under the heading: "The Brady Act serves very important purposes, is most efficiently administered by CLEOs during the interim period, and places a minimal and only temporary burden upon state officers." There is considerable disagreement over the extent of the burden, but we need not pause over that detail. Assuming all the mentioned factors were true, they might be relevant if we were evaluating whether the incidental application to the States of a federal law of general applicability excessively interfered with the functioning of state governments. See, e.g., *Usery* (overruled by *Garcia*) * * *. But where, as here, it is the whole object of the law to direct the functioning of the state executive, and hence to compromise the structural framework of dual sovereignty, such a "balancing" analysis is inappropriate. It is the very principle of separate state sovereignty that such a law offends, and no comparative assessment of the various interests can overcome that fundamental defect. * * *

We adhere to that principle today, and conclude categorically, as we concluded categorically in *New York*: "The Federal Government may not compel the States to enact or administer a federal regulatory program." The mandatory obligation imposed on CLEOs to perform background checks on prospective handgun purchasers plainly runs afoul of that rule. [Accordingly, the Court invalidated those parts of the Brady Act requiring CLEOs to make background checks and to accept notice of the contents of, and a copy of, the completed Brady Form, which the firearms dealer is required to provide to him. The other provisions of the Brady Act have no effect on the plaintiff CLEOs, and their constitutionality is not before the Court.]

[We omit the concurring opinions of **JUSTICES O'CONNOR** and **THOMAS** and the dissenting opinion of **JUSTICE BREYER**.]

JUSTICE STEVENS, joined by **JUSTICE SOUTER**, **JUSTICE GINSBURG**, and **JUSTICE BREYER**, dissenting.

There is not a clause, sentence, or paragraph in the entire text of the Constitution of the United States that supports the proposition that a local police officer can ignore a command contained in a statute enacted by Congress pursuant to an express delegation of power enumerated in Article I. [This was no accident, Justice Stevens argued, because a key goal of the Constitution was to empower the national government.]

Indeed, the historical materials strongly suggest that the Founders intended to enhance the capacity of the federal government by empowering it—as a part of the new authority to make demands directly on individual citizens—to act through local officials. Hamilton made clear that the new Constitution, "by extending the authority of the federal head to the individual citizens of the several States, will enable the government to employ the ordinary magistracy of each, in the execution of its laws." *The Federalist* No. 27, at 180. * * *

More specifically, during the debates concerning the ratification of the Constitution, it was assumed that state agents would act as tax collectors for the federal government. Opponents of the Constitution had repeatedly expressed fears that the new federal government's ability to impose taxes directly on the citizenry would result in an overbearing presence of federal tax collectors in the States. Federalists rejoined that this problem would not arise because, as Hamilton explained, "the United States . . . will make use of the State officers and State regulations for collecting" certain taxes. [*The Federalist*] No. 36. Similarly, Madison made clear that the new central government's power to raise taxes directly from the citizenry would "not be resorted to, except for supplemental purposes of revenue . . . and that the eventual collection, under the immediate authority of the Union, will generally be made by the officers . . . appointed by the several States." *Id.*, No. 45. * * *

Bereft of support in the history of the founding, the Court rests its conclusion on the claim that there is little evidence the National Government actually exercised such a power in the early years of the Republic. This reasoning is misguided in principle and in fact. * * * [W]e have never suggested that the failure of the early Congresses to address the scope of federal power in a particular area or to exercise a particular authority was an argument against its existence. That position, if correct, would undermine most of our post-New Deal Commerce Clause jurisprudence. [More important, the early statutes delegating duties to state judges, such as immigration and naturalization duties, are on point, because in such statutes state judges were performing the same sort of reporting, checking, and housekeeping duties that the sheriffs must do under the Brady Act. E.g., Act of Mar. 26, 1790, ch. 3, § 1, 1 Stat. 103 (requiring state courts to consider immigration applications, specifying that the state courts "shall administer" an oath of loyalty to the United States, and that "the clerk of such court shall record such application"); Act of July 20, 1790, ch. 29, § 3, 1 Stat. 132–133 (requiring state courts to serve, functionally, like contemporary regulatory agencies in certifying the seaworthiness of vessels).]

* * * [T]he majority's opinion consists almost entirely of arguments against the substantial evidence weighing in opposition to its view; the Court's ruling is strikingly lacking in affirmative support. Absent even a modicum of textual foundation for its judicially crafted constitutional rule, there should be a presumption that if the Framers had actually intended such a rule, at least one of them would have mentioned it. * * *

Indeed, the presumption of validity that supports all congressional enactments has added force with respect to policy judgments concerning the impact of a federal statute upon the respective States. The majority points to nothing suggesting that the political safeguards of federalism identified in *Garcia* need be supplemented by a rule, grounded in neither constitutional history nor text, flatly prohibiting the National Government from enlisting state and local officials in the implementation of federal law.

[JUSTICE SOUTER explained in his separate dissenting opinion that his vote was driven by his reading of *The Federalist*.] Hamilton in No. 27 first notes that because the new Constitution would authorize the National Government to bind individuals directly through national law, it could "employ the ordinary magistracy of each [State] in the execution of its laws." *The Federalist* No. 27 (A. Hamilton). Were he to stop here, he would not necessarily be speaking of anything beyond the possibility of cooperative arrangements by agreement. But he then addresses the combined effect of the proposed Supremacy Clause, U.S. Const., Art. VI, cl. 2, and state officers' oath requirement, U.S. Const., Art. VI, cl. 3, and he states that "the Legislatures, Courts and Magistrates of the respective members will be incorporated into the operations of the national government, *as far as its just and constitutional authority extends*; and will be rendered auxiliary to the enforcement of its laws." *The Federalist* No. 27 (emphasis in original). The natural reading of this language is not merely that the officers of the various branches of state governments may be employed in the performance of national functions; Hamilton says that the state governmental machinery "will be incorporated" into the Nation's operation, and because the "auxiliary" status of the state officials will occur because they are "bound by the sanctity of an oath," *id.*, I take him to mean that their auxiliary functions will be the products of their obligations thus undertaken to support federal law, not of their own, or the States', unfettered choices. [In *Federalist* Nos. 36 and 45, Hamilton indicated that the national government can require state officials to assist in the collection of federal revenues. See also *Federalist* No. 44 (Madison).]

In the light of all these passages, I cannot persuade myself that the statements from No. 27 speak of anything less than the authority of the National Government, when exercising an otherwise legitimate power (the commerce power, say), to require state "auxiliaries" to take appropriate action. To be sure, it does not follow that any conceivable requirement may be imposed on any state official. I continue to agree, for example, that Congress may not require a state legislature to enact a regulatory scheme and that *New York v. United States* was rightly decided (even though I now believe its dicta went too far toward immunizing state administration as well as state enactment of such a scheme from congressional mandate); after all, the essence of legislative power, within the limits of legislative jurisdiction, is a discretion not subject to command. But insofar as national law would require nothing from a state officer inconsistent with the power proper to his branch of tripartite state government (say, by obligating a state judge to exercise law enforcement powers), I suppose that the reach of federal law as Hamilton described it would not be exceeded, cf. *Garcia* (without precisely delineating the outer limits of Congress's Commerce Clause power, finding that the statute at issue was not "destructive of state sovereignty").

NOTES ON *PRINTZ*, *FEDERALISM*, AND *ORIGINAL MEANING*

Printz illustrates the importance of starting points. The dissenters presume that when Congress acts within its Commerce Clause power, it is presumptively lawful; the burden is on those challenging the congressional action. The majority presumes that when Congress regulates the states directly, there is cause for concern; the burden is on those defending the congressional action. How do you choose the baseline? The precedents (*FERC v. Mississippi* and *New York v. United States*) cut both ways and are not exactly on point. Some other possibilities:

1.   *Constitutional Structure and the Values of Federalism*. Note Justice Scalia's core principle—the integrity of state governments—is nowhere set

forth in the Constitution, but is teased out of various clauses in the document. Is it fair to compare that methodology with Justice Douglas's teasing a right of privacy out of the *penumbras* of the Bill of Rights (*Griswold*, Chapter 5, § 4A)? At the very least, however, the Constitution unmistakably creates a federal arrangement. Is it threatened by the kind of regulation invalidated in *Printz*? See John F. Manning, *Federalism and the Generality Problem in Constitutional Interpretation*, 122 Harv. L. Rev. 2003 (2009) (criticizing *New York* and *Printz* as inconsistent with a textualist approach to constitutional interpretation).

Are the federalism values identified in our Note at the beginning of this chapter implicated in this kind of commandeering? How might liberty be threatened? Participatory democracy at the local level? Accountability? Efficiency? Justice Thomas's concurring opinion raised the link between the federalism and Second Amendment (right to keep and bear arms) issues in this case. In *District of Columbia v. Heller*, 554 U.S. 570 (2008), the Court recognized an individual right of law-abiding citizens to gun ownership for self-defense. The majority in *Heller* was similar to the one in *Printz* (with Roberts and Alito replacing Rehnquist and O'Connor, respectively), and the four dissenters were the same. Does this right "bear" any relevance to the federalism problem?

Do the values of federalism support a bright-line rule such as that adopted by the Court: No commandeering of state officers, *period*. Or would these values support a balancing approach? Vicki Jackson, *Federalism and the Uses and Limits of Law:* Printz *and Principle*, 111 Harv. L. Rev. 2180, 2200–05 (1998), argues that the Constitution supports clear lines of accountability but sharply disputes, from the perspective of constitutional text and principles, the Court's nondeferential bright-line approach.

2.   *Political Philosophy: The Nature of State Sovereignty*. The majority and dissenting Justices disagreed about the nature of federal and state sovereignty: Justice Scalia emphasized retained state sovereignty, Justice Stevens the supervening national sovereignty. Note that Justice Scalia did not follow Justice Thomas' theory in *U.S. Term Limits* and, instead, quoted Justice Kennedy (the only Justice in the majority for both cases). Kennedy's approach rejected the asymmetry suggested in *McCulloch* and supported an active role for the Court when either national or state sovereignties seek to encroach upon core features of the other. Is *Printz* inconsistent with the *McCulloch-U.S. Term Limits* idea that sovereignty resides wholly in We the People? Were the earlier cases wrongly decided?

Note what was largely absent in the debate about state sovereignty: the *McCulloch-Garcia* argument that, because the states are formally represented in the national government, the Court should leave the protection of their sovereignty to the political process. Justice Stevens made this point in dissent, but the Court ignored it. Justice Breyer's dissent (which we omitted) observed that most federations in the world allow the national government to delegate duties to provincial governments, and some federations (the European

Community, Switzerland) provide that the constituent states and not the national government will ordinarily implement national laws and regulations.

3.   *Original Meaning.* Note also the methodological shift from the *Garcia-National League of Cities* debate to the debate among the Justices in *Printz* and *U.S. Term Limits.* The Justices in the latter cases de-emphasized or ignored the legal-process type arguments of institutional competence that were debated in the former cases. Original meaning arguments have replaced the legal process arguments. All nine Justices made such arguments in *Printz*; original meaning was the keystone of Justice Scalia's opinion for the Court and for Justice Stevens' lead dissent, and it was the only reason Justice Souter believed *New York v. United States* (which he joined) was not applicable. Note that Professor Prakash's leading article, concluded that *New York* was correct, but *Printz* was wrong under the original meaning standard.

Does the debate in *Printz* surmount—or does it confirm—the theoretical difficulties with originalism raised in Chapter 2, § 3A2, namely: (1) for an old document like the Constitution, all the questions are counterfactual—*i.e.*, we attribute conclusions to long-dead people "as if" they had anticipated current states of affairs; (2) there is no reason to believe that the Framers "intended" us to be bound by their original intent or, even if so, by what level of intent (specific intent or general purpose); (3) even if we can "know" how Madison and Hamilton (authors of the always-quoted *Federalist Papers*) would have answered the interpretive puzzle, there is no reliable way to attribute the views of these authors (of blatant propaganda documents!) to other Framers or to the state ratifying conventions. Do the changed-circumstances, intent-about-intent, and aggregation-of-intent argument have extra bite in a case, such as *Printz*, where the Court did not cite to a specific constitutional provision that it was applying?

PROBLEM 7-6:
FEDERALISM VALUES IN THE MARRIAGE EQUALITY CASES

Recall the marriage equality debate from Chapter 4. In 2013, not only did most state marriage laws exclude lesbian and gay couples, but so did federal law. Congress and President Clinton in 1996 enacted the Defense of Marriage Act ("DOMA") to defend marriage against such couples. Section 3, 1 U.S.C. § 7, denied federal economic and other benefits to lawfully married same-sex couples. Several federal courts ruled that DOMA violated the Fifth Amendment rights of validly married lesbian and gay couples—but the Commonwealth of Massachusetts challenged DOMA as a violation of the Tenth Amendment. Under what congressional authority was § 3 enacted? Was § 3 vulnerable to constitutional attack based upon the Court's federalism jurisprudence? What precedents might the state rely on to argue that DOMA § 3 violated the Tenth Amendment? If the Massachusetts and individual couples lawsuits were consolidated, as they were on appeal, how might the *federalism* argument interact with the *equal protection* argument? See

Commonwealth of Massachusetts v. Department of Health and Human Services, 682 F.3d 1 (1st Cir. May 31, 2012) (Boudin, J.).

In ***United States v. Windsor*, 570 U.S. 744 (2013)** (Chapter 4, § 3D), the Supreme Court ruled that DOMA § 3 violated the Fifth Amendment rights of Edie Windsor, a widow whose valid same-sex marriage was disregarded by the IRS. In Part III of his opinion for the Court, **Justice Kennedy** prefaced his discussion of the Fifth Amendment challenge with a discussion of federalism. "By history and tradition the definition and regulation of marriage * * * has been treated as being within the authority and realm of the separate States. Yet it is further established that Congress, in enacting discrete statutes, can make determinations that bear on marital rights and privileges."

By creating a blanket rule that no federal law or regulation referring to "marriage" or "spouse" could include same-sex marriages, DOMA's § 3 was unprecedented in its sweep. In 2013, it affected "a class of persons that the laws of New York, and of 11 other States, have sought to protect." The Court considered this constitutionally "significant," because "regulation of domestic relations" is "an area that has long been regarded as a virtually exclusive province of the States." *Sosna* v. *Iowa*, 419 U.S. 393, 404 (1976). "The definition of marriage is the foundation of the State's broader authority to regulate the subject of domestic relations with respect to the '[p]rotection of offspring, property interests, and the enforcement of marital responsibilities.' *Ibid.* '[T]he states, at the time of the adoption of the Constitution, possessed full power over the subject of marriage and divorce . . . [and] the Constitution delegated no authority to the Government of the United States on the subject of marriage and divorce.' *Haddock* v. *Haddock*, 201 U.S. 562, 575 (1906)."

Justice Kennedy found it "unnecessary to decide whether this federal intrusion on state power was a violation of the Constitution because it disrupted the federal balance. The State's power in defining the marital relation was of central relevance in this case quite apart from principles of federalism. Here the State's decision to give this class of persons the right to marry conferred upon them a dignity and status of immense import. When the State used its historic and essential authority to define the marital relation in this way, its role and its power in making the decision enhanced the recognition, dignity, and protection of the class in their own community. DOMA, because of its reach and extent, departs from this history and tradition of reliance on state law to define marriage." He then delivered the apparent doctrinal punch line: "[D]iscriminations of an unusual character especially suggest careful consideration to determine whether they are obnoxious to the constitutional provision." *Romer* v. *Evans*, 517 U.S. 620, 633 (1996).

Three dissenting Justices (**Chief Justice Roberts** and **Justices Thomas** and **Alito**) opined that Congress clearly had the authority to adopt DOMA (as the Solicitor General had conceded at oral argument) and that in pending challenges to state marriage exclusions the Court's ode of federalism ought to support state defenses of statutes and constitutional amendments hewing to the "traditional" one man, one woman definition of marriage. Also dissenting, **Justice Scalia** (joined by Justice Thomas) agreed that Congress had plenty of authority to adopt DOMA but lambasted the Court for Fifth Amendment analysis that assured success for challenges to state marriage exclusions. Indeed, with the exception of some rulings in Louisiana, every federal court evaluating state exclusions after *Windsor* struck them down (many citing Justice Scalia's sarcastic analysis).

Take seriously the perspective of the Chief Justice. Consider how the values of federalism—liberty, republican deliberation, and regulatory pluralism—might *support* a deferential posture for judges evaluating state exclusions, even if they believe the blanket federal exclusion went too far. Construct a federalism brief for the states in *Obergefell v. Hodges*, 135 S.Ct. 2584 (2015). As you know from Chapter 5, § 4D, Justice Kennedy wrote for the Court in *Obergefell* and pretty much ignored his earlier ode to federalism. Why were the federalism values not sufficient to save the state definitions of marriage? Finally, advise John Roberts on this question: Federalism values suggest some alternative ways to decide *Obergefell*. In other words, set aside the dueling results in those cases—uphold the state exclusions or require marriage equality—and come up with different ways to resolve the controversies. Is there a resolution that protects the equality values of *Romer*, *Lawrence*, and *Windsor* (equality parts of the opinion), while at the same time respecting the federalism values of *Boerne*, *New York*, and *Windsor* (ode to federalism), as well as the democracy values of *Schuette v. Coalition to Defend Affirmative Action*, 572 U.S. 291 (2014), which upheld a ballot initiative addressing the important issue of affirmative action? All of the state constitutional provisions at issue in *Obergefell* had been overwhelmingly endorsed by the voters in elections held in 2004 and 2006. (Hint: there is an obvious solution to this dilemma, but one that all parties and *amici* in *Obergefell* considered anathema.)

Reno v. Condon

528 U.S. 141 (2000)

Congress enacted the Driver's Privacy Protection Act of 1994 (DPPA), 18 U.S.C. §§ 2721–2725 (as amended), to prevent state departments of motor vehicles from disclosing drivers' personal information to third parties, unless drivers have affirmatively consented to such disclosure. South Carolina, whose law allowed such personal information to be available to third parties, challenged the DPPA as violating constitutional principles of federalism. The Supreme Court, in an opinion by **Chief Justice Rehnquist**, unanimously rejected the challenge.

The Court first ruled that the law was within Congress' Commerce Clause powers, because the personal information the DPPA regulates is a "thing in interstate commerce," and therefore is a proper exercise of Congress' Commerce Clause powers under *Lopez*. "The motor vehicle information which the States have historically sold is used by insurers, manufacturers, direct marketers, and others engaged in interstate commerce to contact drivers with customized solicitations. The information is also used in the stream of interstate commerce by various public and private entities for matters related to interstate motoring. Because drivers' information is, in this context, an article of commerce, its sale or release into the interstate stream of business is sufficient to support congressional regulation. We therefore need not address the Government's alternative argument that the States' individual, intrastate activities in gathering, maintaining, and distributing drivers' personal information has a sufficiently substantial impact on interstate commerce to create a constitutional base for federal legislation." (Nor did the Court address the government's argument that the DPPA was also enacted pursuant to Congress' power to enforce the Fourteenth Amendment.)

A statute properly enacted under Congress' Commerce Clause power might still violate the Tenth Amendment, which was construed in *New York* and *Printz* to limit Congress' authority to direct state governmental activities. And the DPPA did impose new duties on state governments, with possible criminal penalties for violations. But the Court ruled that the law did not fall afoul the principles of *New York* or *Printz*. "We think, instead, that this case is governed by our decision in *South Carolina v. Baker*. In *Baker*, we upheld a statute that prohibited States from issuing unregistered bonds because the law 'regulate[d] state activities,' rather than 'seek[ing] to control or influence the manner in which States regulate private parties.' We further noted:

> The NGA [National Governor's Association] nonetheless contends that § 310 has commandeered the state legislative and administrative process because many state legislatures had to amend a substantial number of statutes in order to issue bonds in registered form and because state officials had to devote substantial effort to determine how best to implement a registered bond system. Such "commandeering" is, however, an inevitable consequence of regulating a state activity. Any federal regulation demands compliance. That a State wishing to engage in certain activity must take administrative and sometimes legislative action to comply with federal standards regulating that activity is a commonplace that presents no constitutional defect.

"Like the statute at issue in *Baker*, the DPPA does not require the States in their sovereign capacity to regulate their own citizens. The DPPA regulates the States as the owners of databases. It does not require the South Carolina Legislature to enact any laws or regulations, and it does not require state officials to assist in the enforcement of federal statutes regulating private individuals. We accordingly conclude that the DPPA is consistent with the constitutional principles enunciated in *New York* and *Printz*."

Murphy v. NCAA

138 S.Ct. 1461 (2018)

The Professional and Amateur Sports Protection Act (PASPA) makes it unlawful for a State or its subdivisions "to sponsor, operate, advertise, promote, license, or authorize by law or compact * * * a lottery, sweepstakes, or other betting, gambling, or wagering scheme" based on competitive sporting events, 28 U.S.C. § 3702(1), and for "a person to sponsor, operate, advertise, or promote" those same gambling schemes if done "pursuant to the law or compact of a governmental entity," § 3702(2). PASPA does not make sports gambling itself a federal crime but does allow the Attorney General, as well as professional and amateur sports organizations, to bring civil actions to enjoin violations. § 3703. "Grandfather" provisions allow existing forms of sports gambling to continue in four States, § 3704(a)(1)-(2), and another provision would have permitted New Jersey to set up a sports gambling scheme in Atlantic City within a year of PASPA's enactment, § 3704(a)(3).

Several years later, the New Jersey Legislature more broadly legalized sports gambling, and the NCAA sued to overturn the law as preempted by PASPA. The state responded that § 3702(1) violated the Supreme Court's federalism precedents. In an opinion by **Justice Alito**, the Supreme Court agreed with New Jersey, based upon the anti-commandeering precedents.

"The anticommandeering doctrine may sound arcane, but it is simply the expression of a fundamental structural decision incorporated into the Constitution, *i.e.,* the decision to withhold from Congress the power to issue orders directly to the States. When the original States declared their independence, they claimed the powers inherent in sovereignty—in the words of the Declaration of Independence, the authority 'to do all . . . Acts and Things which Independent States may of right do.' ¶ 32. The Constitution limited but did not abolish the sovereign powers of the States, which retained 'residuary and inviolable sovereignty.' The Federalist No. 39, p. 245 (C. Rossiter ed. 1961). Thus, both the Federal Government and the States wield sovereign powers, and that is why our system of government is said to be one of 'dual sovereignty.' *Gregory v. Ashcroft,* 501 U.S. 452, 457, 111 S.Ct. 2395, 115 L.Ed.2d 410 (1991)."

Justice Alito explained how the anti-commandeering rule is foundational to three great purposes of constitutional federalism: (1) *Liberty.* "[A] healthy balance of power between the States and the Federal Government [reduces] the risk of tyranny and abuse from either front." *New York.* (2) *Political Accountability.* "When Congress itself regulates, the responsibility for the benefits and burdens of the regulation is apparent. Voters who like or dislike the effects of the regulation know who to credit or blame. By contrast, if a State imposes regulations only because it has been commanded to do so by Congress, responsibility is blurred." (3) *Efficiency.* "If Congress enacts a law and requires enforcement by the Executive Branch, it must appropriate the funds needed to administer the program. It is pressured to weigh the expected benefits of the program against its costs. But if Congress can compel the States to enact and enforce its program, Congress need not engage in any such analysis. See, *e.g.,*

E. Young, *Two Cheers for Process Federalism,* 46 Vill. L. Rev. 1349, 1360–61 (2001)."

Section 3702(1) violated the anti-commandeering rule. "That provision unequivocally dictates what a state legislature may and may not do. * * * [S]tate legislatures are put under the direct control of Congress. It is as if federal officers were installed in state legislative chambers and were armed with the authority to stop legislators from voting on any offending proposals. A more direct affront to state sovereignty is not easy to imagine."

The United States defended PASPA as different from earlier commandeering statutes on the ground that it did not require state legislatures to do anything—it just barred them from acting. "This distinction is empty. It was a matter of happenstance that the laws challenged in *New York* and *Printz* commanded 'affirmative' action as opposed to imposing a prohibition. The basic principle—that Congress cannot issue direct orders to state legislatures—applies in either event.

"Here is an illustration. PASPA includes an exemption for States that permitted sports betting at the time of enactment, § 3704, but suppose Congress did not adopt such an exemption. Suppose Congress ordered States with legalized sports betting to take the affirmative step of criminalizing that activity and ordered the remaining States to retain their laws prohibiting sports betting. There is no good reason why the former would intrude more deeply on state sovereignty than the latter." Indeed, the Court also ruled that PASPA's bar to state "licensing" of sports gambling also violated the anti-commandeering rule.

Once most of § 3702(1) falls under the judicial mandate, the Court ruled that § 3702(2) (barring private gambling) and indeed the remainder of PASPA were invalid as well. These remaining provisions were not "severable" from the rest of the statute, because Congress would not have passed the law at all without the state-compulsion provision. If the core of the statute falls, so must the entire statute. Article III does not allow federal judges to create a new law that Congress did not vote on. (Recall that Justices Alito, Thomas, Kennedy, and Scalia would have unvalidated the entire Affordable Care Act once they struck down the individual mandate in *NFIB*.)

Concurring in the Court's opinion, **Justice Thomas** stated that he would revisit the Court's severability precedents, which in his view clash with Article III, because they (a) require judges to rewrite statutes, (b) based upon a hypothetical exercise inconsistent with a strict textual approach to the Constitution, and (c) without proper adversarial contest on that issue. **Justice Ginsburg** (joined by Justices Breyer and Sotomayor) dissented on the severability issue. Consistent with *NFIB*, she would have severed § 3702(1) from the remainder of the statute, which would have barred the spread of legalized sports gambling.

PROBLEM 7-7
HOW FAR DO THE ANTI-COMMANDEERING
PRECEDENTS REACH?

State bonds are debt securities issued by state governments, often to finance large capital projects. The bond holder is entitled to interest and may redeem her investment pursuant to the terms of the bond. Assume that Congress, after many hearings, finds that state bonds are subject to consumer fraud and are also increasingly used to launder money generated by illegal activities. In the Bond Protection Act of 2019, Congress forbids the states to issue any further bonds and requires the states to liquidate their entire bond debt within two years. Relying on *Murphy* and the earlier anti-commandeering precedents, New Jersey sues to enjoin the operation of the Act. What arguments might the United States make to defend the Act? How would the Supreme Court rule?

NOTE ON FEDERAL REGULATION OF STATE PROCESS

In *Jinks v. Richland County*, 538 U.S. 456 (2003), the Court unanimously rejected a commandeering challenge to the application of 28 U.S.C. § 1367(d) to toll a state statute of limitations for 30 days after a voluntary dismissal of a claim brought in federal court under § 1367(a). Congress clearly has the authority to enact laws implementing its authority "[t]o constitute Tribunals inferior to the supreme Court,' U.S. Const., Art. I, § 8, cl. 9, and to assure that those tribunals may fairly and efficiently exercise '[t]he judicial Power of the United States,' Art. III, § 1. Invoking *Printz*, Richland County also maintained that § 1367(d) was not a proper exercise of Congress's Article I powers, because it intruded on state sovereignty over the procedure followed in state courts. The Court observed that statutes of limitations are arguably substantive (clearly so for purposes of *Erie R.R. v. Tompkins*). Without holding that Congress can set the rules of state court procedure, the Court found no Tenth Amendment violation.

Applying much the same analysis as *Jinks*, the Court earlier ruled that Congress has the authority to impose an evidentiary privilege on state as well as federal courts if that privilege is "necessary and proper" to the operation of a federal statutory program seeking to identify and eliminate hazardous road conditions. *Pierce County v. Guillen*, 537 U.S. 129 (2003). But the Court interpreted the federal statute stingily, based upon a presumption that evidentiary privileges should be narrowly construed. As in *Jinks*, this might bespeak a constitutional concern that Congress does not have plenary authority to regulate state court procedures. Could Congress require state courts to follow the following rules as a matter of uniformity in adjudicatory practice?

1.   A rule barring cross-examination of a rape victim based upon her or his previous sexual history. Assume Congress gathers extensive evidence showing that cross-examination of this sort has little bearing on the facts of

rape, has a prejudicial effect on jury deliberations, and deters rape victims from complaining to authorities or supporting prosecution of their assailants.

2. A rule requiring state courts to follow the liberal discovery rules adopted by the U.S. Supreme Court for federal civil practice, Fed. R. Civ. P. 26–37. Assume Congress gathers extensive evidence showing that the liberality of the Federal Rules produces greater fairness in civil litigation and facilitates settlement.

3. A rule requiring states to have jury trials in all cases arising under the common law or under statutes creating common law-type claims for relief (tort, contract, property, etc.). The Seventh Amendment does not apply to the states, and Congress finds that the legitimacy and efficiency added to civil adjudication justifies a statutory jury trial right.

PROBLEM 7-8:
WHAT PRECEDENTS OUGHT TO BE OVERRULED?

Since 1992, the Supreme Court has revived and rethought federalism as a limit on congressional power. In light of this rethinking, which precedents should now be overruled or narrowed? Some candidates:

- *Darby et al.* The Tenth Amendment no longer seems like the "truism" *Darby* said it was. Should *Darby* or *Wickard* be revisited? *McClung*?

- *South Dakota v. Dole.* Does this broad authorization for congressional spending conditions undercut the other precedents?

- *Missouri v. Holland.* Justice Holmes's reasoning might be vulnerable, and the holding seems strongly inconsistent with the New Federalism.

- *Katzenbach v. Morgan.* The Court has already moved away from the reasoning of this precedent. Can § 5 of the reauthorized Voting Rights Act be invalidated without overruling this precedent?

- *Katz.* Should the jurisprudence of *Seminole Tribe* reconsider the Bankruptcy Clause as a basis for abrogating state immunity? Is *Bitzer* too entrenched to be overruled?

- *Hibbs.* Does *Coleman* open the door to overruling *Hibbs*? Should *Tennessee v. Lane* also be reconsidered?

- *FERC v. Mississippi.* Justice O'Connor's dissenting opinion reads like a roadmap for the later federalism jurisprudence.

- *Garcia. Printz* and *New York* ignored *Garcia*, which may be a prelude to an overruling. If *Garcia* falls, does *South Carolina v. Baker* fall too?

- *McCulloch v. Maryland.* It is doubtful that the Court would overrule this constitutional chestnut, but its expansive view of the Necessary and Proper Clause might be questioned.[66] Should *Comstock* be overruled?

Use this exercise as an occasion, first, to figure out what is the principle that best explains the recent federalism precedents and, then, to figure out how that principle applies to the previous precedents, considering the force of *stare decisis*. See *Planned Parenthood v. Casey* (Chapter 5, § 4B). The Justices consistently in the majority of the federalism cases take different approaches to *stare decisis*. In contrast to Justice Thomas, who is the most open to overruling constitutional precedents, Chief Justice Roberts not only follows precedent but sees himself as guided by precedent: *stare decisis* is his primary methodology, not just a limiting condition.

On the other hand, Justice Breyer has been a frequent dissenter in the federalism cases, often decided by 5–4 Courts. Given his pragmatic premises, which precedents should he want to overrule:

- *Lopez* and *Morrison.* Should a pragmatic theory of the Commerce Clause overrule *Morrison* but leave *Lopez* in place?

- *Boerne.* Should this landmark precedent be overruled, or its congruence and proportionality test abandoned? Or should the test be applied more deferentially than it was applied in *Kimel, Garrett,* and *Coleman*? Should any of those precedents be overruled?

- *Seminole Tribe.* If this precedent were overruled, the abrogation of state immunity in *Kimel, Garrett,* and *Coleman* could be justified by Congress's Commerce Clause authority.

- *New York v. United States.* Or should any overruling focus instead on *Printz*, which has a much weaker basis in original meaning?

Like the Chief Justice, however, Justice Breyer is a fan of *stare decisis*: Should that value persuade him against overruling any of these precedents? What strategy might a precedent-following pragmatist adopt?

---

[66] See John C. Yoo, McCulloch v. Maryland, in *Constitutional Stupidities/Constitutional Tragedies* (William N. Eskridge Jr. & Sanford Levinson eds. 1998).

C. SUMMING UP FEDERALISM DOCTRINE: THE AFFORDABLE CARE ACT CASE

NATIONAL FEDERATION OF INDEPENDENT BUSINESS V. SEBELIUS

567 U.S. 519, 132 S.Ct. 2566, 183 L.Ed. 2d 450 (2012)

CHIEF JUSTICE ROBERTS announced the judgment of the Court and delivered the opinion of the Court with respect to Parts I, II, and III-C, an opinion with respect to Part IV, in which JUSTICE BREYER and JUSTICE KAGAN join, and an opinion with respect to Parts III-A, III-B, and III-D.

"State sovereignty is not just an end in itself: Rather, federalism secures to citizens the liberties that derive from the diffusion of sovereign power." *New York v. United States.* Because the police power is controlled by 50 different States instead of one national sovereign, the facets of governing that touch on citizens' daily lives are normally administered by smaller governments closer to the governed. The Framers thus ensured that powers which "in the ordinary course of affairs, concern the lives, liberties, and properties of the people" were held by governments more local and more accountable than a distant federal bureaucracy. The Federalist No. 45, at 293 (J. Madison). The independent power of the States also serves as a check on the power of the Federal Government: "By denying any one government complete jurisdiction over all the concerns of public life, federalism protects the liberty of the individual from arbitrary power." *Bond v. United States.*

This case concerns two powers that the Constitution does grant the Federal Government, but which must be read carefully to avoid creating a general federal authority akin to the police power [namely, Congress's Commerce Clause power and its Tax-and-Spend Clause power, supplemented by Congress's authority under the Necessary and Proper Clause, all of which the Court has applied liberally]. * * *

Our permissive reading of these powers is explained in part by a general reticence to invalidate the acts of the Nation's elected leaders. "Proper respect for a co-ordinate branch of the government" requires that we strike down an Act of Congress only if "the lack of constitutional authority to pass [the] act in question is clearly demonstrated." *United States v. Harris*, 106 U.S. 629, 635 (1883). Members of this Court are vested with the authority to interpret the law; we possess neither the expertise nor the prerogative to make policy judgments. Those decisions are entrusted to our Nation's elected leaders, who can be thrown out of office if the people disagree with them. It is not our job to protect the people from the consequences of their political choices.

Our deference in matters of policy cannot, however, become abdication in matters of law. "The powers of the legislature are defined and limited; and that those limits may not be mistaken, or forgotten, the constitution is written." *Marbury*. Our respect for Congress's policy judgments thus can never extend so far as to disavow restraints on federal power that the Constitution carefully constructed. * * * And there can be no question that it is the responsibility of this Court to enforce the limits on federal power by striking down acts of Congress that transgress those limits. *Marbury*.

The questions before us must be considered against the background of these basic principles.

[**Part I.** The Patient Protection and Affordable Care Act, Pub. L. No. 111–148, 124 Stat. 119 (2010), as amended by the Health Care and Education Reconciliation Act of 2010, Pub. L. No. 111–152, 124 Stat. 1029 (2010) (the "Act" or the "ACA"), expanded health care coverage for Americans. One key provision was the individual mandate, which required most Americans to maintain "minimum essential" health insurance coverage. 26 U.S.C. § 5000A. For individuals who were not exempt, and who did not receive health insurance through an employer or government program, the means of satisfying the requirement was to purchase insurance from a private company. Beginning in 2014, those who did not comply with the mandate must make a "[s]hared responsibility payment" to the Federal Government. § 5000A(b)(1). The Act provided that this "penalty" would be paid with an individual's income taxes, and "shall be assessed and collected in the same manner" as tax penalties. §§ 5000A(c), (g)(1).

[The Act also expanded the Medicaid program. That program offers federal funding to States to assist pregnant women, children, needy families, the blind, the elderly, and the disabled in obtaining medical care. 42 U.S.C. § 1396d(a). The ACA expanded Medicaid coverage by 2014 to include adults with incomes up to 133 percent of the federal poverty level. § 1396a(a)(10)(A)(i)(VIII). The Act increased federal funding to cover the States' costs in expanding Medicaid coverage. § 1396d(y)(1). But if a State did not comply with the Act's new coverage requirements, it might lose not only the federal funding for those requirements, but all of its federal Medicaid funds. § 1396c.

[Twenty-six states, several individuals, and the National Federation of Independent Business (NFIB) brought suit in federal court challenging the constitutionality of the individual mandate and the Medicaid expansion. In **Part II** of his opinion, joined by **JUSTICES GINSBURG, BREYER, SOTOMAYOR,** and **KAGAN,** the **CHIEF JUSTICE** spoke for the Court to hold that the Anti-Injunction Act did not bar litigation of the constitutional attacks on the Act, because Congress labeled the individual mandate as a "penalty" rather than as a "tax." Litigation against the latter is barred, but not litigation against the former.]

[In **Part III.A,** treating the argument that the individual mandate constitutionally rests upon Congress's Commerce Clause authority, the **CHIEF JUSTICE** spoke only for himself but delivered a conclusion with which **JUSTICES SCALIA, KENNEDY, THOMAS,** and **ALITO,** in their Joint Dissent, did not join but implicitly agreed.] According to the Government, the health care market is characterized by a significant cost-shifting problem. Everyone will eventually need health care at a time and to an extent they cannot predict, but if they do not have insurance, they often will not be able to pay for it. Because state and federal laws nonetheless require hospitals to provide a certain degree of care to individuals without regard to their ability to pay, hospitals end up receiving compensation for only a portion of the services they provide. To recoup the losses, hospitals pass on the cost to insurers through higher rates, and insurers, in turn, pass on the cost to policy holders in the form of higher premiums. Congress estimated that the cost of uncompensated care raises family health insurance premiums, on average, by over $1,000 per year. 42 U.S.C. § 18091(2)(F).

In the Affordable Care Act, Congress addressed the problem of those who cannot obtain insurance coverage because of preexisting conditions or other health issues. It did so through the Act's "guaranteed-issue" and "community-rating" provisions. These provisions together prohibit insurance companies from denying coverage to those with such conditions or charging unhealthy individuals higher premiums than healthy individuals.

The guaranteed-issue and community-rating reforms do not, however, address the issue of healthy individuals who choose not to purchase insurance to cover potential healthcare needs. In fact, the reforms sharply exacerbate that problem, by providing an incentive for individuals to delay purchasing health insurance until they become sick, relying on the promise of guaranteed and affordable coverage. The reforms also threaten to impose massive new costs on insurers, who are required to accept unhealthy individuals but prohibited from charging them rates necessary to pay for their coverage. This will lead insurers to significantly increase premiums on everyone.

The individual mandate was Congress's solution to these problems. By requiring that individuals purchase health insurance, the mandate prevents cost-shifting by those who would otherwise go without it. In addition, the mandate forces into the insurance risk pool more healthy individuals, whose premiums on average will be higher than their health care expenses. This allows insurers to subsidize the costs of covering the unhealthy individuals the reforms require them to accept. The Government claims that Congress has power under the Commerce and Necessary and Proper Clauses to enact this solution.

The Government contends that the individual mandate is within Congress's power because the failure to purchase insurance "has a substantial and deleterious effect on interstate commerce" by creating the cost-shifting problem. [The Government invoked the Court's many decisions allowing Congress authority to regulate transactions "affecting" commerce, e.g., *Darby*, and even to aggregate many transactions to create the effect on commerce. *Wickard*.]

Given its expansive scope, it is no surprise that Congress has employed the commerce power in a wide variety of ways to address the pressing needs of the time. But Congress has never attempted to rely on that power to compel individuals not engaged in commerce to purchase an unwanted product. Legislative novelty is not necessarily fatal; there is a first time for everything. But sometimes "the most telling indication of [a] severe constitutional problem . . . is the lack of historical precedent" for Congress's action. *Free Enterprise Fund v. Public Company Accounting Oversight Bd.* [Chapter 8]. At the very least, we should "pause to consider the implications of the Government's arguments" when confronted with such new conceptions of federal power. *Lopez*.

The Constitution grants Congress the power to "*regulate* Commerce." Art. I, § 8, cl. 3 (emphasis added). The power to *regulate* commerce presupposes the existence of commercial activity to be regulated. If the power to "regulate" something included the power to create it, many of the provisions in the Constitution would be superfluous. For example, the Constitution gives Congress the power to "coin Money," in addition to the power to "regulate the Value thereof." *Id.,* cl. 5. And it gives Congress the power to "raise and support Armies" and to "provide and maintain a Navy," in addition to the power to "make Rules for the Government and Regulation of the land and naval Forces." *Id.,* cls. 12–14. If the power to regulate the armed forces or the value of money included the power to bring the subject of the regulation into existence, the specific grant of such powers would have been unnecessary. The language of the Constitution reflects the natural understanding that the power to regulate assumes there is already something to be regulated. [Likewise, the Court's precedents "uniformly" describe the Commerce Clause power as reaching "activity."]

The individual mandate, however, does not regulate existing commercial activity. It instead compels individuals to *become* active in commerce by purchasing a product, on the ground that their failure to do so affects interstate commerce. Construing the Commerce Clause to permit Congress to regulate individuals precisely *because* they are doing nothing would open a new and potentially vast domain to congressional authority.
* * *

Applying the Government's logic to the familiar case of *Wickard v. Filburn* shows how far that logic would carry us from the notion of a government of limited powers. In *Wickard*, the Court famously upheld a federal penalty imposed on a farmer for growing wheat for consumption on his own farm. That amount of wheat caused the farmer to exceed his quota under a program designed to support the price of wheat by limiting supply. The Court rejected the farmer's argument that growing wheat for home consumption was beyond the reach of the commerce power. It did so on the ground that the farmer's decision to grow wheat for his own use allowed him to avoid purchasing wheat in the market. That decision, when considered in the aggregate along with similar decisions of others, would have had a substantial effect on the interstate market for wheat.

Wickard has long been regarded as "perhaps the most far reaching example of Commerce Clause authority over intrastate activity," *Lopez*, but the Government's theory in this case would go much further. Under *Wickard* it is within Congress's power to regulate the market for wheat by supporting its price. But price can be supported by increasing demand as well as by decreasing supply. The aggregated decisions of some consumers not to purchase wheat have a substantial effect on the price of wheat, just as decisions not to purchase health insurance have on the price of insurance. Congress can therefore command that those not buying wheat do so, just as it argues here that it may command that those not buying health insurance do so. The farmer in *Wickard* was at least actively engaged in the production of wheat, and the Government could regulate that activity because of its effect on commerce. The Government's theory here would effectively override that limitation, by establishing that individuals may be regulated under the Commerce Clause whenever enough of them are not doing something the Government would have them do.

Indeed, the Government's logic would justify a mandatory purchase to solve almost any problem. To consider a different example in the health care market, many Americans do not eat a balanced diet. That group makes up a larger percentage of the total population than those without health insurance. The failure of that group to have a healthy diet increases health care costs, to a greater extent than the failure of the uninsured to purchase insurance. Those increased costs are borne in part by other Americans who must pay more, just as the uninsured shift costs to the insured. Congress addressed the insurance problem by ordering everyone to buy insurance. Under the Government's theory, Congress could address the diet problem by ordering everyone to buy vegetables.

[The Chief Justice believed this power to be limitless and, if sanctioned, would constitute a decisive shift in the relationship between the citizenry and the federal government.] The Government regards it as sufficient to trigger Congress's authority that almost all those who are uninsured will, at some unknown point in the future, engage in a health care transaction. Asserting that "[t]here is no temporal limitation in the Commerce Clause," the Government argues that because "[e]veryone subject to this regulation is in or will be in the health care market," they can be "regulated in advance." Tr. of Oral Arg. 109 (Mar. 27, 2012).

The proposition that Congress may dictate the conduct of an individual today because of prophesied future activity finds no support in our precedent. We have said that Congress can anticipate the *effects* on commerce of an economic activity. See, *e.g., Heart of Atlanta Motel*; *McClung*. But we have never permitted Congress to anticipate that activity itself in order to regulate individuals not currently engaged in commerce. * * *

Everyone will likely participate in the markets for food, clothing, transportation, shelter, or energy; that does not authorize Congress to direct them to purchase particular products in those or other markets today. The Commerce Clause is not a general license to regulate an individual from cradle to grave, simply because he will predictably engage in particular transactions. Any police power to regulate individuals as such, as opposed to their activities, remains vested in the States.

The Government argues that the individual mandate can be sustained as a sort of exception to this rule, because health insurance is a unique product. According to the Government, upholding the individual mandate would not justify mandatory purchases of items such as cars or broccoli because, as the Government puts it, "[h]ealth insurance is not purchased for its own sake like a car or broccoli; it is a means of financing health-care consumption and covering universal risks." But cars and broccoli are no more purchased for their "own sake" than health insurance. They are purchased to cover the need for transportation and food.

The Government says that health insurance and healthcare financing are "inherently integrated." But that does not mean the compelled purchase of the first is properly regarded as a regulation of the second. No matter how "inherently integrated" health insurance and health care consumption may be, they are not the same thing: They involve different transactions, entered into at different times, with different providers. And for most of those targeted by the mandate, significant health care needs will be years, or even decades, away. The proximity and degree of connection between the mandate and the subsequent commercial activity is too lacking to justify an exception of the sort urged by the Government. The individual mandate forces individuals into commerce precisely because they elected to refrain from commercial activity. Such a law cannot be sustained under a clause authorizing Congress to "regulate Commerce."

[The Chief Justice maintained that the Necessary and Proper Clause does not save a statute that does not regulate "commerce" to start with.]

Each of our prior cases upholding laws under that Clause involved exercises of authority derivative of, and in service to, a granted power. For example, we have upheld provisions permitting continued confinement of those *already in federal custody* when they could not be safely released, *Comstock*; criminalizing bribes involving organizations *receiving federal funds*, *Sabri v. United States*, 541 U.S. 600, 602, 605 (2004); and tolling state statutes of limitations while cases are *pending in federal court*, *Jinks v. Richland County*. The individual mandate, by contrast, vests Congress with the extraordinary ability to create the necessary predicate to the exercise of an enumerated power.

This is in no way an authority that is "narrow in scope," *Comstock*, or "incidental" to the exercise of the commerce power, *McCulloch*. Rather, such a conception of the Necessary and Proper Clause would work a substantial expansion of federal authority. No longer would Congress be limited to regulating under the Commerce Clause those who by some preexisting activity bring themselves within the sphere of federal regulation. Instead, Congress could reach beyond the natural limit of its authority and draw within its regulatory scope those who otherwise would be outside of it. Even if the individual mandate is "necessary" to the Act's insurance reforms, such an expansion of federal power is not a "proper" means for making those reforms effective.

[In **Part III.B,** the **CHIEF JUSTICE**, speaking only for himself, expressed openness to the Government's alternative argument in support of the individual mandate, that it was an exercise of Congress's authority to tax and spend under Article I, § 8, cl. 1. The Act expresses the mandate as a command, but may the statute also be read as a tax.] The question is not whether that is the most natural interpretation of the mandate, but only whether it is a "fairly possible" one. *Crowell v. Benson*, 285 U.S. 22, 62 (1932). As we have explained, "every reasonable construction must be resorted to, in order to save a statute from unconstitutionality." *Hooper v. California*, 155 U.S. 648, 657 (1895). The Government asks us to interpret the mandate as imposing a tax, if it would otherwise violate the Constitution. Granting the Act the full measure of deference owed to federal statutes, it can be so read, for the reasons set forth below.

[In **Part III.C,** the **CHIEF JUSTICE** spoke for a Court majority, i.e., himself and **JUSTICES GINSBURG, BREYER, SOTOMAYOR,** and **KAGAN.**] The exaction the Affordable Care Act imposes on those without health insurance looks like a tax in many respects. The "[s]hared responsibility payment," as the statute entitles it, is paid into the Treasury by "taxpayer[s]" when they file their tax returns. 26 U.S.C. § 5000A(b). It does not apply to individuals who do not pay federal income taxes because their household income is less than the filing threshold in the Internal Revenue Code. § 5000A(e)(2). For taxpayers who do owe the payment, its amount is determined by such familiar factors as taxable income, number of dependents, and joint filing status. §§ 5000A(b)(3), (c)(2), (c)(4). The requirement to pay is found in the Internal Revenue Code and enforced by the IRS, which * * * must assess and collect it "in the same manner as taxes." This process yields the essential feature of any tax: it produces at least some revenue for the Government. [The Chief Justice pointed out that, in prior cases, the Court had upheld statutes under Congress's taxing power even though the levies had not been identified as taxes.]

Even if the taxing power enables Congress to impose a tax on not obtaining health insurance, any tax must still comply with other requirements in the Constitution. Plaintiffs argue that the shared responsibility payment does not do so, citing Article I, § 9, clause 4. That clause provides: "No Capitation, or other direct, Tax shall be laid, unless in Proportion to the Census or Enumeration herein before directed to be taken." This requirement means that any "direct Tax" must be apportioned so that each State pays in proportion to its population. According to the plaintiffs, if the individual mandate imposes a tax, it is a direct tax, and it is unconstitutional because Congress made no effort to apportion it among the States.

Even when the Direct Tax Clause was written it was unclear what else, other than a capitation (also known as a "head tax" or a "poll tax"), might be a direct tax. See *Springer v. United States*, 102 U.S. 586, 596–598 (1881). Soon after the framing, Congress passed a tax on ownership of carriages, over James Madison's objection that it was an unapportioned direct tax. This Court upheld the tax, in part reasoning that apportioning such a tax would make little sense, because it would have required taxing carriage owners at dramatically different rates depending on how many carriages were in their home State. See *Hylton v. United States*, 3 Dall. 171, 174 (1796) (opinion of Chase, J.). The Court was unanimous, and those Justices who wrote opinions either directly asserted or strongly suggested that only two forms of taxation were direct: capitations and land taxes. [The Chief Justice ruled that a tax on going without health insurance does not fall within any recognized category of direct tax.]

There may, however, be a more fundamental objection to a tax on those who lack health insurance. Even if only a tax, the payment under § 5000A(b) remains a burden that the Federal Government imposes for an omission, not an act. If it is troubling to interpret the Commerce Clause as authorizing Congress to regulate those who abstain from commerce, perhaps it should be similarly troubling to permit Congress to impose a tax for not doing something.

Three considerations allay this concern. First, and most importantly, it is abundantly clear the Constitution does not guarantee that individuals may avoid taxation through inactivity. A capitation, after all, is a tax that everyone must pay simply for existing, and capitations are expressly contemplated by the Constitution. The Court today holds that our Constitution protects us from federal regulation under the Commerce Clause so long as we abstain from the regulated activity. But from its creation, the Constitution has made no such promise with respect to taxes. See Letter from Benjamin Franklin to M. Le Roy (Nov. 13, 1789) ("Our new Constitution is now established . . . but in this world nothing can be said to be certain, except death and taxes"). [Likewise, there is nothing new about congressional deployment of tax incentives to encourage people to move from inactivity to commercial activity by, for example, purchasing homes, which are subsidized by 26 U.S.C. § 163(h).]

Second, Congress's ability to use its taxing power to influence conduct is not without limits. A few of our cases policed these limits aggressively, invalidating punitive exactions obviously designed to regulate behavior otherwise regarded at the time as beyond federal authority. See, *e.g.*, *United States v. Butler*, 297 U.S. 1 (1936); *Drexel Furniture.* More often and more recently we have declined to closely examine the regulatory motive or effect of revenue-raising measures. We have nonetheless maintained that " 'there comes a time in the extension of the penalizing features of the so-called tax when it loses its character as such and becomes a mere penalty with the characteristics of regulation and punishment.' " * * *

Third, although the breadth of Congress's power to tax is greater than its power to regulate commerce, the taxing power does not give Congress the same degree of control over individual behavior. Once we recognize that Congress may regulate a particular decision under the Commerce Clause, the Federal Government can bring its full weight to bear. Congress may simply command individuals to do as it directs. An individual who disobeys may be subjected to criminal sanctions. Those sanctions can include not only fines and imprisonment, but all the attendant consequences of being branded a criminal: deprivation of otherwise protected civil rights, such as the right to bear arms or vote in elections; loss of employment opportunities; social stigma; and severe disabilities in other controversies, such as custody or immigration disputes.

By contrast, Congress's authority under the taxing power is limited to requiring an individual to pay money into the Federal Treasury, no more. If a tax is properly paid, the Government has no power to compel or punish individuals subject to it. We do not make light of the severe burden that taxation—especially taxation motivated by a regulatory purpose—can impose. But imposition of a tax nonetheless leaves an individual with a lawful choice to do or not do a certain act, so long as he is willing to pay a tax levied on that choice.

The Affordable Care Act's requirement that certain individuals pay a financial penalty for not obtaining health insurance may reasonably be characterized as a tax. Because the Constitution permits such a tax, it is not our role to forbid it, or to pass upon its wisdom or fairness. [Speaking only for himself, the CHIEF JUSTICE in Part III.D defended his decision to evaluate the Commerce Clause authority first, because that was the ground upon which Congress itself rested the statute. Only after that ground proved unavailing did the Chief Justice deem it necessary to consider the taxing power argument.]

[In Part IV, the CHIEF JUSTICE spoke for himself and for JUSTICES BREYER and KAGAN.] The States also contend that the Medicaid expansion exceeds Congress's authority under the Spending Clause. They claim that Congress is coercing the States to adopt the changes it wants by threatening to withhold all of a State's Medicaid grants, unless the State accepts the new expanded funding and complies with the conditions that come with it. This, they argue, violates the basic principle that the "Federal Government may not compel the States to enact or administer a federal regulatory program." *New York.*

There is no doubt that the Act dramatically increases state obligations under Medicaid. The current Medicaid program requires States to cover only certain discrete categories of needy individuals—pregnant women, children, needy families, the blind, the elderly, and the disabled. 42 U.S.C. § 1396a(a)(10). There is no mandatory coverage for most childless adults, and the States typically do not offer any such coverage. The States also enjoy considerable flexibility with respect to the coverage levels for parents of needy families. § 1396a(a)(10)(A)(ii). On average States cover only those unemployed parents who make less than 37 percent of the federal poverty level, and only those employed parents who make less than 63 percent of the poverty line.

The Medicaid provisions of the Affordable Care Act, in contrast, require States to expand their Medicaid programs by 2014 to cover *all* individuals under the age of 65 with incomes below 133 percent of the federal poverty line. § 1396a(a)(10)(A)(i)(VIII). The Act also establishes a new "[e]ssential health benefits" package, which States must provide to all new Medicaid recipients—a level sufficient to satisfy a recipient's obligations under the individual mandate. §§ 1396a(k)(1), 1396u–7(b)(5), 18022(b). The Affordable Care Act provides that the Federal Government will pay 100 percent of the costs of covering these newly eligible individuals through 2016. § 1396d(y)(1). In the following years, the federal payment level gradually decreases, to a minimum of 90 percent. *Ibid.* In light of the expansion in coverage mandated by the Act, the Federal Government estimates that its Medicaid spending will increase by approximately $100 billion per year, nearly 40 percent above current levels.

The Spending Clause grants Congress the power "to pay the Debts and provide for the . . . general Welfare of the United States." U.S. Const., Art. I, § 8, cl. 1. We have long recognized that Congress may use this power to grant federal funds to the States, and may condition such a grant upon the States' "taking certain actions that Congress could not require them to take." *College Savings Bank*. Such measures "encourage a State to regulate in a particular way, [and] influenc[e] a State's policy choices." *New York*. The conditions imposed by Congress ensure that the funds are used by the States to "provide for the . . . general Welfare" in the manner Congress intended.

At the same time, our cases have recognized limits on Congress's power under the Spending Clause to secure state compliance with federal objectives. "We have repeatedly characterized . . . Spending Clause legislation as 'much in the nature of a *contract*.'" *Barnes v. Gorman*, 536 U.S. 181, 186 (2002) (quoting *Pennhurst State School and Hospital v. Halderman*, 451 U.S. 1, 17 (1981)). The legitimacy of Congress's exercise of the spending power "thus rests on whether the State voluntarily and knowingly accepts the terms of the 'contract.'" *Pennhurst*. Respecting this limitation is critical to ensuring that Spending Clause legislation does not undermine the status of the States as independent sovereigns in our federal system. * * *

That insight has led this Court to strike down federal legislation that commandeers a State's legislative or administrative apparatus for federal purposes. See, *e.g., Printz* (striking down federal legislation compelling state law enforcement officers to perform federally mandated background checks on handgun purchasers); *New York* (invalidating provisions of an Act that would compel a State to either take title to nuclear waste or enact particular state waste regulations). It has also led us to scrutinize Spending Clause legislation to ensure that Congress is not using financial inducements to exert a "power akin to undue influence." *Steward Machine Co. v. Davis*, 301 U.S. 548, 590 (1937). Congress may use its spending power to create incentives for States to act in accordance with federal policies. But when "pressure turns into compulsion," *ibid.*, the legislation runs contrary to our system of federalism. "[T]he Constitution simply does not give Congress the authority to require the States to regulate." *New York*. That is true whether Congress directly commands a State to regulate or indirectly coerces a State to adopt a federal regulatory system as its own.

Permitting the Federal Government to force the States to implement a federal program would threaten the political accountability key to our federal system. "[W]here the Federal Government directs the States to regulate, it maybe state officials who will bear the brunt of public disapproval, while the federal officials who devised the regulatory program may remain insulated from the electoral ramifications of their decision." *New York*. Spending Clause programs do not pose this danger when a State has a legitimate choice whether to accept the federal conditions in exchange for federal funds. In such a situation, state officials can fairly be held politically accountable for choosing to accept or refuse the federal offer. But when the State has no choice, the Federal Government can achieve its objectives without accountability, just as in *New York* and *Printz*. Indeed, this danger is heightened when Congress acts under the Spending Clause, because Congress can use that power to implement federal policy it could not impose directly under its enumerated powers. * * *

* * * We have upheld Congress's authority to condition the receipt of funds on the States' complying with restrictions on the use of those funds, because that is the means by which Congress ensures that the funds are spent according to its view of the "general Welfare." Conditions that do not here govern the use of the funds, however, cannot be justified on that basis. When, for example, such conditions take the form of threats to terminate other significant independent grants, the conditions are properly viewed as a means of pressuring the States to accept policy changes.

In *South Dakota v. Dole*, we considered a challenge to a federal law that threatened to withhold five percent of a State's federal highway funds if the State did not raise its drinking age to 21. The Court found that the condition was "directly related to one of the main purposes for which highway funds are expended—safe interstate travel." At the same time, the condition was not a restriction on how the highway funds—set aside for specific highway improvement and maintenance efforts—were to be used.

We accordingly asked whether "the financial inducement offered by Congress" was "so coercive as to pass the point at which 'pressure turns into compulsion.'" [*Dole*] (quoting *Steward Machine*). By "financial inducement" the Court meant the threat of losing five percent of highway funds; no new money was offered to the States to raise their drinking ages. We found that the inducement was not impermissibly coercive, because Congress was offering only "relatively mild encouragement to the States." *Dole*. We observed that "all South Dakota would lose if she adheres to her chosen course as to a suitable minimum drinking age is 5%" of her highway funds. In fact, the federal funds at stake constituted less than half of one percent of South Dakota's budget at the time. In consequence, "we conclude[d] that [the] encouragement to state action [was] a valid use of the spending power." Whether to accept the drinking age change "remain[ed] the prerogative of the States not merely in theory but in fact."

In this case, the financial "inducement" Congress has chosen is much more than "relatively mild encouragement"—it is a gun to the head. Section 1396c of the Medicaid Act provides that if a State's Medicaid plan does not comply with the Act's requirements, the Secretary of Health and Human Services may declare that "further payments will not be made to the State." 42 U.S.C. § 1396c. A State that opts out of the Affordable Care Act's expansion in health care coverage thus stands to lose not merely "a relatively small percentage" of its existing Medicaid funding, but *all* of it.

Dole. Medicaid spending accounts for over 20 percent of the average State's total budget, with federal funds covering 50 to 83 percent of those costs. The Federal Government estimates that it will pay out approximately $3.3 trillion between 2010 and 2019 in order to cover the costs of *pre*-expansion Medicaid. In addition, the States have developed intricate statutory and administrative regimes over the course of many decades to implement their objectives under existing Medicaid. It is easy to see how the *Dole* Court could conclude that the threatened loss of less than half of one percent of South Dakota's budget left that State with a "prerogative" to reject Congress's desired policy, "not merely in theory but in fact." The threatened loss of over 10 percent of a State's overall budget, in contrast, is economic dragooning that leaves the States with no real option but to acquiesce in the Medicaid expansion. * * *

[Anticipating this argument], the Government claims that the Medicaid expansion is properly viewed merely as a modification of the existing program because the States agreed that Congress could change the terms of Medicaid when they signed on in the first place. The Government observes that the Social Security Act, which includes the original Medicaid provisions, contains a clause expressly reserving "[t]he right to alter, amend, or repeal any provision" of that statute. 42 U.S.C. § 1304. So it does. But "if Congress intends to impose a condition on the grant of federal moneys, it must do so unambiguously." *Pennhurst*. A State confronted with statutory language reserving the right to "alter" or "amend" the pertinent provisions of the Social Security Act might reasonably assume that Congress was entitled to make adjustments to the Medicaid program as it developed. Congress has in fact done so, sometimes conditioning only the new funding, other times both old and new.

The Medicaid expansion, however, accomplishes a shift in kind, not merely degree. The original program was designed to cover medical services for four particular categories of the needy: the disabled, the blind, the elderly, and needy families with dependent children. See 42 U.S.C. § 1396a(a)(10). Previous amendments to Medicaid eligibility merely altered and expanded the boundaries of these categories. Under the Affordable Care Act, Medicaid is transformed into a program to meet the health care needs of the entire nonelderly population with income below 133 percent of the poverty level. It is no longer a program to care for the neediest among us, but rather an element of a comprehensive national plan to provide universal health insurance coverage.

Indeed, the manner in which the expansion is structured indicates that while Congress may have styled the expansion a mere alteration of existing Medicaid, it recognized it was enlisting the States in a new health care program. Congress created a separate funding provision to cover the costs of providing services to any person made newly eligible by the expansion. While Congress pays 50 to 83 percent of the costs of covering individuals currently enrolled in Medicaid, § 1396d(b), once the expansion is fully implemented Congress will pay 90 percent of the costs for newly eligible persons, § 1396d(y)(1). The conditions on use of the different funds are also distinct. Congress mandated that newly eligible persons receive a level of coverage that is less comprehensive than the traditional Medicaid benefit package. § 1396a(k)(1).

As we have explained, "[t]hough Congress' power to legislate under the spending power is broad, it does not include surprising participating States with post-acceptance or 'retroactive' conditions." *Pennhurst.* A State could hardly anticipate that Congress's reservation of the right to "alter" or "amend" the Medicaid program included the power to transform it so dramatically. * * *

Nothing in our opinion precludes Congress from offering funds under the Affordable Care Act to expand the availability of health care, and requiring that States accepting such funds comply with the conditions on their use. What Congress is not free to do is to penalize States that choose not to participate in that new program by taking away their existing Medicaid funding. Section 1396c gives the Secretary of Health and Human Services the authority to do just that. It allows her to withhold *all* "further [Medicaid] payments . . . to the State" if she determines that the State is out of compliance with any Medicaid requirement, including those contained in the expansion. 42 U.S.C. § 1396c. In light of the Court's holding, the Secretary cannot apply § 1396c to withdraw existing Medicaid funds for failure to comply with the requirements set out in the expansion. [**Eds.** The Joint Dissent of **JUSTICES SCALIA, KENNEDY, THOMAS**, and **ALITO** agreed with the **CHIEF JUSTICE** on this point, but the four dissenters did not join any portion of his opinion.]

That fully remedies the constitutional violation we have identified. The chapter of the United States Code that contains § 1396c includes a severability clause confirming that we need go no further. That clause specifies that "[i]f any provision of this chapter, or the application thereof to any person or circumstance, is held invalid, the remainder of the chapter, and the application of such provision to other persons or circumstances shall not be affected thereby." § 1303. Today's holding does not affect the continued application of § 1396c to the existing Medicaid program. Nor does it affect the Secretary's ability to withdraw funds provided under the Affordable Care Act if a State that has chosen to participate in the expansion fails to comply with the requirements of that Act. * * *

The question remains whether today's holding affects other provisions of the Affordable Care Act. In considering that question, "[w]e seek to determine what Congress would have intended in light of the Court's constitutional holding." *United States v. Booker*, 543 U.S. 220, 246 (2005). Our "touchstone for any decision about remedy is legislative intent, for a court cannot use its remedial powers to circumvent the intent of the legislature." *Ayotte v. Planned Parenthood of Northern New Eng.*, 546 U.S. 320, 330 (2006). The question here is whether Congress would have wanted the rest of the Act to stand, had it known that States would have a genuine choice whether to participate in the new Medicaid expansion. Unless it is "evident" that the answer is no, we must leave the rest of the Act intact. *Champlin Refining Co. v. Corporation Comm'n of Okla.*, 286 U.S. 210, 234 (1932).

We are confident that Congress would have wanted to preserve the rest of the Act. It is fair to say that Congress assumed that every State would participate in the Medicaid expansion, given that States had no real choice but to do so. The States contend that Congress enacted the rest of the Act with such full participation in mind; they point out that Congress made Medicaid a means for satisfying the mandate, 26 U.S.C. § 5000A(f)(1)(A)(ii), and enacted no other plan for providing coverage to many low-income individuals. According to the States, this means that the entire Act must fall.

We disagree. The Court today limits the financial pressure the Secretary may apply to induce States to accept the terms of the Medicaid expansion. As a practical matter, that means States may now choose to reject the expansion; that is the whole point. But that does not mean all or even any will. Some States may indeed decline to participate, either because they are unsure they will be able to afford their share of the new funding obligations, or because they are unwilling to commit the administrative resources necessary to support the expansion. Other States, however, may voluntarily sign up, finding the idea of expanding Medicaid coverage attractive, particularly given the level of federal funding the Act offers at the outset.

We have no way of knowing how many States will accept the terms of the expansion, but we do not believe Congress would have wanted the whole Act to fall, simply because some may choose not to participate. [On this point, the **CHIEF JUSTICE** was joined by **JUSTICES GINSBURG, BREYER, SOTOMAYOR**, and **KAGAN**.] * * *

The Framers created a Federal Government of limited powers, and assigned to this Court the duty of enforcing those limits. The Court does so today. But the Court does not express any opinion on the wisdom of the Affordable Care Act. Under the Constitution, that judgment is reserved to the people. * * *

[**JUSTICE GINSBURG** concurred in much of the Chief Justice's opinion but dissented from the judgment that Congress was not acting properly under its Commerce Clause powers and that the Medicaid cutoff exceeded Congress's Spending Clause authority.]

[**Part II.** Speaking also for **JUSTICES BREYER, SOTOMAYOR,** and **KAGAN, JUSTICE GINSBURG** started with the Framers' goal of replacing the Articles of Confederation with the Constitution of 1787.] What was needed was a "national Government . . . armed with a positive & compleat authority in all cases where uniform measures are necessary." See Letter from James Madison to Edmund Randolph (Apr. 8, 1787), in 9 Papers of James Madison 368, 370 (R. Rutland ed. 1975). See also Letter from George Washington to James Madison (Nov. 30, 1785), in 8 *id.,* at 428, 429 ("We are either a United people, or we are not. If the former, let us, in all matters of general concern act as a nation, which ha[s] national objects to promote, and a national character to support."). The Framers' solution was the Commerce Clause, which, as they perceived it, granted Congress the authority to enact economic legislation "in all Cases for the general Interests of the Union, and also in those Cases to which the States are separately incompetent." 2 Records of the Federal Convention of 1787, pp. 131–132, ¶ 8 (M. Farrand rev. 1966). * * *

* * * Beyond dispute, Congress had a rational basis for concluding that the uninsured, as a class, substantially affect interstate commerce. Those without insurance consume billions of dollars of health-care products and services each year. Those goods are produced, sold, and delivered largely by national and regional companies who routinely transact business across state lines. The uninsured also cross state lines to receive care. Some have medical emergencies while away from home. Others, when sick, go to a neighboring State that provides better care for those who have not prepaid for care.

Not only do those without insurance consume a large amount of health care each year; critically, as earlier explained, their inability to pay for a significant portion of that consumption drives up market prices, foists costs on other consumers, and reduces market efficiency and stability. Given these far-reaching effects on interstate commerce, the decision to forgo insurance is hardly inconsequential or equivalent to "doing nothing"; it is, instead, an economic decision Congress has the authority to address under the Commerce Clause. * * *

[No precedent of the Court supports the Chief Justice's constitutional limitation. Indeed,] contrary to the Chief Justice's contention, our precedent does indeed support "[t]he proposition that Congress may dictate the conduct of an individual today because of prophesied future activity." In *Wickard,* the Court upheld a penalty the Federal Government imposed on a farmer who grew more wheat than he was permitted to grow under the Agricultural Adjustment Act of 1938 (AAA). He could not be penalized, the farmer argued, as he was growing the wheat for home consumption, not for sale on the open market. The Court rejected this argument. Wheat intended for home consumption, the Court noted, "overhangs the market, and if induced by rising prices, tends to flow into the market and check price increases [intended by the AAA]."

Similar reasoning supported the Court's judgment in *Raich,* which upheld Congress' authority to regulate marijuana grown for personal use. Homegrown marijuana substantially affects the interstate market for marijuana, we observed, for "the high demand in the interstate market will [likely] draw such marijuana into that market."

Our decisions thus acknowledge Congress' authority, under the Commerce Clause, to direct the conduct of an individual today (the farmer in *Wickard,* stopped from growing excess wheat; the plaintiff in *Raich,* ordered to cease cultivating marijuana) because of a prophesied future transaction (the eventual sale of that wheat or marijuana in the interstate market). Congress' actions are even more rational in this case, where the future activity (the consumption of medical care) is certain to occur, the sole uncertainty being the time the activity will take place.

[**Part III.** Even if the Commerce Clause were not a sufficient authority for the regulation, Justice Ginsburg maintained that the Necessary and Proper Clause would authorize the individual mandate.] "[A] complex regulatory program . . . can survive a Commerce Clause challenge without a showing that every single facet of the program is independently and directly related to a valid congressional goal. [*Hodel v. Indiana*, 452 U.S. 314 (1981).] * * * It is enough that the challenged provisions are an integral part of the regulatory program and that the regulatory scheme when considered as a whole satisfies this test." *Ibid.* (collecting cases).

Recall that one of Congress' goals in enacting the Affordable Care Act was to eliminate the insurance industry's practice of charging higher prices or denying coverage to individuals with preexisting medical conditions. The commerce power allows Congress to ban this practice, a point no one disputes. See *United States v. South-Eastern Underwriters Assn.,* 322 U.S. 533, 545, 552–553 (1944) (Congress may regulate "the methods by which interstate insurance companies do business.").

Congress knew, however, that simply barring insurance companies from relying on an applicant's medical history would not work in practice. Without the individual mandate, Congress learned, guaranteed-issue and community-rating requirements would trigger an adverse-selection death-spiral in the health-insurance market: Insurance premiums would skyrocket, the number of uninsured would increase, and insurance companies would exit the market. When complemented by an insurance mandate, on the other hand, guaranteed issue and community rating would work as intended, increasing access to insurance and reducing uncompensated care. The minimum coverage provision is thus an "essential par[t] of a larger regulation of economic activity"; without the provision, "the regulatory scheme [w]ould be undercut." *Raich.* Put

differently, the minimum coverage provision, together with the guaranteed-issue and community-rating requirements, is " 'reasonably adapted' to the attainment of a legitimate end under the commerce power": the elimination of pricing and sales practices that take an applicant's medical history into account. See *id.* (Scalia, J., concurring in judgment).
* * *

[**Part V.** Speaking also for **JUSTICE SOTOMAYOR, JUSTICE GINSBURG** dissented from the Court's invalidation of the Act's provision cutting off all Medicaid funds to states declining to expand their programs to meet the new federal standards. Medicaid is an exemplar of "cooperative federalism," as the national government pays half of the states' costs of providing needed medical care to their indigent populations. Between 1965 and 2010, Congress repeatedly expanded the program to include more beneficiaries; at any point, states could opt out of the program. The ACA merely continues this policy of expanding the program (but with even more generous federal participation), with states free to opt out of the program at any point. Contrary to the Chief Justice's opinion, the ACA did not create a "new" program, nor did its new beneficiaries take the states entirely by surprise. The Chief Justice's inquiry into whether the funds cutoff is so drastic as to be "coercive" is an ad hoc judgment that is essentially political, rather than a clear-cut rule or standard that could be judicially administered.]

[Joined by **JUSTICES BREYER, SOTOMAYOR,** and **KAGAN, JUSTICE GINSBURG** concurred with the Chief Justice's judgment that the Medicaid funds cutoff is severable from the remainder of the statute.]

JUSTICE SCALIA, JUSTICE KENNEDY, JUSTICE THOMAS, and **JUSTICE ALITO,** dissenting.

This case is in one respect difficult: it presents two questions of first impression. The first of those is whether failure to engage in economic activity (the purchase of health insurance) is subject to regulation under the Commerce Clause. Failure to act does result in an effect on commerce, and hence might be said to come under this Court's "affecting commerce" criterion of Commerce Clause jurisprudence. But in none of its decisions has this Court extended the Clause that far. The second question is whether the congressional power to tax and spend, U.S. Const., Art. I, § 8, cl. 1, permits the conditioning of a State's continued receipt of all funds under a massive state-administered federal welfare program upon its acceptance of an expansion to that program. Several of our opinions have suggested that the power to tax and spend cannot be used to coerce state administration of a federal program, but we have never found a law enacted under the spending power to be coercive. Those questions are difficult.

The case is easy and straightforward, however, in another respect. What is absolutely clear, affirmed by the text of the 1789 Constitution, by the Tenth Amendment ratified in 1791, and by innumerable cases of ours in the 220 years since, is that there are structural limits upon federal power—upon what it can prescribe with respect to private conduct, and upon what it can impose upon the sovereign States. Whatever may be the conceptual limits upon the Commerce Clause and upon the power to tax and spend, they cannot be such as will enable the Federal Government to regulate all private conduct and to compel the States to function as administrators of federal programs.

That clear principle carries the day here. The striking case of *Wickard v. Filburn,* which held that the economic activity of growing wheat, even for one's own consumption, affected commerce sufficiently that it could be regulated, always has been regarded as the *ne plus ultra* of expansive Commerce Clause jurisprudence. To go beyond that, and to say the *failure* to grow wheat (which is *not* an economic activity, or any activity at all) nonetheless affects commerce and therefore can be federally regulated, is to make mere breathing in and out the basis for federal prescription and to extend federal power to virtually all human activity.

As for the constitutional power to tax and spend for the general welfare: The Court has long since expanded that beyond (what Madison thought it meant) taxing and spending for those aspects of the general welfare that were within the Federal Government's enumerated powers, see *United States v. Butler,* 297 U.S. 1, 65–66 (1936). Thus, we now have sizable federal Departments devoted to subjects not mentioned among Congress' enumerated powers, and only marginally related to commerce: the Department of Education, the Department of Health and Human Services, the Department of Housing and Urban Development. The principal practical obstacle that prevents Congress from using the tax-and-spend power to assume all the general-welfare responsibilities traditionally exercised by the States is the sheer impossibility of managing a Federal Government large enough to administer such a system. That obstacle can be overcome by granting funds to the States, allowing them to administer the program. That is fair and constitutional enough when the States freely agree to have their powers employed and their employees enlisted in the federal scheme. But it is a blatant violation of the constitutional structure when the States have no choice.

The Act before us here exceeds federal power both in mandating the purchase of health insurance and in denying nonconsenting States all Medicaid funding. These parts of the Act are central to its design and operation, and all the Act's other provisions would not have been enacted without them. In our view it must follow that the entire statute is inoperative.

[JUSTICES SCALIA, KENNEDY, THOMAS, and ALITO agreed with the Chief Justice that the Act's individual mandate was not a proper exercise of Congress's Commerce Clause authority, dissented from the Court's interpretation of the Act to be a "tax," dissented from the Court's ruling that the individual mandate is a proper exercise of Congress's Tax Clause authority, agreed with the Chief Justice that the Act's direction to the Secretary to cut off Medicaid funding for noncomplying States was not a proper exercise of Congress's Spending Clause authority, dissented from the Court's ruling that the funding cut-off is severable from the remainder of the Act, and concluded that the entire Act was beyond Congress's constitutional authority: the core of the statute was beyond the powers delegated to Congress in the Constitution, and the peripheral provisions were not severable from the unconstitutional core.]

NOTES ON THE AFFORDABLE CARE ACT CASE

According to his biographer, Chief Justice Roberts was originally the fifth vote to invalidate the ACA as a statute beyond Congress's Article I authority, but he had second thoughts about the wisdom of such a big move on the part of the Court. Joan Biskupic, *The Chief: The Life and Turbulent Times of Chief Justice John Roberts* (2019). Would it seem "partisan" or "illegitimate" for five GOP Justices to sweep away the Democrats' super-statute, in the wake of still-bitter partisan memories of *Bush v. Gore* (2000) and *Citizens United* (2010)? Was there a way to save the statute, yet still assert the Chief's understanding of what the rule of law required? Apparently, the Chief Justice reached out to Justice Kennedy, but he was adamant that the ACA was unconstitutional. Instead, Justices Breyer and Kagan were willing to work with the Chief Justice, and the result was the crazy quilt that you just read.

Whatever the underlying politics, *Independent Business v. Sebelius* is a summary of the Court's jurisprudence of federalist limitations on Congress's powers enumerated in the Constitution. The following notes explore most of the key philosophical and doctrinal issues presented by Chief Justice Roberts's opinion and by the objections raised from the left (Justice Ginsburg) and from the right (the Joint Dissent).

1.   *The Nature of the Federal Arrangement and the Purpose of the Commerce Clause.* There are different visions of the federal arrangement within the Court's debate. Chief Justice Roberts presented the Constitution as a social compact whose point is to protect individual liberty and state autonomy, while at the same time creating a national authority capable of addressing problems arising under the enumerated (and therefore limited) powers of that government. The four Justices (Scalia, Kennedy, Thomas, and Alito) who signed the Joint Dissent seemed to share that general philosophy. Justice Thomas gave even more emphasis than the Chief Justice to state sovereignty concerns. In contrast, Justices Ginsburg, Breyer, Sotomayor, and Kagan emphasized the positive powers granted to the national government, especially the powers to solve the collective action problems that had doomed

the Articles of Confederation. Keep these somewhat different emphases in mind as we walk you through the doctrinal debates among the Justices.

2. *Framing the Commerce Clause Inquiry: How You Ask the Question Drives Your Answer.* The Joint Dissent and Part III.A of the Chief Justice's opinion posed the Commerce Clause question this way: Can Congress compel Americans who are not participating in the health insurance market to purchase health insurance? This way of posing the question generates the broccoli hypothetical: If Congress can "coerce" you to buy health insurance, then there is no stopping point and so Congress can "coerce" you to buy broccoli.

Justice Ginsburg did not accept this way of posing the question. She presented the health care market (that everybody has to participate in) and the health insurance market (more limited, with tens of millions of American unable or unwilling to participate) as functionally inseparable: the existence of free riders or nonparticipants in the latter market creates inefficiencies in that market and soaring costs and inequities in the former market. "Not only do those without insurance consume a large amount of health care each year; * * * their inability to pay for a significant portion of that consumption drives up market prices, foists costs on other consumers, and reduces market efficiency and stability. Given these far-reaching effects on interstate commerce, the decision to forgo insurance is hardly inconsequential or equivalent to 'doing nothing'; it is, instead, an economic decision Congress has the authority to address under the Commerce Clause." Justice Ginsburg's framing had the virtue of understanding the issue the way Congress framed it. Why did the Chief Justice not see the issue this way?

3. *Is There an Activity/Inactivity Limitation on Congress's Commerce Clause Authority?* Accept the Chief Justice's framing of the Commerce Clause inquiry: Why can Congress not require everyone to participate in at least some economic markets? To accept that proposition is *not* to say that Congress's Commerce Clause authority has no limits. That authority is limited by the requirement that Congress can only regulate *economic* activities, see *Lopez*; *Morrison*, and by the bar against commandeering state governments, see *New York v. United States*; *Printz*. The question posed by the ACA is whether yet another limitation hems in Congress's ability to regulate under the aegis of the Commerce Clause.

Justice Ginsburg responded that there was no precedent striking down a congressional enactment for requiring action where people would rather remain inactive. She read *Wickard* for the proposition that Congress can adopt regulations that force people to engage in market transactions they'd rather avoid. If it's not authority for that proposition, is that, again, not a framing judgment? If inaction can always be reframed as action, and vice-versa, does that not suggest difficulties in administering the new action/inaction line for the Commerce Clause power? Consider this variation: If an employer declines to hire a person because of her race, has the employer "acted" (discrimination)? Or is this, too, an example of "inaction" (failing to enter into a contract)? Is Title VII unconstitutional as applied to this kind of "inaction"?

Congress can surely regulate the automobile market, by imposing safety standards on cars to make them more crashworthy. But can Congress *also* not regulate the automobile market, more broadly understood, by requiring all drivers of automobiles to secure insurance? The Chief Justice says that the better parallel would be a congressional statute requiring everyone to purchase automobiles. Isn't the point of "deference" a willingness to let the political process set the policymaking agenda and to frame the question the way it finds productive? Or is re-framing a feature of *Marbury*-style judicial review?

Consider another hypothetical. A communicable but nonfatal disease afflicts a growing number of Americans. A vaccine has the potential to eradicate the disease. Finding that this disease imposes economic costs upon the market, Congress enacts a statute (1) requiring every person within our borders to secure a vaccination (2) from a government-approved doctor, with (3) government subsidies for persons who fall below a minimum income level. Congress relies on its Commerce Clause powers. After *Sebelius,* does Congress have authority to enact such a statute? To strike down the compulsory vaccination law, one might say that Congress is regulating "inactivity," namely, the failure of Americans to secure vaccinations on their own volition. Or one might uphold the law by saying that Congress is regulating "activity," namely, the health consequences imposed upon the body politic by persons who might be carrying the disease.

4.   *Does the Necessary and Proper Clause Allow Congress to "Correct" Personal Inactivity as Ancillary to Its Restructuring of the Health Insurance Market?* The government buttressed its Commerce Clause argument with the Necessary and Proper Clause: Congress has the Commerce Clause authority to structure the market (and thus "commerce") for health insurance; a central reform was to require insurance companies not to discriminate against people with preexisting conditions; but to achieve that commercial regulation without destroying the industry, Congress found the individual mandate to be necessary and proper. Seven Justices found some version of this argument persuasive in *Comstock*. The Chief Justice joined the Court in *Comstock* but says that the individual mandate is not a "proper" exercise of the foregoing Commerce Clause authority. Why?

Consider this analogy. The Copyright Clause gives Congress the power to grant copyrights to "authors" or "writings." Could the Necessary and Proper Clause be used to justify a law requiring people to produce writings, so that Congress could then grant them copyrights? If not, does this suggest a limiting principle? The Necessary and Proper Clause cannot be used to create the predicate (e.g., the economic activity of buying insurance) for the exercise of an enumerated power? How would Justice Ginsburg respond to this puzzle?

5.   *If Congress Does Not Have Commerce Clause Authority to Impose the Individual Mandate, Can the ACA Be Interpreted as a Tax Statute?* The Joint Dissent was astounded by the Court's move (in Part III.C of the Chief Justice's opinion) to interpret the ACA as a tax statute. Such an interpretation was in tension with Part II of the opinion for the Court, holding that the mandate was

a "penalty" and not a "tax" for purposes of the Anti-Injunction Act. Also, the Court had rejected the Chief Justice's strategy previously. After the Court struck down the original child labor law in *Hammer v. Dagenhart,* Congress adopted a tax statute seeking the same regulatory result. Rejecting that strategy, the Court held that a statute that "adopt[s] the criteria of wrongdoing" and then imposes a monetary penalty as the "principal consequence on those who transgress its standard," creates a regulatory penalty, not a tax. *Child Labor Tax Case*, 259 U.S. 20, 38 (1922).

The Joint Dissent said this: "we have never—*never*—treated as a tax an exaction which faces up to the critical difference between a tax and a penalty, and explicitly denominates the exaction a 'penalty.' Eighteen times in § 5000A itself and elsewhere throughout the Act, Congress called the exaction in § 5000A(b) a 'penalty.'" The statutory interpretation rule to avoid unconstitutional interpretations *cannot* be invoked to abandon a century of precedent and to rewrite a statute as completely as the Chief Justice rewrote the ACA to save its constitutionality. In short, the Joint Dissent objected that the Court was strong-arming the statutory language so much that it went well beyond "interpretation" all the way to "judicial legislation."

Is the surgery the Court performs on the ACA justified by some kind of judicial statesmanship? The ACA is the most significant socio-economic legislation since the Civil Rights Act of 1964—and the Chief Justice was loathe to erase decades of political effort (Biskupic, *The Chief*). The Joint Dissent responded: "Judicial tax-writing is particularly troubling. Taxes have never been popular, see, *e.g.,* Stamp Act of 1765, and in part for that reason, the Constitution requires tax increases to originate in the House of Representatives. See Art. I, § 7, cl. 1. That is to say, they must originate in the legislative body most accountable to the people, where legislators must weigh the need for the tax against the terrible price they might pay at their next election, which is never more than two years off." Accord, *Federalist* No. 58 (Madison). "We have no doubt that Congress knew precisely what it was doing when it rejected an earlier version of this legislation that imposed a tax instead of a requirement-with-penalty. Imposing a tax through judicial legislation inverts the constitutional scheme, and places the power to tax in the branch of government least accountable to the citizenry." Is this not a telling point?

6.   *Can the Action-Forcing Mandate Be Constitutional as a Tax if Not as a Regulation of Commerce?* The Joint Dissent objected that the liberty-denying features of the individual mandate are just as objectionable as a tax as they are of a regulation of commerce. If there is an inaction limit on the commerce power, why is there not an inaction limit on the taxing power? Viewed holistically, if Article I is a grant of *limited* power to Congress, you might be reluctant to repackage a failed commercial regulation as a tax, or so the dissenters thought. (On the other hand, the plaintiffs in this case conceded that Congress could tax or prohibit the provision of health care services to anyone who had failed to secure private insurance.)

The Chief Justice responded that the tax power is traditionally used to bestir people from inaction; the home mortgage deduction is one example. But that's a goodie that Congress uses to entice people to buy homes—while the mandate is a penalty used to punish taxpayers for not getting insurance. In Part III.C, the Chief Justice treated subsidies and penalties as functionally interchangeable—but that was precisely Justice Ginsburg's objection to his action-inaction gambit in Part III.A of his opinion (on the Commerce Clause). This is a larger point about the Chief Justice's opinion: it wove back and forth between constitutional formalism (Part II, Part IIII.A, and Part IV's invalidation of the funds cutoff) and functionalism (Part III.B–C and Part IV's treatment of severability), without any constitutional justification, beyond the statesmanship point. Recall that similar criticisms have been made of Chief Justice John Marshall in *Marbury* and *McCulloch*.

7.   *Is the Medicaid Funds Cutoff Provision a Violation of the Spending Clause?* Until this case, the Supreme Court had never *held* that the Spending Clause is violated if Congress "coerces" the states to go along with new strings on money Congress has long offered the states. Seven Justices said that Congress had gone too far in the ACA. Joined only by Justice Sotomayor, Justice Ginsburg argued not: "Given past expansions, plus express statutory warning that Congress may change the requirements participating States must meet, there can be no tenable claim that the ACA fails for lack of notice. Moreover, States have no entitlement to receive any Medicaid funds; they enjoy only the opportunity to accept funds on Congress' terms."

Justice Ginsburg documented the steady stream of federal statutes that had expanded state Medicaid obligations, often very significantly, since 1965. "Future Congresses are not bound by their predecessors' dispositions; they have authority to spend federal revenue as they see fit. The Federal Government, therefore, is not * * * threatening States with the loss of 'existing' funds from one spending program in order to induce them to opt into another program. Congress is simply requiring States to do what States have long been required to do to receive Medicaid funding: comply with the conditions Congress prescribes for participation." How would the Chief Justice respond to this point?

Notice that the most needy of Americans (those who would benefit from the expanded Medicaid program) were placed at risk by the Court's taking away Secretary Sebelius's biggest inducement to secure compliance in the new benefits from all the states. There may be a race to the bottom, as states decline to participate in the new expansion of Medicaid, perhaps openly hoping that poor people will leave their jurisdictions and settle in ones that cooperate. Is there reason to think there will not be a race to the bottom?

8.   *Severability.* This case is now the best citation for the Court's well-established presumption in favor of severability. Notice the odd thought experiment that the majority engaged in: Would the Congress that enacted the ACA have been OK with the Court-revised ACA? With a straight face, five Justices said yes, but that strikes your editors as hard to swallow. It is possible

(but not inevitable) to imagine that the ACA Congress would have been willing to toss out the Medicaid funds cutoff provision to save the statute—but it is hard to imagine that the ACA Congress would have voted for the statute if it were billed as a new *tax*! The Joint Dissent walloped the Court with language demonstrating that the ACA Congress ran away from any mention of new taxation. Did the Court perform judicial surgery that killed the patient, for whom the Court substituted its own Frankenstein version?

9. *The Critical Role That Background Norms Play.* How a judge evaluated the ACA's individual mandate and the new Medicaid program and its broad cutoff provision depended, at least in part, on how she viewed the structure of the Constitution. If she viewed the structure as reflecting a compact among the states to give up limited amounts of their sovereignty (as Justices Thomas, Alito, and perhaps one or more new Justices do), she was going to be highly skeptical: Why ought Congress to have this much power? If the ACA were upheld, the Court would be acquiescing in plenary congressional authority. If she viewed the structure as reflecting a social compact among "We the People" to solve collective action problems that had doomed the Articles of Confederation (as Justices Ginsburg, Breyer, Sotomayor, and Kagan do), then the ACA looked much easier to uphold: health care and insurance are a huge national problem, and so why shouldn't Congress be able to address it through the ACA?

Instead of relying on private insurance or state-administered Medicaid, Congress could have expanded federally-funded and -administered Medicare to cover the entire population. This move, toward "socialized medicine," would have been constitutional under the Spending Clause, according to the analysis provided by all nine Justices. If the Constitution is concerned with excessive national power, does it make sense to adopt constitutional doctrines that favor a larger direct role for the national government? Or is limiting "compromise" solutions such as the ACA desirable because it renders the division of authority between the state and federal governments more transparent and improves political accountability?

Although Medicare and Medicaid have had huge effects on the health care industry, the federal government has left most direct regulation to the states; states have in turn deferred to hospitals and medical associations; and they have devolved authority to individual doctors. *See* Theodore W. Ruger, *Plural Constitutionalism and the Pathologies of American Health Care*, 120 YALE L.J. ONLINE 347 (Mar. 22, 2011). This "old" health care regime is one that the Joint Dissent was protecting, for the ACA is a major "intrusion" of federal "coercive" power into decisions made by individuals or, at most, the states. Professor (now Dean) Ruger argues that the old health care regime is obsolete and that a new regime, placing limits on the doctor-patient decision-making process, is the only way the country can prevent an expensive meltdown of the healthcare payment system.

PROBLEM 7-9:
DOES THE ACA SURVIVE THE REPEAL OF THE MANDATE?

Congress passed the Tax Cuts and Jobs Act of 2017, Public Law 115–97, that (among many things) repealed the penalty (or "tax") to enforce the individual mandate. Ruling in a new lawsuit to invalidate the ACA, a Texas district court took it upon himself to rethink the Supreme Court's decision in *NFIB v. Sebelius*. See *Texas v. United States,* Civil Action No. 4-18-cv-00167-O (S.D. Tex. Dec. 14, 2018). The court's reasoning: "In *NFIB*, the Supreme Court held the Individual Mandate was unconstitutional under the Interstate Commerce Clause but could fairly be read as an exercise of Congress's Tax Power because it triggered a tax. The TCJA eliminated that tax. The Supreme Court's reasoning in *NFIB* * * * thus compels the conclusion that the Individual Mandate may no longer be upheld under the Tax Power. And because the Individual Mandate continues to mandate the purchase of health insurance, it remains unsustainable under the Interstate Commerce Clause— as the Supreme Court already held." (Was this an accurate statement of the Supreme Court's holding in *NFIB*?)

The court found that Congress has repeatedly acted under the assumption that the individual mandate is key to the ACA. For example: "The requirement is an *essential* part of this larger regulation of economic activity, and *the absence of the requirement would undercut Federal regulation* of the health insurance market." § 18091(2)(H) (emphasis added by the court). Hence, the court ruled that he remainder of the statute was not severable, and so the court invalidated the entire law.

Intervening state attorneys general have filed an appeal, and the case seems headed back to the Supreme Court. If it follows the approach advanced in the district court, the Trump Administration will support invalidation of the individual mandate and related provisions of the ACA but will argue that the other provisions of the ACA are severable. The nation's most eminent health care law experts (Abbe Gluck, Jonathan Adler, Nicholas Bagley, et al.) have condemned the decision and would support reversal. If you were advising newly appointed Justices Gorsuch or Kavanaugh on what the rule of law required the Supreme Court to do, what advice would you give?

SECTION 6. NATIONALIST LIMITATIONS UPON STATE REGULATORY AUTHORITY

A. CONSTITUTIONAL PRINCIPLES, POLICIES, AND HISTORY

A central purpose of the Constitution was not just to authorize the federal government to deal with national problems, but also to disable the states from disrupting the plan of a national union. There are at least three policy concerns with state rulemaking embodied in the Constitution.[67] First is the *uniformity policy*: Certain policies need to be uniform throughout the country, and allowing the states to adopt varying regulations would be counterproductive. One of the problems with the Articles of Confederation was that the country did not speak with one voice when it needed to do so. Second, the *common market policy* seeks to integrate the states into one national marketplace. The Articles allegedly contributed to economic Balkanization, and a central goal of the Constitution was to create interstate commercial harmony. Third, is the *policy to avoid trade wars.* Based upon the nation's experience during the Articles of Confederation, the Framers believed that states would discriminate against other states or their citizens in their laws and regulations (Denning, *Confederation-Era Discrimination*). Once one state discriminated against another, the next state would retaliate, perhaps raising the stakes into a full-blown trade war.

These policies suggested to the Framers the need to prevent the states from taking a variety of actions they otherwise might want to take. Apart from the Reconstruction Amendments, the constitutional text provides three types of explicit limits on the states. See Martin Redish & Shane Nugent, *The Dormant Commerce Clause and the Constitutional Balance of Federalism*, 1987 Duke L.J. 569, 591–92. First, the Constitution expressly prohibits the states from enacting certain types of legislation. Thus, Article I, § 10 prevents the states from entering into treaties, coining money, engaging in war, and many other activities. Another total prohibition is found in Article IV, § 2, which bars the states from depriving citizens of other states of their privileges and immunities.

Second, the Constitution contains certain waivable prohibitions on state action. Article I, § 10, cl. 2 provides that "[n]o State shall, without the consent of Congress, lay any Imposts or Duties on Imports or Exports, except what may be absolutely necessary for executing its inspection Laws." Clause 3 provides that "[n]o State shall, without the Consent of Congress, lay any Duty of Tonnage." For these potentially disruptive activities, the states may act only if authorized by Congress. Also under Clause 3, states may not enter into "Agreement[s] or Compact[s]" with one another without the consent of Congress.

---

[67] For thoughtful explications of the framing goals, see Richard B. Collins, *Economic Union as a Constitutional Value*, 63 NYU L. Rev. 43 (1988); Brannon P. Denning, *Reconstructing the Dormant Commerce Clause Doctrine*, 50 Wm. & Mary L. Rev. 417 (2008); Denning, *Confederation-Era Discrimination Against Interstate Commerce and the Legitimacy of the Dormant Commerce Clause Doctrine*, 94 Ky. L.J. 37 (2005); Barry Friedman & Daniel T. Deacon, *A Course Unbroken: The Constitutional Legitimacy of the Dormant Commerce Clause*, 97 Va. L. Rev. 1877 (2011); Donald H. Regan, *The Supreme Court and State Protectionism: Making Sense of the Dormant Commerce Clause*, 84 Mich. L. Rev. 1091 (1986); Norman R. Williams, *The Foundations of the American Common Market*, 84 Notre Dame L. Rev. 409 (2008).

Finally, the constitutional text forecloses state action where it clashes with national regulation. So long as Congress is acting under its enumerated powers, its statutes are superior to state law, according to the Supremacy Clause of Article VI. This is termed federal *preemption* of state law. State law is preempted if it is (1) contrary to the provisions of a federal statute, (2) inconsistent with federal policy, or (3) in an area wholly occupied by federal law (§ 6C3 below).

Together, the Commerce Clause and the Supremacy Clause give Congress the power to override state barriers to interstate trade, as well as the ability to pursue other regulatory goals. But suppose a state attempts to exclude interstate commerce in the *absence* of federal legislation? In that situation, the Commerce Clause is "dormant"—Congress hasn't made active use of its power. But even in this dormant condition, according to longstanding doctrine, the Commerce Clause creates an implicit barrier to protectionist state laws. See Barry Friedman & Daniel T. Deacon, *A Course Unbroken: The Constitutional Legitimacy of the Dormant Commerce Clause,* 97 Va. L. Rev. 1877 (2011). James Madison wrote in 1829 that he considered the Commerce Clause to be "a negative and preventive provision against injustice among the States themselves, rather than as a power to be used for the positive purpose of the General Government." Letter from Madison to J.C. Cabell (13 Feb. 1829), reproduced in III Farrand 478.[68] Consider an even earlier suggestion.

GIBBONS V. OGDEN
22 U.S. (9 Wheat.) 1, 6 L.Ed. 23 (1824)

[In a portion of **CHIEF JUSTICE MARSHALL**'s opinion for the Court that we omitted from § 2 of this chapter, the Chief Justice addressed the argument that] although the power of Congress to regulate commerce with foreign nations, and among the several states, be co-extensive with the subject itself, and have no other limits than are prescribed in the constitution, yet the states may severally exercise the same power, within their respective jurisdictions. In support of this argument, it is said that they possessed it as an inseparable attribute of sovereignty, before the formation of the constitution, and still retain it, except so far as they have surrendered it by that instrument; that this principle results from the nature of the government, and is secured by the tenth amendment; that an affirmative grant of power is not exclusive, unless in its own nature it be such that the continued exercise of it by the former possessor is inconsistent with the grant, and that this is not of that description.

---

[68] Note that this letter was written a generation after the Founding, and that Madison does not say the *Court*, rather than *Congress*, should enforce this negative feature of the Commerce Clause.

The appellant, conceding these postulates, except the last, contends, that full power to regulate a particular subject, implies the whole power, and leaves no residuum; that a grant of the whole is incompatible with the existence of a right in another to any part of it. * * *

The grant of the power to lay and collect taxes is, like the power to regulate commerce, made in general terms, and has never been understood to interfere with the exercise of the same power by the states; and hence has been drawn an argument which has been applied to the question under consideration. But the two grants are not, it is conceived, similar in their terms or their nature. Although many of the powers formerly exercised by the states, are transferred to the government of the Union, yet the State governments remain, and constitute a most important part of our system. The power of taxation is indispensable to their existence, and is a power which, in its own nature, is capable of residing in, and being exercised by, different authorities at the same time. * * * In imposing taxes for State purposes, they are not doing what Congress is empowered to do. Congress is not empowered to tax for those purposes which are within the exclusive province of the states. When, then, each government exercises the power of taxation, neither is exercising the power of the other. But, when a State proceeds to regulate commerce with foreign nations, or among the several States, it is exercising the very power that is granted to Congress, and is doing the very thing which Congress is authorized to do. There is no analogy, then, between the power of taxation and the power of regulating commerce.

In discussing the question, whether this power is still in the States, in the case under consideration, we may dismiss from it the inquiry, whether it is surrendered by the mere grant to Congress, or is retained until Congress shall exercise the power. We may dismiss that inquiry, because it has been exercised, and the regulations which Congress deemed it proper to make, are now in full operation. The sole question is, can a State regulate commerce with foreign nations and among the states, while Congress is regulating it? * * *

It has been contended by the counsel for the appellant, that, as the word "to regulate" implies in its nature, full power over the thing to be regulated, it excludes, necessarily, the action of all others that would perform the same operation on the same thing. That regulation is designed for the entire result, applying to those parts which remain as they were, as well as to those which are altered. It produces a uniform whole, which is as much disturbed and deranged by changing what the regulating power designs to leave untouched, as that on which it has operated.

There is great force in this argument, and the court is not satisfied that it has been refuted.

Since, however, in exercising the power of regulating their own purely internal affairs, whether of trading or police, the states may sometimes enact laws, the validity of which depends on their interfering with, and being contrary to, an act of Congress passed in pursuance of the constitution, the court will enter upon the inquiry, whether the laws of New York, as expounded by the highest tribunal of that State, have, in their application to this case, come into collision with an act of Congress, and deprived a citizen of a right to which that act entitles him. Should this collision exist, it will be immaterial whether those laws were passed in virtue of a concurrent power "to regulate commerce with foreign nations and among the several States," or in virtue of a power to regulate their domestic trade and police. In one case and the other, the acts of New York must yield to the law of Congress; and the decision sustaining the privilege they confer, against a right given by a law of the Union, must be erroneous.

* * * In the exercise of this power [over commerce] Congress has passed "an act for enrolling or licensing ships or vessels to be employed in the coasting trade and fisheries, and for regulating the same." The counsel for the respondent contend that this act does not give the right to sail from port to port, but confines itself to regulating a preexisting right, so far only as to confer certain privileges on enrolled and licensed vessels in its exercise.

It will at once occur, that, when a legislature attaches certain privileges and exemptions to the exercise of a right over which its control is absolute, the law must imply a power to exercise the right. The privileges are gone, if the right itself be annihilated. It would be contrary to all reason, and to the course of human affairs, to say that a State is unable to strip a vessel of the particular privileges attendant on the exercise of a right, and yet may annul the right itself; that the State of New York cannot prevent an enrolled and licensed vessel, proceeding from Elizabethtown, in New Jersey, to New York, from enjoying, in her course, and on her entrance into port, all the privileges conferred by the act of Congress; but can shut her up in her own port, and prohibit altogether her entering the waters and ports of another State. To the court it seems very clear, that the whole act on the subject of the coasting trade, according to those principles which govern the construction of statutes, implies, unequivocally, an authority to license vessels to carry on the coasting trade. * * *

* * * A coasting vessel employed in the transportation of passengers, is as much a portion of the American marine as one employed in the transportation of a cargo; and no reason is perceived why such vessel should be withdrawn from the regulating power of that government, which has been thought best fitted for the purpose generally. The provisions of the law respecting native seamen, and respecting ownership, are as applicable to vessels carrying men as to vessels carrying manufacturers;

and no reason is perceived why the power over the subject should not be placed in the same hands. * * *

[The Court then decreed that "so much of the several laws of the State of New York, as prohibits vessels, licensed according to the laws of the United States, from navigating the waters of the State of New York, by means of fire or steam, is repugnant to the" United States Constitution and void, because these state laws conflicted with the privileges granted by the federal licensing law.]

JUSTICE JOHNSON [concurring].

[The commerce] power must be exclusive; it can reside in but one potentate; and hence, the grant of this power [to Congress] carries with it the whole subject, leaving nothing for the State to act upon. * * * If there was any one object riding over every other in the adoption of the constitution, it was to keep the commercial intercourse among the States free from all invidious and partial restraints. And I cannot overcome the conviction, that if the licensing act was repealed tomorrow, the rights of the appellant to a reversal of the decision complained of, would be as strong as it is under this license.

NOTE ON FEDERALISM AS A LIMIT ON STATE POWER

Analytically, the possibilities for federal/state regulation for interstate commerce are the following:

1. *Mutually exclusive regulation.* Whatever Congress can regulate as *interstate* under the Commerce Clause is closed to the states; whatever the states can regulate as *local* is closed to Congress under the Commerce Clause.

2. *Concurrent regulation.* Congressional and state jurisdiction overlap; each can regulate interstate commerce, but state regulation cannot violate other constitutionally prohibitions (*e.g.*, the Imposts Clause) or interfere with federal regulation (*preemption*).

3. *Authorized concurrent regulation.* The states can regulate interstate commerce, but not if inconsistent with federal statutes or with the negative (i.e., anti-trade war) goals of the Commerce Clause.

Theory 1 is reflects the "dual federalism" idea, whereby state and federal sovereignty is plenary in the respective jurisdiction of each. This is the view announced by Justice Johnson, and it logically creates a negative or *dormant* feature of the Commerce Clause that should be enforced by the Court. Theory 2 does not logically or necessarily entail a dormant feature of the Commerce Clause, because the most obvious limitations on the states are those imposed by or implicit in federal statutes and those specifically enumerated in the

Constitution. Theory 3 necessarily entails a dormant feature as a matter of constitutional policy but could logically be expressed without that feature.

Note that Chief Justice Marshall refrained from deciding which of the three options is embedded in the Constitution, although he did recognize "great force" in Theory 1. Instead, he decided the case as a *preemption* case. (Under all three theories, a congressional enactment properly adopted under the Commerce Clause trumps state policies because of the Supremacy Clause.) In *Willson v. Black-Bird Creek Marsh Co.*, 27 U.S. (2 Pet.) 245 (1829), Chief Justice Marshall continued to fudge the theoretical issue. There, a state law authorized a company to build a dam in a creek that fed into the Delaware River, a major interstate waterway. The dam excluded water from a marsh, thereby enhancing the value of the marshland and "probably improv[ing]" the health of nearby residents. But the dam also obstructed navigation of the creek by federally licensed ships. The Court upheld the state law, categorizing it as a local health measure.

Gibbons and *Black Bird Creek* left open the possibility that the federal commerce power was exclusive and, thus, that states could not regulate interstate commerce. Until the middle of the nineteenth century, the decisions following these precedents engaged in labeling inquiries, invalidating state regulations that were deemed "regulations of interstate commerce" and upholding those "within the local police power." Compare *Mayor of New York v. Miln*, 36 U.S. (11 Pet.) 102 (1837) (upholding a state law requiring ship's masters to report the names and residences of passengers to local authorities, on the ground it was "not a regulation of commerce, but of police"), with *The Passenger Cases*, 48 U.S. (7 How.) 283 (1849) (striking down two state laws requiring ship's masters to pay a tax for each alien on the ship). The theoretical confusion was ameliorated when the Court coalesced into a majority in the following case.

Cooley v. Board of Wardens of the Port of Philadelphia

53 U.S. (12 How.) 299 (1851)

The Court was faced with two statutes: an 1803 Pennsylvania statute regulating the pilots of ships entering and leaving the port of Philadelphia, and a 1789 federal statute providing that pilots should be regulated by state law. The opinion for the Court by **Justice Curtis** adopted Theory 3. Regulations of pilots "constitute regulation of navigation, and consequently of commerce, within the just meaning" of the Commerce Clause (*Gibbons*). Justice Curtis declined to interpret the federal statute as an authorization of state law, in part because Congress could not authorize a violation of the Constitution. Thus the Court was squarely confronted with the question whether the Commerce Clause completely disabled the states from regulating in the area (Theory 1).

The Court rejected Theory 1: "Now the power to regulate commerce embraces a vast field, containing not only many, but exceedingly various subjects, quite unlike in their nature; some imperatively demanding a single uniform rule, operating equally on the commerce of the United States in every port; and some, like the subject now in question, as imperatively demanding that diversity, which alone can meet the local necessities of navigation." Under this standard, the Court upheld the state law, on the ground that the matter was intrinsically "local" in nature, and not an area needing national uniformity. "Whatever subjects of this [commerce] power are in their nature national, or admit only of one uniform system, or plan of regulation may justly be said to be of such a nature as to require exclusive legislation by Congress. That this cannot be affirmed of laws for the regulation of pilots and pilotage is plain," citing the 1789 statute, which thus played a role as a "signification" of the local nature of the regulation, and the value of diversity rather than uniformity in this area.

NOTE ON THE DORMANT COMMERCE CLAUSE AFTER COOLEY

Cooley suggested that the Dormant Commerce Clause inquiry turned on whether the subject matter of the regulation was so local in character as to justify differing treatment around the country, or so national in character as to suggest that a uniform rule is necessary. Unfortunately, drawing a line based on the subject matter of regulation proved difficult, and sometimes controversial. The Court's decision striking down state regulation of railroad rate discrimination in *Wabash, St. Louis & P. Ry. v. Illinois*, 118 U.S. 557 (1886), raised a firestorm of protests from farm states and was the direct impetus for Congress to adopt the Interstate Commerce Act in 1887. Indeed, after 1887, the Court frequently allowed state "safety" regulations for railroads, albeit based upon a theory that such regulations had only an "indirect" and not "direct effect" on interstate commerce. *E.g., Southern Ry. v. King*, 217 U.S. 524 (1910); *Smith v. Alabama*, 124 U.S. 465 (1888). *Cooley's* national/local test was not considered the only approach to these issues, although its conceptual distinction between areas needing national uniformity and those permitting local diversity is an idea that has survived.

Less robust was *Cooley's* suggestion that Congress cannot authorize states to regulate non-local commerce. In *Leisy v. Hardin*, 135 U.S. 100 (1890), the Court invalidated a state seizure of the interstate shipment of beer kegs on the ground that Congress' power to regulate interstate commerce is "plenary and exclusive." Congress thereupon passed a statute authorizing the states to regulate interstate-shipped liquor once it had arrived within their borders. The Court upheld that authorization. *In re Rahrer*, 140 U.S. 545 (1891). By the twentieth century, it became accepted doctrine that Congress could authorize state regulation of interstate commerce.[69] It is now recognized that there is an

---

[69] See *Prudential Ins. Co. v. Benjamin*, 328 U.S. 408 (1946) (reaffirming *Rahrer* and extending its rationale to allow state tax rule discriminating against interstate commerce because it was authorized by Congress); William Cohen, *Congressional Power to Validate Unconstitutional State Laws: A Forgotten Solution to an Old Enigma*, 35 Stan. L. Rev. 387 (1985). As it has done in other areas involving federalism values, the Supreme Court has imposed a clear statement requirement on the exercise of this power: "Congress must manifest its unambiguous intent before a federal statute will be read to permit or approve" what would otherwise be a Dormant Commerce Clause violation. *Wyoming v. Oklahoma*, 502 U.S. 437, 458 (1992).

area of concurrent regulation by the states and Congress. As the Court has expanded Congress' Commerce Clause powers, this area of concurrent authority has become quite large.

The question arises, therefore, as to why the Court continues to enforce a Dormant Commerce Clause once the dual federalism idea (Theory 1) was rejected in *Cooley* and subsequent precedents. The doctrinal answer is that a dormant feature of the Commerce Clause is implicated in Theory 3, the theory tentatively accepted in *Cooley* and firmly entrenched in subsequent cases. But, unlike Theory 1, where a negative feature of the Commerce Clause is logically necessary, Theory 3 involves a negative feature only for functional— constitutional policy—reasons and, more important, says nothing about whether the Court rather than Congress should enforce the negative feature of the Commerce Clause.

NOTES ON WHY THE COURT MIGHT ENFORCE THE "DORMANT" FEATURE OF THE COMMERCE CLAUSE

The issue identified at the end of the previous Note has troubled the Court in recent decades. Hence, the Court and commentators have come up with theories for why the Dormant Commerce Clause is an important part of federalism and why the Court rather than just Congress should enforce the negative feature of the Commerce Clause.

1.   *Economic Union as a Constitutional Value.* Justice Jackson laid out a vision for Dormant Commerce Clause jurisprudence in his opinion for the Court in *H.P. Hood & Sons v. Du Mond*, 336 U.S. 525 (1949):

> [The] principle that our economic unit is the Nation, which alone has the gamut of powers necessary to control the economy, including the vital power of erecting customs barriers against foreign competition, has as its corollary that the states are not separable economic units. * * *

> Our system * * * is that every farmer and every craftsman shall be encouraged to produce by the certainty that he will have free access to every market in the Nation, that no home embargoes will withhold his exports, and no foreign state [within the Nation] will by customs duties or regulations exclude them.

Is this constitutional *law*, enforceable by the Court?

Donald Regan and Richard Collins, among others, maintain that the Dormant Commerce Clause is as law-like as federalism and the right to privacy, for the *principle of economic union* is instinct in the structure of the Constitution.[70] That is, specific provisions in the constitutional text, supported

---

[70] See Donald H. Regan, *The Supreme Court and State Protectionism: Making Sense of the Dormant Commerce Clause*, 84 Mich. L. Rev. 1091 (1986); Richard B. Collins, *Economic Union as a Constitutional Value*, 63 N.Y.U.L. Rev. 43 (1988). For a narrower understanding, see Brannon P. Denning, *Reconstructing the Dormant Commerce Clause Doctrine,* 50 Wm. & Mary L. Rev. 417,

by the overall goals the Framers had in mind when they adopted the Constitution to replace the "Balkanizing" Articles of Confederation, suggest the meta-concept that the Constitution creates a framework for an integrated economic union.[71] Inherent in any such union—even if not explicitly mentioned—is the compelling need to prevent economic Balkanization and protectionism among the states. Hence, as Madison suggested in 1829, the Dormant Commerce Clause is part of the structure of the Constitution. For the same reasons the Court enforces other structural protections, such as federalism, the Court should enforce the structural protections of the Dormant Commerce Clause.

The Dormant Commerce Clause jurisprudence is different from the federalism and privacy areas in that it does not create "nontrumpable" rights—that is, rights that cannot be overridden by the normal political process. While Congress could not have authorized Connecticut to regulate contraceptives (*Griswold*), nor could the states have authorized Congress's violation of the Commerce Clause or Fourteenth Amendment (*New York v. United States*; *Morrison*), Congress can authorize state laws that would otherwise violate the Dormant Commerce Clause. For this reason, Henry Monaghan, *The Supreme Court, 1974 Term—Foreword: Constitutional Common Law*, 89 Harv. L. Rev. 1 (1975), maintains that the Dormant Commerce Clause cases represent "constitutional common law" rather than normal constitutional law. Is such a body of law consistent with *Marbury*'s justifications for judicial review?

2.   *Representation-Reinforcement Role of the Dormant Commerce Clause.* Another justification is suggested by *McCulloch*: State laws may be too protective of the interests of state political *insiders*, at the expense of *outsiders*. The Court might be a useful check on such political dysfunction, because it is not only outside the political process, but it has a national rather than local perspective. This suggestion was fully developed as a justification for activist Dormant Commerce Clause review during the New Deal. The chief articulation was Justice Stone's opinion in *South Carolina State Highway Dep't v. Barnwell Bros.*, 303 U.S. 177 (1938):

> State regulations affecting interstate commerce, whose purpose or effect is to gain for those within the state an advantage at the expense of those without, or burden those out of the state without any corresponding advantage to those within, have been thought to impinge upon the constitutional prohibition even though Congress has not acted.

> Underlying the stated rule has been the thought that when the regulation is of such a character that its burden falls principally upon those without the state, legislative action is not likely to be subjected

---

484–85 (2008) (the core idea is political rather than economic union, and the doctrine should only police discriminatory state policies that can be expected to provoke retaliation).

[71] Compare *Printz v. United States* (§ 5B of this chapter) and *Griswold v. Connecticut* (Chapter 5, § 4A).

to those political restraints which are normally exerted on legislation where it affects adversely some interests within the state.

Recall that later in 1938 Justice Stone also wrote the celebrated *Carolene Products* footnote four, which inspired Professor Ely's representation-reinforcement theory.[72]

Drawing from modern public choice (interest-group) theories of politics, Professor Mark Tushnet advanced a "cost-exporting" rationale for the Dormant Commerce Clause.[73] Interest groups will tend to organize and seek benefits from the political process. The ability of a group to extract *rents* (distributions to the group not justified by overall efficiency) depends in part on the inability of cost-payers to mobilize against the group's lawmaking efforts. One way to assure this is for a group to pursue statutes that "export" the costs to outsiders less well-represented in the local political process. An important role of the Dormant Commerce Clause, therefore, is to prevent widespread rent-seeking by state "insiders" at the expense of state "outsiders" (and obviously also at the expense of the national free market). Dormant Commerce Clause doctrine sets limits on state laws "exporting costs" of regulation to outsiders.

Another way the Court's enforcement of the Dormant Commerce Clause might be representation-reinforcing is that it corrects for congressional inertia. The Commerce and Supremacy Clauses give Congress authority to preempt state laws interfering with interstate commerce, but it is hard for Congress to monitor state violations: The violations are too numerous and too subtle to get on the crowded congressional agenda, and the Article I, § 7 requirements prevent Congress from rectifying most of the violations. The Court is better situated to monitor the violations: Case-by-case adjudication is ideal for sorting out the unjustified discriminations and burdens on commerce, and judicial invalidation of the most serious violations helps Congress conserve its resources while addressing the most thorny problem areas. This kind of representation-reinforcement argument not only justifies the Court's review of state laws burdening commerce, but also justifies the rule that Congress can override the Court and authorize state laws burdening interstate commerce. For recent evidence supporting this line of argument, see Brian Galle, *Kill Quill, Keep the Dormant Commerce Clause History's Lessons on Congressional Control of State Taxation*, 70 Stan. L. Rev. Online 158 (March 2018).

3. *The Commitment Problem with Federalism.* Consider this further passage from Justice Jackson's opinion in *Hood*:

---

[72] Representation-reinforcement theory posits that the role of the Court in constitutional law is to correct for serious defects in the political process (Chapter 2, § 3B). Much of this chapter can be viewed through the prism of representation-reinforcement theory, which was anticipated in some detail by Professor Wechsler's argument that the structures in the Constitution protect the states against federal encroachment and that judicial review is not needed (§ 5B). Cases like *Heart of Atlanta Motel* (§ 2) and *Garcia* (§ 5B) can be viewed as exemplars of Wechsler's insight and illustrations of Ely's theory applied to issues of federalism. Tushnet's theory, described in text, is an effort along similar lines.

[73] Mark V. Tushnet, *Rethinking the Dormant Commerce Clause*, 1979 Wis. L. Rev. 125; see Daniel A. Farber, *State Regulation and the Dormant Commerce Clause*, 3 Const. Comm. 395 (1986).

The material success that has come to inhabitants of the states which make up this federal free trade unit has been the most impressive in the history of commerce, but the established interdependence of the states only emphasizes the necessity of protecting interstate movement of goods against local burdens and repressions. We need only consider the consequences if each of the few states that produce copper, lead, [etc.] should decree that industries located in that state shall have priority. What fantastic rivalries and dislocations and reprisals would ensue if such practices were begun!

The "dislocations and reprisals" problem is not just that the benefits of economic union will be lost and escalating rents will be extracted, but is that such trade wars will threaten the political union itself.

Jenna Bednar and William Eskridge have identified the *commitment problem* as the chief reason for judicial enforcement of the Dormant Commerce Clause.[74] Under this theory, the temptation to cheat on the federal arrangement among the states not only threatens the free market, but undermines the federal arrangement itself. Unless there is a credible deterrent to such cheating, there is a risk that the states will turn on one another, putting pressure on the political stability of the federal arrangement. Bednar and Eskridge maintain, further, that Congress is not a sufficient check on state cheating, for the reasons suggested in the previous note. Case-by-case adjudication seems well designed to regulate such cheating: the interests harmed by the rent-seeking have incentives to bring suit, courts cannot dodge the issue and are well trained in evaluating facts needed to determine whether a state is burdening interstate commerce unjustifiably, and federal judges as national officials would seem impartial enough to resolve matters credibly, such that states are assured that their own cheating and other states' cheating will be fairly handled. For an argument that the Framers anticipated this justification, see Barry Friedman & Daniel T. Deacon, *A Course Unbroken: The Constitutional Legitimacy of the Dormant Commerce Clause,* 97 Va. L. Rev. 1877 (2011).

B. DORMANT COMMERCE CLAUSE DOCTRINE

1. Discrimination Against Interstate Commerce

The key doctrinal precept in the Dormant Commerce Clause jurisprudence is that *overt state discrimination* against interstate commerce is presumptively invalid and can only be sustained if needed to

---

[74] See Jenna Bednar & William N. Eskridge, Jr. *Steadying the Court's "Unsteady Path": A Theory of Judicial Enforcement of Federalism,* 68 S. Cal. L. Rev. 1447 (1995). For a related argument, focusing the Dormant Commerce Clause on discriminatory laws that could be expected to provoke political retaliation, see Brannon P. Denning, *Reconstructing the Dormant Commerce Clause Doctrine,* 50 Wm. & Mary L. Rev. 417, 484–85 (2008).

meet an important state interest.[75] "When a state statute clearly discriminates against interstate commerce, it will be struck down unless the discrimination is demonstrably justified by a valid factor unrelated to economic protectionism. Indeed, when the state statute amounts to simple economic protectionism, a 'virtually per se rule of invalidity' has applied." *Wyoming v. Oklahoma*, 502 U.S. 437, 454–55 (1992). Laws discriminating on their face against interstate commerce on goods or services have included the following kinds:

(a) *Discrimination against outside competition.* The Court has traditionally applied strict scrutiny to laws that impose costs or restrictions on out-of-state (or out-of-area) goods or services. Few laws survive such scrutiny, because the Court usually finds that the local statute is designed to give local businesses artificial competitive advantages over out-of-state businesses, a per se invalid purpose under the Dormant Commerce Clause. In *Welton v. Missouri*, 91 U.S. (1 Otto) 275 (1876), the Court struck down a Missouri law requiring that peddlers of goods "not the growth, produce, or manufacture of the State" obtain a license. The Court ruled that "the very object" of the Commerce Clause was to protect against "discriminating State legislation." E.g., *Crutcher v. Kentucky*, 141 U.S. 47 (1891) (invalidating state law requiring out-of-state express companies to obtain state license); *Buck v. Kuykendall*, 267 U.S. 307 (1925) (similar).

Many of the leading cases involve milk. In *Baldwin v. G.A.F. Seelig*, 294 U.S. 511 (1935), the Court invalidated a New York law that barred importation of out-of-state milk that did not adhere to local price minima. Justice Cardozo's opinion for the Court reasoned that the law "set a barrier to traffic between one state and another as effective as if customs duties, equal to the price differential, had been laid upon the milk," precisely the sort of barrier that triggers trade wars and other reprisals. In *Dean Milk Co. v. City of Madison*, 340 U.S. 349 (1951), the Court invalidated ordinances making it unlawful to sell milk not pasteurized within five miles of the city and to sell, import, receive, or store milk unless from a source inspected by city officials (and within 25 miles of the city). The Court admitted the legitimacy of the state regulation and the dearth of federal statutes regulating the subject but invalidated the ordinances because their "practical effect" was to exclude milk produced and pasteurized out-of-state. "In thus erecting an economic barrier protecting a major local industry against competition from without the State, Madison plainly discriminates against interstate commerce. This it cannot do, even in the exercise of its unquestioned power to protect the health and safety of its people, if reasonable nondiscriminatory alternatives, adequate to serve legitimate local interest, are available." The Court found reasonable

---

[75] The anti-discrimination rule is not limited to state policies, but also applies to policies adopted at the municipal, see *Dean Milk Co. v. Madison*, 340 U.S. 349 (1951), or county level, see *Fort Gratiot Sanitary Landfill, Inc. v. Michigan Dep't Nat. Resources*, 504 U.S. 353 (1992).

alternatives to be available. Compare *Minnesota v. Clover Leaf Creamery Co.*, 449 U.S. 456 (1981) (upholding state ban on selling milk in nonreturnable containers, because it did not on its face or in effect discriminate against interstate commerce).

(b) *Discriminatory hoarding local resources or opportunities.* Statutes trying to prevent resources or businesses from going out-of-state are also immediately suspect under the Dormant Commerce Clause. In *Pennsylvania v. West Virginia*, 262 U.S. 553 (1923), the Court invalidated a West Virginia statute requiring in-state pipeline companies to meet the domestic needs of domestic gas consumers before the companies could export gas to out-of-state customers. Because the law discriminated against interstate commerce, it was invalid, notwithstanding the state's argument that it was merely preserving one of its natural advantages. See also *New England Power Co. v. New Hampshire*, 455 U.S. 331 (1982), invalidating a New Hampshire statute requiring regulatory permission before hydroelectric power could be sold out of state; *Wyoming v. Oklahoma*, 502 U.S. 437 (1992), invalidating an Oklahoma statute requiring power plants to use at least 10% local coal.

Most of the hoarding cases have involved "local processing requirements," which channel business opportunities to in-state or in-area businesses. In a leading decision, *Foster-Fountain Packing Co. v. Haydel*, 278 U.S. 1 (1928), the Court invalidated a Louisiana law prohibiting the exportation of shrimp until the heads and hulls had been removed. The state justified the discrimination on the ground that shrimp hulls and heads were needed as fertilizer in the state, a goal the Court found not credible; the real purpose of the statute was to prevent Mississippi processing plants from competing with those in Louisiana. Other requirements held invalid have included local inspection of meat, *Minnesota v. Barber*, 136 U.S. 313 (1890); local packing of shrimp, *Toomer v. Witsell*, 334 U.S. 385 (1948); and local processing of timber, *South-Central Timber Dev., Inc. v. Wunnicke*, 467 U.S. 82 (1984).

(c) *Discrimination preventing outside burdens from flowing in-state.* This is the trickiest category. In the nineteenth century, the Court was tolerant of state efforts to prevent outside burdens from flowing into the state. For example, the law regulating the importation of potential public charges was sustained in *Milne*. (Because the law regulated immigration, it would not be sustained today. See *Arizona v. United States,* below.) The Court also upheld quarantine laws honestly seeking to prevent the spread of contagious diseases. See *Bowman v. Chicago & Northwestern R.*, 125 U.S. 465 (1888) (leading case); *Kimmish v. Ball*, 129 U.S. 217 (1889); *Sligh v. Kirkwood*, 237 U.S. 52 (1915). Recall the "outlaws of commerce" theory of the Lottery Case and other Commerce Clause precedents in § 2 of this chapter. This kind of discrimination has faced tougher scrutiny in recent cases, starting with the leading decision, which follows.

CITY OF PHILADELPHIA V. NEW JERSEY
437 U.S. 617, 98 S.Ct. 2531, 57 L.Ed.2d 475 (1978)

JUSTICE STEWART delivered the opinion of the Court.

[A New Jersey law prohibited the importation of most "solid or liquid waste which originated or was collected outside the territorial limits of the State." Private landfill operators challenged the statute on preemption and Dormant Commerce Clause grounds. The state supreme court rejected both claims, finding that the statute "advanced vital health and environmental objectives with no economic discrimination against, and with little burden upon, interstate commerce." The Supreme Court reversed on the Dormant Commerce Clause claim.]

All objects of interstate trade merit Commerce Clause protection; none is excluded by definition at the outset. * * * Hence, we reject the state court's suggestion that the banning of "valueless" out-of-state wastes by [the statute] implicates no constitutional protection. Just as Congress has power to regulate the interstate movement of these wastes, States are not free from constitutional scrutiny when they restrict that movement.

Although the Constitution gives Congress the power to regulate commerce among the States, many subjects of potential federal regulation under that power inevitably escape congressional attention "because of their local character and their number and diversity." In the absence of federal legislation, these subjects are open to control by the States so long as they act within the restraints imposed by the Commerce Clause itself. The bounds of these restraints appear nowhere in the words of the Commerce Clause, but have emerged gradually in the decisions of this Court giving effect to its basic purpose. * * *

The opinions of the Court through the years have reflected an alertness to the evils of "economic isolation" and protectionism, while at the same time recognizing that incidental burdens on interstate commerce may be unavoidable when a State legislates to safeguard the health and safety of its people. Thus, where simple economic protectionism is effected by state legislation, a virtually per se rule of invalidity has been erected. The clearest example of such legislation is a law that overtly blocks the flow of interstate commerce at a State's borders. Cf. *Welton v. Missouri.* But where other legislative objectives are credibly advanced and there is no patent discrimination against interstate trade, the Court has adopted a much more flexible approach [described and illustrated in the Subpart 2, *infra*].

The crucial inquiry, therefore, must be directed to determining whether [the statute] is basically a protectionist measure, or whether it can fairly be viewed as a law directed to legitimate local concerns, with effects upon interstate commerce that are only incidental.

The purpose of [the statute] is set out in [it as] follows:

> The Legislature finds and determines that . . . the volume of solid and liquid waste continues to rapidly increase, that the treatment and disposal of these wastes continues to pose an even greater threat to the quality of the environment of New Jersey, that the available and appropriate land fill sites within the State are being diminished, that the environment continues to be threatened by the treatment and disposal of waste which originated or was collected outside the State, and that the public health, safety and welfare require that the treatment and disposal within this State of all wastes generated outside of the State be prohibited.

The New Jersey Supreme Court accepted this statement of the state legislature's purpose. The state court additionally found that New Jersey's existing landfill sites will be exhausted within a few years; that to go on using these sites or to develop new ones will take a heavy environmental toll, both from pollution and from loss of scarce open lands; that new techniques to divert waste from landfills to other methods of disposal and resource recovery processes are under development, but that these changes will require time; and finally, that "the extension of the lifespan of existing landfills, resulting from the exclusion of out-of-state waste, may be of crucial importance in preventing further virgin wetlands or other undeveloped lands from being devoted to landfill purposes." Based on these findings, the court concluded that [the statute] was designed to protect, not the State's economy, but its environment, and that its substantial benefits outweigh its "slight" burden on interstate commerce.

[The parties disagreed over whether the statutory purpose was protectionist or remedial.] This dispute about ultimate legislative purpose need not be resolved, because its resolution would not be relevant to the constitutional issue to be decided in this case. Contrary to the evident assumption of the state court and the parties, the evil of protectionism can reside in legislative means as well as legislative ends. Thus, it does not matter whether the ultimate aim of [the statute] is to reduce the waste disposal costs of residents or to save remaining open lands from pollution, for we assume New Jersey has every right to protect its residents' pocketbooks as well as their environment. And it may be assumed as well that New Jersey may pursue those ends by slowing the flow of *all* waste into the State's remaining landfills, even though interstate commerce may incidentally be affected. But whatever New Jersey's ultimate purpose, it may not be accomplished by discriminating against articles of commerce from outside the State unless there is some reason, apart from their origin, to treat them differently. Both on its face and in its plain effect, [the statute] violates this principle of nondiscrimination.

The Court has consistently found parochial legislation of this kind to be constitutionally invalid, whether the ultimate aim of the legislation was to assure a steady supply of milk by erecting barriers to allegedly ruinous outside competition, *Baldwin v. G.A.F. Selig*; or to create jobs by keeping industry within the State, *Foster-Fountain Packing*; or to preserve the State's financial resources from depletion by fencing out indigent immigrants. *Edwards v. California* [Chapter 5, § 3C]. In each of these cases, a presumably legitimate goal was sought to be achieved by the illegitimate means of isolating the State from the national economy.

Also relevant here are the Court's decisions holding that a State may not accord its own inhabitants a preferred right of access over consumers in other States to natural resources located within its borders. *Pennsylvania v. West Virginia*. These cases stand for the basic principle that a "State is without power to prevent privately owned articles of trade from being shipped and sold in interstate commerce on the ground that they are required to satisfy local demands or because they are needed by the people of the State." *Foster-Fountain Packing Co.*

The New Jersey law at issue in this case falls squarely within the area that the Commerce Clause puts off limits to state regulation. On its face, it imposes on out-of-state commercial interests the full burden of conserving the state's remaining landfill space. It is true that in our previous cases the scarce natural resource was itself the article of commerce, whereas here the scarce resource and the article of commerce are distinct. But that difference is without consequence. In both instances, the State has overtly moved to slow or freeze the flow of commerce for protectionist reasons. It does not matter that the State has shut the article of commerce inside the State in one case and outside the State in the other. What is crucial is the attempt by one State to isolate itself from a problem common to many by erecting a barrier against the movement of interstate trade.

The appellees argue that not all laws which facially discriminate against out-of-state commerce are forbidden protectionist regulations. In particular, they point to quarantine laws, which this Court has repeatedly upheld even though they appear to single out interstate commerce for special treatment. In the appellees' view, [the statute] is analogous to such health-protective measures, since it reduces the exposure of New Jersey residents to the allegedly harmful effects of landfill sites.

It is true that certain quarantine laws have not been considered forbidden protectionist measures, even though they were directed against out-of-state commerce. But those quarantine laws banned the importation of articles such as diseased livestock that required destruction as soon as possible because their very movement risked contagion and other evils. Those laws thus did not discriminate against interstate commerce as such, but simply prevented traffic in noxious articles, whatever their origin.

The New Jersey statute is not such a quarantine law. There has been no claim here that the very movement of waste into or through New Jersey endangers health, or that waste must be disposed of as soon and as close to its point of generation as possible. The harms caused by waste are said to arise after its disposal in landfill sites, and at that point, as New Jersey concedes, there is no basis to distinguish out-of-state waste from domestic waste. If one is inherently harmful, so is the other. Yet New Jersey has banned the former while leaving its landfill sites open to the latter. The New Jersey law blocks the importation of waste in an obvious effort to saddle those outside the State with the entire burden of slowing the flow of refuse into New Jersey's remaining landfill sites. That legislative effort is clearly impermissible under the Commerce Clause of the Constitution.

Today, cities in Pennsylvania and New York find it expedient or necessary to send their waste into New Jersey for disposal, and New Jersey claims the right to close its borders to such traffic. Tomorrow, cities in New Jersey may find it expedient or necessary to send their waste into Pennsylvania or New York for disposal, and those States might then claim the right to close their borders. The Commerce Clause will protect New Jersey in the future, just as it protects her neighbors now, from efforts by one State to isolate itself in the stream of interstate commerce from a problem shared by all. The judgment is reversed.

JUSTICE REHNQUIST, with whom **THE CHIEF JUSTICE [BURGER]** joins, dissenting.

A growing problem in our Nation is the sanitary treatment and disposal of solid waste. For many years, solid waste was incinerated. Because of the significant environmental problems attendant on incineration, however, this method of solid waste disposal has declined in use in many localities, including New Jersey. "Sanitary" landfills have replaced incineration as the principal method of disposing of solid waste. * * * [But] landfills also present extremely serious health and safety problems. First, in New Jersey, "virtually all sanitary landfills can be expected to produce leachate, a noxious and highly polluted liquid which is seldom visible and frequently pollutes . . . ground and surface waters." The natural decomposition process which occurs in landfills also produces large quantities of methane and thereby presents a significant explosion hazard. Landfills can also generate "health hazards caused by rodents, fires and scavenger birds" and, "needless to say, do not help New Jersey's aesthetic appearance nor New Jersey's noise or water or air pollution problems."

The health and safety hazards associated with landfills present appellees with a currently unsolvable dilemma. Other, hopefully safer, methods of disposing of solid wastes are still in the development stage and cannot presently be used. But appellees obviously cannot completely stop the tide of solid waste that its citizens will produce in the interim. For the moment, therefore, appellees must continue to use sanitary landfills to dispose of New Jersey's own solid waste despite the critical environmental problems thereby created.

The question presented in this case is whether New Jersey must also continue to receive and dispose of solid waste from neighboring States, even though these will inexorably increase the health problems discussed above. The Court answers this question in the affirmative. New Jersey must either prohibit *all* landfill operations, leaving itself to cast about for a presently nonexistent solution to the serious problem of disposing of the waste generated within its own borders, or it must accept waste from every portion of the United States, thereby multiplying the health and safety problems which would result if it dealt only with such wastes generated within the State. Because past precedents establish that the Commerce Clause does not present appellees with such a Hobson's choice, I dissent. * * *

* * * I do not see why a State may ban the importation of items whose movement risks contagion, but cannot ban the importation of items which, although they may be transported into the State without undue hazard, will then simply pile up in an ever increasing danger to the public's health and safety. The Commerce Clause was not drawn with a view to having the validity of state laws turn on such pointless distinctions.

* * * [T]he Court implies that the challenged laws must be invalidated because New Jersey has left its landfills open to domestic waste. But, as the Court notes, this Court has repeatedly upheld quarantine laws "even though they appear to single out interstate commerce for special treatment." The fact that New Jersey has left its landfill sites open for domestic waste does not, of course, mean that solid waste is not innately harmful. Nor does it mean that New Jersey prohibits importation of solid waste for reasons other than the health and safety of its population. New Jersey must out of sheer necessity treat and dispose of its solid waste in some fashion, just as it must treat New Jersey cattle suffering from hoof-and-mouth disease. It does not follow that New Jersey must, under the Commerce Clause, accept solid waste or diseased cattle from outside its borders and thereby exacerbate its problems.

NOTES ON CITY OF PHILADELPHIA *AND THE COURT'S* POLICING DISCRIMINATIONS AGAINST COMMERCE

Consider the similarities between *City of Philadelphia* and *Lochner*: A Court dedicated to free market principles in both cases struck down state laws based upon reasoning having only a broad, tenuous connection with the Constitution. If *Lochner* was a failed experiment, which at least could be linked to the Contract Clause, can one justify the *City of Philadelphia* line of cases, which are only inferentially (and some think unpersuasively) linked to the

Commerce Clause, any better?[76] Return to the three justifications for Dormant Commerce Clause enforcement by the Supreme Court and see how they fit here:

1. *Economic Union and Efficiency.* Typically, as in *City of Philadelphia*, the Court simply applies heightened scrutiny to any overt discrimination against interstate commerce, without any analysis whether the particular discrimination might be efficient overall. A simple economic argument would support the efficiency of New Jersey's rule: Waste imposes *externalities* on the public, that is, costs (such as air pollution, stench, and visual blight) that are not internalized in the price charged. Hence, a state prohibition on such goods might be efficient overall, because the benefits (externalities avoided) outweigh the costs (opportunity costs lost by outsiders). Strict scrutiny short-circuits such analysis, because it requires super-efficiency: New Jersey's flat prohibition was invalid under strict scrutiny because it was overbroad; a tax on waste could have solved the externality problem without discriminating against interstate commerce. The super-efficiency required by strict scrutiny is not impossible to establish, see *Maine v. Taylor*, 477 U.S. 131 (1986) (allowing Maine to bar the importation of live baitfish, on the ground that there were proven dangers baitfish parasites would pose to indigenous wild fishes), but it disallows many state regulations that are efficient overall.

The Court warns of a trade (or waste!) war; theories of free trade emphasize that any barriers risk reprisals and new barriers. But set against that possibility is the value of local autonomy—embedded in the Constitution, according to the Court's federalism cases. Local autonomy is just as threatened by outside intrusions and options cut off from higher-level organs such as the Supreme Court, and the Court exposes citizens to what they view as increased risks and insecurities (Heinzerling, *Commercial Constitution,* 237–39). How can the Court compare the risks New Jersey imposes on free trade in waste, with the risks Philadelphia imposes on local autonomy in New Jersey? Does the Constitution provide a basis to differentiate? Or is this just the same kind of value choice the Court made in *Lochner*?

2. *Political Process Defects?* Maybe there is a process defect that can serve as a surrogate for an efficiency or trade war risk. Consider the application of Professor Tushnet's costs-exporting theory to this case. The New Jersey law was probably sought by in-state industrial concerns, whose costs of waste-disposal would be increased by out-of-state competition for New Jersey landfill. The law burdens out-of-state industrial concerns, because it increases

---

[76] For criticisms of *City of Philadelphia* for disabling states from engaging in productive activities such as containing externalities, see Stanley Cox, *Garbage In, Garbage Out: Court Confusion About the Dormant Commerce Clause*, 50 Okla. L. Rev. 155 (1997); Richard A. Epstein, *Waste and the Dormant Commerce Clause*, 3 Green Bag 2d 29 (1999); Christine A. Klein, *The Environmental Commerce Clause*, 27 Harv. Envtl. L. Rev. 1 (2003); Paul McGreal, *The Flawed Economics of the Dormant Commerce Clause*, 39 Wm. & Mary L. Rev. 1191 (1998); Paula C. Murray & David B. Spence, *Fair Weather Federalism and America's Waste Disposal Crisis*, 27 Harv. Envtl. L. Rev. 27 (2003). See generally Lisa Heinzerling, *The Commercial Constitution*, 1995 Sup. Ct. Rev. 217 (making this criticism, but also arguing that the Dormant Commerce Clause jurisprudence is internally incoherent).

their costs of waste disposal. Viewed this way, *City of Philadelphia* seems to fit Tushnet's theory, because in-state industrial concerns are exporting costs to their out-of-state competitors, who will have to pay more for waste disposal. The state's internal political process cannot be expected to prevent this sort of rent-seeking, so we need the Supreme Court to step in.

But this scenario neglects the externality problem: New Jersey's policy is a response to outsiders' exporting their costs to New Jersey; the Court's approach prevents New Jersey from responding except by a highly calibrated and nondiscriminatory measure. Because two other groups are involved in the state law (in-state landfill owners, who bear costs of the regulation, and out-of-state landfill owners, who benefit from the regulation), the cost-bearers are *not* entirely out-of-staters. While landfill owners are probably not a huge group within New Jersey, their compactness and commonality of interest make it likely that they will be well-organized on any issue of landfill regulation and, hence, that their perspective will be heard during the legislative process.

Moreover, if you want to play the cost-benefit game, you should consider long-run costs and benefits. Perhaps the cheapness of New Jersey landfill has discouraged industry in New York and Pennsylvania from developing technologies which dispose of wastes without damage to the environment. New Jersey's law may benefit everyone in the Northeast, as innovation-forcing regulation. While New Jersey's balance of policies may be self-interested, New York and Pennsylvania (with twice as many Senators and more than three times as many Representatives) can go to Congress to obtain a better allocation of costs and benefits. Indeed, why aren't these fatal problems with the representation-reinforcement justification for the Dormant Commerce Clause cases? Determining winners and losers, and costs and benefits, should be left to the political process, which has superior information-gathering capacity. It is no response to say that in many of these cases the losers are badly represented in the regulating state's political process, because they then have recourse to Congress.

3.   *A Commitment Problem?* The Bednar and Eskridge theory relies on a domino effect, whereby any compromise of the national marketplace will trigger state commitment problems and reprisals. But the Court's stringent approach in *City of Philadelphia* does not seem to have discouraged state and local governments from continuing to adopt environmental measures that burden or discriminate against interstate commerce. Does the popularity of environmental regulations suggest that states are willing to make the following counter-commitment: Each state is willing to tolerate some inconvenience because of neighbor state environmental regulations, so long as those regulations are reasonably related to environmental protection and are not pretexts for economic advantage-seeking, and so long as the state can adopt its own reasonable environmental rules. Perhaps Justice Rehnquist was right to dissent in *City of Philadelphia*: The pro-environmental regulations are more like quarantine laws than laws that hoard resources and business opportunities or that protect against interstate competition. By frustrating

legitimate environmental protection efforts, is the Court undermining rather than protecting state enthusiasm for the federal arrangement?

NOTE ON THE POST-PHILADELPHIA WASTE CASES

Following *City of Philadelphia*'s stringent scrutiny, many state and local waste rules and taxes that discriminated on their face against interstate commerce have been declared unconstitutional by the Supreme Court. In *Chemical Waste Management, Inc. v. Hunt*, 504 U.S. 334 (1992), the Court struck down an Alabama law requiring commercial landfill owners to pay the state $25.60 per ton on all hazardous wastes disposed of, plus an additional $72.00 per ton for wastes generated outside Alabama. The Court applied *City of Philadelphia*'s strict scrutiny, because it viewed the additional fee as a facial discrimination against interstate commerce. The additional fee was not justified by any evidence that out-of-state waste was more expensive to deal with, and other, nondiscriminatory methods were available for handling any problems that existed. In *Oregon Waste Systems, Inc. v. Department of Environmental Quality*, 511 U.S. 93 (1994), the Court rejected a surcharge of $2.25 per ton for out-of-state waste, whose differential (three times the charge of $0.85 for in-state waste) the Court found unsupported by evidence of extra regulatory cost. Accord, *Fort Gratiot Sanitary Landfill, Inc. v. Michigan Dept. of Natural Resources*, 504 U.S. 353 (1992) (striking down a similar law discriminating against out-of-county waste).

In *C & A Carbone, Inc. v. Town of Clarkstown*, 511 U.S. 383 (1994), a sharply divided Court struck down a municipal flow-control ordinance requiring all nonhazardous waste to be funneled through a privately operated waste treatment plant, even though it was sometimes cheaper to send it out-of-state. By limiting waste processing to a favored facility within its own jurisdiction, the town discriminated against interstate commerce and fell within the Court's local processing requirement precedents, which have almost always invalidated "laws hoard[ing] a local resource—be it meat, shrimp, or milk—for the benefit of local businesses that treat it. The flow control ordinance has the same design and effect. It hoards solid waste, and the demand to get rid of it, for the benefit of the preferred processing facility. The only conceivable distinction from the cases cited above is that the flow control ordinance favors a single local proprietor. But this difference just makes the protectionist effect of the ordinance more acute," because it "squelches competition in the waste-processing service altogether, leaving no room for investment from outside."

"Discrimination against interstate commerce in favor of local business or investment is per se invalid, save in a narrow class of cases in which the municipality can demonstrate, under rigorous scrutiny, that it has no other means to advance a legitimate local interest." *Amici* argued that the ordinance was needed to ensure safe handling of waste, given the shortage of landfill space and escalating environmental clean-up costs, but Justice Kennedy's opinion for the Court responded that the town could have achieved those safety goals through nondiscriminatory safety regulations. "State and local governments may not use their regulatory power to favor local enterprise by prohibiting patronage of out-of-state competitors or their facilities." Justice Souter's dissenting opinion viewed the regulation as a justified environmental regulation; it was anticompetitive but not protectionist. There was no exporting of costs to other jurisdictions.

UNITED HAULERS ASS'N, INC. V. ONEIDA-HERKIMER SOLID WASTE MANAGEMENT AUTHORITY
550 U.S. 330, 127 S.Ct. 1786, 167 L.Ed.2d 655 (2007)

CHIEF JUSTICE ROBERTS delivered the opinion of the Court.

[Oneida and Herkimer Counties adopted flow control ordinances requiring haulers to bring waste to facilities owned and operated by a state-created public benefit corporation.] We find this difference constitutionally significant. Disposing of trash has been a traditional government activity for years, and laws that favor the government in such areas—but treat every private business, whether in-state or out-of-state, exactly the same—do not discriminate against interstate commerce for purposes of the Commerce Clause. Applying the Commerce Clause test reserved for regulations that do not discriminate against interstate commerce, we uphold these ordinances because any incidental burden they may have on interstate commerce does not outweigh the benefits they confer on the citizens of Oneida and Herkimer Counties. [*Carbone* involved a similar flow-control ordinance, but the processing plant to which the flow was channeled was run by a *private* company, a point emphasized in the *Carbone* opinion.]

The flow control ordinances in this case benefit a clearly public facility, while treating all private companies exactly the same. Because the question is now squarely presented on the facts of the case before us, we decide that such flow control ordinances do not discriminate against interstate commerce for purposes of the dormant Commerce Clause.

Compelling reasons justify treating these laws differently from laws favoring particular private businesses over their competitors. "Conceptually, of course, any notion of discrimination assumes a comparison of substantially similar entities." But States and municipalities are not private businesses—far from it. Unlike private enterprise, government is vested with the responsibility of protecting the health, safety, and welfare of its citizens. * * *

Given these differences, it does not make sense to regard laws favoring local government and laws favoring private industry with equal skepticism. As our local processing cases demonstrate, when a law favors in-state business over out-of-state competition, rigorous scrutiny is appropriate because the law is often the product of "simple economic protectionism." Laws favoring local government, by contrast, may be directed toward any number of legitimate goals unrelated to protectionism. Here the flow control ordinances enable the Counties to pursue particular policies with respect to the handling and treatment of waste generated in the Counties, while allocating the costs of those policies on citizens and businesses according to the volume of waste they generate.

This case

The contrary approach of treating public and private entities the same under the dormant Commerce Clause would lead to unprecedented and unbounded interference by the courts with state and local government. The dormant Commerce Clause is not a roving license for federal courts to decide what activities are appropriate for state and local government to undertake, and what activities must be the province of private market competition. In this case, the citizens of Oneida and Herkimer Counties have chosen the government to provide waste management services, with a limited role for the private sector in arranging for transport of waste from the curb to the public facilities. The citizens could have left the entire matter for the private sector, in which case any regulation they undertook could not discriminate against interstate commerce. But it was also open to them to vest responsibility for the matter with their government, and to adopt flow control ordinances to support the government effort. It is not the office of the Commerce Clause to control the decision of the voters on whether government or the private sector should provide waste management services. "The Commerce Clause significantly limits the ability of States and localities to regulate or otherwise burden the flow of interstate commerce, but it does not elevate free trade above all other values."

The people give the responsibility to the gov.

We should be particularly hesitant to interfere with the Counties' efforts under the guise of the Commerce Clause because "[w]aste disposal is both typically and traditionally a local government function." Congress itself has recognized local government's vital role in waste management, making clear that "collection and disposal of solid wastes should continue to be primarily the function of State, regional, and local agencies." Resource Conservation and Recovery Act of 1976, 42 U.S.C. § 6901(a)(4). The policy of the State of New York favors "displac[ing] competition with regulation or monopoly control" in this area. N.Y. Pub. Auth. Law Ann. § 2049–tt(3). We may or may not agree with that approach, but nothing in the Commerce Clause vests the responsibility for that policy judgment with the Federal Judiciary.

typically a gov function

Finally, it bears mentioning that the most palpable harm imposed by the ordinances—more expensive trash removal—is likely to fall upon the very people who voted for the laws. Our dormant Commerce Clause cases often find discrimination when a State shifts the costs of regulation to other States, because when "the burden of state regulation falls on interests outside the state, it is unlikely to be alleviated by the operation of those political restraints normally exerted when interests within the state are

the burden falls on the people that voted for it

affected." Here, the citizens and businesses of the Counties bear the costs of the ordinances. There is no reason to step in and hand local businesses a victory they could not obtain through the political process.

We hold that the Counties' flow control ordinances, which treat in-state private business interests exactly the same as out-of-state ones, do not "discriminate against interstate commerce" for purposes of the dormant Commerce Clause.

[We omit the opinions of **JUSTICE SCALIA**, concurring in part, and of **JUSTICE THOMAS,** concurring in the judgment. The latter announced that he would jettison the Dormant Commerce Clause entirely; the former repeated that he would follow but not expand on binding precedents.]

JUSTICE ALITO, with whom **JUSTICE STEVENS** and **JUSTICE KENNEDY** join, dissenting.

The fact that the flow control laws at issue discriminate in favor of a government-owned enterprise does not meaningfully distinguish this case from *Carbone*. The preferred facility in *Carbone* was, to be sure, nominally owned by a private contractor who had built the facility on the town's behalf, but it would be misleading to describe the facility as private. In exchange for the contractor's promise to build the facility for the town free of charge and then to sell it to the town five years later for $1, the town guaranteed that, during the first five years of the facility's existence, the contractor would receive "a minimum waste flow of 120,000 tons per year" and that the contractor could charge an above-market tipping fee. If the facility "received less than 120,000 tons in a year, the town [would] make up the tipping fee deficit." To prevent residents, businesses, and trash haulers from taking their waste elsewhere in pursuit of lower tipping fees (leaving the town responsible for covering any shortfall in the contractor's guaranteed revenue stream), the town enacted an ordinance "requir[ing] all nonhazardous solid waste within the town to be deposited at" the preferred facility. * * *

The only real difference between the facility at issue in *Carbone* and its counterpart in this case is that title to the former had not yet formally passed to the municipality. The Court exalts form over substance in adopting a test that turns on this technical distinction, particularly since, barring any obstacle presented by state law, the transaction in *Carbone* could have been restructured to provide for the passage of title at the beginning, rather than the end, of the 5-year period. * * *

In any event, we have never treated discriminatory legislation with greater deference simply because the entity favored by that legislation was a government-owned enterprise. * * *

The fallacy in the Court's approach can be illustrated by comparing a law that discriminates in favor of an in-state facility, owned by a corporation whose shares are publicly held, and a law discriminating in favor of an otherwise identical facility that is owned by the State or municipality. Those who are favored and disfavored by these two laws are essentially the same with one major exception: The law favoring the corporate facility presumably benefits the corporation's shareholders, most of whom are probably not local residents, whereas the law favoring the government-owned facility presumably benefits the people of the enacting State or municipality. I cannot understand why only the former law, and not the latter, should be regarded as a tool of economic protectionism. Nor do I think it is realistic or consistent with our precedents to condemn some discriminatory laws as protectionist while upholding other, equally discriminatory laws as lawful measures designed to serve legitimate local interests unrelated to protectionism.

This is protectionism

NOTES ON UNITED HAULERS AND THE KENTUCKY BONDS CASE

The debate among the Justices in *United Haulers* continued the next Term in *Department of Revenue of Kentucky v. Davis*, 553 U.S. 328 (2008). The issue was whether Kentucky could exempt from state income taxation interest on its own bonds, but not interest on bonds issued by other states. Justice Souter's opinion for the Court upheld the discrimination against out-of-state bonds. The debate among the Justices illuminates some of the issues decided, or not, in *United Haulers*.

1. *Does Government Ownership Make a Decisive Difference?* In *United Haulers,* the Chief Justice distinguished *Carbone* on the ground that the local government, rather than a private firm, owned and operated the waste treatment facility. In *Davis,* Justice Souter made a similar point. If the goal of the Dormant Commerce Clause jurisprudence is protecting free markets and avoiding balkanization or "economic protectionism," why should government ownership make a difference? (Justice Alito raised this concern in his *United Haulers* dissent.) Does public operation provide evidence that the discrimination against interstate commerce is at least founded in a public-regarding purpose? The Chief Justice seemed to think so, a point that Justice Alito vigorously disputed. Relatedly, Justice Souter's *Davis* opinion applied the market participant exception to the Dormant Commerce Clause, but only Justices Stevens and Breyer joined that discussion. In the wake of *United Haulers,* local governments have revised their waste-management plans to centralize them in public agencies and departments, and they are winning in the lower courts. E.g., *C & A Carbone, Inc. v. County of Rockland*, 2014 WL 1202699 (W.D.N.Y. March 24, 2014) (following *United Haulers* to uphold waste plan similar to that struck down in the earlier *Carbone* precedent, but revised to vest enforcement with a public institution).

2. *Balancing.* Although the Justices all claim to be applying *per se* rules and argue about how to categorize the schemes before them, we'd suggest that there is a fair amount of balancing afoot in these cases. When the Court applies

the Dormant Commerce Clause to strike down state or local regulation, the Court is, to at least some extent, nationalizing that regulatory issue. In *United Haulers, amicus* briefs demonstrated that waste processing was an issue of tremendous relevance to local governments. And Congress has said that these issues are best handled at the local level. E.g., Resource Conservation and Recovery Act (RCRA) of 1976, Public Law No. 94–580, 90 Stat. 2795, codified at 42 U.S.C. § 6901(a)(4). Although the *United Haulers* dissenters responded that the Dormant Commerce Clause does not preempt all regulation, just discriminatory rules, the *amici* persuaded a plurality of Justices that monopolizing (i.e., discriminating against commerce) regulation was needed. Justice Souter made the same finding for the Kentucky exemption in *Davis*.

3.   *Debate over the Dormant Commerce Clause Generally.* The Dormant Commerce Clause represents an area of constitutional doctrine where the Court is divided into three camps (and not the usual Republicans versus the Democrats): (1) *The Zealous Enforcer.* Justice Alito zealously enforces the nationwide free market, anti-balkanization norm and is inclined to give the Dormant Commerce Clause precedents a broad reading. (2) *The Anti-Enforcers.* Justices Thomas and Gorsuch object that the Dormant Commerce Clause jurisprudence is blatant judicial activism and ought not be extended one iota or ought to be abrogated. (3) *The Pragmatists.* Other Justices are willing to apply the Dormant Commerce Clause precedents and the anti-balkanization norm, but with an eye to the value of local regulation. They will also consider congressional signals (such as RCRA in *United Haulers*), how widespread a policy is and how long it has been in place, and the apparent motivations for the policy. (Justice Kavanaugh's views are not clear.)

On the whole, the Dormant Commerce Clause has been on the downward slope at the Supreme Court level, with *United Haulers* merely a dramatic example of its decline. Even instances of state or municipal "discriminations" against interstate commerce are not being invalidated unless the Court majority believes there was a protectionist (and not efficiency or conservationist) purpose for the regulation. Daniel Francis, *The Decline of the Dormant Commerce Clause,* 94 Denver L. Rev. 255, 278–92 (2017) (surveying the cases after 1977 and highlighting *United Haulers*); Donald H. Regan, *The Supreme Court and State Protectionism: Making Sense of the Dormant Commerce Clause*, 84 Mich. L. Rev. 1291, 1292–93 (1986) (presciently arguing for precisely this approach to the Dormant Commerce Clause); see generally Kenneth L. Karst, *From* Carbone *to* United Haulers: *The Advocates' Tales*, 2007 Sup. Ct. Rev. 237. With a majority of the Court committed to in this area, why might the Dormant Commerce Clause be slumbering?

NOTE ON STATE TAXATION OF INTERSTATE COMMERCE

What if Oneida County had financed its waste-treatment venture by a special tax applicable only on waste treated outside the town? A complex set of doctrines governs state taxation of interstate commerce. The prevailing approach to "discriminatory" state taxation is *Complete Auto Transit v. Brady*, 430 U.S. 274 (1977). To satisfy the Commerce Clause test, the tax must be "applied to an activity with substantial nexus with the taxing State, [must be] fairly apportioned, [must] not discriminate against interstate commerce, and [must be] fairly related to services provided by the State." Hence, a tax falling only on out-of-state haulers of waste would appear to be unconstitutional.

The Court's recent decisions suggest that the third and fourth prongs tend to collapse when the "discrimination" is in a statute's effect and not on its face: The brunt of a tax can be borne primarily by out-of-staters so long as there is some relationship between the tax and services or burdens on the state. E.g., *Commonwealth Edison v. Montana*, 453 U.S. 609 (1981) (upholding severance tax on coal, most of which is borne by out-of-state shippers and consumers). See also *Armco, Inc. v. Hardesty*, 467 U.S. 638 (1984); *Westinghouse Electric Corp. v. Tully*, 466 U.S. 388 (1984).

Commerce Clause restrictions on state taxation of multistate enterprises promise to remain an important area of constitutional law because of the increasingly multistate, and multinational, incidence of business operations.[77] See *General Motors Corp. v. Tracy*, 519 U.S. 278 (1997); *Barclays Bank PLC v. Franchise Tax Bd.*, 512 U.S. 298 (1994) (upholding state taxation of multinational companies, relying in part on congressional signals of approval).

Comptroller of the Treasury of Maryland v. Wynne

135 S.Ct. 1787 (2015)

Maryland's personal income tax on state residents consists of a "state" income tax and a "county" income tax. Residents who pay income tax to another jurisdiction for income earned in that other jurisdiction are allowed a credit against the "state" tax but not the "county" tax. Nonresidents who earn income from sources within Maryland must pay the "state" income tax, and nonresidents not subject to the county tax must pay a "special nonresident tax" in lieu of the "county" tax. Brian and Karen Wynne were a Maryland married couple with income from many other jurisdictions; they challenged the state's refusal to give them credit against the county tax for similar taxes paid to other jurisdictions.

Justice Alito, writing for a narrowly divided Court, ruled that this tax scheme violated the Dormant Commerce Clause, under the *Complete Auto Transit* standard, refined for tax challenges by what the Court has called the "internal consistency" test. This test, which helps courts identify tax schemes that discriminate against interstate commerce, "looks to the structure of the tax at issue to see whether its identical application by every State in the Union would place interstate commerce at a disadvantage." *Oklahoma Tax Comm'n v. Jefferson Lines, Inc.*, 514 U.S. 179, 185 (1986). By hypothetically assuming

---

[77] See generally Jesse Choper & Tung Yin, *State Taxation and the Dormant Commerce Clause: The Object-Measure Approach*, 1998 Sup. Ct. Rev. 193; Howard Hunter, *Federalism and State Taxation of Multistate Enterprises*, 32 Emory L.J. 89 (1983); Daniel Shaviro, *A Political and Economic Look at Federalism in Taxation*, 90 Mich. L. Rev. 895 (1992).

that every State has the same tax structure, the internal consistency test allows courts to isolate the effect of a defendant State's tax scheme.

"Maryland's income tax scheme fails the internal consistency test. A simple example illustrates the point. Assume that every State imposed the following taxes, which are similar to Maryland's 'county' and 'special nonresident' taxes: (1) a 1.25% tax on income that residents earn in State, (2) a 1.25% tax on income that residents earn in other jurisdictions, and (3) a 1.25% tax on income that nonresidents earn in State. Assume further that two taxpayers, April and Bob, both live in State A, but that April earns her income in State A whereas Bob earns his income in State B. In this circumstance, Bob will pay more income tax than April solely because he earns income interstate. Specifically, April will have to pay a 1.25% tax only once, to State A. But Bob will have to pay a 1.25% tax twice: once to State A, where he resides, and once to State B, where he earns the income.

"Maryland's tax scheme is inherently discriminatory and operates as a tariff. This identity between Maryland's tax and a tariff is fatal because tariffs are '[t]he paradigmatic example of a law discriminating against interstate commerce.' *West Lynn.*" Justice Alito also rejected the argument, posed by the Solicitor General as well as the dissenting Justices, that constitutional scrutiny may be abated because the "discriminatory" tax fell upon state individual residents (insiders) like the Wynnes, rather than out-of-state corporations (outsiders). "The argument is that this Court need not be concerned about state laws that burden the interstate activities of individuals because those individuals can lobby and vote against legislators who support such measures. But if a State's tax unconstitutionally discriminates against interstate commerce, it is invalid regardless of whether the plaintiff is a resident voter or nonresident of the State. This Court has thus entertained and even sustained dormant Commerce Clause challenges by individual residents of the State that imposed the alleged burden on interstate commerce, *Department of Revenue of Ky.* v. *Davis; Granholm* v. *Heald*, 544 U.S. 460, 469 (2005), and we have also sustained such a challenge to a tax whose burden was borne by in-state consumers, *Bacchus Imports, Ltd.* v. *Dias*, 468 U.S. 263, 272 (1984)."

Justice Scalia (joined by Justice Thomas) dissented, on the ground that the "negative Commerce Clause" is a "judicial fraud." It is not grounded in the text or original meaning of the Constitution, and judges should not expand the Dormant Commerce Clause case law any further. Also dissenting, **Justice Thomas** (joined by Justice Scalia) found the negative understanding of the Commerce Clause inconsistent with the Constitution's regulation of state taxation through the Import Export Clause.

Justice Ginsburg (joined by Justices Scalia and Kagan) dissented from the majority's application of the Court's Dormant Commerce Clause precedents. "Today's decision veers from a principle of interstate and international taxation repeatedly acknowledged by this Court: A nation or State 'may tax *all* the income of its residents, even income earned outside the taxing jurisdiction.' *Oklahoma Tax Comm'n* v. *Chickasaw Nation*, 515 U.S. 450, 462–463 (1995). In accord with this principle, the Court has regularly rejected claims that taxes on a resident's out-of-state income violate the Due Process Clause for lack of a sufficient 'connection' to the taxing State. *Quill Corp.* v. *North Dakota*, 504 U.S. 298, 306 (1992). But under dormant Commerce Clause jurisprudence, the Court decides, a State is not really empowered to tax a resident's income from whatever source derived. In taxing personal income, the Court holds, source-based authority, *i.e.,* authority to tax commerce conducted within a State's territory, boxes in the taxing authority of a taxpayer's domicile."

As a general matter, "States have long favored their residents over nonresidents in the provision of local services. See *Reeves, Inc.* v. *Stake*, 447 U.S. 429, 442 (1980) (such favoritism does not violate the Commerce Clause). Excluding nonresidents from these services, this Court has observed, is rational for it is residents 'who fund the state treasury and whom the State was created to serve.' A taxpayer's home State, then, can hardly be faulted for making support of local government activities an obligation of every resident, regardless of any obligations residents may have to *other* States. Residents, moreover, possess political means, not shared by outsiders, to ensure that the power to tax their income is not abused. 'It is not,' this Court has observed, 'a purpose of the Commerce Clause to protect state residents from their own state taxes.' *Goldberg* v. *Sweet*, 488 U.S. 252, 266 (1989). The reason is evident. Residents are 'insider[s] who presumably [are] able to complain about and change the tax through the [State's] political process.' *Ibid.* Nonresidents, by contrast, are not similarly positioned to 'effec[t] legislative change.' *Ibid.* As Chief Justice Marshall, developer of the Court's Commerce Clause jurisprudence, reasoned: 'In imposing a tax the legislature acts upon its constituents. This is in general a sufficient security against erroneous and oppressive taxation.' *McCulloch* v. *Maryland.* The 'people of a State' can thus 'res[t] confidently on the interest of the legislator, and on the influence of the constituents over their representative, to guard them against . . . abuse" of the "right of taxing themselves and their property.' "

Additionally, Justice Ginsburg pointed to the longstanding state adherence to the rule announced in this case, namely, granting tax credits to residents who pay taxes elsewhere. "As Justice Holmes stated over a century ago, in regard to a 'mode of taxation . . . of long standing, . . . the fact that the system has been in force for a very long time is of itself a strong reason . . . for leaving any improvement that may be desired to the legislature.' *Paddell* v. *City of New York*, 211 U.S. 446, 448 (1908). Only recently, this Court followed that sound advice in resisting a dormant Commerce Clause challenge to a taxing practice with a pedigree as enduring as the practice in this case. See *Department of Revenue of Ky.* v. *Davis.* Surely that advice merits application here, where the challenged tax draws support from both historical practice and numerous decisions of this Court."

Query: What distinguishes *Wynne* from *United Haulers*? Brannon Denning, *The Dormant Commerce Clause Wins One: Five Takes on* Wynne *and*

Direct Marketing Association, 2016 Minn. L. Rev. Headnotes 103, interpreted *United Haulers/Wynne* to suggest that the Roberts Court was abandoning active review of waste-management laws and refocusing its scrutiny on state taxation of interstate commerce. Did that mean the Court was going to strike down more state tax laws under the Dormant Commerce Clause? Daniel Francis argues that *Wynne* was an aberration and that Justice Alito is losing the battle to prop up the Dormant Commerce Clause. Francis, *Decline of the Dormant Commerce Clause,* 94 Denver L. Rev. at 290–92. Does the next case bear out his insights, which were published in 2017?

South Dakota v. Wayfair, Inc.

138 S.Ct. 2080 (2018)

In *Quill Corp. v. North Dakota,* 504 U.S. 298 (1992), the Court had reaffirmed that states could not tax a commercial shipment of goods to an in-state consumer, unless the seller had a physical presence in the taxing state. South Dakota wanted to tax internet sales of goods shipped into the state and joined forty other states and the District of Columbia in asking the Court to overrule *Quill.* **Justice Kennedy**'s opinion for the Court did just that.

"*Quill* is flawed on its own terms. First, the physical presence rule is not a necessary interpretation of the requirement that a state tax must be 'applied to an activity with a substantial nexus with the taxing State.' *Complete Auto.* Second, *Quill* creates rather than resolves market distortions. And third, *Quill* imposes the sort of arbitrary, formalistic distinction that the Court's modern Commerce Clause precedents disavow."

The *Quill* majority expressed concern that without the physical presence rule "a state tax might unduly burden interstate commerce" by subjecting retailers to tax-collection obligations in thousands of different taxing jurisdictions. "But the administrative costs of compliance, especially in the modern economy with its Internet technology, are largely unrelated to whether a company happens to have a physical presence in a State. * * * [U]nder *Quill,* a small company with diverse physical presence might be equally or more burdened by compliance costs than a large remote seller. The physical presence rule is a poor proxy for the compliance costs faced by companies that do business in multiple States."

Justice Kennedy noted the goal of the Commerce Clause "to prevent States from engaging in economic discrimination," but it was " 'not the purpose of the [C]ommerce [C]lause to relieve those engaged in interstate commerce from their just share of state tax burden.' *Complete Auto.* And it is certainly not the purpose of the Commerce Clause to permit the Judiciary to create market distortions." Specifically, "*Quill* puts both local businesses and many interstate businesses with physical presence at a competitive disadvantage relative to remote sellers. Remote sellers can avoid the regulatory burdens of tax collection and can offer *de facto* lower prices caused by the widespread failure of consumers to pay the tax on their own. * * * In effect, *Quill* has come to serve as a judicially created tax shelter for businesses that decide to limit their physical presence and still sell their goods and services to a State's consumers—something that has become easier and more prevalent as technology has advanced.

"Worse still, the rule produces an incentive to avoid physical presence in multiple States. Distortions caused by the desire of businesses to avoid tax collection mean that the market may currently lack storefronts, distribution points, and employment centers that otherwise would be efficient or desirable. The Commerce Clause must not prefer interstate commerce only to the point where a merchant physically crosses state borders. Rejecting the physical presence rule is necessary to ensure that artificial competitive advantages are not created by this Court's precedents. This Court should not prevent States from collecting lawful taxes through a physical presence rule that can be satisfied only if there is an employee or a building in the State."

Justice Kennedy explicitly invoked "modern e-commerce" as a reason to overrule *Quill*, because the Internet rendered its physical presence test indeterminate. "For example, a company with a website accessible in South Dakota may be said to have a physical presence in the State via the customers' computers. A website may leave cookies saved to the customers' hard drives, or customers may download the company's app onto their phones. Or a company may lease data storage that is permanently, or even occasionally, located in South Dakota." *Quill*'s bright-line rule looked a lot fuzzier, and its consequences increasingly "arbitrary."

Justice Kennedy gave a deep bow to *stare decisis*, but the rule of law and reliance interests in following precedent were weaker in this case, and countervailing constitutional interests much stronger. "If it becomes apparent that the Court's Commerce Clause decisions prohibit the States from exercising their lawful sovereign powers in our federal system, the Court should be vigilant in correcting the error. While it can be conceded that Congress has the authority to change the physical presence rule, Congress cannot change the constitutional default rule. It is inconsistent with the Court's proper role to ask Congress to address a false constitutional premise of this Court's own creation. Courts have acted as the front line of review in this limited sphere; and hence it is important that their principles be accurate and logical, whether or not Congress can or will act in response. It is currently the Court, and not Congress, that is limiting the lawful prerogatives of the States."

Justice Thomas concurred, with his standing objection to all the "negative commerce clause" precedents. Writing also for Justices Breyer, Sotomayor, and Kagan, **Chief Justice Roberts** dissented. He agreed that *Quill* and *Bellas Hess* were wrongly decided, but he worried that e-commerce had "grown into a significant and vibrant part of our national economy against the backdrop of established rules, including the physical-presence rule. Any alteration to those rules with the potential to disrupt the development of such a critical segment of the economy should be undertaken by Congress. The

Court should not act on this important question of current economic policy, solely to expiate a mistake it made over 50 years ago."

The Chief Justice pointed out that *stare decisis* has much stronger bite in areas where Congress has the authority to regulate. Unlike most other constitutional issues, Congress has full authority to set baselines and override the Court's Dormant Commerce Clause decisions like *Bellas* and *Quill,* and Congress had considered numerous bills to override those precedents between 2001 and 2017. "[B]y suddenly changing the ground rules, the Court may have waylaid Congress's consideration of the issue. Armed with today's decision, state officials can be expected to redirect their attention from working with Congress on a national solution, to securing new tax revenue from remote retailers."

Unlike the majority, the dissenters worried about "the costs that its decision will impose on retailers. Correctly calculating and remitting sales taxes on all e-commerce sales will likely prove baffling for many retailers." Over 10,000 jurisdictions levy sales taxes, each with different tax rates, exempted goods, product definitions, and standards for determining whether an out-of-state seller has a "substantial presence" in the jurisdiction. New Jersey knitters pay sales tax on yarn purchased for art projects, but not on yarn earmarked for sweaters. Texas taxes sales of plain deodorant at 6.25 percent but imposes no tax on deodorant with antiperspirant. Illinois categorizes Twix and Snickers bars—chocolate-and-caramel confections usually displayed side-by-side in the candy aisle—as food and candy, respectively (Twix have flour; Snickers don't), and taxes them differently." The Chief Justice's mind was boggled by all this complexity: Leave it to Congress to figure out the appropriate balance of state taxation and electronic sales.

Your casebook authors are also scholars of legislation, and we feel compelled to note that the Court had waited a quarter century for a gridlocked Congress to work out the political accommodation advocated by the *Wayfair* dissenters. Congress had done nothing, and there was no likelihood of its ever doing anything. See Brian Galle, *Kill Quill, Keep the Dormant Commerce Clause: History's Lessons on Congressional Control of State Taxation*, 70 Stan. L. Rev. Online 158 (March 2018) (detailed examination of congressional attention to this issue, and Congress's hopeless deadlock).

NOTE ON STATE LAWS HAVING EXTRATERRITORIAL EFFECT

The Court identified state laws having extraterritorial effects as a Commerce Clause problem in *Brown-Forman Distillers Corp. v. New York State Liquor Auth.*, 476 U.S. 573 (1986). Under review was a New York law requiring liquor dealers selling wholesale in the state to file a price schedule every month and to sell in New York at the lowest price the distiller charged in any other state for that month. The Court struck it down under the *Baldwin* line of cases: "Economic protectionism is not limited to attempts to convey advantages to local merchants; it may include attempts to give local consumers an advantage over consumers in other States." New York could regulate the sale or even the price of liquor within its borders, but the Commerce Clause sets limits on its ability to "project" its laws into other states by regulating the price to be paid in those states. In *Healy v. Beer Institute*, 491 U.S. 324 (1989), the Court invalidated a Connecticut law requiring beer companies to post prices every month and to certify that the posted prices were no higher than the prices they charged in three neighboring states. Because "the practical effect of the regulation is to control conduct beyond the boundaries of the State," the Court held the law subject to strict scrutiny. Because the "extraterritorial effect" of the law was to prevent "brewers from undertaking competitive pricing in Massachusetts based on prevailing market conditions," it was per se invalid.

It is not exactly clear how far the Court's rule against extraterritorial regulation reaches. Before these alcohol cases, the Due Process and Full Faith and Credit Clauses were the Constitution's mechanisms for reviewing extraterritorial application of state law. See *Allstate Ins. Co. v. Hague*, 449 U.S. 302 (1981). *Allstate* only bars extraterritorial application of state law when there are no meaningful contacts between the regulated activity and the regulating state. In contrast, *Brown-Forman* and *Healy* bar application of state law to extraterritorial economic activity even when it has substantial and harmful effects within the state. Note that *Allstate* construes a written constitutional provision, while *Healy* applies the nontextual Dormant Commerce Clause.[78]

2.   State Rules Burdening Interstate Commerce

In a portion of *United Haulers* that we omitted, the Chief Justice considered a further argument, that the ordinance imposed an undue burden on interstate commerce, and held that it did not. (Only three other Justices joined that part of Roberts's opinion.) He was invoking a line of cases evaluating state regulations having a *disruptive effect* on interstate commerce. Judicial review of local laws with effects on interstate commerce was a feature of the Court's Commerce Clause jurisprudence since *Cooley* and *Willson*. See Francis, *The Decline of the Dormant Commerce Clause,* 94 Denver L. Rev. at 292–98. The modern, post-New Deal Court has struggled with that doctrine, as almost any state law has an effect on interstate commerce. Leading cases involved state regulation of trucks.

For example, in *South Carolina State Highway Dep't v. Barnwell Bros.*, 303 U.S. 177 (1938), the district court invalidated a South Carolina statute forbidding motor trucks whose width exceeded 90 inches and whose weight exceeded 20,000 pounds. The court found that the limitations imposed substantial burdens on interstate commerce, because 85% to 90% of the trucks in interstate commerce were 96 inches wide and weighed more than

---

[78]   For an argument that the Full Faith & Credit Clause should be more aggressively applied, see Kermit Roosevelt III, *The Myth of Choice of Law: Rethinking Conflicts*, 97 Mich. L. Rev. 2448 (1999).

20,000 pounds. Still, the Supreme Court reversed, because the state regulation was at least "fairly debatable."

In *Southern Pacific Co. v. Arizona*, 325 U.S. 761 (1945), however, the Court struck down an Arizona statute forbidding the operation of railroad trains of more than 14 passenger or 70 freight cars. The Court stated its now-classic rendition of the main dormant Commerce Clause inquiry: "Hence the matters for ultimate determination here are the nature and extent of the burden which the state regulation of interstate trains, adopted as a safety measure, imposes on interstate commerce, and whether the relative weights of the state and national interests involved are such as to make inapplicable the rule, generally observed, that the free flow of interstate commerce and its freedom from local restraints in matters requiring uniformity of regulation are interests safeguarded by the Commerce Clause from state interference." The Court concluded that the state went "too far," based upon factual findings that the rule greatly disrupted interstate train schedules and did not significantly enhance safety (because safety gains through shorter trains were more than offset by safety losses due to the larger number of trains). Why the different result from the *Barnwell Bros.* case (both opinions were by Harlan Stone)? The Court emphasized the greater interest states have in highway safety versus the traditional federal interest in train regulation.

After *Southern Pacific*, the Court followed a fact-based balancing test (local benefits versus burden on interstate commerce), which has developed along the following lines: In determining the local benefits, the Court asks whether the state had a rational basis for enacting the law. Safety measures obviously qualify, and indeed carry a presumption of validity. See *Bibb v. Navajo Freight Lines, Inc.*, 359 U.S. 520 (1959). A finding of a legitimate localized purpose does not itself save the state law, however. The Court also evaluates the burden on interstate commerce and balances that against the local benefit. In balancing these interests, the Court considers the comparative impairment of the local and national interests (i.e., is the burden on commerce much more substantial than the benefit to safety, or vice versa?) and the even-handedness of the law (i.e., does it apply quite differently to intrastate transportation than to interstate transportation?). A leading statement of the test is in *Pike v. Bruce Church, Inc.*, 397 U.S. 137 (1970):

> Where the statute regulates evenhandedly to effectuate a legitimate local public interest, and its effects on interstate commerce are only incidental, it will be upheld unless the burden imposed on such commerce is clearly excessive in relation to the putative local benefits. If a legitimate local purpose is found, then the question becomes one of degree. And the extent of the burden that will be tolerated will of course depend on the nature of the

local interest involved, and on whether it could be promoted as well with a lesser impact on interstate activities.

Consider the application of this test in the following controversial case.

KASSEL V. CONSOLIDATED FREIGHTWAYS CORP.

450 U.S. 662, 101 S.Ct. 1309, 67 L.Ed.2d 580 (1981)

JUSTICE POWELL announced the judgment of the Court and delivered an opinion in which JUSTICE WHITE, JUSTICE BLACKMUN, and JUSTICE STEVENS joined.

[Consolidated Freightways Corporation of Delaware is one of the largest common carriers in the country. Consolidated carries commodities through Iowa on Interstate 80, the principal east-west route linking New York, Chicago, and the west coast, and on Interstate 35, a major north-south route. Consolidated mainly uses two kinds of trucks: a *semi*, a 55-foot long, three-axle tractor pulling a 40-foot two-axle trailer; and a *twin* or *double*, a 65-foot long, two-axle tractor pulling a single-axle trailer which, in turn, pulls a single-axle dolly and a second single-axle trailer. Consolidated would like to use 65-foot doubles on many of its trips through Iowa, but the state—alone in the Midwest or West—prohibits the use of 65-foot doubles within its borders.

[Under an Iowa statute, most truck combinations were restricted to 55 feet in length. Doubles, mobile homes, trucks carrying vehicles such as tractors and other farm equipment, and singles hauling livestock were permitted to be as long as 60 feet. Notwithstanding these restrictions, Iowa's statute permitted cities abutting the state line by local ordinance to adopt the length limitations of the adjoining State. Where a city had exercised this option, otherwise oversized trucks were permitted within the city limits and in nearby commercial zones. Also, an Iowa truck manufacturer could obtain a permit to ship trucks that were as large as 70 feet, and permits were available to move oversized mobile homes, provided that the unit was to be moved from a point within Iowa or delivered for an Iowa resident.

[Consolidated challenged the statute as an unconstitutional burden on interstate commerce. Iowa defended the law as a reasonable safety measure. After a fourteen-day trial, the District Court ruled as a matter of fact that the double was as safe on the road as the semi and, more specifically, that the 65-foot double was as safe as, if not safer than, the 60-foot double and the 55-foot semi. "Twins and semis have different characteristics. Twins are more maneuverable, are less sensitive to wind, and create less splash and spray. However, they are more likely than semis to jackknife or upset. They can be backed only for a short distance. The negative characteristics are not such that they render the twin less safe than semis overall. Semis are more stable but are more likely to 'rear end' another vehicle." In light of these findings, the District Court applied the standard in *Raymond Motor Transportation, Inc. v. Rice*, 434 U.S. 429 (1978), and concluded that the state law impermissibly burdened interstate commerce. The Supreme Court affirmed.]

* * * [A] State's power to regulate commerce is never greater than in matters traditionally of local concern. For example, regulations that touch upon safety—especially highway safety—are those that "the Court has been most reluctant to invalidate." *Raymond*. Indeed, "if safety justifications are not illusory, the court will not second-guess legislative judgment about their importance in comparison with related burdens on interstate commerce." *Raymond* (Blackmun, J., concurring). Those who would challenge such bona fide safety regulations must overcome a "strong presumption of validity." *Bibb*.

But the incantation of a purpose to promote the public health or safety does not insulate a state law from Commerce Clause attack. Regulations designed for that salutary purpose nevertheless may further the purpose so marginally, and interfere with commerce so substantially, as to be invalid under the Commerce Clause. In the Court's recent unanimous decision in *Raymond*, we declined to "accept the State's contention that the inquiry under the Commerce Clause is ended without a weighing of the asserted safety purpose against the degree of interference with interstate commerce." This "weighing" by a court requires—and indeed the constitutionality of the state regulation depends on—"a sensitive consideration of the weight and nature of the state regulatory concern in light of the extent of the burden imposed on the course of interstate commerce." * * *

In *Raymond*, the Court held that a Wisconsin statute that precluded the use of 65-foot doubles violated the Commerce Clause. This case is *Raymond* revisited. Here, as in *Raymond*, the State failed to present any persuasive evidence that 65-foot doubles are less safe than 55-foot singles. Moreover, Iowa's law is now out of step with the laws of all other Midwestern and Western States. Iowa thus substantially burdens the interstate flow of goods by truck. In the absence of congressional action to set uniform standards, some burdens associated with state safety regulations must be tolerated. But where, as here, the State's safety interest has been found to be illusory, and its regulations impair significantly the federal interest in efficient and safe interstate transportation, the state law cannot be harmonized with the Commerce Clause. * * *

[Iowa made a more serious effort to support the safety rationale of its law than had been made in *Raymond,* but through its own experience and expert studies Consolidated established that 65-foot doubles were at least as safe overall as 55-foot singles and 60-foot doubles. Indeed, the Iowa

Department of Transportation found that "[s]ixty-five foot twin trailer combinations have *not* been shown by experiences in other states to be less safe than 60-foot twin trailer combinations *or* conventional tractor-semitrailers." Consolidated also demonstrated that Iowa's law added about $12.6 million each year to the costs of trucking companies. Consolidated itself incurred about $2 million per year in increased costs. Finally, there was evidence that Iowa's law might aggravate, rather than ameliorate, the problem of highway accidents. Because 65-foot doubles could carry more freight without added safety concerns, and because the Iowa law would require more highway miles to be driven to transport the same quantity of goods, the district court found that the law tended to *increase* the number of accidents, and to shift the incidence of them from Iowa to other states.]

[Iowa implored the Justices to "defer" to the legislative line-drawing.] The Court normally does accord "special deference" to state highway safety regulations. *Raymond*. This traditional deference "derives in part from the assumption that where such regulations do not discriminate on their face against interstate commerce, their burden usually falls on local economic interests as well as other States' economic interests, thus insuring that a State's own political processes will serve as a check against unduly burdensome regulations." Less deference to the legislative judgment is due, however, where the local regulation bears disproportionately on out-of-state residents and businesses. Such a disproportionate burden is apparent here. Iowa's scheme, although generally banning large doubles from the State, nevertheless has several exemptions that secure to Iowans many of the benefits of large trucks while shunting to neighboring States many of the costs associated with their use.

At the time of trial there were two particularly significant exemptions. First, singles hauling livestock or farm vehicles were permitted to be as long as 60 feet. As the Court of Appeals noted, this provision undoubtedly was helpful to local interests. Cf. *Raymond* (exemption in Wisconsin for milk shippers). Second, cities abutting other States were permitted to enact local ordinances adopting the larger length limitation of the neighboring State. This exemption offered the benefits of longer trucks to individuals and businesses in important border cities without burdening Iowa's highways with interstate through traffic. Cf. *Raymond* (exemption in Wisconsin for shipments from local plants).

The origin of the "border cities exemption" also suggests that Iowa's statute may not have been designed to ban dangerous trucks, but rather to discourage interstate truck traffic. In 1974, the legislature passed a bill that would have permitted 65-foot doubles in the State. Governor Ray vetoed the bill. He said:

> I find sympathy with those who are doing business in our
> state and whose enterprises could gain from increased cargo

carrying ability by trucks. However, with this bill, the Legislature has pursued a course that would benefit only a few Iowa-based companies while providing a great advantage for out-of-state trucking firms and competitors at the expense of our Iowa citizens.

After the veto, the "border cities exemption" was immediately enacted and signed by the Governor.

It is thus far from clear that Iowa was motivated primarily by a judgment that 65-foot doubles are less safe than 55-foot singles. Rather, Iowa seems to have hoped to limit the use of its highways by deflecting some through traffic. * * *

JUSTICE BRENNAN, with whom JUSTICE MARSHALL joins, concurring in the judgment.

Both the opinion of my Brother Powell and the opinion of my Brother Rehnquist are predicated upon the supposition that the constitutionality of a state regulation is determined by the factual record created by the State's lawyers in the trial court. But that supposition cannot be correct, for it would make the constitutionality of state laws and regulations depend on the vagaries of litigation rather than on the judgments made by the State's lawmakers.

In considering a Commerce Clause challenge to a state regulation, the judicial task is to balance the burden imposed on commerce against the local benefits sought to be achieved by the State's *lawmakers*. In determining those benefits, a court should focus ultimately on the regulatory purposes identified by the lawmakers and on the evidence before or available to them that might have supported their judgment. [The actual purpose of the Iowa lawmakers was to discourage interstate truck traffic on Iowa highways, not to improve traffic safety.]

[A 1974 statute] would have increased the maximum length of twin trailer trucks operable in Iowa from 60 to 65 feet. But Governor Ray * * * vetoed the legislation. The legislature did not override the veto, and the present regulation was thus maintained. In his veto, Governor Ray did not rest his decision on the conclusion that 55-foot singles and 60-foot doubles are any safer than 65-foot doubles, or on any other safety consideration inherent in the type or size of the trucks. Rather, his principal concern was that to allow 65-foot doubles would "basically ope[n] our state to literally thousands and thousands more trucks per year." This increase in interstate truck traffic would, in the Governor's estimation, greatly increase highway maintenance costs, which are borne by the citizens of the State, and increase the number of accidents and fatalities within the State. The legislative response was not to override the veto, but to accede to the Governor's action, and in accord with this basic premise, to enact a "border cities exemption." This permitted cities within border areas to allow 65-foot doubles while otherwise maintaining the 60-foot limit throughout the State to discourage interstate truck traffic. * * *

This Court's heightened deference to the judgments of state lawmakers in the field of safety is largely attributable to a judicial disinclination to weigh the interests of safety against other societal interests, such as the economic interest in the free flow of commerce. Thus, "if safety justifications are not illusory, the Court will not second-guess legislative judgment about their importance in *comparison with related burdens on interstate commerce.*" *Raymond* (Blackmun, J., concurring) (emphasis added). Here, the decision of Iowa's lawmakers to promote *Iowa's* safety and other interests at the direct expense of the safety and other interests of neighboring States merits no such deference. No special judicial acuity is demanded to perceive that this sort of parochial legislation violates the Commerce Clause. As Justice Cardozo has written, the Commerce Clause "was framed upon the theory that the peoples of the several states must sink or swim together, and that in the long run prosperity and salvation are in union and not division." *Baldwin v. G.A.F. Seelig, Inc.*

JUSTICE REHNQUIST, with whom THE CHIEF JUSTICE [BURGER] and JUSTICE STEWART join, dissenting. [*Dissent*]

The result in this case suggests, to paraphrase Justice Jackson, that the only state truck-length limit "that is valid is one which this court has not been able to get its hands on." * * *

It is necessary to elaborate somewhat on the facts as presented in the plurality opinion to appreciate fully what the Court does today. Iowa's action in limiting the length of trucks which may travel on its highways is in no sense unusual. Every State in the Union regulates the length of vehicles permitted to use the public roads. [*every state limits length*] Nor is Iowa a renegade in having length limits which operate to exclude the 65-foot doubles favored by Consolidated. These trucks are prohibited in other areas of the country as well, some 17 States and the District of Columbia, including all of New England and most of the Southeast. While pointing out that Consolidated carries commodities through Iowa on Interstate 80, "the principal east-west route linking New York, Chicago, and the west coast," the plurality neglects to note that both Pennsylvania and New Jersey, through which Interstate 80 runs before reaching New York, also ban 65-foot doubles. In short, the persistent effort in the plurality opinion to paint Iowa as an oddity standing alone to block commerce carried in 65-foot doubles is simply not supported by the facts. * * *

The District Court approached the case as if the question were whether Consolidated's 65-foot trucks were as safe as others permitted on Iowa highways, and the Court of Appeals as if its task were to determine if the District Court's factual findings in this regard were "clearly erroneous."

this
rev
issue

The question, however, is whether the Iowa Legislature has acted rationally in regulating vehicle lengths and whether the safety benefits from this regulation are more than slight or problematical. * * * "Since the adoption of one weight or width regulation, rather than another, is a legislative and not a judicial choice, its constitutionality is not to be determined by weighing in the judicial scales the merits of the legislative choice and rejecting it if the weight of evidence presented in court appears to favor a different standard." *Barnwell Brothers.* * * *

It must be emphasized that there is nothing in the laws of nature which make 65-foot doubles an obvious norm. Consolidated operates 65-foot doubles on many of its routes simply because that is the largest size permitted in many States through which Consolidated travels. Doubles can and do come in smaller sizes; indeed, when Iowa adopted the present 60-foot limit in 1963, it was in accord with [American Association of State Highway and Transportation Officials] recommendations. Striking down Iowa's law because Consolidated has made a voluntary business decision to employ 65-foot doubles, a decision based on the actions of other state legislatures, would essentially be compelling Iowa to yield to the policy choices of neighboring States. Under our constitutional scheme, however, there is only one legislative body which can pre-empt the rational policy determination of the Iowa Legislature and that is Congress. Forcing Iowa to yield to the policy choices of neighboring States perverts the primary purpose of the Commerce Clause, that of vesting power to regulate interstate commerce in Congress, where all the States are represented. * * *

don't look
at motive

not
protectionist

Both the plurality and concurring opinions attach great significance to the Governor's veto of a bill passed by the Iowa Legislature permitting 65-foot doubles. Whatever views one may have about the significance of legislative motives, it must be emphasized that the law which the Court strikes down today was not passed to achieve the protectionist goals the plurality and the concurrence ascribe to the Governor. Iowa's 60-foot length limit was established in 1963, at a time when very few States permitted 65-foot doubles. Striking down legislation on the basis of asserted legislative motives is dubious enough, but the plurality and concurrence strike down the legislation involved in this case because of asserted impermissible motives for *not* enacting *other* legislation, motives which could not possibly have been present when the legislation under challenge here was considered and passed. Such action is, so far as I am aware, unprecedented in this Court's history.

NOTES ON KASSEL *AND* JUDICIAL EVALUATION OF STATE *LAWS* BURDENING INTERSTATE COMMERCE

1.   *The Debate About the Legitimacy of Balancing.* The *Pike/Southern Pacific* balancing test recalls the Court's debate in the 1940s over whether or

not the Court is institutionally competent to engage in serious utilitarian (cost-benefit) analysis. Compare the debate between Justices Frankfurter and Black in *Adamson v. California* (Chapter 5, § 1), over whether the Due Process Clause of the Fourteenth Amendment selectively "incorporates" only the most "fundamental" of the Bill of Rights protections and not all of them. Justice Black, who opposed "balancing" in *Adamson*, wrote a scathing dissent in *Southern Pacific*. He found the trial court proceeding in the case "extraordinary" in second-guessing the legislature's evaluation of the costs and benefits in a long-running battle between railroads and railroad workers at the state and national level. "[This] new pattern of trial procedure makes it necessary for a judge to hear all the evidence offered as to why a legislature passed a law and to make findings of fact as to the validity of those reasons. [In] this respect, [this] Court today is acting as a 'super-legislature.' " What would Justice Black have said about the trial record in *Kassel*?

The late Justice Scalia articulated a position similar to that of Justice Black:

> I do not know what qualifies us to make [the] ultimate (and most ineffable) judgment as to whether, given the importance-level x, and effectiveness-level y, the worth of the statute is "outweighed" by impact-on-commerce z. One commentator [Donald Regan] has suggested that * * * we do not in fact mean what we say when we declare that statutes that neither discriminate against commerce nor present a threat of multiple and inconsistent burdens might nonetheless be unconstitutional under a "balancing" test. If he is not correct, he ought to be. As long as a State's [law does] not discriminate against out-of-state interests [on its face], it should survive this Court's scrutiny. [Beyond] that, it is for Congress to prescribe its invalidity.

CTS Corporation v. Dynamics Corporation, 481 U.S. 69 (1987) (Scalia, J., concurring and referencing the prescient analysis of Regan, *Making Sense of the Dormant Commerce Clause*, 84 Mich. L. Rev. 1291).[79] Since 1987, the Court has not invalidated a state law based upon the *Pike* balancing test. See Francis, *The Decline of the Dormant Commerce Clause*, 94 Denver L. Rev. at 299–303.

Is *Kassel* a good example of the perils of judicial balancing? After you read the plurality and concurring opinions, is there any basis for deferring to the state judgment, as Justice Rehnquist argues? The evidence seemed overwhelming that there were no safety reasons supporting Iowa's policy— beyond the stated reason that, if Iowa could shift (export) interstate truck traffic to other states, *Iowa* drivers would be safer, even if at the expense of safety in *Minnesota* or *Missouri* (to which traffic would be diverted). This seems

---

[79] Other commentators agree with Scalia and Regan that the Court is not the best decision maker in these kinds of cases. See Julian Eule, *Laying the Dormant Commerce Clause to Rest*, 91 Yale L.J. 425 (1982); Daniel A. Farber, *State Regulation and the Dormant Commerce Clause*, 3 Const. Comm. 395 (1986); Robert Sedler, *The Negative Commerce Clause as a Restriction on State Regulation and Taxation: An Analysis in Terms of Constitutional Structure*, 31 Wayne St. L. Rev. 885 (1985).

not only irrational, but politically perverse, and a much better example of the Stone/Tushnet representation-reinforcement analysis than the facial discrimination cases such as *City of Philadelphia* and *Carbone*. If you follow Justice Scalia, are you not sacrificing the whole point of the Dormant Commerce Clause, namely, clearing the channels of interstate commerce?

2.   *Congress as a Forum for Curing Discriminatory Effects on Interstate Commerce.* If the ills described in the *Kassel* opinions are genuine and interstate commerce really is being clogged, Congress and the President have incentives to intervene. Handed down in the pre-gridlock era, *Kassel* triggered a response. In 1984, Congress amended the Surface Transportation Act to authorize state governors to petition the Secretary of Transportation to exclude doubles and other oversize vehicles from portions of the interstate highway system if the Secretary were persuaded by state showings of real safety problems.[80] Thus, state safety regulation is preempted, but safety issues are resolved at the national rather than state level and by a flexible fact-finding process that can respond to new evidence and political considerations. Is this not preferable to having the Court balance costs and benefits from case to case? Would the 1984 statute have been enacted without *Kassel*, though?

3.   *The Anomaly of Creeping Unconstitutionality.* Iowa bought itself trouble by building exceptions into the state law that favored in-state interests. The Court has had few cases in which a truly nondiscriminatory state measure has been challenged because it unduly burdens interstate commerce. *Bibb* is perhaps the best example. In that case, Illinois required trucks operating in that state to have contour rear-fender mudguards; 45 states authorized the use of straight mudguards, and Arkansas actually required the straight ones and outlawed the contour ones. The Court concluded that the Illinois law was unconstitutional because it added little to highway safety and seriously disrupted interstate commerce (by requiring a carrier to shift cargo from one kind of carrier to another as state lines were crossed). Self-serving motives can be identified for the Illinois regulation, but the case stands for the proposition that even without them, and even without a clear showing that the regulation had effects favoring in-state interests, state regulation can nonetheless unduly burden the flow of interstate commerce.

Without the in-state exceptions, and Governor Ray's indiscreet veto statement, the Iowa situation was similar to that in *Bibb*: A regulation surely constitutional when it was adopted in 1963 became unconstitutional over time because it fell out of step with the allowances of other midwestern and western states, as Justice Rehnquist's dissent charged. Even Richard Collins, who endorses the Court's balancing approach, has expressed reservations about applying it to invalidate state statutes that burden commerce only because they have grown inconsistent with the laws of other states.[81] Why? Would his

---

[80]   See Tandem Truck Safety Act of 1984, Pub. L. No. 98–554, §§ 102–03, 98 Stat. 2829–30.

[81]   See Richard A. Collins, *Justice Scalia and the Elusive Idea of Discrimination Against Interstate Commerce*, 20 N. Mex. L. Rev. 555 (1990).

rationale apply to *Kassel*, where there was damning evidence concerning the reason Iowa declined to conform to the policy adopted by surrounding states?

PROBLEM 7-10:
SHOULD PIKE AND KASSEL BE OVERRULED?

The Court's overruling *Quill* and the appointment of Neil Gorsuch, who has written skeptically of the Dormant Commerce Clause, see *Direct Marketing Ass'n v. Brohl,* 814 F.3d 1129, 1147–51 (10th Cir. 2016) (Gorsuch, J., concurring), suggest that the Justices might be open to further doctrinal curtailments of the Dormant Commerce Clause. Thoughtful scholars have expressed skepticism that the Court will toss out 200 years of precedent on this subject, but they might be open to narrowing the potentially broad ambit of the Dormant Commerce Clause. E.g., Edward Zelinsky, *Comparing* Wayfair *and* Wynne*: Lessons on the Future of the Dormant Commerce Clause,* Chapman L. Rev. (forthcoming 2018).

One vulnerable line of precedent is *Pike v. Bruce Church* and the many decisions protecting truckers against state regulation, including the *Kassel* plurality opinion. If a state regulation or tax merely burdens but does not discriminate against interstate commerce, should courts apply anything more scrutinizing than the rational basis approach? Whatever arguments against the Dormant Commerce Clause one might pose from the constitutional text, structure, or original meaning, those arguments are much stronger against the *Pike* balancing test that applies even if there is no explicit or intended discrimination against interstate commerce. Compare the Powell and Rehnquist opinions in *Kassel*: Do judges have a comparative advantage in this kind of policy balancing? See Regan, *Making Sense of the Dormant Commerce Clause,* 84 Mich. L. Rev. 1291 (no); Francis, *The Decline of the Dormant Commerce Clause,* 94 Denver L. Rev. at 299–303 (agreeing with Regan and observing that the Court as of 2017 had not struck down state laws based upon the *Pike* balancing approach since 1987).

Note also the obvious contrast between activist judicial review of facially neutral state laws having a *discriminatory effect on interstate commerce* (*Kassel*) and nonactivist judicial review of facially neutral state laws having a *discriminatory effect on racial minorities or women* (*Washington v. Davis* (Chapter 3, § 1B) and *Feeney* (Chapter 4, § 2B)). Can this contrast be defended?

If you were advising a Supreme Court Justice, what would you suggest she do about *Pike*? If *Pike* were overruled, should *Kassel* also be overruled?

3. Exceptions to Dormant Commerce Clause Review

Granholm v. Heald

544 U.S. 460 (2005)

Michigan and New York regulated the sale and importation of wine through three-tier systems requiring separate licenses for producers, wholesalers, and retailers. Their regulatory schemes allowed in-state, but not out-of-state, wineries to make direct sales to consumers. Because this differential treatment explicitly discriminated against interstate commerce by limiting the emerging and significant direct-sale business, **Justice Kennedy**'s opinion for the Court had no difficulty holding it a violation of the Dormant Commerce Clause rule against "differential treatment of in-state and out-of-state economic interests that benefits the former and burdens the latter." Justice Kennedy waxed eloquently against the evils of a "low-level trade war" among the states created by such discriminatory rules, and invoked the virtual "per se rule of invalidity" recognized in *City of Philadelphia*.

No Justice disputed this much of Kennedy's analysis, but **Justice Thomas**'s dissenting opinion (joined by Chief Justice Rehnquist and Justices Stevens and O'Connor) argued that Congress authorized plenary state regulation of liquor in the Webb-Kenyon Act, which prohibits any "shipment or transportation" of alcoholic beverages "into any State" when those beverages are "intended, by any person interested therein, to be received, possessed, sold, or in any manner used . . . in violation of any law of such State." 27 U.S.C. § 122. The Court in *McCormick & Co. v. Brown*, 286 U.S. 131, 139–40 (1932), interpreted the Act to free the states of Dormant Commerce Clause claims, and Congress reenacted the statute in 1935 under this assumption about its meaning.

Justice Kennedy, in turn, did not dispute that Congress can authorize state laws that would otherwise violate the Dormant Commerce Clause but replied with a clear statement rule: the "Webb-Kenyon Act expresses no clear congressional intent to depart from the principle . . . that discrimination against out-of-state goods is disfavored." (*McCormick*, for example, upheld a state law that was nondiscriminatory.) Justice Thomas disagreed. He not only argued that the plain meaning of the statute was clear enough to demonstrate a congressional allowance of plenary state regulation of liquor, but also argued that the legislative history and background of the Act demonstrated a legislative intent to allow discriminatory state laws. The Court ruled in *Scott v. Donald*, 165 U.S. 58 (1897), that earlier congressional authorizing legislation did not allow the states to enact laws discriminating against out-of-state liquor by barring importation for personal use. Justice Thomas relied on legislative history to show that Congress meant to override *Scott* and reinstate the states' plenary authority when it enacted Webb-Kenyon. (Justice Kennedy maintained that the statute left *Scott*'s nondiscrimination holding intact.)

Justice Thomas also argued that the Michigan/New York schemes were saved by Section 2 of the Twenty-First Amendment: "The transportation or importation into any State, Territory, or possession of the United States for delivery or use therein of intoxicating liquors, in violation of the laws thereof, is hereby prohibited." The language is broader than that of Webb-Kenyon and broad enough to authorize discriminatory as well as nondiscriminatory state liquor statutes. Indeed, the Court so held in *State Bd. of Equalization of Cal. v. Young's Market Co.*, 299 U.S. 59 (1936). California law facially discriminated against beer importers and, by extension, out-of-state producers. The Court held that this explicit discrimination against out-of-state beer products came within the terms of the Twenty-First Amendment, and therefore did not run afoul of the Dormant Commerce Clause. The Court reasoned that the Twenty-First Amendment's words are "apt to confer upon the State the power to forbid all importations which do not comply with the conditions which it prescribes." The Court reaffirmed *Young's Market* in subsequent cases, and the states engaged in all manner of discriminatory liquor-regulatory schemes, similar to those in New York and Michigan, and without serious constitutional quarrel after the *Young's Market* cases. (In a separate dissent, **Justice Stevens** personally recalled the context of the Twenty-First Amendment to support Justice Thomas's analysis.)

Justice Kennedy responded that the Court's Twenty-First Amendment jurisprudence took the same turn its Commerce Clause jurisprudence did after the 1930s—toward greater limitations on state authority. In *Bacchus Imports, Ltd. v. Dias*, 468 U.S. 263 (1984), for example, the Court struck down a Hawaii statute exempting local products from the state's 20% excise tax on liquor. The Court held that the Twenty-First Amendment did not implicitly repeal or modify the Commerce Clause and therefore did not authorize state laws amounting to "mere economic protectionism." The Amendment's "central purpose * * * was not to empower States to favor local liquor industries by erecting barriers to competition." Justice Thomas urged the Court to overrule or limit *Bacchus*, not cast aside a century of liquor jurisprudence and the plain meaning of the Twenty-First Amendment.

NOTE ON THE MARKET-PARTICIPANT EXCEPTION

The Court in *City of Philadelphia* noted a possible loophole in the Dormant Commerce Clause, for the Court expressed no opinion regarding a state's power to "restrict to state residents access to state-owned resources [or] to spend state funds solely on behalf of state residents and businesses" (footnote 6 of the Court's opinion). The latter exemption for discretionary state spending is related to the "market participant" exception to the Dormant Commerce Clause the Court recognized in *Hughes v. Alexandria Scrap Corp.*, 426 U.S. 794 (1976). Under this exception, when the state participates as an actor in the market, it can behave in discriminatory ways not permitted when it acts in its regulatory and taxing capacity. In *Alexandria Scrap*, Maryland offered a bounty for abandoned cars, in order to speed up their removal from public spaces, but conditioned the bounty in ways that favored in-state over out-of-state processing of the cars. The Court refused to apply the *Pike* balancing test, because it held that the Dormant Commerce Clause does not cover situations where "the entry by the State itself in the market as a purchaser, in effect, of a potential article of interstate commerce creates a burden upon that commerce if the State restricts its trade to its own citizens or businesses within the State." (Note that this exception might swallow up the rule of *City of*

Philadelphia, as more than 80% of the nation's landfill is owned and operated by state and local governments.[82])

Neither the reach nor the precise rationale for the market participant exception is clear.[83] *Alexandria Scrap*'s rationale was that the Dormant Commerce Clause only targets state regulation of a preexisting market, not state creation of a market on terms the state desires. There is no indication of a constitutional design to limit the ability of the states to spend their own money or to operate in the free market (see Madison's original statement of the dormant principle in the Commerce Clause, as well as the early cases, such as *Gibbons*). When states "act like" private proprietors, they are subject to more restrictions on their activities, and so ought to have at least some of the freedom of action that private proprietors have. But if the Dormant Commerce Clause has essentially been made up by the Court to prevent economic balkanization, why should the state's capacity as a proprietor versus a regulator, or as a spender rather than tax collector of money, make a constitutional difference? For example, if Clarkstown itself had owned the waste treatment plant, should its regulation have been acceptable in *Carbone*? Would it be constitutional for Clarkstown to tax all companies collecting waste, and then use those monies to subsidize the private waste treatment plant? To subsidize a waste treatment plant it owns? See *C.A. Carbone, Inc. v. County of Rockland*, 2014 WL 1202699 (W.D.N.Y. March 24, 2014) (this plan would be constitutional under *United Haulers*); Francis, *The Decline of the Dormant Commerce Clause,* 94 Denver L. Rev. at 303–09 (expanding market participant exception has rendered Justice Alito's *Carbone* decision irrelevant).

Alternatively, the Court said in *Reeves, Inc. v. Stake*, 447 U.S. 429 (1980) (upholding South Dakota's policy of restricting the sale of cement from a state-owned plant to state residents), "the competing considerations in cases involving state proprietary action often will be subtle, complex, politically charged, and difficult to assess under traditional Commerce Clause analysis. Given these factors * * * as a rule, the adjustment of interests in this context is a task better suited for Congress than this Court." This seems at odds with *Kassel* and the activist philosophy of the Dormant Commerce Clause cases generally.

Donald Regan argues that justification of the market participant exception rests upon the functional differences between discriminatory state spending, as opposed to discriminatory state taxes or regulations.[84] Spending

---

[82] See David Pomper, Note, *Recycling* Philadelphia v. New Jersey: *The Dormant Commerce Clause, Postindustrial "Natural" Resources, and the Solid Waste Crisis,* 137 U. Pa. L. Rev. 1309 (1989).

[83] *Alexandria Scrap* has been followed in *White v. Massachusetts Council of Constr. Employers, Inc.*, 460 U.S. 204 (1983), and *Reeves, Inc. v. Stake*, 447 U.S. 429 (1980). The Court in *South-Central Timber Dev. v. Wunnicke*, 467 U.S. 82 (1984), fractured badly on the application of the exception to Alaska's requirement tying the sale of timber owned by the state to processing the timber in Alaska, rather than out-of-state, by purchasers. The Court majority invalidated the state rule, but there was no rationale commanding a majority of the Justices. In *United Haulers*, the Chief Justice mentioned the market participant exception but did not rely on it.

[84] See Regan, *Making Sense of the Dormant Commerce Clause*, 84 Mich. L. Rev. at 1194. For other thoughtful discussions, see Dan T. Coenen, *Untangling the Market-Participant Exemption to*

discriminations are less likely to trigger the prisoners' dilemma of spiraling retaliations that open discriminations and even indirect regulations might trigger. In light of Professor Regan's theory, is the following case wrongly decided, under either the market participant exception or general principles of the Dormant Commerce Clause?

West Lynn Creamery, Inc. v. Healy

512 U.S. 186 (1994)

Massachusetts imposed a nondiscriminatory tax on wholesale milk transactions and used the result to fund cash payments to the state's struggling dairy farmers. The Court, per **Justice Stevens**, held that this scheme, when viewed holistically, had the same economic effect as a tariff. "Its avowed purpose and its undisputed effect are to allow higher cost Massachusetts dairy farmers to compete with lower cost dairy farmers in other States. The 'premium payments' are effectively a tax which makes milk produced out of State more expensive. Although the tax also applies to milk produced in Massachusetts, its effect on Massachusetts producers is entirely (indeed more than) offset by the subsidy provided exclusively to Massachusetts dairy farmers. Like an ordinary tariff, the tax is thus effectively imposed on only out-of-state products. The pricing order thus allows Massachusetts dairy farmers who produce at a higher cost to sell at or below the price charged by lower cost out-of-state producers. This effect renders the program unconstitutional, because it, like a tariff, 'neutralize[s] advantages belonging to the place of origin.'"

The state defended with the argument that each of the components of its program—the nondiscriminatory tax and the discriminatory subsidy—was constitutional. Justice Stevens replied: "However, when a nondiscriminatory tax is coupled with a subsidy to one of the groups hurt by the tax, a state's political processes can no longer be relied upon to prevent legislative abuse, because one of the in-state interests which would otherwise lobby against the tax has been mollified by the subsidy." The state also claimed that the cost of the program was not exported in any sense, for it was borne entirely by in-state consumers (who therefore had political incentives to repeal the program if not in some longer-term public interest). Justice Stevens responded that much the same could be said of a tariff, the classic instance of a Dormant Commerce Clause violation. Moreover, this argument "ignores the fact that Massachusetts dairy farmers are part of an integrated interstate market. The purpose and effect of the pricing order are to divert market share to Massachusetts dairy farmers. This diversion necessarily injures the dairy farmers in neighboring States," making it oversimple to assume that only in-state consumers are harmed.

the Dormant Commerce Clause, 88 Mich. L. Rev. 395 (1989); Jonathan Varat, State "Citizenship" and Interstate Equality, 48 U. Chi. L. Rev. 487 (1981).

In a concurring opinion, **Justice Scalia**, joined by **Justice Thomas**, reiterated his view that Dormant Commerce Clause jurisprudence is illegitimate. Feeling obligated to follow existing precedent, however, he suggested this distinction: A subsidy for in-state businesses can be financed out of general revenue but not through an earmarked tax. "Perhaps, as some commentators contend, that line comports with an important economic reality: a State is less likely to maintain a subsidy when its citizens perceive that the money (in the general fund) is available for any number of competing, non-protectionist purposes."

Chief Justice Rehnquist dissented, in an opinion joined by Justice Blackmun. They objected to the Court's defense of the Dormant Commerce Clause based on supposed interest group alignment. The last time the Court had struck down a tax because of the use to which its revenues was put was in *United States v. Butler*, 297 U.S. 1 (1936), a *Lochner*-era precedent now viewed as discredited.

SHOULD STATE SUBSIDIES BE EXEMPTED FROM DORMANT COMMERCE CLAUSE REGULATION?

A number of commentators agree with Justice Scalia that a subsidy supported by general tax revenues ought not be subjected to Dormant Commerce Clause scrutiny. They have argued that subsidies were not the original concerns of the Framers or the Justices developing the early history of this line of cases, see Dan T. Coenen, *Business Subsidies and the Dormant Commerce Clause*, 107 Yale L.J. 965 (1998); can be socially beneficial, especially when they confer positive externalities on the state and its economy, see Note, *Functional Analysis, Subsidies, and the Dormant Commerce Clause*, 110 Harv. L. Rev. 1537 (1997); and are less likely to have cost-exporting or protectionist effects. See Peter Enrich, *Saving the States from Themselves: Commerce Clause Constraints on State Tax Incentives for Business*, 110 Harv. L. Rev. 377 (1996). Francis, *The Decline of the Dormant Commerce Clause,* 94 Denver L. Rev. at 310–12.

On the other hand, Edward Zelinsky, *Are Tax Benefits Constitutionally Equivalent to Direct Expenditures?*, 112 Harv. L. Rev. 379 (1998), argues that there is no functional difference between a state subsidy for in-state businesses, which Justice Scalia would immunize, and a state tax break for in-state businesses, which is invalid under the Court's interstate taxation cases. Professor Enrich responds that tax incentives are more likely than subsidies to slide through the state appropriations process as special rent-seeking measures and therefore need greater judicial policing. Thus far, the lower courts have declined to apply *West Lynn Creamery* to state subsidy programs not connected to a specific tax. See, e.g., *Cumberland Farms, Inc. v. Mahany*, 943 F. Supp. 83 (D. Me. 1996); cf. Francis, *The Decline of the Dormant Commerce Clause,* 94 Denver L. Rev. at 310–12 (arguing that the subsidy cases are an important feature in the declining Dormant Commerce Clause).

C. SHOULD THE DORMANT COMMERCE CLAUSE BE LAID TO REST? ALTERNATE LIMITATIONS ON THE STATES

Several academic commentators, from a variety of perspectives, have called for laying the Dormant Commerce Clause to rest. See, e.g., Julian Eule, *Laying the Dormant Commerce Clause to Rest*, 91 Yale L.J. 425 (1982); Francis, *The Decline of the Dormant Commerce Clause,* 94 Denver L. Rev. at 316–18; Lisa Heinzerling, *The Commercial Constitution*, 1995 Sup. Ct. Rev. 217; Martin Redish & Shane Nugent, *The Dormant Commerce Clause and the Constitutional Balance of Federalism*, 1987 Duke L.J. 569. The defects of the doctrine: It is not well grounded in either the text or original meaning of the Constitution, asks the Court to make utilitarian (balancing) judgments it is not institutionally competent to perform, and substitutes the Court's market-based policy preferences, *Lochner*-style, for the regulatory preferences of elected state and local representatives. Perhaps in light of this sustained academic criticism, several of the Justices have become increasingly restive as well.

Camps Newfound/Owatonna, Inc. v. Town of Harrison

520 U.S. 564 (1997)

Maine provided a general exemption from real estate taxes for charitable institutions incorporated in the state. Because Camps Newfound/Owatonna was not a Maine company, it could not claim the exemption. In an opinion by **Justice Stevens**, the Court held that (1) Camps' service was clearly in commerce and so triggered the Dormant Commerce Clause jurisprudence; (2) that jurisprudence is fully applicable to not-for-profit as well as profitmaking enterprises; and (3) the statute's facial discrimination against interstate commerce brought it within the rule of *New England Power Co. v. New Hampshire*, 455 U.S. 331, 338 (1982), that "the Commerce Clause * * * precludes a state from mandating that its residents be given a preferred right of access, over out-of-state consumers, to natural resources located within its borders or to the products derived therefrom." See also *City of Philadelphia*. This kind of regulation risked the sort of "economic Balkanization" and retaliatory spiral the Dormant Commerce Clause is supposed to prevent.

Although the ordinance discriminated on its face against interstate commerce, **Justice Scalia** wrote for himself and three other Justices (Rehnquist, Thomas, and Ginsburg) arguing for its validity under the Court's existing jurisprudence, basically because the state ought to be able to encourage charitable uses of state land. On the one hand, Justice Scalia argued that there was no *facial discrimination*, because land gratuitously devoted to relieving the state of its welfare obligations is not *similarly situated* to land not so devoted, and hence there is no discrimination to treat the two kinds of land differently. On the other hand, Justice Scalia argued that encouraging domestic charity ought to be the sort of state interest that would justify a facial discrimination against interstate commerce. If there is a market participant exception, why is there not a domestic charity exception to the Dormant Commerce Clause? Indeed, the Court in *Board of Educ. of Ky. Ann. Conf. of Methodist Episcopal Church v. Illinois*, 203 U.S. 553 (1906), upheld a state inheritance tax allowing exemption to in-state charities but denying a similar exemption to out-of-state charities.

Justice Thomas wrote a separate dissent, joined by Justice Scalia and Chief Justice Rehnquist. Justice Thomas argued that the "negative" Commerce Clause jurisprudence is both *overbroad*, because it brings state laws under judicial scrutiny without any basis in the Constitution and with insufficient regard for judicial policymaking limitations, and *unnecessary*, because the Constitution explicitly regulates state laws that discriminate against interstate commerce or travel. The problem, he said, is that the Constitution mandates a different regulatory regime than the one the Court has created on its own initiative. But see Barry Friedman & Daniel T. Deacon, *A Course Unbroken: The Constitutional Legitimacy of the Dormant Commerce Clause,* 97 Va. L. Rev. 1877 (2011) (disputing Thomas's view, based upon the original meaning of the Commerce Clause as barring state regulations imposing burdens on interstate commerce). The remainder of this subpart discusses the textual limitations the Constitution places on state burdens against interstate commerce and travel.

1. The Import-Export Clause

In his *Camps* dissent, Justice Thomas examined the interpretive regime for evaluating discriminatory taxation under the Import-Export Clause, Article I, § 10, cl. 2: "No State shall, without the Consent of the Congress, lay any Imposts or Duties on Imports or Exports, except what may be absolutely necessary for executing its inspection Laws." Discriminatory state taxation can therefore be invalidated only if the challenger can show that (1) it is an "Impost" or a "Duty" (2) on "Imports or Exports," and (3) not "absolutely necessary for executing its inspection Laws." As with the Dormant Commerce Clause, Congress can authorize the discrimination otherwise prohibited.

The Import-Export Clause has been of little importance, because *Woodruff v. Parham*, 8 Wall. 123 (1868), held that the clause only applies to international trade. Justice Thomas' *Camps* dissent maintained, however, that contemporary usage of the terms Imports or Exports included trade between the states as well as trade between nations. Accord, 1 William Crosskey, *Politics and the Constitution in the History of the United States* 295–323 (1953). In an appropriate case, he would overrule *Woodruff* for that and other reasons. For Justice Thomas, the key inquiry would be whether a state tax is an Impost or Duty, as those terms were used in the eighteenth century.

An Impost was a tax levied on goods at the time of importation. A Duty included such taxes, but had a broader meaning, according to statements by James Wilson (who served on the Committee on Detail) at the Convention. "What seems likely from these descriptions is that a duty, though broader than an impost, was still a tax *on* particular *goods* or written instruments." What were excluded were so-called "direct taxes," such as taxes on real property. See *Federalist* No. 12 (Hamilton) (distinguishing direct taxes, such as property taxes, from indirect taxes, such as imposts, duties, and excises). Because discriminatory property taxes are neither "Imposts" nor "Duties," Justice Thomas concluded that the Maine tax scheme did not violate the Import-Export Clause.

2.   The Privileges and Immunities Clause

Like Justice Thomas in *Camps*, Professor Julian Eule has argued that the Dormant Commerce Clause should be laid to rest. He maintained that the Privileges and Immunities Clause, Article IV, § 2, cl. 1, ought to be the main protection against state burdens on interstate commerce. The main issue under this provision is what are the "Privileges and Immunities" to which the "Citizens of each State" shall be entitled? The leading cases, discussed below, provide some answers to these questions.

The heading case is *Corfield v. Coryell*, 4 Wash. C.C. 371, Fed. Cas. No. 3,230 (1823). A New Jersey statute made it unlawful for any person who was not an inhabitant of the state to gather clams, oysters, or shells in the state's waters. The opinion, by Justice Washington sitting on federal circuit court, dismissed the Privileges and Immunities Clause claim on the ground that the complainant did not have a "privilege" or "immunity" to gather clams. Justice Washington admonished that "it would, in our opinion, be going quite too far to construe the grant of privileges and immunities of citizens, as amounting to a grant of co-tenancy in the common property of the State, to the citizens of all the other states." Hence, the privileges and immunities protected by the clause should be limited to those "which are, in their nature, *fundamental*" and "which belong, of right, to the citizens of all free governments." Among these rights are the "right of a citizen of one State to pass through, or to reside in any other state, for the purposes of trade, agriculture, professional pursuits, or otherwise"; the right "to take, hold, and dispose of property, either real or personal; and an exemption from higher taxes or impositions than are paid by the other citizens of the State."

The leading case today is *United Building & Constr. Trades Coun. of Camden Cnty. v. Mayor and Coun. of Camden,* 465 U.S. 208 (1984). The Court struck down a Camden, New Jersey, ordinance requiring that at least 40% of the employees of contractors and subcontractors working on city construction projects be Camden residents. Justice Rehnquist's opinion for the Court ruled that a policy discriminating solely on the basis of *municipal* residency can violate the P&I Clause. Even though the text of the clause speaks only to state-level discrimination, the Court held that the anti-discrimination and economic integration purposes would be thwarted if the clause did not apply to municipal as well as state exclusions. "Given the Camden ordinance, an out-of-state citizen who ventures into New Jersey will not enjoy the same privileges as the New Jersey citizen residing in Camden."

The Court held that an out-of-state resident's interest in employment on public works contracts in another State is sufficiently "fundamental" to the promotion of interstate harmony so as to "fall within the purview of the Privileges and Immunities Clause." Noting that the market participant exception would have barred relief under the Dormant Commerce Clause, the Court ruled that such an exception did not apply to the P&I Clause. "Thus, the fact that Camden is merely setting conditions on its expenditures for goods and services in the marketplace does not preclude the possibility that those conditions violate the Privileges and Immunities Clause." Accord, *Hicklin v. Orbeck*, 437 U.S. 518 (1978) (striking down an "Alaska Hire" statute containing a resident hiring preference for all employment related to the development of the State's oil and gas resources).

Camden's infringement of the foregoing privilege or immunity of citizenship would be invalid under the clause unless the city could show a "substantial reason" for the difference in treatment. The city urged the policy as a way to arrest the middle class flight from the city and to tie work for the city to commitment in the city. Justice Rehnquist recognized that Camden's policy was not only a valid one, but its ordinance was more appropriately tailored to such a valid policy than, for example, the Alaska Hire statute at issue in *Hicklin*, which covered not only contractors and subcontractors dealing directly with the State's oil and gas, but also suppliers and other tangentially related concerns. Because there was no factual record, however, the case was remanded for further proceedings.

NOTES CONTRASTING THE DORMANT COMMERCE CLAUSE AND THE PRIVILEGES AND IMMUNITIES CLAUSE

Camden rendered the Privileges and Immunities Clause parallel to the Dormant Commerce Clause in one respect: Both apply to municipal and local discriminations as well as statewide ones. In most other respects, however, the two lines of cases follow different doctrinal rules and impose different limitations on states and municipalities. Among them are the following:

1.   *Only Fundamental Rights. Corfield* held that the Privileges and Immunities Clause only protects fundamental privileges naturally belonging to the citizens of any free government. Like *Camden*, most of the recent cases have dealt with state efforts to exclude nonresidents from professional opportunities. See, e.g., *Lunding v. New York Tax Appeals Tribunal*, 522 U.S.

287 (1998) ("right" secured by the P & I Clause is the right of a citizen of one state "to remove to and carry on business in another without being subjected in property or person to taxes more onerous than the citizens of the latter State are subjected to"); *Supreme Court of Virginia v. Friedman*, 487 U.S. 59 (1988) (residency requirement to become member of Virginia bar violates P & I Clause); *Supreme Court of New Hampshire v. Piper*, 470 U.S. 274 (1985) (similar). Compare *Baldwin v. Montana Fish & Game Comm'n*, 436 U.S. 371 (1978) (rejecting challenge to elk-hunting license law imposing higher fees on nonresidents; elk-hunting is not a fundamental right). Can *Camden's* protection of public employment be extended to qualify as a privilege the right to sell products across state boundaries (*Dean Milk Co.*)? The right to nondiscriminatory access to a state's resources (*City of Philadelphia*)? How about the right to drive your truck across the state of Iowa, as part of your business of trucking (*Kassel*)?

2.   *Only "Citizens" (Not Corporations) Are Protected.* Although the clause itself only identifies "Citizens" as protected, *Camden* read the clause broadly to mean "nonresidents." Compare the Fourteenth Amendment, which makes us "citizens" of the states in which we "reside." A more thorny question is whether corporations are protected by the clause. The Supreme Court in *Bank of Augusta v. Earle*, 38 U.S. (13 Pet.) 519 (1839) (Taney, C.J.), held that corporations are not Citizens under the clause. See also *Paul v. Virginia*, 75 U.S. (8 Wall.) 168, 177 (1868). If corporations such as Consolidated Freightways are not Citizens, then surely government units, such as the City of Philadelphia, would not be either. Note that the Court has interpreted "person" in the Fourteenth Amendment to include corporations, e.g., *Railway Express Agency v. New York*, 336 U.S. 106 (1949), and *Camden* was willing to interpret "State" in the Privileges and Immunities Clause to mean "municipality." Should *Earle* be overruled?

3.   *There Must Be Overt Discrimination—Discriminatory Effects Not Policed.* Unlike the Dormant Commerce Clause, the Privileges and Immunities Clause only applies when there is an overt discrimination. As the Court recognized in *Camden*, "[i]t is discrimination against out-of-state residents on matters of fundamental concern which triggers the Clause, not regulation affecting interstate commerce."[85] Hence, cases like *Kassel* (Iowa simply had a different truck-length rule from other states) would probably be decided differently under the Privileges and Immunities Clause, because they do not readily distinguish between state citizens and noncitizens. Indirect burdens on interstate commerce do not count for privileges and immunities purposes.

4.   *No Market Participant Exception.* As the Court held in *Camden*, the Privileges and Immunities Clause has no market participant exception such as that created by *Alexandria Scrap* for the Dormant Commerce Clause. (But the Court seemed willing to allow preferential economic concern for local residents as a valid legislative interest in *Camden*.)

---

[85] See Jonathan Varat, *State "Citizenship" and Interstate Equality*, 48 U. Chi. L. Rev. 487 (1981).

5. *Standard of Review*. Compare the standard of review announced in *Toomer v. Witsell*, 334 U.S. 385 (1948) and applied in *Camden*: Discrimination against citizens of other states can be justified if there is "substantial reason" for the different treatment; the state or city must show that such reasons exist and that the particular discrimination bears a "close relation" to them. This seems like a more lenient standard than the Dormant Commerce Clause standard for overt discrimination against interstate commerce, but stiffer than the *Pike* test for evaluating discriminatory effects. Consider *Lunding, supra*, in which the Court struck down a New York law denying only nonresident taxpayers an income tax deduction for alimony. The Court reaffirmed that state legislatures have "considerable discretion" in drawing local taxing policy, but would be faulted if they violate the Court's rule of "substantial equality."

6. *No Congressional Validation*. The ruling in *Kassel* that Iowa's prohibition of doubles violated the Dormant Commerce Clause was properly overridden by congressionally authorized procedures. But if the Court held that the Iowa law discriminated against out-of-staters under the Privileges and Immunities Clause, presumably Congress could not validate the state law, although (of course) the state could simply reformulate the statute without the discrimination.

3.   The Supremacy Clause and Preemption

Under the Supremacy Clause of Article VI, Congress can enact federal statutes that override, or "preempt," state law. The Court has held that duly authorized regulations promulgated by a federal agency may also have preemptive effect, see *Hillsborough County v. Automated Medical Laboratories*, 471 U.S. 707 (1985). Because today both sovereigns exercise so much regulatory authority over so many things, preemption issues are pervasive, yet they are so complicated by the diversity of their facts that no simple formula for federal preemption is evident. In any event, the Court has repeatedly stated that state regulation can be preempted in three different circumstances. *Murphy v. NCAA*, 138 S.Ct. 1461, 1480–81 (2018).[86]

First, Congress may expressly preempt state law by so stipulating in a federal statute. E.g., *Shaw v. Delta Air Lines*, 463 U.S. 85 (1983). This is but a simple application of the Supremacy Clause: if the federal statute is constitutional and says that state law is preempted, courts must apply the federal rule and not the state law. Likewise, if Congress determines that state regulation should not be preempted by a federal statute, Congress may expressly say so in a "savings clause" in the statute. Not only will the savings clause prevent preemption, but, depending upon the wording of the

---

[86]   *Ray v. Atlantic Richfield Co.*, 435 U.S. 151 (1978) (leading case); see also *Crosby v. National Foreign Trade Council*, 530 U.S. 363 (2000); *Gade v. National Solid Wastes Management Ass'n*, 505 U.S. 88 (1992); *Pacific Gas & Elec. Co. v. State Energy Resources Conservation & Dev. Comm'n*, 461 U.S. 190 (1983).

clause, it may immunize the state regulation from Dormant Commerce Clause attack as well.

Second, even without an explicit preemption provision, a federal statute will preempt state laws whose operation is inconsistent with that of the federal statute. Not surprisingly, a conflict will be found "where compliance with both federal and state regulations is a physical impossibility." *Florida Lime & Avocado Growers, Inc. v. Paul*, 373 U.S. 132, 142–43 (1963). A venerable example is *McDermott v. Wisconsin*, 228 U.S. 115 (1913), where compliance with federal food labeling requirements would have caused the food to have been mislabeled under state law. More difficult to apply is another line of cases, under which the state law is preempted if it "stands as an obstacle to the accomplishment and execution of the full purposes and objectives of Congress." *Hines v. Davidowitz*, 312 U.S. 52, 67 (1941).

Third, federal statutes "occupying the field" comprehensively will preempt state law. "The scheme of federal regulations may be so pervasive as to make reasonable the inference that Congress left no room for the States to supplement it. Or the Act of Congress may touch a field in which the federal interest is so dominant that the federal system will be assumed to preclude enforcement of state laws of the same subject." *Rice v. Santa Fe Elevator Corp.*, 331 U.S. 218, 230 (1947). Note that this approach preempts state law even if it is not in actual conflict with the text or policies of federal law. This massive intrusion on federalism values is not easily assumed by the Court: There is a strong presumption against so-called "field preemption," and it will be found only if "the nature of the regulated subject matter permits no other conclusion, or [if] the Congress has unmistakably so ordained." *Florida Lime, supra*. Nonetheless, for example, the extensive federal regulation of aliens, coupled with the unique federal interest in foreign affairs, led the Court in *Hines, supra*, to hold that a federal statute governing the registration of aliens preempted a state alien registration statute.

ARIZONA V. UNITED STATES

567 U.S. 387, 132 S.Ct. 2492, 183 L.Ed.2d 351 (2012)

JUSTICE KENNEDY delivered the opinion of the Court.

[Responding to rising numbers of immigrants who were in the state illegally, Arizona in 2010 enacted a statute entitled the Support Our Law Enforcement and Safe Neighborhoods Act (also known as S.B. 1070). Its stated purpose is to "discourage and deter the unlawful entry and presence of aliens and economic activity by persons unlawfully present in the United States." The Attorney General challenged four provisions as inconsistent with the Constitution. Two provisions were new state offenses. Section 3 makes failure to comply with federal alien registration requirements a state misdemeanor. Ariz. Rev. Stat. § 13–1509 (West Supp. 2011). Section 5(C) makes it a misdemeanor for an unauthorized alien to seek or engage in work in the State. § 13–2928(C). Two other provisions give specific arrest authority and investigative duties with respect to certain aliens to state and local law enforcement officers. Section 6 authorizes officers to arrest without a warrant a person "the officer has probable cause to believe . . . has committed any public offense that makes the person removable from the United States." § 13–3883(A)(5). Section 2(B) provides that officers who conduct a stop, detention, or arrest must in some circumstances make efforts to verify the person's immigration status with the Federal Government. § 11–1051(B) (West 2012). Writing also for the CHIEF JUSTICE and JUSTICES GINSBURG, BREYER, and SOTOMAYOR, JUSTICE KENNEDY's opinion for the Court found all but § 2(B) preempted.]

The Government of the United States has broad, undoubted power over the subject of immigration and the status of aliens. See *Toll v. Moreno*, 458 U.S. 1, 10 (1982); see generally S. Legomsky & C. Rodríguez, Immigration and Refugee Law and Policy 115–132 (5th ed. 2009). This authority rests, in part, on the National Government's constitutional power to "establish an uniform Rule of Naturalization," U.S. Const., Art. I, § 8, cl. 4, and its inherent power as sovereign to control and conduct relations with foreign nations.

The federal power to determine immigration policy is well settled. Immigration policy can affect trade, investment, tourism, and diplomatic relations for the entire Nation, as well as the perceptions and expectations of aliens in this country who seek the full protection of its laws. Perceived mistreatment of aliens in the United States may lead to harmful reciprocal treatment of American citizens abroad. See Brief for Madeleine K. Albright et al. as *Amici Curiae* 24–30.

It is fundamental that foreign countries concerned about the status, safety, and security of their nationals in the United States must be able to confer and communicate on this subject with one national sovereign, not the 50 separate States. See *Chy Lung v. Freeman*, 92 U.S. 275, 279–280 (1876); see also The Federalist No. 3, p. 39 (C. Rossiter ed. 2003) (J. Jay) (observing that federal power would be necessary in part because "bordering States . . . under the impulse of sudden irritation, and a quick sense of apparent interest or injury" might take action that would undermine foreign relations). This Court has reaffirmed that "[o]ne of the most important and delicate of all international relationships . . . has to do with the protection of the just rights of a country's own nationals when those nationals are in another country." *Hines v. Davidowitz*, 312 U.S. 52, 64 (1941).

Federal governance of immigration and alien status is extensive and complex. Congress has specified categories of aliens who may not be admitted to the United States. See 8 U.S.C. § 1182. Unlawful entry and unlawful reentry into the country are federal offenses. §§ 1325, 1326. Once here, aliens are required to register with the Federal Government and to carry proof of status on their person. See §§ 1301–1306. Failure to do so is a federal misdemeanor. §§ 1304(e), 1306(a). Federal law also authorizes States to deny noncitizens a range of public benefits, § 1622; and it imposes sanctions on employers who hire unauthorized workers, § 1324a.

Congress has specified which aliens may be removed from the United States and the procedures for doing so. Aliens may be removed if they were inadmissible at the time of entry, have been convicted of certain crimes, or meet other criteria set by federal law. See § 1227. Removal is a civil, not criminal, matter. A principal feature of the removal system is the broad discretion exercised by immigration officials. See Brief for Former Commissioners of the United States Immigration and Naturalization Service as *Amici Curiae* 8–13 (hereinafter Brief for Former INS Commissioners). Federal officials, as an initial matter, must decide whether it makes sense to pursue removal at all. If removal proceedings commence, aliens may seek asylum and other discretionary relief allowing them to remain in the country or at least to leave without formal removal. See § 1229a(c)(4); see also, *e.g.,* §§ 1158 (asylum), 1229b (cancellation of removal), 1229c (voluntary departure).

Discretion in the enforcement of immigration law embraces immediate human concerns. Unauthorized workers trying to support their families, for example, likely pose less danger than alien smugglers or aliens who commit a serious crime. The equities of an individual case may turn on many factors, including whether the alien has children born in the United States, long ties to the community, or a record of distinguished military service. Some discretionary decisions involve policy choices that bear on this Nation's international relations. Returning an alien to his own country may be deemed inappropriate even where he has committed a removable offense or fails to meet the criteria for admission. The foreign state may be mired in civil war, complicit in political persecution, or enduring conditions that create a real risk that the alien or his family will be harmed upon return. The dynamic nature of relations with other countries requires the Executive Branch to ensure that enforcement policies are consistent with this Nation's foreign policy with respect to these and other realities. [Justice Kennedy evaluated each challenged provision in light of the federal statutory scheme and the Court's preemption jurisprudence.]

[**Section 3**, where Arizona made it a state crime to violate federal registration requirements.] The Court discussed federal alien-registration requirements in *Hines v. Davidowitz*. In 1940, as international conflict spread, Congress added to federal immigration law a "complete system for alien registration." The new federal law struck a careful balance. It punished an alien's willful failure to register but did not require aliens to carry identification cards. There were also limits on the sharing of registration records and fingerprints. The Court found that Congress intended the federal plan for registration to be a "single integrated and all-embracing system." Because this "complete scheme . . . for the registration of aliens" touched on foreign relations, it did not allow the States to "curtail or complement" federal law or to "enforce additional or auxiliary regulations." As a consequence, the Court ruled that Pennsylvania could not enforce its own alien-registration program.

The present regime of federal regulation is not identical to the statutory framework considered in *Hines*, but it remains comprehensive. Federal law now includes a requirement that aliens carry proof of registration. 8 U.S.C. § 1304(e). Other aspects, however, have stayed the same. Aliens who remain in the country for more than 30 days must apply for registration and be fingerprinted. Compare § 1302(a) with *id.*, § 452(a) (1940 ed.). Detailed information is required, and any change of address has to be reported to the Federal Government. Compare §§ 1304(a), 1305(a) (2006 ed.), with *id.*, §§ 455(a), 456 (1940 ed.). The statute continues to provide penalties for the willful failure to register. Compare § 1306(a) (2006 ed.), with *id.*, § 457 (1940 ed.).

The framework enacted by Congress leads to the conclusion here, as it did in *Hines*, that the Federal Government has occupied the field of alien registration. The federal statutory directives provide a full set of standards governing alien registration, including the punishment for noncompliance. It was designed as a " 'harmonious whole.' " *Hines*. Where Congress occupies an entire field, as it has in the field of alien registration, even complementary state regulation is impermissible. Field preemption reflects a congressional decision to foreclose any state regulation in the area, even if it is parallel to federal standards.

Federal law makes a single sovereign responsible for maintaining a comprehensive and unified system to keep track of aliens within the Nation's borders. If § 3 of the Arizona statute were valid, every State could give itself independent authority to prosecute federal registration violations, "diminish[ing] the [Federal Government]'s control over enforcement" and "detract[ing] from the 'integrated scheme of regulation' created by Congress." *Wisconsin Dept. of Industry v. Gould Inc.*, 475 U.S. 282, 288–289 (1986). Even if a State may make violation of federal law a crime in some instances, it cannot do so in a field (like the field of alien registration) that has been occupied by federal law.

[Section 5C, where Arizona created a new crime, without analogue in federal law, of seeking employment in the United States while one is an illegal immigrant.] The United States contends that the provision upsets the balance struck by the Immigration Reform and Control Act of 1986

(IRCA) and must be preempted as an obstacle to the federal plan of regulation and control.

When there was no comprehensive federal program regulating the employment of unauthorized aliens, this Court found that a State had authority to pass its own laws on the subject. In 1971, for example, California passed a law imposing civil penalties on the employment of aliens who were "not entitled to lawful residence in the United States if such employment would have an adverse effect on lawful resident workers." 1971 Cal. Stats. ch. 1442, § 1(a). The law was upheld against a preemption challenge in *De Canas v. Bica*, 424 U.S. 351 (1976). *De Canas* recognized that "States possess broad authority under their police powers to regulate the employment relationship to protect workers within the State." At that point, however, the Federal Government had expressed no more than "a peripheral concern with [the] employment of illegal entrants."

Current federal law is substantially different from the regime that prevailed when *De Canas* was decided. Congress enacted IRCA as a comprehensive framework for "combating the employment of illegal aliens." *Plastic Compounds, Inc. v. NLRB*, 535 U.S. 137, 147 (2002). The law makes it illegal for employers to knowingly hire, recruit, refer, or continue to employ unauthorized workers. See 8 U.S.C. §§ 1324a(a)(1)(A), (a)(2). It also requires every employer to verify the employment authorization status of prospective employees. See §§ 1324a(a)(1)(B), (b); 8 CFR § 274a.2(b) (2012). These requirements are enforced through criminal penalties and an escalating series of civil penalties tied to the number of times an employer has violated the provisions. See 8 U.S.C. §§ 1324a(e)(4), (f); 8 CFR § 274a.10.

This comprehensive framework does not impose federal criminal sanctions on the employee side (*i.e.,* penalties on aliens who seek or engage in unauthorized work). Under federal law some civil penalties are imposed instead. With certain exceptions, aliens who accept unlawful employment are not eligible to have their status adjusted to that of a lawful permanent resident. See 8 U.S.C. §§ 1255(c)(2), (c)(8). Aliens also may be removed from the country for having engaged in unauthorized work. See § 1227(a)(1)(C)(i); 8 C.F.R. § 214.1(e). In addition to specifying these civil consequences, federal law makes it a crime for unauthorized workers to obtain employment through fraudulent means. See 18 U.S.C. § 1546(b). Congress has made clear, however, that any information employees submit to indicate their work status "may not be used" for purposes other than prosecution under specified federal criminal statutes for fraud, perjury, and related conduct. See 8 U.S.C. §§ 1324a(b)(5), (d)(2)(F)–(G).

The legislative background of IRCA underscores the fact that Congress made a deliberate choice not to impose criminal penalties on aliens who seek, or engage in, unauthorized employment. A commission established by Congress to study immigration policy and to make recommendations concluded these penalties would be "unnecessary and unworkable." U.S. Immigration Policy and the National Interest: The Final Report and Recommendations of the Select Commission on Immigration and Refugee Policy with Supplemental Views by Commissioners 65–66 (1981); see Pub. L. 95–412, § 4, 92 Stat. 907. Proposals to make unauthorized work a criminal offense were debated and discussed during the long process of drafting IRCA. But Congress rejected them. See, *e.g.,* 119 Cong. Rec. 14184 (1973) (statement of Rep. Dennis). In the end, IRCA's framework reflects a considered judgment that making criminals out of aliens engaged in unauthorized work—aliens who already face the possibility of employer exploitation because of their removable status—would be inconsistent with federal policy and objectives.

IRCA's express preemption provision, which in most instances bars States from imposing penalties on employers of unauthorized aliens, is silent about whether additional penalties may be imposed against the employees themselves. See 8 U.S.C. § 1324a(h)(2). But the existence of an "express pre-emption provisio[n] does *not* bar the ordinary working of conflict pre-emption principles" or impose a "special burden" that would make it more difficult to establish the preemption of laws falling outside the clause. *Geier v. American Honda Motor Co.,* 529 U.S. 861, 869–872 (2000).

The ordinary principles of preemption include the well-settled proposition that a state law is preempted where it "stands as an obstacle to the accomplishment and execution of the full purposes and objectives of Congress." *Hines.* Under § 5(C) of S.B. 1070, Arizona law would interfere with the careful balance struck by Congress with respect to unauthorized employment of aliens. Although § 5(C) attempts to achieve one of the same goals as federal law—the deterrence of unlawful employment—it involves a conflict in the method of enforcement. The Court has recognized that a "[c]onflict in technique can be fully as disruptive to the system Congress enacted as conflict in overt policy." *Motor Coach Employees v. Lockridge,* 403 U.S. 274, 287 (1971). The correct instruction to draw from the text, structure, and history of IRCA is that Congress decided it would be inappropriate to impose criminal penalties on aliens who seek or engage in unauthorized employment. It follows that a state law to the contrary is an obstacle to the regulatory system Congress chose.

[Section 6, which authorizes state and local law enforcement officers, without a warrant, to arrest persons where there is probable cause to believe they have committed "public offense[s]" that would render them removable from the United States.] As a general rule, it is not a crime for a removable alien to remain present in the United States. If the police stop someone based on nothing more than possible removability, the usual predicate for an arrest is absent. When an alien is suspected of being removable, a federal official issues an administrative document called a Notice to Appear. See 8 U.S.C. § 1229(a); 8 C.F.R. § 239.1(a) (2012). The form does not authorize an arrest. Instead, it gives the alien information about the proceedings, including the time and date of the removal hearing. See 8 U.S.C. § 1229(a)(1). If an alien fails to appear, an *in absentia* order may direct removal. § 1229a(5)(A).

The federal statutory structure instructs when it is appropriate to arrest an alien during the removal process. For example, the Attorney General can exercise discretion to issue a warrant for an alien's arrest and detention "pending a decision on whether the alien is to be removed from the United States." 8 U.S.C. § 1226(a); see Memorandum from John Morton, Director, ICE [Immigration & Customs Enforcement], to All Field Office Directors et al., Exercising Prosecutorial Discretion Consistent with the Civil Immigration Enforcement Priorities of the Agency for the Apprehension, Detention, and Removal of Aliens (June 17, 2011) (hereinafter 2011 ICE Memorandum) (describing factors informing this and related decisions). And if an alien is ordered removed after a hearing, the Attorney General will issue a warrant. See 8 C.F.R. § 241.2(a)(1). In both instances, the warrants are executed by federal officers who have received training in the enforcement of immigration law. See §§ 241.2(b), 287.5(e)(3). If no federal warrant has been issued, those officers have more limited authority. See 8 U.S.C. § 1357(a). They may arrest an alien for being "in the United States in violation of any [immigration] law or regulation," for example, but only where the alien "is likely to escape before a warrant can be obtained." § 1357(a)(2).

Section 6 attempts to provide state officers even greater authority to arrest aliens on the basis of possible removability than Congress has given to trained federal immigration officers. Under state law, officers who believe an alien is removable by reason of some "public offense" would have the power to conduct an arrest on that basis regardless of whether a federal warrant has issued or the alien is likely to escape. This state authority could be exercised without any input from the Federal Government about whether an arrest is warranted in a particular case. This would allow the State to achieve its own immigration policy. The result could be unnecessary harassment of some aliens (for instance, a veteran, college student, or someone assisting with a criminal investigation) whom federal officials determine should not be removed.

This is not the system Congress created. Federal law specifies limited circumstances in which state officers may perform the functions of an immigration officer. A principal example is when the Attorney General has granted that authority to specific officers in a formal agreement with a state or local government. Officers covered by these agreements are subject to the Attorney General's direction and supervision. § 1357(g)(3). There are significant complexities involved in enforcing federal immigration law, including the determination whether a person is removable. As a result, the agreements reached with the Attorney General must contain written certification that officers have received adequate training to carry out the duties of an immigration officer. * * *

By authorizing state officers to decide whether an alien should be detained for being removable, § 6 violates the principle that the removal process is entrusted to the discretion of the Federal Government. See, *e.g.*, *Reno v. American-Arab Anti-Discrimination Comm.*, 525 U.S. 471, 483–484 (1999); see also Brief for Former INS Commissioners 8–13. A decision on removability requires a determination whether it is appropriate to allow a foreign national to continue living in the United States. Decisions of this nature touch on foreign relations and must be made with one voice. * * *

[Section 2(B), which requires state officers to make a "reasonable attempt . . . to determine the immigration status" of any person they stop, detain, or arrest on some other legitimate basis if "reasonable suspicion exists that the person is an alien and is unlawfully present in the United States."] Three limits are built into the state provision. First, a detainee is presumed not to be an alien unlawfully present in the United States if he or she provides a valid Arizona driver's license or similar identification. Second, officers "may not consider race, color or national origin . . . except to the extent permitted by the United States [and] Arizona Constitution[s]." Third, the provisions must be "implemented in a manner consistent with federal law regulating immigration, protecting the civil rights of all persons and respecting the privileges and immunities of United States citizens." § 11–1051(L) (West 2012). * * *

The United States argues that making status verification mandatory interferes with the federal immigration scheme. It is true that § 2(B) does not allow state officers to consider federal enforcement priorities in deciding whether to contact ICE about someone they have detained. In other words, the officers must make an inquiry even in cases where it seems unlikely that the Attorney General would have the alien removed. This might be the case, for example, when an alien is an elderly veteran with significant and longstanding ties to the community. See 2011 ICE Memorandum 4–5 (mentioning these factors as relevant).

Congress has done nothing to suggest it is inappropriate to communicate with ICE in these situations, however. Indeed, it has encouraged the sharing of information about possible immigration violations. See 8 U.S.C. § 1357(g)(10)(A). A federal statute regulating the public benefits provided to qualified aliens in fact instructs that "no State or local government entity may be prohibited, or in any way restricted, from sending to or receiving from [ICE] information regarding the immigration status, lawful or unlawful, of an alien in the United States." § 1644. The federal scheme thus leaves room for a policy requiring state officials to contact ICE as a routine matter.

Some who support the challenge to § 2(B) argue that, in practice, state officers will be required to delay the release of some detainees for no reason other than to verify their immigration status. Detaining individuals solely to verify their immigration status would raise constitutional concerns. See, e.g., *Arizona v. Johnson*, 555 U.S. 323, 333 (2009); *Illinois v. Caballes*, 543 U.S. 405, 407 (2005) ("A seizure that is justified solely by the interest in issuing a warning ticket to the driver can become unlawful if it is prolonged beyond the time reasonably required to complete that mission"). And it would disrupt the federal framework to put state officers in the position of holding aliens in custody for possible unlawful presence without federal direction and supervision. The program put in place by Congress does not allow state or local officers to adopt this enforcement mechanism.

But § 2(B) could be read to avoid these concerns. To take one example, a person might be stopped for jaywalking in Tucson and be unable to produce identification. The first sentence of § 2(B) instructs officers to make a "reasonable" attempt to verify his immigration status with ICE if there is reasonable suspicion that his presence in the United States is unlawful. The state courts may conclude that, unless the person continues to be suspected of some crime for which he may be detained by state officers, it would not be reasonable to prolong the stop for the immigration inquiry. * * *

However the law is interpreted, if § 2(B) only requires state officers to conduct a status check during the course of an authorized, lawful detention or after a detainee has been released, the provision likely would survive preemption—at least absent some showing that it has other consequences that are adverse to federal law and its objectives. There is no need in this case to address whether reasonable suspicion of illegal entry or another immigration crime would be a legitimate basis for prolonging a detention, or whether this too would be preempted by federal law. [Justice Kennedy ruled that as-applied constitutional questions might be raised once Arizona started enforcing § 2(B).]

[**JUSTICE KAGAN** did not participate in this case.]

[**JUSTICE SCALIA** concurred in part and dissented in part. He would have upheld all four provisions, starting with the premise that the states retain as a matter of sovereignty the independent authority to exclude persons from their territory if they reside there illegally. Justice Scalia viewed the Constitution as a compact among independent sovereigns who gave up only the sovereign powers reflected in the Constitution. Arizona's exercise of its sovereign powers are subject to federal preemption, but the Court is too liberal in finding discretion in federal immigration law. Indeed, President Obama, just days before the decision was handed down, announced that his administration was not going to enforce federal law against most children of illegal aliens. The President has that discretion, but Justice Scalia's mind was "boggled" at the reality that Arizona cannot enforce a federal law the President will not.]

[JUSTICE THOMAS also concurred and dissented and would have upheld all four provisions, based upon the idea that there is no clear conflict between federal immigration statutes and the Arizona statute. Justice Thomas opined that the Court's longstanding "obstacle preemption" jurisprudence is, itself, unconstitutional, for it allows the Court to extrapolate well beyond actual preemption to create an expansive federal law at the expense of state law.]

[JUSTICE ALITO concurred with the Court's upholding § 2(B) and striking down § 3 (based on the *Hines* precedent), but dissented from the Court's striking down § 5(C) (based on the *De Canas* precedent) and § 6.]

NOTES ON THE ARIZONA *IMMIGRATION CASE*

1. *Preemption as a Replacement or Supplement for the Dormant Commerce Clause?* At the very point when the Supreme Court is deeply divided as to the legitimacy of Dormant Commerce Clause review, it is united in its view that Congress can preempt state law. Except for Justice Thomas, see *Wyeth v. Levine*, 555 U.S. 555 (2009) (Thomas, J., concurring in the judgment), the Justices also accept and will vigorously enforce the rule that state laws presenting "obstacles" to the achievement of federal statutory purposes will be preempted. As one might expect, the Justices' votes in particular cases will vary, depending on the particular federal statutory language and legislative purpose, the effect of preemption on business and other interests, and the preemption position articulated by the relevant federal agency. E.g., William N. Eskridge Jr., *Vetogates,* Chevron, *Preemption*, 83 Notre Dame L. Rev. 1441 (2008) (empirical examination of all of the Court's preemption cases, 1984–2006, finding that the Court was especially deferential to agency views rejecting preemption claims and agency views in technical areas such as energy and transportation).

We now inhabit a republic of statutes—federal statutes cover many fields quite exhaustively. Should the Court lay the Dormant Commerce Clause to rest and decide all or almost all the cases based upon a federal statutory analysis? As with immigration, there are many areas of law comprehensively regulated by federal statutes, and obstacle preemption could replace the Court's balancing approach as the mode of analysis. Perhaps a role could remain for the Dormant Commerce Clause precept that states cannot "discriminate" against interstate commerce without a compelling justification—but even in those cases federal statutes tolerating state regulation might play a validating role. See *United Haulers Ass'n, Inc.*

2. *The Decline of Arguments from Independent State Sovereignty?* Recall *U.S. Term Limits v. Thornton*, where four Justices articulated a view that the

union is the compact among still-sovereign states. In *Arizona*, only Justice Scalia started with the assumption that the states only gave up some of their sovereign authority when they joined the union. Justice Scalia provided a detailed account of the original framing discussions and maintained that no state would have ratified the Constitution if its leaders could have foreseen the Court's result in *Arizona*. Justice Thomas probably agreed with this discussion—but no other Justice invoked anything like this line of argument. Five Justices (including Chief Justice Roberts) joined the Court's opinion, which treated the states with respect but rested upon the assumption that the federal government makes the rules for border patrol and illegal immigration. The quintessential common law judge, Justice Alito ruled very narrowly, carefully following precedent and announcing no broad theory of federalism. Should the Arkansas Term Limits (dissenting) view of federalism be retired? Has the Court moved on to a focus on national democratic norms, expressed in congressional enactments and their compromises and presidential decisions about enforcement and further compromise?

3.   *Ethnic Profiling Concerns.* The Court upheld § 2(B) as a matter of preemption analysis. Justice Kennedy made clear that it would be premature to address most of the concerns with § 2(B) at the preliminary injunction stage, when the Court addressed only a *facial* challenge. It is black letter law that the Court is not supposed to strike down a statute on its face unless there is "no set of circumstances" as to which the statute can be constitutionally applied. *United States v. Salerno*, 481 U.S. 739 (1987). The *Salerno* test may be too broadly stated (and the Court often softens the test in practice), but it does reflect the higher bar for facial challenges.

That a statute might be constitutional in a range of circumstances does not mean that it will actually play out that way—and so Justice Kennedy suggested the possibility of *as applied* challenges to the statute, depending on how it is enforce by the state police and interpreted by the state supreme court. Justice Kennedy made the same point in *Gonzales v. Carhart*, the Partial-Birth Abortion Case (Chapter 5).

From the perspective of Latinos, the main concern with § 2(B) is that it will, as a structural matter, create a police regime that overwhelmingly, if not exclusively, focuses on Spanish-speaking Americans and legal (as well as undocumented) immigrants. It is likely that police will apply § 2(B) in a backwards way—first concluding that a "reasonable suspicion exists that the person is an alien and is unlawfully present in the United States," and then detaining or arresting the person for a "legitimate" reason. How can this be, given all the admonitions in the Arizona law and in Justice Kennedy's opinion?

There are, literally, thousands of "legitimate" reasons to stop or detain a person. Your casebook authors, for example, a few years ago observed a Justice of the Supreme Court and his law clerks walking back to Chambers after lunch. The Justice and the law clerks violated jaywalking and other traffic safety laws on no fewer than six street crossings in a ten-minute period. Any one of those actions would have justified a police stop. Few police officers are going to stop "citizens" for illegal jaywalking. But someone who might be an undocumented alien?

So how is the police officer going to determine whether a "reasonable suspicion exists that the person is an alien and is unlawfully present in the United States"? Civil liberties groups worry that Arizona will not control or regulate police officers who entertain such a "suspicion" based upon the person's appearance, linguistic ability, or accent. So Spanish-speaking persons in Arizona might be disproportionately stopped and asked to produce evidence of citizenship or legal immigrant status. The effect may be to create a state-supported caste: One group of citizens and visitors who must *always* stand ready to produce evidence of their legality (Latino Americans and other Latinos), and another group of citizens who can go about their business with the assurance they would not be stopped.

Is this a realistic concern? If so, is there a way to monitor and challenge Arizona's enforcement? Cf. *Washington v. Davis* and related "disparate impact" cases (Chapter 3, § 1). Relatedly, are there procedures or protocols that Arizona can adopt that can reduce or minimize this risk?

PROBLEM 7-11:
WHAT STATE AND LOCAL LAWS SURVIVE ARIZONA V. UNITED STATES?

Consider whether the following state laws or municipal ordinances can be defended after *Arizona v. United States* and the Court's earlier decision in *Chamber of Commerce v. Whiting*, 563 U.S. 582 (2011), which upheld against ICRA preemption attack Arizona's law requiring all employers to use E-Verify, a congressional system verifying immigrant status, and penalizes employers that knowingly employ illegal immigrants. Would the Supreme Court strike down all of these laws, which are based on measures actually adopted by legislators? Which ones might survive?

(a) State law requiring landlords within the city to secure from all tenants proof of citizenship or legal immigrant status. Violation is a municipal offense. *Cf.* 8 U.S.C. § 1324(a)(1)(A)(iv)(b)(iii) (federal immigration bar to encouraging or inducing illegal immigrants to reside in the United States).

(b) State law barring all employers within the state from employing "illegal aliens" and requiring employers to secure from all employees proof of citizenship or legal immigrant status. Violation is a state misdemeanor. *Cf. Whiting* (upholding narrower Arizona law).

(c) State law barring children of illegal aliens from attending public colleges or universities. *Cf. Plyler v. Doe*, 457 U.S. 202 (1982).

(d) State law barring the provision of state or local public "benefits" to "illegal aliens" (as defined in 8 U.S.C. § 1621(a)), with exceptions allowing receipt of the public benefits identified in 8 U.S.C. § 1621(b).

(e)   State law making it a felony for an illegal immigrant to apply for a state license, including a driver's license.

(f)   State law nullifying contracts entered into with illegal immigrants.

In light of *Arizona*, should any of these legal requirements be invalidated?

CHAPTER 8

SEPARATION OF POWERS

■ ■ ■

The Constitution contemplates that the national government will have three branches: Congress, vested with "[a]ll legislative Powers" (Article I); the President, assisted by various Departments, who would carry out the "executive Power" (Article II); and the Supreme Court, and such "inferior courts" as Congress should establish, vested with the "judicial Power" (Article III). These three Articles describe the responsibilities of each branch of the national government, and Article I sets forth procedural and substantive limits on the authority of Congress to legislate. While it sounds simple enough, this scheme has given rise to vexing constitutional quandaries. Some of these quandaries have arisen in response to reformist demands of social movements in the twentieth century. For example, until the 1960s, Congress was completely unresponsive to the equality demands of the civil rights movement—and the policymaking void was filled by the Supreme Court and the President.[1] Hence, the Imperial Presidency (§ 1 of this chapter) and the Political Court (Chapter 9) were in no small part a product of identity politics. The most dramatic separation of powers controversies, however, have involved other activities of Congress and the President, most recently the War on Terrorism (§ 3). The great controversies of the last century have exposed a number of tensions in separation of powers jurisprudence.[2]

In examining these tensions, we start with the text and structure of the Constitution, particularly as explicated in *The Federalist Papers* and illuminated by commentators. Immediately following this conceptual overview is an excerpt from Professor Casper's presentation of the historical background against which the Framers drafted Articles I, II, and

---

[1] By executive orders in the 1940s, President Roosevelt desegregated the federal civil service and President Truman desegregated the armed forces. From the Roosevelt through the Carter Administrations, the Department of Justice engaged in law-inviting activism to support the civil rights movement's constitutional campaigns.

[2] On the structure of the national government, see, e.g., Charles Black, *Structure and Relationship in Constitutional Law* (1969); Mathew E. Glassman, Congressional Research Service, *Separation of Powers: An Overview* (Jan. 8, 2016); Saikrishna Bangalore Prakash, *Imperial from the Beginning: The Constitution and the Original Executive* (2015); John Yoo, *Crisis and Command: A History of Executive Power from George Washington to George W. Bush* (2009); Rebecca Brown, *Separated Powers and Ordered Liberty*, 139 U. Pa. L. Rev. 1513 (1991); Steven G. Calabresi & Saikrishna Prakash, *The President's Power To Execute the Laws*, 104 Yale L.J. 541 (1994); Victoria F. Nourse, *Toward a New Constitutional Anatomy*, 56 Stan. L. Rev. 835 (2004); Peter L. Strauss, *The Place of Agencies in Government: Separation of Powers and the Fourth Branch*, 84 Colum. L. Rev. 573 (1984).

III. The rest of this chapter then explores these tensions in the Supreme Court's application of Articles I–III to cases where an imperial presidency, a greedy Congress, or even both Congress and the President acting in concert have arguably claimed powers they do not have or usurped the powers of another branch. Chapter 9 will explore these tensions in connection with the federal courts' assertion of authority.

1.   *Separation of Powers Versus Checks and Balances.* Read as a unit, the first three Articles of the Constitution have been interpreted to suggest two general organizing principles, which are sometimes in tension with one another. One is separation of powers, the notion that the three branches shall be separate from one another and shall concentrate on their respective functions (described in the "vesting clause" of each Article). A second is checks and balances, the notion that each of the three branches shall have some influence on how the other two branches perform their specialized roles. (A third principle is internal checks. According to Article I, § 7, Congress cannot accomplish its primary task, enacting statutes, unless both chambers agree to the same text and it is presented to the President. There are internal checks within the executive and judicial branches, but they are not mandated by the Constitution.)

Although the Supreme Court and any duly established inferior courts alone exercise the "judicial Power of the United States" (Art. III, § 1), their authority depends upon the cooperation of the other branches. Congress has substantial power over the Court's appellate jurisdiction (Art. III, § 2, cl. 2) and has the power to create the inferior federal courts (Art. III, § 1). The President executes judgments entered by the courts (Art. II, § 1). Moreover, the political branches determine who is a Justice of the Court. The President nominates Justices as well as judges on the "inferior" federal courts, who then must be approved by the Senate (Art. II, § 2, cl. 2). The House has the power to impeach federal judges and Justices (Art. I, § 2, cl. 5), who are removed from office if convicted by the Senate (Art. I, § 3, cl. 6).

Although Congress, and only Congress, exercises "[a]ll legislative Powers" (Art. I, § 1), before a bill becomes a law it must be presented to the President and (with specified exceptions) signed by the President (Art. I, § 7, cl. 2–3). Once a bill does become a law, it may be ineffective if the Supreme Court finds it unconstitutional (Art. VI, § 2, as interpreted in *Marbury* and later cases). The execution and interpretation of the laws are left to the executive and the judiciary. To take a specific example, Congress' power to declare war and regulate the armed forces (Art. I, § 8, cl. 11–14) depends very much on the cooperation of the President, who is the Commander-in-Chief of the armed forces (Art. II, § 2, cl. 1).

Although the President, and only the President, has the "executive Power" (Art. II, § 1), the Constitution makes clear that it is the "Laws" passed by Congress that must be "faithfully" executed (Art. II, § 3). The

President, like Congress, is subject to judicial remedies for violating statutes and the Constitution (Art. VI, § 2, as interpreted in *Marbury*). Additionally, the President's primary officers must meet with the approval of the Senate (Art. II, § 2, cl. 2). Like judges, the President and such officers can be impeached by the House (Art. I, § 2, cl. 5) and removed from office if convicted by the Senate (Art. I, § 3, cl. 6; Art. II, § 4).

The Framers and those defending the Constitution in the ratification debates were well aware of this tension between separation of powers and checks and balances. Rather than resolve the tension, however, they sought to justify it. Invoking Montesquieu's celebrated defense of separation of powers, the Anti-Federalists attacked the Constitution for permitting so much intermixing. James Madison responded in *Federalist* No. 47 (App. 2) that neither Montesquieu nor the British system which inspired Montesquieu contemplated a complete separation. Madison read these sources to suggest that the optimal protection of citizens' liberty lay in a strategy combining separation of powers with checks and balances. A system in which each branch needed some cooperation from another branch before setting policy would protect against arbitrary action better than a system in which the three branches acted entirely on their own and simply competed with one another.

2.   *Ensuring Efficacy Versus Preventing Tyranny.* The main policy emphasized in the ratification debates was the prevention of tyranny, and that policy was argued under both the separation of powers idea and the checks-and-balances idea. Following Montesquieu, *Federalist* No. 47 (App. 2) said: "The accumulation of all powers, legislative, executive, and judiciary, in the same hands, whether of one, a few, or many, and whether hereditary, self-appointed, or elective, may justly be pronounced the very definition of tyranny." The rationale was that the separation of rulemaking from the rule-executing and rule-adjudicating arms of government gives citizens some protection against being persecuted and treated unfairly— there is less danger of factional vendettas. Also important is that when legislators enact statutes, other branches will implement those statutes. The implementation by others, over whom the legislature has no absolute control, has two advantages. See *Federalist* No. 78 (App. 2). On the one hand, legislators will be more reluctant to pass unfair statutes, out of fear that tyrannical laws could be used against them and their supporters. On the other hand, if unjust laws were passed, they might be implemented in ways that avoid their most tyrannical features. Separation of powers strategies are a negative way of protecting against tyranny, by ensuring that circumstances do not unduly encourage it.[3]

---

[3]   See Paul Verkuil, *Separation of Powers, the Rule of Law, and the Idea of Independence*, 39 Wm. & Mary L. Rev. 301 (1989). For a modern critique of the Framers as naïve, see Eric A. Posner & Adrian Vermeule, *The Executive Unbound: After the Madisonian Republic* (2010).

Checks-and-balances strategies represent a more positive way of protecting against tyranny: By requiring the cooperation of more than a single branch to take action, it is more likely that the action will be reasonable and just. This idea is more subtle than the simple insight that "two heads are better than one." The ambitious legislator will be more reluctant to press for tyrannical laws favoring her faction, because her ambition is countered by that of the also ambitious executive, who can be expected to resist arbitrary legislative grabs for power—or who might even turn oppressive laws against their authors. Much of the Framers' attention seems to have been focused on heading off potential legislative tyranny. See *Federalist* Nos. 10, 48 and 51 (App. 2). For this reason, it is particularly hard for Congress to do anything.

While protecting against tyranny was the Framers' most frequently discussed policy, in reaction to the colonists' objection to British rule, they also recognized a policy of ensuring efficacious national governance,[4] because the Framers also operated against their experience with the weak national government of the Articles of Confederation. (This was, after all, the reason for the new Constitution.) Some of the Framers specifically criticized the Articles of Confederation for not providing a national executive and judiciary to implement national policy. James Wilson defended the Constitution's establishment of separate executive functions as needed to respond in "emergencies, in which the man [who] deliberates, is lost." *Federalist* No. 70 defended a strong executive as "essential to the protection of the community against foreign attacks," as well as "the steady administration of the laws; to the protection of property against those irregular and highhanded combinations which sometimes interrupt the ordinary course of justice; to the security of liberty against the enterprises and assaults of ambition, of faction, and of anarchy."

These two policies, against tyranny and in favor of efficacy, are sometimes in tension. Government may run roughshod over the interests of some to accomplish national goals expeditiously. Indeed, expeditious government action typically involves some sacrifice on the part of a minority of the citizenry, a phenomenon reflected in our nation's response to the events of September 11, 2001. Today, therefore, we worry about presidential tyranny more than we worry about legislative tyranny. The congeries of procedural roadblocks to efficacious legislative action have yielded legislative paralysis and encouraged the executive (and sometimes the courts) to take initiatives. The Constitution is quite vague about checks on the imperial presidency, or upon government by judiciary, which the Framers termed the "least dangerous branch." *Federalist* No. 78 (App. 2). Also, governance today is by agencies, which combine rulemaking (legislative), adjudication (judicial), and enforcement (executive) functions

---

[4] See Prakash, *Imperial from the Beginning,* 63–66; Suzanna Sherry, *Separation of Powers: Asking a Different Question,* 30 Wm. & Mary L. Rev. 287 (1989).

in one body. Government by agencies is justified on efficiency grounds, but might not this concentration of functions violate the central limiting precepts of separation of powers as well as checks and balances?

3.　*Political Versus Judicial Enforcement of Separation of Powers.* It is not clear whether the Supreme Court should have much of a role in deciding separation of powers disputes. Recall Herbert Wechsler's "political safeguards" thesis (Chapter 7, §§ 1, 5B): Because political safeguards such as the state representation in the Senate provide sufficient protection for state autonomy, the Supreme Court's power of judicial review should not include the Constitution's federalism-based limits on congressional power. Jesse Choper makes the same kind of argument for separation of powers issues: Where the President is usurping power from Congress, the latter has plenty of political weapons with which to respond; the same is true when Congress seeks to usurp authority from the President. In those cases, and others, the Framers did not expect the Court to intervene, and its intervention is neither necessary nor productive.[5]

Commentators and judges remain deeply divided over the wisdom of judicial review for separation of powers issues. Recall that the first important case of judicial review (*Marbury*) involved a clash between a new President and the outgoing Congress—Jefferson and Secretary Madison were refusing to carry out mandatory duties established by the prior Congress. There was no hue and cry in 1803 that the Supreme Court had "betrayed" the original deal by announcing authority to review the Jefferson Administration's alleged failure to "take Care that the Laws be faithfully executed" (Art. II, § 3). Nor is it clear that the political safeguards will usually mobilize against usurpation. The gravest dangers to the separation of powers come in periods of emergency or alarm—precisely the time when the political organs are least likely to resist. As a relatively insulated branch, the Supreme Court might be most inclined to resist, but perhaps least able to stop, unwarranted assertions of authority.

An open question is the "productivity" of the Supreme Court's intervention in separation of powers disputes. As to that, the proof is in the pudding. We invite you to read the cases in this chapter—especially the cases involving the War on Terror (§ 3)—with these questions in mind: Has the Court developed a coherent body of law limiting the political branches

---

[5]　Compare Jesse H. Choper, *Judicial Review and the National Political Process: A Functional Reconsideration of the Role of the Supreme Court* (1980) (separation of powers issues should be treated as nonjusticiable political questions), with Harold H. Koh, *The National Security Constitution: Sharing Power After the Iran-Contra Affair* (1990) (plenty of issues are appropriate for judicial resolution), and with John Choon Yoo, *The Powers of War and Peace: The Constitution and Foreign Affairs After 9/11* (2005) (urging a highly restrained judicial role in foreign affairs cases, leaving such issues to presidential and congressional accommodation), and John F. Manning, *The Supreme Court, 2013 Term—Foreword: The Means of Constitutional Power*, 124 Harv. L. Rev. 1 (2014) (deferential judicial review built into the Constitution's structure), and with Philip Bobbitt, *Terror and Consent: The Wars for the Twenty-First Century* (2008) (anti-terror measures must be grounded in the rule of law, including judicial review).

along separation of powers lines? Do the cases sensibly mediate the tensions we find in the Constitution's framework for such issues? Do they reach a good balance, substantially protecting liberty without sacrificing efficacy?

4. *Formalist Versus Functionalist Reasoning.* To the extent the Supreme Court does assume an active role in separation of powers conflicts (as it decidedly has), the challenge is how to draw the lines of national responsibilities suitably. There are several different strategies the Court could take if it wants to police the Constitution's boundaries. For example, the Court could strictly enforce the lines apparently drawn in the Constitution, based upon its original meaning.[6] On this view, the President is in charge of all executive functions, and if he tries to make rather than execute law he will be overruled; Congress does all the legislating, and if it tries to meddle in executive functions it will be overruled; the courts do all the adjudicating, and if they try to make policy they will be overruled. This approach has traditionally been considered an example of constitutional *formalism*. It has the advantage of providing rules for national decisionmaking that the Court might find easy to discern and implement: If a practice violates the Constitution's allocation, the Court strikes it down; if a practice does not fall outside that allocation, the Court should permit it and leave the political branches to work out ultimate accommodations. A problem with the formalist approach is that it is not always clear what boundaries and rules for federal government decisionmaking are embodied in the Constitution. Even when the boundaries and rules are clear, they may not be responsive to the ultimate constitutional policies in light of modern conditions (the imperial presidency, independent agencies, and so forth).

In contrast, a *functionalist* approach would sacrifice or soften some of the sharp constitutional lines to permit "necessary" government action, unless such action generally threatens our freedoms.[7] A functionalist approach can be justified on the ground that it subserves the ultimate goal of the Constitution (the "general Welfare") and as such contributes to the overall legitimacy of government. A problem with a functionalist approach is that it is not always clear what situations justify a departure from the apparent commands of the Constitution. A particular case might seem to cry out for deviation, but the proper balance is not just whether a deviation is justified in this case (the costs of enforcing an apparent constitutional line are outweighed by the benefits of deviating this one time), but whether

---

[6] E.g., Prakash, *Imperial from the Beginning*; Stephen G. Calabresi & Kevin H. Rhodes, *The Structural Constitution: Unitary Executive, Plural Judiciary*, 105 Harv. L. Rev. 1153 (1992) (sophisticated theoretical examination of the vesting clauses); John F. Manning, *Textualism as a Nondelegation Doctrine*, 97 Colum. L. Rev. 673 (1997) (similar, for bicameralism).

[7] E.g., Abner Greene, *Checks and Balances in an Era of Presidential Lawmaking*, 61 U. Chi. L. Rev. 123 (1994) (on the fear of aggrandizement); Strauss, *Agencies in Government* (on the nature of the administrative state in light of separation of powers norms).

the deviation's long-term benefits outweigh its long-term costs, including the rule-of-law costs of occasional deviation from formal commands (a President who "gets away with" a usurpation of congressional power one time is more prone to make greater inroads into congressional authority in the future).

Finally, the Court can adopt an approach that is something of a hybrid of the formalist and functional approaches.[8] For example, the Court could decide, for functionalist reasons, that it will enforce some of the constitutional boundaries strictly (bicameralism and presentment) and, for equally functionalist reasons, that it will relax other boundaries to accommodate government in the modern regulatory state (such as allowing independent agencies that are part of neither Congress nor the presidency). Or, it could decide to enforce the textual boundaries and then add some functionalist restrictions of its own.

5. *Horizontal (Functional) Versus Vertical (Political) Approaches.* As described above, both functional and formal perspectives approach separation of powers issues *horizontally*: Which branch is vested with the authority to do something (formalist) or is most capable of doing it (functionalist)? Does a novel arrangement cross institutional lines (formalist) or pose risks of usurpation by the empowered branch (functionalist)? Victoria Nourse argues that we should also consider the issues *vertically*:[9] What constituency does each branch represent, and what incentives does that create for decisionmakers in that branch? What new incentives does a shift in authority from one branch to another create? What new risks does the shift create for the ability of popular majorities to affect policy—or for minority groups or individuals who might be unduly harmed by majority-supported policies?[10] How does the shift affect the nation's overall posture as a representative democracy?

Say the President invaded another country without congressional authorization. As a formal matter, this would ask us to think about whether the President was acting (properly) as the Commander-in-Chief of the armed forces (Art. II, § 2, cl. 1) or was acting to declare war, a power vested in Congress (Art. I, § 8, cl. 11). As a functional matter, one might ask whether such action reflected a good balance between liberty and efficacy: The President would argue that his action was needed as a decisive measure to head off the escalating risk of devastating foreign

---

[8] Many of the cases in this chapter will exemplify both formalist and functionalist arguments. See William N. Eskridge, Jr., *Relationships Between Formalism and Functionalism in Separation of Powers Cases*, 22 Harv. J. L & Pub. Pol'y 21 (1998).

[9] See Victoria F. Nourse, *The Vertical Separation of Powers*, 49 Duke L.J. 749 (1999); Nourse, *Toward a "Due Foundation" for the Separation of Powers: The Federalist Papers as Political Narrative*, 74 Tex. L. Rev. 447 (1996); Nourse, *Toward a New Constitutional Anatomy Structure*, 56 Stan. L. Rev. 835 (2004).

[10] The dual-risk analysis in Nourse's work is taken from Neil Komesar, *Imperfect Alternatives: Choosing Institutions in Law, Economics, and Public Policy* (1994).

attack. His critics would respond that such a drastic and aggressive step should only be taken after deliberation and vote in Congress (which as a practical matter has to fund the enterprise).

A vertical approach to the issue would look at constituencies and incentives. The President has a national constituency, with one person formally responsible for all actions taken under color of that office; Congress contains many members, all representing local (House) or state (Senate) constituencies, with no one person formally responsible for its deliberative actions. If the President acts against a foreign country, there is a risk that he is acting prematurely and without the support of all the constituencies needed for a unified national effort. A congressional declaration addresses those risks much better, but poses the risk of being too slow to respond and too fragmented to respond decisively. This balance of risks could support a rule that the Framers seem to have had in mind (see § 1B): The President may act to repel foreign attacks, but Congress must declare war when there is no immediate danger.

Professor Nourse's theory is an example of a representation-reinforcing theory of separation of powers. (Recall *Carolene Products*, which set forth a representation-reinforcing theory of individual rights (Chapter 2, § 3B), and *Barnwell Brothers*, which set forth such a theory for the Dormant Commerce Clause (Chapter 7, § 6B).) If the Supreme Court is going to play a role in arbitrating separation of powers disputes, this might be an attractive basis for its decisions. Keep the vertical perspective in mind as you read the cases in this chapter.

6. *Fixed Versus Evolving Rules.* Recall the debate in between originalist and evolutive theories of judicial review (Chapter 2, § 3). This debate plays out in distinctive ways for separation of powers issues. On the one hand, the Framers hardly anticipated the Civil War, the New Deal, or the War on Terror; indeed, they failed to anticipate some of the challenges faced by the Washington Administration (1789–97). Not only have events blurred some of the lines suggested by the Constitution, but they have motivated what might be considered major changes in the constitutional balance. Because many separation of powers issues are not justiciable (Chapter 9), much of the evolution has occurred within the political process, with little or no input from the Supreme Court (recall tension #3). The cases in this chapter illustrate the allure of a constitutional rule of *adverse possession*: If Congress (to take the usual example) has acquiesced in a presidential exercise of power over a period of years, that evidence significantly supports the constitutional acceptability of that practice once it reaches the Supreme Court.[11] Recall a similar point made by John

---

[11] Adverse possession theories find support in the concurring and dissenting opinions in the *Steel Seizure Case*, excerpted in Section 1A below and is the explicit basis for much of the presidential authority asserted in Yoo, *Powers of War and Peace*, 9–10. Other original meaning thinkers strongly reject an adverse possession theory of executive power and argue that it remains

Marshall in the opening portion of *McCulloch* (Chapter 7, § 1): Because the political process had come to embrace the legitimacy of the Bank of the United States, it came to the Court cloaked in a strong presumption of constitutionality.

On the other hand, the Framers' thinking about separation of powers issues retains a cogency it does not have for their thinking about free speech, due process, and equal protection. As with federalism cases, original meaning is taken seriously by lawyers and sometimes by politicians in separation of powers cases. So we start at the beginning—the drafting origins of the Constitution's separation of powers, introduced in the following essay. (You should also read *Federalist* Nos. 47 and 78, reproduced in Appendix 2 of this casebook.)

GERHARD CASPER,
An Essay in Separation of Powers: Some Early Versions and Practices
30 Wm. & Mary L. Rev. 211, 212–22 (1989)[12]

Article VI of the Maryland Declaration of Rights of 1776 provided "[t]hat the legislative, executive and judicial powers of government, ought to be forever separate and distinct from each other." Similar formulations appear elsewhere, for instance in the 1776 Virginia Bill of Rights. * * *

Invocation of the phrase "separation of powers" in bills of rights, such as those of Maryland, Massachusetts, New Hampshire, North Carolina, Virginia, and France * * * suggests a common linkage between the concept of liberty and the notion of separation of powers. * * * Montesquieu, perhaps the most frequently cited and most confused and confusing of the writers on separation of powers, provided the classical formulation concerning the linkage:

> When the legislative and executive powers are united in the same person, or in the same body of magistracy, there can be then no liberty; because apprehensions may arise, lest the same monarch or senate should enact tyrannical laws, to execute them in a tyrannical manner.

> Again, there is no liberty, if the power of judging be not separated from the legislative and executive powers. Were it joined with the legislative, the life and liberty of the subject would be exposed to arbitrary control; for the judge would be then the legislator. Were it joined to the executive power, the judge might behave with all the violence of an oppressor.

---

unchanged from 1789. E.g., *NLRB v. Noel Canning*, 134 S.Ct. 2550, 2605 (2014) (Scalia, J., concurring in the judgment); Prakash, *Imperial from the Beginning*.

[12] Copyright © 2000 by the *William and Mary Law Review*. Reprinted with permission.

As put forward by Montesquieu, separation of powers is a functional concept; separation is a necessary, if not a sufficient, condition of liberty. Its absence promotes tyranny. * * *

As one reviews the state constitutions adopted between 1776 and 1787 for the ways in which they implemented separation of powers notions, one is struck by the fact that the particulars display an exceedingly weak version of separation of powers. Most of the constitutions made a conceptual distinction, either explicitly or implicitly, between legislative, executive, and judicial functions, introduced more or less elaborate systems of interbranch ineligibilities, and gave some, although often a modest, measure of independence to the judiciary. The most distinct feature of the constitutions, however, was the dependence of the executive on the legislative branch on four counts. First, only New York, Massachusetts, and New Hampshire provided for the election of governors by voters. In the latter two states, the choice reverted to the legislature if no candidate received a majority of the votes. The other constitutions granted the legislature the power to elect the governor or president, typically on an annual basis. In Pennsylvania the legislature and the "supreme executive council," which was popularly elected, jointly chose the president. Second, only Massachusetts and New York recognized an overridable veto. In New York the veto power was lodged in a council of revision. Third, all states provided for some kind of executive or privy council, generally elected by the legislature. Fourth, states distributed the power of appointments in various ways, but legislative controls predominated.

[These state constitutional arrangements were criticized for intermingling executive, legislative, and judicial powers. The "Essex Result" of 1778, attacking the proposed Massachusetts Constitution, said:] "A little attention to the subject will convince us, that these three powers ought to be in different hands, and independent of one another, and so balanced, and each having that check upon the other, that their independence shall be preserved." * * *

The Bill of Rights of the 1784 New Hampshire Constitution expressed clearly that the doctrine of separation of powers, or for that matter the notion of checks and balances, could not supply neat formulas from which proper governmental organizational arrangements would follow automatically. Article XXXVII of the New Hampshire Bill of Rights displayed a deeper appreciation of the problem than the more barren assertions in all the other state constitutions:

> In the government of this state, the three essential powers thereof, to wit, the legislative, executive and judicial, ought to be kept as separate from and independent of each other, as the nature of a free government will admit, or as is consistent with

that chain of connection that binds the whole fabric of the constitution in one indissoluble bond of union and amity.

This provision, which is still in force, obviously views the separation of powers as essential to free government. However, it also reflects the concept of separate and independent powers as limited by the very notion of free government and by the necessity of maintaining "the whole fabric of the constitution." In short, New Hampshire emphasizes separation, coordination, and cooperation. Its dialectical view of the matter concisely summarizes the difficulties that awaited the federal constitutional convention as it faced the separation of powers "doctrine."

The Articles of Confederation had established a congress of state delegates as the central law-making and governing institution. Although its President, committees, and civil officers partook of an executive quality, and although after 1780 it established a court of appeals for cases of capture, the Confederation can hardly be seen as possessing the characteristics of a tripartite government. On the other hand, one should not overlook the fact that some institutional separation of administrative tasks had evolved, dictated, as it were, by the nature of things, and the need to free the Congress from concerning itself with too much administrative detail.

Although the absence of separation of powers was not generally viewed as the main weakness of the Confederation, Hamilton criticized the Articles as early as July 1783 for "confounding legislative and executive powers in a single body" and for lacking a federal judicature "having cognizance of all matters of general concern." In a draft resolution calling for a convention to amend the Articles, Hamilton wrote that the Confederation's structure was "contrary to the most approved and well founded maxims of free government which require that the legislative executive and judicial authorities should be deposited in distinct and separate hands." Hamilton had intended to submit the resolution to the Continental Congress, but abandoned the project for want of support.

When Randolph opened the substantive deliberations of the 1787 Convention with his enumeration of the defects of the Confederation, he apparently made no reference to separation of powers. The Virginia Plan, submitted the same day, however, implied separation of powers and called for a quadripartite governmental structure: a bicameral legislature, a national executive, a national judiciary (to serve during good behavior), and a council of revision to be composed of the executive and members of the judiciary. The first house of the legislature was to elect the second from a pool of candidates to be nominated by the states, and the legislature was to elect the executive and judiciary. The executive was to enjoy "the Executive rights vested in Congress by the Confederation," but what these rights were not adumbrated.

Other plans for a constitution all presupposed a three-branch structure of government. A resolution "that a national government ought to be established consisting of a supreme legislative, judiciary, and executive" was adopted overwhelmingly in the Committee of the Whole on May 30, the day following submission of the Virginia Plan. In a way, this event was the beginning and the end of the consideration of separation of powers *as such* in the Convention. To be sure, in the subsequent discussions of the structure and powers of the legislative, executive, and judicial branches as well as in the repeated debates concerning a council of revision, the delegates raised many points about the independence of the respective branches, the dangers of encroachments, and the need for checks and balances. What was strikingly absent, however, was anything that might be viewed as a coherent and generally shared view of separation of powers.

The constitutional text itself, although implying the notion of distinct branches, did not invoke the separation of powers as a principle. Some of the state ratifying conventions attempted to remedy this omission in their original proposals for bills of rights to be added to the Constitution. Madison also sought a remedy. * * *

Madison's 1789 proposal for a new Article VII to precede the existing one (which was to be renumbered) was ingenious in the manner in which it formulated a separation of powers doctrine that took account of the constitutional scheme of checks and balances:

> The powers delegated by this constitution, are appropriated to the departments to which they are respectively distributed: so that the legislative department shall never exercise the powers vested in the executive or judicial; nor the executive exercise the powers vested in the legislative or judicial; nor the judicial exercise the powers vested in the legislative or executive departments.

The separation of powers provision of Roger Sherman's draft bill of rights, also dating from the summer of 1789, captured even more clearly the point made by Madison's proposed Article VII:

> The legislative, executive and judiciary powers vested by the Constitution in the respective branches of the Government of the United States shall be exercised according to the distribution therein made, so that neither of said branches shall assume or exercise any of the powers peculiar to either of the other branches.

The House adopted Madison's amendment (with a minor change) despite objections that it was unnecessary and "subversive of the Constitution." Madison supposed "the people would be gratified with the amendment, as it was admitted that the powers ought to be separate and distinct; it might also tend to an explanation of some doubts that might arise respecting the construction of the Constitution." This was an intriguing suggestion: the amendment would provide a principle of interpretation for the Constitution—*in dubio, pro* separation of powers. In fact, Madison had taken this position earlier that year when discussing the removal power. Alas, the Senate rejected the amendment for reasons we shall never know. One can only surmise that the Senate was not eager to adopt separation of powers as an independent doctrine or even as a mere principle of construction for the many and subtle "mixing" decisions of the Framers, some of which benefited the Senate.

Addendum. For an excellent survey of state constitutions at and soon after the Founding, see Peter M. Shane, *The Originalist Myth of the Unitary Executive,* 19 U. Pa. J. Const'l L. 323 (2016) (appendix of separation of powers provisions in early state constitutions, pp. 363–68). Dean Shane documents how state constitutions combined strict separation of powers provisions with authorization of legislative control over specified executive functions. Accord, Jerry Mashaw, *Creating the Administrative Constitution: The Lost One Hundred Years of American Administrative Law* (2012).

In *Executive Power Essentialism and Foreign Affairs*, 102 Mich. L. Rev. 545, 571–85 (2002), Curtis A. Bradley and Martin S. Flaherty make the important point that the early state constitutions reflected important *shifts in political thinking*. The initial wave of state constitutions, adopted during the Revolution, were republican; there were ten such constitutions by 1777. They revealed strong distrust of executive power (associated with King George III) and hence concentrated power in legislatures. Some states had no chief executives; others created governors who shared power with privy councils drawn from or appointed by the legislature. In most states, the power to appoint judges and other officials was vested entirely in the legislature.

Founders such as James Madison were disappointed by the performance of state legislatures under these arrangements, and state constitutions adopted in the 1780s vested less authority in legislatures and more in governors. The Massachusetts Constitution of 1780 made the governor popularly elected; although it defined his powers carefully, the governor had both appointment and veto authority (both missing from most of the other state constitutions in effect during the 1780s). Saikrishna Bangalore Prakash argues in "A King, Under the Title of President," in *Imperial from the Beginning: The Constitution of the Original Executive* 12–35 (2015), that the Framers who assembled in Philadelphia favored a strong executive branch, with many monarchical powers, to provide decisiveness and energy for government responding to crises and challenges. (We shall return to this thesis in Section 2.)

NOTE ON EARLY INTERACTIONS BETWEEN THE
BRANCHES OF THE GOVERNMENT, 1790–1798

In addition to the intellectual and drafting origins of the constitutional separation of powers, early practice might be relevant to discerning the original understanding of Articles I–III.[13] Indeed, the leading players in the early years of the republic were aware that their interactions and points of agreement or compromise would set "precedents" for subsequent practice. At the same time, however, there was often no consensus as to the precise contours or even root theory of separate powers.[14]

An example of both points involved the *Decision of 1789*.[15] In that first year of the Washington Administration, the House of Representatives' consideration of a bill to create a Department of Foreign Affairs turned to this question: Who would have the power to remove the Secretary of that Department? Some representatives thought that removal power must parallel appointment power: the President could remove only with the consent of the Senate (accord, *Federalist* No. 77 (Hamilton)). Others thought that the President, acting alone, should have the power to remove the Secretary—either because it was good policy that Congress in its discretion ought to choose (Representative Madison's original view) *or* because the Constitution required such power to rest with the President alone (Madison's view by the end of the debate). The House and Senate both ultimately voted for a law that indirectly left the removal power with the President alone, but with the basis for that power (the Constitution versus congressional choice) left dangling. On the other hand, the Decision of 1789 did set a precedent followed by subsequent Congresses.

Another precedent-setting episode arose out of a proposal in the House to request the President to initiate an investigation into the destruction of the army command under General St. Clair in Ohio.[16] Hostilities with the Indians had commenced in 1789, and the St. Clair disaster was an incident in that

---

[13] For clashing historical treatments of early practice as shedding light on original understandings, compare Curtis A. Bradley & Martin S. Flaherty, *Executive Power Essentialism and Foreign Affairs*, 102 Mich. L. Rev. 545 (2002), with Saikrishna B. Prakash & Michael Ramsey, *The Executive Power over Foreign Affairs*, 111 Yale L.J. 231 (2001), and Steven G. Calabresi & Saikrishna B. Prakash, *The President's Power to Execute the Laws*, 104 Yale L.J. 541 (1994), with Martin S. Flaherty, *History "Lite" in Modern American Constitutionalism*, 95 Colum. L. Rev. 523 (1995), and Shane, *Originalist Myth of the Unitary Executive*, and William Michael Treanor, *Fame, the Founding and the Power to Declare War*, 82 Cornell L. Rev. 695 (1997), with John C. Yoo, *The Continuation of Politics by Other Means: The Original Understanding of War Powers*, 84 Cal. L. Rev. 167 (1996).

[14] In 1790, John Jay observed that there was agreement that there should be three independent branches, but "how to constitute and ballance them in such a Manner as best to guard against Abuse and Fluctuation, & preserve the constitution from Encroachments, are Points on which there continues to be a great Diversity of opinions, and on which we have all as yet much to learn." Maeva Marcus, *Separation of Powers in the Early National Period*, 30 Wm. & Mary L. Rev. 269, 270 (1989), quoting Jay's Charge to the Grand Jury of the Circuit Court for the District of New York, Apr. 12, 1790.

[15] Casper, *Some Early Versions and Practices*, 234–39; Curtis & Flaherty, *Executive Power Essentialism*, 656–64.

[16] Casper, *Some Early Versions and Practices*, 228–29.

ongoing struggle. Representatives themselves objected that such a request was improper, because it amounted to an encroachment on executive powers, 3 Annals of Cong. 490–94 (1792). The proposal was defeated, and the House instead appointed its own committee of inquiry. President Washington and his cabinet were in agreement that the House acted properly and agreed to cooperate. The President insisted, however, that requests for executive department papers be made directly to the President, who would withhold any information, "the disclosure of which would injure the public." The House in turn followed the President's conditions when it formally requested papers.

During the course of the St. Clair investigation, the Secretary of War and another executive officer asked to present their views directly to the House, which instead asked them to present their views to the investigating committee. As this episode suggests, much thought was given to whether personal interactions among the branches were appropriate. The trend in the Washington Administration was away from face-to-face and informal dealings. Thus, President Washington himself refused a Senate request that he submit appointments in person to the senators, as inconsistent with his vision of the appointments process, and after one face-to-face encounter on a treaty with Native Americans both the President and Congress decided that complex treaty matters were best handled through formal communications.

Nonetheless, there was a great deal of interbranch communication. For example, the statute creating the Treasury Department directed the Secretary "to make report, and give information to either branch of the legislature, in person or in writing (as he may be required), respecting all matters referred to him by the Senate or House of Representatives," 1 Stat. 66. More important, the Washington Administration's foreign policy was conducted with constant coordination with Congress for practical reasons: the Senate was needed to ratify treaties, and both House and Senate were needed for appropriations.[17] Starting in 1790, the administration sought the return of American hostages taken by the Barbary Powers and an arrangement whereby the Powers would cease harassment of American shipping. At most points of his dealings with the Barbary Powers, the President sought to keep Congress apprised of the diplomatic situation and the options being considered (including war), sought or received the advice of either chamber, and acted in conformity with legislative consensus. Over Senate objections, Washington even included the House of Representatives in his consultations about the possibility of a treaty, again for the practical reason that any treaty would involve monetary payments (ransom and tribute) requiring House initiation and approval. The President also demanded, and generally obtained, confidentiality for his messages to Congress and for most legislative deliberations. The careful coordination paid off: a treaty was ratified in 1796, and monies appropriated in 1797, although the House threw off the requirement of confidentiality that year.

---

[17] Casper, *Some Early Versions and Practices*, 242–57.

The Adams Administration handled its big foreign crisis in a similarly cooperative way.[18] French raids on American commerce and a disrespectful demand of tribute from American envoys in 1797 generated outrage in the United States. The Adams Administration refused to pay a penny for tribute and commenced the "Quasi-War" with France in 1798. As had the Washington Administration in its dealings with the Barbary Powers, the Adams Administration needed and obtained Congress's cooperation to fund new ships and armed forces to confront the French. Although some hyperintensive Federalists wanted a formal declaration of war against France, Adams did not ask for, and Congress did not provide, such a declaration; naval hostilities lasted more than two years.

The federal judiciary was likewise attuned to its theoretical independence and the precedential nature of early arrangements. When in 1793 Secretary of State Jefferson asked the Supreme Court for its opinion on legal issues, the Court responded that it would not issue *advisory opinions*. "[T]he three departments of the government [being] in certain respects checks upon each other, and our being judges of a court of last resort, are considerations which accord strong arguments against the propriety of our extrajudicially deciding the questions alluded to, especially as the power given by the Constitution to the President, of calling the heads of departments for opinions, seems to have purposely as well as expressly united to the executive departments."[19] Also, federal judges refused to participate as judges deciding claims for pensions by veterans claiming to have been wounded, pursuant to the Invalid Pensions Act of 1792, 1 Stat. 243, because their findings were only recommendations to the Secretary of War.[20] Yet individual Justices gave their opinions to executive and legislative officials, and judges participated in the pension statute as extrajudicial *commissioners* rather than as judges.[21] Chief Justices John Jay and Oliver Ellsworth served as presidential envoys to negotiate treaties during their tenures, over objections that were dismissed during the confirmation process.

SECTION 1. ISSUES OF EXECUTIVE AGGRANDIZEMENT (IMPERIAL PRESIDENCY)

Although President Washington initially walked on egg shells in his dealings with Congress, and tended to be solicitous of congressional opinions when he took either domestic or foreign affairs initiatives, as time went by he operated more independently, especially in matters of military or foreign policy. This was even truer of his successors. Illustrating

---

[18] Yoo, *Continuation of Politics by Other Means*, 292–93.

[19] Letter from John Jay, James Wilson, John Blair, James Iredell, and William Paterson to George Washington, Aug. 8, 1793, Record Group 59, National Archives, quoted and discussed in *Hart and Wechsler's The Federal Courts and the Federal System* 92–93 (4th ed. 1996); Maeva Marcus & Emily Van Tassel, *Judges and Legislators in the New Federal System 1789–1800*, in *Judges and Legislators: Toward Institutional Comity* 31, 42 (Robert Katzmann ed. 1988).

[20] Marcus, *Early National Period*, 272–73.

[21] *Id.* at 173–75.

aggressive executive department initiatives carried out without the close cooperation of Congress detailed in the previous Note were President Jefferson's doubling the size of the country through his agreement to purchase the Louisiana Territory from France; the "Monroe Doctrine," directing the European powers to leave Western Hemisphere matters to the United States; President Polk's leading us into the Mexican-American War; President Lincoln's leadership during the Civil War, including such bold strokes as the Emancipation Proclamation and such controversial practices as military trials of civilians and suspension of the writ of habeas corpus; President Andrew Johnson's defiance of the Reconstruction Congress and his insistence that the Tenure of Office Act, limiting his ability to discharge cabinet officers, was unconstitutional; President Teddy Roosevelt's deployment of "gunboat diplomacy" to protect American interests in other Western Hemisphere nations; and President Wilson's international role as a founder of the League of Nations (which the Congress then refused to permit our country to join).

Political scientists have suggested an explanation for these remarkable actions: the President has a huge *first mover advantage*, especially in crisis situations such as the Civil War, where the other branches face a double difficulty in opposing the President—they not only have to get their collective act together, but they would usually have to defy public opinion as well.[22] Consistent with this political science wisdom, the growth of the national government witnessed an even bigger growth in presidential power, because there were more problems that activist Presidents could tackle, and We the People usually voted for aggressive rather than passive presidential candidates (both Roosevelts, Truman, Kennedy, Johnson, Nixon, Reagan, etc.).

Political scientists as well as law professors have raised concerns that an "Imperial Presidency" threatens to eclipse the other branches of the national government, as well as the states, and thereby to disrupt the Constitution's system of checks and balances. See Arthur M. Schlesinger, *The Imperial Presidency* (1973); Bruce A. Ackerman, *The Decline and Fall of the American Republic* (2010). In contrast, Saikrishna Bangalore Prakash argues in *Imperial from the Beginning: The Constitution of the Original Executive* (2015) that the original design of Article II was to establish a "King Under the Title of President." *Id.* at 12–27. William Howell and Terry Moe argue that the Constitution undermines the President's ability to get things done; as the only functional branch of the federal government, the Presidency needs to be given the ability to fast-track his proposals through a vetogate-ridden Congress. Howell & Moe,

---

[22] William Howell, *Power without Persuasion: The Politics of Direct Presidential Action* (2003); Terry Moe & William Howell, *The Presidential Power of Unilateral Action*, 15 J.L. Econ. & Org. 132 (1999).

Relic: How the Constitution Undermines Effective Government—and Why We Need a More Powerful Presidency (2016).

This section examines three different contexts in which the Imperial Presidency has raised serious constitutional concerns: the President's alleged usurpation of legislative power in domestic (Part A) and foreign (Part B) affairs, and the President's insistence that his office immunizes him from judicial process applicable to other citizens or even other federal officials (Part C). Interestingly, it was the administration of now-admired President Harry Truman that most dramatically presented the first two issues: Truman committed the United States to the Korean War without a congressional declaration of war and, during the course of the war, seized the steel industry without congressional authorization. The last issue, of privilege and immunity, was pressed by President Richard Nixon's dramatic fall from power in 1974.

As you study the constitutional limitations on presidential power, consider the thesis of Eric A. Posner & Adrian Vermeule, *The Executive Unbound: After the Madisonian Republic* (2010), that constitutional rules have little or no effect on the Presidency and that the only effective limits on presidential power reside in public opinion and elections. Although consistent with the political scientists' first-mover advantage, their work is grounded in the authoritarian philosophy of a Weimar political scientist Carl Schmitt, who argued that chief executives in liberal democracies would always be able to evade or finesse preexisting rules aimed at limiting their authority.

A. THE POST-NEW DEAL FRAMEWORK

YOUNGSTOWN SHEET & TUBE CO. V. SAWYER (THE STEEL SEIZURE CASE)

343 U.S. 579, 72 S.Ct. 863, 96 L.Ed. 1153 (1952)

[The facts of the case were particularly complex.[23] Leading a United Nations-sanctioned peacekeeping force, the United States went to war with North Korea to repel its June 1950 attack on South Korea. Although Congress never declared war, it supported the war effort by authorizing a build-up of our armed forces to 3,500,000 people strong and appropriating unprecedented sums of money for national defense. In 1950, President Truman requested authority to requisition property and to allocate priorities for scarce goods. In Title IV of the Defense Production Act of 1950, Congress not only gave the President the powers requested, but also gave

---

[23] See Maeva Marcus, *Truman and the Steel Seizure Case: The Limits of Presidential Power* (1977); Alan Westin, *The Anatomy of a Constitutional Case* (1958); Henry M. Hart Jr. & Albert M. Sacks, *The Legal Process* 1010–46 (William N. Eskridge Jr. & Philip P. Frickey eds., 1994 [tent. ed. 1958]); Patricia L. Bellia, *The Story of the Steel Seizure Case,* in *Presidential Power Stories* 233 (Christopher Schroeder & Curtis Bradley eds., 2009).

him authority to stabilize wages and prices and to provide for the settlement of labor disputes arising in the defense program. Congress extended the Act in 1951. A Senate committee expressed concern about inflation in some of the defense industries, because of the strain of producing for both military and domestic markets; the committee emphasized the steel industry as the exemplar of this problem. A three-way dispute broke out among the government, the steel companies, and the unions: the unions wanted a wage increase, which the companies wouldn't grant without a hefty price increase, which the government resisted.[24]

[On April 4, 1952, the union announced a nationwide strike to start on April 9. The President was in a bind. During World War II, the War Labor Disputes Act had authorized the President to seize industrial plants threatened with disruptive labor disputes. That authority ended in 1946. Congress replaced it with a more limited authority. The Taft-Hartley Act of 1947 provided: If in his opinion an actual or threatened strike imperiled the nation's health or safety, the President was authorized to appoint a special board to report the facts of the dispute and, if the report failed to induce resolution of the dispute, to seek a district court order enjoining the strike for 80 days, to facilitate efforts at settling the dispute (this is called a "cooling-off order"). President Truman was not willing to invoke the Taft-Hartley Act.[25] Nor was he willing to invoke the Selective Service Act of 1948. Whenever a producer failed to fill an order for goods required by the armed forces for defense purposes within a specified period of time, the Act authorized the President to take immediate possession of the producer's facilities and operate them for the production of the required goods (with "just compensation" to be paid to the producer). Nor was President Truman willing to invoke Title II of the Defense Production Act of 1950, which set up procedures for the President to "acquire by condemnation" facilities necessary for the national defense. A prerequisite to condemnation was an effort by the President to acquire the facilities by negotiation.

---

[24] Pursuant to Title IV, President Truman established an Economic Stabilization Agency. On January 26, 1951, the Agency issued formal wage and price controls, to stem inflationary pressures in the steel industry, among others. On November 1, 1951, the United Steelworkers Union gave notice to the major steel companies that the union intended to demand wage increases at the end of its contract. The companies resisted these demands. On December 22, President Truman referred the union-industry dispute to the Wage Stabilization Board (WSB) for recommendation of a fair solution, also as authorized by the 1950 Act. On March 22, 1952, the WSB recommended a modest wage increase. The union embraced the recommendation; the companies rejected it but pressed the Office of Price Stabilization (OPS) for a price increase (favorable action on prices would have made the companies amenable to a wage increase). On March 28, the OPS suggested a modest price increase, which the companies rejected. On April 3, the companies offered the union a small wage increase, which the union rejected.

[25] In his memoirs, the President claims that both he and Congress assumed that the WSB procedures were supposed to be substitutes for the Taft-Hartley procedures; since he had already exhausted the WSB procedures, Taft-Hartley was not available. See Harry S. Truman, *Memoirs—Years of Trial and Hope* 465–78 (1956) (vol. 2). Also note that the Taft-Hartley Act itself was bitterly opposed by organized labor and enacted over President Truman's veto.

[Hours before the strike was to commence, the President issued Executive Order 10340, 17 Fed. Reg. 3139 (1952), which directed Secretary of Commerce Sawyer to take possession of the steel industry and to keep the mills operating, "in order to assure the continued availability of steel and steel products during the existing emergency." The order invoked "the authority vested in [the President] by the Constitution and laws of the United States, and as President of the United States and Commander in Chief of the armed forces of the United States."

[Executive Order 10340 had the advantage of maintaining production of an important war commodity without offending organized labor, which acquiesced in the order. It had the disadvantage of antagonizing the steel industry, which complied with the order but sued to have it overturned. On April 30, the steel companies obtained a preliminary injunction against the Secretary's action. The court of appeals stayed the effect of the injunction, pending review. In an extraordinary move, the Supreme Court took the case on certiorari on May 3; it was argued on May 12. The Court announced its decision affirming the injunction on June 2, 1952.]

JUSTICE BLACK delivered the opinion of the Court.

We are asked to decide whether the President was acting within his constitutional power when he issued an order directing the Secretary of Commerce to take possession of and operate most of the Nation's steel mills. The mill owners argue that the President's order amounts to lawmaking, a legislative function which the Constitution has expressly confided to the Congress and not to the President. The Government's position is that the order was made on findings of the President that his action was necessary to avert a national catastrophe which would inevitably result from a stoppage of steel production, and that in meeting this grave emergency the President was acting within the aggregate of his constitutional powers as the Nation's Chief Executive and the Commander in Chief of the Armed Forces of the United States. * * *

The President's power, if any, to issue the order must stem either from an act of Congress or from the Constitution itself. There is no statute that expressly authorizes the President to take possession of property as he did here. Nor is there any act of Congress to which our attention has been directed from which such a power can fairly be implied. * * * There are two statutes which do authorize the President to take both personal and real property under certain conditions[, but] these conditions were not met and * * * the President's order was not rooted in either of the statutes. The Government refers to the seizure provisions of one of these statutes * * * as "much too cumbersome, involved, and time-consuming for the crisis which was at hand."

Moreover, the use of the seizure technique to solve labor disputes in order to prevent work stoppages was not only unauthorized by any congressional enactment; prior to this controversy, Congress had refused to adopt that method of settling labor disputes. When the Taft-Hartley Act was under consideration in 1947, Congress rejected an amendment which would have authorized such governmental seizures in cases of emergency. Apparently it was thought that the technique of seizure, like that of compulsory arbitration, would interfere with the process of collective bargaining. * * * Instead, the plan sought to bring about settlements by use of the customary devices of mediation, conciliation, investigation by boards of inquiry, and public reports. In some instances temporary injunctions were authorized to provide cooling-off periods. All this failing, unions were left free to strike. * * *

It is clear that if the President had authority to issue the order he did, it must be found in some provision of the Constitution. And it is not claimed that express constitutional language grants this power to the President. The contention is that presidential power should be implied from the aggregate of his powers under the Constitution. Particular reliance is placed on provisions in Article II which say that "The executive Power shall be vested in a President . . . "; that "he shall take Care that the Laws be faithfully executed"; and that he "shall be Commander in Chief of the Army and Navy of the United States."

The order cannot properly be sustained as an exercise of the President's military power as Commander in Chief of the Armed Forces. The Government attempts to do so by citing a number of cases upholding broad powers in military commanders engaged in day-to-day fighting in a theater of war. Such cases need not concern us here. Even though "theater of war" be an expanding concept, we cannot with faithfulness to our constitutional system hold that the Commander in Chief of the Armed Forces has the ultimate power as such to take possession of private property in order to keep labor disputes from stopping production. This is a job for the Nation's lawmakers, not for its military authorities.

Nor can the seizure order be sustained because of the several constitutional provisions that grant executive power to the President. In the framework of our Constitution, the President's power to see that the laws are faithfully executed refutes the idea that he is to be a lawmaker. The Constitution limits his functions in the lawmaking process to the recommending of laws he thinks wise and the vetoing of laws he thinks bad. And the Constitution is neither silent nor equivocal about who shall make laws which the President is to execute. The first section of the first Article says that "All legislative Powers herein granted shall be vested in a Congress of the United States. . . ." After granting many powers to the Congress, Article I goes on to provide that Congress may "make all Laws which shall be necessary and proper for carrying into Execution the foregoing Powers, and all other Powers vested by this Constitution in the Government of the United States, or in any Department or Officer thereof."

The President's order does not direct that a congressional policy be executed in a manner prescribed by Congress—it directs that a presidential policy be executed in a manner prescribed by the President. * * * The power of Congress to adopt such public policies as those proclaimed by the order is beyond question. It can authorize the taking of private property for public use. It can make laws regulating the relationships between employers and employees, prescribing rules designed to settle labor disputes, and fixing wages and working conditions in certain fields of our economy. The Constitution does not subject this lawmaking power of Congress to presidential or military supervision or control.

It is said that other Presidents without congressional authority have taken possession of private business enterprises in order to settle labor disputes. But even if this be true, Congress has not thereby lost its exclusive constitutional authority to make laws necessary and proper to carry out the powers vested by the Constitution "in the Government of the United States, or any Department or Officer thereof."

The Founders of this Nation entrusted the lawmaking power to the Congress alone in both good and bad times. It would do no good to recall the historical events, the fears of power and the hopes for freedom that lay behind their choice. Such a review would but confirm our holding that this seizure order cannot stand.

JUSTICE FRANKFURTER, concurring.

To be sure, the content of the three authorities of government is not to be derived from an abstract analysis. The areas are partly interacting, not wholly disjointed. The Constitution is a framework for government. Therefore the way the framework has consistently operated fairly establishes that it has operated according to its true nature. Deeply embedded traditional ways of conducting government cannot supplant the Constitution or legislation, but they give meaning to the words of a text or supply them. It is an inadmissibly narrow conception of American constitutional law to confine it to the words of the Constitution and to disregard the gloss which life has written upon them. In short, a systematic, unbroken, executive practice, long pursued to the knowledge of the Congress and never before questioned, engaged in by Presidents who have also sworn to uphold the Constitution, making as it were such exercise of power part of the structure of our government, may be treated as a gloss on "executive Power" vested in the President by § 1 of Art. II. * * *

Down to the World War II period * * * the record is barren of instances comparable to the one before us. Of twelve seizures by President Roosevelt prior to the enactment of the War Labor Disputes Act in June, 1943, three were sanctioned by existing law, and six others were effected after Congress, on December 8, 1941, had declared the existence of a state of war. In this case, reliance on the powers that flow from declared war has been commendably disclaimed by the Solicitor General. Thus the list of executive assertions of the power of seizure in circumstances comparable to the present reduces to three in the six-month period from June to December of 1941. We need not split hairs in comparing those actions to the one before us, though much might be said by way of differentiation. Without passing on their validity, as we are not called upon to do, it suffices to say that these three isolated instances do not add up, either in number, scope, duration or contemporaneous legal justification, to [a systematic and longstanding] executive construction of the Constitution. Nor do they come to us sanctioned by long-continued acquiescence of Congress giving decisive weight to a construction by the Executive of its powers.

A scheme of government like ours no doubt at times feels the lack of power to act with complete, all-embracing, swiftly moving authority. No doubt a government with distributed authority, subject to be challenged in the courts of law, at least long enough to consider and adjudicate the challenge, labors under restrictions from which other governments are free. It has not been our tradition to envy such governments. In any event our government was designed to have such restrictions. The price was deemed not too high in view of the safeguards which these restrictions afford.

JUSTICE JACKSON, concurring in the judgment and opinion of the Court.

A judge, like an executive adviser, may be surprised at the poverty of really useful and unambiguous authority applicable to concrete problems of executive power as they actually present themselves. Just what our forefathers did envision, or would have envisioned had they foreseen modern conditions, must be divined from materials almost as enigmatic as the dreams Joseph was called upon to interpret for Pharaoh. A century and a half of partisan debate and scholarly speculation yields no net result but only supplies more or less apt quotations from respected sources on each side of any question. They largely cancel each other. And court decisions are indecisive because of the judicial practice of dealing with the largest questions in the most narrow way.

The actual art of governing under our Constitution does not and cannot conform to judicial definitions of the power of any of its branches based on isolated clauses or even single Articles torn from context. While the Constitution diffuses power the better to secure liberty, it also contemplates that practice will integrate the dispersed powers into a workable government. It enjoins upon its branches separateness but interdependence, autonomy but reciprocity. Presidential powers are not fixed but fluctuate, depending upon their disjunction or conjunction with those of Congress. We may well begin by a somewhat over-simplified grouping of practical situations in which a President may doubt, or others may challenge, his powers, and by distinguishing roughly the legal consequences of this factor of relativity.

1. When the President acts pursuant to an express or implied authorization of Congress, his authority is at its maximum, for it includes all that he possesses in his own right plus all that Congress can delegate. In these circumstances, and in these only, may he be said (for what it may be worth) to personify the federal sovereignty. If his act is held unconstitutional under these circumstances, it usually means that the Federal Government as an undivided whole lacks power. A seizure executed by the President pursuant to an Act of Congress would be supported by the strongest of presumptions and the widest latitude of judicial interpretation, and the burden of persuasion would rest heavily upon any who might attack it.

2. When the President acts in absence of either a congressional grant or denial of authority, he can only rely upon his own independent powers, but there is a zone of twilight in which he and Congress may have concurrent authority, or in which its distribution is uncertain. Therefore, congressional inertia, indifference or quiescence may sometimes, at least as a practical matter, enable, if not invite, measures on independent presidential responsibility. In this area, any actual test of power is likely to depend on the imperatives of events and contemporary imponderables rather than on abstract theories of law.

3. When the President takes measures incompatible with the expressed or implied will of Congress, his power is at its lowest ebb, for then he can rely only upon his own constitutional powers minus any constitutional powers of Congress over the matter. Courts can sustain exclusive presidential control in such a case only by disabling the Congress from acting upon the subject. Presidential claim to a power at once so conclusive and preclusive must be scrutinized with caution, for what is at stake is the equilibrium established by our constitutional system.

Into which of these classifications does this executive seizure of the steel industry fit? It is eliminated from the first by admission, for it is conceded that no congressional authorization exists for this seizure. * * *

Can it then be defended under flexible tests available to the second category? It seems clearly eliminated from that class because Congress has not left seizure of private property an open field but has covered it by three statutory policies inconsistent with this seizure. * * *

This leaves the current seizure to be justified only by the severe tests under the third grouping, where it can be supported only by any remainder of executive power after subtraction of such powers as Congress may have over the subject. In short, we can sustain the President only by holding that seizure of such strike-bound industries is within his domain and beyond control by Congress. * * *

Possible places in Const.

The Solicitor General seeks the power of seizure in three clauses of the Executive Article, the first reading, "The executive Power shall be vested in a President of the United States of America." Lest I be thought to ① *doesn't work* exaggerate, I quote the interpretation which his brief puts upon it: "In our view, this clause constitutes a grant of all the executive powers of which the Government is capable." If that be true, it is difficult to see why the forefathers bothered to add several specific items, including some trifling ones.

The example of such unlimited executive power that must have most impressed the forefathers was the prerogative exercised by George III, and the description of its evils in the Declaration of Independence leads me to doubt that they were creating their new Executive in his image. Continental European examples were no more appealing. And if we seek instruction from our own times, we can match it only from the executive powers in those governments we disparagingly describe as totalitarian. I cannot accept the view that this clause is a grant in bulk of all conceivable executive power but regard it as an allocation to the presidential office of the generic powers thereafter stated.

The clause on which the Government next relies is that "The President ② *doesn't work* shall be Commander in Chief of the Army and Navy of the United States.".." [J]ust what authority goes with the [title] has plagued presidential advisers who would not waive or narrow it by nonassertion yet cannot say where it begins or ends. It undoubtedly puts the Nation's armed forces under presidential command. Hence, this loose appellation is sometimes advanced as support for any presidential action, internal or external, involving use of force, the idea being that it vests power to do anything, anywhere, that can be done with an army or navy. * * *

There are indications that the Constitution did not contemplate that the title Commander in Chief *of the Army and Navy* will constitute him also Commander in Chief of the country, its industries and its inhabitants. He has no monopoly of "war powers," whatever they are. * * *

The third clause in which the Solicitor General finds seizure powers is ③ *doesn't work* that "he shall take Care that the Laws be faithfully executed..." That authority must be matched against words of the Fifth Amendment that "No person shall be . . . deprived of life, liberty or property, without due process of law. . . ." One gives a governmental authority that reaches so far as there is law, the other gives a private right that authority shall go no farther. These signify about all there is of the principle that ours is a government of laws, not of men, and that we submit ourselves to rulers only if under rules.

The Solicitor General lastly grounds support of the seizure upon nebulous, inherent powers never expressly granted but said to have accrued to the office from the customs and claims of preceding administrations. The plea is for a resulting power to deal with a crisis or an emergency according to the necessities of the case, the unarticulated assumption being that necessity knows no law. * * *

The appeal, however, that we declare the existence of inherent powers *ex necessitate* to meet an emergency asks us to do what many think would be wise, although it is something the forefathers omitted. They knew what emergencies were, knew the pressures they engender for authoritative action, knew, too, how they afford a ready pretext for usurpation. We may also suspect that they suspected that emergency powers would tend to kindle emergencies. Aside from suspension of the privilege of the writ of habeas corpus in time of rebellion or invasion, when the public safety may require it [U.S. Const., Art. I, § 9, cl. 2], they made no express provision for exercise of extraordinary authority because of a crisis. I do not think we rightfully may so amend their work. * * *

In view of the ease, expedition and safety with which Congress can grant and has granted large emergency powers, certainly ample to embrace this crisis, I am quite unimpressed with the argument that we should affirm possession of them without statute. Such power either has no beginning or it has no end. If it exists, it need submit to no legal restraint. I am not alarmed that it would plunge us straightway into dictatorship, but it is at least a step in that wrong direction.

As to whether there is imperative necessity for such powers, it is relevant to note the gap that exists between the President's paper powers and his real powers. The Constitution does not disclose the measure of the actual controls wielded by the modern presidential office. That instrument must be understood as an Eighteenth-Century sketch of a government hoped for, not as a blueprint of the Government that is. Vast accretions of federal power, eroded from that reserved by the States, have magnified the scope of presidential activity. Subtle shifts take place in the centers of real power that do not show on the face of the Constitution.

Executive power has the advantage of concentration in a single head in whose choice the whole Nation has a part, making him the focus of public hopes and expectations. In drama, magnitude and finality his decisions so far over-shadow any others that almost alone he fills the public eye and ear. No other personality in public life can begin to compete with him in access to the public mind through modern methods of communications. By his prestige as head of state and his influence upon public opinion he exerts a leverage upon those who are supposed to check and balance his power which often cancels their effectiveness.

Moreover, rise of the party system has made a significant extraconstitutional supplement to real executive power. No appraisal of his necessities is realistic which overlooks that he heads a political system as well as a legal system. Party loyalties and interests, sometimes more binding than law, extend his effective control into branches of government other than his own and he often may win, as a political leader, what he cannot command under the Constitution. * * *

But I have no illusion that any decision by this Court can keep power in the hands of Congress if it is not wise and timely in meeting its problems. A crisis that challenges the President equally, or perhaps primarily, challenges Congress. If not good law, there was worldly wisdom in the maxim attributed to Napoleon that "The tools belong to the man who can use them." We may say that power to legislate for emergencies belongs in the hands of Congress, but only Congress itself can prevent power from slipping through its fingers.

[The concurring opinions of JUSTICE DOUGLAS, JUSTICE CLARK (concurring only in the judgment), and JUSTICE BURTON are omitted.]

CHIEF JUSTICE VINSON, with whom JUSTICE REED and JUSTICE MINTON join, dissenting.

A review of executive action demonstrates that our Presidents have on many occasions exhibited the leadership contemplated by the Framers when they made the President Commander in Chief, and imposed upon him the trust to "take Care that the Laws be faithfully executed." With or without explicit statutory authorization, Presidents have at such times dealt with national emergencies by acting promptly and resolutely to enforce legislative programs, at least to save those programs until Congress could act. Congress and the courts have responded to such executive initiative with consistent approval. * * *

Without declaration of war, President Lincoln took energetic action with the outbreak of the War Between the States. He summoned troops and paid them out of the Treasury without appropriation therefore. He proclaimed a naval blockade of the Confederacy and seized ships violating that blockade. Congress, far from denying the validity of these acts, gave them express approval. The most striking action of President Lincoln was the Emancipation Proclamation, issued in aid of the successful prosecution of the War Between the States, but wholly without statutory authority.

In an action furnishing a most apt precedent for this case, President Lincoln without statutory authority directed the seizure of rail and telegraph lines leading to Washington. Many months later, Congress recognized and confirmed the power of the President to seize railroads and telegraph lines and provided criminal penalties for interference with Government operation. * * *

President Hayes authorized the wide-spread use of federal troops during the Railroad Strike of 1877. President Cleveland also used the troops in the Pullman Strike of 1895 and his action is of special significance. No statute authorized this action. No call for help had issued from the Governor of Illinois; indeed Governor Altgeld disclaimed the need for supplemental forces. But the President's concern was that federal laws relating to the free flow of interstate commerce and the mails be continuously and faithfully executed without interruption. To further this aim his agent sought and obtained the injunction upheld by this Court in *In re Debs*, 158 U.S. 564 (1895). The Court scrutinized each of the steps taken by the President to insure execution of the "mass of legislation" dealing with commerce and the mails and gave his conduct full approval. Congress likewise took note of this use of Presidential power to forestall apparent obstacles to the faithful execution of the laws. By separate resolutions, both the Senate and the House commended the Executive's action.

President Theodore Roosevelt seriously contemplated seizure of Pennsylvania coal mines if a coal shortage necessitated such action. In his autobiography, President Roosevelt expounded the "Stewardship Theory" of Presidential power, stating that "the executive as subject only to the people, and, under the Constitution, bound to serve the people affirmatively in cases where the Constitution does not explicitly forbid him to render the service." * * *

Beginning with the Bank Holiday Proclamation and continuing through World War II, executive leadership and initiative were characteristic of President Franklin D. Roosevelt's administration. * * * [Before, as well as after, Pearl Harbor and the declaration of war] industrial concerns were seized to avert interruption of needed production. [After war was declared,] the President directed seizure of the Nation's coal mines to remove an obstruction to the effective prosecution of the war.

This is but a cursory summary of executive leadership. But it amply demonstrates that Presidents have taken prompt action to enforce the laws and protect the country whether or not Congress happened to provide in advance for the particular method of execution. * * * [T]he fact that Congress and the courts have consistently recognized and given their support to such executive action indicates that such a power of seizure has been accepted throughout our history.

NOTE ON FRAMEWORKS FOR THINKING ABOUT SEPARATION OF POWERS ISSUES

1. *Theoretical Approaches to Separation of Powers.* Three different conceptual approaches can be gleaned from the opinions in the Steel Seizure Case.

(a) *Formalist Categories (Black).* Justice Black's opinion for the Court, joined by four other Justices (Douglas, Jackson, Frankfurter, and Burton), sets forth a categorical approach. Because the President's action fell under the legislative power defined in Article I and under none of the executive powers defined in Article II, the President was acting *ultra vires* (beyond his authority). This approach has the advantages of simplicity, compliance with a logical structure grounded in the constitutional text, and a clear message for future Presidents. It has the further advantage of taking the text of the Constitution seriously, consistent with the *textualist* and *holistic* theories of judicial review examined in Chapter 2, § 3A. It has the disadvantages of drawing constitutional lines by reference to the distinction between "legislative" and "executive" exercises of authority, of tying the President's hands in times of emergency, and of seeming to render much of the President's historical activities unconstitutional. Is this approach defensible in light of the original expectations of the Framers, reflected in the Philadelphia Convention debates and *The Federalist Papers*? Early practice?[26]

(b) *Constrained Functionalism (Jackson, Frankfurter)*. A second approach is a process-based functional approach which seeks to draw constitutional lines flexibly so as to allow the President to take action in emergencies, but not so flexibly as to ignore congressionally directed procedures for action. This approach is articulated in the concurring opinions of Justices Frankfurter and Jackson. These Justices were leading *legal process* theorists of constitutional law, anticipating the work of Hart, Sacks, Bickel, and Ely (Chapter 2, § 3B). The advantage of this approach is that it allows constitutional authority to evolve as times change, while preserving the original objectives of checks and balances. A disadvantage is that its line-drawing might seem like judicial policymaking unsupported by the Constitution. How would Justice Jackson, for example, defend his scheme as a matter of constitutional *law*?

(c) *Evolutive Functionalism—Constitutional Adverse Possession (Vinson)*. A third approach is a lenient functional approach, which essentially defers to the political branch taking the challenged action, so long as it has some historical precedent. Note the possible conceptual basis for this approach in *pragmatic* or *common law* theories of judicial review (Chapter 2, § 3C). The three dissenters endorsed this approach. They maintained that a long-established practice of executive power and congressional acquiescence provided concrete meaning to the vague constitutional clauses in question. This is a form of constitutional "adverse possession": If the President openly exercises power, with the knowledge and presumably the acquiescence of Congress, then after a certain period of time, the Constitution comes to consider this power as truly the President's. Can this be defended, in light of the background and history of separation of powers? Note that similar arguments prevailed in *McCulloch v. Maryland* (Chapter 7, § 1), but were rejected in *Brown v. Board of Education* (Chapter 2, § 1).

2. *The Jackson Concurrence as the Now-Dominant Approach*. Justice Jackson's concurring opinion has become the most influential of those penned

---

[26] Casper, *Essay on Separation of Powers* (excerpted above), supports a functionalist approach. For a response to Casper and a defense of a categorical approach based on state practice in the 1770s, see Russell Osgood, *Early Versions and Practices of Separation of Powers: A Comment*, 30 Wm. & Mary L. Rev. 279 (1989).

in the Steel Seizure Case and is now the "accepted framework" for analyzing claims of presidential power. *Medellín v. Texas,* 552 U.S. 491, 524–25 (2008); accord, *Hamdan v. Rumsfeld,* 548 U.S. 557, 638 (2006) (Kennedy, J., concurring). Traditionally, commentators have considered the tripartite framework to be an effective constraint on the increasing power of the Imperial Presidency.[27]

Ironically, Jackson was one of the Justices President Truman might have expected to vote his way in the Steel Seizure Case. In 1941, President Roosevelt had ordered seizure of a bomber/airplane factory, to avert a strike-based shutdown. As Attorney General, Jackson defended the seizure as resting upon "the aggregate of the Presidential powers derived from the Constitution itself and from statutes enacted by the Congress." 89 Cong. Rec. 3992 (1941). As a Justice in the Steel Seizure Case, Jackson dismissed this argument. His change in attitude was probably inspired by his experience as the Chief Prosecutor at the Nuremberg Trials of Nazi war criminals.[28] What he saw in his post-mortem of Nazi Germany was the ability of determined totalitarian groups to erode liberty by chipping away at the structural protections of citizens—namely, federalism, separation of powers, and the sanctity of private property. In his oral biography, Jackson opined that "the freedom of the individual to engage in a business economically is a parallel to his freedom of speech and his freedom of action generally. I believe these are protected by a diffusion of power. If you concentrate the power over his living and ways of existence, I don't know whether it is possible to maintain other liberties."[29]

Because it asks how shifting power from Congress to the President poses minoritarian risks to personal (and corporate) liberties, the Jackson opinion might be read as the germ of what Victoria Nourse calls the vertical approach to separation of powers. She would add that the President's decision also posed majoritarian risks, as it dislocated the national economy without sanction from the pluralistic process of congressional legislation (Jackson's Category 3). Unlike the Truman Administration in Steel Seizure, most administrations in subsequent cases have *not* conceded that their actions fell within Category 3 and have, instead, affirmatively argued that their actions fell within statutory authorizations. Thus, many such cases end up being matters of statutory interpretation, where judges as well as politicians need to figure out exactly what Congress has authorized, in order to decide which category the presidential action falls under. If authorized by statute (Category 1), the presidential action is going to prevail. If contrary to statutory authorization (Category 3), the presidential action is going to fail.

---

[27] E.g., Erwin Chemerinsky, *Controlling Inherent Presidential Power: Providing a Framework for Judicial Review,* 56 S. Cal. L. Rev. 863 (1983); William Van Alstyne, *The Role of Congress in Determining Incidental Powers of the President and of the Federal Courts,* 40 Law & Contemp. Probs. 102 (Spring 1976).

[28] See Edward Reisman, "Justice Robert Jackson's Road to *Youngstown Sheet & Tube Co. v. Sawyer:* The Impact of Nuremberg" (Georgetown Univ. Law Center, Feb. 20, 1990).

[29] "Justice Jackson's Story," Jackson Papers, Library of Congress (Madison Building), Container 190, folder 4, pp. 575–76, quoted in Reisman, "Jackson's Road," 16.

The foregoing dynamic has not necessarily been constraining in practice. Edward Swaine, *The Political Economy of Youngstown*, 83 S. Cal. L. Rev. 263 (2010).[30] Once Presidents and their legal advisers understand the framework, they have incentives to avoid Congress entirely, to enlist legislative support indirectly and perhaps fraudulently, and to reinterpret previous statutes aggressively and perhaps disingenuously. Given their first-mover advantages, congressional gridlock, and judicial timidity in foreign affairs, Presidents can get away with a great deal under cover of the Jackson framework, as Professor Swaine demonstrates. Although not citing *Steel Seizure*, the Bush 45 Administration's justification for torture of suspected terrorists as well as the Obama Administration's justification for its drone program worked within Jackson's framework. See Bruce Ackerman & Oona Hathaway, *Limited War and the Constitution: Iraq and the Crisis of Presidential Legality*, 109 Mich. L. Rev. 447 (2009) (Bush 45 Administration unilaterally went beyond Congress's limited authorization for the Iraq War, and the Obama Administration has acquiesced in this illegal unilateralism).

The Court, of course, might head off presidential unilateralism by casting beady eyes on presidential evasions or self-serving statutory constructions (precisely as the Court did in the Steel Seizure Case), but Professor Swaine is not optimistic that the Justices will demonstrate a great deal of political fortitude along these lines. Congress might enact more framework statutes to constrain the President, but such statutes are rare because they are subject to presidential vetoes. Bruce Ackerman suggests an institutional solution: a new Supreme Executive Tribunal, consisting of independent judges, that would subject presidential assertions of authority to a veto at the behest of a legally cogent petition from members of Congress. See Bruce Ackerman, *The Decline and Fall of the American Republic* (2010). Would this be a regime that could successfully enforce the Steel Seizure approach?

Other scholars push back against the authoritarian account of the neo-Schmittians (Posner and Vermeule) or the political realists (Swaine and Hathaway). Jack Goldsmith, who headed OLC during part of the Bush 45 Administration, argues that rule of law pushback significantly narrowed presidential assertions of authority during the Bush 45 Administration. On issues of human torture, due process rights of suspected terrorists, wiretapping, and detention outside the criminal process, congressional and judicial review and rebuke rolled back anti-liberal policy initiatives felt to be needed for the war on terror. See Goldsmith, *Power and Constraint: The Accountable Presidency After 9/11* (2012).

3. *Consequences of the Court's Decision.* When the Supreme Court quickly granted certiorari in the Steel Seizure Case, the industry and union negotiators had just reached tentative agreement as to a settlement at the White House. Upon learning that the Court had granted review and stayed the effect of a takeover, the steel industry backed away from the agreement,

---

[30] Accord, Posner & Vermeule, *Executive Unbound* (Schmittian arguments for why liberal legal restrictions do not constrain the executive branch, especially in emergencies).

according to legal historian Maeva Marcus.[31] After the Court handed the industry its victory on June 2, the union struck for 53 days; with further pressure from the President, the union and industry finally agreed upon a wage increase similar to that fixed by the Wage Stabilization Board months earlier. The strike was the longest and most costly ($400 million in lost wages, 21 million tons in lost steel output) in the country's history. Most current constitutional commentators follow Marcus in believing that the strike did not harm the war effort, but the Truman Administration believed otherwise. The President was wholly unswayed by the Court's justifications, and a leading historian of his administration concludes that the strike did impair the war effort.[32]

National Labor Relations Board v. Noel Canning

134 S.Ct. 2550 (2014)

After failing to secure Senate confirmation of several appointments to the NLRB, Art. II, § 2, cl. 2, President Obama exercised his authority, without Senate advise and consent, "to fill up all Vacancies that may happen during the Recess of the Senate, by granting Commissions which shall expire at the End of the next Session." Art. II, § 2, cl. 3. A company subject to NLRB sanctions challenged the existence of a Board quorum, on the ground that the appointments were not justified by the Recess Appointments Clause. The company claimed that the clause does not allow appointments (1) that were made during intra-session recesses (such as a summer break), (2) that involved vacancies originating when Congress was in session, and (3) that were made during three-day recesses between pro forma sessions of the Senate when no formal business was conducted. **Justice Breyer**'s opinion for the Court started with two important principles:

"First, *the Recess Appointments Clause sets forth a subsidiary, not a primary, method for appointing officers of the United States*. The immediately preceding Clause—Article II, Section 2, Clause 2—provides the primary method of appointment. * * * The Federalist Papers make clear that the Founders intended this method of appointment, requiring Senate approval, to be the norm (at least for principal officers). * * * [T]he need to secure Senate approval provides 'an excellent check upon a spirit of favoritism in the President, and would tend greatly to preventing the appointment of unfit characters from State prejudice, from family connection, from personal attachment, or from a view to popularity.'" *Federalist* No. 76.

"Second, *in interpreting the Clause, we put significant weight upon historical practice*. For one thing, the interpretive questions before us concern the allocation of power between two elected branches of Government. Long ago Chief Justice Marshall wrote that

---

[31] Marcus, *Truman and the Steel Seizure Case,* 147–48.

[32] 2 Harry Truman, *Memoirs* 478 (1956); David McCullough, *Truman* 901–02 (1992).

'a doubtful question, one on which human reason may pause, and the human judgment be suspended, in the decision of which the great principles of liberty are not concerned, but the respective powers of those who are equally the representatives of the people, are to be adjusted; if not put at rest by the practice of the government, ought to receive a considerable impression from that practice.' *McCulloch* v. *Maryland.*

And we later confirmed that '[l]ong settled and established practice is a consideration of great weight in a proper interpretation of constitutional provisions' regulating the relationship between Congress and the President. *The Pocket Veto Case*, 279 U.S. 655, 689 (1929)."

"There is a great deal of history to consider here. Presidents have made recess appointments since the beginning of the Republic. Their frequency suggests that the Senate and President have recognized that recess appointments can be both necessary and appropriate in certain circumstances. We have not previously interpreted the Clause, and, when doing so for the first time in more than 200 years, we must hesitate to upset the compromises and working arrangements that the elected branches of Government themselves have reached." Writing for four Justices concurring only in the judgment, **Justice Scalia** rejected what he called a constitutional principle of "adverse possession" and argued that the original meaning of the Recess Appointments Clause was limited to inter-session appointments and for vacancies that arose during such a recess.

Intra-Session Appointments: OK. Each elected Congress meets for two years. At the end of the first year (session), each chamber will adjourn *sine die* (without specifying a return date) and will reconvene early in the next year (session). The Senate and House also take breaks during each session, especially during holidays and in the summer. Justice Breyer found the constitutional language "the recess of the Senate" ambiguous—it could refer to just inter-session recesses or both intra- and inter-session recesses—and therefore had to be resolved by reference to the purpose and history of the constitutional provision. As to purpose, "the President can ensure the continued functioning of the Federal Government when the Senate is away. The Senate is equally away during both an inter-session and an intra-session recess, and its capacity to participate in the appointments process has nothing to do with the words it uses to signal its departure." As to history, once the Senate started taking frequent intra-session recesses, Presidents made intra-session appointments which were considered constitutional by Attorneys General advising them.

Justice Scalia disputed every bit of this analysis. The original meaning of "recess" was only inter-session breaks—a proposition he considered to be confirmed by the constitutional locution "the recess" and by the use of "adjourn" to refer to breaks during a session in Article I, § 5, cls. 1 & 4. The concurring Justices focused on the purpose of the Appointments Clause generally, which was "to preserve the Senate's role in the appointment process—which the founding generation regarded as a critical protection against 'despotism'—by clearly delineating the times when the President can appoint officers without the Senate's consent. Today's decision seriously undercuts *that* purpose." Indeed, the Recess Appointments Clause, even under the majority's understanding of purpose, was in 2014 an anachronism, as modern transportation and communication assure the President of access to Congress if he or she really needs a speedy confirmation process.

Pre-Recess Vacancies: OK. The Court also held that "Vacancies that may happen during the Recess" included positions that fell vacant before the recess. "We concede that the most natural meaning of 'happens' as applied to a 'vacancy' (at least to a modern ear) is that the vacancy " 'happens' when it initially occurs. But that is not the only possible way to use the word." Justice Breyer quoted a letter from Thomas Jefferson, who said the clause was "certainly susceptible of [two] constructions." Letter to Wilson Cary Nicholas (Jan. 26, 1802), in 36 Papers of Thomas Jefferson 433 (B. Oberg ed., 2009). "It 'may mean "vacancies that may happen to be" or "may happen to fall" ' during a recess."

Relying on advice from their Attorney Generals, early Presidents made recess appointments for pre-recess vacancies, and every President since James Buchanan has done so. In 1863 the Senate Judiciary Committee issued a report declaring that a vacancy "must have its inceptive point after one session has closed and before another session has begun." S. Rep. No. 80, 37th Cong., 3d Sess., p. 3. The same year, Congress passed the Pay Act, which provided that "no money shall be paid * * * as a salary, to any person appointed during the recess of the Senate, to fill a vacancy [which] existed while the Senate was in session." Act of Feb. 9, 1863, § 2, 12 Stat. 646.

Justice Breyer minimized the 1863 Pay Act, on the ground that Presidents kept making such appointments, without further objection from Congress. In 1940, Congress amended the Pay Act to authorize salary payments where (1) the "vacancy arose within thirty days prior to the termination of the session," (2) "at the termination of the session" a nomination was "pending," or (3) a nominee was "rejected by the Senate within thirty days prior to the termination of the session." Act of July 11, 54 Stat. 751. "All three circumstances concern a vacancy that did not initially occur during a recess but happened to exist during that recess. By paying salaries to this kind of recess appointee, the 1940 Senate (and later Senates) in effect supported the President's interpretation of the Clause."

Justice Scalia could not have disagreed more strongly. He agreed that the most "natural" reading of the clause is that the vacancy must be created during the recess. Attorney General Edmund Randolph explicitly said as much to President Washington, a view followed by the Adams Administration as well. See Michael Rappaport, *The Original Meaning of the Recess Appointments Clause,* 52 UCLA L. Rev. 1547 (2005). Few Presidents made such appointments in the first century of the republic—and when they did so, there was sometimes pushback. After President Lincoln appointed David Davis to the Supreme Court through a recess appointment to a preexisting vacancy, a number of Senators strenuously objected.

Congress itself objected when it passed the Pay Act in 1863, a statute Justice Scalia wielded like a Jedi lightsaber. Even as amended, the Pay Act seems disapproving of the practice generally, and certainly regulates it stringently. Senators, including the Republican Senators who participated in *Noel Canning,* have continued to object to the practice. Concluded Justice Scalia: "I can conceive of no sane constitutional theory under which this evidence of 'historical practice'—which is actually evidence of a long-simmering inter-branch conflict—would require us to defer to the views of the Executive Branch."

Appointment During a Three-Day Recess: Not OK. On December 17, 2011, the Senate by unanimous consent adopted a resolution to convene "*pro forma* session[s]" only, with no business transacted, on every Tuesday and Friday from December 20, 2011, through January 20, 2012. At the end of each *pro forma* session, the Senate would adjourn until the following *pro forma* session. The President made the recess appointments in question on January 4, 2012, in between the January 3 and the January 6 *pro forma* sessions. The Court unanimously rejected the Solicitor General's argument that the *pro forma* sessions did not count as sessions, and hence did not break up the periods of recess. "[F]or purposes of the Recess Appointments Clause, the Senate is in session when it says it is, provided that, under its own rules, it retains the capacity to transact Senate business. The Senate met that standard here."

"The standard we apply is consistent with the Constitution's broad delegation of authority to the Senate to determine how and when to conduct its business. The Constitution explicitly empowers the Senate to 'determine the Rules of its Proceedings.' Art. I, § 5, cl. 2. And we have held that 'all matters of method are open to the determination' of the Senate, as long as there is 'a reasonable relation between the mode or method of proceeding established by the rule and the result which is sought to be attained' and the rule does not 'ignore constitutional restraints or violate fundamental rights.' *United States* v. *Ballin*, 144 U.S. 1, 5 (1892)."

The Court ruled that the President could not act when the Senate was in recess or on break for fewer than three days, as the Constitution (Article I, § 5, cl. 4) bars the Senate from adjourning for more than three days without the consent of the House. "[I]n light of historical practice, that a recess of more than 3 days but less than 10 days is presumptively too short to fall within the Clause. We add the word 'presumptively' to leave open the possibility that some very unusual circumstance—a national catastrophe, for instance, that renders the Senate unavailable but calls for an urgent response—could demand the exercise of the recess-appointment power during a shorter break."

Quaere: Is the Court's opinion in *Noel Canning* consistent with the Steel Seizure Case? The Court seems to treat the issue as one falling in Justice Jackson's "twilight zone," where an ambiguous constitutional allocation requires attention to a continuous presidential practice as to which Congress did not object. Is that defensible in light of Justice Scalia's scathing counterattack, invoking the ordinary meaning of the clause, both today and in 1789? How would you vote in the case? (Remember, all nine Justices rejected the appointments, but for different reasons.)

B. FOREIGN RELATIONS AND WAR

The Steel Seizure Case arose in the context of the Korean War. Among the most far-reaching assertions of presidential power are in the context of foreign relations, including presidential commitment of United States military forces abroad and entry into executive agreements with foreign countries. Even as its Justices were at loggerheads with President Roosevelt over the New Deal's domestic program (Chapter 1, § 6; Chapter 7, § 2), the Supreme Court endorsed a broad scope for presidential action in the foreign arena.

Several leading opinions were authored by Justice George Sutherland, who as a senator had set forth a constitutional theory sharply distinguishing between *internal* affairs, where the Constitution's allocation of authority between the states and the national government had to be rigidly enforced, and *external* affairs, where the national government exercised plenary authority (Chapter 7, § 4C). As to the latter, Sutherland suggested a "radically more liberal" rule of construction: the federal government, and its officers, were free to exercise any external powers normally exercised by sovereign states under international law, excepting only those explicitly forbidden by the Constitution, strongly contrary to fundamental constitutional principles, or not "essential" to governance. Sutherland, *Constitutional Power and World Affairs* 47 (1919).

United States v. Curtiss-Wright Export Corp.

299 U.S. 304 (1936)

The Court upheld the President's action against Curtiss-Wright for selling guns to Bolivia. This case was different from the Steel Seizure Case, as Congress had by joint resolution authorized the President to place an embargo on arms sales to Bolivia and Paraguay, but **Justice Sutherland**'s opinion for the Court went beyond the facts. He stated not only that national power over external affairs is inherent and plenary, but also that the President plays a uniquely important role in foreign affairs. "In this vast external realm, with its important, complicated, delicate and manifold problems, the President alone has the power to speak or listen as a representative of the nation. He *makes* treaties with the advice and consent of the Senate; but he alone negotiates."

"It is quite apparent that if, in the maintenance of our international relations, embarrassment—perhaps serious embarrassment—is to be avoided and success for our aims achieved, congressional legislation which is to be made effective through negotiation and inquiry within the international field must often accord to the President a degree of discretion and freedom from statutory restriction which would not be admissible were domestic affairs alone involved." Buttressing this practical basis for presidential discretion was the "overwhelming support" for such broad delegation "which has prevailed almost from the inception of the national government to the present day. * * * Practically every volume of the United States Statutes contains one or more acts or joint resolutions of Congress authorizing action by the President in respect of subjects affecting foreign relations, which either leave the exercise of the power to his unrestricted judgment, or provide a standard far more general than that which has always been considered a requisite with regard to domestic affairs."

Commentators have been impressed by the breadth of Sutherland's reasoning and by his begging the central question in the case: Even if the national government has plenary authority to act in foreign affairs, hasn't the Constitution vested primary national authority in Congress, and not the President? Especially when the President's actions violate a company's liberty of contract, shouldn't it be the deliberative Congress, which is closer to the people, that should make the call?[33] Is the Court's subsequent disposition in the Steel Seizure Case inconsistent with *Curtiss-Wright*? If so, should *Curtiss-Wright* be narrowed—or is there a stronger constitutional basis for its sweeping dicta?

NOTE ON THE VESTING CLAUSE THESIS FOR PRESIDENTIAL PRIMACY IN FOREIGN AFFAIRS

Reviving arguments first made by Thomas Jefferson, Saikrishna B. Prakash and Michael D. Ramsey, *The Executive Power over Foreign Affairs*, 111 Yale L.J. 231 (2001), argue that Article II's Vesting Clause delegates to the President primary authority to manage the nation's foreign relations. The authors make three kinds of arguments for this proposition, to which Curtis A. Bradley & Martin S. Flaherty, *Executive Power Essentialism and Foreign Affairs*, 102 Mich. L. Rev. 545 (2004), provide a detailed historiographical response. Prakash and Ramsey respond and defend their thesis in *Foreign Affairs and the Jeffersonian Executive: A Defense*, 89 Minn. L. Rev. 1591 (2005), as well as Prakash, *Imperial from the Beginning* (2015).

1.　*Text: "Executive" Authority Means Management of Foreign Relations, and All of That Authority Is Vested in the President.* Contrast Article I, which vests Congress only with the "legislative Powers herein granted," with Article II, which vests the President with the "executive Power," simpliciter. Prakash and Ramsey draw from this contrast the notion that the President has *all* powers that the framing era would have considered "executive," and not just

---

[33]　See G. Edward White, *The Constitution and the New Deal* 69–77 (2000); Raoul Berger, *The Presidential Monopoly of Foreign Relations*, 71 Mich. L. Rev. 1, 45–48 (1972); David Levitan, *The Foreign Relations Power: An Analysis of Mr. Justice Sutherland's Theory*, 55 Yale L.J. 467 (1946). The contemporary response to Sutherland's opinion was strongly supportive. E.g., James Garner, *Executive Discretion in the Conduct of Foreign Relations*, 31 Am. J. Int'l L. 289 (1937).

the powers identified in Article II (such as receiving ambassadors). The leading political philosophers who influenced the Framers considered foreign affairs to be "essentially" executive tasks. Montesquieu identified two kinds of executive power, the enforcement of laws and initiation of activities in the foreign affairs arena. Blackstone, the colonists' main source of knowledge about British law and constitutionalism, closely followed Montesquieu in considering the monarch's foreign affairs prerogatives to be "executive" in nature. Under Montesquieu's understanding, Article II's vesting all "executive power" with the President carried with it all foreign affairs power, as the typical American would have understood the matter in 1789.

If the Vesting Clause gives the President plenary authority in foreign affairs, Bradley and Flaherty ask why Article II specifically vests the President with authority to receive ambassadors and to command American military forces in foreign campaigns? A second problem with the Prakash and Ramsey argument is that the Montesquieu-Blackstone model for executive control dominance in matters of foreign affairs was the monarchy—precisely what the Framers were *rejecting* as a model for their Article II President. Prakash's new book sharply disputes that claim and argues that because the Framers assumed George Washington would be the first President, they vested the office with "monarchical" powers. Even if this was the intent of the drafters in Philadelphia, is it likely that the ordinary people in state ratifying conventions had this understanding? Recall the Caspar article excerpted earlier.

Finally, Bradley and Flaherty argue that state constitutions in effect in 1789 are strong evidence against the Foreign Affairs Vesting Thesis. No state constitution gave the governor *all* powers that could be understood as "executive," and *all* the constitutions followed the American approach of enumerating gubernatorial powers in the same way the U.S. Constitution would do in Articles I–III. Prakash and Ramsey recall that states enjoyed foreign affairs power before 1789: Who exercised that authority? Except for South Carolina, which vested treaty-making in both the governor and the legislature, the state constitutions do not tell us which organ exercised foreign affairs authority.

2.   *Drafting and Ratifying the Constitution.* At the Convention, the Virginia Plan was the first comprehensive proposal for a constitution. Its Seventh Resolution, presented by Edmund Randolph, called for the establishment of a national executive; "besides a general authority to execute the National laws, [this executive] ought to enjoy the Executive rights vested in Congress by the Confederation." Because the Confederation Congress (like the Continental Congress) exercised plenary authority over foreign affairs, Prakash and Ramsey argue that this broad understanding of "executive" power (consistent with their reading of Montesquieu-Blackstone) formed the unspoken baseline for subsequent deliberations.

Bradley and Flaherty counter that the Virginia Plan and this undefined resolution were not adopted by the Convention and that most speakers followed the state constitutional practice of focusing on specific grants of authority to the chief executive. In opposing a too-powerful executive, James Wilson said he "did not consider the Prerogatives of the British Monarch as a proper guide in defining the Executive powers. Some of these prerogatives were of a legislative nature. Among others that of war & peace & c. The only powers he conceived strictly Executive were those of executing the laws, and appointing officers." Madison agreed with Wilson that executive powers "do not include the Rights of war & peace & c" and that "the powers should be confined and defined" lest the country be afflicted with the "Evils of elective Monarchies." He moved that the executive be vested with three powers: "to carry into execution the national laws"; "to appoint to offices in cases not otherwise provided for"; and "to execute such powers, not legislative or judiciary in their nature, as may from time to time be delegated by the national legislature." The Committee of the Whole agreed to the motion, deleting the third power as included in the first. Bradley and Flaherty argue that Article II reflects this decision, with the addition of further specified powers. Prakash and Ramsey note that the Convention nonetheless vested the President with "executive Power," essentially the same term used in the Virginia Plan.

Bradley and Flaherty trade quotations from *The Federalist Papers* with Prakash and Ramsey, and we refer the student to those lengthy articles for the exact quotations and their warring constructions. Bradley and Flaherty devote extensive attention to the debates within the state conventions, whose ratification in the name of We the People is the foundation of the Constitution's legitimacy. In Virginia, for example, the defenders of the Constitution said that the President's powers were very limited, the most important of which were to "see the laws executed" and to command the armed forces, while Congress would have the primary responsibility for national defense and foreign affairs. Prakash and Ramsey counter that no one at the Virginia or other state ratifying conventions denied that the Vesting Clause gave the President substantive powers, including residual authority (i.e., authority not delegated to Congress or the Senate) over foreign affairs.

3. *Early Practice: The Washington Administration.* Prakash and Ramsey's strongest evidence comes from officials in the Washington Administration, which took many foreign affairs initiatives that were not clearly sanctioned by the enumerated powers in Article II. In 1790, Secretary of State Thomas Jefferson opined that the President (not Congress) could set diplomatic grades and destinations: "The Constitution . . . has declared that 'the Executive powers shall be vested in the President'. . . . The transaction of business with foreign nations is Executive altogether. It belongs then to the head of that department [Jefferson!], except as to such portion of it as are specially submitted to the Senate. Exceptions are to be construed strictly." In his diary, President Washington said that Representative Madison and Foreign Secretary John Jay concurred with Jefferson. Bradley and Flaherty say that Jefferson was right because of the Presidential Appointments Clause, Article II, § 2 (Jefferson himself disclaimed reliance on that clause, however).

In 1793, President Washington announced a Proclamation of Neutrality in the war then ensuing among Great Britain, France, and other European powers. The Proclamation forbade interference by American ships and citizens in these wars and of course came under attack by partisans of France, namely Jefferson and Madison (by then emerging as an oppositional force within the government). Defending the President, Alexander Hamilton published a series of Letters from Pacificus, the first of which addressed the constitutionality of Washington's Proclamation.[34] Within the national government the executive branch is the "organ of intercourse between the [United States] and foreign Nations." While Congress had the authority to declare war against England or France, in the absence of such declaration, "the duty of the Executive is to preserve Peace till war is declared. * * * The President is charged with the execution of all laws, the laws of Nations as well as the Municipal law * * *. It is consequently bound, by faithfully executing the laws of neutrality, when that is the state of the Nation, to avoid giving a cause of war to foreign Powers."

Madison responded to Pacificus in a series of essays published under the name Helvidius. He argued, first, that the powers of declaring war and making peace were inherently "legislative" in nature and thus "can never fall within a proper definition of executive powers." Madison also argued that the Constitution does not allow concurrent exercise of powers that are purely "legislative" or "executive," and so the President was unconstitutionally invading Congress's power when he issued the Proclamation. (Bradley and Flaherty concede the "weakness" of Madison's argument but maintain that the main weakness, essentialist thinking about what is "executive," is a key weakness of the Foreign Affairs Vesting Thesis itself.)

Based on the foregoing evidence, do you consider the Foreign Affairs Vesting Thesis cogent? Or not? Consider how this thesis or some variation plays out in the following areas of constitutional inquiry.

1. Presidential Authority to Make or Enforce Binding International Commitments

The President has Article II, § 2, cl. 2 power, "by and with the Advice and Consent of the Senate, to make Treaties." If two-thirds of the Senate concur, such a treaty becomes the "Law of the Land" under the Supremacy Clause of Article VI. Presidential practice, ratified by the Supreme Court, has both expanded and contracted this constitutional regime. On the one hand, executive agreements (entered without Senate ratification) may sometimes be the "Law of the Land." See Oona A. Hathaway, *Presidential Power Over International Law: Restoring the Balance*, 119 Yale L.J. 140 (2009). On the other hand, most ratified treaties are *not* the "Law of the Land" without congressional enactment under Article I, § 7 (in addition to Senate ratification under Article II, § 2, cl. 2).

---

[34] Hamilton, Letters of Pacificus No. 1 (June 29, 1793), reprinted in 15 *The Papers of Alexander Hamilton* 33–42 (Harold Syrett & Jacob Cooke eds. 1969).

United States v. Belmont

301 U.S. 324 (1937)

The Court upheld and applied the "Litvinov Agreement" negotiated by President Franklin Roosevelt with the Soviet Union. That agreement assigned to the United States Russian claims against Americans who held funds of Russian companies seized after the Russian Revolution, and the Court held not only that the agreement was legally enforceable but that it also preempted contrary state law. Responding to the argument that only *treaties* agreed to by the Senate pursuant to Article II are the law of the land preempting state law, **Justice Sutherland**'s opinion for the Court ruled that "an international compact, as this was, is not always a treaty which requires the participation of the Senate." But, like treaties, executive agreements trump state law. "[W]hile this rule in respect of treaties is established by the express language of cl. 2, Art. VI of the Constitution, the same rule would result in the case of all international compacts and agreements, from the very fact that complete power over international affairs is in the national government and is not and cannot be subject to any curtailment or interference on the part of the several states. Compare *Curtiss-Wright*. * * * In respect of all international negotiations and compacts, and in respect of our foreign relations generally, state lines disappear."

Postscript. Unlike *Curtiss-Wright*, Justice Sutherland's broad reasoning in *Belmont* called forth much contemporary as well as modern criticism.[35] Even more than *Curtiss-Wright*, *Belmont* permitted matters of private property to be determined by the President and not by Congress. This was not only suspect in light of the Constitution's structure but was contrary to founding era precedent. See *Brown v. United States*, 12 U.S. 110 (1814), where the Marshall Court overruled the President's effort to condemn property owned in this country by citizens of Great Britain during the War of 1812; although the United States could seize such property consistent with international law, Chief Justice Marshall insisted that this authority rested with Congress, not the President. On the other hand, the Foreign Affairs Vesting Thesis might justify the holding of *Belmont*. The Court during World War II reaffirmed and expanded upon Sutherland's views in *United States v. Pink*, 315 U.S. 203 (1942). Is there any limit to the President's authority under this thesis? Note that the Supreme Court in the Steel Seizure Case did consider the Foreign Affairs Vesting Thesis and implicitly rejected it.

---

[35] See Edwin Borchard, *Confiscations, Extraterritorial and Domestic*, 31 Am. J. Int'l L. 675 (1937); Stefan Riesenfeld, *The Power of Congress and the President in International Relations: Three Recent Supreme Court Decisions*, 25 Cal. L. Rev. 643 (1937). See generally White, *Constitution and the New Deal*, 77–85.

Dames & Moore v. Regan

453 U.S. 654 (1981)

On November 4, 1979, Iranian students seized 53 Americans as hostages after taking over the U.S. embassy in Tehran, Iran. In response, President Carter blocked the removal of all Iranian property and assets in the United States, pursuant to congressional authorization in the International Emergency Economic Powers Act (IEEPA). Both before and after the President's blocking of assets, private parties (including petitioner Dames & Moore) had filed lawsuits against Iran and Iranian entities in U.S. courts. On January 20, 1981, the United States and Iran entered into an international agreement, under which the hostages would be released; the U.S. would unblock Iranian assets by July 19, 1981 and allow most of them to return to Iran; and litigation against Iran in U.S. courts would be "terminated," and all cases referred to an Iran-United States Claims Tribunal, which would arbitrate any claims against Iran that were not settled within six months. Presidents Carter and Reagan issued a series of Executive Orders implementing the international agreement, including an order "suspending" the American lawsuits against Iran. But neither President submitted the agreement to the Senate for ratification as a "treaty," nor did they seek implementing legislation from Congress. Dames & Moore had a money judgment against Iran but was unable to enforce it because of the regulations; the district court suspended the lawsuit and referred Dames & Moore to the Iran-U.S. Tribunal. The Supreme Court granted expedited review of the order and affirmed.

Justice Rehnquist's opinion for the Court followed the framework suggested by Justice Jackson's opinion in the Steel Seizure Case. Under the Jackson framework, the President's nullification of attachments and direction that persons holding blocked Iranian assets transfer them to the United States were defensible under Category 1, because these actions were explicitly authorized by Congress: IEEPA § 203 authorized the President pervasively to regulate foreign-owned property subject to the jurisdiction of the United States. Because IEEPA did not authorize suspension of the claims in United States courts, that action was more questionable. Still, under Category 2 of the Jackson framework, the President might have power to act, "where there is no contrary indication of legislative intent and when, as here, there is a history of congressional acquiescence in conduct of the sort engaged in by the President."

Justice Rehnquist pointed to a longstanding practice whereby the executive branch would "espouse" claims of U.S. nationals harmed by foreign state action and thereby negotiate agreements settling the claims of U.S. nationals. Under such agreements, the foreign state would provide a lump sum compensation package, in return for extinguishment of U.S. claims against the state. Typically these arrangements have been executive agreements and not treaties, and oftentimes the U.S. nationals have felt their interests slighted by a negotiation process emphasizing larger goals of national security and foreign policy. Starting with the "Wilmington Packet" in 1799, no fewer than 80 executive agreements were entered into by the President to settle foreign claims. The International Claims Settlement Act of 1949 created a procedure whereby funds resulting from future settlements could be distributed. "By creating a procedure to implement future settlement agreements, Congress placed its stamp of approval on such agreements." Justice Rehnquist also relied on the legislative background of IEEPA, which suggested that " '[n]othing in this act is intended . . . to interfere with the authority of the President to [block assets], or to impede the settlement of claims of U.S. citizens against foreign countries.' "

Justice Powell dissented in part, because he thought there might be a taking of property under the Fifth Amendment (Chapter 5, § 2C).

NOTE ON EXECUTIVE AGREEMENTS AS "LAW OF THE LAND"

Justice Rehnquist's congressional acquiescence argument has some holes. None of the earlier claims settlements was quite like the one in the Iranian Hostages Case, where the President suspended ongoing litigation filed in U.S. courts.[36] After the earlier claims settlements, Congress asserted its authority in a statute setting forth the procedures to be followed when foreign states are sued, namely, the Foreign Sovereign Immunities Act (FSIA). Before 1976, when foreign states were sued in U.S. courts, the Department of State usually filed a statement seeking dismissal on immunity grounds, to which courts deferred. Setting forth legal criteria for federal jurisdiction and immunity, the FSIA was intended to take the Executive out of the business of interfering in such lawsuits. Congress rejected a proposal to make FSIA procedures "subject to * * * future international agreements" in order to "eliminate any possible question" that the FSIA permitted the President to interfere with the new rules.[37] Under this analysis, the President's suspension of lawsuits falls under Jackson's Category 3, where his authority it at its "lowest ebb."

The Court's decision is more defensible under *Curtiss-Wright* and *Belmont* than under the Steel Seizure Case. But those cases were different in material ways. In *Curtiss-Wright* the President was acting in concert with Congress (Jackson's Category 1), and in *Belmont* the President was acting independently to trump state law (Category 2). But as to the suspension of lawsuits issue in *Dames & Moore*, the President was acting on his own and was arguably against the commands of a congressional enactment, rather than just state law

---

[36] In the earlier settlements, the President had frozen foreign assets in this country and used them as a bargaining chip to obtain compensation for U.S. companies whose property in the foreign state had been nationalized; the companies in the earlier instances had not sued foreign states in U.S. courts, because foreign states enjoyed sovereign immunity from lawsuits arising out of their nationalization of assets within their borders. See Lee Marks & John Grabow, *The President's Foreign Economic Powers After* Dames & Moore v. Regan: *Legislation by Acquiescence*, 68 Cornell L. Rev. 68, 87–91 (1982).

[37] Right after the FSIA was adopted, Beverly Carl, *Suing Foreign Governments in American Courts: The United States Foreign Sovereign Immunities Act in Practice*, 33 Sw. L.J. 1009, 1063 (1979), wrote: "Assume American hostages are being held by a foreign government. While negotiating for their release, the United States government wishes to offer as a quid pro quo the termination of pending litigation against that nation within this country. Under the FSIA, the executive would have no such authority * * *."

(Category 3). So *Dames & Moore* might best be justified as an example of the Foreign Affairs Vesting Thesis. See Michael D. Ramsey, *Executive Agreements and the (Non)Treaty Power*, 77 N.C.L. Rev. 133, 207–16 (1998). Does that thesis justify overriding a federal statute (FSIA)? If the President wanted to get around the FSIA, why shouldn't he have to seek legislation from Congress or a treaty from the Senate? In the interim, the President could have sought stays from judges handling claims against Iran; most such cases were already on hold at the request of the Departments of Justice and State.

Justice Powell raised a "vertical" concern: By shifting power to settle foreign claims from Congress and the courts, *Dames & Moore* shifted governmental incentives away from majoritarian deliberation (Congress) and protection of individual rights (courts) toward decisive action during foreign crises (President). This shift threatens liberty and property rights. Is there any limit to the President's power? For example, could the President have traded the Vice-President and his family for the 52 remaining hostages?

Medellín v. Texas

552 U.S. 491 (2008)

In the *Case Concerning Avena and Other Mexican Nationals* (*Mex. v. U. S.*), 2004 I. C. J. 12, the International Court of Justice (ICJ) held that the United States had violated Article 36(1)(b) of the Vienna Convention on Consular Relations by failing to inform 51 Mexican nationals, including petitioner José Ernesto Medellín, of their Vienna Convention rights when they were prosecuted in state criminal proceedings. The ICJ found that those individuals were entitled to review and reconsideration of their U.S. state-court convictions and sentences regardless of their failure to comply with generally applicable state rules governing challenges to criminal convictions.

In *Sanchez-Llamas v. Oregon*, 548 U. S. 331 (2006), the Supreme Court held, contrary to the ICJ's determination, that the Convention did not preclude the application of state default rules. Although the Supremacy Clause of Article VI might be read to render all treaties the "Law of the Land," the Supreme Court has long held that some treaties are not "self-executing," that is, they are not binding law unless implemented through congressional legislation. Self-executing treaties are binding law that would preempt state law, but the Convention, the Court held, was not self-executing. It could only preempt state law if it were adopted through domestic legislation or an equivalent process.

President George W. Bush issued a Memorandum to the Attorney General (Feb. 28, 2005), stating:

> I have determined, pursuant to the authority vested in me as President by the Constitution and the laws of the United States of America, that the United States will discharge its international obligations under the decision of the International Court of Justice in [*Avena*], by having State courts give effect to the decision in

accordance with general principles of comity in cases filed by the 51 Mexican nationals addressed in that decision.

Relying on *Avena* and the President's Memorandum, Medellín filed a second Texas state-court habeas application challenging his state capital murder conviction and death sentence on the ground that he had not been informed of his Vienna Convention rights. The Texas Court of Criminal Appeals dismissed Medellín's application, ruling that neither *Avena* nor the President's Memorandum was binding federal law that could displace the state's limitations on filing successive habeas applications. The court held that the President did not have discretion to implement non-self-executing treaties as binding law on his own authority. The Solicitor General argued that this was inconsistent with *Belmont* and *Dames & Moore*.

The Supreme Court affirmed. Writing for the majority, **Chief Justice Roberts** ruled that the *Avena* judgment was not binding "Law of the Land" pursuant to the Supremacy Clause, Article VI, § 2. To be sure, the judgment was binding on the United States pursuant to its international obligations under Article 94(1) of the United Nations Charter, which provides that "[e]ach Member of the United Nations *undertakes to comply* with the decision of the [ICJ] in any case to which it is a party." 59 Stat. 1051 (emphasis added). The Solicitor General argued that the phrase "undertakes to comply" is not "an acknowledgment that an ICJ decision will have immediate legal effect in the courts of U.N. members," but rather "a *commitment* on the part of U.N. Members to take *future* action through their political branches to comply with an ICJ decision." Brief for United States as *Amicus Curiae*. The Court agreed with this interpretation, and said that the executive department's views were entitled to "great weight."

The President sought to carry out the nation's "commitment" to ICJ judgments through the foregoing Memorandum, which the Solicitor General urged upon the Court as a basis for overturning the Texas conviction. "In this case, the President seeks to vindicate United States interests in ensuring the reciprocal observance of the Vienna Convention, protecting relations with foreign governments, and demonstrating commitment to the role of international law. These interests are plainly compelling. Such considerations, however, do not allow us to set aside first principles. The President's authority to act, as with the exercise of any governmental power, 'must stem either from an act of Congress or from the Constitution itself.' *Youngstown*; *Dames & Moore*."

The Chief Justice followed "Justice Jackson's familiar tripartite scheme," which "provides the accepted framework for evaluating executive action in this area." The Court ruled that the President has no authority to convert a non-self-executing treaty into a self-executing one, but took seriously the argument that the President's Memorandum fit within Jackson's Category 2, the "twilight zone" where longstanding presidential action, accompanied by congressional acquiescence, creates a field for future unilateral executive power. See *Dames & Moore*; *Belmont*. "The President's Memorandum is not supported by a 'particularly longstanding practice' of congressional acquiescence, but rather is what the United States itself has described as 'unprecedented action,' Brief for United States as *Amicus Curiae* in *Sanchez-Llamas*, O.T. 2005, Nos. 05–51 and 04–10566, pp. 29–30. Indeed, the Government has not identified a single instance in which the President has attempted (or Congress has acquiesced in) a Presidential directive issued to state courts, much less one that reaches deep into the heart of the State's police powers and compels state courts to reopen final criminal judgments and set aside neutrally applicable state laws." **Justice Stevens** concurred in the Court's judgment affirming Medellín's conviction.

Justice Breyer, joined by Justice Souter and Justice Ginsburg, dissented, maintaining that Article 94(1) of the U.N. Convention was self-executing and therefore preempted state law and required Texas to follow *Avena.* On the separate issue of the status of the President's Memorandum, Justice Breyer seemed friendly to the Solicitor General's argument that the Memorandum fell close to or within Justice Jackson's "twilight zone" of concurrent authority. "It is difficult to believe that in the exercise of his Article II powers pursuant to a ratified treaty, the President can *never* take action that would result in setting aside state law. Suppose that the President believes it necessary that he implement a treaty provision requiring a prisoner exchange involving someone in state custody in order to avoid a proven military threat. Or suppose he believes it necessary to secure a foreign consul's treaty-based rights to move freely or to contact an arrested foreign national. Does the Constitution require the President in each and every such instance to obtain a special statute authorizing his action? On the other hand, the Constitution must impose significant restrictions upon the President's ability, by invoking Article II treaty-implementation authority, to circumvent ordinary legislative processes and to pre-empt state law as he does so.

"Previously this Court has said little about this question. It has held that the President has a fair amount of authority to make and to implement executive agreements, at least in respect to international claims settlement, and that this authority can require contrary state law to be set aside. See, *e.g.*, *Pink*; *Belmont*. It has made clear that principles of foreign sovereign immunity trump state law and that the Executive, operating without explicit legislative authority, can assert those principles in state court. See *Ex parte Peru*, 318 U. S. 578, 588 (1943). It has also made clear that the Executive has inherent power to bring a lawsuit 'to carry out treaty obligations.' *Sanitary Dist. of Chicago v. United States*, 266 U. S. 405, 425, 426 (1925). But it has reserved judgment as to 'the scope of the President's power to preempt state law pursuant to authority delegated by . . . a ratified treaty'—a fact that helps to explain the majority's inability to find support in precedent for its own conclusions. *Barclays Bank PLC v. Franchise Tax Bd. of Cal.*, 512 U.S. 298, 329 (1994).

"Given the Court's comparative lack of expertise in foreign affairs; given the importance of the Nation's foreign relations; given the difficulty of finding the proper constitutional balance among state and federal, executive and legislative, powers in such matters; and given the likely future importance of this Court's efforts to do so, I would very much hesitate before concluding that the Constitution implicitly sets forth broad prohibitions (or permissions) in this area."

NOTE ON THE *ICJ JUDGMENT* CASE AND THE FOREIGN AFFAIRS VESTING THESIS

1. *Presumption Against Self-Executing Treaties.* The most important doctrinal point of *Medellín* is the Court's stinginess in declining to find that a treaty negotiated by the President and ratified by the Senate is the "Law of the Land," as the Supremacy Clause plainly says. Treaties will be considered self-executing "Law of the Land" only if there is clear evidence that the President and Congress expected them to be enforced through domestic legal mechanisms. But because treaties are typically international agreements that each country "undertakes" to comply, the *Medellín* approach seems to create a "presumption against self-executing treaties," as the dissenting opinion charged. Compare Carlos Manuel Vásquez, *Laughing at Treaties*, 99 Colum. L. Rev. 2154 (1999) (arguing that the Constitution supports a presumption in favor of self-execution), with John Choon Yoo, *Globalism and the Constitution: Treaties, Non-Self-Execution, and the Original Understanding*, 99 Colum. L. Rev. 1955 (1999) (arguing for a constitutional presumption against self-execution). And if a treaty is not self-executing, state law inconsistent with the treaty commitments is not preempted, either by force of the treaty or of presidential directives implementing the treaty.

Medellín may contribute to the decline of treaties as a significant means by which the United States enters into international commitments. As Oona A. Hathaway, *Treaties' End: The Past, Present, and Future of International Lawmaking in the United States*, 117 Yale L.J. 101 (2008), documents, the last hundred years have seen congressional-executive agreements become the overwhelmingly dominant form of international commitment on the part of the United States. Especially in light of *Medellín*, a big difference in relying on congressional-executive agreements is that they will enjoy "Law of the Land" status because they are statutory. Professor Hathaway celebrates the decline of treaties, but other scholars support treaties in light of the text and original meaning of the Constitution. E.g., Peter Spiro, Treaties, *Executive Agreements, and Constitutional Method*, 79 Tex. L. Rev. 961 (2001); John C. Yoo, *Laws as Treaties?: The Constitutionality of Congressional-Executive Agreements*, 99 Mich. L. Rev. 757 (2001).

2. *The Triumph of the Jackson Framework and the Turn Toward Statutory Interpretation.* Presidentialist scholars have sought to entrench the Foreign Affairs Vesting Thesis and to marginalize the Jackson framework as the baseline for separation of powers analysis touching on national security and foreign affairs. *Medellín* unanimously affirms the Jackson framework in a foreign relations context, and the majority explicitly rejects the Foreign Affairs Vesting Thesis as a basis for preempting state law, in seemingly absolute

terms. What is the status of *Dames & Moore* (unilateral presidential override of a federal statute) and *Belmont* (override of state law) after *Medellín*? Neither decision has been overruled, but how can their reasoning stand after *Medellín*?

Medellín is a setback to the Foreign Affairs Vesting Thesis, but alternative defenses of broad presidential power have already come to the forefront. John Yoo, *The Powers of War and Peace: The Constitution and Foreign Affairs After 9/11* (2005), operates within the Jackson framework, arguing that the Constitution only establishes a general structure and leaves the details to be filled in by experience, practice, and acquiescence on the part of legislators and We the People. Thus, many foreign affairs issues fall within Jackson's "zone of twilight," where presidential initiatives plus congressional acquiescence can expand presidential power over time. As *Medellín* suggests (confirming the lesson of Steel Seizure), twilight zone arguments will not be automatically accepted; the President has to show genuine similarity between powers his predecessors have exercised and those he now claims as his own, and perhaps also genuine congressional knowledge and acquiescence (which were not issues in *Medellín*). Scholarship by professional historians such as William Michael Treanor and Martin Flaherty is strongly dubious as to broad presidential claims.[38]

The triumph of the Jackson framework and the proliferation of national security statutes means that, increasingly, debates are going to be about how to interpret congressional enactments—for such interpretation will reveal whether a case is Category 1, where the President wins, or the "lowest ebb" Category 3, where the President loses. As the stakes of statutory interpretation have gone up in separation of powers cases, there has been greater pressure to "constitutionalize" such interpretation through clear statement rules and other canons. Should there be a strong presumption in favor of the President's construction of statutes touching upon foreign and military affairs or national security, arenas where Article II vests the President with special authority?[39]

3.   *Federalism.* Most of the *Medellín* majority Justices support strong presidential power *vis-à-vis* individual rights or congressional power—but here they take a very hard line against presidential authority. The new variable is federalism: the constitutional structure and original meaning preserve a key

---

[38]   E.g., Martin S. Flaherty, *More Real Than Apparent: Separation of Powers, the Rule of Law, and Comparative Executive "Creativity" in* Hamdan v. Rumsfeld, 2005–2006 Cato Sup. Ct. Rev. 51 (skeptical examination of presidential claims for preclusive authority to create military tribunals); William Michael Treanor, *Fame, the Founding, and the Power to Declare War*, 82 Cornell L. Rev. 695 (1997) (skeptical examination of presidential claims for preclusive warmaking authority); see also David J. Barron & Martin S. Lederman, *The Commander in Chief at the Lowest Ebb—A Constitutional History*, 121 Harv. L. Rev. 941 (2008) (skeptical examination of presidential claims for commander-in-chief authority).

[39]   *Department of Navy v. Egan*, 484 U.S. 518, 529 (1988) (suggesting such a deferential approach). Compare Curtis A. Bradley, *War on Terrorism: International Law, Clear Statement Requirements, and Constitutional Design*, 118 Harv. L. Rev. 2683 (2005), with William N. Eskridge Jr. & Lauren E. Baer, *The Continuum of Deference: Supreme Court Treatment of Agency Statutory Interpretation from* Chevron *to* Hamdan, 96 Geo. L.J. 1083 (2008) (arguing that the Supreme Court is too deferential to executive department interpretations generally and that a "special" deference for national security and foreign affairs cases is uncalled for).

role for the states, whose autonomy is protected through constitutional law rules, as well as canons of statutory interpretation. Federalism also helps explain why the Roberts Court takes such a stingy view of the treaty self-execution doctrine: a major effect of self-executing treaties is that they preempt state law, and the presumption against self-execution is one way the Court makes sure that the Senate and the President explicitly take account of the federalism effects when they enter treaties.[40]

2.　President's Commander-in-Chief Authority

Article II, § 2, cl. 1 says: "The President shall be Commander in Chief of the Army and Navy of the United States," etc. If Congress declares war, the President is in charge of the military operations, which Congress funds. This sounds simple enough, but there are dozens of issues that have arisen, many of which remain unresolved to this day. Consider whether the history recounted below sheds any light on the debate over the Foreign Affairs Vesting Thesis; even if not established as a matter of original meaning, the thesis might gain constitutional traction through congressional acquiescence (Steel Seizure; *Dames & Moore*).

Did the Framers create a presidential "commander-in-chief power" that Congress cannot readily regulate? George Washington, the Commander in Chief of the Revolutionary Army (1775–1783), faithfully followed most of the directives issued by the Continental Congress but departed from those directives when the necessities of war warranted. See Logan Beirne, *Blood of Tyrants: George Washington and the Forging of the Presidency* chs. 9–11 (2013) (Washington failed to follow the initial congressional directive of humane treatment of all prisoners, and Congress reversed itself in light of the Commander in Chief's position); *id.,* chs. 24–25 (Washington failed to follow the congressional directive that enemy spies must be tried by court-martial, when he tried Major André by military commission).

As President, Washington hewed pretty carefully to congressional directives, as did his successor, John Adams. Thus, when Congress wanted the country to prepare for possible war against France in 1798, it authorized President Adams to raise an army up to 10,000 men and to seize French vessels and vessels sailing to French ports under specified circumstances, thereby initiating the Quasi-War with France. Pursuant to an order from the Secretary of the Navy, Captain George Little seized a ship sailing *from* a French port. In *Little v. Barreme,* 6 U.S. 170 (1804), the Marshall Court ruled that the seizure was illegal because it did not fall within the terms of the statutory authorizations for the Quasi-War. Under

---

[40] Curtis A. Bradley, *Federalism and the Treaty Power,* 98 Am. J. Int'l L. 341 (2004), and Medellin v. Dretke: *Federalism and International Law,* 43 Colum. J. Transnat'l L. 667 (2005). On Article I, § 7 (and so implicitly Article II, § 2, the treaty power) as a safeguard of state autonomy, see Bradford R. Clark, *Separation of Powers as a Safegurard of Federalism,* 79 Tex. L. Rev. 1321 (2001).

Little, the President's commander-in-chief authority is subject to congressional direction.[41]

After South Carolina seceded in 1861, when Congress was not in session, President Lincoln took bold unilateral action, ordering a naval blockade of the South, calling up the militia, expanding the regular army, and essentially taking the nation to war. The President admitted that some of these actions "were without the authority of law," but justified them as needed to ensure that the "Government was saved [from] overthrow." Cong. Glove, 37th Cong., 2d Sess. 2383 (1862) (message from President Lincoln). Within a month of Lincoln's justifications, Congress ratified Lincoln's actions by statute, except for his suspension of habeas corpus.[42]

Although Lincoln did not assert a preclusive power of the President to act contrary to congressional directives, some of his allies did. Concurring in *Ex parte Milligan,* 71 U.S. 2 (1866), Chief Justice Salmon Chase (Lincoln's Treasury Secretary and his replacement for Chief Justice Taney) rendered a broad construction of Congress's war powers—"except such as interferes with the command of the forces and the conduct of campaigns. That power and duty belong to the President as commander-in-chief." *Id.* at 141. Following this dictum (in a concurring opinion) was a broad statement of presidential power in John Norton Pomeroy, *An Introduction to the Constitutional Law of the United States* §§ 703–706 (1868), which opined that in his role as commander in chief the President cannot be bound by congressional statutes. Thus, "all direct management of warlike operations, all planning and organizing of campaigns, all establishment of blockages, all direction of marches, sieges, battles, and the like, are as much beyond the jurisdiction of the legislature, as they are beyond that of any assemblage of private citizens." *Id.,* § 455. Congress could make general rules, such as setting the size of the army or navy, but could not tell the President exactly how to deploy those troop levels.

The Chase-Pomeroy viewpoint was expressed more broadly in the twentieth century. Presidents such as Theodore Roosevelt, William Howard Taft, and Woodrow Wilson did not challenge the conventional wisdom that Congress could set limits on presidential military decisions. After his presidency, and during his time as a professor at the Yale Law School, however, Taft opined that Congress could *not* prevent the President from deploying the armed forces to respond to an invasion, from deciding how to deploy the armed forces in time of war, or "order battles to be fought on a certain plan." William Howard Taft, *The Boundaries Between the*

---

[41] See David J. Barron & Martin S. Lederman, *The Commander in Chief at the Lowest Ebb— A Constitutional History,* 121 Harv. L. Rev. 941, 944–50, 964–70 (2008); H. Jefferson Powell, *The Founders and the President's Authority over Foreign Affairs,* 40 Wm. & Mary L. Rev. 1471, 1511– 28 (1999).

[42] For detailed examination of Lincoln's actions, his justifications, and after-the-fact congressional ratifications, see Daniel A. Farber, *Lincoln's Constitution* (2003); Barron & Lederman, *Commander in Chief at the Lowest Ebb (History),* 993–1025.

Executive, the Legislative, and the Judicial Branches of the Government, 25 Yale L.J. 599, 610 (1916).

World War II called forth some highly aggressive statutory interpretations by the (Franklin) Roosevelt Administration. During the litigation surrounding the use of military tribunals to try war criminals in 1942, Attorney General Francis Biddle argued to a stunned Supreme Court that during time of war the President had extra-statutory authority to try war criminals: "the Commander-in-Chief, in time of war and to repel an invasion, is not bound by a statute." Transcript of Oral Argument, *Ex parte Quirin*, 317 U.S. 1 (1942). Following Biddle's main argument, the Court held that Congress had authorized the tribunals in that case. In a draft concurring opinion, Justice Jackson suggested that the Court's construction of the statute was required to avoid the serious constitutional question entailed by Congress's interfering with the commander-in-chief power. He questioned Congress's authority to limit the President's ability to deal with "those who come here as belligerents to destroy our institutions." Because no other Justice agreed with these views, Jackson joined the Chief Justice's opinion for the Court with no separate commentary.

After World War II, Congress adopted a series of framework statutes and treaties to govern the nation's military affairs. These included the National Security Act of 1947, the Geneva Conventions of 1949 (ratified in 1955), the Uniform Code of Military Justice of 1950, and the Universal Military Training and Service Act of 1951. President Truman objected to none of this, and in the Steel Seizure Case his Department of Justice said that the President would follow any statute addressing the shortage of war materials. But in the course of the Korean War (1950 onwards), the President asserted a commander-in-chief authority to deploy troops without congressional limitation and to adjust military appropriations to meet changing battlefield needs. Congress did not formally push back against these claims, but did do so in response to President Nixon's conduct of the undeclared War in Vietnam.

Between 1954 and 1975, the United States was involved in the war between North and South Vietnam. There was never a congressionally declared "war," and our involvement came about through a series of presidential decisions, first to send advisers to help the Vietnamese fight "Communist aggression," then to commit U.S. soldiers to help fight the Communists, then to have U.S. soldiers take primary responsibility for the war, then to escalate the war through massive bombing and defoliation in both Vietnams, then to escalate the war into other countries (mainly Cambodia), and then to withdraw. Congress appropriated increasing amounts of money for the President's activities, and the Senate approved presidential authority to respond to events in Indochina through the Gulf of Tonkin Resolution in 1964. During the Nixon Administration, Congress grew more restive with its marginal role and with the unproductive (but still expanding) war effort. One result was the enactment in 1973, over President Nixon's veto, of the War Powers Resolution, Pub. L. No. 93–148, 87 Stat. 555 (1973), codified at 50 U.S.C. §§ 1541 et seq.

Section 2(a) of the Resolution declared its purpose, to "insure that the collective judgment of both the Congress and the President will apply to the introduction of United States Armed Forces into hostilities, or into situations where imminent involvement in hostilities is clearly indicated by the circumstances, and to the continued use of such forces in hostilities or in such situations." 50 U.S.C. § 1541(a).

Section 3 required presidential consultation with Congress "before introducing United States Armed Forces into hostilities or into situations where imminent involvement in hostilities is clearly indicated by the circumstances," and regularly thereafter until hostilities have ended or forces removed. *Id.,* § 1542. Section 4(a) required a written report from the President to Congress "in any case in which United States Armed Forces are introduced—

(1) into hostilities or into situations where imminent involvement in hostilities is clearly indicated by the circumstances;

(2) into the territory, airspace or waters of a foreign nation, while equipped for combat, except for deployments which relate solely to supply, replacement, repair, or training of such forces; or

(3) in numbers which substantially enlarge United States Armed Forces equipped for combat already located in a foreign nation;

Id., § 1543(a). Among other things, the report should include "the estimated scope and duration of the hostilities or involvement." *Id.,* § 1543(a)(C).

Section 5(b) provides: "Within sixty calendar days after a report is submitted or is required to be submitted pursuant to section 4(a)(1), whichever is earlier, the President shall terminate any use of United States Armed Forces with respect to which such report was submitted (or required to be submitted), unless the Congress (1) has declared war or has enacted a specific authorization for such use of United States Armed Forces, (2) has extended by law such sixty-day period, or (3) is physically unable to meet as a result of an armed attack upon the United States. Such sixty-day period shall be extended for not more than an additional thirty days if the President determines and certifies to the Congress in writing that unavoidable military necessity respecting the safety of United States Armed Forces requires the continued use of such armed forces in the course of bringing about a prompt removal of such forces." *Id.,* § 1544(b).

Section 8(c) defines "introduction of United States Armed Forces" to include "the assignment of members of such armed forces to command, coordinate, participate in the movement of, or accompany the regular or irregular military forces of any foreign country or government when such military forces are engaged, or there exists an imminent threat that such forces will become engaged, in hostilities." *Id.*, § 1547(c).

PROBLEM 8-1:
IS THE WAR POWERS RESOLUTION CONSTITUTIONAL?

President Ford notified Congress when he deployed armed force to rescue the merchant ship *Mayaguez* in May 1975. President Carter did not consult with Congress when he tried, unsuccessfully, to rescue the 52 hostages in Iran in April 1980, though he did notify Congress after the mission failed. President Reagan ignored the Resolution when he invaded Grenada in October 1983, to rescue American medical students. In September 1982, President Reagan committed U.S. armed forces to Lebanon but claimed that the Resolution did not apply because the troops were not involved in "hostilities." A year later, several hundred marines died in Beirut. In 1989, the first President Bush notified Congress of military action taken in Panama. The second President Bush in 2002 obtained congressional authorization for the use of force against Iraq. Although there has been a trend toward substantial compliance with the Resolution, no President has conceded its constitutionality.

Scholars are divided on whether the President has constitutional authority to defend the United States preemptively (i.e., by attacking opponents before they can attack us). For example, Dean Eugene Rostow, one of President Johnson's informal advisers during the Vietnam conflict, attacked the Resolution as contrary to traditional practice:[43]

> The pattern against which the [Resolution] protests is old, familiar, and rooted in the nature of things. There is nothing constitutionally illegitimate or even dubious about "undeclared" wars. We and other nations fought them frequently in the eighteenth and nineteenth centuries, as well as in the twentieth. [The Resolution] would turn the clock back to the Articles of Confederation, and destroy the Presidency which it was one of the chief aims of the men in Annapolis and Philadelphia to create.

---

[43] Eugene Rostow, *Great Cases Make Bad Law: The War Powers Act*, 50 Tex. L. Rev. 833, 855–56 (1972). Also arguing for broad presidential power are Eric A. Posner & Adrian Vermeule, *Terror in the Balance: Security, Liberty, and the Courts* (2007); H. Jefferson Powell, *The President's Authority Over Foreign Affairs: An Essay in Constitutional Interpretation* (2002); John C. Yoo, *The Powers of War and Peace: The Constitution and Foreign Affairs After 9/11* (2005); Leonard Ratner, *The Coordinated Warmaking Power—Legislative, Executive, and Judicial Roles*, 44 S. Cal. L. Rev. 461 (1971).

Modern critics of the WPR, most prominently John Yoo, have combined Dean Rostow's pragmatic arguments with the formalist and original meaning arguments supporting the Foreign Affairs Vesting Thesis or some variation.[44]

Among a host of constitutional scholars, Harold Koh and John Hart Ely defend the constitutionality of the Resolution, even while regretting its frequent inefficacy.[45] They maintain that the primacy of Congress in the making of war is one of the few arenas where the Framers of the Constitution operated under a clear consensus and that presidential appropriation of the power to make war is unconstitutional. They invoke both the Black and Jackson opinions in the Steel Seizure Case as precedential authority for their position. Scholars such as these criticize the Resolution as too narrow. Apparently, it does not apply to "covert wars," in which intelligence agents acting under civilian supervision conduct paramilitary activities against foreign governments and to "quick strikes" against foreign powers which can be completed well within the 60-day time span (e.g., President Reagan's strikes against Grenada in 1983, Libya in 1986, and Iran in 1987 and 1988).

Each side resolutely appeals to constitutional text and original meaning.[46] How do these sources cut?

1. *Deliberations at the Philadelphia Convention.* Consider Madison's notes of the debate over the "Declare War" Clause, Art. I, § 8, cl. 11:

"To make war."

Mr. Pinkney [sic] opposed the [vest]ing this power in the Legislature. Its proceedings were too slow. It wd. meet but once a year. The Hs. of Reps. would be too numerous for such deliberations. The Senate would be the best depository, being more acquainted with foreign affairs, and most capable of proper resolutions. * * *

Mr. Butler. The Objections agst the Legislature lie in great degree agst the Senate. He was for vesting the power in the

---

[44] Yoo, *The Powers of War and Peace*; John C. Yoo, *The Continuation of Politics by Other Means: The Original Understanding of War Powers*, 84 Cal. L. Rev. 167 (1996). See also Phillip Trimble, *International Law: United States Foreign Relations* Law 10–46 (2002); Gary Lawson & Guy Seidman, *The Constitution of Empire: Territorial Expansion and American Legal History* (2004); Michael Stokes Paulsen, *Youngstown Goes to War*, 19 Const. Comm. 215, 237–38 (2002).

[45] John Hart Ely, *War and Responsibility: Constitutional Lessons of Vietnam and Its Aftermath* (1993); Harold H. Koh, *The National Security Constitution: Sharing Power After the Iran-Contra Affair* (1990). Also arguing for a larger congressional role are Jacob Javits, *Who Makes War?: The President versus Congress* (1973); Louis Fisher, *Presidential War Power* (1995); Louis Henkin, *Constitutionalism, Democracy, and Foreign Affairs* (1990); Jane Stromseth, *Rethinking War Powers: Congress, the President, and the United Nations*, 81 Geo. L.J. 597 (1993); William Van Alstyne, *Congress, the President, and the Power to Declare War*, 121 U. Pa. L. Rev. 1 (1972).

[46] Leading sources on the original meaning debate are Ely, *War and Responsibility* (arguing for broad congressional authority to regulate foreign military involvements); David J. Barron & Martin S. Lederman, *The Commander in Chief at the Lowest Ebb—Framing the Problem, Doctrine, and Original Understanding*, 121 Harv. L. Rev. 689, 772–800 (2008) (similar); William Michael Treanor, *Fame, the Founding, and the Power to Declare War*, 82 Cornell L. Rev. 695 (1997) (similar); Yoo, *Original Understanding of War Powers* (arguing for narrow congressional authority, with the funding power being the main way the Framers expected Congress to influence military policy).

President, who will have all the requisite qualities, and will not make war but when the Nation will support in.

Mr. M[adison] and Mr. Gerry moved to insert "*declare*," striking out "*make*" war; leaving to the Executive the power to repel sudden attacks.

Mr. Sharman thought it stood very well. The Executive shd. be able to repel and not to commence war. "Make" better than "declare" the latter narrowing the power too much.

Mr. Gerry never expected to hear in a republic a motion to empower the Executive alone to declare war.

Mr. Mason was agst. giving the power of war to the Executive, because not (safely) to be trusted with it; or to the Senate, because not so constructed as to be entitled to it. He was for clogging rather than facilitating war; but for facilitating peace. He preferred "*declare*" to "*make*."

On the motion to insert *declare*—in place of *make* (it was agreed to).

What conclusions would you draw from this discussion and the eventual decision made by the Framers?

Notice that most of the delegates were thinking in functional, institutionalist terms. Thus, they emphasized the President's advantages of speedy response as a reason not to tie his hands when the nation was attacked by another country. There was support for a larger Senate role because it was thought that body would have more experience in foreign affairs. But there was also some voice for popular concerns, especially Butler's confidence that the President, who alone was elected by the entire nation, will be more responsive to national demands for war. Gerry's objection seems to be a popular response: But in a *republic*, it should be the deliberated judgment of localities and states assembled in Congress that must have the final word.

Consider John Yoo's argument that these debates must be read in light of eighteenth century understanding of what *declare war* meant. Blackstone and other eighteenth century legal synthesizers allowed that the monarch could initiate hostilities with other nations; a "declaration of war" was important in escalating *hostilities* to all-out *war*, with broader repercussions for relations between the nations and notice for their citizens that normal intercourse was disrupted. Parliament's increasingly important role focused on funding decisions, allowing elected representatives to veto royally initiated hostilities. The experience in the colonies was similar, with governors generally having control over militias, including the authority to initiate hostilities, but with legislatures exercising some negative authority through appropriations pressure. See Yoo, *Original Understanding of War Powers*, 204–16, 218–35, 242–43.

Jane Stromseth disputes this reading of pre-1789 practice and reads the originalist sources to support the proposition that "the Founders would have expected the President as Commander in Chief and Chief Executive to protect the United States in a dangerous and uncertain world by repelling actual or imminent attacks against the United States, its vessels, and its armed forces, but not, on his own, to go beyond this authority and effectively change the state of the nation from peace to war." Jane Stromseth, *Understanding Constitutional War Powers Today: Why Methodology Matters*, 106 Yale L.J. 845, 860–62 (1996). Her reading receives support from the apparent purpose of the Framers' war clauses. As Madison put it, "[i]n no part of the constitution is more wisdom to be found, than in the clause which confides the question of war or peace to the legislature, and not to the executive department. * * * [T]he trust and the temptation would be too great for any one man. * * * War is in fact the true nurse of executive aggrandizement." Accord, Prakash, *Imperial from the Beginning,* 144–49 (reading the Declare War Clause broadly, based on eighteenth-century practice), 162–70 (congressional authority over the armed forces, and its limitation on the commander-in-chief authority).

2.   *Ratification Debates.* James Wilson defended the Declare War Clause during the Pennsylvania ratifying convention with this argument:

> This system will not hurry us into war; it is calculated to guard against it. It will not be in the power of a single man, or a single body of men, to involve us in such distress; for the important power of declaring war is vested in the legislature at large: * * * nothing but our national interest can draw us into war. [Elliott, *Debates in the Several State Conventions* 528 (1836).]

This statement is cited by most of the scholars who favor congressional initiative to make war. At the Philadelphia Convention, however, Wilson had been the author of the original Make War Clause, whose tilt toward congressional power had been reversed in some part by vote of the Convention.

John Yoo argues that the Federalist position matured after the Pennsylvania debates, and that by the time New York and Virginia ratified the defenders of the Constitution were taking a stronger pro-President position. At the critical Virginia convention, the Federalist response to charges of presidential aggrandizement rested largely upon the argument that Congress's power of the purse was the best practical limit on an imperial presidency. See Yoo, *Original Understanding of War Powers*, 281–86. Writing for the New York delegates, Hamilton in *Federalist* No. 25 deemphasized the significance of a declaration of war, saying it "has of late fallen into disuse."

Legal historians William Treanor, Curtis Bradley, and Martin Flaherty have disputed Yoo's account.[47] Hamilton's *Federalist* No. 69 responded to Anti-Federalist attacks on the strong presidency with the observation that the President's power as Commander-in-Chief was not as plenary as the authority of some governors to control their militias. Anti-Federalist charges that the President would be like the hated King of England were overstated. If the

---

[47]   Bradley & Flaherty, *Presidential Power Essentialism and Foreign Affairs*; Treanor, *Fame, the Founding and the Power to Declare War.*

President were the Commander-in-Chief of the army and navy, Hamilton observed, he lacked the British King's power of "the *declaring* of war and the *raising* and *regulating* of fleets and armies; all which by the Constitution under consideration would appertain to the Legislature." Hamilton's concession was repeated by Federalist James Iredell at the North Carolina convention.

3. *Practice and Precedent.* The Washington and Adams Administrations conducted hostilities in the 1790s without formal declarations of war, but they did seek congressional authorization for deploying the militia or raising a navy before they took action. The Supreme Court entertained several lawsuits in connection with the Quasi-War with France in 1798–1800, including *Little v. Barreme*, 6 U.S. 170 (1804), where Chief Justice Marshall enforced implicit congressional limits on presidential authority. For the first two generations under the Constitution, Presidents dependent upon congressional funds for ships and troops cooperated with Congress when hostilities were planned, but by the middle of the nineteenth century Presidents were more assertive. Also, Presidents throughout the nineteenth century engaged in small-scale military operations against pirates and bandits and to protect American interests abroad.

The Civil War commenced when southern states seceded from the Union and their forces fired on Fort Sumter. President Lincoln responded, inter alia, with a unilateral blockade of southern ports after the South's secession. Although his action was highly controversial, the Supreme Court upheld it in *The Prize Cases*, 67 U.S. (2 Black) 635 (1863). Justice Grier's opinion for the Court interpreted the Constitution to give the President broad discretion when responding to attack:

> By the Constitution, Congress alone has the power to declare a national or foreign war. It cannot declare war against a State, or any number of States, by virtue of any clause in the Constitution. The Constitution confers on the President the Whole Executive power. * * * He has no power to initiate or declare war either against a foreign nation or a domestic State. But by [Acts] of Congress, [he] is authorized to [call] out the militia and use the military and naval forces of the United States in case of invasion by foreign nations, and to suppress insurrection against the government of a State or of the United States.

> If a war be made by invasion of a foreign nation, the President is not only authorized but bound to resist force by force. He does not initiate the war, but is bound to accept the challenge without waiting for any special legislative authority. * * *

> Whether the President in fulfilling his duties, as Commander-in-Chief, in suppressing an insurrection, has met with such armed hostile resistance, and a civil war of such alarming proportions as will compel him to accord to them the character of belligerents, is a question to be decided *by him*, and this Court must be governed by

the decisions and acts of the political department of the Government
to which this power was entrusted.

Four Justices dissented from this opinion, arguing that only Congress could
authorize the blockade. Do *The Prize Cases* provide some support for the
President's executive agreement upheld in *Dames & Moore?*

Altogether, the United States has declared war five times in its history:
the War of 1812, the Mexican-American War (1848), the Spanish-American
War (1898), and World Wars I (1917) and II (1941). The United States has
committed military forces somewhere between 125 and 215 times after the
adoption of the Constitution, but many of those commitments were after
consultation and some kind of authorization by Congress. Consider the
following as-applied challenges:[48]

(a) Invasion of Iraq, 2003. In the wake of the terrorist attacks of
September 11, 2001, charges that Iraq provided support to al-Qaeda, the group
responsible for the 9/11 attacks, were added to charges that Iraq was
developing weapons of mass destruction that could be used against the United
States as well as other countries. In § 3(a) of the Authorization for Use of
Military Force (AUMF) Against Iraq Resolution of 2002, Pub. Law No. 107–
243 (2002), Congress provided: "The President is authorized to use the Armed
Forces of the United States as he determines to be necessary and appropriate
in order to (1) defend the national security of the United States against the
continuing threat posed by Iraq; and (2) enforce all relevant United Nations
Security Council resolutions concerning Iraq." Could the President have
invaded Iraq without the 2002 AUMF? Invoking the AUMF, President Bush
deployed the nation's armed forces to invade Iraq in 2003. Should there have
been a formal declaration of war by Congress? Does the WPR impose additional
requirements on the President? If so, are they constitutional?

(b) Bombing Libya, 2011. Acting in response to a request from the Arab
League, and pursuant to U.N. Security Council Resolutions 1970 and 1973,
President Barack Obama mobilized American military forces on March 19,
2011, to prevent a humanitarian catastrophe, to address the threat posed to
international peace and security by the crisis in Libya, and to protect the
people of Libya from the Qadhafi regime. On March 21, the President notified
Congress that American and allied aircraft had commenced airstrikes against
the regime. Did the President act lawfully when he committed American
soldiers and aircraft to the multilateral military engagement with Libya?
What, if any, obligations did the WPR impose on President Obama in
conducting these operations?

---

[48] For background and analysis relevant to the problems offered here, see Prakash, *Imperial
from the Beginning,* 152–70; Bruce Ackerman & Oona Hathaway, *Limited War and the
Constitution: Iraq and the Crisis of Presidential Legality,* 109 Mich. L. Rev. 447 (2009); Trevor W.
Morrison, *Hostilities,* 1 Journal of Law (1 Pub. L. Misc.) 233–311 (2011) (assembling primary
materials), and *Libya, "Hostilities," and the Process of Executive Branch Legal Interpretations,* 124
Harv. L. Rev. 62 (2011). See also Harold H. Koh, *War Powers Resolution and Humanitarian
Interventions,* 53 Hous. L. Rev. 971 (2016) (defense of the Obama Administration's Libyan bombing
by a central architect).

(c) "Hostilities" in Libya, 2011? On June 14, House Speaker John Boehner informed President Obama that the American participation in the Libyan operations were approaching the 90-day limit (60 days plus a necessity extension of 30 days)—after which the WPR § 5(b) requires the President either to withdraw Americans from the hostilities or to secure congressional authorization for their continuing role. The President responded the next day: "The initial phase of U.S. military involvement in Libya was conducted under the command of the U.S. Africa Command. By April 4, however, the United States had transferred responsibility for the military operations in Libya to NATO and the U.S. involvement ha[d] assumed a supporting role in the coalition's efforts. Since April 4, U.S. participation * * * consisted of: (1) non-kinetic support to the NATO-led operation, including intelligence, logistical support, and search and rescue assistance; (2) aircraft that have assisted in the suppression and destruction of air defenses in support of the no-fly zone; and (3) since April 23, precision strikes by unmanned aerial vehicles against a limited set of clearly defined targets in support of the NATO-led coalition's efforts." Letter from President Barack Obama to House Speaker John Boehner and Senate President Pro Tempore Daniel Inouye (June 15, 2011). The President characterized American involvement as supporting "international efforts to protect civilians and civilian populated areas from the actions of the Qadhafi regime, and to address the threat to international peace and security posed by the crisis in Libya. With the exception of operations to rescue the crew of a U.S. aircraft on March 21, 2011, the United States has deployed no ground forces to Libya." *Id.*

In a report accompanying the letter, the White House explained its view that the American involvement did not constitute "hostilities" under WPR §§ 4(a)(1) and 5(b): "The President is of the view that the current U.S. military operations in Libya are consistent with the War Powers Resolution and do not under that law require further congressional authorization, because U.S. military operations are distinct from the kind of 'hostilities' contemplated by the Resolution's 60 day termination provision. U.S. forces are playing a constrained and supporting role in a multinational coalition, whose operations are both legitimized by and limited to the terms of a United Nations Security Council Resolution that authorizes the use of force solely to protect civilians and civilian populated areas under attack or threat of attack and to enforce a no-fly zone and an arms embargo. U.S. operations do not involve sustained fighting or active exchanges of fire with hostile forces, nor do they involve the presence of U.S. ground troops, U.S. casualties or a serious threat thereof, or any significant chance of escalation into a conflict characterized by those factors." Because the involvement did not constitute "hostilities" under § 4(a)(1), the Administration was not bound by § 5(b)'s requirement of termination without a congressional authorization.

Is President Obama's interpretation of the WPR correct? For a negative assessment, see Dawn Johnsen, *When Responsibilities Collide: Humanitarian Intervention, Shared War Powers, and the Rule of Law*, 53 Hous. L. Rev. 1065 (2016). Compare the defense by Harold H. Koh, *War Powers Resolution and*

Humanitarian Interventions, 53 Hous. L. Rev. 971 (2016). If the President is not correct, and the Libyan engagement did constitute "hostilities," did the WPR limitation period unconstitutionally infringe upon the President's commander-in-chief authority?

3. Presidential Authority in Foreign Relations and Immigration

Zivotofsky v. Kerry

135 S.Ct. 2076 (2015)

Since 1948, the United States, acting through the President, has recognized the state of Israel but has taken no position on the delicate issue of which state has sovereignty over Jerusalem. Consistent with this policy, the State Department will not identify Israel as the nation of citizenship for anyone born in Jerusalem; the passport will simply say "Jerusalem." This was considered objectionable by many supporters of Israel.

In 2002, Congress passed the Foreign Relations Authorization Act, Fiscal Year 2003, 116 Stat. 1350. Section 214 of the Act is titled "United States Policy with Respect to Jerusalem as the Capital of Israel." Section 214(d) allows citizens born in Jerusalem to list their place of birth as "Israel." "For purposes of the registration of birth, certification of nationality, or issuance of a passport of a United States citizen born in the city of Jerusalem, the Secretary shall, upon the request of the citizen or the citizen's legal guardian, record the place of birth as Israel." Did this statutory override of State Department and Presidential policy violate Article II?

Writing for the Court, **Justice Kennedy** applied the Steel Seizure framework and found that the President's assertion of authority fell under Category 3—"measures incompatible with the expressed or implied will of Congress," which can only be allowed when the President's own constitutional authority disables Congress from acting. Unlike the Steel Seizure Case, where President Truman did not satisfy the stringent requirements of Category 3, the Court here upheld the President and ruled that the 2002 statute was invalid because Article II vested the President with exclusive authority to "recognize" foreign states.

The Constitution does not use the term "recognition," but Secretary Kerry relied on the Reception Clause, which directs that the President "shall receive Ambassadors and other public Ministers." Art. II, § 3. The Reception Clause received little attention at the Constitutional Convention, see Reinstein, Recognition: A Case Study on the Original Understanding of Executive Power, 45 U. Rich. L. Rev. 801, 860–862 (2011), and during the ratification debates, Alexander Hamilton claimed that the power to receive ambassadors was "more a matter of dignity than of authority," a ministerial duty largely "without consequence." The Federalist No. 69, p. 420 (C. Rossiter ed. 1961).

"At the time of the founding, however, prominent international scholars suggested that receiving an ambassador was tantamount to recognizing the sovereignty of the sending state. See E. de Vattel, The Law of Nations § 78, p. 461 (1758) (J. Chitty ed. 1853) ('[E]very state, truly possessed of sovereignty, has a right to send ambassadors' and 'to contest their right in this instance' is equivalent to 'contesting their sovereign dignity'); [other sources omitted]. It is a logical and proper inference, then, that a Clause directing the President alone to receive ambassadors would be understood to acknowledge his power to recognize other nations."

"This in fact occurred early in the Nation's history when President Washington recognized the French Revolutionary Government by receiving its ambassador. After this incident the import of the Reception Clause became clear—causing Hamilton to change his earlier view. He wrote that the Reception Clause 'includes th[e power] of judging, in the case of a revolution of government in a foreign country, whether the new rulers are competent organs of the national will, and ought to be recognised, or not.' See A. Hamilton, Pacificus No. 1, in The Letters of Pacificus and Helvidius 5, 13–14 (1845) (reprint 1976) (President 'acknowledged the republic of France, by the reception of its minister'). [S]ee also 3 J. Story, Commentaries on the Constitution of the United States § 1560, p. 416 (1833) ('If the executive receives an ambassador, or other minister, as the representative of a new nation . . . it is an acknowledgment of the sovereign authority *de facto* of such new nation, or party'). As a result, the Reception Clause provides support, although not the sole authority, for the President's power to recognize other nations."

Justice Kennedy found the foregoing inference supported by the President's other Article II powers. The President, "by and with the Advice and Consent of the Senate," is to "make Treaties, provided two thirds of the Senators present concur." Art. II, § 2, cl. 2. Also, "he shall nominate, and by and with the Advice and Consent of the Senate, shall appoint Ambassadors" as well as "other public Ministers and Consuls." *Ibid.*

"As a matter of constitutional structure, these additional powers give the President control over recognition decisions. At international law, recognition may be effected by different means, but each means is dependent upon Presidential power. In addition to receiving an ambassador, recognition may occur on 'the conclusion of a bilateral treaty,' or the 'formal initiation of diplomatic relations,' including the dispatch of an ambassador. The President has the sole power to negotiate treaties, and the Senate may not conclude or ratify a treaty without Presidential action. The President, too, nominates the Nation's ambassadors and dispatches other diplomatic agents. Congress may not send an ambassador without his involvement. Beyond that, the President himself has the power to open diplomatic channels simply by engaging in direct diplomacy with foreign heads of state and their ministers. The Constitution thus assigns the President means to effect recognition on his own initiative. Congress, by contrast, has no constitutional power that would enable it to initiate diplomatic relations with a foreign nation. Because these specific

Clauses confer the recognition power on the President, the Court need not consider whether or to what extent the Vesting Clause, which provides that the 'executive Power' shall be vested in the President, provides further support for the President's action here. Art. II, § 1, cl. 1.

"The text and structure of the Constitution grant the President the power to recognize foreign nations and governments. The question then becomes whether that power is exclusive. The various ways in which the President may unilaterally effect recognition—and the lack of any similar power vested in Congress—suggest that it is. So, too, do functional considerations. Put simply, the Nation must have a single policy regarding which governments are legitimate in the eyes of the United States and which are not. Foreign countries need to know, before entering into diplomatic relations or commerce with the United States, whether their ambassadors will be received; whether their officials will be immune from suit in federal court; and whether they may initiate lawsuits here to vindicate their rights. These assurances cannot be equivocal."

Justice Kennedy also found it significant that "the President since the founding has exercised this unilateral power to recognize new states—and the Court has endorsed the practice. See *Banco Nacional de Cuba v. Sabbatino*, 376 U.S. 398, 410, 84 S.Ct. 923, 11 L.Ed.2d 804 (1964); [*United States v. Pink*, 315 U.S. 203, 229, 62 S.Ct. 552, 86 L.Ed. 796 (1942)]; *Williams v. Suffolk Ins. Co.*, 13 Pet. 415, 420, 10 L.Ed. 226 (1839). Texts and treatises on international law treat the President's word as the final word on recognition. See, *e.g.*, Restatement (Third) of Foreign Relations Law § 204, at 89 ('Under the Constitution of the United States the President has exclusive authority to recognize or not to recognize a foreign state or government'). In light of this authority all six judges who considered this case in the Court of Appeals agreed that the President holds the exclusive recognition power." Justice Kennedy found *Sabbatino* especially relevant, for the Court held that "[p]olitical recognition is exclusively a function of the Executive."

Secretary Kerry urged the Court to define the executive power broadly, namely, "exclusive authority to conduct diplomatic relations," along with "the bulk of foreign-affairs powers." Brief for Respondent 18, 16. The Court refused to go that far. "In a world that is ever more compressed and interdependent, it is essential the congressional role in foreign affairs be understood and respected. For it is Congress that makes laws, and in countless ways its laws will and should shape the Nation's course. The Executive is not free from the ordinary controls and checks of Congress merely because foreign affairs are at issue."

Finally, Justice Kennedy considered the extensive historical record to discern whether there had been congressional acquiescence in the exclusive power claimed by the President and the Secretary of State. As Judge Tatel had remarked in the proceedings below, what is most remarkable is that, since the Washington Administration, the President had openly claimed the exclusive authority to recognize foreign states (or not) and had not been met with a congressional statute to the contrary—until the 2002 law at issue in this case.

Justice Breyer joined the opinion for the Court but noted his view, rejected by the Court in *Zivotofsky v. Clinton*, 132 S.Ct. 1421 (2012), that the controversy was a nonjusticiable political question. See Chapter 9, as well as *Sabbatino*, where the Court ruled that the President's recognition of Cuba was not reviewable.

Justice Thomas concurred in part of the Court's judgment and rejected the Court's constitutional analysis. He argued that the Article II Vesting Clause ("executive power," without qualification) gives the President plenary authority to act in matters of foreign affairs or military deployment. Because Congress's Article I Vesting Clause only gives Congress "[a]ll legislative Powers herein granted," Congress can trump the President only where the Constitution has explicitly authorized congressional action, such as confirming ambassadors and providing funds for foreign affairs and military operations. See Saikrishna Prakash & Michael Ramsey, *The Executive Power Over Foreign Affairs*, 111 Yale L.J. 231, 298–346 (2001). Under his framework, Justice Thomas would have invalidated § 214(d) as applied to passports (fully within the "executive Power" as understood in 1789) but would have applied it to matters of naturalization, fully within Congress's enumerated powers. U.S. Const. art. I, § 8, cl. 4.

In a dissenting opinion, **Chief Justice Roberts** (joined by Justice Alito) noted that this was the first time the Supreme Court has allowed the President to defy an explicit congressional statute regulating foreign affairs. The Court's holding was not properly attentive to the "caution" urged by Justice Jackson in Steel Seizure Category 3 cases.

Justice Scalia (joined by the Chief Justice and Justice Alito) also dissented. In a significant break from Justice Thomas's broad reading of the Article II Vesting Clause, Justice Scalia worked within the analytical structure of a balanced government, where both Congress and the President share foreign affairs authority.

"Congress's power to 'establish an uniform Rule of Naturalization,' Art. I, § 8, cl. 4, enables it to grant American citizenship to someone born abroad. The naturalization power also enables Congress to furnish the people it makes citizens with papers verifying their citizenship—say a consular report of birth abroad (which certifies citizenship of an American born outside the United States) or a passport (which certifies citizenship for purposes of international travel). As the Necessary and Proper Clause confirms, every congressional power 'carries with it all those incidental powers which are necessary to its complete and effectual execution.' *Cohens v. Virginia*, 6 Wheat. 264, 429, 5 L.Ed. 257 (1821). Even on a miserly understanding of Congress's incidental authority, Congress may make grants of citizenship 'effectual' by providing for the issuance of certificates authenticating them.

"One would think that if Congress may grant Zivotofsky a passport and a birth report, it may also require these papers to record his birthplace as 'Israel.' The birthplace specification promotes the document's citizenship-authenticating function by identifying the bearer, distinguishing people with similar names but different birthplaces from each other, helping authorities uncover identity fraud, and facilitating retrieval of the Government's citizenship records."

Having found that Congress possessed constitutional authority to enact § 214(d), Justice Scalia posed the question whether Article II trumps that authority. Without resolving the thorny question of whether Article II trumps Article I, Justice Scalia found no conflict between the legislative and executive powers at issue, because "§ 214(d) has nothing to do with recognition," the core executive power the majority jealously protected. "Section 214(d) does not require the Secretary to make a formal declaration about Israel's sovereignty over Jerusalem. And nobody suggests that international custom infers acceptance of sovereignty from the birthplace designation on a passport or birth report, as it does from bilateral treaties or exchanges of ambassadors. Recognition would preclude the United States (as a matter of international law) from later contesting Israeli sovereignty over Jerusalem. But making a notation in a passport or birth report does not encumber the Republic with any international obligations. It leaves the Nation free (so far as international law is concerned) to change its mind in the future. That would be true even if the statute required *all* passports to list 'Israel.' But in fact it requires only those passports to list 'Israel' for which the citizen (or his guardian) *requests* 'Israel'; all the rest, under the Secretary's policy, list 'Jerusalem.' It is utterly impossible for this deference to private requests to constitute an act that unequivocally manifests an intention to grant recognition.

"Section 214(d) performs a more prosaic function than extending recognition. Just as foreign countries care about what our Government has to say about their borders, so too American citizens often care about what our Government has to say about their identities."

What of the Court's concern that the nation speak in one voice on matters of foreign relations? Nonsense, replied Justice Scalia. There is nothing in the Constitution that says Congress and the President must operate along exactly the same assumptions about foreign relations matters. Consider the President's power "to make Treaties," Art. II, § 2, cl. 2. "There is no question that Congress may, if it wishes, pass laws that openly flout treaties made by the President. Would anyone have dreamt that the President may refuse to carry out such laws—or, to bring the point closer to home, refuse to execute federal courts' judgments under such laws—so that the Executive may 'speak with one voice' about the country's international obligations? To ask is to answer. Today's holding puts the implied power to recognize territorial claims (which the Court infers from the power to recognize states, which it infers from the responsibility to receive ambassadors) on a higher footing than the express power to make treaties."

Justice Scalia concluded: "In the end, the Court's decision does not rest on text or history or precedent. It instead comes down to 'functional considerations'—principally the Court's perception that the Nation 'must speak with one voice' about the status of Jerusalem. The vices of this mode of analysis go beyond mere lack of footing in the Constitution. Functionalism of the sort the Court practices today will *systematically* favor the unitary President over the plural Congress in disputes involving foreign affairs. It is possible that this approach will make for more effective foreign policy, perhaps as effective as that of a monarchy. It is certain that, in the long run, it will erode the structure of separated powers that the People established for the protection of their liberty."

Quaere: Recall Edward Swaine's argument that decisive, initiative-seizing Presidents have deployed the Steel Seizure (Jackson) framework much more successfully than plodding Congress has been. Edward T. Swaine, *The Political Economy of* Youngstown, 83 S. Cal. L. Rev. 263 (2010). But is functionalism always the President's best friend in constitutional theory? Keep that question in mind as you read the other cases in this chapter.

PROBLEM 8-2:
PRESIDENTIAL DEFERRAL OF DEPORTATION
OF UNDOCUMENTED IMMIGRANTS

In June 2012, the Department of Homeland Security ("DHS") implemented the Deferred Action for Childhood Arrivals program ("DACA"). DHS described the program as an exercise of "prosecutorial discretion." The Department would defer action against undocumented immigrants who had come to this country before the age of sixteen and met other criteria; for such persons, the government would also accept applications for work authorization. But the memo disclaimed any new "substantive right, immigration status or pathway to citizenship" for the 1.2 million persons qualifying for DACA.

In November 2014, DHS expanded DACA by making millions more persons eligible for the program and extending the period for employment authorization. DHS also created a new process called Deferred Action for Parents of Americans and Lawful Permanent Residents program ("DAPA"), which applied to individuals who then had a son or daughter who was a U.S. citizen or lawful permanent resident and meet five additional criteria. Although "[d]eferred action does not confer any form of legal status in this country, much less citizenship[,] it [does] mean[ ] that, for a specified period of time, an individual is permitted to be *lawfully present* in the United States," according to the DAPA Memo. Of the approximately 11.3 million undocumented immigrants then in the United States, 4.3 million would be eligible for lawful presence pursuant to DAPA, according to the District Court.

"Lawful presence" is not an enforceable right to remain in the United States and can be revoked at any time, but that classification nevertheless has significant legal consequences. Unlawfully present aliens are generally not eligible to receive federal public benefits or state and local public benefits unless the state otherwise provides, but DAPA-qualified persons granted lawful presence are no longer barred from receiving social security and Medicare benefits, pursuant to the authorizing statutes for the various programs. The Government conceded that, under federal statutory law, an undocumented immigrant "lawfully present" and with a work authorization may obtain a social security number, would accrue social security credit for employment, and would be eligible for earned income tax credits. Some state benefits turn on the distinction. Texas, for example, will not issue driver's licenses to immigrants who are not "lawfully present" but will do so for DAPA-qualified immigrants. Complaining about the extra costs for its driver's license and other state programs, Texas and twenty-five other states brought suit against the federal government and secured a nationwide injunction barring DHS from implementing the DAPA program. (The lawsuit did not challenge DACA.

Does the President have this authority? See *Texas v. United States*, 109 F.3d 134 (5th Cir. Nov. 2015), *aff'd by an equally divided Court*, 136 S.Ct. 2271 (2016).

C. EXECUTIVE PRIVILEGES AND IMMUNITIES

Since the Washington Administration, the President had maintained his privilege to withhold information from Congress or to divulge it under confidential circumstances, in order to protect the national interest. More ambiguous, because much less tested, was the President's amenability to or immunity from legal process. Executive privilege and presidential immunity for misdeeds are grounded in the notion that the needs of the job require compromise with the rule of law. Both issues came to the Supreme Court in cases arising out of alleged violations of law by President Nixon (1969–74). Both issues have recurred, as illustrated by the many legal problems faced by President Clinton (1993–2001) and soon to be faced by President Trump (2017 onward).

UNITED STATES V. NIXON
418 U.S. 683, 94 S.Ct. 3090, 41 L.Ed.2d 1039 (1974)

CHIEF JUSTICE BURGER delivered the opinion of the Court.

[Agents of the Committee to Re-elect the President (CREEP) broke into the Democratic National Headquarters at the Watergate Hotel on June 17, 1972 and were apprehended. They implicated officials in the campaign to reelect President Nixon, and in 1973–74 both Senate and House committees conducted hearings on the Watergate break-in and the apparent effort to cover it up. In May, the President named Archibald Cox as a special prosecutor to investigate any White House involvement in a cover-up. John Dean, former White House Counsel, implicated the President himself in June, and in February 1974 the House authorized the

Judiciary Committee to commence impeachment proceedings against the President.

[On March 1, 1974, a grand jury returned indictments against seven defendants: former Attorney General John Mitchell, White House officials H.R. Haldeman and John Ehrlichman, and four others. Each was charged with conspiracy to defraud the United States and to obstruct justice in the Watergate affair. The President was named as an unindicted co-conspirator in *United States v. Mitchell.* On April 18, upon motion by the special prosecutor, a subpoena was issued by the district court, requiring the President to produce tapes, memoranda, and other writings relating to specified meetings with the President. The President released edited transcripts of some of the tapes in question and on May 1 moved to quash the subpoena on grounds of executive privilege. The district court denied the motion. As in the Steel Seizure Case and the Iranian Hostages Case, the Supreme Court took review before the case had been considered by the court of appeals. The Court affirmed and remanded the case to the district court for examination of the subpoenaed documents.]

* * * [W]e turn to the claim that the subpoena should be quashed because it demands "confidential conversations between a President and his close advisors that it would be inconsistent with the public interest to produce." The first contention is a broad claim that the separation of powers doctrine precludes judicial review of a President's claim of privilege. The second contention is that if he does not prevail on the claim of absolute privilege, the court should hold as a matter of constitutional law that the privilege prevails over the subpoena *duces tecum.* * * *

No holding of the Court has defined the scope of judicial power specifically relating to the enforcement of a subpoena for confidential Presidential communications for use in a criminal prosecution. * * * In a series of cases, the Court interpreted the explicit immunity conferred by express provisions of the Constitution on Members of the House and Senate by the Speech or Debate Clause, U.S. Const., Art. I, § 6. Since this Court has consistently exercised the power to construe and delineate claims arising under express powers, it must follow that the Court has authority to interpret claims with respect to powers alleged to derive from enumerated powers.

Our system of government "requires that federal courts on occasion interpret the Constitution in a manner at variance with the construction given the document by another branch." * * * Notwithstanding the deference each branch must accord the others, the "judicial Power of the United States" vested in the federal courts by Art. III, § 1, of the Constitution can no more be shared with the Executive Branch than the Chief Executive, for example, can share with the Judiciary the veto power, or the Congress share with the Judiciary the power to override a

Presidential veto. Any other conclusion would be contrary to the basic concept of separation of powers and the checks and balances that flow from the scheme of a tripartite government. We therefore reaffirm that it is the province and duty of this Court "to say what the law is" with respect to the claim of privilege presented in this case. *Marbury v. Madison.*

In support of his claim of absolute privilege, the President's counsel urges two grounds, one of which is common to all governments and one of which is peculiar to our system of separation of powers. The first ground is the valid need for protection of communications between high Government officials and those who advise and assist them in the performance of their manifold duties; the importance of this confidentiality is too plain to require further discussion. Human experience teaches that those who expect public dissemination of their remarks may well temper candor with a concern for appearances and for their own interests to the detriment of the decisionmaking process. Whatever the nature of the privilege of confidentiality of Presidential communications in the exercise of Art. II powers, the privilege can be said to derive from the supremacy of each branch within its own assigned area of constitutional duties. Certain powers and privileges flow from the nature of enumerated powers; the protection of the confidentiality of Presidential communications has similar constitutional underpinnings.

The second ground asserted by the President's counsel in support of the claim of absolute privilege rests on the doctrine of separation of powers. Here it is argued that the independence of the Executive Branch within its own sphere, insulates a President from a judicial subpoena in an ongoing criminal prosecution, and thereby protects confidential Presidential communications.

However, neither the doctrine of separation of powers, nor the need for confidentiality of high-level communications, without more, can sustain an absolute, unqualified Presidential privilege of immunity from judicial process under all circumstances. The President's need for complete candor and objectivity from advisers calls for great deference from the courts. However, when the privilege depends solely on the broad, undifferentiated claim of public interest in the confidentiality of such conversations, a confrontation with other values arises. Absent a claim of need to protect military, diplomatic, or sensitive national security secrets, we find it difficult to accept the argument that even the very important interest in confidentiality of Presidential communications is significantly diminished by production of such material for *in camera* inspection with all the protection that a district court will be obliged to provide.

The impediment that an absolute, unqualified privilege would place in the way of the primary constitutional duty of the Judicial Branch to do justice in criminal prosecutions would plainly conflict with the function of the courts under Art. III. In designing the structure of our Government and dividing and allocating the sovereign power among three co-equal branches, the Framers of the Constitution sought to provide a comprehensive system, but the separate powers were not intended to operate with absolute independence. * * * To read the Art. II powers of the President as providing an absolute privilege as against a subpoena essential to enforcement of criminal statutes on no more than a generalized claim of the public interest in confidentiality of nonmilitary and nondiplomatic discussions would upset the constitutional balance of "a workable government" and gravely impair the role of the courts under Art. III. * * *

The expectation of a President to the confidentiality of his conversations and correspondence, like the claim of confidentiality of judicial deliberations, for example, has all the values to which we accord deference for the privacy of all citizens and, added to those values, is the necessity for protection of the public interest in candid, objective, and even blunt or harsh opinions in Presidential decisionmaking. * * * The privilege is fundamental to the operation of Government and inextricably rooted in the separation of powers under the Constitution. In *Nixon v. Sirica*, 159 U.S. App. D.C. 58, 487 F.2d 700 (1973), the Court of Appeals held that such Presidential communications are "presumptively privileged," and this position is accepted by both parties in the present litigation. * * *

But this presumptive privilege must be considered in light of our historic commitment to the rule of law. This is nowhere more profoundly manifest than in our view that "the twofold aim [of criminal justice] is that guilt shall not escape or innocence suffer." We have elected to employ an adversary system of criminal justice in which the parties contest all issues before a court of law. The need to develop all relevant facts in the adversary system is both fundamental and comprehensive. The ends of criminal justice would be defeated if judgments were to be founded on a partial or speculative presentation of the facts. The very integrity of the judicial system and public confidence in the system depend on full disclosure of all the facts, within the framework of the rules of evidence. To ensure that justice is done, it is imperative to the function of courts that compulsory process be available for the production of evidence needed either by the prosecution or by the defense.

Only recently the Court restated the ancient proposition of law, albeit in the context of a grand jury inquiry rather than a trial, "that 'the public . . . has a right to every man's evidence,' except for those persons protected by a constitutional, common-law, or statutory privilege." The privileges referred to by the Court are designed to protect weighty and legitimate competing interests. Thus, the Fifth Amendment to the Constitution provides that no man "shall be compelled in any criminal case to be a witness against himself." And, generally, an attorney or a priest may not be required to disclose what has been revealed in professional confidence. These and other interests are recognized in law by privileges against forced disclosure, established in the Constitution, by statute, or at common law. Whatever their origins, these exceptions to the demand for every man's evidence are not lightly created nor expansively construed, for they are in derogation of the search for truth.

In this case the President challenges a subpoena served on him as a third party requiring the production of materials for use in a criminal prosecution; he does so on the claim that he has a privilege against disclosure of confidential communications. He does not place his claim of privilege on the ground they are military or diplomatic secrets. As to these areas of Art. II duties the courts have traditionally shown the utmost deference to Presidential responsibilities. * * *

No case of the Court, however, has extended this high degree of deference to a President's generalized interest in confidentiality. Nowhere in the Constitution, as we have noted earlier, is there any explicit reference to a privilege of confidentiality, yet to the extent this interest relates to the effective discharge of a President's powers, it is constitutionally based.

The right to the production of all evidence at a criminal trial similarly has constitutional dimensions. The Sixth Amendment explicitly confers upon every defendant in a criminal trial the right "to be confronted with the witnesses against him" and "to have compulsory process for obtaining witnesses in his favor." Moreover, the Fifth Amendment also guarantees that no person shall be deprived of liberty without due process of law. It is the manifest duty of the courts to vindicate those guarantees, and to accomplish that it is essential that all relevant and admissible evidence be produced.

In this case we must weigh the importance of the general privilege of confidentiality of Presidential communications in performance of the President's responsibilities against the inroads of such a privilege on the fair administration of criminal justice. The interest in preserving confidentiality is weighty indeed and entitled to great respect. However, we cannot conclude that advisers will be moved to temper the candor of their remarks by the infrequent occasions of disclosure because of the possibility that such conversations will be called for in the context of a criminal prosecution.

On the other hand, the allowance of the privilege to withhold evidence that is demonstrably relevant in a criminal trial would cut deeply into the guarantee of due process of law and gravely impair the basic function of the courts. A President's acknowledged need for confidentiality in the communications of his office is general in nature, whereas the constitutional need for production of relevant evidence in a criminal proceeding is specific and central to the fair adjudication of a particular criminal case in the administration of justice. Without access to specific facts a criminal prosecution may be totally frustrated. The President's broad interest in confidentiality of communications will not be vitiated by disclosure of a limited number of conversations preliminarily shown to have some bearing on the pending criminal cases.

We conclude that when the ground for asserting privilege as to subpoenaed materials sought for use in a criminal trial is based only on the generalized interest in confidentiality, it cannot prevail over the fundamental demands of due process of law in the fair administration of criminal justice. The generalized assertion of privilege must yield to the demonstrated, specific need for evidence in a pending criminal trial.

[The Court further held that the district court did not err in authorizing the issuance of the subpoena: the court properly treated the material as presumptively privileged, proceeded to find that the Special Prosecutor had made a sufficient showing to rebut the presumption, and ordered an *in camera* examination of the subpoenaed material. In conducting the *in camera* inspection, the district court was instructed:]

Statements that meet the test of admissibility and relevance must be isolated; all other material must be excised. At this stage the District Court is not limited to representations of the Special Prosecutor as to the evidence sought by the subpoena; the material will be available to the District Court. It is elementary that *in camera* inspection of evidence is always a procedure calling for scrupulous protection against any release or publication of material not found by the court, at that stage, probably admissible in evidence and relevant to the issues of the trial for which it is sought. That being true of an ordinary situation, it is obvious that the District Court has a very heavy responsibility to see to it that Presidential conversations, which are either not relevant or not admissible, are accorded that high degree of respect due the President of the United States. Mr. Chief Justice Marshall, sitting as a trial judge in the *Burr* case, was extraordinarily careful to point out that "[i]n no case of this kind would a court be required to proceed against a president as against an ordinary individual." Marshall's statement cannot be read to mean in any sense that a President is above the law, but relates to the singularly unique role under Art. II of a President's communications and activities, related to the performance of duties under that Article. Moreover, a President's communications and activities encompass a vastly wider range of sensitive material than would be true of any "ordinary individual." It is therefore necessary in the public interest to afford Presidential confidentiality the greatest protection consistent with the fair administration of justice. The need for confidentiality even as to idle conversations with associates in which casual reference might be made concerning political leaders within the country or foreign statesmen is too obvious to call for further treatment. We have no doubt that the District Judge will at all times accord to Presidential records

[a] high degree of deference * * * and will discharge his responsibility to see to it that until released to the Special Prosecutor no *in camera* material is revealed to anyone. This burden applies with even greater force to excised material; once the decision is made to excise, the material is restored to its privileged status and should be returned under seal to its lawful custodian.

JUSTICE REHNQUIST took no part in the consideration or decision of these cases.

NOTES ON EXECUTIVE PRIVILEGES AND THE NIXON TAPES CASE

1. *Why Should This Issue Be Resolved by the Court?* There may be something to President Nixon's argument that the Court should have stayed out of this controversy. Essentially, the case involved the creeping paralysis of Nixon's Administration. The Senate Select Committee that had publicized the Watergate affair, the House Judiciary Committee conducting the impeachment inquiry, and the Special Prosecutor all had access to the public documents and were interested in obtaining the subpoenaed transcripts. The President's refusal to release the tapes was of central concern in the impeachment proceedings, and the Nixon Tapes Case seems like a classic instance where the remedy for presidential recalcitrance is the political, and not judicial, process.

On July 27 (two days after the Supreme Court's decision), the House Judiciary Committee voted its first article of impeachment, charging the President with obstruction of justice. On July 29, it adopted a second article, charging the President with abuse of power. On July 30, it adopted a third article of impeachment, charging the President with willful disobedience of subpoenas issued by the Committee. The President released transcripts of the tapes to the public. The transcripts contained the smoking guns linking the President to the Watergate cover-up. President Nixon resigned on August 9. Was the Supreme Court's decision, in the midst of the impeachment process, appropriate? See Gerald Gunther, *Judicial Hegemony and Legislative Autonomy: The* Nixon *Case and the Impeachment Process*, 22 UCLA L. Rev. 30 (1974) (no).

2. *Why Does the President Enjoy Any Executive Privilege?* One of the most striking things about the Chief Justice's opinion is its dismissive attitude toward the Special Prosecutor's argument that there is no constitutional basis for executive privilege. After all, the Speech or Debate Clause, Art. I, § 6, expressly protects Members of Congress against being "questioned" about their legislative activities. Why was there no similar privilege set out in Article II? The Court assumes that such a privilege is relevant and appropriate to the grants of power made to the President. How is that? Would the President not

be able to execute the laws if the President had no privilege against testifying about such activities?[49]

Moreover, history and tradition weigh against the Court's casual treatment of the argument. In Aaron Burr's treason trial in 1807, Chief Justice Marshall (sitting as a circuit judge) ruled that President Jefferson was subject to a subpoena to testify and produce documents relating to presidential activities. In 1818, President Monroe was served with a subpoena to testify about his appointment of Dr. William Barton for a position at the Philadelphia naval hospital. Attorney General William Wirt advised the President that he could be subpoenaed, and the President offered to give his testimony by deposition or (as was ultimately done) by interrogatories. In light of this historical evidence, why should the President have a constitutional privilege against testifying?

3.　*Why Is Executive Privilege Not Absolute?* If there is a constitutionally mandated executive privilege, why is it not absolute, at least as to presidential conversations pertinent to the President's executive duties? Compare other evidentiary privileges: The Fifth Amendment's privilege against self-incrimination is not subject to a balancing test to determine its applicability. If a statement might tend to incriminate you, you have an absolute right not to make it. The rationale is as follows: The purpose of evidentiary privileges is to assure complete and free conversations society wants to encourage (client to counsel, patient to doctor, the President to top advisers). To assure the interlocutors of completely candid discourse, society guarantees that the information will not turn up in trial and cannot be compelled by the government. Hence, the privilege must be absolute. Since the President's conversations with advisers are, according to the Court and received wisdom, so very important to the nation, doesn't this rationale apply with special force?

And what about the Court's "balancing" act? How can the Court balance executive privilege against other interests? Is executive privilege as weighty as the defendants' rights to fair trial? Why can't one's privilege against self-incrimination also be balanced away? The more one engages in this sort of balancing, the more the Court may begin to look like a legislature. See T. Alexander Aleinikoff, *Constitutional Law in the Age of Balancing*, 96 Yale L.J. 943 (1987).

Nixon v. Administrator of General Services

433 U.S. 425 (1977)

The Presidential Recordings and Materials Preservation Act directed the Administrator of General Services (an executive official) to take possession of former President Nixon's presidential papers and tape recordings, screen them

---

[49] Compare Raoul Berger, *Executive Privilege: A Constitutional Myth* (1974), and Norman Dorsen & John Shattuck, *Executive Privilege, the Congress and the Courts*, 35 Ohio St. L.J. 1 (1974) (skeptical of the need for executive immunity), with Akhil Reed Amar & Neal Kumar Katyal, *Executive Privileges and Immunities: The Nixon and Clinton Cases*, 108 Harv. L. Rev. 701 (1995) (big fans).

for personal and private materials (to be returned to the former President), and determine which of the retained materials should be made available to the public. The Court rejected the former President's executive privilege challenge to the law.

Justice Brennan's opinion for the Court invoked the "pragmatic, flexible approach" to separation of powers "expressly affirmed" in the Nixon Tapes Case, and which the Court characterized as "essentially embrac[ing] Mr. Justice Jackson's view" in the Steel Seizure Case. The Court agreed that the seizure of the presidential papers "would adversely affect the ability of future Presidents to obtain the candid advice necessary for effective decisionmaking" but ruled that the seizure would not be "unduly disruptive," that is, would not materially interfere with the President's ability to accomplish the "constitutionally assigned functions" of the office. Such a "limited intrusion into executive confidentiality" was justified by the "substantial public interest" in restoring "public confidence in our political processes by preserving the materials as a source for facilitating a full airing of the events leading to [President Nixon's] resignation."

Justice Rehnquist (who did not participate in the Nixon Tapes Case) dissented on the ground that the Act was a serious intrusion into the President's assurance of freely flowing information in executive decisionmaking and that separation of powers precludes balancing away such intrusions based upon the Court's "potpourri of reasons" why the Act represents good policy. Moreover, Rehnquist argued that the Court's willingness to balance away core powers was starkly inconsistent with the formalist approach in the Steel Seizure Case. "Surely if ever there were a case for 'balancing,' and giving weight to the asserted 'national interest' to sustain government action, it was in [the Steel Seizure Case]."

Chief Justice Burger also dissented on separation of powers grounds: The statute was "an exercise of executive—not legislative—power by the Legislative Branch," inconsistent with the Steel Seizure majority, and it constituted a "sweeping modification of the constitutional privilege and historical practice of confidentiality of every Chief Executive since 1789," inconsistent with the Steel Seizure dissent as well as majority.

PROBLEM 8-3:
EXECUTIVE PRIVILEGE AND CONGRESSIONAL DELIBERATIONS

The Nixon Tapes Case involved a criminal trial proceeding, where the private interest in obtaining presidential materials was particularly strong. Since the Nixon Presidency, most of the invocations of executive privilege have been to prevent congressional committees from examining presidential advisory documents.[50] The Supreme Court has affirmed that Congress has

---

[50] Executive privilege was invoked by President Ford 1 time (against Congress), Carter 1 time (against Congress), President Reagan 3 times (all against Congress), first President Bush 1 time (against Congress), President Clinton 14 times (5 times against Congress), and the second President Bush 3 times (2 against Congress). See CRS Report for Congress: Morton Rosenberg,

oversight authority "to enable it efficiently to exercise a legislative function belonging to it under the Constitution." *McGrain v. Daugherty*, 273 U.S. 135, 160 (1927); accord, *Watkins v. United States*, 354 U.S. 178 (1957). And, of course, the Senate must confirm judicial and high executive branch appointments by the President. In doing so for nominees who have served in the executive branch, senators may request documents relating to the nominee's opinions and advice.

The executive branch has developed a common law of privilege, partly codified in OLC opinions. See Rosenberg, *Presidential Claims of Executive Privilege*, 10–16. The President asserts executive privilege in three areas: (1) state secrets involving foreign and military affairs; (2) law enforcement investigations; and (3) confidential information that reveals the executive's "deliberative process." The Clinton Administration claimed it for *any* communications within the White House or between the White House and agencies and departments. Generally, however, post-Nixon Presidents (including Clinton) have said they will not invoke privilege to block congressional inquiries into fraud, corruption, or other illegal or unethical conduct within the executive branch. *Id.* at 13–14. All post-Nixon administrations have worked out most executive privilege disputes involving Congress informally. But sometimes negotiation does not work.

In 2007, a House committee investigated Attorney General Alberto Gonzales's discharge of several U.S. Attorneys based upon allegations that the discharges were efforts to discipline U.S. Attorneys who did not follow a White House political agenda, including prosecuting Democrats and not Republicans. The committee issued subpoenas to several White House officials, including Chief of Staff Joshua Bolten and former White House Counsel Harriet Miers, to produce relevant documents, including communications (1) internal to the White House; (2) between White House officials and persons outside the executive branch; and (3) between White House and DOJ officials.

On June 27, 2007, the White House invoked executive privilege as to these documents; Bolten and Miers subsequently declined to testify for these reasons. Upon the recommendation of the committee, the House voted to subpoena the witnesses and their documents. On March 10, 2008, the House Counsel filed an action for declaratory judgment and injunction for production of documents against Miers and Bolten. If you were a judge, how would you rule? Jot down your thoughts and then review the following document.

Letter from Acting Attorney General Paul Clement to the President, June 27, 2007. The letter lays out the objections to the Bolten/Miers documents. Our excerpts will focus on the internal White House communications, but the Clement analysis is similar for the other categories. "Among other things, these communications discuss the wisdom of such a

---

Presidential Claims of Executive Privilege: History, Law, Practice and Recent Developments appendix (Updated April 16, 2008). For an excellent case study of a Reagan era investigation of the EPA, see Peter Shane, *Legal Disagreement and Negotiation in a Government of Laws: The Case of Executive Privilege Claims Against Congress*, 71 Minn. L. Rev. 461 (1987).

proposal, specific U.S. Attorneys who could be removed, potential replacement candidates, and possible responses to congressional and media inquiries about the dismissals. These types of internal deliberations among White House officials fall squarely within the scope of executive privilege." Cites are to *Nixon*, D.C. Circuit authority, and previous presidential assertions of executive privilege.

"Under D.C. Circuit precedent, a congressional committee may not overcome an assertion of executive privilege unless it establishes that the documents and information are 'demonstrably critical to the responsible fulfillment of the Committee's functions.' *Senate Select Comm. on Presidential Campaign Activities v. Nixon*, 498 F.2d 725, 731 (D.C. Cir. 1974) (en banc). And those functions must be in furtherance of Congress's legitimate legislative responsibilities. *McGrain*.

"As a threshold matter, it is not at all clear that internal White House communications about the possible dismissal and replacement of U.S. Attorneys fall within the scope of *McGrain* and its progeny. The Supreme Court has held that Congress's oversight powers do not reach 'matters which are within the exclusive province of one of the other branches of the Government.' *Barenblatt v. United States*, 360 U.S. 109, 112 (1959). The Senate has the authority to approve or reject the appointment of officers whose appointment by law requires the advice and consent of the Senate (which has been the case for U.S. Attorneys since the founding of the Republic), but it is for the President to decide whom to nominate to such positions and whether to remove such officers once appointed. [*Public Citizen v. Department of Justice*, 491 U.S. 440, 483 (1989) (Kennedy, J., concurring in the judgment) (Congress cannot impose reporting requirements on the President's decision whom to nominate as judges).] Consequently, there is reason to question whether Congress has oversight authority to investigate deliberations by White House officials concerning proposals to dismiss and replace U.S. Attorneys, because such deliberations necessarily relate to the potential exercise by the President of an authority assigned to him alone."

The Acting Attorney General also opined that the committee had not shown a genuine need for the documents sufficient to override the executive privilege claim. Under *Senate Select Committee,* Congress must "point[ ] to . . . specific legislative decisions that cannot responsibly be made without access to [privileged] materials." DOJ had already turned over 8500 pages of documents relating to its own deliberations concerning the U.S. Attorney resignations. Cf. *History of Refusals by Executive Branch Officials to Provide Information Demanded by Congress*, 6 Op. O.L.C. 751, 758–59, 767 (1982) (refusals by nineteenth-century Presidents to provide *any* information relating to decisions to remove executive branch officials, including a U.S. Attorney in one case).

"In a letter accompanying the subpoenas, the House Committee references the alleged 'written misstatements' and 'false statements' provided by the Department [of Justice] to the Committees about the U.S. Attorney dismissals. * * * This interest does not, however, justify the Committees' demand for White

House documents and information about the U.S. Attorney resignations. Officials in the Department, not officials in the White House, presented the challenged statements, and as noted, the Department has provided unprecedented information to Congress concerning, *inter alia*, the process that led to the Department's statements."[51]

Query: President Trump's second Supreme Court nominee was Judge Brett Kavanaugh, who had served in the Bush 45 White House. The Senate Judiciary Committee requested all documents relating to Judge Kavanaugh's work for the White House Counsel's Office (2001–03)—but the Bush 45 Presidential Archives in early September 2018 announced that it would withhold more than 100,000 pages of documents. (The Archives released more than 415,000 pages of documents, however.)

In a letter sent to the Senate Judiciary Committee, William Burck, who was in charge of compiling documents related to the Bush 45 Presidency, wrote that former President Bush had advised him to err "on the side of transparency and disclosure," but that the Trump White House directed him not to release certain files, citing executive privilege. The documents in question, he wrote, "reflect deliberations and candid advice concerning the selection and nomination of judicial candidates, the confidentiality of which is critical to any president's ability to carry out this core constitutional executive function." The bulk of the documents were internal White House Counsel memoranda on legal and constitutional issues and not direct communications with the President. (Judge Kavanaugh was Secretary to President Bush 45 after 2003, but the Committee did not request documents relating to that position.)

Was this invocation of executive privilege consistent with the White House common law of privilege? With the constitutional case law?

Before the controversy over the Kavanaugh documents, which became moot when the Senate confirmed Judge Kavanaugh to join the Supreme Court, the Trump Administration had taken the position that it would decline any subpoena from Special Counsel Mueller's investigation into Russian interference in the 2016 election. The Administration's position was that the President was too busy to respond to a subpoena and would invoke executive privilege to resist it. Would a court enforce a properly focused subpoena?

---

[51] *In re Sealed Case (Espy)*, 121 F.3d 729 (D.C. Cir. 1997), ruled that departmental deliberations were protected only by a common law deliberative process privilege (not the constitutional privilege) that "disappears altogether when there is any reason to believe government misconduct has occurred." *Judicial Watch, Inc. v. Department of Justice*, 365 F.3d 1108 (D.C. 2004), extended that analysis to require disclosure of departmental documents to a congressional committee investigating presidential abuse of the pardon power. Only departmental documents "solicited and received" by the President are protected by constitutional executive privilege."

Nixon v. Fitzgerald

457 U.S. 731 (1982)

The Court, by a 5–4 vote, applied the Nixon Tapes Case balancing approach to hold former President Nixon absolutely immune from a civil damages lawsuit filed by a Defense Department whistleblower who was allegedly discharged by the President because of what Nixon considered his disloyalty. **Justice Powell**'s opinion for the Court interpreted Article II to assign to the President uniquely important discretionary decisionmaking that would be impaired by allowing his decisions to be second-guessed in damage lawsuits against him individually; decisions such as the Steel Seizure one could still, of course, be challenged in lawsuits for injunctive relief.

Justice Powell also found support in the original understanding at the Philadelphia Convention: Senator Maclay recorded the views of John Adams and Oliver Ellsworth (key Framers) that " 'the President, personally, was not subject to any process whatever,' " as such process " 'would . . . put it in the power of a common justice to exercise any authority over him and stop the whole machine of Government.' " Likewise, Justice Joseph Story's constitutional commentary reasoned in 1833 that the President " 'cannot be liable to arrest, imprisonment, or detention, while he is in the discharge of the duties of his office; and for this purpose his person must be deemed, in civil cases at least, to possess an official inviolability.' " Because civil lawsuits could "distract the President from his public duties, to the detriment of not only the President and his office but also the Nation that the Presidency was designed to serve," the Court found the individual interest in remedy insufficient to justify a civil lawsuit against the President for acts within his official responsibilities. Political remedies, including actual or threatened impeachment, were a sufficient deterrent for presidential misconduct.

The opinion of the Court was ambiguous as to whether the President's immunity was grounded in constitutional common law and, therefore, could be stripped by Congress. **Chief Justice Burger**'s concurring opinion argued that constitutional separation of powers requires the immunity, which, therefore, cannot be taken away.

Justice White wrote one of the most passionate dissents of his career, arguing that the Court's grant of absolute immunity to former President Nixon was inconsistent with the more limited immunity given Members of Congress only for their legislative acts in the Speech and Debate Clause, Art. I, § 6, e.g., *United States v. Brewster*, 408 U.S. 501 (1972) (Senator can be prosecuted for taking bribes); with the limited immunity accorded members of the President's Cabinet in *Butz v. Economou*, 438 U.S. 478 (1978); and with the rule of law articulated in *Marbury v. Madison* (Chapter 2, § 2A). Justice White subjected the historical materials to intense scrutiny and found no evidence sufficient to displace the normal presumption that every citizen is subject to the rule of law. As the President has been repeatedly held amenable to judicial process and even under the Court's analysis subject to criminal prosecution, Justice White found no justification, even under a balancing approach, for carving out damages cases for special immunity.

Clinton v. Jones

520 U.S. 681 (1997)

A unanimous Court rejected President Clinton's claim that a President could invoke *Fitzgerald* immunity to claims that arose before the President took office. Although she brought the lawsuit during Clinton's presidency, Paula Jones alleged that Clinton sexually harassed her when he was governor of Arkansas. The President maintained that the uniqueness of his office, recognized in *Fitzgerald*, demands that he be free of damage lawsuits during his term.

Justice Stevens' opinion for the Court accepted the premise of the President's argument but rejected its conclusion. The core concern of constitutional separation of powers is that one branch of government not usurp the powers or assume the responsibilities of another branch. "[I]n this case there is no suggestion that the Federal Judiciary is being asked to perform any function that might in some way be described as 'executive.' [Jones] is merely asking the courts to exercise their core Article III jurisdiction to decide cases and controversies. Whatever the outcome of this case, there is no possibility that the decision will curtail the scope of the official powers of the Executive Branch. The litigation of questions that relate entirely to the unofficial conduct of the individual who happens to be the President poses no perceptible risk of misallocation of either judicial power or executive power."

Justice Stevens recognized some force to the President's functional argument, that allowing the lawsuit to proceed would impair the President in the performance of his duties. Justice Stevens found little reason to believe that the lawsuit, and the prospect of similar ones in the future, would actually distract the President. (In American history, only three Presidents had been subject to such private actions.) In any event, the impairment claimed by the President was not constitutionally weighty enough to outweigh the judiciary's traditional Article III duties, for two related reasons.

"First, we have long held that when the President takes official action, the Court has the authority to determine whether he has acted within the law. Perhaps the most dramatic example of such a case is our holding that President Truman exceeded his constitutional authority when he issued an order directing the Secretary of Commerce to take possession of and operate most of the Nation's steel mills in order to avert a national catastrophe. *Youngstown*. Despite the serious impact of that decision on the ability of the Executive Branch to accomplish its assigned mission, and the substantial time that the President must necessarily have devoted to the matter as a result of judicial involvement, we exercised our Article III jurisdiction to decide whether his official conduct conformed to the law. * * *

"Second, it is also settled that the President is subject to judicial process in appropriate circumstances. Although Thomas Jefferson apparently thought otherwise, Chief Justice Marshall, when presiding in the treason trial of Aaron Burr, ruled that a subpoena *duces tecum* could be directed to the President. *United States v. Burr*, 25 F. Cas. 30 (No. 14,692d) (C.C.Va. 1807). We unequivocally and emphatically endorsed Marshall's position when we held that President Nixon was obligated to comply with a subpoena commanding him to produce certain tape recordings of his conversations with his aides. *United States v. Nixon*." Justice Stevens noted several other instances where Presidents had responded to court orders requiring testimony, including two cases where President Clinton agreed to give video testimony.

"In sum, '[i]t is settled law that the separation-of-powers doctrine does not bar every exercise of jurisdiction over the President of the United States.' *Fitzgerald*. If the Judiciary may severely burden the Executive Branch by reviewing the legality of the President's official conduct, and if it may direct appropriate process to the President himself, it must follow that the federal courts have power to determine the legality of his unofficial conduct. The burden on the President's time and energy that is a mere by-product of such review surely cannot be considered as onerous as the direct burden imposed by judicial review and the occasional invalidation of his official actions. We therefore hold that the doctrine of separation of powers does not require federal courts to stay all private actions against the President until he leaves office."

The reasons for rejecting such a categorical rule also counseled against a constitutional requirement that the case be stayed during the President's term of office, but Justice Stevens allowed the trial judge substantial discretion. " '[E]specially in cases of extraordinary public moment, [a plaintiff] may be required to submit to delay not immoderate in extent and not oppressive in its consequences if the public welfare or convenience will thereby be promoted.' Although we have rejected the argument that the potential burdens on the President violate separation of powers principles, those burdens are appropriate matters for the District Court to evaluate in its management of the case. The high respect that is owed to the office of the Chief Executive, though not justifying a rule of categorical immunity, is a matter that should inform the conduct of the entire proceeding, including the timing and scope of discovery."

Although viewing the future burdens on the President as more substantial and constitutionally noteworthy, **Justice Breyer** concurred in the judgment.

NOTES ON THE PRESIDENTIAL IMMUNITY CASES

1. *Reconciling the Cases?* Justice Breyer's separate opinion in *Jones* argued that the Court's analysis was inconsistent with the reasoning of *Fitzgerald*. Justice Stevens responded that *Fitzgerald* was distinguishable, as it involved a President's official conduct during his presidency, not conduct before he attained that office. But *Fitzgerald*'s sweeping *claim immunity* deprived a plaintiff of his cause of action altogether, while *Jones' temporal*

immunity would only have postponed a plaintiff's opportunity for her day in court. See Akhil Reed Amar & Neal Kumar Katyal, *Executive Privileges and Immunities: The Nixon and Clinton Cases*, 108 Harv. L. Rev. 701 (1995).

Moreover, *Fitzgerald* involved a case that arose after the President left office, and therefore would not have distracted a sitting President, while *Jones* involved a President busily working away in the Oval Office, actually much more distracted from presidential duties by the lawsuit. Most important, by allowing a lawsuit against a sitting President for personal misdeeds to go forward, the Court was empowering the President's political opponents and perhaps needlessly injecting the federal courts into politics. See Victoria Nourse, *The Vertical Separation of Powers*, 49 Duke L.J. 749, 768–72 (1999). These ideas turn Stevens' distinction on its head: If either President should have gotten a break due to the nature of the office, it should have been sitting President Clinton, who would ultimately have faced his accuser under a temporal immunity, and not former President Nixon, who was freed completely by a claim immunity.

2. *The Ambiguous Role of Original Understanding.* Both Justice Breyer and the *Fitzgerald* majority invoked Justice Story's idea that the President "cannot be liable to arrest, imprisonment, or detention, while he is in the discharge of the duties of his office; and for this purpose his person must be deemed, in civil cases at least, to possess an official inviolability." 3 Joseph Story, *Commentaries on the Constitution of the United States* § 1563, at 418–19 (1833). Note that Story's words support only the temporal immunity involved in *Jones* (no lawsuits while the President is in office), but not the claim immunity involved in *Fitzgerald* (no claim, ever). Amar & Katyal, *Executive Privileges*, 715–18, argue that the same point can be made for the statements by Framers Oliver Ellsworth and John Adams, if you read them in context. Should both *Fitzgerald* and *Jones* be overruled?

Justice Stevens' most telling historical argument for rejecting a temporal immunity (made in a section of the opinion we omitted) was James Wilson's response at Pennsylvania's ratifying convention to charges that the President was a king-in-waiting. Wilson responded that the President is "placed high," but that "not a single privilege is annexed to his character; far from being above the laws, he is amenable to them in his private character as a citizen, and in his public character by impeachment." 2 Elliott, *Debates on the Federal Constitution* 480 (2d ed. 1863). If Wilson's statement is representative of the Framers' sentiments, does that confirm that *Fitzgerald* was wrongly decided? Should the Court revisit its dicta in *United States v. Nixon*, which found an executive privilege for communications within the Oval Office?

3. *Court-Created Immunities, Generally.* The only immunity from judicial process assured in the Constitution is that for Members of Congress in the Speech or Debate Clause, Art. I, § 6. All the other immunities have been created by the Supreme Court, essentially as constitutional common law—inspired by constitutional values but possibly subject to congressional override. In addition to the absolute immunity of the President and the qualified

immunity of Cabinet members and other national executive officials created in *Butz v. Economou*, the Supreme Court has granted absolute immunity from private damage actions to federal judges, *Bradley v. Fisher*, 13 Wall. 335 (1872). All of these immunities, except for those in the Speech or Debate Clause, are creations of judicial policymaking. The maxim *inclusio unius est exclusio alterius* (including one thing in the text suggests the exclusion of all others) augurs against their being constitutional, and there is little if any support for them in the discussions surrounding the adoption of the Constitution. (Judicial immunity might be supported by reference to common law understandings in 1789. Compare the Court's elevation of the states' common law immunity to constitutional principle in Chapter 7, § 4). On the other hand, the functions of the various offices might be severely compromised without such immunities.

The Court's policymaking has been even more open in decisions construing 42 U.S.C. § 1983 (damages action against state officials for violating federal constitutional and statutory rights) to include various immunities for state legislators, *Tenney v. Brandlove*, 341 U.S. 367 (1951) (absolute); state judges, *Pierson v. Ray*, 386 U.S. 547 (1967) (absolute); state executive officials, *Scheuer v. Rhodes*, 416 U.S. 232 (1974) (qualified, for most); state prosecutors, *Imbler v. Pachtman*, 424 U.S. 409 (1976) (absolute for some functions, qualified for others).

PROBLEM 8-4:
SUBJECTING A PRESIDENT TO CRIMINAL PROSECUTION?

On May 17, 2017, the Deputy Attorney General appointed a Special Counsel, Robert S. Mueller III, to investigate wrongdoing in connection with the Russian government's efforts to interfere with the 2016 election. Mueller's office brought prosecutions against a number of defendants and secured convictions against all of them; some defendants traded information and testimony for leniency in sentencing. As we go to press in March 2019, the Special Counsel is winding down his investigation. Assume that Mueller had secured credible evidence that presidential candidate Donald J. Trump conspired with his campaign team and with Russian agents to corrupt the 2016 election and with associates to cover up the conspiracy and the Russians' activities. Consider constitutional issues that might arise:

(a) Federal Criminal Prosecution? Can a sitting President be prosecuted by the Department of Justice for crimes he allegedly committed before becoming President?

(b) Self-Pardon? Can the President pardon himself, thereby freeing him from worry about any kind of future federal prosecution? Under Article II, § 2, the President "shall have power to grant reprieves and pardons for offenses against the United States, except in cases of impeachment." Alexander Hamilton justified the pardon power in *Federalist* No. 74: "Humanity and good policy conspire to dictate, that the benign prerogative of pardoning should be as little as possible fettered or embarrassed. The criminal code of every country partakes so much of necessary severity, that without an easy access to exceptions in favor of unfortunate guilt, justice would wear a countenance too sanguinary and cruel." In *Ex parte Garland,* 71 U.S. 333 (1866), the Supreme Court ruled that the presidential pardon power can be exercised before a federal criminal indictment, during the course of a criminal trial, or after a federal criminal conviction. But can the President pardon himself? Compare Brian C. Kalt, Note, *Pardon Me? The Constitutional Case Against Presidential Self-Pardons,* 106 Yale L.J. 779 (1996), with Prakash, *Imperial from the Beginning,* 107–08.

Does it affect your answer to know that state governors have pardoned themselves? For example, Governor Isaac Stevens of the Washington Territory ordered farmers who were married to Native Americans to leave a certain area. When one judge opened an investigation into this legally questionable move, Stevens closed the court, declared martial law, and had several judges arrested. This was all pretty lawless, and the Governor backed down in the wake of public outrage. After being subject to a fine for contempt of court, and perhaps seeking to head off further penalties, the Governor pardoned himself. See Max Kutner, *No President Has Pardoned Himself, But Governors and a Drunk Mayor Have,* Newsweek, July 24, 2017 (this and other examples). Do state precedents help you answer the self-pardon question?

Margaret Love, who headed the Pardon Office for many years, thinks not. In her view, the original meaning of the pardon power was that exercised by the King of England, from whom the constitutional provision was modeled. Because the pardon power would require the King to step out of his position as sovereign, British monarchs never self-pardoned. See generally Margaret Love, *The Twilight of the Pardon Power,* 100 J.L. & Criminology 1077 (2010).

(c) State Prosecution? If the President can pardon himself to escape federal criminal liability, can a state prosecutor indict a sitting President for state crimes he allegedly committed before becoming President? Can a state prosecutor indict the President for obstruction of justice, if the facts establish that the pardon power was used to cover up crimes? If states cannot prosecute a sitting President, can they prosecute a former President? Can the President pardon himself for violations of state law?

NOTE ON CONGRESS'S IMPEACHMENT POWER: THE CASE OF WILLIAM JEFFERSON CLINTON

President Clinton landed in political hot water after the Court permitted *Jones v. Clinton* to proceed. During his deposition in the case, the President allegedly lied in response to a question whether he had "sex" with a subordinate federal government employee, Monica Lewinsky. Independent Counsel Kenneth Starr investigated this matter as part of his general inquiry of alleged improprieties on the part of President Clinton and reported his evidence and findings to Congress. Under its authority vested by Article I, § 2, cl. 5, the House of Representatives voted several articles of impeachment. A key constitutional issue was this: What kinds of misconduct would justify impeachment (by the House) and removal from office (by the Senate).

Article II, § 4 specifies that the President can be removed from office for "Treason, Bribery, or other high Crimes or Misdemeanors." Few seriously maintained that the President's adultery or his oral sex with a White House intern constituted a "high Crime or Misdemeanor," but the House of Representatives determined that perjury (the original lie) and obstruction of justice (continuing to cover up the lie) did fall into those categories. Were they right? As a textual matter, one would expect an impeachable crime or misdemeanor to be something similarly serious as "Treason" or "Bribery." On the one hand, perjury and obstruction of justice are public crimes (like treason and bribery). On the other hand, they do not reflect betrayal of the President's core executive functions in the same way that treason and bribery do.

There was some deliberation as to this matter during the ratification debates. In *Federalist* No. 70, Hamilton explained that the Convention rejected proposals for a committee-like chief executive; there should be one president, fully accountable to the people. He and the other Federalists understood that it was important to distance the President from Anti-Federalist charges of monarchy, and a chief distinction was that the President would be subject to impeachment.[52] In *Federalist* No. 65, he described the grounds for impeachment as "those offences which derive from the misconduct of public men, in other words, from the abuse or violation of some public trust. They are of a nature which may with peculiar propriety be denominated POLITICAL as they relate chiefly to injuries done immediately to the society itself." At the Virginia Convention, Edmond Randolph asserted that the President could not be impeached for mere errors of judgment. At the North Carolina Convention, James Iredell suggested that the President could be impeached not just for bribery, but also for inducing the Senate to go along with a foreign relations matter based upon presidential misrepresentations. (On the ratification discussions, see 1974 Judiciary Comm. Report 13–17.)

Also potentially relevant to this issue were the English parliamentary standards for impeachment, which were the linguistic basis for "high Crimes and Misdemeanors" in the Impeachment Clause. The kinds of executive misconduct Parliament invoked included misappropriation of funds, abuse of official power, neglect of duty, encroachment on Parliament's prerogatives, and betrayal of public trust (1974 Judiciary Comm. Report 4–7). By the time President Clinton was impeached, the House had impeached one previous

---

[52] There was little dissent from this idea at the Philadelphia Convention. Early on, the delegates unanimously voted to make the executive removable for "malpractice or neglect of duty." In debate, Madison defended impeachment as "indispensable" to defend the community against "the incapacity, negligence or perfidy of the chief magistrate." The main argument against the Impeachment Clause was Charles Pinckney's concern that the legislature would wield impeachment "as a rod over the Executive and by that means effectually destroy his independence." The Impeachment Clause was rewritten to make the President removable for "treason and bribery." George Mason proposed adding "maladministration," but Madison objected that such a vague term would leave the President at the mercy of a politically hostile Senate. Mason withdrew that language and substituted "high crimes and misdemeanors agst. the state," which was adopted, 8–3.

President, one cabinet officer, one senator, and thirteen federal judges. The conduct the House had charged fell into three broad categories: "(1) exceeding the constitutional bounds of the powers of the office in derogation of the powers of another branch of government; (2) behaving in a manner grossly incompatible with the proper function and purpose of the office; and (3) employing the power of the office for an improper purpose or for personal gain." *Id.* at 18; see also 1998 Judiciary Comm. Report 4–14 (post-1974 impeachments of three federal judges included charges of perjury and making false statements in the course of a criminal investigation, filing false income tax returns, and bribery).

Under these criteria, did President Clinton's apparent perjury in his deposition and before the grand jury, as well as alleged obstruction of justice, constitute impeachable offenses? If impeachable offenses, was it constitutionally prudent for the House to have impeached President Clinton for those activities? Does it make a difference to your answer if you knew the Senate would not have convicted Clinton? Indeed, the Senate acquitted on an evenly divided vote (a two-thirds vote would have been required to convict). What precedential principle would you draw from this series of events?[53]

PROBLEM 8-5:
CAN A PRESIDENT BE IMPEACHED FOR ABUSE OF PARDONS?

Assume that Special Prosecutor Mueller brings criminal prosecutions against members of President Donald Trump's family and inner circle. The President pardons all of them. Assume that Mueller has evidence that members of the inner circle made deals with the President that they would not incriminate him if they were pardoned. Once that evidence comes to light, President Trump pardons himself. The Special Prosecutor turns over all of that evidence to the House of Representatives, just as Independent Counsel Kenneth Starr had done in 1998. You are the Counsel to the House Judiciary Committee. If credible, would such evidence justify impeaching President Trump? (As Counsel you do not make the call whether such proceedings should be initiated; the Committee would make that decision.)

SECTION 2. ISSUES OF LEGISLATIVE OVERREACHING

The Framers of the Constitution and their opponents, the Anti-Federalists, felt that Congress, rather than the President, posed the greatest danger to liberty. Hence Congress alone among the three branches is fragmented into two equal bodies (Art. I, § 7), the better to prevent

---

[53] The Senate trial raised another interesting issue: What burden of proof did the House Managers carry in their prosecution of Clinton before the Senate? The managers claimed the Senate should have convicted if persuaded by a preponderance of the evidence, the standard in civil cases. The President's counsel claimed the burden was beyond a reasonable doubt, the standard for criminal cases. As to this issue, what valence would you give the requirement of Article I, § 3, cl. 6 that conviction should require the assent of two-thirds of the Senate?

legislative usurpation by slowing down the Leviathan. In today's government, the many vetogates and hyper-partisan acrimony have produced gridlock, which many political scientists believe to be a bigger problem than the Leviathan problem. E.g., William Howell & Terry Moe, *Relic: How the Constitution Undermines Effective Government—and Why We Need a More Powerful Presidency* (2016).

Separation of powers jurisprudence, of the sort articulated in the Steel Seizure Case, is naturally concerned with direct congressional attacks on the President's exercise of his "executive Power" (Part B) and the Supreme Court's exercise of the "judicial Power" (Part C), but in the modern administrative state a different kind of problem has been Congress' tendency to delegate broad lawmaking powers, often with strings attached (Part A). While the Supreme Court says it has abandoned serious effort to enforce the *nondelegation doctrine* (Congress cannot delegate lawmaking power without clear standards as to the rules to be developed), the Court has indirectly discouraged such delegation by cutting some of the strings, including the legislative veto and the vesting of enforcement discretion in congressionally controlled agents.

As you consider the doctrinal debates surveyed in this section, consider a broader constitutional attack on the modern administrative state. Political leaders, current members of the executive branch, academics, and some judges claim that the modern administrative state—where a lot of lawmaking and adjudication have been ceded by Congress to agencies—has "run amok" (to use the common phrase), at the expense of constitutional liberties and the good of the community. Invoking original constitutional meaning or the Anglo-American constitutional tradition, the scholars and the judges argue that agency lawmaking and adjudication are either completely unconstitutional, e.g., Philip Hamburger, *Is Administrative Law Unlawful?* (2014), or have been taken beyond constitutional limits.[54] Professor Hamburger, for example, argues that the Constitution only allows Congress and the judiciary to issue rules or orders that are legally binding on the citizenry. He relies on an extensive survey of seventeenth-century English common-law judges and their resistance to the bureaucratic tyranny of the Stuart monarchs. A modern-day version of Chief Justice Edward Coke, Professor Hamburger wants to do to modern administrative law what the Whigs did to James II in 1689—depose it and drive it back to the Continent. This raises the stakes of the administrative state debate: Give me liberty, don't give me death by bureaucracy.

If the original meaning of the separate allocation of legislative, executive, and judicial authority by Articles I-III is binding on modern

---

[54] See also Randy Barnett, *Our Republican Constitution* (2016); Philip Hamburger, *The Administrative Threat* (2017); Douglas H. Ginsburg & Steven Menashi, *Our Illiberal Administrative Law*, 10 NYU J.L. & Liberty 475 (2016); Gary Lawson, *Delegation and Original Meaning*, 88 Va. L. Rev. 327 (2002).

judges, an increasing number of federal judges and scholars would dismantle or trim back congressional delegations of (Article I) lawmaking and (Article III) adjudicatory authority to (Article II) agencies. Does longstanding Supreme Court precedent insulate these delegations from constitutional attack? Or curtailment? Most administrative law and constitutional scholars find the argument from original meaning unpersuasive and maintain, further, that agency lawmaking and adjudication are liberty-respecting and essential for governance under the conditions of the modern regulatory state. E.g., Gillian E. Metzger, *The Supreme Court, 2016 Term—Foreword: 1930s Redux: The Administrative State Under Siege,* 131 Harv. L. Rev. 1 (2017). We shall consider their counterarguments in the course of the materials and notes that follow.

A. "EXCESSIVE" CONGRESSIONAL DELEGATIONS AND THE ARTICLE I, SECTION 7 STRUCTURE FOR LAWMAKING

Operating within the framework of state common law, the Framers did not anticipate a great deal of legislating by Congress, but federal statutory law has become the norm, increasingly, since the Civil War. This has posed dilemmas for Members of Congress, dilemmas which are usually resolved by delegation of conflictual issues to other government organs. The traditional explanation for delegation is legislative uncertainty and the availability of administrative expertise. Henry M. Hart Jr. & Albert M. Sacks, *The Legal Process: Basic Problems in the Making and Application of Law* (William N. Eskridge Jr. & Philip P. Frickey eds. 1994 (tent. ed. 1958)). Congress often is called upon to solve problems for which there is no clear solution, or for which the details cannot be surmised. Delegation to a group of expert administrators allows Congress to address the problem, but to allow for the details of the solution to be worked out by people who know what they are doing and who can respond to new information about the problem.

Delegation can also be explained as a consequence of the rational operation of the legislative process.[55] Individual legislators risk fragile political support every time they take policy positions controversial within their districts. Presidents and governors often fall victim to this phenomenon of eroding support, which drives them from office with some regularity. Members of Congress have been better able to avoid such disastrous erosions of popularity, typically by focusing on issues about which their constituents agree and, for conflictual issues, by avoidance, compromise, and delegation of the controversial details to someone else, especially executive departments or independent agencies. The impulse to delegate is reinforced by the difficult processes of lawmaking, whereby

---

[55] See Daniel A. Farber & Philip P. Frickey, *Law and Public Choice: A Critical Introduction* (1991).

numerous veto points (committees, negative chamber vote, filibuster, presidential veto) can kill a measure. These processes of lawmaking drive legislators not only toward compromise and moderate rather than radical changes in the status quo, as the Framers expected, but also toward fudging divisive issues through delegation to other decisionmakers.[56]

The explosion in congressional delegation to agencies raises a host of constitutional problems. First, is there any limit on Congress's authority to delegate *lawmaking* power to agencies? Second, Congress may be more willing to delegate lawmaking power to agencies when it can attach strings to that delegation to allow future Congresses to have some kind of veto or control. Are there constitutional limits to this? Third, Congress has recently been willing to delegate to the President himself the ability to veto specific "lines" of tax and appropriations measures, without having to veto the entire bill. Is this constitutional? The primary constitutional provision relevant to all three of these issues is Article I, Section 7, which sets forth the structure by which Congress creates legislation.[57]

1. The Decline and Potential Revival of the Nondelegation Doctrine

Consistent with Justice Black's opinion for the Court in the Steel Seizure Case, judges and scholars maintain that the constitutional structure and/or its original meaning support the *nondelegation doctrine*.[58] That doctrine posits that Congress cannot, consistent with Article I, delegate lawmaking powers to other groups (the executive, agencies, courts, private groups). Congress can delegate gap-filling authority to agencies and judges so long as Congress makes the important policy choices and lays down "an intelligible principle" to which the implementers must conform. *J.W. Hampton, Jr. & Co. v. United States*, 276 U.S. 394, 409 (1928). Although the nondelegation doctrine has from early in our history been an established constitutional principle, recent evidence suggests that judges have almost never enforced it, either in the nineteenth century (once believed to be its heyday) or since the New Deal. See Keith Whittington &

---

[56] See Victoria F. Nourse, *Misreading Law, Misunderstanding Congress* (2017); Joseph A. Grundfest & A.C. Pritchard, *Statutes with Multiple Personality Disorders: The Value of Ambiguity in Statutory Design and Interpretation*, 54 Stan. L. Rev. 627 (2002); Victoria F. Nourse, *Misunderstanding Congress: Statutory Interpretation, the Supermajoritarian Difficulty, and the Separation of Powers*, 99 Geo. L.J. 1119 (2011).

[57] For constitutional-theoretic introductions, see Bradford R. Clark, *Separation of Powers as a Safeguard of Federalism*, 79 Tex. L. Rev. 1321 (2001); William N. Eskridge Jr. & John Ferejohn, *The Article I, Section 7 Game*, 80 Geo. L.J. 523 (1992); Gary Lawson, *The Weak Nondelegation Doctrine and* American Trucking Associations v. EPA, 2000 BYU L. Rev. 627.

[58] On the nondelegation doctrine as inherent in Article I and reflects its original meaning, see *Wayman v. Southard*, 23 U.S. 1 (1825) (Marshall, C.J.); Philip Hamburger, *Is Administrative Law Unlawful?* (2015); David Schoenbrod, *Power Without Responsibility: How Congress Abuses the People Through Delegation* 181–89 (1993); Steven G. Calabresi & Gary Lawson, *The Rule of Law as a Law of Law*, 90 Notre Dame L. Rev. 483 (2014); Gary Lawson, *Discretion as Delegation: The "Proper" Understanding of the Nondelegation Doctrine*, 73 Geo. Wash. L. Rev. 235 (2005).

Jason Iuliano, *The Myth of the Nondelegation Doctrine*, 165 U. Pa. L. Rev. 379 (2017).

Ironically, the New Deal was both the high point and the collapse of the nondelegation doctrine as a constitutional limit on Congress. In 1935, the Supreme Court used the nondelegation doctrine to invalidate federal legislation in *A.L.A. Schechter Poultry Corp. v. United States*, 295 U.S. 495 (1935). See also *Panama Refining v. Ryan*, 293 U.S. 388 (1935). President Franklin Roosevelt's National Industrial Recovery Act of 1933 authorized committees of management and labor in individual industries to draft codes of "fair competition," subject to Presidential approval, upon a finding that the codes contained no inequitable restrictions upon entry and no attempts to establish a monopoly or suppress small enterprises. The purpose of the statute, enacted during FDR's celebrated first "Hundred Days," was to stabilize wages and prices and restore stability and confidence in American businesses. The statute did so by prohibiting various practices deemed to be "unfair methods of competition."

A unanimous Court in *Schechter* invalidated the "live poultry code." Starting with the axiom that "[t]he Congress is not permitted to abdicate or to transfer to others the essential legislative function with which it is thus vested," the Court found insufficient standards to guide the private groups and the President in implementing the statute. The Court was unpersuaded that the "fair competition" language imposed significant guidance and rejected Congress' justification that the delegation was justified by the knowledge and expertise of industry leaders. The Court emphasized the extraordinary nature of delegating regulatory authority to private groups.

Recall that in *Curtiss-Wright* the Supreme Court had no similar problem with broad congressional delegations to the President as to matters of foreign affairs. The New Deal majority that took control of the Court after 1937–38 relegated the nondelegation doctrine to the constitutional dustbin in domestic affairs cases as well. In *Yakus v. United States*, 321 U.S. 414 (1944), the Court upheld the delegation of price controls during wartime to the Price Administrator, with the only direction being that prices "in his judgment will be generally fair and equitable and will effectuate the purposes of this Act." How is this "fair and equitable" standard any more determinate than the "fair competition" standard of the NIRA? *Yakus* found that the statute "sufficiently marks the field within which the Administrator is to act so that it will be known whether he has kept within it in compliance with the legislative will."

The Economic Stabilization Act of 1970, 84 Stat. 799, did not even have this "fair and equitable" standard when it authorized the President "to issue such orders and regulations as he may deem appropriate to stabilize prices, rents, wages, and salaries at levels not less than those prevailing on

May 25, 1970." Yet when President Nixon exercised that power to freeze wages and prices in 1971, a three-judge court rejected the nondelegation challenge. *Amalgamated Meat Cutters and Butcher Workmen of North American v. Connally*, 337 F. Supp. 737 (D.D.C. 1971). Judge Harold Leventhal constructed standards to guide presidential action from (1) the Act's legislative history, (2) prior price control statutes such as the one upheld in *Yakus*, and (3) principles implicit in the old "fair and equitable" standard used in prior statutes and mentioned in the legislative history.

The nondelegation doctrine continued to draw support from commentators, e.g., Theodore Lowi, *The End of Liberalism* 298 ff. (2d ed. 1979), long after the Supreme Court substantially abandoned it. Some state courts still enforce their version of the nondelegation doctrine. Hans Linde et al., *Legislative and Administrative Processes* 477–78 (2d ed. 1981), suggest several reasons for this: (1) the more slipshod work done by some state legislatures (with fewer staff), (2) the continuing appeal of substantive due process review at the state level, and (3) the dearth of legislative history in many states to guide administrators and judges to fill in details. A common test followed in the states is that of *Thygesen v. Callahan*, 74 Ill. 2d 404, 406–07, 385 N.E.2d 699, 700 (1979), which states that a legislative delegation is only valid if it sufficiently identifies:

(1) The *persons* and *activities* potentially subject to regulation;

(2) the *harm* sought to be prevented; and

(3) the general *means* intended to be available to the administrator to prevent the identified harm.

Commentators suggest that state courts have deployed the nondelegation doctrine more often to strike down legislation, largely because state legislatures have abused the delegation power most egregiously. Whittington & Iuliano, *Myth of the Nondelegation Doctrine,* 405–17.

During the 1980s there was some support at the Supreme Court level for a "revival" of the nondelegation doctrine. *Industrial Union Department, AFL-CIO v. American Petroleum Institute*, 448 U.S. 607 (1980) (Rehnquist, J., dissenting); *American Textile Manufacturers Institute, Inc. v. Donovan*, 452 U.S. 490, 543 (1981) (Rehnquist, J., dissenting). We place "revival" in quotes, because the evidence suggests that "federal courts never posed a significant obstacle to the development of the administrative state and the delegation of extensive policymaking authority to executive officials." Whitington & Iuliano, *Myth of the Nondelegation Doctrine*, 383.

Mistretta v. United States

488 U.S. 361 (1989)

The Supreme Court unanimously rejected a nondelegation challenge to the Sentencing Reform Act of 1984, 18 U.S.C. § 3551 et seq., and 28 U.S.C.

§ 991–998, which charged the United States Sentencing Commission with developing Sentencing Guidelines to assure greater predictability and uniformity in the sentences received for violations of federal criminal law. The Sentencing Reform Act was a relatively easy case, because Congress had set forth its goals on the face of the statute and set limits on the Commission—it could not go beyond the sentencing maxima then provided in the criminal code and was directed to use current average sentences as a "starting point" for constructing the sentencing range, and specified seven factors in formulating categories of offenses and eleven factors in formulating categories of defendants that the Commission was to follow, as well as offender characteristics the Commission could not consider (e.g., race and sex) and aggravating (e.g., violence) and mitigating (e.g., cooperation with the government) circumstances the Commission should consider.

As **Justice Blackmun**'s opinion for the Court put it, "although Congress granted the Commission substantial discretion in formulating guidelines, in actuality it legislated a full hierarchy of punishment—from near maximum imprisonment, to substantial imprisonment, to some imprisonment, to alternatives—and stipulated the most important offense and offender characteristics to place defendants within these categories."

That level of detail easily satisfied the *J.W. Hampton* test, but Justice Blackmun's opinion, joined by then-Chief Justice Rehnquist and six other Justices, closed its discussion with the lenient approach in *Yakus*:

> It is no objection that the determination of facts and the inferences to be drawn from them in light of the statutory standards and declaration of policy call for the exercise of judgment, and for the formulation of subsidiary administrative policy within the prescribed statutory framework. * * * Only if we could say that there is an absence of standards for the guidance of the Administrator's action, so that it would be impossible in a proper proceeding to ascertain whether the will of Congress has been obeyed, would we be justified in overriding its choice of means for effecting its declared purpose. * * *

In a footnote, Justice Blackmun made clear that the earlier cases invoking the nondelegation doctrine would be narrowly read to apply only in cases where Congress made "crimes of acts never before criminalized [*Panama Refining*] or delegate[d] regulatory power to private individuals [*Schechter*]. In recent years, our application of the nondelegation doctrine principally has been limited to the interpretation of statutory texts, and, more particularly, to giving narrow constructions to statutory delegations that might otherwise be thought to be unconstitutional."

Justice Scalia, who dissented on other grounds, agreed with the majority that the statute survived the nondelegation attack.

Whitman v. American Trucking Ass'ns

531 U.S. 457 (2001)

This case involved the Clean Air Act's requirement that the EPA promulgate air quality standards that are, in the Administrator's judgment, "requisite to protect the public health." 42 U.S.C. § 7409(b)(1). Notwithstanding *Mistretta,* the D.C. Circuit ruled that this statutory provision provided the EPA with no "intelligible principle" to guide its exercise of authority and therefore fell athwart the nondelegation doctrine. The Supreme Court reversed, finding the quoted language more than enough of a limiting principle to meet the *Hampton* standard for delegations.

Justice Scalia's opinion for the Court noted that, "even in sweeping regulatory schemes we have never demanded, as the Court of Appeals did here, that statutes provide a 'determinate criterion' for saying 'how much [of the regulated harm] is too much.' " The opinion reaffirmed *Mistretta's* admonition that the Court has " 'almost never felt qualified to second-guess Congress regarding the permissible degree of policy judgment that can be left to those executing or applying the law.' "

Concurring opinions debated the theoretical viability of the nondelegation doctrine. **Justice Thomas** indicated that he would, in an appropriate case, consider judicial enforcement of the nondelegation doctrine. See Gary Lawson, *Delegation and Original Meaning,* 88 Va. L. Rev. 327 (2002). In contrast, **Justice Stevens** argued that nothing in Article I limits Congress's authority to delegate lawmaking power to other officials. See Thomas A. Merrill, *Rethinking Article I, Section 1: From Nondelegation to Exclusive Delegation,* 104 Colum. L. Rev. 2097 (2004).

Justice Scalia's opinion gave concrete meaning to the statutory principle, which the Court interpreted to require the EPA to set air quality standards "not lower or higher than is necessary * * * to protect the public health with an adequate margin of safety." This move suggests that the Court is no longer inclined to enforce the nondelegation doctrine by striking down broadly phrased statutory delegations but might be willing to deploy the nondelegation idea as a principle of statutory construction. See *King v. Burwell,* 135 S.Ct. 2480 (2015); Lisa Schultz Bressman, Schechter Poultry *at the Millennium: A Delegation Doctrine for the Administrative State,* 109 Yale L.J. 1399 (2000).

THE NONDELEGATION DOCTRINE AND CANONS
OF STATUTORY INTERPRETATION

As applied by the Supreme Court, federalism and separation of powers are by most accounts "underenforced constitutional norms": the Court does not invoke them to invalidate congressional enactments nearly as often as it might. One way to give effect to underenforced constitutional norms is through clear statement rules of statutory interpretation. William N. Eskridge Jr. & Philip P. Frickey, *Quasi-Constitutional Law: Clear Statement Rules as Constitutional Lawmaking,* 45 Vand. L. Rev. 593 (1992). After *Mistretta* and *American*

Trucking, the nondelegation doctrine is the most underenforced norm of all. What form might a clear statement approach to the nondelegation doctrine take? Consider some possibilities, and then apply what you know about constitutional law to the following Problems.

First, the Court might presume that broad and vague delegations contain within them a limiting principle that might be discerned from the legislative history and/or the statutory text. This is Judge Leventhal's idea in *Amalgamated Meat*, and Justice Scalia applied that idea in *American Trucking*. As agencies carry out their statutory duties under vague delegations, the Court will hold them accountable to Congress's purpose and will stop them when they go beyond or against that purpose.

Justice Scalia's opinion in *American Trucking* suggests a second nondelegation canon: the Supreme Court will presume that "Congress does not hide elephants in mouseholes." That is, broad and unspecified delegations of authority to an agency do not entitle it to make big public policy changes; agency "lawmaking" is interstitial, carrying out policies set by Congress rather than instituting new policies on its own. See also *FDA v. Brown & Williamson Corp.*, 529 U.S. 120 (2000) (interpreting food and drug law *not* to allow the FDA to unsettle a generation of tobacco regulatory policy); *MCI v. AT&T*, 512 U.S. 218 (1994) (presuming against a major regulatory change when Congress gave the FCC authority to "modify" statutory requirements).

A third nondelegation-based clear statement rule might be the "avoidance canon": presume that Congress does not intend that agencies press broad delegations so far that they create "serious constitutional difficulties" or problems. See *NLRB v. Catholic Bishop of Chicago,* 440 U.S. 490 (1979) (interpreting NLRA narrowly and rejecting aggressive agency assertion of jurisdiction over religious schools). In *Hamdan v. Rumsfeld*, 548 U.S. 557 (2006), the Court interpreted a congressional authorization for the President to create military commissions by importing Geneva Convention protections that avoided possible due process problems with the summary process created by the President. William Kelley, *Justice Scalia, the Nondelegation Doctrine, and Constitutional Argumentation*, 92 Notre Dame L. Rev. 2107 (2017).

PROBLEM 8-6:
THE ATTORNEY GENERAL'S AUTHORITY TO
PREEMPT STATE AID-IN-DYING LAWS

In 1994, Oregon became the first state to legalize assisted suicide when voters approved a ballot measure enacting the Oregon Death With Dignity Act (ODWDA). ODWDA, which survived a 1997 ballot measure seeking its repeal, exempts from civil or criminal liability state-licensed physicians who, in compliance with the specific safeguards in ODWDA, dispense or prescribe a lethal dose of drugs upon the request of a terminally ill patient.

The drugs Oregon physicians prescribe under ODWDA are regulated under a federal statute, the Controlled Substances Act (CSA). 84 Stat. 1242, as amended, 21 U.S.C. § 801 et seq. Congress classified a host of substances when it enacted the CSA, but the statute permits the Attorney General to add, remove, or reschedule substances, but only after making particular findings; on scientific and medical matters he is required to accept the findings of the Secretary of Health and Human Services (Secretary). These proceedings must be on the record after an opportunity for comment. See 21 U.S.C.A. § 811. The drugs used under the ODWDA are listed in Schedule II and can only be used pursuant to a prescription from a registered physician. 21 U.S.C. § 829(a).

To prevent diversion of controlled substances with medical uses, the CSA regulates the activity of physicians. To issue prescriptions of Schedule II drugs, physicians must "obtain from the Attorney General a registration issued in accordance with the rules and regulations promulgated by him." 21 U.S.C. § 822(a)(2). The Attorney General may deny, suspend, or revoke this registration if, as relevant here, the physician's registration would be "inconsistent with the public interest." § 824(a)(4); § 822(a)(2). When deciding whether a practitioner's registration is in the public interest, the Attorney General "shall" consider:

> "(1) The recommendation of the appropriate State licensing board or professional disciplinary authority.

> "(2) The applicant's experience in dispensing, or conducting research with respect to controlled substances.

> "(3) The applicant's conviction record under Federal or State laws relating to the manufacture, distribution, or dispensing of controlled substances.

> "(4) Compliance with applicable State, Federal, or local laws relating to controlled substances.

> "(5) Such other conduct which may threaten the public health and safety." § 823(f).

The CSA also says: "The Attorney General is authorized to promulgate rules and regulations and to charge reasonable fees relating to the registration and control of the manufacture, distribution, and dispensing of controlled substances and to listed chemicals." § 821. "The Attorney General may promulgate and enforce any rules, regulations, and procedures which he may deem necessary and appropriate for the efficient execution of his functions under this subchapter." § 871(b).

On November 9, 2001, Attorney General John Ashcroft issued a Directive announcing that using controlled substances to assist suicide is not a legitimate medical practice and that dispensing or prescribing them for this purpose is unlawful under the CSA. The Directive was not issued through the notice-and-comment process used for legislative rulemaking, and the Attorney General did not seek input from other departments.

Oregon challenges the Attorney General's authority to issue this Directive; Ashcroft maintains that it has been validly issued pursuant to several explicit delegations of authority to him. What are some responses Oregon might make to the latter point? Would the Supreme Court agree? How would Justice Scalia, the Court's biggest critic of excessive delegation, vote in this case? For the debate among the Justices, see *Gonzales v. Oregon*, 546 U.S. 243 (2006); William N. Eskridge Jr., *The Story of* Gonzales v. Oregon: *Death, Deference, Deliberation,* in *Statutory Interpretation Stories* 366–98 (Eskridge, Frickey & Garrett eds. 2011).

PROBLEM 8-7:
AN OPPORTUNITY FOR THE SUPREME COURT TO GIVE TEETH TO THE NONDELEGATION DOCTRINE

Several Justices have complained that the Court's nonenforcement of the nondelegation doctrine, combined with agency incentives, have made administrative lawmaking too easy, at the expense of citizens' liberties and democratic accountability. E.g., *Department of Transp. v. Association of Am. Railroads,* 135 S.Ct. 1225, 1239–40 (2015) (Alito, J., concurring); *id.* at 1246–51 (Thomas, J., concurring in the judgment); *Gutierrez-Brizuela v. Lynch,* 834 F.3d 1142, 1149 (10th Cir. 2016) (Gorsuch, J., concurring).

Consider the case of Herman Avery Gundy. He was convicted of committing sexual assault in Maryland while on supervised release for a prior federal offense. After serving his sentence for the Maryland sex offense, Gundy was to be transferred to federal custody to serve his sentence for violating his supervised release. As a part of this transfer, Gundy received permission to travel unsupervised by bus from Pennsylvania to New York. Gundy made the trip, but did not register as a sex offender in either Maryland or New York, as required by state law.

In January 2013, Gundy was indicted under 18 U.S.C. § 2250, the Sex Offender Notification and Registration Act (SORNA), for traveling from Pennsylvania to New York and then staying in New York without registering as a sex offender. Based on rules developed by the Department of Justice to implement SORNA, he was convicted and sentenced to time served, along with five years of supervised release. The Second Circuit affirmed the conviction. *Gundy v. United States,* 695 Fed. Appx. 639 (2d Cir. June 22, 2017).

Mr. Gundy then sought and secured Supreme Court review of the following point of law: Does SORNA's delegation of authority to the U.S. Attorney General to issue regulations under 42 U.S.C. § 16913 violate the nondelegation doctrine? See *Gundy v. United States,* 138 S.Ct. 1260 (March 3, 2018). The current codification is 34 U.S.C. § 20913(d):

> The Attorney General shall have the authority to specify the applicability of the requirements of this subchapter to sex offenders convicted before the enactment of this chapter or its implementation in a particular jurisdiction, and to prescribe rules for the registration of any such sex offenders and for other categories of sex offenders who

are unable to comply with subsection (b) [relating to the original registration].

How would you resolve the nondelegation challenge? Should the Supreme Court invalidate the delegation? If so, under what constitutional precept? Should the Court revive the nondelegation doctrine as a basis for invalidating a federal statute? If so, what rule or standard should the Court adopt, to guide the lower courts?

2. The Legislative Veto

Unchecked by the judiciary, broad congressional delegations to departments and agencies grew like weeds in a vacant lot during and after the New Deal. Congress has been ambivalent about so much delegation and (especially in periods of divided government) sought to exercise greater control over executive and agency enforcement of the broad statutory mandates. Some control is exercised through legislative oversight and (especially) appropriations pressure,[59] but the frustrations of oversight stimulated interest in the legislative veto. This is a statutory mechanism which renders the initial or continuing implementation of administrative decisions or actions subject to some further form of legislative review or control. Typically, a legislative veto provision of a statute provides that an agency or department must inform a congressional committee of specified actions, that those actions cannot have operative legal effect for a specified period of time, and that they can be nullified by vote of a committee, or of one chamber, or of both chambers of Congress.

The first federal legislative veto was adopted in 1932, over the objections of Attorney General William Mitchell that it was unconstitutional. Between 1932 and 1975, at least 295 legislative vetoes were inserted into 196 different federal statutes (generally over the objections of Presidents or Attorneys General). The use of such vetoes quickened after 1975. See Joseph Cooper, *The Legislative Veto in the 1980s*, in *Congress Reconsidered* 364, 367 (Lawrence Dodd & Bruce Oppenheimer eds. 3d ed.1985) (counting 208 legislative vetoes between 1932 and 1978, and 78 between 1978 and 1982). Legislative veto provisions were attached to some of our nation's most important legislation after 1970, especially laws involving defense and foreign policy (e.g., the War Powers Resolution, reprinted in Section 1), energy and environmental policy (e.g., the Energy Policy and Conservation Act), consumer welfare (e.g., Employee

---

[59] Political scientists have found oversight disappointing in practice, in part because oversight committees can be captured by the same groups that capture the agencies themselves. E.g., Morris Ogul, *Congressional Oversight: Structures and Incentives*, in *Congress Reconsidered* 317 (Lawrence Dodd & Bruce Oppenheimer eds. 2d ed. 1981).

Retirement Income Security Act), and transportation policy (e.g., Regional Rail Reorganization Act of 1973).[60]

State legislatures in the 1970s adopted a similar array of legislative vetoes. The tendency at the state level was to create a committee to advise the legislature, and to suspend operation of agency rules until the legislature could study, and perhaps overturn, them. The states tended to be less ad hoc than Congress, with omnibus veto rules for all state agencies. By 1982, about half the states authorized committee or legislative vetoes of agency regulations; the most popular version of the legislative veto required both chambers to overturn agency rules. See L. Harold Levinson, *Legislative and Executive Veto of Rules of Administrative Agencies: Models and Alternatives*, 24 Wm. & Mary L. Rev. 79, 81–83 (1982).

IMMIGRATION & NATURALIZATION SERVICE v. CHADHA
462 U.S. 919, 103 S.Ct. 2764, 77 L.Ed.2d 317 (1983)

CHIEF JUSTICE BURGER delivered the opinion of the Court.

[Jagdish Chadha, an East Indian born in Kenya who held a British passport, was lawfully admitted to the United States on a nonimmigrant student visa. After his visa expired and he was subject to deportation, an immigration judge, acting on behalf of the Attorney General, concluded that Chadha met the statutory grounds for a suspension of deportation: He had resided continuously in the United States for over seven years, was of good moral character, and would suffer "extreme hardship" if deported. Pursuant to the Immigration and Nationality Act, a report of this suspension of deportation was transmitted to Congress. Under § 244(c)(2) of the Act, one chamber of Congress had the authority to invalidate this decision by adopting a resolution to that effect either in the session of Congress in which the report was submitted or in the following session of Congress.]

On December 12, 1975, Representative Eilberg, Chairman of the Judiciary Subcommittee on Immigration, Citizenship, and International Law, introduced a resolution opposing "the granting of permanent residence in the United States to [six] aliens," including Chadha. The resolution was referred to the House Committee on the Judiciary. On December 16, 1975, the resolution was discharged from further consideration by the House Committee on the Judiciary and submitted to the House of Representatives for a vote. The resolution had not been printed and was not made available to other Members of the House prior to or at the time it was voted on. So far as the record before us shows, the House consideration of the resolution was based on Representative Eilberg's statement from the floor that "[i]t was the feeling of the

---

[60] See Jacob Javits & Joel Klein, *Congressional Oversight and the Legislative Veto: A Constitutional Analysis*, 52 N.Y.U. L. Rev. 455 (1977).

committee, after reviewing 340 cases, that the aliens contained in the resolution [Chadha and five others] did not meet these statutory requirements, particularly as it relates to hardship; and it is the opinion of the committee that their deportation should not be suspended." The resolution was passed without debate or recorded vote.[3] Since the House action was pursuant to § 244(c)(2), the resolution was not treated as an Art. I legislative act; it was not submitted to the Senate or presented to the President for his action. [Following the House action, the immigration judge ordered Chadha deported. By the time the controversy made its way to the Court of Appeals for the Ninth Circuit, the INS had agreed with Chadha and joined his arguments that the House action was unconstitutional. After entertaining briefs amici curiae from both the Senate and the House of Representatives, the Ninth Circuit held that the House action was unconstitutional. The Supreme Court affirmed.]

* * * [T]hat a given law or procedure is efficient, convenient or useful in facilitating functions of the government, standing alone, will not save it if it is contrary to the Constitution. Convenience and efficiency are not the primary objectives—or the hallmarks—of democratic government and our inquiry is sharpened rather than blunted by the fact that Congressional

---

[3]   It is not at all clear whether the House generally, or Subcommittee Chairman Eilberg in particular, correctly understood the relationship between H. Res. 926 and the Attorney General's decision to suspend Chadha's deportation. Exactly one year previous to the House veto of the Attorney General's decision in this case, Representative Eilberg introduced a similar resolution disapproving the Attorney General's suspension of deportation in the case of six other aliens. H. Res. 1518, 93d Cong., 2d Sess. (1974). The following colloquy occurred on the floor of the House:

"Mr. WYLIE. Mr. Speaker, further reserving the right to object, is this procedure to expedite the ongoing operations of the Department of Justice, as far as these people are concerned. Is it in any way contrary to whatever action the Attorney General has taken on the question of deportation; does the gentleman know?

"Mr. EILBERG. Mr. Speaker, the answer is no to the gentleman's final question. These aliens have been found to be deportable and the Special Inquiry Officer's decision denying suspension of deportation has been reversed by the Board of Immigration Appeals. We are complying with the law since all of these decisions have been referred to us for approval or disapproval, and there are hundreds of cases in this category. In these six cases however, we believe it would be grossly improper to allow these people to acquire the status of permanent resident aliens.

"Mr. WYLIE. In other words, the gentleman has been working with the Attorney General's office?

"Mr. EILBERG. Yes.

"Mr. WYLIE. This bill then is in fact a confirmation of what the Attorney General intends to do?

"Mr. EILBERG. The gentleman is correct insofar as it relates to the determination of deportability which has been made by the Department of Justice in each of these cases.

"Mr. WYLIE. Mr. Speaker, I withdraw my reservation of objection." 120 Cong. Rec. 41412 (1974).

Clearly, this was an obfuscation of the effect of a veto under § 244(c)(2). Such a veto in no way constitutes "a confirmation of what the Attorney General intends to do." To the contrary, such a resolution was meant to overrule and set aside, or "veto," the Attorney General's determination that, in a particular case, cancellation of deportation would be appropriate under the standards set forth in § 244(a)(1).

veto provisions are appearing with increasing frequency in statutes which delegate authority to executive and independent agencies * * *.

Explicit and unambiguous provisions of the Constitution prescribe and define the respective functions of the Congress and of the Executive in the legislative process. * * * Article I provides:

> All legislative Powers herein granted shall be vested in a Congress of the United States, which shall consist of a Senate *and* House of Representatives.

Art. I, § 1. (Emphasis added.)

> Every Bill which shall have passed the House of Representatives and the Senate, *shall*, before it becomes a law, be presented to the President of the United States. . . .

Art. I, § 7, cl. 2. (Emphasis added.)

> Every Order, Resolution, or Vote to which the Concurrence of the Senate and House of Representatives may be necessary (except on a question of Adjournment) *shall be* presented to the President of the United States; and before the Same shall take Effect, *shall be* approved by him, or being disapproved by him, *shall be* repassed by two thirds of the Senate and House of Representatives, according to the Rules and Limitations prescribed in the Case of a Bill.

Art. I, § 7, cl. 3. (Emphasis added.)

These provisions of Art. I are integral parts of the constitutional design for the separation of powers. * * *

The decision to provide the President with a limited and qualified power to nullify proposed legislation by veto was based on the profound conviction of the Framers that the powers conferred on Congress were the powers to be most carefully circumscribed. It is beyond doubt that lawmaking was a power to be shared by both Houses and the President. In *The Federalist* No. 73, Hamilton focused on the President's role in making laws:

> If even no propensity had ever discovered itself in the legislative body to invade the rights of the Executive, the rules of just reasoning and theoretic propriety would of themselves teach us that the one ought not to be left to the mercy of the other, but ought to possess a constitutional and effectual power of self-defense. * * *

The President's role in the lawmaking process also reflects the Framers' careful efforts to check whatever propensity a particular Congress might have to enact oppressive, improvident, or ill-considered measures. The President's veto role in the legislative process was described later during public debate on ratification:

> It establishes a salutary check upon the legislative body, calculated to guard the community against the effects of faction, precipitancy, or of any impulse unfriendly to the public good, which may happen to influence a majority of that body. * * * The primary inducement to conferring the power in question upon the Executive is, to enable him to defend himself; the secondary one is to increase the chances in favor of the community against the passing of bad laws, through haste, inadvertence, or design.

The Federalist No. 73 (A. Hamilton). The Court also has observed that the Presentment Clauses serve the important purpose of assuring that a "national" perspective is grafted on the legislative process: "The President is a representative of the people just as the members of the Senate and of the House are, and it may be, at some times, on some subjects, that the President elected by all the people is rather more representative of them all than are the members of either body of the Legislature whose constituencies are local and not countrywide. . . ."

The bicameral requirement of Art. I, §§ 1, 7, was of scarcely less concern to the Framers than was the Presidential veto and indeed the two concepts are interdependent. By providing that no law could take effect without the concurrence of the prescribed majority of the Members of both Houses, the Framers reemphasized their belief, already remarked upon in connection with the Presentment Clauses, that legislation should not be enacted unless it has been carefully and fully considered by the Nation's elected officials. * * *

Hamilton argued that a Congress comprised of a single House was antithetical to the very purposes of the Constitution. Were the Nation to adopt a Constitution providing for only one legislative organ, he warned:

> [W]e shall finally accumulate, in a single body, all the most important prerogatives of sovereignty, and thus entail upon our posterity one of the most execrable forms of government that human infatuation ever contrived. Thus we should create in reality that very tyranny which the adversaries of the new Constitution either are, or affect to be, solicitous to avert.

The Federalist No. 22.

This view was rooted in a general skepticism regarding the fallibility of human nature later commented on by Joseph Story:

> Public bodies, like private persons, are occasionally under the dominion of strong passions and excitements; impatient, irritable, and impetuous. . . . If [a legislature] feels no check but its own will, it rarely has the firmness to insist upon holding a question long

enough under its own view, to see and mark it in all its bearings and relations on society.

These observations are consistent with what many of the Framers expressed, none more cogently than Madison in pointing up the need to divide and disperse power in order to protect liberty:

> In republican government, the legislative authority necessarily predominates. The remedy for this inconveniency is to divide the legislature into different branches; and to render them, by different modes of election and different principles of action, as little connected with each other as the nature of their common functions and their common dependence on the society will admit.

The Federalist No. 51 (sometimes attributed to "Hamilton or Madison" but now generally attributed to Madison).

However familiar, it is useful to recall that apart from their fear that special interests could be favored at the expense of public needs, the Framers were also concerned, although not of one mind, over the apprehensions of the smaller states. Those states feared a commonality of interest among the larger states would work to their disadvantage; representatives of the larger states, on the other hand, were skeptical of a legislature that could pass laws favoring a minority of the people. It need hardly be repeated here that the Great Compromise, under which one House was viewed as representing the people and the other the states, allayed the fears of both the large and small states.

We see therefore that the Framers were acutely conscious that the bicameral requirement and the Presentment Clauses would serve essential constitutional functions. The President's participation in the legislative process was to protect the Executive Branch from Congress and to protect the whole people from improvident laws. The division of the Congress into two distinctive bodies assures that the legislative power would be exercised only after opportunity for full study and debate in separate settings. The President's unilateral veto power, in turn, was limited by the power of two-thirds of both Houses of Congress to overrule a veto thereby precluding final arbitrary action of one person. It emerges clearly that the prescription for legislative action in Art. I, §§ 1, 7, represents the Framers' decision that the legislative power of the Federal Government be exercised in accord with a single, finely wrought and exhaustively considered, procedure.

The Constitution sought to divide the delegated powers of the new Federal Government into three defined categories, Legislative, Executive, and Judicial, to assure, as nearly as possible, that each branch of government would confine itself to its assigned responsibility. The hydraulic pressure inherent within each of the separate Branches to exceed the outer limits of its power, even to accomplish desirable objectives, must be resisted.

* * * When the Executive acts, he presumptively acts in an executive or administrative capacity as defined in Art. II. And when, as here, one House of Congress purports to act, it is presumptively acting within its assigned sphere.

Beginning with its presumption, we must nevertheless establish that the challenged action under § 244(c)(2) is of the kind to which the procedural requirements of Art. I, § 7, apply. Not every action taken by either House is subject to the bicameralism and presentment requirements of Art. I. Whether actions taken by either House are, in law and fact, an exercise of legislative power depends not on their form but upon "whether they contain matter which is properly to be regarded as legislative in its character and effect."

Examination of the action taken here by one House pursuant to § 244(c)(2) reveals that it was essentially legislative in purpose and effect. In purporting to exercise power defined in Art. I, § 8, cl. 4, to "establish an uniform Rule of Naturalization," the House took action that had the purpose and effect of altering the legal rights, duties, and relations of persons, including the Attorney General, Executive Branch officials and Chadha, all outside the Legislative Branch. * * * The one-House veto operated in these cases to overrule the Attorney General and mandate Chadha's deportation; absent the House action, Chadha would remain in the United States. Congress has *acted* and its action has altered Chadha's status.

The legislative character of the one-House veto in these cases is confirmed by the character of the congressional action it supplants. Neither the House of Representatives nor the Senate contends that, absent the veto provision in § 244(c)(2), either of them, or both of them acting together, could effectively require the Attorney General to deport an alien once the Attorney General, in the exercise of legislatively delegated authority,[16] had

---

[16] Congress protests that affirming the Court of Appeals in these cases will sanction "lawmaking by the Attorney General." To be sure, some administrative agency action—rulemaking, for example—may resemble "lawmaking." This Court has referred to agency activity as being "quasi-legislative" in character. Clearly, however, "[i]n the framework of our Constitution, the President's power to see that the laws are faithfully executed refutes the idea that he is to be a lawmaker." *Youngstown.* When the Attorney General performs his duties pursuant to § 244, he does not exercise "legislative" power. The bicameral process is not necessary as a check on the Executive's administration of the laws because his administrative activity cannot reach beyond the limits of the statute that created it—a statute duly enacted pursuant to Art. I, §§ 1, 7. The constitutionality of the Attorney General's execution of the authority delegated to him by § 244 involves only a question of delegation doctrine. The courts, when a case or controversy arises, can always "ascertain whether the will of Congress has been obeyed," and can enforce adherence to statutory standards. It is clear, therefore, that the Attorney General acts in his presumptively Art. II capacity when he administers the Immigration and Nationality Act. Executive action under legislatively delegated authority that might resemble "legislative" action in some respects is not subject to the approval of both Houses of Congress and the President for the reason that the Constitution does not so require. That kind of Executive action is always subject to check by the terms of the legislation that authorized it; and if that authority is exceeded it is open to judicial review as well as the power of Congress to modify or revoke the authority entirely. A one-House veto is clearly legislative in both character and effect and is not so checked; the need for the check

determined the alien should remain in the United States. Without the challenged provision in § 244(c)(2), this could have been achieved, if at all, only by legislation requiring deportation. * * *

The nature of the decision implemented by the one-House veto in these cases further manifests its legislative character. After long experience with the clumsy, time-consuming private bill procedure, Congress made a deliberate choice to delegate to the Executive Branch, and specifically to the Attorney General, the authority to allow deportable aliens to remain in this country in certain specified circumstances. It is not disputed that this choice to delegate authority is precisely the kind of decision that can be implemented only in accordance with the procedures set out in Art. I. Disagreement with the Attorney General's decision on Chadha's deportation—that is, Congress' decision to deport Chadha—no less than Congress' original choice to delegate to the Attorney General the authority to make that decision, involves determinations of policy that Congress can implement in only one way; bicameral passage followed by presentment to the President. Congress must abide by its delegation of authority until that delegation is legislatively altered or revoked.

Finally, we see that when the Framers intended to authorize either House of Congress to act alone and outside of its prescribed bicameral legislative role, they narrowly and precisely defined the procedure for such action. There are four provisions in the Constitution, explicit and unambiguous, by which one House may act alone with the unreviewable force of law, not subject to the President's veto: [the House's power to initiate impeachments, Art. I, § 2, cl. 5; the Senate's power to conduct impeachment trials, Art. I, § 3, cl. 6; the Senate's power to confirm presidential appointments, Art. II, § 2, cl. 2; and the Senate's power to ratify treaties, Art, II, § 2, cl. 2. Chief Justice Burger concluded that these "narrow, explicit, and separately justified" exceptions to bicameralism and presentment "provide further support for the conclusion that congressional authority is not to be implied."]

The veto authorized by § 244(c)(2) doubtless has been in many respects a convenient shortcut; the "sharing" with the Executive by Congress of its authority over aliens in this manner is, on its face, an appealing compromise. In purely practical terms, it is obviously easier for action to be taken by one House without submission to the President; but it is crystal clear from the records of the Convention, contemporaneous writings and debates, that the Framers ranked other values higher than efficiency. The records of the Convention and debates in the States preceding ratification underscore the common desire to define and limit the exercise of the newly created federal powers affecting the states and the people. There is

---

provided by Art. I, §§ 1, 7, is therefore clear. Congress' authority to delegate portions of its power to administrative agencies provides no support for the argument that Congress can constitutionally control administration of the laws by way of a congressional veto.

unmistakable expression of a determination that legislation by the national Congress be a step-by-step, deliberate and deliberative process.

The choices we discern as having been made in the Constitutional Convention impose burdens on governmental processes that often seem clumsy, inefficient, even unworkable, but those hard choices were consciously made by men who had lived under a form of government that permitted arbitrary governmental acts to go unchecked. There is no support in the Constitution or decisions of this Court for the proposition that the cumbersomeness and delays often encountered in complying with explicit constitutional standards may be avoided, either by the Congress or by the President. *See Youngstown*. With all the obvious flaws of delay, untidiness, and potential for abuse, we have not yet found a better way to preserve freedom than by making the exercise of power subject to the carefully crafted restraints spelled out in the Constitution.

[The opinion of **JUSTICE POWELL**, concurring in the judgment, is omitted. Rather than joining an opinion that "apparently will invalidate every use of the legislative veto," Justice Powell opted to decide the case on the ground that "[w]hen Congress finds that a particular person does not satisfy the statutory criteria for permanent residence in the country it has assumed a judicial function in violation of the principle of separation of powers." Justice Powell stressed the Framers' concern about the exercise of unchecked legislative power and noted that the congressional act here was surrounded by none of the traditional procedural protections that accompany adjudication.]

[The dissenting opinion of **JUSTICE REHNQUIST** is also omitted. Justice Rehnquist agreed that the legislative veto was unconstitutional but would not have severed it from the remainder of the law, thereby denying Chadha any relief.]

JUSTICE WHITE, dissenting.

[Justice White first stressed that the decision "sounds the death knell for nearly 200 other statutory provisions in which Congress has reserved a 'legislative veto.'" He then emphasized the utility of the legislative veto in allowing "the President and Congress to resolve major constitutional and policy differences, assur[ing] the accountability of independent regulatory agencies, and preserv[ing] Congress' control over lawmaking."]

The history of the legislative veto also makes clear that it has not been a sword with which Congress has struck out to aggrandize itself at the expense of the other branches—the concerns of Madison and Hamilton. Rather, the veto has been a means of defense, a reservation of ultimate authority necessary if Congress is to fulfill its designated role under Art. I as the Nation's lawmaker. While the President has often objected to particular legislative vetoes, generally those left in the hands of congressional committees, the Executive has more often agreed to legislative review as the price for a broad delegation of authority. To be sure, the President may have preferred unrestricted power, but that could be precisely why Congress thought it essential to retain a check on the exercise of delegated authority. * * *

* * * There is no question but that agency rulemaking is lawmaking in any functional or realistic sense of the term. The Administrative Procedure Act provides that a "rule" is an agency statement "designed to implement, interpret, or prescribe law or policy." When agencies are authorized to prescribe law through substantive rulemaking, the administrator's regulation is not only due deference, but is accorded "legislative effect." These regulations bind courts and officers of the Federal Government, may pre-empt state law, and grant rights to and impose obligations on the public. In sum, they have the force of law.

If Congress may delegate lawmaking power to independent and Executive agencies, it is most difficult to understand Art. I as prohibiting Congress from also reserving a check on legislative power for itself. Absent the veto, the agencies receiving delegations of legislative or quasi-legislative power may issue regulations having the force of law without bicameral approval and without the President's signature. It is thus not apparent why the reservation of a veto over the exercise of that legislative power must be subject to a more exacting test. In both cases, it is enough that the initial statutory authorizations comply with the Art. I requirements. * * *

The central concern of the presentment and bicameralism requirements of Art. I is that when a departure from the legal status quo is undertaken, it is done with the approval of the President and both Houses of Congress—or, in the event of a Presidential veto, a two-thirds majority in both Houses. This interest is fully satisfied by the operation of § 244(c)(2). The President's approval is found in the Attorney General's action in recommending to Congress that the deportation order for a given alien be suspended. The House and the Senate indicate their approval of the Executive's action by not passing a resolution of disapproval within the statutory period. Thus, a change in the legal status quo—the deportability of the alien—is consummated only with the approval of each of the three relevant actors. The disagreement of any one of the three maintains the alien's pre-existing status: the Executive may choose not to recommend suspension; the House and Senate may each veto the recommendation. The effect on the rights and obligations of the affected individuals and upon the legislative system is precisely the same as if a private bill were introduced but failed to receive the necessary approval. "The President and the two Houses enjoy exactly the same say in what the law is to be as would have been true for each without the presence of the one-House veto, and nothing in the law is changed absent the concurrence of the President and a majority in each House." *Atkins v. United States*, 556 F.2d 1028, 1064 (1977), cert. denied, 434 U.S. 1009 (1978).

NOTES ON CHADHA *AND CONSTITUTIONAL FORMALISM*

1. *Is* Chadha *Defensible Constitutional Law?* Many legal academics have been underwhelmed by the Chief Justice's reasoning.[61] Among the questions they have raised: Isn't the legislative veto formally consistent with Article I, § 7, insofar as it is just a condition subsequent of a statute validly adopted by both chambers of Congress, with presentment? The Chief Justice's broad definition of what's "legislative" (and his insistence that all of it be done by both chambers of Congress and presented to the President) seems to cover agency rulemaking itself, which if taken seriously would call into question the constitutionality of the administrative state. Laurence Tribe, *The Legislative Veto Decision: A Law by Any Other Name?*, 21 Harv. J. Legis. 7 (1984), suggests that "the only imaginable justification" for the Court's apparent position is that "the legislature can delegate authority to others *but not to itself.*" Persuasive?

2. *What Survives.* The Court could have written a narrow opinion in *Chadha*, striking down only legislative vetoes that interfered with adjudicatory proceedings (Justice Powell's position), or that permitted a veto upon the vote of only one house. But the Court's opinion seems applicable to virtually all of the legislative vetoes Congress has enacted. See *Process Gas Consumers Group v. Consumer Energy Council of America*, 463 U.S. 1216 (1983) (summarily affirming invalidation of legislative veto of agency rulemaking); *United States Senate v. FTC*, 463 U.S. 1216 (1983) (summarily affirming invalidation of two-house veto of agency rulemaking). On the other hand, lower courts have ruled that *Chadha* did not invalidate "report-and-wait" or "laying over" provisions, holding off the effective date of an agency action until Congress has an opportunity to review it. E.g., *Hechinger v. Metropolitan Washington Airports Auth.*, 36 F.3d 97 (D.C. Cir. 1994).

Also surviving *Chadha* are other mechanisms for legislative influence over agency actions: (a) hearings and informal pressure by congressional oversight committees; (b) refusal by Congress to appropriate monies to wayward agencies, or to appropriate funds subject to substantive conditions (e.g., that the money will not be spent to carry out specified rules or policies); and (c) informal pressure by appropriations subcommittees and language in their committee reports earmarking funds for certain projects or policies and not for others. Jessica Korn, *The Power of Separation: American Constitutionalism and the Myth of the Legislative Veto* 36–37 (1996), reports that not only did all these practices survive intact, but that they had been more efficacious than the legislative veto all along. Another mechanism in recent use

---

[61] See Donald Elliott, INS v. Chadha: *The Administrative Constitution, the Constitution, and the Legislative Veto*, 1983 Sup. Ct. Rev. 125; William N. Eskridge Jr. & John Ferejohn, *The Article I, Section 7 Game*, 80 Geo. L.J. 523 (1992); Girardeau Spann, *Deconstructing the Legislative Veto*, 68 Minn. L. Rev. 473 (1984); Peter L. Strauss, *Was There a Baby in the Bathwater?: A Comment on the Supreme Court's Legislative Veto Decision*, 1983 Duke L.J. 789.

is the Congressional Review Act, which allows Congress to veto regulations using a fast-track procedure, subject to presidential veto.

Political scientist Michael Berry documents that the legislative veto itself survived and indeed flourished in dozens of post-*Chadha* statutes. Berry, *The Modern Legislative Veto: Macropolitical Conflict and the Legacy of* Chadha 279–308 (2016) (list of federal statutes containing legislative vetoes).[62]

3. *Functional Problems with Legislative Vetoes.* While the veto has been defended as a way for Congress to monitor the enforcement of its statutes, it has also been subjected to serious functional criticisms.[63] Madison argued in *Federalist* Nos. 10 and 51 (App. 2) that bicameralism and presentment were mechanisms whereby temporary, perhaps factional, majorities would be prevented from enacting unwise legislation. Modern public choice theory supports Madison's insight. The tendency of the legislature to distribute rents to special interest groups can be ameliorated if the groups must push their rents through two differently constituted chambers, and then must obtain the acquiescence of the President. As the costs and delays of obtaining legislation increase, special interest groups will demand less of it—but they will demand more if some of the vetogates are relaxed.[64] But see William N. Eskridge Jr., *Vetogates and American Public Law*, 31 J.L. Econ. & Org. 756 (April 2012) (because a bill needs supermajorities to pass through the vetogates, sponsors will engage in logrolling, which may increase with rent-seeking).

In one sense, *Chadha* was an easy case, because its veto represented an institutional power grab that posed threats both to popular majorities and to minorities. The one-chamber veto risked creating an "electoral aristocracy." A small group of people (Representative Eilberg's subcommittee) made immigration policy for the entire country. Now there's always that risk in our complex government, but the bicameralism and presentment requirements are forms that minimize the risk—and the Burger opinion essentially rests upon this notion, not on its artificial idea of what's "legislative." Likewise, the Powell opinion rests upon the converse risk, that people like Chadha will be singled out by some faction in Congress and deprived of an important liberty for no publicly stated, judicially reviewable reason. The Constitution says that Congress cannot adopt bills of attainder (Art. I, § 9, cl. 3); what the House did to Chadha came too close to that, and Powell insisted on the Constitution's structural protection for that popular reason.

4. *Encouraging Too Much Delegation?* Perhaps another problem with the legislative veto was that it encouraged Congress to vote for broader and more abstract delegations to agencies and departments. Controversial delegations to a particular, often captured, agency might not have passed but

---

[62] Accord, Louis Fisher, *The Legislative Veto: Invalidated, It Survives,* 56 J.L. & Contemp. Probs. 273 (1993); Darren A. Wheeler, *Actor Preference and the Implementation of* INS v. Chadha, 83 BYU J. Pub. L. 83 (2008).

[63] Stanley Brubaker, *Slouching Toward Constitutional Duty: The Legislative Veto & the Delegation of Authority*, 1 Const. Comm. 81 (1984); Eskridge & Ferejohn, *Article I, Section 7 Game.*

[64] See Harold Bruff, *Legislative Formality, Administrative Rationality*, 63 Tex. L. Rev. 207, 222 (1984).

for legislative veto provisions, which assured dubious legislators that if the agency went too far, a congressional subgroup could reverse unwanted individual decisions. This scheme allows a lot more legislation to be enacted, but greatly exacerbates the already-excessive tendency of Congress to delegate. In this way, *Chadha* may have been the Court's way of saying: We shall not revive the nondelegation doctrine, but we are not going to make it easy for Congress to delegate.

5. *Legislative Veto Challenges Under State Constitutions.* State courts have generally invalidated state legislative vetoes upon the same reasoning as that followed in *Chadha,* e.g., *State ex rel. Stephan v. Kansas House of Representatives,* 236 Kan. 45, 687 P.2d 622 (1984), and indeed some state supreme courts precisely anticipated *Chadha's* reasoning. E.g., *General Assembly of New Jersey v. Byrne,* 90 N.J. 376, 448 A.2d 438 (1982).

The Idaho Supreme Court in *Mead v. Arnell,* 117 Idaho 660, 791 P.2d 410 (1990), upheld a statute allowing the legislature to override agency rules by a concurrent resolution passed by both chambers but not submitted to the governor for veto. The Court explicitly relied on the reasoning in Justice White's *Chadha* dissent. See also *Opinion of the Justices,* 121 N.H. 552, 431 A.2d 783 (1981) (dictum that laying-over requirement was constitutional). In addition, the state constitutions of Arkansas, Connecticut, Iowa, Michigan, Nevada, New Jersey, and South Dakota explicitly authorize their state legislatures to exercise veto authority over agency decisions. Berry, *Modern Legislative Veto,* 211–68 (survey of state practice).

NOTE ON SEVERABILITY

Because unconstitutional legislative vetoes were included in hundreds of federal statutes, *Chadha* triggered lawsuits challenging the constitutionality of the entire statutes in which such vetoes were found. When an unconstitutional provision is "severable" from the remainder of the statute, the Court will not invalidate the statute—which was the approach taken by the Chief Justice in *Chadha* itself (with Justices Rehnquist and White in dissent). The Supreme Court's doctrine regarding severability has followed an unsteady path. Early in the twentieth century, the Court frequently refused to sever unconstitutional portions of regulatory legislation, thereby sweeping the whole statute away. E.g., *Carter v. Carter Coal Co.,* 298 U.S. 238 (1936) (Chapter 7, § 2). The New Deal Court abandoned that practice. Since 1938, the Court has followed a strong presumption of severability and rarely refused to sever unconstitutional provisions from statutes. E.g., See *Heckler v. Mathews,* 465 U.S. 728, 738 & n.5 (1984); *Regan v. Time,* 468 U.S. 641 (1984).

In the leading case, *Alaska Airlines v. Brock,* 480 U.S. 678 (1987), the Court held that an unconstitutional legislative veto provision found in the employee protections title of the Airline Deregulation Act of 1978, 92 Stat. 1705, was severable from the remainder of the title. The Court said:

> * * * In considering this question, in the context of a legislative veto, it is necessary to recognize that the absence of the veto

necessarily alters the balance of powers between the Legislative and Executive Branches of the Federal Government. Thus, it is not only appropriate to evaluate the importance of the veto in the original legislative bargain, but also to consider the nature of the delegated authority that Congress made subject to a veto. Some delegations of power to the Executive or to an independent agency may have been so controversial or so broad that Congress would have been unwilling to make the delegation without a strong oversight mechanism. The final test, for legislative vetoes as well as for other provisions, is the traditional one: the unconstitutional provision must be severed unless the statute created in its absence is legislation Congress would not have enacted.

In *Alaska Airlines,* a unanimous Court severed the legislative veto from the employee protections title, even though that title was the only one out of twenty-five in the statute to have a legislative veto attached to it; there was great concern about the title because it would be administered by the Secretary of Labor, not under the normal oversight responsibility of the transportation committees; a primary House sponsor specifically spoke to the importance of the legislative veto to the employee protection title and no one spoke against it. Contrary to the Court, it seems implausible that Congress would have adopted the title without the legislative veto.

The *Alaska Airlines* presumption of severability seems like a very strong one. Is it the best baseline under separation of powers precepts, however? See Michael Shumsky, *Severability, Inseverability, and the Rule of Law*, 41 Harv. J. Legis. 227 (2004) (no). One might argue that the presumption leaves in force a statute that Congress did not vote for. Recall the ObamaCare Case, *National Federation of Independent Business v. Sebelius,* 132 S.Ct. 2566 (2012) (Chapter 7, § 5), where Chief Justice Roberts's opinion struck down a coercive Medicaid funding condition in the Affordable Care Act. Applying the presumption in favor of severability, the Chief Justice, speaking for the Court on this issue, ruled the unconstitutional condition severable from the remainder of the statute. *Id.* at 2607–08; *id.* at 2630–31 (Ginsburg, J., concurring on this point).

Wouldn't presumptive nullification of the entire statute, or title, often be more appropriate, especially when a key provision is found invalid, so that Congress itself could readjust the statutory scheme? See *Sebelius,* 132 S.Ct. at 2668–76 (Joint Dissent); *Califano v. Westcott,* 443 U.S. 76, 93 (1979) (Powell, J., dissenting). In the ObamaCare Case, the Joint Dissent characterized the Court's severability of a central provision "vast judicial overreaching," because it "creates a debilitated, inoperable version of health-care regulation that Congress did not enact and the public does not expect" and "makes enactment of sensible health-care regulation more difficult." *Sebelius,* 132 S.Ct. at 2676 (Joint Dissent). Does *Chadha* lend support to the dissenters' concerns?

Can the presumption of severability be defended as useful to protect private reliance interests that would be unsettled if entire statutes fell because of the invalidity of minor provisions? Would a presumption of nonseverability impose burdens on Congress that the legislative process could not sustain? Is ObamaCare an example of this concern? See *Sebelius,* 132 S.Ct. at 2630 (Ginsburg, J.) (when striking down an unconstitutional portion of a law, the Court ordinarily "undertakes a salvage operation; it does not demolish the statute").

The presumption of severability was overcome in *Murphy v. National Collegiate Athletic Association,* 138 S.Ct. 1461 (2018). The Court ruled that Professional and Amateur Sports Protection Act (PASPA) prohibiting state authorization of sports gambling violated the anti-commandeering rule of the Constitution. The Court further found that the *Alaska Airlines* presumption was overcome because the statute could not operate as intended without the commandeering provision. Dissenting Justices argued that judicial restraint supported severability, as the Court had done in virtually all its separation of powers cases.

In a concurring opinion, Justice Thomas expressed his "growing discomfort with our modern severability precedents" and urged the Court to reconsider its precedents on the topic. "Those precedents appear to be in tension with traditional limits on judicial authority. Early American courts did not have a severability doctrine. They recognized that the judicial power is, fundamentally, the power to render judgments in individual cases. * * * Thus, when early American courts determined that a statute was unconstitutional, they would simply decline to enforce it in the case before them. * * * [T]here was no 'next step' in which courts inquired into whether the legislature would have preferred no law at all to the constitutional remainder. See Kevin Walsh, *Partial Unconstitutionality,* 85 N.Y.U. L. Rev. 738 (2010).

Justice Thomas's argument is that the original meaning of Article III is inconsistent with *Alasaka Airlines.* Ought *stare decisis* weigh in favor of that established test? Is there a doctrinal mechanism to reconcile precedent with his view of original meaning?

3. The Line Item Veto

Unlike Article I, § 7, the large majority of state constitutions allow their chief executives to veto particular lines or sections of tax and spending bills while signing the remainder into law. Budget-conscious politicians of both parties portrayed the line item veto as a panacea for the universally reviled "out of control federal spending." After *Chadha,* however, advocates of a federal line item veto realized that it was risky to follow the precise approach of the state constitutions. Instead, they took as their model presidential impoundment, allowing the President to "cancel" tax and spending provisions he disapproved. The GOP congressional leadership and a Democrat President bought this rationale. Should the Supreme Court? Jot down your thoughts and read on.

CLINTON V. CITY OF NEW YORK

524 U.S. 417, 118 S.Ct. 2091, 141 L.Ed.2d 393 (1998)

JUSTICE STEVENS delivered the opinion of the Court.

[The Line Item Veto Act, Pub. L. 104–130, 110 Stat. 1200, codified at 2 U.S.C. § 691 et seq., gave the President authority to *cancel* certain spending and tax benefit measures after he has signed them into law. Section 691(a) of the Act provides:

> [T]he President may, with respect to any bill or joint resolution that has been signed into law pursuant to Article I, section 7, of the Constitution of the United States, cancel in whole—
>
> (1) any dollar amount of discretionary budget authority;
>
> (2) any item of new direct spending; or
>
> (3) any limited tax benefit;
>
> if the President—
>
>> (A) determines that such cancellation will—
>>
>>> (i)   reduce the Federal budget deficit;
>>>
>>> (ii) not impair any essential Government functions; and
>>>
>>> (iii) not harm the national interest; and
>>
>> (B) notifies the Congress of such cancellation by transmitting a special message * * * within five calendar days (excluding Sundays) after the enactment of the law [to which the cancellation applies].

The President's *cancellation* under the Act would take effect when the special message notifying Congress of the cancellation was received in the House and Senate. With respect to dollar amounts of discretionary budget authority, a cancellation meant "to rescind." § 691e(4)(A). With respect to new direct spending items or limited tax benefits, a cancellation meant that the relevant legal provision, legal obligation, or budget authority is "prevent[ed] * * * from having legal force or effect." §§ 691e(4)(B), (C). The Act also established expedited procedures in both Houses for the consideration of disapproval bills, § 691d, bills or joint resolutions which, if enacted into law by the familiar procedures set out in Article I, § 7 of the Constitution, would render the President's cancellation null and void, § 691b(a).

[Appellees challenged two of President Clinton's exercises of the cancellation power under the Line Item Veto Act. First, he canceled a provision in the Balanced Budget Act of 1997 that gave New York preferential treatment under Medicaid. The federal government claimed that New York had inappropriately characterized taxes it had collected from Medicaid providers; unless granted a waiver, the state would owe the federal government as much as $2.6 billion. The canceled provision deemed the state's actions permissible and thereby waived the federal government's right to recoupment. New York City and private parties challenged the constitutionality of this cancellation. Second, the President canceled a tax provision in the Taxpayer Relief Act of 1997 that allowed owners of certain food processors to defer paying tax on the gain from the sale of their stock if they sold to eligible farmers' cooperatives. Because few taxpayers could take advantage of the tax expenditure, it was a limited tax benefit eligible for cancellation. An Idaho farmers' cooperative and an individual farmer challenged this second cancellation.]

[In the Court's first opportunity to consider the constitutionality of the line item veto, the Court had determined that the Members of Congress who brought that case lacked standing. See *Raines v. Byrd* (Chapter 9, § 2). In contrast, in this case the Court concluded that the appellees had standing, because they each had a personal stake in having an actual injury redressed by the Court.]

The effect of a cancellation is plainly stated in § 691e, which defines the principal terms used in the Act. With respect to both an item of new direct spending and a limited tax benefit, the cancellation prevents the item "from having legal force or effect."[26] Thus, under the plain text of the statute, the two actions of the President that are challenged in these cases prevented one section of the Balanced Budget Act of 1997 and one section of the Taxpayer Relief Act of 1997 "from having legal force or effect." The remaining provisions of those statutes * * * continue to have the same force and effect as they had when signed into law.

In both legal and practical effect, the President has amended two Acts of Congress by repealing a portion of each. * * * There is no provision in the Constitution that authorizes the President to enact, to amend, or to repeal statutes. * * *

There are important differences between the President's "return" of a bill pursuant to Article I, § 7, and the exercise of the President's cancellation authority pursuant to the Line Item Veto Act. The constitutional return takes place *before* the bill becomes law; the statutory cancellation occurs *after* the bill becomes law. The constitutional return is of the entire bill; the statutory cancellation is of only a part. Although the Constitution expressly authorizes the President to play a role in the process of enacting statutes, it is silent on the subject of unilateral Presidential action that either repeals or amends parts of duly enacted statutes.

---

[26] The term "cancel," used in connection with any dollar amount of discretionary budget authority, means "to rescind.". * * *

There are powerful reasons for construing constitutional silence on this profoundly important issue as equivalent to an express prohibition. The procedures governing the enactment of statutes set forth in the text of Article I were the product of the great debates and compromises that produced the Constitution itself. Familiar historical materials provide abundant support for the conclusion that the power to enact statutes may only "be exercised in accord with a single, finely wrought and exhaustively considered, procedure." *Chadha.* * * * What has emerged in these cases from the President's exercise of his statutory cancellation powers, however, are truncated versions of two bills that passed both Houses of Congress. They are not the product of the "finely wrought" procedure that the Framers designed. * * *

[The government's main defense of this unconventional arrangement was that the substance of the authority to cancel tax and spending items "is, in practical effect, no more and no less than the power to 'decline to spend' specified sums of money, or to 'decline to implement' specified tax measures." Recall our Note on Impoundment in § 1A of this chapter.] The Government has reviewed in some detail the series of statutes in which Congress has given the Executive broad discretion over the expenditure of appropriated funds. For example, the First Congress appropriated "sum[s] not exceeding" specified amounts to be spent on various Government operations. In those statutes, as in later years, the President was given wide discretion with respect to both the amounts to be spent and how the money would be allocated among different functions. It is argued that the Line Item Veto Act merely confers comparable discretionary authority over the expenditure of appropriated funds. The critical difference between this statute and all of its predecessors, however, is that unlike any of them, this Act gives the President the unilateral power to change the text of duly enacted statutes. None of the Act's predecessors could even arguably have been construed to authorize such a change. * * *

If there is to be a new procedure in which the President will play a different role in determining the final text of what may "become a law," such change must come not by legislation but through the amendment procedures set forth in Article V of the Constitution. *Cf. U.S. Term Limits, Inc. v. Thornton* (Chapter 7, § 1).

[JUSTICE KENNEDY's concurring opinion is omitted.]

JUSTICE SCALIA, with whom JUSTICE O'CONNOR joins, and with whom JUSTICE BREYER joins as to Part III, concurring in part and dissenting in part.

As much as the Court goes on about Art. I, § 7, therefore, that provision does not demand the result the Court reaches. It no more categorically prohibits the Executive *reduction* of congressional dispositions in the course of implementing statutes that authorize such reduction, than it categorically prohibits the Executive *augmentation* of congressional dispositions in the course of implementing statutes that authorize such augmentation—generally known as substantive rulemaking. There are, to be sure, limits upon the former just as there are limits upon the latter—and I am prepared to acknowledge that the limits upon the former may be much more severe. Those limits are established, however, not by some categorical prohibition of Art. I, § 7, which our cases conclusively disprove, but by what has come to be known as the doctrine of unconstitutional delegation of legislative authority: When authorized Executive reduction or augmentation is allowed to go too far, it usurps the nondelegable function of Congress and violates the separation of powers. * * *

Insofar as the degree of political, "law-making" power conferred upon the Executive is concerned, there is not a dime's worth of difference between Congress's authorizing the President to *cancel* a spending item, and Congress's authorizing money to be spent on a particular item at the President's discretion. And the latter has been done since the Founding of the Nation. * * *

Certain Presidents have claimed Executive authority to withhold appropriated funds even *absent* an express conferral of discretion to do so. [The action of withholding appropriated funds is often termed "impoundment."] * * * President Nixon, the Mahatma Gandhi of all impounders, asserted at a press conference in 1973 that his "constitutional right" to impound appropriated funds was "absolutely clear." Our decision two years later in *Train v. City of New York,* 420 U.S. 35 (1975), proved him wrong, but it implicitly confirmed that Congress may confer discretion upon the executive to withhold appropriated funds, even funds appropriated for a specific purpose. The statute at issue in *Train* authorized spending "not to exceed" specified sums for certain projects, and directed that such "[s]ums authorized to be appropriated . . . shall be allotted" by the Administrator of the Environmental Protection Agency. Upon enactment of this statute, the President directed the Administrator to allot no more than a certain part of the amount authorized. This Court held, as a matter of statutory interpretation, that the statute *did not grant* the Executive discretion to withhold the funds, but required allotment of the full amount authorized.

The short of the matter is this: Had the Line Item Veto Act authorized the President to "decline to spend" any item of spending contained in the Balanced Budget Act of 1997, there is not the slightest doubt that authorization would have been constitutional. What the Line Item Veto Act does instead—authorizing the President to "cancel" an item of spending— is technically different. But the technical difference does *not* relate to the technicalities of the Presentment Clause, which have been fully complied with; and the doctrine of unconstitutional delegation, which *is* at issue here, is preeminently *not* a doctrine of technicalities. The title of the Line

Item Veto Act, which was perhaps designed to simplify for public comprehension, or perhaps merely to comply with the terms of a campaign pledge, has succeeded in faking out the Supreme Court. The President's action it authorizes in fact is not a line-item veto and thus does not offend Art. I, § 7; and insofar as the substance of that action is concerned, it is no different from what Congress has permitted the President to do since the formation of the Union.

JUSTICE BREYER, with whom JUSTICE O'CONNOR and JUSTICE SCALIA join as to Part III, dissenting.

III. The Court believes that the Act violates the literal text of the Constitution. A simple syllogism captures its basic reasoning:

> Major Premise: The Constitution sets forth an exclusive method for enacting, repealing, or amending laws.

> Minor Premise: The Act authorizes the President to "repea[l] or amen[d]" laws in a different way, namely by announcing a cancellation of a portion of a previously enacted law.

> Conclusion: The Act is inconsistent with the Constitution.

I find this syllogism unconvincing, however, because its Minor Premise is faulty. When the President "canceled" the two appropriation measures now before us, he did not *repeal* any law nor did he *amend* any law. He simply *followed* the law, leaving the statutes, as they are literally written, intact.

To understand why one cannot say, *literally speaking,* that the President has repealed or amended any law, imagine how the provisions of law before us might have been, but were not, written. Imagine that the canceled New York [Medicaid] provision at issue here had instead said the following:

> Section One. Taxes . . . that were collected by the State of New York from a health care provider before June 1, 1997 and for which a waiver of provisions [requiring payment] have been sought . . . are deemed to be permissible health care related taxes . . . *provided however that the President may prevent the just-mentioned provision from having legal force or effect if he determines x, y and z.* (Assume x, y and z to be the same determinations required by the Line Item Veto Act).

Whatever a person might say, or think, about the constitutionality of this imaginary law, there is one thing the English language would prevent one from saying. One could not say that a President who "prevent[s]" the deeming language from "having legal force or effect" has either *repealed* or *amended* this particular hypothetical statute. Rather, the President has *followed* that law to the letter. He has exercised the power it explicitly delegates to him. He has executed the law, not repealed it.

It could make no significant difference to this linguistic point were the italicized proviso to appear, not as part of what I have called Section One, but, instead, at the bottom of the statute page, say referenced by an asterisk, with a statement that it applies to every spending provision in the act next to which a similar asterisk appears. And that being so, it could make no difference if that proviso appeared, instead, in a different, earlier-enacted law, along with legal language that makes it applicable to every future spending provision picked out according to a specified formula.

But, of course, this last-mentioned possibility is this very case. The earlier law, namely, the Line Item Veto Act, says that "the President may ... prevent such [future] budget authority from having legal force or effect." * * * For that reason, one cannot dispose of this case through a purely literal analysis as the majority does. Literally speaking, the President has not "repealed" or "amended" anything. He has simply *executed* a power conferred upon him by Congress, which power is contained in laws that were enacted in compliance with the exclusive method set forth in the Constitution. * * *

* * * This is not the first time that Congress has delegated to the President or to others this kind of power—a contingent power to deny effect to certain statutory language. [E.g.,] 28 U.S.C. § 2072 (Supreme Court is authorized to promulgate rules of practice and procedure in federal courts, and "[a]ll laws in conflict with such rules *shall be of no further force and effect*") (emphasis added); Gramm-Rudman-Hollings Act, § 252(a)(4) (authorizing the President to issue a "final order" that has the effect of "*permanently cancell[ing]*" sequestered amounts in spending statutes in order to achieve budget compliance) (emphasis added).

All of these examples, like the Act, delegate a power to take action that will render statutory provisions "without force or effect." Every one of these examples, like the present Act, delegates the power to choose between alternatives, each of which the statute spells out in some detail. None of these examples delegates a power to "repeal" or "amend" a statute, or to "make" a new law. Nor does the Act. Rather, the delegated power to nullify statutory language was *itself* created and defined by Congress, and included in the statute books on an equal footing with (indeed, as a component part of) the sections that are potentially subject to nullification. * * *

[In Part IV, Justice Breyer rejected arguments based upon separation of powers principles: (1) Has Congress given the President the wrong kind of power, *i.e.*, "non-executive" power? No. (2) Has Congress given the President the power to "encroach" upon Congress' own constitutionally reserved territory? No. (3) Has Congress given the President too much power, violating the nondelegation doctrine? No, because the law provides "intelligible" standards to guide the President.]

NOTES ON CLINTON V. CITY OF NEW YORK

1. *Should Spending and Taxing Cancellations Have Been Treated Differently? Is the President's Impoundment Authority Limited?* The cancellations before the Court concerned a tax provision and a spending provision. From a historical perspective, the taxing provision appears more questionable than the spending provision. As the dissents noted, Presidents have sometimes claimed a power functionally indistinguishable from cancellation—the impoundment authority—to withhold funds that Congress had allocated to government programs in the annual appropriations process. But see *Train v. City of New York,* 420 U.S. 35 (1975) (narrowly interpreting an appropriations statute, to deny the President authority to withhold authorized funds). Is the cancellation power relating to discretionary spending, which consists of appropriated funds that have been the traditional target of presidential impoundments, clearly unconstitutional? If so, is it unconstitutional for the President to impound what he considers unnecessary spending levels? In all cases?[65]

As a formal matter, can one consider the presidential impoundment authority more "executive" than an authority to rescind taxes, which looks more "legislative"? As a functional matter, is the problem of rent-seeking (Congress's dolloping out goodies to special interests) greater for tax statutes than for spending programs? As a matter of popular constitutionalism, does shifting power to the President pose unacceptable new risks to popular majorities or to minorities? As we read him, Justice Breyer would say that the functional and vertical inquiries suggest no big difference, and he would not rest upon the formality of the executive/legislative inquiry (contrary to the Burger approach in *Chadha*).

2. *A Congressional Response?* In May 2018, President Trump asked Congress to pass a law giving him authority to edit congressional spending bills. The media made sport of the President for not knowing that *Clinton v. United States* had taken that off the table, but perhaps the President knew something the media did not. Can you construct a statutory impoundment law that would be constitutional?

What if "to cancel" was defined as "to decline to spend or enforce"? Or could Congress delegate to the President the power to "suspend" or federal spending

---

[65] Notice that the definition of *cancel* is different in the context of discretionary spending. Rather than rendering a provision of law without "legal force and effect," the President "rescinds" an item of discretionary spending when he cancels it. In budget parlance, a rescission is a congressionally authorized impoundment. Under the Impoundment Control Act of 1974, the President wanting to impound authorized funds is supposed to propose to rescind federal spending, but his proposal would not go into effect unless approved by Congress within 45 days. One way to view the Line Item Veto Act's provisions affecting appropriated money is as merely a change in the way Congress authorizes rescissions. Rather than requiring ex post congressional approval, the Line Item Veto Act delegates a continuing power to rescind spending, as long as the President complies with the standards set forth in the Act.

programs if he finds his action would reduce the federal deficit, not impair any essential government functions, and not harm the national interest? See Virginia A. McMurtry, Congressional Research Service, *Item Veto and Expanded Impoundment Proposals: History and Current Status* (June 18, 2010).

Another option is separate enrollment. Using this procedure, Congress would divide an omnibus spending bill into separate bills, formally enrolling each provision allocating funds to particular programs as a separate bill. The group of bills would be passed by Congress (probably using a procedure that would require only one vote to enact the bundle of bills). The President would then have the ability to use his constitutional veto to cancel as many of the programs as he wishes; Congress would have the opportunity to override any veto with a supermajority vote. Are there reasons Congress might not want to follow this approach?

3. *How Significant Was the Cancellation Power?* President Clinton used this new power to cancel relatively small projects, cumulatively worth about $500 million. One explanation for the infrequent use of cancellation is that the effect of the new power occurred primarily during negotiations as Congress drafted and considered spending and tax legislation. Theoretically, the President's role in the content of legislation is determined in part by the possibility that he might veto bills containing provisions he dislikes; even when the veto threat is not carried out, it should influence the bargaining process that goes on in the legislative process. See William N. Eskridge Jr. & John Ferejohn, *The Article I, Section 7 Game*, 80 Geo. L.J. 523 (1992). Thus, except for some symbolic uses of cancellation to score political points with voters, the President might never actually have to cancel or impound funds, because he would have already negotiated deals with members of Congress before the bill reaches his desk.

A vertical perspective, therefore, would be concerned that the item veto reflects a big shift in lawmaking power—away from Congress's state and local constituencies and toward national ones (that elect the President). Evidence from studies of governors' use of their line-item veto power suggests it has little effect on the amount of state spending but allows the executives more influence over the shape of the budget. This latter outcome is more pronounced when the two branches are controlled by different parties. As a matter of the Constitution's balance of representation, therefore, the item veto law significantly altered the Article I, § 7 structure—and the Court was right to strike it down. See Steven G. Calabresi, *Separation of Powers and the Rehnquist Court: The Centrality of* Clinton v. City of New York, 99 Nw. U.L. Rev. 77 (2004) (arguing that the Line Item Veto Case was an implicit revival of the nondelegation doctrine).

B. CONGRESSIONAL AND PRESIDENTIAL POWER TO CONTROL "EXECUTIVE" OFFICIALS

Another way Congress can delegate its cake and eat it too would be to grant authority to officials whom it controls to some extent through power over appointment, removal, or even threat of impeachment. Congress also might attempt to undercut presidential power by making officials removable only for "good cause." The validity of these kinds of arrangements might turn on how tightly the President must be viewed as controlling the *unitary executive* established in Article II, rather than on improper action by legislative subgroups under Article I, § 7. Thus, one might ask the formal question whether Article II assumes a unitary executive; the functional question whether congressional control over executive officials interferes with either the legislative duties of Congress or the executive duties of the President; and the vertical question whether congressional control (or presidential lack of control) over executive officials affects the President's constituency and his incentives to act. The theoretical possibilities are rich. The Supreme Court's precedents in this area are an unruly lot.

Myers v. United States

272 U.S. 52 (1926)

The Court invalidated an 1876 statute preventing the President from discharging postmasters without the consent of the Senate. **Chief Justice Taft**'s opinion for the Court rested in large part on the *Decision of 1789*, whereby a Congress filled with Framers expressed what the Chief Justice felt was a general understanding that the President must have the authority to remove executive department officers, without the need for Senate consent (Note on Early Interactions at the beginning of this chapter). The Chief Justice particularly relied on the position ultimately taken by Representative James Madison in the House, that "[i]f there is any point in which the separation of the Legislative and Executive powers ought to be maintained with great caution, it is that which relates to officers and offices." 1 Annals of Cong. 581 (1789).

Drawing from the discussions at Philadelphia and the Framers' purpose to avoid the weaknesses of the Articles of Confederation, Chief Justice Taft (himself President from 1909 to 1913) viewed the executive as a unitary branch, hierarchically arrayed with the President in command of subordinate officers. The Vesting Clause of Article II was textual evidence of the proposition advanced by Madison and others in the Decision of 1789, that all executive powers were vested in the President and none in Congress. As the British system attested, the power of removal as well as the power of appointment were central features of the executive power.

The history of the Advise and Consent Clause for appointment proved that it was not intended by the Framers to spill over into removal. Typically, James Madison said it best (1 Annals of Cong. 499):

> Vest this [removal] power in the Senate jointly with the President, and you abolish at once that great principle of unity and responsibility in the Executive department, which was intended for the security of liberty and the public good. If the President should possess alone the power of removal from office, those who are employed in the execution of the law will be in their proper situation, and the chain of dependence be preserved; the lowest officers, the middle grade, and the highest, will depend, as they ought, on the President, and the President on the community.

The Court considered the Decision of 1789 dispositive because it offered Madison a chance to speak so clearly, because his views were accepted by a Congress populated by Framers, and because even Hamilton (whose *Federalist* No. 77 supported the necessity of Senate consent for removal as well as appointment) acquiesced in the Madisonian consensus.

Justice Brandeis dissented, arguing that there was no consensus in 1789, but that by 1833, when Joseph Story penned his *Commentaries on the Constitution*, there was a consensus that Congress could require Senate consent for the removal of *inferior* executive officers. Brandeis also pointed out a logical problem in the Chief Justice's opinion: It conceded that Congress under the Appointments Clause (Art. II, § 2, cl. 2) could vest both appointment and removal of postmasters with the Postmaster General, and that Congress could condition removals upon Senate consent. See *United States v. Perkins*, 116 U.S. 483 (1886). If Congress could do this, consistent with Article II, why could it not impose the same condition on removals by the President? If Congress has the power to create the Post Office Department, why does it not have authority, under the Necessary and Proper Clause, to condition removals from office? Also dissenting, in separate opinions, were **Justices Holmes** and **McReynolds**.

Humphrey's Executor v. United States

295 U.S. 602 (1935)

The Court upheld a provision in the Federal Trade Commission Act which permitted removal by the President, but only for "inefficiency, neglect of duty, or malfeasance in office." **Justice Sutherland**'s opinion for the Court reasoned that this limitation was needed to accomplish the goals of the statute. *Myers* was distinguishable, for it involved an "executive officer restricted to the performance of executive functions * * *. Putting aside *dicta*, which may be followed if sufficiently persuasive but which are not controlling, the necessary reach of the decision goes far enough to include all purely executive officers. It goes no farther; much less does it include an officer who occupies no place in the executive department and who exercises no part of the executive power vested by the Constitution in the President."

Justice Sutherland characterized the FTC as "an administrative body created by Congress to carry into effect legislative policies embodied in the statute in accordance with the legislative standard therein prescribed, and to perform other specified duties as a legislative or as a judicial aid. Such a body cannot in any proper sense be characterized as an arm or an eye of the executive." Because the FTC investigates, prosecutes, and adjudicates complaints of unfair trade practices, the Court characterized it as exercising "quasi-legislative or quasi-judicial powers, or as an agency of the legislative or judicqw6eaial departments of the government." In creating such bodies, Congress can set the terms of the commissioners' office and limit the conditions of their removal, the latter to assure their independence of the President. The Supreme Court followed *Humphrey's Executor* in *Wiener v. United States*, 357 U.S. 349 (1958), to uphold congressional restrictions on the President's power to remove members of the War Claims Commission.

Buckley v. Valeo

424 U.S. 1 (1976)

The Federal Election Campaign Act of 1971, as amended in 1974, established the Federal Election Commission (FEC) and charged it with investigating, sanctioning, and rulemaking duties. The eight-member FEC included two members appointed by the President, two by the Speaker of the House, and two by the President *pro tempore* of the Senate. The Supreme Court, in a *per curiam* opinion, found that structure to violate the Appointments Clause (Art. II, § 2, cl. 2). Because the FEC members were "appointee[s] exercising significant authority pursuant to the laws of the United States," they were *Officers of the United States* and had to be appointed according to the terms of the Appointments Clause. The two members appointed by the President raised no difficulty, but the four appointed by Congress had no support in the clause.

The Court added that if the FEC were merely an investigative arm of Congress, the Appointments Clause would not apply. The Commission's enforcement and sanctioning power, however, rendered it something more. So, too, its rulemaking power: "These functions, exercised free from day-to-day supervision of either Congress or the Executive Branch, * * * are of kinds usually performed by independent regulatory agencies or by some department in the Executive Branch under the direction of an Act of Congress." Although under *Humphrey's Executor*, "the President may not insist that such functions be delegated to an appointee of his removable at will, none of them operates merely in aid of congressional authority to legislate or is sufficiently removed from the administration and enforcement of public law to allow it to be performed by the present Commission."

BOWSHER V. SYNAR

478 U.S. 714, 106 S.Ct. 3181, 92 L.Ed.2d 583 (1986)

CHIEF JUSTICE BURGER delivered the opinion of the Court.

[The Gramm-Rudman-Hollings Act sought to eliminate the federal budget deficit. To that end, the Act set a "maximum deficit amount" for federal spending for each of fiscal years 1986 through 1991 (when it would be zero). If in any fiscal year the federal budget deficit exceeded the maximum deficit amount by more than a specified sum, the Act required across-the-board cuts in federal spending to reach the targeted deficit level. Each year, the Directors of the Office of Management and Budget (OMB) and the Congressional Budget Office (CBO) would estimate the amount of the federal budget deficit for the upcoming fiscal year. If that deficit exceeded the maximum targeted deficit amount for that fiscal year by more than a specified amount, the Directors of OMB and CBO would independently calculate, on a program-by-program basis, the budget reductions necessary to ensure that the deficit does not exceed the maximum deficit amount. The Act then required the Directors to report jointly their deficit estimates and budget reduction calculations to the Comptroller General, who would then report his conclusions to the President. The President was required under the Act to issue a "sequestration" order mandating the spending reductions specified by the Comptroller General. After a certain period, the cuts required by the order would be implemented. Anticipating constitutional challenge to these procedures, the Act contained a "fallback" deficit reduction process to take effect in the event the foregoing procedures were invalidated.

[Twelve Members of Congress, the National Treasury Employees Union, and a union member brought suit challenging the Act on separation of powers grounds. A three-judge court invalidated the law, and the Supreme Court affirmed.]

The Constitution does not contemplate an active role for Congress in the supervision of officers charged with the execution of the laws it enacts. The President appoints "Officers of the United States" with the "Advice and Consent of the Senate. . . ." Art. II, § 2. Once the appointment has been made and confirmed, however, the Constitution explicitly provides for removal of Officers of the United States by Congress only upon impeachment by the House of Representatives and conviction by the Senate. An impeachment by the House and trial by the Senate can rest only on "Treason, Bribery or other high Crimes and Misdemeanors." Art. II, § 4. A direct congressional role in the removal of officers charged with the execution of the laws beyond this limited one is inconsistent with separation of powers. * * *

[The Chief Justice reviewed the precedents—*Myers*, *Humphrey's Executor*, and *Wiener*.] In light of these precedents, we conclude that

Congress cannot reserve for itself the power of removal of an officer charged with the execution of the laws except by impeachment. To permit the execution of the laws to be vested in an officer answerable only to Congress would, in practical terms, reserve in Congress control over the execution of the laws. As the District Court observed: "Once an officer is appointed, it is only the authority that can remove him, and not the authority that appointed him, that he must fear and, in the performance of his functions, obey." The structure of the Constitution does not permit Congress to execute the laws; it follows that Congress cannot grant to an officer under its control what it does not possess.

* * * To permit an officer controlled by Congress to execute the laws would be, in essence, to permit a congressional veto. Congress could simply remove, or threaten to remove, an officer for executing the laws in any fashion found to be unsatisfactory to Congress. This kind of congressional control over the execution of the laws, *Chadha* makes clear, is constitutionally impermissible. * * *

Appellants urge that the Comptroller General performs his duties independently and is not subservient to Congress. * * * [T]his contention does not bear close scrutiny.

The critical factor lies in the provisions of the statute defining the Comptroller General's office relating to removability. Although the Comptroller General is nominated by the President from a list of three individuals recommended by the Speaker of the House of Representatives and the President *pro tempore* of the Senate, and confirmed by the Senate, he is removable only at the initiative of Congress. He may be removed not only by impeachment but also by joint resolution of Congress "at any time" resting on any one of the following bases: [(i) permanent disability; (ii) inefficiency; (iii) neglect of duty; (iv) malfeasance; or (v) a felony or conduct involving moral turpitude.] 31 U.S.C. § 703(e)(1)(B). This provision was included, as one Congressman explained in urging passage of the Act, because Congress "felt that [the Comptroller General] should be brought under the sole control of Congress, so that Congress at any moment when it found he was inefficient and was not carrying on the duties of his office as he should and as the Congress expected, could remove him without the long, tedious process of a trial by impeachment." 61 Cong. Rec. 1081 (1921). * * *

* * * [T]he dissent is simply in error to suggest that the political realities reveal that the Comptroller General is free from influence by Congress. The Comptroller General heads the General Accounting Office (GAO), "an instrumentality of the United States Government independent of the executive departments," 31 U.S.C. § 702(a), which was created by Congress in 1921 as part of the Budget and Accounting Act of 1921. Congress created the office because it believed that it "needed an officer,

responsible to it alone, to check upon the application of public funds in accordance with appropriations." H. Mansfield, *The Comptroller General: A Study in the Law and Practice of Financial Administration* 65 (1939). [Additionally, both Congress and the Comptroller General over the years have viewed that office as part of the legislative branch.]

Against this background, we see no escape from the conclusion that, because Congress has retained removal authority over the Comptroller General, he may not be entrusted with executive powers. The remaining question is whether the Comptroller General has been assigned such powers in the Balanced Budget and Emergency Deficit Control Act of 1985. * * *

Appellants suggest that the duties assigned to the Comptroller General in the Act are essentially ministerial and mechanical so that their performance does not constitute "execution of the law" in a meaningful sense. On the contrary, we view these functions as plainly entailing execution of the law in constitutional terms. Interpreting a law enacted by Congress to implement the legislative mandate is the very essence of "execution" of the law. Under § 251, the Comptroller General must exercise judgment concerning facts that affect the application of the Act. He must also interpret the provisions of the Act to determine precisely what budgetary calculations are required. Decisions of that kind are typically made by officers charged with executing a statute.

The executive nature of the Comptroller General's functions under the Act is revealed in § 252(a)(3) which gives the Comptroller General the ultimate authority to determine the budget cuts to be made. Indeed, the Comptroller General commands the President himself to carry out, without the slightest variation (with exceptions not relevant to the constitutional issues presented), the directive of the Comptroller General as to the budget reductions:

> The [Presidential] order *must provide* for reductions in the manner specified in section 251(a)(3), *must incorporate* the provisions of the [Comptroller General's] report submitted under section 251(b), and *must be consistent with such report in all respects.* The President *may not modify or recalculate any of the estimates, determinations, specifications, bases, amounts, or percentages* set forth in the report submitted under section 251(b) in determining the reductions to be specified in the order with respect to programs, projects, and activities, or with respect to budget activities, within an account. . . . "§ 252(a)(3) (emphasis added).

Congress of course initially determined the content of the Balanced Budget and Emergency Deficit Control Act; and undoubtedly the content of the Act determines the nature of the executive duty. However, as

Chadha makes clear, once Congress makes its choice in enacting legislation, its participation ends. Congress can thereafter control the execution of its enactment only indirectly—by passing new legislation. By placing the responsibility for execution of the Balanced Budget and Emergency Deficit Control Act in the hands of an officer who is subject to removal only by itself, Congress in effect has retained control over the execution of the Act and has intruded into the executive function. The Constitution does not permit such intrusion.

JUSTICE STEVENS, with whom JUSTICE MARSHALL joins, concurring in the judgment.

It is not the dormant, carefully circumscribed congressional removal power that represents the primary constitutional evil. Nor do I agree with the conclusion of both the majority and the dissent that the analysis depends on a labeling of the functions assigned to the Comptroller General as "executive powers." Rather, I am convinced that the Comptroller General must be characterized as an agent of Congress because of his longstanding statutory responsibilities; that the powers assigned to him under the Gramm-Rudman-Hollings Act require him to make policy that will bind the Nation; and that, when Congress, or a component or an agent of Congress, seeks to make policy that will bind the Nation, it must follow the procedures mandated by Article I of the Constitution—through passage by both Houses and presentment to the President. In short, Congress may not exercise its fundamental power to formulate national policy by delegating that power to one of its two Houses, to a legislative committee, or to an individual agent of the Congress such as the Speaker of the House of Representatives, the Sergeant at Arms of the Senate, or the Director of the Congressional Budget Office. *Chadha.* That principle, I believe, is applicable to the Comptroller General.

[Justice Stevens noted that the Court did not dispute that it would be constitutional for Congress to delegate to an executive official the authority provided to the Comptroller General in the Act. He saw the "central issue" in the case as follows: "If the delegation to a stranger is permissible, why may not Congress delegate the same responsibilities to one of its own agents?" His response was that intra-congressional delegations violate *Chadha*: "If Congress were free to delegate its policymaking authority to one of its components, or to one of its agents, it would be able to evade 'the carefully crafted restraints spelled out in the Constitution.' *Chadha.* That danger—congressional action that evades constitutional restraints—is not present when Congress delegates lawmaking power to the executive or to an independent agency."]

JUSTICE WHITE, dissenting.

[Justice White complained that the Court had struck down a novel legislative response to an economic crisis based on a removal power found in "a solitary provision of another statute that was passed sixty years ago and has lain dormant since that time." Justice White did not consider the Comptroller's authority under Gramm-Rudman to include substantial policymaking discretion and thought it sensible for Congress to entrust these duties to "an officer who is to the greatest degree possible nonpartisan and independent of the President and his political agenda and who therefore may be relied upon not to allow his calculations to be colored by political considerations." Moreover, he saw no intrusion into executive functions at work in the statute: The appropriation of funds is purely a congressional function, Congress has set a limit on the amount of appropriations, and Congress delegated the mechanics of enforcing the limitation to someone independent of the President.]

[T]he Court baldly mischaracterizes the removal provision when it suggests that it allows Congress to remove the Comptroller for "executing the laws in any fashion found to be unsatisfactory"; in fact, Congress may remove the Comptroller only for one or more of five specified reasons * * *. Second, and more to the point, the Court overlooks or deliberately ignores the decisive difference between the congressional removal provision and the legislative veto struck down in *Chadha*: under the Budget and Accounting Act, Congress may remove the Comptroller only through a joint resolution, which by definition must be passed by both Houses and signed by the President. In other words, a removal of the Comptroller under the statute *satisfies the requirements of bicameralism and presentment laid down in Chadha.* * * *

The practical result of the removal provision is not to render the Comptroller unduly dependent upon or subservient to Congress, but to render him one of the most independent officers in the entire federal establishment. Those who have studied the office agree that the procedural and substantive limits on the power of Congress and the President to remove the Comptroller make dislodging him against his will practically impossible. * * *

* * * The wisdom of vesting "executive" powers in an officer removable by joint resolution may indeed be debatable—as may be the wisdom of the entire scheme of permitting an unelected official to revise the budget enacted by Congress—but such matters are for the most part to be worked out between the Congress and the President through the legislative process, which affords each branch ample opportunity to defend its interests. The Act vesting budget-cutting authority in the Comptroller General represents Congress' judgment that the delegation of such authority to counteract ever-mounting deficits is "necessary and proper" to the exercise of the powers granted the Federal Government by the Constitution; and the President's approval of the statute signifies his unwillingness to reject the choice made by Congress. Under such circumstances, the role of this Court should be limited to determining

whether the Act so alters the balance of authority among the branches of government as to pose a genuine threat to the basic division between the lawmaking power and the power to execute the law. Because I see no such threat, I cannot join the Court in striking down the Act.

[JUSTICE BLACKMUN dissented separately. He would have invalidated the provisions of the 1921 statute allowing Congress to remove the Comptroller General, thereby saving the Gramm-Rudman-Hollings Act.]

NOTES ON MYERS THROUGH BOWSHER: THE SUPREME COURT'S UNSTEADY PATH

1. *The Reasoning of* Bowsher. *Bowsher's* categorization exercise is replete with logical holes and unanswered questions:[66]

(a) *Is the Comptroller an "Executive" Official?* An anomaly of the Court's opinion is its reliance on the idea that anyone who has a hand in enforcing the laws cannot be "controlled" by Congress. The Chief Justice views "control" functionally, but in that event congressional committees often exercise much more effective "control" over agencies than Congress does over the Comptroller, by means of oversight hearings, appropriations measures, and informal pressure. Also, there are plenty of congressional agents who execute the laws. The Capitol Hill Police who patrol the Capitol area, the Sergeant-at-Arms who manages the congressional payroll, and the Capitol Architect who maintains the grounds are all formally controlled by Congress. In a sense they all "execute" statutory directives. Does this violate separation of power precepts? Are these officials materially different from the Comptroller General in their "executive" duties?

(b) *Does Congress "Control" the Comptroller General?* Even if the Comptroller General were an executive official, she could act out her role in the statutory scheme if Congress didn't "control" her. The Court concedes that Congress has never "removed" a Comptroller General under the statute in question, and (as Justice White argued) any removal must be through a Joint Resolution meeting the bicameralism and presentment requirements. Is there any reason to believe that this official would kowtow to Congress under the Gramm-Rudman Act?[67] Aren't the Comptroller's duties under the Act substantially limited by the OMB and CBO projections?

Does *Bowsher* cast constitutional doubt on congressional efforts to control administrative policy except through substantive statutes (e.g., through oversight and appropriations)? For example, § 605 of Public Law No. 99–180, an appropriations measure, disapproved of Department of Justice efforts to

---

[66] *Bowsher* has been the object of intense academic criticism of its strained exercise in categorization. E.g., Abner Greene, *Checks and Balances in an Era of Presidential Lawmaking*, 61 U. Chi. L. Rev. 123 (1994); David Yassky, Note, *A Two-Tiered Theory of Consolidation and Separation of Powers*, 99 Yale L.J. 431 (1989).

[67] Arguing not is Peter L. Strauss, *Formal and Functional Approaches to Separation of Powers Questions—A Foolish Inconsistency?*, 72 Cornell L. Rev. 488 (1987).

liberalize antitrust rules concerning resale price maintenance. It provided that no funds appropriated to the Department of Justice "may be used for any activity to alter the per se prohibition on resale price maintenance in effect under Federal antitrust laws." Included was also a "sense of Congress" condemnation of the Department's "Guidelines" on vertical restraints, on grounds that they violated the Supreme Court's interpretation of the statute. Is § 605 constitutional?

(c) *What Happened to* Chadha? Having just read the Legislative and Line Item Veto Cases, you might think that the Gramm-Rudman Act had the same structural problem. It delegated important law-creating authority to an agent (like a subgroup) of the legislature, without requiring bicameral approval and presentment. Indeed, the Gramm-Rudman Case seems more constitutionally fishy than the Legislative Veto Case, since massive policy choices are potentially being made by a single unelected person. Moreover, if Chief Justice Burger is right that the Comptroller General is under Congress' thumb, there is even greater opportunity for rent-seeking behavior, as various lobbying groups and clusters of Members might pressure the Comptroller General's decisions. But only Justices Marshall and Stevens believed that the Act was invalid because it delegated lawmaking power to a legislative agent. Why did the majority follow a different path?

2. *Theories for Reconciling the Cases.* In *Checks and Balances in an Era of Presidential Lawmaking*, 61 U. Chi. L. Rev. 123, 167 (1994), Abner Greene suggests that the laws in *Bowsher* and *Chadha* were both efforts at self-aggrandizement, and the Court was right to monitor that process defect. But under such a rationale, *Clinton v. New York* ought to come out differently, as Congress was giving away power, without strings attached, in the Line Item Veto Act. Is *Clinton v. New York* wrongly decided?

Victoria F. Nourse, in *The Vertical Separation of Powers*, 49 Duke L.J. 749, 793–95 (1999), argues that the cases can be reconciled through the vertical perspective. Forget the Court's categorization game, and do not end discussion with the aggrandizement problem. Instead, focus on how a shift in power is also a shift in political constituency and in popular accountability. Both *Chadha* and *Bowsher* shifted important federal decisionmaking away from the messy but deliberative *political* process and toward less accountable insiders (*Chadha*) and bureaucrats (*Bowsher*). Both cut the President, and his national constituency, out of important public decisions. *Clinton v. New York* is a harder case, because the line item veto does not take important decisions out of the political process, but does shift power in the other direction, to the President and away from Congress.

3. *Debate over Methodology: Triumph of Formalism?* After *Chadha* and *Bowsher*, one might tentatively conclude that the Supreme Court had opted for a formalist approach to separation of powers: each branch is limited to the particular power granted it in the Constitution, and is not to exercise other powers unless expressly authorized by the Constitution. (Although decided later, *Clinton v, New York* supports this conclusion.) Under such a formalist

approach, does Justice Black's majority opinion in the Steel Seizure Case dominate Justice Jackson's concurring opinion, or can both be characterized as formalist along *Chadha* lines?

NOTE ON THE CONSTITUTIONALITY OF INDEPENDENT AGENCIES

The Chief Justice's opinion in the Gramm-Rudman Case was careful not to cast doubt on the constitutionality of independent agencies, whose officials are not removable by Congress and can only be removed by the President based upon a finding of "just cause."[68] But when the Court's precedents are read together, there might be substantial constitutional doubt about independent agencies, such as the FTC.[69] In short, should *Humphrey's Executor* be overruled? Although *Bowsher* did not take that step, it gave new wind to such arguments by its respectful treatment of *Myers* and its broad understanding of executive functions. If, as *Myers* held, Article II vests the President with plenary authority to supervise the execution of the laws *and*, as *Bowsher* held, execution includes any step in the implementation of a law's policy, then follows that the FTC plays an executive role that must be under the control of the President.

Conversely, if the FTC is not part of the executive branch, where is it? The reasoning in *Humphrey's* treating the FTC as "quasi-legislative" might be questioned after *Bowsher*. In that event, the FTC becomes part of an unenumerated fourth branch of government—the legislative, executive, and judicial branches named in the Constitution are now joined by a "quasi" branch (to use the *Humphrey's* terminology) of independent agencies that are under the actual control of neither Congress nor the President. Forthright defenders of independent agencies such as Peter Strauss make this concession (see our excerpt from his article in Part C), but it seems like a riskier one after *Bowsher*.

Finally, as *Humphrey's* emphasized, many of the independent agencies make legislative rules based upon a broad statutory delegation, initiate enforcement actions, and adjudicate at least some of those actions. The FTC, for example, adjudicates unfair competition complaints brought by its own enforcement division and issues legislative rules. This combination of legislative, executive, and judicial functions in one institution might be said to violate the essential worry of the Framers (based upon Montesquieu) that these powers be separated lest they be (inevitably) abused. For a case against

---

[68] In footnote 4, which we omitted, the Chief Justice rejected the appellants' slippery slope argument that the lower court opinion cast doubt on the constitutional status of independent agencies. "The statutes establishing independent agencies typically specify either that the agency members are removable by the President for specified causes * * * or else do not specify a removal procedure. This case involves nothing like these statutes, but rather a statute that provides for direct congressional involvement over the decision to remove the Comptroller General."

[69] For different points of view, consult Gary Lawson, *The Rise and Rise of the Administrative State*, 107 Harv. L. Rev. 1231 (1994); Geoffrey Miller, *Independent Agencies*, 1986 Sup. Ct. Rev. 41; Peter L. Strauss, *The Place of Agencies in Government: Separation of Powers and the Fourth Branch*, 84 Colum. L. Rev. 573 (1984); Michael Froomkin, Note, *In Defense of Agency Autonomy*, 96 Yale L.J. 787, 799 (1987).

any congressional authorization for agencies to perform "quasi-legislative" or "quasi-judicial" functions, see Philip Hamburger, *Is Administrative Law Unlawful* (2014) (discussed at the beginning of this section).

Peter L. Strauss, *The Place of Agencies in Government: Separation of Powers and the Fourth Branch*

84 Colum. L. Rev. 573, 578–80 (1984)[70]

"[F]or any consideration of the structure given law-administration below the very apex of the governmental structure, the rigid separation of powers compartmentalization of governmental functions should be abandoned in favor of analysis in terms of separation of functions and checks and balances. Almost fifty years of experience has accustomed lawyers and judges to accepting the independent regulatory commissions, in the metaphor, as a 'headless "fourth branch"' of government. Although the resulting theoretical confusion has certainly been noticed, we accept the idea of potent actors in government joining judicial, legislative, and executive functions, yet falling outside the constitutionally described schemata of three named branches embracing among them the entire allocated authority of government. * * * A shorthand way of putting the argument is that we should stop pretending that all our government (as distinct from its highest levels) can be allocated into three neat parts. * * * "From the perspective suggested here, the important fact is that an agency is neither Congress nor President nor Court, but an inferior part of government. Each agency is subject to control relationships with some or all of the three constitutionally named branches, and those relationships give an assurance—functionally similar to that provided by the separation-of-powers notion for the constitutionally named bodies—that they will not pass out of control.[71] Powerful and potentially arbitrary as they may be, the Secretary of Agriculture and the Chairman of the SEC for this reason do not present the threat that led the framers to insist on a splitting of the authority of government at its very top. What we have, then, are three named repositories of authorizing power and control, and an infinity of institutions to which parts of the authority of each may be lent. The three must share the reins of control; means must be found of assuring that no one of them becomes dominant. But it is not terribly important to number or allocate the horses that pull the carriage of government." Strauss then lays out an analytical model along the following lines (pp. 596–97): (1) The formal *separation of powers* idea should govern relationships among the three named actors—Congress, the President, the Supreme Court—but not the inferior bodies and agencies. This formal approach is appropriate for evaluating the President's action in the Steel Seizure Case and presumably in the Line Item and Legislative Veto Cases, but

---

[70] Reprinted by permission of the Columbia Law Review.

[71] Thus, Professor Strauss reads the nondelegation doctrine functionally, as requiring both statutory authorization (a relationship with Congress) and a capacity on the part of the courts to assure legality (a relationship with the courts). The availability of at least limited judicial review, indeed, appears to be identified with increasing frequency as an essential element of the grant of rulemaking authority."

not in *Myers*. (2) The guidepost for structuring agencies should be the fairness ideas derived from *separation of functions*, including clear policy statements to guide and limit agency rulemaking (*Hampton*), especially when citizen liberty is involved (*Mistretta*); relative independence for agencies performing adjudicative and prosecutorial functions (*Chadha* and *Buckley* (independence from Congress), *Humphrey's Executor* (from the President); and avoidance of too many cooks spoiling the broth (*Bowsher*) and conflicts of interest (*Schechter* and *Metropolitan Washington Airports Authority*). (3) The relationship between the President and agencies should be guided by *checks and balances* precepts. "Whatever arrangements are made, one must remain able to characterize the President as the unitary, politically accountable head of all law-administration, sufficiently potent in his own relationships with those who actually perform it to serve as an effective counter to a feared Congress." These theoretical precepts were soon enough put to a practical test in the following decisions.

Morrison v. Olson

487 U.S. 654 (1988)

[In response to the Watergate scandal, Congress adopted the Ethics in Government Act of 1978. Title IV created the office of "Independent Counsel" to investigate and, if appropriate, prosecute certain high-ranking government officials for violations of federal criminal laws. After notification of a possible federal offense, the Attorney General must decide within 90 days whether there are "reasonable grounds to believe that further investigation is warranted." If such reasonable grounds exist, the Attorney General must apply to a Special Division of the U.S. Court of Appeals for the D.C. Circuit for appointment of a special prosecutor; the judicial panel appoints the prosecutor and defines her jurisdiction. The Independent Counsel proceeds until she reports that her job is "completed," *or* the Special Division finds her job completed, *or* the Attorney General removes her (but only for "good cause," as specified in the statute). Defendant Theodore Olson, then head of the Justice Department's Office of Legal Counsel, was accused of providing misleading testimony to a congressional subcommittee. Independent Counsel Alexia Morrison was appointed to investigate. Olson moved to quash her subpoenas on the ground that Title IV was unconstitutional. The court of appeals agreed, but the Supreme Court reversed.

Chief Justice Rehnquist's opinion for the Court first ruled that Morrison's manner of appointment did not violate the Appointments Clause of Article II, which reads as follows:

[The President] shall nominate, and by and with the Advice and Consent of the Senate, shall appoint Ambassadors, other public Ministers and Consuls, Judges of the Supreme Court, and all other Officers of the United States, whose Appointments are not herein otherwise provided for, and which shall be established by Law: but the Congress may by Law vest the Appointment of such inferior

Officers, as they think proper, in the President alone, in the Courts of Law, or in the Heads of Departments. U.S. Const., Art. II, § 2, cl. 2.

The first question was whether Morrison was a "principal" officer whose appointment had to be made by the President. Conceding that the line between "inferior" and "principal" officers is "far from clear, and the Framers provided little guidance into where it should be drawn," the Chief Justice found that Morrison "clearly falls on the 'inferior officer' side of that line," for a variety of reasons: She is subject to removal by the Attorney General for good cause, is empowered by the Act to perform only certain duties and is otherwise to comply with the policies of the Justice Department, and has a limited tenure in an office of strictly limited jurisdiction.

Once the Court found Morrison to be an "inferior" officer, the Appointments Clause, by its plain language, allows Congress to vest her appointment outside the executive branch. What little debate there was over the clause at the Philadelphia Convention or during the ratification debates did nothing to negate the rule suggested by the plain meaning of the clause. Congress's authority is not unlimited, however. In *Ex parte Siebold*, 100 U.S. 371 (1879), the Court suggested that "Congress' decision to vest the appointment power in the courts would be improper if there was some 'incongruity' between the functions normally performed by the courts and the performance of their duty to appoint. In this case, however, we do not think it impermissible for Congress to vest the power to appoint independent counsels in a specially created federal court. * * * We have recognized that courts may appoint private attorneys to act as prosecutor for judicial contempt judgments. * * * [W]e [have] approved court appointment of United States commissioners, who exercised certain limited prosecutorial powers. In *Siebold*, * * * we indicated that judicial appointment of federal marshals, who are 'executive officer[s],' would not be inappropriate."

Chief Justice Rehnquist also rejected Olson's argument that the provisions giving judges the authority to appoint the special prosecutor violate Article III. "[O]nce it is accepted that the Appointments Clause gives Congress the power to vest the appointment of officials such as the independent counsel in the 'courts of Law,' there can be no Article III objection to the Special Division's exercise of that power, as the power itself derives from the Appointments Clause, a source of authority for judicial action that is independent of Article III."

The Court was more troubled by the non-appointment powers vested in the Special Division, including granting extensions for the Attorney General's preliminary investigation; receiving reports from the Attorney General and from the Independent Counsel; referring matters to the Counsel upon request; deciding whether to release the counsel's final report to Congress or the public and determining whether any protective orders should be issued; and terminating an independent counsel when his task is completed. The Chief

Justice found most of the powers given the Special Division passive or ministerial, thereby posing no trespass on the executive branch.

"We are more doubtful about the Special Division's power to terminate the office of the independent counsel. * * * As appellees suggest, the power to terminate, especially when exercised by the Division on its own motion, is 'administrative' to the extent that it requires the Special Division to monitor the progress of proceedings of the independent counsel and come to a decision as to whether the counsel's job is 'completed.' It also is not a power that could be considered typically 'judicial,' as it has few analogues among the court's more traditional powers. Nonetheless, we do not * * * view this provision as a significant judicial encroachment upon executive power or upon the prosecutorial discretion of the independent counsel."

To reinforce that conclusion, the Court imposed upon the Special Division's removal power this limitation: "The termination provisions of the Act do not give the Special Division anything approaching the power to *remove* the counsel while an investigation or court proceeding is still underway—this power is vested solely in the Attorney General. As we see it, 'termination' may occur only when the duties of the counsel are truly 'completed' or 'so substantially completed' that there remains no need for any continuing action by the independent counsel. It is basically a device for removing from the public payroll an independent counsel who has served her purpose, but is unwilling to acknowledge the fact. So construed, the Special Division's power to terminate does not pose a sufficient threat of judicial intrusion into matters that are more properly within the Executive's authority to require that the Act be invalidated as inconsistent with Article III."

Finally, the Chief Justice rejected Olson's objection that the Act violated the Constitution's separation of powers. "Unlike both *Bowsher* and *Myers*, this case does not involve an attempt by Congress itself to gain a role in the removal of executive officials other than its established powers of impeachment and conviction. The Act instead puts the removal power squarely in the hands of the Executive Branch; an independent counsel may be removed from office 'only by the personal action of the Attorney General, and only for good cause.' § 596(a)(1). There is no requirement of congressional approval of the Attorney General's removal decision, though the decision is subject to judicial review. In our view, the removal provisions of the Act make this case more analogous to *Humphrey's Executor* and *Weiner* than to *Myers* or *Bowsher*."

Olson argued that *Humphrey's Executor* was distinguishable because it did not involve officials who performed a "core executive function." When a "purely executive" official is involved, the governing precedent was *Myers*, not *Humphrey's Executor*. The Chief Justice responded: "We undoubtedly did rely on the terms 'quasi-legislative' and 'quasi-judicial' to distinguish the officials involved in *Humphrey's Executor* and *Wiener* from those in *Myers*, but our present considered view is that the determination of whether the Constitution allows Congress to impose a 'good cause'-type restriction on the President's power to remove an official cannot be made to turn on whether or not that official is classified as 'purely executive.' The analysis contained in our removal cases is designed not to define rigid categories of those officials who may or may not be removed at will by the President, but to ensure that Congress does not interfere with the President's exercise of the 'executive Power' and his constitutionally appointed duty to 'take Care that the laws be faithfully executed' under Article II. *Myers* was undoubtedly correct in its holding, and in its broader suggestion that there are some 'purely executive' officials who must be removable by the President at will if he is to be able to accomplish his constitutional role.

"At the other end of the spectrum from *Myers*, the characterization of the agencies in *Humphrey's Executor* and *Wiener* as 'quasi-legislative' or 'quasi-judicial' in large part reflected our judgment that it was not essential to the President's proper execution of his Article II powers that these agencies be headed up by individuals who were removable at will. We do not mean to suggest that an analysis of the functions served by the officials at issue is irrelevant. But the real question is whether the removal restrictions are of such a nature that they impede the President's ability to perform his constitutional duty, and the functions of the officials in question must be analyzed in that light."

The Court ruled that the imposition of a "good cause" standard for removal by itself did not "unduly" trammel the President's executive authority. "[B]ecause the independent counsel may be terminated for 'good cause,' the Executive, through the Attorney General, retains ample authority to assure that the counsel is competently performing her statutory responsibilities in a manner that comports with the provisions of the Act. * * * [T]he legislative history of the removal provision also makes clear that the Attorney General may remove an independent counsel for 'misconduct.' Here, as with the provision of the Act conferring the appointment authority of the independent counsel on the special court, the congressional determination to limit the removal power of the Attorney General was essential, in the view of Congress, to establish the necessary independence of the office. We do not think that this limitation as it presently stands sufficiently deprives the President of control over the independent counsel to interfere impermissibly with his constitutional obligation to ensure the faithful execution of the laws."

Because the Act did not involve an attempt by Congress to increase its own powers at the expense of the President, it was not like either *Bowsher* or *Chadha*. As narrowed by the Court, the statute did not permit "any *judicial* usurpation of properly executive functions." Nor did the Act "impermissibly undermine" the powers of the executive branch, or "disrupt the proper balance between the coordinate branches [by] prevent[ing] the Executive Branch from accomplishing its constitutionally assigned functions." While the Act reduced the amount of control or supervision that the Attorney General and, through him, the President could exercise over the investigation and prosecution of a certain class of alleged criminal activity, "the Act does give the Attorney General several means of supervising or controlling the prosecutorial powers that may be wielded by an independent counsel," such as the power to remove the counsel for "good cause." Also, the Attorney General was not required to request appointment of an Independent Counsel, and if the General did so request, the appointment was limited to the issues identified by the General.

Justice Kennedy did not participate in the case. Among the eight participating Justices, only **Justice Scalia** dissented, and quite ringingly. "Frequently an issue of this sort will come before the Court clad, so to speak, in sheep's clothing: the potential of the asserted principle to effect important change in the equilibrium of power is not immediately evident, and must be discerned by a careful and perceptive analysis. But this wolf comes as a wolf."

Justice Scalia's main objection was grounded in Article II's Vesting Clause, which he argued vests *all* "executive Power" in the President and allows no congressional derogation of the President's complete and exclusive control over the "execution" of the laws. "It seems to me, therefore, that the decision of the Court of Appeals invalidating the present statute must be upheld on fundamental separation-of-powers principles if the following two questions are answered affirmatively: (1) Is the conduct of a criminal prosecution (and of an investigation to decide whether to prosecute) the exercise of purely executive power? (2) Does the statute deprive the President of the United States of exclusive control over the exercise of that power? Surprising to say, the Court appears to concede an affirmative answer to both questions, but seeks to avoid the inevitable conclusion that since the statute vests some purely executive power in a person who is not the President of the United States it is void. * * *

"Is it unthinkable that the President should have such exclusive power, even when alleged crimes by him or his close associates are at issue? No more so than that Congress should have the exclusive power of legislation, even when what is at issue is its own exemption from the burdens of certain laws. See Civil Rights Act of 1964, Title VII, 42 U.S.C. §§ 2000e *et seq.* (prohibiting 'employers,' not defined to include the United States, from discriminating on the basis of race, color, religion, sex or national origin). No more so than that this Court should have the exclusive power to pronounce the final decision on justiciable cases and controversies, even those pertaining to the constitutionality of a statute reducing the salaries of the Justices. A system of separate and coordinate powers necessarily involves an acceptance of exclusive power that can theoretically be abused. * * * The checks against any Branch's abuse of its exclusive powers are twofold: First, retaliation by one of the other Branch's use of *its* exclusive powers: Congress, for example, can impeach the Executive who willfully fails to enforce the laws; the Executive can decline to prosecute under unconstitutional statutes; and the courts can dismiss malicious prosecutions. Second, and ultimately, there is the political check that the people will replace those in the political branches (the branches more 'dangerous to the political rights of the Constitution,' *Federalist* No. 78) who are guilty of abuse. Political pressures produced special prosecutors—for Teapot Dome and for Watergate, for example—long before this statute created the independent counsel."

Justice Scalia bemoaned the Court's willingness to fudge the Constitution's clear jurisdictional rules and substitute some kind of "balancing" approach, whose details are not apparent. "Evidently, the governing standard is to be what might be called the unfettered wisdom of a majority of this Court, revealed to an obedient people on a case-by-case basis. This is not only not the government of laws that the Constitution established; it is not a government of laws at all."

Justice Scalia contended that special prosecutors were in no sense "inferior" officers as they are in no sense subordinate to the President; hence, the statute violates the Appointments Clause even under the Court's functional reading. The Court's functionalism had the further disadvantage, Justice Scalia maintained, of departing from both *Myers* and *Humphrey's Executor*—the latter, by abandoning the "executive-versus-quasi-legislative-officer" distinction, and both precedents by explicitly announcing that some executive officers could be released from any presidential control.

NOTES ON CONSTITUTIONAL FORMALISM AND THE INDEPENDENT COUNSEL CASE

1. *Reconciling the Precedents?* Is there any way to make *Morrison* consistent with *Bowsher*? With *Myers*? With *Buckley*? Note that in *Morrison* the Court approved a congressional plan that deprived the President of control over a "core" executive official. Wasn't that a more drastic congressional intrusion upon the separation of powers than plans to deprive the President of control over a postmaster (*Myers*) or even over budget cuts (*Bowsher*) or federal campaign regulation (*Buckley*)? In this instance, the uncontrollable officer was out to get one of the President's own officials—indeed, perhaps even the President himself! One way to reconcile *Morrison* with the earlier precedents is to read all the cases functionally, as Professor Strauss does in the preceding excerpt.

Another way to reconcile them is suggested by Harold Krent, *Executive Control over Criminal Law Enforcement: Some Lessons from History*, 38 Am. U.L. Rev. 275 (1989), who contends that Justice Scalia misstated the historical record supporting the conclusion that criminal prosecutions are "core" executive functions.[72] Instead, Krent notes, the Attorney General did not preside over a core group of prosecutors until the late nineteenth century; in the early history under the Constitution, criminal prosecutions for violating federal laws were carried out by state prosecutors, private citizens, and district attorneys who reported to no one before 1820. Under Krent's reading, the independent counsel might be viewed as an officer not necessarily "executive" for *Myers* purposes.

---

[72] On the historical record, see Susan Low Bloch, *The Early Role of the Attorney General in Our Constitutional Scheme: In the Beginning There Was Pragmatism*, 1989 Duke L.J. 561; Daniel Reisman, *Deconstructing Justice Scalia's Separation of Powers Jurisprudence: The Preeminent Executive*, 53 Alb. L. Rev. 49 (1988); Stephanie Dangel, Note, *Is Prosecution a Core Executive Function?* Morrison v. Olson *and the Framers' Intent*, 99 Yale L.J. 1069 (1990).

Yet another way to read the cases would rely on the principle against self-aggrandizement. Under this principle, Congress itself cannot exercise direct control over officials "executing" the law (*Myers, Buckley,* and *Bowsher*), but it can authorize someone other than the President to control them (*Morrison*). Now consider this reading of *Humphrey's Executor*: Article II gives the President plenary authority over certain "purely executive" functions, but not over all functions that might be classified as "executive." As to those functions, Congress under the Necessary and Proper Clause, Art. I, § 8, cl. 18, and under the Appointments Clause, Art. II, § 2, cl. 2, may exercise some influence, as a corollary of its own Article I authority as the nation's lawmaker. That influence cannot be through a congressional veto of executive action (*Chadha*) or through congressional control of an executive official (*Bowsher*), because of the self-aggrandizement involved. Similarly, that influence cannot be through congressional control over appointments to the commission (*Buckley*), but it can be through an appointments mechanism set up within the executive or judicial branches of government.

2.   *Terminator Risks.* Motivating Chief Justice Rehnquist's opinion is the Richard Nixon problem: If foxes are guarding the henhouse, who will guard the foxes? So Congress created a hound to monitor the foxes. The independence from political interference needed to solve the Richard Nixon problem was also, unfortunately, independence from practical incentives that have traditionally supported the presumption of innocence accorded accused wrongdoers. A former student analogized the independent counsel to *The Terminator*, a movie in which a futuristic robot is programmed to do nothing but hunt down a designated victim. Like the Terminator, the independent counsel was appointed for one purpose and one purpose only—to track down and get the goods on a designated federal official. She would be given lots of money and eager assistants. Her decision whether to prosecute might be skewed by her own status (she goes out of business if she decides not to prosecute) and, more important, by her freedom from the many other factors prosecutors often have to consider (limited resources and executive enforcement priorities). The suspect stood a good chance of being wiped out financially even if never indicted. See Julie O'Sullivan, *The Independent Counsel Statute: Bad Law, Bad Policy*, 33 Am. Crim. L. Rev. 463 (1996).

Also troubling was that the law shifted responsibility for monitoring the President and his assistants from oversight and impeachment by Congress, with its political constituencies, to relentless investigation and exposure by the Independent Counsel.[73] Is this concern ameliorated by the fact that the Independent Counsel (then and now) operated strictly within the prosecutorial guidelines of the Department of Justice and could be removed, for cause, by the Attorney General?

Contrast the public disgraces of Presidents Nixon and Clinton. Nixon's wrongdoing became public through a process by which his own Department of

---

[73] Nourse, *Vertical Separation*, 773–77; Julie O'Sullivan, *The Interaction Between Impeachment and the Independent Counsel Statute*, 86 Geo. L.J. 2193 (1998).

Justice and Congress exposed links between criminal behavior and the White House. He resigned on the eve of impeachment votes that would have ended his presidency. Clinton's wrongdoing, in contrast, became public through a process by which a perceived political enemy (Republican Independent Counsel Kenneth Starr) gathered evidence and turned it over to a hostile House of Representatives, which impeached him (see the Note on Impeachment above). Whatever the merits of Starr's charges, the public was underwhelmed by them, yet Clinton's impeachment and trial occupied the nation's political process for the better part of a year—to the detriment of Congress's doing its Article I, § 7 job.

3. *Neo-Formalism in Separation of Powers Cases.* It is striking how functionalist the Chief Justice's opinion was in the Independent Counsel Case, and how little support Justice Scalia's powerful dissent garnered. Why was that? One reason may be that formalism does not automatically support the Scalia result, for the reasons raised in Note 1. Or it might be ambivalence about formalism's drawbacks. Its reliance on fitting novel arrangements into old categories has a Procrustean ring to it and, according to legal historiographers such as Martin Flaherty, typically relies on "originalist" analysis that is ahistorical or even amateurish.[74] Historians emphasize complexity and evolution; the legal archaeologist seeking categorical evidence tends to want, and therefore to find, simplicity and stability. The mechanical matchmaking (arrangement and category) of the legal archaeologist conveys a potentially misleading objectivity about constitutional law. Finally, one might find formalism simply inconvenient; a thoroughgoing formalism would make a mess of this century's modern regulatory state, says Strauss.

Nonetheless, formalism itself has a kind of Terminator quality to it: It is well-nigh indestructible—just when you think it has been crushed, it rises and renews pursuit. It seemed dead during the New Deal, but made a dramatic comeback in the Steel Seizure Case. Even after the judiciary embraced the functionalism of the Jackson concurrence (as in the Iranian Hostages Case), formalism came back even stronger in *Chadha* and *Bowsher*. Has *Morrison* been any more fatal? Hardly. If anything, *Morrison* reinvigorated formalism in the academy. Legal scholars feasted on the Chief Justice's opinion like famished dieters.[75] Conservative contempt for *Morrison* fueled sympathy for Gary Lawson's proposal that Supreme Court constitutional opinions should generally not count as binding precedent when they are inconsistent with

---

[74] The point is made generally in Martin S. Flaherty, *History "Lite" in Modern American Constitutionalism*, 95 Colum. L. Rev. 523 (1995), and with specific reference to separation of powers debates in Flaherty, *The Most Dangerous Branch*, 105 Yale L.J. 1725 (1996).

[75] See, e.g., Steven G. Calabresi & Kevin H. Rhodes, *The Structural Constitution: Unitary Executive, Plural Judiciary*, 105 Harv. L. Rev. 1153 (1992); Stephen L. Carter, *From Sick Chicken to Synar: The Evolution and Subsequent De-Evolution of the Separation of Powers*, 1987 B.Y.U. L. Rev. 719; Lee Liberman, Morrison v. Olson: *A Formalistic Perspective on Why the Court Was Wrong*, 38 Am. U.L. Rev. 313 (1989); Thomas A. Merrill, *The Constitutional Principle of Separation of Powers*, 1991 Sup. Ct. Rev. 225; Martin Redish & Elizabeth Cisar, *"If Angels Were to Govern": The Need for Pragmatic Formalism in Separation of Powers Theory*, 1992 Duke L.J. 449.

original meaning.[76] (Justice Thomas, not on the Court for *Morrison*, may be sympathetic to the Lawson thesis.) Correspondingly, the Scalia dissent energized a new generation of neo-formalist constitutional scholarship supporting the idea that Article II creates a "unitary executive" branch. Consider an exemplar of scholarship supporting Justice Scalia's approach.

Steven G. Calabresi & Saikrishna B. Prakash, *The President's Power to Execute the Laws*

104 Yale L.J. 541, 663–64 (1994)[77]

The conclusion to the authors' lengthy article sums up their claims: "First, our Constitution creates a trinity of types of governmental powers and personnel [Arts. I–III]. The constitutional text thus forecloses historical arguments for a headless fourth branch of government. Second, the Vesting Clauses of Article II (and Article III) are general grants of power that are explicated (to different degrees) by the subsequent Sections of those Articles. The Executive Power Clause [Art. II, § 1, cl. 1] in particular gives the President the authority to execute federal law.[78] Third, since the President's grant of 'the executive Power' is exclusive, Congress may not create other entities independent of the President and let them exercise his 'executive Power.' Fourth, the hierarchical structure of Article II is further confirmed by the language of the Take Care [Art. II, § 3], Opinions [Art. II, § 2, cl. 1], and Militia [*ibid.*] Clauses. Finally, the Necessary and Proper Clause does not give Congress any power to deviate from the basic constitutional structure. Congress can no more use that Clause to abolish the unitary Executive than it could use it to abolish the states. The pre-ratification history fully supports these understandings, and little in the post-ratification history calls any of this into question. Indeed, there is more post-ratification evidence to support our textual theories. We should not be surprised that the founding generation read the text according to its 'plain meaning.' * * *

"We can now appreciate our Constitution's elegant simplicity. Our grade school and high school civics teachers were right all along: The Constitution separates our federal government into three branches, each exercising one of three types of powers. * * * The Framers and ratifiers consciously and deliberately chose to put one person in charge of executing *all* federal laws."

---

[76] Gary Lawson, *The Constitutional Case Against Precedent*, 17 Harv. J.L. & Pub. Pol'y 23 (1994); accord, Randy E. Barnett, *Trumping Precedent with Original Meaning: Not As Radical As It Sounds*, 22 Const. Comm. 257 (2005); Michael Stokes Paulsen, *The Intrinsically Corrupting Influence of Precedent*, 22 Const. Comm. 289 (2005).

[77] Reprinted by permission of The Yale Law Journal Company and Fred B. Rothman & Company from *The Yale Law Journal*, Vol. 104, pages 541–665.

[78] *Editors' note*: Calabresi and Prakash contrast the Vesting Clause of Article II, which is a *general grant* of "executive Power"—presumably *all* of it, except as taken away elsewhere in the Constitution—with the Vesting Clause of Article I, which is a *limited grant* of "[a]ll legislative Powers *herein granted*." First articulated by Alexander Hamilton and a holding of *Myers*, this Vesting Clause Thesis is also the starting point for Prakash and Ramsey's Foreign Affairs Vesting Clause Thesis discussed in Section 1B.

In subsequent books and articles, the authors have elaborated on the unitary executive thesis. For example, Professor Prakash's *Imperial from the Very Beginning: The Constitution of the Original Executive* 63 (2015) claims historical support for the proposition that "executive power" in the eighteenth century expansively referred to the "execution of federal law, management of foreign affairs, and direction of executive officers." He relies on the broad use of the term "executive power," in contrast to legislative and judicial powers, and maintains that the Executive Vesting Clause has got to mean something a lot broader than the powers listed in Article II. Steven Calabresi and Christopher Yoo, *The Unitary Executive: Presidential Power from Washington to Bush* (2008) maintain that, starting with George Washington, every President has asserted and exercised broad executive authority along the lines suggested in the Calabresi and Prakash article. Generally, there has either been no congressional pushback, or the pushback has been ineffectual.

NOTE ON THE UNITARY EXECUTIVE THESIS

If accepted, the unitary executive thesis might require reconsidering a number of precedents, including *Humphrey's Executor, Clinton v. Jones,* other presidential immunity or privilege cases (surely *Nixon v. Administrator of General Services*), and perhaps even the Iranian Hostages Case—not to mention the Independent Counsel Case. A thesis that cuts against so much conventional wisdom has stimulated a host of responses over the last two decades.[79] As a matter of constitutional *law*, is the unitary executive thesis valid? Consider a few questions:

Does the original meaning of the Executive Vesting Clause support the Calabresi and Prakash argument that the President must control all "administration"? There is evidence that eighteenth and early nineteenth-century American political thought considered day-to-day administration different from higher-level executive decisionmaking. The leading administrative law historian opines that the Constitution's Framers and the First Congress seem "to have had no fixed general idea about the relationship of the President to administration." Jerry L. Mashaw, *Governmental Practice and Presidential Discretion: Lessons from the Antebellum Republic?*, 45 Willamette L. Rev. 659, 668 (2009).

The unitarists respond that there is no evidence that this practice influenced the Framers (Calabresi & Prakash, *President's Power*, 639–63).

---

[79] In addition to the Strauss article excerpted above, see Martin S. Flaherty, *The Most Dangerous Branch*, 105 Yale L.J. 1725 (1996); Jerry L. Mashaw, *Governmental Practice and Presidential Direction: Lessons from the Antebellum Republic?*, 45 Willamette L. Rev. 659 (2009); Peter M. Shane, *The Originalist Myth of the Unitary Executive*, 19 U. Pa. L. Const'l L. 323 (2016). See also Michael Froomkin, *The Imperial Presidency's New Vestments*, 88 Nw. U.L. Rev. 1346 (1994); Abner Greene, *Checks and Balances in an Era of Presidential Lawmaking*, 61 U. Chi. L. Rev. 123 (1993). For additional historical and analytical support for the unitary executive thesis, see Steven G. Calabresi & Kevin H. Rhodes, *The Structural Constitution: Unitary Executive, Plural Judiciary*, 105 Harv. L. Rev. 1153 (1992); Gary Lawson & Guy Seidman, *The Jeffersonian Treaty Clause*, 2006 U. Ill. L. Rev. 1; Prakash & Ramsey, *Executive Power over Foreign Affairs*, 111 Yale L.J. 231.

Does that matter? Indeed, is the Appointments Clause not evidence that the *public meaning* of the Constitution of 1787 distinguished between core "executive" functions and general "administration" of the law. Historians tell us that the framing generation did not conceptualize governance within the three neat categories modern formalists do (Flaherty, *Most Dangerous Branch*, 1756–77). Indeed, state constitutions both before and after 1787 explicitly announced the separation of legislative, executive, and judicial offices and functions—yet the same constitutions recognized the governor's "executive" powers were subject to legislative structuring. See Peter M. Shane, *The Originalist Myth of the Unitary Executive*, 19 U. Pa. J. Const'l L. 323, 344–52 (2016).

William Van Alstyne, *The Role of Congress in Determining Incidental Powers of the President and of the Federal Courts*, Law & Contemp. Probs. 102 (Spring 1976), argues that the Necessary and Proper Clause of Article I gives Congress a role in defining an administrative structure for execution of the laws. Calabresi & Prakash, *President's Power*, 622–26, respond that such a broad reading of the clause was not contemplated by the Framers, who saw it only as giving Congress flexibility as to *means* and not adding to Congress' authorized powers (*ends*). Is Van Alstyne's reading not supported by the plain meaning of the clause, which vests in Congress authority "[t]o make all Laws which shall be necessary and proper for carrying into Execution [1] the foregoing Powers [in Article I], and [2] all other Powers vested by this Constitution in the Government of the United States, or [3] in any Department or Officer thereof." Notice that there are, actually, three Necessary and Proper Clauses—and that Clause 3 explicitly gives Congress authority to make laws that it believes facilitate the President's faithful execution of congressional enactments. See John Mikhail, *The Necessary and Proper Clauses*, 102 Geo. L.J. 1045 (2014) (largely in accord with VanAlstyne).

The first two points rest upon the original meaning and textualist methodology invoked by Professors Calabresi and Prakash. A third argument would be grounded upon precedent and established practice: Since the New Deal, if not before, Congress has established governmental structures that deny the President direct and exclusive control over administration—contrary to the unitary executive thesis. Although Calabresi & Yoo, *Unitary Executive*, demonstrate that Presidents have not acquiesced in this derogation of their power, the matter is too well-established in our constitutional culture for the country to hew closely to a unitary executive. In other words, Justice Scalia's *Morrison* dissent came 50 years too late—and now *Morrison v. Olson* confirms the rejection of the thesis by our constitutional culture. Or does it?

Free Enterprise Fund, Inc. v. Public Company Accounting Oversight Board

561 U.S. 477 (2010)

The Public Company Accounting Oversight Board was created as part of a series of corporate reforms in the Sarbanes-Oxley Act of 2002. The Board is composed of five members appointed by the Securities and Exchange

Commission (SEC). It is a government-created entity with expansive powers to govern an entire industry. Every accounting firm that audits public companies under the securities laws must register with the Board, pay it an annual fee, and comply with its rules and oversight. The Board may inspect registered firms, initiate formal investigations, and issue severe sanctions in its disciplinary proceedings. The parties stipulated that the Board is a government actor and that its members are *Officers of the United States* who exercise significant authority pursuant to the laws of the United States.

Although the SEC oversees the Board, it can remove Board members only "for good cause shown," §§ 7211(e)(6), 7217(d)(3). The Court assumed, by stipulation of the parties, that the SEC's Commissioners, in turn, cannot themselves be removed by the President except for inefficiency, neglect of duty, or malfeasance in office, the standard in *Humphrey's Executor.* Free Enterprise sought to invalidate the Board, on the grounds that these limits on presidential removal authority violate both the constitutional separation of powers and the Appointments Clause, Art. II, § 2, cl. 2.

Delivering the opinion for the Court, **Chief Justice Roberts** ruled that the limits violate Article II's vesting all "executive" authority in the President. The Chief Justice started with the Decision of 1789 and the Court's precedents, namely, *Myers, Humphrey's Executor, Bowsher,* and *Morrison.* "[W]e have previously upheld limited restrictions on the President's removal power. In those cases, however, only one level of protected tenure separated the President from an officer exercising executive power. It was the President—or a subordinate he could remove at will—who decided whether the officer's conduct merited removal under the good-cause standard. The Act before us does something quite different. It not only protects Board members from removal except for good cause, but withdraws from the President any decision on whether that good cause exists. That decision is vested instead in other tenured officers—the Commissioners—none of whom is subject to the President's direct control. The result is a Board that is not accountable to the President, and a President who is not responsible for the Board.

"The added layer of tenure protection makes a difference. Without a layer of insulation between the Commission and the Board, the Commission could remove a Board member at any time, and therefore would be fully responsible for what the Board does. The President could then hold the Commission to account for its supervision of the Board, to the same extent that he may hold the Commission to account for everything else it does. A second level of tenure protection changes the nature of the President's review. Now the Commission cannot remove a Board member at will. The President therefore cannot hold the Commission fully accountable for the Board's conduct, to the same extent that he may hold the Commission accountable for everything else that it does. The Commissioners are not responsible for the Board's actions. They are only responsible for their own determination of whether the Act's rigorous good-cause standard is met. And even if the President disagrees with their determination, he is powerless to intervene—unless that determination is so unreasonable as to constitute 'inefficiency, neglect of duty, or malfeasance in office.' *Humphrey's Executor*.

"This novel structure does not merely add to the Board's independence, but transforms it. Neither the President, nor anyone directly responsible to him, nor even an officer whose conduct he may review only for good cause, has full control over the Board. The President is stripped of the power our precedents have preserved, and his ability to execute the laws—by holding his subordinates accountable for their conduct—is impaired."

Chief Justice Roberts was concerned that the statute raised slippery slope problems. "If Congress can shelter the bureaucracy behind two layers of good-cause tenure, why not a third? At oral argument, the Government was unwilling to concede that even *five* layers between the President and the Board would be too many. The officers of such an agency—safely encased within a Matryoshka doll of tenure protections—would be immune from Presidential oversight, even as they exercised power in the people's name."

The Chief Justice continued: "The diffusion of power carries with it a diffusion of accountability. The people do not vote for the 'Officers of the United States.' They instead look to the President to guide the 'assistants or deputies . . . subject to his superintendence.' *The Federalist* No. 72 (A. Hamilton). Without a clear and effective chain of command, the public cannot 'determine on whom the blame or the punishment of a pernicious measure, or series of pernicious measures ought really to fall.' *Id.*, No. 70. That is why the Framers sought to ensure that 'those who are employed in the execution of the law will be in their proper situation, and the chain of dependence be preserved; the lowest officers, the middle grade, and the highest, will depend, as they ought, on the President, and the President on the community.' 1 Annals of Cong., at 499 (J. Madison).

"One can have a government that functions without being ruled by functionaries, and a government that benefits from expertise without being ruled by experts. Our Constitution was adopted to enable the people to govern themselves, through their elected leaders. The growth of the Executive Branch, which now wields vast power and touches almost every aspect of daily life, heightens the concern that it may slip from the Executive's control, and thus from that of the people. This concern is largely absent from the dissent's paean to the administrative state."

The Chief Justice rejected Free Enterprise's argument that the unconstitutionality of the removal provisions required the Court to rule that the Board itself was unconstitutional and could no longer operate. Instead, following the lenient test described in our earlier Note on Severability, the Court ruled that the unconstitutional provisions insulating the Board members from SEC removal without cause were severable from the provisions creating the Board and vesting it with duties prescribed in the statute. Henceforth, Board members could be removed by the SEC for any reason. The Chief Justice also rejected Free Enterprise's Appointments Clause challenge to the Board's appointment by the SEC. The Court ruled that Board members were "inferior Officers" and that the SEC (which the Court assumed to be an independent agency) was a "Department" for purposes of Article II, § 2, clause 2. Ironically, the Court's opinion declined to cite *Morrison v. Olson* for this proposition.

Justice Breyer (joined by Justices Ginsburg, Sotomayor, and Kagan) dissented. He started with the observation that Congress's structure for the Board violated no specific provision of the Constitution, in contrast to *Chadha*, for example. In deciding whether the Board's structure, and specifically the removal rules, violated the abstract separation of powers principle, judges have no choice but to be guided by the purposes underlying the separation of powers. Applying such a purposive, or functional, approach, Justice Breyer started with a presumption in favor of the practical judgment made by Congress and the President, that the Board's independence from "political" influence was important for its purpose, to restore public faith in the market. When he signed the Sarbanes-Oxley Act into law, President George W. Bush criticized some of its provisions as unwise or unconstitutional but praised the Board's independence.

Additionally, Justice Breyer argued that the Court's remedy in this case did little to solve the separation of powers concerns with this arrangement. Because the SEC was itself an independent agency, the President might still not "control" the Board even if the SEC could remove its members for any reason—because the President could not remove SEC commissioners except "for cause." Because the Court left *Humphrey's Executor* intact, its remedy in *Free Enterprise* was virtually worthless as a matter of political control and accountability. "In other words, the Court fails to show why *two* layers of "for cause" protection—Layer One insulating the Commissioners from the President, and Layer Two insulating the Board from the Commissioners—impose any more serious limitation upon the *President's* powers than *one* layer." To the contrary, in many situations, the two-layer protections would *enhance* the President's authority, for example where the President approved of what the Board is doing while the SEC wanted to discipline it. The Court's "solution" actually increased the authority of the SEC, not the President, to control the Board.

Justice Breyer argued that the SEC had plenty of authority to control the Board under the statute as written. For example, no Accounting Board rule took effect unless and until the Commission approved it, and the SEC might abrogate, delete, or add to any Board rule and may promulgate its own rules "restricting or directing" the Board's activities. Justice Breyer noted the irony that there is nothing in the enabling statute saying or even suggesting that the SEC's members were protected against removal except "for cause." In order to strike down the SEC's controls over the Board, the Court accepted nonstatutory restrictions on the President's ability to control the SEC. Justice Breyer marveled at the Court's willingness to add language to the statute, at the same time it was removing a statutory provision without any basis in the text of the Constitution.

PHH Corp. v. Consumer Financial Protection Bureau

881 F.3d 75 (D.C. Cir. en banc, Jan. 31, 2018)

In the Dodd-Frank Wall Street Reform and Consumer Protection Act of 2010, P.L. 111–203, Congress established the Consumer Financial Protection Bureau (CFPB). The CFPB is a financial regulator that applies a set of preexisting statutes to financial services marketed "primarily for personal, family, or household purposes." 12 U.S.C. § 5481(5)(A); *see also id.* §§ 5481(4), (6), (15). Congress has historically given a modicum of independence to financial regulators like the Federal Reserve, the FTC, and the Office of the Comptroller of the Currency. Rather than a multi-member commission, the CFPB's chief decision-maker is its Director, who is appointed by the President for a five-year term. The Director in 2017 would have seen his term expire in 2018; the next expiration date would be 2023, and so forth. The Director may be fired only for "inefficiency, neglect of duty, or malfeasance in office," 12 U.S.C. § 5491(c)(3)—the same language the Supreme Court approved for the independent commission in *Humphrey's.*

The Director has a considerable amount of authority. He or she sets the agency's general agenda; determines what proposed rules ought to be advanced for public comment; decides whether to issue a final rule, after notice and comment; manages the agency's budget; and accepts or rejects adjudicatory decisions rendered by administrative law judges (ALJs), who conduct the formal hearings and draft proposed orders and decisions. PHH was a company sanctioned by the CFPB, based upon an agency adjudication presided over by an ALJ appointed by the Chief ALJ within the SEC (pursuant to an agreement between the SEC and the CFPB) and applying consumer-protective rules promulgated by the Director. Its main argument was that the order was inconsistent with the regulatory statute, but PHH also argued that the decision-making structure of the agency violated the Constitution's separation of powers and/or Article II.

Speaking for a majority of six judges, **Judge Pillard** authored the opinion for the court. The Court of Appeals was bound by *Humphrey's Executor,* and Judge Pillard found the CFPB constitutionally indistinguishable from the FTC, whose "for cause" removal provision was upheld in that case. The challengers claimed that decision-making by a single Director made the CFPB constitutionally vulnerable, but Judge Pillard found that agency structure "neither unprecedented nor constitutionally significant."

As historical precedents for "sole-headed financial regulators," Judge Pillard cited "the Comptroller of the Treasury, dating back to [1789]; and the Office of the Comptroller of the Currency, established in [1863]. Other examples of single-headed independent agencies included the Social Security Administration, which was placed under a single director in 1994, and the Office of Special Counsel established under a sole director in 1978, the same year as the Office of Independent Counsel upheld in *Morrison.* Judge Pillard distinguished cases like *Myers* on the ground that "the functions of the CFPB and its Director are not core executive functions, such as those entrusted to a

Secretary of State or other Cabinet officer who we assume must directly answer to the President's will. Rather, the CFPB is one of a number of federal financial regulators—including the Federal Trade Commission, the Federal Reserve, the Federal Deposit Insurance Corporation, and others—that have long been permissibly afforded a degree of independence.

In short, Judge Pillard found "nothing constitutionally suspect about the CFPB's leadership structure. *Morrison* and *Humphrey's Executor* stand in the way of any holding to the contrary. And there is no reason to assume an agency headed by an individual will be less responsive to presidential supervision than one headed by a group. It is surely more difficult to fire and replace several people than one. And, if anything, the Bureau's consolidation of regulatory authority that had been shared among many separate independent agencies allows the President more efficiently to oversee the faithful execution of consumer protection laws. Decisional responsibility is clear now that there is one, publicly identifiable face of the CFPB who stands to account—to the President, the Congress, and the people—for all its consumer protection actions. The fact that the Director stands alone atop the agency means he cannot avoid scrutiny through finger-pointing, buck-passing, or sheer anonymity. What is more, in choosing a replacement, the President is unhampered by partisan balance or *ex-officio* requirements; the successor replaces the agency's leadership wholesale. Nothing about the CFPB stands out to give us pause that it—distinct from other financial regulators or independent agencies more generally—is constitutionally defective."

Writing also for Judge Rogers, **Judge Wilkins** wrote a concurring opinion, adding that "removal restrictions of officers performing adjudicatory functions intrude far less on the separation of powers than removal restrictions of officers who perform purely executive functions." Also, Congress created a new entity, the Financial Stability Oversight Council, with veto power over any rule promulgated by the Director that the Council believed would "put the safety and soundness of the United States banking system or the stability of the financial system of the United States at risk." 12 U.S.C. § 5513. Any member of the Council can file a petition to stay or revoke a rule, which can be granted with a two-thirds majority vote. "Thus, if the Director's decisionmaking goes awry on a critical rulemaking, a multi-member body of experts can step in. Significantly, a supermajority of persons on the Council are designated by the President."

Judge Griffith concurred in the judgment of the en banc Court. He opined that *Humphrey's* and *Morrison* were inconsistent with the text and original meaning of Article II, but that only the Supreme Court could overrule those precedents. In any event, he asked an antecedent question: "How difficult is it for the President to remove the Director? The President may remove the CFPB Director for 'inefficiency, neglect of duty, or malfeasance in office.' After reviewing these removal grounds, I conclude they provide only a minimal restriction on the President's removal power, even permitting him to remove the Director for ineffective policy choices. Therefore, I agree that the CFPB's structure does not impermissibly interfere with the President's ability to perform his constitutional duties." If the President's removal authority could be exercised by a finding that the CFPB Director has not been producing the policy desired by the President and his supporters, then the constitutional conflict between the statute and Article II lost most if not all of its edge.

Writing also for Judge Randolph, **Judge (now Justice) Kavanaugh** issued the principal dissenting opinion: "This is a case about executive power and individual liberty," he opened, with a bang. "To prevent tyranny and protect individual liberty, the Framers of the Constitution separated the legislative, executive, and judicial powers of the new national government. To further safeguard liberty, the Framers insisted upon accountability for the exercise of executive power. The Framers lodged full responsibility for the executive power in a President of the United States, who is elected by and accountable to the people. The first 15 words of Article II speak with unmistakable clarity about who controls the executive power: 'The executive Power shall be vested in a President of the United States of America.' U.S. Const. art. II, § 1. And Article II assigns the President alone the authority and responsibility to 'take Care that the Laws be faithfully executed.' *Id.* § 3. The purpose 'of the separation and equilibration of powers in general, and of the unitary Executive in particular, was not merely to assure effective government but to preserve individual freedom.' *Morrison v. Olson* (Scalia, J., dissenting)."

Judge Kavanaugh described the process by which the Court in *Humphrey's Executor* retreated from the unitary executive holding of *Myers v. United States*. *Humphrey's* was read to have ratified the constitutional legitimacy of this "headless fourth branch" of the federal government. "To mitigate the risk to individual liberty, the independent agencies historically have been headed by *multiple* commissioners or board members. In the Supreme Court's words, each independent agency has traditionally been established as a 'body of experts appointed by law and informed by experience.' *Humphrey's Executor*. Multi-member independent agencies do not concentrate all power in one unaccountable individual, but instead divide and disperse power across multiple commissioners or board members. The multi-member structure thereby reduces the risk of arbitrary decisionmaking and abuse of power, and helps protect individual liberty.

"In other words, the heads of *executive* agencies are accountable to and checked by the President; and the heads of *independent* agencies, although not accountable to or checked by the President, are at least accountable to and checked by their fellow commissioners or board members. No independent agency exercising substantial executive authority has ever been headed by *a single person*."

Judge Kavanaugh would draw the constitutional line in this case: "Because the CFPB is an independent agency headed by a single Director and not by a multi-member commission, the Director of the CFPB possesses more unilateral authority—that is, authority to take action on one's own, subject to no check—than any single commissioner or board member in any other independent agency in the U.S. Government. Indeed, other than the President, the Director enjoys more unilateral authority than any other official in any of the three branches of the U.S. Government." Because this structure was, according to Judge Kavanaugh, unprecedented, a direct threat to liberty, and inconsistent with Article II's baseline of agency accountability to the elected President, he would invalidate it.

"In traditional multi-member agencies, the President may designate the chair of the agency, and the President may remove a chair at will from the chair position. (Of course, the President may not remove that official from the commission or board altogether, only from the position as chair.) By contrast, the CFPB has only one Director, and the President may not designate a new Director until the former Director leaves office or the Director's term expires. That structure diminishes the President's power to influence the direction of the CFPB, as compared to the President's power to influence the direction of traditional multi-member independent agencies." Indeed, Judge Kavanaugh argued, the CFPB involves a greater invasion of presidential power than the structure invalidated in *Free Enterprise Fund*.

"[A]s the Supreme Court indicated in *Free Enterprise Fund*, an independent agency's structure violates Article II when it is not historically rooted and when it causes an *additional* diminution of Presidential control beyond that caused by a traditional independent agency. * * * The CFPB's single-Director structure contravenes that diminution principle. As a result of the CFPB's novel single-Director structure and the five-year fixed term for the Director, a President may be stuck for years—or even for his or her entire four-year term—with a single Director who was appointed by a prior President and who has different policy views.

By disabling the President from supervising and directing the Director of the CFPB, the Dodd-Frank Act contravenes the Supreme Court's statement in *Free Enterprise*: "Congress cannot reduce the Chief Magistrate to a cajoler-in-chief." Following the Chief Justice's lead in *Free Enterprise*, Judge Kavanaugh urged his colleagues to strike down the Dodd-Frank "for cause" limitation, but sever it from the remainder of Title X. Thus, the CFPB would continue to operate with a single Director, but he or she would be removable at will by the President.

Judge Henderson wrote a broader dissenting opinion. "If forced to expand the *Humphrey's Executor* exception, I would limit it to an agency that answers in *some* meaningful way to the policy oversight of at least one political branch." The CFPB did not come close to such an agency, because of its budgetary autonomy (freeing it from congressional control) as well as its political autonomy (freeing it from presidential control). Unlike Judge Kavanaugh, Judge Henderson would not have severed that provision from the remainder of Title X, and so her constitutional ruling would abrogate the agency's authority altogether. "Above all else, the 111th Congress wanted the CFPB to be independent: free, that is, from industry influence and the changing political tides that come with accountability to the President. Severing section 5491(c)(3) would yield an executive agency entirely at odds with the legislative design. In my view, the Congress would not have enacted Title X in its current form absent for-cause removal protection. I believe, therefore, that the appropriate remedy for the CFPB's Article II problem is to invalidate Title X in its entirety."

Judge Randolph joined Judge Kavanaugh's dissenting opinion and penned an additional reason for rejecting the result here. After the CFPB's enforcement unit filed a Notice of Charges, an ALJ held a nine-day hearing and issued a recommended decision, concluding that PHH had violated the real estate settlement law. The Director affirmed the ALJ's recommended decision. "I believe the ALJ who presided over the hearing was an 'inferior Officer' within the meaning of Article II, section 2, clause 2 of the Constitution. That constitutional provision requires 'inferior Officers' to be appointed by the President, the 'Courts of Law,' or the 'Heads of Departments.' This ALJ was not so appointed. Pursuant to an agreement between the CFPB and the Securities and Exchange Commission, the SEC's Chief Administrative Law Judge assigned him to the case. In addition to the unconstitutional structure of the CFPB, this violation of the Appointments Clause rendered the proceedings against PHH unconstitutional." Judge Randolph found the case the same as *Freytag v. Commissioner of Internal Revenue*, 501 U.S. 868 (1991).

NOTE: SHOULD THE COURT OVERRULE ONE OF ITS REMOVAL PRECEDENTS?

Should the Supreme Court overrule one of its removal precedents? Professors Calabresi and Yoo argue that *Free Enterprise* frees the Court to overrule *Morrison v. Olson*. See Steven G. Calabresi & Christopher S. Yoo, *Remove* Morrison v. Olson, 62 Vand. L. Rev. En Banc 103 (2012). If it adopted the unitary executive thesis, the Court could also overrule *Humphrey's Executor* and reaffirm *Myers* as the super-precedent. Such a move would have the advantage of bringing coherence and simplicity to the Court's removal jurisprudence. Would it have the disadvantage of being inconsistent with the Appointments Clause? Or good governance?

As an alternative, one might follow Justice Brandeis's *Myers* dissent, which suggests that the Constitution's text answers the removal question. Under the Appointments Clause, U.S. Const., Art. II, § 2, cl. 2, Congress has special latitude in structuring "inferior Officers," such as the postmaster in *Myers*, the FTC Commissioner in *Humphrey's*, the Independent Counsel in *Morrison*, and the SEC Commissioners as well as the Board in *Free Enterprise*. But for "major Officers" such as cabinet officials and top executive branch officials, Congress cannot limit the President's removal authority. General separation of powers principles, such as the anti-aggrandizement one in *Chadha*, suggest the further precept that Congress cannot condition any removal upon the express consent of the Senate or House. Why not adopt the foregoing framework—and confine *Myers* to its facts and overrule *Free Enterprise*?

Another approach is suggested by Kirti Datla & Richard Revesz, *Deconstructing Independent Agencies (and Executive Agencies)*, 98 Cornell L. Rev. 769, 818 (2013). Previous scholars had established that there is no single criterion distinguishing "independent" from "executive" agencies. In practice, all agencies are both influenced by the President's priorities and operate independently of it. Hence, Datla and Revesz would downgrade the distinction between independent and executive agencies. Inconsistent with dicta in *Humphrey's Executor*, they would presumptively treat all agencies as executive ones under the plenary direction of the President—but they would follow and indeed expand *Humphrey's Executor* to allow reasonable, non-aggrandizing congressional limits on presidential control of agencies. Would the Court have to overrule *Myers*? *Free Enterprise*?

PROBLEM 8-8:
PRESIDENTIAL REVIEW OF INDEPENDENT AGENCY RULES

In the last generation, the White House has imposed administrative review by the Office of Information and Regulatory Affairs (OIRA) significant rules propounded by executive agencies. OIRA can veto such rules and typically demands important changes in proposed directives. As you know from *Free Enterprise*, Congress has directed the SEC to issue hundreds of legislative rules, having pervasive effects on American businesses. Previous executive orders have not brought the SEC within OIRA's ambit, presumably because of constitutional concerns with presidential control over independent agencies such as the SEC. Assume that the President wants to expand OIRA review to include these SEC rules. Can he constitutionally exercise this authority over the SEC? Is there a way to do that without overruling *Humphrey's Executor*?

C. CONGRESSIONAL STRUCTURING OF ADJUDICATION

Just as the modern regulatory state has pressed against the limits arguably imposed upon "legislative" and "executive" powers purportedly allocated in Articles I and II, so has it challenged limits arguably imposed on the "judicial Power" in Article III. The core feature of Article III is that the adjudications specified in § 2 be handled (or reviewed) by judges with assurances of independence—namely service for life "during good Behaviour" and with "Compensation, which shall not be diminished during their Continuance in Office" (§ 1).[80] Chapter 9 examines the self-imposed limits the Court has developed from Article III to restrain its own potentially self-aggrandizing exercise of power and the limits placed on Congress's ability to strip Article III courts of jurisdiction. The remainder of this section examines the limits Article III places on Congress: (1) May

---

[80] We do not treat the Good Behaviour and Compensation Clauses in this casebook. They are discussed in *Federalist* Nos. 78 and 79 (Hamilton). Leading cases on each are *United States ex rel. Toth v. Quarles*, 350 U.S. 11 (1955) (Good Behaviour); *United States v. Will*, 449 U.S. 200 (1980) (Compensation).

Congress assign Article III judges extrajudicial tasks? (2) May Congress assign adjudicative tasks to non-Article III judges? (3) Can Congress alter valid Article III judgments?

1.　Assigning Article III Judges Nonjudicial Duties

Mistretta v. United States

488 U.S. 361 (1989)

In the Sentencing Reform Act of 1984, codified as 18 U.S.C. § 3551 *et seq.* and 28 U.S.C. §§ 991–998, Congress created the United States Sentencing Guidelines Commission "as an independent commission in the judicial branch of the United States." 28 U.S.C. § 991(a). It has seven members appointed by the President and confirmed by the Senate. At least three members must be federal judges "selected after considering a list of six judges recommended to the President by the Judicial Conference of the United States." Members of the Commission are subject to removal by the President "only for neglect of duty or malfeasance in office or for other good cause shown."

After upholding the statute's delegation of authority to craft sentencing guidelines (§ 2A of this chapter), the Court rejected arguments that the Commission's composition and placement violated the separation of powers and Article III. **Justice Blackmun**'s opinion for the Court invoked the Nixon Cases and *Federalist* No. 47 (App. 2) for the proposition that "the Framers did not require—and indeed rejected—the notion that the three Branches must be entirely separate and distinct. * * * In a passage now commonplace in our cases, Justice Jackson summarized the pragmatic, flexible view of differentiated governmental power to which we are heir," when he said the Constitution " 'enjoins upon its branches separateness but interdependence, autonomy but reciprocity.' " Steel Seizure Case (Jackson, J., concurring).

"It is this concern of encroachment and aggrandizement that has animated our separation-of-powers jurisprudence and aroused our vigilance against the 'hydraulic pressure inherent within each of the separate Branches to exceed the outer limits of its power.' Buckley v. Valeo. Accordingly, we have not hesitated to strike down provisions of law that either accrete to a single Branch powers more appropriately diffused among separate Branches or that undermine the authority and independence of one or another coordinate Branch. * * * Bowsher; Chadha. By the same token, we have upheld statutory provisions that to some degree commingle the functions of the Branches, but that pose no danger of either aggrandizement or encroachment. Morrison." Three issues were discussed: (1) the location of the Commission within the judicial branch, (2) the assignment of nonjudicial duties to Article III judges, and (3) excessive presidential control.

1.　*The Location-of-the-Commission Issue.* To "ensure the independence of the Judicial Branch by precluding debilitating entanglements between the Judiciary and the two political Branches, and prevent the Judiciary from encroaching into areas reserved for the other Branches," the Court has refused to allow judges to issue advisory opinions or handle matters that are not justiciable (see Chapter 9, § 1). In *Morrison*, the Court repeated what it first said in *Buckley*, that " 'executive or administrative duties of a nonjudicial nature may not be imposed on judges holding office under Art. III.' "

But there is a "twilight area" in which the activities of the separate branches might properly overlap—including rulemaking authority for federal rules governing procedure ceded by Congress to the Supreme Court. *Sibbach v. Wilson & Co.*, 312 U.S. 1 (1941), construing the Rules Enabling Act, 28 U.S.C. § 2072. "[C]onsistent with the separation of powers, Congress may delegate to the Judicial Branch nonadjudicatory functions that do not trench upon the prerogatives of another Branch and are appropriate to the central mission of the Judiciary," pursuant to its powers under the Necessary and Proper Clause. See *Wayman v. Southard*, 23 U.S. (10 Wheat.) 1 (1825) (Marshall, C.J.). Justice Blackmun concluded that Congress had not vested in the judicial branch any powers more appropriately performed by other branches—sentencing is, after all, primarily a judicial function, despite the role of the executive branch in investigating the defendant and proposing sentences. Thus, the power to create rules for sentencing was found sufficiently similar to the longstanding power to create rules for practice and procedure to sustain Congress' discretion to place the Commission in the judicial branch of government.

Mistretta argued that the sentencing guidelines are *substantive,* in contrast to the *procedural* nature of prior judicial rulemaking. "Although the Guidelines are intended to have substantive effects on public behavior (as do the rules of procedure), they do not bind or regulate the primary conduct of the public or vest in the Judicial Branch the legislative responsibility for establishing minimum and maximum penalties for every crime. They do no more than fetter the discretion of sentencing judges to do what they have done for generations—impose sentences within the broad limits established by Congress. Given their limited reach, the special role of the Judicial Branch in the field of sentencing, and the fact that the Guidelines are promulgated by an independent agency and not a court, it follows that as a matter of 'practical consequences' the location of the Sentencing Commission within the Judicial Branch simply leaves with the Judiciary what long has belonged to it."

2.   *The Extralegal-Job-for-Judges Issue.* Although the Court found the requirement of judicial service on the Commission "somewhat troublesome," it ruled that such participation did not interfere with the independent functioning of the judiciary. In light of the Incompatibility Clause prohibiting certain kinds of extralegislative service by Members of Congress (Art. I, § 6, cl. 2), Justice Blackmun found it significant that the Constitution did not limit extrajudicial service by federal judges, a matter that was debated, inconclusively, at the Philadelphia Convention.

Remarkably, the first three Chief Justices also served in other capacities during their judicial terms: John Jay as Ambassador to England (where he negotiated the infamous Jay Treaty), Oliver Ellsworth as Minister to France, and John Marshall as Secretary of State (briefly overlapping with his initial service as Chief Justice) and member of the Sinking Fund Commission—all positions requiring Senate confirmation. Although some objected to Jay's double service, their objections were rebuffed in the Senate, as they had been at the Philadelphia Convention. "[A]t a minimum, both the Executive and Legislative Branches acquiesced in the assumption of extrajudicial duties by judges. * * * This contemporaneous practice by the Founders themselves is significant evidence that the constitutional principle of separation of powers does not absolutely prohibit extrajudicial service." After the founding period, federal judges have frequently performed nonjudicial roles with the consent of the political branches. Judicial service on the Sentencing Commission was similar to prior service that had been ratified by history and political acquiescence and shown not to undermine the independence of the judiciary.

Because the "legitimacy of the Judicial Branch ultimately depends on its reputation for impartiality and nonpartisanship," the Court was "somewhat more troubled by [Mistretta's] argument that the Judiciary's entanglement in the political work of the Commission undermines public confidence in the disinterestedness of the Judicial Branch." Still, the Court rejected this challenge, too, because "the Sentencing Commission is devoted exclusively to the development of rules to rationalize a process that has been and will continue to be performed exclusively by the Judicial Branch. In our view, this is an essentially neutral endeavor and one in which judicial participation is peculiarly appropriate."

3. *The Presidential-Control-Power Issue.* The Court also concluded that the President's power to appoint and remove for cause did not threaten judicial independence. The appointment power might be used as a carrot to get judges to do the President's bidding, but the President already has a better carrot in his ability to elevate lower federal judges to higher judicial positions, ultimately to the Supreme Court. The removal power, but only for cause, "poses a similarly negligible threat to judicial independence," because a judge removed from the Commission would retain her Article III job. *Bowsher* was a different case, as it involved self-aggrandizement: "Congress was accreting to itself," and not giving away, "the power to control the functions of another Branch."

Justice Scalia, in another solo dissent, objected that the problem with the statute was not a commingling of functions, but the creation of a whole new branch of government, "a sort of junior-varsity Congress." He argued that "because the scope of delegation is largely uncontrollable by the courts, we must be particularly rigorous in preserving the Constitution's structural restrictions that deter excessive delegation. The major one, it seems to me, is that the power to make law cannot be exercised by anyone other than Congress, except in conjunction with the lawful exercise of executive or judicial power.

"The whole theory of *lawful* congressional 'delegation' is not that Congress is sometimes too busy or too divided and can therefore assign its responsibility of making law to someone else; but rather that a certain degree of discretion, and thus of lawmaking, *inheres* in most executive or judicial action, and it is up to Congress, by the relative specificity or generality of its statutory commands, to determine—up to a point—how small or how large that degree shall be. Thus, the courts could be given the power to say precisely what constitutes a 'restraint of trade,' or to adopt rules of procedure, or to prescribe by rule the manner in which their officers shall execute their judgments, because that 'lawmaking' was ancillary to their exercise of judicial powers. * * * Or to take examples closer to the case before us: Trial judges could be given the power to determine what factors justify a greater or lesser sentence within the statutorily prescribed limits because that was ancillary to their exercise of the judicial power of pronouncing sentence upon individual defendants. * * *

"The lawmaking function of the Sentencing Commission is completely divorced from any responsibility for execution of the law or adjudication of private rights under the law. * * * The power to make law at issue here, in other words, is not ancillary but quite naked. The situation is no different in principle from what would exist if Congress gave the same power of writing sentencing laws to a congressional agency such as the General Accounting Office, or to members of its staff.

"The delegation of lawmaking authority to the Commission is, in short, unsupported by any legitimating theory to explain why it is not a delegation of legislative power. * * * The only governmental power the Commission possesses is the power to make law; and it is not the Congress." Justice Scalia found "no place within our constitutional system for an agency created by Congress to exercise no governmental power other than the making of laws.

"Today's decision follows the regrettable tendency of our recent separation-of-powers jurisprudence to treat the Constitution as though it were no more than a generalized prescription that the functions of the Branches should not be commingled too much—how much is too much to be determined, case-by-case, by this Court. * * * In designing [the constitutional] structure, the framers *themselves* considered how much commingling was, in the generality of things, acceptable, and set forth their conclusions in the document."

NOTE ON MISTRETTA AND JUNIOR VARSITY LAWMAKERS

The Sentencing Commission was the next step, after the Independent Counsel and the quasi-legislative FTC, in the sort of functional commingling tolerated by pragmatic theories of separation of powers, such as Professor Strauss's (§ 2B). This time, however, the independent agency was "placed" in the judicial branch, although it otherwise looked just like an executive branch agency: The Commissioners were appointed and could be removed by the President, the Attorney General and the Chair of the U.S. Parole Commission were ex officio members, and the guidelines were expected to have legal force much like those promulgated by executive and quasi-legislative agencies.[81] The President's essential control over this matter was potentially troubling, because it vested the prosecutorial and sentencing functions in the same hands. How would a unitary executive theorist, such as Steven Calabresi or Saikrishna Prakash, evaluate this arrangement? Are there functional concerns sufficient to disturb a pragmatist like Strauss?

An originalist concern arises from the parallel between the Sentencing Commission and the proposed and rejected Council of Revision. At the Philadelphia Convention, a Council of Revision, consisting of members of the judicial and executive branches, was proposed as an organ to veto legislation passed by both chambers of Congress. The Council was rejected, as an "improper coalition between the Executive and the Judiciary." Was the Sentencing Commission a similarly "improper coalition" between the two branches? On the other hand, a proposal to prohibit Supreme Court Justices from holding other offices was made at the Philadelphia Convention but was never reported out of the Committee of Detail. See Lewis Liman, Note, *The Constitutional Infirmities of the United States Sentencing Commission*, 96 Yale L.J. 1363, 1379 n.120 (1987) (arguing against the Sentencing Commission).

2.   Assigning Adjudicative Tasks to Non-Article III Judges

One problem addressed by the modern regulatory state has been the insufficiency of traditional adjudication as a way of resolving many cases and controversies. For example, the states in the early twentieth century shifted workplace injury cases from common law courts to state workers' compensation agencies, which were considered more reliable, efficient, and expert forums for handling these claims. The federal government in the first third of the century created federal agencies which conducted formal adjudications affecting the rights of private parties. For example, the Interstate Commerce Commission was transformed into an essentially adjudicatory body, where rates and service requirements were hashed out in a trial-like setting, but within an agency (not a court) and presided over by hearing examiners (not Article III judges).

In response, private interests argued that they had a constitutional right to have their claims adjudicated by the independent Article III judiciary, and not by civil servants without constitutional assurances of independence. The Supreme Court rejected these arguments in *Crowell v. Benson*, 285 U.S. 22 (1932), holding that agencies adjudicating regulatory claims were essentially handling matters of "public rights," and not simply "private rights." Hence, Congress ought to have flexibility to send these controversies to special Article I tribunals. Decided on the eve of the New Deal, *Crowell* was a magna carta for agency adjudications, which

---

[81]   Relying on the Sixth Amendment, the Court has ruled that the Sentencing Guidelines are not legally binding on sentencing judges. See *United States v. Booker*, 543 U.S. 220 (2005).

proliferated in the expanding regulatory state. The Court reaffirmed and expanded upon *Crowell* in *Glidden v. Zdanok*, 370 U.S. 530 (1962), which held that judges on the Court of Customs and Patent Appeals were essentially Article I creations and therefore did not have to have the life tenure and protection against wage cuts assured to Article III judges. Consider the recent cases in light of further congressional innovations and the separation of powers jurisprudence developed in this chapter.

Northern Pipeline Co. v. Marathon Pipe Line Co.

458 U.S. 50 (1982)

The Bankruptcy Reform Act of 1978 established new Bankruptcy Courts in each federal judicial district. Bankruptcy judges—appointed for 14-year terms, removable under specified conditions, and with no protection against salary diminution—had plenary jurisdiction over all civil proceedings arising under the Bankruptcy Act, which meant that Article I judges would be adjudicating not just federal regulatory claims, but also state law issues.[82] The Court invalidated the statute insofar as it empowered Article I judges to resolve contract disputes.

Justice Brennan delivered the judgment of the Court, but only three other Justices joined his plurality opinion. Article III, § 1, seems to prohibit the vesting of *any* judicial functions with officials who are not Article III judges having life tenure and salary protection. Following historical practice revealing negligible threats to separation of powers concerns, the Court has recognized three exceptions to Article III's rule: territorial courts, e.g., *American Ins. Co. v. Canter*, 1 Pet. 511 (1828); courts-martial, e.g., *Dynes v. Hoover*, 20 How. 65 (1857); and courts that adjudicate certain disputes concerning "public rights," e.g., *Crowell v. Benson*. The public rights doctrine "extends only to matters arising 'between the Government and persons subject to its authority in connection with the performance of the constitutional functions of the executive or legislative departments,' *Crowell*, and only to matters that historically could have been determined exclusively by those departments. * * * In contrast, 'the liability of one individual to another under the law as defined,' *Crowell*, is a matter of private rights," that *must* be heard by Article III tribunals, for they "lie at the core of the historically recognized judicial power."

Defining "private rights" to include contract rights, grounded in state common law, independent of the federal regulatory statute, Justice Brennan concluded that bankruptcy judges were assigned adjudicatory tasks that could only be given to Article III judges and, therefore, were created in derogation of Article III. That the bankruptcy judges' factfinding was reviewable by an

---

[82] The 1978 Act required the judges to interpret contracts involving the bankrupt under state law, and then to modify the rights of the parties along lines directed by the new federal law, as part of Congress' chosen method for restructuring debtor-creditor relations. On the 1978 Act and its constitutional problems, see Thomas Krattenmaker, *Article III and Judicial Independence: Why the New Bankruptcy Courts Are Unconstitutional*, 70 Geo. L.J. 297 (1981).

Article III judge did not save the statute. While Congress has discretion to assign factfinding functions to an administrative adjunct created to aid in the adjudication of congressionally created rights (*Crowell*), it has less discretion when the underlying rights are not created by Congress, such as state common law and federal constitutional rights. See Steel Seizure Case (Frankfurter, J., concurring).

Justices Rehnquist and **O'Connor** concurred only in the Court's judgment. They believed that the lawsuit before them, essentially raising only state law claims, was one that non-Article III courts had never exercised jurisdiction over, and so that kind of lawsuit could not be heard by the new bankruptcy courts. Writing for three Justices, **Justice White** dissented.

Commodity Futures Trading Commission v. Schor

478 U.S. 833 (1986)

The Commodity Exchange Act (as interpreted by the Court) empowered the Commodity Futures Trading Commission (CFTC) to entertain state law counterclaims in adjudicatory proceedings in which disgruntled customers sought compensation from professional commodity brokers for the brokers' violation of the statute or CFTC regulations. **Justice O'Connor**'s opinion for the Court held that this delegation of adjudicatory authority over state law counterclaims did not violate the core purposes of Article III.

Justice O'Connor followed the pragmatic approach of the Court's decision in *Thomas v. Union Carbide Agricultural Products Co.*, 473 U.S. 568 (1985) (upholding a statutory requirement shifting private disputes from Article III courts to binding arbitration) and not the formalist approach of the *Northern Pipeline* plurality: " '[P]ractical attention to substance rather than doctrinaire reliance on formal categories should inform application of Article III,' " she ruled, quoting *Thomas*. Thus, the inquiry turned on the purposes of Article III.

"Article III, § 1, serves both to protect 'the role of the independent judiciary within the constitutional scheme of tripartite government,' *Thomas*, and to safeguard litigants' 'right to have claims decided before judges who are free from potential domination by other branches of government.' Although our cases have provided us with little occasion to discuss the nature or significance of this latter safeguard, our prior discussions of Article III, § 1's guarantee of an independent and impartial adjudication by the federal judiciary of matters within the judicial power of the United States intimated that this guarantee serves to protect primarily personal rather than structural interests. *Northern Pipeline* (Rehnquist, J., concurring in the judgment); *id.* (White, J., dissenting).

"Our precedents also demonstrate, however, that Article III does not confer on litigants an absolute right to the plenary consideration of every nature of claim by an Article III court. See, e.g., *Thomas*; *Crowell*. Moreover, as a personal right, Article III's guarantee of an impartial and independent federal adjudication is subject to waiver, just as are other personal constitutional rights that dictate the procedures by which civil and criminal matters must be tried." The Court held that Schor had waived his right to Article III adjudication of counterclaims against him by electing to proceed before the CFTC rather than suing the broker in federal district court, where he had a private right of action."

The structural interest served by Article III—assurance of the integrity of the Judicial Branch, *Northern Pipeline* (plurality)—could not be waived by the parties, of course. Again, Justice O'Connor insisted that the Court would not "adopt formalistic and unbending rules" that "might also unduly constrict Congress' ability to take needed and innovative action pursuant to its Article I powers. Thus, in reviewing Article III challenges, we have weighed a number of factors, [namely,] the extent to which the 'essential attributes of judicial power' are reserved to Article III courts, and, conversely, the extent to which the non-Article III forum exercises the range of jurisdiction and powers normally vested only in Article III courts, the origins and importance of the right to be adjudicated, and the concerns that drove Congress to depart from the requirements of Article III. See, e.g., *Thomas*; *Northern Pipeline*. * * *

"The CFTC, like the agency in *Crowell*, deals only with a 'particularized area of law,' whereas the jurisdiction of the bankruptcy courts found unconstitutional in *Northern Pipeline* extended broadly to 'all civil proceedings arising under title 11 or arising in or *related to* cases under title 11.' CFTC orders, like those of the agency in *Crowell*, but unlike those of the bankruptcy courts under the 1978 Act, are enforceable only by order of the district court. CFTC orders are also reviewed under the same 'weight of the evidence' standard sustained in *Crowell*, rather than the more deferential standard found lacking in *Northern Pipeline*. The legal rulings of the CFTC, like the legal determinations of the agency in *Crowell*, are subject to *de novo* review. Finally, the CFTC, unlike the bankruptcy courts under the 1978 Act, does not exercise 'all ordinary powers of district courts,' and thus may not, for instance, preside over jury trials or issue writs of habeas corpus."

Although the nature of the private right was owed some weight in the balance, it was negligible in this case, because of (1) the choice Schor had in going to the CFTC rather than federal court to press his statutory claims, per se evidence that Congress was not trying to displace Article III tribunals with administrative ones; (2) the obvious efficiency reasons for allowing the CFTC to adjudicate ancillary state claims, and the tight fit between this limited authority to hear counterclaims and the statutory purpose (the counterclaims must arise out of the same transaction or occurrence as the federal statutory claim); and (3) the dearth of evidence that Congress was trying either to aggrandize its own power or diminish the power of the independent judiciary.

Justice Brennan spoke for only two dissenters, defending the approach he developed in *Northern Pipeline*. "The Court requires that the legislative interest in convenience and efficiency be weighed against the competing interest in judicial independence. In doing so, the Court pits an interest the benefits of which are immediate, concrete, and easily understood against one, the benefits of which are almost entirely prophylactic, and thus often seem remote and not worth the cost in any single case. Thus, while this balancing creates the illusion of objectivity and ineluctability, in fact the result was foreordained, because the balance is weighted against judicial independence. The danger of the Court's balancing approach is, of course, that as individual cases accumulate in which the Court finds that the short-term benefits of efficiency outweigh the long-term benefits of judicial independence, the protections of Article III will be eviscerated."

NOTE ON SCHOR

After *Schor,* the Court seems committed to a balancing approach that is highly deferential to congressional judgments about the value of administrative, rather than judge-based, adjudication. See also Richard Fallon, *Of Legislative Courts, Administrative Agencies and Article III*, 101 Harv. L. Rev. 915 (1988). Note the contrast between the deferential balancing approach the Court has taken to Article III in *Mistretta* and *Schor,* and the nondeferential, rule-based approach the Court has taken in cases where Congress has allegedly invaded turf claimed by the President (*Myers* and *Free Enterprise*) or the states (the post-*Lopez* federalism cases). See Steven G. Calabresi, *Separation of Powers and the Rehnquist Court: The Centrality of Clinton v. City of New York*, 99 Nw. U.L. Rev. 77 (2004). Why has the Court taken such different approaches to enforcing structural guarantees? Consider yet another example of a deferential approach.

Ex Parte Quirin

317 U.S. 1 (1942)

The defendants, one American citizen and several aliens, were convicted by Article II military tribunals of violating the law of war. The defendants, "being enemies of the United States and acting for * * * the German Reich, a belligerent enemy nation, secretly and covertly passed, in civilian dress, contrary to the law of war, through the military and naval lines and defenses of the United States * * * for the purpose of committing * * * hostile acts, and, in particular, to destroy certain war industries, war utilities and war materials within the United States." They brought a writ of habeas corpus objecting to the constitutionality of the tribunals and procedures under which they were convicted and sentenced to death. **Chief Justice Stone**'s opinion for the Court ruled that the writ was properly before the Court and that military commission decisions could be set aside by courts on habeas petition when there is "clear conviction that they are in conflict with the Constitution or laws of Congress constitutionally enacted." Even during war, the courts have a duty "to preserve unimpaired the constitutional safeguards of civil liberty." On the merits, however, the Chief Justice ruled the convictions to have been validly obtained.

Articles of War adopted by statute authorized the President to establish "military commissions * * * appointed by military command as an appropriate tribunal for the trial and punishment of offenses against the law of war not ordinarily tried by court martial." [Article 16.] The President was also authorized to establish procedures for those commissions. "By universal agreement and practice, the law of war draws a distinction between the armed forces and the peaceful populations of belligerent nations and also between those who are lawful and unlawful combatants. Lawful combatants are subject to capture and detention as prisoners of war by opposing military forces. Unlawful combatants are likewise subject to capture and detention, but in addition they are subject to trial and punishment by military tribunals for acts which render their belligerency unlawful. The spy who secretly and without uniform passes the military lines of a belligerent in time of war, seeking to gather military information and communicate it to the enemy, or an enemy combatant who without uniform comes secretly through the lines for the purpose of waging war by destruction of life or property, are familiar examples of belligerents who are generally deemed not to be entitled to the status of prisoners of war, but to be offenders against the law of war subject to trial and punishment by military tribunals." This was the practice of the United States before the adoption of the Constitution, throughout the nineteenth century, and during World War I.

"By a long course of practical administrative construction by its military authorities, our Government has likewise recognized that those who during time of war pass surreptitiously from enemy territory into our own, discarding their uniforms upon entry, for the commission of hostile acts involving destruction of life or property, have the status of unlawful combatants punishable as such by military commission." The Court found that defendants' conduct fell within this violation of the law of war. That one of the defendants was an American citizen "does not relieve him from the consequences of a belligerency which is unlawful because in violation of the law of war. Citizens who associate themselves with the military arm of the enemy government, and with its aid, guidance and direction enter this country bent on hostile acts are enemy belligerents within the meaning of the Hague Convention and the law of war." The American defendant objected that his conviction was inconsistent with *Ex parte Milligan*, 71 U.S. (4 Wall.) 2 (1866), a Civil War case where the Court ruled that the law of war "can never be applied to citizens in states which have upheld the authority of the government, and where the courts are open and their process unobstructed." The Court distinguished *Milligan* as a case where the defendant had no association with the armed forces of a belligerent.

Defendants also contended that they had been convicted without grand jury indictment or a jury trial on the issues of fact, as required by the Fifth and Sixth Amendments. The Court ruled that these constitutional guarantees were "procedures unknown to military tribunals," at the time of the nation's founding. "Section 2 of the Act of Congress of April 10, 1806, 2 Stat. 371, derived from the Resolution of the Continental Congress of August 21, 1776, imposed the death penalty on alien spies 'according to the law and usage of nations, by sentence of a general court martial'. This enactment must be regarded as a contemporary construction of both Article III, and the Amendments as not foreclosing trial by military tribunals, without a jury, of offenses against the law of war committed by enemies not in or associated with our Armed Forces. It is a construction of the Constitution which has been followed since the founding of our government, and is now continued in the 82nd Article of War. Such a construction is entitled to the greatest respect."

Finally, the Court addressed the seeming inconsistency between the summary procedures of the commissions and several of the Articles of War enacted by Congress. "We need not inquire whether Congress may restrict the power of the Commander in Chief to deal with enemy belligerents. For the Court is unanimous in its conclusion that the Articles in question could not at any stage of the proceedings afford any basis for issuing the writ. But a majority of the full Court are not agreed on the appropriate grounds for decision. Some members of the Court are of opinion that Congress did not intend the Articles of War to govern a Presidential military commission convened for the determination of questions relating to admitted enemy invaders and that the context of the Articles makes clear that they should not be construed to apply in that class of cases. Others are of the view that—even though this trial is subject to whatever provisions of the Articles of War Congress has in terms made applicable to 'commissions'—the particular Articles in question, rightly construed, do not foreclose the procedure prescribed by the President or that shown to have been employed by the Commission in a trial of offenses against the law of war and the 81st and 82nd Articles of War, by a military commission appointed by the President."

Historical Notes. *Quirin* was heard under an expedited schedule, and the Court delivered its judgment affirming the defendants' sentences immediately. The written opinion, excerpted above, was delivered several months after the saboteurs had been executed. Chief Justice Stone and his colleagues found the result somewhat harder to justify on paper than they had anticipated, and his opinion for the Court went through several drastic revisions. Some Justices were disturbed by the haste and post-hoc rationalization features of this case. For an excellent account, see David Danelski, *The Saboteurs' Case*, 1996 J. Sup. Ct. Hist. 61 (1996).

For a different historical perspective, consider Logan Beirne, *Blood of Tyrants: George Washington and the Forging of the Presidency* ch. 24 (2013), who demonstrates that George Washington, the Commander in Chief of the Revolutionary Army, used a military commission to try and execute Major John André, a British spy who conspired with Benedict Arnold to turn over West Point to the British. Washington's action was in conflict with an explicit directive from the Continental Congress. Does this historical precedent suggest a constitutional argument that President Roosevelt had independent Article II authority to create and operate the *Quirin* commission? Beirne also reports that, consistent with congressional directives, Washington tried an accused *American* conspirator (Joshua Hett Smith) through a regular court-martial. *Id.* ch. 25. (Smith was acquitted, to the surprise of all.) Does this early precedent suggest that the American conspirator in *Quirin* ought not have been summarily tried by military commission?

Lucia v. Securities and Exchange Commission

138 S.Ct. 2044 (2018)

One way the SEC administers the nation's securities laws is by instituting an administrative proceeding against an alleged wrongdoer. Typically, the Commission delegates the task of presiding over such a proceeding to one of the agency's ALJs, all selected by the agency's staff and not appointed by the Commission. An ALJ assigned to hear an SEC enforcement action has the "authority to do all things necessary and appropriate" to ensure a "fair and orderly" adversarial proceeding. 17 C.F.R. §§ 201.111, 200.14(a). After a hearing ends, the ALJ issues an initial decision. The Commission can review that decision, but if it opts against review, it issues an order that the initial decision has become final. See § 201.360(d). The initial decision is then "deemed the action of the Commission." 15 U.S.C. § 78d–1(c).

Raymond Lucia was charged with violating certain securities laws. ALJ Cameron Elliot conducted the hearing and issued an initial decision concluding that Lucia had violated the law and imposing sanctions. On appeal to the SEC, Lucia objected that the ALJ was an "Officer of the United States" who had not been properly appointed. The SEC disagreed and ruled that an ALJ is just an "employee" of the agency, not an "Officer." Under Supreme Court precedent, to qualify as an Officer, rather than an employee, an individual must occupy a "continuing" position established by law and must "exercis[e] significant authority pursuant to the laws of the United States."

In *Freytag v. Commissioner,* 501 U.S. 868 (1991), the Supreme Court applied this framework to "special trial judges" (STJs) of the United States Tax Court. STJs could issue the final decision of the Tax Court in "comparatively narrow and minor matters." In major matters, they could preside over the hearing but could not issue a final decision. Instead, they were to "prepare proposed findings and an opinion" for a regular Tax Court judge to consider. The proceeding challenged in *Freytag* was a major one. The losing parties argued on appeal that the STJ who presided over their hearing was not constitutionally appointed.

Freytag held that STJs were Officers for purposes of the Appointments Clause. Such persons occupied a "continuing office established by law" and exercised "significant" authority" pursuant to the laws of the United States. The Tax Court argued that STJs were employees in all cases in which they could not enter a final decision. But the focus on finality "ignore[d] the significance of the duties and discretion that [STJs] possess." STJs "take testimony, conduct trials, rule on the admissibility of evidence, and have the power to enforce compliance with discovery orders. * * * [I]n the course of carrying out these important functions," STJs "exercise significant discretion."

Agreeing with Lucia, **Justice Kagan**'s opinion for the Court followed *Freytag* and ruled that the SEC's ALJs are "Officers" who had to be appointed by one of the bodies listed in the Appointments Clause. Like the Tax Court's STJs, the SEC's ALJs hold a continuing office established by law. SEC ALJs "receive[ ] a career appointment," 5 C.F.R. § 930.204(a), to a position created by statute, see 5 U.S.C. §§ 556–557, 5372, 3105. And they exercise the same "significant discretion" when carrying out the same "important functions" as STJs do. Both sets of officials have all the authority needed to ensure fair and orderly adversarial hearings—indeed, nearly all the tools of federal trial judges. The Commission's ALJs, like the Tax Court's STJs, "take testimony," "conduct trials," "rule on the admissibility of evidence," and "have the power to enforce compliance with discovery orders." So point for point from *Freytag*'s list, SEC ALJs have equivalent duties and powers as STJs in conducting adversarial inquiries.[83]

Moreover, at the close of those proceedings, SEC ALJs issue decisions much like that in *Freytag*. STJs prepare proposed findings and an opinion adjudicating charges and assessing tax liabilities. Similarly, the Commission's ALJs issue initial decisions containing factual findings, legal conclusions, and appropriate remedies. And what happens next reveals that the ALJ can play the more autonomous role. In a major Tax Court case, a regular Tax Court judge must always review an STJ's opinion, and that opinion comes to nothing unless the regular judge adopts it. By contrast, the SEC can decide against reviewing an ALJ's decision, and when it does so the ALJ's decision itself "becomes final" and is "deemed the action of the Commission."

Writing also for Justices Ginsburg and Sotomayor, **Justice Breyer** would have resolved the case on statutory rather than constitutional grounds. Dissenting, **Justice Sotomayor** (joined by Justice Ginsburg) would have interpreted the "significant authority" requirement to exclude agency personnel (such as the SEC ALJs) who did not have the authority to issue final, binding decisions.

3.   Congressional Attempts to Alter Valid Article III Judgments

[This topic is examined in Chapter 9, § 4. See the excerpts and notes for *Plaut v. Spendthrift Farm, Inc.*, 514 U.S. 211 (1996).]

SECTION 3. SEPARATION OF POWERS, DUE PROCESS, RELIGION, AND THE WAR ON TERROR

Philip Bobbitt, *Terror and Consent: The Wars for the Twenty-First Century* (2008)

Professor Bobbitt has served as a foreign policy or national security adviser in the administrations of six Presidents. *Terror and Consent* is a synthesis of constitutionalism, political history, and practical executive experience that provides some valuable lessons for understanding the constitutional separation of powers showdowns between the Bush 45, Obama,

---

[83] The Supreme Court's opinion vindicates the point of law made by Judge Randolph's dissenting opinion in *PHH Corp. v. CFPB*, excerpted above.

and Trump Administrations and civil libertarians that have followed the terrorist attacks on the World Trade Center and the Pentagon on 9/11/2001. (The cases and notes that follow will give the student a chronology of legal events that accompany the American response, loosely termed our "War Against Terrorism.") Consider several themes of Bobbitt's book.

The New Face of War (Chapter 1 of *Terror and Consent*). Western civilization has always faced "terrorism," or unconventional violent tactics for assaulting superior conventional forces. Different eras have known different kinds of terrorists, from the mercenaries of the Renaissance to the pirates of the early modern period to the national liberation movements of the twentieth century. In each era, terrorism represents an attempted disruption of the dominant form of constitutionalism, while at the same time mimicking its structure and characteristics. The current era is that of the *market state*. In contrast to the nation state, which advances the collective goals of a self-identified cohesive national community, the market state creates conditions conducive to individual self-fulfillment. The former is centralized, the latter decentralized, like a market. The terrorism characteristic of our current age (e.g., al Qaeda or the Islamic State) rejects the consumerism and materialism of the market state, but its characteristic structure mimics that state: decentralized and networked.

In this brave new world of stateless networked terrorism, it is hard to know who the "enemy" is. In nation-state war, the typical prisoner was easy to identify as the enemy, and he was entitled to decent treatment under the Geneva Conventions of 1949, but few judicial protections under the Constitution; in the war on terror, the typical prisoner is someone the United States *suspects* is a collaborator with a designated terrorist organization. The state would like to treat him worse that it treats POWs, in order to find out where his allegiance lies and to uncover other cells, but such a stance is morally vulnerable because of the risk that the detainee is actually an innocent bystander.

The Rule of Law as a Limitation and a Weapon in the War on Terror (Chapters 4 & 7). Bobbitt characterizes the United States and its allies as *states of consent*. Not only is the government accountable to We the People and so is vigorous in protecting our security, but the government is accountable to the rule of law and so is vigorous in setting forth bright-line rules that we all must obey, including government actors. Terrorism is the opposite: "*Terrorism is the pursuit of political goals through the use of violence against noncombatants in order to persuade them from doing what they have a lawful right to do.*" (P. 352, emphasis in original.)

Bobbitt endorses "a counterterrorist strategy that scrupulously and transparently respects international standards [and] a positive vision of societies built around democracy, human rights, and the rule of law— something that people can be *for*—to accompany the important but partial vision of being *against* terrorism." (P. 356.) For Bobbitt, law provides several examples of what states of consent are and should be fighting *for*. One is inalienable rights, those that cannot be given or taken away. "Because consent is not merely a matter of saying Yes, but also of having the option of saying No, consent depends upon the availability of alternatives. Inalienability is one way—the law's way—of creating the necessity of citizens having to choose among alternatives." (P. 183.) Another is the creation of governing rules through a process that is democratic, open, and deliberative. In discussing such a process, Bobbitt assumes but does not defend the proposition that Congress must ratify major changes in American anti-terrorist policy.

Bobbitt considers this an attractive political philosophy to offer world populations, and this is an advantage that states of consent have against terrorism. The goal of states of consent, therefore, is not just to protect their citizens against harm and violence, but also to do so within the parameters of the rule of law. Hence, Bobbitt is strongly opposed to separating law from (anti-terrorist) strategy (p. 237).

The Constitutional Relationship Between Rights and Powers (Chapters 5–8). From the ACLU to the Cato Institute, Americans of most political persuasions tend to understand state power and individual rights as a zero-sum game: when one gains traction, the other loses. Bobbitt revives the Hobbesian understanding of the state as *necessarily* limiting men's liberties "as they might not hurt, but assist one another, and join together against a common enemy." Hobbes, *Leviathan* ch. 26 (1651). Like Hamilton in *Federalist* No. 1, Bobbitt insists upon the *interdependence* rather than competition between the "vigor of government" and the "security of liberty" (Hamilton's words).

Bobbitt insists that this kind of synergy can only be effectuated if the war on terror is conducted with a proper appreciation for *strategy*: the rational connection between lawful ends and rational means. Thus, he denounces the unlawful torture of suspected terrorists: the end is at best ambiguous, as torture is in tension with the rule of law, and the means is ineffective, as torture rarely secures useful information. At the same time, Bobbitt would expand government power to gather electronic information, insist upon a more cooperative structure for intelligence agencies, regularize procedures for detention and interrogation, and expand cooperative relationships with other governments and NGOs (Chapter 6). He endorses preemptive strikes: Are we better off after the preclusive strike against al Qaeda in Afghanistan after 9/11?

Normatively, Bobbitt insists upon the *duty of consequentialism*—"that is, any contemplated course of action must be measured in terms of the foreseeable costs and benefits that are its result and not against any absolute or categorical rule, including those regarding intentions" (p. 361). Thus, Bobbitt does not flinch from the "ticking bomb scenario": if Jack Bauer thinks that the malefactor he has captured can provide him with a valuable lead toward finding a ticking time bomb that will blow up Los Angeles, Jack must do what is required to extract that information, pronto. Including torture, presumably torture leading toward serious bodily injury or death. "It is an easy question" (p. 362). But this assumes Jack is sure the captive has relevant information.

At the same time, Bobbitt links this consequentialist philosophy to his rule of law institutionalism: "The states of consent must develop rules that define what terrorism is, who is a terrorist, and what states can lawfully do to fight terrorists and terrorism. * * * At the same time, we must * * * jettison nonconstitutional rules like those against information acquisition from the private sector of data voluntarily provided, and also many rules against data sharing among agencies. We must develop new practices like the requirement of national identity cards, including biometrics when these become reliable; increased CCTV surveillance of transportation, energy, and communication hubs; sophisticated data mining as well as standards for the detention of terrorist combatants on a noncriminal basis. We must do this because an open society depends upon a government strong enough and foresighted enough to protect individual rights." (P. 394.) Chapter 8 contains a more detailed set of pro-active proposals for restructuring the government and improving our capacity for preventing and responding to terrorist attacks.

HAMDI V. RUMSFELD
542 U.S. 507, 124 S.Ct. 2633, 159 L.Ed.2d 578 (2004)

[After the terrorist attacks of 9/11, Congress passed a resolution—the Authorization for Use of Military Force (AUMF)—authorizing the President to "use all necessary and appropriate force" against "nations, organizations, or persons" that he determines "planned, authorized, committed, or aided" in the attacks. As part of this response, President Bush 45 ordered an invasion of Afghanistan to attack al Qaeda and the Taliban regime that had harbored al Qaeda. Hamdi, an American citizen, was captured in Afghanistan and after some intermediate stops was detained at a naval brig in Charleston, S.C. No charges were brought against him. His father filed a habeas corpus petition on his behalf and asserted that Hamdi went to Afghanistan to do "relief work" less than two months before September 11 and could not have received military training. In response to the petition, the government filed a declaration from Michael Mobbs, a Defense Department official. The Mobbs Declaration alleged various details regarding Hamdi's trip to Afghanistan, his affiliation there with a Taliban unit, and his subsequent surrender of an assault rifle.

[Writing for a plurality, Justice O'Connor, ruled that Hamdi was entitled to some form of due process hearing. See *Mathews v. Eldridge* (Chapter 5, § 6). Four other Justices would have held his detention squarely unlawful. Two of those Justices joined portions of O'Connor's opinion in order to provide a majority for some disposition of the case. Justice Thomas agreed with the government's view that the Mobbs Declaration had provided a sufficient basis for indefinite detention.]

JUSTICE O'CONNOR announced the judgment of the Court and delivered an opinion, in which the CHIEF JUSTICE, JUSTICE KENNEDY, and JUSTICE BREYER join.

We hold that although Congress authorized the detention of combatants in the narrow circumstances alleged here, due process demands that a citizen held in the United States as an enemy combatant be given a meaningful opportunity to contest the factual basis for that detention before a neutral decisionmaker. * * *

The threshold question before us is whether the Executive has the authority to detain citizens who qualify as "enemy combatants." * * * [F]or purposes of this case, the "enemy combatant" that it is seeking to detain is an individual who, it alleges, was " 'part of or supporting forces hostile to the United States or coalition partners' " in Afghanistan and who " 'engaged in an armed conflict against the United States' " there. We therefore answer only the narrow question before us: whether the detention of citizens falling within that definition is authorized.

The Government maintains that no explicit congressional authorization is required, because the Executive possesses plenary authority to detain pursuant to Article II of the Constitution. We do not reach the question whether Article II provides such authority, however, because we agree with the Government's alternative position, that Congress has in fact authorized Hamdi's detention, through the AUMF.

Our analysis on that point, set forth below, substantially overlaps with our analysis of Hamdi's principal argument for the illegality of his detention. He posits that his detention is forbidden by 18 U.S.C. § 4001(a). Section 4001(a) states that "[n]o citizen shall be imprisoned or otherwise detained by the United States except pursuant to an Act of Congress." Congress passed § 4001(a) in 1971 as part of a bill to repeal the Emergency Detention Act of 1950, which provided procedures for executive detention, during times of emergency, of individuals deemed likely to engage in espionage or sabotage. Congress was particularly concerned about the possibility that the Act could be used to reprise the Japanese internment camps of World War II. The Government again presses two alternative positions. First, it argues that § 4001(a), in light of its legislative history and its location in Title 18, applies only to "the control of civilian prisons and related detentions," not to military detentions. Second, it maintains that § 4001(a) is satisfied, because Hamdi is being detained "pursuant to an Act of Congress"—the AUMF. [Justice O'Connor sustained the second argument and so did not address the first.] * * *

The capture and detention of lawful combatants and the capture, detention, and trial of unlawful combatants, by "universal agreement and practice," are "important incident[s] of war." *Ex parte Quirin.* The purpose of detention is to prevent captured individuals from returning to the field of battle and taking up arms once again.

There is no bar to this Nation's holding one of its own citizens as an enemy combatant. In *Quirin,* one of the detainees, Haupt, alleged that he was a naturalized United States citizen. We held that "[c]itizens who associate themselves with the military arm of the enemy government, and with its aid, guidance and direction enter this country bent on hostile acts, are enemy belligerents within the meaning of . . . the law of war." While Haupt was tried for violations of the law of war, nothing in *Quirin* suggests that his citizenship would have precluded his mere detention for the duration of the relevant hostilities. Nor can we see any reason for drawing such a line here. A citizen, no less than an alien, can be "part of or supporting forces hostile to the United States or coalition partners" and "engaged in an armed conflict against the United States"; such a citizen, if released, would pose the same threat of returning to the front during the ongoing conflict.

In light of these principles, it is of no moment that the AUMF does not use specific language of detention. Because detention to prevent a combatant's return to the battlefield is a fundamental incident of waging war, in permitting the use of "necessary and appropriate force," Congress has clearly and unmistakably authorized detention in the narrow circumstances considered here.

Hamdi objects, nevertheless, that Congress has not authorized the *indefinite* detention to which he is now subject. The Government responds that "the detention of enemy combatants during World War II was just as 'indefinite' while that war was being fought." We take Hamdi's objection to be not to the lack of certainty regarding the date on which the conflict will end, but to the substantial prospect of perpetual detention. We recognize that the national security underpinnings of the "war on terror," although crucially important, are broad and malleable. As the Government concedes, "given its unconventional nature, the current conflict is unlikely to end with a formal cease-fire agreement." The prospect Hamdi raises is therefore not far-fetched. If the Government does not consider this unconventional war won for two generations, and if it maintains during that time that Hamdi might, if released, rejoin forces fighting against the United States, then the position it has taken throughout the litigation of this case suggests that Hamdi's detention could last for the rest of his life.

It is a clearly established principle of the law of war that detention may last no longer than active hostilities. [Citing the Geneva Convention and other international materials.]

Hamdi contends that the AUMF does not authorize indefinite or perpetual detention. Certainly, we agree that indefinite detention for the purpose of interrogation is not authorized. Further, we understand

Congress' grant of authority for the use of "necessary and appropriate force" to include the authority to detain for the duration of the relevant conflict, and our understanding is based on longstanding law-of-war principles. If the practical circumstances of a given conflict are entirely unlike those of the conflicts that informed the development of the law of war, that understanding may unravel. But that is not the situation we face as of this date. Active combat operations against Taliban fighters apparently are ongoing in Afghanistan. The United States may detain, for the duration of these hostilities, individuals legitimately determined to be Taliban combatants who "engaged in an armed conflict against the United States." If the record establishes that United States troops are still involved in active combat in Afghanistan, those detentions are part of the exercise of "necessary and appropriate force," and therefore are authorized by the AUMF.

Ex parte Milligan, 4 Wall. 2 (1866), does not undermine our holding about the Government's authority to seize enemy combatants, as we define that term today. In that case, the Court made repeated reference to the fact that its inquiry into whether the military tribunal had jurisdiction to try and punish Milligan turned in large part on the fact that Milligan was not a prisoner of war, but a resident of Indiana arrested while at home there. That fact was central to its conclusion. Had Milligan been captured while he was assisting Confederate soldiers by carrying a rifle against Union troops on a Confederate battlefield, the holding of the Court might well have been different. The Court's repeated explanations that Milligan was not a prisoner of war suggest that had these different circumstances been present he could have been detained under military authority for the duration of the conflict, whether or not he was a citizen.[14]

Moreover, as Justice Scalia acknowledges, the Court in *Ex parte Quirin*, dismissed the language of *Milligan* that the petitioners had suggested prevented them from being subject to military process. * * * Haupt * * * was accused of being a spy. The Court in *Quirin* found him "subject to trial and punishment by [a] military tribunal[ ]" for those acts, and held that his citizenship did not change this result. * * *

Even in cases in which the detention of enemy combatants is legally authorized, there remains the question of what process is constitutionally due to a citizen who disputes his enemy-combatant status. Hamdi argues that he is owed a meaningful and timely hearing and that "extra-judicial detention [that] begins and ends with the submission of an affidavit based on third-hand hearsay" does not comport with the Fifth and Fourteenth

---

[14] Here the basis asserted for detention by the military is that Hamdi was carrying a weapon against American troops on a foreign battlefield; that is, that he was an enemy combatant. The legal category of enemy combatant has not been elaborated upon in great detail. The permissible bounds of the category will be defined by the lower courts as subsequent cases are presented to them.

Amendments. The Government counters that any more process than was provided below would be both unworkable and "constitutionally intolerable." Our resolution of this dispute requires a careful examination both of the writ of habeas corpus, which Hamdi now seeks to employ as a mechanism of judicial review, and of the Due Process Clause, which informs the procedural contours of that mechanism in this instance. * * *

[The government] asks us to hold that, given both the flexibility of the habeas mechanism and the circumstances presented in this case, the presentation of the Mobbs Declaration to the habeas court completed the required factual development. * * *

[To fit within the AUMF authorization, Hamdi would need to be "part of or supporting forces hostile to the United States or coalition partners" and "engaged in an armed conflict against the United States."] Under the Government's most extreme rendition of this argument, "[r]espect for separation of powers and the limited institutional capabilities of courts in matters of military decision-making in connection with an ongoing conflict" ought to eliminate entirely any individual process, restricting the courts to investigating only whether legal authorization exists for the broader detention scheme. At most, the Government argues, courts should review its determination that a citizen is an enemy combatant under a very deferential "some evidence" standard. Under this review, a court would assume the accuracy of the Government's articulated basis for Hamdi's detention, as set forth in the Mobbs Declaration, and assess only whether that articulated basis was a legitimate one.

In response, Hamdi emphasizes that this Court consistently has recognized that an individual challenging his detention may not be held at the will of the Executive without recourse to some proceeding before a neutral tribunal to determine whether the Executive's asserted justifications for that detention have basis in fact and warrant in law. * * * The District Court, agreeing with Hamdi, apparently believed that the appropriate process would approach the process that accompanies a criminal trial. It therefore disapproved of the hearsay nature of the Mobbs Declaration and anticipated quite extensive discovery of various military affairs. Anything less, it concluded, would not be "meaningful judicial review."

Both of these positions highlight legitimate concerns. And both emphasize the tension that often exists between the autonomy that the Government asserts is necessary in order to pursue effectively a particular goal and the process that a citizen contends he is due before he is deprived of a constitutional right. The ordinary mechanism that we use for balancing such serious competing interests, and for determining the procedures that are necessary to ensure that a citizen is not "deprived of life, liberty, or property, without due process of law," is the test that we articulated in

Mathews v. Eldridge [Chapter 5, § 6]. *Mathews* dictates that the process due in any given instance is determined by weighing "the private interest that will be affected by the official action" against the Government's asserted interest, "including the function involved" and the burdens the Government would face in providing greater process. The *Mathews* calculus then contemplates a judicious balancing of these concerns, through an analysis of "the risk of an erroneous deprivation" of the private interest if the process were reduced and the "probable value, if any, of additional or substitute safeguards." We take each of these steps in turn. [The Court discussed the gravity of the government's interest in national security and the significance of the right to be free from arbitrary detention.]

Striking the proper constitutional balance here is of great importance to the Nation during this period of ongoing combat. But it is equally vital that our calculus not give short shrift to the values that this country holds dear or to the privilege that is American citizenship. It is during our most challenging and uncertain moments that our Nation's commitment to due process is most severely tested; and it is in those times that we must preserve our commitment at home to the principles for which we fight abroad.

With due recognition of these competing concerns, we believe that neither the process proposed by the Government nor the process apparently envisioned by the District Court below strikes the proper constitutional balance when a United States citizen is detained in the United States as an enemy combatant. That is, "the risk of erroneous deprivation" of a detainee's liberty interest is unacceptably high under the Government's proposed rule, while some of the "additional or substitute procedural safeguards" suggested by the District Court are unwarranted in light of their limited "probable value" and the burdens they may impose on the military in such cases.

We therefore hold that a citizen-detainee seeking to challenge his classification as an enemy combatant must receive notice of the factual basis for his classification, and a fair opportunity to rebut the Government's factual assertions before a neutral decisionmaker. These essential constitutional promises may not be eroded.

At the same time, the exigencies of the circumstances may demand that, aside from these core elements, enemy combatant proceedings may be tailored to alleviate their uncommon potential to burden the Executive at a time of ongoing military conflict. Hearsay, for example, may need to be accepted as the most reliable available evidence from the Government in such a proceeding. Likewise, the Constitution would not be offended by a presumption in favor of the Government's evidence, so long as that presumption remained a rebuttable one and fair opportunity for rebuttal were provided. Thus, once the Government puts forth credible evidence that the habeas petitioner meets the enemy-combatant criteria, the onus could shift to the petitioner to rebut that evidence with more persuasive evidence that he falls outside the criteria. A burden-shifting scheme of this sort would meet the goal of ensuring that the errant tourist, embedded journalist, or local aid worker has a chance to prove military error while giving due regard to the Executive once it has put forth meaningful support for its conclusion that the detainee is in fact an enemy combatant. In the words of *Mathews,* process of this sort would sufficiently address the "risk of erroneous deprivation" of a detainee's liberty interest while eliminating certain procedures that have questionable additional value in light of the burden on the Government. * * *

In sum, while the full protections that accompany challenges to detentions in other settings may prove unworkable and inappropriate in the enemy-combatant setting, the threats to military operations posed by a basic system of independent review are not so weighty as to trump a citizen's core rights to challenge meaningfully the Government's case and to be heard by an impartial adjudicator.

In so holding, we necessarily reject the Government's assertion that separation of powers principles mandate a heavily circumscribed role for the courts in such circumstances. Indeed, the position that the courts must forgo any examination of the individual case and focus exclusively on the legality of the broader detention scheme cannot be mandated by any reasonable view of separation of powers, as this approach serves only to *condense* power into a single branch of government. We have long since made clear that a state of war is not a blank check for the President when it comes to the rights of the Nation's citizens. Whatever power the United States Constitution envisions for the Executive in its exchanges with other nations or with enemy organizations in times of conflict, it most assuredly envisions a role for all three branches when individual liberties are at stake. Likewise, we have made clear that, unless Congress acts to suspend it, the Great Writ of habeas corpus allows the Judicial Branch to play a necessary role in maintaining this delicate balance of governance, serving as an important judicial check on the Executive's discretion in the realm of detentions. Thus, while we do not question that our due process assessment must pay keen attention to the particular burdens faced by the Executive in the context of military action, it would turn our system of checks and balances on its head to suggest that a citizen could not make his way to court with a challenge to the factual basis for his detention by his government, simply because the Executive opposes making available such a challenge. Absent suspension of the writ by Congress, a citizen detained as an enemy combatant is entitled to this process.

Because we conclude that due process demands some system for a citizen detainee to refute his classification, the proposed "some evidence" standard is inadequate. Any process in which the Executive's factual assertions go wholly unchallenged or are simply presumed correct without any opportunity for the alleged combatant to demonstrate otherwise falls constitutionally short. As the Government itself has recognized, we have utilized the "some evidence" standard in the past as a standard of review, not as a standard of proof. That is, it primarily has been employed by courts in examining an administrative record developed after an adversarial proceeding—one with process at least of the sort that we today hold is constitutionally mandated in the citizen enemy-combatant setting. This standard therefore is ill suited to the situation in which a habeas petitioner has received no prior proceedings before any tribunal and had no prior opportunity to rebut the Executive's factual assertions before a neutral decisionmaker.

Today we are faced only with such a case. Aside from unspecified "screening" processes, and military interrogations in which the Government suggests Hamdi could have contested his classification, Hamdi has received no process. An interrogation by one's captor, however effective an intelligence-gathering tool, hardly constitutes a constitutionally adequate factfinding before a neutral decisionmaker. * * * Plainly, the "process" Hamdi has received is not that to which he is entitled under the Due Process Clause.

JUSTICE SOUTER, joined by **JUSTICE GINSBURG**, concurring in part, dissenting in part, and concurring in the judgment.

[Justice Souter would have followed the plain terms of the Non-Detention Act. The statute was passed in order to supersede a previous statute, the Emergency Detention Act of 1950, which had authorized the Attorney General to detain anyone reasonably thought likely to engage in espionage or sabotage during national emergencies. Justice Souter rejected the government's arguments that § 4001(a) did not even apply to wartime military detentions or that the AUMF provided a blanket exemption for all terrorism-related detentions. Even if the Government were correct, that the AUMF authorized detentions authorized by the laws of war, the Government failed to show that it was detaining Hamdi in accord with the laws of war. The detention probably did not comply with the Geneva Convention, which gave detainees like Hamdi the right to a hearing before a neutral tribunal, which the Government had not provided.]

Since the Government has given no reason either to deflect the application of § 4001(a) or to hold it to be satisfied, I need to go no further; the Government hints of a constitutional challenge to the statute, but it presents none here. I will, however, stray across the line between statutory and constitutional territory just far enough to note the weakness of the Government's mixed claim of inherent, extrastatutory authority under a combination of Article II of the Constitution and the usages of war. It is in fact in this connection that the Government developed its argument that the exercise of war powers justifies the detention, and what I have just said about its inadequacy applies here as well. Beyond that, it is instructive to recall Justice Jackson's observation that the President is not Commander in Chief of the country, only of the military.

There may be room for one qualification to Justice Jackson's statement, however: in a moment of genuine emergency, when the Government must act with no time for deliberation, the Executive may be able to detain a citizen if there is reason to fear he is an imminent threat to the safety of the Nation and its people (though I doubt there is any want of statutory authority). This case, however, does not present that question, because an emergency power of necessity must at least be limited by the emergency; Hamdi has been locked up for over two years. Cf. *Ex parte Milligan* (martial law justified only by "actual and present" necessity as in a genuine invasion that closes civilian courts).

[In principle, Justice Souter said he would vote to hold the detention illegal. "Since this disposition does not command a majority of the Court, however, the need to give practical effect to the conclusions of eight members of the Court rejecting the Government's position calls for me to join with the plurality in ordering remand on terms closest to those I would impose." He added, however, that it "should go without saying that in joining with the plurality to produce a judgment, I do not adopt the plurality's resolution of constitutional issues that I would not reach."]

JUSTICE SCALIA, with whom **JUSTICE STEVENS** joins, dissenting.

Where the Government accuses a citizen of waging war against it, our constitutional tradition has been to prosecute him in federal court for treason or some other crime. Where the exigencies of war prevent that, the Constitution's Suspension Clause, Art. I, § 9, cl. 2, allows Congress to relax the usual protections temporarily. Absent suspension, however, the Executive's assertion of military exigency has not been thought sufficient to permit detention without charge. No one contends that the congressional Authorization for Use of Military Force, on which the Government relies to justify its actions here, is an implementation of the Suspension Clause. Accordingly, I would reverse the decision below.

The very core of liberty secured by our Anglo-Saxon system of separated powers has been freedom from indefinite imprisonment at the will of the Executive. Blackstone stated this principle clearly:

> "Of great importance to the public is the preservation of this personal liberty: for if once it were left in the power of any, the highest, magistrate to imprison arbitrarily whomever he or his officers thought proper . . . there would soon be an end of all other rights and immunities. . . . To bereave a man of life, or by violence to confiscate his estate, without accusation or trial, would be so

gross and notorious an act of despotism, as must at once convey the alarm of tyranny throughout the whole kingdom. But confinement of the person, by secretly hurrying him to gaol, where his sufferings are unknown or forgotten; is a less public, a less striking, and therefore a more dangerous engine of arbitrary government. * * * "

These words were well known to the Founders. Hamilton quoted from this very passage in The Federalist No. 84. The two ideas central to Blackstone's understanding—due process as the right secured, and habeas corpus as the instrument by which due process could be insisted upon by a citizen illegally imprisoned—found expression in the Constitution's Due Process and Suspension Clauses. See Amdt. 5; Art. I, § 9, cl. 2.

The gist of the Due Process Clause, as understood at the founding and since, was to force the Government to follow those common-law procedures traditionally deemed necessary before depriving a person of life, liberty, or property. When a citizen was deprived of liberty because of alleged criminal conduct, those procedures typically required committal by a magistrate followed by indictment and trial. * * *

Justice O'Connor, writing for a plurality of this Court, asserts that captured enemy combatants (other than those suspected of war crimes) have traditionally been detained until the cessation of hostilities and then released. That is probably an accurate description of wartime practice with respect to enemy *aliens*. The tradition with respect to American citizens, however, has been quite different. Citizens aiding the enemy have been treated as traitors subject to the criminal process. * * *

There are times when military exigency renders resort to the traditional criminal process impracticable. English law accommodated such exigencies by allowing legislative suspension of the writ of habeas corpus for brief periods. * * * Where the Executive has not pursued the usual course of charge, committal, and conviction, it has historically secured the Legislature's explicit approval of a suspension. [While legislative suspension of the writ *or* criminal prosecutions have been the only traditional means for citizens who levy war against their country, Justice Scalia considered the possibility that "the Constitution does not *require* a choice between these alternatives."]

I believe, however, that substantial evidence does refute that possibility. First, the text of the 1679 Habeas Corpus Act makes clear that indefinite imprisonment on reasonable suspicion is not an available option of treatment for those accused of aiding the enemy, absent a suspension of the writ. In the United States, this Act was read as "enforc[ing] the common law," and shaped the early understanding of the scope of the writ. [Section] 7 of the Act specifically addressed those committed for high treason, and provided a remedy if they were not *indicted and tried* by the second succeeding court term. That remedy was *not* a bobtailed judicial inquiry into whether there were reasonable grounds to believe the prisoner had taken up arms against the King. Rather, if the prisoner was not indicted and tried within the prescribed time, "he shall be discharged from his Imprisonment." The Act does not contain any exception for wartime. That omission is conspicuous, since § 7 explicitly addresses the offense of "High Treason," which often involved offenses of a military nature. * * *

Further evidence comes from this Court's decision in *Ex parte Milligan.* There, the Court issued the writ to an American citizen who had been tried by military commission for offenses that included conspiring to overthrow the Government, seize munitions, and liberate prisoners of war. The Court rejected in no uncertain terms the Government's assertion that military jurisdiction was proper "under the 'laws and usages of war' ":

> "It can serve no useful purpose to inquire what those laws and usages are, whence they originated, where found, and on whom they operate; they can never be applied to citizens in states which have upheld the authority of the government, and where the courts are open and their process unobstructed."

Milligan is not exactly this case, of course, since the petitioner was threatened with death, not merely imprisonment. But the reasoning and conclusion of *Milligan* logically cover the present case. The Government justifies imprisonment of Hamdi on principles of the law of war and admits that, absent the war, it would have no such authority. But if the law of war cannot be applied to citizens where courts are open, then Hamdi's imprisonment without criminal trial is no less unlawful than Milligan's trial by military tribunal. * * *

The Government argues that our more recent jurisprudence ratifies its indefinite imprisonment of a citizen within the territorial jurisdiction of federal courts. It places primary reliance upon *Ex parte Quirin,* a World War II case upholding the trial by military commission of eight German saboteurs, one of whom, Hans Haupt, was a U.S. citizen. The case was not this Court's finest hour. The Court upheld the commission and denied relief in a brief *per curiam* issued the day after oral argument concluded; a week later the Government carried out the commission's death sentence upon six saboteurs, including Haupt. The Court eventually explained its reasoning in a written opinion issued several months later.

[Justice Scalia argued that *Quirin* misread *Milligan* and was wrong in principle.] But even if *Quirin* gave a correct description of *Milligan,* or made an irrevocable revision of it, *Quirin* would still not justify denial of the writ here. In *Quirin* it was uncontested that the petitioners were members of enemy forces. They were "*admitted* enemy invaders," and it was "undisputed" that they had landed in the United States in service of German forces. The specific holding of the Court was only that, "upon the *conceded* facts," the petitioners were "plainly within [the] boundaries" of military jurisdiction. But where those jurisdictional facts are *not* conceded—where the petitioner insists that he is *not* a belligerent—*Quirin* left the pre-existing law in place: Absent suspension of the writ, a citizen held where the courts are open is entitled either to criminal trial or to a judicial decree requiring his release. * * *

It follows from what I have said that Hamdi is entitled to a habeas decree requiring his release unless (1) criminal proceedings are promptly brought, or (2) Congress has suspended the writ of habeas corpus. A suspension of the writ could, of course, lay down conditions for continued detention, similar to those that today's opinion prescribes under the Due Process Clause. But there is a world of difference between the people's representatives' determining the need for that suspension (and prescribing the conditions for it), and this Court's doing so. * * *

There is a certain harmony of approach in the plurality's making up for Congress's failure to invoke the Suspension Clause and its making up for the Executive's failure to apply what it says are needed procedures—an approach that reflects what might be called a Mr. Fix-it Mentality. The plurality seems to view it as its mission to Make Everything Come Out Right, rather than merely to decree the consequences, as far as individual rights are concerned, of the other two branches' actions and omissions. Has the Legislature failed to suspend the writ in the current dire emergency? Well, we will remedy that failure by prescribing the reasonable conditions that a suspension should have included. And has the Executive failed to live up to those reasonable conditions? Well, we will ourselves make that failure good, so that this dangerous fellow (if he is dangerous) need not be set free. The problem with this approach is not only that it steps out of the courts' modest and limited role in a democratic society; but that by repeatedly doing what it thinks the political branches ought to do it encourages their lassitude and saps the vitality of government by the people. * * *

JUSTICE THOMAS, dissenting.

The Executive Branch, acting pursuant to the powers vested in the President by the Constitution and with explicit congressional approval, has determined that Yaser Hamdi is an enemy combatant and should be detained. This detention falls squarely within the Federal Government's war powers, and we lack the expertise and capacity to second-guess that decision. * * * I do not think that the Federal Government's war powers can be balanced away by this Court. Arguably, Congress could provide for additional procedural protections, but until it does, we have no right to insist upon them. But even if I were to agree with the general approach the plurality takes, I could not accept the particulars. The plurality utterly fails to account for the Government's compelling interests and for our own institutional inability to weigh competing concerns correctly. I respectfully dissent. * * *

Although the President very well may have inherent authority to detain those arrayed against our troops, I agree with the plurality that we need not decide that question because Congress has authorized the President to do so. [Justice Thomas sharply disagreed with the Court's judgment that the AUMF's authorization was not indefinite and was limited by the Geneva Convention.]

Accordingly, I conclude that the Government's detention of Hamdi as an enemy combatant does not violate the Constitution. By detaining Hamdi, the President, in the prosecution of a war and authorized by Congress, has acted well within his authority. Hamdi thereby received all the process to which he was due under the circumstances. I therefore believe that this is no occasion to balance the competing interests, as the plurality unconvincingly attempts to do.

Companion Cases. On the same day the Court announced *Hamdi*, the Justices handed down two other opinions. In *Rumsfeld v. Padilla*, 542 U.S. 426 (2004), the Court ruled that an American citizen accused of being an enemy combatant had to bring his habeas suit in the jurisdiction (South Carolina) where he was incarcerated. Four Justices dissented, arguing that Padilla ought to be able to sue the Secretary of Defense in New York City. In *Rasul v. Rumsfeld*, 542 U.S. (2004), excerpted below, the Court ruled that accused enemy combatants detained in American facilities in Guantanamo Bay, Cuba, could bring habeas corpus lawsuits.

NOTES ON HAMDI AND THE WAR ON TERROR

1.   *The Three Issues in* Hamdi. As usefully framed by Jenny S. Martinez, *Process and Substance in the "War on Terror,"* 108 Colum. L. Rev. 1013, 1045–48 (2008), there are, analytically, three issues for the Court to resolve. *First*, does the federal government have the authority to detain American citizens indefinitely without a criminal charge or a congressional suspension of habeas? This is the issue addressed by Justices Scalia and Stevens, and they correctly said that this issue should be answered by analysis of constitutional structure as well as history, which they provided. But they alone opined that the federal government did not have the power to detain without criminal process or habeas suspension. What could have persuaded the majority otherwise? Does Professor Bobbitt's book suggest a line of analysis for the majority?

Second, does the President have the authority to detain American citizens? On this issue, the Court was divided 5–4, with Justices Souter and Ginsburg joining Stevens and Scalia in saying no. The plurality Justices (Rehnquist, O'Connor, Kennedy, Breyer) asserted that Congress conferred authority on the President in the AUMF, and so the President was operating on the firm terrain of Jackson's Category 1. Souter and Ginsburg disagreed and believed that the President was operating in Category 3 ("lowest ebb"), because he was acting contrary to statute (the Non-Detention Act, § 4001(a)). Justice Thomas agreed with the plurality and viewed this as a Category 1 case, but he also believed that the President has inherent Article II authority to detain citizens, and so would be prepared to treat this as a Category 2 case or perhaps even Category 3, where the President's commander-in-chief authority trumps the Non-Detention Act or requires that the Act be construed narrowly.

Third, what process is constitutionally owed to detained citizens who dispute their enemy combatant status? On this issue Justices Souter and Ginsburg went along with Justice O'Connor's plurality opinion, because they wanted an authoritative judgment for the Bush-Cheney Administration to obey. Justice Thomas disagreed; he asserted that once the political branches have determined the proper process for suspected enemies, the Court cannot second-guess it. Justices Scalia and Stevens complained about the plurality's Mr. Fix-It Mentality and would not have balanced away citizens' rights.

2.　*Should the Court Be (Very) Reluctant to Second-Guess the President?* All the Justices except Thomas second-guessed the President's judgment on Hamdi's detention. There are three kinds of arguments in favor of some judicial monitoring of these detentions. First is the Bobbitt argument: the rule of law demands that the President, even in a national emergency, must respect citizens' presumptive liberty. It is decisions like *Hamdi* that distinguish our state of consent and the rule of law from the state of terror represented by al Qaeda. All eight second-guessing Justices believed that either statutory or constitutional rules prevent indefinite detention. The variety of viewpoints is striking, however: Was there a clear rule of law applicable here?

Second is a Steel Seizure argument: the Court should require the President to follow the processes established by Congress. This is consistent with both the Constitution and democratic accountability. But just four Justices (Stevens, Scalia, Souter, Ginsburg) gave this argument any bite. The Non-Detention Act seems pretty sweeping and clear, while the AUMF says nothing about detention. Why does the plurality cut back on a clear congressional command—and then stick its neck out by imposing constitutionally required process on the Administration?

A third kind of argument might support the majority: representation-reinforcing judicial review of the sort laid out in Chapter 2, § 3B. When the United States feels itself under attack or insecure, "the individuals whose rights are sacrificed are not those who make the laws, but minorities, dissidents, and noncitizens. In those circumstances, 'we' are making a decision to sacrifice 'their' rights—not a very prudent way to balance the competing interests." Geoffrey Stone, *Perilous Times* 531 (2004). Ethnic minorities such as Hamdi, accused of heinous associations in a time of fear and patriotic ferment, are in danger of being scapegoated by the political process. Only independent judges can slow the juggernaut and seek more measured treatment. Perhaps more cynically, it is important in emotional times of crisis that the Supreme Court rhetorically reassure everyone (especially minorities) that there is one institution dedicated to ensuring people are treated fairly by the government. The Administration was holding Yaser Hamdi for years with no credible evidence that he was an "enemy" of any sort, and the government indeed released him soon after the Supreme Court's decision.

It is striking that conservative and liberal Justices alike joined in rebuking the Administration—especially in light of several serious arguments in favor of the Administration's (and Justice Thomas's) position that the Supreme Court should defer to the President's judgment here. To begin with, if you accept Prakash and Ramsey's Foreign Affairs Vesting Thesis, Article II vests the President with duties as the primary organ for the United States in matters of national security as well as foreign affairs. This thesis would be an argument for reading the AUMF broadly to create an exception to the Non-Detention Act, as the *Hamdi* majority does, but it is not as good an argument for a narrow reading of the Due Process Clause, which applies to the government generally.

Second, the Foreign Affairs Vesting Clause argument can be buttressed in this case by the President's explicit commander-in-chief authority. Implicit in the commander-in-chief power is the authority to take needed action against the "enemy," without judicial second-guessing. While Justice Scalia shrinks from this precedent, *Quirin* is a citation for this idea. A la Bobbitt, the President might say that *Quirin* provides the rule of law cover for updating presidential power to deal with a new kind of enemy—not the treasonous citizen betraying his country, but the enemy within, the Trojan Horse technically living in our state of consent but whose loyalty is to a state of terror.

The Civil War cases are less supportive. President Lincoln issued an order authorizing his generals to detain citizens without conforming to normal process. Numerous individuals were held pursuant to this order, in one case in defiance of a habeas opinion by Chief Justice Taney in *Ex parte Merryman*, 17 F. Cas. 144 (C.C.D. Md. 1861). Responding to Taney, Lincoln said he could not allow "all the laws but one" to remain unexecuted merely to uphold the habeas law. Lincoln also justified his action under the Suspension Clause: when Congress is not in session, the President himself has the authority to suspend habeas during national emergencies. In 1861, Congress declined to ratify this detention without habeas; when it did so in 1863, Congress required military commanders to discharge detainees, apart from prisoners of war, in states where courts were operating unimpaired and required officers to obey judicial orders in those states. The President accepted the 1863 statute but construed it narrowly. In *Ex parte Milligan*, 71 U.S. 2 (1866), the Supreme Court rejected the President's narrowing construction and directed that the detainee was entitled to habeas release.[84] Since the habeas suspension no longer applied, there had been no question about Milligan's right to file for the writ; only about the legality of his trial and sentence.

---

[84] For detailed examinations of Lincoln's suspension of habeas, see Daniel A. Farber, *Lincoln's Constitution* (2003); David J. Barron & Martin S. Lederman, *The Commander in Chief at the Lowest Ebb—A Constitutional History*, 121 Harv. L. Rev. 941, 998–1000, 1004–08 (2008).

A third line of support for the President is pragmatic. Politically, the President's inherent first-mover advantage is most powerful in times of national emergency or threat (such as 9/11), and the Supreme Court's institutional weakness is even more on display in such circumstances. Political scientists "find that judges are less likely to overturn presidents who appointed them to the bench, presidents who enjoy strong public approval ratings, and policies that involve foreign affairs." William Howell, *Power without Persuasion: The Politics of Direct Presidential Action* 151 (2003). Unfortunately for President Bush, he appointed no member of the *Hamdi* Court, the fact that a citizen was detained gave the case a domestic feature that worked against his position, and the Court was deliberating in *Hamdi* just as news reports documented (with photos) American abuse of Iraqi prisoners at Abu Ghraib prison. In light of the international black eye the United States acquired from Abu Ghraib, *Hamdi*'s mild affirmation of the rule of law was not likely to embroil the Court in controversy.

Some legal pragmatists worry that the Supreme Court has nothing to add when the country is making calculations about security and liberty. Institutionally, the President is the best decisionmaker in times of emergency, because he has access to information and experts on terrorism and can act quickly and in a tailored way to new threats.[85] But Stephen Holmes reminds us that, under conditions of uncertainty, decisionmakers make fewer mistakes when they hew to time-tested rules and protocols, rather than ad hoc judgments; the value of judges in cases like *Hamdi* is to impose rule-following protocols on executive decisionmakers and to empower rule-abiding executive agencies such as the Office of Legal Counsel. Stephen Holmes, *In Case of Emergency: Misunderstanding Tradeoffs in the War on Terror*, 97 Calif. L. Rev. 301 (2009).

President-boosters are skeptical that rules or protocols effectively constrain the President in times of crisis. Agreeing with these skeptics, Professor Posner adds that the rule of law rarely entails nothing but bright-line rules; any legal regime, whether judicial or executive, will consist of both rules and standards. And when new circumstances present themselves (as they do in times of crisis), the most rule-like regime will call forth exceptions. See Eric A. Posner, *Deference to the Executive in the United States After September 11*, 35 Harv. J.L. & Pub. Pol'y 213 (2012). A broader implication of Posner's thinking is that liberal democracies cannot effectively limit the authority of a strong chief executive, especially in times of "emergency."

3.　*Congress's Response on the Issue of Detention.* In the National Defense Authorization Act for Fiscal Year 2012, P.L. 112–81 (2011), Congress responded to the detention issue in *Hamdi*. Section 1021(a) "affirms that the authority of the President to use all necessary and appropriate force pursuant to the Authorization for Use of Military Force includes the authority for the

---

[85] On institutional defects of the judiciary in foreign affairs matters, see Neil Komesar, *Imperfect Alternatives: Choosing Institutions in Law, Economics, and Public Policy* (1994); Eric A. Posner & Adrian Vermeule, *Terror in the Balance: Security, Liberty, and the Courts* (2007); John Yoo, *Judicial Review and the War on Terrorism*, 72 Geo. Wash. L. Rev. 427 (2003).

Armed Forces of the United States to detain covered persons pending disposition under the law of war." Section 1021(b) defines "covered persons" as follows:

> (1) A person who planned, authorized, committed, or aided the terrorist attacks that occurred on September 11, 2001, or harbored those responsible for those attacks.
>
> (2) A person who was a part of or substantially supported al-Qaeda, the Taliban, or associated forces that are engaged in hostilities against the United States or its coalition partners, including any person who has committed a belligerent act or has directly supported such hostilities in aid of such enemy forces.

Section 1021(d) said this: "Nothing in this section is intended to limit or expand the authority of the President or the scope of the Authorization for Use of Military Force." Section 1021(e): "Nothing in this section shall be construed to affect existing law or authorities relating to the detention of United States citizens, lawful resident aliens of the United States, or any other persons who are captured or arrested in the United States."

When he signed the 2011 Act into law, President Barack Obama opined that § 1021 did not appreciably increase his authority, beyond what he already had under Article II and the 2001 AUMF. Do you agree? Does § 1021 authorize the President to detain American citizens (like Mr. Hamdi) if it considers them "a part of or substantially support[ing] al-Qaeda, the Taliban," and other hostile forces? Does § 1021 authorize the President to detain noncitizens who "substantially supported" those terrorist groups by leaking classified intelligence information? The Second Circuit answered "no" to the first question and ducked the second in *Hedges v. Obama*, 724 F.3d 170 (2 Cir. 2013), cert. denied, 572 U.S. 1087 (2014). See generally Oona Hathaway et al., *The Power to Detain: Detention of Terrorism Suspects After 9/11,* 38 Yale J. Int'l L. 123, 14344 (2013).

PROBLEM 8-9:
CRIMINAL RESPONSIBILITY FOR TORTURE OF PRISONERS?

At the same time the Supreme Court was deliberating in *Hamdi*, the media reported that U.S. soldiers engaged in abusive practices against Iraqis in Abu Ghraib prison, including various forms of sexual humiliation; the piling up of naked bodies in pyramids; beatings; food and sleep deprivation; and other abuses. Assume that some of the above practices are "torture" in violation of the Convention Against Torture and the criminal statute implementing the Convention, 18 U.S.C. § 2340A. Jack Bauer, a U.S. soldier who committed these offenses, is prosecuted in the United States.

Bauer's attorney argues that his client was acting under Department of Defense imperatives to extract useful information from "suspected terrorists." Hence, Bauer was acting reasonably pursuant to policies that can be traced back to Secretary of Defense Rumsfeld and, through him, to the President.

Assume that Bauer can make this connection. Does he have a valid constitutional argument that his prosecution for torture violates the constitutional separation of powers? In formulating your answer, consider (a) the Commander-in-Chief Clause, as well as other relevant provisions of the Constitution; (b) presidential practice under the Commander-in-Chief Clause;[86] and (c) Supreme Court precedent such as *The Prize Cases*, 67 U.S. 635 (1862), discussed in the Note on the War Powers Resolution. Jot down your thoughts, and now read the following executive department memorandum. If you were a judge, would you accept or reject Jack Bauer's constitutional defense to the torture prosecution?

Memorandum from Jay S. Bybee, Assistant Attorney General, to Alberto R. Gonzales, Counsel to the President, *Re: Standards of Conduct for Interrogation under 18 U.S.C. §§ 2340–2340A*

(Aug. 1, 2002)

This memorandum from the Office of Legal Counsel evaluated the limitations allegedly imposed on executive branch interrogation of prisoners taken in the "war on terrorism," by the Convention Against Torture and its implementing legislation. The memorandum advised the President that the anti-torture convention and legislation only "proscribe[ ] acts inflicting, and that are specifically intended to inflict, severe pain or suffering, whether mental or physical. Those acts must be of an extreme nature [to violate the Convention and statute]. We further conclude that certain acts may be cruel, inhuman, or degrading, but still not produce pain and suffering of the requisite intensity to fall within [the statutory] proscription against torture." In a later section, the memorandum also suggested that executive branch personnel engaged in torture out of "necessity" or in "self-defense" (of the country) would have defenses to prosecution for admitted torture of enemy combatants.

"Even if an interrogation method arguably were to violate [the anti-torture statute], the statute would be unconstitutional if it impermissibly encroached on the President's constitutional power to conduct a military campaign. As Commander-in-Chief, the President has the constitutional authority to order interrogations of enemy combatants to gain intelligence information concerning the military plans of the enemy. The demands of the Commander-in-Chief power are especially pronounced in the middle of a war in which the nation has already suffered a direct attack. In such a case, the information gained from interrogations may prevent future attacks by foreign enemies. Any effort to apply [the statute] in a manner that interferes with the

---

[86] George Washington was Commander in Chief both before and after there was a Constitution. According to Logan Beirne, *Blood of Tyrants: George Washington and the Forging of the Presidency* (2013), General Washington during the Revolution authorized torture of British agents and prisoners and considered such orders part of his authority as the American Commander in Chief; Beirne also argues that the Continental Congress eventually found it necessary to vest General Washington with virtually plenary authority to conduct the war. Barron & Lederman, *The Commander in Chief at the Lowest Ebb*, 772–81, argue that General Washington was always faithful to specific directives of the Congress.

President's direction of such core war matters as the detention and interrogation of enemy combatants thus would be unconstitutional." Bybee opined that "the President enjoys complete discretion in the exercise of his Commander-in-Chief authority and in conducting operations against hostile forces." Accordingly, he concluded that the anti-torture statute and convention do not limit the President's authority in any way.

" * * * The President's constitutional power to protect the security of the United States and the lives and safety of its people must be understood in light of the Founders' intention to create a federal government 'cloathed with all the powers requisite to the complete execution of its trust.' *The Federalist* No. 23 (Alexander Hamilton). Foremost among the objectives committed to that trust by the Constitution is the security of the nation. As Hamilton explained in arguing for the Constitution's adoption, because 'the circumstances which may affect the public safety' are not 'reducible within certain determinate limits,'

> it must be admitted, as a necessary consequence, that there can be no limitation of that authority, which is to provide for the defence and protection of the community, in any matter essential to its efficacy."
> *Id.* * * *

"The text, structure and history of the Constitution establish that the Founders entrusted the President with the primary responsibility, and therefore the power, to ensure the security of the United States in situations of grave and unforeseen emergencies. The decision to deploy military force in the defense of United States interests is expressly placed under Presidential authority by the Vesting Clause, U.S. Const. Art. I, § 1, cl. 1, and by the Commander-in-Chief Clause, *id.*, § 2, cl. 1. This Office has long understood the Commander-in-Chief Clause in particular as an affirmative grant of authority to the President. *See, e.g.,* Memorandum for Charles W. Colson, Special Counsel to the President, from William H. Rehnquist, Assistant Attorney General, Office of Legal Counsel, *Re: The President and the War Power: South Vietnam and the Cambodian Sanctuaries* (May 22, 1970). The Framers understood the Clause as investing the President with the fullest range of power understood at the time of the ratification of the Constitution as belonging to the military commander. In addition, the structure of the Constitution demonstrates that any power traditionally understood as pertaining to the executive—which includes the conduct of warfare and the defense of the nation—unless expressly assigned in the Constitution to Congress, is vested in the President. Article II, Section 1 makes this clear by stating that the 'executive Power shall be vested in a President of the United States of America.' That sweeping grant vests in the President an unenumerated 'executive power' and contrasts with the specific enumeration of the powers—those 'herein'—granted to Congress in Article I. The implications of constitutional text and structure are confirmed by the practical consideration that national security decisions require the unity in purpose and energy in action that characterize the Presidency rather than Congress.

"As the Supreme Court has recognized, the Commander-in-Chief power and the President's obligation to protect the nation imply the ancillary powers necessary to their successful exercise. 'The first of the enumerated powers of the President is that he shall be Commander-in-Chief of the Army and Navy of the United States. And, of course, the grant of war power includes all that is necessary and proper for carrying those powers into execution.' *Johnson v. Eisentrager*, 339 U.S. 763, 788 (1950). In wartime, it is for the President alone to decide what methods to use to best prevail against the enemy. *See, e.g.,* Rehnquist Memorandum * * *. The President's complete discretion in exercising the Commander-in-Chief power has been recognized by the courts. In the *Prize Cases*, for example, the Court explained that whether the President 'in fulfilling his duties as Commander in Chief' had appropriately responded to the rebellion of the southern states was a question 'to be *decided by him*' and which the Court could not question, but must leave to 'the political department of the Government to which this power was entrusted.'

"One of the core functions of the Commander in Chief is that of capturing, detaining, and interrogating members of the enemy. [Six lines crossed out in the public version of this memorandum.] It is well settled that the President may seize and detain enemy combatants, at least for the duration of the conflict, and the laws of war make clear that prisoners may be interrogated for information concerning the enemy, its strength, and its plans. Numerous Presidents have ordered the capture, detention, and questioning of enemy combatants during virtually every major conflict in the Nation's history, including recent conflicts such as the Gulf, Vietnam, and Korean wars. Recognizing this authority, Congress has never attempted to restrict or interfere with the President's authority on this score.

"Any effort by Congress to regulate the interrogation of battlefield combatants would violate the Constitution's sole vesting of the Commander-in-Chief authority in the President. * * * It may be the case that only successful interrogations can provide the information necessary to prevent the success of covert terrorist attacks upon the United States and its citizens. Congress can no more interfere with the President's conduct of the interrogation of enemy combatants than it can dictate strategic or tactical decisions on the battlefield. Just as statutes that order the President to conduct warfare in a certain manner or for specific goals would be unconstitutional, so too are laws that seek to prevent the President from gaining the intelligence he believes necessary to prevent attacks upon the United States."

Postscript. The OLC subsequently withdrew this memorandum, in part because of its narrow interpretation of what is "torture," Jack Goldsmith, *The Terror Presidency: Law and Judgment Inside the Bush Administration* 141–62 (2007), but has not backed away from the proposition that there is a core Commander-in-Chief power that Congress cannot regulate. Does Article II authorize the President to order suspected terrorists to be tortured under certain circumstances? If so, is there any limit to that authority?

Rasul v. Bush

542 U.S. 466 (2004)

Several non-citizen detainees at Guantanamo Bay, Cuba brought habeas corpus actions seeking release from what they charged was illegal detention. The government persuaded the lower court to dismiss these habeas petitions based upon *Johnson v. Eisentrager*, 339 U.S. 763 (1950). In that case, the Supreme Court ruled that prisoners detained by the Americans in Landsberg Prison in post-war occupied Germany were beyond the habeas jurisdiction of the federal judiciary. The Court said that the prisoners "at no relevant time were within any territory over which the United States is sovereign, and the scenes of their offense, their capture, their trial and their punishment were all beyond the territorial jurisdiction of any court of the United States." But the Court also emphasized the difficulties of ordering the government to produce the prisoners in a habeas corpus proceeding in the United States, for that "would require allocation of shipping space, guarding personnel, billeting and rations" and would damage the prestige of military commanders at a sensitive time.

Justice Stevens' opinion for the Court rejected the government's argument and ruled that statutory habeas jurisdiction extends to territories (such as Guantanamo) where the United States holds plenary and exclusive territorial jurisdiction, even if not ultimate sovereignty. Cuba has never exercised practical control over Guantanamo; from Cuban independence to the present, the United States has exercised practical control, but not sovereign control, pursuant to a long-term lease from Cuba. Justice Stevens distinguished *Eisentrager* on three grounds: (1) its complainants had been adjudicated enemy combatants, while Rasul and his colleagues insisted that they were not; (2) Landsberg Prison was far away from this country, and it would have been inconvenient to bring them here for a habeas proceeding, while Guantanamo is close at hand; and (3) Guantanamo is territory over which the United States has exclusive and plenary control. Justice Stevens's opinion also announced that *Eisentrager*'s interpretation of the habeas statute had been implicitly overruled by a subsequent Supreme Court decision.

Concurring only in the judgment, **Justice Kennedy** maintained that *Eisentrager* had not been overruled. Moreover, *Eisentrager* stands for the correct proposition that there is a "realm of political authority over military affairs where the judiciary may not enter," and which must be left to the political branches. But the Guantanamo detentions, although implicitly authorized by Congress, see *Hamdi*, were not within that realm, and Justice Kennedy concluded that these detentions fell outside the *Eisentrager* realm, in part because the United States exercises plenary control over Guantanamo Bay and in part because there had not been an authoritative determination of Rasul's status as an enemy combatant.

Writing for three dissenters, **Justice Scalia** assailed the majority opinion as a "wrenching departure from precedent." He relied on *Eisentrager* and claimed that it could not legitimately be distinguished from the Guantanamo cases. Additionally, Justice Scalia relied on the presumption that the Constitution does not apply extraterritorially, except under some circumstances to United States citizens (like Hamdi, but not Rasul).

NOTE ON THE NEW STATUTORY PROCESSES FOR GUANTANAMO DETAINEES

1. *Post-*Hamdi *Process for Detainees Seeking Release.* To satisfy the Court's judgment in *Hamdi*, the Bush-Cheney Administration established Combat Status Review Tribunals (CSRTs) to determine whether Hamdi and all other Guantanamo detainees should continue to be detained as suspected enemy combatants. Memorandum of the Secretary of the Navy, Implementation of Combatant Status Review Tribunal Procedures for Enemy Combatants Detained at Guantanamo Bay Naval Base (July 29, 2004). The tribunals followed the procedures of Army Regulation 190–8, *Enemy Prisoners of War, Retained Personnel, Civilian Internees and Other Detainees* (Dep't of Army, Nov. 11, 1997), which in turn follows the procedures outlined in the Geneva Convention. The process provided detainees with notice of the unclassified basis for his being considered an enemy combatant and opportunity to testify and present evidence to the CSRT, consisting of three military officers sworn to render an impartial decision and not involved in the detention or interrogation of the detainee. Each detainee was provided a "personal representative" who was charged with helping the detainee present his evidence. The decision of the tribunal was subject to mandatory review by the CSRT Legal Advisor and then the CSRT Director. As of November 2007, thirty-eight detainees were released pursuant to findings of their tribunals; another fifty-five (including Hamdi) were released after Department of Defense administrative review. Together, this was more than 25% of the detainees.

After *Rasul,* dozens of Guantanamo detainees filed habeas petitions. Section 1005(e) of the Detainee Treatment Act of 2005 (DTA) amended the habeas law, 28 U.S.C. § 2241, to provide that "no court, justice, or judge shall have jurisdiction to hear or consider . . . an application for a writ of habeas corpus filed by or on behalf of an alien detained by the Department of Defense at Guantanamo Bay, Cuba." 119 Stat. 2742. Section 1005(e) further provided that the Court of Appeals for the District of Columbia Circuit should have "exclusive" jurisdiction to review decisions of Department of Defense military commissions. The Supreme Court in *Hamdan v. Rumsfeld*, 548 U.S. 557 (2006), ruled that § 1005(e) did not apply to habeas petitions brought before the effective date of the statute.

2. *Military Commissions to Try Accused Enemy Combatants for Violations of the Law of War.* Soon after setting up the detention camp at Guantanamo, the Bush 45 Administration established, by executive order, military commissions to try detainees for war crimes, similar to the tribunal in *Quirin*, and with possible death penalties (such as those meted out in *Quirin*). In *Hamdan*, the Supreme Court ruled that the President's military

commissions were unlawful: its procedures were legally insufficient, because they were contrary to congressional enactments, primarily the Uniform Code of Military Justice (UCMJ). All eight participating *Hamdan* Justices followed and applied the Jackson framework from the *Steel Seizure Cases*. The Court (Justices Stevens, Kennedy, Souter, Ginsburg, Breyer) ruled that the Administration's deployment of a military commission in Hamdan's case fell within Jackson's Category 3, namely, that this was "incompatible with the expressed or implied will of Congress." The dissenters (Justices Scalia, Thomas, Alito), in contrast, found the matter to fall within Category 1, where the President's "authority is at its maximum, for it includes all that he possesses in his own right plus all that Congress can delegate." (Chief Justice Roberts did not participate, because he had joined the lower court opinion the Court was reversing.)

The *Quirin* Court had ruled that Congress in the Articles of War had authorized the President to try the Nazi saboteurs by military commission. Even though UCMJ Article 21 was a reenactment of the Article upon which *Quirin* had relied (Congress was aware of that and approved of *Quirin*), the *Hamdan* Court ruled that the UCMJ, adopted in 1950, did not authorize the post-9/11 military commissions. Justice Stevens offered three reasons: (1) Article 21 authorizes military commissions to try "offenders or offenses" that "by statute or by the law of war may be tried by" such commissions. The government could point to no statute, and conspiracy to commit war crimes is not a recognized violation of the law of war. In contrast, the sabotage in *Quirin* was an accepted violation of the law of war. This reason commanded only a plurality of the eight-Justice Court, but the other two commanded a majority. (2) The military commissions did not comport with UCMJ Article 36(b), which requires uniformity in procedural rules under the UCMJ unless "impracticable." The Court ruled that Article 36(b) creates a baseline whereby the court-martial procedures presumptively apply to military commissions; the Administration's relaxed evidentiary rules and its failure to give the defendant access to all the evidence against him were important departures from the court-martial rules that the Administration could not justify. (3) Until Hamdan is judged to be an enemy combatant, the 1949 Geneva Conventions require that he be subject to punishment only by a "regularly constituted court affording all the judicial guarantees which are recognized as indispensable by civilized peoples."

3. *Military Commissions Act of 2006 and a Tougher Statutory Restriction on Jurisdiction.* Four of the *Hamdan* majority Justices opined that Congress could speak more clearly if it chose, and Congress promptly did so, authorizing military commissions to try war crimes allegedly committed by the Guantanamo detainees and setting forth detailed procedural rules for those commissions. Some of the rules were similar to those followed in courts martial, but with many notable exceptions, including the admissibility of hearsay and (under some tightly defined circumstances) evidence obtained by coercion, the composition of the jury and the appointment of a presiding officer, and so forth. Note that military commissions are different from CSRTs: the

latter (responding to *Hamdi*) provide a process by which detained persons can challenge their continued detention and seek release; the former (responding to *Hamdan*) provide a process by which the government can seek penalties against detained persons for violating the law of war.

Section 7(a) of the Military Commissions Act of 2006 (MCA) further amended 28 U.S.C. § 2241(e) to read as follows:

> (1) No court, justice, or judge shall have jurisdiction to hear or consider an application for a writ of habeas corpus filed by or on behalf of an alien detained by the United States who has been determined by the United States to have been properly detained as an enemy combatant or is awaiting such determination.

> (2) Except as provided in [DTA §§ 1005(e)(2) and (e)(3)] no court, justice, or judge shall have jurisdiction to hear or consider any other action against the United States or its agents relating to any aspect of the detention, transfer, treatment, trial, or conditions of confinement of an alien who is or was detained by the United States and has been determined by the United States to have been properly detained as an enemy combatant or is awaiting such determination.

Section 7(b) provided that the amended language added by § 7(a) "shall take effect on the date of the enactment of this Act, and shall apply to all cases, without exception, pending on or after the date of the enactment of this Act which relate to any aspect of the detention, transfer, treatment, trial, or conditions of detention of an alien detained by the United States since September 11, 2001."

The purpose of § 7 was to cut off habeas for all Guantanamo Bay detainees. Senator Arlen Specter, the Chair of the Judiciary Committee and a sponsor of the MCA, opposed the inclusion of § 7 and argued that it was an unconstitutional deprivation of habeas rights. Notwithstanding this argument, the Senate narrowly voted to add § 7.

Boumediene v. Bush

553 U.S. 723 (2008)

In consolidated appeals, Lakhdar Boumediene and other accused terrorists detained by the United States at Guantanamo argued that federal courts could continue to hear their habeas petitions, either because § 7 did not by its literal terms apply to them or because § 7 was unconstitutional as applied to their habeas appeals. In his opinion for the Court, **Justice Kennedy** relied on the litigation background and the legislative history of MCA to interpret § 7 as applicable to these appeals. The question then was whether the Suspension Clause guaranteed a habeas forum to noncitizens held at Guantanamo and adjudged by CSRTs to be enemy combatants.

"The Framers viewed freedom from unlawful restraint as a fundamental precept of liberty, and they understood the writ of habeas corpus as a vital instrument to secure that freedom. Experience taught, however, that the common-law writ all too often had been insufficient to guard against the abuse of monarchial power. That history counseled the necessity for specific language in the Constitution to secure the writ and ensure its place in our legal system." Justice Kennedy provided a brief history of the English writ, which enjoyed a roller-coaster deployment, as often suspended or laxly enforced as actually applied. "That the Framers considered the writ a vital instrument for the protection of individual liberty is evident from the care taken to specify the limited grounds for its suspension" in Art. I, § 9, cl. 2.

The ratification debates indicated that the Framers deemed the writ of habeas corpus to be "an essential mechanism in the separation-of-powers scheme." For example, a "resolution passed by the New York ratifying convention made clear its understanding that the Clause not only protects against arbitrary suspensions of the writ but also guarantees an affirmative right to judicial inquiry into the causes of detention." Alexander Hamilton elaborated in *The Federalist* No. 84:

> "[T]he practice of arbitrary imprisonments, have been, in all ages, the favorite and most formidable instruments of tyranny. The observations of the judicious Blackstone . . . are well worthy of recital: 'To bereave a man of life . . . or by violence to confiscate his estate, without accusation or trial, would be so gross and notorious an act of despotism as must at once convey the alarm of tyranny throughout the whole nation; but confinement of the person, by secretly hurrying him to jail, where his sufferings are unknown or forgotten, is a less public, a less striking, and therefore a *more dangerous engine* of arbitrary government.' And as a remedy for this fatal evil he is everywhere peculiarly emphatical in his encomiums on the *habeas corpus* act, which in one place he calls 'the *bulwark* of the British Constitution.' " (quoting Blackstone).

Quoting *Hamdi,* the Court held that the Habeas Clause "ensures that, except during periods of formal suspension, the Judiciary will have a time-tested device, the writ, to maintain the 'delicate balance of governance' that is itself the surest safeguard of liberty. The Clause protects the rights of the detained by affirming the duty and authority of the Judiciary to call the jailer to account. The separation-of-powers doctrine, and the history that influenced its design, therefore must inform the reach and purpose of the Suspension Clause."

Justice Kennedy also examined founding-era materials to determine whether the writ could be denied because the prisoner was an alien or held outside the national boundaries. Rejecting cases presented by counsel for both Boumediene and the Administration, Justice Kennedy found no relevant founding-era precedent. Cf. *Brown v. Board of Education* ("although these sources cast some light, it is not enough to resolve the problem with which we are faced. At best, they are inconclusive").

Justice Kennedy looked to the Court's precedents to see if the writ could only be issued to noncitizens held in territory subject to the de jure, and not just de facto, sovereignty of the United States. Between 1901 and 1904, the Court adjudicated a series of *Insular Cases* involving the application of American law to former Spanish colonies (Puerto Rico, Cuba, Philippines). He summarized the holdings of those cases: "the Constitution has independent force in these territories, a force not contingent upon acts of legislative grace," but dependent upon practical considerations varying from case to case. See Christina Duffy Burnett, *United States: American Expansion and Territorial Deannexation*, 72 U. Chi. L. Rev. 797 (2005). As the Court later made clear, "the real issue in the Insular Cases was not whether the Constitution extended to the Philippines or Porto Rico when we went there, but which of its provisions were applicable by way of limitation upon the exercise of executive and legislative power in dealing with new conditions and requirements." *Balzac v. Porto Rico*, 258 U.S. 298, 312 (1922). "[T]he Court took for granted that even in unincorporated Territories the Government of the United States was bound to provide to noncitizen inhabitants 'guaranties of certain fundamental personal rights declared in the Constitution.'"

The Court rejected the Government's broad reading of *Johnson v. Eisentrager*, 339 U.S. 763 (1950), including its reasoning that, "at no relevant time were within any territory over which the United States is sovereign, and [that] the scenes of their offense, their capture, their trial and their punishment were all beyond the territorial jurisdiction of any court of the United States." That language could not support a rule that the Suspension Clause does not apply to any detention outside the United States: (1) other reasoning in *Eisentrager* emphasized practical concerns; (2) in *Eisentrager*, unlike this case, the United States lacked both de jure sovereignty *and* de facto authority over Landsberg Prison; and (3) the Insular Cases required a narrower reading.

Also, the Government's reading "raises troubling separation-of-powers concerns as well. * * * The necessary implication of the argument is that by surrendering formal sovereignty over any unincorporated territory to a third party, while at the same time entering into a lease that grants total control over the territory back to the United States, it would be possible for the political branches to govern without legal constraint. Our basic charter cannot be contracted away like this."

Based upon precedent, the Court found three factors to be relevant in determining the reach of the Suspension Clause: (1) the citizenship and status of the detainee and the adequacy of the process through which that status determination was made; (2) the nature of the sites where apprehension and then detention took place; and (3) the practical obstacles inherent in resolving the prisoner's entitlement to the writ. Given these factors, the Guantanamo detainees were not similarly situated to the Landsberg detainees of *Eisentrager*: (1) Although both were noncitizens, the Guantanamo detainees had not been afforded the trial-type process of military commissions given the detainees in Landsberg. (2) Although both were held outside the de jure sovereign territory of the United States, Guantanamo was subject to American plenary and exclusive control as a practical matter. (3) The costs of habeas consideration for the Guantanamo detainees were modest in comparison with the costs of habeas proceedings for the Landsberg ones.

The Court considered the argument that the D.C. Circuit appeals process provided by § 1005(e) of the DTA was an adequate substitute for habeas and ruled that it was not. While not offering a "comprehensive" procedural roadmap, the Court ruled that "the privilege of habeas corpus entitles the prisoner to a meaningful opportunity to demonstrate that he is being held pursuant to 'the erroneous application or interpretation' of relevant law. And the habeas court must have the power to order the conditional release of an individual unlawfully detained—though release need not be the exclusive remedy and is not the appropriate one in every case in which the writ is granted. These are the easily identified attributes of any constitutionally adequate habeas corpus proceeding. But, depending on the circumstances, more may be required." For example, "habeas courts in this country routinely allowed prisoners to introduce exculpatory evidence that was either unknown or previously unavailable to the prisoner."

The Court examined the process afforded by the CSRTs and found it insufficient. "The most relevant [process deficiency] for our purposes are the constraints upon the detainee's ability to rebut the factual basis for the Government's assertion that he is an enemy combatant. [A]t the CSRT stage the detainee has limited means to find or present evidence to challenge the Government's case against him. He does not have the assistance of counsel and may not be aware of the most critical allegations that the Government relied upon to order his detention. The detainee can confront witnesses that testify during the CSRT proceedings. But given that there are in effect no limits on the admission of hearsay evidence—the only requirement is that the tribunal deem the evidence "relevant and helpful"—the detainee's opportunity to question witnesses is likely to be more theoretical than real."

"Although we make no judgment as to whether the CSRTs, as currently constituted, satisfy due process standards, we agree with petitioners that, even when all the parties involved in this process act with diligence and in good faith, there is considerable risk of error in the tribunal's findings of fact. * * * And given that the consequence of error may be detention of persons for the duration of hostilities that may last a generation or more, this is a risk too significant to ignore.

"For the writ of habeas corpus, or its substitute, to function as an effective and proper remedy in this context, the court that conducts the habeas proceeding must have the means to correct errors that occurred during the CSRT proceedings. This includes some authority to assess the sufficiency of the Government's evidence against the detainee. It also must have the authority to admit and consider relevant exculpatory evidence that was not introduced during the earlier proceeding. Federal habeas petitioners long have had the means to supplement the record on review, even in the postconviction habeas setting. Here that opportunity is constitutionally required."

Chief Justice Roberts and **Justice Scalia** issued sharply-worded dissenting opinions. Concurring **Justice Souter** responded to some of their concerns.

NOTES ON BOUMEDIENE AND THE APPLICATION OF HABEAS TO NONCITIZEN DETAINEES

1. *Does Habeas Protect Noncitizens Held Outside American Sovereign Jurisdiction?* Justice Scalia's dissenting opinion presented three arguments why habeas does not so extend. (a) *Original Meaning.* When the Constitution of 1789 included the Suspension Clause, Justice Scalia maintained that the Framers would have assumed that the habeas remedy would have extended *no further* than it had already extended in 1789. Like the Court, Justice Scalia found no case where habeas had been extended to protect a noncitizen held by the Crown outside territories under the Crown's sovereign jurisdiction. The Court started from a different baseline, whereby habeas is available in all cases (and perhaps more) where it might have been available in 1789. Which is the more defensible baseline? Justice Scalia also relied on the Habeas Corpus Act of 1679, which was then adopted in several of the colonies and whose text seemed to contemplate a geographical limitation to England and territories it controlled. For a different understanding of the history, based upon original research, see Amanda L. Tyler, *Habeas Corpus in Wartime: From the Tower of London to Guantanamo Bay* (2017).

(b) *Precedent.* Justice Scalia maintained that *Eisentrager* had settled the issue, because Justice Jackson's opinion for the Court had rested upon his conclusion that there was no historical precedent for extending the writ to a noncitizen held outside the United States. Justice Kennedy responded that Justice Jackson also gave functional reasons for not extending habeas to the Landsberg prisoners, to which Justice Scalia replied that, under a functional approach, the Guantanamo detainees ought to have been entitled to *less* process than the Landsberg ones, not more: "The prisoners in *Eisentrager* were *prosecuted* for crimes after the cessation of hostilities; the prisoners here are enemy combatants *detained* during an ongoing conflict. The category of prisoner comparable to these detainees are not the *Eisentrager* criminal defendants, but the more than 400,000 prisoners of war detained in the United States alone during World War II." Justice Souter's concurring opinion emphasized that the Court's interpretation of *Eisentrager* in *Rasul* was also entitled to *stare decisis* effect, and that interpretation supported the Court.

(c) *Constitutional Text.* Under Article I, § 9, cl. 1, habeas can be suspended only "in Cases of Rebellion or Invasion." Justice Scalia argued: "The latter case (invasion) is plainly limited to the territory of the United States; and while it is conceivable that a rebellion could be mounted by American citizens abroad, surely the overwhelming majority of its occurrences would be domestic. If the extraterritorial scope of habeas turned on flexible, 'functional' considerations, as the Court holds, why would the Constitution limit its suspension almost entirely to instances of domestic crisis? Surely there is an even greater justification for suspension in foreign lands where the United States might hold prisoners of war during an ongoing conflict. And correspondingly, there is less threat to liberty when the Government suspends the writ's (supposed) application in foreign lands, where even on the most extreme view prisoners are entitled to fewer constitutional rights. It makes no sense, therefore, for the Constitution generally to forbid suspension of the writ abroad if indeed the writ has application there." Is this a cogent argument?

2.   *Has Congress Provided an Adequate Substitute for Habeas?* Chief Justice Roberts's dissenting opinion argued that the process was more than adequate. Properly understood, the way the political process presented the matter, Congress was replacing the collateral review of a habeas trial court + federal appeals court review with the collateral review of a CSRT + federal appeals court review. What is wrong with that, given the traditional flexibility of habeas *and* the *Hamdi* Court's balancing test for detainees? Under the DTA and the Department's post-*Hamdi* regulations, a detainee has the following rights (in the Chief Justice's language):

1.   "to present evidence that he has been wrongfully detained," including witnesses who are reasonably available, documentary evidence, the detainee's own testimony;

2.   access to a "personal representative" who may review "classified information" and explain its gist to the detainee, help the detainee arrange for witnesses, assist the detainee's preparation of his case, and even aid the detainee in presenting his evidence to the tribunal;

3.   appellate review of the sufficiency of the evidence justifying continued detention, as well as the constitutionality of the process the tribunal followed; the D.C. Circuit has the authority to direct the release of a detainee whose CSRT proceeding was unlawful.

"The DTA provides more opportunity and more process, in fact, than that afforded prisoners of war or any other alleged enemy combatants in history."

The Court's primary objection to this process was that the detainee could not present newly discovered exculpatory evidence to the D.C. Circuit, evidence that well might be missed by the incarcerated detainee and his vaguely defined "personal representative." But the Chief Justice responded that (a) the D.C. Circuit had the authority to remand the case to the CSRT for further proceedings in light of newly discovered evidence; (b) the Department of Defense authority in charge of Guantanamo conducted her own reviews of detainee status (most of the detainees thus far released had been pursuant to such administrative review) and could consider such evidence; and (c) DOD regulations affirmatively entitled the detainee to a new CSRT if there were new evidence that was material to the legality of his detention.

3.   *Consequentialist Arguments: What Happens Next?* Interestingly, three leading conservative jurists traded consequentialist arguments that revealed, for each jurist, why he voted the way he did in this case.

Justice Kennedy concluded his opinion with some rhetoric we have omitted: "Security depends upon a sophisticated intelligence apparatus and the ability of our Armed Forces to act and to interdict. There are further considerations, however. Security subsists, too, in fidelity to freedom's first principles. Chief among these are freedom from arbitrary and unlawful restraint and the personal liberty that is secured by adherence to the separation of powers. It is from these principles that the judicial authority to consider petitions for habeas corpus relief derives. * * * Within the Constitution's separation-of-powers structure, few exercises of judicial power are as legitimate or as necessary as the responsibility to hear challenges to the authority of the Executive to imprison a person. Some of these petitioners have been in custody for six years with no definitive judicial determination as to the legality of their detention. Their access to the writ is a necessity to determine the lawfulness of their status, even if, in the end, they do not obtain the relief they seek." Recall Bobbitt's analysis that opened this section.

Justice Scalia started his opinion with this: "America is at war with radical Islamists. * * * The game of bait-and-switch that today's opinion plays upon the Nation's Commander in Chief will make the war harder on us. It will almost certainly cause more Americans to be killed. * * * At least 30 of those prisoners hitherto released from Guantanamo Bay have returned to the battlefield. Some have been captured or killed. But others have succeeded in carrying on their atrocities against innocent civilians. In one case, a detainee released from Guantanamo Bay masterminded the kidnapping of two Chinese dam workers, one of whom was later shot to death when used as a human shield against Pakistani commandoes. Another former detainee promptly resumed his post as a senior Taliban commander and murdered a United Nations engineer and three Afghan soldiers. Still another murdered an Afghan judge. It was reported only last month that a released detainee carried out a suicide bombing against Iraqi soldiers in Mosul, Iraq."

Chief Justice Roberts ended his opinion thus: "So who has won? Not the detainees. The Court's analysis leaves them with only the prospect of further litigation to determine the content of their new habeas right, followed by further litigation to resolve their particular cases, followed by further litigation before the D. C. Circuit—where they could have started had they invoked the DTA procedure. Not Congress, whose attempt to 'determine—through democratic means—how best' to balance the security of the American people with the detainees' liberty interests, has been unceremoniously brushed aside. Not the Great Writ, whose majesty is hardly enhanced by its extension to a jurisdictionally quirky outpost, with no tangible benefit to anyone. Not the rule of law, unless by that is meant the rule of lawyers, who will now arguably have a greater role than military and intelligence officials in shaping policy for alien enemy combatants. And certainly not the American people, who today lose a bit more control over the conduct of this Nation's foreign policy to unelected, politically unaccountable judges."

There is a more pragmatic, and less dramatic, way of thinking about the consequences of the *Boumediene* and *Hamdi* line of cases. This is the *proceduralization of enemy detention*. The old model of prisoners of war held without process (*Eisentrager*) has given way to a new model of suspected terrorists who are entitled to some process (*Hamdi* and *Boumediene*). The big change is not that the latter are held at Guantanamo (*Boumediene*) or within the United States (*Rasul*), or that they are sometimes citizens (*Hamdi*). The big change is rampant ambiguity as to who is the "enemy." Now that the War on Terror has formally delinked "enemy" from "nation state," it is often hard to tell who is (potential) "ally" and who is (secret) "enemy." The Bush 45 Administration thought that the President needed leeway to hold suspected enemies with no judicial monitoring, see the Bybee Memorandum (2002), while the critics believed that judicial monitoring is needed to assure that the rule of law is followed. See Bobbitt, *Terror and Consent*; Christina Duffy Burnett, *A Convenient Constitution? Extraterritoriality After* Boumediene, 109 Colum. L. Rev. 973 (2009) (arguing that the Court should have laid down a harder rule for treatment of alleged enemy combatants).

PROBLEM 8-10:
PRESIDENT TRUMP'S ANTI-TERROR AUTHORITY

In 2016, Donald J. Trump was elected President on a platform of tougher protection of the homeland. Consider the constitutionality of three presidential responses to homeland security. The first one, below, is largely hypothetical, the second and third ones draw from President Trump's exercise of the powers of his office. Would any of the following policies violate the Constitution?

(a) *Indefinite Detention.* Like President Obama, President Trump has condemned Australian computer programmer Julian Assange (now a citizen of Ecuador, whose London embassy gave him asylum). Assange's "Wikileaks" have included embarrassing and classified information, including the 2010 *Collateral Murder* video (April 2010) showing American soldiers fatally shooting 18 people from a helicopter in Iraq, as well as classified government war logs for the wars in Afghanistan and Iraq, as well as classified diplomatic cables. Both Administrations consider Assange's actions to be criminal offenses—but assume the Trump Administration somehow gets ahold of Assange and detains him indefinitely in Guantanamo. Consider the following constitutional and statutory issues:

- Can the President and his successors detain Assange for the rest of his life? Does the Constitution or any statute assure Assange of some kind of process? Is § 1021 of the 2011 Defense Authorization Act relevant? If so, how should it be interpreted?

- Can the President issue an executive order denying Assange the right to file a writ of habeas corpus?

- In various tweets, President Trump has asserted authority to direct officials to torture suspected terrorists if required by national security. Can the President authorize officials to waterboard Assange, in order to secure information about our government's leaks of classified information? The Bybee Memorandum suggests that he can, but the Department of Justice has withdrawn it: Should its analysis be revived? Is it constitutionally sound?

Set aside issues of justiciability, which we shall develop in the next chapter. Would the Supreme Court allow these various actions?

(b) *Funding a Wall on the Border with Mexico.* A central theme of Trump's successful presidential campaign was that, if elected, he would build a tall, secure "wall" between the United States and Mexico. He claimed that Mexico would pay for the wall, but Mexico has not been forthcoming on that front. As of March 2019, Congress has not enacted sufficient appropriations to pay for such a wall, which would cost $20–100 billion, depending on the quality and height of the wall. On February 15, 2019, President Trump declared a national emergency, pursuant to the National Emergencies Act of 1976, P.L. 94–412, 50 U.S.C. § 1621 (authorizing the President to declare a national emergency but not defining "emergency"). The national emergency was premised upon the President's representation that the nation was being flooded with illegal drugs and "gangs" entering through unprotected portions of the Mexican border. Official as well as unofficial sources establish that almost all illegal drugs enter the United States through protected ports of entry. Congress can veto the declaration through a joint resolution (presented to the President) that must be considered under fast-track procedures set forth in 50 U.S.C. § 1622. Congress did pass such blocking legislation, but President Trump vetoed it, so the state of emergency continued (as we went to press in March 2019).

Based upon the emergency, the President also announced his intention to divert $3.6 billion from funds appropriated for defense construction to help finance a wall between the United States and Mexico. When Congress declares war or the President declares a national emergency that "requires the use of the armed forces, the Secretary of Defense, without regard to any other provision of law, may undertake military construction projects, and may authorize the Secretaries of the military departments to undertake military construction projects, not otherwise authorized by law that are necessary to support such use of the armed forces." 10 U.S.C. § 2808(a). The Bush-Cheney Administration had accessed such funds after declaring a national emergency in the wake of 9/11. Other funding sources for the wall do not depend upon the declaration of an emergency. In February, Congress itself appropriated $1.375 billion for construction of the wall.

Assume that the President spends the $3.6 billion in military construction funds and that its legality is justiciable (Chapter 9): Does it violate the Constitution?

(c) *The [Muslim] Travel Bans.* Another central theme of Trump's 2016 presidential campaign was that he would ban immigration of Muslims into the United States, on the ground that Islam, by his lights, is an extremist and violent religion and that Muslims pose an unusually high threat of terrorist activities. Until May 2017, the candidate's website said this: "Donald J. Trump is calling for a total and complete shutdown of Muslims entering the United States until our country's representatives can figure out what is going on. According to Pew Research, among others, there is great hatred towards Americans by large segments of the Muslim population."

A week after his inauguration, the President issued Travel Ban 1.0, which was withdrawn after a barrage of injunctions issued by judges all over the country. The President replaced it with Travel Ban 2.0: "Protecting the Nation From Foreign Terrorist Entry Into the United States." Exec. Order No. 13780, 82 Fed. Reg. 13209 (Mar. 6, 2017). The White House Press Secretary told reporters that, by issuing the second executive order, President Trump "continue[d] to deliver on * * * his most significant campaign promises." That statement was consistent with President Trump's own declaration that "I keep my campaign promises, and our citizens will be very happy when they see the result."

Travel Ban 2.0 announced a 90-day ban on travel into the United States for nationals of six majority-Muslim countries: Iran, Libya, Somalia, Sudan, Syria, and Yemen. (Travel Ban 1.0 also included Iraq.) The order explained:

> Each of these countries is a state sponsor of terrorism, has been significantly compromised by terrorist organizations, or contains active conflict zones. Any of these circumstances diminishes the foreign government's willingness or ability to share or validate important information about individuals seeking to travel to the United States. Moreover, the significant presence in each of these countries of terrorist organizations, their members, and others exposed to those organizations increases the chance that conditions will be exploited to enable terrorist operatives or sympathizers to travel to the United States. Finally, once foreign nationals from these countries are admitted to the United States, it is often difficult to remove them, because many of these countries typically delay issuing, or refuse to issue, travel documents.

Based on the conditions of these six countries, "the risk of erroneously permitting entry of a national of one of these countries who intends to commit terrorist acts or otherwise harm the national security of the United States is unacceptably high."

Travel Ban 2.0 exempted lawful permanent residents, dual citizens traveling under a passport issued by a country not on the banned list, asylum-seekers, and refugees already admitted to the United States. The executive order also provided that consular officers or Customs and Border Protection officials could exercise discretion in authorizing case-by-case waivers to issue visas and grant entry during the suspension period, and offered examples of when waivers "could be appropriate."

Like Travel Ban 1.0, Travel Ban 2.0 was issued pursuant to authority vested in the President by § 212(f) of the Immigration and Nationalization Act of 1952:

> Whenever the President finds that the entry of any aliens or of any class of aliens into the United States would be detrimental to the interests of the United States, he may by proclamation, and for such period as he shall deem necessary, suspend the entry of all aliens or any class of aliens as immigrants or nonimmigrants, or impose on the entry of aliens any restrictions he may deem to be appropriate.

8 U.S.C. § 1182(f). Added by a later amendment to the 1952 Act, section 1182(a)(3) requires that immigration officials bar entry into this country to an alien for whom there is "reasonable ground to believe" that he or she "is likely to engage after entry in any [specifically defined] terrorist activity," 8 U.S.C. § 1182(a)(3)(B)(i)(II).

Contemporaneous to enacting the Civil Rights Act of 1964, Congress amended the INA in 1965 to eliminate the "national origins system as the basis for the selection of immigrants to the United States." H.R. Rep. No. 89–745, at 8 (1965). Section 1152(a)(1)(A) says this:

> [N]o person shall receive any preference or priority or be discriminated against in the issuance of an immigrant visa because of the person's race, sex, nationality, place of birth, or place of residence.

8 U.S.C. § 1152(a)(1)(A). In addition, the Establishment Clause of the First Amendment has been read to bar the federal government from penalizing religious minorities in domestic statutes and regulations. See Chapter 6, § 6 of this Casebook for a detailed analysis.

What is the biggest constitutional problem with Travel Ban 2.0? What would be the President's best argument in response? What is the proper constitutional analysis for each colorable challenge? How should a court have ruled? Compare *Hawaii v. Trump*, 859 F.3d 741 (9th Cir. 2017), cert. granted, 137 S.Ct. 2080 (June 2017) (negative evaluation), with Josh Blackman, *Immigration and National Security*, 2018 Cato Sup. Ct. Rev. 29 (history and constitutional defense of Travel Bans 1.0, 2.0, and 3.0).

TRUMP V. HAWAII
___ U.S. ___, 138 S.Ct. 2392, 201 L.Ed.2d 775 (2018)

CHIEF JUSTICE ROBERTS delivered the opinion of the Court. * * *

[After several judicial rebuffs to Travel Ban 2.0, President Trump in September 2017 replaced it with Travel Ban 3.0. Proclamation No. 9645 placed entry restrictions on the nationals of eight foreign states whose systems for managing and sharing information about their nationals the President deemed inadequate. Foreign states were selected for inclusion in the new travel ban based on a risk review undertaken by DHA, the State Department, and intelligence agencies. DHS identified countries having deficient information-sharing practices and presenting national security concerns. After the State Department made diplomatic efforts to encourage foreign governments to improve their practices, the Acting Secretary of Homeland Security concluded that eight countries—Chad, Iran, Iraq, Libya, North Korea, Syria, Venezuela, and Yemen—remained deficient. She recommended entry restrictions for certain nationals from all of those countries but Iraq, which had a close cooperative relationship with the U.S. She also recommended including Somalia, which met the information-sharing component of the baseline standards but had other special risk factors, such as a significant terrorist presence.

[After consulting with Cabinet members, the President adopted the recommendations and issued the Proclamation as Travel Ban 3.0. Invoking his authority under §§ 1182(f) and 1185(a), the President determined that certain restrictions were necessary to "prevent the entry of those foreign nationals about whom the United States Government lacks sufficient information" and "elicit improved identity-management and information-sharing protocols and practices from foreign governments." The Proclamation imposed a range of entry restrictions that vary based on the "distinct circumstances" in each of the eight countries. It exempted lawful permanent residents and provided case-by-case waivers under certain circumstances. It also directed DHS to assess on a continuing basis whether the restrictions should be modified or continued, and to report to the President every 180 days. At the completion of the first such review period, the President determined that Chad had sufficiently improved its practices, and he lifted restrictions on its nationals.]

Plaintiffs—the State of Hawaii, three individuals with foreign relatives affected by the entry suspension, and the Muslim Association of Hawaii—argue that the Proclamation violates the Immigration and Nationality Act (INA) and the Establishment Clause. The District Court granted a nationwide preliminary injunction barring enforcement of the restrictions. The Ninth Circuit affirmed, concluding that the Proclamation contravened two provisions of the INA: § 1182(f), which authorizes the President to "suspend the entry of all aliens or any class of aliens" whenever he "finds" that their entry "would be detrimental to the interests of the United States," and § 1152(a)(1)(A), which provides that "no person shall . . . be discriminated against in the issuance of an immigrant visa because of the person's race, sex, nationality, place of birth, or place of residence." * * *

The text of § 1182(f) states:

"Whenever the President finds that the entry of any aliens or of any class of aliens into the United States would be detrimental to the interests of the United States, he may by proclamation, and for such period as he shall deem necessary, suspend the entry of all aliens or any class of aliens as immigrants or nonimmigrants, or impose on the entry of aliens any restrictions he may deem to be appropriate."

By its terms, § 1182(f) exudes deference to the President in every clause. It entrusts to the President the decisions whether and when to suspend entry ("[w]henever [he] finds that the entry" of aliens "would be detrimental" to the national interest); whose entry to suspend ("all aliens or any class of aliens"); for how long ("for such period as he shall deem necessary"); and on what conditions ("any restrictions he may deem to be appropriate"). It is therefore unsurprising that we have previously observed that § 1182(f) vests the President with "ample power" to impose entry restrictions in addition to those elsewhere enumerated in the INA. [*Sale v. Haitian Centers Council, Inc.,* 509 U.S. 155 (1993).]

The Proclamation falls well within this comprehensive delegation. The sole prerequisite set forth in § 1182(f) is that the President "find[ ]" that the entry of the covered aliens "would be detrimental to the interests of the United States." The President has undoubtedly fulfilled that requirement here. He first ordered DHS and other agencies to conduct a comprehensive evaluation of every single country's compliance with the information and risk assessment baseline. The President then issued a Proclamation setting forth extensive findings describing how deficiencies in the practices of select foreign governments—several of which are state sponsors of terrorism—deprive the Government of "sufficient information to assess the risks [those countries' nationals] pose to the United States." Proclamation § 1(h)(i). Based on that review, the President found that it was in the national interest to restrict entry of aliens who could not be vetted with adequate information—both to protect national security and public safety, and to induce improvement by their home countries. The Proclamation therefore "craft[ed] . . . country-specific restrictions that would be most likely to encourage cooperation given each country's distinct circumstances," while securing the Nation "until such time as improvements occur." *Ibid.*

Plaintiffs believe that these findings are insufficient. They argue, as an initial matter, that the Proclamation fails to provide a persuasive rationale for why nationality alone renders the covered foreign nationals a security risk. And they further discount the President's stated concern about deficient vetting because the Proclamation allows many aliens from the designated countries to enter on nonimmigrant visas.

Such arguments are grounded on the premise that § 1182(f) not only requires the President to *make* a finding that entry "would be detrimental to the interests of the United States," but also to explain that finding with sufficient detail to enable judicial review. That premise is questionable. See *Webster v. Doe,* 486 U.S. 592, 600 (1988) (concluding that a statute authorizing the CIA Director to terminate an employee when the Director "shall deem such termination necessary or advisable in the interests of the United States" forecloses "any meaningful judicial standard of review"). But even assuming that some form of review is appropriate, plaintiffs' attacks on the sufficiency of the President's findings cannot be sustained. The 12-page Proclamation—which thoroughly describes the process, agency evaluations, and recommendations underlying the President's chosen restrictions—is more detailed than any prior order a President has issued under § 1182(f).

Moreover, plaintiffs' request for a searching inquiry into the persuasiveness of the President's justifications is inconsistent with the broad statutory text and the deference traditionally accorded the President in this sphere. "Whether the President's chosen method" of addressing perceived risks is justified from a policy perspective is "irrelevant to the scope of his [§ 1182(f)] authority." *Sale.* And when the President adopts "a preventive measure . . . in the context of international affairs and national security," he is "not required to conclusively link all of the pieces in the puzzle before [courts] grant weight to [his] empirical conclusions." *Holder v. Humanitarian Law Project,* 561 U.S. 1, 35 (2010). * * *

For more than a century, this Court has recognized that the admission and exclusion of foreign nationals is a "fundamental sovereign attribute exercised by the Government's political departments largely immune from judicial control." *Fiallo v. Bell,* 430 U.S. 787, 792 (1977). Because decisions in these matters may implicate "relations with foreign powers," or involve "classifications defined in the light of changing political and economic circumstances," such judgments "are frequently of a character more appropriate to either the Legislature or the Executive." *Mathews v. Diaz,* 426 U.S. 67, 81 (1976).

Nonetheless, although foreign nationals seeking admission have no constitutional right to entry, this Court has engaged in a circumscribed judicial inquiry when the denial of a visa allegedly burdens the constitutional rights of a U.S. citizen. In *Kleindienst v. Mandel,* [408 U.S. 753 (1972),] the Attorney General denied admission to a Belgian journalist and self-described "revolutionary Marxist," Ernest Mandel, who had been invited to speak at a conference at Stanford University. The professors who wished to hear Mandel speak challenged that decision under the First Amendment, and we acknowledged that their constitutional "right to receive information" was implicated. But we limited our review to whether the Executive gave a "facially legitimate and bona fide" reason for its action. Given the authority of the political branches over admission, we held that "when the Executive exercises this [delegated] power negatively on the basis of a facially legitimate and bona fide reason, the courts will neither look behind the exercise of that discretion, nor test it by balancing its justification" against the asserted constitutional interests of U.S. citizens.

The upshot of our cases in this context is clear: "Any rule of constitutional law that would inhibit the flexibility" of the President "to respond to changing world conditions should be adopted only with the greatest caution," and our inquiry into matters of entry and national security is highly constrained. *Mathews*. We need not define the precise contours of that inquiry in this case. A conventional application of *Mandel,* asking only whether the policy is facially legitimate and bona fide, would put an end to our review. But the Government has suggested that it may be appropriate here for the inquiry to extend beyond the facial neutrality of the order. See Tr. of Oral Arg. 16–17, 25–27 (describing *Mandel* as "the starting point" of the analysis). For our purposes today, we assume that we may look behind the face of the Proclamation to the extent of applying rational basis review. That standard of review considers whether the entry policy is plausibly related to the Government's stated objective to protect the country and improve vetting processes. See *Railroad Retirement Bd. v. Fritz,* 449 U.S. 166, 179 (1980). As a result, we may consider plaintiffs' extrinsic evidence, but will uphold the policy so long as it can reasonably be understood to result from a justification independent of unconstitutional grounds. * * *

The Proclamation is expressly premised on legitimate purposes: preventing entry of nationals who cannot be adequately vetted and inducing other nations to improve their practices. The text says nothing about religion. Plaintiffs and the dissent nonetheless emphasize that five of the seven nations currently included in the Proclamation have Muslim-majority populations. Yet that fact alone does not support an inference of religious hostility, given that the policy covers just 8% of the world's Muslim population and is limited to countries that were previously designated by Congress or prior administrations as posing national security risks. See 8 U.S.C. § 1187(a)(12)(A) (identifying Syria and state sponsors of terrorism such as Iran as "countr[ies] or area[s] of concern" for purposes of administering the Visa Waiver Program); Dept. of Homeland Security, DHS Announces Further Travel Restrictions for the Visa Waiver Program (Feb. 18, 2016) (designating Libya, Somalia, and Yemen as additional countries of concern). * * *

Finally, the dissent invokes *Korematsu v. United States,* 323 U.S. 214 (1944). Whatever rhetorical advantage the dissent may see in doing so, *Korematsu* has nothing to do with this case. The forcible relocation of U.S. citizens to concentration camps, solely and explicitly on the basis of race, is objectively unlawful and outside the scope of Presidential authority. But it is wholly inapt to liken that morally repugnant order to a facially neutral policy denying certain foreign nationals the privilege of admission. The entry suspension is an act that is well within executive authority and could have been taken by any other President—the only question is evaluating the actions of this particular President in promulgating an otherwise valid Proclamation.

The dissent's reference to *Korematsu,* however, affords this Court the opportunity to make express what is already obvious: *Korematsu* was gravely wrong the day it was decided, has been overruled in the court of history, and—to be clear—"has no place in law under the Constitution." [*Korematsu,*] 323 U.S. at 248 (Jackson, J., dissenting). * * *

[We omit the concurring opinions of **JUSTICE KENNEDY** and **JUSTICE THOMAS**. Based on his reading of the original meaning of Article III, the latter objected to the nationwide injunction issued by the district courts in these cases.]

[**JUSTICE BREYER**, joined by **JUSTICE KAGAN**, dissented. In their view, "the Proclamation's elaborate system of exemptions and waivers" were relevant. They would provide "case-by-case consideration of persons who may qualify for visas despite the Proclamation's general ban. Those persons include lawful permanent residents, asylum seekers, refugees, students, children, and numerous others." Briefs filed in the case suggest that that system was not being applied, and these Justices would have remanded the case for district court hearings on this issue. If the record could not be enriched in that way, these Justices agreed with Justice Sotomayor's constitutional objection.]

JUSTICE SOTOMAYOR, joined by **JUSTICE GINSBURG**, dissented.

The United States of America is a Nation built upon the promise of religious liberty. Our Founders honored that core promise by embedding the principle of religious neutrality in the First Amendment. The Court's decision today fails to safeguard that fundamental principle. It leaves undisturbed a policy first advertised openly and unequivocally as a "total and complete shutdown of Muslims entering the United States" because the policy now masquerades behind a facade of national-security concerns. But this repackaging does little to cleanse Presidential Proclamation No. 9645 of the appearance of discrimination that the President's words have created. Based on the evidence in the record, a reasonable observer would conclude that the Proclamation was motivated by anti-Muslim animus. That alone suffices to show that plaintiffs are likely to succeed on the merits of their Establishment Clause claim. The majority holds otherwise by ignoring the facts, misconstruing our legal precedent, and turning a blind eye to the pain and suffering the Proclamation inflicts upon countless families and individuals, many of whom are United States citizens.

Because that troubling result runs contrary to the Constitution and our precedent, I dissent. * * *

The Establishment Clause forbids government policies "respecting an establishment of religion." U.S. Const., Amdt. 1. The "clearest command" of the Establishment Clause is that the Government cannot favor or disfavor one religion over another. *Larson v. Valente,* 456 U.S. 228, 244 (1982); *Church of Lukumi Babalu Aye, Inc. v. Hialeah,* 508 U.S. 520, 532 (1993). Consistent with that clear command, this Court has long acknowledged that governmental actions that favor one religion "inevitabl[y]" foster "the hatred, disrespect and even contempt of those who [hold] contrary beliefs." *Engel v. Vitale,* 370 U.S. 421, 431 (1962). That is so, this Court has held, because such acts send messages to members of minority faiths " 'that they are outsiders, not full members of the political community.' " *Santa Fe Independent School Dist. v. Doe,* 530 U.S. 290, 309 (2000). To guard against this serious harm, the Framers mandated a strict "principle of denominational neutrality." *Larson.*

"When the government acts with the ostensible and predominant purpose" of disfavoring a particular religion, "it violates that central Establishment Clause value of official religious neutrality, there being no neutrality when the government's ostensible object is to take sides." *McCreary County v. American Civil Liberties Union of Ky.,* 545 U.S. 844, 860 (2005). To determine whether plaintiffs have proved an Establishment Clause violation, the Court asks whether a reasonable observer would view the government action as enacted for the purpose of disfavoring a religion. See *id.*

In answering that question, this Court has generally considered the text of the government policy, its operation, and any available evidence regarding "the historical background of the decision under challenge, the specific series of events leading to the enactment or official policy in question, and the legislative or administrative history, including contemporaneous statements made by" the decisionmaker. *Lukumi; McCreary.*

[Justice Sotomayor recounted the history of the President's religion-based justification for a travel ban. Our quotations in Problem 8-10(c) are taken from her dissenting opinion, which cited much more evidence that President Trump openly boasted that his travel bans were fulfilling his campaign promise to ban Muslims seeking to enter the country; the majority did not dispute the accuracy or attribution of any of the quotations.]

Taking all the relevant evidence together, a reasonable observer would conclude that the Proclamation was driven primarily by anti-Muslim animus, rather than by the Government's asserted national-security justifications. Even before being sworn into office, then-candidate Trump stated that "Islam hates us," warned that "[w]e're having problems with the Muslims, and we're having problems with Muslims coming into the country," promised to enact a "total and complete shutdown of Muslims entering the United States," and instructed one of his advisers to find a "lega[l]" way to enact a Muslim ban. The President continued to make similar statements well after his inauguration * * *.

Moreover, despite several opportunities to do so, President Trump has never disavowed any of his prior statements about Islam. Instead, he has continued to make remarks that a reasonable observer would view as an unrelenting attack on the Muslim religion and its followers. Given President Trump's failure to correct the reasonable perception of his apparent hostility toward the Islamic faith, it is unsurprising that the President's lawyers have, at every step in the lower courts, failed in their attempts to launder the Proclamation of its discriminatory taint. * * *

In light of the Government's suggestion "that it may be appropriate here for the inquiry to extend beyond the facial neutrality of the order," the majority rightly declines to apply *Mandel's* "narrow standard of review" and "assume[s] that we may look behind the face of the Proclamation." In doing so, however, the Court, without explanation or precedential support, limits its review of the Proclamation to rational-basis scrutiny. That approach is perplexing, given that in other Establishment Clause cases, including those involving claims of religious animus or discrimination, this Court has applied a more stringent standard of review. As explained above, the Proclamation is plainly unconstitutional under that heightened standard.

But even under rational-basis review, the Proclamation must fall. That is so because the Proclamation is " 'divorced from any factual context from which we could discern a relationship to legitimate state interests,' and 'its sheer breadth [is] so discontinuous with the reasons offered for it' " that the policy is " 'inexplicable by anything but animus.' " [Opinion for the Court] (quoting *Romer*); see also *Cleburne v. Cleburne Living Center, Inc.,* 473 U.S. 432, 448 (1985) (recognizing that classifications predicated on discriminatory animus can never be legitimate because the Government has no legitimate interest in exploiting "mere negative attitudes, or fear" toward a disfavored group). The President's statements, which the majority utterly fails to address in its legal analysis, strongly support the conclusion that the Proclamation was issued to express hostility toward Muslims and exclude them from the country. Given the overwhelming record evidence of anti-Muslim animus, it simply cannot be said that the Proclamation has a legitimate basis.

The majority insists that the Proclamation furthers two interrelated national-security interests: "preventing entry of nationals who cannot be adequately vetted and inducing other nations to improve their practices."

But the Court offers insufficient support for its view "that the entry suspension has a legitimate grounding in [those] national security concerns, quite apart from any religious hostility." Indeed, even a cursory review of the Government's asserted national-security rationale reveals that the Proclamation is nothing more than a " 'religious gerrymander.' " *Lukumi.*

The majority first emphasizes that the Proclamation "says nothing about religion." Even so, the Proclamation, just like its predecessors, overwhelmingly targets Muslim-majority nations. Given the record here, including all the President's statements linking the Proclamation to his apparent hostility toward Muslims, it is of no moment that the Proclamation also includes minor restrictions on two non-Muslim majority countries, North Korea and Venezuela, or that the Government has removed a few Muslim-majority countries from the list of covered countries since EO-1 was issued. Consideration of the entire record supports the conclusion that the inclusion of North Korea and Venezuela, and the removal of other countries, simply reflect subtle efforts to start "talking territory instead of Muslim," precisely so the Executive Branch could evade criticism or legal consequences for the Proclamation's otherwise clear targeting of Muslims. The Proclamation's effect on North Korea and Venezuela, for example, is insubstantial, if not entirely symbolic. A prior sanctions order already restricts entry of North Korean nationals, see Exec. Order No. 13810, 82 Fed. Reg. 44705 (2017), and the Proclamation targets only a handful of Venezuelan government officials and their immediate family members, 82 Fed. Reg. 45166. As such, the President's inclusion of North Korea and Venezuela does little to mitigate the anti-Muslim animus that permeates the Proclamation.

[Justice Sotomayor also contended that Congress had already provided procedures that were a better-tailored mechanism for protecting national security concerns. Even after opportunity for briefing in the various court challenges, President Trump had not demonstrated how the broad travel ban added anything to national security. The failure to make such a showing was further evidence that EO3 was, like EO1 and EO2, nothing more than a mechanism to implement Trump's repeated promises of a Muslim travel ban.]

Today's holding is all the more troubling given the stark parallels between the reasoning of this case and that of *Korematsu v. United States,* 323 U.S. 214 (1944). In *Korematsu,* the Court gave "a pass [to] an odious, gravely injurious racial classification" authorized by an executive order. *Adarand Constructors, Inc. v. Peña,* 515 U.S. 200, 275 (1995) (Ginsburg, J., dissenting). As here, the Government invoked an ill-defined national-security threat to justify an exclusionary policy of sweeping proportion. As here, the exclusion order was rooted in dangerous stereotypes about, inter alia, a particular group's supposed inability to assimilate and desire to harm the United States. As here, the Government was unwilling to reveal its own intelligence agencies' views of the alleged security concerns to the very citizens it purported to protect. And as here, there was strong evidence that impermissible hostility and animus motivated the Government's policy. * * *

NOTES ON THE TRAVEL BAN CASE AND JUDICIAL REVIEW OF PRESIDENTIAL AUTHORITY TOUCHING NATIONAL SECURITY

1. *Justiciability Issues.* In the travel ban cases, the courts had to determine whether there was an Article III case or controversy. The Trump Administration maintained that the plaintiffs' statutory claims (under the INA) were nonjusticiable. Based on the doctrine of consular nonreviewability, the Administration argued that because aliens have no "claim of right" to enter the United States, and because exclusion of aliens is "a fundamental act of sovereignty" by the political branches, review of an exclusion decision "is not within the province of any court, unless expressly authorized by law." *United States ex rel. Knauff v. Shaughnessy,* 338 U.S. 537, 542–43 (1950). The INA itself sets forth a comprehensive framework for review of orders of removal, but authorizes judicial review only for aliens physically present in the United State. Without dissent, the Chief Justice sidestepped that issue, which did not affect the Court's jurisdiction, and declined to resolve it.

As Chapter 9 will note, many Establishment Clause cases are dismissed because the plaintiffs cannot claim an individuated harm, which is fatal under the Court's Article III "standing" jurisprudence. Also, noncitizens trying to enter the country may not have standing to assert constitutional rights of their own. For those reasons, the plaintiffs were not the people directly subject to the travel ban, but were instead their American relatives. In *Trump v. Hawaii,* the Chief Justice's opinion held, without dissent, that American relatives of excluded foreign visitors had standing to sue.

2. *Which Jackson Category?* As in *Steel Seizure,* a central debate in the Travel Ban Cases was whether the President's action was at its "lowest ebb," because contrary to specific direction from Congress, acting through statutes that were on point and disregarded by the President. As is commonly the case now, the *Steel Seizure* constitutional authority issue boiled down to a series of statutory interpretation issues: If the President is acting pursuant to an explicit congressional delegation—as he did in *Curtiss-Wright*—the Supreme Court will uphold his action against separation of powers claims.

The lower courts found that the President went beyond his congressionally delegated authority in § 1182(f) and, further, contravened the anti-discrimination rule of § 1152(a)(1)(A). The Chief Justice's opinion rejected those findings and ruled, without explicit dissent, that the Proclamation complied with the former and was not at war with the latter. The Ninth Circuit applied normal principles of statutory interpretation to find a clash between Travel Ban 3.0 and the immigration statutes—but the President argued that judges should defer to his interpretation of the laws (meaning broad interpretation of the delegations and avoidance of hard restrictions). Should the Court have been even more deferential than the Chief Justice was, before determining the direct conflict found here? Compare Josh Blackman, *Immigration and National Security*, 2018 Cato Sup. Ct. Rev. 29 (yes), with David Cole, *Trump's Travel Bans—Look Beyond the Text*, N.Y. Rev. Books, May 11, 2017 (no).

Plaintiffs also maintained that Travel Ban 3.0 (like its predecessors) violated the Religion Clauses. Even though it disclaims discrimination based on religion and does not have an explicit religion-based allowance (as the Travel Ban 1.0 did), plaintiffs argued that the President's own statements confirmed the inference (from the named Muslim countries) that the order favors Christianity over Islam, thereby effecting an establishment of religion. (Because the plaintiffs were not immigrants who were themselves allegedly excluded, but were instead their American relatives, there were no free exercise claims.)

Ought a judge be able to use the dozens of anti-Muslim statements made by presidential candidate Trump to show religion-based animus? Statements by President Trump showing such animus or referring to his campaign statements and promises? See Katherine Shaw, *Beyond the Bully Pulpit: Presidential Speech in the Courts*, 96 Tex. L. Rev. 1 (2017), who argues that presidential speech should generally not be probative, except in cases where it evidences a clear intent to enter the legal (and not just political) arena, or involves foreign relations or national security, or is relevant to government purpose as a proper constitutional inquiry.

For Religion Clause claims, purpose is a central inquiry. Just weeks before the Court decided the Travel Ban Cases, it applied the Religion Clauses to invalidate a state commission order against a baker who invoked conscience reasons not to cater a gay wedding. Justice Kennedy's opinion for a 7–2 Court in *Masterpiece Cakeshop, Ltd. v. Colorado Civil Rights Commission,* 138 S.Ct. 1719 (June 2, 2018), which is excerpted in Chapter 6, found a violation of state neutrality required by the Religion Clauses based upon statements by two of the seven commissioners, who endorsed the view that religious beliefs cannot legitimately be carried into the public sphere or commercial domain, disparaged the baker's faith as despicable and characterized it as merely rhetorical, and compared his invocation of his sincerely held religious beliefs to defenses of slavery and the Holocaust. No other commissioners endorsed or objected to the comments. The Court also relied on the commission's disparate treatment of cases where bakers objected on nonreligious grounds to making cakes with objectionable messages. The evidence of anti-religious animus seems much stronger in the Travel Ban Cases: What might be a constitutional basis for reading the evidence so differently?

3. *Should the President Get a Bounce from the National Security Context?* Although sidestepping the *Mandell* dicta suggesting essentially no judicial review, the Chief Justice's majority opinion read the Constitution and the Court's national security precedents to support a significant interpretive

thumb on the scales in favor of the President's interpretation of both immigration statutes and the Constitution. That explains the difference between the Court majorities in the Travel Ban Cases and the Cakeshop Case, but is this a constitutionally defensible interpretive norm? In support of such a norm are a number of constitutional precedents, as well as the sovereignty theory evoked in *Mandel*. Institutionally, the Supreme Court has been concerned that it does not have much to add to our government's politically volatile immigration policy. And some Justices believe that such policies are political questions for which serious judicial review would be inconsistent with Article III as well as Articles I and II.

On the other hand, scholars have praised the Court for more modest interventions, as when the Justices have trimmed back presidential or agency overreaching through narrow interpretations of the immigration laws. E.g., Philip Frickey, *Getting from Joe to Gene (McCarthy): The Avoidance Canon, Legal Process Theory, and Narrowing Statutory Interpretation in the Early Warren Court*, 93 Calif. L. Rev. 397 (2005). Why should the Roberts Court not have followed that approach in the Travel Ban Cases? Justice Breyer's dissenting opinion offered a similar legal process strategy for mild judicial pushback. Accord, Shirin Sinnar, *Procedural Experimentation and National Security in the Courts*, 106 Calif. L. Rev. 991 (2018) (nondeferential review, coupled with procedural protections for national security interests, might be optimal).

Quare: Would Travel Ban 2.0 have been constitutional under the Court's approach in *Trump v. Hawaii*? Consult Problem 8-10(c), where we describe Travel Ban 2.0.

Assume that a flat travel ban limited to Muslims would violate the Establishment Clause. Notice how the President gets to have his cake and eat it too. He gets credit with his electoral base for banning Muslims from the country—while at the same time he is able to sell Travel Ban 3.0 to the Court. To do so, he engages in three devices: (1) *contracting* the ban, by focusing only on certain majority-Muslim countries and dramatically omitting Iraq; (2) *expanding the ban,* by dropping the allowance for Christian refugees; and (3) *resequencing the ban,* by enlisting DHS and State to provide factual support or institutional cover (depending on your perspective). We owe these moves to Professor Leo Katz, who argues that rules of law can never constrain actors who are willing to go through an effort to evade the law. Is constitutional law toothless, or does it draw lines that have practical benefits? Or, to put it another way, is Travel Ban 3.0 less objectionable than Travel Bans 1.0 and 2.0? Is Katz right that constitutional rules offer no constraint?

Consider one more hypothetical:

Assume that President Trump issues a Travel Ban 4.0 to supplement Ban 3.0. Under Travel Ban 4.0, "no visa may be issued to any person of Arab descent." The President adopts this additional travel ban after securing a report from DHS finding that "persons of Arab descent have a greater proclivity toward terrorist activity than any other racial or ethnic group." The

President consults with his Cabinet. In his televised signing statement and in official presidential tweets, the President says, "Arabs are bad news. Almost all of them." Does *Trump v. Hawaii* require a court to uphold this hypothetical Travel Ban 4.0?

CHAPTER 9

LIMITS ON THE JUDICIAL POWER

■ ■ ■

The preceding two chapters explored the Supreme Court's role in policing the boundaries between Congress and the President, and those between the federal and state governments. But the Court has also evolved an elaborate set of doctrines to police the boundaries between the federal judiciary itself and other organs of government. Besides being an important part of the constitutional structure, these doctrines are essential working tools for any lawyer who litigates in federal court. These doctrines are sufficiently complex and recondite to require separate courses on federal jurisdiction. This chapter will merely present the outlines of some of the major doctrines and consider how they relate to more general issues of constitutional interpretation.

Article III of the Constitution establishes and rather vaguely defines the authority of the federal judiciary. We will discuss in turn three different kinds of limitations on federal courts' power to hear certain controversies, which have been teased out of Article III. First, the Supreme Court has held that the "judicial Power" granted in Article III does not permit courts to adjudicate lawsuits raising essentially "political questions" that are best left to resolution by the legislative (Article I) and executive (Article II) branches. Second, Article III, § 2's limitation of federal jurisdiction to "Cases" or "Controversies" has been read to establish other limits on the justiciability of certain types of lawsuits—primarily those where the plaintiff does not have a sufficient stake in the outcome. Third, the remedial powers granted federal courts in Article III limit the kinds of relief available to plaintiffs.

The civil rights cases of the second half of the twentieth century transformed the Court's justiciability doctrines. Matters that judges had traditionally left to state and local administrators—voting practices, public education, management of state institutions (e.g., prisons)—came under ever-closer scrutiny of federal judges. Specifically, federal courts came to adjudicate an increasing array of "political" matters. They heard litigants whose cases were arguably premature or who sought remedies on behalf of (future) beneficiaries as well as themselves. Most dramatically, they sometimes issued "structural injunctions" that went beyond relief ordinarily granted by courts of equity by forcing states and localities to restructure their governmental institutions and by retaining authority to oversee whether the restructuring was carried out and actually achieved its remedial purposes. See generally Owen Fiss, *The Civil Rights Injunction* (1978). The Warren and early Burger Courts encouraged such activism in support of the national campaign against southern apartheid. The apotheosis of the new model was *Swann* (Chapter 2, § 2C1), where the Court affirmed an ambitious injunction that restructured a city-county school system. Although the civil rights cases generally (and the *Brown II* cases in particular) inspired the era of relaxed limits on judicial authority, the relaxation extended beyond the race cases to litigation involving the antiwar movement, environmental challenges to state and private pollution, challenges to the rules and administration of public welfare programs, and vote dilution claims of all sorts.

Beginning with the Burger Court, however, the Justices have reasserted some—but by no means all—traditional limits on the exercise of the "judicial Power" granted them by Article III. Under Chief Justices Rehnquist and Roberts, the tendency toward restricting access to the courts has continued, but the Court's path has been unsteady. Justice Scalia was at the forefront of efforts to restrict judicial access. Other Justices, however, continue to support broader access in order to maintain what they view as the Court's proper role under *Marbury* in enforcing the Constitution.

In this chapter, we will consider how the Court views the scope of Article III jurisdiction and judicial remedies, as well as efforts by Congress to restrict the courts' jurisdiction and remedial authority.

SECTION 1. THE POLITICAL QUESTION DOCTRINE

The "political question doctrine" posits that some constitutional issues are not justiciable because the issue is committed to the political branches of government (Congress and the President). Recall the suggestion in *Marbury* that, where the President or another executive branch official had "legal discretion," the judiciary would not grant relief. The modern way of putting this is to say that the issue is political and not legal, or that there are "no judicially cognizable standards" by which a court could resolve the dispute. The constitutional basis for the political question doctrine is usually said to be separation of powers.

The leading modern political question case, *Baker v. Carr*, excerpted below, presents a sharp debate between the majority and dissenting opinions over the source and ambit of the political question doctrine. Much of the debate in *Baker v. Carr* concerns the meaning of prior cases, especially decisions holding nonjusticiable questions arising under Article IV, § 4 (referred to as the "Guarantee Clause," the "Guaranty Clause," or the "Republican Form of Government Clause"). As background to *Baker v. Carr*, we first describe some key earlier cases.

Luther v. Borden

7 How. (48 U.S.) 1 (1849)

Rhode Island was in a condition amounting to civil war: Some citizens who were disenfranchised under the original colonial charter went into rebellion, seeking a new and more democratic state constitution. The government organized under the colonial charter imposed martial law and gave its soldiers various police powers. The issue in the case was whether the soldiers had committed a trespass when breaking into a private home. This issue turned in part on whether the original charter government was still in power, or whether the insurgents had established a new legitimate government, thereby revoking the old government's authority to impose martial law. The Court held that a federal court could not determine which of two competing state governments was legitimate. The Court thought that a court was not equipped to consider this problem, and it also took solace in the wording of the Guarantee Clause. The clause suggests that Congress has the authority to decide this question, and any congressional resolution should not be subject to second-guessing by any other branch. This holding turned out to be very important after the Civil War, when it gave the Reconstruction Congress the final authority to decide which southern states had reestablished lawful governments. Note that *Luther* may not necessarily hold that all Guarantee Clause claims are nonjusticiable. Narrowly understood, the case may merely stand for the proposition that some questions under the clause are beyond judicial resolution.[1]

Giles v. Harris

189 U.S. 475 (1903)

The case involved a claim that Montgomery County, Alabama unlawfully refused to register more than 5,000 qualified African-American voters. Although "traditional limits of proceedings in equity have not embraced a remedy for political wrongs," **Justice Holmes'** opinion for the Court assumed that the circuit court had jurisdiction, but ruled that the court properly declined to issue an injunction to remedy the wrongs. The main reasons were

---

[1] The Court did not read *Luther* narrowly in later cases, however. In *Pacific States Tel. & Tel. Co. v. Oregon*, 223 U.S. 118 (1912), Oregon's adoption of direct democracy, by which the voters could directly make law, allegedly violated the Guarantee Clause's requirement that states possess a "republican form of government." (Essentially, the argument would be that a "republican" government requires a representative legislative process, not direct democracy.) The Court held the issue nonjusticiable, concluding that the federal courts had no judicially manageable standards to determine when a state government loses the label of "republican."

In the heyday of the Progressive Era, in which direct democracy was a popular governmental reform, it is not surprising that the Court in this case was reluctant to adjudicate its compatibility with the Guarantee Clause. Whatever might be the practical utility of its outcome, however, *Pacific States Tel. & Tel.* broadly suggested that federal courts could not hear any claim that a state government failed to be "republican."

that popular opinion would defeat the injunction, rendering it pointless, and that only the national political process could truly assure enforcement of voting rights under these circumstances, making the injunction unnecessary. Justice Holmes suggested that the lower court had essentially no "practical power to deal with the people of the state in a body. The [complaint] imports that the great mass of the white population intends to keep the blacks from voting. To meet such an intent something more than ordering the plaintiff's name to be inscribed upon the lists of 1902 will be needed. * * * Unless we are prepared to supervise the voting in that state by officers of the court, it seems to us that all that the plaintiff could get from equity would be an empty form. Apart from damages to the individual, relief from a great political wrong, if done, as alleged, by the people of a state and the state itself, must be given by them or by the legislative and political department of the government of the United States."

To the extent that both *Luther* and *Giles* are considered political question cases (which may not be true of *Giles*), they suggest that the doctrine is an amalgam of several different concerns about the exercise of the "judicial Power": (1) *constitutional*, arising out of the Constitution's allocation of authority to other branches of government; (2) *pragmatic*, relating to the competence of the judiciary to develop and apply rules and principles of law to the matter; and (3) *administrability*, relating to the courts' supposed incapacity to administer a remedy.[2] All three policies came into play when the Court first considered the issue of legislative apportionment.

Colegrove v. Green

328 U.S. 549 (1946)

Illinois had not redrawn its congressional districts for four decades despite major population shifts. Illinois voters living in districts with much greater population than some other districts brought suit, objecting to the dilution of their vote on "one person, one vote" grounds. The state argued that *Giles* precluded equitable relief in this "political" matter. Writing for a plurality and invoking *Giles*, **Justice Frankfurter** reasoned from the constitutional structure and the greater institutional competence of the political branches that "courts ought not to enter this political thicket." Although not cited, *Giles*

---

[2] See William Eskridge, Jr., *Some Effects of Identity-Based Social Movements on Constitutional Law in the Twentieth Century*, 100 Mich. L. Rev. 2062 (2002). For a more elaborate typology, see Louis Henkin, *Is There a "Political Question" Doctrine?*, 85 Yale L.J. 597 (1976). For a simpler typology, see Rachel Barkow, *More Supreme Than Court? The Fall of the Political Question Doctrine and the Rise of Judicial Supremacy*, 102 Colum. L. Rev. 237 (2002) (emphasizing the "prudential" features of the political question doctrine). For an argument that the political question doctrine is merely an institutional safety valve, with no principled evolution, see Fritz Scharpf, Judicial Review and the Political Question: *A Functional Analysis*, 75 Yale L.J. 517 (1966).

was even more central to **Justice Rutledge**'s concurring opinion, which argued that voting matters were not political questions in the constitutional sense, but posed "delicate" issues of remedy and enforcement such that judges should exercise their equitable discretion to refrain from issuing relief. Citing cases where the NAACP had successfully challenged exclusionary voting practices in damage actions (rather than *Giles* injunction suits), e.g., *Nixon v. Herndon*, 273 U.S. 536 (1927), three dissenting Justices (**Black**, **Douglas**, and **Murphy**) conceded that "voting is part of elections and that elections are 'political,'" but it does not follow that "courts are impotent in connection with evasions of all 'political' rights."

The Court's ultimate willingness to adjudicate these kinds of claims was influenced by its experience with the school desegregation cases, culminating in *Cooper v. Aaron* (Chapter 2, § 2B). Counsel for the Little Rock School Board extensively quoted *Giles* to support his assertion that desegregation orders could not be issued by federal judges when the people of the state were massively unwilling to go along. Given the Court's commitment to *Brown* and the district's underlying (but never directly asserted) challenge to its duty to follow that precedent, this was an argument that even Justice Frankfurter summarily dismissed. The Court did not even mention the *Giles* issue in its landmark opinion, which held that local opposition was no justification for a federal judge to delay entry of an injunction enforcing constitutional rights. This new attitude toward judicial authority was also in evidence in 1960, when the Court returned to the issue of political boundaries.

Gomillion v. Lightfoot

364 U.S. 339 (1960)

The NAACP challenged an Alabama statute altering the city limits of Tuskegee, to the effect that virtually all the black voters were moved outside the new limits. The challengers recognized that *Colegrove* was a problem for their lawsuit. The ACLU's brief distinguished between the constitutional dimension of the political question doctrine and the pragmatic-administrability dimension. The Court's prior cases, starting with *Herndon*, made clear that the first was no barrier. Nor was the second, because Congress in 1957 had explicitly authorized federal courts to exercise jurisdiction in voting rights cases. Unmentioned but also relevant was the Solicitor General's participation in the case, suggesting that the Eisenhower Administration would back the Court (as it had done in *Cooper*). Distinguishing *Colegrove* and ignoring *Giles*, Justice Frankfurter's opinion for a unanimous Court saw the challenged law as just the same as *Herndon*: a subterfuge to deny people of color their rights to vote and therefore no different from any other individual rights case. Notwithstanding Frankfurter's cautious opinion, *Gomillion* was a doctrinal fulcrum for the Court to reconsider *Colegrove* two years later in the following case.

BAKER V. CARR

369 U.S. 186, 82 S.Ct. 691, 7 L.Ed.2d 663 (1962)

JUSTICE BRENNAN delivered the opinion of the Court.

[The Tennessee legislature had not been reapportioned since 1901. The state's demographics had changed dramatically since then. Plaintiffs, who lived in urban and suburban legislative districts that had many more voters than rural districts, claimed that their votes were diluted in violation of the Equal Protection Clause. They sought an injunction prohibiting elections under the current scheme and either a reapportionment of legislative seats in accordance with population or "at-large elections" for the legislature. The district court denied relief, holding the controversy a "political question" under *Colegrove*.]

Of course the mere fact that the suit seeks protection of a political right does not mean it presents a political question. Such an objection "is little more than a play upon words." *Herndon.* Rather, it is argued that apportionment cases, whatever the actual wording of the complaint, can involve no federal constitutional right except one resting on the guaranty of a republican form of government, and that complaints based on that clause have been held to present political questions which are nonjusticiable. * * *

We have said that "In determining whether a question falls within [the political question] category, the appropriateness under our system of government of attributing finality to the action of the political departments and also the lack of satisfactory criteria for a judicial determination are dominant considerations." The nonjusticiability of a political question is primarily a function of the separation of powers. Much confusion results from the capacity of the "political question" label to obscure the need for case-by-case inquiry. Deciding whether a matter has in any measure been committed by the Constitution to another branch of government, or whether the action of that branch exceeds whatever authority has been committed, is itself a delicate exercise in constitutional interpretation, and is a responsibility of this Court as ultimate interpreter of the Constitution. * * *

Foreign relations: There are sweeping statements to the effect that all questions touching foreign relations are political questions. Not only does resolution of such issues frequently turn on standards that defy judicial application, or involve the exercise of a discretion demonstrably committed to the executive or legislature; but many such questions uniquely demand single-voiced statement of the Government's views. Yet it is error to suppose that every case or controversy which touches foreign relations lies beyond judicial cognizance. Our cases in this field seem invariably to show a discriminating analysis of the particular question posed, in terms of the history of its management by the political branches, of its susceptibility to judicial handling in the light of its nature and posture in the specific case, and of the possible consequences of judicial action. * * *

It is apparent that several formulations which vary slightly according to the settings in which the questions arise may describe a political question, although each has one or more elements which identify it as essentially a function of the separation of powers. Prominent on the surface of any case held to involve a political question is found a textually demonstrable constitutional commitment of the issue to a coordinate political department; or a lack of judicially discoverable and manageable standards for resolving it; or the impossibility of deciding without an initial policy determination of a kind clearly for nonjudicial discretion; or the impossibility of a court's undertaking independent resolution without expressing lack of the respect due coordinate branches of government; or an unusual need for unquestioning adherence to a political decision already made; or the potentiality of embarrassment from multifarious pronouncements by various departments on one question.

Unless one of these formulations is inextricable from the case at bar, there should be no dismissal for nonjusticiability on the ground of a political question's presence. The doctrine of which we treat is one of "political questions," not one of "political cases." * * *

But it is argued that this case shares the characteristics of decisions that constitute a category not yet considered, cases concerning the Constitution's guaranty of a republican form of government. * * * Guaranty Clause claims involve those elements which define a "political question," and for that reason and no other, they are nonjusticiable. In particular, * * * the nonjusticiability of such claims has nothing to do with their touching upon matters of state governmental organization. * * *

Clearly, several factors were thought by the Court in *Luther* to make the question there "political": the commitment to the other branches of the decision as to which is the lawful state government; the unambiguous action by the President, in recognizing the charter government as the lawful authority; the need for finality in the executive's decision; and the lack of criteria by which a court could determine which form of government was republican.

But the only significance that *Luther* could have for our immediate purposes is in its holding that the Guaranty Clause is not a repository of judicially manageable standards which a court could utilize independently in order to identify a State's lawful government. The Court has since refused to resort to the Guaranty Clause—which alone had been invoked for the purpose—as the source of a constitutional standard for invalidating state action. [Citing nine cases.]

Just as the Court has consistently held that a challenge to state action based on the Guaranty Clause presents no justiciable question so has it held, and for the same reasons, that challenges to congressional action on the ground of inconsistency with that clause present no justiciable question. * * *

We come, finally, to the ultimate inquiry whether our precedents as to what constitutes a nonjusticiable "political question" bring the case before us under the umbrella of that doctrine. A natural beginning is to note whether any of the common characteristics which we have been able to identify and label descriptively are present. We find none: The question here is the consistency of state action with the Federal Constitution. We have no question decided, or to be decided, by a political branch of government coequal with this Court. Nor do we risk embarrassment of our government abroad, or grave disturbance at home if we take issue with Tennessee as to the constitutionality of her action here challenged. Nor need the appellants, in order to succeed in this action, ask the Court to enter upon policy determinations for which judicially manageable standards are lacking. Judicial standards under the Equal Protection Clause are well developed and familiar, and it has been open to courts since the enactment of the Fourteenth Amendment to determine, if on the particular facts they must, that a discrimination reflects *no* policy, but simply arbitrary and capricious action.

JUSTICE FRANKFURTER, whom JUSTICE HARLAN joins, dissenting.

From its earliest opinions this Court has consistently recognized a class of controversies which do not lend themselves to judicial standards and judicial remedies. * * *

The present case involves all of the elements that have made the Guarantee Clause cases non-justiciable. It is, in effect, a Guarantee Clause claim masquerading under a different label. But it cannot make the case more fit for judicial action that appellants invoke the Fourteenth Amendment rather than Art. IV, § 4, where, in fact, the gist of their complaint is the same—unless it can be found that the Fourteenth Amendment speaks with greater particularity to their situation. We have been admonished to avoid "the tyranny of labels." Art. IV, § 4, is not committed by express constitutional terms to Congress. It is the nature of the controversies arising under it, nothing else, which has made it judicially unenforceable. * * * But where judicial competence is wanting, it cannot be created by invoking one clause of the Constitution rather than another.

[Justice Frankfurter concluded that the plaintiffs' complaint "is simply that the representatives are not sufficiently numerous or powerful," and federal judicial consideration of it "will add a virulent source of friction and tension in federal-state relations."]

[Concurring opinions by JUSTICES DOUGLAS, CLARK, and STEWART are omitted. JUSTICE CLARK stressed that Tennessee's apportionment scheme was "a topsy turvical of gigantic proportions," for which there was no political remedy because the beneficiaries of the "crazy quilt" system had a vested interest in keeping their advantage—they controlled the Assembly and hence could block any legislative change, and Tennessee had no initiative or referendum by which the voters could change the apportionment directly. A dissenting opinion by **JUSTICE HARLAN**, arguing that no federal constitutional right was at stake, is also omitted. **JUSTICE WHITTAKER** did not participate in this case.]

NOTE ON BAKER V. CARR

The substantive rules governing reapportionment are discussed in Chapter 5, § 3A. Justice Brennan's *Baker* opinion was revolutionary. It not only overruled *Colegrove* and ushered in a generation of voting rights litigation, but its mode of analysis reconfigured the political question doctrine. Notice that Brennan's list of six factors the Court should consider in deciding whether an issue is a political question emphasized the pragmatic (factors 2–6) rather than constitutional (factor 1) dimensions of the doctrine and, within the pragmatic dimension, emphasized competence to discern rules of law rather than administrability concerns. Indeed, *Baker* can be read as narrowing the kinds of administrability concerns courts ought to consider and as decisively rejecting *Giles*'s holding that problems with enforcement are a reason for refusing to exercise jurisdiction. Powerfully supporting this reading of *Baker* are the dozens of post-1962 voting and school desegregation cases, where the Court has affirmed or required federal court civil rights injunctions in the face of strong popular and official opposition. Even more dramatic have been the orders entered in other institutional reform litigation, especially in the many lawsuits seeking structural reform of state prison systems, a topic to which we will return later in the chapter.[3] Consider other contexts in which federal courts have considered the applicability of the post-*Baker* political question doctrine.

NOTES ON THE POLITICAL QUESTION DOCTRINE SINCE BAKER

1.   *Exclusion of Members of Congress.* The House of Representatives in 1967 refused to seat Representative Adam Clayton Powell based upon a resolution asserting that he had "wrongfully diverted House funds for the use of others and himself" and had made "false reports on expenditures of foreign currency to the Committee on House Administration." Arguing that he met all the formal requirements of Article I, § 2, cl. 2, and had been overwhelmingly reelected by his constituents after full ventilation of these charges, Representative Powell sued to be seated. The House Speaker invoked Article I, § 5, cl. 1, that "each House shall be the Judge of the * * * Qualifications of its

---

[3]   See Malcolm Feeley & Edward Rubin, *Judicial Policy Making and the Modern State: How the Courts Reformed America's Prisons* (1998) (institutional analysis of federal judicial decrees requiring detailed plans for reorganization of state prisons, often over intense local opposition).

own Members." This is a textual commitment of the issue to another branch under *Baker v. Carr,* argued Speaker McCormack. He also asserted that judicial resolution of the claim would yield a "potentially embarrassing confrontation between coordinate branches."

Chief Justice Warren, writing for the Court in *Powell v. McCormack*, 395 U.S. 486 (1969), held the controversy justiciable:

> Our system of government requires that federal courts on occasion interpret the Constitution in a manner at variance with the construction given the document by another branch. The alleged conflict that such an adjudication may cause cannot justify the courts' avoiding their constitutional responsibility.

> Nor are any of the other formulations of a political question "inextricable from the case at bar." *Baker v. Carr.* Petitioners seek a determination that the House was without power to exclude Powell from the 90th Congress, which, we have seen, requires an interpretation of the Constitution—a determination for which clearly there are "judicially * * * manageable standards." Finally, a judicial resolution of petitioners' claim will not result in "multifarious pronouncements by various departments on one question." For [it] is the responsibility of this Court to act as the ultimate interpreter of the Constitution. *Marbury*.

2. *Adjudicating Expropriations by Foreign Countries.* Shortly after *Baker v. Carr,* the Supreme Court held in *Banco Nacional de Cuba v. Sabbatino,* 376 U.S. 398 (1964), that foreign expropriations of the property of U.S. citizens are nonjusticiable "acts of state." The Court gave two reasons for nonjusticiability: There was no accepted standard in international law for determining when nationalizations require just compensation for those who lose their property, and the usual remedy was for the executive branch to "espouse" its nationals' claims through diplomacy (as the United States was doing in response to Cuba's expropriations after Fidel Castro took power). Justice Harlan, a dissenter in *Baker v. Carr*, wrote the opinion for a unanimous Court. Is this holding consistent with *Baker*?

In response, Congress enacted the *Sabbatino* Amendment to the Foreign Assistance Act of 1964, Pub. L. No. 88–63, § 301(d)(4), 78 Stat. 1009, 1013, codified at 22 U.S.C. § 2370(e)(2), which directs courts to adjudicate claims that foreign state expropriations violate international law, unless the President states officially that such an adjudication in the particular case would inhibit the executive's conduct of foreign policy. Is this statute constitutional in requiring courts to adjudicate what they believe to be political questions? See *Banco Nacional de Cuba v. First National City Bank*, 431 F.2d 394 (2d Cir. 1970), *rev'd on other grounds*, 406 U.S. 759 (1972) (avoiding the constitutional question by construing statute narrowly).

The plurality opinion for four Justices in *Alfred Dunhill of London, Inc. v. Republic of Cuba*, 425 U.S. 682 (1976), sought to create a "commercial exception" for the act of state doctrine, rendering it inapplicable to "purely commercial operations" of a foreign state; four Justices dissented from the exception, and the fifth (Justice Stevens) expressed no view on it. Courts relied on *Dunhill* and other exceptions to adjudicate claims by American companies that the Islamic Republic of Iran owed them "just compensation" when it nationalized their Iranian subsidiaries and properties after the Shah was overthrown in 1979. Recall from *Dames & Moore* (Chapter 8, § 1B) that the President used the claims against Iran as a bargaining chip in his negotiations for the return of 52 hostages held in Tehran, and that the claims were referred to an international claims tribunal, one of the traditional means of resolving foreign nationalization claims. In light of this context, were American courts wise in distinguishing *Sabbatino*? See William Eskridge, Jr., *The Iranian Nationalization Cases*, 22 Harv. Int'l L.J. 525 (1981) (no).

3. *The Constitutionality of the Vietnam War.* During the 1950s and early 1960s, the executive branch eased the country into the Vietnam War, and after 1964 rather rapidly escalated involvement to mammoth proportions. There was never a formal congressional declaration of war, though in August 1964 the Senate did pass the Gulf of Tonkin Resolution (with only two Senators dissenting), which broadly approved of the President's responding to Communist aggression in Vietnam. The ambiguous nature of this "war," the ultimately staggering commitment of people and resources to its conduct, and the perception by the late 1960s that this was a losing effort all made the war legally as well as politically controversial.[4]

The Supreme Court ducked the legal issues, e.g., *Mora v. McNamara*, 389 U.S. 934 (1967) (denying certiorari on case raising issue of legality of the war, over dissents by Justices Douglas and Stewart), but they percolated quite actively in the courts of appeals. In *Orlando v. Laird*, 443 F.2d 1039 (2d Cir.), *cert. denied*, 404 U.S. 869 (1971), the Second Circuit held that the question whether or not Congress was required to take *some* action to authorize the Vietnam War was not a political question under *Baker v. Carr*, because it was possible to discern judicially manageable standards. The *Orlando* court found that Congress had authorized the President to commit military forces at various points, specifically in the Gulf of Tonkin Resolution and in continuing appropriations measures.

But in *DaCosta v. Laird*, 448 F.2d 1368 (2d Cir. 1971), *cert. denied*, 405 U.S. 979 (1972), the same court refused to adjudicate the claim that Congress' repeal of the Gulf of Tonkin Resolution removed the congressional authorization found sufficient (and justiciable) in *Orlando*. The Court relied on dicta in *Orlando* that the means by which Congress and the President cooperated in prosecuting the war was a political question. It extended that

---

[4] See John Hart Ely, *The American War in Indochina, Part I: The (Troubled) Constitutionality of the War They Told Us About*, 42 Stan. L. Rev. 877 (1990); John Hart Ely, *The American War In Indochina, Part II: The Unconstitutionality of the War They Didn't Tell Us About*, 42 Stan. L. Rev. 1093 (1990); Michael Tigar, *The "Political Question" Doctrine and Foreign Relations*, 17 UCLA L. Rev. 1135 (1970); Lawrence Velvel, *The War in Viet Nam: Unconstitutional, Justiciable, and Jurisdictionally Attackable*, 16 Kan. L. Rev. 449 (1968).

dicta to hold that "the method and means by which they mutually participate in winding down the conflict and in disengaging the nation from it, is also a political question." The Second Circuit later found to be political questions the President's unilateral decision to escalate the bombing of North Vietnam in 1973, see *DaCosta v. Laird*, 471 F.2d 1146 (1973), and the President's decision to continue military operations in Cambodia notwithstanding specific congressional directives to remove all U.S. forces from that country. See *Holtzman v. Schlesinger*, 484 F.2d 1307 (2d Cir. 1973), *cert. denied*, 416 U.S. 936 (1974). Are these decisions consistent with *Baker*?

4. *Treaty Termination*. By *per curiam* order without opinion, *Goldwater v. Carter*, 444 U.S. 996 (1979), reversed a lower court decision that the President had the authority to terminate a Senate-approved treaty with Taiwan without congressional approval. Justice Rehnquist (joined by Chief Justice Burger and Justices Stewart and Stevens) wrote a separate opinion arguing that the issue of treaty termination is a political question, because "while the Constitution is express as to the manner in which the Senate shall participate in the ratification of a treaty, it is silent as to that body's participation in the abrogation of a treaty, and the fact that different termination procedures may be appropriate for different treaties." Note the similarity to the Second Circuit's reasoning in *DaCosta*. Is this argument consistent with *Powell v. McCormack*? *Baker v. Carr*?

Justice Powell, concurring in the judgment on grounds that the dispute was not ripe for adjudication, rejected Justice Rehnquist's position, arguing that Article II, § 2 and Article VI provide plenty of constitutional text from which "judicially discoverable and manageable standards" can be discerned. "Interpretation of the Constitution does not imply lack of respect for a coordinate branch. If the President and Congress had reached irreconcilable positions, final disposition of the question presented by this case would eliminate, rather than create, multiple constitutional interpretations. The specter of the Federal Government brought to a halt because of the mutual intransigence of the President and the Congress would require this Court to provide a resolution pursuant to our duty 'to say what the law is.'"

Justice Brennan dissented from the *per curiam* opinion, finding no political question and arguing in favor of the President's power to terminate treaties. According to Brennan, the political question doctrine "does not pertain when a court is faced with an *antecedent* question whether a particular branch has been constitutionally designated as the repository of political decisionmaking power. The issue of decisionmaking authority must be resolved as a matter of constitutional law, not political discretion; accordingly, it falls within the competence of the courts."

5. *Reapportionment and Gerrymandering*. Every ten years the allocation of House of Representatives seats to the states is recalculated, and this triggers political battles over how many seats each state will get (the Census numbers not being beyond question) and how new districts will be drawn in each state (even states keeping the same number of seats have to

reconfigure their districts so that they will be roughly equal). *Baker v. Carr* seems to have allowed these controversies to grow and flourish in the courts.

A unanimous Supreme Court in *United States Department of Commerce v. Montana*, 503 U.S. 442 (1992), held justiciable Montana's claim that the congressionally adopted method for computing House representation unfairly short-changed it under Article I, § 2, providing that Representatives shall be apportioned among the States "according to their respective Numbers." Relying on *Baker* and *Bandemer*, the Court simply said that "the interpretation of the apportionment provisions of the Constitution is well within the competence of the Judiciary," and then proceeded to a complex mathematical defense of Congress' chosen means of apportionment. Interestingly, the Court cited two leading sources advocating abolition of the political question doctrine, though it cited them for innocuous propositions. *Id.* at 1425 nn.36 & 37, citing Louis Henkin, *Is There a "Political Question" Doctrine?*, 85 Yale L.J. 597 (1976), and Martin Redish, *The Federal Courts in the Political Order* (1991).

NIXON v. UNITED STATES
506 U.S. 224, 113 S.Ct. 732, 122 L.Ed.2d 1 (1993)

CHIEF JUSTICE REHNQUIST delivered the opinion of the Court.

[The House of Representatives impeached Walter Nixon, a federal district judge, following his federal conviction and imprisonment for making false statements to a federal grand jury. Pursuant to Senate Rule XI, the Senate delegated much of its role in trying the impeachment to a committee of Senators. After receiving evidence and hearing testimony, the committee presented the full Senate with a transcript of the proceedings and a report specifying the uncontested facts and summarizing the evidence concerning the contested facts. Nixon and the House impeachment managers submitted briefs to the full Senate and were allowed to deliver arguments from the Senate floor. Nixon was also allowed to make a personal appeal to the Senate. Following his conviction by the Senate and his removal from office, Nixon brought this action, contending that his impeachment was unconstitutional because the full Senate did not take part in the evidentiary hearing. The lower courts dismissed the action on the ground that it was nonjusticiable.]

A controversy is nonjusticiable—*i.e.*, involves a political question—where there is "a textually demonstrable constitutional commitment of the issue to a coordinate political department; or a lack of judicially discoverable and manageable standards for resolving it. . . ." *Baker v. Carr.* But the courts must, in the first instance, interpret the text in question and determine whether and to what extent the issue is textually committed. As the discussion that follows makes clear, the concept of a textual commitment to a coordinate political department is not completely separate from the concept of a lack of judicially discoverable and manageable standards for resolving it; the lack of judicially manageable standards may strengthen the conclusion that there is a textually demonstrable commitment to a coordinate branch.

In this case, we must examine Art. I, § 3, cl. 6, to determine the scope of authority conferred upon the Senate by the Framers regarding impeachment. It provides:

> The Senate shall have the sole Power to try all Impeachments. When sitting for that Purpose, they shall be on Oath or Affirmation. When the President of the United States is tried, the Chief Justice shall preside: And no Person shall be convicted without the Concurrence of two thirds of the Members present.

The language and structure of this Clause are revealing. The first sentence is a grant of authority to the Senate, and the word "sole" indicates that this authority is reposed in the Senate and nowhere else. The next two sentences specify requirements to which the Senate proceedings shall conform: The Senate shall be on oath or affirmation, a two-thirds vote is required to convict, and when the President is tried the Chief Justice shall preside.

Petitioner argues that the word "try" in the first sentence imposes by implication an additional requirement on the Senate in that the proceedings must be in the nature of a judicial trial. From there petitioner goes on to argue that this limitation precludes the Senate from delegating to a select committee the task of hearing the testimony of witnesses[.] * * * Petitioner concludes from this that courts may review whether or not the Senate "tried" him before convicting him.

There are several difficulties with this position which lead us ultimately to reject it. The word "try," both in 1787 and later, has considerably broader meanings than those to which petitioner would limit it. Older dictionaries define try as "[t]o examine" or "[t]o examine as a judge." See 2 S. Johnson, A Dictionary of the English Language (1785). In more modern usage the term has various meanings. For example, try can mean "to examine or investigate judicially," "to conduct the trial of," or "to put to the test by experiment, investigation, or trial." Webster's Third New International Dictionary 2457 (1971). Petitioner submits that "try," as contained in T. Sheridan, Dictionary of the English Language (1796), means "to examine as a judge; to bring before a judicial tribunal." Based on the variety of definitions, however, we cannot say that the Framers used the word "try" as an implied limitation on the method by which the Senate might proceed in trying impeachments. "As a rule the Constitution speaks in general terms, leaving Congress to deal with subsidiary matters of detail as the public interests and changing conditions may require[.]"

The conclusion that the use of the word "try" in the first sentence of the Impeachment Trial Clause lacks sufficient precision to afford any judicially manageable standard of review of the Senate's actions is fortified by the existence of the three very specific requirements that the Constitution does impose on the Senate when trying impeachments: The Members must be under oath, a two-thirds vote is required to convict, and the Chief Justice presides when the President is tried. These limitations are quite precise, and their nature suggests that the Framers did not intend to impose additional limitations on the form of the Senate proceedings by the use of the word "try" in the first sentence.

Petitioner devotes only two pages in his brief to negating the significance of the word "sole" in the first sentence of Clause 6. As noted above, that sentence provides that "[t]he Senate shall have the sole Power to try all Impeachments." We think that the word "sole" is of considerable significance. Indeed, the word "sole" appears only one other time in the Constitution—with respect to the House of Representatives' "*sole* Power of Impeachment." Art. I, § 2, cl. 5 (emphasis added). The commonsense meaning of the word "sole" is that the Senate alone shall have authority to determine whether an individual should be acquitted or convicted. The dictionary definition bears this out. "Sole" is defined as "having no companion," "solitary," "being the only one," and "functioning . . . independently and without assistance or interference." Webster's Third New International Dictionary 2168 (1971). If the courts may review the actions of the Senate in order to determine whether that body "tried" an impeached official, it is difficult to see how the Senate would be "functioning . . . independently and without assistance or interference." * * *

The history and contemporary understanding of the impeachment provisions support our reading of the constitutional language. The parties do not offer evidence of a single word in the history of the Constitutional Convention or in contemporary commentary that even alludes to the possibility of judicial review in the context of the impeachment powers. This silence is quite meaningful in light of the several explicit references to the availability of judicial review as a check on the Legislature's power with respect to bills of attainder, *ex post facto* laws, and statutes. See The Federalist No. 78 ("Limitations . . . can be preserved in practice no other way than through the medium of the courts of justice").

The Framers labored over the question of where the impeachment power should lie. Significantly, in at least two considered scenarios the power was placed with the Federal Judiciary. Indeed, Madison and the Committee of Detail proposed that the Supreme Court should have the power to determine impeachments. Despite these proposals, the Convention ultimately decided that the Senate would have "the sole Power to try all Impeachments." Art. I, § 3, cl. 6. According to Alexander Hamilton, the Senate was the "most fit depositary of this important trust" because its Members are representatives of the people. See The Federalist

No. 65. The Supreme Court was not the proper body because the Framers "doubted whether the members of that tribunal would, at all times, be endowed with so eminent a portion of fortitude as would be called for in the execution of so difficult a task" or whether the Court "would possess the degree of credit and authority" to carry out its judgment if it conflicted with the accusation brought by the Legislature—the people's representative. See *id.* In addition, the Framers believed the Court was too small in number: "The awful discretion, which a court of impeachments must necessarily have, to doom to honor or to infamy the most confidential and the most distinguished characters of the community, forbids the commitment of the trust to a small number of persons." *Id.*

There are two additional reasons why the Judiciary, and the Supreme Court in particular, were not chosen to have any role in impeachments. First, the Framers recognized that most likely there would be two sets of proceedings for individuals who commit impeachable offenses—the impeachment trial and a separate criminal trial. In fact, the Constitution explicitly provides for two separate proceedings. See Art. I, § 3, cl. 7. The Framers deliberately separated the two forums to avoid raising the specter of bias and to ensure independent judgments[.] * * * Certainly judicial review of the Senate's "trial" would introduce the same risk of bias as would participation in the trial itself.

Second, judicial review would be inconsistent with the Framers' insistence that our system be one of checks and balances. In our constitutional system, impeachment was designed to be the *only* check on the Judicial Branch by the Legislature. On the topic of judicial accountability, Hamilton wrote:

> The precautions for their responsibility are comprised in the article respecting impeachments. They are liable to be impeached for mal-conduct by the house of representatives, and tried by the senate, and if convicted, may be dismissed from office and disqualified for holding any other. *This is the only provision on the point, which is consistent with the necessary independence of the judicial character, and is the only one which we find in our own constitution in respect to our own judges.* [The *Federalist* No. 79 (emphasis added).]

Judicial involvement in impeachment proceedings, even if only for purposes of judicial review, is counterintuitive because it would eviscerate the "important constitutional check" placed on the Judiciary by the Framers. See *id.*, No. 81. Nixon's argument would place final reviewing authority with respect to impeachments in the hands of the same body that the impeachment process is meant to regulate.

Nevertheless, Nixon argues that judicial review is necessary in order to place a check on the Legislature. Nixon fears that if the Senate is given unreviewable authority to interpret the Impeachment Trial Clause, there is a grave risk that the Senate will usurp judicial power. The Framers anticipated this objection and created two constitutional safeguards to keep the Senate in check. The first safeguard is that the whole of the impeachment power is divided between the two legislative bodies, with the House given the right to accuse and the Senate given the right to judge. * * * The second safeguard is the two-thirds supermajority vote requirement. * * *

In addition to the textual commitment argument, we are persuaded that the lack of finality and the difficulty of fashioning relief counsel against justiciability. We agree with the Court of Appeals that opening the door of judicial review to the procedures used by the Senate in trying impeachments would "expose the political life of the country to months, or perhaps years, of chaos." This lack of finality would manifest itself most dramatically if the President were impeached. The legitimacy of any successor, and hence his effectiveness, would be impaired severely, not merely while the judicial process was running its course, but during any retrial that a differently constituted Senate might conduct if its first judgment of conviction were invalidated. Equally uncertain is the question of what relief a court may give other than simply setting aside the judgment of conviction. Could it order the reinstatement of a convicted federal judge, or order Congress to create an additional judgeship if the seat had been filled in the interim?

Petitioner finally contends that a holding of nonjusticiability cannot be reconciled with our opinion in *Powell v. McCormack*, 395 U.S. 486 (1969). The relevant issue in *Powell* was whether courts could review the House of Representatives' conclusion that Powell was "unqualified" to sit as a Member because he had been accused of misappropriating public funds and abusing the process of the New York courts. We stated that the question of justiciability turned on whether the Constitution committed authority to the House to judge its Members' qualifications, and if so, the extent of that commitment. Article I, § 5 provides that "Each House shall be the Judge of the Elections, Returns and Qualifications of its own Members." In turn, Art. I, § 2 specifies three requirements for membership in the House: The candidate must be at least 25 years of age, a citizen of the United States for no less than seven years, and an inhabitant of the State he is chosen to represent. We held that, in light of the three requirements specified in the Constitution, the word "qualifications"—of which the House was to be the Judge—was of a precise, limited nature.

Our conclusion in *Powell* was based on the fixed meaning of "[q]ualifications" set forth in Art. I, § 2. The claim by the House that its power to "be the Judge of the Elections, Returns and Qualifications of its own Members" was a textual commitment of unreviewable authority was defeated by the existence of this separate provision specifying the only qualifications which might be imposed for House membership. The decision as to whether a Member satisfied these qualifications *was* placed with the House, but the decision as to what these qualifications consisted of was not.

In the case before us, there is no separate provision of the Constitution which could be defeated by allowing the Senate final authority to determine the meaning of the word "try" in the Impeachment Trial Clause. We agree with Nixon that courts possess power to review either legislative or executive action that transgresses identifiable textual limits. As we have made clear, "whether the action of [either the Legislative or Executive Branch] exceeds whatever authority has been committed, is itself a delicate exercise in constitutional interpretation, and is a responsibility of this Court as ultimate interpreter of the Constitution." *Baker v. Carr.* But we conclude, after exercising that delicate responsibility, that the word "try" in the Impeachment Clause does not provide an identifiable textual limit on the authority which is committed to the Senate.

[The concurring opinion of **JUSTICE STEVENS** is omitted.]

JUSTICE WHITE, with whom **JUSTICE BLACKMUN** joins, concurring in the judgment.

[T]he Court's willingness to abandon its obligation to review the constitutionality of legislative acts merely on the strength of the word "sole" is perplexing. Consider, by comparison, the treatment of Art. I, § 1, which grants "All legislative powers" to the House and Senate. As used in that context "all" is nearly synonymous with "sole"—both connote entire and exclusive authority. Yet the Court has never thought it would unduly interfere with the operation of the Legislative Branch to entertain difficult and important questions as to the extent of the legislative power. * * *

What the relevant history mainly reveals is deep ambivalence among many of the Framers over the very institution of impeachment, which, by its nature, is not easily reconciled with our system of checks and balances. As they clearly recognized, the branch of the Federal Government which is possessed of the authority to try impeachments, by having final say over the membership of each branch, holds a potentially unanswerable power over the others. In addition, that branch, insofar as it is called upon to try not only members of other branches, but also its own, will have the advantage of being the judge of its own members' causes.

The historical evidence reveals above all else that the Framers were deeply concerned about placing in any branch the "awful discretion, which a court of impeachments must necessarily have." The *Federalist* No. 65. Viewed against this history, the discord between the majority's position and the basic principles of checks and balances underlying the Constitution's separation of powers is clear. In essence, the majority suggests that the Framers conferred upon Congress a potential tool of legislative dominance yet at the same time rendered Congress' exercise of that power one of the very few areas of legislative authority immune from any judicial review. While the majority rejects petitioner's justiciability argument as espousing a view "inconsistent with the Framers' insistence that our system be one of checks and balances," it is the Court's finding of nonjusticiability that truly upsets the Framers' careful design. In a truly balanced system, impeachments tried by the Senate would serve as a means of controlling the largely unaccountable Judiciary, even as judicial review would ensure that the Senate adhered to a minimal set of procedural standards in conducting impeachment trials.

[**JUSTICE SOUTER**, concurring in the judgment, argued that the political-question doctrine is "deriv[ed] in large part from prudential concerns about the respect we owe the political departments." Although agreeing with the majority that the issue in this case was a political question, Justice Souter opined that "[i]f the Senate were to act in a manner seriously threatening the integrity of its results, convicting, say, upon a coin toss, * * * judicial interference might well be appropriate. In such circumstances, the Senate's action might be so far beyond the scope of its constitutional authority, and the consequent impact on the Republic so great, as to merit a judicial response despite the prudential concerns that would ordinarily counsel silence."]

Zivotofsky v. Clinton

566 U.S. 189 (2012)

Congress enacted a statute providing that Americans born in Jerusalem may elect to have "Israel" listed as the place of birth on their passports. The State Department declined to follow that law, citing its longstanding policy of not taking a position on the political status of Jerusalem. The court of appeals held that the validity of the statute was a political question. The Supreme Court reversed, in an opinion by **Chief Justice Roberts**:

> In this case, determining the constitutionality of § 214(d) involves deciding whether the statute impermissibly intrudes upon Presidential powers under the Constitution. If so, the law must be invalidated and Zivotofsky's case should be dismissed for failure to state a claim. If, on the other hand, the statute does not trench on the President's powers, then the Secretary must be ordered to issue Zivotofsky a passport that complies with § 214(d). Either way, the political question doctrine is not implicated. "No policy underlying the political question doctrine suggests that Congress or the Executive . . . can decide the constitutionality of a statute; that is a decision for the courts."

The Court concluded that determining the constitutionality of a statute is not a task committed to one of the political branches and that the deciding of the constitutional issue did not involve judicially unmanageable standards: "Resolution of Zivotofsky's claim demands careful examination of the textual, structural, and historical evidence put forward by the parties regarding the nature of the statute and of the passport and recognition powers. This is what courts do. The political question doctrine poses no bar to judicial review of this case."

Justice Alito, concurring, said that some constitutional challenges to statutes might involve political questions, but that this was not such a case. In a concurring opinion joined in part by **Justice Breyer**, **Justice Sotomayor** suggested that the majority's analysis was too simplistic. In particular, she argued that the Court had failed to consider—

Baker v. Carr factors:

> The final three *Baker* factors address circumstances in which prudence may counsel against a court's resolution of an issue presented. Courts should be particularly cautious before forgoing adjudication of a dispute on the basis that judicial intervention risks "embarrassment from multifarious pronouncements by various departments on one question," would express a "lack of the respect due coordinate branches of government," or because there exists an "unusual need for unquestioning adherence to a political decision already made."

Nevertheless, Justice Sotomayor concluded that the additional factors did not make this case a political question.

In dissent, **Justice Breyer** disagreed with Justice Sotomayor's conclusion while sharing her concern about the final three factors. Stressing the delicate international issues presented by the case, he argued that that "this case is unusual both in its minimal need for judicial intervention and in its more serious risk that intervention will bring about "embarrassment," show lack of "respect" for the other branches, and potentially disrupt sound foreign policy decisionmaking."

Query whether the final three *Baker* factors are still relevant after *Zivotofsky*. The following two problems give you the opportunity to explore the application of the political question doctrine.

PROBLEM 9-1:
THE CASE OF THE GULF WAR

On August 2, 1990, Iraqi troops invaded Kuwait. Within ten days, the United States responded with an embargo and military blockade against all shipments into Iraq or Kuwait. On November 8, President George H.W. Bush announced a significant increase in U.S. troops in the Gulf, which he accomplished under his Article II powers as Commander in Chief, but over objections in Congress that he should have followed the procedures of the War Powers Resolution (Chapter 8, § 1B). On November 29, the United Nations passed a Resolution sanctioning the use of "all necessary means" to force Iraq out of Kuwait if there were not a voluntary withdrawal by January 15, 1991. Immediately after that, two lawsuits (one by U.S. soldiers and one by 54

Members of Congress) were filed to enjoin the President from committing troops to a war against Iraq without first obtaining a congressional declaration of war or, at least, without formally reporting to Congress pursuant to the War Powers Resolution. Was this lawsuit a nonjusticiable political question? Compare *Ange v. Bush*, 752 F. Supp. 509 (D.D.C. 1990) (yes), with *Dellums v. Bush*, 752 F. Supp. 1141 (D.D.C. 1990) (no).

PROBLEM 9-2:
THE CASE OF THE SENATE-ORIGINATED REVENUE BILL

The Victims of Crime Act of 1984 established a Crime Victims Fund, 98 Stat. 2170, 42 U.S.C. § 10601(a), as a federal source of funds for programs to compensate crime victims. One source of money for the Fund is a provision requiring "special assessments" to be made against criminals, with the money going into the Fund, up to $100 million, with any amount beyond that going into the general federal Treasury. 42 U.S.C. § 10601. The statute also amended the federal criminal code to require, *inter alia*, courts to impose a special assessment on any person convicted of a federal misdemeanor. 18 U.S.C. § 3013. Defendant, convicted of a misdemeanor and assessed $50 under the statute, challenges its constitutionality. His argument is that the bill that was to become the 1985 statute originated in the Senate, in violation of the Origination Clause of the Constitution, Article I, § 7, cl. 1, which says: "All Bills for raising Revenue shall originate in the House of Representatives." Is this claim a nonjusticiable political question? See *United States v. Munoz-Flores*, 495 U.S. 385 (1990); *Millard v. Roberts*, 202 U.S. 429, 436–37 (1906).

A NOTE ON POLITICAL QUESTIONS
AND THE GUARANTEE CLAUSE

Baker and other cases are often understood to preclude justiciability of all claims, whether individual or structural, raised under the Guarantee Clause. The Supreme Court suggested at one point, however, that it might entertain a reconsideration of this issue for structural federalism issues. In *New York v. United States* (Chapter 7, § 5C), the Court rejected federalism-based challenges to certain provisions of a federal statute regulating the disposal of low-level radioactive waste. In addition to the typical arguments (that the statute exceeded Congress' Article I powers or violated the Tenth Amendment), New York contended that the statute violated the Guarantee Clause. Justice O'Connor's majority opinion acknowledged that at least one post-*Baker* case, as well as several commentators, have suggested that not all Guarantee Clause questions should be nonjusticiable. She continued:

> We need not resolve this difficult question [of justiciability] today. * * * The twin threats imposed by the first two challenged provisions of the Act—that New York may miss out on a share of federal spending or that those generating radioactive waste within New York may lose out-of-state disposal outlets—do not pose any realistic risk of altering the form or the method of functioning of New

York's government. Thus even indulging the assumption that the Guarantee Clause provides a basis upon which a State or its subdivisions may sue to enjoin the enforcement of a federal statute, petitioners have not made out such a claim in this case.

One way to understand *New York v. United States* is to suggest that the policies of the Guarantee Clause provide the underlying rationale for the Court's Article I/Tenth Amendment rule in *New York v. United States*. On this reading, issues directly arising under the Guarantee Clause can remain nonjusticiable, while the policies of this clause may provide a theory to assist the Court in its difficult line-drawing exercises under Article I and the Tenth Amendment.

SECTION 2. "CASES" OR "CONTROVERSIES"

One can imagine a legal system in which any citizen who cares enough to litigate could obtain a hearing about whether government officials have violated the law. That has never been our system. Instead, courts are limited to hearing cases in which the plaintiff has some more definite personal connection with an alleged violation of law. The easiest cases are those in which the government action directly deprives the plaintiff of some specific legal right. In *Marbury*, for example, the plaintiff claimed to have the right to a specific government job that was being illegally withheld by the defendant. *Marbury* indicates the traditional willingness of courts to intervene in such situations. But today, government actions often affect the interests of millions of people with varying degrees of directness and tangibility, and courts have struggled to draw a line between purely partisan or ideological disputes and concrete legal controversies.

Ultimately, the effort to draw this line is rooted in the language of Article III itself. The "judicial Power" in Article III extends only to "Cases" or "Controversies" enumerated in § 2. These are abstract terms, and the judicial opinions defining them often serve to obscure rather than elucidate their meaning. But the basics are easy to understand.

The power of the federal courts is "judicial"—it is not "legislative," as is Congress' (Article I, § 1), nor is it "executive," as is the President's (Article II, § 1). If courts go beyond the "judicial" function, they invade the provinces of Congress and the President. But what is the judicial function? Article III defines it in terms of hearing "Cases" or "Controversies." These terms—which are essentially synonymous except that perhaps the latter refers only to civil cases—seem to encompass only adversarial lawsuits, not merely questions that somebody might have about what the law is.

Thus, limiting the power of federal judges to hear only adversarial lawsuits has at least two complementary justifications. As a functional matter, judges have experience and training in handling a live controversy between adverse parties adjudicated by our adversary system, but have no special expertise in considering abstract policy questions. Moreover, an adversarial dispute ensures that the courts will have a full basis for making a decision. As a formal matter, when judges reach beyond the adversarial situation and consider abstract policy questions, they arguably violate the separation of powers—they invade the legislative or executive domains.

The Framers considered, but rejected, allowing "Each branch of the Legislature, as well as the supreme Executive [the] authority to require the opinions of the supreme Judicial Court upon important questions of law, and upon solemn occasions."[5] Consistent with this, in a 1793 exchange of letters, the Supreme Court refused to provide President Washington advice on a legal question he had posed. The Justices concluded that, under the separation of powers, in a merely advisory situation any declaration of law the Court uttered would exceed the powers of the judiciary and invade the province of other branches.[6] A year before, in refusing to provide legal advice to Congress and the Secretary of War, the Justices quoted language from a letter that a circuit court had written to the President referring to limitations based in part on the judicial function " '[N]either the Legislative nor the Executive branches can constitutionally assign to the judicial any duties, but such as are properly judicial, and to be performed in a judicial manner.' "[7] Since these early precedents, the federal courts have refused to issue advisory opinions, requiring instead an actual case or controversy between adversary parties before invoking their Article III powers.

In this part, we will examine the most important doctrines limiting federal judicial power under Article III: standing, ripeness, and mootness. Each of these doctrines is quite murky at the margin, but each at its core is easy to understand. To use a simple example, suppose that law students think that Mr. Bill, their admittedly eccentric professor in the required first-year constitutional law course, graded their exams arbitrarily. They are considering filing complaints with the law school grievance committee. Consider the differing arguments that one of the students could make, and the responses available.

Standing. Michael, who received an A+, may think that Mr. Bill was wacko in giving him that grade (he claims to have learned "less than zero" in the course), but he has no "standing" to file a grievance—he suffered no

---

⁵ See, e.g., Daniel Farber & Suzanna Sherry, *A History of the American Constitution* 86–87 (2nd ed. 2005).

⁶ Chief Justice Jay wrote:

[T]he lines of separation [are] drawn by the Constitution between the three departments of the government. These being in certain respects checks upon each other, and our being judges in a court in the last resort, are considerations which afford strong arguments against the propriety of our extra-judicially deciding the questions [previously asked], especially as the power given by the Constitution to the President, of calling on the heads of departments for opinions [see Article II, § 2], seems to have been *purposely* as well as expressly united to the *executive* departments.

3 Henry Johnston, Correspondence and Public Papers of John Jay 486–89 (1891).

⁷ *Hayburn's Case*, 2 U.S. 408 (1792).

harm from Mr. Bill's supposed wackiness. When the grievance committee throws out his grievance, it could couch its decision in the separation of powers—Mr. Bill's supposedly arbitrary award of an A+ to Michael may be something implicating the executive powers of the school (the Dean should investigate) or its legislative assembly (the faculty should investigate), but it is not appropriate for the grievance committee to take up the abstract issue of Mr. Bill's eccentricities. More likely, however, the grievance committee will justify denying his grievance on functional grounds: Michael has no concrete injury to grieve, and considering his complaints will waste the committee's time and force it to consider abstract possibilities. In other words, the committee could rule "no harm, no foul," or "if you want to grouse, go on a talk show" (or see the Dean, which has certain similarities).

Ripeness. Michael responds that he'll forego any direct complaint about his grade in constitutional law. But he thinks that he would like to take the law school's elective on international trade law, which unfortunately is taught only by Mr. Bill, and he fears that he'll get nailed this time when Mr. Bill grades that exam. This grievance would also almost certainly be denied. The most obvious reason is that the complaint comes far too early—it is not "ripe" for consideration—and therefore is far too abstract. Mr. Bill may never offer the course while Michael is a student (Michael might graduate before the course is offered again, Mr. Bill might get hit by a truck in the interim). If Mr. Bill does offer it, Michael might decide not to take it (it could be offered at the same time as a course offered by Ms. Suzanna, Michael's favorite professor, for which Michael would opt). If Michael does take Mr. Bill's course, he might get another A+, or Mr. Bill might not be wacky, or . . . well, you get the idea. Again, if the grievance committee heard this complaint, it would be stepping into a domain more appropriate for other institutional actors (the Dean, the faculty assembly), and it would be undertaking review of a complaint that it has no functional capacity to adjudicate.

Mootness. Michael restrains his litigious self and files no grievance based on his experience in constitutional law with Mr. Bill. Later, he takes administrative law from Mr. Bill, who in the interim has completely fallen off the deep end. Mr. Bill gives a mid-term exam (itself a sign of lunacy) and then admits to the class that he graded it by throwing the bluebooks down the stairs, awarding proportionally higher grades the farther down a bluebook ended up. Michael's bluebook landed on the second step and he receives a D- for the midterm exam. Michael files a grievance. He certainly has standing, his complaint seems ripe—but then Mr. Bill announces in class that he has had a change of heart (after a stern talk from the Dean) and will grade the exams carefully. He does so, and Michael gets another

A+. His complaint has been "mooted" by Mr. Bill's subsequent action—it has been rendered no longer timely, and again too abstract.[8]

These examples are designed to suggest that there is a common-sense basis for notions of standing, ripeness, and mootness related to formal institutional responsibilities (which in constitutional law travel under the label of separation of powers) and to functional capacities. Now let us turn to a more legalistic assessment situating case or controversy requirements in our adversary system and translating the common-sense concerns noted above into their constitutional analogues.

The various case or controversy requirements reflect four different types of concerns. First, these requirements make for more reliable adjudicative decisions. If the plaintiff truly suffers an injury and the injury continues to hurt her, she will most likely press her case vigorously, and the defendant will respond in kind. This assures the sort of adversarial clash that the Anglo-American system of litigation traditionally assumed produces well-informed results (perhaps even "truth"). By forcing the focus onto concrete, individual grievances rather than generalized political disputes, these requirements afford the Court a richer factual context for its deliberation and the possibility of writing a narrowly tailored decision. This means constitutional law develops incrementally, without sweeping pronouncements that might go too far and erode the Court's legitimacy.

Second, these requirements reflect the Court's understanding of its role within the Constitution's scheme of separation of powers. This strand of case or controversy policy is intimately related to the political question doctrine discussed in the previous part.[9] Under this policy, the "judicial Power" is not a roving authority to do good and *make* law. While courts do make law "interstitially" (filling the gaps left by the legislature), they should only do so as needed to resolve a concrete problem affecting

---

[8]   Ripeness and mootness are usually both problems of timing—the complaint comes too early (not ripe) or too late (now moot). Assume that Susan, whose application to the law school has not yet been granted or denied, wants to complain that the school does not offer a course in international trade law. Her complaint is obviously not ripe—she may never be admitted, or even if admitted might decide to go to another law school, and so on. Assume that she is admitted and forgets about this matter until she has graduated, and then files a grievance complaining about the failure to offer the course. Her complaint obviously comes too late—it is moot.

Note how at least simple examples of the justiciability doctrine, like this one and the one involving Michael in the text, suggest that one virtue of the doctrine is that people who complain in the abstract—regardless of whether they are mere whiners or virtuous do-gooders—are forced to complain to institutions that are designed to consider abstract complaints (executive and legislative bodies), but also usually have the capacity to respond by ignoring them. In contrast, at least in theory, if federal courts have jurisdiction, they generally have the duty to render a decision rather than ignore or avoid the case. See generally, e.g., David Shapiro, *Jurisdiction and Discretion*, 60 N.Y.U. L. Rev. 543 (1985). This is another, quite important, aspect of the "judicial function" under Article III that may support limiting access to the federal courts.

[9]   Note in this regard that, until *Nixon*, the last time the Supreme Court had dismissed a case as a nonjusticiable political question was *Gilligan v. Morgan*, 413 U.S. 1, 10–12 (1973). With the virtual abandonment of the political question doctrine at the Supreme Court level after the 1970s, some of the separation-of-powers concerns reflected in the political question doctrine have floated over into other doctrines, especially standing.

individuals. What the "judicial Power" is *not*, but what *is* included in the "legislative Powers" of Article I, is the power to rearrange the rights and duties of groups of people; to create legal rules and standards without reference to an established authority or tradition; or to deal with problems which a mere judicial order cannot resolve or which are committed to the political branches of government. See generally *Valley Forge Christian College v. Americans United*, 454 U.S. 464 (1982), for a more complete statement of this philosophy.

Third, these requirements allow the Court to avoid confronting issues it is not ready to decide. The Court might choose not to speak for purely political reasons. Recall from Chapter 2 that at Justice Frankfurter's urging in the early 1950s, the Court put off the segregation issue (over the objections of Justices Black and Douglas) until it could reach a consensus and perhaps devise the most politically acceptable way of framing a decree. This philosophy inspired Professor Alexander Bickel, Justice Frankfurter's law clerk during the 1952 Term, to develop his theory extolling the Court's "passive virtues"—its willingness to defer resolution of hotly disputed constitutional issues—discussed above in connection with the political question doctrine.

Fourth, the presence of a specific plaintiff may help define the issues more precisely and allow for a focused remedy. In contrast, the absence of any directly harmed plaintiffs makes the issues far more abstract and lends itself to sweeping (and possibly vague) remedies. To use our earlier analogy, a complaint that a teacher's grading is arbitrary, set free from any complaint by an affected student, would require a grievance committee to identify appropriate grading systems, order the teacher to comply, and then engage in on-going monitoring for violations. This is much more intrusive that reversing individual grades.

Set against these values are the values enshrined in *Marbury*, namely, the obligation of the Court to say what the law is and to refuse to give effect to laws inconsistent with the Constitution. See also *The Federalist* No. 78 (Alexander Hamilton) (App. 2). Professor Martin Redish assailed the passive virtues, and especially standing restrictions, in *The Federal Courts in the Political Order: Judicial Jurisdiction and American Political Theory* (1991), arguing that these restrictions are not apparent from the text and structure of Article III, needlessly displace constitutional debate from substance to procedure, and keep important issues of constitutional interpretation from the courts. He also argued that the private law model of adjudication (an adversarial clash between a person directly harmed and a person directly causing harm) is not appropriate for the sort of public controversies involved in constitutional cases. This latter point was forcefully argued in Owen Fiss, *The Civil Rights Injunction* (1978), and Abram Chayes, *The Supreme Court, 1981 Term—Foreword: Public Law Litigation and the Burger Court*, 96 Harv. L. Rev. 4 (1982).

Consider the values and the costs of the passive virtues as we survey the doctrinal lay of the land for the three main passive virtues that have been teased out of the case or controversy requirement of Article III.

Mootness. Under traditional doctrine, " 'federal courts are without power to decide questions that cannot affect the rights of litigants in the case before them.' The inability of the federal judiciary 'to review moot cases derives from the requirement of Article III of the constitution under which the exercise of judicial power depends upon the existence of a case or controversy.' " *DeFunis v. Odegaard*, 416 U.S. 312 (1974) (*per curiam*). Any number of things might moot a case: Plaintiff no longer objects to defendant's conduct, defendant agrees to conform with plaintiff's demands, or the passage of time renders the court unable to grant plaintiff the remedy she seeks. In *DeFunis*, the Court found plaintiff's claim that he had been unconstitutionally denied admission to the University of Washington Law School (on the ground that the state law school's affirmative preferences for minority applicants gave his place to someone less well "qualified") moot because the school later admitted plaintiff and he was about to graduate when the matter reached the Court. Nothing the Court might rule would affect DeFunis' rights: If the Supreme Court agreed with the district court, which had ordered DeFunis admitted, obviously DeFunis would get his degree. But everyone in the case also agreed that he would get his degree even if the Supreme Court held that the law school had acted lawfully. Over the objections of four Justices, the Court held that the case did not present a justiciable case or controversy.

The standards enunciated in *DeFunis* often do not apply in the context of public law litigation, such as the desegregation cases. As a technical matter, parties usually litigate most such cases as class actions (*DeFunis* was not a class action, a point emphasized by the Court). This often seems to insulate a lawsuit against mootness problems. Even though the class representative's claim may become moot, other class members' claims usually remain alive. See *United States Parole Commission v. Geraghty*, 445 U.S. 388 (1980). As a class representative's claim expires, a fresh class representative may replace her.

The class action strategy might not work where the challenged public policy, like a state residency requirement for voting, has a short time fuse requiring constant rollover of the entire class. Thus, just because a class action can continue even though the case becomes moot as to a single class representative, *Sosna v. Iowa*, 419 U.S. 393 (1975), a mootness objection is not saved simply because the plaintiffs denominate their case a class action if the original class members are subject to the same mootness issue, *Hall v. Beals*, 396 U.S. 45 (1969). In response to this seemingly inequitable dilemma which favors defendants with the resources to stall litigation until the plaintiff's claim expires, the Court will sometimes hear a case notwithstanding its mootness where an issue is "capable of repetition yet evading review," because the lawsuit's duration systematically tends to moot individual grievances. *Southern Pacific Terminal Co. v. ICC*, 219 U.S. 498, 515 (1911).

The landmark abortion rights case, *Roe v. Wade* (Chapter 5, § 4B), provides a useful example of this phenomenon. There the Court decided the case even though Ms. Roe had already borne her child, holding that so long as some member of the class remained capable of asserting a claim against the Texas law (e.g., some member of the class could seek to have or aid in an abortion), the case remained justiciable. Realistically, it is unlikely that an abortion case could reach the Supreme Court in time to be heard; the gestation period for litigation is much longer than nine months! Later, the Court further broadened this, even in suits not filed as class actions, where an otherwise moot issue is capable of repetition among the same litigants. *First National Bank v. Bellotti*, 435 U.S. 765 (1978).

Ripeness. In an effort to keep the judiciary from overstepping its Article III jurisdiction over cases and controversies, ripeness doctrine seeks to avoid "premature adjudication." *Pacific Gas & Electric Co. v. State Energy Resources Conservation & Development Commission*, 461 U.S. 190 (1983). Under traditional doctrine, "[d]etermination of the scope and constitutionality of legislation in advance of its immediate adverse effect in the context of a concrete case involves too remote and abstract an inquiry for the proper exercise of the judicial function." *International Longshoremen's & Warehousemen's Union, Local 37 v. Boyd*, 347 U.S. 222 (1954). In the leading case of *United Public Workers v. Mitchell*, 330 U.S. 75 (1947), government workers brought suit challenging provisions of the Hatch Act prohibiting their participation in political campaigns. While the Court found that one employee who had violated the Act had a ripe claim, those who merely wished to undertake political activities, but had not yet done so, were barred from adjudication. The Court said that the power of judicial review "arises only when the interests of litigants require the use of this judicial authority for their protection against actual interference. A hypothetical threat is not enough." Justice Douglas dissented on this issue, reasoning that it was unfair to government employees to require them to risk incurring the statute's penalties in order to challenge it.

In a host of cases, however, the Supreme Court has adjudicated important constitutional issues without demanding actual prosecutions. For example, in *Adler v. Board of Education*, 342 U.S. 485 (1952), the Court upheld New York's Feinberg Law, excluding "subversive persons" from employment in the public school system, without demanding that any of the plaintiffs had been prosecuted for violating the statute. The majority opinion did not even mention ripeness, even though Justice Frankfurter hotly dissented on ripeness grounds, citing *Mitchell*. In other cases, the Court has considered "hardship to the parties" and "fitness of the issues" in adjudicating controversies where there had been no actual prosecution. E.g., *Abbott Laboratories v. Gardner*, 387 U.S. 136 (1967).

As with mootness, plaintiffs alleging ongoing patterns of constitutional violations have sometimes been able to sue without proving that particular plaintiffs have been subject to the practices in question. In *Lankford v. Gelston*, 364 F.2d 197 (4th Cir. 1966), Judge Sobeloff held that African-American families in Baltimore were entitled to injunctive relief against the police department to prevent future violations of the families' privacy rights. The district court had refused relief, because it was satisfied that new police procedures were a good-faith effort to deal with the pattern of unjustified searches of black persons' homes. Judge Sobeloff disagreed, based upon the "vast demonstration of disregard of private rights" and the persistence of "[a] sense of impending crisis in police-community relations."

The Supreme Court, however, did not follow this reasoning in refusing to hear (on ripeness grounds) challenges of ongoing discriminatory law enforcement in *O'Shea v. Littleton*, 414 U.S. 488 (1974). The Court refused to "conclude that the case or controversy requirement is satisfied by general assertions or inferences that in the course of their activities [plaintiffs] will be prosecuted for violating valid criminal laws." Sharply dissenting, Justice Douglas (joined by Justices Brennan and Marshall) said that the complaint alleged "a more pervasive scheme for suppression of Blacks and their civil rights than I have ever seen," in which a judge and magistrate were alleged to have consistently denied African Americans fair bonds, jury fees, and sentences. See also *Los Angeles v. Lyons*, 461 U.S. 95 (1983) (refusing to adjudicate the discriminatory use of chokeholds by Los Angeles police, based upon plaintiff's lack of standing to obtain an injunction against the practice, even though it had been applied to his own neck); *Rizzo v. Goode*, 423 U.S. 362 (1976) (refusing to adjudicate discriminatory police practices in Philadelphia for similar reasons). On the other hand, in *Duke Power Co. v. Carolina Environmental Study Group, Inc.*, 438 U.S. 59 (1978), the Court heard a case challenging the constitutionality of a federally mandated ceiling on liability for nuclear disasters, notwithstanding the absence of such a disaster and its future unlikelihood.

The right-to-privacy cases in Chapter 5, § 4, have had a particularly roller-coaster history with ripeness doctrine. In *Poe v. Ullman*, Justice Frankfurter's opinion for the Court dismissed challenges to Connecticut's prohibition against the use of contraceptives because none of the plaintiffs had been prosecuted and, given the state's general lack of interest in enforcing the statute, seemed unlikely to be prosecuted. In *Griswold v. Connecticut*, plaintiffs (according to Tom Emerson, who argued the case) orchestrated a cooked-up arrest and were able to escape ripeness problems. In *Bowers v. Hardwick*, the Court upheld Georgia's sodomy law even though charges against plaintiff had been dropped, and there was little if any indication that he would be prosecuted in the future.

Standing. According to the doctrines associated with standing, a plaintiff must have "a personal stake in the outcome of a controversy as to assure that concrete adverseness which sharpens the presentation of issues upon which the court so largely depends for illumination of difficult constitutional questions." *Baker v. Carr.* In a sense, this is the most basic requirement: Roughly speaking, a case isn't ripe if the plaintiff does not yet have a sufficiently clear personal stake, and it's moot if the plaintiff no longer has a personal stake.

The traditional law of standing required the plaintiff to show that she had suffered a legal injury, typically to a right protected under common law. More recently, the Supreme Court has defined the law of standing more realistically to require that the plaintiff in a case or controversy be someone who has suffered only an "injury in fact," an actual injury to her interests, *and* who is within the "zone of interests" meant to be protected by constitutional or statutory provisions. *Association of Data Processing Service Organizations v. Camp,* 397 U.S. 150 (1970). The Supreme Court considers the injury in fact component of standing a constitutional requirement of Article III, but the zone of interests component only a prudential concern inspired by Article III. *Valley Forge Christian College, supra.* Therefore, the key concept is what constitutes an injury in fact.

The Supreme Court has broken injury in fact into three inquiries: (1) whether plaintiff has suffered an actual injury, (2) whether plaintiff's injury is the result of defendant's conduct, and (3) whether plaintiff's injury can be redressed by the judicial relief she requests. *Los Angeles v. Lyons,* 461 U.S. 95 (1983). If a showing of any of these three elements is lacking, the court will dismiss the suit for lack of constitutional standing. There is considerable dispute about whether this three-part test leads to coherent results or advances significant societal goals. See, e.g., *American Bottom Conservancy v. U.S. Army Corps of Engineers,* 650 F.3d 652, 655 (7th Cir. 2011) (Posner, J.) ("Some of the most frequently mentioned grounds for the constitutional doctrine of standing are tenuous"); Heather Elliott, *The Functions of Standing,* 61 Stan. L. Rev. 459 (2008).

The requirement of actual injury is often pretty easy for a plaintiff to satisfy, since the Court will recognize not only economic injury, but also aesthetic, environmental, and certain emotional injuries as well. For example, in *Duke Power, supra,* the Court found standing for an environmental group challenging the liability limits for a local nuclear reactor. The Court found the possibility of environmental and thermal pollution to be an actual injury, as well as plaintiffs' "generalized concern about exposure to radiation and the apprehension flowing from the uncertainty about the health and genetic consequences of even small emissions like those concededly emitted by nuclear power plants." See also *United States v. SCRAP*, 412 U.S. 669 (1973).

Once a plaintiff has satisfactorily demonstrated that she suffered an injury in fact, she must prove a causal link between her injury and the defendant's conduct. In constitutional cases, the plaintiff must show that her injury is "fairly traceable" to a specific government action. In *Warth v. Seldin*, 422 U.S. 490 (1975), the Court denied standing to low-income and minority individuals who claimed to have been denied housing opportunities because of a town's exclusionary zoning ordinance. The Court held that the plaintiffs had not properly asserted that "absent [the town's] restrictive zone practices, there [was] a substantial probability that they would have been able to purchase and lease in Penfield," since they were unable to show that any developer who would build housing suitable to their needs and resources was being excluded by the zoning law. But a black plaintiff, who wished to purchase specific housing that a developer wished to build but could not under existing zoning laws, was held to have standing to challenge the law as racially discriminatory. *Village of Arlington Heights v. Metropolitan Housing Development*, 429 U.S. 252 (1977).

The third element required to demonstrate a personal stake in litigation is the ability of the court to correct the perceived wrong. To have standing, litigants must demonstrate that there is a "substantial likelihood" that they will benefit from the requested relief. In *Warth*, the Court questioned whether judicial redress was possible, holding that the plaintiffs had failed to show that "if the court affords the relief requested, the asserted liability of petitioners will be removed." Similarly, in *Simon v. Eastern Kentucky Welfare Rights Organization*, 426 U.S. 26 (1976), the Court denied standing to indigents and allied organizations challenging an IRS policy giving tax exemptions to nonprofit hospitals which limited access of poor people to their emergency room services. The Court found no standing because it would only be "speculative" whether the desired relief would actually change the hospitals' emergency room services to the poor.

We will now focus on standing doctrine. We begin with a cluster of cases applying the three-part test that is now the core of standing doctrine. These case are followed by a Note on the special problems posed when standing claims are based on the plaintiff's role in the lawmaking process. We then close this section with a discussion of Congress's ability to expand the rules of standing.

Northeastern Florida Chapter of the Associated General Contractors of America v. Jacksonville

508 U.S. 656 (1993)

In 1984, Jacksonville, Florida, "enacted an ordinance entitled 'Minority Business Enterprise Participation,' which required that 10% of the amount spent on city contracts be set aside each fiscal year for so-called 'Minority Business Enterprises' (MBE's). An MBE was defined as a business whose ownership was at least 51% 'minority' or female, and a 'minority' was in turn defined as a person who is or considers himself to be black, Spanish-speaking, Oriental, Indian, Eskimo, Aleut, or handicapped. Once projects were earmarked for MBE bidding by the city's chief purchasing officer, they were 'deemed reserved for minority business enterprises only.' "

The ordinance was challenged by an association of individuals and firms in the construction industry who did business in Jacksonville and did not qualify as MBEs under the city's ordinance. The Eleventh Circuit held that the association lacked standing, because it "has not demonstrated that, but for the program, any [association] member would have bid successfully for any of these contracts." The Supreme Court reversed. **Justice Thomas**'s opinion for the Court stated that the Court had frequently allowed standing for persons challenging discrimination, as in *Bakke* (Chapter 3, § 3A), where a twice-rejected white male applicant claimed that a medical school's admissions program, which reserved 16 of the 100 places in the entering class for minority applicants, was inconsistent with equal protection guarantees. See also *Turner v. Fouche*, 396 U.S. 346 (1970) (plaintiff had standing to challenge a Georgia law limiting school-board membership to property owners even though there was no allegation that plaintiff would have been appointed "but for" the property requirement); *Clements v. Fashing*, 457 U.S. 957 (1982) (allowing lawsuit against "automatic resignation" provision of the Texas Constitution, which requires the immediate resignation of some state officeholders upon their announcement of a candidacy for another office, and finding standing because plaintiffs had alleged that they would have announced their candidacy were it not for the consequences of doing so).

"Singly and collectively, these cases stand for the following proposition: When the government erects a barrier that makes it more difficult for members of one group to obtain a benefit than it is for members of another group, a member of the former group seeking to challenge the barrier need not allege that he would have obtained the benefit but for the barrier in order to establish standing. The 'injury in fact' in an equal protection case of this variety is the denial of equal treatment resulting from the imposition of the barrier, not the ultimate inability to obtain the benefit. And in the context of a challenge to a set-aside program, the 'injury in fact' is the inability to compete on an equal footing in the bidding process, not the loss of a contract."

NOTE ON TAXPAYER STANDING

The plaintiffs in *Allen* did not sue as taxpayers seeking full enforcement of federal tax law, or objecting to the way their tax dollars are being used. The problem with asserting federal taxpayer standing is the difficulty in proving a causal relationship between general governmental tax policies and specific injuries to individuals. Once collected, revenues become aggregated, losing their individual identity and connection to specific taxpayers. In *Frothingham v. Mellon*, 262 U.S. 447 (1923), the Court declined to hear a challenge to the Federal Maternity Act, which conditioned appropriations to states on compliance with provisions of the Act aimed at reducing maternal and infant mortality. The Court denied standing, stating: "The party who invokes the [judicial] power must be able to show that he has sustained or is immediately in danger of sustaining some direct injury as a result of the statute's enforcement, and not merely that he suffers in some indefinite way in common with people generally."

In *Flast v. Cohen*, 392 U.S. 83 (1968), on the other hand, the Court held that federal taxpayer standing could be recognized in those limited circumstances where litigants (1) challenge a specific exercise of the government's taxing or spending power, which (2) they contend is a violation of the constitutional limitations on the taxing or spending power. It is not enough to challenge appropriations incidental to federal regulations. *Flast* stands as an exception to the general rule that disfavors taxpayer standing, and it probably applies only to Establishment Clause violations (*Flast* dealt with a challenge to aid to religious schools). The *Flast* decision was severely limited in *Valley Forge Christian College v. Americans United*, 454 U.S. 464 (1982). There, taxpayers challenged a federal grant of surplus funds and a land transfer to a parochial college as violating the Establishment Clause. The Court refused standing, holding that the challenge was to an administrative agency's actions, not congressional legislation as in *Flast*. The Court denied standing to challenge the land transfer since it was made pursuant to the Property Clause of Article IV, not under the Article I spending power.

The Court again limited *Flast* in *Arizona Christian School Tuition Organization v. Winn*, 563 U.S. 125 (2011), holding that *Flast* did not apply to tax credits for contributions to organizations that fund scholarships for students at private schools. **Justice Kennedy**'s opinion for the Court reasoned that a tax credit simply amounts to a failure by the state to collect a tax, and thus cannot be considered to extract funds from taxpayers for a government expenditure. Although the Court had decided establishment clause cases involving tax expenditures on multiple occasions, none of the cases had discussed the standing issue, and Justice Kennedy considered the issue still open.

NOTE ON THIRD-PARTY STANDING

Sometimes one party asserts standing on the basis of another party's legal injury. This is known as third-party standing or *jus tertii*. Generally, no one has the right to press another's claim. For example, in *Tileston v. Ullman*, 318 U.S. 44 (1943) (per curiam), the Court ruled that a doctor had no standing to press the liberty and privacy claims of his patients, who wished to have access to contraceptives that were illegal in Connecticut.

But exceptions have been recognized over the years. For instance, where it is difficult for the rightful plaintiff to assert her legal right, another plaintiff *with standing to sue in his own right* may also press her claim. Thus, the doctrine of *jus tertii* is not a rule of constitutional law required by Article III (because plaintiff has standing on her own), but is a judicially created prudential limitation—"a salutary 'rule of self-restraint' designed to minimize unwarranted intervention into controversies where the applicable constitutional questions are ill-defined and speculative." *Craig v. Boren* (Chapter 4, § 2B1). Recall that *Craig* involved a state law forbidding the sale of 3.2% beer to males below twenty-one years of age, but allowing its sale to females aged eighteen and older. *Craig* allowed a beer seller to challenge the law as a violation of the rights of potential eighteen-year-old male customers: (1) the seller had standing in her own right because she suffered injury in fact flowing from the statute (her choice was either to obey the statute and forego beer sales to young males or to sell to them and risk sanctions and the loss of her beer license); and (2) the seller was ideally situated to assert the rights of the young males, for she had strong reasons to oppose the law, and compliance with the law would operate to violate the rights of third parties. In addition, see, e.g., *Singleton v. Wulff*, 428 U.S. 106 (1976) (physician may raise privacy rights of patients in challenging restrictive abortion law).

A striking issue of third-party standing was posed by *Bush v. Gore* (Chapter 5, § 3A), where a presidential candidate was allowed to litigate the equal protection rights of voters with "spoiled" ballots. The Court did not even mention the standing issue. Did Bush have standing under *Craig v. Boren*? How is Bush's case different from *Tileston*?

Certain organizations may also press the claims of their members. Third-party standing has been granted in such cases where the organization's members have suffered an injury in fact sufficient to give them standing, but where the litigation is relevant to the entire organization. See, e.g., *Hunt v. Washington State Apple Advertising Commission*, 432 U.S. 333 (1977); *NAACP v. Alabama*, 357 U.S. 449 (1958).

Given the incoherence of standing doctrine and the anomalous policy consequences of it, some scholars have advocated its abolition or amelioration. E.g., Mark Tushnet, *The New Law of Standing: A Plea for Abandonment*, 62 Cornell L. Rev. 663 (1977). If not abandoned, could the law of standing be more narrowly formulated, as *McKenna* might suggest? Or perhaps politely ignored or excepted from, as the mootness and ripeness cases might suggest?

LUJAN V. DEFENDERS OF WILDLIFE
504 U.S. 555, 112 S.Ct. 2130, 119 L.Ed.2d 351 (1992)

JUSTICE SCALIA delivered the opinion of the Court with respect to Parts I, II, III-A, and IV, and an opinion with respect to Part III-B in which THE CHIEF JUSTICE, JUSTICE WHITE, and JUSTICE THOMAS join.

[The Endangered Species Act of 1973 (ESA) seeks to protect species of animals against threats to their continuing existence caused by humans. Endangered or threatened species are identified by a periodic list compiled by the Secretary of the Interior. Section 7(a)(2) of the Act then provides that each federal agency must ensure that "any action authorized, funded, or carried out by that agency * * * is not likely to jeopardize the continued existence of any endangered species or any threatened species or result in the destruction or adverse modification of the habitat of such species." The Secretary by regulation determined that § 7 is only applicable to species and habitats within the territorial borders of the United States or on the High Seas. Plaintiffs, organizations dedicated to wildlife conservation and other environmental causes, obtained an injunction requiring the Secretary to promulgate a revised regulation applying § 7 extraterritorially.]

While the Constitution of the United States divides all power conferred upon the Federal Government into "legislative Powers," Art. I, § 1, "[t]he executive Power," Art. II, § 1, and "[t]he judicial Power," Art. III, § 1, it does not attempt to define those terms. To be sure, it limits the jurisdiction of federal courts to "Cases" and "Controversies," but an executive inquiry can bear the name "case" (the Hoffa case) and a legislative dispute can bear the name "controversy" (the Smoot-Hawley controversy). Obviously, then, the Constitution's central mechanism of separation of powers depends largely upon common understanding of what activities are appropriate to legislatures, to executives, and to courts. In The Federalist No. 48, Madison expressed the view that "[i]t is not infrequently a question of real nicety in legislative bodies whether the operation of a particular measure will, or will not, extend beyond the legislative sphere," whereas "the executive power [is] restrained within a narrower compass and . . . more simple in its nature," and "the judiciary [is] described by landmarks still less uncertain." One of those landmarks, setting apart the "Cases" and "Controversies" that are of the justiciable sort referred to in Article III—"serv[ing] to identify those disputes which are appropriately resolved through the judicial process"—is the doctrine of standing. Though some of its elements express merely prudential considerations that are part of judicial self-government, the core component of standing is an essential and unchanging part of the case-or-controversy requirement of Article III.

Over the years, our cases have established that the irreducible constitutional minimum of standing contains three elements: First, the plaintiff must have suffered an "injury in fact"—an invasion of a legally-protected interest which is (a) concrete and particularized, and (b) "actual or imminent, not 'conjectural' or 'hypothetical.' " Second, there must be a causal connection between the injury and the conduct complained of—the injury has to be "fairly ... trace[able] to the challenged action of the defendant, and not ... th[e] result [of] the independent action of some third party not before the court." Third, it must be "likely," as opposed to merely "speculative," that the injury will be "redressed by a favorable decision." * * *

We think the Court of Appeals failed to apply the foregoing principles in denying the Secretary's motion for summary judgment. Respondents had not made the requisite demonstration of (at least) injury and redressability.

A. Respondents' claim to injury is that the lack of consultation with respect to certain funded activities abroad "increase[s] the rate of extinction of endangered and threatened species." * * * To survive the Secretary's summary judgment motion, respondents had to submit affidavits or other evidence showing, through specific facts, not only that listed species were in fact being threatened by funded activities abroad, but also that one or more of respondents' members would thereby be "directly" affected apart from their " 'special interest' in th[e] subject."

[The affidavits alleged that two members, Kelly and Skilbred, had visited two project areas in the past and intended to return in the future to observe endangered species.]

[The affidavits] plainly contain no facts * * * showing how damage to the species will produce "imminent" injury to Mss. Kelly and Skilbred. That the women "had visited" the areas of the projects before the projects commenced proves nothing. As we have said in a related context, " '[p]ast exposure to illegal conduct does not in itself show a present case or controversy regarding injunctive relief ... if unaccompanied by any continuing, present adverse effects.' " And the affiants' profession of an "inten[t]" to return to the places they had visited before—where they will presumably, this time, be deprived of the opportunity to observe animals of the endangered species—is simply not enough. * * *

[Justice Scalia's opinion then identifies and rejects plaintiffs' "novel standing theories." Their "ecosystem nexus" theory proposed that any person who uses *any* part of a "contiguous ecosystem" adversely affected by a funded activity has standing even if the activity is located a great distance away. The Court rejected this theory as inconsistent with precedent holding that a plaintiff claiming injury from environmental damage must use the area affected by the challenged activity and not an area roughly "in the vicinity" of it. Plaintiffs' "animal nexus" theory asserted that anyone who has an interest in studying or seeing the endangered animals anywhere on the globe has standing; similar was their "vocational nexus" theory, under which anyone with a professional interest in such animals can sue.] This is beyond all reason. * * * It goes beyond the limit * * * and into pure speculation and fantasy, to say that anyone who observes or works with an endangered species, anywhere in the world, is appreciably harmed by a single project affecting some portion of that species with which he has no more specific connection. * * *

The Court of Appeals found that respondents had standing for an additional reason: because they had suffered a "procedural injury." The so-called "citizen-suit" provision of the ESA provides, in pertinent part, that "any person may commence a civil suit on his own behalf (A) to enjoin any person, including the United States and any other governmental instrumentality or agency . . . who is alleged to be in violation of any provision of this chapter." The court held that, because § 7(a)(2) requires interagency consultation, the citizen-suit provision creates a "procedural righ[t]" to consultation in all "persons"—so that *anyone* can file suit in federal court to challenge the Secretary's (or presumably any other official's) failure to follow the assertedly correct consultative procedure, notwithstanding their inability to allege any discrete injury flowing from that failure. To understand the remarkable nature of this holding one must be clear about what it does *not* rest upon: This is not a case where plaintiffs are seeking to enforce a procedural requirement the disregard of which could impair a separate concrete interest of theirs (*e.g.*, the procedural requirement for a hearing prior to denial of their license application, or the procedural requirement for an environmental impact statement before a federal facility is constructed next door to them). Nor is it simply a case where concrete injury has been suffered by many persons, as in mass fraud or mass tort situations. Nor, finally, is it the unusual case in which Congress has created a concrete private interest in the outcome of a suit against a private party for the government's benefit, by providing a cash bounty for the victorious plaintiff. Rather, the court held that the injury-in-fact requirement had been satisfied by congressional conferral upon *all* persons of an abstract, self-contained, noninstrumental "right" to have the Executive observe the procedures required by law. We reject this view. * * *

* * * "The province of the court," as Chief Justice Marshall said in *Marbury v. Madison*, "is, solely, to decide on the rights of individuals." Vindicating the *public* interest (including the public interest in government observance of the Constitution and laws) is the function of Congress and the Chief Executive. The question presented here is whether the public interest in proper administration of the laws (specifically, in agencies' observance of a particular, statutorily prescribed procedure) can be converted into an individual right by a statute that denominates it as such, and that permits all citizens (or, for that matter, a subclass of citizens who suffer no distinctive concrete harm) to sue. If the concrete injury

requirement has the separation-of-powers significance we have always said, the answer must be obvious: To permit Congress to convert the undifferentiated public interest in executive officers' compliance with the law into an "individual right" vindicable in the courts is to permit Congress to transfer from the President to the courts the Chief Executive's most important constitutional duty, to "take Care that the Laws be faithfully executed," Art. II, § 3. It would enable the courts, with the permission of Congress, "to assume a position of authority over the governmental acts of another and co-equal department," and to become " 'virtually continuing monitors of the wisdom and soundness of Executive action.' " We have always rejected that vision of our role * * *.

JUSTICE KENNEDY, with whom **JUSTICE SOUTER** joins, concurring in part and concurring in the judgment.

[I] join Part IV of the Court's opinion with the following observations. As government programs and policies become more complex and far-reaching, we must be sensitive to the articulation of new rights of action that do not have clear analogs in our common-law tradition. Modern litigation has progressed far from the paradigm of Marbury suing Madison to get his commission, or Ogden seeking an injunction to halt Gibbons' steamboat operations. *Gibbons v. Ogden*, 9 Wheat. 1 (1824). In my view, Congress has the power to define injuries and articulate chains of causation that will give rise to a case or controversy where none existed before, and I do not read the Court's opinion to suggest a contrary view. In exercising this power, however, Congress must at the very least identify the injury it seeks to vindicate and relate the injury to the class of persons entitled to bring suit. The citizen-suit provision of the Endangered Species Act does not meet these minimal requirements, because while the statute purports to confer a right on "any person . . . to enjoin . . . the United States and any other governmental instrumentality or agency. . . who is alleged to be in violation of any provision of this chapter," it does not of its own force establish that there is an injury in "any person" by virtue of any "violation." 16 U.S.C. § 1540(g)(1)(A).

[**JUSTICE STEVENS** concurred in the judgment; he rejected the plurality opinion's analysis of standing but found the Secretary's regulation a correct interpretation of the statute and so concurred in the reversal of the lower courts' orders. **JUSTICE BLACKMUN**, joined by **JUSTICE O'CONNOR**, dissented from the Court's holding that there was no standing.]

NOTES ON DEFENDERS OF WILDLIFE AND STANDING TO ENFORCE STATUTES

1.   *The Court's Environmental Standing Precedents*. The leading case is *Sierra Club v. Morton*, 405 U.S. 727 (1972), in which the environmental group

sued to overturn the Forest Service's approval of a private resort, which would allegedly have despoiled natural wooded areas. Over Justice Douglas' celebrated dissent arguing that "trees have standing," the Court held that the organization or its members would have to show a particularized injury to them (including aesthetic injury to members who had been to the forest and wanted to go back).

The Court indicated that the *Sierra Club* test might be easy to satisfy in *United States v. SCRAP*, 412 U.S. 669 (1973), where the Court held that environmental groups (in that case, a bunch of students) could challenge Interstate Commerce Commission rate policies. The injury in fact claimed was this: Higher rates proposed by the ICC would allegedly increase the use of non-recyclable goods, which would lead to the use of more resources to produce the goods, which in turn would further deplete forests that the plaintiffs enjoyed. Does this characterization of the plaintiffs' injury seem too attenuated?

In *Duke Power Company v. Carolina Environmental Study Group, Inc.*, discussed above, the Court found that an environmental group had standing to challenge the constitutionality of federal limits on tort liability of nuclear power plants for meltdowns and other disasters. Relying on *SCRAP*, the Court held that plaintiffs had the requisite "personal stake" in the controversy because of their "direct and present injury" by reason of the alleged aesthetic and thermal pollution of their neighborhood by the nuclear plant. The Court did not reach the issue of whether their "fear and apprehension" of a nuclear disaster would, alone, justify their standing to sue.

The Supreme Court signaled a more restrictive application of *Sierra Club* in *Lujan v. National Wildlife Federation*, 497 U.S. 871 (1990), which prevented the Federation from challenging the Bureau of Land Management's failure to follow congressionally mandated procedures. Those procedures were required for reviewing executive orders withdrawing public lands from resource development. Justice Scalia's opinion for the Court faulted the Federation for not providing *Sierra Club*-type affidavits alleging that its members used the very lands in question, not just those in the vicinity, and also for challenging the entire BLM program and not just its review of the lands directly affecting Federation members.

2.   *Procedural Injuries, Citizen Suits, and Original Intent.* The Court in *Defenders of Wildlife* brushes aside the claim of procedural standing, calling it nothing more than "an abstract, self-contained, noninstrumental 'right' to have the Executive observe the procedures required by law." Are such "noninstrumental rights" ever a basis for standing? What about the right to a decisionmaking process free of racial motivation, which the Court found a sufficient basis for standing in *Northeastern Florida Contractors* and in *Shaw v. Reno* (Chapter 3, § 3E)?

Cass Sunstein, *What's Standing After* Lujan? *Of Citizen Suits, "Injuries," and Article III*, 91 Mich. L. Rev. 163 (1992), argues that *Defenders of Wildlife* seems to contract Article III standing limits well beyond the boundaries assumed by the Framers of the Constitution. According to Sunstein, the strict injury-in-fact requirement of standing is of relatively recent origin, and giving it such bite against Congress' efforts to recognize regulatory interests subserved by citizen suits is inconsistent with the Framers' understanding that Congress would have such authority. Practice at the time of the Constitution's framing was tolerant of congressional authorization for citizens to seek mandamus against officials violating the law and to seek *qui tam* relief for private violations—actions that would not be allowed under a strict reading of *Defenders of Wildlife*. How might Justice Scalia respond? Cf. Harold Krent & Ethan Shenkman, *Of Citizen Suits and Citizen Sunstein*, 91 Mich. L. Rev. 1793 (1993) (arguing that allowing citizen suits would interfere with the ability of the President to "take Care" that the laws be faithfully executed). For further exploration of the history of standing, see Elizabeth Magill, *Standing for the Public: A Lost History*, 95 Va. L. Rev. 1131 (2009); Daniel Ho and Erica Ross, *Did Liberal Justices Invent the Standing Doctrine? An Empirical Study of the Evolution of Standing, 1921–2006* (2010).

    3. *Separation of Powers Concerns with the New Standing.* Justice Blackmun's dissenting opinion in *Defenders of Wildlife* expressed concern that the new rigidity in applying standing precepts to environmental statutes would shift power away from Congress to the President. It seems obvious that Congress sets policy both by the substantive rules and by the procedures through which policy is implemented. Hence, when Congress delegates rulemaking power to agencies it does not control (and which are often now controlled by a President of a different political party), it typically "hard wires" into the statute procedures that will press the agency toward the policy equilibrium desired by Congress.[10] The use of process to direct agencies toward substantive results has been particularly popular in environmental statutes, such as the National Environmental Policy Act, which requires agencies to consider the environmental impact of their activities.

    Procedural obligations can be as important as substantive obligations in the modern regulatory state, and judicial review to enforce both types of obligations is necessary if one accepts the premise of legislative supremacy, as Article I implicitly does.[11] The problem, highlighted in *Defenders of Wildlife*, is that if you take a narrow, private-law view of standing it is harder to find plaintiffs who can enforce procedural obligations. They run into problems of particularity and redressability—it's hard for plaintiffs to show that they are affected by every single procedural violation they challenge, and it's also hard for such plaintiffs to show that following the right procedures will help them.

    Justice Blackmun concluded: "It is to be hoped that over time the Court will acknowledge that some classes of procedural duties are so enmeshed with the prevention of substantive, concrete harm that an individual plaintiff may

---

    [10] Matthew McCubbins, Roger Noll & Barry Weingast, *Administrative Procedures as Instruments of Control*, 3 J.L. Econ. & Org. 243 (1987); see also Jonathan Macey, *Separated Powers and Positive Political Theory: The Tug of War Over Administrative Agencies*, 80 Geo. L.J. 671 (1992).

    [11] See Daniel Farber, Politics and Procedure in Environmental Law, 8 J. L. Econ. & Org. 59, 76–78 (1992).

be able to demonstrate a sufficient likelihood of injury just through the breach of that procedural duty."

FEDERAL ELECTION COMMISSION V. AKINS
524 U.S. 11, 118 S.Ct. 1777, 141 L.Ed.2d 10 (1998)

Plaintiffs challenged the Commission's determination that the American Israel Public Affairs Committee (AIPAC) was not a "political committee" under the federal election laws and therefore was not covered by various disclosure requirements. In an opinion by **Justice Breyer**, the Court held that the plaintiffs had standing. Their injury in fact consisted of "their inability to obtain information" such as lists of donors that, on their view of the law, "the statute requires that AIPAC make public." The Court "found no reason to doubt their claim that the information would help them (and others to whom they would communicate it) to evaluate candidates for public office, especially candidates who received assistance from AIPAC, and to evaluate the role that AIPAC's financial assistance might play in a specific election." This "injury consequently seems concrete and particular." The government argued, however, that this was an undifferentiated injury shared by the voters generally, and hence not a basis for standing. The Court found it irrelevant, however, that the injury was shared generally: "Often the fact that an interest is abstract and the fact that it is widely shared go hand in hand. But their association is not invariable, and where a harm is concrete, though widely shared, the Court has found 'injury in fact.'" Thus, "the informational injury at issue here, directly related to voting, the most basic of political rights, is sufficiently concrete and specific such that the fact that it is widely shared does not deprive Congress of constitutional power to authorize its vindication in the federal courts."

JUSTICE SCALIA dissented, joined by **JUSTICES O'CONNOR** and **THOMAS**. He viewed the Court's rejection of the "widely shared" test with alarm:

> The provision of law at issue in this case is an extraordinary one, conferring upon a private person the ability to bring an Executive agency into court to compel its enforcement of the law against a third party.

> * * * If provisions such as the present one were commonplace, the role of the Executive Branch in our system of separated and equilibrated powers would be greatly reduced, and that of the Judiciary greatly expanded.

> Because this provision is so extraordinary, we should be particularly careful not to expand it beyond its fair meaning. In my view the Court's opinion does that. Indeed, it expands the meaning beyond what the Constitution permits.

Justice Scalia stressed that a "system in which the citizenry at large could sue to compel Executive compliance with the law would be a system in which the courts, rather than the President, are given the primary responsibility to 'take Care that the Laws be faithfully executed,' Art. II, § 3." The barrier to this system of judicial control has been that "the common understanding of the interest necessary to sustain suit has included the requirement * * * that the complained-of injury be particularized and differentiated, rather than common to all the electorate."

2. Besides criticizing the majority for being inconsistent with *Defenders of Wildlife*, Justice Scalia predicted sweeping consequences:

> If today's decision is correct, it is within the power of Congress to authorize any interested person to manage (through the courts) the Executive's enforcement of any law that includes a requirement for the filing and public availability of a piece of paper. This is not the system we have had, and is not the system we should desire.

In short, Justice Scalia concluded, the statute as construed by the majority "unconstitutionally transfers from the Executive to the courts the responsibility to 'take Care that the Laws be faithfully executed.'"

Was Justice Scalia correct in his implication that *Akins* overruled the Article II, separation of powers theory of *Defenders of Wildlife*? Putting aside the question whether this is "the system we have had," was he correct that this "is not the system we should desire"?

MASSACHUSETTS V. EPA
549 U.S. 497, 127 S.Ct. 1438, 167 L.Ed.2d 248 (2007)

JUSTICE STEVENS delivered the opinion of the Court.

[States, local governments, and environmental organizations petitioned for review of an order of the Environmental Protection Agency (EPA) denying a petition for rulemaking to regulate greenhouse gas emissions from motor vehicles under the Clean Air Act. The statute mandates such regulations if certain prerequisites are met. A divided panel of the D.C. Circuit ruled in favor of the EPA, in part on the basis of questions about the petitioners' standing.]

A well-documented rise in global temperatures has coincided with a significant increase in the concentration of carbon dioxide in the atmosphere. Respected scientists believe the two trends are related. For when carbon dioxide is released into the atmosphere, it acts like the ceiling of a greenhouse, trapping solar energy and retarding the escape of reflected heat. It is therefore a species—the most important species—of a "greenhouse gas."

Calling global warming "the most pressing environmental challenge of our time," a group of States, local governments, and private organizations, alleged in a petition for certiorari that the Environmental Protection Agency (EPA) has abdicated its responsibility under the Clean Air Act to regulate the emissions of four greenhouse gases, including carbon dioxide. Specifically, petitioners asked us to answer two questions concerning the meaning of § 202(a)(1) of the Act: whether EPA has the statutory authority to regulate greenhouse gas emissions from new motor vehicles; and if so, whether its stated reasons for refusing to do so are consistent with the statute. * * *

Article III of the Constitution limits federal-court jurisdiction to "Cases" and "Controversies." Those two words confine "the business of federal courts to questions presented in an adversary context and in a form historically viewed as capable of resolution through the judicial process." It is therefore familiar learning that no justiciable "controversy" exists when parties seek adjudication of a political question, when they ask for an advisory opinion, or when the question sought to be adjudicated has been mooted by subsequent developments. This case suffers from none of these defects.

The parties' dispute turns on the proper construction of a congressional statute, a question eminently suitable to resolution in federal court. Congress has moreover authorized this type of challenge to EPA action. That authorization is of critical importance to the standing inquiry: "Congress has the power to define injuries and articulate chains of causation that will give rise to a case or controversy where none existed before." "In exercising this power, however, Congress must at the very least identify the injury it seeks to vindicate and relate the injury to the class of persons entitled to bring suit." We will not, therefore, "entertain citizen suits to vindicate the public's nonconcrete interest in the proper administration of the laws." [The three preceding sentences are quotations from Justice Kennedy's *Lujan* concurrence.]

EPA maintains that because greenhouse gas emissions inflict widespread harm, the doctrine of standing presents an insuperable jurisdictional obstacle. We do not agree. At bottom, "the gist of the question of standing" is whether petitioners have "such a personal stake in the outcome of the controversy as to assure that concrete adverseness which sharpens the presentation of issues upon which the court so largely depends for illumination." *Baker v. Carr.* As Justice Kennedy explained in his Lujan concurrence:

While it does not matter how many persons have been injured by the challenged action, the party bringing suit must show that the action injures him in a concrete and personal way. This requirement is not just an empty formality. It preserves the vitality of the adversarial process by assuring both that the parties before the court have an actual, as opposed to professed, stake in the outcome, and that the legal questions presented . . . will be resolved, not in the rarified atmosphere of a debating society, but in a concrete factual context conducive to a realistic appreciation of the consequences of judicial action.

To ensure the proper adversarial presentation, Lujan holds that a litigant must demonstrate that it has suffered a concrete and particularized injury that is either actual or imminent, that the injury is fairly traceable to the defendant, and that it is likely that a favorable decision will redress that injury. See *id*. However, a litigant to whom Congress has "accorded a procedural right to protect his concrete interests"—here, the right to challenge agency action unlawfully withheld—"can assert that right without meeting all the normal standards for redressability and immediacy." When a litigant is vested with a procedural right, that litigant has standing if there is some possibility that the requested relief will prompt the injury-causing party to reconsider the decision that allegedly harmed the litigant.

Only one of the petitioners needs to have standing to permit us to consider the petition for review. We stress here, as did Judge Tatel below, the special position and interest of Massachusetts. It is of considerable relevance that the party seeking review here is a sovereign State and not, as it was in Lujan, a private individual. * * *

When a State enters the Union, it surrenders certain sovereign prerogatives. Massachusetts cannot invade Rhode Island to force reductions in greenhouse gas emissions, it cannot negotiate an emissions treaty with China or India, and in some circumstances the exercise of its police powers to reduce in-state motor-vehicle emissions might well be pre-empted.

These sovereign prerogatives are now lodged in the Federal Government, and Congress has ordered EPA to protect Massachusetts (among others) by prescribing standards applicable to the "emission of any air pollutant from any class or classes of new motor vehicle engines, which in [the Administrator's] judgment cause, or contribute to, air pollution which may reasonably be anticipated to endanger public health or welfare." 42 U.S.C. § 7521(a)(1). Congress has moreover recognized a concomitant procedural right to challenge the rejection of its rulemaking petition as arbitrary and capricious. 42 U.S.C. § 7607(b)(1). Given that procedural right and Massachusetts' stake in protecting its quasi-sovereign interests, the Commonwealth is entitled to special solicitude in our standing analysis.

With that in mind, it is clear that petitioners' submissions as they pertain to Massachusetts have satisfied the most demanding standards of the adversarial process. EPA's steadfast refusal to regulate greenhouse gas emissions presents a risk of harm to Massachusetts that is both "actual" and "imminent." There is, moreover, a "substantial likelihood that the judicial relief requested" will prompt EPA to take steps to reduce that risk.

The Injury

The harms associated with climate change are serious and well recognized. Indeed, the NRC Report itself—which EPA regards as an "objective and independent assessment of the relevant science"—identifies a number of environmental changes that have already inflicted significant harms, including "the global retreat of mountain glaciers, reduction in snow-cover extent, the earlier spring melting of rivers and lakes, [and] the accelerated rate of rise of sea levels during the 20th century relative to the past few thousand years. . . ." ["NRC" refers to the National Research Council of the National Academy of Sciences.] * * *

That these climate-change risks are "widely shared" does not minimize Massachusetts' interest in the outcome of this litigation. According to petitioners' unchallenged affidavits, global sea levels rose somewhere between 10 and 20 centimeters over the 20th century as a result of global warming. These rising seas have already begun to swallow Massachusetts' coastal land. Because the Commonwealth "owns a substantial portion of the state's coastal property," it has alleged a particularized injury in its capacity as a landowner. The severity of that injury will only increase over the course of the next century: If sea levels continue to rise as predicted, one Massachusetts official believes that a significant fraction of coastal property will be "either permanently lost through inundation or temporarily lost through periodic storm surge and flooding events." Remediation costs alone, petitioners allege, could run well into the hundreds of millions of dollars.

Causation

EPA does not dispute the existence of a causal connection between man-made greenhouse gas emissions and global warming. At a minimum, therefore, EPA's refusal to regulate such emissions "contributes" to Massachusetts' injuries.

EPA nevertheless maintains that its decision not to regulate greenhouse gas emissions from new motor vehicles contributes so insignificantly to petitioners' injuries that the agency cannot be haled into federal court to answer for them. For the same reason, EPA does not believe that any realistic possibility exists that the relief petitioners seek would mitigate global climate change and remedy their injuries. That is especially so because predicted increases in greenhouse gas emissions from developing nations, particularly China and India, are likely to offset any marginal domestic decrease.

But EPA overstates its case. Its argument rests on the erroneous assumption that a small incremental step, because it is incremental, can never be attacked in a federal judicial forum. Yet accepting that premise would doom most challenges to regulatory action. Agencies, like legislatures, do not generally resolve massive problems in one fell regulatory swoop. They instead whittle away at them over time, refining their preferred approach as circumstances change and as they develop a more-nuanced understanding of how best to proceed. That a first step might be tentative does not by itself support the notion that federal courts lack jurisdiction to determine whether that step conforms to law.

And reducing domestic automobile emissions is hardly a tentative step. Even leaving aside the other greenhouse gases, the United States transportation sector emits an enormous quantity of carbon dioxide into the atmosphere—according to the MacCracken affidavit, more than 1.7 billion metric tons in 1999 alone. That accounts for more than 6% of worldwide carbon dioxide emissions. * * *

The Remedy

While it may be true that regulating motor-vehicle emissions will not by itself reverse global warming, it by no means follows that we lack jurisdiction to decide whether EPA has a duty to take steps to slow or reduce it. Because of the enormity of the potential consequences associated with man-made climate change, the fact that the effectiveness of a remedy might be delayed during the (relatively short) time it takes for a new motor-vehicle fleet to replace an older one is essentially irrelevant. Nor is it dispositive that developing countries such as China and India are poised to increase greenhouse gas emissions substantially over the next century: A reduction in domestic emissions would slow the pace of global emissions increases, no matter what happens elsewhere.

We moreover attach considerable significance to EPA's "agree[ment] with the President that 'we must address the issue of global climate change,'" and to EPA's ardent support for various voluntary emission-reduction programs. As Judge Tatel observed in dissent below, "EPA would presumably not bother with such efforts if it thought emissions reductions would have no discernable impact on future global warming."

In sum—at least according to petitioners' uncontested affidavits—the rise in sea levels associated with global warming has already harmed and will continue to harm Massachusetts. The risk of catastrophic harm, though remote, is nevertheless real. That risk would be reduced to some extent if petitioners received the relief they seek. We therefore hold that petitioners have standing to challenge the EPA's denial of their rulemaking petition.

[On the merits, the Court held that EPA did have authority to regulate greenhouse gases from vehicles and that EPA had relied on impermissible factors in deciding against regulation. The Court remanded for further consideration by the agency under the correct statutory standards. On remand, the agency decided that greenhouse gases were covered by the statute and issued a series of regulations dealing with them.]

CHIEF JUSTICE ROBERTS, with whom JUSTICE SCALIA, JUSTICE THOMAS, and JUSTICE ALITO join, dissenting.

Global warming may be a "crisis," even "the most pressing environmental problem of our time." Pet. for Cert. 26, 22. Indeed, it may ultimately affect nearly everyone on the planet in some potentially adverse way, and it may be that governments have done too little to address it. It is not a problem, however, that has escaped the attention of policymakers in the Executive and Legislative Branches of our Government, who continue to consider regulatory, legislative, and treaty-based means of addressing global climate change.

Apparently dissatisfied with the pace of progress on this issue in the elected branches, petitioners have come to the courts claiming broad-ranging injury, and attempting to tie that injury to the Government's alleged failure to comply with a rather narrow statutory provision. I would reject these challenges as nonjusticiable. Such a conclusion involves no judgment on whether global warming exists, what causes it, or the extent of the problem. Nor does it render petitioners without recourse. This Court's standing jurisprudence simply recognizes that redress of grievances of the sort at issue here "is the function of Congress and the Chief Executive," not the federal courts. Lujan. I would vacate the judgment below and remand for dismissal of the petitions for review.

* * *

It is not at all clear how the Court's "special solicitude" for Massachusetts plays out in the standing analysis, except as an implicit concession that petitioners cannot establish standing on traditional terms. But the status of Massachusetts as a State cannot compensate for petitioners' failure to demonstrate injury in fact, causation, and redressability.

When the Court actually applies the three-part test, it focuses, as did the dissent below, on the State's asserted loss of coastal land as the injury in fact. If petitioners rely on loss of land as the Article III injury, however, they must ground the rest of the standing analysis in that specific injury.

* * * Without "particularized injury, there can be no confidence of 'a real need to exercise the power of judicial review' or that relief can be framed 'no broader than required by the precise facts to which the court's ruling would be applied.' "

The very concept of global warming seems inconsistent with this particularization requirement. Global warming is a phenomenon "harmful to humanity at large," and the redress petitioners seek is focused no more on them than on the public generally—it is literally to change the atmosphere around the world.

If petitioners' particularized injury is loss of coastal land, it is also that injury that must be "actual or imminent, not conjectural or hypothetical," "real and immediate," and "certainly impending." * * *

The Court's sleight-of-hand is in failing to link up the different elements of the three-part standing test. What must be likely to be redressed is the particular injury in fact. The injury the Court looks to is the asserted loss of land. The Court contends that regulating domestic motor vehicle emissions will reduce carbon dioxide in the atmosphere, and therefore redress Massachusetts's injury. But even if regulation does reduce emissions—to some indeterminate degree, given events elsewhere in the world—the Court never explains why that makes it likely that the injury in fact—the loss of land—will be redressed. Schoolchildren know that a kingdom might be lost "all for the want of a horseshoe nail," but "likely" redressability is a different matter. The realities make it pure conjecture to suppose that EPA regulation of new automobile emissions will likely prevent the loss of Massachusetts coastal land. * * *

When dealing with legal doctrine phrased in terms of what is "fairly" traceable or "likely" to be redressed, it is perhaps not surprising that the matter is subject to some debate. But in considering how loosely or rigorously to define those adverbs, it is vital to keep in mind the purpose of the inquiry. The limitation of the judicial power to cases and controversies "is crucial in maintaining the tripartite allocation of power set forth in the Constitution." In my view, the Court today—addressing Article III's "core component of standing"—fails to take this limitation seriously.

NOTES ON MASSACHUSETTS V. EPA

1. *Is* Lujan *Still Standing?* The *Mass. v. EPA* majority purports to distinguish *Lujan*, but the Court clearly bases its ruling much more on the Kennedy concurrence than on the Scalia opinion. Is Justice Scalia's opinion in *Lujan* still good law after *Massachusetts v. EPA.*?

2. *The Federalism Overlay on Standing Doctrine.* Justice Stevens makes much of the sovereign status of the state and its implication for the state's claim of standing. The result might be to empower the states to challenge federal actions that would otherwise be immune from suit by private parties. Is this a healthy reinforcement of the states' role in the federalist system, or is it an invitation to litigate questions that are essentially political disagreements rather than live controversies? Putting that question aside, to what extent is the state's status determinative of the outcome? Is the holding limited to state-initiated litigation, or has the Court relaxed standing requirements across the board?

3. *Counting to Five.* Justice Stevens seems to have done a remarkable job of corralling Justice Kennedy's vote—note how frequently he refers to Kennedy's *Lujan* performance as the gold standard in standing doctrine. If there is a retirement from the liberal side of the Court, however, the *Mass. v. EPA* majority may not hold up very long, depending on the next judicial appointment. Thus, Chief Justice Roberts' view could yet become the law. Could the Chief Justice's concerns be addressed by new scientific evidence, firming up the causal connections and demonstrating precisely how the EPA's actions (or refusal to act) affect the plaintiffs? Or under his view, are climate change claims inherently nonjusticiable, regardless of the specific factual showing made by plaintiffs?

SUMMERS V. EARTH ISLAND INSTITUTE
555 U.S. 488, 129 S.Ct. 1142, 173 L.Ed.2d 1 (2009)

The plaintiff contended that the U.S. Forest Service had unlawfully exempted small sales of timber from fire-damaged public lands from the public participation required for larger timber sales. The case began as a challenge to the sale of a particular parcel but that challenge was settled. However, the parties continued to contest the validity of the Forest Service's exemption as applied to large numbers of other parcels. The plaintiff based its standing on an affidavit by a member named Bensman who used national forest lands in many locations frequently, alleging that he was likely to encounter one of the tracts of land in question. **JUSTICE SCALIA** held that this affidavit did not suffice to demonstrate injury in fact:

> The National Forests occupy more than 190 million acres, an area larger than Texas. There may be a chance, but is hardly a likelihood, that Bensman's wanderings will bring him to a parcel about to be affected by a project unlawfully subject to the regulations. Indeed, without further specification it is impossible to tell *which* projects are (in respondents' view) unlawfully subject to the regulations. * * * Accepting an intention to visit the National Forests as adequate to confer standing to challenge any Government action affecting any portion of those forests would be tantamount to eliminating the requirement of concrete, particularized injury in fact. * * *

> The dissent proposes a hitherto unheard-of test for organizational standing: whether, accepting the organization's self-description of the activities of its members, there is a statistical probability that some of those members are threatened with concrete injury. Since, for example, the Sierra Club asserts in its pleadings that it has more than " '700,000 members nationwide, including thousands of members in California' " who " 'use and enjoy the Sequoia National Forest,' " it is probable (according to the dissent) that some (unidentified) members have

planned to visit some (unidentified) small parcels affected by the Forest Service's procedures and will suffer (unidentified) concrete harm as a result. This novel approach to the law of organizational standing would make a mockery of our prior cases, which have required plaintiff-organizations to make specific allegations establishing that at least one identified member had suffered or would suffer harm.

A concurring opinion by **JUSTICE KENNEDY** remarked that "[t]his case would present different considerations if Congress had sought to provide redress for a concrete injury 'giv[ing] rise to a case or controversy where none existed before.'"

In dissent, **JUSTICE BREYER**, joined by **JUSTICES STEVENS, SOUTER,** and **GINSBURG**, argued that the Court was ignoring the scope of the government's activities:

> The Bensman affidavit does not say *which particular* sites will be affected by future Forest Service projects, but the Service itself has conceded that it will conduct thousands of exempted projects in the future. Why is more specificity needed to show a "realistic" threat that a project will impact land Bensman uses? To know, virtually for certain, that snow will fall in New England this winter is not to know the name of each particular town where it is bound to arrive. The law of standing does not require the latter kind of specificity. How could it? * * *

Suppose that the government banned logging on small tracts. To have standing, would a logging company have to identify the specific tracts that it would otherwise have liked to log and show that it would have at least had a good chance of winning the bids for the specific tracts? Or would it be enough to show that it had logged many such tracts in the past and planned to continue to do so in the future? If the latter showing would be enough, why isn't the company required to meet the same standard of specificity as an environmental organization?

CLAPPER V. AMNESTY INTERNATIONAL
568 U.S. 398, 133 S.Ct. 1138, 185 L.Ed.2d 264 (2013)

JUSTICE ALITO delivered the opinion of the Court.

In 1978, after years of debate, Congress enacted the Foreign Intelligence Surveillance Act (FISA) to authorize and regulate certain governmental electronic surveillance of communications for foreign intelligence purposes. * * *

When Congress enacted the FISA Amendments Act of 2008 (FISA Amendments Act), it left much of FISA intact, but it "established a new and independent source of intelligence collection authority, beyond that granted in traditional FISA." As relevant here, § 702 of FISA, which was enacted as part of the FISA Amendments Act, supplements pre-existing FISA authority by creating a new framework under which the Government may seek the FISC's authorization of certain foreign intelligence surveillance targeting the communications of non-U.S. persons located abroad. Unlike traditional FISA surveillance, § 1881a does not require the Government to demonstrate probable cause that the target of the electronic surveillance is a foreign power or agent of a foreign power. And, unlike traditional FISA, § 1881a does not require the Government to specify the nature and location of each of the particular facilities or places at which the electronic surveillance will occur. * * *

Respondents are attorneys and human rights, labor, legal, and media organizations whose work allegedly requires them to engage in sensitive and sometimes privileged telephone and e-mail communications with colleagues, clients, sources, and other individuals located abroad. Respondents believe that some of the people with whom they exchange foreign intelligence information are likely targets of surveillance under § 1881a. Specifically, respondents claim that they communicate by telephone and e-mail with people the Government "believes or believed to be associated with terrorist organizations," "people located in geographic areas that are a special focus" of the Government's counterterrorism or diplomatic efforts, and activists who oppose governments that are supported by the United States Government. * * *

Respondents assert that they can establish injury in fact that is fairly traceable to § 1881a because there is an objectively reasonable likelihood that their communications with their foreign contacts will be intercepted under § 1881a at some point in the future. This argument fails. As an initial matter, the Second Circuit's "objectively reasonable likelihood" standard is inconsistent with our requirement that "threatened injury must be certainly impending to constitute injury in fact. Furthermore, respondents' argument rests on their highly speculative fear that: (1) the Government will decide to target the communications of non-U.S. persons with whom they communicate; (2) in doing so, the Government will choose to invoke its authority under § 1881a rather than utilizing another method of surveillance; (3) the Article III judges who serve on the Foreign Intelligence Surveillance Court will conclude that the Government's proposed surveillance procedures satisfy § 1881a's many safeguards and are consistent with the Fourth Amendment; (4) the Government will succeed in intercepting the communications of respondents' contacts; and (5) respondents will be parties to the particular communications that the Government intercepts. As discussed below, respondents' theory of standing, which relies on a highly attenuated chain of possibilities, does not satisfy the requirement that threatened injury must be certainly impending. * * *

Second, even if respondents could demonstrate that the targeting of their foreign contacts is imminent, respondents can only speculate as to whether the Government will seek to use § 1881a-authorized surveillance (rather than other methods) to do so. The Government has numerous other methods of conducting surveillance, none of which is challenged here. * * *

Third, even if respondents could show that the Government will seek the Foreign Intelligence Surveillance Court's authorization to acquire the communications of respondents' foreign contacts under § 1881a, respondents can only speculate as to whether that court will authorize such surveillance. In the past, we have been reluctant to endorse standing theories that require guesswork as to how independent decisionmakers will exercise their judgment. * * *

Fourth, even if the Government were to obtain the Foreign Intelligence Surveillance Court's approval to target respondents' foreign contacts under § 1881a, it is unclear whether the Government would succeed in acquiring the communications of respondents' foreign contacts. And fifth, even if the Government were to conduct surveillance of respondents' foreign contacts, respondents can only speculate as to whether their own communications with their foreign contacts would be incidentally acquired.

Respondents' alternative argument—namely, that they can establish standing based on the measures that they have undertaken to avoid § 1881a-authorized surveillance—fares no better. Respondents assert that they are suffering ongoing injuries that are fairly traceable to § 1881a because the risk of surveillance under § 1881a requires them to take costly and burdensome measures to protect the confidentiality of their communications. Respondents claim, for instance, that the threat of surveillance sometimes compels them to avoid certain e-mail and phone conversations, to "tal[k] in generalities rather than specifics," or to travel so that they can have in-person conversations. * * *

Respondents incorrectly maintain that "[t]he kinds of injuries incurred here—injuries incurred because of [respondents'] reasonable efforts to avoid greater injuries that are otherwise likely to flow from the conduct they challenge—are the same kinds of injuries that this Court held to support standing in cases such as" *Laidlaw* * * * As an initial matter, none of these cases holds or even suggests that plaintiffs can establish standing simply by claiming that they experienced a "chilling effect" that resulted from a governmental policy that does not regulate, constrain, or compel any action on their part. Moreover, each of these cases was very different from the present case.

In *Laidlaw*, plaintiffs' standing was based on "the proposition that a company's continuous and pervasive illegal discharges of pollutants into a river would cause nearby residents to curtail their recreational use of that waterway and would subject them to other economic and aesthetic harms."

Because the unlawful discharges of pollutants were "concededly ongoing," the only issue was whether "nearby residents"—who were members of the organizational plaintiffs—acted reasonably in refraining from using the polluted area. *Laidlaw* is therefore quite unlike the present case, in which it is not "concede[d]" that respondents would be subject to unlawful surveillance but for their decision to take preventive measures. *Laidlaw* would resemble this case only if (1) it were undisputed that the Government was using § 1881a-authorized surveillance to acquire respondents' communications and (2) the sole dispute concerned the reasonableness of respondents' preventive measures.

JUSTICE BREYER, with whom **JUSTICE GINSBURG, SOTOMAYOR**, and **JUSTICE KAGAN** join, dissenting.

The plaintiffs' standing depends upon the likelihood that the Government, acting under the authority of § 1881a, can obtain court approval for its surveillance of electronic communications between places within the United States and targets in foreign territories by showing the court (1) that "a significant purpose of the acquisition is to obtain foreign intelligence information," and (2) that it will use general targeting and privacy-intrusion minimization procedures of a kind that the court had previously approved.

Several considerations, based upon the record along with commonsense inferences, convince me that there is a very high likelihood that Government, acting under the authority of § 1881a, will intercept at least some of the communications just described. First, the plaintiffs have engaged, and continue to engage, in electronic communications of a kind that the 2008 amendment, but not the prior Act, authorizes the Government to intercept. These communications include discussions with family members of those detained at Guantanamo, friends and acquaintances of those persons, and investigators, experts and others with knowledge of circumstances related to terrorist activities. These persons are foreigners located outside the United States. They are not "foreign power[s]" or "agent[s] of . . . foreign power[s]." And the plaintiffs state that they exchange with these persons "foreign intelligence information," defined to include information that "relates to" "international terrorism" and "the national defense or the security of the United States."

Second, the plaintiffs have a strong motive to engage in, and the Government has a strong motive to listen to, conversations of the kind described. A lawyer representing a client normally seeks to learn the circumstances surrounding the crime (or the civil wrong) of which the client is accused. A fair reading of the affidavit of Scott McKay, for example, taken together with elementary considerations of a lawyer's obligation to his client, indicates that McKay will engage in conversations that concern what suspected foreign terrorists, such as his client, have done; in conversations that concern his clients' families, colleagues, and contacts; in conversations that concern what those persons (or those connected to them) have said and done, at least in relation to terrorist activities; in conversations that concern the political, social, and commercial environments in which the suspected terrorists have lived and worked; and so forth. Journalists and human rights workers have strong similar motives to conduct conversations of this kind. * * *

The majority more plausibly says that the plaintiffs have failed to show that the threatened harm is "certainly impending." But, as the majority appears to concede, certainty is not, and never has been, the touchstone of standing. The future is inherently uncertain. Yet federal courts frequently entertain actions for injunctions and for declaratory relief aimed at preventing future activities that are reasonably likely or highly likely, but not absolutely certain, to take place. And that degree of certainty is all that is needed to support standing here. * * *

NOTES ON CLAPPER

1.   *The Plaintiffs' Dilemma.* The Court faults the plaintiffs for being unable to show that their calls have been intercepted under authority of § 1881a. But the possible existence of any surveillance of their calls, let alone the legal basis invoked by the agency in particular cases, is top secret, so there's no way the plaintiffs can offer direct evidence. Yet the Court won't let them establish their standing indirectly, so they seem to have no way of protesting what could well be a violation of their constitutional rights.

2.   *What About* Laidlaw? Is it fair to say that the majority distinguishes *Laidlaw* on the ground that in *Laidlaw*, there was no doubt that the defendant's conduct was taking place, and the only issue was the impact on the plaintiffs, whereas here it was unclear whether the conduct was even taking place? Doesn't that really go to the fairly traceable requirement rather than injury in fact?

3.   *What Is "Imminent"?* Imminent seems to carry an implication of certainty and immediacy. *Susan B. Anthony List v. Driehaus*, 573 U.S. 149 (2014), makes it clear that neither temporal proximity nor certainty is required in order to obtain standing. Ohio has a law prohibiting false statements in connection with elections. The lead plaintiff was accused by a candidate of making such statements, and the candidate filed a complaint with the Ohio Elections Commission. When the candidate lost, however, the complaint was dropped. The Court nevertheless held that the plaintiff had standing to challenge the law because it said it intended to make similar statements about other candidates in the future elections, and if doing so could then face the burden of defending administrative proceedings as well as possible criminal charges. It was enough that the plaintiff established "an intention to engage in a course of conduct arguably affected with a constitutional interest, but

proscribed by statute, and there exists a credible threat of prosecution thereunder."

NOTE ON STANDING CLAIMS BASED ON POLITICAL ROLES

Raines v. Byrd, 521 U.S. 811 (1997), illustrates the difficulties that are posed when plaintiffs claim standing, not on the basis of private injuries, but on the basis of their roles in the lawmaking process. Raines involved a challenge to federal legislation authorizing a "line item veto." Rather than having to veto an entire appropriations or tax bill, the President was authorized to "cancel" certain provisions within the bill. The President could do so by sending a "special message" to Congress, which could override his action only by passing a new "disapproval bill" through the normal Article I procedures. The suit was brought by legislators who had voted against the bill and argued that it violated the Presentment Clause of Article I, § 7. The Supreme Court ordered the complaint dismissed for lack of standing.

The majority opinion was by **Chief Justice Rehnquist.** He began by stressing that the existence of a case or controversy is a "bedrock requirement," one element of which is standing. The Court has "always insisted on strict compliance with this jurisdictional standing requirement," and the "standing inquiry has been especially rigorous when reaching the merits of the dispute would force us to decide whether an action taken by one of the other two branches of the Federal Government was unconstitutional." Stressing the "overriding and time-honored concern about keeping the Judiciary's power within its proper constitutional sphere," he called for a careful inquiry to determine whether the plaintiffs' claimed injury is "personal, particularized, concrete, and otherwise judicially cognizable."

The Chief Justice distinguished *Coleman v. Miller*, 307 U.S. 433 (1939), in which a narrow majority had granted state legislators standing. In *Coleman*, half of the members of the Kansas Senate had voted not to ratify the proposed Child Labor Amendment, but the lieutenant governor cast the deciding vote in favor of the amendment. Thus, Rehnquist said, *Coleman* "stands (at most) for the proposition that legislators whose votes would have been sufficient to defeat (or enact) a specific legislative act have standing to sue if that legislative action goes into effect (or does not go into effect), on the ground that their votes have been completely nullified." Hence, to "uphold standing here would require a drastic extension of *Coleman*. We are unwilling to take that step." In closing, the Court noted that the plaintiffs alleged no injury to themselves as individuals and "the institutional injury they allege is wholly abstract and widely dispersed." The Court "attach[ed] some importance to the fact" that the plaintiffs did not have formal authority to represent either branch of Congress. It also noted, without specifying whether these facts were decisive, that "our conclusion neither deprives Members of Congress of an adequate remedy (since they may repeal the Act or exempt appropriations bills from its reach), nor forecloses the Act from constitutional challenge (by someone who suffers judicially cognizable injury as a result of the Act)."

Concurring, **Justice Souter** (joined by **Justice Ginsburg**) found the standing issue "fairly debatable" in its own right. Hence, "it behooves us to resolve the question under more general separation-of-powers principles underlying our standing requirements." Souter remarked that a dispute "involving only officials, and the official interests of those, who serve in the branches of the National Government" is far removed "from the model of the traditional common-law cause of action at the conceptual core of the case-or-controversy requirement." In essence, the case presented "an interbranch controversy about calibrating the legislative and executive powers, as well as an intrabranch dispute between segments of Congress itself." "Intervention in such a controversy" would embroil "the federal courts in a power contest nearly at the height of its political tension."

Justices Stevens and **Breyer** dissented. Justice Breyer argued that the statute deprived legislators of the right to vote "for or against the truncated measure that survives the exercise of the President's cancellation authority." Because the right to cast such a vote is guaranteed by Article I, legislators should have standing to protest the violation of that right. Justice Breyer phrased the issue as whether the case "is so different in form from those 'matters that were the traditional concern of the courts at Westminster' that it falls outside the scope of Article III's judicial power." In any event, he said, he did not find *Coleman* distinguishable.

In two cases involving the issue of same-sex marriage, the Justices found themselves deeply divided over standing.

Hollingsworth v. Perry

570 U.S. 693 (2013)

The original sponsors of a ballot initiative banning same-sex marriage attempted to appeal a ruling striking down the measure when the state of California refused to do so. The state of California, in response to a certified question by the federal court of appeals, ruled that the sponsors had the authority to defend the initiative's validity. The sponsors argued that consequently they should be allowed to sue as agents of the people of California, playing the same role as a state attorney general. **CHIEF JUSTICE ROBERTS** delivered the opinion of the Court rejecting this claim:

> [T]he most basic features of an agency relationship are missing here. Agency requires more than mere authorization to assert a particular interest. "An essential element of agency is the principal's right to control the agent's actions." Yet petitioners answer to no one; they decide for themselves, with no review, what arguments to make and how to make them. Unlike California's attorney general, they are not elected at regular intervals—or elected at all. See Cal. Const., Art. V, § 11. No provision provides for their removal. As one *amicus* explains, "the proponents apparently have an unelected appointment

for an unspecified period of time as defenders of the initiative, however and to whatever extent they choose to defend it."

In conclusion, the majority said, "[w]e have never before upheld the standing of a private party to defend the constitutionality of a state statute when state officials have chosen not to. We decline to do so for the first time here."

JUSTICE KENNEDY dissented along with **JUSTICE ALITO**, and **JUSTICE SOTOMAYOR**. The dissenters argued that the Court should respect the state court's determination that the initiative's proponents could act as representatives of the state. In the dissenters' view, it is especially appropriate to allow proponents to defend an initiative since one of the purposes of the initiative process is to bypass state officials who may be resistant to the policies embodied in initiatives.

United States v. Windsor

570 U.S. 744 (2013)

This case involved a challenge by a surviving spouse in a same-sex marriage. The marriage was recognized by New York law, but the federal government refused to recognize it for estate tax purposes because of the Defense of Marriage Act (DOMA). The federal government declined to defend DOMA on appeal but continued to enforce the statute pending judicial resolution of the issue. The Bipartisan Legal Advisory Group (BLAG) of the House of Representatives voted to intervene in the litigation to defend the constitutionality of § 3 of DOMA. The Court also appointed a law professor to act as amicus on the jurisdictional issue, since all the parties agreed the Court had jurisdiction.] The question before the Court was whether there was a live case or controversy notwithstanding the position of the federal government.

JUSTICE KENNEDY delivered the opinion of the Court. He held that the standing determination in *Chadha*, where the government had also failed to defend the statute, was controlling:

> This Court confronted a comparable case in *INS* v. *Chadha*, 462 U.S. 919 (1983). A statute by its terms allowed one House of Congress to order the Immigration and Naturalization Service (INS) to deport the respondent Chadha. There, as here, the Executive determined that the statute was unconstitutional, and "the INS presented the Executive's views on the constitutionality of the House action to the Court of Appeals." The INS, however, continued to abide by the statute, and "the INS brief to the Court of Appeals did not alter the agency's decision to comply with the House action ordering deportation of Chadha." This Court held "that the INS was sufficiently aggrieved by the Court of Appeals decision prohibiting it from taking action it would otherwise take," regardless of whether the agency welcomed the judgment. The necessity of a "case or controversy" to satisfy Article III was defined as a requirement that the Court's " 'decision will have real meaning: if we rule for Chadha,

he will not be deported; if we uphold [the statute], the INS will execute its order and deport him.'"

This conclusion was not dictum. It was a necessary predicate to the Court's holding that "prior to Congress' intervention, there was adequate Art. III adverseness." The holdings of cases are instructive, and the words of *Chadha* make clear its holding that the refusal of the Executive to provide the relief sought suffices to preserve a justiciable dispute as required by Article III. In short, even where "the Government largely agree[s] with the opposing party on the merits of the controversy," there is sufficient adverseness and an "adequate basis for jurisdiction in the fact that the Government intended to enforce the challenged law against that party."

* * *

Justice Scalia, along with **Justices Thomas** and **Chief Justice Roberts,** rejected the Court's analysis. They argued that since the surviving spouse won in the trial court and the government no longer contested the decision, there was no longer a case or controversy. **JUSTICE ALITO** also dissented on the basis of standing. He argued that the United States was no longer a proper party since it did not contest the trial court decision. He found the standing of the Bipartisan Legal Advisory Group of the House of Representatives (BLAG) a much more difficult question. It is also a significantly closer question than whether the interveners in *Hollingsworth* v. *Perry*—which the Court also decides the same day— have standing to appeal. He argued that Congress as a whole was the only party that had standing in *Chadha*, making that case distinguishable from *Windsor*.

Case	Justices Finding Standing	Justices Finding No Standing
Hollingsworth v. Perry	Kennedy, Thomas, Alito, Sotomayor	Roberts, Scalia, Ginsburg, Kagan, Breyer
United States v. Windsor	Kennedy, Breyer, Kagan, Ginsburg, Sotomayor, Alito (as to interveners)	Scalia, Thomas, Roberts, Alito (as to the government)

Thus, there are four groups of Justices:

    1.   *Finding standing in both cases*: Kennedy, Sotomayor, Alito (but only as to the interveners in *Windsor*, not the government).

    2.   *Finding standing in neither case*: Scalia and Roberts.

    3.   *Finding standing in* Windsor *but not in* Hollingsworth: Breyer, Kagan, and Ginsburg.

    4.   *Finding standing in* Hollingsworth *but not in* Windsor: Thomas.

The peculiar, shifting configurations of votes in these two cases are indicative of the grave difficulties that the Court has encountered in cases where lawmakers claim standing to attack or defend a law. One might argue in favor of either of two clearcut position. The first is that such claims do not constitute injuries in fact and should not provide standing. The second is that these claims should provide standing whenever analogous claims would do so in the private sector—for instance, one might analogize voters to shareholders and legislators to members of a company's board of directors. But there are no signs that the Court is likely to settle on a clear-cut approach for the class of standing cases.

PROBLEM 9-3:
CAN CONGRESS SUE THE PRESIDENT?

    The House of Representatives filed suit in late 2014 against President Obama, claiming that he unlawfully delayed implementation of part of the health care law and also unlawfully funded part of the law in violation of the Appropriation Clause. (That clause provides: "No Money shall be drawn from the Treasury, but in Consequence of Appropriations made by Law.") Does the House have standing? In this connection, consider *Arizona State Legislature v. Arizona Independent Redistricting Comm'n*, ___ U.S. ___, 135 S.Ct. 2652 (2015), where the Court held that the state legislature had standing to challenge a popular initiative stripping it of its control over reapportionment. The legislature challenged the initiative, which transferred control over districting to an independent commission, as a violation of the Elections Clause. That clause grants control of federal election procedures in each state to the "Legislature thereof," subject to Congressional override. The Court rejected the constitutional claim on the merits, holding that the state initiative validly placed legislative control over redistricting in the commission. Justice Scalia argued in dissent that the legislature lacked standing. But according to the Court, the legislature did have standing because the effect of the initiative was to nullify any vote it might hold on districting, "now or in the future," depriving it of its preexisting legal powers. A footnote reserved the question of Congressional standing:

>   The case before us does not touch or concern the question whether Congress has standing to bring a suit against the President. There is no federal analogue to Arizona's initiative power, and a suit between Congress and the President would raise separation-of-powers concerns absent here. The Court's standing analysis, we have noted, has been "especially rigorous when reaching the merits of the dispute would force [the Court] to decide whether an action taken by one of the other two branches of the Federal Government was unconstitutional." *Raines v. Byrd,* 521 U.S. 811, 819–820, 117 S.Ct. 2312, 138 L.Ed.2d 849 (1997).

In light of *Windsor* and *Arizona State Legislature*, should the House be granted standing against the President? Which of the House's legal claims has better prospects of surviving a standing challenge? Does the case present a political question?

Given the difficulties surrounding standing law, it is tempting to think that Congress might be able to intervene. Justice Scalia's opinion in *Defenders of Wildlife* suggests that Congress has little or no power to expand standing. Justice Kennedy's concurring opinion seemed to point in the opposite direction. The following case is the Court's most recent encounter with the issue.

SPOKEO, INC. V. ROBINS
___ U.S. ___, 136 S.Ct. 1540, 194 L.Ed.2d 635 (2016)

JUSTICE ALITO delivered the opinion of the Court.

This case presents the question whether respondent Robins has standing to maintain an action in federal court against petitioner Spokeo under the Fair Credit Reporting Act of 1970 (FCRA or Act).

Spokeo operates a "people search engine." If an individual visits Spokeo's Web site and inputs a person's name, a phone number, or an e-mail address, Spokeo conducts a computerized search in a wide variety of databases and provides information about the subject of the search. Spokeo performed such a search for information about Robins, and some of the information it gathered and then disseminated was incorrect. When Robins learned of these inaccuracies, he filed a complaint on his own behalf and on behalf of a class of similarly situated individuals.

The District Court dismissed Robins' complaint for lack of standing, but a panel of the Ninth Circuit reversed. The Ninth Circuit noted, first, that Robins had alleged that "Spokeo violated *his* statutory rights, not just the statutory rights of other people," and, second, that "Robins's personal interests in the handling of his credit information are individualized rather than collective." Based on these two observations, the Ninth Circuit held that Robins had adequately alleged injury in fact, a requirement for standing under Article III of the Constitution.

This analysis was incomplete. As we have explained in our prior opinions, the injury-in-fact requirement requires a plaintiff to allege an injury that is both "concrete *and* particularized." The Ninth Circuit's analysis focused on the second characteristic (particularity), but it overlooked the first (concreteness). We therefore vacate the decision below and remand for the Ninth Circuit to consider *both* aspects of the injury-in-fact requirement.

The Constitution confers limited authority on each branch of the Federal Government. It vests Congress with enumerated "legislative Powers," Art. I, § 1; it confers upon the President "[t]he executive Power," Art. II, § 1, cl. 1; and it endows the federal courts with "[t]he judicial Power of the United States," Art. III, § 1. In order to remain faithful to this tripartite structure, the power of the Federal Judiciary may not be permitted to intrude upon the powers given to the other branches.

Although the Constitution does not fully explain what is meant by "[t]he judicial Power of the United States," Art. III, § 1, it does specify that this power extends only to "Cases" and "Controversies," Art. III, § 2. And " '[n]o principle is more fundamental to the judiciary's proper role in our system of government than the constitutional limitation of federal-court jurisdiction to actual cases or controversies.' "

Standing to sue is a doctrine rooted in the traditional understanding of a case or controversy. The doctrine developed in our case law to ensure that federal courts do not exceed their authority as it has been traditionally understood. The doctrine limits the category of litigants empowered to maintain a lawsuit in federal court to seek redress for a legal wrong. In this way, "[t]he law of Article III standing . . . serves to prevent the judicial process from being used to usurp the powers of the political branches," and confines the federal courts to a properly judicial role.

Our cases have established that the "irreducible constitutional minimum" of standing consists of three elements. The plaintiff must have

(1) suffered an injury in fact, (2) that is fairly traceable to the challenged conduct of the defendant, and (3) that is likely to be redressed by a favorable judicial decision. The plaintiff, as the party invoking federal jurisdiction, bears the burden of establishing these elements. Where, as here, a case is at the pleading stage, the plaintiff must "clearly . . . allege facts demonstrating" each element.

This case primarily concerns injury in fact, the "[f]irst and foremost" of standing's three elements. Injury in fact is a constitutional requirement, and "[i]t is settled that Congress cannot erase Article III's standing requirements by statutorily granting the right to sue to a plaintiff who would not otherwise have standing."

To establish injury in fact, a plaintiff must show that he or she suffered "an invasion of a legally protected interest" that is "concrete and particularized" and "actual or imminent, not conjectural or hypothetical." We discuss the particularization and concreteness requirements below.

For an injury to be "particularized," it "must affect the plaintiff in a personal and individual way."

Particularization is necessary to establish injury in fact, but it is not sufficient. An injury in fact must also be "concrete." Under the Ninth

Circuit's analysis, however, that independent requirement was elided. As previously noted, the Ninth Circuit concluded that Robins' complaint alleges "concrete, *de facto*" injuries for essentially two reasons. First, the court noted that Robins "alleges that Spokeo violated *his* statutory rights, not just the statutory rights of other people." Second, the court wrote that "Robins's personal interests in the handling of his credit information are *individualized rather than collective.*" Both of these observations concern particularization, not concreteness. We have made it clear time and time again that an injury in fact must be both concrete *and* particularized.

A "concrete" injury must be "*de facto*"; that is, it must actually exist. See Black's Law Dictionary 479 (9th ed. 2009). When we have used the adjective "concrete," we have meant to convey the usual meaning of the term—"real," and not "abstract." Webster's Third New International Dictionary 472 (1971); Random House Dictionary of the English Language 305 (1967). Concreteness, therefore, is quite different from particularization.

"Concrete" is not, however, necessarily synonymous with "tangible." Although tangible injuries are perhaps easier to recognize, we have confirmed in many of our previous cases that intangible injuries can nevertheless be concrete.

In determining whether an intangible harm constitutes injury in fact, both history and the judgment of Congress play important roles. Because the doctrine of standing derives from the case-or-controversy requirement, and because that requirement in turn is grounded in historical practice, it is instructive to consider whether an alleged intangible harm has a close relationship to a harm that has traditionally been regarded as providing a basis for a lawsuit in English or American courts. In addition. Congress is well positioned to identify intangible harms that meet minimum Article III requirements, its judgment is also instructive and important. Thus, we said in *Lujan* that Congress may "elevat[e] to the status of legally cognizable injuries concrete, *de facto* injuries that were previously inadequate in law." Similarly, Justice Kennedy's concurrence in that case explained that "Congress has the power to define injuries and articulate chains of causation that will give rise to a case or controversy where none existed before."

Congress' role in identifying and elevating intangible harms does not mean that a plaintiff automatically satisfies the injury-in-fact requirement whenever a statute grants a person a statutory right and purports to authorize that person to sue to vindicate that right. Article III standing requires a concrete injury even in the context of a statutory violation. For that reason, Robins could not, for example, allege a bare procedural violation, divorced from any concrete harm, and satisfy the injury-in-fact requirement of Article III.

This does not mean, however, that the risk of real harm cannot satisfy the requirement of concreteness. For example, the law has long permitted recovery by certain tort victims even if their harms may be difficult to prove or measure. *See, e.g.,* Restatement (First) of Torts §§ 569 (libel), 570 (slander *per se*) (1938). Just as the common law permitted suit in such instances, the violation of a procedural right granted by statute can be sufficient in some circumstances to constitute injury in fact. In other words, a plaintiff in such a case need not allege any *additional* harm beyond the one Congress has identified.

In the context of this particular case, these general principles tell us two things: On the one hand, Congress plainly sought to curb the dissemination of false information by adopting procedures designed to decrease that risk. On the other hand, Robins cannot satisfy the demands of Article III by alleging a bare procedural violation. A violation of one of the FCRA's procedural requirements may result in no harm. For example, even if a consumer reporting agency fails to provide the required notice to a user of the agency's consumer information, that information regardless may be entirely accurate. In addition, not all inaccuracies cause harm or present any material risk of harm. An example that comes readily to mind is an incorrect zip code. It is difficult to imagine how the dissemination of an incorrect zip code, without more, could work any concrete harm.

Because the Ninth Circuit failed to fully appreciate the distinction between concreteness and particularization, its standing analysis was incomplete. It did not address the question framed by our discussion, namely, whether the particular procedural violations alleged in this case entail a degree of risk sufficient to meet the concreteness requirement. We take no position as to whether the Ninth Circuit's ultimate conclusion— that Robins adequately alleged an injury in fact—was correct.

NOTES ON SPOKEO

1   *What Decision on Remand?* In dissent, Justice Ginsburg argued that the complaint easily satisfied the concreteness requirement:

> In particular, Robins alleged that Spokeo posted "a picture . . . purport[ing] to be an image of Robins [that] was not in fact [of him]," and incorrectly reported that Robins "was in his 50s, . . . married, . . . employed in a professional or technical field, and . . . has children." Robins further alleged that Spokeo's profile of him continues to misrepresent "that he has a graduate degree, that his economic health is 'Very Strong[,]' and that his wealth level [is in] the 'Top 10%.'" Spokeo displayed that erroneous information, Robins asserts, when he was "out of work" and "actively seeking employment." Because of the misinformation, Robins stated, he encountered "[imminent and ongoing] actual harm to [his] employment prospects." . . . Spokeo's report made him appear overqualified for jobs he might

have gained, expectant of a higher salary than employers would be willing to pay, and less mobile because of family responsibilities.

As you read the Court's opinion, are these allegations sufficient?

2.   *How Far Can Congress Expand Standing After Spokeo?* The Court quotes with approval Justice Kennedy's language in *Lujan* to the effect that Congress can provide remedies for injuries that were previously unrecognized by the law and that it can also identify chains of causation that will then qualify legally as traceable. In terms of the concreteness requirement, the Court says, "[B]ecause Congress is well positioned to identify intangible harms that meet minimum Article III requirements, its judgment is also instructive and important." But how does Congress go about identifying such intangible harms? Is it sufficient if a statute grants standing for redress of a type of harm or does Congress have to make some specific finding about concreteness? What are the limits on the idea of concreteness? For instance, could Congress find that a reasonable fear of government surveillance is a concrete harm? Could it grant standing to challenge a threat to an endangered species to any scientist who studies the species or works professionally with members of the species?

NOTES

1.   *What Decision on Remand?* In dissent, Justice Ginsburg argued that the complaint easily satisfied the concreteness requirement:

> In particular, Robins alleged that Spokeo posted "a picture . . . purport[ing] to be an image of Robins [that] was not in fact [of him]," and incorrectly reported that Robins "was in his 50s, . . . married, . . . employed in a professional or technical field, and . . . has children." Robins further alleged that Spokeo's profile of him continues to misrepresent "that he has a graduate degree, that his economic health is 'Very Strong[,]' and that his wealth level [is in] the 'Top 10%.' " Spokeo displayed that erroneous information, Robins asserts, when he was "out of work" and "actively seeking employment." Because of the misinformation, Robins stated, he encountered "[imminent and ongoing] actual harm to [his] employment prospects." As Robins elaborated on brief, Spokeo's report made him appear overqualified for jobs he might have gained, expectant of a higher salary than employers would be willing to pay, and less mobile because of family responsibilities.

As you read the Court's opinion, are these allegations sufficient?

2.   *How Far Can Congress Expand Standing After* Spokeo? The Court quotes with approval Justice Kennedy's language in *Lujan* to the effect that Congress can provide remedies for injuries that were previously unrecognized by the law and that it can also identify chains of causation that will then qualify legally as traceable. In terms of the concreteness requirement, the Court says, "because Congress is well positioned to identify intangible harms that meet minimum Article III requirements, its judgment is also instructive

and important." But how does Congress go about identifying such intangible harms? Is it sufficient if a statute grants standing for redress of a type of harm or does Congress have to make some specific finding about concreteness? What are the limits on the idea of concreteness? For instance, could Congress find that a reasonable fear of government surveillance is a concrete harm? Could it grant standing to challenge a threat to an endangered species to any scientist who studies the species or works professionally with members of the species?

SECTION 3. REMEDIAL LIMITATIONS

One factor in the Court's standing test is whether a court could provide a remedy for the plaintiff's injury. Thus, the ability to issue a remedy is key to the Court's conception of the judicial power. On the other hand, the standing decisions also reflect concerns about overextending the remedial power and thereby trespassing on the domain of the other governmental institutions. Two cases school desegregation cases from Missouri provide a good introduction to the issues.

Missouri v. Jenkins (*Jenkins II*)

495 U.S. 33 (1990)

In 1977, the Kansas City, Missouri, School District (KCMSD) and a class of KCMSD students sued the state of Missouri for operating a segregated school system in Kansas City. The district judge realigned KCMSD as a party defendant and found in 1984 that the state and district had violated *Brown*. According to the judge, the state intentionally allowed the city school system to deteriorate; as a result, the district's "physical facilities have literally rotted" and educational services were substandard in an increasingly all-black system. In 1985, the district court ordered a far-reaching remedy, as summarized by the court of appeals:

> The magnet plan provided that by 1991–92 every high school and middle school in the KCMSD and about half the elementary schools would become magnet schools with one or more distinctive themes, such as foreign languages, performing arts, and math and science. The elementary magnets were to be located at selected sites throughout KCMSD, with at least one magnet in each area of the KCMSD.

The district court also ordered a capital improvements program for KCMSD totaling some $260 million. The principal capital improvement plan called for the closing of some eighteen KCMSD school facilities, construction of seventeen new facilities and renovation of others.

One purpose of the remedy was to draw white students back into the public school system; another was to give minority students an educational experience of the same quality they would have received but for the results of segregation.

After some further proceedings, the case reached the Supreme Court, which did not pass on the validity of the remedy but only on the method of financing it. In an opinion by **Justice White**, the Court held that the district judge had erred in ordering an increase in the local property tax. The district judge had resorted to this extreme remedy because the school district was unable to afford the required actions, and under state law KCMSD was unable to increase the tax levy itself. The Supreme Court held that this was too intrusive a remedy; instead, the district court should have enjoined the operation of the state tax laws that interfered with the school district's efforts to raise taxes. Such an injunction would be proper under Article III and the Tenth Amendment, because the Court had repeatedly ruled that federal courts could issue writs of mandamus to compel local governments to levy taxes to satisfy their debt obligations. E.g., *Von Hoffman v. City of Quincy*, 4 Wall. 535 (1866).

Speaking for four Justices who concurred in the judgment, **Justice Kennedy** objected that "[t]oday's casual embrace of taxation imposed by the unelected, life-tenured Federal Judiciary disregards fundamental precepts for the democratic control of public institutions." He added that the expense was not surprising, given the scope of the remedy. "It comes as no surprise that the cost of this approach to the remedy far exceeded KCMSD's budget, or for that matter, its authority to tax. A few examples are illustrative. Programs such as a 'performing arts middle school,' a 'technical magnet high school' that 'will offer programs ranging from heating and air conditioning to cosmetology to robotics,' were approved. The plan also included a '25 acre farm and 25 acre wildlife area' for science study." The district court had rejected a renovation program proposed by the state because if would not achieve "suburban comparability or the visual attractiveness sought by the Court as it would result in floor coverings with unsightly sections of mismatched carpeting and tile, and individual walls possessing different shades of paint." Justice Kennedy objected to such a micromanaged approach.

NOTES ON JENKINS II AND STRUCTURAL INJUNCTIONS

1. *Case or Controversy Problems.* Under *Warth v. Seldin* and *Allen v. Wright*, plaintiffs must show a concrete injury that can be remedied by a federal court, in order to meet the Article III requirements for Case or Controversy standing. What, precisely, was the injury suffered by the plaintiffs in *Jenkins II*? Was it differentiated enough from that of others to satisfy *Allen*? Would a court order likely remedy the injury?

The foregoing questions can probably be answered in the affirmative; standing was not an issue in the case, so far as we can tell. Consider this twist, however. By the time the Supreme Court upheld the remedy, 1990, the original plaintiffs had all graduated from the KCMSD system. Presumably, they were replaced by fresh plaintiffs, to prevent the case from becoming moot, but given the accustomed time lag between lawsuit and remedy in these kinds of cases, the practical reality is that the original plaintiffs know that they will never benefit from any judicial remedy and that they are surrogates for future schoolchildren in the KCMSD. Does this reality create any Article III problems?

Justice Kennedy charged that the plaintiffs and the school district maintained a "friendly adversary" relationship (unsurprisingly, as they had originally been co-plaintiffs). This surely informed his objection that the remedy was unduly lavish, for it looked like the KCMSD officials were cooperating, at some level, with plaintiffs to achieve greater funding for their school system. It is not unusual in structural reform legislation for the interests of aggrieved plaintiffs (*e.g.*, prisoners) and institutional defendants (*e.g.*, prison administrators) to align against those of unnamed third parties— taxpayers or the legislature itself. Does this structural dilemma unduly threaten the integrity of Article III adjudication?

2.   *Separation of Powers and Federalism Problems.* Related to the Article III problems are separation of powers and even federalism ones. First, was it appropriate for the *federal government* to intrude into the details of state decisionmaking? A central value of federalism is local autonomy in making decisions and policy affecting the community. While it is surely appropriate for the national government to enforce individuals' Fourteenth Amendment rights, it may not be appropriate for the national government to micromanage the state's response to a constitutional violation. In *Freeman v. Pitts* (Chapter 2, § 2C), Justice Kennedy's opinion for the Court said that *Brown II* remedies carried a heavy price in local official accountability for managerial decisions. See also the commandeering and Eleventh Amendment cases in Chapter 7.

Second, was it appropriate for a *federal court* to be making essentially "political" judgments in its remedial order? Justice Kennedy objected that taxation is not a judicial function. "In our system 'the legislative department alone has access to the pockets of the people,' *The Federalist* No. 48 (Madison), for it is the Legislature that is accountable to them and represents their will." In other cases, critics of structural injunctions attack federal courts for trying to solve polycentric problems, which are best left to the political process, which has the financial and factfinding resources to address them.[12]

Third, was it appropriate for a federal court to *concentrate in one institution* (itself) several constitutional functions? The trial judge in *Jenkins* was not only making big money decisions about how to structure the KCMSD, but was also directing the creation of a mini-bureaucracy to implement its program, including the hiring of a "public information specialist" to solicit community support for the district court desegregation plan. Is this the sort of concentration of governmental functions that Madison and Montesquieu warned were the very essence of tyranny? See *Federalist* No. 47 (App. 2).

---

[12]   See Lon Fuller, *The Forms and Limits of Adjudication*, 92 Harv. L. Rev. 353 (1978), for an argument that courts are not appropriate institutions to resolve "polycentric" disputes, namely, disputes that involve interconnected social, economic, and political dimensions. Compare the response by Owen Fiss, *The Supreme Court, 1978 Term—Foreword: The Forms of Justice*, 93 Harv. L. Rev. 1 (1979).

3. *Practical Problems.* The district court program was carried into effect, paid for largely by the state of Missouri. Yet in the early years of the new program, only 200 suburban white students transferred into the district, even though the district was spending over 75% above the state average per pupil; test scores for KCMSD students remained steady or declined; and African-American parents became disgruntled by efforts to reserve places for white students.[13]

The Court took up the *Jenkins* litigation again five years after *Jenkins II.*

Missouri v. Jenkins (*Jenkins III*)

515 U.S. 70 (1995)

The Supreme Court evaluated two remedial issues not included in the grant of certiorari for *Jenkins II.* A narrow Court majority, in an opinion by **Chief Justice Rehnquist**, overturned several features of the district court's remedial orders. The district court's efforts to attract (white) students from outside the school district were beyond the scope of the constitutional violation. The Court in *Milliken v. Bradley*, 418 U.S. 717 (1974), had held that interdistrict relief could not be fashioned under *Brown II* unless there was a factual finding that surrounding school districts had been guilty of constitutional violations. For similar reasons, the Chief Justice ruled that the district court had erred in requiring across-the-board salary increases for teachers and staff in pursuit of the court's effort to attract white students from the suburbs. The Court also faulted the district court for requiring the state to continue to fund the magnet school programs so long as student achievement scores were below national norms at many grade levels. The Court remanded the case to the district court to reconsider the scope of its remedial jurisdiction under *Freeman v. Pitts* (Chapter 2, § 2C2): Has the effect of prior de jure segregation been remedied to the extent practicable? The Chief Justice sharply hinted that the district court should speed up the return of the school system to local authorities.

Writing also for **Justices Stevens**, **Ginsburg**, and **Breyer**, **Justice Souter** dissented. He objected to the Court's disinclination to defer to the district court's remedy (as the Court had generally done from *Swann* onward) and to its disregard of findings of fact made by the trial court. There was no interdistrict remedy of the sort disapproved in *Milliken*, where the trial court had ordered busing across districts, thereby imposing a direct judicial order on districts found not liable; in this case, there was only a candid effort to attract children from various districts. **Justice Ginsburg** also dissented separately: "The Court stresses that the present remedial programs have been in place for seven years. But compared to more than two centuries of firmly entrenched

---

[13] Arlynn Leiber Presser, *Broken Dreams*, ABA Journal 60, 63 (May 1991). For an argument in favor of aggressive judicial efforts to enforce state educational standards that would advance the goals of *Brown*, see James Liebman, *Implementing* Brown *in the Nineties: Political Reconstruction, Liberal Recollection, and Litigatively Enforced Legislative Reform*, 76 Va. L. Rev. 349 (1990).

official discrimination, the experience with the desegregation remedies ordered by the District Court has been evanescent."

Justice Thomas wrote a concurring opinion that forcefully rejected the proposition that all-black school systems are constitutionally questionable. Under *Freeman*, he wrote, trial courts cannot conflate voluntary white flight with state-imposed apartheid. Missouri had required school segregation until 1954. For a court to find that continuing school segregation 30 or 40 years later is a vestige of pre-1954 state law, the court must find more than continuing patterns of same-race schools. The district court had no basis for such a finding, and Justice Thomas charged that its opinion rested instead on racial stereotypes. "It never ceases to amaze me that the courts are so willing to assume that anything that is predominantly black must be inferior." Justice Thomas specifically scorned the social science data noted in footnote 11 of *Brown I*, and he insisted that *Brown I* should rest upon sounder foundations:

> Segregation was not unconstitutional because it might have caused psychological feelings of inferiority. * * * Regardless of the relative quality of the schools, segregation violated the Constitution because the State classified students based on their race. * * * But neutral policies, such as local school assignments, do not offend the Constitution when individual private choices concerning work or residence produce schools with high black populations. *Keyes*. The Constitution does not prevent individuals from choosing to live together, to work together, or to send their children to school together, so long as the State does not interfere with their choices on the basis of race.

Justice Thomas was confident that "there is no reason to think that black students cannot learn as well when surrounded by members of their own race as when they are in an integrated environment."

Justice Thomas continued by arguing that the district court not only violated the substantive limits of the Equal Protection Clause by its overly race-conscious approach to the case, but also violated the procedural limits of Articles I–III and the Tenth Amendment by its intrusive remedies. Here, Justice Thomas issued what amounted to a constitutional indictment of the structural injunction: (1) It is inconsistent with the Framers' intent to limit the reach of courts' equity powers. See *Federalist* No. 78 (Hamilton) (App. 2) (responding to Anti-Federalist attacks that federal courts would have potentially expansive equity powers, and insisting that the use of equitable remedies would be reserved for "extraordinary cases").[14] (2) When federal courts micromanage local school districts, they abridge the federalism precepts

---

[14] Contrast, however, Theodore Eisenberg & Stephen Yeazell, *The Ordinary and the Extraordinary in Institutional Litigation*, 93 Harv. L. Rev. 465 (1980), showing that traditional judicial proceedings in the areas of wills and trusts, antitrust and monopoly, and so forth have required the judiciary to retain jurisdiction for long periods of time and to engage in ongoing compliance review. They maintain that these prior practices serve as a justifying parallel for the structural injunction. For a reply, see John Yoo, *Who Measures the Chancellor's Foot? The Inherent Remedial Authority of the Federal Courts*, 84 Calif. L. Rev. 1121, 1162–66 (1996).

of the Tenth Amendment and, potentially, the Eleventh Amendment as well. (3) When federal courts direct managerial decisions, they are appropriating executive powers explicitly withheld from them in Article III (compare Article II).

BROWN V. PLATA

536 U.S. 493, 131 S.Ct. 1910, 179 L.Ed.2d 969 (2011)

JUSTICE KENNEDY delivered the opinion of the Court.

The degree of overcrowding in California's prisons is exceptional. California's prisons are designed to house a population just under 80,000, but at the time of the three judge court's decision the population was almost double that. The State's prisons had operated at around 200% of design capacity for at least 11 years. Prisoners are crammed into spaces neither designed nor intended to house inmates. As many as 200 prisoners may live in a gymnasium, monitored by as few as two or three correctional officers. As many as 54 prisoners may share a single toilet. [Eds. Unless otherwise noted, the factual assertions in the Court's opinion cite to the record on appeal and designated appendices.]

Prisoners in California with serious mental illness do not receive minimal, adequate care. Because of a shortage of treatment beds, suicidal inmates may be held for prolonged periods in telephone-booth sized cages without toilets. * * * In 2006, the suicide rate in California's prisons was nearly 80% higher than the national average for prison populations; and a court appointed Special Master found that 72.1% of suicides involved "some measure of inadequate assessment, treatment, or intervention, and were therefore most probably foreseeable and/or preventable."

Prisoners suffering from physical illness also receive severely deficient care. California's prisons were designed to meet the medical needs of a population at 100% of design capacity and so have only half the clinical space needed to treat the current population. * * *

[These conditions triggered class action lawsuits claiming that California state prisoners with mental or physical illnesses were incarcerated in a system that violated their Eighth Amendment rights to be free of "cruel and unusual punishment." The state did not dispute the existence of constitutional violations and cooperated in remedial programs to improve conditions for inmates with mental and physical illnesses. After almost a decade of remedial programs, however, special masters concluded that conditions were deteriorating, in large part because of increased overcrowding in the state prisons. Pursuant to the Prison Litigation Reform Act of 1996, 18 U.S.C. § 3626 [PLRA], a three-judge court was convened to develop a factual record that could be the basis for a remedy. The three-judge court ordered California to reduce its prison population to 137.5% of the prisons' design capacity within two years.]

Courts faced with the sensitive task of remedying unconstitutional prison conditions must consider a range of available options, including appointment of special masters or receivers and the possibility of consent decrees. When necessary to ensure compliance with a constitutional mandate, courts may enter orders placing limits on a prison's population. By its terms, the PLRA restricts the circumstances in which a court may enter an order "that has the purpose or effect of reducing or limiting the prison population." 18 U. S. C. § 3626(g)(4). [For example, the PLRA requires that such an order be grounded upon a finding that prison overcrowding is the "primary cause" of the constitutional violation. *Id.* § 3626(a)(3)(E)(i). After extensive fact finding, the three-judge court made the findings required by the PLRA, and the Supreme Court ruled that those findings were amply supported by the record.]

[California argued that overcrowding could not be the "primary cause" of the constitutional violations, because additional measures would have to be taken to help ill inmates even if overcrowding were reduced. The Court ruled that the PLRA was still satisfied.] Courts should presume that Congress was sensitive to the real-world problems faced by those who would remedy constitutional violations in the prisons and that Congress did not leave prisoners without a remedy for violations of their constitutional rights. A reading of the PLRA that would render population limits unavailable in practice would raise serious constitutional concerns. A finding that overcrowding is the "primary cause" of a violation is therefore permissible, despite the fact that additional steps will be required to remedy the violation. * * *

The PLRA states that no prospective relief shall issue with respect to prison conditions unless it is narrowly drawn, extends no further than necessary to correct the violation of a federal right, and is the least intrusive means necessary to correct the violation. 18 U. S. C. § 3626(a). When determining whether these requirements are met, courts must "give substantial weight to any adverse impact on public safety or the operation of a criminal justice system." *Ibid.* [The Court found that this PLRA requirement was met, even though the remedy—reduction of overcrowding—would benefit all prisoners and not just those with mental or physical illnesses. Likewise, the Court was satisfied that the PLRA requirement that any remedial order minimize threats to public safety was met by the three-judge court's detailed factual findings and the flexibility it afforded the state to figure out the best means for meeting the 137 percent requirement.]

JUSTICE SCALIA, joined by **JUSTICE THOMAS,** dissenting.

One would think that, before allowing the decree of a federal district court to release 46,000 convicted felons, this Court would bend every effort to read the law in such a way as to avoid that outrageous result. Today, quite to the contrary, the Court disregards stringently drawn provisions of the governing statute, and traditional constitutional limitations upon the power of a federal judge, in order to uphold the absurd.

The proceedings that led to this result were a judicial travesty. I dissent because the institutional reform the District Court has undertaken violates the terms of the governing statute, ignores bedrock limitations on the power of Article III judges, and takes federal courts wildly beyond their institutional capacity. * * *

The drawbacks of structural injunctions have been described at great length elsewhere. See, *e.g., Missouri* v. *Jenkins*, 515 U.S. 70, 124–133 (1995) (Thomas, J., concurring); Horowitz, *Decreeing Organizational Change: Judicial Supervision of Public Institutions*, 1983 Duke L. J. 1265. This case illustrates one of their most pernicious aspects: that they force judges to engage in a form of factfinding-as-policymaking that is outside the traditional judicial role. The factfinding judges traditionally engage in involves the determination of past or present facts based (except for a limited set of materials of which courts may take "judicial notice") exclusively upon a closed trial record. That is one reason why a district judge's factual findings are entitled to clear-error review: because having viewed the trial first hand he is in a better position to evaluate the evidence than a judge reviewing a cold record. In a very limited category of cases, judges have also traditionally been called upon to make some predictive judgments: which custody will best serve the interests of the child, for example, or whether a particular one-shot injunction will remedy the plaintiff's grievance. When a judge manages a structural injunction, however, he will inevitably be required to make very broad empirical predictions necessarily based in large part upon policy views—the sort of predictions regularly made by legislators and executive officials, but inappropriate for the Third Branch. * * *

[T]he idea that the three District Judges in this case relied solely on the credibility of the testifying expert witnesses is fanciful. *Of course* they were relying largely on their own beliefs about penology and recidivism. And *of course* different district judges, of different policy views, would have "found" that rehabilitation would not work and that releasing prisoners would increase the crime rate. I am not saying that the District Judges rendered their factual findings in bad faith. I am saying that it is impossible for judges to make "factual findings" without inserting their own policy judgments, when the factual findings *are* policy judgments.

[We omit the separate dissenting opinion of **JUSTICE ALITO** (joined by **CHIEF JUSTICE ROBERTS**), who argued that the three-judge court order in this case was a "perfect example" of what the PLRA was enacted to prevent.]

NOTES ON BROWN AND ARTICLE III

This casebook began with *Brown [v. Board]* and our penultimate case is *Brown [v. Plata]*. Ironically, the 2011 *Brown v. Plata* decision dramatically highlights Article III issues with the structural injunctions that ultimately flowed from the Court's 1954 and 1955 decisions in *Brown v. Board of Education* (Chapter 2 of the Casebook). See Owen Fiss, *The Civil Rights Injunction* (1978); *Missouri v. Jenkins II & III* (Casebook, pages 1423–1428). The new *Brown* case provides a useful opportunity to revisit the methodological and theoretical issues arising from the old *Brown* cases.

Issues of constitutional theory are also richly illustrated by the two lines of *Brown* decisions (separated by more than half a century). Original meaning theories of constitutional law, such as those espoused by Justices Scalia and Thomas and former Judge Bork, are most skeptical of the structural injunctions in those cases. Representation-reinforcement theories, such as the one articulated by Dean John Hart Ely and probably accepted in part by Justice Breyer, support the role of federal courts as checks on political processes when they are most prone to deny human rights.

Social movement theories, surely reflected in the career of Justice Ginsburg, argue that the Supreme Court follows as well as leads the political process. Although the PLRA was enacted to limit the discretion of federal courts imposing rules on state prison systems, the law is also notable in its acceptance of the structural injunction and the willingness of even conservative lawmakers to work within the structural injunction framework.

Finally, consider the jurisprudential angle. Justices Scalia and Thomas are the Court's leading textualists, in both statutory interpretation and constitutional review. Yet they demand that both the PLRA statute and constitutional Article III be read to avoid the absurdities that they find in and flowing from the Court's opinion. Indeed, Justice Scalia insisted that the Supreme Court should "bend" the law to avoid absurdities. See generally Jane S. Schacter, *"Text or Consequences?,"* 76 Brooklyn L. Rev. 1007 (2011) (detecting this as a general trend in Justice Scalia's statutory jurisprudence).

In contrast, the Court's pragmatists (mainly Justice Breyer, but also Justice Kennedy sometimes) could not have been more procedurally correct and lawlike. Carefully adhering to the PLRA's requirements and making virtually impregnable factual findings (many of which the state did not dispute), the three-judge court was behaving like a classic Article III tribunal—and Justice Kennedy's opinion reads like a textbook example of factually deferential appellate review.

What should the student of constitutional law make of this anomalous juxtaposition of absurdity-obsessed textualists and procedurally fastidious pragmatists?

The *Boumediene* case provides us an important opportunity to examine the Court's role in our system of government. One issue involved in the case was whether detainees needed to exhaust the procedures provided by Congress before seeking habeas relief. As we will see, the Justices were divided about whether the courts should defer to the congressional scheme of remedies.

BOUMEDIENE V. BUSH

553 U.S. 723, 128 S.Ct. 2229, 171 L.Ed.2d 41 (2008)

JUSTICE KENNEDY delivered the opinion for the Court.

[Striking down § 7 of the Military Commissions Act, which barred habeas relief for accused terrorists detained at Guantanamo Bay, Justice Kennedy defended the Court's decision not to require the detainees to exhaust their remedies with the D.C. Circuit.]

[VI.A.]   The Government argues petitioners must seek review of their CSRT determinations in the Court of Appeals before they can proceed with their habeas corpus actions in the District Court. As noted earlier, in other contexts and for prudential reasons this Court has required exhaustion of alternative remedies before a prisoner can seek federal habeas relief. Most of these cases were brought by prisoners in state custody, and thus involved federalism concerns that are not relevant here. But we have extended this rule to require defendants in courts-martial to exhaust their military appeals before proceeding with a federal habeas corpus action. * * *

In cases involving foreign citizens detained abroad by the Executive, it likely would be both an impractical and unprecedented extension of judicial power to assume that habeas corpus would be available at the moment the prisoner is taken into custody. If and when habeas corpus jurisdiction applies, as it does in these cases, then proper deference can be accorded to reasonable procedures for screening and initial detention under lawful and proper conditions of confinement and treatment for a reasonable period of time. Domestic exigencies, furthermore, might also impose such onerous burdens on the Government that here, too, the Judicial Branch would be required to devise sensible rules for staying habeas corpus proceedings until the Government can comply with its requirements in a responsible way. Cf. *Ex parte Milligan*, 4 Wall., at 127 ("If, in foreign invasion or civil war, the courts are actually closed, and it is impossible to administer criminal justice according to law, *then*, on the theatre of active military operations, where war really prevails, there is a necessity to furnish a substitute for the civil authority, thus overthrown, to preserve the safety of the army and society; and as no power is left but the military, it is allowed to govern by martial rule until the laws can have their free course"). Here, as is true with detainees apprehended abroad, a relevant consideration in determining the courts' role is whether there are suitable alternative processes in place to protect against the arbitrary exercise of governmental power.

The cases before us, however, do not involve detainees who have been held for a short period of time while awaiting their CSRT determinations.

Were that the case, or were it probable that the Court of Appeals could complete a prompt review of their applications, the case for requiring temporary abstention or exhaustion of alternative remedies would be much stronger. These qualifications no longer pertain here. In some of these cases six years have elapsed without the judicial oversight that habeas corpus or an adequate substitute demands. And there has been no showing that the Executive faces such onerous burdens that it cannot respond to habeas corpus actions. To require these detainees to complete DTA review before proceeding with their habeas corpus actions would be to require additional months, if not years, of delay. The first DTA review applications were filed over a year ago, but no decisions on the merits have been issued. While some delay in fashioning new procedures is unavoidable, the costs of delay can no longer be borne by those who are held in custody. The detainees in these cases are entitled to a prompt habeas corpus hearing.

* * * Our holding with regard to exhaustion should not be read to imply that a habeas court should intervene the moment an enemy combatant steps foot in a territory where the writ runs. The Executive is entitled to a reasonable period of time to determine a detainee's status before a court entertains that detainee's habeas corpus petition. The CSRT process is the mechanism Congress and the President set up to deal with these issues. Except in cases of undue delay, federal courts should refrain from entertaining an enemy combatant's habeas corpus petition at least until after the Department, acting via the CSRT, has had a chance to review his status.

[The Court remanded the cases to the District Court to determine whether the writ of habeas corpus should be granted.]

CHIEF JUSTICE ROBERTS, with whom **JUSTICE SCALIA**, **JUSTICE THOMAS**, and **JUSTICE ALITO** join, dissenting.

Today the Court strikes down as inadequate the most generous set of procedural protections ever afforded aliens detained by this country as enemy combatants. The political branches crafted these procedures amidst an ongoing military conflict, after much careful investigation and thorough debate. The Court rejects them today out of hand, without bothering to say what due process rights the detainees possess, without explaining how the statute fails to vindicate those rights, and before a single petitioner has even attempted to avail himself of the law's operation. And to what effect? The majority merely replaces a review system designed by the people's representatives with a set of shapeless procedures to be defined by federal courts at some future date. One cannot help but think, after surveying the modest practical results of the majority's ambitious opinion, that this decision is not really about the detainees at all, but about control of federal policy regarding enemy combatants.

* * * The critical threshold question in these cases * * * is whether the system the political branches designed protects whatever rights the detainees may possess. If so, there is no need for any additional process, whether called "habeas" or something else.

Congress entrusted that threshold question in the first instance to the Court of Appeals for the District of Columbia Circuit, as the Constitution surely allows Congress to do. See Detainee Treatment Act of 2005 (DTA), § 1005(e)(2)(A), 119 Stat. 2742. But before the D.C. Circuit has addressed the issue, the Court cashiers the statute, and without answering this critical threshold question itself. The Court does eventually get around to asking whether review under the DTA is, as the Court frames it, an "adequate substitute" for habeas, but even then its opinion fails to determine what rights the detainees possess and whether the DTA system satisfies them. The majority instead compares the undefined DTA process to an equally undefined habeas right—one that is to be given shape only in the future by district courts on a case-by-case basis. This whole approach is misguided.

It is also fruitless. How the detainees' claims will be decided now that the DTA is gone is anybody's guess. But the habeas process the Court mandates will most likely end up looking a lot like the DTA system it replaces, as the district court judges shaping it will have to reconcile review of the prisoners' detention with the undoubted need to protect the American people from the terrorist threat—precisely the challenge Congress undertook in drafting the DTA. All that today's opinion has done is shift responsibility for those sensitive foreign policy and national security decisions from the elected branches to the Federal Judiciary.

I believe the system the political branches constructed adequately protects any constitutional rights aliens captured abroad and detained as enemy combatants may enjoy. I therefore would dismiss these cases on that ground.

NOTE ON BOUMEDIENE AND PRUDENTIAL LIMITS

The Chief Justice's dissent did not argue that the Court was violating Article III by deploying the "judicial Power" in something that was not a "Case or Controversy" under Article III. Instead, the Chief Justice was invoking the *prudential* feature of the Court's justiciability doctrines—in this case, the exhaustion doctrine for military criminal processes. The traditional defense of prudential justiciability is that best articulated by Alexander M. Bickel's *The Least Dangerous Branch: The Supreme Court at the Bar of Politics* (1962). Bickel's "passive virtues" theory defended judicial abstention from the perspective of the Court's own institutional limitations: the Court should typically not adjudicate complicated issues involving national policy when the Justices did not have sufficient information to make a confident decision, when they were unable to implement their will directly and were unwilling to invest years of judicial monitoring to do so, or when popular opinion was overwhelmingly aligned against them.

It is likely that the Chief Justice found much wisdom in such concerns, and his insistence that the legal issues were not ripe sounds highly Bickelian: good adjudication and careful resolution of thorny issues require complete procedural correctness, and no cutting of corners. It seems to us that the Chief Justice was making a broader point and was thinking outside of Article III. In the *Brown II* cases, the Supreme Court invoked principles of federalism to require lower courts to trim back their desegregation remedies. In the Guantanamo Cases, the dissenters are invoking principles of separation of powers to trim back habeas remedies.

In contrast, the majority opinion places more emphasis on the role of the courts as guardians of the constitutional order and on the need to provide effective remedies for constitutional violations. The tension between these visions—one stressing the rule of law, the other the separation of powers— runs throughout the cases in this chapter.

SECTION 4. CONGRESSIONAL CONTROL OF JURISDICTION

Boumedienne involved an effort by Congress to restrict a judicial remedy and replace it with a more limited one. As we will see in this section, Congress has also attempted to modify the role of Article III judges in other ways or replace them with other decision makerx.

Plaut v. Spendthrift Farm, Inc.

514 U.S. 211 (1996)

The federal district court dismissed plaintiffs' securities fraud suit, with prejudice, following a Supreme Court decision setting a statute of limitations that plaintiffs' filing did not meet. After the judgment became final, Congress added a new § 27A to the Securities Act, which provides for reinstatement of securities fraud lawsuits, on motion, that had been commenced before the Supreme Court decision but dismissed thereafter as time barred. The district court refused to reopen the judgment, on the ground that the new statute was unconstitutional. The Supreme Court, in an opinion by **Justice Scalia**, affirmed.

"Our decisions to date have identified two types of legislation that require federal courts to exercise the judicial power in a manner that Article III forbids. The first appears in *United States v. Klein*, 13 Wall. 128 (1872), where we refused to give effect to a statute that was said '[t]o prescribe rules of decision to the Judicial Department of the government in cases pending before it.' Whatever the precise scope of *Klein*, however, later decisions have made clear that its prohibition does not take hold when Congress 'amend[s] applicable law.' Section 27A(b) indisputably does set out substantive legal standards for the Judiciary to apply, and in that sense changes the law (even if solely retroactively). The second type of unconstitutional restriction upon the exercise of judicial power identified by past cases is exemplified by *Hayburn's Case*, 2 Dall. 409 (1792), which stands for the principle that Congress cannot vest review of the decisions of Article III courts in officials of the Executive Branch. Yet under any application of 27A(b) only courts are involved; no officials of other departments sit in direct review of their decisions. Section 27A(b) therefore offends neither of these previously established prohibitions.

"We think, however, that § 27A(b) offends a postulate of Article III just as deeply rooted in our law as those we have mentioned. Article III establishes a 'judicial department' with the 'province and duty . . . to say what the law is' in particular cases and controversies. *Marbury*. The record of history shows that the Framers crafted this charter of the judicial department with an expressed understanding that it gives the Federal Judiciary the power, not merely to rule on cases, but to decide them, subject to review only by superior courts in the Article III hierarchy—with an understanding, in short, that 'a judgment conclusively resolves the case' because 'a "judicial Power" is one to render dispositive judgments.' Easterbrook, *Presidential Review*, 40 Case W. Res. L. Rev. 905, 926 (1990). By retroactively commanding the federal courts to reopen final judgments, Congress has violated this fundamental principle."

Justice Scalia reviewed the background of Article III. During the colonial and revolutionary period, legislatures regularly decided essentially private controversies and set aside court judgments. This practice became even more common in the 1780s, and fell under increasingly critical scrutiny. "This sense of a sharp necessity to separate the legislative from the judicial power, prompted by the crescendo of legislative interference with private judgments of the courts, triumphed among the Framers of the new Federal Constitution. See Corwin, *The Progress of Constitutional Theory Between the Declaration of Independence and the Meeting of the Philadelphia Convention*, 30 Am. Hist. Rev. 511, 514–517 (1925). The Convention made the critical decision to establish a judicial department independent of the Legislative Branch by providing that 'the judicial Power of the United States shall be vested in one supreme Court, and in such inferior Courts as the Congress may from time to time ordain and establish.' Before and during the debates on ratification, Madison, Jefferson, and Hamilton each wrote of the factional disorders and disarray that the system of legislative equity had produced in the years before the framing; and each thought that the separation of the legislative from the judicial power in the new Constitution would cure them." See *Federalist* No. 48 (Madison) (noting the phenomenon).

Explaining Article III and the value of judicial independence, Hamilton wrote in *Federalist* No. 81:

> It is not true . . . that the parliament of Great Britain, or the legislatures of the particular states, can rectify the exceptionable decisions of their respective courts, in any other sense than might be done by a future legislature of the United States. The theory neither

of the British, nor the state constitutions, authorises the revisal of a judicial sentence, by a legislative act. . . . A legislature without exceeding its province cannot reverse a determination once made, in a particular case; though it may prescribe a new rule for future cases.

"Judicial decisions in the period immediately after ratification of the Constitution confirm the understanding that it forbade interference with the final judgments of courts." Justice Scalia invoked dicta in *Calder v. Bull*, 3 Dall. 386 (1798), and a number of contemporaneous state cases for the proposition that the power to grant new trials was properly a judicial and not a legislative power. By the middle of the nineteenth century, this was conventional wisdom among American lawyers and judges. According to this understanding of the "judicial Power," only judges and not legislators could make the decision to reopen judgments, and § 27A was therefore a congressional encroachment upon the "judicial Power."

Justice Breyer concurred in the judgment, on the ground that "its exclusively retroactive effect, its application to a limited number of individuals, and its reopening of closed judgments" combined to yield an unconstitutional usurpation. **Justice Stevens**, joined by Justice Ginsburg, dissented. Congress has the authority to override a Supreme Court decision interpreting a federal statute and to make the override rule applicable retroactively. E.g., *Sampeyreac v. United States*, 7 Pet. 222, 239 (1833) (very similar to present case). Under such a statute, courts would routinely reopen judgments. Why can Congress not make the process of reopening judgments more orderly and uniform? It had done so at least once, and the Court allowed it against constitutional attack. *United States v. Sioux Nation*, 448 U.S. 371 (1980).

"The Court has drawn the wrong lesson from the Framers' disapproval of colonial legislatures' appellate review of judicial decisions. The Framers rejected that practice, not out of a mechanistic solicitude for 'final judgments,' but because they believed the impartial application of rules of law, rather than the will of the majority, must govern the disposition of individual cases and controversies. Any legislative interference in the adjudication of the merits of a particular case carries the risk that political power will supplant evenhanded justice, whether the interference occurs before or after the entry of final judgment. Cf. *Klein*; *Hayburn's Case*. Section 27A(b) neither commands the reinstatement of any particular case nor directs any result on the merits. Congress recently granted a special benefit to a single litigant in a pending civil rights case, but the Court saw no need even to grant certiorari to review that disturbing legislative favor. In an ironic counterpoint, the Court today places a higher priority on protecting the Republic from the restoration to a large class of litigants of the opportunity to have Article III courts resolve the merits of their claims."

PROBLEM 9-4:
CONGRESSIONAL EFFORTS TO STRIP FEDERAL COURTS
OF AUTHORITY TO REQUIRE BUSING AS A
REMEDY FOR BROWN *VIOLATIONS*

Recall *Swann* (Chapter 2, § 2C), in which the Supreme Court upheld an order requiring busing and other aggressive remedies for *Brown* violations. Federal court-required busing to achieve unitary school systems was extremely controversial, and proposals abounded in Congress to thwart it. In light of the Court's later decision in *Plaut*, it is notable that no one proposed that Congress vacate *Brown II* judgments and direct district judges to implement *Brown* without recourse to busing as a remedy.

Even in 1971, such legislation would have been problematic under *United States v. Klein*, 80 U.S. (13 Wall.) 128 (1872). The Court had previously held that a presidential pardon was admissible evidence for southerners seeking to regain confiscated property upon a showing they had not been disloyal during the Civil War. Congress responded with an 1870 statute making pardons inadmissible as proof of loyalty and, instead, conclusive evidence of disloyalty. The statute further provided that "in all cases where judgment shall have been heretofore rendered in the Court of Claims in favor of any claimant, on any other proof of loyalty then such as is above required and provided, * * * the Supreme Court shall, on appeal, have no further jurisdiction of the cause, and shall dismiss the same for want of jurisdiction." In such cases, the court of claims was required, on remand, to dismiss the claimant's petition for restitution of his or her property. In *Klein*, Chief Justice Chase refused to follow the 1870 statute, as it was an unconstitutional congressional usurpation of both the judicial power to adjudicate cases or controversies and of the executive power to grant pardons.

Three different kinds of proposals were floated in Congress to respond, politically, to *Swann*:

1. *Constitutional Amendment.* On four occasions, the Constitution has been amended to override a Supreme Court interpretation of the Constitution.[15] A steady stream of political leaders called for amendments to overturn *Swann*, usually by restricting federal courts' remedial options in school desegregation cases. E.g., H.R.J. Res. 56, 97th Cong., 2d Sess. (1982). None was ever recommended by the requisite two-thirds vote of each chamber of Congress.

---

[15] The Eleventh Amendment (1798), insulating states from many federal court lawsuits, was a reaction to *Chisholm v. Georgia*, 2 U.S. (2 Dall.) 419 (1793). The Fourteenth Amendment (1868) specifically overrode *Dred Scott* (1857). The Sixteenth Amendment (1913) granting the federal government the authority to lay income taxes, overrode the Supreme Court's decision in *Pollock v. Farmers' Loan & Trust Co.*, 157 U.S. 429 (1895), which had invalidated the federal income tax. Finally, the Twenty-Sixth Amendment (1971) giving eighteen-year-olds the right to vote in state and national elections, overrode that part of *Oregon v. Mitchell*, 400 U.S. 112 (1970), which invalidated Congress' power to set voting-age rules for state elections.

2. *Legislation to Curtail Constitutional Decisions.* Congress also may respond to Supreme Court decisions through normal legislation. Congress may have some room to resist Supreme Court decisions it dislikes. *Swann* stimulated some legislation of this sort. The Educational Amendments of 1972, 20 U.S.C. §§ 1651–1656, denied the use of federal money to bus students for racial balance. The Equal Education Opportunities Act of 1974 (EEOA) prohibited any "court, department, or agency of the United States [from ordering] transportation of any student to a school other than the school closest or next closest to his place of residence which provides the appropriate grade level, and type of education for such student." 20 U.S.C. § 1714. The EEOA seems at or beyond the constitutional boundary, but federal judges interpreted it to apply only to cases not raising constitutional violations. E.g., *Drummond v. Acree*, 409 U.S. 1228 (1972) (Powell, Circuit Justice). That is, of course, a problem with ordinary legislation: The Court can narrowly construe it or invalidate it.

3. *Limitations on Jurisdiction.* Another strategy relies on Congress' authority under Article III to regulate federal jurisdiction.[16] While the Supreme Court has been loath to interpret federal statutes to eliminate a federal forum for constitutional adjudication, e.g., *Webster v. Doe*, 486 U.S. 592 (1988), Article III's text suggests that Congress has some discretion. Article III, § 1 states that the "[t]he judicial Power * * * shall be vested in one supreme Court, and in such inferior Courts as the Congress may from time to time ordain and establish." Article III, § 2, par. 2, provides that the Supreme Court "shall" have original jurisdiction over cases affecting ambassadors and other public ministers and cases in which a state is a party. "In all other Cases before mentioned [in paragraph 1], the supreme Court shall have appellate jurisdiction . . . with such Exceptions, and under such Regulations as the Congress shall make."

The text of Article III suggests three ways Congress might try to curtail *Swann*—all of which have been proposed and deliberated in Congress: (1) Restrict or eliminate the Supreme Court's appellate jurisdiction in school desegregation cases. This approach receives some support from the leading Supreme Court case on this topic (excerpted below). (2) Restrict or eliminate the jurisdiction of lower federal courts in school desegregation cases. (3) Restrict or eliminate the jurisdiction of any federal court (lower federal courts' original jurisdiction as well as the Supreme Court's appellate jurisdiction) in school desegregation cases. This third approach has been the one most often proposed by legislative opponents of *Swann*. Some bills went even further and sought to restrict jurisdiction of any court in the United States (including state courts).

---

[16] See Richard H. Fallon Jr. et al., *Hart and Wechsler's The Federal Courts and the Federal System* (6th ed. 2010) (classic exploration of Congress' power to restrict federal jurisdiction); Michael Perry, *The Constitution, the Courts, and Human Rights* 128–37 (1982) (arguing that this is the ultimate and most workable political check on the Court's constitutional lawmaking authority).

For each of these strategies—including the abrogation of jurisdiction in any court, state or federal—ask yourself the following questions: First, what is the argument for Congress' constitutional authority to enact each type of jurisdiction limitation? Second, what constitutional counterarguments might be constructed, and would they prevail? Third, even if Congress has the constitutional authority to adopt any or all of the different strategies, what policy problems accompany each strategy?

Some scholars argue from the Vesting Clause's mandatory language— "The judicial Power * * * *shall be vested*"—that there is an irreducible minimum of jurisdiction Congress must vest in the Supreme Court and/or inferior federal courts.[17] Others emphasize that the Ordain and Establish Clause gives Congress seemingly total discretion whether even to create inferior federal courts and that the Exceptions Clause gives Congress arguably unlimited power to restrict the appellate jurisdiction of the Supreme Court.[18] The challenge for the former group of (mandatory jurisdiction) scholars is to explain how the Vesting Clause can avoid the cumulative trumping of the Ordain and Establish and the Exceptions Clauses. The challenge for the latter group of (discretionary jurisdiction) scholars is to explain how the judiciary can perform its core function if Congress can take away all its jurisdiction.

EX PARTE MCCARDLE
74 U.S. (7 Wall.) 506, 19 L.Ed. 264 (1869)

CHIEF JUSTICE CHASE delivered the opinion of the Court.

[McCardle was a civilian being held for trial by military commission in Mississippi for allegedly publishing "incendiary and libellous" articles in his newspaper in violation of federal Reconstruction statutes. The federal circuit court denied his application for habeas corpus, and he appealed to the Supreme Court. McCardle relied on a February 5, 1867 federal statute providing the Supreme Court with appellate jurisdiction in habeas corpus cases. The case was argued in the Supreme Court in early March 1868. On March 27, 1868, Congress enacted a statute that provided "[t]hat so much of the act of February 5, 1867 * * * as authorized an appeal from the judgment of the Circuit Court to the Supreme Court of the United States, or the exercise of any such jurisdiction by said Supreme Court, on appeals which have been, or may hereafter be taken, be, and the same is hereby repealed."]

---

[17] See Akhil Reed Amar, *A Neo-Federalist View of Article III: Separating the Two Tiers of Federal Jurisdiction*, 65 B.U.L. Rev. 205 (1985); Robert Clinton, *A Mandatory View of Federal Court Jurisdiction: A Guided Quest for the Original Understanding of Article III*, 132 U. Pa. L. Rev. 741 (1984); Lawrence Gene Sager, *The Supreme Court, 1980 Term—Foreword: Constitutional Limitations on Congress' Authority To Regulate the Jurisdiction of the Federal Courts*, 95 Harv. L. Rev. 17 (1981).

[18] See Paul Bator, *Congressional Power over the Jurisdiction of the Federal Courts*, 27 Vill. L. Rev. 1030 (1982); Gerald Gunther, *Congressional Power to Curtail Federal Court Jurisdiction: An Opinionated Guide to the Ongoing Debate*, 36 Stan. L. Rev. 895 (1984).

The first question necessarily is that of jurisdiction; for, if the act of March, 1868, takes away the jurisdiction defined by the act of February, 1867, it is useless, if not improper, to enter into any discussion of other questions.

It is quite true, as was argued by the counsel for the petitioner, that the appellate jurisdiction of this court is not derived from acts of Congress. It is, strictly speaking, conferred by the Constitution. But it is conferred "with such exceptions and under such regulations as Congress shall make."

It is unnecessary to consider whether, if Congress had made no exceptions and no regulations, this court might not have exercised general appellate jurisdiction under rules prescribed by itself. For among the earliest acts of the first Congress, at its first session, was the act of September 24th, 1789, to establish the judicial courts of the United States. That act provided for the organization of this court, and prescribed regulations for the exercise of its jurisdiction. * * *

The principle that the affirmation of appellate jurisdiction implies the negation of all such jurisdiction not affirmed having been thus established, it was an almost necessary consequence that acts of Congress, providing for the exercise of jurisdiction, should come to be spoken of as acts granting jurisdiction, and not as acts making exceptions to the constitutional grant of it.

The exception to appellate jurisdiction in the case before us, however, is not an inference from the affirmation of other appellate jurisdiction. It is made in terms. The provision of the act of 1867, affirming the appellate jurisdiction of this court in cases of *habeas corpus* is expressly repealed. It is hardly possible to imagine a plainer instance of positive exception.

We are not at liberty to inquire into the motives of the legislature. We can only examine into its power under the Constitution; and the power to make exceptions to the appellate jurisdiction of this court is given by express words.

What, then, is the effect of the repealing act upon the case before us? We cannot doubt as to this. Without jurisdiction the court cannot proceed at all in any cause. Jurisdiction is power to declare the law, and when it ceases to exist, the only function remaining to the court is that of announcing the fact and dismissing the cause. * * *

[T]he general rule, supported by the best elementary writers, is, that "when an act of the legislature is repealed, it must be considered, except as to transactions past and closed, as if it never existed." * * * [N]o judgment [can] be rendered in a suit after the repeal of the act under which it was brought and prosecuted.

It is quite clear, therefore, that this court cannot proceed to pronounce judgment in this case, for it has no longer jurisdiction of the appeal; and judicial duty is not less fitly performed by declining ungranted jurisdiction than in exercising firmly that which the Constitution and the laws confer.

Counsel seem to have supposed, if effect be given to the repealing act in question, that the whole appellate power of the court, in cases of *habeas corpus*, is denied. But this is an error. The act of 1868 does not except from that jurisdiction any cases but appeals from Circuit Courts under the act of 1867. It does not affect the jurisdiction which was previously exercised.

Felker v. Turpin

518 U.S. 651 (1996)

This case was a reprise of *McCardle*. The Anti-Terrorism and Effective Death Penalty Act of 1996 placed new limitations on petitions for habeas corpus. Especially in death penalty cases, it is common for prisoners to file successive habeas petitions, repeating earlier claims or attempting to raise new but untimely ones. The relevant provisions of the statute do not affect a prisoner's first habeas petition, but sharply limit subsequent petitions, which can only be heard if a special appellate panel grants a motion for leave to file the petition. The statute provides that the special panel's decision whether or not to grant leave is not appealable and not subject to a writ of certiorari to the Supreme Court. A prisoner on death row attempted to file a second petition for habeas relief, but the special court ruled that he had not met the statutory requirements. The issue before the Court was whether Congress had unconstitutionally eliminated the Supreme Court's jurisdiction. The Court unanimously held that it still had the power to hear the cases on an *original* writ of habeas corpus—that is, as a petition directly to the Court, rather than as a petition seeking review of a lower court order. (Recall that *Marbury v. Madison* was the flip side of this situation.) The Court also held that the limitations on second and later writs are not an unconstitutional "suspension of the writ."

NOTES ON MCCARDLE AND CONGRESS'S AUTHORITY TO RESTRICT THE SUPREME COURT'S JURISDICTION

McCardle can be read broadly, for the proposition that the Exceptions Clause empowers Congress to limit the Supreme Court's jurisdiction over cases of a certain type, even if they raise constitutional issues. But does *McCardle* have to be read to sanction an unlimited congressional power? Consider possible limitations:

1. *The Court's "Essential Role."* Henry M Hart Jr., *The Power of Congress to Limit the Jurisdiction of Federal Courts: An Exercise in Dialectic*, 66 Harv. L. Rev. 1362, 1365 (1953), argued for a narrow reading of *McCardle* and posited: "The measure [of Congress' power under the Exceptions Clause] is simply that the exceptions must not be such as will destroy the essential role of the Supreme Court in the constitutional plan. *McCardle*, you will remember, meets that test. The circuit courts of the United States were still open in

habeas corpus. And the Supreme Court itself could still entertain petitions for the writ which were filed with it in the first instance." What is the Court's "essential role in the constitutional plan"? Leonard Ratner argues that the Court's essential roles are "(1) to provide a tribunal for the ultimate resolution of inconsistent or conflicting interpretations of federal law by state or federal courts, and (2) to provide a tribunal for maintaining the supremacy of federal law when it conflicts with state law or is challenged by state authority."[19] Would a bill cutting off the Supreme Court's appellate jurisdiction in school desegregation cases violate these "essential roles"? Consider similar "essential roles" limitations suggested but not found to be violated by the Court's opinions in *Morrison, Schor,* and *Mistretta,* albeit with little discussion of precisely what would violate the judiciary's core functions or its independent role (as dissenting Justices in each case duly noted).

2.   *Bitter with the Sweet.* There is a political check on Congress' ability to restrict the Supreme Court's appellate jurisdiction: If the Court cannot review lower court decisions in school desegregation cases, for example, the results will be unpredictable—some state and federal courts might order massive busing, and then the Court is not available to check lower court excesses. (Even if Congress can strip lower federal courts as well as the Supreme Court of jurisdiction, the Supremacy Clause of Article VI seems to assure that state courts would remain as a forum for federal constitutional cases.) Of course, then Congress might say the Court can review those cases, but it cannot order busing in any case. But this might fall afoul *United States v. Klein* (described in Problem 9-3). *Klein* might be read for the proposition that Congress must take the bitter with the sweet: If it allows the Supreme Court to take jurisdiction over a class of cases to assure uniformity (the sweet), it may not tell the Court how it has to decide the cases (the bitter).

3.   *How Broadly Should* McCardle *Be Read?* Read broadly, *Klein* seems somewhat inconsistent with *McCardle*, even though both were written by Chief Justice Chase. If so, you might want to read *Klein* more narrowly—or reconsider the correctness of some of the language in *McCardle*, which may have read too much into the Exceptions Clause. For example, there is no indication in the original discussions that the Framers imagined that the Exceptions Clause would enable Congress to curtail the Court's appellate jurisdiction as a way to prevent decision on substantive grounds. See William Van Alstyne, *A Critical Guide to* Ex Parte McCardle, 15 Ariz. L. Rev. 229, 263–64 (1973). Moreover, a broad reading of *McCardle* raises questions of equal protection, ex post facto penalization, and due process. Could *McCardle* be read more narrowly (particularly in light of the final paragraph of the opinion)?

---

[19] Leonard Ratner, *Congressional Power over the Appellate Jurisdiction of the Supreme Court,* 109 U. Pa. L. Rev. 157, 160–61 (1960). Critical of the Hart argument and rejecting an "essential roles" limit is Martin Redish, *Federal Jurisdiction: Tensions in the Allocation of Judicial Power* 27–28 (2d ed. 1990).

NOTE ON CONGRESS'S POWER TO RESTRICT THE JURISDICTION OF INFERIOR FEDERAL COURTS

If Congress has discretion not to create inferior federal courts at all under the Ordain and Establish Clause, does it not also have the authority to limit their jurisdiction in just about any way it desires? This is a familiar form of argument: The greater power includes the lesser power. Is there any way around it?

Justice Story said in *Martin v. Hunter's Lessee*, 14 U.S. (1 Wheat.) 304 (1816), that the language of Article III "is manifestly designed to be mandatory upon the legislature. Its obligatory force is so imperative, that congress could not, without a violation of its duty, have refused to carry it into operation. * * * If, then, it is a duty of congress to vest the judicial power of the United States, it is a duty to vest the whole judicial power." Justice Story argued that Congress was therefore required to establish the Supreme Court, and also at least some inferior federal courts. Because the Supreme Court only has original jurisdiction in two types of cases, its appellate jurisdiction is needed to exercise the other kinds of judicial power listed in Article III, § 2 (and, according to Justice Story, mandatory kinds of jurisdiction). Therefore:

> [I]f in any of the cases enumerated in [Art. III, § 2 of] the constitution, the state courts did not then possess jurisdiction, the appellate jurisdiction of the supreme court (admitting that it could act on state courts) could not reach those cases, and, consequently, the injunction of the constitution, that the judicial power "shall be vested," would be disobeyed. It would seem, therefore, to follow, that congress are bound to create some inferior courts, in which to vest all that jurisdiction which, under the constitution, is exclusively vested in the United States, and of which the supreme court cannot take original cognizance.

Justice Story's expansive dictum has been controversial. Many scholars argue that giving Congress discretion whether to create inferior federal courts at all was a deliberate compromise (some Framers favored mandatory inferior courts, some none at all). E.g., Henry M. Hart Jr. & Herbert Wechsler, *The Federal Courts and the Federal System* 11–12 (2d ed. 1973). The Judiciary Act of 1789 vested the federal judiciary with less than the jurisdiction authorized by Article III: it gave no general federal question jurisdiction, limited diversity jurisdiction to lawsuits involving more than $500, and did not authorize Supreme Court review of all federal questions.

Subsequent cases have not accepted the import of the *Martin v. Hunter's Lessee* dictum. In *Sheldon v. Sill*, 49 U.S. (8 How.) 441 (1850), for example, the Court held that a circuit court has no jurisdiction over a case meeting the constitutional but not the narrower statutory requirements. "[C]ongress may withhold from any court of its creation jurisdiction of any of the enumerated controversies. Courts created by statute can have no jurisdiction but such as the statute confers." If the *Sill* statement is credited, can Congress preclude federal jurisdiction over just one kind of federal question case—school desegregation—or preclude jurisdiction to issue just one kind of remedy? Is the latter not tantamount to an unconstitutional congressional interference in civil rights? Or is it only Congress' exercise of its own Fourteenth Amendment, § 5 powers? Note here that any such statute would leave state courts with authority to enter busing orders.

Akhil Amar has suggested a synthesis of the Story and Hart arguments.[20] Hart was right that Congress cannot deprive the judiciary of its "essential role" in our constitutional system, but wrong to focus only on the Supreme Court. Story was right that Congress is obliged to vest some effective federal jurisdiction in the judiciary, but wrong to insist that Congress had to create inferior federal courts for such a purpose. In short, Amar argues that Congress cannot, consistent with the Vesting Clause and the central role of the Article III judiciary, give full effect to the Exceptions Clause and the Ordain and Establish Clause in the same constitutional subject matter. This thesis finds support in the Court's dicta in *Mistretta* and other cases, to the effect that Congress cannot deprive the Judicial Branch of its core functions, and with suggestions in prior cases that there must be some judicial forum to challenge unconstitutional actions. E.g., *Estep v. United States*, 327 U.S. 114 (1946). Responses?

Note the parallel between the broad Vesting Clauses in Articles II and III (executive and judicial power, apparently all of it, *shall be vested* in President and Supreme Court/inferior courts), especially in contrast to the more narrow one in Article I (only legislative powers *herein granted* shall be vested in Congress). Steven G. Calabresi & Kevin H. Rhodes, *The Structural Constitution: Unitary Executive, Plural Judiciary*, 105 Harv. L. Rev. 1153 (1992), note the parallel between Amar's argument against jurisdiction-stripping—the Exceptions and Ordain and Establish Clauses in Article III must be read narrowly in light of its broad and mandatory Vesting Clause—and Justice Scalia's argument in *Morrison*—the Appointments Clause in Article II must be read narrowly in light of its broad and mandatory Vesting Clause. But the Supreme Court in *Morrison* rejected the Scalia reading of Article II. Is there a better reason for the same Court to accept the Amar reading of Article II?

CONCLUDING THOUGHTS ON THE SUPREME COURT AND AMERICAN SOCIETY

The cases in this chapter illustrate profound ambiguities of judicial review.[21] The Court is both reluctant to enter the political process openly (e.g., *Nixon v. United States* and *Allen v. Wright*) yet is itself an inevitable player in

---

[20] Starting with Amar, *Neo-Federalist View of Article III*, and continuing with follow-up articles, e.g., Akhil Reed Amar, *The Two-Tiered Structure of the Judiciary Act of 1789*, 138 U. Pa. L. Rev. 1499 (1990), and responses to attacks, e.g., Akhil Reed Amar, *Reports of My Death Are Greatly Exaggerated: A Reply*, 138 U. Pa. L. Rev. 1651 (1990).

[21] This theme is developed in Alexander Bickel, *The Least Dangerous Branch* (1962); William Eskridge, Jr. & Philip Frickey, *The Supreme Court, 1993 Term—Foreword: Law as Equilibrium*, 108 Harv. L. Rev. 26 (1994).

the political process by which public policy emerges in the United States (*Baker v. Carr* and the *Jenkins* decisions). The Court is both the "least dangerous branch" (*Federalist* No. 78) and the one subject to the fewest short-term constraints, both propositions evidenced in the Kansas City *Jenkins* desegregation litigation. (Indeed, at times, the Court may seem to some to be the most powerful and *least* constrained political actor, see *Bush v. Gore*.) *Brown*, the case with which we began this casebook, may be evidence of these apparently contradictory propositions.

In *The Hollow Hope: Can Courts Bring About Social Change* (1991), Gerald Rosenberg argues that courts are able to produce significant social reform only when supported by ample legal precedent developed over time in a common-law-like way, by substantial backing and follow-up from Congress and the President, and by approval or at least acquiescence from the general public. Specifically, he maintains that the desegregation decisions surveyed in Chapter 2 had little or no positive effect on actual school segregation until Congress and the President became actively engaged in the 1960s. Rosenberg's critics respond that the Court had great importance in signaling national support for civil rights activists and in putting desegregation on the national agenda through the *Brown* decision.[22] Both Rosenberg and some of his critics agree that *Brown* was a focal point for opposition in the South and may have hardened attitudes both for and against desegregation. Of course, there is no way of knowing the possible effect of a 1954 decision reaffirming *Plessy*, which might have been the alternative to *Brown*.

In the 2008 edition of his book, Rosenberg argued that the public reaction to gay marriage rulings confirmed his pessimistic view of the judicial role in social change. The story is still unfolding, but at least seems more complex and nuanced than Rosenberg's portrayal. Although gay marriage is a divisive issue, gay marriage advocates were aware of the potential for backlash and adjusted their strategies accordingly. It is at least arguable that judicial rulings in states like Massachusetts and Vermont gave society the chance to learn about the human dimensions of the issue. They may then have paved the way for greater acceptance of same-sex marriage and civil unions nationally. If so, the lesson is that the relationship between the courts and social change is more complicated and context-dependent than Rosenberg suggests.[23]

A similar story of agenda-setting, negative or positive feedback from the political process, and judicial retreat or accommodation can be told for most of the other big issues covered in this casebook: affirmative action (Chapter 3, § 3); equal rights for women (Chapter 4, §§ 2–3); freedom of contract (Chapter 5, § 2B); one person, one vote (Chapter 5, § 3A); the right of a woman to choose

---

[22] E.g., Neal Devins, Book Review, 80 Calif. L. Rev. 1027 (1992); David Garrow, *Hopelessly Hollow History: Revisionist Devaluing of* Brown v. Board of Education, 80 Va. L. Rev. 151 (1994); Michael Klarman, *Civil Rights Law: Who Made It and How Much Did It Matter?*, 83 Geo. L.J. 433 (1994).

[23] For the counterpoint to Rosenberg's view, see William N. Eskridge Jr., *Backlash Politics: How Constitutional Litigation Has Advanced Marriage Equality in the United States*, 93 B.U. L. Rev. ___ (2013).

abortion (Chapter 5, § 4B); flagburning and other offensive or even hate speech (Chapter 6, §§ 1–2); school prayer (Chapter 6, § 6B); the reach of Congress' power under the Commerce Clause (Chapter 7, § 2); and executive privileges (Chapter 8, § 1C) as well as congressional power to delegate rulemaking but with strings attached (Chapter 8, § 2). We wonder how this interplay will work out in the context of new Supreme Court initiatives such as enforcement of the Second Amendment and support for corporate political activity. As we have seen, there have also been important interactions between the Court and the other branches in the terrorism context.

Justices are necessarily products of their times, and cases do not come before them unless issues are first conceptualized as constitutional and litigants are motivated to bring them to court. Thus, to understand and appreciate the larger shifts in constitutional law—not just the formal amendments or major constitutional "moments"—the student needs to consider also the larger shifts in American politics and society, such as urbanization and the revolution in transportation and communications, the antislavery movement and reconstruction after the Civil War, the struggle between big business and organized labor, the pervasively regulatory state whose engine is agencies rather than courts, the civil rights revolution for people of color, the apparent worldwide dominance of market capitalism, the imperial presidency, the entry of fundamentalist sects into the political process, the women's and later gay liberation movements; and the tea party revolt against government regulation. Many of these social and political changes are still in progress, and others are joining them.

Constitutional law in the Constitution's third century will have to account for developments such as the Internet and changes in the mass media, globalization, the nation's increasing racial heterogeneity, divided government, the growing political dominance of suburbs, revolutionary technologies such as cloning, and so forth.

Finally, think about how the law in general and the Supreme Court in particular influence these social and political developments, albeit often in ways that are not intended. Rosenberg argues that *Brown* itself created a new and hardened political dynamic, where resistance to "judicial activism" became a rallying cry. To what extent did the Court's Establishment Clause and abortion-rights activism fuel the creation of the "religious right" as a coherent and powerful political movement? Did *Bowers v. Hardwick* (Chapter 5, § 4C) help fuel a more aggressive gay rights movement? Has the Court's race and gender jurisprudence affected people's choices when they form families, make hiring decisions, and speak out in public discourse? Has the Court's new activism as to issues of federalism contributed to localism as a public value?

Early in the previous century, the Supreme Court decided the *Lochner* case. No one then could have foreseen the following hundred years of Supreme Court jurisprudence, or the forces that repeatedly transformed the political landscape during the remainder of the century. No doubt this third century of constitutionalism will bring similar surprises. But unless we profoundly alter our existing practices, the Supreme Court will continue to play a key role in society's responses to these changes.

APPENDIX 1

THE CONSTITUTION OF THE UNITED STATES

■ ■ ■

PREAMBLE

We the People of the United States, in Order to form a more perfect Union, establish Justice, insure domestic Tranquility, provide for the common defence, promote the general Welfare, and secure the Blessings of Liberty to ourselves and our Posterity, do ordain and establish this Constitution for the United States of America.

ARTICLE I

Section 1. All legislative Powers herein granted shall be vested in a Congress of the United States, which shall consist of a Senate and House of Representatives.

Section 2. [1] The House of Representatives shall be composed of Members chosen every second Year by the People of the several States, and the Electors in each State shall have the Qualifications requisite for Electors of the most numerous Branch of the State Legislature.

[2] No Person shall be a Representative who shall not have attained to the Age of twenty five Years, and been seven Years a Citizen of the United States, and who shall not, when elected, be an Inhabitant of that State in which he shall be chosen.

[3] Representatives and direct Taxes shall be apportioned among the several States which may be included within this Union, according to their respective Numbers, which shall be determined by adding to the whole Number of free Persons, including those bound to Service for a Term of Years, and excluding Indians not taxed, three fifths of all other Persons. The actual Enumeration shall be made within three Years after the first Meeting of the Congress of the United States, and within every subsequent Term of ten Years, in such Manner as they shall by Law direct. The Number of Representatives shall not exceed one for every thirty Thousand, but each State shall have at Least one Representative; and until such enumeration shall be made, the State of New Hampshire shall be entitled to chuse three, Massachusetts eight, Rhode Island and Providence Plantations one, Connecticut five, New York six, New Jersey four,

Pennsylvania eight, Delaware one, Maryland six, Virginia ten, North Carolina five, South Carolina five, and Georgia three.

[4]   When vacancies happen in the Representation from any State, the Executive Authority thereof shall issue Writs of Election to fill such Vacancies

[5]   The House of Representatives shall chuse their Speaker and other Officers; and shall have the sole Power of Impeachment.

Section 3. [1] The Senate of the United States shall be composed of two Senators from each State, chosen by the Legislature thereof, for six Years; and each Senator shall have one Vote.

[2]   Immediately after they shall be assembled in Consequence of the first Election, they shall be divided as equally as may be into three Classes. The Seats of the Senators of the first Class shall be vacated at the Expiration of the second Year, of the second Class at the Expiration of the fourth Year, and of the third Class at the Expiration of the sixth Year, so that one third may be chosen every second Year; and if Vacancies happen by Resignation, or otherwise, during the Recess of the Legislature of any State, the Executive thereof may make temporary Appointments until the next Meeting of the Legislature, which shall then fill such Vacancies.

[3]   No Person shall be a Senator who shall not have attained to the Age of thirty Years, and been nine Years a Citizen of the United States, and who shall not, when elected, be an Inhabitant of that State for which he shall be chosen.

[4]   The Vice President of the United States shall be President of the Senate, but shall have no Vote, unless they be equally divided.

[5]   The Senate shall chuse their other Officers, and also a President pro tempore, in the Absence of the Vice President, or when he shall exercise the Office of President of the United States.

[6]   The Senate shall have the sole Power to try all Impeachments. When sitting for that Purpose, they shall be on Oath or Affirmation. When the President of the United States is tried, the Chief Justice shall preside: And no Person shall be convicted without the Concurrence of two thirds of the Members present.

[7]   Judgment in Cases of Impeachment shall not extend further than to removal from Office, and disqualification to hold and enjoy any Office of honor, Trust, or Profit under the United States: but the Party convicted shall nevertheless be liable and subject to Indictment, Trial, Judgment, and Punishment, according to Law.

Section 4. [1] The Times, Places and Manner of holding Elections for Senators and Representatives, shall be prescribed in each State by the

Legislature thereof; but the Congress may at any time by Law make or alter such Regulations, except as to the Places of chusing Senators.

[2]   The Congress shall assemble at least once in every Year, and such Meeting shall be on the first Monday in December, unless they shall by Law appoint a different Day.

Section 5. [1] Each House shall be the Judge of the Elections, Returns, and Qualifications of its own Members, and a Majority of each shall constitute a Quorum to do Business; but a smaller Number may adjourn from day to day, and may be authorized to compel the Attendance of absent Members, in such Manner, and under such Penalties as each House may provide.

[2]   Each House may determine the Rules of its Proceedings, punish its Members for disorderly Behaviour, and, with the Concurrence of two thirds, expel a Member.

[3]   Each House shall keep a Journal of its Proceedings, and from time to time publish the same, excepting such Parts as may in their Judgment require Secrecy; and the Yeas and Nays of the Members of either House on any question shall, at the Desire of one fifth of those Present, be entered on the Journal.

[4]   Neither House, during the Session of Congress, shall without the Consent of the other, adjourn for more than three days, nor to any other Place than that in which the two Houses shall be sitting.

Section 6. [1] The Senators and Representatives shall receive a Compensation for their Services, to be ascertained by Law, and paid out of the Treasury of the United States. They shall in all Cases, except Treason, Felony, and Breach of the Peace, be privileged from Arrest during their Attendance at the Session of their respective Houses, and in going to and returning from the same; and for any Speech or Debate in either House, they shall not be questioned in any other Place.

[2]   No Senator or Representative shall, during the Time for which he was elected, be appointed to any civil Office under the Authority of the United States, which shall have been created, or the Emoluments whereof shall have been encreased during such time; and no Person holding any Office under the United States, shall be a Member of either House during his Continuance in Office.

Section 7. [1] All Bills for raising Revenue shall originate in the House of Representatives; but the Senate may propose or concur with Amendments as on other Bills.

[2]   Every Bill which shall have passed the House of Representatives and the Senate, shall, before it become a Law, be presented to the President of the United States; If he approve he shall sign it, but if not he shall return

it, with his Objections to that House in which it shall have originated, who shall enter the Objections at large on their Journal, and proceed to reconsider it. If after such Reconsideration two thirds of that House shall agree to pass the Bill, it shall be sent, together with the Objections, to the other House, by which it shall likewise be reconsidered, and if approved by two thirds of that House, it shall become a Law. But in all such Cases the Votes of both Houses shall be determined by Yeas and Nays, and the Names of the Persons voting for and against the Bill shall be entered on the Journal of each House respectively. If any Bill shall not be returned by the President within ten Days (Sundays excepted) after it shall have been presented to him, the Same shall be a Law, in like Manner as if he had signed it, unless the Congress by their Adjournment prevent its Return, in which Case it shall not be a Law.

[3] Every Order, Resolution, or Vote to which the Concurrence of the Senate and House of Representatives may be necessary (except on a question of Adjournment) shall be presented to the President of the United States; and before the Same shall take Effect, shall be approved by him, or being disapproved by him, shall be repassed by two thirds of the Senate and House of Representatives, according to the Rules and Limitations prescribed in the Case of a Bill.

Section 8. [1] The Congress shall have Power To lay and collect Taxes, Duties, Imposts and Excises, to pay the Debts and provide for the common Defence and general Welfare of the United States; but all Duties, Imposts and Excises shall be uniform throughout the United States;

[2] To borrow Money on the credit of the United States;

[3] To regulate Commerce with foreign Nations, and among the several States, and with the Indian Tribes;

[4] To establish an uniform Rule of Naturalization, and uniform Laws on the subject of Bankruptcies throughout the United States;

[5] To coin Money, regulate the Value thereof, and of foreign Coin, and fix the Standard of Weights and Measures;

[6] To provide for the Punishment of counterfeiting the Securities and current Coin of the United States;

[7] To establish Post Offices and Post Roads;

[8] To promote the Progress of Science and useful Arts, by securing for limited Times to Authors and Inventors the exclusive Right to their respective Writings and Discoveries;

[9] To constitute Tribunals inferior to the supreme Court;

[10] To define and punish Piracies and Felonies committed on the high Seas, and Offences against the Law of Nations;

[11] To declare War, grant Letters of Marque and Reprisal, and make Rules concerning Captures on Land and Water;

[12] To raise and support Armies, but no Appropriation of Money to that Use shall be for a longer Term than two Years;

[13] To provide and maintain a Navy;

[14] To make Rules for the Government and Regulation of the land and naval Forces;

[15] To provide for calling forth the Militia to execute the Laws of the Union, suppress Insurrections and repel Invasions;

[16] To provide for organizing, arming, and disciplining, the Militia, and for governing such Part of them as may be employed in the Service of the United States, reserving to the States respectively, the Appointment of the Officers, and the Authority of training the Militia according to the discipline prescribed by Congress;

[17] To exercise exclusive Legislation in all Cases whatsoever, over such District (not exceeding ten Miles square) as may, by Cession of particular States and the Acceptance of Congress, become the Seat of the Government of the United States, and to exercise like Authority over all Places purchased by the Consent of the Legislature of the State in which the Same shall be, for the Erection of Forts, Magazines, Arsenals, dock-Yards, and other needful Buildings;—And

[18] To make all Laws which shall be necessary and proper for carrying into Execution the foregoing Powers, and all other Powers vested by this Constitution in the Government of the United States, or in any Department or Officer thereof.

Section 9. [1] The Migration or Importation of such Persons as any of the States now existing shall think proper to admit, shall not be prohibited by the Congress prior to the Year one thousand eight hundred and eight, but a Tax or duty may be imposed on such Importation, not exceeding ten dollars for each Person.

[2] The Privilege of the Writ of Habeas Corpus shall not be suspended, unless when in Cases of Rebellion or Invasion the public Safety may require it.

[3] No Bill of Attainder or ex post facto Law shall be passed.

[4] No Capitation, or other direct, Tax shall be laid, unless in Proportion to the Census or Enumeration herein before directed to be taken.

[5] No Tax or Duty shall be laid on Articles exported from any State.

[6] No Preference shall be given by any Regulation of Commerce or Revenue to the Ports of one State over those of another: nor shall Vessels

bound to, or from, one State, be obliged to enter, clear, or pay Duties in another.

[7] No Money shall be drawn from the Treasury, but in Consequence of Appropriations made by Law; and a regular Statement and Account of the Receipts and Expenditures of all public Money shall be published from time to time.

[8] No Title of Nobility shall be granted by the United States: And no Person holding any Office of Profit or Trust under them, shall, without the Consent of the Congress, accept of any present, Emolument, Office, or Title, of any kind whatever, from any King, Prince, or foreign State.

Section 10. [1] No State shall enter into any Treaty, Alliance, or Confederation; grant Letters of Marque and Reprisal; coin Money; emit Bills of Credit; make any Thing but gold and silver Coin a Tender in Payment of Debts; pass any Bill of Attainder, ex post facto Law, or Law impairing the Obligation of Contracts, or grant any Title of Nobility.

[2] No State shall, without the Consent of the Congress, lay any Imposts or Duties on Imports or Exports, except what may be absolutely necessary for executing its inspection Laws: and the net Produce of all Duties and Imposts, laid by any State on Imports or Exports, shall be for the Use of the Treasury of the United States; and all such Laws shall be subject to the Revision and Controul of the Congress.

[3] No State shall, without the Consent of Congress, lay any Duty of Tonnage, keep Troops, or Ships of War in time of Peace, enter into any Agreement or Compact with another State, or with a foreign Power, or engage in War, unless actually invaded, or in such imminent Danger as will not admit of delay.

ARTICLE II

Section 1. [1] The executive Power shall be vested in a President of the United States of America. He shall hold his Office during the Term of four Years, and, together with the Vice President, chosen for the same Term, be elected, as follows:

[2] Each State shall appoint, in such Manner as the Legislature thereof may direct, a Number of Electors, equal to the whole Number of Senators and Representatives to which the State may be entitled in the Congress: but no Senator or Representative, or Person holding an Office of Trust or Profit under the United States, shall be appointed an Elector.

[3] The electors shall meet in their respective States, and vote by ballot for two Persons, of whom one at least shall not be an Inhabitant of the same State with themselves. And they shall make a List of all the Persons voted for, and of the Number of Votes for each; which List they shall sign and certify, and transmit sealed to the Seat of the Government

of the United States, directed to the President of the Senate. The President of the Senate shall, in the Presence of the Senate and House of Representatives, open all the Certificates, and the Votes shall then be counted. The Person having the greatest Number of Votes shall be the President, if such Number be a Majority of the whole Number of Electors appointed; and if there be more than one who have such Majority, and have an equal Number of Votes, then the House of Representatives shall immediately chuse by Ballot one of them for President; and if no Person have a Majority, then from the five highest on the List the said House shall in like Manner chuse the President. But in chusing the President, the Votes shall be taken by States, the Representation from each State having one Vote; A quorum for this Purpose shall consist of a Member or Members from two thirds of the States, and a Majority of all the States shall be necessary to a Choice. In every Case, after the Choice of the President, the Person having the greatest Number of Votes of the Electors shall be the Vice President. But if there should remain two or more who have equal Votes, the Senate shall chuse from them by Ballot the Vice-President.

[4] The Congress may determine the Time of chusing the Electors, and the Day on which they shall give their Votes; which Day shall be the same throughout the United States.

[5] No Person except a natural born Citizen, or a Citizen of the United States, at the time of the Adoption of this Constitution, shall be eligible to the Office of President; neither shall any Person be eligible to that Office who shall not have attained to the Age of thirty five Years, and been fourteen Years a Resident within the United States.

[6] In Case of the Removal of the President from Office, or of his Death, Resignation, or Inability to discharge the Powers and Duties of the said Office, the Same shall devolve on the Vice President, and the Congress may by Law provide for the Case of Removal, Death, Resignation or Inability, both of the President and Vice President, declaring what Officer shall then act as President, and such Officer shall act accordingly, until the Disability be removed, or a President shall be elected.

[7] The President shall, at stated Times, receive for his Services, a Compensation, which shall neither be encreased nor diminished during the Period for which he shall have been elected, and he shall not receive within that Period any other Emolument from the United States, or any of them.

[8] Before he enter on the Execution of his Office, he shall take the following Oath or Affirmation: "I do solemnly swear (or affirm) that I will faithfully execute the Office of President of the United States, and will to the best of my Ability, preserve, protect and defend the Constitution of the United States."

Section 2. [1] The President shall be Commander in Chief of the Army and Navy of the United States, and of the Militia of the several States, when called into the actual Service of the United States; he may require the Opinion, in writing, of the principal Officer in each of the executive Departments, upon any Subject relating to the Duties of their respective Offices, and he shall have Power to grant Reprieves and Pardons for Offenses against the United States, except in Cases of Impeachment.

[2] He shall have Power, by and with the Advice and Consent of the Senate, to make Treaties, provided two thirds of the Senators present concur; and he shall nominate, and by and with the Advice and Consent of the Senate, shall appoint Ambassadors, other public Ministers and Consuls, Judges of the supreme Court, and all other Officers of the United States, whose Appointments are not herein otherwise provided for, and which shall be established by Law: but the Congress may by Law vest the Appointment of such inferior Officers, as they think proper, in the President alone, in the Courts of Law, or in the Heads of Departments.

[3] The President shall have Power to fill up all Vacancies that may happen during the Recess of the Senate, by granting Commissions which shall expire at the End of their next Session.

Section 3. He shall from time to time give to the Congress Information of the State of the Union, and recommend to their Consideration such Measures as he shall judge necessary and expedient; he may, on extraordinary Occasions, convene both Houses, or either of them, and in Case of Disagreement between them, with Respect to the Time of Adjournment, he may adjourn them to such Time as he shall think proper; he shall receive Ambassadors and other public Ministers; he shall take Care that the Laws be faithfully executed, and shall Commission all the Officers of the United States.

Section 4. The President, Vice President and all civil Officers of the United States, shall be removed from Office on Impeachment for, and Conviction of, Treason, Bribery, or other high Crimes and Misdemeanors.

ARTICLE III

Section 1. The judicial Power of the United States, shall be vested in one supreme Court, and in such inferior Courts as the Congress may from time to time ordain and establish. The Judges, both of the supreme and inferior Courts, shall hold their Offices during good Behaviour, and shall, at stated Times, receive for their Services, a Compensation, which shall not be diminished during their Continuance in Office.

Section 2. [1] The judicial Power shall extend to all Cases, in Law and Equity, arising under this Constitution, the Laws of the United States, and Treaties made, or which shall be made, under their Authority;—to all Cases affecting Ambassadors, other public Ministers and Consuls;—to all Cases of admiralty and maritime Jurisdiction;—to Controversies to which the United States shall be a Party;—to Controversies between two or more

States;—between a State and Citizens of another State;—between Citizens of different States;—between Citizens of the same State claiming Lands under Grants of different States, and between a State, or the Citizens thereof, and foreign States, Citizens or Subjects.

[2]   In all Cases affecting Ambassadors, other public Ministers and Consuls, and those in which a State shall be Party, the supreme Court shall have original Jurisdiction. In all the other Cases before mentioned, the supreme Court shall have appellate Jurisdiction, both as to Law and Fact, with such Exceptions, and under such Regulations as the Congress shall make.

[3]   The Trial of all Crimes, except in Cases of Impeachment, shall be by Jury; and such Trial shall be held in the State where the said Crimes shall have been committed; but when not committed within any State, the Trial shall be at such Place or Places as the Congress may by Law have directed.

Section 3. [1] Treason against the United States, shall consist only in levying War against them, or in adhering to their Enemies, giving them Aid and Comfort. No Person shall be convicted of Treason unless on the Testimony of two Witnesses to the same overt Act, or on Confession in open Court.

[2]   The Congress shall have Power to declare the Punishment of Treason, but no Attainder of Treason shall work Corruption of Blood, or Forfeiture except during the Life of the Person attainted.

ARTICLE IV

Section 1. Full Faith and Credit shall be given in each State to the public Acts, Records, and judicial Proceedings of every other State. And the Congress may by general Laws prescribe the Manner in which such Acts, Records and Proceedings shall be proved, and the Effect thereof.

Section 2. [1] The Citizens of each State shall be entitled to all Privileges and Immunities of Citizens in the several States.

[2]   A person charged in any State with Treason, Felony, or other Crime, who shall flee from Justice, and be found in another State, shall on Demand of the executive Authority of the State from which he fled, be delivered up, to be removed to the State having Jurisdiction of the Crime.

[3]   No Person held to Service or Labour in one State, under the Laws thereof, escaping into another, shall, in Consequence of any Law or Regulation therein, be discharged from such Service or Labour, but shall be delivered up on Claim of the Party to whom such Service or Labour may be due.

Section 3. [1] New States may be admitted by the Congress into this Union; but no new State shall be formed or erected within the Jurisdiction of any other State; nor any State be formed by the Junction of two or more States, or Parts of States, without the Consent of the Legislatures of the States concerned as well as of the Congress.

[2] The Congress shall have Power to dispose of and make all needful Rules and Regulations respecting the Territory or other Property belonging to the United States; and nothing in this Constitution shall be so construed as to Prejudice any Claims of the United States, or of any particular State.

Section 4. The United States shall guarantee to every State in this Union a Republican Form of Government, and shall protect each of them against Invasion; and on Application of the Legislature, or of the Executive (when the Legislature cannot be convened) against domestic Violence.

ARTICLE V

The Congress, whenever two thirds of both Houses shall deem it necessary, shall propose Amendments to this Constitution, or on the Application of the Legislatures of two thirds of the several States, shall call a Convention for proposing Amendments, which, in either Case, shall be valid to all Intents and Purposes, as Part of this Constitution, when ratified by the Legislatures of three fourths of the several States, or by Conventions in three fourths thereof, as the one or the other Mode of Ratification may be proposed by the Congress; Provided that no Amendment which may be made prior to the Year One thousand eight hundred and eight shall in any Manner affect the first and fourth Clauses in the Ninth Section of the first Article; and that no State, without its Consent, shall be deprived of its equal Suffrage in the Senate.

ARTICLE VI

[1] All Debts contracted and Engagements entered into, before the Adoption of this Constitution, shall be as valid against the United States under this Constitution, as under the Confederation.

[2] This Constitution, and the Laws of the United States which shall be made in Pursuance thereof; and all Treaties made, or which shall be made, under the Authority of the United States, shall be the supreme Law of the Land; and the Judges in every State shall be bound thereby, any Thing in the Constitution or Laws of any State to the Contrary notwithstanding.

[3] The Senators and Representatives before mentioned, and the Members of the several State Legislatures, and all executive and judicial Officers, both of the United States and of the several States, shall be bound by Oath or Affirmation, to support this Constitution; but no religious Test shall ever be required as a Qualification to any Office or public Trust under the United States.

ARTICLE VII

The Ratification of the Conventions of nine States, shall be sufficient for the Establishment of this Constitution between the States so ratifying the Same.

ARTICLES IN ADDITION TO, AND AMENDMENT OF, THE CONSTITUTION OF THE UNITED STATES OF AMERICA, PROPOSED BY CONGRESS, AND RATIFIED BY THE LEGISLATURES OF THE SEVERAL STATES, PURSUANT TO THE FIFTH ARTICLE OF THE ORIGINAL CONSTITUTION.

AMENDMENT I [1791]

Congress shall make no law respecting an establishment of religion, or prohibiting the free exercise thereof; or abridging the freedom of speech, or of the press; or the right of the people peaceably to assemble, and to petition the Government for a redress of grievances.

AMENDMENT II [1791]

A well regulated Militia, being necessary to the security of a free State, the right of the people to keep and bear Arms, shall not be infringed.

AMENDMENT III [1791]

No Soldier shall, in time of peace be quartered in any house, without the consent of the Owner, nor in time of war, but in a manner to be prescribed by law.

AMENDMENT IV [1791]

The right of the people to be secure in their persons, houses, papers, and effects, against unreasonable searches and seizures, shall not be violated, and no Warrants shall issue, but upon probable cause, supported by Oath or affirmation, and particularly describing the place to be searched, and the persons or things to be seized.

AMENDMENT V [1791]

No person shall be held to answer for a capital, or otherwise infamous crime, unless on a presentment or indictment of a Grand Jury, except in cases arising in the land or naval forces, or in the Militia, when in actual service in time of War or public danger; nor shall any person be subject for the same offence to be twice put in jeopardy of life or limb; nor shall be compelled in any criminal case to be a witness against himself, nor be deprived of life, liberty, or property, without due process of law; nor shall private property be taken for public use, without just compensation.

AMENDMENT VI [1791]

In all criminal prosecutions, the accused shall enjoy the right to a speedy and public trial, by an impartial jury of the State and district wherein the crime shall have been committed, which district shall have been previously ascertained by law, and to be informed of the nature and cause of the accusation; to be confronted with the witnesses against him; to have compulsory process for obtaining witnesses in his favor, and to have the Assistance of Counsel for his defence.

AMENDMENT VII [1791]

In Suits at common law, where the value in controversy shall exceed twenty dollars, the right of trial by jury shall be preserved, and no fact tried by a jury, shall be otherwise re-examined in any Court of the United States, than according to the rules of the common law.

AMENDMENT VIII [1791]

Excessive bail shall not be required, nor excessive fines imposed, nor cruel and unusual punishments inflicted.

AMENDMENT IX [1791]

The enumeration in the Constitution, of certain rights, shall not be construed to deny or disparage others retained by the people.

AMENDMENT X [1791]

The powers not delegated to the United States by the Constitution, nor prohibited by it to the States, are reserved to the States respectively, or to the people.

AMENDMENT XI [1798]

The Judicial power of the United States shall not be construed to extend to any suit in law or equity, commenced or prosecuted against one of the United States by Citizens of another State, or by Citizens or Subjects of any Foreign State.

AMENDMENT XII [1804]

The Electors shall meet in their respective states and vote by ballot for President and Vice-President, one of whom, at least, shall not be an inhabitant of the same state with themselves; they shall name in their ballots the person voted for as President, and in distinct ballots the person voted for as Vice-President, and they shall make distinct lists of all persons voted for as President, and of all persons voted for as Vice-President, and of the number of votes for each, which lists they shall sign and certify, and transmit sealed to the seat of the government of the United States, directed to the President of the Senate;—The President of the Senate shall, in the presence of the Senate and House of Representatives, open all the certificates and the votes shall then be counted;—The person having the greatest number of votes for President, shall be the President, if such number be a majority of the whole number of Electors appointed; and if no person have such majority, then from the persons having the highest numbers not exceeding three on the list of those voted for as President, the House of Representatives shall choose immediately, by ballot, the President. But in choosing the President, the votes shall be taken by states, the representation from each state having one vote; a quorum for this purpose shall consist of a member or members from two-thirds of the states, and a majority of all the states shall be necessary to a choice. And if the House of Representatives shall not choose a President whenever the right of choice shall devolve upon them, before the fourth day of March next following, then the Vice-President shall act as President, as in the case of the death or other constitutional disability of the President. The person having the greatest number of votes as Vice-President, shall be the Vice-President, if such number be a majority of the whole number of Electors appointed, and if no person have a majority, then from the two highest numbers on the list, the Senate shall choose the Vice-President; a quorum for the purpose shall consist of two-thirds of the whole number of Senators, and a majority of the whole number shall be necessary to a choice. But no person constitutionally ineligible to the office of President shall be eligible to that of Vice-President of the United States.

AMENDMENT XIII [1865]

Section 1. Neither slavery nor involuntary servitude, except as a punishment for crime whereof the party shall have been duly convicted, shall exist within the United States, or any place subject to their jurisdiction.

abolish slavery

Section 2. Congress shall have power to enforce this article by appropriate legislation.

AMENDMENT XIV [1868]

Section 1. All persons born or naturalized in the United States, and subject to the jurisdiction thereof, are citizens of the United States and of the State wherein they reside. No State shall make or enforce any law which shall abridge the privileges or immunities of citizens of the United States; nor shall any State deprive any person of life, liberty, or property, without due process of law; nor deny to any person within its jurisdiction the equal protection of the laws.

equal protection clause

Section 2. Representatives shall be apportioned among the several States according to their respective numbers, counting the whole number of persons in each State, excluding Indians not taxed. But when the right to vote at any election for the choice of electors for President and Vice President of the United States, Representatives in Congress, the Executive and Judicial officers of a State, or the members of the Legislature thereof, is denied to any of the male inhabitants of such State, being twenty-one years of age, and citizens of the United States, or in any way abridged, except for participation in rebellion, or other crime, the basis of representation therein shall be reduced in the proportion which the number of such male citizens shall bear to the whole number of male citizens twenty-one years of age in such State.

Section 3. No person shall be a Senator or Representative in Congress, or elector of President and Vice President, or hold any office, civil or military, under the United States, or under any State, who, having previously taken an oath, as a member of Congress, or as an officer of the United States, or as a member of any State legislature, or as an executive or judicial officer of any State, to support the Constitution of the United States, shall have engaged in insurrection or rebellion against the same, or given aid or comfort to the enemies thereof. But Congress may by a vote of two-thirds of each House, remove such disability.

Section 4. The validity of the public debt of the United States, authorized by law, including debts incurred for payment of pensions and bounties for services in suppressing insurrection or rebellion, shall not be questioned. But neither the United States nor any State shall assume or pay any debt or obligation incurred in aid of insurrection or rebellion against the United States, or any claim for the loss or emancipation of any slave; but all such debts, obligations and claims shall be held illegal and void.

Section 5. The Congress shall have power to enforce, by appropriate legislation, the provisions of this article.

AMENDMENT XV [1870]

Section 1. The right of citizens of the United States to vote shall not be denied or abridged by the United States or by any State on account of race, color, or previous condition of servitude.

Section 2. The Congress shall have power to enforce this article by appropriate legislation.

AMENDMENT XVI [1913]

The Congress shall have power to lay and collect taxes on incomes, from whatever source derived, without apportionment among the several States, and without regard to any census or enumeration.

AMENDMENT XVII [1913]

[1] The Senate of the United States shall be composed of two Senators from each State, elected by the people thereof, for six years; and each Senator shall have one vote. The electors in each State shall have the qualifications requisite for electors of the most numerous branch of the State legislatures.

[2] When vacancies happen in the representation of any State in the Senate, the executive authority of such State shall issue writs of election to fill such vacancies: *Provided*, That the legislature of any State may

empower the executive thereof to make temporary appointments until the people fill the vacancies by election as the legislature may direct.

[3] This amendment shall not be so construed as to affect the election or term of any Senator chosen before it becomes valid as part of the Constitution.

AMENDMENT XVIII [1919]

Section 1. After one year from the ratification of this article the manufacture, sale, or transportation of intoxicating liquors within, the importation thereof into, or the exportation thereof from the United States and all territory subject to the jurisdiction thereof for beverage purposes is hereby prohibited.

Section 2. The Congress and the several States shall have concurrent power to enforce this article by appropriate legislation.

Section 3. This article shall be inoperative unless it shall have been ratified as an amendment to the Constitution by the legislatures of the several States, as provided in the Constitution, within seven years from the date of the submission hereof to the States by the Congress.

AMENDMENT XIX [1920]

[1] The right of citizens of the United States to vote shall not be denied or abridged by the United States or by any State on account of sex.

[2] Congress shall have power to enforce this article by appropriate legislation.

AMENDMENT XX [1933]

Section 1. The terms of the President and Vice President shall end at noon on the 20th day of January, and the terms of Senators and Representatives at noon on the 3d day of January, of the years in which such terms would have ended if this article had not been ratified; and the terms of their successors shall then begin.

Section 2. The Congress shall assemble at least once in every year, and such meeting shall begin at noon on the 3d day of January, unless they shall by law appoint a different day.

Section 3. If, at the time fixed for the beginning of the term of the President, the President elect shall have died, the Vice President elect shall become President. If a President shall not have been chosen before the time fixed for the beginning of his term, or if the President elect shall have failed to qualify, then the Vice President elect shall act as President until a President shall have qualified; and the Congress may by law provide for the case wherein neither a President elect nor a Vice President elect shall have qualified, declaring who shall then act as President, or the manner in which one who is to act shall be selected, and such person shall act accordingly until a President or Vice President shall have qualified.

Section 4. The Congress may by law provide for the case of the death of any of the persons from whom the House of Representatives may choose a President whenever the right of choice shall have devolved upon them, and for the case of the death of any of the persons from whom the Senate may choose a Vice President whenever the right of choice shall have devolved upon them.

Section 5. Sections 1 and 2 shall take effect on the 15th day of October following the ratification of this article.

Section 6. This article shall be inoperative unless it shall have been ratified as an amendment to the Constitution by the legislatures of three-fourths of the several States within seven years from the date of its submission.

AMENDMENT XXI [1933]

Section 1. The eighteenth article of amendment to the Constitution of the United States is hereby repealed.

Section 2. The transportation or importation into any State, Territory, or possession of the United States for delivery or use therein of intoxicating liquors, in violation of the laws thereof, is hereby prohibited.

Section 3. This article shall be inoperative unless it shall have been ratified as an amendment to the Constitution by conventions in the several States, as provided in the Constitution, within seven years from the date of the submission hereof to the States by the Congress.

AMENDMENT XXII [1951]

Section 1. No person shall be elected to the office of the President more than twice, and no person who has held the office of President, or acted as President, for more than two years of a term to which some other person was elected President shall be elected to the office of the President more than once. But this Article shall not apply to any person holding the office of President when this Article was proposed by the Congress, and shall not prevent any person who may be holding the office of President, or acting as President, during the term within which this Article becomes operative from holding the office of President or acting as President during the remainder of such term.

Section 2. This article shall be inoperative unless it shall have been ratified as an amendment to the Constitution by the legislatures of three-fourths of the several States within seven years from the date of its submission to the States by the Congress.

AMENDMENT XXIII [1961]

Section 1. The District constituting the seat of Government of the United States shall appoint in such manner as the Congress may direct:

A number of electors of President and Vice President equal to the whole number of Senators and Representatives in Congress to which the District would be entitled if it were a State, but in no event more than the least populous State; they shall be in addition to those appointed by the States, but they shall be considered, for the purposes of the election of President and Vice President, to be electors appointed by a State; and they shall meet in the District and perform such duties as provided by the twelfth article of amendment.

Section 2. The Congress shall have power to enforce this article by appropriate legislation.

AMENDMENT XXIV [1964]

Section 1. The right of citizens of the United States to vote in any primary or other election for President or Vice President, for electors for President or Vice President, or for Senator or Representative in Congress, shall not be denied or abridged by the United States or any State by reason of failure to pay any poll tax or other tax.

Section 2. The Congress shall have power to enforce this article by appropriate legislation.

AMENDMENT XXV [1967]

Section 1. In case of the removal of the President from office or of his death or resignation, the Vice President shall become President.

Section 2. Whenever there is a vacancy in the office of the Vice President, the President shall nominate a Vice President who shall take office upon confirmation by a majority vote of both Houses of Congress.

Section 3. Whenever the President transmits to the President pro tempore of the Senate and the Speaker of the House of Representatives his written declaration that he is unable to discharge the powers and duties of his office, and until he transmits to them a written declaration to the contrary, such powers and duties shall be discharged by the Vice President as Acting President.

Section 4. Whenever the Vice President and a majority of either the principal officers of the executive departments or of such other body as Congress may by law provide, transmit to the President pro tempore of the Senate and the Speaker of the House of Representatives their written declaration that the President is unable to discharge the powers and duties of his office, the Vice President shall immediately assume the powers and duties of the office as Acting President.

Thereafter, when the President transmits to the President pro tempore of the Senate and the Speaker of the House of Representatives his written declaration that no inability exists, he shall resume the powers and duties of his office unless the Vice President and a majority of either the principal officers of the executive department or of such other body as Congress may by law provide, transmit within four days to the President pro tempore of the Senate and the Speaker of the House of Representatives their written declaration that the President is unable to discharge the powers and duties of his office. Thereupon Congress shall decide the issue, assembling within forty-eight hours for that purpose if not in session. If the Congress, within twenty-one days after receipt of the latter written declaration, or, if Congress is not in session, within twenty-one days after Congress is required to assemble, determines by two-thirds vote of both Houses that the President is unable to discharge the powers and duties of his office, the Vice President shall continue to discharge the same as Acting President; otherwise, the President shall resume the powers and duties of his office.

AMENDMENT XXVI [1971]

Section 1. The right of citizens of the United States, who are eighteen years of age or older, to vote shall not be denied or abridged by the United States or by any State on account of age.

Section 2. The Congress shall have power to enforce this article by appropriate legislation.

AMENDMENT XXVII [1992][1]

No law, varying the compensation for the services of the Senators and Representatives, shall take effect, until an election of Representatives shall have intervened.

---

[1]   *Editors' note*: For questions about the validity of the ratification of this amendment, see pp. 1268–1269, *supra*.

APPENDIX 2

CONSTITUTIONAL RATIFICATION MATERIALS

■ ■ ■

Letter of George Washington, President of the Federal Convention, to the President of Congress, Transmitting the Constitution[1]

In Convention, September 17, 1787.

Sir,

We have now the honor to submit to the consideration of the United States in Congress assembled, that Constitution which has appeared to us the most adviseable

The friends of our country have long seen and desired, that the power of making war, peace, and treaties, that of levying money and regulating commerce, and the correspondent executive and judicial authorities should be fully and effectually vested in the general government of the Union: But the impropriety of delegating such extensive trust to one body of men is evident—Hence results the necessity of a different organization.

It is obviously impracticable in the federal government of these states, to secure all rights of independent sovereignty to each, and yet provide for the interest and safety of all: Individuals entering into society, must give up a share of liberty to preserve the rest. The magnitude of the sacrifice must depend as well on situation and circumstance, as on the object to be obtained. It is at all times difficult to draw with precision the line between those rights which must be surrendered, and those which may be reserved; and on the present occasion this difficulty was increased by a difference among the several states as to their situation, extent, habits, and particular interests.

In all our deliberations on this subject we kept steadily in our view, that which appears to us the greatest interest of every true American, the consolidation of our Union, in which is involved our prosperity, felicity, safety, perhaps our national existence. This important consideration, seriously and deeply impressed on our minds, led each state in the Convention to be less rigid on points of inferior magnitude, than might

---

[1] From Daniel Farber, The Constitution's Forgotten Cover Letter: An Essay on the New Federalism and the Original Understanding, 94 Mich. L. Rev. 615 (1995).

have been otherwise expected; and thus the Constitution, which we now present, is the result of a spirit of amity, and of that mutual deference and concession which the peculiarity of our political situation rendered indispensible.

That it will meet the full and entire approbation of every state is not perhaps to be expected; but each will doubtless consider, that had her interest been alone consulted, the consequences might have been particularly disagreeable or injurious to others; that it is liable to as few exceptions as could reasonably have been expected, we hope and believe; that it may promote the lasting welfare of that country so dear to us all, and secure her freedom and happiness, is our most ardent wish.

With great respect, We have the honor to be, Sir,

Your Excellency's

most obedient and humble servants,

George Washington, *President*

By unanimous Order of the Convention.

His Excellency the President of Congress.

Federalist No. 10[2]

Madison

Among the numerous advantages promised by a well-constructed Union, none deserves to be more accurately developed than its tendency to break and control the violence of faction. The friend of popular governments never finds himself so much alarmed for their character and fare, as when he contemplates their propensity to this dangerous vice.

By a faction, I understand a number of citizens, whether amounting to a majority or minority of the whole, who are united and actuated by some common impulse of passion, or of interest, adverse to the rights of other citizens, or to the permanent and aggregate interests of the community.

There are two methods of curing the mischiefs of faction: the one, by removing its causes; the other, by controlling its effects.

There are again two methods of removing the causes of faction: the one, by destroying the liberty which is essential to its existence; the other, by giving to every citizen the same opinions, the same passions, and the same interests.

It could never be more truly said than of the first remedy, that it was worse than the disease. Liberty is to faction what air is to fire, an aliment without which it instantly expires. But it could not be less folly to abolish

---

[2] As excerpted in Daniel Farber & Suzanna Sherry, *A History of the American Constitution* (1990).

liberty, which is essential to political life, because it nourishes faction, than it would be to wish the annihilation of air, which is essential to animal life, because it imparts to fire its destructive agency.

The second expedient is as impracticable as the first would be unwise. As long as the reason of man continues fallible, and he is at liberty to exercise it, different opinions will be formed. As long as the connection subsists between his reason and his self-love, his opinions and his passions will have a reciprocal influence on each other; and the former will be objects to which the latter will attach themselves. The diversity in the faculties of men, from which the rights of property originate, is not less an insuperable obstacle to a uniformity of interests. The protection of these faculties is the first object of government. From the protection of different and unequal faculties of acquiring property, the possession of different degrees and kinds of property immediately results; and from the influence of these on the sentiments and views of the respective proprietors, ensues a division of the society into different interests and parties.

The latent causes of faction are thus sown in the nature of man; and we see them everywhere brought into different degrees of activity, according to the different circumstances of civil society. A zeal for different opinions concerning religion, concerning government, and many other points, as well of speculation as of practice; an attachment to different leaders ambitiously contending for pre-eminence and power; or to persons of other descriptions whose fortunes have been interesting to the human passions, have, in turn, divided mankind into parties, inflamed them with mutual animosity, and rendered them much more disposed to vex and oppress each other than to co-operate for their common good. So strong is this propensity of mankind to fall into mutual animosities, that where no substantial occasion presents itself, the most frivolous and fanciful distinctions have been sufficient to kindle their unfriendly passions and excite their most violent conflicts. But the most common and durable source of factions has been the various and unequal distribution of property. Those who hold and those who are without property have ever formed distinct interests in society. Those who are creditors, and those who are debtors, fall under a like discrimination. A landed interest, a manufacturing interest, a mercantile interest, a moneyed interest, with many lesser interests, grow up of necessity in civilized nations, and divide them into different classes, actuated by different sentiments and views. The regulation of these various and interfering interests forms the principal task of modern legislation, and involves the spirit of party and faction in the necessary and ordinary operations of the government.

No man is allowed to be a judge in his own cause, because his interest would certainly bias his judgment, and, not improbably, corrupt his integrity. With equal, nay with greater reason, a body of men are unfit to be both judges and parties at the same time; yet what are many of the most important acts of legislation, but so many judicial determinations, not indeed concerning the rights of single persons, but concerning the rights of large bodies of citizens? And what are the different classes of legislators but advocates and parties to the causes which they determine? Is a law proposed concerning private debts? It is a question to which the creditors are parties on one side and the debtors on the other. Justice ought to hold the balance between them. Yet the parties are, and must be, themselves the judges; and the most numerous party, or, in other words, the most powerful faction must be expected to prevail. Shall domestic manufactures be encouraged, and in what degree, by restrictions on foreign manufactures? are questions which would be differently decided by the landed and the manufacturing classes, and probably by neither with a sole regard to justice and the public good. The apportionment of taxes on the various descriptions of property is an act which seems to require the most exact impartiality; yet there is, perhaps, no legislative act in which greater opportunity and temptation are given to a predominant party to trample on the rules of justice. Every shilling with which they overburden the inferior number, is a shilling saved to their own pockets.

It is in vain to say that enlightened statesmen will be able to adjust these clashing interests, and render them all subservient to the public good. Enlightened statesmen will not always be at the helm. Nor, in many cases, can such an adjustment be made at all without taking into view indirect and remote considerations, which will rarely prevail over the immediate interest which one party may find in disregarding the rights of another or the good of the whole.

The inference to which we are brought is, that the *causes* of faction cannot be removed, and that relief is only to be sought in the means of controlling its *effects*.

If a faction consists of less than a majority, relief is supplied by the republican principle, which enables the majority to defeat its sinister views by regular vote. It may clog the administration, it may convulse the society; but it will be unable to execute and mask its violence under the forms of the Constitution. When a majority is included in a faction, the form of popular government, on the other hand, enables it to sacrifice to its ruling passion or interest both the public good and the rights of other citizens. To secure the public good and private rights against the danger of such a faction, and at the same time to preserve the spirit and the form of popular government, is then the great object to which our inquiries are directed. Let me add that it is the great desideratum by which this form of government can be rescued from the opprobrium under which it has so long labored, and be recommended to the esteem and adoption of mankind.

By what means is this object attainable? Evidently by one of two only. Either the existence of the same passion or interest in a majority at the same time must be prevented, or the majority, having such coexistent passion or interest, must be rendered, by their number and local situation, unable to concert and carry into effect schemes of oppression. If the impulse and the opportunity be suffered to coincide, we well know that neither moral nor religious motives can be relied on as an adequate control. They are not found to be such on the injustice and violence of individuals, and lose their efficacy in proportion to the number combined together, that is, in proportion as their efficacy becomes needful.

From this view of the subject it may be concluded that a pure democracy, by which I mean a society consisting of a small number of citizens, who assemble and administer the government in person, can admit of no cure for the mischiefs of faction. A common passion or interest will, in almost every case, be felt by a majority of the whole; a communication and concert result from the form of government itself; and there is nothing to check the inducements to sacrifice the weaker party or an obnoxious individual. Hence it is that such democracies have ever been spectacles of turbulence and contention; have ever been found incompatible with personal security or the rights of property; and have in general been as short in their lives as they have been violent in their deaths. Theoretic politicians, who have patronized this species of government, have erroneously supposed that by reducing mankind to a perfect equality in their political rights, they would, at the same time, be perfectly equalized and assimilated in their possessions, their opinions, and their passions.

A republic, by which I mean a government in which the scheme of representation takes place, opens a different prospect, and promises the cure for which we are seeking. Let us examine the points in which it varies from pure democracy, and we shall comprehend both the nature of the cure and the efficacy which it must derive from the Union.

The two great points of difference between a democracy and a republic are: first, the delegation of the government, in the latter, to a small number of citizens elected by the rest; secondly, the greater number of citizens, and greater sphere of country, over which the latter may be extended.

The effect of the first difference is, on the one hand, to refine and enlarge the public views, by passing them through the medium of a chosen body of citizens, whose wisdom may best discern the true interest of their country, and whose patriotism and love of justice will be least likely to sacrifice it to temporary or partial considerations.

On the other hand, the effect may be inverted. Men of factious tempers, of local prejudices, or of sinister designs, may, by intrigue, by corruption, or by other means, first obtain the suffrages, and then betray the interests, of the people. The question resulting is, whether small or extensive republics are more favorable to the election of proper guardians of the public weal; and it is clearly decided in favor of the latter[.]

[T]he greater number of citizens and extent of territory which may be brought within the compass of republican than of democratic government . . . [is the] circumstance principally which renders factious combinations less to be dreaded in the former than in the latter. The smaller the society the fewer probably will be the distinct parties and interests composing it; the fewer the distinct parties and interests, the more frequently will a majority be found of the same party; and the smaller the number of individuals composing a majority, and the smaller the compass within which they are placed, the more easily will they concert and execute their plans of oppression. Extend the sphere, and you take in a greater variety of parties and interests; you make it less probable that a majority of the whole will have a common motive to invade the rights of other citizens; or if such a common motive exists, it will be more difficult for all who feel it to discover their own strength, and to act in unison with each other. Besides other impediments, it may be remarked that, where there is a consciousness of unjust or dishonorable purposes, communication is always checked by distrust in proportion to the number whose concurrence is necessary.

Hence, it clearly appears, that the same advantage which a republic has over a democracy, in controlling the effects of faction, is enjoyed by a large over a small republic,—is enjoyed by the Union over the States composing it. Does the advantage consist in the substitution of representatives whose enlightened views and virtuous sentiments render them superior to local prejudices and to schemes of injustice? It will not be denied that the representation of the Union will be most likely to possess these requisite endowments. Does it consist in the greater security afforded by a greater variety of parties, against the event of any one party being able to outnumber and oppress the rest? In an equal degree does the increased variety of parties comprised within the Union, increase this security. Does it, in fine, consist in the greater obstacles opposed to the concert and accomplishment of the secret wishes of an unjust and interested majority? Here, again, the extent of the Union gives it the most palpable advantage.

The influence of factious leaders may kindle a flame within their particular States, but will be unable to spread a general conflagration through the other States. A religious sect may degenerate into a political faction in a part of the Confederacy; but the variety of sects dispersed over the entire face of it must secure the national councils against any danger from that source. A rage for paper money, for an abolition of debts, for an equal division of property, or for any other improper or wicked project, will be less apt to pervade the whole body of the Union than a particular member of it; in the same proportion as such a malady is more likely to taint a particular county or district, than an entire State.

In the extent and proper structure of the Union, therefore, we behold a republican remedy for the diseases most incident to republican government. And according to the degree of pleasure and pride we feel in being republicans, ought to be our zeal in cherishing the spirit and supporting the character of Federalists.

Federalist No. 47[3]

Madison

One of the principal objections inculcated by the more respectable adversaries to the Constitution is its supposed violation of the political maxim that the legislative, executive, and judiciary departments ought to be separate and distinct. In the structure of the federal government no regard, it is said, seems to have been paid to this essential precaution in favor of liberty. The several departments of power are distributed and blended in such a manner as at once to destroy all symmetry and beauty of form, and to expose some of the essential parts of the edifice to the danger of being crushed by the disproportionate weight of other parts.

No political truth is certainly of greater intrinsic value, or is stamped with the authority of more enlightened patrons of liberty than that on which the objection is founded. The accumulation of all powers, legislative, executive, and judiciary, in the same hands, whether of one, a few, or many, and whether hereditary, self-appointed, or elective, may justly be pronounced the very definition of tyranny. Were the federal Constitution, therefore, really chargeable with this accumulation of power, or with a mixture of powers, having a dangerous tendency to such an accumulation, no further arguments would be necessary to inspire a universal reprobation of the system. I persuade myself, however, that it will be made apparent to everyone that the charge cannot be supported, and that the maxim on which it relies has been totally misconceived and misapplied. In order to form correct ideas on this important subject it will be proper to investigate the sense in which the preservation of liberty requires that the three great departments of power should be separate and distinct.

The oracle who is always consulted and cited on this subject is the celebrated Montesquieu. If he be not the author of this invaluable precept in the science of politics, he has the merit at least of displaying and recommending it most effectually to the attention of mankind. Let us endeavor, in the first place, to ascertain his meaning on this point.

The British Constitution was to Montesquieu what Homer has been to the didactic writers on epic poetry. As the latter have considered the work of the immortal bard as the perfect model from which the principles and rules of the epic art were to be drawn, and by which all similar works were to be judged, so this great political critic appears to have viewed the

---

[3]   Edited for the present volume.

Constitution of England as the standard, or to use his own expression, as the mirror of political liberty; and to have delivered, in the form of elementary truths, the several characteristic principles of that particular system. That we may be sure, then, not to mistake his meaning in this case, let us recur to the source from which the maxim was drawn.

On the slightest view of the British Constitution we must perceive that the legislative, executive, and judiciary departments are by no means totally separate and distinct from each other. The executive magistrate forms an integral part of the legislative authority. He alone has the prerogative of making treaties with foreign sovereigns which, when made, have, under certain limitations, the force of legislative acts. All the members of the judiciary department are appointed by him, can be removed by him on the address of the two Houses of Parliament, and form when he pleases to consult them, one of his constitutional councils. One branch of the legislative department forms also a great constitutional council to the executive chief, as, on another hand, it is the sole depositary of judicial power in cases of impeachment, and is invested with the supreme appellate jurisdiction in all other cases. The judges, again, are so far connected with the legislative department as often to attend and participate in its deliberations, though not admitted to a legislative vote.

From these facts, by which Montesquieu was guided, it may clearly be inferred that in saying "There can be no liberty where the legislative and executive powers are united in the same person, or body of magistrates," or, "if the power of judging be not separated from the legislative and executive powers," he did not mean that these departments ought to have no partial agency in, or no control over, the acts of each other. His meaning, as his own words import, and still more conclusively as illustrated by the example in his eye, can amount to no more than this, that where the whole power of one department is exercised by the same hands which possess the whole power of another department, the fundamental principles of a free constitution are subverted. This would have been the case in the constitution examined by him, if the king, who is the sole executive magistrate, had possessed also the complete legislative power, or the supreme administration of justice; or if the entire legislative body had possessed the supreme judiciary, or the supreme executive authority. This, however, is not among the vices of that constitution. * * *

If we look into the constitutions of the several States we find that, notwithstanding the emphatical and, in some instances, the unqualified terms in which this axiom has been laid down, there is not a single instance in which the several departments of power have been kept absolutely separate and distinct. New Hampshire, whose constitution was the last formed, seems to have been fully aware of the impossibility and inexpediency of avoiding any mixture whatever of these departments, and has qualified the doctrine by declaring "that the legislative, executive, and judiciary powers ought to be kept as separate from, and independent of, each other *as the nature of a free government will admit; or as is consistent with that chain of connection that binds the whole fabric of the constitution in one indissoluble bond of unity and amity.*" Her constitution accordingly mixes these departments in several respects. The Senate, which is a branch of the legislative department, is also a judicial tribunal for the trial of impeachments. The President, who is the head of the executive department, is the presiding member also of the Senate; and, besides an equal vote in all cases, has a casting vote in case of a tie. The executive head is himself eventually elective every year by the legislative department, and his council is every year chosen by and from the members of the same department. Several of the officers of state are also appointed by the legislature. And the members of the judiciary department are appointed by the executive department. [Madison discusses other state constitutions, all of which mix legislative, executive, and judicial power in this way.]

In citing these cases, in which the legislative, executive, and judiciary departments have not been kept totally separate and distinct, I wish not to be regarded as an advocate for the particular organizations of the several State governments. I am fully aware that among the many excellent principles which they exemplify they carry strong marks of the haste, and still stronger of the inexperience, under which they were framed. It is but too obvious that in some instances the fundamental principle under consideration has been violated by too great a mixture, and even an actual consolidation of the different powers; and that in no instance has a competent provision been made for maintaining in practice the separation delineated on paper. What I have wished to evince is that the charge brought against the proposed Constitution of violating a sacred maxim of free government is warranted neither by the real meaning annexed to that maxim by its author, nor by the sense in which it has hitherto been understood in America. * * *

Federalist No. 51[4]

Madison

In order to lay a due foundation for that separate and distinct exercise of the different powers of government, which to a certain extent is admitted on all hands to be essential to the preservation of liberty, it is evident that each department should have a will of its own; and consequently should be so constituted that the members of each should have as little agency as possible in the appointment of the members of the others. Were this principle rigorously adhered to, it would require that all the appointments for the supreme executive, legislative, and judiciary magistracies should be

---

[4]   As excerpted in Daniel Farber & Suzanna Sherry, *A History of the American Constitution* (1990).

drawn from the same fountain of authority, the people, through channels having no communication whatever with one another. Perhaps such a plan of constructing the several departments would be less difficult in practice than it may in contemplation appear. Some difficulties, however, and some additional expense would attend the execution of it. Some deviations, therefore, from the principle must be admitted. In the constitution of the judiciary department in particular, it might be inexpedient to insist rigorously on the principle: first, because peculiar qualifications being essential in the members, the primary consideration ought to be to select that mode of choice which best secures these qualifications; secondly, because the permanent tenure by which the appointments are held in that department, must soon destroy all sense of dependence on the authority conferring them.

It is equally evident, that the members of each department should be as little dependent as possible on those of the others, for the emoluments annexed to their offices. Were the executive magistrate, or the judges, not independent of the legislature in this particular, their independence in every other would be merely nominal.

But the great security against a gradual concentration of the several powers in the same department, consists in giving to those who administer each department the necessary constitutional means and personal motives to resist encroachments of the others. The provision for defence must in this, as in all other cases, be made commensurate to the danger of attack. Ambition must be made to counteract ambition. The interest of the man must be connected with the constitutional rights of the place. It may be a reflection on human nature, that such devices should be necessary to control the abuses of government. But what is government itself, but the greatest of all reflections on human nature? If men were angels, no government would be necessary. If angels were to govern men, neither external nor internal controls on government would be necessary. In framing a government which is to be administered by men over men, the great difficulty lies in this: you must first enable the government to control the governed; and in the next place oblige it to control itself. A dependence on the people is, no doubt, the primary control on the government; but experience has taught mankind the necessity of auxiliary precautions.

This policy of supplying, by opposite and rival interests, the defect of better motives, might be traced through the whole system of human affairs, private as well as public. We see it particularly displayed in all the subordinate distributions of power, where the constant aim is to divide and arrange the several offices in such a manner as that each may be a check on the other—that the private interest of every individual may be a sentinel over the public rights. These inventions of prudence cannot be less requisite in the distribution of the supreme powers of the State.

But it is not possible to give to each department an equal power of self-defence. In republican government, the legislative authority necessarily predominates. The remedy for this inconveniency is to divide the legislature into different branches; and to render them, by different modes of election and different principles of action, as little connected with each other as the nature of their common functions and their common dependence on the society will admit. It may even be necessary to guard against dangerous encroachments by still further precautions. As the weight of the legislative authority requires that it should be thus divided, the weakness of the executive may require, on the other hand, that it should be fortified.

In a single republic, all the power surrendered by the people is submitted to the administration of a single government; and the usurpations are guarded against by a division of the government into distinct and separate departments. In the compound republic of America, the power surrendered by the people is first divided between two distinct governments, and then the portion allotted to each subdivided among distinct and separate departments. Hence a double security arises to the rights of the people. The different governments will control each other, at the same time that each will be controlled by itself.

Federalist No. 78[5]

Hamilton

Whoever attentively considers the different departments of power must perceive, that, in a government in which they are separated from each other, the judiciary, from the nature of its functions, will always be the least dangerous to the political rights of the Constitution; because it will be least in a capacity to annoy or injure them. The Executive not only dispenses the honors, but holds the sword of the community. The legislature not only commands the purse, but prescribes the rules by which the duties and rights of every citizen are to be regulated. The judiciary, on the contrary, has no influence over either the sword or the purse; no direction either of the strength or of the wealth of the society; and can take no active resolution whatever. It may truly be said to have neither FORCE nor WILL, but merely judgment; and must ultimately depend upon the aid of the executive arm even for the efficacy of its judgments.

This simple view of the matter suggests several important consequences. It proves incontestably, that the judiciary is beyond comparison the weakest of the three departments of power;[6] That it can never attack with success either of the other two; and that all possible care

---

[5]   As excerpted in Daniel Farber & Suzanna Sherry, *A History of the American Constitution* (1990).

[6]   The celebrated Montesquieu, speaking of them, says: "Of the three powers above mentioned, the judiciary is next to nothing."—"Spirit of Laws," vol. i., page 186.—PUBLIUS.

is requisite to enable it to defend itself against their attacks. It equally proves, that though individual oppression may now and then proceed from the courts of justice, the general liberty of the people can never be endangered from that quarter; I mean so long as the judiciary remains truly distinct from both the legislature and the Executive. For I agree, that "there is no liberty, if the power of judging be not separated from the legislative and executive powers."[7] And it proves, in the last place, that as liberty can have nothing to fear from the judiciary alone, but would have every thing to fear from its union with either of the other departments; that as all the effects of such a union must ensue from a dependence of the former on the latter, notwithstanding a nominal and apparent separation; that as, from the natural feebleness of the judiciary, it is in continual jeopardy of being overpowered, awed, or influenced by its coordinate branches; and that as nothing can contribute so much to its firmness and independence as permanency in office, this quality may therefore be justly regarded as an indispensable ingredient in its constitution, and, in a great measure, as the citadel of the public justice and the public security.

The complete independence of the courts of justice is peculiarly essential in a limited Constitution. By a limited Constitution, I understand one which contains certain specified exceptions to the legislative authority; for instance, as that it shall pass no bills of attainder, no *ex-post-facto* laws, and the like. Limitations of this kind can be preserved in practice no other way than through the medium of courts of justice, whose duty it must be to declare all acts contrary to the manifest tenor of the Constitution void. Without this, all the reservations of particular rights or privileges would amount to nothing.

Some perplexity respecting the rights of the courts to pronounce legislative acts void, because contrary to the constitution, has arisen from an imagination that the doctrine would imply a superiority of the judiciary to the legislative power. It is urged that the authority which can declare the acts of another void, must necessarily be superior to the one whose acts may be declared void. As this doctrine is of great importance in all the American constitutions, a brief discussion of the ground on which it rests cannot be unacceptable.

There is no position which depends on clearer principles, than that every act of a delegated authority, contrary to the tenor of the commission under which it is exercised, is void. No legislative act, therefore, contrary to the Constitution, can be valid. To deny this, would be to affirm, that the deputy is greater than his principal; that the servant is above his master; that the representatives of the people are superior to the people themselves; that men acting by virtue of powers, may do not only what their powers do not authorize, but what they forbid.

---

[7]   *Idem.* page 181.—PUBLIUS.

If it be said that the legislative body are themselves the constitutional judges of their own powers, and that the construction they put upon them is conclusive upon the other departments, it may be answered, that this cannot be the natural presumption, where it is not to be collected from any particular provisions in the Constitution. It is not otherwise to be supposed, that the Constitution could intend to enable the representatives of the people to substitute their *will* to that of their constituents. It is far more rational to suppose, that the courts were designed to be an intermediate body between the people and the legislature, in order, among other things, to keep the latter within the limits assigned to their authority. The interpretation of the laws is the proper and peculiar province of the courts. A constitution is, in fact, and must be regarded by the judges, as a fundamental law. It therefore belongs to them to ascertain its meaning, as well as the meaning of any particular act proceeding from the legislative body. If there should happen to be an irreconcilable variance between the two, that which has the superior obligation and validity ought, of course, to be preferred; or, in other words, the Constitution ought to be preferred to the statute, the intention of the people to the intention of their agents.

Nor does this conclusion by any means suppose a superiority of the judicial to the legislative power. It only supposes that the power of the people is superior to both; and that where the will of the legislature, declared in its statutes, stands in opposition to that of the people, declared in the Constitution, the judges ought to be governed by the latter rather than the former. They ought to regulate their decisions by the fundamental laws, rather than by those which are not fundamental.

INDEX

References are to Pages